THE LAW OF BANKRUPTCY

Third Edition

by

Charles Jordan Tabb
Mildred Van Voorhis Jones Chair in Law
University of Illinois College of Law

HORNBOOK SERIES®

Mat #41529910

© 1997 FOUNDATION PRESS
© 2009 THOMSON REUTERS/FOUNDATION PRESS
© 2014 LEG, Inc. d/b/a West Academic
    444 Cedar Street, Suite 700
    St. Paul, MN 55101
    1-877-888-1330

ISBN: 978–0–314–29017–5

Dedication

(To the third edition, 2013)

To my parents, Bill and Jeanne Tabb,

Two great lawyers and legal minds,

who taught me to love and respect the law

Dedication

(To the second edition, 2009)

To the law students at the University of Illinois,

whom I have had the privilege of teaching for the past quarter century

Dedication

(To the first edition, 1997)

To Linda,

My wife, friend, and inspiration

and to our dear children,

Rebecca, Natalie, Charles, and John

Preface to the Third Edition

When I published the First Edition of this treatise in 1997, bankruptcy had become ubiquitous in the United States, with filings eclipsing one million new cases every year. In the interim between the First and Second Editions, Congress passed the Bankruptcy Abuse Prevention and Consumer Protection Act of 2005, which in many ways substantially revised the Bankruptcy Code of 1978, and which made bankruptcy much more difficult for individual consumer debtors. Sadly, that law was premised largely on a mistaken belief of widespread debtor abuse. Shortly before the Second Edition was published in 2009, the Great Recession of 2008 wreaked economic havoc around the world. We have yet to recover fully.

In the United States, the federal bankruptcy law remains the primary vehicle for dealing with the consequences of economic disaster, whether corporate or personal, large or small. Since the publication of the Second Edition, we have witnessed the once-unimaginable bankruptcies of General Motors and Chrysler, and have seen those companies saved and restored to financial health through the creative use of the bankruptcy law. The bankruptcy courts are still sorting through the economic ruins left by the biggest fraudster in history, Bernie Madoff. Notwithstanding the congressional belief that the 2005 amendments would curb consumer filings, over a million individual consumer cases are still filed every year.

The goal of this book remains the same as in the First and Second Editions: to explain and explore in depth in a single volume both the basic principles and the nuances of the bankruptcy law in the United States. That law is extraordinarily complex. This book is intended to serve as a primary and comprehensive resource on bankruptcy law for law students, law professors, attorneys, and judges.

With this Third Edition, I am pleased to be joining the team at West Publishing. I have nothing but heartfelt gratitude to and fond memories of the wonderful people at Foundation Press, which published the First and Second Editions. I look forward to publishing many future editions with West.

CHARLES JORDAN TABB

Champaign, Illinois
June 2013

Preface to the Second Edition

When I published the first edition of this treatise in 1997, bankruptcy had eclipsed its legal boundaries and had become a social and cultural phenomenon. In the dozen years since, that trend has become even more pronounced and entrenched. Bankruptcy is in the news on a daily basis. In the wake of the cataclysmic worldwide economic collapse in the fall of 2008, "bankruptcy" is a word known (and feared) universally. Not since the Great Depression came crashing down almost 80 years ago has the world experienced such a financial disaster. Bankruptcy is the principal legal mechanism through which the fallout from such economic calamity is handled, whether it be Lehman Brothers addressing over $600 billion in debts, United Airlines trying to salvage its business, or our individual friends, relatives, and neighbors seeking refuge in bankruptcy court. Over one million new bankruptcy cases are filed every single year, and that number is rapidly increasing. It is a virtual certainty that every person in the United States knows someone who has filed for bankruptcy.

The goal of this book remains the same as in the first edition: to explain and explore in depth in a single volume both the basic principles and the nuances of the bankruptcy law in the United States. That law is extraordinarily complex, and became even more so with the enactment of the Bankruptcy Abuse Prevention and Consumer Protection Act of 2005, a bill over 500 pages long, which amended the existing Bankruptcy Code in myriad ways. This Second Edition analyzes the many changes effected by BAPCPA, while carrying forward the fundamental explanations of the core principles of United States bankruptcy law. This book is intended to serve as a primary and comprehensive resource on bankruptcy law for law students, law professors, attorneys, and judges.

CHARLES JORDAN TABB

Champaign, Illinois
March 2009

Preface to the First Edition

Bankruptcy happens. A lot. In the year preceding the publication of this treatise, over one million new bankruptcy cases were filed in the federal courts. Bankruptcy is by far the most frequent form of federal court proceeding. About one out of 90 households in the nation filed bankruptcy last year; in some areas, the ratio was closer to one out of 25. Bankruptcy court is the forum in which financially distressed consumers, celebrities, family farmers, agribusinesses, partnerships, small businesses, and huge multinational corporations attempt to address and resolve their difficulties. A student graduating from law school today is virtually certain to encounter the specter of bankruptcy in their legal career.

The sophisticated United States bankruptcy law, the most progressive in the world, offers flexible solutions for the myriad problems attendant to a debtor's financial crisis. The bankruptcy law is based on two cornerstones: fairness to all creditors, and a fresh start for honest debtors. Different chapters of the Bankruptcy Code implement those core principles in ways tailored to the particularized needs of the debtor and the debtor's creditors. An individual debtor may obtain an immediate discharge of debts in exchange for turning over her nonexempt property for the benefit of her creditors in chapter 7; or that individual may repay her debts over time, in chapter 13, and obtain even more complete relief. Family farmers are provided special help in keeping their family farm in chapter 12. Even municipalities may restructure their debts in bankruptcy, under chapter 9. For business debtors of every sort and description, chapter 11 is a primary mechanism for them to reorder their financial affairs.

Many lawyers and law students have perception that bankruptcy law is a narrow and difficult "specialty." Perhaps the "difficult" part is on target, although this book is intended to unveil at least some of the mysteries of bankruptcy law. Nothing could be further from the truth, though, than to think of bankruptcy law as "narrow" in its focus. Indeed, bankruptcy may be the last haven for the legal generalist. The whole panorama of the law flashes through the bankruptcy arena. Issues involving contracts, sales of goods, real property, personal property, taxes, leases, mortgages, security interests, labor, pensions, torts, products liability, environmental concerns, alimony and support, and even the Constitution arise under bankruptcy's broad umbrella.

This book undertakes in a single volume to explain and explore the basic principles and the nuances of bankruptcy law in the United States. It is intended to be a resource for students taking any law school course, basic or advanced, involving bankruptcy. The book also is written so that attorneys and judges may obtain insights into the operation of the bankruptcy law. A law student should be able to use this treatise in his or her legal career. I have found the study of bankruptcy law to be endlessly fascinating and challenging; in this book I have tried to share some of my discoveries.

CHARLES JORDAN TABB

Champaign, Illinois
July 1997

Acknowledgments to the Third Edition

In the Acknowledgments to the First Edition, I spoke first and foremost of my debt of gratitude to my family. I repeat and reaffirm that debt here. Most importantly, I thank my wife Linda, my best friend and biggest supporter. This book—indeed, my entire career—would not have been possible without her love, support, and encouragement. Linda and I are very fortunate to have four wonderful children, Rebecca, Natalie, Charles, and John. In the Second Edition, I had the good fortune to work with two of our children as research assistants, Rebecca (J.D., Stanford, 2009), and Natalie (B.A., Stanford, 2008). In this Third Edition, I again was gratified to have the opportunity to work with another of our children, Charles Jr. (B.A., University of Illinois, 2011).

As in the Second Edition, I owe a huge debt to my friend, former student, colleague, and co-author, Professor Ralph Brubaker of the University of Illinois College of Law. Ralph and I have published together three editions of a casebook on bankruptcy law, and in this Third Edition (as in the Second), I have drawn generously on the many insights that Ralph and I have jointly developed in writing our casebook and the accompanying teacher's manual. I also am grateful to another friend, former student, and colleague, Professor Robert Lawless of the University of Illinois College of Law, whose expertise in bankruptcy law has been enormously helpful.

I especially want to thank my long-time Administrative Assistant, Sally Cook. Sally is so competent, a consummate professional, and also a friend. It is my privilege to be able to work with her.

This Third Edition is very much the product of a fantastic team of research assistants, to whom I am especially grateful. Thank you all for your brilliant and dedicated work. I noted above that my son Charles Tabb Jr. provided valuable research assistance, and I thank him.

I also have had the chance to work with many outstanding students at the University of Illinois College of Law, who helped turn this Third Edition from a dream into reality. I want to single out Jamie Netznik (J.D. 2013), who was my primary research assistant and who coordinated and oversaw the entire project. The simple truth is that I could not have published this book without Jamie's help. Her work was extraordinary, far above and beyond the call of duty.

In addition to Jamie, nine outstanding students in the J.D. classes of 2013 and 2014 did excellent research work on this treatise. Every one of them handled at the least an entire chapter. From the class of 2013, I was honored to be assisted by (in alphabetical order): Dannia Altemimei; David Bauer; Hannah Costigan-Cowles; Kelly Kono; James Liu; and Amy Timm. From the class of 2014, able research help was provided by Kristin Isaacson; Robbie McLellarn; and Kristi Osentoski.

Finally, I owe a considerable debt of gratitude to two generous benefactors of the University of Illinois College of Law, whose endowed gifts enabled me to enjoy the robust research support exemplified in the long list of outstanding research assistants noted just above. First, Alice Curtis Campbell, an alumna of the College of Law, generously endowed the professorship to which I was named in 2002, and which I held until 2012. Alice and her husband Robert have also become valued friends. Second, the family of Mildred Van Voorhis Jones endowed the chair to which I was named in 2012. I also am very grateful for the support of the University of Illinois College of Law, under the able leadership of my friends and former Deans, Thomas Mengler, Heidi Hurd, and Ralph Brubaker, and current Dean Bruce Smith.

CHARLES JORDAN TABB

Champaign, Illinois
June 2013

Acknowledgments to the Second Edition

In the Acknowledgments to the First Edition, I spoke of the fact that I began that work in the "latter days of the Bush Administration." Little did I know then that there would be a second "Bush Administration"—and that this Second Edition would not be completed until after the second President Bush left office. Much has happened in the world of bankruptcy law since the publication of the First Edition in 1997, the most notable event being, of course, the enactment of the Bankruptcy Abuse Prevention and Consumer Protection Act of 2005. This Second Edition, finished in the late winter of 2009, completely revises and updates the First Edition, taking into account not only BAPCPA but also a dozen years of case law developments. As this book goes to press, the United States is suffering from its most cataclysmic economic collapse since the Great Depression. Bankruptcy, unfortunately, is a very timely and important topic. Legislative initiatives to further revise the bankruptcy law are on the table as this book is being published.

In the Acknowledgments to the First Edition, I spoke first and foremost of my debt of gratitude to my family, and I repeat and reaffirm that debt here. My wife Linda has been my biggest supporter and source of encouragement, and I thank her from the bottom of my heart. I also am very fortunate to have four wonderful children, Rebecca, Natalie, Charles, and John. This Second Edition has been especially meaningful to me in that two of my research assistants have been my daughters, Rebecca (J.D., Stanford, 2009), and Natalie (B.A., Stanford, 2008).

I owe a huge debt to my friend, former student, colleague, and co-author, Professor Ralph Brubaker of the University of Illinois College of Law. Ralph and I have published together two editions of a casebook on bankruptcy law, and in this Second Edition I have drawn generously on the many insights that Ralph and I have jointly developed in writing our casebook and the accompanying teacher's manual. I also am grateful to another friend, former student, and colleague, Professor Robert Lawless of the University of Illinois College of Law, whose expertise in bankruptcy law has been enormously helpful.

This Second Edition is very much a product of an extraordinary team of research assistants, to whom I am especially grateful. Thank you all for your brilliant and dedicated work. I noted above that my daughters Rebecca Tabb and Natalie Tabb provided valuable research assistance. After the enactment of BAPCPA I had many able students at the University of Illinois College of Law who worked diligently and ably to help bring this Second Edition to fruition. Jillian McClelland (J.D. 2007) co-authored an article with me that informed many of the revisions pertaining to the "means test." I want to thank the following superb research assistants who helped to implement the BAPCPA changes as well as case law through 2008: Aubrey Meyers (J.D. 2009); Benjamin Christenson (J.D. 2010); Katy Dixon (J.D. 2010); Laurel Hennenfent (J.D. 2010); Anna Kaluzny (J.D. 2010); Andrea Krejczyk (J.D. 2010); Raghav Krishnapriyan

(J.D. 2010, University of California); Richard Nowak (J.D. 2010); Elizabeth Rodgers (J.D. 2010); Katherine Shah (J.D. 2010); and Tyrone Thomas (J.D. 2010).

Prior to the 2005 enactment of BAPCPA, another excellent team of research assistants did excellent work updating the treatise from 1997 to 2004. They are: James Antonopolous (J.D. 2003); Jason Bohm (J.D. 2003); Jeffrey Davis (J.D. 2003); David Deschler (J.D. 2004); Joseph DiRago (J.D. 2004); Wendy Dodson (J.D. 2001); David Gemperle (J.D. 2003); Kristen Jacobsen (J.D. 2004); Mi–Seon Kim (J.D. 2004); Matthew Kuenning (J.D. 2003); Kristen Laughridge (J.D. 2004); Christopher Leasor (J.D. 2004); Tyler Mertes (J.D. 2004); Anthony Moeller (J.D. 2004); Linda Salfisberg (J.D. 2003); Peter Sgro (J.D. 2004); Matthew Sostrin (J.D. 2003); Cynthia Stencel (J.D. 2004); Jeffrey Stotler (J.D. 2004); Erin Sylvester (J.D. 2004); Aaron Van Getson (J.D. 2003); Kevin Van Hout (J.D. 2003); and Andrew Wool (J.D. 2004).

Finally, I owe a considerable debt of gratitude to Alice Curtis Campbell, an alumna of the University of Illinois College of Law, who generously endowed the professorship to which I was named in 2002. Alice and her husband Robert have also become valued friends. In the years since being invested as the holder of the Alice Curtis Campbell Professorship, in working on this book, I have benefited enormously from the research support provided by that Professorship, as is evident from the fact that I have been able to utilize the Campbell funds to employ 36 research assistants! I also am very grateful for the support of the University of Illinois College of Law, under the able leadership of my friends and former Deans, Thomas Mengler and Heidi Hurd, and Interim Dean Ralph Brubaker.

CHARLES JORDAN TABB

Champaign, Illinois
March 2009

Acknowledgments to the First Edition

This book has been "in the works" for a long time. I undertook to write a comprehensive one-volume treatise on the law of bankruptcy back in the latter days of the Bush Administration, with the encouragement of Harold R. Eriv, then the President of Foundation Press. I thank Harold for giving me this opportunity. Harold's successor at the helm of Foundation Press, Richard T. Fenton, gave me constant and unwavering support throughout his tenure there, for which I thank him. It was a pleasure working with both of them.

My biggest debt of gratitude is to my family, and especially to my dear wife Linda. Without her this book would never have been possible. She has kept me going through the good times and bad. For these many years, Linda and our wonderful children, Rebecca, Natalie, Charles, and John, have exhibited the patience of Job in bearing with me as I have put in long hours laboring over this book. My heartfelt thanks goes to each of them. This book is at least half theirs.

Being a lawyer is in my blood. My original inspiration to study law came from my parents, William H. Tabb and Jeanne J. Tabb, both of whom were members of the bar. Bill Tabb was a brilliant trial lawyer, and a man of conscience and integrity. Jeanne Tabb gave me a love for the academic side of the law. They both instilled in me the deepest respect for the rule of law, and an appreciation of the importance of law in the life of our country. My maternal grandfather, Murray J. Jordan, was a dedicated trial lawyer. John E. Smith, my father-in-law, is a fine real estate lawyer; it has been a pleasure to get to know him. And last but certainly not least, I want to acknowledge my older brother, W. Murray Tabb, my lifelong friend. He too is a professor of law, and has written many scholarly books and articles.

It is great privilege to be on the faculty of the University of Illinois College of Law. The administration, under Dean Thomas M. Mengler and his predecessor, Richard Schmalbeck, has been unfailingly supportive of my research efforts. The law library, under the able tutelage of Richard Surles, has responded favorably to every request I have made. My colleagues have given me welcome encouragement. I gratefully acknowledge the research support provided by the Ross and Helen Workman research grants.

Summary of Contents

THE LAW OF BANKRUPTCY

Third Edition

Chapter 1

OVERVIEW OF BANKRUPTCY

A. THE NATURE AND PURPOSES OF BANKRUPTCY RELIEF

§ 1.1   Liquidation Bankruptcy

Bankruptcy. It is the most dreaded word in the world of commerce. But what is "bankruptcy"? The United States Constitution gives Congress the power to enact uniform laws on "the subject of bankruptcies."[1] A federal bankruptcy law has been in effect since 1898.[2] Somewhat surprisingly, that federal law, the United States Bankruptcy Code,[3] does not define the term "bankruptcy." Indeed, considerable effort has been expended in ascertaining what falls within "the subject of bankruptcies."[4] In common understanding, "bankruptcy" suggests financial ruin or death. The term is associated with "going bankrupt," which suggests a debtor who cannot pay its debts, and loses everything. While the laymen's view contains a kernel of truth, it is incomplete. Missing is the notion of financial rebirth. Legally, "bankruptcy" is a type of court proceeding designed to settle the financial affairs of a "bankrupt" debtor.[5] The goals of a bankruptcy case are twofold: resolving the competing claims of multiple creditors, *and* freeing the debtor from its financial past. After passing through the crucible of bankruptcy, the debtor and its creditors must move on.

The etymology of the word "bankrupt" suggests its original meaning. One view is that the word derives from the Latin words *"bancus,"* meaning table or counter, and *"ruptus,"* meaning broken. A merchant trader who went broke in medieval days would break his trading table, graphically signifying that he was out of business. Another suggestion is that the word comes from the French words *"banque,"* meaning bench, and *"route,"* meaning a trace; thus, a ruined trader would remove his trading bench without leaving a trace.[6]

---

[1]   U.S. Const. art. I, § 8, cl. 4.

[2]   The Bankruptcy Act of 1898, ch. 541, 30 Stat. 544 (repealed 1978), governed from 1898 until October 1, 1979, the effective date of the Bankruptcy Reform Act of 1978, Pub. L. No. 95–598, 92 Stat. 2549. In the 1800s federal bankruptcy laws were in effect from 1800 to 1803 (Bankruptcy Act of 1800, ch. 19, 2 Stat. 19 (repealed 1803)); 1841 to 1843 (Bankruptcy Act of 1841, ch. 9, 5 Stat. 440 (repealed 1843)); and 1867 to 1878 (Bankruptcy Act of 1867, ch. 176, 14 Stat. 517 (repealed 1878)).

[3]   The Bankruptcy Code is title 11 of the United States Code. This book will refer to it as the "Code," and cites to the Code will omit the reference to title 11, using section numbers only.

[4]   See § 1.10.b. For an attempt to define bankruptcy, see Max Radin, The Nature of Bankruptcy, 89 U. Pa. L. Rev. 1 (1940).

[5]   Prior to the 1978 Bankruptcy Code, such a debtor was and always had been called a "bankrupt." By congressional fiat, however, the term "bankrupt" was legislated out of proper legal usage. Now a bankrupt is just a "debtor."

[6]   F. Regis Noel, History of the Bankruptcy Law 10–11 (1919); William Blackstone, Commentaries *471 n.(e). The Italian equivalent was *"bancarotta."* Radin, supra note 4, at 1 n.1.

Bankruptcy laws in the United States have evolved considerably since the first federal bankruptcy law was passed in 1800. The term "bankruptcy" at that time had a very specific technical meaning. A bankruptcy law was one intended principally for the relief of creditors of a merchant trader who had committed an "act of bankruptcy," and a bankruptcy case could only be brought by creditors against the merchant debtor. An "insolvency" law, by contrast, was conceived as a debtor relief law, and could be commenced by the impoverished individual debtor.[7]

Today in the United States the distinction between the two terms has largely evaporated. The term "bankruptcy" has come to encompass both the notions of a remedy for creditors and of debtor relief. The current Bankruptcy Code encompasses a wide spectrum of possible measures. These range from straight liquidation bankruptcy (chapter 7), to the reorganization of businesses (chapter 11), to the adjustment of family farmer debts (chapter 12), to the adjustment of the debts of individual consumers (chapter 13), and even to the adjustment of the debts of a municipality (chapter 9). Cross-border cases are dealt with in chapter 15. All of these varied forms of relief fall within "the subject of bankruptcies."

The most common type of bankruptcy case is a *liquidation* bankruptcy case (also called "straight" bankruptcy), governed by chapter 7 of the Code. In a chapter 7 liquidation case, the debtor's existing assets are sold, or "liquidated," and the net proceeds are distributed to creditors. For individual debtors, any "exempt" property is returned to them rather than being sold for the benefit of creditors. An independent party, the bankruptcy trustee, supervises the process of collecting the debtor's assets (the bankruptcy "estate," § 541(a)), liquidating those assets, returning exempt property, § 522, and making distribution to creditors. § 704. While this bankruptcy process is pending, creditors are enjoined, or "stayed," from attempting to collect their claims from the estate or from the debtor. § 362(a). Instead, those creditors will be paid only out of the estate in an orderly manner pursuant to the process overseen by the trustee. With some exceptions, creditors are treated equally, on a pro rata basis. § 726(b). In other words, if (as is usually the case) the debtor does not have enough property to pay all of its creditors in full, then each creditor takes the same proportionate share of those assets. The exceptions to equal treatment of creditors are twofold. First, *secured* creditors are paid the value of their collateral, before unsecured creditors are paid. Second, out of the residue of the estate remaining after secured creditors are paid, some unsecured creditors have been awarded *priority* in payment by Congress, and must be paid before non-priority unsecured creditors. §§ 507(a), 726(a)(1).

The debtor, in exchange for giving up its existing property for immediate distribution, is in most cases relieved of any further legal obligation to pay its prior debts. § 727(b). An individual debtor thus may keep his future earnings for himself, free from the claims of his pre-bankruptcy creditors. This extraordinary benefit is called a *"discharge"* of debts. A corporation is not technically discharged, but the point is moot, since a corporation just dissolves after bankruptcy.

---

[7]   Sturges v. Crowninshield, 17 U.S. (4 Wheat.) 122, 194–95 (1819).

Liquidation bankruptcy cases serve two independent purposes: relief of debtors, and equitable treatment of creditors. The former is the one most people would think of first, but actually is less central to the essence of a bankruptcy case. "Bankruptcy" could exist without any form of debtor relief, and indeed did so for a considerable period of time. The first bankruptcy law in Anglo–American jurisprudence, enacted in 1543,[8] did not discharge debtors from their debts at all. The discharge did not exist until 1706 in England,[9] and even then was designed primarily as a way to encourage merchant debtors to cooperate in disclosing and turning over their assets for distribution to creditors in the bankruptcy case.[10] The first United States bankruptcy law, passed in 1800, did not allow debtors to file bankruptcy voluntarily and take advantage of the discharge.[11] Only creditors could commence a bankruptcy case, and then only against merchant debtors. The 1841 Act was the first to offer debtors the option of voluntary bankruptcy and ready access to a discharge, and those voluntary discharge doors were opened to all debtors, merchant and non-merchant alike.[12]

Today, however, the goal of providing a financial "fresh start" for "honest but unfortunate debtors"[13] has become entrenched in our bankruptcy law. The two main aspects of the fresh start for *individual* debtors are (1) the discharge of debts, which frees up a debtor's future earnings, and (2) exemption laws, which permit a debtor to keep a minimally necessary amount of her current property. This fresh start allows hopelessly insolvent individuals to get out from under the weight of their debts and resume productive lives as contributing members of society. The debtor would have less incentive to work if her creditors could reach the fruits of her labors. The bankruptcy discharge frees up the product of an individual debtor's human capital, allowing that debtor to keep her future earnings. The discharge provides a sort of social safety net, helping to avoid the creation of a perpetual debtor underclass.[14]

---

[8]   34 & 35 Henry 8, c. 4 (1542). Scholars debate whether royal assent actually occurred in 1542 or 1543, but the legal fiction at the time dated all laws from the beginning of the session. See http://bankruptcy andinsolvency.blogspot.com/2010/03/hobs–1542–statute-dating-act-against.html. See also Emily Kadens, The Last Bankrupt Hanged: Balancing Incentives in the Development of Bankruptcy Law, 59 Duke L.J. 1229, 1236–37 (2010).

[9]   4 Anne, c. 17 (1705). While officially dated 1705, there is no doubt that this law was actually enacted in 1706. See John C. McCoid, II, Discharge: The Most Important Development in Bankruptcy History, 70 Am. Bankr. L.J. 163, 163–69 (1996); see also Kadens, supra note 8, at 1261.

[10]   See Charles J. Tabb, The Historical Evolution of the Bankruptcy Discharge, 65 Am. Bankr. L.J. 325, 333–39 (1991). See also Kadens, supra note 8; McCoid, supra note 9.

[11]   See generally Bruce H. Mann, Republic of Debtors: Bankruptcy in the Age of American Independence (2002).

[12]   See John C. McCoid, II, The Origins of Voluntary Bankruptcy, 5 Bankr. Dev. J. 361 (1988).

[13]   Local Loan Co. v. Hunt, 292 U.S. 234, 244 (1934).

[14]   For discussions of the fresh start policy, see chapter 10, and especially § 10.3; see also Barry Adler, Ben Polak & Alan Schwartz, Regulating Consumer Bankruptcy: A Theoretical Inquiry, 29 J. Legal Stud. 585 (2000); Margaret Howard, A Theory of Discharge in Consumer Bankruptcy, 48 Ohio St. L.J. 1047 (1987); Richard M. Hynes, Why (Consumer) Bankruptcy?, 56 Ala. L. Rev. 121 (2004); Thomas H. Jackson, The Fresh–Start Policy in Bankruptcy Law, 98 Harv. L. Rev. 1393 (1985); Charles J. Tabb, The Scope of the Fresh Start in Bankruptcy: Collateral Conversions and the Dischargeability Debate, 59 Geo. Wash. L. Rev. 56 (1990). Scholars have questioned how well the bankruptcy law achieves its intended fresh start goal. See Katherine Porter & Dr. Deborah Thorne, The Failure of Bankruptcy's Fresh Start, 92 Cornell L. Rev. 67 (2006).

The primary justification for a bankruptcy law is not the fresh start, laudatory though that goal may be. Rather, the core function of bankruptcy is as a *collective creditors' remedy* that furthers the goals of efficiency and of distributive justice.

State law provides individual creditors with remedies to collect their debts from recalcitrant debtors: execution, garnishment, and so forth.[15] Under state collection law, creditors are able to invoke the power of the state to seize the assets of defaulting debtors in order to satisfy their claims. These state-law collection remedies focus on the dispute between one specific creditor and the debtor. As to the relative rights of creditors versus each other with respect to the debtor's assets, the central premise is that "first in time is first in right." In other words, the creditor who acts first to have the sheriff seize the debtor's assets will be paid first. Accordingly, state collection law is sometimes referred to as "the race of diligence," or "grab law."

"Grab law" works relatively well either when (1) the debtor is solvent, i.e., has enough assets to satisfy all of its creditors in full, or (2) when the debtor has only one creditor. The relative priority between creditors as to the debtor's property is not an important issue in either of those scenarios. When the debtor is insolvent, however, and has multiple creditors, state collection law fails to serve the interests of the creditor body as a whole. Under the race of diligence, the first creditors who grab the debtor's assets will be paid in full. Those who come later in time will get nothing. As a matter of distributive justice, this all-or-nothing result leaves much to be desired. Instead, the more equitable result when all creditors cannot be paid in full is for the creditors to *share* the debtor's property on a *pro rata* basis, with each creditor receiving partial payment for their claim. Each creditor thus also shares part of the loss from the debtor's collective default.[16]

The equitable solution of pro rata sharing through utilization of a collective remedy also is more efficient than state collection law.[17] In a race system, every creditor would have to spend time and money in an attempt to grab the debtor's assets before other creditors exhaust the insufficient asset pool. If a creditor did not join in the race, it would be certain to recover nothing. The other creditors would take everything. If a creditor did race, it might (or might not) prevail. The critical point, though, is that every creditor would have an incentive to race. Accordingly, viewed from the perspective of the body of creditors as a whole, some of the expenses of racing would be wasted, reducing the average recovery to creditors.

A simple example illustrates the point. Assume that the debtor has $1000 in assets, but $2000 in liabilities (for simplicity, assume four creditors each with claims of $500). Assume further that the expense for each creditor to invoke state collection procedures, i.e., of "racing," is $100. If each creditor races, then the net recovery for the

---

[15] See § 1.3.

[16] The importance of the "sharing" concept is examined in Thomas H. Jackson & Robert E. Scott, On the Nature of Bankruptcy: An Essay on Bankruptcy Sharing and the Creditors' Bargain, 75 Va. L. Rev. 155 (1989).

[17] See Thomas H. Jackson, Bankruptcy, Non–Bankruptcy Entitlements, and the Creditors' Bargain, 91 Yale L.J. 857 (1982).

creditors, *as a group*, will be only $\underline{\$600}$.[18] Thus, the average recovery per creditor will only be $150 ($600 divided by four). Although two of the creditors actually will be paid in full, minus their expenses, before the race no creditor could know whether it would be one of the two winners, or instead one of the two losers who would spend the collection costs and yet come up empty-handed. Viewed *ex ante*, then, each creditor may assume only a $\underline{\$150}$ projected recovery.

If, however, the four creditors could cooperate and agree not to race, they could save $300 as a group. How so? Acting collectively, the creditors would only have to spend the $100 in collection costs *once*—by the representative or agent acting on the behalf of the creditor group. A total of $\underline{\$900}$ would be available for distribution.[19] Each creditor would be paid $\underline{\$225}$. This collective solution thus increases the projected average recovery for each creditor. Acting rationally, then, the four creditors should agree in advance to work together and utilize a collective approach.

So why don't the creditors just do that voluntarily? Who needs a bankruptcy procedure? The problem is one of *compulsion*. Unless all four creditors are legally bound to the collective remedy, it would be possible for any one of the creditors to *renege* on the agreement and pursue collection individually. That reneging creditor then could recover its claim in full, and would be better off than with the partial payment it would get under the collective remedy. In the example above, that creditor would recover a net of $400 (the $500 on its claim, less the $100 in collection costs), as opposed to the $225 it would receive from the group process. The remaining three creditors then would be worse off than under a pure race system. Knowing that the possibility of a defector exists, each of the four creditors would again have an incentive to race, notwithstanding the agreement. The creditors as a group would be back to square one, with each spending $100 in collection costs.

The solution to this problem is to *bind* all four creditors to the collective remedy. If none of the creditors can renege and opt out of the collective remedy, then there is no reason for them to incur the collection costs personally. The creditor group will incur the costs only once, and split the remaining assets equally. The bankruptcy law offers just such a compulsory collective remedy. An "automatic stay" (a statutory injunction) blocks all individual creditor collection efforts. § 362. If an individual creditor tries to ignore the automatic stay and recover assets for itself, it will not work—the creditor will have to give the money back. §§ 362, 549. The bankruptcy trustee acts as the representative of the creditors in collecting the debtor's assets, liquidating them, and distributing the net proceeds to the creditors on a pro rata basis.

§ 1.2 Rehabilitation Cases

Liquidation of a debtor's assets through chapter 7, while both a just and efficient means for distributing those assets, may not always be the optimal solution for either the debtor or the creditors. A liquidation is necessarily limited to the distribution of the

---

[18] This calculation is: $1000 [debtor's assets] minus $400 [four "racing" creditors multiplied by $100 each in expenses] = $600.

[19] This calculation is: $1000 [debtor's assets] minus $100 [one collection cost multiplied by $100] = $900.

debtor's then-existing property. If the debtor, whether an individual or a business entity, has a positive future earning capacity, it may make more sense economically to permit the debtor to retain its property and pay its creditors out of those future earnings. As long as the present value of those payments exceeds the distribution that creditors would receive in an immediate chapter 7 liquidation, and assuming that the risk that debtor will default on the future payments is low, then the creditors as a group may be better off in a reorganization than in a liquidation. Again, though, absent some form of binding compulsion, such as a bankruptcy case, the risk of defectors undermining a collective agreement remains. But with such compulsion in place, all may benefit from capturing a going-concern surplus out of the debtor's future positive earnings.

The debtor also may fare better under a payment plan than in a straight liquidation. If the debtor is a business entity, then a reorganization or rehabilitation may help keep the business operating and preserve value for the residual owners. An individual debtor who proceeds under a rehabilitation plan may be able to keep more of her property, such as her home or the family farm, and preserve a better credit rating.

The Bankruptcy Code contains four chapters that offer some form of rehabilitation of the debtor rather than liquidation. For businesses, chapter 11 permits a reorganization of the enterprise. For individuals with regular income and less than a certain amount of debt,[20] chapter 13 allows the adjustment of their debts through a repayment plan of three to five years. Chapter 12 provides family farmers and, as of 2005, family fishermen, with a means of relief very similar to that provided by chapter 13. As with chapter 13, a debt limit is imposed in chapter 12.[21] Finally, chapter 9 authorizes the adjustment of the debts of a municipality.

In the 1980s and 1990s, some scholars questioned the wisdom of chapter 11, the business reorganization chapter.[22] Others rose to defend chapter 11.[23] The traditional

---

[20]   Originally, the chapter 13 debt ceiling was $100,000 in unsecured debts and $350,000 in secured debts. The Bankruptcy Reform Act of 1994 increased the ceilings to $250,000 in unsecured and $750,000 in secured debts. The debt ceiling is indexed to changes in the Consumer Price Index, with adjustments to occur automatically every three years. § 103(b)(1). The most recent indexing, as of April 1, 2013, raised the debt limits to $383,175 in unsecured and $1,149,525 in secured debts. § 109(e).

[21]   For family farmers, the debt limit was raised in 2005 and then indexed most recently in 2013 to $4,031,575, which encompasses all debts, secured and unsecured. § 101(18). For family fishermen, the debt ceiling is $1,868,200, again all-inclusive. § 101(19A). Both of those amounts are indexed, to adjust every three years, with April 1, 2016 the next pending adjustment. § 103(b)(1).

[22]   Those questioning the justifications for chapter 11 included Thomas H. Jackson, The Logic and Limits of Bankruptcy Law, ch. 9, "Reconsidering Reorganizations," 209–24 (1986); Barry E. Adler, Financial and Political Theories of American Corporate Bankruptcy, 45 Stan. L. Rev. 311 (1993); Douglas G. Baird, The Uneasy Case for Corporate Reorganizations, 15 J. Legal Stud. 127 (1986); Michael Bradley & Michael Rosenzweig, The Untenable Case for Chapter 11, 101 Yale L.J. 1043 (1992). Substantial revisions to the form of chapter 11 have been proposed as well. See Lucian A. Bebchuk, A New Approach to Corporate Reorganizations, 101 Harv. L. Rev. 775 (1988); Mark J. Roe, Bankruptcy and Debt: A New Model for Corporate Reorganizations, 83 Colum. L. Rev. 527 (1983).

[23]   Defenders of chapter 11 included Hon. Frank H. Easterbrook, Is Corporate Bankruptcy Efficient?, 27 J. Fin. Econ. 411 (1990); Donald R. Korobkin, The Unwarranted Case Against Corporate Reorganization: A Reply to Bradley and Rosenzweig, 78 Iowa L. Rev. 669 (1993); Lynn LoPucki, Strange Visions in a Strange World: A Reply to Professors Bradley and Rosenzweig, 91 Mich. L. Rev. 79 (1992); Charles J. Tabb, The Future of Chapter 11, 44 S.C. L. Rev. 791 (1993); Elizabeth Warren, The Untenable Case for the Repeal of Chapter 11, 102 Yale L.J. 437 (1992).

view supporting chapter 11 was expressed as follows in the legislative history to the 1978 Bankruptcy Code:

> The purpose of a business reorganization case, unlike a liquidation case, is to restructure a business's finances so that it may continue to operate, provide its employees with jobs, pay its creditors, and provide a return for its stockholders. The premise of a business reorganization is that assets that are used for production in the industry for which they were designed are more valuable than those same assets sold for scrap.[24]

In short, under the traditional view, chapter 11 rests on the notion "that a business is worth more alive than dead—i.e., it is worth more as a going concern than in a forced sale liquidation."[25] The Supreme Court has cited this policy justification with approval.[26] The pro-reorganization view also recognizes that a wide array of parties have a legitimate interest in the successful reorganization of a large company—creditors, stockholders, employees, and the community at large.

Those commentators who have questioned chapter 11 do so for several reasons. One is that however meritorious the theory might be, the reality is that chapter 11 has failed to achieve its stated goals at an acceptable cost.[27] Another criticism is that the premise that a going concern surplus can be reaped only in a reorganization is flawed; the same value, critics argue, sometimes could be achieved in a liquidation.[28] And in fact, today it has become a commonplace for chapter 11 reorganizations to proceed via a quick sale of all assets under § 363 rather than pursuant to a traditional drawn-out negotiated plan of reorganization.[29] But the sale alternative can never be more than that, an alternative; many cases still require extended restructuring under court supervision.[30] Furthermore, skeptics charge that considering goals other than pure value maximization and optimal asset deployment is an inappropriate use of bankruptcy policy. Finally, some view chapter 11 as a weak "second-best" political compromise that should be replaced with a free market contract-based structure.[31] Each of these charges has been challenged; the debate continues.[32] For now, both Congress and the Supreme Court appear to be satisfied with the traditional justification.

---

[24] H.R. Rep. No. 95–595, 95th Cong., 1st Sess., at 220 (1977).

[25] Tabb, supra note 23, at 804; see also Lynn M. LoPucki & William C. Whitford, Corporate Governance in the Bankruptcy Reorganization of Large, Publicly Held Companies, 141 U. Pa. L. Rev. 669, 758 (1993); Elizabeth Warren, Bankruptcy Policymaking in an Imperfect World, 92 Mich. L. Rev. 336 (1993).

[26] See United States v. Whiting Pools, Inc., 462 U.S. 198, 203 (1983).

[27] Bradley & Rosenzweig, supra note 22.

[28] Jackson, supra note 22; Baird, supra note 22.

[29] See Ralph Brubaker & Charles J. Tabb, Bankruptcy Reorganizations and the Troubling Legacy of Chrysler and GM, 2010 U. Ill. L. Rev. 1375, 1377–78 (2010). Chrysler went through bankruptcy in 41 days and General Motors in 39 days. See also § 5.17.

[30] Thus, for example, United Airlines went through chapter 11 successfully in just under three years.

[31] Adler, supra note 22.

[32] A useful early review of the debate and a critique of the reform proposals is found in David A. Skeel, Jr., Markets, Courts, and the Brave New World of Bankruptcy Theory, 1993 Wis. L. Rev. 465 (1993).

Whatever the theoretical arguments, the reality is that many financially distressed businesses do attempt to work out some form of restructuring with their creditors instead of simply liquidating. This restructuring can be and often is achieved outside of the bankruptcy court, through a workout agreement.[33] Perhaps the relevant question to ask in assessing the wisdom of chapter 11 is not whether reorganization per se is a good idea, for debtors and creditors seem to take that as a given, but rather why reorganization ever would need to take place *under court supervision*.[34]

The answer to that question follows from an understanding of why consensual out-of-court workouts fail. A primary reason that workouts do not succeed is that dissenting creditors cannot be bound to the restructuring agreement. A dissenting creditor is free to ignore the workout and try to collect more for itself. Thus, a dissenter may proceed with its own state law collection remedies against the debtor, such as levying against the debtor's assets. Seizing the debtor's assets obviously could impair the debtor's ability to continue in business and thereby would undermine the workout. Such collection efforts can be prevented outside of bankruptcy only by paying off the renegade creditor. In short, a "holdout problem" arises: even if a workout would be better for the creditors as a group, a holdout creditor can effectively extort more than its fair share from the debtor by threatening to levy on the debtor's assets and scuttle the whole reorganization. Knowing that such a possibility exists, all creditors naturally want to be the preferred holdout.

The solution to the holdout problem is twofold. First, dissenting creditors must be enjoined from exercising their state law collection remedies against the debtor. Second, the dissenters must be bound to the terms of the reorganization plan. In a word— compulsion is needed. Some type of court process is needed to implement these two remedies. When corporate reorganizations were first undertaken in earnest in the late nineteenth century to save the railroads, the means used was the equity receivership.[35] Today, the means of choice is chapter 11. A chapter 11 bankruptcy reorganization contains both a stay provision, § 362, and a rule binding dissenters to the terms of the plan agreed to by the bulk of creditors. § 1141(a). Even if chapter 11 were repealed, some mechanism that permitted business reorganizations using the two provisions just described likely would take the place of chapter 11.

Chapter 13, by comparison, is designed for the rehabilitation of the individual consumer debtor. The choice for such a debtor normally is whether to file chapter 7 or chapter 13. Unsecured creditors might prefer for a debtor to proceed under chapter 13 if they would be paid more over time under the chapter 13 repayment plan than in an immediate chapter 7 liquidation. However, creditors cannot compel a debtor to proceed under chapter 13; resort to chapter 13 is entirely optional with the debtor. § 303(a).

---

[33] See Stuart C. Gilson et al., Troubled Debt Restructurings: An Empirical Study of Private Reorganization of Firms in Default, 27 J. Fin. Econ. 315, 345 (1990) (estimating that half of all corporate restructuring occur out of court). See § 1.4.

[34] For a fuller discussion, see Tabb, supra note 23, at 804–07.

[35] See David A. Skeel, Jr., Debt's Dominion: A History of Bankruptcy Law in America, ch. 2, "Railroad Receivership and the Elite Reorganization Bar," 48–70 (2001).

From the debtor's perspective, chapter 13 might make sense in cases in which the debtor wants to retain his property.[36] In a chapter 7 liquidation, the debtor must surrender all of his nonexempt assets to the trustee to be sold, with distribution of the net proceeds to creditors; the debtor would get to keep only his exempt property. Furthermore, even exempt property that is subject to unavoidable liens might be lost to the secured creditor if adequate protection cannot be offered. In chapter 13, however, the debtor may keep all of his property—exempt or nonexempt, secured or unsecured—by proposing a repayment plan that meets the requirements of that chapter. Chapter 13 has proven to be an especially useful vehicle for debtors to retain property subject to valid liens. In a chapter 7 case, such property often would have to be turned over to the lienholder, unless the debtor can work out a reaffirmation agreement with the secured creditor. In crafting the original Bankruptcy Code in 1978, Congress expressed the view that a debtor who chooses chapter 13 will have a better credit rating than a debtor who elects the chapter 7 route, and that most debtors would prefer chapter 13 in order "to avoid the stigma attached to straight bankruptcy and to retain the pride attendant on being able to meet one's obligations."[37]

Congressional optimism as to the good intentions of debtors aside, the reality is that an individual debtor who has few current assets but some future earning capacity normally would prefer an immediate chapter 7 liquidation over a chapter 13 payment plan, so that she may keep the future earnings for herself, free from her creditors. Such a debtor has little to lose in giving up her existing property and much to gain from insulating her future earnings from creditors. In this common situation, the interests of the debtor and the creditors directly conflict.

In the 1978 Bankruptcy Code and for over a quarter century thereafter, Congress equivocated in resolving this conflict. The congressional hope always has been that debtors would opt for chapter 13 if feasible. Prior to 2005, Congress took a carrot[38] and stick[39] approach to "encourage" debtors to choose chapter 13 over chapter 7. Yet, Congress shirked from actually compelling individual debtors to proceed under a chapter 13 repayment plan, reasoning that such an approach smacked of involuntary servitude and would be unworkable as well.[40] Still, throughout that quarter century,

---

[36]   Some scholars argue that chapter 13 is almost never a prudent choice for a well-informed debtor. See, e.g., William C. Whitford, Has the Time Come to Repeal Chapter 13?, 65 Ind. L.J. 85 (1989).

[37]   H.R. Rep. No. 95–595, 95th Cong., 1st Sess., at 118 (1977).

[38]   One example of the inducement for a debtor to choose chapter 13 prior to 2005 was the so-called "superdischarge" under former § 1328(a), pursuant to which a debtor could discharge some types of debts in a chapter 13 repayment plan (such as fraud) that she could not discharge in chapter 7. In the 2005 amendments, Congress largely eliminated the superdischarge. Now, almost all of the discharge exceptions apply in chapter 13 as well as in chapter 7.

[39]   The most prominent stick Congress created to be used against debtors who seek to avoid paying creditors even when they have the ability to pay was the "substantial abuse" test of former § 707(b), enacted in 1984, which permitted a court to dismiss a chapter 7 case if it found that allowing the debtor to have relief under chapter 7 would be a substantial abuse. The clear intent was that such a debtor would then have to proceed under a chapter 13 repayment plan if he wanted bankruptcy relief. While courts looked to the "totality of the circumstances" to determine substantial abuse, a debtor's future payment capacity was found by the courts to be a significant factor in assessing that "totality." See, e.g., In re Green, 934 F.2d 568, 572–73 (4th Cir. 1991).

[40]   H.R. Rep. No. 95–595, 95th Cong., 1st Sess., at 120–21 (1977).

Congress repeatedly amended the bankruptcy law to favor creditors at the expense of debtors, and made the chapter 13 option less available and less attractive to debtors.[41]

Finally, in 2005, in the Bankruptcy Abuse Prevention and Consumer Protection Act,[42] Congress decided that if an individual consumer debtor has a sufficient projected future repayment capacity, such a debtor should be barred entirely from proceeding under chapter 7. The mechanism for removing such a debtor from chapter 7 is the "abuse" test of § 707(b),[43] which utilizes a complicated "means test" to ascertain presumptive abuse. § 707(b)(2). That test seeks to calculate a debtor's excess future income over allowable expenses, and if a debtor appears to be a so-called "can pay" debtor, with too much projected excess income, he is kicked out of chapter 7 unless he can demonstrate "special circumstances." In addition, even if a debtor is not a presumptive abuser based on the formulaic means test, he can be kicked out of chapter 7 if the facts show the debtor's bad faith or if the totality of the circumstances warrant dismissal. § 707(b)(3). Note that Congress still has not taken the final plunge and allowed creditors to file an involuntary chapter 13 case directly against individual debtors.[44] However, if a debtor fails the means test of § 707(b) and thus is disqualified from proceeding under chapter 7, if that debtor desires bankruptcy relief, "voluntarily" converting to chapter 13 is that debtor's only viable option.

Chapter 12 is a modified form of chapter 13 dressed up to help alleviate the plight of family farmers. Family farmers are permitted to keep their land if they make payments under a three-to-five year plan that complies with the requirements spelled out in the Code. §§ 1222, 1225. Chapter 12 was not a part of the Bankruptcy Code as enacted in 1978. Instead, chapter 12 was born in 1986, in response to a farm crisis.[45]

While a family farmer in theory could use either chapter 13 or chapter 11 to restructure his obligations, Congress believed that neither chapter adequately addressed the needs of family farmers.[46] So, a new chapter came into being, "to give family farmers facing bankruptcy a fighting chance to reorganize their debts and keep their land."[47] Chapter 12 has a higher debt limit than chapter 13.[48] Many of the legal

---

[41]   For example, Congress repeatedly added to the list of debts that were not dischargeable in chapter 13. Debtors also were now required to commit all of their "projected disposable income" to payments under the plan if the trustee or an unsecured creditor objects to the plan. § 1325(b)(1). This is sometimes called the "best efforts" test.

[42]   Pub. L. No. 109–8, 119 Stat. 23 (2005).

[43]   See § 2.15.

[44]   Curiously, and inconsistently, Congress did amend the law in 2005 to permit involuntary *chapter 11* cases to be filed against individual debtors with the same capacity to capture that debtor's future earnings that always before led Congress to shy away from involuntary chapter 13 cases. See 11 U.S.C. § 1115. See also Margaret Howard, Bankruptcy Bondage, 2009 U. Ill. L. Rev. 191.

[45]   Bankruptcy Judges, United States Trustees, and Family Farmer Bankruptcy Act of 1986, Pub. L. No. 99–554, 100 Stat. 3088 (1986).

[46]   The Joint Explanatory Statement of the Conference Committee that hammered out the final version of the 1986 bill elaborated:

> Most family farmers have too much debt to qualify as debtors under Chapter 13 and are thus limited to relief under Chapter 11. Unfortunately, family farmers have found Chapter 11 needlessly complicated, unduly time-consuming, inordinately expensive and, in too many cases, unworkable.

132 Cong. Rec. H8998 (daily ed. Oct. 2, 1986).

[47]   Id. at H8999.

hurdles that proved difficult for farmers to overcome in chapter 11 are absent from chapter 12. Originally chapter 12 was to terminate ("sunset") on October 1, 1993. The sunset date was later extended to October 1, 1998.[49] In 2005 it was made permanent under BAPCPA, and family fishermen were also made eligible debtors.[50]

B. ALTERNATIVES TO BANKRUPTCY

§ 1.3　　State Collection Law

a. *Introduction: General Principles*

The remedy of bankruptcy does not exist in a vacuum. One of the salient features of debt collection in the United States today is that bankruptcy coexists with a separate, well-developed state law system for debt collection. These state law procedures have evolved from roots in the common law.[51] Differences between the bankruptcy remedy and the remedies afforded by state law raise the possibility of forum shopping by creditors or debtors seeking to invoke the more favorable law.[52] As discussed above in § 1.1, bankruptcy and state collection law operate from diametrically opposed initial premises. Bankruptcy seeks to enhance the collective welfare of the entire *group* of creditors, using a presumption of inter-creditor equality as a starting point.

State collection law, conversely, hinges on the premise that "first in time is first in right." Its primary focus is on the rights of the particular, individual creditor, not on the group of creditors as a whole. As between creditors, the first to obtain an enforceable *in rem* claim or right against the debtor's assets usually will prevail in a "*priority*" dispute. This type of *in rem* claim or right is commonly referred to as a "*lien*."[53] A priority dispute arises when two or more non-debtor parties (usually either creditors of the debtor or purchasers of the debtor's assets) each assert a claim against the debtor's assets. If the debtor does not have sufficient assets to pay all the competing claimants in full, deciding which ones get paid first assumes paramount importance. A claimant at the end of the line may get nothing at all.

An important question that pervades the state law of collection is determining exactly *when* a creditor acquires a lien, for that date typically will fix the creditor's

---

[48]　Section 109(f) limits eligibility for chapter 12 to "family farmers." Under § 101(18), a family farmer is defined, in pertinent part, as an "individual or individual and spouse engaged in a farming operation whose aggregate debts do not exceed $4,031,575." For "family fishermen," who were added to those eligible to use chapter 12 in 2005, the debt limit as of the 2013 indexing is $1,868,200. § 101(19A). In chapter 13 the debt ceiling (as of 2013) is $383,175 in unsecured debts and $1,149,525 in secured debts. § 109(e). Before the 1994 Act, however, the difference in the debt ceilings in chapters 12 and 13 was much more dramatic, with a chapter 13 limit of $100,000 in unsecured debt and $350,000 in secured debt.

[49]　Pub. L. No. 103–65, 107 Stat. 311 (1993).

[50]　Pub. L. No. 109–8, 119 Stat. 23 (2005).

[51]　See Stefan A. Riesenfeld, Enforcement of Money Judgements in Early American History, 71 Mich. L. Rev. 691 (1973); Stefan A. Riesenfeld, Collection of Money Judgments in American Law—A Historical Inventory and Prospectus, 42 Iowa L. Rev. 155 (1957).

[52]　See generally Douglas G. Baird, Loss Distribution, Forum Shopping, and Bankruptcy: A Reply to Warren, 54 U. Chi. L. Rev. 815 (1987).

[53]　The Code defines a "lien" as a "charge against or interest in property to secure payment of a debt or performance of an obligation." § 101(37).

priority status to the debtor's property vis-à-vis competing third party claimants. Obtaining a lien also moves the creditor closer to the goal of realizing on its claim. For example, a lien may be enforced by sale of the encumbered property, with the net proceeds (after deducting the expenses of the sale) paid to the creditor in satisfaction of its claim.

These liens are normally acquired in the course of invoking judicial collection procedures, and are for that reason generically called *"judicial liens."*[54] A wide variety of judicial liens exist: execution liens, judgment liens, garnishment liens, attachment liens, and so forth. The creditor also may in some circumstances obtain a lien against the debtor's property through the operation of a state statute. These types of liens are called *"statutory liens."*[55] A common example is a mechanics and materialmens' lien, which gives a mechanic or a materialman a lien on the property worked on or supplied until paid.

Note that a creditor does not have to wait until payment problems develop to seek a lien against a debtor. With the debtor's agreement, the creditor may obtain a lien on the debtor's assets (the "collateral") at the outset of the credit relationship, or at any time thereafter. This consensual lien on collateral secures repayment of the debt, and thus the creditor is called a *"secured"* creditor. If the debtor does not pay, the secured creditor can get paid out of the collateral. If the debtor gives the creditor a lien on personal property, Article 9 of the Uniform Commercial Code governs. The creditor's lien is referred to as a *"security interest."* If the collateral is real property, the creditor has a mortgage or deed of trust.[56] These types of consensual liens, if properly *"perfected"* under state law (typically by recordation or possession), are normally enforced not only against the debtor, but also against subsequent third party claimants, as well as in bankruptcy. A secured creditor holding such a consensual lien often may be able to enforce its lien by "foreclosure," without having to go through the judicial procedures that an unsecured creditor must follow to collect. Consensual secured creditors, because of their priority and enforcement rights, stand on vastly superior footing to unsecured creditors in dealing with a debtor who does not or cannot voluntarily repay its debts in full.

An unsecured creditor, by definition, does not have collateral standing behind its claim. All that it has are the rights (1) to have a court decide that the debtor owes it money, by entry of a *"judgment"* in a lawsuit by the creditor seeking money, and (2) to invoke the power of the state to seize the nonexempt property of the debtor to satisfy that judgment if the debtor fails to pay voluntarily. A judgment in a court of law is not

---

[54] Judicial liens are given effect as secured claims in bankruptcy cases. The Code defines a "judicial lien" as a "lien obtained by judgment, levy, sequestration, or other legal or equitable process or proceeding." § 101(36).

[55] Statutory liens also are treated as secured claims in bankruptcy, unless avoided by the trustee under § 545. A "statutory lien" is defined in part by the Code as a "lien arising solely by force of a statute on specified circumstances or conditions." § 101(53).

[56] The Code refers to all types of a "lien created by an agreement" as a "security interest," § 101(51), including thereby real property mortgages as well as personal property security interests under Article 9. In Uniform Commercial Code lingo, however, a security interest is limited to "an interest in personal property or fixtures which secures payment or performance of an obligation," U.C.C. § 1–201(37), and thus excludes pure real property mortgages.

a court order directing the debtor to pay, in the sense of a "decree" of a court of equity. An equitable decree is directed personally to the affected party, and is enforceable through the exercise of the court's power of contempt. For example, a debtor who fails to heed a decree to pay alimony may be jailed for contempt, whereas a judgment debtor in a court of law who fails to pay a judgment usually may not be jailed. All that can happen is that the judgment debtor's property may be taken away by officers of the state and sold to pay off the judgment.

A money judgment in a court of law has three aspects. First, it is "*executable*," which is the technical term for the consequence just described, i.e., that the judgment gives the judgment creditor the right to use legal process to have the debtor's property seized and sold in order to satisfy the judgment. Second, a money judgment is "*lienable*," which means that a judgment creditor may use the judicial process to obtain a lien on property of the debtor to secure the payment of the judgment debt. Third, a judgment for money is "*actionable*," meaning that a judgment creditor may bring an action asserting the judgment itself as the basis for the lawsuit. This latter facet of a judgment may be important if the judgment creditor is seeking to enforce its judgment against property that the debtor owns in a state other than the one in which the judgment was entered. Unless the other state has a statute similar to the Uniform Enforcement of Foreign Judgments Act, which allows registration of the judgment of a sister state, the creditor must bring a new action in the second state. That second action will be predicated on the judgment entered in the first state, rather than the original underlying debt. All that the creditor must assert in the second action is the first judgment.

Before proceeding to the discussion of the various formal state procedures for collection of debts, a caveat is in order. The vast majority of debts are collected through nonjudicial means. Debtors make decisions about which debts to pay first, based on their own unique circumstances and their own balancing of the costs and benefits of paying one debt versus another. Creditors attempt to "persuade" debtors to pay their claim voluntarily, relieving the creditor of the need to go to court. The formal state judicial procedures serve as a backdrop to this whole process of balancing and persuasion, establishing the parameters of what the parties may do absent agreement. Limits on the informal collection process are established (1) by state tort law causes of action (e.g., abuse of process, defamation, invasion of privacy, intentional infliction of emotional distress),[57] and (2) by the federal Fair Debt Collection Practices Act, which was enacted in 1977 and became effective in March 1978.[58]

b. *Execution*

The primary formal legal means for the enforcement of a money judgment is through the process of *execution*. In a broader sense, the term "execution" is sometimes used to describe any and all means to enforce a money judgment, i.e., enforcing a judgment is by definition "execution." Technically, and as used here, execution has a less global meaning. Execution in this narrower sense comprehends the legal process

---

[57]   See Michael M. Greenfield, Coercive Collection Tactics—An Analysis of the Interests and the Remedies, 1972 Wash. U. L. Rev. 1 (1972).

[58]   15 U.S.C. § 1692. The FDCPA is title VIII, §§ 801–818, of the Consumer Credit Protection Act.

by which a creditor with a judgment causes the sheriff to seize and sell property in the hands of the debtor and apply the net proceeds against the creditor's judgment. In a few states execution is still known by its original common law name of "*fi fa*," which is a shorthand reference to the common law writ of "*fieri facias*," from which modern execution procedure is derived.

Execution procedure is statutory in virtually all states today, notwithstanding its origin in the common law writ of *fi fa*. The essentials of execution procedure are similar from state to state, although there are differences in some of the statutory specifics. The steps in execution are:

(1) **rendition** or **entry** of a final money judgment;

(2) **issuance** of the writ of execution;

(3) **delivery** of the writ of execution to the sheriff;

(4) **levy** on the debtor's property by the sheriff;

(5) **sale** of the property levied upon at execution sale; and

(6) **distribution** of the net proceeds of the sale to the judgment creditor.

Step One: Final Money Judgment. The first step for an unsecured creditor seeking to collect from a recalcitrant debtor is to obtain a final money judgment. Until the creditor gets such a judgment, it cannot seize the debtor's property to satisfy an outstanding debt. Nor does an unsecured creditor have any *in rem* claims against any of the debtor's assets, and attendant priority rights in that property, until it goes through the execution process. By contrast, upon the debtor's default, a "secured" creditor is allowed to seize the debtor's property (the "collateral" for the debt) and sell it at foreclosure, without having to waste the time and money to go through the courts. Furthermore, the secured creditor's property and priority rights in the collateral are established at the outset of the secured credit relationship.

There is some division in the states as to whether the creditor's right to invoke the execution process commences when the court itself *renders* judgment (the old common law rule), or when the clerk of the court formally *enters* the rendered judgment on the docket (the practice under Rule 58(a) of the Federal Rules of Civil Procedure). Most states now look to "entry" as the operative trigger. Note that an appeal does not preclude execution on the appealed judgment unless the appellant obtains a supersedeas bond. Some types of judgments, such as child support, are payable in installments, and execution may only proceed with regard to installments that have come due.

Step Two: Issuance of Writ. The clerk of the court in which the judgment is entered must *issue* a "*writ of execution*" on the request of the judgment creditor. This is a purely ministerial act. Note that in some states the formal writ of execution has been abolished, and the clerk of the court instead would simply issue a certified copy of the judgment to the judgment creditor. There is no difference in legal effect.

A writ of execution is a powerful legal instrument. It both commands and empowers the sheriff to seize enough nonexempt assets of the judgment debtor to satisfy the judgment. This process is known as *"levy."* In order to levy, the sheriff must assert dominion and control over the debtor's property. The writ further requires the sheriff to report back within a limited time period, typically ranging from 60 to 180 days (as specified by state statute). This deadline is known as the *"return date"* of the writ. After the return date passes, the sheriff no longer has any legal authority to execute on the judgment. The creditor then would have to obtain another writ of execution. The sheriff has no authority to seize exempt property, and will be liable to the debtor if he does.

The creditor may have to wait to request a writ of execution for a short initial period of time after the judgment is entered in order to permit the judgment debtor adequate time and opportunity to pursue various common post-judgment motions, such as a motion for a new trial or to amend the judgment. This waiting period ranges from 10 to 30 days, as specified by rule or statute.

The only other time constraint on the judgment creditor in seeking the issuance of a writ of execution is that the judgment must not be *"dormant."* At common law a judgment became dormant a year and a day after the court signed the judgment. In all states today the period for dormancy has been lengthened considerably by statute, with most periods in the range of five to ten years. In a number of states a creditor may postpone dormancy indefinitely if it seeks execution during the statutory period Conversely, other states shorten the dormancy period if no attempt is made by the judgment creditor to enforce the judgment within a shorter time period. Practices differ widely between states, and are governed entirely by rule or statute; the moral for a lawyer is to check the governing provision carefully in their own jurisdiction.

The creditor also may be able to avoid the bar of dormancy by *"revival"* of the original judgment or by *"renewal"* of that judgment. At common law revival occurred through a writ of *"scire facias"* ("scary face" to generations of law students) and renewal through the bringing of an action on the original judgment. The states have retained the concepts of revival and renewal, but have adopted widely varying rules on issues such as the manner in which revival or renewal may be invoked, the priority status of a judgment after revival or renewal, and the limits on how often and for how long those remedies may be available. Note that even with revival and renewal available, a judgment creditor may lose its priority status on the original judgment vis-à-vis other claimants if it allows that judgment to become dormant. Some states also limit the number of times a dormant judgment may be revived or renewed.

Assuming that the judgment is not dormant, the clerk has a duty to issue a writ of execution if requested to do so by the judgment creditor. The clerk enjoys no discretion on this matter. It is a purely ministerial act, and can be compelled by mandamus. Within the statutory life of the judgment there are no limits on the number of execution writs that the creditor may seek. The only restriction is that subsequent writs[59] may not be issued while another writ in favor of that creditor is outstanding.

---

[59]　The second writ is usually called an "alias" writ and all writs thereafter are known as "pluries" writs.

Thus, a diligent judgment creditor may, and should, try repeatedly to collect via the execution process.

Step Three: Delivery of Writ. Following the issuance of the writ of execution by the clerk, the writ is delivered to the sheriff so that its mandate may be carried out. Such delivery is a routine, ministerial matter, but in a minority of states delivery has important legal consequences. It is at that moment that an *"execution lien"* is created in favor of the judgment creditor against all of the debtor's nonexempt property subject to execution. The fixing of this execution lien gives the creditor priority rights in the encumbered property versus competing claimants whose rights in the property date from a later point in time. In effect, the judgment creditor at that moment becomes a "secured" creditor, with its "collateral" being all of the debtor's nonexempt property subject to execution.

However, the execution lien that arises in the minority of states upon the delivery of the writ of execution to the sheriff is still tentative or *contingent*. It may be lost, with attendant loss of priority and *in rem* rights. The creditor's execution lien at this point is said to be *"inchoate,"* meaning imperfect or unfinished. The obvious question, then, is how does this tentative, contingent, inchoate lien become fixed and perfected (i.e., *"choate"*[60])? The answer: the sheriff must **levy** pursuant to that writ, and must do so before the writ's return date. If levy does occur, the effective date of the judgment creditor's execution lien "relates back" to the earlier date when the writ was delivered to the sheriff. That is, the lien's operative date for priority purposes then would be the date of delivery of the writ to the sheriff.

However, if the return date passes without a levy, or if the sheriff returns the writ of execution *"nulla bona,"* meaning execution was attempted and no property was found, then the inchoate execution lien expires, and the judgment creditor loses any rights it had pursuant to that writ. The judgment creditor then is back to square one, and must try again to execute, obtaining the issuance of a new writ of execution, delivery, and so forth.

Even in the majority of states that do not date the execution lien from the date of delivery of the writ to the sheriff, delivery is still a necessary and important step in the execution process. The reason is that the sheriff cannot levy until he has the writ in his possession.

Step Four: Levy and return. The key step in the execution process is levy. *"Levy"* is the sheriff's seizure of the debtor's non-exempt property in order to satisfy a judgment. To levy, the sheriff must assert dominion and control over the subject property. Furthermore, as noted above, this levy must occur before the *"return date"* of the writ (normally somewhere from 60 to 180 days). In other words, the sheriff's legal power to levy only exists during the life of that particular writ of execution. If the writ

---

[60] A "choate" lien is one as to which nothing more needs to be done to make it enforceable, as contrasted to an "inchoate" lien. Normally choateness requires that the identity of the lienor, the property subject to the lien, and the amount of the lien are all established. In execution, the sheriff's levy fixes the identity of the property subject to the lien. Linguistically, "choate" is an improper backward formulation from "inchoate," see Bryan A. Garner, A Dictionary of Modern Legal Usage 112 (1987), but is commonly used.

expires, then the judgment creditor would have to get a new writ issued. Until a sheriff actually levies on the debtor's property, the judgment creditor really has made no progress in enforcing its judgment. Once levy occurs, however, that creditor has something tangible and of value that can be sold to help satisfy its judgment.

The judgment creditor often plays an active and cooperative role in the execution process. In particular, a diligent judgment creditor may engage in post-judgment discovery in an attempt to find particular assets of the debtor subject to execution. Once nonexempt assets are discovered, the judgment creditor then can give specific instructions to the sheriff to facilitate the chances of a successful levy. All states have extensive rules governing and authorizing such supplementary discovery proceedings in aid of execution.

The legal effect of the sheriff's levy is to bring the seized property "*in custodia legis,*" i.e., in the custody of the law. In a majority of states, the judgment creditor's *execution lien* arises at the instant of the levy. That lien applies to the property actually seized by the sheriff by the levy. Thus, levy not only captures property of the debtor that can be used to pay off the judgment, but it also gives the judgment creditor important *in rem* and priority rights good against the debtor and the world. In minority states, as noted earlier, the "inchoate" execution lien becomes "choate" upon levy (but remember, the operative date of the lien then relates back to the time of delivery of the writ to the sheriff).

The sheriff must "make return" to the issuing court on the writ of execution by the return date, either announcing a levy or a *nulla bona* return. If the latter, the creditor will have to obtain another writ of execution.

A sheriff has no authority to levy on "*exempt*" property. All states allow an individual debtor to retain some of his property for himself and his family, even if his general unsecured creditors are not paid. Exemption laws are based on notions of fundamental decency and also practicality. As a society, we do not want debtors and their families to be thrown in the street, homeless and penniless and without food and clothing. The state then would have to step in and care for the debtor as a ward of the state. Furthermore, it makes sense for a debtor to be allowed to retain the means to make a living and thereby be a more productive member of society. A farmer who lost his tractor would have a hard time farming.[61] The theory sounds good; however, the reality is that exemption laws as enacted often depart substantially from what a prudential theory would dictate, and vary widely between states. Some are exceedingly (overly?) generous, while others offer debtors little.

In practice, the existence of exemption laws and the prohibition against a sheriff levying on exempt property make it more difficult for a judgment creditor to execute

---

[61] Note, though, that exemption laws do not stop seizure of exempt property by a *secured* creditor. Thus, if a farmer buys a tractor from John Deere on credit and grants Deere a security interest in that tractor, if the debtor does not pay, Deere could still repossess and sell the tractor, any exemption laws notwithstanding. The debtor's initial grant of the security interest in the tractor is effectively a *waiver* of any exemption rights. Furthermore, the secured creditor effectively enabled the debtor to buy the property in the first place, so it is not considered unfair to allow the creditor to seize that property. The exemption law would protect the tractor from execution levy by any other creditor, however.

successfully. The sheriff would be liable to the debtor if he levies on exempt property, perhaps even for multiple damages. Thus, a judgment creditor may need to get a court order that certain of the debtor's property is not exempt and directing the debtor to turn over that property to the sheriff before the sheriff will levy on disputed property. Alternatively, a judgment creditor may offer to indemnify the sheriff against any liability the sheriff would face for wrongful levy.

Step Five: Sale. If the sheriff has made a levy, the next step of the execution process is the *sale* of the levied property by the sheriff. Execution sales are notorious for bringing very low prices. This is a serious problem, because the debtor loses the property upon the execution sale and yet only receives a credit against the outstanding judgment in the amount of the net sale price.

This sale should proceed without undue delay after the sheriff levies on the property. If the judgment creditor instructs the sheriff to delay the sale, the creditor's execution lien may become "dormant" during the period of delay. The practical ramification of this form of dormancy is that the creditor loses its priority rights vis-à-vis competing claimants whose rights to the property arise during the dormancy period. Assuming that no dormancy occurs, the sale will be scheduled and conducted in accordance with statutory directives.

As noted, a persistent problem with execution sales is that the sale price may be outrageously low compared to the probable value of the property. Most execution sales are poorly attended, and competitive bidding is lacking. A common scenario is for the judgment creditor to bid in the amount of the judgment, even if that amount is substantially less than the fair market value of the property. One reason for this problem is that the purchaser at an execution sale is not protected against latent defects in the debtor's title; instead, the purchaser only gets whatever title the debtor had. No warranties of title run to the purchaser. If the title proves defective, the majority view is that the execution purchaser is not entitled to a return of the purchase price paid. The disappointed purchaser's only recourse is to go against the judgment debtor. A few states, however, do permit the purchaser to recover the purchase price paid if the title fails.

States have tried a variety of means to counter low execution sale prices. One is the use of "appraisal" statutes, in which the property to be sold is appraised before the sale. This appraised value then is either treated (1) as the minimum amount that must be credited against the judgment, no matter what the actual sale price, or (2) as an "upset price," meaning that the sale will be invalid if it does not bring a certain percentage of the appraised value.

Another means of redress is an action brought by the debtor to "set aside" the sale. This a largely toothless remedy, however, since the rule is that the sale will not be set aside in equity based on "mere inadequacy" of the sale price. Either procedural irregularities in connection with the sale must be shown as well, or the price inadequacy must be so extreme as to "shock the conscience." It has been noted "that judges' consciences are not easily shocked."[62]

Other states allow "redemption" rights as a way to counter the low sale price problem. A redemption right is a statutory right to purchase the property sold at execution within a specified time period, usually at the purchase price. In essence, redemption is a right of first refusal. The judgment debtor is given the primary right to redeem. In some states, if the debtor fails to exercise the right, other parties, particularly creditors holding junior liens against the property that would be cut off by the sale, have a subsidiary redemption right. Redemption statutes, however, may do more harm than good, as they often further depress execution sales prices, because the execution purchaser will not be able to take good title to the property until the redemption period expires.

An issue in execution sales is whether a sale at a very low price relative to the fair market value of the property can be set aside as a fraudulent transfer, if the sale occurs at a time when the judgment debtor is insolvent. Historically, states had not permitted such attacks, but in the 1980s and 1990s a series of decisions raised the possibility of such an attack. In 1994, however, in a case involving the foreclosure sale of real property under a deed of trust, the United States Supreme Court held that fraudulent transfer law is not a legitimate means of upsetting the foreclosure if that foreclosure complied with state law procedural requirements.[63] The reasoning of that case should apply to execution sales as well. Thus, as long as proper *procedures* are followed, an execution sale should be safe from fraudulent transfer attack, no matter how low the sale price.

Step Six: Distribution. After the execution sale has been completed, the proceeds of the sale are distributed. First the costs and expenses of the sale itself must be paid out of the sale proceeds. The judgment creditor is then paid next, up to the amount of the judgment. What if there are other liens on the property sold at the execution sale? Typically, liens *senior* to the judgment creditor's execution lien are not adversely affected by the sale. Instead, those liens follow the property into the hands of the execution purchaser, although in some states the senior lienors are paid out of the sale proceeds before the judgment creditor is paid. Liens *junior* to the execution creditor, by comparison, are cut off by the sale without compensation. Any proceeds remaining after payment of sales expenses, senior creditors, and the judgment creditor are paid to the judgment debtor.

A word on priority disputes. One of the most important issues that may arise in connection with execution liens is determining who has priority as between competing claimants for the same property of the debtor. Thus, for example, two execution lien creditors may be seeking priority in the same property. Or an execution lien creditor may be competing with a purchaser of the debtor's property. Or an Article 9 secured creditor may assert a right in property of the debtor in competition with an execution lien creditor. The key to resolving all of these priority disputes is to ascertain the

---

[62]   Charles J. Tabb & Ralph Brubaker, Bankruptcy Law: Principles, Policies, and Practice 17 (3d ed. 2010).

[63]   BFP v. Resolution Trust Corp., 511 U.S. 531 (1994). See also § 6.41.

precise point in time when each contestant's rights are deemed to arise for priority purposes. Then, whoever is "first in time" wins the priority dispute.

For the execution lien creditor, the majority rule is that its priority rights arise and are fixed at the moment the sheriff levies on the debtor's property. In a minority of states, recall that the execution lien creditor's priority rights date earlier, at the time the writ of execution is delivered to the sheriff, assuming that a levy is timely made. So, for two competing execution lien creditors, resolving a priority dispute usually turns simply on who is first to levy (majority) or obtain delivery of their writ (minority).

If the competing claimant is an Article 9 secured creditor, the key point in time is when that secured creditor "perfects" its security interest under Article 9. Perfection requires some form of public notice, usually the filing of a "financing statement" in a public office. An execution lien creditor will enjoy priority against an "unperfected" secured creditor, but would lose to a secured creditor who had already perfected before the execution lien arose. U.C.C. § 9–317(a)(2)(A). Thus, in most states, the question will be whether the judgment creditor obtained levy before the secured creditor perfected.

Finally, a purchaser of property from the debtor takes whatever rights the debtor had at the time of the sale. Thus, if the debtor's property is already subject to an execution lien at the time of the sale, then the execution lien creditor would have priority over the purchaser. The purchaser would take subject to the lien, meaning that the execution lien creditor could complete the execution process by sale and distribution. In majority states, which require levy for an execution lien to arise, this result is fair, because by definition the debtor would no longer have dominion and control over the property that the sheriff had seized. All the purchaser would need to do to protect itself is ask to see the property.

c. *Judgment Liens*

Another important component of the collection process under state law is the "*judgment lien.*" A judgment lien is an encumbrance binding some of the property of the judgment debtor and giving the judgment creditor the right to have that property sold to satisfy the judgment. In most jurisdictions a judgment lien operates only against the debtor's real property.

The judgment lien is a useful anachronism. It derived from the common law writ of "*elegit,*" which gave the judgment creditor a lien for a term of years on half of the debtor's real property. The judgment was paid out of the rents and profits of the land during the judicially established term. Although the writ of elegit has disappeared, the vestigial judgment lien still survives in statutory form.

Separate and distinct from the execution lien, the judgment lien possesses certain characteristics that provide a judgment creditor with a helpful remedy against the debtor. The judgment lien may enhance the creditor's rank in a priority dispute with competing creditors, in two respects: (1) it may attach at an earlier point in time than an execution lien (because the execution lien must wait for a sheriff's levy), and (2) a judgment lien attaches automatically to after-acquired property of the judgment debtor.

Creation of a judgment lien is simple. In many states the manner of creation differs depending on whether or not the affected land of the debtor is located in the *same county* in which the judgment was obtained. For real property that *is* in the county where the judgment was docketed, the statutes of a majority of states fix a judgment lien on that real property at the instant the judgment is *docketed* by the clerk of the court.[64] In such a situation, the judgment creditor does not have to do anything to obtain the fixing of the judgment lien. Thus, the creditor's priority status as to in-county land automatically will date from the moment of docketing. In a small handful of states, the judgment lien arises even earlier for in-county land, at the time the judgment is rendered by the court.

In a growing but still minority number of jurisdictions, however, the judgment lien is not created at the time of docketing. Instead, in those states the judgment lien does not arise until the judgment creditor files a notice of the judgment in the *real estate records* for the county in which the land is located.[65] This developing rule is designed to protect third parties who might deal with the land by affording them a meaningful opportunity to learn of the judgment lien's existence before they act to their detriment. Under the majority rule, which dates the lien from docketing, third parties cannot realistically protect themselves. They would have the near-impossible burden of checking the judgment dockets as well as the real estate records in order to ascertain the state of the debtor's title.

For the debtor's real property located outside of the county in which the judgment is entered, the almost universal rule is that the judgment lien is not created until the judgment creditor files a notice in the real estate records of that county. Otherwise third parties who deal with the debtor would have the truly impossible burden of checking the judgment dockets for the entire state to find any judgment liens.

If the judgment debtor has real property located in *another state*, two possible avenues are open to the judgment creditor, depending on the jurisdiction. If the state has adopted the Uniform Enforcement of Foreign Judgments Act, the creditor may simply *register* the original judgment in the second state, with that registration having the force of a judgment in State 2. The judgment lien then is created in the same manner as for any other judgment (by filing a notice in the real estate records). If, however, the other state does not have the UEFJA, then the creditor must file a *new*

---

[64] New York is the most prominent example of the majority view, which dates the judgment lien from docketing:

> McKinney's CPLR § 5203. Priorities and liens upon real property. (a) Priority and lien on docketing judgment.

> No transfer of an interest of the judgment debtor in real property, against which property a money judgment may be enforced, is effective against the judgment creditor either from the time of the docketing of the judgment with the clerk of the county in which the property is located until ten years after filing of the judgment-roll, or from the time of the filing with such clerk of a notice of levy pursuant to an execution until the execution is returned.

[65] California is a leading example of this emerging minority approach, which dates a judgment lien only from the time of recordation:

> CCCP § 697.310. Creation and duration of judgment lien on real property generally

> (a) Except as otherwise provided by statute, a judgment lien on real property is created under this section by recording an abstract of a money judgment with the county recorder.

lawsuit in State 2, based on the judgment in State 1. Recall that one attribute of a money judgment is that it is "actionable." The creditor then will get a judgment lien on real property located in State 2 based on the State 2 judgment.

A judgment lien is said to be a *"general"* lien. This vague term means that the judgment creditor does not actually have an estate or interest as such in any specific real property of the debtor. Rather, what the judgment creditor has is a right against all of the debtor's real property subject to the lien, to have that property sold to satisfy the judgment. That right is persistent, however: if the judgment debtor sells the property subject to the creditor's judgment lien, the judgment lien follows the real estate into the hands of the purchaser. The practical import is that the judgment creditor would still have the right to have the encumbered property sold, even in the hands of the third-party purchaser. This right underscores the importance of the notice to third parties in conjunction with the creation of the judgment lien, and explains the trend towards requiring registration in the real estate records for all judgment liens. The judgment lien does not attach, however, to the proceeds of the sale in the hands of the judgment debtor. Of course, the creditor would still be free to attempt to reach those proceeds through the execution process.

What property is subject to a judgment lien? Statutes govern this question. Recall that an execution lien can reach any non-exempt property upon which the sheriff actually levies. The judgment lien is fundamentally different. Reflecting its historical origins in the writ of elegit, the judgment lien reaches *only real property* in a majority of states, whereas an execution lien can reach real and personal property. In a few states, though, a judgment lien can reach personal property as well.

Note also that what is required of the judgment creditor to fix a judgment lien on specific property of the debtor's is radically different than for an execution lien. Actually levying on the property is unnecessary. Instead, the judgment lien will attach to the debtor's real property that is located in a county in which the necessary action has been taken, *viz.*, either docketing the judgment or filing a notice of the judgment in the real estate records.

Exempt property normally is free from the clutches of a judgment lien. Thus, for example, the debtor's homestead will not be encumbered by a subsequent judgment lien. However, if the property later loses its homestead character during the life of the judgment lien, the lien will attach at that later time.

Perhaps the most important aspect of the judgment lien is that it reaches *after-acquired* property of the debtor during the life of the judgment lien. The life of a judgment lien, specified by statute, normally runs between five and ten years. To illustrate, assume that a debtor does not own any property in the county in which a judgment is rendered (X County, for simplicity's sake) at the time the judgment is entered. Five years later, the debtor inherits real property in X County, without having yet paid the outstanding judgment. Without the creditor having to do anything new,[66]

---

[66]   This assertion assumes that the requisite action to perfect a judgment lien has been taken, be it the docketing of the judgment (which would have been done by the clerk of the court) or, in states where required, filing a notice of the judgment in the real estate records.

the creditor will obtain a judgment lien on the debtor's newly inherited real property in X County at the instant the debtor acquires that interest. To acquire an execution lien, by contrast, the sheriff must actually levy on specific property of the debtor pursuant to the writ of execution. For land outside of the county in which the judgment was obtained, the creditor still can take advantage of the after-acquired feature, but must have filed or must now file a notice of judgment in the real estate records of that county.

A judgment lien also attaches to subsequent *increases in the value* of property subject to the lien. This rule applies whether the increase is due solely to market conditions or due to the making of improvements on the land. This feature of the judgment lien applies even if the property is in the hands of a third party successor to the debtor's title.

The *priority* status of a judgment lien often is critical, and often is one of the most important benefits of the judgment lien for the judgment creditor. The priority ranking of the judgment lien dates from the instant the lien is created, which can be quite early (and certainly earlier than for an execution lien). Recall that for land in the county where the judgment is entered, a judgment lien arises either when the judgment is docketed (majority rule) or when the creditor files a notice in the real estate records (minority rule), depending on the state. For land outside the county, a real estate records filing is required. As against most third parties, either purchasers or lienholders, the priority rule is the familiar one that "first in time" wins. In other words, a judgment lien would prevail over a subsequent purchaser, mortgagee, or judgment lienholder. The only important exception is for a "purchase-money" mortgagee, who is a creditor that loaned the very money used by the landholder to buy or improve the subject property.

The priority rules change a bit with regard to after-acquired property. Assume, for example, that Creditor 1 and Creditor 2 each obtain a judgment against the debtor in X County, with Creditor 1 obtaining its judgment before Creditor 2, and that both creditors take all steps necessary to create a judgment lien (docketing or filing a notice). However, assume that the debtor does not own any real property in X County at the time either of those judgments is entered or the formal lien creation steps are taken. Subsequently, the debtor acquires real estate in X County, during the life of the judgments. The majority rule is that the judgment liens of Creditor 1 and Creditor 2 are of equal rank. The theory supporting that result is that neither creditor had a judgment lien until the debtor acquired an interest in real estate in X County, and accordingly both creditors acquired their lien at the exact same instant, namely the instant the debtor acquired the property. Under the majority rule, this equal ranking is not disturbed even if one of the creditors proceeds first to enforce its judgment lien. Under a small minority view, even if the liens as to the after-acquired property were initially of equal rank, priority will be given to the creditor who enforces its lien first.

A judgment lien may be *enforced* by execution or, in some states, simply by a direct foreclosure action. Under this latter option, the judgment creditor files a lawsuit requesting foreclosure of its judgment lien, and the court orders the sheriff to conduct the foreclosure sale.

Unlike an execution lien, which requires the creditor to proceed with dispatch to enforce the lien by sale, a judgment lien will not become dormant if not enforced promptly. In other words, the judgment lien creditor will not lose its priority as to the subject property if it delays enforcement.

A judgment lien will only terminate if one of three events occurs: (1) the underlying judgment is satisfied; (2) the judgment creditor files a release of lien, or (3) the statutory limitation period on the life of the judgment lien expires. Even if the judgment debtor files bankruptcy, the lien will be enforceable as a secured claim in the bankruptcy case. If the judgment debtor dies, the lien still persists against the property.

d. *Garnishment*

Garnishment allows a judgment creditor to reach property of the judgment debtor in the hands of a *third party*, providing an important supplement to the execution process. Garnishment most often is utilized either (1) to seize a debtor's bank account or (2) to place a charge against the debtor's future wages. A garnishment action may take place after the entry of judgment or prior to judgment, as a provisional remedy conceptually linked to attachment. The discussion in this section will focus on the use of garnishment as a post-judgment collection device.

A garnishment action is ancillary to the main action for the collection of the debt. The garnishment action is primarily between the judgment creditor, known as the "*garnishor,*" and the third party claimed to hold property of or owe a debt to the debtor, known as the "*garnishee.*" For example, if a creditor attempts to garnish a debtor's bank account, the bank would be the garnishee; in a wage garnishment, the employer who owes wages to the debtor would be the garnishee. The judgment debtor typically is not even a party to the garnishment, although intervention by the debtor may be allowed in some states.

Garnishment procedure proceeds as follows. The garnishor-creditor starts the process by filing an affidavit alleging that the garnishee holds property of or owes a debt to the debtor. In post-judgment garnishment, the garnishor also would allege that it had an unsatisfied judgment against the debtor. In some states, the garnishor also has to file a bond, especially in a pre-judgment garnishment. The clerk of the court then issues a writ of garnishment, or "summons," which is then delivered to the sheriff, who must serve the summons on the garnishee. A few jurisdictions also require the summons to be served on the debtor. Those jurisdictions that require service on the debtor usually also allow the debtor to file a bond of its own and replevy the garnished property. The garnishee then must answer.

The garnishee may raise several possible defenses in its answer: (1) deny that it holds property of or owes a debt to the debtor; (2) admit that it owes the debtor a debt or holds the debtor's property, but nevertheless deny liability on the ground that it has defenses or a right of setoff against the debtor; or (3) admit that it owes a debt to the debtor or holds the debtor's property, but deny liability on the ground that the debt or property is exempt as to the debtor. If the garnishee denies liability, the ball is back in the garnishor's court, who may either "controvert" the answer and file a "traverse," or give up and let the garnishment lapse. If the garnishor controverts the garnishee's answer denying liability, a trial is held. The issue is whether the garnishee holds property of or owes a non-exempt debt to the debtor.

Garnishment is premised on a *subrogation* theory. In other words, the garnishor-creditor "steps into the debtor's shoes" vis-à-vis the garnishee. The garnishor thus is "subrogated" to the rights of the judgment debtor against the garnishee as of the time the writ of garnishment is served. A corollary of this subrogation principle is that the garnishor acquires no greater rights against the garnishee than the debtor had. A simple test of the garnishee's liability to the garnishor is to ask whether the debtor could successfully maintain suit against the garnishee for the debt or property. If so, then the garnishor enjoys the same rights as the debtor; if not, the garnishor loses.

This subrogation principle suggests some timing restrictions on garnishment. The critical measuring point in time is the instant the writ or summons of garnishment is *served* on the garnishee. On service, a *"garnishment lien"* is created against any nonexempt debt the garnishee owes to the debtor and against any of the debtor's nonexempt property that the garnishee holds. In essence, the garnishor-creditor captures sums due from the garnishee to the debtor at that point in time, up to the amount of the judgment. The garnishee would be liable to the garnishor if it failed to hold such captured sums for the garnishor's benefit.

Taking a snapshot of the garnishee's liability to the debtor at the moment the writ is served limits the garnishor's recovery in several circumstances. First, to the extent the debt is reduced or the debtor's property returned *before* the writ is served, nothing is captured by the garnishor. For example, if a garnishee-bank honored a check drawn on a debtor's bank account even a minute before the sheriff served the writ of garnishment, the garnishment would not capture the amount of the check. A bank account is just a debt owing from the bank to the depositor. Once a check is honored, the amount owed by the bank to the depositor is correspondingly reduced.

Second, the garnishment might not capture debts from the garnishee to the debtor that arise *after* service of the writ. For example, continuing with the bank account situation, if a deposit is made a minute after the garnishment writ is served, that subsequent deposit might not be subject to the garnishment. The states are divided on this question. Some do allow a garnishment to attach to post-service debts, but many others do not. Even in states where the garnishment lien reaches post-service property or debts, that reach is limited, terminating at a specific point in time (typically either (1) when the garnishee answers, or (2) at the latest, at the time of trial in the garnishment action.

A particularly important practical consequence of the subsequent debt limitation is that unearned wages are not garnishable, absent special statutory treatment. The rationale is that at the time the writ of garnishment is served, the employer-garnishee does not yet owe a debt to the judgment debtor for wages that have not yet been earned. This restriction obviously would limit the utility of wage garnishment greatly, for the creditor-garnishor would have to obtain garnishments every single pay period. Also, once the wages have been actually paid over to the debtor-employee, the garnishment would not work, because the employer would no longer owe a debt to the debtor for those wages. Accordingly, to facilitate wage garnishment, most states have passed special "wage garnishment" or "wage deduction" laws, which allow the judgment creditor to reach future wages in the manner and extent specified in the statute. These special wage garnishment laws enable the judgment creditor to garnish all future wages by service of a single garnishment summons on the debtor's employer, thereby greatly easing the creditor's task. Thereafter, until the judgment is satisfied, in each pay period the employer will pay a portion of the debtor's wages directly to the judgment creditor.

Wage garnishments are carefully limited by both federal and state law, in order to protect the debtor and his or her family from undue hardship. Importantly, these laws place a ceiling on the amount of wages that may be garnished. Federal law limits the amount of wages that can be garnished to the lesser of (1) 25% of the debtor's disposable earnings or (2) the amount by which the debtor's disposable earnings exceed 30 times the federal minimum wage.[67] An exception is made for support orders, where up to 65% of disposable earnings may be garnished.[68] The federal law also prohibits employers from firing an employee solely because of a garnishment.[69]

State wage garnishment laws also impose limits on garnishment amounts. While those state laws may not be less protective of debtors than the federal law, because of the Supremacy Clause, they may afford debtors *more* protection. The federal statute expressly allows states to enact more protective garnishment laws.[70] So, for example, where the federal law permits garnishing up to the lesser of 25% of disposable wages or the amount disposable earnings exceed 30 times the minimum wage, a state could enact a law that limited garnishment to the lesser of 15% of disposable earnings or the amount disposable earnings exceed 45 times the minimum wage.[71] In that situation, a judgment creditor would only be able to garnish up to the more restrictive state law ceilings.

The garnishee has clearly defined rights and duties. With respect to the garnishor, the garnishee's paramount duty is to turn over to the garnishor any property or debt that is subject to the garnishment lien, up to the amount of the judgment. If the garnishee fails to do so, it will be personally liable to the judgment creditor to the extent of its default.

The garnishee's rights and duties as regards the judgment debtor also may be affected by the garnishment. If the garnishee is compelled to turn money or property over to the garnishor, then the normal result is that the garnishee's liability to the debtor is reduced in a like amount. In other words, the basic rule is that the garnishee is not subject to double liability. This is fair to the debtor, even though the debtor did not participate in the garnishment action, because the debtor's liability to the judgment creditor-garnishor on the judgment is reduced in the amount that the garnishee paid. For example, assume that the debtor has $800 in a bank account at Bank, and owes $1,500 on a judgment to Creditor. Creditor garnishes the account, and

---

[67] Consumer Credit Protection Act, Pub. L. No. 90–321, tit. III, § 303(a), 82 Stat. 146 (codified at 15 U.S.C. § 1673(a)).

[68] Id. § 303(b); 15 U.S.C. § 1673(b).

[69] Id. § 304; 15 U.S.C. § 1674.

[70] Id. § 307; 15 U.S.C. § 1677.

[71] See 735 ILCS 5/12–803 (Illinois).

Bank pays the $800 to Creditor. The result is: Bank owes nothing to Debtor on the bank account, and Debtor owes $700 to Creditor.

An exception to this rule is if the garnishee has a statutory duty either to give notice to the debtor of the pendency of the garnishment action or to assert known exemptions of the debtor, but fails to do so. Again, this exception makes sense, because the garnishee's failure has potentially prejudiced the debtor.

While a debtor may be bound to the outcome of a garnishment action in which the garnishee ends up paying over money or property to the judgment creditor, as explained above, the opposite is not necessarily true. A judgment in the garnishment action that the garnishee is not liable to the garnishor, on the ground that the garnishee is not liable to the debtor, will not bar a subsequent suit by the debtor against the garnishee. The reason is that judgments only bind parties, and the debtor usually will not be a party to the garnishment action. The only exception would be if the debtor intervened and became a party to the garnishment action.

Similarly, a third party who is not a party to the garnishment action will not be bound by a judgment in that action. Therefore, a third party who claims a superior right to the property or debt garnished could assert a claim against the garnishee in a later action, even if the garnishee is compelled to pay the garnishor. To protect itself against such possible double liability, the garnishee should interplead in the garnishment action any third party that may be asserting a competing claim to the garnished property, so that all parties will be bound to the garnishment judgment.

e.   *Attachment and Other Prejudgment Remedies*

Winning a lawsuit is small consolation if the creditor discovers that the debtor has become judgment-proof while the case was pending. The normal post-judgment remedies of execution and garnishment do little good if there are no assets left for the sheriff to seize. Accordingly, a creditor who has filed a lawsuit and who fears that the debtor may dissipate his assets during the case may seek to take advantage of a provisional pre-judgment remedy. These remedies serve the function of securing any possible judgment that the creditor might later win by preventing the debtor from dissipating his property during the case. They are said to be *"provisional"* remedies because they only have continuing effect if the creditor ultimately prevails in the lawsuit. Common examples of provisional prejudgment remedies include attachment, garnishment, replevin (or sequestration), and *lis pendens*. In rare cases a creditor may be able to obtain an equitable decree enjoining the debtor from transferring assets, or appointing a receiver pendente lite to take over the debtor's property during the case.

It bears emphasis that the utilization of prejudgment remedies remains the exception, and not the rule. The direct effect of a prejudgment remedy is to tie up the debtor's property during the pendency of the lawsuit and deprive the debtor of the free use of that property, all before a court of law has ruled that the debtor owes anything to the creditor. In the face of a strong legal tradition favoring a property owner's right to use and alienate its property, compelling justifications must be put forth to support the imposition of restraints on those rights.

Virtually all of the prejudgment remedies currently in use have roots in the common law. However, today those remedies are almost entirely creatures of *statute*. The creditor must strictly comply with the statutory provisions, which define clear boundaries on the availability of any particular provisional remedy. In addition, a series of Supreme Court cases decided from 1969 to 1975 imposed significant constitutional procedural due process limits on pre-judgment remedies.[72]

In *attachment*, the sheriff, acting pursuant to a writ of attachment, levies upon the debtor's nonexempt property, bringing that property *in custodia legis*. The seized property is then retained as security for the payment of any judgment that the creditor-plaintiff might later win in the underlying lawsuit. If the creditor wins the lawsuit, it can then execute against the seized property to satisfy its judgment. Prejudgment *garnishment* is a close cousin of attachment; the only difference is that the property of the debtor that is seized is in the hands of a third party (garnishee) rather than the debtor. For example, the debtor's bank account might be the subject of garnishment; the bank (garnishee) owes a debt (the amount of the account) to the debtor-defendant. Upon garnishment, the bank now would hold that debt for the possible benefit of the garnishor-creditor.

Replevin (or *sequestration*) differs from attachment and garnishment in that the plaintiff is alleging a right superior to the debtor to the very property seized. For example, a secured creditor holding an Article 9 security interest in collateral might seek to replevy that collateral upon the debtor's default. In attachment or garnishment, by contrast, there is nothing special about the particular property taken; any nonexempt property of the debtor will serve the security function as well.

Lis pendens, which means "a suit pending," imposes a cloud on the title to property that is itself the subject of litigation, binding the world to the result of that litigation.

Attachment and *garnishment* are the most common provisional remedies. A plaintiff usually will attempt to invoke these remedies unilaterally, without notifying the debtor in advance. Indeed, prior notice would be inherently at odds with the very basis for the remedy itself, *viz.*, that the debtor will get rid of the property once it learns of the lawsuit. It is this *ex parte* feature of attachment, garnishment, and other prejudgment remedies that raises the due process concerns addressed by the Supreme Court. The Court did not mandate prior notice to the debtor in all cases; instead, all the Court required was a fair accommodation of the debtor's property interest.

Attachment and garnishment proceedings are begun when the creditor-plaintiff files an affidavit with the court requesting the issuance of a writ of attachment or garnishment in conjunction with a pending lawsuit seeking money damages. The plaintiff must file a bond with the affidavit to protect the absent debtor-defendant. Attachment and garnishment are purely ancillary proceedings; they exist solely to

---

[72]   N. Georgia Finishing Co. v. Di–Chem, Inc., 419 U.S. 601 (1975) (commercial garnishment held unconstitutional); Mitchell v. W.T. Grant Co., 416 U.S. 600 (1974) (sequestration statute upheld); Fuentes v. Shevin, 407 U.S. 67 (1972) (replevin unconstitutional); Sniadach v. Family Fin. Corp., 395 U.S. 337 (1969) (wage garnishment law unconstitutional).

protect the plaintiff's ability to realize on a judgment in a pending suit. By contrast, a replevin action, which addresses the relative rights of the parties to a specific item of property, may stand alone.

The plaintiff's affidavit must recite facts showing the probable existence of a statutory ground supporting the relief sought. Conclusory allegations will not suffice. The most common statutory grounds are (1) that there is a real risk that the debtor will dispose of its property during the pendency of the case or (2) that the defendant is a nonresident. In some states special types of claims, such as those alleging fraud, or for necessaries, also may support the issuance of a writ of attachment or garnishment.

The writ must be issued by the court. Before the Supreme Court cases, the norm was for the clerk of the court to issue the writ. However, that series of cases made clear that close control and oversight by the responsible judicial officer was necessary to protect the rights of the absent defendant. Before the court will issue the writ, a hearing will be held, usually without the debtor present, as noted above. The plaintiff must convince the court both (1) that it is likely to prevail on the merits of the main case and (2) that one of the statutory grounds exists to support the attachment or garnishment.

If the court issues the writ, the writ is delivered to the sheriff. The sheriff's job then is to seize or levy on sufficient property of the debtor to ensure that any judgment that the plaintiff might later obtain could be satisfied. Levy in this context is the same as in execution. Namely, the sheriff must assert dominion and control over the levied property. In a garnishment, the writ is served not on the debtor but on the third party alleged to owe a debt to the debtor (a bank or an employer, for example).

The effect of levy is to bring the property "*in custodia legis*" and to create a lien of attachment or garnishment on the property seized. At that point the lien is said to be "inchoate." The creation of the lien is of critical importance to the priority status of the plaintiff creditor. If the creditor subsequently does prevail in the underlying lawsuit, its priority right to the seized property will relate back to and date from the time the lien was created by levy. The inchoate lien is made choate by the subsequent entry of judgment. In practical terms, this means that a third party who obtains rights in the levied property during the interim between the levy and the entry of a judgment will lose to the creditor holding the attachment or garnishment lien. The intervening third party takes subject to the prior attachment or garnishment. If the principal lawsuit is dismissed or if the defendant prevails, then the attachment or garnishment is dissolved.

A lawsuit may take a long time to be resolved. To alleviate hardships to the debtor stemming from the deprivation of its property during that lengthy period, the debtor may be able to recover that property before the termination of the lawsuit. This can be done by the debtor posting a bond. The bond in effect replaces the seized property as security for any possible future judgment in that action.

A debtor also may try to recover attached or garnished property by quashing or vacating the attachment or garnishment. The court will grant a motion to quash either on a showing (1) that the plaintiff is not likely to prevail on the merits of the lawsuit or (2) that the attachment or garnishment itself is defective, either procedurally or substantively. If a debtor is successful in quashing an attachment or garnishment, it will get its property back and also may be able to recover damages for wrongful attachment. In many states a debtor will prevail in a wrongful attachment action even if the plaintiff creditor had probable cause and acted in good faith.

A plaintiff pondering the use of attachment or garnishment must carefully weigh the possible costs and benefits of following that course. On the plus side, the security of a prospective judgment is enhanced, and the creditor's priority status is improved versus third parties. As a practical matter, the creditor also may obtain enormous leverage over the debtor, putting great pressure on the debtor to acquiesce to the creditor's demands. However, seeking attachment or garnishment is a risky business. The attempt may not be successful, but will certainly involve expenditures of time and money. The prospect of liability for wrongful attachment exists. Even if the creditor succeeds in attaching or garnishing property of the debtor, the victory may be a pyrrhic one. The debtor may be left with no realistic alternative but to file bankruptcy. In a bankruptcy case, the attachment or garnishment will be set aside as a preference if effected within 90 days before the bankruptcy filing. 11 U.S.C. § 547. The plaintiff then will be relegated to the status of a general unsecured creditor, entitled only to its pro rata share of the residue of the debtor's nonexempt assets. The debtor's personal liability for the debt normally will be discharged.

A creditor concerned about the possibility of a debtor rendering itself judgment-proof and yet also worried about the inadequacies of the traditional prejudgment remedies just discussed might seek to obtain an *injunction* from the court in which the suit is brought, specifically prohibiting the debtor from transferring specified assets pending the outcome of the lawsuit. An example where such an asset-freeze injunction might be useful is where some of the debtor's most significant assets are located outside of the jurisdiction of the local courts. In that situation, the local sheriff cannot seize the assets in a prejudgment attachment or garnishment. However, an equitable decree compelling the debtor-defendant not to transfer the assets would lie within the court's jurisdiction. This strategy has become well-accepted in England, and is known as a "*Mareva*" injunction, based on the 1975 English case of that name. Today the English practice is based on a statute.

The United States Supreme Court had the opportunity to embrace *Mareva* injunctions. Instead, in *Grupo Mexicano De DeSarrollo, S.A. v. Alliance Bond Fund, Inc.,*[73] the Court held that such an injunction lies outside of the equitable jurisdiction of the federal courts. Accordingly, after *Grupo Mexicano*, a federal court has no power under its own jurisdiction to issue such an injunction. State courts are still free to issue such injunctions. Note too that if state law authorizes such injunctions, then under Rule 64 of the Federal Rules of Civil Procedure, the federal courts sitting in that state would have like power.

The facts to support granting a *Mareva* injunction could hardly have been stronger in *Grupo Mexicano*. Grupo Mexicano (GMD) was a subcontractor for the building of toll roads in Mexico. GMD became insolvent; it owed about $250 million in notes primarily

---

[73]   527 U.S. 308 (1999).

to American investors and $450 million in debt to Mexican creditors. The toll roads were doing poorly and the Mexican government issued Toll Road Notes as a rescue program. GMD had a right to receive $309 million of these Toll Road Notes, which was its only substantial asset. GMD decided that it would pay this money entirely to the Mexican creditors, leaving nothing for the American note holders. GMD defaulted on its notes to the American creditors.

Accordingly, the American note holders sued in federal court in New York. GMD had consented to personal jurisdiction there. The American creditors asserted that by the time they obtained a money judgment, all of the debtor's assets would already have been paid out to the Mexican creditors, and their judgment would be worthless. Normally the appropriate prejudgment remedy to secure a debtor's rights to payments would be to garnish that debt in the hands of the third party who owes the debt to the debtor. In this case, however, garnishment would not work, because the New York courts could not obtain personal jurisdiction over the Mexican parties who owed GMD the $309 million. Since GMD itself had consented to personal jurisdiction in New York, though, an injunction ordering GMD not to make any payments to other creditors until the pending lawsuit was resolved (i.e., a *Mareva* injunction) conceivably could work.

Unfortunately for the American creditors, the Supreme Court held that the federal court's inherent equitable powers did not allow such injunctions under Rule 65 of the Federal Rules of Civil Procedure. The Court reasoned that federal jurisdiction in equity is limited to what was recognized in England at the time of the separation of the two countries in the eighteenth century, and at that time such asset-freeze injunctions were unknown. Nor could the American creditors prevail under FRCP Rule 64, since New York state law did not authorize asset-freeze injunctions either.

What recourse could there then be for the American creditors, facing the imminent threat of an insolvent foreign debtor making preferential payments to other creditors, and rendering their own claims worthless? In a word—bankruptcy! The essence of a bankruptcy case, as explained earlier,[74] is precisely to address such collective-action problems in the case of an insolvent debtor. In a bankruptcy case, transfers that prefer some creditors over others are prohibited, and if made shortly before bankruptcy can be recaptured from the preferred creditor. The only answer, then for the American creditors would be to initiate a bankruptcy case against GMD, either in the United States or, more likely, in Mexico.

§ 1.4 Workouts (Compositions and Extensions)

Many debtors are able to work out their financial problems by agreement with their creditors outside of court. Studies show that approximately half of all business restructurings take place pursuant to a voluntary workout.[75] A "workout" agreement typically consists of a "composition" agreement, an "extension" agreement, or, most often, both. A *composition* is a contract between the debtor and two or more creditors, pursuant to which all of the participating creditors agree to accept less than full

---

[74] See § 1.1.

[75] Stuart C. Gilson et al., Troubled Debt Restructurings: An Empirical Study of Private Reorganization of Firms in Default, 27 J. Fin. Econ. 315, 345 (1990).

payment on their claim in full satisfaction of the debt. An *extension* is a contract between the debtor and two or more creditors, pursuant to which all of the participating creditors agree to extend the time for repayment of their claim. When a composition and an extension are combined, creditors agree to accept less than full payment over an extended period of time.

A workout agreement is binding on all creditors who agree to its terms. Payment by the debtor in accordance with the terms of the agreement will forever discharge the creditors' claims. This discharge rule does not contradict the venerable contracts rule of *Foakes v. Beer*,[76] a case in which the House of Lords held that the necessary consideration to support a discharge of a duty was lacking when the creditor agreed to accept payment of less than the full amount of an undisputed, liquidated debt. In a workout agreement, consideration is found in the mutual promises of the two (or more) creditors to each other to accept less than full payment and to forbear from further collection efforts against the debtor. It is for this technical reason that a workout agreement needs at least two creditors. A handful of states, however, have rejected the rule of *Foakes v. Beer* outright, and will enforce the agreement of even a single creditor to accept less than full payment as a discharge of the debtor's duty.[77]

In some circumstances a creditor may be able to avoid the binding effect of a workout agreement. One such case is when the debtor promises a secret preference to one of the agreeing creditors. For example, assume that the debtor reaches an agreement with creditors A, B, C, and D to pay each creditor 25% of its claim. Secretly, however, the debtor has promised to pay A an additional 5% to persuade A to sign the workout agreement. The claims of creditors B, C, and D will not be discharged even if the debtor makes the promised 25% payment. If, however, the workout agreement itself contains the additional 5% payment promised to A, with the full knowledge of B, C, and D, then all of the participants will be bound to those terms. Creditors are permitted to agree to unequal treatment; they just have to know that they are doing so.

Creditors also will not be bound to a workout agreement if any conditions precedent in the agreement are not satisfied. A common condition is that all creditors, or a specified percentage of creditors in number or amount, agree to the terms of the workout agreement. The reason for such a condition is that a workout agreement is not binding on creditors who do not agree to its terms. Nonassenting creditors are free to pursue their state law collection remedies and levy on the debtor's assets. If too many creditors refuse to assent to the agreement, i.e., "hold out," then the viability of the restructuring of the debtor's business that the workout is intended to accomplish might be threatened. Furthermore, assenting creditors feel that it is unfair for them to accept less than full payment while other creditors are paid in full. To protect themselves, assenting creditors must include an express condition in the workout agreement requiring a set percentage of accepting creditor participants. The courts will not imply such a condition, and will discharge the claims of the agreeing creditors even if other creditors refuse to assent to the workout.

---

[76]   L.R. 9 A.C. 605 (H.L. 1884).

[77]   E. Allan Farnsworth, Farnsworth on Contracts 552 (3d ed. 2004).

An important question in a workout agreement is what happens to the creditors' claims if the debtor defaults before fully performing under the agreement. The issue is whether the creditors are free to pursue collection of their full original claim, or whether they are limited to recovering only the balance of the smaller amount specified in the workout agreement. Consider the hypothetical in which four creditors agree to take 25% in the workout agreement. Assume that the debtor pays 20% (i.e., 80% of the 25%) and then defaults. May the creditors attempt to collect only the remaining 5% due under the workout, or the 80% left under their original claim? In contract law terms, the question is whether the workout agreement itself was intended to be a substituted contract and work a novation of the original claim, or whether it was just an accord, with discharge of the full claim dependent on performance or satisfaction. The intention of the contracting parties governs. Accordingly, if creditors want to be sure that their original claims will not be discharged until the workout terms have been fully performed, they should put an express condition in the agreement to that effect. If they do so, that condition will be given effect. Absent an express condition, a court must try to ascertain the intentions of the parties from all facts and circumstances.

As mentioned earlier, a workout agreement is not binding on creditors who do not agree to its terms. Those nonassenting creditors are free to pursue all of their state law collection remedies, and perhaps collect in full. This inability to bind dissenting creditors is one of the biggest weaknesses of the out-of-court workout and is one of the main reasons why chapter 11 of the Bankruptcy Code is needed. In chapter 11, dissenting creditors are bound to the terms of the reorganization plan agreed to by the requisite majority of creditors. § 1141(a).

In many cases the availability of chapter 11 facilitates the out-of-court workout without the need to actually resort to chapter 11. Potential holdout creditors, knowing that the debtor could file chapter 11 and bind them even if they dissent, will relent and agree to the out-of-court workout. Another risk prospective holdout creditors may face is that the debtor may give a lien on all of its assets for the benefit of the creditors participating in the workout, leaving nothing for nonparticipants. Furthermore, those creditors who do not agree to the workout forfeit the opportunity to be paid voluntarily by the debtor pursuant to the workout agreement.

§ 1.5　　Assignment for the Benefit of Creditors

An assignment for the benefit of creditors ("assignment" or "A/B/C") is a state law alternative to a liquidation bankruptcy under chapter 7. In an assignment the debtor makes a voluntary transfer of all of its nonexempt assets to an assignee in trust for the purpose of liquidating the assets and distributing the proceeds to creditors on a pro rata basis. Creditors do not have to consent to an A/B/C for it to be effective. Their claims against the debtor will not be discharged, however.

Assignments originated at common law, but now are governed by statute in most states. These statutes may be mandatory, replacing common law assignments entirely, or permissive, allowing common law assignments to continue. In addition to specifying applicable procedures in detail, state assignment statutes usually prohibit preferences to creditors and award priority to favored creditors (e.g., for taxes or wages). State laws may not provide for the discharge of debts, however, or condition a creditor's participation in a distribution upon the granting of a discharge. Such laws are preempted by the federal government's exercise of its power to enact a uniform bankruptcy law.[78]

Creditors may override an A/B/C by filing a bankruptcy case against the debtor. The making of a general assignment by the debtor is a ground for involuntary bankruptcy. § 303(h)(2). The bankruptcy court could, however, abstain from taking the bankruptcy case and dismiss the case if it believes that doing so would better serve the interests of creditors and the debtor. § 305(a)(1). Creditors might want to proceed in bankruptcy rather than under an A/B/C for several reasons. They may not trust the assignee chosen by the debtor, preferring an independent bankruptcy trustee. Also, the Bankruptcy Code gives the trustee greater powers than does state law to avoid pre-bankruptcy transfers, such as preferences, and thereby bring additional property into the estate to be distributed to all creditors. In addition, the United States has a lower priority in payment in a bankruptcy case than it does under an assignment, allowing other creditors to take a larger piece of the pie.[79]

Assignments are most often used by corporate debtors rather than individuals. The compelling reason why individual debtors rarely use assignments is that they do not receive a discharge of debts in an assignment, but typically are discharged in a bankruptcy case. Thus, if an assignment is used, creditors may still pursue collection from the debtor afterwards to the extent that the distribution in the assignment did not satisfy their claims in full. A corporate debtor, however, does not care about a discharge if it is liquidating, because after liquidation there will be nothing left but a corporate shell. A corporate debtor may prefer to liquidate through an assignment rather than bankruptcy because of the ease and simplicity of the assignment process and the freedom from court oversight.

In common law assignments, debtors have attempted to obtain releases from creditors by offering preferences to releasing creditors, thus hoping to realize the functional equivalent of a discharge without having to go through bankruptcy. This tactic may open the door to a successful attack on the assignment itself by other creditors as a fraudulent transfer. At common law, preferences to some creditors in the assignment have been permitted, as long as the preference was not conditioned on the granting of a release. If a preferential A/B/C is attempted, however, there is a high likelihood that nonpreferred creditors will petition for involuntary bankruptcy. If bankruptcy relief is ordered, the trustee in bankruptcy will be able to recapture the preferences, assuming they were made in the statutory period of vulnerability (*viz.*, 90 days for non-insiders, one year for insiders, § 547(b)(4)).

The procedure in an A/B/C is quite similar to a chapter 7 bankruptcy case. The debtor triggers the assignment by making a written assignment or transfer of all of its nonexempt property to the "assignee." The assignee, the functional equivalent of a bankruptcy trustee, takes legal title to the assets, which he holds as a fiduciary for the benefit of all general creditors. The debtor also normally schedules its assets and

---

[78] Int'l Shoe Co. v. Pinkus, 278 U.S. 261 (1929).

[79] In bankruptcy, tax claims are granted an eighth priority. § 507(a)(8). Other government claims may not enjoy any priority at all. Under an A/B/C, however, claims of the United States are entitled to first priority in payment. Rev. Stat. § 3466 (codified at 31 U.S.C. § 3713).

liabilities. Notice of the assignment is mailed to all creditors listed by the debtor, who are invited to file claims with the assignee and to attend a meeting of creditors. The assignee sells the assets and distributes the net proceeds to creditors holding approved claims. Secured creditors are paid first out of their collateral. Next to be paid are the expenses of administering the assignment; then the statutory priorities under non-bankruptcy federal and state law (recall that the United States has first priority); and the residue is distributed pro rata to nonpriority, unsecured creditors. In the highly unlikely event that any money remains, it is paid to the debtor.

Once a debtor makes an assignment, creditors are precluded from attempting to levy on the assigned assets. Those assets are brought in custodia legis by the assignment and are held in trust by the assignee. Thus, an assignment trumps individual state law collection remedies, such as execution and garnishment. Creditors must wait for distribution from the assignee.

Secured creditors face a risk from an A/B/C. Under Article 9 of the Uniform Commercial Code, an assignee is treated as a "lien creditor."[80] As a lien creditor, an assignee has priority over an unperfected security interest.[81] Typically, a security interest is not perfected until the secured creditor files a financing statement in the public records.[82] The practical effect of these rules is that collateral subject to an unperfected security interest will be distributed to general unsecured creditors in the assignment, free of the security interest. The ex-secured creditor will take only a pro rata share of that distribution, as an unsecured creditor. A perfected secured creditor is safe, however; the assignee takes title subject to all valid and perfected liens and security interests. The same rules regarding the enforceability and vulnerability of security interests apply in a bankruptcy case.

Creditors unhappy about an A/B/C may be able to upset it. As mentioned, the making of an assignment is a ground for involuntary bankruptcy. The creditors also may attempt to set aside the assignment as a fraudulent transfer. Fraudulent transfers are transfers by the debtor that hinder, delay, or defraud creditors in collecting their debts. In one sense, an assignment always hinders and delays creditors, because it blocks their ability to invoke their state law collection remedies. Yet, the normal rule is that an assignment is not a fraudulent conveyance per se, because the property transferred under an assignment is by definition held for the benefit of all creditors.

Exceptions to the general rule of validity exist, however. One exception, noted above, is when the debtor offers preferential treatment to creditors who will grant a release. An assignment by a solvent debtor also has been held fraudulent, because all creditors would have been able to obtain full payment through the use of individual collection remedies. The assignment then only serves to delay collection. Partial assignments, in which the debtor holds back a portion of its property, have been found

---

[80]   U.C.C. § 9–102(a)(52)(B).

[81]   U.C.C. § 9–317(a)(2)(A).

[82]   U.C.C. §§ 9–308(a), 9–310(a). For some types of collateral a security interest may be perfected by possession of the collateral by the secured party. U.C.C. § 9–313. In other cases perfection is automatic, without the secured party having to do anything. U.C.C. § 9–309.

fraudulent as to creditors, as have assignments that attempted to exclude some creditors. Courts also have set aside assignments when the debtor attempted to reserve too many rights and exercise too much control, such as the power to revoke the assignment, to designate the use of the assigned property, or to delay the liquidation process. In these cases, courts say that the assignment is being used for the benefit of the debtor, and not for creditors.

C. THE HISTORY OF BANKRUPTCY LEGISLATION

§ 1.6   Prior to 1978

a. *English Antecedents*

The framers of the United States Constitution had the English bankruptcy system in mind when they included the power to enact "uniform laws on the subject of bankruptcies" in the Article I powers of the legislative branch.[83] The first United States bankruptcy law, passed in 1800, virtually copied the existing English law. United States bankruptcy laws thus have their conceptual origins in English bankruptcy law prior to 1800.

Early English law had a distinctly pro-creditor orientation, and was noteworthy for its harsh treatment of defaulting debtors. Imprisonment for debt was the order of the day, from the time of the Statute of Merchants in 1285,[84] until Dickens' time in the mid-nineteenth century. The common law writ of "capias" authorized "body execution," i.e., seizure of the body of the debtor, to be held until payment of the debt.

English law was not unique in its lack of solicitude for debtors, however. History's annals are replete with tales of draconian treatment of debtors, with punishments including forfeiture of all property, relinquishment of the consortium of a spouse,

---

[83]   U.S. Const. Art. 1, § 8, cl. 4. For discussions of various aspects of the history of the United States bankruptcy laws, see Edward J. Balleisen, Navigating Failure: Bankruptcy and Commercial Society in Antebellum America (2001); Peter J. Coleman, Debtors and Creditors in America: Insolvency, Imprisonment for Debt, and Bankruptcy (1974); Bruce H. Mann, Republic of Debtors: Bankruptcy in the Age of American Independence (2002); F. Regis Noel, History of the Bankruptcy Law (1919); Scott A. Sandage, Born Losers: A History of Failure in America (2005); David H. Skeel, Jr., Debt's Dominion: A History of Bankruptcy Law in America (2001); Charles Warren, Bankruptcy in United States History (1935); Vern Countryman, A History of American Bankruptcy Law, 81 Com. L.J. 226 (1976); Lawrence P. King, An Ode to the Bankruptcy Lawr, 81 Com. L.J. 234 (1976); Kenneth N. Klee, Legislative History of the New Bankruptcy Law, 28 DePaul L. Rev. 941 (1979); Kurt H. Nadelmann, On the Origin of the Bankruptcy Clause, 1 Am. J. Legal Hist. 215 (1957); Stefan Riesenfeld, The Evolution of Modern Bankruptcy Law, 31 Minn. L. Rev. 401 (1947); Charles J. Tabb, The History of the Bankruptcy Laws in the United States, 3 Am. Bankr. Inst. L. Rev. 5 (1995). Good discussions of the development of the English system are found in Jay Cohen, The History of Imprisonment for Debt and its Relation to the Development of Discharge in Bankruptcy, 3 J. Legal Hist. 153 (1982); Ian P.H. Duffy, English Bankrupts, 1571–1861, 24 Am. J. Legal Hist. 283 (1980); Emily Kadens, The Last Bankrupt Hanged: Balancing Incentives in the Development of Bankruptcy Law, 59 Duke L.J. 1229 (2010) (hereafter "Last Bankrupt Hanged"); Emily Kadens, The Pitkin Affair: A Study of Fraud in Early English Bankruptcy, 84 Am. Bankr. L.J. 483 (2010) (hereafter "Pitkin Affair"); Louis E. Levinthal, The Early History of English Bankruptcy, 67 U. Pa. L. Rev. 1 (1919); Michael Quilter, Daniel Defoe: Bankrupt and Bankruptcy Reformer, 25 J. Legal Hist. 53, 68 (2004).

[84]   13 Edw. 1, stat. 3 (1285); see also Statute of Acton Burnell, 11 Edw. 1 (1283); Statute of Westminster II, 13 Edw. 1, stat. 1, cc. 11, 18, 45 (1285).

imprisonment, and death.[85] In Rome creditors were apparently authorized to carve up the body of the debtor, although scholars debate the extent to which that law was actually utilized.

As commerce expanded, the need for a collective procedure to collect debts became evident. In 1543, during the reign of Henry VIII, the first bankruptcy law was passed in England.[86] This first law, entitled "An act against such persons as do make bankrupts," viewed debtors as criminals, and placed additional remedies in the hands of creditors. Only creditors could commence a bankruptcy proceeding, and debtors could be imprisoned for committing fraudulent acts of bankruptcy. The debtor's assets were seized, appraised, and sold, and the proceeds distributed pro rata to creditors. A discharge of debts was unheard of.

The first comprehensive bankruptcy law was passed in 1571 during the reign of Queen Elizabeth I.[87] Over the next two centuries, Parliament periodically amended the bankruptcy laws, in each instance enhancing the power of the bankruptcy commissioner to reach more of the debtor's assets, and increasing the penalties against debtors. For example, the commissioner was given the power to break into the debtor's house or shop to seize the debtor's property.[88] A debtor could be pilloried and have his ear cut off.[89] During this long period, bankruptcy remained an involuntary remedy against debtors to be used by creditors and could only be invoked against debtors who were merchant traders. These limitations on bankruptcy relief persisted until the nineteenth century.

Perhaps the most notable English bankruptcy law passed in this era was the Statute of Anne in 1706.[90] This law introduced the discharge of debts for the benefit of a debtor who cooperated in the bankruptcy proceeding.[91] At the same time, however, the Statute of Anne raised the stakes even higher for uncooperative debtors by providing for the death penalty for fraudulent bankrupts.[92] While the quasi-criminal nature of bankruptcy remained, the Statute of Anne established the roots of a more humanitarian legislative attitude toward honest but unfortunate debtors.

The 1732 Statute of George II was the English bankruptcy law in effect at the time of the United States Constitution and the passage of the first United States bankruptcy law in 1800.[93] As noted above, the English law served in many respects as

---

[85] For example, when yellow fever spread throughout Philadelphia in 1798, the city moved its criminal prisoners to a jail outside of the city, while leaving the imprisoned debtors behind in the wake of the contagion. Mann, supra note 83, ch. 3.

[86] 34 & 35 Hen. 8, c. 4 (1542). The official year in the record is based on the custom at the time to date all parliamentary laws from the beginning of the session, regardless of when actually enacted.

[87] 13 Eliz., c. 7 (1570).

[88] 21 Jac. 1, c. 19, § 8 (1623).

[89] 1 Jac. 1, c. 15, § 9 (1604).

[90] 4 Anne, c. 17 (1705).

[91] Id. § 7. See also John C. McCoid, II, Discharge: The Most Important Development in Bankruptcy History, 70 Am. Bankr. L.J. 163 (1996); see also Kadens, Pitkin Affair, supra note 83; Kadens, Last Bankrupt Hanged, supra note 83.

[92] 4 Anne, c. 17 §§ 1, 18 (1705). See also Kadens, Last Bankrupt Hanged, supra note 83. The English terminology for the death penalty was that the criminal "shall suffer as a felon, without benefit of clergy."

[93] 5 Geo. 2, c. 30 (1732).

the model for the 1800 Act. The carrot-and-stick approach of prior laws was continued: a discharge for the debtor who cooperated and death for the fraudulent debtor. Bankruptcy remained an involuntary proceeding available only against traders.

A separate set of "insolvency" laws addressed the concerns of debtor relief more directly. These laws dealt with relief from debts and release from imprisonment. In this early English period, such laws were only infrequently in force, becoming much more common in the nineteenth century. In the legal lexicon of the day, "bankruptcy" was understood to deal principally with collective creditor actions regarding financially ruined merchant traders, while "insolvency" focused instead on the relief of individual debtors.

b.   *The Constitution and American Bankruptcy Law Prior to 1898*

The subject of bankruptcy received only passing attention from the framers at the Constitutional Convention of 1787.[94] The bankruptcy clause, empowering Congress to "pass uniform laws on the subject of bankruptcies," was inserted in Article I, § 8, after very little debate. In the colonial era many of the states had comprehensive laws regulating debtor-creditor relations.[95] A federal bankruptcy law was apparently believed necessary because of the problems for commerce and for nonresident creditors stemming from varying and discriminatory state laws. James Madison described the perceived purpose of the Bankruptcy Clause in No. 42 of The Federalist:

> The power of establishing uniform laws of bankruptcy is so intimately connected with the regulation of commerce, and will prevent so many frauds where the parties or their property may lie or be removed into different states that the expediency of it seems not likely to be drawn into question.

For over a century after the Constitution, however, the Bankruptcy Clause remained largely unexercised. A federal bankruptcy law was in existence only from 1800 to 1803,[96] from 1841 to 1843,[97] and from 1867 to 1878.[98] Permanent federal bankruptcy legislation did not go into effect until 1898. In each instance, the federal legislation followed a major financial disaster: the Act of 1800 followed the Panic of 1797; the Act of 1841 came after the Panic of 1837; the 1867 Act followed the Panic of 1857 and the Civil War; and finally the 1898 Act was passed in the wake of the Panic of 1893.

The states picked up the slack and continued to regulate debtor-creditor relations and bankruptcy and insolvency during this lengthy era of federal inaction. In some important respects state relief was limited. For example, the Supreme Court held in

---

[94]   See Coleman, supra note 83, ch. 2; Mann, supra note 83, ch. 6; Nadelmann, supra note 83; Noel, supra note 83, ch. 4; Warren, supra note 83, at 4–7; Frank R. Kennedy, Bankruptcy and the Constitution, 33 U. Mich. L. Quad. 40 (Spring 1989).

[95]   The standard reference on this subject is Coleman, supra note 83. See also Noel, supra note 83, ch. 3.

[96]   Bankruptcy Act of 1800, ch. 19, 2 Stat. 19, repealed ch. 6, 2 Stat. 248 (1803).

[97]   Bankruptcy Act of 1841, ch. 9, 5 Stat. 440, repealed ch. 82, 5 Stat. 614 (1843).

[98]   Bankruptcy Act of 1867, ch. 176, 14 Stat. 517, repealed ch. 160, 20 Stat. 99 (1878).

Sturges v. Crowninshield[99] that because of the prohibition on impairing the obligation of contracts, states could not constitutionally provide for the discharge of debts incurred prior to the legislative enactment, and held that states could not discharge the debts due a citizen of another state in *Ogden v. Saunders*.[100] *Ogden* did hold, however, that states could discharge future debts (that is, debts incurred after the passage of the state bankruptcy law) against citizens of the same state.

Voluntary bankruptcy came into being with the passage of the Bankruptcy Act of 1841.[101] For the first time a financially troubled debtor could file for bankruptcy and receive a discharge. Nor was this relief limited to merchant debtors; eligibility was extended to "all persons whatsoever owing debts."[102] Considerable debate focused on whether such a law even fell within the "subject of bankruptcies," but ultimately Congress's power was upheld.

From the viewpoint of creditors, the 1841 law was a dismal failure. Many thousands of debtors were discharged, minimal dividends were paid to creditors, and administrative fees were high. The law was repealed after little more than a year of operation.[103]

In the meantime, the lengthy era of widespread use of imprisonment for debt had come to an end. The practice was abolished at the federal level in 1833, and many states followed suit in the 1830s and 1840s. In England, general abolition of the practice did not come until 1869. Today only vestiges of "body execution" remain, usually in cases where the debtor is perceived to be morally culpable, such as a debt for fraud, or for alimony or child support.

After the Panic of 1857 and the Civil War, overwhelming pressure for another federal bankruptcy law led to the enactment of the Bankruptcy Act of 1867.[104] In time, this law too proved a failure and was eventually repealed in 1878.[105] Criticisms levied by creditors included small dividends, high fees and expenses, and lengthy delays. Northern creditors who had hoped to use the bankruptcy law to facilitate collection from Southern debtors were disappointed.

Nor did debtors do very well under the 1867 law. Due to the inclusion of numerous grounds for denying discharge, only about one-third of the debtors received a discharge. The 1867 law, however, did allow debtors to elect the benefit of generous state exemption laws as an alternative to the federal scheme. This utilization of state exemption laws in a federal bankruptcy case has continued to the present.[106]

---

[99]   17 U.S. (4 Wheat.) 122 (1819).

[100]   25 U.S. (12 Wheat.) 213 (1827).

[101]   Ch. 9, 5 Stat. 440 (1841) (repealed 1843). See John C. McCoid, II, The Origins of Voluntary Bankruptcy, 5 Bankr. Dev. J. 361 (1988).

[102]   Ch. 9, § 1, 5 Stat. 441.

[103]   Ch. 82, 5 Stat. 614 (1843).

[104]   Ch. 176, 14 Stat. 517 (1867) (repealed 1878).

[105]   Ch. 160, 20 Stat. 99 (1878).

[106]   For a thoughtful analysis of this issue, see Judith S. Koffler, The Bankruptcy Clause and Exemption Laws: A Reexamination of the Doctrine of Geographic Uniformity, 58 N.Y.U. L. Rev. 22 (1983).

A major innovation, the composition agreement, was introduced into the bankruptcy law in 1874.[107] The forerunner of modern reorganization provisions, the composition agreement allowed the debtor to propose payment of a certain percentage of his debts over time in full discharge of those debts, while also keeping his property. If the proposed composition was accepted by a majority in number and three-fourths in value of the creditors, it was binding on all creditors, including dissenters. The new composition law also was held to be within the "subject of bankruptcies," further expanding the scope of the Bankruptcy Clause. Of course, the composition law died with the rest of the bankruptcy law upon its repeal in 1878.

The twenty years following the repeal of the bankruptcy act in 1878 marked the final period of federal absence from the bankruptcy scene. One last attempt was made to solve bankruptcy and insolvency problems at the state level, and again these efforts did not succeed. The Panics of 1884 and 1893 highlighted the inability of the states to deal effectively with national financial problems.

In another development, federal and state courts entered the reorganization business with the equity receivership. Use of this device blossomed in the late 1800s in attempts to keep the railroads running. Court-supervised receiverships were the predominant means of corporate reorganization for about a half century, until new federal reorganization laws were enacted during the Depression.

c.   Bankruptcy Act of 1898

The Bankruptcy Act of 1898[108] marked the beginning of the era of permanent federal bankruptcy legislation. The 1898 Act remained in effect for eighty years, until it was replaced by the Bankruptcy Reform Act of 1978.[109] During the course of its existence, the 1898 Act was amended numerous times, with the most important amendment being the Chandler Act of 1938.[110]

The 1898 Act ushered in the modern era of liberal debtor treatment in United States bankruptcy laws. While the earlier laws had allowed a debtor a discharge, many restrictions had been hedged in around that privilege. Included were requirements that a specified percentage of creditors consent to the granting of the discharge and that a minimum dividend be paid to creditors as a condition of the discharge.[111] The 1898 Act abolished those restrictions, and also strictly limited the number of grounds for denying the discharge.

Since 1898, legislative inroads have been made on the scope of the discharge, with new grounds for denial and for exception to discharge being added from time to time.

---

[107]   Ch. 390, § 17, 18 Stat. 182–84 (1874) (repealed 1878).

[108]   Ch. 541, 30 Stat. 544 (1898) (repealed 1978). See David H. Skeel, Jr., The Genius of the 1898 Bankruptcy Act, 15 Bankr. Dev. J. 321 (1999); Charles Jordan Tabb, A Century of Regress or Progress? A Political History of Bankruptcy Legislation in 1898 and 1998, 15 Bankr. Dev. J. 343 (1999).

[109]   Pub. L. No. 95–598, 92 Stat. 2549 (1978).

[110]   Ch. 575, 52 Stat. 840 (1938) (repealed 1978).

[111]   See Charles Jordan Tabb, The Historical Evolution of the Bankruptcy Discharge, 65 Am. Bankr. L.J. 325 (1991).

In 1970, Congress enacted a new dischargeability law,[112] which significantly enhanced the debtor's ability to protect and enforce the discharge. The law made the discharge self-executing, rather than just an affirmative defense, and channeled common dischargeability litigation exclusively into the bankruptcy court.[113]

Much of the 1898 Act, however, was directed not at debtor relief, but at facilitating the equitable and efficient administration and distribution of the debtor's property to creditors. Creditors exercised significant control over the process through the power to elect the trustee and creditors' committees. The federal district courts sat as "courts of bankruptcy," but the bulk of the judicial and administrative work was done by "referees in bankruptcy," who were appointed by the district courts. Referees became "bankruptcy judges" in 1973.

Provision was made for reorganization in lieu of liquidation as well. Section 12 of the original 1898 Act authorized compositions much along the lines of the 1874 law. After the Depression came crashing down in 1929, Congress passed several amendments that favored rehabilitation under the auspices of the bankruptcy laws. The Supreme Court that infuriated President Roosevelt so much held some of these acts unconstitutional, but ultimately Congress was able to enact revised versions that passed constitutional muster.

A 1933 law made compositions more readily and widely available in § 74, authorized agricultural compositions in § 75, and permitted railroads to reorganize under § 77.[114] Corporate reorganizations were allowed by § 77B just a year later.[115] Also in 1934, Congress introduced a reorganization law for municipalities in chapter IX.[116] The Supreme Court overturned this law in 1936.[117] The Frazier–Lemke Act was passed in 1934 as well, giving farmers under § 75 greater ability to keep their farms.[118] In 1935, the Supreme Court struck down this act on the ground that it violated the Fifth Amendment property rights of the mortgagee.[119] In just a few weeks Congress responded by passing a revised amendment to § 75,[120] which then survived judicial review. In a crucial decision, the Supreme Court also upheld the constitutionality of § 77, the railroad reorganization section.[121]

---

[112] Pub. L. No. 91–467, 84 Stat. 990 (1970).

[113] See Vern Countryman, The New Dischargeability Law, 45 Am. Bankr. L.J. 1 (1971).

[114] Ch. 204, 47 Stat. 1467 (1933).

[115] Ch. 424, 48 Stat. 911 (1934).

[116] Ch. 345, 48 Stat. 798 (1934).

[117] Ashton v. Cameron Cnty. Water Improvement Dist. No. 1, 298 U.S. 513 (1936).

[118] Ch. 869, 48 Stat. 1289 (1934).

[119] Louisville Joint Stock Bank v. Radford, 295 U.S. 555 (1935). For analyses of the constitutional issue, see James S. Rogers, The Impairment of Secured Creditors' Rights in Reorganization: A Study of the Relationship Between the Fifth Amendment and the Bankruptcy Clause, 96 Harv. L. Rev. 973 (1983); Charles J. Tabb, Credit Bidding, Security, and the Obsolescence of Chapter 11, 2013 U. Ill. L. Rev. 103 (2013).

[120] Ch. 792, 49 Stat. 942 (1935).

[121] Cont'l Illinois Bank & Trust Co. v. Chicago, Rock Island & Pac. Ry. Co., 294 U.S. 648 (1935).

The fury of bankruptcy legislation in the 1930s came to a head in 1938 with the passage of the Chandler Act.[122] The Chandler Act substantially revised many of the provisions of the 1898 Act. Perhaps most significant, however, was the reworking of the recently enacted reorganization provisions into the form that prevailed for the next 40 years. Chapter X governed corporate reorganizations, chapter XI dealt with arrangements, chapter XII applied to real property arrangements, and chapter XIII provided for wage earners' plans. Over the next forty years, Congress continued to amend the bankruptcy laws, but only as to specific and discrete issues.

Bankruptcy procedure was governed in substantial part by sections of the 1898 Act. Under the authority of § 30 of the 1898 Act, the Supreme Court from time to time passed "General Orders in Bankruptcy" to further govern procedure. In 1960, an Advisory Committee on Bankruptcy Rules was established. In 1964, Congress authorized the promulgation of rules of bankruptcy procedure by the Supreme Court.[123] These rules took effect in 1973. Special rules for the various rehabilitation chapters came into being in the years following.

In 1970, Congress created the Commission on the Bankruptcy Laws of the United States to study and report on the existing law.[124] The Commission filed its two-part report in 1973.[125] Five years later, almost a decade of study and debate about bankruptcy reform culminated when the Bankruptcy Reform Act of 1978 replaced the 1898 Act with the Bankruptcy Code.[126]

§ 1.7 Bankruptcy Reform Act of 1978

The Bankruptcy Reform Act of 1978[127] was the first comprehensive reform of the federal bankruptcy law in 40 years, and replaced the law that had been in effect since the end of the nineteenth century. When enacted, the 1978 Act was unique in the history of the nation's bankruptcy legislation in that it was the first that was not passed as a response to a severe economic depression. The Bankruptcy Code, created by the 1978 Act, governs bankruptcy law in the United States today. As will be discussed in the following sections, the Code has been the subject of a number of amendments in the years since 1978, most notably in the Bankruptcy Abuse Prevention and Consumer Protection Act of 2005.[128]

The bankruptcy reform process that led to the passage of the Bankruptcy Reform Act took a decade.[129] The process began in 1968, when Senator Quentin Burdick

---

[122] Ch. 575, 52 Stat. 840 (1938).

[123] Pub. L. No. 88–623, 78 Stat. 100 (1964) (codified at 28 U.S.C. § 2075).

[124] Pub. L. No. 91–354, 84 Stat. 468 (1970).

[125] Report of the Commission on the Bankruptcy Laws of the United States, pts. I and II, H.R. Doc. No. 93–137, 93d Cong., 1st Sess. (1973).

[126] Pub. L. No. 95–598, 92 Stat. 2549 (1978).

[127] Pub. L. No. 95–598, 92 Stat. 2549 (1978). This law is referred to as BRA, the 1978 Act, The Reform Act, or, most often, the Bankruptcy Code, or just "the Code".

[128] Pub. L. No. 109–8, 119 Stat. 23 (2005). See § 1.9.

[129] For helpful analyses of the legislative history of the Bankruptcy Reform Act, see Kenneth N. Klee, Legislative History of the New Bankruptcy Law, 28 DePaul L. Rev. 941 (1979); Eric A. Posner, The Political Economy of the Bankruptcy Act of 1978, 96 Mich. L. Rev. 47 (1997).

chaired hearings before a subcommittee of the Senate Judiciary Committee to determine whether a bankruptcy review commission should be formed. As mentioned in the preceding section, Congress created such a review commission in 1970,[130] charged with the mission to "study, analyze, evaluate, and recommend changes to the [1898] Act . . . in order for such Act to reflect and adequately meet the demands of present technical, financial, and commercial activity."[131]

The Commission, under the able guidance of Professor Frank Kennedy as Executive Director, filed its two-part report in July 1973.[132] Part I contained a series of reports and recommendations, and Part II consisted of a draft bankruptcy statute, which then was introduced as a bill in both the House and Senate.[133] The "Commission Bill" recommended many substantial changes from prior law, including the expansion of the jurisdiction of bankruptcy judges, the creation of a Bankruptcy Administration to handle all administrative matters, the consolidation of all of the business reorganization chapters into a single chapter, and greater protection of the rights of consumer debtors on a uniform basis.

A competing bill was drafted by the National Conference of Bankruptcy Judges. The "Judges' Bill" was also introduced in both the House and Senate.[134] In 1975 and 1976, Congressman Don Edwards presided over thirty-five days of hearings on the two bills.[135] Senator Burdick presided over twenty-one days of hearings in the Senate on the companion bills in 1975.[136] From 1973 to 1978, the bankruptcy reform bills underwent numerous metamorphoses, and were the subject of extensive commentary and debate.

Committee reports regarding then extant versions of the bill were printed in 1977 by the House[137] and in 1978 by the Senate.[138] While these reports are of great assistance as legislative history in construing the Bankruptcy Code, in some instances the reports speak to a provision which was later changed in the final bill that became law. There was not a conference report on the 1978 Act, due to the exigencies of time. Instead, the floor leaders of the bill, Congressman Edwards and Senator DeConcini, issued a joint explanatory statement as to the compromise bill that became law, which

---

[130]   Pub. L. No. 91–354, 84 Stat. 468 (1970).

[131]   84 Stat. 468.

[132]   Report of the Commission on the Bankruptcy Laws of the United States, pts. I and II, H.R. Doc. No. 93–137, 93d Cong., 1st Sess. (1973). In 1971, while the Commission was engaged in its work, a useful study of bankruptcy was published by the Brookings Institution. David T. Stanley & Marjorie Girth, Bankruptcy: Problem, Process, Reform (1971).

[133]   H.R. 10,792, 93d Cong., 1st Sess. (1973); S. 4026, 93d Cong., 1st Sess. (1973). The bills were reintroduced in the 94th Congress as H.R. 31 and S. 236.

[134]   H.R. 32, 94th Cong., 1st Sess. (1975); S. 235, 94th Cong., 1st Sess. (1975).

[135]   Hearings on H.R. 31 & H.R. 32 before the Subcomm. on Civil & Constitutional Rights of the House Comm. on the Judiciary, 94th Cong., 1st & 2d Sess. (1975–1976).

[136]   Hearings on S. 235 & 236 before the Subcomm. on Improvements in Judicial Machinery of the Senate Comm. on the Judiciary, 94th Cong., 1st Sess. (1975).

[137]   H.R. Rep. No. 95–595, 95th Cong., 1st Sess. (1977). This report accompanied H.R. 8200, which was reported favorably by the House Judiciary Committee in September 1977.

[138]   S. Rep. No. 95–989, 95th Cong., 2d Sess. (1978). This report accompanied S. 2266, which was reported favorably by the Senate Judiciary Committee in July 1978. The Senate Finance Committee also published a report on S. 2266. S. Rep. No. 1106, 95th Cong., 2d Sess. (1978).

was printed in the Congressional Record.[139] That joint statement often is treated by courts as essentially equivalent to a conference report.

A major point of debate in the bankruptcy bill concerned the status of the bankruptcy judges. A key aspect of the reform was to enlarge substantially the jurisdiction of the bankruptcy courts, so that bankruptcy judges could hear virtually any matter arising in or related to the bankruptcy case. One of the major perceived weaknesses of the 1898 Act was the splintered jurisdictional scheme, in which bankruptcy referees (renamed judges in 1973) could only hear certain core bankruptcy matters, within their so-called "summary" jurisdiction. "Plenary" matters, by contrast, could only be heard either by Article III district judges or by state court judges of general jurisdiction. Drawing the line between summary and plenary jurisdiction was both difficult and wasteful.[140] Everyone agreed that creating a unified jurisdictional system would be a substantial improvement.

What everyone did not agree on was the status of the judges who would exercise that enlarged jurisdiction. The options were (1) to keep the bankruptcy judges as non-Article III adjuncts to the federal district court judges, or (2) to make the bankruptcy judges Article III judges in their own right, with the constitutional guarantees of life tenure and protection against diminution in salary. The latter course would eliminate the constitutional concern over non-Article III bankruptcy judges exercising the judicial power of the United States in derogation of Article III and would enhance the status of the bankruptcy bench. The House favored giving bankruptcy judges Article III status, while the Senate steadfastly opposed such a course. Chief Justice Burger lobbied against the creation of Article III bankruptcy judges. In the end the Senate prevailed: while bankruptcy judges were given jurisdiction over all matters arising in, under, or related to bankruptcy cases, they remained adjuncts of the district court, without the protections of Article III. This choice proved improvident, however, for the Supreme Court held in 1982 in *Northern Pipeline Construction Co. v. Marathon Pipe Line Co.*[141] that the 1978 Act unconstitutionally gave Article III powers to non-Article III judges. When Congress went back to the well in 1984 in an attempt to fix the *Marathon* problem, it opted yet again for a split jurisdiction, which again proved inefficacious, as the Supreme Court in 2011 struck down as unconstitutional a part of the jurisdiction assigned to non-Article III bankruptcy judges in *Stern v. Marshall.*[142]

A decade of study and debate came to a conclusion when President Carter signed the Bankruptcy Reform Act of 1978 into law on November 6, 1978. The law took effect, for the most part, on October 1, 1979.[143] Some of the provisions, in particular those affecting the bankruptcy courts, were to be phased in over a five-year transition

---

[139] 124 Cong. Rec. H11,047–117 (daily ed. Sept. 28, 1978); 124 Cong. Rec. S17,403–34 (daily ed. Oct. 6, 1978).

[140] See generally Ralph Brubaker, A "Summary" Statutory and Constitutional Theory of Bankruptcy Judges' Core Jurisdiction After Stern v. Marshall, 86 Am. Bankr. L.J. 121 (2012); Ralph Brubaker, On the Nature of Federal Bankruptcy Jurisdiction: A General Statutory and Constitutional Theory, 41 Wm. & Mary L. Rev. 743 (2000).

[141] 458 U.S. 50 (1982).

[142] 131 S.Ct. 2594 (2011).

[143] Pub. L. No. 95–598, tit. IV, § 402, 92 Stat. 2682 (1978).

period.[144] The *Marathon* decision, however, upset these plans, and required Congress to go back to the drawing board, a development discussed in the following section.

§ 1.8   Legislation from 1978 to 2005

The passage of the Bankruptcy Reform Act of 1978 did not put an end to congressional tinkering with bankruptcy legislation, culminating in a substantial revision in 2005. Several factors have spurred Congress into almost nonstop consideration of the federal bankruptcy laws since 1978. First, and most importantly, the consumer credit industry, unhappy with skyrocketing bankruptcy filings and mounting bad debt losses, steadily lobbied for amendments providing for harsher treatment of debtors, until they achieved success in 2005[145].

Second, Congress responded to several significant court decisions handed down by the Supreme Court as well as by lower courts.[146] Third, the farm crisis of the early 1980s prompted a call for relief for family farmers; the enactment of chapter 12 in 1986 was the result. Fourth, the bankruptcy court has unexpectedly become the forum in which many difficult social problems have been aired.[147] Fifth, special interest groups have tried to persuade Congress to amend the Code in ways favoring their interests.[148] Finally, the exponential growth in the number of bankruptcy cases since the enactment

---

[144] Id. §§ 402(b), 404–07.

[145] See § 1.9.

[146] The most important, of course, were the *Marathon* and *Bildisco* cases discussed in this section. They were not alone, though, in prompting Congressional action. For example, Congress overturned the Supreme Court's decision in *Pennsylvania Department of Public Welfare v. Davenport*, 495 U.S. 552 (1990), that a debtor's criminal restitution obligation could be discharged in chapter 13. Pub. L. No. 101–581, 104 Stat. 2865 (1990) (dischargeability of certain debts); Pub. L. No. 101–647, 104 Stat. 4916 (1990) (duplicative dischargeability provisions to Pub. L. No. 101–581; federal depository institutions).

Meanwhile, the Fourth Circuit issued a controversial holding in 1985 in *Lubrizol Enterprises, Inc. v. Richmond Metal Finishers, Inc.,* 756 F.2d 1043 (4th Cir. 1985), that a debtor could reject a technology licensing agreement and thereby deprive the licensee of the right to use the licensed technology. Congress effectively overruled this holding by adding a new § 365(n) to the Code, which permitted licensees to retain the use of intellectual property even after rejection of a licensing agreement. An Act to keep secure the rights of intellectual property licensors and licensees which come under the protection of title 11 of the United States Code, the Bankruptcy Code, Pub. L. No. 100–506, 102 Stat. 2538 (1988).

[147] For example, Congress addressed the savings and loan crisis by amendments designed to protect the rights of federal depository institutions. Pub. L. No. 101–647, 104 Stat. 4916 (1990).

In July 1986, LTV Corporation filed chapter 11 and stopped paying medical and life insurance benefits for retired employees. That fall Congress responded with a joint resolution that required the continued payment of benefits. House Joint Resolution, Continuing Appropriations, 1987, Pub. L. No. 99–591, 100 Stat. 3341 (1986); Declaration of Taking Act Amendments, Pub. L. No. 99–656, 100 Stat. 3668 (1986). In June 1988 permanent legislation to protect retirees' benefits was passed. Retiree Benefits Bankruptcy Protection Act of 1988, Pub. L. No. 100–334, 102 Stat. 610 (1988). The 1988 legislation created new § 1114, governing the payment of insurance benefits to retired employees, and added a requirement that a plan could be confirmed only if it provided for the continued payment of retiree benefits. § 1129(a)(13).

[148] To illustrate: a provision regarding airport leases, passed in 1992, was intended solely to protect the St. Louis airport in connection with the TWA bankruptcy case. Pub. L. No. 102–365, 106 Stat. 972 (1992). The oil and gas industry obtained the passage of an amendment affecting farmout agreements, excluding property covered by such an agreement from the bankruptcy estate. Pub. L. No. 102–486, 106 Stat. 2776 (1992). Some other examples include Pub. L. No. 101–311, 104 Stat. 267 (1990) (swap agreements and forward contracts); Pub. L. No. 101–508, 104 Stat. 1388 (1990) (educational loans).

of the 1978 Act impeded the administration of those cases and clogged the bankruptcy courts.[149]

The first major bump in the road for the new Bankruptcy Code came soon after its enactment. On June 28, 1982, the Supreme Court rendered a decision in *Northern Pipeline Construction Co. v. Marathon Pipe Line Co.*[150] that forced Congress's hand.[151] In *Marathon*, the Court held that the broad grant of jurisdiction to the bankruptcy courts in the 1978 Act violated Article III of the Constitution by vesting non-Article III bankruptcy judges with too much of the "judicial power" of the United States. The Court further held that the unconstitutional portion of the jurisdictional grant could not be severed from the constitutional portion, thus condemning the entire bankruptcy court system and requiring Congress to redo the jurisdictional and court scheme. The Court did avoid wholesale disaster by deciding that its holding of unconstitutionality should only apply prospectively, thus validating actions taken by bankruptcy courts under the Code to that date. To give Congress time to fix the broken court system, the *Marathon* Court stayed its judgment until October 4, 1982, and later extended the stay until December 24, 1982.

Surprisingly, Congress did not act to amend the bankruptcy court system before the expiration of the *Marathon* stay on Christmas Eve 1982, instead delaying a response until July 1984. In the 18–month interregnum in which no federal statute governed the operation of the bankruptcy courts, the Judicial Conference of the United States stepped into the breach by proposing a model "Emergency Rule." Adopted as a local rule by all United States District Courts, the Emergency Rule used a bifurcated jurisdictional scheme, with some core bankruptcy matters heard by bankruptcy judges on reference from the district courts and the remaining matters heard in the district courts. Although many doubts were raised as to the constitutionality of the Emergency Rule,[152] the circuit courts upheld the Rule, and the Supreme Court refused to decide the Rule's validity.

The Supreme Court's decision in February 1984 in *National Labor Relations Board v. Bildisco & Bildisco*[153] finally triggered congressional action. In *Bildisco*, the Court held that a chapter 11 debtor in possession could reject its collective bargaining agreement in bankruptcy and that the debtor did not commit an unfair labor practice by unilaterally modifying that labor contract. The resulting furor pushed Congress into speedy action, and the jurisdictional problem was fixed along with the labor problem. The consumer credit industry and other special interest groups took advantage of the congressional activity and seized the opportunity to obtain desired changes in the Bankruptcy Code.

---

[149] In addition to the major court system overhaul effected in 1984, as discussed in the text below, some systemic amendments include Pub. L. No. 101–509, 104 Stat. 1452 (1990) (compensation of standing trustees); Pub. L. No. 101–650, 104 Stat. 5105 (1990) (judicial improvements).

[150] 458 U.S. 50 (1982).

[151] For a discussion of *Marathon* and post-*Marathon* events, see § 4.2.

[152] See, e.g., Vern Countryman, Emergency Rule Compounds Emergency, 57 Am. Bankr. L.J. 1 (1983).

[153] 465 U.S. 513 (1984).

The result was the Bankruptcy Amendments and Federal Judgeship Act of 1984 (BAFJA),[154] a major piece of legislation, which contained three titles. Title I, on "Bankruptcy Jurisdiction and Procedure," tried to fix the *Marathon* problem by revamping the bankruptcy system. The long-running debate of the 1970s over whether the bankruptcy judges should have comprehensive jurisdiction, and if so, whether they should be made Article III judges, was replayed. This time, however, the *Marathon* decision prevented Congress from having it both ways, i.e., comprehensive jurisdiction but without Article III status. One or the other had to go. The House again favored Article III status and unified jurisdiction, and the Senate favored non-Article III status and bifurcated jurisdiction. The Senate won, but their victory ultimately proved to be pyrrhic. As will be discussed in more detail in Chapter 4, the jurisdictional and court scheme established by BAFJA created the bankruptcy courts as units of the district court. Bankruptcy courts hear cases and proceedings in bankruptcy only by reference from the district courts. BAFJA made a distinction between "core" bankruptcy matters, in which the bankruptcy court can enter a final order, and "non-core" matters, which are reviewable de novo by the district court.[155] Unfortunately, Congress again failed to satisfy fully the Article III commands, leaving too much authority to bankruptcy judges in the "core" category. In 2011, in *Stern v. Marshall*, the Supreme Court held that the 1984 amendments unconstitutionally empowered the non-Article III bankruptcy judge to enter a final order on a state law counterclaim that is not resolved in the process of ruling on the creditor's claim.[156]

Title III of the 1984 law contained a series of amendments to the Bankruptcy Code itself.[157] In Subtitle J, Congress responded to the *Bildisco* decision by enacting a new § 1113 to govern the rejection of collective bargaining agreements. Some special interest groups shared in the bounty of the 1984 amendments. For example, lessors of commercial real estate obtained substantial beneficial changes in Subtitle C, the Leasehold Management Amendments.

The consumer credit industry got many of the items on its wish list in Subtitle A of Title III, the "Consumer Credit Amendments." These amendments, based on the hotly debated premise that many consumer debtors were abusing the bankruptcy laws,[158] tightened the reins on consumer debtors.[159] As it turned out, however, the credit industry soon became dissatisfied with the 1984 changes, and lobbied hard for

---

[154] Pub. L. No. 98–353, 98 Stat. 333 (1984). This act is known as "BAFJA," the acronym derived from the act's full name.

[155] 28 U.S.C. § 157(b), (c).

[156] 131 S.Ct. 2594, 2620 (2011).

[157] Title II of BAFJA created additional judgeships.

[158] Much of the fuel for the consumer credit industry's fire was provided by a study financed by the industry itself, the Consumer Bankruptcy Study, by the Credit Research Center, Krannert Graduate School of Management, Purdue University (1982) (known as the "Purdue Study"). The Purdue Study concluded that at least a third of consumer debtors could repay a significant portion of their debts. This study was severely criticized, however. See, e.g., Teresa A. Sullivan, Elizabeth Warren, and Jay Lawrence Westbrook, As We Forgive Our Debtors: Bankruptcy and Consumer Credit in America ch. 12 (1989).

[159] For a review of these 1984 amendments, see Karen Gross, Preserving a Fresh Start for the Individual Debtor: The Case for Narrow Construction of the Consumer Credit Amendments, 135 U. Pa. L. Rev. 59 (1986).

further amendments to make things harder for consumer debtors, finally achieving victory in 2005.

The farm crisis motivated Congress to pass yet another significant bankruptcy bill just over two years after BAFJA became law. In October 1986, the Bankruptcy Judges, United States Trustees, and Family Farmer Bankruptcy Act of 1986 was enacted.[160] The 1986 legislation created chapter 12, designed specifically for "family farmers." The avowed purpose of chapter 12 was to make it easier for such farmers to keep their farms and pay their creditors over time. Chapter 12 was not enacted as permanent legislation, but was to sunset in seven years. The sunset period was extended several times, and finally chapter 12 was made a permanent part of the Bankruptcy Code in the 2005 amendments, effective July 1, 2005.

The 1986 bill also made the United States trustee system permanent, on a nationwide basis. Congress had instituted the system as a pilot program in a few judicial districts in the 1978 Act. The United States trustee performs many of the administrative and supervisory tasks in a bankruptcy case, enabling the bankruptcy judge to serve more exclusively in a judicial role, free from many of the administrative burdens that judges carried under the Act.

In 1994 Congress passed a major bankruptcy bill. The Bankruptcy Reform Act of 1994[161] was significant on two counts. First, and most importantly, Congress created a second National Bankruptcy Review Commission, just less than a quarter century after the first Commission was established in 1970. The 1994 Commission was charged with the duty of studying the Code and submitting a report in two years suggesting proposed reforms. Congress made clear, however, that it was "generally satisfied with the basic framework" of the current Code, and that the Commission should therefore focus on "reviewing, improving, and updating the Code in ways which do not disturb the fundamental tenets and balance of current law." As it turned out, however, the political reality was that the consumer credit industry used the advent of the second Review Commission as an opportunity to lobby for a fundamental rethinking and retrenchment of the rights of individual consumer debtors. As the next section will discuss, while the Commission itself in its 1997 Report rejected the anti-debtor views pushed by the credit industry, the industry proved more successful in persuading Congress, leading to the drastic 2005 amendments.

The second significant aspect of the Bankruptcy Reform Act of 1994 was that Congress made a number of substantive amendments to the Bankruptcy Code. This feature of the bill was somewhat paradoxical, given the concurrent creation of a Review Commission charged with the responsibility of studying the Code and suggesting amendments thereto. Nevertheless, the 1994 Act made literally scores of changes in the bankruptcy law. Congress took the opportunity to resolve numerous specific issues that had arisen under the 1978 law and to overrule many court decisions. Special emphasis was also placed on means of improving bankruptcy administration.

---

[160]   Pub. L. No. 99–554, 100 Stat. 3088 (1986).

[161]   Pub. L. No. 103–394, 108 Stat. 4106 (1994).

§ 1.9   The Bankruptcy Abuse Prevention and Consumer Protection Act of 2005 and Beyond

On April 20, 2005, President Bush signed into law the Bankruptcy Abuse Prevention and Consumer Protection Act of 2005 (BAPCPA).[162] Weighing in at a hefty 514 pages, BAPCPA marked the culmination of years of feverish and well-funded lobbying efforts by the consumer credit industry to crack down on consumer debtors.[163] Relying on an unproven but oft-repeated premise of rampant debtor abuse, the focal point of the reform effort was to make bankruptcy more difficult for individual consumer debtors. The credit industry asserted that way too many people were filing bankruptcy,[164] and that many of those who filed could have made payments to their creditors, but chose not to do so. The many dramatic and draconian anti-debtor amendments are found in Title III, titled "Discouraging Bankruptcy Abuse." BAPCPA did much, much more than "discourage bankruptcy abuse"—indeed, only 75 of its 514 pages comprise Title III. But there is no doubt that the law would never have come to pass but for the imperative to enact Title III's anti-debtor provisions.

The principal thrust of the reform was to change the fundamental nature of consumer bankruptcy in the United States as it had existed since 1898.[165] Before BAPCPA, individual debtors had enjoyed a largely unfettered right to choose between filing under chapters 7 and 13.[166] The only "fetter" was the "substantial abuse" test of § 707(b), which had been enacted in 1984 in response to earlier credit industry cries of foul. In chapter 7, in exchange for turning over all non-exempt assets, the debtor receives an immediate discharge from his past debts (and thus is able to enjoy his future earnings free from creditors' pre-bankruptcy claims). In chapter 13, a debtor can retain his property, but must make payments to creditors out of future earnings for three to five years. Choosing a chapter 13 repayment plan is entirely voluntary for debtors; creditors cannot file an involuntary chapter 13 against an individual debtor. Not surprisingly, debtors generally prefer chapter 7 over 13, whereas creditors think that more debtors could and should proceed under chapter 13. The creditors' belief long has been that large numbers of debtors had the "means" to make substantial payments to creditors out of future earnings, but simply chose not to do so.[167] That choice, creditors asserted, was an abuse. Furthermore, that abuse was costing every American $400 a year, they claimed.[168] While the "substantial abuse" test of § 707(b) that had

---

[162]   Pub. L. No. 109–8, 119 Stat. 23 (2005).

[163]   The definitive source detailing the history of BAPCA is Susan Jensen, A Legislative History of the Bankruptcy Abuse Prevention and Consumer Protection Act of 2005, 79 Am. Bankr. L.J. 485 (2005). Jensen was intimately involved in the reform process from 1994 to 2005, serving as General Counsel to the National Bankruptcy Reform Commission and then as Majority Counsel to the House subcommittee that produced the ultimate bankruptcy bill.

[164]   Filings rose from 331,264 in 1980 (the first year under the Code) to over 1.4 million in 1997, when the Commission filed its Report.

[165]   See Tabb, Death, supra note 165, at 1–2.

[166]   Id. at 6–8.

[167]   As it had in 1982, the credit industry commissioned studies that purported to show that a substantial numbers of consumer debtors could repay a significant portion of their debts. These studies, however, were sharply criticized by several researchers. See Jensen, supra note 165, at 502–504.

[168]   Elizabeth Warren, among others, showed convincingly that the claimed $400 "tax" was a complete fabrication, with no basis in reality. Elizabeth Warren, The Phantom $400, 13 J. Bankr. L. & Prac. 77 (2004). But it made for a persuasive and memorable sound-bite for reform advocates.

been enacted in 1984 in theory could lead to the dismissal of a chapter 7 case filed by a debtor with future "can-pay" ability, the consumer credit industry believed that test had become largely a dead letter.

The central effort, then, was to impose a "means test" as a gatekeeping device to chapter 7 for individual consumer debtors. If, according to a strict formula, a debtor had the means to pay a certain amount to creditors out of future income, then the court would be required to dismiss the debtor's chapter 7 case. While the debtor could not be required to file chapter 13, the only choices such a debtor would be left with would be to forgo bankruptcy altogether or to "voluntarily" file chapter 13. The proposed new system was labeled "needs-based" bankruptcy, the idea being that only those with the requisite need should be eligible for traditional chapter 7 bankruptcy relief. Lobbying efforts by the "National Consumer Bankruptcy Coalition"[169] seeking to introduce needs-based bankruptcy began again in earnest in 1991.[170] Fourteen long years later, President Bush signed BAPCPA into law, and the credit industry's long-sought victory was complete.

The history of the enactment of BAPCPA is lengthy, tortured, and at times astonishing. With overwhelming support in Congress for the basic reform concept of moving to needs-based bankruptcy, an idea first embraced in the 102nd Congress did not come to pass until the 109th Congress. Along the way the various proposed bills were waylaid by the September 11 terrorist attacks,[171] the Lewinsky sex scandal, a pocket veto by President Clinton, an anthrax scare, an abortion controversy, a senator's defection from his party, and more.[172]

When the 103rd Congress passed the Bankruptcy Reform Act of 1994, which created a second National Bankruptcy Review Commission, reform proponents believed that they had a prime opportunity to get their cherished reforms before Congress, and with the imprimatur of a bipartisan blue-ribbon commission. The Commission worked diligently under the able leadership of Brady Williamson, a Wisconsin attorney, as Chair,[173] and Professor (now Senator) Elizabeth Warren as Reporter. The Commission convened numerous working groups and held 21 national and regional hearings and public meetings over 35 days from May 1996 through

---

[169] The NCBC included such financial powerhouses as the American Bankers Association, Visa, and Mastercard, and other influential pro-business groups, including the U.S. Chamber of Commerce. This group later renamed itself the Consumer Bankruptcy Reform Coalition.

[170] The credit industry had consistently sought means testing since at least 1968, prior to the first Bankruptcy Review Commission. In the 1970s, that plea fell on deaf ears, as the first Review Commission and Congress flatly rejected any requirement that individual debtors be forced to pay creditors out of future earnings.

[171] The House and Senate conferees were scheduled to meet on the then-pending reform bills (which had passed each house by huge margins) on September 12, 2001. After the terrorist attacks, the conference was postponed indefinitely.

[172] Susan Jensen's section headings in her definitive article on the history of the 2005 law give a flavor of the colorful history: "(I) Seeds of Reform Are Planted: 103rd and 104th Congresses (1993–1996); (II) Congressional Consideration of Reforms Begins: 105th Congress (1997–1998); (III) Reforms Nearly Accomplished: 106th Congress (1999–2000); (IV) Terrorism, Anthrax, Abortion, Power Shifts, and Lloyd's of London: 107th Congress (2001–2002); (V) Seventh Time a Charm or Frozen Coffee?: 108th Congress (2003 to 2004); (VI) Finish Line Finally Crossed: 109th Congress (2005–2006)." Jensen, supra note 165.

[173] The first Chairman, Rep. Mike Synar, died during the process.

August 1997. On October 20, 1997, the Commission filed its Final Report.[174] The Report, over a thousand pages in length, made 172 separate recommendations to Congress, covering virtually every area of bankruptcy. Many of those recommendations eventually became law in BAPCPA.

With all that, what is perhaps most notable about the 1997 Commission Report is what it did *not* recommend, namely, needs-based bankruptcy and a means test. The Report states:

> The Commission conducted an intensive review of consumer bankruptcy that resulted in a full set of recommendations, but the proposals contemplate no change in the basic structure of consumer bankruptcy. Access to Chapter 7 and to Chapter 13, the central feature of the consumer bankruptcy system for nearly 60 years, should be preserved.[175]

This endorsement of the traditional consumer bankruptcy system was stillborn when filed. Seeing that the Commission was not going to adopt means testing, the credit industry turned instead directly to Congress. A month before the Commission filed its report, a bill adopting means testing was introduced in the House.[176] The very next day after the Commission Report was filed, a bill was introduced in the Senate embodying means testing.[177] The Commission's more debtor-friendly proposals regarding consumer bankruptcy were never seriously considered by Congress, although hearings on the Commission Report were held in the fall of 1997.[178] In February 1998, Rep. George Gekas, Chairman of the House subcommittee, introduced H.R. 3150,[179] a more comprehensive omnibus bill, which also embodied means testing. H.R. 3150 became the template for reform that carried through to the eventual bill (S. 256) that was enacted into law in 2005. Extensive hearings were then held on this and related bills in the spring of 1998.[180]

For the next seven years, bankruptcy reform followed an uneven course through Congress, sometimes coming to the brink of passage only to fall short, sometimes diverted by unforeseeable events, but always with substantial support in Congress. While President Clinton held office, he blocked any attempt to enact overly harsh anti-debtor amendments, and once pocket vetoed a bill. Once President Bush was elected, that obstacle was removed, as he fully supported the most extreme measures of bankruptcy reform, but the Republicans were deadlocked 50–50 in the Senate in his

---

[174] National Bankruptcy Review Commission, Final Report: "Bankruptcy: The Next Twenty Years" (Oct. 20, 1997), at http://govinfo.library.unt.edu/nbrc/reporttitlepg.html.

[175] Id. at 91. Four Commissioners dissented from the consumer recommendations, and two dissenting commissioners advocated means testing in a separate dissent.

[176] H.R. 2500, 105th Cong. (1997).

[177] S. 1301, 105th Cong. (1997).

[178] See, e.g., National Bankruptcy Review Commission Report: Hearings Before the Subcomm. on Commercial and Administrative Law of the H. Comm. on the Judiciary, 105th Cong. (1997).

[179] H.R. 3150, 105th Cong. (1998).

[180] Bankruptcy Reform Act of 1998: Responsible Borrower Protection Act and Consumer Lenders and Borrowers Bankruptcy Accountability Act of 1998—Parts I–IV: Hearings on H.R. 3150, H.R. 2500, and H.R. 3146 Before the Subcomm. on Commercial and Administrative Law of the H. Comm. on the Judiciary, 105th Cong. (1998).

first term, and lost control when Senator Jeffords left the party to caucus with the Democrats. In hindsight, it is apparent that the final die in favor of the bill was cast with the 2002 elections, when Republicans regained control of the Senate (they already held the House and the Presidency), giving them full control over the legislative agenda. After another session of congressional maneuvering, the bankruptcy bill finally came to pass. On February 1, 2005, Senator Grassley introduced S. 256, the "Bankruptcy Abuse Prevention and Consumer Protection Act of 2005."[181] The Senate passed the bill by a vote of 74 to 25 just over a month later.[182] The House then took up S. 256, and issued a lengthy committee report on that bill.[183] In April the House passed S. 256 by a vote of 302 to 126.[184] President Bush signed the bill into law on April 20, 2005. The effective date of the new law was October 17, 2005.

The reform process of the 1997–2005 era differed markedly from that of the 1970s in important ways. Non-partisan bankruptcy professionals (judges, attorneys, professors), who had played a major role in the 1970s, were largely ignored by Congress. Their place was taken by a handful of lobbyists who represented the credit industry, and who had the ear of key congressman and their staffs. Campaign contributions by the credit industry, totaling millions of dollars, were funneled to critical members of Congress and to President Bush.

BAPCPA, in its 514 pages, made hundreds of changes to the Bankruptcy Code in addition to the provision for means testing consumer debtors. Many of those amendments followed recommendations of the 1997 Commission Report, and many are beneficial advances in the law. An example is the adoption of chapter 15, for cross-border cases. At the same time, the basic structure of the Bankruptcy Code was not disturbed. The 2005 law did not repeal the 1978 Bankruptcy Reform Act. The only truly major structural change in the law came in the reshaping of consumer bankruptcy, as discussed above. The 2005 law did not change the status of bankruptcy judges, even though the Commission had recommended giving them Article III status.

At this point in time, major bankruptcy reform seems unlikely to surface again for some years to come, although the catastrophic economic recession of 2008 and the election and reelection of Barack Obama (who had voted against BAPCPA as a Senator from Illinois) as President may trigger specific reforms designed to ameliorate some of the dismal conditions facing debtors. For example, the Obama Administration has recommended that Congress create a mechanism for debtors to discharge certain student debts by filing for bankruptcy relief, under limited circumstances. The Obama Administration has also promoted legislation regarding home mortgages, in order to address the recent foreclosure crisis. The administration introduced the Home Affordable Mortgage Program (HAMP) in March 2009, which was designed to aid homeowners in modifying mortgages they cannot afford.[185] However, HAMP has been

---

[181] S. 256, 109th Cong. (2005).

[182] 151 Cong. Rec. S2474 (daily ed. Mar. 10, 2005).

[183] H.R. Rep. No 109–31, 109th Cong., 1st Sess. (2005).

[184] 151 Cong. Rec. H2074–76 (daily ed. Apr. 14, 2005).

[185] HAMP gives various incentives to participating lenders to modify the home mortgages of eligible debtors, rather than allowing the bankruptcy court to modify the mortgage. Lenders that participate in HAMP are required to consider granting a loan modification before foreclosing on debtor's home if the debtor

largely unsuccessful; commentators continue to suggest that a better solution to the mortgage crisis would be to allow modification of home mortgages in bankruptcy,[186] though Congress appears disinclined to do so.

D. THE SOURCES OF CURRENT BANKRUPTCY LAW

§ 1.10   United States Constitution

a.   *Introduction*

Article I, § 8, clause 4 of the United States Constitution (the "Bankruptcy Clause") gives Congress the power to establish "uniform laws on the subject of bankruptcies." As noted earlier, the framers gave little attention to the subject of bankruptcy at the Constitutional Convention of 1787.[187] The need for a federal bankruptcy law was believed to stem from potential interstate commerce problems. The idea of a bankruptcy law as a means of providing a fresh start for distressed debtors was foreign to the framers. Rather, the framers believed that without a federal bankruptcy law, the ability of nonresident creditors to collect their debts from debtors in other states might be impaired, thereby hindering interstate commerce to the detriment of the nation. Nonresident creditors might be discriminated against by local state laws, and also might have difficulty in reaching property of the debtor located in or removed to another state.[188]

The Bankruptcy Clause (and congressional enactments pursuant thereto) has raised several constitutional issues. BAPCPA presents a host of new constitutional questions,[189] which are still slowly percolating through the courts. The first constitutional issues that arose concerned identifying the appropriate scope of the Bankruptcy Clause itself. Thus, the courts had to determine what comprises the "subject of bankruptcies" within the constitutional grant.[190] Secondly, the question has

---

or the trustee makes a request. If the debtor is found eligible under HAMP, the lender must modify the loan pursuant to certain guidelines. HAMP is limited in that the debtor must satisfy certain criteria to be eligible, and not all lenders participate in the program. Lenders who do not participate are not reprimanded.

[186] E.g., Adam Levitin, Resolving the Foreclosure Crisis: Modification of Mortgages in Bankruptcy, 2009 Wisc. L. Rev. 565 (2009). See also Jean Braucher, Humpty Dumpty and the Foreclosure Crisis: Lessons from the Lackluster First Year of the Home Affordable Modification Program (HAMP), 52 Ariz. L. Rev. 727 (2010).

[187] See, e.g., Kurt H. Nadelmann, On the Origin of the Bankruptcy Clause, 1 Am. J. Legal Hist. 215 (1957). See also Frank R. Kennedy, Bankruptcy and the Constitution, 33 U. Mich. L. Quad. 40 (Spring 1989).

[188] James Madison's explained the purpose of the Bankruptcy Clause in number 42 of the Federalist Papers:

> The power of establishing uniform laws of bankruptcy is so intimately connected with the regulation of commerce, and will prevent so many frauds where the parties or their property may lie or be removed into different states that the expediency of it seems not likely to be drawn into question.

[189] See Hon. Samuel L. Bufford & Erwin Chemerinsky, Constitutional Problems in the 2005 Bankruptcy Amendments, 82 Am. Bankr. L.J. 1 (2008); Erwin Chemerinsky, Constitutional Issues Posed in the Bankruptcy Abuse Prevention and Consumer Protection Act of 2005, 79 Am. Bankr. L.J. 571 (2005).

[189] See Hon. Samuel L. Bufford & Erwin Chemerinsky, Constitutional Problems in the 2005 Bankruptcy Amendments, 82 Am. Bankr. L.J. 1 (2008); Erwin Chemerinsky, Constitutional Issues Posed in the Bankruptcy Abuse Prevention and Consumer Protection Act of 2005, 79 Am. Bankr. L.J. 571 (2005).

[190] See Thomas E. Plank, The Constitutional Limits of Bankruptcy, 63 Tenn. L. Rev. 487 (1996); see also Kennedy, supra note 187. See § 1.10.b.

arisen as to whether a bankruptcy law is a "uniform" law as required by the constitutional grant.[191]

A second set of problems implicates federalism issues. For example, a question that has arisen is determining when a state debtor-creditor law is preempted by Congress's exercise of its powers under the Bankruptcy Clause.[192] The provision for municipal bankruptcy (under chapter 9) poses concerns about federal encroachment on state sovereignty to regulate municipalities.[193] Some of the regulations imposed on attorneys (as "debt relief agencies") in BAPCPA[194] may raise Tenth Amendment and separation of powers questions, as they intrude on traditional state regulation of attorneys.[195]

Finally, courts have had to sort out the relationship between the Bankruptcy Clause and other provisions in the Constitution. To what extent is the operation of the Bankruptcy Clause constrained by other constitutional rights and limitations? Issues have arisen regarding the Fifth Amendment Takings Clause;[196] Article III;[197] the Seventh Amendment right to jury trial;[198] the Eleventh Amendment;[199] the First Amendment guarantee of freedom of speech;[200] and the Thirteenth Amendment prohibition of involuntary servitude.[201]

b.   The "Subject of Bankruptcies"

The first constitutional issue that arose in interpreting the Bankruptcy Clause was determining what constituted the permissible limits of *the subject of bankruptcies.* The constitutional framers probably well understood the scope of the "subject of bankruptcies." The model they undoubtedly had in mind was the one that existed in England at that time. "Bankruptcy" at the time of the Constitution was well-

---

[191] See Judith S. Koffler, The Bankruptcy Clause and Exemption Laws: A Reexamination of the Doctrine of Geographic Uniformity, 58 N.Y.U. L. Rev. 22 (1983); see also Kennedy, supra note 187. See § 1.10.c.

[192] Int'l Shoe Co. v. Pinkus, 278 U.S. 261 (1929). See also § 1.10.d.

[193] The first legislation providing for municipal bankruptcy was struck down by the Supreme Court on state sovereignty grounds. Ashton v. Cameron Cnty. Water Improvement Dist., 298 U.S. 513 (1936).

[194] See 11 U.S.C. §§ 526–528.

[195] See Bufford & Chemerinsky, supra note 189, at 22–27; Chemerinsky, supra note 189, at 580–83.

[196] James S. Rogers, The Impairment of Secured Creditors' Rights in Reorganization: A Study of the Relationship Between the Fifth Amendment and the Bankruptcy Clause, 96 Harv. L. Rev. 973 (1983). See also § 1.10.e.(1).

[197] See, e.g., Stern v. Marshall, 131 S.Ct. 2594 (2011); N. Pipeline Constr. Co. v. Marathon Pipe Line Co., 458 U.S. 50 (1982). See also §§ 1.8, 1.10.c(6), 4.2.

[198] Granfinanciera, S.A. v. Nordberg, 492 U.S. 33 (1989). See § 1.10.e.(2).

[199] Cent. Virginia Cmty. Coll. v. Katz, 546 U.S. 356 (2006). See also § 1.10.e.(3).

[200] BAPCPA in particular raised serious concerns about the constitutionality of restrictions on attorney advertising, the content of attorneys' advice to clients, and disclosures required of debt relief agencies. See Bufford & Chemerinsky, supra note 189, at 14–22; Chemerinsky, supra note 189, at 572–80. The Supreme Court ruled on the issue in 2010. Milavetz, Gallop, & Milavetz, P.A. v. United States, 130 S.Ct. 1324 (2010) (holding that when narrowly construed, § 526(a)(4) is not impermissibly vague in violation of the First Amendment).

[201] See Margaret Howard, Bankruptcy Bondage, 2009 U. Ill. L. Rev. 191; Robert J. Keach, Dead Man Filing Redux: Is the New Individual Chapter Eleven Unconstitutional?, 13 Am. Bankr. Inst. L. Rev. 483 (2005). See also § 1.10.e.(4).

understood to mean a collective collection remedy that creditors alone could invoke involuntarily against a merchant trader who had committed an "act of bankruptcy." Debtors had no right to institute a voluntary bankruptcy case. By contrast, an "insolvency" law was one that a financially distressed debtor could invoke to obtain relief.[202]

As the forms of available bankruptcy relief enacted by Congress evolved over time, questions were raised as to whether the newer types of relief fell within the constitutional grant of power over the subject of bankruptcies. While this is an academically interesting and indeed debatable question, the reality is that the Supreme Court has regularly rejected these challenges. The Court without exception has declined to limit the reach of the bankruptcy power to the conception of bankruptcy existing at the time of the Constitution.

The first major expansion in the concept of a bankruptcy law came with the adoption of (1) voluntary bankruptcy for (2) non-merchant debtors in the Bankruptcy Act of 1841.[203] Under the traditional understanding, "voluntary bankruptcy" would have been an oxymoron. The constitutionality of the law was challenged by John Calhoun and Thomas Benton, among others, and defended by Daniel Webster and Joseph Story,[204] the latter being the chief architect of the 1841 Act. The Supreme Court never decided the constitutional question, although Justice Catron sitting on circuit did uphold the constitutionality of the new law in 1843.[205] Justice Catron's broad definition of the scope of the Bankruptcy Clause has been quoted with approval by the Supreme Court:

> I hold, it [the bankruptcy power] extends to all cases where the law causes to be distributed the property of the debtor among his creditors; this is its least limit. Its greatest, is a discharge of the debtor from his contracts. And all intermediate legislation, affecting substance and form, but tending to further the great end of the subject—distribution and discharge—are in the competency and discretion of Congress.[206]

After the 1841 Act, the question of the legitimacy of voluntary bankruptcy for non-merchants was settled in the affirmative, never to be questioned again.

The authorization for composition agreements, contained in the 1874 amendments to the 1867 Act, represented the next significant expansion in the scope of the subject

---

[202] See Sturges v. Crowninshield, 17 U.S. 194 (1819). Justice Marshall in *Sturges* did emphasize, however, that the historical distinction between bankruptcy laws and insolvency laws did not necessarily define the limits of the constitutional grant.

[203] Ch. 9, 5 Stat. 441 (1841) (repealed 1843). See John C. McCoid, II, The Origins of Voluntary Bankruptcy, 5 Bankr. Dev. J. 362 (1988).

[204] Story had argued that voluntary bankruptcy was constitutional in his 1833 Commentaries on the Constitution. Joseph Story, Commentaries on the Constitution of the United States § 543 (abridged ed. Boston 1833).

[205] In re Klein, appended in notes to Nelson v. Carland, 42 U.S. (1 How.) 265, 277 (1843).

[206] Id. (quoting Louisville Joint Stock Land Bank v. Radford, 295 U.S. 555, 588 n.18 (1935)). See also Ashton v. Cameron Cnty. Water Improvement Dist., 298 U.S. 513, 536 (1936) (citing *Klein* with approval).

of bankruptcies.[207] The composition agreement, if accepted by the requisite percentage of creditors, allowed the debtor to retain his or her property and discharge the debts by paying the amounts specified in the composition. Although the Supreme Court never directly passed on the constitutionality of the composition provision, the lower courts found that it was constitutional.[208] In an 1881 case, the Supreme Court recognized that the composition provision was a proceeding "in bankruptcy," and thus had to be applied consistently with the other provisions of the bankruptcy law.[209]

The Depression of the 1930s produced a spate of bankruptcy legislation. Although the Supreme Court overturned two acts during this period on other grounds, the Court continued to reaffirm the expansive scope of the bankruptcy power.[210] In *Continental Illinois National Bank & Trust Co. v. Chicago, Rock Island & Pacific Railway Co.,*[211] the Court upheld the provisions of § 77, permitting railroad reorganizations, as within the scope of the Bankruptcy Clause. In the 1970s the Court again held that a railroad reorganization law fell within the subject of bankruptcies.[212]

Today virtually any law that addresses the relationship between creditors and a financially distressed debtor, and readjusts the respective rights of those parties, is considered to fall within the "subject of bankruptcies." According to the Supreme Court, "bankruptcy" covers the "subject of the relations between an insolvent or nonpaying or fraudulent debtor and his creditors, extending to his and their relief."[213]

c. *Uniformity*

A second major constitutional bankruptcy issue that has arisen is whether a given law is a "uniform" bankruptcy law within the meaning of the Bankruptcy Clause. "Uniformity" is problematic in the bankruptcy context because (1) most laws governing the substance of the debtor-creditor relationship are *state* laws; (2) these state laws are incorporated into and applied in the federal Bankruptcy Code; and (3) these state laws are not necessarily uniform. Strictly speaking, then, "true" or "personal" uniformity does not exist in bankruptcy, in the sense that debtors and creditors in different states may be treated differently on similar facts. For example, a debtor in California might be liable in bankruptcy on a claim for breach of a cohabitation agreement, while a Vermont debtor might not be liable on such a claim on identical facts. A debtor in Florida may be able to exempt a palatial homestead, while a Pennsylvania debtor may

---

[207] Ch. 390, § 17, 18 Stat. 182–84 (1874) (repealed 1878).

[208] See, e.g., In re Reiman, 20 F. Cas. 490 (S.D.N.Y. 1874) (No. 11,673).

[209] Wilson v. Mudge, 103 U.S. (13 Otto) 217 (1881). The Court held that a debt based on fraud could not be discharged in a composition when the defrauded creditor did not assent.

[210] In the two cases in which it struck down bankruptcy legislation, the Court did not do so on the ground that the legislation exceeded the scope of the bankruptcy power, but rather that the exercise of the bankruptcy power had to yield to other constitutional demands. See Ashton v. Cameron Cnty. Water Improvement Dist., 298 U.S. 513 (1936) (State sovereignty); Louisville Joint Stock Land Bank v. Radford, 295 U.S. 555 (1935) (Fifth Amendment).

[211] 294 U.S. 648 (1935).

[212] Blanchette v. Connecticut Gen. Ins. Corp. (Regional Rail Reorganization Act Cases), 419 U.S. 102 (1974).

[213] See Wright v. Union Cent. Life Ins. Co., 304 U.S. 502, 513–514 (1938); Cont'l Illinois Nat'l Bank & Trust Co. v. Chicago, Rock Island & Pac. Ry. Co., 294 U.S. 648, 672–73 (1935). The Supreme Court adopted this quote from *In re Reiman*, 20 F. Cas. 490 (S.D.N.Y. 1874) (No. 11,673).

be entitled to almost no homestead exemption. Does this destroy bankruptcy uniformity?

The short answer, perhaps surprisingly, is no.[214] According to a landmark Supreme Court decision in 1902, *Hanover National Bank v. Moyses*,[215] all that the Constitution requires is "geographical" uniformity, rather than personal uniformity. In *Moyses,* the Court upheld the incorporation of state exemption laws in the 1898 Bankruptcy Act. Geographical uniformity in this context, the Court observed, was satisfied "when the trustee takes in each state whatever would have been available to the creditor if the bankrupt law had not been passed."[216]

Thus, a bankruptcy law is uniform when (1) the substantive law applied in a bankruptcy case conforms to that applied outside of bankruptcy under state law; (2) the same law is applied to all debtors within a state and to their creditors; and (3) Congress uniformly delegates to the states the power to fix those laws. The fact that debtors and creditors in different states may receive different treatment does not render the law unconstitutional.

In 1918, the Court reaffirmed the *Moyses* principle in a case involving the use of state fraudulent conveyance laws in bankruptcy.[217] More recently, the lower courts have followed *Moyses* in upholding the exemption provisions of the 1978 Bankruptcy Code against uniformity challenges.[218] The Supreme Court has not addressed the issue. The Court continues to affirm, however, that "the uniformity requirement is not a straightjacket that forbids Congress to distinguish among classes of debtors, nor does it prohibit Congress from recognizing that state laws do not treat commercial transactions in a uniform manner."[219]

A uniformity issue is also presented when Congress passes a "bankruptcy" law that is not available to debtors across the country. Private bankruptcy laws for particular debtors are not permitted. In recent years the Supreme Court has twice confronted this problem with regard to special railroad legislation, with different results. In the 1974 *Regional Rail Reorganization Cases*,[220] the Court upheld the Regional Rail Reorganization Act even though the law was restricted in its application to the railroads of a single geographic region. The saving grace in the law stemmed from the reality that all of the railroads then operating under the bankruptcy laws were in that region; even if the statute had been drafted to be of general applicability, its operation and effect would have been unchanged. According to the Court in *Railway*

---

[214] See Koffler, supra note 191; see also Daniel A. Austin, Bankruptcy and the Myth of "Uniform Laws," 42 Seton Hall L. Rev. 1081 (2012). The answer is surprising in part because "uniformity" is given a much stricter meaning when applied to other constitutional powers, such as naturalization and taxation.

[215] 186 U.S. 181 (1902).

[216] Id. at 190. The Court noted that "[t]he general operation of the law is uniform although it may result in certain particulars differently in different states." Id.

[217] Stellwagen v. Clum, 245 U.S. 605 (1918).

[218] See, e.g., In re Sullivan, 680 F.2d 1131 (7th Cir.), cert. denied, 459 U.S. 992 (1982).

[219] Ry. Labor Execs. Ass'n v. Gibbons, 455 U.S. 457, 469 (1982).

[220] Blanchette v. Connecticut Gen. Ins. Corp. (The Regional Rail Reorganization Cases), 419 U.S. 102 (1974).

Labor Executives Association v. Gibbons,[221] however, Congress did overreach in passing a private bankruptcy law that affected only the employees of the Rock Island Railroad.

A puzzling uniformity issue has arisen with regard to the incorporation of state exemption laws—a question on which the courts, following *Moyses*, have had little troubling finding constitutionally satisfactory uniformity—when the wrinkle is added that the state enacts a *bankruptcy-specific* exemption law, available *only* to state residents in a bankruptcy case itself, but not available to state residents outside of bankruptcy. In such a situation, the conceptual linchpins of *Moyses,* of state-wide "geographic" uniformity and the incorporation of non-bankruptcy laws of general applicability, seem to be lacking, and some courts accordingly have (I would argue correctly) found them unconstitutional.[222] However, at least two courts of appeals have nonetheless found satisfactory uniformity, taking the view that congressional delegation of the exemption power to the states in § 522 gave the states essentially unlimited power to enact bankruptcy exemption laws as they saw fit.[223] According to those courts, virtually the only uniformity restraint is that Congress may not pass a private bankruptcy law.

The enactment of the "means test" in § 707(b) in 2005 may raise serious uniformity issues,[224] notwithstanding the historical leniency of the Supreme Court on bankruptcy uniformity. First, several aspects of the means test, and safe harbors pertinent thereto, differentiate between debtors of different states based on income differentials between states.[225] Standing alone, that aspect of "non-uniform" treatment may be found to be constitutionally permissible under *Moyses* and *Stellwagen*, since differences between states are tolerated under the "geographical" uniformity doctrine, as long as all debtors within a state are treated alike. Having said that, though, the *raison d'être* of those decisions is lacking in the means test context. In *Moyses* and *Stellwagen*, the Court gave effect to matters of *state law* (exemptions and fraudulent conveyances, respectively) that impacted the treatment of debtors and creditors generally, and were simply imported into the federal bankruptcy realm. The Court did not find the constitutional uniformity mandate to be offended when the same debtor-creditor rules that pertained under state law were extended to bankruptcy, even though that meant outcomes might vary between states. In the means test provisions utilizing different state incomes to reach different results, by comparison, the state income medians lack any independent state law force in regulating the debtor-creditor relationship; instead, the only debtor-creditor function is in the federal bankruptcy realm, and yet debtors are treated non-uniformly.

---

[221] 455 U.S. 457 (1982).

[222] See, e.g., In re Schafer, 455 B.R. 590 (B.A.P. 6th Cir. 2011), rev'd, 689 F.3d 601 (6th Cir. 2012); In re Mata, 115 B.R. 288 (Bankr. D. Colo. 1990); In re Lennen, 71 B.R. 80 (Bankr. N.D. Cal. 1987); In re Reynolds, 24 B.R. 344 (Bankr. S.D. Ohio 1982).

[223] *Schafer*, supra note 222, 689 F.3d 601; In re Kulp, 949 F.2d 1106 (10th Cir. 1991).

[224] See Butford & Chemerinsky, supra note 189, at 39–45; Chemerinsky, supra note 189, at 592–94.

[225] For example, questions of who can bring an action against the debtor, and whether the debtor enjoys a safe harbor, turn on whether the debtor's family income is below the median income for the state in which the debtor resides. 11 U.S.C. § 707(b)(6), (7). Accordingly, two debtors with the same income who live in different states could be treated differently, depending on the median incomes for those states.

Troubling as the income median differences might be, another aspect of the means test is even more likely to contravene even the permissive geographic uniformity doctrine, since debtors *within the same state* are treated differently. The computation of the means test requires reference to specified expense allowances,[226] in order to determine how much disposable income the debtor has to make payments to creditors. For the housing and utilities allowance, the amounts allotted to debtors to claim as a deduction *vary by county* within the state.[227] Thus, like debtors who happen to live in different counties are treated differently under the means test within the very same state. Nor does this differential treatment have any grounding in underlying state law that governs the affairs of debtors and creditors; rather, it is purely a creature of federal law. A similar problem exists for the transportation allowance for those states that contain a "Metropolitan Statistical Area," as the transportation allowance is different for debtors within the state depending on whether they live in the MSA.[228] Finally, for cases filed before February 1, 2008, the amount of expenses allowed under the National Standards (for food, clothing, etc.) differed depending on the debtor's income level. That is, debtors of the same family size were given larger deductions for food and clothing if they had higher incomes. This distinction caused non-uniformity for debtors within the same states and without any justification or basis in underlying state law. All of these non-uniform applications to like debtors within the same state should be vulnerable to a constitutional uniformity challenge. If the Court holds otherwise, then truly the uniformity "requirement" in the Bankruptcy Clause has been rendered utterly meaningless.[229]

d. *Preemption*

A third constitutional question raised by the Bankruptcy Clause is preemption. Preemption is a pervasive problem in the federal system, and bankruptcy is no different. In the bankruptcy context, preemption questions fall within two basic categories. The first category includes the more global question of whether a state law is a "bankruptcy" law and thus generally preempted by Congress's exercise of its power

---

[226] 11 U.S.C. § 707(b)(2)(a)(2)(i). See § 2.15(c). The United States Trustee website maintains helpful links: http://www.justice.gov/ust/eo/bapcpa/20130501/meanstesting.htm.

[227] For an example that illustrates the county-by-county disparate treatment, consider Illinois: http://www.justice.gov/ust/eo/bapcpa/20130501/bci_data/housing_charts/irs_housing_charts_IL.htm.

[228] To use Illinois again as an example, debtors located in the Chicago MSA (defined by county) are given a larger operating costs transportation allowance than other Illinois debtors. http://www.justice.gov/ust/eo/bapcpa/20130501/bci_data/IRS_Trans_Exp_Stds_MW.htm.

[229] Only one Court of Appeals has addressed the uniformity requirement under BAPCPA to date. In *Schultz v. United States*, 529 F.3d 343 (6th Cir. 2008), the court decided a uniformity issue in chapter 13. Under new § 1325(b)(4), Schultz was forced to pay all of his projected disposable income over a five-year period, rather than a three-year period, because his income was more than the median for Tennessee. Schultz's income would have been below the median in five states, thus subjecting him to worse treatment because he lived in Tennessee instead of one of those other states. The Sixth Circuit saw no distinction between differences in state exemption law or fraudulent conveyance law, as approved by *Moyses* and *Stellwagen*, and differences in state median income. The fact that fraudulent conveyance and exemption laws have independent application outside of bankruptcy, whereas "state median income" does not in terms of regulating the debtor-creditor relationship, was a distinction the court failed to grasp. The court also analogized to the *Regional Rail Reorganization Cases*, which it read as allowing Congress to take into account differences in regions and to address geographically isolated problems, saying that with the median income provisions Congress was addressing the problem of different costs of living across the states. The court added that it was also addressing the "identical" provisions of the chapter 7 means test, though it did not address whether intrastate differences could be treated the same as interstate differences.

under the Bankruptcy Clause. The second category encompasses whether a particular state statute conflicts with some specific aspect of the federal bankruptcy law.

For much of the nineteenth century, Congress left the bankruptcy power unexercised. The Supreme Court decided in *Sturges v. Crowninshield* in 1819 that the mere existence of the Bankruptcy Clause did not in and of itself preempt state legislation on bankruptcy and insolvency issues, if Congress had not passed a bankruptcy law.[230] Thus, states were free to fill this vacuum with bankruptcy and insolvency laws of their own, subject, however, to the independent constitutional limitation that states may not impair the obligation of contracts. Many states did enact such bankruptcy and insolvency laws. Since 1898, however, a federal bankruptcy law has occupied the field. In 1929 in *International Shoe Co. v. Pinkus*,[231] the Supreme Court struck down an Arkansas insolvency law that forced creditors to stipulate to the debtor's discharge in order to share in the distribution of the debtor's property. In sweeping language, the Court held that states were precluded from enacting competing bankruptcy legislation.[232] Although state laws governing assignments for the benefit of creditors are permitted, such laws may not provide for a discharge of debts, and in other respects may be preempted by the federal Bankruptcy Code.[233]

Preemption questions occasionally arise regarding whether specific state legislation might conflict with the federal scheme spelled out in the Bankruptcy Code. The form of analysis here is not peculiar to the bankruptcy field, but follows standard constitutional preemption doctrine. Under the Supremacy Clause, of course, the federal law controls in the event of conflict. Resolution of the issue can be tricky in bankruptcy, however. One problem concerns the widespread use of state laws in bankruptcy cases. For example, Congress has authorized the states to pass exemption laws that will be available to bankruptcy debtors. § 522(b). The state exemption law itself, then, obviously is not preempted in its entirety. In some particulars, however, a state's exemption law may conflict with the federal scheme and to that extent may be preempted.[234] Generally, though, courts have been very lenient in upholding state exemption laws as applied in bankruptcy.

---

[230] 17 U.S. (4 Wheat.) 122, 192–96 (1819). Chief Justice Marshall observed that "[i]t is not the mere existence of the power, but its exercise, which is incompatible with the exercise of the same power by the states." Id. at 196.

[231] 278 U.S. 261 (1929).

[232] "The power of Congress to establish uniform laws on the subject of bankruptcies is paramount. . . . In respect of bankruptcies the intention of Congress is plain. The national purpose to establish uniformity necessarily excludes state regulation. It is apparent . . . that intolerable inconsistencies and confusion would result if that [Arkansas] insolvency law be given effect while the national [Bankruptcy] Act is in force. Congress did not intend to give insolvent debtors seeking discharge, or their creditors seeking to collect claims, choice between the relief provided by the Bankruptcy Act and that specified in state insolvency laws. . . . It is clear that the provisions of the Arkansas law governing the distribution of property of insolvents for the payment of their debts and providing for their discharge . . . are within the field entered by Congress when it passed the Bankruptcy Act, and therefore such provisions must be held to have been superseded."

278 U.S. at 265–66.

[233] See, e.g., Sherwood Partners, Inc. v. Lycos, 394 F.3d 1198 (9th Cir. 2005) (holding that a state law preference statute could not be asserted by an assignee for the benefit of creditors due to federal preemption).

[234] For example, § 522(f) permits the avoidance of certain liens that impair exemptions; states thus may not define exemptions so as to preclude lien avoidance.

Recently, for example, the Sixth Circuit was faced with whether a bankruptcy-specific state exemption statute was preempted by federal bankruptcy law. The preceding section noted the problems such statutes raise under the uniformity test. In *In re Schafer*,[235] a Michigan debtor was given the option under state law to elect from (1) the federal bankruptcy homestead exemption, (2) the general state homestead exemption, or (3) a state homestead exemption available exclusively for debtors in bankruptcy, which far exceeded the other two available exemptions. The debtor, of course, elected the greater bankruptcy-specific state exemption, and the trustee objected on the grounds that such exemptions were unconstitutional under the Bankruptcy Clause (because nonuniform) and under the Supremacy Clause.

The court found that the bankruptcy-specific exemption was constitutional. As noted above, the court did not find a violation of uniformity, reasoning that only private bankruptcy laws are forbidden. On the supremacy question, the court reasoned that under the "plain meaning" of § 522, Congress had not expressed a desire to restrict state authority in the field. Further, the court also emphasized that the state bankruptcy-specific exemptions did not in any way impede the policies and purposes of the national bankruptcy law, and in fact promoted the federal policy of allowing the debtor a "fresh start."[236]

Another problem arises in defining the scope of the federal interest and the extent of state interference in cases of indirect conflict. The best-known example is the Supreme Court's decision in *Perez v. Campbell*,[237] holding that an Arizona driver's responsibility statute was invalid under the Supremacy Clause as conflicting with the federal fresh start policy manifested in the bankruptcy discharge. The offending law required suspension of a debtor's driver's license as long as a judgment arising out of the operation of a motor vehicle remained unsatisfied, even if that debtor obtained a discharge of the debt in bankruptcy. Yet, cases after *Perez* have upheld other state driver's responsibility laws as applied against bankruptcy debtors when those laws interfered less directly with the federal scheme. Drawing the line is not easy.

e. *Reconciling Competing Constitutional Provisions*

(1) Fifth Amendment

A final type of constitutional issue that has arisen is determining when Congress's exercise of its powers under the Bankruptcy Clause conflicts with other provisions of the Constitution. The Supreme Court has held that the reach of Bankruptcy Clause is limited by other constitutional provisions, such as the Fifth Amendment, the Seventh Amendment, the Eleventh Amendment, and Article III. In each instance, defining the appropriate constitutional accommodation has proved an elusive (and illusive?) task.

The Fifth Amendment prohibitions against the taking of private property without just compensation and without due process of law limit the Bankruptcy Clause. In

---

[235] 689 F.3d 601 (6th Cir. 2012).

[236] Id. at 616.

[237] 402 U.S. 637 (1971).

Louisville Joint Stock Land Bank v. Radford,[238] the Supreme Court struck down the Frazier–Lemke Act, a Depression era bankruptcy law designed to alleviate the plight of farmers, on the ground that it deprived mortgagors of their collateral without just compensation. Yet, just two years later, the Court upheld a very slightly revised version of the invalidated law in *Wright v. Vinton Branch.*[239] The very next year the Court again read narrowly the Fifth Amendment limitation on the Bankruptcy Clause in *Wright v. Union Central Life Insurance Co.*[240] In 1982, however, the Supreme Court in *United States v. Security Industrial Bank*[241] squelched any speculation that it had abandoned *Radford*, citing that decision with approval for the proposition that the Fifth Amendment limits the bankruptcy power. To avoid a constitutional problem, the Court construed the lien avoidance provisions in § 522(f) of the 1978 Code as only applying prospectively.[242] The Court also cited *Radford* with approval in *Dewsnup v. Timm*, in rejecting lien stripping under § 506(d) in the chapter 7 context.[243] The net result of the Court's decisions in this area is that the rights of a secured creditor in a bankruptcy case must be protected against a Fifth Amendment taking, but only to the extent of preserving the principal value of the creditor's property claim (in the collateral held by the debtor).[244] Of course, a necessary prerequisite to any Fifth Amendment claim in this context is a lien on some collateral that is also property of the estate.[245]

(2) Seventh Amendment

The Seventh Amendment provision preserving the right to a trial by jury in suits at common law also applies in bankruptcy. In 1966, the Supreme Court cast doubt on that proposition with its decision in *Katchen v. Landy*[246] that a creditor who was sued for the recovery of a preference did not have a jury trial right when the creditor had filed a claim against the estate. In 1989, the Supreme Court removed the doubts when it held in *Granfinanciera, S.A. v. Nordberg*[247] that a trustee's suit to recover a fraudulent conveyance in bankruptcy was subject to the defendant's right to trial by jury. The next year, the Court in *Langenkamp v. Culp*[248] concluded that both *Katchen* and *Granfinanciera* were still good law, holding that a creditor has a jury trial right when sued for a preference (under *Granfinanciera*), but that the creditor lost that right when it filed a claim against the estate (under *Katchen*). In 2011, the Supreme Court drew heavily on the underlying precepts of all of these jury trial cases in holding in *Stern v. Marshall* that the bankruptcy court could not constitutionally enter a final

---

[238]   295 U.S. 555 (1935).

[239]   300 U.S. 440 (1937).

[240]   304 U.S. 502 (1938).

[241]   459 U.S. 70 (1982).

[242]   The Court's decision was criticized by Rogers, supra note 196.

[243]   502 U.S. 410, 419 (1992).

[244]   For an extended discussion of these cases, see Charles J. Tabb, Credit Bidding, Security, and the Obsolescence of Chapter 11, 2013 U. Ill. L. Rev. 103 (2013).

[245]   E.g., In re Motors Liquidation Co., 430 B.R. 65 (S.D.N.Y. 2010); In re Chrysler LLC, 405 B.R. 84 (Bankr. S.D.N.Y. 2009).

[246]   382 U.S. 323 (1966).

[247]   492 U.S. 33 (1989). See also § 4.8.a.

[248]   498 U.S. 42 (1990).

order on a state law counterclaim that was not necessarily resolved in the claims allowance process.[249] The parameters of the jury trial right and the power of a non-Article III court to adjudicate were largely synonymous, the Court suggested. Given the *Stern* holding (and reasoning), that indicates strongly that the jury trial cases all remain good law.

The Court in *Granfinanciera* left open the question whether a non-Article III bankruptcy judge could preside over a constitutionally mandated jury trial. The concern is whether doing so constitutes an exercise of "the essential attributes of judicial power," which the Court in *Marathon Pipe Line* and in *Granfinanciera* had suggested could only be done by an Article III court in the federal system. Prior to 1994 most courts of appeals dodged the difficult constitutional question by ruling that bankruptcy courts did not have the statutory authority to preside over a jury trial. Although the Court initially granted certiorari on the question in the case of *In re Ben Cooper* out of the Second Circuit, it remanded on an unrelated procedural issue and then refused to grant certiorari again.[250] In the Bankruptcy Reform Act of 1994, Congress forced the courts to reach the constitutional question by conferring express statutory authority to conduct jury trials on bankruptcy judges.[251]

A recent case in the Eighth Circuit raised the issue of whether the Supreme Court's 2011 ruling in *Stern v. Marshall*[252] impacted the line of Seventh Amendment cases, and concluded, as I have argued here, that *Stern* only reinforced those jury trial cases. In *Pearson Education Inc. v. Almgren,*[253] creditors filed a proof of claim regarding a copyright infringement claim, and sought a jury trial to determine the amount of damages for their infringement claim. They lost. The Eighth Circuit drew heavily upon *Katchen* and *Langenkamp* to conclude that while there otherwise would be a Seventh Amendment right to a jury trial, the creditors waived this right by filing a proof of claim.

However, the creditors argued that *Stern* "casts doubt on the continued viability" of the *Katchen* and *Langenkamp* line.[254] The Eighth Circuit rejected this argument, noting that *Stern* "expressly distinguished" *Katchen* and *Langenkamp* as cases where resolution of the cause of action was necessarily a part of the allowance process itself—a distinction similarly critical to drawing the line as to the bankruptcy court's power to enter a final order notwithstanding the dictates of Article III. The Eighth Circuit concluded that the copyright claim at hand was just such a case: a determination of the amount of damages to be awarded was necessary for determining the allowability of the claim.[255]

---

[249] 131 S.Ct. 2594, 2620 (2011).

[250] 896 F.2d 1394 (2d Cir.), cert. granted, 497 U.S. 1023, vacated and remanded, 498 U.S. 964 (1990), decision on remand, 924 F.2d 36 (2d Cir.), cert. denied, 500 U.S. 928 (1991). The Second Circuit was the only circuit court to hold that bankruptcy judges had the statutory and constitutional authority to conduct a jury trial.

[251] Bankruptcy Reform Act of 1994, Pub. L. No. 103–394, § 112, 108 Stat. 4106.

[252] 131 S.Ct. 2594 (2011).

[253] 685 F.3d 691 (8th Cir. 2012).

[254] Id. at 694.

[255] Id. at 695.

(3) Eleventh Amendment

The spectrum of an expansive state immunity from bankruptcy proceedings under the Eleventh Amendment haunted the bankruptcy world for a decade, from 1996 to 2006. Today peace and harmony (if not judicial consistency) have been restored, and states acting as creditors (again) are, at Congress' whim, subject to the full force of the federal bankruptcy power, notwithstanding the Eleventh Amendment. To jump to the end of the story, the Supreme Court's 2006 decision in *Central Virginia Community College v. Katz*[256] held that the Bankruptcy Clause stands (alone, apparently) as an Article I exception to state sovereign immunity under the Eleventh Amendment.[257] Thus, after *Katz*, Congress has the power pursuant to the Bankruptcy Clause to subject states in their capacity as creditors of bankruptcy debtors to the full force of the Code, including the discharge injunction, the automatic stay, turnover of assets, preference recovery, and so forth. In § 106, Congress has exercised that power. One more vote the other way in *Katz*,[258] however, and states could have ignored bankruptcy with impunity and thumbed their noses (holding the sovereign immunity card) at any attempts by bankruptcy trustees to sue them and recover for the state's violation of bankruptcy orders.

The Eleventh Amendment stands for the propositions that there can be no suit of a sovereign without its consent, and that each state is sovereign.[259] Under the Eleventh Amendment, this state sovereignty must be respected in the federal system. Thus, absent some exception, states cannot be sued in federal court without their consent. Until 1996, however, it had generally been assumed that the Eleventh Amendment posed no meaningful limitation on the conduct of proceedings in bankruptcy. That comforting assumption was obliterated in 1996 in a non-bankruptcy case. The Supreme Court held in *Seminole Tribe of Florida v. Florida*[260] that Congress could not rely on its Article I powers to extend Article III jurisdiction against states that would otherwise violate the Eleventh Amendment.[261] The Court made it clear in dicta that the rationale of its decision applied equally to Congress's Article I bankruptcy power, which meant that states were immune from suit under the Code. The Code's purported abrogation of

---

[256] 546 U.S. 356 (2006).

[257] The American Bankruptcy Institute Law Review devoted an entire symposium issue (volume 15, issue 1, Summer 2007) to the *Katz* decision. Included in that symposium are the following: G. Ray Warner, Introduction, at 1; Richard Lieb, Federal Supremacy and State Sovereignty: The Supreme Court's Early Jurisprudence, at 3; Martin H. Redish & Daniel M. Greenfield, Bankruptcy Sovereign Immunity and the Dilemma of Principled Decision Making: The Curious Case of *Central Virginia Community College v. Katz*, at 13; Thomas E. Plank, State Sovereignty in Bankruptcy After *Katz*, at 59; Ralph Brubaker, Explaining *Katz's* New Bankruptcy Exception to State Sovereign Immunity: The Bankruptcy Power as a Federal Forum Power, at 95; Randolph J. Haines, Federalism Principles in Bankruptcy After *Katz*, at 135; Susan M. Freeman & Marvin C. Ruth, The Scope of Bankruptcy Ancillary Jurisdiction After *Katz* as Informed by Pre–*Katz* Ancillary Jurisdiction Cases, at 155.

[258] Justice Alito took Justice O'Connor's seat just 8 days after the *Katz* opinion was handed down. One suspects strongly that had Justice Alito been on the Court for the *Katz* decision, he would have voted with the four conservative dissenting Justices (Thomas wrote the opinion, joined by Scalia, Roberts, and Kennedy).

[259] See, e.g., Hans v. Louisiana, 134 U.S. 1 (1890).

[260] 517 U.S. 44 (1996).

[261] The Article I power at issue in *Seminole Tribe* was the Indian Commerce Clause.

state sovereign immunity in § 106 thus would be unenforceable as applied to states in light of the Eleventh Amendment.

A shred of hope remained. While *Seminole Tribe* made it clear that Congress could not subject states to suit in *federal* court, nevertheless the Eleventh Amendment had never been interpreted to provide states with immunity from suit in their own *state* courts. Thus, a malfeasant state entity that violated bankruptcy orders arguably could be sued by the bankruptcy trustee for recovery in state court. That hope was shattered in 1999 when the Supreme Court in *Alden v. Maine*[262] extended the states' Eleventh Amendment immunity to suits in state court as well.[263]

The threat of *Seminole Tribe* coupled with *Alden* to the integrity of the bankruptcy system was manifest. States as creditors apparently could rely on the immunity of the Eleventh Amendment to ignore the bankruptcy system, and thus to violate the automatic stay, ignore discharges, take preferences without fear of recovery, and otherwise wreak havoc on the carefully structured bankruptcy scheme. This was a huge problem in bankruptcy, because state entities often are significant creditors. States would get a better deal than any other creditor, to the detriment of those other creditors and to the debtor alike.

Just when it appeared that all hope was lost, in 2004 the Court created an incongruous exception to sovereign immunity for bankruptcy in *Tennessee Student Assistance Corp. v. Hood*.[264] In that case the debtor (Hood) brought an adversary proceeding against the State of Tennessee alleging that student loans held by Tennessee imposed an undue hardship on her and therefore were dischargeable in bankruptcy. Tennessee, of course, objected to jurisdiction in bankruptcy on Eleventh Amendment grounds. What Eleventh Amendment problem?, the Supreme Court amazingly responded. Why no problem? Because, the Court asserted, the Eleventh Amendment only gives states immunity from the assertion of *personal* jurisdiction against nonconsenting states, whereas the bankruptcy dischargeability proceeding was purely an *in rem* proceeding.[265] The Court thus dodged directly deciding whether Congress may invoke the Bankruptcy Clause to abrogate sovereign immunity.

But what if a bankruptcy trustee were suing a state entity in bankruptcy court to recover money damages? For example, what if the trustee were suing a state to set aside and recover a preference? In such a case the *in rem* dodge of *Hood* would not work, and the conflict between the Eleventh Amendment and Article I would be inescapable. On such facts, *Seminole Tribe* plainly seemed to say that the Eleventh Amendment would prevail.

---

[262] 527 U.S. 706 (1999).

[263] A useful article written after *Seminole Tribe* and *Alden* is Kenneth N. Klee, James O. Johnston, & Eric Winston, State Defiance of Bankruptcy Law, 52 Vand. L. Rev. 1527 (1999).

[264] 541 U.S. 440 (2004).

[265] For a superb critique of the Court's controversial decision in *Hood*, see Ralph Brubaker, From Fictionalism to Functionalism in State Sovereign Immunity: The Bankruptcy Discharge as Statutory *Ex Parte Young* Relief After *Hood*, 13 Am. Bankr. Inst. L. Rev. 59 (2005).

Just such a case was presented to the Court in *Central Virginia Community College v. Katz*.[266] Katz was a court-appointed liquidation supervisor seeking to avoid and recover money damages for preferential transfers from the debtor bookstore to four state colleges in Virginia. The state asserted its Eleventh Amendment immunity from suit. Now there was no escaping the issue. Relying on the history of the Constitutional Convention, the Supreme Court held that the Eleventh Amendment did not apply in the bankruptcy context; that is, the Court held that the Article I Bankruptcy Clause constituted an exception to the Eleventh Amendment.[267] The Court at least had the decency to admit that it had suggested otherwise in *Seminole Tribe*. The majority reasoned that the states had agreed at the time of the ratification of the Constitution not to exercise their sovereign immunity when it touches upon bankruptcy proceedings, which in substance are essentially *in rem* in nature (even, apparently, when the particular matter in question is a suit for the recovery of money damages).[268] According to the Court, the states' sovereign immunity thus was abrogated as to virtually everything connected with bankruptcy proceedings in the "plan of the Convention" itself. Bottom line: states can be sued in federal bankruptcy court, just like any other creditor. The decision is consonant with pre-*Seminole Tribe* law and in effect rolls back that decision in the bankruptcy sphere.

As applied, however, the bottom-line holding of *Katz* may become somewhat muddled, and the protection for debtors against state actions less substantial than first believed. For example, in a recent Eleventh Circuit case,[269] the state allegedly violated both the automatic stay and the discharge injunction, and the debtor sought to have the state sanctioned for contempt, but lost. The Court of Appeals did hold that bankruptcy courts have the power after *Katz* to issue orders "ancillary to *in rem* jurisdiction," that is, orders that are needed to carry out the court's *in rem* jurisdiction.[270] While an action for violation of the automatic stay could indeed in theory be such an action ancillary to the court's *in rem* jurisdiction and thus trump sovereign immunity, the court further found that the case at hand fell outside of *Katz's in rem* nexus. The reason was that the contempt action was brought four years after the alleged stay violation and thus "the automatic stay had already accomplished its purpose of preserving the assets of the estate by the time that Diaz brought this suit, and it was no longer necessary or even operative to assist the bankruptcy court in exercising its *in rem* jurisdiction."[271] Thus the court found that there was no

---

[266] 546 U.S. 356 (2006).

[267] Id. at 378–79.

[268] The Court stated:

> The power to enact bankruptcy legislation was understood to carry with it the power to subordinate state sovereignty, albeit within a limited sphere. . . . The ineluctable conclusion, then, is that States agreed in the plan of the Convention not to assert any sovereign immunity defense they might have had in proceedings brought pursuant to "Laws on the subject of Bankruptcies". . . . In ratifying the Bankruptcy Clause, the States acquiesced in a subordination of whatever sovereign immunity they might otherwise have asserted in proceedings necessary to effectuate the *in rem* jurisdiction of the bankruptcy courts."

Id. at 377–78.

[269] In re Diaz, 647 F.3d 1073 (11th Cir. 2011).

[270] Id. at 1084.

[271] Id. at 1086. The court found that there was no sovereign immunity as to the post-discharge collection claims, as it is still necessary to effectuate the *in rem* jurisdiction of the bankruptcy court because

jurisdiction to bring the action against the state for violation of the automatic stay, in the face of the state's assertion of sovereign immunity.

(4) Thirteenth Amendment

The Thirteenth Amendment prohibits slavery and involuntary servitude, except as punishment for a crime for which the person has been convicted. Debt peonage—compulsory service tied to the repayment of a debt—falls within the constitutional prohibition.[272] How might the Thirteenth Amendment debt peonage ban be implicated in a bankruptcy case? The concern is that if creditors could (1) file an *involuntary* bankruptcy case against an individual debtor *and* then (2) in that case capture the debtor's *future earnings*, the debtor would effectively be in debt bondage to his creditors pursuant to a federal statute, enforceable by orders of the bankruptcy court.

Until 2005, the suspect combination was unavailable in bankruptcy. Creditors could file an involuntary case against an individual debtor under chapter 7 or chapter 11, but in neither of those chapters could the debtor's future earnings be reached as part of the bankruptcy estate. Under the exception clause to § 541(a)(6), property of the estate does not include "earnings from services performed by an individual debtor after the commencement of the case."

Chapter 13, by contrast, specifically does bring into the bankruptcy estate "earnings from services performed by the debtor after the commencement of the case." § 1306(a)(2). Indeed, such post petition earnings typically are the means by which a debtor funds payments under his chapter 13 plan; the debtor's plan must "provide for the submission of all or such portion of future earnings or other future income of the debtor to the supervision and control of the trustee as is necessary for the execution of the plan." § 1322(a)(1). However, creditors cannot file an *involuntary* chapter 13 case against a debtor.[273] § 303(a). A debtor who chooses to repay his creditors voluntarily under a chapter 13 plan cannot then raise a Thirteenth Amendment complaint of "involuntary" servitude.

In the bankruptcy reforms of the late 1960s and 1970s, the credit industry had renewed its push to persuade Congress to authorize creditors to impose mandatory chapter 13 payment plans against bankrupt debtors with some future payment capacity. In that era, Congress rebuffed those efforts and made a considered choice to keep chapter 13 purely voluntary, at least in part because of concerns that doing otherwise would contravene the Thirteenth Amendment. The 1977 House Report that accompanied the bill that became the 1978 Code notes, "[t]hough it has never been

---

the discharge injunction is integral to the debtor's "fresh start." However, the state prevailed on the underlying claim, on the ground that the support claims being collected were nondischargeable. Id. at 1087–90.

[272] E.g., Bailey v. State of Alabama, 219 U.S. 219 (1911); Clyatt v. United States, 197 U.S. 207 (1905).

[273] The conversion rules likewise prevent anyone other than the debtor from converting a case under another chapter to a case under chapter 13. See §§ 706(c), 1112(d).

tested in the wage earner context, it has been suggested that a mandatory chapter 13, by forcing an individual to work for creditors, would violate this prohibition."[274]

The Supreme Court has never had occasion to opine directly on whether compulsory debt repayment in bankruptcy would be unconstitutional. In *Toibb v. Radloff*, however, in deciding that individual debtors were eligible for relief under chapter 11, the Court in dicta gave at least some credence to the constitutional worry that supported Congress' decision in 1978 not to permit compulsory repayment plans.[275]

In 2005, in BAPCPA, Congress for the first time did enact what *Toibb* had suggested was potentially suspect, namely, a "comparable provision in Chapter 11 requiring a debtor to pay future wages to a creditor."[276] § 1115(a)(2). This legislation was passed at the behest of the credit industry. Essentially, the chapter 13 future wage rules were copied into chapter 11.[277]

Yet, at the same time that Congress incorporated all of the chapter 13 future wage inclusion rules into chapter 11, it did *not* likewise carry forward the prohibition against involuntary cases being brought against an individual debtor under chapter 11.

Thus, as Professor Howard points out:

Taken together, these provisions allow creditors to use an involuntary bankruptcy to reach a debtor's future income—the very statutory configuration that has raised

---

[274] H.R. Rep. No. 95–595, 95th Cong., 1st Sess., at 120 (1977). The constitutional discomfort—and the statements then made cannot be described any more strongly—played only a partial role in Congress' rejection of compulsory chapter 13. Congress also felt that forcing a debtor to work for his creditors would be impractical and simply would not work. Id.

[275] Responding to an argument that allowing individual chapter 11 cases might undermine a congressional scheme that individuals attempting repayment would go only into chapter 13, the Court said:

> In any event, the argument overlooks Congress' primary concern about a debtor's being forced into bankruptcy under Chapter 13: that such a debtor, whose future wages are not exempt from the bankruptcy estate, § 1322(a)(1), would be compelled to toil for the benefit of creditors in violation of the Thirteenth Amendment's involuntary servitude prohibition. See H.R. Rep. No. 95–595, at 120. Because there is no comparable provision in Chapter 11 requiring a debtor to pay future wages to a creditor, Congress' concern about imposing involuntary servitude on a Chapter 13 debtor is not relevant to a Chapter 11 reorganization.

501 U.S. 157, 165–66 (1991).

[276] An excellent analysis of the new chapter 11 provisions and the Thirteenth Amendment concerns thereby implicated is found in Howard, supra note 201.

[277] Thus, for example, new § 1115(a)(2) tracks § 1306(a)(2) and brings into the estate "earnings from services performed by the debtor after the commencement of the case." The plan-inclusion rule of § 1322(a)(1) was copied into § 1123(a)(8). BAPCPA also added § 1129(a)(15)(B), which follows § 1325(b)(1)(B) in requiring as a condition of plan confirmation that a debtor devote his "projected disposable income" for the next five years to the plan. Professor Howard further explains how the new rules interact with existing chapter 11 rules to trap a debtor into involuntary future income repayment:

> These new provisions, obviously, operate in conjunction with preexisting chapter 11 rules: first, individual consumer debtors are eligible for chapter 11; second, involuntary cases are permissible under chapter 11; third, individual chapter 11 debtors cannot convert an involuntary case to another chapter; fourth, chapter 11 plans have no statutory maximum time limit and can be extended on a creditor's motion; fifth, unlike in chapter 13, creditors can propose a plan in chapter 11 if the debtor has not; and, finally, debtors in involuntary cases do not have an absolute right to dismiss the case.

Howard, supra note 201, 2009 U. Ill. L. Rev. at 198.

thirteenth amendment concerns for years—and does so under circumstances from which the debtor cannot easily escape by seeking conversion or dismissal. Thus, the constitutional question is no longer theoretical in chapter 11. Now the question of such a statute's constitutionality under the thirteenth amendment is ripe.[278]

So, with the issue now ripe—is there really a Thirteenth Amendment involuntary servitude problem with the new chapter 11 rules that might permit creditors to bring an involuntary case and thereby possibly capture a debtor's future wages? To date, no court has ruled directly on the question,[279] but a New Jersey bankruptcy court granted the debtor's motion to convert to chapter 7 based on the doctrine of constitutional avoidance, finding that otherwise there would be a serious possibility of a Thirteenth Amendment violation.[280]

The essence of a Thirteenth Amendment claim is *compulsion*. As the Supreme Court stated in the leading case of *Bailey v. Alabama*, "[t]he essence of the thing is compulsory service in payment of a debt. A peon is one who is compelled to work for his creditor until his debt is paid."[281]

What, then, is the nature of the compulsion required? In *United States v. Kozminski*, the Supreme Court determined after a careful historical analysis that "our precedents clearly define a Thirteenth Amendment prohibition of involuntary servitude enforced by the use or threatened use of physical or legal coercion."[282] Nor has the Court been quick to find sufficient "physical or legal coercion," except in patently obvious cases—most of which involved actual physical deprivation of liberty.

The only possible hook for sustaining a Thirteenth Amendment charge in the involuntary chapter 11 context is "legal" coercion. Many scholars have observed that an involuntary bankruptcy regime that would capture a debtor's future earnings looks a lot like—and indeed is probably constitutionally indistinguishable from—the familiar non-bankruptcy remedy of *garnishment* of a debtor's wages.[283] And garnishment has never been thought to raise Thirteenth Amendment problems. The debtor is not in any constitutionally infirm way *forced* to work—if he does choose to work, though, his creditors get a share of those wages. The same can be said for the new involuntary chapter 11 regime—the debtor can simply choose not to work for his creditors. If he does so his plan will fail, and he will not receive a discharge, but that is not enough of a "legal" coercion to raise constitutional angst. Only if a frustrated bankruptcy court entered a coercive order compelling the debtor to work in order to fund a plan, with the sanction for non-compliance being incarceration for civil contempt, would the

---

[278] Id. at 198–99.

[279] Rather, courts avoid answering this question by holding it is not ripe for review, as the hardships of requiring debtors to work and pay projected disposable income into a plan had not yet occurred. See, e.g., In re Gordon, 465 B.R. 683 (Bankr. N.D. Ga. 2012).

[280] In re Clemente, 409 B.R. 288 (Bankr. D.N.J. 2009).

[281] 219 U.S. 219, 242 (1911).

[282] 487 U.S. 931, 944 (1988).

[283] Howard, supra note 201, 2009 U. Ill. L. Rev. at 217–218 (citing sources).

Thirteenth Amendment be implicated.[284] Of course, with the bankruptcy court's hands thus tied, the new involuntary chapter 11 provisions may not do as much for the credit industry as they had hoped, since a recalcitrant debtor can frustrate collection by working less or not at all. Thus, notwithstanding the oft-repeated concern about an involuntary servitude problem with an involuntary chapter 11 (or chapter 13, for that matter) case, in fact on close analysis such a fear appears unwarranted, assuming that bankruptcy judges can restrain themselves from issuing plainly unconstitutional coercive orders.

(5) First Amendment

Until the 2005 amendments, Congress had been able to pass bankruptcy laws without offending the First Amendment, and then the Supreme Court saved Congress from itself. That record came to a halt when Congress added § 526(a)(4) to the Code. On its face, that section prohibits a "debt relief agency" from "advis[ing] an assisted person or prospective assisted person to incur more debt in contemplation of such person filing a case under this title." The definition of "debt relief agency" in § 101(12A) appears to include attorneys. The constitutional issue, then, is that § 526(a)(4) purports to prohibit attorneys from giving even legally permissible advice to their clients, which would render the provision overbroad and thus facially unconstitutional.

The issue went to the Supreme Court, which held that "narrowly construed," the provision is constitutional.[285] In *Milavetz,* petitioners argued that the over breadth of § 526(a)(4) would chill protected speech, and thus was unconstitutionally vague under the First Amendment. Milavetz argued that the notion of "abusive prefiling conduct" is too indefinite to adequately put attorneys on notice of what is prohibited without stifling protected speech as well. The Supreme Court, however, rejected this broad reading of the statute, and limited § 526(a)(4) to prohibit "a debt relief agency only from advising a debtor to incur more debt because the debtor is filing for bankruptcy, rather than for a valid purpose."[286] Having supposedly cabined the scope of the seemingly broader language Congress used, the Court then rejected the vagueness challenge, reasoning: "it is hard to see how a rule that narrowly prohibits an attorney from affirmatively advising a client to commit this type of abusive prefiling conduct could chill attorney speech or inhibit the attorney-client relationship."[287] The Court emphasized that an attorney could advise a debtor to incur more debt without running afoul of § 526(a)(4), even if bankruptcy might soon follow, just not if that advice was "principally motivated by that likelihood."[288]

Apparently the Court believed that it would be self-evident (enough) to debtor's attorneys what motivated their advice to avoid chilling protected speech. Anyone with any experience advising financially distressed individuals can appreciate just how fatuous an assumption the Court indulged. The problem is that the imminent necessity for a debtor to file bankruptcy, and what that reality will entail, inextricably permeates

---

[284] Id. at 220–24.

[285] Milavetz, Gallop & Milavetz, P.A. v. United States, 559 U.S. 229 (2010).

[286] Id. at 243.

[287] Id. at 248.

[288] Id. at 248 n.6.

all of the advice the attorney might offer; at the very least then, almost all advice the attorney gives is *partially* motivated by the prospective bankruptcy. How to tell when that mix tips to "principally motivated" often is virtually impossible. Say, for example, a debtor with a paid-off car with 200,000 miles needs to file chapter 13. That debtor could buy a new car now and incur secured debt, before filing, and doing so would have significant effects (almost all in the debtor's favor) on the shape of the impending chapter 13 case. The debtor does not *have* to have a new car, but obviously could use one, and buying it now—*before* filing—is a fine idea. Is that prohibited advice? Who knows? The Court *seemed* to put an interpretive thumb on the scales in the debtor's favor,[289] but is that enough to overcome the vagueness problem?

(6) Article III

Although all of the foregoing constitutional decisions have been significant, each pales next to the Supreme Court's Article III decisions. First was the Court's 1982 decision in *Northern Pipeline Construction Co. v. Marathon Pipe Line Co.*[290] that the bankruptcy jurisdictional and court system instituted in the 1978 Bankruptcy Reform Act unconstitutionally violated Article III. The Court concluded that bankruptcy judges, who did not enjoy the Article III guarantees of life tenure and protection against diminution in salary, could not exercise the judicial power of the United States to the extent authorized by the 1978 Act. *Marathon* involved the bankruptcy court's power to issue a final order in traditional state law breach of contract case. In 1984, Congress tried to cure the *Marathon* problem by enacting a revised jurisdictional scheme. However, they failed again to clear the Article III hurdle. In 2011 the Supreme Court finally ruled on the revised system in *Stern v. Marshall*,[291] holding that the new scheme still vests too much power in the hands of non-Article III bankruptcy judges. In *Stern*, the Court concluded that the statutory designation of the power to hear and determine a state law counterclaim as "core," thus allowing the bankruptcy judge to issue a final order, contravened Article III when that determination was not necessarily resolved in the claims allowance process.[292] Nevertheless, the bankruptcy court system remains intact because the new jurisdictional scheme gives final adjudicative authority to the district courts in cases where that is required. The trick is figuring out which cases do and which do not require that the article II court (or a state court of general jurisdiction) issue the final order.

§ 1.11   Title 11, United States Code

The substantive law of bankruptcy is found in title 11 of the United States Code, commonly referred to as the "Bankruptcy Code." As discussed in earlier sections, the Bankruptcy Code was first enacted as part of the Bankruptcy Reform Act of 1978,[293] which replaced the Bankruptcy Act of 1898 (the "Act"). The Code applies to all

---

[289] Thus, the Court observed: "[t]hus, advice to refinance a mortgage or purchase a reliable car prior to filing because doing so will reduce the debtor's interest rates or improve his ability to repay is not prohibited, as the promise of enhanced financial prospects, rather than the anticipated filing, is the impelling cause." Id.

[290] 458 U.S. 50 (1982). See also § 4.2.

[291] 131 S.Ct. 2594 (2011). See also § 4.2.

[292] 131 S.Ct. at 2620.

[293] Pub. L. No. 95–598, 92 Stat. 2549 (1978).

bankruptcy cases filed on or after October 1, 1979. The Code has been amended several times since 1978, most prominently in 1984,[294] 1986,[295] 1994,[296] and 2005.[297]

The Code is comprised of nine "chapters." These chapters followed odd numbers (1, 3, 5, 7, 9, 11, and 13)[298] in the 1978 Reform Act; the odd number trend was broken with the addition of chapter 12 for family farmers in 1986. Chapter 15 (for ancillary and cross-border cases) was added in 2005. The section numbers in title 11 all begin with the number of the chapter in which they are found, for easy reference. For example, § 105 (dealing with the power of the court) is found in chapter 1; § 727 (discharge) in chapter 7; and § 1129 (plan confirmation) in chapter 11. The old Bankruptcy Act in effect prior to the Code used Roman numerals to denote chapters (e.g., chapter VII, chapter XI); the Roman convention has been abandoned in favor of Arabic numerals in the Code. The word "chapter" is sometimes capitalized when used in conjunction with the chapter number (e.g., Chapter 11), although the proper usage as found in title 11 itself is not to capitalize "chapter" (e.g., chapter 11).

The chapters in the Bankruptcy Code are of two types. The first type of chapter contains provisions of *general applicability* in the most common types of bankruptcy cases (i.e., chapters 7, 11, 12, and 13), excluding chapters 9 and 15.[299] Those generally applicable chapters are chapters 1, 3, and 5. § 103(a). Thus, § 105, dealing with the power of the court, would apply in every bankruptcy case. So too would § 362 (automatic stay) and § 541 (property of the estate).

The other type of chapter specifies a particular type of bankruptcy case. The case chapters within this category are chapters 7, 9, 11, 12, 13, and 15. The provisions of each chapter apply exclusively to those cases under that chapter.[300] The six case chapters offer different types of bankruptcy relief. The most common type of case (about 70% of all cases) is chapter 7, providing for a liquidation or sale of the debtor's assets and distribution of the net proceeds to creditors.

---

[294] Bankruptcy Amendments and Federal Judgeship Act of 1984, Pub. L. No. 98–353, 98 Stat. 333. This amendment revamped the bankruptcy court system after the *Marathon Pipe Line* decision that held the 1978 system unconstitutional.

[295] Bankruptcy Judges, United States Trustees, and Family Farmer Bankruptcy Act of 1986, Pub. L. No. 99–554, 100 Stat. 3088. This amendment added chapter 12 for family farmer debtors.

[296] Bankruptcy Reform Act of 1994, Pub. L. No. 103–394, 108 Stat. 4106. The 1994 Act created a second Bankruptcy Review Commission and enacted scores of substantive amendments.

[297] Pub. L. No. 109–8, 119 Stat. 23 (2005).

[298] The Bankruptcy Reform Act of 1978 also had a chapter 15 (no relation to the chapter 15 enacted in 2005), which provided special rules for those pilot districts in which the United States trustee program was being tested. When the United States trustee program was made permanent and nationwide in 1986, chapter 15 was repealed and the United States trustee provisions were incorporated throughout the entire Code.

[299] For chapter 9 cases, involving municipal debtors, only chapters 1 and 9 apply, along with the specific sections listed in § 901. § 103(f).

For chapter 15 cross-border and ancillary cases, chapters 1 and 15 apply, along with a handful of sections listed in § 103(a). See § 103(a).

[300] Section 103(b) (chapter 7), § 103(f) (chapter 9), § 103(g) (chapter 11), § 103(i) (chapter 13), § 103(j) (chapter 12); § 103(k) (chapter 15) (note that few sections in chapter 15 apply in all cases, see § 103(k)(1), (2)).

Four of the case chapters (9, 11, 12, and 13) provide for some form of rehabilitation of the debtor, as opposed to a straight liquidation. In these chapters the debtor (or a trustee) usually retains the property of the debtor and pays creditors over time out of future earnings. Of these cases the most commonly used is chapter 13, which authorizes the adjustment of the debts of an individual debtor with regular income and a relatively small amount of debt. Chapter 13 is usually perceived to be the alternative to chapter 7 for consumer debtors. Cases filed by noncommercial debtors account for about 95% of all cases filed.[301]

Chapter 12 is a chapter 13 near-clone that is available to family farmers and family fishermen. Chapter 11 is the basic business reorganization chapter.[302] Chapter 9, which is seldom invoked, permits the adjustment of the debts of a municipality.

Chapter 15 is *sui generis*. It covers cross-border and ancillary cases, where a foreign proceeding is also pending. A chapter 15 case might be a "main proceeding," in which a significant liquidation or reorganization is attempted, or it might be purely ancillary and "non-main," involving perhaps nothing more than the turnover of a single asset located in the United States to a foreign proceeding.

Subchapters of the case chapters provide for some special types of cases. Like the provisions of the chapters, the provisions of the subchapters apply only to the special case covered. Stockbroker liquidation is governed by subchapter III of chapter 7, § 103(c); commodity broker liquidation by subchapter IV of chapter 7, § 103(d); and clearing bank liquidation by subchapter V of chapter 7. § 103(e). Railroad reorganizations are dealt with by subchapter IV of chapter 11. § 103(g).

§ 1.12   Other Federal Statutory Law: Titles 28 and 18

Title 11 does not comprehend the entire universe of federal statutes applicable to bankruptcy cases and proceedings. Important provisions are also found in title 28, dealing with the Judicial Code, and title 18, regarding Crimes and Criminal Procedure. In addition, the Internal Revenue Code, title 26, contains several provisions applicable to bankruptcy. Scattered provisions relevant to bankruptcy cases appear elsewhere in the United States Code.[303]

Title 28 governs the organization of the bankruptcy courts and the jurisdiction and venue provisions applicable to bankruptcy cases. Titled "Bankruptcy Judges," chapter 6 in §§ 151 through 158 of title 28 addresses such crucial matters as the designation of the bankruptcy courts as a unit of the district court (§ 151); the jurisdiction of bankruptcy judges (§ 157, vaguely entitled "Procedures"); and bankruptcy appeals

---

[301] To illustrate, in 2012, a total of 1,221,091 cases were filed. Of those, 1,181,016 were noncommercial filings, and 40,075 were commercial cases. On the chapter breakdown, in 2012, chapter 7 cases comprised about 70% of the cases, chapter 13 close to 30%, and chapter 11 a shade under one percent. Only 512 cases were filed under chapter 12, just 121 under chapter 15 and 20 under chapter 9.

[302] Note, however, that eligibility for relief under chapter 11 is not strictly limited to business debtors, but that individual consumers can proceed under that chapter if otherwise eligible. See, e.g., Toibb v. Radloff, 501 U.S. 157 (1991).

[303] For example, provisions making certain types of student loans nondischargeable in bankruptcy are found in the statutes dealing with those student loan programs, rather than in the Code. See Higher Education Act of 1965, § 439A, 20 U.S.C. § 1087–3; Public Health Service Act, § 733(g), 42 U.S.C. § 294f.

(§ 158). Section 1334 grants federal jurisdiction over bankruptcy cases and proceedings to the district court. Venue is covered in §§ 1408 to 1412, and removal is dealt with in § 1452. Chapter 39 covers the treatment of United States trustees, as an arm of the Department of Justice, in §§ 581 through 589b. Section 959 makes bankruptcy trustees suable and requires them to manage property in accordance with state law. Bankruptcy fees are prescribed by § 1930. Bankruptcy rules are authorized by § 2075.

Bankruptcy crimes are spelled out in §§ 151 through 157 of title 18. Section 152 largely tracks several of the grounds for denial of a chapter 7 discharge found in § 727(a) of the Bankruptcy Code, except that a heightened *mens rea* of "knowingly and fraudulently" is required, and of course the standard of proof is the criminal standard. The punishment for a § 152 bankruptcy crime is a fine or up to five years in prison or both. In addition, § 153 provides for a fine or up to five years imprisonment for embezzlement by a trustee. In 1994, two new bankruptcy crimes were added in §§ 156 and 157.[304] Section 157 makes "bankruptcy fraud," defined broadly, a federal crime punishable by up to five years imprisonment and a fine.

The relevant provisions of the Internal Revenue Code applicable to bankruptcy were primarily added by the Bankruptcy Tax Act of 1980.[305] This act addressed such basic issues as the tax treatment of discharge of indebtedness,[306] rules relating to the bankruptcy cases of individual debtor-taxpayers,[307] provisions for corporate reorganizations,[308] and tax procedures applicable to bankruptcy-related rules.[309]

§ 1.13   Federal Rules of Bankruptcy Procedure and Official Forms

Of great practical importance in bankruptcy cases and proceedings are the procedural rules and official forms promulgated by the Supreme Court. The "Federal Rules of Bankruptcy Procedure" and the "Official Bankruptcy Forms" "govern procedure in cases under title 11." The Bankruptcy Rules "shall be construed to secure the just, speedy, and inexpensive determination of every case and proceeding." Bankr. Rule 1001.

Congress delegated the power to prescribe official rules and forms to the Supreme Court in 28 U.S.C. § 2075 of the Rules Enabling Act: "The Supreme Court shall have the power to prescribe by general rules, the forms of process, writs, pleadings, and motions, and the practice and procedure in cases under Title 11." In reality, the Supreme Court has little real input into the rules and forms that ultimately become law. The Justices of that Court most assuredly do not sit around pontificating on the merits or demerits of possible changes in the Bankruptcy Rules.

---

[304] Bankruptcy Reform Act of 1994, Pub. L. No. 103–394, § 312, 108 Stat. 4106.

[305] Pub. L. No. 96–589, 94 Stat. 3389 (1980).

[306] Bankruptcy Tax Act of 1980, § 2, amending §§ 108 and 1017 of the Internal Revenue Code.

[307] Id. § 3, amending §§ 1398 and 1399 of the Internal Revenue Code.

[308] Id. § 4, amending §§ 368, 354, 355, and 370 of the Internal Revenue Code.

[309] Id. § 6, amending numerous sections of the Internal Revenue Code, including §§ 6012, 6213, and 6503.

Instead, the bulk of the work in drafting and revising the Rules falls to the Advisory Committee on Bankruptcy Rules. The members of the Advisory Committee, which is composed primarily of prominent federal judges, law professors, and lawyers, are appointed by the Chief Justice. The Advisory Committee helps the Judicial Conference of the United States carry out its statutory obligation to "carry on a continuous study of the operation and effect of the general rules of practice and procedure." 28 U.S.C. § 331. The Advisory Committee does this by meeting at least twice a year and considering and proposing possible changes to the rules and official forms. The Advisory Committee also publishes "Notes" to accompany rules changes.

The recommendations of the Advisory Committee then are forwarded to the Standing Committee, which coordinates the work of all of the advisory committees. If the Standing Committee approves a suggested change, the proposal is published and public comment is invited. The Advisory Committee then evaluates the public comments and gives final approval (or not) to a proposed amendment. That proposal then must be approved by the Standing Committee, then the Judicial Conference, and then the Supreme Court. The Supreme Court transmits rules changes to Congress on May 1. Congress then has three months to override the proposed Bankruptcy Rule; if Congress fails to act, the rule goes into effect on December 1.

The Rules Enabling Act in 28 U.S.C. § 2075 specifies that "[s]uch rules shall not abridge, enlarge, or modify any substantive right." Thus, if a Bankruptcy Rule contravenes a provision of the Bankruptcy Code itself, then the Code provision will control. To illustrate, an earlier version of Rule 3002 required a "proof of claim" to be filed within 90 days of the first meeting of creditors in chapter 7, 12, or 13 cases for the creditor's claim to be "allowed." In bankruptcy, only "allowed" claims are permitted to share in the distribution of assets of the bankruptcy estate. Thus, applying that version of Rule 3002 on its face, it appeared that a tardily filed claim could never be paid in bankruptcy. However, § 726 of the Bankruptcy Code, which deals with the order in which the assets of the bankruptcy estate are distributed, expressly contemplates the payment of some "allowed" claims that are "tardily" filed. The Rule thus appeared to contradict the Code. As such, pursuant to 28 U.S.C. § 2075, the Code would control, and literal effect would not be given to the disallowance provision in Rule 3002.[310]

Too much should not be made of the limitation imposed by § 2075, however. The current Bankruptcy Code, unlike the Bankruptcy Act that it replaced, deals very little with issues of procedure. Thus, the field is open for the Bankruptcy Rules to dictate the procedure that will be applicable in bankruptcy cases and proceedings. The importance of procedure in bankruptcy can hardly be overstated. In many respects the bankruptcy system is at its core concerned primarily with the procedures by which the assets of bankrupt debtors will be liquidated or reorganized, rather than with a substantive readjustment of rights. Indeed, a course in bankruptcy could perhaps fairly be labeled "Advanced Civil Procedure."

---

[310] See In re Hausladen, 146 B.R. 557 (Bankr. D. Minn. 1992). In the 1994 reform bill, Congress amended § 502 and § 726, stating that it was "overruling *In re Hausladen*," although it is not certain that Congress accomplished its stated objective. However, Rule 3002 was amended in 1996 to eliminate any conflict.

The Bankruptcy Rules are divided into nine parts, and follow a standardized numbering system. The first number is the number of the part of the Rules in which that Rule falls, the second number is "0," and then the third and fourth numbers are the number of the Rule in that part. For example, Part VII governs "adversary proceedings," which essentially are civil lawsuits being litigated in connection with a bankruptcy case. The Part VII rules all are in the "7000" series. The fourth rule in Part VII is Rule 7004; number 36 is Rule 7036.

The Federal Rules of Civil Procedure also are important in some bankruptcy proceedings, particularly those involving litigation. In particular, many of the Civil Rules apply in "adversary proceedings," the bankruptcy moniker for what would be thought of as typical litigation. The Part VII rules accomplish this by incorporating the Civil Rule by reference. For example, Rule 7036 mentioned above, provides simply that "Rule 36 F.R.Civ.P. applies in adversary proceedings." Any change in Rule 36 of the Federal Rules of Civil Procedure, then, would automatically apply in adversary proceedings as well. Not all of the Part VII rules incorporate the Civil Rule, however. Rule 7004, also noted above, only partially adopts Rule 4 of the Civil Rules, utilizing instead somewhat different rules regarding service of process that are believed to be more appropriate for bankruptcy cases.

Some of the Civil Rules are also made applicable to "contested matters" by Bankruptcy Rule 9014. A contested matter is basically some form of bankruptcy litigation other than an adversary proceeding. A motion for relief from the automatic stay is an example. While some of the Civil Rules are applied to contested matters, Rule 9014 generally provides for a more informal procedure than would be followed under the Civil Rules.

Other of the Civil Rules are incorporated generally into bankruptcy proceedings by some of the Bankruptcy Rules in Part IX (the 9000 series). Part IX deals with "general provisions," which are applicable in all bankruptcy cases and proceedings. As an illustration, Rule 9016 incorporates Civil Rule 45 (dealing with a subpoena) into bankruptcy cases.

The Federal Rules of Evidence apply in bankruptcy cases. Bankruptcy Rule 9017, which is of general applicability, incorporates the evidence rules in their entirety. Having said that, as a practical matter one should bear in mind that in many bankruptcy courts this rule is honored in the breach.

Much of what happens in the bankruptcy court is not litigation in the traditional "A v. B" sense. Rather, bankruptcy proceedings often implicate the rights of numerous parties. For such quintessential bankruptcy proceedings, special rules applicable only in bankruptcy are a necessity. An illustration would be the procedures associated with the confirmation of a plan of reorganization under chapter 11. A whole series of Bankruptcy Rules (in the 3000 series) govern the plan confirmation process.

The Bankruptcy Rules also specify that "Official Bankruptcy Forms" are obligatory and must generally be followed, but with some leeway. The standard is one of substantial compliance; Rule 9009 states that "the Official Forms prescribed by the Judicial Conference of the United States shall be observed and used with alterations as may be appropriate." That rule goes on to provide that "[f]orms may be combined and their contents rearranged to permit economies in their use." Many local courts and clerks' offices have seized on the opening offered by Rule 9009 to develop and use forms that vary slightly from the Official Forms. In some cases this local experimentation has proven useful in testing different forms. In other instances, however, the local variants have been found wanting. The most notable example of the latter result is a 1993 Supreme Court decision which partly based its holding on the insufficiency of a local form that gave notice of the chapter 11 filing and the bar date for filing claims.[311]

In addition to the Official Forms, additional forms may be issued by the Director of the Administrative Office of the United States Courts (AOUSC). Currently many of these "Procedural Forms" have been issued. Unlike Official Forms, Procedural Forms are not binding. In the words of the Advisory Committee Note to Rule 9009, Procedural Forms are offered for "the guidance of the bar."

§ 1.14   Local Court Rules

Local court rules are also of considerable practical importance in the daily practice in the bankruptcy courts. Local rules are made by the district judges (or bankruptcy judges if authorized by the district judges) and apply to all bankruptcy cases in a particular federal judicial district. Bankruptcy Rule 9029 authorizes local rules, imposing limitations only that local rules (1) must not be inconsistent with the national Bankruptcy Rules, i.e., the national Rules control, and (2) may not prohibit or limit the use of Official Forms.

Rule 8018, dealing with bankruptcy appeals, contains a similar authorization allowing local rules regarding appeals. The local rules for bankruptcy appeals would be made either by the district judges or the circuit council, if the council has established a "bankruptcy appellate panel." The principal limitation under Rule 8018 is that the local appellate rules may not be inconsistent with the national Bankruptcy Rules dealing with appeals.

In 1995 Rules 9029 and 8018 were amended to: (1) require local rules to be consistent with Acts of Congress as well as with the national rules; (2) require local rules to conform to any uniform numbering system prescribed by the Judicial Conference; and (3) provide that a local rule that imposes a requirement of form must not be enforced in a way that causes a party to lose rights because of a non-willful failure to comply. In addition, the amendments to Rules 8018 and 9029 give a judge the power to regulate practice in any manner consistent with federal law, the Bankruptcy Rules, the Official Forms, and any local rules. However, no sanction or disadvantage could be imposed for noncompliance with such a regulation unless the alleged violator was furnished with actual notice of the requirement in the particular case.

§ 1.15   State Law

The Bankruptcy Code is a federal law, codified in title 11 of the United States Code. The substantive law applied in bankruptcy cases, however, is in the greater part

---

[311] Pioneer Inv. Servs. Co. v. Brunswick Assocs. Ltd. P'ship, 507 U.S. 380 (1993).

governed by state law.[312] Indeed, apart from diversity cases, it is probably safe to say that state law plays a more important role in bankruptcy cases and proceedings than in any other form of action in federal court. In short, a competent practitioner in bankruptcy court must be well-versed in applicable state laws.

This feature of bankruptcy cases tells much about the nature of bankruptcy itself. Bankruptcy is primarily a remedial device designed to deal with the problem of multiple defaults, to provide a forum to sort out efficiently the rights of numerous creditors and other parties in interest in a collective proceeding. In so doing, however, bankruptcy largely takes the debtor's property and the claims against that property as it finds them.

The Supreme Court in *Butner v. United States* stated the general rule and explained the justifications for that rule:

> Congress has generally left the determination of property rights in the assets of a bankrupt's estate to state law. Property interests are created and defined by state law. Unless some federal interest requires a different result, there is no reason why such interests should be analyzed differently simply because an interested party is involved in a bankruptcy proceeding. Uniform treatment of property interests by both federal and state courts within a State serves to reduce uncertainty, to discourage forum shopping, and to prevent a party from receiving "a windfall by reason of the happenstance of bankruptcy."[313]

First, then, "property of the estate," defined by § 541(a) of the Code, is almost entirely defined by the underlying state law. The general definitional section, § 541(a)(1), includes in property of the estate "all legal or equitable interests of the debtor in property." Those interests are determined by reference to state law. To be sure, what constitutes "property" for bankruptcy purposes is said to be in the final analysis a question of federal law rather than state law.[314] The federal question is a matter of labeling; i.e., if an interest possesses certain attributes, the question of whether that interest will be labeled "property" for purposes of a federal bankruptcy case is a question of federal law. However, state law determines whether a particular interest possesses the attributes of "property" in the first instance.

State law also is crucial to the question of what property may be exempted from the bankruptcy estate. The Code incorporates state exemption laws, making those state exemption laws available to bankruptcy debtors. § 522(b)(3). In states that have not "opted out" of the federal exemptions offered by § 522(d), debtors may choose either the federal exemption scheme or the exemption scheme of the state of their residence. A substantial majority (35) of the states have elected not to permit their debtors to use the federal exemptions, thus limiting debtors to the state exemption laws. Under the

---

[312] The most comprehensive discussion of the importance of state law in bankruptcy cases is found in Professor Vern Countryman's two-part article, The Use of State Law in Bankruptcy Cases (part 1), 47 N.Y.U. L. Rev. 407 (1972), (part 2), 47 N.Y.U. L. Rev. 631 (1972). Professor Countryman's study, undertaken as part of the work of the Bankruptcy Commission, addressed the law under the old Bankruptcy Act, not the current Code, but nonetheless remains valuable today.

[313] 440 U.S. 48, 54–55 (1979).

[314] See Chicago Bd. of Trade v. Johnson, 264 U.S. 1 (1924).

Bankruptcy Act of 1898, the Supreme Court upheld the delegation of bankruptcy exemption law to the states against constitutional challenges.[315] Thus, for example, debtors residing in Florida or Texas have exceedingly generous exemptions available to them in bankruptcy, while debtors in other states have far less.

Just as the scope of the property included in the bankruptcy estate is largely determined by state law, so too is the determination of the claims made against that property primarily an issue of state law. A bankruptcy "claim" is defined as a "right to payment." § 101(5). Whether a right to payment against the debtor exists is a state law question. Furthermore, a claim will not be "allowed" in a bankruptcy case if "such claim is unenforceable against the debtor and property of the debtor, under any agreement or applicable law." § 502(b)(1). Thus, whether a creditor may assert a claim payable out of the bankruptcy estate is mostly governed by state law. However, there are some exceptions to this general rule, whereby overriding federal interests expressly limit bankruptcy claims.[316]

The same general rule of deference to state law applies to claimants asserting a property interest in assets of the estate. The most common illustration of this principle is for security interests or liens on estate property. The validity of security interests and liens is again a state law problem. Thus, if a creditor can establish that it had a valid and perfected security interest in the debtor's property at the time of the bankruptcy filing, that creditor has a secured claim in the bankruptcy case and is entitled to be paid at least the value of its collateral in the bankruptcy case. The security interest may be tested in bankruptcy pursuant to the trustee's "strong-arm power," § 544(a), which allows the bankruptcy trustee to avoid a security interest that was unperfected at the time bankruptcy was filed, and thus which was subject to being defeated by a lien creditor.[317] Indeed, the vast majority of case law construing Article 9 of the Uniform Commercial Code occurs in the bankruptcy courts pursuant to litigation over the perfected status of asserted security interests. For our purposes, however, the important point is that the outcome of such litigation depends on a construction of a state law, here the UCC, not some federal law.

Another important avoiding power of the bankruptcy trustee that also incorporates state law is the trustee's power to set aside pre-bankruptcy fraudulent conveyances. The Bankruptcy Code does have an independent fraudulent transfer provision, § 548 (which not coincidentally draws heavily on the Uniform Fraudulent Transfer Act). Even more directly, however, under § 544(b) the trustee is empowered to invoke state law in order to avoid any transfer or interest "that is voidable under applicable law by a creditor holding an unsecured claim." Under state law such unsecured creditors typically may set aside fraudulent conveyances, and thus by virtue of § 544(b) that same power passes to the bankruptcy trustee. Section 544(b) is a particular advantage for the trustee when the state fraudulent conveyance law has a broader reach than would § 548, the Bankruptcy Code fraud provision.

---

[315] Hanover Nat'l Bank v. Moyses, 186 U.S. 181 (1902).

[316] For example, in § 502(b)(6), a landlord under a long-term real property lease can only recover part of its claim against the estate, so that the landlord's claim will not consume an excessive share of the estate, leaving little for the other creditors.

[317] See UCC § 9–317(a)(2).

Other forms of property interests in bankruptcy that also depend substantially on state law are executory contracts and unexpired leases. Section 365, a very long (too long) section, governs executory contracts and unexpired leases in bankruptcy. In some respects § 365 alters state law. For example, in bankruptcy a contract may be assigned by the estate, thus relieving the estate of any further liability on the contract, § 365(k), whereas under state law the assignor normally would remain liable. Another example is that clauses that would prohibit the assignment of the contract, or that would terminate the contract on the filing of bankruptcy, are not enforceable in bankruptcy. § 365(b), (c), (e), (f). Having said that, state law still must be consulted on the fundamental questions of (1) whether there is a contract at all; (2) what the duties and rights of the parties are under that contract; and (3) what constitutes a breach of that contract. These issues assume considerable importance because of the bankruptcy law principle that an executory contract must be assumed or rejected "*cum onere*," meaning that the trustee's decision whether to take on the obligations and benefits of the contract is an all-or-nothing proposition. In other words, the trustee must take all of the burdens of the contract along with the benefits of that contract.

A final illustration of the central importance of state law in bankruptcy cases is found in the exceptions to a bankruptcy discharge specified in § 523(a) of the Code. Section 523(a) spells out a number of different types of debts that will not be discharged in a bankruptcy case, such as debts based on fraud, or fiduciary defalcation, or willful and malicious injury. State law is important here because a bankruptcy court will give collateral estoppel effect to litigation in state court. Thus, for example, if a creditor obtains a judgment against a debtor in state court based on a necessary finding of fraud, that judgment will not be discharged under § 523(a)(2), and the debtor will be collaterally estopped from relitigating the fraud question in the bankruptcy case.[318]

E. THE PARTICIPANTS IN A BANKRUPTCY CASE

§ 1.16 Debtor

The "debtor" is defined in the Code as the "person or municipality concerning which a case under this title has been commenced." § 101(13). In other words, the debtor is the subject of the bankruptcy case. In olden days, the debtor was referred to as the "bankrupt," but that usage has been banished from the official lexicon. "Person" and "municipality" are defined terms of art. A "person" is not, as one might intuitively expect, simply a human being. Instead, "person" is defined as including an "individual, partnership, and corporation, but does not include [a] governmental unit." § 101(41). The first two categories of persons, individuals and partnerships, are self-explanatory. The meaning of "corporation" is less self-evident, and the Code definition must be consulted. § 101(9). Ascertaining what types of entities constitute "corporations" for the purposes of bankruptcy eligibility has proven a difficult task in many instances.

Nor is a "municipality" within the meaning of the Code exactly what one might expect, i.e., a town or city. The category is much broader, meaning a "political

---

[318] See Grogan v. Garner, 498 U.S. 279 (1991).

subdivision or public agency or instrumentality of a State." § 101(40). Thus, many varieties of public bodies might qualify as "debtors," from Orange County to Detroit to irrigation districts.

The mere fact that an entity is a "debtor" as defined in the Code does not guarantee that they will be eligible for bankruptcy relief. Additional eligibility requirements are set out in § 109 of the Code. Thus, being a "debtor" is a necessary but not sufficient requirement.

§ 1.17   Debtor in Possession

The "debtor in possession," commonly known as the "DIP," is an odd hybrid creature unique to chapter 11 reorganization cases. The debtor in possession is defined as "debtor except when a person that has qualified under section 322 of this title is serving as trustee in the case." § 1101(1). In plain English, that means that the DIP is the chapter 11 debtor, but also must perform the duties of the bankruptcy trustee. In other words, upon the filing of a chapter 11 case, the debtor assumes two mantles. The first is as debtor *qua* debtor; the second is as debtor *qua* trustee. The debtor is itself, of course, and is also the fiduciary representative of the bankruptcy estate. All duties of the trustee (except investigating the debtor!) fall on the shoulders of the debtor as the DIP. § 1107(a). The debtor ceases to be DIP only in the relatively rare event that an independent trustee is appointed for cause under § 1104. One of the critical policy decisions that Congress made in the 1978 Code was to leave the debtor in possession as the norm. In so doing Congress adopted the approach of old chapter XI and rejected the requirement of an independent trustee imposed by old chapter X.

§ 1.18   Creditor

A "creditor" is much what a layperson would expect, but with some important qualifications. The basic definition of "creditor" is an "entity that has a claim against the debtor that arose at the time of or before the order for relief concerning the debtor."[319] § 101(10). This definition makes sense: the "debtor" owes money to a "creditor."

Two aspects of this definition, however, require further scrutiny. First, the definition includes a time component. Only pre-bankruptcy claims are dealt with as part of the bankruptcy case. Any post-bankruptcy claims are normally excluded. Having said that, in some cases it is difficult to fix the time when a claim arises for bankruptcy purposes.

Second, the creditor must have a "claim," and "claim" itself is a carefully defined term of art. § 101(5). The essence of the definition of "claim" is that the creditor must have a "right to payment." Congress intended to sweep broadly here, and defined right to payment expansively, providing that the creditor has a qualifying right to payment "whether or not such right is reduced to judgment, liquidated, unliquidated, fixed,

---

[319] The definition of creditor also includes entities that have certain types of claims that actually arise after the bankruptcy case begins, but are deemed for purposes of the bankruptcy case to arise prior to the case, so that they may be dealt with as part of the bankruptcy. "Creditor" also includes an entity that has a community claim.

contingent, matured, unmatured, disputed, undisputed, legal, equitable, secured, or unsecured." § 101(5)(A).

Congress also swept in as part of the claim definition the "right to an equitable remedy for breach of performance if such breach gives rise to a right to payment." § 101(5)(B). In other words, the holder of an equitable remedy against the debtor, typically a right of specific performance or an injunction, may also have a "claim." This usually is important with respect to the question of discharge, because only claims may be discharged. The problem has arisen most often in the environmental cases, with the issue being whether the debtor may escape a clean-up injunction by discharging that injunction as a bankruptcy claim. The most famous case on this point is the Supreme Court's 1985 decision in *Ohio v. Kovacs*,[320] in which the Court held that an individual's clean-up obligation was a dischargeable bankruptcy claim.

§ 1.19   Trustee

In the interest of abject confusion, there are actually several different types of "trustees" in cases under the Code. The type of trustee depends on which chapter the case is under. The clearest way to distinguish between the various forms of trustees is to focus on the statutory duties placed on the particular trustee.

All trustees, no matter under which chapter, do share some common characteristics. Most centrally, trustees are representatives of the bankruptcy estate, § 323(a), and as such are fiduciaries. To qualify a person must post a bond in favor of the United States, "conditioned on the faithful performance of [their] official duties." § 322(a). As the estate representative, the trustee has the capacity to sue and be sued. § 323(b). For example, the trustee will prosecute causes of action belonging to the estate, and normally brings suits invoking the Code's "avoiding powers," seeking to recover fraudulent transfers, preferences, and so forth. Trustees are paid out of estate assets up to statutorily specified limits. § 326.

The traditional "trustee" superintends a liquidation bankruptcy under chapter 7. The core duties of a chapter 7 trustee are to collect the assets of the estate, liquidate those assets, object to any improper claims of creditors, and file a final report and accounting so that the liquidated estate assets can be distributed on a pro rata basis to creditors. § 704. In performing these functions the bankruptcy trustee is closely akin to an assignee in an assignment for the benefit of creditors. The trustee also is primarily responsible for policing the debtor's entitlement to the benefits of bankruptcy relief. As such the trustee is charged with the duty of investigating the financial affairs of the debtor and objecting to the debtor's discharge if advisable.

In chapter 7 creditors retain a measure of control over the trustee, in that they have the right to elect the trustee. § 702. This right, however, goes unexercised in the vast majority of cases, in which instance a trustee is appointed by the United States trustee from a panel of prospective private trustees. § 701.

---

[320]   469 U.S. 274 (1985).

The duties of a trustee in all of the reorganization chapters (11, 12, and 13) vary from those of a chapter 7 trustee in many respects, the most notable of which is that the trustee in those chapters usually does not liquidate the assets of the estate. Although liquidation is theoretically possible in chapter 11, the normal premise of the reorganization chapters is the opposite of liquidation: the debtor retains its assets and pays off creditors over time pursuant to the terms of a plan confirmed by the court. Accordingly, it would make little sense for the trustee in those chapters to liquidate assets of the estate.

So what functions do trustees perform under the reorganization chapters? In chapter 11, a trustee is not appointed in every case. Retention of the debtor as debtor in possession is the standard. Cause for the appointment of a trustee must be shown. § 1104(a). If a trustee is appointed, the trustee takes over the role of the debtor in possession. As such the trustee has two overriding responsibilities: operate the debtor's business during the pendency of the chapter 11 bankruptcy case, and formulate and file a plan of reorganization. § 1106(a). In order to perform these duties, the trustee may investigate the debtor's business and financial affairs.

In chapter 11 an examiner may be appointed instead of a trustee. § 1104(c). The examiner's duty usually is to perform an investigation as directed by the court. § 1106(b). The examiner does not usually operate the debtor's business or file a plan. Appointment of an examiner does not divest the debtor from its status as debtor in possession. The court does however have the flexibility to authorize the examiner to perform a broader range of duties than just to investigate.

In chapters 12 and 13 the trustee is a much different creature. In those chapters the United States trustee normally appoints a single individual to serve as "standing trustee" in all cases under that chapter in the entire judicial district. §§ 1202(a), 1302(a). The primary function of the chapter 12 or 13 trustee is to serve as the disbursing agent for monies paid by the debtor under the plan. In other words, the debtor makes their monthly plan payment to the trustee, who then turns around and makes distribution to each individual creditor. §§ 1226, 1326. The trustee also is called upon to ensure that the debtor begins making timely payments and to advise and assist the debtor in performance under the plan. The chapter 12 or 13 trustee does not, however, take possession of the debtor's property, run the debtor's business, or propose a plan.

A trustee under chapter 12 or chapter 13 has some additional duties beyond serving as disbursing agent. §§ 1202, 1302. Many of the duties of a chapter 7 trustee are also imposed on chapter 12 and 13 trustees, such as the duty to examine and object to claims, to investigate the debtor's financial affairs, and to object when advisable to the debtor's discharge. The trustee also is given standing to appear and be heard at hearings on the value of secured property, the confirmation of the plan, or the modification of a confirmed plan.

§ 1.20   United States Bankruptcy Judge

The United States Bankruptcy Judge is the judicial officer that presides over a bankruptcy case. Bankruptcy judges are not Article III judges with lifetime tenure, but instead "serve as judicial officers of the United States district court." 28 U.S.C.

§ 152(a)(1). Thus, bankruptcy judges function as a unit of the Article III district court, 28 U.S.C. § 151, i.e., as an adjunct to the district court. The bankruptcy judges themselves are appointed for fourteen-year terms by the court of appeals for the circuit. 28 U.S.C. § 152(a)(1).

The fact that bankruptcy judges are *not* Article III judges is noteworthy, to put it mildly. One of the major points of debate leading up to the enactment of the Bankruptcy Reform Act of 1978 was whether bankruptcy judges should be made Article III judges. The House of Representatives favored such a move, which its supporters believed would enhance the quality of the bankruptcy bench and end the manifold problems associated with the splintered bankruptcy jurisdictional scheme. The Senate and the Judicial Conference of the United States (with Chief Justice Burger leading the way) opposed extending Article III status to bankruptcy judges, not wanting to diminish the prestige of existing Article III judges, establish a precedent of "specialized" Article III courts, or saddle the judiciary with several hundred lifetime judges in the event bankruptcy filings declined. In the end, bankruptcy judges were not given Article III status, but they were vested with broad jurisdictional powers. In 1982 the Supreme Court held in *Northern Pipeline Construction Co. v. Marathon Pipe Line Co.*[321] that non-Article III bankruptcy judges could not constitutionally exercise the expansive jurisdiction vested in them by the 1978 Code.

Congress responded to that decision in 1984 by limiting the jurisdiction of bankruptcy judges and keeping bankruptcy judges as non-Article III adjuncts of the district court. Under the current system, bankruptcy judges, sitting as a "unit" of the district court, "hear and determine" bankruptcy cases and proceedings in those cases by reference from the district court. 28 U.S.C. § 157. All districts have standing orders referring all bankruptcy cases to the bankruptcy court. The district judge has the power to "withdraw" the reference of a case or proceeding from the bankruptcy judge, however, and some proceedings must be withdrawn to the district court. 28 U.S.C. § 157(d). A distinction is made between "core proceedings," in which a bankruptcy judge may enter final orders which are reviewable only on appeal, and non-core proceedings, in which the bankruptcy judge must submit proposed findings of fact and conclusions of law to the district court for de novo review. 28 U.S.C. § 157(b), (c). Unfortunately, in 2011, the Court again cabined the scope of judicial authority exercisable by the non-Article III bankruptcy judges in *Stern v. Marshall.*[322] In that case the Court held that bankruptcy judges could not constitutionally enter final orders as to all of the statutorily designated "core" categories.[323] Thus, post-*Stern*, the core/noncore distinction has both a statutory and a constitutional dimension; some statutory "core" proceedings cannot be resolved by the entry of a final order by the bankruptcy judge. That in turn leaves a bit of a conundrum as to what should be done with the statutory but unconstitutional core matters, although bankruptcy courts likely will simply submit proposed findings and conclusions to the district court (per the noncore procedure of § 157(c)), notwithstanding the fact that subsection (c) on its

---

[321] 458 U.S. 50 (1982).

[322] 131 S.Ct. 2594 (2011).

[323] Id. at 2620. The Court held that 28 U.S.C. § 157(b)(2)(C) could not constitutionally grant bankruptcy judges the power to enter final orders on all state law counterclaims.

face appears to be limited to proceedings that are "not a core proceeding,"[324] raising the spectre of a jurisdictional vacuum.

The function of a bankruptcy judge is to serve as a *judge*. While that statement may appear at first blush to be a tautology, it signifies a substantial reorientation of the role of bankruptcy judges in the 1970s. Until 1973 bankruptcy judges were known as "referees" in bankruptcy. In addition to their judicial role, referees actively participated in the *administration* of bankruptcy cases. The referee presided over the meeting of creditors, met with parties throughout the case, and assumed an active posture in the management of the case. While referees were often able to "move cases along," concerns were expressed that the neutrality of the referee as judge might be compromised by their active administrative role, as well as over the practical difficulties inherent in adequately carrying out both administrative and judicial functions as caseloads increased. A conscious decision thus was made in the reform of the 1970s to separate the judicial and administrative roles, with the bankruptcy judge assuming the judicial mantle and the office of the United States trustee carrying out the administrative functions.

§ 1.21   United States Trustee

The "United States trustee" should *not* be confused with the "trustee" that serves as representative of the bankruptcy estate. Perhaps a more accurate term would be "Bankruptcy Administrator."[325] United States trustees are a part of the Department of Justice and are appointed by and under the supervision of the Attorney General. 28 U.S.C. §§ 581(a), 586(c). The activities of the United States trustees are coordinated by the Executive Office for United States Trustees, under the leadership of the Director.

The core duty of U.S. trustees is to carry out the *administrative* functions connected with bankruptcy cases. This delegation of power is part of the division of judicial and administrative responsibilities implemented in 1978. Thus, among the duties given to U.S. trustees are: to establish panels of private trustees that can serve in bankruptcy cases; appoint those trustees, and appoint standing trustees in chapters 12 and 13; review fee applications; ensure that reports are filed and fees are paid; monitor plans in reorganization cases; appoint and monitor creditors' committees; monitor the progress of bankruptcy cases; conduct required bankruptcy audits, and so on. 28 U.S.C. § 586(a).

The United States trustee program was created as a pilot program in selected districts in the 1978 Act. In 1986 the program was made permanent and established nationwide (excepting Alabama and North Carolina).[326] There are twenty-one U.S. trustee regions.

---

[324] See, e.g., In re Ortiz, 464 B.R. 807 (Bankr. E.D. Wis. 2012).

[325] The term was suggested by the 1973 Bankruptcy Commission report, and is used in the separate administrative programs in place in Alabama and North Carolina.

[326] The Bankruptcy Judges, United States Trustees, and Family Farmer Bankruptcy Act, Pub. L. No. 99–554, 100 Stat. 3088 (1986).

§ 1.22   Committees

In chapter 7 cases the trustee carries the laboring oar in overseeing the liquidation and distribution of the estate on behalf of the body of unsecured creditors. The creditors themselves do little in the lion's share of cases, although the unsecured creditors in rare cases may elect a creditors' committee to consult with and make recommendations to the trustee and otherwise assist in administration of the estate. § 705. Usually such creditor intervention only occurs in complex or controversial cases involving substantial assets.

In chapter 11 reorganization cases the story is much different. The norm in chapter 11 is to leave the debtor in control as debtor in possession. Appointment of a trustee is the exception. There is thus a need for an independent entity to function as a counterweight to the debtor in chapter 11 cases, and to represent directly the interests of creditors. The official committee of unsecured creditors fills that need. The Code mandates the appointment of a creditors' committee in all chapter 11 cases, excepting only "small business"[327] cases. § 1102(a). Additional committees may be created or the composition of current committees modified if "necessary to assure adequate representation of creditors or of equity security holders." § 1102(a)(2), (4).

The duties of a chapter 11 committee are broad. § 1103(c). The committee may consult with the debtor or trustee, and has standing to appear and be heard on any issue in the case. § 1109(b). The committee plays a particularly important role in the formulation and confirmation of a reorganization plan. The committee negotiates directly with the debtor (or trustee if one is appointed) over the terms of a plan on behalf of the class of creditors or equity holders represented. The committee then corresponds with the class members about the plan and collects votes. The class normally follows the committee's recommendation on whether to accept or reject a plan.

The creditor's committee also may investigate the debtor's business and financial affairs. Based upon that investigation the committee may seek the appointment of a trustee or examiner, move that the case be dismissed or converted to chapter 7, seek permission to file their own plan, or take other action.

Members of a committee have a fiduciary responsibility to their constituents. Much of the work of the committee is conducted through professionals retained by the committee, especially through counsel to the committee. § 1103(a). The professionals retained by the committee are paid out of the bankruptcy estate on an administrative priority basis. The members of the committee are also entitled to reimbursement for expenses incurred in performing official committee duties.[328] § 503(b)(3)(F).

---

[327] A "small business" is defined as one with less than $2,490,925 in noncontingent debts. § 101(51D). Businesses whose primary activity is owning or operating real property are excluded from the definition, even if they satisfy the debt ceiling.

[328] This provision was added to the Code in 1994, to resolve a split in the case law over the issue of whether committee members were entitled to expense reimbursement.

The United States trustee appoints the members of the committee. The Code establishes a presumption that the seven largest unsecured creditors (or equity security holders) will be appointed, § 1102(b), but in practice the United States trustee has considerable discretion to depart from that norm. This preference for the largest creditors reflects the realities (1) that those parties may be most interested in the outcome of the bankruptcy case and thus most dedicated to performing the duties of the committee and (2) that the committee will be trying to negotiate a consensual plan of reorganization and thus for the case to succeed will need to have the support of the largest creditors.

A creditors' committee formed prior to the commencement of the bankruptcy case also may be continued as the official committee in the bankruptcy case. The Code demands that such a committee have been "fairly chosen" and that it be "representative" of the different types of claims to be represented. § 1102(b)(1). Such a pre-bankruptcy creditors' committee may have been formed in connection with attempts to put together an out-of-court workout arrangement. In such instances it is efficient to take advantage of the case expertise already gained by the existing committee.

Committees are not used in chapters 12 and 13. The plan in those chapters is neither negotiated nor voted on, so there is no role for a committee to play regarding the plan. The standing trustee is called upon to investigate the debtor when appropriate and to monitor the debtor's preparation, filing, confirmation, and performance under the plan. Individual creditors are still free to appear and be heard.

F. OVERVIEW OF TYPES OF BANKRUPTCY CASES

§ 1.23   Chapter 7: Liquidation

A chapter 7 liquidation bankruptcy case is the norm. The majority of all bankruptcy filings, about two-thirds, are liquidation bankruptcies under chapter 7. Furthermore, bankruptcy as originally conceived contemplated the liquidation of the debtor's assets. Even today, when one speaks of a "bankruptcy" case, the common understanding is of a chapter 7 case. Chapter 7 is sometimes referred to as "straight" bankruptcy.

Basically, in chapter 7 the bankruptcy trustee liquidates (sells) the debtor's nonexempt assets and distributes the net proceeds of those assets to creditors holding allowed claims. The debtor is allowed to keep exempt assets, and, if the debtor is an individual, is usually discharged from pre-bankruptcy claims. This discharge gives the individual debtor a financial "fresh start" in life.

A chapter 7 case is commenced by the filing of a petition.[329] The petition in almost all cases is filed by the debtor; those cases are called "voluntary." In a voluntary case the filing of the petition operates automatically as an "order for relief." § 301. The debtor presents the petition and the statutorily prescribed filing fee, the clerk of the bankruptcy court stamps the debtor's petition, and relief is thereby ordered by

---

[329] §§ 301 (voluntary), 302 (joint), 303 (involuntary).

operation of law. The bankruptcy judge does not even participate in the process. Yet, the order for relief has the force and effect of a court order and is good against the world.

An involuntary case, by contrast, is commenced by the filing of an involuntary petition by creditors of the debtor. § 303(b). Normally at least three creditors must join in the petition. The petitioning creditors bear the burden of proving one of the statutory grounds for involuntary relief. The most common ground is that the debtor is generally not paying its debts as they come due. § 303(h)(1). The filing of the involuntary petition commences the bankruptcy case, but does not constitute an order for relief. In an involuntary case, the court must order relief after proof of a statutory ground. While involuntary petitions are only rarely filed, the fact that creditors have the right to seek such relief gives creditors some leverage in negotiating with financially distressed debtors.

The commencement of the case by the filing of the petition has at least two important automatic legal consequences. First, commencement creates a bankruptcy "estate," comprised of all of the debtor's property at the time of filing. § 541(a). Thus, the instant a bankruptcy petition is filed, the debtor's property is transformed into "property of the estate." That property no longer belongs to the debtor, although some estate property may later be returned to the debtor either as exempt property, § 522, or by abandonment. § 554. Property that the debtor acquires after the bankruptcy filing will remain property of the debtor (subject to a few narrow exceptions). Property of the estate is an important concept in chapter 7, for that property is what will be liquidated and distributed to the debtor's pre-bankruptcy creditors.

The second important consequence of commencement is the imposition of an "automatic stay" against all collection actions. § 362(a). The automatic stay is a statutory injunction that stops all creditor actions to collect prepetition debts from the debtor or to proceed against property of the debtor or the estate. The court does not have to issue the injunction, and the injunction need not be served on creditors to be effective. The filing of the petition alone is enough. The automatic stay is a temporary measure, designed to preserve the status quo as of the time of the bankruptcy filing, so that the bankruptcy case can proceed in an orderly fashion under the supervision of the bankruptcy court. Actions taken in violation of the stay are held to be void by most courts, and creditors can be assessed damages for violating the stay.

Congress added a significant gatekeeping rule to chapter 7 in 1984 and then substantially changed it in 2005 for individual debtors with primarily consumer debts. After the 2005 change, such debtors must pass an initial screening for "abuse," with a presumption of abuse being raised if the debtor fails a "means test" that calculates the debtor's debt repayment capacity. § 707(b). The idea behind the change was that individual consumer debtors with a repayment capacity of at least $100 per month (now indexed up to about $125) should not be allowed to obtain an immediate discharge of debts without having to repay anything to creditors out of their future income. If such a debtor wants bankruptcy relief, Congress wanted to force those debtors to elect to proceed under a chapter 13 repayment plan. Chapter 7 is no longer an option for these "can-pay" individuals.

Soon after the case is commenced and relief is ordered the liquidation process gets underway. The trustee first must collect the property of the estate. § 704(1). This collection process is facilitated by statutory directives admonishing the debtor, § 521(4), and third parties, § 542, to turn over property of the estate to the trustee. If they fail to do so the trustee can bring suit to compel the turnover. The debtor also must file schedules listing all of their property interests and executory contracts, as well as the property the debtor is claiming as exempt. Rule 1007. The debtor also must file a statement of affairs, which among other things gives the trustee further information about possible property interests that the trustee might seek to recover for the benefit of the estate. For example, the statement may indicate that preferential payments were made to certain creditors or that potentially fraudulent transfers were made. Finally, a creditors' meeting is held soon after the commencement of the case. § 341. Among the purposes of that meeting is to give the trustee a chance to examine the debtor and make further inquiry into the possible existence of property interests that could be recovered for the estate.

The trustee then must liquidate the estate that has been collected. Before beginning to sell assets, the trustee will first look to see if any property should be removed from the estate and returned to any party. Thus, the trustee will review the debtor's schedule of exempt assets, and if no objections are filed the debtor will keep those exempt assets, free from the claims of his creditors. The trustee also will review the schedules to see if any of the property of the estate is subject to a valid lien. If certain property is subject to a valid lien securing a claim that exceeds the value of the collateral, the trustee will "abandon" the property to the secured creditor. § 554. There is no reason for the trustee to go to the trouble of selling that property and turning all of the proceeds over to the secured creditor, because there would be no benefit to the estate. In lieu of abandonment the trustee may agree to an order lifting the automatic stay to let the secured party sell the collateral. However, if the debtor does have equity in the property, the trustee may choose to sell the property himself, pay the secured creditor the amount of their lien out of the proceeds, and keep the balance for the benefit of the estate. The trustee also may choose to abandon other property that would simply be burdensome to administer and would not benefit the estate.

All property of the estate that is not exempted by the debtor or abandoned by the trustee or otherwise released to a third party then must be reduced to money by the trustee. § 704(1). In the vast majority of chapter 7 cases there will not be any assets left to liquidate. These are called "no-asset" cases, in the sense that there are "no assets" to distribute to the unsecured creditors of the debtor. In such cases there is no reason for creditors to file claims. The trustee will file a final report and account, § 704(9), and the case will be closed. § 350(a). The debtor (if an individual) will typically be granted a discharge of their debts that arose prior to the order for relief.[330]

In the cases in which assets remain to be liquidated, the trustee will undertake to sell those assets. The Code (§ 363) and Rules (Rule 6004) give the trustee broad powers to sell property. Notice must be given to all creditors, who have the opportunity to

---

[330] § 727(a), (b); Rule 4004(c). Recall that in a voluntary chapter 7 case, the order for relief occurs at the time of filing the petition, while in an involuntary case the order for relief must be entered by the court sometime after filing.

object and demand a hearing. Absent objection the sale will go forward without a formal hearing. The sale may be either by public auction or by private sale. The trustee is given substantial discretion to choose the method that will maximize the return to the estate. The trustee is also given the power in certain circumstances to sell property free and clear of liens or free and clear of the interests of co-owners such as tenants in common, subject of course to the requirement that the lienholder or co-owner be paid their share of the net proceeds. § 363(f)–(k).

Once the estate is reduced to money, the trustee must make distribution to creditors. As mentioned above, secured creditors will either be given their collateral or will be paid the value of that collateral. Unsecured creditors holding allowed claims will then be paid in the order specified by statute. § 726. To hold an allowed claim a creditor must file a proof of claim with the clerk in the bankruptcy case. §§ 501, 502. To be timely, the proof of claim must be filed within 90 days after the date set for the first meeting of creditors. Rule 3002(c). A proof of claim is a written statement that sets forth the basis and amount of the creditor's claim. Rule 3001(a). The trustee then must review all filed claims and object to any that appear improper. § 704(5); Rule 3007. Absent objection the claim will be allowed as filed, § 502(a); if an objection is lodged the bankruptcy court must resolve the dispute. Claims are normally allowed to the extent that they are valid and enforceable under state law, unless they contradict some special bankruptcy policy. § 502(b). Claims are determined as of the date the bankruptcy case is filed. § 502(a).

Those unsecured creditors whose claims are allowed are then paid according to the statutory priority scheme. § 726. First in the distributive ladder are those claims entitled to priority under the Code. §§ 726(a)(1), 507(a). Section 507(a) specifies ten types of claims that Congress for varying policy reasons has elevated above other unsecured claims in the payment line. Priority claims are strictly statutory; the courts have no power to create new priority categories based on their notions of equity. The first priority traditionally was for administrative claims, which are the expenses of operating the bankruptcy case itself. § 503(b). In 2005, domestic support obligations were awarded first priority, and administrative expenses were moved to the second priority.

The remaining priority categories are for different categories of claims that arose before the order for relief that have been singled out by Congress for preferred treatment. These include such things as unpaid wage claims of employees, child support claims, tax claims, and even the claims of fishermen. The rationale for awarding priority in each instance is not always self-evident. As with administrative claims, all claims in one priority category must be paid in full before any payment may be made to claims in the following priority category. § 726(b).

After all statutory priority claims are paid in full, distribution is made to the remaining unsecured non-priority creditors who hold general unsecured claims. § 726(a)(2). The driving distributive principle is equality, measured on a pro rata basis. Thus, if as is usually the case, the estate is not large enough to pay all unsecured creditors the full amount of their claims, those creditors will each be paid the same percentage share on their claims. § 726(b). To illustrate, assume that the estate has $10,000 left to distribute to non-priority unsecured claims that total $100,000. Each of those claims will then be paid ten percent (i.e., $10,000/$100,000) of the amount of their allowed claim. Thus, a claim of $20,000 would be paid a distribution of $2,000, and a claim of $500 would be paid $50. This principle of equality of distribution to similarly situated claims is one of the cardinal bankruptcy doctrines, and defines one of the essential differences between bankruptcy law and non-bankruptcy collection law. Recall that outside of bankruptcy the operative premise is "first in time," with payment being made to creditors in the order in which they are able to grab the debtor's assets.

The distribution of the assets of the bankruptcy estate to creditors on an equitable basis by a neutral agent (the trustee) is one of the core functions of bankruptcy. The other primary function of bankruptcy law, applicable to individual debtors, is to afford "honest but unfortunate debtors" a chance at a fresh start in life, free from the burden of their debts. This chance is offered in part by allowing debtors to retain exempt assets, but even more fundamentally by the "discharge" of pre-bankruptcy debts. The discharge permanently bars creditors from collecting prepetition debts; it is enforced by a statutory injunction.[331] Most individual debtors who file under chapter 7 do so to take advantage of the discharge.

Not all debtors receive a complete discharge, however. Some debtors are denied a discharge entirely, § 727(a), and others have particular debts excepted from the discharge. § 523(a). Complete denial of the discharge usually is based on the commission of some act by the debtor that undermines the purpose and function of the bankruptcy case. For example, if a debtor hides assets and refuses to turn those assets over to the bankruptcy trustee, or transfers property to a relative shortly before filing bankruptcy, the discharge would be denied. § 727(a)(2). The exclusion of specific debts only from the discharge usually is based either on the blameworthiness of the debtor with regard to the creation of that debt itself—for example, the debt was based on an intentional tort, § 523(a)(6), or fraud, § 523(a)(2)—or on the worthiness of the creditor; thus tax claims, § 523(a)(1), and domestic support obligations, § 523(a)(5), are excluded from discharge.

The Bankruptcy Rules specify the procedures for the granting of a discharge in chapter 7 cases. A complaint objecting to the discharge must be filed (or an extension of time sought) fairly soon after the beginning of the case, i.e., within 60 days after the first meeting of creditors. Rule 4004. The trustee is required to investigate the debtor's financial affairs and object to the debtor's discharge "if advisable." § 704(a)(4), (6). Creditors or the United States trustee also may object to the discharge. § 727(c). If no objection is filed, the rule directs the court to grant the discharge "forthwith." Rule 4004(c). Thus, the debtor may well receive his discharge long before the liquidation and distribution of the estate has been completed. If a complaint is filed, a civil lawsuit is commenced (called an "adversary proceeding," Rule 7001, in bankruptcy cases), and a trial will be held in the bankruptcy court. The party objecting to the discharge will have the burden of proving one of the statutory grounds by a preponderance of the evidence. Rule 4005.

---

[331] §§ 524(a), 727(b). Technically, debts that arose before the order for relief are discharged, but in voluntary cases the order for relief occurs simultaneously with the filing of the petition.

A creditor also may file a complaint objecting to the discharge of their debt under one of the statutory exceptions to the discharge. A few of the statutory grounds must be brought in a lawsuit filed with the bankruptcy court within the same short time limits (60 days after the first creditors' meeting) specified for filing objections to the discharge. § 523(c)(1), Rule 4007(c). All of the other grounds may be raised at any time, Rule 4007(b), and may be and often are brought in the state courts.

The debtor may waive his or her discharge, in full or in part. A complete waiver of discharge may only be done in a writing executed by the debtor after the commencement of the bankruptcy case and with the approval of the bankruptcy court. § 727(a)(10). These stringent protections are designed to protect debtors from overreaching creditors and from their own improvidence. Partial waiver of discharge usually comes in the form of a reaffirmation agreement, in which the debtor agrees to pay a debt that otherwise would be discharged. These reaffirmation agreements are only enforceable if the parties jump through a number of statutory hoops, § 524(c), again the purpose being to protect debtors from their own folly. Debtors are permitted to make voluntary payment of discharged debts, § 524(f), but of course they cannot be compelled to do so.

§ 1.24 Chapter 11: Reorganization

Chapter 11 is the general business reorganization chapter of the Bankruptcy Code. The premise underlying chapter 11 is that everyone—creditors, stockholders, employees, the community at large—is better off if a salvageable business can be rescued. The hope is to reap the premium of going concern value over liquidation value. The same benefits can sometimes be achieved in an out-of-court workout; in many other cases, however, court protection is needed to hold off creditors while a settlement is being negotiated, and to bind dissenting creditors to that settlement. Chapter 11 offers that cocoon of federal court protection while the restructuring plan is being worked out.

The ultimate goal of chapter 11 is to confirm a plan for working out the debtor's financial obligations. Most confirmed plans are consensual, in that the terms are agreed to by the requisite majorities of the different classes of creditors and equity holders. In rare cases a plan is "crammed down" over the objection of a dissenting class. § 1129(b). The plan negotiation process takes time, however—perhaps even several years. Obviously the debtor's business cannot be allowed to die on the vine while the plan is being worked out; thus much of chapter 11 law and practice concerns the operation of the debtor's business during the pendency of the reorganization case.

While the primary function and purpose of chapter 11 is to reorganize business entities, the reach of the chapter is broader, on two scores. First, chapter 11 relief is not limited to business entities; individual debtors are eligible for chapter 11 relief.[332] With the increased debt ceilings for chapter 13 introduced by the 1994 amendments, however, and as indexed upward every three years, fewer individual debtors are likely

---

[332] Toibb v. Radloff, 501 U.S. 157 (1991). Recent data shows that approximately 14% of all chapter 11 cases are filed by individuals.

to need to file under chapter 11 for this reason.[333] Second, liquidation of the debtor's assets may be effectuated in chapter 11. § 1123(b)(4). A debtor may choose to liquidate in chapter 11 because of a desire to retain control of the liquidation process. Sales of all of the debtor's assets in chapter 11 have become much more common in recent years.

A chapter 11 case is commenced in the same way as a chapter 7 case. The debtor may file a voluntary petition, § 301, or at least three unsecured creditors may file an involuntary petition. § 303(b). Again, entry of the order for relief is automatic in a voluntary case, whereas in an involuntary case the bankruptcy court will only order relief upon proof of one of the statutory grounds. Sometimes creditors who are disgruntled with the progress of a workout agreement under state law will file an involuntary chapter 11 and move for the appointment of a trustee.

Most of the litigation at the filing stage involves a creditor moving to dismiss the chapter 11 case on the ground that it was filed in "bad faith." Even though the Code does not expressly contain a good faith filing requirement, the courts have implied one.[334] The paradigmatic situation is when a single asset real estate debtor files bankruptcy on the eve of a scheduled foreclosure of property, thus automatically staying that foreclosure. Absent a realistic prospect of the debtor successfully reorganizing, the court will dismiss the case in such circumstances. Even if the debtor has not acted in bad faith, creditors may move to dismiss the case or to convert it to a chapter 7 liquidation case if they believe that the chapter 11 case is unlikely to succeed, fearing a dissipation of the debtor's assets in a futile chapter 11 attempt. § 1112(b).

In most instances, however, the debtor is afforded at least an opportunity to reorganize in chapter 11. Reorganization may entail the restructuring of both the debtor's business itself and the financial obligations of the debtor. Until a reorganization plan is confirmed by the bankruptcy court, however, the debtor's business operations must be continued. No special court order is needed to authorize continued operation of the debtor's business; instead, such authorization is automatically conferred by statute. § 1108. As noted above, the debtor may in some cases operate while under the protection of chapter 11 for extended periods. In some respects the operation of a debtor's business in chapter 11 proceeds as "business as usual" but in many other respects special limiting rules are applied.

One critical point is that the norm is to leave the debtor's management in control as the "debtor in possession" (DIP). §§ 1101(1), 1107(a). A trustee is only appointed in unusual cases, if cause is shown, or if the appointment is in the best interests of creditors or equity holders. § 1104(a). The Code thus adopted the practice followed in old chapter XI under the prior Bankruptcy Act and rejected the chapter X rule that

---

[333] Before the 1994 amendments, a debtor was eligible to file for relief under chapter 13 only if he owed unsecured debts of no more than $100,000 and secured debts of no more than $350,000. In 1994 those limits were raised to $250,000 in unsecured debts and $750,000 in secured debts, and by 2013 the limits were $383,175, and $1,149,525. § 109(e).

[334] See, e.g., In re Laguna Assocs. Ltd. P'ship, 30 F.3d 734 (6th Cir. 1994); In re Little Creek Dev. Co., 779 F.2d 1068 (5th Cir. 1986); In re Premier Auto. Servs., Inc., 492 F.3d 274 (4th Cir. 2007); In re SGL Carbon Corp., 200 F.3d 154 (3d Cir. 1999). See also Lawrence Ponoroff & F. Stephen Knippenberg, The Implied Good Faith Requirement: Sentinel of an Evolving Bankruptcy Policy, 85 Nw. U. L. Rev. 919 (1991).

required the appointment of an independent trustee in all cases. The premises underlying the decision to leave the debtor in charge as DIP were (1) to encourage debtors to file chapter 11 while their business could still be saved and (2) to avoid the cost, delay, and disruption that would occur if a trustee were always appointed, while still preserving the option of using an independent trustee if the circumstances dictate the need for one. In practice the courts have been extremely reluctant to appoint trustees, thus giving considerable power and control to debtor management.

The debtor's business operations continue uninterrupted by the chapter 11 filing. The DIP may enter into transactions in the "ordinary course of business" without the need for court approval. §§ 363(c)(1), 364(a). The DIP thus may use, sell, or lease property, extend or obtain credit, and so forth. The authorization to operate the business carries with it the authorization to engage in transactions normally incident to that business. Creditors are on notice that the DIP may enter into such ordinary course transactions. However, transactions that are not in the ordinary course of business may only be undertaken with court approval, after creditors are given specific notice and the opportunity to object and be heard. §§ 363(b)(1), 364(b). The debtor's freedom of operation thus is curtailed. Normally, however, the court will approve non-ordinary course transactions if satisfied that the DIP has properly exercised its business judgment. If the court is concerned about the manner in which the DIP is running the business, the court can appoint a trustee or it can enter an order restricting in any way the debtor's power to transact business.

The debtor's executory contracts and unexpired leases continue in effect after the chapter 11 filing, and the other party to the contract or lease must continue to perform.[335] The DIP must pay as an administrative expense for benefits received under such contracts and leases post-petition, but, with some exceptions, § 365(d)(3), (5), is not bound to perform under those contracts unless and until it chooses to formally assume the contract or lease. The DIP may be able to postpone the decision whether to assume until the time of confirmation of the plan, §§ 365(d)(2), 1123(b)(2), except for nonresidential real property leases, § 365(d)(4), which have a shorter time limit. The DIP may elect instead to reject the contracts or leases, subject to court approval. § 365(a). The power to shed unfavorable contracts is a distinct attraction of chapter 11 for many business debtors. Another option for the DIP is to assign valuable contracts to third parties and reap the profit. § 365(f). Furthermore, unlike state law, on assignment the debtor is freed from all further obligations to perform under the contract. § 365(k).

The DIP is authorized to obtain credit or borrow money. § 364. Ordinary course credit transactions need not be approved by the court, but all borrowing or obtaining of credit out of the ordinary course must be approved by the court, after notice to creditors and the opportunity for a hearing. Substantial incentives are available to entice lenders to loan money or extend credit to a DIP in chapter 11. The creditor may be offered an administrative priority on a par with other first priority claims, or may if necessary be offered a "superpriority," i.e., a priority even over all other administrative claims. § 364(c)(1). Furthermore, liens may be granted on property of the estate to

---

[335] See, e.g., In re Whitcomb & Keller Mortg. Co., 715 F.2d 375 (7th Cir. 1983).

secure chapter 11 loans. Indeed, if sufficient need is proven, the new chapter 11 lender may even be given a "priming" lien on estate property, i.e., a first lien that subordinates prior lienholders. § 364(d). Some form of "adequate protection" must then be given to the displaced lienholder.

One significant advantage of chapter 11 is that the DIP does not have to pay interest during the pendency of the case. The filing of the bankruptcy case stops the accruing of interest. § 502(b)(2). Only if the debtor is solvent will that postpetition interest have to be repaid pursuant to the reorganization plan. The suspension of interest payments is a major boon to chapter 11 business debtors, and may afford the debtor a considerable business advantage over competitors.

One exception to the rule that post-filing interest does not accrue is for secured creditors, but only to the extent that the secured creditor is "oversecured." § 506(b). To illustrate, assume that a creditor is owed $10,000 at the time the debtor files chapter 11, and that the debt is secured by collateral worth $11,000. The first $1,000 of postpetition interest does accrue and becomes part of the creditor's secured claim, until that claim equals the value of the collateral (i.e., $11,000). The secured creditor is not entitled to pendency interest thereafter, however, and never is entitled to such interest if it is undersecured.[336] The only protection for the secured creditor is against diminution in the value of its collateral. Thus, the DIP would only have to pay the secured creditor during the case for the actual amount of depreciation of the collateral, but would not have to pay for the time value of that asset.

A DIP still must comply with the law, however, even in chapter 11. 28 U.S.C. § 959(b). Thus, for example, the DIP is not free to pollute, or to engage in anticompetitive behavior or unfair labor practices. The policy favoring the reorganization of business enterprises does not trump otherwise valid laws. Having said that, however, in some instances bankruptcy policies may allow the DIP to skirt close to the line and engage in otherwise dubious practices solely because of their chapter 11 status. For example, a DIP may be able to reject an unfavorable collective bargaining agreement even though it could not do so under the federal labor laws.[337]

The debtor cannot remain in chapter 11 in perpetuity. Eventually the debtor will either have to confirm a plan and emerge from chapter 11, or have its case dismissed or converted to chapter 7. The plan of reorganization is usually arrived at through negotiations with major classes of creditors and equity security holders. Achieving a consensual plan is of paramount importance to most debtors. All impaired classes will vote on the plan. § 1126. For the plan to be confirmed at least one impaired class must accept the plan, § 1129(a)(10), and every impaired class must either accept the plan or be "crammed down." § 1129(a)(8), (b). Cram down can only occur if the court finds that the plan is "fair and equitable" and "does not discriminate unfairly." § 1129(b). These terms of art in reorganization law require application of the "absolute priority" rule, which means as a practical matter that equity must be eliminated unless unsecured creditors are paid in full. Furthermore, cram down requires a full valuation of the

---

[336] See United Sav. Ass'n v. Timbers of Inwood Forest Assocs., Ltd., 484 U.S. 365 (1988).
[337] See NLRB v. Bildisco & Bildisco, 465 U.S. 513 (1984).

debtor, which can be costly and time-consuming. However, cram down can be avoided entirely by a consensual plan.

The dynamics of plan negotiation can be complex. The primary negotiating body for unsecured creditors is the official creditors' committee. § 1103(c)(3). If the creditors' committee is "on board" with the plan, a positive vote by the unsecured creditors is virtually assured; the opposite proposition also is usually true. One form of leverage that creditors can assert is to withhold consent to the terms proposed by the debtor and thereby threaten to invoke the absolute priority rule.

A crucial question, though, is who has the right to file a plan and seek confirmation of that plan. Competing concerns are at play. On the one hand, if the debtor retains forever the exclusive right to file a plan, it has considerable leverage to force acceptance of its proposed terms. Recall that creditors are not paid interest during the pendency of the case. The debtor thus can simply "wait out" the creditors, who lose money each day the case drags on. The only counters the creditors have to such a tactic are to move for the appointment of a trustee, seek to convert the case to chapter 7 or to dismiss the case entirely, or veto any plan the debtor proposes. They would not have the power to propose a plan themselves.

While permanent exclusivity in favor of the debtor thus causes problems, so too would countervailing difficulties arise if the debtor had no exclusive right to file a plan. One concern is that debtors would be reluctant to file chapter 11 in the first place, and thus might bypass a viable opportunity to save the business before it is too late. Furthermore, once in chapter 11, an absence of exclusivity might contribute to a breakdown of negotiations, with every interested group simply going off and filing their own plan. Consensus might then never be realized.

The balance struck by Congress is to give the debtor an initial exclusive period of 120 days to file a plan (and 180 days to obtain acceptances), but thereafter to permit any party in interest to file a plan, unless the court for cause extends the debtor's exclusivity. § 1121(b), (c). This compromise affords the debtor the first chance to put an acceptable plan together, with all parties more or less forced to the bargaining table, but does not permit the debtor to stall creditors into submission. If a trustee is appointed the exclusive period is terminated, § 1121(c)(1), which is logical because one of the primary duties of a trustee is to formulate a plan. In practice the congressional compromise has broken down somewhat, because courts routinely grant debtors extensions of the exclusive period. Thus, prior to 2005, in many cases a practice of de facto permanent debtor exclusivity developed. In 2005, Congress imposed an absolute deadline on the debtor's exclusive right to file a plan of 18 months, and 20 months to obtain acceptances. § 1121(d)(2).

Once a plan is filed the proponent of the plan will solicit votes on the plan. Another central premise of chapter 11 is informed suffrage. Those parties who are entitled to vote on the plan must be given adequate information about the debtor's financial situation and the prospects for the proposed plan. This is accomplished by requiring the plan proponent to obtain court approval of a "disclosure statement" that contains such information before soliciting votes. The approved disclosure statement then will be sent to all parties who will be voting on the plan. § 1125; Rules 3016, 3017.

Votes on the plan will then be collected and tabulated. Voting is by "classes." Only claims or interests that are "substantially similar" may be placed in the same class. § 1122(a). Note, however, that the Code does not require all substantially similar claims to be placed in the same class; judicial guidelines for separate classification of similar claims have been developed. The plan might not affect the legal rights of some classes; these classes are "unimpaired" and are deemed to accept the plan; they do not vote. §§ 1124, 1126(f). For voting classes, acceptance occurs if the plan is accepted by at least two-thirds in amount and a majority in number of allowed claims that actually vote. § 1126(c). Non-voting claims are not counted. A class of interests must accept by a vote of two-thirds in amount of those allowed interests voting. § 1126(d).

A plan will not necessarily be confirmed by the bankruptcy court even if it is accepted by all classes. Sixteen statutory requirements must be satisfied before a plan can be confirmed. § 1129(a)(1)–(16). In fact, the only one of those requirements that is not mandatory is an affirmative vote by all classes; the plan proponent in that event could still seek to confirm the plan under the cram down provision. § 1129(a)(8), (b). The bankruptcy court must hold a confirmation hearing, after notice to all creditors and parties in interest, who may object to the plan. § 1128; Rule 3020(b).

Many different policies are embodied in the confirmation requirements. Two are worthy of note in this overview: the court must find that the plan is feasible, and the plan must be in the "best interests" of creditors. "Feasibility" means that the bankruptcy court must find that "confirmation of the plan is not likely to be followed by the liquidation, or the need for further financial reorganization, of the debtor." § 1129(a)(11). Persuasive evidence that the debtor has reasonable prospects of successfully implementing the plan and maintaining a viable business thus must be introduced at the confirmation hearing. The court has an independent responsibility to make a feasibility finding even if all classes of creditors vote to accept the plan.

The "best interests" test means that every creditor must receive at least as much under the chapter 11 plan as it would if the debtor were liquidated under chapter 7. § 1129(a)(7). Such a showing establishes that confirmation of the chapter 11 plan is in the "best interests" of all creditors, as compared with the liquidation alternative. This test helps to protect the interests of those creditors who vote against the plan from the tyranny of the accepting majority. Congress concluded that a dissenting creditor has no right to insist on more than its liquidation share, even though the dissenter may not agree with the manner in which the going concern premium over liquidation is allocated. The plan proponent must put on evidence of a hypothetical chapter 7 liquidation analysis at the confirmation hearing. The value of the distribution that creditors will receive under the chapter 11 plan must be discounted to present value for a valid comparison to be made. For example, if a creditor would receive $500 right now in chapter 7, the best interests test would not be satisfied by a plan that proposed to pay that creditor $100 a year for five years, because the present value of that $500 payment stream would be less than $500.

Confirmation of the plan has a profound legal effect. § 1141. The old obligations of the debtor are replaced with the obligations specified in the plan. The terms of the plan are binding on the debtor and all creditors and equity holders. § 1141(a). This binding effect applies whether or not the affected party voted in favor of the plan. The ability to bind dissenting creditors is one of the primary advantages of chapter 11 over out-of-court workouts. Furthermore, in cases involving corporate or partnership debtors, confirmation of the plan discharges all debts that arose before the date of confirmation. § 1141(d)(1). This is true whether or not the creditor filed a proof of claim, had its claim allowed, or voted in favor of the plan. The absolute discharge language of the Code will in some cases have to bow to the dictates of due process; creditors who have no notice of the bankruptcy case cannot be discharged.[338] Individual debtors cannot discharge debts in chapter 11 if those debts would be excepted from the discharge in chapter 7, § 1141(d)(2), and do not receive a general discharge until they complete performance under the plan, or are excused from doing so. § 1141(d)(5). If a debtor liquidates in chapter 11, and does not continue in business, then the chapter 7 rules on discharge (§ 727(a)) are applied with equal force in the chapter 11 case. § 1141(d)(3).

Once confirmed a plan is difficult to attack. Even if the confirmation order is appealed directly, the appeal may become moot if the debtor makes substantial distributions under the terms of the plan. Collateral attack is extremely difficult. The doctrine of *res judicata* has been applied with rigor in this area.[339] The only way to undo a confirmed plan is to move to revoke the order of confirmation on the ground that the order was procured by fraud. § 1144. Such a motion may only be brought within 180 days after entry of the confirmation order.

Confirmation is not the end of the case. The reorganized debtor still has to perform under the terms of the plan. Many disputes and problems may arise in the years that may be required to complete performance. It is common for the order of confirmation to provide for the bankruptcy court to retain broad post-confirmation jurisdiction over disputes involving the debtor and the implementation of the plan.[340] If the debtor has difficulty in performing under the plan, it may seek to modify the plan. Otherwise plan claimants have the right to enforce their claims under the plan against the debtor by actions in state court. However, for corporate and partnership debtors, modification is only possible if the plan has not been substantially consummated. §§ 1101(2), 1127(b). If the debtor's difficulties are more extreme, it might seek to convert to chapter 7 and liquidate, or it might file a second chapter 11 case, called a "serial" filing.[341]

§ 1.25 Chapter 13: Adjustment of Debts of an Individual with Regular Income

Chapter 13 is intended to function as the primary rehabilitation chapter for individual consumer debtors. For such debtors the choice normally is between liquidation under chapter 7 and rehabilitation under chapter 13, rather than between reorganization under chapter 11 or under chapter 13.[342] In chapter 13 the debtor

---

[338] See, e.g., Reliable Elec. Co. v. Olson Constr. Co., 726 F.2d 620 (10th Cir. 1984); In re Big O Movers & Storage, Inc., 326 B.R. 434 (Bankr. N.D. Ill. 2005).

[339] See Stoll v. Gottlieb, 305 U.S. 165 (1938).

[340] See Frank R. Kennedy & Gerald K. Smith, Postconfirmation Issues: The Effects of Confirmation and Postconfirmation Proceedings, 44 S.C. L. Rev. 621 (1993).

[341] See, e.g., In re Jartran, Inc., 886 F.2d 859 (7th Cir. 1989).

[342] See § 12.3 for a comparison of the merits of chapter 13 against chapter 7 and chapter 11.

retains his property and pays creditors pursuant to a court-approved plan over three to five years.

In theory, both the debtor and his creditors may be benefited through the choice of chapter 13 over chapter 7.[343] Creditors are likely to be repaid a larger percentage of their claim in a repayment plan than in a straight liquidation; indeed, a chapter 13 plan must provide that creditors will be paid at least as much as in a chapter 7 liquidation. § 1325(a)(4). For the debtor, chapter 13 offers a chance to retain non-exempt property, whereas in chapter 7 that property would have to be turned over to the trustee for distribution to creditors. Thus a debtor who hopes to keep his house and car, and who cannot work out a reaffirmation with his secured creditor, may prefer to proceed under chapter 13.[344] Furthermore, the debtor may emerge from chapter 13 with a better credit rating than if he had liquidated under chapter 7.

In many instances, however, a debtor would prefer to liquidate immediately under chapter 7 rather than pay creditors more money for several years under chapter 13. The prototypical debtor who would prefer chapter 7 is one with few non-exempt assets but significant future earning capacity. Such a debtor would lose little in relinquishing his existing property, but would gain the unfettered enjoyment of his future earnings, because of the discharge of pre-bankruptcy debts. Congress has stopped short of compelling such debtors to proceed under chapter 13, concluding that involuntary payment plans border on involuntary servitude, and are unlikely to succeed anyway if the debtor is recalcitrant.[345]

In 2005, however, Congress made a major change in the law by taking away the chapter 7 option for individual consumer debtors with enough future repayment capacity. Under the "means test," such a "can-pay" debtor would face dismissal of his chapter 7 case as an "abuse." § 707(b). That debtor then would either have to forgo bankruptcy relief or proceed under chapter 13.

Chapter 13 still nominally remains purely voluntary with the debtor. An involuntary case cannot be commenced against a debtor under chapter 13, § 303(a), and a case cannot be converted from another chapter to chapter 13 against the debtor's wishes. §§ 706(c), 1112(d). Furthermore, the debtor is generally free to change his mind after voluntarily filing chapter 13 and move either to dismiss the case or convert it to chapter 7. § 1307(a), (b).

Aside from the "means test," Congress has tried to influence debtors to "choose" chapter 13. As first enacted in 1978, the Code offered debtors significant inducements to select chapter 13, by making that chapter more attractive in some respects than chapter 7. For example, a debtor could receive a "superdischarge" in chapter 13, § 1328(a), pursuant to which a debtor who completed payments under the chapter 13 plan could discharge some types of debts that would not be dischargeable in chapter 7,

---

[343] H.R. Rep. No. 95–595, 95th Cong., 1st Sess., at 118 (1977).

[344] The benefit of chapter 13 in this regard would be even more compelling for a debtor if the debtor could modify her home mortgage, which currently is prohibited, § 1322(b)(2), but which could change in President Obama's second term.

[345] Id. at 120–21.

such as a debt based on fraud. However, since the enactment of the 1978 Act, Congress has steadily chipped away at the superdischarge, and in the 2005 amendments virtually eliminated it altogether. This move was consistent with the adoption of the means test in chapter 7; rather than try to "persuade" debtors with repayment capacity to pick chapter 13 over chapter 7, Congress simply took away the chapter 7 option. Congress also remains committed to the notion that many right-thinking debtors will still choose chapter 13, especially if they have all of the facts.[346]

Eligibility for chapter 13 relief is limited in several important respects. § 109(e). First, only individual debtors are eligible. Thus, corporate and partnership debtors cannot obtain relief under chapter 13. An individual who runs a business as sole proprietor would be eligible, however. Second, the individual debtor must have "regular income." § 101(30). The purpose of this requirement is to limit chapter 13 to those debtors whose income is sufficiently stable and regular to permit the debtor to make payments under the chapter 13 plan. Finally, only debtors with a limited amount of debt may go under the expedited procedures of chapter 13. Until 1994, the debt ceiling for chapter 13 eligibility was $100,000 in unsecured debts and $350,000 in secured debts. A debtor with larger debts in either category was relegated either to liquidation bankruptcy under chapter 7 or to the more complicated reorganization procedures of chapter 11. In the Bankruptcy Reform Act of 1994 Congress substantially expanded the availability of chapter 13 relief by increasing the debt limits to $250,000 in unsecured debts and $750,000 in secured debts, and by 2013 the limits had increased to $383,175 (unsecured) and $1,149,525 (secured), and will increase every three years as indexed. § 104(b)(1).

The debtor normally remains in possession of his property, which becomes "property of the estate." § 1306. Postpetition earnings are also insulated from creditor collection efforts. Creditors are stayed from attempting to collect their debts from the debtor or his property during the case. Furthermore, creditors are even stayed from pursuing a codebtor of the debtor on consumer debts, unless the bankruptcy court lifts the stay. § 1301. This codebtor stay protects the debtor from indirect pressure and thus allows the debtor a better opportunity to pay all creditors in an orderly manner under the terms of a plan.

While a trustee serves in each case, the chapter 13 trustee does not take possession of or liquidate the debtor's property, run the debtor's business, or propose a plan. The main duties of the chapter 13 trustee are to serve as the disbursing agent for plan payments, and to monitor the debtor's filing of and performance under the plan. § 1302. The trustee also may examine the debtor's affairs, object to the discharge, and appear and be heard on issues that arise during the case. Usually one individual is appointed to serve as "standing trustee" for all chapter 13 cases in an entire judicial district.

---

[346] For instance, § 341(d) requires the trustee to inform the debtor at the chapter 7 meeting of creditors of the effect of chapter 7 on the debtor's credit and that the debtor could file under another chapter. The not-so-subtle message that the debtor is supposed to come away with is that chapter 13 is preferable to chapter 7. Furthermore, in 2005 Congress added a requirement that an individual debtor get credit counseling before filing bankruptcy. § 109(h). The hope was that debtors could work out a repayment arrangement with their creditors without having to file bankruptcy, and if they did have to file they would be aware of the supposed benefits of chapter 13.

The chapter 13 process emphasizes speed and simplicity. The debtor may file his proposed chapter 13 plan with the bankruptcy petition itself, and in any event must file the plan within 14 days of the filing of the petition. Rule 3015(b). The debtor then must commence making payments to the trustee within 30 days after filing the plan or the date of the order for relief, whichever is earlier. § 1326(a)(1). The trustee holds the payments until the plan is confirmed, and after confirmation distributes payments to creditors under the plan. All creditors are given 28 days notice of the time fixed for filing objections to the plan and the hearing on confirmation. Rule 2002(b). While creditors are entitled to object to confirmation, § 1324, they do not vote on the plan, unlike in chapter 11. The absence of creditor voting obviates the need for a disclosure statement, which is required in chapter 11, and largely eliminates negotiations between the debtor and creditors over the terms of the plan. Instead, the debtor proposes the terms of the plan, which are then tested against statutory standards. If the court finds that the statutory tests are met, it will confirm the plan.

The Code specifies in considerable detail: (1) what provisions are required to be in the plan, § 1322(a); (2) what provisions are permitted to be in the plan, § 1322(b); and (3) what standards must be met to support confirmation of the plan. § 1325. Since creditors do not vote on the plan, these statutory provisions serve instead to protect the rights and interests of the creditors, while still offering meaningful relief to the debtor.

For unsecured creditors, the first basic protection is that they must receive at least as much under the chapter 13 plan as they would in a liquidation under chapter 7. § 1325(a)(4). This is known as the "best interests" test, in that the chapter 13 case can only be said to be in the creditors' best interests if they are paid as much as in chapter 7.

A second protection for unsecured creditors, added in 1984 and modified in 2005, is the "projected disposable income" test, also called the "best efforts" test. § 1325(b). That provision requires the debtor to commit all "projected disposable income," as defined in the Code, to payments under the plan for the "applicable commitment period." That period will be either three years or five years, depending on whether the debtor's family income is above or below the income median for the state in which the debtor resides. § 1325(b)(4). Above-median debtors must make payments for the longer five-year period. The projected disposable income test was added in 1984 to stop the perceived abuse of a debtor receiving the enhanced benefits of chapter 13 (such as the superdischarge) without paying more than a nominal amount to unsecured creditors. Until the disposable income test was added to the Code, courts would sometimes police against that abuse by holding that a zero-payment or low-payment plan was not proposed in "good faith," and thus was not confirmable. § 1325(a)(3).

The protection for secured creditors rests on a different basis. The basic premise is that, unless it agrees to the contrary, the holder of the secured claim must receive under the plan at least the value of its secured claim, which normally is the value of their collateral. § 1325(a)(5). The debtor can achieve this result either (1) by turning the collateral over to the secured creditor or (2) by paying the creditor over time a series of payments which, when reduced to present value, are equal to the collateral value. Note, however, that the plan payments do not have to be equal in amount to the payments specified in the original contract, for two reasons. First, payments are computed based on the collateral value, not the total outstanding debt, so if the collateral is worth less than the total debt the payments will correspondingly be lower. Second, the interest rate used to calculate the payments need not be the contract rate, but only a market rate sufficient to discount the payments to present value. If that market discount rate is lower than the contracted-for interest rate, plan payments again will be lower.

Furthermore, the debtor is permitted to cure defaults and to modify the rights of secured creditors. § 1322(b)(2), (3), (5). This power to cure defaults has been interpreted broadly. Even where a creditor has already rightfully accelerated a debt, i.e., declared the entire balance immediately due and owing after the debtor's default, the debtor in chapter 13 may "deaccelerate" and thereby reinstate the original time schedule for payments.

A special protective rule is included for mortgagees whose claim is secured only by a security interest in the debtor's principal residence. § 1322(b)(2). The rights of those creditors may not be modified, although defaults may be cured. This statutory protection was interpreted by the Supreme Court in the case of *Nobelman v. American Savings Bank*[347] to prohibit "bifurcation" of the creditor's claim into a secured claim (which could not be modified) and an unsecured claim (which could). For example, if the total debt is $80,000, but the home is worth only $60,000, the creditor has a $60,000 secured claim and a $20,000 unsecured claim. The Court in *Nobelman* concluded that the prohibition against modification extended to the entire $80,000 debt, not just the $60,000 portion attributable to the secured debt. One limitation on this special protective rule is that it applies only in situations where the creditor's only security interest is in the debtor's principal residence; in other words, if the creditor has additional security (such as in personal property), it forfeits the protection of the special rule.

A second exception to the normal rule whereby under-secured claims can be bifurcated (and likely then paid off only at the lower collateral value) was added in 2005 in the so-called "hanging paragraph"[348] of § 1325(a). The primary target of the hanging paragraph is a "910" claim—that is, a purchase-money secured claim in a motor vehicle acquired for the personal use of the debtor within 910 days prior to the bankruptcy filing. For such a claim, the 2005 amendment simply says that "section 506 shall not apply."[349] The intention was to keep debtors from stripping down under-secured claims on their car if the car was purchased within 910 days of bankruptcy. Thus, for example, before 2005, a debtor who owed $10,000 on a car that was only worth $8,000 at the time of filing bankruptcy could keep the car and pay the secured creditor only $8,000 on the secured claim. The unsecured balance of $2,000 would be paid, if at all, with other unsecured claims. The 2005 amendment forces the debtor to

---

[347] 508 U.S. 324 (1993).

[348] So named because the enacting legislation simply provided that the provision be added at the end of § 1325(a), without further specification. Pub. L. No. 109–8, § 306(b) (2005).

[349] Because of this language, and its effects, application of the hanging paragraph is plagued by many interpretive difficulties. To give just one example—what happens when the debtor simply surrenders the car to the creditor? Does the creditor then still retain an unsecured claim? See, e.g., In re Wright, 492 F.3d 829 (7th Cir. 2007). However, the main intent of Congress was as stated in the text—to prevent a debtor from keeping a recently-purchased car and paying less than the debt owed.

pay the creditor the full $10,000 if he wants to keep the car. In addition to secured claims on motor vehicles purchased within 910 days of bankruptcy, the hanging paragraph precludes application of § 506 to any type of collateral, not just vehicles, for a debt incurred within one year of bankruptcy.

The terms of the confirmed plan bind the debtor and all creditors. § 1327(a). After confirmation the debtor will perform under the plan for the three-to-five year life of the plan. If the debtor completes performance under the plan, he will then receive a full discharge. § 1328(a). Until 2005, the full-compliance discharge (or "superdischarge") in chapter 13 substantially exceeded the scope of a chapter 7 discharge, by permitting the discharge of a number of types of debts (e.g., for fraud) that would not be dischargeable in chapter 7. After the 2005 amendments, however, the only meaningful type of debt that would be dischargeable under chapter 13 that is not dischargeable in chapter 7 is for a non-fraudulent tax claim under § 523(a)(1)(A). Even if the debtor is unable to complete performance under the plan, the court still may grant the debtor a "hardship" discharge in appropriate circumstances. § 1328(b), (c). The hardship discharge, however, is limited to the scope of the chapter 7 discharge.

The plan also may be modified, either before, § 1323, or after, § 1329, confirmation of the plan. Before confirmation only the debtor may modify the plan. Court approval of the modification at that juncture is not necessary, because the modified plan still must meet the confirmation requirements. After confirmation but before the completion of plan payments the debtor, the chapter 13 trustee, or the holder of an unsecured claim may move to modify the plan. The proposed modification may be to increase or to decrease the payments under the plan, depending on the circumstances. Courts have differed on the showing necessary to support a post-confirmation modification. If the plan is modified and the debtor completes performance under the modified plan, the debtor will receive a full-compliance discharge.

§ 1.26 Chapter 12: Adjustment of Debts of a Family Farmer with Regular Annual Income

Chapter 12 was added to the Code in 1986 as a temporary emergency chapter to provide relief to family farmers.[350] The enactment of chapter 12 continued a long history of special bankruptcy treatment for farmers, the most notable examples of which were the Frazier–Lemke Acts enacted during the Great Depression.[351] The "sunset" period by which chapter 12 was to expire was extended several times. Chapter 12 became a permanent part of the Code effective July 1, 2005, as part of the

---

[350] Bankruptcy Judges, United States Trustees, and Family Farmer Bankruptcy Act of 1986, Pub. L. No. 99–554, 100 Stat. 3088 (1986).

[351] Congress enacted the first Frazier–Lemke Act in 1934. Ch. 869, 48 Stat. 1289 (1934). The Supreme Court, however, struck down that law as a violation of the Fifth Amendment rights of mortgagees. Louisville Joint Stock Land Bank v. Radford, 295 U.S. 555 (1935). Congress then enacted the second Frazier–Lemke Act in response to the *Radford* decision, Ch. 792, 49 Stat. 942 (1935). The Supreme Court then upheld the constitutionality of the second act. Wright v. Vinton Branch, 300 U.S. 440 (1937); Wright v. Union Cent. Life Ins. Co., 311 U.S. 273 (1940).

Bankruptcy Abuse Prevention and Consumer Protection Act of 2005 (BAPCPA).[352] Additionally, BAPCPA expanded chapter 12 to include family fishermen.

In essence chapter 12 is a chapter 13 clone tailored to fit family farmers (and now fishermen). For farmers who are ineligible for chapter 13 (mainly due to debts exceeding the eligibility limit), chapter 12 offers significant advantages over chapter 11 if they are hoping to save the family farm. Having said that, relatively few chapter 12 cases are filed.[353]

Bankruptcy is a purely voluntary remedy for farmers and fishermen. § 303(a). Creditors are prohibited not only from filing an involuntary chapter 12 case against a family farmer or family fishermen, but are also prohibited from filing involuntary bankruptcy against a farmer or family farmer under *any* chapter. This special concern that farmers not be forced into bankruptcy against their will dates all the way back to the nineteenth century. Creditors also cannot place a family farmer or fisherman in chapter 12 by seeking conversion to that chapter of a case voluntarily filed by the debtor under chapter 7, 11, or 13, unless the debtor consents to the conversion to chapter 12. §§ 706(c), 1112(d), 1307(e). Furthermore, a family farmer or fisherman who voluntarily files under chapter 12 has an absolute right to convert to chapter 7 or to dismiss the case entirely.[354]

As in chapter 13, a chapter 12 debtor presumptively remains in possession of his property as debtor in possession. § 1203. Thus, a family farmer who files for relief under chapter 12 continues to operate his farm and the fisherman his fishing operation. However, the debtor may be dispossessed for cause, such as fraud, dishonesty, incompetence, or gross mismanagement. § 1204(a). The debtor, as well as certain codebtors of the debtor, § 1201, are protected by an automatic stay against collection efforts.

Also like chapter 13, and unlike chapter 11, a trustee is appointed in every chapter 12 case. § 1202(a). That trustee, however, only takes possession of the debtor's property in the unusual case where the debtor is divested of possession for cause. In the normal case, the chapter 12 trustee serves primarily as a disbursing agent for plan payments, monitors the debtor's performance under the plan, and appears and is heard at any hearing on the valuation of collateral, confirmation or modification of the plan, or the sale of property. § 1202(b). If appropriate the trustee may conduct an examination of the debtor or object to discharge. In most districts the United States trustee appoints a single individual to serve as standing trustee in all chapter 12 cases in that district.

The eligibility requirements for chapter 12 are strictly defined. Only a "family farmer or family fisherman with regular annual income" may obtain relief under chapter 12. § 109(f). The "regular annual income" part of the rule is taken directly from chapter 13, and as in chapter 13 is defined functionally; the test is whether the

---

[352] Pub. L. No. 109–8, § 1001, 119 Stat. 185 (2005).

[353] In 2012, for example, only 512 chapter 12 cases were filed.

[354] Section 1208(a), (b). The courts are divided, however, on the issue of whether the debtor's absolute right to dismiss under § 1208(b) must give way to a creditor's motion to convert a chapter 12 case to chapter 7 under § 1208(d) based on the alleged fraud of the debtor.

farmer's income is sufficiently stable and regular to permit the debtor to make payments under the plan. §§ 101(19), (19B). Given the seasonal nature of farm and fishery income, courts give farmer debtors considerable leeway on this score, and one expects they will do the same for fishermen. The more critical limitation on eligibility is that the debtor must be either a "family farmer" or a "family fisherman." Both terms are carefully defined, with several independent limitations designed to exclude the large "agribusiness" or major commercial fishery from chapter 12. §§ 101(18), (19A).

For farmers, a debt ceiling of $1.5 million originally was imposed. That limit includes secured and unsecured debts alike; no differentiation is made, as in the chapter 13 debt ceiling. The chapter 12 debt limit for farmers has been increased substantially; as of 2013, the debt ceiling stood at $4,031,575. That amount is indexed every three years. § 104(b)(1). Even the lower original debt limit of $1.5 million was much greater when enacted in 1986 than the then-existing chapter 13 limits,[355] and thus opened up relief to many farmer debtors. A farmer debtor with debts exceeding $4,031,575 will still have to proceed under chapter 11. A second restriction is that the debtor must either be an individual or a business entity in which a single extended family owns a majority interest. Third, at least 80 percent of the debtor's debts (excluding the debt on the principal residence) must be attributable to "farming operations" (which is broadly defined in § 101(21)). Finally, at least half of the debtor's gross income must come from that farming operation.

The extension of eligibility to family fishermen in 2005 carried with it a host of definitional limits on that eligibility. § 101(19A). Most are similar to the restrictions on family farmers, such as the 80% and 50% rules. Notably, though, for family fishermen the debt limit was enacted at $1.5 million (the pre–2005 amount for family farmers), and after indexing in 2013 went only to $1,868,200, so it now stands much lower than for family farmers.

The chapter 12 process largely tracks the simplified and expeditious chapter 13 scheme rather than the more cumbersome chapter 11 provisions. The debtor may file the plan with the petition, Rule 3015(a), and in any event must do so within 90 days unless granted an extension by the court because of "circumstances for which the debtor should not justly be held accountable." § 1221. This time for filing is greater than in chapter 13 but less than that allowed in chapter 11. Only the debtor may file a plan in chapter 12.

Creditors will receive 21 days notice of the time for filing objections to confirmation and of the confirmation hearing. Rule 2002(a)(8). Unlike chapter 11, but like chapter 13, creditors do not receive a disclosure statement in chapter 12 and are not entitled to vote on the plan. There are no committees of creditors and no negotiation on the plan. If the plan meets the statutory requirements it will be

---

[355] Before the 1994 amendments, chapter 13 eligibility was restricted to debtors with no more than $100,000 in unsecured and $350,000 in secured debts, so the chapter 12 limit of $1.5 million more than tripled the overall ceiling. The disparity was reduced by the 1994 amendment that increased the ceiling in chapter 13 to $250,000 in unsecured and $750,000 in secured debts. However, the subsequent substantial increase in the chapter 12 debt ceiling has again opened up chapter 12 to many farmers who would not qualify for chapter 13 relief.

confirmed. The confirmation hearing must be concluded within 45 days after the plan is filed, unless the court extends the time for cause. § 1224.

The statutory provisions on what terms are required to be in the plan, § 1222(a), what terms are permitted to be in the plan, § 1222(b), and what requirements must be satisfied for the plan to be confirmed, § 1225, are similar to but not identical with the chapter 13 rules. Chapter 12 (like chapter 13) permits the debtor to write down the secured debt to the value of the collateral. §§ 1225(a)(5), 1222(b)(2), (3). This is a very significant right indeed in an era of depressed farm values. One important difference is that a family farmer in chapter 12 may pay off the restructured secured debt over a period of time exceeding the plan period of three to five years. § 1222(b)(9). Also, chapter 12 does not contain the restrictions on restructuring home mortgages or new car loans that are in chapter 13 (in § 1322(b)(2) and § 1325(a)).

The basic protections for unsecured creditors, as in chapter 13, are the best interests test, which entitles a creditor to receive at least as much in chapter 13 as it would in a chapter 7 liquidation, § 1225(a)(4), and the projected disposable income test, which requires the debtor to commit all disposable income to plan payments for three years. § 1225(b). As to the latter rule, Congress when it enacted chapter 12 made a small concession to creditors beyond what chapter 13 demanded, allowing the court to require the debtor to pay all disposable income for more than three years, up to an outside limit of five years. However, when Congress amended chapter 13 in 2005 to make a five-year commitment period mandatory for consumer debtors with incomes above the state median, it did not enact any similar rule in chapter 12.

The chapter 12 rules are very different from the chapter 11 requirements in a number of ways that greatly benefit the farmer or fisherman debtor. For example, the "absolute priority" rule in chapter 11, which prohibits the debtor from retaining any property (e.g., the farm) over the objection of a class of unsecured creditors unless that class is paid in full, § 1129(b)(2)(B), is not included in chapter 12. The difficulties the absolute priority rule pose for a farmer debtor were highlighted in a Supreme Court case that held that the farmer's promise to contribute future labor to the farming operation did not justify a departure from the absolute priority rule that would allow the farmer to keep his farm.[356] In addition, in chapter 12 special rules are included to make it easier to effect a sale of farmland, farm equipment, or property used to carry out a commercial fishing operation, free and clear of liens, § 1206, and to provide "adequate protection" to a secured creditor by paying a market rent. § 1205.

Confirmation of the plan does not discharge the debtor, as in chapter 11. Instead, the debtor receives a discharge only upon the completion of payments under the plan, § 1228(a), as in chapter 13. However, the chapter 12 discharge is not the "super discharge" provided for in chapter 13; instead, all debts that would be nondischargeable in chapter 7 are similarly nondischargeable in chapter 12. § 1228(a)(2), (c)(2). A debtor who is unable to complete performance under the plan

---

[356] Norwest Bank Worthington v. Ahlers, 485 U.S. 197 (1988). Even though the case was decided after chapter 12 became part of the Code, the case had originally been filed under chapter 11 prior to the enactment of chapter 12.

may attempt to modify the plan, § 1229, and then complete performance under the modified plan, or may request a hardship discharge without modification. § 1228(b).

The right to request modification is not limited to the debtor, however, but extends to unsecured creditors and the trustee as well. § 1229(a). Thus a debtor may find that the payments called for in the plan will be increased or extended against the debtor's wishes. In this respect chapter 12 is less favorable to the debtor than chapter 11. Overall, however, for most family farmers and now family fishermen, chapter 12 may be preferable to relief under any other chapter of the Code.

§ 1.27   Special Types of Cases

a.   *Introduction*

The Code authorizes six special types of cases: stockbroker liquidation;[357] commodity broker liquidation;[358] clearing bank liquidation;[359] adjustment of debts of a municipality (chapter 9);[360] railroad reorganization;[361] and cross-border and ancillary cases.[362] Each is fairly rare. While there are many thousands of filings of the more common types of cases each year (except for chapter 12, which is rarely invoked), the specialty categories may be invoked only a handful of times each year. Sometimes, however, these cases can be extremely important; the Orange County, California, chapter 9 filing in 1994 is a prominent example, as is the 2013 filing by the city of Detroit.

The particular rules governing these specialty cases apply only to cases under those chapters or subchapters. Thus, the provisions of subchapter III of chapter 7 apply only to stockbroker cases, § 103(c); the provisions of subchapter IV of chapter 7 apply only to commodity broker cases, § 103(d); the provisions of subchapter V of chapter 7 apply only to clearing bank liquidations, § 103(e); the provisions of subchapter IV of chapter 11 apply only to railroad reorganizations. § 103(h); and (with a handful of exceptions) chapter 15's provisions apply only in chapter 15 cases. § 103(k). Furthermore, some of the Code's generally applicable provisions do not apply in municipality cases, §§ 103(a), (f), 901, or in railroad reorganizations. §§ 103(a), 1161.

b.   *Stockbroker, Commodity Broker, and Clearing Bank Liquidations*

The two special liquidation subchapters for brokers are creations of the Bankruptcy Reform Act of 1978. The 1898 Act did not contain any special liquidation procedures for brokers. Yet, those cases present unique problems that demand specialized treatment. The markets in which securities and commodities are traded are complex and highly regulated. For those markets to function efficiently and effectively, careful attention must be given to the treatment of margin payments, forward

---

[357]   Subchapter III of chapter 7, §§ 741–753.

[358]   Subchapter IV of chapter 7, §§ 761–767.

[359]   Subchapter V of chapter 7, §§ 781–784.

[360]   Sections 901–946.

[361]   Subchapter IV of chapter 11, §§ 1161–1174.

[362]   Chapter 15, §§ 1501–1532.

contracts, and the protection of customer property in the event of insolvency. Any doubts on that score were eliminated with the infamous case of Bernie Madoff. For securities brokers, Congress enacted a separate statute in 1970, the Securities Investor Protection Act (SIPA).[363] The liquidation of a stockbroker will take place under SIPA, not the Bankruptcy Code, if the Securities Investor Protection Corporation (SIPC) applies for a protective decree under SIPA. § 742. If not, the liquidation will go forward under the Code. For commodity brokers, many of the special rules in subchapter IV of chapter 7 were enacted in response to recommendations of the Commodity Futures Trading Commission (CFTC). The CFTC voiced the concern that commodity customers be given priority in property traceable to a futures commission merchant. The provisions of the Bankruptcy Code regarding commodity broker liquidation are supplemented by detailed federal regulations promulgated by the CFTC pursuant to statutory authority under the Commodity Exchange Act. 17 CFR §§ 190.01–190.10.

In 2000, Congress added a new subchapter V to Chapter 7 for clearing bank liquidations.[364] Historically, banks and other depository institutions had never been eligible for relief under the federal bankruptcy laws, and that exclusion was carried forward in the Bankruptcy Code. § 109(b)(2), (3). The 2000 law created a very narrow exception to that policy for certain "clearing banks," which are defined to include only "an uninsured State member bank, or a corporation organized under section 25A of the Federal Reserve Act, which operates, or operates as, a multilateral clearing organization pursuant to section 409 of the Federal Deposit Insurance Corporation Improvement Act of 1991." § 781(3). Such a clearing bank may be a chapter 7 debtor if a petition is filed at the direction of the Board of Governors of the Federal Reserve System. § 109(b)(2). This amendment was enacted as part of a broader congressional scheme to provide for and regulate multilateral clearing organizations, including resolution of their failures. The provisions in subchapter V (§§ 781–784) apply only in such cases. The provisions in chapters 1, 3, and 5, and in subchapters I and II of chapter 7, do generally apply to clearing bank liquidations.

c. *Chapter 9: Adjustment of Debts of a Municipality*

Unlike the more recently enacted broker and clearing bank provisions, both municipal bankruptcy and railroad reorganizations claim a longer lineage. Each can trace direct statutory roots to the Great Depression.[365] The provisions for municipal bankruptcy were significantly amended in 1976 to make it feasible for large cities to file bankruptcy,[366] prompted by concerns over the financial problems of New York City.

---

[363] Pub. L. No. 91–598, 84 Stat. 1636 (codified at 15 U.S.C. §§ 78aaa–78lll).

[364] Pub. L. No. 106–554, 114 Stat. 2763 (2000).

[365] Ch. 204, 47 Stat. 1467 (1933) (enacting § 77 to govern the reorganization of railroads), amended by ch. 774, 49 Stat. 911 (1935); Ch. 345, 48 Stat. 798 (1934) (enacting chapter IX for municipalities). Although the Supreme Court struck down the first municipal bankruptcy law, a slightly revised chapter IX was then upheld by the Court. United States v. Bekins, 304 U.S. 27 (1938). The Court also upheld the railroad reorganization provision. Cont'l Illinois Bank & Trust Co. v. Chicago, Rock Island & Pac. Ry. Co., 294 U.S. 648 (1935).

[366] Pub. L. No. 94–260, 90 Stat. 315 (1976).

After being streamlined in the 1978 Code, chapter 9 was again amended substantially in 1988.[367]

Chapter 9 is a unique creature. Unlike in the other case chapters, Congress has had to draft chapter 9 with due accommodation for the Tenth Amendment sovereignty of the states, which extends to state control of municipalities.[368] Thus, liquidation of a municipality is not contemplated by the Bankruptcy Code; liquidation would require action by the state legislature. The chapter 9 debtor operates largely free from court and creditor constraints with regard to the use of property or revenues and the exercise of political and governmental powers.[369] Furthermore, state law must authorize the municipality to be a debtor under chapter 9. § 109(c)(2).

Eligibility for chapter 9 relief is narrowly circumscribed. § 109(c). As noted, state law must authorize the municipality to be a debtor, although most cases have not required specific authorization, but have allowed implied authority to suffice. The entity must be a "municipality," which is defined as a "political subdivision or public agency or instrumentality of a State." § 101(40). This definition thus does not limit relief to towns or cities; instead, entities such as school districts and sanitation districts have properly filed under chapter 9.[370] A third eligibility requirement is that the municipality must be insolvent. § 901(c)(3). Chapter 9 is the only Code chapter that requires insolvency of the debtor.[371] The municipality also must desire to effect a plan to adjust its debts, and finally must engage in good faith prepetition negotiations with creditors, unless doing so would be impractical. Furthermore, a chapter 9 case may be dismissed if, after objection by creditors, the court finds that the debtor did not file the petition in good faith. § 921(c).

The plan confirmation process in chapter 9 is similar to that in chapter 11.[372] The debtor files a plan, a disclosure statement is approved by the court and sent to creditors, creditors vote, objections to confirmation may be filed, and the court holds a confirmation hearing. One difference from chapter 11 is that only the debtor may file a plan in a chapter 9 case. § 941. Also, the "best interests" of creditors test is not gauged by comparison to the projected dividend in a liquidation, but by an overall reasonableness inquiry that considers many factors, including the extent the municipality uses its taxing power. As in chapter 11, the court must conclude that the proposed plan is feasible. § 943(b)(7). The court's primary input in a chapter 9 case

---

[367] Municipal Bankruptcy Amendments, Pub. L. No. 100–597, 102 Stat. 3028 (1988).

[368] The Supreme Court held that the first municipal bankruptcy law was an unconstitutional infringement of the state's Tenth Amendment powers. Ashton v. Cameron Cnty. Water Improvement Dist. No. 1, 298 U.S. 513 (1936).

[369] Section 903 (reservation of State power to control municipalities), § 904 (limitation on jurisdiction and powers of court), § 901(a) (not incorporating § 363 on use of property and § 541 on property of estate).

[370] However, one bankruptcy court barred a drainage district from chapter 9 relief where Illinois law did not explicitly authorize such an entity to be a debtor. In re Slocum Lake Drainage Dist. of Lake Cnty., 336 B.R. 387 (Bankr. N.D. Ill 2006).

[371] Failure to meet this test prompted the 1991 dismissal of the bankruptcy filing of Bridgeport, Connecticut. In re City of Bridgeport, 129 B.R. 332 (Bankr. D. Conn. 1991).

[372] See § 901(a) (incorporating many of the chapter 11 provisions relating to confirmation of the plan); Fed. R. Bankr. P. 3013–3014, 3016–3021 (rules on plan process applied to chapters 9 and 11).

comes at two points—the decision to permit the filing to go forward initially, and the decision whether to confirm the plan.

d. Railroad Reorganizations

Railroad reorganizations historically may be said to be the father of modern reorganization law. The federal equity receivership was devised in the late nineteenth century as a means to keep the railroads running. Some of the principles developed in those receiverships continue to apply to cases under the Code today. § 1171(b). Railroads have long been afforded singular treatment under reorganization laws, either in equity courts or by statute. Courts and the Congress have identified a strong public interest in railroads. That emphasis on the public interest continues today. The Code specifically requires the court and the bankruptcy trustee to "consider the public interest" in applying most of the special railroad reorganization rules, including confirmation of the plan. § 1165.

The subchapter for railroad reorganizations is found in chapter 11, and most of the generally applicable rules of that chapter apply with equal force in railroad cases. §§ 103(a), (f), 1161. There are some important exceptions, however. Most notable is that in railroad cases a trustee must always be appointed. § 1163. Thus, those provisions of chapter 11 relating to the discretionary appointment of a trustee and the role of the debtor in possession have no place in railroad reorganizations. Another difference is that an unsecured creditors' committee is not appointed in a railroad case, because the most important creditor constituency usually is the secured creditors.

The provisions of the railroad reorganization subchapter apply only to railroad cases. § 103(h). The provision for direct consideration of the public interest has been noted. The Interstate Commerce Commission, the Department of Transportation, and corresponding state agencies are explicitly given the right to be heard. § 1164. Special rules govern matters such as the treatment of the rights of secured creditors in rolling stock equipment, § 1168; the rejection of a lease of a railroad line, § 1169; the abandonment of a railroad line, § 1170; priority claims, § 1171; the contents of the plan, § 1172; and the requirements for confirmation of a plan. § 1173. In addition, subject to a few exceptions, the provisions of the Interstate Commerce Act are binding on a railroad in reorganization. § 1166. An outside time limit of five years to achieve confirmation of a plan is imposed, failing which the court must order the trustee to liquidate the debtor. § 1174.

From time to time Congress has enacted special supplementary legislation to deal with particular rail crises. Examples include: (1) the Emergency Rail Services Act of 1970;[373] (2) the Regional Rail Reorganization Acts of 1973 and 1975;[374] (3) the Rock Island Railroad Employee Assistance Act;[375] and (4) the Milwaukee Road Restructuring Act.[376] While most of this special legislation has been upheld, the Supreme Court did hold part of the Rock Island act to be unconstitutional on the

---

[373] 45 U.S.C. §§ 661–668.

[374] 31 U.S.C. § 9101; 45 U.S.C. §§ 701–797m.

[375] 45 U.S.C. §§ 1001–1018.

[376] 45 U.S.C. §§ 901–922.

ground that it applied only to that one railroad and therefore was not a "uniform" law on the subject of bankruptcies.[377]

e. *Chapter 15: Ancillary and Other Cross–Border Cases*

In 2005, Congress enacted chapter 15, a new case chapter, for "Ancillary and Other Cross-Border Cases."[378] Chapter 15 is designed to deal with the burgeoning problem of multinational insolvencies, where debtors have assets and creditors in more than one country.[379] Chapter 15 replaces § 304 of the 1978 Bankruptcy Code, which had covered "cases ancillary to foreign proceedings." Section 304 cases were, as the section title indicates, entirely *ancillary* in nature. Under § 304, a foreign representative of a foreign insolvency proceeding could file a petition in the United States seeking various forms of relief in the United States to assist in that foreign proceeding.[380] For example, the foreign debtor might have assets located in the United States, which the foreign representative would want to recover so that those assets could be administered in the home country proceeding.

While in many respects chapter 15 continues aspects of the law existing under § 304, it is more comprehensive, and does change or clarify some aspects of prior law.[381] Further, not only is its scope broader, but much that had previously been left solely to judicial development or discretion is now codified. As provided in § 1501(b), Chapter 15

"applies where:

---

[377] Ry. Labor Execs.' Assoc. v. Gibbons, 455 U.S. 457 (1982).

[378] Pub. L. No. 109–8, tit. VIII, §§ 801–802 (2005).

[379] Two excellent books addressing this topic are, Samuel L. Bufford et. al., International Insolvency (2001), and Bob Wessels et. al., International Cooperation in Bankruptcy and Insolvency Matters (2009). See also Jay Lawrence Westbrook, Multinational Enterprises in General Default: Chapter 15, The ALI Principles, and the EU Insolvency Regulation, 76 Am. Bankr. L.J. 1 (2002).

    As my co-author Professor Brubaker and I have explained:

> Today, many firms have assets, interests, and creditors in multiple countries. When such a firm becomes financially distressed and needs bankruptcy relief (either liquidation or reorganization), many difficult issues arise. Which country or countries will conduct bankruptcy proceedings regarding that firm? What assets will be administered in those proceedings? Which countries' laws will apply? How will creditors be treated? Will the orders of foreign courts be recognized and enforced? Will foreign representatives have access to the courts in other countries? The list goes on and on.

Charles J. Tabb & Ralph Brubaker, Bankruptcy Law: Principles, Policies, and Practice 821 (3d ed. 2010).

[380] Professor Jay Westbrook, one of the leading American scholars in the field of international bankruptcy, observed about § 304:

> That section for the first time codified United States notions of comity and cooperation with foreign courts in bankruptcy matters. It provided a mechanism for a foreign trustee appointed in a main proceeding to initiate a United States ancillary case in which the trustee could seek injunctions, turnover of assets, and other relief in aid of the proceedings in the debtor's home country.

Jay Lawrence Westbrook, Chapter 15 at Last, 79 Am. Bankr. L.J. 713, 718–19 (2005).

    The 1997 Commission Report, which recommended adoption of chapter 15, noted that § 304 "for the first time gave the courts explicit authority to recognize foreign insolvency proceedings, to cooperate with those proceedings, and, when appropriate, to transfer assets from the United States to a foreign proceeding in the debtor's home country." National Bankruptcy Review Commission Final Report, Bankruptcy: The Next Twenty Years, at 354 (1997).

[381] See Westbrook, supra note 380, at 725–28, for a summary of significant changes from pre-2005 law. See also Commission Report, supra note 380, at 362–63.

(1) Assistance is sought in the United States by a foreign court or a foreign representative in connection with a foreign proceeding;

(2) Assistance is sought in a foreign country in connection with a case under this title;

(3) A foreign proceeding and a case under this title with respect to the same debtor are pending concurrently; or

(4) Creditors or other interested persons in a foreign country have an interest in requesting the commencement of, or participating in, a case or proceeding under this title."

Some sense of the coverage of chapter 15 can be seen by looking at its subchapters. "General Provisions" are found in subchapter I (§§ 1502–1508). Subchapter II (§§ 1509–1514) deals with "Access of foreign representatives and creditors to this court." The subject of subchapter III (§§ 1515–1524) is "Recognition of a foreign proceeding and relief." In practice, this may prove to be the most important subchapter. The provisions of subchapter IV (§§ 1525–1527) deal with "Cooperation with foreign courts and foreign representatives." "Concurrent proceedings" are the topic covered by subchapter V (§§ 1528–1532).

Chapter 15, with minor changes,[382] incorporates the Model Law on Cross–Border Insolvency proposed in 1997 by the United Nations Commission on International Trade Law (UNCITRAL).[383] By adopting the UNCITRAL Model Law, the United States furthered its position as a world leader in the development of cross-border insolvency.[384] The European Union promulgated a Regulation on Insolvency, effective in 2002, that governs multinational bankruptcies involving EU member states,[385] but has not adopted the UNCITRAL Model Law for cases involving EU member states and

---

[382] Perhaps the most significant departure from the Model Law is the exclusion of consumer cases. See § 1501(c)(2). See also Commission Report, supra note 380, at 364–65.

[383] The UNCITRAL promulgaters explained the purpose of the Model Law:

The Model Law is designed to assist States to equip their insolvency laws with a modern, harmonized and fair framework to address more effectively instances of cross-border insolvency. Those instances include cases where the insolvent debtor has assets in more than one State or where some of the creditors of the debtor are not from the State where the insolvency proceeding is taking place. The Model Law respects the differences among national procedural laws and does not attempt a substantive unification of insolvency law. It offers solutions that help in several significant ways, including: foreign assistance for an insolvency proceeding taking place in the enacting State; foreign representative's access to courts of the enacting State; recognition of foreign proceedings; cross-border cooperation; and coordination of concurrent proceedings.

See http://www.uncitral.org/uncitral/en/uncitral_texts/insolvency/1997Model.html.

[384] Great Britain followed the U.S. lead, adopting the Model Law on April 6, 2006. Japan is another major economic power that has adopted the Model Law. See Tabb & Brubaker, supra note 379, at 821. The National Bankruptcy Review Commission believed that "the principal benefit to the United States from adopting the Model Law will lie in the effect of its adoption on other jurisdictions. . . . [I]ts adoption of the Model Law is probably essential to the Law's widespread adoption by other countries." Commission Report, supra note 24, at 361.

[385] Council Regulation (EC) No1346/2000 of 29 May 2000 on insolvency proceedings [Official Journal L 160 of 30.06.2000].

non-member states. Other law reform efforts in the international insolvency arena have been ongoing.[386]

Chapter 15 is certainly not the only source of law on the subject of cross-border insolvency. Judicial principles of *"comity,"* long-developed by courts as part of international law, continue to be important. "Comity" has been defined by the Supreme Court as "the recognition which one nation allows within its territory to the legislative, executive or judicial acts of another nation, having due regard both to international duty and convenience, and to the rights of its own citizens or of other persons who are under the protection of its laws."[387] The importance of comity in the realm of transnational insolvency was emphasized as far back as 1883 in a foundational decision by the Supreme Court.[388] A modern example of the exercise of comity to facilitate the administration of an exceedingly complex multinational case is that involving the Maxwell Communications empire, with substantial contacts in Great Britain and the United States. The primary administration of that case went forward in England, with close cooperation and assistance from courts in the United States, where a parallel chapter 11 case was conducted.[389] Even after the enactment of chapter 15, courts in the United States often will have to exercise their wise discretion regarding comity.

To understand the problems unique to transnational insolvency, a student must appreciate the crucial distinction between and meaning of the core competing theories of "universalism" and "territorialism."[390] Historically, the prevailing approach has been *"territorialism,"* also known pejoratively (albeit accurately) as the "grab rule."[391] Under territorialism, each country will "grab" whatever assets of the debtor are located within that country and administer those assets in accordance with their own local insolvency law, and possibly favoring local creditors. Even if a debtor has its home base in another country, and a comprehensive bankruptcy proceeding is conducted in that home country, the remote "grabbing" jurisdiction would ignore pleas to turn over the assets

---

[386] See Bufford, supra note 379, and Wessels, supra note 379, for comprehensive discussions. Professor Brubaker and I have noted that:

"The American Law Institute (ALI) agreed in 2002 to "Principles of Cooperation in Transnational Insolvency Cases Among the Members of the North American Free Trade Agreement," i.e., as between the United States, Canada, and Mexico. The Cross–Border Insolvency Concordat was developed in 1995 by Committee J of the Section of Business law of the International Bar Association. Courts may, and do, adopt principles of the Concordat on a case-by-case basis."

Tabb & Brubaker, supra note 379, at 822.

[387] Hilton v. Guyot, 159 U.S. 113, 164 (1895).

[388] See Canada S. Ry. Co. v. Gebhard, 109 U.S. 527 (1883).

[389] See Maxwell Commc'ns Corp. PLC v. Société Générale (In re Maxwell Commc'ns Corp. PLC), 93 F.3d 1036 (2d Cir. 1996). See also Jay Lawrence Westbrook, The Lessons of *Maxwell Communications*, 64 Fordham L. Rev. 2531 (1996).

[390] See Tabb & Brubaker, supra note 379, at 822–23, for an exposition of the distinction.

[391] See Commission Report, supra note 380, at 353. Professor Lynn LoPucki is the leading modern critic of universalism and advocate of what he calls "cooperative territorialism." See, e.g., Lynn M. LoPucki, The Case for Cooperative Territorialism in International Bankruptcy, 98 Mich. L. Rev. 2216 (2000). Also by LoPucki, see Cooperation in International Bankruptcy: A Post–Universalist Approach, 84 Cornell L. Rev. 696 (1999); Global and Out of Control, 79 Am. Bankr. L.J. 79 (2005); Universalism Unravels, 79 Am. Bankr. L.J. 143 (2005). Professor Tung likewise is critical of universalism as unworkable. See Frederick Tung, Is International Bankruptcy Possible?, 23 Mich. J. Intl. L. 31 (2001).

within its boundaries and control for administration abroad. In short, in territorialism, all assets are administered in the country where located, under local law.

By contrast, under *"universalism,"* the ideal is a single, comprehensive, "universal" bankruptcy proceeding conducted (preferably) in the debtor's home country, with all assets in the world turned over to and administered in that single proceeding, for the benefit of all creditors worldwide, in accordance with the law deemed most appropriate under choice of law rules.[392] Territorialism is criticized by universalist proponents as being both inefficient and unfair. A "modified" universalism would depart from the "pure" form just described by permitting ancillary or secondary administrations of local assets in some instances, where necessary to accommodate important domestic concerns. Even under modified universalism, though, the dominant administration is in the home country, and the presumption is that most assets will be turned over to that country and most creditors' claims administered in that proceeding. The trend, exemplified by the Model Law and the EU Regulation, is toward *modified universalism*. As a practical political matter, there are too many important differences in domestic insolvency laws worldwide for a pure universalist approach to be adopted in the near future.

Chapter 15, in keeping with this trend, adopts a modified universalist approach. Thus, if a "foreign main proceeding" has been commenced and if the foreign representative petitions the United States courts for recognition (§§ 1504, 1515), then, subject to some procedural safeguards (§§ 1515(b)–(d), 1516), "recognition" of the foreign proceeding is mandatory. § 1517. Upon such recognition, an automatic stay goes into effect in the United States protecting the debtor's assets from seizure, other rules are triggered empowering the foreign representative to deal with and operate the U.S. assets in the same manner as a local trustee, and the foreign representative is given full access to U.S. courts. §§ 1520, 1509.

However, on the critical question of whether assets located in the United States *must* be turned over for administration abroad in the foreign main proceeding, the answer is "no." Instead, under § 1521(b), the United States court in which the foreign representative has commenced a chapter 15 case is given discretion whether to turn over assets. Under that section, the court *"may"* "entrust the distribution of all or part of the debtor's assets located in the United States to the foreign representative or another person . . . , *provided that the court is satisfied that the interests of creditors in the United States are sufficiently protected."* Note that the U.S. court is required to consider the interests of U.S. creditors. The question of course will be, what constitutes a "sufficient" protection of those creditors? At the extreme, a court might say that if a U.S. creditor would get *anything* less in the foreign proceeding than it would under

---

[392] The leading advocates of universalism are Professors Jay Lawrence Westbrook and Andrew Guzman. By Guzman, see International Bankruptcy: In Defense of Universalism, 98 Mich. L. Rev. 2177 (2000); An Economic Analysis of Transnational Bankruptcies, 42 J.L. & Econ. 775 (1999) (with Lucian A. Bebchuk). By Westbrook, see a Global Solution to Multinational Default, 98 Mich. L. Rev. 2276 (2000); Theory and Pragmatism in Global Insolvencies: Choice of Law and Choice of Forum, 65 Am. Bankr. L.J. 457 (1991). Another defender of universalism is Judge Samuel Bufford. See, e.g., Hon. Samuel L. Bufford, Global Venue Controls Are Coming: A Reply to Professor LoPucki, 79 Am. Bankr. L.J. 105 (2005).

U.S. law, that fact alone would be enough to deny turnover.[393] A less extreme view would be to accept some differences in the specific treatment of particular creditors, as long as the basic premises underlying the foreign insolvency law are compatible with U.S. law, and the foreign proceeding is fair and equitable.[394] At the very least § 1521(b) mandates that the foreign distribution scheme not discriminate in favor of local creditors, to the detriment of foreign (including U.S.) creditors.

A further statutory limitation on pure universalism is found in the "public policy" exception of § 1506: "Nothing in this chapter prevents the court from refusing to take an action governed by this chapter if the action would be manifestly contrary to the public policy of the United States." Section 1506 codifies the long-standing judicial approach taken in deciding whether to extend comity to foreign proceedings.

An important question in transnational insolvency cases is determining the proper forum for a "main proceeding." Many important consequences follow. Significantly, if an insolvency proceeding is commenced in a country that is found to be improper by the courts of another country, that second country likely will deny recognition of the foreign proceeding and will refuse to cooperate with that proceeding. See § 1517. Of course, in a strictly territorialist regime, identifying a main proceeding would not be important, because no one cooperates with anyone else anyway. But under the modified universalism of chapter 15, main proceedings are centrally important.

A threshold question is what even constitutes a "foreign proceeding" to which chapter 15 could apply. The 2005 law amended the definition of "*foreign proceeding*" in § 101(23), to be "a collective judicial or administrative proceeding in a foreign country, including an interim proceeding, under a law relating to insolvency or adjustment of debt in which proceeding the assets and affairs of the debtor are subject to control or supervision by a foreign court, for the purpose of reorganization or liquidation." This definition is broad, reaching virtually any collective proceeding relating to insolvency or debt adjustment.

Assuming that a proceeding is a "foreign proceeding," the critical issue will be whether it is "*main*" or "*non-main*." A main proceeding is "[a] primary, full-blown insolvency proceeding in which claims are filed, distribution made, and so forth. A "non-main" proceeding is, believe it or not, a proceeding that is not a main proceeding."[395] The foreign representative of a foreign main proceeding has substantially greater rights than for a non-main proceeding. For example, in a main proceeding, upon recognition, an automatic stay goes into effect, but for a non-main proceeding, the court must affirmatively grant an injunction. See §§ 1520, 1521. Furthermore, a United States court is much more likely to award discretionary relief under § 1521 with respect to a foreign main proceeding than for a foreign non-main

---

[393] For a case denying turnover under § 304 on the basis that the creditor's claim would be treated as secured under U.S. law but as unsecured under the foreign (Canadian) law, see In re Toga Mfg. Ltd., 28 B.R. 165 (Bankr. E.D. Mich. 1983).

[394] For an example of such a case, where the court ordered turnover of assets to the Bahamas under § 304, even though U.S. creditors who had attached assets in the U.S. would lose their preferential claims and thus recover less, see *In re Culmer*, 25 B.R. 621 (Bankr. S.D.N.Y. 1982).

[395] Tabb & Brubaker, supra note 379, at 823.

proceeding. For example, while theoretically possible, it is highly unlikely that a United States court would entrust assets located in the United States to a foreign representative for a non-main proceeding under § 1521(b).

The dispositive test for locating a main proceeding is identifying the country where the debtor has the *"center of main interests"* (known as "COMI"). See § 1502(4). While COMI is not defined under chapter 15 or the Model Law, instead being left to case development, some guidance can be found in the EU Regulation, which also utilizes a COMI test. The EU Regulation establishes a presumption that the place of the registered office (which under U.S. law would be the place of incorporation) is the COMI. However, the EU preamble also states that "the 'centre of main interests' should correspond to the place where the debtor conducts the administration of his interests on a regular basis and is therefore ascertainable by third parties." In some (many?) cases, the situs suggested by the EU preamble might well differ from the place of the registered office. Perhaps the most trenchant criticisms Professor LoPucki and others have leveled at the modified universalism embraced by chapter 15 is that the debtor's COMI is both indeterminate and manipulable, thereby allowing the debtor to forum shop on a worldwide level for favorable laws.[396] Some controversial decisions in the EU upholding dubious assertions of a debtor's COMI lend some credence to the critics' charges. Defenders of universalism are more sanguine that a debtor's COMI can be both identified fairly and accurately and regulated more readily against manipulation.[397]

A "non-main" proceeding may only be in a country where the debtor has an "establishment." § 1502(5). An "establishment" is defined as "any place of operations where the debtor carries out a *non-transitory economic activity*." § 1502(2). If a United States court finds that a debtor lacks the sufficient connection to sustain a foreign non-main proceeding, then recognition will be denied and the foreign representative will get no assistance from chapter 15.

Identifying a debtor's COMI has recently become an issue in the context of investment funds. The issue is that while many funds are registered as an LLC outside of the United States, such organizations tend to be shell companies conducting no actual operations and holding no assets overseas.[398] In such cases where the debtor fund is in reality operated and controlled in the United States, courts will tend to find that a foreign COMI has not been established despite offshore registration.[399] However, it is a highly fact-specific determination; when the fund maintains at least some operations offshore, the court may determine that the fund has a foreign COMI.[400]

---

[396] See sources cited in note 391, supra.

[397] See sources cited in note 392, supra.

[398] E.g., In re Bear Stearns High–Grade Structured Credit Strategies Master Fund, Ltd., 389 B.R. 325 (S.D.N.Y. 2008) (holding that although the fund was registered in the Cayman Islands, the COMI was not located in the Cayman Islands since the investment manager, books and records, and all assets were located in the United States).

[399] Id.

[400] E.g., In re Millennium Global Emerging Credit Master Fund Ltd., 458 B.R. 63 (Bankr. S.D.N.Y. 2011) (holding that a fund's COMI was located in Bermuda where, among other factors, two of the three

It is worth noting that with regard to the filing of a "main" bankruptcy case *in the United States*, chapter 15 is not controlling. Instead, eligibility to be a debtor under title 11 of the Bankruptcy Code requires only that the debtor be a "person" (defined in § 101(41) as an "individual, partnership, or corporation") that "resides or has a domicile, a place of business, or property in the United States." § 109(a). Thus, if the debtor has even a small amount of property in the United States, or any place of business, it would be eligible to file a full bankruptcy case in the United States bankruptcy courts, likely under either chapter 11 or chapter 7. The only recourse if the United States connection is too small, or if a foreign main proceeding has already been commenced in another country, would be for the United States bankruptcy court to *abstain* from hearing the case under § 305. Abstention may be granted if "the purposes of chapter 15 would be best served by such dismissal or suspension," § 305(a)(2)(B); if a "petition under section 1515 for recognition of a foreign proceeding has been granted," § 305(a)(2)(A); or "if the interests of creditors and the debtor would be better served by such dismissal or suspension," § 305(a)(1). Abstention by a United States bankruptcy court is permissive, not mandatory.

---

directors of the fund were located in Bermuda and exercised significant control over fund decisions and Bermuda was "reasonably ascertainable by third parties" as the COMI).

Chapter 2

INVOKING BANKRUPTCY RELIEF

§ 2.1   Introduction

One of the most fundamental issues of bankruptcy policy is what sort of bankruptcy relief, if any, should be available for a particular debtor. A second question in framing a bankruptcy law is who may trigger bankruptcy relief. A third basic issue is what showing is necessary to commence a bankruptcy case. Each of these gate-keeping questions goes to the core of a bankruptcy system, defining in large part what goals that system is supposed to (and will be able to) accomplish.

The United States Code authorizes six different types of bankruptcy cases. The Code designates these cases by "chapter": chapter 7 (liquidation); chapter 9 (adjustment of debts of a municipality); chapter 11 (reorganization); chapter 12 (adjustment of debts of a family farmer or family fisherman with regular annual income);[1] chapter 13 (adjustment of debts of an individual with regular income); and chapter 15 (ancillary and other cross-border cases).[2]

Of those, chapter 7 and 13 cases are by far the most common. To get a sense of this, consider the case statistics for the calendar year 2012. In that year, a total of 1,221,091 cases were filed.[3] Of those, 69% were chapter 7 cases (843,545); 30% were filed under chapter 13 (366,532); chapter 11 filings comprised just 0.8% of the total (10,361); and the rest were negligible—chapter 12 (512), chapter 9 (19 filings), and chapter 15 (121 filings). The current chapter 13 filing rate is about the same as in 2004, the last full calendar year pre-BAPCPA, when chapter 13 cases accounted for 28% of all filings,[4] which suggests that Congress may have missed the mark in enacting the Bankruptcy Abuse Prevention and Consumer Protection Act of 2005, since one of their primary goals was to push more consumer debtors out of chapter 7 and into chapter 13. Now that initial filing dislocations have corrected, in the longer term it has not worked out that way (just as many critics of BAPCPA predicted!).

On the first fundamental question—*what debtors are eligible* for what sort of bankruptcy relief—the Code contains detailed rules in § 109 that govern debtor eligibility under each case chapter.[5]

---

[1]   Chapter 12 did not become a permanent part of the Code until 2005. It was enacted originally as a temporary measure in 1986.

[2]   Chapter 15 was added to the Code in 2005. In enacting chapter 15, the United States adopted the 1997 UNCITRAL Model Law on Cross–Border Insolvency. Chapter 15 replaced § 304.

[3]   See   http://www.uscourts.gov/uscourts/Statistics/BankruptcyStatistics/BankruptcyFilings/2012/1212_f2.pdf

[4]   In 2004, of 1,597,462 total filings, 449,129 were under chapter 13.

[5]   See §§ 2.2, 2.3. The exception is chapter 15, on ancillary and cross-border cases, which contains its own eligibility rules.

The second core question is *who may trigger* bankruptcy relief. A bankruptcy case can be commenced either by the debtor or by the debtor's creditors. Historically (meaning a long, long time ago), creditor commencement was the norm, but today almost all cases are begun by debtors. A *"voluntary"* bankruptcy case is commenced *by the debtor*, § 301, or jointly by the debtor and the debtor's spouse. § 302. An eligible debtor commences a case under a particular chapter (e.g., chapter 7, 9, 11, 12, or 13) simply by filing a bankruptcy petition under that chapter.[6] Filing the petition has profound effects: it triggers an automatic stay against all sorts of creditor collection actions, § 362(a), and creates a bankruptcy "estate," comprised of all the debtor's property. § 541(a).

In a voluntary case, the filing of the petition not only commences the case, it also automatically constitutes the *"order for relief."* The entry of the order for relief is the operative date for many of the important consequences of bankruptcy. For example, in a chapter 7 case, a trustee is appointed after the entry of the order for relief, § 701, and only debts that arise before the order for relief are discharged. § 727(b).

Commencing a voluntary case is not difficult.[7] The bankruptcy petition must conform to Official Form 1.[8] In addition to paying the required filing fee, 28 U.S.C. § 1930(a), Rule 1006(a), the debtor also must disclose certain financial information in reports that must be filed with the petition or soon thereafter: a list of creditors, schedules of assets and liabilities, a schedule of current income and expenditures, a schedule of executory contracts and leases, a statement of financial affairs, and more. Rule 1007.

Regarding the third basic issue regarding the invocation of bankruptcy relief— *what showing* is necessary to trigger bankruptcy—the answer for voluntary cases is, perhaps surprisingly, almost nothing. Debtors do not have to state that they are insolvent, or indeed make any averment regarding their financial status, troubles, or need for relief. The relatively minimal screening in voluntary cases comes not at the point of commencement, but rather through the process of dismissal. The policy in the United States since the enactment of the Bankruptcy Act of 1898 has been one of open access to the bankruptcy system for debtors. Some inroads on that policy were made in the BAPCPA amendments in 2005, but the fundamental orientation remains one of ready access to bankruptcy relief.

An *"involuntary"* case, by contrast, is commenced *by creditors* of the debtor, not by the debtor. § 303(b). In other words, from the debtor's perspective, bankruptcy relief is involuntary. While bankruptcy relief in its original conception was only available at the behest of creditors, today the overwhelming norm (far in excess of 99% of all cases) is voluntary bankruptcy.[9]

---

[6]   A chapter 15 case is commenced when a foreign representative files a petition for recognition of a foreign proceeding. §§ 1504, 1509, 1515.

[7]   See § 2.4.

[8]   See http://www.uscourts.gov/uscourts/RulesAndPolicies/rules/BK_Forms_Current/B_001.pdf.

[9]   See Susan Block–Lieb, Why Creditors File So Few Involuntary Petitions and Why the Number is Not Too Small, 57 Brook. L. Rev. 803 (1991).

Petitioning creditors' access to bankruptcy relief is much more limited in involuntary cases than for a petitioning debtor in voluntary cases, in two ways. First, the order for relief is *not* entered automatically upon creditors filing the petition. Instead, the petitioning creditors must establish one of the statutory grounds supporting relief.[10] § 303(h). Although some bankruptcy consequences are triggered by the filing of the involuntary petition alone (e.g., an automatic stay goes into effect, § 362(a), and a bankruptcy estate is created, § 541(a)), the full operation of the case must await the entry of the order for relief.

Second, involuntary relief is not available for all chapters,[11] or against all types of debtors.[12] Involuntary bankruptcy is only permitted in cases under chapter 7 or chapter 11, § 303(a); thus, only debtors may commence a case—voluntarily—under chapter 9, 12 or 13. Nor is involuntary relief allowed against farmers, family farmers, or corporations that are "not a moneyed, business, or commercial corporation." § 303(b).

While a case must always be commenced under a particular chapter, there is no guarantee that it will remain in that chapter until the completion of the case. Instead, a case may be *converted* from one chapter to another. For example, a case may be commenced as a reorganization under chapter 11, but subsequently may be converted to a liquidation under chapter 7. The conversion could run the other way as well—from chapter 7 to chapter 11. Each chapter contains special rules that specify the grounds for and limits on conversion from that chapter.[13] There are significant differences in the governing conversion rules depending on whether the request to convert is made by the debtor (i.e., is voluntary), or by someone other than the debtor, such as the trustee or a creditor (i.e., is involuntary).[14] Other provisions of the Code and Federal Rules of Bankruptcy Procedure govern the effects of conversion.[15] § 348; Rule 1019. Of necessity, the conversion rules are harmonized with the commencement rules, so that only the same sorts of debtors can end up in the same bankruptcy chapter on the same sort of showing by the same triggering party, whether done at the outset of the case or later via conversion.

A case may not make it all the way through the bankruptcy process; the bankruptcy judge may *dismiss* the case. The most rigorous screening for bankruptcy relief comes through the operation of the rules on dismissal. In voluntary cases, debtors have almost complete license to commence a case; however, whether that debtor is able to continue the case and obtain full relief thereunder is subject to more constraints. Different rules govern dismissal of cases under the respective chapters.[16] § 707 (chapter 7), § 1112 (chapter 11), § 1208 (chapter 12), § 1307 (chapter 13). As with conversion, dismissal may be voluntary, on request of the debtor, or involuntary, on request of someone other than the debtor. Different standards govern in each instance. In most instances, the bankruptcy judge may choose whether to convert or to dismiss a

---

[10] See § 2.9.

[11] See § 2.6.

[12] See § 2.7.

[13] See § 706 (chapter 7); § 1112 (chapter 11); § 1208 (chapter 12); § 1307 (chapter 13).

[14] See §§ 2.20, 2.21.

[15] See § 2.22.

[16] See §§ 2.13—2.17.

particular case. Special rules dictate the effects of the dismissal of a case.[17] § 349. The judge also may decide to abstain from hearing a case.[18] § 305.

A. GENERALLY APPLICABLE REQUIREMENTS

§ 2.2   Eligible Debtors—Chapter Requirements

Not all debtors are eligible for bankruptcy relief. Some debtors are eligible for relief under some but not all of the case chapters. Congress spelled out these eligibility rules in § 109, as supplemented by the definitional provisions in § 101. Eligibility is dealt with in § 109 primarily on a chapter-by-chapter basis. Congress also has included two sets of eligibility rules that depend on the debtor's behavior, seeking to curb serial filings and to mandate credit counseling for individual debtors.[19] § 109(g), (h).

In all cases (excepting chapters 9 and 15), two threshold requirements for eligibility must be satisfied. § 109(a). First, the debtor must be a *person.* Second, the debtor must have some *connection to the United States* (a domicile, place of business, or property). Notably absent is any requirement that the debtor be insolvent, or indeed that the debtor even owe any debts.

"Person" is a defined term in the Code. It "includes individual, partnership, and corporation." § 101(41). Expressly excluded from this definition is a governmental unit, which thus may only file, if eligible, under chapter 9. Excluded by implication are estates and trusts, which are included in the broader definition of "entity," § 101(15), but which are not included in the definition of person.

Why is a probate estate excluded from bankruptcy relief? The state probate process itself provides for a mandatory collective proceeding that deals with all creditor claims against that estate. There is no pressing need to displace the state process with a federal bankruptcy scheme. Furthermore, there is no "fresh start" policy for the deceased debtor (at least none within the purview of earthly legislatures).

The Code does not define "individual," but the term refers to a natural person, i.e., a living, breathing human being. "Partnership" likewise is not defined in the Code, so courts look to state partnership law to determine what constitutes a partnership. Note that a partnership as an entity must file for bankruptcy relief apart from the individual general partners.

"Corporation" is a defined term in the Code, defined broadly to include almost every type of limited liability organization with corporate-like powers other than limited partnerships. § 101(9). Thus, for example, business trusts, joint-stock companies, labor unions, and cooperatives have been held to qualify as a corporation.[20] Courts have balked, however, at extending the definition to trusts that do not carry on

---

[17]   See § 2.18.

[18]   See § 2.19.

[19]   See § 2.3.

[20]   See, e.g., In re Kenneth Allen Knight Trust, 303 F.3d 671 (6th Cir. 2002) (business trust); In re Chateaugay Corp., 104 B.R. 626 (S.D.N.Y. 1989) (labor union); In re Schatz Fed. Bearings Co., Inc., 5 B.R. 543 (Bankr. S.D.N.Y. 1980) (joint-stock).

an active business, but which are utilized more as investment or financing vehicles.[21] In such a situation, a basic justification for allowing bankruptcy relief at all[22]—to provide an efficient and fair collective creditors' remedy—is lacking.

Chapter 7 eligibility is governed by § 109(b). All persons with a sufficient nexus to the United States are eligible for bankruptcy relief under chapter 7, excepting only certain narrowly defined classes of debtors. First, a railroad may not file under chapter 7. § 109(b)(1). Railroads instead may only seek bankruptcy relief under a special subchapter of chapter 11. Second, domestic and foreign insurance companies, banks, and similar regulated financial institutions are ineligible for chapter 7 relief.[23] § 109(b)(2), (3). Congress chose to defer to the governing regulatory laws for the liquidation of those types of institutions. In some cases it may be difficult to determine whether an entity falls within an excluded class. To give one example, a health maintenance organization (HMO) is part insurance company and part healthcare provider. In those borderline instances, the courts largely defer to the classification provided by the applicable non-bankruptcy regulatory law.[24]

Eligibility under chapter 9 is narrowly limited. § 109(c). The debtor must be a "municipality," which is defined as a "political subdivision or public agency or instrumentality of a state." § 101(40). Because of the special sovereignty interests of the state, the debtor also must be specifically authorized by state law to be a bankruptcy debtor. Unlike the other chapters, insolvency is required before a municipality debtor may file under chapter 9, and the debtor not only must intend to adjust its debts, but also must have negotiated with its creditors to that end.

In chapter 11 cases, the eligibility rules from chapter 7 are incorporated by reference. § 109(d). In almost all cases, then, a debtor who may file under chapter 7 also may file under chapter 11. Thus, an individual, partnership, or corporation with a connection to the United States may file under chapter 11, while insurance companies and banks are excluded. The only statutory divergences in the eligibility requirements between chapters 7 and 11 are that a stockbroker, commodity broker, or clearing bank may file under chapter 7 but not under chapter 11, and a railroad may file under chapter 11 but not chapter 7. Special subchapters in chapter 7 govern liquidation cases for stockbrokers, commodity brokers, and clearing banks. Prior to 1991 some courts had permitted only business debtors to have access to chapter 11, thereby excluding individual consumer debtors. In 1991 the Supreme Court held in *Toibb v. Radloff* that the plain language of the Code did authorize individual non-business debtors to proceed under chapter 11.[25]

---

[21]   See, e.g., In re Secured Equip. Trust of E. Air Lines, Inc., 38 F.3d 86 (2d Cir. 1994). A divided Second Circuit held that a trust that purchased and leased back $500 million in airplanes to Eastern Air Lines in return for rent payments did not constitute a "business trust" and thus was not a "corporation" eligible for bankruptcy relief.

[22]   See §§ 1.1, 1.2.

[23]   A very limited exception for clearing banks was enacted in subchapter V of chapter 7 in 2000. Pub. L. No. 106–554, 114 Stat. 2763 (2000). See also § 1.27(b).

[24]   See In re Estate of Medcare HMO, 998 F.2d 436 (7th Cir. 1993) (HMO classified under state law as a domestic insurance company and thus ineligible for bankruptcy).

[25]   501 U.S. 157 (1991).

The eligibility requirements for chapter 13 are more stringent than in chapters 7 and 11. § 109(e). Chapter 13 is the successor to the old "wage earner" chapter XIII of the Bankruptcy Act, and its lineage shows. First, *only individuals* are eligible, thus excluding partnerships and corporations. Furthermore, stockbrokers and commodity brokers are excluded.

Second, the individual debtor must have "regular income," which is defined functionally to mean that the individual must have income that is "sufficiently stable and regular to enable such individual to make payments under a plan." § 101(30). There is little point in embarking on a chapter 13 case that is doomed to fail from the outset. However, courts have been fairly lenient to debtors on the "regular income" question, finding a congressional intent in favor of chapter 13 relief.

Third, a debt ceiling restricts chapter 13 eligibility to individuals with unsecured debts of less than $383,175 and secured debts of less than $1,149,525 (both amounts as of 2013).[26] Only noncontingent and liquidated debts are counted. Congress decided that the simplified and streamlined procedures of chapter 13 should be available only in relatively small cases. What is "relatively small" changes over time with inflation, however, and the debt limits originally imposed in 1978 ($100,000 unsecured, $350,000 secured) eventually became too low. These debt limits accordingly were increased substantially by the 1994 amendments, and now are adjusted every three years.[27] In joint cases for spouses the debt ceiling is not doubled. In such a case, only one of the joint debtors needs to have a "regular income."

Chapter 12 eligibility extends to debtors who qualify as a "family farmer" or a "family fisherman," and who have "regular annual income." § 109(f). The regular income requirement embodies the same principle as in chapter 13, focusing on the debtor's ability to make payments under a plan. The only difference is that *annual* income is taken into account in chapter 12, given the nature of the farming (or fishing) business. § 101(19), (19B). Unlike chapter 13, a "family farmer" or "fisherman" debtor may be a partnership or a corporation, and not just an individual. Congress tried to capture the ideas of a "family farmer" and a "family fisherman" in complicated statutory definitions.[28]

---

[26]   See § 109(e).

[27]   Most recent adjustments were effective as of April 1, 2013, with the next adjustment due in 2016. See § 104(b)(1).

[28]   See § 101(18) (family farmer); § 101(19A) (family fisherman). Consider the "family farmer" definition. For individuals, the debtor (plus their spouse in a joint case): (1) must be engaged in a "farming operation" (defined in § 101(21)); (2) must not have aggregate debts exceeding $4,031,575; (3) must have not less than 50% of their noncontingent, liquidated debts attributable to the farming operation; and (4) must have received more than half of their gross income in the taxable year or the second and third taxable years preceding bankruptcy from that farming operation. § 101(18)(A).

  If the "family farmer" debtor is a corporation or partnership: (1) one family must own more than half of the equity; (2) that family must conduct the farming operation; (3) more than 80% of the asset value must be attributable to the farming operation; (4) the aggregate debts must not exceed $4,031,575; (5) 50% of the noncontingent, liquidated debts must arise out of the farming operation; and (6) the stock, if any, must not be publicly traded. § 101(18)(B).

  While "commercial fishing operation" does not contain any limits for debt totals, but rather just entity characteristics, § 101(7A), the "family fisherman" definition for individuals or individual and spouse debtors

Chapter 15 was added to the Code in 2005. It largely incorporates the UNCITRAL Model Law on Cross–Border Insolvency. § 1501(a). None of the debtor eligibility rules in § 109 apply in chapter 15 cases. Instead, chapter 15 contains its own eligibility rules. A "debtor" is "an entity that is the subject of a foreign proceeding." § 1502(1). Note that in chapter 15 the broader term "entity" is used. A "foreign proceeding" is one of two types: a "foreign main proceeding," which is a foreign proceeding pending where the debtor has its "center of main interests," § 1501(4), or a "foreign nonmain proceeding," which is a foreign proceeding that is not a main proceeding and which is pending in a country where the debtor has an "establishment." § 1501(5).

Chapter 15 does not apply to individual debtors who have debts within the chapter 13 debt limits, and who are either United States citizens or lawful resident aliens. § 1501(c)(2). This exclusion is a departure from the UNCITRAL Model Law, on which chapter 15 is based. The reason for the exclusion is that the United States domestic bankruptcy law has detailed, special rules applicable only to individual consumer debtors, whereas the Model Law is designed principally for business and commercial debts, and therefore the use of chapter 15 against resident United States consumers would be unjust.[29] The residence requirement prevents consumer debtors from other countries from fleeing to the United States as a safe haven from their own country's foreign debt enforcement.

Chapter 15 also does not apply to entities identified by exclusion in § 109(b) (i.e., railroads, domestic insurance companies, and banks), except that foreign insurance companies are not excluded. § 1501(c)(1). Additionally, chapter 15 does not apply to stockbrokers, commodity brokers, or entities subject to a proceeding under the Securities Investor Protection Act of 1970. § 1501(c)(3).

§ 2.3   Eligible Debtors—Serial Filings, Credit Counseling

The remaining debtor eligibility requirements are not chapter specific. Instead, they apply across the board, to cases under all chapters (except 9 and 15), and are of a different nature than the particular chapter requirements. These final requirements focus on debtor *behavior*, rather than debtor characteristics. One such limitation seeks to curb abusive serial filings by individual debtors or family farmers. § 109(g). The other, added in 2005, imposes a requirement of pre-bankruptcy credit counseling for individual debtors. § 109(h).

a.   Serial Filings

The first such limitation on the availability of voluntary bankruptcy relief is imposed to stop the abuse of frequent filings by a single debtor. A bankruptcy filing automatically triggers a stay against creditor collection efforts, such as foreclosures on collateral. § 362(a). In the early years of the Code, some clever debtors took advantage of this feature of the law by filing a voluntary bankruptcy case on the eve of a

---

contains a debt limit of $1,868,200 and requires at least 80% of debts arise from a commercial fishing operation owned or operated by the debtor. § 101(19A).

[29] See Nat'l Bankr. Review Comm'n Final Report, Bankruptcy: The Next Twenty Years, Final Report § 2.2.5 at 364–65 (Oct. 20, 1997), available at http://govinfo.library.unt.edu/nbrc/reporttitlepg.html.

foreclosure, without intending to go through with the bankruptcy case. The debtor would make no effort to proceed with the case, and if the creditor filed for relief from the stay or for dismissal of the case, the debtor would either voluntarily dismiss the case or not oppose a dismissal by the court. However, after dismissal, when the creditor again was about to foreclose, the debtor would file another bankruptcy case and again trigger an automatic stay against the creditor's foreclosure. This cycle would be repeated over and over, with the net result being that the creditor could never foreclose, and yet the debtor never had to suffer the ultimate slings and arrows of bankruptcy fortune. Under § 109(g), which Congress added to the Code in 1984, no individual or family farmer debtor is eligible for bankruptcy relief if (1) they were a debtor in a case pending within the prior 180 days, and (2) the case was dismissed by the court for the debtor's willful failure to abide by court orders or to prosecute the case, or was dismissed voluntarily by the debtor after the creditor moved for relief from the stay.

A question that has arisen is whether a debtor's ineligibility under § 109(g) is *jurisdictional*. If it is, as some courts have held,[30] then the case is void *ab initio*,[31] and no automatic stay ever goes into effect. Under this view, if a creditor believes that a filing is plainly in contravention of § 109(g), the creditor could ignore the automatic stay with impunity and proceed with foreclosure. Other courts take the competing position that § 109(g) is not jurisdictional, so that a filing in violation of that provision does still commence a case, and trigger the automatic stay.[32] This position is consistent with that taken by courts regarding the other debtor eligibility rules in § 109, which consistently are held not to be jurisdictional.[33] Only after the bankruptcy court makes a determination that the statutory test was breached can the case then be dismissed.[34] Even under this approach, the bankruptcy court has the power to annul the stay with retroactive effect and thereby validate a foreclosure that occurred after the filing but prior to dismissal.[35] The creditor, however, could not know at the time of foreclosure that the blessing of retroactive annulment would be forthcoming, and thus would be proceeding with the foreclosure at its own risk. Alternatively, a court may strike an

---

[30] See, e.g., McKay v. Alliance Mortg. Corp. (In re McKay), 268 B.R. 908 (Bankr. W.D. Va. 2001); In re Hollberg, 208 B.R. 775 (Bankr. D.D.C. 1997); In re Prud'Homme, 161 B.R. 747 (Bankr. E.D.N.Y. 1993); Miller v. First Fed. Sav. & Loan Ass'n of Monessen, 143 B.R. 815 (Bankr. W.D. Pa. 1992).

[31] Black's Law Dictionary defines void *ab initio* as "[n]ull from the beginning." (9th ed. 2009).

[32] See, e.g., In re Willis, 411 B.R. 455 (Bankr. S.D. Ga. 2007); In re Ross, 338 B.R. 134 (Bankr. N.D. Ga. 2006); In re Seaman, 340 B.R. 698 (Bankr. E.D.N.Y. 2006).

[33] See, e.g., In re Gosset, 369 B.R. 361 (Bankr. N.D. Ill. 2007) (regarding § 109(h) and chapter 7 eligibility); In re Hawkins, 340 B.R. 642 (Bankr. D.D.C. 2006) ("Because Congress singled out § 109(g) for exemption from the automatic stay only with respect to liens or security interests in real property, the court must infer that bankruptcy cases commenced in violation of the other sub-parts of § 109 . . . give rise to the automatic stay."); Rudd v. Laughlin, 866 F.2d 1040 (8th Cir. 1989) (regarding § 109(e) and chapter 13 eligibility); In re Hamilton Creek Metro. Dist., 143 F.3d 1381 (10th Cir. 1998) (regarding § 109(c) and chapter 9 eligibility). But see In re Salazar, 339 B.R. 622 (Bankr. S.D. Tex. 2006) (holding that "[b]oth logic and statute dictate that no automatic stay arises on the filing of a petition by an ineligible person," regarding § 109(h) and chapter 13 eligibility).

[34] See, e.g., In re Durham, 461 B.R. 139 (Bankr. D. Mass. 2011) ("Thus until the court rules on eligibility, the filing of a petition by an individually possibly ineligible under § 109(g) effectively commences a bankruptcy case."); In re Seaman, 340 B.R. 698 (Bankr. E.D.N.Y. 2006).

[35] See, e.g., In re Ross, 338 B.R. 134 (Bankr. N.D. Ga. 2006) (discussing that a court may reach the same result as the void *ab initio* courts by annulling the automatic stay under § 362(d)); Casse v. Key Bank N.A. (In re Casse), 198 F.3d 327 (2d Cir. 1999).

ineligible debtor's petition, rather than dismissing it, leaving the question open as to whether the automatic stay arose upon the filing of petition.[36]

b. Credit Counseling

The second behavioral limitation on debtor eligibility—the credit counseling requirement—was added to the Code with BAPCPA in 2005. Under § 109(h), an individual debtor must receive credit counseling from an approved nonprofit budget and credit counseling agency "during the 180–day period preceding the date of filing of the petition by such individual."[37] § 109(h)(1). Under this rule, an individual debtor is barred from filing under *any* chapter if he does not obtain this pre-bankruptcy counseling, unless the court waives the requirement.[38]

The stated congressional hope was that this would operate as a *debtor protection* provision: if a financially distressed debtor gets credit counseling before he files bankruptcy, that debtor can make a more informed choice as to whether filing bankruptcy really is in his best interests.[39] Given how the provision has been operating in practice, individual debtors probably would prefer that Congress not do them any more favors. A cynic might argue that Congress never meant to protect consumer debtors at all, but rather intended to erect yet another barrier to obtaining bankruptcy relief. So far, the real-world effects of § 109(h) have been closer to the cynical view than to the stated purpose.[40] The new provision has also spawned a flood of litigation, as courts try to make sense of its confusing intricacies.

For example, some issues have arisen concerning whether a debtor has adequately complied with the counseling requirement. To illustrate, one question courts confront is what constitutes a sufficient "certificate" of compliance with the credit-counseling requirement that the debtor must file under § 521(b).[41] In particular, courts have divided over whether the debtor must make a declaration under penalty of perjury under 28 U.S.C. § 1746.[42] If such a formal declaration is required, debtors face yet another "trap for the unwary," and could face dismissal of their case *even if* they got

---

[36] In re Gossett, 369 B.R. 361 (Bankr. N.D. Ill. 2007) ("If the petition is stricken or declared void *ab initio*, a question arises as to whether the automatic stay arose upon the filing of the petition." (citing *In re Rios*, 336 B.R. 177, 180 n.2 (Bankr. S.D.N.Y. 2005))).

[37] This requirement has survived a constitutional challenge as a denial of access to the courts. See In re Headquist, 342 B.R. 295 (B.A.P. 8th Cir. 2006).

[38] Note that an additional "debtor education" provision requires completion of an instructional course in personal financial management *during* the bankruptcy case, with failure to do so also carrying a big penalty—denial of discharge. § 727(a)(11) (chapter 7); § 1328(g)(1) (chapter 13).

[39] H.R. Rep. No. 109–31 (pt. 1), 109th Cong., 1st Sess., at 18 (2005). Congress noted in particular that debtors might want to be informed of the negative impact on their credit if they file bankruptcy.

[40] In fact, one court referred to the § 109(h) credit counseling requirement as "[o]ne of the more absurd provisions of [the Code]." In re Sosa, 336 B.R. 113 (Bankr. W.D. Tex. 2005).

[41] See, e.g., In re Dixon, 338 B.R. 383 (B.A.P. 8th Cir. 2006) (noting the uncertainty of the "sufficiency" requirement in § 521(b), holding that the fairest reading of the statute is to allow courts discretion to determine sufficiency, and only allow reversal for clear error).

[42] Compare In re Miller, 336 B.R. 232 (Bankr. W.D. Pa. 2006) (must comply with § 1746), with In re Talib, 335 B.R. 417 (Bankr. W.D. Mo. 2005) (need not comply with § 1746). See also In re Wallert, 332 B.R. 884 (Bankr. D. Minn. 2005) (noting the difference between certificate and certification in §§ 109(h) and 521(b), and that § 109(h) requires a "certification," which requires meeting the form standard in 28 U.S.C. § 1746).

the requisite counseling and *even if* they notified the court of that fact in a timely manner.[43] Such a draconian result would seem to be at odds with the supposed "debtor protective" purpose underlying the requirement.

Another puzzle is what has been called the problem of the "lost day." The issue is whether a debtor can obtain the required filing on the *day of* the petition, but before the time of filing. For example, assume that a debtor gets counseling at 9 a.m. and then files bankruptcy at noon, along with the requisite certificate. The problem is that the statute literally says that the debtor must be counseled during the "180–day period *preceding the date* of the filing of the petition." § 109(h)(1). Some courts accordingly have held that same-day counseling is inadequate, concluding that it does not precede the "date" of the filing.[44] Such a result, however (1) makes little sense as a policy matter—a same-day counseled debtor still is "warned" in time to make an informed choice before plunging into the bankruptcy abyss; (2) is not dictated by the legislative history, which says only that the debtor "should have the opportunity to learn about the consequences of bankruptcy . . . *before* they decide to file for bankruptcy relief,"[45] which is fully consistent with same-day counseling; and (3) is not required by the statute itself, as "date" is sometimes defined in dictionaries (a Court favorite!) and construed in statutes to mean an exact time, and not just a day. Such considerations, along with the stated congressional purpose to protect debtors via the counseling requirement, have led other courts to allow same-day counseling, as long as it precedes the exact time of filing.[46]

The literal statutory text suggests another timing problem: a debtor who is counseled *too soon, viz.,* more than 180 days before bankruptcy, also may fall short of § 109(h)'s requirements. The statute requires counseling to occur "during" the 180–day pre-bankruptcy period. The legislative history states that the counseling must occur "within" the 180–day period.[47] Here, then, it appears that early counseling may be

---

[43] In fact, this is exactly what happened in *In re Miller*, 336 B.R. 232 (Bankr. W.D. Pa. 2006). Here, the court had "no doubt that [the debtor] received and completed the briefing required by § 109(h)(1)." However, the court held that because the debtor's certificate filed was in the form of a fax, it did not meet § 521(b)'s requirements. The court treated the fax instead as a motion to allow a reasonable period of time for the debtor to obtain the required certificate, or, alternatively, as a motion to compel the credit-counseling agency to deliver or file the certificate due to the debtor.

[44] See, e.g., In re Gossett, 369 B.R. 361 (Bankr. N.D. Ill. 2007); In re Cole, 347 B.R. 70 (Bankr. E.D. Tenn. 2006); In re Murphy, 342 B.R. 671 (Bankr. D.D.C. 2006).

[45] See note 39, *supra*. In another place, the House Report states that the debtor must receive counseling "in the 180–day period *preceding the filing* of a bankruptcy case." H.R. Rep. No. 109–31 (pt. 1) at 54 (emphasis added). Noticeably missing from the italicized text is the additional, and critical, statutory phrase "the date of." Indeed, Judge Teel sitting in the Bankruptcy Court for the District of Columbia held that under BAPCPA, a debtor must obtain credit counseling at least one calendar day prior to the petition date in In re Mills, 341 B.R. 106 (Bankr. D.D.C. 2006). However, a year later, Judge Teel reversed his *Mills* opinion, explaining that "I am now convinced that in § 109(h), Congress failed to accord the term "date" (in the clause "date of filing of the petition") its usual meaning of calendar day, and instead intended "date" to mean the moment of the filing of the petition. In re Barbaran, 365 B.R. 333, 334 (Bankr. D.D.C. 2007).

[46] See, e.g., In re Warren, 339 B.R. 475 (Bankr. E.D. Ark. 2006).

[47] H.R. Rep. No. 109–31 (pt. 1), 109th Cong., 1st Sess., at 54 (2005).

unavoidably fatal,[48] although some sympathetic courts nonetheless have found such counseling to be sufficient as consonant with the "spirit" of the law.[49]

Sometimes, however, a debtor does not obtain pre-bankruptcy counseling at all. What then? There are four possible grounds for *waiver* of the credit counseling requirement: (1) the debtor demonstrates "exigent circumstances that merit a waiver," § 109(h)(3); (2) the debtor cannot complete the requirements because the debtor is incapacitated or disabled, § 109(h)(4); (3) the debtor is on active military duty in a military combat zone, § 109(h)(4); or (4) the United States Trustee determines that such counseling services are not reasonably available in the individual's district, § 109(h)(2). Of these, the most common and most important is the "exigent circumstances" excuse.

Two common scenarios have arisen. Both involve imminent foreclosures, with the debtor urgently time-pressed to file bankruptcy in order to trigger the automatic stay and stop the foreclosure. Consider hypothetical Debtor Smith, whose home is scheduled to be sold at foreclosure on November 1 at 10:00 a.m. In scenario number 1, the debtor files bankruptcy on October 31—prior to the scheduled foreclosure—without previously (1) obtaining or (2) even requesting pre-bankruptcy credit counseling, either out of ignorance or desperation.[50]

In scenario number 2, while the debtor does not obtain the counseling prior to filing, he did request it, only to discover that he could not receive the counseling in time to stop the foreclosure, and thus files bankruptcy and requests an "exigent circumstances" waiver.[51] So, for example, assume that instead of filing bankruptcy immediately, Debtor Smith goes to see an attorney on October 31—the day before the scheduled foreclosure—and the attorney gives Smith a nasty Halloween scare by telling him about the counseling requirement. Debtor Smith then calls an approved counseling agency to ask for counseling but learns to his chagrin that they cannot counsel him until the following week—*after* the foreclosure will have been completed. So Debtor Smith goes ahead and files bankruptcy at 9:00 a.m. on November 1, just before the foreclosure is scheduled.

In scenario number 1, the debtor clearly has failed to comply with the credit counseling requirement, and, unfortunately, also is ineligible for a waiver, since he did not at least *request* counseling prior to filing bankruptcy. See § 109(h)(3)(A)(ii). Thus, his bankruptcy case should not go forward in its present incarnation.

But what exactly is the *remedy* for noncompliance with § 109(h)? Should the case simply be *dismissed*?[52] Or should the court *strike* the case or petition, reasoning that failure to comply with § 109(h) is jurisdictional, rendering the noncompliant filing a

---

[48]   See, e.g., In re Giles, 361 B.R. 212 (Bankr. D. Utah 2007).

[49]   See, e.g., In re Bricksin, 346 B.R. 497 (Bankr. N.D. Cal. 2006).

[50]   E.g., In re Sosa, 336 B.R. 113 (Bankr. W.D. Tex. 2005).

[51]   E.g., Dixon v. LaBarge (In re Dixon), 338 B.R. 383 (B.A.P. 8th Cir. 2006).

[52]   See, e.g., In re Ross, 338 B.R. 134 (Bankr. N.D. Ga. 2006).

nullity, and thus void *ab initio*?[53] On this question the debate—and the split—in the courts reprises that under § 109(g), discussed above.[54]

A "Catch–22" problem is present here: no matter what remedy is adopted for noncompliance with § 109(h), the debtor has a serious problem. One might think that it should not matter, because the debtor could simply file a new bankruptcy petition, after satisfying the credit counseling prerequisite to filing. This new case would again trigger an automatic stay and stop foreclosure. If the court *dismissed* the first case, though, the trap for the debtor is § 362(c)(3) (also added in 2005), which provides that in a subsequent case filed within one year after *dismissal* of an earlier case, the automatic stay will terminate after 30 days unless the debtor can demonstrate that the later filing was in "good faith as to the creditors to be stayed." Thus, by failing to comply with the credit counseling requirement in the first case, the debtor may lose forever any hope of effectively invoking the automatic stay within the next year.[55]

Conversely, if the court tries to avoid the § 362(c)(3) trap by *striking* the case or petition in the first case because of the debtor's noncompliance with § 109(h), rather than *dismissing* that case, the problem then would be that logically no stay ever went into effect in the first case. It was as if no case had ever been commenced at all; no case, no stay.[56] Legally, it would be no different than if the Debtor had filed his bankruptcy petition with the cashier at Burger King. Thus, in Debtor Smith's case, if the home mortgagee went ahead with the scheduled foreclosure at 10:00 a.m. on November 1, notwithstanding the apparent pendency of the case that Smith filed just before the scheduled foreclosure but that later was "stricken," that foreclosure would be valid. However, if the defective pre-foreclosure filing was not void *ab initio*, but did effectively commence a case that was not dismissed until later, the automatic stay would have been in effect at 10:00 a.m. on November 1, the purported foreclosure sale would have violated the stay, and that sale would be void. As with § 109(g), the bankruptcy court still would have the power to annul the stay with retroactive effect and validate the earlier foreclosure,[57] but such retroactive validation certainly would not be automatic or routine.

The better view, I believe (and also the majority view[58]), is that noncompliance with § 109(h) is *not* jurisdictional. When a debtor files a petition (with the federal

---

[53]   See, e.g., In re Hubbard, 333 B.R. 377 (Bankr. S.D. Tex. 2005).

[54]   See § 2.3.a.

[55]   One court reasoned that whether the petition is "stricken" or "dismissed" for failure to comply with § 109(h), the consequence would be the same. The court explained that a *case* dismissed under a provision such as § 707 brings a different result than a *petition* dismissed under § 109(h); a dismissal of a petition amounts to a dismissal of a "case" prior to the case's commencement. Accordingly, the court held that a petition dismissed under § 109 would not create a case "pending within the preceding 1–year period" under § 362(c)(3). In re Salazar, 339 B.R. 622 (Bankr. S.D. Tex. 2006). However, few courts have followed the *Salazar* reasoning.

[56]   E.g., In re Rios, 336 B.R. 177 (Bankr. S.D.N.Y. 2005). At least one court has held that even if the petition is stricken, and thus no "case" is commenced, a stay still goes into effect. See In re Thompson, 344 B.R. 899 (Bankr. S.D. Ind. 2006). While debtors surely would be pleased with this handy escape from the Catch–22 problem, *Thompson* surely must be wrong.

[57]   See *Casse*, supra note 35, 198 F.3d 327 (case under § 109(g)).

[58]   Early, post-BAPCPA cases are collected and discussed in *In re Seaman*, 340 B.R. 698 (Bankr. E.D.N.Y. 2006).

bankruptcy court, not Burger King), he does invoke the jurisdiction of the federal courts, commencing a bankruptcy case, and an automatic stay goes into effect. There may be a flaw in the filing (such as noncompliance with § 109(h)), but that can only be determined by the bankruptcy court. The other eligibility provisions of § 109 have almost universally been construed (excepting a few misguided court decisions under § 109(g)) not to be jurisdictional.[59] Section 109(h) should be treated in like manner.

Assuming that compliance with § 109(h) is not jurisdictional, a lurking possibility is that in particularly sympathetic cases the United States trustee simply may never move to dismiss the case. The case then could proceed.

The most commonly litigated situation under § 109(h) is proving to be that of scenario number 2: debtor does not get pre-bankruptcy counseling, but requests a bankruptcy court waiver for "exigent circumstances" under § 109(h)(3). This waiver provision actually has three elements: (1) the debtor describes "exigent circumstances that merit a waiver"; (2) the debtor requested credit counseling services from an approved agency but was unable to get those services within the next seven days; and (3) the debtor's certification is "satisfactory to the court." § 109(h)(3)(A)(i)–(iii). Starting at the end, it is not at all clear what the third element, that the certification by the debtor be "satisfactory to the court," adds to the first two: if the debtor can demonstrate meritorious exigent circumstances and the debtor requested but was unable to obtain a timely briefing, what reason might there be for the court to remain unsatisfied?

One trap for the unwary in this waiver provision is the second prong—that the debtor be unable to obtain counseling within seven days after the request. This is in addition to the trap that the debtor must *request* counseling *prior* to bankruptcy, so the ignorant debtor who files bankruptcy blissfully but fatally unaware of the counseling requirement cannot obtain a waiver, no matter how meritorious his exigent circumstances might be. The 7–day trap can catch even a debtor who does learn of the counseling requirement prior to filing bankruptcy, if they only learn of it within seven days of the scheduled foreclosure. Consider the hypothetical under scenario 2 for our unfortunate Debtor Smith, who goes to see an attorney on October 31, the day before the scheduled November 1 foreclosure. Assume that Smith then calls a counseling agency, which tells him "fine, we can counsel you in six days, on November 6." Smith would be out of luck—he cannot file bankruptcy until after he gets the counseling on November 6, but the foreclosure will happen on November 1. Smith cannot file bankruptcy before the November 1 foreclosure and get a waiver under § 109(h)(3) because he cannot satisfy the condition that he requested but was unable to obtain counseling within seven days.[60] Yet it is entirely understandable that a debtor would wait until shortly before the scheduled foreclosure to see an attorney; an average consumer debtor likely would not know about the counseling requirement and certainly would be unlikely to know of the 7–day rule.

---

[59]   See cases cited in notes 32 and 33, supra.

[60]   E.g., *Talib*, supra note 42, 335 B.R. 417. Some courts have taken an even more onerous view of the 7–day provision, requiring the debtor to *request* the briefing at least 7 days before the bankruptcy filing. That view is arguably erroneous, in light of the statutory wording in § 109(h)(1), which only requires the debtor to get counseling in the 180–day period "preceding the date" of the bankruptcy filing.

If the debtor is able to escape the 7–day timing trap, the question still remains as to what it means to be "unable to obtain" the counseling services. Several interpretive questions lurk. Is it enough for a debtor to make the request of only one agency? A literal reading of the statute suggests that the answer is "yes," since it says the debtor must request counseling from "an" agency. But what if there were a readily available agency from which the debtor could obtain timely counseling—is the debtor excused just because the first agency they asked was too busy? In such a case the court might bar the debtor by finding that the "exigent circumstances" do not "merit a waiver."

Consider another issue: what does it mean to be "unable"? For instance, what if the agency that the debtor contacts says that it can provide counseling within the 7–day period via the Internet (which the statute allows), but the debtor claims he has no access to a computer?[61] Should the court be able to ask if the debtor could use the public library to access the Internet? His attorney's office?

Even if the debtor satisfies the inability prong of the waiver provision, he still will have to establish meritorious exigent circumstances. In most cases, the fact of exigency is probably going to be obvious—debtor is trying to stop a foreclosure, and if he has to wait for counseling, it will be too late. The hypothetical facing our poor Debtor Smith is common fare. When he calls the agency on October 31, he needs to get counseling and file bankruptcy before 10:00 a.m. the next day, when his home mortgage will be foreclosed. But do those exigent circumstances "merit a waiver"?

The problem here is deciding how to deal with the procrastinating debtor. The debtor presumably received notice of the scheduled foreclosure sale some number of days in advance. The court is likely to ask why the debtor waited so long to do something, and many courts have turned a deaf ear to the procrastinating debtor's plea, concluding that the debtor created his own exigency.[62] One can imagine other courts taking a more sympathetic tack.[63] A debtor who waits until the day before a foreclosure to contact an attorney, even if he has had 20 or 30 days' notice of the foreclosure, probably had no idea that he had thereby squandered any legal rights. It is very unlikely that most individuals are aware of the rule in § 109(h) or its 7–day component. As far as that debtor knows, he is acting in a timely manner. It seems harsh to punish such an unwitting and understandably ignorant debtor—particularly when, if Congress is to be believed, the counseling requirement was put in the Code for the debtor's own protection!

The Code contains very detailed rules regulating approved counseling agencies, and the services they must provide. § 111. Prospective debtors must obtain counseling from an agency that has been *approved* by the United States trustee. §§ 109(h)(1), 111(b)–(c). The bankruptcy clerk must maintain a publicly available list of approved agencies. § 111(a)(1). Regarding fees, the agency shall "if a fee is charged for counseling services, charge a reasonable fee, *and provide services without regard to ability to pay the fee.*" § 111(c)(2)(B). If a debtor is unable to pay the agency, the agency would have

---

[61] E.g., *Dixon*, supra note 41, 338 B.R. 383.

[62] See id.

[63] See, e.g., In re Giambrone, 365 B.R. 386 (Bankr. W.D.N.Y. 2007); In re Cleaver, 333 B.R. 430 (Bankr. S.D. Ohio 2005).

an administrative expense claim under § 503(b) to the extent the fees charged by it were reasonable.[64]

It is not evident how rigorous (or helpful?) the mandated counseling actually is for prospective debtors; one may wonder whether the supposed benefit to debtors outweighs the detriments they suffer. The briefing must "outline[ ] the opportunities for available credit counseling and assist[ ] such individual in performing a related budget analysis." § 109(h)(1). This briefing can be conducted via the telephone or the Internet. § 109(h)(1). To be approved, an agency must show that it can "provide adequate counseling with respect to a client's credit problems that includes an analysis of such client's current financial condition, factors that caused such financial condition, and how such client can develop a plan to respond to the problems without incurring negative amortization of debt." § 111(c)(2)(E). Ironically, then, the statutorily mandated content of the necessary counseling does *not* require the sort of warnings about the dire impact of filing bankruptcy on a debtor's credit that the legislative history so piously trumpeted as justification for the new requirement. Furthermore, individualized counseling is not mandated; group counseling is sufficient. § 109(h)(1). In sum, a debtor may get group counseling over the Internet, with no warnings about the impact of bankruptcy on their credit—but if they do not obtain such meaningful and helpful counseling, they are ineligible or bankruptcy—it is, Congress tells us, for their own good!

B. VOLUNTARY CASES

§ 2.4   Mechanics of Filing

How does a debtor commence a voluntary bankruptcy case? It is simple. File a "petition." And, perhaps, pay the filing fee (subject to two exceptions). That is all. Section 301 provides:

> (a) A voluntary case under a chapter of this title is commenced by the filing with the bankruptcy court of a petition under such chapter by an entity that may be a debtor under such chapter.

> (b) The commencement of a voluntary case under a chapter of this title constitutes an order for relief under such chapter.

For a joint case, the individual debtor and that individual's "spouse" commence a case by filing a single petition. § 302. Who qualifies as a "spouse" is determined by state law.[65]

The debtor should use Form 1 of the Official Bankruptcy Forms for the petition.[66] The debtor files the petition with the "clerk." Rule 1002(a). The "clerk" is the

---

[64]   In re Miller, 336 B.R. 232 (Bankr. W.D. Pa. 2006).

[65]   See, e.g., In re Balas, 449 B.R. 567 (Bankr. C.D. Cal. 2011) (holding that same-sex couple consisting of debtors legally married under state law were eligible to file joint petition, notwithstanding provisions of the Defense of Marriage Act, 1 U.S.C. § 7, which defines marriage as a legal union between one man and one woman).

bankruptcy clerk for the district. Rule 9001(3). The bankruptcy courts are deemed to be "always open," Rule 5001(a), which means that a petition can be filed at any time, day or night. If the clerk's office happens to be closed, the petition can be filed with a bankruptcy judge.[67]

The petition either must be verified or contain an unsworn declaration as provided by 28 U.S.C. § 1746. Rule 1008. Thus, the debtor must sign the petition and declare under penalty of perjury that the information provided is true and correct. It is a bankruptcy crime to knowingly and fraudulently make a false declaration, 18 U.S.C. § 152(3), punishable by a fine, up to 5 years imprisonment, or both. Note that the debtor's attorney would not be in a position to make this declaration, because the attorney would not have personal knowledge of the information contained in the petition.[68] However, the debtor's attorney does have to sign the petition as attorney of record. Rule 9011(a).

For a corporate or partnership debtor, an authorized agent of the debtor must sign the petition, stating that the information provided is true and correct and that the signatory has been authorized to file the petition on behalf of the debtor. Determining who is authorized to file bankruptcy on behalf of a corporation or a partnership is a matter of state corporate or partnership laws. Note that for a partnership, a *voluntary* petition requires the consent of *all* of the general partners. If any general partner does not consent, the case has to be commenced as an *involuntary* petition by the consenting partners. The non-consenting partners may oppose the filing. § 303(b)(3); Rule 1004.

The petition must be accompanied by the filing fee, with two exceptions. Rule 1006(a). The first exception is that an individual debtor may apply for permission to pay the filing fee in up to four installments. 28 U.S.C. § 1930(a)(7); Rule 1006(b)(1); Official Form 3A.[69]

What if the debtor believes he is too poor to pay the fee, even in installments? Before the 2005 Act, tough luck: the federal *in forma pauperis* statute, 28 U.S.C. § 1915, did not apply in bankruptcy. In *United States v. Kras*,[70] the Supreme Court in 1973 upheld the constitutionality of the mandatory fee scheme, concluding that due process does not require that indigent debtors have access to a discharge in bankruptcy. The 2005 Act for the first time permits (but apparently does not require) the district court or bankruptcy court to waive the filing fee for an individual debtor in a chapter 7 case whose income is less than 150% of the income official poverty line, if the court also determines that the debtor cannot pay the filing fee in installments. 28

---

[66] Available at http://www.uscourts.gov/uscourts/RulesAndPolicies/rules/BK_Forms_Current/B_001.pdf.

[67] The author filed a case with a bankruptcy judge at 11:00 p.m. while the judge was on a treadmill at a health club (he—the judge—was not happy). This unusual action was necessary to capture newly discovered preferential transfers made by the debtor exactly 90 days earlier.

[68] Although some courts permit an agent of the debtor, including an attorney, to make this declaration. See, e.g., In re Bestway Prods., Inc., 151 B.R. 530 (Bankr. E.D. Cal. 1993).

[69] Form 3A available at: http://www.uscourts.gov/uscourts/RulesAndPolicies/rules/BK_Forms_1207/B_003A_1207f.pdf.

[70] 409 U.S. 434 (1973). The Court distinguished its holding in *Boddie v. Connecticut*, 401 U.S. 371 (1971), that due process did require giving indigents access to state courts to obtain a divorce.

U.S.C. § 1930(f)(1). Thus, the second exception to the rule that the petition must be accompanied by the filing fee is that a voluntary chapter 7 petition filed by an individual debtor will be accepted if accompanied by a waiver request. Rule 1006(c); Official Form 3B.[71]

The required fees, which are specified in 28 U.S.C. § 1930(a), differ by chapter. Trustee fees and administrative fees are also imposed. The filing fees are: chapter 7—$245; chapter 9—$1,167; chapter 11 (not a railroad)—$1,167; chapter (railroad)—$1,000; chapter 12—$200; chapter 13—$235; chapter 15—$1,167.

The most onerous part of commencing a voluntary bankruptcy case for the debtor is amassing all sorts of financial and other information that must be filed at or near the time of commencement. § 521. The debtor must file numerous lists, schedules, and statements. Most of these must either be filed with the petition or, if a list of creditors is filed with the petition, within 14 days of the petition date. Rule 1007(c).

The documents required of *all* debtors include:

- List of creditors (with names and addresses), must be filed with thepetition. § 521(a)(1)(A), Rule 1007(a)(1).

- Schedules of assets and liabilities, within 14 days of the petition. § 521(a)(1)(B)(i), Rule 1007(b)(1)(A), (c), Official Form 6, Schedules A, B, D, E, and F.

- Schedule of executory contracts and unexpired leases, within 14 days of the petition. Rule 1007(b)(1)(C), (c); Official Form 6, Schedule G.

- Statement of financial affairs, within 14 days of the petition. § 521(a)(1)(B)(iii), Rule 1007(b)(1)(D), (c); Official Form 7.

- Schedule of current income and current expenditures, within 14 days of the petition. § 521(a)(1)(B)(ii); Rule 1007(b)(1)(B), (c); Official Form 6, Schedules I & J

- In a chapter 9 or 11 case, a list of the creditors holding the 20 largest unsecured claims (with names, addresses, and claim amounts), with the petition. Rule 1007(d), Official Form 4.

- In a chapter 11 case, a list of equity security holders, within 14 days of the petition. Rule 1007(a)(3).

In addition, *individual* debtors must file all of the following. As is evident, the paperwork burden is daunting:

---

[71] Form 3B available at: http://www.uscourts.gov/uscourts/RulesAndPolicies/rules/BK_Forms _Current/B_003B.pdf.

- Statement of current monthly net income, itemized to show calculation, within 14 days of petition. § 521(a)(1)(B)(v); Rule 1007(b)(4)–(6); Official Form 22.

- Statement disclosing any changes in income or expenses reasonably expected to occur in the twelve months following the filing of the petition. § 521(a)(1)(B)(vi).

- Schedule of property claimed as exempt, with the schedule of assets, within 14 days of petition.[72] § 522(l); Rule 4003(a); Official Form 6, Schedule C.

- Statement of intention with respect to property securing a consumer debt, within the earlier of 30 days of the petition, or the date of the meeting of creditors. § 521(a)(2); Rule 1007(b)(2); Official Form 8.

- With the statement of the debtor's financial affairs, if § 342(b) applies, debtor must file a certificate of either (i) an attorney that delivered the appropriate notice of § 342(b) or (ii) of debtor that such notice was received and read by debtor in case no attorney indicated, and no bankruptcy petition preparer signed the petition. § 521(a)(1)(B)(iii).

- Certificate from the approved nonprofit budget and credit counseling agency that provided the debtor services under § 109(h) describing the services provided to the debtor, along with a copy of the debt repayment plan, if any, developed under § 109(h); must be filed with the petition. § 521(b); Rule 1007(b)(3).

- Copies of all payment advices or other evidence of payment received from any employer in the 60 days preceding the filing date, within 14 days of petition. § 521(a)(1)(B)(iv); Rule 1007(b)(1)(E).

- Record of any interest that a debtor has in an educational individual retirement account or under a qualified State tuition program, within 14 days of petition. § 521(c); Rule 1007(b)(1)(F).

- Copy of Federal income tax return for the most recent tax year preceding the filing for which the return was filed, not later than 7 days before the date first set for the first meeting of creditors, to the trustee. § 521(e)(2)(A).

- At the request of the court, U.S. trustee or any party in interest in case under chapter 7, 11, 13 for an individual debtor, debtor shall, at the same time filed with the taxing authority, file (1) each tax return for tax years ending while the case is pending; (2) tax returns filed for three years preceding the filing that are filed while the case is pending; (3) any amendments to returns. § 521(f).

---

[72] If the debtor fails to file exemptions within 14 days of the petition, a dependent of the debtor may file within 30 days of the petition. Rule 4003(a). "Dependent" includes the debtor's spouse, whether or not actually dependent. § 522(a)(1).

- At the request of the U.S. trustee or trustee, debtor shall provide photo identification that establishes the identity of the debtor. § 521(h).

- Statement regarding completion of course in personal financial management, within 60 days of first date set for meeting of creditors in chapter 7 and no later than the last payment in a chapter 13 case. §§ 727(a)(11), 1328(g); Rule 1007(b)(7), (c).

§ 2.5   Effects of Filing

a.   *Generally*

The filing of a voluntary petition has momentous and instantaneous legal consequences. Filing the petition with the bankruptcy clerk "constitutes an order for relief." § 301. In simple terms, this means that a full bankruptcy case begins at the instant the clerk takes the debtor's petition and filing fee and stamps "filed" on the petition. Legally, it is exactly as if the bankruptcy judge entered an order decreeing the debtor a bankrupt and finding that bankruptcy relief should proceed.

Several immediate consequences are triggered by the petition filing. First, a bankruptcy "estate" is created.[73] § 541(a). This bankruptcy estate is comprised of all of the debtor's legal and equitable interests in property as of the time of the filing of the petition. § 541(a)(1). Effectively, then, filing a bankruptcy petition transfers all of the debtor's property to the newly established bankruptcy estate. The estate is a separate legal entity, and the bankruptcy trustee acts as representative of the estate. § 323(a). Estate property is within the exclusive jurisdiction of the federal bankruptcy court. 28 U.S.C. § 1334(e).

Second, upon the filing of a bankruptcy petition an "automatic stay" is effectuated. § 362(a). The automatic stay is explored in more depth in Chapter 3. The automatic stay is a federal statutory injunction. All collection efforts on pre-bankruptcy debts are halted immediately and automatically. The stay also protects estate property. In short, the stay protects the debtor and other creditors alike, preserving the status quo during the pendency of the bankruptcy case to allow the orderly resolution of the debtor's financial affairs, under court supervision. Chaos is replaced by order (hopefully). The stay is good against the world and is effective without personal notice. Actions taken in violation of the stay are void. Thus, for example, if Debtor files a bankruptcy petition at 11:59 a.m. with the bankruptcy clerk, and a foreclosure sale of the debtor's property occurs a minute later at high noon, that sale is void and of no effect, whether or not notice of the filing was given to the foreclosing creditor. If the creditor did have notice, however, they also would be potentially liable for sanctions.[74]

Third, a debtor is protected from the termination of utility services.[75] § 366. After the filing of a petition, a utility may not cut off service unless the debtor fails to provide

---

[73]   See § 2.5.b.

[74]   See, e.g., In re Crawford, 476 B.R. 83 (Bankr. S.D.N.Y. 2012) (holding that punitive damage available for stay violations if malice or bad faith is found).

[75]   See § 2.5.d.

adequate assurance of future payment within 20 days. § 366(b). The fact that the debtor has not paid a pre-bankruptcy debt is not a permissible reason for a utility to discontinue services. § 366(a). In 2005, Congress defined "assurance of payment," listing six forms of acceptable security for future utility services. § 366(c)(1)(A). Notably, the promise of an administrative expense priority does *not* qualify as an acceptable assurance. § 366(c)(1)(B). In chapter 11 cases, the 2005 law also empowered the utility to discontinue services within 30 days if it did not receive payment assurances that it judged to be satisfactory, thereby shifting the burden to the debtor to get a court order compelling continued provision of services. §§ 366(c)(2), (3).

Fourth, a bankruptcy filing extends certain time periods.[76] § 108. This gives the trustee time to assess the estate's situation. Also, the bar erected by the automatic stay necessitates carrying over time periods that otherwise would expire. Statutes of limitation for actions that could have been brought by the debtor are tolled; the trustee is given two years to bring the action on behalf of the estate. § 108(a). Under § 108(b), a trustee is given a 60–day grace period in which to take any action other than filing a lawsuit. Finally, any statute of limitations for creditors to sue the debtor is extended until 30 days after the automatic stay is terminated. § 108(c).

b.   Creation of Estate

The commencement of a bankruptcy case creates an "estate." § 541(a). This rule applies both in voluntary cases (§ 301, individual; § 302, joint), and involuntary cases. § 303. A case is "commenced" by the filing of the bankruptcy petition. While the filing of the petition and the entry of the order for relief occur simultaneously in voluntary cases, in involuntary cases the commencement of the case precedes the entry of the order for relief. Thus, in involuntary cases an estate is created even though the court has not yet ordered bankruptcy relief.

The bankruptcy estate is comprised initially of all of the debtor's interests in property at the time the case begins.[77] § 541(a)(1). During the pendency of the case some types of property that are acquired by the debtor or the estate also will become part of the estate.[78] § 541(a)(3)–(7). Special rules in chapters 12 and 13, and for individual debtors in chapter 11, bring additional postpetition property into the estate.[79] §§ 1115, 1207(a), 1306(a). Some forms of property will be excluded from the estate initially.[80] § 541(b)–(d). Other estate property may be removed during the case, either by exemption by the debtor,[81] § 522, or by abandonment by the trustee.[82] § 554.

The estate is a separate and distinct legal entity. The bankruptcy trustee is the representative of the estate. § 323(a). In chapter 11 cases, the debtor in possession serves the function of the trustee unless displaced by court order. § 1107(a). In all of

---

[76]   See § 2.5.e.

[77]   See § 5.2.

[78]   See § 5.3.

[79]   See § 5.4.

[80]   See §§ 5.6–5.10.

[81]   See § 5.11.

[82]   See § 5.14.

the rehabilitation cases, the debtor remains in possession of estate property unless the court orders otherwise. §§ 1101(1) and 1107(a) (chapter 11), § 1207(b) (chapter 12), § 1306(b) (chapter 13). In a liquidation case under chapter 7, however, property of the estate must be turned over to the trustee by the debtor, § 521(4), or by a third party in possession of estate property.[83] § 542. The trustee then will administer the estate, abandoning valueless property, and liquidating the remainder and distributing the net proceeds to creditors.

The district court has exclusive jurisdiction over property of the estate. 28 U.S.C. § 1334(e)(1). This jurisdiction is normally exercised by the bankruptcy court by reference from the district court. 28 U.S.C. § 157. Creditors are stayed from proceeding against property of the estate,[84] § 362(a)(2)–(4), unless the stay terminates or the bankruptcy court grants the creditor relief from the stay.[85] § 362(d). Strict limits are placed on the freedom of the debtor or trustee to use, sell, or lease estate property in the bankruptcy case. § 363. For activities outside of the ordinary course of business, court permission must be obtained.[86] § 363(b). The court will be careful to ensure that other parties with an interest in the property will be adequately protected before granting such permission. § 363(e). If the debtor's business has authorization from the court to operate, transactions respecting estate property may be entered into in the ordinary course of business without notice or a hearing.[87] § 363(c)(1). In such cases, the authorization to operate the debtor's business necessarily carries with it the implicit authorization to conduct ordinary course affairs as part of that business operation.

If property of the estate is transferred without court authorization, the bankruptcy trustee has the power to avoid the transfer and recover that property for the estate.[88] §§ 549, 550. Some narrow exceptions to this rule protect certain good faith parties who give value. §§ 549(c), 550(b). In general, though, all of the Code provisions regarding the bankruptcy estate work together to promote a coordinated and unified administration of estate property under the auspices of the trustee and the bankruptcy court.

c. Debtor's Duties

The filing of a bankruptcy case imposes a number of duties on the debtor. Performance of each of these duties facilitates the administration and processing of the bankruptcy case. The debtor's cooperation is essential. These duties arise even if the case was commenced as an involuntary case.

Most of the debtor's duties are spelled out in § 521. First, the debtor must file financial information pertinent to the bankruptcy case.[89] § 521(a)(1); Rule 1007; Official Forms 6, 7. These papers include: a list of creditors; schedules of assets and

---

[83]   See § 5.12.

[84]   See § 3.6.

[85]   See Chapter 3, part D.

[86]   See § 5.17.

[87]   See § 5.16.

[88]   See Chapter 6, part G.

[89]   See § 2.4.

liabilities; a schedule of current income and current expenditures; a schedule of executory contracts and leases; and a statement of the debtor's financial affairs. All of these must be filed with the voluntary petition or within 14 days. Rule 1007(b), (c). In an involuntary case, the debtor does not have to file these papers with the petition, which of course is filed by creditors, but instead must only file the lists and schedules if bankruptcy relief is ordered; in that event, the debtor is given 14 days to file the papers. The debtor in a voluntary or involuntary case may request an extension of time to file the required information. Rule 1007(a)(5). If the debtor does not file these papers, another party may prepare and file them and be reimbursed out of the estate. Rule 1007(k).

In 2005, Congress added a number of reporting duties to the list for *individual* debtors. The debtor must file copies of all payment advices from his employer received within 60 days of filing the petition. § 521(a)(1)(B)(iv); Rule 1007(b)(1)(E). The debtor also must file an itemized statement of monthly net income, § 521(a)(1)(B)(v); Rule 1007(b)(4)–(6); Official Form 22, along with any projected changes over the next twelve months. § 521(a)(1)(B)(vi). These documents help the United States trustee and the court determine whether the new "means test" provisions apply to the debtor. The debtor also must file the certificate of pre-bankruptcy credit counseling, and any budget plan developed.[90] § 521(b); Rule 1007(b)(3). Another document the debtor must file is a record of any educational IRA owned by the debtor. § 521(c); Rule 1007(b)(1)(F). The debtor must provide the trustee a copy of his most recent federal income tax return no later than seven days before the first meeting of creditors. § 521(e)(2)(A). During the case, the debtor likewise must provide the trustee with a copy of any current income tax returns he files, at the request of any party in interest (including the court or trustee). § 521(f). If the trustee so requests, the debtor must provide documentation that proves his identity, such as a passport or driver's license. § 521(h).

For individual debtors in a chapter 7 or 13 case, the sanction for failing to file much of the required information (especially the financial schedules and statements, and payment advices) is harsh indeed—*automatic dismissal* of the case on the 46th day. § 521(i)(1). Courts have puzzled over what it means for dismissal to be "automatic," particularly where such dismissal may be dependent on the determination of underlying facts, but some conclude that they must try to give effect to the plain statutory language.[91] For these courts, nothing in § 521(i)(2) (which requires the court to enter a dismissal order within seven days in cases within subsection (i)(1) if a party in interest requests dismissal) impliedly undercuts the automatic dismissal mandate.[92] Instead, they construe that provision simply to allow parties in interest to obtain some certainty regarding the *fait accompli* of dismissal. Other courts, though, take the position that "automatic dismissal" is not necessarily so "automatic" after all, given the

---

[90]   See § 2.3.b.

[91]   E.g., In re Wilkinson, 346 B.R. 539 (Bankr. D. Utah 2006).

[92]   See In re Hall, 368 B.R. 595 (Bankr. W.D. Tex. 2007) (when debtor sought confirmation of his automatic dismissal under § 521, the court looked into and found bad faith by the debtor, so they conditioned the dismissal with a two year bar date for filing); In re Fawson, 338 B.R. 505 (Bankr. D. Utah 2006) ("If the case were not dismissed under § 521(i)(1) until a party in interest made a[ ] request, then what effect would the automatic dismissal language of § 521(i)(1) have? None."). But see In re Jackson, 348 B.R. 487 (Bankr. S.D. Iowa 2006).(holding that it should not have entered sua sponte order dismissing case, where no party in interest requested dismissal under § 521(i)(2)).

opportunities for court involvement in § 521, and read the request for dismissal provision in (i)(2) as qualifying the supposedly "automatic" nature of the dismissal under (i)(1).[93] Courts worry too about the chaos that might result from an "automatic" dismissal, when the case proceeds and actions are taken (assets sold, plans confirmed, discharges granted, and so forth) *after* the case supposedly evaporated in a puff of automatic dismissal smoke. The debtor can request a 45–day extension, but he must do so within the original 45–day time period. § 521(i)(3). The court does have the power to decline to dismiss the case if it finds that the debtor tried in good faith to comply and the best interests of creditors would be served by administering the bankruptcy case. § 521(i)(4).

The sanction for failing to provide tax returns to the trustee in a timely manner is not automatic dismissal, but nevertheless the Code mandates that the court "shall" dismiss, § 521(e)(2)(A), subject only to the ability to grant leniency if the debtor "demonstrates that the failure to so comply is due to circumstances beyond the control of the debtor." § 521(e)(2)(B). An intriguing issue that has arisen is whether the *trustee* has the power to exercise "prosecutorial discretion" and waive the debtor's noncompliance.[94] While a hyper-literal reading of the statutory text might suggest otherwise, it is hard to fathom why the very party to whom a document is to be provided lacks the power to say "never mind"—and especially to say "just get it to me later."

In 1984 Congress added a new duty, requiring an individual debtor in a chapter 7 case to file a "statement of intention" with regard to consumer debts secured by property of the estate. Rule 1007(b)(2); Official Form 8. This statement is to be filed within 30 days of the filing of the petition (or the date of the meeting of creditors, if earlier), unless the court extends the time. § 521(a)(2)(A). The intention to be stated is "with respect to the retention or surrender of such property and, if applicable, specifying that such property is claimed as exempt, that the debtor intends to redeem such property, or that the debtor intends to reaffirm debts secured by such property." § 521(2)(A).

Before the 2005 amendments, the Code provided that the debtor "shall perform his intention" within 45 days after filing the statement. However, the statute went on to state that "nothing in subparagraphs (A) and (B) of this paragraph shall alter the debtor's or the trustee's rights with regard to such property." The cumulative effect of these provisions caused a split in the courts. One view was that the three listed options for the debtor—exempt, redeem, or reaffirm—were exclusive and mandatory, and that

---

[93] See, e.g., In re Warren, 568 F.3d 1113 (9th Cir. 2009) (reasoning that if § 521(i)(1) were automatic and no requests from creditors necessary, then manipulative debtors could abuse the system by getting an automatic dismissal); In re Acosta–Rivera, 557 F.3d 8 (1st Cir. 2009) (explaining that § 521(i)(1)'s "automatic dismissal" is a misnomer, because it typically happens after a party in interest requests); In re Parker, 351 B.R. 790 (Bankr. N.D. Ga. 2006). The court's power to dismiss on request of a party in interest under § 521(i)(2) is one such provision, see *Jackson,* supra note 92. Some judges ponder the mystery of why or how a court can dismiss a case that has already been automatically dismissed. Also, the need to file the information required under § 521(a)(1) is excused if "the court orders otherwise." § 521(a)(1)(B). The facts in *Parker* were hardly sympathetic for the debtor; the *debtor* himself was urging automatic dismissal, since the case had taken an ugly turn—the trustee was selling the debtor's $180,000 "fantasy houseboat."

[94] Compare In re Duffus, 339 B.R. 746 (Bankr. D. Or. 2006) (trustee may waive), with In re Norton, 347 B.R. 291 (Bankr. E.D. Tenn. 2006) (trustee may not waive).

the debtor was required to select one of the three.[95] This was true even if the debtor was not in default on his payments on the secured debt at the time of filing. A competing view (called "ride-through") permitted a debtor who was current on the secured debt to continue making scheduled payments as an alternative to selecting one of the three choices in § 521(a)(2).[96] Under this approach, the debtor's statutory choices were not considered to be exclusive.

In 2005, Congress attempted to resolve the debate in favor of secured creditors and against individual debtors. The amendments specify, as before, that if an individual chapter 7 debtor intends to retain estate property securing a debt, the debtor must either redeem or reaffirm. § 521(a)(2)(A)–(C); Rule 1007(b)(2). Furthermore, the debtor must perform his stated intention within 30 days after the first date set for the meeting of creditors, unless the court extends the time. § 521(a)(2)(B). Those rules were in the pre–2005 law, however (except that the time given to perform a stated intention was reduced from 45 to 30 days), and thus in and of themselves do not eliminate "ride-through." The operative changes come in the new enforcement rules. Failure of the debtor to comply may result in a lifting of the automatic stay, allowing the secured creditor to repossess and foreclose.[97] § 362(h)(1). But what happens when a debtor files a statement of intention to retain collateral and continue to make payments, timely enters into and files a reaffirmation agreement, but the court denies the reaffirmation agreement because it constitutes an undue hardship on the debtor? Clearly the debtor fails to technically comply with § 362(h). Nonetheless, one court held that this scenario constituted "substantial compliance" with §§ 521(a)(2) and 362(h), as to permit a "ride through."[98]

Furthermore, in a related (and confusingly overlapping) provision, Congress added a separate provision instituting a *45–day* rule (measured from "after the first meeting of creditors") for personal property collateral securing the purchase price. § 521(a)(6). Failure to comply with subsection (6), however, does not in and of itself result in termination of the stay; nothing in § 362(h) addresses failure to comply with § 521(a)(6), and only mentions § 521(a)(2). However, one court used § 362(d)(1) (allowing courts to grant relief from the stay "for cause, including the lack of adequate protection of an interest in property") to hold that the automatic stay "terminated by operation of law" when the debtor failed to file his reaffirmation agreement with regards to a car secured by debt within 45–days.[99] Additionally, such failure does validate a bankruptcy default clause in the underlying agreement, enhancing the secured creditor's chances of successfully moving for relief from the stay. How Congress

---

[95]   E.g., In re Edwards, 901 F.2d 1383 (7th Cir. 1989).

[96]   E.g., In re Belanger, 962 F.2d 345 (4th Cir. 1992).

[97]   See, e.g., In re Miller, 443 B.R. 54, 58 (Bankr. D. Del. 2011) (explaining that the BAPCPA amendments to § 521(a)(2) did not eliminate the "ride through" option, but that § 362(h) requires the debtor to "perform accordingly" regarding his or her surrender/reaffirm/redeem/assume indication, or else the automatic stay terminates).

[98]   In re Baker, 400 B.R. 136, 139 (Bankr. D. Del. 2009).

[99]   In re Visnicky, 401 B.R. 61, 65 (Bankr. D.R.I. 2009) (holding the automatic stay was terminated on the 45th day from the first meeting of the creditors, where the debtor filed 7 days late).

intended the 30–day rule and 45–day rule to interact is unclear, and will be discussed in more detail in a subsequent section.[100]

The debtor also has a duty to cooperate with the trustee as is necessary to enable the trustee to perform the trustee's duties. § 521(a)(3). This general duty of cooperation is supplemented by the specific directive that the debtor must surrender any property to the trustee as well as any recorded information that relates to property of the estate. § 521(a)(4). The Code makes clear that this turnover duty is not excused even if the debtor attempts to claim a privilege against self-incrimination.[101] The courts have held that the surrender of estate property and records is not testimonial, and therefore does not implicate the Fifth Amendment.[102] Some debtors try circumventing this by giving their attorneys any records or information they wish to shield with the attorney-client privilege.[103] One court held that under certain circumstances, the trustee held the attorney-client privilege, and therefore had the power to waive it instead of an individual debtor.[104] In cases involving corporate debtors, the Supreme Court held that the trustee controls the corporation's attorney-client privilege, and thus has the ability to waive it.[105]

The Bankruptcy Rules flesh out the debtor's duties of cooperation with the trustee in more detail, and also prescribe duties in addition to the ones found in the Code. Rule 4002. If the debtor is uncooperative, the trustee may obtain a court order directing the debtor to cooperate. If the debtor ignores that court order, her discharge may be denied under § 727(a)(6)(A).

The debtor also has a duty to attend at least one and possibly two hearings. First, the debtor must attend the initial meeting of creditors. § 343. The purpose of the creditors' meeting under § 341(a) is to permit the trustee and creditors to examine the debtor under oath. § 343. The debtor's failure to attend the creditors' meeting may result in the dismissal of the case.[106] Second, the debtor may be required to attend a discharge hearing under § 524(d). § 521(a)(5). The court has discretion whether to make the debtor attend that hearing. If the debtor is seeking to reaffirm a debt, the court may require the debtor to attend a reaffirmation hearing. § 524(d). Finally, during the case the court may order the debtor to appear and submit to an

---

[100] See Chapter 7, part E.

[101] Section 521(a)(4) requires a debtor to turn over all property of the estate, including all recorded information, regardless of whether immunity is granted under § 541, which incorporates Part V of Title 18, titled "Immunity of Witnesses." 18 U.S.C. § 6002.

[102] See, e.g., In re Crabtree, 39 B.R. 726 (Bankr. E.D. Tenn. 1984) (holding that involuntary debtor may not decline statutory duty to surrender estate assets on basis of Fifth Amendment privilege); In re Ross, 156 B.R. 272 (Bankr. D. Idaho 1993) (holding that Fifth Amendment privilege did not apply to debtors in voluntary case who filed all statement of financial affairs and schedules with only their attorney's compensation details, and the statement "[e]ach Debtor refuses to answer this question or each of these questions on the grounds that it may tend to incriminate them").

[103] See, e.g., In re Butcher, 38 B.R. 796 (Bankr. E.D. Tenn. 1984).

[104] In re Fairbanks, 135 B.R. 717 (Bankr. D.N.H. 1991).

[105] Commodity Futures Trading Comm'n v. Weintraub, 471 U.S. 343 (1985).

[106] Some courts allow debtors to appear at § 341 meetings through counsel. See, e.g., In re Dinova, 212 B.R. 437 (B.A.P. 2d Cir. 1997) (holding that debtor's failure to appear in person at initial or adjourned meeting of creditors did not constitute "cause" for dismissal under § 707(a), given that the debtor appeared through counsel).

examination. Rule 4002(a)(1). Failure of the debtor to comply with this court order will be a basis for denial of the debtor's discharge. § 727(a)(6).

d. Protection Against Loss of Utility Services

For many individual consumer debtors, one of the most important provisions of the Code is the protection against the loss of utility services in § 366. For example, an individual residing in a small apartment in Minnesota in the dead of winter has a substantial interest in keeping the utility company from cutting off the heat to her apartment. Utility companies have considerable leverage in collecting unpaid bills; they can simply discontinue service and refuse to resume service until the outstanding debt is paid. Furthermore, many utilities enjoy monopoly power, so affected customers do not have the option of seeking alternative service from another provider. By exercising its leverage, the utility company also can obtain an advantage over competing creditors of the debtor. On the other side, a utility company does not want to and should not have to provide free utility service; it is not an eleemosynary institution. Section 366 seeks to balance these competing interests of the debtor, the utility company, and the other creditors in a fair and equitable manner.

This balancing is implemented in two steps. First, the utility is precluded initially from altering, refusing, or discontinuing service to the debtor or trustee or discriminating against the debtor or trustee solely because of the bankruptcy filing or the failure to pay an outstanding pre-bankruptcy debt. § 366(a). Thus, a debtor has the power to stop an impending utility service termination simply by filing a bankruptcy petition.

Second, however, the utility is protected as well. The rule against terminations refers to non-payment of *prepetition* debts; it does not preclude the utility from terminating services if the debtor does not pay for *postpetition* services. Furthermore, the debtor or the trustee only has a 20–day grace period after filing within which to provide the utility with adequate "assurance of payment" for future services. If such assurances are not provided in that time, the utility is then permitted to alter, refuse, or discontinue further service. § 366(b). It may not terminate services prior to the expiration of the 20–day period, however. In a chapter 11 case, the utility has somewhat greater rights; it has the power to discontinue services within the 30–day period beginning on the petition date if it does not receive assurance of payment "that is satisfactory to the utility." § 366(c)(2). The debtor or trustee then must go to court and contest the utility's determination.

The burden is on the debtor or trustee to provide the assurances. Any party in interest may request a modification of the assurances given. § 366(b), (c)(3)(A). The Code indicates that assurances should be "in the form of a deposit or other security." For cases under chapter 11, governed by subsection (c), Congress in 2005 added a detailed definition of "assurance of payment" in § 366(c)(1), requiring a cash deposit, a letter of credit, a certificate of deposit, a surety bond, a prepayment, or another form of security, mutually agreed upon. Congress did not adopt the House proposal that adequate assurances could be established by the promise of nothing more than an administrative expense priority for postpetition services.[107] For chapter 11 cases, Congress made explicit that administrative priority did not suffice. § 366(c)(1)(B).

For a deposit to be "adequate" the courts may require that it equal the amount of one or perhaps two average monthly bills.[108] Courts look to applicable state public utility regulations in determining the adequacy of deposits, and also tend to enforce such regulations as ceilings on deposit amounts. Additionally, some courts, in computing the amount, consider the length of time it would take a utility to terminate service if a debtor misses a billing cycle.[109] A prepetition deposit normally may not be applied as security toward the postpetition services, because it secures prepetition bills.[110] The courts are divided over whether assurances must be given under § 366(b) if the debtor is current on her account at the time of the bankruptcy filing.[111] While some courts have excused the debtor or trustee from providing assurances in this situation, there is no language in the Code that supports such an exclusion. In chapter 11 cases, the thrust of the pro-utility 2005 amendments, and especially the tenor of § 366(c)(2), which gives the utility power in the first instance to determine whether the assurances are adequate, strongly cut against any such exclusion.

It is critical to emphasize that the assurances need go only to the payment for *postpetition* services. The utility has no right to insist on the payment of *prepetition* debts.[112] As to those debts, the utility is simply a general creditor, and may seek payment only through the bankruptcy distribution. § 502. It may not condition the provision of postpetition service on payment of the prepetition debt. By contrast, note that bankruptcy courts in chapter 11 cases have permitted some other creditors with leverage (such as key employees or critical suppliers) to insist on the payment of prepetition claims as a condition of providing postpetition services to the estate, under the "doctrine of necessity," i.e., "critical vendor" orders.[113] Section 366(a) closes that door to utility companies. Note, though, that in chapter 11 cases, the 2005 amendments specifically authorize the utility to set off its claim against a prepetition security deposit, and indeed to do so "without notice or order of the court."[114] § 366(c)(4).

---

[107] H.R. Rep. No. 95–595, 95th Cong., 1st Sess., at 350 (1977).

[108] See, e.g., In re Bedford Town Condo., 427 B.R. 380 (Bankr. D. Md. 2010) (utility requiring adequate assurance deposit of twice the debtor's average monthly service expense).

[109] See, e.g., In re Weisel, 400 B.R. 457 (Bankr. W.D. Pa. 2009).

[110] See, e.g., In re Utica Floor Maint., Inc., 25 B.R. 1010 (N.D.N.Y. 1982).

[111] Compare In re Demp, 22 B.R. 331 (Bankr. E.D. Pa. 1982) ("In such a case as this where the debtor has a history of prompt and complete payment, in addition to being completely current in the prepetition utility payments, a cash deposit would be unnecessary."), with In re 499 W. Warren St. Assocs. Ltd. P'ship, 138 B.R. 363 (Bankr. N.D.N.Y. 1991) (holding that utility could demand assurance regardless of status of debtor's prepetition account).

[112] See, e.g., In re Jones, 369 B.R. 745 (B.A.P. 1st Cir. 2007) (utility may not refuse to furnish service because of prepetition debt).

[113] See § 11.12. The doctrine of necessity is criticized in Charles J. Tabb, Emergency Preferential Orders in Bankruptcy Reorganizations, 65 Am. Bankr. L.J. 75 (1991). The Seventh Circuit questioned the legitimacy of critical vendor orders in *In re Kmart Corp.*, 359 F.3d 866 (7th Cir. 2004).

[114] Some courts had allowed this practice even before the 2005 amendments, and outside of chapter 11 cases. See, e.g., In re McMahon, 129 F.3d 93 (2d Cir. 1997) (allowing utility to apply prepetition deposit to prepetition debt in a chapter 13 case, postpetition); Brooks Shoe Mfg. Co., Inc. v. United Tel. Co., 39 B.R. 980 (Bankr. E.D. Pa. 1984) (same, but in chapter 11).

One issue that sometimes arises is what constitutes a "utility" within the meaning of § 366.[115] The term is not defined in the Code. The legislative history suggests that Congress' focus was on the monopoly position of most traditional utilities, such as electric, gas, water, and telephone companies.[116] As technology improves, however, some traditional utilities may lose monopoly power; if so, much of the reason for the special protections of § 366 may be eliminated.

e.   Extension of Time

The filing of a bankruptcy case interrupts the normal course of financial affairs for the debtor and the debtor's creditors. The automatic stay in § 362(a) prevents creditors from continuing collection efforts or from interfering with estate property. A trustee takes over the property of the estate from the debtor in chapter 7, and needs time to assess the debtor's assets and liabilities. § 704. Even in the rehabilitation chapters, where the debtor presumptively retains possession of property, significant new burdens and limitations weigh on the debtor, and may impede the debtor from taking prompt action. Meanwhile, however, as Chaucer once observed, "time and tide wait for no man." What is to be done if a statute of limitations is about to expire when the bankruptcy case is filed, or if a redemption period is about to run? Section 108 of the Code extends the "legal" time for parties affected by the bankruptcy case to protect their rights and discharge their duties (but the tide still rolls on).

Section 108 has three parts. Subsection (a) tolls the statute of limitations for actions that could have been brought *by the debtor*, and gives the trustee two years after the order for relief to bring the action on behalf of the estate. Subsection (b) allows the trustee 60 days after the order for relief to take an action other than the bringing of a lawsuit, namely, to "file any pleading, demand, notice, or proof of claim or loss, cure a default, or perform any other similar act." Finally, the statute of limitations *for creditors* to bring actions against the debtor is extended by subsection (c) for 30 days after notice of the termination of the automatic stay. The times provided in § 108 only apply if necessary to extend the time to act; all three subsections provide that a longer non-bankruptcy time period will still control.

The provisions of subsections (a) and (b) are intended to afford the trustee time to review the debtor's financial situation and determine what actions to take, and thereby to preserve for the benefit of the estate all potentially valuable assets. For example, at the time of the bankruptcy filing, the debtor may have a possible cause of action against a third party, but the non-bankruptcy statute of limitations may be scheduled to expire within a few days of the bankruptcy filing. It would be unrealistic to expect the trustee to file the lawsuit on behalf of the estate before the statute runs, and yet the estate should not be deprived of that cause of action. In such a situation, § 108(a) gives the trustee two years to file.

---

[115] See, e.g., In re Darby, 470 F.3d 573 (5th Cir. 2006) (holding that provider of cable television does not qualify as a utility); In re Erving Indus., Inc., 432 B.R. 354 (Bankr. D. Mass. 2010) (distinguishing between electricity seller and deliverer, and holding the former is not a utility); In re Hobbs, 20 B.R. 488 (Bankr. E.D. Pa. 1982) (holding that condo association is a utility when it receives electricity from an electric company, and in turn sells it to the debtor).

[116] H.R. Rep. No. 95–595, 95th Cong., 1st Sess., at 350 (1977); S. Rep. No. 95–989, 95th Cong., 2d Sess., at 60 (1978).

To provide another example, the debtor's real property may have been sold prior to bankruptcy, giving the debtor a statutory right to redeem that property. If a bankruptcy case is filed and relief ordered before the redemption period has run, the trustee is given 60 days to exercise the redemption right on behalf of the estate.[117] § 108(b). The question has been raised whether the automatic stay of § 362(a) more generally stays the running of time, but almost all courts have concluded that the stay does not apply to the mere running of time, leaving § 108 as the sole source of authority to extend time.[118]

Attending to the precise language of § 108(a) and (b) reveals some limitations on the reach of those sections, and also raises some questions. Those subsections authorize the "trustee" to act. Thus, in a chapter 7 case, only the trustee, and not the debtor personally, obtains the benefit of the extension. In chapters 11 and 12, the debtor acting in its capacity as debtor in possession has the powers of the trustee, §§ 1107(a), 1203, and accordingly is the party privileged to act within the extended time periods. In chapter 13, the situation is murkier, because the debtor does not have all of the powers of the trustee. Some courts thus conclude that the plain meaning of the Code prohibits the debtor from invoking the time extensions of § 108;[119] other courts, however, recognizing the practical utility of allowing the debtor to bring actions in lieu of the chapter 13 trustee, ignore the statutory restrictions.[120]

Under subsection (a), only actions that "the debtor" could have commenced are covered. This limitation means that the trustee does not have the benefit of a time extension for actions that could have been commenced by creditors, even if the trustee now is empowered to bring such actions for the benefit of the entire estate. The most important example is § 544(b), which gives the trustee the power to bring avoidance actions maintainable by unsecured creditors.[121] The primary use of § 544(b) is to invoke state fraudulent transfer law. Furthermore, § 108(a) does not extend the time for bringing any action, which is created by the Code itself. This point applies to most avoiding powers of the trustee. For those actions, the governing statutes of limitations are § 546(a) (for the bringing of the avoidance action) and § 550(f) (for the bringing of an action to recover an avoided transfer).

---

[117]   E.g., Canney v. Merchs. Bank (In re Canney), 284 F.3d 362 (2d Cir. 2002).

[118]   See, e.g., In re Glenn, 760 F.2d 1428 (6th Cir. 1985) (since § 362 does not mention running of time, and § 108 explicitly does, § 108 governs the issue of tolling time); Johnson v. First Nat'l Bank, 719 F.2d 270 (8th Cir. 1983) (holding that Congress only intended § 362 to prohibit certain types of affirmative actions).

[119]   See, e.g., Estate of Carr v. United States, 482 F. Supp.2d 842 (W.D. Tex. 2007) (holding that chapter 13 debtor is not allowed to invoke § 108 time extension); In re Ranasingh, 341 B.R. 556 (Bankr. E.D. Va. 2006) (same). For related authority in chapter 11 cases, see Cunningham v. Healthco, Inc., 824 F.2d 1448 (5th Cir. 1987) (stating that, with regards to a chapter 11 case, "[w]hile a debtor-in-possession is entitled to § 108's tolling period, however, a debtor is not"); United States v. C.I.T. Constr. Inc. of Texas, 944 F.2d 253 (5th Cir. 1991) (holding that in a chapter 11 case, noting that because purpose of § 108 is to benefit the estate, post-confirmation debtors may not invoke powers of extension because their interest diverges from those of creditors).

[120]   See, e.g., Thomas v. GMAC Res. Funding Corp., 309 B.R. 453 (D. Md. 2004) (allowing chapter 13 debtor to invoke extension); In re McConnell, 390 B.R. 170 (Bankr. W.D. Pa. 2008) (permitting chapter 13 debtor to use § 108 extension because they are acting as a "debtor-in-possession"); In re Gaskins, 98 B.R. 328 (Bankr. E.D. Tenn. 1989) (allowing chapter 13 debtor § 108 powers when their suit benefitted the estate).

[121]   See § 6.5.

A trustee is not limited to the times delineated in § 108(b) in acting with regard to an "executory contract." Instead, the more specific rules of § 365, which govern executory contracts and unexpired leases, would govern. For example, the time within which a default in the contract must be cured would be controlled by § 365, not § 108(b).

If a bankruptcy case is converted from one chapter to another, no new time extensions are generated. The tolling in subsections (a) and (b) is triggered by and measured from the date of the entry of the order for relief. Conversion of a case does not effect a change in the date of the order for relief. § 348(a).

Section 108(c) serves to protect the interests of creditors who are stayed by § 362(a) from bringing actions against the debtor or property of the debtor or the estate. Under § 108(c), stayed parties are given 30 days to commence or continue an action after notice of the termination of the stay, unless of course the non-bankruptcy limitation period is even longer. Note that strictly speaking the running of the limitations period is not tolled or suspended during the pendency of the bankruptcy case, but rather only a 30–day grace period is given after the bar of the automatic stay is lifted. Section 108(c) does not toll the running of time periods on a contract,[122] and on its face does not generally afford creditors extensions of time other than for filing lawsuits. In other words, creditors are not given a corollary section to § 108(b).

Some of the more complex applications of § 108(c) come in the area of taxes. Many provisions in both the Internal Revenue Code and in the Code are keyed to particular time periods; the problem is integrating those rules. The legislative history makes clear that the Internal Revenue Code's six-month suspension period for the collection of taxes after the taxpayer's assets are removed from court control applies in addition to the 30–day extension offered by § 108(c).[123] The Supreme Court held in *Young v. United States* that the time periods in § 507(a)(8), which govern whether the tax will be treated as a priority claim and whether the tax will be excepted from discharge under § 523(a)(1), are equitably tolled during the pendency of a bankruptcy case while the automatic stay is in effect.[124] Because of the equitable tolling doctrine, the Court did not have to decide whether § 108(c) applied.

---

[122] See, e.g., Moody v. Amoco Oil Co., 734 F.2d 1200 (7th Cir. 1984), cert. denied, 469 U.S. 982 (1984) ("Section 108(b) does not apply to curing defaults in executor contracts. Section 365 specifically governs the time for curing defaults in executor contracts, and thus, it controls. . . . "). But see In re Empire Equities Capital Corp., 405 B.R. 687 (Bankr. S.D.N.Y. 2009) (holding that the time for a debtor to exercise an option in a contract had not yet expired as of commencement of the case, and was extended by § 108).

[123] 124 Cong. Rec. S17,426 (daily ed. Oct. 6, 1978); 124 Cong. Rec. H11,109 (daily ed. Sept. 28, 1978). See also 26 U.S.C. § 6503(b) (Internal Revenue Code provision).

[124] 535 U.S. 43 (2002).

C. INVOLUNTARY CASES

§ 2.6   Limitations on Involuntary Relief: Available Chapters

An involuntary case can be commenced only under chapter 7 or chapter 11. § 303(a). By implication, involuntary cases cannot be commenced under chapters 9, 12, or 13. The conversion rules reinforce these limitations.[125]

One of the long-running debates in bankruptcy policy has been whether creditors should be able to force individual debtors to repay their debts in bankruptcy out of future earnings. Major lobbying efforts were made in the 1920s, 1960s, and then continuously from 1982 to 2005 by the consumer credit industry, seeking either some form of compulsory repayment scheme or at the very least denial of bankruptcy relief to "can-pay" debtors who refuse to commit future earnings to repay their debts. Until 2005, Congress generally rebuffed this idea. However, in 1984 Congress gave creditors half a loaf by adding the "substantial abuse" ground for dismissing chapter 7 filings. § 707(b) (1984). The idea was that a debtor who could repay a substantial portion of his debts would be denied access to chapter 7, leaving the debtor with the option either to proceed "voluntarily" under chapter 13 or to forego bankruptcy relief altogether. This principle was strengthened substantially in 2005, with the substitution of the broader "abuse" test for the old "substantial abuse" test in § 707(b), and the enactment of a formalized "means test" as a trigger for a presumption of such "abuse."[126] The new version of § 707(b) specifically contemplates that a debtor who fails the abuse test will either face dismissal of his chapter 7 case, or, "with the debtor's consent," conversion to chapter 11 or chapter 13. § 707(b)(1). That being said, though, the debtor still retains a choice, even if it is an unpleasant one.

Even under the law as revised in 2005, an individual debtor retains control over the choice to proceed under chapter 13. The reasons why Congress has consistently rejected a compulsory chapter 13 scheme were explained in the legislative history to the 1978 Code.[127] First is the concern that coercing unwilling debtors to repay debts out of future income might contravene the prohibition against involuntary servitude in the Thirteenth Amendment. Constitutional qualms aside, Congress further doubted that involuntary chapter 13 cases would work. A debtor who does not want to work for the benefit of his creditors and perform under a chapter 13 plan is not likely to do so. Empirical studies have shown that the failure rate for even voluntary chapter 13 cases is quite high, lending credence to the congressional concern that involuntary chapter 13 cases would be "preordained to fail."[128]

When Congress added chapter 12 to the Code in 1986, it patterned that chapter after chapter 13. Chapter 12 similarly requires a debtor to commit to paying all projected disposable income over a three-to-five-year period to creditors. The reasons for not permitting involuntary chapter 13 filings therefore apply with equal force to

---

[125] For example, § 706(c) does not allow conversion from chapter 7 to chapter 12 or 13 without debtor request; a similar provision is found in § 1112(d) for conversion from chapter 11.

[126] See § 2.15.

[127] H.R. Rep. No. 95–595, 95th Cong., 1st Sess., at 120 (1977).

[128] Id.

cases under chapter 12, and Congress accordingly prohibited involuntary chapter 12 cases.

In the 2005 amendments, however, Congress for the first time departed from its policy against subjecting individual debtors to involuntary bankruptcy proceedings in which the debtor's future earnings are brought into the bankruptcy estate. The vehicle for this sea change was chapter 11. While involuntary chapter 11 cases have always been allowed as against individual debtors, until 2005 the postpetition earnings of those individual debtors were not brought into the bankruptcy estate, thus obviating any Thirteenth Amendment concern.[129] Such earnings were excluded from the estate under § 541(a)(6). Chapter 11, in short, lacked any analogue to § 1306(a)(2), which brings an individual debtor's postpetition earnings into the bankruptcy estate. In 2005, however, Congress added § 1115(a)(2), which copies the chapter 13 postpetition-earnings inclusion. The chapter 11 amendments also require (analogously to chapter 13) that an individual debtor devote all projected disposable income to the plan for five years if any unsecured creditor objects, § 1129(a)(15), and postpone entry of the discharge until the individual debtor has completed plan payments. § 1141(d)(5). The combined force of these new rules is to allow a creditor to force an individual debtor involuntarily into chapter 11 and capture all of the debtor's disposable income for the benefit of creditors for five years. The only remedy for noncompliance appears to be denial of discharge and possible dismissal of the case. The post–2005 chapter 11 involuntary rules for individual debtors, in sum, present precisely the regime that Congress has previously rejected as being unwise as a policy matter, and possibly as suspect under the Thirteenth Amendment. Courts have addressed the constitutionality of § 1115, but none have ruled definitively either way.[130] The weak link in the constitutional argument for debtors, though, is whether sufficient "compulsion" exists. Absent compulsion, the new chapter 11 rules seem little different from wage garnishments, which have never been considered constitutionally suspect.[131]

In light of the shift in 2005, one wonders why Congress stopped short of permitting involuntary cases under chapters 12 and 13. Nothing in those chapters would be any more constitutionally vulnerable than the new chapter 11 regime. On policy grounds, involuntary chapter 11 cases against individual debtors may be even more "preordained to fail" than chapter 13, since in chapter 11 creditors can propose plans and creditors are entitled to vote, whereas in chapter 13 the debtor retains the exclusive right to propose a plan and creditors do not vote. §§ 1121, 1321.

The concerns under chapter 9 are of a different stripe. First, an involuntary chapter 9 case might invade state sovereignty in violation of the Tenth Amendment.

---

[129]   The Supreme Court noted this point in *Toibb v. Radloff*, 501 U.S. 157, 165–66 (1991).

[130]   See, e.g., In re Gordon, 465 B.R. 683 (Bankr. N.D. Ga. 2012) (declining to rule on constitutionality of § 1115 because it was not "ripe for review"); In re Marciano, 459 B.R. 27 (B.A.P. 9th Cir. 2011) (same); In re Clemente, 409 B.R. 288 (Bankr. D.N.J. 2009) (debtor raised constitutionality of § 1115, but court invoked doctrine of constitutional avoidance to convert the debtors case to a chapter 7); Misuraca v. U.S. Tr., 2009 WL 1212471 (D. Ariz. May 4, 2009) (declining to rule on debtor's argument that *Radloff* dicta counsels that involuntary chapter 11 cases are unconstitutional, because the issues was not "ripe for review").

[131]   For a more extended analysis of the constitutional issue, see § 1.10. See also Margaret Howard, Bankruptcy Bondage, 2009 U. Ill. L. Rev. 191 (2009); Robert J. Keach, Dead Man Filing Redux: Is the New Individual Chapter Eleven Unconstitutional?, 13 Am. Bankr. Inst. L. Rev. 483 (2005).

Second, as a policy matter Congress did not think that "the fate of a municipality, governed by officials elected by the people . . . [should] be determined by a small number of creditors."[132]

§ 2.7   Limitations on Involuntary Relief: Eligible Debtors

Not every debtor who is eligible for voluntary relief is a permissible target of an involuntary case. Eligibility under § 109 is thus a necessary but not a sufficient condition to involuntary eligibility. Two types of debtors are immunized from involuntary petitions: (1) a farmer or a family farmer, and (2) a non-profit corporation. § 303(a). For those types of debtors, the choice to file bankruptcy is purely voluntary, no matter what the chapter.

Note, though, that most courts hold that a debtor must raise its exempt status as an affirmative defense to the involuntary filing, or the defense is waived.[133] In other words, the debtor's status is not jurisdictional.

In addition, an involuntary case may not be filed against joint debtors.[134] The only provision in the Code for joint cases is § 302, which speaks only of voluntary filings by an individual debtor and "such individual's spouse." § 302(a). Additionally, the legislative history of this section stated "[a] joint case is a *voluntary* bankruptcy case concerning a wife and husband."[135] Under § 303(a), by contrast, involuntary cases may be commenced only against "a person" who is an eligible debtor under the relevant chapter; that section is deafeningly silent as to any mention of permission to file also against a spouse. If petitioning creditors attempt to file a joint involuntary, the proper remedy is to dismiss the case as against the spouse.[136] However, some courts procedurally "cure" this defect by severing the joint involuntary case into two individual involuntary cases.[137]

Farmers (and family farmers) are excluded because of the practical concern that the cyclical nature of a farmer's business may expose even a relatively successful farmer to proof that the farmer is not paying his debts as they come due, and thus to the threat of involuntary bankruptcy. Thus, "one drought year or one year of low prices, as a result of which the farmer is temporarily unable to pay his creditors, should not subject him to involuntary bankruptcy."[138] Eleemosynary institutions, such as "churches, schools, and charitable organizations and foundations" (as the legislative

---

[132] H.R. Rep. No. 95–595, 95th Cong., 1st Sess., at 321–22 (1977).

[133] See, e.g., In re Marlar, 432 F.3d 813 (8th Cir. 2005); McCloy v. Silverthorne (In re McCloy), 296 F.3d 370 (5th Cir. 2002).

[134] See King v. Fidelity Nat'l Bank, 712 F.2d 188 (5th Cir. 1983), cert. denied, 465 U.S. 1029 (1984).

[135] H.R. Rep. No. 95–595, 95th Cong., 1st Sess., at 321 (1977); S. Rep. No. 95–989, 95th Cong., 1st Sess., at 32 (1978) (emphasis added).

[136] See, e.g., In re Calloway, 70 B.R. 175 (Bankr. N.D. Ind. 1986); In re Jones, 112 B.R. 770 (Bankr. E.D. Va. 1990); In re Busick, 719 F.2d 922 (7th Cir. 1983).

[137] See, e.g., In re Bowshier, 313 B.R. 232 (Bankr. S.D. Ohio 2004); In re Gale, 177 B.R. 531 (Bankr. E.D. Mich. 1995). See also In re Benny, 842 F.2d 1147 (9th Cir. 1988) (acknowledging that it lacked jurisdiction over involuntary joint petition, but finding jurisdictional defect cured when the couple voluntarily converted to chapter 11).

[138] H.R. Rep. No. 95–595, 95th Cong., 1st Sess., at 322 (1977).

history describes them),[139] likewise have long enjoyed an exemption from involuntary bankruptcy. Note, though, that the actual Code language (a "corporation that is not a moneyed, business, or commercial corporation") is not narrowly restricted to charitable institutions, notwithstanding the legislative history. For example, a country club would seem to qualify as an institution free from the threat of involuntary bankruptcy.

A possible de facto exemption from involuntary bankruptcy exists for an individual debtor who had a case dismissed in the prior 180 days in circumstances that would render that debtor ineligible to "be a debtor under this title" under § 109(g).[140] Nothing in the statutory language of § 109(g) limits its reach to voluntary cases, even though that was obviously the intent of Congress when it enacted the section in 1984 to curb abusive serial filings. If the literal reading holds, a debtor actually could concoct a personal immunity from bankruptcy for 180 days by intentionally tripping the § 109(g) bar.

The same problem does not exist regarding debtor ineligibility due to failure to obtain pre-bankruptcy credit counseling under § 109(h). According to the statutory language, the counseling requirement only applies for the 180–day period "preceding the date of filing *by such individual.*" That trigger, by definition, can never occur in an involuntary case. Nor logically could it: how would the debtor be prescient enough to go get *pre*-bankruptcy counseling in an involuntary case? And if the requirement were to apply in an involuntary case, then we would have the absurd result that involuntary cases against individual debtors would be impossible.

The conversion rules are consistent with the prohibition against involuntary cases against farmers and charities. Thus, a chapter 11 case may not be converted to chapter 7 absent a request by the farmer or not-for-profit debtor. § 1112(c). Nor may a chapter 13 case be converted to one under chapter 7, 11, or 12 unless the debtor farmer requests conversion. § 1307(e). No conversion prohibition is needed in chapter 13 for non-profit corporations, because corporations are ineligible for chapter 13 relief in the first place. Note, however, that a family farmer in chapter 12 does not enjoy absolute immunity from conversion to chapter 7 against his wishes; such relief is possible on a showing of fraud in connection with the case. § 1208(d).

§ 2.8   Limitations on Involuntary Relief: Eligible Petitioning Creditors

Involuntary cases are available because the debtor's self-interest in "pulling the trigger" and filing a bankruptcy case may not always mirror the creditors' need for a collective proceeding. Left solely to its own devices, the debtor may wait and act too late—or not at all—thereby forfeiting the potential benefits of the collective proceeding for the entire group of creditors. To avoid this problem, the bankruptcy law has always

---

[139] Id.

[140] See § 2.3.a. The court in *In re Corto*, 1995 WL 643372 (W.D.N.Y. 1995), dismissed an involuntary filed within 180 days after a dismissal that triggered § 109(g). However, the court also found that the involuntary filing was collusive and in bad faith (among the petitioners were the debtor's mother and son) and affirmed the bankruptcy court's dismissal on that basis. However, dicta in the court's opinion supported the view that the debtor could not be a debtor in any case within 180 days—whether voluntary or involuntary.

permitted creditors to take matters into their own hands and file a bankruptcy petition in appropriate circumstances. The goal is to make it easy for creditors to commence a bankruptcy case when needed, but to prevent creditors from improperly using the threat of involuntary bankruptcy as leverage against the debtor to obtain unwarranted advantages. The difficulty is in reconciling and balancing these often conflicting aims.

Section 303 governs involuntary filings. That section contains many checks and balances designed to implement the policies of allowing ready access but preventing creditor abuse. Most important are: (1) the limitations in § 303(b) on which parties are eligible to petition the court for involuntary relief, discussed in this section, and (2) the substantive grounds in § 303(h) for determining whether bankruptcy relief should be ordered, discussed in the next section.[141]

Eligibility to petition for involuntary bankruptcy is limited in three major respects:

(1) the petitioner must be a creditor (or represent creditors as an indenture trustee);

(2) the petitioners' claims must satisfy certain tests in nature and amount; and

(3) a minimum number of eligible petitioners must join in the request for relief. § 303(b).

First, only a creditor—the "holder of a claim"—may serve as a petitioning party. The only exception is for an indenture trustee who represents such a creditor. Thus, an impartial watchdog group (the United States trustee, for example) would lack standing to petition for involuntary bankruptcy. The creditor requirement establishes a self-interested nexus to the bankruptcy case, and thereby may help to police against misuse of the process.

A petitioning creditor must also be an "entity." Entity is broadly defined in the Code, encompassing "person, estate, trust, governmental unit, and United States trustee." § 101(15). Recall that only a "person" may be an eligible debtor. § 109(a). Thus, the class of prospective petitioning creditors is broader than the class of eligible debtors.

The second type of limitation on who is eligible to participate as a petitioning creditor concerns the nature and amount of the claims held by the petitioner. To begin with, a monetary floor is imposed. Not only must petitioners have a pecuniary stake in the outcome of the case to have standing, but that stake must be sufficiently substantial. For cases filed after April 1, 2013, all of the petitioning creditors counted together must hold a total of at least $15,325 in unsecured claims.[142]

---

[141] See § 2.9.

[142] Indexed adjustments to the dollar minimum are made every three years; the next adjustment is due in 2016. § 104(b). As originally enacted in 1978, the floor was $5,000.

Note that the Code does not require *each* petitioner to hold $15,325 in claims, but only that the entire group must claim that amount in the *aggregate*. § 303(b)(2). Furthermore, only *unsecured* claims count toward the dollar amount. This restriction is imposed because creditors with security are protected financially up to the value of their collateral, and (in theory at least) should not be affected by the outcome of the collective proceeding. Unsecured creditors, however, are directly impacted by the collective proceeding. If the debtor is insolvent, unsecured creditors are the primary residual stakeholders.

Note that the Code language does permit a secured creditor to count as one of the requisite number of petitioners. The only restriction is that the unsecured *total* of the petitioning creditors as a group meet the unsecured debt floor; there is no textual requirement that each such creditor hold an unsecured claim. Some courts, however, bar a *fully secured* creditor from counting as a petitioning creditor, and thus only count a secured creditor as a petitioner if that creditor's claim is unsecured at least in part, or if the creditor waives its security.[143] Clearly, the secured portion of the creditor's claim will not count toward the required total unsecured dollar amount. An undersecured claim is bifurcated into a secured portion and an unsecured portion, and only the unsecured portion is counted to satisfy the dollar requirement. To illustrate, a creditor with a total claim of $8,000, secured by collateral worth $5,000, has a $5,000 secured claim and a $3,000 unsecured claim ($8,000–$5,000), see § 506(a)(1); the $3,000 unsecured portion counts against the overall required floor.

The next important limitation is that a qualifying claim may not be "contingent as to liability." § 303(b)(1). Note that this requirement is more restrictive than the definition of "claim" found in the Code. § 101(5). A claim is considered contingent as to liability when the debtor's obligation to pay depends upon the occurrence of an extrinsic future event, reasonably within the contemplation of the debtor and the creditor at the time the claim arose.[144] The classic illustration is a guaranty on which the principal obligor has not yet defaulted. The guarantor's duty to pay is contingent on the principal's default; if that eventuality has not come to pass, the guarantor may not serve as a petitioning creditor. A claim is not "contingent," however, simply because it is unmatured, if no further events have to transpire for the duty to pay to arise, other than the passage of time. Nor is a claim contingent because it is not yet liquidated (a tort claim, for instance), or even because it is disputed by the debtor. The contingency must go to the fact of liability to be disqualifying; contingency merely as to amount will not bar the creditor.

The treatment of *disputed* claims has been a source of substantial controversy. Under the Code as originally enacted in 1978, creditors holding disputed claims were eligible to serve as petitioning creditors. This approach was consistent with the general policy Congress embraced in the 1978 reform to make it easier for creditors to bring an involuntary case. Courts would engage in a very limited preliminary inquiry to ensure that there was some potential basis to the creditor's claim; if there was, the creditor's

---

[143] See, e.g., In re James Plaza Joint Venture, 67 B.R. 445 (Bankr. S.D. Tex. 1986).

[144] The leading formulation of this test is found in *In re All Media Properties, Inc.*, 5 B.R. 126 (Bankr. S.D. Tex. 1980).

eligibility would be upheld.[145] Congress soon changed course, however, and in 1984 decided that this approach tilted the scales too heavily against the debtor, enabling creditors with disputed claims to use the threat of bankruptcy as a club to collect their claims.

In 1984 Congress thus changed § 303(b) to exclude from eligibility as a petitioning creditor the holder of a claim that is "the subject of a bona fide dispute." Congress did not define bona fide dispute, however. Note that the same "bona fide dispute" textual limitation is found in § 303(h)(1), which is one of the grounds for granting involuntary relief.[146] Although the same text is used in subsections (b) and (h) of § 303, it is important to recognize that the role of the bona fide dispute limitation differs in the two places.[147] Under subsection (b), if a sufficient "dispute" is found, the creditor is completely disqualified from serving as a petitioning creditor. In subsection (h), by comparison, the question is whether the disputed debt will count or not in the calculation of whether the debtor "generally not paying" its debts.

The game now is how to ascertain what constitutes a "bona fide dispute," and how that issue should be decided.[148] What are the competing policy concerns? On the one hand, a debtor should not be able to escape involuntary relief by the simple expedient of "disputing" the claim of every petitioning creditor. On the other hand, the bankruptcy court should not have to conduct a full trial on the merits of the petitioners' claims in order to decide the eligibility issue. After all, one of the functions of a bankruptcy case is to resolve creditors' claims; it does not make much sense to do that at the outset, in deciding whether to even have a bankruptcy case.

Courts accordingly must conduct a preliminary investigation into the merits of the claim if a dispute is alleged. The difference is the default rule. Before 1984, if the creditor had a colorable basis for its claim, they could be counted as a petitioning creditor. Now, if the debtor has a plausible basis in law or fact for disputing the claim, the creditor is barred. Courts require some objective basis in law or fact for disputing the claim to be asserted; the debtor's subjective belief in the invalidity of the claim is not enough.[149] The standard for applying the objective test often is framed in summary judgment terms. Many courts also invoke a burden-shifting approach, first requiring the petitioning creditor to establish a prima facie case for the validity of its claim, with the burden then shifting to the debtor to raise a bona fide dispute in fact or law.

The bar got higher for putative petitioning creditors in disputed debt cases in 2005. Congress amended § 303(b)(1) to exclude as eligible petitioning creditors a creditor whose claim is the subject of a bona fide dispute *as to liability or amount.* This change may prove most significant where the debtor asserts a counterclaim to the

---

[145] E.g., In re Covey, 650 F.2d 877 (7th Cir. 1981).

[146] See § 2.9.

[147] See In re Seko Invs., 156 F.3d 1005 (9th Cir. 1998); In re Focus Media, Inc., 378 F.3d 916 (9th Cir. 2004).

[148] An excellent discussion of this issue (under an earlier version of the Code) is found in Lawrence Ponoroff, Involuntary Bankruptcy and the Bone Fides of a Bona Fide Dispute, 65 Ind. L.J. 315 (1990).

[149] E.g., In re AMC Investors, LLC, 406 B.R. 478 (Bankr. D. Del. 2009). Even then, the counterclaim has to arise out of the same transaction or occurrence as the principal claim. See In re Seko Invs., 156 F.3d 1005 (9th Cir. 1998).

creditor's claim, but that counterclaim is for less than the full amount claimed by the petitioning creditor. Before 2005, a counterclaim would only disqualify the petitioner if it would serve as a complete defense to the claim. Now, however, *any* objectively colorable counterclaim or defense, no matter how small the amount involved, may knock out a putative petitioning creditor. One wonders if—and if so, why—Congress *really* meant for any objectively bona fide dispute as to amount, even if for a trifling sum, to disqualify an otherwise meritorious petitioning creditor. Assume, for example, that Debtor admittedly owes $25,000 for the purchase price of equipment it purchased from Creditor. Debtor, however, asserts a warranty counterclaim for $500. Even if Debtor were to prevail, it still then would owe Creditor $24,500. The 2005 amendments, though, seem to indicate that Creditor cannot serve as a petitioner, because there is a "bona fide dispute" as to whether it is owed $24,500 or $25,000.[150] Perhaps this is one of those "surely that can't be the law" situations.

The other significant petitioning creditor requirement is that the statutory minimum number of eligible petitioners must join in the request for relief. The rule is: if the debtor has 12 or more creditors, three petitioners are required; if less than 12, one petitioner will suffice. § 303(b)(1), (2). Why three? Strength in numbers. Requiring multiple petitioners limits the power of any one creditor to threaten a debtor with involuntary bankruptcy, and lends credibility to the actual necessity for the filing. If few creditors exist, however, there is less danger of harmful abuse, and obtaining three petitioners might be difficult.

The three-creditor rule may not be skirted by assigning claims to entities willing to join as petitioners. If a petitioning creditor acquired its claim by assignment, it must sign a statement affirming that "the claim was not transferred for the purpose of commencing the case." Rule 1003(a).

Twelve is not always twelve, however. It is quite possible that all creditors of the debtor might not be counted toward the 12–creditor total. Excluded are employees of the debtor, insiders of the debtor, and the transferees of transfers that would be voidable in bankruptcy (e.g., the recipients of preferences or fraudulent transfers shortly before the bankruptcy filing). § 303(b)(2). The rationale for these exclusions is that such entities would be unlikely to favor a bankruptcy filing and thus would probably not join as petitioning creditors; accordingly, it would be unfair to count them against the creditor total to the prejudice of parties who might be interested in filing. Some courts have also carved out a "de minimis" exception and do not count the holders of small recurring claims (such as utility bills),[151] although there is no statutory basis in the Code for that approach.

A problem under the numerosity requirement has been the question of when it is permissible for creditors to *join* later as petitioners and cure an initial deficiency in

---

[150] One court found that the sole creditor of a corporation had a claim subject to a bona fide dispute when the potential magnitude of the claim varied by hundreds of thousands of dollars, even though the petitioner asserted that its claim was so large that no matter the resolution of the dispute it would be in excess of $13,475 (now $15,325). See In re Mountain Dairies, Inc., 372 B.R. 623 (Bankr. S.D.N.Y. 2007).

[151] See, e.g., In re Smith, 243 B.R. 169 (Bankr. N.D. Ga. 1999); In re Smith, 123 B.R. 423 (Bankr. M.D. Fla. 1990). But see In re Fischer, 202 B.R. 341 (Bankr. E.D.N.Y. 1996) (holding *de minimis* claims should not be excluded for determining number of petitioning creditors).

number. The three-creditor rule is not jurisdictional, and can be waived, even if the debtor has twelve or more creditors. The Code provides that, before a case is dismissed, an eligible creditor "may join in the petition with the same effect as if such joining creditor were [an original] petitioning creditor." § 303(c). That joinder will then cure any numerical deficiency. Furthermore, the Bankruptcy Rules state that "the court shall afford a reasonable opportunity for other creditors to join" if fewer than three creditors file originally and the debtor's answer shows that there are twelve or more creditors. Rule 1003(b). Do these provisions for free joinder thus mean that a single creditor may file an involuntary petition with impunity, and hope to persuade additional creditors to join later? Not necessarily. Some courts hold that a single-creditor petition is permissible only if that petitioner had a good faith but mistaken belief that the debtor had fewer than twelve qualifying creditors.[152] If the petitioner knew the debtor had twelve or more creditors, joinder will not be permitted (notwithstanding the language of § 303(c)), the case will be dismissed, and the petitioner will be liable for the debtor's damages.[153] A competing view rejects this bar-to-joinder doctrine, however, and permits free joinder irrespective of the initial petitioner's state of mind.[154]

Partnership cases are governed by a special rule. § 303(b)(3). All general partners normally must consent to the filing of a voluntary case on behalf of the partnership. Rule 1004(a). If fewer than all of the general partners file a bankruptcy petition on behalf of the partnership, the case is treated as an involuntary petition, § 303(b)(3)(A), and the non-filing general partners may contest the entry of involuntary relief. The other basis for an involuntary filing is that if bankruptcy relief has been ordered against all of the general partners in their individual capacity, an involuntary filing may be made against the partnership itself by one general partner or the trustee of a general partner, or just by the holder of a claim against the partnership. § 303(b)(3)(B).

§ 2.9   Grounds for Involuntary Relief

The heart of the involuntary bankruptcy rules is found in the substantive grounds for ordering bankruptcy relief. The bases upon which creditors can put a debtor into bankruptcy against its wishes define in a fundamental way the precise balance of power between the debtor and creditors, and dictate whether access to bankruptcy will be granted readily or only in extreme cases. Furthermore, the extent to which creditors have the power to choose the bankruptcy option impacts the dealings between the debtor and creditors outside of bankruptcy. The threat of involuntary bankruptcy has been described as a "fleet in being,"[155] the analogy being to the added negotiating power held by a country that can call on a powerful naval fleet if negotiations fail. Thus, if creditors can easily place a debtor into involuntary bankruptcy, the

---

[152] See, e.g., In re Smith, 243 B.R. 169 (Bankr. N.D. Ga. 1999).

[153] E.g., Basin Elec. Power Coop. v. Midwest Processing Co., 769 F.2d 483 (8th Cir. 1985), cert. denied, 474 U.S. 1083 (1986). Accord Atlas Mach. & Iron Works, Inc. v. Bethlehem Steel Corp., 986 F.2d 709 (4th Cir. 1992).

[154] E.g., In re Kidwell, 158 B.R. 203 (Bankr. E.D. Cal. 1993). Accord Fetner v. Hagerty, 99 F.3d 1180 (D.C. Cir. 1997).

[155] Hearings on H.R. 31 and H.R. 32 Before the Subcomm. On Civil and Constitutional Rights of the House Comm. On the Judiciary, 94th Cong., 1st Sess., Ser. 27, pt. 1, at 396 (1975) (describing the process as a "force towards mutual accommodation").

negotiations that are carried out in the shadow of bankruptcy are shaped by the rules that would potentially apply in the event bankruptcy is invoked. Ideally, the grounds for involuntary bankruptcy would be precisely tailored, so that creditors could place into bankruptcy all debtors who belonged there, and none who did not.

Under the prior Bankruptcy Act (and every Anglo–American bankruptcy law since 1543, for that matter), creditors could place a debtor into involuntary bankruptcy only on proof that the debtor had committed an "*act of bankruptcy*" in the preceding four months. Bankruptcy Act of 1898, § 3. Acts of bankruptcy included such things as making a fraudulent conveyance, giving a preference, or making an assignment for the benefit of creditors. These acts supposedly signified a debtor whose financial affairs were "in extremis" and whose creditors were at risk. In practice, however, acts of bankruptcy served as a poor indicator of the need for bankruptcy relief, and discovery and proof of the requisite acts were difficult. Many debtors who needed to be in bankruptcy either escaped bankruptcy altogether, or did not go in until long after effective relief was possible. In the 1978 Code, Congress finally took to heart the longstanding criticisms of the whole concept of acts of bankruptcy,[156] and in a single dramatic stroke abolished acts of bankruptcy as the basis for an adjudication of involuntary bankruptcy.[157]

In place of acts of bankruptcy, Congress provided two alternative grounds for involuntary bankruptcy in § 303(h): (1) that the debtor is generally not paying its debts as they become due, or (2) that a custodian was appointed for substantially all of the debtor's assets within the preceding 120 days. This dramatic change in the law was designed to make it easier for creditors to commence an involuntary bankruptcy case, and simplified the proof needed for involuntary bankruptcy. The new grounds attempt to capture more precisely the situations in which a collective bankruptcy proceeding would be necessary and beneficial, namely, when the debtor's financial failure has become general, affecting the body of creditors as a whole. Proof of a pervasive failure to pay debts as they come due in theory signifies such a general financial failure.

The second ground, appointment of a custodian, is but a specific illustration of the probable existence of the first ground; as the legislative history notes, "If a custodian of all or substantially all of the property of the debtor has been appointed, this paragraph creates an irrebuttable presumption that the debtor is unable to pay its debts as they mature."[158] In addition, the second ground gives creditors the right to have a collective proceeding regarding the debtor conducted in the bankruptcy court and under the federal bankruptcy laws. Thus, creditors are usually able to preempt a non-bankruptcy collective proceeding, which leads to the result that such non-bankruptcy proceedings often end up largely mirroring bankruptcy cases; otherwise, disadvantaged creditors would be able to throw the matter into bankruptcy court. This right of creditors is limited in part by the possibility that the bankruptcy court might abstain from hearing

---

[156] See, e.g., Report of the Comm. on the Bankr. Laws, H.R. Doc. No. 137, 93d Cong., 1st Sess. 186–89 (pt. I) (1973); Israel Treiman,Acts of Bankruptcy: A Medieval Concept in Modern Bankruptcy Law, 52 Harv. L. Rev. 189 (1938).

[157] H.R. Rep. No. 95–595, 95th Cong., 1st Sess., at 321 (1977) ("This bill abolishes the concept of Acts of Bankruptcy. The only basis for an involuntary case will be the inability of the debtor to meet its debts.").

[158] H.R. Rep. No. 95–595, 95th Cong., 1st Sess., at 323 (1977).

the bankruptcy case under § 305, if doing so would better serve the interests of creditors and the debtor.[159] Courts typically only abstain in rare cases,[160] however, such as when an out-of-court proceeding is almost completed.[161]

Most of the difficult litigation comes in applying the first ground, that the debtor is generally not paying its debts as they become due.[162] This test is a variant of the venerable "equity insolvency" test used in numerous commercial law settings. The only difference is that the traditional formulation of equity insolvency focuses on the debtor's *ability* to pay, while the Code limits its inquiry to whether the debtor is *in fact* paying its debts.

Several common problems arise in applying this test. First, § 303(h)(1) excludes from the debt-paying calculation debts that "are the subject of a bona fide dispute." In 2005, Congress added the further limitation that unpaid debts cannot be counted against the debtor if the dispute concerns "liability or amount." What constitutes a bona fide dispute is far from clear.[163] The same limitation is encountered in determining whether a creditor is eligible to petition for involuntary bankruptcy under § 303(b), although, as noted in the preceding section,[164] the two provisions serve different functions, and courts do not necessarily interpret them in the same way.[165] Second, courts have struggled to ascertain when a failure to pay debts has become sufficiently "general" to justify ordering bankruptcy relief.

The disputed debt situation implicates conflicting concerns. On the one hand, if disputed debts are counted as debts that the debtor is "not paying," the debtor may be pressured into paying debts that it does not believe it owes just to avoid being thrown into bankruptcy. On the other hand, if the debtor can dream up enough of a dispute to disqualify the debt from the involuntary bankruptcy calculation, the debtor can steer clear of bankruptcy court even if the debtor is in fact a prime candidate for a collective proceeding. At the extremes, there is no question how to resolve the problem: a debt that is obviously not owed should not be counted, and a debt that is owed should count. The problem is how to deal with the gray area in the middle, and to balance the competing interests of the debtor and the body of creditors.[166]

Also of concern is how much court effort should be devoted to deciding the disputed debt question. While in theory the bankruptcy court could actually adjudicate

---

[159] See § 2.19.

[160] See, e.g., In re Century/ML Cable Venture, 294 B.R. 9 (Bankr. S.D.N.Y. 2003) ("[Abstention] is a form of extraordinary relief . . . that should only be utilized under extraordinary circumstances.").

[161] In fact, one court stated that courts should *only* abstain if the debtor and its creditors are able to work out a less expensive out-of-court arrangement. In re Gurley, 222 B.R. 124 (Bankr. W.D. Tenn. 1998).

[162] In re Green Hills Dev. Co., LLC, 445 B.R. 647 (Bankr. S.D. Miss. 2011) ("The Code does not define the term "generally not paying," and courts have had to fashion their own definition.").

[163] See Lawrence Ponoroff, Involuntary Bankruptcy and the Bone Fides of a Bona Fide Dispute, 65 Ind. L.J. 315 (1990).

[164] See § 2.8.

[165] See, e.g., In re Seko Invs., 156 F.3d 1005 (9th Cir. 1998).

[166] One court attempted to balance both interests by: (1) deciding whether a debt is included in the calculation to begin with, considering the reasons why the debtor disputed the debt; and (2) once the debt amount is calculated, not considering reasons why debt is not being paid when determining whether debtor is generally paying debts as they become due. In re R.N. Salem Corp., 29 B.R. 424 (Bankr. S.D. Ohio 1983).

every disputed claim, and definitively cast each claim into the "valid claim" or "invalid claim" category, and then make the "generally not paying" calculation, to do so would require the expenditure of enormous judicial resources. Even more fundamentally, such an approach would usurp a considerable part of the function of the bankruptcy case: much of what goes on in a bankruptcy case involves the determination of claims. Accordingly, bankruptcy courts typically conduct only a preliminary, summary inquiry into the merits of the dispute over a particular debt.[167]

The decision by Congress in 1978 to make involuntary bankruptcy relief more readily available would suggest that the default rule should be in favor of counting the disputed debt as one that is not being paid, and thus in favor of the interest of creditors in commencing the proceeding. Until 1984, the courts generally did count disputed debts, unless: (1) the dispute went to the very existence of the claim, and not just the amount; (2) resolution of the dispute would not require substantial litigation; and (3) the debtor's interest in avoiding relief outweighed the creditors' interest in a rapid determination.[168]

In 1984, however, Congress changed its mind, and expressly excluded from the "generally not paying" calculation those debts that are the subject of a bona fide dispute. Congress was concerned that the previous approach gave creditors too much power and confronted debtors with an unfair dilemma. The 1984 amendment effectively changed the default rule in the case of a dispute. Now, if the debtor disputes a debt, most courts will conduct something like a mini-trial to determine the bona fides of the dispute, both on the law and the facts; if the debtor's dispute survives this preliminary inquiry, the debt will be excluded.

The 2005 amendment, which added the further qualification that a disputed debt cannot be counted if the dispute goes to "liability *or amount*," strengthens the debtor's hand even further. As with the like amendment to the petitioning creditor eligibility rule in § 303(b), courts will have to decide if Congress really intended to exclude an entire debt from the "generally not paying" calculation if the debtor disputes some part of that debt but admits liability. Consider the example used in the preceding section, where Debtor admittedly owes Creditor $25,000 for the unpaid purchase price of equipment, but Debtor also asserts a disputed $500 warranty counterclaim regarding that equipment. The only "bona fide dispute," then, goes to Debtor's counterclaim, and thus whether Debtor is "not paying" a debt of $24,500 or a debt of $25,000. The most sensible result would be to count the undisputed unpaid amount of $24,500 against the debtor in making the "generally not paying" calculation. Before the 2005 amendment, that certainly would have been the result. But the language of the Code after 2005 might not permit any part of the partially disputed debt to be counted. The statute says that involuntary relief is to be ordered "if the debtor is generally not paying such debtor's debts as such debts become due *unless such debts are the subject of a bona fide dispute as to . . . amount.*" That language suggests complete exclusion of "such debts" that are disputed only "as to amount." Possibly a court could try to escape this

---

[167] See., e.g., In re Byrd, 357 F.3d 433 (4th Cir. 2004) ("The bankruptcy court need not resolve the merits of the bona fide dispute, but simply determine whether one exists.").

[168] E.g., In re Covey, 650 F.2d 877 (7th Cir. 1981).

incongruous result by treating the purchase price debt and the warranty counterclaim as distinct "such debts," but the problem with that sleight of hand is that they really are not readily severable: they arise out of the same transaction, and the amount Debtor owes Creditor for the purchase price is inextricably bound up in the resolution of the counterclaim.[169]

An even more obvious example in which it appears that post–2005 the Debtor would not have a disputed debt counted against it is where the debt is for an unliquidated tort claim and liability is conceded, but the amount of damages has not been determined and is disputed. Assume, for example, that Debtor negligently damaged Creditor's property, and admits liability for such negligence, but no judgment has been entered, and Debtor refuses to pay Creditor anything and disputes the amount of damages. On such facts, the unpaid debt almost certainly cannot be counted in the "generally not paying" calculation.

Most contested involuntary petitions turn on the issue of whether the debtor's failure to pay undisputed debts when due is *general*." Courts look at a number of factors, but eschew any strict mathematical tests as to the necessary percentage or amount of unpaid debts.[170] Preliminarily, the petitioning creditors must establish when the debtor's debts are "due," considering the terms and practices of the relevant industry. Then, courts will weigh: (1) the number and percentage of unpaid debts; (2) the amount of those unpaid debts, both in total dollars and in proportion to the total debt outstanding; (3) the average age of the unpaid debts, i.e., how long they have gone unpaid; and (4) the debtor's overall conduct of its financial affairs.[171] Typically the debtor's failure to pay a single debt will not suffice, although nonpayment of one debt could be enough if that single debt comprises a sufficiently large percentage of the total debts.[172] The calculation of "generally not paying" is made as of the time of the filing of the bankruptcy petition.[173] Thus, the debtor cannot escape entry of an order for bankruptcy relief by paying debts postpetition; this rule also limits any incentive for creditors to use an involuntary filing as a means to coerce a debtor into paying a debt.

§ 2.10 Operations in the "Gap"

In a voluntary bankruptcy case, the filing of the petition by the debtor instantaneously and automatically constitutes the entry of the "order for relief," meaning that the bankruptcy case will proceed. § 301. The same is not true in an

---

[169] But see In re Skyworks Ventures, Inc., 431 B.R. 573 (Bankr. D.N.J. 2010) (citing pre-BAPCPA cases for the contention that claims are not subject to a bona fide dispute simply because of an unrelated counterclaim against a petitioning creditor, unless the counterclaim arises out of the same transaction as the underlying claim).

[170] See, e.g., In re Norris, 183 B.R. 437 (Bankr. W.D. La. 1995) (rejecting a pure mathematical test to determine whether debtor was generally paying its debts as they became due). But see In re ELRS Loss Mitigation, LLC, 325 B.R. 604 (Bankr. N.D. Okla. 2005).

[171] See In re Harmsen, 320 B.R. 188 (B.A.P. 10th Cir. 2005) (noting that Congress, by not defining the term "generally," avoids a mechanical test and allows courts the ability to deal with a variety of situations as they are presented).

[172] See, e.g., In re Euro–American Lodging Corp, 357 B.R. 700 (Bankr. S.D.N.Y. 2007). See also Fed. Fin. Co. v. DeKaron Corp., 261 B.R. 61 (S.D. Fla. 2001) (addressing situation where debtor only had one outstanding creditor, thus holding it possible to be found "not generally paying" its debts as they came due).

[173] See, e.g., In re VitaminSpice, 472 B.R. 282 (Bankr. E.D. Pa. 2012).

involuntary case; the filing of the petition by the creditors does not constitute the entry of an order for relief. Instead, the bankruptcy court will only order relief after proof of one of the substantive grounds in § 303(h), or if the petition is not timely controverted by the debtor. In other words, in an involuntary case the commencement of the case, by the filing of the petition, is separated in theory and in time from the entry of the order for relief by the court. This separation creates a "gap" period. The Code spells out the respective rights of the debtor and the creditors during this gap period.

Although filing an involuntary petition against a debtor does not automatically constitute an "order for relief," the mere filing of the involuntary petition does "commence" the bankruptcy case, which causes some important consequences. § 303(b). First, creditor collection actions are automatically stayed. § 362(a). Second, the debtor's property becomes "property of the estate." § 541(a). The ramifications of these results are discussed in subsequent chapters.

The debtor's interest during the gap period is to be allowed to continue with business as usual. Prior to the entry of an order for relief by the court, nothing has been proven; the mere fact that the petitioning creditors have alleged that this debtor should be in bankruptcy does not make it so. The default rule during the gap period is in the debtor's favor: the debtor may continue to operate its business without the need for court authorization, and the debtor may use, acquire, or dispose of property freely, as if the case had not been commenced. § 303(f). The rules in § 363 limiting the ability of the trustee (or debtor in possession) to use, sell, or lease property of the bankruptcy estate do not apply during the gap period.

The debtor's freedom during the gap period may not be absolute, however. The petitioning creditors may have commenced the involuntary case in part because of a concern that the debtor would dissipate assets, make preferential transfers, or in some other way pose a financial risk to creditors that could best be dealt with under the auspices of a collective bankruptcy proceeding. If the debtor retains complete freedom to deal with its property during the gap period, the creditors' fears that motivated the involuntary filing might be realized before the court can order relief; colloquially, the belated entry of the order for relief would then be analogous to "locking the barn after the horse is gone." Such a result would undermine the point of the whole shift in the 1978 Code to make it easier for creditors to bring an involuntary case at an earlier point in time, when effective relief can still be given.

Congress resolved this concern by giving the bankruptcy court the power to enter orders limiting the debtor's freedom of action during the gap period. § 303(f). If the court does nothing, the rule, as stated above, is that the debtor may continue its business without interruption and deal freely with its property. However, on proof of the need for a limiting order, usually on the ground that there is some danger to assets, the court has the power to restrict the debtor's freedom, as necessary, to run its business and manage its property. § 303(g). For example, the court may require prior court approval of expenditures over a certain amount, or of transactions outside the ordinary course of business.

In some cases, even a limiting order may not be enough to mollify the creditors' reasonable fears and adequately guard against the risk to creditors posed by the debtor's continued possession of its property and management of its business. In a chapter 7 case, if "necessary to preserve the property of the estate or to prevent loss to the estate," the court may order the appointment of a trustee to take possession of the property and to operate the debtor's business. § 303(g).[174] A trustee also may be appointed in an involuntary chapter 11 case, on proof of one of the grounds for a trustee found in chapter 11 itself, such as "cause, including fraud, dishonesty, incompetence, or gross mismanagement." § 1104(a)(1).

Since the dispossession of the debtor prior to proof of a ground for involuntary bankruptcy is an extreme measure, a trustee may only be appointed on request of a party in interest, after notice to the debtor, the petitioning creditors, and the United States trustee, and a hearing. § 303(g), Rule 2001(a). Furthermore, the movant must furnish a bond in an amount approved by the court, conditioned to indemnify the debtor for possible monetary recoveries under § 303(i) if the case is dismissed. Rule 2001(b). Even after a trustee is appointed and takes possession of the property, the debtor may recover the property by posting a bond conditioned on accounting for and delivering that property (or its value) to a trustee if an order for relief is subsequently entered. § 303(g).

Creditors thus may be protected during the gap period from a danger to the debtor's property or business. Another issue of importance to creditors during the gap period concerns the rights they have with regard to claims which are paid or incurred in that time. Note that creditors often may not even be aware that an involuntary petition has been filed, and recall that the presumptive rule is that the debtor may continue to operate its business. The Code thus must attempt to deal fairly with individual creditors that do business with the debtor during the gap, but still preserve the rights of the entire body of creditors in the event bankruptcy relief is ordered.

A creditor who extends credit during the gap period to the debtor in the ordinary course of the debtor's business or financial affairs is deemed to have a claim against the bankruptcy estate, § 502(f), and is granted a third priority in the payment of claims out of the estate in the event an order for relief later is entered. § 507(a)(3). The only types of expense that will be paid ahead of the creditor's third priority gap claim are first priority domestic support obligations, § 507(a)(1), and second priority administrative expenses that arise during the administration of the bankruptcy case itself, after the entry of the order for relief. §§ 507(a)(2), 503(b).

This protection only extends to claims that actually arise after the commencement of the case by the filing of the involuntary petition. If the creditor's claim arose *before* the bankruptcy petition was filed, the creditor has only a general unsecured claim, and will not be entitled to priority in the bankruptcy distribution. Furthermore, if such a prepetition claim is actually paid during the involuntary gap period, the creditor will have to return that payment to the bankruptcy estate if an order for relief later is entered. § 549(a), (b). Otherwise that creditor would be better off than other prepetition general creditors who were not paid during the gap period. If a transferee of estate property during the gap period gives value in exchange for that property, however, it

---

[174] If the putative debtor is also an individual, the activities that form a basis for appointment of a trustee mi also result in a denial of discharge. See 11 U.S.C. § 707(a)(2)–(4).

will not have to return the property to the estate if relief is ordered.[175] § 549(b). The satisfaction of an antecedent debt does not constitute new value, however.[176]

§ 2.11 Procedure in Involuntary Cases

The order for relief is not entered automatically in an involuntary case. Relief will only be ordered if the debtor fails to timely controvert the involuntary petition, or if the petitioning creditors prove the existence of one of the substantive grounds for involuntary relief. § 303(h).

Most involuntary cases are commenced by the filing of the petition by the petitioning creditors. § 303(b)(1), (2). The petition is filed with the bankruptcy clerk, Rule 1002(a), and must be accompanied by the prescribed filing fee. Rule 1006(a). The petitioners must verify the petition's allegations under penalty of perjury. In a case involving a partnership debtor, the case is commenced by the filing of a petition by fewer than all of the general partners. § 303(b)(3). In an international case, the estate's foreign representative in the foreign proceeding concerning the debtor may file a petition to commence an involuntary case in the United States against the debtor. § 303(b)(4).

After the petition is filed the clerk issues a summons for service. The summons, along with a copy of the petition, is then served on the debtor. Rule 1010. Service may be in person or by mail, and nationwide service is authorized. Rule 7004. In rare cases, service by publication is allowed. In a partnership case, the petitioning partners must send a copy of the petition to nonpetitioning general partners, and the clerk issues a summons, which is then served on the nonpetitioners. Rule 1004.

The debtor has 21 days after service to file a responsive pleading contesting the petition. Rule 1011(a), (b). In partnership cases, a nonpetitioning general partner may contest the petition. Rule 1011(a). Note that the petition may not be challenged by any of the following: other creditors (even though some creditors might have an incentive to avoid a bankruptcy case, such as those who have received a preference); a custodian of the debtor's assets (who might prefer that the nonbankruptcy receivership continue); the Securities and Exchange Commission; or the United States trustee (who does receive a copy of the petition, Rule 1002(b)). Intervention by interested parties is permitted in accordance with Federal Rule of Civil Procedure 24, however.

The Bankruptcy Rules limit what can be pled in the answer to the petition. Rule 1011. Defenses and objections to the allegations of the petition itself can of course be pled. Rule 1011(b). These defenses typically would go to the substantive allegations peculiar to § 303. Thus, for example, the debtor could assert that it was generally paying its debts as they became due. Federal Rule of Civil Procedure 12(b) defenses may be asserted, and will extend the time for the responsive pleading in accordance

---

[175] Note that § 549(b) does not require a simultaneous exchange of value for estate property. E.g., In re Pucci Shoes, Inc., 120 F.3d 38, 41 (4th Cir. 1997) ("The plain language of § 549(b) imposes no requirement that the value provided and the property of the bankruptcy estate be exchanged simultaneously. Instead, § 549(b) requires only that the property and the value be exchanged during the gap period.")

[176] See, e.g., In re Williams Contract Furniture, Inc., 148 B.R. 805 (Bankr. E.D. Va. 1992).

with Civil Rule 12(a). Rule 1011(c). The answer may not assert a claim against a petitioning creditor, except for the purpose of defeating the petition. Rule 1011(d). No other pleadings are permitted, except the court may order a reply to an answer. Rule 1011(e).

If fewer than three creditors file the involuntary petition under § 303(b)(2), the debtor might answer that it has a total of twelve or more creditors, thus necessitating three petitioning creditors. The debtor in its answer must then file a list of all of its creditors, including their addresses, a brief statement of the nature of the claims, and the amount thereof. Rule 1003(b). If it appears that there are twelve or more creditors, then Rule 1003(b) provides that "the court shall afford a reasonable opportunity for other creditors to join in the petition," which would cure the defect in the number of petitioning creditors as permitted by § 303(c). The debtor's disclosure of the names and addresses of its creditors gives the original petitioning creditors useful information to solicit joining petitioners. Recall, however, that some courts bar joinder in this situation if the original petitioners did not have a reasonable, good faith belief that the debtor had fewer than twelve creditors.[177]

The parties may engage in discovery in accordance with the Federal Rules of Civil Procedure that govern discovery. Rule 1018. In addition, a special Bankruptcy Rule allows the court to order the examination of any entity, at any time, on such conditions as the court may impose. Rule 2004.

Speed is of the essence in resolving the merits of a contested involuntary petition. If bankruptcy relief is appropriate, then sooner is better than later. One of the primary goals of Congress in rewriting the involuntary provisions in 1978 was to permit creditors to trigger a bankruptcy case as early as possible, in order to facilitate the possibility of efficacious relief. Furthermore, if bankruptcy relief is not merited, then it is in the debtor's interest to be out from under the cloud of bankruptcy as soon as possible. Accordingly, the Rules direct the bankruptcy court to "determine the issues of a contested petition at the earliest practicable time and forthwith enter an order for relief, dismiss the petition, or enter any other appropriate order." Rule 1013(a). In the event a responsive pleading is not filed within the time specified by the Rules, the court must enter an order for relief "on the next day, or as soon thereafter as practicable." Rule 1013(b).

Under the prior Bankruptcy Act, a debtor against whom an involuntary petition was filed had a right to a jury trial. Bankruptcy Act of 1898, § 19. The Code withdrew the debtor's absolute entitlement to trial by jury. Now, the statute expressly provides that the "district court may order the issues arising under [§ 303] to be tried without a jury." 28 U.S.C. § 1411(b). Thus, a jury trial is only granted in the exercise of the court's discretion. Because of the need for expedition in deciding involuntary petitions, and because of the doubts surrounding whether the non-Article III bankruptcy judge

---

[177] See § 2.8. Compare Basin Elec. Power Coop. v. Midwest Processing Co., 769 F.2d 483 (8th Cir. 1985), cert. denied, 474 U.S. 1083 (1986) (joinder barred), with In re FKF Madison Park Group Owner, LLC, 435 B.R. 906 (Bankr. D. Del. 2010) (joinder permitted); In re Kidwell, 158 B.R. 203 (Bankr. E.D. Cal. 1993) (same).

may conduct a jury trial,[178] involuntary cases are almost invariably tried without a jury. This approach does not offend the Seventh Amendment, because the adjudication of an involuntary petition is a form of equitable relief, rather than an action at law.

§ 2.12   Ramifications When Bankruptcy Relief Is Not Ordered

After an involuntary petition is filed, there are two possible ultimate outcomes: the court may dismiss the petition, or the court may enter an order for relief. § 303(h), (i), (j), Rule 1013. In the latter event, the bankruptcy case goes forward. If the court dismisses the petition, however, the bankruptcy case is terminated, with all of the accompanying effects of dismissal, such as the revesting of property.[179] § 349.

The petition might be dismissed either because of (1) a successful contest by the debtor or (2) the consent of all parties, subject to court approval. One way the debtor may achieve a dismissal is by challenging the petitioning creditors themselves, by showing that the eligibility requirements in § 303(b) have not been satisfied. For example, the debtor may establish that one of the necessary petitioners held a disputed claim, or may show that the initial filing was by fewer than the required three petitioners and in bad faith. If the petitioners' eligibility stands up, the debtor still may defeat the petition if the petitioning creditors fail to carry their burden of proving one of the substantive grounds for relief in § 303(h).[180] Thus, if the petitioners cannot prove that the debtor was generally not paying its debts as they became due, or that a general custodian was appointed, the court will dismiss the petition.

In rare cases the court will dismiss or suspend the case even if the petitioners were eligible and could prove a ground for relief. Such a dismissal or suspension, called abstention, must be predicated on a finding that "the interests of creditors and the debtor would be better served" by dismissal.[181] § 305(a)(1). For example, a court might abstain if an out-of-court workout has been almost completed, and a handful of creditors who are dissatisfied with the terms of the workout file an involuntary petition.

The petitioning creditors may agree to dismiss the petition. Significantly, though, the petitioners do not have an unfettered right to dismiss, as they would in a standard civil lawsuit. In a real sense, once an involuntary petition is filed, the petitioning creditors lose ultimate control of the process. Since bankruptcy is a collective proceeding, for the benefit of the entire body of creditors, the creditors who choose to petition for bankruptcy are acting as representatives of all creditors. If a petitioner fails to prosecute a petition, or moves to dismiss the petition, or even if all petitioners join with the debtor to request dismissal, dismissal will not automatically be granted. Before the court will dismiss the case, 21 days' notice must be sent out to all creditors and the United States trustee. § 303(j); Rules 1017(a), 2002(a)(4), (k). Any noticed party may then appear at the hearing on dismissal and oppose dismissal. This limitation on voluntary dismissal prevents creditors from using involuntary

---

[178] See § 4.8.b.

[179] See § 2.18.

[180] See § 2.9.

[181] See § 2.19.

bankruptcy as a means to collect a contested debt. Furthermore, creditors should be aware that abusing the bankruptcy system to obtain an advantage is a federal crime, punishable by up to 5 years in prison and a fine. 18 U.S.C. § 152.

If all petitioners and the debtor consent to dismissal, and the court orders dismissal after notice as described above, the bankruptcy case is over and the petitioners are not subject to any sanctions.[182] If, however, the court dismisses the petition on any basis other than the consent of the debtor and all the petitioning creditors, then monetary sanctions might be imposed against the petitioners. § 303(i). This remedy thus is available if the debtor successfully contests an involuntary petition, or if the petition is dismissed for want of prosecution or on motion of a petitioner. Monetary sanctions will not be imposed if the debtor waives the right to such judgment. In addition, the court will not enter judgment under § 303(i) if the court chooses to abstain from hearing the bankruptcy case under § 305(a)(1). Otherwise, however, the court has discretion to award the debtor its costs and reasonable attorney's fees, even against a petitioner that filed the petition in good faith. § 303(i)(1). If the debtor can prove that a petitioner acted in bad faith, the court then may enter judgment for any damages proximately caused by the filing, as well as punitive damages. § 303(i)(2). The remedies specified in § 303(i) are cumulative. Actual damages might include loss of business caused by the bankruptcy filing.[183] Prior to dismissal of the petition, the court, on a showing of cause, may order the petitioners to post a bond to indemnify the debtor for possible later recoveries under § 303(i). § 303(e).

In 2005, Congress added new protections for individual debtors if an involuntary case is dismissed. § 303(l). In such a case, the court may prohibit consumer reporting agencies from making any consumer report that contains information regarding the involuntary filing. § 303(l)(2). The idea is that individuals should not have their credit hurt because of an unsuccessful attempt to throw them into involuntary bankruptcy. In addition, if the petition is "false or contains any materially false, fictitious, or fraudulent statement," the court on the debtor's motion shall seal all court records relating to the petition. § 303(l)(1). Finally, the debtor can move to have the court expunge all records relating to the involuntary petition, upon a showing of good cause. § 303(l)(3). This relief can only be ordered after the expiration of the statute of limitations for bankruptcy crimes under Title 18. Congress was apparently motivated in part to create these new protections for dismissed involuntary debtors by the example of one tax protestor filing involuntary bankruptcy petitions against 36 local officials in Wisconsin, which caused numerous credit problems for the victims.[184]

---

[182] But note, one court held that the mere fact that a petitioning creditor acquiesced in a putative debtors' motion to dismiss an involuntary petition filed against it did not automatically preclude an award of attorney fees against the creditor, on the theory that the dismissal was "on consent" of all parties. In re Express Car & Truck Rental, Inc., 440 B.R. 422 (Bankr. E.D. Pa. 2010).

[183] H.R. Rep. No. 95–595, 95th Cong., 1st Sess., at 324 (1977).

[184] H.R. Rep. No. 109–31 (pt. 1), 109th Cong., 1st Sess., at 85 (2005).

D. DISMISSAL

§ 2.13   Dismissal: Overview

Other than some modest eligibility rules,[185] there are very few restrictions on a debtor's ability to commence a bankruptcy case on a voluntary basis. The debtor generally is free to file, whether or not there is much to be gained from a collective proceeding for the debtor. In the United States system, the real sorting of whether bankruptcy relief is warranted in voluntary cases comes not through the eligibility rules, but through dismissal. In involuntary cases, § 303 has detailed screening mechanisms in place to determine whether bankruptcy relief should be ordered in the first place.[186]

For individual debtors, the question usually is whether they in fact need the "fresh start" that the bankruptcy discharge can provide, and, related thereto, whether they should have to repay creditors out of future earnings in order to receive the discharge blessing. In 2005, Congress added more stringent tests for "abuse" to screen out of chapter 7 those individual debtors with sufficient payment capacity.[187] Otherwise, individual debtors are subject to dismissal principally only for "cause."[188] In addition, in BAPCPA Congress created some new dismissal provisions in § 521 designed to put teeth in the requirements that individual debtors file various financial schedules and other information at the outset of the case.[189]

Corporate debtors, being inanimate creations of the law, do not need a fresh start in the way that human beings do. There is no reason to permit corporate debtors to stall and harm creditors by resorting to bankruptcy unless a collective proceeding offers sufficient offsetting benefits to the body of creditors as a whole. The court's power to dismiss a case permits that balancing analysis to be made. The normal testing ground for such contests is in chapter 11.[190]

In some cases, even when a case is properly commenced and even when "cause" for dismissal is not obviously present, the bankruptcy judge still may have a sense that it nevertheless would be in the "interests of creditors and the debtor" if the bankruptcy case not go forward. The Code grants the court the discretionary, and indeed unreviewable, power to abstain from hearing a bankruptcy case in just such a situation.[191] § 305.

§ 2.14   Dismissal of a Chapter 7 Case: For Cause

A chapter 7 liquidation case may be dismissed outright. The 1978 Code as originally enacted only authorized dismissal for *"cause."* § 707(a). The 1984

---

[185] See §§ 2.2, 2.3.

[186] See §§ 2.6–2.9.

[187] See § 2.15.

[188] See § 2.14 (chapter 7), § 2.16 (chapter 13).

[189] See § 2.5.c.

[190] See § 2.17.

[191] See § 2.19.

amendments added a provision permitting the court to dismiss the case of an individual consumer debtor on a showing of "substantial abuse," § 707(b), which was then changed in 2005 simply to "*abuse*," as discussed in the next section.[192]

The debtor does not have an absolute right to dismiss a chapter 7 case, but must establish cause just like any other movant.[193] This restriction limits the possibility that the debtor will be able to abuse the system, as for example by filing bankruptcy on the eve of foreclosure just to take advantage of the automatic stay, and then dismissing the case. Note that the utility of this tactic is further weakened by the eligibility restriction under § 109(g) that makes such a debtor ineligible to file bankruptcy for 180 days.[194]

Furthermore, a debtor usually has to live with his choice of filing dates for the purpose of discharging debts or claiming exemptions. Courts have declined to find cause for dismissal when the debtor wants to dismiss and then refile in order to gain some legal advantage—e.g., to discharge a debt that arose after the original filing, render dischargeable a previously nondischargeable debt, or file an exemption under state law.[195] In short, a debtor will be permitted to dismiss voluntarily only if no creditors will suffer "legal prejudice" because of the dismissal[196]—and since almost any reason a debtor would have to dismiss would prejudice some creditor, the debtor's voluntary dismissal option in reality is a humble one indeed.

The Code does not define "cause." The meaning of the term must be developed and applied on a case-by-case basis. Three nonexclusive illustrations of cause are listed in the statute: unreasonable delay that is also prejudicial to creditors; the nonpayment of required fees; and, only on the motion of the United States trustee, the failure to file required schedules and lists of creditors. § 707(a)(1)–(3). Each of these statutory grounds describes the minimum degree of debtor cooperation in the case necessary to support a filing.

Before the 2005 amendments, the federal "*in forma pauperis*" statute, 28 U.S.C. § 1915, did not apply in bankruptcy. The Supreme Court upheld the constitutionality of the scheme requiring all debtors to pay a filing fee as a condition to access to bankruptcy.[197] The Bankruptcy Rules long have authorized the court to permit the filing fee to be paid in installments. Rule 1006(b); see Official Form 3A. Congress first implemented a pilot program for *in forma pauperis* filings in a few selected districts. Then, the 2005 Act for the first time permitted (but did not require) the district court or bankruptcy court to waive the filing fee for an individual debtor whose income is less

---

[192] See § 2.15.

[193] E.g., In re Underwood, 24 B.R. 570 (S.D. W.Va. 1982).

[194] See § 2.3.a.

[195] E.g., *Underwood,* supra note 193. See also In re Leach, 130 B.R. 855 (B.A.P. 9th Cir. 1991); Gill v. Hall (In re Hall), 15 B.R. 913 (B.A.P. 9th Cir. 1981). But see In re Hull, 339 B.R. 304 (Bankr. E.D.N.Y. 2006) (allowing first-time pro se debtor to dismiss her case when she misunderstood consequences of filing for chapter 7 relief, including fact that her personal injury cause of action was estate property that the trustee could administer for benefit of creditors).

[196] E.g., *Hall,* supra note 195.

[197] United States v. Kras, 409 U.S. 434 (1973).

than 150% of the official poverty line, if the court also determines that the debtor cannot pay the filing fee in installments.[198] 28 U.S.C. § 1930(f).

The courts are free to develop additional grounds for dismissal, and have done so. Prior to the 2005 amendments, some courts held that a lack of *good faith* in filing constituted "cause" for dismissal.[199] For example, the Third Circuit upheld the dismissal of a debtor's chapter 7 case for bad faith, reasoning that the debtor could have repaid his creditors in full, but instead had timed his bankruptcy filing so that he could keep for himself his share of soon-to-be-dissolved tenancy by the entirety property.[200] The Ninth Circuit, however, went the other way, and held that there is no implicit good faith filing requirement in chapter 7.[201]

In 2005, Congress for the first time specifically inserted a "bad faith" dismissal ground in the Code in chapter 7 cases. However, Congress placed this bad faith dismissal ground in *subsection (b)* of § 707 (in § 707(b)(3)(A)), as a species of the "abuse" test, rather than in subsection (a). This placement may restrain courts from treating "bad faith" as an unstated species of "cause" under § 707(a), as the Third Circuit had done, and instead to test bad faith only under § 707(b). Addressing bad faith solely under § 707(b) carries with it all the baggage of that long subsection. For example, subsection (b) applies only to an individual debtor with primarily consumer debts. § 707(b)(1). Also, for a debtor with family income below the state median, only the U.S. trustee or the bankruptcy judge—and thus, *not* a creditor or the case trustee— may bring a dismissal motion under that subsection. § 707(b)(6). Furthermore, on the merits, "abuse" (under subsection (b)) seems to be a more demanding standard than "cause" (under subsection (a)).

Despite Congress placing "bad faith" in § 707(b), and not subsection (a), the Third Circuit continues to find bad faith as cause to dismiss under § 707(a),[202] while the Ninth Circuit continues to refuse to dismiss a case for "bad faith" under subsection (a).[203] Some lower courts have circumvented (ignored?) this statutory change, holding that filing a chapter 7 petition *requires* "good faith" to begin with, such that a lack of "good faith" is grounds for dismissal under § 707(a).[204]

Even more clearly, the debtor's ability to pay some portion of his debts out of future income should no longer be treated as cause for dismissal under § 707(a). Even the Third Circuit, which allowed consideration of a debtor's income and expenses in considering dismissal for bad faith under § 707(a), acknowledged that ability to pay cannot be the exclusive or primary reason to dismiss for cause.[205] The Code took this

---

[198]   See Rule 1006(c), Official Form 3B.

[199]   E.g., In re Zick, 931 F.2d 1124 (6th Cir. 1991).

[200]   Tamecki v. Frank (In re Tamecki), 229 F.3d 205 (3d Cir. 2000).

[201]   Neary v. Padilla (In re Padilla), 222 F.3d 1184 (9th Cir. 2000).

[202]   In re Perlin, 497 F.3d 364 (3d Cir. 2007). See also In re Piazza, 719 F.3d 1253 (11th Cir. 2013); In re Parikh, 456 B.R. 4 (Bankr. E.D.N.Y. 2011); In re Mohr, 425 B.R. 457 (Bankr. S.D. Ohio 2010).

[203]   In re Sherman, 491 F.3d 948 (9th Cir. 2007). See also In re Lobera, 454 B.R. 824 (Bankr. D.N.M. 2011); In re Adolph, 441 B.R. 909 (Bankr. N.D. Ill. 2011).

[204]   See, e.g., In re Rahim, 449 B.R. 527 (E.D. Mich. 2011); In re Carr, 344 B.R. 776 (Bankr. N.D. W. Va. 2006).

[205]   *Perlin*, supra note 202, 497 F.3d 364.

position from the start. Indeed, the legislative history to the 1978 Code demonstrates congressional intent on this point.[206] Thus, under the Code as originally enacted, a debtor could choose to liquidate under chapter 7, even if the debtor's projected future income would have permitted the debtor to pay more to creditors under one of the rehabilitation chapters. As will be seen in the next section, Congress changed course on this policy decision, first with the amendment in 1984 adding the substantial abuse ground for dismissal in § 707(b), and then again in 2005 with the "abuse" provision and the "means test" presumption, meant to keep "can pay" debtors out of chapter 7 liquidation. Such alleged "can-pay" debtors will have their future payment capacity tested under the carefully crafted scheme in subsection (b), rather than the generic "cause" assessment under subsection (a).

Another option for creditors and other parties in interest is to convert a debtor's chapter 7 case to chapter 11, against the debtor's wishes. § 706(b). Once converted, the debtor does not have an absolute right to convert back to chapter 7. § 1112(a)(3). Conversion on motion of a party in interest to chapter 12 or 13 is not allowed, however, unless the debtor consents. § 706(c).

Dismissal of a bankruptcy case is of potential interest to all creditors. Normally, all creditors must receive 21 days notice of the hearing to dismiss the case, Rules 1017(a), 2002(a)(4), and will have the opportunity to object. The exception is for dismissal for failure to pay the filing fee, which does not require prior notice. Rule 1017(b). However, creditors will be notified of the dismissal after the fact. Also note that special procedural rules apply to a dismissal for abuse. Rule 1017(e).

§ 2.15   Dismissal of a Chapter 7 Case: "Abuse" and the Means Test[207]

a.   Introduction

The consumer credit industry has asserted for decades that many consumer debtors with the ability to repay some or all of their debts out of future income nevertheless file under chapter 7 and seek an immediate discharge of their debts, thus escaping having to pay anything to creditors. Creditors cannot force such debtors involuntarily into chapter 13, however. § 303(a). The policy question is what should be done with these supposed "can-pay" debtors. Under the Code as originally enacted in 1978, debtors were free to choose chapter 7 even if they had repayment capacity. As explained in the preceding section, Congress clearly did not intend for future

---

[206] See S. Rep. No. 95–989, 95th Cong., 2d Sess., at 94 (1978) ("The section does not contemplate, however, that the ability of the debtor to repay his debts in whole or in part constitutes adequate cause for dismissal. To permit dismissal on that ground would be to enact a non-uniform mandatory chapter 13, in lieu of the remedy of bankruptcy.").

[207] Much of the version of § 2.15 in the Second Edition was originally published in a symposium article in the *Southern Illinois University Law Journal* that I wrote with Jillian McClelland. See Charles J. Tabb & Jillian K. McClelland, Living With the Means Test, 31 S. Ill. U. L.J. 463 (2007). In the Third Edition, substantial changes have been made to reflect new developments. Note that I have not attempted herein to put quotation marks on all passages taken from that earlier work.

An excellent discussion of the means test can be found in Hon. Eugene Wedoff, Means Testing in the New § 707(b), 79 Am. Bankr. L.J. 231 (2005).

repayment ability to constitute "cause" for dismissal of a chapter 7 case under § 707(a).[208]

That policy choice did not sit well with the consumer credit industry, however, which lobbied almost from the moment the ink was dry on the 1978 Reform Act to persuade Congress to change its position and exclude can-pay debtors from chapter 7. In 1984, Congress added § 707(b) in response to these complaints. As enacted in 1984, § 707(b) empowered the bankruptcy court to dismiss the chapter 7 case of an individual debtor with primarily consumer debts if the court found that the filing was a *"substantial abuse"* of chapter 7. In a legislative compromise (or stalemate?), Congress did not define "substantial abuse," and the legislative history contained conflicting evidence of the extent that Congress intended for future repayment ability to support dismissal for substantial abuse. Clearly, though, a debtor's future repayment ability was intended to be at least a *permissible* consideration in a dismissal determination after 1984 under § 707(b). If a court did dismiss a debtor's chapter 7 case, that debtor was left with the options to forego bankruptcy relief altogether or to proceed "voluntarily" under chapter 13.

Soon, however, the consumer credit industry became disenchanted with the "substantial abuse" test. Procedural constraints, substantive vagueness, and substantial judicial discretion resulted in many fewer dismissals than the credit industry believed were warranted. In their opinion, many can-pay debtors still could and did proceed under chapter 7, and thus the law needed to be amended to catch those debtors. Others, though, debunked the notion of a large class of prospective can-pay chapter 7 debtors, and opposed changes in the law that that would inflict a harsher regime on consumer debtors.[209] In a closely divided vote, the 1997 National Bankruptcy Review Commission rejected the credit industry's proposals for reform.[210]

The solution sought by the consumer credit industry? Institute a mechanical, and strict, *"means test"* to calculate net income available to pay creditors, and then exclude from chapter 7 those consumer debtors with sufficient projected future repayment capacity. Part and parcel of the desired reforms was to strip most of the discretion away from bankruptcy judges and *require* dismissal if the debtor projects to have at least a specified minimum amount of excess income, according to the means test calculation. The consumer credit industry lobbied hard and spent freely to obtain passage of such a means test, and, while they failed to persuade the majority of the 1997 Review Commission, they had better luck with Congress. In April 2005 Congress enacted and President Bush signed into law the Bankruptcy Abuse Prevention and

---

[208] S. Rep. No. 95–989, 95th Cong., 2d Sess., at 94 (1978).

[209] For example, a leading non-partisan study found only a 3.6% can-pay pool. Taking the New Consumer Bankruptcy Model for a Test Drive: Means–Testing Real Chapter 7 Debtors, 7 Am. Bankr. Inst. L. Rev. 27 (1999). See generally Charles Jordan Tabb, The Death of Consumer Bankruptcy in the United States?, 18 Bankr. Dev. J. 1 (2001).

[210] See National Bankruptcy Review Commission Final Report, Bankruptcy: The Next Twenty Years, at 89–91 (1997). Four commissioners dissented. The fullest explication of the means test proposal is in the Additional Dissent to Recommendations for Reform of Consumer Bankruptcy Law (submitted by Hon. Edith H. Jones and James I. Shepherd).

Consumer Protection Act of 2005 (BAPCPA), effective for cases filed on or after October 17, 2005.[211] The basic approach of those dismissal provisions is as follows.

Under BAPCPA, the old substantial abuse test of § 707(b) is replaced by a new *"abuse"* test. § 707(b)(1). An excruciatingly detailed *"means test"* in § 707(b)(2)(A) spells out what level of excess income constitutes *presumptive* abuse, and how to calculate that excess income.[212] If presumptive abuse is found, then dismissal of the chapter 7 filing is required unless the debtor can prove *"special circumstances,"* thereby rebutting the presumption.[213] § 707(b)(2)(B). If a presumption of abuse does not arise or is rebutted, the court still may dismiss the case as an abuse, considering whether the debtor filed the petition in *bad faith*, and looking at the *"totality of the circumstances."*[214] § 707(b)(3).

In considering dismissal for "abuse" under § 707(b)(1), the following are helpful markers:

1.   Dismissal for abuse under § 707(b)(1) is possible only for an *individual* debtor.

2.   That individual debtor's debts must be primarily *consumer debts*.[215] These first two limitations continue those found under the prior "substantial abuse" dismissal rule.

3.   Abuse under § 707(b)(1) can be established in two alternative ways: first, either via an unrebutted presumption of abuse under § 707(b)(2), or second, through the "bad faith" or "totality of the circumstances" tests under § 707(b)(3).

4.   Only debtors whose combined family income is higher than the *state median family income* for their household size[216] are potentially subject to a presumption of abuse under the means test. § 707(b)(7). The U.S. trustee's office maintains, and periodically updates, a website that lists income medians, by "family" size.[217] However, *all* debtors, even those with a median family income below the state median, have to calculate the means test in their schedule of current income and expenditures. § 707(b)(2)(C); Rule 1007(b)(4)–(6); Official Form B22A. Debtors with family incomes

---

[211] Bankruptcy Abuse Prevention and Consumer Protection Act of 2005, Pub. L. No. 109–8, 119 Stat. 23 (2005).

[212] See § 2.15.c.(1).

[213] See § 2.15.c.(4).

[214] See § 2.15.d.

[215] See § 2.15.b.

[216] What constitutes a "household" has proven to be a very difficult issue in many cases where, for example, children or step-children are involved, and only live in the house with the debtor part of the time. See, e.g., Johnson v. Zimmer, 686 F.3d 224 (4th Cir. 2012) (adopting the "economic unit" test and counting split-time dependents as fractions of a person).

[217] For cases filed on and after May 1, 2013, the state medians for each "family" size can be found at: http://www.justice.gov/ust/eo/bapcpa/20130501/bci_data/median_income_table.htm. Thus, for example, the Table shows that in Illinois the single earner income median is $47,485, and the median income for a family of four is $80,776. Note the problematic curiosity that the statute speaks of "household" size, but then a median "family" income, § 707(b)(7), with cases struggling with the possibility that "household" and "family" are not necessarily synonymous. The state medians are updated regularly.

below the state median, while protected from a presumption of abuse, still are subject to possible dismissal for abuse on the grounds of "bad faith" or the "totality of the circumstances" under § 707(b)(3).

5.   The "means test" calculates the debtor's income available to repay creditors under the following *formula*, § 707(b)(2)(A)(i):

a)   Compute the debtor's "current monthly income," § 101(10A);[218]

b)   Subtract the following expenses:[219]

(i)   *living expenses*, calculated by reference to Internal Revenue Service collection guidelines for delinquent taxpayers, § 707(b)(2)(A)(ii)(I);

(ii)   projected payments for 60 months on actual *secured* debts, § 707(b)(2)(A)(iii);

(iii) projected payments for 60 months on actual *priority* debts, § 707(b)(2)(A)(iv); and

(iv)   a miscellany of special interest expenses, charitable contributions, and administrative charges, § 707(b)(2)(A)(ii)(II)–(V), § 707(b)(1).

c)   Multiply by the resulting net total by 60 (for 60 months).

6.   A *presumption of abuse* arises under § 707(b)(2) if the total available income derived from the foregoing means test calculation is:

Not less than the *lesser* of:

(I) $7,475, <u>or</u> 25% of the debtor's nonpriority unsecured claims, whichever is *greater*, § 707(b)(2)(A)(i)(I)

or

(II) $12,475, § 707(b)(2)(A)(i)(II).

Thus, the range of repayment capacity that may demonstrate presumptive abuse ranges from a low of $7,475 (i.e., about $124.59 per month for 60 months) to a high of $12,475 (i.e., about $207.92 per month).[220]

7.   The debtor may *rebut* the presumption of abuse by proving "*special circumstances*" that require an adjustment of the available income calculation sufficient to bring the debtor below the presumptive abuse triggers.[221] The debtor must

---

[218]   See § 2.15.c.(2).

[219]   See § 2.15.c.(3).

[220]   The dollar amounts in § 707(b) are indexed and adjusted every three years. § 104(b). The next adjustment will be made on April 1, 2016.

[221]   See § 2.15.c.(4).

show that he has "no reasonable alternative" but to make the adjustment and must document the special circumstances. § 707(b)(2)(B).

BAPCPA also enacted detailed procedural rules and standing requirements, concerning who may bring what types of motions to dismiss, against what categories of debtors, and in what manner.[222] § 707(b)(6), (7). Furthermore, BAPCPA added rules allowing the possibility of sanctions against a debtor's counsel for filing a petition under chapter 7 that is later dismissed for "abuse."[223] § 707(b)(4). Conversely, debtors may recover costs in certain circumstances where an unsuccessful dismissal motion is brought. § 707(b)(5).

b.   Scope of the Abuse Test

The new "abuse" test of § 707(b)(1) does not apply to all debtors. Following in the footsteps of its predecessor, the "substantial abuse" test, two significant limitations cabin its scope. First, the abuse test only applies to an *individual* debtor.[224] Accordingly, corporate debtors and partnership debtors are not subject to dismissal for "abuse" in chapter 7, but only are subject to dismissal for "cause" under § 707(a).

Second, the test applies only to a debtor who has "primarily *consumer* debts." § 707(b)(1). Thus, even an individual debtor is not subject to dismissal for "abuse" if he has primarily business debts. The definition for "consumer debt" is a familiar one in commercial law: it is a debt "incurred by an individual primarily for a personal, family, or household purpose." § 101(8).

The reach of the "presumption" of abuse via the means test in § 707(b)(2) is limited even further. That is, even if an individual debtor has primarily consumer debts, he nevertheless still may be protected from the means test by a *safe harbor*. The most important safe harbor from the means test is for debtors with low total income. If the debtor and the debtor's spouse together have "current monthly income" that is *below the state median income* for a household of the same size, they cannot be subjected to a motion for dismissal under § 707(b)(2). § 707(b)(7). Another safe harbor is for disabled veterans whose indebtedness occurred primarily while the individual was on active duty or performing a homeland defense activity. § 707(b)(2)(D).

Note, though, that immunity from a possible presumption of abuse under § 707(b)(2) does *not* mean that an individual consumer debtor is immune to dismissal for abuse under § 707(b)(1); it only means that *no presumption* of abuse can be raised. Such a debtor is still vulnerable to dismissal for abuse based on § 707(b)(3), on a showing either of "bad faith" or the "totality of the circumstances."[225]

In determining whether a debtor's family income falls below the applicable state median, the first step is to determine the debtor's income.[226] This calculation is made

---

[222]   See § 2.15.e.

[223]   See § 2.15.f.

[224]   Note that courts apply the means test to joint debtors as well. See e.g., In re Lapke, 428 B.R. 839 (B.A.P. 8th Cir. 2010).

[225]   See § 2.15.d.

[226]   See § 2.15.c.(2).

by multiplying the debtor's "current monthly income," defined in § 101(10A), by twelve, thus generating an annualized income. This test looks back in time, at the income the debtor received in the six full months prior to the bankruptcy filing. All income, even if not taxable, is included in this calculation, excepting only Social Security benefits.[227]

Next, the income received by the debtor's spouse must be added to the debtor's current monthly income. This addition must be made even if the case is not a joint filing. § 707(b)(7)(A). The only exception from this requirement is if the debtor is separated from his spouse. § 707(b)(7)(B). However, courts have grappled with what to do in the cases that involve domestic partners, rather than legally married spouses. For example, one court held that the debtor did not have to include all of his domestic partner's income under § 707(b)(7), even though they were part of the same two-person household, where the debtor and his partner maintained separate finances, had no access to each other's income, and owned no common property. However, the court *did* include the $900 per month that the partner regularly contributed towards household expenses as part of the debtor's "current monthly income" itself under § 101(10)(A)(B).[228]

After the debtor's income (plus spousal income) is computed, the next step is to compare that annualized income figure with the state median family income for the same household size. "*Median family income*" is defined as "the median family income calculated and reported by the Bureau of the Census" in the most recent year, or as adjusted for inflation using the Consumer Price Index in years no state medians are reported by the Census Bureau. § 101(39A). As noted above, the U.S. trustee's office maintains a website that lists income medians by state and family size (up to four people).[229] If there are more than 4 people in the debtor's household,[230] the applicable state median is computed by taking the highest median income in the state for a family of four people or less[231] and adding $675 per month (i.e., $8,100 per year) for each extra person. § 707(b)(7)(A). So, for example, assume a debtor lived in Illinois in a 6–person household; the relevant median would be $80,776 (family of four) plus $16,200 (for people five and six), for a total median income of $96,976. Thus, if that debtor's total income, with his spouse, is less than $96,976, no motion can be brought alleging a presumption of abuse under § 707(b)(2). That debtor's only worry would be a motion under § 707(b)(3) alleging abuse based on bad faith in filing or because of the totality of the circumstances.

---

[227] 11 U.S.C. § 101(10A)(B). In 1983, Congress specifically exempted social security benefits from "the operation of any bankruptcy or insolvency law." 42 U.S.C. § 407(a).

[228] In re Epperson, 409 B.R. 503 (Bankr. D. Ariz. 2009).

[229] See http://www.justice.gov/ust/eo/bapcpa/20130501/bci_data/median_income_table.htm.

[230] Above I noted the problem that "household" does not necessarily have a meaning synonymous to "family." See supra notes 216 and 217 and accompanying text.

[231] Almost always, the highest such median is the one for a family of four people; in the tables applicable to cases filed on or after May 1, 2013, that rule of thumb held true in all states.

c. *Presumption of Abuse*

(1) The Statutory Formula

The "means test" under § 707(b)(2) provides a detailed and mechanical method for determining whether an individual debtor with primarily consumer debts has sufficient excess income available to pay to his creditors.[232] If a debtor fails the means test, a presumption of abuse is raised, and unless the debtor can rebut the presumption, the chapter 7 case must be dismissed or, with the debtor's consent, be converted to chapter 13. The means test is the cornerstone of the consumer credit industry's long-sought consumer bankruptcy reforms.

The two principal components of the means test are, not surprisingly, figuring out the debtor's *income* and *expenses*. Once a debtor's income and allowable expense deductions have been calculated, it is possible to determine whether a presumption of abuse exists. § 707(b)(2)(A)(i). Official Form B22A provides a detailed form to follow in making the computation.

There are six steps in all:

1. Compute the debtor's "current monthly income."[233] See § 101(10A).

2. Subtract all permitted monthly deductions,[234] see § 707(b)(2)(A)(ii)–(iv), thereby computing a net monthly income (i.e., the debtor's supposed repayment capacity).

3. Multiply that net monthly income by 60 (representing the number of months in the five years the debtor would have to devote excess income to pay his unsecured creditors in a chapter 13 case). This figure is the debtor's total projected repayment capacity.

4. Figure out the statutory trigger amount for presumptive abuse. This amount varies depending on the amount of the debtor's nonpriority unsecured debt. The exact statutory formula is:

the *lesser* of—

(1) 25% of the debtor's nonpriority unsecured claims *or* $7,475, whichever is *greater*

or

(2) $12,475.[235]

---

[232] See Wedoff, supra note 207, for a very helpful analysis of the means test.

[233] See § 2.15.c.(2).

[234] See § 2.15.c.(3).

[235] The dollar amounts in § 707(b) are indexed and adjusted every three years. § 104(b). The next adjustment will be made on April 1, 2016.

5.   If #3 is greater than or equal to #4, then the debtor flunks the means test. That is, if the debtor's projected repayment capacity (#3) is not less than the statutory trigger amount (#4), then abuse is presumed. § 707(b)(2)(A)(i).

6.   If debtor fails the means test, he can try to rebut the presumption of abuse.[236]

A convenient shorthand method of applying the means test is to divide debtors into three tiers, depending on the *total amount of unsecured debt* that is not entitled to priority.[237]

• **Tier One**: *Debtor has $29,900 or less in nonpriority unsecured debt*. Abuse is presumed if the debtor's total projected repayment capacity (step #3) is at least $7,475 (or, on a monthly basis, $124.59).[238]

• **Tier Two**: *Debtor has nonpriority unsecured debts between $29,900 and $49,900*. Abuse is presumed if the debtor's total projected repayment capacity (step #3) is at least 25% of the debtor's unsecured debts.[239] The repayment range for this tier is between $7,475 and $12,475 (i.e., between $124.59 and $207.91 per month).

• **Tier Three**: *Debtor has more than $49,900 in nonpriority unsecured debt*. Abuse is presumed if the debtor's total projected repayment capacity (step #3) is at least $12,475 (or $207.92 a month).[240]

Another rule of thumb for applying the means test is to think of "trigger points."[241] Since $7,475 is the minimum amount that can trigger a presumption of abuse, and $7,475 divided by 60 months is $124.583, if a debtor's repayment capacity is *$124.58 or less* a month, the presumption of abuse *never* arises. Conversely, since any repayment capacity of $12,475 or more always triggers the presumption, and since $12,475 divided by 60 months is $207.916, the presumption of abuse *always* arises if a debtor's monthly repayment capacity is $207.92 or more. For a repayment capacity between $124.59 and $207.91, the outcome depends on the amount of nonpriority unsecured debt. In tabular form, these trigger points are as follows:

---

[236] See § 2.15.c.(4).

[237] Judge Wedoff came up with this helpful rule of thumb. See supra note 1. The specific dollar tier levels (or trigger points) will change every three years with indexing under § 104(b). See supra note 235.

[238] The $7,475 figure controls in this unsecured debt range because it is (1) >= 25% of unsecured debt (for debt < $29,900, 25% of that debt must be < $7,475), and is (2) less than $12,475.

[239] In this debt range, the 25% rule applies, because (1) 25% of anything over $29,900 in debt will be greater than $7,475, and (2) 25% of anything less than $49,900 in debt is less than $12,475.

[240] The $12,475 figure governs here because the statutory abuse trigger can never exceed $12,475, and for any debt over $49,900, the 25% rule would give an amount greater than $12,475 (and obviously greater than $7,475 as well). It is irrelevant how much unsecured debt the debtor actually has.

[241] See Wedoff, supra note 207.

Debtor's Monthly Repayment Capacity: "Current Monthly Income" Minus Deductions	Presumption of Abuse
Less than $124.59	Never Arises
$124.59 – $207.91	(1) Arises if nonpriority unsecured debt ≤ $29,900; (2) If nonpriority unsecured debts > $29,900, arises if repayment capacity ≥ 25% of unsecured debts
More than $207.91	Always Arises

Note how small a margin a debtor has under the means test. A difference of just $83.34 of excess income a month (less than three dollars a day) could be the difference between a presumption of abuse *never* arising ($124.58) and *always* arising ($207.92)!

Consider some examples. Assume Debtor has current monthly income of $6,840 (step #1), allowed deductions of $6,700 a month (step #2), and nonpriority unsecured debts of $32,000. Abuse is presumed. How do we know? Step #3 reveals that Debtor's total repayment capacity is $8,400.[242] Step #4 gives a statutory trigger presumption amount of $8,000.[243] Under step #5, we compare the total repayment capacity ($8,400) with the statutory presumption trigger ($8,000), and since the repayment capacity is larger, Debtor is a presumptive abuser. As a shortcut, since this is a "tier two" debtor ($32,000 in nonpriority unsecured debts falls between $29,900 and $49,900), the operative statutory presumption trigger is 25% of the $32,000 nonpriority unsecured debt.

As a second example, assume Debtor has $10,000 in unsecured debt, income of $5,500 a month and allowed deductions of $5,400 per month. This debtor has net monthly income of $100 a month, or $6,000 over 60 months. Since that projected repayment capacity is less than $7,475 total (or $124.59 per month), she is not presumed to be an abuser, no matter what amount of unsecured debt she has. This debtor, note, could repay 60% of her nonpriority unsecured debt ($6,000 of $10,000)— but nevertheless is not a presumed abuser, since her repayment capacity falls below $124.59 a month. Of course, it is possible that this debtor still could be vulnerable to dismissal for abuse based on the totality of the circumstances, or bad faith, under § 707(b)(3).

Final example. Debtor has current monthly income of $7,010, and allowed deductions of $6,800 (and thus a monthly repayment capacity of $210), and nonpriority unsecured debts of $600,000. Debtor is a presumed abuser, since he has a monthly

---

[242] 60 months multiplied by $140 a month ($6840 income – $6700 deductions) = $8400.

[243] Take the lesser of (1) 25% of nonpriority unsecured debts [$32,000] = [$8,000] or $7,475, whichever is greater [thus, $8,000] or (2) $12,475, and thus $8,000.

repayment capacity greater than $207.91. Note that this debtor could repay about 2% of his unsecured debts ($12,600 of $600,000), but is still a presumed abuser.

(2) Calculating Income

The first step in applying the means test is to compute the debtor's *"current monthly income"* (CMI). This income figure is used for two purposes: (1) to determine whether the debtor's income falls below the relevant state median family income, in which case the debtor is immune from a presumption of abuse, § 707(b)(7), and (2) if the debtor is not within the below-median income safe harbor, to calculate whether the debtor's projected repayment capacity is sufficient to trigger a presumption of abuse. § 707(b)(2)(A)(i). In chapter 13, "current monthly income" is used to compute the "projected disposable income" that a debtor must contribute to plan payments. § 1325(b)(1)(B), (2).

Note that the need to compute "current monthly income" always arises in the first instance. Even if the debtor might fall within the below-median safe harbor, the only way to determine that fact is to calculate the debtor's income. The Code requires *all* individual debtors—even those whose income falls below the state median—to file a means test calculation with their schedule of current income and expenditures. § 707(b)(2)(C). Thus, all individual chapter 7 debtors must file Form B22A.

So, what exactly is *"current monthly income"*? The term is defined in § 101(10A). That definition has two parts. The first part, in subsection (A), defines it as the *"average monthly income"* the debtor *"receives"* from all sources, whether or not it is "taxable income," derived during the six-month period *prior* to bankruptcy. In a joint case, the spouse's income is included under subsection (A). Thus, by definition only *historical* income is relevant in calculating CMI, which is used to determine whether the debtor can repay his creditors in the *future*.

The relevant time period actually is the six-month period that ends on the last day of the calendar month immediately preceding the date of the filing. § 101(10A)(A)(i). Thus, the partial month in which the debtor files the case is excluded. For example, if Debtor files on September 30, his income for the months of (looking backward) August, July, June, May, April, and March will be counted; September income will be excluded. If Debtor waits a day, though, and files on October 1, September income comes in and March income falls out.

Under § 101(10A)(A), only "income" will be counted. Note that the Code does not define "income." Courts should look to interpretations of the Internal Revenue Code as to what constitutes "income."[244] While some courts have read § 101(10A) very expansively, invoking snappy aphorisms such as "§ 101(10A) . . . include[s] *every dime*

---

[244] See, e.g., In re Curcio, 387 B.R. 278 (Bankr. N.D. Fla. 2008) (holding that neither tax refund nor proceeds from sale of property constituted CMI). But see Blausey v. U.S. Trustee, 552 F.3d 1124 (9th Cir. 2009) (holding that looking to the Internal Revenue Code to determine "income" is inappropriate when Congress specifically stated "without regard to whether such income is taxable income" in § 101(10A)(A).

a debtor gets during the relevant period except for those specifically excluded,"[245] such a reading seems plainly wrong. "Income" is a narrower concept; according to the Supreme Court in the tax realm, "income" encompasses "accessions to wealth, clearly realized, and over which the taxpayers have complete dominion."[246]

Note also that under subsection (A) the debtor must have "received" the income during the relevant six-month pre-bankruptcy period. While in many instances determining the time of receipt will not be a problem, there will be cases where the time of the debtor's actual receipt of the money may differ from the time the income is deemed earned. In such cases, courts will have to determine how literally Congress intended the direction to count CMI based upon the time of "receipt" to be taken. Most courts hold that wages earned but not paid during this period are not counted towards a debtor's CMI.[247] This of course also means that income earned outside of the six-month period, but received during the six-month period, goes towards CMI.[248]

Cases involving debtors taking distributions from retirement plans[249] highlight this problem even more: is the income taken as a distribution to be counted under CMI when earned or when the distribution is taken? Or what about a year-end bonus received by the debtor within the six-month period, but attributable to the entire preceding year's work? Does the entire bonus count as CMI? The statutory language suggests that it does,[250] but such a result is unfair to a debtor, whose apparent repayment capacity would be greater than what it actually is.[251] Under the awkward BAPCPA scheme, such a debtor could only seek to rebut a presumption of abuse by alleging "special circumstances."[252]

The second part of the definition, in subsection (B), brings in any "*amount*" paid by any entity other than the debtor (or in a joint case the debtor and debtor's spouse) "on a regular basis for the household expenses" of the debtor and his dependents. Note the use of the term "amount" rather than "income," thus indicating that items that would be excluded from the meaning of "income" (such as child support) nevertheless may

---

[245] In re DeThample, 390 B.R. 716 (Bankr. D. Kan. 2008) (holding that disbursement debtor received from her 401(k) plan constituted CMI). Contra Simon v. Zittel, 2008 WL 750346 (Bankr. S.D. Ill. March 19, 2008); In re Wayman, 351 B.R. 808 (Bankr. E.D. Tex. 2006).

[246] C.I.R. v. Glenshaw Glass Co., 348 U.S. 426, 431 (1955) (holding that punitive damages are income).

[247] See, e.g., In re Arnoux, 442 B.R. 769 (Bankr. E.D. Wash. 2010); In re Meade, 420 B.R. 291 (Bankr. W.D. Va. 2009). But see In re Robrock, 430 B.R. 197 (Bankr. D. Minn. 2010) (holding that although income must be derived from employment during the six-month period, timing of its actual receipt is irrelevant, as long as the debtor ultimately does receive it).

[248] See, e.g., In re Burrell, 399 B.R. 620 (Bankr. C.D. Ill. 2008).

[249] See cases at note 245 supra.

[250] See In re Katz, 451 B.R. 512 (Bankr. C.D. Cal. 2011).

[251] See In re Meade, 420 B.R. 291 (Bankr. W.D. Va. 2009) (prorating the debtor's bonus to comport with the six-month look-back period).

[252] Of course, the absurdity could run the other way: the debtor could have received her year-end bonus prior to the six-month period, and thus escape having any part of the bonus count as CMI. See In re Beasley, 342 B.R. 280 (Bankr. C.D. Ill. 2006).

count as an "amount" and thus if paid regularly, would be included in "current monthly income."[253]

Attribution problems arise in single-filing cases filed by a married debtor, in determining what amounts the debtor's non-filing spouse regularly contributes to the payment of household expenses.[254] The statute is clear in a single-filing case by a married debtor that the non-filing spouse's income is *not* automatically included in CMI under subsection (B), but is counted only if paid regularly toward household expenses. So, for example, what if bills are paid out of a joint account, into which both spouses deposit wages? Courts may have to adopt tracing presumptions to determine how to attribute as between the spouses the past payments out of that account. In cases where another relative (or a really good friend!) helps the debtor out occasionally with expenses, the issue will be how "regular" the contributions need to be to qualify.

The only statutory exclusions from current monthly income are for Social Security benefits and payments received by victims of war crimes, crimes against humanity, or terrorism. § 101(10A)(B). The most important, of course, is the exclusion for Social Security benefits, which will be critical for many elderly debtors.[255]

Using a purely historical approach to project future repayment capacity is fraught with problems. The past is not necessarily prologue; income may go up, and it may go down. Nothing in the means test calculation itself allows such adjustments to be made, no matter how certain the impending future departure from historical income.

For example, a debtor could be laid off prior to bankruptcy, but his past income would still count as "current monthly income." If that historic income pushes the debtor over the presumptive abuse trigger, the debtor's only hope to avoid dismissal is to try to *rebut* the presumption of abuse. Conversely, the definition of current monthly income does not account for prospective future increases in earnings, however likely. Thus, a law student whose six-month pre-bankruptcy historical income was small but who has accepted a job with a big city law firm for $150,000 would not have to count that future salary in the means test calculation. The only way to attack such a debtor for "abuse" would be under "bad faith" or the "totality of the circumstances" under § 707(b)(3).

Using an historical approach also creates a perverse incentive for a debtor contemplating the possibility of bankruptcy to keep his income low. For example, a debtor who had previously worked overtime might be well advised to stop overtime work for the six months prior to bankruptcy to lower his income. If both spouses had

---

[253] See, e.g., In re Coverstone, 461 B.R. 629 (Bankr. D. Idaho 2011) (noting that adult daughter's contributions to the debtors would have been included had they occurred during the six-month look-back period); *Epperson*, supra note 228.

[254] See *Epperson*, supra note 228.

[255] Note a drafting error: the exclusion for these benefits appears *only* in subsection (B), which includes amounts paid by others for household expenses, and does not cross-reference subsection (A), which includes all income received by the debtor, from all sources. Read literally, then, these exclusions would not apply to income received by the debtor under subsection (A), and indeed would never apply at all, because such exclusions would never arise as to contributions by others. The legislative history indicates that Congress clearly intended a blanket exclusion from "current monthly income" for these benefits. See H.R. 109–31 (pt. 1), 109th Cong., 1st Sess., at 13 n.60, 52 (2005).

worked, perhaps one spouse should stop working during all or part of the six-month pre-bankruptcy period, if it would make a difference in passing or failing the means test. While courts can try to police such planning behavior through "bad faith" or "totality" assessments under § 707(b)(3), such enforcement will be difficult and erratic, and debtors still gain an advantage in escaping the presumption of abuse under § 707(b)(2).

The Supreme Court in *Hamilton v. Lanning* addressed this issue in the context of chapter 13 cases.[256] In *Lanning*, the Court acknowledged that income may fluctuate, and a debtor's repayment capacity may change, and when those changes are "know or virtually certain," a court may account for them at the time of plan confirmation. However, the *Lanning* Court based its decision on an interpretation of the term "projected disposable income" in § 1325(b)(1)(B), a term that is not in § 707(b). Thus, *Lanning* arguably only controls chapter 13 cases, and not chapter 7, and this is the majority view in the courts.[257] Still, some courts in chapter 7 see *Lanning* as a general grant by the Supreme Court to depart from the mechanical framework of the means test, and to substitute their own discretionary assessment of the debtor's actual future repayment capacity.[258] However, it is hard to see how the statute could bend enough for such judicial discretion to be exercised in raising a presumption of abuse under § 707(b)(2); instead, the court should only consider these apparent changes as "bad faith" or "totality" grounds for establishing "abuse" under § 707(b)(3).

(3) Calculating Expenses

A debtor cannot pay *all* of his monthly income to his creditors. People of necessity must incur living expenses. A core aspect of the means test is the determination of what expense deductions will be allowed to consumer debtors. In BAPCPA, Congress provided very detailed (and sometimes confusing) rules governing permitted expense deductions. § 707(b)(2)(A)(ii), (iii), and (iv). The second step in the means test calculation is to subtract these expenses from a debtor's "current monthly income" to arrive at the debtor's monthly disposable income. See Official Form B22A, Part V. The allowed deductions fall into three broad categories: (1) living expenses, § 707(b)(2)(A)(ii); (2) secured debt payments, § 707(b)(2)(A)(iii); and (3) priority debt payments, § 707(b)(2)(A)(iv).

However, before turning to a close examination of the very dense thicket of the particulars of the means test expense categories, it is important to step back and note the potentially broad and overarching impact of, curiously enough, a second chapter 13 case, in addition to *Lanning*: the Supreme Court's 2011 decision in *Ransom v. FIA Card Services, N.A.*[259] In *Ransom*, the debtor sought to claim an ownership expense deduction for his vehicle, even though he owned it free and clear. The issue turned on

---

[256] 130 S.Ct. 2464 (2010).

[257] See, e.g., In re Rivers, 466 B.R. 558 (Bankr. M.D. Fla. 2012); In re Grinkmeyer, 456 B.R. 385 (Bankr. S.D. Ind. 2011); In re Sonntav, 2011 WL 3902999 (Bankr. N.D. W. Va. Sept. 6, 2011); In re Ng, 2011 WL 576067 (Bankr. D. Haw. Feb. 9, 2011).

[258] See e.g., In re Fredman, 471 B.R. 540, (Bankr. S.D. Ill. 2012). See also In re Peterlin, 457 B.R. 630 (Bankr. N.D. Ohio 2011) (using the "known or virtually certain" test).

[259] 131 S.Ct. 716 (2011).

an interpretation of a chapter 7 means test expense provision, § 707(b)(2)(A)(ii)(I), which provides that, "[t]he debtor's monthly expenses shall be the debtor's *applicable* monthly expense amounts specified under the National Standards and Local Standards." This language raises the question of "what does it mean for expenses to be applicable?" The Court held that for an expense to be applicable means for it to be "appropriate, relevant, suitable, or fit,"[260] thus requiring the debtor *actually to incur* the expense. Thus, the Court rebuffed the debtor's attempt at claiming ownership expense in his fully owned vehicle as an "amount specified" in the relevant Standard, holding that "[a] debtor who does not make loan or lease payments may not take the car-ownership deduction."[261] The Court thought it important that the expense deductions allowed should bear a close "correspondence to an individual debtor's financial circumstances."[262]

Nor did the Court rest only on its preferred parsing of the text, but invoked the policy behind BAPCPA to support an interpretation favoring creditors over the debtor. Justice Kagan found in the legislative history a congressional directive that consumer debtors should pay all they can to their creditors.[263] Notably, Justice Kagan never mentioned the "fresh start" policy of consumer bankruptcy. Lower courts have gotten the Supreme Court's "make debtors pay" message. For example, the Sixth Circuit observed, "as the Supreme Court recognized in both *Ransom* and *Lanning*, the legislative history makes clear that the focus of Congress in enacting BAPCPA was on maximizing the amount of disposable income that debtors would pay to creditors."[264]

Ransom thus has provided two guideposts for how means test expenses should be determined by a court, in cases where the statute is not crystal clear. First, to the extent possible, unless doing so would do violence to clear statutory text, the debtor's allowed expenses must align with their actual expenses as much as possible. The problem with this view, though, is that Congress *did* provide, in excruciating detail, a largely mechanical schedule of permissible expenses, some of which are based directly on the debtor's actual expenses, but others of which are not. It is thus very difficult to correlate claimed expenses to actual expenses in all instances.

Second, as noted, the Court gave weight to a perceived legislative policy that the Code should be interpreted in such a way as to make the debtors pay as much as they can to creditors.[265] Put more informally: tie goes to the creditor. *Ransom*'s emphasis on maximizing creditor recoveries has already had an influence in the lower courts, as noted.[266]

---

[260] Id. at 724.

[261] Id. at 721.

[262] Id. at 724.

[263] Id. at 721.

[264] Baud v. Carroll, 634 F.3d 327 (6th Cir. 2011) ("[I]n which the Supreme Court relied on BAPCPA's purpose of ensuring that debtors repay the maximum they can afford."). See also § 1325(b)(1)(B).

[265] In Justice Kagan's words, "the statute's purpose—to ensure that debtors pay creditors the maximum they can afford—is best achieved by interpreting the means test, consistent with the statutory text, to reflect a debtor's ability to afford repayment." *Ransom*, 131 S.Ct. at 720.

[266] See, e.g., In re Quigley, 673 F.3d 269 (4th Cir. 2012) (holding debtor could not deduct payments for ATV when she did not plan on making them); see also *Baud*, supra note 264.

Note that although *Ransom* was a chapter 13 case, the decision centered on an interpretation of § 707(b)(2)(A)(ii), because § 1325(b)(3) refers back to § 707(b)(2). Naturally, this poses the question of whether *Ransom*—both as to the narrow issue implicated as well as the broader principles announced—applies to chapter 7 cases. Obviously, the means test functions differently in chapters 7 and 13. In chapter 7, the means test is designed to screen for abuse, and either push "abusive" debtors into chapter 13 or out of bankruptcy altogether. One court has described the means test in chapter 7 as a "snapshot" of the debtor's financial situation as of the petition date.[267] Conversely, chapter 13 uses the means test as a baseline to determine "projected disposable income," in order to calculate monthly payments to creditors during the duration of the plan. In short, in chapter 13 the debtor actually is going to have to make payments to creditors, so correspondence to the debtor's actual financial circumstances makes more intuitive sense. Indeed, this sense largely motivated the Court's chapter 13 decision in *Lanning* that adjustments had to be made in calculating projected disposable income for changes that were "known or virtually certain."[268] The same pragmatic imperative is not as compelling in chapter 7, but the statutory text remains the same, of course, in either chapter. Some courts have applied *Ransom* to chapter 7 cases,[269] while others have declined to do so.[270] In the final analysis, the Court's pro-creditor thumb on the scales is likely to play a role in the interpretation of the means test expense categories, even in chapter 7. Let us now turn from the big picture to the dense statutory thicket.

(a) Living Expenses

The first category of permitted deductions is for the debtor's monthly living expenses (other than secured debt payments and priority debt payments). This first category itself can be divided into two basic types of expenses:

(1) those provided by the Internal Revenue Service's Collection Financial Standards, § 707(b)(2)(A)(ii)(I), see Official Form B22A, Part V, Subpart A, and

(2) a hodge-podge of miscellaneous expenses, § 707(b)(2)(A)(ii)(II)–(V), see Official Form B22A, Part V, Subpart B.

1.   Internal Revenue Service Collection Financial Standards

The Internal Revenue Service uses Collection Financial Standards when it arranges payment plans with delinquent taxpayers.[271] The IRS defines these allowable necessary expenses as:

[E]xpenses that are necessary to provide for a taxpayer's and his or her family's health and welfare and/or production of income. The expenses must be

---

[267] *Rivers*, supra note 257.

[268] Hamilton v. Lanning, 130 S.Ct. 2464, 2478 (2010).

[269] See, e.g., In re Fredman, 471 B.R. 540, (Bankr. S.D. Ill. 2012); In re Wilson, 454 B.R. 155 (Bankr. D. Colo. 2011); In re Thompson, 457 B.R. 872 (Bankr. M.D. Fla. 2011).

[270] In re Grinkmeyer, 456 B.R. 385 (Bankr. S.D. Ind. 2011).

[271] See http://www.irs.gov/individuals/article/0,,id=96543,00.html.

reasonable. The total necessary expenses establish the minimum a taxpayer and family needs to live.[272]

Congress's incorporation of the IRS Collection Standards into the bankruptcy law is remarkable. The implicit premise of the means test is that consumer debtors who end up in bankruptcy deserve to be treated just like income tax evaders, and should only be allowed to live on the minimum necessary expenses for five years while they repay their debts.

The allowed IRS living expenses fall into three categories:

(1) National Standards;

(2) Local Standards; and

(3) Other Necessary Expenses.

The U.S. Trustee's office maintains a web site for use in applying the bankruptcy means test, and updates the IRS allowed amounts for use in bankruptcy on a periodic basis.[273]

An important preliminary question in computing the deductions under the Standards is whether debtors are limited to their *actual* expenses, or whether they may deduct higher amounts as *"specified"* in the Standards. § 707(b)(2)(A)(ii)(I). Before *Ransom*,[274] there was a consensus understanding on this question; courts routinely held that a debtor could deduct the "applicable monthly expense amounts specified" by the IRS under the National Standards and Local Standards, even if the debtor's actual expenses were less than the amounts specified.[275] If the debtor's expenses were higher than the IRS Standards in those categories, they were limited to the "amounts specified" by the IRS.[276] Debtors always are limited to their actual expenses under "Other Necessary Expenses."

Unfortunately, the *Ransom* decision cast into doubt whether debtors may claim the "amounts specified" for the National and Local Standards when their actual expenses are less.[277] The Court clearly held that the debtor may not claim any ownership expense in a category when the debtor has no such expenses.[278] But what if

---

[272] Internal Revenue Manual, § 5.15.1.7 (see http://www.irs.gov/irm/part5/irm_05-015-001.html#d0e1470) (emphasis in original).

[273] See http://www.justice.gov/ust/eo/bapcpa/20130501/meanstesting.htm (Applicable to cases filed on and after May 1, 2013). This data is updated periodically, whenever the underlying IRS standards are updated.

[274] 131 S.Ct. 716 (2011). See supra notes 259–70 and accompanying text.

[275] *Ransom*, 131 S.Ct. at 731–32. The Code partially departs from the IRS approach here. The IRS allows specified amounts for the National Standards, as does the Code, but differs from the Code as to Local Standards, for which the IRS numbers serve as caps; if the debtor's expenses are lower, they are limited to their actual expenses.

[276] If the debtor has secured debts that exceed the IRS Standards, he may claim the higher secured debt expense under that deduction category. See § 707(b)(2)(A)(iii).

[277] *Ransom* did confirm that debtors may only claim the "amounts specified" when their actual expenses are *higher*. 131 S.Ct. at 727.

[278] Id. at 730.

the debtor does have *some* expense in the category, but less than the Standard? In footnote 8, the Court "decline[d] to resolve the issue."[279] The problem for the majority in *Ransom* was rationalizing their underlying premise that a debtor's actual expenses should closely match his claimed expenses with the reality that there cannot be a perfect match between actual and claimed expenses, as, for instance, when a debtor's actual expenses either exceed or fall below, possibly even far below, the statutory limit. The question left for courts is how closely should they align actual and claimed expenses—and on what statutory basis can such line-drawing distinctions be based? Are debtors allowed to claim the full amount when their expenses are below a threshold amount? What is that threshold amount? There is no apparent answer;[280] so far, some lower courts have opted for the previous practice of allowing the debtor to claim the full amount specified as long as the debtor had *some* expense in that category,[281] while at least one other court chose to limit the amount based on the actual expense.[282]

The better view, I submit, and the one clearly mandated by the Code, is that as long as a debtor has some expense in a category under the National or Local Standards (thus rendering the expense category "applicable" to him), he should be able to claim the full amount specified under the relevant standard, even if his actual expenses are less. If those expenses exceed the amount specified, though, the debtor indisputably is capped at the specified amount. For Other Necessary Expenses, of course, the debtor always is limited to actual expenses.

A. NATIONAL STANDARDS

The *National Standards* establish allowances for six categories of expenses: food, housekeeping supplies, apparel and services, personal care products and services, out-of-pocket health care costs, and miscellaneous. As the name suggests, these Standards are established on a national basis.[283] As noted above, the allowances are fixed, irrespective of the debtor's actual expenses. However, under § 707(b)(2)(A)(ii)(I), debtors may request an additional allowance of 5% of the National Standard

---

[279] Id. at 727 n.8.

[280] The United States Government had an interesting take on this issue in their *amicus curiae* brief for *Ransom*. See Brief of the United States as Amicus Curiae Supporting Respondent, 2010 WL 3232490 (2010). According to the view of the U.S. Government, the best way to strike a balance between precision and ease of administration is to require "a debtor who invokes that deduction to establish the existence, but not the exact amount, of a vehicle loan or lease payment."

[281] In re O'Neill Miranda, 449 B.R. 182 (Bankr. D.P.R. 2011); In re Scott, 457 B.R. 740 (Bankr. S.D. Ill. 2011).

[282] In re Hargis, 451 B.R. 174 (Bankr. D. Utah 2011).

[283] See http://www.justice.gov/ust/eo/bapcpa/20130501/bci_data/national_expense_standards.htm (applicable to cases filed on and after May 1, 2013).

allowances "for food and clothing,"[284] if such an increase is demonstrated to be "reasonable and necessary"—whatever that means![285] The Code provides no guidance.

The amounts allowed under the National Standards increase as the debtor's family size increases.[286] The out-of-pocket healthcare expense also varies depending on whether a given family member is over age 65.[287] As an example, consider the following monthly table, for a family of four:

Item	Allowance
Food	$777
Housekeeping supplies	$74
Apparel & services	$244
Personal care	$70
Miscellaneous	$300
Out-of-Pocket Health Care	$240
Total	$1,705

For families larger than four people, a total per-person additional allotment is provided: $281 (for everything except healthcare which is listed separately), which can be added to the amount allowed for a family of four. So a family of five, all under age 65, would get $2,046 ($1,705 from the table for four, above, plus $281 and an additional $60 healthcare allowance).

The website maintained by the U.S. Trustee's office also provides a corollary table with the potential extra 5% for food and clothing provided for each family size. The table simply adds together the amounts allowed for "food" and for "apparel & services" for each income category, and then takes 5% of that total. So, for example, for a family of 4 the food allowance of $777 is added to the apparel & services amount of $244, for a total of $1,021, and 5% of that is rounded to $51.

---

[284] The National Standard does not have a category for "clothing," which is the term used in the Code. There is a category for "apparel and services," which must be the intended referent, even though it is broader than just "clothing" since it includes "services."

[285] See, e.g., In re Gregory, 452 B.R. 895 (Bankr. M.D. Pa. 2011) (denied joint debtors an additional food allowance, finding that their daughter's unhappiness "with the food options available at her school" hardly qualified as both "reasonable and necessary" under § 707(b)(2)(A)(ii)).

[286] Specific tables are provided for family sizes of 1, 2, 3, and 4 people.

[287] Family members over 65 are allowed $144 while those under are allowed $60, for cases filed on and after May 1, 2013. See http://www.justice.gov/ust/eo/bapcpa/20130501/bci_data/national_oop_healthcare.htm.

B. LOCAL STANDARDS

The second set of IRS Collection Standards is the *Local Standards*. The Local Standards establish allowances for two categories of necessary expenses:

(1) housing and utilities (which are provided for each county within a state), and

(2) transportation (which is provided on a regional basis).

This data is also found on the U.S. Trustee website.[288] The applicable locations (county or region) are determined by where the debtor resides as of the date of the order for relief. Recall that the debtor is (probably—thanks for the uncertainty, *Ransom*) allowed to deduct the "amount specified" in the Local Standards, even if his actual expenses are lower, *if* that expense is "applicable" to the debtor.[289]

The housing and utilities allowance is broken down into two components: (1) non-mortgage expenses, and (2) mortgage or rent expenses. The allowance is further differentiated by family size. The amounts allowed are updated periodically. For example, in Champaign County, Illinois, for a case filed on and after May 1, 2013, the allowances for a single debtor would be $417 in non-mortgage expenses and $904 for mortgage or rent (a total of $1,321), whereas a debtor who has a family of 4 people would be entitled to $576 in non-mortgage expenses and $1,246 for mortgage or rent (a total of $1,822).

Looking at the tables, one can see a huge potential for manipulating the outcome of the means test by moving prior to filing bankruptcy. If the Champaign debtor with a family of 4 were to move to Cook County (i.e., Chicago) and then file bankruptcy, her $1,822 housing allowance would jump to $2,516 ($662 non-mortgage and $1,854 mortgage or rent)—a difference of $694 per month, and thus a total additional deduction over the 60–month means test calculation period of $41,640 on housing alone. Transportation allowances, discussed below, also would jump higher. Recall also that the debtor's income is computed on an historical basis, so even if the move to Cook County were for a more lucrative job, the debtor would not have to count those increased future wages in the means test. Such "planning" maneuvers might help the debtor pass the means test and escape a presumption of abuse under § 707(b)(2), leaving only the possible attack of "bad faith" or the "totality of the circumstances" as a basis for abuse, under § 707(b)(3).

This in-state differentiation by county of housing deductions for purposes of the federal bankruptcy means test poses a serious constitutional issue of uniformity.[290]

---

[288] For example, the transportation allowance for the Midwest region is found at: http://www.justice.gov/ust/eo/bapcpa/20130501/bci_data/IRS_Trans_Exp_Stds_MW.htm.

For housing and utilities, an Illinois debtor would look at: http://www.justice.gov/ust/eo/bapcpa/20130501/bci_data/housing_charts/irs_housing_charts_IL.htm.

[289] *Ransom,* 131 S.Ct. at 726.

[290] See § 1.10.c. See also Hon. Samuel L. Bufford & Erwin Chemerinsky, Constitutional Problems in the 2005 Bankruptcy Amendments, 82 Am. Bankr. L.J. 1, 39–45 (2008); Erwin Chemerinsky, Constitutional Issues Posed in the Bankruptcy Abuse Prevention and Consumer Protection Act of 2005, 79 Am. Bankr. L.J. 571, 592–94 (2005).

While the Supreme Court has upheld what it calls "geographical" uniformity,[291] those decisions were based on the idea that the constitutional grant to enact "uniform" laws on the subject of bankruptcies was not offended when the in-bankruptcy outcome mirrored results that would obtain outside of bankruptcy under state law "if the bankrupt law had not been passed."[292] The means test expense deduction differences, by contrast, create non-uniform results in federal bankruptcy cases (1) *within* states, not just between states, and, perhaps even more tellingly, (2) *not* based on underlying state laws of general applicability to creditors and debtors.[293] However, the Sixth Circuit held that the absence of either of these two justifications for allowing non-uniform results did not present a constitutional problem under another means test provision, effectively concluding that in the bankruptcy context the "uniformity" test was almost meaningless.[294] A similar constitutional problem of uniformity plagues the transportation deduction, to be discussed next, for the same reasons.

The transportation allowance has three components:

(1) ownership costs;

(2) operating costs; and

(3) public transportation costs.

Different allowances are provided depending on whether the debtor has no car, one car, or two cars. Two cars is the maximum for which allowances may be claimed, even if the debtor actually owns more than two cars.

The *ownership* cost is based on a national standard. The national allowance is $517 for each car, up to the two-car maximum. Obviously, if the debtor owns no cars, he does not get an ownership expense deduction, or an operating cost deduction.

Before the 2011 *Ransom* decision,[295] a long-debated issue was whether a debtor who owns a car free and clear could nevertheless claim the "ownership cost" deduction. Following *Ransom*'s holding that the ownership deduction is "applicable" only to debtors with current loan or lease payments on their car, debtors who own their vehicle outright cannot claim the ownership deduction.

Perhaps at first blush it seems fair that only those incurring an expense related to the ownership of their car should be allowed an ownership deduction, but recall that

---

[291] Hanover Nat'l Bank v. Moyses, 186 U.S. 181 (1902) (allowing use of state exemption laws in bankruptcy). See also Stellwagen v. Clum, 245 U.S. 605 (1918) (allowing use of state fraudulent conveyance laws in bankruptcy).

[292] *Moyses,* supra note 291.

[293] The only Court of Appeals to address the uniformity issue found these provisions to be uniform; the case was determined by a uniformity issue in chapter 13, which the court thought identical to the chapter 7 issues. Schultz v. United States 529 F.3d 343 (6th Cir. 2008). The court noted the existence of the differences within states, but did not subject them to any separate analysis.

[294] Id. See also In rc Cox, 393 B.R. 681 (Bankr. W.D. Mo. 2008) (objective standards for expense deductions rather than actual expenses was rationally related to congressional purpose and did not violate debtor's equal protection rights).

[295] 131 S.Ct. 716 (2011). See supra notes 259–70, 274–82 and accompanying text.

the means test is designed to be a mechanical, standardized test, one that allows for some over-allowances and under-allowances. The particular subsection at issue distinguishes between Other Necessary Expenses, where only the debtor's *actual* expenses are allowed, and the National and Local Standards, which permit the debtor to deduct the "*amount specified*" in the relevant standard, if "applicable." Justice Scalia argued that "applicable" here should mean that the debtor owns a car, not that the debtor owns a car *and* has an actual ownership expense.[296] Attempting to correct for inexact matches between claimed and actual expenses is a fool's errand under the means test as currently enacted. For example, even after *Ransom*, it is still possible (indeed, likely) that a debtor who owes a mere $1 a month can claim the full $517 ownership deduction. The Court in *Ransom* expressly left that question open.[297] However, if the debtor pays off that last dollar, according to *Ransom*, the debtor can no longer claim the $517 deduction. Justice Scalia pointed out this absurdity, among others, in his dissent in *Ransom*.[298]

There is no question, however, nor has there ever been, that if a debtor's actual expenses are *higher* than the relevant standard, the debtor's ownership cost deduction for transportation is capped at the "amount specified" in the standard.[299] Note, though, that the debtor may be able still to claim some or all of that higher expense separately under the secured debt expense deduction authorized in § 707(b)(2)(iii).

Operating costs are provided on a regional basis for either one car or two cars. For example, in the Midwest region, our Champaign debtor, who does not reside in a MSA (Metropolitan Statistical Area), would be allotted the basic Midwest region allowance of $212 for one car and $424 for two cars.[300] Thus, if our hypothetical Champaign debtor had one car, she would be permitted a total transportation deduction of $729 per month ($517 ownership cost for the first car, and $212 operating cost for one car). This assumes that she has no provable public transportation costs; if she does, then those would be added as well. If that debtor had a second car, she could claim twice as much—$1,458. Even without considering secured debt expenses, that debtor thus would enjoy an additional deduction of $729 per month attributable solely to the second car (and thus an additional $43,740 expense deduction for the 60–month means test computation).

The *public transportation* allowance of $182 is also calculated on a national basis. A debtor who does not own any cars is entitled to claim the whole public transportation allowance without showing actual expenses. A debtor who also is claiming a deduction for operating expenses for a car may try to claim all or part of the public transportation allowance as well, but may not do so as a matter of right. Instead, such a debtor must show actual necessary expenditures.

---

[296] 131 S.Ct. at 731 (Scalia, J., dissenting).

[297] Id. at 727 n.8 (Kagan, J., majority). See supra notes 281–82 and accompanying text.

[298] Id. at 732 (Scalia, J., dissenting).

[299] *Ransom*, 131 S.Ct. at 727.

[300] See http://www.justice.gov/ust/eo/bapcpa/20130501/bci_data/IRS_Trans_Exp_Stds_MW.htm.

A debtor in a MSA typically enjoys a larger operating cost and public transportation cost deduction than a debtor who does not. For example, a debtor in the Chicago MSA would be allowed $262 for one car and $524 for two cars—$50 and $100 more than the basic Midwest region allowance.

An important question in applying the means test is how the allowances for the Local Standards under § 707(b)(2)(A)(ii)(I) interact with the deduction for secured debt payments under § 707(b)(2)(A)(iii). The issue is whether the debtor can "double count"—that is, may she claim deductions for *both* the full amount specified for ownership costs in the Local Standards *and* for the entire secured debt for housing and cars (that will come due in the 60–month period)? Notwithstanding reputable authority to the contrary, I think not. The Code states:

> "*Notwithstanding any other provision of this clause, the monthly expenses of the debtor shall not include any payments of debt.*" § 707(b)(2)(A)(ii)(I).

The most plausible interpretation of this provision is to require the debtor to subtract from the IRS Standards all payments on secured debts that otherwise would fall within the IRS categories.[301] That is, a debtor would have to subtract "any payments of debt" from the ownership portion of the transportation allowance and from the mortgage portion of the housing allowance under § 707(b)(2)(A)(ii)(I). The debtor then could claim the full secured debt deduction under § 707(b)(2)(A)(iii). That way, the secured debt for the mortgage and car loans would be counted once. Since the debtor only has to make those payments once, this approach makes logical sense as well as giving meaning to the statutory language quoted above.

Recall, though, subject to the possible *Ransom* uncertainty, that a debtor *is* entitled to the full Local Standard allowances for housing and for transportation "specified" in the IRS Standards—even if the specified allowances are higher than the debtor's actual expenses, as long as that expense is "applicable" to the debtor. Thus, if the debtor's secured debt payment is *less* than the ownership portion of the Local Standard, then under the IRS Standard the debtor would get the net balance left after subtracting the secured debt payment.[302] The full secured debt payment then would be claimed as a deduction under the secured debt part of the means test. For example, assume a debtor owns one car, on which she has a $350 monthly secured debt obligation. Since the ownership cost allowance for a debtor's first car is $517 under the Local Standard, that debtor would get a net transportation ownership allowance under the Local Standard of $167 ($517 as "specified" minus the $350 secured debt obligation). She then would deduct the $350 secured debt obligation under § 707(b)(2)(A)(iii), giving her a total expense deduction under the means test for the ownership cost of her one car of exactly $517 (just as the Local Standard allows): $167 under the Local Standard plus $350 for secured debt. However, if no subtraction for secured debt were required, this debtor would enjoy a total means test deduction for the ownership portion of her car of $867: $517 under the Local Standard and $350 for secured debt. I do not believe Congress so intended.

---

[301]   This is the approach taken in Official Form B22A, Part V, Subpart A.

[302]   If the secured debt obligation were *greater* than the Local Standard ownership cost allowance, the subtraction would simply zero out the Local Standard ownership cost allowance—it would not require a negative assessment against the debtor for the balance. That debtor just would not have a Local Standard ownership cost deduction. Official Form B22A makes this clear. See, e.g., In re Scott, 457 B.R. 740 (Bankr. S.D. Ill. 2011); In re Hardacre, 338 B.R. 718 (Bankr. N.D. Tex. 2006).

There is a competing view, which argues that secured debt payments do *not* have to be deducted from the amount "specified" in the standard.[303] The argument rests on a proffered strict reading of the statutory text (with a dash of policy thrown in). Essentially the pitch is twofold. First, the deduction for secured debt payments is in a separate subsection of § 707(b)(2)(A) from the deduction for IRS Collection Standards. Second, the amounts deducted under the Standards are "amounts specified" and are not "payments for debts" and thus do not fall within the statutory prohibition against including any payments for debts. Under this view, the debt payment prohibition would apply *only* to the "Other Necessary Expenses" Standard, which does not specify an amount but looks to the actual expenses of the debtor. The courts, however, have not embraced this position, but instead follow the "no double-counting" approach argued for above and adopted by the Official Form.

C. OTHER NECESSARY EXPENSES

The final category of IRS expenses that a debtor may deduct under the means test is called *Other Necessary Expenses.*" Unlike the allowances for expenses under the National Standards and the Local Standards, there is no question that only *actual* expenses of the debtor are permitted as Other Necessary Expenses. In this category, no set allowance is specified by the IRS. The IRS test is a basic one: expenses are allowed *"if they meet the necessary expense test—they must provide for the health and welfare of the taxpayer and/or his or her family or they must be for the production of income."*[304] Examples in the Internal Revenue Manual of possibly allowable "other" expenses include child care, education (if required for the debtor's job),[305] life insurance, court-ordered payments such as alimony or child support,[306] mandatory payroll deductions, and income and social security taxes.[307] For many debtors, the income tax expense will be the largest. Note that § 707(b)(2)(A)(ii)(I) specifically provides that "reasonably necessary health insurance, disability insurance, and health savings account expenses" may be counted as deductions in this category.

The bankruptcy judge will have to exercise discretion to determine how much to allow to the debtor as "Other Necessary Expenses." This is of course inescapable for such a category, but it flies in the face of one the primary goals of the means test, which was to take as much discretion as possible out of the hands of the bankruptcy judges and institute a mechanical test instead.

---

[303] See, e.g., Henry J. Sommer, Trying to Make Sense Out of Nonsense: Representing Consumers Under the Bankruptcy Abuse Prevention and Consumer Protection Act of 2005, 79 Am. Bankr. L.J. 191, 197–99 (2005).

[304] Internal Revenue Manual § 5.15.1.10, #1 (at http://www.irs.gov/irm/part5/irm_05-015-001.html#d0e1954) (emphasis added).

[305] One court allowed a debtor to deduct internet expenses, which were needed for employment related matters. In re Williams, 424 B.R. 207 (Bankr. W.D. Va. 2010).

[306] One court found that childcare expenses were not reasonable when the debtor-wife, who was unemployed, had time to care for her child. In re Reed, 422 B.R. 214 (C.D. Cal. 2009).

[307] Official Form B22A lists these categories, among others, in lines 25–32.

2. *Miscellaneous Living Expenses*

In addition to the expenses a debtor may deduct under the IRS Collection Financial Standards under § 707(b)(2)(A)(ii)(I), Congress included a laundry list of other types of potentially deductible expenses.[308] § 707(b)(2)(A)(ii)(I)–(V). There is little rhyme or reason to the inclusions. In no particular order, they include:

• *Expenses for protection from family violence.* A debtor may deduct "reasonably necessary expenses incurred to maintain the safety of the debtor and the debtor's family from family violence." § 707(b)(2)(A)(ii)(I)

• *Continued contributions for the care of family or household members.*[309] A debtor may claim expenses for the "care and support" of an "elderly, chronically ill, or disabled" member of the debtor's household or member of the debtor's immediate family (including parents, grandparents, siblings, children, and grandchildren of the debtor, dependents of the debtor and spouse of the debtor in a joint case). § 707(b)(2)(A)(ii)(II). To be allowed, these expenses must satisfy a host of qualifiers: they must be actual, continuing, reasonable, and necessary.

• *Actual expenses of administering a chapter 13 plan.* For debtors eligible for chapter 13, the debtor can deduct actual administrative expenses of administering a chapter 13 case in the district where the debtor resides. § 707(b)(2)(A)(ii)(III). This deduction is consistent with the theory underlying the means test, since a desire to move "can-pay" debtors into chapter 13 must take into account the realities of a prospective chapter 13 case. The U.S. Trustee's office publishes schedules of permissible chapter 13 expenses.[310] The debtor is capped by statute at deducting 10% of the projected plan payments, but a smaller percentage may be scheduled, depending on the judicial district.

• *School expenses.* The debtor is allowed to claim actual expenses, up to $1,875, per minor child per year (i.e., about $156 per month), for the debtor's minor children (i.e., less than 18 years old) to attend a private or public elementary or secondary school. § 707(b)(2)(A)(ii)(IV). The debtor must document the expense and explain why it is "reasonable and necessary," as well as why the expense is not already accounted for in the IRS Standards.

• *Additional home energy costs.* If a debtor's actual home energy costs are higher than those allowed by the IRS Local Standards for housing and utilities, the debtor may be able to deduct her actual expenses, provided she documents them and shows why the extra expense is reasonable and necessary.[311] § 707(b)(2)(A)(ii)(V).

---

[308] These expenses are listed in Official Form B22A, Part V, Subpart B.

[309] Debtors have tried to fit expenses paid to their children in college here, to no avail. See, e.g., In re Linville, 446 B.R. 522 (Bankr. D.N.M. 2011); In re Williams, 424 B.R. 207 (Bankr. W.D. Va. 2010); In re Harris, 415 B.R. 756 (Bankr. E.D. Cal. 2009).

[310] See http://www.justice.gov/ust/eo/bapcpa/20130501/bci_data/ch13_exp_mult.htm.

[311] See, e.g., In re Barbutes, 436 B.R. 518 (Bankr. M.D. Tenn. 2010) (holding that debtor whose home had "special maintenance needs," thus requiring high utility bills, could deduct the higher utility amounts).

• *Extra 5% for food and clothing*. As explained above in connection with the deduction for food and clothing under the IRS National Standards, a debtor may be entitled to up to an extra 5% for food and clothing, provided she can demonstrate that such a bump is "reasonable and necessary." § 707(b)(2)(A)(ii)(I).

• *Charitable Contributions*. When the bankruptcy court is considering whether to dismiss a case for abuse under § 707(b)(1), "the court may not take into consideration whether a debtor has made, or continues to make," charitable monetary contributions to a qualified religious or charitable organization. § 707(b)(1). This limitation was in § 707(b) prior to BAPCPA. Significantly, note that the charitable contributions exclusion does not place any dollar limit on the amount of charitable contributions that a debtor may count under the means test calculation. The only limits are: (1) it must be a "charitable contribution";[312] (2) it must be made to a qualified (i.e., tax exempt) religious or charitable organization;[313] and (3) it must be rooted in the debtor's pre-bankruptcy past— that is, it must be a contribution that the debtor "has made, or continues to make." § 707(b)(1). Thus, a debtor cannot "get religion" after filing bankruptcy and escape the clutches of the means test. But if the contemplation of bankruptcy triggered the debtor's charitable impulses, so that the debtor actually made contributions prior to filing, that hurdle is surmounted.

(b) Secured Debt Payments

The second major category of deductions under the means test is for secured debt payments. The debtor may subtract the average monthly payments on account of secured debts that are to come due over the five-year period of a chapter 13 plan. § 707(b)(2)(A)(iii). The debtor first must compute the total payments scheduled as contractually due to secured creditors in the 60 months following the date of the petition. § 707(b)(2)(A)(iii)(I). Next, the debtor must add payments necessary to retain possession of her primary residence, motor vehicle, and any other necessary property. § 707(b)(2)(A)(iii)(II). The second category is typically for payments to cure arrearages. The total of the two categories then is divided by 60 to give the average monthly obligation for secured debts.

The secured debt deduction makes sense on the same rationale as the deduction for prospective chapter 13 administrative expenses. Secured creditors are entitled to insist on full payment out of their collateral in chapter 13. If the premise of the means test is to bar from chapter 7 those debtors who could succeed in chapter 13, then the chapter 7 means test calculus must take the realities of chapter 13 into account.

One point to note about the secured debt deduction is that it discriminates against renters. Those who rent a home or apartment, or those who lease a car rather than making secured debt payments on the car, would be entitled under the means test to deduct only the limited amount specified by the IRS Standards for housing and for

---

[312] See 11 U.S.C. § 548(d)(3). The limiting aspects of that definition are that it must be made by a natural person, be made in cash or a financial instrument (thus no in-kind contributions will count), and must meet the Internal Revenue Code's definition of "charitable contribution" in § 170(c).

[313] See 11 U.S.C. § 548(d)(4).

transportation, even if the rent were higher than specified in the Standard. A debtor who has mortgage or car debt, however, would be entitled to deduct his entire secured debt, even if larger than the Standard.

Another problem with the secured debt deduction is one of perverse incentives. Without question, in making the means test calculation, the debtor is *rewarded* for having larger amounts of secured debt. The means test itself contains no limitations on the secured debt deduction, other than that the projected expenses be actual. Thus, there are no restrictions as to the amount of the secured debt, its necessity, or the circumstances under which the debt was incurred. The only way that such concerns might be addressed is through a "bad faith" or totality" dismissal under § 707(b)(3). The Supreme Court took note of this, stating that the means test "enhances incentives to incur additional debt prior to filing, as payments on secured debts offset a debtor's monthly income under the formula."[314]

Consider a case of two hypothetical debtors, who are virtual clones: their current monthly income is the same; they are allowed the same monthly expense deductions; their priority claim deductions are the same; and their total unsecured nonpriority debt is the same. However, Debtor One has more secured debt than does Debtor Two; Debtor One has scheduled monthly payments on a $800,000 home, a motor home, and a boat.[315] Assume further that this secured debt differential is outcome-determinative regarding the means test: Debtor One passes the means test because of her higher level of secured debt, but Debtor Two, who has less secured debt, flunks the means test. Thus, the debtor with *less* debt is the one found to be a presumed abuser!

Several secured debt pre-bankruptcy planning strategies might help a debtor pass the means test. She could incur additional secured debt in the pre-bankruptcy period. Prior to bankruptcy, she could pay more on her *un*secured debts, at the expense of her *secured* debts, leaving her with more secured debt when the means test is computed. Finally, the debtor could let payments on her primary residence or motor vehicle lapse, since she could subtract any payments required to cure arrearages. None of these strategies can be policed through the means test. As noted above, the only check on such behavior is through a discretionary "bad faith" or "totality" assessment under § 707(b)(3).

Courts debate whether a debtor can deduct scheduled secured debt payments for property that the debtor intends to *surrender* to the secured creditor but which has not been returned when the case is filed (or even by the time the motion to dismiss is filed). There are three general approaches. Some courts allow the deduction.[316] They read the statute literally—until surrender and a corresponding release of lien by the creditor, the secured debt payments are "scheduled as contractually due" under

---

[314] Milavetz, Gallop & Milavetz, P.A. v. U.S., 130 S.Ct. 1324, 1336 (2010).

[315] A debtor *did* actually owe all of those secured debts in one case. Nevertheless, the court ruled that this was not an abuse warranting dismissal. In re Jensen, 407 B.R. 378 (Bankr. C.D. Cal. 2009).

[316] See, e.g., In re Rivers, 466 B.R. 558 (Bankr. M.D. Fla. 2012); In re Grinkmeyer, 456 B.R. 385 (Bankr. S.D. Ind. 2011).

§ 707(b)(2)(A)(iii)(I) and thus must be subtracted.[317] Conversely, other courts read the "scheduled" language to refer to the documents accompanying the bankruptcy petition.[318] Under this interpretation, any property that the debtor states an intention to surrender is no longer "scheduled" within the meaning of the statute. Finally, a third approach is to consider the state of the property at the time of the motion to dismiss: if it has already been surrendered, then the future payments on it cannot be claimed as secured debt expenses, but if it has not yet been surrendered, the scheduled payments can be subtracted from income, notwithstanding the debtor's stated intention to surrender.[319] That the statute fairly can be (perhaps must be?) read to permit a debtor to deduct future secured debt expenses that are "scheduled" even though the debtor has stated in court documents an intention to surrender that very collateral is yet another case in point of the problematic drafting that plagued BAPCPA.

The debate concerning the deductibility of secured mortgage payments the debtor intends to surrender is a debate in which the question of *Ransom*'s application to chapter 7 cases comes naturally. After all, the dual focus in *Ransom* on maximizing creditor recoveries and allowing debtors to claim only actually incurred expenses argues against allowing debtors this deduction if the debtor plans to surrender the collateral. Yet, the question remains whether *Ransom* properly fits into a chapter 7 analysis, especially here. One preliminary issue is that *Ransom* concerned § 707(b)(2)(A)(ii)(I) and the word "applicable," whereas secured debt payments are mentioned in § 707(b)(2)(A)(iii), where the word "applicable" is not found. Indeed, one court relied on this statutory difference to preclude *Ransom*'s application.[320] Other courts have found that *Ransom* did not apply to chapter 7 debtors intending to surrender properties,[321] while others have concluded that *Ransom* does apply.[322] Remember that even if *Ransom* is found not to apply, the debtor still has to clear the § 707(b)(3) "totality of the circumstances" and "bad faith" hurdles.[323]

(c) Priority Claims

The third and final category of deductions is for the debtor's unsecured debts that are entitled to priority. § 707(b)(2)(A)(iv). Priority claims include such debts as domestic support obligations, administrative expenses, and pre-petition taxes. § 507(a). Under the means test, a debtor is allowed to subtract from current monthly income all

---

[317] See, e.g., In re Lindstrom, 381 B.R. 303 (Bankr. D. Colo. 2007); In re Walker, 2006 WL 1314125 (Bankr. N.D. Ga. May 1, 2006).

[318] See, e.g., In re Fredman, 471 B.R. 540 (Bankr. S.D. Ill. 2012); In re Thompson, 457 B.R. 872 (Bankr. M.D. Fla. 2011); In re Rudler, 576 F.3d 37 (1st Cir. 2009); In re Skaggs, 349 B.R. 594 (Bankr. E.D. Mo. 2006).

[319] See, e.g., In re Vecera, 430 B.R. 840 (Bankr. S.D. Ind. 2010); In re Singletary, 354 B.R. 455 (Bankr. S.D. Tex. 2006); In re Nockerts, 357 B.R. 497 (Bankr. E.D. Wis. 2006).

[320] In re Sonntag, 2011 WL 3902999 (Bankr. N.D. W. Va. Sept. 6, 2011).

[321] *Grinkmeyer*, supra note 316.

[322] *Fredman*, see supra note 318. *Fredman* not only finds that *Ransom* can be grafted onto chapter 7 cases to "look forward," but also cites *Ransom*'s reasoning that cases should be decided in favor of creditors as support for its conclusion that the debtors cannot claim the mortgage expense deduction for property they intend to surrender.

[323] In *Grinkmeyer*, supra note 316, the court found abuse under subsection (b)(3).

of his expenses for payment of all priority claims (including priority child support and alimony claims). The monthly deduction amount is determined by summing the total priority debt and then dividing by 60 (again, to replicate the 60–month chapter 13 payment period).

The logic of the priority claim deduction is similar to that for secured debt. To confirm a chapter 13 plan, a debtor must provide for the payment in full of all priority claims. § 1322(a)(2). Thus, to assess whether a debtor is a presumptive chapter 7 "abuser" on the theory that the debtor instead could confirm and complete a chapter 13 plan, that debtor has to be allowed to deduct all payments he would be required to make in that hypothetical chapter 13. In one case the debtors tried to deduct their student loan payments, since they are not dischargeable. However, the court denied this classification, as it does not fit in any category listed in § 507, which governs priority.[324]

The problem with the priority claim deduction mirrors that of the secured debt deduction, namely, creating perverse incentives. The more priority debt a debtor has, the better that debtor's chances of passing the means test. Thus, a debtor who is contemplating filing chapter 7 and whose monthly net income is close to the presumptive abuse trigger point would be better off *not* to pay priority claims prior to bankruptcy, and to pay his nonpriority debt instead. Yet, priority claims typically are the ones that Congress cares most should be paid, such as alimony and child support. The means test deduction gives debtors exactly the opposite incentive.

(4) Rebuttal of Presumption of Abuse

Congress sought to create as mechanical a means test as possible in BAPCPA to exclude supposed "can pay" debtors from chapter 7. One of the primary complaints the consumer credit industry had about the operation of the prior "substantial abuse" test was that it gave too much discretion to bankruptcy judges—discretion they exercised way too often, in the industry's view, in favor of consumer debtors. Thus, a key aspect of the 2005 reforms was to curb the bankruptcy judges' discretion in finding "abuse." Nevertheless, it would have been impossible to eliminate all discretion, without sacrificing substantial justice in many individual cases. Without a discretionary safety valve permitting individualized adjustments, a debtor who lost her job shortly before bankruptcy might fail the means test based on historical income from a job she no longer had. A debtor with unavoidably high medical expenses due to a serious medical condition would be deemed to have income available to repay creditors when in reality she did not. Thus, to ensure that these sorts of debtors are not unfairly denied access to chapter 7, Congress added a provision allowing a debtor to rebut the presumption of abuse.

Section 707(b)(2)(B) outlines the guidelines for rebuttal. To rebut, the debtor must demonstrate *"special circumstances"* showing "that justify additional expenses or adjustments of current monthly income." Furthermore, the debtor must show that he had *"no reasonable alternative"* but to make the adjustments attributable to the special circumstances. § 707(b)(2)(B)(i). Rebuttal of the presumption of abuse is successful if

---

[324] In re Thompson, 457 B.R. 872 (Bankr. M.D. Fla. 2011).

the adjustments that decrease income or increase expenses suffice to bring the monthly net income below the applicable presumptive-abuse trigger point. § 707(b)(2)(B)(iv).

What might qualify as "special circumstances"? Of necessity, this will be an intensely fact-driven inquiry.[325] The Code specifically cites a serious medical condition or a call or order to active duty in the armed services as examples. But almost anything could qualify, as long as the debtor can show necessity, reasonableness, and lack of a reasonable alternative. So, for example, a rural Iowa debtor was able to claim the operating expenses on a second car, since "at any given time, one of the vehicles may be inoperable due to a deer collision."[326]

Procedurally, the debtor is required to itemize each additional expense or reduction in income, and must provide documentation. The debtor also bears the burden of explaining in detail why the adjustments are "necessary and reasonable." § 707(b)(2)(B)(ii). The debtor must attest under oath to the accuracy of these statements. § 707(b)(2)(B)(iii).

d. Finding Abuse without a Presumption

An individual debtor with primarily consumer debts may survive the means test and escape the triggering of a presumption of abuse under § 707(b)(2) for several reasons. The debtor may have "current monthly income" below the relevant state family income median, and thus not be subject to means test scrutiny at all. § 707(b)(7). Even if the debtor's income is above the state median, once the means test calculation is performed, that debtor's net income may fall below the presumptive abuse trigger point. § 707(b)(2)(A)(i). Finally, even if the debtor is subject to the means test, and even if the debtor's net income exceeds the presumptive abuse trigger, that debtor might successfully *rebut* the presumption of abuse. § 707(b)(2)(B). Is such a means test survivor then completely immune to dismissal for abuse under § 707(b)(1)?

The answer is no. The presumption of abuse is just that—a presumption; nothing more, nothing less. For individual debtors with primarily consumer debts, the dismissal test under § 707(b) is a single one: *abuse*, under § 707(b)(1). The means test under subsection (2) serves simply to trigger a presumption of abuse. However, even if

---

[325] See, e.g., In re Fetcher, 456 B.R. 65 (Bankr. D. Mont. 2011) (new luxury vehicle not a special circumstance); In re Tuss, 360 B.R. 684 (Bankr. D. Mont. 2007) (debtor's job requiring him to be away from home for long periods of time, thus incurring restaurant and rental bills, were not a special circumstance); In re Littman, 370 B.R. 820 (Bankr. D. Idaho 2007) (child support debt was a special circumstance); In re Blair, 214 B.R. 257 (Bankr. D. Me. 1997) (debtor's poor health was not special circumstance when no evidence indicating chapter 13 proceeding would be deleterious to their health).

Courts have been all over the map on whether student loans constitute a special circumstance. See, e.g., In re Sanders, 454 B.R. 855 (Bankr. M.D. Ala. 2011) (student loan obligations were special circumstance); In re Johnson, 446 B.R. 921 (Bankr. E.D. Wis. 2011) (student loan debt incurred as part of shift in career from working as nurse to seeking employment as attorney, because of weight issues precluding her success from working as a nurse, did not qualify as special circumstance); In re Haman, 366 B.R. 307 (Bankr. D. Del. 2007) (debtor's nondischargeable obligation as co-signer on her son's student loans qualified as special circumstance).

[326] In re Batzkiel, 349 B.R. 581 (Bankr. N.D. Iowa 2006). The debtor could not afford to turn in any more deer collision claims to his insurance company (he had four in one year!), or his car insurance would have been cancelled. The debtor also was allowed a large additional gas allowance, since he and his wife had to commute round-trip to work 40 and 70 miles respectively.

there is no presumption of abuse, the core issue of, and possibility of, "abuse" remains. Any doubt on this score is eliminated conclusively by § 707(b)(3). In that subsection, Congress makes clear that the court may determine "whether the granting of relief would be an abuse" under subsection (b)(1) even "in a case in which the presumption . . . does not arise or is rebutted."

The grounds a court should consider in making that determination of abuse are spelled out as well: first, whether the debtor filed in *"bad faith,"* § 707(b)(3)(A); and second, whether the *"totality of the circumstances* . . . of the debtor's financial situation" shows abuse. § 707(b)(3)(B). The "bad faith" ground was introduced explicitly in the Code in chapter 7 cases for the first time in 2005; previously, courts had invoked bad faith in filing as a species of "cause" for dismissal under § 707(a).[327] Notably, this change means that a dismissal motion based on bad faith now is subject to all of the procedural constraints in § 707(b) (including the fact that only the United States Trustee or the court may bring a dismissal motion against debtors with income below the state median family income).[328]

In the 2005 amendments, Congress expressly identified one factor the court should consider as relevant to the "totality of the circumstances" test: where the debtor seeks to reject a personal services contract and the financial need for such rejection. Dismissal seems a blunt instrument to deal with such a case; simply denying an unmeritorious rejection motion would seem more appropriate.

The *"totality of the circumstances"* test was used by many courts under the pre–2005 law to determine "substantial abuse."[329] The factors relevant to this "totality" determination included: (1) the triggering reason for the bankruptcy filing (e.g., whether the petition was filed as a consequence of illness, disability, unemployment, or some other calamity); (2) the debtor's immediate pre-bankruptcy financial behavior (e.g., whether the debtor made substantial eve-of-bankruptcy credit purchases, or obtained large cash advances); (3) whether the debtor was forthcoming in the bankruptcy case, by filing an accurate statement of income and expenses; (4) the debtor's projected future financial behavior (e.g., whether the proposed budget is excessive or extravagant); and (5) whether the petition was filed in good faith. How much should courts applying § 707(b)(3)(B) draw upon the pre–2005 "totality" precedents? Obviously, at least the last factor (good faith) is duplicative of the alternative ground in current § 707(b)(3)(A) and should not also be considered as part of the current totality of the circumstances test.

The most controversial question under subsection (3) is whether the debtor's ability to repay his debts in the future can be considered, either as part of the totality of the circumstances calculus or as relevant to a showing of bad faith. Prior to 2005, when courts had *only* the undefined "substantial abuse" test and utilized the totality of the circumstances analysis to determine substantial abuse, they obviously could and did consider a debtor's ability to pay as one factor. BAPCPA, however, radically

---

[327] See § 2.14.

[328] 11 U.S.C. § 707(b)(6). See also § 2.15.e.

[329] E.g., Green v. Staples (In re Green), 934 F.2d 568 (4th Cir. 1991).

changed this statutory scheme with the introduction of the extremely detailed means test as a formalized mechanism to test for abuse based on repayment ability. Accordingly, some have argued that under this revised scheme, Congress intended for the means test presumption in subsection (2) to be the *only* test of repayment ability, and that the more general tests of "bad faith" and "totality of the circumstances" in subsection (3) should not be interpreted to permit a second "can-pay" screening review.[330] Since Congress enacted an exhaustive *rule* to measure repayment ability in the means test, driven by a clear motivation to restrict judicial discretion on this question, it would be wrong, the argument goes, to retain a vague *standard* that also addresses the identical "can-pay debtor" problem. Instead, according to this school of thought, those subsection (3) tests should deal only with "serious debtor misconduct" other than simply repayment ability.[331]

A competing view, however, and the one that has been adopted by most courts, does not read the means test as the exclusive basis for testing repayment prospects.[332] Instead, courts can and should consider a debtor's payment ability under subsection (3) as well.[333] Nothing in the statute specifically states that the means test is the exclusive repayment screening mechanism, and indeed the statutory structure suggests that subsections (2) and (3) are simply two different and complementary ways of getting at the same core issue of "abuse" under subsection (1): subsection (2) generates a presumption of abuse in certain circumstances, while subsection (3) allows for a more generalized assessment of abuse without a presumption.[334] Congress in 2005 was most concerned with stopping the supposed abuse of debtors with significant repayment ability getting a discharge without having to make future payments to creditors, and the non-exclusivity approach furthers that purpose.

Note that under the exclusivity view, debtors with incomes in the preceding six months below the state median would *never* be susceptible to dismissal for abuse based on repayment ability, even if they could easily repay their debts out of future income. It is hard to imagine that the 109th Congress in BAPCPA actually intended to eliminate the possibility of dismissal based on future can-pay ability for a substantial class of debtors. At least in the case of these below-median debtors, who are not subject to the means test under subsection (2) at all, courts are holding that future payment capacity can be a basis for dismissal under subsection (3).[335] So, for example, a debtor whose six-

---

[330] See Marianne B. Culhane & Michaela M. White, Catching Can–Pay Debtors: Is the Means Test the Only Way?, 13 Am. Bankr. Inst. L. Rev. 665 (2005); Sommer, supra note 303, at 203.

[331] Culhane & White, supra note 330.

[332] See, e.g., Calhoun v. U.S. Tr., 650 F.3d 338 (4th Cir. 2011); In re Lanza, 450 B.R. 81 (Bankr. M.D. Pa. 2011); In re Lavin, 424 B.R. 558 (Bankr. M.D. Fla. 2010); In re Crink, 402 B.R. 159 (Bankr. M.D.N.C. 2009); In re Davis, 378 B.R. 539 (Bankr. N.D. Ohio 2007); In re Pennington, 348 B.R. 647 (Bankr. D. Del. 2006); In re Pak, 343 B.R. 239 (Bankr. N.D. Cal. 2006); In re Richie, 353 B.R. 569 (Bankr. E.D. Wis. 2006).

[333] The leading advocate of this view is Judge Eugene Wedoff. See Hon. Eugene R. Wedoff, Judicial Discretion to Find Abuse Under § 707(b)(3), 25 Am. Bankr. Inst. J. 1 (2006); Hon. Eugene R. Wedoff, Means Testing in the New § 707(b), 79 Am Bankr. L. Rev. 231, 236 (2005).

[334] A comparison could be made to the fraud exception to discharge in § 523(a), which creates a presumption of fraud in certain circumstances, but even when no presumption arises, it is open to an objecting creditor to try to prove fraud.

[335] See cases in supra note 332. But see In re Nockerts, 357 B.R. 497 (Bankr. E.D. Wis. 2006) (holding that an above median debtor who passed the means test cannot be dismissed under section (3) totality for ability to pay alone).

months' pre-bankruptcy historical income was low, and thus below the state median, but who currently has a job paying over $100,000 per year and could easily repay creditors, would be vulnerable to a "totality" dismissal under subsection (3).[336]

One class of cases that subsection (3) will help police for abuse are those in which the debtor through aggressive planning tries to game the means test in order to escape the presumption of abuse. So, for example, the debtor could either artificially depress historic income (quit a job, work fewer hours, and so forth) or inflate expenses on the eve of bankruptcy, especially by taking on secured debt or not paying priority debt. Recently, the Supreme Court referenced this type of pre-bankruptcy planning, referring to it as "abusive per se."[337] If a debtor owns a paid-off car, and trades it in and buys a Mercedes with an $800 a month secured debt payment the week before filing bankruptcy in order to reduce his net income below the presumptive abuse dollar trigger in § 707(b)(2)(A)(i), that debtor still will face the possibility of dismissal for abuse under subsection (3).[338] Interestingly, even those who advocate that the means test in subsection (2) should be the exclusive mechanism for dismissing the cases of debtors with repayment capacity would nevertheless allow a court to use subsection (3) to catch what they call "means test cheaters."[339] Of course, what is "cheating" and what is just permissible good planning is likely to be controversial.

e. Procedure

Prior to BAPCPA, the consumer credit industry believed that the "substantial abuse" test had become a virtual dead letter, both substantively and, equally as importantly, procedurally. One of the major reform goals in 2005 was to put serious bite in the abuse test for "can pay" debtors, on both the substantive and procedural fronts. The substantive fix, of course, was the means test and related provisions. The essential procedural change was to impose a presumptive directive for the United States trustee to file a motion to dismiss (or convert to chapter 13) if the debtor fails the means test. Under prior law, filing a dismissal motion was discretionary, and the exercise of that discretion effectively was unreviewable. No more.

Several new provisions of the Code work together to force the filing of the dismissal or conversion motion when a debtor fails the means test. Step one requires the debtor to provide the necessary information by filing with her schedules a statement of her "current monthly income" and the means test calculations that show whether or not a presumption of abuse arises. § 707(b)(2)(C); Official Form B22A. The obligation to file Form B22A applies to all individual debtors with primarily consumer debts, even if the debtor would not be subject to the means test, because of below-median income. Failure to file the statement within the time allotted is itself grounds for dismissal of the case. § 521(i)(1).

---

[336] *Pak*, supra note 332, 343 B.R. 239.

[337] Milavetz, Gallop & Milavetz, P.A. v. United States, 130 S.Ct. 1324, 1336 (2010).

[338] A related situation arose in a case where the abuse presumption arose, but the debtor tried to argue that her monthly $805.76 Mercedes payments warranted "special circumstances" that should suffice to rebut the presumption. However, the court did not buy the debtor's argument, finding that the debtor did have a "reasonable alternative," and dismissed the case. In re Fechter, 456 B.R. 65 (Bankr. D. Mont. 2011).

[339] See Culhane and White, supra note 330.

Once the debtor has filed the means test calculation and other required documents and schedules, step two requires the United States trustee to review the debtor's materials and file with the court a statement as to whether the debtor's case would be presumed to be an abuse under § 707(b). § 704(b)(1)(A). The United States trustee must file this statement not later than ten days after the date of the first meeting of creditors.[340] The court then must provide a copy of this statement to all creditors within seven days after receiving it. § 704(b)(1)(B).

Step three is triggered if the United States trustee determines that the debtor's case should be presumed to be an abuse under § 707(b) *and* the debtor's current monthly income multiplied by twelve is *above* the applicable state income median. In such a case, the United States trustee must act not later than 30 days after filing the statement under § 704(b)(1)(A) that the presumption of abuse has arisen. Within that 30–day period, the United States trustee is required *either* to file a motion to dismiss or convert under § 707(b), *or* to file a statement setting forth the reasons why the U.S. trustee does not believe such a motion is appropriate. § 704(b)(2). Neither the Code nor the legislative history give any examples as to what sorts of reasons might support finding that a dismissal or conversion motion is inappropriate. A case where the presumption of abuse would likely be rebutted because of "special circumstances"[341] would seem to be precisely the sort of situation where the U.S. trustee should refrain from filing an abuse motion.

This is not the end of the story, however. Standing to bring abuse motions was greatly expanded in 2005. If the United States trustee decides not to file a motion to dismiss or convert, other parties still have standing to file such a motion. Amended § 707(b)(1) allows not only the court or the United States trustee, but also the chapter 7 trustee or any party in interest, to file an abuse motion. This check on the United States trustee's discretion was an important cog in the credit industry reform package. Parties in interest have standing to file an abuse motion under § 707(b)(1) based either on the presumption of abuse under subsection (2) or because of bad faith or if warranted by the totality of the circumstances under subsection (3). It is likely that parties in interest first will wait to see if the U.S. trustee brings a motion.

The broadened standing rule of § 707(b)(1) only applies, though, if the debtor's income is *above* the applicable state median for the same family size. If the debtor's income (as augmented by the income of the debtor's spouse) is *below* the applicable state median, no one—not the judge, U.S. trustee, chapter 7 trustee, or any party in interest—has standing to file a motion to dismiss or convert based on the means test presumption of § 707(b)(2). § 707(b)(7). Note that this is true even if the means test calculation shows that the debtor has disposable income above the presumptive trigger amount. Furthermore, in a below-median income case, the only parties with standing to file a motion to dismiss or convert under § 707(b)(3) are the judge and the United

---

[340] The Code is unclear as to exactly when the 10–day period begins to run—is it from the first date *set* for the meeting of creditors, or from the *conclusion* of the meeting? Logic supports the latter, since if the original meeting is continued for some reason, the U.S. trustee may not have sufficient information to make a determination.

[341] See § 2.15.c.(4).

States trustee. § 707(b)(6). In short, for below-median debtors, the case trustee and individual creditors are denied standing to bring an abuse motion.

All creditors will receive notice if a presumption of abuse arises. As noted above, if the United States trustee's statement indicates that the presumption of abuse has arisen, all creditors must be notified within seven days. § 704(b)(1)(B). Additionally, if the presumption of abuse arises in an individual case, the clerk must notify all creditors in writing not later than ten days after the date of the filing of the petition. § 342(d).

If the presumption of abuse arises and a motion is filed to dismiss or convert, then the burden shifts to the debtor to rebut the presumption of abuse by demonstrating special circumstances. § 707(b)(2)(B). The debtor must document and justify those special circumstances.

The Code still appears to leave the ultimate question of whether to dismiss or (with the debtor's consent) convert a case for abuse to the discretion of the judge, since § 707(b)(1) provides that the court "may" dismiss or convert. However, given the presumption under § 707(b)(2) and the history of the enactment, Congress surely intended for judges to grant the motion to dismiss (or convert to chapter 13 with the debtor's consent) in cases where there is an unrebutted presumption of abuse and where the motion is filed by the United States trustee.

It is not as clear what the court should do if the United States trustee chooses *not* to file a dismissal motion as "not appropriate" under § 704(b)(2), even though the debtor fails the means test, and a party in interest then files such a motion. Under § 707(b)(2)(A)(i), the court "shall presume abuse exists" if the debtor fails the means test, leaving only the possibility of debtor rebuttal under § 707(b)(3). But surely some weight should be given to the United States trustee's decision not to file a dismissal motion. However, how to do so is unstated.

f. Sanctions

One controversial new provision under revised § 707(b) authorizes the court to impose sanctions against debtor's counsel if the case is dismissed or converted as an abuse under § 707(b) on motion of the trustee,[342] and the court finds that the attorney violated Rule 9011. § 707(b)(4). The court or any party in interest may move for sanctions in such cases.

The sanctions authorized are twofold. First, the court may order the debtor's attorney to reimburse the trustee for all reasonable costs the trustee incurred in prosecuting a motion under § 707(b), including reasonable attorney's fees. § 707(b)(4)(A). Second, the court may award a civil penalty against the debtor's attorney, payable to the chapter 7 trustee or United States trustee. § 707(b)(4)(B).

---

[342] Note that this rule does not apply in the common case where a United States trustee files the motion, or if a party in interest files, but instead only if the "trustee" files the motion.

In the form finally enacted, the sanctions provisions actually add little to prior law, since Rule 9011 already provided for the possibility of sanctions to be imposed in egregious cases. Earlier versions of the reform legislation, though, would have greatly expanded the exposure of debtor's attorneys, and prompted much wailing and gnashing of teeth, and indeed still color the perception of the sanctions rules actually enacted.

Rule 9011 is the bankruptcy equivalent to Federal Rule of Civil Procedure 11, and authorizes a court to impose sanctions against an attorney who commences a frivolous action with unsupported allegations or files inappropriate documents in violation of the rule. After BAPCPA, if an individual debtor's case is dismissed as abusive under § 707(b), the debtor's attorney *could* be sanctioned for filing what is tantamount to a frivolous lawsuit. However, the imposition of sanctions is unlikely unless the attorney's defalcation was severe. Under Rule 9011 (and Federal Rule of Civil Procedure 11), an attorney may rely upon objectively reasonable representations by a client, and only has a duty to investigate available documents.[343]

The new sanctions legislation provides that the signature of a debtor's attorney constitutes a certification that the attorney has "performed a reasonable investigation" and determined that "the petition, pleading or written motion is well grounded in fact and is warranted by existing law or a good faith argument for the extension, modification or reversal of existing law." § 707(b)(4)(C). These standards are almost identical to those of Rule 9011.[344]

Further, the attorney's signature constitutes a certification that the attorney has "determined" that the petition "does not constitute an abuse under paragraph (1)." § 707(b)(4)(C)(ii)(II). Here again, careful attention to the precise language of the statute should defuse the "sky is falling" fears that the legislation first prompted. The worry was that the debtor's attorney was certifying that the case was not an abuse, and thus if the case were dismissed as an abuse, then, *ipso facto,* the attorney would be open to sanction for making an invalid certification. That, however, is not what the statute says; it provides only that the attorney is certifying that he has *determined* that the case is not an abuse, which could still be a truthful and accurate certification even if the case were dismissed as an abuse. It would only be if the attorney actually believed that the case was an abuse, but filed under chapter 7 anyway, that the attorney's certification would be false.

Additionally, the signature certifies that the attorney "has no knowledge" after an inquiry that information contained in the schedules filed with the petition is incorrect. § 707(b)(4)(D). This provision has caused some concern that attorneys effectively are guarantors of the accuracy of the debtor's schedules. Such a worry seems overblown. Importantly, for a violation to occur, the statute requires that the attorney have actual *knowledge* that the information is wrong. As one commentator observed, "this is a pretty low standard that any honest attorney should meet,"[345] noting that even a suspicion or belief that the schedules are inaccurate would not be enough. Nor is the

---

[343] See Sommer, supra note 303, at 205.

[344] Id. at 204.

[345] Id. at 206.

debtor's attorney actually compelled to conduct an inquiry beyond what Rule 9011 already would have demanded; instead, the statute only speaks to what an attorney knows if the attorney does conduct an inquiry, and asks the attorney not to lie to the court.

Having said all that, since perception often becomes reality, the sense in the field is that the sanctions rules may have made it more difficult—or at least more expensive—for debtors to file under chapter 7 in cases that fall close to the abuse line. Whether required or not, the reality is that many attorneys are conducting more exhaustive (and expensive) independent investigations into the truth of the representations their debtor clients make to them. For example, it has been reported that many debtor's attorneys now are hiring appraisers to value the debtor's property.[346] Certainly debtor's attorneys' fees in consumer chapter 7 cases have increased dramatically since BAPCPA became law, and the perceived risk of sanctions could be one contributing cause.

More troubling are some of the provisions regulating *"debt relief agencies."* Of particular concern is § 526(a)(4), which prohibits a debt relief agency from "advis[ing] an assisted person or prospective assisted person to incur more debt in contemplation of such person filing a case under this title." Congress inserted this provision in an effort to stop abusive manipulation of the bankruptcy process. The concern is that if this prohibition is applied as written to attorneys, it would impinge on the First Amendment rights of attorneys by precluding them from giving even legally permissible advice to their clients. It also would also infringe upon the states' traditional power to regulate attorneys. The problem is that the statute is very broadly written; it bans advising the incurrence of *any* debt, even lawful debts or debts that the debtor fully intends to repay.[347] As one court observed, "[i]ncurring debt on the eve of bankruptcy can scarcely be considered *malum in se.*"[348]

The pertinent Code definitions,[349] on their face, seem to include attorneys who give bankruptcy advice as "debt relief agencies," and the legislative history is consistent with that view. In *Milavetz, Gallop & Millavetz, P.A. v. U.S.*, the Supreme Court so held.[350] In *Milavetz*, a law firm challenged the application of § 526(a)(4), arguing that the section prohibited even constitutionally protected speech, and was also too vague. The Court rebuffed the challenge.

---

[346] See, e.g., Dean A. James Elliot, et al, Ethics Panel: If I Knew Then What I Know Know—Lessons in Ethics and Professional Responsibility for New Bankruptcy and Insolvency Practitioners, 27 Emory Bankr. Dev. J. 313 (2011).

[347] See Chemerinsky, supra note 290, at 578.

[348] Milavetz, Gallop & Milavetz, P.A. v. United States, 355 B.R. 758 (D. Minn. 2006).

[349] A "debt relief agency" is defined as "any person who provides any bankruptcy assistance to an assisted person in return for the payment of money or other valuable consideration." § 101(12A). "Bankruptcy assistance," in turn, is defined in § 101(4A) to mean "any goods or services sold or otherwise provided to an assisted person with the express or implied purpose of providing information, advice, counsel, document preparation, or filing, or attendance at a creditors' meeting or appearing in a case or proceeding on behalf of another or providing legal representation with respect to a case or proceeding under this title."

[350] 130 S.Ct. 1324, 1331–33 (2010).

First, Justice Sotomayer, writing for the Court, did hold that attorneys were within the statutory target group as a "debt relief agency" under § 101(12A); accordingly, law firms and their attorneys must avoid giving their clients any of the prohibited advice found in § 526(a)(4).

The Supreme Court then addressed the First Amendment concern, and found no violation. The Court so held by first narrowly construing the language of § 526(a)(4), and then by concluding that this narrowly construed language was not unconstitutionally vague. On the question of the scope of the statutory prohibition, the Court determined that only advising *abusive* behavior is forbidden, i.e., it read the statute "to forbid only advice to undertake actions to abuse the bankruptcy system."[351] Thus, according to the Court, "§ 526(a)(4) prohibits a debt relief agency only from advising a debtor to incur more debt because the debtor is filing for bankruptcy, rather than for a valid purpose."[352] As such, what was prohibited by the statute as narrowly construed was constitutionally permissible.

However, that still left the question of vagueness: could an attorney sufficiently distinguish what was and what was not prohibited? The Court found no vagueness problem, based on its reading of the statute that "the prohibited advice is not defined in terms of abusive pre-filing conduct but rather the incurrence of additional debt when the impelling reason is the anticipation of bankruptcy."[353] According to the Court, "it is hard to see how a rule that narrowly prohibits an attorney from affirmatively advising a client to commit this type of abusive prefiling conduct could chill attorney speech or inhibit the attorney-client relationship. Our construction of § 526(a)(4) to prevent only advice principally motivated by the prospect of bankruptcy further ensures that professionals cannot unknowingly run afoul of its proscription."[354]

The Second Circuit construed *Milavetz* as only directly prohibiting a debt relief agency from advising a debtor to incur more debt in contemplation of filing for bankruptcy, further noting that "[t]he Supreme Court rejected a broad reading of the provision that would prohibit any discussion of the advantages, disadvantages, or legality of incurring more debt."[355] Accordingly, the Second Circuit held that as long as attorneys do not affirmatively advise their clients to incur more debt in contemplation of bankruptcy, they are free to talk about the incurrence of debt.

However, it remains to be seen how broadly or narrowly courts apply *Milavetz*. It is also not evident how easily debtor's attorneys will be able to determine in advance what is proscribed by § 526(a)(4), notwithstanding the Court's blithe assertions to the contrary. For example, assume a debtor is about to file for chapter 7 bankruptcy, and owns her car free and clear, but it is an old junker, and likely will need to be replaced fairly soon. The debtor's attorney, reviewing the debtor's financial situation, realizes that the debtor will pass the means test if she incurs secured debt to buy a replacement car, but will fail it and be presumptively an abuser if she does not. Also, of course,

---

[351] Id. at 1334.
[352] Id. at 1336.
[353] Id. at 1338.
[354] Id.
[355] Adams v. Zenas Zelotes, Esq., 606 F.3d 34 (2d Cir. 2010).

having a new car is better than not having one for the debtor's financial future, bankruptcy aside. Is it a violation to tell the debtor to buy the car? Perhaps not, perhaps so; according to the Court, the attorney must somehow divine the "primary motivation" for the incurring of debt.[356] Here, of course, the motive is mixed, and inextricably so.

§ 2.16   Dismissal of a Chapter 13 (or Chapter 12) Case

Chapter 13 and its near-clone, chapter 12, are designed for the benefit of both the debtor and the creditors: for the debtor, who may be able to retain property he otherwise would not be able to keep, and who may emerge with better credit; and for creditors, who may get paid more than in a liquidation. These lofty theoretical aspirations often are not realized in practice, however; many cases filed under chapter 13 fail, or are used by debtors for illicit purposes. In such instances, the proper remedy is dismissal of the case, or perhaps conversion to liquidation bankruptcy under chapter 7.

The debtor has an absolute statutory right to dismiss a case originally commenced under chapter 12 or chapter 13 "at any time." §§ 1208(b), 1307(b). This dismissal right is consistent with the principle that proceeding under either chapter 12 or 13 is entirely voluntary with the debtor. Thus, the debtor is allowed to bail out at any time (at least as long as the debtor is in good faith, as discussed below). Furthermore, the debtor may not waive this dismissal right. The only express *statutory* limitation on the debtor's right to dismiss is if the case has previously been converted to chapter 12 or 13, and this conversion was at the request of the debtor.

A controversy has arisen over whether the debtor's seemingly absolute statutory dismissal right is limited implicitly by the right of a party in interest to seek conversion of the case to chapter 7, and by a debtor's bad faith efforts to sabotage that conversion-request privilege. Conversion from chapter 13 to chapter 7 may be sought for cause, § 1307(c), and conversion from chapter 12 to chapter 7 may be requested if the debtor has committed fraud in connection with the chapter 12 case. § 1208(d). The concern is that if the debtor may exercise the right to dismiss even after a conversion motion has been filed, the meaningfulness of the conversion remedy would be substantially undermined. For example, a debtor could commit fraud in connection with the chapter 12 case, and if that fraud is then discovered and a motion to convert to a liquidation bankruptcy case is filed, the debtor could prevent liquidation simply by dismissing the case. To avoid the possibility of such debtor abuse, some courts have not allowed a debtor to dismiss after a conversion motion has been filed.[357] Other courts, however, while sympathetic to the policy problem, have felt constrained to follow the

---

[356]   130 S.Ct. at 1338 n.6:

We emphasize that awareness of the possibility of bankruptcy is insufficient to trigger § 526(a)(4)'s prohibition. Instead, that provision proscribes only advice to incur more debt that is principally motivated by that likelihood. Thus, advice to refinance a mortgage or purchase a reliable car prior to filing because doing so will reduce the debtor's interest rates or improve his ability to repay is not prohibited, as the promise of enhanced financial prospects, rather than the anticipated filing, is the impelling cause.

[357]   E.g., In re Graven, 936 F.2d 378 (8th Cir. 1991) (chapter 12); In re Jacobsen, 609 F.3d 647 (5th Cir. 2010) (chapter 13).

apparently unqualified language of the Code, §§ 1208(b), 1307(b), which says that the court "shall" dismiss the case when the debtor "at any time" requests dismissal.[358] Courts in this camp have pointed out that other remedies, such as dismissal with prejudice, may be brought to bear against misbehaving debtors.[359]

The force of the "plain meaning" statutory command has been undermined, though, by the Supreme Court's 2007 *Marrama* decision,[360] which allowed courts to refuse to grant a seemingly absolute statutory right to *convert* from chapter 7 to chapter 13 under § 706(a) when the debtor acted in bad faith. If an unwritten "bad faith" qualification limits a debtor's statutorily unfettered conversion right in that context, courts by analogy could pencil in a similar "bad faith" limitation on the debtor's "absolute" dismissal right as well. The *Marrama* Court emphasized that the debtor's specific statutory power to convert was limited both by § 105(a)'s overarching delegation of power to bankruptcy judges to take any action necessary "to prevent an abuse of process" in a bankruptcy case, as well as by "the inherent power of every federal court to sanction 'abusive litigation practices.'"[361] That same logic suggests that the bankruptcy courts would have the power to block abusive attempted dismissals by malfeasing debtors under §§ 1208(b) or 1307(b).[362]

In both chapters 12 and 13, provision is made for the case to be dismissed on a showing of "cause." §§ 1208(c), 1307(c). Virtually identical nonexclusive lists of factors indicative of cause are included. Each list provides that cause includes such things as unreasonable and prejudicial delay by the debtor; continuing loss to the estate and the unlikelihood of successful rehabilitation; nonpayment of fees; and numerous instances of plan failure, such as failure to file a plan on time, denial of confirmation of a plan, and material default under a plan. In 2005, Congress added to this list the debtor's failure to pay a domestic support obligation that first becomes payable post-petition. §§ 1208(c)(10), 1307(c)(11). In addition, chapter 12 permits dismissal for "gross mismanagement." § 1208(c)(1). Because of the similarity of the lists, case authority under one chapter should be relevant authority for cases under the other chapter.

The list of factors that might constitute "cause" is not exclusive. The predicate to the list is the word "including," which the Code's own internal rules of construction state is "not limiting." § 102(3). Courts have been confronted with abuses from debtors that do not fall neatly within any of the enumerated categories. In those cases, the

---

[358] E.g., In re Davenport, 175 B.R. 355 (Bankr. E.D. Cal. 1994) (chapter 12); In re Barbieri, 199 F.3d 616 (2d Cir. 1999) (chapter 13).

[359] E.g., In re Procel, 467 B.R. 297, 306 (Bankr. S.D.N.Y. 2012) (citing *Barbieri* for the "numerous sanctions and other remedies that bankruptcy courts have the discretion to apply in order to prevent abuses of the bankruptcy process").

[360] Marrama v. Citizens Bank of Massachusetts, 549 U.S. 365 (2007). See discussion in § 2.20.

[361] 549 U.S. at 375–76.

[362] Indeed, one court stated that "[a]lthough the plain language of 11 U.S.C. § 1307(b) can be read to confer an absolute right to dismiss, the Supreme Court's decision[ ] compels us to hold that the right to dismiss under 11 U.S.C. § 1307(b) is subject to a limited exception for bad-faith conduct or abuse of the bankruptcy process . . . " *Jacobsen*, supra note 1, 609 F.3d at 647. See also In re Williamson, 414 B.R. 886 (Bankr. S.D. Ga. 2008) (same, but for § 1208(b)). But see In re Procel, 467 B.R. 297, 308 (S.D.N.Y. 2012) ("*Marrama* was silent as to the absolute right to voluntarily dismiss under § 1307(b), and thus is arguably reconcilable with *Barbieri* [which holds an absolute right to dismiss].").

courts have not hesitated to dismiss.[363] They have announced long laundry lists of relevant factors, and have emphasized the intensely fact-specific nature of the inquiry.

In *Marrama*, the Court gave its stamp of approval to this approach, discussing favorably the many lower court decisions embracing a general "bad faith" ground for dismissal under § 1307(c).[364] The Court stated: "Nothing in the text of either § 706 or § 1307(c) (or the legislative history of either provision) limits the authority of the court to take appropriate action in response to fraudulent conduct by the atypical litigant who has demonstrated that he is not entitled to the relief available to the typical debtor."[365]

The standard for a bad-faith dismissal is a high one, though—and higher than what is required to establish bad faith at the time of *confirmation* of a plan under § 1325(a)(3). In a footnote, the *Marrama* court explained:

> We have no occasion here to articulate with precision what conduct qualifies as "bad faith" sufficient to permit a bankruptcy judge to dismiss a Chapter 13 case or to deny conversion from Chapter 7. It suffices to emphasize that the debtor's conduct must, in fact, be atypical. Limiting dismissal or denial of conversion to extraordinary cases is particularly appropriate in light of the fact that lack of good faith in proposing a Chapter 13 plan is an express statutory ground for denying plan confirmation.[366]

One debtor stratagem has been to attempt a so-called "chapter 20" case, in which the debtor files a chapter 7 case and then follows with filing a chapter 13 case. By doing this, the debtor eliminates personal liability on their secured debt in the chapter 7 case, and then uses their chapter 13 plan to restructure the secured debt. The Supreme Court in *Johnson v. Home State Bank*[367] held that the debtor in such a "chapter 20" case was not necessarily precluded from filing the chapter 13 case and seeking confirmation of the chapter 13 plan, after filing under chapter 7. Instead, each separate case must be tested against a good faith standard. Recently, courts have grappled with the issue of whether these "chapter 20" debtors may strip off unsecured liens, regardless of whether the debtor is eligible to receive a discharge.[368]

In 2005, Congress added another dismissal ground in chapter 13. § 1307(e). One of the new obligations imposed on chapter 13 debtors in BAPCPA is to file all tax returns for the past four years' tax periods with the appropriate taxing authorities, by the day

---

[363] See, e.g., In re Michels, 305 B.R. 868 (B.A.P. 8th Cir. 2004) (holding that dismissal was proper "on any basis supported by the record," even if the reason did not appear in the enumerated list in § 1208).

[364] 549 U.S. at 372–74.

[365] Id. at 374–75.

[366] Id. at 375 n.11.

[367] 501 U.S. 78 (1991). The specific issue before the Court was whether the secured creditor in the chapter 13 case held a "claim" that could potentially be dealt with in the chapter 13 plan. The Supreme Court held that it did have a claim, noting that the "claim" definition was not the appropriate battleground to fight the good faith issue.

[368] Compare Victorio v. Billingslea, 470 B.R. 545 (Bankr. S.D. Cal. 2012) (chapter 20 debtors may not permanently strip off junior liens absent a discharge or payment in full), with Frazier v. Real Time Resolutions, Inc., 469 B.R. 889 (Bankr. E.D. Cal. 2012) (no discharge is required to effectuate strip-off of junior lien).

before the creditors meeting. § 1308(a). Extensions may be granted for up to 120 days. § 1308(b). The purpose of this requirement is to provide taxing authorities with the information they need to file a proof of claim. If the debtor fails to file the required returns, then on request of a party in interest (e.g., the taxing authority) or the United States trustee, the court shall either dismiss the case or convert it to chapter 7, whichever is in the best interest of creditors and the estate. § 1307(e). Filing the tax returns required by § 1308 is also a condition of confirmation of a chapter 13 plan. § 1325(a)(9).

One difference between chapters 12 and 13 is the scope of relief available to the court on a showing of cause. In chapter 13 the court has the discretion to dismiss *or* to convert to chapter 7, whichever it believes is in the best interests of creditors and the estate. § 1307(c). In chapter 12, however, no conversion option is given merely on proof of cause. § 1208(c). The only basis for conversion of a chapter 12 case against the debtor's wishes to chapter 7 is that the debtor committed fraud in connection with the case. § 1208(d).

Another issue is whether the bankruptcy court has the power to dismiss a chapter 12 or chapter 13 case *sua sponte*. At first blush, the Code language in the dismissal sections of chapters 12 and 13 suggests that the court lacks such authority, since dismissal is allowed "on request of a party in interest." It is accepted now, though, that the inherent right of a court to protect against abuses of its jurisdiction permits *sua sponte* dismissal. This view is supported by a 1986 amendment to § 105(a), which provides that "[n]o provision of this title providing for the raising of an issue by a party in interest shall be construed to preclude the court from, *sua sponte,* taking any action or making any determination necessary or appropriate to enforce or implement court orders or rules, or to prevent an abuse of process." On those grounds, then, a court apparently may act on its own motion to dismiss a case under chapter 12 or 13.[369]

§ 2.17   Dismissal of a Chapter 11 Case

For "cause" shown the bankruptcy court may dismiss a chapter 11 case as an alternative to converting the case to chapter 7. § 1112(b)(1). The choice lies within the discretion of the court, based on a determination of what is in the best interests of the creditors and the estate. In addition, the court may dismiss on motion of the United States trustee if the debtor fails to file in a timely manner the required schedules and lists of creditors. § 1112(e).

The debtor does not have an absolute right to dismiss a chapter 11 case, as it does in chapter 12 or chapter 13. Instead, the debtor must request dismissal for cause under § 1112(b), on the same basis as anyone else. This restriction applies whether or not the debtor chose initially to be in chapter 11. If the debtor is unwilling to go forward with the reorganization of its business and the proposal and confirmation of a plan, the court may appoint a trustee to take over. § 1104(a).

---

[369] In fact, some courts have held just that. See, e.g., In re Pretzer, 96 B.R. 790 (Bankr. N.D. Ohio 1989) (§ 1208); In re Eilderts, 389 B.R. 682 (Bankr. N.D. Iowa 2008) (§ 1307). But see In re Jackson, 348 B.R. 487 (Bankr. S.D. Iowa 2006) (not dismissing *sua sponte* because it "cannot confer upon itself the right to act when Congress specifically designated another entity to fulfill a particular task," with regards to § 1307).

As with cases under chapters 12 and 13, there has been some debate over whether the court may act *sua sponte* to dismiss a chapter 11 case.[370] The statute on its face appears to require a motion by a party in interest or the United States trustee. § 1112(b)(1), (e). However, as discussed in the preceding section, the court almost certainly does have the power to dismiss a chapter 11 case *sua sponte*. The 1986 amendment to § 105(a) makes clear that bankruptcy judges always may take any action or make any determination necessary to "enforce or implement court orders or rules, or to prevent an abuse of process." Even aside from this statutory provision, such probably was the proper view all along, since courts have an inherent equitable power to protect their own jurisdiction from abuse.

In any event, dismissal is a cataclysmic event that requires prior notice to all creditors, as well as the United States trustee. Rule 2002(a)(5), (k). Equity security holders are typically notified as well. Rule 2002(d)(4). Interested parties may appear and be heard on the issue of the desirability of dismissal. The hearing must be within thirty days of the motion, and the court must decide the motion within fifteen days after the hearing. § 1112(b)(3).

The critical substantive issue is what constitutes grounds for dismissal of the chapter 11 case. As noted above, the debtor's failure to file required schedules will support dismissal. § 1112(e).

Most dismissal cases, however, fall under the more general heading of "cause" under § 1112(b)(1). Section 1112(b) was altered by BAPCPA to be more restrictive on debtors and give less discretion to the court. While the old version of § 1112(b) said the court "may" dismiss, the new version, in § 1112(b)(1), says the court "*shall*" dismiss "absent unusual circumstances." The debtor or another party in interest is given the opportunity to avoid dismissal by showing that there is reasonable likelihood that a plan will be confirmed or that the debtor's actions that amount to cause were justified or can be cured by the court. § 1112(b)(2).

The statute lists sixteen examples of what might be adequate cause for dismissal (or conversion to chapter 7), § 1112(b)(4)(A)–(P), but the list is not intended to be exhaustive or exclusive. Most of the listed grounds speak to the failure of the chapter 11 case. The ultimate goal of a chapter 11 case is the confirmation and consummation of a feasible plan of reorganization. If that goal is not likely to be achieved, or at an acceptable cost, then the most sensible course for all interested parties is to abort the chapter 11 proceeding.

Accordingly, the grounds for dismissal or conversion include "substantial or continuing loss to or diminution of the estate and the absence of a reasonable likelihood of rehabilitation." § 1112(b)(4)(A). Chapter 11 is not free; a chapter 11 case of any size will generate substantial administrative expenses, see § 503(b), which must be paid ahead of general unsecured claims. In an unsuccessful chapter 11 case that lingers on and on, unsecured creditors will be worse off than they would have been if

---

[370] Compare In re Starmark Clinics, LP, 388 B.R. 729 (Bankr. S.D. Tex. 2008) (court may act *sua sponte*), with In re Gusam Rest., 737 F.2d 274 (2d Cir. 1984) (court may not act *sua sponte*). Note that the latter decision was before the 1986 amendment to § 105(a) referred to in the text.

the debtor had liquidated immediately or had not filed chapter 11 at all. A well-known case demonstrating this simple reality is the Eastern Airlines debacle,[371] in which the debtor spent hundreds of millions of dollars in a futile attempt to reorganize.

Of course, hindsight is "20–20," and the task for the court is to make an informed judgment on the prospects of a successful rehabilitation as the case proceeds. If Eastern Airlines could have been saved, thousands of jobs would have been preserved, and the creditors would have been paid more. As a practical matter, the timing of a motion to dismiss is crucial. During the early stages of a case, the court is likely to indulge a strong presumption in favor of giving the debtor a chance to reorganize. This tendency is especially pronounced during the time (initially 120 days, § 1121(b)) when the debtor has the exclusive right to file a plan. As the case drags on, however, the court may lose patience with the debtor and be more willing to dismiss or convert. The court's denial of a motion to dismiss is not *res judicata* of a later motion seeking the same relief.

Other listed illustrative grounds for dismissal similarly point to a chapter 11 failure. Examples include: gross mismanagement of the estate, § 1112(b)(4)(B); failure to follow the requirements and orders of the court and the Code, § 1112(b)(4)(E), (F), (G); failure to propose or to confirm a plan, or the revocation of a confirmation order, § 1112(b)(4)(J), (L); and the failure to carry out a plan. § 1112(b)(4)(M), (N), (O). Also, nonpayment of fees is a basis for dismissal or conversion, as is the failure to pay tax or domestic support obligations that arise after filing. § 1112(b)(4)(I), (K), (P).

The interrelationship between the statutory grounds for dismissal and the grounds for relief from the stay in § 362(d) are noteworthy. "Cause" is a basis for relief in both. §§ 1112(b)(1), 362(d)(1). The lack of reasonable prospects for a successful reorganization may support the granting of relief under both sections, in conjunction with other factors.[372] If relief from the stay is granted, a secured creditor might be permitted to foreclose on crucial assets, thus effectively spelling the end of the reorganization effort. Procedurally there is a major difference between a motion for stay relief and one to dismiss; comprehensive notice must be given to all creditors only of the motion to dismiss.[373] This significant procedural distinction has led some courts to suggest that allegations that the reorganization is not feasible should be tested solely on motions to dismiss, and not on stay motions, in order to protect the rights of the entire body of creditors.[374] However, the Supreme Court in dictum has approved the feasibility test in the stay context.[375]

---

[371] In re E. Airlines, Inc., No. 89 B 10449 (Bankr. S.D.N.Y. March 9, 1989).

[372] See § 1112(b)(4)(A) ("absence of a reasonable likelihood of rehabilitation" and "substantial or continuing loss to or diminution of the estate"), § 362(d)(2) (property "not necessary to an effective reorganization" and debtor lacks equity in the property).

[373] Compare Fed. R. Bankr. P. 2002(a)(4) (dismissal: all creditors), with Fed. R. Bankr. P. 4001(a) (stay: committees only, or twenty largest creditors).

[374] E.g., In re Koopmans, 22 B.R. 395 (Bankr. D. Utah 1982).

[375] United Sav. Ass'n v. Timbers of Inwood Forest Assocs., Ltd., 484 U.S. 365 (1988).

Perhaps the most controversial issue concerning the dismissal of chapter 11 cases has been the propriety of dismissing a case as a "bad faith" filing.[376] The threshold question is whether a bankruptcy court even has the *power* to dismiss for a lack of good faith. The argument against doing so is that: (1) bad faith is not listed as one of the statutory examples of cause for dismissal in § 1112(b)(4); (2) prior reorganization statutes (e.g., chapter X) expressly required a finding that the filing was in good faith, supporting an inference that the omission in § 1112(b)(4) was intentional and not inadvertent; (3) good faith is listed specifically as a requirement of confirmation of a plan in § 1129(a)(3), reinforcing the inference that Congress meant to test good faith only at the end of a chapter 11 case, rather than the outset; (4) the statutory listing of illustrative grounds for "cause" for dismissal in § 1112(b)(4) encompass most of the types of "bad faith" that had been recognized by courts under the prior Bankruptcy Act; and (5) Congress in enacting the Code expressed a strong policy in favor of access to chapter 11 and encouraging reorganization efforts.[377]

Notwithstanding the foregoing arguments, most courts under the Code have concluded that access to chapter 11 is limited by an implicit good faith requirement.[378] The reasoning of the Supreme Court's 2007 decision in the chapter 13 context in *Marrama*[379] strongly supports the view that bankruptcy judges retain the inherent power to dismiss a filing under any chapter, including chapter 11, for bad faith.[380]

The fight then comes in defining what good faith means, as applied in a particular case.[381] In one notable case, the court held that the chapter 11 bankruptcy filing by a large corporation in an attempt to deal with the flood of asbestos cases was in good faith, stating that "Manville is a real business with real creditors in pressing need of

---

[376] See Ali M.M. Mojdehi & Janet Dean Gertz, The Implicit "Good Faith" Requirement in Chapter 11 Liquidations: A Rule in Search of a Rationale?, 14 Am. Bankr. Inst. L. Rev. 143 (2006); Janet Flaccus, Have Eight Circuits Shorted? Good Faith and Chapter 11 Petitions, 67 Am. Bankr. L.J. 401 (1993); Lawrence Ponoroff & F. Stephen Knippenberg, The Implied Good Faith Filing Requirement: Sentinel of an Evolving Bankruptcy Policy, 85 Nw. U. L. Rev. 919 (1991).

[377] See, e.g., In re Victoria Ltd. P'ship, 187 B.R. 54 (Bankr. D. Mass. 1995).

[378] See In re G.S. Distrib., Inc., 331 B.R. 552 (Bankr. S.D.N.Y. 2005); In re Phoenix Piccadilly, Ltd., 849 F.2d 1393, 1394 (11th Cir. 1988). E.g., In re Detienne Ltd. P'ship, 342 B.R. 318 (Bankr. D. Mont. 2006) (dismissing a chapter 11 case that was "virtually identical" to one dismissed less than one month before). The leading early Code case to so conclude, after a lengthy historical analysis, was *In re Victory Construction Co.*, 9 B.R. 549 (Bankr. C.D. Cal. 1981). Judge Ordin held in that case that the debtor had filed in bad faith because it was seeking to create a new business in chapter 11, not to rehabilitate an existing business.

[379] Marrama v. Citizens Bank of Massachusetts, 549 U.S. 365 (2007). The Court noted that an express good faith requirement exists for confirmation of a plan (as is also true in chapter 11), but found no inference that thereby suggested the courts lacked the power to dismiss prior to confirmation to police against abusive debtor behavior.

[380] See In re Attack Props., LLC, 478 B.R. 337, 343 (N.D. Ill. 2012) (noting that the statutory list of circumstances that will constitute "cause" for dismissal of a chapter 11 case is not exhaustive, and "courts may find 'cause' for other equitable reasons"); Clear Blue Water, LLC v. Oyster Bay Mgmt. Co., LLC, 476 B.R. 60, 67 (E.D.N.Y. 2012) (holding that dismissal of a chapter 11 petition for lack of good faith is theoretically proper).

[381] See Bruce H. White & William L. Medford, Dismissals of Bankruptcies Filed in Bad Faith: What's the Standard?, 23–10 Am. Bankr. Inst. J. 26 (2005). See also *Clear Blue Water*, supra note 380, 76 B.R. at 69 (providing examples of bad faith dismissals: "(1) the filing of false or misleading information; (2) persistent failure to comply with court orders, rules, or procedures; (3) the use of bankruptcy process to escape familial obligations; (4) the secretion of property and other efforts to avoid the disclosure of assets; (5) the use of bankruptcy as a vehicle to resolve disputes solely between equity participants; and (6) the "new debtor syndrome," in which property is transferred solely for the purpose of commencing a bankruptcy case").

economic reorganization."[382] Similarly, filing chapter 11 for the purpose of seeking rejection of a collective bargaining agreement was held to be permissible in the first Continental Airlines case, when the debtor had an ongoing business and real financial problems.

The prototypical bad faith case is one in which a debtor with only a single asset (often a limited partnership created to own an office building, apartment complex, etc.) files chapter 11 on the eve of foreclosure of their property, seeking to invoke the automatic stay and thereby frustrate the secured creditor's ability to foreclose.[383] If the debtor has a legitimate prospect and intention of reorganizing, dismissal may be denied even in such a case; courts, however, are suspicious of such eleventh hour filings.[384] These types of cases often implicate the "new debtor syndrome," where the debtor was formed on the brink of foreclosure as a means of delaying the secured creditor.[385] As courts are wont to do, a long laundry list of factors relevant to the good faith issue has been developed.[386]

The mere fact that a debtor is seeking to liquidate is not by itself grounds for dismissing a chapter 11 case, because liquidation is permitted in chapter 11.[387] Neither is there an absolute requirement that the debtor be operating a business, if some benefit can be obtained in chapter 11. The Supreme Court has held that an individual consumer debtor may file chapter 11.[388]

§ 2.18   Effects of Dismissal

The guiding principles regarding the effect of the dismissal of a bankruptcy case, under any chapter, are that "the basic purpose of [§ 349] is to undo the bankruptcy case, as far as practicable," subject to the limitation that "the court will make the appropriate orders to protect rights acquired in reliance on the bankruptcy case."[389] Thus, dismissal of a bankruptcy case is normally without prejudice to the debtor's right

---

[382]   In re Johns–Manville Corp., 36 B.R. 727 (Bankr. S.D.N.Y. 1984).

[383]   E.g., *Phoenix Piccadilly*, supra note 378, 849 F.2d 1393.

[384]   See, e.g. In re Primestone Inv. Partners L.P., 272 B.R. 554 (D. Del. 2002) (dismissal proper, even though the debtor did not do anything inherently improper, when they filed sixteen hours before foreclosure was scheduled, and case involved essentially a two party dispute between the debtor and its lender).

[385]   In re Duvar Apt., Inc., 205 B.R. 196 (B.A.P. 9th Cir. 1996) (it is proper to lift automatic stay in a case of new debtor syndrome). E.g., In re Little Creek Dev. Co., 779 F.2d 1068 (5th Cir. 1986).

[386]   The list includes the following indicia of bad faith, which are relevant to but not dispositive of the determination: (1) the debtor only has one asset; (2) the debtor has few unsecured creditors whose claims are small in relation to those of the secured creditors; (3) the debtor's one asset is the subject of a foreclosure action as a result of arrearages or default on the debt; (4) the debtor's financial condition is, in essence, a two party dispute between the debtor and secured creditors which can be resolved in the pending state foreclosure action; (5) the timing of the debtor's filing evidences an intent to delay or frustrate the legitimate efforts of the debtor's secured creditors to enforce their rights; (6) the debtor has little or no cash flow; (7) the debtor can't meet current expenses including the payment of personal property and real estate taxes; and (8) the debtor has no employees. See In re C–TC 9th Ave. P'ship, 113 F.3d 1304, 1311 (2d Cir. 1997) (citation omitted).

[387]   But note that liquidation might be grounds for conversion. See In re Vaughan, 429 B.R. 14 (Bankr. D.N.M. 2010) (conversion proper when only purpose of chapter 11 is liquidation, which is more easily done in chapter 7).

[388]   Toibb v. Radloff, 501 U.S. 157 (1991).

[389]   H.R. Rep. No. 95–595, 95th Cong., 1st Sess., at 338 (1977).

to obtain future bankruptcy relief, § 349(a); avoided transfers are reinstated, § 349(b)(1); and property is revested in the pre-bankruptcy owner, § 349(b)(3). Reliance parties (such as good faith purchasers of estate property) should be protected by court order.

Of considerable interest to the debtor is whether dismissal of a case will in any way preclude the debtor from (1) later filing bankruptcy and (2) discharging debts. The Code's default rule is that dismissal neither blocks a subsequent discharge of dischargeable debts nor prevents a subsequent bankruptcy filing. § 349(a). However, that default rule is modified somewhat by statutory exceptions and in some respects may be overridden by court order for cause.[390]

If a case is dismissed before a discharge is granted, then the eight-year discharge bar of § 727(a)(8) and (9) is not triggered. Of course, if dismissal follows the entry of discharge in the first case, then the eight-year limitation is operative. The essential point is this: nothing in the original dismissal in and of itself inherently prevents a later discharge. § 349(a). The court is given the power, however, to enter a dismissal order *with prejudice* to the debtor's ability to discharge debts in a subsequent case. The mere fact that dismissal was ordered for "cause" does not likewise dictate that cause exists to make that dismissal with prejudice and thus preclude later discharge. The norm is for dismissals to be without prejudice. To dismiss with prejudice, and block a debtor from later discharging debts that were covered by the dismissed case, courts have required a showing of egregious bad faith conduct by the debtor that was prejudicial to creditors.[391]

What about refiling after dismissal? Again, the default rule in § 349(a) is that dismissal, without anything else, does not keep a debtor from filing bankruptcy subsequently. The Code does provide one exception to this rule, as § 109(g) imposes an express statutory limitation on the debtor's ability to refile a bankruptcy case after a previous dismissal. Section 109(g) was added to the Code in 1984 to deal with abusive repetitive filings. That section only applies to individuals or family farmer debtors, and the ban on refiling only lasts for 180 days. The ban is triggered if (1) the court dismissed the case for the debtor's willful failure to abide by court orders or to appear to prosecute the case, or (2) the debtor voluntarily dismissed the case after a motion for relief from the stay was filed. Section 109(g) limits the debtor's ability to keep creditors at bay indefinitely by repeatedly invoking the bankruptcy stay without ever going through a bankruptcy distribution. Now creditors have a six-month window after a dismissal of the type described in § 109(g) in which to foreclose or otherwise collect from the debtor. Note that dismissal of the bankruptcy case automatically terminates the automatic stay. § 362(c)(2)(B).

The question has arisen whether § 109(g) is the *only* basis upon which a debtor can be barred from refiling after a dismissal. Closely related thereto is the issue whether a debtor may be blocked from refiling for more than the 180 days provided

---

[390] See, e.g., In re Casse, 198 F.3d 327, 340 (2d Cir. 1999) ("[A] debtor may be prejudiced from filing subsequent bankruptcy petitions under two circumstances: (1) if the court, for cause, so orders, or (2) if the terms of § 109(g) apply to debtors' case.").

[391] See, e.g., In re Frieouf, 938 F.2d 1099 (10th Cir. 1991), cert. denied, 502 U.S. 1091 (1992).

under § 109(g). The problem is deciphering the last clause of § 349(a), which provides, "nor does the dismissal of a case under this title prejudice the debtor with regard to the filing of a subsequent petition under this title, except as provided in section 109(g) of this title." Plainly that language says that dismissal does not always and automatically prejudice a debtor from subsequent filing. But does the opposite inference hold? The question is whether that "except" clause is to be read as the exclusive predicate for barring future filings. Many courts have concluded that it is not.[392] Those courts assert that, upon dismissal under § 349(a) and dependent on a sufficient showing of egregious cause, they have the inherent equitable power to bar the debtor from filing a subsequent bankruptcy case, on grounds other than and for periods greater than specified in § 109(g). The Tenth Circuit, however, held that the only defensible grammatical reading of § 349(a) was that the court lacked the power to enjoin a later filing for any reason other than, or for a period longer than, provided in § 109(g).[393] My sense, again, is that the rationale of the 2007 Supreme Court decision in *Marrama*[394] should support the view that dismissal with prejudice to subsequent filing is possible apart from § 109(g). *Marrama* espouses a very expansive view of the breadth of a bankruptcy court's inherent equitable powers to police for debtor abuse and keep bad faith debtors out of the bankruptcy system, and shows a disinclination to draw negative inferences from specific statutory grants that might cabin in that equitable power.

Another major impact of dismissal of a bankruptcy case is that transfers that were avoided during the case are reinstated, § 349(b)(1), and money or property recovered for the benefit of the estate is returned. § 349(b)(2). For example, assume that during the case a creditor is adjudged to have received a preference, and is ordered to pay the amount of the preference to the bankruptcy trustee. Dismissal of the case unwinds that order: the money paid by the creditor to the trustee must be refunded to the creditor, and the preferential transaction is now validated.[395] If a new bankruptcy case is later filed, the preferential transfer will only be set aside if made within the reach-back period as judged from the time of the second filing. To take another example, if a lien on property is avoided in the bankruptcy case, when the case is dismissed that lien will reattach to the collateral.

Note, however, that not every order entered in the bankruptcy case is reversed by dismissal, but only those made pursuant to the sections listed in § 349. Thus, for example, if an executory contract or unexpired lease is rejected in the bankruptcy case, a later dismissal of the case will not revive that contract.[396] If § 552 prevents a creditor's lien from attaching to property acquired by the estate postpetition, dismissal

---

[392] See, e.g., In re Mehlhose, 469 B.R. 694 (Bankr. E.D. Mich. 2012).

[393] *Frieouf,* supra note 391, 938 F.2d 1099. Note that one lower court in the Tenth Circuit narrowly construed *Frieouf* to dismissals warranted under § 109(g), and held that a dismissal justified under § 349(a) allows a court to dismiss with prejudice in excess of 180 days. Interestingly enough, this case arose before the holding in *Marrama.* In re Norton, 319 B.R. 671 (Bankr. D. Utah 2005).

[394] 549 U.S. 365 (2007).

[395] See In re Sadler, 935 F.2d 918 (7th Cir. 1991).

[396] See In re BSL Operating Corp., 57 B.R. 945 (Bankr. S.D.N.Y. 1986).

will not retroactively confer a lien on that creditor, even though the creditor would have had a lien if no bankruptcy case had ever been filed.[397]

Property of the estate revests upon dismissal in the entity in which that property was vested immediately prior to the filing of the bankruptcy petition. § 349(b)(3). Often this provision means that the debtor regains its property, because most property of the estate is derived from the debtor. In chapter 12 and 13 cases this principle may extend to postpetition monies of the debtor delivered to the trustee for distribution to creditors pursuant to the plan. Upon dismissal those monies should be returned to the debtor, and should not be paid over to creditors.[398]

In some instances, however, an entity other than the debtor may have had the superior possessory right prior to filing. For example, a secured party that had rightfully repossessed collateral before bankruptcy may have to turn that property over to the trustee in bankruptcy under § 542(a). On dismissal, that property arguably should revert to the secured party, not to the debtor.

The general rule that property of the estate revests often calls for court action to protect parties that relied in good faith on orders of the bankruptcy court. For example, a sale of estate property during bankruptcy to a good faith purchaser normally should not be disturbed on dismissal, and the court has the authority to enter such a protective order limiting the effect of dismissal.[399] § 349(b). Actions taken in reliance on plan confirmation orders, such as the distribution of property, similarly are leading candidates for protective orders.

The effect of dismissal of a case following confirmation of a plan has caused many interpretive difficulties. Courts sometimes differentiate between confirmation under chapter 11, in which the debtor's discharge is effective immediately for corporate and partnership debtors, and under chapters 12 or 13, in which the debtor is discharged only after it performs under the plan. In chapter 11 cases, courts may ascribe a permanently binding effect to the plan's provisions, even if dismissal then ensues, but in chapters 12 or 13 the court may find that dismissal operates to vacate the confirmation order.[400] Even if the confirmation order is not held to be permanently binding, some aspects of that order may be given *res judicata* effect even after a dismissal.

A crucial issue is what happens on dismissal to a secured claim that was written down to a judicially determined value in the plan, with the payment terms restructured under the plan. Dismissal is often held to erase the writing down of the

---

[397] See In re Newton, 64 B.R. 790 (Bankr. C.D. Ill. 1986).

[398] See In re Tran, 309 B.R. 330 (B.A.P. 1st Cir. 2004). But see In re Parker, 400 B.R. 55 (Bankr. E.D. Pa. 2009) (holding that pre-confirmation funds paid by debtor to trustee for distribution to creditors did not revest in the debtor after case was dismissed).

[399] H.R. Rep. No. 95–595, 95th Cong., 1st Sess., at 338 (1977).

[400] See In re Nash, 765 F.2d 1410 (9th Cir. 1985) (chapter 13); In re Keener, 268 B.R. 912 (Bankr. N.D. Tex. 2001) (chapter 12).

secured claim, with the original terms of the secured debt accordingly restored.[401] The issue is complicated, though, if the debtor fully pays off the restructured secured debt prior to dismissal; in that event, some courts have found that the creditor's lien is permanently eradicated.[402]

A final question that often arises is the extent to which the bankruptcy court after dismissal retains jurisdiction over proceedings related to the bankruptcy case.[403] The presumptive rule is that the court's jurisdiction over all related proceedings evaporates with the dismissal of the overall case. That presumption, however, is not absolute. The bankruptcy court has the discretion to retain jurisdiction over adversary proceedings or other related matters, even after dismissal.[404]

§ 2.19 Abstention

Parties petitioning for bankruptcy relief do not have an absolute right to have the case administered under the aegis of the bankruptcy court, even if the case meets all of the threshold requirements for bankruptcy adjudication. The bankruptcy court is given the power to abstain from hearing a case under § 305(a). Specifically, the court has the discretion to dismiss or suspend all proceedings in a case. The bankruptcy court itself thus is designated as the final arbiter of the appropriateness of bankruptcy relief. *Sua sponte* action is permitted, although only after notice and a hearing.

The decision of the bankruptcy court on the abstention question is largely final. The Code expressly prohibits review (by appeal or otherwise) of the bankruptcy court's decision to abstain or not to abstain by either the court of appeals or the Supreme Court. § 305(c). The courts have determined that the congressional command on this issue must be given full effect, and have refused to carve out any judicial exceptions to the prohibition on review. Note, however, that the statute does not preclude review by the district court of the abstention order. In fact, several courts have held explicitly that bankruptcy judges may not enter unreviewable abstention orders, but that any such orders are subject to district court review.[405]

Given the nearly complete finality of the abstention decision, and the major import of denying access to the bankruptcy forum in facially meritorious cases, bankruptcy courts exercise their abstention power very sparingly, with great caution and restraint. The Code specifies two situations in which abstention is appropriate. First, the court may dismiss or suspend bankruptcy proceedings if "the interests of creditors and the debtor would be better served." § 305(a)(1). The second situation involves chapter 15 cases. Where a petition for recognition of a foreign proceeding has been granted under

---

[401] See H.R. Rep. No. 95–595, 95th Cong., 1st Sess., at 337–38 (1997) ("The basic purpose of [§ 349(b)] is to undo the bankruptcy case, as far as practicable, and restore all property rights to the position in which they were found at the commencement of the case.").

[402] See, e.g., In re Castro, 285 B.R. 703 (Bankr. D. Ariz. 2002) (holding that conversion or dismissal of case following satisfaction of creditor's stripped lien fully releases the undersecured creditor's lien).

[403] See In re Statistical Tabulating Corp., Inc., 60 F.3d 1286 (7th Cir. 1995) (noting that "generally dismissal of bankruptcy proceeding results in dismissal of related proceedings. . . . ").

[404] E.g., In re Carraher, 971 F.2d 327 (9th Cir. 1992); In re Morris, 950 F.2d 153 (11th Cir. 1992).

[405] See, e.g., In re Goerg, 930 F.2d 1563 (11th Cir. 1991).

§ 1515, abstention is called for if "the purposes of chapter 15 . . . would be best served" by abstention. § 305(a)(2). The purposes of chapter 15 are spelled out in § 1501(a).[406]

The statutory standard of "best interests of creditors and the debtor" is intentionally vague, leaving much to the sound discretion of the bankruptcy judge. Abstention may occur in a voluntary case or in an involuntary case. At first blush, the statutory standard appears to be either counterintuitive or paternalistic—how could it be in the best interests of creditors and the debtor to dismiss or suspend the case when either the debtor (voluntary case) or the requisite number of petitioning creditors (involuntary case) has obviously decided that it must be in their best interest to proceed in bankruptcy court? Otherwise the petitioners would never have filed the bankruptcy petition.

Consider first the involuntary case. The paradigmatic candidate for abstention that Congress had in mind was when a "few recalcitrant creditors" file an involuntary bankruptcy petition in an attempt to derail an otherwise promising out-of-court workout.[407] The best interests of "creditors" suggests more of a utilitarian "greater good" analysis, considering the welfare of the creditors as a group, not a determination that every single creditor will be better off outside of bankruptcy. Indeed, in some cases a few creditors will be demonstrably worse off in bankruptcy than not, or vice versa. For example, the court may refuse to order abstention because of the need to recover preferential transfers. While the entire group of creditors may be benefited by the preference recovery, the preferred creditor who will have to pay the money back obviously is not. Care must be taken, however, not to fall into a simple majoritarian trap in deciding to abstain or not to abstain; often the need to protect the valid rights of dissenting creditors may be a compelling reason to proceed in bankruptcy. To follow up on a variant of the example just given, if a majority of creditors received preferential transfers while the debtor was insolvent, the non-preferred creditors should not be foreclosed from bankruptcy relief simply because they are in the minority.

In weighing the comparative benefit of the non-bankruptcy option, courts take into account such factors as how far along the out-of-court proceedings are, what cost savings are likely if abstention is ordered, how the rights of the parties will be affected, what remedies would be available to the parties outside of bankruptcy, and so forth.[408] Courts do not require that the prospective non-bankruptcy distribution exactly mirror the bankruptcy scheme, but at the same time they will not abstain if creditors would be

---

[406] The objectives of chapter 15 include providing an effective mechanism for promoting cooperation between U.S. and foreign courts; greater legal certainty; fair and efficient administration of cross-border cases; protecting and maximizing the value of the debtor's assets; and facilitating the rescue of financially troubled businesses. § 1501(a)(1)–(5). Prior to BAPCPA, the court was directed to consider the factors listed in § 304(c) (repealed by BAPCPA), which were that the "court shall be guided by what will best assure an economical and expeditious administration of such estate, consistent with": (1) just treatment of all creditors; (2) protection of U.S. creditors against prejudice and inconvenience; (3) prevention of fraudulent or preferential dispositions; (4) distribution "substantially" in accord with the U.S. bankruptcy scheme; (5) comity; and (6) the opportunity for a fresh start.

[407] H.R. Rep. No. 95–595, 95th Cong., 1st Sess., at 325; S. Rep. No. 95–989, 95th Cong., 2d Sess., at 36 (1978).

[408] See, e.g., In re Mountain Dairies, Inc., 372 B.R. 623 (Bankr. S.D.N.Y. 2007) (as an alternative holding court abstained in involuntary case that was a essentially a two-party dispute for which the parties had adequate remedies in state court; court stated that "the bankruptcy court is not a collection agency").

seriously prejudiced outside of bankruptcy. One point of importance is that abstention under § 305 does not subject petitioning creditors in an involuntary case to a claim for damages, as would be true if the involuntary case were dismissed for failure to prove the case.[409]

In some instances abstention may even be appropriate in a voluntary case, filed by the debtor. Here the facial oddity of concluding that abstention is in the best interest of "the debtor" is most striking, since the debtor evidently disagrees. The hurdle is not insurmountable, however, as courts have abstained in voluntary cases. Perhaps the best-known example is the case of *In re Colonial Ford*.[410] The debtor had entered into a workout agreement with its major creditors, pursuant to which the creditors compromised their claims and gave the debtor nine months to sell or refinance its car dealership, in exchange for the debtor's agreement that a decree of foreclosure would be entered if the debtor's efforts proved unavailing. The debtor was not able to sell or refinance, but then filed chapter 11 bankruptcy before the foreclosure could occur. The bankruptcy court abstained from the bankruptcy case. Judge Mabey rejected as "astigmatic" the debtor's argument that its interests were not served by dismissal. The court emphasized that § 305(a) reinforces the policy in favor of workouts, and that this policy helps debtors by inducing creditors to be willing to enter into workout agreements in the first place. If a debtor could always renege on a workout by filing bankruptcy, creditors would be wary of compromising their claims in the first place, and debtors generally would be worse off. Thus, viewing debtors as a group, and considering the ex ante effects of the abstention decision, the court was able to conclude that the best interests of creditors and the debtor were served by dismissal.

E. CONVERSION

§ 2.20   Voluntary Conversion

The fact that a case is commenced originally under one chapter does not guarantee that it will remain there. The Code authorizes the conversion of a case from one chapter to another. The conversion rules differ depending upon whether conversion is requested by the debtor, i.e., is voluntary, or by someone other than the debtor, i.e., is involuntary. This section discusses voluntary conversion, while the next section addresses involuntary conversion.[411]

The rules governing conversion on the request of the debtor are chapter-specific, depending both on the chapter the debtor currently is in and the chapter to which the debtor is seeking to convert. These rules are found in the statutory sections for the chapter from which the debtor is requesting conversion. If the debtor is in chapter 7, § 706 applies. A chapter 7 debtor has an absolute one-time right to convert from chapter 7 to chapter 11, 12, or 13, § 706(a), assuming of course that the debtor is also eligible for relief under the chapter to which conversion is sought. § 706(d). This rule encourages the debtor to attempt to repay a larger percentage of their debts out of future income under a repayment plan. The only statutory exception to the debtor's

---

[409] H.R. Rep. No. 95–595, 95th Cong., 1st Sess., at 324 (1977).

[410] 24 B.R. 1014 (Bankr. D. Utah 1982).

[411] See § 2.21.

absolute conversion right is if the case had previously been converted from another chapter to chapter 7. The debtor cannot waive the right to convert. § 706(a).

A judicial "bad faith" exception to the debtor's apparently absolute right to convert from chapter 7 has developed in the courts. A typical scenario in these cases is that a debtor files chapter 7 and fraudulently attempts to hide the value of assets from the trustee. When the trustee catches on to the debtor's game and seeks to sell the property and thus capture its value for the benefit of the estate, the debtor attempts to convert under § 706(a) to chapter 13 in order to retain the property through the plan. Some courts have denied conversion based on the debtor's bad faith, notwithstanding the seemingly absolute language of the statute.

The Supreme Court endorsed this view in the *Marrama* case in 2007.[412] The Court gave two independent reasons for its decision. First, and most dubiously, the Court got around the apparently absolute language of § 706(a) by reasoning that the malfeasing debtor was subject to immediate dismissal if converted to chapter 13, and therefore was not a person who "may be a debtor under such chapter" (meaning the converted-to chapter, here chapter 13) as required by § 706(d).[413] The Court's reasoning on this point is almost certainly wrong; the "may be a debtor" limitation in § 706(d) refers to whether the debtor is *eligible* for relief in the target chapter under § 109, and a debtor's threshold eligibility for relief under a chapter is distinct from the question of that debtor's susceptibility to dismissal under the chapter. Conflating the two is erroneous and fosters confusion.

The Court's second basis for its holding was that even if the language in § 706(a) is on its face absolute and unqualified, that provision is trumped by the inherent power of courts to guard against an abuse of process. The courts' power in this context is found both in the particular specification in the Code in § 105(a) that a bankruptcy court may take any action "necessary or appropriate to . . . prevent an abuse of process," as well as in "the inherent power of every federal court to sanction 'abusive litigation practices.'"[414] This second ground is much more defensible, and does less violence to the Code's scheme.

Note that the fact that the debtor may convert the chapter 7 case to another chapter does not require the court to permit the case to remain indefinitely in the new chapter. Indeed, as the *Marrama* Court reasoned, that power of dismissal or conversion after conversion can be short-circuited and conversion barred in the first instance. Once in the new chapter, the case becomes subject to the conversion and dismissal rules of that chapter.[415]

---

[412] Marrama v. Citizens Bank of Massachusetts, 549 U.S. 365 (2007).

[413] Id. at 372–74.

[414] Id. at 375–76.

[415] For example, in *In re Bowman*, 181 B.R. 836 (Bankr. D. Md. 1995), the chapter 7 debtor requested conversion to chapter 11 because she did not want the trustee to accept an offer to settle a lawsuit, even though that settlement would allow all of her creditors to be paid in full. The debtor thought the suit was worth more, and any extra amounts she could extract would go to her, since the offer already on the table would pay the creditors in full. After conversion the debtor, as chapter 11 debtor in possession, planned to reject the settlement offer. Finding this plan to be a breach of the debtor's fiduciary duty to her creditors, the

A debtor who is in chapter 11 may convert to chapter 7, § 1112(a), or to chapter 12 or 13, § 1112(d), again assuming that the debtor is eligible for relief under the chapter to which conversion is sought. The debtor's right to convert from chapter 11 to chapter 7 is absolute if the debtor is in chapter 11 voluntarily, and if the debtor has not been dispossessed by a trustee. However, the debtor may only convert on a showing of "cause" under § 1112(b)(1), in three situations: (1) if the debtor is not serving as debtor in possession, i.e., a trustee has been appointed; (2) if the chapter 11 case was commenced as an involuntary case; or (3) if the case was converted to chapter 11 at the request of someone other than the debtor. § 1112(a)(1)–(3). The debtor should not be able to frustrate the desire of its creditors to effectuate a reorganization by converting to liquidation under chapter 7.

If the debtor wishes to convert from chapter 11 to another rehabilitation chapter (either 12 or 13), different rules apply. § 1112(d). The primary limitation is that the conversion must take place before the debtor is discharged under § 1141(d), § 1112(d)(2), which typically means that the conversion must occur before the chapter 11 plan is confirmed. Also, if conversion to chapter 12 is sought, the conversion must be "equitable," § 1112(d)(3), a limitation added in the 1986 amendments to guard against debtors abusing the provisions of chapter 12 to the prejudice of their creditors.

The rules governing conversion at the request of the debtor from chapters 12 and 13 are quite similar, although not completely identical. The similarity in rules is to be expected, since chapter 12 was modeled after chapter 13, and both are intended to be entirely voluntary with the debtor. Congress believed that imposing an involuntary repayment plan on a debtor would be both unlikely to work and potentially in violation of the constitutional prohibition against involuntary servitude.[416] Thus, in both chapter 12 and chapter 13, the debtor has an absolute right to convert to chapter 7 "at any time," and may not waive this right. §§ 1208(a), 1307(a). The debtor's right to convert applies even in the situation where someone other than the debtor moves for dismissal of the chapter 12 or 13 case, see §§ 1208(c), (d), 1307(c), and the debtor then moves to convert to chapter 7 while the dismissal motion is pending.

There is no provision for conversion from chapter 12 to another rehabilitation chapter, i.e., to 11 or 13. Congress took the view that chapter 12 provided more relief to family farmers than either chapter 11 or 13, and that allowing conversion would just foster delay.[417] Prior courts have exercised their equitable power to permit a debtor who filed under chapter 12 in good faith but who was ineligible for chapter 12 relief to convert to chapter 11 or 13.[418] More recent courts have consistently ruled, however, that the plain language of the Code does not permit such a conversion.[419]

---

court allowed the debtor to exercise her absolute right to convert under § 706(a), but then immediately converted the case back to chapter 7 for cause under § 1112(b). The independent chapter 7 trustee then could accept the settlement on behalf of all creditors. Under the reasoning of *Marrama*, however, it seems that courts may now simply deny conversion in the first instance if the result would be immediate conversion back to chapter 7.

[416] H.R. Rep. No. 95–595, 95th Cong., 1st Sess., at 120 (1977).

[417] 172 Cong. Rec. S5557 (daily ed. May 7, 1986) (statement of Sen. Grassley).

[418] E.g., In re Orr, 71 B.R. 639 (Bankr. E.D.N.C. 1987).

[419] E.g., In re Stumbo, 301 B.R. 34 (Bankr. S.D. Iowa 2002).

For conversion from chapter 13 to either chapter 11 or 12, the Code does not provide a special rule for requests by the debtor; instead, the debtor must move for such conversion as a party in interest. § 1307(d). The Code does not specify a legal standard to govern the request to convert from chapter 13 to 11 or 12, committing the question to the sound discretion of the bankruptcy judge. The debtor thus does not have an absolute right to convert to chapter 11 or 12 from chapter 13. The only formal restriction on such a conversion is that the request must come before the chapter 13 plan is confirmed. Also, of course, the debtor must be eligible under the chapter to which they are seeking to go. § 1307(f).

§ 2.21   Involuntary Conversion

The right to request conversion of a case from one chapter to another does not reside exclusively in the debtor. The Code also affords that right to any "party in interest" (which includes any creditor, a committee, a trustee, any equity security holder, and others) and to the United States trustee. Thus, a bankruptcy case may be converted to a particular chapter against the debtor's wishes. Once in bankruptcy, then, a debtor does not have absolute control over the chapter in which the case will proceed.

The involuntary conversion rules are more limited than the rules for voluntary conversion, in several respects. First, involuntary conversion is never a matter of right, as it often is for the debtor. Some showing (which varies depending on the chapter) must be made to support the conversion motion. Second, the debtor may in some instances be able to trump a conversion motion by requesting outright dismissal of the bankruptcy case. Finally, the involuntary conversion rules mirror the restrictions on filing an involuntary petition.

Taking the last point first, recall that an involuntary petition may not be filed under chapter 12 or chapter 13, and may not be filed against a farmer or a not-for-profit corporation.[420] § 303(a). Similarly, conversion from chapter 7 or 11 to chapter 12 or 13 is prohibited, except on the debtor's request or consent. §§ 706(c), 1112(d)(1).

Farmers also are protected. A chapter 11 case involving a debtor who is a farmer (or a non-profit corporation) may not be converted to chapter 7 other than on the debtor's motion. § 1112(c). Similarly, a chapter 13 case of a farmer debtor may not be converted to chapter 7, 11, or 12 against the debtor's wishes. § 1307(f). Slightly more flexibility is permitted in chapter 12; a case involving a family farmer debtor may be converted to chapter 7 on a showing that the debtor has committed fraud in connection with the case. § 1208(d). Note, however, that some courts have concluded that the debtor may avoid this conversion to a liquidation case by exercising its absolute right to dismiss the case under § 1208(b).[421] Other courts give precedence to the conversion motion, reasoning that debtor fraud must not be countenanced.[422] The Supreme Court's *Marrama* 2007 decision,[423] while in another context, lends support to the view that a

---

[420]   See §§ 2.6, 2.7.

[421]   See, e.g., In re Davenport, 175 B.R. 355 (Bankr. E.D. Cal. 1994).

[422]   See, e.g., In re Graven, 936 F.2d 378 (8th Cir. 1991).

[423]   549 U.S. 365 (2007).

debtor's apparently clear statutory right might give way to the court's inherent power to prevent fraud and abuse of process.

In another respect farmers are not given full chapter choice. The Code does not protect a farmer who originally seeks liquidation under chapter 7 from an involuntary conversion to chapter 11.

Conversion on the request of a party in interest or the United States trustee is never a matter of right. Court approval is always required. §§ 706(b), 1112(b), (e), 1208(d), 1307(c). The different chapters from which conversion is sought specify different rules that the court must apply in exercising its discretion whether to grant conversion. The rule in converting from chapter 7 is entirely silent on the legal standard to be applied by the bankruptcy court, and thus the matter is within the sound discretion of the court.[424]

The provision for involuntary conversion from chapter 11 to chapter 7 is much more explicit regarding what must be shown to support conversion. § 1112(b)(1). The statutory ground is "cause," and the Code then lists sixteen nonexclusive illustrations of what might constitute "cause." § 1112(b)(4). Most of these envision a situation where the reorganization has failed or is likely to fail, and thus continuing in chapter 11 would be a wasted effort. On proof of cause, the court has the discretion either to convert the case to chapter 7 or to dismiss the case entirely, "whichever is in the best interests of creditors and the estate." § 1112(b)(1). In addition, conversion or dismissal on motion of the United States trustee is authorized if the debtor fails to timely file its lists of creditors, schedules, and statement of affairs. § 1112(e). Note that the 2005 amendments withdrew from the United States trustee the standing to seek conversion or dismissal under § 1112(b)(1) for cause. Now only a "party in interest" has standing under § 1112(b)(1).

The most often litigated ground for conversion or dismissal that is not expressly listed in the Code is for a bad faith filing. For example, a debtor with no objective hope of reorganizing may file chapter 11 on the eve of a foreclosure, seeking merely to delay the inevitable.

The rule in chapter 13 for involuntary conversion to chapter 7 or dismissal, § 1307(c), is very similar to the analogous chapter 11 provision, § 1112(b)(1). Again, the legal standard is "cause," and again the Code contains a nonexclusive laundry list of factors that might constitute cause. § 1307(c)(1)–(11). These factors, as in chapter 11, generally involve the present or prospective failure of the rehabilitation effort.

A chapter 13 case also may be converted to chapter 11 or 12, and there is no requirement that cause for such conversion be established. § 1307(d). The matter rests within the court's discretion. Such a conversion might be ordered if the debtor had debt in excess of the chapter 13 eligibility amount. The only substantive limitation is that conversion must occur before the debtor's chapter 13 plan is confirmed.

---

[424] See In re Texas Extrusion Corp., 844 F.2d 1142 (5th Cir.), cert. denied, 488 U.S. 926 (1988).

The rule for involuntary conversion in chapter 12 is much more limited than in chapters 11 and 13. In chapter 12, only dismissal of the case is authorized on a showing of cause. § 1208(c). The court is not permitted to choose to convert the case to chapter 7 for cause, as it may in chapter 11 or chapter 13. Instead, the only basis for converting a chapter 12 case to chapter 7 against the debtor's wishes is on proof that the debtor committed fraud in connection with the case. § 1208(d).

§ 2.22   Effects of Conversion

The legal rules governing the effects of a conversion of a case from one chapter to another are somewhat complicated.[425] § 348; Rule 1019. In part the complexity arises because of the nature of a converted case. Conversion does not create a new bankruptcy "case"; the case after conversion is the same case that existed before, just under another chapter. All bankruptcy cases, no matter what the chapter, share some common features. Having said that, there also are critical differences between the various chapters of the Code; many of the special rules and consequences of each chapter are *sui generis*. The challenge is to identify those aspects of the bankruptcy case that are common to the different chapters, and thus suggest continuity in treatment, and those that are specific to the particular chapter, and thus dictate treating the conversion as triggering a new set of rules.

The baseline rule as to the legal effect of conversion has two components: first, the conversion constitutes an order for relief under the chapter to which the case is converted, but second, subject to some stated exceptions, § 348(b), (c), the conversion does not change the date of the filing of the petition, the commencement of the case, or the order for relief. § 348(a). The second part of the rule recognizes the reality of the continuity of the overall bankruptcy case; the first part, especially in conjunction with some of the stated exceptions, gives effect to the need for rules specifically geared to the post-conversion chapter. Specific examples may serve to make the point.

Obviously, one of the most crucial aspects of a bankruptcy case is dealing with claims. Questions that usually arise include determining which claims should participate in the bankruptcy distribution, and the means by which those claims are able to participate, and deciding which claims are discharged. The simplest example is a claim that arises before the original bankruptcy filing. That claim is treated as a prepetition claim throughout the bankruptcy case, prior to conversion and after conversion, and accordingly will share in a distribution if the claim is allowed, and will be discharged. Normally the holder of such a claim will not need to take any new action in the converted case. For example, if a proof of claim with regard to such a prepetition claim is filed in the case before conversion, the creditor will not have to refile the proof of claim after conversion. The original filing will still suffice after conversion. Rule 1019(3).

However, caution must be exercised. In a chapter 11 case, a creditor's claim will be allowed without the need for filing a proof of claim if the claim is scheduled and is not listed as disputed, contingent, or unliquidated. § 1111(a)(1). The "deemed" filing from

---

[425] See generally David Epstein, Consequences of Converting a Bankruptcy Case, 60 Am. Bankr. L.J. 339 (1986).

the chapter 11 case will not carry forward into the chapter 7 case after conversion. The creditor must file a proof of claim after conversion in order for its claim to be allowed. The creditor will be mailed notice of the conversion, alerting it to the need to file a proof of claim. § 348(c); Rule 2002(f)(2).

The situation gets a bit trickier when the creditor's claim arises after the bankruptcy case is commenced, but prior to the conversion. The normal rule is that the date of the bankruptcy filing serves as the critical point of cleavage for claims; generally speaking, only those claims that arise prior to bankruptcy are paid in the bankruptcy case and are discharged by the bankruptcy. Postpetition claims (with a few exceptions) neither share in the bankruptcy distribution nor are affected by the bankruptcy discharge. The most important exception is for expenses of the administration of the bankruptcy case, which are afforded second priority in the bankruptcy distribution. §§ 507(a)(2), 503(b).

In the event of a conversion, which date is operative for claim allowance and for discharge: the date of the original bankruptcy filing, or the date of the conversion? Answer: the date of conversion. Thus, postpetition, pre-conversion claims are dealt with in the converted bankruptcy case; they are treated as a prepetition claim and thus may share in any distribution, § 348(d), but they also are discharged. §§ 348(b), 727(b). Notice will be sent to the holders of those claims, who then have an opportunity to file a proof of claim. Rule 1019(6). Administrative expense claims arising in the superseded case prior to conversion do not lose their priority entitlement, but they come behind administrative expense claims that arise in the superseding chapter 7 case. § 726(b).

Conversion affects the status of the representative of the bankruptcy estate in the superseded case. The service of a trustee or examiner is automatically terminated by conversion, § 348(e), and the trustee or debtor in possession in the superseded case must turn over all records and estate property and file a detailed accounting. Rule 1019(4), (5). In a conversion to chapter 7, a trustee will be appointed promptly after the conversion order. §§ 348(b), 701(a).

The effect of conversion on the identification of what property is included as property of the estate can be a difficult problem in those cases where the bankruptcy estate includes property acquired or earned postpetition by the debtor. This occurs in chapter 13, § 1306(a); chapter 12, § 1207; and, after the 2005 amendments, in chapter 11 cases involving individual debtors, § 1115(a). Before turning to those hard cases, though, it is helpful to understand how the issue would be resolved in those cases where there is not a rule bringing postpetition property acquired by the debtor into the estate. For example, that would be the situation in a chapter 11 case involving a corporate debtor. The rule is that property of the estate in the superseding case (i.e., the post-conversion case) does *not* include property acquired by the debtor after the initial bankruptcy filing up to the time of the conversion. Property of the estate is defined as of the commencement of the case, § 541(a)(1), and the baseline conversion rule is that conversion does not change the date of the commencement of the case. § 348(a). Note that some types of property interests that are acquired postpetition do come into the estate, but those special inclusive rules apply irrespective of whether a conversion has taken place, i.e., the property would become part of the estate even if a conversion never happened.

The more difficult scenario with regard to defining the scope of the post-conversion estate is when the pre-conversion case is in a chapter that does bring into the estate property acquired by the debtor after the filing. This is the rule in chapter 13, chapter 12, and chapter 11 cases regarding an individual debtor. The issue is whether the property acquired by the debtor postpetition and pre-conversion should be included in the estate after conversion. Here is the basic problem: if those postpetition acquisitions are included in the estate, the debtor may be worse off than if he had not filed chapter 13 (for example) in the first place. This problem arises in particular with respect to postpetition wages earned by an individual debtor, which, but for the special inclusive rule, would be excluded from the estate. § 541(a)(6). On the other side of the balance, however, is the fact that the debtor can discharge debts that arise postpetition and pre-confirmation, as noted above. Furthermore, an exclusionary rule may afford the debtor the opportunity to engage in strategic opportunistic behavior.

Prior to the 1994 amendments, the majority view in the cases was that the post-conversion estate included all property of the debtor or estate as of the date of conversion. For example, the Eighth Circuit held that undistributed funds held by the chapter 13 trustee prior to conversion to chapter 7 remained property of the post-conversion estate.[426] Similarly, the Seventh Circuit held that an inheritance acquired by the chapter 13 debtor more than 180 days after the original filing became property of the estate under § 1306, and remained so after conversion to chapter 7, notwithstanding the fact that the inherited property would not have been property of the estate if the case had been filed under chapter 7.[427] Other courts disagreed, however, and excluded such postpetition property from the post-conversion estate.[428]

In the 1994 amendments Congress resolved the split in the case law for chapter 13 cases, deciding the issue largely in the debtor's favor. This rule—which applies only when the superseded case was under chapter 13—relates back the time of the determination of estate property to the original filing date. § 348(f)(1). Thus, only estate property as of the date of the filing of the petition that is still in the debtor's possession or control is included in the estate. An exception is made if the debtor converts from chapter 13 in bad faith, with the result then being that all property of the estate as of the date of conversion is included in the post-conversion estate. § 348(f)(2). This restriction is intended to prevent overt debtor abuse while still encouraging a debtor to file under chapter 13.

As noted, the same problem of what happens to property acquired postpetition and pre-conversion exists in chapter 12, which also has a special rule including postpetition acquisitions in the estate. § 1207. Just as in conversions from chapter 13, the cases have split over whether the conversion from chapter 12 revests that postpetition property in the debtor, or whether the property remains in the estate. Congress did not address the chapter 12 problem in the 1994 amendments, with the amendatory language in § 348(f) limited to conversions from chapter 13.

---

[426] Resendez v. Lindquist, 691 F.2d 397 (8th Cir. 1982).

[427] In re Lybrook, 951 F.2d 136 (7th Cir. 1991).

[428] E.g., In re Young, 66 F.3d 376 (1st Cir. 1995).

The 2005 amendments included a postpetition property inclusive rule in individual chapter 11 cases, § 1115(a), that tracks the chapter 13 rule in § 1306(a). Thus, for an individual debtor, exactly the same problem would arise whether that debtor originally (i.e., prior to conversion) was in chapter 13 or chapter 11. However, when Congress added § 1115(a), it did not at the same time amend § 348(f)(1), which continues to apply only in chapter 13 cases. Thus, courts will have to develop case law to resolve the problem of whether the property acquired postpetition and pre-conversion in chapter 11 by an individual debtor will or will not be property of the bankruptcy estate after a conversion.[429] The chapter 11 problem is even more difficult than it was under chapter 13 pre–1994 because an individual debtor can be subjected to bankruptcy involuntarily under chapter 11, and thus could have the postpetition property inclusive rule imposed on him against his will, whereas at least under chapter 13 the debtor was making a choice to proceed initially under chapter 13.

Conversion also may trigger the running of some new time periods. For example, upon conversion to chapter 7, creditors are given new time to file claims, file a complaint objecting to discharge, or file a complaint objecting to the dischargeability of a debt. Rule 1019(2). Courts have split over whether to allow additional time for the trustee or creditors to object to the debtor's claimed exemptions after a conversion to chapter 7.[430] Courts also disagree whether a debtor may claim exemptions as of the date of the conversion, without being bound to the exemptions claimed in the superseded case.[431]

Furthermore, after the 2005 amendments added a means test and dismissal for abuse under § 707(b) in chapter 7 cases involving individual debtors with primarily consumer debts, correlative procedural changes needed to be made in the Bankruptcy Rules to allow for the possibility of filing motions to dismiss a converted chapter 7 case for abuse. Accordingly, under Bankruptcy Rule 1019(2), a new time period for filing a motion under § 707(b) arises upon conversion to chapter 7 in cases involving individual consumer debtors. The only exception is if the case had originally been converted from chapter 7 to chapter 11, 12, or 13, and then was reconverted back to chapter 7. In that situation, no new time period to seek dismissal arises.

The 2005 amendments added rules protecting secured creditors in cases converted from chapter 13. The concern was that secured creditors would have their secured claims written down to a lower judicially determined collateral value in chapter 13 and paid off (or down) at the reduced value (under § 1325(a)(5)), and then the debtor would

---

[429] See, e.g, In re Sundale, Ltd., 471 B.R. 300 (Bankr. S.D. Fla. 2012) (holding that in absence of express provision in debtors' confirmed chapter 11 plan, upon conversion to chapter 7, assets that had vested in reorganized debtors on confirmation did not revest in estate to be distributed by chapter 7 trustee); In re Evans, 464 B.R. 429 (Bankr. D. Colo. 2011) (holding that debtor's postpetition earnings included in chapter 11 estate reverted back to debtor and not property of chapter 7 estate);

[430] Compare In re Fonke, 321 B.R. 199 (Bankr. S.D. Tex. 2005) (deadline to object to exemptions did not recommence when case converted), with In re Bace, 364 B.R. 166 (Bankr. S.D.N.Y. 2007) (time for objecting to exemptions runs from conclusion of post-conversion meeting of creditors).

[431] E.g., In re Lindberg, 735 F.2d 1087 (8th Cir.), cert. denied, 469 U.S. 1073 (1984) (holding debtors can claim exemptions from conversion date). But see In re Alexander, 236 F.3d 431 (8th Cir. 2001) (holding debtors are bound by original petition for claiming exemptions); In re Stamm, 222 F.3d 216 (5th Cir. 2000) (same).

convert to chapter 7 and keep the collateral free and clear of the creditor's lien. The debtor thereby could discharge his unsecured debts without paying them under a chapter 13 plan, and keep collateral at a reduced valuation. Note that the debtor could not accomplish this result if he originally filed under chapter 7, because (other than the limited redemption rule of § 722), the debtor cannot strip down a secured claim to a lower judicially fixed value and retain the collateral at that lower amount.[432] In chapter 7, the only way a debtor could keep collateral (other than redemption) would be to persuade the creditor to agree to a reaffirmation of the debt, but then the creditor could protect itself by the terms of the reaffirmation agreement.

The 2005 law took away this "chapter 13 write down and then convert" option from debtors in § 348(f)(1), by amending subsection (B) and adding a new subsection (C). Prior to amendment, § 348(f)(2) provided that (1) valuations of property and of allowed secured claims in the pre-conversion chapter 13 case would apply in the converted case, and (2) that an allowed secured claim would be reduced by the amounts paid in the chapter 13 case. So, for example, assume that Debtor owed Creditor $10,000 on a claim secured by Collateral, and that in the pre-conversion chapter 13 case the court valued the Collateral at $6,000 and Debtor paid Creditor $6,000 on the secured claim. Debtor then converts to chapter 7. Prior to 2005, Creditor has no secured claim remaining after conversion—the $6,000 valuation stands, and that amount was reduced by the $6,000 paid, meaning Debtor can now enjoy the Collateral free and clear of Creditor's lien.

The 2005 amendments change the result in this case. First, under § 348(f)(1)(B), valuations made in the chapter 13 case do not apply once the case is converted to chapter 7. Second, the provision that the creditor's allowed secured claim is reduced by payments made in the chapter 13 case does not apply when conversion is to chapter 7. Thus, in our hypothetical, the Debtor could not argue that (1) the Creditor's Collateral was valued at $6,000 or (2) that the $6,000 paid to Creditor paid off the allowed secured claim.

Note that under § 348(f)(1)(B) as amended, the old rule does still apply in cases converted from chapter 13 to chapter 11 or chapter 12. Thus, a judicial strip down of collateral in chapter 13 pre-conversion apparently will still work when the debtor converts to chapter 11 or 12, rather than chapter 7. However, as will be discussed below, how this rule squares with new § 348(f)(1)(C) is confusing.

To eliminate any doubt that a debtor cannot keep collateral free and clear when a debtor converts from chapter 13 to chapter 7 and pays only the stripped-down amount, Congress also added § 348(f)(1)(C), which on its face covers *all* cases converted from chapter 13, not just conversions to chapter 7. This new provision does two things. First, it states that a creditor's claim will continue to be secured by its collateral "unless the full amount of such claim determined under applicable nonbankruptcy law has been paid in full." § 348(f)(1)(C)(i). In our hypothetical, this means that Debtor must pay Creditor $10,000—the total amount of the debt—rather than just the $6,000 judicially appraised amount, to pay off the secured claim. The amendment underscores this point

---

[432] Dewsnup v. Timm, 502 U.S. 410 (1992).

by adding that this rule applies "notwithstanding any valuation or determination of the amount of an allowed secured claim made for the purposes of the case under chapter 13."

Second, the new rule provides that any pre-bankruptcy default "shall have the effect given under nonbankruptcy law" unless that default "has been fully cured under the plan at the time of conversion." § 348(f)(1)(C)(ii). This prevents a debtor from reinstating a debt under chapter 13 and then keeping that reinstatement in effect following conversion unless the debtor completes the cure contemplated.

A point of confusion under the 2005 changes is how the rules will be applied when a chapter 13 case is converted to chapter 11 or 12. On the one hand, the old rule in § 348(f)(1)(B) supposedly still applies to conversions to chapter 11 or 12, meaning that valuations made in the pre-conversion chapter 13 case are still valid and that amounts paid on that secured claim in chapter 13 count. So, in our hypothetical, it appears to say that the $6,000 valuation would hold, meaning that the Creditor's allowed secured claim was $6,000, and that the $6,000 in payments would reduce that secured claim, which by my math leaves an allowed secured claim of $0. That seemingly should mean that Debtor could keep the Collateral free and clear of any lien by Creditor, without paying another cent to Creditor. However, on the other hand, flying in the face of that result is § 348(f)(1)(C)(i), which states, as described above, that in all cases converted from chapter 13 (apparently to any chapter), Creditor keeps its lien to secure its "claim" until it is paid the full amount of the debt, "notwithstanding any valuation" made in the chapter 13 case. If subsection (C) is given effect as written in conversions from chapter 13 to chapter 11 or 12, it is hard to see how subsection (B) will have any effect. Creditor would have an allowed secured claim of $0 (under subsection B), but under subsection (C) would retain a security interest to secure its "claim" (the remaining $4,000 left when $6,000 is paid on the total $10,000 claim) until paid in full.

F. SUBSTANTIVE CONSOLIDATION

§ 2.23   Effects of Substantive Consolidation

The bankruptcy court has the equitable power to order the substantive consolidation of the bankruptcy cases of separate debtors. The grounds on which substantive consolidation may be ordered are examined in the next section. This section discusses the effects of substantive consolidation. Except for the provision regarding spouses, § 302, and the provision listing the required contents of a chapter 11 plan, § 1123(a)(5)(C) ("provide adequate means for the plan's implementation, such as . . . merger or consolidation of the debtor with one or more persons"), no statutory provision governs either the grounds for or the effects of substantive consolidation. The law of substantive consolidation thus has been developed by the courts.

A distinction should be drawn between "*substantive*" consolidation, which affects the substantive rights of the parties, and "*procedural*" consolidation, which does not. In procedural consolidation, commonly called "joint administration,"[433] the court directs

---

[433] Consolidation and joint administration are provided for in Rule 1015. Technically, "consolidation" refers only to Rule 1015(a), which authorizes the procedural consolidation of two or more petitions involving

that the bankruptcy cases of related debtors be dealt with as a unit with regard to procedural and administrative matters. The purpose is to save time and money. For example, a single set of notices may be sent out, a single case docket kept, and a joint claims docket maintained. If conflicts of interests do not pose a problem, the same trustee could even be appointed for the jointly administered cases, subject to the right of creditors to elect separate trustees. Rule 2009.

For spouses, consolidation may be either procedural or substantive, depending on the court's order. A court order is necessary to effect a substantive consolidation; the mere filing of a joint case does not automatically effectuate a substantive consolidation of those cases. The Code expressly authorizes consolidation of the joint cases of spouses, but does not specify a standard. § 302(b). Spouses are required to elect the same set of exemptions, i.e., state or federal. § 522(b); Rule 1015(b). In community property or marital property states, additional rules govern the treatment of spousal cases. E.g., §§ 541(a)(2) (property of estate), 524(a)(3) (discharge injunction).

Substantive consolidation dramatically alters the rights of creditors and the debtors. In essence, the estates of multiple debtors are merged or combined, on both the asset and debt side of the ledger. That is, the assets of the consolidated debtors are pooled into one estate, and the claims of the creditors of the consolidated debtors are directed against that single pooled fund. All creditor claims are paid out of the consolidated estate.[434] This also means that "[s]ubstantive consolidation has the effect of eliminating duplicative claims filed against related debtors by creditors uncertain as to where the liability should be allocated."[435] In the seminal case on substantive consolidation, the Supreme Court recognized that consolidation of different but related estates is a vital tool in accomplishing the fundamental purpose of bankruptcy.[436] In so holding, the Court made clear that the "power of the bankruptcy court to subordinate or to adjudicate equities arising out of the relationship between the several creditors is complete."[437]

This pooling effect means that substantive consolidation almost inevitably prejudices the creditors of one of the consolidated debtors in favor of creditors of another consolidated debtor. A simple example will illustrate the point. Assume that Debtor A has $100,000 in assets and $200,000 in allowed unsecured debts. Without consolidation, creditors of Debtor A thus would receive 50 cents on the dollar on their claims. Assume further that Debtor B has $100,000 in assets and $400,000 in debts; B creditors would be paid 25% without consolidation. After substantive consolidation, the

---

the same debtor in the same court. "Joint administration" is dealt with in Rule 1015(b), and may be invoked when there are petitions pending in the same court involving different but related debtors, namely: (1) husband and wife; (2) partnership and a general partner; (3) two or more general partners; or (4) a debtor and an affiliate. However, in common parlance the terms "procedural consolidation" and "joint administration" are used interchangeably. The critical point is that these purely administrative or procedural mechanisms differ fundamentally from substantive consolidation.

[434] As a practical effect, in chapter 11 cases, courts do not need to conduct separate liquidation analyses for each debtor that was consolidated in determining whether the "best interests of creditors" test is satisfied. See In re Jennifer Convertibles, Inc., 447 B.R. 713, 724 (Bankr. S.D.N.Y. 2011).

[435] In re AHF Dev., Ltd., 462 B.R. 186, 197 (Bankr. N.D. Tex. 2011).

[436] Sampsell v. Imperial Paper & Color Corp., 313 U.S. 215 (1941).

[437] Id. at 219.

estate has $200,000 in assets, and $600,000 in debts. Each creditor will be paid one-third on their claims. The creditors of Debtor A (the less insolvent of the two debtors) are made worse off because of the consolidation (their dividend drops from one-half to one-third), but B creditors gain correspondingly (increasing their take from one-fourth to one-third). This apparent prejudice to A creditors dictates the cautious approach courts take to substantive consolidation and influences the grounds upon which consolidation will be ordered. As will be seen below,[438] courts usually will only substantively consolidate debtors in two situations: first, if creditors treated the debtors as a single economic unit, and thus did not really rely on their separateness, or, second, if the cost of not consolidating would exceed the prejudice from doing so.

Further complicating the situation is that the claims of the consolidated debtors against each other must be cancelled. In other words, intercompany claims are eliminated.[439] Thus, in our example, if Debtor A had loaned Debtor B $20,000, prior to consolidation, that liability would be reflected as an asset on A's balance sheet and a liability on B's; but upon consolidation, it would be nonsense to say that consolidated Debtor A–B owed itself $20,000. This cancellation would further prejudice the creditors of A. In cases involving the consolidation of corporate groups, such intercompany claims may be common.

Consolidation also will have an effect in chapter 11 cases on plan voting. The creditors of the consolidated debtors will be combined for purposes of voting on the plan.[440] This merging of voting constituencies alters the extent of the voice that creditors have over the outcome of the vote. Creditors of a smaller debtor who had a controlling say in that debtor's chapter 11 case might hold only a small minority of voting claims in the consolidated case. Conversely, creditors holding a narrow majority of the votes of the largest pre-consolidation debtor might lose control after consolidation. The plans could address this problem by placing the creditors of different debtors into different classes.

Courts have sometimes countenanced "hybrid" substantive consolidation, which actually has several possible meanings. One possibility is to consolidate all related debtors, but to confer a priority in distribution on those creditors who would be prejudiced otherwise by the consolidation. This prejudice might occur because those creditors had claims against the more solvent pre-consolidation debtor (e.g., Debtor A in our example above), or because a secured creditor lost its security in the consolidation.[441] Consolidation also might be limited to prevent the security interest of

---

[438] See § 2.24.

[439] See In re Owens Corning, 419 F.3d 195, 205 (3d Cir. 2005) (explaining that substantive consolidation causes inter-entity liabilities to be erased); In re Source Enters., Inc., 392 B.R. 541, 551 (S.D.N.Y. 2008) ("Substantive consolidation results . . . [in eliminating] inter company claims.").

[440] See, e.g., In re Raymond Prof'l Group, Inc., 438 B.R. 130, 138 (Bankr. N.D. Ill. 2010) ("Substantive consolidation usually results in . . . combining the creditors of the [consolidated] companies for purposes of voting on reorganization plans.").

[441] For example, in In re Gulfco Inv. Corp., 593 F.2d 921 (10th Cir. 1979), a creditor of the parent debtor held a security interest in stock of the subsidiary corporation, which stock was cancelled by the consolidation.

a secured creditor from expanding to capture previously unencumbered assets.[442] Another form of hybrid consolidation is when the court orders the consolidation of less than all of the debtors in a related group, in order to prevent unfairness to creditors who relied on the separate identity of their debtor.[443] Additionally, the court may order less than complete consolidation to limit the effect of the consolidation order, such as consolidating for the limited purpose of voting and distribution under a parent entity's plan.[444]

A problem arises when the consolidated debtors filed (or had filed against them) their bankruptcy petitions at different times. Which petition date controls? The answer may be crucial for a number of reasons, especially in applying the trustee's avoiding powers. For example, transfers made within 90 days before bankruptcy are vulnerable as preferences. § 547. If a transfer was made to a creditor of Debtor A, which then filed bankruptcy more than 90 days later, but Debtor A's case was later consolidated with Debtor B, which filed bankruptcy less than 90 days after the transfer, is the transfer within the preference period? If the earlier petition date of Debtor B is used, such a result is possible. In effect, the consolidation would be given retroactive effect. Some courts take the position that the earliest petition date should govern.[445] Others, however, insist on weighing the overall fairness to all affected parties in ascertaining the governing petition date.[446] Under this latter view, giving retroactive effect to consolidation (often referred to as consolidation with *nunc pro tunc*, or "now is then") should be an extraordinary remedy used only sparingly.[447]

§ 2.24 Grounds for Substantive Consolidation

The law of substantive consolidation has been crafted by the courts in the exercise of their equitable powers.[448] As the preceding section demonstrates, the impact of an order substantively consolidating separate debtors in bankruptcy can be momentous. What, then, are the bases on which a court will enter such an order? While commentators have debated whether substantive consolidation should be available only in rare cases or as a matter of course,[449] most courts have taken the view that consolidation is an extraordinary remedy that should be sparingly invoked, because of

---

[442] In re Cont'l Vending Mach. Corp., 517 F.2d 997 (2d Cir. 1975) (consolidating assets and liabilities for purposes of dealing with unsecured creditors but not secured creditors), cert. denied, 424 U.S. 913 (1976).

[443] E.g., In re Flora Mir Candy Corp., 432 F.2d 1060 (2d Cir. 1970).

[444] In re Asarco LLC, 420 B.R. 314, 368 (Bankr. S.D. Tex. 2009) ("By entry of this order, the Debtors shall be deemed consolidated under the Parent's Plan, solely for the limited purpose of voting and distribution under the Parent's plan.").

[445] E.g., In re Baker & Getty Fin. Servs., Inc., 974 F.2d 712 (6th Cir. 1992).

[446] E.g., In re Auto-Train Corp., 810 F.2d 270 (D.C. Cir. 1987).

[447] Id. at 275; In re Bonham, 229 F.3d 750, 772 (9th Cir. 2000).

[448] Because the law of substantive consolidation does not depend on any provision of the Code but on general principles of equity; decisions under the prior Bankruptcy Act continue to have force today. See 11 U.S.C. § 105(a).

[449] This debate reached a peak in a trilogy of law review articles by Jonathan Landers (who favored more routine consolidation) and Richard Posner (who disagreed). See Jonathan Landers, A Unified Approach to Parent, Subsidiary, and Affiliate Questions in Bankruptcy, 42 U. Chi. L. Rev. 589 (1975); Richard A. Posner, The Rights of Creditors of Affiliated Corporations, 43 U. Chi. L. Rev. 499 (1976); Jonathan Landers, Another Word on Parents, Subsidiaries and Affiliates in Bankruptcy, 43 U. Chi. L. Rev. 527 (1976).

the potential prejudice to some creditors.[450] Some courts however, have recognized that perhaps the traditional cautious attitude should be softened because of the increasingly widespread use of corporate groups.[451]

At bottom, the decision whether or not to order substantive consolidation hinges on a balancing test, weighing the prejudice of consolidation against that of continued separate existence; in other words, consolidation is warranted only if the unsecured creditors as a group will thereby enjoy a net benefit.[452] The balance must tilt heavily in favor of the consolidation.[453] Courts have noted several factors as pertinent to the balancing equation: (1) whether the related debtors have consolidated financial statements; (2) unity of ownership and interest; (3) existence of intercorporate guarantees; (4) degree of difficulty in establishing separate assets and liabilities; (5) occurrence of asset transfers without regard to corporate formalities; (6) commingling of assets and operations; and (7) the profitability of consolidation at a single location.[454]

The foregoing factors need not all be shown. Indeed, the cases in which consolidation has been ordered tend to boil down into two basic types; the factors listed above tend to describe specific characteristics of those cases.[455] The first type of situation in which consolidation may be ordered is where the creditors of the related entities have dealt with the entities as a single economic unit, and have not relied on their separate identity when extending credit.[456] In such a situation, consolidation is not unfair to creditors, because those creditors did not rely on separateness; to the contrary, creditor expectations are being given effect. The flip side of the same point is that courts are wary of consolidating when creditors have relied on the separate identity of their debtor when extending credit.[457]

Some courts have approached this issue through a burden-shifting approach. If substantial inter-debtor identity is shown, and consolidation is needed to avoid some harm or realize some benefit, then a presumption arises in favor of consolidation. The burden then shifts to the party objecting to consolidation to show the harm from consolidation—normally, that they relied on the separate identity of their debtor and will receive a smaller dividend in a consolidation. Upon such a showing, consolidation should only be ordered on clear proof that the equities weigh heavily in favor of

---

[450] The Second Circuit has been especially notable for its strict stand on substantive consolidation. See, e.g., FDIC v. Colonial Realty Co., 966 F.2d 57 (2d Cir. 1992); In re Augie/Restivo Baking Co., 860 F.2d 515 (2d Cir. 1988); In re Flora Mir Candy Corp., 432 F.2d 1060 (2d Cir. 1970). More recently, the Third Circuit added its voice to this side of the debate. In re Owens Corning, 419 F.3d 195 (3rd Cir. 2005).

[451] E.g., Eastgroup Props. v. S. Motel Assocs., Ltd., 935 F.2d 245 (11th Cir. 1991). See also In re Brentwood Golf Club, LLC, 329 B.R. 802 (Bankr. E.D. Mich. 2005).

[452] See In re Hemingway Transp., Inc., 954 F.2d 1 (1st Cir. 1992). See also In re AHF Dev., Ltd., 462 B.R. 186 (Bankr. N.D. Tex. 2011); In re Century Elecs. Mfg., Inc., 310 B.R. 485 (Bankr. D. Mass. 2004).

[453] *Flora Mir Candy*, supra note 450, 432 F.2d 1060.

[454] *Eastgroup Properties*, supra note 451, 935 F.2d at 249.

[455] See *Augie/Restivo Baking*, supra note 450, 860 F.2d 515. See also In re Archdiocese of Milwaukee, 483 B.R. 693, 700 (Bankr. E.D. Wis. 2012) (describing the *Augie/Restivo Baking* test for substantive consolidation as a "two critical factor" focus: (1) whether creditors dealt with the entities as a single economic unit and did not rely on their separate identity in extending credit, and (2) whether the affairs of the debtors were so entangled that consolidation would benefit all creditors).

[456] E.g., Soviero v. Franklin Nat'l Bank, 328 F.2d 446 (2d Cir. 1964).

[457] See *Flora Mir Candy*, supra note 450, 432 F.2d 1060.

consolidation.[458] Adversely affected creditors also might be afforded a priority to remedy the harm they otherwise would suffer.

The second type of case in which consolidation may be ordered is when the financial affairs of the affiliated debtors are hopelessly entangled and intertwined.[459] In such a case, consolidation as a practical matter will benefit everyone, because the cost of untangling the debtors' assets and liabilities would consume so much of the combined estates. Indeed, in some cases consolidation may be the only realistic option, if unraveling the mess would be impossible.

In extraordinary or compelling circumstances, courts may even consolidate a debtor with a non-debtor.[460] The leading case is *Sampsell v. Imperial Paper & Color Corp.*, in which the Supreme Court approved the consolidation of the estate of an individual debtor with a non-debtor corporation of which the individual was the principal stockholder. The evidence showed that the individual had conveyed his assets to the corporation in an attempt to shield them from his creditors.

---

[458] See *Owens Corning*, supra note 450, 419 F.3d at 212; *Eastgroup Properties*, supra note 451, 935 F.2d at 249; In re Auto–Train Corp., 810 F.2d 270, 276 (D.C. Cir. 1987); In re World Access, Inc. 301 B.R. 217, 272–73 (Bankr. N.D. Ill. 2003).

[459] The leading case announcing this concept is *Chemical Bank New York Trust Co. v. Kheel*, 369 F.2d 845 (2d Cir. 1966).

[460] Compare In re Pearlman, 462 B.R. 849, 854 (Bankr. M.D. Fla. 2012) ("Substantive consolidation is purely a bankruptcy remedy, and does not extent to consolidation of assets and affairs of a non-debtor."), with In re S & G Fin. Servs. of S. Florida, Inc., 451 B.R. 573, 582 (Bankr. S.D. Fla. 2011) ("[I]t is well within this Court's equitable powers to allow substantive consolidation of entities under appropriate circumstances, whether or not all of those entities are debtors in bankruptcy.").

Chapter 3

THE AUTOMATIC STAY

A. INTRODUCTION

§ 3.1   Function of the Automatic Stay

An integral structural component of a bankruptcy case is the *"automatic stay"* against creditor collection actions. § 362(a). The stay is akin to a statutory injunction. It arises automatically upon the filing of a bankruptcy petition.

The stay is essential to the effective realization and implementation of the two core functions of a bankruptcy case: the equitable treatment of multiple creditor claims, and the provision of a financial fresh start for an honest debtor. Creditors are precluded from getting a jump on their fellow creditors, and the debtor is given a respite from creditor collection efforts. Instead of an uncontrolled self-help scramble for the debtor's assets, creditor claims must be dealt with in an orderly manner under the supervision and control of the bankruptcy court. The stay seeks to preserve the status quo as of the date the bankruptcy case is commenced, until such time as the bankruptcy court can act. As the legislative history explains:

> The automatic stay is one of the fundamental debtor protections provided by the bankruptcy laws. It gives the debtor a breathing spell from his creditors. . . . The automatic stay also provides creditor protection. Without it, certain creditors would be able to pursue their own remedies against the debtor's property. Those who acted first would obtain payment of the claims in preference to and to the detriment of other creditors.[1]

The § 362 stay is necessary because a bankruptcy case takes time to process.[2] If a bankruptcy case somehow could be wrapped up in one magical instant, the stay would be unnecessary. By its very nature, the stay serves only to provide *interim* protection for creditors and the debtor during the pendency of the bankruptcy case. Once a discharge is granted, a permanent statutory injunction against the collection of discharged claims comes into effect, § 524(a); at that point the need for an interim stay disappears, and that stay is terminated by operation of law. § 362(c)(2). Similarly, once property ceases to be property of the bankruptcy estate, the reason for the interim stay disappears, because the race of diligence by creditors no longer would undermine the operation of the collective proceeding.

---

[1]   H.R. Rep. No. 95–595, 95th Cong., 1st Sess., at 340 (1977).

[2]   See Thomas H. Jackson, Of Liquidation, Continuation, and Delay: An Analysis of Bankruptcy Policy and Nonbankruptcy Rules, 60 Am. Bankr. L.J. 399 (1986).

The stay is neither absolute nor permanent. As noted above, when the underlying reasons for the stay cease to apply, the stay terminates automatically.[3] The court also may decide to grant an aggrieved party *relief from the stay* under § 362(d), if fulfilling the purposes of the bankruptcy case no longer requires maintaining the stay of acts against property, § 362(d)(2), or if the need to protect the moving party becomes paramount.[4] § 362(d)(1).

Finally, not every action against the debtor or the debtor's property is stayed in the first instance. Instead, in some cases Congress decided that other policies, such as the state's interest in enforcing its criminal or environmental laws, are more important than those behind the bankruptcy stay. Congress excluded such cases from the scope of the automatic stay, § 362(b), even if the action otherwise would fall within the prohibitions described in § 362(a). In such an instance, the debtor bears the affirmative burden of obtaining an injunction from the court.[5] By contrast, for an action that is initially stayed under § 362(a) and not excepted under § 362(b), the stayed party bears the onus of going to court and obtaining relief from the stay.[6] The difference is in the default rule.

§ 3.2   Enforcing the Automatic Stay

The automatic stay of § 362(a) is extremely powerful and effective; it is not something with which creditors should trifle. The stay, while essentially a statutory injunction in effect, is unlike an injunction in at least two critical respects. First, the debtor does not have to do anything to trigger the stay, other than file a bankruptcy petition commencing a case. Thus, the debtor does not have to go to court to request injunctive relief. The imposition of the stay is *automatic* (thus the name). Second, the stay is effective against the world without the necessity of serving notice of the stay on affected parties. In all important respects, then, the stay is self-executing.

The practical importance of the automatic creation of the stay cannot be overemphasized. The debtor has the legal power to stop creditor actions in an instant. For example, a scheduled foreclosure sale must be cancelled; an imminent repossession must be halted; and an ongoing lawsuit must stop dead in its tracks. The debtor, with the right to file a bankruptcy petition and invoke the stay, in effect holds a trump card.

Once in place, the stay looms as an impenetrable barrier to unilateral creditor activity. If a creditor wants to avoid the operation of the stay, it must obtain

---

[3]   See § 3.15.

[4]   See § 3.17.

[5]   See, e.g., In re Storozhenko, 459 B.R. 693, 696 (Bankr. E.D. Mich. 2011) ("The nondischargeable debts listed in [§ 362(b)] are not automatically stayed by the filing of a bankruptcy petition. The burden is on the debtor or trustee to affirmatively seek injunctive relief from the enforcement of these debts." (quoting In re Embry, 10 F.3d 401, 404 (6th Cir. 1993))).

Generally, the debtor will file an adversary proceeding for an injunction and a determination that a particular creditor's actions do not fall within the § 362(b) stay exceptions. See, e.g., In re Bertuccio, 414 B.R. 604 (N.D. Cal. 2008); In re Gandy, 327 B.R. 796 (S.D. Tex. 2005); In re First Alliance Mortg. Co., 264 B.R. 634 (C.D. Cal. 2001).

[6]   E.g., In re Palmdale Hills Prop., LLC, 654 F.3d 868, 876 (9th Cir. 2011) (stating that acts not within § 362(b) are not barred completely, but require the creditor to bring an adversary proceeding or otherwise file for relief from stay).

permission from the bankruptcy court. What happens, however, if a creditor decides to take matters into its own hands, and acts in violation of the stay without first receiving the blessing of the court? For example, assume that after the debtor files bankruptcy and thereby triggers the stay, the creditor goes ahead with the scheduled foreclosure sale, or repossesses the debtor's property, or obtains a default judgment. What is the remedy?

The prevailing rule is that all acts taken in violation of the automatic stay are null and void *ab initio*, and without legal effect.[7] The foreclosure sale would be ineffective, the repossessed property would have to be returned, and the judgment would be nugatory. The creditor in each instance thus would lack any incentive to ignore the stay in the hope that its actions will not be challenged.

A minority view holds that acts taken in violation of the stay are voidable only, and not void.[8] The dispute between the courts on this point is in some respects a matter of semantics, and in others speaks to a real difference in judicial attitude toward the enforcement of the stay. The primary argument made for the "voidable" view is that § 362(d), which authorizes the court to grant relief from the stay, provides that the court may "annul" the stay, thereby according retroactive validity to an earlier action taken in contravention of the stay. These courts explain that a "void" action cannot later be ratified or validated (by "annulling"), while a voidable action can. When the Supreme Court in 1940 stated in *Kalb v. Feuerstein*[9] that actions violative of the stay were "void," the bankruptcy statute did not empower the judge to "annul" the stay, as it does now. Some courts suggest that perhaps a better word to describe the effect of a violative act would be "invalid."[10]

Another argument in favor of the voidable view rests on the fact that § 549 empowers the trustee to avoid and recover unauthorized postpetition transfers of estate property. The claim is that this power would be unnecessary if all such transfers were already void under § 362. Most courts have rejected this argument, however, pointing out that § 549 complements § 362, and applies to transactions (such as a sale of property to a non-creditor) that are not expressly prohibited elsewhere in the Code.[11]

If all that were at stake in the void-voidable debate was the legal terminology used, the outcome would be unimportant. By whatever name, the rule everywhere would be that an action taken in violation of the stay would not be given any legal

---

[7] E.g., Acands, Inc. v. Travelers Cas. & Sur. Co., 435 F.3d 252 (3d Cir. 2006); In re Wardrobe, 559 F.3d 932, 934 (9th Cir. 2009) (citing In re Schwartz, 954 F.2d 569, 571 (9th Cir. 1992)); Ellis v. Consol. Diesel Elec. Corp., 894 F.2d 371 (10th Cir. 1990); Mann v. Chase Manhattan Mortg. Corp., 316 F.3d 1 (1st Cir. 2003); In re Vitale, 469 B.R. 595 (Bankr. W.D. Pa. 2012).

This doctrine stems from the Supreme Court's decision in *Kalb v. Feuerstein*, 308 U.S. 433 (1940), in which the Court held that a real property foreclosure was void.

[8] E.g., Bronson v. United States, 46 F.3d 1573 (Fed. Cir. 1995); In re Coho Res., Inc., 345 F.3d 338 (5th Cir. 2003).

[9] 308 U.S. 433 (1940).

[10] See Easley v. Pettibone Michigan Corp., 990 F.2d 905 (6th Cir. 1993); In re Bazzi, 481 B.R. 397 (Bankr. E.D. Mich. 2012); In re Tyson, 450 B.R. 754 (Bankr. W.D. Tenn. 2011).

[11] E.g., 40235 Washington St. Corp. v. Lusardi, 329 F.3d 1076 (9th Cir. 2003); In re Tippett, 542 F.3d 684 (9th Cir. 2008); In re Beery, 452 B.R. 825 (Bankr. D.N.M. 2011); In re Garcia, 109 B.R. 335 (N.D. Ill. 1989).

effect unless the bankruptcy court later retroactively validated the action on motion of the creditor. If nothing is done, the act would be invalid. Danger lurks, though, if the void/voidable distinction reflects a difference in which party bears the burden of going forward. As the First Circuit explained in holding, correctly, that violations of the automatic stay should be deemed "void," even though the stay can still be annulled and the "void" actions retroactively validated:

> This semantic difference has practical consequences because the characterization of an infringing action as "void" or "voidable" influences the burden of going forward. Treating an action taken in contravention of the automatic stay as void places the burden of validating the action after the fact squarely on the shoulders of the offending creditor. In contrast, treating an action taken in contravention of the automatic stay as voidable places the burden of challenging the action on the offended debtor. We think that the former paradigm, rather than the latter, best harmonizes with the nature of the automatic stay and the important purposes that it serves.[12]

Placing the burden on the debtor to act, rather than on the creditor, adopts a premise of "no harm, no foul." This view is plainly wrong, and would contradict the policy behind the *automatic* stay. A creditor would have some incentive to ignore the stay under the "voidable" view. Whatever term is used, the proper result should be that acts that violate the stay do not have any operative legal effect unless the bankruptcy court subsequently annuls the stay for cause shown.

A creditor who violates the automatic stay also may be liable for damages. There are two possible bases for a damages claim: the court's power to punish for contempt, and the statutory remedy provided in § 362(k). As to the first, the bankruptcy stay is analogous to an injunction, and disobedience of an injunction historically has been punishable by contempt sanctions. The leading case establishing that contempt was a viable means of redressing a knowing violation of the stay was the 1976 Second Circuit decision in *Fidelity Mortgage Investors v. Camelia Builders, Inc.*,[13] decided under the previous Bankruptcy Act. Indeed, even until 1984, after the enactment of the Code, contempt was the only means by which stay violations could be punished.

In 1984 Congress added § 362(k), which states, in operative part: "an individual injured by a willful violation of a stay provided by this section shall recover actual damages, including costs and attorneys' fees, and, in appropriate cases, may recover punitive damages." § 362(k)(1). In cases within its scope, § 362(k)(1) affords a private right of action to proper plaintiffs. Significantly, proof of the grounds necessary for contempt is not required to establish a right to relief under § 362(k). Instead, strict liability is imposed upon proof of a willful violation. The court is mandated to grant relief if the statute applies.

---

[12] In re Soares, 107 F.3d 969, 976 (1st Cir. 1997). See also In re Myers, 491 F.3d 120, 127 (3d Cir. 2007) (holding that "actions in violation of the stay, although void (as opposed to voidable), may be revitalized in appropriate circumstances by retroactive annulment of the stay").

[13] 550 F.2d 47 (2d Cir. 1976), cert. denied, 429 U.S. 1093 (1977).

In 2005, a safe harbor against punitive damages was added in § 362(k)(2) in certain cases involving individual debtors, in conjunction with the addition of § 362(h). The new provisions give teeth to the requirement in § 521(a)(2) that, with respect to personal property subject to a lien, the debtor within a short time period must both file a "statement of intention" regarding what he plans to do with the subject property (e.g., redeem, reaffirm, or surrender) and then carry out the stated intention.[14] Under § 362(h), if the debtor fails to act within the required time periods, the stay automatically terminates. But what if the creditor believes that the debtor failed to act as required by § 521(a)(2), and thus assumes that the stay has terminated under § 362(h), and accordingly proceeds to seize the subject property, but in fact is in error? Certainly the creditor has violated the stay. What is the sanction? According to § 362(k)(2), if the creditor acted "in the good faith belief that subsection (h) applied to the debtor," then only actual damages may be recovered.

Some question has been raised as to whether § 362(k)(1) has displaced the contempt power. While a minority of courts have held the statute displaces contempt power,[15] a substantial majority conclude that contempt remains as an alternative means of punishing stay violations.[16] In cases within the scope of § 362(k)(1), the issue is largely academic, because the injured party (usually the debtor) ordinarily may obtain all the relief under § 362(k)(1) that it could under contempt.[17] However, as discussed below, § 362(k)(1) may have a limited reach, and for cases that lie outside of § 362(k)(1), contempt will be the only available avenue for sanctioning violations. Additionally, if a debtor seeking to recover damages under § 362(k)(1) does not have to prove his case by clear and convincing evidence; the "clear and convincing standard applies only when [a] debtor seeks adjudication of contempt for violation of automatic stay."[18]

The interpretive scope question under § 362(k)(1) is whether Congress really meant to limit the pool of prospective plaintiffs to *"individuals"*, as the statutory language appears to indicate. Usage elsewhere in the Code indicates that "individuals" refers to natural persons—human beings—and not to corporations, partnerships, the government, and other legal entities. The definition of "person" in § 101(41) "includes individual, partnership, and corporation," obviously contemplating that corporations and partnerships must be something different from "individuals." Because of this "plain" statutory reading, a majority of courts have restricted § 362(k) to living,

---

[14]   See § 7.28.

[15]   E.g., In re Rimsat, Ltd., 208 B.R. 910 (Bankr. N.D. Ind. 1997).

[16]   E.g., In re Gordon Props, LLC, 460 B.R. 681 (Bankr. E.D. Va. 2011); In re Johnston, 321 B.R. 262 (D. Ariz. 2005).

[17]   Note that proceeding under a civil contempt or § 362(k) theory might affect the type of damages available. Compare In re Repine, 536 F.3d 512 (5th Cir. 2008) (holding emotional injury damages proper under § 362(k)), with McBride v. Coleman, 955 F.2d 571 (8th Cir. 1992) (holding that civil contempt is not an appropriate vehicle for awarding emotional distress damages).

[18]   In re Florio, 229 B.R. 606, 608 (S.D.N.Y. 1999). See also In re Johnson, 501 F.3d 1163, 1170 (10th Cir. 2007) ("Accordingly, we hold that willful violations of an automatic stay [under § 362(k)] must be proven by a preponderance of the evidence.").

breathing, human beings,[19] meaning therefore that a corporate debtor injured by a willful stay violation would have no recourse under § 362(k)(1). Such an entity would have to proceed under a contempt theory. Some courts, however, take an expansive view of "individual," and do not limit § 362(k)(1) to natural persons.[20] These courts reason that the narrow view lacks any logical justification, that corporate or partnership debtors are as deserving as individual debtors of a remedy for willful stay violations, and that Congress accordingly must not have intended to use "individual" in the same technical sense as elsewhere in the Code. Nice try, but the statute just does not read that way; "individual" indisputably is a term of art in the Code, and means humans, not companies. Courts also disagree whether a trustee may bring an action to recover damages for willful violations of stay.[21]

A party other than an "individual" who is injured by a stay violation is not remediless, however. As noted earlier, the remedy of *contempt* remains, in virtually all courts, as a form of redress for a stay violation. The major difference between contempt and the statutory sanction in § 362(k)(1) is that the decision whether to impose sanctions for contempt lies within the discretion of the court, and is not mandatory. Relief under § 362(k)(1), by comparison, is a matter of right if a sufficient showing is made.[22] A creditor will be held in contempt only if it has knowledge of the pendency of the bankruptcy case, and yet still undertakes intentional actions in violation of the stay. Thus, the creditor may escape punishment for contempt if it can show that it proceeded on a good faith belief that its action was valid, or if it can show that the action was inadvertent.[23] In other words, courts do not impose damages for all violations of the automatic stay, "but only those that are within its statutory definition, i.e., 'deliberate' actions that are 'willful.'"[24]

Some doubt has been expressed as to whether a bankruptcy judge, who is not an Article III judge, has the power to punish for contempt. The "power" question actually has several layers: first, does the bankruptcy court have the inherent equitable power to sanction for contempt; second, does § 105(a) purport to convey such a power to bankruptcy judges; and, finally, is the exercise of contempt powers by a non-Article III

---

[19] E.g., In re Spookyworld, Inc., 346 F.3d 1 (1st Cir. 2003); In re Jove Eng'g, Inc. v. IRS, 92 F.3d 1539 (11th Cir. 1996); In re Chateaugay Corp., 920 F.2d 183 (2d Cir. 1990); In re C.W. Mining Co., 477 B.R. 176 (B.A.P. 10th Cir. 2012).

[20] E.g., In re Atl. Bus. & Cmty. Corp., 901 F.2d 325 (3d Cir. 1990); Budget Serv. Co. v. Better Homes of Virginia, Inc., 804 F.2d 289 (4th Cir. 1986). See also St. Paul Fire & Marine Ins. Co. v. Labuzan, 579 F.3d 533 (5th Cir. 2009) (holding that principals, in their capacity as creditors, and not owners/equity holders of a company, had standing to pursue damages under § 362(k)).

[21] Compare In re Howard, 428 B.R. 335 (Bankr. W.D. Pa. 2010) (holding that a trustee has standing regarding § 362(k)), with In re Glenn, 379 B.R. 760 (Bankr. N.D. Ill. 2007) (holding that the trustee was not the kind of individual § 362 provides a remedy for).

[22] 11 U.S.C. § 362(k) ("[A]n individual injured by any willful violation of a stay provided by this section *shall* recover actual damages." (emphasis added)). Additionally, note that debtors have an "unequivocal statutory right" to prove actual damages after a willful violation of automatic stay. In re Vazquez Laboy, 647 F.3d 367 (1st Cir. 2011).

[23] For example, a debtor-landlord's former tenants commenced a state court action to compel the debtor to refund their security deposit after commencement of the debtor's chapter 13 case, but did not receive notice of the bankruptcy case until the debtor filed an answer in state court. Accordingly, the court held that this "mere technical violation" did not give rise to damages. In re Kline, 424 B.R. 516 (Bankr. D.N.M. 2010).

[24] E.g., In re Bernstein, 447 B.R. 684, 704 (Bankr. D. Conn. 2011).

bankruptcy court constitutional? If the bankruptcy judge lacks the contempt power, then the contempt proceeding must be certified to the Article III district court judge. With regard to *civil* contempt, an early division in the case law as to whether the bankruptcy judge had the power to act[25] has been settled in favor of finding such authority.[26] More controversial is the issue of whether bankruptcy judges may enter an order of *criminal* contempt.[27] The better view is that they do not. Bankruptcy courts unquestionably do have the power to award damages under the specific statutory authorization of § 362(k)(1), however.

One might worry about whether the Supreme Court's decision in *Stern v. Marshall*,[28] which circumscribed (to an unknown and much-debated extent) the scope of the Article I bankruptcy court's constitutional powers, undercuts this settled jurisprudence, on the basis that issuing contempt orders is a fundamental aspect of the exercise of judicial power, which historically had not been part of the arsenal of the bankruptcy judge's summary powers. If so, a bankruptcy judge would not be able to enter a final order of contempt (even civil), but must seek the district court's blessing of the contempt order.[29] Cutting the other way, in favor of the bankruptcy court having constitutional power to enter a final order of civil contempt for a stay violation, is the argument that the automatic stay is solely a creature of the bankruptcy case and thus an action seeking contempt for violation of the stay could have no independent existence outside of bankruptcy;[30] instead, it is part and parcel of the core bankruptcy case itself.

Liability under § 362(k)(1) is more readily established than under a contempt theory. The statutory predicate is a "*willful violation*" of the stay. What constitutes "willful" action has been discussed in innumerable cases. The primary requirement is that the creditor (or other defendant) (1) must have had *knowledge* of the pendency of the bankruptcy case, and (2) must have had the *intent* to commit the proscribed act.[31]

---

[25] Compare In re Sequoia Auto Brokers, Ltd., 827 F.2d 1281 (9th Cir. 1987) (no power), with In re Skinner, 917 F.2d 444 (10th Cir. 1990) (has power).

[26] See, e.g., In re Dyer, 322 F.3d 1178 (9th Cir. 2003); Caldwell v. Unified Capital Corp. (In re Rainbow Magazine, Inc., 77 F.3d 278 (9th Cir. 1996) (stating that recent developments had superseded the circuit's earlier decision in *Sequoia Auto Brokers*, 827 F.2d 1281).

[27] The cases are collected in *Dyer*, supra note 26, 322 F.3d at 1193 n.15. See also Cox v. Zale Delaware, Inc., 239 F.3d 901, 917 (7th Cir. 2001) ("Since punitive damages are punitive, and it is punitive purpose that distinguishes criminal from civil contempt, section [363(k)] implies that bankruptcy judges do have some criminal contempt power. . . . ").

[28] 131 S.Ct. 2594 (2011). See also §§ 4.2.g, 4.4; Ralph Brubaker, A "Summary" Statutory and Constitutional Theory of Bankruptcy Judges' Core Jurisdiction After *Stern v. Marshall*, 86 Am. Bankr. L.J. 121 (2012).

[29] See In re Brown, 481 B.R. 351, 354 n.1 (Bankr. W.D. Pa. 2012) ("This Court has subject matter jurisdiction. . . . However, if the [District Court] determines pursuant to the rationale set forth in *Stern*[ ] that this Court does not have the authority to enter final judgment, then the Memorandum Opinion and Order entered shall constitute the Court's proposed findings of fact and conclusions of law and recommendation to the District Court.").

[30] E.g., In re Mele, 486 B.R. 546 (Bankr. N.D. Ga. 2013); In re Brown, 481 B.R. 351 (Bankr. W.D. Pa. 2012).

[31] E.g., In re Waldo, 417 B.R. 854, 890 (Bankr. E.D. Tenn. 2009) ("A violation of the automatic stay is willful if the creditor deliberately carried out the prohibited act with knowledge of the debtor's bankruptcy case." (citing In re Printup, 264 B.R. 169, 173 (Bankr. E.D. Tenn. 2001)).

Significantly, a specific intent to violate the stay is not required.[32] Indeed, knowledge of the existence of the automatic stay itself is not necessary to establish liability; knowledge of the bankruptcy case constructively imputes notice of the stay as well.[33] However, note that courts are split whether a debtor's oral notice of his bankruptcy case to a creditor is enough to satisfy the "knowledge" element in § 362(k), or whether written confirmation of the bankruptcy petition filing is required.[34]

A purely innocent stay violation will not subject the creditor to damages, however, even though the action taken will be void (or "invalid"), as discussed above.[35] For example, assume that a creditor completes a foreclosure sale of collateral belonging to the debtor shortly after the bankruptcy petition is filed, *before* learning of the existence of the bankruptcy case. While the sale is indisputably a violation of the stay, see § 362(a)(4), (5), the creditor has not acted "willfully" and therefore will not be liable for damages under § 362(k)(1). The sale is ineffective however.

In some circumstances a creditor may have to take affirmative steps to undo a stay violation after learning of the bankruptcy filing in order to avoid liability under § 362(k)(1). For example, assume that a creditor repossesses collateral after the debtor filed bankruptcy, but without knowing of the bankruptcy case. While the initial repossession would be impermissible, the innocent creditor would not be subject to § 362(k)(1) damages. Once the creditor finds out about the pendency of the bankruptcy case, however, the creditor must promptly return the repossessed property to the bankruptcy trustee, or it will then be held liable for a willful violation because of its continued retention of possession.

The statute provides that *"actual damages"* shall be recovered by the injured individual.[36] The most common form of damages awarded are costs and attorneys' fees incurred by the injured party in seeking to remedy the stay violation. These damages should be recoverable even if no other damages are proven. Other actual damages caused by the violation would of course also be recoverable, assuming they can be proven with the requisite certainty. Additionally, in "appropriate circumstances . . . *punitive damages*" may be awarded as well. § 362(k)(1). However, mere willfulness is not enough to support an award of punitive damages; instead, courts require proof that

---

[32]   For example, where a creditor's stay violation was a product of a clerical or ministerial error by its employee, the court nonetheless found the stay violation "willful." See In re Nixon, 419 B.R. 281 (Bankr. E.D. Pa. 2009).

[33]   See, e.g., In re Tyson, 450 B.R. 754, 766 (Bankr. W.D. Tenn. 2011) ("It is irrelevant to a court faced with imposing § 362(k) sanction whether a defendant actually intended to violate the automatic stay . . . [s]o long as the defendant had knowledge of the bankruptcy case and took a deliberate act in violation of the automatic stay. . . . "); In re Theokary, 444 B.R. 306, 322 (Bankr. E.D. Pa. 2011) ("Knowledge of the existence of the bankruptcy case is treated as knowledge of the automatic stay for these purposes.").

[34]   Compare In re Johnson, 478 B.R. 235 (Bankr. S.D. Miss. 2012) (holding oral notice is sufficient to trigger "knowledge"), with In re Collier, 410 B.R. 464 (Bankr. E.D. Tex. 2009) (holding that a creditor must receive written confirmation before being charged with "knowledge"). See also In re Henley, 480 B.R. 708 (Bankr. S.D. Tex. 2012) (holding that notifying a creditors' attorney of debtor's intention to file bankruptcy was not notice of stay to hold such creditors liable or violation of stay).

[35]   See cases cited supra note 7.

[36]   Chapter 11 and 13 debtors should be aware that a court might require him or her to turn over any damages received, as being part of the estate. E.g., In re Crouser, 476 B.R. 340 (Bankr. S.D. Ga. 2012) (holding that chapter 13 debtor must turn over settlement proceeds received from a creditor who willfully violated the stay, due to the expanded definition of estate property in § 1306).

the creditor acted with heightened culpability, such as "egregious, intentional misconduct."[37] Factors a court might consider when determining what actions warrant punitive damages include the nature of the creditor's conduct, the nature and extent of harm to the debtor, the creditor's ability to pay damages, the level of sophistication of the creditor, the creditor's motives, and any provocation by the debtor.[38]

For example, a creditor who exhibits a pattern of defying the stay in multiple cases, or who seeks to humiliate or embarrass the debtor, might be subjected to punitive damages. To illustrate, the Eighth Circuit permitted the debtor to recover punitive damages when the creditor not only refused to turn over property requested by the debtor, but also attempted to have the debtor excommunicated from his church for having declared bankruptcy.[39]

While the creditor's good faith belief that its behavior is permitted would not protect it from liability for actual damages, such a belief would be a defense to the imposition of punitive damages. In addition, as explained above, § 362(k)(2) protects a creditor against an award of punitive damages and limits its exposure to actual damages if the creditor had a good faith belief that § 362(h) applied to an individual debtor.[40]

Until the 1994 amendments, a loophole in the enforcement of § 362(k)(1) was that governmental units could assert sovereign immunity as a defense to an action to collect damages for willful stay violations. Two Supreme Court cases held that § 106 of the Code did not effectively waive sovereign immunity so as to permit an award of damages, unless the government specifically waived its immunity in the particular case, such as by filing a proof of claim.[41] In the 1994 amendments, however, Congress made clear that sovereign immunity could not be raised as a defense to a damages action under § 362(k)(1). Doubt as to the viability of that congressional abrogation with regard to *state* governments was raised by the Supreme Court's 1996 decision in *Seminole Tribe of Florida v. Florida*,[42] which held that Congress did not have the power under its Article I powers to abrogate the Eleventh Amendment immunity of a state without the state's consent. In 2006, however, the Supreme Court in *Katz* reversed course and held that the Bankruptcy Clause (alone, apparently, among Article I powers) trumped the Eleventh Amendment, and thus state sovereign immunity is not a barrier in bankruptcy cases.[43] States as creditors are therefore

---

[37]   E.g., In re Knaus, 889 F.2d 773 (8th Cir. 1989); In re Repine, 536 F.3d 512 (5th Cir. 2008); In re Johnson, 478 B.R. 235 (Bankr. S.D. Miss. 2012).

[38]   See, e.g., In re Anderson, 430 B.R. 882, 889 (Bankr. S.D. Iowa 2010).

[39]   *Knaus*, supra note 9, 889 F.2d 773. Contrast this case with *In re Pearce*, 400 B.R. 126 (Bankr. N.D. Iowa 2009), where the court held that a creditor's contact with a prosecutor and police about a debtor's unpaid debt did not warrant punitive damages.

[40]   See supra note 14 and accompanying text.

[41]   United States v. Nordic Vill., Inc., 503 U.S. 30 (1992); Hoffman v. Connecticut Dep't of Income Maint., 492 U.S. 96 (1989).

[42]   517 U.S. 44 (1996).

[43]   Cent. Virginia Cmty. Coll. v. Katz, 546 U.S. 356 (2006).

subject to the imposition of monetary sanctions under § 362(k)(1) just like any other creditor who willfully violates the stay.[44]

B. SCOPE OF THE STAY: ACTS STAYED UNDER § 362(a)

§ 3.3   Collecting Prepetition Debts

The critical first step in assessing an automatic stay issue is to ascertain whether the action in question is within one of the categories of acts stayed under § 362(a). If the act does not fall within § 362(a), then the inquiry is at an end. There is only a need to consider exceptions to the stay under § 362(b), or relief from the stay under § 362(d), if § 362(a) applies in the first instance. Subsection (a) of § 362 contains eight subparagraphs that describe the acts that are stayed. This listing of eight areas is exclusive; if an act does not come within at least one of those eight, it is not stayed. In that event, the court would have to enter an injunction in order to stay the action. Note that there is some overlap between the various subparts of § 362(a), i.e., an action may be stayed under more than one subpart. Only one subparagraph need apply, however, for the stay to operate. Because of the central importance of the stay to the entire bankruptcy system, courts have liberally interpreted the provisions of § 362(a), broadly extending its coverage to all close cases. If one of the subparts of § 362(a) applies, the next step is to turn to the long list of exceptions to the stay in § 362(b). If an exception is operative, then the stay again will not bar the activity in question.

In considering what acts are stayed under § 362(a), it is helpful to focus initially on first principles: why is there a stay in the first place, and what is the stay designed to accomplish? The stay allows the orderly management of the collective proceeding through which creditors will be paid equitably, and affords the debtor protection from collection efforts.[45] To implement these goals, then, the stay should block (1) attempts to collect pre-bankruptcy debts by individual creditors and (2) efforts to interfere with property of the bankruptcy estate. Those types of actions, if unchecked, would impede the bankruptcy process. The various subparts of § 362(a) implement these basic goals.

One type of activity that must be stayed is the collection of prepetition debts by specific creditors. The concern is that these creditors will continue the "race of diligence" and attempt to grab part of the debtor's assets to satisfy their claim, without going through the bankruptcy process. The concern is not with the substantive entitlements of the creditor; the claim asserted may well be valid. Rather, the problem is with the procedural means by which the creditor seeks to collect. Once the bankruptcy case is filed, the creditor's collection efforts must be channeled through the formal bankruptcy proceeding. The creditor must go through the court to collect, either by filing a claim in the bankruptcy case and being paid out of the bankruptcy distribution, or by obtaining court permission to go forward with independent collection efforts.

---

[44]   But see In re Diquez, 477 B.R. 257 (Bankr. S.D. Fla. 2012) (holding that the Florida Department of Business and Professional Regulation and the Florida Construction Industry Licensing Board were arms of state, protected from suit by Florida's Eleventh Amendment immunity). Notably, this case never once mentioned *Katz*.

[45]   See § 3.1.

Several subsections of § 362(a) implement this basic rule against efforts by "all entities"[46] to collect prepetition claims. Subsection (1) stays all formal proceedings against the debtor to recover prepetition claims. Subsection (2) stays the enforcement of a prepetition judgment. Actions to enforce liens against either property of the estate or the debtor are stayed under subsections (4) and (5), respectively.[47] Setoffs of prepetition debts are forbidden by subsection (7).[48] Finally, a catch-all provision, subsection (6), stays "any act" to collect a prepetition claim.[49]

Section 362(a)(1) stays:

[T]he commencement or continuation, including the issuance or employment of process, of a judicial, administrative, or other action or proceeding against the debtor that was or could have been commenced before the commencement of the case under this title, or to recover a claim against the debtor that arose before the commencement of the case under this title.

Two categories of proceedings are stayed under this subsection: (1) all proceedings against the debtor that either were commenced prepetition or that could have been commenced prepetition, and (2) all proceedings to recover a prepetition claim against the debtor. This section examines the latter category, and the next section of the book discusses the former. Several important points about § 362(a)(1) must be noted. First, it applies to the "commencement or continuation" of a proceeding. Second, a wide variety of proceedings are embraced. Third, for the claim recovery portion of § 362(a)(1) to apply, the creditor must be attempting to recover a "claim" as defined in § 101(5). Finally, the timing of the claim is critical: the stay only applies to claims that arose before the filing of the bankruptcy case.

The most obvious application of § 362(a)(1) would be to stay a creditor from filing a lawsuit against the debtor after the bankruptcy filing in order to recover on a prepetition claim. Such a filing would indeed be proscribed as a "commencement . . . of a judicial . . . proceeding." The reach of subsection (1) is much broader, though. Also stayed is the "continuation" of proceedings that were commenced prior to the bankruptcy case. Thus, there is no benefit to the creditor to "win the race to the courthouse" and file its lawsuit before the debtor files bankruptcy. The stay will still apply.

In some cases a creditor (or even a third party![50]) may even be obligated to take affirmative steps after bankruptcy to stop an ongoing proceeding. For example, if a

---

[46] "Entity" is a broad term that includes "person [itself defined to include "individual, partnership, and corporation," § 101(41)], estate, trust, governmental unit, and United States trustee." 11 U.S.C. § 101(15).

[47] See § 3.5.

[48] See § 3.7.

[49] See § 3.8.

[50] In re Tyson, 450 B.R. 754 (Bankr. W.D. Tenn. 2011) (holding that the purchaser in a postpetition foreclosure sale—which violated the stay—violated the automatic stay themselves when they refused to cooperate in voiding the foreclosure sale). But see In re TLB Equip., LLC, 479 B.R. 464 (Bankr. S.D. Ohio 2012) (holding no violation of the stay occurred when defendant repossessed the debtor's property prepetition and sold it postpetition).

creditor initiates a garnishment action prior to bankruptcy, the garnishment will continue in effect until the debt is paid, without the need for the creditor to do anything more. Postpetition passivity is not a defense, however; if the creditor does not take steps to halt that ongoing garnishment, it will violate the stay.[51]

The "continuation" provision also poses problems in cases in which the debtor is one of multiple parties to a lawsuit that is pending at the time the bankruptcy case is filed. The action cannot go forward with the debtor as a party, but the debtor's filing does not operate as a stay against the non-debtor parties. The usual solution is to sever the debtor from the case and then go forward against the non-debtor parties. Note that some courts extend the stay in these circumstances over non-debtor defendants if a suit against the non-debtor is essentially a suit against the debtor, or if the proceeding would have an adverse impact on the debtor's ability to reorganize successfully.[52]

The legislative intention was to extend the stay to a wide range of proceedings.[53] Thus, while a traditional lawsuit would be stayed, so too would the stay apply to an arbitration proceeding, or a hearing before an administrative agency. If the proceeding does not pose a threat to the bankruptcy administration, the bankruptcy court may lift the stay under § 362(d)(1), but that decision is for the bankruptcy judge to make, not the other litigants or the non-bankruptcy forum.

An important limitation on the scope of the stay under the second clause of § 362(a)(1) is that the creditor must be seeking to recover on a "*claim*," and that claim must arise before the bankruptcy filing. "Claim" is defined in § 101(5):[54]

> "[C]laim" means—(A) right to payment, whether or not such right is reduced to judgment, liquidated, unliquidated, fixed, contingent, matured, unmatured, disputed, undisputed, legal, equitable, secured, or unsecured; or (B) right to an equitable remedy for breach of performance if such breach gives rise to a right to payment. . . .

This definition of claim is intentionally broad. The intent of Congress was "that all legal obligations of the debtor, no matter how remote or contingent, will be able to be dealt with in the bankruptcy case."[55] To be "dealt with in the bankruptcy case," collection activities on claims must be stayed. As both the Code and the legislative history make clear, a creditor has a "claim" and will be stayed even if its right to be

---

[51]   In re Russell, 441 B.R. 859 (Bankr. N.D. Ohio 2010); In re Scroggin, 364 B.R. 772 (B.A.P. 10th Cir. 2007). But see In re Henson, 477 B.R. 786 (Bankr. D. Colo. 2012) (distinguishing between taking additional steps to collect a debt from allowing a prepetition action to collect a debt continue, and holding that the latter does not violate the stay).

[52]   E.g., Rivera–Olivera v. Antares Oil Servs., 482 B.R. 44 (Bankr. D.P.R. 2012). See also In re Gander Partners LLC, 432 B.R. 781 (Bankr. N.D. Ill. 2010) (issuing an injunction to prevent a creditor from pursuing state court lawsuits against third-party guarantors of debtors' debt). But see Kreisler v. Goldberg, 478 F.3d 209 (4th Cir. 2007) (denying stay protection for a suit against the debtor's wholly-owned non-debtor subsidiary).

[53]   See H.R. Rep. No. 95–595, 95th Cong., 1st Sess., at 340 (1977).

[54]   See § 7.1.

[55]   H.R. Rep. No. 95–595, 95th Cong., 1st Sess., at 309 (1977).

paid at the time bankruptcy is filed is unliquidated, or contingent, or unmatured, or disputed.

To illustrate, a creditor with a tort claim that arose prepetition but which has not been reduced to judgment by the time of bankruptcy still would have a claim—*"unliquidated"*—that would be stayed. A guarantor or surety of an obligation of the debtor has a claim—*"contingent"*—even if the contingency that would trigger the creditor's guaranty obligation (the debtor's default) has not occurred prior to bankruptcy. A creditor with a note of the debtor that was executed before bankruptcy but which is scheduled to come due after bankruptcy has a claim—*"unmatured."* And a bankruptcy claim exists if it arose prior to bankruptcy even if the debtor contests the validity and amount of that claim—*"disputed"*.

The date of the bankruptcy filing serves as the point of cleavage; actions rooted in the pre-bankruptcy past are subject to the bankruptcy case, and are stayed, but those that are connected to the post-bankruptcy world are not. Courts are fond of quipping that the debtor is entitled to a "fresh start, but not a head start."

Sometimes it is hard to pinpoint exactly when a claim arises, however.[56] This difficulty has been especially pronounced in tort and environmental cases. A prominent example is the Fourth Circuit decision in *Grady v. A.H. Robins Co.*[57] The creditor, Rebecca Grady, had a Dalkon Shield intrauterine device inserted *before* Robins filed bankruptcy. However, Grady did not manifest injury until *after* the filing. The court held that Grady's claim arose prior to bankruptcy and therefore was stayed. The court explained that the claim arose when Robins engaged in the tortious conduct.

Note, though, that courts since *Robins* have been careful not to go too far with a pure "conduct" test to determine when a claim arises. Indeed, in *Robins* the tort victim also was *exposed* to the defective product prior to bankruptcy. The same problem has been encountered in environmental cases, with regard to when the environmental agency's claim against the debtor for cleanup costs arises. The difficulty occurs in situations in which the debtor engages in conduct that leads to pollution prior to the bankruptcy filing, but the responsible governmental agency does not discover the pollution until after filing.

The trend in the courts has been to adopt a "relationship" test in tort and environmental[58] cases to determine when a claim arises. Under this approach, the debtor and the claimant must have had some relationship, "such as contact, exposure, impact, or privity," at the time the bankruptcy petition was filed. In *Robins*, Rebecca Grady still would have a claim under the relationship test, because she was exposed to the defective product prior to bankruptcy. If she had not yet been exposed, however, she would not have a claim, even if Robins had already engaged in the operative conduct of manufacturing and selling the defective and dangerous product. A variant of the "relationship" test is the "fair contemplation" test, often used in environmental

---

[56]   See § 7.2.

[57]   839 F.2d 198 (4th Cir. 1988).

[58]   See, e.g., In re Jensen, 995 F.2d 925 (9th Cir. 1993). See also In re Ritter Ranch Dev., L.L.C., 255 B.R. 760 (B.A.P. 9th Cir. 2000).

cases, with the operative principle being that the affected governmental unit must have had "fair contemplation" of the fact of the debtor's environmental violation at the time of the bankruptcy filing. If the environmental agency has notice of the pollution, it would have a claim. However, if the government does not have notice of a pollution problem, no claim would have arisen—and the stay would not apply. Thus, unknown pre-bankruptcy pollution by a debtor would not trigger a claim under this view.

A completely different approach to determining when a claim arises for purposes of the stay was adopted by the Third Circuit in the case of *In re M. Frenville Co.*[59] The *Frenville* court linked the time when a bankruptcy claim arises to the time the claim could have been brought under state law. In that case, an accounting firm sued the debtor after bankruptcy as a third-party defendant, seeking contribution or indemnity. The Third Circuit held that the action was not stayed. The court relied on the fact that the accounting firm could not have sued the debtor under state law until after bankruptcy, when the accounting firm itself was sued. The circuit court reasoned that the firm did not have a "right to payment" until its state law claim was ripe. The Third Circuit's approach accordingly has been described as the "accrued state law theory," meaning that a claim only arises when an action has accrued against the debtor under state law. However, the *Frenville* approach has been roundly criticized and finally in 2010 was overruled by the Third Circuit itself in the *Grossman* case. All of the operative facts that gave rise to the contribution or indemnity claim occurred prior to bankruptcy, in connection with the preparation of the debtor's financial statements. Under the federal bankruptcy definition of "claim," that should have been sufficient.

Of course, even if the timing problem is not fatal, the creditor still will only be stayed if it has a "claim." While the legislative history certainly suggests that Congress intended a broad definition, the affected entity still must have a *"right to payment"* in order to have a "claim." Many of the problem cases have involved § 101(5)(B), which classifies an equitable remedy as a "claim" if there is an alternative right to payment.[60] The courts have had considerable difficulty with the environmental cases.[61] The issue usually is whether an order directing the debtor to clean up polluted property is a "claim." Does the environmental agency have a "right to payment"? Note that even if a cleanup order is classified as a claim initially, the enforcement of the order might be excepted from the stay under § 362(b)(4) as a permissible exercise of the government's police and regulatory powers.[62]

The environmental cases are a mess (so to speak). In *Ohio v. Kovacs*,[63] the Supreme Court held that a cleanup order was a dischargeable claim. In that case, however, the debtor had been dispossessed by a receiver, and could not personally effect the cleanup. The only performance sought from the debtor was the payment of money. Subsequent cases have seized on this fact to distinguish *Kovacs*, and many courts have held that an injunction directing the debtor itself to clean up a site is not a

---

[59] 744 F.2d 332 (3d Cir. 1984), cert. denied, 469 U.S. 1160 (1985), (overruled by In re Grossman's Inc., 607 F.3d 114 (3d Cir. 2010)).

[60] See § 7.3.a.

[61] See § 7.3.b.

[62] See § 3.11.

[63] 469 U.S. 274 (1985).

claim that is stayed or dischargeable. As the Second Circuit explained in *In re Chateaugay Corp.*,[64] the governmental environmental agency may not have the option to accept monetary payment from the debtor in lieu of cleaning up. That court did hold, however, that the agency's right to be reimbursed for response costs that it incurs or is likely to incur constitutes a claim. Other courts have been even more reluctant to find any sort of "claim" in the environmental area, thereby permitting the government to ignore both the stay and the discharge.[65]

The prohibition against attempting to collect on prepetition claims is reinforced by § 362(a)(2), which stays "the enforcement, against the debtor or against property of the estate, of a judgment obtained before commencement of the case under this title." Thus, a judgment creditor would be stayed from proceeding with execution and levy against property of the debtor or the estate to enforce the judgment, or from garnishing the debtor's wages. The judgment creditor would have a claim that would be dealt with in the bankruptcy case. If that creditor had obtained a valid and unavoidable judicial lien prior to bankruptcy, then it would be treated as a secured creditor. An exception to the stay permits the enforcement of prepetition judgments other than money judgments by a governmental unit to enforce the government's police or regulatory powers. § 362(b)(4).

§ 3.4   Proceedings Against Debtor

The "breathing spell" for the debtor provided by the automatic stay extends beyond merely freeing the debtor from creditor efforts to collect prepetition debts, although that is the central concern. All entities are also stayed from "the commencement or continuation . . . of a judicial, administrative, or other action or proceeding against the debtor that was or could have been commenced before the commencement of the case." § 362(a)(1).

Note that this provision does *not* also require that the proceeding be linked to the collection of a debt. The only requirements are that: (1) it be some form of "proceeding"; (2) it be against the debtor, and (3) it either actually was commenced before bankruptcy or at least could have been brought in that time period. The legislative history makes clear that the sweep of this provision is broad, covering "all proceedings . . . , including arbitration, license revocation, administrative, and judicial proceedings," and that the proceedings need not be before "government tribunals."[66] For example, a non-judicial contractual procedure to reduce the number of the debtor's landing slots was held to violate § 362(a)(1).[67]

Sometimes a question arises whether a proceeding is "against" the debtor. The stay does not operate against proceedings "by" the debtor. Many courts have grappled with this issue when the debtor appeals from an adverse judgment in a case commenced before bankruptcy. The resolution is to focus on the status of the debtor as

---

[64]   944 F.2d 997 (2d Cir. 1991).

[65]   See, e.g., In re Torwico Elecs., Inc., 8 F.3d 146 (3d Cir. 1993).

[66]   H.R. Rep. No. 95–595, 95th Cong., 1st Sess., at 340 (1977); S. Rep. No. 95–989, 95th Cong. 2d Sess., at 50 (1978).

[67]   In re Am. Cent. Airlines, Inc. 52 B.R. 567 (Bankr. N.D. Iowa 1985).

either aggressor or defender at the inception of the case, not whether the debtor is appellant or appellee. If the original action was against the debtor, then the appeal is stayed as a continuation of that action, even if the debtor brings the appeal.[68] This rule applies even when the original action against the debtor was a counterclaim by the creditor, if the appeal is of a judgment on that counterclaim.[69] However, if the debtor brought the original action, the stay does not apply when the debtor later appeals a judgment on the debtor's original claim.[70]

The broad scope of § 362(a)(1), if not qualified by any exclusions, would operate to stay many types of proceedings against the debtor that should not be stayed in the normal course of events. Bankruptcy is not the only show in town; other important societal policies must be implemented, and the filing of a bankruptcy case may sometimes impede the realization of those policies. Accordingly, some of the most important exceptions to the automatic stay in § 362(b) permit certain types of proceedings against the debtor to go forward even if a bankruptcy case is filed. The burden then falls on the debtor to obtain an injunction from the bankruptcy court against the continuation of the excluded proceeding. So, for example, a criminal action against the debtor will go forward even if the debtor files bankruptcy, § 362(b)(1); the state's interest in enforcing its criminal laws is paramount.[71] Many domestic relations matters, such as the establishment of paternity; the establishment or modification of an order for a domestic support obligation; a proceeding concerning child custody or visitation; and a proceeding concerning marriage dissolution, are not stayed. § 362(b)(2)(A). An action by a governmental unit to enforce its police or regulatory powers will not be stayed.[72] § 362(b)(4). Other examples could be given.[73] Thus, to properly understand the scope of the stay, it is crucial to remember that subsections (a) and (b) must be read together.

Also, even if a proceeding is stayed under (a) and is not expressly excepted from the stay under (b), relief from the stay still might be obtained from the bankruptcy court under subsection (d). If the proceeding would not interfere with realization of the goals of the bankruptcy case, the court is likely to grant the requested relief. Indeed, the legislative history contemplates that stay relief should be granted routinely to permit actions to go forward "before specialized or non-governmental tribunals . . . in their place of origin, when no great prejudice to the bankruptcy estate would result."[74] By funneling the matter through the bankruptcy court, though, Congress has given that court the chance to exercise appropriate oversight of all matters affecting the debtor or the estate.

---

[68]   E.g., Ass'n of St. Croix Condominium Owners v. St. Croix Hotel Corp., 682 F.2d 446 (3d Cir. 1982); (TW Telecom Holdings Inc., v. Carolina Internet Ltd., 661 F.3d 495 (11th Cir. 2011).

[69]   E.g., Parker v. Bain, 68 F.3d 1131 (9th Cir. 1995).

[70]   E.g., Carley Capital Grp. v. Fireman's Fund Ins. Co., 889 F.2d 1126 (D.C. Cir. 1989).

[71]   See § 3.10.

[72]   See §§ 3.11, 3.12.

[73]   E.g., § 362(b)(8), (9), (12)–(16), (22)–(23).

[74]   H.R. Rep. No. 95–595, 95th Cong., 1st Sess., at 341 (1977); S. Rep. No. 95–989, 95th Cong., 2d Sess., at 50 (1978).

Section 362(a)(8) also stays "the commencement or continuation of a proceeding before the United States Tax Court concerning" the debtor. This prohibition is consistent with the power of the bankruptcy court to determine tax liability under § 505. Subsection (a)(8) was amended in 2005 to distinguish between corporate and individual debtors; as to the former, all actions are stayed regarding the corporate debtor's tax liability for a taxable period the bankruptcy court may determine, whereas with regard to individual debtors, the stay applies only regarding taxable periods that ended prior to bankruptcy. Note that not all governmental actions directed toward tax collection are automatically stayed. Thus, for example, § 362(b)(9) excepts from the stay a tax audit, the issuance of a notice of tax deficiency, a demand for tax returns, or the assessment of a tax.

§ 3.5   Lien Creation, Perfection and Enforcement

Another essential component of the automatic stay is the prohibition against the creation, perfection, or enforcement of liens against property of the estate, § 362(a)(4), or against property of the debtor to the extent the lien secures a prepetition claim. § 362(a)(5). Without this part of the stay, creditors could obtain preferential treatment by converting unsecured claims into secured claims, could obtain early payment on secured claims and possibly undermine a prospective reorganization, could interfere with the bankruptcy court's exclusive jurisdiction over estate property, and could undermine the debtor's discharge.

To illustrate, assume the debtor has three unsecured creditors, A, B, and C, each of whom is owed $10,000, and assume further that the debtor has $15,000 in unencumbered property. Outside of bankruptcy, state collection law gives precedence to the first creditor to act to seize the debtor's property or to obtain a lien against that property. Thus, if Creditor A were able to obtain a judicial lien against the debtor's property, A would have a secured claim, and ultimately would be paid in full, leaving Creditors B and C to divide up the remaining $5,000. Bankruptcy is designed to stop this race of diligence and substitute collective action for the benefit of the entire creditor group. Once the debtor files bankruptcy, creditor A cannot obtain a lien; in short, the stay serves to freeze the status quo as of the time of the bankruptcy filing.

Note that the stay in § 362(a)(4) and (5) is broad. It applies not only to acts to "*create*" a lien, but also to acts to "*perfect*" or to "*enforce*" a lien. For example, assume that Creditor A in the above example did have a security interest in the debtor's property prior to bankruptcy, but had not yet perfected that security interest when the debtor filed bankruptcy. The automatic stay would prevent A from taking the steps necessary to perfect the security interest after the bankruptcy filing. A's lien would remain unperfected. As such, it could be avoided by the bankruptcy trustee under § 544(a)(1).[75]

Even if Creditor A had a perfected lien prior to bankruptcy, it could not decide to go forward with the enforcement of the lien by foreclosure after bankruptcy. In fact, one of the most common reasons for a bankruptcy filing is to stop an impending

---

[75]   See § 6.3.

foreclosure. While Creditor A would retain its secured status in the bankruptcy case, the bankruptcy court would have to grant A permission to proceed with the enforcement of its lien under § 362(d). The interests of the debtor and the creditor group as a whole might dictate against allowing A to foreclose at once. For example, the collateral subject to A's lien might be necessary to an effective reorganization of the debtor, and it might be possible for the debtor to provide A with adequate protection of A's interest. If so, the stay against foreclosure should be continued. Even if not, the decision to lift the stay is for the court to make, not for the creditor acting in its own self-interest.

The stay against lien enforcement applies even if the creditor has already taken preliminary steps to foreclose its lien, including repossessing the collateral. The Supreme Court established in *United States v. Whiting Pools, Inc.*[76] that a secured creditor who has rightfully repossessed collateral prior to a chapter 11 bankruptcy filing cannot foreclose, and must turn that property over to the debtor in possession.

"Lien" is defined broadly in the Code as a "charge against or interest in property to secure payment of a debt or performance of an obligation." § 101(37). This sweeping definition includes consensual liens (i.e., those that arise by agreement, § 101(51)),[77] statutory liens (i.e., those arising solely by force of statute, § 101(53)), and judicial liens (i.e., those arising through the judicial process "by judgment, levy, [or] sequestration," § 101(36)).

The extension of the lien enforcement stay to acts against property of the debtor in § 362(a)(5) is necessary to give full effect to the debtor's discharge. Section 362(a)(4) already stays lien enforcement efforts against estate property. That provision does not help the debtor, however, with regard to property that is not included within the estate, such as property that the debtor acquires after bankruptcy, exempt property, or abandoned property. Section 362(a)(5) thus supplements the reach of (a)(4). The point of the discharge is to prevent attempts by creditors to collect dischargeable debts from the debtor. The discharge is limited to debts that arose prior to bankruptcy. § 727(b). One way to collect a debt is to obtain and enforce a lien against the debtor's property. Thus, if a creditor could create or enforce a lien against property of the debtor to collect a prepetition debt, the debtor would lose the benefit of the discharge as to that debt. Section 362(a)(5) forestalls such efforts. Consistent with its purpose of protecting the discharge, § 362(a)(5) only applies to lien enforcement efforts directed at the collection of prepetition debts. For debts that arise after bankruptcy, the debtor receives no special protection because of the pendency of the bankruptcy case.

An important exception to the stay against lien enforcement efforts against the debtor's property is § 362(b)(2)(B), which permits "the collection of a domestic support obligation from property that is not property of the estate." This rule is consistent with the provision that nondischargeable debts for domestic support obligations may be enforced against exempt property. § 522(c)(1).

---

[76]   462 U.S. 198 (1983). See § 5.13.

[77]   These are defined in the Code as "security interests," § 101(51), but cover all types of consensual liens, including not only Article 9 "security interests" in personal property, but also consensual mortgages in land.

The lien enforcement provisions of the automatic stay are subject to several other exceptions in § 362(b). Probably the most important in practice is the exception in § 362(b)(3), which allows the postpetition perfection of liens when that perfection has a retroactive effect under non-bankruptcy law.[78] The most common example is a purchase money security interest (PMSI), where Article 9 of the Uniform Commercial Code gives the secured creditor a grace period within which to perfect the PMSI and still maintain priority over intervening lien creditors. UCC § 9–317(e). If the debtor files bankruptcy during that grace period, § 362(b)(3) permits the secured party to go ahead and perfect its PMSI, and that perfection is given retroactive effect under § 546(b).

Some other exceptions to the stay deserve note. The stay does not apply to the commencement of an action to foreclose a HUD mortgage, if the mortgage was insured under the National Housing Act and covers property consisting of five or more living units. § 362(b)(8). The foreclosure by the Secretary of Transportation of ship mortgages under the Merchant Marine Act is allowed. § 362(b)(12), (13). The 1994 Amendments overruled several cases and added an exception permitting the creation or perfection of an ad valorem property tax that comes due after the filing of the petition. § 362(b)(18).

The 2005 amendments added an exception in § 362(b)(20) for the enforcement of a lien against real property following entry of a stay relief order under § 362(d)(4). So too in 2005 did Congress add an exception allowing enforcement of a lien in real property if the debtor is ineligible under § 109(g) or if the case was filed in violation of a prior bankruptcy court order prohibiting a bankruptcy filing. § 362(b)(21). These changes were part of a series of amendments designed to stop abusive serial filing tactics.[79]

§ 3.6   Acts Against Property of the Estate

The filing of a bankruptcy petition automatically creates an "estate." § 541(a). That estate is comprised initially of all of the debtor's interests in property as of the date of the bankruptcy filing. § 541(a)(1). The federal court has exclusive jurisdiction of all property of the bankruptcy estate. 28 U.S.C. § 1334(e). One of the core functions of a bankruptcy case is to administer property of the estate in an orderly manner, and to make an equitable distribution of that property to creditors. In order "to prevent dismemberment of the estate" and to ensure that the bankruptcy case "proceed[s] in an orderly fashion,"[80] all entities are stayed from taking "any act to obtain possession of property of the estate or of property from the estate or to exercise control over property of the estate." § 362(a)(3). An entity that wants to obtain possession of or exercise control over estate property may do so only if given permission by the bankruptcy court. Creditor self-help is prohibited.

The reach of § 362(a)(3) is quite broad. To begin with, "any act" regarding estate property is stayed. Furthermore, property of the estate is broadly defined in § 541(a).[81] In addition, the stay applies not only to acts to obtain possession of property of the

---

[78]   See § 3.13.

[79]   See § 3.16.

[80]   H.R. Rep. No. 95–595, 95th Cong., 1st Sess., at 341 (1977).

[81]   See §§ 5.2, 5.3.

estate, but also to acts to "exercise control over" estate property. Finally, the stay reaches acts to obtain property "from" the estate, even if that property does not belong to the estate, but is only in the possession of the estate.

The stay against interfering with estate property in § 362(a)(3) goes hand-in-hand with other provisions of the Bankruptcy Code dealing with estate property. Entities in possession of property of the estate must turn that property over to the bankruptcy trustee. §§ 542, 543. The trustee then may use, sell, or lease that property in the bankruptcy case, subject to the obligation to provide adequate protection to parties with an interest in the property. § 363. If the trustee cannot provide adequate protection, then the entity with an interest is entitled to relief from the automatic stay. § 362(d)(1). If the trustee does not perceive any benefit to the bankruptcy process to continue administering the property, the trustee may abandon the property. § 554.

These statutory interactions have generated substantial controversy in the following common scenario. Prior to bankruptcy, following a default by debtor, creditor lawfully repossesses collateral (often an automobile) from the debtor. After debtor files bankruptcy (typically a reorganization chapter, often chapter 13), debtor demands immediate return of the property. Creditor says it will gladly turn the property over— just as soon as it receives the "adequate protection" to which it is entitled. Until then, though, creditor says it will maintain the status quo by holding onto the collateral. Is creditor's refusal to turn over the collateral in this situation and on those terms a violation of the stay under § 362(a)(3)?

Most courts that have considered the issue hold—wrongly, I believe—that the creditor has violated the stay by withholding possession.[82] These courts reason that the creditor violates § 362(a)(3) by exercising control over property of the estate. The fact that creditor already has possession when bankruptcy is filed precludes any argument that the creditor has violated the stay under § 362(a)(3) by an act "to obtain possession" of property. But what about the "exercise control over property" clause, which Congress added to the Code in 1984? While at first blush that seems to be a plausible basis for finding a stay violation on these facts, one difficulty is identifying what constitutes the "property" over which the creditor supposedly is wrongfully exercising control. The answer cannot simply be "the collateral." Why not? Because the creditor is *rightfully in possession* the collateral when bankruptcy is filed. Of the proverbial property "bundle of sticks," at least one stick—possession—belongs to the creditor at the time of filing. Courts who rule against the creditor on these facts conclude, however, based on some loose dictum in the Supreme Court's decision in *United States v. Whiting Pools, Inc.*,[83] that upon the filing of the bankruptcy case, the turnover provision in § 542(a) gives the bankruptcy estate—not the creditor—the possessory interest in the collateral. With the

---

[82]   A leading case adopting the majority view is *Thompson v. General Motors Acceptance Corp.*, 566 F.3d 699 (7th Cir. 2009). For one of the best presentations of the arguments pro and con (in the majority and dissent), see TranSouth Fin. Corp. v. Sharon (In re Sharon), 234 B.R. 676 (B.A.P. 6th Cir. 1999). See also Unified People's Fed. Credit Union v. Yates (In re Yates), 332 B.R. 1 (B.A.P. 10th Cir. 2005). Contra In re Young, 193 B.R. 620 (Bankr. D.D.C. 1996).

[83]   462 U.S. 198 (1983). The Supreme Court stated: "In effect, § 542(a) grants to the estate a possessory interest in certain property of the debtor that was not held by the debtor at the commencement of reorganization proceedings." Id. at 207. The Court's holding, though, emphasized that the secured creditor was entitled to adequate protection in exchange for possession. See note 5, infra, and § 5.13.

creditor's possessory right thereby supplanted, these courts reason, continued retention of possession by the creditor violates the stay. In sum, these courts hold that the creditor's turnover obligation is immediate and self-executing once bankruptcy is filed.

The problem with this reasoning is that it completely ignores the central role of "adequate protection" in the Code's scheme. When the *Whiting Pools* court stated that § 542(a) gives the estate a possessory interest, it did so on the clear understanding that the *quid pro quo* for turnover is the provision of adequate protection to the to-be-dispossessed creditor.[84] Properly read, § 542(a) is *not* self-executing; adequate protection must be provided in exchange for turnover. Section 542(a) says only that an entity must turn over "property that the trustee may use . . . under section 363," and under § 363, in turn, the trustee may only use property in which a party has a lien on the condition that the trustee afford the lienholder "adequate protection" of its lien interest. § 363(e). Once a court determines that adequate protection has been offered, then, and only then, must the creditor turn over the property.[85] To hold that a secured creditor must turn over rightfully repossessed collateral immediately upon the filing of the petition, before it is given adequate protection, negates the creditor's adequate protection rights and undermines the Code's carefully drawn balance of power between a secured creditor and the debtor.[86]

In addition to the situation just discussed, the breadth of the (a)(3) stay can be seen by looking at some other examples. Consider the case where the debtor holds a leasehold interest in property. When the debtor files bankruptcy, the non-debtor lessor is stayed from taking any act to terminate that lease or to retake possession of the leased property. This is true even if the debtor is in default on the lease and the lessor would have the right outside of bankruptcy to terminate the lease and evict the debtor. That leasehold may be a valuable property right. The bankruptcy trustee is afforded an opportunity to evaluate the worth of that leasehold to the estate and to take appropriate steps to capture that value for the estate. The lessor's remedy is to petition the bankruptcy court for relief from the stay—not to act unilaterally. The stay applies under (3) even if the debtor at the time of bankruptcy holds only a tenancy by sufferance.[87] The Second Circuit has held that the stay even applies to prevent a non-

---

[84] Indeed, in the very next sentence after the always-quoted sentence in note 83, supra, the Supreme Court went on to say: "The Bankruptcy Code provides secured creditors various rights, including the right to adequate protection, and these rights replace the protection afforded by possession." 462 U.S. at 207.

[85] The estate's property interest in possession arises under § 541(a)(7) following a turnover order under § 542(a). Technically, then, the Supreme Court's broad statement that § 542(a) grants a possessory interest to the estate is at best incomplete and at worst mischievously misleading. While that loose statement made no difference in the *Whiting Pools* case itself, it has led subsequent courts to misapply § 362(a)(3) in the context discussed in the text.

[86] The difficulties with the majority view are underscored by the fact that after turnover, the secured creditor could move immediately for relief from the stay on the ground that it is entitled to adequate protection, § 362(d)(1), and the court must grant stay relief—and give the collateral back to the secured creditor!—if adequate protection is not provided. It makes more sense to read these various provisions together and make a single decision up front whether to compel turnover and what sort of adequate protection to require in return.

[87] In re Atlantic Bus. & Cmty. Corp., 901 F.2d 325 (3d Cir. 1990).

debtor lessor from terminating the lease of a non-debtor prime tenant, when doing so would adversely affect the interests of the debtor subtenant.[88]

If the debtor's property interest has been finally and completely terminated prior to the bankruptcy filing, the stay will not apply.[89] In that event, there is no interference with "property of the estate." All steps necessary to termination must have been completed prior to bankruptcy, however. Even then, the non-debtor party will be stayed from taking possession of property back from the debtor, but should be able to obtain relief from the stay in order to do so.

Some exceptions apply to leases. For a lease of nonresidential real property, § 362(b)(10) excepts from the stay "any act by a lessor . . . under a lease . . . that has terminated by the expiration of the stated term of the lease before the commencement of or during a case under this title to obtain possession of such property." Note that this stay exception applies only to commercial leases, and only when the lease terminated by expiration of the stated term. For residential leases, two exceptions were added in 2005. Under § 362(b)(22), the lessor can continue an eviction action if it obtained a judgment for possession of the premises prior to bankruptcy. This right, in turn, is subject to an exceedingly detailed provision in § 362(l), also added in 2005, which spells out very specifically the operative dates, procedures, and rights of the lessor and debtor.[90] The second personal property lease exception, also new in 2005, permits the lessor to pursue eviction based on endangerment to the premises or the illegal use of controlled substances on the property. § 362(b)(23). Again, this exception is subject to a detailed provision covering the procedures to be followed and the rights of the lessor and debtor. § 362(m).

A situation that has generated controversy is whether the stay applies under § 362(a)(3) to prevent a non-debtor from terminating or cancelling a contract with the debtor. To give one example, the debtor may at the time of filing have an insurance policy in force, and the insurance company may seek to cancel the policy on the giving of notice, in accordance with the terms of the contract. Most courts have held that cancellation of a contract with the debtor, even as authorized by the contract, is stayed.[91] Their reasoning is that the debtor's contract rights are a form of property and that cancellation of the contract would deprive the debtor of that property. If the non-debtor wishes to enforce its termination rights, it must do so with the blessing of the bankruptcy court. Care must be taken by the bankruptcy court in these cases not to give the bankruptcy estate greater rights in the contract than the debtor would have had outside of bankruptcy. As discussed below, an important question in the insurance

---

[88]   In re 48th St. Steakhouse, Inc., 835 F.2d 427 (2d Cir. 1987), cert. denied, 485 U.S. 1035 (1988).

[89]   E.g., In re Mann, 907 F.2d 923 (9th Cir. 1990); Boone Coal & Timber Co. v. Polan, 787 F.2d 1056 (6th Cir. 1986).

[90]   Indeed, one wonders why Congress felt impelled to legislate so specifically on this matter rather than leaving the administration of the dispute to the sound discretion of the bankruptcy judge.

[91]   See, e.g., In re Computer Commc'ns, Inc., 824 F.2d 725 (9th Cir. 1987); In re Minoco Grp. of Cos., 799 F.2d 517 (9th Cir. 1986).

policy cases is whether the estate or debtor has any property interest in the proceeds of the policy; if not, then the stay will not apply.[92]

If the termination of the contract is automatic and self-executing, without the need for any action by the non-debtor party, the stay will not prevent that termination.[93] In that situation, there is no "act" to be stayed. Furthermore, the automatic termination provision limits the extent of the property interest held by the estate. Note, however, that special rules applicable to executory contracts and leases in § 365 will override certain contractual termination provisions that are contrary to bankruptcy policy, such as clauses that would terminate the contract if the debtor files bankruptcy. See § 365(e)(1). Apart from those special rules, however, the general principle applies that the estate only succeeds to the rights that the debtor had. In one case, for example, the First Circuit held that the FAA did not violate the stay when it terminated the debtor airline's right to landing slots, when it did so in accordance with mandatory federal rules governing the use and allocation of those landing slots.[94]

Courts have been quite willing in borderline cases to find that the non-debtor party has committed an "act" with regard to estate property. The stay applies even if the non-debtor did not act coercively; for example, a creditor that merely accepted a voluntary postpetition payment of estate funds by the debtor was held to have violated the stay.[95] Courts have not permitted creditors to "hold" funds of the debtor.[96] This rule has even been applied when the creditor implemented the hold prior to the bankruptcy filing; the passive continuation of the hold was held to violate the stay.[97]

Often the inquiry in cases assessing whether the stay has been violated under § 362(a)(3) turns on whether the estate has an interest in property that is affected by the creditor's actions. This determination depends on the application of § 541(a). The courts in this area have also resolved close calls in favor of the application of the automatic stay. If the estate's interest is very remote, then relief can be granted by the court or adequate protection can be awarded with little difficulty.

Many cases have addressed the question of whether creditors can continue to pursue actions against non-debtor insurance companies on insurance policies held by the debtor. This issue has been of great importance in mass tort cases. The courts usually find that the stay is applicable, reasoning that the insurance policy is a valuable asset of the estate, and that some creditors should not be allowed to deplete the pool of money available under that policy to the detriment of all other creditors.[98]

---

[92]   In re Pintlar Corp., 124 F.3d 1310 (9th Cir. 1997).

[93]   E.g., Cntys. Contracting & Constr. Co. v. Constitution Life Ins. Co., 855 F.2d 1054 (3d Cir. 1988); Hazen First State Bank v. Speight, 888 F.2d 574 (8th Cir. 1989).

[94]   In re Gull Air, Inc., 890 F.2d 1255 (1st Cir. 1989).

[95]   In re Germansen Decorating, Inc., 149 B.R. 517 (Bankr. N.D. Ill. 1992).

[96]   SBA v. Rinehart, 887 F.2d 165 (8th Cir. 1989).

[97]   Knaus v. Concordia Lumber Co. (In re Knaus), 889 F.2d 773 (8th Cir. 1989).

[98]   See, e.g., A.H. Robins Co. v. Piccinin, 788 F.2d 994 (4th Cir.), cert. denied, 479 U.S. 876 (1986); In re Johns–Manville Corp., 40 B.R. 219 (S.D.N.Y. 1984).

However, as noted above, if neither the debtor nor the estate has a direct interest in the proceeds of the policy, then the stay is not applicable.[99]

In a similar vein, creditors have not been allowed in their individual right to pursue causes of action against third parties that would be available to the estate. The potential recovery under that cause of action belongs to the estate. Examples where this issue arises include fraudulent conveyance claims[100] and corporate alter ego actions.[101]

Actions by creditors against third parties are not stayed, however, if the action does not affect estate property. For example, most courts have permitted creditors who are beneficiaries of a letter of credit to make a draw on the credit against the issuing bank even after the debtor-customer files bankruptcy.[102] The letter of credit is a separate contract, independent of the underlying debt between the debtor and creditor, and the property being claimed by the creditor-beneficiary is that of the non-debtor issuing bank, not that of the debtor's estate.

§ 3.7   Setoffs, Freezes and Recoupment

One of the most powerful state law remedies of a creditor is the right of setoff. The right of setoff exists when the creditor and the debtor owe mutual debts to each other. The most common example involves a bank-creditor and a customer-debtor, where the customer has a checking account at the bank and has also taken out a loan from the bank. The bank owes a debt to the customer in the amount of the balance in the checking account; the customer owes a debt to the bank for the unpaid loan balance. If the debtor defaults on the loan, the bank may exercise its setoff right simply by deducting the loan balance due from the amount owing on the checking account. For example, if the debtor has $5,000 in the checking account, and defaults on a $8,000 loan, the bank may setoff the checking account debt against the loan, leaving a balance of $3,000 due on the loan and reducing the checking account to zero.

The Bankruptcy Code has several interrelated provisions that deal with the effect of the setoff right in bankruptcy cases. As a starting premise, the right of setoff is preserved in bankruptcy. § 553(a). Furthermore, the creditor is deemed to have a secured claim in the bankruptcy case in the amount subject to setoff. § 506(a)(1). In the example given above, prior to setoff the creditor would have a $5,000 secured claim and a $3,000 unsecured claim. The checking account is in effect collateral for the loan. A creditor with a setoff right may assert that right as a defense to turnover under § 542(b); in our example, the bank would not have to pay over $5,000 of the balance in the checking account to the bankruptcy trustee. In addition, when the "collateral" subject to the setoff right is a cash equivalent, such as a bank account, special rules limit the bankruptcy trustee's ability to use that "cash collateral." § 363(c)(2). The

---

[99]   See *Pintlar*, supra note 92, 124 F.3d 1310.

[100] E.g., In re Sherk, 918 F.2d 1170 (5th Cir. 1990).

[101] E.g., In re S.I. Acquisition, Inc., 817 F.2d 1142 (5th Cir. 1987). A useful discussion can be found in *Baillie Lumber Co. v. Thompson (In re Icarus Holding, LLC)*, 391 F.3d 1315 (11th Cir. 2004).

[102] E.g., In re Prime Motor Inns, Inc., 130 B.R. 610 (S.D. Fla. 1991). But see In re Twist Cap, Inc., 1 B.R. 284 (Bankr. M.D. Fla. 1979) (court enjoined draw on letter).

trustee may use cash collateral only with the creditor's consent or with permission of the bankruptcy court, which will only be granted if the creditor is afforded "adequate protection." § 363(e).

The provisions just noted all favor the creditor. As a policy matter, this pro-creditor outcome is somewhat controversial, because the creditor is effectively preferred over other creditors to the extent of the setoff right.[103] To illustrate, assume in our example that unsecured creditors will be paid a 25% dividend in the bankruptcy case. If the bank's setoff right were not honored, the bank would receive $2,000 (25% of $8,000). With the setoff right intact, the bank will receive $5,750 (the $5,000 subject to setoff, plus 25% of the remaining $3,000). In short, the creditor with a setoff right is paid in full to the extent of that right, instead of the percentage dividend payable to general creditors. As a policy matter, the Supreme Court decreed long ago that this result should be permitted in order to avoid "the absurdity of making A pay B when B owes A."[104]

In certain important respects, the setoff right is restricted in bankruptcy. Some of these limitations are discussed later in the book.[105] For example, a creditor may not exercise or obtain a setoff right in the time period shortly prior to the bankruptcy case so as to improve its position vis-à-vis other creditors. §§ 553(a)(2),(3), (b).

For purposes of this chapter, the important limitation on the creditor's freedom of action is that the creditor is stayed from "the setoff of any debt owing to the debtor that arose before the commencement of the case under this title against any claim against the debtor." § 362(a)(7). In our ongoing example, while the bank would retain its setoff right after the debtor files bankruptcy, the bank would be stayed from actually effectuating that setoff. If the bank wants to set off, it must obtain relief from the stay. This limitation is consistent with the treatment of other secured claims in bankruptcy. The secured creditor thus retains the benefit of its lien or setoff right, but is stayed from enforcing that lien or setoff "pending an orderly examination of the debtor's and creditor's rights."[106]

The most difficult question under § 362(a)(7) has been determining whether the stay applies to an administrative "freeze" or "hold" of the debtor's checking account by the bank. The issue arises when the debtor seeks to withdraw money from the checking account or a check drawn on the account is presented after the bankruptcy petition is filed. The problem for the bank is that it will lose its setoff right if the money is

---

[103] See John C. McCoid, II, Setoff: Why Bankruptcy Priority?, 75 Va. L. Rev. 15 (1989). Professor McCoid, as always, captured the problem precisely, id. at 15:

> Between solvent parties, setoff makes perfect sense. If you owe me $10 and I owe you $7, it is certainly efficient for you simply to pay me $3; it also avoids the possibility of my default after you have paid what you owe me. Striking that balance affects no one else. If, however, one of us is insolvent and has other creditors, the sense of this solution is less obvious. It is hardly news that setoff, whether it takes place postbankruptcy or in the period immediately preceding bankruptcy, is preferential in effect. A creditor who owes money to his debtor receives, to the extent of the debtor's claim against him, 100 cents on the dollar from his claim against the debtor, while other creditors receive less.

[104] Studley v. Boylston Nat'l. Bank, 229 U.S. 523, 528 (1913).

[105] See §§ 6.27–6.28.

[106] H.R. Rep. No. 95–595, 95th Cong., 1st Sess., at 342 (1977).

released; the right of setoff under state law continues only to the extent mutual debts are still owing between the creditor and debtor. Note also that the "cash collateral" in the account may not legally be used without the consent either of the bank or the bankruptcy court. The response of many banks in this situation has been to freeze the account, and not to honor any checks drawn on the account or to permit any monies to be withdrawn. The bank does not actually effect the setoff; the prior balance in the account remains outstanding, but may not be accessed without court permission. By taking this action the bank preserves its right of setoff—but, until 1995, it also ran the risk of violating the stay; thus, courts described this scenario as the "banker's dilemma."

Before 1995, one line of cases had held that the bank violated the stay by freezing the debtor's account.[107] A similar issue arose in cases where the IRS refused to refund a debtor's tax overpayment.[108] These courts reasoned that the bank's unilateral action in placing a hold on the account was "tantamount to the exercise of a right of setoff"[109] that "effectively deprives the debtor of the use of the funds." Furthermore, they concluded that the bank's action was an exercise of control over estate property, in violation of § 362(a)(3). The bank's proper recourse was to apply to the bankruptcy court for emergency relief from the stay or for an injunction against the debtor. A competing line of authority held that the bank's action in placing a hold on the debtor's account did not amount to a setoff and did not violate the stay.[110]

In 1995 the Supreme Court settled the issue in favor of the banks in *Citizens Bank of Maryland v. Strumpf*,[111] holding that an administrative freeze did not violate the stay. In a unanimous opinion, the Court held that the freeze was not a "setoff" as typically understood under state law, because the bank did not intend to permanently reduce the debtor's account balance by its actions. Thus, the § 362(a)(7) stay did not apply by its terms. The Court further stated that federal law determines whether a "setoff" has occurred under § 362(a)(7), and dictates the same conclusion—that a freeze is not a setoff. This result is necessary to give effect to other sections of the Code, which excuse a creditor from paying over a debt subject to setoff, § 542(b), and which recognize the general right of setoff. § 553(a). The Court also could have pointed to the prohibition against the debtor using cash collateral without permission, § 363(c)(2), and to the treatment of the setoff right as a secured claim. § 506(a)(1). The Court likewise declined to find that the bank had violated either § 362(a)(3) or (6), concluding that the bank had not exercised control over any "property" of the debtor, but had simply refused to perform a promise to pay a debt. In *Strumpf*, the Court did not decide how long the bank could leave the freeze in place, emphasizing that the hold there was only temporary, until the bank could seek relief from the stay from the bankruptcy

---

[107] E.g., In re Patterson, 967 F.2d 505 (11th Cir. 1992).

[108] E.g., United States v. Norton, 717 F.2d 767 (3d Cir. 1983).

[109] Citizens Bank of Maryland v. Strumpf, 37 F.3d 155, 158 (4th Cir. 1994), rev'd, 516 U.S. 16 (1995).

[110] E.g., In re Edgins, 36 B.R. 480 (B.A.P. 9th Cir. 1984).

[111] 516 U.S. 16 (1995).

court. Courts applying *Strumpf* accordingly have held that while a temporary hold is permissible, an indefinite freeze violates the stay.[112]

The stay against setoff only applies to *prepetition* debts. If the debts both arise postpetition, the creditor will not be stayed from exercising its right of setoff. Applying this rule in practice will require the courts to identify the time the debts arise. In making that identification, courts should remember that a debt is deemed to exist for purposes of the Bankruptcy Code even if the right to payment is "unliquidated," "contingent," "unmatured," or "disputed," § 101(5), and that Congress intended to bring "all legal obligations of the debtor, no matter how remote or contingent"[113] within the purview of the bankruptcy case.

The stay under § 362(a)(7) will not apply if the creditor is asserting a right of *"recoupment"* on a claim.[114] Recoupment is distinguishable from setoff in that in recoupment the debts must arise out of the *same transaction*. Courts have narrowly construed the doctrine of recoupment in bankruptcy because of the concern that the creditor will obtain an advantage over other creditors.[115] An example of recoupment is where the creditor makes advance payments on a contract, and the debtor later asserts rights under the same contract. Under the equitable doctrine of recoupment, the creditor is allowed to raise its prior payments as a defense to the debtor's claim. In one case, for instance, advance royalties were paid to a musician before the musician filed bankruptcy.[116] After bankruptcy, the sale of records generated a claim for royalties by the musician's bankruptcy estate. The recording company was permitted to recoup the advance royalties paid against the claim for subsequent royalties. A common recoupment scenario arises in the Medicare context, involving health care providers whose relationship with the federal government involves ongoing Medicare reimbursements and credits. Most courts have allowed the government to recoup in this setting.[117]

Several exceptions to the stay under subsection (b) permit setoff in specific narrowly defined situations. § 362(b)(6), (7), (17), (26), (27). Virtually all of these exceptions concern sophisticated financial contracts, and were enacted by Congress to ensure the integrity of those financial markets and to protect the participants. Thus, for example, subsection (b)(6) permits setoff in the case of securities contracts (see also § 555) and commodities and forward contracts (see also § 556). Subsection (7) allows setoff for repurchase agreements (see also § 559). Setoff under swap agreements (see also § 560) is covered by subsection (b)(17). In 2005 Congress added a provision, § 362(b)(27), allowing setoff under master netting agreements (see also § 561).

---

[112] See, e.g., In re Kleinsmith, 361 B.R. 504 (Bankr. S.D. Iowa 2006) (stay violated when creditor maintained hold on debtor's account for a year and a half after the bankruptcy filing and never sought stay relief to pursue setoff).

[113] H.R. Rep. No. 95–595, 95th Cong., 1st Sess., at 309 (1977).

[114] See, e.g., In re Slater Health Ctr., 398 F.3d 98 (1st Cir. 2005); In re Holford, 896 F.2d 176 (5th Cir. 1990); In re B & L Oil Co., 782 F.2d 155 (10th Cir. 1986).

[115] See, e.g., Westinghouse Credit Corp. v. D'Urso, 278 F.3d 138 (2d Cir. 2002) (denying recoupment obligations arising from discrete and independent units in single contract).

[116] Waldschmidt v. C.B.S., Inc., 14 B.R. 309 (M.D. Tenn. 1981).

[117] E.g., *Slater Health Center*, supra note 114, 398 F.3d 98. Contra, In re Univ. Med. Ctr., 973 F.2d 1065 (3d Cir. 1992).

The final stay exception allowing setoff was also added in 2005, and permits the government to set off an income tax refund pertaining to a pre-bankruptcy taxable period against a pre-bankruptcy income tax liability. § 362(b)(26). This last exception mooted the controversy over whether the government's "hold" of a refund violated the stay, as discussed above. Now the government is free to proceed with setoff.

§ 3.8   Catch-All Provision

The intention of Congress to implement a pervasive stay against all conceivable creditor collection efforts is demonstrated by § 362(a)(6), which stays "any act to collect, assess, or recover a claim against the debtor that arose before the commencement of the case under this title." The legislative history to the Code emphasizes the congressional concern that "sophisticated creditors" might take advantage of "inexperienced, frightened, or ill-counseled debtors" and coerce them into repaying dischargeable debts, thus evading the purpose of bankruptcy to afford debtors a fresh start.[118] Subsection (6) responds to this concern by staying all formal and informal actions to collect prepetition debts. Courts have broadly construed this catch-all provision.

Most fundamentally, § 362(a)(6) fills a useful gap by outlawing informal collection efforts, such as dunning letters or phone calls demanding payment of prepetition debts. Creditors must leave the debtor alone once the debtor files bankruptcy. This freedom from harassment gives the debtor the "breathing spell" from his or her creditors that Congress viewed as a central purpose of the automatic stay.

This prohibition against even informal contact with the debtor raises a problem of coordination with other provisions that bear on the scope of the debtor's fresh start. A debtor is permitted to repay voluntarily an otherwise dischargeable debt. § 524(f). Thus, if the debtor makes a voluntary payment, the creditor may keep the money without violating the Bankruptcy Code. Even more saliently, a debtor is allowed to reaffirm a dischargeable debt, subject to certain procedural limitations. § 524(c), (d). The debtor's promise to pay a reaffirmed debt is enforceable by the creditor notwithstanding the discharge.

Given these provisions, may the creditor contact the debtor and request either voluntary payment or reaffirmation? Reading § 362(a)(6) literally, and taking to heart its underlying purposes as expressed in the legislative history, the answer should be no; to avoid a stay violation the initiative must come from the debtor. Otherwise, "[i]nexperienced, frightened, or ill-counseled debtors may succumb to suggestions to repay notwithstanding their bankruptcy," thereby allowing "evasion of the purpose of the bankruptcy laws by sophisticated creditors."[119] Many courts, however, have found no stay violation if the creditor "merely" sends a request (typically in a standard form letter) for reaffirmation. Instead, these courts require something more, such as a threat, coercion or harassment.[120] These holdings are in line with a broader, and I

---

[118] H.R. Rep. No. 95–595, 95th Cong., 1st Sess., at 342 (1977).

[119] Id.

[120] See, e.g., Pertuso v. Ford Motor Credit Co., 233 F.3d 417 (6th Cir. 2000); In re Duke, 79 F.3d 43 (7th Cir. 1996).

believe regrettable, trend to read § 362(a)(6) not as a prohibition of all contact between creditor and debtor, but only to prevent specific harassment.[121] Furthermore, even if the contact were of the type that might otherwise violate the stay if made directly with the debtor, some courts have held that a creditor does not violate the stay if it contacts the debtor's attorney, rather than the debtor.[122]

Courts also have struggled in applying § 362(a)(6) in situations where the creditor has the power to exert leverage against the debtor, by engaging in otherwise legal behavior that might coerce the debtor into repaying a dischargeable debt. For example, what happens if a physician that has not been paid by the debtor declines to provide further treatment;[123] or if a key supplier refuses to ship more goods to the debtor;[124] or a university withholds the debtor's transcript?[125] In each instance the creditor is acting within its legal rights to refuse to provide the item sought. Yet, if the debtor were to pay the unpaid debt, one suspects that the physician might resume treatment, the supplier might ship goods, and the university might release the transcript. Faced with this situation, courts have attempted to divine the creditor's motive in asserting its legal rights. If the court believes that the creditor is trying to coerce payment of the prepetition debt, the court will hold that the creditor has violated the automatic stay. Furthermore, the court may even order the creditor to provide the goods or services requested by the debtor on a current basis.[126] If, however, the court takes a more benign view of the creditor's motives, it may find no stay violation.[127]

In some cases creditors have given vent to their anger at the debtor's default, and have engaged in conspicuous conduct and speech condemning the debtor's default. By so indulging themselves, the creditors may violate the stay under (a)(6)—although pure speech may find constitutional protection in the First Amendment. In *In re Reed*,[128] Judge Mabey held that an unpaid creditor violated the stay when he dumped garbage on the debtor's lawn. The court in *In re Sechuan City, Inc.*[129] similarly condemned the actions of the creditor in posting signs in the hotel lobby proclaiming that the debtor restaurant was a deadbeat and urging people not to patronize it. The evidence showed that the creditor hoped to embarrass and humiliate the debtor into paying the debt. The court did not believe that actions by the creditor that contravened § 362(a)(6) fell within the ambit of speech protected by the First Amendment. In another case, however, where the creditor parked a display truck outside the debtor's business

---

[121] See, e.g, In re Connor, 366 B.R. 133 (Bankr. D. Haw. 2007) (no stay violation by sending monthly loan statements while debtor in chapter 13, but violation occurred once debtor converted to chapter 7).

[122] See United States ex. rel. Farmers Home Admin. v. Nelson, 969 F.2d 626 (8th Cir. 1992).

[123] In re Olson, 38 B.R. 515 (Bankr. N.D. Iowa 1984).

[124] In re Sportfame of Ohio, Inc., 40 B.R. 47 (Bankr. N.D. Ohio 1984).

[125] In re Walker, 336 B.R. 534 (Bankr. M.D. Fla. 2005); In re Merchant, 958 F.2d 738 (6th Cir. 1992). See also In re Parker, 334 B.R. 529 (Bankr. D. Mass. 2005).

[126] For a strong criticism of such judicial activism, see Daniel Keating, Offensive Uses of the Bankruptcy Stay, 45 Vand. L. Rev. 71 (1992).

[127] E.g., In re Jamo, 283 F.3d 392 (1st Cir. 2002); In re Brown, 851 F.2d 81 (3d Cir. 1988).

[128] 11 B.R. 258 (Bankr. D. Utah 1981).

[129] 96 B.R. 37 (Bankr. E.D. Pa. 1989).

making a similar "deadbeat" announcement, the court held that the creditor's "speech" was constitutionally protected.[130]

§ 3.9 Application to Nondebtor Parties

The automatic stay does not normally apply to actions against nondebtor parties. Section 362(a)(1), for instance, stays actions "against the debtor," and § 362(a)(6) stays any act to collect a prepetition claim "against the debtor." The purposes of the stay, to protect the debtor from harassment and to preserve the property of the estate to permit an orderly distribution, are not typically implicated by proceedings against a nondebtor.

Thus, the stay will not apply to a suit against nondebtor general partners of a debtor partnership.[131] Nor will the stay stop actions versus guarantors of a debt of the debtor. A lawsuit brought initially against multiple defendants, including the debtor, may still proceed against the nondebtor co-defendants after the debtor files bankruptcy.[132] A beneficiary is permitted to make a draw against the issuer of a letter of credit after the debtor-customer files bankruptcy.[133] Similarly, a proceeding against a surety of the debtor may continue unless affirmatively enjoined by the court.[134]

In very limited circumstances, however, actions against nondebtors may be stayed. One such situation is where there is an "identity of interest" between the nondebtor and the debtor. Stated otherwise, if the debtor should be considered the real party in interest, the action nominally against the nondebtor but effectively against the debtor should be stayed. The most prominent example is the case of *A.H. Robins Co. v. Piccinin.*[135] The Fourth Circuit held that the stay applied to actions against third parties who were entitled to indemnification from the debtor.[136] Other courts have made clear that this exception does not apply if the third party is independently liable, but only if their liability is derivative of the debtor.[137] The Second Circuit has held that "[t]he automatic stay can apply to non-debtors, but normally does so only when a claim against the non-debtor will have an immediate adverse economic consequence for the debtor's estate."[138]

---

[130] In re Stonegate Sec. Serv., Ltd., 56 B.R. 1014 (N.D. Ill. 1986).

[131] E.g., Patton v. Bearden, 8 F.3d 343 (6th Cir. 1993).

[132] E.g., In re Delta Air Lines, 310 F.3d 953 (6th Cir. 2002); Lynch v. Johns–Manville Sales Corp., 710 F.2d 1194 (6th Cir. 1983).

[133] E.g., In re Prime Motor Inns, Inc., 130 B.R. 610 (S.D. Fla. 1991).

[134] Two circuit courts reached the conclusion that the automatic stay did not apply to the action against the surety in the *Celotex Corp.* case. See Willis v. Celotex Corp., 978 F.2d 146 (4th Cir. 1992), cert. denied, 507 U.S. 1030 (1993); Edwards v. Armstrong World Indus., Inc., 6 F.3d 312 (5th Cir. 1993), rev'd on other grounds, 514 U.S. 300 (1995). Those courts parted company on the appropriateness of the injunction, on the bankruptcy court's jurisdiction to issue the injunction, and on the permissibility of collaterally attacking the injunction order; the Supreme Court sided with the Fourth Circuit and prohibited the collateral attack.

[135] 788 F.2d 994 (4th Cir.), cert. denied, 479 U.S. 876 (1986).

[136] Id. at 999. The Fourth Circuit reaffirmed this exception in *Kreisler v. Goldberg*, 478 F.3d 209 (4th Cir. 2007).

[137] See In re Lockard, 884 F.2d 1171 (9th Cir. 1989).

[138] Queenie, Ltd. v. Nygard Int'l., 321 F.3d 282, 287 (2d Cir. 2003) (stay applies when suit is against wholly owned subsidiary of debtor).

A second exception to the general rule is in cases where the action against the third party will interfere with property of the bankruptcy estate or the debtor. In such a situation, the stay under § 362(a)(3) will be operative.[139] In the *Robins* case, the court further held that a suit against a nondebtor insurer was stayed because the insurance policy itself was property of the estate.[140] An action to terminate the lease of a nondebtor prime tenant was held to be stayed in another case, where the effect would have been to terminate the debtor's sublease.[141] Where the debtor makes a fraudulent conveyance to a third party, creditors may not pursue the third party after bankruptcy, because the fraudulent conveyance cause of action is property of the bankruptcy estate.[142]

In cases under chapter 12 and chapter 13, a direct statutory stay of actions against codebtors is provided with regard to consumer debts.[143] § 1201, 1301. The purpose of the codebtor stay in these consumer cases is to "protect a debtor . . . from indirect pressures" from his creditors.[144] A debtor whose elderly grandmother has cosigned his note on a consumer debt might go ahead and pay the creditor in order to keep the creditor from hounding grandma; the codebtor stay stops the action against grandma during the bankruptcy case. However, the creditor "does not lose the benefit of his bargain"; after the bankruptcy case, or if the creditor can obtain relief from the stay, the creditor may pursue its substantive rights against the codebtor.

Even if the automatic stay of § 362(a) does not apply to the action against the nondebtor third party, the bankruptcy court still may issue an injunction against such a proceeding under its general equitable powers under § 105(a). The Supreme Court observed in *Celotex Corp. v. Edwards* that the bankruptcy court has jurisdiction to issue such an injunction if the injunction could have a *"conceivable effect"* on the bankruptcy case.[145] In *Celotex*, the bankruptcy court had issued an injunction prohibiting creditors from executing on supersedeas bonds against independent sureties, on the ground that execution would have an adverse effect on the debtor's reorganization. Other courts have also upheld third-party injunctions premised on the need to protect the debtor's chances of reorganizing under chapter 11.[146] This interference with the rights of one nondebtor against another nondebtor should not be ordered, however, except in "unusual circumstances" where the benefit to the reorganization clearly outweighs the detriment to the enjoined party.

---

[139]   See § 3.6.

[140]   *Robins*, supra note 135, 788 F.2d at 1001.

[141]   In re 48th St. Steakhouse, Inc., 835 F.2d 427 (2d Cir. 1987), cert. denied, 485 U.S. 1035 (1988).

[142]   E.g., In re Sherk, 918 F.2d 1170 (5th Cir. 1990).

[143]   See §§ 12.8, 13.5.

[144]   H.R. Rep. No. 95–595, 95th Cong., 1st Sess., at 426 (1977).

[145]   514 U.S. 300 (1995).

[146]   E.g., In re Eagle–Picher Indus., Inc., 963 F.2d 855 (6th Cir. 1992); In re Drexel Burnham Lambert Grp., 960 F.2d 285 (2d Cir. 1992), cert. dismissed, 506 U.S. 1088 (1993).

C. SCOPE OF THE STAY: ACTS EXCEPTED UNDER § 362(b)

§ 3.10   Criminal Actions Against Debtor

Not all actions that fall within the ambit of § 362(a) are automatically stayed. Ascertaining whether the stay applies also requires consulting § 362(b), which specifies a long list of exceptions to the stay. If an action is excepted from the stay under any of the provisions of subsection (b), the burden is on the debtor to obtain an injunction against that action from the bankruptcy court. The exclusions in (b) implement a wide array of disparate policy objectives.

One of the most important of those policy objectives is that a bankruptcy case should not be permitted to interfere with the operation of essential governmental functions. The interests of the body politic in furthering the common weal presumptively outweigh the interests of the debtor in obtaining a fresh start or the interests of creditors in equitable collection proceedings. This premise is codified most generally in § 362(b)(4), which exempts from the stay "the commencement or continuation of an action or proceeding by a governmental unit to enforce such governmental unit's police or regulatory power."[147] A more specific instance of the same broad policy is § 362(b)(1), which excludes from the stay "the commencement or continuation of a criminal action or proceeding against the debtor." As the legislative history emphasizes, "the bankruptcy laws are not a haven for criminal offenders."[148]

The exclusion in § 362(b)(1) for criminal proceedings most often counters the stay provision in § 362(a)(1) for the commencement or continuation of proceedings against the debtor that could have been brought prior to bankruptcy,[149] although other provisions in § 362(a) also arguably might block criminal actions without the (b)(1) exception. In most cases, the application of § 362(b)(1) is simple and straightforward. A debtor standing trial for murder cannot bring that trial to a halt by filing a bankruptcy petition.

The hard cases arise, however, when the criminal action carries with it the incidental but unmistakable overtones of debt collection. This can happen when the criminal law in some manner requires the debtor to make restitution to a victimized creditor. A common example is a bad check case, where the debtor-criminal's "sentence" often is to make good on the check. Allowing the criminal proceeding to go forward might well result in the creditor being paid in preference to other creditors, and in contravention of the debtor's fresh start. Indeed, the primary motivation for the criminal action in the first place may be to compel the debtor to pay a debt. The difficult balancing task for the courts in these cases is to protect the state's interest in the unfettered operation of its criminal justice system while not permitting the state criminal law to be used as a convenient means of evading the federal bankruptcy law.

Even in such quasi-collection cases, § 362(b)(1) applies on its face. If the action against the debtor is brought pursuant to the state criminal laws, the literal language

---

[147]   See §§ 3.11, 3.12.

[148]   H.R. Rep. No. 95–595, 95th Cong., 1st Sess., at 342 (1977).

[149]   See § 3.4.

of (b)(1) operates to except that proceeding from the automatic stay. While some courts have read § 362(b)(1) to be limited by a "debt collection" exception, wherein the stay will still apply if the criminal action is motivated by a primary purpose to collect a debt,[150] the better (and majority) view is that subsection (b)(1) is unqualified, and applies to exclude from the bankruptcy stay any criminal proceeding, irrespective of the underlying prosecutorial purpose.[151]

That subsection (b)(1) applies to exclude the criminal proceeding from the automatic stay does not, however, necessarily preclude a federal bankruptcy court from issuing an injunction against the commencement or continuation of the criminal action. Accordingly, the battle will be joined when the debtor asks the bankruptcy court to issue such an injunction. The courts agree that the bankruptcy court has the power to issue such an injunction under § 105(a). The question is one of application.

The starting point in answering that question must be the Supreme Court's 1971 decision in *Younger v. Harris*.[152] In sweeping language, the Court reaffirmed the longstanding policy against federal courts enjoining state proceedings except in special and extraordinary circumstances, in keeping with "our federalism." *Younger* only allows an injunction to be issued if the movant can demonstrate a "great and immediate danger" of irreparable injury to his federally protected rights, and if the danger cannot be eliminated by a defense in a single criminal prosecution.[153] An exception applies if the movant can show that the criminal proceeding was brought in bad faith or for purposes of harassment.[154]

A handful of bankruptcy and district courts have issued injunctions against state criminal proceedings in bankruptcy cases, reasoning that the "primary motivation" of the action was to collect a debt.[155] The overwhelming trend in the courts of appeals, however, has been to deny such injunctions. For example, in *Barnette v. Evans*,[156] the debtor issued $37,000 in bad checks to an auto dealer, and was prosecuted criminally. The state criminal law mandated full restitution to the creditor. The Eleventh Circuit overturned the issuance of an injunction against the continuation of the criminal action, holding that the strict *Younger* tests were not satisfied. The debtor's interest in receiving a discharge was not a sufficient federally protected right (especially since discharge of the debt might well be denied anyway under § 523(a)), and the creditor's "motivation" in seeking collection did not by itself constitute bad faith or harassment. Furthermore, the debtor could raise bad faith as a defense in the criminal action itself. Several circuit courts have also held that the revocation of the debtor-criminal's probation and ensuing incarceration of the debtor for failure to make restitution

---

[150] E.g., In re Dovell, 311 B.R. 492 (Bankr. S.D. Ohio 2004).

[151] See In re Gruntz, 202 F.3d 1074 (9th Cir. 2000).

[152] 401 U.S. 37 (1971).

[153] Id. at 46.

[154] Id. at 49–50.

[155] E.g., In re Penny, 414 F. Supp. 1113 (W.D.N.C. 1976) (under Bankruptcy Act); In re Curly, 25 B.R. 260 (Bankr. E.D. Pa. 1982) (alternatively held § 362(b)(1) inapplicable because of debt collection purpose).

[156] 673 F.2d 1250 (11th Cir. 1982).

payments ordered as a condition of probation did not violate the bankruptcy stay and should not be enjoined.[157]

The Supreme Court's 1986 decision in *Kelly v. Robinson*[158] further cemented the view that state criminal actions should not be interfered with just to accommodate a supposed bankruptcy interest. In *Kelly*, the Court held that a criminal restitution obligation was not dischargeable under § 523(a)(7), relying heavily on the policy of federal deference to the operation of the state criminal justice system. The Court so held notwithstanding apparently clear statutory language in the Bankruptcy Code to the contrary. After *Kelly*, the courts have readily concluded that debtors do not have a cognizable federal interest in avoiding criminal restitution, and that seeking restitution is not bad faith or harassment within the meaning of the *Younger* exception.[159] While the Court's 1990 holding in *Pennsylvania Department of Public Welfare v. Davenport*[160] that a criminal restitution obligation is a debt potentially dischargeable in a chapter 13 case might suggest some retreat from the strong policy of deference indicated by *Younger* and *Kelly*, the rapid amendment of the Code in 1991 to overrule the result in *Davenport*[161] signals congressional approval of the deferential approach. Cases decided post–1991 confirm that, almost without constraint, the states remain free to use restitution in criminal cases notwithstanding the happenstance of bankruptcy.[162]

§ 3.11   Environmental Pollution Cases

One of the most vexing and persistent problems under the Bankruptcy Code has been the application of the environmental protection laws in cases involving polluting debtors. Congress certainly did not intend for bankruptcy to be either a haven for polluters or a license to pollute. However, care must be taken by the courts not to afford an unintended preference in the bankruptcy distribution to governmental environmental protection agencies acting in their status as a creditor. Courts often must navigate this fine line in the context of the automatic stay.

As originally enacted in 1978, two subsections of § 362(b) were pertinent to the inquiry. Subsection (b)(4) excluded from the automatic stay "the commencement or continuation of an action or proceeding by a governmental unit to enforce such governmental unit's police or regulatory power." The next subsection, (b)(5), further excepted from the stay "the enforcement of a judgment" obtained in an action to enforce that police or regulatory power, but then "excepted from the exception" an action to enforce a money judgment. In 1998, Congress combined former subsections (b)(4) and (b)(5) into a single subsection (b)(4); however, no substantive changes in prior law were

---

[157] See, e.g., Hucke v. Oregon, 992 F.2d 950 (9th Cir.), cert. denied, 510 U.S. 862 (1993), overruled on other grounds, In re Gruntz, 202 F.3d 1074 (9th Cir. 2000); United States v. Caddell, 830 F.2d 36 (5th Cir. 1987).

[158] 479 U.S. 36 (1986).

[159] See Fussell v. Price, 928 F.2d 712 (5th Cir. 1991), cert. denied, 502 U.S. 1107 (1992); *Caddell*, supra note 157, 830 F.2d 36.

[160] 495 U.S. 552 (1990).

[161] An exception to the chapter 13 discharge was added for criminal restitution obligations in § 1328(a)(3).

[162] See *Hucke*, supra note 157, 992 F.2d 950.

intended. The legislative history makes clear that environmental protection is one of the prototypical exercises of the government's police or regulatory power to which these sections were intended to apply.[163]

The concern that a governmental unit acting as a creditor will use the police power exception as a means of indirectly capturing a preference over other creditors is addressed by the "exception to the exception" referred to above. The stay exclusion allowing the government to enforce a judgment to enforce its police power is itself qualified: the government is only permitted to enforce a judgment *other than a money judgment.*" In other words, the government is stayed from enforcing a "money judgment," even if that money judgment is connected with the government's police and regulatory powers. In seeking to collect money, the government must stand in the bankruptcy distribution line with all of the other creditors of the debtor. As the legislative history explains:

> Since the assets of the debtor are in the possession and control of the bankruptcy court, and since they constitute a fund out of which all creditors are entitled to share, enforcement by a governmental unit of a money judgment would give it preferential treatment to the detriment of all other creditors.[164]

Stating the rules is one thing; applying them is another. Courts, as they are wont to do, have devised various tests in an attempt to divine whether the government's actions fall within the exception (thus permitting the government to act) or within the exception-to-the-exception (thus prohibiting the government from acting). The most commonly used tests are (1) the *"pecuniary purpose"* test, which asks if the government is acting primarily to protect its pecuniary interest or to protect the public safety, and (2) the *"public policy"* test, which distinguishes between actions to adjudicate private rights and those to effectuate public policy.[165] In the environmental cases, the resolution is almost invariably in the government's favor, no matter what test is used.

Several different fact patterns illustrate the application of § 362(b)(4) in the environmental context. In one common type of case, the government brings an action against the debtor to recover costs that the government has incurred in cleaning up polluted property. The courts usually allow such an action to proceed notwithstanding the stay, up to the point of assessing and fixing the damages, but do not allow the government to execute on the judgment obtained.[166]

Another fairly easy case is where the debtor continues in possession of its property, and the government obtains an injunction ordering the debtor to cease polluting. A bankruptcy debtor must obey the environmental laws just like everybody else. Thus, neither the obtaining nor the enforcement of that prohibitory injunction would be stayed.

---

[163] H.R. Rep. No. 95–595, 95th Cong., 1st Sess., at 343 (1977).

[164] Id.

[165] See Lockyer v. Mirant Corp., 398 F.3d 1098 (9th Cir. 2005); Chao v. Hosp. Staffing Servs., Inc., 270 F.3d 374 (6th Cir. 2001); In re Commerce Oil Co., 847 F.2d 291 (6th Cir. 1988).

[166] E.g., City of New York v. Exxon, 932 F.2d 1020 (2d Cir. 1991); United States v. Nicolet, Inc., 857 F.2d 202 (3d Cir. 1988); *Commerce Oil,* supra note 165, 847 F.2d 291.

The hardest case is when the government seeks to obtain a mandatory injunction ordering the debtor to clean up past pollution. Note that the government could itself effect the cleanup, and then sue the debtor to recover those response costs—but recall that the actual collection of any money judgment for response costs would be stayed under the "exception to the exception." To the extent the government can make the debtor do the cleanup, the government will not have to spend that money itself, and will in effect have obtained a priority over other creditors in the amount of saved response costs. Nevertheless, when the debtor is continuing in possession of the polluted site as a chapter 11 debtor in possession, the government properly is permitted to compel the debtor to bring the site into compliance with the environmental laws.[167] A debtor in possession or trustee operating a business is required by 28 U.S.C. § 959(b) to "manage and operate the property in his possession according to the requirements of the valid laws of the State."

Does that same logic hold, however, when the debtor is not continuing in business under chapter 11, but is liquidating under chapter 7? The Third Circuit confronted this issue in the well-known case of *Penn Terra Ltd. v. Department of Environmental Resources*.[168] Prior to bankruptcy, a corporate debtor entered into a consent order requiring the debtor to bring its coal mines into compliance with the relevant Pennsylvania statutes. The debtor did not complete the reclamation work, however, but instead ceased operations and filed chapter 7. The total cost of the cleanup exceeded the total assets of the debtor. The Pennsylvania Department of Environmental Resources brought an action in state court to compel the bankruptcy trustee to abide by the consent order and expend the remaining assets of the estate in doing the reclamation work. In a debatable decision, the Third Circuit held that the action to compel the trustee to spend the estate's money was not the "enforcement of . . . a money judgment," either in form or substance, and thus was not stayed. The court instead characterized the proceeding as "an equitable action to prevent future harm."[169] The practical effect of the court's holding, however, was to give the government's cleanup claim a de facto priority over all other creditors of the debtor. Once the trustee spent the limited assets of the estate on the cleanup, there would be nothing left for anyone else.

§ 3.12   Other Police Power Activities

The range of police power activities by a governmental unit exempted from the automatic stay extends far beyond the environmental protection area[170] and the enforcement of the criminal laws.[171] The legislative history states that the exception in (b)(4) would apply "where a governmental unit is suing a debtor to prevent or stop violation of fraud, environmental protection, consumer protection, safety, or similar police or regulatory laws, or attempting to fix damages for violation of such a law."[172]

---

[167]   In re Commonwealth Oil Refining Co., 805 F.2d 1175 (5th Cir. 1986), cert. denied, 483 U.S. 1005 (1987).

[168]   733 F.2d 267 (3d Cir. 1984).

[169]   Id. at 277–79.

[170]   See § 3.11.

[171]   See § 3.10.

[172]   H.R. Rep. No. 95–595, 95th Cong., 1st Sess., at 343 (1977).

As a matter of first principles, the filing of bankruptcy by itself should not excuse compliance with other laws, absent a compelling bankruptcy-specific justification. However, the government should not be able to use the guise of "police or regulatory laws" as a cover for obtaining preferential treatment in its status as a creditor of the debtor. The sponsors of the 1978 Code stated that the exception "is intended to be given a narrow construction in order to permit governmental units to pursue actions to protect the public health and safety and not to apply to actions by a governmental unit to protect a pecuniary interest."[173]

Notwithstanding the sponsors' admonition to give the exception a narrow construction, the courts have excluded a wide range of governmental actions from the stay. The Supreme Court held that an administrative proceeding against a financial holding company by the Board of Governors of the Federal Reserve System fell squarely within § 362(b)(4) in *Board of Governors, FRS v. MCorp Financial, Inc.*[174] A number of circuit court decisions have held that the NLRB may obtain the entry of a back pay award for violation of the labor laws.[175] However, the NLRB cannot actually enforce that back pay order, because of the prohibition against enforcing a money judgment.[176] Enforcement would have to be sought in the bankruptcy court. The Secretary of Labor has been permitted to enforce an injunction against the sale of "hot goods" produced in violation of the Fair Labor Standards Act, even though the practical effect would be to coerce the payment of back wages.[177] The EEOC is not stayed from enforcing the requirements of Title VII.[178] Nor is the SEC precluded from enforcing the securities laws.[179] The list goes on and on.

In some cases, however, the courts do find that the protection of the government's pecuniary interest is paramount and that the stay therefore applies. This has come up particularly in instances where the regulatory law in question itself purports to define the rights of affected creditors and speaks directly to the proper means of liquidating and distributing the debtor's assets. Courts have little trouble finding that such laws do not directly affect public "health, welfare, morals and safety," and should be stayed.[180]

Even if the regulatory law itself does implicate a legitimate governmental police power, the issue may arise whether the government is seeking the "enforcement of . . . a money judgment," which then would be stayed. A leading case is the Second Circuit's decision in *SEC v. Brennan.*[181] The debtor, Brennan, was found to have committed a

---

[173] 124 Cong. Rec. H11,092 (daily ed. Sept. 28, 1978) (statement of Rep. Edwards); 124 Cong. Rec. S17,409 (daily ed. Oct. 6, 1978) (statement of Sen. DeConcini).

[174] 502 U.S. 32 (1991).

[175] E.g., N.L.R.B. v. P*I*E Nationwide, Inc., 923 F.2d 506 (7th Cir. 1991); N.L.R.B. v. Evans Plumbing Co., 639 F.2d 291 (5th Cir. 1981).

[176] See N.L.R.B. v. Cont'l Hagen Corp., 932 F.2d 828 (9th Cir. 1991).

[177] Brock v. Rusco Indus., Inc., 842 F.2d 270 (11th Cir. 1988), cert. denied, 488 U.S. 889 (1989).

[178] E.g., E.E.O.C. v. Rath Packing Co., 787 F.2d 318 (8th Cir.), cert. denied, 479 U.S. 910 (1986).

[179] S.E.C. v. First Fin. Grp., 645 F.2d 429 (5th Cir. 1981).

[180] E.g., In re Cash Currency Exch., Inc., 762 F.2d 542 (7th Cir. 1985); Missouri v. U.S. Bankr. Court for the E.D. of Ark., 647 F.2d 768 (8th Cir. 1981), cert. denied, 454 U.S. 1162 (1982).

[181] 230 F.3d 65 (2d Cir. 2000).

massive securities fraud and ordered to disgorge $75 million. Brennan responded by filing chapter 11 and moving millions of dollars in assets to off-shore havens. The SEC, in turn, obtained an order in federal district court directing Brennan to repatriate the assets to the registry of the court, to be held while the New Jersey bankruptcy court sorted out how those assets should be handled in the pending bankruptcy case.

The Second Circuit held that the repatriation order constituted the "enforcement of a money judgment" and therefore violated the stay. Up through the moment of the entry of the $75 million judgment, the SEC unquestionably was acting squarely within its police and regulatory powers and was not stayed. For the Second Circuit majority, however, once the money judgment had been entered, anything beyond that point necessarily constituted the impermissible enforcement of that money judgment. Fixing liability, the court said, did vindicate the public interest; once liability was fixed, however, "the government necessarily acts only to vindicate its own interest in collecting its judgment. Except in an indirect and attenuated manner, it is no longer attempting to deter wrongful conduct. It is therefore no longer acting in its 'police or regulatory' capacity."[182]

Judge Calabresi dissented, emphasizing that the repatriation order did not enhance the government's recovery prospects vis-à-vis other creditors, since the order only brought the assets back into a U.S. court, where those assets could be distributed to the entire body of creditors in accordance with the bankruptcy law's distribution scheme.[183] In his view, the "exception to the exception" should only be read to prohibit the government acting as a creditor from getting the jump on competing creditors. For the Second Circuit majority, the focus instead was on whether the government's action was necessary to vindicate public policy.[184]

The question of whether the action is being brought by a "governmental unit" sometimes arises. In cases involving administrative agencies, the courts uniformly find the requirement met. The issue gets more difficult when the plaintiff is a private entity acting in the role of a "private attorney general" to enforce some public law. The Seventh Circuit held that a private person who brought a motion for sanctions under Rule 11 qualified as a "governmental unit" on a private attorney general theory.[185] Other courts have not been willing to take that step, however.[186]

Normally a bankruptcy court is free to enjoin an action that is excepted from the stay under § 362(b). In the area of governmental regulatory powers, however, other federal statutes sometimes may prohibit the entry of injunctions. For example, a

---

[182] Id. at 73.

[183] Id. at 78–79 (Calabresi, J., dissenting).

[184] It is also worth noting an important undercurrent that could have affected the court's decision. Prior to obtaining the repatriation order in the federal district court, the SEC had sought such a repatriation order from the bankruptcy court itself, which that court had denied. The Second Circuit thus was dealing with the spectre of another court interfering with the bankruptcy court's administrative control of estate property.

[185] Alpern v. Lieb, 11 F.3d 689 (7th Cir. 1993).

[186] See In re Revere Copper & Brass, Inc., 29 B.R. 584 (Bankr. S.D.N.Y.), aff'd, 32 B.R. 725 (S.D.N.Y. 1983) (Clean Water Act).

bankruptcy court may not enjoin a labor strike.[187] In *MCorp*, the Supreme Court pointed out that the courts lacked injunctive power under the Financial Institutions Supervisory Act.[188]

§ 3.13   Retroactive Perfection

One of the primary applications of the automatic stay is to stop the creation, perfection, or enforcement of liens against property of the estate, § 362(a)(4), or against property of the debtor to the extent the lien secures the payment of a prepetition claim, § 362(a)(5).[189] Otherwise, unsecured creditors could enhance their standing vis-à-vis the remaining pool of unsecured creditors by achieving secured status.

In some situations, however, the broad stay of § 362(a)(4) and (5), if left unqualified, would actually operate to make certain creditors *worse* off than they would have been outside of bankruptcy. Such a result would run counter to the purposes of the stay, which is meant only to preserve the status quo and maintain the place of creditors in the chain of distribution as of the time of the bankruptcy filing. The problem arises when a creditor could perfect a lien outside of bankruptcy with retroactive effect, i.e., when the creditor's perfected status would be good against competing prior lien creditors. Section 362(b)(3) provides an exception to the stay of § 362(a)(4) and (5) to allow such a creditor to perfect its lien postpetition without hindrance by the automatic stay.

Two other sections of the Code, § 544(a) and § 546(b), bear directly on the issue. Section 544(a), called the "strong-arm" power, gives the bankruptcy trustee the right to "avoid" (set aside) certain interests that are unperfected or unrecorded as of the time the bankruptcy case is commenced.[190] For example, a creditor holding an unperfected security interest in property of the debtor when bankruptcy is filed will lose its security interest and will be relegated to the ranks of unsecured creditors. § 544(a)(1). The trustee is given the status of a "lien creditor," UCC § 9–102(a)(52)(C), 11 U.S.C. § 544(a)(1), and a lien creditor usually takes priority over a security interest that is unperfected. UCC §§ 9–317(a)(2). The trustee is also accorded the status of a bona fide purchaser of real property, and as such will normally be able to avoid an unrecorded real property interest. § 544(a)(3).

Non-bankruptcy law, however, recognizes some exceptions where a lien creditor or bona fide purchaser would not defeat an unperfected or unrecorded interest as of a particular point in time. These exceptions share a common feature: they accord *retroactive effect* to the perfection or recordation of the lien or interest, which is good against intervening parties. Section 546(b) recognizes the validity in bankruptcy of such non-bankruptcy retroactive perfection rules. The most common of these non-bankruptcy retroactive perfection rules are for purchase money security interests in personal property and for mechanics' and materialmens' liens.

---

[187]   E.g., In re Crowe & Assocs., Inc., 713 F.2d 211 (6th Cir. 1983).

[188]   H.R. Rep. No. 95–595, 95th Cong., 1st Sess., at 426 (1977).

[189]   See § 3.5.

[190]   See §§ 6.3, 6.4.

An example involving a purchase money security interest will illustrate the point. Assume that on March 1 Creditor loans Debtor $5,000 to enable Debtor to buy a machine, Debtor uses the money to buy the machine, and Debtor signs a security agreement giving Creditor a security interest in the machine. Creditor's security interest "attaches" on March 1, UCC § 9–203(a), (b), but will not be perfected until Creditor files a financing statement. UCC §§ 9–310(a). As mentioned above, normally a "lien creditor" (which includes the bankruptcy trustee) will take priority over an unperfected security interest in collateral. § 9–317(a)(2). However, as the holder of a "purchase money security interest," UCC § 9–103(a), Creditor is afforded a grace period of 20 days to perfect its security interest and still maintain priority in the collateral over any lien creditors whose rights attach in the interim. UCC § 9–317(e). Thus, if Creditor perfects by filing a financing statement by March 21 (20 days after March 1), it will defeat any lien creditors who acquire their lien status between March 1 and March 21. In effect, once Creditor perfects (if by the 20–day deadline of March 21), its perfected status is deemed to "relate back" to the time its security interest first attached—here, to March 1.

What happens, however, if the Debtor files bankruptcy after March 1 and before March 21, and before Creditor has filed a financing statement to perfect its security interest? As of the time Debtor files bankruptcy, Creditor has not yet perfected, and thus is vulnerable to losing its security interest under § 544(a)(1). However, as explained above, under non-bankruptcy law (the UCC), Creditor should have until March 21 to perfect. If Creditor does perfect by March 21, its perfection will relate back to March 1, prior to bankruptcy, and thus will be immune from attack under § 544(a)(1). Section 546(b)(1) gives effect to that non-bankruptcy right. The problem, however, is that § 362(a)(4) by itself would stay Creditor from perfecting its security interest. Section 362(b)(3) saves the day for Creditor in this situation, by permitting Creditor to go ahead and perfect its security interest notwithstanding the stay. Without § 362(b)(3), § 546(b) would be a dead letter, and creditors with retroactive perfection rights outside of bankruptcy would lose those rights if bankruptcy intervened.

The application of § 362(b)(3) and § 546(b) is not limited to purchase money security interests; any non-bankruptcy law which permits perfection with retroactive effect is covered. As noted above, one common example is mechanics' and materialmens' liens.[191] In those cases, state law usually allows a mechanic who has performed work or a materialman who has provided materials to file a notice of lien within a statutory grace period thereafter, with the perfection of the lien then relating back to the time the services were performed or the materials supplied. State environmental liens to secure cleanup costs also may provide for retroactive priority.[192]

Note that § 362(b)(3) also permits the maintenance or continuation of liens that have previously been perfected. For example, a secured creditor can continue perfection in collateral under Article 9 of the UCC by filing a continuation statement. UCC § 9–

---

[191] See, e.g., In re Yobe Elec., Inc., 728 F.2d 207 (3d Cir. 1984).

[192] See, e.g., In re 229 Main St. Ltd. P'ship, 262 F.3d 1 (1st Cir. 2001); In re Perona Bros., Inc., 186 B.R. 833 (D.N.J. 1995).

515(d), (e). The automatic stay will not prevent the filing of a continuation statement. However, § 362(b)(3) only permits acts to perfect a lien or maintain perfection; it does not permit a secured creditor to enforce a lien. Such enforcement would be an improper interference with property of the bankruptcy estate. Relief from the stay must still be obtained before enforcement will be allowed.

Section 362(b)(3) also applies to permit a creditor to take acts to perfect a transfer within the grace period allowed by § 547(e)(2)(A). Section 547 governs the avoidance of preferential transfers, and subsection (e) speaks to the time when a transfer is deemed to be made. The timing of the transfer is important both to determine whether the transfer was made within the preference period and whether the transfer was made on account of an antecedent debt. Under (e)(2)(A), a transfer is deemed made when it became effective between the transferor and transferee, if it is perfected within a 30–day grace period. If bankruptcy is filed during the running of that 30–day grace period, § 362(b)(3) will allow the creditor to perfect its interest and thus perhaps to avoid preference liability. Note, however, that the creditor still might be exposed to avoidance of its interest under the strong-arm clause of § 544(a).

§ 3.14　Other Exceptions

The exceptions to the stay for criminal actions, police power activities, and retroactive perfection just scratch the surface of the statutory list of actions excluded from the reach of the automatic stay. Section 362(b) has proven to be one of the more fertile areas for special interest legislation in the Code. After the passage of the 1994 Amendments to the Code, a total of 18 separate provisions graced § 362(b). With the 2005 amendments, the number of stay exceptions had grown yet again, totaling 28 as of 2008. Three-fourths of these have been added since 1978, and several of the original exceptions have been expanded as well.

Two of the exceptions merit comment here, those relating to domestic relations issues, § 362(b)(2), and activities by taxing authorities, § 362(b)(9). As to the former, a fundamental policy of our federal system has been a position of presumptive noninterference in domestic relations issues, resolution of which is vested almost exclusively in the states. The federal bankruptcy law does have a number of provisions that bear on domestic relations questions, but those statutes usually adopt a "hands off" approach. In other words, for the most part a debtor cannot circumvent his obligations under state domestic relations laws by filing a bankruptcy case. Debts for domestic support obligations are not dischargeable, § 523(a)(5), a prohibition that applies in chapter 13 cases as well, § 1328(a)(2). Even property settlement debts are nondischargeable. § 523(a)(15). Furthermore, the debtor's exempt property may be liable for alimony and support debts. § 522(c)(1). A debtor may not avoid a judicial lien that secures domestic support obligations even if that lien impairs an exemption. § 522(f)(1)(A).

This deferential approach to state domestic relations issues is reflected in the exclusions from the automatic stay in § 362(b)(2). Perhaps most significantly, a creditor is not stayed from "the collection of a domestic support obligation[193] from property that

---

[193]　Defined in § 101(14A).

is not property of the estate." § 362(b)(2)(B). The family debt creditor is stayed from collecting against property of the estate; as to that property, the creditor must wait with all other creditors for a pro rata distribution of estate assets in the bankruptcy case. In the meantime, however, the creditor is free to pursue the debtor's assets, which the debtor obtains either by exemption, abandonment, or from postpetition earnings. Recall that such a debt is excluded from discharge, § 523(a)(5), and may be enforced against exempt property, § 522(c)(1). Expedition in collection may be necessary to avoid hardship to the debtor's ex-spouse or to the debtor's children. Since collection is limited to non-estate assets, other creditors of the debtor are not prejudiced.[194]

Numerous domestic relations actions are excepted from the stay. The 2005 amendments in particular greatly expanded the number of domestic relations matters excluded from the bankruptcy stay. Indeed, after 2005 probably a safe rule of thumb is to assume a domestic relations matter probably is not affected by bankruptcy. The additional domestic relations stay exclusions include:

- the commencement or continuation of civil[195] actions or proceedings:

  - To establish paternity, § 362(b)(2)(A)(i);

  - To establish an order for domestic support obligations, or to modify an existing order, § 362(b)(2)(A)(ii);

  - Concerning child custody or visitation, § 362(b)(2)(A)(iii);

  - For the dissolution of a marriage as long as it does not determine the division of property that is property of the estate, § 362(b)(2)(A)(iv);

  - Regarding domestic violence, § 362(b)(2)(A)(v).

- a number of methods to facilitate collection of domestic support obligations; several of these reference the Social Security Act (title 42, § 666):

  - Withholding of income that is property of the estate or property of the debtor for payment of a domestic support obligation, § 362(b)(2)(C);

  - Withholding or revoking a license, § 362(b)(2)(D);

  - Reporting overdue support, § 362(b)(2)(E);

  - Intercepting a tax refund, § 362(b)(2)(F);

  - Enforcing a medical obligation, § 362(b)(2)(G).

---

[194] H.R. Rep. No. 95–595, 95th Cong., 1st Sess., at 343 (1977).

[195] The modifier "civil" was added in 2005. Criminal actions are of course already excepted from the stay under § 362(b)(1). See § 3.10.

Another important stay exception affects tax collection. Some latitude in the automatic stay is afforded to taxing authorities by § 362(b)(9). The breadth of the exception was expanded considerably in the 1994 Amendments. Now the government is permitted to take most of the preliminary steps necessary to the fixing of a tax liability against the debtor and the imposition of a tax lien on the debtor's property, but still may not complete the tax collection process without relief from the stay. Thus, the government is allowed to:

- conduct an audit to determine tax liability, § 362(b)(9)(A);

- issue a notice of tax deficiency, § 362(b)(9)(B);

- make a demand for tax returns, § 362(b)(9)(C); and, finally,

- to make an assessment for any tax and issue a notice and demand for payment of the assessment, § 362(b)(9)(D).

Under this latter provision the government will not have a tax lien attach to property by reason of the assessment unless (1) the debt in question is not dischargeable (under § 523(a)(1)) and (2) the affected property is that of the debtor, not of the estate. Allowing the government to make a tax assessment during the pendency of the bankruptcy case will be advantageous in chapter 11, where the plan must provide for full payment of a priority tax claim within five years after the date of the bankruptcy order for relief. § 1129(a)(9)(C). The provision permitting the government to issue the notice of tax deficiency fulfills the precondition to the debtor's ability to bring a proceeding in Tax Court. Note, however, that relief from the stay must be obtained to proceed with a Tax Court action. § 362(a)(8).

The government's ability to collect tax debts was further facilitated in the 2005 amendments by the addition of § 362(b)(26), which allows the government to set off a tax refund with respect to a pre-bankruptcy taxable period against a prepetition tax liability. Even if the applicable nonbankruptcy law does not allow a setoff because the tax liability is still being contested, under subsection (b)(26) the government can hold the tax refund, rather than turn it over, pending the resolution of the tax liability.

The many, many remaining (and ever-growing) exceptions typically address very specific special interest matters. A number of these were added in 2005 as part of a larger package of amendments addressing particular problems. Some of the new exceptions may be quite important in the narrow realm in which they operate, but are not of consuming interest in a general study of bankruptcy. Those interested can consult § 362(b) as well as, where applicable, the legislative history to the 2005 amendments[196] to learn more about the exceptions for:

- setoffs under various sophisticated financial contracts, including commodity contracts, forward contracts, or securities contracts (§ 362(b)(6)); repurchase agreements (§ 362(b)(7)); swap agreements (§ 362(b)(17)); and master netting agreements (§ 362(b)(27)). Note that

---

[196] H.R. Rep. No. 109–31 (pt. 1), 109th Cong., 1st Sess. (2005).

the court does not even have the power to issue a stay with regard to actions covered by these provisions, see § 362(o);

- foreclosure of mortgages by HUD (§ 362(b)(8)), or of ship mortgages (§§ 362(b)(12), (13));

- actions to retake possession of leased premises, either with regard to expired nonresidential real property leases (§ 362(b)(10)); or to residential leases, either where the lessor obtained a judgment for possession prior to bankruptcy (§ 362(b)(22)) or where the property is endangered or there is illegal use of controlled substances (§ 362(b)(23));

- presentment and dishonor of a negotiable instrument, § 362(b)(11);

- accreditation and licensing of an educational institution (§§ 362(b)(14), (15)), and the participation of such institutions in guaranty programs, (§ 362(b)(16));

- the creation or perfection of statutory liens for ad valorem property taxes that come due postpetition, § 362(b)(18);

- withholding and collection of a debtor's wages under a pension plan, to the extent the amounts withheld are used for payment of certain loans, § 362(b)(19);

- acts to enforce liens, in cases involving abusive serial filings (§§ 362(b)(20), (21));[197]

- unavoidable transfers, § 362(b)(24);

§ 8.1 actions by securities self-regulatory organizations to enforce their regulatory powers, § 362(b)(25); and

- exclusion of the debtor from participation in Medicare and other federal health care programs, § 362(b)(28).

D. TERMINATION OF STAY AND RELIEF FROM STAY

§ 3.15   Automatic Termination under § 362(c): The Basic Provisions

The automatic stay is not intended to be permanent. Its function is to preserve the status quo on a temporary basis, during the pendency of the bankruptcy case, in order to permit the collective proceeding to go forward in an orderly manner. The stay will terminate automatically under § 362(c), by operation of law, when the reason for its existence no longer applies. In addition, a creditor may obtain relief from the stay from the court at earlier time under § 362(d), if an appropriate showing is made.[198]

---

[197] See § 3.16.

[198] See § 3.17.

Section 362(c) is divided into four subsections. Until 2005, there were just two: subsection (1) governs when the stay terminates with respect to acts against property of the estate, and subsection (2) controls the expiration of the stay as to all acts other than those affecting estate property. This section addresses the original provisions for automatic termination, subsections (1) and (2).

Subsections (3) and (4) were added in 2005 to handle serial filings and discourage bad faith repeat filings.[199] Subsection (3) deals with debtors who have filed one prior bankruptcy case in the year before the current bankruptcy, while subsection (4) is concerned with debtors who have filed more than one prior bankruptcy case in the previous year (other than a case refiled under a chapter other than chapter 7 after dismissal under section 707(b)[200]). Another "termination" provision (§ 362(h)) speaks to the situation where the debtor either fails to file or perform a statement of intention with respect to personal property collateral as required by § 521(a)(2). Finally, 2005 also saw the introduction of a rule negating the stay in small business cases where a prior case was dismissed in the prior two years. § 362(n). The following section of the book examines those provisions, and related 2005 amendments, in more detail.[201]

For acts against property of the estate, the stay will continue in effect until that property ceases to be property of the estate. § 362(c)(1). This rule helps to implement the bankruptcy court's exclusive jurisdiction over estate property. The stay will remain in effect for estate property even after the expiration of the time limits spelled out in (c)(2), as long as that property remains in the estate.[202] Acts against property of the estate that are stayed are spelled out in § 362(a)(?) (the enforcement of judgments against that property), § 362(a)(3) (any act to obtain possession of or to exercise control over estate property), and § 362(a)(4) (any act to create, perfect, or enforce a lien against property of the estate).

Property may pass out of the estate in a variety of ways. The property may be abandoned (§ 554), sold (§ 363), or exempted (§ 522). A word of caution must be raised, however. If the property passes out of the estate and then to the debtor, the stay still may be in force. Recall that prepetition judgments may not be enforced against the debtor, § 362(a)(2), and a creditor may not take any act to create, perfect, or enforce a lien that secures a prepetition claim against the debtor's property. § 362(a)(5). Property could pass from the estate to the debtor if the property is abandoned, since the normal rule is that abandoned property revests in the entity that had the possessory interest prior to bankruptcy. Thus, a secured creditor would not be able to foreclose a lien on collateral if the trustee abandoned the encumbered property, because the (a)(5) stay would still be in effect. Relief from the stay under § 362(d) still would have to be obtained. Similarly, if the debtor exempts property, the stay may still be in effect.

For all acts other than those affecting property of the estate, the stay will terminate automatically at the earliest of the time when the case is closed, dismissed,

---

[199] H.R. Rep. No. 109–31 (pt. 1), 109th Cong., 1st Sess., at 69 (2005).

[200] This exception to the rule in subsection (4) was added in 2010. See Pub. L. No. 111–327, 124 Stat 3557.

[201] See § 3.16.

[202] See In re Pace, 159 B.R. 890 (B.A.P. 9th Cir. 1993), aff'd in part, 56 F.3d 1170 (9th Cir. 1995).

or the debtor's discharge is either granted or denied. § 362(c)(2). If the case is dismissed, of course, there is no reason to continue the bankruptcy stay. Otherwise, the earliest time when the stay is likely to terminate is when the discharge decision occurs. That determination normally occurs before the case is closed. Note that in chapter 7 cases the automatic termination only occurs for individual debtors; the (c)(2) rule would not make any sense for corporate or partnership debtors, who cannot receive a discharge. § 727(a)(1). In chapter 7 cases, objections to discharge must be filed early in the proceeding, within 60 days after the first meeting of creditors. If no objection is filed, the court "shall forthwith" grant the discharge. Rule 4004.

This early automatic termination of the stay under § 362 does not mean, however, that creditors then have carte blanche to resume collection efforts as to prepetition debts. Once the discharge is granted, a permanent statutory injunction against the collection of discharged debts goes into effect.[203] § 524(a). Thus, at no point in time may creditors attempt to collect discharged debts: until the discharge decision is made, the § 362 stay operates; thereafter, the § 524 stay is in effect. However, if the court denies the debtor's discharge under § 727(a), the stay will terminate and creditors may attempt to collect their debts. Recall, though, that creditors may not go against estate property as long as that property remains in the estate.

One question that has arisen is whether the stay terminates as to a specific debt when a creditor obtains a determination from the bankruptcy court that the particular debt is not dischargeable under § 523(a). The statutory language in § 362(c)(2)(C) provides that the stay terminates when "a discharge is granted or denied." A number of bankruptcy courts have concluded that the plain meaning of that language is that the stay only terminates if the discharge is denied generally under § 727(a), and not when only a particular debt is excepted from the discharge under § 523(a). The Sixth Circuit held otherwise, however, deciding that a creditor did not violate the stay when it garnished the debtor's bank account after the bankruptcy court held that the debt was nondischargeable under § 523(a)(2).[204] The court saw no reason to make the creditor wait to collect from non-estate assets.

In rehabilitation cases, the discharge may be entered at a much later stage of the case than in chapter 7. In chapter 11 cases involving corporate or partnership debtors, the confirmation of the reorganization plan discharges prior debts. § 1141(d)(1). Confirmation may not occur, however, for many months or even years after the filing of the case. In chapters 12 and 13, and in chapter 11 cases involving individual debtors, the discharge normally will not be entered until the debtor completes performance under the plan, or obtains a hardship discharge excusing nonperformance. §§ 1141(d)(5), 1228(a), (c), 1328(a), (c). Thus, the stay will remain in effect during the entire time the debtor is performing under the plan. Note also that in chapter 12 (§ 1207(a)) and 13 cases (§ 1306(a)) as well as chapter 11 cases involving individual debtors (§ 1115(a)), the estate includes property acquired postpetition and postpetition earnings of the debtor during this time period, and the stay against acts affecting property of the estate therefore will be in effect as well.

---

[203] See § 10.31.

[204] In re Embry, 10 F.3d 401 (6th Cir. 1993).

§ 3.16   Combating Abusive Serial Filings

The very characteristic that makes the automatic stay so effective and useful—its automatic self-executing nature—also invites abuse. Debtors figured out long ago that they could use the stay to frustrate a particular creditor's exercise of state-law remedies.[205] In particular, debtors have been able to stop repeatedly—effectively indefinitely—a mortgagee's attempts to foreclose on a particular piece of real property, and a landlord's attempts to evict a residential tenant. And they can do this without having to suffer through a full bankruptcy case.

How do debtors manage this trick? Simple, really. A debtor facing foreclosure on his home files what is called a "face sheet" petition, which contains the minimum information necessary to trigger a bankruptcy case. Once the petition is filed, the stay goes into effect, automatically, instantaneously, and good against the world. Under § 362(a)(4), the mortgagee's foreclosure action is stayed immediately. For a "good faith" debtor, who needs bankruptcy relief, this dramatic legal consequence is seen as a positive good, and indeed as a cornerstone of our bankruptcy system. But what if the debtor is in "bad faith," and has no intention of going through with the bankruptcy case? Assume that the debtor does not file schedules or take any other action necessary to prosecute his bankruptcy case to conclusion. The case then will be dismissed in due course. But the bad faith debtor does not care about the dismissal; that debtor got what he wanted—the initial benefit of the automatic stay, which stopped the foreclosure. Being "automatic," the stay cannot distinguish between good faith and abusive debtors. All who file a petition got the benefit of the automatic stay. Under state foreclosure law, the mortgagee will have to start over, beginning anew the foreclosure proceedings. What then? Once the foreclosure gets close to fruition, after the running of statutorily mandated time periods and such, the abusive debtor simply files another "face sheet" petition, to the same effect, and the sequence repeats itself, possibly in perpetuity. Obviously, something must be done to counteract such abusive serial filings.

The 1984 amendments first tried to combat abusive serial filings, in § 109(g).[206] Under that provision, an individual or family farmer debtor is conclusively precluded from being an "eligible" bankruptcy debtor if he was a debtor in a bankruptcy case pending within the preceding 180 days that "was dismissed by the court for willful failure of the debtor to abide by orders of the court, or to appear before the court in proper prosecution of the case." § 109(g)(1). This provision will stop some of the serial filing abuses noted above, but not all. Note that this ban applies only if the *court* dismisses the case. That may take care of a bad faith debtor who initially files under chapter 7, because a debtor does not have an absolute right to dismiss a chapter 7 case. However, a debtor *does* have an absolute right to dismiss under chapter 13, § 1307(b) (as long as the case had not previously been converted to chapter 13 from another chapter), so a debtor could evade the reach of § 109(g)(1) simply by filing under chapter 13, and then himself voluntarily dismissing the case. *See* § 1307(b). To prevent that

---

[205] See Laura B. Bartell, Staying the Serial Filer—Interpreting the New Exploding Stay Provisions of § 362(c)(3) of the Bankruptcy Code, 82 Am. Bankr. L.J. 201 (2008); Kimberly L. Nelson, Abusive Filings: Can Courts Stop the Abuse Within the Confines of the Bankruptcy Code?, 17 Emory Bankr. Dev. J. 331 (2000); Final Report of the Bankruptcy Foreclosure Scam Task Force, 32 Loy. L.A. L. Rev. 1063 (1999).

[206] See discussion of § 109(g) in § 2.3.a.

abuse, § 109(g)(2) also imposes a 180–day eligibility ban if a debtor voluntarily dismisses his case after a creditor files a motion for relief from the stay. A diligent mortgagee, then, whose pending foreclosure is frustrated by a debtor's bankruptcy filing, should file a motion for relief from stay as soon as possible. Then, if the debtor dismisses the case, that debtor will be ineligible for bankruptcy relief for 180 days, and the mortgagee can try to complete foreclosure in that time period.

Clever debtors continued to find ways to frustrate creditors, notwithstanding § 109(g), so the 2005 amendments enacted a number of additional provisions designed to curb abusive serial filings. Even if a debtor were not "eligible" under § 109(g), most courts have held that a filing by such a debtor is not a jurisdictional defect, and that means that the debtor still gets the benefit of the stay, even if only for a short while— which is all the debtor needs to make the mortgagee start over in foreclosure. To counter this problem, in 2005 Congress enacted § 362(b)(21)(A), which creates a new stay exception, so that a bankruptcy petition filed in violation of the 180–day refiling bar of § 109(g) does not give rise to an automatic stay at all.

The refiling ban of § 109(g) will not always apply. The bankruptcy court has the power (under the majority view) to dismiss the first case "with prejudice" and judicially impose a ban on refiling under § 349(a) in addition to anything dictated by § 109(g).[207] In that situation, another stay exception added in 2005, § 362(b)(21)(B), provides that no stay goes into effect if the debtor files a subsequent petition "in violation of a bankruptcy court order in a prior case . . . prohibiting the debtor from being a debtor in another case."

Congress also added two provisions for automatic termination of the stay in 2005 in serial filing cases. These rules further complement § 109(g) and also relieve the bankruptcy court of the need to enter a dismissal with prejudice in the original case. First consider newly enacted § 362(c)(3). That section applies if an individual or joint debtor's chapter 7, 11, or 13 case was commenced within *one year* of the dismissal of an earlier case. The section applies even if the new filing is involuntary. Nor are there any limitations such as those found in § 109(g). If case #1 was dismissed within the preceding year, then § 362(c)(3) is triggered in case #2 filed within the year. The only exception is if case #1 was dismissed under § 707(b) (the "abuse" provision[208]), and then refiled under another chapter after dismissal.

This new rule adds bite to the requirement in § 109(h) that an individual debtor get prepetition credit counseling in order to be eligible for bankruptcy relief. Assume that a debtor files a case without getting the required prepetition credit counseling under § 109(h), and thus has his case dismissed on the ground that he is an ineligible debtor. That debtor then gets the required counseling, and (within a year) tries again, filing a new bankruptcy case. Section 362(c)(3) will apply in the new case.[209]

---

[207] See § 2.18.

[208] See § 2.15.

[209] See § 2.3.b. This feature of the 2005 law has prompted some judicial anger at the harshness of that law. See, e.g., In re Sosa, 336 B.R. 113 (Bankr. W.D. Tex. 2005).

If § 362(c)(3) is triggered, then the automatic stay in the second case will terminate by operation of law *30 days* after the petition filing, § 362(c)(3)(A), unless the court specifically finds, after motion by a party in interest (presumably the debtor), that case #2 was filed in "good faith." § 362(c)(3)(B). The court must hold the hearing within the 30–day period, and must find good faith by "clear and convincing evidence." If the court so finds, then it can continue the automatic stay in effect "as to any or all creditors." In essence, § 362(c)(3) reverses the burden of going forward from normal stay practice, establishing as a default rule that the stay will terminate at the 30–day mark unless the debtor obtains a ruling to keep the stay in effect.

In practice under § 362(c)(3), it will be of paramount importance to identify what constitutes "good faith." Congress spelled out a detailed set of presumptions, identifying various circumstances that would *not* be "good faith." § 362(c)(3)(C)(i)–(ii). If a presumption arises, the debtor has the burden of rebutting that presumption by clear and convincing evidence. The presumption of "not in good faith" as to all creditors is triggered if any of the following apply:

- more than one case involving the debtor was pending in the prior year, § 362(c)(3)(C)(i)(I);

- a previous case was dismissed within the 1–year period based on the debtor's failure to file necessary documents, even if that failure was inadvertent, unless caused by the debtor's attorney's negligence, § 362(c)(3)(C)(i)(II)(aa);

- a previous case was dismissed after the debtor failed to provide adequate protection as ordered by the court, § 362(c)(3)(C)(i)(II)(bb);

- a previous case was dismissed after the debtor failed to perform the terms of a confirmed plan, § 362(c)(3)(C)(i)(II)(cc);

- there has not been a substantial change in the debtor's financial or personal affairs since the dismissal of the next most previous case, § 362(c)(3)(C)(i)(III);

- it does not appear that the new case under chapter 7 will be concluded with a discharge, § 362(c)(3)(C)(i)(III)(aa); or

- it does not appear that the new case under chapter 11 or chapter 13 will be concluded with a confirmed plan that the debtor will fully perform, § 362(c)(3)(C)(i)(III)(bb).

Furthermore, a presumption of "not in good faith" as to a particular creditor is triggered if that creditor had filed an action in the prior case (most likely for relief from the stay) and that action was either still pending or had been resolved by some form of stay relief. § 362(c)(3)(C)(ii). Under this provision, apparently, if the creditor and debtor agree to an adequate protection order after the creditor files for relief from stay, and the case is then dismissed, if the debtor refiles within a year then the stay presumptively will terminate as to that creditor after 30 days. The debtor can only keep the stay in effect by proving his good faith by clear and convincing evidence. That is a pretty big stick to give secured creditors.

If the subsequent case is filed on the heels of *two* dismissals within the previous year [and, as added in 2010, unless the case was refiled under a chapter other than chapter 7 after dismissal under § 707(b)], § 362(c)(4)(A)(i) provides that the "stay . . . shall not go into effect upon the filing of the later case." In the 2–dismissal situation under subsection (c)(4), there is no 30–day grace period, as there is in the 1–dismissal case under subsection (c)(3). The starting point in the 2–dismissal case is *no stay at all.* Rather, the only way a stay will *ever* go into effect is if a party in interest (i.e., the debtor) files a request within 30 days and at the hearing proves that the new case was filed in "good faith." § 362(c)(4)(B). Even if the court so orders, the stay is only effective from that point forward, § 362(c)(4)(C), suggesting that the court does not have the power to retroactively impose the stay. Thus, if the creditor can complete foreclosure before the court can rule on the debtor's "I filed in good faith" motion, then the creditor wins, and there is nothing the debtor can do about it. As was the case with subsection (c)(3), under subsection (c)(4) Congress lists a slew of circumstances (essentially mirroring those under subsection (3)) that will trigger a presumption that the new case was not filed in good faith. § 362(c)(4)(D).

Creditors who want comfort that the draconian provisions of § 362(c)(3) or (c)(4) really are operative in their favor in a particular case can get a confirmatory order from the court that the stay has terminated. § 362(j). See also § 362(c)(4)(A)(ii). With such an order in hand, the creditor can complete a foreclosure sale with peace of mind.

The 2005 amendments also enacted a provision for automatic dismissal of "face sheet" petitions. If an individual debtor fails to file financial schedules, statements, and certificates required by § 521(a)(1) within 45 days after the petition date, the case will be *automatically* dismissed on the 46th day.[210] § 521(i)(1). The debtor may request up to an additional 45 days to file such information and thereby prevent automatic dismissal, but must justify that extension to the court's satisfaction. § 521(i)(3). Even if the debtor fails to file the required documents, the court has the power to prevent automatic dismissal on a request by the trustee, if (1) the best interests of creditors would be served by administration of the case (e.g., because the debtor's estate has substantial nonexempt assets) and (2) the debtor attempted in good faith to provide evidence of all employer payments received within 60 days before the petition date. § 521(i)(4). If a case is automatically dismissed for failure to file required information, the court must enter an order confirming the dismissal upon request of any party in interest "not later than 7 days after such request." § 521(i)(2).

Another provision combating serial filings was added in 2005 in "small business" cases. § 362(n). If § 362(n) is triggered, then the stay "does not apply." A "small business" case is a defined term, see §§ 101(51C), (51D), applying to debtors who are engaged in commercial or business activities (other than owning or operating real property) with total debts of no more than $2,490,925 (indexed as of April 2013) and where there is no unsecured creditors committee. Congress identified four situations where the serial filing stay bar would apply in the small business context:

- the debtor is a debtor in another pending small business case, § 362(n)(1)(A);

---

[210] See § 2.5.c.

- the debtor was a debtor in a small business case that was dismissed in the preceding two years, § 362(n)(1)(B);

- the debtor was a debtor in a small business case in which a plan was confirmed in the preceding two years, § 362(n)(1)(C); or

- the debtor acquired substantially all of the assets or business of a small business debtor otherwise covered in the three preceding subsections, unless the debtor can prove it acted in good faith and not for the purpose of evading the serial filing bar, § 362(n)(1)(D).

If the present case was filed involuntarily against the debtor, the bar of § 362(n)(1) does not apply, unless the debtor acted collusively with the petitioning creditors. § 362(n)(2)(A). For voluntary cases, the only way a debtor who falls within the ambit of subsection (n)(1) can avoid the bar of that section and enjoy the benefit of a stay is to prove to the court that the current filing was due to unforeseeable circumstances beyond the debtor's control, § 362(n)(2)(B)(i), *and* it is more likely than not that the court will confirm a feasible plan—and not a liquidating plan—within a reasonable time. § 362(n)(2)(B)(ii).

In Rem Stay Relief

Even the detailed and extensive "serial filing" rules just discussed can be evaded by what is known as the "fractional interest transfer" scheme. The way this scheme works is that a homeowner facing foreclosure transfers small fractional interests in the home to numerous other people. One of those people (Debtor #1) will then file a "face sheet" bankruptcy petition, staying (even if only briefly) foreclosure of that person's small fractional interest in the home. While the interest as to which foreclosure is stayed may be small, the impact is not. Since the mortgagee now cannot transfer 100% ownership of the home in a foreclosure sale, effectively *all* of the foreclosure proceedings are stopped. Nor would it help to ban or limit the effect of any bankruptcy refiling by Debtor #1. Debtor #2 could then step up and do the same thing, and then Debtor #3, and on and on—indeed, there would be a virtually endless supply of transferee-debtors available, in succession, to stop the foreclosure proceedings through subsequent bankruptcy filings.

The courts devised a response to the fractional interest transfer scheme, known as *in rem* stay relief, in which they would enter an order that limited the effect of any future stays, as against the *property*, rather than with respect to any particular debtor. Then, whoever filed, the prior *in rem* order would vitiate the stay. The 2005 amendments expressly validated this practice in § 362(d)(4). This provision allows relief from the stay of an act against real property if "the filing of the petition was part of a scheme to delay, hinder, or defraud creditors," involving either (A) transfer of any interest in the real property without the consent of the secured creditor, or (B) multiple bankruptcy filings affecting the same real property. The remedy is critical: if stay relief is granted under subsection (d)(4), and if the stay relief order is recorded in the appropriate public records for the giving of "notices of interests or liens in real property," then the stay relief order "shall be binding in any other case under this title purporting to affect such real property filed not later than 2 years after" the *in rem* stay relief order. Furthermore, a stay exception in § 362(b)(20) makes explicit that during this 2–year period, a bankruptcy filing by *any* person will not stay "any act to enforce any lien against or security interest in . . . such real property," unless the debtor in the subsequent case obtains "relief from such [*in rem*] order based upon changed circumstances or for other good cause shown, after notice and a hearing."

§ 3.17   Introduction to Relief from the Stay under § 362(d)

Automatic termination of the stay under § 362(c)(1) and (2)[211] provides a useful default rule. In practice, however, creditors with a security interest in collateral held by a debtor in possession or trustee are rarely content to bide their time and wait until the bankruptcy case runs its course to seek recourse to their collateral. In chapter 11 cases in particular, the stay could remain in effect for a very long time before it would terminate by operation of law under § 362(c). Creditors and other affected parties need not wait for automatic termination. A stayed creditor may ask the bankruptcy court for earlier relief from the automatic stay upon proof of one of the grounds specified in § 362(d). Stay relief motions are one of the most common forms of litigation under the entire Bankruptcy Code. Most of those actions involve a secured creditor seeking stay relief so that it may foreclose on its collateral.

The grounds for relief from the stay reflect a carefully considered congressional attempt to balance fairly the interests of the secured creditor against the goals of the bankruptcy proceeding. The secured creditor's interest is to realize as much as it can on its collateral as quickly as possible. However, absolute protection of that interest often might prevent full realization of the potential benefit of the bankruptcy proceeding. This tension is seen most clearly in a chapter 11 reorganization case. In chapter 11, the usual hope is to reorganize the debtor's business in order to capture the full going concern value of that business for creditors and stockholders and also to preserve jobs. If a secured creditor is allowed to repossess and foreclose on collateral that is indispensable to the debtor's business, the policy in favor of reorganization will be undermined.

Assume, for example, that the secured creditor holds a security interest in the inventory of a debtor toy store. If the secured creditor is allowed to repossess and sell that inventory, the debtor probably will be out of business and any chance of reorganization will be lost (and some children may have a less than merry Christmas). And yet, the secured creditor has a legitimate interest in realizing on the value of its security interest in that inventory. The desire to foster the debtor's chances for reorganizing should not come at the expense of the secured creditor.

The resolution of this tension is found in § 362(d). Congress and the Supreme Court have recognized that the secured creditor has a property interest in collateral that is deserving of protection, both under the Fifth Amendment and as a matter of policy.[212] But, the Court has only recognized the secured creditor's interest in receiving

---

[211] See § 3.15.

[212] H.R. Rep. No. 95–595, 95th Cong., 1st Sess., at 339 (1977) (citing Wright v. Union Cent. Life Ins. Co., 311 U.S. 273 (1940), and Louisville Joint Stock Land Bank v. Radford, 295 U.S. 555 (1935)). See also United States v. Sec. Indus. Bank, 459 U.S. 70 (1982). See generally Charles J. Tabb, Credit Bidding, Security, and the Obsolescence of Chapter 11, 2013 U. Ill. L. Rev. 103 (2013).

the *value* of its collateral, rather than the exact rights for which it originally bargained. That the creditor might be delayed in receiving that value, or might have to reap that value through alternative procedures, has been held not to be objectionable.

Two fundamental premises drive the stay relief decision with regard to secured creditors. First, relief will be granted if no bankruptcy policy necessitates interfering with the secured creditor's non-bankruptcy right to repossess and foreclose.[213] § 362(d)(2). In other words, there must be a good bankruptcy reason to keep the stay in place. Second, even if there is a legitimate bankruptcy interest to be served by staying the secured creditor from exercising its rights—such as promoting the chance for a successful reorganization—relief from the stay still will be granted if the secured creditor's interest in the collateral is not "adequately protected." § 362(d)(1). In a sense, then, the secured creditor's interest is given precedence.

The full extent of that precedence depends on the exact meaning of *"adequate protection,"* a term of art in the Bankruptcy Code that is dealt with in § 361. A fuller discussion of the meaning of adequate protection is found in the following sections.[214] Basically, adequate protection demands that the value of the secured creditor's collateral position should not be allowed to decline because of the stay. In a momentous 1988 decision, the Supreme Court held in *United Savings Association v. Timbers of Inwood Forest Associates, Ltd.*[215] that a secured creditor is not entitled to receive compensation for delay in foreclosure as part of adequate protection.[216] In this respect, the broader policy interest in promoting reorganizations is given priority over the secured creditor's interest in foreclosing expeditiously. Returning to the toy store hypothetical, adequate protection will be found if the secured creditor retains a security interest in a constant level of toy inventory (probably through replacement liens), assuming that the inventory is properly insured and maintained and that taxes are paid.

Stay relief also may be granted if no bankruptcy reason exists to keep the stay in place. This idea is embodied in § 362(d)(2), which provides that relief should be granted if (A) the debtor does not have equity in the property,[217] *and* (B) the property is not necessary to an effective reorganization. In a chapter 7 liquidation case, obviously only part (A) of this test is applicable. In chapter 7, if the debtor does not have any equity in the property, there is no reason for the bankruptcy trustee to administer the encumbered property. All of the proceeds from the sale of that property will go to the secured creditor in any event. Nothing will be left for general creditors. In such a case, the trustee should agree to an order abandoning the collateral to the secured creditor and lifting the stay to allow foreclosure.

In a chapter 11 case, however, the mere fact that the debtor lacks equity in the property does not mean that a bankruptcy purpose would not be served by keeping the stay in place. Equity in the collateral only matters if the property is being sold; in

---

[213]　See § 3.21.

[214]　See §§ 3.18–3.20.

[215]　484 U.S. 365 (1988).

[216]　See § 3.19.

[217]　See § 3.22.

chapter 11, however, the likelihood is that the debtor (as debtor in possession) will want to retain the collateral and use it in operating its business. In chapter 11 cases, stay relief will not be granted solely on a showing that the debtor lacks equity, under § 362(d)(2)(A). Proof also must be made that the property is not necessary to an effective reorganization, under § 362(d)(2)(B). If the debtor does need the collateral in order to reorganize, a bankruptcy reason exists to stay foreclosure. This is the "necessity" component of (d)(2)(B).[218] Keeping the stay in place because the debtor needs the property in order to be able to reorganize only makes sense, of course, if a successful reorganization is a realistic possibility. If it is not, the secured creditor should not be stayed any longer. This latter notion embodies the "feasibility" facet of (d)(2)(B).[219]

In the 1994 Amendments, a third ground for relief from the stay was added to deal with the special case of single asset real estate.[220] Section 362(d)(3) embodies aspects of both of the basic principles enunciated above; first, that a bankruptcy reason must support the maintenance of the stay, and second, that the secured creditor must be protected in the interim. The rules of (d)(3) only apply to a creditor whose claim is secured by an interest in "single asset real estate." § 101(51B). Under (d)(3), the court must grant relief from the stay 90 days after filing or 30 days after the court determines the debtor is subject to this subsection, whichever is later, unless one of two events occurs. First, if the debtor files a plan that "has a reasonable possibility of being confirmed within a reasonable time," § 362(d)(3)(A), relief may be denied. This rule merely makes explicit the "feasibility" test that is implicit in subsection (d)(2)(B). Second, relief may be denied if the debtor begins making monthly interest payments to the secured creditor. § 362(d)(3)(B). These payments offer some interim protection to the affected creditor.

The burden of proving the grounds for relief from the stay are divided between the movant and the party resisting relief (e.g., the trustee or debtor in possession). § 362(g). The movant has the burden of proving that the debtor does not have equity in property under § 362(d)(2)(A). On all other issues, the party opposing relief has the burden of proof. This means that the trustee or debtor in possession would have to prove adequate protection under § 362(d)(1), necessity and feasibility under § 362(d)(2)(B), and either the filing of a feasible plan or the commencement of interest payments under § 362(d)(3).

The procedures governing the resolution of a motion for relief from stay are designed to compel a quick response. Congress sought to protect secured creditors from the situation under pre-Code law where a motion for relief from the stay often would languish on the bankruptcy court's docket. Relief delayed in practice effectively may mean relief denied. To counter this problem, several procedural provisions were placed in the Code itself, which is highly unusual, because very few procedural rules are included in the Code. Section 362(e)(1) provides that the stay will terminate by operation of law 30 days after a request for relief from the stay of an act against

---

[218] See § 3.23.

[219] See § 3.24.

[220] See § 3.25.

property is filed, unless the court orders the stay continued in effect after notice and a hearing. If the court chooses to treat this initial hearing as a preliminary hearing rather than a final hearing, the court must find a "reasonable likelihood" that the party opposing relief will prevail at the final hearing. The statute goes on to require that the final hearing be concluded no later than 30 days after the conclusion of the preliminary hearing, unless the parties agree to extend the time or the court finds "compelling circumstances" requiring an extension of time. In cases where the debtor is an individual, § 362(e)(2) provides that the stay will terminate by operation of law 60 days after a request for relief from the stay. This rule will not apply if the court makes a final decision during the 60–day period. § 362(e)(2)(A). The 60–day period can be extended, either by agreement of all parties in interest, § 362(e)(2)(B)(i), or by the court for a specific period of time as is required for "good cause." § 362(e)(2)(B)(ii).

In addition, in emergency situations a creditor may obtain *ex parte* relief from the stay. § 362(f). Such relief may only be granted in order to "prevent irreparable damage" to the creditor's property interest, if "such damage" will occur if the normal time procedures are followed.

If a ground for relief is established, the Code mandates that relief be ordered, stating that the court "shall" grant relief. § 362(d). However, the court has considerable discretion in choosing the exact form of relief to award; it does not necessarily have to lift the stay completely. Instead, the relief to be granted may include "terminating, annulling, modifying, or conditioning" the stay. Thus, for example, the court may order that the stay will be lifted if the debtor does not satisfy stated conditions, such as making certain adequate protection payments, or granting designated replacement liens, or filing a plan by a set date, and so on. This flexibility permits the court to take an active role in managing the case.

If relief is denied, the game is not necessarily up for the secured creditor. A determination by the court that stay relief is not warranted at a particular stage of the bankruptcy case is not given *res judicata* effect.[221] The secured creditor is free to try again later. This tactic is common in practice. In reorganization cases bankruptcy courts often are inclined to give the debtor a chance to reorganize, and thus may deny a motion for stay relief brought early in the case. However, the same motion renewed six months or a year later may find a more receptive court, if the debtor has made little progress in the interim towards effectuating a reorganization.

Relief from the stay is not limited to cases involving secured creditors, although those cases comprise the bulk of the decisions. In other situations good "cause" may exist to lift the stay. § 362(d)(1). This may be the case in particular with regard to the stay of all proceedings against the debtor under § 362(a)(1).[222] Sometimes those proceedings have little if anything to do with the bankruptcy proceeding, other than the happenstance that the debtor is involved, and the stay should be lifted. Some examples given in the legislative history include divorce or child custody cases,[223]

---

[221] S.Rep. No. 989, 95th Cong., 2d Sess., at 54 (1978).

[222] See § 3.4.

[223] After the 2005 amendments, these two situations are now covered under 362(b)(2) and exempt from the stay. See § 362(b)(2)(A)(iii), (iv).

probate proceedings in which the debtor is the executor or administrator of the estate of another, proceedings in which the debtor is acting as a fiduciary and not in his or her personal capacity, and actions involving postpetition activities of the debtor.[224]

§ 3.18 Adequate Protection: Basic Applications

"Adequate protection" is the fundamental right bestowed on secured creditors by the Bankruptcy Code. It is through the invocation of "adequate protection" that secured creditors are enabled to insist on the recognition in bankruptcy of the value of their secured claim. See § 361. Bankruptcy does not create that secured claim, however. The nature and extent of a secured creditor's interest in collateral is established by applicable nonbankruptcy law. Thus, for example, state law will govern whether a creditor has a security interest in certain personal property, and what priority that creditor has in the collateral. State law will control the incidents of mortgages and deeds of trust in realty. The Internal Revenue Code reigns supreme over federal tax liens. But when it comes to actually *enforcing* a secured claim in bankruptcy, the bankruptcy concept of "adequate protection" controls the play of the game. At bottom, adequate protection replaces the secured creditor's nonbankruptcy *remedies* during the pendency of the bankruptcy case and defines how the creditor may preserve its secured claim for that interim period.

Adequate protection plays a central coordinating role in calibrating the treatment of secured creditors in bankruptcy cases, and the utilization of the creditor's collateral by the trustee or debtor in possession. In effect, it is the glue that holds together the multiple sections affecting the rights of a secured creditor. Several provisions of the Code are implicated. Section 363 governs the use, sale, or lease of estate property by the trustee or debtor in possession.[225] On request of the affected secured creditor who has a lien on that estate property, the court shall prohibit or condition that use, sale, or lease in order to assure that the creditor's interest is adequately protected. § 363(e). If the creditor has already repossessed the collateral prior to bankruptcy, the court may order the creditor to turn over the collateral to the trustee under § 542(a), thus enabling the estate to use, sell, or lease the property under 363—but only if adequate protection is given.[226] Meanwhile, any attempts by the secured creditor to enforce its lien are stayed under § 362(a)—but relief from the stay will be given under § 362(d)(1) unless the creditor receives adequate protection. Finally, if the estate wants to borrow money and grant the new lender a senior lien on property that is already subject to a lien, that may only be done if the subordinated lender is afforded adequate protection.[227] § 364(d).

---

[224] H.R. Rep. No. 95–595, 95th Cong., 1st Sess., at 343–44 (1977).

[225] See §§ 5.16–5.18.

[226] United States v. Whiting Pools, Inc., 462 U.S. 198, 207 (1983). Note, though, that the courts disagree on whether or not adequate protection must be given *before* (or contemporaneously with) turnover, or whether instead it suffices if adequate protection is given after turnover is made. The prevailing trend in the courts is that adequate protection need not be given at or before turnover; that is, a secured creditor who has repossessed collateral before bankruptcy must turn over the property to the debtor without first receiving adequate protection as the quid pro quo. See, e.g., Thompson v. Gen. Motors Acceptance Corp., 566 F.3d 699 (7th Cir. 2009). See §§ 5.12, 5.13.

[227] See § 11.10.c.

The concept of adequate protection rests on twin pillars. First, the Supreme Court repeatedly has recognized that a secured creditor's lien interest is an interest in property entitled to protection under the Fifth Amendment.[228] This constitutional imperative is the bedrock on which the adequate protection concept rests and the source from which it is derived.[229]

Second Congress emphasized that the principles embodied by adequate protection are not to be limited to the constitutional minimum, but reflect important considerations of bankruptcy policy. That policy is that "[s]ecured creditors should not be deprived of the benefit of their bargain."[230] Congress did not intend, though, that the secured creditor should receive the benefit of the literal and exact bargain which it could have enforced under non-bankruptcy law, because such enforcement might interfere with the realization of the goals of bankruptcy. For example, if a secured creditor were permitted to foreclose on essential collateral early in the case, an otherwise feasible reorganization might be torpedoed. The aim, then, is to provide *alternative* means of giving the secured creditor "in *value* essentially what he bargained for."[231] By doing so, the best of all possible worlds can be achieved: the reorganization is given a chance to succeed, and the secured creditor gets the value of its security.

So, what exactly *is* adequate protection, *what* is protected, and *from* what is the protection offered? Section 361 is the governing section. But no definition of adequate protection is given. Instead, three illustrative means of providing that protection are described in § 361(1), (2), and (3), discussed below. This congressional vagueness was intentional. The legislative history left the explication of adequate protection to "case-by-case interpretation and development. It is expected that the courts will apply the concept in light of [the] facts of each case and general equitable principles."[232] As one learned judge explained:

> Congress was aware of the turbulent rivalry of interests in reorganization. It needed a concept which would mediate polarities. But a carefully calibrated concept, subject to a brittle construction, could not accommodate the 'infinite number of variations possible in dealings between debtors and creditors.' This problem required, not a formula, but a calculus, open-textured, pliant, and versatile.[233]

According to the language of the Bankruptcy Code, *what* is protected by the concept of "adequate protection" is "an interest of an entity in property." § 361. In

---

[228] See, e.g., Wright v. Union Cent. Life Ins. Co., 311 U.S. 273 (1940); Louisville Joint Stock Land Bank v. Radford, 295 U.S. 555 (1935). See generally Charles J. Tabb, Credit Bidding, Security, and the Obsolescence of Chapter 11, 2013 U. Ill. L. Rev. 103 (2013).

[229] See S. Rep. No. 95–989, 95th Cong., 2d Sess., at 49 (1978); H.R. Rep. No. 95–595, 95th Cong., 1st Sess., at 339 (1977).

[230] See S. Rep. No. 95–989, 95th Cong., 2d Sess., at 53 (1978); H.R. Rep. No. 95–595, 95th Cong., 1st Sess., at 339 (1977).

[231] H.R. Rep. No. 95–595, 95th Cong., 1st Sess., at 339 (1977).

[232] Id.

[233] Bankers Life Ins. Co. v. Alyucan Interstate Corp. (In re Alyucan Interstate Corp.), 12 B.R. 803, 805 (Bankr. D. Utah 1981).

laymen's terms, in the case of a secured creditor this language refers to the creditor's security interest in the collateral. The statutory language does not fully resolve, however, the important question of what *aspects* of the creditor's "interest in property" deserve protection. At a minimum, the *value* of that interest must be preserved during the pendency of bankruptcy. In plain terms, the creditor's collateral value must be maintained.[234]

That interest must be protected *from* "a decrease in the value" caused by the imposition of the bankruptcy case, during the pendency of the case. § 361. For example, the § 362 stay may prevent immediate foreclosure, and § 363 may authorize the estate to use the collateral. Just as the automatic stay is designed to preserve the status quo for all interested parties during the life of the bankruptcy case, so too is adequate protection the creditor's temporary palliative while the bankruptcy case is in effect. Adequate protection is necessary because bankruptcy cases cannot be resolved in an instant, and in the interim rights might be adversely affected.

An example will illustrate the concept of adequate protection. Assume that Creditor has a valid security interest in a fleet of Zambonis (ice resurfacing machines, for the uninitiated), to secure a debt of $500,000. Debtor uses the Zambonis to resurface ice rinks in a region. At the time Debtor files chapter 11, the Zambonis have a value of $500,000. The Debtor is in default on its payments to Creditor, and thus Creditor would have the right outside of bankruptcy to foreclose its security interest. U.C.C. §§ 9–601, 9–610. Debtor plans to keep operating its business in chapter 11, and hopes and intends to keep using the Zambonis. Creditor requests adequate protection. How should this motion be resolved?

The baseline protection for Creditor is to maintain a value package of $500,000, the value the collateral had at the time the Debtor filed chapter 11. It is common ground that Creditor must at the very least receive adequate protection to compensate it for any *depreciation* in the value of its collateral.[235] For example, if the rate of depreciation were $5,000 per month, Creditor would have to receive adequate protection compensation of $5,000 per month for that decline. That compensation would preserve the $500,000 collateral value. If such protection were not forthcoming, Creditor would be entitled to relief from the stay to proceed with foreclosure of its security interest, and Debtor would be prohibited from using the Zambonis.

A significant preliminary difficulty should be noted: where did the figures of $500,000 in total collateral value, and a rate of depreciation of $5,000 per month come from? These initial factual determinations will largely drive the Creditor's "adequate protection." As one might perceive, reasonable people can differ over such things as the value of property and the rate of depreciation of that property. In real cases, expert testimony is utilized; indeed, these cases often boil down to "dueling experts" on the two sides.

---

[234] See United Savings Ass'n v. Timbers of Inwood Forest Assocs., Ltd., 484 U.S. 365, 372 (1988).
[235] See id. at 370.

Even the appropriate legal *standard* of valuation is left undecided. Congress intentionally chose not to require courts to use either forced sale liquidation value, on the one extreme, or full going concern value, on the other extreme.[236] Room is afforded for the parties to negotiate and for the court to invoke equitable considerations based on the particular facts of the case.

Assuming that valuation issues are resolved, the question then becomes, by what *means* will the adequate protection be effected? As noted above, § 361 describes three nonexclusive means for providing protection. First, the trustee or debtor in possession may make *cash payments* to the affected creditor. § 361(1). In the hypothetical, the amount of the payment required would be $5,000 per month, to make up for the depreciation. Note that the amount of the adequate protection payment is *not* necessarily the same as the monthly payments that Debtor would have owed to Creditor under the original terms of the loan.[237] Adequate protection is tied to changes in the value of the *collateral*, not to the amount of the *debt*.[238] Indeed, if the collateral is not depreciating in value at all, or if the collateral is worth more than the debt, it is possible that no adequate protection payment would have to be made.

A second possible means of providing adequate protection is to grant the affected Creditor additional or replacement *liens* on other collateral to make up for the decrease in value of the original collateral. § 361(2). As the Supreme Court has made clear, the secured creditor is only entitled to protection of the *value* of its collateral, not to its rights in any specific items of collateral.[239] In our hypothetical, assume that Debtor also owned real estate worth $800,000, which was subject to a single mortgage that secured a $600,000 debt. Adequate protection could be provided to the Creditor with the security interest in the Zambonis by giving it a second mortgage on the real estate. The $200,000 in equity remaining after recognition of the first mortgage would afford ample protection for Creditor for the $5,000 monthly depreciation of the Zambonis for a considerable time.

The third means of adequate protection identified in the Code is to grant the affected Creditor other, unspecified relief that will result in the Creditor realizing the "*indubitable equivalent*" of its secured interest. § 361(3). This rather quaint language is taken from Learned Hand's opinion long, long ago in the case of *In re Murel Holding Corp.*[240] As will be seen below, the adoption of this phrase perhaps caused more harm than good in the early years of the Code.[241] Be that as it may, what Congress had in mind in § 361(3) was to include in the Code a flexible catch-all provision for adequate protection that courts could invoke. An example given in the legislative history is a

---

[236] S. Rep. No. 95–989, 95th Cong., 2d Sess., at 54 (1978); H.R. Rep. No. 95–595, 95th Cong., 1st Sess., at 339 (1977).

[237] See S. Rep. No. 95–989, 95th Cong., 2d Sess., at 54 (1978) ("The periodic payments would be to compensate for the depreciation and might, but need not necessarily, be in the same amount as payments due on the secured obligation.").

[238] See *Alyucan*, supra note 233, 12 B.R. at 808.

[239] See *Wright*, supra note 228, 311 U.S. 273.

[240] 75 F.2d 941 (2d Cir. 1935).

[241] See § 3.19.

guarantee by a financially responsible third party.[242] Thus, if Warren Buffet[243] were to guarantee the payment of Creditor's secured claim, Creditor probably could cease worrying about any risk of nonpayment resulting from the $5,000 per month in depreciation.

Could the Debtor offer Creditor as adequate protection the promise of an *administrative priority* for the $5,000 a month depreciation? Under the prior Bankruptcy Act, such a result was possible,[244] and the House included the provision of an administrative priority as a means of adequate protection.[245] The Senate, however, rejected the promise of an administrative priority as a means of adequate protection "because such protection is too uncertain to be meaningful."[246] The uncertainty is whether all priority claims will be paid in full, which they occasionally are not; the secured creditor would be asked to trade the certainty of full payment out of its collateral for the hope of payment as an unsecured priority creditor. In the final compromise the Senate position prevailed.[247] Thus, § 361(3) specifically excludes the grant of an administrative priority under § 503(b)(1) as a permissible method of adequate protection.

Note that there is still one scenario in which the secured creditor could end up with a priority claim in lieu of its secured claim. That result could occur if adequate protection is provided initially, but later unfortunately proves to have been *inadequate*. § 507(b). To the extent of the inadequacy, the secured creditor is given a "superpriority" claim under § 507(b).[248] For example, in the hypothetical, assume that the Zambonis were sold for $410,000 ten months after Debtor commenced paying monthly adequate protection payments of $5,000. Creditor would have suffered an unexpected $40,000 loss: the actual loss in value of the collateral was $90,000 (a decline from $500,000 to $410,000), whereas the parties had expected and provided for only a $50,000 decline. The $40,000 shortfall would be entitled to superpriority (i.e., priority even over other second priority administrative expenses under § 507(a)(2)).[249]

The courts have struggled to give proper effect to § 507(b), which is not a model of precise draftsmanship. Among the problems with § 507(b) are that it appears to apply only if the trustee actually provides adequate protection, meaning that a creditor would be remediless if it were denied adequate protection altogether at the outset. In addition, § 507(b) seems to require as a predicate that the creditor have a claim that is independently valid as an administrative priority under § 507(a)(2) and § 503(b), raising the possibility that the creditor will not be protected if the debtor does not use

---

[242]   See H.R. Rep. No. 95–595, 95th Cong., 1st Sess., at 340 (1977).

[243]   According to Forbes, while Buffett had been the richest person in the world in 2008, when I penned the previous edition of this treatise, by late 2012 he had dropped to third place—but with $44 billion in net worth (now worth $53.5 billion as of March 2013), he's still probably a safe bet as a guarantor.

[244]   See In re Yale Express Sys., Inc., 384 F.2d 990 (2d Cir. 1967).

[245]   H.R. Rep. No. 95–595, 95th Cong., 1st Sess., at 340 (1977).

[246]   S. Rep. No. 95–989, 95th Cong., 2d Sess., at 54 (1978).

[247]   124 Cong. Rec. H11,092 (daily ed. Sept. 28, 1978) (remarks of Rep. Edwards).

[248]   See id. at H11,095.

[249]   See, e.g., In re Scopac, 624 F.3d 274 (5th Cir. 2010); Grundy Nat'l Bank v. Rife, 876 F.2d 361 (4th Cir. 1989).

the collateral at all.[250] Note also that the Code was amended in 2005, dropping § 507(b) superpriority claims behind newly established first priority claims for domestic support obligations. Now, under § 507(b), the superpriority is only over other priority claims under the now-demoted second priority, § 507(a)(2).

The catch-all provision in § 361(3) does give the court the ability to go beyond the mere provision of cash payments or replacement liens in approving the form of adequate protection that is best tailored to the situation before it. Indeed, a secured creditor would rarely be content *only* with either cash or liens, because there are other risks besides depreciation to the maintenance of the value of its security. For example, in our hypothetical, the Creditor would insist that the Zambonis be insured, that they be properly maintained and used, that all taxes be paid, and so forth. Otherwise the Creditor's collateral would be at risk.

During the first decade the Code was in place, the raging debate was whether the creditor's protectable "interest in property" under § 361 *also* included the right to immediate foreclosure. In practical terms, the issue was whether the secured creditor was entitled to compensation for the *time value* of its lien interest. This question arose in two contexts.

First, for an "*oversecured*" creditor, the issue was whether adequate protection gave the creditor the right to maintain the "*equity cushion*." The equity cushion is simply the amount by which the value of the collateral exceeds the total debt. For example, assume in our hypothetical that the Zambonis were worth $600,000, rather than $500,000, and that the debt at the time of filing was $500,000. Creditor would have an equity cushion of $100,000. As time passes, and the Creditor is stayed from foreclosing, that cushion will erode from both ends: the collateral will depreciate, and the debt will increase as interest accrues. Eventually, the cushion will disappear altogether. Does adequate protection mandate the preservation of the cushion? This question is explored in more depth below.[251] The short answer is "no," i.e., the equity cushion does not have to be maintained.

Note, however, that an equity cushion alone can serve to provide adequate protection for a limited period of time. In the hypothetical just described ($600,000 collateral value, $500,000 debt), Creditor will be fully protected and assured of full payment on its claim for several months, even if no payments, additional liens, or other "indubitable equivalents" are provided. Assuming depreciation of $5,000 per month, and interest accrual of $4,000 per month, the $100,000 cushion will not erode for eleven months. If Debtor plans to complete the reorganization process in six months, for instance, the $100,000 cushion by itself should afford Creditor adequate protection.

The second major battlefield in which the "time value" dispute was fought during the Code's first decade was in the case of an "*undersecured*" creditor.[252] In our hypothetical, assume now that the value of the Zambonis at the time of bankruptcy was $400,000, with the debt still $500,000. Now Creditor faces a shortfall of $100,000.

---

[250] See, e.g., Ford Motor Credit Co. v. Dobbins, 35 F.3d 860 (4th Cir. 1994).

[251] See § 3.20.

[252] See § 3.19.

Outside of bankruptcy, since Debtor is in default, Creditor would be entitled to foreclose right away, meaning that Creditor would gain prompt access to the $400,000. Presumably Creditor then could earn an appropriate market return on that $400,000. In bankruptcy, however, Creditor will be stayed from foreclosing, and while stayed will not be able to realize the time value of that $400,000. Does adequate protection entitle Creditor to that time value? In 1988 the Supreme Court definitively answered that question in the negative, holding in *United Savings Association v. Timbers of Inwood Forest Associates, Ltd.*[253] that an undersecured creditor is not entitled to compensation for delay in foreclosing as part of adequate protection. It is to a fuller discussion of that problem that I now turn.

§ 3.19 Adequate Protection: *Timbers* and Opportunity Cost

Perhaps the most hotly debated topic during the first decade the Code was in effect was whether adequate protection entitled an undersecured creditor to compensation for the opportunity cost incurred because of delay in foreclosing during the pendency of a bankruptcy case.[254] In substance, the undersecured creditor wanted to be paid postpetition interest, albeit computed with respect to the value of the collateral rather than the principal debt. The question assumed enormous importance in reorganization cases, where the secured creditor's principal debt and the collateral value could be quite large, and the delay suffered during the reorganization might continue for many months or even years. The issue was settled by the 1988 decision of the Supreme Court in *United Savings Association v. Timbers of Inwood Forest Associates, Ltd.,*[255] holding that adequate protection does not require the payment of opportunity costs or postpetition interest to undersecured creditors.

The basic facts in *Timbers* neatly illustrate the paradigmatic fact situation in which the issue arose.[256] The debtor operated an apartment project in Houston, Texas; the bank loaned the money and held a lien on the apartments, along with an assignment of rents. The debtor filed chapter 11 in March 1985, and the bank moved for relief from stay two weeks later, arguing that it was not adequately protected.[257] The total amount of the debt was just over $4.3 million; the value of the collateral was between $2.65 and $4.25 million, depending on whose appraiser was to be believed. The courts used the higher $4.25 million figure. The collateral was not depreciating in value; if anything, it was appreciating, if only slightly. Presumably taxes and insurance were being paid. The debtor had agreed to pay the postpetition rents from

---

[253] 484 U.S. 365 (1988).

[254] Dozens of law review articles were written on the issue. Perhaps the most heard (although ultimately unheeded) voices were those of Professors Baird and Jackson. See Douglas G. Baird & Thomas H. Jackson, Corporate Reorganizations and the Treatment of Diverse Ownership Interests: A Comment on Adequate Protection of Secured Creditors in Bankruptcy, 51 U. Chi. L Rev. (1984). Baird and Jackson argued that secured creditors should be compensated for the time value of their interests. For a sampling of other articles, see H. Miles Cohn, Protecting Secured Creditors Against the Costs of Delay in Bankruptcy: Timbers of Inwood Forest and Its Aftermath, 6 Bankr. Dev. J. 147 (1989) (Cohn represented the losing petitioning creditor before the Supreme Court); Raymond T. Nimmer, Secured Creditors and the Automatic Stay: Variable Bargain Models of Fairness, 68 Minn. L. Rev. 1 (1983); 'Note, Adequate Protection' and the Availability of Postpetition Interest to Undersecured Creditors in Bankruptcy, 100 Harv. L. Rev. 1106 (1987).

[255] 484 U.S. 365 (1988).

[256] The facts are discussed at id. at 368–69.

[257] Note that the bank did not seek relief under § 362(d)(2).

the project to the bank. Apart from the time-value/opportunity-cost issue, then, the bank was adequately protected—its collateral was safe and was not declining in value.

The bank argued, however, that it was *not* adequately protected, on the ground that it was being denied the time value of its money. Outside of bankruptcy, the bank asserted, it would have the right to proceed immediately with foreclosure of its lien. Once it had completed foreclosure, the bank would have the $4.25 million in proceeds from the sale of the collateral, which it then could reinvest and earn a market return. The market rate of return was about 12% per annum at the time. At that rate, the bank was losing $42,500 per month ($510,000 per year) due to the imposition of the automatic stay and the delay in foreclosing due to bankruptcy.

The bank argued that adequate protection under § 361 was designed to protect the secured creditor's "interest in property," and that the right to proceed with foreclosure upon the debtor's default was one of the bundle of sticks comprising the bank's "interest." That the full value of the bank's "interest" deserved protection under § 361 was underscored, the bank claimed, by the passage in the legislative history that secured creditors are to receive the "benefit of their bargain."[258] Its bargain included the right to immediate foreclosure. Not only that, the use of the term of art "indubitable equivalent" in § 361(3) connoted that adequate protection has a time value component, since the phrase was lifted from the plan confirmation setting, where it undeniably requires payment of time value. Furthermore, the bank asserted that the Bankruptcy Code as a general principle does not impose the costs of reorganization on secured creditors.

As a normative matter, the argument made in support of the view that compensation for delay should be paid[259] rested on the premise that a reorganization is run for the potential benefit of the residual claimants, *viz.*, the unsecured creditors and equity holders. Secured creditors have their collateral; they do not care about the reorganization and will not share in the upside if the reorganization succeeds. Fundamentally, then, it is unfair to burden them with reorganization costs. Furthermore, the bank argued that it was inefficient to impose reorganization costs on the secured creditors, because doing so would skew the resolution of the issue of how best to deploy the debtor's assets in favor of attempting reorganization. The reason for this inherent pro-reorganization bias is that the residual owners of the business would not have to pay all costs normally incident to the chosen asset deployment. If time-value compensation is denied, the debtor in effect has an interest-free loan for the duration of the bankruptcy reorganization. The inefficiency and inequity of denying compensation to an undersecured creditor is highlighted by the fact that a chapter 11 debtor *would* have to pay current expenses for rent, if it had leased the property instead of purchasing it, and would have to pay current debt if it were to purchase property *during* the reorganization. In effect, proponents of time-value compensation urged viewing that compensation as a form of administrative expense that should be paid in return for the use of property.

---

[258] See S. Rep. No. 95–989, 95th Cong., 2d Sess., at 53 (1978); H.R. Rep. No. 95–595, 95th Cong., 1st Sess., at 339 (1977).

[259] This position was argued most forcefully by Professors Baird and Jackson, supra note 254.

The bankruptcy court agreed with the bank's position, which reflected the growing trend in the courts.[260] The bankruptcy court conditioned the continuance of the stay on the debtor's payment to the bank of monthly payments of 12% per annum on the projected realizable foreclosure value of the collateral of $4.25 million, beginning in six months (the approximate time it would take to foreclose outside of bankruptcy). The court ruled that the postpetition rents could be applied toward this payment of $42,500 per month. The district court affirmed the bankruptcy court, but the Fifth Circuit, sitting en banc, reversed.[261]

The Supreme Court granted certiorari to resolve the split in the circuits. The Court had to determine "whether undersecured creditors are entitled to compensation under 11 U.S.C. § 362(d)(1) for the delay caused by the automatic stay in foreclosing on their collateral."[262] Affirming the Court of Appeals, the Supreme Court unanimously held that undersecured creditors are not entitled to such compensation.[263]

Writing for the Court, Justice Scalia focused on the precise meaning of the secured creditor's "interest in property" for purposes of adequate protection. The fundamental issue is whether the secured creditor has a protectable property interest in the right to take immediate possession of the collateral and foreclose.[264] If it does, then obviously compensation must be paid if the secured creditor is restrained and delayed from exercising that property right.[265] Justice Scalia began by noting that the term "interest in property" does not normally conjure up the idea of "right to immediate foreclosure," but acknowledged that such a meaning is at least conceivable.[266] Viewed in isolation, then, the phrase lacks a dispositive "plain" meaning.

That ambiguity is clarified, however, by consideration of the rest of the Bankruptcy Code. Justice Scalia observed that "[s]tatutory construction is a holistic endeavor."[267] The other terms of the Code affecting the rights of a secured creditor pointed the Court emphatically towards the conclusion that time-value compensation is not provided for undersecured creditors.

First, the term "interest in property" is used elsewhere in the Code, including in § 506(a), where it defines the amount of a creditor's allowed secured claim. In that context, the term obviously means the value of the creditor's lien *without* taking into account the right to immediate foreclosure. The Court thought it likely that the same term would have the same meaning in § 361 as well.[268]

---

[260] The leading case at the time requiring payment of time value to undersecured creditors was *In re Am. Mariner Indus., Inc.*, 734 F.2d 426 (9th Cir. 1984).

[261] 808 F.2d 363 (5th Cir. 1987), aff'd, 484 U.S. 365 (1988).

[262] *Timbers*, supra note 255, 484 U.S. at 369.

[263] Id. at 382.

[264] See Charles Jordan Tabb & Robert M. Lawless, Of Commas, Gerunds, and Conjunctions: The Bankruptcy Jurisprudence of the Rehnquist Court, 42 Syracuse L. Rev. 823, 835 (1991).

[265] *Timbers*, supra note 255, 484 U.S. at 370–71.

[266] Id. at 371.

[267] Id.

[268] Id. at 371–72.

This suspicion was raised almost to a certitude by consideration of the Code's rules governing the allowance of postpetition interest on claims. The general rule is that creditors are denied postpetition interest. § 502(b)(2). Secured creditors are expressly excepted from this general rule *only* to the extent that they are *over*secured.[269] § 506(b). To grant an *under*secured creditor postpetition compensation for lost time value would in essence have the same economic effect as allowing interest. Doing so would render the Code's carefully drawn postpetition interest rules largely superfluous. The Court found such an outcome "implausible even in the abstract, but even more so in light of the historical principles of bankruptcy law," which denied postpetition interest to undersecured creditors.[270] Allowing a *de facto* interest claim for undersecured creditors also would be structurally inconsistent with § 552, which recognizes a secured creditor's lien against property acquired postpetition only in the limited circumstance in which that property represents proceeds or rents of the prepetition collateral.[271]

The Court also found persuasive the interaction between § 362(d)(1) and (d)(2), and stated that the bank's proffered reading "makes nonsense" of the latter.[272] Under § 362(d)(2), stay relief is warranted if the debtor lacks equity in the property (subsection (A)), and the "property is not necessary to an effective reorganization" (subsection (B)). Justice Scalia opined that giving relief from the stay to an undersecured creditor under § 362(d)(1) simply because of the lack of equity and the nonpayment of postpetition interest "renders § 362(d)(2) a practical nullity and a theoretical absurdity."[273] The occasion to prove the necessity of the property to an effective reorganization would disappear, except in cases where the secured creditor's collateral was not depreciating and the creditor was being paid postpetition interest, but still wanted to foreclose. The Court could not imagine "why Congress would want to provide relief for such an obstreperous and thoroughly unharmed creditor."[274]

On this point, the Court may have misperceived the focus of § 362(d)(2). The question under that section is not *why* relief should be given to the secured creditor, but *why not*. Outside of bankruptcy the creditor would have the right to foreclose on the debtor's default. Section 362(d)(2) asks if there is a bankruptcy reason to interfere with the creditor's non-bankruptcy law entitlements. If the debtor has no equity, and if the property is not needed for an effective reorganization, there is no such reason, and foreclosure should be allowed, irrespective of whether the creditor is harmed or not.

One of the most significant passages in the Court's opinion with respect to the practical impact of the decision came in dictum in connection with the Court's musings about the application and role of § 362(d)(2). Given its holding that a chapter 11 debtor did not have to pay anything to undersecured creditors for the privilege of delay, the Court apparently felt the need to rebut the charge "that undersecured creditors will face inordinate and extortionate delay."[275] The answer came in the Court's perception

---

[269] See § 7.31.

[270] *Timbers*, supra note 255, 484 U.S. at 372–74.

[271] Id. at 374.

[272] Id. at 374–75.

[273] Id. at 375.

[274] Id.

[275] Id.

(or perhaps admonition) that bankruptcy courts can, do and should aggressively manage their chapter 11 cases, and light a fire under debtors to move the case forward to conclusion.[276] Interpreting the provision in § 362(d)(2)(B) regarding whether the "property is necessary to an effective reorganization," the Court suggested that the showing required is "that the property is essential for an effective reorganization *that is in prospect*."[277] In other words, the debtor must prove that there is "a reasonable possibility of a successful reorganization within a reasonable time."[278]

The Court found the bank's remaining arguments unpersuasive as well. The reference to "indubitable equivalent" in § 361(3) does not require payment of interest, as the bank suggested, just because that term is also used in the plan confirmation context, where interest undeniably is mandated. The Court explained that the contexts are different; rights are finally fixed on confirmation, whereas adequate protection is only a temporary measure. Furthermore, interest is required at confirmation not because of the "indubitable equivalent" phrase, but because of the language in § 1129(b)(2)(A) requiring the calculation of the present value of the stream of payments to the secured creditor as of the "effective date" of the plan.[279]

Nor did the Court agree that the Code contained a "general principle" excusing secured creditors from having to bear any of the costs of the reorganization.[280] It is true that administrative expenses do not have priority over secured claims, and cannot be paid out of the secured creditor's collateral.[281] § 506(c). But, the Court explained, "[t]hat secured creditors do not bear one kind of reorganization cost hardly means that they bear none of them."[282] Instead, the Court reaffirmed the continuing validity of the general historical approach to the treatment of secured creditors, whereby postpetition interest is allowed only to the extent the creditor is oversecured. Under pre-Code law, undersecured creditors did not receive compensation for lost opportunity costs. The Court implicitly ratified this partial allocation of reorganization costs to secured creditors, largely ignoring in the process the normative arguments outlined earlier that it is unfair and inefficient to cast those burdens onto secured creditors.

The Court found the legislative history insufficient to countermand the statutory language, the structure of the Code, and the history of non-compensation.[283] The bank relied almost entirely on the "benefit of their bargain" language in the House and Senate Reports. Dismissing those references as "generalizations," Justice Scalia pointed out that the legislative history actually worked against the bank, since it did not contain even a hint that Congress intended to change the well-settled pre-Code law that denied compensation to undersecured creditors.[284]

---

[276] Id. at 375–76.

[277] Id. at 376 (emphasis in original).

[278] Id.

[279] Id. at 377–78.

[280] Id. at 378–79.

[281] See § 7.31.

[282] *Timbers*, supra note 255, 484 U.S. at 379.

[283] Id. at 379–82.

[284] Id. at 380.

After *Timbers*, then, a secured creditor is not entitled as part of adequate protection to compensation for lost opportunity costs resulting from a delay in foreclosure. As noted above, this outcome results in a chapter 11 debtor gaining the interest-free use of the creditor's collateral during the pendency of the reorganization. Obviously, such a benefit enhances the debtor's chances of reorganizing. At the same time, debtors must reckon with the Court's dictum that debtors must prove a "reasonable possibility of a successful reorganization within a reasonable time."[285] Bankruptcy judges, aware that secured creditors are in economic terms unquestionably being harmed by the delay ensuing from the pendency of the chapter 11 case, may be less patient with debtors, and demand a stronger showing of feasibility at an earlier stage of the case than otherwise might have been true.[286]

In some situations, the "no compensation" rule of *Timbers* will not be fully operative. For cases involving "*single asset real estate,*" stay relief will be granted unless the debtor within 90 days after the bankruptcy filing (or, if later, 30 days after the court determines that subsection (d)(3) applies) either files a feasible plan or begins making monthly interest payments.[287] § 362(d)(3). In chapter 12 cases involving family farmers, § 1205 governs the provision of adequate protection, rather than § 361.[288] Under § 1205(b)(3), the debtor may have to pay "reasonable rent" for the use of the farmland.

§ 3.20   Adequate Protection: Equity Cushion

The Supreme Court's decision in *United Savings Association v. Timbers of Inwood Forest Associates, Ltd.*[289] examined the question of whether an *under*secured creditor is entitled to compensation for the time value of money as a component of adequate protection. The Court said no. A related but factually converse situation concerns whether adequate protection entitles an *over*secured creditor to preserve its *equity cushion* during the pendency of the bankruptcy case.

An "equity cushion" is the amount (judged either in dollar or percentage terms) by which the value of the collateral exceeds the amount of the debt. For example, assume that Creditor is owed a debt of $500,000, with interest of 12% per annum. Simple interest thus is accruing at a rate of $5,000 per month. Assume further that the collateral securing the debt is valued at $600,000, and is not declining in value. Creditor has an equity cushion of $100,000 in dollar terms ($600,000 minus $500,000) and a cushion of 20% in percentage terms ($100,000 cushion versus $500,000 debt). Viewed another way, the collateral-to-debt ratio is 1.2 to 1 ($600,000 to $500,000).

The problem is this: as time elapses, interest will accrue on the debt, and the debt accordingly will get larger. To the extent the creditor is oversecured, the postpetition interest that accrues on the debt will become part of the secured claim itself.[290]

---

[285] Id. at 376.

[286] See Tabb & Lawless, supra note 264, at 838.

[287] See § 3.25.

[288] See § 13.13.

[289] 484 U.S. 365 (1988). See § 3.19.

[290] See § 7.31.

§ 506(b). Eventually, the "equity cushion" will disappear altogether. In the hypothetical, the $100,000 cushion will be gone entirely in 20 months, with interest accruing at $5,000 per month. The legal question is: may the creditor insist that postpetition interest be paid in order to prevent the cushion from evaporating? Although the equity cushion question obviously is a spiritual cousin to the *Timbers* issue, since each implicates the time value of money as applied to secured creditors in bankruptcy, the *Timbers* holding does not directly dispose of the factually distinguishable equity cushion situation.

In the early years that the Code was in place, the bankruptcy courts routinely held that secured creditors *were* entitled to adequate protection of their equity cushion. The basic theoretical justification for that result was that (1) adequate protection should afford the secured creditor the "benefit of their bargain,"[291] and (2) an integral part of that "bargain" was the equity cushion itself. In other words, the secured creditor did not just bargain for certain collateral; the creditor also bargained for the value of that collateral to remain a safe percentage above the amount of the debt.

Creditors do not want to risk any possibility of a collateral shortfall, and thus intentionally build in a margin for error. Many secured lending agreements do provide that if the amount of the debt gets "out of ratio" to the collateral value, the obligation is in default and the creditor has the right to call the loan and foreclose immediately. For example, in our hypothetical, the Creditor's agreement with Debtor might provide that if the collateral-to-debt ratio falls below 1.2 to 1, Creditor could declare a default and foreclose. Thus, with a collateral value of $600,000, any debt amount over $500,000 would be a default situation. But is this aspect of the credit agreement part of the creditor's "interest in property" that is deserving of adequate protection in bankruptcy?

The leading case that reversed the trend and rejected the view that an oversecured creditor is entitled to preserve its equity cushion as part of adequate protection was the decision of Judge Ralph Mabey in *Bankers Life Insurance Co. v. Alyucan Interstate Corp. (In re Alyucan Interstate Corp.)*.[292] In *Alyucan*, the secured creditor's collateral was valued at $1.425 million, securing a debt of just under $1.3 million on the date bankruptcy was filed. Thus, on the date of the petition, the creditor had an equity cushion of $127,000. Interest was accruing at about $8,000 per month; by the time of the hearing on the creditor's motion for relief from stay, the debt had increased by $33,000, reducing the cushion to $94,000. The collateral value was stable. If no adequate protection payments were made, the equity cushion would disappear in just under a year. The issue was whether the chapter 11 debtor had to make those postpetition interest payments. Judge Mabey said no.

The core reason that the *Alyucan* court rejected a cushion analysis was that such an approach misperceives the proper focus of adequate protection. Fundamentally, "the 'interest in property' entitled to protection is not measured by the amount of the debt but by the value of the lien."[293] If the value of the creditor's collateral position is not

---

[291] See S. Rep. No. 95–989, 95th Cong., 2d Sess., at 53 (1978); H.R. Rep. No. 95–595, 95th Cong., 1st Sess., at 339 (1977).

[292] 12 B.R. 803 (Bankr. D. Utah 1981).

[293] Id. at 808.

threatened, adequate protection is not necessary. The pro-cushion courts, by comparison, included the right to maintain a certain collateral-to-debt ratio as part of the creditor's protectable property interest.

The rationale of *Timbers*, decided seven years after *Alyucan*, is consistent with that of *Alyucan*. In each instance the basic issue is whether the secured creditor, be it undersecured or oversecured, should be protected against delay. Money does have time value. A secured creditor who is forced to wait until the close of the bankruptcy case to get its money is in an economic sense indisputably worse off than a secured creditor who gets paid at the outset of the case. The payment of postpetition interest would rectify that loss. The bankruptcy concept of "adequate protection," however, was not intended by Congress and has not been interpreted by the Supreme Court to make such amends to the delayed secured creditor. Instead, adequate protection focuses only on preservation of the value of the creditor's collateral throughout the case. The only concession made to the secured creditor with regard to the time value of money is that if the creditor is oversecured, its allowed secured claim will include postpetition interest, to the extent of the excess security. § 506(b). Apart from that express exception, however, the secured creditor must suffer the pangs of bankruptcy delay, just like all other creditors. Adequate protection for that delay is not required.[294]

§ 3.21 Stay Relief under § 362(d)(2): Overview

Relief from the stay may be granted even in cases where the creditor is adequately protected, and thus "cause" cannot be established under § 362(d)(1).[295] An alternative ground for relief from the stay, applicable *only* "with respect to a stay of an act against property," is found in § 362(d)(2). In other words, a creditor who is seeking stay relief in order to proceed with an act against property may obtain the desired relief if it proves *either* that it is not adequately protected (under (d)(1)), *or* that it is entitled to relief on the grounds stated in § 362(d)(2).

Under § 362(d)(2), two things must be established in order for the creditor to prevail. First, the creditor must prove that "the debtor does not have an equity in such property."[296] § 362(d)(2)(A). The creditor bears the burden of proof on this issue. § 362(g)(1). Second, even if the creditor does prove that the debtor lacks equity, stay relief will not be granted unless "the property is not necessary to an effective reorganization." § 362(d)(2)(B). The party opposing stay relief, who typically would be either the trustee or, in a reorganization case, the debtor in possession, bears the burden of proof under § 362(d)(2)(B). § 362(g)(2). In effect, if the creditor can prove the debtor's lack of equity, the burden shifts to the debtor in possession or trustee to justify continuance of the stay on the ground that the estate needs to retain the collateral in order to be able to successfully reorganize. This second test itself has two components:

---

[294] See, e.g., Orix Credit Alliance, Inc. v. Delta Res., Inc. (In re Delta Res., Inc.), 54 F.3d 722 (11th Cir. 1995).

[295] See §§ 3.18–3.20.

[296] See § 3.22.

first, that the debtor actually *needs* the collateral in question;[297] and second, that a successful reorganization is *feasible*.[298]

The emphasis in subsection (1) of § 362(d) is on whether the interests of the creditor are being unfairly put at risk by the continuation of the bankruptcy case. In subsection (2) of § 362(d) the focus is exactly the opposite. Here, a valid reason must be given for interfering with the creditor's nonbankruptcy rights. The right the creditor usually is interested in enforcing is the right to foreclose its lien. The reason for continuing to stay the creditor from foreclosure could be that some equity could be realized in the property, or it could be that the property will aid in the achievement of a successful rehabilitation. Absent either justification, though, the stay should be lifted, and the creditor should be allowed to go forward with foreclosure.

Section 362(d)(2) was designed specifically "to solve the problem of real property mortgage foreclosures of property where the bankruptcy petition is filed on the eve of foreclosure."[299] In its application, though, § 362(d)(2) extends to a request for relief from stay with respect to an act against any type of property, real or personal. For example, a creditor with a security interest in personal property could invoke § 362(d)(2).

§ 3.22   Stay Relief under § 362(d)(2): Lack of Equity in the Property

The first element that must be established for a secured creditor to obtain relief from the stay under § 362(d)(2) is that the "debtor does not have an equity in such property." § 362(d)(2)(A). The creditor who is seeking relief bears the burden of proof on the equity issue. § 362(g)(1).

The rationale behind this test is that a bankruptcy purpose would be served by denying the creditor relief from stay if the debtor has equity. If the bankruptcy trustee were to sell the property in which the debtor has equity, by definition there would be something left over for the estate. This surplus then could either be distributed to the general creditors of the estate, in a liquidation, or used by the debtor in its business, in a reorganization. Indeed, in a reorganization the debtor could simply retain the property and provide the secured creditor with adequate protection. Accordingly, it is worth having the trustee (or debtor in possession) conduct the sale (or forgo the sale), in order to enhance the likelihood of maximizing the return to the estate. If the sale were left to the secured creditor, by comparison, that creditor would have no incentive to attempt to obtain a sale price over and above the creditor's own debt. Having the trustee conduct the sale will not harm the fully secured creditor, who will be paid in full.

How is the issue of the debtor's equity computed? A simple mathematical comparison must be made between:

(1)   the value of the *debtor's interest* in the property,

---

[297] See § 3.23.

[298] See § 3.24.

[299] 124 Cong. Rec. H11,092–93 (daily ed. Sept. 28, 1978) (remarks of Rep. Edwards).

and

(2) the total dollar value of *all liens* on the property securing claims against the
     debtor.

If (1) is greater than (2), the debtor has equity, and the creditor cannot get stay relief
under § 362(d)(2). However, if (2) is greater than (1), then the movant creditor has
successfully carried its burden of proof under subsection (d)(2)(A), and will be entitled
to stay relief if it also prevails under subsection (d)(2)(B).

An example will illustrate the point. Assume that Debtor has Property, which has
a value of $100,000. Creditor One has the senior lien against the Property, securing a
debt of $80,000. Creditor Two has a junior lien against the Property, securing a debt of
$30,000. Creditor One moves for relief from the stay. Is § 362(d)(2)(A) satisfied? The
answer is yes. The two secured debts of $80,000 and $30,000 together total $110,000
and thus are greater than the $100,000 value of the Property. Debtor has no equity in
the Property. If Creditor can also win under subsection (d)(2)(B), it will get stay relief.
If, however, the Property were valued at $120,000, for example, Debtor would have
equity, and Creditor would lose its stay relief motion under subsection (d)(2).

Note that equity is computed from the perspective of the *debtor*, not from the
perspective of the creditor who is petitioning for relief.[300] Indeed, under the original
hypothetical, as to Creditor One, there is equity of $20,000 ($100,000 value versus
$80,000 debt). That, however, is not the point of subsection (d)(2). Concerns about
protecting the creditor are addressed in subsection (d)(1). Indeed, the $20,000 cushion
above Creditor One's debt would be relevant to establishing that Creditor One was
adequately protected.[301] Instead, the focus under subsection (d)(2) is to ask if it would
be of any benefit *to the estate* to keep the stay in place, and if the *debtor* has no equity,
the answer is no, for the reasons explained above.

Law students tend to share a misconception that a debtor must have "equity" in
property to the extent that the debtor has made payments on the secured debt. Wrong.
Not true. Why not? The reason this logic is fallacious is that it ignores the facts (1) that
the value of the collateral may have declined and (2) that interest will have accrued on
the debt, in a combined amount that exceeds the amount of payments made. A debtor
who puts $1,000 down to purchase property, and makes principal payments of $4,000,
will not have any equity if the property has declined more than $5,000 in value. Also, it
is possible that the property may have become encumbered by other liens, including
involuntary liens such as judicial liens or tax liens.

In the hypothetical above, a value of $100,000 for the property was assumed. As
one might imagine, in the real world arriving at the proper valuation of property is not
so easy. Each party will bring their own expert appraiser in to testify, and the

---

[300] See, e.g., In re Dowding, 124 Fed. Appx. 921 (6th Cir. 2005); Nantucket Investors II v. California
Fed. Bank (In re Indian Palms Assocs.), 61 F.3d 197 (3d Cir. 1995); Stewart v. Gurley, 745 F.2d 1194 (9th
Cir. 1984).

[301] See, e.g., In re Mellor, 734 F.2d 1396 (9th Cir. 1984); In re Indian Palms Assocs., Ltd., 61 F.3d 197
(3d Cir. 1995).

bankruptcy judge will have to weigh the competing evidence (sometimes they simply split the difference!). The Code does not even specify a particular standard of valuation that courts must apply in every instance. The only statutory guidance is in § 506(a)(1), which vaguely admonishes courts to determine value "in light of the purpose of the valuation and of the proposed disposition or use of such property, and in conjunction with any hearing on such disposition or use . . . affecting such creditor's interest." The legislative history emphasizes that the bankruptcy court should not always adopt either a forced sale liquidation value or a full going concern value; rather, the court should assess the equities of the particular case in determining how to allocate the difference between the polar extremes.[302]

One modification in the approach to valuation of property was made in 2005. If the debtor is (1) an individual; (2) the case is under chapter 7 or chapter 13; and (3) the property is personal property, then the value of the creditor's secured claim is based on "replacement value" (as of the date of the petition), "without deduction for costs of sale or marketing."[303] § 506(a)(2). The intent was to give the secured creditor the benefit of the higher replacement value, rather than a lower liquidation value. While using a higher valuation does benefit a secured creditor if a debtor is trying to keep property by paying off the secured creditor (either pursuant to a reorganization plan or by redemption), the secured creditor actually might be worse off in the stay relief context. The reason that this amendment could hurt a secured creditor moving for relief under § 362(d)(2) is that if the collateral has a higher valuation, that accordingly increases the possibility that the debtor will have equity, thus defeating the stay relief motion under subsection (d)(2)(A).

In making the valuation assessment (under § 506(a)(1), where the court still enjoys discretion), courts tend to give considerable weight to the "proposed disposition or use" of the property. As just discussed, if § 506(a)(2) applies, courts must use replacement value. Otherwise, though, they remain free to value property under the broader guidelines of subsection (a)(1). How do courts exercise this discretion in practice? If the property will be sold, there is a greater tendency to use a liquidation value.[304] If, however, the debtor plans to retain the property and use it in its business, courts gravitate more to going concern value.[305] Some concern has been expressed that valuing the property at the higher going concern level is unfair to secured creditors, because it ignores the fact that from the perspective of the secured creditor, collateral is only important if the creditor has to foreclose—in which case only the lower liquidation value will be meaningful. Forceful though that argument may be in some contexts, it forgets the point that the role of § 362(d)(2) is to ask why the estate needs to resist stay relief, not whether the creditor is protected. If the focus is on the estate's need, then it is perfectly logical to use a value that mirrors the estate's projected deployment of the collateral. Whether the creditor is adequately protected is the bailiwick of § 362(d)(1).

---

[302] See S. Rep. No. 95–989, 95th Cong., 2d Sess., at 54, 68 (1978).

[303] Furthermore, if the property is acquired for "personal, family, or household purposes," then replacement value is specified to be "the price a retail merchant would charge."

[304] See, e.g., In re McElwee, 449 B.R. 669 (Bankr. M.D. Pa. 2011).

[305] See, e.g., In re Pelham Enters., 376 B.R. 684 (Bankr. N.D. Ill. 2007); In re SK Foods, L.P., 487 B.R. 257 (Bankr. E.D. Cal. 2013)

Note that a value determination at the stay relief hearing will not be binding and given *res judicata* effect later in the case.[306] Having said that, the parties must be sensitive to the reality that judges have memories. Even if the judge is not legally bound to follow her earlier determination of value, a party arguing for a different value than it argued for earlier in the case will have to do some serious explaining to the judge. Bearing this in mind, each side has to weigh competing considerations. For the secured creditor, a low valuation might be preferred early in the case at the stay relief hearing, because a low value might help prove the debtor's lack of equity. In addition, if the property has a low value, the debtor may not be able to prove the existence of an equity cushion that would suffice as adequate protection. But, at the conclusion of a reorganization case, the secured creditor inevitably will want a high value, because the creditor is entitled in the plan to be paid the value of its collateral.

For the trustee or debtor in possession, the incentives are, of course, exactly reversed. The trustee or DIP will want a high value at the stay hearing, both to show the presence of equity under § 362(d)(2)(a) and to establish adequate protection via a cushion under § 362(d)(1). At the end of the case, at confirmation, the DIP would prefer a lower collateral valuation, thereby allowing the plan to be confirmed with lower payments to the secured creditor.

Proof by a secured creditor that a debtor lacks equity in the property is not necessarily dispositive of the lift stay issue. Even if the debtor lacks equity, stay relief will be denied if the debtor needs the property for a successful reorganization.[307] In other words, proof of a lack of equity is a necessary but not sufficient condition to obtaining relief from the stay under § 362(d)(2) in a reorganization or debt adjustment case. In a chapter 7 liquidation case, however, equity will be the only real issue, because by definition there is not going to be a reorganization.

§ 3.23   Stay Relief under § 362(d)(2): Necessity

If a party who is seeking relief from the stay under § 362(d)(2) with respect to an act against property can prove that the debtor does not have an equity in that property,[308] the requested relief will be granted unless the opponent can show that the property is "necessary to an effective reorganization." § 362(d)(2)(B). The burden of proving necessity to an effective reorganization is on the trustee (or debtor in possession). § 362(g)(2). This issue almost always arises in the context of a secured creditor's attempt to obtain permission from the bankruptcy court to proceed with foreclosure of its lien. The usual opponent is the debtor in possession in a chapter 11 case, who typically plans to retain and use the collateral in its business.

In chapter 7 liquidation cases, § 362(d)(2)(B) by definition is not in issue. If the secured creditor in a chapter 7 case proves the debtor's lack of equity, stay relief should be granted. Some question has arisen in the courts as to whether § 362(d)(2)(B) is applicable to debt adjustment cases under chapter 12 or chapter 13. Although a few decisions hold that it is not applicable, narrowly reading the reference to

---

[306] S. Rep. No. 95–989, 95th Cong., 2d Sess., at 54, 68 (1978).

[307] See §§ 3.23–3.24.

[308] See § 3.22.

"reorganization" in subsection (d)(2)(B), the majority and better view is that (d)(2)(B) does apply in chapter 12 and chapter 13 cases.[309] The debtor in those chapters normally retains possession and control of its property, and may need to use that property in order to perform under the plan. Indeed, it is even possible that § 362(d)(2)(B) will apply in a chapter 11 *liquidation*, because one form of "reorganization" that is permitted under chapter 11 is to liquidate the debtor's assets.

The test in § 362(d)(2)(B) has two components: *necessity* and *feasibility*.[310] Each spears to the larger question of whether any bankruptcy purpose would be served in forestalling the secured creditor from proceeding with foreclosure. In order to retain the benefit of the stay and keep the secured creditor at bay, the resisting debtor in possession must show *both* prongs. In other words, if the debtor fails to show either that the property is necessary or that a successful reorganization is a realistic possibility, the secured creditor should be given permission to foreclose (assuming of course proof of the "no equity" ground under subsection (d)(2)(A)).

The *necessity* prong is almost never an issue in reorganization cases. In virtually every chapter 11 case, the debtor in possession obviously needs to retain and use its property if it is to have any chance of reorganizing. While "feasibility" may be and virtually always is debated,[311] the "necessity" of the property usually is self-evident. Indeed, the very fact that the debtor in possession is opposing the secured creditor's motion for stay relief suggests rather strongly that the debtor at least believes that the property is necessary. The debtor may be mistaken, of course, and the ultimate determination of need is for the court.

In some situations, however, necessity may not be a foregone conclusion. One such case could be where the property that is subject to the creditor's lien is fungible, at least in the sense of being readily replaceable and available. To give an example, for a considerable period of time in the 1980s the available supply of oil rigs greatly exceeded the demand. Anyone who wanted an oil rig could readily obtain one, and at a substantial discount price. In such a setting, assume that a debtor has an oil rig that is subject to a creditor's security interest. Is *that* rig really necessary to the debtor? The secured creditor could make a plausible argument that the particular rig in which it has a security interest is not necessary to the debtor, and it therefore should be allowed to foreclose, because the debtor could purchase a replacement rig with no difficulty.

Notwithstanding the intuitive appeal of this reasoning, courts have not been receptive to the creditor's plea. For one thing, the debtor would incur transaction costs in replacing the rig. However, in a market glut situation, those costs might be quite small. Much more important is the fact that the debtor would have to pay real money for the new rig, and if it did not pay cash, it would have to pay interest. By comparison,

---

[309] See, e.g., In re Timmer, 423 B.R. 870 (Bankr. N.D. Iowa 2010); In re Huggins, 357 B.R. 180 (Bankr. D. Mass. 2006).

[310] Some courts have questioned whether § 362(d)(2)(B) includes a feasibility test, arguing that it should be read only to require proof of necessity. See Empire Enters., Inc. v. Koopmans (In re Koopmans), 22 B.R. 395 (Bankr. D. Utah 1982). This issue is explored in more detail in § 3.24. The overwhelmingly prevailing view, though, is that feasibility must be proven.

[311] See § 3.24.

the debtor might not have to pay current dollars for the use of the old rig. If the old rig was not declining in value, and the rig was adequately insured and maintained, the secured creditor might be adequately protected. And, under the rule announced by the Supreme Court in *United Savings Association v. Timbers of Inwood Forest Associates, Ltd.*,[312] the secured creditor would not be compensated for the cost of delay. In this light, the "necessity" of the particular rig is that it alone can qualify for the special benefits flowing from the no-compensation *Timbers* rule.

Another situation in which the secured creditor might make a cogent argument that collateral is not "necessary" to an effective reorganization is where the debtor is not planning on actually using the property in its business operations. This might be the case, for instance, if the debtor is retaining the property simply as an investment. Examples might include undeveloped land or oil and gas reserves. In such a scenario, the secured creditor could argue that there is nothing special and unique about its collateral as an investment. Other investments are available to the debtor. Nor should the debtor be able to argue that this particular investment property has a unique value—even if the property is in fact unique. Economically, if the markets are working properly, the price for which the property could be sold should fairly reflect the property's fair market value. The courts have rejected arguments by the debtor that the secured creditor would not do anything more with the property; to resist relief from the stay under § 362(d)(2), the debtor must explain why it needs the property, not how the creditor is unharmed or what the creditor would or would not do with the property.[313]

Aside from these relatively rare circumstances, however, necessity usually is easily established in a reorganization or debt adjustment case. The fighting issue in those cases is almost always over the other prong of § 362(d)(2)(B)—feasibility of the reorganization effort. It is to that question that I now turn.

§ 3.24 Relief under § 362(d)(2): Prospect of a Successful Reorganization

Relief will be granted with respect to a stay of an act against property under § 362(d)(2) if the debtor does not have an equity in the property,[314] § 362(d)(2)(A), and if the property is not necessary to an effective reorganization. § 362(d)(2)(B). Under subsection (d)(2)(B), the party opposing relief from the stay—usually the trustee or the debtor in possession—bears the burden of proving (§ 362(g)(2)) both the necessity of the property to the reorganization effort,[315] *and* that a successful reorganization is *feasible*. The latter element is examined in this section.

As a threshold matter, there has been some dispute in the courts over whether § 362(d)(2)(B) does in fact require the debtor in possession or trustee to prove feasibility at a stay relief hearing. The leading case holding that *only necessity* must be

---

[312]   484 U.S. 365 (1988). See § 3.19.

[313]   See, e.g., In re Playa Dev. Corp., 68 B.R. 549 (Bankr. W.D. Tex. 1986); In re Greiman, 45 B.R. 574 (Bankr. N.D. Iowa 1984); In re BBT, 11 B.R. 224 (Bankr. D. Nev. 1981).

[314]   See § 3.22.

[315]   See § 3.23.

established is the early Code case of *In re Koopmans*.[316] The statutory language in (d)(2)(B) arguably is ambiguous: it provides that the property must be "necessary to an effective reorganization." While a superficial glance at this phraseology might suggest that the debtor in possession must prove both that the property is "necessary" and that an "effective reorganization" is possible, a closer examination of the language reveals another possible reading—that the DIP must prove only that if a reorganization is to be effective, this property will be necessary. Indeed, the statute says nothing in § 362(d)(2)(B) about proving the likelihood that the reorganization will succeed. This congressional silence in § 362 is all the more telling in light of the fact that elsewhere in the Code Congress demonstrated that it did know how to craft a feasibility test. In § 1112(b)(4)(A), Congress specified that a chapter 11 case could be dismissed or converted to chapter 7 on proof of "substantial or continuing loss to or diminution of the estate and the *absence of a reasonable likelihood of rehabilitation.*"

Judge Mabey argued in *Koopmans* that the differences in the language of § 362(d)(2)(B) and § 1112(b) were anything but accidental. To begin with, the history of stay litigation and the evolution of § 362(d)(2)(B) in the reform process leading up to the enactment of the Code in 1978 suggest that necessity and feasibility should not be linked.[317] But even more significant, perhaps, is the difference in the roles of and procedures governing stay relief under § 362(d) and dismissal or conversion under § 1112(b).[318] The stay relief section is essentially a two-party affair, between the secured creditor and the debtor in possession (or trustee). Although notice of a stay relief motion must be served on an official creditors' committee, Rule 4001(a), the hearing generally will only involve the creditor and the debtor. The issues at the hearing will be whether the creditor is protected and whether the debtor can demonstrate a good reason to interfere with the creditor's non-bankruptcy remedies. By contrast, a motion to dismiss or convert the case under § 1112(b) must be served on *all* creditors. Rule 2002(a)(4). The noticed creditors, whose interests obviously would be directly implicated by conversion or dismissal, have a right to be heard on the matter. The issue of the debtor's reorganization prospects is fair game for all interested parties, not just the one secured creditor. Yet, if relief effectively could be granted for the same reasons at a stay relief hearing, the affected creditors would not be heard.

The "necessity only" advocates of § 362(d)(2)(B) further support their position by pointing out that the chapter 11 process is designed only to put the debtor to its proof of reorganization prospects at the *conclusion* of the case, not at the outset. In the 1978 reforms, Congress abandoned the requirement under old chapter X that the debtor make a preliminary showing to the court of good faith, which was construed to carry with it the need to prove reasonable prospects of reorganization. Under the Code, even the power to dismiss or convert under § 1112(b) will only be triggered if the debtor's absence of reorganization prospects is accompanied by "substantial or continuing loss to or diminution of the estate." The negative inference is that the case should not be dismissed solely because a reorganization may not be likely, if there is no ongoing loss.

---

[316] Empire Enters., Inc. v. Koopmans (In re Koopmans), 22 B.R. 395 (Bankr. D. Utah 1982).

[317] Id. at 397–400.

[318] Id. at 400–01.

Instead, the only time the debtor must prove feasibility is at *confirmation*.[319] See § 1129(a)(11).

Notwithstanding the considerable force of the arguments made in *Koopmans*, today the prevailing view is that the debtor in possession must prove under § 362(d)(2)(B) that there is "*a reasonable possibility of a successful reorganization within a reasonable time*." In its 1988 decision in *United Savings Association v. Timbers of Inwood Forest Associates, Ltd.*,[320] the Supreme Court approved in dictum the feasibility test of subsection (d)(2)(B) as just quoted.[321] According to the Court, "what [§ 362(d)(2)(B)] requires is not merely a showing that if there is conceivably to be an effective reorganization, this property will be needed for it; but that the property is essential for an effective reorganization *that is in prospect*."[322] In so proclaiming, the Court did not even consider the powerful arguments outlined above that would support reading subsection (d)(2)(B) to demand only proof of necessity. Instead, the Court was driven to its dictum as a means of defending its holding that an undersecured creditor was not entitled to compensation for delay during the pendency of the case. The Court's point was that the harm to the delayed creditor would not be that great, since it would not be held up for an inordinate amount of time. The Court observed that stay relief often is given within a year of the bankruptcy filing, and may even be granted in the first months of the case if there is a "lack of any realistic prospect" of reorganization success.[323]

Assuming that lower courts will follow the Supreme Court's dictum in *Timbers* and require the party opposing a stay relief request under § 362(d)(2) to prove feasibility as well as necessity, the question becomes how the feasibility test will be applied in practice. The first point of importance is that the nature and extent of the proof required of the debtor in possession will vary depending on the time frame. In chapter 11, the debtor in possession generally has the exclusive right to propose a reorganization plan for the first 120 days of the case.[324] § 1121(b). In these first few months of the case, bankruptcy courts tend to be very lenient to the debtor with regard to the quality of the proof of feasibility they will demand. Courts recognize that the debtor should be given at least some time to try to put a plan together. The Supreme Court in *Timbers* noted this tendency with apparent approval.[325] In these early days, the bankruptcy court is almost certain to give the debtor a chance; only if the court perceives that the situation is hopeless or that the filing was a bad faith attempt to forestall foreclosure will an early lift stay motion be granted. However, after the debtor has been in chapter 11 for many months, the court's patience may begin to wear thin, and the secured creditor's chances of obtaining a favorable ruling on the lift stay motion will increase steadily. At some point, the court will demand concrete and persuasive evidence of rehabilitation prospects. Note that the court's ruling against the

---

[319] See § 11.28.

[320] 484 U.S. 365 (1988). See § 3.19.

[321] 484 U.S. at 376.

[322] Id. at 375–76 (emphasis in original).

[323] Id. at 376.

[324] See § 11.15.

[325] 484 U.S. at 376.

creditor early in the case will not be *res judicata* of a later stay relief motion, because the circumstances may have changed. As a tactical matter, the secured creditor thus is not harmed by bringing a lift stay motion early in the case. Even though the court is likely to deny the motion then, the issue of the debtor's reorganization prospects will have come to the judge's attention, and when the creditor renews the motion later, the judge at the subsequent hearing might be more sensitive to the creditor's plight and less forgiving of the debtor's failure to make tangible progress towards reorganization.

What sort of evidence will be relevant to the merits of the issue of the likelihood of a successful reorganization? To begin with, the bankruptcy court will insist on some actual evidence of reorganization prospects, rather than just the debtor's unsupported and self-serving assertions of vague hopes and dreams. Courts want to see verifiable research, documentation, sensible and realistic projections, and financial analysis.[326] Beyond this, the nature of the proof may depend more on the business practicalities of the case than on legalities. Factors the court might weigh in the balance include the general state of the economy, the trends in the debtor's particular industry, market conditions, competition, the ability of debtor's management, the availability of sufficient working capital, and so forth. Remember that the debtor does not have to prove that the reorganization definitely will succeed; at this point in the case it only must establish a "reasonable possibility" of success.[327]

Whether the debtor is likely to be able to turn around its business is not, however, always the only issue regarding feasibility. A secured creditor also might be able to prevail on the feasibility issue if it can prove that *legally* the debtor will never be able to confirm a plan of reorganization. This proof could be made if the secured creditor itself has the power to veto any reorganization plan proposed by the debtor by the expedient of voting against such a plan. For example, the secured creditor might have this power if it held a controlling interest in a class and could not be "crammed down" under § 1129(b).[328] Thus, in these cases the hearing on the motion to lift the stay under § 362(d)(2) may become a sort of preliminary confirmation hearing.

§ 3.25   Stay Relief under § 362(d)(3) for Single Asset Real Estate

A third ground for relief from the automatic stay was added to the Code in the 1994 Amendments.[329] Section 362(d)(3) was added in response to the pleas of secured lenders. For years lenders had complained bitterly about what they perceived to be the abuses inflicted on them in bankruptcy cases involving "single asset real estate" ("SARE") debtors. As the name suggests, these debtors have only one major asset—real estate. For example, a limited partnership might be formed to purchase an apartment building, an office park, or the like. Often these single asset debtors are little more than investment vehicles, used to take advantage of various tax shelters. In many of the cases the secured lender is the only significant creditor. The debtor often files

---

[326] See, e.g., Pegasus Agency, Inc. v. Grammatikakis (In re Pegasus Agency, Inc.), 101 F.3d 882 (2d Cir. 1996); In re Teron Trace, No. 09–82889, 2010 WL 2025530, at *1, *8 (Bankr. N.D. Ga. Jan. 28, 2010).

[327] *Timbers*, 484 U.S. at 366.

[328] See §§ 11.30–11.34 for a discussion of cram down.

[329] Bankruptcy Reform Act of 1994, Pub. L. No. 103–394, § 218, 108 Stat. 4128 (1994).

bankruptcy on the eve of foreclosure of the lender's mortgage or deed of trust, invoking the automatic stay. The only real dispute the debtor has is with this secured lender.

Even though § 362(d)(2) was enacted in large part to deal with the problem of eve-of-foreclosure filings,[330] secured creditors found stay relief hard to obtain, with courts inclined to give the debtor a chance to reorganize. In the 1978 reforms, the Senate wanted to include a provision excluding "single asset real estate" from the property potentially necessary to an effective reorganization under § 362(d)(2)(B),[331] but that exclusion was not included in the final bill. And even worse, the creditor's relief might be delayed for many months or even years while the debtor wallowed in chapter 11.

This unpleasant situation for lenders became almost intolerable in 1988 when the Supreme Court held in *United Savings Association v. Timbers of Inwood Forest Associates, Ltd.*,[332] that an undersecured creditor was not entitled as part of adequate protection to compensation for the time value of their money lost due to bankruptcy delay. Because of *Timbers*, and because postpetition interest generally does not have to be paid, debtors did not even have to pay for the privilege of delay while they were in bankruptcy. The ability to squeeze lenders through lengthy uncompensated delays gave debtors leverage to coerce favorable reorganization agreements by lenders.

Section 362(d)(3) offers substantial succor to stayed secured creditors in single asset real estate cases. Within a few months of the petition date, in order to keep the stay in effect the debtor *either* must file a feasible plan or start making monthly interest payments. The debtor is initially given 90 days to act (or, if later, 30 days after the court determines that the debtor is subject to § 362(d)(3)). For cause shown, the debtor can obtain an extension from the court.

The feasibility prong, § 362(d)(3)(A), tracks the dictum in *Timbers* on feasibility: the debtor must file a plan "that has a reasonable possibility of being confirmed within a reasonable time." The same considerations that go into a feasibility decision under § 362(d)(2)(B)[333] should be given effect under (d)(3) as well. Thus, the debtor must offer more than vague hopes or dreams, and must present some concrete evidence of why and how the plan could work. At the same time, all details do not have to be settled; the feasibility imperative is less onerous at this early stage of the case than it would be at the time of plan confirmation, at the end of the case.

If the debtor does not file a feasible plan within the required time period, it will have to pay the secured creditor for the privilege of further delay. § 362(d)(3)(B). It is this aspect of § 362(d)(3) that alters for secured creditors the result of the *Timbers* case. If a debtor is lingering in chapter 11, the secured creditor will be entitled to be paid monthly interest. Note that the interest payments required under § 362(d)(3)(B) are calculated based on the *collateral* value, not the debt, so an undersecured creditor will not necessarily receive full interest compensation. However, the only harm to the creditor from the bankruptcy stay is based on the collateral value, for it is only that

---

[330] See 124 Cong. Rec. H11,092–93 (daily ed. Sept. 28, 1978) (remarks of Rep. Edwards).

[331] See S. Rep. No. 95–989, 95th Cong., 2d Sess., at 53 (1978).

[332] 484 U.S. 365 (1988). See § 3.19.

[333] See § 3.24.

value that the creditor could realize on foreclosure outside of bankruptcy. The rate of interest is to be pegged at the "then applicable nondefault contract rate of interest on the value of the creditor's interest in the real estate." § 362(d)(3)(B)(ii). Prior to the 2005 amendments, a "current fair market rate" of interest was used, rather than the contract rate.

The catch with regard to § 362(d)(3) is that it is not uniformly available. Only a creditor who is stayed from enforcing a lien against "single asset real estate" may take advantage of subsection (d)(3). Thus, ascertaining the meaning of "single asset real estate" assumes primary importance; indeed, almost all of the litigation under the new section has been to determine whether certain property falls within the definition. Section 101(51B) defines *"single asset real estate"* as

> real property constituting a single property or project, other than residential real property with fewer than 4 residential units, which generates substantially all of the gross income of a debtor who is not a family farmer and on which no substantial business is being conducted by a debtor other than the business of operating the real property and activities incidental thereto.

Even a casual perusal of the single asset real estate definition reveals that it is a well-spring of uncertainty and ambiguity. What does "the business of operating the real property" entail? What is a "substantial" "other" business that is not "incidental"?[334] What is a "single property or project"? In putting flesh on these unsteady statutory bones, the courts have drawn on the considerable jurisprudence that developed prior to 1994 in cases in which the "single asset real estate" red flag was raised.[335] Many single asset real estate decisions addressed whether the case should be dismissed for "bad faith."[336] The concert of "single asset real estate" came to have a fairly well-understood meaning in bankruptcy parlance.

Courts (prior to 2005) identified four criteria for SARE that inhere in the statutory definition:

> First, real property constituting a single property or project, other than residential real property with fewer than 4 residential units, falls within the scope of section 101(51B). Second, that real property must generate substantially all of the income of the debtor. Third, the debtor must not be involved in any substantial business other than the operation of its real property and the activities incidental thereto. Fourth, the debtor's aggregate non-contingent liquidated secured debt must be less than $4,000,000.[337]

These criteria, developed in cases soon after the passage of the 1994 amendment, continue to influence courts today. The only exception is that the last criteria—the $4

---

[334] See Ad Hoc Grp. of Timber Noteholders v. Pac. Lumber Co. (In re Scotia Pac. Co.), 508 F.3d 214 (5th Cir. 2007); Kara Homes, Inc. v. Nat'l City Bank (In re Kara Homes, Inc.), 363 B.R. 399 (Bankr. D.N.J. 2007).

[335] See *Scotia Pacific,* supra note 6; *Kara Homes,* supra note 334; In re CBJ Dev., Inc., 202 B.R. 467 (B.A.P. 9th Cir. 1996); In re Kkemko, Inc., 181 B.R. 47 (Bankr. S.D. Ohio 1995).

[336] See, e.g., In re Costa Bonita Beach Resort, Inc., 479 B.R. 14 (Bankr. D.P.R. 2012).

[337] In re Philmont Dev. Co., 181 B.R. 220, 223 (Bankr. E.D. Pa. 1995).

million secured debt ceiling—was repealed in 2005. Today, a debtor will qualify as a SARE no matter how much debt it has, if it meets the three remaining criteria.[338] Another 2005 amendment excluded "family farmers" from the definition.

At a minimum, Congress meant to subject passive tax-shelter type real estate investments to the stay relief rule of subsection (d)(3). Courts give great weight to whether the core of the business is a "passive" real estate investment, where the debtor simply collects income.[339] If so, it is a SARE. The seminal and oft-cited case of *In re Kkemko, Inc.*, after looking closely at the history of the passage of the 1994 law, observed, "The drafters and promulgators of § 101(51B) were working in a bankruptcy context, and we have no doubt that their intention in using the phrase "single asset real estate" grew out of the common usage of that term in bankruptcy. By it, they meant a building or buildings which were intended to be income producing, or raw land."[340]

Thus, if the debtor's only business is to collect rents from an apartment building or office park, and the property is not residential realty with less than 4 units, the special rule of § 362(d)(3) certainly will apply. Even if the debtor's only asset is undeveloped raw land, the courts generally find subsection (d)(3) applicable. A 2007 decision went so far as to hold that a debtor whose business consisted of purchasing real estate and then developing and selling single family homes and condominiums on that real estate was a SARE.[341] That decision, though, surely skates out on the thinnest interpretive ice. One could debate whether the non-passive acts of planning, developing, and selling the homes and condominiums was merely "operating the real property" and activities incidental thereto. § 101(51B). Just because the debtor's activities are based on and flow from the real estate itself does not necessarily mean that it will qualify, if the debtor is conducting a "substantial business" other than just owning and operating the real estate. Thus, a Fifth Circuit case held that a company that planned, grew, harvested, and sold timber was not a SARE.[342] The court found that the active, as opposed to passive, management of the timber operations took the debtor out of the SARE definition. Distinguishing the home development case discussed above, the court emphasized that such timber management activities could be conducted as a business independent of the ownership of the underlying real estate.

Many cases have grappled with the SARE issue when the debtor's "single asset" includes an active operating business, such as a shopping center, golf course, or hotel. Courts in such cases inevitably find that the debtor is doing more than merely

---

[338] See *Kara Homes*, supra note 334.

[339] See, e.g., In re Prairie Hills Golf & Ski Club, Inc., 255 B.R. 228 (Bankr. D. Neb. 2000) (holding that golf and ski club was not SARE because was not simply a "passive" real estate investment); see also *Kara Homes*, supra note 334; In re Club Golf Partners, 2007 WL 1176010 (Bankr. E.D. Tex. Feb. 15, 2007).

[340] *Kkemko*, supra note 335, 181 B.R. at 51.

[341] *Kara Homes*, supra note 334.

[342] *Scotia Pacific*, supra note 334.

"operating the real property and activities incidental" thereto, and will not force such a debtor to comply with the dictates of § 362(d)(3).[343] § 101(51B).

---

[343] See, e.g., In re Whispering Pines Estate, Inc., 341 B.R. 134 (Bankr. D.N.H. 2006) (hotel); In re Larry Goodwin Golf, Inc., 219 B.R. 391 (Bankr. M.D.N.C. 1997) (golf course); *Kkemko*, supra note 335 (marina).

Chapter 4

JURISDICTION AND PROCEDURE

§ 4.1   The Nature of the Problem

One of the most difficult and persistent problems Congress has faced in dealing with the bankruptcy system has been to find a workable approach to issues of jurisdiction and procedure. There are several reasons for this nagging difficulty. First is sheer volume: many more bankruptcy cases are processed in the federal court system than any other type of case. The number of bankruptcy cases has grown dramatically since the passage of the Code in 1978. Over a million new bankruptcy cases are filed every year.

Second is the unique nature of bankruptcy cases. A bankruptcy case is composed of many different types of matters and "proceedings." These proceedings range in complexity from uncontested administrative tasks to full-scale adversarial litigation. Traditional civil lawsuits of the "A versus B" variety comprise only a small portion of a typical bankruptcy "case."[1]

At one end of the spectrum of complexity of bankruptcy proceedings are routine administrative matters. These are the functions that inhere in the implementation of the bankruptcy process. Typically, these matters do not involve any litigation at all. Examples include sending notices, appointing a trustee in a liquidation case, approving the liquidation of estate property, mailing distributions to creditors, and approving a final accounting.

In the middle of the scale are the adjudications of disputes concerning "core" bankruptcy issues that arise only because of the pendency of the bankruptcy.[2] See 28 U.S.C. § 157(b)(2). Depending on the subject, these core matters may be litigated either as a "*contested matter*," Rule 9014, which often is somewhat less formal than classic civil litigation, or as an "*adversary proceeding*," Rule 7001, which is a full-blown civil lawsuit. Illustrations of contested matters include motions for relief from the stay, objections to claims, objections to exemptions, motions to sell property, and objections to confirmation of a plan. These contested matters might implicate issues only of bankruptcy law, such as a stay relief motion or a contested plan confirmation. Or, the contested matter might raise non-bankruptcy law questions, such as the merits of a creditor's claim or of the debtor's exemption under state law. Adversary proceedings on core matters include such disputes as objections to the debtor's discharge or an action to recover a preference.

---

[1]   See, e.g. Douglas G. Baird & Edward R. Morrison, Adversary Proceedings in Bankruptcy: A Sideshow, 79 Am. Bankr. L.J. 915 (2005); Rafael I. Pardo & Kathryn A. Watts, The Structural Exceptionalism of Bankruptcy Administration, 60 UCLA L. Rev. 384 (2012); Elizabeth Warren, Vanishing Trials: The New Age of American Law, 79 Am. Bankr. L.J. 915 (2005); Elizabeth Warren, Vanishing Trials: The Bankruptcy Experience, 1 J. Emp. Legal Stud. 913 (2004).

[2]   See § 4.4.

Finally, on the far end of the spectrum of the types of matters that may be heard in a bankruptcy case are those issues that are unrelated to the bankruptcy case except for the happenstance that the debtor is a party to the lawsuit, or that the outcome of the suit might affect the debtor or the bankruptcy case. In other words, these *"related matters"* or "non-core" proceedings would exist even if there were no bankruptcy case.[3] A suit brought by the bankruptcy trustee against a third party for breach of a pre-bankruptcy contract with the debtor is but one example of a related matter. These related matters are adjudicated entirely in the form of conventional civil litigation.

The challenge for Congress is threefold. First, it must identify the most appropriate forums to vest with the responsibility for handling the different types of proceedings in a bankruptcy case. Second, in allocating bankruptcy jurisdiction to these forums, Congress should seek to promote efficiency in administration and to minimize controversy and confusion over the question of forum identification. Third, the allocation of jurisdiction must comply with constitutional limits—no small matter in the wake of the Supreme Court's monumental decision in 2011 in *Stern v. Marshall*,[4] which significantly curtailed the scope of matters that could be finally adjudicated by a non-Article III bankruptcy court.[5]

The initial question is which judicial or administrative body should be responsible for processing a particular type of proceeding in the bankruptcy case. The main possible candidates to deal with the range of questions that could arise in a bankruptcy case are: (1) the state courts; (2) an administrative agency; (3) a specialized federal court that deals only with bankruptcy cases, e.g., a "bankruptcy court;" and (4) the federal courts of general jurisdiction.

The state courts are a logical forum to decide the purely state law questions that arise in a bankruptcy case. Examples include the validity of claims lodged against the debtor's estate, or exemptions claimed by the debtor. The state courts are a poor choice, however, to adjudge the numerous complex issues of federal bankruptcy law. An administrative agency could ably process the routine administrative matters, but might be less well-suited to preside over significant litigation. A specialized bankruptcy court would be able to develop expertise in deciding core bankruptcy issues, and could devote itself entirely to processing the immense bankruptcy case load. The difficulty for a specialized bankruptcy court, however, lies in handling litigation that is only tangentially related to the bankruptcy case. That difficulty became even more imposing after *Stern* was decided. That related, non-core litigation could be dealt with by the federal district courts, but those courts do not have the time or interest to do all of the bankruptcy work.

The current system has allocated parts of the jurisdictional pie to each of the aforementioned bodies, as will be discussed more fully in the following sections. In daily practice, however, the great bulk of the work in a bankruptcy case is handled by the United States Bankruptcy Court, the specialized federal forum. As will be seen,

---

[3]   See § 4.5.

[4]   131 S.Ct. 2594 (2011).

[5]   See infra § 4.2.g.

political and constitutional difficulties nevertheless have prevented complete consolidation of all bankruptcy-related issues into that single forum.

§ 4.2　History

a.　Introduction

Perhaps the most debated and most controversial aspect of the Bankruptcy Reform Act of 1978 concerned the change in the bankruptcy court system. The change effected in 1978 had a short life: in 1982 the Supreme Court struck down the new jurisdictional scheme as unconstitutional in *Northern Pipeline Construction Co. v. Marathon Pipe Line Co.*[6] For two years thereafter, the bankruptcy courts operated in a statutory vacuum under the questionable aegis of the "Emergency Rule," a model rule proposed by the Judicial Conference and adopted as a local rule by all district courts. In 1984, Congress finally responded to the *Marathon* case, instituting a revised court system in the Bankruptcy Judges and Federal Judgeship Act (BAFJA).[7] The scheme enacted in BAFJA is still in effect today, although the exact scope of a bankruptcy court's authority under BAFJA is once again in question as a result of *Stern v. Marshall*.[8] That decision struck down as unconstitutional part of the BAJFA scheme that granted bankruptcy courts the power to enter a final order as to a traditional state law cause of action brought as a counterclaim to a filed proof of claim, and not necessarily resolved in ruling on that proof of claim.[9]

b.　The Bankruptcy Act of 1898

To make sense of the bizarre saga of bankruptcy jurisdiction, some understanding of history before 1978 is necessary. Indeed, after the *Stern* decision, the importance of history is more important than ever, as it appears the Court effectively constitutionalized the jurisdictional scheme under the Bankruptcy Act of 1898. Under that prior Bankruptcy Act, a "reference" system was used. Jurisdiction over bankruptcy cases was vested in the federal district courts. However, the district courts appointed subordinate judicial officers as "referees" to handle the bulk of matters that arose in a bankruptcy case, subject to review by the district court. Reference of the entire bankruptcy case to the referee was automatic, although the district judge could "withdraw" the reference. The referee's title was changed to "United States Bankruptcy Judge" in 1973.

One major problem under the 1898 Act was that the jurisdiction of the courts of bankruptcy was limited to "*summary* jurisdiction." Bankruptcy Act of 1898, § 2a. Summary jurisdiction extended only over: (1) property in the actual or constructive possession of the bankruptcy court; (2) the debtor; and (3) persons who consented to the court's jurisdiction (popularly known as "jurisdiction by ambush"). All other matters had to be adjudicated in a non-bankruptcy federal court or state court of competent

---

[6]　458 U.S. 50 (1982).

[7]　Pub. L. No. 98–353, 98 Stat. 333 (1984).

[8]　131 S.Ct. 2594 (2011).

[9]　Id. at 2620.

jurisdiction in a *"plenary"* lawsuit. Id. § 23.[10] This divided summary/plenary jurisdictional scheme was widely condemned as cumbersome and inefficient, because it (1) prevented the bankruptcy judge with charge over the bankruptcy case from deciding many issues of importance to that case, and (2) engendered considerable preliminary litigation over which court had jurisdiction.

A second problem under the Act was that the bankruptcy judges had to perform many administrative tasks in addition to their judicial duties. This dual role was considered burdensome to the judge, and also created concerns about the judge's impartiality and objectivity. Furthermore, the subordinate position of a bankruptcy judge was not considered very prestigious, raising concerns that the most able candidates would not be attracted to the bankruptcy bench.

c.   The Bankruptcy Reform Act of 1978

The decade-long reform effort that culminated in the passage of the Bankruptcy Reform Act of 1978 addressed the problems with bankruptcy jurisdiction by:

(1)   Unifying the jurisdiction over all matters arising in a bankruptcy case in an independent bankruptcy court;

(2)   Separating the judicial and administrative functions of the bankruptcy judge; and, finally,

(3)   Enhancing the prestige of bankruptcy judges.

The not-so-good old days of splintered jurisdiction, dual roles, and second-class status were to end. In creating this independent bankruptcy court, Congress had to decide whether to make the new bankruptcy judges Article III judges, with the constitutional protections of life tenure and against diminution in salary. The constitutional question was whether an untenured non-Article III bankruptcy judge could exercise the "judicial power of the United States" to the degree contemplated by the new unified jurisdictional provisions. The issue of Article III status proved to be the shoal on which the carefully concocted 1978 scheme ultimately foundered in *Marathon*, and then again, even after supposedly being fixed in 1984, in *Stern*.

The House of Representatives undertook its own study of the constitutional question, and solicited the opinions of leading constitutional scholars. The House concluded that "the Constitution suggests that an independent bankruptcy court must be created under Article III."[11] The House also believed that making bankruptcy judges Article III judges would attract the best possible candidates. Accordingly, the House bill (H.R. 8200) constituted the bankruptcy court as an Article III court. The Senate, however, opposed giving Article III status to bankruptcy judges, an opposition encouraged by Chief Justice Burger and the Judicial Conference of the United States.[12]

---

[10]   See Ralph Brubaker, On the Nature of Federal Bankruptcy Jurisdiction: A General Statutory and Constitutional Theory, 41 Wm. & Mary L. Rev. 743, 765–90 (2000).

[11]   H.R. Rep. No. 95–595, 95th Cong., 1st Sess., at 39 (1977).

[12]   See Vern Countryman, Scrambling to Define Bankruptcy Jurisdiction: The Chief Justice, the Judicial Conference, and the Legislative Process, 22 Harv. J. on Legis. 1, 10–11 (1985).

The sitting Article III judges did not want to expand their ranks to include the bankruptcy specialists. The Senate bill (S. 2266) created the bankruptcy courts as non-Article III adjuncts of the district court. The Senate took the view that it was constitutional for "the expanded jurisdiction vested in the U.S. district courts [to] be delegated by statute for exercise exclusively by bankruptcy judges, subject always to review, as under present law, by the district courts."[13] In the end the Senate's position prevailed. Unfortunately, it turned out that the House was right and the Senate was wrong on the constitutional question. As I noted:

> Congress attempted to have its cake and eat it too. Congress had the cake by creating an independent bankruptcy court with jurisdiction over virtually all matters encompassed by the broad umbrella of a bankruptcy case. . . . Congress ate the cake by refusing to give Article III status to the new bankruptcy judges who were to exercise this pervasive jurisdiction.[14]

Section 241(a) of the 1978 Act contained the new jurisdictional provisions, which were to be codified in the Judicial Code at 28 U.S.C. § 1471. Subsections (a) and (b) initially conferred original jurisdiction over bankruptcy cases and proceedings on the district courts, but then § 1471(c) provided that:

> The bankruptcy court for the district in which a case under title 11 is commenced shall exercise all of the jurisdiction conferred by this section on the district courts.

The only role assigned to the Article III district court was to review final orders of the bankruptcy courts on appeal. The bankruptcy judges were to be appointed for 14–year terms by the President on recommendation of the circuit court councils. This new system was to be phased in over a five-year transition period.

The Senate also refused to go along with the House's plan to create a United States trustee system to handle the great bulk of administrative matters. Instead, a pilot program for United States trustees was established in a few districts. The House had the last laugh on this issue, however; legislation in 1986 finally made the United States trustee program a permanent, nationwide feature of the bankruptcy system.[15]

Notwithstanding the substantial doubts and controversy over the constitutionality of the new bankruptcy court system, few observers believed that the Supreme Court would ever actually take the drastic step of holding that system unconstitutional. The ramifications of doing so could be extreme, and the Court's Article III precedents were a hopeless maze. The optimists were proven wrong, however.

d. *Northern Pipeline Construction Co. v. Marathon Pipe Line Co.*

Northern Pipeline Construction Co. filed a chapter 11 case in Minnesota. Two months later, Northern Pipeline, as debtor in possession, filed an adversary proceeding

---

[13] S. Rep. No. 95–989, 95th Cong., 2d Sess., at 16 (1978).

[14] Charles J. Tabb, The Bankruptcy Reform Act in the Supreme Court, 49 U. Pitt. L. Rev. 477, 486 (1988).

[15] Except in Alabama and North Carolina, which use a "Bankruptcy Administrator."

against Marathon Pipe Line Co. in the Minnesota bankruptcy court, seeking over $2 million in damages based on breach of contract and other state law claims. Marathon moved to dismiss, alleging that the bankruptcy court's asserted jurisdiction under § 241(a) of the Bankruptcy Reform Act contravened the requirement of Article III that the "judicial power of the United States" be exercised by tenured judges. The bankruptcy court denied the motion to dismiss,[16] but the district court granted the motion and held that the 1978 Act's jurisdictional provisions were unconstitutional.[17] Since the United States had intervened to argue for the constitutionality of the challenged law, and the Act was held unconstitutional, appeal as of right was authorized directly to the Supreme Court.

On June 28, 1982, the Supreme Court affirmed the holding of unconstitutionality.[18] Justice Brennan wrote the plurality opinion for four Justices.[19] Justice Rehnquist concurred, and was joined by Justice O'Connor. Three Justices dissented, with the primary dissent by Justice White.[20]

The Supreme Court actually decided four matters in *Marathon*:

1.   Most significantly, the Court held that the jurisdictional provisions of the 1978 Act were unconstitutional under Article III, as applied to state law claims against a nonconsenting party.[21]

2.   The Court decided that the unconstitutional portion of the jurisdictional grant to the bankruptcy courts could not be severed from the rest of the jurisdictional provisions, which might be constitutionally valid.[22]

3.   The Court applied its holdings on the merits prospectively only,[23] thereby validating all actions taken by the bankruptcy courts during the prior three years under the 1978 Act.

4.   Finally, the Court stayed its judgment until October 4, 1982,[24] to give Congress time to cure the constitutional defect. When Congress failed to do so, the Court extended the stay again until December 24, 1982,[25] but did not grant any further extensions.

The principal issue before the Court was the constitutionality of the jurisdictional system enacted in the 1978 Act. The constitutional problem can be summarized as follows:

---

[16]   6 B.R. 928 (Bankr. D. Minn. 1980).

[17]   12 B.R. 946 (D. Minn. 1981).

[18]   458 U.S. 50 (1982).

[19]   Joining the plurality opinion were Justices Marshall, Blackmun, and Stevens.

[20]   Justice White's dissenting opinion was joined by Chief Justice Burger and Justice Powell. The Chief Justice also wrote a short separate dissent.

[21]   458 U.S. at 87 (Brennan, J., plurality); id. at 91 (Rehnquist, J., concurring).

[22]   Id. at 87 n.40 (Brennan, J., plurality); id. at 91–92 (Rehnquist, J., concurring).

[23]   Id. at 88 (Brennan, J., plurality); id. at 92 (Rehnquist, J., concurring).

[24]   Id. at 88 (Brennan, J., plurality); id. at 92 (Rehnquist, J., concurring).

[25]   459 U.S. 813 (1982).

• Article III, § 1 provides that "[t]he judicial Power of the United States" shall be vested in the Supreme Court and in such inferior courts as Congress may establish;

• Article III then provides that the judges of the Supreme Court *and* of the inferior courts "shall hold their Offices during good Behaviour, and shall . . . receive for their Services, a Compensation, which shall not be diminished during their Continuance in Office";

• The bankruptcy judges established in the 1978 Bankruptcy Reform Act did not enjoy the protections mandated by Article III; and yet

• The bankruptcy judge in *Marathon* was exercising the "judicial power of the United States" by adjudicating a state law breach of contract claim in connection with Northern Pipeline's reorganization.

Two main arguments were advanced to uphold the constitutionality of the Bankruptcy Reform Act system. The first was that the bankruptcy courts validly exercised authority as "legislative courts" or "Article I courts." The second was that the bankruptcy courts were acting only as adjuncts of the Article III district courts, and thus the command of Article III was satisfied. The Supreme Court rejected both assertions.

The "legislative courts" argument rested on the premise that Congress may invoke the authority derived from its enumerated Article I powers, together with the Necessary and Proper Clause (Article I, § 8, cl. 18), to create specialized tribunals to hear and decide matters arising within the scope of the particular Article I power.[26] Thus, pursuant to the Bankruptcy Clause (Art. I, § 8, cl. 4), advocates of the constitutionality of the bankruptcy system argued that Congress could create an Article I Bankruptcy Court to deal with bankruptcy as a "specialized area having particularized needs and warranting distinctive treatment."[27] Ever since 1828, the Court had rejected the "absolutist" view of Article III that *only* tenured federal judges could hear cases involving any part of the judicial power of the United States.[28] Indeed, as recently as 1973 the Court had held that the legislative courts rationale permitted the creation of non-Article III courts to decide cases arising in the District of Columbia.[29]

The plurality opinion rejected this reading of the legislative courts precedents, and refused to accept the principle that Congress had a broad power to create non-Article III courts pursuant to any of its Article I powers. Instead, Justice Brennan synthesized the legislative courts precedents as falling exclusively within three narrowly defined categories, in each of which an extraordinary grant of power had already been made to the legislative branch: (1) courts-martial; (2) territorial courts; and (3) public rights.

---

[26] A masterful analysis of the whole problem is presented in James E. Pfander, Article I Tribunals, Article III Courts, and the Judicial Power of the United States, 118 Harv. L. Rev. 643 (2004).

[27] Palmore v. United States, 411 U.S. 389, 408 (1973).

[28] The seminal case is *American Ins. Co. v. Canter*, 26 U.S. (1 Pet.) 511 (1828).

[29] *Palmore*, supra note 27, 411 U.S. 389.

Only the last category had any potential applicability in bankruptcy. While Justice Brennan acknowledged that in some circumstances "the restructuring of debtor-creditor relations" arguably might be classified as falling within the area of public rights, the instant case, involving nothing more than a state law breach of contract dispute, was a quintessential *private* rights matter. Accordingly, in the federal system, a tenured Article III judge had to decide that dispute.[30] The concurring opinion neither agreed with nor disputed the plurality's tidy three-category synthesis; rather, the two concurring Justices concluded simply that the present case went far beyond any of the precedents and had to be heard by an Article III judge.[31] Justice Rehnquist also noted that some matters in a bankruptcy case might be covered by the public rights doctrine, but stated that this state law breach of contract case was not one of them.

Justice White in dissent argued that the crucial question, not addressed by either the plurality or the concurrence, was "why bankruptcy courts can not qualify as Article I courts in their own right."[32] He could find no abstract principle for distinguishing between Article I courts and Article III courts, and urged the adoption of a balancing test. Under that test, Congress should weigh the values embodied by Article III against the legislative interest in creating the specialized Article I court. Justice White argued that the great volume of bankruptcy cases, the special expertise involved, the history of *de facto* delegation of bankruptcy jurisdiction to referees, and the opportunity for appellate review by an Article III court all supported his conclusion that the Court should have held that a specialized untenured bankruptcy court was constitutional.[33]

The second argument, that the bankruptcy courts were permissible "adjuncts" of the Article III district courts, fared no better. The Court's analysis on this question is extremely important, because in the 1984 corrective legislation Congress took the adjunct approach. The issue is whether the *"essential attributes of the judicial power"* are retained by the Article III tribunal. The precedents demonstrated that the Article III court does not have to retain *all* adjudicative functions in order to satisfy the constitutional command.[34]

The 1978 Bankruptcy Reform Act, however, effectively vested *all* jurisdiction over bankruptcy cases and proceedings in the bankruptcy courts. This result was achieved through a two-step scheme: first, jurisdiction was vested in the Article III district courts; but then second, the non-Article III bankruptcy courts were empowered to exercise all of that jurisdiction. The Article III district courts retained *only* the power to review final decisions of the bankruptcy court on appeal. The three dissenters believed that retention of appellate review was enough to comply with Article III.[35] The

---

[30]   458 U.S. at 71–72.

[31]   Id. at 90–91 (Rehnquist, J., concurring).

[32]   Id. at 105 (White, J., dissenting).

[33]   Id. at 113–18.

[34]   In *Crowell v. Benson*, 285 U.S. 22 (1932), the Court upheld the use of an administrative agency to make initial findings of fact with regard to admiralty employee compensation claims. In *United States v. Raddatz*, 447 U.S. 667 (1980), the Court sustained the use of magistrates to make determinations on pretrial motions.

[35]   458 U.S. at 116 (White, J., dissenting).

plurality and concurrence disagreed.[36] Having rejected that assertion, it was apparent to those six Justices that the bankruptcy court was not an adjunct of the district court at all, and thus the adjunct argument had to fail.[37] The Court did not give any guidance on what *would* be enough control by the Article III court, leaving the constitutional fate of any future congressional reforms up in the air. That lack of guidance turned out to be unfortunate, as the 1984 reforms were overturned in part in 2011 in the *Stern* case.

In dictum, the plurality went on to express doubts as to whether even a true adjunct could exercise adjudicatory functions with regard to rights that were not of congressional creation, such as the state law claims before the Court.[38] If that reasoning were to be accepted by a majority of the Court, the adjunct approach would not work in bankruptcy at all, because a large percentage of matters heard in bankruptcy are rooted in state law rights, as Justice White pointed out in his dissent.[39] Fortunately, the Court has not yet embraced this suggestion of the *Marathon* plurality. Indeed, even in *Stern* the Court did not go that far.

e. The Emergency Rule

In *Marathon Pipe Line*, the Supreme Court avoided immediate wholesale disaster and gave Congress a chance to remedy the constitutional defect by complementing its primary holding of unconstitutionality with the additional holdings (1) that the decision should operate prospectively only, and (2) that the judgment should be stayed for several months. Until corrective legislation could be implemented, then, the bankruptcy system was to continue with business as usual, in the decidedly quirky posture of cases and proceedings being decided pursuant to a scheme that had already been held unconstitutional by the Supreme Court. This odd limbo period, which supposedly was to last only three months,[40] ultimately remained in effect for over two years![41] Congress got hung up by (1) a renewed debate over whether to grant Article III status to the bankruptcy judges in order to cure the constitutional problem, and (2) the lobbying efforts of hordes of special interest groups (and especially the consumer credit industry), who sought to add their own pet bankruptcy amendments to the necessary bankruptcy jurisdictional reforms.

When the first *Marathon* stay expired on October 4, 1982, the Supreme Court granted an extension until December 24, 1982. As Christmas Eve of 1982 approached, however, it was becoming abundantly clear that Congress was not going to pass remedial legislation before the deadline. The Supreme Court refused to extend the stay again. The real prospect loomed that the bankruptcy courts would shut down on Christmas Day and that chaos would ensue. Into the breach stepped the Judicial

---

[36]   Id. at 86 n.39 (Brennan, J., plurality); id. at 91 (Rehnquist, J., concurring).

[37]   Id. at 86 (Brennan, J., plurality); id. at 91 (Rehnquist, J., concurring).

[38]   Id. at 80–84 (Brennan, J., plurality).

[39]   Id. at 96–100 (White, J., dissenting).

[40]   The initial stay granted by the Supreme Court in *Marathon* was until October 4, 1982; the *Marathon* decision was handed down on June 28, 1982.

[41]   This period extended from the date of the *Marathon* decision, June 28, 1982, until the effective date of the corrective legislation in BAFJA, which was July 10, 1984.

Conference of the United States, which drafted and circulated a proposed model rule suitable for adoption as a local rule by all United States District Courts. Known universally in bankruptcy lore as the "Emergency Rule," this rule provided a means to keep the bankruptcy system operating until such time as Congress could pass a new statute fixing the *Marathon* problem. The district courts across the nation gratefully seized the Emergency Rule lifeline and adopted it as a local rule.

Leading bankruptcy scholars condemned the Emergency Rule as "invalid and unworkable."[42] In essence, the Emergency Rule did by local rule what Congress had expressly refused to do in 1978 (permit bankruptcy jurisdiction to reside ultimately in the district courts) and what the Supreme Court had held was unconstitutional in *Marathon* (permit untenured judges to exercise in fact virtually all of the bankruptcy jurisdiction). Notwithstanding these telling concerns, no circuit court ever held the Emergency Rule invalid.[43] The Supreme Court steadfastly refused to hear challenges to the Emergency Rule, denying original writs of prohibition and mandamus attacking the Rule and denying petitions for certiorari in circuit court cases upholding the Rule.[44] Heartened by the Emergency Rule's resistance to challenge, Congress followed the same basic scheme in the 1984 jurisdictional reforms.[45]

The cornerstone of the Emergency Rule was the implementation of a *reference system* of bankruptcy cases and proceedings from the district judges to the bankruptcy judges. The idea for such a system came from the late unlamented Bankruptcy Act of 1898. The initial premise (almost certainly wrong) was that residual federal bankruptcy jurisdiction persisted in the *district* courts even after the 1978 Bankruptcy Reform Act and the decision in *Marathon Pipe Line*. Then, the Emergency Rule made an initial blanket reference of *all* of the district court's jurisdiction over bankruptcy cases and proceedings to the bankruptcy judges. Without more, the Rule indisputably would have been invalid under *Marathon*.

Several aspects of the Emergency Rule attempted to correct the constitutional impediment, by reserving some measure of control over bankruptcy cases and proceedings in the hands of the district judges. The Supreme Court had indicated that the command of Article III would not be violated as long as the "essential attributes of the judicial power" remained in the Article III district judges. The "attributes" retained by Article III district judges and denied to the non-Article III bankruptcy judges under the Emergency Rule were the following:

1.   The district judge could *withdraw* the reference to the bankruptcy judge, and hear and decide all or part of any bankruptcy case or proceeding in the first instance.

---

[42]   See, e.g., Vern Countryman, Emergency Rule Compounds Emergency, 57 Am. Bankr. L.J. 1, 3 (1983); Lawrence P. King, The Unmaking of a Bankruptcy Court: Aftermath of *Northern Pipeline v. Marathon*, 40 Wash. & Lee L. Rev. 99, 116 (1983).

[43]   Only a hardened cynic would note the fact that representatives of these same judges, in the Judicial Conference, had proposed the Emergency Rule in the first place.

[44]   See Tabb, supra note 14, at 576 n. 400, for citation to cases.

[45]   See §§ 4.3–4.6.

2.   In a "related" proceeding (defined as a proceeding that could have been brought in a state or federal court in the absence of bankruptcy[46]), the bankruptcy judge could not enter a final order (unless all parties consented), but was authorized only to submit *proposed* findings of fact and conclusions of law to the district judge, who had the power to review those findings and conclusions *de novo*, and in doing so "need give no deference to the findings of the bankruptcy judge."

3.   In all proceedings, even those in which the bankruptcy judge was permitted to enter a final order, a party had the right to object specifically to the bankruptcy judge's findings and conclusions, with *de novo* review then available in the district court.

4.   The bankruptcy judge on his own motion could certify that a judgment or order had to be approved by the district judge.

5.   The bankruptcy judge could not enjoin a court, punish a criminal contempt, hear an appeal, or conduct a jury trial.

In the year and a half that the Emergency Rule was in place, it worked surprisingly well. The dire predictions that the provisions for *de novo* review of the bankruptcy judge's actions by the district court would be inefficient and cumbersome did not materialize in most cases. Instead, bankruptcy practice continued on much as before, with the bankruptcy judges deciding almost everything and with review by the district judges usually being little more than a cursory "rubber stamp" procedure. Of course, that de facto reality suggested a serious question as to the validity of the Emergency Rule in light of *Marathon*; but after the whole system came so close to the precipice of disaster in 1982, almost no one had the desire to press too hard on such legal niceties.

f.   The Bankruptcy Amendments and Federal Judgeship Act of 1984

The Supreme Court's 1982 decision in *Marathon*, holding the bankruptcy jurisdictional scheme unconstitutional, obviously demanded a congressional response. Two years elapsed, however, before Congress finally passed the Bankruptcy Amendments and Federal Judgeship Act of 1984 (known by its acronym of "BAFJA"),[47] which was signed into law by President Reagan on July 10, 1984. The battle over the status of bankruptcy judges that had been fought in the 1970s was replayed.

This time, however, in the wake of *Marathon*, Congress had only two realistic choices (or so one would have thought): (1) give Article III status to the bankruptcy judges, who then would be able constitutionally to exercise all of a pervasive, unified federal bankruptcy jurisdiction, or (2) not give the bankruptcy judges Article III status, which would necessitate dividing bankruptcy jurisdiction between the district court and the bankruptcy judges. The 1978 "solution," in which bankruptcy judges were not

---

[46]   For example, the breach of contract suit involved in *Marathon* would have been a "related proceeding" under this definition.

[47]   Pub. L. No. 98–353, 98 Stat. 333 (1984).

given Article III status but were given all of the bankruptcy jurisdiction, was no longer possible after *Marathon*. The option of having the existing Article III district court judges exercise all of the bankruptcy jurisdiction, while of course constitutionally permissible, was unrealistic because district judges did not have the time, interest, or expertise to deal with the mass of bankruptcy cases and proceedings.

The logical and sensible choice would have been to make bankruptcy judges Article III judges.[48] Congress did not take that tack, however. Bowing to the determined lobbying efforts of the sitting Article III judges, spearheaded by Chief Justice Burger and the Judicial Conference, Congress chose to deny yet again Article III status to bankruptcy judges, and to return to a complex and confusing system of splintered jurisdiction akin to that which had been used (and roundly condemned) under the pre–1978 Bankruptcy Act.[49]

Under BAFJA, bankruptcy judges are constituted as a *"unit"* of the district court, and are designated to serve as "judicial officers" of the district court. 28 U.S.C. §§ 151, 152(a)(1). Bankruptcy judges are appointed by the judges of the United States court of appeals for the circuit for terms of 14 years, and may be removed only for incompetence, misconduct, neglect of duty, or physical or mental disability. 28 U.S.C. § 152(a)(1), (e). The salary of bankruptcy judges is 92 percent of the salary of the district court judges. 28 U.S.C. § 153(a).

The fundamental limitation on jurisdictional exercise imposed on the non-Article III bankruptcy courts by BAFJA in order to address the constitutional problem was to distinguish between the power exercised by bankruptcy judges in "core" proceedings, on the one hand, and non-core proceedings, on the other. In a "core" proceeding, the bankruptcy judge was given the power to "hear and determine" the matter. 28 U.S.C. § 157(b)(1). In plain English, that means the bankruptcy judge could issue a final order, reviewable only on appeal by the Article III district court, with appropriate deference given to findings of fact. Core proceedings supposedly were those matters at the heart—the core—of the bankruptcy process, and which accordingly (hopefully, prayerfully) would pass constitutional muster.[50] The jurisdictional statute did not define core proceedings, but provided a non-exclusive list of illustrative core proceedings. 28 U.S.C. § 157(b)(2). Roughly, core matters were designed to cover that part of the bankruptcy jurisdictional grant to the federal courts in 28 U.S.C. § 1334(b) for those proceedings either "arising under" title 11 or "arising in" cases under title 11, the federal bankruptcy law. As it turned out, though, in *Stern* the Supreme Court held that the listing of core proceedings was overinclusive, exceeding the constitutional bounds.[51] For proceedings that were not core proceedings, conversely, BAFJA provided that the bankruptcy judge was only given the power to "hear" the matter.[52] 28 U.S.C. § 157(c)(1). Again reverting to the English translation, the telling absence of "and

---

[48] Not everyone agrees. See, e.g., Thomas E. Plank, Why Bankruptcy Judges Need Not and Should Not Be Article III Judges, 72 Am. Bankr. L.J. 567 (1998).

[49] See § 4.3. For a comprehensive review of jurisdiction under BAFJA, see Lawrence P. King, Jurisdiction and Procedure Under the Bankruptcy Amendments of 1984, 38 Vand. L. Rev. 675 (1985).

[50] See § 4.4.

[51] See 4.2.g.

[52] See § 4.5.

determine" meant that the non-Article III bankruptcy judge could not issue a final order. Instead, the judge could only "submit proposed findings of fact and conclusions of law to the district court," id., which would then issue the final order. Although the name "related" proceeding was not used in the statute (as it had been in the Emergency Rule), it evidently was the intent of Congress that the non-core proceedings covered by § 157(c) would encompass that part of the jurisdictional grant in § 1334(b) for proceedings "related to cases under title 11."

g.   *Stern v. Marshall*

In 2011, the Supreme Court threw a major wrench into the BAJFA jurisdictional scheme when it ruled 5–4 in *Stern v. Marshall* that "[t]he Bankruptcy Court below lacked the constitutional authority to enter a final judgment on a state law counterclaim that is not resolved in the process of ruling on a creditor's proof of claim."[53] Why is that so problematic for the BAFJA scheme? The counterclaim at issue was designated as "core" (28 U.S.C. § 157(b)(2)(C)), and accordingly the bankruptcy court supposedly could enter a final order. *Stern* thus calls into question the legitimacy of the constitutional authority allocated to bankruptcy judges under the core/non-core divide in BAFJA.

While Chief Justice Roberts protested that "our decision today does not change all that much" and does "not . . . meaningfully change[ ] the division of labor" between the bankruptcy and district court, since "the question presented here is a 'narrow' one,"[54] the Court's own analysis belies those protestations. Many lower courts have thus chosen not to take the Court at its word but have relied instead on the Court's analysis to find that bankruptcy courts cannot enter final orders in many "core" areas that it previously was thought they could. A prominent example is the decision of the Ninth Circuit that a bankruptcy judge cannot enter a final order in a fraudulent transfer action.[55] Even worse, the Sixth Circuit has held that the Article III defect cannot be waived, even with litigant consent.[56] Some courts, though, have adopted the "narrow

---

[53]   131 S.Ct. 2594, 2620 (2011). Chief Justice Roberts wrote the opinion for the Court, joined by the conservative block of Justices Scalia, Thomas, Alito, and Kennedy. Justice Breyer dissented, joined by Justices Ginsburg, Sotomayor, and Kagan. Justice Scalia filed a separate concurring opinion as well.

Numerous scholars have written about *Stern*. A superb analysis can be found in Ralph Brubaker, A "Summary" Statutory and Constitutional Theory of Bankruptcy Judges' Core Jurisdiction After *Stern v. Marshall*, 86 Am. Bankr. L.J. 121, 134 (2012). There are many, many other valuable pieces, just a sampling of which includes Douglas G. Baird, Blue Collar Constitutional Law, 86 Am. Bankr. L.J. 3, 16 (2012); Eric G. Behrens, *Stern v. Marshall*: The Supreme Court's Continuing Erosion of Bankruptcy Court Jurisdiction and Article I Courts, 85 Am. Bankr. L.J. 387 (2011); Susan Block–Lieb, What Congress Had to Say: Legislative History as a Rehearsal of Congressional Response to *Stern v. Marshall*, 86 Am. Bankr. L.J. 55 (2012); Erwin Chemerinsky, Formalism Without a Foundation: *Stern v. Marshall*, 2011 Sup. Ct. Rev. 183 (2011); Troy A. McKenzie, Getting to the Core of *Stern v. Marshall*: History, Expertise, and Separation of Powers, 86 Am. Bankr. L.J. 23 (2012).

[54]   131 S.Ct. at 2620.

[55]   Exec. Benefits Ins. Agency v. Arkison (In re Bellingham Ins. Agency, Inc.), 702 F.3d 553, 564 (9th Cir. 2012).

[56]   Waldman v. Stone, 698 F.3d 910 (6th Cir. 2012).

interpretation" of *Stern* and have concluded that the Court's holding is indeed limited to the specific circumstances at issue there.[57]

Stern arose out of facts that would fall under the category of "you can't make this stuff up"[58] or perhaps "truth is stranger than fiction;"[59] at the very least, it's the stuff of a Dickens novel, an allusion which Chief Justice Roberts himself evokes.[60] When Vickie Lynn Marshall, much more famously known as *Playboy* Playmate Anna Nicole Smith, was but 25 she married an 89–year old Texas billionaire, J. Howard Marshall, who she met while working at a strip club. When he died a few months later, having failed to follow through on what she claimed was his promise to give her half of his estate, she got into a legal battle over his estate with his son, E. Pierce Marshall. Vickie sued in Texas probate court, claiming that Pierce fraudulently induced the old man to sign a living trust that excluded Vickie. While the Texas probate proceeding was pending, Vickie filed chapter 11 in California. Pierce filed a proof of claim in her bankruptcy case, alleging that she had defamed him by telling the press about how he tricked his dad into cutting her out; she in turn objected to Pierce's claim and also filed a compulsory counterclaim against Pierce, alleging tortious interference with a gift, asking for just a few hundred million dollars in damages.[61] Importantly (as it turned out), resolution of Pierce's proof of claim would not necessarily resolve all (or even most) of the dispositive issues on Vickie's tort cause of action.

The bankruptcy court granted Vickie summary judgment on Pierce's defamation claim, disallowing the claim in its entirety, and then the bankruptcy court tried Vickie's tortious interference counterclaim, treating it as a "core" proceeding under 28 U.S.C. § 157(b)(2)(C). After trial, the bankruptcy court purported to enter a final order, ruling for Vickie in the amount of about $425 million.[62] On appeal, the district court affirmed liability but reduced the damages to just under $90 million.[63]

The reason that the core/non-core issue was relevant was because of the parallel litigation proceeding in Texas probate court administering J. Howard's estate. After the bankruptcy court's judgment, but before the district court ruling, the Texas probate court ruled the other way, holding in Pierce's favor that he was not liable to Vickie for tortious interference. With conflicting judgments from collateral courts, resolving those conflicting judgments was a matter of preclusion principles—which court had entered the first "final" judgment? If the bankruptcy court did not have the authority legally to enter a "final" judgment, then the Texas probate court's judgment against Vickie would be first in time, and the California district court would have to give preclusive effect to the Texas judgment. Whether the bankruptcy court had entered the first "final"

---

[57]   See, e.g., In re Direct Response Media, Inc. (Bankr. D. Del. 2012) (bankruptcy court has constitutional core jurisdiction over preference and fraudulent transfer claims); In re USDigital, Inc., 461 B.R. 276 (Bankr. D. Del. 2011) (equitable subordination).

[58]   See, e.g., Dave Barry, Dave Barry is Not Making This Up (1994).

[59]   The origin of that phrase has been variously attributed, including Lord Byron (in *Don Juan*) and Mark Twain. I suspect both would have found the facts in *Stern* fascinating.

[60]   131 S.Ct. at 2600.

[61]   Id., at 2601 (citing Marshall v. Marshall, 547 U.S. 293 (2006)).

[62]   253 B.R. 550 (Bankr. C.D. Cal. 2000).

[63]   275 B.R. 5 (C.D. Cal. 2002).

judgment turned on whether Vickie's counterclaim was a "core" proceeding under the bankruptcy jurisdictional statute, and as to which it was constitutional for the non-Article III bankruptcy judge to enter a final judgment.

Accordingly, Pierce raised a post-trial motion in the California bankruptcy court that the counterclaim brought by Vickie matter was not a "core proceeding." The bankruptcy court held that it was core under the statute (and that such exercise was permissible),[64] but the district court[65] and court of appeals[66] (after one run up to the Supreme Court on another issue) each concluded (albeit by somewhat different reasoning) that the counterclaim was not "core" under the statute, since holding otherwise would have raised a serious constitutional problem. The Ninth Circuit then held that preclusion dictated giving deference to the Texas judgment. The Supreme Court granted certiorari.

Two issues had to be decided by the Court: "(1) whether the Bankruptcy Court had the statutory authority under 28 U.S.C. § 157(b) to issue a final judgment on Vickie's counterclaim; and (2) if so, whether conferring that authority on the Bankruptcy Court is constitutional."[67] The Supreme Court's answers were: "We conclude that, although the Bankruptcy Court had the statutory authority to enter judgment on Vickie's counterclaim, it lacked the constitutional authority to do so."[68] Since it was unconstitutional for the non-Article III bankruptcy judge to purport to enter a final judgment on Vickie's counterclaim, the Texas probate court's judgment was given preclusive effect, denying Vickie any relief on her tortious interference counterclaim against Pierce.

If the Court had affirmed the Ninth Circuit on issue one, and held that the bankruptcy court simply lacked *statutory* authority to enter a final order on the counterclaim, the case would indeed have been of only modest importance and a mild annoyance in bankruptcy litigation, and would have stood for little more than an exercise in statutory interpretation. But by deciding that statutory authority did exist, and then squarely deciding the constitutional issue, the Supreme Court threw the legitimacy of much of the core jurisdiction of the bankruptcy courts into confusion and doubt.

The Court first held that section 157(b)(2)(C) *did* purport to confer *statutory* authority for the bankruptcy court to issue a final order on Vickie's counterclaim.[69] They saw no way to read the statute otherwise. The Court reasoned that the phrases "arising under" and "arising in" found in § 157(b) are most plausibly read "as simply describing what core proceedings are: matters arising under Title 11 or in a Title 11 case."[70] The Court concluded, "In this case, we do not think the plain text of § 157(b)(2)(C) leaves any room for the canon of avoidance. We would have to 'rewrite'

---

[64]   257 B.R. 35 (Bankr. C.D. Cal. 2000).

[65]   264 B.R. 609 (C.D. Cal. 2001).

[66]   600 F.3d 1037 (9th Cir. 2010).

[67]   131 S.Ct. at 2600.

[68]   Id. at 2601.

[69]   Id. at 2605.

[70]   Id. at 2604.

the statute, not interpret it, to bypass the constitutional issue § 157(b)(2)(C) presents."[71]

Turning of necessity then to the constitutional question, the Court concluded "[a]lthough we conclude that § 157(b)(2)(C) permits the Bankruptcy Court to enter final judgment on Vickie's counterclaim, Article III of the Constitution does not."[72] Why not? Chief Justice Roberts explained that "[i]t is clear that the Bankruptcy Court in this case exercised the 'judicial power of the United States' in purporting to resolve and enter final judgment on a state common law claim, just as the court did in *Northern Pipeline*."[73] The Court rejected the two principal arguments put forward to support constitutionality, the public rights theory[74] and the adjunct theory.[75] Furthermore, the Court rejected the notion that Pierce had somehow "consented" to final adjudication in the bankruptcy court by filing a proof of claim, as "he had nowhere else to go if he wished to recover from Vickie's estate."[76]

Most observers had thought that *Northern Pipeline's* force had been largely undermined by two cases decided soon after it, *Thomas v. Union Carbide*[77] and *Commodity Futures Trading Commission v. Schor*.[78] In *Stern,* however, the Court read those decisions narrowly, and effectively resurrected *Northern Pipeline*, harmonizing that case with *Thomas* and *Schor*, divining a unifying principle for the "public rights" exception that "limit[s] the exception to cases in which the claim at issue derives from a federal regulatory scheme, or in which resolution of the claim by an expert government agency is deemed essential to a limited regulatory objective within the agency's authority."[79] Against that test, Vickie's state law tort claim looked to be out of luck, and indeed it was: the Court concluded that "Vickie's claimed right to relief does not flow from a federal statutory scheme, as in *Thomas*," and "is not 'completely dependent upon' adjudication of a claim created by federal law, as in *Schor*."[80]

Instead, and very significantly, the Court relied on *Granfinanciera S.A. v. Nordberg*,[81] explicitly extending its Seventh Amendment jury trial rationale to Article III. The Court in *Granfinanciera* had taken a limited view of the public rights exception in finding that the right to a jury trial in bankruptcy obtained even as to designated "core" proceedings, if the cause of action in question was a private, rather than public, right—and concluded that fraudulent conveyance actions were private. However, before *Stern,* the common assumption was that *Granfinanciera* was just a Seventh Amendment case, with no necessary relevance to the Article III question. *Stern* changed that. Thus, *Stern v. Marshall* can be seen as "the Article III counterpart

---

[71]   Id. at 2605.

[72]   Id. at 2608.

[73]   Id. at 2611.

[74]   Id. at 2611–15.

[75]   Id. at 2618–19.

[76]   Id. at 2614–15 & n. 8.

[77]   473 U.S. 568 (1985).

[78]   478 U.S. 833 (1986).

[79]   *Stern*, 131 S.Ct. at 2613.

[80]   Id. at 2614.

[81]   492 U.S. 33 (1989). See § 4.8.a.

to the *Granfinanciera* Seventh Amendment decision in fully equating bankruptcy litigants' Seventh Amendment right to a jury trial in federal bankruptcy proceedings with their right to a final judgment from an Article III judge."[82] A common thread running through *Northern Pipeline, Granfinanciera,* and *Stern*, militating in each instance for a "private" rights classification, is that each was an action "at common law that simply attempts to augment the bankruptcy estate."[83] Plainly, many of the designated "core" provisions in 28 U.S.C. § 157(b)(2) are of the same ilk, and thus under the *Stern* reasoning may likewise be suspect.

But isn't a battle over the bankruptcy estate itself within the permitted jurisdictional bailiwick, however limited, of the non-Article III bankruptcy courts? And if a creditor subjects itself to the bankruptcy court's jurisdiction by seeking a share of that bankruptcy estate by filing a proof of claim, then isn't it the case that actions connected with that claims resolution—such as the trustee filing a counterclaim— likewise fall within the safe womb of constitutional bankruptcy court jurisdiction? The Court's own precedents seemed to support such a result, especially *Katchen v. Landy*[84] and *Langenkamp v. Culp*.[85] The Court in *Stern*, though, decided that the result did *not* change because Pierce had filed a proof of claim and that Vickie had then brought a *compulsory* counterclaim to that proof of claim.

Instead, constitutional comfort may be found for a counterclaim only if that claim will "necessarily be resolved in the claims allowance process."[86] Here, however, "there was never any reason to believe that the process of adjudicating Pierce's proof of claim would necessarily resolve Vickie's counterclaim.[87] The Court distinguished *Katchen v. Landy*, which involved a voidable preference claim "brought by the bankruptcy trustee against a creditor who had filed a proof of claim in the bankruptcy proceeding."[88] The difference was that in *Katchen*, "it was not possible for the referee to rule on the creditor's proof of claim without first resolving the voidable preference issue."[89] As Professor Brubaker explains, under "§ 57g of the 1898 Act—providing that even an otherwise valid creditor claim must be disallowed unless and until the creditor disgorges in its entirety any voidable preference received by the creditor—the referee did have summary jurisdiction to finally adjudicate the trustee's preference counterclaim under those circumstances, as a necessary incident to its summary jurisdiction to allow or disallow the creditor's claim against the estate."[90] In *Stern*, ruling on the counterclaim could not have been necessary to rule on the proof of claim because the bankruptcy court had already ruled against Pierce on his defamation claim on summary judgment.

---

[82]   Brubaker, *supra* note 53, at 151.

[83]   *Stern*, 131 S.Ct. at 2616.

[84]   382 U.S. 323 (1966).

[85]   498 U.S. 42 (1990).

[86]   *Stern*, 131 S.Ct. at 2618.

[87]   Id. at 2617.

[88]   Id. at 2616.

[89]   Id.

[90]   Brubaker, supra note 53, at 167–68.

After *Stern,* then, we are left with the critical question: what *is* the extent of the constitutional limit, applicable (apparently) both to Seventh Amendment and Article III questions? The *Stern* Court never says so precisely, but did leave some clues, especially in explaining why Vickie's state law tort counterclaim did *not* qualify for the public rights exception. Considering especially the reaffirmed precedents of *Northern Pipeline* (traditional state law contract claim not public right) and *Granfinanciera* (fraudulent conveyance action, as "quintessentially suits at common law," not public right),[91] as well as the exceptions recognized (and distinguished) in *Katchen* and *Langenkamp,* the central thesis of the Court can be found in the following passage:

> Vickie's claim . . . is in no way derived from or dependent upon bankruptcy law; it is a state tort action that exists without regard to any bankruptcy proceeding. . . . Congress may not bypass Article III simply because a proceeding may have *some* bearing on a bankruptcy case; the question is whether the action at issue stems from the bankruptcy itself or would necessarily be resolved in the claims allowance process.[92]

In another passage, the Court stated: "Here Vickie's claim is a state law action independent of the federal bankruptcy law and not necessarily resolvable by a ruling on the creditor's proof of claim in bankruptcy."[93] And in conclusion, the Court held: "The Bankruptcy Court below lacked the constitutional authority to enter a final judgment on a state law counterclaim that is not resolved in the process of ruling on a creditor's proof of claim."[94]

It appears, then, that the following are relevant criteria:

- Is the claim one that is "quintessentially a suit at common law"? Another way to look at this is whether it is a state law action that is independent of the bankruptcy law. If so, it is likely to be a private right, with the jury trial right obtaining and Article III status required to enter a final order.

- As to the prior point, the claim is even more certainly a private right if it is seeking to augment the estate.

- By contrast, is that claim derived from (or does it stem from) or is it dependent on the bankruptcy itself? If so, that favors finding a public right.

- Would the action "necessarily be resolved in the claims allowance process"? If so, again, a jury trial right would not exist, and a non-Article III bankruptcy court can enter a final order.

The Court also rejected, with little hesitation, the contention that bankruptcy courts can be considered "adjuncts" of the district courts.[95] The reason is factual and

---

[91]   *Stern,* 131 S. Ct. at 2614.

[92]   Id. at 2618.

[93]   Id. at 2611.

[94]   Id. at 2620.

[95]   Id. at 2618.

functional: they aren't, at least not when they are entering a final order! The *Stern* Court explained that "it is still the bankruptcy court itself that exercises the essential attributes of judicial power over a matter such as Vickie's counterclaim."[96] Since a bankruptcy court has the power to enter "'appropriate orders and judgments'— including final judgments—subject to review only if a party chooses to appeal . . . a bankruptcy court can no more be deemed a mere 'adjunct' to the district court than a district court can be deemed such an 'adjunct' of the court of appeals."[97]

In dissent, Justice Breyer noted that the Court's reading of Article III casts into doubt the entirety of the administrative state.[98] Moreover, Justice Breyer accuses the majority of putting too much emphasis on a plurality opinion in *Northern Pipeline* rather than subsequent majority opinions in *Thomas* and *Schor*. Instead, Justice Breyer would have applied the balancing approach in *Schor*, and found the "delegation of adjudicatory authority before us constitutional."[99] In a nutshell, the dissent favored a pragmatic, sensible approach, while the majority lapsed into myopic formalism.

Where are we now? The most cogent summary is from Professor Brubaker, who asserts:

> Although certainly not definitively established, the best reading of the Court's cumulative jurisprudence regarding non-Article III bankruptcy adjudications is that the Court's jurisprudence under the Bankruptcy Act of 1898 (the "1898 Act") demarcating the boundaries between so-called "summary" referee jurisdiction and "plenary" suits at law and in equity has essentially been constitutionalized. Consequently, the current statute is constitutionally suspect to the extent it authorizes non-Article III bankruptcy judges to enter final orders and judgments in any bankruptcy proceeding that would not indisputably have been a summary matter appropriate for final adjudication by a non-Article III referee under the 1898 Act.[100]

Below, in discussing core proceedings,[101] we will explore how Professor Brubaker's analysis plays out in a number of common scenarios. It must be noted, though, that already *Stern* has spawned hundreds and hundreds of confusing and inconsistent decisions, as lower courts try to make sense of the puzzling analysis embraced by the Supreme Court. Only time will tell what the proper resolution is of the myriad of possible types of cases that may implicate *Stern*.

§ 4.3   Jurisdiction and Powers of the District Court and Bankruptcy Judges

The jurisdictional scheme implemented by BAFJA in 1984 and still in effect today is based on a *reference* of bankruptcy cases and proceedings from the Article III district

---

[96] Id.

[97] Id. at 2619.

[98] Id. at 2623 (Breyer, J., dissenting).

[99] Id. at 2626.

[100] Brubaker, supra note 53, at 122.

[101] See § 4.4.

court to the non-Article III bankruptcy judges. Federal jurisdiction in bankruptcy is governed by 28 U.S.C. § 1334. Subsection (a) of § 1334 gives the district courts "original and exclusive jurisdiction of all cases under title 11." The "case" is the entire chapter 7, 9, 11, 12, 13, or 15 case involving the debtor. Jurisdiction over bankruptcy "*proceedings*," which are discrete disputes that arise within the context of the overall "case," is addressed by 28 U.S.C. § 1334(b). That subsection confers on the district courts "original but not exclusive jurisdiction of all civil proceedings arising under title 11, or arising in or related to cases under title 11."[102] The 1978 Reform Act contained provisions identical to current § 1334(a) and (b) (denominated as § 1471(a) and (b) in 1978), but went on in § 1471(c) to provide that the *bankruptcy* court would exercise all of the jurisdiction conferred on the district courts in subsections (a) and (b). It was this block transfer of all of the district court's bankruptcy jurisdiction to the untenured bankruptcy judges that the Supreme Court found unconstitutional in *Marathon*. Accordingly, in the corrective legislation enacted in 1984, Congress did *not* include in § 1334 any provision automatically transferring all federal bankruptcy jurisdiction to the non-Article III bankruptcy judges.

Another component of federal bankruptcy jurisdiction is specified in 28 U.S.C. § 1334(e). Subsection (e)(1) gives the district court "exclusive jurisdiction of all of the property, wherever located, of the debtor as of the commencement of such case, and of property of the estate." This section makes clear that a bankruptcy case is in many respects an *in rem* proceeding, with one of its primary goals being the equitable and coordinated resolution of all claims against the bankruptcy estate. All of the debtor's property at the time of filing and all property that comes into the estate thereafter is brought *in custodia legis*, under the supervision and control of the federal court. Note that under § 1334(e)(1), the district court's jurisdiction is *exclusive*, unlike the grant of jurisdiction in subsection (b) as to "proceedings," which is original but not exclusive. Thus, no other court can exercise jurisdiction over property of the bankruptcy estate.

A second exclusive jurisdictional grant to the district court was added in 2005. Under new 28 U.S.C. § 1334(e)(2), the district court has exclusive jurisdiction "over all claims or causes of action that involve construction of section 327 of title 11, United States Code, or rules relating to disclosure requirements under section 327." Section 327 of the Bankruptcy Code contains the rules regarding the employment of professional persons in bankruptcy cases.

The absence of a direct statutory jurisdictional grant to the bankruptcy judges akin to § 1471(c) of the 1978 Act, in order to dodge the *Marathon* problem, is a bit misleading. Notably, it does *not* mean that Congress in BAFJA did not provide the means for bankruptcy judges to hear virtually all matters that arise in a bankruptcy case. District judges, who are given bankruptcy jurisdiction under § 1334, most assuredly do not want to exercise that jurisdiction in the bulk of cases. Congress attempted to achieve the daunting task of conferring most bankruptcy jurisdiction on the bankruptcy judges without appearing to do so in one of the most deceivingly innocuously labeled sections in the entire United States Code, 28 U.S.C. § 157, called

---

[102] In 2005, an exception was carved out of the grant of original but not exclusive jurisdiction over proceedings in subsection (b), to give the district court exclusive jurisdiction under subsection (e)(2) over proceedings involving the employment of professional persons under Bankruptcy Code § 327.

simply "Procedures." This section on "Procedures" governs the allocation of judicial power over bankruptcy matters as between the bankruptcy judges and the district court. As discussed above, though, this solution to the division of labor between district courts and bankruptcy courts was called into question by *Stern v. Marshall*.[103]

Subsection (a) of § 157 authorizes the reference of "any or all" bankruptcy cases and proceedings from the district court to the bankruptcy judges. The reference in § 157(a) is permissive ("may"), not mandatory. However, not surprisingly, every single district court in the country has availed itself of the option offered by subsection (a) and has entered a standing local order that initially refers *all* bankruptcy cases and proceedings to the bankruptcy judges. Thus, the default rule is that every bankruptcy case is filed with and heard in the *bankruptcy* court, and every bankruptcy proceeding is heard in the first instance by the bankruptcy judge. So far, the system in substance (if not form) looks a lot like the constitutionally defective 1978 law.

To deal with the constitutional problem, however, Congress could not permit the non-Article III bankruptcy judges to enter final orders in all types of bankruptcy proceedings. At a minimum, state law claims of the type involved in the *Marathon* case itself could not be finally adjudicated before the untenured bankruptcy judge. The solution Congress devised in § 157 was to bifurcate the universe of bankruptcy proceedings into two categories: (1) "*core* proceedings," and (2) "*non-core* proceedings" (also called "*related*" proceedings). The crucial distinction between the two, intended specifically to cure the constitutional infirmity identified in *Marathon*, is that bankruptcy judges are given authority to enter final orders in core proceedings, but not in non-core proceedings (absent consent). 28 U.S.C. § 157(b), (c). Unfortunately, as we learned in *Stern*, Congress again transgressed constitutionally, with at least some of the supposedly "core" matters being the types of suits that cannot be finally resolved by a non-Article III bankruptcy court.

Core proceedings are identified in § 157(b)(2).[104] That subsection lists 16 nonexclusive examples of proceedings that are considered "core." These proceedings are those that supposedly form the "core" of the bankruptcy process; they implicate quintessential bankruptcy functions, such as the liquidation of the debtor's assets and the adjustment of the debtor-creditor relationship. Core proceedings are those that "arise under" title 11 or "arise in" a case under title 11. 28 U.S.C. § 157(b)(1). For example, a hearing to resolve a motion for relief from the automatic stay of § 362 is a core proceeding; it could only arise in the context of a bankruptcy case. Bankruptcy judges are given the authority to determine whether or not a proceeding is a core proceeding. 28 U.S.C. § 157(b)(3).

Bankruptcy judges are authorized by § 157(b)(1) to "*hear and determine*" all "cases under title 11" and all "core proceedings arising under title 11, or arising in a case under title 11," that are referred by the district court, and to "enter appropriate orders and judgments." Review of these orders and judgments is only on appeal, pursuant to 28 U.S.C. §§ 158, 1291, or 1292. In other words, bankruptcy judges have the power to

---

[103] 131 S.Ct. 2594 (2011). See § 4.2.g. See also § 4.4.

[104] For more discussion of core proceedings, see § 4.4.

enter final orders in core proceedings. The bankruptcy judge's findings are entitled to the normal deference given to trial level courts, *viz.*, review of fact findings under a "clearly erroneous" standard. In this respect the jurisdictional rules under BAFJA give more authority to the bankruptcy judges than did the Emergency Rule. Under the Rule, even core proceedings were subject to possible *de novo* review by the district court on objection by a party, with no deference required to be given to the bankruptcy judge's findings.

One type of proceeding is expressly carved out from the definition of core proceedings and is reserved to the district courts: personal injury tort and wrongful death claims. 28 U.S.C. § 157(b)(2)(B). These proceedings must be tried in the district court, 28 U.S.C. § 157(b)(5), and are not subject to the provisions for mandatory abstention in 28 U.S.C. § 1334(c)(2). 28 U.S.C. § 157(b)(4). These rules are the product of a successful lobbying campaign by the plaintiff's tort bar to keep the trial of their lawsuits out of the hands of bankruptcy judges.

Those proceedings that fall within the ambit of bankruptcy jurisdiction under § 1334(b) but which are not core proceedings are referred to as "non-core" or "related" proceedings, and are dealt with in 28 U.S.C. § 157(c).[105] Bankruptcy jurisdiction under § 1334(b) extends to proceedings "arising under" title 11 or "arising in" a title 11 case, and to proceedings "related to" the title 11 case. The "arising under" and "arising in" categories are core proceedings; the "related to" category encompasses non-core proceedings. Unfortunately, Congress did not define "related proceeding" in the 1984 legislation. The Emergency Rule had defined such a proceeding as a "civil proceeding that could have been brought in district court or state court absent a petition in bankruptcy." The breach of contract claim brought by the debtor in possession in *Marathon* would be an example of such a non-core, related proceeding. These are the types of proceedings in which the connection to the core bankruptcy function is the most attenuated and the constitutionality of having an untenured judge resolve the case is the most problematic.

Accordingly, in BAFJA Congress did not authorize bankruptcy judges to "hear and determine" non-core related proceedings, as it did for core proceedings. Bankruptcy judges may not enter a final order reviewable only on appeal in these non-core proceedings (subject to an exception noted below). Instead, the role of a bankruptcy judge in a non-core proceeding is analogous to that of a special master. The bankruptcy judge may "*hear*" (but not "determine") the proceeding and then "shall submit *proposed* findings of fact and conclusions of law to the district court." 28 U.S.C. § 157(c)(1). The district court then will enter the final order or judgment, after "considering" the proposed findings and conclusions submitted by the bankruptcy judge and "after reviewing de novo those matters to which any party has timely and specifically objected." The statute does not elaborate on the extent of the deference to be given by the district court when "considering" the proposed submissions. The concern often has been voiced that the district courts will do little more than give a rubber stamp seal of approval to the bankruptcy judge's proposals, meaning that the extent of the control exercised by the Article III court will usually be more theoretical than real. Yet that

---

[105] For more discussion of related proceedings, see § 4.5.

theoretical reed is a primary basis for circumventing the constitutional difficulty identified in *Marathon*.

Unfortunately, *Stern v. Marshall* has created a *third* category of proceedings, not contemplated or intended by Congress in 1984. Those are proceedings—such as the state law tort counterclaim in *Stern*—which are *statutorily* core (under § 157(b)) but as to which the bankruptcy judge may not *constitutionally* render final judgment.[106] At first blush, that result might suggest a statutory gap, since core and non-core proceedings were defined to be mutually exclusive of each other, with the bankruptcy judge to "hear and determine" core proceedings under subsection (b) and then only to "hear a proceeding that is *not* a core proceeding" under subsection (c). Some courts accordingly have expressed doubt as to whether the bankruptcy courts have any authority to *do anything* in such gap cases: they cannot constitutionally hear and determine the case under *Stern*, and, so the argument goes, have no statutory authority to "hear" the case under subsection (c).[107] Surely, though, that argument is misguided. The Ninth Circuit cogently rejected such a view, concluding that "the power to 'hear and determine' a proceeding surely encompasses the power to hear the proceeding and submit proposed findings of fact and conclusions of law to the district court."[108]

The exception that permits bankruptcy judges to "hear and determine" even non-core related proceedings is if all of the parties to the proceeding give their *consent*. 28 U.S.C. § 157(c)(2). In that event, the bankruptcy judge may enter a final order reviewable only on appeal under § 158.

However, the constitutionality of the provision authorizing bankruptcy judges to hear and determine related proceedings with party consent is debatable. The de facto effect of the consent rule, when coupled with the comprehensive initial reference to the bankruptcy judge, is to confer subject matter jurisdiction over related proceedings to the non-Article III bankruptcy judge. Yet, subject matter jurisdiction cannot be conferred by consent. This objection should apply with full force to Article III jurisdictional concerns, which are rooted in the structural concept of separation of powers. Following this line of thinking, the Sixth Circuit held that a litigant cannot waive its constitutional right to have a final judgment entered by an Article III judge.[109] In short, on this view, consent to have a non-Article III bankruptcy judge hear and determine the type of matters that *Stern* found to require Article III adjudication is not possible. If that is true, then obviously section 157(c)(2) is unconstitutional. However, it is not clear that the Sixth Circuit got it right.[110] Notably, in *Stern v. Marshall*, even though the Court found that the bankruptcy court did not have constitutional authority to issue the final order, it also opined that the allocation of authority to enter a final judgment does not implicate questions of subject matter

---

[106] Exec. Benefits Ins. Agency v. Arkinson (In re Bellingham Ins. Agency, Inc.), 702 F.3d 553, 565 (9th Cir. 2012); Douglas G. Baird, Blue Collar Constitutional Law, 86 Am. Bankr. L.J. 3, 16 (2012).

[107] See Ortiz v. Aurora Health Care, Inc. (In re Ortiz), 665 F.3d 906, 915 (7th Cir. 2011).

[108] *Bellingham*, supra note 106, 702 F.3d at 565.

[109] Waldman v. Stone, 698 F.3d 910, 918 (6th Cir. 2012).

[110] See Ralph Brubaker, The Constitutionality of Litigant Consent to Non–Article III Bankruptcy Adjudications, 32 Bankr. L. Letter 1 (Dec. 2012).

jurisdiction.[111] Moreover, a consent-based magistrate system has been upheld by the courts. The Ninth Circuit, accordingly, has held that even though a litigant has a constitutional right to have a fraudulent conveyance action finally determined by an Article III court, the litigant can (and in that case, did) waive that right.[112]

Another "attribute" of the judicial power over bankruptcy proceedings that the 1984 Amendments gave to the Article III district courts is the power to *withdraw* the § 157(a) reference of all or part of a case or proceeding from the bankruptcy court.[113] 28 U.S.C. § 157(d). This withdrawal power was designed to shore up the constitutionality of the bankruptcy jurisdictional scheme. If the district court withdraws the reference of a case or proceeding, that court then will hear and enter a final order in the withdrawn matter. The notion of withdrawal was utilized by the Emergency Rule. Withdrawal is determined by the district court.

Another limitation on the power of bankruptcy judges is with regard to their authority to conduct a jury trial.[114] The Supreme Court held in *Granfinanciera, S.A. v. Nordberg*[115] that the Seventh Amendment right to a jury trial applies in bankruptcy, but did not address the question of whether the non-Article III bankruptcy judge could preside over that trial. After *Granfinanciera*, all the courts of appeal that considered the question, except for the Second Circuit, concluded that bankruptcy judges did not have the statutory authority to conduct a jury trial after 1984, and many further suggested that such a power would be constitutionally suspect.[116] In the 1994 Amendments, Congress added 28 U.S.C. § 157(e), which authorizes the bankruptcy judge to "conduct the jury trial if specially designated to exercise such jurisdiction by the district court and with the express consent of all the parties."

Somewhat surprisingly, the 1984 legislation did not address whether the bankruptcy judges have the powers (1) to enjoin another court, or (2) to punish for either civil or criminal contempt. If those powers exist, a further question is whether the proceeding is a core or non-core proceeding. The Emergency Rule had specifically prohibited bankruptcy judges from enjoining a court and from punishing criminal contempt. The case law since BAFJA has been divided on both the injunction and contempt questions. Most courts have concluded that bankruptcy judges may punish for civil contempt.[117] Query, though, whether *Stern's* narrower view of the constitutionally legitimate powers of the non-Article III bankruptcy judge might call these holdings into question. Punishment for contempt arguably is an "essential

---

[111]   131 S.Ct. at 2607.

[112]   *Bellingham*, 702 F.3d at 566–70.

[113]   See § 4.6.

[114]   See § 4.8.b.

[115]   492 U.S. 33 (1989). See § 4.8.a.

[116]   See, e.g., In re United Missouri Bank, N.A., 901 F.2d 1449 (8th Cir. 1990). Contra, In re Ben Cooper, Inc., 896 F.2d 1394 (2d Cir.), vacated on other grounds and remanded, 498 U.S. 964 (1990), reinstated, 924 F.2d 36 (2d Cir.), cert. denied, 500 U.S. 928 (1991).

[117]   See, e.g., In re Terrebonne Fuel & Lube, Inc., 108 F.3d 609 (5th Cir. 1997) (has power to punish for contempt); In re Skinner, 917 F.2d 444 (10th Cir. 1990) (same). Contra In re Sequoia Auto Brokers, Ltd., 827 F.2d 1281 (9th Cir. 1987) (not have contempt power). However, the Ninth Circuit retreated from *Sequoia* in *In re Rainbow Magazine, Inc.*, 77 F.3d 278 (9th Cir. 1996). See also In re Hercules Enters., Inc., 387 F.3d 1024 (9th Cir. 2004).

attribute of judicial power." Few courts have been willing to allow bankruptcy judges to punish criminal contempt, however.[118] Those courts finding a contempt power usually cite as authority § 105(a) of the Code, which states that "[t]he court may issue any order, process, or judgment that is necessary or appropriate to carry out the provisions of this title."[119]

Another question on which the courts are divided that has arisen with some frequency in applying other federal statutes is whether bankruptcy courts are "courts of the United States." For example, this issue may be implicated in a proceeding to recover attorneys' fees under the Equal Access to Justice Act[120] or the Internal Revenue Code[121] or to sanction counsel for litigation abuses under 28 U.S.C. § 1927. Courts that exclude bankruptcy courts from this category do so because the bankruptcy judges do not have Article III status.[122] The prevailing view, though, runs the other way, reasoning that bankruptcy judges are "units" of the Article III district court and are "judicial officers" of the district court.[123]

The jurisdiction of the federal district courts over bankruptcy proceedings is limited by 28 U.S.C. § 1334(c), which provides for the district court to *abstain* from hearing certain types of proceedings that implicate state law.[124] Recall that federal jurisdiction over bankruptcy proceedings is not exclusive. 28 U.S.C. § 1334(b). Section 1334(c) speaks to the allocation of judicial power as between the state and federal courts, rather than between the district and bankruptcy courts in the federal system. Abstention may be *permissive*, under § 1334(c)(1), or *mandatory*, under § 1334(c)(2).

§ 4.4   Core Proceedings

Bankruptcy judges are authorized by 28 U.S.C. § 157(b) to *"hear and determine"* all "core proceedings" in a bankruptcy case. The practical significance of this grant of power is that the bankruptcy judge will enter a *final order* in the core proceeding, subject only to review on appeal by an Article III judge. In non-core related proceedings, by contrast, the bankruptcy judge may not enter a final order absent the consent of the parties.[125]

---

[118] See, e.g., *Terrebonne Fuel and Lube*, supra note 16, 108 F.3d 609; In re Power Recovery Sys., Inc., 950 F.2d 798 (1st Cir. 1991); In re Hipp, Inc., 895 F.2d 1503 (5th Cir. 1990). But see In re Ragar, 3 F.3d 1174 (8th Cir. 1993) (bankruptcy court could punish for criminal contempt, subject to defendant's opportunity to seek de novo review by district court).

[119] For a good discussion of the contempt issue, concluding that bankruptcy judges cannot constitutionally exercise the contempt power, see Laura B. Bartell, Contempt of the Bankruptcy Court—A New Look, 1996 U. Ill. L. Rev. 1 (1996).

[120] 28 U.S.C. § 2412.

[121] 26 U.S.C. § 7430.

[122] See, e.g., In re Brickell Inv. Corp., 922 F.2d 696 (11th Cir. 1991) (interpreting 26 U.S.C. § 7430).

[123] See, e.g., United States v. Yochum (In re Yochum), 89 F.3d 661 (9th Cir. 1996) (rejecting *Brickell*); Grewe v. United States (In re Grewe), 4 F.3d 299 (4th Cir. 1993) (interpreting 26 U.S.C. § 7430); O'Connor v. U.S. Dep't of Energy, 942 F.2d 771 (10th Cir. 1991) (interpreting 28 U.S.C. § 2412).

[124] See § 4.7.

[125] This assumes, of course, that consent to the exercise of jurisdiction is upheld, which as the previous section explained, is a subject of some debate. Compare Exec. Benefits Ins. Agency v. Arkinson (In re Bellingham Ins. Agency, Inc.), 702 F.3d 553, 566–70 (9th Cir. 2012) (consent valid), with Waldman v. Stone, 698 F.3d 910, 918 (6th Cir. 2012) (consent invalid).

Core proceedings are those that *"arise under"* title 11 or *"arise in"* a title 11 case. 28 U.S.C. § 157(b)(1). Proceedings that are *"related to"* a title 11 case are classified as non-core. 28 U.S.C. § 157(c)(1). In theory, core proceedings are those that are integrally bound up in the bankruptcy process, i.e., they go to the "core" of the bankruptcy function. A popular test, espoused by the Fifth Circuit in *Wood* and cited favorably by many courts, classifies a proceeding as core if it "invokes a substantive right provided by title 11 or . . . by its nature, could arise only in the context of a bankruptcy case."[126] Other courts, though, have found the latter part of that test unduly restrictive, as explained below.

The *Wood* court elucidated the difference in "arising under" and "arising in" jurisdiction—the two facets of core proceedings—as follows:

> "Congress used the phrase "arising under title 11" to describe those proceedings that involve a cause of action created or determined by a statutory provision of title 11. Apparently, the phrase was taken from 28 U.S.C. § 1331, conferring federal question jurisdiction in which it carries a similar and well-accepted meaning. The meaning of "arising in" proceedings is less clear, but seems to be a reference to those "administrative" matters that arise *only* in bankruptcy cases. In other words, "arising in" proceedings are those that are not based on any right expressly created by title 11, but nevertheless, would have no existence outside of the bankruptcy."[127]

Note, though, that the leading scholar on federal bankruptcy jurisdiction, Professor Brubaker, after an exhaustive historical analysis, ascribes importantly different meanings to these terms, with the crucial difference being with respect to "arising in" jurisdiction:

> "'Arising under'" and 'arising in' proceedings, therefore, can be seen as *statutory* grants of federal jurisdiction over all *constitutional* federal question claims "arising" during the administration of a bankruptcy case—claims created by the Bankruptcy Code ("arising under") and claims by and against a bankruptcy estate ("arising in")."[128]

At least with regard to *post*-petition based disputes, two circuits have adopted a view of "arising in" jurisdiction more in line with Professor Brubaker's reading, and have found that actions involving a contract with the estate or an estate asset to be "core."[129] In holding the estate's suit to collect a debt from the post-petition sale of an estate asset to be core, even though the recovery of a contract claim is by its nature based on state law, the First Circuit observed that "It is the nature of the proceeding—its relation to the basic function of the bankruptcy court—not the state or federal basis

---

[126] In re Wood, 825 F.2d 90, 97 (5th Cir. 1987).

[127] Id. at 96–97.

[128] Ralph Brubaker, On the Nature of Federal Bankruptcy Jurisdiction: A General Statutory and Constitutional Theory, 41 Wm. & Mary L. Rev. 743, 856 (2000) (emphasis in original).

[129] See In re Ben Cooper, Inc., 896 F.2d 1394, 1399 (2d Cir.), certiorari granted and judgment vacated, 498 U.S. 964 (1990), opinion reinstated, 924 F.2d 36 (2d Cir.1991); In re Arnold Print Works, Inc., 815 F.2d 165 (1st Cir. 1987); see also In re Harris 590 F.3d 730, 740 (9th Cir. 2009) (citing In re Arnold, 815 F.2d 165).

for the claim, that makes the difference here."[130] The statute does make clear that a determination that a proceeding is not a core proceeding should not be based solely on the fact that its resolution may be affected by state law. 28 U.S.C. § 157(b)(3).

However defined, what is clear is that as to such matters, untenured bankruptcy judges have the *statutory* authority to enter final orders. The question then is whether they also have the *constitutional* authority, as delineated in *Stern* and *Marathon*. As *Stern* made manifest, the fact that a matter is statutorily core does not dictate that it will necessarily pass constitutional muster, Resolution of the statutory question, though, is bound up in, although not dispositive of, the constitutional inquiry. Courts have construed congressional intent in BAFJA as attempting to allocate statutory jurisdiction as between bankruptcy and district judges so as to comply with the constitutional commands of *Marathon*, and, indeed, to press that allocation up the outer limit of constitutionality. Yet, we saw in *Stern* that the Supreme Court declined to read the statutory grant of core proceedings as necessarily coextensive with the constitutional limits.[131] Indeed, as discussed below, even with such professed congressional constraint, the Supreme Court ruled that Congress has crossed the constitutional line by defining the scope of core proceedings too broadly.[132]

To provide more detailed guidance as to what constitutes a core proceeding, Congress provided a nonexclusive list in 28 U.S.C. § 157(b)(2). This list includes matters involving:

- administration of the estate, § 157(b)(2)(A);

- allowance or disallowance of claims or exemptions, and estimation of claims, § 157(b)(2)(B);

- counterclaims by the estate against persons filing claims, § 157(b)(2)(C);[133]

- obtaining of credit, § 157(b)(2)(D);

- turnover of estate property, § 157(b)(2)(E);

- preferences, § 157(b)(2)(F);

- relief from the automatic stay, § 157(b)(2)(G);

- fraudulent conveyances, § 157(b)(2)(H);

- dischargeability of debts, § 157(b)(2)(I);

- discharge objections, § 157(b)(2)(J);

---

[130] *Arnold Print Works*, supra note 129, 815 F.2d at 169.

[131] Stern v. Marshall, 131 S.Ct. 2594, 2604–05 (2011).

[132] Long before *Stern*, commentators had raised questions about the constitutionality of the broad scope of core proceedings. See, e.g., Lawrence P. King, Jurisdiction and Procedure Under the Bankruptcy Amendments of 1984, 38 Vand. L. Rev. 675, 687–93 (1985).

[133] This, of course, was the provision that was held unconstitutional as applied to the counterclaim at issue in *Stern*. 131 S.Ct. at 2620.

- the validity, extent, or priority of liens, § 157(b)(2)(K);

- confirmation of plans, § 157(b)(2)(L);

- use or lease of property, § 157(b)(2)(M);

- sale of property, § 157(b)(2)(N);

- "other proceedings affecting the liquidation of the assets of the estate or the adjustment of the debtor-creditor . . . relationship," § 157(b)(2)(O), and

- recognition of foreign proceedings and other matters under chapter 15 (this category was added in 2005), § 157(b)(2)(P).

These 16 types of core proceedings can be grouped informally into four major categories: (1) administrative matters; (2) avoiding powers; (3) matters affecting property of the estate; and (4) catch-all.

Those listings that implicate matters of bankruptcy administration are: (A), administration of the estate; (B), allowance of claims and exemptions; (D), credit; (G), stay relief; (I) and (J), discharge; and (L), plan confirmation. Indeed, subsection (A) by itself is probably broad enough to subsume all of the other listed administrative categories. These administrative proceedings would not exist absent a bankruptcy case, and lie at the heart of bankruptcy jurisdiction.

A critical starting point in assessing what parts of the statutory designation of core proceedings in section 157(b) remain constitutionally permissible after *Stern* is to emphasize that all matters having to do with the allowance of claims against the bankruptcy estate may be finally decided by the non-Article III bankruptcy judge. Indeed, the Court's very holding that denied the bankruptcy court's constitutional power to issue a final order on Vickie's counterclaim emphasized that the counterclaim was "not resolved in the process of ruling on a creditor's proof of claim."[134] Obviously the inference is that if the counterclaim *had* been resolved in the process of ruling on the proof of claim, then all would be well constitutionally, even with the non-Article III bankruptcy judge issuing the final judgment. And that could only be true because the proof of claim allowance process itself fell within the bankruptcy judge's permitted powers. Further, the Court's obvious approval of the holdings in both *Katchen*[135] and *Langenkamp*,[136] both of which treated preference counterclaims to filed proofs of claim as matters of private right within the bankruptcy court's permissible jurisdiction, and the fact that it went to great pains to distinguish those cases from Vickie's case because resolution of the proof of claim filed against Vickie's estate would not dispose of her

---

[134] Id.

[135] 382 U.S. 323 (1966).

[136] 498 U.S. 42 (1990).

counterclaim,[137] all point ineluctably to a conclusion that claims allowance proceedings even after *Stern* may be finally determined by non-Article III bankruptcy judges.[138]

Two of the trustee's avoiding powers are specifically listed in § 157(b)(2), namely, the powers to set aside and recover preferences, § 157(b)(2)(F), and fraudulent conveyances, § 157(b)(2)(H). Other avoiding powers, such as the § 544(a) "strong-arm" power, while not included in § 157(b)(2), are considered core proceedings as well. The constitutionality of the bankruptcy judge "hearing and determining" *all* avoidance actions is highly questionable after *Stern v. Marshall.* The Ninth Circuit has squarely held that preference and fraudulent transfer avoidance actions may not be finally adjudicated by the non-Article III bankruptcy court.[139] *Stern* seems to demand that result, especially as to fraudulent conveyance actions. Yet, other lower courts have disagreed, taking a "narrow interpretation" of Stern, and limiting it to its specific facts, and thus have held that a bankruptcy court may enter a final order in preference and fraudulent transfer actions.[140]

Under the law under the pre–1978 Bankruptcy Act, which the *Stern* Court seemingly constitutionalized,[141] actions by the trustee to recover preferences and fraudulent conveyances had to be brought as "plenary" proceedings in a state court or federal district court with jurisdiction unless the defendant "consented" to the summary jurisdiction of the bankruptcy court. Such consent would be found, for example, if the defendant had filed a proof of claim in the bankruptcy case.[142]

These also are precisely the sort of estate-augmenting actions that the Supreme Court found questionable in *Stern.*[143] Indeed, the *Stern* Court explicitly linked the scope of Article III to the scope of the jury trial right, and invoked *Granfinanciera*[144]—a fraudulent conveyance case—to argue that such a "quintessential[ ] suit[ ] at common law" would be a matter of private rather than public right, and as such could be finally determined only by an Article III court.[145]

Under the current system, however, core jurisdiction lies in the bankruptcy court for all avoidance actions even if the defendant has not filed a claim or otherwise consented. In *Stern,* the Court held that *even though* the creditor had filed a proof of claim, Article III still demanded adjudication by an Article III judge unless the estate's counterclaim against the creditor would "necessarily be resolved in the claims

---

[137] *Stern,* 131 S.Ct. at 2615–18.

[138] As Professor Brubaker explains: "The *Stern v. Marshall* Court's willingness to regard and treat both *Katchen v. Landy* and *Langenkamp v. Culp* as if they were binding precedent for purposes of Article III means that bankruptcy judges' core jurisdiction in claims allowance proceedings appears constitutionally sound." Ralph Brubaker, A "Summary" Statutory and Constitutional Theory of Bankruptcy Judges' Core Jurisdiction After *Stern v. Marshall,* 86 Am. Bankr. L.J. 121, 173 (2012).

[139] *Bellingham,* supra note 125, 702 F.3d at 565–66.

[140] See, e.g., In re Direct Response Media, Inc., 466 B.R. 626, 644 (Bankr. D. Del. 2012).

[141] Brubaker, supra note 138, at 122.

[142] See Katchen v. Landy, 382 U.S. 323 (1966).

[143] 131 S.Ct. at 2618.

[144] Granfinanciera, S.A. v. Nordberg, 492 U.S. 33 (1989).

[145] *Stern,* 131 S.Ct. at 2614.

allowance process"[146]—and concluded that factually such was not the case there. Note, though, that if resolution of the creditor's proof of claim *does* necessarily resolve the fraudulent transfer counterclaim, with "nothing remain[ing] for adjudication," then the bankruptcy court may not only finally determine the fraudulent transfer claim, but may award affirmative relief as well.[147] That is basically what happened in *Katchen*. The outcome, then, is case-specific, depending on whether the bankruptcy court's constitutionally permissible final resolution of the issue of allowance of the creditor's proof of claim will or will not also resolve the estate's counterclaim against the creditor, be it for avoidance and recovery of a fraudulent conveyance, avoidance under the strong-arm clause of § 544(a),[148] or for a state law tort claim.

With regard to those avoiding powers that are created entirely by Congress, such as preferences under § 547, the chances are greater that the untenured bankruptcy judge may constitutionally hear and determine the proceeding. The argument supporting that conclusion is that preference avoidance is solely a creature of the federal Bankruptcy Code, and a preference action would not exist but for the bankruptcy. In the *Marathon* case, the plurality opinion indicated that Congress had considerably more discretion to assign the determination of congressionally created rights to a non-Article III forum.[149] In *Stern* the Court reaffirmed that view,[150] and even distinguished *Katchen*[151] and *Langenkamp*[152] in part because in those cases—unlike in Vickie's—"the trustee bringing the preference action was asserting a right of recovery created by federal bankruptcy law."[153] Under this view, a preference action, which is created by § 547 of the Bankruptcy Code and does not exist outside of bankruptcy, could be decided by a bankruptcy judge. And yet, the *Stern* Court in discussing *Katchen* and *Langenkamp*—both preference cases—*also* distinguished them from the case before it because resolution of the claims allowance issue in those cases would of necessity also dispose of the preference claim. Indeed, the Court in *Stern* apparently embraced (and as Professor Brubaker has argued, seemingly constitutionalized[154]) the plenary/summary divide under the 1898 Act, and indisputably under that Act, a preference action not brought as a counterclaim had to be brought as a plenary action.

Regardless of how preference claims are decided, however, the power to set aside fraudulent conveyances is *not* created solely by federal bankruptcy law. State law has authorized the avoidance of fraudulent conveyances since colonial times. In other words, a fraudulent conveyance action can be brought even if a bankruptcy case is

---

[146] Id. at 2615–18.

[147] In re Global Technovations, Inc., 694 F.3d 705, 722–23 (6th Cir. 2012).

[148] For example, the Bankruptcy Court for the Southern District of New York had a fascinating case involving competing claims to a painting by Botticelli. Resolution of a lift stay motion, strong-arm clause avoidance, and a proof of claim all were intertwined. Since determination of the proof of claim would resolve also the avoidance claim, the judge held that final determination by a bankruptcy court was constitutionally permissible. In re Salander O'Reilly Galleries, 453 B.R. 106 (Bankr. S.D.N.Y. 2011).

[149] 458 U.S. 50, 83–84 (1982) (Brennan, J., plurality).

[150] 131 S.Ct. at 2613–14.

[151] 382 U.S. 323 (1966).

[152] 498 U.S. 42 (1990).

[153] *Stern*, 131 S.Ct. at 2618.

[154] Brubaker, supra note 138, at 122.

never filed. While § 548 creates a fraudulent conveyance avoiding power in bankruptcy, § 544(b) of the Code also permits the bankruptcy trustee to invoke the rights of unsecured creditors to set aside fraudulent conveyances under state law. Accordingly, the constitutionality of the non-Article III bankruptcy judge entering a final order in a fraudulent conveyance action (especially under § 544(b)) was uncertain even before *Stern*, and I believe after *Stern* is definitely foreclosed. This uncertainty was underscored by the Supreme Court's holding in *Granfinanciera, S.A. v. Nordberg*[155] that the jury trial right under the Seventh Amendment applies in a fraudulent conveyance action brought in a bankruptcy case. The Court in *Granfinanciera* declined to take the view that all core proceedings in a bankruptcy case are somehow imbued with the "equitable" character of the bankruptcy; instead, some proceedings (such as the fraudulent conveyance action at issue) retain their essential character as "quintessentially suits at common law."[156] In *Stern*, as discussed before, the Court explicitly adopted the rationale of *Granfinanciera* from the Seventh Amendment world and transported it, lock, stock, and barrel, to the Article III realm.

The third category of core proceedings are those that affect the property of the estate. The district court has *exclusive* jurisdiction over estate property. 28 U.S.C. § 1334(e)(1). The apparent intent of Congress in defining core proceedings to include most types of controversies involving estate property is to have the bankruptcy judge exercise the jurisdiction conferred on the district courts by § 1334(e). Those subsections of § 157(b)(2) relating to property of the estate are: (E), orders to turn over estate property; (K), determinations of the validity, extent, or priority of liens; (M), orders approving the use or lease of property; and (N), orders approving the sale of property

The most controversy in applying these provisions has been with regard to the turnover provision, § 157(b)(2)(E). The debate is whether an action to collect a prepetition contract debt owing to the debtor should be classified as a core proceeding or a non-core proceeding. On the face of the statute, such an action could plausibly be deemed core: a debt owing to the debtor at the time the case commences is property of the estate, § 541(a)(1), and must be paid over to the trustee, § 542(b). Further, the estate (represented by the trustee or debtor in possession) is a party to such a suit. Professor Brubaker asserts that an historical appreciation of the development of the bankruptcy jurisdictional regime indicates that *Marathon*-type claims (suits by the estate on a debtor's prepetition state law claim) should be construed to fall within the meaning of "arising in" jurisdiction.[157] The reasoning of *Stern* shows that BAFJA failed to fix the *Marathon* problem: the very breach of contract action that the *Marathon* Court held could not constitutionally be determined by a non-Article III bankruptcy judge would yet again be assigned under § 157(b)(1) to the untenured bankruptcy judge. Thus, indulging in the presumption that Congress intended to comply with the constitutional commands of Article III as outlined by the Supreme Court, most courts have held that actions by the trustee to collect prepetition debts are not core proceedings.[158] Such plainly was the espoused intent of Congress in 1984. In enacting

---

[155]   492 U.S. 33 (1989). See § 4.8.a.

[156]   492 U.S. at 56.

[157]   Brubaker, supra note 128, at 856.

[158]   See, e.g., In re Orion Pictures Corp., 4 F.3d 1095 (2d Cir. 1993).

§ 157 in 1984, Congress drew inspiration from the repeated statements in dicta by Justice Brennan in his plurality opinion in *Marathon* that the suit before the Court fell within "related to" jurisdiction. Even though Justice Brennan likely was wrong,[159] his "throwaway dicta"[160] has now become the law.

Having said that, though, one must be cognizant of the fact that *some* turnover claims by the estate to collect debts are so routine and uncontested that they might in fact fall within the bankruptcy court's constitutionally permissible core jurisdiction. How so? The reason is that in *Stern* the Court embraced (resurrected?) as a dispositive method of analysis the summary/plenary divide under the 1898 Act. And under that Act, claims by the estate to recover a pre-petition debt as to which no meaningful defense was raised were considered to fall within the summary jurisdiction of the bankruptcy court. Only actions brought against an "adverse claimant" had to be brought in a plenary suit. The magic that made this happen was that such uncontested claims were deemed to be within the *constructive possession* of the bankruptcy court.[161]

Even if suits by the estate to collect *pre*-petition debts are held to be non-core in order to comply with *Marathon*, the same constraint does not apply to suits to collect accounts that arise *post*-petition pursuant to a transaction involving the bankruptcy estate. Such actions have been held to be "core" within the meaning of the statutory grant in § 157.[162] Furthermore, that classification has been held to be constitutional under *Marathon*[163] and likewise should be permissible under *Stern*. Courts have pointed out that even under the 1898 Act, suits by the estate representative to collect post-petition claims fell within the summary jurisdiction of the federal court.

The catch-all provisions in § 157(b)(2) are also open to interpretation and controversy. One such omnibus provision is subsection (A), referring to matters involving the administration of the estate, discussed above. Another is subsection (O), which designates as core every proceeding "affecting the liquidation of the assets of the estate" as well as those affecting "the adjustment of the debtor-creditor relationship." These expansively worded phrases could be read to comprehend virtually any proceeding that in any way relates to the bankruptcy case. Such a broad interpretation would run afoul of *Marathon*, and therefore is not likely to reflect congressional intent. Congress intended, however, to expand the bankruptcy judge's power to hear and determine core proceedings to the outer limits of constitutional authority.

In ascertaining those outer limits, courts have historically taken note of the fact that the Supreme Court itself had read the *Marathon* decision narrowly. For example, in *Thomas v. Union Carbide Agricultural Products Co.*, the Court observed that *Marathon* "establishes only that Congress may not vest in a non-Article III court the power to adjudicate, render final judgment, and issue binding orders in a traditional contract action arising under state law, without consent of the litigants, and subject

---

[159] See Brubaker, supra note 128, at 857–59.

[160] Id. at 856.

[161] Brubaker, supra note 138, at 128.

[162] See *Arnold Print Works*, supra note 129, 815 F.2d at 168–69.

[163] Id. at 169–70.

only to ordinary appellate review."[164] This view of *Marathon* tracks more closely the concurring opinion in that case; it does not embrace the more restrictive view of the plurality. The Court reaffirmed its narrow view of *Marathon* in *Commodity Futures Trading Commission v. Schor*.[165] However, this approach has been called into question by the reaffirmation of *Marathon* in *Stern*, though some courts have relied on self-limiting language in *Stern* to continue construing the constitutional limit broadly.[166]

Until *Stern*, the 1984 amendments revived the concept of "jurisdiction by ambush" in § 157(b)(2)(C), which classifies a counterclaim by the estate against a person who files a claim against the estate as a core proceeding. In other words, if a creditor files a claim against the estate, *any* counterclaim the estate has against that creditor could have been brought as a core proceeding as to which the bankruptcy judge could issue a final order. Note that the statute does not limit its reach to compulsory counterclaims, but presumably would extend to permissive counterclaims as well. Nor is it limited on its face to counterclaims necessarily resolved in the claims allowance process (the fatal flaw in *Stern*). The basic premise of subsection (C) is that the non-debtor party has consented to the jurisdiction of the bankruptcy court by filing the proof of claim. This idea is derived from a 1966 Supreme Court decision, *Katchen v. Landy*,[167] which held that the filing of a proof of claim submitted the creditor to the summary jurisdiction of the bankruptcy court with regard to a preference action. In *Schor*, a 1986 non-bankruptcy case, the Court upheld in very limited circumstances the constitutionality of having a non-Article III forum adjudicate state law counterclaims.[168] However, as discussed above, in *Stern*, while the Court reaffirmed the vitality of *Katchen*, nevertheless it limited its reach, and declined to find constitutional authority for a non-Article III bankruptcy judge to issue a final order on a traditional state law tort claim that was not necessarily resolved in ruling on the proof of claim.[169] Nor did the mere fact that Pierce filed a proof of claim somehow signify his consent to adjudication by the bankruptcy court.[170] Plainly, then, post-*Stern* § 157(b)(2)(C) cannot be given literal effect in all cases without violating the commands of Article III. Therefore, if the debtor has a prepetition state law claim against a party, such as the contract claim involved in *Marathon*, the tort claim in *Stern*, or the fraudulent conveyance claim in *Granfinanciera*, the filing of a proof of claim by that non-debtor party would not automatically obviate the non-waivable constitutional objection to having an untenured judge hear and determine the private state law claim. Instead, after *Stern*,

---

[164]   473 U.S. 568, 584 (1985).

[165]   478 U.S. 833 (1986).

[166]   E.g. In re AFY, Inc., 461 B.R. 541, 547–48 (B.A.P. 8th Cir. 2012) ("Unless and until the Supreme Court visits other provisions of Section 157(b)(2), we take the Supreme Court at its word and hold that the balance of the authority granted to bankruptcy judges by Congress in 28 U.S.C. § 157(b)(2) is constitutional."); Kurz v. EMAK Worldwide, 464 B.R. 635, 645 n.6 (D. Del. 2011); Feuerbacher v. Moser, No. 4:11–CV–272, 2012 WL 1070138, at *6 (E.D. Tex. March 29, 2012) (*Stern* does not extend *Granfinanciera* to Article III division of authority between bankruptcy and district court.).

[167]   382 U.S. 323 (1966).

[168]   478 U.S. 833 (1986).

[169]   131 S.Ct. at 2620.

[170]   Id. at 2614 ("Pierce did not truly consent to resolution of Vickie's claim in the bankruptcy court proceedings.")

such a counterclaim can be finally adjudicated by the bankruptcy court only if resolving the proof of claim necessarily also disposes of the counterclaim.[171]

§ 4.5   Related Proceedings

Bankruptcy jurisdiction extends not only to proceedings that "arise under" title 11 and those that "arise in" a title 11 case,[172] but also to proceedings that are *related to* a case under title 11. 28 U.S.C. § 1334(b). Proceedings that are "related to" a bankruptcy case are referred to as "related" or "non-core" proceedings. In terms of the allocation of judicial power between the district judge and the bankruptcy judge, only the district judge has the power to enter a final order in a related proceeding. The bankruptcy judge may "hear" the non-core, related matter, but may only submit proposed findings of fact and conclusions of law to the district judge. 28 U.S.C. § 157(c)(1). If the parties *consent*, however, the bankruptcy judge may hear and determine the related proceeding, i.e., enter a final order reviewable only on appeal. 28 U.S.C. § 157(c)(2). As noted in the preceding sections, doubt has been expressed as to the constitutionality of litigant consent,[173] although I believe that the better view, based on what the Supreme Court said in *Stern*, is that a litigant's right to Article III adjudication can be waived.[174] These limits on the untenured bankruptcy judge's powers in related proceedings were designed to alleviate the Article III constitutional problem identified in the *Marathon Pipe Line* case.[175] Of course, *Stern* showed that Congress still put too much in the "core" basket.

The issue of the proper scope of related proceedings arises in two ways. One is in ascertaining whether a proceeding is "core" or "non-core" (i.e., "related"). The two types of proceedings are mutually exclusive. The bankruptcy judge may enter a final order in a core proceeding, but not in a related proceeding, unless the parties consent. Thus, this first inquiry concerns the allocation of jurisdiction as between Article III federal district judges and non-Article III federal bankruptcy judges. The second scenario in which the question arises is in determining whether federal bankruptcy jurisdiction exists at all. "Related to" jurisdiction represents the outer limits of federal bankruptcy jurisdiction under 28 U.S.C. § 1334. If a proceeding is not related to the bankruptcy case, federal bankruptcy jurisdiction does not exist. This second inquiry speaks to the allocation of judicial power as between the federal and state courts. Note that the reenactment of the jurisdictional scheme in 1984 in BAFJA did nothing to change the answer to the second question; the scope of federal bankruptcy jurisdiction under

---

[171] See In re Global Technovations, Inc., 694 F.3d 705, 722–23 (6th Cir. 2012). See also *Bellingham*, 702 F.3d at 564 ("the dispositive distinction between the claims in *Stern* and *Katchen* was that in *Katchen*, the trustee's preference action 'would necessarily be resolved in the claims allowance process' because the defendant had filed a proof of claim against the bankruptcy estate.") (Quoting *Stern*, 131 S.Ct. at 2618); Brubaker, supra note 138, at 171.

[172] See § 4.3.

[173] Compare Exec. Benefits Ins. Agency v. Arkinson (In re Bellingham Ins. Agency, Inc.), 702 F.3d 553, 566–70 (9th Cir. 2012) (consent valid) with Waldman v. Stone, 698 F.3d 910, 918 (6th Cir. 2012) (consent invalid).

[174] The Court noted that the allocation of authority to enter a final judgment does not implicate questions of subject matter jurisdiction. 131 S.Ct. 2594, 2607 (2011). See Ralph Brubaker, The Constitutionality of Litigant Consent to Non–Article III Bankruptcy Adjudications, 32 Bankr. L. Letter 1 (Dec. 2012). Moreover, a consent-based magistrate system has been upheld by the courts.

[175] 458 U.S. 50 (1982). See § 4.2.d.

§ 1334 remained the same as it had been under the 1978 law in § 1471. What was changed in 1984 was the answer to the first question, regarding the distribution of jurisdiction as between district judges and bankruptcy judges, under § 157.

Congress in its infinite wisdom did not choose in BAFJA to define either core proceedings or related proceedings. The Emergency Rule (which governed during the period between *Marathon* and BAFJA), defined a related proceeding as a civil proceeding that could have been brought in federal district court or state court absent the bankruptcy case. Such a definition may be helpful in answering the question of whether an action already falling within the federal bankruptcy jurisdiction is to be heard and determined by the district judge or the bankruptcy judge (under § 157), but helps not at all in delineating the scope of federal bankruptcy jurisdiction as between the federal courts and state courts (under § 1334).

So what is the ultimate scope of federal bankruptcy jurisdiction under § 1334? In defining the outer boundary of bankruptcy jurisdiction, the Third Circuit in *Pacor, Inc. v. Higgins*[176] announced the leading test of related proceedings:

> The test for determining whether a civil proceeding is related to bankruptcy is whether the outcome of the proceeding could *conceivably have any effect* on the estate being administered in bankruptcy. . . . An action is related to bankruptcy if the outcome could alter the debtor's rights, liabilities, options, or freedom of action (either positively or negatively) and which in any way impacts upon the handling and administration of the bankrupt estate.

Courts since *Pacor* have emphasized that the *"conceivable effect"* test is quite broad, and does not require showing that the proceeding is likely to or probably will affect the bankruptcy case; all that must be shown is a *conceivable* or potential effect.[177] In some types of cases, the effect on the bankruptcy case is evident, and jurisdiction plainly lies. For example, an action by the bankruptcy estate asserting a prepetition state law cause of action for breach of contract against a non-debtor party— such as the case in *Marathon*—would be a related proceeding.[178] In other cases, however, when the bankruptcy estate is neither implicated directly in nor a party to the suit, and the action at issue concerns only third parties, the case for federal bankruptcy jurisdiction is more attenuated. The issue often arises when the estate seeks to enjoin an action between two other parties, arguing that the resolution of that third-party dispute will have a collateral effect on the bankruptcy case. In those instances, bankruptcy jurisdiction may still lie, but only if the effect can be demonstrated.

---

[176] 743 F.2d 984, 994 (3d Cir. 1984) (emphasis added); Nuveen Mun. Trust v. Withumsmith Brown, 692 F.3d 283 (3d. Cir. 2012) (citing *Pacor*, 743 F.2d 984 (3d Cir. 1984)).

[177] In re Wood, 825 F.2d 90, 94 (5th Cir. 1987); Halper v. Halper, 164 F.3d 830 (3d. Cir. 1999); In re G–I Holdings Inc., 278 B.R. 376 (Bankr. D. N.J. 2002)

[178] E.g., In re Orion Pictures Corp., 4 F.3d 1095 (2d Cir. 1993). Recall, though, that Professor Brubaker has argued convincingly that properly understood, *Marathon* is an illustration of "arising in" jurisdiction, not "related to" jurisdiction." Ralph Brubaker, On the Nature of Federal Bankruptcy Jurisdiction: A General Statutory and Constitutional Theory, 41 Wm. & Mary L. Rev. 743, 856 (2000).

The Supreme Court in *Celotex Corp. v. Edwards* summarized the law as follows: "Proceedings "related to" the bankruptcy include (1) causes of action owned by the debtor which become property of the estate pursuant to 11 U.S.C. § 541, and (2) suits between third parties which have an effect on the bankruptcy estate."[179] While the *Celotex* Court cautioned that the reach of bankruptcy jurisdiction was "not limitless," it also approved the *Pacor* view that Congress intended to provide bankruptcy jurisdiction of "some breadth" that would "grant comprehensive jurisdiction to the bankruptcy courts so that they might deal efficiently and expeditiously with all matters connected with the bankruptcy estate."[180] Furthermore, on the "actions speak louder than words" theory, the Court's actual decision in that case indicated a very expansive approach to bankruptcy jurisdiction. In *Celotex*, the debtor in a chapter 11 case obtained an injunction in the bankruptcy court prohibiting a judgment creditor from executing on a supersedeas bond *against a third party surety*. The Supreme Court concluded that the entry of that injunction fell within the federal court's "related to" jurisdiction, because execution on the bond might have impacted negatively on the debtor's prospects for reorganization.[181]

Note that the Court so held even though the action was not against the debtor, and did not directly affect property of the bankruptcy estate. The bankruptcy court had found that if execution on the bond were permitted, the surety (and others like it) would attempt to realize on insurance proceeds that the debtor had deposited as collateral to secure the bond. The debtor's reorganization prospects, however, depended on effecting a global settlement of all insurance-related obligations. Such a settlement would not be possible if the sureties acted against those insurance proceeds. The Court in *Celotex* noted in dicta that the reach of bankruptcy jurisdiction might be greater in a chapter 11 case than in chapter 7.[182]

Prior to *Celotex,* a number of lower courts similarly had concluded that bankruptcy jurisdiction existed over a third party injunction entered in order to promote the debtor's chances of reorganizing. For example, in a number of the mass tort cases, suits against insurers and other third parties were enjoined on the theory that doing so would facilitate the reorganization.[183] If, however, the injunction would not have a conceivable effect on the bankruptcy, then jurisdiction would not lie.

A common type of case in which the courts have refused to find "related to" jurisdiction is where the suit is between two non-debtor parties, and does not have even an indirect effect on estate property.[184] If the debtor is not a party and property of the estate is not at issue, the courts are extremely reluctant to find jurisdiction. Courts emphasize that even under the "conceivable effect" test, the matter at issue must have

---

[179]   514 U.S. 300, 307–08 n.5 (1995).

[180]   Id. at 308.

[181]   Id. at 309–10.

[182]   Id. at 310.

[183]   E.g., MacArthur Co. v. Johns–Manville Corp., 837 F.2d 89 (2d Cir.), cert. denied, 488 U.S. 868 (1988); A.H. Robins Co. v. Piccinin, 788 F.2d 994 (4th Cir.), cert. denied, 479 U.S. 876 (1986).

[184]   E.g., Specialty Mills, Inc. v. Citizens State Bank, 51 F.3d 770 (8th Cir. 1995); In re Walker, 51 F.3d 562 (5th Cir. 1995).

some identifiable "nexus" to the bankruptcy case.[185] These courts are sensitive to the federalism concerns that underlie the appropriate interpretation of the scope of any federal jurisdictional statute.

The *Pacor* "conceivable effect" test has enjoyed surprising staying power. Conceptually, though, the test is essentially incoherent and meaningless, and offers no real insight into how to resolve particular cases.[186] Obviously the test cannot be applied according to its literal terms, because then the jurisdiction in bankruptcy would be virtually limitless. Courts are left to guess on an ad hoc basis what is too much of a jurisdictional grab to stomach in any particular case, and accordingly results are hard to predict. Sadly, courts could achieve much more coherent and predictable results if they recognized that "related to" jurisdiction in bankruptcy is nothing more than a form of supplemental jurisdiction, a well-understood and well-formed procedural doctrine.[187]

Whether jurisdiction lies in a suit against the bankruptcy trustee depends on whether the trustee is being sued in his official or personal capacity, and whether estate property is implicated. If the suit is only against the trustee individually, and does not seek recovery against estate property, jurisdiction does not exist, even if the action is predicated on acts committed by the trustee in the performance of his duties.[188] However, if the trustee is sued in his official capacity and if assets of the estate are vulnerable to recovery, the action is maintainable under bankruptcy jurisdiction.[189]

A case that is based on *post*-petition acts also may lie outside of the ambit of federal jurisdiction. If the case is under chapter 7, and the claim is by the debtor, then the cause of action is not property of the estate, and the outcome could not have an effect on the estate. Any recovery will go only to the debtor. Accordingly, bankruptcy jurisdiction will not exist.[190] However, if the action is by the trustee on behalf of the estate, then any recovery will become property of the estate, and accordingly the action will be within the ambit of bankruptcy jurisdiction.[191]

§ 4.6   Withdrawal of the Reference

One of the basic components of the bankruptcy jurisdictional scheme enacted in 1984 in response to *Marathon* was to give the Article III district judge the power to *withdraw* the reference of a proceeding to the bankruptcy judge. 28 U.S.C. § 157(d). The district court's withdrawal power is part of the effort to alleviate the constitutional difficulty of having an untenured bankruptcy judge exercise judicial power. Recall that

---

[185] In re Lemco Gypsum, Inc., 910 F.2d 784, 787 (11th Cir. 1990); In re Hospitality Ventures/LaVista, 358 B.R. 462 (Bankr. N.D. Ga. 2007)

[186] Professor Brubaker has thoroughly demonstrated the manifold shortcomings of the *Pacor* test. See Brubaker, supra note 178, 41 Wm. & Mary L. Rev. at 869–903.

[187] Id. at 755, 921–33.

[188] E.g., In re Guild & Gallery Plus, Inc., 72 F.3d 1171 (3d Cir. 1996).

[189] See Robinson v. Michigan Consol. Gas Co., 918 F.2d 579 (6th Cir. 1990).

[190] E.g., In re Boone, 52 F.3d 958 (11th Cir. 1995); In re Bobroff, 766 F.2d 797 (3d Cir. 1985).

[191] E.g., In re Arnold Print Works, Inc., 815 F.2d 165 (1st Cir. 1987).

under § 157(b)(1), proceedings in bankruptcy may initially be referred to the bankruptcy judge by the district judge, and that in practice all district courts have entered a standing order of general reference. The idea behind § 157(d) is that more of the "essential attributes" of judicial power reside in the tenured district judge if that judge retains the power to decide a matter in the first instance, even if in any particular instance that power might go unexercised. Of course, given that the right to withdraw is almost never exercised in fact, in *Stern* the Court concluded that the mere potentiality of withdrawal was not a relevant factor supporting the constitutionality of the bankruptcy system.[192]

Withdrawal of the reference under § 157(d) can be either *permissive* or *mandatory*. Permissive withdrawal of the reference is predicated on a showing of "cause," and may be done on timely motion of a party or on the court's own motion. Neither the statute nor the legislative history provides any guidance as to what might constitute "cause." The mere fact that a proceeding is a related proceeding in which the bankruptcy court cannot enter a final order under § 157(c) is not necessarily enough; otherwise, a party would have the power to make § 157(c) a dead letter simply by filing a motion for permissive withdrawal of the reference. Yet, the district court may give weight to notions of judicial economy, efficiency, and expedition in exercising its discretion whether to withdraw the proceeding. For example, if a jury trial has been demanded, and the bankruptcy court has not been authorized to conduct such a trial under § 157(e), the district court is likely to withdraw the reference of that proceeding.

The withdrawal motion is decided by the district court. Some question has been raised as to when a motion is "timely," as the statute requires. The concern is over possible litigation gamesmanship. Some courts require the motion to withdraw to be "made as promptly as possible in light of developments of the bankruptcy proceeding,"[193] while other courts allow greater delay in filing the motion, as long as no prejudice would result.[194] Another procedural question is whether the court must determine whether the proceeding is core or non-core before making the withdrawal decision; the cases have gone both ways.[195] However, withdrawal under § 157(d) is not limited to non-core proceedings, but may be invoked in core matters as well.[196] Even after *Stern v. Marshall*, courts have been reluctant to withdraw the reference, relying on the Court's language that the decision was "narrow" and it "does not 'meaningfully change[ ] the division of labor between bankruptcy courts and district courts.'"[197] The recent trend has been toward allowing bankruptcy judges to at least enter proposed findings of fact and conclusions of law, rather than withdrawing the reference at the outset.[198]

---

[192]   131 S. Ct. 2594, 2618 (2011).

[193]   In re Baldwin–United Corp., 57 B.R. 751 (S.D. Ohio 1985).

[194]   E.g., In re New York Trap Rock Corp., 158 B.R. 574 (S.D.N.Y. 1993).

[195]   Compare In re Orion Pictures Corp., 4 F.3d 1095 (2d Cir. 1993) (must decide before), with In re Delaware & Hudson Ry. Co., 122 B.R. 887 (D. Del. 1991) (do not have to decide before).

[196]   E.g., In re White Motor Corp., 42 B.R. 693 (N.D. Ohio 1984).

[197]   In re Extended Stay, Inc., 466 B.R. 188, 199 (S.D.N.Y. 2011).

[198]   In re Lehman Bros. Holdings Inc., 469 B.R. 415, 432 (Bankr. S.D.N.Y. 2012).

The most confusion and difficulty under § 157(d) has arisen in cases applying the mandatory withdrawal provision. *Mandatory* withdrawal of the reference is triggered by the motion of a party when:

> resolution of the proceeding requires consideration of both title 11 and other laws of the United States regulating organizations or activities affecting interstate commerce. 28 U.S.C. § 157(d).

Most courts have narrowly construed this mandatory withdrawal provision, notwithstanding the expansive language used. Almost every federal law "affects" interstate commerce to some degree. The legislative history indicates that courts are being faithful to congressional intent in giving § 157(d) a narrow construction.[199] Also, few district courts favor adjudicating bankruptcy-related cases that could be tried in the bankruptcy court.

Note that withdrawal is mandated only if the non-bankruptcy federal law that is implicated regulates interstate commerce. Examples given in the legislative history include the National Labor Relations Act and the Securities and Exchange Act of 1934.[200] Furthermore, § 157(d) states that "resolution" of the proceeding must "require" consideration of the Bankruptcy Code and that other federal law. In giving effect to this statute, courts have disputed whether *both* the Bankruptcy Code and non-Code federal laws must be relevant to the outcome of the case, and if so, how material each law must be to the resolution. The language of the statute plainly seems to demand that both laws be involved, and many cases have so held.[201] However, other courts have departed from the statutory language, and have not insisted on a showing that provisions of the Bankruptcy Code will bear materially on the dispute, especially if resolution of the case will require a "substantial and material" consideration of the non-bankruptcy federal law.[202] Some courts have held that withdrawal is only mandatory if novel questions are raised with regard to the non-bankruptcy law, as opposed to routine applications of that law.[203] This view is hard to square with the statutory language.

§ 4.7   Abstention and the Role of the State Courts

Although bankruptcy is a matter within the jurisdiction of the federal courts, 28 U.S.C. § 1334, that does not mean that every bankruptcy proceeding will ultimately be litigated in a federal forum. Many of the substantive issues implicated in a bankruptcy case are based on non-bankruptcy state law.[204] Accordingly, Congress has given the state courts *concurrent* jurisdiction over all *proceedings* in bankruptcy, with one exception. The exception, added in 2005, gives the district courts exclusive jurisdiction

---

[199] 130 Cong. Rec. H1849, H1850 (daily ed. March 21, 1984) (remarks of Rep. Kramer and Rep. Kastenmeier).

[200] Id. at H1850 (remarks of Rep. Kastenmeier).

[201] E.g., In re Nat'l Gypsum Co., 134 B.R. 188 (N.D. Tex. 1991).

[202] E.g., In re Johns–Manville Corp., 63 B.R. 600 (S.D.N.Y. 1986).

[203] E.g., In re Ionosphere Clubs, Inc., 922 F.2d 984 (2d Cir. 1990).

[204] See Vern Countryman, The Use of State Law in Bankruptcy Cases (pt. I), 47 N.Y.U. L. Rev. 407 (1972); id. (pt. II), 47 N.Y.U. L. Rev. 631 (1972).

over proceedings relating to the employment of professional persons under Code § 327. Under 28 U.S.C. § 1334(b), the federal district courts are granted original but *not exclusive* jurisdiction over all civil proceedings arising under title 11 or arising in or related to a title 11 case. The district court's exclusive jurisdiction extends only to bankruptcy cases, § 1334(a); to property of the estate, § 1334(e)(1), and to proceedings involving the employment of professional persons under § 327. § 1334(e)(2).

Many different types of proceedings connected with a bankruptcy case may be heard in a state court. Ordinary civil litigation involving common state law questions, such as breach of contract or tort actions, may be prime candidates for resolution in a state forum. Domestic relations issues are almost invariably dealt with in the state courts. Even some bankruptcy-specific issues, such as the dischargeability of specific debts under § 523(a), may be decided in state court.[205]

Congress has provided a formal means for the federal courts to defer in favor of state courts in 28 U.S.C. § 1334(c), which allows the district court (or bankruptcy court on reference) to *abstain* from hearing a proceeding over which bankruptcy jurisdiction otherwise would exist. Upon abstention, the proceeding will be decided in a state court of appropriate jurisdiction. Abstention under § 1334(c) is of two types: *permissive* abstention, under § 1334(c)(1), and *mandatory* abstention, under § 1334(c)(2). Permissive abstention is available for all types of proceedings subject to bankruptcy jurisdiction, i.e., for core and for non-core proceedings; mandatory abstention, however, is only applicable to non-core related proceedings. One exception to permissive abstention was added in 2005: the federal court may not abstain with respect to proceedings in a case under chapter 15, which deals with cross-border and ancillary cases.

The standard for permissive (or discretionary) abstention is "in the interest of justice, or in the interest of comity with State courts or respect for State law." 28 U.S.C. § 1334(c)(1). Discretionary abstention remains the exception and not the rule, and is granted in only a small number of cases.[206] The concept of discretionary abstention by the federal courts in favor of the state courts may be traced to the Supreme Court's 1940 decision in *Thompson v. Magnolia Petroleum Co.*[207] In *Thompson*, the Court held that abstention was appropriate in cases involving "unsettled questions of state law," such as the issue in that case of the proper interpretation of documents of conveyance under Illinois real property law. In such cases, the state court, which has the greater interest and expertise, is the more appropriate forum for resolution. Not all courts applying § 1334(c)(1) have strictly required that the state law issue be "unsettled," but some may allow abstention even on routine state law matters if the state courts can dispose of the case expeditiously, without delaying the bankruptcy administration. While permissive abstention is available both for core and related proceedings, the bankruptcy courts are more likely to abstain in related proceedings that have only a remote connection to the bankruptcy

---

[205] Only three of the twenty-one discharge exceptions in § 523(a) must be litigated in the bankruptcy court. 11 U.S.C. § 523(c)(1) (bankruptcy court must decide exceptions in § 523(a)(2), (4), and (6)).

[206] See In re Chicago, Milwaukee, St. Paul & Pac. R.R. Co., 6 F.3d 1184 (7th Cir. 1993); In re Phelps Techs., Inc., 238 B.R. 819 (Bankr. W.D. Mo. 1999).

[207] 309 U.S. 478 (1940).

case, but a primary nexus to state law. As courts are wont to do, lengthy laundry lists of factors relevant to the permissive abstention decision have been developed.[208]

Section 1334(c)(2) provides for mandatory abstention of certain civil proceedings which are "related to" a title 11 case. Mandatory abstention will be ordered only if *all* of the statutory elements are met:

1. Timely motion of a party.

2. Proceeding is based upon a state law claim or cause of action.

3. Proceeding is related to the bankruptcy.

4. The only basis for federal jurisdiction is § 1334.

5. Action is commenced in state court.

6. Action "can be timely adjudicated" in the state court.

Note, however, that even if abstention is not mandated under § 1334(c)(2), permissive abstention is still possible under § 1334(c)(1).

A close examination of the elements required for mandatory abstention reveals many possible shoals on which the abstention motion may run aground. First, abstention is not mandated if federal jurisdiction exists on any basis other than § 1334, such as federal question jurisdiction, 28 U.S.C. § 1331, or diversity of citizenship. 28 U.S.C. § 1332. Second, core proceedings are not subject to mandatory abstention.[209] Accordingly, even if an action otherwise satisfies the requirements of § 1334(c)(2), if a party files a proof of claim in the bankruptcy case and thereby converts the matter to a core proceeding, mandatory abstention will be defeated. Third, most courts have given literal effect to the statutory language and have demanded that the state court action actually be "commenced" *prior* to the initiation of the bankruptcy case. Finally, even if all of the other elements are met, the federal court can decline to abstain if it concludes that the state court action cannot be "timely adjudicated." This open-ended test permits the court to compare how long it would take to try the case in the state court versus the federal court, and to weigh the importance of a speedy determination in

---

[208] For example, the court in *In re Tucson Estates, Inc.*, 912 F.2d 1162 (9th Cir. 1990) approved the following list:

> (1) the effect or lack thereof on the efficient administration of the estate if a Court recommends abstention, (2) the extent to which state law issues predominate over bankruptcy issues, (3) the difficulty or unsettled nature of the applicable law, (4) the presence of a related proceeding commenced in state court or other nonbankruptcy court, (5) the jurisdictional basis, if any, other than 28 U.S.C. § 1334, (6) the degree of relatedness or remoteness of the proceeding to the main bankruptcy case, (7) the substance rather than form of an asserted "core" proceeding, (8) the feasibility of severing state law claims from core bankruptcy matters to allow judgments to be entered in state court with enforcement left to the bankruptcy court, (9) the burden on the bankruptcy court's docket, (10) the likelihood that the commencement of the proceeding in bankruptcy court involves forum shopping by one of the parties, (11) the existence of a right to a jury trial, and (12) the presence in the proceeding of nondebtor parties.

[209] See In re S.G. Phillips Constr., 45 F.3d 702 (2d Cir. 1995); In re Petrie Retail, Inc., 304 F.3d 223 (2d Cir. 2002).

administering the bankruptcy case. Furthermore, even if the bankruptcy court finds that abstention is appropriate, the automatic stay will not necessarily be lifted to permit immediate adjudication in the state court.[210]

Section 1334(d), as amended by the Bankruptcy Reform Act of 1994,[211] limits the reviewability of decisions by the federal district court or bankruptcy court to abstain or not to abstain. Review of abstention decisions by appeal or otherwise is not allowed in the court of appeals or in the Supreme Court. The only exception, added in 1994, is for decisions not to abstain on the basis of mandatory abstention under § 1334(c)(2). Thus, all decisions to abstain or not to abstain under permissive abstention and all decisions to abstain under mandatory abstention are appealable only to the district court or to the Bankruptcy Appellate Panel. Notwithstanding the statutory bar, some courts of appeals have concluded that they have the authority to review mandatory abstention decisions for the limited purpose of ensuring that the statutory prerequisites for abstention are met.[212] It should be noted that an abstention decision under § 1334(d) does not automatically lift the stay under § 362 to permit a state court proceeding to go forward.[213]

There is one major exception to the mandatory abstention rules. Under 28 U.S.C. § 157(b)(4), personal injury tort and wrongful death claims against the estate are not subject to mandatory abstention. Instead, § 157(b)(5) provides that the district court "shall" order that such claims be tried in the district court in which the bankruptcy case is pending or in which the claim arose. Notwithstanding the mandatory language of § 157(b)(5), a number of courts have held that the federal court retains the power to abstain on a permissive basis under § 1334(c)(1) and thereby leave a personal injury tort or wrongful death claim in the state court.[214]

§ 4.8 Jury Trials in Bankruptcy

a. *Right to Jury Trial*

The Seventh Amendment gives litigants a constitutional right to a jury trial in the circumstances described therein:

> In Suits at common law, where the value in controversy shall exceed twenty dollars, the right of trial by jury shall be preserved, and no fact tried by a jury shall be otherwise re-examined in any Court of the United States, than according to the rules of the common law.

---

[210] See In re Conejo Enters., Inc., 96 F.3d 346 (9th Cir. 1996); In re Jefferson Cnty., Ala., 484 B.R. 427 (Bankr. N.D. Ala. 2012).

[211] Pub. L. No. 103–394, § 104(b), 108 Stat. 4106 (1994).

[212] E.g., *S.G. Phillips Construction*, supra note 209, 45 F.3d 702.

[213] E.g., Pursifull v. Eakin, 814 F.2d 1501 (10th Cir. 1987).

[214] See, e.g., In re Pan Am. Corp., 950 F.2d 839 (2d Cir. 1991); In re White Motor Corp., 761 F.2d 270 (6th Cir. 1985); Podkolzin v. Amboy Bus Co., Inc., 402 B.R. 539 (Bankr. E.D.N.Y. 2009).

One of the most difficult questions in bankruptcy practice has been the application of the Seventh Amendment.[215] Two major issues predominate: first, does the *right* to a jury trial persist in bankruptcy; and second, if a litigant has a right to a jury trial, may the *bankruptcy judge* conduct that trial? The short answers are: to the first issue—yes, the right to jury trial continues in bankruptcy;[216] and to the second issue—yes, by statute (28 U.S.C. § 157(e)), if the parties expressly consent and the district court specially designates the bankruptcy judge to do so, *unless* the Constitution forbids an untenured federal bankruptcy judge from exercising that jurisdiction.

The right to a jury trial can be conferred by *statute*. If a statutory jury trial right is conferred, there is no need to reach the issue of the application of the Seventh Amendment. In the Bankruptcy Reform Act of 1978, Congress included a relatively broad statutory jury trial grant in former 28 U.S.C. § 1480. However, the Supreme Court's 1982 decision in *Northern Pipeline Construction Co. v. Marathon Pipe Line Co.*,[217] that the bankruptcy jurisdictional system violated Article III, spelled doom for § 1480. In the 1984 Amendments passed in response to *Marathon Pipe Line*, Congress repealed § 1480 and enacted a more limited provision, 28 U.S.C. § 1411, in its stead.

Section 1411(b) makes clear that there is not a jury trial right in the trial of an involuntary petition under § 303. Section 1411(a) provides that the Judicial Code and the Bankruptcy Code "do not affect any right to trial by jury that an individual has under applicable nonbankruptcy law with regard to a personal injury or wrongful death tort claim." While the exact parameters of § 1411(a) are not entirely clear, that section does *not* confer a statutory jury trial right for contract claims and for preference and fraudulent conveyance actions. In such cases, any jury trial entitlement must be founded on the Seventh Amendment.

With regard to the threshold question of whether the Seventh Amendment right to a jury trial applies in bankruptcy proceedings, one plausibly might turn the question around and ask why the Seventh Amendment would *not* apply in bankruptcy. What is so different about bankruptcy? The reason is this: the Seventh Amendment only applies to "suits at *common law*." By inference, the constitutional right to a jury trial does not apply to proceedings in *equity*. Prior to the 1978 reform legislation, it was generally assumed (although perhaps erroneously)[218] that the bankruptcy court was

---

[215] A number of excellent articles have probed the bankruptcy jury trial issue. For articles written prior to the Supreme Court's decision in *Granfinanciera, S.A. v. Nordberg*, 492 U.S. 33 (1989), discussed below, see Conrad K. Cyr, The Right to Jury Trial in Bankruptcy: Which Judge is to Preside?, 63 Am. Bankr. L.J. 53 (1989); S. Elizabeth Gibson, Jury Trials in Bankruptcy: Obeying the Commands of Article III and the Seventh Amendment, 72 Minn. L. Rev. 967 (1988); G. Ray Warner, *Katchen* Up in Bankruptcy: The New Jury Trial Right, 63 Am. Bankr. L.J. 1 (1989). Articles written after *Granfinanciera* include Douglas G. Baird, Jury Trials After Granfinanciera, 65 Am. Bankr. L.J. 1 (1991); S. Elizabeth Gibson, Jury Trials and Core Proceedings: The Bankruptcy Judge's Uncertain Authority, 65 Am. Bankr. L.J. 143 (1991); John E. Matthews, The Right to Jury Trial in Bankruptcy Courts: Constitutional Implications in the Wake of Granfinanciera, S.A. v. Nordberg, 65 Am. Bankr. L.J. 43 (1991); John C. McCoid, II, Right to Jury Trial in Bankruptcy: Granfinanciera, S.A. v. Nordberg, 65 Am. Bankr. L.J. 15 (1991); Robert G. Skelton & Donald F. Harris, Bankruptcy Jurisdiction and Jury Trials: The Constitutional Nightmare Continues, 8 Bankr. Dev. J. 469 (1991).

[216] Granfinanciera, S.A. v. Nordberg, 492 U.S. 33 (1989).

[217] 458 U.S. 50 (1982). See § 4.2.d.

[218] See McCoid, supra note 215, at 28–40.

entirely a "court of equity," and therefore all proceedings in bankruptcy were "equitable" in character and not subject to the Seventh Amendment. This perception of the bankruptcy court as a court of equity originated in a statement in dictum by the Supreme Court in the 1881 case of *Barton v. Barbour*.[219]

Under the 1898 Bankruptcy Act, two major decisions of the Supreme Court addressed the jury trial right in bankruptcy. In *Schoenthal v. Irving Trust Co.*,[220] the bankruptcy trustee sued in equity in district court to recover a preference from a creditor who had not filed a claim against the bankruptcy estate. The Supreme Court held that the trustee had an adequate remedy at law and therefore the suit had to proceed at law, meaning that the creditor had a Seventh Amendment jury trial right. Under the jurisdictional scheme in effect at that time, however, a suit to recover a preference was not within the summary jurisdiction of the district court sitting in bankruptcy, but had to be brought as a separate, plenary action, to which the Seventh Amendment plainly applied.

The 1966 case of *Katchen v. Landy*[221] presented a different picture. In *Katchen*, the creditor filed a claim against the bankruptcy estate. When the trustee counterclaimed for the return of a preference, the creditor asserted the right to a jury trial under the Seventh Amendment. The Supreme Court held that the creditor did *not* have a jury trial right on the trustee's preference counterclaim. Under the 1898 Act, the creditor could not be paid a dividend out of the bankruptcy estate until he returned the preference. Thus, resolution of the preference issue was integrally connected with the equitable process of administering the bankruptcy estate, and the jury trial right was lost. The preference issue had been subsumed within the summary jurisdiction of the bankruptcy court by the creditor's act of filing a claim.

The 1978 reform legislation unified the jurisdiction of the bankruptcy court, and abandoned the distinction between summary and plenary jurisdiction that helped explain the differing results in *Schoenthal* and *Katchen*. In light of this unified jurisdiction, which was continued in the 1984 Amendments (albeit in the district courts rather than the bankruptcy courts), some commentators argued that the theoretical underpinnings of *Katchen* had been removed, and that the Seventh Amendment did apply to claims of a legal nature brought in bankruptcy cases.[222] Others, however, clung to the notion that the bankruptcy court was purely a court of equity, and that the Seventh Amendment therefore did not apply.[223]

The Supreme Court settled the debate in 1989 in *Granfinanciera, S.A. v. Nordberg*.[224] In the 1984 Amendments, Congress had characterized suits to recover fraudulent conveyances as "core proceedings" in which the non-Article III bankruptcy judge could enter a final order. 28 U.S.C. § 157(b)(2)(H). The issue in *Granfinanciera*

---

[219]   104 U.S. 126 (1881).

[220]   287 U.S. 92 (1932).

[221]   382 U.S. 323 (1966).

[222]   See Gibson, supra note 215, 72 Minn. L. Rev. at 1025; Warner, supra note 215, at 4.

[223]   E.g., Lawrence P. King, Jurisdiction and Procedure Under the Bankruptcy Amendments of 1984, 38 Vand. L. Rev. 675, 703–04 (1985).

[224]   492 U.S. 33 (1989).

was "whether a person who has not submitted a claim against a bankruptcy estate has a right to a jury trial when sued by the trustee in bankruptcy to recover an allegedly fraudulent monetary transfer."[225]

The Court held "that the Seventh Amendment entitles such a person to a trial by jury, notwithstanding Congress' designation of fraudulent conveyance actions as 'core proceedings.'"[226] In so holding, the *Granfinanciera* Court refused to accept a simplistic "everything in bankruptcy is equitable" approach. Instead, the Court insisted on examining the legal or equitable nature of the precise issue in question, even if that issue happened to arise in the context of a bankruptcy case, and even if Congress had labeled the matter as "core."

The Supreme Court followed a three-step form of analysis in *Granfinanciera*.[227] Step one is to compare the statutory action to 18th-century actions in England prior to the merger of law and equity, to determine whether the current action would have been brought at law or in equity. The Court concluded that the action to recover a fraudulent conveyance would have been brought at law.[228] The second step, which is more important than the first, is to examine the remedy sought, and to determine whether it is legal or equitable.[229] Here, too, the Court concluded that the remedy of money damages is legal in nature.[230]

The third and final stage of the Seventh Amendment analysis is to "decide whether Congress may assign and has assigned resolution of the relevant claim to a non Article III adjudicative body that does not use a jury as a factfinder."[231] The Court has held that Congress may create new statutory rights and assign their adjudication to administrative agencies, without violating the Seventh Amendment.[232] This power, though, only exists in cases involving "public rights." In earlier cases the Court had intimated that some aspects of federal bankruptcy cases might implicate public rights.

In *Granfinanciera*, however, the Court concluded that the trustee's right to recover a fraudulent conveyance was a "private" right, not a public right.[233] Congress lacked the power to eliminate the creditor's jury trial right merely by relabeling the cause of action as a "core proceeding" in bankruptcy and assigning that action to a specialized court of equity.[234] Thus, the defendant retained its Seventh Amendment jury trial right. The Court explained that *Schoenthal* and *Katchen* could be explained

---

[225] Id. at 36.

[226] Id.

[227] Id. at 42.

[228] Id. at 43–47.

[229] Id. at 42.

[230] Id. at 47–49.

[231] Id. at 42.

[232] Atlas Roofing Co. v. Occupational Safety & Health Review Comm'n, 430 U.S. 442 (1977).

[233] 492 U.S. at 55.

[234] Id. at 60–61.

as holding that the creditor's right to a jury trial of a preference action depended on whether the creditor submitted a claim against the bankruptcy estate.[235]

The Court in *Granfinanciera* held only that the creditor was entitled to a jury trial. The Court emphasized that it was *not* deciding whether § 1411 permitted bankruptcy courts to conduct jury trials, *or* whether it would violate either Article III or the Seventh Amendment for the non-Article III bankruptcy judge to conduct a jury trial.[236] As the next subsection will discuss, the statutory issue has been resolved, but the constitutional question remains.

Since the Court in *Granfinanciera* was careful to limit both its holding and its justification to the situation in which the creditor does not file a claim against the bankruptcy estate, the logical question after *Granfinanciera* was whether a creditor would forfeit its Seventh Amendment right if it did file a claim. The Court answered this question in the affirmative in 1990 in *Langenkamp v. Culp*.[237] By filing a claim in bankruptcy, the creditor triggers the bankruptcy court's equitable jurisdiction to allow and disallow claims, and subjects himself to the bankruptcy court's equitable power. An ensuing preference counterclaim "becomes part of the claims-allowance process which is triable only in equity."[238]

Thus, after *Granfinanciera* and *Langenkamp*, a creditor who is sued in bankruptcy for the recovery of a fraudulent conveyance or preference is entitled to a jury trial if the creditor has not filed a claim, but loses its jury trial right if it has filed a claim. In *Stern* the Supreme Court reaffirmed the holdings in both *Granfinanciera* and in *Langenkamp*, and indeed extended their premises from the Seventh Amendment context to Article III.[239] This means that a creditor cannot have it both ways; it must choose whether to file a claim or to retain its jury trial right. Courts have not allowed creditors to file "conditional" claims in which they insist that they have not waived their right to a jury trial,[240] nor have courts allowed creditors to postpone the filing of a claim until after the completion of the jury trial of an adversary proceeding.[241] However, if the creditor *withdraws* a filed proof of claim before the trustee brings the action against the creditor, courts have allowed the creditor to assert its right to a jury trial.[242]

Today, if a creditor does not file a claim in the bankruptcy case, the scope of the creditor's jury trial right if sued by the trustee depends on whether the remedy sought by the trustee is legal or equitable in nature and whether that action would have been brought in the courts of law in 18th-century England. The possibility that an action

---

[235] Id. at 58.

[236] Id. at 64.

[237] 498 U.S. 42 (1990).

[238] Id. at 44.

[239] 131 S.Ct. 2594, 2614–18 (2011).

[240] E.g., Travellers Int'l AG v. Robinson, 982 F.2d 96 (3d Cir. 1992); In re EXDS, Inc., 301 B.R. 436 (Bankr. D. Del. 2003).

[241] E.g., In re Hooker Inv., Inc., 937 F.2d 833 (2d Cir. 1991); In re Millenium Seacarriers, Inc., 419 F.3d 83 (2d Cir. 2005).

[242] E.g., Smith v. Dowden, 47 F.3d 940 (8th Cir. 1995); In re Christou, 448 B.R. 859 (Bankr. N.D. Ga. 2011).

would be classified as implicating "public rights" and thus not subject to the Seventh Amendment has been narrowly circumscribed by the Court. The Court in *Granfinanciera* explained that the "public/private rights" analysis is the same under the Seventh Amendment and Article III.[243] *Stern* agreed.[244] Thus, Article III precedents (such as *Marathon Pipe Line*[245] and *Stern*) also help delineate the scope of a litigant's Seventh Amendment rights, and vice versa.

For example, traditional state law actions for torts or for breach of contract in which legal relief is sought (such as money damages) would entitle the defendant to invoke the Seventh Amendment. Much of the "related to" or "non-core" jurisdiction in bankruptcy cases is of this sort. And, as *Granfinanciera* itself illustrates, the mere fact that Congress has classified a proceeding as "core" under § 157(b)(2) does not necessarily mean that the Seventh Amendment is inapplicable. If the relief sought is legal and if private rights only are implicated, the defendant retains a right to a jury trial. *Stern*'s reasoning further confirms that result.

Granfinanciera and its progeny examined whether a party who is sued *by* the bankruptcy trustee on behalf of the estate is entitled to a jury trial. A distinct and difficult issue that the courts have not completely resolved is whether the *debtor* or the *trustee* also is entitled to a jury trial under the Seventh Amendment. For example, assume that a creditor files a claim against the estate, and the debtor as DIP or the trustee files a counterclaim against the creditor that is legal in nature. Although the creditor cannot insist on a jury trial (under *Langenkamp*), may the debtor or trustee invoke the Seventh Amendment?

The most extreme view is that the debtor (and inferentially the trustee) forfeits *any* right to a jury trial by commencing a bankruptcy case.[246] The filing of the petition is viewed as a global waiver of the Seventh Amendment right with regard to any proceeding that later arises in that bankruptcy case. Under this approach, the debtor loses the right to a jury trial irrespective of whether the creditor has filed a claim.

A less extreme approach is to link the jury trial right of the debtor to that of the creditor. Under this view, if the creditor has filed a claim and thereby given up its own jury trial right, the debtor or trustee likewise lose their jury trial rights with regard to any counterclaims against the creditor. But if the creditor has not filed a claim at all, the debtor and trustee retain full Seventh Amendment entitlements for legal claims brought against the creditor.[247]

Most protective of the debtor's and trustee's Seventh Amendment rights is the view that the jury trial right is lost only with regard to counterclaims against a creditor that are closely connected to the issue of the allowance of the creditor's own

---

[243] 492 U.S. 33, 53–54 (1989).

[244] 131 S.Ct. at 2614, 2618.

[245] 458 U.S. 50 (1982). See § 4.2.d.

[246] E.g., In re McLaren, 3 F.3d 958 (6th Cir. 1993); In re Hallahan, 936 F.2d 1496 (7th Cir. 1991); Charlotte Commercial Grp., Inc. v. Fleet Nat'l Bank (In re Charlotte Commercial Grp., Inc.), 288 B.R. 715 (Bankr. M.D.N.C. 2003).

[247] E.g., In re Jensen, 946 F.2d 369 (5th Cir. 1991).

claim.[248] This approach interprets the distinction between *Granfinanciera* and *Langenkamp* as resting on the premise that the filing of the creditor's claim converts all integrally related proceedings (including legal counterclaims) into part of the equitable claims allowance process, rather than on the idea that the creditor "waived" its Seventh Amendment rights. Even within this third school, courts evince different attitudes as to how close the connection must be between the creditor's filed claim and the trustee's or debtor's counterclaim.[249] For example, in one case attorneys filed a claim for postpetition legal fees, and the debtor objected to the fees and separately sued for malpractice. Over a vigorous dissent, the Third Circuit held that the debtor was not entitled to a jury trial on the legal malpractice claim.[250]

b.   Power of Bankruptcy Judge to Conduct Jury Trial

The Supreme Court made clear in *Granfinanciera, S.A. v. Nordberg*[251] that the Seventh Amendment right to trial by jury in suits at common law applies in proceedings in bankruptcy. The Court left open, however, the question of whether that jury trial could be conducted by the non-Article III *bankruptcy judge*.[252] This question breaks down into two subsidiary issues: (1) is there any *statutory* authority for bankruptcy judges to conduct jury trials; and (2) if so, is the exercise of that authority consistent with the Constitution?

Prior to the 1994 Amendments, the answers to both issues were unclear. The 1994 Amendments resolved the statutory question, conferring a limited authority on bankruptcy judges to supervise jury trials in 28 U.S.C. § 157(e). The constitutional question is still open, however.

Before 1994, all but one of the courts of appeals that considered the matter found no statutory authority for the bankruptcy judge to conduct a jury trial in any type of proceeding, core or non-core.[253] Several of these courts expressed grave doubts that the untenured bankruptcy judge could constitutionally exercise such authority, and then resolved the statutory issue in a way that avoided the constitutional problem.[254] Only the Second Circuit held that the bankruptcy judge had both the statutory and constitutional authority to conduct a jury trial.[255] In that case, the Supreme Court initially granted certiorari, remanded on a technical procedural question, and then, after the Second Circuit on remand reaffirmed its holding that the bankruptcy judge

---

[248] E.g., Billing v. Ravin, Greenberg & Zackin, P.A., 22 F.3d 1242 (3d Cir. 1994); Germain v. Connecticut Nat'l Bank, 988 F.2d 1323 (2d Cir. 1993).

[249] Compare *Germain*, 988 F.2d 1323 (close connection required) with *Billing*, 22 F.3d 1242 (looser connection suffices).

[250] *Billing,* supra note 34, 22 F.3d 1242.

[251] 492 U.S. 33 (1989).

[252] Id. at 64.

[253] In re Clay, 35 F.3d 190 (5th Cir. 1994); In re Stansbury Poplar Place, Inc., 13 F.3d 122 (4th Cir. 1993); In re Grabill Corp., 967 F.2d 1152 (7th Cir. 1992); In re Baker & Getty Fin. Servs., 954 F.2d 1169 (6th Cir. 1992); In re Kaiser Steel Corp., 911 F.2d 380 (10th Cir. 1990); In re United Missouri Bank, N.A., 901 F.2d 1449 (8th Cir. 1990).

[254] E.g., *Clay*, supra note 253, 35 F.3d 190.

[255] In re Ben Cooper, Inc., 896 F.2d 1394 (2d Cir.), vacated on other grounds and remanded, 498 U.S. 964 (1990), reinstated, 924 F.2d 36 (2d Cir.), cert. denied, 500 U.S. 928 (1991).

could conduct a jury trial, the Supreme Court inexplicably denied the second certiorari writ.

The courts agree that any possible authority of the bankruptcy judge to conduct a jury trial is limited to *core* proceedings. In *non-core* related proceedings, the bankruptcy judge cannot conduct a jury trial because of the conflict between 28 U.S.C. § 157(c) and the Reexamination Clause of the Seventh Amendment.[256] The Reexamination Clause provides that "no fact tried by a jury shall be otherwise re-examined in any Court of the United States, than according to the rules of the common law." Those "rules of the common law" contemplate traditional appellate review, with deference to findings of fact made by the jury under a clearly erroneous standard of review. In a non-core related proceeding, however, the district court is empowered to review de novo, with no deference, any findings of fact to which objection is made. 28 U.S.C. § 157(c)(1).

The statutory void regarding the bankruptcy judge's power to conduct a jury trial was filled in 1994 with the enactment of 28 U.S.C. § 157(e), which provides:

> If the right to a jury trial applies in a proceeding that may be heard under this section by a bankruptcy judge, the bankruptcy judge may conduct the jury trial if specially designated to exercise such jurisdiction by the district court and with the express consent of all the parties.

This statute contains two restrictions. First, the district court must "specially designate" the bankruptcy judge to conduct the jury trial. The statute does not specify whether this designation must be made in each individual case, or whether a district court can enter a blanket designation order.

The second limitation is that all of the parties to the action must "expressly consent" to the conduct of the jury trial by the bankruptcy judge. Failure to object is not enough; the affirmative consent of every party to the action must be obtained. If all parties consent, and the requisite designation is made, the statutory authority for the bankruptcy judge to supervise the jury trial is clear. Conversely, if any party refuses to consent, the bankruptcy judge will not be allowed to supervise the jury trial. If a timely jury trial demand is made and consent is withheld, the district court either will have to withdraw the reference of the proceeding and try the case itself, or withdraw the reference, abstain, and send the case to state court for trial.

The unanswered constitutional question is whether § 157(e) passes muster in a case where all of the parties have consented. Is the fact of consent enough to remove the constitutional difficulties inherent in having a non-Article III judge conduct a jury trial? Apart from consent, the constitutional problem stems from the linkage that the

---

[256] See, e.g., In re Orion Pictures Corp., 4 F.3d 1095 (2d Cir. 1993); In re Cinematronics, Inc., 916 F.2d 1444 (9th Cir. 1990); Beard v. Braunstein, 914 F.2d 434 (3d Cir. 1990).

Court identified between Article III and the Seventh Amendment in *Granfinanciera*,[257] and again reiterated in *Stern*.[258] The *Granfinanciera* Court explained:

> [T]he question whether the Seventh Amendment permits Congress to assign its adjudication to a tribunal that does not employ juries as factfinders requires the same answer as the question whether Article III allows Congress to assign adjudication of that cause of action to a non-Article III tribunal. For if a statutory cause of action . . . is not a "public right" for Article III purposes, then Congress may not assign its adjudication to a specialized non-Article III court lacking the "essential attributes of the judicial power." And if the action must be tried under the auspices of an Article III court, then the Seventh Amendment affords the parties a right to a jury trial whenever the cause of action is legal in nature. Conversely, if Congress may assign the adjudication of a statutory cause of action to a non-Article III tribunal, then the Seventh Amendment poses no independent bar to the adjudication of that action by a nonjury factfinder.[259]

This linkage leads to a "catch–22 . . . : "if bankruptcy judges do not have the essential attributes of judicial power, they cannot satisfy the seventh amendment; if they do, they are in violation of Article III."[260] A proceeding involving only a "private right" that is legal in nature thus would appear to give rise to a jury trial right under the Seventh Amendment, with the necessity of adjudication by an Article III court. While the de novo review by the Article III district court of the non-Article III bankruptcy judge's findings and conclusions contemplated by 28 U.S.C. § 157(c) might cure the Article III problem, such a reexamination is not permissible under the Seventh Amendment's Reexamination Clause. In short, absent consent of the parties, the constitutionality of an untenured bankruptcy judge presiding over the jury trial of a private right is dubious. Nothing in *Stern* suggests otherwise.

Does consent change the constitutional outcome? Congress modeled § 157(e) after the magistrate jury trial provision, 28 U.S.C. § 636(c), which also requires special designation by the district court and the consent of all parties. Numerous courts of appeals have upheld the constitutionality of § 636(c).[261] And courts that questioned the constitutionality of allowing a bankruptcy judge to conduct a jury trial prior to the 1994 Amendments suggested that the constitutional problem might go away if the parties consented.[262] To the extent that Article III is viewed as a protection for litigants, the idea that those protected parties can waive their constitutional rights makes sense.

However, Article III is not just a mechanism for affording litigants an impartial decision maker. Article III is at bottom a structural limitation on the form of government, necessary to implement the system of checks and balances contemplated

---

[257]   492 U.S. 33 (1989).

[258]   131 S.Ct. at 2614, 2618.

[259]   Id. at 53–54.

[260]   Matthews, supra note 215, at 69.

[261]   See, e.g., Pacemaker Diagnostic Clinic of Am., Inc. v. Instromedix, Inc., 725 F.2d 537 (9th Cir.), cert. denied, 469 U.S. 824 (1984).

[262]   E.g., *Clay*, supra note 253, 35 F.3d 190.

by the separation of powers; viewed in that perspective, the consent of the litigants would not seem to matter.[263] Language in the Supreme Court's 1986 decision in a non-bankruptcy case, *Commodity Futures Trading Commission v. Schor*,[264] supports the view that litigant consent cannot cure the structural violation:

> Article III, § 1, not only preserves to litigants their interest in an impartial and independent federal adjudication of claims within the judicial power of the United States, but also serves as "an inseparable element of the constitutional system of checks and balances." . . . To the extent that this structural principle is implicated in a given case, the parties cannot by consent cure the constitutional difficulty for the same reason that the parties by consent cannot confer on federal courts subject-matter jurisdiction. . . . Whenever these Article III limitations are at issue, notions of consent and waiver cannot be dispositive because the limitations serve institutional interests that the parties cannot be expected to protect.[265]

Unless the Supreme Court speaks further on the subject, however, it is likely that the lower courts, weary of constitutional haggling over bankruptcy matters, will uphold the constitutionality of § 157(e) based on the precedent of the magistrate cases.[266] *Stern* does not really speak directly to the issue, other than to equate the Seventh Amendment jurisprudence to that under Article III, as already noted, and as *Granfinanciera* also had done. Having said that, faithful adherence to the Court's statements in *Marathon Pipe Line, Schor*, and *Granfinanciera* could lead to the plausible conclusion that § 157(e) is unconstitutional.

§ 4.9   Personal Jurisdiction

One of the most notable aspects of bankruptcy procedure is that nationwide service of process is available in proceedings within bankruptcy subject matter jurisdiction under § 1334(b). Rule 7004(d). Importantly, this means that a defendant in an adversary proceeding in bankruptcy is subject to personal jurisdiction in a distant forum even if that defendant does not have "minimum contacts" with that forum.[267] In other words, the dictates of *International Shoe Co. v. Washington*[268] do not apply in bankruptcy proceedings. Instead, the defendant only needs to have minimum contacts with the United States as a whole; this idea had been referred to as an "aggregate contacts" test.

---

[263] See Baird, supra note 215, at 12 n.36; Gibson, supra note 215, 65 Am. Bankr. L.J. at 167 n.166.

[264] 478 U.S. 833 (1986).

[265] Id. at 850–51. In dissent Justice Brennan was even more explicit, stating that "consent is irrelevant to Article III analysis." Id. at 867 (Brennan, J., dissenting).

[266] See, e.g., In re Blackwell ex rel. Estate of I.G. Servs., Ltd., 267 B.R. 724 (Bankr. W.D. Tex. 2001) (allowing bankruptcy judges to conduct jury trials based on § 157(e), which was modeled on similar statute to allow magistrates to conduct jury trials). Most cases do not mention the precedent of magistrate cases, but simply acknowledge that the bankruptcy judge can conduct a jury trial with consent from all parties and the district court.

[267] E.g., In re Outlet Co. Stores, Inc., 82 B.R. 694, (Bankr. S.D.N.Y. 1988); In re DeLorean Motor Co., 49 B.R. 900 (Bankr. E.D. Mich. 1985).

[268] 326 U.S. 310 (1945).

The constitutionality of this system has been consistently upheld,[269] notwithstanding the criticisms of commentators who believe that "traditional notions of fair play and substantial justice" (under *International Shoe* and its progeny) should require minimum contacts with the forum state even in a bankruptcy case.[270] In cases involving foreign defendants, courts have differed over whether an "aggregate contacts" approach is authorized under Rule 7004(e) and state long-arm statutes, or whether minimum contacts with the forum state are required.[271]

§ 4.10   Venue

Where do bankruptcy cases happen? Bankruptcy cases are filed and processed in the federal courts. The United States District Courts are vested with "original and exclusive jurisdiction of all cases under title 11." 28 U.S.C. § 1334(a). In addition, the federal district courts have "original but not exclusive jurisdiction of all civil proceedings arising under title 11, or arising in or related to cases under title 11." 28 U.S.C. § 1334(b). Typically, though, the district courts themselves do not actually exercise this jurisdiction. Instead, by *reference* from the district courts, 28 U.S.C. § 157(a), the federal *bankruptcy* judges exercise the bulk of the federal bankruptcy jurisdiction. 28 U.S.C. § 157(b), (c). Federal bankruptcy judges are not Article III judges, but instead serve as a "unit" of the district court, known collectively as the "bankruptcy court." 28 U.S.C. § 151. In the real world, then, bankruptcy cases are handled by the bankruptcy courts, with the bankruptcy judges, bankruptcy clerks, bankruptcy trustees, and other bankruptcy personnel doing the work.[272]

So the bankruptcy courts are the place where bankruptcy happens. *Which* bankruptcy court? This, of course, is a question of *venue*. There are actually two distinct venue questions in the bankruptcy context: the venue of a bankruptcy "case"[273] and the venue for bankruptcy "proceedings."[274] The "case," of course, is the entire bankruptcy matter involving the debtor. "Proceedings" are particular matters that arise within the larger "case." So, for example, when United Airlines filed bankruptcy, its "case" was the entire matter pending before the federal court in the Northern District of Illinois. A preference action brought against a creditor in that case would be called a "proceeding." The venue of bankruptcy "cases" under title 11 is governed by 28 U.S.C. § 1408. The venue of "proceedings" within a "case" is prescribed by 28 U.S.C. § 1409.

a.   Venue of Cases

The venue of a bankruptcy "case" is governed by 28 U.S.C. § 1408, which provides:

---

[269]   E.g., In re Park Nursing Ctr., Inc., 766 F.2d 261 (6th Cir. 1985).

[270]   See Jeffrey T. Ferriell, The Perils of Nationwide Service of Process in a Bankruptcy Context, 48 Wash. & Lee L. Rev. 1199 (1991); Note, Bankruptcy and the Limits of Federal Jurisdiction, 95 Harv. L. Rev. 703 (1982).

[271]   Compare In re Ace Pecan Co., 143 B.R. 696 (Bankr. N.D. Ill. 1992) (aggregate contacts approved), with In re Old Elec. Inc., 142 B.R. 189 (Bankr. N.D. Ohio 1992) (aggregate contacts approach not approved).

[272]   See § 4.3.

[273]   See § 4.10.a.

[274]   See § 4.10.b.

a case under title 11 may be commenced in the district court for the district—

(1) in which the domicile, residence, principal place of business in the United States, or principal assets in the United States, of the person or entity that is the subject of such case have been located for the one hundred and eighty days immediately preceding such commencement, or for a longer portion of such one-hundred-and-eighty-day period than the domicile, residence, or principal place of business, in the United States, or principal assets in the United States, of such person were located in any other district; or

(2) in which there is pending a case under title 11 concerning such person's affiliate, general partner, or partnership.

Thus, there are two alternatives for the venue of a case: direct venue for the particular debtor, under § 1408(1), or affiliate venue, under § 1408(2). Under the first, a debtor has the option under § 1408(1) to commence a bankruptcy case in the district where *any* of the following have been located for the greater part of the 180 days before the bankruptcy filing:

- domicile

- residence

- principal place of business in the United States, or

- principal assets in the United States.

If the debtor's domicile, residence, principal place of business, or principal assets were located in more than one district during the 180–day period, venue is proper in the district in which the venue determinant was located for the longer portion of the 180 days. This rule prevents a debtor from relocating shortly before filing bankruptcy and thereby obtaining the benefit of a preferred forum.

For *individual* debtors, venue normally is the location of the debtor's "domicile" or "residence." The place of the debtor's employment usually is not considered a "principal place of business" for venue purposes.[275] For example, a debtor who lives in Connecticut and commutes to work in New York City would have to file in Connecticut, and may not file in New York. The rules for an individual who is a general partner of a partnership are discussed below.

Importantly, a *corporate* debtor may choose *any* of the statutory alternatives. This rule is broader than the law under the pre–1978 Bankruptcy Act, which limited the venue for a corporate debtor to the location of the principal place of business or principal assets.[276]

---

[275] E.g., Barnes v. Whelan, 689 F.2d 193 (D.C. Cir. 1982); In re Berryhill, 182 B.R. 29 (Bankr. W.D. Tenn. 1995).

[276] Fed. R. Bankr. P. 116(a)(2) (1973) (abrogated).

Of the most significance is the rule that authorizes a corporation to file a bankruptcy case where it is "domiciled." A corporation is "domiciled" in the state of incorporation. For example, if XYZ Corp. is incorporated in Delaware, but its principal place of business and principal assets are located elsewhere, Delaware still is a proper venue choice for a bankruptcy filing. This single change in the law led to a dramatic, and controversial,[277] boom in the 1990s in the use of Delaware as a venue for large corporate reorganizations. Critics have raised the concern that corporate debtors are engaging in harmful forum shopping.[278] The 1997 Report of the National Bankruptcy Review Commission recommended abolishing domicile—and thus the state of incorporation—as a venue option for a corporate debtor.[279] However, Congress in the 2005 amendments chose to ignore this recommendation, and left intact the corporate venue option in the state of incorporation.

Determining the "residence" of a corporation for purposes of § 1408(1) is a bit trickier, and has not been definitively resolved. One possible resolution is to analogize to the general federal venue statute for diversity cases, which provides that a corporation "resides" in and may be sued in any judicial district in which it is subject to personal jurisdiction. 28 U.S.C. § 1391(c). Under this rule, a corporation resides in any jurisdiction in which it is incorporated or is licensed to do business or is doing business. However, § 1391(c) has been held to apply only to corporate defendants, and not to corporate plaintiffs, who instead reside only in the state of incorporation. If residence is given the same meaning in § 1408(1) as in § 1391(c) for corporate defendants, a corporation could file bankruptcy in a jurisdiction in which it was licensed to do business or was doing business, even if it was incorporated in another state and had its principal place of business and principal assets elsewhere. If not, residence will not add anything to the state of incorporation as a venue choice.

A corporate debtor has yet another option. Under 28 U.S.C. § 1408(2), a corporation may file in any district in which there is pending a case under title 11 concerning an *affiliate* of the corporation. "Affiliate" is defined in § 101(2) of the Code

---

[277] Scholars have divided over whether the Delaware (state of incorporation) option is beneficial or not. Among those arrayed against, led most vociferously by Professor Lynn LoPucki, are: Lynn M. LoPucki, Courting Failure: How Competition for Big Cases is Corrupting the Bankruptcy Courts (University of Michigan Press 2005); Theodore Eisenberg & Lynn M. LoPucki, Shopping for Judges: An Empirical Analysis of Venue Choice in Large Chapter 11 Reorganizations, 84 Cornell L. Rev. 967 (1999); Lynn M. LoPucki & Joseph W. Doherty, Why Are Delaware and New York Bankruptcy Reorganizations Failing?, 55 Vand. L. Rev. 1933 (2002); Lynn M. LoPucki & Sara D. Kalin, The Failure of Public Company Bankruptcies in Delaware and New York: Empirical Evidence of a "Race to the Bottom," 54 Vand. L. Rev. 232 (2001); Lynn M. LoPucki & William C. Whitford, Venue Choice and Forum Shopping in the Bankruptcy Reorganization of Large, Publicly Held Companies, 1991 Wisc. L. Rev. 11. Those in favor are led by Professors David Skeel, Bob Rasmussen, and Randall Thomas: Robert K. Rasmussen and Randall S. Thomas, Whither the Race? A Comment on the Effects of the Delawarization of Corporate Reorganizations, 54 Vand. L. Rev. 283 (2001); Robert K. Rasmussen and Randall S. Thomas, Timing Matters: Promoting Forum Shopping by Insolvent Corporations, 94 Nw. U. L. Rev. 1357 (2000); David A. Skeel, Jr., What's So Bad About Delaware?, 54 Vand. L. Rev. 309 (2001); David A. Skeel, Jr., Bankruptcy Judges and Bankruptcy Venue: Some Thoughts on Delaware, 1 Del. L. Rev. 1 (1998). Marcus Cole does not fit neatly in either camp. Marcus Cole, "Delaware is Not a State": Are We Witnessing Jurisdictional Competition in Bankruptcy?, 55 Vand. L. Rev. 1845 (2002). Stephen Lubben asks whether the answer even matters. Stephen J. Lubben, Delaware's Irrelevance, 16 Am. Bankr. Inst. L. Rev. 267 (2008).

[278] See LoPucki, Courting Failure, supra note 277.

[279] National Bankruptcy Review Commission Final Report, Bankruptcy: The Next Twenty Years, § 3.1.5, at 770, 782–84 (1997).

as (A) an entity that owns 20% or more of the voting securities of the debtor, or (B) a corporation of which 20% or more of the voting securities are owned by the debtor, or by an entity that controls 20% or more of the debtor. Under this broad definition, virtually any other corporation in a corporate group, be it a parent, subsidiary, or sister corporation, would be considered an "affiliate" for venue purposes. The purpose of this rule is to permit a coordinated filing of all members of a corporate group in the same jurisdiction.

This affiliate venue rule often gives the members of a corporate group considerable venue choice. Once one affiliate files first in the preferred forum based on the rules in § 1408(1), under § 1408(2) any other affiliated corporation—even the affiliate's *parent* corporation—may file in that forum as well, even if that second filing corporation itself has none of the venue ties under § 1408(1). A notorious example is the Enron case. Although Enron had its headquarters and principal place of business in Houston, Texas (with the "crooked "E" prominently displayed), and was incorporated in Oregon, a relatively small affiliate filed first in New York, enabling Enron to file in New York under § 1408(2). Exactly the same scenario played out in the Eastern Airlines case: although Eastern was headquartered in Miami, its affiliated frequent flyers' club sank the venue "hook" in New York, allowing Eastern to file in New York as well. Such opportunities for forum shopping have led to criticism of the "tail-wagging-the-dog" rule of § 1408(2).[280]

The 1997 National Bankruptcy Review Commission recommended that Congress amend § 1408(2) to reduce the possibility of forum shopping through use of the affiliate hook.[281] Under the Commission Recommendation, a corporation could only follow its corporate *parent* into an otherwise improper venue; thus, the parent itself (e.g., Eastern Airlines, Enron) could *not* follow a subsidiary. Congress, however, also ignored this recommendation, and made no changes to the case venue rules in the 2005 amendments.

A final possibility for a corporate debtor to file in a desired location is to ignore the venue rules, file in an improper venue, and hope that no one objects. Venue is a waivable defect and is not jurisdictional, and a defect in venue may not be raised by the court on its own motion. Rule 1014(a)(2). Indeed, even if a motion to transfer to the proper venue is made, it is not certain that the court must grant the request.[282]

For partnership debtors, the normal venue choice under § 1408(1) will be either the principal place of business or the location of the principal assets. Although the preferred view is that a partnership does not have a "residence" for bankruptcy venue purposes, it is possible to analogize to the diversity rules and argue that a partnership resides in any judicial district in which it is doing business. Domicile is not meaningful in the partnership context.

Under § 1408(2), a partnership may file in a district where a case is already pending concerning a general partner. Under the same section, a general partner may

---

[280] See supra notes 277–79 and accompanying text.

[281] Commission Report, supra note 279, § 3.1.5, at 770–71, 774–75.

[282] See § 4.10.c.

choose to file in any district where a case concerning the partnership or any other general partner is pending, in addition to the generally applicable venue rules under § 1408(1).

The venue of ancillary and other cross-border cases under chapter 15 is governed by a special venue rule, 28 U.S.C. § 1410. A chapter 15 case may be commenced in the district court for the district in which the debtor has its principal place of business or principal assets in the United States. § 1410(1). If, however, the debtor does not have a principal place of business or assets in the United States, the chapter 15 case may be brought wherever there is an action pending in federal or state court in the United States against the debtor. § 1410(2). Lacking either of those venue grounds, venue may be placed wherever "consistent with the interests of justice and the convenience of the parties," considering "the relief sought by the foreign representative." § 1410(3).

b.   Venue of Proceedings

The venue of proceedings in a bankruptcy case is governed by 28 U.S.C. § 1409. A "proceeding" is an individual lawsuit within the overall case. The district court has original but not exclusive jurisdiction over all civil proceedings "arising under" title 11 or "arising in or related to" a title 11 case. 28 U.S.C. § 1334(b). Section 1409 has five subsections that specify the proper venue for different types of proceedings. Filing in an improper venue is not necessarily fatal to the plaintiff's case, however, because the defendant must object to the improper venue or the defense will be waived.

The general rule for the venue of proceedings in bankruptcy is found in § 1409(a). That section provides for a "home court" default venue: the district court in which the case is pending is a proper venue for a proceeding arising under title 11 or arising in or related to a case under title 11. The home court rule is subject to two exceptions noted below. The ability to bring virtually all bankruptcy proceedings in the debtor's home court is a significant advantage for the estate, especially when coupled with nationwide service of process.[283] Note, though, that § 1409(a) does not expressly state that proceedings may "only" be brought in the home bankruptcy court. This lack of specificity leaves open the possibility of a non-debtor party bringing suit against the estate in a distant forum.

The trustee has an additional venue option if she is commencing a proceeding as *successor* to the debtor or creditors under § 541 or § 544(b). For example, the trustee may bring a fraudulent conveyance action under § 544(b) as successor to an actual unsecured creditor. In such a situation, the trustee is entitled to sue in the district court for the district where the state or federal court sits in which the debtor or creditors to whom the trustee is succeeding could have brought the action outside of bankruptcy. 28 U.S.C. § 1409(c).

The venue rules of § 1409(a) and (c) are subject to an exception for small debts, to protect distant defendants. Under § 1409(b), as amended in 2005 and adjusted for indexing in 2013, if the trustee is suing on a consumer debt of less than $18,675, is suing a non-insider on a debt (other than a consumer debt) of less than $12,475, or is

---

[283]   See § 4.9.

suing anybody else for $1,250 or less, the trustee may file suit only in the district where the *defendant resides*. In other words, "home court" suits are barred in such small-dollar proceedings. The 2005 amendments[284] embraced the recommendation of the 1997 Commission Report,[285] which itself was adopted from a recommendation in the 1997 Preference Survey Report by the American Bankruptcy Institute.[286] Prior to 2005, the "small-debt" exception was small indeed: the dollar amounts were less than $1,000 for any debt and $5,000 for consumer debts. The original purpose of this rule was to "prevent unfairness to distant debtors of the estate, where the cost of defending would be greater than the cost of paying the debt owed."[287] The 2005 amendment simply expanded the scope of that protection, recognizing that the original dollar amounts had become far too low to afford the protection intended. After BAPCPA, the original $1,000 amount (indexed to $1,250) applies only to insiders sued for business debts. Note that the dollar amounts will be indexed every three years; the last indexing was in 2013.

One caveat should be noted about § 1409(b) as applied to preference actions, and any other action that arises "under" title 11. Read literally, the statutory language in § 1409(b) only applies to a "proceeding arising in or related to" a case. A small number of courts have held that the omission of a reference to arising "under" in § 1409(b) means that it does *not* apply to preference actions, which arise "under" § 547 of title 11.[288] Other courts, however, disagree, and conclude that § 1409(b) *does* apply to defendants in an "arising under" proceeding.[289] The upshot of the strict interpretation is that the preference suit then could be commenced in the debtor's home court under § 1409(a), which could be far, far away from where the preference defendant resides. The only problem with this interpretation is that it surely is not what Congress intended. Indeed, the Commission Recommendation that Congress adopted in 2005 was entitled "Venue of *Preference* Actions under 28 U.S.C. § 1409."[290] The commission, in turn, drew its recommendation from the ABI *Preference* Survey Report. Indeed, virtually all of the "small debt" cases reported under § 1409(b) are preference cases, which would mean that the 2005 amendments were almost pointless, if the strict interpretation view is to be believed. While it is unfortunate that the pre–2005 case law split over the scope of § 1409(b) was not plainly settled in the text of the 2005 amendments, the clear legislative history of the amendment reveals that Congress believed it was endorsing the view that § 1409(b) *does* apply to "arising under" suits, such as preference proceedings.

---

[284] See discussion in Charles J. Tabb, The Brave New World of Bankruptcy Preferences, 13 Am. Bankr. Inst. L. Rev. 425, 428, 437–39 (2005).

[285] Commission Report, supra note 279, § 3.2.2, at 799–800.

[286] American Bankruptcy Institute Task Force on Preferences, Preference Survey Report 30–31 (1997) (Charles J. Tabb, Reporter).

[287] H.R. Rep. No. 95–595, 95th Cong., 1st Sess., at 446 (1977).

[288] See In re Guilmette, 202 B.R. 9 (Bankr. N.D.N.Y. 1996); In re Van Huffel Tube Corp., 71 B.R. 155 (Bankr. N.D. Ohio 1987).

[289] E.g., In re Little Lake Indus., Inc., 158 B.R. 478 (B.A.P. 9th Cir. 1993); In re Nukote Int'l, Inc., 457 B.R. 668 (Bankr. M.D. Tenn. 2011).

[290] See Commission Report, supra note 279, § 3.2.2, at 799 (emphasis added).

Note that the § 1409(b) exception to home court venue only applies to small claims brought *by* the trustee *against* a third party and *not* to creditor claims against the estate. There is no small "claims" exception to home court venue. Creditors still must file their claims in the home bankruptcy court, and any objections to claims disputed by the trustee will be litigated in that home court.

The applicable rule for proceedings brought by the trustee based on claims arising *after* the bankruptcy filing from the operation of the debtor's business is found in 28 U.S.C. § 1409(d). The trustee is subject to applicable non-bankruptcy venue rules in such a situation. The "home court" rule of subsection (a) does not apply. The trustee thus might have to sue the defendant where the defendant resides. See 28 U.S.C. § 1391(c). If the shoe is on the other foot, and the estate is being sued based on a postpetition claim, the plaintiff has a choice: venue is proper either in the district where the bankruptcy case is pending, or where the suit could have been brought outside of bankruptcy. 28 U.S.C. § 1409(e).

c. *Change of Venue*

The district court has the power to change the venue of a case or a proceeding. 28 U.S.C. § 1412. Under that section, the district court may transfer the case or proceeding to a district court for another district, "in the interest of justice or for the convenience of the parties." Whether the *bankruptcy* court also has the authority to order a change of venue pursuant to its referred powers in 28 U.S.C. § 157 is a matter of dispute; the majority view is that a motion for venue transfer is a core proceeding that may be heard and determined by the bankruptcy court.

If a case is filed in an *improper* venue, and a party in interest objects, the only options the court has are to dismiss the case, or to transfer the case to another district. 28 U.S.C. § 1406; Rule 1014(a)(2). Prior to the 1984 Amendments, a statute then in effect (28 U.S.C. § 1477(a)) gave the court the power to retain an improperly venued bankruptcy case. However, that statute was repealed in 1984. Note, though, that if no objection is filed, the case still may proceed in the wrong venue. In short, improper venue can be waived.

Even if a case is filed in a *proper* venue, the court has the power to transfer the case to another district. 28 U.S.C. § 1412; Rule 1014(a)(1). The court may not act *sua sponte*, however; it may order a transfer only if a party in interest files a timely motion.

Whether venue originally was proper or improper, the court may transfer the case under § 1412 and Rule 1014(a) to "any other district." Neither the statute nor the rule requires the transfer to be to a district in which venue is proper. The standard to be applied by the court in both proper and improper venue cases is "the interest of justice and the convenience of the parties." 28 U.S.C. § 1412; Rule 1014(a). Factors the court might consider include the proximity to the court of the debtor, the proximity of creditors, the proximity of necessary witnesses, the location of the debtor's assets, the economy and efficiency of estate administration, and connections with related debtors.

A peculiar problem that sometimes occurs is that two or more petitions concerning the same debtor or related debtors may be pending in different districts at the same time. This could happen, for example, if the debtor filed a voluntary petition in one district and creditors filed an involuntary petition in another district. In cases involving related debtors (such as a debtor and an affiliate), one debtor could file in one district and the affiliate in another district. Because there are multiple bases for venue, it is even possible that venue would be proper in all of the cases. The court in which the *first petition* is filed has the power to determine the district or districts in which the cases should proceed. While that court is making its decision, all proceedings on the other petitions are to be stayed. Rule 1014(b).

§ 4.11   Removal and Remand

a. *Removal*

The Judicial Code provides for the removal of claims related to bankruptcy cases, 28 U.S.C. § 1452(a), and for the remand of removed claims. 28 U.S.C. § 1452(b). A party has the power to remove "any claim or cause of action in a civil proceeding" to the district court where the civil action is pending, *if* the district court has jurisdiction of the claim or cause of action under 28 U.S.C. § 1334. 28 U.S.C. § 1452(a).

This statute contains two limitations on the removal power. First, only a *civil* proceeding may be removed. Second, federal jurisdiction must exist in bankruptcy. Bankruptcy jurisdiction under § 1334 extends to proceedings that arise under title 11 or that arise in or are related to a case under title 11.[291]

The bankruptcy removal statute also contains two exceptions to the removal power. One is for a proceeding before the United States Tax Court. The other is for a civil action by a governmental unit to enforce its police or regulatory power. 28 U.S.C. § 1452(a). The scope of the "police or regulatory power" provision should be coextensive with the exception to the automatic stay in § 362(b)(4).[292]

Removal from state court to the federal district court also can be effected pursuant to the general federal removal statute, 28 U.S.C. § 1441. The Supreme Court made clear in 1995 in *Things Remembered, Inc. v. Petrarca*[293] that removal to a district court exercising bankruptcy jurisdiction can take place under either § 1452 or § 1441, or both.

The procedure for removal under § 1452 is governed by Bankruptcy Rule 9027. If removal is effected under § 1441, then the procedures of § 1446 must be followed. The notice of removal must be filed in the district and division where the action to be removed is pending, Rule 9027(a)(1), rather than in the district where the bankruptcy case is pending. The notice of removal must contain a "short and plain statement of the facts" which support removal, and a statement of whether the proceeding is core or non-core. The Rule specifies the time limits for filing the notice of removal. Rule 9027(a)(2), (3). The notice must be served on all parties to the removed action. Rule 9027(b). "Promptly" after the party files the notice of removal, that party must file a copy of the notice with the clerk of the non-bankruptcy court from which the action was

---

[291] See §§ 4.4, 4.5.

[292] See §§ 3.10–3.12.

[293] 516 U.S. 124 (1995).

removed. Removal is automatically effective when that copy of the notice is filed. Rule 9027(c). Once removal is effected, the parties may not proceed in the court from which the action was removed unless and until the action is remanded.

Removal is to the district court. 28 U.S.C. § 1452(a). However, if there is a general reference order to the bankruptcy judges in that district pursuant to 28 U.S.C. § 157(a), the bankruptcy judge will conduct the removed proceeding. Rule 9027(e).

b. *Remand*

The court to which a claim or cause of action has been removed pursuant to the bankruptcy removal statute, 28 U.S.C. § 1452(a), may remand the removed claim to the court of origin pursuant to 28 U.S.C. § 1452(b). Remand is the sole remedy for an improper removal. However, remand is possible even if removal was proper. Under § 1452(b), remand may be ordered "on any equitable ground."

Remand also may be ordered under 28 U.S.C. § 1447. Under § 1447(c), remand may be ordered based on "any defect in removal procedure" or a lack of subject matter jurisdiction. The Supreme Court held in *Things Remembered, Inc. v. Petrarca*[294] that § 1447 applies to bankruptcy cases, rejecting the argument that § 1452 is the exclusive statute governing removal and remand of proceedings based on bankruptcy jurisdiction. Thus, in *Things Remembered*, untimely removal (a "defect in removal procedure") was held to be a proper basis for remanding a bankruptcy proceeding.

Under Rule 9027(d), a motion for remand is a contested matter under Rule 9014 that may be heard and determined by the bankruptcy judge. The 1991 amendments to the Bankruptcy Rules resolved a split in the case law over whether remand had to be ordered by the district court, or whether the bankruptcy judge also had remand authority.

The bankruptcy judge's remand order may be appealed to the district court or bankruptcy appellate panel, but no further. If the district court orders the remand in the first instance, no appeal is possible. The statute specifies that the remand order "is not reviewable by appeal or otherwise by the court of appeals . . . or by the Supreme Court." 28 U.S.C. § 1452(b). Similarly, if remand is ordered pursuant to 28 U.S.C. § 1447(c), the remand order is "not reviewable on appeal or otherwise." 28 U.S.C. § 1447(d). In *Things Remembered*, the Supreme Court held that § 1447(d) prohibits an appeal to the court of appeals of a remand order in a proceeding based on bankruptcy jurisdiction.[295]

If remand is sought "on any equitable ground" under § 1452(b), the bankruptcy court will consider a number of factors. These include: (1) the most economical use of judicial resources; (2) the likelihood of prejudice to the involuntarily removed parties; (3) forum non conveniens; (4) the extent that the matter involves questions of state law that the state court would be better able to answer; (5) comity; (6) whether the possibility of inconsistent results is reduced by remand; and (7) the expertise of the

---

[294] Id.

[295] Id.

court in which the matter originally was pending.[296] On balance, federal courts generally favor retaining matters within their jurisdiction unless compelling reasons support remand.

§ 4.12   Appeals

The appellate system in bankruptcy cases and proceedings is more complicated than for other types of civil litigation in the federal courts for two basic reasons. First, there is an added tier of courts: the bankruptcy court is interposed in the court hierarchy at the rung below the district court. Adding to the complication is the fact that the district court can act either as the first-level trial court (if it withdraws the reference to the bankruptcy judge, 28 U.S.C. § 157(d)), *or* as an appellate court (if the bankruptcy judge hears the case by reference, 28 U.S.C. § 157(a)–(c)). Second, many bankruptcy proceedings are not readily comparable to self-contained traditional civil litigation of the "A versus B" variety. Bankruptcy proceedings may involve many interested parties, and they take place within the umbrella of the overall bankruptcy case, which itself may not be finally resolved for years. The unique nature of bankruptcy proceedings makes it more difficult to apply concepts of "finality" that are so fundamental to appellate practice.

a.   *Route of Appeals*

Appeals of bankruptcy cases and proceedings are governed specifically by 28 U.S.C. § 158. In addition, the general federal appeals provisions in 28 U.S.C. §§ 1291 and 1292 apply to orders entered by the district courts in bankruptcy matters.[297]

The first point of importance with regard to appeals in bankruptcy is to identify the *route* of the appeal. In other words, to which courts may appeal be made? The answer to this question depends first on which court "hears and determines" the bankruptcy proceeding in the first instance. While jurisdiction of bankruptcy cases and proceedings is lodged in the federal *district* courts, 28 U.S.C. § 1334(a) and (b), the vast majority of bankruptcy cases and proceedings are referred to the *bankruptcy* judges for the district for initial determination. 28 U.S.C. § 157(a). The district court may, however, withdraw the reference and act as the trial court.[298] 28 U.S.C. § 157(d).

Proceedings that are referred to the bankruptcy judge may be divided into core[299] and non-core[300] proceedings. If the proceeding is a *core* proceeding under 28 U.S.C. § 157(b), the bankruptcy judge may "hear and determine" the action and enter appropriate orders and judgments (assuming that doing so complies with the constitutional limits of Article III), which will be subject to review only on appeal under 28 U.S.C. § 158. The bankruptcy judge thus functions in every practical respect as the trial court in a core proceeding.

---

[296] E.g., In re Cont'l Holdings, Inc., 158 B.R. 442 (Bankr. N.D. Ohio 1993); Unico Holdings Inc., v. Nutramax Prods., Inc., 264 B.R. 779 (Bankr. S.D. Fla 2001).

[297] Connecticut Nat'l Bank v. Germain, 503 U.S. 249 (1992).

[298] See § 4.6.

[299] See § 4.4.

[300] See § 4.5.

If the proceeding is a non-core related matter, however, the bankruptcy judge may only submit proposed findings of fact and conclusions of law to the district court, subject to *de novo* review. 28 U.S.C. § 157(c)(1). The district court then would be the court that enters the appealable orders and judgments. The bankruptcy judge's function in a non-core proceeding is analogous to that of a special master. If, however, all of the parties consent, the bankruptcy judge may enter orders and judgments in a non-core proceeding that will be subject to review only on appeal under § 158 (again, assuming that such consent is consonant with the commands of Article III).

To summarize, the bankruptcy court acts as the trial court in (1) referred core proceedings, and (2) referred non-core proceedings in which all parties consent. The district court acts as the trial court in (1) proceedings in which the reference is withdrawn, and (2) referred non-core proceedings in which the parties do not consent to the bankruptcy judge acting as the trial court.

If the bankruptcy court acts as the trial court, appeals are governed by 28 U.S.C. § 158. The appeal will be made to:

1.   The district court, § 158(a);

2.   The bankruptcy appellate panel service for the circuit ("BAP"), § 158(b), (c); or

3.   The court of appeals, via either

      a.   Appeals from final judgments of the district court or BAP, § 158(d)(1), or

      b.   Direct appeal, § 158(d)(2).

The district court for the judicial district in which the bankruptcy judge is serving has jurisdiction under § 158(a) to hear appeals from the bankruptcy judge of:

1.   Final judgments, orders, and decrees, § 158(a)(1);

2.   Interlocutory orders and decrees issued under Code § 1121(d), increasing or reducing the exclusive period for a debtor to file a chapter 11 plan of reorganization, § 158(a)(2); and

3.   Other interlocutory orders and decrees, with leave of court, § 158(a)(3).

The primary alternative to appeal from the bankruptcy court to the district court is to appeal from the bankruptcy judge to the bankruptcy appellate panel service for the circuit, commonly known as the "BAP." A BAP is composed of bankruptcy judges for the circuit who are appointed by the judicial council for the circuit. The judicial council for the circuit must act to establish a BAP, and even if it does so, the district judges for a district must authorize the BAP to hear appeals originating in that district. In practice these limitations meant that originally the BAP concept was largely stillborn. Until 1994, only the Ninth Circuit had a BAP. The 1994 Amendments, however, require the judicial council to establish a BAP for the circuit, unless the council finds that there are insufficient judicial resources available or that undue delay or increased cost would result. § 158(b)(1).

Even if a BAP is established by the judicial council and authorized by the district judges, an appeal from the orders or judgments of a bankruptcy judge may only be made to the BAP "with the consent of all the parties." § 158(b)(1). Thus, any one of the parties may prevent the appeal to a BAP. Congress probably included this consent provision in an abundance of Article III caution. However, the burden is placed on the parties to object; under § 158(c)(1), the appeal from the bankruptcy judge's order "shall be heard" by the BAP panel unless the appellant elects otherwise at the time of filing the appeal or the other party opts out within 30 days after service of the notice of appeal. If the appeal does go to the BAP, it will be heard by a three-judge panel. § 158(b)(5).

The second level of appeal from the judgment of the district court sitting on appeal or the BAP is to the court of appeals. If the judgment or order appealed from is *final*, then the court of appeals has jurisdiction to hear the appeal under § 158(d)(1). That section is silent, however, on whether the court of appeals has jurisdiction to hear appeals of *interlocutory* bankruptcy court orders that are first appealed to the district court or BAP. Prior to 1992, many courts concluded that the negative inference to be drawn from § 158(d)'s limitation to final orders was that the court of appeals lacked jurisdiction over appeals of interlocutory bankruptcy court orders that were first appealed to the district court.

The Supreme Court held otherwise in 1992 in *Connecticut National Bank v. Germain*.[301] The Court concluded that an appeal could be taken to the court of appeals of an interlocutory bankruptcy court order that was first appealed to the district court, pursuant to 28 U.S.C. § 1292(b), which is the general federal statute authorizing appeals from interlocutory district court orders. According to the *Germain* Court, § 158(d) and § 1292 complement each other; in other words, § 158 is not the exclusive section governing bankruptcy appeals. After *Germain,* appeals from the district court to the court of appeals may be based (1) on either § 158(d)(1) or § 1291 for final orders, and (2) on § 1292 for interlocutory orders.

Note, though, that a statutory gap still remains with regard to the appeal of interlocutory bankruptcy court orders. If the initial appeal of the interlocutory order is to the BAP, rather than to the district court, there is no provision for further appeal to the court of appeals. Section 158(d)(1) only grants the court of appeals jurisdiction to hear appeals of final orders, and § 1292 only permits review of interlocutory orders of the district court.

If the district court decides a bankruptcy case or proceeding while sitting as the trial court, rather than on appeal, the general federal appeals statutes will apply. Section 1291 authorizes the appeal of final district court orders to the court of appeals, and § 1292 authorizes the appeals of interlocutory district court orders in limited circumstances.

Until 2005, there was no direct appeal from the bankruptcy court to the court of appeals. The 1978 legislation did permit such direct appeal to the circuit court, but

---

[301] 503 U.S. 249 (1992).

that provision was repealed in 1984. In 2005 Congress restored direct appeal to the court of appeals. Under § 158(d)(2)(A), the appropriate court of appeals has jurisdiction of appeals described in § 158(a). That reference incorporates appeals from final judgments (§ 158(a)(1)), all interlocutory orders under § 1121(d) altering time periods (§ 158(a)(2)), and other interlocutory orders with leave of court (§ 158(a)(3)).

Direct appeals are not granted routinely. First, some authorized entity must certify a direct appeal to the court of appeals; second, that certification must be based on one of three listed statutory grounds, see § 158(d)(2)(A)(i)–(iii); and, third, the court of appeals itself must authorize the direct appeal. § 158(d)(2)(A).

Certification of a direct appeal can be made by the bankruptcy court, district court, or BAP acting on its own motion or on request of a party litigant, § 158(d)(2)(A), (B)(i), or solely by the litigants if all join in the request. § 158(d)(2)(A). If only a majority of appellants and a majority of appellees want a direct appeal, then they must request certification from the bankruptcy court, district court, or BAP, which then would make the certification. § 158(d)(2)(B). In the latter instance, it is not clear what discretion, if any, the certifying court enjoys; the statute simply says that upon receipt of a request from the requisite majority of litigants, the court "shall" make the certification. The parties must request the certification within 60 days after the entry of the order appealed from. § 158(d)(2)(E). If certification is made by a court, the parties are entitled to supplement the certification with a "short statement" explaining the basis for the certification. § 158(d)(2)(C). A Bankruptcy Rule governs direct appeals to the Court of Appeals. Rule 8001(f).

Note that a direct appeal in and of itself does *not* stay any proceeding. Instead, some court (either the relevant bankruptcy court, district court, or BAP, or the court of appeals in which the appeal is pending) must issue a stay of the proceeding pending the appeal. § 158(d)(2)(D). If the order appealed from is of the type as to which an appeal could soon be rendered moot, then an affected party would want to request the issuance of such a stay.

The exclusive statutory grounds for granting a direct appeal are:

1. The judgment appealed from involves a question of law as to which there is no controlling circuit or Supreme Court precedent, § 158(d)(2)(A)(i);

2. The judgment appealed from "involves a matter of public importance," § 158(d)(2)(A)(i);

3. The judgment involves a question of law "requiring resolution of conflicting opinions," § 158(d)(2)(A)(ii); or

4. Immediate appeal "may materially advance the progress of the case," § 158(d)(2)(A)(iii).

In light of the numerous (and often quite confusing) 2005 amendments to the Bankruptcy Code, for the first few years post–2005 the first and third grounds above (no controlling precedent, conflicting opinions) served as fairly regular predicates for direct appeal.[302]

Whether a proceeding originates in the bankruptcy court or the district court, the final level of appeal is to the Supreme Court of the United States. Appeal to the Supreme Court from the court of appeals is by writ of certiorari. 28 U.S.C. § 1254(1). Of course, the decision to grant certiorari is discretionary with the Supreme Court.

The procedures that govern the appeal of orders of the bankruptcy court to the district court or BAP are the same as for appeals to the court of appeals in civil proceedings generally. 28 U.S.C. § 158(c)(2). The time for taking bankruptcy appeals is governed by Bankruptcy Rule 8002. The most important difference between bankruptcy appeals and other civil appeals is that a notice of appeal of a bankruptcy order must be filed within 10 days of the entry of the order appealed from, Rule 8002(a), as compared to 30 days for other civil proceedings. Fed. R. App. P. 4(a). The shortened time period for taking a bankruptcy appeal reflects the need for speed in the administration of bankruptcy cases. Other aspects of bankruptcy appellate practice are governed by Part VIII of the Bankruptcy Rules, Rules 8001–8019.

b. *Final and Interlocutory Orders*

The distinction between "final" and "interlocutory" orders is a cornerstone of federal appellate practice. Parties normally have a right to appeal in the first instance an order or judgment that is final, but do not usually have appeal as of right of an order that is interlocutory. Furthermore, the failure to appeal a final order in a timely manner forecloses later attacks on that order, but the same bar does not apply to interlocutory orders. Thus, it may be critical to ascertain whether an order is final or interlocutory.

This distinction between the appealability of final and interlocutory orders is applied to bankruptcy proceedings. A final order or decree of a bankruptcy judge is appealable as of right to the district court, 28 U.S.C. § 158(a)(1), or to the bankruptcy appellate panel service (BAP), 28 U.S.C. § 158(b), (c), if one is established and the parties consent. Interlocutory bankruptcy court orders, by comparison, are only appealable "with leave of the court." 28 U.S.C. § 158(a)(3). The only exception is for appeals of interlocutory orders extending or reducing the debtor's exclusive period to file a plan, which are appealable as of right. 28 U.S.C. § 158(a)(2). If the district court decides the bankruptcy proceeding as the trial court, appeal of final orders may be had as of right to the court of appeals. 28 U.S.C. § 1291. Interlocutory district court orders are appealable only in limited situations under 28 U.S.C. § 1292.

Determining which orders are "final" for the purposes of appeal in bankruptcy cases and proceedings has proven to be an enormous problem.[303] The difficulty is traceable to multiple causes: (1) many types of bankruptcy proceedings are not "A

---

[302] See, e.g., Tidewater Fin. Co. v. Kenney, 531 F.3d 312 (4th Cir. 2008) (granting direct appeal to decide novel issue interpreting "hanging paragraph" in § 1325(a)(5)).

[303] An excellent article discussing this problem is John P. Hennigan, Jr., Toward Regularizing Appealability in Bankruptcy, 12 Bankr. Dev. J. 583 (1996).

versus B" types of matters, but are more administrative in character, and implicate the interests of many diverse parties, not all of whom are clearly adverse;[304] (2) some bankruptcy orders are not given *res judicata* effect, but can be relitigated without prejudice at a later date;[305] and, finally, (3) numerous bankruptcy "proceedings" take place within the context of the overall bankruptcy "case."

On the last point, even if one proceeding is resolved, others may well remain pending. In ordinary civil actions, finality typically is reached only when every claim has been fully concluded as to every party.[306] Under this approach, no order entered in a bankruptcy proceeding would be final until all proceedings in the case and the case itself were finally resolved. Applying the traditional civil notion of finality in bankruptcy would be disastrous, however, as it would preclude the timely appeal of most bankruptcy orders, could prejudice litigants, and might lead to inefficient and wasteful results. Thus, finality in bankruptcy is more readily found than for normal civil litigation. Courts speak of "flexible" and "pragmatic" finality in bankruptcy proceedings.

Having said that, it is difficult to define the concept or describe the parameters of finality in bankruptcy. "Flexibility" and "pragmatism" are hard to capture in a neat and tidy test. There is general agreement that the relevant "judicial unit" for determining finality is the individual *proceeding*, rather than the overall bankruptcy case. In other words, an order in a bankruptcy case is final if it "finally disposes of discrete disputes" within the case, even if other "discrete disputes" have not been resolved.[307] The task is to define finality with regard to individual proceedings. Generally, an order is considered "final" if it "ends the litigation and leaves nothing for the court to do but execute the judgment."[308] An interlocutory order, by contrast, might not fully resolve all issues before the court, or might require the court to conduct further significant non-ministerial proceedings.

To illustrate, an order allowing a claim is considered final, even though the exact amount that the allowed claim will receive will not be settled until later in the case. In the leading case of *In re Saco Local Development Corp.*,[309] the First Circuit, in an opinion by Judge Breyer, held that an order granting priority status to a claim was final. With regard to the particular discrete dispute over priority, nothing more remained to be done; the litigation had, to paraphrase the musical *Oklahoma*, "gone about as far as it could go."

In other bankruptcy situations, the finality of the order is readily apparent under this approach. The resolution of any type of adversary proceeding, either by dismissal or resolution on the merits, would plainly qualify as final. The disposition of many contested matters also would be final, if nothing remained to be done with regard to

---

[304] An example would be an order authorizing the trustee to incur debt.

[305] A motion for relief from stay is an example.

[306] See Sears, Roebuck & Co. v. Mackey, 351 U.S. 427 (1956).

[307] In re Saco Local Dev. Corp., 711 F.2d 441 (1st Cir. 1983); Howard Delivery Serv., Inc. v. Zurich Am. Ins. Co., 547 U.S. 651 (2006).

[308] Catlin v. United States, 324 U.S. 65 (1945).

[309] 711 F.2d 441 (1st Cir. 1983).

the matter. For example, orders granting relief from the automatic stay are universally held to be final. Orders that globally resolve the overall case also would be final. Included would be orders dismissing the bankruptcy case, or confirming a reorganization plan.

By comparison, if further proceedings are required or possible, the order will be considered interlocutory. An order denying confirmation of a plan, for example, would not be final, because another plan could be proposed. An order approving a disclosure statement is not final, because that approval is just one step leading to confirmation of a plan.

Other orders fall into the gray area, and courts differ on whether and in what circumstances those orders should be classified as final or interlocutory. One prominent example is an order *denying* a movant relief from the stay, as contrasted with an order granting relief, which is always considered final.[310] Another area of dispute is with regard to orders of the district court *remanding* a final bankruptcy court order.[311]

Under the ancient authority of *Forgay v. Conrad*,[312] finality will be found if immediate appeal is necessary to prevent irreparable injury to a litigant. In that case, the court entered an immediately enforceable order requiring Forgay to deliver to Conrad assets that had been fraudulently transferred, and also ordered further proceedings, including an accounting. Under normal finality rules, the order for further proceedings would have defeated finality; however, in order to prevent irreparable injury to Forgay, the Court treated as final the part of the order requiring the delivery of property.

The *Forgay* principle supports the finality of many types of bankruptcy orders. Since a bankruptcy case is intimately concerned with the collection, utilization, liquidation, and distribution of assets, many of the orders therein bear on those subjects. Thus, for example, orders to turn over property to the trustee, granting or denying exemption claims, permitting the use of cash collateral, authorizing the sale of property, approving the rejection of an executory contract, lifting the automatic stay to permit foreclosure, and the like are final under the *Forgay* doctrine.

Another important qualification to the finality rule is the "collateral order" doctrine announced in *Cohen v. Beneficial Industrial Loan Corp.*[313] As restated by the Supreme Court, that doctrine permits direct appeal of an order if three elements exist: "the order must conclusively determine the disputed question, resolve an important

---

[310] Compare In re Sonnax Indus., Inc., 907 F.2d 1280 (2d Cir. 1990) (denial of stay relief is final) and Banc of Am. Commer. Fin. Corp. v. CGE Shattuck, LLC (In re CGE Shattuck, LLC), 255 B.R. 334 (BAP 10th Cir. 2000) (same), with In re West Elec., Inc., 852 F.2d 79 (3d Cir. 1988) (not always final) and Caterpillar Fin. Servs. Corp. v. Braunstein (In re Henriquez), 261 B.R. 67 (B.A.P. 1st Cir. 2001) (same).

[311] Compare In re Marin Motor Oil, Inc., 689 F.2d 445 (3d Cir. 1982), cert. denied, 459 U.S. 1206 (1983) (final), with In re Riggsby, 745 F.2d 1153 (7th Cir. 1984) (not final). Courts following *Riggsby* make an exception for a "ministerial" remand, and find the remand order to be final when the lower court on remand is instructed to carry out only ministerial functions. E.g., In re Stoecker, 5 F.3d 1022 (7th Cir. 1993).

[312] 47 U.S. (6 How.) 201 (1848).

[313] 337 U.S. 541 (1949).

issue completely separate from the merits of the action, and be effectively unreviewable on appeal from a final judgment."[314] Examples where the collateral order has been applied in bankruptcy are orders continuing the automatic stay in effect or denying an entity the right to invoke an exception to the stay.[315]

An illustration of the liberalized finality rules in bankruptcy is the appealability of an order appointing a trustee in a chapter 11 case. Even though the trustee appointment could be appealed at the conclusion of the case, most courts of appeals have held that the appointment order is immediately appealable.[316] These courts reason that the dispossessed debtor otherwise would have no effective relief.

Even if an order is interlocutory, appeal is sometimes possible. A bankruptcy court order extending or reducing the exclusive period for the debtor to file a chapter 11 plan is immediately appealable as of right. 28 U.S.C. § 158(a)(2). Other interlocutory orders are appealable "with leave of the court." 28 U.S.C. § 158(a)(3). The statute does not make clear whether leave must be granted by the reviewing court or the originating court; while the majority of cases hold that it is the reviewing court that must grant leave, there is authority to the contrary. The statute also does not specify any standards for the reviewing court to apply in exercising its discretion whether to grant such leave. Many courts have filled this void by applying the standard in 28 U.S.C. § 1292(b), discussed in the next paragraph, but they are not statutorily required to do so.

The statute authorizing appeals of interlocutory orders from the district courts to the court of appeals is quite specific with regard to when leave should be granted. 28 U.S.C. § 1292. Pursuant to the Supreme Court's decision in *Connecticut National Bank v. Germain*,[317] § 1292 applies to appeals of interlocutory orders from the district court, whether the district court is sitting as a trial court or as an appellate court. Under § 1292(a)(1), the courts of appeals have jurisdiction of appeals of interlocutory orders "granting, continuing, modifying, refusing or dissolving injunctions, or refusing to dissolve or modify injunctions." Section 1292(b) provides for the certification of the appeal of an interlocutory order by the district judge if the judge "shall be of the opinion that such order involves a controlling question of law as to which there is substantial ground for difference of opinion and that an immediate appeal from the order may materially advance the ultimate termination of the litigation."

c. *Statutory Bars to Appellate Review*

Three types of bankruptcy orders are immunized from review by the court of appeals or the Supreme Court:

---

[314] Coopers & Lybrand v. Livesay, 437 U.S. 463, 468 (1978).

[315] E.g., Eddleman v. U.S. Dep't of Labor, 923 F.2d 782 (10th Cir. 1991); In re Looney, 823 F.2d 788 (4th Cir.), cert. denied, 484 U.S. 977 (1987).

[316] See, e.g., In re Cajun Elec. Power Coop., Inc., 69 F.3d 746 (5th Cir. 1995). Contra In re Cash Currency Exch., Inc., 762 F.2d 542 (7th Cir. 1985).

[317] 503 U.S. 249 (1992).

1. A decision to abstain or not to abstain from exercising jurisdiction over a bankruptcy proceeding. 28 U.S.C. § 1334(d). This bar does not extend to mandatory abstention from a proceeding under § 1334(c)(2).

2. An order remanding a claim or cause of action removed under 28 U.S.C. § 1452(a), or a decision not to remand. 28 U.S.C. § 1452(b).

3. An order abstaining from hearing a bankruptcy under 11 U.S.C. § 305(a) by dismissing the case or suspending all proceedings in the case. 11 U.S.C. § 305(c).

For these orders, appellate review is only available by the district court or bankruptcy appellate panel service. The common thread of these statutes is that they address whether the matter should go forward in the bankruptcy court or in another forum.

Chapter 5

PROPERTY OF THE ESTATE

A. INCLUSIONS IN THE ESTATE: § 541(a)

§ 5.1 The Nature and Importance of Property of the Estate

The filing of a bankruptcy petition commencing a case creates an "estate." § 541(a). An estate is created immediately upon filing in cases under chapters 7, 11, 12, and 13, § 103(a), in voluntary and involuntary cases, and for all types of debtors. This general rule does not apply under chapters 9 and 15.[1]

The bankruptcy "estate" is a separate and distinct legal entity. It is comprised initially of all of the debtor's property at the time the case is commenced.[2] § 541(a)(1). In addition, some property interests acquired by the debtor or the estate after the bankruptcy filing are brought into the estate.[3] § 541(a)(3)–(7). For example, the estate may be enhanced by the recapture of property from third parties, through the exercise of the trustee's "avoiding powers."[4] § 541(a)(3).

The bankruptcy trustee is the representative of the estate. § 323(a). Unlike pre-Code law, the trustee does not take "title" to estate property. In a chapter 7 case, the trustee does take possession of property of the estate. The debtor is required to surrender that property to the trustee, § 521(a)(4), and third parties in possession of estate property must turn over that property to the trustee, subject to some qualifications. §§ 542, 543. In reorganization cases, the debtor retains possession of estate property unless displaced by the court. § 1107(a) (chapter 11), § 1207(b) (chapter 12), § 1306(b) (chapter 13). The trustee (or debtor in possession) is permitted to use, sell, or lease estate property, although for transactions outside of the ordinary course of business, court approval is required.[5] § 363(b), (c).

In cases under chapter 12 or chapter 13, and (as of 2005) in chapter 11 cases involving an individual debtor, all of the debtor's earnings and property acquisitions during the pendency of the case are brought into the estate.[6] §§ 1115(a), 1207(a), 1306(a). In chapter 7 cases, however, earnings attributable to an individual debtor's

---

[1] The general rule does not apply to municipal debtors under chapter 9. Section 541 is not made applicable to chapter 9 cases, § 901(a), and "property of the estate" in a chapter 9 case is defined to mean "property of the debtor." § 902(1).

Nor does the general rule apply in chapter 15 ancillary and cross-border cases. Those cases are commenced by filing a petition for recognition under § 1515. See § 1504. The bankruptcy court will deal with particular property of the debtor depending on the relief sought by the foreign representative.

[2] See § 5.2.

[3] See § 5.3.

[4] See Chapter 6 for a full discussion of the avoiding powers of the trustee.

[5] See § 5.16, 5.17.

[6] See § 5.4.

postpetition services are excluded from the estate, in order to facilitate the debtor's "fresh start."[7] § 541(a)(6).

Exempt property is not automatically excluded from the estate at the outset of the case, as it was under prior law,[8] even though that exempt property may be an important component of a debtor's fresh start. Instead, even property that could be claimed as exempt is initially included in the bankruptcy estate.[9] The burden is placed on the debtor to claim his or her exemptions under § 522, thereby taking that property out of the estate.[10]

Property of the debtor is included in the estate even if that property is in the possession of another party at the time the case is commenced. See § 541(a) ("by whomever held"). As noted above, the trustee may be able to recover possession of that property from the possessor, pursuant to the "turnover" provisions of § 542 and § 543.[11]

Executory contracts and leases are a special form of estate property.[12] While those contracts and leases constitute assets of the debtor, the asset that inheres in the contract may only be realized upon performance of a correlative obligation; in short, the asset is coupled with a liability. The special case of executory contracts and leases is governed not by § 541, but by a separate Code provision, § 365.

Some types of property interests are excluded from the bankruptcy estate.[13] § 541(b)–(d). Many of these "exclusions" are but the flip side of the rule that the debtor's property passes into the estate. By inference, that which is *not* property of the debtor does not become estate property. For example, property in which the debtor holds only legal title, and not equitable title, becomes property of the estate only to the extent of the debtor's legal title.[14] § 541(d). The corpus of a trust as to which the debtor is the trustee is an illustration of this limitation.

In addition, some types of property that creditors could not reach outside of bankruptcy, such as the debtor's beneficial interest in a spendthrift trust or in a qualified pension plan, are kept out of the bankruptcy estate as well.[15] § 541(c)(2). The Code does not, however, embody a general rule limiting the estate to property that would be reachable by creditors outside of bankruptcy. Indeed, most non-bankruptcy transfer restrictions are invalidated by the Code, and the debtor's property passes into the estate notwithstanding the restriction.[16] § 541(c)(1).

---

[7]   See § 5.9.

[8]   See Lockwood v. Exch. Bank, 190 U.S. 294 (1903) (applying Act § 70a) (superseded by 11 U.S.C. § 522).

[9]   See § 5.11.

[10]   See Chapter 9 for a detailed discussion of exemptions.

[11]   See §§ 5.12, 5.13.

[12]   See Chapter 8 for a detailed discussion of executory contracts and leases.

[13]   See §§ 5.6–5.11.

[14]   See § 5.8.

[15]   See § 5.7.

[16]   See id.

Some property that passes into the estate is burdensome, and not worth the trustee's time and expense to administer. For example, the debtor may own an asset that is fully encumbered. In such instances, the trustee has the power to "abandon" the property.[17] § 554. Once abandoned, the property ceases to be a part of the estate. It then reverts to the party who held the possessory interest immediately prior to filing. Note, though, that the Supreme Court has imposed a limit on the trustee's power to abandon polluted property.[18]

What constitutes "property" within the meaning of § 541 is a question of federal law.[19] Having said that, the Supreme Court has recognized that "property interests are created and defined by state law."[20] In other words, even in a federal bankruptcy case, the nature and characteristics of estate property depend upon the law that created the property interest in question.[21]

The fundamental importance of "property of the estate" in a bankruptcy case is that it establishes the "what" in the core question of "who gets what" in the bankruptcy distribution. In a liquidation case under chapter 7, the property of the estate is what the debtor gives up and what the debtor's creditors will receive. The trustee is charged with the duty to convert estate property to cash, § 704(a)(1), and to distribute that cash to creditors in accordance with the bankruptcy distributive priority scheme. Exempt property, if claimed as exempt, is returned to the debtor and is not distributed to creditors.

Even though reorganization cases (11, 12, and 13) normally contemplate a rehabilitation of the debtor's affairs, not a liquidation of estate property, identifying what is included as property of the estate remains of primary importance. The baseline dividend which creditors are entitled to receive pursuant to a confirmed reorganization plan is computed by reference to the amount of estate property that would be available for distribution if that property were liquidated under chapter 7. § 1129(a)(7) (chapter 11); § 1225(a)(4) (chapter 12); § 1325(a)(4) (chapter 13). In short, creditors may insist that the plan provide them with at least as much as they would receive in a liquidation. This is known as the "best interests of creditors" test, because a reorganization plan is not in the creditors' "best interests" if those creditors would be paid more in a chapter 7 liquidation. What creditors would receive in a liquidation is the net proceeds of the liquidated property of the estate.

Because property of the estate is central to the bankruptcy distributional scheme, the Code contains several provisions designed to protect the creditors' interests in that property during the pendency of the case. First, actions against property of the estate are automatically stayed.[22] § 362(a)(2)–(4). Second, the trustee must obtain court permission to use, sell, or lease property of the estate outside of the ordinary course of business. § 363(b)(1).

---

[17] See § 5.14.

[18] Midlantic Nat'l Bank v. New Jersey Dep't of Envtl. Protection, 474 U.S. 494 (1986). See § 5.15.

[19] Bd. of Trade of City of Chicago v. Johnson, 264 U.S. 1 (1924).

[20] Butner v. United States, 440 U.S. 48, 55 (1979).

[21] See § 5.5.

[22] See § 3.6.

Finally, the district court retains exclusive jurisdiction over property of the estate. 28 U.S.C. § 1334(e)(1). The federal court has the power to restrain anyone from interfering in any way with that property. Bankruptcy, at its core, is an *in rem* proceeding.

§ 5.2   The Basic Inclusive Provision: § 541(a)(1)

The primary inclusive provision establishing the scope of property of the estate is § 541(a)(1), which brings into the estate:

all legal or equitable interests of the debtor in property as of the commencement of the case.

As this expansive statutory language suggests, Congress intended that property of the estate have a very broad scope.[23] The encompassing reach of the bankruptcy estate mirrors the sweeping definition of "claim" in § 101(5).[24] In each instance Congress operated from the baseline premise that, to the extent reasonably possible, the bankruptcy case should settle all of the debtor's financial affairs as of the time of the bankruptcy filing. Virtually all of the debtor's property is swept into the estate, and is then applied toward all of the debtor's existing legal obligations.

The definition of estate property in § 541(a) is not limitless, however. Three critical aspects of that definition point to limitations on the scope of property of the estate:

- it must be "property"

- "of the debtor"

- "as of the commencement of the case."

The "property" requirement

The threshold requirement is that only "interests in property" can be included in the estate under § 541(a). Whether something is classified as "property" is a question of *federal* law, not state law.[25] As noted above, the federal policy is inclusionary. The legislative history explains that § 541(a) "includes all kinds of property, including tangible or intangible property, causes of action, and all other forms of property currently specified in section 70a of the Bankruptcy Act."[26] The Supreme Court has emphasized that "the term 'property' has been construed most generously and an interest is not outside its reach because it is novel or contingent or because enjoyment must be postponed."[27]

---

[23]   H.R. Rep. No. 95–595, 95th Cong., 1st Sess., at 367 (1977).

[24]   See § 7.1.

[25]   Bd. of Trade of City of Chicago v. Johnson, 264 U.S. 1 (1924).

[26]   H.R. Rep. No. 95–595, 95th Cong., 1st Sess., at 367 (1977).

[27]   Segal v. Rochelle, 382 U.S. 375, 379 (1966).

The famous case of *Board of Trade of City of Chicago v. Johnson* aptly demonstrates that federal law governs the classification question.[28] At issue in that case was the status in bankruptcy of the bankrupt debtor's seat on the Chicago Board of Trade. The Supreme Court of Illinois previously had held that the seat did not qualify as "property" under Illinois state law, because of various limiting attributes. The United States Supreme Court explained that this interpretation did not bind the federal courts sitting in bankruptcy, and proceeded to hold that the seat was in fact "property" for the purposes of the bankruptcy case. However, as will be discussed below,[29] the trustee's victory proved hollow, because the Court went on to hold that state law did define the nature and characteristics of the "property" interest. The state law prevented the sale of the seat until all claims of other members of the exchange against the debtor were fully satisfied, leaving no residual value for the trustee to recover for the entire body of creditors.

Given the intended broad scope of "property of the estate" in § 541(a), almost all imaginable interests might qualify. The fact that creditors are not able to levy on the "property" under state law will not preclude that property from coming into the bankruptcy estate. In this respect the Code goes beyond the prior Act. Under the Code, creditors may be able to reach more assets in bankruptcy than they would have been able to reach outside of bankruptcy.

Nor does the fact that state law restricts the transferability of the interest necessarily preclude the interest from being classified as property of the estate. Again, the Code goes beyond the Act on this issue. To give one example, in many states tort causes of action are not transferable. Under the Code, the bankruptcy estate nevertheless will include the cause of action.[30] The bankruptcy trustee will be able to attempt to collect from the alleged tortfeasor on behalf of the estate. However, the trustee will not be able to transfer the cause of action to a third party in derogation of the state law.

At the fringes, some interests of the debtor might not be classified as property. For example, in the first Braniff Airways reorganization case, the Fifth Circuit held that the debtor's landing slots were not "property" within the meaning of § 541(a), and thus could not be dealt with in the bankruptcy case.[31] The court's decision may be misguided, however; other courts have held that landing slots are property of the estate.[32] The *Braniff* court arguably conflated the distinct questions of (1) whether an interest is property, and (2) if so, what attributes inhere in that property interest. The landing slots could be classified as property of the estate (answering question 1), but yet subject to FAA regulation with regard to transferability and other attributes (answering question 2). In other words, the fact that the debtor did not have all of the "bundle of sticks" in the landing slots did not mean that the debtor had no sticks at all.

---

[28]   264 U.S. 1 (1924).

[29]   See § 5.5.

[30]   See, e.g., In re Cottrell, 876 F.2d 540 (6th Cir. 1989); Sierra Switchboard Co. v. Westinghouse Elec. Corp., 789 F.2d 705 (9th Cir. 1986); Tilley v. Anixter Inc., 332 B.R. 501 (D. Conn. 2005).

[31]   In re Braniff Airways, Inc., 700 F.2d 935 (5th Cir. 1983).

[32]   E.g., In re Am. Cent. Airlines, Inc., 52 B.R. 567 (Bankr. N.D. Iowa 1985). See also In re Gull Air, Inc., 890 F.2d 1255 (1st Cir. 1989).

The intent of § 541(a)(1) is that the estate gets all of the debtor's sticks, however few or many that might be.

Of course, the debtor may have no legally cognizable and enforceable "sticks" at all, holding nothing more than a mere expectancy or hope. If so, the estate does not succeed to any "property". One example is where the debtor prior to bankruptcy has a right to renew season tickets to sporting events, subject, however, to the team's preemptive privilege not to renew the tickets. If the debtor has no legal right under state law to prevent the team from declining to renew, some courts have concluded that there is no property right at all that passes into the bankruptcy estate.[33] Other courts, though, have still found a contingent property interest, albeit one limited by the team's nonrenewal power.[34]

The property must be that "of the debtor"

A second definitional and also limiting aspect of the property of the estate calculus in § 541(a)(1) is that the interest in property must be that "of the debtor." *All* property of the debtor at the time of bankruptcy is included. Thus, whether the debtor holds a fee simple, a joint interest, a leasehold, a naked possessory right, legal title only— whatever the debtor has comes into the estate. The other side of that coin, though, is that *only* what the debtor has comes into the estate. To the extent that the debtor's interest in property is limited, so too is the estate's interest limited.[35]

Thus, if the debtor had a fee simple, the estate gets a fee simple; if the debtor had a tenancy in common, the estate succeeds to the debtor's tenancy interest; if the debtor had a leasehold for a term of years, the estate obtains a leasehold for a term of years; if the debtor's interest is subject to a valid lien, the estate takes subject to that lien; and so on. This fundamental restriction on the scope of property of the estate recognizes the obvious truth that creditors of the debtor generally are only entitled to satisfy their claims out of the debtor's property.

For example, assume that at the time of bankruptcy Debtor was an equal tenant in common of Blackacre with CoTenant. Blackacre was worth $100,000. Debtor had granted a valid mortgage on her interest in Blackacre to Bank to secure a $40,000 debt. Also, Debtor and CoTenant had granted X an easement on Blackacre. Debtor's bankruptcy estate would include exactly what Debtor had: a half interest in Blackacre (worth $50,000), subject to a $40,000 mortgage in favor of Bank and to X's easement.

This limitation is codified in part in § 541(d), which provides that "property in which the debtor holds, as of the commencement of the case, only legal title and not an equitable interest, . . . becomes property of the estate . . . only to the extent of the debtor's legal title to such property, but not to the extent of any equitable interest in such property that the debtor does not hold." Thus, for example, if at the time of the

---

[33]　E.g., In re Harrell, 73 F.3d 218 (9th Cir. 1996) (Phoenix Suns tickets). See also In re Liehman, 208 B.R. 38 (Bankr. N D. Ill. 1997) (Chicago Bulls tickets)

[34]　E.g., In re I.D. Craig Serv. Corp., 138 B.R. 490 (Bankr W.D. Pa. 1992) (Pittsburgh Steelers tickets). See also In re Nejberger, 934 F.2d 1300 (3d Cir. 1991) (liquor license).

[35]　124 Cong. Rec. H11,096 (daily ed. Sept. 28, 1978) (remarks of Rep. Edwards).

bankruptcy filing the debtor was the trustee of an express trust, the beneficial interest in the trust corpus would not become part of the estate. Instead, that beneficial interest would remain the sole property of the trust beneficiaries, free from the claims of the debtor's creditors.[36]

The limitation on the reach of estate property identified in § 541(d) is not absolute, however. It is possible that the bankruptcy trustee may be able to invoke an avoiding power and capture for the estate the interest held by the nondebtor party. This scenario arises most often in the context of the "strong arm" clause in § 544(a), which gives the trustee the powers of a hypothetical lien creditor or of a bona fide purchaser.[37] Upon avoidance and recovery (under § 550), the recovered property comes into the bankruptcy estate. § 541(a)(3).

Note that the practical effect of finding that another entity has a *property* right that is superior to that of the debtor (and thus the estate) is to accord that entity *priority* over creditors of the debtor in the bankruptcy distribution. That property claimant is entitled to recover its property in full before any distribution is made to creditors. Such a result is not surprising and indeed seems only fair when the property indisputably belongs to that nondebtor party. Peter's property should not have to answer for Paula's debts.

A problem sometimes arises, though, in drawing the line between a "property" interest and a "priority" claim. If Peter asserts a "constructive trust" in Paula's property, does Peter have a property claim that should be honored in bankruptcy, or is Peter simply attempting to invoke state remedial law to circumvent the federal bankruptcy priority scheme in Paula's bankruptcy case? In a leading (although arguably misguided) opinion, the Sixth Circuit refused to give effect to a constructive trust in bankruptcy, unless the trust had been decreed by a state court prior to the commencement of the bankruptcy case.[38]

Statutes that purport to create a "trust" in property held by a debtor run into the same quagmire. For example, if a state statute imposes a "trust" on funds held by a general contractor, does that statute permissibly create a property interest in a trust that must be respected in bankruptcy, or impermissibly attempt to reorder bankruptcy priorities in favor of the "beneficiaries"? One statutory claimant has been largely successful in upholding the "trust" characterization in bankruptcy: the Internal Revenue Service. The Supreme Court has held that "trust-fund" taxes (such as withholding taxes) are property of the government, not the debtor, even if held by the debtor in a commingled account.[39]

---

[36] See § 5.8 for more discussion.

[37] See §§ 6.3, 6.4.

[38] In re Omegas Grp., Inc., 16 F.3d 1443 (6th Cir. 1994).

[39] Begier v. IRS, 496 U.S. 53 (1990) (payments of trust-fund taxes made by debtor to IRS during preference period were not avoidable under § 547, because the property transferred was not property of the debtor, but was held by debtor in trust for IRS). But see, In re Appalachian Oil Co., Inc., 471 B.R. 199, 215 n.7 (Bankr. E.D. Tenn. 2012) (noting that most courts have limited *Begier* to § 7501 trust-fund taxes, although a few, including the Third Circuit Court of Appeals, see *City of Farrell v. Sharon Steel Corp.*, 41 F.3d 92, 98–99 (3rd Cir. 1994), have extended its holding to other types of trust-fund taxes).

The timing restriction: "as of the commencement of the case"

The final important facet in delimiting the scope of the bankruptcy estate is one of timing. The estate succeeds to all of the debtor's interests in property "as of the commencement of the case." In other words, the instant of the bankruptcy filing is the magic moment at which the extent of the estate initially is determined. Section 541(a)(1) takes a snapshot of the debtor's assets at the moment of filing, bringing all of those assets into the estate.

This timing rule effects a sharp cleavage between the prepetition and postpetition worlds with regard to estate property. An identical temporal provision governs the determination of claims against the estate.[40] § 502(b). Thus, a bankruptcy case settles the debtor's financial affairs, assets and liabilities alike, as of the time of the filing of the case.

To illustrate, if a debtor's property interest terminates the day before bankruptcy is filed, that property will not become part of the estate. The estate would get exactly what the debtor had—nothing. For example, if Debtor had a lease on Blackacre that expired on May 15, and Debtor filed bankruptcy on May 16, the estate would not acquire any leasehold interest.

The only exception to the foregoing would be if the trustee were able to recapture property transferred prior to bankruptcy pursuant to the avoiding powers. For example, if Debtor made a fraudulent transfer of Blackacre six months before bankruptcy, the trustee would be able to recover Blackacre (or its value) for the estate.[41] §§ 544(b), 548, 550, 541(a)(3).

If the debtor retains any vestige of a property interest at the moment of the bankruptcy filing, that interest passes into the estate. For example, if a debtor retains a right of redemption in property that has been sold, the estate succeeds to and will be entitled to exercise that redemption right. In a case where a secured creditor validly repossessed the debtor's collateral prior to bankruptcy, the Supreme Court held that, until final foreclosure, the debtor nevertheless had a sufficient residual property interest upon which to base a turnover order against the secured creditor.[42]

Similarly, as a beginning premise, if the debtor acquires property *after* the bankruptcy filing, the debtor is entitled to retain that property for itself, free from its pre-bankruptcy creditors. The debtor's privilege to keep property acquired postpetition is an integral part of the debtor's "fresh start."

The exclusion of postpetition property from the estate is far from absolute, however, as will be discussed below.[43] For example, postpetition proceeds of estate property come into the estate, *unless* they are attributable to the postpetition services of an individual chapter 7 debtor. § 541(a)(6). Property acquired by the estate

---

[40]   See § 7.2.

[41]   See § 6.29.

[42]   United States v. Whiting Pools, Inc., 462 U.S. 198 (1983). See § 5.13.

[43]   See §§ 5.3–5.4, 5.9.

postpetition becomes part of the estate. § 541(a)(7). Thus, for corporate and partnership debtors, virtually all property acquired postpetition during the pendency of the case comes into the estate. This makes sense, because only human beings receive a "fresh start." In chapters 11, 12 and 13, however, in which the debtor undertakes to pay its creditors over a period of time, *individual* debtors can defer their fresh start: an ongoing "perpetual estate" is created during the pendency of the bankruptcy. §§ 1115(a), 1207(a), 1306(a).

The most significant timing problem with regard to property of the estate does not concern the legal rules, which are relatively straightforward, but the *application* of those rules. Fixing the exact moment at which a property right arises can be quite difficult in some cases. The debtor's (and thus the estate's) full enjoyment of and entitlement to that property interest may be connected to and dependent on events that transpire over an extended period of time that straddles the bankruptcy filing date. In such an instance, what property interest, if any, did the debtor have at the time the bankruptcy case was filed?

As an initial proposition, it is important to note that property passes into the estate even if that interest is unliquidated, unmatured, or contingent, or if enjoyment will be postponed. For both the allowance of claims against the debtor and the inclusion of property, bankruptcy serves to accelerate the debtor's financial affairs down to the date of the bankruptcy filing.

To give a simple example, assume that Debtor files bankruptcy on April 1. Debtor is the holder of a promissory note that will mature on June 1. The Debtor's right to be paid on the note on June 1 becomes property of the estate, even though the obligor will not have to pay the trustee until the note's maturity date. The promise to pay the note was made before bankruptcy, and thus is property of the Debtor. Similarly, if the Debtor has an unliquidated tort cause of action against Tortfeasor on the date of bankruptcy, the right to attempt to liquidate and collect that cause of action passes into the estate. The alleged tortious behavior against the Debtor occurred prior to bankruptcy, and thus is part of the Debtor's asset sheet at the time of bankruptcy. A Debtor who purchases a lottery ticket on Thursday, files bankruptcy on Friday, and wins the lottery on Saturday will be disappointed to learn that his lottery ticket became property of the estate, and thus the winnings will go into the estate as well.

In some cases, though, the question of the very existence of a property interest depends on events in both the pre-bankruptcy *and* post-bankruptcy period. The leading case illustrating this problem is the Supreme Court decision in *Segal v. Rochelle*.[44] In *Segal*, the issue was whether a tax loss-carryback refund for a taxable year that ended postpetition, but which was attributable to losses incurred by the debtors prepetition, constituted property of the estate. The debtors filed bankruptcy on September 27, having suffered losses prior to that date. Under the Internal Revenue Code, however, the tax refund could not be claimed until the end of the taxable year, which for the debtors was the end of the calendar year. The debtors wanted to apply the loss-carryback refund against taxes they had paid in the preceding two years. The trustee

---

[44]   382 U.S. 375 (1966).

argued that the refund belonged to the estate. The Supreme Court held for the trustee, concluding that the refund was property of the estate. The Court reasoned that the refund was "sufficiently rooted in the pre-bankruptcy past and so little entangled with the bankrupts' ability to make an unencumbered fresh start that it should be regarded as 'property.'"[45]

The quoted rationale contains two distinct points. The first focuses on timing, the second on the fresh start policy. The latter concern, that an individual debtor fully enjoy a financial fresh start, is protected in large part by the exclusion of property attributable to postpetition services in chapter 7 cases.[46] § 541(a)(6). Concerning the temporal issue, the *Segal* Court demanded that the property interest at issue be "sufficiently rooted in the pre-bankruptcy past" to justify characterization as property of the debtor at the time of bankruptcy. The problem is one of attribution, linking the property interest to events. In the *Segal* case, the Court found that the "rooting" requirement was met, since all the losses that gave rise to the refund claim occurred prior to bankruptcy.

If a court believes, though, that critically necessary "roots" arise after filing, it may exclude property from the estate. The question is whether there is enough of a pre-bankruptcy root to say that as of the time of bankruptcy there was a "contingent" property interest, or instead whether the debtor at the time of filing had nothing more than a mere hope or expectation. This has come up numerous times when legislation is passed *post*-petition that provides benefits to a debtor based on *pre*-petition events. Is it more telling for the property of the estate analysis that as of the time of bankruptcy the legislation had not yet been passed, or that the underlying events had already occurred? A fair reading of *Segal* suggests that the latter should control, and that the property should be included. In these cases one could argue, based on *Segal*, that the debtor had a *contingent* property interest when he filed bankruptcy. When the contingency then came to pass postpetition, the property would belong to the bankruptcy estate. Alternatively, in some scenarios (where the debtor had something pre-bankruptcy, such as a crop that was then lost), a reasonable case could be made that the postpetition payments constituted "proceeds" of prepetition property under § 541(a)(6).[47]

Most courts, though, have gone the other way, and have excluded the property from the estate. For those courts, the fact that the authorizing legislation had not yet been passed at the time of bankruptcy meant that the debtor did not have a "contingent" property interest at all. For example, the Ninth Circuit held that federally created fishing quota rights were not property of the estate when the governing regulations were not promulgated until after the debtor filed bankruptcy, even though the value of those quota rights was based entirely on the debtor's pre-bankruptcy fishing history.[48] Similarly, several circuits have determined that crop loss assistance payments paid to a debtor postpetition, pursuant to legislation enacted postpetition,

---

[45]   Id. at 380.

[46]   See § 5.9.

[47]   See § 5.3.

[48]   Sliney v. Battley (In re Schmitz), 270 F.3d 1254 (9th Cir. 2001).

were not estate property, even though the payments constituted compensation for *pre*-petition crop losses.[49] A handful of decisions have gone the other way, and have concluded that such postpetition compensatory schemes for *pre*-bankruptcy losses do constitute estate property.[50] In so holding the courts either bring the property in as property as of commencement of the case under § 541(a)(1) or, depending on the circumstances, as proceeds of prepetition property, under § 541(a)(6).

Community property.

Community property presents special concerns in determining which property of the debtor will go into the bankruptcy estate. The problem is that the debtor and the debtor's spouse together hold an integrated and entire interest in the whole; the marital unit owns the property, not either spouse individually. If only one spouse files bankruptcy, however, it becomes necessary to identify which community property goes into the bankruptcy estate. The governing section is § 541(a)(2). Under that section, community property passes into the debtor's bankruptcy estate to the extent that it is:

- subject to the debtor's sole, equal, or joint management and control, § 541(a)(2)(A), or

- liable for an allowable claim against the debtor, or for a joint claim to the extent the interest is liable. § 541(a)(2)(B).

§ 5.3   Inclusions of Postpetition Property

The bankruptcy estate initially is comprised of all of the legal and equitable interests in property that the debtor had at the time of the commencement of the bankruptcy case.[51] § 541(a)(1). Except for cases under chapters 12 and 13, and for individual debtors under chapter 11,[52] the United States bankruptcy law generally does not provide for a "perpetual" bankruptcy estate that remains open to capture all postpetition property acquired by the debtor or the estate. However, neither is the door to entry into the estate closed permanently the instant after the bankruptcy filing. In five specific situations, postpetition property is added to the estate:

1. The trustee recovers property for the benefit of the estate pursuant to the avoiding powers, or another enumerated Code section, § 541(a)(3);

2. Property is preserved for the benefit of the estate or ordered transferred to the estate, § 541(a)(4);

---

[49]   In re Bracewell, 454 F.3d 1234 (11th Cir. 2006); In re Burgess, 438 F.3d 493 (5th Cir. 2006); In re Vote, 276 F.3d 1024 (8th Cir. 2002).

[50]   See, e.g., FarmPro Servs., Inc. v. Brown, 276 B.R. 620 (D.N.D. 2002). See also In re Lemos, 243 B.R. 96 (Bankr. D. Idaho 1999). The judge who issued the *Lemos* decision subsequently acknowledged (based on cases such as *Vote*, supra note 49) that "the legal landscape has changed markedly," and thus recanted. In re Stallings, 290 B.R. 777, 781 (Bankr. D. Idaho 2003).

[51]   See § 5.2.

[52]   See § 5.4.

3.   The debtor gets a "windfall" by inheritance, divorce, or life insurance within 180 days after the filing, § 541(a)(5);

4.   The property is proceeds of estate property, § 541(a)(6); and

5.   The estate acquires property, § 541(a)(7).

Trustee recovery

One means by which postpetition property may be added to the estate is through the recovery of property by the bankruptcy trustee performing her statutory duties. § 541(a)(3). In a variety of circumstances the trustee is empowered to bring back into the estate property that rightfully belongs there. This power exists with regard to: (1) property recovered pursuant to the trustee's avoiding powers under § 550; (2) recaptured setoffs, § 553; (3) excessive retainers paid to the debtor's attorney prior to bankruptcy, § 329(b); (4) property subject to a bankruptcy sale that is set aside as improper, § 363(n); (5) property in the hands of a custodian at the time of bankruptcy, § 543; and (6) property recovered from the general partners of a partnership debtor, § 723.

For example, assume that the day before filing bankruptcy the debtor made a preferential payment of $10,000 to Creditor A. That payment obviously reduced the debtor's total asset balance by $10,000. If the payment had not been made, the amount of the debtor's property that would have been included in the estate under § 541(a)(1) would have been $10,000 greater. Assuming that the transfer to Creditor A is avoidable under § 547, the trustee will be entitled to recover $10,000 from Creditor A under § 550. The $10,000 recovered as a preference from A then becomes property of the estate under § 541(a)(3). Upon payment of the $10,000 to the trustee, Creditor A's claim against the estate is increased by $10,000. In effect, the preferential transfer is unwound: the transferred property is restored to the estate, and the Creditor's claim is reinstated.

Preserved property

A similar principle of restoring to the estate that to which it is rightfully entitled underlies the rule in § 541(a)(4) that the estate includes property preserved for the benefit of or ordered transferred to the estate under § 510(c) or § 551. Section 510(c) codifies the doctrine of equitable subordination, and § 551 provides for the automatic preservation of avoided transfers for the benefit of the estate. Without the automatic inclusive rule of § 541(a)(4), the subordination or avoidance would not serve its purpose; the wrongful depletion of the estate would go unremedied.

For example, assume that prior to bankruptcy the Debtor owns Blackacre, which is then worth $25,000. Within the preference period, Creditor A obtains a judicial lien on Blackacre to secure a debt of $5,000. Debtor subsequently grants a mortgage on Blackacre to Creditor B to secure a $20,000 loan. Outside of bankruptcy, Creditor A's judicial lien would have priority over Creditor B's mortgage. Unfortunately, Blackacre drops in value to $20,000 by the time Debtor files bankruptcy. In the bankruptcy case the trustee avoids Creditor A's senior judicial lien as a preference under § 547. Creditor B's $20,000 mortgage, however, is valid in bankruptcy. Without preservation of the avoided transfer to Creditor A for the benefit of the estate under § 551, and inclusion of that preserved interest in the estate under § 541(a)(4), Creditor B's previously junior mortgage would swallow up all value in Blackacre, leaving nothing for the general creditors of the estate. Instead, the estate succeeds to Creditor A's senior position to the extent of A's avoided $5,000 interest. That $5,000 interest in Blackacre becomes property of the estate under § 541(a)(4). Creditor B remains in the identical junior position it was in all along, except now it is junior to the estate rather than to Creditor A.

Windfall clause

With regard to property acquired by the debtor, the baseline rule, discussed above, is that the time of the bankruptcy filing serves as the point of demarcation between property that is included in the estate and property that is not. If the debtor has a property interest at the time of filing, that interest goes into the estate under § 541(a)(1); if the debtor acquires the interest after the filing, the property is the debtor's to keep. Assume, for example, that the Debtor's rich Uncle gives the Debtor a car the day before the Debtor files bankruptcy; the car becomes property of the estate. If the Uncle delays making the gift until the day after the filing, however, the Debtor has a "free ride," so to speak. The postpetition windfall may be enjoyed by the Debtor free from his or her creditors.

In some situations, though, the Code brings postpetition "windfalls" acquired by the debtor within 180 days after the filing into the estate.[53] § 541(a)(5). The common thread in these provisions (although not a required element of proof) is that the debtor often may be able to anticipate the windfall. The rule of inclusion in the estate thus attempts to minimize any incentive of the debtor to race to file bankruptcy just before receiving the windfall. As a matter of basic fairness, Congress does not want debtors to be able to manipulate the timing of events to the detriment of creditors. Section 541(a)(5) brings into the estate property that the debtor acquires or becomes entitled to acquire within 180 days after filing by:

- bequest, devise, or inheritance,

- a property settlement agreement or a divorce decree, or

- a life insurance policy or death benefit plan.

For example, if Debtor's rich Uncle has executed a will that leaves $100,000 to Debtor, and Debtor knows that Uncle is on his deathbed, Debtor might be inclined to file bankruptcy before Uncle "shuffles off [his] mortal coil" if § 541(a)(5) were not on the books. Under § 541(a)(5), however, if Uncle dies within 180 days of the filing, Debtor's inheritance will come into the estate. The same would hold true if Debtor were to acquire the property as the beneficiary of a life insurance policy or a death benefit plan.

---

[53] See Adam J. Hirsch, Inheritance and Bankruptcy: The Meaning of the Fresh Start, 45 Hastings L.J. 175 (1994).

Interestingly, though, § 541(a)(5) as drafted does not appear to reach property that the debtor might acquire pursuant to other forms of common "will substitutes," such a living trust.[54] Nor would trust income paid to a debtor beneficiary during the 180–day period be brought into the estate, because that income payment is not payable by "bequest, devise, or inheritance."[55] Of course, if the debtor actually acquires an interest in property prior to bankruptcy (such as a contingent remainder, for example), as opposed to a mere expectancy, the property interest will be included in the estate under the general inclusive rule of § 541(a)(1).[56]

The windfall clause of § 541(a)(5) may not help creditors much, although in some cases it might serve to deprive debtors of the property as well. The reason is that able counsel often will be able to draft around the capture rules of subsection (5). After the debtor files bankruptcy, the instrument that would have provided the windfall to the debtor (e.g., the will, the life insurance policy beneficiary designation, etc.) can be revised to eliminate the debtor's expectancy. Indeed, it may even be possible to structure the wealth transmission so that the debtor still takes the property, but free from the strictures of § 541(a)(5). For example, the Uncle could revoke his will after the debtor files bankruptcy, then execute a living trust, naming the debtor as remainderman. However, if adequate planning is not done in advance, § 541(a)(5) will apply. For example, one court held that a debtor could not disclaim an inheritance received within the 180–day period.[57]

Proceeds of estate property

An important inclusion in property of the estate is for the postpetition "proceeds, product, offspring, rents, or profits of or from property of the estate." § 541(a)(6). Subsection (6) reflects the economic reality that the proceeds or product of a property interest may be an intrinsic part of that property's current value. In a sense, § 541(a)(6) in many cases arguably is but a specification of the general inclusive rule of § 541(a)(1).

A common example is nonresidential real property. The "value" of real property may be computed by capitalizing the projected future income stream from that property. If the debtor owns an apartment building at the time bankruptcy is filed, the future rents that would be paid by tenants represent the core value of the property. Those future rents would be included in the debtor's bankruptcy estate under § 541(a)(6) as they come due.

Another aspect of the proceeds rule of subsection (6) is that it captures any *substitutions* in value for the original estate property. For example, assume that the estate succeeds to a truck that the debtor owned at the time of filing. During the case,

---

[54]   E.g., In re Crandall, 173 B.R. 836 (Bankr. D. Conn. 1994) (although court did find that debtor's beneficial interest in a revocable trust came into the bankruptcy estate under § 541(a)(1)).

[55]   In re Newman, 903 F.2d 1150 (7th Cir. 1990); In re Eley, 331 B.R. 353 (Bankr. S.D. Ohio 2005).

[56]   See *Crandall*, supra note 54, 173 B.R. 836. In re Schmitt, 215 B.R. 417 (B.A.P. 9th Cir. 1997), disagreed with the *Crandall* court's conclusion that subsection (a)(1) captured the debtor's interest in a revocable trust.

[57]   In re Chenoweth, 3 F.3d 1111 (7th Cir. 1993).

while the truck was estate property, the truck is accidentally destroyed in a fire. The insurance proceeds, which represent the substituted value of the original estate property, would become property of the estate under § 541(a)(6).

The "proceeds" rule § 541(a)(6) is not restricted to cases in which the proceeds represent an intrinsic part of or a substitution for the property's value at the time of bankruptcy, however. *Any* property that is a product of the original estate property potentially falls within the ambit of subsection (6) (subject to the individual services exclusion noted below). As the legislative history makes plain, the proceeds rule of subsection (6) is a broad one.[58] Another way of conceptualizing the extent of the rule is to view the filing of the bankruptcy case as a transfer of all of the debtor's property to the new owner, the bankruptcy estate. The estate as owner is entitled to any proceeds of the property it owns.

This rule extends both to increases in the value of estate property and to accessions to that property. For example, assume that the debtor's stock in a corporation becomes property of the estate. The estate would enjoy both the increases in the market value of that stock and any dividends on the stock.

The principal difficulty with § 541(a)(6) comes in applying the exclusion for postpetition proceeds that "are earnings from services performed by an individual debtor after the commencement of the case." To the extent that the proceeds are the product of an individual debtor's services, those proceeds are not included as property of the estate in a chapter 7 case.[59] Instead, the individual debtor is privileged to retain those proceeds for himself or herself, free from the claims of creditors. The individual debtor's right to retain the postpetition product of his or her "human capital" lies at the very core of the notion of a "fresh start" in bankruptcy.

While the concept makes sense, applying the rule can be quite difficult. As will be explored in more detail in a later section, the problem often is one of *attribution*. Proceeds may be realized after the filing of the bankruptcy case that are attributable in part *both* to property that the debtor held at the time of the bankruptcy filing *and* to the debtor's postpetition services. Assume that the debtor has a contract to write a novel, and completes half of the novel before filing bankruptcy, then completes the book after filing. To what extent should the postpetition royalties be included in the bankruptcy estate? Courts have struggled to value the property held at the time of filing and the postpetition services, but such an undertaking appears necessary.

Estate acquisition

The final category of property acquired postpetition that is included in the bankruptcy estate is for property that is acquired *by the estate*. § 541(a)(7). The estate as the acquiring party is the logical owner of what it obtains. The legislative history

---

[58] H.R. Rep. No. 95–595, 95th Cong., 1st Sess., at 368 (1977).

[59] See § 5.9.

gives the example of the estate entering into a contract; that postpetition contract is property of the estate.[60]

In a sense, this rule is simply an extended and relaxed version of the proceeds rule of subsection (6), not requiring any proof of tracing or attribution. If the estate, as opposed to the debtor, acquires property during the bankruptcy case, at some level the estate's ability to do so must be traceable to original estate property: all that the estate starts out with is the property of the estate as of the commencement of the case. In cases involving debtors who are not individuals, i.e., corporate or partnership debtors, in which the individual earnings exclusion of § 541(a)(6) by definition cannot apply, presumptively all postpetition acquisitions will come into the estate.

§ 5.4   Expanded Estate in Chapters 11, 12 and 13

The presumption in chapter 7 bankruptcy cases is against a "perpetual" bankruptcy estate, in which the estate includes all property acquired by the debtor after the filing of the bankruptcy petition. Instead, the general rule is that the extent of the estate is fixed at the time of the bankruptcy filing, and that any property that the debtor acquires after filing belongs to the debtor. For individual debtors, the right to retain property acquired after bankruptcy is a cornerstone of the debtor's fresh start.

However, the presumption against a perpetual estate does not apply in cases under chapter 12 or chapter 13, or in cases involving individual debtors under chapter 11. In those cases, the governing rule is that all postpetition property acquired during the pendency of the case, whether by the debtor or by the estate, becomes property of the estate. §§ 1115(a), 1207(a), 1306(a). This rule extends even to postpetition earnings of the debtor. In short, a debtor who elects to proceed voluntarily under chapter 12 or chapter 13, or an individual in chapter 11 either voluntarily or involuntarily, must defer the full enjoyment of their fresh start until the conclusion of the bankruptcy case. Note, though, that the debtor remains in possession of estate property in chapters 11, 12 and 13, §§ 1115(b), 1207(b), 1306(b), unlike the situation in chapter 7, in which the debtor must relinquish possession of estate property to the trustee. § 521(a)(4).

Specifically, the expanded estate in chapters 11, 12 and 13 includes:

- all property of the kind specified in § 541 that the debtor acquires *after* the commencement of the case and *before* the case is closed, dismissed, or converted, §§ 1115(a)(1), 1207(a)(1), 1306(a)(1), and

- all earnings from postpetition services performed by the debtor after the commencement of the case and before the case is closed, dismissed, or converted, §§ 1115(a)(2), 1207(a)(2), 1306(a)(2).

The expanded estate in chapters 11, 12 and 13 can be important for a variety of reasons. One is that the automatic stay protects creditors from taking any action against property of the estate. § 362(a)(3), (4). This protective rule applies even if the creditor's claim arose after the commencement of the case.

---

[60]   124 Cong. Rec. H11,097 (daily ed. Sept. 28, 1978) (remarks of Rep. Edwards).

The supposed benefit to the debtor from the automatic stay may turn out to be more of a hindrance, however, because it will be more difficult for the debtor to obtain postpetition credit. Ameliorating this problem is the provision in § 1327(b) that confirmation of the debtor's plan vests all property of the estate in the debtor, unless the plan provides otherwise. Confirmation occurs at a very early stage in a chapter 13 case, and thus the literal reading of § 1327(b) suggests that the stay will not continue to apply to bar the collection of postpetition claims.[61] A debtor could elect, though, to maintain the stay in effect by providing specifically in the plan that estate property will not vest in the debtor upon confirmation.

A second potentially important consequence of the expanded estate in chapters 11, 12 and 13 concerns the effect of a *conversion* of the case to another chapter.[62] The problem (for the debtor) is this: property acquired postpetition and pre-conversion that becomes property of the estate only because of the special rules governing in chapters 11, 12 and chapter 13 may be included in the estate after conversion. As such, it will be distributed to creditors in a chapter 7 case, and will establish the basis for the required minimum distribution to creditors in a chapter 11 case. Yet, if the debtor had originally filed under chapter 7, that postpetition property would not have been included in the estate, and thus would not have been subject to creditors' claims. By initially attempting to proceed under chapter 11, 12 or 13, then, the debtor may end up *worse* off. For example, an individual chapter 7 debtor's postpetition earnings would be excluded from the estate under § 541(a)(6), but will be included in the estate in chapters 11, 12 and 13 pursuant to § 1115(a)(2), 1207(a)(2) and § 1306(a)(2).

The 1994 Amendments addressed this problem in the chapter 13 setting, but said nothing about the situation in chapter 12. When the expanded estate was enacted for individual chapter 11 debtors in 2005, Congress again did not clarify the conversion rule. When the case before conversion was under chapter 13, property of the estate after conversion will *only* consist of property of the estate as of the date of the filing of the petition—excluding therefore property acquired postpetition and pre-conversion—and which remains in the possession and under the control of the debtor on the date of conversion. § 348(f)(1)(A). However, if the debtor converts in bad faith, the property of the estate in the converted case will consist of the property of the estate as of the date of conversion, rather than the date of filing. § 348(f)(2). Whether courts will read a similar rule into chapter 12 cases or individual chapter 11 cases remains to be seen.

§ 5.5   The Role of Non-Bankruptcy Law in Defining Property of the Estate

What constitutes "property of the estate" within the meaning of § 541 ultimately is a *federal* question.[63] The fact that state law might not call an interest "property" is not binding on the federal courts in a bankruptcy case. That being said, however, the more critical point is that *state* law plays the paramount role in defining the underlying

---

[61]   The collection of prepetition claims will still be stayed. §§ 362(a)(1), (2), (6), 524(a)(1), (2). Such claims may not be collected even against property of the debtor; indeed, that prohibition is necessary to effectuate the discharge.

[62]   For a more detailed discussion of the effects of conversion, see § 2.22.

[63]   Bd. of Trade of City of Chicago v. Johnson, 264 U.S. 1 (1924).

nature and characteristics of estate property. As the Supreme Court recognized in the leading case of *Butner v. United States*, "property interests are created and defined by state law."[64] In short, while state law labels are not controlling, the *attributes* given to property by state law generally are recognized and given effect in federal bankruptcy cases.

Why do the federal courts sitting in bankruptcy give effect to the state law attributes of property? The Supreme Court in *Butner* explained that "uniform treatment of property interests by both state and federal courts within a state serves to reduce uncertainty, to discourage forum shopping, and to prevent a party from receiving 'a windfall merely by reason of the happenstance of bankruptcy.'"[65]

This explanation is grounded in the fact that bankruptcy in large part is a *procedural* device utilized to distribute the debtor's property in an equitable manner to multiple creditors with competing claims. Apart from the independent "fresh start" policy, the remedy of bankruptcy exists principally because of the collective action problem inherent in resolving the claims of numerous creditors. Presumptively, the *substantive* rights of the debtor and others in property and the substantive validity of claims against the debtor do not and should not vary just because as a matter of procedure the payment of claims is being done on a collective rather than an individual basis. If the rule were otherwise, some parties would be benefited by a bankruptcy proceeding and others harmed, without any policy justification relevant to the reasons for having bankruptcy in the first place. Those favored would have an incentive to seek recourse to bankruptcy relief solely to capture those benefits. As the *Butner* court noted, "unless some federal interest requires a different result, there is no reason why such interests [in property] should be analyzed differently simply because an interested party is involved in a bankruptcy proceeding."[66]

The federal utilization of state law property attributes is illustrated by another venerable Supreme Court precedent, *Board of Trade of City of Chicago v. Johnson*.[67] In that case, the debtor held a seat on the Chicago Board of Trade. At the time the debtor filed bankruptcy, the membership was worth $10,500. Under state law, creditors could not levy on the seat or compel its sale. Under the rules of the exchange, a member could voluntarily transfer his seat upon payment of a transfer fee. However, those rules also prohibited transfer of the seat if the holder of the membership owed outstanding debts to other members of the exchange and one of those creditors objected to the transfer. In other words, the debtor-member would have to pay the claims of all creditor-members before he could transfer the membership. In the case, the debtor owed $60,000 to other members of the exchange, and objections to transfer were filed.

The issues facing the court were twofold: first, was the debtor's membership on the exchange property of the bankruptcy estate; and second, if so, was that property subject to or free from the prior claims of the other members of the exchange? The

---

[64]   440 U.S. 48, 55 (1979).

[65]   Id.

[66]   Id.

[67]   264 U.S. 1 (1924).

difficulty with the first question was that Illinois law, which governed the exchange, did not recognize the membership as "property," given that creditors could not levy on the seat and that transfer was so limited. The Supreme Court declined to be bound by the state law label, however, and concluded that as a matter of federal bankruptcy law the seat was "property."[68] Thus, the membership did pass into the debtor's bankruptcy estate.

Even though the membership was property of the estate, the second question remained. Did the bankruptcy trustee take the seat free from or subject to the claims of the other members of the exchange? In short, the issue was whether the federal court should give effect to the state law attributes of the property that limited the debtor's transfer rights. Under state law, the seat could not be sold until the $60,000 in member claims were satisfied in full. Applying that restriction would render the seat valueless for general creditors in bankruptcy, since the seat was only worth $10,500.

The Supreme Court held that the state law limitation must be honored in bankruptcy. The creditors' right to block a transfer of the seat until their claims had been paid was analogous to a lien, the Court concluded. That "lien," the Court observed "is inherent in the property in its creation."[69] As such, the limitation must be respected in bankruptcy. The estate gets what the debtor has—no more, no less. General creditors of the debtor would not have been able to realize any value on the seat outside of bankruptcy until the "lien-like" claims of exchange members were first satisfied, and bankruptcy did not expand the rights of those general creditors vis-à-vis exchange members.

The same result would obtain today under the Code. The debtor's seat on the exchange would pass into the estate initially, notwithstanding the transfer restrictions. Section 541(c)(1) makes clear that an interest of the debtor in property becomes property of the estate notwithstanding provisions under non-bankruptcy law that restrict the transfer of that interest.[70] That rule only answers the first question, namely, whether the interest becomes property of the estate. Once the interest is in the estate, though, the state law restrictions on transfer will apply and preclude the trustee from dealing with the property in derogation of the state law limitations. The estate gets the debtor's membership, but the trustee acting on behalf of the estate cannot sell the seat until the claims of objecting member creditors are paid.

Federal deference to state law property attributes applies "unless some federal interest requires a different result," according to the Supreme Court in *Butner v. United States*.[71] There is a strong "federal interest" in the application of the distributional priority scheme spelled out in the federal Bankruptcy Code. If a state attempts to impose its own schedule of priorities in bankruptcy, that attempt will fail under the Supremacy Clause. A state law that provides that a debtor's property must be distributed in a certain order thus will not be enforceable in bankruptcy. The

---

[68]   Id. at 9–11.

[69]   Id. at 15.

[70]   See § 5.6.

[71]   440 U.S. 48, 55 (1979).

trouble arises, however, when the state priority rules are effectuated *indirectly,* by adroit definition of the characteristics of the debtor's interests in property. Recognition of a creditor's "lien-like" property interest has the practical effect of affording *priority* to that creditor in the distribution of the debtor's assets. Thus, the members of the exchange in the *Chicago Board of Trade* case effectively were given a priority claim to the debtor's membership over general creditors of the debtor by the Court's willingness to honor the state law transfer restriction.

At what point does the state's permissible delineation of property attributes cross the line and become an impermissible intrusion into the federal prerogative to establish the priority of claims? At a minimum, the state law must be "*bankruptcy neutral.*" In other words, to be given effect in bankruptcy, a state law defining the characteristics of property must apply across the board, in or out of bankruptcy. A law that gives lien or priority rights to certain creditors *only* in the event of bankruptcy would not pass muster. Such a law plainly is not a definition of the nature of the property interest, but a blatant attempt to prescribe priorities.

Sometimes, though, a state law is bankruptcy neutral, and yet still clearly creates priority entitlements favoring certain creditors, but does so pursuant to the definition and creation of the property interest. Perhaps the best example is the liquor license transfer cases. In virtually all states, liquor licenses exist and are granted only with the blessing of the state government. An integral part of the licensee's property interest in the license is the power to *transfer* that license. Many states condition the licensee's power to transfer the license upon prior payment of all outstanding taxes and other debts to the state itself. When the debtor-licensee files bankruptcy, the issue is whether the trustee may sell the license without first paying the back taxes to the state.

The courts are divided. One view is that the transfer restriction is a valid state law limitation on the extent of the debtor's property interest, which must be respected in bankruptcy.[72] Thus, transfer is only permissible if the back taxes are first paid. Cases in this line invariably invoke the spirit of the *Chicago Board of Trade* case. Other courts, though, are more troubled by what they perceive to be in substance a state attempt to designate priorities, even if in form the designation is dressed up in "property" garb. Courts taking this view do not give effect to the transfer restriction, and permit the trustee to transfer the liquor license without paying state taxes.[73] The state as a creditor is required to get in the distribution line with everyone else.

One way to resolve the problem may be to analogize to statutory liens. That is, the property transfer restriction could be given effect only in those situations in which a state statutory lien is enforceable in bankruptcy. Section 545 explicitly regulates statutory liens, and permits the trustee to avoid those liens in certain circumstances.[74] Avoidance is authorized if the lien is triggered only in the event of bankruptcy or insolvency, or if a bona fide purchaser could defeat the lien. In addition, tax liens are

---

[72]   See, e.g., In re Farmers Mkts., Inc., 792 F.2d 1400 (9th Cir. 1986).

[73]   See, e.g., In re Terwilliger's Catering Plus, Inc., 86 B.R. 937 (Bankr. S.D. Ohio 1988), aff'd on other grounds, 911 F.2d 1168 (6th Cir. 1990).

[74]   See §§ 6.49–6.51.

subordinated under § 724(b) to higher priority claims.[75] The rationale for analogizing to statutory liens is that the state could accomplish the identical goal of priority payment for its own claims either through the mechanism of a transfer restriction or a statutory lien on the license.

B. EXCLUSIONS FROM THE ESTATE

§ 5.6   Transfer Restrictions

The scope of property of the estate is broad. The Code embodies a strong congressional policy favoring maximization of the size of the estate so that creditors may be paid as much as possible on their claims. However, the maximization policy is not inevitably afforded superiority. Other policies sometimes take precedence. Not every conceivable interest of the debtor in property is always included in the estate. Exclusions from the estate may serve to minimize forum shopping by creditors, recognize superior equitable entitlements of third parties,[76] or promote the debtor's interest in receiving a fresh start.[77]

As a general principle, creditors should not be able to recover more assets inside a bankruptcy case than they could outside of bankruptcy, solely because of the "happenstance of bankruptcy." Such a result would encourage forum shopping; creditors might seek recourse to bankruptcy relief solely to grab more assets, without any independent justification for the maintenance of a bankruptcy case. Furthermore, there are no evident distributive justice concerns that would warrant such a departure from non-bankruptcy norms, attainable only in the bankruptcy setting. A "bankruptcy only" rule should find support in a bankruptcy-specific policy. Congress could decide that a debtor who wanted the benefit of a discharge of debts, a radical form of relief available only in a federal bankruptcy case, would have to relinquish extra property to creditors as the *quid pro quo* for the discharge. While conceptually imaginable, there is no evidence at all that Congress intended such a tradeoff.

A logical corollary of the foregoing principle is that creditors should not have *fewer* assets available to them in a bankruptcy case than they would outside of bankruptcy. This corollary means that "*ipso facto*" clauses are not enforceable in bankruptcy. § 541(c)(1)(B). An ipso facto clause purports to terminate or forfeit a debtor's property interest upon the filing of bankruptcy, or upon the occurrence of certain conditions of financial distress that signal the likelihood of an impending bankruptcy. Property thus will come into the estate notwithstanding the existence of an ipso facto clause.

In one respect creditors may be able to reach more assets of the debtor in bankruptcy than they could outside. Under § 541(c)(1)(A), non-bankruptcy restrictions on the transfer of property will not prevent the debtor's property from going into the estate. In other words, the debtor's property will pass into the estate, notwithstanding

---

[75]   A 2005 amendment to § 724(b) created an exception to this subordination rule for ad valorem taxes. See generally § 6.52.

[76]   See § 5.8.

[77]   See § 5.9, 5.11.

the existence of transfer restrictions. That property will then be available for liquidation and distribution to creditors.

The exception is not entirely inconsistent with the general principle, however. Once the property is in the estate, the trustee as representative of the estate normally will still be bound by the restriction, and will not be permitted to transfer the property in violation of the condition. For example, state law may not allow tort causes of action to be transferred. Because of § 541(c)(1)(A), such a cause of action will become property of the estate, but then the trustee will not be able to transfer the cause of action. All that the trustee would be able to do would be to prosecute the action on behalf of the estate. Furthermore, § 541(c)(1)(A) often makes sense because the justification for the non-bankruptcy transfer restriction may not apply in bankruptcy.

The rule in subsection (c)(1) overriding non-bankruptcy transfer restrictions is subject to one major exception, however, which is codified in § 541(c)(2). Property subject to a transfer restriction that is within the scope of subsection (c)(2) is excluded from the bankruptcy estate in the first instance. The debtor thus is free to retain such property free from the claims of his or her prebankruptcy creditors. In cases involving debtor pension plans, the (c)(2) exclusion has proven to be of tremendous importance and has generated enormous controversy, leading ultimately to a decision by the United States Supreme Court.[78] The next section explores the mysteries of § 541(c)(2), especially as applied to pension plans, along with other sections that protect a debtor's retirement assets.

§ 5.7   Retirement Assets

As noted in the preceding section, § 541(c)(2) constitutes an exception to the general rule that property transfer restrictions are ignored in bankruptcy. The most important application of subsection (c)(2) has been with respect to retirement assets. A major holding of the Supreme Court in 1992 dealt with this question. Since then, subsequent Supreme Court precedent and congressional legislation have served to provide comprehensive protection for an individual debtor's retirement assets. By one means or another, a debtor can keep for herself virtually all of her retirement assets in bankruptcy.

Let us begin with an examination of § 541(c)(2) and the key Supreme Court case interpreting that section. Given that the Supreme Court found the language of § 541(c)(2) dispositive in the pension plan case to be discussed below, the logical starting point in the analysis is with the language of (c)(2):

> "A restriction on the transfer of a beneficial interest of the debtor in a trust that is enforceable under applicable nonbankruptcy law is enforceable in a case under this title."

The legislative history "explained" this provision in the following excerpt from the House Report, which also is quoted verbatim because of the central role that history came to play in the interpretive debate:

---

[78]   Patterson v. Shumate, 504 U.S. 753 (1992).

"Paragraph (2) of subsection (c), however, preserves restrictions on transfer of a spendthrift trust to the extent that the restriction is *enforceable under applicable nonbankruptcy law.*"[79]

At a minimum, then, Congress intended for § 541(c)(2) to exclude from the estate the debtor's beneficial interest in a spendthrift trust, if the spendthrift restriction would be enforceable against creditors under state law. A "spendthrift" provision prevents the voluntary or involuntary alienation of the beneficiary's future benefits under the trust. Subject to some exceptions (such as debts for necessaries and alimony and support claims), many states generally enforce spendthrift trusts.[80] The effect is that a creditor of a debtor-beneficiary cannot presently reach the debtor's future rights to trust income or principal, but must wait until distribution is actually made to the debtor. Section 541(c)(2) thus follows the general principle that creditors can reach only those assets in bankruptcy that they could reach outside of bankruptcy—not more and not less. The prospectively inalienable interests of the debtor-beneficiary of a spendthrift trust do not become property of the estate.

However, state law recognizes an important exception to the general rule that spendthrift provisions are usually valid against creditors: a "self-settled" spendthrift trust is not enforceable. A self-settled trust is one in which the debtor creates the trust for his own benefit; that is, the debtor is both settlor *and* beneficiary. A debtor may not immunize his own property from the claims of creditors and yet retain the beneficial interest in that property.

With this background in mind, consider the pension plan problem. Pension plans became extremely widespread after the enactment of ERISA in 1974.[81] After the enactment of the Bankruptcy Code in 1978, bankruptcy courts increasingly faced the issue of whether a debtor's interest in a pension plan becomes property of the bankruptcy estate. The stakes can be high. The Supreme Court case of *Patterson v. Shumate*[82] is illustrative. Joseph Shumate, the president and chairman of the Coleman Furniture Company, had $250,000 in the company's pension plan at the time he filed bankruptcy under chapter 7. Was that quarter of a million dollars part of the bankruptcy estate (in which case it would be distributed to Shumate's creditors) or did Shumate retain that pension plan interest free from his creditors? The answer lies in part in the interpretation of § 541(c)(2), in conjunction with ERISA. After the 2005 amendments, § 541(b)(7) also will be relevant, as explained below.

Virtually all pension plans under ERISA are "qualified." Shumate's plan was no exception. A requirement to "qualify" for favorable tax treatment under ERISA is that the "pension plan shall provide that benefits provided under the plan may not be

---

[79] H.R. Rep. No. 95–595, 95th Cong., 1st Sess., at 369 (1977) (emphasis added). The Senate version of the bill limited the exclusion to that income reasonably necessary for support. S. Rep. No. 95–989, 95th Cong., 2d Sess., at 83 (1978). Congress ultimately went with the House version. 124 Cong. Rec. H11,096 (daily ed. Sept. 28, 1978) (remarks of Rep. Edwards).

[80] See Paul G. Haskell, Preface to Wills, Trusts and Administration 209–13 (1987); Broadway Nat'l Bank v. Adams, 133 Mass. 170 (1882).

[81] Employee Retirement Income Security Act, codified at 29 U.S.C. § 1001 et seq.

[82] 504 U.S. 753 (1992).

assigned or alienated."[83] Much like spendthrift trusts, this "anti-alienation" provision prevents creditors of the employee from reaching the employee's benefits prior to distribution to the employee.

However, if § 541(c)(2) *only* excludes trust transfer restrictions that meet the exacting standards of state spendthrift trust law, pension benefits often will fall short, even if "ERISA-qualified," and therefore will be included in the estate. The reason is that the pension benefits, at least in part, may be "self-settled," i.e., the debtor-employee himself makes the contributions to the pension plan. As explained above, state law does not insulate self-settled spendthrift trusts from the claims of the debtor's creditors. In the early years of the Code, every court of appeals to consider the question held that ERISA pension plans were not protected by § 541(c)(2), and the debtor's benefits in the pension plan must be included in the estate.[84]

Those courts relied on two main arguments. First, they read the language in the legislative history, quoted above, as indicative of a congressional intent to limit the scope of the § 541(c)(2) exclusion to trusts that would qualify as enforceable spendthrift trusts under state law. Second, those courts used a "surplusage" argument. Section 522(d)(10)(E) permits a debtor to *exempt* from the estate their right to receive payments under pension plans, but only to the extent reasonably necessary for the support of the debtor and the debtor's dependents. An exemption is only relevant, however, if the property to be exempted otherwise would be property of the bankruptcy estate. Thus, the exemption right in § 522(d)(10)(E) would be superfluous if the debtor's pension plan assets already were excluded from the estate under § 541(c)(2).

The tide turned in 1990, however, with a decision of the Fourth Circuit holding that an ERISA-qualified pension plan was excluded from the estate by the plain language of § 541(c)(2).[85] Three other circuits soon followed suit,[86] setting the stage for the Supreme Court to resolve the split. Joseph Shumate's quarter-million dollar case provided the Court with an opportunity to act.

The Supreme Court held for the debtor in a unanimous opinion.[87] The Court ruled that the debtor's $250,000 in the ERISA-qualifed plan was excluded from the bankruptcy estate by § 541(c)(2). The basis for the Court's decision was summed up in one sentence: "In our view, the plain language of the Bankruptcy Code and ERISA is our determinant."[88] Section 541(c)(2), quoted earlier, enforces a trust transfer restriction that is "enforceable under applicable nonbankruptcy law" by keeping the trust property subject to the restriction out of the estate. ERISA is such an "applicable nonbankruptcy law," the Court concluded, finding no textual support for limiting

---

[83]   ERISA § 206(d)(1), 29 U.S.C. § 1056(d)(1).

[84]   See In re Daniel, 771 F.2d 1352 (9th Cir. 1985), cert. denied, 475 U.S. 1016 (1986); In re Lichstrahl, 750 F.2d 1488 (11th Cir. 1985); In re Graham, 726 F.2d 1268 (8th Cir. 1984); In re Goff, 706 F.2d 574 (5th Cir. 1983).

[85]   In re Moore, 907 F.2d 1476 (4th Cir. 1990).

[86]   In re Harline, 950 F.2d 669 (10th Cir. 1991); Velis v. Kardanis, 949 F.2d 78 (3d Cir. 1991); In re Lucas, 924 F.2d 597 (6th Cir.), cert. denied, 500 U.S. 959 (1991).

[87]   504 U.S. 753 (1992).

[88]   Id. at 757.

applicable law to *state* law.[89] Furthermore, the ERISA-mandated anti-alienation provision in the pension plan is "enforceable" under ERISA.[90] Thus, on a plain reading of the statutory text, the anti-alienation provision appeared to the Court to fall squarely within the operation of § 541(c)(2).

The bankruptcy trustee argued, however, that the Court should not give effect to the Code's plain meaning, but should limit the § 541(c)(2) exclusion to transfer restrictions that would be enforceable under state spendthrift trust law. The trustee's burden of establishing such a meaning was "exceptionally heavy," the Court noted, "given the clarity of the statutory text."[91] The trustee attempted to carry that burden by raising the legislative history and surplusage arguments that early circuit court decisions had found telling. The Supreme Court was persuaded by neither.

The Court doubted whether resort to legislative history was even warranted in the face of the clear statutory language. Regardless, the history was not conclusive enough to overcome the statutory text. All that the House Report indicated was that spendthrift trusts were within the exclusion of (c)(2); those statements did not support the further assertion that *only* spendthrift trusts were covered.[92]

Nor was the surplusage argument persuasive to the Court. Such an argument falls apart if some meaning and function can still be ascribed to the allegedly superfluous statute, here the exemption provided by § 522(d)(10)(E). The Court concluded that § 522(d)(10)(E) was not superfluous even if ERISA-qualified pension plans were excluded from the estate under § 541(c)(2), because a number of other pension plans do not contain enforceable transfer restrictions and thus would not be covered by § 541(c)(2). For such plans, the exemption provision would play an important role.[93] The Court cited individual retirement accounts (IRAs) as an example, presaging its later decision in *Rousey v. Jacoway*.[94]

The trustee's last-ditch appeal to the bankruptcy policy of estate maximization predictably fell on deaf ears. Doubting the usefulness of vague "policy" claims generally, especially in the face of a clear statute, the Court nevertheless found at least two countervailing policies. One was the ERISA goal of protecting and preserving pension benefits for workers, on a uniform national basis.[95] The other was the principle that bankruptcy should not effect a change in the substantive entitlements of creditors, by allowing them to reach property that they could not reach outside of bankruptcy. Otherwise uniformity would collapse and forum shopping would be a concern. As the Court explained, "declining to recognize any exceptions to that provision within the bankruptcy context minimizes the possibility that creditors will engage in strategic manipulation of the bankruptcy laws in order to gain access to otherwise inaccessible

---

[89] Id. at 758–59.
[90] Id. at 759–60.
[91] Id. at 760.
[92] Id. at 761–62.
[93] Id. at 762–63.
[94] 544 U.S. 320 (2005).
[95] 504 U.S. at 764–65.

funds."[96] The anti-alienation provision in Shumate's pension plan effectively would keep creditors at bay absent a bankruptcy case, and under § 541(c)(2) had to be given identical effect in bankruptcy.

Patterson v. Shumate settled, obviously, the issue of whether ERISA-qualified pension plans are included in the estate. Under § 541(c)(2), they are not. Subsequent courts have concluded that the *Patterson* Court must be taken at its word, dictating that even voluntary after-tax contributions to which the debtor has immediate access must be excluded from the estate, assuming that the plan contains an enforceable anti-alienation clause.[97] Left unanswered by *Patterson*, however, was what happens to the debtor's interests in pension and retirement plans that do *not* contain the sort of anti-alienation provision present in *Patterson*. This issue arises, for example, with regard to individual retirement accounts (IRAs), which are not "ERISA-qualified," lacking enforceable restrictions on transfer. There are a host of other retirement asset vehicles, with differing characteristics.

Absent more, unrestricted plans (like IRAs) would become property of the debtor's estate under § 541(a). Without any restriction on the transfer of the debtor's beneficial interest, such plans fail to satisfy the requisites of § 541(c)(2) for exclusion from the estate.[98] The debtor's interest in such an unrestricted plan could only be excluded from the estate if exempt under § 522 or if otherwise excluded under § 541(b).

Complicating the situation is the fact that many states have enacted statutes that make the debtor's interests in all types of pension and retirement plans exempt from the claims of creditors. The question that courts have had to face is whether such a state exemption law operates to exclude the debtor's beneficial interest in a covered plan from the bankruptcy estate under § 541(c)(2). Some courts have said no, concluding that the transfer restriction must be contained in the plan or trust itself rather than in an independent state exemption law.[99] Those courts also worry about federal preemption of the state law. Other courts, though, have held that state laws exempting pension plans from the claims of creditors are "applicable nonbankruptcy law" transfer restrictions within the meaning of § 541(c)(2).[100] Given the presence of a separate section of the Code that covers exemptions from the bankruptcy estate, it is unlikely that Congress intended for a state exemption to be given effect through the back door of § 541(c)(2). Of course, if the debtor is entitled to elect state exemptions in bankruptcy under § 522, then the debtor need not worry about the applicability of § 541(c)(2), since she can simply claim the retirement assets as exempt under the state law.

---

[96]   Id. at 764.

[97]   See, e.g., In re Conner, 73 F.3d 258 (9th Cir.), cert. denied, 519 U.S. 817 (1996); see also In re Rueter, 11 F.3d 850 (9th Cir. 1993); IRS v. Snyder, 343 F.3d 1171 (9th Cir. 2003); In re Kunz, 309 B.R. 795 (B.A.P. 10th Cir. 2003).

[98]   See, e.g., In re Walker, 959 F.2d 894 (10th Cir. 1992).

[99]   See, e.g., In re Van Nostrand, 183 B.R. 82 (Bankr. D.N.J. 1995); In re Snyder, 206 B.R. 347 (Bankr. M.D. Pa. 1996).

[100]   See In re Yuhas, 104 F.3d 612 (3d Cir. 1997).

The debtor's ability to exclude retirement assets from the bankruptcy estate was expanded and clarified in 2005, with a Supreme Court decision and the enactment of § 541(b)(7) as well as a new exemption. Under § 541(b)(7), property of the estate does not include any amount withheld by an employer from an employee's wages or accepts from an employee for payment as contributions (1) to an employee benefit plan under ERISA (the *Patterson* situation), (2) to a plan under IRC §§ 457 or 403(b), or (3) to a health insurance plan. With regard to wages withheld for contributions to an ERISA plan, § 541(b)(7) moots in part the precise issue in *Patterson*. For such retirement assets, there now is no need to resort to the § 541(c)(2) exclusion, since § 541(b)(7) accomplishes the same result. Furthermore, subsection (b)(7) goes beyond *Patterson* by removing from the estate non-ERISA retirement assets under IRC § 457 and IRC § 403(b), as well as contributions to a health insurance plan. Note, though, that subsection (b)(7) does not apply to any amounts an *employer contributes* to an employee's pension plan, and to that extent the analysis of *Patterson* remains relevant. If the employer's contribution is to an ERISA-qualified plan, then § 541(c)(2) continues to exclude that amount from the estate under *Patterson*.

In determining what property is in the bankruptcy estate, it is important to consider not only § 541, but to examine the possibility that the property may be *exempted* under § 522. That is, even if an asset would initially come into the estate under § 541, an individual debtor still might get the enjoyment of that property by exempting that property under § 522. On the exemption front, both Supreme Court case law and the 2005 legislation offer debtors greater ability to keep retirement assets. First, in 2005 the Supreme Court held in *Rousey v. Jacoway*[101] that assets in an IRA—which cannot be excluded under § 541(c)(2) since IRAs do not contain enforceable transfer restrictions—nevertheless could be exempted under § 522(d)(10)(E), thereby embracing dicta by the *Patterson* Court. Prior to *Rousey*, there had been uncertainty whether IRAs were covered by § 522(d)(10)(E). Note, though, that an exemption under § 522(d)(10)(E) is not necessarily for the full amount in the pension plan, but is limited to the amount reasonably necessary for the support of the debtor or the debtor's dependents.

Rousey was decided less than two weeks before the enactment of BAPCPA in 2005, and that legislation rendered *Rousey*'s actual holding largely unimportant, by creating new exemptions that offer substantial protection for many retirement assets. Under new § 522(b)(3)(C) and § 522(d)(12), *all* tax-exempt retirement funds under IRC §§ 401, 403, 408, 408A, 414, 457, or 501(a) are exempt in bankruptcy.[102] Importantly, these 2005 exemptions apply to Individual Retirement Accounts under IRC §§ 408 or 408A.

---

[101] 544 U.S. 320 (2005).

[102] The legislative history of the BAPCPA offers this explanation of the intent of the 2005 law:

Sec. 224. Protection of Retirement Savings in Bankruptcy. The intent of section 224 is to expand the protection for tax-favored retirement plans or arrangements that may not be already protected under Bankruptcy Code section 541(c)(2) pursuant to *Patterson v. Shumate,* or other state or Federal law. Subsection (a) of section 224 of the Act amends section 522 of the Bankruptcy Code to permit a debtor to exempt certain retirement funds to the extent those monies are in a fund or account that is exempt from taxation under section 401, 403, 408, 408A, 414, 457, or 501(a) of the Internal Revenue Code and that have received a favorable determination pursuant to Internal Revenue Code section 7805 that is in effect as of the date of the commencement of the case.

H.R. Rep. No. 109–31 (pt. 1), 109th Cong., 1st Sess., at 63 (2005).

The only limitation on IRA exemptions is a generous one: as of 2013 (and subject thereafter to tri-annual indexing), an individual debtor could exempt $1,245,475, and a couple filing jointly could exempt twice that amount ($2,490,950). § 522(n). There is no need to demonstrate necessity for support, as under § 522(d)(10)(E).

To summarize the byzantine state of retirement asset protection in bankruptcy after 2005:

1.   The full amount of an ERISA-qualified plan (whether based on amounts withheld from the employees' wages or on employer contributions) is excluded from the estate under § 541(c)(2), on the authority of *Patterson,* and also, for amounts withheld from an employees' wages, under § 541(b)(7).

2.   The full amount of contributions withheld from an employee's wages is excluded for ERISA plans, plans under IRC §§ 457 and 403(b), and health insurance plans.

3.   The full amount of all tax-exempt funds under IRC §§ 401, 403, 414, 457, or 501(a) is exempted from the estate under § 522(b)(3)(C) and § 522(d)(12).

4.   For a tax-exempt IRA under IRC §§ 408 and 408A, $1,245,475 (individual debtor) or $2,490,950 (couple) is exempt under §§ 522(b)(3)(C), 522(d)(12), and 522(n).

5.   Any right to receive "a payment under a stock bonus, pension, profitsharing, annuity, or similar plan or contract on account of illness, disability, death, age, or length of service" may be exempted under § 522(d)(10)(E), but only "to the extent reasonably necessary for the support of the debtor and any dependent of the debtor."

6.   State exemptions of retirement assets may be available in states that do not require debtors to choose the federal exemption scheme, or, even in states that do not permit a debtor to elect state exemptions, the debtor might (depending on the jurisdiction) be able to invoke the state exemption scheme as a "transfer restriction" under § 541(c)(2).

§ 5.8   Non–Debtor Equitable Interests

A fundamental defining principle of property of the estate is that the estate succeeds to whatever interests in property the debtor had at the time the bankruptcy case is commenced.[103] § 541(a)(1). The corollary to that principle is that the estate does *not* include property interests held by entities other than the debtor; i.e., the estate is comprised of all interests of the debtor in property, *and nothing more.*

The limiting premise just noted in many circumstances may be nothing more than an obvious tautology. This truism is most evident in cases in which the debtor has no property interest at all. If Bill files for bankruptcy, it would be absurd for Sam's property to be brought into Bill's estate. Bill's creditors have no right to be paid out of Sam's property.

---

[103]   See § 5.2.

The same general rule should still govern when the debtor has a *partial* interest in property, but does not enjoy the entire fee simple absolute. As the legislative history explains, "to the extent such an interest [in property] is limited in the hands of the debtor, it is equally limited in the hands of the estate."[104] Thus, for example, if Bill and Sam own Blackacre as tenants in common, and Bill files bankruptcy, only Bill's tenancy interest passes into the estate. Sam, of course, retains his tenancy interest, free from the clutches of Bill's creditors. If Sam loans Bill his car for the day, and Bill drives the car down to the federal courthouse to file bankruptcy, the car will not become property of Bill's estate, except to the extent of Bill's mere possessory interest.

This limiting principle applies as well when the legal title and equitable title are divided, with the debtor holding one but not the other. Thus, if the debtor is the beneficiary of a trust, the debtor's equitable beneficial interest in the trust will become estate property (subject to enforceable transfer restrictions),[105] but the legal title will not.

Conversely, if the debtor is the trustee of a trust but not the beneficiary, and thus holds the legal but not the equitable title, only the legal title will become property of the estate. The equitable beneficial interest in favor of the nondebtor remains outside the estate. For example, if Bill were the trustee of an express trust for the benefit of Sam, Sam's beneficial interest in the trust res would not be in Bill's estate. Section 541(d) expressly recognizes this exclusion of the nondebtor party's equitable interest from the estate where the debtor holds only the legal title at the time of the commencement of the case. The particular instance that Congress had in mind, as reflected both in the language of § 541(d) itself and in the legislative history,[106] is where the debtor sells a mortgage but retains the legal title to the mortgage for servicing. This exclusion was thought necessary to protect the integrity of the secondary mortgage market.

The principal difficulty that has arisen in connection with the foregoing general limitation on the scope of property of the estate is in harmonizing that limitation with the trustee's strong-arm avoiding power under § 544(a)(3).[107] That avoiding power permits the bankruptcy trustee to avoid and recover for the estate unrecorded interests that would be vulnerable to a bona fide purchaser for value outside of bankruptcy. For example, if the debtor has secretly granted a mortgage to a third party, but the mortgagee fails to record the mortgage, the trustee would be able to avoid the mortgage under § 544(a)(3). This strong-arm power is justified as a means of defeating secret liens and enforcing the debtor's ostensible ownership in favor of the debtor's creditors. The direct effect of § 544(a)(3) is to bring into the estate equitable interests held by third parties.

Perhaps one has little sympathy for the plight of a third party who has colluded with a debtor to mislead creditors by keeping liens and conveyances secret, and then

---

[104] 124 Cong. Rec. H11,096 (daily ed. Sept. 28, 1978) (remarks of Rep. Edwards).

[105] See § 5.6.

[106] 124 Cong. Rec. H11,096 (daily ed. Sept. 28, 1978) (remarks of Rep. Edwards).

[107] See §§ 6.3, 6.4 for a discussion of the strong-arm power.

discovers that it cannot enforce its secret interest when the debtor files bankruptcy. The sympathy meter tilts sharply the other way, though, when the third party has been defrauded by the debtor, and the only reason the third party's interest is vulnerable under § 544(a)(3) is the debtor's fraudulent failure to record the true state of the property's ownership. In *Belisle v. Plunkett*,[108] for example, the debtor raised money for various real estate investments from five partnerships, but then purchased and recorded the property in his own name, rather than in the name of the partnerships. Under non-bankruptcy law, the defrauded investors would have been entitled to impose a constructive trust on the property. The bankruptcy trustee in *Belisle* successfully set aside the investors' equitable interests under § 544(a)(3), however, notwithstanding the investors' fervent pleas that § 541(d) required recognition of their equitable interests. Some courts have expressed the view that § 541(d) should "prevail" over § 544(a)(3) in such circumstances.[109]

The *Belisle* view that the strong-arm power of § 544(a)(3) is not constrained by § 541(d) now commands a clear majority of courts. Indeed, a close reading of § 541(d) lends further support to this view: that provision only excludes property from the estate *under* § 541(a)(1) or (2), whereas it is § 541(a)(3) that brings into the estate property that is captured through the exercise of the trustee's avoiding powers (such as the strong-arm clause).

The whole supposed "conflict" between § 541(d) and § 544(a)(3) in these constructive trust cases would disappear entirely if the Sixth Circuit's approach to constructive trusts in bankruptcy were followed. In *In re Omegas Group, Inc.*,[110] the Sixth Circuit concluded that constructive trusts do not automatically create the type of equitable interest in property that must be respected under § 541(d). Unlike an express trust, a constructive trust is only a remedial device, and according to the Sixth Circuit, no "property" interest exists in favor of the "beneficiaries" until a court has actually ordered the imposition of the constructive trust.

§ 5.9   Earnings from Individual Debtor's Postpetition Services

The postpetition proceeds of property of the estate are included in the estate pursuant to § 541(a)(6).[111] This general rule of inclusion is subject to an important exception in liquidation cases involving individual debtors under chapter 7, however. Postpetition proceeds are *not* included in the bankruptcy estate to the extent those proceeds are earnings from services performed by an individual debtor after the commencement of the case. As discussed earlier,[112] this exclusion for post-petition earnings by an individual debtor is not applicable in cases under chapters 11, 12, or 13; in those cases, the debtor's post-petition earnings are brought into the estate. §§ 1115(a)(2); 1207(a)(2), 1306(a)(2).

---

[108] 877 F.2d 512 (7th Cir.), cert. denied, 493 U.S. 893 (1989).

[109] See, e.g., In re Quality Holstein Leasing, 752 F.2d 1009 (5th Cir. 1985).

[110] 16 F.3d 1443 (6th Cir. 1994).

[111] See § 5.3.

[112] See § 5.4.

Together with the discharge from prior debts, the exclusion from the estate in § 541(a)(6) for the postpetition earnings of an individual debtor lies at the core of the "fresh start" policy in bankruptcy. The essence of the fresh start concept is that an individual debtor should have "a new opportunity in life with a clear field for future effort."[113] The "field" would be anything but "clear" if the debtor's *future* earnings were subject to the payment of pre-bankruptcy debt. Thus, American bankruptcy law has long taken the view that the date of the bankruptcy filing operates as the critical point of cleavage: anything the debtor earns *before* bankruptcy is fair game for payment to the debtor's pre-bankruptcy creditors, and comes into the estate; but an individual debtor's earnings *after* bankruptcy belong to the debtor alone, free from the clutches of the debtor's creditors.

This exclusionary rule for the postpetition earnings of an individual debtor is fairly easy to state, and has an appealing ring of clarity and certainty. Unfortunately, the application of the exclusion often is quite difficult. Some cases are pleasingly simple. For example, assume that the debtor takes a new job after filing bankruptcy. There is no dispute that the debtor's postpetition earnings from that job would not come into the bankruptcy estate. Those earnings have no connection at all to the debtor's pre-bankruptcy world; they plainly fall entirely on the postpetition side of the wall.

The problems arise, though, when the debtor's earnings do have some link to the pre-bankruptcy era as well as the postpetition world. When the postpetition earnings have a foot on both sides of the bankruptcy filing date, the challenge in applying § 541(a)(6) is one of *attribution*. How much of the earnings should be allocated to the pre-bankruptcy time period (and thus be counted as part of the bankruptcy estate), and how much should be attributed to the time after the bankruptcy filing (and thus excluded from the estate)?

A simple example, with three variants, demonstrates the problem. Assume that prior to bankruptcy Debtor enters into a contract with Books, Inc. to publish Debtor's novel. In scenario one, assume that Debtor has completely written the book before filing bankruptcy, but then files bankruptcy before the book is sold. In this situation, none of the postpetition royalties from book sales are attributable to Debtor's postpetition services; all of the Debtor's work was performed prior to bankruptcy. Thus, under the inclusive rule of § 541(a)(6), all of the postpetition royalties are included in the estate.

Now consider a second scenario. Debtor has the book contract before filing, but files bankruptcy before writing a single word. Debtor then writes the entire book after the bankruptcy filing. Now, the exclusionary rule of § 541(a)(6) kicks in; none of the postpetition royalties are included in the estate, because all of the Debtor's services were performed after bankruptcy.

You can guess what scenario three is going to be. The Debtor writes part of the book before filing bankruptcy, and then finishes the writing after the filing. Now

---

[113] Local Loan Co. v. Hunt, 292 U.S. 234, 244 (1934).

neither of the polar extremes governs; the postpetition royalties are neither obviously included nor excluded from the estate. The Debtor might argue that all of the royalties should be excluded, urging a "but-for" sort of allocation, *viz.*, no royalties would be possible without a finished book, and the book was only finished by virtue of the Debtor's postpetition exertions. That reasoning must be wrong, though; surely even an unfinished book might have some market value—think of Dickens' unfinished novel *The Mystery of Edwin Drood*. As a bankruptcy policy matter, creditors should enjoy that value. Furthermore, going down the "all-or-nothing" road would open the door to some fairly obvious possibilities for manipulation and abuse by the Debtor, who could reap all of the royalties by the simple expedient of filing bankruptcy at any time before final completion of the manuscript. The fairest result, and the result probably commanded by the Code, would be to allocate some of the royalties to the prepetition period, thus including that portion in the estate, and some of the royalties to the postpetition period, and thus excluded from the estate.

Stating the preferred outcome is a lot simpler than actually performing the economic allocation between the services performed in the pre- and post-bankruptcy worlds, however. In the example being considered, it is doubtful that future royalties on the sale of a book can rationally be allocated on a pro rata "per page" basis, or on an imputed hourly wage for authors. Staying with Dickens—how much of the royalties from his classic *A Tale of Two Cities* should be attributed to the unforgettable opening line, "It was the best of times, it was the worst of times," as compared with Sidney Carton's line at the end of the book as he eloquently went to his death uttering "It is a far, far better thing that I do, than I have ever done"? Alas, though, the difficulty of making the allocation does not, however, excuse bankruptcy courts from the necessity of doing so.

Adding to the quagmire is the fact that the quantum of post-bankruptcy proceeds realized may hinge not only on the debtor's pre- and postpetition services, but also on many other economic factors. The Ninth Circuit case of *In re FitzSimmons*[114] is illustrative. In that case, the debtor was an attorney who operated as a sole proprietor. The question was how much of the postpetition earnings of the law practice were included in the estate as proceeds under § 541(a)(6).[115] The debtor, of course, argued that all of the law firm's post-bankruptcy revenues were attributable to his own services, and thus none of those earnings should be included in the estate. The Ninth Circuit, however, pointed out that at least some of those earnings were attributable to the firm's "invested capital, accounts receivable, good will, employment contracts with the firm's staff, client relationships, fee agreements," and so forth. The truth of the Ninth Circuit's reasoning can be grasped by recognizing that surely FitzSimmons could have sold his law business for some amount of money even if he were to bow out of the business entirely and just go fishing. That amount of money that he hypothetically could have sold it for is what belongs to the estate. To the extent the postpetition earnings emanated from those factors, rather than the personal services performed by

---

[114]　725 F.2d 1208 (9th Cir. 1984).

[115]　Note that after the 2005 amendments, in a chapter 11 case, the individual debtor's post-petition earnings would be brought into the estate under § 1115(a)(2), thus making unnecessary the attribution exercise discussed in the text. If the case were brought under chapter 7, however, the issue remains.

the debtor, the court concluded that the earnings should be included in the bankruptcy estate.

The challenge of applying § 541(a)(6) can get even worse. The Fourth Circuit case of *In re Andrews*[116] raised the intriguing question of whether a debtor can claim the benefit of the exclusionary rule of § 541(a)(6) by *not* working. The debtor in that case sold his ready-mix concrete business before he filed chapter 7. The sale agreement called for the buyers to pay the debtor a million dollars over four years in exchange for the debtor's promise not to compete with the buyer. At the time the debtor filed bankruptcy, $250,000 remained unpaid under the noncompetition agreement.

The issue was whether the postpetition payments were property of the estate. Without question, those payments were "rooted in the pre-bankruptcy past,"[117] as they were provided for in the prepetition sale agreement, and thus were potentially includible in the estate. The difficulty, though, was that the debtor had to "earn" the $250,000 payment after bankruptcy by not competing. This forbearance from working, the debtor argued, was the functional and economic equivalent of performing services in the specific context of a noncompetition agreement. The Fourth Circuit held against the debtor, reasoning that the statutory exclusion in § 541(a)(6) for earnings from services performed required the debtor to perform actual work, not to forbear from working.

Yet, the court may have discounted the fresh start policy too much. In substance, the payments under the noncompetition agreement might be characterized as a direct substitute for the earnings the debtor could have realized by engaging in the ready-mix concrete business. That business had been the debtor's livelihood, and could have been again after bankruptcy, but for the noncompetition agreement. By enforcing the noncompetition agreement after bankruptcy, and depriving the debtor of the compensation promised in return, the court may have been denying the debtor the "clear field for future effort"[118] contemplated by the fresh start doctrine; indeed, the court effectively made the debtor get off the "field" the debtor knew best.

A couple of final caveats about the exclusionary rule of § 541(a)(6) should be noted. First, the rule excluding earnings attributable to postpetition services applies only to *individual* debtors. Only a human being is offered a "fresh start" in life under the bankruptcy laws. Inanimate debtors such as corporations and partnerships may perform work postpetition (through agents, obviously), but will not be able to invoke the § 541(a)(6) exclusion.

Second, by electing to proceed under chapter 12 or chapter 13 the debtor relinquishes the privilege of excluding postpetition earnings from the estate.[119] §§ 1207(a)(2), 1306(a)(2). This inclusion of postpetition earnings in the expanded estate in chapters 12 or 13 is part of the *quid pro quo* the debtor must accept in exchange for the special benefits offered by those chapters. Recall, though, that a debtor's choice to

---

[116] 80 F.3d 906 (4th Cir. 1996).

[117] See Segal v. Rochelle, 382 U.S. 375 (1966).

[118] See Local Loan Co. v. Hunt, 292 U.S. 234, 244 (1934).

[119] See § 5.4.

proceed under chapter 12 or chapter 13 is entirely voluntary: the Code does not permit creditors to bring an involuntary case under those chapters, § 303(a); does not allow involuntary conversion to those chapters, §§ 706(c), 1112(d); and gives the debtor an absolute right to dismiss a case under those chapters. §§ 1208(b), 1307(b).

The same cannot be said, however, for chapter 11 cases involving individual debtors. The 2005 amendments extended the "perpetual estate" concept to chapter 11 cases of individual debtors, § 1115(a), intending thereby to mimic the chapter 13 result, and prevent individual debtors from getting a better deal in chapter 11 than they could in chapter 13. However, unlike chapter 13 (or 12), a debtor does *not* enjoy an unfettered choice to be in chapter 11. Creditors can throw a debtor into chapter 11 involuntarily, § 303(a); creditors can move to convert a case to chapter 11 against the debtor's wishes, § 706(a); the debtor does not enjoy an absolute right to dismiss a chapter 11 case, § 1112(b)(1); and a debtor does not have an absolute right to convert to chapter 7 if the chapter 11 case was begun involuntarily or converted to chapter 11 involuntarily. § 1112(a)(2), (3). Thus, after 2005, an individual debtor who is forced into chapter 11 is not getting much of a "deal" with the inclusion of post-petition earnings in the estate. Whether such capture of post-bankruptcy earnings is constitutional under the Thirteenth Amendment is discussed in chapter 1;[120] notwithstanding much historical rhetoric of doubt on that score, close analysis suggests that there likely is no constitutional violation.

§ 5.10   Other Limitations and Exclusions

The sweeping inclusionary rules for property of the estate in § 541(a) are subject to a handful of rather narrow exclusions in § 541(b). Most of these limiting rules have been added to the Code since its original enactment in 1978, in response to the specific concerns of particular interest groups.

The only original portion of § 541(b) is now found in subsection (b)(1) of § 541. That provision states that property of the estate does not include "any power that the debtor may exercise solely for the benefit of an entity other than the debtor." Perhaps the most obvious example is a power of appointment, in which the debtor is given the power to "appoint," i.e., to designate, the takers of the property covered by the power.

If the debtor is not permitted to appoint to himself, the power is said to be "special." Under § 541(b)(1), the property covered by the debtor's special power will not become property of the debtor's bankruptcy estate. This result makes sense; the debtor could never reach the assets covered by the power, and there is no reason to give the debtor's creditors any greater rights. In short, this limitation is but a specific example of the general policy against altering non-bankruptcy distributive results. If property covered by a special power were brought into the bankruptcy estate, the debtor's creditors would receive a "windfall by reason of the happenstance of bankruptcy."

The negative inference from § 541(b)(1), in conjunction with the expansive coverage of § 541(a)(1), suggests that property of the estate *does* include a power that the debtor is permitted to exercise for the debtor's own benefit. This result obtains even

---

[120]   See § 1.10.e.(4).

if the debtor's exercise of the power is discretionary or if other possible takers exist. An example would be a "general" power of appointment, which allows the donee of the power to appoint to himself. The general power would become property of the estate, and the bankruptcy trustee then could exercise the power on behalf of the estate, appointing the estate as the taker of the property. The same line of argument would suggest that a debtor's power to revoke a trust would become property of the estate, allowing the bankruptcy trustee to revoke the trust and capture the trust res for the bankruptcy estate.

In some instances, however, courts have been reluctant to find that a debtor's power is exercisable by the bankruptcy trustee for the benefit of the bankruptcy estate. For example, in the case of *In re McCourt*,[121] the court refused to allow the trustee to compel a debtor to exercise his statutory right to elect against the will of the debtor's deceased wife. If the debtor had elected against the will, the debtor's bankruptcy estate would have become entitled to a larger share of the decedent's probate estate. The court concluded, though, that the right of election was not "property" at all, but was "personal" to the husband-debtor, and thus was not within the debtor's estate. The court arguably did not give enough weight to the fact that the right of election itself was a valuable right that might be classified as "property" under the supreme *federal* law in § 541(a)(1), no matter how that privilege might be labeled under state law.

The rest of § 541(b) is an eclectic collection of narrow carveouts from the estate. One of the provisions added as part of the 1984 leasehold amendments was § 541(b)(2), which excludes from the estate the interest of a debtor as lessee under a nonresidential real property lease that has terminated at the expiration of the stated term of the lease. For example, if Debtor Co. is the lessee of a commercial lease that expires on May 1, and the Debtor files bankruptcy on June 1, the Debtor's expired leasehold interest will not become estate property. If the lease expires after the bankruptcy filing, the estate will cease to include the leasehold interest upon expiration. Thus, if the Debtor files on June 1, and the lease expires on July 1, the leasehold ceases to be in the estate as of July 1. Note, though, that § 541(b)(2) only applies to leases that expire at the end of a stated term; a purported contractual termination of the lease based on the happening of some extrinsic event (such as the bankruptcy filing) might be nullified as an impermissible "ipso facto" clause under § 365(e)(1).[122] Note also that the lessor's right to evict the holdover debtor still will be governed by the Code's automatic stay provisions in § 362, although in 2005 Congress added two exclusions form the stay to make it easier for landlords to evict tenants in certain situations. §§ 362(b)(22), 362(b)(23), 362(l), 362(m).[123]

The third exclusion is quite narrow. Added in 1990, § 541(b)(3) removes from the estate the debtor's eligibility to participate in programs authorized by the Higher Education Act, as well as the debtor's accreditation or licensing as an educational institution. Thus, if Yale Law School filed bankruptcy, its trustee could not sell its accreditation to the Hillary Clinton School of Law.

---

[121] 12 B.R. 587 (Bankr. S.D.N.Y. 1981). Accord, In re Brand, 251 B.R. 912 (Bankr. S.D. Fla. 2000).

[122] See § 8.17.

[123] See § 3.14.

The two parts of the fourth exclusion address specific problems germane to the oil and gas industry. Under § 541(b)(4)(A), the debtor's interest in liquid or gaseous hydrocarbons is excluded to the extent that the debtor has transferred the interest pursuant to a farmout agreement. This rule was added in 1992 to overcome a problem created by a technical application of the strong-arm avoiding power of § 544(a)(3), which otherwise would bring the farmed-out interest back into the estate. Similarly, production payments in oil and gas leases that are sold by the debtor were carved out of the estate by Congress in 1994 by the addition of § 541(b)(4)(B).

Section 541(b)(5) was added in 1994, and renumbered as § 541(b)(9) in 2005. That provision removes from the estate the cash proceeds of a money order sold within fourteen days of the bankruptcy filing pursuant to an agreement that prohibits the commingling of the proceeds with the debtor's property, even if those proceeds are in fact commingled. Obviously, this fifth exclusion was intended to remedy a very narrow problem.

In 2005, Congress added four new exclusions to property of the estate. § 541(b)(5)–(8). One of the exclusions, § 541(b)(7), adds to the debtor's protection of retirement assets, as discussed in a previous section.[124] Under § 541(b)(7), estate property does not include any amount that an employer withholds from an employee's wages or accepts from an employee for payment as contributions (1) to an employee benefit plan under ERISA, (2) to a plan under IRC §§ 457 or 403(b), or (3) to a health insurance plan.

New section § 541(b)(5) takes out of the estate funds placed in an educational Individual Retirement Account[125] under IRC § 530(b)(1) for a child or grandchild (or stepchild or stepgrandchild) of the debtor. However, the debtor cannot make this contribution on the "eve" of bankruptcy and still keep it out of the estate—instead, only contributions made at least a year before the bankruptcy filing are excluded. For funds placed in the account from 365 to 720 days before bankruptcy, the exclusion is limited to $6,225 per beneficiary (and indexed every three years).[126] § 541(b)(5)(C). Apparently, funds contributed more than two years before bankruptcy are not limited in amount, other than what is imposed under the IRC. The new exclusion does not apply to "excess contributions" under IRC § 4973(e), § 541(b)(5)(B)(ii), and also is not available for funds pledged or promised to any entity in connection with a credit extension. § 541(b)(5)(B)(i).

A virtually identical exclusion was added in 2005 for funds used to purchase a tuition credit or certificate under IRC § 529(b)(1)(A) under a qualified state tuition program. § 541(b)(6). As with the educational IRA, to qualify such funds must be contributed at least 365 days before the debtor's bankruptcy filing. Other limitations that track those for educational IRAs are that the subsection (b)(6) exclusion only applies to accounts established for a child, stepchild, grandchild, or stepgrandchild of the debtor for the taxable year in which the funds were contributed, § 541(b)(6)(A), and for contributions made in year two before bankruptcy (i.e., between 365 and 720 days

---

[124] See § 5.7.

[125] Such an account actually is now called a "Coverdell Education Savings Account" by the IRS.

[126] This amount is indexed every three years, most recently in 2013.

before), a $6,225 cap (as indexed) applies. § 541(b)(6)(C). Furthermore, the limitation on contributions in IRC § 529(b)(7) carries over to the bankruptcy exclusion as well, which is capped in like amount. § 541(b)(6)(B).

The final 2005 addition to the subsection (b) estate carveouts is § 541(b)(8), which appears to be directed at property a debtor has pawned. The exclusion applies to tangible personal property that a debtor has sold or pledged as collateral for a loan or money advance from a person licensed to make such loans, when: the pledgee is in possession of the property, § 541(b)(8)(A); the debtor is not obligated to pay the money back or redeem the collateral, § 541(b)(8)(B); and in fact neither the debtor nor the trustee has redeemed the property. § 541(b)(8)(C). If the debtor has actually exercised a redemption right, then of course the redeemed property would come into the estate. This carveout also is subject to the trustee's avoiding powers, which means that if the trustee can avoid the pledgee's interest, then the property would be brought into the estate under § 541(a)(3). For example, under Article 9 of the UCC or other state laws, in some situations a "lien creditor" might be able to defeat the interests of a pledgee; if so, then the trustee's strong-arm power in § 544(a)(1) would allow the trustee in bankruptcy to set aside the pledgee's interest as well, and under § 541(a)(3) the pledged property would then be brought into the bankruptcy estate. If not, however, then the likely intent of Congress was to leave the pawn shop unaffected by the debtor's intervening bankruptcy, so that the pawn shop could go ahead and sell the debtor's unredeemed property.[127]

§ 5.11   Exempt Property

One of the core policies of the Bankruptcy Code is to give an individual debtor a "fresh start" in life after going through bankruptcy. This fresh start is effectuated in three primary ways. First, the debtor is discharged from pre-bankruptcy debts.[128] § 727(b). Second, the debtor in a chapter 7 case is permitted to keep property that he earns after the bankruptcy filing as a result of postpetition services.[129] § 541(a)(6). Third, the debtor is allowed to retain as exempt from creditors certain property that he or already owned at the time of bankruptcy.[130] § 522(b).

The exemption portion of the fresh start policy is effectuated by excluding exempt property from the bankruptcy estate. This policy is not limited to bankruptcy cases;

---

[127] One problem, though, is that doing so could be considered "any act to collect" a prepetition claim against the debtor, which would be stayed under § 362(a)(6), meaning that the pawn shop would have to request stay relief under § 362(d) in order to proceed to dispose of the pawned property. But when the pawn shop requests stay relief, the bankruptcy court might be hesitant since the pawn shop actually does not have a "secured claim" in the bankruptcy case—an unintended result of the exclusion, under § 541(b)(8), of the pledged property from the estate, because under § 506 a creditor can have a "secured claim" only in property in which the estate has an interest! Probably the best course for a bankruptcy court faced with this curious circular problem is to go ahead and grant stay relief to permit the pawn shop to dispose of the pledged property, as long as the trustee does not have a plausible avoidance case, because in that situation the pledged property could not be sold for the benefit of estate creditors—due to the § 541(b)(8) exclusion—so there is no reason to interfere with the pawn shop's non-bankruptcy rights. Was this whole subsection really necessary?

[128] See Chapter 10.

[129] See § 5.9.

[130] See Chapter 9.

outside of bankruptcy, all states allow individual debtors to keep some property from their creditors, even if the creditors go unpaid. Thus, for example, a debtor might be allowed to keep his home, a car, the tools of his trade, a family Bible, and so forth. The rationale behind allowing debtors to keep exempt property is founded on notions of both humanity and pragmatism; not only might debtors who retain some essential property be more productive and not become wards of the state, their fundamental human dignity is respected and preserved. In a bankruptcy case, the practical consequence of granting exemptions is that the exempted property is not ultimately part of the estate, and thus instead of that property being sold and the proceeds distributed to creditors, the debtor is allowed to keep the exempt property for himself. Furthermore, with but a few exceptions, creditors with pre-bankruptcy debts also may not attempt to collect their debts after bankruptcy from that property reserved to the debtor as exempt in the bankruptcy case. § 522(c).

Under the Bankruptcy Act in effect prior to the enactment of the current Code in 1978, the exemption part of the fresh start policy was implemented by *automatically* excluding exempt property from the bankruptcy estate. Under § 70a of the Act, the bankruptcy trustee was "vested by operation of law with the title of the bankrupt as of the date of the filing of the petition . . . *except insofar as it is to property which is held to be exempt.*" The Supreme Court in the early Act case of *Lockwood v. Exchange Bank*[131] interpreted this language to mean that exempt property never passed into the bankruptcy estate in the first instance.

In the 1978 Code Congress decided to overrule *Lockwood*.[132] Exempt property is not excluded from the estate at the outset. Instead, under the broad inclusive provision of § 541(a)(1), *all* interests of the debtor in property as of the commencement of the case, *including* exempt property, initially are brought into the bankruptcy estate. It is then up to the debtor (or a dependent of the debtor if the debtor fails to act) to file a list of property that he or she claims as exempt under § 522(b).[133] § 522(l), Rule 4003(a). Thus, property that is not claimed as exempt will remain in the estate, even if it was within the coverage of an applicable exemption law. If an exemption is claimed, that property will be excluded from the estate if no party in interest timely objects.[134] If a timely objection is filed, the bankruptcy court will determine the merits of the exemption claim.

C. TURNOVER

§ 5.12 Basic Principles

As previous sections have explained, the scope of property of the estate under § 541 is quite broad. Virtually all of the debtor's interests in property as of the

---

[131] 190 U.S. 294, 299–300 (1903).

[132] H.R. Rep. No. 95–595, 95th Cong., 1st Sess., at 368 (1977).

[133] See § 9.6.

[134] Taylor v. Freeland & Kronz, 503 U.S. 638 (1992). Even though the Supreme Court "updated" *Taylor* in *Schwab v. Reilly*, 130 S.Ct. 2652 (2010) (we cannot say the Court "overruled" *Taylor* since Justice Thomas swore they were not), nothing in the reasoning of *Schwab* undermines this part of *Taylor*, that what is claimed as exempt *is* exempt if not objected to in timely fashion. Instead, *Schwab* quibbled about how to determine what it was that the debtor had claimed as exempt in the first place. See § 9.6.

commencement of the bankruptcy case become part of the estate,[135] and in some instances postpetition property is added to the estate.[136] In conjunction with the expansive definition of "claim," the idea behind the inclusive approach to property of the estate is to permit the broadest possible relief for the debtor and for the debtor's creditors in the bankruptcy case itself.

Identifying property as part of the estate is not a sterile academic exercise; a real function is thereby served. In a liquidation case, the trustee must collect property of the estate and convert that property to cash, § 704(a)(1), and then distribute the net proceeds to claimants. An individual debtor, meanwhile, may claim some of the estate property as exempt.[137] § 522. In a reorganization case, the debtor in possession typically will use or sell property of the estate in an effort to reorganize.

In order for the estate representative (i.e., the trustee or debtor in possession) to be able to carry out the particular bankruptcy functions associated with property of the estate, it is generally necessary for the representative to have *possession* of the property. A chapter 7 trustee will need to have possession of property of the estate before she can liquidate that property. A chapter 11 debtor in possession will only be able to use property in its business if it has possession of that property.

In most cases the great majority of estate property will be in the possession of the debtor at the time of the bankruptcy filing. In a chapter 7 case, one of the basic duties of the debtor is to surrender to the trustee all property of the estate that the debtor has, along with any documents relating to that property. § 521(a)(4). In a chapter 11 case, where the norm is for the debtor to remain in possession, the debtor does not literally turn over property of the estate to itself, but simply continues in possession of the property. If a chapter 11 trustee is appointed in place of the debtor in possession, though, the debtor then must turn over estate property to the trustee in accordance with § 521(a)(4).

Sometimes, property of the estate will be in the hands of a third party at the time the bankruptcy case is commenced (or thereafter), rather than in the possession of the debtor. The fact that the property is not in the debtor's possession does not affect the property's status as property of the estate. The introductory clause to § 541(a) clearly provides that the estate is comprised of the described types of property, "wherever located and *by whomever held*." The *turnover* rules found in § 542 and § 543 require a third party in possession of estate property to surrender that property to the bankruptcy trustee or debtor in possession, as the case may be, under the terms and conditions provided in those sections. Following the turnover, the estate representative will be able to carry out its prescribed statutory duties with respect to the estate property.

---

[135] See § 5.2.

[136] See §§ 5.3, 5.4.

[137] See § 5.11; see Chapter 9 for more detailed discussion of exemptions.

General turnover requirement

The basic requirement for turnover of estate property by a third party to the trustee is found in § 542(a). The general premise of that section is that an entity in possession of estate property must turn that property over to the trustee if doing so would serve some bankruptcy-related function. Otherwise, there is no reason to upset the status quo. The duty to turn over property to the trustee is continuing, applying throughout the case. The rule in § 542(a) applies to any "entity" (other than a "custodian," to whom the special rules of § 543 apply) in "possession, custody, or control" of property of the estate. In addition to turning the property over to the trustee, the third party must account for the property or its value.

The limitations on the turnover requirement bespeak its function and role. Property must be turned over *only* in one of two situations: first, when the trustee could use, sell, or lease the property under § 363; or second, if the debtor could exempt the property under § 522. Furthermore, the duty to turn over the property is excused if the "property is of inconsequential value or benefit to the estate." § 542(a).

This last provision dovetails with the abandonment rule in § 554, which authorizes the trustee to abandon property of the estate when such property is burdensome or of inconsequential value or benefit to the estate.[138] The premise in § 542(a) is to save a step; there is no point in requiring a party to turn property over to the trustee, if the trustee then would just abandon the property under § 554. Note, though, that turnover is excused only if the property does not have any value *or* benefit to the estate. For example, even if there were no equity in property subject to a lien, turnover would still be required if the debtor could use that property in its business.

The debtor exemption provision is self-explanatory. If the debtor could claim an exemption in property under § 522, a third party in possession of the property must turn over the property so the debtor will be able to claim the exempt property.

Most turnover cases are predicated on the possibility that the trustee could use, sell, or lease the property under § 363. That section gives the trustee (or debtor in possession) broad powers to deal with property of the estate.[139] Included are the powers to liquidate property of the estate by a chapter 7 trustee (sale), as well as to utilize estate property by a chapter 11 debtor in possession in its business (use or lease). Note, however, that the reference in § 542(a) to § 363 incorporates all of the requirements and limitations on the use, sale, or lease of estate property in § 363 itself.

For example, property in which a third party also has an interest may only be used, sold, or leased under § 363 if that third party is given *adequate protection* of its interest in the property.[140] § 363(e). Therefore, turnover should not be required if the interests of a third party would not be adequately protected. As with the linkage to the abandonment section, there is no reason to force a third party to turn over property to the trustee if the trustee would be unable to use, sell, or lease that property. It is worth

---

[138] See § 5.14.

[139] See §§ 5.16–5.18.

[140] See §§ 3.18–3.20 for a discussion of adequate protection.

noting that a turnover motion often is countered by a motion seeking relief from the automatic stay, which could be based on a failure of adequate protection, § 362(d)(1), or on a showing that the debtor had no equity in the property and that the property is not necessary to an effective reorganization. § 362(d)(2). Logically, the bankruptcy judge should dispose of the turnover and stay relief motions at the same hearing; the same substantive issues will be dispositive of both.

Note, though, that the adequate protection limitation on the turnover doctrine has been substantially undermined by a substantial line of case authority that requires a secured creditor rightfully in possession of collateral that it had repossessed prior to bankruptcy because of the debtor's default to turn over that collateral to a chapter 11 or chapter 13 debtor *before* receiving adequate protection.[141] The theory courts embrace is that withholding possession pending receipt of adequate protection constitutes a violation of the automatic stay under § 362(a)(3) as an exercise of control over property of the estate. These courts deny that the creditor has the right to insist on adequate protection *prior to* or *contemporaneous with* turning over the property. Instead, those courts read the turnover rule of § 542(a) as essentially a self-executing grant of an absolute possessory right to the representative of the bankruptcy estate. Such a reading, though, completely ignores the limitations found in § 542(a) (and by reference § 363(e)) regarding adequate protection.

A special facet of turnover is commanded by § 542(e). That section authorizes the court to order an attorney, accountant or other person that holds recorded information relating to the debtor's property or financial affairs to turn those documents over to the trustee. This rule is expressly made subject to any applicable privilege, however. Section 542(e) was intended to deprive attorneys and accountants of the leverage they had to obtain payment of their fees in preference to other creditors by asserting a "lien" on the documents in their possession.[142]

Payment of debts to trustee

Sometimes a third party does not hold tangible property of the debtor, but owes a debt to the debtor. For example, if the debtor has a bank account, the bank owes a debt to the debtor in the amount of the net balance in the account. After the bankruptcy filing, that debt becomes property of the estate. Instead of making payment to the debtor, therefore, the third party should pay the debt to the representative of the estate. § 542(b). In the example, the bank should pay the balance in the account to the trustee. This requirement only applies to debts that are matured, payable on demand, or payable on order.

The duty to pay over matured debts to the trustee is subject to one very important exception. The obligor does not have to pay the debt to the trustee to the extent the debt may be set off under § 553. That is, if the obligor has an offsetting claim *against*

---

[141] See, e.g., Thompson v. Gen. Motors Acceptance Corp., 566 F.3d 699 (7th Cir. 2009); Unified People's Fed. Credit Union v. Yates (In re Yates), 332 B.R. 1 (B.A.P. 10th Cir. 2005); TranSouth Fin. Corp. v. Sharon (In re Sharon), 234 B.R. 676 (B.A.P. 6th Cir. 1999). Contra, In re Young, 193 B.R. 620 (Bankr. D.D.C. 1996). See discussion in §§ 3.6, 5.13.

[142] H.R. Rep. No. 95–595, 95th Cong., 1st Sess., at 369–70 (1977).

the debtor, it is entitled to assert its right of offset as a defense to turnover. For example, assume that Debtor has $5000 in an account at Bank, but owes Bank $3000 on a loan. Bank would not have to pay the full $5000 that it owes Debtor to the trustee, but could invoke the setoff rules and reduce its payment obligation under § 542(b) to $2,000 (i.e., $5,000 minus $3,000). Note, though, that the Bank still would be stayed from actually effecting the setoff.[143] The Supreme Court in a case in 1995 emphasized the interdependence of the turnover requirement and the setoff rules.[144] Under that case, the creditor enjoying the setoff right would not violate the stay by placing an administrative "hold" or "freeze" on the debtor's account, and would not have to turn over the debt to the bankruptcy trustee, but could not go forward with an actual setoff unless and until the bankruptcy court lifted the stay.

Exceptions to turnover requirement

The turnover requirements of § 542(a) and (b) are subject to two exceptions. The first exception, § 542(c), codifies the result of the 1966 Supreme Court case of *Bank of Marin v. England*.[145] The situation is this: after a debtor-depositor files bankruptcy, the debtor's bank honors a check drawn on the debtor's account prior to bankruptcy, not knowing that the debtor had filed bankruptcy in the meantime. If the bank were aware of the bankruptcy filing, there would not be a problem; the bank would simply dishonor the check and pay the entire balance in the account over to the trustee, pursuant to § 542(b). However, banks handle literally thousands of items, and it would be totally impractical for banks to investigate to see if drawers had filed bankruptcy before honoring checks presented for payment. Yet if banks were not afforded a safe harbor from the turnover requirement, a bank presented with a debtor-drawer's check would have to pay twice: once to the payee, and once to the trustee.

The Supreme Court in *Bank of Marin* simply carved out an equitable exception to the statutory provisions of the prior Act, observing that "we do not read these statutory words with the ease of a computer,"[146] and let the bank off the hook. In the 1978 Code, Congress chose to give statutory recognition to the *Bank of Marin* rule. Under § 542(c), an entity is excused from turnover if it (1) has neither actual notice nor actual knowledge of the commencement of the case, and (2) transfers property of the estate or pays a debt in good faith. Note, though, that the trustee still may recover the amount paid to the *payee* of the check, under § 549.[147]

The second exception protects life insurance companies that are required to make automatic premium loans from property that otherwise might be property of the estate.[148] § 542(d). Thus, if a life insurance contract: (1) was entered into prior to bankruptcy and is property of the estate; (2) requires a transfer of property to pay a premium or to carry out a nonforfeiture insurance option; and (3) the transfer must be

---

[143] See § 3.7.

[144] Citizens Bank of Maryland v. Strumpf, 516 U.S. 16, 19–20 (1995).

[145] 385 U.S. 99 (1966).

[146] Id. at 103.

[147] See § 6.47.

[148] H.R. Rep. No. 95–595, 95th Cong., 1st Sess., at 369 (1977).

made automatically; then (4) the transfer is given effect as long as it was made in good faith.

Turnover by a custodian

A separate section governs the turnover of property by a custodian. § 543. A "custodian" is defined in § 101(11) as a receiver or trustee of the debtor's property appointed in a non-bankruptcy case, an assignee for the benefit of creditors, or a trustee, receiver, or agent appointed or authorized under a contract or applicable law to take charge of the debtor's property to enforce a lien or to administer the property for the benefit of creditors. For example, assume that two months before filing bankruptcy Debtor made a general assignment for the benefit of creditors, transferring legal title to his property to X as assignee. Upon the filing of bankruptcy, X would be classified as a custodian, and the turnover rules of § 543 would apply to X. However, a secured creditor who takes possession of collateral, intending to foreclose on a lien, is not considered a "custodian," but instead is governed by the general turnover rules of § 542.[149]

The custodian turnover rules differ in some respects from the general rules of § 542. The basic requirements are that the custodian (1) deliver to the trustee any property of the debtor in the custodian's possession, custody, or control on the date the custodian learns of the bankruptcy filing, and (2) file an accounting of any property of the debtor that came into the custodian's possession at any time. § 543(b). In addition, once the custodian learns of the case, the custodian is prohibited from disbursing or otherwise administering the debtor's property, except as is necessary to preserve that property. § 543(a). In short, the bankruptcy case generally supersedes the nonbankruptcy custodianship.

The only exceptions would be if the bankruptcy court expressly permits the custodian to continue in possession, on the ground that the interests of creditors or equity holders would be better served, or if the custodian is an assignee for the benefit of creditors that was appointed or took possession of the debtor's property more than 120 days before bankruptcy. § 543(d). In the latter instance, the bankruptcy court might abstain from hearing the bankruptcy case at all under § 305(a), leaving the administration in the hands of the custodian-assignee.

The custodian may have made disbursements of the debtor's property, otherwise administered that property, or incurred obligations during the time when it was in charge of the debtor's property. The bankruptcy court is authorized to exercise some oversight over the propriety of the custodian's actions. As noted above, the custodian must file an accounting. If the custodian made any improper or excessive disbursements that were not in accordance with applicable law or authorized by a court, the custodian may be surcharged. However, assignees for the benefit of creditors who took possession or were appointed more than 120 days prior to bankruptcy are excepted from this rule. § 543(c)(3). The bankruptcy court is authorized to enter orders protecting entities who have dealt with the custodian. § 543(c)(1). Finally, the court

---

[149]   United States v. Whiting Pools, Inc., 462 U.S. 198 (1983).

may approve the payment of reasonable compensation to and the reimbursement of expenses incurred by the custodian. § 543(c)(2).

§ 5.13   Against a Rightful Possessor: *Whiting Pools* and Beyond

The most significant issue regarding the scope of the Code's turnover provisions came before the United States Supreme Court in 1983, in the case of *United States v. Whiting Pools, Inc.*[150] The question before the Court was whether a secured creditor who had rightfully repossessed collateral prior to the bankruptcy filing had to turn over the repossessed property to the debtor in possession in a chapter 11 case. A unanimous Court held that § 542(a) did require the secured creditor to turn over the property to the estate, subject only to the limitations specified in that section. According to the Court, the Code replaces the secured creditor's non-bankruptcy procedural right of possession with the right to "adequate protection."[151] The court's ruling is important, because it gives debtors the power in bankruptcy to reverse a repossession of collateral, thereby dramatically altering the balance of power between a debtor and secured creditor.

The debtor, Whiting Pools, Inc., defaulted on federal tax obligations, and a federal tax lien attached to all of the debtor's property. Pursuant to the levy and distraint provisions of the Internal Revenue Code, the Internal Revenue Service seized all of the tangible personal property of the debtor. The very next day the debtor filed for relief under chapter 11 and was continued as debtor in possession. The IRS moved for relief from the automatic stay under § 362(d) so that it could proceed with a tax sale of the repossessed property. The debtor counterclaimed for turnover of the seized property pursuant to § 542(a). The debtor planned to use the property to reorganize its swimming pool business.

Under the provisions of the Internal Revenue Code, the IRS was rightfully in possession of the debtor's property that was subject to the tax lien. The seizure of the items had not, however, operated to transfer title to the IRS; a tax sale was still required to terminate the debtor's ownership. The debtor, conversely, had no right to possession at the time it filed chapter 11; instead, the only rights remaining in the debtor were to notice of the tax sale, to any surplus proceeds remaining after the sale, and to redeem the property by paying the tax debt in full.

The IRS argued that turnover was not authorized under the Code, urging a literal interpretation of the statutory provisions, in light of the fundamental principle that the estate succeeds to no greater rights than the debtor had at the time of filing bankruptcy. Here, since the debtor at the time of bankruptcy had no right to possession of the collateral, the estate likewise had no possessory right, and could not circumvent that limitation by invoking the turnover statute. Under § 542(a), a third party must turn over "property that the trustee may use, sell, or lease under § 363." Section 363, in turn, provides that the trustee may use "property of the estate." Finally, "property of the estate" under § 541(a) extends only to "interests of the debtor in property." Following the logic of this statutory trail, the Service argued that the debtor's "interest

---

[150] 462 U.S. 198 (1983).

[151] Id. at 206–07.

in property" did not include the right to possession, and thus turnover was not appropriate.[152]

The Supreme Court rejected the government's argument and held that turnover was required, even though the debtor did not have a possessory right at the time bankruptcy was filed. The Court concluded that § 542(a) operated to give the estate a possessory interest in any property in which the debtor had an interest.[153] *The quid pro quo* given to the secured creditor was the right to "adequate protection." Described by § 361, "adequate protection" limits the trustee's power to use estate property, § 363(e), and a secured creditor is entitled to resist turnover and obtain relief from the stay if adequate protection is not provided.[154] § 362(d)(1). The scheme contemplated by the Code, the Court determined, requires the secured creditor to assert its right to adequate protection before the bankruptcy court, rather than relying on the remedies of possession and foreclosure afforded by non-bankruptcy law.

In addition to the comfort it drew from the broad scope of the definition of property of the estate, the Court relied upon history and policy to support its conclusion. Case law prior to the enactment of the Code had compelled secured creditors to turn over repossessed collateral to reorganizing debtors,[155] and Congress had evidenced no desire to alter that result. Extensive testimony before Congress in hearings leading up to the enactment of the 1978 Code emphasized the necessity of a turnover requirement to help debtors to reorganize. The Court agreed that the reorganization policy would be frustrated unless turnover by repossessing lienholders was required.[156]

Indeed, it is interesting to note that the Supreme Court carefully limited its holding to chapter 11 cases, because of its partial reliance on the reorganization policy.[157] Cases after *Whiting Pools* have speculated over whether the turnover rule of that case should be extended beyond the chapter 11 context. After some initial disagreement, most courts have extended the requirement even to chapter 7 liquidation cases.[158] There is no statutory support for limiting turnover by a secured creditor to the chapter 11 setting. The only question in a chapter 7 case is whether the statutory turnover requirements (can be exempted by debtor, or trustee can use, sell, or lease) would be applicable. Chapter 13 cases routinely require turnover.

The first section of the Court's opinion in *Whiting Pools* can be and has been applied with equal force to private secured creditors operating under Article 9 of the

---

[152] This line of argument had been adopted by the Fourth Circuit in *Cross Electric Co. v. United States*, 664 F.2d 1218 (4th Cir. 1981).

[153] 462 U.S. at 207. As discussed in § 3.6, this statement by the Court has been misconstrued by many courts to require a secured creditor to turn over rightfully repossessed collateral *even before* receiving adequate protection, on pain of violating the automatic stay in § 362(a)(3) if turnover is delayed pending receipt of adequate protection. See, e.g., Thompson v. Gen. Motors Acceptance Corp., 566 F.3d 699 (7th Cir. 2009); TranSouth Fin. Corp. v. Sharon (In re Sharon), 234 B.R. 676 (B.A.P. 6th Cir. 1999).

[154] See § 3.18–3.20.

[155] The leading pre-Code case was *Reconstruction Fin. Corp. v. Kaplan*, 185 F.2d 791 (1st Cir. 1950).

[156] *Whiting Pools*, supra note 150, 462 U.S. at 208–09.

[157] Id. at 208–09 n.17.

[158] See, e.g., In re Gerwer, 898 F.2d 730 (9th Cir. 1990); In re Velichko, 473 B.R. 64 (Bankr. S.D.N.Y. 2012).

Uniform Commercial Code. The only reservation the Court made with regard to Article 9 security interests was to note that turnover might not be required if the third party's possessory interest was independent of the creditor's remedies, giving the example of a pledge of collateral.[159] Nevertheless, some lower courts after *Whiting Pools* have held that even a pledgee is subject to turnover, notwithstanding the Court's dictum.[160]

The Court in *Whiting Pools* still had to consider whether turnover should be denied because the IRS was the creditor involved. A Supreme Court case under the Act, *Phelps v. United States*,[161] had refused to order turnover against the IRS, suggesting in dictum that an IRS levy left no substantial property rights in the debtor. The Supreme Court in *Whiting Pools* distinguished the holding of *Phelps*, explaining that the decision there rested on the bankruptcy court's limited "summary" jurisdiction over property under the Act, whereas the Code had granted sweeping jurisdiction to the bankruptcy courts. The Court disavowed the troublesome dictum, emphasizing that a levy by the IRS does not transfer title to the government and terminate the debtor's ownership; only upon completion of the tax sale is the debtor's title eliminated and the turnover privilege lost.[162]

The Court's holding in *Whiting Pools* resolved most aspects of the turnover controversy with regard to tangible personal property. Less certain, however, was what would happen if the IRS seized *intangible* property, such as a bank account or accounts receivable. Those situations might require a different result. The levy on an intangible such as a bank account might effectively transfer ownership from the debtor to the government, cutting off the right to turnover. The issue turns on the proper interpretation of the governing non-bankruptcy law. Courts have divided on this question.[163]

The primary persisting problem in applying the turnover rules with respect to secured creditors has been whether a secured creditor who rightfully repossessed prior to bankruptcy violates the automatic stay of § 362(a)(3) by conditioning turnover on the prior or contemporaneous receipt of adequate protection, or whether the creditor must immediately turn the collateral over to the trustee or debtor (in chapter 11 and 13) and then ask for adequate protection. This question was discussed in detail in the automatic stay chapter.[164] Most courts have held that the secured creditor does violate the stay.[165] As explained in chapter 3, however, I believe that this line of cases improperly ignores the explicit requirements of the turnover provision itself, which in § 542(a) only requires turnover of property the trustee can use, sell, or lease under § 363, which then incorporates the adequate protection requirement in § 363(e).

---

[159] *Whiting Pools*, supra note 150, 462 U.S. at 206–07 n.14.

[160] See, e.g., *Gerwer*, supra note 158, 898 F.2d 730.

[161] 421 U.S. 330 (1975).

[162] *Whiting Pools*, supra note 150, 462 U.S. at 210–11.

[163] Compare In re Brown, 126 B.R. 767 (N.D. Ill. 1991) (no turnover of bank account), with In re Metro Press, Inc., 139 B.R. 763 (Bankr. D. Mass. 1992) (turnover available even for bank account). Courts that have not allowed turnover of a levied bank account differ on whether the same prohibition applies to accounts receivable. Compare *Brown*, 126 B.R. at 767 (allowing turnover of account receivable), with In re Sigmund London, Inc., 139 B.R. 765 (Bankr. E.D.N.Y. 1992) (not allowing turnover of account receivable).

[164] See § 3.6.

[165] See, e.g., *Thompson*, supra note 153, 566 F.3d 699; *Sharon*, supra note 153, 234 B.R. 767.

Nothing in the *Whiting Pools* decision is inconsistent with allowing a secured creditor to demand adequate protection prior to or contemporaneous with turnover; indeed, in that case itself, the dueling motions in the bankruptcy court were for turnover and stay relief. The Court only decided whether turnover could *ever* be ordered against a rightful possessor; in holding that such a remedy was possible, it did not hold that turnover could be commanded without complying with the statutory requisites for turnover in § 542(a).

A final remaining problem with a turnover action is the impact of a sovereign immunity defense by a governmental creditor. Prior to the 1994 Amendments, the Supreme Court held that Congress had not clearly waived sovereign immunity in § 106 for either the federal government[166] or for the states.[167] The sovereign immunity issue had not been raised in *Whiting Pools*. In 1994 Congress amended § 106, making clear its intention to abrogate sovereign immunity. For suits against the federal government, § 106 thus clears the way for turnover actions. As against state governments, however, a decade of uncertainty was ushered in with the Supreme Court's 1996 decision in *Seminole Tribe of Florida v. Florida*[168] that Congress lacked the power under Article I to abrogate the states' Eleventh Amendment immunity against suits by private persons (such as a bankruptcy trustee). Although *Seminole Tribe* was decided with reference to another Article I power, the Supreme Court made clear in that opinion that its rationale extended to other Article I powers of Congress, including the Bankruptcy Clause. A decade later, however, the Supreme Court reversed course and in 2006 held in *Central Virginia Community College v. Katz*[169] that the Bankruptcy Clause trumps state sovereign immunity under the Eleventh Amendment. Thus, after *Katz,* state governments also can be compelled to turn over property to the bankruptcy trustee, notwithstanding any assertion of sovereign immunity.

D. ABANDONED PROPERTY

§ 5.14   Basic Principles

The filing of a bankruptcy petition commencing a bankruptcy case automatically creates an estate comprised of all of the debtor's interests in property.[170] § 541(a). The bankruptcy trustee, as representative of the estate, has a statutory duty to administer the property of the estate. § 704(a)(1), (a)(2). If that property is worth something to the unsecured creditors of the estate, the trustee will liquidate the property and distribute the net proceeds to creditors in the order of their claim priorities. In a business case, some property that lacks equity still may be valuable to the estate if it contributes to the operation of the debtor's business.

Not all estate property is valuable to the general creditors of the estate, however. In other words, some property of the estate may lack equity and may not be helpful to business operations. In those instances, there is no benefit to the general creditors of

---

[166] United States v. Nordic Vill., Inc., 503 U.S. 30 (1992).

[167] Hoffman v. Connecticut Dep't of Income Maint., 492 U.S. 96 (1989).

[168] 517 U.S. 44 (1996).

[169] 546 U.S. 356 (2006).

[170] See § 5.2.

the estate for the trustee to continue to administer the property. Continued administration would simply be a wasteful drain of time and money.

The Code accordingly permits the trustee to *abandon* any property of the estate that is (1) *burdensome* to the estate, or (2) of *inconsequential value and benefit* to the estate. § 554(a), (b). Section 554 codifies the abandonment power for the first time, but courts under previous bankruptcy laws recognized such a power as inherent in the bankruptcy process. The legal effect of abandonment is to remove the property from the estate. Once abandoned, the property is no longer property of the estate, and no longer must be administered by the trustee. Abandonment of the property effectively permits the residual beneficiaries of the estate to cut their losses.

Abandonment is "to any party with a possessory interest in the property abandoned."[171] Normally this means that the property is abandoned to the debtor, because the debtor usually had possession of the property at the time bankruptcy was filed. However, if the reason the property is being abandoned is that it is subject to a lien that secures a debt greater than the property's value, the trustee may simply abandon the property directly to the lienholder.[172]

The trustee may only abandon property of the estate "after notice and a hearing." § 554(a), (b). In Code lingo, this does not necessarily mean that the court must hold an actual hearing. Instead, notice must be given as is appropriate in the circumstances, and the noticed parties must have an opportunity to request a hearing. § 102(1). Notice is sent to all creditors. Rule 6007(a). If no one requests a hearing within fourteen days, though, the court may order the abandonment without holding a hearing. A party in interest is also entitled to ask the court to order the trustee to abandon property of the estate, even if the trustee has not filed an abandonment motion. § 554(b), Rule 6007(b).

A few examples will illustrate the normal operation of the abandonment provision. Assume that at the time of the bankruptcy filing Debtor is in possession of a tractor with a fair market value of $50,000. The tractor is subject to a security interest to secure a debt to Bank. If Debtor files under chapter 7, the trustee's decision whether to abandon the tractor will turn on whether the debt to Bank is greater or less than the tractor's $50,000 value. If the Bank debt is only $40,000, for example, the trustee will not abandon the tractor, but will sell it for $50,000, pay off Bank's debt, and put the remaining $10,000 in proceeds (less any sale costs) in the estate for distribution to general creditors. If, however, the debt to Bank is greater than $50,000, there is no reason for the trustee to bother selling the tractor; all of the proceeds will just go to Bank. The trustee thus will file a motion to abandon the tractor to the Bank.

If Debtor files for relief under one of the reorganization chapters (11, 12, or 13), however, the analysis changes. Even if the tractor is worth less than the debt to Bank, the tractor still may have a use value in the hands of the debtor in the operation of the

---

[171] H.R. Rep. No. 95–595, 95th Cong., 1st Sess., at 377 (1977); S. Rep. No. 95–989, 95th Cong., 2d Sess., at 92 (1978).

[172] As a note of caution to the lienholder, the lienholder still would not be free to foreclose its lien without getting relief from the automatic stay, because the stay also blocks the enforcement of liens against property of the debtor with regard to prebankruptcy debts. § 362(a)(5). See § 3.5.

debtor's farming business. The debtor may want to retain and use the tractor, and in return pay Bank "adequate protection" for that use. §§ 363(e), 361. Thus, the Debtor as debtor in possession might not want to abandon the tractor. If, however, Debtor had more tractors than it needed to run its farming business, it might move to abandon this tractor.

§ 5.15   Polluted Property: *Midlantic* and Its Progeny

The biggest controversy under the Code in the application of § 554 has been with respect to attempts to abandon polluted property. The concern has been to reconcile the supposedly competing commands of the bankruptcy and environmental laws. The controversy culminated in a decision of the United States Supreme Court in 1986 in *Midlantic National Bank v. New Jersey Department of Environmental Protection.*[173]

In *Midlantic*, a bare majority of five Justices held in favor of the environmental laws, subject to important qualifications. The Court's precise holding was that a chapter 7 "trustee may not abandon property in contravention of a state statute or regulation that is reasonably designed to protect the public health or safety from identified hazards."[174] In a crucial footnote, Justice Powell for the majority elaborated that "the abandonment power is not to be fettered by laws or regulations not reasonably calculated to protect the public health or safety from *imminent and identifiable harm.*"[175] After *Midlantic*, the fighting issue in the environmental abandonment cases has been whether the projected harm from abandoning the contaminated property is "imminent and identifiable." If not, abandonment is allowed.[176]

Midlantic involved a liquidating corporate debtor, Quanta Resources Corp. After briefly attempting to reorganize in chapter 11, Quanta, a waste oil processor, converted to chapter 7 precisely because of its inability to comply with the state environmental laws and clean up prebankruptcy contamination at its two plants. The cost of cleanup exceeded the value of the property. Accordingly, the trustee moved to abandon the sites under § 554(a). The states admitted that the statutory requirements for abandonment were satisfied, *viz.*, the property was burdensome to the estate and of inconsequential value and benefit to the estate. However, the states objected to the abandonment on the ground that it would contravene the environmental laws, asserting that § 554(a) was subject to an unwritten exception that required compliance with state police power regulations. The trustee countered that § 554(a) created an absolute and unqualified power to abandon property of the estate if the statutory requisites were met, as they were here.

The Supreme Court agreed by a narrow margin with the qualified abandonment view. Justice Rehnquist wrote an opinion for four dissenters that read § 554 as

---

[173] 474 U.S. 494 (1986).

[174] Id. at 507.

[175] Id. at 507 n.9 (emphasis added).

[176] See, e.g., In re L.F. Jennings Oil Co., 4 F.3d 887 (10th Cir. 1993), cert. denied sub. nom. New Mexico Envtl. Dep't v. Franco, 511 U.S. 1005 (1994) (abandonment proper, no imminent and identifiable harm); In re Smith–Douglass, Inc., 856 F.2d 12 (4th Cir. 1988) (same).

absolute and unqualified.[177] The heart of Justice Powell's reasoning for the majority, by contrast, was that the pre-Code judge-made abandonment power was subject to an exception requiring adherence to police power regulations, and that when Congress codified the abandonment rule in § 554 in 1978, it presumably intended to carry forward this exception as well.[178] The majority insisted that the plausibility of this presumed intention is buttressed by other evidence of congressional sensitivity to environmental concerns, even in bankruptcy cases.[179] The Court recognized the importance of the bankruptcy policy favoring the expeditious and equitable distribution of estate assets, however, and accordingly settled on the compromise noted above: the bankruptcy abandonment power is qualified by the need to comply with the environmental laws, but only in egregious cases where the environmental risk is "imminent and identifiable."[180] Before authorizing abandonment of contaminated sites, the bankruptcy court must formulate conditions that will adequately protect the public's health and safety.

The practical effect of the *Midlantic* decision is to give the government a de facto *priority* over all other creditors for its claim for response costs. This follows even though the Court disavowed making any decision on the priority question.[181] Notwithstanding the Court's protestations, its holding effectively compels a priority result. If abandonment is prohibited, a bankruptcy trustee must expend estate assets to clean up contaminated property, even if doing so will not result in any benefit or value to the estate. The environmental laws require the party in possession of a polluted site to clean up that property; absent abandonment, the estate retains possession. The dollars spent cleaning up the sites then are no longer available for distribution to general creditors. Conversely, if abandonment is allowed, the government will have to pay for the cleanup itself, and then will file a request for reimbursement in the bankruptcy case.

The dissenting Justices saw this clearly, observing that "barring abandonment and forcing a cleanup would effectively place [the states'] interest in protecting the public fisc ahead of the claims of other creditors."[182] Numerous cases decided after *Midlantic* confirm the inevitable priority consequence of a no-abandonment decision.[183] While one might fairly debate as a policy matter whether priority status is merited for environmental claims, nothing in the Code's priority section (§ 507) indicates that Congress intended that result.

---

[177] 474 U.S. at 507–17 (Rehnquist, J., dissenting).

[178] Id. at 500–01 (Powell, J., majority).

[179] Id. at 502–06. The Court pointed out that an exception to the automatic stay permits the enforcement of police and regulatory powers, § 362(b)(4); that a trustee managing and operating the property of a bankrupt debtor must comply with state laws, 28 U.S.C. § 959(b); and, finally, that Congress has enacted major environmental legislation (RCRA and CERCLA) since the 1978 Code was passed.

[180] 474 U.S. at 507 & n.9.

[181] Id. at 498 n.2. The state of New York had already cleaned up one of the sites, and sought reimbursement for its costs as an administrative priority. The Court noted that this issue was not before it.

[182] Id. at 516–17 (Rehnquist, J., dissenting).

[183] See, e.g., In re Chateaugay Corp., 944 F.2d 997 (2d Cir. 1991); In re Wall Tube & Metal Prods. Co., 831 F.2d 118 (6th Cir. 1987).

The only way to escape this box is for the court to allow abandonment of a contaminated site on the ground that the harm is not "imminent and identifiable." As might be expected, the courts have differed over whether to read this qualification broadly or narrowly. One approach is to defer almost entirely to the judgment of the state or federal environmental agency, and to prohibit abandonment if the government objects. This view essentially requires full compliance with the environmental laws.[184]

The competing approach gives much more weight to bankruptcy policy, with courts insisting on a clear showing of a serious and immediate risk to the public health or safety.[185] The more fact of noncompliance with the environmental laws is plainly not enough. Courts adopting this view take into account a variety of factors, including the immediacy of the risk of public exposure, the magnitude of that risk, the cost of cleaning up and the funds available in the estate to defray those costs, and whether the environmental agency has already taken steps to deal with the problem. This more restrictive reading of the *Midlantic* opinion seems more faithful to the spirit and letter of the Court's narrow holding.

E.   TRUSTEE'S POWER TO USE, SELL, OR LEASE PROPERTY

§ 5.16   In the Ordinary Course of Business

The representative of the bankruptcy estate often needs to use, sell, or lease property of the estate in carrying out their responsibilities. For example, the trustee in a chapter 7 liquidation case will, by definition, have to sell estate property in the course of liquidating the estate. See § 704(a)(1). A chapter 11 debtor in possession that is attempting to reorganize its business obviously needs to be able to use its property if it is to continue business operations. Section 363 governs the use, sale, or lease of property of the estate by the trustee (or debtor in possession).

The important question under § 363 is not *whether* the trustee may use, sell, or lease estate property. Such powers are essential to the bankruptcy process. The real issue is what *conditions* restrict the trustee's exercise of those powers. Those conditions are spelled out in detail in § 363. As do the other administrative powers of the trustee in the Code, § 363 attempts to strike an efficient and just balance between the needs of the bankruptcy estate and the rights of all interested parties. Both substantive and procedural matters are implicated in this delicate balancing operation.

The statutory authorization for the trustee to use, sell, or lease estate property is found in subsections (b) and (c) of § 363. The principal point of distinction in these subsections concerns a question of *procedure, viz.,* is the trustee required to obtain court approval of the proposed use, sale, or lease of property, after notice and a hearing? The answer depends primarily on whether the proposed transaction is in the *ordinary course of business*. If it is *not* in the ordinary course, then the trustee may use, sell, or lease the property only "after notice and a hearing." § 363(b)(1). If, however, the

---

[184] See, e.g., *Wall Tube*, supra note 183, 831 F.2d 118; In re Peerless Plating Co., 70 B.R. 943 (Bankr. W.D. Mich. 1987).

[185] See, e.g., In re Smith–Douglass, Inc., 856 F.2d 12 (4th Cir. 1988); In re FCX, Inc., 96 B.R. 49 (Bankr. E.D.N.C. 1989); In re Franklin Signal Corp., 65 B.R. 268 (Bankr. D. Minn. 1986).

trustee is authorized to operate the debtor's business, then ordinary course transactions are authorized "without notice or a hearing." § 363(c)(1). The only exception to the ordinary course rule is for "cash collateral," which the trustee may use, sell, or lease only in accordance with the strict requirements of § 363(c)(2)–(4).[186]

Initially, note that the general authorization for the trustee to operate the debtor's business carries with it the further *implied* substantive authorization to engage in all subsidiary transactions and activities necessary and essential to that business operation. The use, sale, or lease of property is a common type of business activity. In all reorganization cases, continued business operation is permitted as a matter of course, unless the court orders otherwise. See § 1108 (chapter 11); § 1203 (chapter 12); § 1304(b) (chapter 13). If a creditor or a committee wants to limit the trustee's operating authority, the burden is on them to ask the court to impose restrictions.

For activities that are substantively authorized, the question then becomes what *procedural* guidelines govern the grant of authority. The two primary possibilities are that the specific activity may be authorized (1) without notice and a hearing or (2) after notice and a hearing. As noted above, the determinant is whether the matter falls within the ordinary course of the debtor's business. Only if it does not is notice and a hearing required.

The ordinary course of business rule in § 363(b) and (c) is premised on notions of (1) efficiency and (2) presumptive consent and approval. First, it would be extremely wasteful and burdensome if the trustee or debtor in possession had to send out notice and request specific authorization from the court for every single transaction, no matter how routine. Second, there is no reason to believe that interested creditors who are not opposed to continued business operations in general would want to have the opportunity to be heard on such ordinary course matters. Nor would a court be likely to prohibit an ordinary course activity, assuming general authority for operations. Any creditor or court opposition to an ordinary course transaction really would be an objection to the more fundamental question of whether the business should be continued, and on what terms. Accordingly, such concerns should be raised and decided in that broader setting, not with regard to each routine transaction. In short, giving notice and an opportunity for a hearing with regard to ordinary course matters would serve no useful purpose.

For transactions outside of the ordinary course of business, however, giving notice and an opportunity for a hearing would serve some function. It is likely that creditors would want to have prior notice and the chance to be heard before the trustee takes extraordinary steps. Acquiescence in the continued operation of the debtor's business would not necessarily imply approval of non-ordinary course transactions.

Defining the ordinary course of business, then, appears to turn largely on the question of whether the transaction is one as to which creditors presumably would want prior notice and the opportunity to be heard. Courts have distilled the ordinary course inquiry into two complementary tests: first, whether the proposed transaction is

---

[186] See § 5.18.

ordinary compared to other businesses in the industry (the "horizontal dimension" test), and second, whether the transaction is ordinary compared to the debtor's own prepetition operations (the "vertical dimension" test).[187] Each test in its own way focuses on the reasonable expectations of the debtor's creditors. The horizontal test is objective in nature, with its industry-wide perspective, while the vertical test is subjective, focusing on the specific situation of this debtor.

Even if a transaction is not in the ordinary course, an actual court hearing will not always be required. The Code provides that the trustee may take the requested action "after notice and a hearing." § 363(b)(1). In the special parlance of the Code, "after notice and a hearing" is a defined term of art. It means "such notice as is appropriate in the particular circumstances and such opportunity for a hearing as is appropriate in the particular circumstances," § 102(1)(A), but further recognizes that an act may be taken without a hearing if notice is given, and either no party in interest timely requests a hearing or an emergency dictates dispensing with a prior hearing. § 102(1)(B). The Bankruptcy Rules implement this "negative notice" approach, dispensing with the need for a hearing if no objection to a proposed use, sale, or lease is filed and served after notice is given. Rule 6004(e).

The procedural constraints on the trustee's authority to use, sell, or lease estate property are not the only limitations found in § 363. Numerous provisions require the protection of the rights of other parties with an interest in the subject property. These rules apply to both ordinary course and non-ordinary course transactions. Most fundamentally, an entity with an interest in property that the trustee proposes to use, sell, or lease is entitled to demand *adequate protection* of its interest. § 363(e). The court is required to prohibit or condition the trustee's use, sale, or lease of estate property as is necessary to provide adequate protection. What constitutes adequate protection is dealt with by § 361.[188] This issue normally arises with respect to secured parties, who are entitled to maintain and preserve the value of their collateral during the bankruptcy case. The trustee has the burden of proving adequate protection. § 363(p)(1). Furthermore, any use, sale, or lease of property under § 363 must be consistent with any relief from the automatic stay granted under § 362. § 363(d)(2).

The treatment and manner of protection of particular types of non-debtor property interests are dealt with by a series of specialized rules in § 363. Examples include dower and curtesy rights (§ 363(g)); tenancies (§ 363(h)); and community property interests (§ 363(i)). The property subject to these non-debtor interests typically can be sold by the trustee under certain conditions, but with protection of the non-debtor interest. See § 363(j). In 2005 Congress added provisions designed to enhance the protection of the privacy of consumers who have dealt with the debtor. §§ 363(b)(1), 332. These are discussed in the next section.

If property of the estate is being sold, a creditor who has a lien on that property is entitled to "credit bid" at the sale. See § 363(k). Credit bidding means that the secured creditor does not have to hand over actual cash if it is the successful bidder, but can

---

[187] See In re Lavigne, 114 F.3d 379 (2d Cir. 1997); In re Dant & Russell, Inc., 853 F.2d 700 (9th Cir. 1988); In re Atlanta Retail, 287 B.R. 849 (Bankr. N.D. Ga. 2002).

[188] See §§ 3.18–3.20 for a discussion of adequate protection.

simply "credit" the sale price against the claim it holds against the debtor. The right to credit bid can be denied only if the bankruptcy court finds "cause." In 2012, the Supreme Court held that the secured creditor's right to credit bid cannot be circumvented by selling the property pursuant to a "cram down" reorganization plan in chapter 11.[189] Instead, the Court held that the operative cram down rule in such a situation is § 1129(b)(2)(A)(ii), which specifically incorporates the credit bidding protection from § 363(k).[190] Thus, whether collateral is sold in a § 363 sale or under a plan, a secured creditor may credit bid unless the court denies that right based on a specific showing of cause.

One type of non-bankruptcy limitation on the debtor's interest in property is *not* honored under § 363. "Ipso facto" clauses are not given effect. Those clauses would affect or give an option to a non-debtor party to effect a forfeiture, modification, or termination of the debtor's interest, conditioned on the filing of bankruptcy, or the occurrence of insolvency or a financial condition. The Code consistently overrides the effect of ipso facto clauses, and § 363 is no exception.

§ 5.17 Sales Outside of the Ordinary Course of Business

One of the most common transactions a trustee engages in with regard to property of the estate is the sale of property. In chapter 7 cases, liquidation of estate property is the statutorily-mandated norm. § 704(a)(1). In chapter 11 cases, the debtor in possession often will sell some of the property of the estate, either in an attempt to raise working capital or to streamline operations. Liquidation of the entire estate is also permitted in chapter 11. § 1123(b)(4). In debt adjustment cases under chapter 12 or 13, some estate property may be sold as well.

Recent years have witnessed an even more dramatic and widely used innovation: the practical effectuation of a chapter 11 reorganization, not via a confirmed plan (except as a *fait accompli* after the fact of a sale), but through a sale of all of the debtor's assets under § 363(b). These § 363 sales have been called "the new 'chapter 3' reorganization."[191] Many have noted the ubiquity of the "363 sale" method of reorganization, with varying attitudes as to whether that is a good thing or not.[192] The swift and dramatic sale/reorganizations of General Motors[193] and Chrysler[194] in 2009

---

[189] RadLax Gateway Hotel, LLC v. Amalgamated Bank, 132 S.Ct. 2065 (2012). See Charles J. Tabb, Credit Bidding, Security, and the Obsolescence of Chapter 11, 2013 U. Ill. L. Rev. 103 (2013).

[190] *RadLax*, 132 S.Ct. at 2072.

[191] Charles J. Tabb & Ralph Brubaker, Bankruptcy Law: Principles, Policies, and Practice 719 (3d ed. 2010).

[192] See, e.g., Ralph Brubaker & Charles Jordan Tabb, Bankruptcy Reorganization and the Troubling Legacy of *Chrysler* and *GM*, 2010 U. Ill. L. Rev. 1375 (2010). See also Barry E. Adler, A Reassessment of Bankruptcy Reorganization After *Chrysler* and *General Motors*, 18 Am. Bankr. Inst. L. Rev. 305 (2010); Douglas G. Baird & Robert K. Rasmussen, The End of Bankruptcy, 55 Stan. L. Rev. 751 (2002); Stephen J, Lubben, No Big Deal: The *GM* and *Chrysler* Cases in Context, 83 Am. Bankr. L.J. 531 (2009); Stephen J. Lubben, The "New and Improved" Chapter 11, 93 Ky. L.J. 839 (2005); Mark J. Roe & David Skeel, Assessing the *Chrysler* Bankruptcy, 108 Mich. L. Rev. 727 (2010); David A. Skeel, Jr., Creditors' Ball: The "New" New Corporate Governance in Chapter 11, 152 U. Pa. L. Rev. 927 (2003)

[193] In re Gen. Motors Corp. 407 B.R. 463 (Bankr. S.D.N.Y. 2009).

[194] In re Chrysler LLC, 405 B.R. 84, 111 (Bankr. S.D.N.Y. 2009), aff'd, 576 F.3d 108, 123–26 (2d Cir. 2009), vacated as moot sub. nom. Ind. State Police Pension Trust v. Chrysler LLC, 130 S.Ct. 1015 (2009).

are the poster children for this sea change.[195] More will be said below about this form of "chapter 3 reorganization."

Sales of property in bankruptcy cases may occur either in or out of the ordinary course of business. Consider, for example, a hypothetical chapter 11 debtor whose primary business is the operation of a chain of retail shoe stores. Each shoe sold by each store is a sale of estate property, and obviously is in the ordinary course of business.[196] See § 363(c)(1). Such sales may be made without notice and a hearing. If the debtor wants to sell an entire store, however, notice of that sale would have to be given to parties in interest, with an opportunity to object. § 363(b)(1). Such a major transaction would not fall within the ordinary course of business. It would be out of the ordinary as measured both by what is normal in the industry (the horizontal dimension test), and by what was normal for this debtor before bankruptcy (the vertical dimension test).[197] This section explores some of the rules regulating sales out of the ordinary course of business.

Procedures

A sale out of the ordinary course of business may only be approved "after notice and a hearing." § 363(b)(1). Under the Code's terminology, "after notice and a hearing" only requires appropriate notice to be given, with the *opportunity* for noticed parties to request a hearing. § 102(1). If no noticed party requests a hearing, the court probably will enter the order authorizing the sale without holding an actual hearing. Rule 6004(o). The Bankruptcy Rules implement this negative notice approach for sales of property. Under Rule 2002(a)(2) and (k), 21 days' notice of the proposed sale must be given to the debtor, the trustee, all creditors and indenture trustees, and the United States trustee. The court may shorten the notice period, however, and also may order that notice be given to official committees instead of to all creditors. See Rule 2002(i). The content of the notice must state whether the sale is to be public or private, and must include the time and place of any public sale, the terms and conditions of any private sale, and the time fixed for filing objections. A general description of the property to be sold is sufficient. Rule 2002(c)(1). For sales of property worth less than $2,500, the trustee may give general notice of intent to sell such property. Rule 6004(d). Objections to proposed sales normally must be filed and served at least seven days ahead of time. Rule 6004(b). If an objection is filed, a hearing will be held. The dispute is treated as a "contested matter" under Rule 9014.

In cases under chapter 11 or chapter 12, the plan proponent has the alternative of providing *in the plan* for the sale of all or part of the property of the estate. §§ 1123(a)(5)(D), 1123(b)(4) (chapter 11); § 1222(b)(8) (chapter 12). In plan sale cases, of course, the proponent must comply with all of the applicable confirmation provisions.

---

[195] For discussion of these cases, see Brubaker & Tabb, supra note 192; see also Adler, supra note 192; Douglas G. Baird, Lessons from the Automobile Reorganizations, 4 J. Leg. Analysis 271 (2012); Lubben, *No Big Deal,* supra note 192, Roe & Skeel, supra note 192; A. Joseph Warburton, Understanding the Bankruptcies of Chrysler and General Motors: A Primer, 60 Syracuse L. Rev. 531 (2010).

[196] See § 5.16.

[197] See In re Lavigne, 114 F.3d 379 (2d Cir. 1997); In re Dant & Russell, Inc., 853 F.2d 700 (9th Cir. 1988).

Because of the greater complexity of plan sales, the trustee or debtor in possession may attempt to effect a sale of substantially all property of the estate under § 363(b)(1), as noted previously. The legitimacy of such sales is discussed below.

Once a sale has been approved, opponents of the sale who want to appeal the authorization should obtain a stay of the sale pending the appeal. If a stay is not obtained, and the sale is then made, the appeal will be mooted if effective relief no longer can be given by the appellate court.[198] Under § 363(m), a good faith purchaser is protected from the effects of an appellate reversal or modification of a sale authorization. This protection for good faith purchasers in § 363(m) mirrors the protection given for good faith extenders of credit in § 364(e), and encourages participation in bankruptcy sales. In plan sale cases, mootness also will apply with respect to the implementation of the plan.

However, under § 363(n), a collusive sale can be set aside by the trustee. Alternatively, the trustee may recover the value lost through the collusive sale, along with costs and attorneys' fees, and punitive damages in cases involving willfulness. A sale is subject to avoidance or recapture under § 363(n) only if the sale price was "controlled" by an agreement among potential bidders. A showing only that the sales price was adversely affected by the agreement will not be enough.[199]

Sales free and clear of other interests

Property in which the estate has an interest also may be subject to the interests of other entities. For example, a creditor may have a lien on estate property. Or, a non-debtor party may hold a tenancy interest in the property, or the estate property may be subject to a dower or curtesy right. In these situations, the interests of the estate and the non-debtor party might conflict most directly. The estate's interest is to realize the maximum value for its interest; yet, the non-debtor party's own property rights must be respected, both as a matter of policy and as a constitutional imperative. In certain situations, the Code permits a sale to be made free and clear of the interests of the non-debtor party. § 363(f)–(i).

The presumptive rule is that any sale of estate property is *subject to* the interests of non-debtor parties. In other words, a sale free and clear must be predicated on a specific statutory grant of power. The general section authorizing free and clear sales is § 363(f). Subsection (f) lists five situations in which a free and clear sale may be made. This list is exclusive, permitting a free and clear sale only if one of the following can be proven:

1.   A free and clear sale would be permitted under applicable nonbankruptcy law, § 363(f)(1);

2.   The other party consents, § 363(f)(2);

---

[198]   See, e.g., In re Nashville Senior Living, LLC, 620 F.3d 584 (6th Cir. 2010); In re WestPoint Stevens, Inc., 600 F.3d 231 (2d Cir. 2010); In re Stadium Mgmt. Corp., 895 F.2d 845 (1st Cir. 1990).

[199]   See In re New York Trap Rock Corp., 42 F.3d 747 (2d Cir. 1994); In re Sunnyside Timber LLC, 413 B.R.352 (Bankr. W.D. La. 2009).

3.   The other interest is a lien, and the sales price is greater than the aggregate value of all liens on the property, § 363(f)(3);

4.   The other party's interest is in bona fide dispute, § 363(f)(4); or

5.   The other party could be compelled to accept a money satisfaction of their interest in a legal or equitable proceeding, § 363(f)(5).

To illustrate the application of § 363(f), consider the common example of estate property subject to a valid lien. Assume that the Debtor owned Blackacre at the time she filed bankruptcy. Blackacre is worth $50,000, but is subject to a first mortgage in favor of Bank to secure a debt of $40,000. Under § 363(f)(3), the trustee could sell Blackacre free and clear of Bank's interest for any price greater than $40,000. Note, though, that unless the court ordered otherwise, Bank itself could bid at the sale, and could "credit bid"—i.e., offset its claim against the purchase price of the property. § 363(k). The lienholder's right to bid in at a sale is also honored in a sale to be made pursuant to a chapter 11 plan.[200] § 1129(b)(2)(A)(ii).

If, however, the hypothetical is changed to add a junior lienholder with a claim of $15,000 secured by Blackacre, a sale free and clear of Bank's interest could not be authorized under § 363(f)(3), unless the sales price exceeded the total value of both liens—Bank's $40,000 first lien and the $15,000 junior lien. The fact that the sale price exceeded the Bank's lien would not suffice. For the free and clear sale to be authorized, another provision of subsection (f) would have to apply. A plausible candidate might be subsection (f)(5), because under non-bankruptcy law, a junior security interest would be terminated by a foreclosure by a senior lienholder.

However, some concern over whether (f)(5) works in such a case was raised in an important judicial decision that gave a narrow reading to § 363(f)(5), the 2008 *Clear Channel* decision of the Ninth Circuit Bankruptcy Appellate Panel.[201] In *Clear Channel*, a senior lender that was owed over $40 million purchased estate property by a credit bid of $41.4 million under § 363(k) and took the property free and clear of a junior lien, which got nothing. The bankruptcy court ruled that the free-and-clear sale was authorized under § 363(f)(5), reasoning that on the facts the junior lienholder could be "crammed down" for no value in a reorganization plan, which qualified as the "legal or equitable proceeding" in which the junior lienholder "could be compelled . . . to accept a money satisfaction." The BAP reversed, holding broadly that § 363(f)(5) does not "permit a secured creditor to credit bid its debt and purchase estate property, taking title free and clear of valid, nonconsenting junior liens."[202] The BAP took the position that there must be some *independent* legal or equitable proceeding *other than* a bankruptcy case in which the junior interest could be forced to take money in

---

[200]   This right was reaffirmed by the Supreme Court in *RadLax Gateway Hotel, LLC v. Amalgamated Bank*, 132 S.Ct. 2065 (2012). See Charles J. Tabb, Credit Bidding, Security, and the Obsolescence of Chapter 11, 2013 U. Ill. L. Rev. 103 (2013).

[201]   Clear Channel Outdoor, Inc. v. Knupfer (In re PW, LLC), 391 B.R. 25 (B.A.P. 9th Cir. 2008). See also Robert M. Lawless, BAP Prohibits Sale Free and Clear of an Underwater Junior Lien, 28 Bankr. L. Letter 1 (Oct. 2008); Joel H. Levitin, et. al., Ninth Circuit BAP Dresses Down Lienstripping: Could This Be the Last Dance for 363 Sales?, 27 Am. Bankr. Inst. J. 1 (Oct. 2008).

[202]   *Clear Channel*, supra note 201, 391 B.R. at 29.

exchange for its lien, and rejected the view that the chapter 11 plan confirmation process could qualify as that "proceeding," finding such reasoning circular.[203] Curiously, though, the court did *not* consider the possibility of a state law foreclosure proceeding as the requisite "proceeding" in which the junior lien could be compelled to accept a money satisfaction of its lien even if for less than full payment, even though "the word "foreclosure" means exactly that—the foreclosure of junior interests."[204] The appellate court may have been worried about the absence of a factual record at the bankruptcy court regarding the hypothetical state law foreclosure proceeding. It thus would seem that, notwithstanding the dire "sky is falling" concerns expressed that *Clear Channel* sounds a death knell for § 363 sales when there is a nonconsenting junior lien and the price is less than the amount of all liens, a qualifying free-and-clear sale still could be made under § 363(f)(5) by relying on a state law foreclosure proceeding as the requisite "legal or equitable proceeding" in which the junior lien could be compelled to accept a money satisfaction, as long as an adequate factual record was made.

Non-debtor parties with a tenancy interest are given even greater protection than lienholders. Consider a hypothetical, in which the Debtor owns Blackacre as a tenant in common with Other Party. Purchaser offers the trustee $50,000 for Blackacre, but insists on buying the entire parcel. Given the unique configuration of the property, it is impracticable to partition Blackacre, and even if partition were possible, the trustee could not readily obtain offers of equivalent value for the Debtor's interest. Other Party, however, will not consent to the sale. What happens?

Under § 363(h), the trustee could sell Blackacre free and clear of the tenancy interest of Other Party, but only if strict conditions are satisfied: partition must be impracticable, § 363(h)(1); sale of the estate's undivided interest must realize significantly less for the estate than would a free and clear sale, § 363(h)(2); and, finally, the benefit to the estate must outweigh the detriment to Other Party. § 363(h)(3). Also, this option is not available for property "used in the production, transmission, or distribution, for sale, of electric energy or of natural or synthetic gas for heat, light, or power." § 363(h)(4). Even if all of those conditions are met, the Other Party is given a right of first refusal to purchase the property at the proposed sale price. § 363(i). If Other Party does not exercise the first refusal right, then the sale to Purchaser will be consummated, and Other Party will be given its share of the net sales proceeds. § 363(j).

Even if a sale of estate property is authorized free and clear of all interests under § 363(f), or in a confirmed plan, some interests still might survive. For example, in situations in which *successor liability* would be imposed under applicable non-bankruptcy law, a number of courts have recognized such liability, even following a purported "free and clear" bankruptcy sale.[205] Such successor liability might be recognized, for instance, in a case involving injury to a future victim from a defective

---

[203] Id. at 45–46.

[204] Lawless, supra note 201.

[205] See, e.g., Chicago Truck Drivers, Helpers, & Warehouse Workers Union Pension Fund v. Tasemkin, Inc., 59 F.3d 48 (7th Cir. 1995); In re Savage Indus., Inc., 43 F.3d 714 (1st Cir. 1994); In re Grumman Olson Indus., Inc., 467 B.R. 694 (S.D.N.Y. 2012).

product.[206] These courts typically take the view that a successor liability claim is not an "interest in property" at all, and thus nothing in 363(f) would allow the purchaser to take free and clear of the non-property successor liability claim. The prevailing trend in the cases, though, illustrated in *Chrysler*[207] and *General Motors*,[208] follows the lead of the Third Circuit in the *TWA* case,[209] and finds that a successor liability claim is an interest in property and that a § 363(f) free and clear sale purchaser does take free of successor liability claims.[210] Professor Brubaker has argued that the prevailing view has it right: "When the predecessor transfers all assets, ceases operations, and dissolves *in bankruptcy*, though, it is perfectly legitimate to say that, to the extent federal bankruptcy law provides claimants equitable recourse against the predecessor's bankruptcy estate, federal bankruptcy law must also be taken to have fully preempted claimants' nonbankruptcy successor liability remedies."[211] Professor Kuney, however, sharply disagrees.[212] Either way, of course, the mandates of constitutional Due Process must be accorded to those claimants whose successor liability claims are supposedly to be expunged, and if it is not, then of course the claimants retain their successor liability rights.[213]

A particularly troubling question is whether the trustee can sell a lease or an intellectual property license "free and clear" under § 363(f) and strip the non-debtor lessee or licensee of the right to continue using the leased or licensed property—even though special protections in the section governing executory contracts and leases appears to preclude precisely such a result. Thus, 365(h) allows a non-debtor tenant to elect to remain in possession ever after the lease is rejected, and 365(n) provides similar succor to a non-debtor licensee of intellectual property.[214] One would think that the canon of interpretation that the specific controls the general would dictate that the carefully crafted and narrowly tailored protections in § 365 would control over the broad coverage of § 363(f), especially in light of the strong congressional purpose to safeguard the rights of non-debtor tenants and licensees. And indeed until 2003 virtually every court held that § 365(h) or § 365(n) allowed the non-debtor tenant or licensee to retain its property notwithstanding a free and clear sale. In 2003, however, the Seventh Circuit sent shock waves through the bankruptcy, leasing, and intellectual property communities with its holding in *Precision Industries, Inc. v. Qualitech Steel*

---

[206] See, e.g., *Savage Industries*, supra note 205, 43 F.3d 714 (firearms); In re Fairchild Aircraft Corp., 184 B.R. 910 (Bankr. W.D. Tex. 1995), vacated on other grounds, 220 B.R. 909 (Bankr. W.D. Tex. 1998) (airplanes).

[207] In re Chrysler LLC, 405 B.R. 84, 111 (Bankr. S.D.N.Y. 2009), aff'd, 576 F.3d 108, 123–26 (2d Cir. 2009), vacated as moot sub. nom. Ind. State Police Pension Trust v. Chrysler LLC, 130 S.Ct. 1015 (2009).

[208] In re Gen. Motors Corp. 407 B.R. 463, 500–06 (Bankr. S.D.N.Y. 2009).

[209] 322 F.3d 283 (3d Cir. 2003). The Third Circuit, in turn, relied heavily on a similar holding of the Fourth Circuit in *United Mine Workers of America 1992 Benefit Plan v. Leckie Smokeless Coal Co. (In re Leckie Smokeless Coal Co.)*, 99 F.3d 573 (4th Cir. 1996).

[210] See George W. Kuney, Misinterpreting Bankruptcy Code Section 363(f) and Undermining the Chapter 11 Process, 76 Am. Bankr. L.J. 235 (2002); Ralph Brubaker, Successor Liability and Bankruptcy Sales: Free and Clear of What?, 23 Bankr. L. Letter No. 6, 12 (June 2003).

[211] Brubaker, supra note 210, at 12 (emphasis in original).

[212] Kuney, supra note 210, at 286–87.

[213] See, e.g., Zerand–Bernal Grp., Inc. v. Cox, 23 F.3d 159, 163–64 (7th Cir. 1994).

[214] See § 8.10.

SBQ, LLC[215] that a § 363(f) free and clear sale did in fact strip the non-debtor lessee of its leasehold interest, thereby trumping § 365(h). If the lessee wanted protection, the court opined, it could have asked for adequate protection under § 363(e). As has been cogently explained by others,[216] for the reasons noted above the decision in *Qualitech Steel* seems misguided. A number of courts have declined to follow the Seventh Circuit's approach, with perhaps the best-known decision being that of the Massachusetts bankruptcy court in *In re Haskell L.P.*[217]

Sale of substantially all assets outside of plan

As noted above, a sale of property of the estate generally can be effected *either* during the pendency of the case, pursuant to § 363, *or* pursuant to a plan in chapter 11 or 12. A § 363 sale need only comply with the notice and hearing provisions of that section and the relevant Bankruptcy Rules, and is usually judged under a lenient "business judgment" standard. A chapter 11 plan may only be confirmed, though, if the rigorous provisions for disclosure, voting, and confirmation are satisfied. Thus, there is some incentive to effect sales under § 363.

Cutting the other way, though, is the Supreme Court's 2008 decision in *Florida Department of Revenue v. Piccadilly Cafeterias, Inc.*[218] The Court in *Piccadilly* held that the stamp-tax exemption in § 1146(a) applies only to transfers made under a confirmed plan, and not to pre-plan sales. That decision thus creates an incentive for plan sales rather than § 363 sales if the stamp tax is a significant factor. While *Piccadilly* may be somewhat at odds with the realities of reorganization practice, where pre-plan sales are quite common, the fairest reading of the statute in question supported the Court's holding. On a broader level, *Piccadilly* suggests that the Supreme Court may not be willing to endorse practices that conflict with the Code simply because doing so might better promote reorganization efforts.

A difficult and important question that a number of courts have faced is whether a § 363 sale is permitted, and if so on what terms, if the trustee or debtor in possession is seeking to sell *all* or substantially all of the property of the estate. While liquidation is permitted in chapter 11 cases, § 1123(b)(4), a § 363 sale of all assets would effectively end the case, without affording all interested parties the more complete chapter 11 protections of disclosure, the right to vote, and the numerous confirmation requirements. May the chapter 11 process be circumvented in this manner? This raises "the new 'chapter 3' reorganization" issue noted at the beginning of this chapter. Have § 363 sales become the "new normal" in chapter 11—and if so, should they?[219]

---

[215] 327 F.3d 537 (7th Cir. 2003).

[216] See Michael St. Patrick Baxter, Section 363 Sales Free and Clear of Interests: Why the Seventh Circuit Erred in *Precision Industries v. Qualitech Steel*, 59 Bus. Law. 475 (2004).

[217] 321 B.R. 1 (Bankr. D. Mass. 2005). See also In re Zota Petroleums, LLC, 482 B.R. 154 (Bankr. E.D. Va. 2012).

[218] 554 U.S. 33 (2008).

[219] See Brubaker & Tabb, 2010 U. Ill. L. Rev. 1375, and the other articles cited in notes 192 and 195 supra.

In thinking about this problem, it is useful to keep separate two distinct issues in the "sale versus plan" debate over how to implement an all–asset sale. Much of the confusion and puzzlement in this area arises because courts conflate the two.[220] Those issues are, first, how should the debtor's assets best be *deployed* so as to maximize value, and second, how should that value be *distributed*? As Professor Baird astutely noted years ago, "how much a particular [stakeholder] gets should have *nothing* to do with how a firm's assets are deployed."[221] Nothing in the asset deployment issue should be considered suspect or gauged by more rigorous standards if done pursuant to a sale as opposed to a reorganization; the worry arises only if the sale effects and dictates final and irreversible distributional outcomes.[222] If Debtor Co. can realize the greatest value for its épée manufacturing plant by selling it to the Home Shopping Network, that strategy for maximization is equally compelling in either the sale or plan context. The biggest reason for empowering creditor enfranchisement via the chapter 11 plan vote concerns distributional questions, not deployment decisions. Significant deference would be given to the *business* decision by the DIP (or trustee) that selling to HSN is the best play in terms of maximizing value. The only worry about a sale would be if the sale procedures were unduly expedited or were structured in such a way that (1) neither stakeholders nor the bankruptcy court could meaningfully ascertain if the HSN sale was indeed the maximal means of capturing value or (2) prospective realistic bidders were foreclosed from effectively participating.[223] As to the first problem, the bankruptcy court can supervise the sale process to ensure meaningful disclosure to and input by stakeholders; as to the second, nothing about a plan versus a sale would necessitate any differences in the bidding structure, and the court again must exercise sound discretion to facilitate competitive bidding.

But if the hypothetical HSN deal is contingent on one stakeholder group getting more than their aliquot share of the sale proceeds, that raises a legitimate distributional concern. The plan confirmation standards and the governing case law contain detailed rules on how and when reorganization value can be distributed in derogation of strict non-bankruptcy priority entitlements,[224] whereas § 363 does not. As Professor Brubaker and I explain, the most troubling aspect of the auto bankruptcies (to us, at least) was how they opened up the possibility of allowing the use of a § 363 sale to do an end run around the settled distributional constraints in chapter 11 plans—a possibility that we argue was realized in the General Motors case.[225] Indeed, in the all-asset sale realm, it is a red herring for courts to try to divine if something is *really* a sale or whether it is actually a reorganization, and then to have anything turn

[220] Indeed, the conflation of deployment and distributional issues plagues chapter 11 in numerous settings. See generally John D. Ayer, Bankruptcy as an Essentially Contested Concept: The Case of the One–Asset Case, 44 S.C. L. Rev. 863, 870 n. 20 (1993).

[221] Douglas G. Baird, Loss Distribution, Forum Shopping, and Bankruptcy: A Reply to Warren, 54 U. Chi. L. Rev. 815, 820 (1987) (emphasis in original).

[222] Brubaker & Tabb, supra note 192, at 1378, 1406.

[223] Indeed, one of the common criticisms of *GM* and *Chrysler* is precisely that the sale procedures were not designed in a way to foster robust competitive bidding and maximize value. See Adler, supra note 192, at 307, 312; Roe & Skeel, supra note 192, at 746–51; see also Douglas G. Baird, supra note 195, at 280–81, 297–98.

[224] See §§ 11.30–11.34.

[225] Brubaker & Tabb, supra note 192, at 1379–80.

on the answer. The focus instead should be on ensuring that distributional entitlements and norms are protected, whether the format is a sale or plan.[226]

The case law, sadly, is not as neat and tidy as my synthesis with Professor Brubaker would dictate. The standard analysis proceeds on two levels, although, having said that, courts sometimes unfortunately tend to merge the two. The first question is whether an all-asset sale outside of the plan context can be justified at all; that is, what would be the harm in just waiting for the plan? Why sell now?, in short. Secondly, assuming that an adequate "sell now"justification can be established, courts look to the *terms* of the sale and will find the supposed "sale" to be "objectionable as a *sub rosa* plan if the sale itself seeks to allocate or dictate the distribution of sale proceeds among different classes of creditors."[227] Brubaker and I think the *sub rosa* plan framework is an inexact way to capture the critical question, noted above, of whether distributional entitlements are being sufficiently preserved.[228]

As to the first issue of justification, all courts agree that a pre-plan sale of all estate assets is permitted under some circumstances. What they do not agree on is what the requisite circumstances are. One view is that a § 363 all-asset sale can be justified only in the event of a genuine *emergency*, which would prevent the proponent from complying with the time-consuming chapter 11 confirmation procedures.[229] Such a situation might exist because either the assets are perishable or because the purchase offer is immutably time-sensitive.

Today, however, the overwhelming majority approach rejects the "emergency only" view. The leading case is the Second Circuit's decision in *In re Lionel Corp.*[230] The courts in the auto cases reaffirmed the continuing validity of *Lionel* and its "good business reason" test, described below.[231] In *Lionel,* the debtor in possession sought permission under § 363(b) to sell its single most valuable asset, a controlling stock interest in a profitable subsidiary, for $50 million cash. Testimony was offered to show that the sale price was fair, but also that the asset was not "wasting away" due to the passage of time. Apparently the only reason for proceeding under § 363(b) instead of under a plan was the creditors' committee's insistence on such a course of action.

The Second Circuit reversed the sale authorization. In doing so the *Lionel* court chose what it viewed as a middle course. The court rejected the strict "emergency" approach, concluding that the statute did not require such a standard, and that giving the bankruptcy judge considerable flexibility was a wiser policy than "shackling" the judge through a narrow emergency test.[232] At the same time, though, the court

---

[226] Id. at 1379.

[227] In re Gen. Motors Corp., 407 B.R. 463, 495 (Bankr. S.D.N.Y. 2009).

[228] Brubaker & Tabb, supra note 192, at 1390–91.

[229] See, e.g., In re White Motor Credit Corp., 14 B.R. 584 (Bankr. N.D. Ohio 1981).

[230] 722 F.2d 1063 (2d Cir. 1983). The Second Circuit test was adopted in other circuits. See, e.g., Stephens Indus. v. McClung, 789 F.2d 386, 389–90 (6th Cir.1986); Inst. Creditors of Cont'l Air Lines, Inc. v. Cont'l Air Lines, Inc. (In re Cont'l Air Lines, Inc.), 780 F.2d 1223, 1226 (5th Cir.1986).

[231] See *Chrysler,* 405 B.R. 84, 94–96, aff'd, 576 F.3d 108, at 116–17; *GM,* 407 B.R.463, at 487–91.

[232] Id. at 1069.

eschewed an "anything goes" delegation of *carte blanche* authority to the bankruptcy judge.[233]

Instead, according to the Second Circuit the proper test for judging whether to approve a proposed preplan sale of all or substantially all of the estate assets is whether the sale proponent offers a *"good business reason"* for the sale.[234] In the case itself, the court decided that bowing to the wishes of an insistent creditors' committee did not meet that standard.[235]

What factors might a court consider in assessing whether a "good business reason" justifies an early sale? The *Lionel* court offered some suggestions for guidance:[236]

* the proportionate value of the asset to the estate as a whole;

* the amount of time elapsed since the filing;

* the likelihood that a plan will be proposed and confirmed in the near future;

* the effect of the proposed sale on future reorganization plans;

* how the proceeds to be received from the sale compare to any appraisals of the property to be sold; and

* most importantly—whether the asset is increasing or decreasing in value.

Numerous subsequent cases have reaffirmed the "good business reason" test. Best known are the *Chrysler* and *General Motors* cases. In the wake of the auto cases, the justification ground often is captured by the metaphor of a "melting ice cube," seizing upon language used in those cases. But a "melting ice cube" test, if taken seriously, sounds a lot more like an "emergency" test. Such was not intended; there is no doubt that the "good business reason" test was embraced fully and remains alive and well.

Ironically, in light of *Lionel,* the reality in the auto cases was that the sale was being done at the insistence of and to appease a major creditor: the United States government. But since the government was providing the necessary billions of dollars of funding; was, it appears, the only show in town; and that liquidation with cataclysmic consequences for the U.S. economy was the only evident alternative, the courts approved the sales. Thus, for example, in *Chrysler* the Second Circuit observed:

> With its revenues sinking, its factories dark, and its massive debts growing, Chrysler fit the paradigm of the melting ice cube. Going concern value was being reduced each passing day that it produced no cars, yet was obliged to pay rents, overhead, and salaries. Consistent with an underlying purpose of the Bankruptcy

---

[233] Id.

[234] Id. at 1071.

[235] Id.

[236] Id.

Code—maximizing the value of the bankrupt estate—it was no abuse of discretion to determine that the Sale prevented further, unnecessary losses.[237]

Similarly, the bankruptcy judge in the *General Motors* case concluded: "it is hard to imagine circumstances that could more strongly justify an immediate 363 sale. . . . GM, with no liquidity of its own and the need to quickly address consumer and fleet owner doubt, does not have the luxury of selling its business under a plan. . . . [T]he only alternative to an immediate sale is liquidation."[238]

Professor Baird has suggested a more demanding standard than *Lionel*'s good business reason test; his proposed approach makes eminent sense:

> In deciding whether to approve a sale, the bankruptcy judge should not defer to the business judgment of the debtor. Rather, the bankruptcy judge should make an independent assessment of whether the proposed sale is the course that maximizes the value of whatever is being sold for the benefit of the estate. The burden of proof should remain on the proponent of the sale. While the proponent need not show that the business or assets are "melting" in order to justify the sale, she should have to show that a sale of the business or asset—in the time frame proposed and in the manner proposed—is the most sensible course.
>
> This is a stronger standard than under current law, where the sale proponent has to do more than show that there is a sensible business reason for the sale. She should have to show that the sale is a good idea for all concerned in the time frame proposed and in the manner proposed. The benchmark for testing the reasonableness of the manner proposed for the sale should be that the sale is being conducted in a fashion that is consistent with the way a prudent person would do it if trading on her own account.[239]

Assuming that justification for the sale can be established, the question remains whether the proposed "sale" is in reality a "reorganization" masquerading in "sale" clothing, or, stated otherwise, is a *sub rosa* plan. As explained above, Professor Brubaker and I urge that this way of framing the issue is not very illuminating; the better approach is to ask directly if chapter 11's distributional norms and entitlements are being carefully preserved and protected, regardless of whether the transaction is cast as a sale or a plan. But courts tread the "masquerading" or *sub rosa* path, and thus so too must we.

The leading early Code case was *In re Braniff Airways, Inc.*,[240] in which the Fifth Circuit reversed a § 363(b) sale authorization on the ground that the transaction was "much more than the 'use, sale, or lease' of Braniff's property authorized by § 363(b)."[241] The so-called sale to Pacific Southwest Airlines "would provide for Braniff's transfer of cash, airplanes and equipment, terminal leases and landing slots

---

[237] 576 F.3d at 119.

[238] 407 B.R. at 491, 493.

[239] Baird, supra note 195, at 296.

[240] 700 F.2d 935 (5th Cir. 1983).

[241] Id. at 939.

to PSA in return for travel scrip, unsecured notes, and a profit participation in PSA's proposed operation" and "would also require significant restructuring of the rights of Braniff creditors."[242] The terms of the PSA sale "had the practical effect of dictating some of the terms of any future reorganization plan."[243] Such evasion of the plan confirmation rules could not be evaded by calling a "plan" a "sale," the Fifth Circuit concluded:

> The debtor and the Bankruptcy Court should not be able to short circuit the requirements of Chapter 11 for confirmation of a reorganization plan by establishing the terms of the plan *sub rosa* in connection with a sale of assets.[244]

If the courts conscientiously pay attention to whether distributional outcomes are dictated by the terms of the sale itself, as *Braniff* suggests, then looking at the distributional problem in "*sub rosa*" lingo is unnecessarily confusing but not dangerous. What is dangerous, though, is if courts follow a misguided explanation of *sub rosa* doctrine in the *Chrysler* case, and which was then relied upon to alter distributional entitlements in *GM*. Compounding the mistake, this misstep on the second issue was justified under the banner of *Lionel's* "good business reason" test.

In explaining why the *Chrysler* plan was not a *sub rosa* reorganization, the bankruptcy judge made the following astonishing statement: "*The allocation of ownership interests in the new enterprise is irrelevant to the estates' economic interests.*"[245] The judge was explaining why it was perfectly fine that value in New Chrysler, the reorganized enterprise, was distributed in accordance with the demands of the purchaser (at the insistence of the U.S. government, which was putting up the money).

The statement, though, is patently wrong, and flies directly in the face of long-established reorganization doctrine, tracing back to the foundational case of *Northern Pacific Railway Co. v. Boyd.*[246] In *Boyd*, the argument was made that it was perfectly fine to squeeze out unsecured creditors, and let the old shareholders (whose priority ranking should have come after the unsecured creditors) retain ownership in the reorganized enterprise, because those unsecured creditors were out of the money anyway; why should they care "if worthless stock in the new company was given for worthless stock in the old"?[247] The Supreme Court, though, laid the cornerstone of the absolute priority rule and established the "fixed principle" that has governed reorganizations ever since, which is that any and all value in the reorganized enterprise is "a right of property out of which the creditors were entitled to be paid."[248] This principle respects the distributional priority order established by non-bankruptcy rights (i.e., creditors are entitled to get paid before stockholders). In short, *Boyd* (and its progeny) made it clear that a "'purchaser,' acting under the guise of a 'sale' of the

---

[242] Id.

[243] Id. at 940.

[244] Id.

[245] *Chrysler,* 405 B.R. at 99.

[246] 228 U.S.482 (1913). See § 11.31.

[247] 228 U.S. at 507.

[248] Id. at 508.

debtor's property to it, was *not* free to dole out interests in the new 'purchasing' entity to the debtor's creditors and shareholders in whatever manner the 'purchaser' wanted."[249]

On the facts in *Chrysler*, there was no harm in the court's misstatement, because *all* of the value in the enterprise belonged as a priority matter to the senior secured lenders, who were vastly undersecured, and the sale was to an independent outside party, who wanted to give some extra value (via debt assumption) to selected creditors.[250] In short, "Not one penny of value of the Debtors' assets is going to anyone other than the First–Lien Lenders."[251] If there were more money to be had in *Chrysler*, the senior lenders had every incentive to take it.

In *General Motors*, though, the facts were critically different; there was no pre-bankruptcy undersecured lender who controlled the entire reorganization value, and the sale was not to an independent third party, but was a "self-sale," i.e., an internal restructuring. Instead, the bankruptcy judge's adoption of the idea that "the allocation of ownership interests in the new enterprise is irrelevant to the estates' economic interests" allowed value in the "new enterprise" to be diverted unequally to pre-bankruptcy claimants of equal priority ranking.[252] UAW retirees got a much bigger share of the pie than did similarly ranked unsecured creditors. While in a plan such "discrimination" could be approved in a cram down plan on a sufficient showing of necessity,[253] under the § 363 sale analysis in *GM* the issue is not even addressed, because the court was under the mistaken impression that it did not apply. Instead, the court there stated that "'the purchaser was free to provide ownership interests in the new entity as it saw fit' and that 'the purchaser's allocation of value in its own enterprise did not elevate its measures into a *sub rosa* plan.'"[254] If so, as Brubaker and I argue, "then *anything goes*. There are no limits; the § 363 sale assumes irrefutable and uncontestable omnipotence."[255] The court's analysis is directly at odds with *Boyd,* and would permit an end run around all of the distributional protections embedded in the plan confirmation context simply by casting the transaction as a sale.

Even worse, the Second Circuit in *Chrysler* collapsed the *sub rosa* plan test— which as just discussed had been egregiously misstated—into the *Lionel* "good business

---

[249]   Brubaker & Tabb, supra note 192, at 1402–03.

[250]   Thus, if those lenders chose to accept the terms of a reorganization plan that allowed some other stakeholders to receive value (in the form of debt assumption by New Chrysler), then absent something nefarious, it could only be because those lenders did not believe that that value formed any part of the debtor's worth, but was independent value over and above that of the debtor, which the purchaser would pay only to keep certain critical parties committed to the future of the enterprise. Brubaker & Tabb, supra note 192, at 1399. Others have suggested that the reason instead was more in the vein of economic blackmail by the U.S. government, which dangled TARP money in front of the senior lenders on the condition that they cave in to the government's demands in the auto cases. E.g., Roe & Skeel, supra note 192, at 743–46. If proven, of course, such a finding would undermine the legitimacy of the lender's consent and thus the sale. The only problem in *Chrysler* was that the judge simply did not find that the allegation had been factually proven. 405 B.R. at 103–04.

[251]   405 B.R. at 98.

[252]   *General Motors,* 407 B.R. at 495–98.

[253]   Brubaker & Tabb, supra note 192, at 1403.

[254]   Id. at 1402, quoting *General Motors,* 407 B.R. at 497.

[255]   Brubaker & Tabb, supra note 192, at 1404.

reason" analysis, saying that an allegation that a sale really is an impermissible *sub rosa* plan can be dealt with "using the analysis set forth in *Lionel* in order to determine whether there was a good business reason for the sale," and rejected the *sub rosa* plan challenge as nothing more than a "complaint that the Sale does not pass the discretionary, multifarious *Lionel* test."[256] If that approach is right, then "*sub rosa* plan doctrine has no independent content at all and thus provides no meaningful check on parties' distribution of the value of a new 'purchaser' entity in whatever manner the most powerful interests in control of the process devise."[257] In effect, then, the same exigencies that justify holding an immediate sale rather than waiting for a plan *also* would "warrant distributing that value amongst creditors and shareholders without any apparent restriction."[258]

Section 363 sales are here to stay. One can only hope that future courts will not make the analytical mistakes just discussed, and instead will hold to the previously established doctrine, and keep appropriately distinct the issues of justification for the sale and distribution of value. If the latter is implicated, then plan protections (substantive and procedural) are required. In sum, the prevailing doctrine is as follows. The combined effect of *Lionel* and *Braniff* is that a preplan sale of all or substantially all of the debtor's assets under § 363(b) may only be approved if (1) a good business reason supports the sale request, after equitably weighing a number of pertinent factors, and (2) the sale is really just a sale, and not a disguised reorganization plan. Courts would be even better advised to recognize that even these factors mask the more critical issues of (1) whether the sale is the best way to maximize asset value, and, if so, (2) whether the sale requires distribution of that value to stakeholders in contravention of established norms and entitlements.

Credit Bidding

If a sale of collateral is made, the lienholder has a very significant protection: it may "credit bid" at the sale. § 363(k). Credit bidding means that the lienholder does not have to bid cash, but can bid its existing claim against the debtor. If it wins the auction, then it simply offsets its sale bid against its claim. So, for example, assume Lienholder has a claim of $100,000 against Collateral, which Trustee auctions off in the bankruptcy case. Lienholder wins the auction with a bid of $60,000. What happens? Lienholder gets the Collateral, as the winning purchaser at the bankruptcy sale, and "pays" the bankruptcy estate by reducing its claim (now unsecured) from $100,000 to $40,000. In short, Lienholder "credits" the sale price against its existing claim; as the statutory text of § 363(k) says, "if the holder of such claim purchases such property, such holder may offset such claim against the purchase price of such property." Lienholder does *not* have to fork over $60 grand in cash to the trustee. Notably, Lienholder could keep upping its credit bid all the way up to its $100,000 claim without committing any cash to the auction table. Any other bidder would have to go up to $100,001 in cold hard cash to win the auction if the Lienholder so chose.

---

[256]   576 F.3d at 117–18.

[257]   Brubaker & Tabb, supra note 192, at 1405.

[258]   Id.

Indeed, it is for this reason that debtors sometimes complain that credit bidding "chills" bankruptcy collateral sales.

Credit bidding was put into the Bankruptcy Code in 1978 as a way to protect secured creditors from being cashed out at a sale for a price they felt was too low. The credit bidding right works hand in glove with the "§ 1111(b) election," which is designed to keep a secured lienholder from being crammed down at what it believes is too a low price when the debtor keeps the collateral.[259] If the debtor is not retaining the collateral, then the § 1111(b) election is not operative, but instead the credit bidding right kicks in.[260] Thus, "when its collateral is being sold . . . the fundamental protection for a secured creditor . . . is to show up at the sale and submit its own bid if it does not think that the bidding at the sale is bringing what the collateral is actually worth."[261] As the Supreme Court observed, "The ability to credit-bid helps to protect a creditor against the risk that its collateral will be sold at a depressed price. It enables the creditor to purchase the collateral for what it considers the fair market price (up to the amount of its security interest) without committing additional cash to protect the loan."[262]

The right to credit bid under § 363(k) is not absolute. The bankruptcy court may preclude credit bidding for "cause." The statute does not specify what constitutes "cause," however, and very few cases have explored the issue. An oft-quoted statement is that "it is intended to be a flexible concept enabling a court to fashion an appropriate remedy on a case-by-case basis."[263] If either the lienholder's claim or priority status is being contested (for example, it is being attacked as a fraudulent conveyance, or there is a dispute as to the priority status of the lien in question), then cause might exist.[264] Similarly, if the secured creditor engaged in egregious misconduct, cause might be found. One common argument that has been made by debtors is that credit bidding chills participation by other bidders, and thus depresses the price that can be achieved at the auction, and therefore this chilling constitutes cause. This argument likely will be made even more often in the wake of the Supreme Court's 2012 *RadLAX* decision, discussed below.[265] However, so far courts have not been receptive to the argument,[266] and perhaps appropriately so; the whole point of the credit bidding right is to give the secured creditor a firm safeguard against a low-ball sale. If "chilling" is accepted as an exception, then that might be the proverbial exception that swallows the rule, because it is *always* the case that other prospective bidders would be cognizant of the possibility of being trumped by a credit bid, and thus may be reluctant to do the due diligence

---

[259] Charles J. Tabb, Credit Bidding, Security, and the Obsolescence of Chapter 11, 2013 U. Ill. L. Rev. 103, 120–23 (2013). See § 11.32.

[260] Kenneth N. Klee, All You Ever Wanted to Know About Cram Down Under the New Bankruptcy Code, 53 Am. Bankr. L.J. 133, 153 (1979).

[261] Tabb, supra note 259, at 122.

[262] RadLAX Gateway Hotel, LLC v. Amalgamated Bank, 132 S.Ct. 2065, 2070 n. 2 (2012).

[263] In re NJ Affordable Homes Corp., 2006 WL 2128624, at *16 (Bankr. D.N.J. June 29, 2006).

[264] See, e.g., In re Takeout Taxi Holdings, Inc., 307 B.R. 525, 536 (Bankr. E.D. Va. 2004); In re Diebart Bancroft, 1993 WL 21423, at *5 (E.D. La. Jan. 26, 1993).

[265] Tabb, supra note 259, at 138–39. See 132 S.Ct. 2065.

[266] For example, in *RadLAX,* the debtors had argued "chilling" as a cause basis for denying credit bidding, and had lost on the facts before the bankruptcy court. In re River Road Hotel Partners, LLC, 2010 WL 6634603, at *1–2 (Bankr. N.D. Ill. 2010). That issue was not appealed to the Supreme Court.

required to submit a bid. Also, though, secured creditors would argue that it makes no sense to say that bidding is chilled, except to the extent that others might be dissuaded from trying to get a huge bargain; if a fair price is being bid for the collateral by others, the lienholder would be thrilled and would not trump others' bids by credit bidding at a price *over* what it believed the collateral to be worth.

Until 2012, some cases—most notably the Third Circuit's 2010 decision in *Philadelphia Newspapers*[267]—had raised the spectre of a secured creditor being denied the right to credit bid pursuant to a sale under a "cram down" *plan*, even though the cram down confirmation rules in chapter 11 appeared to incorporate § 363(k)'s sale rules, with its correlative credit bid right by reference. § 1129(b)(2)(A)(ii). However, cases like *Philadelphia Newspapers* circumvented credit bidding by confirming the plan under the alternative "indubitable equivalent" standard, in § 1129(b)(2)(A)(iii).[268]

In 2012, however, the Supreme Court rejected this "indubitable equivalent" circumvention, holding in *RadLAX Gateway Hotel, LLC v. Amalgamated Bank*[269] that "the RadLAX debtors may not obtain confirmation of a Chapter 11 cramdown plan that provides for the sale of collateral free and clear of the Bank's lien, but does not permit the Bank to credit-bid at the sale."[270] In short, the Court concluded that if collateral was being sold free and clear, then the § 363(k) credit bid right existed, whether that sale was being effected outside of a plan under § 363 or under a plan via the cramdown rules. Accordingly, after *RadLAX*, the only way a secured creditor would not have the right to credit bid if its collateral is being sold is if the bankruptcy court finds specific "cause" to deny that right.

Consumer privacy protection

In 2005 Congress added provisions designed to enhance the protection of the privacy of consumers who have dealt with the debtor. Under amended § 363(b)(1), restrictions are placed on the trustee's ability to sell or lease the "personally identifiable information" of individuals. This protection is triggered if the debtor in connection with the offering of a product or service has disclosed to an individual a policy prohibiting the transfer of such personally identifiable information to unaffiliated parties, and that policy is still in effect when the bankruptcy case is commenced. In that situation, the trustee's sale or lease of the personally identifiable information is possible only if either (1) made in accord with that disclosed policy, § 363(b)(1)(A), or (2) the court approves the sale or lease after the appointment of a "consumer privacy ombudsman" under § 332, who is charged with making a presentation to the court that takes into account a list of balancing factors, § 332(b),

---

[267] In re Philadelphia Newspapers LLC, 599 F.3d 298 (3d Cir. 2010). See also Bank of N.Y. Trust Co. v. Official Unsecured Creditors' Comm. (In re Pac. Lumber Co.), 584 F.3d 229 (5th Cir. 2009). The Seventh Circuit then disagreed in *River Road Hotel Partners LLC v. Amalgamated Bank,* 651 F.3d 642 (7th Cir. 20110), aff'd, 132 S.Ct. 2065 (2012). For discussion of *Philadelphia Newspapers, Pacific Lumber,* and *River Road,* see Tabb, supra note 259, at 125–36. The Seventh Circuit's decision was then affirmed by the Supreme Court in *RadLAX*.

[268] 599 F.3d at 304–10, 318.

[269] 132 S.Ct. 2065 (2012). For discussion of the Supreme Court decision, see Tabb, supra note 259, at 136–38.

[270] 132 S.Ct. at 2073.

and the court's "due consideration" of the factors, § 363(b)(1)(B)(i), and determination that the sale or lease will not violate applicable non-bankruptcy law. § 363(b)(1)(B)(ii).

§ 5.18   Use of Cash Collateral

The Code's general rules in § 363 governing the trustee's power to use, sell, or lease property are subject to special limitations for property that is classified as "cash collateral." § 363(c)(2)–(4). For cash collateral, the interest of the non-debtor party in the property is given significantly greater protection than is the case for other forms of property interests. The reason for this heightened protection is that the risk of loss to the secured creditor is so immediate and grave; cash collateral can be dissipated by the trustee or debtor in possession almost instantaneously, causing severe and perhaps irreversible prejudice to the non-debtor secured party. In effect, the Code grants a creditor with a security interest in cash collateral the benefit of an immediate and automatic temporary restraining order.

The cash collateral rules

What are the special protective rules for cash collateral? The trustee or debtor in possession must segregate and account for any cash collateral in its possession, custody, or control. § 363(c)(4). Even more significantly, the trustee or DIP is absolutely prohibited from using, selling, or leasing the cash collateral unless *prior permission* is obtained from either (1) the entity with the interest in the cash collateral (i.e., the secured creditor), § 363(c)(2)(A), or (2) the court. § 363(c)(2)(B). In other words, unless the secured creditor consents to the use of the cash collateral (usually pursuant to a detailed agreed cash collateral order), the trustee or DIP must go to court and ask for authorization. The dispositive issue at a cash collateral hearing is almost invariably whether the secured creditor's interest in the cash collateral is being adequately protected. See §§ 363(e), 361. This whole scheme reverses the normal procedure, in which the trustee is free to use estate property, and the secured creditor has the burden of requesting adequate protection. For cash collateral, the trustee has the burden to ask for permission before using the property. The reason for the role reversal is that the cash collateral could be spent before the creditor could obtain relief.

In many chapter 11 cases the DIP's need for cash collateral at the outset of the case is compelling. For example, the DIP might need to make a payroll, and the payroll account might be cash collateral. Section 363(c)(3) provides a specialized hearing procedure that enables the DIP to obtain emergency relief, and yet also safeguards the critical interests of the secured creditor. It is not unusual for a contested cash collateral hearing to be the first significant action in a chapter 11 case.

Under § 363(c)(3), the hearing "shall be scheduled in accordance with the needs of the debtor." Furthermore, the statute requires the court to "act promptly on any request for authorization" to use cash collateral. The cash collateral hearing can be either a preliminary hearing or a final hearing. If the court treats it as a preliminary hearing, the court may authorize the use of the cash collateral "if there is a reasonable likelihood that the trustee will prevail at the final hearing." The final hearing may be commenced no earlier than 14 days after service of the motion for permission to use cash collateral. Relief may be granted at a preliminary hearing prior to 14 days, "but the court may authorize the use of only that amount of cash collateral as is necessary to avoid immediate and irreparable harm to the estate pending a final hearing." Rule 4001(b)(2). Thus, in the payroll example, the debtor might be authorized at a preliminary hearing to make a payroll that comes due before the expiration of the 14–day period, but no more.

The definition of "cash collateral"

The special rules just described only apply to "cash collateral." Thus, the threshold inquiry always is to *define* what constitutes cash collateral. After substantial debate over the proper scope of the protected category, the drafters of the 1978 Code defined cash collateral in § 363(a) as follows:

> 'cash collateral' means cash, negotiable instruments, documents of title, securities, deposit accounts, or other cash equivalents whenever acquired in which the estate and an entity other than the estate have an interest.

In adopting this definition, Congress chose the narrower definition proposed by the Senate over the broader category of "soft collateral" that the House favored.[271] Soft collateral also would have included inventory, accounts, contract rights, and general intangibles, which are not covered by the current definition. Instead, only cash and various cash equivalents fall within the protected class. A common example would be a collateral account at a bank. The choice of the narrower definition affords greater flexibility to the trustee or debtor in possession.

Note, though, that the definition clearly encompasses cash collateral "whenever acquired." This means that if property becomes "cash collateral" during the pendency of the bankruptcy case, it immediately becomes subject to the special cash collateral rules.[272] For example, assume that Debtor operates retail stores, selling xylophones. Seventh Bank provides the financing for Debtor, and has a perfected security interest in inventory and accounts, and also requires Debtor to deposit the proceeds of inventory and accounts in a special bank account. The inventory of xylophones does not qualify as cash collateral. Now, assume that the debtor sells 500 xylophones to Buyer on credit, generating an account receivable. That account also is not cash collateral. However, once Buyer pays the money to Debtor on account, and those proceeds are deposited in the collateral account, the proceeds are transformed into "cash collateral."

One of the most difficult and important issues with regard to cash collateral is ascertaining whether a creditor has a security interest at all in the *proceeds*. If it does, then the special cash collateral rules apply. If not, however, the creditor does not even have a lien on the proceeds. The problem often arises where the creditor has a prepetition security interest, and is seeking to claim postpetition proceeds as being subject to that security interest.

---

[271] See 124 Cong. Rec. S17,409 (daily ed. Oct. 6, 1978) (remarks of Sen. DeConcini); 124 Cong. Rec. H11,093 (daily ed. Sept. 28, 1978) (remarks of Rep. Edwards). Compare S. Rep. No. 95–989, 95th Cong., 2d Sess., at 55 (1978) with H.R. Rep. No. 95–595, 95th Cong., 1st Sess., at 344–45 (1977).

[272] See, e.g., United Virginia Bank v. Slab Fork Coal Co. (In re Slab Fork Coal Co.), 784 F.2d 1188 (4th Cir.), cert. denied, 477 U.S. 905 (1986).

This scenario arises frequently in real estate cases, involving properties such as a hotel or apartment building, where the real estate generates a stream of rents. The fight is over whether the creditor has a security interest in postpetition rents. Under § 552(a), the general rule is that property acquired by the estate or the debtor after the filing of the bankruptcy petition is not subject to a prepetition security interest. In short, bankruptcy cuts off floating liens. However, under § 552(b)(1), an exception to the general rule recognizes that the creditor's prepetition security interest can extend to "proceeds, products, offspring, or profits" of the prepetition collateral. The exception for postpetition "rents" was moved to a new § 552(b)(2) in the 1994 Amendments, with the intent of Congress being to make it easier for a hotel lender to perfect its security interest in postpetition rents. Under applicable state law, it often was difficult for a lender to perfect its claim to rents once the debtor filed bankruptcy.[273]

Adequate protection

Assuming that the creditor does have a valid security interest in the property, that the property qualifies as "cash collateral," that the creditor does not consent to the debtor's use of the cash collateral, and that the debtor files a request for court authorization, the critical issue for the court to decide will be whether the creditor's interest is adequately protected. Adequate protection is required by § 363(e), and is dealt with by § 361.[274]

The trustee or debtor in possession has the burden of proving adequate protection. § 363(p)(1). Having said that, the pro-debtor and pro-reorganization biases held by many bankruptcy courts may dispose the court favorably toward giving the debtor a chance to reorganize; that chance may be available only if the debtor is authorized to use cash collateral. Yet, the Code commands the court to protect the interests of the secured creditor. The court's task in reconciling these conflicting goals often is a daunting one, requiring the judge to make critical forecasts of the course of future events, at an early stage of the case when little information is available.

To a secured creditor, the proposition that anything can be an "adequate" replacement for cash is incredible. Yet, courts do permit debtors to use cash collateral. Probably the most sympathetic case for authorizing the use of cash collateral is when the cash will be used to finance the completion of work in process, and the creditor is given a replacement lien in the work to-be-completed. The foundational case is the 1950 chapter X reorganization of the Waltham Watch Company. In *Reconstruction Finance Corp. v. Kaplan (In re Waltham Watch Co.)*,[275] the trustees who took over the watch company were permitted to use cash collateral to complete the assembly of thousands of watches. The court found that the expenditure of $260,000 would increase the value of the inventory by $760,000.

Sometimes, though, the trade forced on the secured creditor of the bird-in-the-hand cash collateral for the replacement lien on the two-in-the-bush collateral to be

---

[273] The foundational case was Butner v. United States, 440 U.S. 48 (1979), in which the Supreme Court held that creditors must comply with state law procedures to obtain perfected interest in rents.

[274] See § 3.18–3.20.

[275] 185 F.2d 791 (1st Cir. 1950).

produced is less concrete and certain than finishing the assembly of watches. Examples where courts have allowed debtors to "bank on the come" with the secured creditor's cash include the planting of crops, with the creditor receiving a replacement lien in the crops to be grown,[276] and the drilling of oil and gas wells, with the creditor receiving a lien on the proceeds of the wells to be drilled.[277] In the common situation of retail businesses, courts often find adequate protection in the form of replacement liens in future inventory and receivables, perhaps also requiring some modest current regular payments.[278]

The court is much more likely to find that the creditor is adequately protected if there is an "equity cushion," i.e., if the value of the collateral exceeds the amount of the debt.[279] In making the equity cushion calculation, the court may have to value other collateral of the creditor. For example, the creditor might have a security interest in inventory and in cash collateral; the equity cushion computation would depend on the value ascribed to the inventory (the value of the cash usually is obvious). The outcome of that valuation might depend on whether the court uses a higher going concern value or a lower liquidation value. The Code gives the court wide latitude in making that determination, see § 506(a)(1); often the court will choose depending in part on its assessment of the likelihood that the debtor will be able to continue in business and reorganize successfully.

It is important to remember that an adequate protection decision is not set in concrete. Courts frequently give the debtor permission to use cash collateral for a relatively short period of time, such as 30 or 60 days, and then require the debtor to come back later for further permission, enabling the court to assess at the subsequent hearing the progress of the case and the adequacy of the protection previously given. Finally, even if adequate protection turns out to have been inadequate, the secured creditor may have a superpriority claim for the shortfall under § 507(b).

---

[276] See In re Sheehan, 38 B.R. 859 (Bankr. D.S.D. 1984). But see In re Martin, 761 F.2d 472 (8th Cir. 1985) (remanding finding that replacement lien on crops constituted adequate protection).

[277] See MBank Dallas, N.A. v. O'Connor (In re O'Connor), 808 F.2d 1393 (10th Cir. 1987).

[278] See, e.g., Chrysler Credit Corp. v. Ruggiere (In re George Ruggiere Chrysler–Plymouth, Inc.), 727 F.2d 1017 (11th Cir. 1984) (car dealership).

[279] See § 3.20. See, e.g., Worcester Cnty. Nat'l Bank v. Xinde Int'l, Inc. (In re Xinde Int'l, Inc.), 13 B.R. 212 (Bankr. D. Mass. 1981); see also Drake v. Franklin Equip. Co. (In re Franklin Equip. Co.), 416 B.R. 483 (Bankr. E.D. Va. 2009).

Chapter 6

THE TRUSTEE'S AVOIDING POWERS

A. INTRODUCTION

§ 6.1   The Meaning and Consequences of Avoidance

Some of the most utilized, analyzed, and criticized provisions of the Bankruptcy Code are the "avoiding powers" of the bankruptcy trustee. These avoiding powers (and corollary provisions) are found primarily in §§ 544 through 553.[1] They apply to cases under all chapters (except 15). § 103(a). The avoiding powers help implement the core principles of bankruptcy, as discussed in the next section.

What does it mean to say that the trustee has the power to "*avoid*" a transfer or obligation? "Avoidance" means that the transfer or obligation in question is being set aside, or invalidated, pursuant to a court order. The effect of avoidance depends on whether the transfer or obligation being avoided is (1) an outright transfer of property, or (2) a lien. If an outright transfer is avoided, the trustee will then attempt to recover either the specific property transferred, or its value, under § 550. If a lien is avoided, however, then in most cases the lien simply is nullified; the formerly secured creditor is relegated to unsecured status, and the property is freed from the encumbrance. Alternatively, the lienholder may retain the lien, and pay the trustee the value of the lien.

"Avoidance" is a concept that is distinct from "*recovery*." A transfer is *avoided* under one of the specific avoiding powers, such as § 547 for preferences, § 548 for fraudulent conveyances, and so forth. Avoidance is a judicial declaration that the transfer should be invalidated or set aside. Avoiding a transfer, however, by itself does not bring money or value into the bankruptcy estate. The only exception is when a lien is avoided. As noted above, avoidance frees the property from the lien, allowing the full value of the property to be dealt with as property of the bankruptcy estate. Otherwise, after avoidance the trustee still must bring an action to *recover* either the transferred property itself or the value of that property. Section 550 governs recovery.

The first option for recovery is for the trustee to proceed against either:

· the *initial transferee* of the avoided transfer

or

· the entity *for whose benefit* the transfer was made (subject to some exceptions). § 550(a)(1).

---

[1]   See § 6.2 for an overview of the different avoiding powers of the trustee.

Alternatively, the second option is for the trustee to recover from a *subsequent* transferee[2] of the initial transferee. § 550(a)(2). However, such a secondary transferee is protected to the extent that it took for value, in good faith, and without knowledge of the voidability of the transfer. § 550(b)(1). In addition, under the principle of derivative title, any transferee taking from or through a protected transferee is similarly protected, on the condition that it took in good faith. § 550(b)(2). In any event, the trustee is only entitled to a single satisfaction. § 550(d).

The liability of the *initial* transferee, unlike that of a subsequent transferee, is absolute. The rationale for the difference is that the initial transferee, who actually deals with the debtor transferor, should be in a better position to monitor the *bona fides* of the initial transfer. Because of this legal difference, determining whether a transferee is the initial or a subsequent transferee can be critically important, and sometimes difficult.[3] The hard cases are ones where nominally the initial transfer from the debtor goes to a third party before passing to the defendant transferee, but it is debatable whether that third party intermediary had sufficient independent dominion and control over the property transferred to count as a "transferee" for purposes of avoidance.[4] If that third party does have sufficient dominion and control, then it will be liable as the "initial" transferee, and the defendant will be a subsequent transferee and thus eligible for protection from recovery under § 550(b)(1) if it took in good faith, without knowledge of voidability, and for value. If, however, the third party does not count as the initial transferee, then the defendant transferee will be the "initial" transferee and its liability for recovery will be absolute. In making this determination, courts try to give effect to substance, not form.

A further exception to the recovery rules was added in 1994 to change the result in the infamous "*Deprizio*" case.[5] In *Deprizio*, the Seventh Circuit permitted the trustee to *recover* under § 550(a)(1) from a non-insider "initial transferee" as to whom the transfer was *not* avoidable,[6] when the transfer was avoided as to an insider. Now, under § 550(c), which overturns the *Deprizio* result, the trustee no longer is able to recover from a non-insider transferee based upon a transfer made more than 90 days before bankruptcy that is avoided only as against an insider. In 2005, a further amendment was made in an attempt to rectify a problem remaining after the 1994 change, to provide that when a transfer is avoided as an insider preference more than 90 days before bankruptcy, even the *avoidance* of the transfer applies only against the insider, and not the innocent non-insider. § 547(i). This change was necessary to protect non-insiders in cases where no "recovery" was sought, *viz.*., the avoidance of a

---

[2]   The subsequent transferee could be either the "immediate" or a "mediate" (meaning, after the "immediate") transferee from the initial transferee.

[3]   See, e.g., In re TOUSA, Inc., 680 F.3d 1298 (11th Cir. 2012); Schafer v. Las Vegas Hilton Corp. (In re Video Depot, Ltd.), 127 F.3d 1195 (9th Cir. 1997).

[4]   See *Schafer*, supra note 3; Bonded Fin. Servs., Inc. v. European Am. Bank, 838 F.2d 890, 891 (7th Cir. 1988); Goldman Sachs Execution & Clearing, L.P. v. Official Unsecured Creditors' Comm. of Bayou Grp., LLC, 491 Fed.Appx. 201 (2d Cir. 2012). See also In re Harwell, 628 F.3d 1312 (11th Cir. 2010) (holding that an attorney could be an initial transferee of a fraudulent transfer where the attorney temporarily held settlement proceeds in trust for the client and was not an "innocent participant" in the transfers).

[5]   Levit v. Ingersoll Rand Fin. Corp., 874 F.2d 1186 (7th Cir. 1989). See discussion in §§ 6.12, 6.26.

[6]   Recovery could not be had against the non-insider because the transfer was made outside the 90–day preference period. See § 6.15.

lien that was transferred to a non-insider but which benefited an insider (typically a guarantor). In such a situation, § 550(c), which only offers the non-insider immunity from "recovery," would not help the non-insider.

If property is recovered from an entity under § 550, that entity will have a claim against the estate in that amount, assuming that the claim otherwise would be allowable. § 502(h). In essence, the idea is to restore the *status quo ante*. For example, assume that Creditor X had a $5,000 claim against the Debtor, and was paid in full the day before bankruptcy. If that payment is avoided as a preference under § 547, and recovery is ordered under § 550, Creditor X will have to pay the $5,000 back to the trustee, but, upon doing so, will again have its $5,000 claim against the estate. § 502(d).

Another concept that plays a part in the avoidance scheme is the *preservation* of an avoided transfer.[7] Under § 551, a transfer that is avoided is "preserved" for the benefit of the estate. This rule ensures that the bankruptcy estate (and thus the creditors of the debtor) will actually reap the benefits of avoidance. A simple example illustrates this point. Assume that property of the estate worth $15,000 is subject to two liens: a senior lien that secures a debt of $10,000, and a junior lien that secures a $20,000 debt. Assume further that the senior lien, but not the junior lien, is avoided by the trustee. What happens? Without preservation of the avoided transfer, the previously junior lienholder would become the senior lien, and nothing would be left for the estate;[8] the entire $15,000 in collateral value would go to the unavoided junior lien. With § 551, however, the estate takes the place of the avoided senior lien. In other words, the estate now would be entitled to the first $10,000 of value in the property (the amount avoided), and the junior lien takes the remainder. Furthermore, unlike an action for recovery, preservation of an avoided transfer occurs automatically.[9]

Property recovered and preserved by the trustee under § 550 and § 551 does not always end up in the estate. If the debtor would have had a valid exemption claim if the property had not been transferred, the debtor will still be able to claim that exemption after recovery of the property. § 522(g). The debtor only has this exemption right, however, if the transfer was not voluntarily made and the debtor did not conceal the transfer.[10]

A transfer that is subject to one of the avoiding powers is not void, but is only *voidable*. In other words, the trustee must bring a lawsuit to avoid the transfer under one of the statutory avoiding powers. The proceeding to avoid the transfer must be brought before the expiration of the statute of limitations in § 546(a) (except that a transfer to avoid a postpetition transfer under § 549 is subject to a special statute of

---

[7] See generally John C. McCoid, II, Preservation of Avoided Transfers and Liens, 77 Va. L. Rev. 1091 (1991).

[8] See H.R. Rep. No. 95–595, 95th Cong., 1st Sess., at 376 (1977).

[9] See, e.g., In re Trout, 609 F.3d 1106, 1108 (10th Cir. 2010).

[10] See, e.g., In re Duncan, 329 F.3d 1195 (10th Cir. 2003).

limitations in § 549(d)).[11] In a chapter 11 case, the debtor in possession has the power to bring avoiding actions. § 1107(a). Interested parties other than the trustee (or debtor in possession), such as the official creditors' committee in chapter 11, have standing to bring an avoidance action on behalf of the estate only if authorized to do so by the court, in the same vein as in a derivative action.[12] Also, the debtor is given a limited authority to exercise avoiding powers in the trustee's stead if the debtor would then be able to claim an exemption in the property recovered. § 522(h).

Prior to the 1994 amendments, the statute of limitations in § 546(a) produced enormous confusion in the courts. One issue that had divided the courts in chapter 11 cases was whether the statute began to run at the inception of the case, or only when a trustee was appointed under § 1104(a).[13] Although the statutory language triggering the limitations period referred to the "appointment" of a trustee (thus favoring the latter interpretation), a majority of the courts of appeals considering the issue instead held that the period began to run at commencement. These courts reasoned that since a trustee is not routinely appointed in chapter 11 cases, and since the debtor in possession is vested with the rights and powers of a trustee, § 1107(a), including the power to bring avoidance actions, the reference to "trustee" in § 546(a) should be read to include the debtor in possession.

Another problem in applying § 546(a) arose when cases were *converted* from one chapter to another, usually from chapter 11 to chapter 7. The question was whether a new limitations period was triggered by the appointment of a new trustee in the superseding case. Again the courts were divided, although the courts of appeals agreed that conversion did not give rise to a new limitations period.[14]

These issues were settled by the 1994 amendments to § 546(a)(1). Under the amended version, the limitations period for actions under §§ 544, 545, 547, 548, or 553 is the *later* of:

- two years after the entry of the order for relief,

or

- one year after the appointment or election of the first trustee appointed or elected under any chapter, *if* that appointment or election occurs before the

---

[11] More specifically, the limitation periods in § 546 end at midnight on the applicable anniversary date (either two years after the entry of the order of relief, or one year after the appointment or election of the first trustee). See, e.g, In re Raynor, 617 F.3d 1065 (8th Cir. 2010).

[12] See, e.g., In re Trailer Source, Inc., 555 F.3d 231 (6th Cir. 2009); Official Comm. of Unsecured Creditors of Cybergenics Corp. ex. rel. Cybergenics Corp. v. Chinery, 330 F.3d 548 (3d Cir. 2003); In re Commodore Intl. Ltd., 262 F.3d 96 (2d Cir. 2001). See also In re Racing Servs., Inc., 540 F.3d 892 (8th Cir. 2008) (holding that a creditor may bring a derivative suit where the trustee consents or does not oppose such suit).

[13] Compare In re Maxway Corp., 27 F.3d 980 (4th Cir. 1994) (only begins to run when trustee appointed), with In re Century Brass Prods., Inc., 22 F.3d 37 (2d Cir. 1994) (begins to run upon filing of case).

[14] Compare In re MS55, Inc., 477 F.3d 1131 (10th Cir. 2007) (no new limitations period), with In re Ajayem Lumber Corp., 145 B.R. 813 (Bankr. S.D.N.Y. 1992) (new limitations period triggered).

expiration of the two year period following entry of the order for relief. § 546(a)(1).

In any event, the action may not be brought after the time the bankruptcy case is closed or dismissed. § 546(a)(2).

Thus, under the amended version of § 546(a)(1), the two-year limitations period will begin to run in a chapter 11 case when the order for relief is entered (i.e., at the commencement of the case in a voluntary case), *but* if an actual trustee (*not* the debtor in possession) is appointed or elected before that two-year period expires, that trustee will have an additional year to file an avoidance action. The same rule will govern in converted cases: if conversion occurs and a trustee is appointed for the first time in the chapter 7 case, that trustee will have a year to bring an action, but only if that trustee is appointed or elected within two years of the initial entry of the order for relief.[15] Thus, the absolute latest an avoidance action could conceivably be brought is three years after the order for relief—if a trustee is appointed or elected exactly two years after the order for relief, that trustee gets another year to file. The time limit cannot exceed three years, because if a trustee is first appointed or elected even one day more than two years after the entry of the order for relief, that trustee would not get more time; the limitations period would have expired at the two-year mark.

As noted earlier, a separate limitations period applies to actions to avoid *post*-petition transfers under § 549. The need for this different period stems from the fact that the transfer to be avoided by definition occurs *after* the commencement of the case. It would be nonsensical to bind the trustee to a limitations period that began to run before the offending transfer was even made. Instead, the trustee is given two years after the date of the transfer to sue, but in any event always must bring the action before the bankruptcy case is closed or dismissed. § 549(d).

A further limitations period applies to actions to *recover* an avoided transfer under § 550. Recall that avoidance of the transfer and recovery of the property transferred (or its value) are distinct concepts; recovery can only occur after a transfer has first been avoided. The trustee must bring the *recovery* action within one year of the time the transfer is avoided, and before the case is closed or dismissed. § 550(f).

A final restriction on the trustee's avoiding powers under §§ 544(a), 545, 547, and 549 (thus excluding fraudulent transfers under §§ 548 and 544(b)) is the seller's right of reclamation, as spelled out in § 546(c).[16] As amended in 2005, § 546(c)(1) provides that the enumerated avoiding powers are subject to the right of a seller of goods to reclaim goods sold in the ordinary course of business and within 45 days of bankruptcy to a debtor who was insolvent when it received the goods. The seller must give written notice within a specified time period of its demand to reclaim. The 2005 changes in the statute (1) deleted explicit reference to non-bankruptcy reclamation rights; (2) added a 45–day reclamation period; and (3) made explicit that the seller's reclamation right was subject to prior secured claims. The deletion of the reference to non-bankruptcy

---

[15] See, e.g., In re Draiman, 714 F.3d 462 (7th Cir. 2013).

[16] See § 7.37.

reclamation rights has caused some confusion as to whether Congress thus meant to create for the first time an independent, free-standing federal bankruptcy right of reclamation. Before 2005, there was no question that a seller had to rely on a non-bankruptcy reclamation right (such as U.C.C. § 2–702); all that former § 546(c) did was acknowledge the legitimacy of such non-bankruptcy claims in the context of a federal bankruptcy case, and impose some limits on the enforcement of those rights. The better view is that sellers still must look to non-bankruptcy law as the source of their reclamation right, but may take advantage of the longer 45–day period provided in § 546(c)(1).

§ 6.2   Overview of Trustee's Avoiding Powers

The Bankruptcy Code contains a series of avoiding powers, which are designed to accomplish a variety of policy goals. To understand what purposes and functions the avoiding powers serve, one must first look at the underlying purposes of bankruptcy.

Bankruptcy is a collective proceeding designed to address, in an equitable manner, the special problems that exist when a debtor has multiple creditors and insufficient assets to pay all creditors in full. From the viewpoint of creditors, the underlying goals of a bankruptcy case are to deal with all creditors on an equitable basis, and to maximize the value of the estate available for distribution to the entire body of creditors. The avoiding powers of the bankruptcy trustee are designed to help implement these fundamental bankruptcy policies, by setting aside certain types of transfers that might interfere with the realization of these goals, and by recapturing the value of those avoided transfers for the benefit of the estate.[17] Furthermore, the potential availability of the avoiding powers in a bankruptcy case may influence the behavior of parties operating in the shadow of bankruptcy.

A primary bankruptcy policy is *equality of distribution* among similarly situated creditors. Bankruptcy's scheme of pro rata distribution replaces the "race of diligence" that governs outside of bankruptcy, pursuant to which creditors who act first to satisfy their claims are paid first; "first in time is first in right" is a descriptive maxim of non-bankruptcy collection law. Yet the transition from the race paradigm that is effective under non-bankruptcy law to the equality paradigm that is operative inside of bankruptcy is not always easily effectuated. Either the debtor or certain creditors may see bankruptcy coming, and attempt to move quickly to avoid the bankruptcy distributional scheme. Transfers preferring some creditors may even be made after the commencement of the bankruptcy case.

Accordingly, several of the avoiding powers attempt to preserve the equality principle in bankruptcy by unwinding transfers that would subvert equality. For example, § 547 allows the trustee to avoid preferential transfers made shortly before the commencement of the bankruptcy case that otherwise would allow the creditor to receive more than its fair share of the debtor's assets.[18] Section 549 carries this same principle over into the post-filing period.[19] Under § 553(b), the trustee may recover an

---

[17]   See generally Thomas H. Jackson, Avoiding Powers in Bankruptcy, 36 Stan. L. Rev. 725 (1984).

[18]   See §§ 6.7–6.8.

[19]   See § 6.47.

amount set off by a creditor in the immediate pre-bankruptcy period to the extent that the setoff enabled the creditor to improve its position.[20] Section 545(1) authorizes the avoidance of certain statutory liens that become effective only in the event of insolvency or bankruptcy.[21] In sum, all of these avoiding powers are designed to prevent creditors or the debtor from opting out of the bankruptcy system of equal distribution.

Bankruptcy, as an equitable proceeding, seeks to promote fairness among creditors and honesty in the debtor's dealings with creditors. Some of the avoiding powers are directed at promoting these principles. One evil that commercial law long has sought to guard against is *secret* liens and interests. The problem is one of ostensible ownership. The debtor may convey property or grant a lien on collateral to some entity without recording it in the public records. Creditors then may do business with the debtor under the false impression that the debtor has unfettered ownership of the secretly conveyed or encumbered assets. In the equitable bankruptcy proceeding, the *ostensible* state of the debtor's affairs is rendered the *actual* state of affairs by operation of the avoiding powers. Thus, the "strong-arm" clause, § 544(a), empowers the trustee to avoid liens and conveyances that have not been perfected or recorded by the time the bankruptcy case is filed.[22] Section 545(2) embodies a similar rule with regard to unrecorded statutory liens.[23] A secret lien that is recorded shortly before bankruptcy may be avoided as a preference under § 547.[24]

Some types of transfers may be avoided even apart from a collective bankruptcy proceeding. The focus of these powers, then, cannot be to protect the rights of creditors as against each other, for that policy inheres only in a collective proceeding such as bankruptcy. Rather, the impetus for these non-bankruptcy avoiding powers is to ensure that the debtor deal fairly with its creditors. That concern exists in or out of bankruptcy. For over 400 years, the principle means by which the law has effectuated this policy is through fraudulent conveyance law.[25] Creditors may set aside fraudulent transfers by the debtor under state law outside of bankruptcy. If a bankruptcy case is commenced, the power of creditors to set aside fraudulent conveyances passes to the trustee under § 544(b), so that the fruits of avoidance may be enjoyed by all creditors.[26] In addition, the Bankruptcy Code contains a separate provision authorizing the trustee to avoid fraudulent transfers. § 548.[27]

Finally, the *debtor,* and not the trustee, is vested with limited avoiding powers designed to protect the debtor's exemptions.[28] § 522(f). The debtor may avoid the fixing of a lien on the debtor's property, if that lien impairs an exemption to which the debtor

---

[20]   See § 6.28.

[21]   See § 6.49.

[22]   See §§ 6.3, 6.4.

[23]   See § 6.51.

[24]   See § 6.9.

[25]   See §§ 6.29–6.46.

[26]   See §§ 6.5, 6.29.

[27]   See § 6.29.

[28]   See §§ 9.7–9.11.

otherwise would have been entitled, and if the lien is either a judicial lien or a nonpossessory, nonpurchase-money security interest in items such as household goods.

B. THE STRONG ARM CLAUSE: § 544(a)

§ 6.3   The Trustee as a Hypothetical Lien Creditor

One of the most important of the trustee's avoiding powers is the *"strong arm"* clause, codified in § 544(a).[29] The strong arm clause gives the bankruptcy trustee the power to avoid some types of unrecorded, i.e., *secret,* liens and conveyances. Unrecorded interests implicate the problem of ostensible ownership. The concern is that creditors will do business with the debtor under the mistaken impression that the debtor has a larger pool of assets backing the enterprise than is really the case. When the debtor goes bankrupt, the trustee may use the strong arm clause to preclude entities holding secret interests from asserting those claims to the detriment of the theoretically misled creditors. Note, however, that § 544(a) does not require proof of actual reliance or detriment; any unrecorded interest that is vulnerable under the statute may be avoided.

Section 544(a) has three subsections, each vesting the bankruptcy trustee with somewhat different powers. Under § 544(a)(1), the trustee is given the powers of a *judicial lien creditor*; under subsection (2), the trustee has the rights of an *unsatisfied execution creditor*; and under (3), the trustee is imbued with the status of a *bona fide purchaser of real property*. The first and the third are by far the most important of these powers. The second power only has independent utility if state law gives unsatisfied execution creditors greater rights than standard judicial lien creditors. Under subsection (1), discussed in this section, the trustee will be able to avoid *unperfected security interests in personal property*; under § 544(a)(3), discussed in the following section, *unrecorded real property conveyances* may be set aside.

Several critical points bear on the application of § 544(a) under any of the subsections. First, the strong arm power focuses on the situation at the time that the bankruptcy case is *commenced*, i.e., the time that the bankruptcy petition is filed. An interest that is sufficiently recorded or perfected at any time before the bankruptcy filing will not be vulnerable under the strong arm clause (although avoidance as a preference under § 547 still may be possible). At the same time, postpetition recordation will not save an interest from avoidance under § 544(a), with one exception discussed below.

Second, the trustee is given the rights and powers of a *hypothetical* lien creditor, execution creditor, or bona fide purchaser. That is, there does not have to be any *actual* lien creditor, execution creditor, or bona fide purchaser in existence in order for the trustee to proceed under § 544(a). By contrast, § 544(b), which permits the trustee to invoke state fraudulent conveyance laws,[30] requires the trustee to find an actual

---

[29] See generally David G. Carlson, The Trustee's Strong Arm Power Under the Bankruptcy Code, 43 S.C. L. Rev. 841 (1992); John C. McCoid, II, Bankruptcy, the Avoiding Powers, and Unperfected Security Interests, 59 Am. Bankr. L.J. 175 (1985).

[30] See § 6.5.

unsecured creditor who would have the power to set aside the transfer under non-bankruptcy law.

A third important general principle under § 544(a) is that any actual *knowledge* that the trustee (or debtor in possession) or any creditor may have is irrelevant. The trustee is conclusively deemed *not* to have knowledge. Thus, for example, if the priority between a bona fide purchaser and the holder of an unrecorded conveyance turns on whether the purchaser had actual knowledge of the existence of the unrecorded interest, the trustee would be deemed *not* to have knowledge, *even if* the trustee actually does know of the unrecorded interest. This rule has proven to be most pertinent in chapter 11 cases in which the debtor in possession, invoking its powers as trustee, is seeking to avoid the secret interest; having made the secret transfer in question, the debtor (now serving as debtor in possession) obviously knows of the existence of that interest.

Fourth, application of the strong arm clause will require the court to look to non-bankruptcy law, usually *state law*. The outcome under § 544(a) will depend on who would have priority under the governing non-bankruptcy law in a battle between (1) the holder of the secret interest and (2) a lien creditor (under § 544(a)(1)), an unsatisfied execution creditor (§ 544(a)(2)), or a bona fide purchaser (§ 544(a)(3)). In the vast majority of cases, the governing law in cases under subsection (1) will be Article 9 of the Uniform Commercial Code, which governs priority disputes between a lien creditor and the holder of an unperfected security interest. Under subsection (3), the state real property recording law normally will be the governing body of law.

The foregoing principles apply, as noted, to all subsections of the strong arm power. The individual subsections serve specific purposes as well. Subsection (1) focuses on secret liens or unrecorded interests in *personal* property. By far the most important, although not the exclusive, application of § 544(a)(1) is with regard to security interests in personal property under Article 9 of the Uniform Commercial Code. Bankruptcy in general and the strong arm clause in particular are the crucibles in which "perfection" under Article 9 is most often tested.

To understand how § 544(a)(1) operates to permit the avoidance of unperfected security interests, some understanding of Article 9 priority rules is necessary. First, the difference between the concepts of "*attachment*" and "*perfection*" must be understood. A security interest in personal property is enforceable by the secured party *against the debtor* once the security interest has "attached" under U.C.C. § 9–203. Attachment occurs once the debtor has agreed to grant a security interest in the collateral (and has properly memorialized that agreement), value has been given, and the debtor has rights in the collateral. U.C.C. § 9–203(b)(1)–(3). Perfection is not required for attachment. Perfection is required, however, to give the secured party the fullest protection that it can have *against third parties*—including the bankruptcy trustee. Perfection most often is accomplished by the filing of a "financing statement" in the public records of the state. See U.C.C. § 9–310(a) and Part 5 (Filing) of Article 9. An "unperfected security interest" is a security interest that has attached but which has not been perfected.

The critical priority rule in Article 9 that is given effect in bankruptcy via § 544(a)(1) is the rule of U.C.C. § 9–317(a)(2):

A security interest . . . is subordinate to the rights of . . . a person that becomes a lien creditor before . . . the security interest . . . is perfected.

In other words, a lien creditor takes priority over an unperfected security interest. Applying this critical rule to the bankruptcy strong arm clause leads inexorably to the result that the bankruptcy trustee, who is given the rights and powers of a *lien creditor* under § 544(a)(1), will be able to avoid a security interest that is *unperfected* at the time the bankruptcy case is commenced. By inference, the trustee using the strong arm clause will not be able to avoid a security interest that is perfected as of the commencement of bankruptcy. The decisive issue, then, always will be whether the security interest was perfected at the instant the bankruptcy case was filed.

Consider a simple illustration. On March 1, Debtor grants Creditor a security interest in property, and the security interest attaches. On March 10, Debtor files bankruptcy. Creditor has not perfected its security interest by March 10. The trustee in Debtor's bankruptcy case will be able to avoid Creditor's security interest under § 544(a)(1). The effect will be that the security interest will be eliminated, and Creditor will become an unsecured creditor. The property that had been subject to Creditor's security interest now will be available for distribution to the general creditors as property of the bankruptcy estate, unencumbered by any lien in favor of Creditor. If, however, Creditor had perfected its security interest on March 9, before the bankruptcy filing, its security interest could not have been avoided under the strong arm clause.

What is the justification for the rule embodied in § 544(a)(1)? That rule effectively gives the debtor's general unsecured creditors the benefit of the rights of a lien creditor, even though none of those unsecured creditors in fact has actually become a lien creditor by the time of the bankruptcy filing. As the statute is written, this is not a problem; remember that the trustee's power of avoidance under § 544(a)(1) does not depend on the existence of any *actual* lien creditors. But why is the statute written that way? If bankruptcy had not intervened, there would have been a priority race under Article 9 (U.C.C. § 9–317(a)(2)) between the holder of the unperfected security interest and all of the unsecured creditors that had not yet obtained a judicial lien. The winner would be the first party to take the required action: if the unperfected secured creditor perfected before any unsecured creditor obtained a judicial lien, the secured creditor would win; but if an unsecured creditor became a lien creditor before the secured party perfected, that lien creditor would win. The bankruptcy filing interrupts that race, before a "winner" is determined; after filing, the secured party cannot perfect and unsecured creditors cannot obtain judicial liens. § 362(a). Section 544(a)(1) in effect declares that the unresolved race is a "tie": the collateral goes back into the bankruptcy estate, where it will be shared equally by all unsecured creditors and by the formerly secured creditor.

The strong arm clause in § 544(a)(1) also is motivated by an antipathy towards secret liens. The worry is that the general creditors of the debtor will be misled into extending credit on an unsecured basis by the absence of any public record of the secured creditor's security interest. If the secured creditor nevertheless could enforce that unrecorded security interest against the collateral in the event of the debtor's bankruptcy, the misled general creditors would be harmed. Assets that they assumed would be available to pay off their claims if the debtor defaulted would not be, and their recovery would be diminished. By denying enforcement in bankruptcy to such an unrecorded security interest, the general creditors are protected against what is sometimes considered almost a species of fraud.

That account is a long-held and oft-repeated justification, but has some serious explanatory weaknesses. More pointedly, it makes for a nice story, but it just isn't true. Note first that there is no requirement in § 544(a)(1) that any actual unsecured creditors of the debtor be misled by the incomplete state of the public record. Indeed, there is not even a requirement that there *be* any unsecured creditors in order for the trustee to take advantage of the strong arm power. In short, no proof of actual reliance by unsecured creditors on the absence of any public filing is required. Nor is this a situation where we believe that general creditors usually do check the public record, but simply excuse proof of what we believe is likely true but hard to prove in bankruptcy. Quite the contrary—the reality is that most unsecured creditors would not check for Article 9 filings before extending unsecured credit. Furthermore, by extending unsecured credit in the first place, the general creditors have assumed a non-trivial risk that they will lose to an unperfected secured creditor outside of bankruptcy. Under Article 9, even an unperfected secured creditor is entitled to enforce its security interest against the collateral upon the debtor's default. U.C.C. §§ 9–201(a), 9–601(a). Be all that as it may, though, the anti-secret lien mantra is alive, well, and powerful.

The timing rule of § 544(a), *viz.*, that the outcome is determined as of the moment the bankruptcy case is filed, is subject to one important exception. Non-bankruptcy *relation back rules* of general applicability are given effect in bankruptcy under § 544(a). § 546(b). In other words, if a non-bankruptcy rule would permit subsequent perfection of a lien to be effective against prior intervening parties, i.e., would "relate back" the perfection to a point in time before the intervening party's interest arose, then bankruptcy will time that perfection as of the earlier relation back point. Thus, § 544(a) uses "legal fiction" time, rather than calendar time.

The most common example of this relation back rule is for "purchase money security interests." Another common example is for mechanics' and materialmens' liens. A "purchase money" security interest is one in which the collateral subject to the security interest was purchased by the debtor with the money loaned by the secured creditor, i.e., the creditor loaned the debtor the "purchase money," and is granted a security interest in the property purchased. U.C.C. § 9–103. Under U.C.C. § 9–317(e), the secured party is given a *grace period* of 20 days to perfect the security interest after the debtor receives delivery of the collateral. If the secured party perfects before the expiration of the 20–day grace period, the secured party will take priority over the rights of a lien creditor which arise between the time the security interest attached and the time of perfection. In short, the perfection is deemed to "relate back" to the time of attachment. That relation back is effective both outside of bankruptcy and also in bankruptcy, to escape the clutches of the strong arm power.

The example used earlier will illustrate the point. The Creditor's security interest attached on March 1, and the Debtor filed bankruptcy on March 10. If Creditor has a *purchase money* security interest, Creditor will be able to perfect at any time until March 21, within the twenty-day grace period of U.C.C. § 9–317(e), and the effective date of Creditor's perfection then will be deemed to relate back to March 1. As of the date bankruptcy was filed, then, Creditor will be deemed to be perfected, and the trustee will not be able to avoid Creditor's security interest under § 544(a)(1). Note that the postpetition perfection of the security interest would not violate the automatic stay.[31] § 362(b)(3).

§ 6.4 The Trustee as Hypothetical Bona Fide Purchaser

The trustee's strong arm power enables the trustee to set aside unrecorded real estate interests under § 544(a)(3). That section vests the trustee with the rights and powers of a bona fide purchaser (BFP) of real property. Thus, if under applicable non-bankruptcy law a BFP would prevail over an unrecorded interest, that unrecorded interest may be avoided under § 544(a)(3). Thus, for example, an improperly executed mortgage may be vulnerable under subsection (3).[32] As is true with the strong arm clause generally,[33] subsection (3) is applied as of the time of the commencement of the case; the trustee is endowed with hypothetical BFP status, irrespective of whether an actual BFP exists, and any actual knowledge of the trustee, debtor in possession, or any creditor is ignored. Unlike the trustee's power as a hypothetical lien creditor, which had long antecedents under the bankruptcy law, the provision in § 544(a)(3) conferring the powers of a BFP on the trustee was an innovation of the 1978 Code.[34]

The justification for the strong arm clause as embodied in § 544(a)(3) is even more difficult to pinpoint than its counterpart in subsection (a)(1). Under the other parts of the strong arm clause, the trustee, acting as the representative of general unsecured creditors, exercises a power that general creditors conceivably could have exercised outside of bankruptcy. Recall from the preceding section that a general unsecured creditor conceivably *could* defeat an unperfected security interest under non-bankruptcy law, if the general creditor acquired a judicial lien before the secured party perfected its security interest. U.C.C. § 9–317(a)(2). With regard to unrecorded interests in real estate, however, general unsecured creditors normally are *not* within the class of parties protected by state recording laws. Those laws instead usually only give precedence to the rights of *purchasers*, not to unsecured creditors. It is possible, through an execution sale, that the rights of a general creditor could eventually lead to a "purchase" of the property, but § 544(a)(3) is not limited to such narrow circumstances. In short, § 544(a)(3) appears to give unsecured creditors the power to reach interests in property that they could not have reached outside of bankruptcy. Among other problems, this fact may lead to forum shopping, as general creditors will have an incentive to commence a bankruptcy case solely to take advantage of § 544(a)(3)'s extended reach. The probable intention of Congress in enacting § 544(a)(3) was to deal broadly with the whole problem of ostensible ownership and secret liens. The historic antipathy towards secret liens likely reared its head, on the unthinking assumption that secret liens on real estate should be avoided in the same way that secret liens on personal property already were avoided. As just noted, though, under non-bankruptcy law there is a critical difference between the two, in that unsecured creditors can readily defeat an unrecorded security interest in personal property (by

---

[31] See § 3.13.

[32] See, e.g., In re Huffman, 408 F.3d 290 (6th Cir. 2005).

[33] See § 6.3.

[34] S. Rep. No. 95–989, 95th Cong., 2d Sess., at 85 (1978).

becoming a "lien creditor"), but generally cannot defeat an unrecorded real estate interest. The basic difficulty with § 544(a)(3), then, is that there is no obvious bankruptcy policy that dictates resolving the secret lien/ostensible ownership issue differently inside a bankruptcy case than it is under non-bankruptcy law.

Two types of problems have arisen in applying § 544(a)(3). The first has to do with the issue of the relevance of *knowledge*. Under applicable non-bankruptcy law, the outcome of a priority dispute between a purchaser and the holder of an unrecorded interest may turn on whether that particular purchaser had actual knowledge of the unrecorded interest. Assume that a debtor grants a mortgage, but the mortgage is not recorded. The debtor then files chapter 11, and is continued as debtor in possession. Then the debtor acting in its capacity as debtor in possession, exercising its powers as a trustee, see § 1107(a), seeks to avoid the unrecorded mortgage as a hypothetical BFP under § 544(a)(3). The mortgagee counters that the debtor cannot set aside the mortgage, because the debtor has actual knowledge of the mortgage that it granted. If state law would give the mortgagee priority over a purchaser with knowledge, some courts in this type of case have held that the unrecorded interest cannot be avoided under § 544(a)(3).[35]

This result, however, is plainly erroneous, as most courts have recognized.[36] It ignores the express statutory language in § 544(a) that the section is to be applied "without regard to any knowledge of the trustee or of any creditor," and the fact that under § 1107(a) a debtor in possession has all of the rights and powers of a trustee. If this interpretation were correct, the result would be that the unrecorded interest could not be set aside as long as the debtor remains in possession, but then could be avoided if a trustee were appointed to replace the debtor in possession.

Courts must at the same time be careful not to be overly zealous in applying the "without knowledge" rule. All that the rule means is that the *actual* knowledge of any particular entity will not be relevant. It does not mean that knowledge attributed to the entire world must be ignored. This issue comes up in cases in which *constructive* notice is important. For example, assume that the debtor conveys an interest in real estate to a purchaser, and the purchaser fails to record the conveyance. However, the purchaser takes up residence on the conveyed property. Under state law, this "clear and open possession" would suffice to provide notice to the world of the purchaser's interest, and would preclude any entity from qualifying as a BFP with a superior entitlement to the property. In such a case, the trustee should not be able to avoid the unrecorded conveyance.[37]

The other type of case in which § 544(a)(3) has produced controversy is when the debtor holds legal title only to the property in question, as a trustee or nominee, subject to the equitable interests of the beneficiaries. A basic principle of bankruptcy

---

[35]   See, e.g., In re Hartman Paving, 745 F.2d 307 (4th Cir. 1984).

[36]   See, e.g., In re Probasco, 839 F.2d 1352 (9th Cir. 1988); In re Sandy Ridge Oil Co., 807 F.2d 1332 (7th Cir. 1986).

[37]   See, e.g., McCannon v. Marston, 679 F.2d 13 (3d Cir. 1982). See also In re Codrington, 691 F.3d 1336 (11th Cir. 2012) (certifying to the Georgia Supreme Court whether a security deed lacking a required component still provides constructive notice as to prevent a trustee from avoiding the conveyance).

law is that only the debtor's legal interest becomes property of the bankruptcy estate; the equitable interest remains outside of the estate. § 541(d).[38] The problem arises if the debtor's limited status as holder of the legal title only is not reflected in the public records, and if applicable non-bankruptcy law would permit the debtor to convey the property to a BFP free of the unrecorded equitable interests. In such a situation, a straightforward application of § 544(a)(3) would appear to permit the bankruptcy trustee to avoid the equitable interests as well.

Some courts have perceived a "conflict" between § 541(d) and § 544(a)(3) in this type of case. They then conclude that § 541(d) must prevail, and deny avoidance.[39] The prevailing view, however, is that avoidance under § 544(a)(3) should still be permitted.[40] Nothing in § 544(a)(3) suggests a limitation on its operation to accommodate § 541(d). Indeed, a careful reading of § 541(d) shows that it only excludes property from the estate under § 541(a)(1) and (2); under § 541(a)(3), the estate includes property recovered by the trustee under § 550. Avoidance has been ordered even when the debtor holds the property pursuant to a constructive trust, as a result of having defrauded investors.[41] The potential "conflict" would be eliminated in many cases, however, if courts adopt the view of the Sixth Circuit that constructive trusts are remedial devices only, and do not automatically convey the type of equitable interest in property that must be respected in bankruptcy under § 541(d).[42]

C. THE TRUSTEE AS SUCCESSOR TO ACTUAL CREDITORS: § 544(b)

§ 6.5 The Application of § 544(b)

Section 544(b)(1) gives the trustee the powers of actual unsecured creditors to avoid transfers under applicable non-bankruptcy law.[43] In essence, the trustee succeeds to the rights of a creditor with the power to avoid a transfer, for the benefit of the entire bankruptcy estate. Section 544(b)(1) applies if two criteria are met: (1) a creditor exists who has the power under applicable non-bankruptcy law to avoid a transfer, and (2) that creditor holds an allowable unsecured claim in the bankruptcy case. The most important application of § 544(b)(1), by far, is to add *state* fraudulent conveyance laws to the arsenal of the trustee's avoiding powers. Pleasingly short, § 544(b)(1) provides in principal part:

[T]he trustee may avoid any transfer of an interest of the debtor in property or any obligation incurred by the debtor that is voidable under applicable law by a

---

[38] See § 5.8.

[39] See, e.g., In re Quality Holstein Leasing, 752 F.2d 1009 (5th Cir. 1985).

[40] See Belisle v. Plunkett, 877 F.2d 512 (7th Cir.), cert. denied, 493 U.S. 893 (1989); In re Day 443 B.R. 338 (Bankr. D.N.J. 2011). See generally Carlos J. Cuevas, Bankruptcy Code Section 544(a) and Constructive Trusts: The Trustee's Strong Arm Powers Should Prevail, 21 Seton Hall L. Rev. 678 (1991); Jeffrey Davis, Equitable Liens and Constructive Trusts in Bankruptcy: Judicial Values and the Limits of Bankruptcy Distribution Policy, 41 Fla. L. Rev. 1 (1989).

[41] *Belisle,* supra note 40, 877 F.2d 512.

[42] In re Omegas Grp., Inc., 16 F.3d 1443 (6th Cir. 1994). See generally Emily Sherwin, Constructive Trusts in Bankruptcy, 1989 U. Ill. L. Rev. 297 (1989).

[43] S. Rep. No. 95–989, 95th Cong., 2d Sess., at 85 (1978).

creditor holding an unsecured claim that is allowable under section 502 of this title.

Section 544(b)(1) differs from the strong arm power of § 544(a)[44] in several critical respects. First, under subsection (b)(1) there must be an *actual* creditor with a power of avoidance into whose shoes the trustee can step; under subsection (a), by contrast, the trustee has the power of a hypothetical creditor without knowledge. Second, section (b)(1) only applies to transfers that are voidable by *unsecured* creditors; under (a), the trustee is given the powers of a "lien creditor,"[45] § 544(a)(1), and a bona fide purchaser,[46] § 544(a)(3). Finally, the timing focus of the two sections is different: subsection (b)(1) permits the avoidance of transfers that occurred *prior* to the bankruptcy filing, while subsection (a) allows a trustee to avoid liens and conveyances that are unrecorded at the instant the bankruptcy case is filed.

In one important regard subsections (a) and (b) of § 544 are similar. The substantive power of avoidance in each case depends on applicable non-bankruptcy law, which usually is state law. Recall that under § 544(a)(1), avoidance turns on the application of state laws governing the rights of "lien creditors" (primarily Article 9), and that § 544(a)(3) requires an inquiry into state real estate recording statutes.

Under § 544(b)(1), any "applicable law" that would permit an *unsecured* creditor to avoid a transaction may be invoked by the trustee in bankruptcy. The most significant of these is the fraudulent conveyance laws of the states. Some states have adopted the Uniform Fraudulent Transfer Act (UFTA), promulgated in 1985; a few still have the Uniform Fraudulent Conveyance Act (UFCA), circa 1918; and still others have some vestige of the ancient Statute of Elizabeth.[47]

Fraudulent conveyance laws are not the only "applicable" laws potentially available to the trustee under § 544(b). Bulk sales laws are still in force in a number of states, such as the old version of UCC § 6–107, giving unsecured creditors the power to avoid certain bulk transfers.[48] The consignment provision of Article 2, § 2–326, also affords an avoidance right to unsecured creditors. Finally, some states have their own *preference* laws, which may vary in particulars from § 547, the Code's preference section. The courts have differed on whether a state preference law is available to the trustee under § 544(b)(1).[49] The concern expressed is whether a state preference law,

---

[44]   See §§ 6.3, 6.4.

[45]   See § 6.3.

[46]   See § 6.4.

[47]   See § 6.29.

[48]   The Permanent Editorial Board of the Uniform Commercial Code recommended the repeal of Article 6 as being unnecessary in today's marketplace. For states that want to retain a bulk sales law, however, an Alternative B to Article 6 is still offered. Even under that law, though, the current recommended version of UCC § 6–107 does not authorize an unsecured creditor to avoid the transfer. Nevertheless, some states may have the old § 6–107 still in effect, and if they do, that law could be used in § 544(b)(1).

[49]   Compare In re Rexplore Drilling, 971 F.2d 1219 (6th Cir. 1992) (trustee may assert state preference law), with Copter, Inc. v. Gladwin Leasing, Inc., 725 F.2d 37 (3d Cir. 1984) (trustee may not assert state preference law). The Ninth Circuit in *Sherwood Partners, Inc. v. Lycos, Inc.*, 394 F.3d 1198 (9th Cir. 2005), a decision holding that a state law preference statute could not be enforced by an assignee for the benefit of creditors outside of bankruptcy, on the ground that the state law was preempted by the Code, nevertheless

which by its very nature addresses issues inherent in *collective* proceedings, conflicts with the federal preference scheme and therefore is preempted.[50] By contrast, fraudulent conveyance laws, which apply whether or not a collective proceeding exists, pose no similar threat. That being said, the better and prevailing view is that state preference laws can be incorporated into § 544(b)(1) (assuming, of course, that the preference power can be invoked by an unsecured creditor under state law[51]). Such state laws complement the bankruptcy trustee's power to avoid preferences under § 547, and no substantial threat to the federal scheme is presented since the bankruptcy trustee retains discretion whether to bring the avoidance action under § 544(b)(1).

The unsecured creditor limitation in § 544(b)(1) excludes some types of transfers from that section's reach. The trustee cannot invoke non-bankruptcy avoidance powers that are not exercisable by unsecured creditors. For example, a law that gives rights only to *secured* creditors (such as lien creditors), would not be available to the trustee under § 544(b)(1). Section 9–317(a)(2) of the Uniform Commercial Code is an example. To illustrate, assume that the Debtor granted a security interest to Creditor One six months prior to bankruptcy, but Creditor One did not perfect that security interest for two more months. During that delay, Creditor Two obtained an execution lien against the collateral subject to the unperfected security interest. Creditor Two would have priority over Creditor One. U.C.C. § 9–317(a)(2). However, the trustee could not step into the shoes of Creditor Two under § 544(b)(1) and avoid the security interest of Creditor One, because Creditor Two is a secured creditor.[52] For similar reasons, state real estate recording statutes would not be available under § 544(b)(1), because unsecured creditors are not in the protected class. Only purchasers and encumbrancers normally are entitled to invoke the benefit of recording statutes.

Another limitation of § 544(b)(1), noted above, is that the trustee must be able to identify an *actual* unsecured creditor of the debtor, still existing at the time of the bankruptcy filing, who would be able to void the transfer in question under applicable law. If there is no such creditor, § 544(b)(1) will not be available to the trustee. If such a creditor exists, the trustee takes over the avoidance action from that creditor, and asserts it for the benefit of all creditors. Indeed, the trustee (or debtor in possession) has *exclusive* standing to assert the creditor's avoidance action under § 544(b)(1).[53] Significantly, under the venerable precedent of the 1931 Supreme Court decision in

---

approved *Rexplore* on the ground that incorporation of state avoidance laws into the bankruptcy trustee's arsenal of powers helped effectuate the incentives behind § 544(b). Id. at 1205 n.7.

[50] See *Rexplore*, supra note 49, 971 F.2d 1219, 1225–26 (Merritt, J., dissenting).

[51] See *Sherwood*, supra note 49, 394 F.3d 1198, expressing concern in dicta as to whether a state law under which an action could be brought only by an assignee for the benefit of creditors would qualify.

[52] Note that Creditor One's security interest also could not be avoided under either § 544(a)(1), because it was perfected prior to bankruptcy, see § 6.3, or under § 547, because it was perfected more than 90 days prior to bankruptcy. § 547(b)(4)(A). See § 6.15. The latter point assumes that Creditor One is not an insider; if it were, then the preference period would be one year, rather than 90 days. § 547(b)(4)(B).

[53] See, e.g., Flip Mfg. Corp. v. McElhone, 841 F.2d 531 (4th Cir. 1988). If, however, the trustee abandons or unjustifiably refuses to pursue the cause of action, the creditor then will be entitled to bring the action, with court permission. See, e.g., In re Trailer Source, Inc., 555 F.3d 231 (6th Cir. 2009); Unisys Corp. v. Dataware Prods., Inc., 848 F.2d 311 (1st Cir. 1988).

Moore v. Bay,[54] the extent of the trustee's avoidance will *not* be limited to the amount the creditor could have avoided; instead, the entire transfer will be avoided.

The fact that the trustee's powers under § 544(b)(1) are entirely derivative of an actual creditor with avoidance power necessitates an inquiry into the *standing* rules of the "applicable law" being utilized. An example will help illustrate the point. Under most state fraudulent conveyance laws, transfers that are *constructively* fraudulent may only be attacked by "present" creditors,[55] i.e., creditors whose claims arose before the time the alleged fraudulent transfer was made. UFCA § 4; UFTA § 5. Actual fraud, by contrast, can be challenged by present *or future* creditors.

Thus, assume that the trustee alleges that the debtor made a constructively fraudulent transfer within the meaning of UFTA § 5(a) on June 2, 2002, and the debtor filed bankruptcy on June 1, 2006. In order to use § 544(b)(1), the trustee will have to identify an unsecured creditor of the debtor in the bankruptcy case who also was a creditor when the challenged transfer was made, almost four years earlier. Only such a creditor would qualify as a "present" creditor. A creditor whose claim arose in 2005, for example, would not suffice. If, however, the trustee alleges actual fraud under UFTA § 4(a)(1), creditors whose claims arose after June 2, 2002, i.e., future creditors, could be used as the qualifying creditor. The 2005 creditor would count.

Given that the only state avoidance law of broad application available to unsecured creditors is the fraudulent conveyance law, *and* that the Bankruptcy Code already has a provision permitting the avoidance of fraudulent transfers (§ 548), one may wonder what benefit, if any, § 544(b)(1) is to the trustee. Stated otherwise, what does § 544(b)(1) do that § 548 cannot do?

Most significantly, state fraudulent conveyance laws may have a longer reach-back period than the bankruptcy law analogue. The bankruptcy fraudulent transfer provision (with one exception) only reaches transfers made within *two years* of bankruptcy. § 548(a)(1). Until the 2005 amendments, this federal reach-back was only one year. In the example used above, the 2002 transfer could not be attacked under § 548 in the 2006 bankruptcy case. The UFTA, however, permits most types of fraudulent transfers to be challenged up to *four years* after they are made. UFTA § 9. The 2002 transfer therefore could be attacked via § 544(b)(1). New York's fraudulent conveyance law, which obviously is very important given New York's prominence in commercial transactions, has a *six-year* reach back period.[56] Note also that the trustee in bankruptcy would not be restrained by the original state statute of limitations, as long as the bankruptcy case was filed before the state statute expired; the trustee would have the full time to file an avoidance action allowed by § 546(a).[57]

The one exception where the federal fraudulent transfer provision has a longer reach-back period than state laws is with regard to the provision enacted in 2005 to

---

[54]   284 U.S. 4 (1931). See § 6.6 for discussion of *Moore v. Bay* and its application.

[55]   See § 6.45.

[56]   N.Y. McKinney's CPLR § 213(8). Furthermore, the running of the limitation period is suspended if the fraud is not readily discoverable.

[57]   See, e.g., In re Acequia, Inc., 34 F.3d 800 (9th Cir. 1994).

permit avoidance of asset protection trusts in certain situations. Under § 548(e)(1), that avoidance power applies to transfers made within *ten years* of bankruptcy.

A second possible benefit of § 544(b)(1) is that the state law being invoked might reach certain types of transfers that § 548 would not. The discussion above identified some state laws other than fraudulent conveyance laws that give avoiding powers to unsecured creditors (e.g., bulk sales, consignments, preferences). Even in the area of fraudulent transfers alone, § 544(b)(1) may give the trustee added powers. While state fraudulent transfer laws are for the most part quite similar in coverage to § 548, the two may not be identical. For example, the definition of "insolvency" under the state law may be broader than under the Bankruptcy Code,[58] allowing the trustee to allege constructive fraud in more situations under the state law (and therefore under § 544(b)(1)). Another example involves "insider preferences." Under state fraudulent conveyance laws (and thus § 544(b)(1)), an insider preference may be vulnerable in a broad range of circumstances.[59] By comparison, the power to set aside insider preferences under § 548 is much more limited. While the 2005 law added a new variant of constructive fraud for insider preferences, § 548(a)(1)(B)(ii)(IV), that new section applies only to transfers to an insider made in connection with an employment contract and not in the ordinary course of business.

An exception to the general power of avoidance in § 544(b) was added in 1998.[60] Responding to a series of controversial court decisions that had held that pre-bankruptcy transfers by a debtor to charity (usually to a church) were voidable as fraudulent conveyances, Congress in the 1998 law intended to exempt most transfers to charitable organizations from attack as a constructively fraudulent conveyance, subject to certain limitations. See § 548(a)(2). As part of that law, the general rule of original § 544(b) was made subject to an exception for transfers of charitable contributions in new § 544(b)(2), and original § 544(b) was renumbered as § 544(b)(1). The exclusion in § 544(b)(2) applies to transfers of "charitable contributions," as defined in § 548(d)(3), and tracks the exclusion in the federal fraudulent conveyance provision, aligning § 544(b)(2) to exclusions under § 548(a)(1)(B) by reason of § 548(a)(2).

§ 6.6   The Impact of § 544(b): The Continuing Life of *Moore v. Bay*

At the age of 90, Justice Holmes for the Supreme Court wrote a cryptic one-page opinion in the 1931 case of *Moore v. Bay*.[61] One commentator has observed, "[s]urely the Supreme Court's decision in *Moore v. Bay* is the most notorious, in both senses of

---

[58]   Compare UFTA § 2 with Bankruptcy Code § 101(32). Under the UFTA, "equity" insolvency (debtor is not paying her debts as they come due) raises a presumption of "balance sheet" insolvency (debts exceed assets); also, balance sheet insolvency may be proven directly. The Code only uses a balance sheet test.

[59]   Under the UFTA, insider preferences are fraudulent if the debtor was insolvent at the time of the transfer and the insider had reasonable cause to believe the debtor was insolvent. UFTA § 5(b). Under the UFCA, a similar result could be reached by construction of §§ 3 and 4. Section 4 permits the avoidance of conveyances when the debtor is insolvent, if made "without a fair consideration." In turn, "fair consideration" is defined in § 3(a) to require "good faith" on the part of the transferee (the insider).

[60]   Pub. L. No. 105–183, § 3(b), 112 Stat. 518 (1998). See § 6.42.

[61]   284 U.S. 4 (1931).

that word, of all bankruptcy decisions."[62] Another called it a "famous—or infamous—case."[63] A prominent Harvard professor at the time the opinion was handed down called it "one of the most glaring misconstructions to be encountered in the history of Anglo–American law."[64] Scholars and courts have expressed confusion over exactly what the Supreme Court held in *Moore*. Yet, Congress in 1978 embraced *Moore v. Bay* in § 544(b); rejecting the recommendation of the Bankruptcy Review Commission to overrule *Moore*, Congress made plain that the Code followed that decision.[65]

So what is all of the fuss about? The ultimate question is the *extent* of avoidance possible under § 544(b). A corollary issue is the scope of *distribution* of any recoveries. The difficulty stems from the fact that § 544(b) gives the trustee only rights derived from actual unsecured creditors. What happens if a transfer is voidable by some unsecured creditors, but not others?

An example will demonstrate the problem. Assume that the Debtor has a total of $10,000 in unsecured claims when it files bankruptcy. Some time prior to bankruptcy, Debtor makes a transfer of property worth $5,000 to Party X. Under state law, that transfer would be avoidable by Creditor Group A,[66] with total claims of $1,000. However, the rest of the Debtor's creditors, whom we will call Creditor Group B, with total claims of $9,000, could not have avoided the transfer to X under state law.[67] When Debtor files bankruptcy, the trustee, deriving its rights from Creditor Group A, will seek to avoid the transfer to X under § 544(b)(1).

Two issues arise. First, will the trustee be able to set aside the transfer to X only to the extent that Group A creditors could have done so under state law (i.e., $1,000), or, will the trustee be able to set aside the transfer to X in its *entirety* (i.e., all $5,000)? Second, whatever the extent of the avoidance, will the proceeds recovered by the trustee be *distributed* only to creditors in Group A (those who had the avoidance power under state law), or to *all* creditors, including those in Group B who did not have an avoidance power?

Moore v. Bay involved similar (albeit more complicated) facts, arising from a delay in the recordation of a chattel mortgage. Under state law, creditors whose claims arose before recordation had priority over the mortgagee, while those whose claims arose after did not. The lower courts held that avoidance was possible only up to the amount of claims held by the Group A creditors, and that distribution should go only to those Group A creditors.[68] The Supreme Court reversed.[69] Commentators have quibbled

---

[62]   John C. McCoid, II, *Moore v. Bay*: An Exercise in Choice of Law, 1990 Ann. Surv. Bankr. L. 157, 157.

[63]   Thomas H. Jackson, Avoiding Powers in Bankruptcy, 36 Stan. L. Rev. 725, 742 (1984). For Jackson's discussion of the case and § 544(b), see id. at 742–50.

[64]   James A. MacLachlan, Handbook of the Law of Bankruptcy, § 284, at 330 (1956), quoted in McCoid, supra note 2, at 157.

[65]   S. Rep. No. 95–989, 95th Cong., 2d Sess., at 85 (1978).

[66]   Assume, for example, that those creditors had present claims at the time of the transfer to X, and were invoking a constructive fraud provision such as UFTA § 5(a).

[67]   Assume that B creditors had future claims that arose after the time of the transfer to X.

[68]   In re Sassard & Kimball, 45 F.2d 449 (9th Cir.), rev'd, 284 U.S. 4 (1931).

[69]   284 U.S. 4 (1931).

about whether the Court reversed on both the extent-of-avoidance issue and the distribution issue, or just on the latter.[70] Whoever is right, the almost universal *perception* has been that the Supreme Court was reversing on *both* issues.

In short, under our hypothetical, the result in *Moore v. Bay* (and thus § 544(b)(1)) is as follows. The answer to the first issue (extent of avoidance) is that the entire $5,000 transfer will be avoided, even though the derivative creditor group to whom the trustee is succeeding had only $1,000 in claims. The answer to the second question (distribution) is that *all* creditors of the estate share in the distribution of that $5,000, even those who could not have avoided the transfer. Lest you think I am being outrageous in dreaming up hypotheticals, I am not; for example, in one case under the prior Bankruptcy Act, the bankruptcy trustee invoked a claim for $4.64 to set aside a chattel mortgage of $1,678.[71] Such was the outcome that Congress said it wanted to keep in the current Bankruptcy Code. The main criticisms of *Moore v. Bay* have been that it is unfair, redistributive, and alters non-bankruptcy rights, without adequate justification. Complete avoidance affords a windfall to the body of creditors (at X's expense) by permitting them to capture property that they could not have reached outside of bankruptcy. In effect, the trustee is given a license by § 544(b) to rob Peter (X) to pay Paul (general creditors).

D. PREFERENCES

§ 6.7 The Reasons for Preference Law

Perhaps the most significant of the trustee's avoiding powers is that found in § 547, which empowers the trustee to set aside preferential transfers. Not only is the preference provision the most litigated of the bankruptcy avoiding powers (by a considerable margin), it is notable because it permits the trustee to upset a wide range of settled pre-bankruptcy transactions that were perfectly legal when made. The great importance of finality in commercial transactions suggests that good explanations indeed must be offered to justify ignoring the policy of repose.[72]

Before exploring those justifications, however, it would be useful to know what a preference is. Generally speaking, a preference is a transfer that favors one creditor over others. Consider a greatly simplified example. Debtor has three creditors—X, Y, and Z—each of whom it owes $30,000 (and thus $90,000 total). Debtor only has $30,000 in assets. Debtor is thus insolvent. The day before Debtor files bankruptcy, it pays X in full. This payment is not a fraudulent conveyance (unless motivated by an actually fraudulent intent), because the satisfaction of X's debt is "value" given in exchange for the payment. § 548(d)(2)(A). X has, however, been preferred over Y and Z. If X is permitted to keep the money, it will be paid in full, and Y and Z will receive nothing. If X is compelled to return the money to the bankruptcy trustee, however, then X, Y, and Z each will receive $10,000.

---

[70] Compare Jackson, supra note 63, at 744–48 (possibly only distribution issue) with McCoid, supra note 62, at 161 62 (both issues).

[71] Mercantile Trust Co. v. Kahn, 203 F.2d 449 (8th Cir. 1953).

[72] See John C. McCoid, II, Bankruptcy, Preferences, and Efficiency: An Expression of Doubt, 67 Va. L. Rev. 249, 269–70 (1981); Charles J. Tabb, Rethinking Preferences, 43 S.C. L. Rev. 981, 1026–27 (1992).

One of the cardinal principles of bankruptcy is equality of distribution to similarly situated creditors. § 726(b). Bankruptcy as a collective proceeding seeks to promote fair and equitable treatment between multiple creditors. The pre-bankruptcy payment to X, if not undone, will frustrate the bankruptcy distributional scheme. At bottom, then, preference law seeks to prevent that frustration, and give full effect to the distributive norms operative in the bankruptcy collective proceeding.[73] As the legislative history explains:

> The preference provisions facilitate the prime bankruptcy policy of equality of distribution among creditors of the debtor. Any creditor that received a greater payment than others of his class is required to disgorge so that all may share equally.[74]

One might wonder why preservation of the bankruptcy scheme of equality requires unwinding transfers that take place *prior* to bankruptcy. Should we not just take debtors (and creditors) as we find them? If the debtor's insolvency and the bankruptcy case occurred at the exact same instant, there would be no need for a preference law. The operative premise under state collection law is "first in time is first in right." The diligent creditor gets paid first. This premise is unobjectionable *if* the debtor is solvent, because then by definition all creditors eventually will be paid in full. If the debtor is *insolvent*, however, the state law paradigm fails to achieve distributive justice. Paying X in full directly harms Y and Z. The difficulty, then, that preference law addresses, is making the *transition* from the state law regime of "grab law" to the bankruptcy norm of equality of distribution.[75] If the debtor becomes insolvent prior to bankruptcy, and makes transfers during the pre-bankruptcy period of insolvency, bankruptcy equality is subverted.

If preservation of the bankruptcy distributional scheme after the onset of insolvency in the pre-bankruptcy period were *all* that preference law attempted to do, that law would be simpler and more coherent. Preference law would require disgorgement of all transfers benefiting creditors after the debtor became insolvent. However, preference law has never adopted that course. One reason is the desire for repose, noted above.

Another is that framers of preference policy have adhered for hundreds of years to the basic view that not all preferences are evil, and have tried in different ways to distinguish between "good" and "bad" preferences, with only the latter subject to avoidance.[76] For a long time, the distinction drawn was based largely on the *intent* of either the debtor or the creditor. In doing so, the policy makers have conflated the *occasion* for preferential behavior with the *harm* caused, and have made the former a requirement for avoidance. Today, seeds of this tendency remain in the preference law,

---

[73] See Vern Countryman, The Concept of a Voidable Preference in Bankruptcy, 38 Vand. L. Rev. 713, 748 (1985).

[74] H.R. Rep. No. 95–595, 95th Cong., 1st Sess., at 177–78 (1977).

[75] See Thomas H. Jackson, Avoiding Powers in Bankruptcy, 36 Stan. L. Rev. 725, 756–60 (1984). Professor Jackson elaborated on the ideas in this article in his book, The Logic and Limits of Bankruptcy Law (1986), in Chapter 6, "Prebankruptcy Opt–Out Activity and the Role of Preference Law," at 123–27.

[76] See Tabb, supra note 72, at 981–83.

primarily in the exceptions of § 547(c)—most significantly, in the exception for transfers in the ordinary course of business.[77] § 547(c)(2).

Preferences often occur because the debtor and perhaps some creditors will see financial disaster looming on the horizon. A debtor who cannot pay all creditors in full, as in our example, may choose to pay selected creditors first. These creditors may be those with whom the debtor has an additional relationship (Grandma), or expects to deal with in the future (the family doctor or a key supplier), or whose collection actions the debtor most expects and dreads ("broken kneecap" collectors).[78] In the example used above, the Debtor must have had some reason to choose to pay X in full before paying Y and Z anything. In short, the debtor herself intentionally may attempt to alter the bankruptcy distribution scheme. For a long period in the early history of the preference laws, the law actually required proof of such a subjective intention to prefer on the part of the debtor.[79] England still does. Now, however, the law does not require such proof directly. Evidence that the debtor acted in the "ordinary course" of its business or financial affairs in making the transfer will, however, immunize the transfer from avoidance. § 547(c)(2).

Creditors, too, may see bankruptcy coming, and act expeditiously to improve their position vis-à-vis other creditors. Word of the debtor's financial distress may trigger a frenzy of collection activities by creditors who do not want to be left behind in the race for the debtor's assets. The legislative history describes this phenomenon as creditors "racing to the courthouse to dismember the debtor during his slide into bankruptcy."[80] A run on the bank is a useful analogy.[81] The harm from this run on the debtor's assets is that any chance that the debtor may have had to work his way out of financial difficulty may be lost. All creditors as a group are then prejudiced, because the debtor loses the opportunity to maximize the value of its assets. The total asset pool available for distribution to creditors is smaller. If all creditors would work together cooperatively, however, the value of the debtor's assets would be maximized. Furthermore, those unlucky creditors who lose out in the bank run do not even get a share of the smaller pool of assets. The traditional view has been that preference law helps to *deter* this "race of diligence" by telling creditors that they will be forced to disgorge the spoils of victory in the race.[82]

One response to the concern of creditor racing has been to require some proof that the preferred creditor had *knowledge* of the debtor's insolvency. The Bankruptcy Act in effect prior to 1978 expressly required proof that the creditor had "reasonable cause to believe the debtor was insolvent at the time of the transfer."[83] This approach might make sense if the focus of the preference law were only to deter the race for the debtor's

---

[77] See § 6.18.

[78] See McCoid, supra note 72, at 260 n.75.

[79] See id. at 250–57; Tabb, supra note 72, at 997–1005.

[80] H.R. Rep. No. 95–595, 95th Cong., 1st Sess., at 177 (1977).

[81] Remember the scene from the movie "It's a Wonderful Life" where the depositors in Jimmy Stewart's little bank get wind that the bank may be insolvent, and rush to the bank in a mob-like scene, desperately trying to withdraw their money? Jimmy, of course, saves the day.

[82] H.R. Rep. No. 95–595, 95th Cong., 1st Sess., at 177–78 (1977).

[83] Bankruptcy Act of 1898, § 60b.

assets, because only a creditor who knows the debtor is insolvent will be motivated to race. Bank runs do not occur unless depositors are worried that the bank will fail.

The 1978 Code purported to discard this premise, however. The Act's "reasonable cause to believe" requirement was eliminated. The House Report explained the seemingly dramatic shift as follows:

> Whether or not a creditor knows or believes that his debtor is sliding into bankruptcy is important if the only purpose of the preference section is to deter the race. However, a creditor's state of mind has nothing whatsoever to do with the policy of equality of distribution, and whether or not he knows of the debtor's insolvency does little to comfort other creditors similarly situated who will receive that much less from the debtor's estate as a result of the prebankruptcy transfer to the preferred creditor. To argue that the creditor's state of mind is an important element of a preference and that creditors should not be required to disgorge what they took in supposed ignorance is to ignore the strong bankruptcy policy of equality among creditors. Finally, the requirement that the trustee prove the state of mind of his opponent is nearly insurmountable. . . . The amount of litigation it causes is too great.[84]

This passage in the legislative history strongly states that the preference policy of equality is to prevail over that of deterrence. Yet, as things worked out, deterrence gained the dominant position over equality.[85] The primary reason, as will be explored in more detail in a later section,[86] is the ordinary course exception. While the subjective state of mind of the debtor and creditor may not be directly determinative, as they were in the past, preference liability will not be found unless the transfer was made out of the ordinary course, no matter how much that transfer may destroy equality. § 547(c)(2). Only "unusual action" by the debtor or creditors[87]—what has been called "opt out" activity[88]—will be subject to avoidance.

This opt out activity can take two forms, both of which are vulnerable to preference attack under § 547. One is the "last minute grab" by the creditor,[89] whereby the creditor seizes assets of the debtor shortly before bankruptcy. The other is the last minute perfection of a previously secret lien. Although at first blush the second form of activity may not appear to implicate opt out behavior, some have argued that it does.[90] In each instance the creditor is precluded from improving its position vis-à-vis general creditors shortly before bankruptcy, when the debtor is insolvent. The holder of an unperfected lien should not be allowed to perfect its lien at a time when general creditors are precluded (by the anti-last-minute-grab rule) from obtaining a lien

---

[84] H.R. Rep. No. 95–595, 95th Cong., 1st Sess., at 178 (1977).

[85] See Tabb, supra note 72, at 994–95.

[86] See § 6.18.

[87] H.R. Rep. No. 95–595, 95th Cong., 1st Sess., at 373 (1977).

[88] Jackson, supra note 75, at 759.

[89] See id. at 760.

[90] Id. at 764.

themselves. Otherwise the holder of the secret lien "would be playing with a stacked deck."[91]

The apparent primacy of the policy of discouraging opt out behavior as a determinant of the shape of the preference law is troubling. One reason is that the equality policy is eviscerated, as the excerpt from the legislative history quoted above explains. As a normative matter, Professor Countryman argues persuasively that it should not "be the purpose of a preference law to punish 'bad' and absolve 'good' creditors, but to preserve the bankruptcy distribution policy."[92] In short, "fault-based criteria make little sense."[93]

The legitimacy of deterrence as a justification for the preference law has been drawn into question on practical grounds as well, as explained by Professor McCoid and others.[94] Deterrence may not work. The major problem is that the only sanction of the bankruptcy preference law is that the preferred creditor will have to give back the money or property transferred or its value. Except to the extent that the creditor has expended resources to obtain the preference in the first place, that creditor is no worse off after returning the preference than it would have been if the preference had never been received. And the preferred creditor may well end up much better off if it receives a preference, because recapture of the preference is not certain: bankruptcy may not be filed for more than 90 days; or, the trustee may not bring a preference action; or, the creditor may prevail in the preference litigation. In short, a rational creditor may choose to take the preference.

Resolving the tensions revealed by an identification of the often-conflicting underlying premises of the preference law is no easy task. Some have suggested repealing the preference law entirely;[95] others have proposed enforcing equality more strictly;[96] and still others have suggested focusing more exclusively on countering opt out behavior.[97] None of these alternatives has been embraced in the Code; indeed, § 547 as currently drafted does not further a coherent policy. The student dealing with § 547 is left to wade through the dense jungle of § 547 without a working compass.

§ 6.8   Overview of § 547

Section 547 authorizes the avoidance of preferential transfers. Two essential steps are required to analyze whether a challenged transfer may be avoided under § 547. First, the trustee must prove the existence of all of the *elements* of a voidable preference under subsection (b).[98] Second, if the trustee establishes a prima facie case

---

[91] Id. at 764 n.117.

[92] Countryman, supra note 73, at 824.

[93] Tabb, supra note 72, at 1035.

[94] See McCoid, supra note 72, at 263–65. See also David G. Carlson, Security Interests in the Crucible of Voidable Preference Law, 1995 U. Ill. L. Rev. 211, 216 (1995); Countryman, supra note 73, at 748; Bruce R. Kraus, Note, Preferential Transfers and the Value of the Insolvent Firm, 87 Yale L.J. 1449, 1458 (1978); Tabb, supra note 72, at 990–92.

[95] McCoid, supra note 72, at 270–73.

[96] See Kraus, supra note 94, at 1459; Tabb, supra note 72, at 1029.

[97] Jackson, supra note 75, at 765.

[98] See §§ 6.10–6.16.

for avoidance under (b), the burden then shifts to the targeted creditor to go forward with proof of any of the safe harbors, or *exceptions*, to preference liability under subsection (c).[99] § 547(g). Subsections (h) and (i)—both added in the 2005 amendments—also provide exceptions to preference liability,[100] but Congress in the 2005 law failed to specify whether the trustee or the defendant creditor bears the burden of proof under those subsections.

The *elements* of a preference in § 547(b) are:

- a transfer, § 547(b);

- of property of the debtor, § 547(b);

- to or for the benefit of a creditor, § 547(b)(1);

- for or on account of an antecedent debt, § 547(b)(2);

- made while the debtor was insolvent, § 547(b)(3), (f),

- made during the preference period of 90 days, or one year for insiders, § 547(b)(4); and

- that enables the creditor to receive more than it would have in a hypothetical chapter 7 liquidation, § 547(b)(5).

The *safe harbors* or *exceptions* to preference liability available under § 547(c) are for:

- contemporaneous exchanges of new value, § 547(c)(1);

- ordinary course transfers, § 547(c)(2);

- enabling loans, § 547(c)(3);

- subsequent advances of new value, § 547(c)(4);

- floating liens, § 547(c)(5);

- statutory liens, § 547(c)(6);

- domestic relations obligations, § 547(c)(7);

- transfers less than $600 in an individual consumer case, § 547(c)(8); and

- transfers less than $6,225 in a non-consumer case, § 547(c)(9)

Additionally, BAPCPA immunized transfers made as part of an alternative repayment schedule created by an approved nonprofit budgeting and credit counseling

---

[99]   See §§ 6.17–6.24. Although the introductory clause to § 547(b) only states that it is subject to subsections (c) and (i), subsection (h), added in 2005, also provides an exception to preference liability.

[100]   See §§ 6.25–6.26.

agency.[101] § 547(h). Curiously, Congress did not include that safe harbor in the list of exceptions in subsection (c).

Some of the other subsections of § 547 aid in the interpretation of parts of (b) and (c). A few definitions are provided in subsection (a).[102] A presumption that the debtor was insolvent for the 90 days prior to bankruptcy, § 547(f), helps the trustee to prove that the debtor was insolvent when the transfer was made.[103] § 547(b)(3). Subsection (e) includes critical timing rules that specify when a transfer is deemed to be made, a matter of considerable importance for applying several of the elements in (b) and exceptions in (c).[104] Finally, § 547(d) permits the avoidance of a transfer to a surety that secures the reimbursement of a bond to dissolve a judicial lien that itself would have been avoidable.

Once a transfer is "avoided" under § 547, the trustee must attempt to "recover" that transfer under § 550. The most noteworthy aspect of § 550 as it relates to preferences is the 1994 amendment that added § 550(c). Under § 550(c), a preference to an insider made more than 90 days before bankruptcy cannot be recovered from a non-insider transferee. This amendment was intended to overrule the result in the Seventh Circuit's decision in *Levit v. Ingersoll Rand Financial Corp.*[105] (known as the *Deprizio* case), which had allowed such a recovery. However, § 550(c) did not afford complete protection to non-culpable non-insiders, since it established the point of protection at *recovery,* rather than at *avoidance,* which does the non-insider little good if no "recovery" is sought. The paradigmatic example is when a lien is avoided; no "recovery" is needed, because the remedy is simply to annul the lien. Accordingly, in 2005 Congress added § 547(i) to provide complete protection for an innocent non-insider on a transfer between 90 days and one year before bankruptcy, by immunizing the non-insider even from *avoidance.*[106] Thus, for such a non-insider, the lien that was transferred to it cannot be set aside, thanks to § 547(i).

§ 6.9   Time When a Transfer Is Deemed Made

A crucial issue that pervades preference litigation is to determine *when* a transfer is made. The timing question can arise in the following situations:

- Was the transfer made on account of an antecedent debt owed by the debtor before the transfer was made? § 547(b)(2).

- Was the transfer made while the debtor was insolvent? § 547(b)(3).

- Was the transfer made during the preference period? § 547(b)(4).

---

[101] See § 6.25.

[102] The terms defined are "inventory," § 547(a)(1); "new value," § 547(a)(2); and "receivable," § 547(a)(3); in addition, § 547(a)(4) states when a tax debt is incurred.

[103] See § 6.14

[104] See § 6.9.

[105] 874 F.2d 1186 (7th Cir. 1989). See discussion in §§ 6.12, 6.26.

[106] See § 6.26.

- Was the transfer in fact a substantially contemporaneous exchange for new value? § 547(c)(1).

- Was the transfer made in the ordinary course of business? § 547(c)(2).

- Was the transferred security interest perfected within the 30–day grace period for enabling loans? § 547(c)(3).

- Was new value given after the transfer? § 547(c)(4).

- When is a transfer made of a security interest in inventory and receivables? § 547(c)(5).

The provision that governs when a transfer is deemed made for purposes of the preference law is § 547(e). With the exception of an issue involving payment by check, discussed below, identifying the time of a transfer when the debtor makes an outright payment to a creditor is rarely problematic—the transfer occurs when the payment is made. Difficulties arise, however, when the transfer is of a lien or security interest. In that situation, the transfer time could be fixed at either of two different points—when the transfer is *effective* as between the debtor and the creditor, or when the transfer is *perfected* as against third parties. Perfection typically requires the filing of some sort of public notice. Because of the policy against "secret" liens, Congress in subsection (e) has picked the time of perfection as the time of transfer, but subject to a 30–day grace period. Thus, a creditor cannot take a security interest long before bankruptcy, keep it secret from third parties for more than 30 days, perfect the security interest just before the debtor files, and still remain invulnerable to preference attack. More specifically, the rule of § 547(e)(2) can be summed up as follows:

A transfer is deemed made when it takes effect between the transferor and transferee, if it is perfected within thirty days of that time, § 547(e)(2)(A), but if it is not perfected within thirty days, the transfer is deemed made when perfected. § 547(e)(2)(B).

Because of the central place of perfection in the timing analysis, it is necessary to know when perfection occurs for preference purposes. For transfers of real property, § 547(e)(1)(A) provides that the transfer is perfected when a bona fide purchaser of the property from the debtor could not acquire an interest superior to the transferee. Typically, to perfect against a "bfp" of realty under state law, a transferee must file a notice in the real estate records of the county where the real estate is located. For personal property and fixtures, perfection occurs when the transfer would be valid against a contract creditor who acquires a judicial lien. § 547(e)(1)(B). For the vast world of Article 9 security interests, this is when the security interest is perfected under Article 9. See U.C.C. § 9–317(a)(2)(A). In most cases, Article 9 perfection is accomplished by filing a financing statement. U.C.C. § 9–310(a).

Identifying the time of perfection under § 547(e)(1) is a matter implicating both state and federal law, as explained in the Supreme Court's 1998 decision in *Fidelity*

Financial Services, Inc. v. Fink.[107] While the specification of the underlying acts needed to perfect is determined by state law, the timing question itself is a matter of *federal* law.[108] The facts in *Fink* demonstrate how this dichotomy plays out. In that case, to perfect its security interest in a motor vehicle under Missouri law, the creditor had to mail in certain documents to the director of revenue. Also under Missouri law, if the creditor performed the necessary acts within 30 days, it was deemed perfected (retroactively) as of day one. The creditor performed the acts required on day 21. When the creditor sought to invoke the protection of the enabling loan safe harbor of § 547(c)(3), which at that time gave the creditor 20 days to perfect (sadly, one day less than what the creditor did!), the determinative issue was when the creditor "perfected" for purposes of § 547(c)(3)(B)—on day 21, or day 1? That, in turn, depended on an interpretation of the timing rule of § 547(e)(1)(B). The Supreme Court held that, while state law spelled out the acts needed to perfect (*viz.*, mail certain documents to director of revenue), the federal bankruptcy law controlled the question of *when* the performance of those acts constituted "perfection." Under § 547(e)(1)(B), that time was when final necessary acts were performed (when the documents were mailed, and thus on day 21), and not at the time when the creditor would have been deemed perfected under state law (via relation-back, on day one).[109]

The operation of the rules of § 547(e)(2) can be illustrated by some examples. Assume that Debtor grants Creditor a valid security interest in Collateral on May 1; in Article 9 parlance, the security interest "attaches" on that date. U.C.C. § 9–203(a), (b). Upon attachment, the security interest is enforceable by Creditor against the Debtor. U.C.C. §§ 9–201(a), 9–203(a). For the purposes of the preference law, the time of attachment (May 1) is when the security interest "takes effect" between the Debtor-transferor and the Creditor-transferee. However, when the transfer of that security interest will be deemed to be made for the purposes of the preference law depends on when Creditor perfects the security interest.

Assume first that Creditor perfects on May 11, ten days after attachment. Since perfection occurred within thirty days of the time the transfer took effect between Debtor and Creditor, the transfer of the security interest is deemed to have been made back when the original transfer took effect, i.e., on May 1, the date of attachment. § 547(e)(2)(A). In other words, upon perfection within thirty days, the time of the transfer relates back to when the transfer first took effect between the Debtor and Creditor. Significantly, note that this thirty-day relation back rule for preferences is *not* limited to purchase money security interests, as is the case under Article 9. See U.C.C. § 9–317(e). I will say more on this oddity below.

Now assume that the Creditor delays perfection of the security interest for more than thirty days after attachment, and does not perfect until June 1 (day 31). The transfer now is deemed to be made on the date of perfection (June 1), since perfection occurred more than thirty days after the transfer first took effect. § 547(e)(2)(B). If the Creditor had not perfected by the later of the filing of the bankruptcy or the 30 day

---

[107]   522 U.S. 211 (1998).

[108]   Id. at 216.

[109]   Id. at 215–16. At that time, subsection (e) had only a 10-day grace period.

period after attachment, the transfer is deemed made immediately before the filing of the bankruptcy petition. § 547(e)(2)(C).

The delay in perfection could prove calamitous for the Creditor. One ramification is that the transfer is now considered made for an antecedent debt.[110] § 547(b)(2). Even if the debt was incurred on May 1, at the time of attachment, the transfer of the security interest for preference purposes does not occur until June 1, the time of perfection. This situation is called a "false" preference—but it is just as avoidable as a "true" preference.

Yet another ill effect of the delay (for Creditor) is that the transfer now may fall within the 90–day preference reach-back period. § 547(b)(4)(A). For example, assume that Debtor files bankruptcy on August 30. The transfer date, when Creditor perfected on June 1, is exactly 90 days before the bankruptcy filing—and thus within the preference period. The fact that the transfer first took effect between the Debtor and Creditor upon attachment on May 1, 121 days before bankruptcy, is irrelevant.

The curious thing about the rule of § 547(e)(2)(A) is that it is not limited to purchase money security interests (PMSI) or enabling loans. Indeed, another provision, § 547(c)(3), specifically protects a PMSI or enabling loan.[111] The curiosity is that § 547(e)(2)(A) provides non-PMSI secured creditors with more protection than they would enjoy under non-bankruptcy law.[112] Under Article 9, a non-PMSI secured creditor would not enjoy relation-back rights against intervening lien creditors if it delayed perfecting. U.C.C. §§ 9 317(a)(2)(A), 9 317(e). Why then give such protection to non-PMSI secured creditors in bankruptcy, and open up an opportunity for the use of secret liens?

To see the impact of this rule, let us revisit and modify the above hypothetical.[113] On May 1, Debtor borrows money from Creditor. As security, assume that Debtor grants Creditor a security interest in a jet ski that Debtor already owns. Thus, Creditor's security interest is not a PMSI under Article 9. Creditor does not perfect its security interest right away. However, Creditor subsequently learns that Debtor is about to file bankruptcy, and rushes to perfect its security interest on May 30. On May 31, Debtor files bankruptcy. Is Creditor's security interest in the jet ski a voidable preference?

After the 2005 amendments, the answer is no. Under amended section 547(e)(2)(A), since Creditor perfected within 30 days of when the security interest attached (on Day 29), the transfer is deemed to have been made at the time the transfer took effect between the transferor and transferee (May 1), and thus there is no "antecedent debt" under § 547(b)(2), and thus no preference.

---

[110] See § 6.13. See, e.g., In re Lazarus, 478 F.3d 12, 14–15 (1st Cir. 2007) (mortgage deemed transferred when recorded 14 days after granted, greater than then 10–day rule in § 547(e)(2)(B), and this for antecedent debt and avoidable as preference).

[111] See § 6.19.

[112] See Charles J. Tabb, The Brave New World of Bankruptcy Preferences, 13 Am. Bankr. Inst. L. Rev. 425, 448–49 (2005).

[113] The hypothetical is taken from id. at 448.

The timing rule of § 547(e)(2)(A) allows creditors holding unperfected security interests in cases like the above hypothetical to engage in "preferential" behavior by perfecting a previously unperfected security interest within the preference period, as long as they do so within 30 days after the security interest attached.[114] Note that Creditor's intent is irrelevant. It is difficult to justify the rule of § 547(e)(2)(A) in its present form, which gives unperfected secured creditors greater rights than they would have under state law and allows them to improve their position on the eve of bankruptcy. Prior to 2005, the same result was possible under § 547(e)(2), but the grace period was a mere 10 days, leaving little room for such creditor opt-out behavior. The reasoning behind that 10–day grace period when it was first introduced into the bankruptcy law in 1950 was to give a diligent secured creditor a brief amount of time to perfect its security interest in situations where prior or contemporaneous perfection was not possible or feasible.[115] Today the rule is an anachronism for Article 9 security interests, since prior or contemporaneous perfection is routinely allowed. Even if the original 10–day period could still be justified (which is open to doubt), certainly it seems that 30 days is excessive.

Another timing rule, of importance primarily for floating liens in inventory and receivables, is § 547(e)(3). That section provides that a transfer is not made until the debtor acquires rights in the property transferred. Along with the antecedent debt provision, § 547(b)(2), subsection (e)(3) overrules some pre-Code cases that sought to protect a secured creditor with a floating lien by adroit interpretation of the rules on transfers and timing.[116] Now the secured creditor can find protection only in the safe harbor of § 547(c)(5).[117]

Delays in perfecting security interests and in recording real property transfers have not been the only source of difficulty in construing the timing rules of § 547. Cases involving a transfer by *check* have also proved troublesome. The quandary in a check case is whether the transfer occurs when the check is *delivered* to the creditor-payee or when the check is *honored* by the drawee bank. If the payee simply holds onto the check, and waits to cash it or deposit it until shortly before bankruptcy, it is easy to see an argument in favor of using the honor date, because the payee's actions smack of "secret lien" behavior. But what if the payee promptly submits a delivered check for honor, but honor occurs (as it will) some period of time after the check was delivered to the payee? Now is the delivery date or honor date controlling? The answer could matter both for purposes of establishing an antecedent debt and also for whether the transfer occurred within the preference period. The only guidance in the legislative history supports using the delivery date: "payment of a debt by means of a check is equivalent to a cash payment, unless the check is dishonored. Payment is considered to be made when the check is delivered for purposes of sections 547(c)(1) and (2)."[118] Relying on this statement in the legislative history, and on policy arguments, the courts of appeals

---

[114] See id. at 449.

[115] See Vern Countryman, The Concept of a Voidable Preference in Bankruptcy, 38 Vand. L. Rev. 713, 754 n. 222 (1985).

[116] S. Rep. No. 95–989, 95th Cong., 2d Sess., at 89 (1978).

[117] See § 6.21.

[118] 124 Cong. Rec. H11,097 (daily ed. Sept. 28, 1978) (statement of Rep. Edwards).

prior to 1992 unanimously agreed that the delivery date should be used, at least for the preference exceptions in § 547(c).[119]

In 1992, however, the Supreme Court held in *Barnhill v. Johnson*[120] that a transfer by check does not occur until the check is *honored* for purposes of determining whether the transfer was made within the 90–day preference period under § 547(b)(4). In that case, the check had been delivered to the creditor 92 days before bankruptcy, and was honored exactly 90 days before. The Court, although admitting that the definition and timing of a transfer under the Bankruptcy Code are matters of federal law, nevertheless gave content to the federal transfer rules by looking at state law.[121] Under U.C.C. Article 3, the delivery of a check to a payee does not amount to an assignment of the funds in the account. Many a slip is possible between delivery and honor. The holder of the check does not acquire any rights against the drawee bank until the bank honors the check. Thus, honor is the moment of transfer.

The majority of the Supreme Court in *Barnhill* did not believe that § 547(e)(2) dictated a different result, even though the check was honored (and thus "perfected"?) within ten days (the operative grace period under subsection (e)(2) at that time). The dissenters argued that if the check was honored within ten days (as it was in the case), then the time of transfer would relate back to the time of delivery.[122] The majority declined to accept this argument by concluding that no "transfer" takes effect even between the debtor and the creditor at the time of delivery, and thus there is nothing to relate back *to* under (e)(2).[123] The Court also declined to adopt a theory that delivery of the check was a "conditional" transfer; in reality, the Court said, there was no transfer at all until the moment of honor.[124]

The Court still had to contend with the legislative history and the unbroken line of circuit court precedent supporting a delivery date for the preference exceptions under § 547(c). The majority dodged that problem by rejecting the underlying premise that the *same* timing rule had to govern both subsection (b) and (c). The case before the Court involved (b), not (c), and thus the law applicable to (c) was irrelevant. Indeed, the Court was careful to point out that it was taking no position on when a transfer by check occurred under (c).[125] The Court's treatment of this question raised the intriguing possibility that the *same* check could be deemed to have been transferred at two *different* times, for purposes of the same preference lawsuit: at the time of honor, under subsection (b); and then at the time of delivery, under subsection (c). Courts after *Barnhill* have made this possibility a reality.[126]

A final timing issue bears mention. That is the treatment of *garnishment* cases. In a garnishment, a notice or writ of garnishment is served on the garnishee, usually

---

[119] E.g., Braniff Airways, Inc. v. Midwest Corp., 873 F.2d 805 (5th Cir. 1989).

[120] 503 U.S. 393 (1992).

[121] Id. at 398–99.

[122] Id. at 403 (Stevens, J., dissenting).

[123] Id. at 401 (Rehnquist, J., majority).

[124] Id. at 400–01.

[125] Id. at 402 n.9.

[126] See, e.g., In re Nat'l Enters. Inc., 174 B.R. 429 (Bankr. E.D. Va. 1994) (delivery date for § 547(c)(4)).

either a bank or an employer. Service of the notice usually creates a perfected lien of garnishment. That perfected lien, under the law of some states, might reach subsequent wages earned by the debtor-employee or deposits made by the debtor-depositor. The question in the garnishment cases is whether the "transfer" occurs for preference purposes when the writ is served and thus perfected, or at a later time.

One area of debate is whether the transfer date should be deferred until a final order of garnishment is entered. A number of courts have held that the time of transfer should not be deferred. Looking at § 547(e)(2)'s emphasis on when a transfer is "perfected," those courts have concluded that the time of service of the writ, which creates the perfected lien, controls.[127] The Seventh Circuit disagreed in an opinion by Judge Posner, and found that the transfer did not take place until the final order of garnishment was entered.[128] The court relied on *Barnhill*, noting that a garnishment (like a delivered check) is tentative until a final order is entered (which is akin to honor). Furthermore, preference policy supported the later date, because using that date would prevent the debtor from effecting an unrecoverable preference by depositing funds in the garnished account shortly before bankruptcy.

Courts also have struggled over whether the transfer in a garnishment can take place before the debtor earns wages. Two pre-*Barnhill* circuit court decisions under the Code held that the transfer took place upon service of the writ.[129] Thereafter, the garnished interest passed directly to the garnishor, those courts concluded, and was never the debtor's property. This analysis seems flawed, however. Under § 547(e)(3), a transfer is not made until the debtor acquires rights in the property. No wages at all are owed by the employer until the debtor performs the work; if the debtor performs the work during the preference period, then logically that should be when the transfer is deemed to occur. Post–*Barnhill*, the trend in the courts has been to hold that the transfer occurs for preference purposes only when the wages are earned.[130]

§ 6.10   Elements of a Preference: Transfer

The first element of a preference is that there must have been a "transfer" of an interest of the debtor in property. § 547(b). The next section discusses the parameters of the requirement that the transfer be of the *debtor's* property; this section explains the meaning of *transfer*. The Code defines "transfer" in § 101(54):

The term "transfer" means

(A)   the creation of a lien;

(B)   the retention of title as security interest;

(C)   the foreclosure of a debtor's equity of redemption; or

---

[127]   E.g., In re Battery One–Stop Ltd., 36 F.3d 493 (6th Cir. 1994).

[128]   In re Freedom Grp., Inc., 50 F.3d 408 (7th Cir. 1995).

[129]   In re Coppie, 728 F.2d 951 (7th Cir. 1984), cert. denied, 469 U.S. 1105 (1985); In re Riddervold, 647 F.2d 342 (2d 1981).

[130]   E.g., In re Morehead, 249 F.3d 445 (6th Cir. 2001).

(D) each mode, direct or indirect, absolute or conditional, voluntary or involuntary, of disposing of or parting with

(i)   property; or

(ii) an interest in property

As the catch-all language in subsection (D) demonstrates, Congress intended that "the definition of transfer [be] as broad as possible."[131] Tautologically, the legislative history explains that "any transfer of an interest in property is a transfer."[132] Note that the definition includes the transfer of a security interest or lien. Thus, a creditor who receives *security* during the preference period is just as vulnerable to preference avoidance as the recipient of an outright payment.

The definition of transfer also includes *involuntary* transfers. An involuntary transfer is one initiated by the transferee creditor, rather than by the debtor. Thus, under § 547 the trustee may be able to avoid collection actions taken by a creditor prior to bankruptcy, such as a levy of execution on the debtor's property. The debtor need not be a willing participant in the creditor's activities. Historically, by comparison, preference law for centuries required proof of the debtor's complicity in the transfer, such as a showing of the debtor's "intent to prefer" the creditor.[133] As noted earlier, such is still the case in England. The trustee's power to reach involuntary transfers is crucial to the accomplishment of one of the central goals of preference law, which is to stop the pre-bankruptcy "race of diligence" by creditors.[134]

In some cases, though, a "transfer" is lacking. One example is in the case of a floating lien in inventory or receivables, the subject of a safe harbor in § 547(c)(5). That provision imposes a two-point improvement-in-position test, as discussed more fully in a later section.[135] The thrust of the idea behind (c)(5) is that an undersecured creditor with a security interest in inventory or receivables is only subject to preference liability to the extent its deficiency (i.e., the amount by which the debt exceeds the value of the collateral) decreases during the preference period. However, there is no preference at all absent a transfer of the debtor's property, even if the creditor's deficiency decreases. If no new collateral is obtained, and the creditor's deficiency decreases because of an increase in the value of the existing collateral, there is no transfer and thus no preference.

Note that it is possible, though, for a preference to occur without the creditor obtaining new collateral, if the debtor transfers her property to increase the value of the collateral. A classic hypothetical to demonstrate the point is the proverbial "fat pig"

---

[131] 95th Cong., 2d Sess., at 27 (1978). The original legislative history remains valid, even though the definition of "transfer" was amended in 2005. Subsection (D) continues the core of the previous definition. Most of the 2005 changes were cosmetic; for example, subsections (B) and (C) were simply broken out into distinct subsections. Nor did the addition of subsection (A) effect a change of substance, as lien transfers were already treated as "transfers."

[132] Id.

[133] See Charles J. Tabb, Rethinking Preferences, 43 S.C. L. Rev. 981, 995–1008 (1992).

[134] See H.R. Rep. No. 95–595, 95th Cong., 1st Sess., at 177 (1977).

[135] See § 6.21.

case, where the debtor spends money to feed a pig that is subject to the creditor's security interest. As the pig fattens from eating, the value of the pig increases; yet, there has not been a transfer of a new pig. The "transfer" that is subject to avoidance, however, is the money the debtor spent on pig feed.

The Supreme Court in *Barnhill v. Johnson*[136] declined the invitation to give "conditional" transfer an expansive meaning in deciding when a transfer by check occurs, as discussed in the preceding section. The creditor argued that the transfer occurred when the check was delivered. One reason urged by the creditor was that the delivery of the check transferred to the creditor-payee a "conditional" interest in the property in the debtor-drawer's bank account, the condition being that the drawee bank would honor the check. The Court concluded that under state law, no interest in the account was transferred until the moment of honor. Until that moment the debtor retained full control over the account, and various third parties could obtain priority over the payee in the account. A contrary result, the Court suggested, "would accomplish a near-limitless expansion of the term 'conditional.'"[137]

Another situation in which the courts have not found a "transfer" is when the debtor's property interest is terminated or extinguished. For example, a debtor-purchaser of real estate may forfeit her down payment upon default. Is the forfeiture a preference to the seller? The Seventh Circuit thought not, concluding that the extinguishment of the debtor's interest was not a transfer.[138] A similar question arises when a valuable contract is terminated upon the debtor's default.

§ 6.11 Elements of a Preference: Property of Debtor

A threshold limitation on the scope of the preference section is that the trustee may only avoid as a preference a "transfer of an interest of the debtor in property." § 547(b). If the property transferred is not that of the debtor, the rationales for preference avoidance collapse. Maintaining inter-creditor equality is a relevant concern only with regard to the debtor's property, for it is only out of that property that the debtor's creditors normally can expect to be paid. For similar reasons, the race of diligence only matters when creditors are racing for the same pot of assets, and the risk of driving the debtor into bankruptcy only exists with regard to the debtor's assets. In short, the legal concern with preferences is not that one creditor of the debtor gets paid while others do not, but that the payment to that creditor is to the corresponding prejudice of the other creditors.

One would think that applying the rule limiting preference avoidance to transfers of the debtor's property would be quite simple and easy. Often it is. But in a surprising number of cases, the issue of whether property of the debtor was transferred is anything but obvious.

---

[136] 503 U.S. 393 (1992). See § 6.9 for further discussion.
[137] 503 U.S. at 401.
[138] In re Wey, 854 F.2d 196 (7th Cir. 1988).

Consider a simple example first. Debtor owes money to Creditors A to Z. Debtor's Mother chooses to pay Creditor Q, the family doctor. That payment is not a preference. Q was not paid with Debtor's property. This result does not offend the purpose of the preference laws, because Debtor's other creditors have no legal claim against Mother. Q may be fortunate, but the other creditors have no cause to complain.

Now make the problem a bit trickier. Assume that Mother pays Q, and then asserts Q's claim against Debtor. Is this a preference? The answer is still no. All that has happened is that one creditor has been substituted for another. In a more formal business context, the same result would occur if the creditor were a beneficiary of a letter of credit, and was paid by the issuer of that letter of credit. The payment would come out of the issuer's property, not the debtor's. Neither the total amount of claims against Debtor nor the amount of property available to satisfy those claims has changed at all.

Note, though, that the foregoing conclusion only holds if the substituted creditor is also an unsecured creditor. If an unsecured creditor is paid and replaced by a creditor holding security for the debt against the debtor, a preference has occurred.[139] The debtor's other creditors are prejudiced, because the new secured creditor will be paid out of its collateral before the unsecured creditors will be paid. There thus is less of the debtor's property left for the remaining unsecured creditors. In this situation the preference is limited to the extent of the security given.[140]

Change the facts a bit. Now, instead of Mother paying Creditor Q directly, Mother gives the money to Debtor, with clear instructions to pay the money over to Q. Debtor does so. Should the result (no preference) change just because the money passed through Debtor's hands from the benefactor to the creditor? The creditor will argue that the two transactions are identical in substance, with only the form differing, and that the result should not change. The trustee, seeking to recover the payment to Q, will argue that once Mother gave the money to Debtor, the money became Debtor's property, and thus within the ambit of the preference law. Even though technically the trustee's argument has merit, as some courts have noted,[141] the courts nevertheless have carved out a judicial exception to the "debtor property" rule, called the "*earmarking*" doctrine.[142] Defining the exact parameters of that doctrine has been a matter of considerable debate in the courts, with some taking a more restrictive view, limiting the doctrine to the situation where the party providing the funds for payment is a co-debtor with the debtor on the debt paid.[143] Under the more permissive form of this doctrine, if any third party—even if not a co-debtor—loans money to a debtor that is "earmarked" for payment to a creditor, and the debtor transfers those earmarked funds to the creditor, no preference occurs. Equitably, the courts conclude, the property transferred was not really the debtor's, but that of the third party (e.g., Mother). The debtor's estate available for distribution to other creditors has not been diminished by

---

[139] See, e.g., In re Compton Corp., 831 F.2d 586 (5th Cir. 1987).

[140] See, e.g., In re Hartley, 825 F.2d 1067 (6th Cir. 1987), cert. denied, 489 U.S. 1077 (1989).

[141] See In re Bohlen Enters., Ltd., 859 F.2d 561 (8th Cir. 1988).

[142] E.g., Adams v. Anderson (In re Superior Stamp & Coin Co.), 223 F.3d 1004 (9th Cir. 2000).

[143] E.g., In re Moses, 256 B.R. 641 (B.A.P. 10th Cir. 2000). A useful discussion of the various lines of case authority is presented in *In re Marshall*, 550 F.3d 1251 (10th Cir. 2008).

the transfer of the earmarked funds. While "diminution of the estate" is not a statutory requirement for preference avoidance, many courts have consistently applied that concept, and find no preference if there is no diminution.[144] If the debtor has unfettered control over the use of the funds, though, or if the debtor fails to abide by the third party's earmarking instructions, then the doctrine will not be applied, even under more liberal versions of the doctrine.

Recently, courts have grappled with the earmarking doctrine in the context of the so-called convenience check cases. The facts are illustrated by *In re Wells*.[145] In that case, the debtor withdrew funds from one credit card issuer using convenience checks in order to pay off the balance owed to a second credit card company. The trustee sought to avoid the transfer as a preference. The second credit card company argued that under the earmarking doctrine the transfer was not of "property of the debtor," and thus not a preference.[146]

The court held that the earmarking doctrine was inapplicable, utilizing a "control of funds" test. Since the funds were not designated by the creditor to pay off a specific debt, debtor was free to use the convenience checks for any reason. Thus the debtor exercised control over the funds in such a manner that she had an ownership interest in the funds. The transfer was deemed a preference because it was, in fact, a transfer of property of the debtor.[147]

Such a rationale is also illustrated by the Tenth Circuit in *Parks v. FIA Card Services, N.A. (In re Marshall)*.[148] In that case, the debtor directed one credit card company (whom for convenience we will call A) to pay off another credit card company (B) through a balance transfer of $38,000. Once that happened, A had become a creditor of the Debtor, and B had been paid off. Notably, in this scenario, the funds never involved actual possession of the funds by the Debtor; the money went directly from A to B. When the trustee attempted to capture the transfer of funds from B as a preference, B of course argued that it was not paid with the Debtor's property at all; rather, it was paid by a direct transfer from credit card company A. All that happened, B asserted, was that A effectively had purchased B's claim, which is perfectly fine and not avoidable as a preference. Simply substituting one creditor for another does not diminish the estate in any way or involve any transfer of the Debtor's property. Even if somehow this transaction were construed as involving a transfer of Debtor's property, B argued, the earmarking defense would apply, since A committed the funds for the sole purpose of paying off B. Balance transfers work that way by their very nature. The trustee, though, argued that in substance this was effectively a loan from A to Debtor, which loan proceeds Debtor then chose to pay to B, which is clearly a preference. The result should not change, the trustee argued, just because Debtor told A to pay the loan directly to B rather than passing the loan proceeds through Debtor's hands en route to

---

[144] See, e.g., Warsco v. Preferred Tech. Group, 258 F.3d 557, 565 & n. 11 (7th Cir. 2001); Campbell v. Hanover Ins. Co., 457 B.R. 452, 457 (W.D.N.C. 2011).

[145] 382 B.R. 355 (B.A.P. 6th Cir. 2008).

[146] Id. at 360.

[147] Id. at 360–61.

[148] 550 F.3d 1251 (10th Cir. 2008).

B. Nor did earmarking apply because the Debtor was the one who directed the payment, not A.

The court agreed with the trustee's view of the transaction, which is followed by a majority of courts, and found that Debtor's draw on its line of credit with A was in substance a loan from A to Debtor, and thus there had been a transfer of property (the loan proceeds) of the Debtor to B. It was no different, the court said, than if Debtor had drawn on its line of credit from A, deposited the funds into its own account, and then transferred the funds to B.[149] Having construed the transaction in that way, the court had little trouble concluding that Debtor had exercised "dominion and control" over the funds by directing the use of the funds. Although there was no actual possession by Debtor, the court pointed to Debtor's control of the funds to find constructive possession. The court also found that the transfer *did* diminish the estate, because for an instant (once the balance transfer was approved by A and before funds were paid to B), the Debtor had the property. The earmarking defense did not apply, the court said, because that requires the party making the payment (A here) to be the one requiring the limited and directed use of the funds, whereas here Debtor made the decision to make the transfer to B.

Ultimately, the "control of funds" approach utilized by courts in cases such as *Marshall* and *Wells* places the focus on the intent and control of the creditor. If the creditor intended to designate a payment, and so limited it, then the debtor would likely not have sufficient control over the funds to constitute property of the debtor for preference purposes. In such scenarios, courts apply the legal fiction that the funds were never really under debtor's control. If, however, the debtor is not constrained in its use of funds, courts tend to find the earmarking doctrine inapplicable. Legal fictions can be a wonderful thing.

This shift may also represent a turn away from the "diminution of the estate" approach, or at least from an intellectually honest application of that test. In this line of cases, where the funds were drawn from one line of credit and placed in another, the general body of creditors never *really* had access to or a right to such funds. From the perspective of the body of creditors, cases like *Marshall* are more like the case where one creditor buys the claim of and is substituted for another; in short, nothing has changed for the other creditors: the debtor had the same amount of money before and after the transfer, and had the same amount of debts. As explained above, though, many courts have employed the legal fiction that the funds did in fact belong to the estate at least momentarily in order to satisfy the "diminution of the estate" test.[150] That is a conclusion rather than a reason, though; as I said, legal fictions can be a wonderful thing.

One must ask, though, whether avoidance in cases like this serves any meaningful bankruptcy function. As I explained, the reality is that nothing has changed for other creditors. The debtor's financial balance sheet of assets and debts is *exactly* the same before and after the balance transfer. Who has been harmed in reality? Note, too, that

---

[149] Id. at 1257.

[150] See, e.g., id. at 1258–59.

the effect of the *Marshall* decision is to give the other creditors a windfall. Why? The estate now has $38,000 more than it had before the balance transfer happened (the money recovered from B). It also has $38,000 more in claims (now both B and A have claims, whereas before the balance transfer only B had a claim), but since the estate is likely insolvent, with everyone by definition only getting cents-on-the-dollar for their claims, adding $38,000 to the estate in 100–cent dollars (the money recovered from B) is a good trade indeed for the less–than–100–cent dollars in the new $38,000 claim.

A form of the earmarking doctrine has also recently been discussed in a number of refinancing transactions cases, where a new mortgagee takes the place of the first one. This scenario is illustrated in *In re Lazarus*.[151] In that case, debtor refinanced her mortgage with a new lender before filing bankruptcy, and the trustee sought to avoid the mortgage of the new lender, which was vulnerable to preference attack because the mortgagee had delayed too long in recording its mortgage. However, the new lender argued that the transfer of the mortgage nevertheless was not a preference since it did not involve a transfer of property of the debtor—certainly a non-obvious argument at first blush since the debtor granted the new lender a mortgage! Undeterred, the lender argued that the refinancing in substance was a transfer of a mortgage interest *from the former mortgagee* to the new lender, not from the debtor. The court rejected the earmarking doctrine. Instead, the court held that what had occurred was a series of multiple transactions, with the debtor being much more than a "bailee" or conduit passing property of one creditor through to another; rather, the debtor had a sufficient independent interest in the property mortgaged for it to be treated as her property for preference purposes.[152] The court distinguished this scenario from a case where third party creditors engage in a transfer, while the debtor remains a passive party. Rather, the debtor extinguished the initial mortgage then created a new mortgage with the refinancer, and thus transferred an interest in property.[153]

Another type of case in which the "debtor property" requirement has proved troublesome is where the creditor who receives the transfer defends by arguing that the debtor was returning to the creditor property that the debtor held *in trust* for the creditor. If the creditor is correct in its assertion of a valid trust, and the debtor only holds legal title to the property, subject to the equitable title of the creditor beneficiary, the creditor's defense would be valid. If the transfer were not made, and the debtor filed bankruptcy, the creditor as beneficiary of a trust would be entitled to the return of its trust property.[154] That property would not be available for distribution to the debtor's other creditors. Property held by a debtor as trustee is not subject to the claims of creditors of the debtor in its individual capacity. § 541(d). Returning trust property to its beneficial owners thus does not contravene the bankruptcy distributional scheme, and if done prior to bankruptcy, likewise should not be recoverable as a preference.

---

[151]   478 F.3d 12 (1st Cir. 2007).

[152]   Id. at 15–16.

[153]   See also, In re Lee, 530 F.3d 458 (6th Cir. 2008) (following the rationale of *In re Lazarus*).

[154]   See §§ 5.8, 7.35–7.36.

The challenge for the creditor is proving the existence of a valid trust that would be immune from the claims of the debtor's other creditors. Meeting this challenge may require the creditor to prove the elements of either an express or constructive trust under applicable non-bankruptcy law. Among other things, the creditor may have to trace the funds in which it asserts a trust.[155] Tracing can be a serious problem if trust property is commingled with the debtor's general funds. Furthermore, if the creditor is trying to assert a constructive trust, rather than an express trust, it will be constrained by the equitable limits of that doctrine. In a Supreme Court case involving victims of the infamous fraud perpetrated by Charles Ponzi (the originator of the notorious "Ponzi" scheme), the Court denied a constructive trust argument both because of tracing issues and also because the equitable commands of that remedy were not satisfied when all claimants were victims of the same fraud.[156]

An interesting application of the trust exclusion is the Supreme Court case of *Begier v. I.R.S.*[157] The dispute in *Begier* centered on payments made by the debtor to the Internal Revenue Service during the preference period for overdue withholding and excise taxes. These taxes are called "trust-fund" taxes because they are subjected to a statutory trust in favor of the IRS by the Internal Revenue Code. 26 U.S.C. § 7501. The problem for the IRS was proving that the monies paid to it were the monies held in trust, rather than the debtor's property; a considerable portion of the payments (almost a million dollars) was made out of the debtor's general operating accounts. Common law tracing rules would have been of little help to the government. The Court nevertheless held for the IRS, concluding that the property transferred was the trust property, not the debtor's property. Therefore no preference had occurred. According to the Court, the debtor's voluntary act of paying the taxes was sufficient to identify the funds held in trust.

Begier is not a panacea for all creditors asserting trust claims as a defense to a preference action. Indeed, the benefit of the extraordinarily generous tracing rule used in that case probably is limited to taxing authorities. In other contexts, courts continue to show much less sympathy to creditors seeking to avoid preference liability by claiming that the debtor did not have the equitable beneficial interest in the property transferred. For example, in the massive bankruptcy case of *In re Southmark Corp.*,[158] all of the cash transactions of a large corporate group were handled by a unified cash management system held in the parent corporation's name. Records were kept of the credits and debits of the many related corporations who formed the corporate group. The former president of one of the subsidiaries was paid over $200,000 for an antecedent debt out of the parent's account, but the records charged the payment against the subsidiary against whom the creditor had the claim. The Fifth Circuit still held that the payment was a preference in the parent's bankruptcy, because the subsidiary did not have an enforceable trust claim in the cash management system

---

[155] See, e.g., In re Unicom Computer Corp., 13 F.3d 321 (9th Cir. 1994). In *Unicom*, funds were deposited in the debtor's account by mistake, and then remitted to the proper party within the preference period. The court found no preference, concluding that state law imposed a constructive trust on the mistaken deposit and that the funds were traced.

[156] See Cunningham v. Brown, 265 U.S. 1 (1924).

[157] 496 U.S. 53 (1990).

[158] 49 F.3d 1111 (5th Cir. 1995).

under state law. All of the money in the account was subject to the claims of creditors, and the payment to the former employee thus diminished the amount that could be paid to other creditors.

A final issue of interest with regard to the requirement that the transfer be of property of the debtor is whether a preference occurs if the debtor transfers *exempt* property to the creditor. On the surface, the statutory requirement appears to be satisfied: the property transferred indisputably was that of the debtor. Most courts under the Code accordingly hold that a transfer of exempt property is still a preference.[159] But does this make sense? By definition, creditors of the debtor cannot satisfy their claims out of exempt property. If the debtor filed bankruptcy and claimed the property as exempt, that property would not be distributed to her creditors. One could argue, then, that a transfer of exempt property does not violate the purpose of the preference law;[160] the transfer to the one creditor does not diminish the funds that would be available for other creditors. Those other creditors are not prejudiced, because they had no claim to the exempt property in the first place. An analogy could be drawn to the earmarking doctrine; in both cases, payment comes from a source that is not subject to general creditor claims. In response, courts finding preference liability when exempt property is transferred point out that the preferred creditor has no standing to assert the debtor's exemptions. Exemptions are personal to the debtor, and by choosing to pay a creditor rather than claim an exemption, the debtor has effectively waived the exemption.

§ 6.12 Elements of a Preference: To or for Benefit of Creditor

A transfer of the debtor's property may only be avoided as a preference if the transfer was "to or for the benefit of a creditor." § 547(b)(1). Two important aspects of preference law are implemented by this requirement. First, the law condemns both *direct* preferences ("to" a creditor) and *indirect* preferences ("for the benefit of" a creditor). Second, the preferred party must have the status of a "*creditor.*"

Taking the latter point first, the requirement that the party preferred be a "creditor" makes sense in view of the role of preference law. The core concerns of preference law are to assure equitable treatment of similarly situated *creditors* of the debtor when the debtor is insolvent shortly before bankruptcy, and to discourage those creditors from racing for the debtor's assets. A transfer to or for the benefit of a person who is not a "creditor" implicates neither concern. A non-creditor has no right to share in the debtor's assets at all. Such an apparently gratuitous transfer by an insolvent debtor to a non-creditor might constitute a fraudulent conveyance,[161] but it is not a preference.[162]

---

[159] E.g., Tavenner v. Smoot, 257 F.3d 401 (4th Cir. 2001); In re Noblit, 72 F.3d 757 (9th Cir. 1995).

[160] See Thomas H. Jackson, The Logic and Limits of Bankruptcy Law 133–34 (1986).

[161] See John C. McCoid, II, Corporate Preferences to Insiders, 43 S.C.L. Rev. 805, 808 (1992). See §§ 6.33–6.36.

[162] One commentator has suggested that the "creditor" requirement should be eliminated for preferences, at least those involving insiders. Peter A. Alces, Rethinking Professor Westbrook's Two Thoughts About Insider Preferences, 77 Minn. L. Rev. 605, 629–33 (1993).

The "creditor" requirement performs both an exclusionary and an inclusionary role. The exclusionary feature was just noted: transfers to or for the benefit of non-creditors fall outside the realm of preference avoidance. Having said that, it is important to remember the inclusive breadth of who is considered a "creditor" under the Bankruptcy Code. A "creditor" is defined as an "entity that has a *claim* against the debtor that arose at the time of or before the order for relief concerning the debtor." § 101(10)(A). "Claim," in turn, is defined very broadly as a "right to payment, whether or not such right is reduced to judgment, liquidated, unliquidated, fixed, contingent, matured, unmatured, disputed, undisputed, legal, equitable, secured, or unsecured,"[163] § 101(5)(A), or as a "right to an equitable remedy" for a breach that gives rise to such a right to payment.[164] § 101(5)(B). The legislative history emphasizes congressional intent that use of "this broadest possible definition . . . contemplates that all legal obligations of the debtor, no matter how remote or contingent, will be able to be dealt with in the bankruptcy case."[165]

"Direct" and "indirect" preferences can be illustrated by a simple example. Assume that Creditor loans Debtor $10,000. Guarantor, the president of Debtor, guarantees payment of the loan. The week before filing bankruptcy, Debtor pays Creditor $10,000, the balance due on the loan. The payment is a transfer "to" Creditor, and is a direct preference as to Creditor.

The payment to Creditor also eliminates the contingent liability that Guarantor had on the guaranty. If Debtor had not paid Creditor, Guarantor would have been called upon to pay Creditor. Thus, Debtor's payment to Creditor was "for the benefit of" Guarantor, and is an indirect preference as to Guarantor. Guarantor also qualifies as a "creditor" holding a "claim" within the meaning of the Bankruptcy Code. If Guarantor had been required to pay Creditor, she would have had a claim back against Debtor, the primary obligor, for reimbursement.

In the foregoing example, the payment from Debtor to Creditor is preferential *both* as to the direct *and* the indirect beneficiaries of that transfer. In terms of the *remedy* available, the bankruptcy trustee would be able to recover the preference from *either* the direct beneficiary of the preference, Creditor, or the indirect beneficiary, Guarantor. § 550(a)(1). Of course, the trustee is only entitled to a single satisfaction. § 550(d).

The interesting problem involving indirect preferences is whether recovery may be had from the direct beneficiary of the transfer when the transfer is preferential *only* as to the indirect beneficiary. This issue has arisen most often in the following situation: the indirect beneficiary is an *insider* and the transfer to the direct beneficiary, who is not an insider, is made during the extended preference period for insiders.[166] For

---

[163] See § 7.1.

[164] See § 7.3.

[165] S. Rep. No. 95–989, 95th Cong., 2d Sess., at 22 (1978); H.R. Rep. No. 95–595, 95th Cong., 1st Sess., at 309 (1977).

[166] Numerous commentators have written about the issues raised by insider preferences. A sampling includes Peter A. Alces, supra note 2; Donald W. Baker, Repayment of Loans Guaranteed by Insiders as Avoidable Preferences in Bankruptcy: *Deprizio* and Its Aftermath, 23 UCC L.J. 115 (1990); Peter L. Borowitz, Waiving Subrogation Rights and Conjuring Up Demons in Response to Deprizio, 45 Bus. Law.

example, in our hypothetical, assume that Debtor paid Creditor nine months before the bankruptcy filing while insolvent. The preference period for non-insider creditors is only 90 days, § 547(b)(4)(A), but for insiders the preference period is extended to one year before bankruptcy.[167] § 547(b)(4)(B). Since Creditor is not an insider, the transfer nine months before bankruptcy would not be a preference *as to Creditor*; that transfer would not fall within the 90–day preference period. However, that transfer to Creditor would be a preference *as to Guarantor*. As the president of the Debtor, Guarantor would qualify as an "insider" of the Debtor, § 101(31)(B), and thus the longer one-year preference period would apply. As discussed above, the transfer to Creditor would be "for the benefit of" Guarantor, because it eliminates Guarantor's contingent liability.

The question that has caused enormous controversy is what the *remedy* is in this case. Specifically, the question is whether the value of the avoided transfer can be *recovered* from the non-insider to whom the transfer was made, even though the transfer was not *avoidable* as to that creditor. The problem is this: the recovery section for avoided transfers provides that the trustee may recover the value of an avoided transfer "from the *initial transferee* of such transfer *or* the entity for whose benefit the transfer was made." § 550(a)(1). In our example, the "initial transferee" is the non-insider (Creditor), and the "entity for whose benefit the transfer was made" is the insider (Guarantor). The trustee without question can recover from the insider, as to whom the transfer was preferential. But § 550(a)(1), read literally and in isolation from § 547, appears to give the trustee the option to recover instead from the non-insider, as the "initial transferee."

In a decision that prompted a firestorm of debate, the Seventh Circuit in 1989 held in *Levit v. Ingersoll Rand Financial Corp. (In re V.N. Deprizio Construction Corp.)*,[168] on facts similar to the foregoing, that § 550(a)(1) should be given a literal and isolated reading. *Deprizio* held that recovery could be had from the non-insider creditor who was the initial transferee, even though the transfer was not a preference as to that non-insider, but only as to the insider. Nor did the court find this result absurd; as a policy matter, the court speculated that the insider guarantor might well cause the debtor to pay the guaranteed debt in preference to other creditors, who did not enjoy an insider guarantee.

Not liking this result, though, Congress amended the Code in 1994 by adding § 550(c), which overturns the precise result in *Deprizio*. Under § 550(c), no *recovery* may be had from a non-insider as to whom the transfer was not avoidable, for transfers made between 90 days and one year before bankruptcy. While § 550(c) solved the exact problem raised by the *Deprizio* facts, it did not provide complete protection for innocent non-insiders in all situations. For example, § 550(c) is no help to non-insiders where the trustee is not seeking any recovery—as would be the case where the trustee was avoiding a lien. To fix *that* problem, Congress again amended the Code in 2005, adding

---

2151 (1990); Robert F. Higgins & David E. Peterson, Is There a One–Year Preference Period for Non–Insiders?, 64 Am. Bankr. L.J. 383 (1990); John C. McCoid, II, supra note 1; Thomas E. Pitts, Jr., Insider Guarantees and the Law of Preferences, 55 Am. Bankr. L.J. 343 (1981); Jay L. Westbrook, Two Thoughts About Insider Preferences, 76 Minn. L. Rev. 73 (1991).

[167] See § 6.15.

[168] 874 F.2d 1186 (7th Cir. 1989).

§ 547(i), which immunizes a non-insider from *avoidance* where the transfer was made between 90 days and one year before bankruptcy. As will be discussed in a subsequent section that examines the *Deprizio* case and the two attempted "fixes" in more detail,[169] while non-insiders now have substantial protection against being harmed by avoidance of a transfer as a preference "for the benefit of" an insider, that protection still is not complete. They still are at risk with regard to indirect preferences made within the 90–day preference period, since both § 550(c) and § 547(i) only apply to transfers made between 90 days and one year before bankruptcy.

In another respect the *Deprizio* result, and subsequent attempted circumventions of that result by market participants, illustrate the significance of the limitation in § 547(b)(1) to avoidance of transfers to or for the benefit of a *creditor*. Note that even the much-maligned *Deprizio* holding is only possible if the insider is a "creditor." Indeed, in the *Deprizio* case itself, the court did not allow recovery with regard to payments made by the debtor for taxes and for pension and welfare obligations; in each instance, the court determined that the insider did not have a "claim" against the debtor.[170] If the insider is not a creditor, then the transfer outside of 90 days is not an avoidable preference at all: not as to the non-insider, because made more than 90 days before bankruptcy, § 547(b)(4)(A), and not as to the insider, because of a failure to satisfy the creditor requirement, § 547(b)(1). With the transfer unavoidable, the issue of recovery under § 550 falls by the wayside.

After *Deprizio*, bank lenders (the most common non-insider "victim" of the *Deprizio* situation) seized on the "creditor" requirement and attempted to get around the *Deprizio* result by careful drafting of the initial loan documents. The key was to have the insider guarantor *waive* any claim of reimbursement that it might have against the debtor if called upon to pay the guaranteed obligation.[171] If the insider did not have a contingent "right to payment" from the debtor, then it would not have a "claim" under § 101(5), would not be a "creditor," and § 547(b)(1) would not be satisfied. Some courts agreed with this argument and declined to find liability if the insider had waived its claims against the debtor.[172]

As many commentators explained, the "waiver" approach was not foolproof.[173] Courts might ignore the waiver as a formal evasion of the *Deprizio* rule, and find that the insider still was a "creditor";[174] the waiver might expose the lender to the risk of equitable subordination; and, finally, the waiver scheme might be attacked as a fraudulent conveyance. As a matter of policy, having the insider waive the right of reimbursement from the debtor made worse the equitable concerns that troubled the

---

[169] See § 6.26.

[170] Deprizio, supra note 168, 874 F.2d at 1191–94.

[171] See Baker, supra note 166, at 145–47.

[172] E.g., In re Ne. Contracting Co., 187 B.R. 420 (Bankr. D. Conn. 1995); In re Fastrans, Inc., 142 B.R. 241 (Bankr. E.D. Tenn. 1992).

[173] See id.; see also Alces, supra note 162, at 626–27; Borowitz, supra note 166, at 2155–68; David I. Katzen, Deprizio and Bankruptcy Code Section 550: Extended Preference Exposure Via Insider Guarantees, and Other Perils of Initial Transferee Liability, 45 Bus. Law. 511, 530–31 (1990).

[174] E.g., In re USA Detergents, Inc., 418 B.R. 533 (Bankr. D. Del. 2009); In re Pro Page Partners, LLC, 292 B.R. 622 (Bankr. E.D. Tenn. 2003); In re Telesphere Commc'ns, Inc., 229 B.R. 173 (Bankr. N.D. Ill. 1999).

Seventh Circuit. Without any possibility of reimbursement from the debtor, the insider guarantor would make every effort to see to it that the debtor paid the guaranteed obligation in preference to all other debts.

One final aspect of the indirect preference issue bears mention. In some cases, the courts have had to ascertain what constitutes a "benefit" within the meaning of § 547(b)(1). For example, assume that Guarantor only guarantees $50,000 of a total debt of $75,000 to Creditor, and that Debtor pays $20,000 to Creditor, reducing the total debt to $55,000. Although Guarantor still has a contingent liability of $50,000, Guarantor arguably is *indirectly* benefited by reducing the likelihood that it will be called on to fulfill the guaranty. The First Circuit concluded that this type of indirect benefit was not enough to support avoidance under § 547(b).[175] That court concluded that only a direct and immediate dollar-for-dollar reduction in the liability of the guarantor counts as a "benefit."

§ 6.13   Elements of a Preference: Antecedent Debt

A transfer of the debtor's property to or for the benefit of a creditor is only a preference if that transfer was made "for or on account of an *antecedent debt* owed by the debtor before such transfer was made." § 547(b)(2). Application of (b)(2) thus requires: (1) determining when the debt was incurred; (2) determining when the transfer was made; and (3) comparing the time of the former to the latter. Only if the debt was incurred prior to the transfer is preference liability possible. Furthermore, the transfer must be "for or on account of" the debt.[176]

The rationales for a preference law[177] support limiting the scope of avoidance to transfers for antecedent debts. This point can be demonstrated by considering an example where the transfer is *not* made for an antecedent debt. Assume that a month before she files bankruptcy, Debtor pays cash for a chain saw to use in her business. Allowing Chain Saw Seller to keep the cash does not contravene the equality principle, because Seller gave full value in exchange for the payment by Debtor; prior to that purchase, Seller was not a creditor of Debtor at all. The "race to the courthouse" concern is not implicated, for the simple reason that Seller has nothing to race for prior to the sale; again, Seller was not a creditor. Indeed, the idea that the preference law should discourage "opt out" activity by creditors that might precipitate the debtor's "slide into bankruptcy" has a flip side; the law should encourage people to do business on normal terms with financially distressed debtors. If cash sales such as the one posited were subject to avoidance, potential sellers would be wary of doing business at all with debtors in financial trouble. Preference law is concerned only with existing creditors trying to improve their position vis-à-vis other creditors, not with people negotiating the original terms of a transaction with the debtor. If the bargain negotiated is too "hard," perhaps fraudulent conveyance law might be relevant, but preference law is not.

---

[175]   In re Erin Food Serv., Inc., 980 F.2d 792 (1st Cir. 1992).

[176]   See, e.g., Warsco v. Preferred Tech. Group, 258 F.3d 557, 569 (7th Cir. 2001).

[177]   See § 6.7.

Applying the antecedent debt rule necessitates ascertaining the exact time that the transfer was made by the debtor, as noted. Performing that task, in turn, requires consideration of the timing rules of § 547(e). These crucial rules were discussed in detail in an earlier section.[178] At this juncture, it is important to recall that in some situations application of the timing rules of (e) might result in finding a technical satisfaction of the antecedent debt requirement of (b)(2). This occurs because the transfer is not deemed made until perfected, subject to a thirty-day grace period. § 547(e)(2). The most important example is a delay in the perfection of a security interest or mortgage.[179]

For example, assume that the Debtor in our hypothetical did not pay cash for the chain saw, but instead bought it on credit, and granted Seller a security interest in the chain saw to secure payment of the balance of the purchase price. As between Debtor and Seller, the transfer of the interest in the chain saw and the grant of the security interest occurred at the same time. Yet, if Seller delays too long in perfecting that security interest, its security interest might be avoided as a preference. This aspect of the preference law enforces the policy against secret liens.

Not all of the cases in which the timing rules of (e) result in the technical creation of an antecedent debt implicate the legitimate concerns of the preference law. The means by which those transactions are excluded from preference avoidance is not through a strained interpretation of the timing rules or the requirement of antecedence, but through specific preference exceptions in § 547(c). For example, if the Debtor pays for the chain saw by means of a check rather than with cash, and the check is honored, the contemporaneous exchange exception of § 547(c)(1) will offer a safe harbor from avoidance.[180] Even intended extensions of credit may be insulated from preference avoidance if the debtor makes payments in the ordinary course of business.[181] § 547(c)(2).

In applying the antecedent debt test, it is important to remember that under the Code a "debt" is considered to exist even if it is still unliquidated, unmatured, disputed, or contingent. § 101(5)(A). Furthermore, the debt arises when value is provided to the debtor, either by the rendition of services, the delivery of goods, or the like—not when a bill or invoice is sent to the debtor. Thus, for example, when a law firm provides legal services to the debtor, the debt is deemed to arise, and any payment thereafter is on account of an "antecedent debt" for preference law purposes.[182] Note, though, that this construction of the antecedent debt requirement does not then necessarily mean that preference liability will invariably be imposed in such situations. If payment is soon forthcoming after the bill is sent, and in a routine manner, the creditor is likely to escape preference liability either under the safe harbor for substantially

---

[178] See § 6.9.

[179] See, e.g., In re Lazarus, 478 F.3d 12, 14–15 (1st Cir. 2007) (delay in recordation of a mortgage renders transfer of mortgage for antecedent debt).

[180] See § 6.17. This example is given in the legislative history. See 124 Cong. Rec. H11,097 (daily ed. Sept. 28, 1978) (statement of Rep. Edwards).

[181] See § 6.18.

[182] See, e.g., In re First Jersey Secs., Inc., 180 F.3d 504, 511–12 (3d Cir. 1999).

contemporaneous exchanges,[183] 547(c)(1), or the one for transfers in the ordinary course of business.[184] § 547(c)(2).

§ 6.14   Elements of a Preference: Made While Debtor Insolvent

A transfer to a creditor is only a potential preference if "made while the debtor was insolvent." § 547(b)(3). Only if the debtor was insolvent at the time of the transfer are the preference policy concerns of equality and deterrence[185] applicable. A solvent debtor by definition has enough assets to pay *all* creditors in full. If a solvent debtor pays one creditor, equality is not defeated, because other creditors likewise should be able to obtain full payment. Nor will the creditors of a solvent debtor have reason to race to the courthouse to grab their share of the debtor's assets; there should be plenty for everyone.

The insolvency issue is determined as of the date the transfer is made. Therefore, even if the debtor later becomes insolvent, and is insolvent at the time of bankruptcy, a creditor who was paid while the debtor was still solvent is immune from preference liability. This immunity exists even if none of the debtor's other creditors were paid thereafter; theoretically, at least, those creditors could have obtained full payment from the then-solvent debtor.

The timing rules of § 547(e)[186] are important to the insolvency determination. The focus will not necessarily be on whether the debtor was solvent when the transfer took effect between the debtor and the creditor, but on the debtor's solvency at the time that the transfer was *deemed* made under subsection (e). To revisit prior discussions, a transfer under (e) may not be deemed made until it is perfected.

For example, assume that Debtor purchases a chain saw on credit from Seller on June 1, and on that same date grants Seller a security interest to secure payment of the balance due. At that time, Debtor is solvent. Seller, however, does not perfect until July 15. The transfer of the security interest will be deemed to have been made on July 15, the date of perfection. § 547(e)(2)(B). If Debtor has become insolvent by July 15, § 547(b)(3) will be satisfied, and Seller will be subject to possible preference liability. This rule makes sense, however (if one accepts the anti-secret lien policy), because it prevents Seller from taking a lien, keeping it secret from the world, and then perfecting that lien only after the debtor develops financial trouble and becomes insolvent.

Under pre-Code law, the requirement that the trustee prove that the debtor was insolvent at the time of the transfer presented a significant practical barrier to preference avoidance. As the House Report explains:

Given the state of most debtor's books and records, such a task is nearly impossible. Given the financial condition of nearly all debtors in the three months

---

[183]   See § 6.17.

[184]   See § 6.18

[185]   See § 6.7.

[186]   See § 6.9.

before bankruptcy, the task is also generally not worth the effort. Rarely is a debtor solvent during the three months before bankruptcy. Thus, the preference section requires the trustee to prove a fact that nearly always exists yet never can be proved with certainty. . . . Because of the difficulty of proof, creditors are not deterred from the race of diligence, and the policy of equality is defeated.[187]

The solution the 1978 Code adopted to this problem was to create a *presumption* of insolvency during the 90–day preference period for non-insiders. § 547(f). Although the trustee retains the ultimate burden of proving insolvency, the presumption of insolvency in subsection (f) shifts to the creditor the burden of going forward with sufficient evidence to overcome the presumption. If the debtor's books and records are a hopeless mess, the creditor will not be able to rebut the presumption. Note that the presumption only applies for 90 days, however. If the trustee is attempting to avoid a transfer to an insider made during the extended preference period of one year, § 547(b)(4)(B), more than 90 days before bankruptcy, the trustee will have to prove insolvency without the aid of a presumption.

In commercial law, "insolvency" may have several possible meanings. The Bankruptcy Code uses a "balance sheet" test of insolvency. Thus, proof that the debtor is generally not paying its debts as they come due, or is unable to pay its debts as they come due (variants of the "equity" insolvency test), are not relevant to the determination of whether a debtor was insolvent for preference purposes.[188] Instead, a debtor is "insolvent" if "the sum of such entity's debts is greater than all of such entity's property, at a fair valuation." § 101(32)(A). Giving meaning to "fair valuation" requires the court to select a standard of valuation. In cases involving business debtors, courts usually utilize going concern value, in light of prevailing market conditions.[189]

Note also that the asset side of the ledger does not include either exempt property or property that the debtor transferred with actual fraudulent intent. § 101(32)(A)(i), (ii). For most consumer debtors, the exclusion of exempt property makes a finding of insolvency likely. For a partnership debtor, the definition of insolvency also takes into account the non-partnership net worth of each general partner. § 101(32)(B).

§ 6.15 Elements of a Preference: Within Preference Period

A creditor is not subject to preference liability for all transfers received after the debtor becomes insolvent, although such a rule would be defensible, and, some have urged, even advisable.[190] Instead, preference avoidance is only possible for transfers made during a limited statutory period prior to the bankruptcy filing. As a general rule, the "preference period" is *ninety days* before the bankruptcy. § 547(b)(4)(A). Thus,

---

[187] H.R. Rep. No. 95–595, 95th Cong., 1st Sess., at 178 (1977).

[188] The only exception is for a municipality debtor, for whom an equity insolvency test is used in lieu of a balance sheet test. § 101(32)(C).

[189] E.g., In re Lamar Haddox Contractor, 40 F.3d 118 (5th Cir. 1994); In re Taxman Clothing Co., 905 F.2d 166 (7th Cir. 1990); In re Am. Classic Voyages Co., 367 B.R. 500 (Bankr. D. Del. 2007).

[190] See Bruce R. Kraus, Note, Preferential Transfers and the Value of the Insolvent Firm, 87 Yale L.J. 1449, 1459–63 (1978).

even if all other elements of a preference are proved, if the transfer was made to the creditor 91 days prior to bankruptcy, the creditor is absolutely protected.

The only exception is for transfers to or for the benefit of *insiders*, as to whom the preference period is extended to *one year*. § 547(b)(4)(B). The rationale for the longer period for insiders is that they may be in a better position than other creditors to see the debtor's bankruptcy looming in the distance. If not subjected to a longer reach-back period, an insider would have an unfair advantage in starting the race of diligence for the debtor's assets before other creditors. Furthermore, an insider may be able to keep the debtor out of bankruptcy for a relatively short period of time (such as 91 days), and thereby insulate any transfers it might receive from the debtor, but forestalling bankruptcy for a financially troubled debtor for over a year would be much more difficult.

Considerable litigation has arisen as to what constitutes an "insider" for preference purposes. The Bankruptcy Code provides a definition of "insider" in § 101(31), but the definition states that the term "includes" certain statutory categories. This leaves open the possibility that a person or entity be deemed a non-statutory insider, and thus qualifies for the extended one-year preference period.

Many courts engage in a highly fact specific analysis in determining whether a creditor is a non-statutory insider. Insider status may be premised upon ownership or ability to control the debtor, but a creditor can refute this if the evidence shows that it dealt with the debtor on an arm's length basis. For individual debtors, the litigation is even more fact specific. For example, a debtor's estranged wife may be considered an insider,[191] while a debtor's future husband may not be considered an insider.[192]

In contrast to the fact-based approach, some courts have adopted a "per se" approach. Under this approach, a relationship can give rise to insider status based on similarity to the insider relationships enumerated in the statute.

In re Longview Aluminum, L.L.C.[193] illustrates this type of analysis. In *In re Longview Aluminum,* the creditor was a 12% stakeholder and a member of the board of managers of the debtor limited liability company. Creditor argued, however, that since he lacked access to business records of the company (due to a dispute with another manager) he could not exercise the control over the debtor required of an insider.

The court in *In re Longview Aluminum* followed the construct that statutory lists should also include analogous categories. Thus the articulated test for determining whether a creditor is a non-statutory insider is whether its relationship to the debtor is "similar to or has characteristics of any of the defined relationships."[194] The court found that LLC members hold positions analogous to corporate directors, an insider position enumerated in the statute. Thus, the actual limitations on the creditor's control of the debtor did not matter; the creditor was deemed an insider since the position held was

---

[191] E.g., In re Paschall, 2009 WL 1528845 (E.D. Va. June 1, 2009).

[192] E.g., In re Farson, 387 B.R. 784 (Bankr. D. Idaho 2008).

[193] 657 F.3d 507 (7th Cir. 2011).

[194] Id. at 510.

analogous to an enumerated insider position, and thus *per se* a category of non-statutory insider status.

Fixing an absolute cutoff period for preference liability implicates once again the need to ascertain exactly when a transfer is made. Section 547(e) must be consulted.[195] As discussed in earlier sections, § 547(e) may postpone the time a transfer is deemed to be made until that transfer is perfected. Thus, a creditor who takes a security interest outside of the preference period, but who does not perfect until during the preference period, may have that security interest avoided as a preference.

An example of the importance of timing with regard to the application of the preference period is the Supreme Court case of *Barnhill v. Johnson*.[196] In *Barnhill*, the debtor delivered a check to the creditor 92 days before bankruptcy, and the check was honored on the ninetieth day. By deciding that the honor date should control, the Supreme Court exposed the creditor to preference liability.

Limiting preference liability to transfers made a relatively short time prior to bankruptcy is derived historically from the notion that only transfers motivated by a "bad" intention should be set aside. Thus, at earlier stages of our jurisprudence, only if a debtor made a transfer "in contemplation" of bankruptcy or with an "intent to prefer" was the transfer voidable. It was a natural step to presume that all transfers made within a short defined period prior to bankruptcy were tainted with the proscribed intention. From there it was again a natural progression to substitute a bright-line rule for an open-ended standard.

Today, the motives of the debtor and creditor are no longer strictly relevant to preference liability, and thus the original justifications for the limited preference period are more dubious. In 1978, Congress eliminated the requirement in prior law that the creditor have "reasonable cause to believe the debtor was insolvent."[197] Yet seeds of the earlier idea remain; the notion persists that only transfers made during the debtor's immediate "slide into bankruptcy," as creditors race to grab the failing debtor's assets, should be vulnerable.[198] A transfer made long before bankruptcy, even if the debtor also was insolvent at that time, may not have been motivated by a "race of diligence." It is worth noting that the elimination of the "reasonable cause to believe" requirement in 1978 was part of a tradeoff; in the same reform bill, Congress shortened the reach-back period in 1978 from four months to 90 days.

If the equality premise behind preference law is given precedence over that of deterrence, the fact that a transfer was not made during the debtor's final pre-bankruptcy slide should not matter, as long as it came when the debtor was already insolvent. Furthermore, the fixed time limit rule may create perverse incentives for

---

[195] See § 6.9.

[196] 503 U.S. 393 (1992).

[197] See Bankruptcy Act of 1898, § 60b. For discussion of the reasons for eliminating this requirement, see H.R. Rep. No. 95–595, 95th Cong., 1st Sess., at 178 (1977).

Congress initially did retain the "reasonable cause to believe" requirement for preferences to an insider made more than 90 days before bankruptcy. However, this provision was repealed in 1984.

[198] See H.R. Rep. No. 95–595, 95th Cong., 1st Sess., at 177–78 (1977).

creditors that actually harm debtors; "the rule invites creditors to keep debtors out of bankruptcy for the statutory period and then to abandon them summarily."[199]

However, even if equality is accorded the upper hand normatively, the limited preference reach-back period can be justified by the interests of *certainty* and *finality*.[200] Repose is crucial to commercial transactions, and preferences by their very nature upset that repose. A cutoff period protects finality absolutely for transfers made beyond the period chosen. Furthermore, preference litigation is simplified; counting days is relatively straightforward. A non-insider creditor who receives a transfer from a distressed debtor knows without question that it will be entitled to keep that transfer if 91 days elapse and the debtor does not go into bankruptcy. That creditor then will be free to use the transferred property without worry of subsequent recapture.[201] And, other creditors know that they must commence an involuntary bankruptcy case within 90 days of a significant transfer to another creditor if they hope to recapture that transfer.

§ 6.16   Elements of a Preference: Preferential Effect

The final element that the trustee must prove to establish a prima facie case for avoiding a transfer as a preference is that the transfer had a "preferential effect," or, as it is otherwise described, that the transfer allowed the creditor to recover a "greater amount" on its claim than it would have without the payment. § 547(b)(5). More precisely, § 547(b)(5) imposes a hypothetical chapter 7 liquidation test. A comparison must be made between:

- what the creditor *actually* received or will receive, counting both the challenged transfer and any projected bankruptcy distribution, and

- what the creditor *hypothetically* would have received in a chapter 7 bankruptcy case, if the transfer had not been made. § 547(b)(5)(A)–(C).

The transfer will satisfy subsection (b)(5) if the amount actually and projected to be received is greater than the amount that hypothetically would have been received.

A useful rule of thumb is that the preferential effect test of § 547(b)(5) will always be met unless:

- the creditor's class would be paid 100 cents on the dollar in bankruptcy, or

- the creditor was fully secured.

The first rule of thumb is that the preferential effect test will be satisfied unless the allegedly preferred creditor's class would be paid in full in a bankruptcy

---

[199] Kraus, supra note 190, at 1457.

[200] See Charles J. Tabb, Rethinking Preferences, 43 S.C. L. Rev. 981, 1026–28, 1034 (1992).

[201] See John C. McCoid, II, Bankruptcy, Preferences, and Efficiency: An Expression of Doubt, 67 Va. L. Rev. 249, 267–68 (1981), for a discussion of the costs incident to a creditor's uncertainty as to whether it will be able to keep transferred property.

distribution.[202] The reason, as Justice Brandeis explained in the foundational case of *Palmer Clay Products v. Brown*,[203] is that the preferred creditor will receive *both* the pre-bankruptcy preference (at 100¢ on the dollar), *and* the bankruptcy distribution (at something less than 100¢), whereas the non-preferred creditors in the same class will receive only the bankruptcy distribution of less than 100¢ on the dollar.[204] Justice Brandeis used the example of a pre-bankruptcy payment of $1,000 on a $10,000 claim, with a projected bankruptcy distribution of 50 percent. The preferred creditor's total actual recovery (without avoidance) will be $5,500: the $1,000 preference, plus $4,500 in bankruptcy (50% of the $9,000 claim remaining after the payment of the preference). If the preference had not been made, the creditor would have received only $5,000: 50% of the entire $10,000. The $500 difference is attributable to the fact that the creditor was paid in full for the $1,000 preference, but would have received only half of the $1,000 in bankruptcy. If the trustee avoids and recovers the $1,000 payment, the creditor will be paid $5,000 in the bankruptcy.

Applying the hypothetical chapter 7 test will require the court to utilize all of the particular rules governing chapter 7 distributions.[205] Thus, for example, the order of distribution mandated by § 726 will have to be applied. Note that in a hypothetical chapter 7 liquidation, the amount of claims against the estate and the total value of property available for distribution might be different than is true in the actual bankruptcy case under another chapter. For example, more contracts and leases might be rejected in a chapter 7, where the debtor's business is not being continued, than in a chapter 11; accordingly, the hypothetical amount of unsecured claims would be increased. Similarly, estate property may not bring full going concern value in a chapter 7, but might be saleable only at a lower liquidation price.[206] Also, the fees that would be paid to the chapter 7 trustee would have to be computed.

Another important question is *when* the hypothetical distribution is to take place. The Code does not answer that question. Again, case law has followed the direction of the Supreme Court in *Palmer Clay Products* that the date of the bankruptcy filing should control, not the date of the challenged transfer. Only by looking at the actual state of affairs at the time of bankruptcy can it be determined if the creditor was effectively preferred.[207]

The second rule of thumb in applying the preferential effect test is that a transfer to a *fully secured* creditor is not a preference.[208] The reason is that even if the challenged transfer had not been made, such a creditor would have been paid in full in a chapter 7 bankruptcy case. To illustrate, assume that Creditor is owed $5,000, and

---

[202] Palmer Clay Prods. v. Brown, 297 U.S. 227, 229 (1936). See also Vern Countryman, The Concept of a Voidable Preference in Bankruptcy, 38 Vand. L. Rev. 713, 723–24, 736–38 (1985).

[203] 297 U.S. 227 (1936).

[204] Id. at 229.

[205] See Countryman, supra note 202, at 733–35. For an extensive discussion of the application of § 547(b)(5), especially as it relates to secured creditors, see David G. Carlson, Security Interests in the Crucible of Voidable Preference Law, 1995 U. Ill. L. Rev. 211, 256–79.

[206] See Carlson, supra note 205, at 257, 267–69.

[207] *Palmer Clay Products*, supra note 202, 297 U.S. at 229.

[208] See Countryman, supra note 202, at 739–40.

has collateral worth $6,000 securing that claim. A payment by Debtor to Creditor during the preference period while Debtor is insolvent will not be a preference, because Creditor would have received payment of the entire $5,000 claim even if the pre-bankruptcy transfer had not been made.

Note, though, that the fact that the creditor was fully secured at the time of the transfer may not be a complete defense, for at least two possible reasons. First, the timing rule of *Palmer Clay Products* requires a valuation of the collateral at the time of bankruptcy, not the time of the payment. Conceivably, the creditor could have been fully secured when the payment was made, but if the collateral declined in value, the creditor could have become undersecured. In the example used above, assume that the collateral was worth $6,000 when the payment was made, but was worth only $3,000 when bankruptcy occurred. In that event, Creditor would not have been paid in full in the bankruptcy case. Second, the valuation standard may change. The creditor may only be fully secured if a going concern value is utilized, rather than a liquidation value; yet, in conducting the hypothetical chapter 7 analysis, the court may adopt the lower liquidation amount.

A corollary of the second rule of thumb is that a transfer to a creditor who is only *partially secured* will have a preferential effect under § 547(b)(5).[209] The reason is that the payment will be allocated to the *unsecured* portion of the claim; undersecured creditors will not usually release collateral until full payment has been made. For example, assume that a payment of $1,000 is made to a Creditor with a $5,000 claim, secured by collateral worth $3,000. Under § 506(a)(1), Creditor's claim is "bifurcated" into two claims: a secured claim for the value of the collateral (here, $3,000), and an unsecured claim for the balance (here, $2,000—the $5,000 total minus the $3,000 secured claim). The $1,000 payment will be attributed to the $2,000 unsecured claim. After the payment, the Creditor still will retain the collateral (worth $3,000), and will have a $1,000 unsecured claim. The preferential effect can be demonstrated, assuming that unsecured claims would be paid 50% in bankruptcy. In our example, without avoidance Creditor will actually receive $4,500 (the $1,000 payment, plus $3,000 for the secured claim, plus $500 for the 50% payout on the remaining $1,000 unsecured claim). If the payment had not been made, Creditor would have received only $4,000 ($3,000 for the secured claim, plus $1,000 for the 50% payout on the $2,000 unsecured claim)

The only exception to the rule that a transfer to a partially secured creditor will be a preference is when the creditor is paid out of its own collateral.[210] In that situation, the creditor by definition relinquishes that portion of the collateral, and the value of its secured claim is diminished in like amount. A common example is when the creditor forecloses on collateral.

An interesting result may be produced in the foreclosure context. For example, a creditor will typically credit bid on its collateral in a routine home foreclosure. If the

---

[209] See, e.g., Barash v. Pub. Fin. Corp., 658 F.2d 504 (7th Cir. 1981); In re Imagine Fulfillment Servs., LLC, 489 B.R. 136 (Bankr. C.D. Cal. 2013); In re Qimonda Richmond, LLC, 467 B.R. 318 (Bankr. D. Del. 2012).

[210] See Countryman, supra note 202, at 742–43.

property is in fact worth more than the secured debt owed to the creditor, the court may find that the creditor has received more than it would have in a hypothetical chapter 7.[211] In fraudulent conveyance actions, the purchase price in a foreclosure sale will generally be deemed "reasonably equivalent value" of the property as long as proper foreclosure procedures are followed. Some courts decline to extend this logic to the preference context. The underlying rationale is that the interpretation of "reasonably equivalent value" in the fraudulent conveyance cases dealt with the term specifically in the fraudulent conveyance provision, and thus does not extend to preference actions.

The test of preferential effect is measured by the amount that the creditor would have been paid in the hypothetical chapter 7 case *out of the estate*. The question is whether that creditor has been preferred over other creditors with respect to the distribution that would have been made in bankruptcy. Thus, the fact that the preferred creditor might have been paid anyway from some other source is irrelevant to the preference analysis. For example, the fact that a debt is not dischargeable, meaning that the creditor may attempt to collect from the debtor after bankruptcy, does not change the fact that the creditor was preferred over other creditors in the distribution of the debtor's assets in bankruptcy.[212]

Another situation where this issue could arise is when the creditor is the beneficiary under a letter of credit, and is paid by the debtor during the preference period. The creditor will argue that even if it had not been paid by the debtor, it would have been paid by the issuer of the letter of credit. Courts, however, have rejected this argument.[213] The debtor's other creditors, who lack similar recourse against the independent issuer of the credit, are prejudiced when the creditor is paid out of the debtor's assets, reducing the amount available for others, and violating the equality principle. The only possible theory for the creditor to avoid liability in such a case is the substantially contemporaneous exchange exception in § 547(c)(1).[214] If the issuer released collateral of the debtor in the amount paid to the creditor beneficiary of the letter of credit, which would constitute an exchange of new value for the payment to the creditor.[215]

A final problem is whether the hypothetical chapter 7 test in § 547(b)(5) can take into account *actual postpetition* events. Nothing on the face of the statute suggests that the court may temper its commanded flight of fantasy with reality. In some instances, however, not doing so might lead to absurd results that would conflict with other provisions of the Code.

A prime example is where the trustee or debtor in possession actually assumes an executory contract or unexpired lease in the bankruptcy case, after the debtor made payments to the other party to the contract or lease during the preference period. May

---

[211] See, e.g., In re Whittle Dev., Inc., 463 B.R. 796 (Bankr. N.D. Tex. 2011); In re Villarreal, 413 B.R. 633 (Bankr. S.D. Tex. 2009).

[212] See Countryman, supra note 202, at 736 n.135.

[213] See, e.g. In re Powerine Oil Co., 59 F.3d 969 (9th Cir. 1995).

[214] See § 6.17.

[215] See, e.g., In re Fuel Oil Supply & Terminaling, Inc., 837 F.2d 224 (5th Cir. 1988).

the trustee then recover the pre-bankruptcy payments as a preference? The trustee will argue that § 547(b)(5) requires the court to hypothesize what would have happened in a chapter 7 case. And, in that hypothetical chapter 7 case, the contract or lease might have been rejected, rather than assumed. If so, the payments made shortly before bankruptcy might have been recoverable as preferences. The problem is that allowing the trustee to recover prepetition payments made on a contract or lease that in fact was later assumed would be inconsistent with the treatment of assumed contracts in § 365. The other party to an assumed contract is entitled to be paid in full; as a condition of assumption, defaults must be cured, § 365(b)(1)(A), and future obligations are entitled to administrative priority. Implicitly, then, that party also should be permitted to retain prepetition payments made on that contract. Recognizing that the hypothetical test of § 547(b)(5) should not be interpreted in a way that would undermine executory contract doctrine, courts have taken postpetition events into account in the contract assumption cases, and by doing so have not allowed preference avoidance.[216]

§ 6.17 Safe Harbors: Contemporaneous Exchange

The first exception to preference liability is for contemporaneous exchanges for new value. § 547(c)(1). The justification for the contemporaneous exchange exception is related to the avoidance requirement that the transfer be on account of an antecedent debt.[217] § 547(b)(2). Payment of a contemporaneous debt is not proscribed by the preference laws. None of the evils which § 547 seeks to redress are implicated in such a case; the debtor's other creditors are not prejudiced unfairly, and there is no "race" for the debtor's assets. Even an insolvent debtor is permitted to buy a hammer or get a haircut, without the hardware store or the barber being forced to disgorge the payment. Indeed, if the law were otherwise, insolvent debtors effectively would be foreclosed from engaging in financial transactions at all.

The need to protect such contemporaneous transactions is not fully satisfied by limiting preference avoidance to payments on antecedent debts under § 547(b)(2). The reason is that even though some types of transactions may be intended by the debtor and the creditor to be essentially contemporaneous, the practical reality is that minor delays might occur. As a technical legal matter, the debt may be deemed to arise slightly before the payment on that debt, i.e., an antecedent debt may be created.

For example, the "transfer" of the debtor's property when payment is made by check does not actually occur until the check is honored a day or two after the check is delivered to the creditor, and yet the parties did not intend a credit transaction. The payment by check is intended to serve as the functional equivalent of a cash payment.[218] Without a safe harbor such as § 547(c)(1), however, such unintended and insignificant delays would expose the creditor to preference avoidance. It makes no sense to make the debtor hand the barber a few pennies with each snip of the scissors, or to make debtors pay always with cash instead of by check. Section 547(c)(1) provides

---

[216] E.g., In re Superior Toy & Mfg. Co., 78 F.3d 1169 (7th Cir. 1996); In re LCO Enters., 12 F.3d 938 (9th Cir. 1993).

[217] See § 6.13.

[218] See H.R. Rep. No. 95–595, 95th Cong., 1st Sess., at 373 (1977).

that safe harbor. Thus, a payment by check for a current debt is not preferential (assuming, of course, that the check is honored).[219]

Two elements must be satisfied for the contemporaneous exchange exception to apply. First, the debtor and the creditor must *intend* to make a contemporaneous exchange for new value. § 547(c)(1)(A). Second, the transfer must *in fact* be a substantially contemporaneous exchange. § 547(c)(1)(B). If either the intent or the fact is lacking, the creditor will not be able to take advantage of the (c)(1) safe harbor.

These two elements of § 547(c)(1) are derived from two old Supreme Court cases. The intent prong comes from *National City Bank v. Hotchkiss*.[220] In that case, a creditor made an unsecured loan to a debtor-stockbroker at 10 a.m. That very same day the market fell, the broker was suspended by the stock exchange, and the creditor, learning of these unfortunate developments, demanded and received a pledge of collateral to secure the now-precarious debt. Bankruptcy was filed still later that same eventful day. The Supreme Court, by Justice Holmes, held that the collateral pledge was an avoidable transfer. Under current § 547(c)(1), the result would be the same: even though the *actual* time elapsed between the making of the loan and the transfer of security was but a few hours, at the time the parties entered into the original transaction they did not *intend* to provide for the contemporaneous transfer of collateral.

The second element of § 547(c)(1) is that the exchange must in fact be substantially contemporaneous. This prong is derived from *Dean v. Davis*.[221] In that case, the debtor and creditor intended to enter into a secured loan at the outset, unlike in *Hotchkiss*. However, in *Dean* the mortgage was not actually executed until seven days later, and was recorded on the eighth day. This short delay, the Supreme Court held (by Justice Brandeis), was permissible, and the mortgage could not be avoided as a preference.

Problems have arisen in applying the second element, that the transfer must in fact be substantially contemporaneous. Courts have recognized that precise temporal equivalence is not required; some flexibility must be permitted, in view of the use of the term "substantially" in the statute. Thus, for example, a two-to-three week delay in transferring collateral has been upheld against preference attack.[222]

The biggest difficulty has been in cases similar to *Dean v. Davis*, *viz.*, those involving a delay in the perfection or recordation of a security interest or mortgage. Ironically, in the face of the subsection's historical roots in *Dean*, many courts have refused to apply the contemporaneous exchange safe harbor in this setting at all, or

---

[219] E.g., Velde v. Kirsch, 543 F.3d 469 (8th Cir. 2008); In re Standard Food Servs., Inc., 723 F.2d 820 (11th Cir. 1984). If a check is subsequently dishonored, then the creditor is usually deprived of the contemporaneous exchange affirmative defense. See, e.g., Endo Steel, Inc. v. Janas (In re JWJ Contracting Co.), 371 F.3d 1079, 1082 (9th Cir. 2004); In re Barefoot, 952 F.2d 795 (4th Cir. 1991). But see In re Philip Servs. Corp., 359 B.R. 616 (Bankr. S.D. Tex. 2006).

[220] 231 U.S. 50 (1913).

[221] 242 U.S. 438 (1917).

[222] See Pine Top Ins. Co. v. Bank of Am. Nat'l Trust & Sav. Ass'n, 969 F.2d 321 (7th Cir. 1992). See also In re Hedrick, 524 F.3d 1175 (11th Cir. 2008) (eight-day delay upheld as contemporanous).

have limited the temporal reach of the section to the time period specified in § 547(e)(2).[223] Consider an example. On day one, Creditor loans Debtor money, and Debtor grants Creditor a security interest to secure the loan. Due to an inadvertent mistake in filing the financing statement, the security interest is not perfected until day 35.[224] Under § 547(e)(2)(B), the transfer of the security interest is deemed to occur at the time of perfection (i.e., on day 35) and thus is a transfer for an antecedent debt (which was created on day one). But can the creditor deflect preference avoidance by arguing that perfection on day 35 was "substantially contemporaneous," and thus protected under § 547(c)(1)?

One line of authority has held against the creditor on these facts as a matter of law, reasoning that § 547(e)(2) contemplates only a 30–day grace period (10 days before 2005) to perfect security interests. Allowing a longer time period to suffice under (c)(1) would effectively permit an end run around (e)(2), these courts believe.[225] In the context of lien perfection cases, those courts limit (c)(1) to the time period allowed under (e)(2); effectively, then, (c)(1) is useless for the secured creditor. Furthermore, if the transaction involves an enabling loan (or PMSI), those courts are even more likely to relegate the creditor to the defense provided by § 547(c)(3). Central to their analysis is an invocation of the statutory construction canon that the more specific (here, subsections (e)(2) and/or (c)(3)) controls the general (here, subsection (c)(1)).[226]

A competing view rejects such a bright-line test, and assesses the issue of substantial contemporaneity on a flexible case-by-case basis, without being necessarily constrained by the subsection (e)(2) time period.[227] At least in non-enabling loan cases, the more flexible view appears to be more faithful to the statutory scheme and to the historical development of the (c)(1) exception, and if properly applied does not undermine the purposes of the preference law. As one court explained, "Where there is a reasonable and plausible explanation for the delay, there should be no concern that a creditor was recording a secret lien in anticipation of a bankruptcy."[228] The hypothetical above, where the creditor attempted to perfect promptly but the delay occurred solely through inadvertence, is illustrative of this point. Recall too that to qualify for the (c)(1) exception, the transfer must not only in fact be substantially contemporaneous, but also must have been *intended* to be so, which significantly limits the ability of a creditor to use secret liens and engage in preferential opt-out behavior.

However, note that if the case involves an enabling loan or PMSI, even courts in the "be flexible" camp may relegate the creditor to the defense provided by subsection

---

[223] That time period was 10 days until 2005, when it was expanded to 30 days. Many of the important cases under the Code arose because of the short 10–day grace period of original subsection (e)(2)(A). As a practical matter, the longer 30–day period should take care of the vast majority of delayed perfection cases.

[224] This was what happened in *In re Dorholt, Inc.*, 224 F.3d 871 (8th Cir. 2000). The delay there was 16 days—longer than the then-applicable 10–day grace period of § 547(e)(2).

[225] See, e.g., In re Lazarus, 478 F.3d 12, 17 (1st Cir. 2007); In re Arnett, 731 F.2d 358 (6th Cir. 1984).

[226] *Lazarus*, supra note 225, 478 F.3d at 18–19.

[227] See, e.g., In re Hedrick, 524 F.3d 1175, 1186–87 (11th Cir. 2008), amended in part by In re Hedrick, 529 F.3d 1126 (11th Cir. 2008); *Dorholt*, supra note 224, 224 F.3d at 873.

[228] In re Marino, 193 B.R. 907, 915 (B.A.P. 9th Cir. 1996), aff'd, 117 F.3d 1425 (9th Cir. 1997).

(c)(3), which specifically governs enabling loans.[229] In that situation, the intuition of many courts is that the interpretive canon of "the specific controls the general" is harder to ignore, and the concern is greater that applying subsection (c)(1) where the creditor fails to qualify for protection under (c)(3) effectively renders (c)(3) superfluous. Interestingly, in the Supreme Court case of *Fidelity Financial Services, Inc. v. Fink*,[230] where the creditor on an enabling loan attempted to perfect on day 21 (within the state law relation-back period of 30 days, but outside of the then-applicable federal enabling loan period of 20 days), the Supreme Court did not even mention the possibility that subsection (c)(1) might apply to save the creditor; instead, the case was decided (against the creditor) entirely under subsection (c)(3).

While intellectually intriguing, the issue became considerably less critical after the 2005 expansion of the subsection (e)(2) grace period from 10 days to 30 days. Now many delayed perfection cases simply will not be preferences at all (because there is no antecedent debt under § 547(b)(2)) given the 30–day grace period of § 547(e)(2)(A).[231] Furthermore, for enabling loans, the expansion from 20 days to 30 days to perfect in § 547(c)(3)(B) should cover virtually all cases where a secured creditor attempted to perfect in accordance with state law.[232] As matters now stand, a creditor who delays perfection is only vulnerable to preference attack in the fairly rare instances where the delay runs beyond 30 days. And in that situation, even if the creditor acted in all good faith and intended to effect a substantially contemporaneous transfer, and even if a court were inclined to take a flexible view of § 547(c)(1) and apply it to a delayed perfection case, the creditor likely would have a significant problem satisfying the requirement in § 547(c)(1)(B) that the transfer was "in fact" substantially contemporaneous. In the hypothetical above, no matter how innocent, or unlucky, the creditor was, it is hard to say that 35 days is in fact substantially contemporaneous.

A situation in which § 547(c)(1) has been found to apply is in "substitution of collateral" cases. For example, assume that in the original transaction, Creditor loans Debtor money, Debtor grants Creditor a security interest in a Stradivarius violin to secure the debt, and Creditor promptly perfects. Sometime later, within the preference period, Debtor wishes to trade its Stradivarius in for a Guarnerius violin of comparable value. Creditor agrees to release its security interest in the Stradivarius if Debtor will grant Creditor a security interest in the Guarnerius, and each party does so. Is the transfer of the security interest in the Guarnerius a preference? The antecedent debt

---

[229] Thus, for example, in the Eleventh Circuit, a creditor is limited to subsection (c)(3) and cannot use subsection (c)(1) in an enabling loan case, see *In re Davis*, 734 F.2d 604 (11th Cir. 1984), but is free to invoke subsection (c)(1) in a non-enabling loan case. See *Hedrick*, supra note 227, 524 F.3d at 1185 n.4, 1186–87.

[230] 522 U.S. 211 (1998). See §§ 6.9, 6.19 for more discussion of this case.

[231] See § 6.9.

[232] Thus, for example, on the facts in *Fink*, where state law gave the creditor 30 days to perfect but the then-existing version of subsection (c)(3)(B) only allowed 20 days, and the creditor perfected on day 21 (and thus lost its preference case), the creditor now would be protected by the 30–day grace period of both subsections (e)(2)(A) and (c)(3)(B). Indeed, for purchase money security interests, the real harshness of the bankruptcy law was greatly alleviated with the 1994 amendment that changed the subsection (c)(3)(B) grace period from 10 days to 20 days. That change brought the federal law into line with the state law grace period of 20 days for a PMSI under Article 9. Before the 1994 amendment, a PMSI secured creditor who perfected between day 11 and 20, as allowed by state law, would lose under § 547(c)(3)(B), and, as the text above explains, would find little solace from the courts in attempting to invoke the substantially contemporaneous exchange exception of § 547(c)(1).

limitation will not help Creditor, because the security interest in the Guarnerius will secure the original debt. Yet the substitution of one item of collateral for another has neither made Creditor better off nor harmed the other creditors of Debtor. Recognizing that preference avoidance would be improper and unfair in such cases, courts have protected Creditor to the extent that the value of the security interest released matches the value of the substituted collateral transferred to Creditor. Under the Code, Creditor's release of the security interest in the Stradivarius is "new value" given in exchange for the new security interest in the Guarnerius. § 547(a)(2), (c)(1). Of course, if the newly acquired collateral is more valuable than the released collateral, a preference will exist to the extent of the increased value, assuming that all other preference elements are met.

§ 6.18 Safe Harbors: Ordinary Course Transfers

By far the most significant exception to preference liability is for *ordinary course* transfers. § 547(c)(2). In almost every preference case against an unsecured creditor, the creditor defendant attempts to and often can make at least a colorable showing of ordinary course; at a minimum, the creditor should be able to get past summary judgment. A 1997 national preference survey conducted by the American Bankruptcy Institute, for which I served as Reporter, found that the ordinary course defense was raised in 73.4% of all preference cases.[233] The ordinary course exception breeds and feeds litigation. Its underlying purposes are problematic and its application is plagued by confusion.

a. *Purposes of the Ordinary Course Exception*

Beyond the enormous practical implications of the ordinary course exception, on a conceptual level the safe harbor for ordinary course transfers defines the fundamental parameters of preference liability. The assertion that preference law is worried primarily about preserving the bankruptcy distributional scheme that is predicated on *equality* between creditors[234] cannot realistically be made in the face of the ordinary course exception.[235] Indeed, Professor Countryman observed that "the exception creates a huge gap in the policy underlying section 547," and went on to add that "the exception is completely at war with the concept of a preference and has no rational confining limits."[236]

Consider a simple example.[237] Debtor has five creditors, A, B, C, D, and E, and owes each of them $10,000. Assume that each debt was incurred in the ordinary course of business. Debtor is hopelessly insolvent, with total assets of only $12,000. However,

---

[233] American Bankruptcy Institute Task Force on Preferences, Preference Survey Project, at 8, 17 (1997) (Tabb, C., Reporter) (hereafter "ABI Report"), available at http://www.abiworld.org/Content/NavigationMenu/NewsRoom/BankruptcyResearchCenter/BankruptcyReportsResearchandTestimony/ABI/Report_on_the_ABI_P1.htm.

[234] See H.R. Rep. No. 95–595, 95th Cong., 1st Sess., at 177–78 (1977).

[235] I have observed that the exception as written and applied "swallows up any realistic supposition that equality matters." Charles J. Tabb, Rethinking Preferences, 43 S.C. L. Rev. 981, 986 (1992).

[236] Vern Countryman, The Concept of a Voidable Preference in Bankruptcy, 38 Vand. L. Rev. 713, 775, 776 (1985).

[237] A similar example is used in Tabb, supra note 235, at 986.

Debtor still maintains hope that it can work out its financial difficulties. Two weeks before filing for relief under chapter 11, Debtor pays Creditor A in full, on ordinary business terms and during the normal trade cycle of 30 days. Debtor retains the remaining $2,000 for use in its business, and pays nothing to Creditors B, C, D, and E. Debtor's chapter 11 case fails, having consumed the last $2,000 in assets, and the case is converted to chapter 7. The chapter 7 trustee sues A to recover the $10,000 as a preference.

The equality paradigm would suggest that A should have to return the money. Then all five of Debtor's creditors could be paid an equal portion of their debts; here, $2,000 each. If the transfer to A had never been made, each of the five creditors would have received $2,000 in the ensuing bankruptcy distribution. If A is allowed to retain the $10,000, however, the other creditors will receive nothing. The pre-bankruptcy transfer to A by an insolvent Debtor will have effectively undermined the bankruptcy distributional scheme. Yet, on the facts as given, Creditor A almost certainly will be allowed to retain the $10,000 payment. As will be explained below, the safe harbor of § 547(c)(2) appears to be satisfied.

Given that it eviscerates equality and permits circumvention of the bankruptcy scheme of distribution, what is the justification for the ordinary course exception? The legislative history to the 1978 Code explained:

> The purpose of the exception is to leave undisturbed normal financial relations, because it does not detract from the general policy of the preference section to discourage unusual action by either the debtor or his creditors during the debtor's slide into bankruptcy.[238]

In other words, the *deterrence* rationale of preference law is given predominant emphasis. Payment of a debt in the ordinary course of business does not implicate that concern. Under this view, only extraordinary behavior by creditors who are seeking to "opt out" of the bankruptcy scheme should be condemned by preference law.[239]

The idea that only opt out behavior should be sanctioned by preference law is a continuation of the ancient idea that preference law should be concerned with the *culpability* of the debtor or creditor.[240] Under pre-Code law, this notion was embodied in the requirement that the creditor have "reasonable cause to believe that the debtor is insolvent" at the time of the transfer. Bankruptcy Act § 60b. That a transfer was made in the ordinary course of business tended to disprove such a state of mind on the part of the creditor. In 1978 Congress eliminated the "reasonable cause to believe" test, citing the difficulty of proving the creditor's mental state and the irrelevance of the creditor's intentions to the goal of equal distribution.[241] Yet, by creating the ordinary course exception in the 1978 law, Congress indirectly resurrected the same core principle of culpability.

---

[238] S. Rep. No. 95–989, 95th Cong., 2d Sess., at 88 (1978); H.R. Rep. No. 95–595, 95th Cong., 1st Sess., at 373 (1977).

[239] See Thomas H. Jackson, The Logic and Limits of Bankruptcy Law 125 (1986).

[240] See Tabb, supra note 235, at 981–83, 994–1010.

[241] H.R. Rep. No. 95–595, 95th Cong., 1st Sess., at 178 (1977).

The ordinary course exception as enacted in 1978 also may have had roots in the judicially created "current expenses" rule.[242] The idea was that payment of current expenses does not really diminish the debtor's estate and is not for an antecedent debt, when the entire transaction—the credit extension and payment—is viewed as a unit. However, a strict application of the preference timing rules might have the effect of treating as "antecedent" some debts that were never intended to be credit extensions, except on a technical level.[243] Why § 547(c)(2) was needed to protect such creditors is unclear, though, in light of the contemporaneous exchange exception of subsection (c)(1).[244]

The principle of the current expenses rule was reflected in the requirement in the original 1978 version of the ordinary course exception that the transfer had to be made within 45 days after the debt was incurred. From 1978 until 1984, considerable litigation focused on exactly when a debt was "incurred." As will be seen, though, the repeal of the 45–day limit in 1984 eliminated this issue. Without a 45–day rule, or something like it, the current expenses rationale no longer can support the ordinary course exception.

The reference in the legislative history to the preservation of normal financial relations suggests a related justification for the ordinary course exception, that allowing creditors to retain ordinary course payments actually *encourages* them to do business on a credit basis with a financially distressed debtor. As a result, the debtor may be able to stay afloat and avoid bankruptcy entirely, or at least will be in stronger financial condition when it does go into bankruptcy.[245] In essence, the argument is that the debtor's creditors as a group are benefited by the resulting maximization of the value of the debtor's assets. The preference of a few creditors is then accepted as a price worth paying.

Some commentators have questioned the legitimacy of the incentive rationale for the ordinary course exception.[246] In fact, the ordinary course safe harbor may create exactly the opposite incentive: a creditor who gets paid in the ordinary course need not cooperate further with the debtor or extend any more credit; if the debtor goes into bankruptcy, that creditor will be able to keep the payment. Furthermore, other creditors may have an incentive not to extend credit, because of the risk that an unrecoverable preference will be paid to someone else. Finally, the subsequent advance

---

[242] See Lissa L. Broome, Payments on Long–Term Debt as Voidable Preferences: The Impact of the 1984 Bankruptcy Amendments, 1987 Duke L.J. 78, 89–91; Countryman, supra note 236, at 767–69.

[243] See C. Robert Morris, Jr., Bankruptcy Law Reform: Preferences, Secret Liens and Floating Liens, 54 Minn. L. Rev. 737, 762–63 (1970). See § 6.13. An example is In re First Jersey Securities, Inc., 180 F.3d 504 (3d Cir. 1999), where the court found that an "antecedent debt" arises when a law firm performs services for a client, not when it sends the bill. In that case, however, the payment by the debtor was extraordinary (securities delivered, rather than cash paid), so the court found the transfer to be an avoidable preference.

[244] See § 6.17.

[245] The Supreme Court appeared to accept this argument in *Union Bank v. Wolas*, 502 U.S. 151, 161–62 (1991).

[246] See Tabb, supra note 235, at 1022–26. See also Michael J. Herbert, The Trustee Versus the Trade Creditor: A Critique of Section 547(c)(1), (2) & (4) of the Bankruptcy Code, 17 U. Rich. L. Rev. 667 (1983); Bruce R. Kraus, Note, Preferential Transfers and the Value of the Insolvent Firm, 87 Yale L.J. 1449, 1458 (1978).

exception in § 547(c)(4)[247] already protects creditors who do extend further credit to a debtor.

At bottom, the rationale for the ordinary course exception may rest on the basic principle of *finality* or repose for commercial transactions, in conjunction with the idea of culpability.[248] The baseline premise arguably should be to leave settled commercial transactions alone, unless a good reason can be given to unwind that completed transaction. Recovering virtually every transfer made by an insolvent debtor for 90 days prior to bankruptcy might impose staggering costs. If creditors have not engaged in opt out activity, and are simply paid as a matter of routine in the ordinary course, they have done nothing "wrong," and should be protected. This view, though, pays homage to deterrence, not equality, as the driving principle behind the preference law, and insists that culpability should matter. The discussion in an earlier section questioned whether deterrence was a valid justification for the preference law, however, and whether it made sense to test preferences by whether they were good or evil.[249] Anyway, if the real concern is repose, the preference law might be better served by other mechanisms: a shorter preference period, a broader safe harbor for all small transfers,[250] or, most dramatically, by repeal.[251] Whatever the merits of these suggestions, though, the reality is that the ordinary course exception exists, and is often the decisive issue in preference litigation. It is to the question of the application of that exception that I now turn.

b.   *Application of the Ordinary Course Exception*[252]

As discussed in the preceding subsection, the wisdom of qualifying a preference law with an ordinary course safe harbor is open to question. However, even if in theory the concept is thought to be wise, a significant practical problem remains: how do you gauge what is in the "ordinary course"? Can an "ordinary course" exception be applied with enough consistency, clarity, and economy to be worth the effort? Before the 2005 amendments, the answer may well have been "no"—the 1997 ABI Report indicated that regular participants in the bankruptcy system believed strongly that the exception "was not working well in practice."[253] According to that report, "[t]he biggest problems are that no one knows what it means, and not surprisingly in light of that perception, the application of the defense is inconsistent."[254] The main need identified was "for greater clarity in this area.[255] Seeking more consistency and clarity, in 2005 Congress made a dramatic, and simple, change—it changed an "and" to an "or." The meaning of, reasons for, and impact of that change are discussed below.

---

[247]   See § 6.20.

[248]   See Morris, supra note 243, at 738; Tabb, supra note 235, at 1026–27.

[249]   See § 6.7.

[250]   See § 6.24. In 2005 Congress did dramatically expand the protection for small transfers, creating a new safe harbor in business debtor cases of $5,000, since indexed up to $6,225 as of 2013. See § 547(c)(9).

[251]   See Tabb, supra note 235, at 984; Countryman, supra note 236, at 775–76.

[252]   The discussion in § 6.18.b. draws heavily on Charles J. Tabb, The Brave New World of Bankruptcy Preferences, 13 Am. Bankr. Inst. L. Rev. 425, 440–45 (2005).

[253]   ABI Report, supra note 233, at 23.

[254]   Id.

[255]   Id. at 29.

To see how the exception might apply, consider the following Hypothetical #1. Debtor, who is insolvent, has three main trade suppliers, X, Y, and Z. The standard credit term in the industry is payment in 30 days without penalty. For several years, Debtor routinely has paid all three within the 30–day period by checks drawn on the general corporate account. Debtor's business falls on hard times, though, and Debtor is late in paying Creditor X for nine months, and X accepts those late payments without complaint. Debtor remains current on payments to Y and Z. X, Y, and Z all continue shipping goods on credit to Debtor. A week before Debtor files bankruptcy, it again pays Y and Z by standard check within the 30–day period, but does not pay X. Creditor X learns of the payments to Y and Z, and also discovers that Debtor is on the brink of bankruptcy. X immediately calls Debtor, and insists that Debtor deliver a cashier's check for all overdue amounts the next day, or X will discontinue shipments to Debtor. Debtor complies with X's demand. If Debtor's bankruptcy trustee sues X, Y, and Z to recover all payments made within the 90–day preference period, what result?

To answer that question, let us first consider how the analysis would have proceeded prior to the 2005 amendments. Before 2005, § 547(c)(2) required a creditor defendant seeking to escape preference liability under the ordinary course exception to prove three things:

(1) that the debt was "incurred by the debtor in the ordinary course of business or financial affairs of the debtor and the transferee," (§ 547(c)(2)(A) (pre–2005 Amendment numbering));

(2) that the transfer was "made in the ordinary course of business or financial affairs of the debtor and the transferee" (§ 547(c)(2)(B) (pre–2005 Amendment numbering));

and[256]

(3) the transfer was "made according to ordinary business terms" (§ 547(c)(2)(C) (pre–2005 Amendment numbering)).

The change made in 2005 was simple—the conjunctive "and" between the second and third tests was changed to the disjunctive "or." That is, as explained below, after 2005 the creditor would have to prove the first element and then *either* the second or third, whereas before 2005 the creditor had to prove all three.

The courts have uniformly interpreted the second test to require proof of conformity to what is ordinary *subjectively*, that is, as between the debtor and *this particular transferee*. What was less obvious was what the third test added to the second. What does "made according to ordinary business terms" mean? "Ordinary" *for whom*? Some courts, particularly in the earlier years under the Code, effectively ignored the third test, and held for the creditor based almost entirely upon the proof of compliance with the subjective standard alone. Beginning in 1992, though, several circuit courts concluded that the third test must have some content independent of the second, and thus must command some sort of proof of compliance with an industry-

---

[256] This is the "and" that was changed to an "or" in 2005.

wide *objective* test.[257] Thus, until 2005, a preference defendant had to prevail on *both* the subjective and objective tests in order to escape preference liability.[258]

In Hypothetical #1, the facts appear to show that for all three creditors all the debts paid were *incurred* in the ordinary course of business, thus satisfying the first element. The question then became whether the payments were made in the ordinary course of business of the debtor and the particular creditors (the subjective test), *and* according to ordinary business terms (the objective test). Creditors Y and Z appear to be covered by the exception, for all payments made. The payments made by Debtor to Y and to Z within the preference period were paid in the same time frame, the same manner, and on the same terms as had been the routine practice for years, both in the industry at large (the objective test) and within Debtor's own business and prior dealings with Y and Z (the subjective test). Even the payments made a week before bankruptcy followed the normal pattern.

Creditor X is on shakier ground. The trustee almost certainly would have been able to recover the final payment made to X, in the last week before bankruptcy. That payment was made in response to a demand and threat by X, and on different terms than before. It thus failed both the subjective and the objective tests. The more interesting question was with regard to the three late payments to X made in the preference period (even though X was paid late for nine months, only the last three—before the eve-of-bankruptcy payment—fell within the 90–day preference period). Unlike the final payment, the three previous payments were not made in response to pressure from X, and were made by a standard check, not a cashier's check. Even though the payments were made late, X would try to argue that the subjective practice as between Debtor and X—followed for a substantial period of nine months—was for Debtor to pay late. Thus X would argue that the late payments satisfied the subjective test. Indeed, many cases found that even late payments could qualify for protection.[259] Where X would have run into certain trouble, though, was in satisfying the industry-wide *objective* test. Recall that X had to prove compliance with both the subjective and objective tests to prevail.

That proof burden often could be daunting—sufficiently daunting, many creditors believed, that trustees were able to bludgeon creditors into capitulating at the very least into settling dubious preference claims. In practice, trade creditors were extremely upset with how the ordinary course exception functioned. That sentiment was captured in the recommendation in the ABI Report that the exception be modified to afford more meaningful protection to creditors and to provide greater clarity and consistency.

---

[257] See, e.g., Advo–Sys., Inc. v. Maxway Corp., 37 F.3d 1044 (4th Cir. 1994); In re Molded Acoustical Prods., Inc., 18 F.3d 217 (3d Cir. 1994); In re U.S.A. Inns of Eureka Springs, Ark., Inc., 9 F.3d 680 (8th Cir. 1993); In re Tolona Pizza Prods. Corp., 3 F.3d 1029 (7th Cir. 1993); In re Fred Hawes Org., Inc., 957 F.2d 239 (6th Cir. 1992).

[258] National Bankruptcy Review Commission, Final Report, Bankruptcy: The Next Twenty Years, § 3.2.3, at 801 (1997).

[259] See, e.g., In re Yurika Foods Corp., 888 F.2d 42 (6th Cir. 1989).

The Commission Report heeded this plea and recommended that the conjunctive test be replaced with a *disjunctive* test, in which the preference defendant could prevail by showing *either* conformity to prior conduct between the parties *or* conformity to industry standards.[260] The former was to be given precedence: "the conduct between the parties should prevail to the extent that there was sufficient prepetition conduct to establish a course of dealing"; only "[i]n the event there is not sufficient prepetition conduct to establish a course of dealing, then industry standards should supply the ordinary course benchmark."[261] According to that Report, this approach would eliminate the need for a preference defendant to prove elusive industry standards, and it is "more accurate to rely on the relationship between the parties."[262]

In 2005, Congress adopted the proposed Commission Recommendation verbatim.[263] By the simple expedient of changing "and" to "or," Congress effected a major change in the ordinary course exception and significantly altered the balance of power in preference litigation, in favor of defendant creditors. Assuming that the debt was incurred in the ordinary course (as before), a creditor now will prevail by proving *either* that the transfer was subjectively ordinary, as between the debtor and that transferee, § 547(b)(2)(A), *or* that the transfer was objectively ordinary, measured against the industry, § 547(b)(2)(B). Thus, in Hypothetical #1, if Creditor X could prove that the parties had established a sufficient course of dealing wherein late payments were the norm, X possibly could escape preference liability for all of the payments (except the final one made on unusual terms in response to pressure by X), even if those late payments fell well outside industry practices.

After the 2005 amendment, the most likely practical consequence is that the preference litigation in this area will focus primarily on the issue of conformity with the subjective prior course of dealing between the parties. The hard-to-prove objective industry test is likely to be raised only in rare cases, usually where there was insufficient pre-petition conduct between the parties to establish a course of dealing. That certainly was the intent of the Commission Recommendation, as noted above.

However, it is worth observing that the statutory language by its terms does not limit use of the objective industry test to those situations where the parties lack a subjective course of dealing. Instead, on the face of the statute the use of the objective industry test would appear to be equally available even if the parties *do* have a course of dealing. That opens up the possibility that a creditor could prevail even if the transfer at issue does not conform to the parties' course of dealing, but did conform to the industry standard. In other words, if the parties' course of dealing was more demanding than the industry standard, and the challenged transfer failed to conform to that stricter standard, it still might be possible for the defendant to prevail under subsection (c)(2) by showing conformity to the laxer industry standard.

---

[260] Commission Report, supra note 258, § 3.2.3, at 802.

[261] Id.

[262] Id.

[263] To make the disjunctive between tests two and three work, Congress had to move test one (old subsection (A)) up into the prefatory clause, and renumber old tests two and three as subsections (A) and (B), with the all-powerful "or" between them.

To see this, consider Hypothetical #2. Assume that the invoices used by Creditor require payment in 20 days, but Creditor and Debtor have a well-established course of dealing allowing payment between 30 and 35 days. Assume further that the norm in the industry is to allow payment in 50–60 days (whereas Creditor and Debtor have a stricter 30–35 day practice). During the preference period, the three challenged transfers from debtor to Creditor each are made 55 days after invoicing. Thus, Creditor and Debtor *have* departed from their own pre-petition course of dealing, in a manner that raises red flags about the possibility that there is disfavored preferential behavior occurring. But the parties are easily covered by the looser industry standard.

In such a case, can Creditor escape preference liability by showing conformity with that laxer industry standard? While the apparent intent of the amendment (as expressed in the Commission Report) would suggest not, with the intent being that the objective standard be used only where prior conduct between the parties was lacking, the statutory language plainly seems to permit such a fall-back defense for the Creditor. It is hard to argue that the statutory word "*or*" used in § 547(c)(2) is ambiguous. The word "or" signifies equally available alternative options. Courts still might balk at finding "ordinariness" in cases such as Hypothetical #2, but to do so would do violence to the statutory language.

The other sort of case that is likely to arise where the 2005 change would be significant is the opposite of the one just posited. That is, even if a transfer is "extraordinary" as judged against ascertainable industry standards, under the new law the creditor appears to be protected if the transfer did not depart from the prior practices of the parties. Consider Hypothetical #3, a variant of the one used above. Assume that the invoices require payment in 20 days, and Creditor and Debtor have a practice of 40–45 days for payment. But in Hypothetical #3, add the fact that the industry standard (which we will assume is easily established) requires strict compliance with the 20–day invoice terms. Creditor, however, gets paid at days 43, 40, and 45 during the preference period. What result?

Here the answer under the new law surely is that Creditor wins. The clear purpose of the Commission Recommendation that led directly to the 2005 amendment was, as quoted earlier but which bears repeating, "that the conduct between the parties should prevail to the extent that there was sufficient prepetition conduct to establish a course of dealing."[264] In Hypothetical #3, we have such a course of conduct, and Creditor and Debtor conformed to it. Now the statutory disjunctive language *and* the statutory purpose are in harmony and point inexorably to an outcome in which Creditor wins. Our intuition in this hypothetical is that such is not really a bad result; if the idea behind the ordinary course exception is in fact "to leave undisturbed normal financial relations," then that idea finds fulfillment in a case such as this hypothetical.

Note, though, that this intuition also rests on the unstated premise that Creditor and Debtor probably were *not* trying to "manipulate their course of conduct prepetition"[265] with an eye to a possible future bankruptcy proceeding in such a way as

---

[264] Commission Report, supra note 258, § 3.2.3, at 802.
[265] Id.

to give Creditor an advantage over other competing creditors. Instead we assume that Creditor simply was not as rigorous as its peers in holding the line against Debtor. But what if Creditor's motivation was not so benign? In the leading pre–2005 case of *In re Tolona Pizza Products Corp.*,[266] Judge Posner identified a justification for the objective industry test as serving "to allay the concern of creditors that one or more of their number may have worked out a special deal with the debtor, before the preference period, designed to put that creditor ahead of the others in the event of bankruptcy."[267] What if *that* is what was going on—will the new disjunctive test be any safeguard?

This concern is nicely illustrated by Hypothetical #4, based on the Fifth Circuit case of *Gulf City Seafoods Inc. v. Ludwig Shrimp Co. (In re Gulf City Seafoods, Inc.).*[268] Creditor and Debtor had an unusual, but consistent and longstanding payment practice. When Debtor placed an order for goods with Creditor, Debtor would immediately send a check in payment of the delivery with the order. Normally, Creditor would hold the check for several weeks after delivering the ordered goods to Debtor before presenting the check to Debtor's bank for payment. By having checks in hand, though, Creditor gained an advantage vis-à-vis other creditors by being able to seek payment earlier than normal if the prospects for payment worsened. Within the preference period, $72,000 in checks to Creditor cleared Debtor's bank account. Each of these checks was paid by Debtor's bank within 40 to 45 days after the delivery of goods for which they paid—fully consistent with the parties' longstanding, established days-to-payment history and well within the industry norm for days to payment. Are those payments to Creditor avoidable?

Before 2005, Creditor faced a serious risk of losing the ordinary course defense in a case such as this one, because the Creditor's deal (getting checks in hand in advance of the normal time for payment, as a form of payment security) was not ordinary for the industry—even if, as it happened, Creditor did not actually present the "security" checks early. As a matter of policy, why should this Creditor be allowed to put in place such a special deal that gave it the option to get a jump on other creditors if the debtor's financial affairs turned ugly?

But under the new law, since Creditor put its special deal in place well before the actual onset of the debtor's insolvency and then bankruptcy, and the parties then adhered to that special deal so as to create a course of dealing, Creditor might be able to prevail by proving conformity to subjective ordinary course, under § 547(c)(2)(A). The fact of non-conformity to industry standards supposedly would be irrelevant. Taking the statutory language at face value, Hypotheticals 3 and 4 should come out the same way, in Creditor's favor. But is that a good result? While we are not bothered in #3 because we doubt that Creditor has engaged in intentional behavior to give it an advantage over other creditors, such is not the case in #4. If Creditor wins under #4, as the statutory language suggests, the violence to the preference policies of equality *and* deterrence seems manifest. But it is hard to see how courts can hold against the Creditor in such a situation. Indeed, not only does the statutory language favor

---

[266] 3 F.3d 1029 (7th Cir. 1993).

[267] Id. at 1032.

[268] 296 F.3d 363 (5th Cir. 2002).

Creditor, but the Commission Report specifically considered as a "competing consideration" to its Recommendation for adoption of a disjunctive test the possibility that parties would engage in pre-petition manipulative behavior in framing their own course of conduct,[269] but nevertheless went forward with the Recommendation.

As noted, most ordinary course cases under the new law will turn on an assessment of whether the parties complied with their own subjective prior course of dealing, under subsection (c)(2)(A). That exercise will require the creditor-defendant to put on evidence of prior payment practices between the parties, and how the challenged transfers are sufficiently similar to warrant protection.

In some cases, though, there will not be a sufficient course of dealing between the parties, and the creditor will be left to argue compliance with the objective industry test under subsection (c)(2)(B). In those cases, questions will arise with regard to (1) what is the relevant industry; (2) what the "ordinary business terms" of that industry were; and (3) whether the transfers to the creditor-defendant were close enough to those ordinary business terms to enjoy protection from avoidance. Prior to 2005, while courts had established that proof of compliance with this objective industry standard was required, they had then been quite lenient in finding compliance with that standard. What is unclear post–2005 is whether courts will be similarly lenient in cases where the *only* thing the creditor must prove to escape liability (other than of course that the incurrence of the debt was ordinary) is compliance with the objective industry standard, as an *alternative* to—rather than in *addition* to—conformity to the subjective course of dealing between the parties.

Leading the way in establishing a lax industry test pre–2005 was the Seventh Circuit's *Tolona Pizza* decision.[270] The Seventh Circuit, recognizing that there may be a wide variety of acceptable practices in an industry, and further noting the difficulty of defining the pertinent industry, decided that creditors do not have to establish a "single, uniform set of business terms" under the objective test. Instead, the court concluded that:

> '[O]rdinary business terms' refers to the *range* of terms that encompasses the practices in which firms similar in some general way to the creditor in question engage, and that only dealings so idiosyncratic as to fall outside that broad range should be deemed extraordinary and therefore outside the scope of subsection [(B)].[271]

Under that exceedingly generous test, the court had little trouble finding in favor of the creditor.[272] Remember, though, that the creditor in *Tolona Pizza,* decided pre–

---

[269] Commission Report, supra note 258, at 802.

[270] 3 F.3d 1029 (7th Cir. 1993).

[271] Id. at 1033.

[272] The facts in Tolona were that the debtor, a pizza maker, had issued eight checks totaling $46,000 to its sausage supplier during the preference period. These payments were made from 12 to 32 days after the invoice date, with the average being 22 days. This was actually an improvement from prior years, when the debtor had paid the supplier an average of 26 days after invoice. The invoices required payment within seven days, but no one in the industry ever enforced that provision. Instead, the actual norm in the industry was about a 21–day grace period, and allowances of up to 30 days were not uncommon. The Seventh Circuit had

2005, did *also* have to prove compliance with the subjective test. One wonders, as noted above, whether such abundant generosity to creditors in framing the parameters of the objective test will still obtain when that is the only test the creditor must prove.[273]

Furthermore, as the Third Circuit noted in reference to the *Tolona Pizza* test, "[w]hile this test is deferential, it is not non-existent."[274] A creditor-defendant still must show *some* conformity to an established industry practice. Thus, for example, a law firm that received securities, not cash, in payment of legal services was held not to satisfy the "ordinary business terms" test.[275]

An interesting interpretive question that has come up with some frequency under the objective test is how to characterize the nature of the comparison group of firms with which the debtor is to be compared. The classic illustration of this is in cases such as *Arrow Electronics, Inc. v. Justus (In re Kaypro)*,[276] which raised the question of whether payments under a debt restructuring agreement that was executed when the debtor was in financial distress could possibly qualify for the ordinary course exception. The Ninth Circuit in *Kaypro* reversed a lower court holding that payments under a restructuring agreement as a matter of law could not be in the ordinary course, opting instead for a case-by-case assessment. It could only do so, though, by defining the benchmark for ordinariness as what is done *by firms in financial distress*. Since the court found testimony in the record that it was common in the industry for financially distressed debtors to enter restructuring agreements, it found that there was at least a triable issue of fact on the ordinary course question. But that surely cannot be what Congress intended when it said the purpose of the exception was "to leave undisturbed normal financial relations."[277] It meant, surely, what is normal for firms *whether or not* they are in dire financial straits, not what they do only when under the gun. It is perfectly "normal" when debtors are on the brink of bankruptcy for the debtor and some of their creditors to take all sorts of actions that are at the core of what we would describe as obviously proscribed preferential behavior—paying off favored creditors, pressuring the debtor to pay, enter restructuring agreements, and so forth. To define "ordinary course" to include that sort of behavior would mean that the exception would completely swallow up the rule.

---

no difficulty in finding that the payments by the debtor to the supplier fell well within the range of industry norms, and thus satisfied subsection (C). A dissenting judge would have deferred to the bankruptcy judge's contrary finding of fact, which was based on an admission by an official of the supplier that the leniency shown to the debtor fell outside the common industry practice.

[273] For example, one recent case out of the district of Delaware continued to follow the broad Tolona Pizza test in applying the post–2005 version of the statute, noting that, "Because Congress did not intend to upset commercial dealings with distressed parties, the 'ordinary business terms' test of section 547(c)(2)(B) is necessarily a broad one, and the evidentiary standard is not formidable." In re Am. Home Mortg. Holdings, Inc., 476 B.R. 124 (Bankr. D. Del. 2012). However, in this case, debtor did in fact prove the subjective prong as well, though it was not required to do so.

[274] In re First Jersey Secs., Inc., 180 F.3d 504, 513 (3d Cir. 1999).

[275] Id.

[276] 218 F.3d 1070 (9th Cir. 2000).

[277] S. Rep. No. 95–989, 95th Cong., 2d Sess., at 88 (1978); H.R. Rep. No. 95–595, 95th Cong., 1st Sess., at 373 (1977).

Another issue that has arisen under the ordinary course exception is whether payments on *long-term* debt can qualify for protection.[278] For example, assume that on June 1, 2007, Debtor borrows $1,000,000 at 10% interest from Creditor, to be repaid over ten years in equal monthly installments of $13,567. The Debtor files bankruptcy on June 1, 2013, having made the scheduled monthly payments in each of the three months prior to bankruptcy, for a total of about $50,700. Can the Creditor protect those payments under the ordinary course exception?

Prior to 1984, the answer clearly was *no*. As originally enacted in 1978, the ordinary course exception only protected payments made within 45 days after the debt was incurred. In the example, the long-term debt was incurred outside of the 45–day period, at least with regard to the principal.[279] In 1984, however, Congress repealed the 45–day limitation in § 547(c)(2), in response to pressure from issuers of commercial paper with maturities in excess of 45 days and trade creditors in industries with payment cycles longer than 45 days.[280] The question was whether the repeal of the 45–day rule had suddenly opened the door of the ordinary course exception to long-term debt payments.

The Supreme Court answered the question in the affirmative in *Union Bank v. Wolas*.[281] The Court held "that payments on long-term debt . . . may qualify for the ordinary course of business exception to the trustee's power to avoid preferential transfers."[282] The *Wolas* Court did not decide whether the requirements of § 547(c)(2) actually were satisfied in the case; thus, a court would be free to conclude that a long-term debt was not "incurred" in the ordinary course, or paid in the ordinary course, or according to ordinary business terms. In the example given above, a court might well decide that a million dollar loan was not an "ordinary course" transaction. Instead, the Court in *Wolas* held only that a *per se* exclusion of long-term debt repayments from the ordinary course safe harbor was not warranted. Nothing in the text of § 547(c)(2) supports such a blanket prohibition.

§ 6.19 Safe Harbors: Enabling Loans (and More Timing Problems)[283]

The third exception to preference liability is for security interests for "*enabling loans*." § 547(c)(3). An "enabling loan" is just what the name suggests: a loan by a creditor that enables the debtor to purchase the collateral itself. If the debtor grants the creditor a security interest in the very property purchased, the protection of § 547(c)(3) may be triggered. A security interest for an enabling loan is one type of "*purchase money security interest*" (PMSI) under Article 9 of the Uniform Commercial Code. U.C.C. § 9–103(a)(2). As will be explained below, the requirements of § 547(c)(3)

---

[278] The most comprehensive analysis of the question prior to the Supreme Court's decision in *Union Bank v. Wolas*, 502 U.S. 151 (1991), was the article by Professor Broome, supra note 242.

[279] There was some dispute whether the interest debt was incurred at the outset of the transaction, or only as time elapsed.

[280] Pub. L. No. 98–353, § 462(c), 98 Stat. 378 (1984). The legislative history is discussed in Broome, supra note 242, at 99–112.

[281] 502 U.S. 151 (1991).

[282] Id. at 162.

[283] The discussion in § 6.19 draws heavily on Charles J. Tabb, The Brave New World of Bankruptcy Preferences, 13 Am. Bankr. Inst. L. Rev. 425, 445–49 (2005).

are similar but not identical to those imposed by the Uniform Commercial Code for purchase money security interests. Significantly, though, the Supreme Court has made clear that the construction of subsection (c)(3) is a matter of *federal* law, not state law,[284] notwithstanding the obvious derivation of (c)(3) from the UCC.

To qualify for the safe harbor of § 547(c)(3), the security interest transferred to the creditor must satisfy all of the following tests:

- it must secure new value given at or after the signing of a security agreement that describes the collateral, § 547(c)(3)(A)(i);

- the new value must be given by or on behalf of the secured party, § 547(c)(3)(A)(ii);

- the new value must be given to enable the debtor to acquire the collateral, § 547(c)(3)(A)(iii);

- the debtor must in fact use the new value to acquire the collateral, § 547(c)(3)(A)(iv); and

- the security interest must be perfected on or before 30 days after the debtor receives possession of the collateral, § 547(c)(3)(B).

To understand how § 547(c)(3) works, what role it plays, how it has been amended since 1978, and why, some review of the Code's treatment of transfers of liens as possible preferences is necessary. In particular, an understanding of how subsection (c)(3) interacts with the timing rules of § 547(e)(2) and with Article 9 of the Uniform Commercial Code is essential.

In determining when the transfer of a security interest or lien is "made" for bankruptcy purposes, two times are possible: when the security interest first becomes *effective* between the debtor and the secured party, or when it is *perfected* as against third parties. Perfection normally requires the filing of some sort of public notice of the existence of the security interest.[285] In effect, "secret" liens (i.e., those not publicly noticed and thus not perfected) can be trumped by third parties. This policy against secret liens is enforced in bankruptcy both by the strong-arm clause, § 544(a), which allows the trustee to avoid liens that are unperfected at the time of the bankruptcy filing,[286] and by the timing rules of the preference statute, § 547(e), which give the trustee the power to set aside some security interests where perfection is delayed until the pre-bankruptcy preference period.[287] As discussed in an earlier section,[288] the bankruptcy preference law generally uses *perfection* as the operative time.

---

[284] Fidelity Fin. Servs., Inc. v. Fink, 522 U.S. 211 (1998).

[285] See, e.g., U.C.C. § 9–310(a).

[286] See § 6.3.

[287] See § 6.9.

[288] See id.

Importantly, though, this use of the time of perfection as the time of transfer is not an absolute. Secured creditors are given some leeway to perfect, without being subject to avoidance as a bankruptcy preference. Prior to the 2005 amendments, secured creditors had a *10–day grace period* in which to perfect. Under the pre–2005 version of § 547(e)(2), a transfer was deemed "made" when it became effective between the debtor and secured party *if* perfected within 10 days of that time, but if it was not perfected within 10 days, then the transfer of the security interest was deemed made when it was perfected. The timing rule in subsection (e)(2) applied (as it still does) to all security interests, whether "purchase money" or not. Note that the grace period ran from when the security interest first became *effective* as between the parties; the significance of that point is explained below.

The § 547(e)(2) timing rule, though, by itself would not provide complete protection for a PMSI, in two distinct situations. The first, and the one that led to the adoption of § 547(c)(3) originally in 1978, is where a lender makes an "enabling loan" to a debtor, and the debtor subsequently uses the money loaned to acquire collateral. Absent any preference law safe harbor, the lender in such a case still would be subject to preference avoidance of the lien in the subsequently-acquired collateral, since without more that lien would be deemed to be transferred on account of an "antecedent debt" under § 547(b)(2). This result obtains because the "debt" would be deemed to arise back when the money was first loaned,[289] while the transfer of the lien would not occur until the debtor acquired the collateral and the lien thus became "effective." Note that this would be the case even if there were no delay in perfection.

For example, assume that Lender loans Debtor $25,000 on May 1 to enable Debtor to purchase certain equipment, Debtor grants Lender a security interest in that equipment, and Lender immediately perfects its security interest. On June 1 Debtor concludes the purchase of the equipment. Under the UCC, the security interest in the equipment does not "attach" until June 1, when the Debtor has acquired rights in the collateral. U.C.C. § 9–203(b). So too, then, the transfer of the security interest in the equipment to lender under § 547(e)(2) would be deemed to occur on June 1, when the security interest first became effective as between Lender and Debtor. The debt, though, arose on May 1, when the loan was made, and May 1 is antecedent to June 1.

The Code as originally enacted in 1978 contained an "enabling loan" exception in § 547(c)(3) to protect the enabling lender in such a situation. Under original subsection (c)(3), an enabling lender was protected from preference avoidance of its security interest if it perfected the security interest on or before 10 days after it attached.[290] Thus, in a case like the example above, Lender would have been protected, since attachment occurred on June 1 (when the Debtor acquired rights in the collateral) and as of June 1 the security interest was already perfected. Today, even after amendments to § 547(c)(3) in 1984, 1994, and 2005, the result in the classic "enabling loan" situation remains the same—Lender wins, assuming it perfected on or before the expiration of the stated grace period. Today, that grace period is 30 days (rather than the original 10

---

[289] See § 6.13.

[290] See Vern Countryman, The Concept of a Voidable Preference in Bankruptcy, 38 Vand, L. Rev. 713, 776–79 (1985).

days). As applied, and in concept, § 547(c)(3) has been unexceptional and easily applied in the forgoing situation, for which it was intended.

All the action and intrigue in the application of § 547(c)(3) has come in the second situation where the timing rules of § 547(e)(2) standing alone fail to provide complete protection for a PMSI—the delayed perfection cases. Ironically, the history of the subsection (c)(3) exception shows that Congress did not originally intend for subsection (c)(3) to apply at all in the delayed perfection scenario,[291] yet over time that provision has come to play a critical role in such cases. Perhaps unsurprisingly, given that as conceived the provision was not even intended to address delayed perfection problems, but has instead transmogrified to do so in fits and starts via case law and legislative evolution, the law as it now stands does an imperfect job of protecting secured creditors from preference avoidance when they delay perfection in a manner permitted by state law.

Here is the crux of the problem. Under non-bankruptcy law, a secured creditor with a PMSI is given a grace period to perfect and yet still prevail over third parties whose interests arise in the interim between the time the security interest was created and the time it was perfected. Under these special rules, the PMSI effectively "relates back" for priority purposes to the earlier time of creation. Most notably, under § 9–317(e) of the UCC, a PMSI is valid against intervening interests if perfected within 20 days after the debtor receives delivery of the collateral. The problem for bankruptcy preference purposes is that the 20–day UCC grace period runs from the time the debtor *receives delivery of the collateral*, which could be *later* than when the security interest first became *effective* ("attached") between the debtor and secured party under UCC § 9–203(b). In bankruptcy, though, the timing rule of § 547(e)(2) uses the potentially earlier time when the security interest first became effective. Thus (pre–2005), without more, under § 547(e)(2) alone, a PMSI perfected within 20 days after the debtor received possession of the collateral but more than 10 days after the security interest attached would have been vulnerable to preference attack.

To see this possibility, consider the following example. Assume that on May 1 Creditor loans money to Debtor to enable Debtor to purchase Collateral, and Debtor at the same time signs a security agreement that grants Creditor a security interest in the Collateral. Also on May 1, Debtor purchases the Collateral, and thereby acquires rights in the collateral. Under Article 9 of the UCC, Creditor's security interest thus "attaches" on May 1; on that date, the Debtor had signed a security agreement, the Creditor had given value, and the Debtor had rights in the collateral. U.C.C. § 9–203(b). Assume next that the Collateral is shipped from the seller's warehouse in Maine on May 15, and arrives at the Debtor's place of business in California on May 20. Creditor perfects its security interest on May 28 by filing a financing statement. Since Creditor perfected its security interest within 20 days after the debtor received delivery of the Collateral on May 20, under state law Creditor's security interest would be valid even against lien creditors whose rights arose between the time of attachment on May 1 and the time of perfection on May 28. U.C.C. § 9–317(e). For state law

---

[291] See id.

purposes, the priority status of Creditor's security interest is deemed to relate back from perfection to the time of attachment.

Under § 547(e)(2) alone, however, Creditor would have been vulnerable to preference attack in this example prior to 2005. The transfer of the security interest under subsection (e)(2) was deemed to be made when perfected (May 28), unless it was perfected within 10 days after the transfer "takes effect" between the Debtor and Creditor. The transfer took effect between Debtor and Creditor when it attached, on May 1—well outside of the pre–2005 10–day grace period of subsection (e)(2). Thus, the transfer of the security interest for purposes of § 547 would have been deemed to be made on May 28. That transfer then would be for an antecedent debt, since the loan was made on May 1. Therefore, without an applicable preference exception, the security interest could be avoided. Yet, the actions of the Debtor and Creditor are perfectly in compliance with state law and do not implicate any of the evils with which preference law is concerned.

As originally enacted in 1978, the enabling loan safe harbor of § 547(c)(3) would not have helped Creditor in this case. The reason is that, as explained above, the original form of subsection (c)(3) used the time of attachment as the trigger date for the running of the grace period to perfect, just like subsection (e)(2). That drafting was not inadvertent, since the provision was targeted at the enabling loan problem, not the delayed perfection problem. In 1984, though, Congress (with little explanation) for the first time sought to make subsection (c)(3) applicable to *both* the enabling loan situation *and* the delayed perfection case. It did so by changing (c)(3)'s trigger point for the running of the then–10–day grace period from the time of *attachment* to the time when the debtor *receives possession* of the collateral. By tying the running of the grace period to the same trigger date as under the UCC, Congress sought to protect a PMSI secured creditor from federal bankruptcy preference avoidance if that creditor would have been protected under the UCC. The 10–day grace period to perfect in the 1984 version of § 547(c)(3) corresponded with the then-prevailing grace period for a PMSI in UCC Article 9.

In the hypothetical above, Creditor would have prevailed under § 547(c)(3) after the 1984 amendment changed the grace period trigger point. With the trigger now when the Debtor received possession of the collateral (on May 20), rather than when the security interest attached (May 1), Creditor's perfection on May 28 fell within the safe harbor of subsection (c)(3).

However, a serious problem soon developed. The UCC grace period was extended to 20 days, and thus the 10–day grace period in subsection (c)(3) became useless for a PMSI perfected between 11 and 20 days after the debtor received possession of the collateral, even though state law would have given relation-back effect to perfection between days 11 and 20. For example, if the hypothetical above is changed so that Creditor perfects on June 5 (rather than May 28), under the 1984 version of the law Creditor would have lost.[292] Perfection occurred 16 days after the Debtor received possession of the collateral—within the time allowed by state law, but more than the

---

[292] E.g., In re Hamilton, 892 F.2d 1230 (5th Cir. 1990).

time allowed under the federal safe harbor in subsection (c)(3). The courts held that the shorter grace period in the federal bankruptcy law controlled over state law.

Congress responded to this problem in the 1994 Bankruptcy Act by amending subsection (c)(3), this time to provide for a 20–day grace period,[293] again intending to mirror the UCC time period.[294] On the specific facts of our hypothetical, Creditor now would win—perfection on day 16 (on June 5) after the Debtor received possession (on May 20) would fall within the 20–day grace period of the 1994 version of § 547(c)(3). Notably, though, Congress did *not* amend the law by simply incorporating grace periods effective under non-bankruptcy law, as it did elsewhere in the Code,[295] but again specified an independent federal time period for perfection. As I predicted in the first edition of this treatise,[296] this 1994 Congressional amendment left open exactly the same problem as before if the applicable state law grace period was *longer* than 20 days, because then the secured party would not find succor in either § 547(e)(2)'s 10–day rule or § 547(c)(3)'s 20–day rule.

That prediction came true in *Fidelity Financial Services, Inc. v. Fink*, decided by the Supreme Court in 1998.[297] Missouri law gave a secured party *thirty* days to perfect a security interest in a motor vehicle. The secured party mailed in the necessary perfection papers on day 21, and argued that it should be protected from preference avoidance because it complied with the Missouri law. The Supreme Court rejected this plea, emphasizing that the time periods in § 547(e)(2) on time-of-transfer and § 547(c)(3) for enabling loans are *federal* time periods and do not depend on or incorporate the underlying state law. With that said, the Court had little trouble finding that "21" was more than "20," and that the creditor accordingly was not protected by the enabling loan exception.

Showing little in the way of a learning curve, Congress has gone and done it again. In 2005, Congress amended § 547(c)(3) yet again, this time putting in a *thirty*-day grace period for enabling loans in place of the prior 20–day period.[298] Once again, though, it did not incorporate non-bankruptcy law grace periods, but used a specific federal time period. The new 30–day federal bankruptcy rule is good and well for secured creditors in states (like Missouri) with a 30–day state law perfection rule. So, on the exact facts of *Fink*, the outcome will be different now. But if state law provides a grace period to perfect longer than 30 days, it will be, as the saying goes, *déjà vu* all over again. Secured creditors will *not* have the full state law period to perfect and still be immune from preference attack. Instead, they will have only the 30–day period of new § 547(c)(3)(B). As a matter of policy, it is difficult to conceive of a coherent bankruptcy policy reason why secured creditors who comply fully with governing non-bankruptcy laws and who would prevail in a priority battle with intervening lien creditors and purchasers under that non-bankruptcy law should lose in the

---

[293] Pub. L. No. 103–394, § 203, 108 Stat. 4121 (1994).

[294] 140 Cong. Rec. H10,767 (daily ed. Oct. 4, 1994).

[295] E.g., 11 U.S.C. § 546(b)(1)(A) (non-bankruptcy relation-back periods given effect).

[296] Charles Jordan Tabb, The Law of Bankruptcy § 6.19, at 391 (1997).

[297] 522 U.S. 211 (1998).

[298] Pub. L. No. 109–8, § 1222, 119 Stat. 196 (2005).

happenstance that the debtor files bankruptcy. Doing so gives a windfall to the debtor's other creditors, a windfall those creditors could not possibly have obtained outside of bankruptcy.

Note, too, that § 547(c)(3) is not exactly identical to § 9–317(e) and § 9–103 of the Uniform Commercial Code.[299] Thus, a careful creditor must be cognizant of the technical requirements of both the U.C.C. and § 547(c)(3). For example, subsection (c)(3) only applies if the creditor gives new value "at or after" the signing of the security agreement. Yet, under Article 9, there is no prohibition on the creditor giving the value before the security agreement is signed. Thus, in the hypothetical used throughout this section, if the Creditor made the loan on May 1, and the Debtor signed the security agreement on May 2, by its terms § 547(c)(3) would not apply.

Finally, one must remember that § 547(c)(3) does not preclude preference avoidance for every situation in which perfection of a security interest is delayed. To give one example, that safe harbor only applies to an enabling loan. Thus, in our hypothetical, if Debtor had granted Creditor a security interest in Collateral that Debtor already owned, subsection (c)(3) would not apply.

§ 6.20   Safe Harbors: Subsequent Advances of New Value

Subsequent advances of new value from the creditor to the debtor are credited against prior preferential transfers. § 547(c)(4). In effect, the creditor's preference liability is reduced to the extent the creditor returns value to the debtor after receiving a preference. This protection for the creditor is justified on the ground that the debtor's estate has been replenished to the extent of the new value, and thus other creditors have not been harmed. Also, the "subsequent advance" exception is thought to encourage creditors to continue doing business with a financially troubled debtor. In practice, § 547(c)(4) has been applied most often in a trade credit situation, involving ongoing extensions of credit on open account.

The requirements of § 547(c)(4) are as follows:

- after a preferential transfer, the creditor gives new value to or for the benefit of the debtor, § 547(c)(4);

- that new value is not secured by an otherwise unavoidable security interest, § 547(c)(4)(A); and

- the debtor does not make an otherwise unavoidable transfer to or for the benefit of the creditor on account of that new value, § 547(c)(4)(B).

Consider the following example. At the beginning of the 90–day preference period on February 1, Debtor (DR) owes $10,000 to Creditor (CR), a trade supplier. Within the preference period, the following transactions occur:

---

[299] See David G. Carlson, Security Interests in the Crucible of Voidable Preference Law, 1995 U. Ill. L. Rev. 211, 299–300 (1995).

DR → CR (payment) CR → DR (credit shipment)

March 1: $10,000

April 1: $8,000

On these facts, the preference would be only $2,000. The $10,000 payment on March 1 from Debtor to Creditor would qualify as a preference in its entirety at the time made, assuming that all § 547(b) elements were met and no other exceptions in § 547(c) applied. However, when Creditor shipped $8,000 worth of goods to Debtor on credit a month later, Creditor gave "new value"[300] to Debtor. That new value was unsecured, and Debtor did not make an unavoidable transfer to Creditor on account of that $8,000 shipment. Therefore, under § 547(c)(4), the $8,000 must be deducted from Creditor's preference liability, leaving only $2,000 that may be avoided.

Now change the facts. Assume again that Debtor owes Creditor $10,000 on February 1, the beginning of the preference period. Within the preference period, the following transactions take place:

DR → CR (payment) CR → DR (credit shipment)

March 1: $8,000

April 1: $10,000

Creditor's preference liability on these facts (again assuming that § 547(b) is met and no other exceptions in (c) apply) is not $2,000, as before, but the entire $10,000 payment made by Debtor to Creditor on April 1. Why does Creditor not get credit under § 547(c)(4) in this hypothetical for the $8,000 extension of new credit during the preference period? The answer is that the extension of new value here came before the preferential transfer. A creditor is allowed a deduction under (c)(4) only for *subsequent* advances of new value.

The foregoing examples expose a misconception about § 547(c)(4). That provision does *not* codify a "net result" rule. The source of the confusion is the legislative history to the Code, which states that "the fourth exception codifies the net result rule in section 60c of current law."[301] A true "net result" rule would add up (1) all transfers from the debtor to the creditor during the preference period, and (2) all extensions of new value from the creditor to the debtor during that period, without regard to chronology, and then (3) net out the totals. Under a net result rule, both of the examples would result in a net preference of $2,000 ($10,000 from Debtor to Creditor, minus $8,000 from Creditor to Debtor). Under § 547(c)(4) as enacted, though, timing *does* matter; a creditor may only take advantage of new value given *after* the

---

[300] "New value" is defined in § 547(a)(2) in part as "money or money's worth in goods, services, or new credit."

[301] S. Rep. No. 95–989, 95th Cong., 2d Sess., at 88 (1978); H.R. Rep. No. 95–595, 95th Cong., 1st Sess., at 374 (1977).

preferential transfer from the debtor.[302] Fortunately, courts have interpreted the statute as written, rather than as described in the legislative history.[303]

Because timing does matter under § 547(c)(4), it may be critical to ascertain exactly when a transfer is made by the debtor and when new value is extended by the creditor. The creditor must extend the new value *after* the debtor's transfer in order to prevail under the new value defense. On the question of when the creditor's new value is extended, courts look at the time the creditor *ships* the goods, not when the debtor receives them.[304] This makes sense, because the point of the exception is to encourage the creditor to act.

Identifying the precise time that a debtor pays the creditor also can be an issue. Consider a "check straddle" case. Assume again that Debtor owes Creditor $10,000 at the beginning of the preference period on February 1. Within the preference period, the following transactions occur:

	DR → CR (payment)	CR → DR (credit shipment)
April 1:	$10,000 check delivered	
April 2:		$8,000
April 3:	check honored	

Whether Creditor will be allowed to take advantage of the § 547(c)(4) defense depends on whether the transfer by the Debtor is deemed to have taken place when the check was *delivered* on April 1, or when it was *honored* on April 3. If the transfer was effective upon delivery, the defense is available, because the extension of new value came thereafter (on April 2); if, however, the transfer did not occur until honor, the defense is lost. In terms of the reasons for the (c)(4) defense and the probable motivations of the parties, the delivery date should be utilized. On these facts, the creditor apparently was prompted to extend new credit by the delivery of the check, and should get credit for that new value. Prior to 1992, the courts uniformly took that view and used the delivery date in normal check transactions under subsection (c). One exception was if the debtor gave the creditor a post-dated check, in which case the debtor's payment was not considered made until the date of the check arrived.[305]

In 1992, the unbroken line of authority that the delivery date controlled for purposes of applying the preference exceptions in § 547(c) was cast into doubt when the Supreme Court held in *Barnhill v. Johnson*[306] that, for purposes of whether a transfer

---

[302] The statement in the legislative history is not only inaccurate in describing the statute as written, it also errs in describing the rule of § 60c of the Act as a net result rule. As has been explained, "no 'net result' rule has existed since 1903, and the rule never was applicable to old section 60c." Vern Countryman, The Concept of a Voidable Preference in Bankruptcy, 38 Vand. L. Rev. 713, 783 (1985).

[303] See, e.g., In re Fulghum Constr. Corp., 706 F.2d 171 (6th Cir.), cert. denied, 464 U.S. 935 (1983).

[304] See, e.g., In re Eleva, Inc., 235 B.R. 486 (B.A.P. 9th Cir. 1999).

[305] See, e.g., In re New York City Shoes, Inc., 880 F.2d 679 (3d Cir. 1989).

[306] 503 U.S. 393 (1992).

by check was made within the preference period under § 547(b)(4), the date of *honor* controls, rather than the date of delivery. The Court was careful to limit its holding to § 547(b), though, and left open the possibility that a different time of transfer by check could be found under subsection (c), where the timing issues may implicate different policy questions. Post–*Barnhill,* courts have taken advantage of this opening left by the Court, and continue to hold that the date of delivery of the check controls under subsection (c)(4).[307] As one court explained, since subsection (c)(4) is "intended to encourage creditors to continue doing business with a troubled enterprise, generally creditors should be allowed to rely on receipt of a check rather than waiting for it to be honored."[308] Otherwise, trade suppliers doing business with a financially distressed debtor would have to wait to extend new credit until cash has been paid or a check has been honored, which actually would harm, not help, the debtor. This result then means that the same check could be deemed to have been transferred at two different times, depending on which subsection of the law is at issue.

A final problem has confronted the courts in interpreting § 547(c)(4). The difficulty arises when the debtor makes payments to the creditor after the creditor has extended new value. The issue is whether the new value given by the creditor must "remain unpaid." If part of the rationale for the (c)(4) exception is that the creditor has restored part of the earlier preference to the debtor, then at first blush logic would suggest that the rationale disappears when the debtor in turn repays the creditor for what had been restored.

As is often the case with the law, however, the precise answer to the question of whether the new value must remain unpaid is subtler. A careful reading of the statute reveals that the answer is: *it depends.* What it depends on is whether the debtor made "an otherwise unavoidable transfer to or for the benefit of the creditor" "on account of" the new value. § 547(c)(4)(B). If the debtor did make an unavoidable transfer on account of the new value, then that new value cannot be credited under (c)(4). However, even if the debtor "paid" the creditor for the new value, if that payment *itself* is avoidable, then the creditor may use the new value without deduction. In essence, avoidance of the "payment" means that the creditor effectively did *not* get paid for the new value; instead, it will have to remit the payment back to the estate. Some examples might help.

Assume again that Debtor owes Creditor $10,000 at the beginning of the preference period on February 1. The following transactions then take place:

---

[307] The leading case is In re Tennessee Chem. Co., 112 F.3d 234 (6th Cir. 1997).

[308] In re Nat'l Enters., Inc., 174 B.R. 429, 433 (Bankr. E.D. Va. 1994) (quoting In re Bob Grissett Golf Shoppes, Inc., 78 B.R. 787, 791 (Bankr. E.D. Va. 1987)).

	DR → CR (payment)	CR → DR (credit shipment)
March 1:	$10,000	
April 1:		$8,000
April 15:	$6,000	

Analysis of the result under the foregoing facts depends on the status of the April 15 payment of $6,000. Assume first that the April 15 payment *is* avoidable as a preference. In that event, the entire $8,000 in new value given on April 1 may be used as a credit under § 547(c)(4) with regard to the March 1 preferential transfer of $10,000. The reason is that the debtor "did not make an otherwise unavoidable transfer" on account of that new value, § 547(c)(4)(B); instead, it made an *avoidable* transfer. Thus, the total preference will be $8,000: $2,000 of the March 1 transfer ($10,000 minus $8,000), *plus* the $6,000 transferred on April 15.

If a court mistakenly required the April 1 new value to "remain unpaid" without considering the voidability of the later payment, the $6,000 payment on April 15 would mean that only $2,000 of the $8,000 in new value could be used as a defense under (c)(4). If so, the creditor's total preference liability would increase to $14,000: $8,000 of the March 1 transfer ($10,000 minus only $2,000), plus $6,000 for the April 15 transfer. But such an outcome would be patently unfair to the creditor; the $6,000 payment on April 15 would be counted *twice*: once to decrease the available (c)(4) defense for the April 1 new value, and once as a preference in its own right. Strictly applying the statutory language of § 547(c)(4)(B) as written avoids the double counting trap. Fortunately, the clear trend in the case law has been to apply the statute properly, and to look beyond the simplistic question of whether the new value "remains unpaid."[309] Still, some courts cling to the demonstrably incorrect "remains unpaid" formulation.[310]

Now assume that the April 15 payment is not avoidable. For example, that payment might be protected by the "ordinary course of business" exception in § 547(c)(2). Post–2005, as of 2013 (as indexed) any transfer in a business case less than $6,225 is immune under the expanded "small preference" safe harbor in § 547(c)(9).[311] If the debtor's subsequent transfer is not avoidable, the requirement of § 547(c)(4)(B) is not met; by its terms, the debtor did "make an otherwise unavoidable transfer" for part of the new value. The safe harbor of subsection (c)(4) now is only available to the extent of $2,000 (the total $8,000 in new value minus the $6,000 unavoidable transfer). The

---

[309] The leading case is In re IRFM, Inc., 52 F.3d 228 (9th Cir. 1995).

[310] See, e.g., In re GGSI Liquidation, Inc., 313 B.R. 770 (Bankr. N.D. Ill. 2004) (stating that *In re Prescott*, 805 F.2d 719 (7th Cir. 1986), which adopted the "remains unpaid" formulation, is still the law in the Seventh Circuit).

[311] See § 6.24.

total preference again will be $8,000: the March 1 $10,000 transfer, minus the $2,000 deducted under (c)(4) from the April 1 transfer, and nothing for the April 15 transfer.

Illustrating the correct interpretation of the statutory language as explained above is a case out of the District of Delaware, which rejected the "remains unpaid" formulation for the reasons noted. In *In re Pillowtex Corp.*,[312] the court concluded that the plain meaning interpretation of § 547(c)(4) did *not* require that the subsequent advance of new value "remain unpaid." The court found that the statute was unambiguous on its face. Further, the court reasoned that the "remains unpaid" formulation is contrary to the main purposes of § 547(c)(4). First, if the subsequent new value defense is intended to encourage creditors to continue to extend credit to a failing debtor, the "remains unpaid" approach counteracts this by essentially increasing the losses of any creditor who continues to extend value throughout the preference period. The example given above shows how this would happen. Second, the approach utilized in *Pillowtex* serves to treat creditors fairly by protecting creditors who do continue to replenish the debtor's estate after receiving a preferential transfer.

One further problem should be noted. There may be numerous payments and shipments in a running account situation. The question has arisen under § 547(c)(4) whether the new value given by the creditor can be used to offset only the immediately preceding preferential payment, or whether that new value can be applied against earlier preferences as well. Although there is case authority both ways, the better view and apparent trend is to hold that the new value can be applied broadly to any previous preferential transfer, even those that did not immediately precede the extension of new value.[313]

Another issue that arises is what may constitute "new" value. Specifically, courts have struggled with whether performance of an existing contractual obligation may constitute "new" value for purposes of § 547(c)(4). The issue is well illustrated in *In re Globe Building Materials, Inc.*,[314] where the court found that performance of an existing contractual duty could not constitute new value. In this case, creditor shipped component parts to debtor pursuant to a contractual agreement after debtor made a payment under the contract. The trustee brought a preference action to avoid the payment, and creditor argued that the shipment of the component parts acted as a "subsequent new value" defense to the prior payment.

The court held that creditor had no defense, as "the "new value" claimed by the creditor was merely a preexisting contractual obligation with the debtor.[315] Since debtor was not in default under the contract, the court reasoned that the creditor was under a contractual obligation to provide the component parts, and thus did not provide anything of "new" value to the estate. The court further reasoned that the purpose of § 547(c)(4) is to reward creditors who voluntarily extend new value to the

---

[312] 416 B.R. 123 (Bankr. D. Del. 2009).

[313] E.g., In re Micro Innovations Corp., 185 F.3d 329 (5th Cir. 1999); *IRFM*, supra note 309, 52 F.3d 228.

[314] 484 F.3d 946 (7th Cir. 2007).

[315] Id. at 950 ("But under the contract the parties actually had, [the creditor's] delivery during the preference period of equipment components it was obliged to furnish does not constitute 'new value.'").

estate in circumstances where such an extension is not required, and thus the purpose of the defense is not met in the context of a pre-existing contractual relationship.

The court thus drew a bright line rule where performance of an existing contractual duty could never constitute subsequent new value. Other courts have declined to follow such a bright line approach, instead holding that even performance of a contractual obligation may constitute subsequent new value where debtor is in some way provided with "money's worth."[316]

§ 6.21 Safe Harbors: Floating Liens

The fifth safe harbor from preference liability offers some protection for secured creditors with "floating liens" in inventory and receivables. § 547(c)(5). A lien is said to "float" when it attaches to property acquired by the debtor after the initial security transaction. Subsection (c)(5) exempts from avoidance a floating lien that attaches to inventory or receivables during the preference period, except to the extent that the creditor has improved its position during the preference period. Thus, the fifth exception requires a comparison of the creditor's security position at the beginning of the preference period with its position at the time of bankruptcy. The fifth exception, in conjunction with the timing rule of § 547(e)(3), solves a difficult problem that perplexed courts under the prior Act.[317]

The difficulty is created by the fact that, for inventory and for receivables, the collateral by its very nature "turns over," i.e., the old collateral is replaced by new collateral. For example, assume that Debtor runs a chain of stores that sell boomerangs. On May 1, 2010, Debtor borrows $100,000 from Creditor to finance, on a "floor plan" basis, all of the inventory of boomerangs. To secure the debt, Debtor grants Creditor a security interest in all present and after-acquired inventory and receivables. Debtor uses the loan proceeds to purchase the initial stock of inventory. As the store operations continue, Debtor sells boomerangs for cash and on account. The sales and the collections of receivables generate cash, which Debtor uses to purchase new inventory of boomerangs. Eventually, Debtor has completely "turned over" the original inventory, i.e., none of the boomerangs on the shelves were part of the original stock in May 2010, when the debt to Creditor was created.

At all times, Creditor has a security interest in the Debtor's current inventory and receivables. Under Article 9, the creditor's security interest "floats" to attach to the replacement collateral. U.C.C. § 9–204(a). Yet, with regard to any specific items of collateral, Creditor's security interest cannot actually attach and become enforceable

---

[316] See, e.g., S. Tech. Coll., Inc. v. Hood, 89 F.3d 1381 (8th Cir. 1996) (holding that allowing debtors to continue to occupy premises under a lease constituted "new value" as it allowed debtors to resume operations).

[317] In the early years of the Code, many scholars helpfully plumbed the mysteries of the floating lien preference problem. For a sampling, see Irving A. Breitowitz, Article 9 Security Interests as Voidable Preferences: Part II: The Floating Lien, 4 Cardozo L. Rev. 1 (1982); David G. Carlson, Security Interests in the Crucible of Voidable Preference Law, 1995 U. Ill. L. Rev. 211, 309–48 (1995); Neil Cohen, "Value" Judgments: Account Receivable Financing and Voidable Preferences Under the New Bankruptcy Code, 66 Minn. L. Rev. 639 (1982); Vern Countryman, The Concept of a Voidable Preference in Bankruptcy, 38 Vand. L. Rev. 713, 790–801 (1985); Richard F. Duncan, Preferential Transfers, the Floating Lien, and Section 547(c)(5) of the Bankruptcy Reform Act of 1978, 36 Ark. L. Rev. 1 (1982).

against the debtor until the debtor has rights in that collateral. U.C.C. § 9–203(a), (b)(2). Thus, the security interest in the replacement collateral is not officially transferred to the secured creditor until the debtor acquires the collateral.

Assume that the boomerang business turns out to be a little slower than Debtor had expected. On May 1, 2013, Debtor files bankruptcy. Ninety days before Debtor filed, the debt to Creditor was $70,000, and the value of the inventory and receivables securing that debt was $50,000. During the 90 days before bankruptcy, all of the Debtor's inventory and receivables turned over, and Creditor's security interest floated to attach to the new collateral. Thus, all of the Creditor's collateral as of the date of bankruptcy was acquired by Debtor in the 90–day preference period. At the time of filing bankruptcy, the collateral still was worth $50,000.

The problem is this. The transfer of the security interest to Creditor does not occur until the Debtor acquires rights in the collateral, as noted above. U.C.C. § 9–203(a), (b)(2). All of that collateral was acquired by Debtor in the preference period. Thus, for preference purposes, Debtor effectively transferred $50,000 worth of collateral to Creditor during the preference period. Yet, the debt from Debtor to Creditor was created three years back, at the inception of the transaction. That debt thus is deemed to be "antecedent" to the transfer of the collateral to Creditor. Without some saving rule, the entire security interest of Creditor would be avoided as a preference. Such a result would undermine a common form of commercial financing and would be patently unfair, since Creditor had not improved its position at all during the preference period. Creditor had $50,000 in collateral at the start of the period *and* when bankruptcy was filed.

Under pre-Code law, courts invoked various theories to escape the artificial antecedent debt problem created by floating liens. None was entirely satisfactory. The two leading cases, decided in 1969, both upheld the creditor's floating lien. The Ninth Circuit held for the creditor in *DuBay v. Williams*.[318] In that case, the Ninth Circuit concluded that the "transfer" of the security interest occurred for preference purposes when the creditor *perfected* the security interest by filing a financing statement, not later when the debtor acquired the collateral.[319] On this theory, in our example the transfer would be deemed to have occurred back in May 2010, at the outset of the transaction.

In *Grain Merchants v. Union Bank*,[320] the Seventh Circuit suggested several rationales for upholding the creditor's lien. One was the "relaxed substitution of collateral" theory. Under § 547(c)(1), a creditor is protected from preference attack if one item of collateral is substituted for another; the release of the lien on the original collateral is "new value" for the transfer of the security interest in the replacement. A strict substitution approach does not work well for floating liens, though, because it is difficult to trace the replacement-item-for-released-item linkage. The Seventh Circuit simply ignored the practical linkage problem. A second theory offered by the Seventh

---

[318] 417 F.2d 1277 (9th Cir. 1969).

[319] Professor Countryman derisively calls this the "Abracadabra" or "The Transfer Occurred Before It Occurred" theory. See Countryman, supra note 317, at 793.

[320] 408 F.2d 209 (7th Cir.), cert. denied, 396 U.S. 827 (1969).

Circuit was the "entity" theory, or, more colorfully, the "Mississippi River" theory. This view posits that the creditor has a security interest, not in specific items of collateral, but in the "entity" that is the debtor's inventory or receivables. An analogy is drawn to the Mississippi River: the specific molecules of water present from time to time vary, but it is still the Mississippi River. Just so, the creditor's security interest may vary from time to time with regard to the precise items of collateral covered, but the "collateral" viewed as an entity is still the same. Under this view, the Creditor in our example got a security interest in the inventory and receivables in May 2010, and still had the "same" security interest when bankruptcy ensued.

Drawing on the work of a committee of the National Bankruptcy Conference chaired by Professor Grant Gilmore, Congress in the 1978 Code overruled *DuBay* and *Grain Merchants*.[321] Under § 547(e)(3), the "transfer" of the security interest does not occur until the debtor acquires rights in the collateral. Thus, in our example, the Creditor's security interest would be deemed to be transferred during the preference period for an antecedent debt, and assuming the other elements are met, would be vulnerable to avoidance in its entirety under § 547(b). The extent of protection depends entirely on § 547(c)(5).

Section 547(c)(5) utilizes a *two-point improvement-in-position test*. The security interest in inventory and receivables is only avoided to the extent that the creditor improves its position from point one to point two. Interim fluctuations are ignored. *Point One* is the beginning of the preference period. § 547(c)(5)(A).[322] *Point Two* is the date of bankruptcy. The comparison between these two points focuses on the extent that the creditor is undersecured, i.e., the amount that the debt exceeds the value of the collateral. A preference only will be found to the extent that the creditor's unsecured claim gets smaller, i.e., its deficiency decreases, from point one to point two.

Thus, the formula for § 547(c)(5) is:

Point One deficiency (debt minus collateral value)

minus

Point Two deficiency (debt minus collateral value)

= *amount avoided*

Consider some examples. First, in the hypothetical used above, application of the statutory test yields the following result:

---

[321] S. Rep. No. 95–989, 95th Cong., 2d Sess., at 88 (1978); H.R. Rep. No. 95–595, 95th Cong., 1st Sess., at 374 (1977).

[322] The only exception is if the creditor does not make the loan until a later date; in that event, the date new value is first extended will be point one. § 547(c)(5)(B).

	Debt	minus	Collateral Value	=	Deficiency
Point One (day 90):	$70,000	–	$50,000	=	$20,000
Point Two (bankruptcy):	$70,000	–	$50,000	=	$20,000

Since the deficiency is the same at both points, there is no preference.

Now assume that the amount of the Creditor's collateral value does increase during the preference period:

	Debt	minus	Collateral Value	=	Deficiency
Point One (day 90):	$70,000	–	$50,000	=	$20,000
Point Two (bankruptcy):	$70,000	–	$55,000	=	$15,000

In this example, the preference is $5,000, which is the difference between the $20,000 deficiency at Point One and the $15,000 deficiency at Point Two. The Creditor has improved its position by that $5,000 amount. Upon avoidance of the $5,000 preference, Creditor will be relegated to a collateral position of $50,000, and again will have a $20,000 deficiency.

A creditor who is fully secured at point one will be completely protected from avoidance by § 547(c)(5). By definition, that creditor cannot improve its position. The following example illustrates the point.

	Debt	minus	Collateral Value	=	Deficiency
Point One (day 90):	$70,000	–	$70,000	=	none
Point Two (bankruptcy):	$70,000	–	$80,000	=	none

The fact that Creditor received $10,000 more in collateral during the preference period does not matter. The Creditor can only get paid in full.

Interim fluctuations in collateral value during the preference period are ignored. The test in § 547(c)(5) looks *only* to the two points. Thus, a buildup in the creditor's collateral position shortly before bankruptcy is not a preference, if the creditor is only restored to the position it enjoyed at the outset of the preference period. This is true even if the creditor engaged in seemingly "preferential" behavior. For example, a creditor whose collateral position drops dramatically might demand a restoration of the collateral value. Section 547(c)(5) opts for a relatively simple rule that affords rough justice. To illustrate, there is no preference in the following example:

	Debt	minus	Collateral Value	=	Deficiency
Point One (day 90):	$70,000	–	$50,000	=	$20,000
Ten days before bankruptcy:	$70,000	–	$10,000	=	$60,000
Point Two (bankruptcy):	$70,000	–	$50,000	=	$20,000

A refinement on § 547(c)(5) is that the reduction in the creditor's deficiency must be "to the prejudice of other creditors holding unsecured claims." The focus of the preference law is not on whether this particular creditor is better off than before, but whether that creditor is better off *at the expense* of other unsecured creditors. This qualification means that the formula stated on the preceding page cannot be applied mechanically in all cases; even if application of the formula indicates a presumptive preference, it is possible that the creditor may escape liability in whole or in part. For example, the increase in collateral value from point one to point two may be attributable entirely to an increase in the market value of collateral that was purchased at a lower price. That increase in value is not a preference, because it does not harm other creditors.

In applying the two-point improvement-in-position test, one must be careful to take all circumstances into account when computing the debt. For example, consider what happens if the debtor makes a payment on the debt during the preference period, as follows:

	Debt	minus	Collateral Value	=	Deficiency
Point One (day 90):	$70,000	–	$50,000	=	$20,000
Point Two (bankruptcy):	$55,000	–	$50,000	=	$5,000

A simple application of the two-point test might suggest that the creditor has received a $15,000 preference, because the deficiency decreased from $20,000 to $5,000. However, note that the decrease occurred because of a decline in the amount of the debt, and not because of an increase in the amount of collateral. One must then explore how the debt was decreased. If the debtor made a $15,000 payment on that debt, it may be that the payment itself will be avoidable as a preference. If so, the creditor will have to return that $15,000 to the estate, §§ 550, 502(d), and will have a claim for the $15,000 returned. § 502(h). Upon that repayment to the trustee, the creditor's total claim (i.e., the "debt") will be $70,000 ($55,000 plus $15,000), not just $55,000. Thus, the deficiency at Point Two of the test under § 547(c)(5) really should be calculated to be $20,000, not $5,000—and thus no avoidance is permitted under (c)(5). Otherwise, the $15,000 payment would in effect be counted against the creditor twice.

In applying § 547(c)(5), it is necessary to compute the *value* of the creditor's collateral. Making that calculation requires the selection of a *standard* of valuation for the collateral. For example, it would make a substantial difference whether the collateral is valued at retail or wholesale price. Congress did not specify any particular standard, leaving the matter to the courts. A leading case on valuation is the Seventh Circuit's decision in *In re Ebbler Furniture & Appliances, Inc.*[323] The *Ebbler* court used the historical wholesale *cost* to the debtor, rather than the higher retail value of "cost plus" a mark-up, because the parties themselves had used cost to value the inventory. The court did not mandate the use of cost in all cases, however, but concluded that value had to be determined on a case-by-case basis. Judge Easterbrook concurred and argued that wholesale *always* would be the proper measure, because that is all that the secured creditor itself could ever realize by foreclosure. The difference between wholesale and retail is attributable to the value added by the debtor's business operations.

A final reminder about the operation of § 547(c)(5) is that it only applies to security interests in *inventory* and *receivables*. The reason is that only those types of collateral turn over by their very nature, and thus need the type of protection offered by (c)(5). For other types of collateral, such as equipment, a security interest in after-acquired property would be vulnerable to preference attack. Of course, the creditor could attempt to defend under a safe harbor other than subsection (c)(5). For example, the creditor might attempt to prove a substitution of collateral that would be protected by the contemporaneous exchange exception of § 547(c)(1).

§ 6.22   Safe Harbors: Statutory Liens

The sixth preference safe harbor is for "the fixing of a statutory lien that is not avoidable under section 545." § 547(c)(6). First, what *is* a statutory lien? The Code defines a "statutory lien" as a "lien arising *solely* by force of a *statute* on specified circumstances or conditions." § 101(53). The most important example, by far, is the federal tax lien. 26 U.S.C. § 6321. A myriad of other statutory liens exist as well: mechanics' & materialmen's lien (known as "M & M" liens), landlord's lien, attorney's lien, and so on.

Note that the definition of statutory lien states that the term "does not include security interest or judicial lien." § 101(53). A "security interest" in Bankruptcy Code parlance is a "lien created by agreement," § 101(51), such as an Article 9 security interest or a real estate mortgage. A "judicial lien" is a "lien obtained by judgment, levy, sequestration, or other legal or equitable process or proceeding," § 101(36), such as an execution lien or garnishment lien. Thus, if the creation of the lien is dependent either on agreement or on taking judicial action, that lien does not qualify as a statutory lien.

The purpose of § 547(c)(6) is to "except statutory liens validated under section 545 from preference attack."[324] Section 545 permits the avoidance of certain types of statutory liens.[325] Congress thus intended for § 545 to be exclusive of § 547 as a means

---

[323]   804 F.2d 87 (7th Cir. 1986).

[324]   S. Rep. No. 95–989, 95th Cong., 2d Sess., at 88 (1978); H.R. Rep. No. 95–595, 95th Cong., 1st Sess., at 374 (1977).

[325]   See §§ 6.49–6.53.

of challenging statutory liens; if the lien survives § 545, the trustee is not entitled to a second bite at the avoidance apple under § 547.[326]

For example, assume that Danny's Drywall Co. installs drywall on a construction project for Debtor, but Danny is not paid. Danny takes the steps necessary under state law to obtain and perfect a M & M lien. Less than 90 days later, Debtor files bankruptcy. If Danny's M & M lien is valid under § 545, the trustee cannot set it aside under § 547.

A curious aspect of § 547(c)(6) is that it protects only the "fixing" of a statutory lien. Payments made on an already "fixed" statutory lien are not expressly excepted. Indeed, the 1978 Code as enacted dropped language in an earlier version of the bill that would have protected such payments.[327] This omission in particular makes payments or levies on a federal tax lien vulnerable under § 547, because the hypothetical chapter 7 distribution analysis required by § 547(b)(5) would bring into play the tax lien subordination rule in § 724(b).[328] Note, though, that to the extent a fixed lien is released as payments are made, the contemporaneous exchange exception[329] would provide a safe harbor from preference avoidance.

§ 6.23   Safe Harbors: Domestic Support Obligations

The seventh exception to preference liability was added to the Code in 1994 as part of a package of amendments designed to protect child support and alimony and maintenance claimants.[330] It was amended in 2005 as part of yet another package of amendments favoring such claimants.[331] Section 547(c)(7) insulates from preference avoidance "bona fide" payments of debts for a *domestic support obligation*," which as of 2005 became a defined term in § 101(14A). This exception protects payments on debts in the nature of alimony, maintenance, or support (§ 101(14A)(B)) that are payable to the debtor's spouse, former spouse, or child. § 101(14A)(A)(i).

Also included, for the first time in 2005, are payments of the same type to a "governmental unit." § 101(14A)(A)(ii). The addition of government assignees as a permitted recipient of protected payments is the most significant substantive change effected by the 2005 amendments. Before 2005, assignees of family support debts could not invoke the preference exception. The exception was purely personal to the claimant. Under the 2005 amendment, the assignee prohibition was continued only for non-governmental assignees (unless voluntarily assigned by the spouse or child for the purpose of collection). § 101(14A)(D). These changes brought the preference exception for family support debts in line with the discharge exception for such debts (§ 523(a)(5)).

---

[326] See Vern Countryman, The Concept of a Voidable Preference in Bankruptcy, 38 Vand. L. Rev. 713, 803 (1985).

[327] 124 Cong. Rec. H11,097 (daily ed. Sept. 28, 1978) (statement of Rep. Edwards).

[328] See Countryman, supra note 326, at 806–11.

[329] See § 6.17.

[330] Pub. L. No. 103–394, § 304(f), 108 Stat. 4133 (1994).

[331] Pub. L. No. 109–8, § 217, 119 Stat. 55 (2005).

For example, assume that Darryl Deadbeat falls $5,000 behind on his child support payments. A week before he files bankruptcy, Darryl pays the $5,000 in overdue child support. Section 547(c)(7) prevents the payment from being avoided as a preference. This is true whether the payment is made to the child (or the child's guardian), a governmental unit to whom the debt had been assigned, or a collection agency.

As of 2005, the preference safe harbor in § 547(c)(7) mirrors exactly the exception to discharge in § 523(a)(5), with the identical reference to "domestic support obligations" (under § 101(14A)) as the protected type of debt. Thus, if a debt is of the type that would be excepted from discharge under § 523(a)(5), it also will not be a preference for the debtor to make a payment on that debt during the pre-bankruptcy preference period. Furthermore, with some qualifications, debts owed for "domestic support obligations" were given first priority in payment by the 2005 amendments. § 507(a)(1). Thus, even if Darryl had not made the $5,000 payment prior to bankruptcy, that debt would not have been dischargeable in bankruptcy, and would have been entitled to first priority in the bankruptcy distribution. Also, efforts to collect such a debt are excepted from the automatic stay. § 362(b)(2)(B). The idea is to facilitate as fully as possible the payment of "domestic support obligations," with no interference by (and indeed the assistance of) the bankruptcy proceedings.

To be protected, though, the debt must be *in the nature of* alimony, maintenance, or support, § 101(14A)(B). This limitation excludes debts that are nothing more than a division of assets under a property settlement agreement. There is an enormous amount of case law under the discharge exception speaking to the question of whether a debt is in the nature of alimony, maintenance, or support or instead is merely a division of assets. That case law should be relevant under the preference exception as well. While the definition of "domestic support obligation" can include debts established in a property settlement agreement, § 101(14A)((C)(i), it *also* requires that the debt be "in the nature of" alimony, maintenance, or support. The intent is that the *nature* of the debt control, not its source.

§ 6.24 Safe Harbors: Small Transfers[332]

The final preference exceptions are for relatively small amounts transferred. The thought is that when such small amounts are at stake, it is not worth undermining the finality of settled transactions or incurring the time and expense of litigating. Of course, if the trustee believes that the preference litigation is not worth the cost, she always has had the discretion not to bring the preference action in the first place. A more salient justification is that preference defendants may feel pressured to settle in cases with few dollars at stake, even if they believe they have a meritorious defense, in order to avoid a Pyrrhic victory, in which the cost of defense would be greater than the liability averted.[333]

---

[332] The discussion in § 6.24. draws heavily on Charles J. Tabb, The Brave New World of Bankruptcy Preferences, 13 Am. Bankr. Inst. L. Rev. 425, 427, 430–37 (2005).

[333] A 1997 national preference law study conducted by the ABI (for which I served as the Reporter) observed:

An easy, clean solution to this problem is simply to set a floor dollar amount below which the creditor defendant has an absolute defense to a successful preference action. Doing so, of course, seriously undermines the rationales for having a preference law in the first place,[334] as discussed below. After 2005, there are two such safe harbors for small transfers.

The first is in cases involving individual consumer debtors. § 547(c)(8). To establish a safe harbor under subsection (c)(8), the creditor must establish: (1) that the debtor is an individual; (2) whose debts are primarily consumer debts; and (3) that the aggregate value of all property that constitutes or is affected by such transfer is less than $600. This small preference exception was added by the 1984 amendments.[335]

The second, enacted in 2005,[336] extends the small dollar safe harbor to non-consumer (i.e., business) cases, but dramatically increases the amount of the safe harbor for those cases. Section 547(c)(9) precludes the trustee from avoiding as a preference a transfer "if, in a case filed by a debtor whose debts are not primarily consumer debts, the aggregate value of all property that constitutes or is affected by such transfer is less than $5,000." The dollar amount of the safe harbor in subsection (c)(9) was indexed up to $6,225 in 2013, and will continue to be indexed tri-annually.

It bears noting here that another 2005 amendment directly affects the economic imperatives of the sort of preference litigation to which § 547(c)(9) was directed. The pressure on the creditor defendant to settle often came from a combination of the facts that (1) a small amount of dollars was at stake and (2) the preference suit was brought in a court far from where the creditor was located, in the debtor's "home court." Problem 1 is addressed by § 547(c)(9). Problem 2 was addressed in 2005 by the amendment of the venue rules in 28 U.S.C. § 1409(b).[337] Now, a defendant in a suit on a consumer debt of less than $18,675 or on a business debt of less than $12,475 (assuming the defendant is not an insider of the debtor) is entitled to be sued in the district in which they reside, rather than where the bankruptcy case is pending.

The impact of the addition of subsection (c)(9) is momentous: it ends all preference liability in business cases for transfers of less than $6,225. The creditor defendant need not prove that the transfer was in the "ordinary course of business,"[338] that it provided

---

A . . . significant and pervasive problem identified is that creditors often feel pressured into making nuisance settlements, even if the action is of dubious validity. . . . One of the common problems identified in the survey responses was that of coercive preference litigation. . . . When suits are brought for very small amounts, the pressure on the preference defendant to settle is enormous.

American Bankruptcy Institute Task Force on Preferences, Preference Survey Project, at 25 (1997) (Tabb, C., Reporter) (hereafter "ABI Report"), available at http://www.abiworld.org/Content/NavigationMenu/ NewsRoom/BankruptcyResearchCenter/BankruptcyReportsResearchandTestimony/ABI/ Report_on_the_ABI_P1.htm.

[334] See § 6.7.

[335] As originally enacted, the exception was found in § 547(c)(7). With the addition of the exception for payments on certain domestic relations debts in 1994, the small consumer exception was renumbered as (c)(8).

[336] Pub. L. No. 109–8, § 409(3), 119 Stat. 106 (2005).

[337] See § 4.10.b.

[338] See § 6.18.

"new value,"[339] or was a "substantially contemporaneous exchange,"[340] or anything else—if the creditor can show that (1) the debtor had primarily non-consumer debts, and (2) "such transfer" was less than $6,225, then the creditor wins, period. Indeed, in such cases, it is hard to imagine why the trustee would even bother to bring the preference lawsuit in the first place, since the creditor has an absolute, and easily provable, defense.

Thus, in a business case, an insolvent debtor on the eve of bankruptcy is free to pick and choose with impunity which debts to pay in preference to others, as long as the preferred debt is less than $6,225—not an insignificant amount in many cases. A creditor owed less than $6,225 by a business debtor can pressure the debtor to pay to its heart's content, free from any nagging worry about possible preference recapture. On the bright side, finality is enhanced—if a creditor of a business debtor is paid a debt of less than $6,225, it knows it will get to keep the payment, even if the debtor soon goes into bankruptcy. Indisputably, though, § 547(c)(9) creates a gaping hole in the conception of preference liability.

Establishing a floor minimum amount is hardly a new idea. The first Bankruptcy Review Commission in 1973 suggested a $1,000 floor for transfers to non-insiders, in consumer and non-consumer cases alike.[341] However, Congress ignored the first Review Commission's recommendation for a floor amount in the 1978 Code, preferring instead to defer to the discretion of trustees in making the cost-benefit assessment. The problem with that thinking, though, is that the cost calculus is not symmetrical between preference plaintiff and defendant, especially given the "home court" venue advantage then enjoyed by the bankruptcy trustee; the trustee-plaintiff could bring greater economic pressure to bear on the creditor-defendant to settle than the trustee would suffer if the creditor called the trustee's bluff and contested the suit.

In 1984 Congress took a small first step along the small-preference-safe-harbor path, adding the $600 safe harbor applicable only in consumer cases, now codified in § 547(c)(8). The push for that amendment came from the consumer credit industry, which was worried that the then-existing 45–day rule that was originally part of the ordinary course exception unfairly exposed consumer credit providers with a greater-than-45-day credit cycle to preference liability.[342] On course, since the 45–day limit in § 547(c)(2) itself also was repealed in 1984, the proffered logic for the new small consumer preference exception was stillborn.

Notably, the 1984 exception did *not* apply to non-consumer cases, notwithstanding the first Review Commission's recommendation for a small preference exception applicable to *all* types of cases. When a driving motivation for the exception is viewed

---

[339] See § 6.20.

[340] See § 6.17.

[341] Report of the Commission on the Bankruptcy Laws of the United States, H.R. Doc. No. 197, 93d Cong., 1st Sess. Pt. II, § 4–607(b)(1), at 166 (1973). See also Charles Jordan Tabb, Rethinking Preferences, 43 S.C.L. Rev. 981, 1033 (1992)

[342] See Vern Countryman, The Concept of a Voidable Preference in Bankruptcy, 38 Vand. L. Rev. 713, 814 (1985). The original ordinary course exception required the transfer to be made within 45 days of when the debt was incurred.

as anti-nuisance suit protection, as the 1997 ABI Report and both the first and second Commission Reports contemplate, then little reason exists to differentiate between the types of cases in principle. A nuisance suit is a nuisance suit, whether the debtor be a consumer or a business. In 2005, Congress finally grasped this point.

One might still draw the *dollar amount* threshold differently for business and consumer cases, if the perception is that the interests of other creditors as well as the case dynamics are sufficiently different. The current system, as explained, uses a $600 floor in consumer cases (§ 547(c)(8)) and a $6,225 floor in non-consumer cases. § 547(c)(9). This differentiation might be defensible in that prospective preference recoveries between $600 and $6,225 may be significant assets of the estate in consumer cases, but much less important in most business cases. Whether that statement is in fact true is at bottom an empirical question. The work of Professors Lawless and Warren suggests that small business cases are much more prevalent than believed,[343] which suggests that the negative impact of the $6,225 floor might be higher than anticipated. We will have to wait and see whether Congress has found just the right balance between the need for trade creditors to be freed from coercive nuisance litigation in small cases, on the one hand, and the need to promote the preference goals of equality and deterrence, on the other.

Whatever the theoretical merits of the small preference exceptions, in practice the main questions that might arise are (1) whether the debtor had primarily consumer or non-consumer debts—since the safe harbor in the consumer situation is a mere $600, as contrasted with the significantly larger $6,225 immunity threshold in business cases, and (2) how "such transfer" will be determined—in particular, whether the trustee can *aggregate* a series of transfers that individually are less than $6,225 but together total more than $6,225 (under subsection (c)(9)) or $600 (under (c)(8)).

The first issue—is the nature of the debtor's debts primarily "consumer" or not—is a familiar one in commercial law. In the Bankruptcy Code, "consumer debt" is defined in § 101(8) as a "debt incurred by an individual primarily for personal, family, or household purpose." This is the standard test used throughout commercial law. In the Bankruptcy Code, the same "primarily consumer debts" formulation is used in the § 707(b) abuse test,[344] and the considerable case law under that section should be relevant in the preference context as well.

The first thing to note is that in all cases where the debtor is a *business entity* (i.e., a corporation or a partnership), all preference defendants will qualify for the more generous $6,225 safe harbor of § 547(c)(9), since by definition only an *individual* can incur a "consumer debt." Questions about whether the $600 or $6,225 safe harbor is the proper one thus can arise only where the debtor is an individual. In that event, the tasks then will be (1) to identify the character of the debts incurred, which under the Code definition requires an examination of the *purpose* for which the debt was incurred—was it for "personal, family, or household purposes"?—and then (2) to assess, among the universe of debts so characterized, whether the consumer or the non-

---

[343] See Robert M. Lawless and Elizabeth Warren, The Myth of the Disappearing Business Bankruptcy, 93 Cal. L. Rev. 745, 746–48 (2005).

[344] See § 2.15.b.

consumer debts comprise the "primary" part. The difficult cases likely will be those involving individual small business owners, who have a mixture of business and consumer debts.

One problem that courts have encountered in applying the small preference exception concerns the second question—whether a series of otherwise preferential transfers can be *aggregated* to exceed the dollar ceiling (of $600 or $6,225, depending on the subsection at issue). Consider the following hypothetical. Creditor regularly ships goods on credit to Debtor. The invoices require payment within 20 days; however, for a period of several years Debtor routinely pays Creditor between 30 and 35 days. In the 90 days before Debtor files bankruptcy, Debtor makes three payments aggregating $6,300 on account to Creditor: $2,100 on Day 80 (33 days after shipment); $2,100 on Day 50 (30 days after shipment); and $2,100 on Day 15 (35 days after shipment). After Debtor files bankruptcy, the bankruptcy trustee sues Creditor to recover $6,300 as a preference. While Creditor believes it has an obviously valid "ordinary course" defense under § 547(c)(2), it would be cleaner (and more susceptible to summary judgment!) if Creditor could show that as a matter of law under § 547(c)(9), the three transfers cannot be aggregated. Since each transfer by itself is plainly less than $6,225, Creditor then indisputably would win.

The 1997 Review Commission, in recommending that Congress enact a $5,000 safe harbor in business cases, did so in part in the belief that the recommended $5,000 figure would be based on an *aggregation* of transfers made during the preference period.[345] Apparently, the Commission contemplated that in a case like the forgoing hypothetical, the defendant would *not* be protected by the new safe harbor. Is that assumption accurate?

The same pertinent statutory language appears in both the prior small preference exception of $600 for consumer cases and the new safe harbor, so judicial precedent under the prior safe harbor would be relevant.[346] The statutory language *favoring* aggregation is that the statute says "*aggregate value* of all property transferred," which implies that multiple transfers may be added together. Cutting the other way, though, is the statutory reference to "*such* transfer," as well as the predicate in subsection (c) of § 547 that a trustee may not avoid "*a* transfer." Read literally, the latter references seem to point to a singular limitation to *one* transfer, thus precluding aggregation in a case such as the above hypothetical. The "aggregate value of all property transferred" language could be explained as consistent with this singular "transfer" language in the situation where the debtor makes multiple but coordinated transfers as an intended single act of payment on a debt.

For example, in the hypothetical, assume that on Day 80, instead of giving Creditor a check for $2,100, Debtor returned goods worth $1,100 and sent a check for $1000 to repay the single outstanding debt of $2,100. One might say that the operative "aggregate" transfer was $2,100. That, however, is a much different matter than saying that the distinct transfers over a 65–day period on Days 80, 50 and 15 were "such

---

[345] National Bankruptcy Review Commission, Final Report, Bankruptcy: The Next Twenty Years, at 798 (1997).

[346] See In re Bay Area Glass, Inc., 454 B.R. 86, 90–92 (B.A.P. 9th Cir. 2011).

transfer" or "a transfer." Such an interpretation of the statute is hard to square with the statutory language. As Professor Coles–Bjerre observed, "aggregation within a transfer—whatever those bounds may be—is different from aggregation across transfers."[347]

One might try to assuage this concern, as many courts do, by invoking the rule of construction that "the singular includes the plural,"[348] § 102(7), although it is questionable whether that rule of construction can do that much work in this context. However, the generous (for trustees) "aggregation" reading is responsive to and consistent with the policy concern of alleviating coercive preference litigation pressure, as gauged by the amount in controversy. The preference defendant who received three transfers totaling $6,300 and is sued for avoidance and recovery of all three is no different from a defendant who receives a single $6,300 transfer. We are sure that the latter creditor is not protected by § 547(c)(9); is there any meaningful reason to treat the former, who receives three transfers, differently? Indeed, eschewing an aggregation approach opens up the possibility of extreme manipulation to avoid the constraints of the preference law—a business debtor in theory then could make an endless series of $6,224 payments to preferred creditors, all entirely immune to recapture.

Whatever the nuances of the statute and policy, the cases now run almost entirely in favor of allowing aggregation.[349] My suspicion is that courts anxious to avoid undue evisceration of preference policy will continue to so hold, especially as emboldened by the Commission commentary.

Note, though, that if aggregation is allowed, a creditor such as the one envisaged in our hypothetical would suffer a severe penalty from the receipt of the final transfer in a series of transfers that pushes the creditor's aggregate total over the $6,225 mark. Our Creditor who has received two transfers of $4,200 would, at that point, be immune from preference liability under § 547(c)(9), even with aggregation. Upon receipt of the final $2,100 transfer, though, Creditor loses its § 547(c)(9) defense entirely. Note that invocation of the $6,225 safe harbor (as well as the $600 safe harbor) is an all-or-nothing situation; it is not a *credit* against preference liability.[350] The statute states that "a trustee may not avoid . . . a transfer" if the property transferred is less than $6,225 (or $600 under (c)(8)). Thus, assuming aggregation is allowed, our Creditor who had received $6,300 in transfers would be potentially liable for the full $6,300 in preferences, not just the $75 extra over the $6,225 safe harbor. Prior to any bankruptcy, ultra-cautious creditors of a financially distressed debtor thus might need to keep their own running total of potentially preferential payments received within the past 90 days and either refuse or remit back to the debtor offered transfers that would push them over $6,224. Thus in the hypothetical, our Creditor would still be completely protected (even assuming the aggregation view is followed) if it received a

---

[347] Andrea Coles–Bjerre, Bankruptcy Theory and the Acceptance of Ambiguity, 80 Am. Bankr. L.J. 327, 355 n.85 (2006).

[348] See, e.g., In re Transcon. Refrigerated Lines, Inc., 438 B.R. 520, 522 (Bankr. M.D. Pa. 2010).

[349] The leading case is still *In re Hailes*, 77 F.3d 873 (5th Cir. 1996) (allow aggregation under § 547(c)(8)). For more recent cases, see *Transcontinental Refrigerated*, supra note 17; In re Robles, 2007 WL 1792320 (Bankr. D. Idaho 2007); In re Maus, 282 B.R. 836 (Bankr. N.D. Ohio 2002).

[350] See *Bay Area Glass*, supra note 346, 454 B.R. at 90.

third transfer of only $2,024 (for a total of $6,224), rather than $2,100 (for a total of $6,300). Get the extra few dollars, though, and the entire aggregation of transfers of $6,300 is potentially avoidable.

Another interesting and related question is the extent to which the $6,225 safe harbor will be applied in conjunction with other preference defenses, especially the subsequent advance for new value defense of § 547(c)(4).[351] Consider a second hypothetical. Creditor is a trade supplier of Debtor. On May 1, Debtor's total debt to Creditor is $10,000. On May 1, Debtor pays Creditor $8,000 on the $10,000 outstanding balance (assume that this payment does not qualify for "ordinary course" protection). On May 15, Creditor ships $3,500 in goods to Debtor on credit; assume that this $3,500 transfer would otherwise qualify for the "new value" defense of subsection (c)(4). On July 1, Debtor files bankruptcy. How much, if any, is Creditor's preference liability? $4,500? Zero?

Before 2005, the analysis was straightforward: the initial transfer of $8,000 was a preference (assuming no other valid defense such as ordinary course); then the Creditor gets a credit under subsection (c)(4) of $3,500 for the value of goods shipped, reducing the net preference to $4,500. After the 2005 Act, can Creditor now add on the $6,225 small preference defense of subsection (c)(9) to eliminate liability for this remaining $4,500 amount? Reading the statute literally, the answer seems to be "no," since subsection (c)(9) refers to "such transfer" as being less than $6,225 as the trigger for the safe harbor, and in context, "such transfer" plainly means the total $8,000 payment, *not* the net liability after the application of the new value defense. Any doubt on that score should be erased by noting that the identical language "such transfer" is used in the new value exception itself, in (c)(4), and therein clearly refers to the original total amount transferred (here, the $8,000), before any crediting for new value given by the creditor. One wonders, though, whether courts will give this literal reading to the Code, when the effect would be to treat differently two creditors who otherwise have an identical preference "liability" of < $6,225, one of whose "liability" is entirely forgiven under § 547(c)(9) because that is the entire amount of the transfer, and the other of whom is held liable since the "liability" of < $6,225 arose only after netting out new value given. If such piggy-backing of defenses is allowed, then a creditor whose net preference liability is above the $6,225 mark can escape all preference liability by making a qualifying "new value" transfer to the debtor on the eve of bankruptcy in a sufficient amount to drop the net liability to less than $6,225— and thus to zero! That prospect of gaming may incline courts to give the statute its literal reading and not allow piggy-backing.

§ 6.25 Safe Harbors: Alternative Repayment Schedule Payments[352]

One of the main goals of the 2005 bankruptcy amendments was to encourage debtors to get credit counseling *prior* to bankruptcy and, as a result, to enter into consensual repayment plans with their creditors. Congress hoped that individual debtors would be persuaded to make voluntary payments and if possible forgo

---

[351] See § 6.20.

[352] The discussion in § 6.25. draws heavily on Charles J. Tabb, The Brave New World of Bankruptcy Preferences, 13 Am. Bankr. Inst. L. Rev. 425, 449–53 (2005).

bankruptcy relief entirely. Several amendments seek to implement these goals. The most direct such "encouragement" is § 109(h)'s bar to an individual debtor filing bankruptcy altogether unless she had received credit counseling from an approved agency in the 180 days prior to bankruptcy.[353] Further, an incentive was added for debtors to propose alternative repayment schedules prior to bankruptcy, in that a creditor who unreasonably refuses to negotiate a reasonable repayment plan on an unsecured consumer debt that meets certain criteria may have its claim reduced by not more than 20 percent, under § 502(k).

Finally, pertinent to the present topic, a safe harbor was added to the preference law in § 547(h)[354] for transfers made as part of an alternative repayment schedule that was created by an approved nonprofit budgeting and credit counseling agency. This provision offers a carrot to *creditors* to agree to such repayment plans, since by doing so they would gain immunity from preference attack for payments made to them under such plans in the event of a subsequent bankruptcy. Note that these last two amendments, regarding the claim reduction and the preference safe harbor, were enacted as part of the same section in BAPCPA, titled "Promotion of Alternative Dispute Resolution."[355]

Application of the new safe harbor in § 547(h) is fairly straightforward, but requires some attention to technical aspects of that provision. The first point of note is that the statutory protection applies on its face only to repayment schedules "created by an approved nonprofit budgeting and credit counseling agency." Apparently, then, it will not avail the creditor to agree to a repayment plan that does *not* have the blessing of an approved agency. Why this restriction is included is puzzling, if the intent of Congress is, as the title to the enacting BAPCPA section says, "promotion of alternative dispute resolution." Would it not serve the congressional purpose just as well for the debtor and creditor to agree on their own to a repayment plan? Requiring the approval of an agency increases transaction costs. Note, of course, that even if the repayment plan does not qualify for protection under subsection (h), it still may pass muster as an "ordinary course" payment under subsection (c)(2).[356]

Perhaps Congress intended the requirement that the repayment schedule be created by an approved credit counseling agency to be a means to prevent debtors and favored creditors from cooking up special deals, whereby only the favored creditors would get paid. The agency may serve as a check on such blatantly preferential deals, and might insist that the debtor propose repayment ratably to all unsecured creditors. If that is the hidden agenda, though, it would have been easy for Congress simply to impose such a ratable treatment substantive requirement on qualifying repayment schedules.

---

[353] See § 2.3.b.

[354] For reasons known only to Congress, this safe harbor was not added to the other safe harbors in subsection (c) of § 547.

[355] 109 P.L. 8, § 201, 119 Stat. 42 (2005).

[356] See, e.g., Arrow Elecs., Inc. v. Justus (In re Kaypro), 218 F.3d 1070 (9th Cir. 2000) (payments made pursuant to restructuring agreement are not per se excluded from ordinary course protection).

Second, the statute is unclear as to the extent (if any) of the intended linkage between § 502(k)'s claim reduction provision and § 547(h)'s preference safe harbor for transfers pursuant to alternative repayment plans. On the face of the statute, none appear. Section 547(h) appears to cover, without limitation, "a transfer . . . made as part of an alternative repayment schedule." The only restriction is the one noted above, that the plan must be created by an approved agency. "Alternative repayment schedule" is not defined in the Code. The only detailed description of such a schedule is found in § 502(k), which, as mentioned above, was enacted as part of the same section of BAPCPA as § 547(h). Nothing in § 547(h), though, purports to limit its coverage to "alternative repayment schedules" that have the following characteristics, which *are* found in § 502(k): (1) only *consumer* debts; (2) debtor proposed plan more than 60 days before bankruptcy; (3) debtor proposed payment of at least 60 percent of the debt over the original repayment period or a reasonable extension thereof; and (4) no part of the debt is nondischargeable. Nor is § 547(h) limited to transfers by *individual* debtors, as is the eligibility bar of § 109(h). Under a plain meaning reading, then, none of those limiting characteristics would limit the scope of coverage of § 547(h). But is it possible that Congress intended for those other sections that speak to the role of credit counseling agencies and the creation of alternative repayment schedules to be read *in pari materia* with § 547(h)? Is it necessarily inherent in the very concept of "credit counseling" (or at least as contemplated in the 2005 amendments to the Bankruptcy Code) that it be regarding consumer debts, and for individual debtors?

As a policy matter, one wonders about the continuing emasculation of the supposed *equality* goal of the preference law. It is getting more and more difficult to say with a straight face that the bankruptcy preference law even *has* a paradigm of equality. Section 547(h) cuts at the very heart of equality. The direct effect of § 547(h) is that creditors who get paid under an alternative repayment schedule get to keep their money, even if other unsecured creditors go unpaid, at a time when the debtor is insolvent. There is no statutory requirement that alternative repayment plans must propose ratable treatment for all unsecured creditors in order to qualify for protection under § 547(h), although perhaps that would be enforced indirectly through the credit counseling agency approval requirement, as suggested above. Furthermore, even if the approved alternative repayment schedule itself provides for ratable payment of all unsecured creditors, there is nothing in the statutory safe harbor that requires the debtor to *perform* on such a basis. That is, assume a hypothetical, under which an alternative repayment plan calls for payment of 60% of unsecured debts to Creditors A, B, and C, but Debtor only pays Creditor A; Creditors B and C get nothing. May Creditor A invoke the safe harbor of § 547(h)? It would appear so.

Nor is § 547(h) necessarily consonant with the other purported principal goal of the preference law, that of *deterring* the proverbial "race to the courthouse." Why not? Demanding creditors may exert coercive pressure on a financially troubled debtor (i) to create an alternative repayment schedule in the first place, and (ii) to pay them in preference to other creditors pursuant to a created schedule, without forfeiting the protection of § 547(h). Revisit the above hypothetical. Assume further that Debtor had not made any payments to any of Creditors A, B, or C pursuant to the created alternative repayment schedule; that Creditor A learned that Debtor was going to file bankruptcy imminently; that Creditor A thereupon insisted that Debtor pay A everything Debtor owed A under the repayment schedule, "or else"; and Debtor did then pay A, but not B or C. Is Creditor A protected by § 547(h)? The answer appears to be "yes"—nothing in that section requires payments to be made "in the ordinary course" or in any other way keeps the creditor from engaging in avowedly preferential behavior.

§ 6.26   Safe Harbors: (Still) Trying to Fix *Deprizio*

The "indirect preference" problem, which is possible because a transfer can be preferential if made "to *or for the benefit of*" a creditor, § 547(b)(1),[357] led to one of the most infamous decisions under the Bankruptcy Code, the 1989 Seventh Circuit decision in *Levit v. Ingersoll Rand Financial Corp.*,[358] known universally as the "*Deprizio*" case (which was the debtor's name). Congress has now tried twice (in 1994 and 2005) to fix the *Deprizio* problem. While Congress is making headway, it still has not completely solved the problem.[359]

Assume that a transfer is made directly *to* a party and that transfer is also "for the benefit of" another party—the classic "indirect" preference. This could happen, for example, if payment is made on a guaranteed debt. While that transfer obviously benefits the party who receives the payment, it also benefits the guarantor, albeit indirectly. Why? The reason is that the guarantor's contingent liability—to pay the debt if the debtor does not—is discharged by the debtor's payment. So, in an indirect preference case where the transfer is avoidable as to both the direct and the indirect beneficiaries, the trustee has a choice—recover from either one. § 550(a)(1). But what happens if the transfer is avoidable *only* as to the guarantor? This would happen, for example, if the payment was made more than 90 days but less than one year before bankruptcy, and the guarantor was an insider but the direct transferee was not. The non-insider would not be vulnerable to preference avoidance, because the transfer to it was made outside the preference period of 90 days for non-insiders. § 547(b)(4). But may *recovery* still be had from the direct transferee under § 550? Furthermore, even if no recovery may be had, is it possible that avoidance of the transfer could harm the innocent non-insider? Although logic would suggest that if the non-insider is not personally subject to preference avoidance, no negative legal consequences should befall it, such has not been the case.

In *Deprizio*, the Seventh Circuit held that the trustee *could* recover under § 550(a)(1) from the non-insider initial transferee in the guaranty situation described above, even though the preference was not avoidable as to that non-insider. The *Deprizio* court applied the plain meaning of that section, which says that the trustee may recover from the "initial transferee" (the non-insider) *or* "the entity for whose benefit such transfer was made" (the insider guarantor"). The Seventh Circuit assumed that the disjunctive "or" indeed meant that the trustee could recover from either one.

---

[357] See § 6.12.

[358] 874 F.2d 1186 (7th Cir. 1989).

[359] For a discussion of this issue, see Charles J. Tabb, The Brave New World of Bankruptcy Preferences, 13 Am. Bankr. Inst. L. Rev. 425, 453–55 (2005). Much of the discussion in this section draws on that work.

Some courts, by comparison, had declined to give § 550(a)(1) literal effect, for several reasons.[360] First, these courts simply could not believe that Congress had intended to effect such a radical change from pre-Code law, which had never allowed recovery from a party against whom the transfer was not preferential.[361] Further, courts and commentators have pointed out ambiguities and inconsistencies that result from divorcing avoidance from recovery entirely.[362] The inequity of allowing recovery from a party as to whom a transfer was not avoidable has been a common complaint about the *Deprizio* result. The non-insider creditor is worse off, courts have noted, solely because there was a guarantee. Other courts had absolved the non-insider of liability under § 550 by construing the transfer from the debtor as involving two conceptually distinct transfers: a direct transfer of "money" to the non-insider, and a second indirect transfer of "benefit" to the insider. Under the "two transfer" theory, recovery could only be had with regard to the transfer avoided.

The *Deprizio* court, however, found all of these escape hatches unconvincing. The "two transfer" theory did not comport with the statutory language or the legislative history, the court concluded. "Transfer" is defined in the Code from the perspective of the debtor transferor, and a single payment is but a single "transfer."[363] The Seventh Circuit further observed that it was not inequitable to allow recovery from the non-insider solely because it had taken a guarantee. On the contrary, the payment to the non-insider very possibly may have been made precisely because an insider was secondarily liable for that debt, and made sure that the guaranteed debt was paid first. The non-insider thus may have benefited during the extended preference period from the insider's exposure.[364] Most circuit courts that confronted the issue after *Deprizio* concurred with the conclusion of the Seventh Circuit.[365]

There was considerable consternation in the aftermath of *Deprizio*. Some lenders sought to get around the *Deprizio* result by having guarantors waive any right of reimbursement against the debtor if called upon to honor the guaranty, which would strip the guarantor of "creditor" status and thus preclude preference liability.[366] More directly, lenders who argued that it was unfair to make them worse off because they had obtained a guaranty sought to overturn the decision legislatively. Congress, agreeing that the *Deprizio* outcome was both unfortunate and unintended, amended

---

[360] See, e.g., In re Midwestern Cos., Inc., 102 B.R. 169 (W.D. Mo. 1989); In re Performance Commc'ns, Inc., 126 B.R. 473 (Bankr. W.D. Pa. 1991); In re Mercon Indus., Inc., 37 B.R. 549 (Bankr. E.D. Pa. 1984).

[361] A review of the historical development of § 550(a)(1) suggests that Congress was simply attempting to make explicit in the statute what had been only implicit under the prior Act, *viz.*, that recovery could be had from an indirect beneficiary of a preference. But it had never been held under prior law that recovery of a preference could be had from a party as to whom the transfer was not avoidable, and nothing in the legislative history to the 1978 Code suggests that Congress thought it was effecting such a sea change in the law.

[362] For example, the preference defenses in § 547(c) refer to "such creditor," meaning the creditor as to whom the transfer was preferential under § 547(b), not the non-insider from whom recovery is sought. Giving (c) its natural reading, though, suggests that the non-insider would not be able to raise its own defenses (such as that the payment was made in the ordinary course of business).

[363] *Deprizio*, supra note 358, 874 F.2d at 1195–96.

[364] Id. at 1198.

[365] See, e.g., In re C & L Cartage Co., 899 F.2d 1490 (6th Cir. 1990); In re Robinson Bros. Drilling, Inc., 877 F.2d 32 (10th Cir. 1989).

[366] See § 6.12.

the recovery section in 1994 in an attempt to reverse *Deprizio*. It did so by adding § 550(c), which precludes recovery from a non-insider transferee on the precise facts of that case, namely, when avoidance occurs under § 547(b) as to a transfer made between 90 days and one year before bankruptcy and which was for the benefit of an insider.[367] The legislative history states that the amendment "overrules the *Deprizio* line of cases and clarifies that non-insider transferees should not be subject to the preference provisions of the Bankruptcy Code beyond the 90–day statutory period."[368]

However, the 1994 "fix" was incomplete, for two reasons. First, § 550(c) does not help the non-insider when no "recovery" is required at all. Second, that section does not apply to transfers made on indirect preferences within the 90–day period. Instead, § 550(c) only covers the specific factual case of the recovery of insider preferential payments during the extended preference period.

Consider the "no recovery" problem first. The prototypical example would be where a *lien* is being avoided.[369] In that situation, no "recovery" is necessary; the lien is simply set aside. This effect can be seen in the following hypothetical. Debtor owes Creditor, a non-insider, $20,000 on an unsecured debt. Guarantor, an insider, has guaranteed Debtor's debt to Creditor. Nine months before filing bankruptcy, Debtor (while insolvent) grants Creditor *a lien* on collateral worth $20,000. While that transfer of the lien benefited Creditor, of course, it is not avoidable as a preference *as against Creditor*, since Creditor is not an insider and the transfer was made more than 90 days before bankruptcy. § 547(b)(4). However, that lien transfer *also* indirectly benefits Guarantor, by reducing the likelihood that Guarantor will be called upon to honor its secondary obligation to Creditor. The transfer of the lien thus is "for the benefit of" Guarantor even though directly "to" Creditor. Since Guarantor is an insider, and thus subject to the longer one-year preference period, § 547(b)(4)(B), the lien can be avoided. In this situation, § 550(c) is of no help to Creditor, because nothing is being "recovered." The lien is just avoided.

In the 2005 amendments, Congress tried to fix this problem, adding § 547(i) for cases such as the above hypothetical.[370] The new provision, which is located in the *avoidance* section (547) rather than in the *recovery* section (550), protects Creditor on these facts. The new safe harbor provides that, "[i]f the trustee avoids under subsection (b) a transfer made between 90 days and 1 year before the date of the filing of the petition, by the debtor to an entity that is not an insider for the benefit of a creditor that is an insider, such transfer shall be considered to be *avoided under this section only with respect to the creditor that is an insider*." (Emphasis added.) In short, under § 547(i), avoidance is effective only with respect to insider-Guarantor, not as to non-insider Creditor, and thus Creditor can keep its lien. By placing the safe harbor at the point of *avoidance* (for the non-insider) rather than at the point of recovery, complete protection is afforded the non-insider in such a case. The consequence is that the lien

---

[367]   Bankruptcy Reform Act of 1994, § 202, Pub. L. No. 103–394, 108 Stat. 4121 (1994).

[368]   140 Cong. Rec. H10,767 (daily ed. Oct. 4, 1994).

[369]   See H.R. Rep. No. 109–31, 109th Cong., 1st Sess. (pt. 1), at 143–44 (2005) (discussing § 1213 of BAPCPA).

[370]   Pub. L. No. 109–8, § 1213(2), 119 Stat. 194–95 (2005), codified at 11 U.S.C. § 547(i).

itself (held by the protected non-insider Creditor) remains valid, and the vulnerable insider will have to pay the trustee the value of the lien.

All that is well and good. But even the 2005 "fix" does not solve all indirect preference problems. The reason is that, even though that amendment moved the safe harbor point back from recovery to avoidance, it did so *only* for indirect preferences that occur beyond the 90–day preference period. If a party were the direct transferee of an indirect preference *within* the 90–day period that was not avoidable as to them but which was avoidable as to someone else, neither § 550(c) nor § 547(i) would protect them, since both of those sections by their terms apply only to transfers made between 90 days and one year before bankruptcy.

This point is illustrated by the following example. Assume that Creditor One loans Debtor $10,000, and takes a first mortgage on Blackacre as security. Creditor Two loans Debtor $10,000 also, and takes a second mortgage on Blackacre. Real estate values drop, and Blackacre declines in value to only $15,000. During the 90–day preference period, Debtor pays Creditor One $5,000 in scheduled debt payments. These payments are not a preference as to Creditor One, because it is fully secured. There is thus no "preferential effect."[371] § 547(b)(5). However, the payment to One indirectly benefits Creditor Two, by freeing up collateral to secure Two's debt. Before the payment to One, Creditor Two was only partially secured, with only $5,000 in collateral value available over and above One's $10,000 first mortgage debt. After the $5,000 payment to One, however, Two became fully secured. Thus, the payment to One is a preference as to Two.

Applying the reasoning of *Deprizio*, the bankruptcy trustee would be able to "avoid" the transfer under § 547 as a preference to Creditor Two, and then "recover" the $5,000 payment *from Creditor One*. Creditor One was the "initial transferee" under § 550(a)(1). Nothing in § 550(c) or in § 547(i) will save Creditor One, because by their terms both those sections apply only to a transfer made between 90 days and one year before bankruptcy, and which benefits an insider. The payment to One satisfies neither criterion. Thus, even after both the 1994 Amendments and the 2005 Amendments, the absurd situation exists that a fully secured creditor who does not have an insider guaranty may be forced to disgorge payments made on its debt. Note too that this case does not even have the possible taint (or justification?) that the creditor against whom the transfer was not avoidable nevertheless may have gotten some subtle benefit, as was argued in *Deprizio* due to the fact of the insider guaranty (*viz.*, that the insider may have influenced the making of the payment on the debt he had guaranteed). Here, Creditor One is not even indirectly benefited and indeed has no control over or role in the fact that Debtor granted a second mortgage. So, Congress still may have some work to do.

---

[371] See § 6.16.

E.   SETOFFS

§ 6.27   Nature of Setoff

A powerful remedy for a creditor is the right of *setoff*, alternatively called "offset." The right of setoff exists when a creditor and a debtor owe mutual debts to each other. Setoff permits the mutual debts to be netted out. The most common example involves a bank and a customer, where the customer has a checking or savings account at the bank, and also has borrowed money from the bank. In this situation, the bank owes a debt to the customer in the amount of the balance in the account; the customer owes a debt to the bank for the unpaid balance of the loan. This scenario may be depicted as follows:

	Creditor	Debtor
Account:	Customer	Bank
Loan:	Bank	Customer

For example, assume that Customer borrows $5,000 from Bank, and maintains (perhaps at Bank's insistence) a checking account with a balance of $6,000. Bank owes Customer a debt of $6,000 on the account; Customer owes Bank a debt of $5,000 on the loan. If Customer defaults on the loan, Bank's remedy is breathtakingly simple: Bank simply sets off the account balance against the loan debt. After Bank exercises the right of setoff, Bank owes Customer only $1,000 ($6,000 minus $5,000), and Customer owes Bank nothing. In effect, Bank paid $5,000 of the debt it owed Customer to itself, to satisfy the debt Customer owed to Bank.

Procedurally, exercising a setoff right is incredibly easy. Bank does not have to go to court to obtain permission; Bank does not have to get Customer's consent; indeed, Bank probably does not even have to notify Customer in advance. All that Bank needs to do to effect the setoff is to make a book entry in the bank's records, reflecting the fact that the Customer's account balance has been reduced by the amount set off. Today, a few strokes on the Bank's computer keyboard will get the job done. Note, though, that the Bank actually must take an action to reduce Customer's account. The Supreme Court has held that a setoff does not occur when the Bank merely places a "hold" or "freeze" on the Customer's account.[372]

As the above example illustrates, the right of setoff is in practical effect a form of *security* for the creditor. The Customer's checking account is akin to collateral for the Bank's loan. When making the loan initially, the Bank may require the Customer to open an account to serve as a "compensating balance" for the loan amount. In effect, exercising a setoff right is like foreclosing on collateral, except easier. The character of

---

[372] Citizens Bank of Maryland v. Strumpf, 516 U.S. 16 (1995).

setoff as security is recognized in the Bankruptcy Code, which deems a setoff right to be a secured claim up to the amount subject to setoff.[373] § 506(a)(1).

The right of setoff is grounded in general principles of equity. The right does not depend on a statute for its existence, although some states may have statutory provisions dealing with setoff. Nor must the creditor contract in advance for the setoff right; the debtor's agreement to setoff is unnecessary. If mutual debts exist between the same parties, acting in the same right and capacity, the right of setoff arises automatically. Note also that the mutual debts do not have to arise out of the same transaction in order for the setoff right to exist.

If the mutual debts between the parties do arise out of the same transaction, the governing doctrine is called *recoupment*, not setoff. The right to recoup debts within a single transaction is even more powerful, and subject to fewer restrictions, than is the right of setoff. In bankruptcy, recoupment is permitted even in situations where setoff might be prohibited. The equitable compulsion to permit a netting out of debts within the same transaction is powerful. A common example of recoupment is where advance payments are made on a contract, to be credited against later obligations.

§ 6.28   Setoff in Bankruptcy: § 553

The Bankruptcy Code itself does not create a right of setoff. However, if a setoff right exists outside of bankruptcy, that right generally is enforceable in the bankruptcy case. A few exceptions do apply, as discussed below. The operative provision is § 553(a), which provides in part:

> [T]his title does not affect any right of a creditor to offset a mutual debt owing by such creditor to the debtor that arose before the commencement of the case under this title against a claim of such creditor against the debtor that arose before the commencement of the case.

In addition, the amount subject to the creditor's right of setoff is treated as a *secured* claim. § 506(a)(1). As such, the creditor will be entitled to receive payment in full on its claim up to the amount subject to setoff. Furthermore, a creditor with a setoff right is entitled to assert that right as a defense against turnover; it will not have to pay to the trustee the debt it owes to the debtor. § 542(b).

Some critics have questioned the fairness of affording such preferential treatment to one class of creditors.[374] The Supreme Court long ago justified the rule that recognizes setoff rights in bankruptcy with the rather unhelpful conclusory observation that doing so avoids "the absurdity of making A pay B when B owes A."[375] Why it is absurd to deal separately and distinctly with the debts owed by a bankruptcy debtor, on the one hand, and the property of that debtor, on the other, is not clear, however—especially since enforcing a setoff right permits the creditor to be treated better than

---

[373] See § 6.28.

[374] See, e.g., John C. McCoid, II, Setoff: Why Bankruptcy Priority?, 75 Va. L. Rev. 15 (1989).

[375] Studley v. Boylston Nat'l Bank of Boston, 229 U.S. 523, 528 (1913), quoted in Citizens Bank of Maryland v. Strumpf, 516 U.S. 16, 18 (1995).

other creditors, violating the bankruptcy norm of equality. Perhaps, though, if setoff rights (especially for banks) are deemed in standard commercial practice to be the functional equivalent of collateral, the creditor should be dealt with in bankruptcy in the same manner as any other secured creditor.

An example will illustrate the preferential impact of enforcing a creditor's setoff right in bankruptcy. Assume first that Creditor has a $10,000 claim against Debtor, and that Creditor owes Debtor $8,000. Under state law, Creditor would have a right of setoff for $8,000, and a general unsecured claim for the $2,000 balance.[376] If Debtor were solvent, Creditor should recover a net of $2,000 (the $10,000 claim minus the $8,000 debt). This situation could be depicted as follows:

Amount Debtor owes Creditor	= $10,000
Amount Creditor owes Debtor	= $8,000
Creditor's non-bankruptcy recovery	= $2,000

Now assume further that Debtor is deeply insolvent, and its unsecured creditors will receive a dividend of 10% in the bankruptcy case. If Creditor were not entitled to enforce its right of setoff in bankruptcy, it would have to pay the entire $8,000 debt over to the Trustee, and would receive a dividend of only $1,000 on its own claim (10% of $10,000). Creditor thus would end up $7,000 in the hole, as follows:

Amount of bankruptcy dividend (10% of $10,000)	= $1,000
Amount Creditor must pay Trustee	= $8,000
Creditor's bankruptcy recovery without setoff	= minus $7,000

However, since its setoff right is recognized in bankruptcy, § 553(a), Creditor will not be required to pay the $8,000 to the Trustee, § 542(b), and will be deemed to be secured in that amount. Creditor will retain a $2,000 unsecured claim. § 506(a)(1). Creditor's net recovery thus will be a positive $200 (nothing due on the $8,000 subject to setoff, plus 10% of the $2,000 balance), as follows:

Amount of bankruptcy dividend (10% of $2,000)	= $200
Amount Creditor must pay Trustee	= $0
Creditor's bankruptcy recovery with setoff	= $200

In essence, Creditor is allowed to "pay" the $8,000 subject to setoff directly to itself, rather than paying the Trustee in full and then receiving a dime per dollar back in return. Enforcing the right of setoff thus permits Creditor to trade "bankruptcy" dollars (here worth 10¢) for 100¢ dollars for the entire $8,000 amount subject to setoff. Creditor therefore ends up $7,200 better off.

The creditor will be stayed from actually exercising the setoff right in bankruptcy, unless it can persuade the court to grant it relief from the stay.[377] § 362(a)(7). Also, the

---

[376] See § 6.27.

[377] See § 3.7.

trustee or debtor in possession can use property subject to a setoff right under § 363. However, if the property subject to setoff is a deposit account, as is so often the case, the creditor will be entitled to special treatment as the holder of "cash collateral." The trustee or DIP will be prohibited from using that cash collateral unless the creditor consents or the court grants prior permission.[378] § 363(c)(2). Such permission will be forthcoming only if the trustee can provide adequate protection for the use of the cash collateral. § 363(e).

As noted above, the creditor's right to enforce its setoff right in bankruptcy is subject to certain exceptions and limitations. These qualifications seek to prevent creditors from taking unfair advantage of the setoff "loophole." In some respects the setoff exceptions in § 553 address the same concerns as the preference law. The restrictions in § 553 are:

- the debts must be "mutual," § 553(a);

- both debts must arise prior to bankruptcy, § 553(a);

- the creditor's claim must not be disallowed, § 553(a)(1);

- the creditor may not acquire its claim within 90 days of bankruptcy while the debtor is insolvent, § 553(a)(2);

- the creditor's debt may not be "built up" for the purpose of obtaining a setoff right during the 90 days before bankruptcy, while the debtor is insolvent, § 553(a)(3); and

- a setoff actually exercised by the creditor during the 90 days before bankruptcy may be recovered by the trustee to the extent the creditor improves its position during the 90–day period until the time of setoff. § 553(b)(1).

Note that the 2005 amendments, as part of a package of "Financial Contract Provisions"[379] dealing with issues involving various sophisticated financial agreements (swap agreements, repurchase agreements, securities contracts, forward contracts, commodities contracts, and master netting agreements), excepted those agreements from the last three setoff restrictions noted above.

The first limitation is that the debts must be *mutual*. Mutuality is a well-understood term of art in this context: it means that the debts must be between the same *parties*, acting in the same right or *capacity*. The party requirement means that "debtor" must owe "creditor," and "creditor" must owe "debtor." To begin with, this limitation precludes "triangular" setoffs, in which A owes B, B owes Debtor, and Debtor owes A. A does not have a setoff right, because A does not owe a debt to Debtor, and B lacks such a right because Debtor owes nothing to B.[380] Even where the parties have an

---

[378] See § 5.18.

[379] Pub. L. No. 109–8, tit. IX, §§ 901–911, 119 Stat. 146–185 (2005).

[380] See, e.g., In re Elcona Homes Corp., 863 F.2d 483 (7th Cir. 1988).

agreement allowing for triangular setoff, such provisions are generally unenforceable in bankruptcy.[381]

In some cases the party mutuality issue is whether two *related* entities should be counted as a *single* entity for setoff purposes. For example, Debtor may owe a debt to Parent Corporation, and Subsidiary Corporation may owe a debt to Debtor. Whether a setoff right exists depends on whether Parent and Subsidiary will be treated as a single entity; the usual result is that they are not, and setoff is denied. A common problem is whether different agencies of the United States should be deemed to be a single entity for setoff purposes. For instance, the Internal Revenue Service may owe the debtor a tax refund, while the debtor owes a loan debt to the Small Business Administration. Since they both are agencies of the "United States," are the IRS and the SBA a single entity for setoff purposes? The trend in the circuit courts has been to treat the various agencies of the United States as a unitary creditor for the purposes of allowing setoff.[382]

The *capacity* requirement recognizes that a single entity may act in different legal roles. Only when the entity is acting in the same role as both debtor and creditor does the logic and fairness of allowing setoff apply. This requirement will not be met, for instance, if the debtor is acting as a fiduciary with regard to one of the debts. For example, assume that Debtor owes Bank a debt on a loan. Debtor also maintains a deposit account at Bank, meaning that Bank owes Debtor a debt for the balance of the account. Without more, this would be a classic setoff situation. However, if Debtor's account is held in Debtor's capacity as the trustee of a trust, or as executor of an estate, or the like, mutuality is lost. While the debt that Debtor owes Bank is in the Debtor's individual capacity, the debt that Bank owes to Debtor is in the Debtor's fiduciary capacity. It would be unfair to allow Bank to setoff against the deposit account, because the money in that account does not really belong to Debtor.

The second limitation on the setoff right is that both of the mutual debts must arise *prior* to the commencement of the bankruptcy case. In a sense, this restriction is a particular application of the mutuality requirement; the bankruptcy filing erects a legal wall between the rights and obligations of the pre-bankruptcy debtor and those of the post-bankruptcy debtor. Thus, if a creditor has a prepetition claim against the debtor, it will not be allowed to offset that claim against a postpetition debt it owes to the debtor.[383] In applying this timing rule, one should remember that the Code's definition of "claim" is quite broad, § 101(5), and includes contingent, disputed, and unmatured claims.

Note, though, that a creditor may be allowed to *recoup* prepetition advances to a debtor against a debtor's claim for postpetition payments. In recoupment, though, the mutual debts must arise out of the *same transaction*, unlike in setoff. For example, in a case involving a musician, the recording company made advance royalty payments to

---

[381] E.g., In re Lehman Bros. Inc., 458 B.R. 134, 136–37 (S.D.N.Y. 2011) (noting that "[c]ontractual provisions that purport to create synthetic mutuality are not a substitute for the real thing").

[382] E.g., United States v. Maxwell, 157 F.3d 1099 (7th Cir. 1998); In re Hal, Inc., 122 F.3d 851 (9th Cir. 1997); In re Turner, 84 F.3d 1294 (10th Cir. 1995).

[383] E.g., Cooper–Jarrett, Inc. v. Cent. Transp., Inc., 726 F.2d 93 (3d Cir. 1984).

the musician prior to bankruptcy. After the musician filed bankruptcy, the sale of records generated a claim for royalties by the debtor's bankruptcy estate under the same contract. Applying the doctrine of recoupment, the court allowed the recording company to apply the prepetition advances against the postpetition royalty debt.[384] Courts have narrowly construed the recoupment doctrine, though, due to a concern that the creditor will obtain better treatment than other creditors.[385] The essential question is whether it would be inequitable to deny recoupment.

Another issue is whether a creditor who proves that the mutual debts arise out of the same transaction may nevertheless be denied recoupment based on the equities of the case. Recently, the Eighth Circuit held that while the court must weigh the facts and equities in determining whether the debts do in fact arise out of the same transaction, if they do, it then would be inappropriate for the court to apply a separate "balancing of the equities" test to deny recovery.[386]

A third restriction on setoff in bankruptcy is that a creditor cannot offset a claim that is *disallowed*. § 553(a)(1). Otherwise, the creditor could effectively circumvent the disallowance rules of § 502(b)[387] by means of a setoff. Assume, for instance, that Creditor has a claim of $5,000, but the claim is unenforceable outside of bankruptcy because of the statute of frauds, and thus would be disallowed in bankruptcy. § 502(b)(1). Creditor also owes Debtor $7,000. Creditor cannot pay the trustee only $2,000, asserting that it has a $5,000 setoff right. Creditor must pay the entire $7,000.

The remaining three restrictions on the enforceability of setoffs in bankruptcy are related conceptually to preferences. Each blocks a creditor from gaining an advantage over other creditors through clever maneuvering of the setoff rules within the 90 days prior to bankruptcy. The first "preference-like" setoff limitation is that the creditor cannot *acquire* its claim against the debtor after 90 days before the bankruptcy filing, while the debtor is insolvent. § 553(a)(2). Otherwise creditors could buy up claims at a discount and then in effect obtain full value for those claims by way of offset in bankruptcy.

For example, assume that Debtor is insolvent, and its unsecured creditors will recover only 10% on their claims. Assume also that P owes Debtor $5,000, and that Debtor owes Q $5,000. As things stand, P will have to pay the full $5,000 to Debtor, and Q will recover only $500 from Debtor. If, however, Q sells its claim against Debtor to P, P would be able (without § 553(a)(2)) to offset the entire debt to Debtor, and pay Debtor nothing. Q would be willing to sell its claim to P for anything more than the $500 it currently stands to recover, and P would be willing to pay Q anything less than the $5,000 it would have to pay. Allowing the Q-to-P transfer to create an enforceable

---

[384] Waldschmidt v. C.B.S., Inc., 14 B.R. 309 (M.D. Tenn. 1981).

[385] See, e.g., In re Univ. Med. Ctr., 973 F.2d 1065 (3d Cir. 1992) (withholding interim payments due for postpetition services in order to collect prepetition overpayment was a setoff that violated stay, rather than recoupment). Some courts have taken a broader view of the "same transaction" requirement for recoupment than the *University Medical Center* court. See, e.g., In re TLC Hosps., Inc., 224 F.3d 1008 (9th Cir. 2000).

[386] In re Terry, 687 F.3d 961 (8th Cir. 2012). Accord In re Slater Health Ctr., Inc., 398 F.3d 98, 104 (1st Cir. 2005).

[387] See § 7.5.

setoff right would harm the other creditors of Debtor by depriving them of up to $4,500 (the $5,000 P would not have to pay Debtor's estate, less the $500 the estate would not have to pay Q). Section 553(a)(2) prevents this result; P cannot setoff the claim acquired from Q against its own debt to Debtor. Note that § 553(c), like § 547(f) for preferences, creates a presumption that the debtor is insolvent for the 90 days before bankruptcy.

The flip side of the same problem occurs if the debt the creditor owes to the debtor is built up during the 90 days before bankruptcy, at a time when the debtor is insolvent. Section 553(a)(3) precludes setoff if the creditor's debt to the debtor was incurred after 90 days before the date of filing, when the debtor was insolvent, and for the purpose of obtaining a right of setoff. The concern that § 553(a)(3) addresses is the same as a buildup of collateral to secure a debt, which is dealt with by § 547. The main difference is that § 553(a)(3) requires proof that the *purpose* of the buildup was to obtain a right of setoff, whereas § 547 does not require proof of subjective intent. However, the ordinary course of business exception, § 547(c)(2), probably provides somewhat analogous protection.

To illustrate § 553(a)(3), assume that Bank Five makes a $10,000 loan to Debtor, and requires Debtor to open a compensating balance account with $12,000 in the account. Debtor falls into financial difficulties and becomes insolvent, and the account balance drops to $2,000. At this point in time, Bank Five's setoff right would be only $2,000; the remainder of its $8,000 claim is effectively unsecured. Bank Five demands that Debtor make additional deposits in the account. Debtor responds by making a deposit of $8,000, increasing the balance in Bank Five to $10,000. Now the setoff right fully secures the Bank's $10,000 claim. A week later Debtor files bankruptcy. Under § 553(a)(3), Bank Five cannot assert a right of setoff with regard to the $8,000 deposited a week before bankruptcy; it will only have a setoff right for $2,000. Bank Five is effectively prevented from improving its position at the expense of other unsecured creditors on the eve of the bankruptcy filing.

But what would happen if Bank Five moved quickly, and, after Debtor built back up the account balance, Bank Five actually exercised its setoff right *before* Debtor filed bankruptcy? Now § 553(a)(3) will not apply; that section only limits the creditor's ability to assert a setoff right *after* the bankruptcy has been filed. Aware of the possibility that a creditor might beat the debtor to the punch and set off before the debtor files, Congress enacted § 553(b). Under § 553(b), the trustee may recover from the creditor a setoff made within 90 days of bankruptcy that allowed the creditor to improve its position at the expense of other creditors by reducing the amount of its insufficiency. The kinship of § 553(b) to § 547(c)(5)'s improvement-in-position test[388] is apparent.

Section 553(b), like § 547(c)(5), utilizes a two-point improvement-in-position test. Point one is either 90 days before the bankruptcy filing, or the first date thereafter on which the creditor has an insufficiency. Point two is the date the creditor actually sets off the debt. The trustee may recover the amount by which the insufficiency at point

---

[388] See § 6.21.

two is less than the insufficiency at point one. An "insufficiency" exists if the debt the creditor owes to the debtor is less than the debt the debtor owes to the creditor. In the common bank-customer situation, the creditor owes a debt to the debtor for the amount of the account balance, and the debtor owes a debt to the bank for the loan balance.

In the example used above, the Debtor owed Bank Five $10,000. The first insufficiency within the 90 days before bankruptcy occurred when the debtor's account balance dropped to $2,000, creating an insufficiency of $8,000 at point one. Assume that Debtor made a deposit that built the account balance back up to $10,000 a week before bankruptcy, and the day after Debtor's deposit, Bank Five set off the debt in full. At point two (the date of setoff), the insufficiency was zero. Thus, Bank Five improved its position by $8,000 from point one to point two, and under § 553(b), the trustee can recover that $8,000 from Bank Five.

F. FRAUDULENT TRANSFERS

§ 6.29 Overview of Fraudulent Transfer Law

The purpose of the law of "fraudulent transfers," also known as "fraudulent conveyances," is to protect creditors from unfair transactions that hamper their efforts to collect from the debtor.[389] The focus is not on the rights of creditors vis-à-vis other creditors, as is true of preference law,[390] but on the rights of creditors vis-à-vis the debtor.[391] Fraudulent transfer law permits creditors (or the bankruptcy trustee acting on behalf of creditors) to set aside transfers that place the debtor's property out of the reach of creditors and thereby hinder the efforts of creditors to get paid.

Originally, fraudulent conveyance law was premised on a norm of debtor misbehavior.[392] A transfer could be set aside as fraudulent only if the debtor acted with *actual fraudulent intent* in making the transfer.[393] Today, however, with the advent of the notion of *constructive* fraud,[394] in which a transfer may be avoided whether or not the debtor subjectively had a wrongful intent, the parameters of fraudulent conveyance law are much broader. Any transfer that might injure the debtor's creditors potentially may fall within the ambit of the fraudulent transfer laws. Without a purely fault-based premise as a limiting principle, defining the outer limits of the fraudulent conveyance laws has proven quite difficult. Fraudulent transfer law has been extended to areas as

---

[389] The classic work on the law of fraudulent transfers is Garrard Glenn, Fraudulent Conveyances and Preferences (rev. ed. 1940). Unfortunately, that work has not been updated since 1940. A more recent useful study is Peter A. Alces, The Law of Fraudulent Transactions (1989). Among the innumerable law review articles on the subject, interesting commentary on the nature of fraudulent transfer law can be found in Douglas G. Baird & Thomas H. Jackson, Fraudulent Conveyance Law and Its Proper Domain, 38 Vand. L. Rev. 829 (1985); David Gray Carlson, The Logical Structures of Fraudulent Transfers and Equitable Subordination, 45 Wm. & Mary L. Rev. 157 (2003); David Gray Carlson, Is Fraudulent Conveyance Law Efficient?, 9 Cardozo L. Rev. 643 (1987); Robert C. Clark, The Duties of the Corporate Debtor to Its Creditors, 90 Harv. L. Rev. 505 (1977).

[390] See § 6.7.

[391] See Thomas H. Jackson, Avoiding Powers in Bankruptcy, 36 Stan. L. Rev. 725, 777 (1984).

[392] See John C. McCoid, II, Constructively Fraudulent Conveyances: Transfers for Inadequate Consideration, 62 Tex. L. Rev. 639, 656 (1983).

[393] 13 Eliz., ch. 5 (1571).

[394] See § 6.33.

diverse as leveraged buyouts,[395] corporate group transactions,[396] and mortgage foreclosures.[397]

While the power to set aside fraudulent transfers is part of the arsenal of the trustee's avoiding powers in bankruptcy, § 548, and is often invoked in that setting, fraudulent transfer law is not limited to the bankruptcy arena. Creditors may attack fraudulent dispositions outside of bankruptcy as well, as they have done for centuries. Indeed, the basic premise of the law of fraudulent conveyances, to protect creditors from harmful transfers by the debtor, is not conceptually linked to the collective action problem that bankruptcy addresses. Even a single creditor can be prejudiced by a debtor's fraudulent transfers.

Fraudulent transfer laws are found both in the Bankruptcy Code and in the law of every state. The substantive and remedial provisions of these laws overlap in many respects, but they are not identical. Section 548 is the special Bankruptcy Code provision governing the avoidance of fraudulent transfers and obligations. The bankruptcy trustee also may invoke state fraudulent transfer law under § 544(b),[398] as long as there is at least one actual unsecured creditor in existence at the time of bankruptcy who would have been able to attack the transfer under the state law.

State law follows one of three models. The most common by far, in force in 43 states, the District of Columbia, and the Virgin islands as of 2013,[399] is the *Uniform Fraudulent Transfer Act* ("UFTA"),[400] which was promulgated in 1984 by the National Conference of Commissioners on Uniform State Laws ("NCCUSL"). The UFTA replaced the *Uniform Fraudulent Conveyance Act* ("UFCA"),[401] which had been promulgated in 1918, as the recommended uniform act. As of 2013, only two states (New York and Maryland) still have the UFCA on the books.[402] But for the fact that the important commercial state of New York still follows the UFCA,[403] it would be little more than an historical curiosity today. Finally, five states (as of 2012)[404] still follow either the civil law (Louisiana) or some version of the fountainhead of modern fraudulent conveyance law, the Statute of 13 Elizabeth,[405] enacted in 1571.

---

[395] See § 6.39.

[396] See § 6.40.

[397] See § 6.41.

[398] See § 6.5.

[399] See http://www.uniformlaws.org/LegislativeFactSheet.aspx?title=Fraudulent%20Transfer%20Act.

[400] Available at http://www.uniformlaws.org/shared/docs/fraudulent%20transfer/ufta_final_84.pdf (hereafter "UFTA Complete Act").

[401] 7A (pt. II) Uniform Laws Annotated 248 (2006) (hereafter "ULA"). For a discussion of the UFCA, see James A. McLaughlin, Application of the Uniform Fraudulent Conveyance Act, 46 Harv. L. Rev. 404 (1933). Professor McLaughlin stated that Professor Samuel Williston (of contracts fame) served as reporter for the UFCA. However, the prefatory note to the UFCA states that Professor William Draper Lewis served as reporter. ULA, supra, at 246. Life is full of mystery.

[402] ULA, supra note 401, at 246, & id. (Supp. 2012).

[403] See N.Y. McKinney's DCD §§ 270–81 (2012).

[404] The states that, as of 2012, have neither the UFTA nor the UFCA in force are Alaska, Kentucky, Louisiana, South Carolina, and Virginia. See sources cited notes 399, 401, and 402 supra.

[405] 13 Eliz., ch. 5 (1571).

The historical progression of the fraudulent conveyance laws teaches us important lessons about the current shape of those laws. The start of it all was the aforementioned Statute of 13 Elizabeth in 1571, which condemned conveyances made by the debtor with the actual intent to hinder, delay, or defraud creditors. This statute thus required proof of *actual fraudulent intent* on the part of the debtor. Since debtors rarely broadcast their fraudulent intentions, the courts over time identified "*badges of fraud*," which are circumstantial factors believed to be indicia of the debtor's actual fraudulent intent.[406] Still, the need to prove the subjective intention of the debtor in all cases was viewed as a shortcoming of fraudulent conveyance law.

The "objectification" of the law in this area received a substantial boost from the UFCA, promulgated in 1918, and eventually adopted in half of the states. The major contribution of the UFCA was the creation of causes of action for several types of *constructive* fraud. Today, actual fraud[407] and constructive fraud[408] are the two basic types of fraudulent transfers. In constructive fraud, the subjective intention of the debtor need not be proven. Instead, proof of certain objective facts conclusively establishes the fraud, irrespective of the debtor's intent. The UFCA served as the model for the fraudulent conveyance provision in the pre-Code Bankruptcy Act, § 67d, as amended in the Chandler Act of 1938.[409]

The next major step in the evolution of fraudulent transfer law came with the enactment of § 548 of the Bankruptcy Reform Act of 1978, which is the current Bankruptcy Code. Section 548 differed in several important respects from the UFCA (and § 67d of the Bankruptcy Act). This created a dissonance between the then-dominant state fraudulent transfer law (as of 1978, still the UFCA) and the bankruptcy provision. Motivated in part by a desire to bring the uniform state law and the bankruptcy law into closer correspondence,[410] in 1984 the NCCUSL withdrew the UFCA and replaced it with the UFTA. The UFTA tracks § 548 of the Bankruptcy Code much more closely than did the UFCA. Even still, § 548 and the UFTA do differ in some respects. With the 2005 bankruptcy amendments, the divergence between § 548 and the UFTA increased.

Other bodies of law address some of the same concerns as the fraudulent transfer laws.[411] A creditor's claim may be *equitably subordinated* to the claims of other creditors if the creditor has collaborated with or manipulated the debtor in ways that harm the body of creditors as a whole.[412] If a corporate debtor is used as an alter ego of its principal, or is inadequately capitalized, creditors of the debtor may be able to "*pierce the corporate veil*" and reach assets of the principal.[413] Furthermore, state

---

[406] See § 6.32.

[407] Id.

[408] See §§ 6.33–6.41.

[409] Act of June 22, 1938, ch. 575, § 67d, 52 Stat. 877 (repealed 1979).

[410] UFTA Complete Act, supra note 400, at 4. See http://www.uniformlaws.org/shared/docs/fraudulent%20transfer/ufta_final_84.pdf.

[411] The seminal work exploring these connections is the article by Professor Clark, supra note 389.

[412] See § 7.21; Clark, supra note 389, at 517–36; see also Alces, supra note 389, ¶ 5.01[4][e][i], at 5–28 to –29.

[413] See Alces, supra note 389, ¶ 5.01[4][e][ii], at 5–29 to –30.

corporate laws restrict certain distributions of dividends to shareholders that would harm the general creditors of the corporate debtor.[414]

The Uniform Commercial Code ("UCC") also contains provisions affecting transactions that might implicate concerns similar to those covered by the fraudulent conveyance laws. For example, UCC § 2–402(2) recognizes that retention of possession of goods by a seller might be fraudulent in some circumstances. Article 6 (in those states where it is still in effect)[415] imposes requirements to protect creditors when a bulk sale of a debtor's assets takes place. The fraudulent conveyance laws and the UCC provisions are designed to coexist and to operate independently of the other. Neither displaces or preempts the other; also, compliance with one does not insure protection under the other.[416]

When analyzing a fraudulent transfer question, two issues must be addressed. The first is to determine *whether the transfer at issue is a fraudulent transfer*. As noted above, the transfer may be challenged as either actually fraudulent or constructively fraudulent. This first step also requires identifying a party with standing to challenge the transaction.[417] If the transfer is not fraudulent, the inquiry ends. If, however, the transfer is fraudulent, the second question is to determine *the rights and remedies* of the affected parties; in other words, what are the incidents or effects of finding that a challenged transfer is fraudulent?[418]

§ 6.30   Transfer of Property of Debtor

A party seeking to avoid any type of fraudulent transfer, actual or constructive, must first prove that a "*transfer*" was made[419] of *property* of the *debtor*.[420] A similar requirement applies for preferences.[421] Alternatively, the plaintiff must prove that the debtor incurred an "*obligation*."[422] As discussed in the next section, it also will be necessary to pinpoint *when* the transfer was made or the obligation was incurred,[423] because fraudulent transfers and obligations may only be set aside for a limited period of time.

This first element of proof may be broken down into separate inquiries. To begin with, a "transfer" must occur. Under all of the fraudulent transfer laws, the term

---

[414] See Model Business Corp. Act § 6.40. See Alces, supra note 389, ¶ 5.01[4][e][iii], at 5–30 to –32.

[415] The Official Version of the UCC now recommends that Article 6 be repealed.

[416] See Comment 8, UFTA § 4, UFTA Complete Act, supra note 400.

[417] See § 6.45.

[418] See §§ 6.43–6.44, 6.46.

[419] I use the passive tense intentionally, since the offending transfer can be effected either voluntarily by the debtor or triggered involuntarily by the action of a third party.

[420] 11 U.S.C. § 548(a); UFTA §§ 4(a), 5(a); UFCA §§ 4–8.

[421] See §§ 6.10–6.11.

[422] Hereafter in this section, this alternative proof to the transfer requirement, that an obligation was incurred, will not be mentioned for the sake of simplicity and convenience. Of course, that omission should not be read to imply that the "obligation" avenue of proof is not available in proper cases.

[423] See § 6.31.

"transfer" (or "conveyance"[424]) is given an extraordinarily broad meaning. The purpose is to reach every conceivable means or form of transferring an interest in property, recognizing that parties with fraud in their hearts can be quite creative and imaginative. The Bankruptcy Code defines "transfer" in § 101(54) as follows:

The term "transfer" means

(A) the creation of a lien

(B) the retention of title as a security interest

(C) the foreclosure of a debtor's equity of redemption; or

(D) each mode, direct or indirect, absolute or conditional, voluntary or involuntary, of disposing of or parting with

(i) property; or

(ii) an interest in property.

As the catch-all language in subsection (D) shows, Congress intended that "the definition of transfer [be] as broad as possible."[425] As the legislative history emphasizes, "*any* transfer of an interest in property is a transfer."[426]

The definition of "transfer" in § 1(12) of the UFTA[427] is very similar in substance, and prior to the 2005 bankruptcy amendment, Code § 101(54) was almost verbatim—which is not surprising, since the UFTA definition was derived directly from the original Bankruptcy Code definition.[428] The UFCA definition of "conveyance" in § 1 likewise is quite broad.[429]

In the vast majority of cases, the "transfer" requirement will not be an issue and is clearly satisfied. The most obvious case is where the debtor makes an outright transfer

---

[424] Under the Statute of Elizabeth and the UFCA, the term "conveyance" is used. The UFTA and the Code replace "conveyance" with "transfer." The change in language was adopted to eliminate any possible connotation that "conveyance" might suggest that either (1) involuntary transfers or (2) transfers of personal property are not covered; they are. The semantic shift has not made any difference in the substance of the law.

[425] S. Rep. No. 95–989, 95th Cong., 2d Sess., at 27 (1978). The original 1978 legislative history remains relevant, even though the definition of "transfer" was amended in 2005. Subsection (D) continues the core of the previous definition. The 2005 changes were mostly stylistic; for example, subsections (B) and (C) were simply broken out into distinct subsections. While new, the addition of subsection (A) did not change the law, as lien transfers were already treated as "transfers."

[426] Id. (emphasis added).

[427] "'Transfer' means every mode, direct or indirect, absolute or conditional, voluntary or involuntary, of disposing of or parting with an asset or an interest in an asset, and includes payment of money, release, lease, and creation of a lien or other encumbrance." UFTA § 1(12).

[428] See http://www.uniformlaws.org/shared/docs/fraudulent%20transfer/ufta_final_84.pdf, Comment 12, UFTA § 1 (2013) (hereafter "UFTA Complete Act").

[429] "'Conveyance' includes every payment of money, assignment, release, transfer, lease, mortgage or pledge of tangible or intangible property, and also the creation of any lien or encumbrance." UFCA § 1. Although that definition does not expressly refer to involuntary transfers, the courts have construed that provision to reach involuntary dispositions. UFTA Complete Act § 1, cmt. 12, supra note 10.

of an asset—for example, Debtor quitclaims Blackacre to Grandma. Transfers for security also are covered—for example, Debtor grants a mortgage on Blackacre (worth $10,000) to Grandma to secure a $100 debt. Involuntary transfers are included. This point has had special significance in the context of foreclosures. Thus, if Grandma forecloses on the mortgage, the foreclosure itself qualifies as a "transfer."[430] If a debtor collusively permits a judgment to be entered against him, and stands by as execution is levied, that too would count as a transfer.

Like the "transfer" element, the "*property*" wing of the first requirement is broadly defined and usually is obviously satisfied. While the Bankruptcy Code itself does not define "property," the intended breadth of the term "property" is seen by the UFTA definition: "'Property' means *anything that may be the subject of ownership*." UFTA § 1(10). The comment to the UFTA explains further that "property includes both real and personal property, whether tangible or intangible, and any interest in property, whether legal or equitable."[431] Thus, property would include not only Blackacre, but also a patent, a cause of action, a power of appointment, a contingent remainder, and so forth.

Ascertaining whether something constitutes "property" requires an examination of the applicable *non-bankruptcy law* that creates that "something." A fundamental principle in bankruptcy cases is that deference is given to the underlying non-bankruptcy law (usually state law) with regard to the creation and recognition of property interests. The attributes of that interest must be determined by state law.[432]

An important difference between the UFTA and the Bankruptcy Code should be noted. Under the Code, § 548 requires the transfer of "*property*"; the UFTA, however, speaks of the transfer of an "*asset*." The difference is substantive, not merely linguistic. Under the UFTA, the definition of "asset" does *not* include property to the extent that property is either *exempt* or subject to a valid *lien*. UFTA § 1(2). Thus, under the UFTA, it is not fraudulent to transfer either exempt property or encumbered property. The rationale is that general creditors of the debtor could not realize on either type of property anyway, and thus the debtor's transfer of that unattainable property cannot harm general creditors. The Bankruptcy Code, though, does not include such a blanket exclusion, leaving open the possibility of a fraudulent transfer attack. Under the Code, exempt property will still become property of the estate under § 541(a), and thus subject to distribution to creditors, unless the debtor formally claims an exemption. A debtor's voluntary transfer of exempt property prior to bankruptcy thus could be viewed as an implicit waiver of the exemption right.

Occasionally, the "transfer" of "property" issue poses a serious obstacle. One example is where the debtor renounces an inheritance. In that situation, the legal fiction under state law typically is that the debtor is deemed never to have "had" the property in the first place; thus, the renunciation relates back prior to the testator's

---

[430] Note, though, that the mortgage foreclosure may not be a fraudulent transfer, if "reasonably equivalent value" is deemed to have been given in exchange. See § 6.41.

[431] UFTA § 1, UFTA Complete Act, cmt. 10, supra note 428.

[432] See Butner v. United States, 440 U.S. 48 (1979); Bd. of Trade of City of Chicago v. Johnson, 264 U.S. 1 (1924). See also § 5.5.

death for all purposes. Can a debtor "transfer" something he never had? The courts have gone both ways. The prevailing view, adopted by several courts of appeals, gives literal effect to the state law "debtor-never-had-it" fiction just noted, and finds no transfer of property.[433] The contrary view is that functionally the debtor took an action that deprived his estate of property that would have been included in the estate if the action had not been taken. When the rights of third parties are implicated by such an action, the legal fiction of relation back must be ignored, and a transfer of property found, these courts reason.[434]

Many of the leading bankruptcy cases finding "no transfer" were decided before the Supreme Court's 1999 decision in *Drye v. United States*,[435] a non-bankruptcy case in which the Court held that a taxpayer's disclaimer of an inheritance is ineffective to defeat a federal tax lien, even if the state law treats disclaimer as if the taxpayer never had the property. The federal tax law trumps state law, the Court concluded. Even post-*Drye*, though, courts have continued to hold in the bankruptcy context that a debtor's pre-bankruptcy disclaimer is effective, is not a "transfer," and thus cannot be avoided as fraudulent.[436] Those courts reason that in bankruptcy the Supreme Court has held (in *Butner v. United States*[437]) that federal law generally defers to state law in defining what constitutes an interest in property, and thus if a debtor's disclaimer is not "property" under state law, then the same must be true in bankruptcy. While possibly reaching the right result, those cases may misread the Court's "property" jurisprudence in bankruptcy cases. In fact, the Supreme Court has held (in *Board of Trade of City of Chicago v. Johnson*)[438] that what constitutes "property" for bankruptcy purposes is indeed a question of *federal* law, and in that case the Court held that a seat on the Chicago Board of Trade was "property" in bankruptcy even though Illinois state law concluded that it was not property. What the *Butner* Court actually held was that the *attributes* of the property interest in the bankruptcy case are governed by state law. The pertinent question for fraudulent transfer analysis in bankruptcy, therefore, arguably should be whether disclaimer would be held effective under state law *as against creditors* of the disclaiming party in circumstances that suggest fraud. In *Chicago Board of Trade*, the Court held that the state law "lien-like" claims of the debtor's creditors on the Board of Trade that constrained the debtor's ability to transfer the property under state law had to be given effect in bankruptcy as well. The Supreme Court's 1994 bankruptcy decision in *BFP v. Resolution Trust Corp.*,[439] that a mortgage foreclosure generally should not be avoidable as a fraudulent transfer in bankruptcy if it cannot be so avoided under state law, supports the approach of deciding the disclaimer question in similar fashion.

---

[433] E.g., In re Laughlin, 602 F.3d 417 (5th Cir. 2010); In re Simpson, 36 F.3d 450 (5th Cir. 1994); In re Atchison, 925 F.2d 209 (7th Cir. 1991).

[434] Perhaps the best known case taking this position is Justice Traynor's opinion in *In re Kalt's Estate*, 16 Cal. 2d 807, 108 P. 2d 401 (Cal. 1940). For more recent expositions of this view, see In re Schmidt, 362 B.R. 318 (Bankr. W.D. Tex. 2007); In re Kloubec, 247 B.R. 246 (Bankr. N.D. Iowa 2000), aff'd on other grounds, 268 B.R. 173 (N.D. Iowa 2001); In re Brajkovic, 151 B.R. 402 (Bankr. W.D. Tex. 1993).

[435] 528 U.S. 49 (1999).

[436] See, e.g., *Laughlin*, supra note 433, 602 F.3d 417; In re Costas, 346 B.R. 198 (B.A.P. 9th Cir. 2006).

[437] 440 U.S. 48 (1979). See § 5.5.

[438] 264 U.S. 1 (1924). See § 5.5.

[439] 511 U.S. 531 (1994).

Another situation where a transfer of property might not be found is where an executory contract or lease to which the debtor is a party is terminated. For example, in one case the non-debtor party to a baseball park concession agreement terminated that contract on the debtor's default, as permitted by the contract terms.[440] The effect of the termination was to deprive the debtor of valuable concession privileges it otherwise would have enjoyed. Although the court concluded that a "transfer" of "property" had taken place, it nonetheless declined to find that the termination was a fraudulent conveyance, reasoning that proscribing such a termination did not fall within the purposes of the fraudulent conveyance laws. Along the lines discussed in the preceding paragraph, the court perhaps could have taken the view that the debtor's "property" interest represented by the contract only had realizable value to the extent the debtor performed its side of the bargain—which it did not do. In other words, a salient attribute of the debtor's contractual interest was that the interest could be terminated upon the debtor's nonperformance. Other courts have held, though, that the termination of a lease or contract in accordance with its terms and applicable law is a fraudulent transfer.[441] The UFTA rejects this view, however, and provides that a transfer is *not* voidable under the constructive fraud provisions if it results from the termination of a lease upon default. UFTA § 8(e).

§ 6.31   Time of Transfer

Determining the time that a transfer is deemed to be "made" is critical to the application of the fraudulent transfer laws. Transfers may only be set aside for a limited period of time after they are made. An obligation may only be avoided for a limited period after it is incurred. A transfer made or obligation incurred prior to the beginning of the statutory reach-back period is invulnerable to attack as fraudulent. Furthermore, a common type of constructive fraud case requires proof that the debtor was insolvent at the time of the transfer. § 548(a)(1)(B)(ii)(I).

Under the Bankruptcy Code's fraudulent transfer provision, transfers may only be avoided if made within *two years* of the filing of the bankruptcy petition. § 548(a)(1). For example, if Debtor made a transfer of Blackacre to Grandma in January 2010, and Debtor filed bankruptcy in February 2012, the bankruptcy trustee could not use § 548 to set aside the Blackacre-to-Grandma transfer. That transfer was made more than two years before the bankruptcy filing.

The reach-back period under the UFTA is considerably longer. For most types of fraudulent transfers, an action may be brought under the UFTA within *four years* of the time the transfer is made.[442] UFTA § 9. New York law goes even further back, calling for a *six-year* period of vulnerability (and even tolling that if the fraud was not readily discoverable).[443] This extended reach-back period is one of the main advantages of using state fraudulent conveyance law under § 544(b), instead of § 548, to challenge a transfer in a bankruptcy case. An action seeking to avoid the Blackacre-to-Grandma

---

[440] In re Metro Water & Coffee Servs., Inc., 157 B.R. 742 (Bankr. W.D.N.Y. 1993).

[441] E.g., In re Farris, 415 F. Supp. 33 (W.D. Okla. 1976).

[442] The only exception is for an insider preference under § 5(b), which may only be challenged for one year. UFTA § 9(c).

[443] N.Y. McKinney's DCD § 213(8).

transfer in Debtor's bankruptcy case would be timely under the UFTA, as incorporated by § 544(b).

Note, though, that the bankruptcy trustee may only invoke state law under § 544(b) if there is an actual unsecured creditor in existence at the time of bankruptcy who would have standing under state law to avoid the transfer. For transfers that took place almost four years in the past, and which may only be challenged by a "present" creditor (i.e., someone who was a creditor at the time the transfer was made),[444] the trustee may have difficulty finding such a "live" creditor to use as the entree to § 544(b).

If the UFCA is the applicable state fraudulent conveyance law, it must be noted that the UFCA does not have its own limitations period. State limitations periods of general applicability will govern. These periods range from three to six years (with the important commercial law state of New York being in the six-year camp, as noted).

As is the case with the preference law,[445] § 547(e), the drafters of the fraudulent transfer laws were concerned with the danger posed to general creditors by *secret* conveyances by the debtor. The problem is one of ostensible ownership. People might do business with a debtor relying on the debtor's apparent ownership of certain assets. If the debtor in actuality has secretly conveyed those assets to someone else, but has retained the appearance of ownership, reliance parties might be misled to their detriment. The law's solution to the ostensible ownership problem long has been to give effect to outward appearances, and to make real, for legal purposes, what was ostensible. In short, secret conveyances will not be honored as against third parties who do business with the debtor. The transfer by the debtor will be deemed to be made for the purposes of applying the fraudulent transfer laws only when that transfer is made a matter of public knowledge. Thus, § 548(d)(1) provides that:

> [A] transfer is made when such transfer is so perfected that a bona fide purchaser from the debtor against whom applicable law permits such transfer to be perfected cannot acquire an interest in the property transferred that is superior to the interest in such property of the transferee.

To see the impact of § 548(d)(1), let us revisit the Blackacre-to-Grandma example. Assume that Debtor deeded Blackacre to Grandma in January 2010. However, Debtor also asked Grandma not to record the deed right away. A party searching title thus would assume that Debtor still owned Blackacre, not Grandma. A few days before Debtor filed bankruptcy in February 2012, he told Grandma that he was going to file, and suggested that she go ahead and record her deed, which she did. The trustee then files an action under § 548 to avoid the transfer to Grandma; she defends on the ground that the transfer was made more than two years before bankruptcy. Who wins? The trustee. Under § 548(d)(1), the transfer is not deemed to be made until Grandma

---

[444] See § 6.45.

[445] See § 6.9.

actually recorded the deed,[446] because it was not until that time that the transfer to her would defeat the claim of a bona fide purchaser. This rule obviates the secret transfer problem.[447]

The time-of-transfer rule also could be important in determining whether the debtor was *insolvent at the time of the transfer*, as required for one type of constructive fraud. § 548(a)(1)(B)(ii)(I). Assume, in the above hypothetical, that when Debtor deeded Blackacre to Grandma in January 2010, Debtor was still solvent. That fact will not help Debtor or Grandma escape the clutches of the fraudulent transfer law, since the time the transfer is deemed made is deferred until recordation of the deed. Thus, if Debtor had become insolvent by the time Grandma recorded the deed in February 2012, the insolvency requirement will be satisfied.

§ 6.32   Actual Fraud: Fraudulent Intent

Since the passage of the Statute of 13 Elizabeth in 1571, a transfer by a debtor has been considered fraudulent and subject to avoidance if made by the debtor with "*actual intent to hinder, delay, or defraud*" any creditor. Today the result is the same: actual fraud is a basis for avoidance. See Bankruptcy Code § 548(a)(1)(A); UFTA § 4(a)(1); UFCA § 7.

Proof of actual fraud requires proof of the *subjective intention of the debtor* in making the transfer. The party seeking to set aside the transfer bears the burden of proof, and in many states, they must carry that burden by "clear and convincing evidence." As one might expect, debtors rarely announce their fraudulent intentions for the world to hear. At a very early stage, courts began to rely on circumstantial evidence to establish the debtor's subjective fraudulent state of mind. These circumstantial factors came to be known as "*badges of fraud.*"

There is no magic combination or requisite number of "badges" needed to establish actual fraud. Rather, the weight to be given to the badges identified in any particular case depends on all of the facts and circumstances of that case, and the inferences to be drawn from the badges are strong or weak depending on the number and nature of the badges present. Courts over time began to recognize certain badges as highly suspicious and almost presumptively indicative of the debtor's fraud. At the same time, the absence of important badges may help to negate a finding of fraudulent intent.

The foundational fraudulent conveyance case was *Twyne's Case*, decided in 1601 by the Star Chamber.[448] Ironically, the case may have involved nothing more than a preference; yet, its place in legal history is secure. Pierce, the debtor, owed £400 to

---

[446] If Grandma did not record the deed before bankruptcy was filed, the transfer would be deemed to be made immediately before the bankruptcy petition was filed. § 548(d)(1). This rule allows the trustee to challenge the transfer under § 548(a).

[447] The UFTA rule is similar. UFTA § 6. The main difference is that the UFTA fixes the time when a transfer of personal property is made at the time a judicial lien creditor cannot acquire a superior interest. UFTA § 6(1)(ii). The bona fide purchaser test is utilized only for real property and fixtures. UFTA § 6(1)(i). Interestingly, the Code's preference timing rules also use a lien creditor test for personal property. § 547(e)(1)(B). The reason for using a bona fide purchaser test for transfers of all types of property in § 548(d)(1), including personal property, is not explained in the legislative history to the Code.

[448] 3 Coke Rep. 80b, 76 Eng. Rep. 809 (Star Chamber 1601).

Twyne and £200 to a mysterious "C". C brought an action against Pierce on the debt. While that action was pending, Pierce secretly transferred all of his property, worth some £300, to Twyne by a deed of gift. Notwithstanding the transfer, Pierce retained possession of some of his sheep and treated them as his own. C obtained judgment against Pierce, but when the sheriff went to levy on the sheep, friends of Pierce prevented him from levying, claiming that the sheep belonged to Twyne, not Pierce. C then sued Twyne to set aside the conveyance, so that C could levy on the property.

C won. Lord Coke for the court held that the transfer from Pierce to Twyne was actually fraudulent under the Statute of 13 Elizabeth. The court based its holding on six badges of fraud:

1. The gift was general, of all of Pierce's property, without excepting even his apparel or anything of necessity.

2. Pierce retained possession of the property supposedly transferred, and treated it as his own.

3. The transfer was made in secret.

4. The transfer was made while C's suit was pending against Pierce.

5. Twyne held the property in trust for Pierce.

6. The deed contained a recital that the gift was bona fide.[449]

Courts ever since have used similar badges of fraud to identify actual fraudulent intent. Of the badges in *Twyne's Case*, the first four especially have been given great weight in subsequent cases: a transfer of all of the debtor's property; retention of possession by the debtor; a secret disposition; and a transfer while a lawsuit was pending.

Badges not present in *Twyne's Case* that have been found significant in many cases over the centuries include: transfer to a family member or another "insider"; a gift transfer, or a transfer for less than full consideration; and the insolvency of the debtor at the time the transfer was made. The UFTA contains a helpful "laundry list" of eleven commonly recognized badges of fraud.[450] § 4(b). The list is not intended to be

---

[449] The sixth "badge" raises a concern analogous to the Shakespearean quote in Hamlet, "The lady doth protest too much, methinks." The drafters of the UFTA took the view, however, that "recitals of 'good faith' can no longer be regarded as significant evidence of a fraudulent intent." Comment 5, UFTA § 4, http://www.uniformlaws.org/shared/docs/fraudulent%20transfer/ufta_final_84.pdf.

[450] UFTA § 4(b) provides that consideration may be given to whether: (1) the transfer was to an insider (which would include a relative); (2) the debtor retained possession or control; (3) the transfer was concealed; (4) the transfer was made pending a lawsuit; (5) substantially all of the debtor's property was conveyed; (6) the debtor absconded; (7) the debtor removed or concealed assets; (8) the debtor received less than reasonably equivalent value for the property transferred; (9) the debtor was insolvent or became insolvent; (10) the transfer occurred shortly before or after a substantial debt was incurred; and (11) the debtor transferred the essential assets of the business to a lienor who transferred the assets to an insider.

exclusive. Some of the factors in combination (e.g., a gift by an insolvent) will trigger a finding of constructive fraud, irrespective of actual intent.[451]

Transfers to relatives in particular have been viewed with great suspicion and have been closely scrutinized. The hypothetical used in an earlier section, where Debtor conveys Blackacre to Grandma, is an example. In some jurisdictions the presence of this factor may trigger a presumption of fraud, shifting the burden of going forward to the transferee to establish the legitimacy of the transaction. Grandma may have to show that she paid a reasonably equivalent value for Blackacre, for example.

One type of case where courts invariably find actual fraudulent intent is where the debtor has been running a "Ponzi" scheme.[452] In a Ponzi scheme, the debtor never makes any real investments, but simply uses later investments to pay "returns" to earlier investors. As the District Judge observed in one of the cases arising out of Bernie Madoff's infamous Ponzi scheme, "Since it is undisputed that Madoff's Ponzi scheme began more than two years before the filing of the bankruptcy petition and continued to almost the very day of filing, it is patent that all of Madoff Securities' transfers during the two-year period were made with actual intent to defraud present and future creditors, *i.e.,* those left holding the bag when the scheme was uncovered."[453]

The badge of fraud for retention of possession by the debtor in the past wreaked some havoc with normal commercial transactions. In 1925, the Supreme Court held in *Benedict v. Ratner*[454] that a security transaction was fraudulent and voidable because the debtor retained possession of the collateral. Such a rule, if followed, would undermine modern commercial secured financing, where debtors routinely retain possession of collateral. The rule of *Benedict v. Ratner* has been overridden by § 9–205 of the Uniform Commercial Code, which permits a debtor to retain collateral without any imputation of fraud. Similarly, UCC § 2–402(2) permits a merchant seller to retain possession of goods sold in the current course of trade and in good faith, for a commercially reasonable period of time, without a suggestion of fraud.

The 2005 bankruptcy amendments added a new category of actual fraud for transfers to self-settled asset protection trusts. § 548(e). The most important aspect of the new provision, and the only important way that it departs from the existing actual fraud provision in § 548(a)(1)(A), is that it gives the trustee an extraordinary *10–year reach-back period.* § 548(e)(1). The elements of this avoiding power are:

- transfer of an interest of the debtor in property, § 548(e)(1);

- made on or within 10 years before the bankruptcy filing, § 548(e)(1);

- made to a self-settled trust or similar device, § 548(e)(1)(A);

---

[451] See §§ 6.33–6.36.

[452] See, e.g., In re Agric. Research & Tech. Grp., Inc., 916 F.2d 528, 535 (9th Cir. 1990).

[453] Picard v. Katz, 462 B.R. 447, 453 (S.D.N.Y. 2011).

[454] 268 U.S. 353 (1925).

- transfer made by the debtor, § 548(e)(1)(B);

- debtor is a beneficiary of the trust, § 548(e)(1)(C); and

- actual fraudulent intent of the debtor, § 548(e)(1)(D).

The addition of § 548(e) allows the federal bankruptcy trustee to avoid so-called "Alaska trusts" (so named after the state that pioneered them in 1997), and permits bankruptcy avoidance (for a very long time period) even though the assets in such a self-settled trust might be difficult to attack under state law. By so doing, the federal bankruptcy law has, at least to some extent, reinstated the traditional result, wherein a debtor was unable to place his own property beyond the reach of his creditors. In a self-settled trust, a debtor transfers his own property—which if not exempt would of course be subject to the claims of his creditors—to a trustee to be held in trust for the benefit of the debtor, under terms that make it difficult for the debtor's creditors to reach the trust res in order to satisfy their claims. Historically, such a transfer had been completely ineffective against the debtor's creditors, irrespective of the debtor's subjective intention. Beginning in 1997, though, some states (most notably Alaska) passed legislation overturning that result, so that a creditor could reach the trust corpus only upon proof of actual fraud, and then only for a four-year period.[455] While § 548(e) also requires proof of the debtor's actual fraud, it extends the period of vulnerability to 10 years if the debtor files bankruptcy. Note also that the debtor's actual fraudulent intent that exposes the transfer to avoidance under subsection (e) can be directed at present *or future* creditors, i.e., those whose claims do not arise until *after* the transfer was made. One wonders how lenient bankruptcy courts might be in inferring such a fraudulent intention from the mere fact of setting up such a trust, since one of the most obvious reasons to do so is to insulate one's property from the claims of creditors.

§ 6.33   Constructive Fraud: Overview

The promulgation of the UFCA in 1918 marked a watershed in the evolution of fraudulent conveyance law. The objectification of the law, developed over the centuries by courts through the invocation of "badges of fraud" as a means of inferring actual fraudulent intent, was given formal recognition. For the first time, proof of certain specified facts conclusively established that the transfer at issue was a fraudulent conveyance, irrespective of the actual subjective intention of the debtor. This type of fraudulent conveyance has come to be known as *constructive* fraud.

As a normative matter, the justification for permitting transfers to be set aside on the basis of constructive fraud has been somewhat difficult to pinpoint.[456] This difficulty has led to great confusion and uncertainty in fixing the outer limits of the

---

[455] See Stewart E. Sterk, Asset Protection Trusts: Trust Law's Race to the Bottom?, 85 Cornell L. Rev. 1035 (2000). There is no evidence that Sarah Palin had anything to do with this legislation.

[456] For thoughtful discussions, see Douglas G. Baird & Thomas H. Jackson, Fraudulent Conveyance Law and Its Proper Domain, 38 Vand. L. Rev. 829 (1985); John C. McCoid, II, Constructively Fraudulent Conveyances: Transfers for Inadequate Consideration, 62 Tex. L. Rev. 639 (1983). A classic discussion of the normative underpinnings of fraudulent conveyance law is Robert C. Clark, The Duties of the Corporate Debtor to Its Creditors, 90 Harv. L. Rev. 505 (1977).

fraudulent transfer laws. In modern times, this problem has cropped up in numerous areas: leveraged buyouts,[457] corporate group transactions,[458] and mortgage foreclosures,[459] to name a few.

Two entirely distinct principles appear to be at work. The first is that constructive fraud may serve as a useful surrogate for actual fraud.[460] Actual fraudulent intent often is hard to prove. Yet, in cases where the existence of that wrongful subjective intention is so likely, and has been found to exist so often in cases down through the centuries, it may be more efficient to create a per se rule of avoidance rather than to litigate the issue of intent in every case. In essence, this rationale for constructive fraud simply takes the notion of "badges of fraud" one step further, and conclusively infers fraud in defined circumstances.

This first justification for constructive fraud does not, however, fully explain the reach of constructive fraud, either as codified or applied in the last century. Many cases fall squarely within the scope of constructive fraud even though there is no hint or even possibility of debtor misbehavior. The second rationale for constructive fraud, and probably the dominant one today, is that some transfers by their very nature injure creditors of the debtor.[461] These transfers are inherently objectionable, and should be set aside.[462] The focus of constructive fraud, then, is on the *victims*—the creditors— rather than on the debtor.[463] Under this theory, constructive fraud is a form of strict liability designed to redress creditor injury.

Three different forms of constructive fraud have been recognized in every fraudulent transfer statute since the adoption of the UFCA in 1918. They are:

1. A transfer in exchange for less than reasonably equivalent value by a debtor who is insolvent or who is rendered insolvent by the transfer.[464]

2. A transfer in exchange for less than reasonably equivalent value by a debtor with unreasonably small capital remaining after the transfer.[465]

3. A transfer in exchange for less than reasonably equivalent value by a debtor who is about to incur debts beyond the debtor's ability to pay as they mature.[466]

---

[457] See § 6.39.

[458] See § 6.40.

[459] See § 6.41.

[460] See Baird & Jackson, supra note 456, at 830–31; McCoid, supra note 456, at 656–57.

[461] This justification motivated the drafters of the UFCA. The Prefatory Note to the UFCA states, "There are many conveyances which wrong creditors where an intent to defraud on the part of the debtor does not in fact exist." 7A (pt. II) Uniform Laws Annotated, UFCA Prefatory Note, at 247 (2006).

[462] See Baird & Jackson, supra note 456, at 831–32.

[463] See McCoid, supra note 456, at 657–58.

[464] 11 U.S.C. § 548(a)(1)(B)(i) & (ii)(I); UFTA § 5(a); UFCA § 4.

[465] 11 U.S.C. § 548(a)(1)(B)(i) & (ii)(II); UFTA § 4(a)(2)(i); UFCA § 5.

[466] 11 U.S.C. § 548(a)(1)(B)(i) & (ii)(III); UFTA § 4(a)(2)(ii); UFCA § 6.

These three types of constructive fraud share in common a focus on the amount of consideration the debtor received in exchange for the transfer. Under the UFCA, this comparative value element is called *"fair consideration."* UFCA § 3. The Bankruptcy Code, § 548(a)(1)(B)(i), and the UFTA, §§ 4(a)(2), 5(a), use the phrase *"reasonably equivalent value."* The next section explores the meaning of "reasonably equivalent value" and "fair consideration" in more detail, and explains the differences in those terms.[467] The need for the value to be received "in exchange" for the transfer is important in some constructive fraud cases, and also is explored below.[468]

Another type of constructive fraud is recognized by the UFCA, involving conveyances of partnership property. UFCA § 8. The Bankruptcy Code also contains a special rule for transfers of partnership property. § 548(b). The drafters of the UFTA, however, chose not to include a special partnership rule. The differences in these approaches is discussed in a later section.[469]

The UFTA contains a provision addressing yet another form of constructive fraud, namely, a preference to an insider. UFTA § 5(b). Prior to 2005, neither the UFCA nor the Bankruptcy Code contained such a rule. However, the 2005 bankruptcy amendments added a narrow provision for constructive fraud involving insiders. § 548(a)(1)(B)(i) & (ii)(IV). Under the new provision, a transfer to or for the benefit of an insider under an employment contract is vulnerable if not made in the ordinary course of business and if the debtor received less than a reasonably equivalent value in exchange. The UFCA addresses the problem of insider preferences indirectly, through the definition of "fair consideration." UFCA § 3. The special case of insider preferences is examined below.[470]

The most important of the constructive fraud actions ever since 1918 has been for transfers for less than equivalent value by an insolvent debtor. Professor Clark captured the core concept behind this type of constructive fraud neatly in a memorable aphorism: "be just before you are generous."[471] The following sections examine in more detail the components of this constructive fraud action: (1) that the debtor received less than reasonably equivalent value;[472] (2) in exchange for the property transferred or obligation incurred;[473] and (3) the debtor was insolvent at the time of the transfer or was rendered insolvent by the transfer.[474]

As Professor McCoid has pointed out, this form of constructive fraud has merged what historically had been treated as two distinct concepts: first, a pure *gift* by an insolvent debtor, in which no consideration is received in exchange (what is sometimes

---

[467] See § 6.34.

[468] See § 6.35.

[469] See § 6.37.

[470] See § 6.38.

[471] Clark, supra note 456, at 510. Professor Clark went on to assert that a "debtor has a moral duty in transferring his property to give *primacy* to so-called legal obligations, . . . as opposed to the interests of self, family, friends, shareholders, and shrewder or more powerful bargaining parties." Id. at 510–11 (emphasis in original). He labeled this norm the "ideal of Respect." Id. at 511.

[472] See § 6.34.

[473] See § 6.35.

[474] See § 6.36.

called a "voluntary" conveyance); and second, a transfer by an insolvent debtor for value, but which value is *inadequate* in comparison to the value of the property transferred.[475] It is this second type, transfers by an insolvent for inadequate consideration, which has proven troublesome when applied to various common modern financial transactions.[476]

The other two main types of constructive fraud, *viz.*, for transfers for less than a reasonably equivalent value by a debtor (1) with unreasonably small capital remaining, or (2) who is about to incur debts beyond his ability to pay as they mature, have been far less important in the application of the fraudulent conveyance laws.[477] For many decades these forms of action have been largely the long-lost cousins of fraudulent conveyance law. In more recent times, however, these actions have enjoyed an upsurge of importance, as they have been invoked to challenge modern corporate transactions, such as leveraged buyouts.[478]

§ 6.34 Constructive Fraud: Less than Reasonably Equivalent Value

A required showing of almost every type of constructive fraud action is that the debtor "received less than a *reasonably equivalent value* in exchange for such transfer or obligation." Bankruptcy Code § 548(a)(1)((B)(i); UFTA §§ 4(a)(2), 5(a). That showing, when linked with proof that the debtor was insolvent, had unreasonably small capital, or was about to incur debts beyond his ability to pay as they mature, will conclusively establish constructive fraud. In modern fraudulent transfer law, many of the most difficult battles have been fought over what constitutes "reasonably equivalent value." In subsequent sections, some of the most frequently fought and critical battles will be examined, including: leveraged buyouts,[479] corporate group transactions,[480] and mortgage foreclosures.[481]

The UFCA uses the term "fair consideration" to capture the value element, rather than "reasonably equivalent value." UFCA § 3. The two phrases are not identical. The UFCA term *"fair consideration"* embodies two separate elements: first, that the value received in exchange for the property conveyed was a *fair equivalent*; and second, that the exchange was made in *good faith*. The good faith referred to is that of the *transferee*. In short, under the UFCA, the consideration received must be "fair" in both an objective value sense and in a subjective moral sense. Neither the UFTA nor the Bankruptcy Code contains the "good faith" component, choosing instead to measure value equivalency solely from the standpoint of objective values exchanged.

---

[475] McCoid, supra note 456, at 642–43.

[476] See §§ 6.39–6.41.

[477] For an excellent article, see Bruce A. Markell, Toward True and Plain Dealing: A Theory of Fraudulent Transfers Involving Unreasonably Small Capital, 21 Ind. L. Rev. 469 (1988).

[478] See § 6.39.

[479] See § 6.39.

[480] See § 6.40.

[481] See § 6.41.

The difference has been important primarily when the transferee is a relative or other insider of the debtor. Thus, as will be discussed in a later section,[482] a preference by the debtor to an insider may be challenged under the UFCA on the basis that the transferee did not act in "good faith," and thus did not give a "fair consideration." The UFTA chooses to deal with the insider preference problem directly, creating a separate constructive fraud action for such cases. UFTA § 5(b). The Bankruptcy Code, by contrast, does not identify the insider preference problem as a type of fraudulent conveyance at all, except in the limited context of employment contracts outside the ordinary course of business. § 548(a)(1)(B)(ii)(IV).

The comparative value element in all of the primary statutes—Bankruptcy Code, UFTA, and UFCA—has two subsidiary facets: first, "*value*" must be given; and second, that value must be "*reasonably equivalent*," or a "fair equivalent," to the property transferred. "*Value*" is defined in the Bankruptcy Code as "property, or satisfaction or securing of a present or antecedent debt of the debtor, but does not include an unperformed promise to furnish support to the debtor or to a relative of the debtor." § 548(d)(2)(A). The UFTA has a similar although not identical definition of "value." UFTA § 3(a). "Reasonably equivalent" is not defined in any of the statutes, but is left to judicial interpretation. The courts do not require an exact mathematical equivalence, but weigh all of the circumstances of the case.

The easiest cases are those in which the debtor plainly receives no value whatsoever in exchange; in short, the debtor makes an outright *gift*. If Debtor deeds Blackacre, worth $100,000, to his daughter "in consideration of your love and affection," Debtor has not received reasonably equivalent value in exchange. Nor would it matter if a nominal consideration were given in exchange; reasonably equivalent value still would be found lacking.

It is often said that value must be measured from the perspective of the *creditors* of the debtor, and not from the debtor's perspective. The reason for this approach is that constructive fraud seeks to redress a wrong against creditors, namely, the removal of leviable assets from the debtor's estate. Illustrative of this view is the Comment to the UFTA section on value: "'Value' is to be determined in light of the purpose of the Act to protect a debtor's estate from being depleted to the prejudice of the debtor's unsecured creditors. Consideration having no utility from a creditor's viewpoint does not satisfy the statutory definition."[483]

Thus, in the example given above, the Debtor's estate was depleted by $100,000 when he conveyed Blackacre to his daughter and received only "love and affection" in return; as much as we all value the love of our children, creditors profit not at all from such familial affections. In terms of the definition of "value," love and affection do not constitute "property."

This creditor-oriented focus dictates another aspect of the value determination in fraudulent conveyance law, which is that "reasonably equivalent value" is not

---

[482] See § 6.38.

[483] See http://www.uniformlaws.org/shared/docs/fraudulent%20transfer/ufta_final_84.pdf, UFTA § 3, cmt. 2 (2013).

synonymous with "consideration" in the contract law sense of the word. In other words, that something would count as a valid consideration sufficient to support a contract does not necessarily mean that it would qualify as reasonably equivalent value under the fraudulent transfer laws. The purposes served by the two concepts are distinct. Contract consideration does not take into account the impact on third party rights, and does not make quantitative comparisons, whereas the concept of reasonably equivalent value under the fraudulent transfer laws serves both functions. In our example, if Debtor did not make a gift of Blackacre to his daughter, but instead sold her Blackacre (worth $100,000) for $25,000, reasonably equivalent value still would be found lacking under the fraudulent transfer laws. Debtor's estate, from the viewpoint of his creditors, would be depleted by $75,000.

Care must be taken, however, not to get too carried away with the "creditor's perspective" measuring stick of value under the fraudulent transfer laws. It is most assuredly *not* the case that the debtor always must have the same quantum of leviable assets after the exchange as she did before the exchange. Perhaps the most obvious example of this point is where the debtor *consumes* goods or services in exchange for hard cash. To illustrate, assume that Debtor goes to Chez François and spends $200 on a lovely dinner. Before the dinner, Debtor had $200 more from which creditors might collect than she did after the dinner. Yet, the fraudulent transfer laws nevertheless hold that the Debtor did receive "value."

This result can be explained as a requirement that "value" be calculated by reference to an *objective market* determinant of value, rather than a pure "what's-left-for-creditors" inquiry. The question is whether the debtor received something with a measurable economic benefit. Under the definition of "value", the debtor must either receive "property" or must satisfy or secure a debt. Paying for dinner is the satisfaction of a present debt. Requiring the debtor to make fair market transactions provides some objective protection for creditors that debtors will behave in a manner that will not unfairly deplete their estate in the normal course of affairs, while at the same time giving debtors some freedom to live their lives as they choose. Creditors who want to collect from a debtor may need to monitor their debtor's activities, and move quickly if they find the debtor is enjoying too much of the "good life" at the creditors' expense. The interests of creditors and that of the debtor are perpetually in tension, and the fraudulent transfer law is content to allow each side some leeway; only when the debtor acts in a way that tilts the scales too heavily and unfairly against the creditors will the transfer be subject to avoidance.

An example of the competing interests of creditors and debtors is where the debtor gambles away assets. For example, assume that Debtor has $100,000 in debts, and $100,000 in nonexempt assets. At this point, Debtor's creditors would be paid in full, but there is nothing left over for Debtor. Moral qualms aside, Debtor would have every incentive to take her $100,000 to Las Vegas and try her luck gambling. Debtor will enjoy all of the upside if she wins, and the creditors will bear all of the downside if she loses. Yet, for the purposes of the fraudulent transfer laws, Debtor receives "value" for her bets, namely, the value of the chance that she will win.[484] If Debtor pays $100 for a one-in-ten chance to win $1000, she has gotten an exact value equivalence.[485]

The gambling example also illustrates another aspect of "value," which is that value must be *measured at the time the transfer is made*. That Debtor may have lost her one-in-ten bet does not mean that she received nothing of value in exchange; before the chance was played, Debtor had a ten percent possibility of receiving $1,000, and thus *at that time* received a $100 value. A party attacking a transfer is not allowed to use "20–20 hindsight."[486] In commercial transactions, a debtor may make an investment that turns out after the fact to have been a poor one. Debtor may buy Blackacre for $100,000, only to find that the real estate market soon collapses, dropping Blackacre's value to a fraction of that amount. However, the value of what the debtor received must be determined from the perspective of what was known at the time of the transfer.

The courts will draw a line beyond which they will not let debtors go in making transfers that do not result in any quantifiable economic benefit to either the debtor or her creditors. An example is where a debtor makes contributions to her church. The intangible benefits the debtor may receive in connection with church membership have been held not to count as "value" under the fraudulent conveyance laws.[487] Courts have concluded that the debtor has not received "property" and has not satisfied or secured a debt. Some argue, though, that the religious contribution situation is akin to the "consumption" cases; a debtor who contributes to her church arguably is "consuming" religious benefits just as is a debtor who spends money at a fine restaurant. The crucial difference between the two for fraudulent transfer purposes, though, is exposed by the objective market test: a church will let you worship even if you do not pay, but your chances of getting a free meal at a restaurant are nonexistent. Note, though, that it is theoretically possible for a charitable contribution to satisfy an enforceable contractual debt, if the debtor has made a binding charitable subscription.[488] In bankruptcy cases, Congress has specifically immunized qualifying charitable contributions (as defined in § 548(d)(3)) from attack as a constructively fraudulent transfer, in the Religious Liberty and Charitable Donation Protection Act of 1998.[489] §§ 548(a)(2), 544(b)(2).

---

[484] See, e.g., In re Chomakos, 69 F.3d 769 (6th Cir. 1995).

[485] The ex ante value of a 10% chance to win $1000 is computed as $1000 x .1 = $100.

[486] See In re TOUSA, Inc., 680 F.3d 1298, 1312 (11th Cir. 2012) ("The Transeastern Lenders and New Lenders attack this finding as 'hindsight reasoning . . . at its most extreme,' but the bankruptcy court based its extensive findings on a thorough review of public knowledge available [at the time the transfer was made].").

[487] See In re Newman, 183 B.R. 239 (Bankr. D. Kan. 1995), aff'd, 203 B.R. 468 (D. Kan. 1996). Contra In re Moses, 59 B.R. 815 (Bankr. N.D. Ga. 1986).

[488] See Rest. (Second) of Contracts § 90(2) (1981).

[489] Pub. L. No. 105–183, §§ 2, 3, 112 Stat. 517 (1998). See § 6.42. The 1998 legislation was prompted by the uproar surrounding the controversial case of Christians v. Crystal Evangelical Free Church (In re Young), 148 B.R. 886 (Bankr. D. Minn. 1992), aff'd, 152 B.R. 969 (D. Minn. 1993), rev'd, 82 F.3d 1407 (8th Cir. 1996), vacated and remanded, 521 U.S. 1114 (1997), reinstated, 141 F.3d 854 (8th Cir.), cert. denied, 525 U.S. 811 (1998). At the circuit level, the *Young* case debated whether the Religious Freedom Restoration Act (RFRA) effectively modified the bankruptcy law's fraudulent conveyance provisions, and if so, whether RFRA was constitutional, a question prompted by the Supreme Court's decision in City of Boerne v. Flores, 521 U.S. 507 (1997), that RFRA was unconstitutional as applied to the states. By directly amending the Bankruptcy Code in the 1998 law, Congress rendered less important the issue of the constitutionality of RFRA as applied in the bankruptcy fraudulent transfer setting. However, nothing in that law or in any of the

While creating immunity in the specific instance, that legislation did not alter the underlying theory upon which courts prior to 1998 had acted. Getting to go to church is wonderful, but it still is not "value" for fraudulent transfer purposes. In fraudulent transfer actions under state law, creditors remain free to challenge charitable contributions by insolvent debtors.

As noted above, the satisfaction or securing of a present or antecedent debt of the debtor does qualify as value. § 548(d)(2)(A). While such a transfer may deplete the asset side of the debtor's balance sheet, and in that respect be harmful to creditors, it also will reduce the total of the debtor's liabilities, and correspondingly benefit creditors. Creditors may have fewer assets from which to collect, but they also will have fewer competitors for that asset pool. In short, a *preference* by a debtor is a transfer for a reasonably equivalent value.

The transfer of security by a debtor for a debt is given for reasonably equivalent value. This result holds even if the value of the collateral greatly exceeds the debt. For example, assume that Debtor grants Creditor a mortgage on Blackacre, worth $100,000, to secure a debt of only $5,000. Even though the value of the collateral transferred is twenty times greater than the debt, Creditor will only be entitled to a single satisfaction of the debt. Thus, the realizable value of the mortgage on Blackacre to Creditor is only $5,000.

A troublesome issue with regard to "value" has been whether an unperformed promise to provide future services qualifies. While Debtor's gift of Blackacre to his daughter clearly does not count as "value," his transfer of Blackacre to his daughter in exchange for her promise to support him for the rest of his life cannot as readily be dismissed as valueless. If she does fulfill her promise, Debtor undoubtedly will have received something of concrete value. The concern, though, is that the unperformed promise may be nothing more than a cover for what is in reality a gift. If the daughter does not perform, will Debtor or his estate really sue her for breach of contract?

The Bankruptcy Code resolves the issue by defining "value" to *exclude* "an unperformed promise to furnish support to the debtor or a relative of the debtor." Thus, the daughter's promise would not count as value. What, though, if the Debtor transferred Blackacre to a nursing home in exchange for a promise of lifetime care? This transaction raises fewer suspicions than the transfer to daughter; it is more likely that the parties intended a real exchange transaction for value. Yet, the Bankruptcy Code definition of value may exclude the nursing home's promise as well as that of the daughter. By contrast, the UFTA definition of "value" does include an unperformed promise to furnish support if made "in the ordinary course of the promisor's business."

Note that the "future services" exclusion in the definition of value in both the Bankruptcy Code and the UFTA is by its terms limited to promises to furnish support. Many cases proclaim that all promises to provide future services are excluded, but the statutory definitions do not support such a broad prohibition.

---

many court decisions detracted from the conclusion that the debtors did not receive "value" in exchange for their contributions to their church.

§ 6.35   Constructive Fraud: In Exchange

The value equivalency prong of a constructive fraud case is not satisfied solely by proof that the debtor received reasonably equivalent value for the property transferred or the obligation incurred. In addition, that value must be received *in exchange* for the property or obligation. In short, there must be a *quid pro quo* aspect to the transaction. Proof of an exchange substantiates the market-based legitimacy of the transaction. Absent such an exchange component to the deal, creditors justifiably could complain that the debtor need not have parted with property or incurred an obligation in the first place. The debtor would have been able to receive the value from the transferee without giving up anything in return.

Most of the time, proof of exchange follows readily if reasonably equivalent value is established. In market transactions, few entities are willing to give up something for nothing. In certain types of cases, though, the exchange element may be problematic. Often the value element itself is dubious in these cases, but the lack of an exchange is more readily established.

Probably the most prominent example in recent years of a situation in which exchange has been found lacking is in the church contribution cases. The Eighth Circuit decision in *Christians v. Crystal Evangelical Free Church (In re Young)*[490] is illustrative. The debtors tithed over $13,000 to their church in the year preceding their bankruptcy filing, in keeping with their sincerely held religious beliefs. The church did not require members to tithe in order to attend worship or otherwise take advantage of the services offered by the church. Defending the fraudulent transfer action brought by the bankruptcy trustee, the church argued that the exchange element could be satisfied by proving a "nexus" between the contributions and the services made available. That nexus existed, in that contributions made by the debtors and other parishioners made it possible for the church to offer the services. The Eighth Circuit declined to read the exchange element so broadly, however. According to the *Young* court, the fact that the debtors were not *required* to contribute in order to partake of the church's offerings was fatal. One could counter, though, that the court's narrow "tit-for-tat" view ignores the economic realities that govern the affairs of a shared enterprise and creates free rider problems for that enterprise. If none of the parishioners contributed to the church, the church would not be able to provide any services.

---

[490] 82 F.3d 1407 (8th Cir. 1996) vacated and remanded, 521 U.S. 1114 (1997), reinstated, 141 F.3d 854 (8th Cir.), cert. denied, 525 U.S. 811 (1998). The *Young* court also expressed doubt as to whether "value" was present, but because it held no exchange was made, it chose not to decide the value issue. Ultimately, though, the court in *Young* held that the debtor's contributions to the church could not be avoided as fraudulent transfers, because of the command of the Religious Freedom Restoration Act. The court concluded that avoidance of the debtor's tithes to the church would substantially burden the debtor's religious practices, and that there was not a compelling governmental interest to justify that burden. The enactment of the Religious Liberty and Charitable Donation Protection Act of 1998, Pub. L. No. 105–183, §§ 2, 3, 112 Stat. 517 (1998), amended the Bankruptcy Code by exempting qualifying charitable contributions from attack as a constructively fraudulent transfer, thus mooting the specific issue in *Young*. See §§ 6.34 n. 10, 6.42. The analysis in *Young* on the "exchange" issue remains relevant for analyzing similar cases under non-bankruptcy law or in bankruptcy but not involving qualifying charitable contributions.

§ 6.36   Constructive Fraud: Insolvent

Proving that the debtor did not receive reasonably equivalent value in exchange for the property transferred or obligation incurred is not enough to establish constructive fraud." The party seeking to avoid the transfer must prove something more, a "plus" factor. Solvent and financially healthy debtors are perfectly free to make gifts or other transfers for inadequate consideration, without their creditors having reason to complain.

The trustee or creditor must prove one of the following four "plus" factors, in addition to showing that the transfer was made in exchange for less than a reasonably equivalent value:

1. That the debtor was insolvent on the date the transfer was made or the obligation was incurred, or was rendered insolvent by the transfer or obligation, Bankruptcy, Code § 548(a)(1)(B)(ii)(I), UFTA § 5(a), UFCA § 4;

2. That the debtor was engaged in or was about to engage in a business or a transaction, for which the property remaining with the debtor was an unreasonably small capital, Bankruptcy Code § 548(a)(1)(B)(ii)(II), UFTA § 4(a)(2)(i), UFCA § 5; or

3. That the debtor intended to incur or believed that it would incur debts beyond the debtor's ability to pay as they matured, Bankruptcy Code § 548(a)(1)(B)(ii)(III), UFTA § 4(a)(2)(ii), UFCA § 6.

4. That the transfer was made to or for the benefit of an insider under an employment contract, and not in the ordinary course of business. Bankruptcy Code § 548(a)(1)(B)(ii)(IV).

Of these factors, the most important by far is the first, that the debtor was *insolvent* at the time of the transfer or became insolvent as a result of the transfer. There are two basic types of insolvency recognized in the law:

- *"balance sheet"* insolvency, and

- *"equity"* insolvency.

"Balance sheet" insolvency focuses, as the name suggests, on the debtor's balance sheet: if debts exceed assets, the debtor is insolvent. "Equity" insolvency, by contrast, looks to the debtor's ongoing operations. If the debtor is generally not paying its debts as they come due, it is insolvent in the equity sense. A variant of the equity test asks whether the debtor has the ability to pay its debts as they come due.

Fraudulent transfer law primarily utilizes a *balance sheet test* in judging the debtor's insolvency. The Bankruptcy Code defines "insolvent" in § 101(32)(A) as a "financial condition such that the sum of such entity's debts is greater than all of such entity's property, at a fair valuation."

The asset side of the equation is refined by excluding property that was fraudulently transferred. § 101(32)(A)(i). Exempt property is also excluded, because the debtor's creditors would not be able to collect their debts out of that property. § 101(32)(A)(ii). The UFTA definition is functionally identical. UFTA §§ 2(a), 1(2). In addition, under the UFTA, to the extent a debt is secured by a lien, a deduction is made from both the asset and debt sides of the ledger. UFTA §§ 2(e), 1(2)(i). Under the UFCA, a person is insolvent when the "present fair salable value of his assets is less than the amount that will be required to pay his probable liability on his existing debts as they become absolute and matured." UFCA § 2(1).

Although the insolvency test is labeled a "balance sheet" test, courts do not blindly accept the numbers presented on the debtor's balance sheet. Book value or historical cost figures will not be dispositive. The reference to "fair valuation" in the Bankruptcy Code and UFTA, and to "present fair salable value" in the UFCA, signifies that courts should look behind the numbers and examine the actual realizable market worth of the debtor's assets and the likely debt exposure as debts come due. Contingent debts (such as guarantees) should be estimated, based on the probability that the debtor will be called upon to pay.

In partnership cases, a slightly different definition is used, because each general partner is individually liable for partnership debts. The Code defines insolvency for partnership debtors in § 101(32)(B) as a

[F]inancial condition such that the sum of such partnership's debts is greater than the aggregate of, at a fair valuation—(i) all of such partnership's property . . . and (ii) the sum of the excess of the value of each general partner's nonpartnership property . . . over such partner's nonpartnership debts.

The same exclusions are made as for non-partnership debtors, i.e., for property that is exempt or that was fraudulently transferred.

Proof of insolvency may be difficult. In theory, the trustee or creditor must prove the debtor's insolvency at the exact moment the challenged transfer was made or the obligation was incurred. Since the party with the burden of proof is not in possession of and did not keep the debtor's financial records, and also because the debtor's records often are a hopeless mess, reconstructing the financial condition of the debtor at a specific point in the past can be problematic. Unlike preference cases, see § 547(f), the Code does not give the trustee the benefit of a presumption of insolvency for fraudulent transfer cases.

One means by which the trustee may be able to carry his proof burden is through "projection" or "retrojection." In other words, the trustee proves the debtor's financial condition at a point in time either shortly before or after the time of the transfer, and then works forward or back, as the case may be. Recognizing the difficulty of the trustee's proof, courts may be somewhat receptive to such extrapolations.

Another avenue for establishing balance sheet insolvency at a precise moment in time is with the benefit of a presumption. The UFTA explicitly recognizes that a debtor who is not generally paying his debts as they become due is presumed to be insolvent. UFTA § 2(b). This presumption is rebuttable. Although the UFCA and the Bankruptcy Code do not contain such an express provision, the courts may fashion a similar rule. Other presumptions have been recognized as well. In a number of jurisdictions, such as

New York, a presumption of insolvency is created by proof that the debtor made a transfer for less than fair consideration, especially if the transferee was a family member. Other jurisdictions, such as California, presume the debtor is insolvent if she has failed to pay several outstanding judgments.

Proof of insolvency is easy in Ponzi scheme cases, assuming that the transfer in question was made after the Ponzi scheme became operative. The reason is that *by definition* a debtor who is running a Ponzi scheme is insolvent.[491] As the Supreme Court explained in *Cunningham v. Brown*, the case involving *the* Charles Ponzi himself, "He was always insolvent, and became daily more so, the more his business succeeded. He made no investments of any kind, so that all the money he had at any time was solely the result of loans by his dupes."[492]

To prove that the debtor was insolvent at the time the transfer was made, it is necessary to identify the time of transfer.[493] Recall that under § 548(d)(1), a transfer is not deemed to be made until it is perfected as against a bona fide purchaser, which typically is when the transfer is recorded in the public records. Thus, a debtor might make a transfer that is effective as between the debtor and the transferee at a time when the debtor is solvent, but if the transferee does not record the transfer until the debtor has become insolvent, the transfer will be vulnerable to avoidance as constructively fraudulent.

§ 6.37   Partnership Debtors

Transfers by partnership debtors raise special concerns. The unique feature of a partnership, of course, is that the general partners are not only responsible for the management of the partnership, but also are individually liable for the debts of the partnership. As such, a general partner of a partnership is the quintessential insider. The question that the drafters of the fraudulent transfer laws have grappled with is whether a distinct category of constructive fraud should be created to deal with transfers by partnership debtors. The Bankruptcy Code, § 548(b), and the UFCA, § 8, do contain a special partnership rule; the UFTA does not.

The scenario that has caused the most concern is where the partnership makes a transfer to or incurs an obligation to a general partner, if the partnership is insolvent at the time of the transfer or is rendered insolvent by the transfer. The legitimacy of such a transfer to a general partner is inherently suspect. The Bankruptcy Code makes such a transfer or obligation constructively fraudulent, if made or incurred within two years of the bankruptcy filing. § 548(b). The UFCA has a similar rule, without the two-year limitation. UFCA § 8(a). Note that these rules do not require proof that the transfer was for less than reasonably equivalent value or fair consideration;[494] that the

---

[491] E.g., Warfield v. Byron, 436 F.3d 551, 558 (5th Cir. 2006).

[492] 265 U.S. 1, 8 (1924).

[493] See § 6.31.

[494] The UFCA does specify that a transfer of partnership property or the incurring of an obligation by a partnership, while the debtor is insolvent or which renders the debtor insolvent, is fraudulent if made to a person not a partner without fair consideration to the partnership. UFCA § 8(b). The UFTA does not include such a particularized rule, rejecting such a provision as "redundant" of the rule that makes a transfer by any debtor fraudulent if made in exchange for less than reasonably equivalent value while insolvent. Prefatory

transfer was to a partner, while the debtor was insolvent, is enough to establish constructive fraud.

The UFTA, however, takes the position that "so categorical a condemnation of a partnership transaction with a partner may unfairly prejudice the interests of a partner's separate creditors."[495] Under the UFTA, a transfer to a general partner while the debtor was insolvent still could be found to be fraudulent if: (1) actual fraudulent intent is shown, § 4(a)(1); (2) the debtor did not receive a reasonably equivalent value in exchange, § 5(a); or (3) the transfer was for an antecedent debt, and the partner (as an "insider of the partnership, see § 1(7)(3)(A)) had reasonable cause to believe that the debtor was insolvent, § 5(b).

In analyzing a transfer by a partnership debtor under the foregoing rules, the special definition of "insolvency" for partnership debtors must be borne in mind.[496] See Bankruptcy Code § 101(32)(B); UFTA § 2(c); UFCA § 2(2). The asset side of the balance sheet for a partnership debtor includes not only the assets of the partnership, but also the net worth of each general partner, exclusive of partnership debts.

§ 6.38   Insider Preferences

Consider a simple example. Debtor has $15,000 in assets, and three creditors, X, Y, and Z, each of whom it owes $10,000. Six months before filing bankruptcy, Debtor pays the debt to Creditor X in full. Is this transfer by an insolvent debtor to one creditor in preference to other creditors a fraudulent conveyance?

The received wisdom long has been that "a preference is not a fraudulent conveyance." Fraudulent conveyance law is concerned with transfers of the debtor's property that prejudice the creditors of the debtor *as a group*, not with the relative claims of the individual members of the creditor group *inter se*. A transfer of the debtor's property that satisfies the valid claim of a creditor—i.e., a preference—by definition does not harm the creditor group, although of course one member of that group is primarily benefited. The debtor has received value in exchange for the transfer, namely, a reduction in liabilities. § 548(d)(2)(A). Although other creditors will have fewer assets of the debtor to pursue, they also will have fewer creditor competitors for that diminished asset pool.

Yet, notwithstanding the law's longstanding differentiation between preferences on the one hand and fraudulent conveyances on the other, the line between the two has been blurred in the case of a preference *to an insider*. In the above example, assume further that the debt to Creditor X is guaranteed by Paula President, the president and CEO of Debtor, and the debts to Y and Z are not guaranteed. Now, the payment to Creditor X not only prefers X over Y and Z, it also has the effect of extinguishing the potential liability of the insider Paula on the guarantee. The transfer thus is an indirect preference as to the insider.

Note to the UFTA, See http://www.uniformlaws.org/shared/docs/fraudulent%20transfer/ufta_final_84.pdf (2013).

[495] Id.

[496] See § 6.36.

Although courts and commentators have struggled to explain exactly why,[497] insider preferences have generated a sense of unease and suspicion, a sense that has given rise to the treatment of insider preferences as a form of constructively fraudulent conveyance. The notion persists that it is somehow unfair for an insider such as Paula to use her position of power and control over the Debtor's affairs to direct the payment of the debt that she has guaranteed in preference to the debts owed other creditors. The Prefatory Note to the UFTA explains in conclusory fashion that "an insolvent debtor is obliged to pay debts to creditors not related to him before paying those who are insiders."[498]

Until 2005, the Bankruptcy Code did not treat a preference to an insider as a fraudulent transfer. In 2005, a small inroad was made, as Congress added a species of constructive fraud for transfers to or for the benefit of an insider under an employment contract, not in the ordinary course of business, and for which the debtor did not receive reasonably equivalent value in exchange. § 548(a)(1)(B)(i) & (ii)(IV). This change was targeted at egregious cases of "golden parachutes" bestowed on a debtor's top executives. Otherwise, the Code contains no provisions similar to those in the UFTA or UFCA, discussed below. Instead, the Code's focus traditionally has been to permit the avoidance of a preference to an insider as a *preference* under § 547, but not as a fraudulent conveyance under § 548. Preferences to insiders can be set aside for a longer period of time than preferences to non-insiders; the standard 90–day reach-back period is extended to *one year* for insider preferences.[499] § 547(b)(4)(B). The trustee does not have the benefit of a presumption of insolvency for the extended period, however, as she would during the 90–day period. § 547(f). In addition, under the 1994 amendments to the Code, an indirect preference made more than 90 days before bankruptcy, such as that in our example, cannot be *recovered* from a non-insider initial transferee. § 550(c). As of 2005, an insider preference made beyond the 90–day period cannot even be avoided as to the non-insider. § 547(i). In our example, then, the transfer to Creditor X six months before bankruptcy could be avoided as an indirect preference to the insider, Paula President, and recovery could be had from Paula, but not from Creditor X.

State fraudulent conveyance law goes beyond the Bankruptcy Code in permitting the avoidance of a preference to an insider as a fraudulent conveyance in certain circumstances (and not limited to the narrow employment contract situation). Not only is this point extremely important outside of bankruptcy, where preferences are normally unassailable, it also has relevance in bankruptcy cases as well. A bankruptcy trustee is able to invoke state fraudulent conveyance laws under § 544(b)(1), assuming

---

[497] One of the most thoughtful articles exploring the normative justifications for avoiding preferences to insiders as fraudulent transfers is John C. McCoid, II, Corporate Preferences to Insiders, 43 S.C. L. Rev. 805 (1992). Professor McCoid ultimately concludes that an insider preference should not be treated as a fraudulent conveyance any more than any other preference. Id. at 813–19. Instead, he suggests attacking such transfers as a breach of the insider's fiduciary duty to the corporation itself. Id. at 830–31. For another view, see Andrew J. Nussbaum, Comment, Insider Preferences and the Problem of Self–Dealing Under the Bankruptcy Code, 57 U. Chi. L. Rev. 603 (1990).

[498] Prefatory Note to the UFTA, See http://www.uniformlaws.org/shared/docs/fraudulent%20transfer/ufta_final_84.pdf (2013).

[499] See § 6.15.

that a creditor exists who would have the power under the state law to avoid the transfer.[500]

Given the direct power in § 547 to avoid insider preferences made up to a year before bankruptcy, it might seem that the power to avoid the transfer as a fraudulent transfer under § 544(b)(1) is unnecessary overkill. The potential to set aside an insider preference under § 544(b)(1) is, however, much more than a matter of academic interest. To begin with, the trustee might have a greater chance of avoiding the transfer, because the safe harbors of § 547(c) will not be available in the § 544(b)(1) fraudulent transfer action.[501] Having said that, avoidance under § 544(b)(1) will require proof of elements not required under § 547(b). Still, there may be transactions that are voidable under § 544(b)(1) but not under § 547. Furthermore, the trustee's ability to recover from the non-insider initial transferee (Creditor X) will not be restricted by § 550(c), which provides a safe harbor for non-insiders when an indirect preference to an insider is avoided *under* § 547. That safe harbor by its terms does not apply if the avoidance is under § 544(b)(1) as a fraudulent conveyance. Nor would the avoidance bar of § 547(i) regarding non-insiders avail the non-insider under § 544(b)(1).

Turning, then, to the state fraudulent conveyance law with regard to insider preferences, both the UFTA and UFCA provide means for upsetting such a transfer. The route taken by the UFTA is more direct: it creates a fraudulent transfer cause of action specifically for insider preferences. UFTA § 5(b). Such a transfer is fraudulent as to creditors whose claims arose before the transfer was made, § 5(b), and may be attacked for one year after the transfer was made. § 9(c). The elements of that action are that:

- the transfer was made to an insider;

- for an antecedent debt;

- the debtor was insolvent at the time of the transfer; and

- the insider had reasonable cause to believe that the debtor was insolvent.

In applying these elements, the UFTA's definitions must be consulted. "Insider" is defined broadly in UFTA § 1(7), and "insolvency" is dealt with in UFTA § 2.[502] "Debt" is defined broadly, in keeping with the similar expansive definition in the Bankruptcy Code. UFTA §§ 1(5), 1(3); see Bankruptcy Code § 101(5). In our hypothetical, Paula President would qualify as an insider, the debtor was insolvent at the time of the transfer, and the contingent debt of Paula would count as a debt. Furthermore, that debt arose at the time the guarantee was made, and thus was antecedent to the time of

---

[500] See § 6.5.

[501] This assertion must be qualified in an action predicated on the UFTA. As discussed in the text below, the UFTA provides safe harbors from the avoidance of insider preferences on several grounds analogous to safe harbors of § 547(c), including the ordinary course of business exception, see § 6.18, § 547(c)(2), and the subsequent advance for new value exception, see § 6.20, § 547(c)(4). See also UFTA § 8(f).

[502] See § 6.36.

the transfer. Recall also that a transfer is not "made" until it is perfected against third parties.[503] UFTA § 6.

A preference to an insider by an insolvent debtor is not always deemed a fraudulent transfer, however; the insider also must have had "reasonable cause to believe that the debtor was insolvent" at the time of the transfer. This requirement is taken directly from the bankruptcy preference law under the prior Bankruptcy Act, a requirement that initially was carried over under the 1978 Bankruptcy Code for insider preferences. However, the Bankruptcy Code dropped the "reasonable cause to believe" test in 1984. The extensive pre-1984 bankruptcy case law on the question of when an insider has such "reasonable cause" should remain relevant in the application of UFTA § 5(b) today. Note that the party challenging the transfer does not need to prove the actual state of mind of the insider, but only what that insider had "*reasonable cause*" to know. In cases where a debtor is plainly insolvent, as in our hypothetical, courts will be leery of the insider's protestations that it did not know or even have reason to know of the debtor's embarrassed circumstances.

The UFTA does provide three safe harbors that immunize a transfer from avoidance under § 5(b). A transfer is not voidable as an insider preference:

- to the extent the insider gave new value to or for the benefit of the debtor after the transfer was made, unless the new value was secured by a valid lien. UFTA § 8(f)(1). This safe harbor is drawn from § 547(c)(4) of the Bankruptcy Code.[504]

- if the transfer was made in the ordinary course of business or financial affairs of the debtor and the insider. UFTA § 8(f)(2). This safe harbor is drawn from § 547(c)(2) of the Bankruptcy Code.[505]

- if made pursuant to a good faith effort to rehabilitate the debtor and the transfer secured present value given for that purpose as well as an antecedent debt of the debtor. UFTA § 8(f)(3).

The UFCA takes a less direct route to permit the avoidance of a preference to an insider as a constructively fraudulent conveyance. One element of most types of constructive fraud under the UFCA is that the debtor did not receive "fair consideration" in exchange for the transfer. For example, a transfer for less than fair consideration by an insolvent debtor is voidable. UFCA § 4. "Fair consideration," in turn, is defined to include two facets, *both* of which must be present: first, that the value given to the debtor was a "*fair equivalent*" to that conveyed by the debtor; and second, that the transfer was "*in good faith*." UFCA § 3(a).

The "good faith" prong is the hook that permits the avoidance of a preference to an insider. Even if the debtor receives a "fair equivalent," "fair consideration" still will be found lacking if the transferee did not act "in good faith." In the case of an insider preference, courts have held that it is not good faith for an insider to cause the debtor

---

[503] See § 6.31.

[504] See § 6.20.

[505] See § 6.18.

to pay the debt owed to the insider in preference to other debts.[506] But, as one noted commentator has observed, "why the payment of a legitimate obligation is not a good faith transaction is not immediately apparent.... To say that it involves taking unconscionable advantage of other creditors begs the question."[507] Although such criticisms undoubtedly help explain why the UFTA and Bankruptcy Code dropped the "good faith" test, that test remains viable in and out of bankruptcy in jurisdictions with the UFCA in force—most prominently, by far, including the state of New York.[508] And, in the substantial majority of states with the UFTA in effect, the subjective "good faith" test of the UFCA has simply been replaced with the objective "reasonable cause to believe the debtor was insolvent" test. One suspects that most cases would come out the same way under either test: an insider who does not even have reasonable cause to believe the debtor was insolvent might not be found to have acted in bad faith in taking a preference, and vice versa.

§ 6.39　Leveraged Buyouts

One of the most notable and controversial developments in fraudulent conveyance law in the late twentieth century was the extension of that law to invalidate transfers and obligations undertaken as part of a *leveraged buyout* ("LBO"). The seminal case that signaled the entry of fraudulent conveyance law into the LBO domain was reported in a triad of decisions in 1983 and 1984 by a Pennsylvania district court, setting aside a lender's mortgages as fraudulent conveyances in *United States v. Gleneagles Investment Co.*[509] These decisions were largely affirmed by the Third Circuit in *United States v. Tabor Court Realty Corp.*[510] in 1986. The *Gleneagles/Tabor Court* case and others like it spawned a flood of commentary in the literature.[511] With some cooling of the LBO craze in the 1990s, the fraudulent conveyance issue likewise cooled; but the basic problem remains.

A leveraged buyout can take a myriad of different forms. The precise form, however, probably does not make a significant legal difference, as courts have been diligent in LBO cases to collapse complex transactions in order to ensure that substance prevails over form. The essence of a leveraged buyout is that investors "buy out" existing stockholders of a target company with mostly borrowed money (the "leverage"), and use the target's own assets to secure the debt. The target will guarantee or endorse the debt to the lenders. The target, then, takes on a substantial secured debt, and gets no direct benefit in return. All that the target company gets is

---

[506]　See, e.g, Bullard v. Aluminum Co. of Am., 468 F.2d 11 (7th Cir. 1972).

[507]　McCoid, supra note 497, at 817.

[508]　New York has adopted a per se rule: "Transfers to a controlling shareholder, officer or director of an insolvent corporation are deemed to be lacking in good faith and are presumptively fraudulent." CIT Group/Commercial Servs., Inc. v. 160–09 Jamaica Ave. Ltd. P'ship, 808 N.Y.S.2d 187, 190 (N.Y. 2006).

[509]　565 F. Supp. 556 (M.D. Pa. 1983); 571 F. Supp. 935 (M.D. Pa. 1983); 584 F. Supp. 671 (M.D. Pa. 1984).

[510]　803 F.2d 1288 (3d Cir. 1986), cert. denied, 483 U.S. 1005 (1987).

[511]　A sampling of the commentary includes Douglas G. Baird & Thomas H. Jackson, Fraudulent Conveyance Law and Its Proper Domain, 38 Vand. L. Rev. 829, 850–54 (1985); David G. Carlson, Leveraged Buyouts in Bankruptcy, 20 Ga. L. Rev. 73 (1985); Emily L. Sherwin, Creditors' Rights Against Participants in a Leveraged Buyout, 72 Minn. L. Rev. 449 (1988); Kathryn V. Smyser, Going Private and Going Under: Leveraged Buyouts and the Fraudulent Conveyance Problem, 63 Ind. L.J. 781 (1988); James F. Queenan, Jr., The Collapsed Leveraged Buyout and the Trustee in Bankruptcy, 11 Cardozo L. Rev. 1 (1989).

new management. The direct beneficiaries of the LBO are the old stockholders, who are cashed out (usually at a handsome price), and the new owners, who are enabled to purchase a company with other people's money.

An LBO converts equity into debt. This conversion of equity into debt often can be financially burdensome for the target company. The debt has to be paid, of course. Interest payments on an LBO debt can be very hard for a company to service out of ongoing operations. If the drain becomes too great, and the company goes bankrupt, the brunt of the loss falls on the unsecured creditors of the target company. The unencumbered assets of the company that would have been available to pay unsecured creditors prior to the LBO are pledged to repay the secured debt undertaken in the LBO, and thus are no longer available to unsecured creditors when the company fails.

Consider an example. Mary Mover and Sam Shaker are high-ranking executives of Target Corp., a sleepy medical products firm. Target Corp. has no secured debt, $20 million in unsecured debt, and assets estimated to be worth $30 million, and thus an estimated equity of $10 million. Mover and Shaker decide to buy out Target and take it private, believing that the company would make huge profits if it refocused its business (under their tutelage, of course) on the biotechnology business. Mover and Shaker agree to buy all of the existing stock for $10 million, putting up $1 million of their own money and borrowing $9 million from Lender. They also agree to give Lender a security interest in all of Target's assets, and to have Target guarantee payment of the $9 million debt to lender. The old stockholders then are cashed out for $10 million, and Mover and Shaker take control of Target. After the LBO, Target has total debt of $29 million ($20 million unsecured plus $9 million secured) and assets estimated to be worth $30 million, leaving a razor-thin equity of at most $1 million. Target ultimately fails to compete successfully in the biotechnology business, and goes bankrupt. The bankruptcy trustee challenges the LBO as a fraudulent transfer.

The LBO can be attacked on the basis of actual fraud or constructive fraud, as was demonstrated by the *Gleneagles/Tabor Court* case.[512] *Actual fraud* requires proof an intent to "hinder, delay or defraud" creditors. The argument is that the unsecured creditors of Target were hindered by the virtual elimination of the debtor's equity and the creation of senior secured debt in its place. The counter is that Mover and Shaker reasonably believed that after the LBO they would be able to convert Target into a stunningly successful company, and that Lender shared their belief. If things had worked out as Lender and Mover and Shaker had expected, creditors would not have been hindered in the slightest. A court will be more likely to find actual fraud if it finds that, at the time the transaction took place, the acquirer and lender knew or should have known that they were imposing an unreasonable risk on the debtor's unsecured creditors.[513]

Even if the court agrees that actual fraudulent intent was not present, the LBO can be challenged on the basis of *constructive fraud*. The first component of constructive fraud is that the debtor did not receive *"reasonably equivalent value"* (or

---

[512] See 565 F. Supp. 556 (M.D. Pa. 1983), aff'd, 803 F.2d 1288 (3d Cir. 1986).

[513] See Barry L. Zaretsky, Fraudulent Transfer Law as the Arbiter of Unreasonable Risk, 46 S.C.L. Rev. 1165 (1995).

"fair consideration") in exchange for the transfers.[514] The courts have readily found this element to be satisfied in LBO transactions. Indeed, in some cases the issue is not even contested. In the example, Target transfers a security interest in all of its assets to Lender to secure a $9 million debt, yet ultimately (once the transaction is collapsed) receives none of that consideration in return. The only direct beneficiaries are the old shareholders and the new owners.

Those defending the LBO will argue that Target received *indirect* benefits, in the form of brilliant new management by Mover and Shaker. In the corporate world, there is no doubt that the identity of the managers can be extremely valuable. Corporate America is replete with examples where new management came in and completely revitalized the company, creating massive amounts of wealth, to the benefit of stockholders, employees, and creditors. If Mover and Shaker's biotechnology gamble had paid off, no one would have complained. The problem, of course, is that the fraudulent conveyance issue only arises in cases where the gamble has *not* paid off. It is extremely difficult to persuade a court of the indirect "value added" from new management when the company has failed under the supervision of those new managers. However, the proper time to measure the "value" received by the debtor is *at the time of the LBO*, when the transfers all took place, based on reasonable projections from information then available. In theory, value could be found as of that time, even though hindsight later proved that the value was ephemeral. One could analogize this situation to placing a bet on a horse. Before the race is run, that bet has value. If the horse wins the race, the bet will pay off at a premium. But if the horse loses, all is lost. The ultimate theoretical question in LBO cases is whether it is fair to the unsecured creditors of the Target to bet the company on the new management. If a beaten-down plow horse is entered in the Kentucky Derby, even viewed *ex ante* its odds of winning are bad indeed. If the new management looks more like the plow horse than Secretariat, creditors may rightly complain.

Even if reasonably equivalent value is not found, the LBO transaction will not necessarily be voidable as constructively fraudulent. A financially sound company is free to take gambles without receiving fair value. Its creditors will not be harmed if the gamble fails, because the debtor still will have plenty of money to pay everyone in full. Creditors are harmed, however, if a financially shaky debtor takes an ill-advised gamble; if the gamble does not pay off, the creditors may not get paid. The second element of constructive fraud identifies which debtors are deemed to be too weak financially to engage in transactions in which the debtor does not receive reasonably equivalent value in exchange. Thus, along with a lack of reasonably equivalent value, any one of the following elements must be proven to establish that an LBO was constructively fraudulent:

- the debtor target was *insolvent* on the date of the LBO, or *became insolvent* as a result of the LBO, Bankruptcy Code § 548(a)(1)(B)(ii)(I); UFTA § 5(a); UFCA § 4;

---

[514] See § 6.34.

- the debtor was engaged in or about to engage in a business or transaction for which the property remaining with the debtor was an *unreasonably small capital*, Bankruptcy Code § 548(a)(1)(B)(ii)(II); UFTA § 4(a)(2)(i); UFCA § 5; or

- the debtor intended to incur or believed it would *incur debts that would be beyond its ability to pay* as the debts matured, Bankruptcy Code § 548(a)(1)(B)(ii)(III); UFTA § 4(a)(2)(ii); UFCA § 6.

In our hypothetical, Lender and Mover and Shaker did not believe that the debtor Target would be rendered insolvent by the LBO. Their calculations showed equity of $1 million remaining after the LBO ($30 million in assets, $29 million in debt). It has become common to insist on a solvency opinion prior to entering into an LBO. Of course, what the parties may have believed to be true will not be binding on a court that later reviews the transaction pursuant to a fraudulent conveyance challenge. The court may value the assets at a lower amount; in the example, if the court values the assets at anything less than $29 million (not a great reach from $30 million), the debtor would be insolvent, and constructive fraud would be established. Where the debtor subsequently fails, and its assets bring a relatively low price in an ensuing liquidation, an LBO defendant may have trouble convincing the court to apply a higher "going concern" valuation standard to the assets at the time of the LBO.

As a practical matter, if the acquirer puts down a fairly substantial part of the purchase price, the court is very unlikely to collapse the transaction and avoid the LBO as a fraudulent transfer. So, for example, in one case the acquirer invested 47% of its own money, and the court refused to find fraud.[515] In that decision, the court contrasted the situation in *Tabor Court Realty*, where the acquirer invested only 8% of its own money.[516]

Even if the court does not find that the debtor was rendered insolvent by the LBO, the transaction still can be set aside if the debtor was about to engage in a business with an "unreasonably small capital."[517] The UFTA uses a slightly different phrase, permitting avoidance if "the remaining assets of the debtor were unreasonably small in relation to the business or transaction." UFTA § 4(a)(2)(ii). Neither the Bankruptcy Code nor either of the uniform acts explain or define when the remaining assets or capital are "unreasonably small." The courts have concluded that the term contemplates a financial condition just short of insolvency, where the debtor has an inability to generate sufficient profits to sustain ongoing operations.[518] In making this inquiry, the cases look to the reasonableness of the financial projections made at the time of the LBO, the availability of credit to the debtor, prior and subsequent operating performance, comparative capital structures in the industry, and the like. The basic

---

[515] Official Comm. of Unsecured Creditors of Grand Eagle Cos., Inc. v. ASEA Brown Boverie, Inc., 313 B.R. 219 (N.D. Ohio 2004).

[516] Id. at 231.

[517] For a helpful discussion of this provision, see Bruce A. Markell, Toward True and Plain Dealing: A Theory of Fraudulent Transfers Involving Unreasonably Small Capital, 21 Ind. L. Rev. 469 (1988).

[518] See, e.g., Boyer v. Crown Stock Distrib., Inc., 587 F.3d 787 (7th Cir. 2009); Moody v. Sec. Pac. Bus. Credit, Inc., 971 F.2d 1056 (3d Cir. 1992).

issue is whether the court believes that it was reasonably foreseeable at the time of the transaction that the debtor would fail.

The initial remedial focus in the LBO cases was on attacking the transfer of the security interests *to the Lender*. Even if the LBO is found to be a fraudulent transfer, the Lender will not be vulnerable if it took its security interest in *good faith* and for *value given to the debtor*.[519] Bankruptcy Code § 548(c); UFTA § 8(a); UFCA § 9(1). An initial and significant problem for the Lender is whether the value was given "to the debtor," as expressly required by the Bankruptcy Code. As explained above, part of the reason an LBO is suspect in the first place is because the debtor does not retain the value; that value "passes through" the debtor to the old stockholders. Even if the Lender can surmount the value-to-the-debtor hurdle, it will have to establish that it acted in good faith. Where a financial institution is considering loaning millions of dollars in an LBO, courts believe that a reasonable lender would familiarize itself with the details of the debtor target's financial situation before making the loan. If that inquiry should reveal to the lender that the debtor is on shaky ground financially, good faith may be found lacking.

Lenders are not the only parties to an LBO that may be challenged. The *selling stockholders* also have been named as defendants in LBO fraudulent transfer suits. The allegation is that the debtor did not receive reasonably equivalent value in exchange for the payments to the shareholders. The party seeking to avoid the transaction wants to recover the money paid to the old stockholders.[520] These payments are analogous to redemptions of stock, which are illegal under corporate law when the corporation is insolvent.

The case law has been quite confused in this area.[521] It is fair to say that courts generally are more hesitant to impose liability on the old stockholders than on the lender. A further distinction has been made by the courts between "innocent" shareholders, who presumably are unaware of the source of the funds, and controlling insider shareholders, who know exactly what is going on.[522] This distinction has been criticized, however, because if the transferees (the selling shareholders) have not given value, there is no statutory basis in the fraudulent transfer laws for insulating them from liability. As the Seventh Circuit observed in *Boyer,* "[t]he reluctance of the courts in the decisions we cited is not easy to square with the language of the Uniform Fraudulent Transfer Act."[523]

---

[519] See § 6.43.

[520] See, e.g., *Boyer,* supra note 518, 587 F.3d 787.

[521] For discussion of the issue, see Michael L. Cook et. al., The Judicially Created "Innocent Shareholder" Defense to Constructive Fraudulent Transfer Liability in Failed Leveraged Buyouts, 43 S.C. L. Rev. 777 (1992); Gerald K. Smith & Frank R. Kennedy, Fraudulent Transfers and Obligations: Issues of Current Interest, 43 S.C. L. Rev. 709, 751–67 (1992).

[522] See, e.g., Kupetz v. Wolf, 845 F.2d 842 (9th Cir. 1988); Wieboldt Stores, Inc. v. Schottenstein, 94 B.R. 488 (N.D. Ill. 1988).

[523] 587 F.3d at 792.

In LBO cases involving publicly owned corporations, and possibly even privately held companies,[524] selling shareholders may be immunized from a constructive fraud challenge by Bankruptcy Code § 546(e). Actual fraud is expressly excepted from the § 546(e) safe harbor, however. That section prevents a trustee from avoiding a "settlement payment" that is "made by or to a . . . stockbroker, financial institution, financial participant, or securities clearing agency." "Settlement payment" is defined broadly in § 741(8). The courts have taken different views as to whether § 546(e) should apply to a failed LBO, but the majority view now appears to tilt in favor of applying the safe harbor to selling shareholders as well as to stockbrokers.[525] The most debate comes in those cases involving "purely private securities transactions that do not involve a financial intermediary."[526]

§ 6.40   Corporate Group Transactions

Much of the business in America today is done through corporate "groups" involving multiple interrelated corporations. While corporate separateness is usually carefully observed as a matter of formalities, the corporate group often functions in practice as an integrated unit. In some circumstances this functional integration can trigger fraudulent conveyance concerns. Property may be transferred or obligations may be incurred by one member of the group in order to help the group as a whole, but without that member receiving a direct beneficial value in return.

The fraudulent conveyance problem in corporate group transactions has been most pronounced in the context of *intercorporate guaranties*.[527] A lender may be unwilling to make a substantial loan to one member of the corporate group based solely on the credit worthiness of that entity, but may insist on obtaining a guaranty or collateral, or both, from one or more affiliated members of the overall enterprise. In an intercorporate guaranty, then, one corporation guarantees the debt of another

---

[524] See, e.g., Contemporary Indus. Corp. v. Frost, 564 F.3d 981 (8th Cir. 2009); QSI Holdings, Inc. v. Alford, 571 F.3d 545 (6th Cir. 2009). Contra Kapila v. Espirito Santo Bank, 374 B.R. 333, 345–46 (Bankr. S.D. Fla.2007) (direct purchase of stock from shareholders in LBO); Norstan Apparel Shops, Inc. v. Lattman, 367 B.R. 68, 77 (Bankr. E.D.N.Y. 2007) (same); Zahn v. Yucaipa Capital Fund, 218 B.R. 656, 676 (D.R.I. 1998); Jewel Recovery L.P. v. Gordon, 196 B.R. 348, 353 (N.D. Tex. 1996) (same); Wieboldt Stores, Inc. v. Schottenstein, 131 B.R. 655, 664–65 (N.D. Ill. 1991) (same) (cases cited in *In re Enron Creditors Recovery Corp.*, 422 B.R. 423, 432 (S.D.N.Y. 2009)).

[525] The leading early cases were a pair of Tenth Circuit decisions in the Kaiser Steel bankruptcy. Kaiser Steel Corp. v. Charles Schwab & Co., 913 F.2d 846 (10th Cir. 1990) (section 546(e) applies to stockholder who is stockbroker); Kaiser Steel Corp. v. Pearl Brewing Co., 952 F.2d 1230 (10th Cir. 1991), cert. denied, 505 U.S. 1213 (1992) (section 546(e) applies to stockholder who is represented by a stockbroker). Several circuit courts have followed *Kaiser Steel*. See, e.g., *Contemporary Industries*, supra note 524, 564 F.3d 981; *QSI Holdings*, supra note 524, 571 F.3d 545; In re Resorts Int'l, Inc., 181 F.3d 505 (3d Cir. 1999); but see Munford v. Valuation Research Corp. (In re Munford, Inc.), 98 F.3d 604 (11th Cir. 1996) (section 546(e) does not apply to selling stockholders); *Wieboldt Stores*, supra note 16, 131 B.R. 655 (N.D. Ill. 1991) (same). Some commentators have advocated the position adopted in *Munford* and *Wieboldt Stores*, but they appear to be fighting a losing battle. See, e.g., Neil M. Garfinkel, Comment, No Way Out: Section 546(e) is No Escape for the Public Shareholder of a Failed LBO, 1991 Colum. Bus. L. Rev. 51.

[526] In re Enron Creditors Recovery Corp., 422 B.R. 423, 432 (S.D.N.Y. 2009).

[527] Much has been written about this issue. See, e.g., Peter A. Alces, Generic Fraud and the Uniform Fraudulent Transfer Act, 9 Cardozo L. Rev. 743 (1987); Phillip I. Blumberg, Intragroup (Upstream, Cross–Stream, and Downstream) Guaranties Under the Uniform Fraudulent Transfer Act, 9 Cardozo L. Rev. 685 (1987); William H. Coquillette, Guaranty of and Security for the Debt of a Parent Corporation by a Subsidiary Corporation, 30 Case W. Res. L. Rev. 433 (1980); Robert J. Rosenberg, Intragroup Guaranties and the Law of Fraudulent Conveyances: Lender Beware, 125 U. Pa. L. Rev. 235 (1976).

corporation in the group, and also may grant security to the lender to secure that debt. This arrangement can be set up in different ways. If a parent guarantees the debt of a subsidiary, it is called a "downstream" guaranty; if a subsidiary guarantees the debt of the parent, it is an "upstream" guaranty; and if one affiliate guarantees the debt of another affiliate, it is known as a "cross-stream" guaranty.

The problem is simple (although the solution is not): the guarantor has incurred a contingent obligation to the lender (the guaranteed debt), but has not directly received any tangible value in exchange, since the loan was made to the other corporation as primary obligor. The debt side of the guarantor's balance sheet has gone up, without a corresponding increase on the asset side. Thus, it is doubtful whether the debtor received "reasonably equivalent value" in exchange for incurring the guaranty obligation. If the guarantor is insolvent at the time the guaranty is made, or is rendered insolvent by the guaranty, or is left with unreasonably small capital, a fraudulent conveyance attack seeking to set aside the guaranty to the lender might succeed. The leading case establishing that an intercorporate guaranty potentially is vulnerable as a fraudulent conveyance is the Second Circuit's decision in *Rubin v. Manufacturers Hanover Trust Co.*[528]

But the mere fact that the guarantor does not receive the value from the transaction directly does not necessarily mean that the guarantor has not received any value at all. What makes the application of the fraudulent conveyance laws to intercorporate guaranties so tricky is that the guarantor may have received *indirect* economic benefits from the loan to the affiliated corporation. The entire corporate group, including the guarantor, may prosper from the loan. Indeed, the guaranty probably would not have been made if the guarantor did not believe as much. But how much benefit? To say that the guarantor may have received "value" does not mean that the value received was "reasonably equivalent" to the obligation incurred. The only situation that should be relatively simple is the downstream guaranty (parent guarantees debt of subsidiary), because the parent will benefit directly from the enhanced value of the subsidiary.

The real problem, then is to make the mathematical comparison between the value given and received. Often neither is readily measurable. On the value-received side of the ledger, the court must try to compute the amount of the indirect economic benefit to the debtor-guarantor. On the other side, the amount of liability incurred must be measured. In the case of a guaranty, that liability is less than the face amount of the principal debt, unless there is a 100% chance that the primary obligor will default instantly. If not, the court must weigh the probability that the guarantor will be called upon to pay the debt, and as of what point in time.

This problem implicates another important issue in the intercorporate guaranty cases, which is determining the point in time at which the debtor's exposure should be measured. The *Rubin* case appears to support valuing the guarantor's debt only when money is actually advanced to the primary obligor. The UFTA rejects this position,

---

[528]   661 F.2d 979 (2d Cir. 1981). Although this case was decided under the prior Bankruptcy Act, its analysis should remain persuasive under the similar provisions of the Code and the state fraudulent conveyance laws.

though, and adopts the view that the obligation on the guaranty is incurred when the written guaranty is delivered to the obligee. UFTA § 6(5). Picking this earlier time will invariably be beneficial to the fraudulent conveyance defendant, because the debtor is more likely to have been solvent at an earlier time, the risk of default by the primary obligor is probably lower at that time, and also because the statute of limitations is more likely to have run when bankruptcy ensues.

The Eleventh Circuit recently grappled with many of these issues in the case of *In re TOUSA, Inc.*[529] Just before the housing bubble burst, TOUSA, Inc., was the thirteenth largest homebuilding enterprise in the country,[530] and had several subsidiaries that guaranteed a revolving line of credit, as well as over $1 billion of public bonds issued by TOUSA. Furthermore, the bond debt and loan agreements provided that in the event of bankrupt cy or a judgment against TOUSA for more than $10 million, all outstanding debt would be immediately due. As the housing market began to crumble, TOUSA defaulted on several loan obligations and the Transeastern Lenders initiated a lawsuit against TOUSA alleging damages of over $2 billion.[531] The lawsuit was eventually settled for around $421 million plus expenses and fees, but financing this settlement required $500 million of new debt to be incurred in a loan from New Lenders, which was secured by liens on the assets of both TOUSA *and* its subsidiaries. Significantly, the case thus "involve[d] a transfer of liens by subsidiaries of TOUSA, Inc., to secure the payment of a debt owed only by their parent, TOUSA."[532]

Six months later TOUSA and the subsidiaries filed bankruptcy under chapter 11. The Unsecured Creditors' Committee sued to avoid the transfer of the liens by the subsidiaries to the New Lenders, and to compel the Transeastern Lenders to disgorge over $400 million of the funds paid to them in the settlement, and won.[533] The bankruptcy court determined that the subsidiaries did not receive "reasonably equivalent value," because they had not received an "enforceable entitlement to some tangible or intangible article."[534] Furthermore, receiving a chance to avoid bankruptcy did not provide value, because the court determined bankruptcy was "inevitable."[535] The Eleventh Circuit upheld the decision of the bankruptcy court, reversing the district court,[536] noting that transfers made in an effort to avoid bankruptcy are not always justified. As the court wryly noted, "[t]he opportunity to avoid bankruptcy does not free a company to pay any price or bear any burden."[537] However, the court declined to decide whether a chance to avoid of bankruptcy can *ever* constitute "reasonably

---

[529] 680 F.3d 1298 (11th Cir. 2012).

[530] Id. at 1301 ("As of 2006, TOUSA, Inc. was the thirteenth largest homebuilding enterprise in the country. . . . ").

[531] Id. at 1302 ("In December 2006, the Transeastern Lenders sued TOUSA, and in January 2007, the Transeastern Lenders alleged that TOUSA was responsible for damages of over $2 billion.").

[532] Id. at 1301.

[533] Id.

[534] In re TOUSA, Inc., 422 B.R. 783, 868 n.55 (Bankr. S.D. Fla. 2009).

[535] Id. at 869.

[536] 444 B.R. 613 (S.D. Fla. 2011).

[537] 680 F.3d at 1313.

equivalent value."[538] The court also held that the Transeastern Lenders were a party "for whose benefit" the liens were transferred under § 550(a).[539]

In the final analysis, the difficulty of computing "reasonably equivalent value" in indirect benefit situations could lead to one of three approaches. Two of these are "throw-up-your-hands" solutions, but on opposite extremes. The first is to ignore any alleged indirect benefits, and to insist that the debtor receive tangible, direct value. The second is to deem that any plausible indirect benefits to the debtor conclusively establish "reasonably equivalent value." There is some authority for each of these positions. The course commanded by courts such as the Second Circuit in *Rubin* is the difficult middle road: while indirect benefits may be counted as value for fraudulent conveyance purposes, a comparison must be made between the value received and the debt incurred. However, mathematical precision is not required, but only a rough equivalence—but that rough equivalence cuts both ways. In *TOUSA*, for example, the Eleventh Circuit ultimately decided that *even if* the intangible value of possibly avoiding bankruptcy for the corporate group did constitute a legally cognizable value, on the facts it should defer to the bankruptcy court's finding that there was just no way that intangible value was "reasonably equivalent"—indeed, was at best "nowhere close"—to the obligations incurred.[540] Perhaps only if the apparent value received by the debtor is disproportionately small as compared to the obligation incurred will the court find a lack of reasonably equivalent value, as in *TOUSA*. If coupled with proof of the debtor's insolvency (or, alternatively, unreasonably small capital, or incurring debts beyond the debtor's ability to pay), the transaction will then be held to be constructively fraudulent.

§ 6.41 Mortgage Foreclosure Sales: Of *BFP*

One of the most controversial questions in commercial law from 1980 until 1994 was whether a mortgage foreclosure sale could be set aside as a constructively fraudulent conveyance. This issue burst upon the legal scene with the 1980 decision of the Fifth Circuit in *Durrett v. Washington National Insurance Co.*[541] that a mortgage foreclosure sale could be set aside as a fraudulent conveyance, if the debtor was insolvent and the sale price was too far below the property's fair market value. After fourteen years of furious debate in the courts and in the academic journals,[542] the

---

[538] Id. at 1311 ("We decline to decide whether the possible avoidance of bankruptcy can confer 'value' because the bankruptcy court found that, even if all the purported benefits of the transaction were legally cognizable, they did not confer reasonably equivalent value.").

[539] Id. at 1313–15. See also § 6.1.

[540] 680 F.3d at 1311–12.

[541] 621 F.2d 201 (5th Cir. 1980).

[542] For a sampling of the numerous articles participating in the debate, see Douglas G. Baird & Thomas H. Jackson, Fraudulent Conveyance Law and Its Proper Domain, 38 Vand. L. Rev. 829 (1985); Cynthia L. DeReamer, Upsetting the Law of Transfer: Mortgage Foreclosures as Fraudulent Conveyances Under the Bankruptcy Code, 63 Am. Bankr. L.J. 321 (1989); Scott B. Ehrlich, Avoidance of Foreclosure Sales as Fraudulent Conveyances: Accommodating State and Federal Objectives, 71 Va. L. Rev. 933 (1985); William H. Henning, An Analysis of *Durrett* and Its Impact on Real and Personal Property Foreclosures: Some Proposed Modifications, 62 N.C. L. Rev. 257 (1985); Frank R. Kennedy, Involuntary Fraudulent Transfers, 9 Cardozo L. Rev. 531 (1987); Barry L. Zaretsky, Fraudulent Transfer Law as the Arbiter of Unreasonable Risk, 46 S.C. L. Rev. 1165 (1995).

Supreme Court settled the question in 1994 in *BFP v. Resolution Trust Corp.*[543] In *BFP*, the Court held that a mortgage foreclosure sale could *not* be set aside as a fraudulent conveyance under § 548(a)(2) if the sale was noncollusive and was regularly conducted in accordance with state law foreclosure procedures. According to the Court, the price received at such a sale was conclusively deemed to be for "reasonably equivalent value."

The facts in *BFP* illustrate the problem. In 1987, the debtor (BFP) borrowed money from Imperial Savings in order to buy a home, and in return granted Imperial a deed of trust as security. In 1989, after BFP defaulted, Imperial foreclosed, and the home was sold at a noncollusive, regularly conducted foreclosure sale for $433,000. Less than a year later, BFP filed chapter 11, and sought to set aside the foreclosure sale as a constructively fraudulent conveyance under § 548(a)(2) [since renumbered as § 548(a)(1)(B)]. The only issue was whether the sale had been for a "reasonably equivalent value." There was no dispute that all of the other elements required to establish constructive fraud had been proven: (1) a transfer of the debtor's property had occurred, (2) within a year of the bankruptcy filing (the reach-back period prior to 2005), (3) when the debtor was insolvent. BFP argued that the sale of the property for $433,000 was not for reasonably equivalent value, alleging that the fair market value of the property at the time of the sale was actually $725,000. BFP hoped to set aside the sale and capture the equity of almost $300,000 for the benefit of the estate.

The approach of the Fifth Circuit in *Durrett* had been to compare the foreclosure sale price with the appraised fair market value, and to determine if the former was close enough to the latter. In *Durrett* itself, the sale (for about $115,000) yielded about 57% of the fair market value (estimated at $200,000). That percentage, the Fifth Circuit concluded, was not close enough; it had not found any cases that allowed a sale for less than 70% of fair market value to stand. On the *Durrett* analysis, the sale in *BFP* probably would have been avoided, since the sale price was only about 60% of fair market value.

Durrett put the issue on the table squarely. One preliminary issue was whether the "transfer" in question was the foreclosure sale itself, or whether the operative transfer occurred back when the original mortgage or deed of trust was granted. If the earlier date applied, the transfer would probably fall outside of the one-year avoidance period in § 548 (extended to two years in 2005), and also would be for reasonably equivalent value, in the form of the initial loan. The Ninth Circuit had taken this view in the *Madrid* case.[544] A second issue was whether fraudulent conveyance law should be applied to set aside an *involuntary* transfer, or whether only transfers made voluntarily by the debtor should be subject to avoidance.

These preliminary issues were settled by the 1984 Amendments to the Bankruptcy Code in favor of possible avoidance. The definition of "transfer" was amended to include "foreclosure of the debtor's equity of redemption," § 101(54)(C), thus clarifying that the foreclosure sale itself was a potentially avoidable transfer. The Ninth Circuit's *Madrid*

---

[543] 511 U.S. 531 (1994).

[544] In re Madrid, 725 F.2d 1197 (9th Cir.), cert. denied, 469 U.S. 833 (1984).

approach thus was put out of court. Furthermore, the 1984 changes made clear that § 548 applied even if the debtor "involuntarily" made a transfer. What is also telling about the 1984 law is what Congress did *not* enact. At one time a draft bill included a provision that "reasonably equivalent value" would be conclusively established if an interest was acquired at a regularly conducted, noncollusive foreclosure sale. This proposal was taken from the Bankruptcy Appellate Panel decision in the *Madrid* case.[545] The UFTA, promulgated in 1984, does include such a safe harbor rule for noncollusive foreclosure sales. UFTA § 3(b). However, Congress in 1984 did not enact that provision in the Bankruptcy Code.

The courts continued to struggle with the problem after 1984. One approach that attracted some following was that of the Seventh Circuit in *In re Bundles*.[546] The *Bundles* court adopted a "totality of the circumstances" test. Under this view, the court would recognize a *rebuttable* presumption that the foreclosure sale price was for reasonably equivalent value. However, that presumption could be rebutted by consideration of all of the facts and circumstances—including a comparison of the sale price with the fair market value. If the shortfall was substantial, the likelihood that the presumption would be rebutted and the sale set aside would be increased.

The Supreme Court decided the *BFP* case against this background. In a 5–4 decision, the Court upheld the foreclosure sale against attack as a constructively fraudulent conveyance under § 548(a)(2). The Court held that the foreclosure sale price must *conclusively* be deemed to constitute "reasonably equivalent value," assuming that the sale was noncollusive and regularly conducted in compliance with state law.[547] In short, the Court read into § 548 the very provision that Congress had considered but had not enacted in 1984—the safe harbor found in § 3(b) of the UFTA for regularly conducted, noncollusive foreclosure sales.

Justice Scalia's opinion for the *BFP* Court rests on two primary supporting rationales. The first is that "fair market value" cannot serve as the benchmark for making the value comparison. By definition fair market value does not make sense in the forced sale context; the Court stated that "it is the very *antithesis* of forced-sale value."[548] Fair market value presupposes conditions that simply do not exist in a foreclosure sale. Property that must be sold at foreclosure "is simply *worth less*."[549] In essence, the Court felt that it would be pointless to compare the apple of fair market value with the orange of a foreclosure sale.

The Court did consider whether a value comparison could still be made by comparing the actual foreclosure sale price with a "reasonable" or "fair" projected forced sale price, rather than with full fair market value.[550] This alternative approach

---

[545] In re Madrid, 21 B.R. 424 (B.A.P. 9th Cir. 1982), aff'd on other grounds, 725 F.2d 1197 (9th Cir.), cert. denied, 469 U.S. 833 (1984).

[546] 856 F.2d 815 (7th Cir. 1988).

[547] BFP v. Resolution Trust Corp., 511 U.S. 531, 545 (1994).

[548] Id. at 537 (emphasis in original).

[549] Id. at 539 (emphasis in original). For a persuasive criticism of the Court's reasoning, see Robert M. Lawless & Stephen P. Ferris, Economics and the Rhetoric of Valuation, 5 J. Bankr. L. & Prac. 3 (1995).

[550] *BFP*, 511 U.S. at 540.

would recognize the reality that foreclosure sales rarely command full market value, and yet still permit a substantive comparison of values to be made. But the Court rejected this alternative as well, concluding that it would require the bankruptcy courts to make policy judgments that they have no authority to make. Having no appropriate benchmark to which to compare the foreclosure sale price, the Court concluded that the only option left was simply to embrace the foreclosure price itself as conclusive evidence of the property's value. The dissenting Justices, by contrast, argued that it was apparent to any "ordinary speaker of English" that the term "reasonably equivalent value" commanded that a comparison be made between the foreclosure sale price and the property's value, and that the sale should be set aside if former was substantially less than the latter.[551]

The second major linchpin of the *BFP* holding was *federalism*. The Court deferred to the state's strong interest in preserving and regulating the security of titles to real estate, absent a clearly expressed federal policy to the contrary.[552] Justice Scalia found it telling that foreclosure law and fraudulent conveyance law had "enjoyed over 400 years of peaceful coexistence," and he presumed that Congress would have used clearer language than "reasonably equivalent value" to upset that "ancient harmony."[553] The Court did not give any special consideration to the federal bankruptcy policy of maximizing the value of the estate available for creditors, a policy the dissent would have elevated over that of protecting the state's interest in real estate titles.[554]

The Court's holding effectively insulates mortgage foreclosure sales from fraudulent conveyance attack, as long as the foreclosing creditor jumps through the procedural hoops prescribed by the state foreclosure laws. The *BFP* decision is also likely to have an impact even beyond its facts. For example, in one post-*BFP* case, the Fifth Circuit relied on *BFP to* uphold a state tax foreclosure sale that yielded a price of $325, when the property soon was resold for over $39,000—over 120 times the sale price.[555] It is also possible that the rationale of *BFP* that fraudulent conveyance law should not readily be extended into previously uncharted waters could be extended to protect many types of complex corporate transactions from fraudulent conveyance attacks,[556] given that those types of transactions historically have not been challenged under the fraudulent conveyance laws.

§ 6.42   Safe Harbor for Charitable Contributions

One of the most controversial bankruptcy issues that exploded in the 1990s concerned the avoidance of contributions by debtors to their church as constructively fraudulent transfers.[557] The case that became the poster child for the debate was (and

---

[551] Id. at 552 (Souter, J., dissenting).

[552] Id. at 542–43 (Scalia, J., majority).

[553] Id. at 543.

[554] Id. at 562–65 (Souter, J., dissenting).

[555] In re T.F. Stone Co., 72 F.3d 466 (5th Cir. 1995).

[556] See §§ 6.39–6.40.

[557] For a thoughtful essay, see Daniel Keating, Bankruptcy, Tithing, and the Pocket Picking Paradigm of Free Exercise, 1996 U. Ill. L. Rev. 1041. Other useful contributions include Mary Jo Newborn Wiggins, A Statute of Disbelief? Clashing Ethical Imperatives in Fraudulent Transfer Law, 48 S.C.L. Rev. 771 (1997);

as comedian Dave Barry would say, I am not making this up), *Christians v. Crystal Evangelical Free Church (In re Young)*.[558] The stipulated facts of that case were:

> In the year immediately preceding the debtors' filing, the debtors made contributions to Crystal Evangelical Free Church. These contributions totaled $13,450 and were made while the debtors were insolvent. The debtors were active church members. As a supplement to their tithing, the debtors held numerous positions in the church and had served as officers of the day. The debtors regularly attended church services, actively participated in the church's programs and were welcomed on the premises at any time. These accommodations were available to the debtors whether they financially supported the church or not. At no time did the church require the debtors to pay any membership or attendance fee. However, the church does teach that people should offer regular contributions to the church. The debtors respected those teachings and made several purely voluntary contributions. However, the debtors did not receive money or tangible property in exchange for their contributions.[559]

The issue initially facing the *Young* court in 1992 was whether the debtors' contributions to the church in the year preceding bankruptcy could be avoided as fraudulent transfers, as transfers by a debtor who was insolvent and did not receive reasonably equivalent value in exchange. With insolvency stipulated, the only question was whether the debtors received "reasonably equivalent value in exchange" for their contributions. That question actually has two components—whether the debtors received "reasonably equivalent value" and whether that value was received "in exchange" for the contributions.[560] As discussed in earlier sections,[561] the answers to both parts favor avoidance, and the bankruptcy court so held,[562] a holding affirmed by the district court.[563] "Value," for fraudulent transfer purposes, requires that the debtor either receive "property" or satisfy a debt (§ 548(d)(2)(A))—in short, that objective, market-based, tangible economic benefit be demonstrated—and the receipt of intangible benefits associated with worship do not qualify.[564] Even if by some stretch "value" in the fraudulent transfer sense could be shown, the "in exchange" requirement could not, since the debtors would have been allowed to receive exactly the same benefits even if they had not contributed.[565] In short, there was no "pay to pray"

Todd J. Zywicki, Rewrite the Bankruptcy Laws, Not the Scriptures: Protecting a Bankruptcy Debtor's Right to Tithe, 1998 Wis. L. Rev. 1223.

[558] 148 B.R. 886 (Bankr. D. Minn. 1992), aff'd, 152 B.R. 969 (D. Minn. 1993), rev'd, 82 F.3d 1407 (8th Cir. 1996), vacated and remanded, 521 U.S. 1114 (1997), reinstated, 141 F.3d 854 (8th Cir.), cert. denied, 525 U.S. 811 (1998). The church was not being assailed by bands of "Christians," but was sued by the bankruptcy trustee, named, believe it or not, Julia Christians.

[559] 148 B.R. at 888.

[560] Id. at 890.

[561] See §§ 6.34–6.35.

[562] 148 B.R. at 897.

[563] 152 B.R. 969 (D. Minn. 1993).

[564] 148 B.R. at 890–95. A couple of reported cases have held otherwise, but the reasoning of those cases is suspect under traditional fraudulent transfer doctrine. See, e.g., In re Moses, 59 B.R. 815 (Bankr. N.D. Ga. 1986) (again, I cannot make up these case names).

[565] 148 B.R. at 895.

requirement. Thus, the holdings of the bankruptcy and district courts in *Young* were well within the mainstream of standard fraudulent transfer doctrine.

The plot thickened considerably in 1993, when Congress passed the Religious Freedom Restoration Act ("RFRA"),[566] one of the more amazing pieces of legislation in our long history. In RFRA, as it was known, Congress attempted to legislate to restore earlier Supreme Court case law on free exercise. Unhappy with the Court's 1990 decision in *Employment Division v. Smith*,[567] which made it very difficult to challenge successfully on First Amendment grounds facially neutral laws of general application that incidentally burdened religious exercise (such as, for example, fraudulent transfer laws!), Congress expressly stated its purpose in RFRA to restore the more demanding "compelling interest" test announced in *Shebert v. Verner*[568] and *Wisconsin v. Yoder*.[569] 42 U.S.C. § 2000bb(b)(1). Debtors whose religious donations were attacked as fraudulent transfers had a plausible claim that RFRA trumped the bankruptcy avoiding power.

By the time *Young* was appealed to the Eighth Circuit, RFRA had been enacted, and the issue shifted not only to whether the lower courts' fraudulent transfer holding was correct, but also whether RFRA precluded fraudulent transfer avoidance under § 548. In a remarkable development, on the day oral argument was scheduled in the Eight Circuit, President Clinton ordered the Justice Department to withdraw its *amicus* brief supporting the trustee's position in favor of avoidance.[570] The Eighth Circuit then held that, while absent RFRA the debtors' contributions to their church likely would be voidable fraudulent transfers, RFRA nevertheless dictated reversal, since to avoid the debtors' church donations impermissibly burdened their religious exercise rights.[571] The Supreme Court subsequently held that RFRA was unconstitutional as applied to the *states* in *City of Boerne v. Flores*.[572] In light of *Flores*, the Supreme Court vacated the Eighth Circuit's decision in *Young* and remanded for reconsideration.[573] Upon remand, the Eighth Circuit reinstated its earlier decision, concluding that RFRA was constitutional as applied to *federal* laws, including the Bankruptcy Code.[574] The Supreme Court then denied *certiorari*,[575] finally ending the epic case. The church got to keep the debtors' donations.

Smelling a political opportunity, though, and with the bit between its teeth, the Clinton Administration sought to codify a safe harbor from fraudulent transfer avoidance for charitable contributions in the bankruptcy law. The result was the

---

[566]　Pub. L. No. 103–141, 107 Stat. 1488 (1993) (codified at 42 U.S.C. § 2000bb).

[567]　494 U.S. 872 (1990).

[568]　374 U.S. 398 (1963).

[569]　406 U.S. 205 (1972).

[570]　N.Y. Times, Sept. 16, 1994, at B18; Wall St. J., Sept. 16, 1994, at B5.

[571]　82 F.3d 1407 (8th Cir. 1996).

[572]　521 U.S. 507(1997).

[573]　521 U.S. 1114 (1997).

[574]　141 F.3d 854 (8th Cir. 1998).

[575]　525 U.S. 811 (1998).

Religious Liberty and Charitable Donation Protection Act of 1998.[576] The 1998 law amended § 548 and § 544(b), specifically immunizing a qualifying "charitable contribution" (as defined in § 548(d)(3)) from attack as a constructively fraudulent transfer. §§ 548(a)(2), 544(b)(2). The defendant will have the burden of proving that the defense applies.[577] In fraudulent transfer actions under *state* law, creditors remain free to challenge charitable contributions by insolvent debtors.

In charitable contribution cases, the avoidance game now turns primarily on the application of the 1998 amendments. If the defendant does not have a successful defense under the 1998 law, then of course the defendant is still entitled to raise First Amendment defenses. In that respect, *Young* remains potentially relevant.

Several aspects of the 1998 law deserve attention. The first point to note is that the safe harbor applies only to challenges based on *constructive* fraud. The statute provides in § 548(a)(2) that qualifying charitable transfers are "not considered to be a transfers covered under paragraph (1)(B)" of § 548(a)(1)—which is the subsection for *constructive* fraud. The safe harbor has no applicability to a challenge based on *actual* fraud § 548(a)(1)*(A)*. An interesting question is how willing courts will be to infer actual fraudulent intent based on "badges of fraud" that mirror the constructive fraud elements of proof. So, for example, it would seem questionable for a court to infer actual fraud based on proof that an insolvent debtor made gratuitous transfers to his church—precisely the sort of activity immunized in its incarnation as constructive fraud. Having said that, certainly it seems that no *per se* bar should be imposed to prevent a court from finding actual fraud in such cases. One can imagine, for example, in a situation in which an insolvent debtor who has never given one red cent to charity suddenly gives 15% of his gross annual income (the standard ceiling amount protected under § 548(a)(2)(A)) to charity the day before he files bankruptcy, the court might well be tempted to infer actual fraudulent intent.

The safe harbor for charitable contributions applies to § 544(b) as well.[578] As amended, the avoiding power is found in § 544(b)(1), and the safe harbor in § 544(b)(2). The wording of subsection (b)(2) appears to reflect an intent to incorporate the same limitation to protect only *constructive* fraud challenges. The statute provides that subsection (b)(1) "shall not apply to a transfer of a charitable contribution . . . *that is not covered under section 548(a)(1)(B)*, by reason of section 548(a)(2)." Since § 548(a)(1)(B) is the constructive fraud avoidance section, it is highly likely that Congress meant to immunize only constructive fraud challenges under § 544(b) as well. Note, though, that this is not the only way the statute could be read. If the *same* transfer could potentially be challenged as *both* actually fraudulent and constructively fraudulent, then a literal reading of the statute would be that subsection (b)(1) would

---

[576]   Pub. L. No. 105–183, §§ 2, 3, 112 Stat. 517 (1998). For commentary, see Thomas M. Walsh, Note, *Religious Liberty and Charitable Donation Act of 1998: Putting the Fear of God Into Bankruptcy Creditors*, 7 Am. Bankr. Inst. L. Rev. 235 (1999); Lawrence A. Reicher, Comment, *Drafting Glitches in the Religious Liberty and Charitable Donation Protection Act of 1998: Amend § 548(a)(2) of the Bankruptcy Code*, 24 Emory Bankr. Dev. J. 159 (2008).

[577]   E.g., Geltzer v. The Universal Church, 2005 WL 6124844 at *4 (E.D.N.Y. Feb. 22, 2005), aff'd, 463 F.2d 218 (2d Cir. 2006), cert. denied, 549 U.S. 1113 (2007).

[578]   See § 6.5.

"not apply to *a transfer*" that is not covered under § 548(a)(1)(B), meaning that the singular "a transfer" would enjoy total protection from attack under § 544(b)(1), even as actually fraudulent.

Another question in applying the safe harbor of § 544(b)(2) arises out of the reference to § 548, which brings within the 544(b)(2) protection only transfers not covered under § 548(a)(1)(B) "by reason of section 548(a)(2)"—the charitable contribution safe harbor. Does that then mean that if a transfer is not covered under § 548(a)(1)(B) for any *other* reason—such as, for example, that it occurred more than two years before bankruptcy—then the safe harbor does not apply under § 544(b)? For example, what if under state law a transfer to charity could be attacked three years before bankruptcy as constructively fraudulent? Would the trustee then be free under § 544(b)(1) to seek avoidance? One suspects that the answer must be "surely not," given the clear Congressional intent to protect charitable contributions, but the statutory language is inelegant at best.

The safe harbor for charitable contributions is not unlimited. Protection is limited in three significant ways:

1.   character:

2.   recipient; and

3.   amount

First, only a "*charitable contribution*" is eligible for protection. That term is defined in the Bankruptcy Code. § 548(d)(3). That definition has three components:

*   the contribution must satisfy the test for "charitable contribution" in § 170(c) of the Internal Revenue Code;

*   the contribution must be made by a natural person, § 548(d)(3)(A); and

*   the contribution must be either a "financial instrument"[579] or cash, § 548(d)(3)(B).

Thus, a transfer by a corporate debtor will not qualify. Only human debtors can make qualifying contributions. Furthermore, a transfer of property that is not cash or sufficiently cash-like will not qualify. Shares of stock do qualify. "Hard" assets do not, though. So, for example, if a financially distressed debtor is thinking of donating his car to his church, the church should have him sell the car and contribute the cash proceeds instead.

The second limitation is that the contribution must be made to a proper recipient: a "*qualified religious or charitable entity or organization.*" § 548(d)(4). Notably, the recipient category is much broader than just religious organizations, which, as

---

[579] The Code incorporates the IRS definition in § 731(c)(2)(C):

The term "financial instrument" includes stocks and other equity interests, evidences of indebtedness, options, forward or futures contracts, notional principal contracts, and derivatives.

discussed above, is where all the fuss started, and where the First Amendment Free Exercise concerns arose. No one would say a person has a First Amendment right to give to United Way. Organizations that are qualified are determined by reference to the Internal Revenue Code. Included are all organizations designated in either § 170(c)(1) or § 170(c)(2) of the IRC. § 548(d)(4)(A), (B). This reference incorporates gifts to governmental entities, if for "exclusively public purposes." IRC § 170(c)(1). The reference to IRC § 170(c)(2) brings in contributions to a "corporation, trust, or community chest, fund, or foundation"—thus, *not* to an individual—if that recipient is "organized and operated exclusively for religious, charitable, scientific, literary, or educational purposes, or to foster national or international amateur sports competition." These categories are long-standing ones in tax law (if not always easily applied) and have been the subject of decades of interpretation, all of which will be relevant in the bankruptcy context as well.

The final limitation on the charitable contribution safe harbor is on the *amount* that can be immunized. The standard limitation is 15% of the "gross annual income" of the debtor, for the year in which the challenged contribution was made. § 548(a)(2)(A). The 15% part is easy enough to grasp. Less clear is exactly what Congress intended by "gross annual income." The term is not defined in the Bankruptcy Code, and, unlike various other aspects of the 1998 charitable contribution legislation, does not reference the Internal Revenue Code. Did Congress contemplate something akin to "adjusted gross income," a well-understood tax law term? If so, one wonders why Congress did not just say so. If not, we are left to speculate as to how the two terms differ.[580]

The safe harbor amount is not necessarily always limited to 15%. A greater amount will be protected if it can be shown that the amount given "was consistent with the practices of the debtor in making charitable contributions." § 548(a)(2)(B). Courts should not have too much difficulty applying this fact-based test, which requires a comparison of the amount and percentage of the challenged contribution with the debtor's previous charitable giving practices.[581]

Some interpretive questions lurk in § 548(a)(2). The first, and probably the most important, is whether the 15% cap applies to *each recipient*, or whether it limits what *the debtor* can give, free from constructive fraud attack, in a given year. For example, assume that Debtor gives 15% to Church and 15% to United Way. Are both Church and United Way safe under § 548(a)(2)? According to the Second Circuit in *Universal Church v. Geltzer*,[582] the answer is "no"—Congress intended an *overall* cap of 15%, not 15% for each entity. In so holding, the Second Circuit relied heavily on legislative history,[583] on the statutory construction rule in the Code that "the singular includes the plural," § 102(7), and on policy. If the 15% cap is applied to each entity to whom the

---

[580] See In re Lewis, 401 B.R. 431 (Bankr. C.D. Cal. 2009) (analyzing meaning of "gross annual income" when debtor operated a business).

[581] See, e.g., Jacobson v. Church of Manalapan, Inc. (In re Jackson), 249 B.R. 373 (Bankr. D.N.J. 2000).

[582] 463 F.2d 218 (2d Cir. 2006), cert. denied, 549 U.S. 1113 (2007). The other leading case, *In re Zohdi*, 234 B.R. 371, 376 & n. 8 (Bankr. M.D. La. 1999), took the opposite view in dictum, and opined that aggregation was not proper under § 548(a)(2).

[583] See H.R. Rep. No. 105–556, 105th Cong., 2d Sess., at 9 (1998).

debtor made transfers, then a debtor of course could far exceed the 15% total figure; indeed, a debtor could give away all of her money to qualified charities, just not more than 15% to any single one. Remember, though, that if a debtor were to give away all of her money to a combination of charities on the eve of bankruptcy, that might be indicative of *actual* fraud, which is not immunized.

The *Geltzer* approach is not free of problems. The court's holding may be correct if the only question is whether all transfers *to the same entity* should be aggregated, but not if the question is, as in the example above, whether transfers *to multiple entities* should be aggregated. The statutory language and the structure of avoidance litigation support allowing aggregation to the same entity but not to multiple entities. First, the language of the statute speaks to "that contribution" "to a qualified entity" not exceeding the 15% figure. While the reference to "that contribution" could be explained away by the "singular includes the plural" rule of construction, and allow aggregation of multiple contributions to a single entity, the same sort of parlor trick is not possible to allow aggregation of entities as fraudulent transfer defendants. As a structural matter, the trustee must bring a fraudulent transfer action against a specific entity and try to recover from that entity, and that defendant singularly is then entitled to raise affirmative defenses on its own behalf. Total aggregation across entities would undermine that litigation reality. This difficulty can be seen if one tries to apply the "total aggregation" approach in practice. What happens in the example above, where the Debtor gave 15% to Church and 15% to United Way? Does neither defendant get the defense at all? Only the first recipient, or recipients up to the point where the debtor hits the 15% mark (a sort of FIFO approach)? Do they enjoy a pro rata share of the 15% cap? None of the possible solutions make sense.

The second question about the application of the 15% ceiling is what happens if the contribution *exceeds* 15%—is the *entire* transfer then avoidable, or just the amount in excess of 15%? For example, assume Debtor, with an annual gross income of $100,000, gives $16,000 to Church. Does Church lose the entire $16,000, or just the $1,000 over and above the 15% safe harbor? The statutory language suggests that if the 15% ceiling is surpassed, then the entire transfer is vulnerable. It says that a transfer is "not a transfer covered" under § 548(a)(1)(B) if the amount of the contribution does not exceed 15 percent. The obvious negative inference is that if it *does* exceed 15%, then the contribution *is* a "transfer covered." There is no "to the extent" language, but instead simply a dichotomous transfer-is-covered-or-not approach. Having said that, as a policy matter it is hard to see why Congress would impose such a draconian all-or-nothing approach. Yet, the preference law's dollar safe harbors are interpreted in an all-or-nothing way,[584] so at least a similar construction of § 548(a)(2) would have a "foolish consistency" going for it. The courts are split, with some opting for the plain textual reading that if the 15% mark is crossed, the entire transfer is avoidable,[585] and others choosing the "but that would be stupid" policy road,

---

[584] See 11 U.S.C. § 547(c)(8), (9). See also § 6.24.

[585] See, *e.g., Zohdi*, supra note 582, 234 B.R. at 375.

which immunizes up to 15% no matter what, with the excess above 15% the only part of the transfer that is vulnerable.[586]

§ 6.43   Liability and Protection of Transferees

Establishing that a fraudulent transfer was made may not be enough to enable a trustee or creditor to recover the property that was fraudulently transferred. The interests of the debtor's defrauded creditors in collecting on their claims must be balanced against the legitimate expectations and interests of innocent transferees. A cardinal rule of fraudulent conveyance law from the earliest days of the Statute of Elizabeth has been that a *good faith purchaser for value is protected from recovery*, even though a fraudulent transfer was made. This principle continues in full force and effect today. Bankruptcy Code §§ 548(c); UFTA § 8(a); UFCA § 9(1). The precise manner of implementation differs, however, under the Bankruptcy Code and the state fraudulent transfer laws.

Under the Bankruptcy Code, a transferee that takes for value and in good faith is protected "to the extent that such transferee gave value to the debtor." § 548(c). Note that the transfer is still voidable, assuming that § 548(a) or (b) is satisfied. If the transferee is the *initial* transferee, it is not completely immunized from recovery, in the way that a subsequent transferee would be, even if it gave value and took in good faith. § 550(a), (b). Under the UFTA, by contrast, a transfer is "not voidable" against a person who took in good faith and for reasonably equivalent value. UFTA § 8(a). Similarly, under the UFCA, the right to set aside the transfer does not apply against a "purchaser for fair consideration without knowledge of the fraud." UFCA § 9(1).

The difference between these rules is important in situations where the asset appreciates in value after the transfer. To illustrate this difference, assume that Debtor transfers Blackacre to X for $50,000, which is the fair market value of Blackacre at the time of the transfer. Assume also that Debtor has an actually fraudulent intent to convert his leviable asset, Blackacre, to cash, and then to hide that cash from his creditors. X, however, knows nothing of Debtor's nefarious scheme, but takes Blackacre in good faith. After the transfer, the value of Blackacre appreciates substantially, to $80,000. Under the UFTA and the UFCA, X would be entitled to retain Blackacre. If Debtor files bankruptcy, however, the trustee could avoid the transfer. X would be entitled only to a lien on Blackacre to secure her payment of $50,000. The appreciation in value would go to the bankruptcy estate, not to X.

For transferees after the initial transferee, protection is complete both in and out of bankruptcy if the transferee takes for value and in good faith. Bankruptcy Code § 550(b)(1); UFTA § 8(a); UFCA § 9(1). For example, assume that Debtor fraudulently gives Blackacre to X for nothing, that X then sells Blackacre to Y for its then-market value of $60,000, and that Y was in good faith. Y will be immune from recovery, and will be able to retain Blackacre, even if Blackacre appreciates in value thereafter.

Transferees who take property after a protected good faith purchaser for value may be protected by the concept of "derivative title," or the "shelter" principle, even if

---

[586]   See, e.g., In re McGough, 467 B.R. 220, 226 (B.A.P. 10th Cir. 2012).

they did not themselves give value. Bankruptcy Code § 550(b)(2); UFTA § 8(a), (b)(2); UFCA § 9(1). For example, in the hypothetical in the preceding paragraph, assume that after Y purchased Blackacre for $60,000, Y gave Blackacre to his daughter as a wedding present. The daughter, who derives her title from the protected purchaser Y, is likewise entitled to protection. Under the Bankruptcy Code, the subsequent transferee is only protected if she took in good faith, § 550(b)(2); the UFTA and UFCA, by contrast, do not expressly require the sheltered transferee to take in good faith. UFTA § 8(a), (b)(2); UFCA § 9(1).

If any transferee (other than a sheltered transferee) takes in good faith, but gives less than fair value, she will be protected in her own right only to the extent of the value given. This partial safe harbor rule is the same in and out of bankruptcy. Bankruptcy Code § 548(c); UFTA § 8(d); UFCA § 9(2). For example, if X paid $35,000 for Blackacre, she would have a lien on Blackacre to secure the $35,000, but the balance would pass into the bankruptcy estate.

This principle of partial protection has proven important in Ponzi scheme cases, where the fraudulent debtor pays a fortunate early investor a "return" that includes both (1) payment in full of the investor's original investment plus (2) a purely fictitious "profit." Even if the investor who got paid was entirely in good faith, she is not protected for the portion of the payment attributable to the false profits,[587] because she gave no "value" for that supposed profit (which of course in reality does not exist at all), but only gave value for the principal.[588] As for the part of the payment attributable to the investment made, the investor did give value,[589] and the analysis of whether she is protected will then focus on whether the transferee took in "good faith."[590]

If the transferee does not take in good faith, she forfeits all protection, even to the extent she gave value.[591] The trustee or avoiding creditor will be able to recover either the transferred property or its value from the transferee, and the transferee will not have a lien for value given. The transferee's only recourse will be against the debtor. Note, too, that the issues of good faith and adequate value may be linked. The fact that a transferee gave substantially less than fair value for property may raise suspicions about the transferee's good faith. At some point a "good deal" becomes simply "too good to be true."

Usually issues of "good faith" in the law are determined subjectively, *viz.,* did *this* particular person in fact act honestly and purely?[592] This is sometimes called (derisively, one suspects) a "pure heart, empty head" test. But it is *not* the good faith test used for judging the protection of transferees under fraudulent transfer law. One

---

[587] The temptation to work in a bad pun analogizing to false "prophets" was almost irresistible here. I am trying to refrain.

[588] See, e.g., Picard v. Katz, 462 B.R. 447, 453 (S.D.N.Y. 2011); see also Donell v. Kowell, 533 F.3d 762, 770, 777–78 (9th Cir. 2008); Scholes v. Lehmann, 56 F.3d 750, 757–58 (7th Cir. 1995).

[589] E.g., *Donell*, supra note 588, 533 F.3d at 777.

[590] See *Katz*, supra note 588, 462 B.R. at 453–54.

[591] See, e.g., In re Agric. Research & Tech. Grp. Inc., 916 F.2d 528, 535 (9th Cir. 1990).

[592] I am compelled to cite the catch phrase from the television series "Friday Night Lights," where the Coach says, "clear eyes; full hearts" and the players respond, "can't lose!"

non-obvious point about fraudulent transfer law is that the "good faith" of the transferee typically is measured by an *objective* rather than by a *subjective* standard. Generally, to be in "good faith," the transferee must not *know or have reason to know* of the fraudulent nature of the disposition.[593] As one court noted, "if the circumstances would place a reasonable person on inquiry of a debtor's fraudulent purpose, and a *diligent* inquiry would have discovered the fraudulent purpose,"[594] then the transferee is not in good faith. The hard cases, as one might suspect, are the "reason to know" cases. What facts suffice to put the transferee on "inquiry notice" that "something is rotten in the state of Denmark," to borrow from the Bard?[595] What exactly would a diligent inquiry have uncovered? Proving a counterfactual is always a problematic exercise.

There is one exception to the objective approach to good faith. In cases involving the transfer of or settlements for *securities*, where the safe harbor of § 546(e) potentially applies and the interest of protecting the smooth functioning of securities markets must also be weighed, some courts have adopted a more stringent and subjective "willful blindness" test.[596]

A transferee can lack the saving good faith even if, in an ethical sense, the transferee has not done anything inherently immoral, deplorable, or deserving of opprobrium. It is not a moral judgment; it has to do only with the smooth functioning of commerce. We protect parties who take in "good faith" and for "value" because if we did not, then commercial certainty and finality would collapse, even though allowing the transferee to keep the fruits of an otherwise fraudulent transaction likely harms other creditors. But protect we must, else every transaction potentially would rest on a bed of sand. However, if a transferee knows or has reason to know that something may be fishy before taking the transfer, the imperative to trump other innocent victims falls by the wayside. So, as one court explained:

> Where the rule of law holds that an investor may not be able to establish his statutory good faith defense because he requested redemption of his investment after becoming aware of a "red flag" putting him on "inquiry notice" of possible infirmity in his investment, that does not necessarily entail a finding or carry an imputation that he was guilty of any sort of *mala fides* or otherwise deserving of opprobrium. To the contrary, any rational investor or financial advisor, on inquiry notice of a warning signal respecting an investment, would be entirely justified in requesting or recommending redemption and could not be criticized for doing so. . . . But if he does so, the courts have held that he cannot invoke the good faith defense under Section 548(c).[597]

---

[593] See, e.g., Shauer v. Alterton, 151 U.S. 607, 621 (1894).

[594] See *Agricultural Research*, supra note 591, 916 F.2d at 536 (emphasis in original).

[595] Hamlet, Act 1, Scene 4. (And yes, seeing the ghost of Hamlet's father would trigger inquiry notice, as it certainly did for Hamlet). As an aside, this line was *not* spoken by Hamlet, but by Marcellus.

[596] See *Katz*, supra note 588, 462 B.R. at 455–56.

[597] In re Bayou Group LLC, 396 B.R. 810, 848 (Bankr. S.D.N.Y. 2008), aff'd in part, rev'd in part, 439 B.R. 284 (S.D.N.Y. 2010).

§ 6.44   Remedies of Creditor or Trustee

Obtaining a decree from the court that the debtor made a fraudulent transfer may constitute a moral victory for a creditor or bankruptcy trustee, but by itself does not enhance the pot of assets available for distribution to that creditor or to the group of creditors. As a practical matter, creditors can only collect on their claims to the extent that there is a *remedy* for the fraudulent transfer. A right without a remedy is hollow indeed.

Any consideration of the remedies available for a fraudulent transfer must begin with the recognition that good faith transferees for value are protected, at least to the extent they gave value.[598] Bankruptcy Code §§ 548(c), 550(b); UFTA § 8; UFCA § 9. Thus, the following discussion of remedies only applies to the extent that the transferee is not insulated. Furthermore, even if the transferee is not within the protected class, the transferee may have disposed of the property itself and may be judgment-proof.[599]

The fundamental remedy for a fraudulent transfer is to *avoid,* or *set aside,* that transfer. Bankruptcy Code § 548(a), (b); UFTA § 7(a)(1); UFCA §§ 9(1)(a), 10(c). In other words, the transfer is disregarded, and the creditor then is free to pursue its normal collection remedies against the property. For example, assume that Debtor fraudulently transferred his priceless Rembrandt painting to X, and that X was not a good faith purchaser for value. If Creditor A obtained a court order setting aside the transfer from Debtor to X as fraudulent, A could then proceed to levy on the painting.

The remedy for a fraudulent *obligation* is even simpler: just annul or invalidate the debtor's obligation. It has been observed that "the remedy for fraudulent obligations is always adequate."[600] This is true for obligations because, unlike the case of fraudulent *transfers,* nothing needs to be recaptured from anyone. For example, assume that Debtor fraudulently incurred an obligation to purchase a $100 painting from X for $10,000. If that obligation were found to be fraudulent, it would be unenforceable.

Once a transfer has been set aside as fraudulent, *recovery* may be had of either (1) the property transferred, or, if the court so orders, (2) the value of the property. Bankruptcy Code § 550(a); UFTA § 8(b). In the above example, assume that the Rembrandt painting had a market value of $10 million. The primary remedy is recover the painting itself. In a bankruptcy case, the painting would then be property of the estate. Outside of bankruptcy, the avoiding creditor (A, in our example) would be able to levy execution on the painting. Of course, the creditor will only be able to collect up to the amount of her claim.

If the property itself cannot be recovered, or if for some other reason recovery of the property would not be practical or beneficial, then the trustee or creditor may

---

[598] See § 6.43.

[599] See Gerald K. Smith & Frank R. Kennedy, Fraudulent Transfers and Obligations: Issues of Current Interest, 43 S.C. L. Rev. 709, 710 (1992) ("the remedy for fraudulent transfers is often inadequate").

[600] Id.

recover the value of the property from the transferee. In a bankruptcy case, the transferee would pay the full value of the painting ($10 million) to the trustee. Outside of bankruptcy, the creditor's recovery will be limited to the amount of her claim, if less than the value of the transferred property. UFTA § 8(b).

An example of a situation in which a money judgment was entered against the transferee as a remedy for a fraudulent conveyance, in lieu of recovery of the property itself, is *Alan Drey Co. v. Generation, Inc.*[601] In that case, the debtor, a magazine publisher, fraudulently sold its only substantial asset, its subscription list, to McGraw–Hill. The value of the list, of course, was in the names. If the list itself had been recovered, it might have been difficult to sell the list for full value to a third party purchaser, because McGraw–Hill already knew the names. The court allowed the creditor to recover a money judgment against McGraw–Hill, up to the amount of the creditor's claim.

A substantial amount of time may elapse between the time the property is transferred to the transferee and the time the transfer is set aside as fraudulent. Unsurprisingly, the value of the property may change, perhaps dramatically, during that time period. Who reaps the benefit and who bears the risk of these fluctuations in value? As might be expected, given that recovery may only be had from a "guilty" transferee (i.e., one not a good faith purchaser for value), the trustee or avoiding creditor usually enjoys the upside and the guilty transferee suffers the downside. The law on this point is a "heads-I-win-tails-you-lose" proposition, as viewed from the standpoint of the bankruptcy trustee or the avoiding creditor. For example, if the Rembrandt painting were worth $10 million when transferred, and has doubled in value to $20 million, the bankruptcy trustee still is entitled to recover the painting itself, now worth $20 million. § 550(a). If, however, the painting were stolen from the transferee, and cannot be found, the transferee still will be held liable for the full value of the property at the time of the transfer, $10 million.

In cases where the court authorizes the recovery of the value of the property, rather than the property itself, the value is normally fixed as of the time of the transfer. However, equitable adjustments may have to be made in the amount recovered because of post-transfer events. UFTA § 8(c). The value may have been enhanced by improvements made by the transferee, or by the discharge of valid liens; the transferee should receive a credit for those increases in value. The Bankruptcy Code recognizes a similar protective rule, but only for a "good faith" transferee. § 550(e). As noted in the preceding paragraph, though, the opposite is also true; if the property declines in value after the time of the transfer, the transferee will remain liable for the full original value at the time of the transfer.

Some have questioned the efficiency of fraudulent conveyance law, since the transferee will not be liable for more than the value of the property transferred.[602] In our hypothetical, all that the transferee X will have to do is give the Rembrandt back. X thus may have little reason beyond moral compunction to refrain from participating

---

[601]   22 Ill. App. 3d 611, 317 N.E.2d 673 (1974).

[602]   See David G. Carlson, Is Fraudulent Conveyance Law Efficient?, 9 Cardozo L. Rev. 643 (1987).

in the fraudulent transfer. The transferee may, however, be liable for the creditor's costs incurred in setting aside the transfer. Nor is the debtor's liability increased beyond what it owed before the transfer, although there are other possible negative ramifications for the debtor that might create disincentives for the debtor to make a fraudulent transfer.

Outside of bankruptcy, a creditor who challenges a transfer as fraudulent may have an alternative remedy to setting aside the transfer: simply ignore the transfer and levy directly on the transferred property, or its traceable proceeds. UFTA § 7(b); UFCA § 9(1)(b). As a practical matter, the creditor will probably have to indemnify the sheriff against possible conversion liability before the sheriff will proceed to levy directly. Under the UFTA, the creditor may only levy directly if it has a judgment and the court so orders. UFTA § 7(b). Under the UFCA, creditors with "matured" claims may levy directly. UFCA § 9(1)((b). A "matured" claim includes claims reduced to judgment as well as contract claims that have come due. The UFCA rule thus is broader than its UFTA counterpart. A claim is unmatured if it is a contract claim that has not yet come due, or if it is a tort claim that has not been reduced to judgment.

Other equitable remedies may be available to the creditor. The creditor may obtain an injunction preventing the transferee from disposing of or transferring the subject property. Alternatively, a receiver may be appointed for the transferred property. UFTA § 7(a)(3), UFCA § 10(a), (b). Under the UFCA, these remedies are listed only under the section for remedies available to creditors whose claims are unmatured, UFCA § 10, perhaps supporting an inference that creditors with matured claims cannot invoke these remedies. Such a distinction between the holders of matured and unmatured claims makes no sense, however, and the courts have allowed creditors with matured claims to utilize these remedies as well. The UFTA drops the distinction between matured and unmatured claims entirely.

§ 6.45 Standing

A fraudulent transfer is a wrong against creditors. Outside of bankruptcy, creditors thus are the parties invested with standing to challenge transfers as fraudulent. However, the rules on which types of creditors have standing to bring a fraudulent transfer action vary depending on the basis being asserted for avoiding the transfer.

In bankruptcy cases, the trustee as representative of all creditors has exclusive standing to bring fraudulent transfer actions on behalf of the estate. § 548(a), (b). Even where the trustee's fraudulent transfer cause of action is derivative of actual creditors under § 544(b)(1), the trustee has the exclusive standing to bring the avoidance action. An individual creditor or a creditors' committee could bring an action only if the trustee failed to act and the court authorized the creditor suit on behalf of the estate. The state law standing rules are relevant under § 544(b)(1), however, because the trustee must be able to identify an actual creditor who would have standing to avoid the transfer.

Under the original Statute of Elizabeth, the *equitable* nature of fraudulent conveyance actions affected the standing rules. A creditor could not bring an action in equity to set aside a transfer as fraudulent unless that creditor had first obtained a judgment against the debtor and execution on that judgment had been returned unsatisfied. Only then could it be said that the creditor's legal remedies were "inadequate," which at that time was a prerequisite to proceeding in equity. Today, however, after the merger of law and equity and the relaxation of pleading rules, a creditor may join in a single action a claim seeking a money judgment with a plea to set aside a transfer as fraudulent.

Under modern state fraudulent conveyance laws, the standing rules divide the world into two categories of creditors: *present* creditors and *future* creditors. "Present" creditors are those whose claims arose at or before the time of the transfer in question; "future" creditors are those whose claims arose after the challenged transfer. In other words, the classification of "present" and "future" creditors speaks to when the creditor's claim arose in comparison to the time of the challenged fraudulent transfer.

"Present" creditors have standing to raise every type of fraudulent transfer cause of action under both the UFTA and the UFCA. UFTA §§ 4, 5; UFCA §§ 4–7. A present creditor may invoke actual fraud as well as all types of constructive fraud in challenging a transfer.

The standing rights of "future" creditors are more limited. Such creditors cannot challenge a transfer as constructively fraudulent on the important ground that it was made for less than reasonably equivalent value (or fair consideration) while the debtor was insolvent. UFTA § 5(a); UFCA § 4. Only present creditors have standing to raise that particular type of constructive fraud. In addition, under the UFTA, future creditors may not attack an insider preference. UFTA § 5(b).

Future creditors may challenge a transfer on the ground that it was: (1) actually fraudulent, UFTA § 4(a)(1); UFCA § 7; (2) constructively fraudulent as an exchange for less than reasonably equivalent value or fair consideration, leaving the debtor with unreasonably small capital, UFTA § 4(a)(2)(i); UFCA § 5; or (3) constructively fraudulent as an exchange for less than reasonably equivalent value or fair consideration, when the debtor intended to incur debts beyond his ability to pay as they became due, UFTA § 4(a)(2)(ii); UFCA § 6. In each of those situations, the harm caused by the debtor's fraudulent transfer is considered to be ongoing, negatively impacting future creditors as well as present creditors.

In making the timing comparison between when the claim arose and when the transfer was made or the obligation was incurred, some salient points must be borne in mind about the timing of both claims and transfers. The definition of "claim" is exceedingly broad under all of the fraudulent transfer laws. Bankruptcy Code § 101(5); UFTA § 1(3); UFCA § 1. A claim is a "right to payment," even if that right has not been reduced to judgment, or is unliquidated, contingent, unmatured, or disputed. In short, a creditor may be deemed to have a "claim" long before the payment on that claim would actually be due and owing.

On the other side of the timing comparison fence, a "transfer" is not deemed to be made until it is perfected against third parties. Bankruptcy Code § 548(d)(1); UFTA § 6. Thus, even if the debtor has made a transfer to a third party, the effective date of that transfer will be postponed until the transfer is recorded. That postponement may bring many additional creditors within the class of "present" creditors.

§ 6.46   Impact on Debtor

The law of fraudulent conveyances is concerned primarily with the rights of third parties. The ultimate issue in most cases is whether defrauded creditors of the debtor will be able to recover property or its value in the hands of a third party transferee. It has been pointed out that "transferees, not debtors, bear the brunt of the invalidation of fraudulent conveyances."[603] So what is the impact on the *debtor* of making a fraudulent conveyance? If David Debtor shows up in your office, explains that he is being hounded by his creditors, and would prefer for his sister Sarah in Alaska to have his property instead of his creditors, what do you tell him?

First, of course, you tell the debtor that "it would be wrong" to engage in a fraudulent transaction. If the debtor is not overly weighed down by moral scruples, however, what do you tell him? As the preceding sections have explained, the attempted fraud will not be successful if the transfer to Sarah is discovered. Creditors (or the bankruptcy trustee, if the debtor files bankruptcy) will be able to set aside the conveyance as fraudulent, and recover the property or its value from the transferee. To that, however, the debtor might respond that his creditors will certainly get the property right now if he does nothing, but if he transfers it, there is at least a chance that they will not get the property. In other words, how can he be any worse off by transferring the property than he already is?

As a matter of economics, the debtor's liability to the creditors might increase. In addition to recovering the principal amount of the debts owed, the creditors will be able to recover the costs incurred in discovering and setting aside the fraudulent conveyance, along with interest. Attorney's fees may be recoverable in some states. Furthermore, in some jurisdictions the debtor may be subjected to liability for punitive damages, upon proof that his actions were willful, wanton, and malicious.

If the debtor files bankruptcy, he might not be able to obtain a *discharge* of his debts.[604] Bankruptcy Code § 727(a)(2). The discharge bar is triggered if the debtor makes a transfer with actual fraudulent intent within a year of the bankruptcy filing. However, constructive fraud will not suffice to deny the discharge. The discharge prohibition for actual fraud is permanent; if Debtor files a subsequent bankruptcy case, the debts that were not discharged in the earlier case because of his actual fraud will continue to be excluded from discharge.[605] § 523(a)(10).

If the prospects of increased liability and loss of discharge do not trouble the debtor, a final factor might tip the scales. In a number of states the debtor also may be subject to *criminal* liability, usually punishable by a fine, if he makes an actual fraudulent transfer.

Assume, however, that David Debtor ignores your advice and makes the fraudulent transfer to his sister Sarah, with her agreement to reconvey the property to

---

[603] John C. McCoid, II, Constructively Fraudulent Conveyances: Transfers for Inadequate Consideration, 62 Tex. L. Rev. 639, 658 (1983).

[604] See § 10.5.

[605] See § 10.25.

him if his trouble with his creditors goes away. By some miracle or stroke of good fortune, Debtor is able to pay off his creditors. He then requests Sarah to reconvey the property back to him, but she refuses. Can the debtor enforce the transferee's agreement to reconvey? The general rule is that the debtor cannot enforce such an agreement, because of his "unclean hands" and the public policy against encouraging fraud. Even if she does reconvey the property back to him, the property will still be subject to the liens of any of the transferee's creditors that attached to the property while in her hands.

G. POSTPETITION TRANSFERS: § 549

§ 6.47 General Rule of Avoidance

The need to preserve the bankruptcy estate and to protect the norm of equality of distribution between similarly situated creditors does not cease when the bankruptcy case is filed. Without protective rules, a debtor could effectively undermine the integrity of the estate and the bankruptcy distributional system by making unauthorized transfers of estate property after the commencement of the bankruptcy case. In a chapter 7 case, there is inevitably some lapse of time after a bankruptcy filing before the independent trustee takes possession of property of the estate from the debtor, and in the reorganization chapters, the debtor typically retains possession of estate property throughout the case. In involuntary cases, a debtor almost always retains its property during the gap between the filing of the petition and the entry of the order for relief. Thus, in many situations the debtor will have an opportunity to make improper transfers. Or, a creditor might attempt to seize estate property after the filing.

The section that protects the bankruptcy estate and preserves equality *after* filing is § 549. That provision empowers the trustee to avoid an unauthorized transfer of property of the estate made after the commencement of the case. § 549(a). The key point in time is the filing of the petition. Filing commences the case, even in an involuntary case. §§ 301, 303(b). Filing also transforms all of the debtor's property into property of the estate. § 541(a)(1). Thus, from the instant a bankruptcy petition is filed, voluntary or involuntary, transfers of what had been the debtor's property are prohibited, unless they fall within one of the statutory exceptions.[606]

If the postpetition transfer is avoided under § 549(a), the transferee will have to return the property or its value to the trustee. § 550(a). Upon doing so, the transferee will be left with an unsecured claim against the estate. § 502(h). The debtor, of course, will have to remit to the trustee any proceeds it collected from the transfer of estate property, and will be liable to the estate for conversion.

For example, assume that Debtor files chapter 7 on May 1. On May 2, Debtor sells his car to P for $5,000. Debtor takes the money and goes on a cruise to ease the pain of filing bankruptcy. The trustee will be able to avoid the transfer of the car to P, and P either will have to give the car back to the trustee or pay the trustee $5,000. P then

---

[606] See § 6.48.

will have a $5,000 unsecured claim against the estate. The result is the same whether or not P knew of the bankruptcy filing.

§ 6.48   Exceptions

In some situations it would be unfair to the transferee and counterproductive to the smooth and orderly operation of the bankruptcy case to avoid a postpetition transfer of estate property. Sometimes estate property must be transferred. Thus, § 549 carves out several exceptions to the general rule of avoidance, in order to provide for cases in which either fairness or the functioning of the bankruptcy process demands that postpetition transfers of estate property be protected. These exceptions are for:

- transfers that are *authorized*, either by the Bankruptcy Code or by the court, § 549(a)(2);

- transfers made during the "gap" period in an involuntary case between the filing of the petition and the entry of the order for relief, to the extent the transferee gave post-bankruptcy value, § 549(b); and

- transfers of real property to a good faith purchaser for value without knowledge of the case, which are recorded in the real estate records before notice of the bankruptcy case is filed in those records, § 549(c).

The first exception, for authorized transfers, is the most obvious. It would be absurd to permit the avoidance of transfers of estate property that are authorized. For example, the trustee may have to sell property of the estate as part of her duty to liquidate the estate and make a distribution.

Most transfers of estate property are authorized pursuant to § 363. Note that express court permission for a transfer often is not required. Transfers in the ordinary course of business are permitted without court approval, assuming that the operation of the debtor's business is authorized. § 363(c)(1). In chapter 11 cases, continued operation will be the norm. § 1108. Even for transfers outside of the ordinary course, notice of a proposed sale will be sent to interested parties, but if no one objects, the court will not hold a hearing. Rule 6004(e).

However, not all authorized transfers are exempt from avoidance. There are two "exceptions to the exception" that authorized transfers are protected. § 549(a)(2)(A). The first is for transfers in involuntary cases during the gap period, which are authorized only under § 303(f). A special safe harbor for such transfers is created by § 549(b), discussed below.

The second is for situations where a party that holds property of the estate makes a transfer that is protected under § 542(c). Under § 542(c), an entity that does not have actual notice or knowledge of the case may in good faith transfer property of the estate or pay a debt owing to the debtor to someone other than the trustee. The entity making the transfer is protected. However, the *transferee* is not protected. § 549(a)(2)(A).

For example, a check drawn on the debtor's bank account may be presented to the drawee bank for payment before the bank learns of the debtor's bankruptcy filing. Technically, the debtor's bankruptcy filing converts their bank account into property of the estate, and if the bank knew of the bankruptcy, it should not honor the check. As a practical matter, though, it would be an impossible burden for banks to check the bankruptcy filings for every single drawer of a check that is presented to the bank for payment. Under the prior Bankruptcy Act, the Supreme Court recognized this practical problem, and carved out an equitable exception to the statute to protect the bank.[607] Under the Code, § 542(c) protects the transferor bank. However, because of § 549(a)(2)(A), the transferee to whom payment is made on the check will not be protected. The trustee is authorized to recover the payment of estate property from that transferee.

The second major exception to the general principle that all postpetition transfers may be avoided is for *involuntary* cases. § 549(b). Normally, after an involuntary petition is filed, and before an order for relief is entered, the debtor is permitted to retain possession of and to deal with its property, and to operate its business. § 303(f). However, the filing of the petition does convert the debtor's property into estate property, § 541(a)(1), even in an involuntary case and prior to the entry of the order for relief. The issue is the extent to which transferees that deal with the debtor during this gap period should be protected from avoidance under § 549.

The answer to this question is to protect gap period transferees to the extent that they *give value* after the bankruptcy filing in exchange for the transfer. The protective rule applies whether or not the transferee knows of the bankruptcy filing; the only issue is whether it gave postpetition value in exchange. Value is defined to include services, but does not include the satisfaction of a prepetition debt.

For example, assume that an involuntary petition is filed against Debtor on May 1. On May 2 Debtor buys a car from P and pays P $5,000. P is protected under § 549(b).

Now assume that Debtor buys a car from P on April 1, and puts $1,000 down. An involuntary petition is filed against Debtor on May 1. On May 2 Debtor pays P the $4,000 balance for the car. The transfer of $4,000 to P will be avoided; it is not protected by § 549(b), because the transfer was for a prepetition debt Debtor owed to P. P will have to return the $4,000 to the estate, and file a claim for $4,000.

The final exception to the general rule of avoidance is for certain transfers of real estate. The basic idea is that purchasers of real estate are entitled to rely on the real estate records. There is no similar safe harbor in § 549 for purchasers of personal property. The transferee will be protected from avoidance under § 549(c) if:

- the transferee purchased in good faith;

- the transferee did not have knowledge of the commencement of the bankruptcy case;

- the transferee gave "present fair equivalent value" for the property; and

---

[607]   Bank of Marin v. England, 385 U.S. 99 (1966).

- the transfer occurs and is properly recorded in the real estate records of the county[608] where the property is located *before* a copy or notice of the bankruptcy filing is filed in the same real estate records.

For example, assume that Debtor files bankruptcy on May 1. On May 2, Debtor sells Orangeacre, located in Z County, to P, for $40,000, which is the "fair equivalent value" of the land. P does not know Debtor filed bankruptcy. P records the transfer in the real estate records of Z County on May 5. On May 10, a copy of the bankruptcy petition is filed in those real estate records. P is protected by § 549(c); the trustee cannot avoid the transfer of Orangeacre.

If, however, a copy of the bankruptcy petition had been filed in the Z County real estate records before P recorded on May 5, or if P had known of Debtor's bankruptcy filing, P would not have been protected. If P filed first, and did not know of the bankruptcy, but gave less than fair equivalent value for the property, the transfer would have been avoided. P would, however, be protected by a lien to the extent of the present value given.

H. STATUTORY LIENS: § 545

§ 6.49   History and Overview

Of the different types of liens, only "statutory liens" are the subject of a special avoiding power in bankruptcy cases. § 545. But why? It is important to remember that in our bankruptcy system, the initial premise is that property rights and entitlements (such as liens) that are valid and enforceable outside of bankruptcy are given effect in bankruptcy as well. A statutory lien is just one type of lien. Is there something unique about statutory liens that suggests that they need special treatment?[609] Probably not. Section 545 instead is just a convenient gathering place for addressing a variety of policy concerns that happen to be implicated by different types of statutory liens. It might be said that there is less there than meets the eye.

What is a "statutory lien"? The definition in § 101(53) provides that the term 'statutory lien' means a

lien arising solely by force of a statute on specified circumstances or conditions, or lien of distress for rent, whether or not statutory, but does not include security interest or judicial lien, whether or not such interest or lien is provided by or is dependent on a statute and whether or not such interest or lien is made fully effective by statute.

---

[608] The statute specifically requires the transfer to be "so perfected that a bona fide purchaser of such property, against whom applicable law permits such transfer to be perfected, could not acquire an interest that is superior to such good faith purchaser." Almost invariably, the moment at which that perfection occurs is when the transfer is recorded in the real estate records of the county.

[609] For good discussions of the subject, see Thomas H. Jackson, Statutory Liens and Constructive Trusts in Bankruptcy: Undoing the Confusion, 61 Am. Bankr. L.J. 287 (1987); John C. McCoid, II, Statutory Liens in Bankruptcy, 68 Am. Bankr. L.J. 269 (1994).

Note that this definition operates in considerable part by *exclusion*. A statutory lien cannot be either a "security interest," meaning a lien created by agreement, § 101(51), or a "judicial lien," meaning a lien created through the judicial process. § 101(36). Thus, statutory liens do *not* include such liens as Article 9 security interests, mortgages, execution liens, garnishment liens, and so forth. Those exclusions occupy a very large percentage of the world of liens. The definition in § 101(53) makes clear that consensual liens and judicial liens are not to be considered statutory liens, *even if* the validity or enforceability of the lien depends on a statute. Thus, if a lien is at all traceable back to an agreement or to the invocation of the judicial process, it is not a statutory lien.

Instead, a "statutory" lien within the meaning of the Bankruptcy Code is one of two types: first, a lien that arises "solely by force of a statute on specified circumstances or conditions"; and second, liens for rent. Note that liens for distress of rent are classified as statutory liens even if not statutory; thus, a common law landlord's lien for rent would fall within the definition. All other common law liens are not covered by § 545. The most common type of lien that arises solely by force of a statute is the ubiquitous federal tax lien. 26 U.S.C. § 6321. Other types of statutory liens may protect particular classes of creditors: mechanics and materialmen, artisans, attorneys, innkeepers, and so forth.

The treatment of statutory liens in bankruptcy has changed considerably over time. Until 1938, statutory liens were routinely enforced in bankruptcy. In the Chandler Act of 1938, certain limitations were imposed.[610] Significantly, that Act for the first time struck down state-created priorities, a rule now found in § 545(1).[611] Another amendment followed in 1952,[612] and another in 1966.[613] The basic scheme of the 1966 amendments continues in effect in the Code today.

The Code's approach to statutory liens may be summed up as follows:

Statutory liens are valid and fully enforceable, unless they are:

1. A state-created priority, dressed up to look like a lien, § 545(1);[614]

2. Not enforceable against a bona fide purchaser, § 545(2);[615] or

3. A lien for rent, § 545(3), (4).[616]

Tax liens are partially unenforceable under the bona fide purchaser test of § 545(2), and are subordinated as provided in § 724(b).[617]

---

[610] See McCoid, supra note 609, at 277–81, for a discussion of the history of the Chandler Act provisions.

[611] See § 6.50.

[612] Act of July 7, 1952, 66 Stat. 427 (1952).

[613] Act of July 5, 1966, 80 Stat. 268 (1966).

[614] See § 6.50.

[615] See § 6.51.

[616] See § 6.53.

The possibility of avoiding a statutory lien under other Code provisions must be borne in mind. For example, the provision in § 545(2) giving the trustee the status of a bona fide purchaser overlaps considerably with § 544(a)(3). One important distinction for statutory liens, though, is that they are not voidable as *preferences*.[618] § 547(c)(6).

§ 6.50   Disguised State Priorities

The first type of statutory lien that may be avoided by the trustee is a lien that is really a disguised state-created priority. The bankruptcy distributional scheme is a matter of *federal* law. Accordingly, the allocation of priorities as between creditors is a matter of federal law, within the exclusive province of Congress. If a state attempts to designate a certain class of claimants as deserving of priority in bankruptcy, that attempt will be blocked by § 545(1) and, in part, § 545(2).

Yet, in a sense states are permitted to influence the order in which a debtor's assets are distributed, and in a very basic way. State law serves as the baseline that dictates which creditors have claims, and in what amount, and which of those claimants have liens on assets of the debtor. A state law that gives a creditor an unavoidable lien on certain property of the debtor would directly impact the outcome of a distribution in bankruptcy. The whole point of a "lien" in bankruptcy is that it affects the priority in which claims will be paid. How can it be that state law defines property entitlements that will be respected in bankruptcy, but that bankruptcy priorities are a matter of federal law? Are we talking out of both sides of our mouth?

The answer is that a state statutory lien that has a priority effect will be enforced in bankruptcy if it is *bankruptcy-neutral*. In other words, the state is authorized to create liens or other property entitlements, as long as those entitlements are enforceable across-the-board, in or out of bankruptcy. What § 545(1) is directed at are state priorities that are designed to operate *only* in the event of bankruptcy. Whether labeled a "lien," a "priority," or a "gazebo," such a state statute would be a blatant attempt by the state to alter the federal priority scheme. A state statute that always gives environmental cleanup costs a lien on the debtor's assets would be enforced in bankruptcy; a state statute that gives such costs a lien on the debtor's assets "in the event the debtor becomes insolvent or files bankruptcy" would not be given effect.

Section 545(1) implements this policy against state-created disguised priorities by allowing the trustee to avoid the fixing of a statutory lien on property of the debtor to the extent that the lien first becomes effective against the debtor upon the occurrence of some triggering event that signifies comprehensive financial disaster. The designated triggers are: a bankruptcy case is commenced; a non-bankruptcy insolvency proceeding is commenced; a custodian is appointed or authorized to take possession of the debtor's property; the debtor becomes insolvent; the debtor's financial condition fails to meet a specified standard; or execution is levied against property of the debtor at the instance of someone other than the holder of the statutory lien.

---

[617] See § 6.52.

[618] See § 6.22.

Because a prohibition similar to § 545(1) has been on the books since 1938, the occasion for invoking that avoidance power is quite rare. States have largely gotten out of the business of trying to alter bankruptcy priorities by statute, because they know that such an effort will be futile.

§ 6.51   Bona Fide Purchaser Test

The second type of statutory lien that is avoidable by the trustee is one that "is not perfected or enforceable at the time of the commencement of the case against a bona fide purchaser that purchases such property, whether or not such a purchaser exists." § 545(2). An exception to the "bona fide purchaser" test was added in 2005 to excludes "purchasers" under § 6323 of the Internal Revenue Code (or similar local laws), a limitation principally relevant to clarifying an issue regarding tax liens.[619] Although the general rule of § 545(2) appears to be designed to help implement the general Code policy against "secret" liens, it actually originated as part and parcel of the proscription against hidden priorities.[620] The idea was that if the statutory "lien" was in fact so tenuous that it could be defeated by a bona fide purchaser, it probably was nothing more than an attempt to reorder priorities as between creditors. Only if the governmental body that creates the statutory "lien" is willing to make that lien substantial enough to defeat the competing claim of a bona fide purchaser will that lien be enforceable in a bankruptcy case.

Notwithstanding its origin, however, § 545(2) does have the effect of striking down *unperfected* statutory liens.[621] The main practical importance of the section may be with regard to tax liens. As discussed in the next section, federal tax liens will be avoidable under § 545(2) if notice of the lien is not filed at all or in the proper place.

Section 545(2) overlaps in large part with the strong-arm power in § 544(a)(3), which gives the trustee the power of a hypothetical bona fide purchaser of real property.[622] As does § 544(a)(3), § 545(2) focuses on the time the bankruptcy case is commenced to test whether the asserted statutory lien would defeat a bona fide purchaser. Also like § 544(a)(3), the trustee's power in § 545(2) does not depend on the existence of an *actual* bona fide purchaser.

The two sections are not identical, however. For one thing, § 545(2) is not limited to real property, as is § 544(a)(3). Thus, a statutory lien on *personal* property that would be vulnerable to a bona fide purchaser is at risk under § 545(2).[623] A second notable difference is that § 544(a)(3) does not require the impossible, while § 545(2) does. Section 544(a)(3) only gives the trustee the rights of a bona fide purchaser "against whom applicable law permits such transfer to be perfected." No such

---

[619] See § 6.52.

[620] See John C. McCoid, II, Statutory Liens in Bankruptcy, 68 Am. Bankr. L.J. 269, 274 (1994). An influential article that helped shape the statutory lien rules explained this point. Frank R. Kennedy, Statutory Liens in Bankruptcy, 39 Minn. L. Rev. 697, 733 (1955).

[621] See, e.g., In re Globe Bldg. Materials, Inc., 328 B.R. 769 (Bankr. N.D. Ind. 2004) (wage lien avoided).

[622] See § 6.4.

[623] So, for example, the Wisconsin wage lien statute that was at issue in *Globe*, supra note 3, applied to all real and personal property of a debtor.

limitation is found in § 545(2) for statutory liens. This distinction can be important in cases where a bona fide purchaser would defeat even a fully perfected and noticed statutory lien, or where the statutory lien on its face does not provide any means by which it can be perfected.[624]

In considering the timing question, the importance of § 546(b)(1) must be borne in mind. That section allows a creditor to perfect a lien after the bankruptcy filing with retroactive effect if the applicable non-bankruptcy law would relate back the effectiveness of the perfected lien. If the lien's effectiveness relates back to a point in time prior to the bankruptcy filing, § 545(2) will not permit avoidance. Note that neither § 545(2) nor § 546(b)(1) imposes an outside time limit within which the post-bankruptcy perfection must occur, although of course the creditor must act within any time limits required by the non-bankruptcy perfection law.

The most common example of such a statutory lien probably is a mechanic's and materialmen's (M & M) lien.[625] Typically such liens can be perfected by the filing of a notice for some period of time after the unpaid work is performed, and upon filing, the lien's effectiveness will relate back to the time the work was done. If the work was done prior to bankruptcy, the M & M lien will be unavoidable in bankruptcy even if the requisite notice of perfection is not filed until after the commencement of bankruptcy. If the notice is not filed within the time required by state law, however, the lien will be avoidable.

The law that creates the statutory lien must be consulted to determine what steps a creditor must take in order to perfect its lien against a bona fide purchaser. The bankruptcy law thus incorporates the non-bankruptcy law perfection requirements, if any. For example, if state law does not impose any formal perfection requirements, but makes a statutory lien enforceable against a bona fide purchaser even without the creditor taking any steps to perfect, neither must any steps be taken for the lien to be enforceable in bankruptcy.[626] The lack of any independent filing requirement to make a statutory lien valid in bankruptcy substantially limits the practical importance of § 545(2), since many state statutory liens do not require any type of recordation. State law also will govern whether a bona fide purchaser would defeat the challenged lien;[627] if so, and if unperfected, then avoidance under § 545(2) will follow.

An intriguing question that is not clearly answered by the Code is whether the trustee's hypothetical bona fide purchaser status in § 545(2) also carries with it "hypothetical possession." For a variety of statutory liens, the non-bankruptcy law that creates the statutory lien gives priority to a purchaser only if that purchaser also takes possession of the subject property before learning of the statutory lien. Recall that under § 545(2), no actual purchaser need exist; the trustee is given the status of a

---

[624] See, e.g., In re Nicolescu, 311 B.R. 27 (Bankr. D. Conn. 2004).

[625] See e.g., In re Orndorff Constr., Inc., 394 B.R. 372 (Bankr. M.D.N.C. 2008).

[626] See, e.g., In re Loretto Winery, Ltd., 898 F.2d 715 (9th Cir. 1990). Some courts have rejected the approach of *Loretto Winery*, insisting that some sort of public notice must be given to immunize a statutory lien from avoidance under § 545(2). See, e.g., In re TWA Inc. Post Confirmation Estate, 312 B.R. 759, 764 & n. 3 (Bankr. D. Del. 2004).

[627] E.g., *Globe*, supra note 621.

hypothetical purchaser. The question then is how far to carry the trustee's hypothetical status—does it also impute possession to the trustee? The courts have disagreed.

§ 6.52   Tax Liens

What to do with tax liens in bankruptcy has been the subject of almost endless controversy. The government obviously has an interest in the collection of taxes; yet, the concern is that without any restriction imposed, tax liens might consume a disproportionate share of the bankruptcy estate, to the detriment of other creditors. The Code's resolution is to allow the avoidance of tax liens to the extent a bona fide purchaser would take free of the lien, § 545(2), and to subordinate a tax lien to higher priority claims. § 724(b).

Under the federal tax lien statute, the United States obtains a lien for the amount of the tax on all of the debtor-taxpayer's property if the debtor neglects or refuses to pay the tax after demand. 26 U.S.C. § 6321. The lien arises at the time the assessment is made. 26 U.S.C. § 6322. The lien is not valid against any purchaser or judgment lien creditor until notice of the lien is filed in the proper place. 26 U.S.C. § 6323(a). Thus, the trustee will be able to avoid an unfiled federal tax lien under § 545(2) or § 544(a).

Even if the government files the required notice of the federal tax lien, that lien is not enforceable against purchasers of certain types of property.[628] 26 U.S.C. § 6323(b). This limitation raises the issue of whether the trustee in bankruptcy has the power under § 545(2) to avoid even a properly filed federal tax lien with regard to those types of property. While some bankruptcy courts have so held, several circuit courts have held that the trustee could not avoid a filed tax lien under § 545(2), declining to give the trustee the requisite status of a "purchaser" under § 6323(b).[629] Any doubts on this question were settled by the 2005 amendments, which added an exception to § 545(2), denying the bankruptcy trustee the status of a "purchaser" under § 6323, thus embracing the "no avoidance" holdings of the courts of appeals. The 2005 amendment also extends to "any other similar provision of State or local law."

Even if it is not avoided, the tax lien may be partially subordinated under § 724(b). Under that section, property that is subject to a tax lien will first be distributed to claims with a higher priority than the tax claim secured by the lien. An exception to this subordination rule was added in 2005, for unavoidable tax liens connected with an ad valorem tax. Many prepetition taxes are accorded eighth priority in § 507(a)(8).[630] Therefore (except for the ad valorem exception just noted), claims in the first seven priority classes will be paid first out of the property subject to the tax lien, but only up to the amount of the tax claim. After the payment of that amount to the higher priority claims, distribution will be made out of any residue to the tax claim. This subordination provision does not benefit the holders of general unsecured non-priority claims, though, since the subordination is only to claims with a priority higher than that of the tax claim.

---

[628] Examples of excluded property include securities, household goods, and motor vehicles.

[629] See In re Berg, 121 F.3d 535 (9th Cir. 1997); In re Walter, 45 F.3d 1023 (6th Cir. 1995).

[630] See § 7.21.

§ 6.53 Landlord's Liens for Rent

The most straightforward part of § 545 is the authorization for the trustee to avoid the fixing of a statutory lien "for rent," § 545(3), or "a lien of distress for rent." § 545(4). Recall that the definition of "statutory lien" extends to a "lien of distress for rent, whether or not statutory." § 101(53). Thus, even a common law landlord's lien falls within the trustee's avoiding power. The concern that motivated § 545(3) and § 545(4) was that if statutory liens for rent were enforced in bankruptcy, the landlord's claim might consume too much of the estate.

The avoiding power in § 545(3) and (4) only applies with respect to *statutory* landlord's liens. The definition of "statutory lien" excludes "security interests," § 101(53), which are liens created by agreement. § 101(51). A lien is deemed to be "statutory" only if it is created *solely* by force of statute. Thus, if the lease agreement itself grants a security interest to the landlord, the landlord's lien will not be avoidable under § 545(3) and (4). Other avoiding powers still might be utilized to avoid the landlord's security interest, however.

Chapter 7

THE PAYMENT OF CLAIMS

A. ALLOWANCE OF CLAIMS

§ 7.1 Basic Principles

One of the most important concepts in the entire Bankruptcy Code is that of a *"claim."* Bankruptcy, at its core, is about the treatment and disposition of the "claims" of creditors. Claims are paid (if also allowed), and claims are discharged. What happens to claims in bankruptcy largely determines the extent of the relief afforded to the debtor and to creditors.

Classifying a creditor's rights against the debtor as a "claim" cognizable in bankruptcy has three primary ramifications. *First,* only claims may be *paid* in the bankruptcy distribution. This is true whether the case is a liquidation under chapter 7,[1] or a reorganization under chapter 11,[2] chapter 12,[3] or chapter 13.[4] The claim also must be *"allowed"* in order for the creditor to participate in the distribution. An allowed claim is a claim that is properly filed and that is substantively valid.[5] §§ 501, 502. Furthermore, in a chapter 11 case, only a creditor holding an allowed claim is entitled to *vote* on the reorganization plan.[6] § 1126(a).

Second, only claims are *discharged.*[7] Again, this rule applies with equal force to discharges granted in chapter 7 liquidations (§ 727(b)), or pursuant to confirmed plans under chapter 11 (§ 1141(d)),[8] chapter 12 (§ 1228),[9] or chapter 13 (§ 1328).[10] The effect of a discharge is that the holder of the claim is permanently enjoined by statute from making any attempt to collect the discharged debt from the debtor.[11] § 524(a).

Third, the holder of a claim is *stayed* during the case from taking any action to collect its claim from the estate or from the debtor.[12] § 362(a). The application of the automatic stay against claims dovetails with the two other effects of claim status just described. The prohibition against independent collection efforts during the pendency

---

[1] See § 726(a); § 7.25.

[2] See §§ 1123(a)(1)–(4), 1129(a)(7), 1129(b)(2). See § 7.26.

[3] See §§ 1222(a), (b), 1225(a)(4), (5). See § 7.26.

[4] See §§ 1322(a), (b), 1325(a)(4), (5). See § 7.26.

[5] See §§ 7.4, 7.5.

[6] See § 11.21.

[7] See § 10.2.

[8] See § 10.37.

[9] See § 10.39.

[10] See § 10.38.

[11] See § 10.31.

[12] See § 3.3.

of bankruptcy, coupled with the permanent discharge injunction, effectively limits a creditor to distributions made in the bankruptcy case.

To summarize, a "claim" may share in the bankruptcy distribution and is subject to being discharged. Conversely, if a creditor does not have a claim, that creditor is excluded from the bankruptcy payout, but also is not discharged or stayed. The ramifications of a "no-claim" finding depend on (1) whether the debtor is an individual, and (2) whether the bankruptcy case is a liquidation or a reorganization.

For an *individual* debtor, a determination that a creditor lacks a bankruptcy "claim" will be doubly disastrous. To begin with, the debtor's obligations to the creditor will not be discharged, and thus will continue after the bankruptcy case. Nor will the creditor's collection efforts against the debtor be stayed. The individual debtor accordingly will lose the benefit of the "fresh start" so central to bankruptcy policy. Furthermore, the obligations that the debtor owes to the "no-claim" creditor will not be reduced at all by any bankruptcy distribution. Therefore, the creditor will be able to enforce all of its legal rights against the debtor after bankruptcy. These negative consequences for an individual debtor will occur irrespective of whether the case is a liquidation or a reorganization, because in either event the debtor continues to exist after bankruptcy.

If the debtor is *not* an individual, the effect of finding that a creditor does not have a claim depends on whether the bankruptcy case is a liquidation or a reorganization. If the case is a liquidation, the creditor will be out of luck. The creditor's *only* chance to get paid anything by the debtor will be pursuant to the bankruptcy distribution, since the debtor will cease to exist after bankruptcy.[13] Therefore, without an allowed claim, no bankruptcy payment will be made. However, if the debtor is reorganizing, the "no-claim" creditor will be counting its blessings, and the debtor will be adversely impacted. Although the creditor still will not be paid anything in the bankruptcy case itself, the creditor holding undischarged rights nevertheless will be able to pursue those rights *in full* against the reorganized debtor after the bankruptcy case is over.

Because of the significant negative consequences to either the debtor or the creditor that occur if a creditor's rights against a debtor are not classified as a claim, Congress decided in the 1978 Code to give "claim" the "broadest possible definition."[14] As the legislative history emphasized, use of this broad definition was a "significant departure" from prior law.[15] In liquidation cases under the old Act, claims had to be "provable" in order to be paid a bankruptcy dividend or to be dischargeable. Contingent and unliquidated claims were not provable under § 63a of the Act. For example, a tort claim against the debtor that had not been fixed at the time of bankruptcy would not be provable; the creditor would not share in the bankruptcy distribution and the debtor

---

[13]   Note that the creditor may still have an opportunity to collect from parties other than the debtor. For example, if the debtor is a partnership, the creditor will have independent recourse against the general partners. For corporate or partnership debtors, the creditor may have a right of recourse against secondary obligors, such as guarantors or sureties.

[14]   H.R. Rep. No. 95–595, 95th Cong., 1st Sess., at 309 (1977); S. Rep. No. 95–989, 95th Cong., 2d Sess., at 22 (1978).

[15]   Id.

would not be discharged from that claim. The result was incomplete relief for both the debtor and the creditor.[16]

Congress abolished the concept of provability in 1978.[17] The purpose of the broad definition of "claim" in § 101(5) was "that all legal obligations of the debtor, no matter how remote or contingent, will be able to be dealt with in the bankruptcy case. It permits the broadest possible relief in the bankruptcy court."[18]

The *definition* of "claim" in § 101(5)(A) is:

right to payment, whether or not such right is reduced to judgment, liquidated, unliquidated, fixed, contingent, matured, unmatured, disputed, undisputed, legal, equitable, secured, or unsecured.

Under this definition, a creditor with a *"right to payment"* has a bankruptcy claim even if that right to payment is *unliquidated*, or *contingent*, or *unmatured*, or *disputed*. For example, the tort victim in the example given above would have a claim under the Code, even if their claim was not fixed or liquidated at the time bankruptcy was filed. That claim will then be fixed in the bankruptcy case. If the trustee disputes the claim's validity or amount, the dispute will be resolved in the bankruptcy case. If the fixing of a contingent or unliquidated claim would "unduly delay the administration of the case," the bankruptcy court is authorized to *estimate* the amount of the claim for the purpose of allowance.[19] § 502(c)(1).

Even a right to an *equitable remedy* can constitute a claim under the Code.[20] Examples might include an *injunction* or a right to *specific performance*. The right to an equitable remedy is considered a claim under § 101(5)(B) if the debtor's breach "gives rise to a right to payment." The legislative history gives the example of a judgment for specific performance that under state law might give the creditor an alternative right to the payment of money if performance is refused.[21] The real importance of § 101(5)(B) is that the debtor can discharge the equitable remedy in bankruptcy, and thus be freed from the constraints of the injunction or other equitable decree. This provision has generated controversy with regard to environmental injunctions and covenants not to compete.

The Supreme Court has taken Congress at its word, and on numerous occasions has given an extremely broad construction to "claim" (and correspondingly to "debt," which simply means "liability on a claim," see § 101(12)). In *Ohio v. Kovacs*,[22] the Court held that an individual debtor's environmental cleanup obligation constituted a claim. All that the state was seeking from the debtor, the Court explained, was the payment

---

[16]   See H.R. Rep. No. 95–595, 95th Cong., 1st Sess., at 180 (1977).

[17]   Id.

[18]   Id. at 309; S. Rep. No. 95–989, 95th Cong., 2d Sess., at 22 (1978). In another passage, the House Report explained that the "law will permit a complete settlement of the affairs of a bankrupt debtor, and a complete discharge and fresh start." H.R. Rep. No. 95–595, 95th Cong., 1st Sess., at 180 (1977).

[19]   See § 7.4.

[20]   See § 7.3.

[21]   124 Cong. Rec. H11,090 (daily ed. Sept. 28, 1978) (statement of Rep. Edwards).

[22]   469 U.S. 274 (1985).

of money, and thus the government had a bankruptcy claim. Therefore, the resulting "debt" was dischargeable. In *Pennsylvania Department of Public Welfare v. Davenport*,[23] the Court held that a criminal restitution obligation constituted a claim, thus enabling the debtor to discharge the restitution debt pursuant to a chapter 13 plan.[24] In so holding, the *Davenport* Court reversed course from dictum in the earlier case of *Kelly v. Robinson*[25] that had suggested that a restitution obligation was not a debt. Finally, in *Johnson v. Home State Bank*,[26] the Supreme Court held that a lienholder who only had *in rem* rights against property of the debtor had a claim. In *Johnson*, the debtor's *in personam* liability had been discharged in a previous bankruptcy case under chapter 7. The debtor then filed a chapter 13 case,[27] and sought to modify the remaining *in rem* mortgage obligation in a chapter 13 plan. The Court held that such an action was at least theoretically permissible,[28] given that the creditor still had a "claim."

Not all "claims" are entitled to be share in the bankruptcy distribution, or to vote on a chapter 11 plan. In order to receive a bankruptcy dividend or vote on a plan, a claim also must be *"allowed."* "Allowance" is a term of art in the Bankruptcy Code. See § 502. It refers to those claims that are filtered through the bankruptcy process and found to be meritorious. In order to be allowed, a claim must satisfy both procedural[29] and substantive[30] criteria.

As a procedural matter, a *"proof of claim"* must be either filed or deemed filed under § 501. A proof of claim is defined as "a written statement setting forth a creditor's claim." Rule 3001(a). The filing of proofs of claims permits the bankruptcy trustee and creditors to review filed claims and object to those claims believed to be invalid. A filed claim is deemed allowed, unless a party in interest objects. § 502(a). If an objection is filed, the bankruptcy court must resolve the dispute. § 502(b). If a claim is contingent or unliquidated, and fixing or liquidating the claim would "unduly delay" the administration of the case, the bankruptcy court must *estimate* the claim for purpose of allowance. § 502(c)(1).

As a substantive matter, the Code sets out a number of grounds for disallowing claims to which an objection is made. § 502(b), (d), (e). To begin with, the claim must be valid under non-bankruptcy law. § 502(b)(1). Even if the claim is valid outside of bankruptcy, that claim may be disallowed in whole or in part in the bankruptcy case because of the application of specific bankruptcy policies. For example, as a general rule claims for unmatured postpetition interest are disallowed, because of the principle

---

[23]   495 U.S. 552 (1990).

[24]   Congress overruled the result in *Davenport* with regard to the dischargeability of a criminal restitution obligation in chapter 13 in 1990, by adding § 1328(a)(3) to the Code. Congress did not, however, upset the Court's specific holding that a restitution obligation constituted a claim.

[25]   479 U.S. 36 (1986).

[26]   501 U.S. 78 (1991).

[27]   The sequence of filing a chapter 7 case and then a chapter 13 case is known colloquially as a "chapter 20" case.

[28]   The creditor still would be allowed to argue that the entire "chapter 20" scheme constituted "bad faith" under the particular circumstances, thus blocking confirmation under § 1325(a)(3). See § 12.15.

[29]   See § 7.4.

[30]   See § 7.5.

that bankruptcy accelerates all obligations down to the date of the bankruptcy filing. § 502(b)(2). Some claims, such as those arising out of the termination of a real property lease or an employment contract, are limited as a matter of distributive justice in order to prevent the claimant from taking an excessively large share of the bankruptcy distribution. See § 502(b)(6), (7).

Claims are generally allowed in the amount owing "as of the date of the filing of the petition." § 502(b). In short, claims are fixed as of the outset of the case. Recall, though, that a claim may be allowable even if it has not yet matured or even if it is still contingent at the time the case is commenced. § 101(5)(A). As long as the operative events giving rise to that claim have taken place prior to the filing of the bankruptcy case, the claim will participate in the bankruptcy administration. Bankruptcy thus accelerates claims. As just mentioned, creditors do not usually receive postpetition interest on their claims. To illustrate, assume that a creditor is owed a principal debt of $1,000, payable on June 1 with 8 percent interest, and that the debtor files bankruptcy on May 1. The creditor would have a claim for $1,000, but would not be entitled to interest for the month of May.

In some cases, fixing the timing of a claim may prove difficult.[31] The problems usually arise when some but not all of the events giving rise to the claim have occurred when bankruptcy is filed. If all that must happen after the bankruptcy filing for the claim to come due is for time to pass, as for an unmatured claim, or for a contingency to be removed, as in a suretyship situation, the creditor clearly has a bankruptcy claim. The hard cases are those in which the link between the debtor's conduct and the creditor's claim is more attenuated. Tort and environmental cases have proven especially troublesome. Consider, for example, a mass tort case, in which the debtor engages in conduct before bankruptcy, such as producing a defective product, but the victims are not actually injured until after bankruptcy. Is there a claim? The courts have struggled to resolve this type of case.

§ 7.2   Timing Problems

Claims are allowed in bankruptcy cases in the amount owing "as of the date of the filing of the petition." § 502(b). In other words, bankruptcy claims are calculated as of the beginning of the case. A claim that comes due before bankruptcy would be allowed in the principal amount due, plus interest accrued up to the date of bankruptcy. However, postpetition interest is ordinarily not allowed. § 502(b)(2).

Claims that have not matured or been fixed or liquidated as of the beginning of the case often are allowed. Congress intentionally defined "claim" broadly, so that all of the debtor's legal obligations could be addressed in the bankruptcy case.[32] Thus, the definition of claim in § 101(5) includes a "right to payment" even if that right is unmatured, contingent, disputed, or unliquidated at the time bankruptcy is filed. As long as the operative events underlying the claim took place prior to bankruptcy, the creditor has a claim for bankruptcy purposes. The bankruptcy court may have to

---

[31]   See § 7.2.

[32]   See § 7.1.

estimate the unliquidated or contingent claim for purposes of allowance, if fixing the claim would unduly delay the administration of the bankruptcy case. § 502(c)(1).

Consider several common examples of legal obligations that are treated as claims in bankruptcy even though they may not be fully matured and fixed as of the date the bankruptcy case is commenced. Assume that Debtor files bankruptcy on April 1. Creditor is the holder of a promissory note issued on March 1, and which is due and payable on May 1. Creditor has a claim, even though that claim is *"unmatured."* Creditor's claim arose before bankruptcy, when the note was issued.

Now assume that Creditor C has a claim against the Debtor that arose before bankruptcy. G, a third party, guaranteed Debtor's debt to Creditor prior to bankruptcy. Debtor is the primary obligor, and G is the secondary obligor; that is, only if Debtor defaults will G be called upon to pay C. Assume that when Debtor files bankruptcy, it has not yet defaulted on the debt to C. Creditor C of course has a claim against Debtor, but so too does G. G's claim against Debtor is *"contingent,"* the contingency being whether Debtor defaults. If Debtor defaults, and G has to pay C, then G would have a right of reimbursement against Debtor.

Next, assume that Debtor drives her car through a red light on March 1 and crashes into Creditor's car. Debtor files bankruptcy on April 1. Creditor has an *"unliquidated"* claim against Debtor based on the alleged tort.

However, if Debtor files bankruptcy on April 1 and runs into Creditor's car on April 2, Creditor would not have a claim in bankruptcy. Creditor's claim now would be deemed to arise after the bankruptcy filing. The date of the bankruptcy filing serves as the point of cleavage; actions rooted in the pre-bankruptcy past are subject to the bankruptcy case, but those that are connected to the post-bankruptcy world generally are not.

Sometimes is hard to pinpoint exactly when a claim arises, however. The problem usually arises when some of the events that give rise to the claim occur before bankruptcy, but other essential predicates to the debtor's liability under non-bankruptcy law have not yet taken place at the time of bankruptcy. This scenario has been especially notable in tort and environmental cases.

A classic illustration is the well-known case of *Grady v. A.H. Robins Co.*[33] Rebecca Grady purchased a Dalkon Shield intrauterine device and had it inserted *before* Robins filed bankruptcy. Shortly *after* Robins filed (later the same day, in fact), Grady manifested the first symptoms of illness attributable to the IUD. She later sued Robins for her injuries in district court. The issue was whether her claim against Robins arose before bankruptcy, in which event her lawsuit would be stayed, or after the bankruptcy filing, in which case it would not be stayed. Grady argued that her claim arose after bankruptcy, on the theory that she could not have brought an action against Robins under state law until she discovered her injury.

---

[33]   839 F.2d 198 (4th Cir. 1988).

The Fourth Circuit court held for Robins, however, concluding that Grady's claim arose prior to bankruptcy and therefore was stayed. The court explained that the claim arose when Robins engaged in the tortious conduct. Section 362(a)(1) stays proceedings that could have been brought before bankruptcy—which this one could not, because she had not yet discovered her injury—*and* proceedings to recover claims that arose before bankruptcy, even if no proceeding could have been brought at that time.

Note, though, that the court's holding also meant that Rebecca Grady would be entitled to (1) vote on the Robins plan, see § 1126(a), and (2) participate in distributions under that plan. At the same time, her claim would be discharged by confirmation of the plan. § 1141(d). In essence, the court's finding that she had a bankruptcy "claim" served to channel the processing of Grady's right to payment through the bankruptcy case. This channeling implements the congressional intent of providing the most complete relief possible to the debtor and to creditors in the bankruptcy case.

The *Robins* court decided not to follow the reasoning of the Third Circuit in the case of *In re M. Frenville Co.*[34] In *Frenville*, an accounting firm brought an action against the debtor after bankruptcy as a third-party defendant, seeking contribution or indemnity. The accounting firm had been sued postpetition by several banks for alleged misdeeds committed in connection with the preparation of financial statements for the debtor prior to bankruptcy. The Third Circuit held that the third-party action against the debtor was not a "claim" and thus was not stayed. The court reasoned that the accounting firm could not have brought its action against the debtor prior to bankruptcy, because under state law the contribution and indemnity action could only be brought after the main action was filed (by the banks against the accounting firm), which occurred post-bankruptcy. For the same reason, the court stated that the accounting firm did not have a "right to payment" necessary for a bankruptcy "claim" against the debtor prior to bankruptcy.

The Third Circuit's approach has been described as the "*accrued state law theory*," meaning that a claim only arises when an action has accrued against the debtor under state law. *Frenville* has been widely condemned on the ground that it improperly elevates state law over federal law.[35] While state law governs the question of whether a cause of action exists, the issue of *when* that claim is cognizable for purposes of a federal bankruptcy case is a matter of federal law.

The proper result would be to hold that the accounting firm had a prepetition claim against the debtor that arose when the conduct of preparing the financial statements took place, and thus the third-party action against the debtor should have been stayed. At the same time, that claim for contribution and indemnity should have been entitled to participate in the bankruptcy distribution and should have been dischargeable. The *Frenville* approach frustrates the intent of Congress to provide complete relief to the debtor and to creditors in a bankruptcy case.

---

[34] 744 F.2d 332 (3d Cir. 1984), cert. denied, 469 U.S. 1160 (1985).

[35] See In re Grossman's Inc., 607 F.3d 114, 121 (3d Cir. 2010) ("Courts have declined to follow *Frenville* because of its apparent conflict with the Bankruptcy Code's expansive treatment of the term 'claim.'").

The Third Circuit finally abandoned its position in *Frenville* in 2010, holding in *In re Grossman's Inc.* as follows:

> Irrespective of the title used, there seems to be something approaching a consensus among the courts that a prerequisite for recognizing a "claim" is that the claimant's exposure to a product giving rise to the "claim" occurred pre-petition, even though the injury manifested after the reorganization. We agree and hold that a "claim" arises when an individual is exposed pre-petition to a product or other conduct giving rise to an injury, which underlies a "right to payment" under the Bankruptcy Code.[36]

While the "accrued state law" view never inspired a following, and now has even been abandoned by the Third Circuit, courts since *Robins* also have been careful not to go too far with a pure "*conduct*" test to determine when a claim arises. Note that in *Robins* the tort victim also was *exposed* to the defective product prior to bankruptcy. To highlight the distinction, consider whether Rebecca Grady would have had a "claim" if the IUD had been manufactured by Robins prepetition, but it had not been sold to her and inserted until after the bankruptcy filing. In that event, the particular claimant would have had no connection with the debtor and would not have been exposed to the debtor's defective product at all prior to bankruptcy. Her connection to the debtor would be too attenuated (nonexistent, in fact) to fairly suggest that she should be subjected to the bankruptcy proceedings. An attempt to bind her, as a future tort claimant, to that bankruptcy also would raise serious due process questions.[37]

The same dilemma has been encountered in environmental cases, in determining when the environmental agency's claim against the debtor for cleanup costs arises. Assume that the debtor engages in conduct that leads to pollution prior to the bankruptcy filing. For example, assume that the debtor improperly disposes of a storage tank containing toxic pollutants. When the debtor files bankruptcy, however, the environmental agency may have no notice whatsoever of the debtor's actions. On a strict debtor "conduct" approach, the agency's claim for cleanup costs would arise prepetition.

The trend in the courts has been to adopt a "*pre-bankruptcy relationship*" test in tort[38] and environmental[39] cases to determine when a claim arises. Often the impetus for doing so has been to avoid due process problems that might arise under a pure "conduct" test. Perhaps a cleaner approach in these cases would be to acknowledge that a "claim" does exist under the Bankruptcy Code's "claim" definition, but then to decline

---

[36] Id. at 125 (holding that asbestos victims' claims arose when they were exposed to the asbestos decades earlier, but also recognizing Due Process limitations).

[37] See, e.g., Jones v. Chemetron Corp., 212 F.3d 199 (3d Cir. 2000); In re Chateaugay Corporation, 944 F.2d 997, 1003 (2nd. Cir. 1991); see also *Grossman's*, supra note 35, 607 F.3d at 125–28 (remanding for consideration of whether asbestos victims' claims were discharged by chapter 11 plan given due process constraints).

[38] E.g., Epstein v. Official Comm. of Unsecured Creditors of Piper Aircraft Corp., 58 F.3d 1573 (11th Cir. 1995).

[39] E.g., In re Jensen, 995 F.2d 925 (9th Cir. 1993), see also *Chateaugay*, supra note 37, 944 F.2d at 1004–05 (government's unincurred CERCLA response costs for debtor's prepetition releases is a "contingent" claim).

to enforce the consequences (such as discharge) against the claimant on due process grounds.[40] Nevertheless, most courts now embrace the "relationship" test. Under this approach, the debtor and the claimant must have had some relationship, *"such as contact, exposure, impact, or privity,"* at the time the bankruptcy petition was filed. In *Robins*, Rebecca Grady still would have a claim under the relationship test, because she was exposed to the defective IUD prior to bankruptcy. If an environmental agency had notice of the pollution at the time of bankruptcy (demonstrated, for example, by the agency listing the site as a problem spot), it would have a claim.[41] If, however, the agency did not have notice of a pollution problem, or if the tort victim had not yet been exposed to injury, no bankruptcy "claim" would have arisen. This approach is sometimes called the *"fair contemplation"* test,[42] the reference being to what the creditor fairly could have known.

Some chapter 11 cases have required a "relationship" between the debtor and the claimant as a prerequisite to a claim, but have pushed back the point in time by which that relationship must be established, from the time of the filing of the case to the *time of confirmation* of the plan. An example is *Piper Aircraft Corp. v. Calabro*.[43] Lori Calabro's parents were killed when a plane manufactured prepetition by the debtor crashed after the filing of the petition, but prior to confirmation of the plan. Calabro as executor of the estate sued the debtor and argued that the claim arose postpetition, when the crash occurred, and thus was not stayed.

The bankruptcy court held that the claim was stayed and must be dealt with in the bankruptcy proceeding. The court explained that while the debtor's prepetition conduct in manufacturing the plane was not enough by itself to sustain a claim, because the pool of potential claimants was not sufficiently identifiable at that time, the postpetition, pre-confirmation crash eliminated that problem in time to permit that claim to be processed in the chapter 11 case. This approach would not work in a chapter 7 case, where presumably the dividing line must be left at the time of the bankruptcy filing.

§ 7.3   Equitable Remedies

a. Introduction

The Code's expansive approach to the definition of "claim" in bankruptcy is underscored by the recognition that even an *equitable remedy* can qualify as a claim. § 101(5)(B). Accordingly, the holder of the equitable remedy may be paid in the bankruptcy case on its "claim." In addition, the claimant's right to enforce the equitable remedy after the conclusion of the bankruptcy case may be barred by the discharge.

Section 101(5)(B) provides:

---

[40]   E.g., *Chemetron*, supra note 37.

[41]   For example, in *Chateaugay*, the Second Circuit pointed out that the EPA was "acutely aware" of the debtor's prepetition releases. 944 F.2d at 1005.

[42]   See In re Zilog, Inc., 450 F.3d 996 (9th Cir. 2006) (extending "fair contemplation" test to sex discrimination claims).

[43]   169 B.R. 766 (Bankr. S.D. Fla. 1994).

"claim" means—. . . (B) right to an equitable remedy for breach of performance if such breach gives rise to a right to payment, whether or not such right to an equitable remedy is reduced to judgment, fixed, contingent, matured, unmatured, disputed, undisputed, secured, or unsecured.

The original reform bill as passed by the House would have classified an equitable remedy as a claim even if the claimant did *not* have a correlative right to payment.[44] As enacted, however, the statutory definition plainly requires the claimant to have a *"right to payment."* Thus, equitable remedies that cannot be satisfied under applicable non-bankruptcy law by the payment of money are not claims and are not subject to the discharge.[45] The claimant's right to the payment of money is satisfied if the right to payment is an *alternative* to the equitable remedy.[46] The example given in the congressional explanation of the Code is a right to specific performance that can be satisfied by the payment of money in the event performance is refused.[47]

The critical inquiry, then, is whether the non-bankruptcy law that gives rise to the equitable remedy gives the holder of that equitable remedy the right to be paid money in lieu of equitable enforcement. This issue has been tested most critically in the areas of (1) environmental cleanup orders[48] and (2) injunctions to enforce covenants not to compete.[49]

The courts have not spoken with a unified (or clear) voice in either area. However, the predominant trend has been to find the existence of a claim only when the holder of the equitable remedy clearly has the right outside of bankruptcy to accept money in lieu of performance.[50] The courts have been reluctant to permit debtors to use the bankruptcy discharge as a convenient way to dodge the need to comply with injunctive orders. Only if the debtor could in effect "buy its way out" of the injunction outside of bankruptcy will it be able to use the bankruptcy discharge in like manner to eliminate the injunction. For example, some courts have held that an agency's right to reimbursement for the cost of cleaning up prepetition pollution damage is a dischargeable claim, but a court injunction to stop polluting in the future is not a dischargeable claim.[51] Of course, if the bankruptcy court does find that the equitable remedy constitutes a "claim" that is dischargeable in bankruptcy, the court also will have to estimate or liquidate the amount of that claim for the purpose of allowance, see § 502(c)(2), thereby permitting the claimant to share in the bankruptcy distribution.

---

[44]   H.R. Rep. No. 95–595, 95th Cong., 1st Sess., at 309 (1977); S. Rep. No. 95–989, 95th Cong., 2d Sess., at 22 (1978).

[45]   124 Cong. Rec. H11,090 (daily ed. Sept. 28, 1978) (statement of Rep. Edwards).

[46]   Id.

[47]   Id.

[48]   See, e.g., Ohio v. Kovacs, 469 U.S. 274 (1985); In re Chateaugay Corp., 944 F.2d 997 (2d. Cir. 1991). See § 7.3.b.

[49]   See, e.g., In re Udell, 18 F.3d 403 (7th Cir. 1994); Rederford v. US Airways, Inc., 589 F.3d 30 (1st Cir. 2009). See § 7.3.c.

[50]   See, e.g., *Chateaugay*, supra note 36, 944 F.2d at 1008.

[51]   See In re Mark IV Indus., Inc., 459 B.R. 173, 188 (S.D.N.Y. 2011).

b.   *Environmental Injunctions*

The environmental cases have come in many shapes and sizes. However, at the core a common fact pattern emerges. Prior to bankruptcy, the Debtor releases or threatens to release toxic wastes. Also prior to bankruptcy, the responsible state or federal government environmental agency orders the Debtor to clean up the pollution. The Debtor then files bankruptcy before complying with the cleanup order. The issue is whether the cleanup order is a "claim."[52]

Any discussion of this issue must begin with the Supreme Court's 1985 decision in *Ohio v. Kovacs*.[53] In *Kovacs*, the Court held that the debtor's cleanup obligation constituted a dischargeable claim.[54] In the wake of *Kovacs*, there was considerable wailing and gnashing of teeth to the effect that the Supreme Court had eviscerated the environmental laws in bankruptcy. However, the predictions of the death of environmental law in the forum of bankruptcy, like the reports of Mark Twain's death, have proven to be greatly exaggerated. The limited reach of the *Kovacs* holding may be attributed to two reasons—the unusual factual setting of *Kovacs*, and Justice White's careful notation in that opinion of what the Court was *not* deciding.[55]

The core facts in *Kovacs* were as follows. William Kovacs was the principal of a corporation that violated Ohio's environmental laws. Prior to bankruptcy, Kovacs agreed to a stipulation, both individually and on behalf of the corporation, which enjoined further pollution, ordered the payment of a fine, and further ordered the cleanup of existing pollution. When no cleanup was made, the state of Ohio appointed a receiver to take possession of the site and remove the pollution. Kovacs then filed a personal bankruptcy case.[56] After the bankruptcy filing, the state attempted to compel Kovacs to pay money to help defray the costs of cleanup. The state also sought a declaration that the cleanup obligation was not a "debt" that was dischargeable in his bankruptcy case.

The state lost. The Supreme Court affirmed the Sixth Circuit's decision that the state had a "claim" arising from William Kovacs' cleanup obligation. The critical fact leading to the Court's holding was that "the only performance sought from Kovacs was the payment of money."[57] As a practical matter, the state of Ohio had a "right to payment" from Kovacs after it had taken over the cleanup operation. By dispossessing Kovacs from the site through the appointment of a receiver, the state of Ohio had effectively prevented Kovacs and his corporation from actually *performing* the cleanup. Later decisions have seized on this important fact, and have found *Kovacs* to be

---

[52]   For a thoughtful early analysis of this problem, see Douglas G. Baird & Thomas H. Jackson, *Kovacs* and Toxic Wastes in Bankruptcy, 36 Stan. L. Rev. 1199 (1984). Professor Kathryn Heidt wrote extensively on the whole area of environmental claims in bankruptcy. Much of her work was brought together in an excellent book, Environmental Obligations in Bankruptcy (1993).

[53]   469 U.S. 274 (1985).

[54]   Id. at 283.

[55]   Id. at 284–85.

[56]   He initially filed under chapter 11, but converted to chapter 7. Id. at 276 n. 1.

[57]   Id. at 283.

inapplicable when the debtor is in possession of the site and is able to effect the cleanup.[58]

The limited reach of the *Kovacs* decision was underscored by the Court itself. The Court emphasized that anyone in possession of a site must comply with applicable environmental laws, even while in bankruptcy: "Plainly, that person or firm may not maintain a nuisance, pollute the waters of the State, or refuse to remove the source of such conditions."[59] Furthermore, the Court reiterated that the discharge did *not* apply to "the injunction against bringing further toxic wastes on the premises or against any conduct that will contribute to the pollution of the site."[60] In short, the only obligation of the debtor that the Court held could be discharged was the order to clean up pre-bankruptcy pollution, and that obligation was a "claim" and thus subject to discharge only because the debtor had been prevented by the State's appointment of a receiver to take possession of the site from actually removing the toxic wastes himself.

The Court also noted that other avenues of enforcement remained viable. The discharge did not shield the debtor from criminal prosecution. If a fine or penalty had been imposed for the violation, that obligation would be excepted from the discharge under § 523(a)(7).[61] Finally, as Justice O'Connor pointed out in an important concurring opinion, if the state had obtained a *lien* on the debtor's property to secure the cleanup obligation prior to bankruptcy, that lien would not be dischargeable in bankruptcy.[62]

Not long before the Supreme Court's decision in *Kovacs*, Professors Baird and Jackson had published an influential article arguing for an expansive interpretation of the definition of "claim" in the environmental context.[63] The approach favored by Baird and Jackson was based on the normative principle that bankruptcy should mirror non-bankruptcy outcomes as much as is reasonably possible. Applying this premise, they asked whether a debtor could effectively escape the obligation by going out of business. That is, in their view whether an environmental obligation is a "claim" should hinge on whether that obligation depends upon the debtor's continued existence. If the obligation would disappear if the debtor ceased operations, they would not classify it as a claim. But, if the obligation would continue to have consequences even after the debtor went out of business, that obligation should be classified as a claim. Applying this paradigm, Baird and Jackson argued that in most cases an order to clean up prepetition pollution should be treated as a claim, whereas an injunction to cease polluting would not be a claim.[64] In addition to mirroring non-bankruptcy results, this approach would further congressional intent in § 101(5)(B) by permitting the bankruptcy case to deal with all of the obligations arising out of the debtor's pre-bankruptcy existence, including the debtor's release of toxic wastes.

---

[58] See, e.g., *Chateaugay*, supra note 36, 944 F.2d at 1007–08.

[59] *Kovacs,* supra note 36, 469 U.S. at 285.

[60] Id.

[61] Id. at 283. See § 10.22.

[62] 469 U.S. at 286 (O'Connor, J., concurring).

[63] See Baird & Jackson, supra note 40.

[64] Some cases have so held. *See* In re Mark IV Indus., Inc., 459 B.R. 173, 188 (S.D.N.Y. 2011).

While the Baird and Jackson approach has been widely discussed by the courts, it has not been adopted in its entirety by any court. Some decisions, such as that of the Sixth Circuit in *United States v. Whizco*,[65] have reached results consistent with the Baird and Jackson theory. In *Whizco*, the court held that a mandatory restoration order under the Surface Mining Control and Reclamation Act was a claim, even though the government did not have the option of suing the debtor for the cost of restoration. The court reasoned that the debtor had to expend money to remedy conditions that were created prior to bankruptcy, and that obligation should be considered a debt.

Starkly opposing *Whizco* is the Second Circuit's leading decision in *In re Chateaugay Corp.*[66] In *Chateaugay*, the court held that a mandatory injunction to clean up prepetition pollution is *not* a claim and is thus not dischargeable unless it *exclusively* requires the removal of previously deposited wastes.[67] In other words, under *Chateaugay*, a cleanup injunction is not a "claim" at all if it has the *dual* purposes of removing accumulated wastes *and* ameliorating ongoing pollution. As the Second Circuit recognized, under their test most cleanup injunctions will "fall on the non-claim side of the line,"[68] because the removal of previously deposited wastes almost always has the concomitant effect of stopping further pollution from those very wastes. The court emphasized that under CERCLA, the government does not have the option to accept money from the debtor in exchange for the debtor's privilege to continue polluting, and therefore does not have a "right" to payment. Admittedly, the government could remove the wastes itself and then sue the debtor for the response costs—in which case the government undoubtedly *would* have a claim—but until that path is taken, no bankruptcy claim exists.

The courts have tended to favor the more restrictive *Chateaugay* approach, although in differing degrees. The Seventh Circuit upheld an order by the Environmental Protection Agency directing the bankruptcy debtor to stop releasing hazardous wastes *and* to expend funds to remedy the damage already done.[69] The crucial factor to the court was that the threat from the prior releases was ongoing; the court characterized the obligation to clean up as one that "ran with the land," and thus continued to bind the debtor as the current owner or operator. The Seventh Circuit did hold, though, that the government had a dischargeable claim to the extent it sought only to recover money to pay for pre-bankruptcy acts. Under this view, the obligations of a debtor who was *not* the current owner or operator of the site would be discharged.

The most extreme example of a disinclination to find that a cleanup obligation is a claim, particularly when the prior pollution poses a continuing threat to the environment, is the Third Circuit's decision in *In re Torwico Electronics, Inc.*[70] In *Torwico*, the court effectively ignored *Kovacs* and went beyond even the Second Circuit and the Seventh Circuit, holding that an order directing the debtor to pay for the

---

[65]   841 F.2d 147 (6th Cir. 1988).

[66]   944 F.2d 997 (2d Cir. 1991).

[67]   Id. at 1008.

[68]   Id.

[69]   In re CMC Heartland Partners, 966 F.2d 1143 (7th Cir. 1992).

[70]   8 F.3d 146 (3d Cir. 1993), cert. denied, 511 U.S. 1046 (1994).

cleanup of pre-bankruptcy pollution did not give rise to a claim—even though the debtor was no longer in possession of the site and even though under applicable statutes the government could have elected to clean up the site and recover its costs. Under *Torwico*, the only way an environmental obligation could be a claim is if the government actually cleaned up the site and then sued the debtor for reimbursement of those costs. Most commentators have been extremely critical of *Torwico*, arguing that it completely undermines important bankruptcy principles.[71]

c.   *Covenants Not to Compete and Specific Performance*

The issue of when an equitable remedy constitutes a claim under § 101(5)(B) is important in a number of settings other than the environmental arena. Prominent examples include covenants not to compete and specific performance. The analysis under covenants not to compete is complicated by the intrusion of the bankruptcy "fresh start" policy; the individual debtor wants to earn a livelihood be engaging after bankruptcy in the very occupation that would be enjoined by injunctive enforcement of the covenant. With regard to specific performance, the concern is that allowing specific performance will contravene the bankruptcy principle of equality of distribution.

Under non-bankruptcy law, noncompete agreements often are enforced against former employees by means of a prohibitory injunction for the duration of the agreed period. Under applicable state law, the employer may but usually does not have an alternative right to the payment of money damages. The relevant issue is whether the employee who is subject to the noncompete provision can escape the force of that clause by filing bankruptcy and discharging their obligation under the covenant. Such an outcome will only be possible if the covenant gives rise to a bankruptcy "claim," which then could be discharged in bankruptcy. If the court finds that a claim exists, then it will also have to estimate that claim for the purpose of allowance.

An interesting illustration of the problems raised by covenants not to compete is found in the Seventh Circuit's decision in *In re Udell*.[72] The debtor had agreed not to compete within 50 miles of Fort Wayne with an Indiana carpet dealer for three years after leaving its employ. In addition, the covenant provided that the employer would be entitled to recover liquidated damages of $25,000 if the employee breached the covenant. The debtor did breach; he left the carpet dealer and bought a competing store within the proscribed radius. The carpet company sued Udell, seeking both a prohibitory injunction and recovery of the liquidated damages. A state court issued a preliminary injunction. After Udell filed chapter 13, the employer sought relief from the stay to enforce the injunction. The employer won.

Resolution of the case required the court to parse the language of § 101(5)(B) carefully. That section provides in relevant part that a claim means a "right to an equitable remedy for breach of performance if such breach gives rise to a right to payment." The critical issue in the case was whether there had to be a connection

---

[71]   E.g., Kathryn R. Heidt, Undermining Bankruptcy Law and Policy: *Torwico Electronics, Inc. v. New Jersey Department of Environmental Protection*, 56 U. Pitt. L. Rev. 627 (1995).

[72]   18 F.3d 403 (7th Cir. 1994). Accord, Kennedy v. Medicap Pharmacies, Inc., 267 F.3d 493 (6th Cir. 2001); In re Stone Res., Inc., 458 B.R. 823 (E.D. Penn. 2011).

between the equitable remedy and the right to payment. The debtor argued that no such nexus was required; the plain language of the statute requires only that "such breach" give rise to the right to payment, not that the equitable remedy itself be subject to a right to payment. Here, Udell argued, the same breach of the covenant gave rise *both* to the injunctive right *and* to the claim for liquidated damages, and thus satisfied the literal requirements of the statute.

The Seventh Circuit, however, looking at the legislative history and at the environmental cases, concluded that there must be some *connection* between the right to payment and the equitable remedy for the equitable remedy to qualify as a claim under § 101(5)(B). In other words, if the right to damages and the injunctive remedy are cumulative and independent, meaning that the injunction itself could not be satisfied under state law by the payment of damages, then the equitable remedy will not be classified as a bankruptcy "claim." Any other result would be "absurd," according to the concurring judge.[73]

The *Udell* court did not consider the broader policy question of whether enforcing a covenant not to compete via an injunction that prevents the debtor from engaging in his chosen occupation violates the bankruptcy fresh start policy. Barry Udell's most productive utilization of his skills may have been selling carpet in the Fort Wayne area; to deny him that privilege at least to some extent may hinder his post-bankruptcy economic productivity. The question is whether the harm to the employer from not enforcing the injunction outweighs the intrusion on the debtor's fresh start. Lurking, too, is the concern that estimation of the amount of the employer's "claim" (which must be done if a claim is found to exist under § 101(5)(B)) may be quite difficult. Indeed, non-bankruptcy law might provide that the injunction may only be issued upon proof that legal damages cannot be proven with sufficient certainty.

The remedy of specific performance also might be classified as a claim. As mentioned earlier, the legislative history expressly cites specific performance as an example of the type of equitable remedy for which there might be an alternative right of payment, and which thus would be treated as a claim.[74] As is the case with injunctions to enforce covenants not to compete, there may be a serious legal and practical problem if the specific performance remedy is classified as a claim—under non-bankruptcy law, the right to specific performance might be awarded precisely because monetary damages cannot readily be calculated. However, the problem as a matter of bankruptcy policy is that enforcing an award of specific performance effectively gives the claimant a larger share of the estate than other creditors, who are limited to their pro rata share out of the residue of the estate. The creditor who receives specific performance is paid in full.

§ 7.4   Allowance Process

In order for the holder of a claim to participate in a bankruptcy distribution or to vote on a chapter 11 plan, the claim must be "*allowed*." Allowance contains both procedural and substantive elements. This section explains the process by which a

---

[73]   *Udell*, supra note 60, 18 F.3d at 411–12 (Flaum, J., concurring).

[74]   124 Cong. Rec. H11,090 (daily ed. Sept. 28, 1978) (remarks of Rep. Edwards).

claim is allowed. The next section discusses the various grounds upon which a claim may be disallowed.[75]

The first requisite for the allowance of a claim is that a *proof of claim* must be filed. See § 501, Rule 3002. Note, however, that a proof of claim needs to be filed only if some purpose would be served by the allowance of the claim.[76] For example, the vast majority of chapter 7 cases are "no asset" cases in which no distribution will be made to unsecured creditors. In those cases, there is no reason for a creditor to file a proof of claim.

Indeed, filing a proof of claim may not be innocuous. By filing a claim, a creditor voluntarily subjects itself to the equitable jurisdiction of the bankruptcy court. Doing so could cause the creditor to forfeit its right to a jury trial under the Seventh Amendment.[77] Furthermore, filing a claim may open the creditor up to the resolution of a counterclaim as a core proceeding in the bankruptcy court, see 28 U.S.C. § 157(b)(2)(C), although in *Stern v. Marshall* the Supreme Court held that the non-Article III bankruptcy court "lacked the constitutional authority to enter a final judgment on a state law counterclaim that is not resolved in the process of ruling on a creditor's proof of claim."[78]

A "proof of claim" is defined in the Rules as "a written statement setting forth a creditor's claim." Rule 3001(a). The proof of claim typically will conform to Official Form 10.[79] However, in limited circumstances the courts have permitted "informal" writings such as letters to suffice as a proof of claim. The proof of claim is supposed to be filed with the clerk of the court. Rules 3002(b), 5005(a).

A proof of claim is almost always filed by the holder of the claim (i.e., the creditor). See § 501(a). The claim also may be filed by an indenture trustee. § 501(a). In limited circumstances, however, another entity may file a proof of claim on behalf of a creditor who has not timely filed a claim. § 501(b), (c). Such a non-creditor usually will file on behalf of the creditor if that non-creditor has a pecuniary stake in the creditor receiving a distribution in the bankruptcy case. For example, an entity that is liable with the debtor to the creditor, or that has secured such creditor, would want the creditor to be paid as much as possible out of the bankruptcy estate, reducing thereby the amount that they will owe the creditor. § 501(b), Rule 3005. The creditor, however, might not have much of an incentive to file the proof of claim, if it has a solvent codebtor, surety, or guarantor to whom it can look for payment.

A proof of claim also may be filed on behalf of the creditor by the debtor or the trustee. § 501(c), Rule 3004. The debtor might want to do this if the creditor's claim would be nondischargeable in the bankruptcy case under § 523(a). The creditor thus

---

[75]   See § 7.5.

[76]   See S. Rep. No. 95–989, 95th Cong., 2d Sess., at 61 (1978); H.R. Rep. No. 95–595, 95th Cong., 1st Sess., at 351 (1977).

[77]   See Langenkamp v. Culp, 498 U.S. 42 (1990).

[78]   131 S.Ct. 2594, 2620 (2011). See § 4.2.g.

[79]   The form can be found at: http://www.uscourts.gov/uscourts/RulesAndPolicies/rules/BK_Forms_Current/B_010_04–13.pdf.

would be entitled to try to collect its claim from the debtor after the bankruptcy case is over. In such a situation the debtor would want the creditor's claim to be reduced by a distribution from the bankruptcy estate. Note, though, that if the debtor has filed a claim on behalf of a creditor, the creditor is permitted to change the amount of the claim; it is not bound by the debtor's filing.[80]

Some dispute has arisen over whether the list of parties in § 501 who may file claims is exclusive. The issue usually has come up in cases involving the filing of a proof of claim on behalf of an entire class. Examples where such a class claim might be useful include large products liability or securities fraud cases. The circuit courts remain divided on the permissibility of class proof of claims, with a majority allowing class claims.[81]

The only exception to the general requirement that a proof of claim must be filed in order for a claim to be allowed is in chapter 11 cases. In chapter 11, a proof of claim is *deemed* filed if the claim is listed in the bankruptcy schedules, unless the claim is scheduled as disputed, contingent, or unliquidated. § 1111(a), Rule 3003(b). Thus, a creditor in a chapter 11 case whose claim is scheduled and not listed as disputed, contingent, or unliquidated does not need to file a proof of claim; the scheduling of the claim serves that function. The creditor only needs to file a proof of claim if the claim is listed as disputed, contingent, or unliquidated, or if the creditor disagrees with the amount in which the claim was scheduled. In large chapter 11 cases involving hundreds or thousands of creditors, the deemed filing rule is extremely efficient, saving considerable cost and paperwork.

A word of caution is in order to creditors who rely on a deemed filing, in the event the chapter 11 case converts to chapter 7. The deemed filing will not suffice in the superseding chapter 7 case. Only claims actually filed by creditors before conversion will be valid in the chapter 7 case. Rule 1019(3). The creditor will receive notice of the conversion, however, and of the date by which claims must be filed.

In order for a creditor to file a proof of claim, the creditor obviously must be aware that a bankruptcy case has been filed. The debtor initiates the process of notification by filing a schedule of creditors. Notice of the filing of the case is then mailed to all scheduled creditors. See Rule 2002(a), (f); Official Form 9.[82] That notice informs the creditor whether it needs to file a proof of claim, and if so, in what court and by what date. This initial notice also will inform the creditor of the date and place of the first meeting of creditors, and of any deadlines for filing complaints objecting to the debtor's discharge or to the dischargeability of a particular debt.

---

[80]   See In re Kolstad, 928 F.2d 171 (5th Cir.), cert. denied, 502 U.S. 958 (1991).

[81]   The leading case permitting class claims is In re American Reserve Corp., 840 F.2d 487 (7th Cir. 1988). Accord, In re Birting Fisheries, Inc., 92 F.3d 939 (9th Cir. 1996); Reid v. White Motor Corp., 886 F.2d 1462 (6th Cir. 1989), cert. denied, 494 U.S. 1080 (1990); In re Charter Co., 876 F.2d 866 (11th Cir. 1989), cert. dismissed, 496 U.S. 944 (1990). The minority view, that class claims are not permissible, is led by In re Standard Metals Corp., 817 F.2d 625, vacated and rev'd in part on other grounds, 839 F.2d 1383 (10th Cir. 1987), cert. dismissed, 488 U.S. 881 (1988). Accord, In re FIRSTPLUS Fin., Inc., 248 B.R. 60 (Bankr. N.D. Tex. 2000).

[82]   For example, the Official Form for Chapter 7 cases for an individual debtor is found at: http://www.uscourts.gov/uscourts/RulesAndPolicies/rules/BK_Forms_Current/B_009A.pdf.

If the creditor is not listed or scheduled, and thus does not receive notice of the bankruptcy case in time to file a proof of claim, its claim will not be discharged.[83] See § 523(a)(3). It would be unfair—indeed, probably a denial of due process—to discharge a debt owed to a creditor if the creditor had no notice of the bankruptcy case and thus no opportunity to participate in that case. However, the creditor who does not receive notice and thus does not file a proof of claim still cannot participate in the bankruptcy distribution, because it will not have an "allowed" claim. Note that even if the creditor's claim is not scheduled, if the creditor still has knowledge or actual notice of the case, its claim will be discharged. Furthermore, in the large majority of cases in which no assets are available for distribution, the failure to schedule a creditor probably will not preclude the discharge of that creditor's claim, because there is no need to file claims at all.

The Code generally does not specify the *time* within which a proof of claim must be filed, instead leaving that matter to the Bankruptcy Rules. The only exceptions are for (1) claims of governmental units, which are timely filed if filed before 180 days after the date of the order for relief, and (2) tax claims of governmental units in chapter 13 cases filed within 60 days after the date a required return is filed under § 1308. § 502(b)(9). The timing requirement for all other claims is provided by the Bankruptcy Rules. See Rule 3002. In cases under chapter 7, chapter 12, or chapter 13, the general rule is that a proof of claim is "timely filed" if it is filed not later than 90 days after the first date set for the § 341 meeting of creditors. Rule 3002(c). This date will be specified in the initial notice mailed to creditors. It is important to note that the 90–day clock starts running from the *first* date set for the creditors meeting; even if that meeting is continued to a later date, the time to file claims is not extended.

A priority claim that is timely filed will share in the first tier of distribution, § 726(a)(1), and a nonpriority claim that is timely filed will participate in the second tier. Tardily filed claims generally are relegated to the third tier under § 726(a)(3).

Prior to 1994, an enormous controversy existed in the courts over the *effect* of a tardy filing. The language of Rule 3002 at that time indicated that timely filing was required for the claim to be *allowed* at all. Many courts gave this Rule its literal effect, and disallowed tardily filed claims. A revolution was triggered, however, by the case of *In re Hausladen*,[84] which held that tardy filing does not mandate disallowance under the provisions of the Code; to the extent Rule 3002 provided otherwise, that Rule had to yield to the Code. Under *Hausladen*, tardy filing might dictate subordinating a claim to the second or third tier of distribution under § 726(a), but nothing more. The controversy proved especially heated with regard to tardily filed *priority* claims. Eventually some, but not all, circuit courts adopted the view that a priority claim had to be allowed and paid in the first tier of distribution under § 726(a)(1), even if not timely filed.[85]

[83] See § 10.18.

[84] 146 B.R. 557 (Bankr. D. Minn. 1992).

[85] See In re Vecchio, 20 F.3d 555 (2d Cir. 1994). Contra, In re Waindel, 65 F.3d 1307 (5th Cir. 1995). The Sixth Circuit limited the application of this rule to priority creditors who did not have notice of the claims filing bar date. In re Century Boat Co., 986 F.2d 154 (6th Cir. 1993).

The problem of what to do with tardily filed claims was dealt with in the 1994 Amendments. Under new § 502(b)(9) as amended, a claim is disallowed if proof of the claim is not timely filed, *except* to the extent the tardy filing is permitted under § 726(a)(1), (2), or (3). The intent of Congress was to overrule the result of *Hausladen*.[86] Note that the disallowance is not complete, due to the exception clause. Reference to § 726(a)(1) reveals that a tardily filed priority claim still may be allowed and paid in the first tier if proof is filed before the earlier of the date on which the trustee commences distribution or within 10 days after the trustee's final report is mailed to creditors. For nonpriority claims, a tardily-filed claim will still be paid in the second tier if the creditor filed late because it did not have notice of the case, and the proof of claim was still filed in time to permit payment. § 726(a)(2)(C).

The time for filing proofs of claim in chapter 11 cases is handled somewhat differently than for the other chapters. To begin with, recall that there is no need for a creditor to even file a proof of claim in chapter 11 if their claim is listed accurately and is not scheduled as disputed, contingent, or unliquidated. See § 1111(a). In addition, negotiations over the chapter 11 plan may delay proceedings for many months or even years, making it unnecessary and indeed unwise to establish a claims bar date at a very early stage of the case. Instead, considerable flexibility is preserved in chapter 11 cases. The court will fix the date by which claims must be filed. Rule 3003(c)(3).

A proof of claim that is filed under § 501 is *deemed allowed*. § 502(a). In other words, if no one objects to the filed claim, the claim will be allowed. No hearing on the validity or amount of the claim will be held. In effect, the filing of the claim establishes a prima facie case of validity.[87] Rule 3001(f). The chapter 7 trustee is charged, however, with the duty of examining proofs of claim and objecting to any claim that is improper. § 704(5). Standing to object to a claim is not limited to the trustee, but is extended to any party in interest. § 502(a). Until an objection is filed (or the creditor participates significantly in the case), the creditor may withdraw a filed claim as of right. Rule 3006.

If an objection is filed, the court will have to determine the validity of the claim and fix the amount of the claim as of the date of the filing of the petition. § 502(b). Since matters regarding the allowance or disallowance of claims are classified as "core proceedings," see 28 U.S.C. § 157(b)(2)(B), the bankruptcy court will usually be the forum in which claims objections are resolved. The primary exception is for the liquidation or estimation of contingent or unliquidated personal injury tort or wrongful death claims, which for purposes of distribution must be fixed in the district court (or in state court). 28 U.S.C. § 157(b)(2)(B), (b)(5). The bankruptcy court also could elect to abstain from hearing the matter, and permit the claim to be tried in a non-bankruptcy forum—but this option is rarely chosen.

In a major change from pre-Code law, the current Code *requires* the court to fix or estimate all claims, even if doing so will be difficult. § 502(c)(1). Under prior law, unliquidated and contingent claims often were not "provable," which excluded them

---

[86]   See 140 Cong. Rec. H10,768 (Oct. 4, 1994).

[87]   See S. Rep. No. 95–989, 95th Cong., 2d Sess. 62 (1978); H.R. Rep. No. 95–595, 95th Cong., 1st Sess. 352 (1977).

from the bankruptcy process. In keeping with the basic policy decision to resolve all of the debtor's legal obligations in the bankruptcy case, even unliquidated and contingent claims must be estimated and then dealt with in the bankruptcy proceeding.

The process by which a claims objection is to be resolved, or by which a claims estimation is to be effected, is not specified in either the Code or the Rules. Considerable leeway has been afforded to the courts in fashioning a claims resolution procedure. While a full-scale trial on the merits is of course possible, and for personal injury and wrongful death cases probably is mandated, most courts resolve claim objections pursuant to a more *summary* claims allowance process. For example, a court might allow only a specified amount of time for the hearing, and might limit the number of witnesses that may be called, the number of exhibits that may be introduced, and so forth. Challenges to summary claims resolution procedures on due process grounds have proven fruitless. The bankruptcy court also has the option of only temporarily fixing the claim for a limited purpose (such as voting on the plan), leaving the final resolution of the claim for a non-bankruptcy forum.

A filed claim is prima facie evidence of the validity and amount of a claim in the absence of an objection. Rule 3001(f). If an objection is filed, the burdens of production and proof in the claims litigation are governed by the non-bankruptcy law (usually state law) under which the claim originates.[88] Once the court has entered an order allowing or disallowing a claim, a party in interest may move for reconsideration. Rule 3008. Reconsideration must be predicated on a showing of cause. § 502(j).

A claim objection also may be resolved by a settlement or compromise between the creditor and the objecting party (usually the trustee). However, the court must approve the settlement or compromise, after notice to creditors. Rule 9019(a).

§ 7.5 Grounds for Disallowance

If a proof of claim is filed, and an objection to the claim is made, the court will have to determine the validity and amount of the claim as of the date of the filing of the petition. § 502(b). In making this determination, the court must apply the grounds for disallowance specified in subsections (1) through (9) of § 502(b). Those delineated grounds, along with the provisions in subsections (d), (e), and (k), are the exclusive bases for disallowing a claim. The court may not invoke its own notions of equity to disallow a claim for any other reason.

The reasons for which a claim may be disallowed under § 502(b) may be divided into three rough categories: (1) the timing of the claim; (2) substantive non-bankruptcy objections; and (3) bankruptcy-specific policies.

First, *timing* matters. A claim is only allowed in "the amount of such claim . . . as of the date of the filing of the petition." § 502(b). In other words, as a general rule, a claim that arises *after* the bankruptcy filing is not allowed. As discussed in an earlier section,[89] this does not mean that a claim will be disallowed just because it is

---

[88] Raleigh v. Illinois Dept. of Revenue, 530 U.S. 15 (2000).
[89] See § 7.2.

unmatured, unliquidated, contingent, or disputed at the time of filing, as long as the creditor had a "right to payment" at that time. In such a case, the court must estimate the amount owing on the petition date. § 502(b), (c). Bankruptcy thus serves to accelerate claims. If, however, the debtor's legal obligation is not rooted in the pre-bankruptcy period, but instead arises postpetition, the claim will be disallowed.

The limitation to claims extant as of the bankruptcy filing is subject to several exceptions for claims that actually arise during the pendency of the bankruptcy case, but which are deemed for bankruptcy purposes to have arisen prior to bankruptcy. These claims are discussed in the next section.[90] Examples would be claims arising from the rejection of an executory contract, § 502(g), or from the recovery of property pursuant to the trustee's avoiding powers, § 502(h).

Second, bankruptcy does not confer on creditors new substantive rights or claims against a debtor. At its core, bankruptcy remains a *procedural* mechanism for sorting out claims that are established under *non*-bankruptcy law. If an entity does not have an enforceable claim against a debtor outside of bankruptcy, nothing about the debtor filing bankruptcy will change that result. This deference to the underlying non-bankruptcy law to determine *claims* against the debtor mirrors the deference to non-bankruptcy law to ascertain *property* rights of the debtor.[91] As the Supreme Court explained in the leading case of *Vanston Bondholders Protective Committee v. Green*, "What claims of creditors are valid and subsisting obligations against the bankrupt at the time a petition in bankruptcy is filed, is a question which, in the absence of overruling federal law, is to be determined by reference to state law."[92] This fundamental policy is implemented by § 502(b)(1), which requires the court to disallow a claim that "is unenforceable against the debtor or property of the debtor, under any agreement or applicable law for a reason other than because such claim is contingent or unmatured." Examples given in the legislative history are claims unenforceable because of usury, unconscionability, or failure of consideration.[93] Other examples might include the expiration of the statute of limitations, a material breach, or the nonoccurrence of a condition. In short, the bankruptcy estate succeeds to all defenses that the debtor could have raised against the creditor's claim. § 558.

An intriguing issue that tests the limits of the principles just discussed is whether a creditor may claim as part of its unsecured claim in bankruptcy a claim for *attorneys' fees* incurred in collecting on its claim (including collection efforts incurred postpetition, during the bankruptcy case), assuming that those fees are authorized under the creditor's contract with the debtor and permitted under state law. Some courts have held that the creditor's claim may include the contractually authorized attorney's fees, even if the fees are incurred in litigating bankruptcy matters, such as a nondischargeability action.[94] The Ninth Circuit, however, had adopted the "*Fobian* rule," which carved out a judicial exception to the general rule allowing contractual

---

[90]   See § 7.6.

[91]   Butner v. United States, 440 U.S. 48 (1979). See § 5.5.

[92]   329 U.S. 156, 161 (1946).

[93]   S. Rep. No. 95–989, 95th Cong., 2d Sess. 62 (1978); H.R. Rep. No. 95–595, 95th Cong., 1st Sess. 352 (1977).

[94]   E.g., In re Alport, 144 F.3d 1163, 1168 (11th Cir. 1998).

attorney's fees, "where the litigated issues involve not basic contract enforcement questions, but issues peculiar to federal bankruptcy law."[95] In 2007, the Supreme Court abrogated *Fobian* in *Travelers Casualty & Surety Co. of America v. Pacific Gas & Electric Co*,[96] concluding that "[t]he absence of textual support is fatal for the *Fobian* rule."[97] The Court stated:

> "We generally presume that claims enforceable under applicable state law will be allowed in bankruptcy unless they are expressly disallowed. See 11 U.S.C. § 502(b). Neither the court below nor PG & E has offered any reason why the fact that the attorney's fees in this case were incurred litigating issues of federal bankruptcy law overcomes that presumption."[98]

Unfortunately, however, *Travelers* is considerably less dispositive than appears at first blush, since the Court decided *only* that the state-federal dichotomy on which *Fobian* rested was unpersuasive. There are at least two other plausible bases for disallowing a claim for postpetition attorneys' fees incurred by an unsecured creditor—that the fees were incurred *postpetition*, and that the fees were incurred by an *unsecured* creditor. Neither of those issues had been raised below, though, so the Court refused to consider them.[99]

The third general category of grounds for the disallowance of claims—the implementation of bankruptcy-specific policies—is the broadest, and covers a variety of procedural and substantive matters. In summary, the following types of claims may be disallowed:

- a claim for unmatured interest, § 502(b)(2);

- a claim for a tax assessed against property of the estate, to the extent the claim exceeds the value of the estate's interest in the property, § 502(b)(3);

- a claim for the services of an insider or an attorney of the debtor in excess of the reasonable value of those services, § 502(b)(4);

- unmatured (i.e., postpetition) claims for domestic support obligations that are nondischargeable under § 523(a)(5);

- a landlord's rent claim, in excess of a specified ceiling, § 502(b)(6);

- an employee's termination claim, in excess of a specified ceiling, § 502(b)(7);

---

[95] In re Fobian, 951 F.2d 1149, 1153 (9th Cir. 1991), cert. denied, 505 U.S. 1221 (1992), abrogated, Travelers Cas. & Sur. Co. of America v. Pacific Gas & Elec. Co., 549 U.S. 443 (2007).

[96] 549 U.S. 443 (2007).

[97] Id. at 452.

[98] Id.

[99] Id. at 456: "Accordingly, we express no opinion with regard to whether, following the demise of the *Fobian* rule, other principles of bankruptcy law might provide an independent basis for disallowing Travelers' claim for attorney's fees. We conclude only that the Court of Appeals erred in disallowing that claim based on the fact that the fees at issue were incurred litigating issues of bankruptcy law." For analysis of *Travelers* and its impact, see Mark S. Scarberry, Interpreting Bankruptcy Code Sections 502 and 506: Post–Petition Attorneys' Fees in a Post–Travelers World, 15 Am. Bankr. Inst. L. Rev. 611 (2007).

- certain employment tax claims, relating to reduced tax credits upon late payment of the tax, § 502(b)(8);

- tardily filed claims, § 502(b)(9);

- the claim of a transferee of an avoidable transfer if the transferee has not paid the amount for which it is liable or turned over the property, § 502(d);

- a claim for reimbursement or contribution that is contingent or as to which a right of subrogation is asserted, § 502(e); and

- a stated percentage of the amount of a claim for a consumer debt if the creditor unreasonably refused to negotiate an alternative repayment schedule for the debt, § 502(k).

Some of these provisions merit further comment. The rule that postpetition interest is disallowed is fundamental. § 502(b)(2). Bankruptcy accelerates all obligations down to the date of the bankruptcy filing, and stops the running of interest. The relative rights of creditors are deemed to be fixed, for the most part, at the instant of bankruptcy. In effect, § 502(b)(2) establishes an irrebuttable presumption that the discount rate (i.e., the rate necessary to discount future sums to present value) is identical to the contractual interest rate.[100] This presumption holds even if the actual contract rates for different creditors vary.

The only exceptions to the no-interest rule are for (1) *oversecured* claims, which are entitled to recover postpetition interest up to the amount of their excess security,[101] § 506(b), and (2) *solvent* estates, in which event interest is paid at the legal rate on all unsecured claims under § 726(a)(5), before any distribution is made to the debtor. A secured creditor who is delayed from foreclosing is not entitled to interest under the guise of adequate protection.[102]

Another significant disallowance rule is § 502(b)(6), for the claim of a lessor for damages resulting from the termination of a lease of real property. That provision sets a ceiling on the amount of the landlord's claim, to prevent that claim from consuming a disproportionately large share of the estate, to the detriment of other creditors. In addition, the concern is that the amounts of a lessor's damages for breach of a long-term real estate lease are very difficult to prove with any certainty. In effect, then, § 502(b)(6) redistributes some of the uncertain entitlement of the real estate lessor to other creditors. Note that a personal property lessor's damages claim is not subjected to the cap.

The amount of the § 502(b)(6) ceiling depends on the remaining term of the lease. The lessor's allowable claim cannot exceed the *greater of:*

---

[100] S. Rep. No. 95–989, 95th Cong., 2d Sess. 63 (1978); H.R. Rep. No. 95–595, 95th Cong., 1st Sess. 353 (1977).

[101] See § 7.31.

[102] See § 3.19.

(1) one year's reserved rent or

(2) 15% of the remaining term, not to exceed three years' rent. § 502(b)(6)(A).

The "remaining term" is counted from the earlier of the date the bankruptcy petition was filed or the date the lessor retook the premises. In addition, the cap includes any unpaid rent due under the lease, but without acceleration, at that earlier date.

To calculate the cap under § 502(b)(6), the first step is to compute 15% of the remaining lease term. If that number is less than one year, then the cap will be the minimum of one year's reserved rent. For example, if the remaining lease term is five years (60 months), 15% of the term would be nine months; since that is less than one year, the lessor's cap is one year's rent. A shorthand rule of thumb is that any remaining lease term of less than 80 months (i.e., six and 2/3 years) will yield a one-year cap.[103]

If the 15% calculation yields a number exceeding 12 months (which, as just noted, will be true for any remaining lease term in excess of 80 months), then the cap will be that 15% number—but only up to three years (36 months). In other words, the lessor's allowed claim cannot ever exceed three years' rent plus unpaid rent already due. The three-year maximum will be reached when the remaining lease term is 20 years.[104] Thus, for any remaining lease term of 20 years or more, the lessor's cap will be three years. To give another example, if the remaining lease term were 10 years, the cap would be 18 months' (1.5 years) rent.

Note that the real estate lessor is not necessarily entitled to have its claim allowed in the amount determined by the § 502(b)(6) computation just described; that figure is just the maximum that can be allowed. The trustee could argue that the actual damages of the lessor are lower, for many possible reasons. For example, the lessor might be able to mitigate its damages by reletting the premises to a new tenant. To the extent that non-bankruptcy law would render the lessor's claim unenforceable to the extent of that mitigation, § 502(b)(1), discussed above, would dictate disallowance in bankruptcy.

In one important situation § 502(b)(6) will not apply at all. That is where the lease was first assumed by the trustee or debtor in possession, and then rejected. The damages from the rejection of an assumed lease are entitled to administrative expense priority under § 503. The § 502 rules apply only to general claims allowed under § 501, and thus do not limit § 503 administrative expenses.[105]

The 2005 amendments made one significant change to the rule discussed in the preceding paragraph, with regard to a previously assumed lease of nonresidential real property (e.g., a commercial real estate lease). Under new § 503(b)(7), the lessor's administrative expense claim is limited to all monetary sums due under the lease for *two years* after the post-assumption rejection of the lease (or, if later, the surrender of

---

[103] To calculate this, multiply 80 months by 15%, which yields 12 months, i.e., exactly one year.

[104] To calculate this, multiply 20 years by 15%, which yields three years.

[105] See In re Klein Sleep Prods., Inc., 78 F.3d 18 (2d Cir. 1996).

the premises). The only reduction in the amount allowed as an administrative expense is for those amounts the lessor actually recoups by reletting. To the extent the lessor's claim exceeds the amount of the two-year cap, that excess claim is treated as a prepetition, nonpriority claim, otherwise limited by the ceiling in § 502(b)(6).

A contract damages limitation is also imposed for employee termination claims. § 502(b)(7). The employee-creditor is restricted to the compensation provided by the contract (again, without acceleration) for *one year* following the earlier of the filing of the bankruptcy or the termination of performance under the contract. § 502(b)(7)(A). In addition, the employee is entitled to any unpaid compensation due at the earlier date. § 502(b)(7)(B). The justifications for this rule are the same as for lessor claims, *viz.*, (1) to prevent a discharged employee's claim from taking an excessively large share of the estate, and (2) to minimize problems in computing damages with sufficient certainty. As is true with lessor claims, § 502(b)(7) imposes a ceiling; it does not create an entitlement. The employee's damages might be substantially less than the cap, depending on possible mitigation deductions.

Section 502(b)(9) disallows a claim that is not timely filed. An exception is made for claims that may be tardily filed pursuant to subsections (1), (2), or (3) of § 726(a). A claim of a governmental unit is timely filed if filed within 180 days after the order for relief, or any longer period permitted by the Bankruptcy Rules. Also, as amended in 2005, a governmental tax claim is timely in a chapter 13 case if filed within 60 days after the date a required return is filed under § 1308. As discussed in the preceding section,[106] the addition of § 502(b)(9) in 1994 helped resolve the difficult issue of the effect of a tardy filing.

The disallowance rule of § 502(d) helps put some teeth into the avoiding power and turnover recovery provisions. The rule comes into play when an entity both has an otherwise allowable claim against the estate and is the subject of an avoidance or turnover action. If either (1) property is recoverable from the entity under the turnover rules (§§ 542 and 543), the avoiding power liability section (§ 550), or the setoff provision (§ 553), or (2) the entity is the transferee of a transfer avoidable under one of the Code's avoiding powers, then the entity's claim will be disallowed under § 502(d) unless it turns over the property or pays the amount for which it is liable. In effect, § 502(d) establishes a *quid pro quo*: a creditor who wants to have its claim allowed must cooperate. Stated the other way, a creditor cannot resist turnover or refuse payment of an avoidance liability and at the same time have its own claim allowed.

Section 502(e) requires disallowance in certain situations involving contribution or reimbursement claims. The basic premise of § 502(e) is that the claim of a codebtor, surety, or guarantor of the debtor for reimbursement or contribution must be disallowed unless the claim of the creditor on that obligation has been paid in full. This rule "prevents competition between a creditor and his guarantor from the limited proceeds in the estate."[107] There can only be a single recovery from the estate on one claim. Thus, if the claim for reimbursement or contribution is still contingent, the

---

[106] See § 7.4.

[107] S. Rep. No. 95–989, 95th Cong., 2d Sess. 65 (1978); H.R. Rep. No. 95–595, 95th Cong., 1st Sess. 354 (1977).

claim will be disallowed. § 502(e)(1)(B). Once the claim becomes fixed (normally by the payment of the creditor by the codebtor, surety, or guarantor), the reimbursement or contribution claim will be allowed. § 502(e)(2). At that point, double recovery from the estate is no longer possible, since the contribution or reimbursement claim cannot become fixed while the primary creditor still has an unsatisfied claim against the estate.

If the primary creditor's claim is disallowed, so too must the claim of the codebtor or surety be disallowed. § 502(e)(1)(A). Finally, if the codebtor or surety asserts a right of subrogation to the creditor's claim under § 509, then the reimbursement or contribution claim will not be allowed. § 502(e)(1)(C). Otherwise the codebtor, surety, or guarantor could recover twice; once in its own right, and once by subrogation. It must choose between proceeding under § 502(e) and under § 509.

Although undoubtedly drafted with contract-based contribution obligations in mind, § 502(e)(1) has become quite important with regard to contingent contribution claims in environmental cases. This situation is possible because both the debtor and another entity could be potentially responsible parties for response costs under CERCLA. The First Circuit has concluded that § 502(e)(1)(B) by its plain language must be applied to disallow a contingent contribution claim under CERCLA.[108] However, the court also held that § 502(e)(1)(B) disallowance would not be triggered until a surrogate claim was filed on behalf of the primary creditor, the EPA. The contribution claimant thus could have its own liability to the EPA reduced by the amount of any bankruptcy distribution to the EPA.

Hoping to encourage debtors and creditors to work together in an effort to restructure debts *prior* to a debtor filing for bankruptcy, Congress enacted a number of amendments in 2005 relevant to that goal. Part of that package bears on claim allowance. Under § 502(k), the bankruptcy court is directed to reduce a creditor's allowable claim by up to 20 percent, if the court finds that the creditor unreasonably refused to negotiate a reasonable alternative repayment schedule for a consumer debt that was proposed on behalf of the debtor by an approved nonprofit budget and credit counseling agency. There are several qualifications to this provision. First, it has no application if any portion of the consumer debt at issue is nondischargeable under § 523(a). Second, it only applies to the extent that the proposed restructuring was made at least 60 days before the petition date and proposed to pay at least 60 percent of the amount of the debt over a reasonable period of time. Third, the debtor has an elevated burden of proving, by clear and convincing evidence, that the creditor unreasonably "refused to consider" the debtor's proposal.

§ 7.6   Treatment of Certain Postpetition Claims

The normal rule is that claims are fixed as of the date of the filing of the bankruptcy petition. If an objection is made to a filed proof of claim, the court must determine the amount of the claim as of the petition date. § 502(b). A "creditor" is

---

[108]   In re Hemingway Transp., Inc., 993 F.2d 915 (1st Cir.), cert. denied, 510 U.S. 914 (1993).

defined in part as an "entity that has a claim against the debtor that arose at the time of or before the order for relief." § 101(10)(A).

These timing rules are incomplete, however. They only tell part of the story. The reason is this. Actions are taken during the bankruptcy case—which of necessity occurs after the filing of the petition—that give rise to claims that in the furtherance of sound bankruptcy policy should be treated on a par with prepetition claims. If these types of claims were considered to arise postpetition (i.e., when they really do arise), then (1) the claims usually would not be discharged, which would undercut an individual debtor's fresh start and would hamper a business debtor's reorganization chances, and (2) the claims would either be paid (a) as an administrative priority, which would deplete the estate at the expense of general creditors, (b) by the debtor post-bankruptcy, causing fresh start or reorganization problems, or (c) not at all, which would be unfair to the claimant.

The solution? Use a legal fiction; simply deem the postpetition claims to have arisen *prior* to bankruptcy. Legal time does not have to follow calendar time. This neat trick of relating back postpetition claims to the prepetition period applies to the following types of claims:

- reimbursement or contribution claims that become fixed after the commencement of the case, § 502(e)(2);[109]

- in involuntary cases, claims that arise in the ordinary course of the debtor's business or financial affairs in the "gap," i.e., after the commencement of the case and before the earlier of the appointment of a trustee or the entry of the order for relief, § 502(f);[110]

- claims arising from the rejection of an executory contract or unexpired lease that has not been assumed, § 502(g)(1);[111]

- claims arising from the rejection or the termination or acceleration of a financial contract under § 562, see § 502(g)(2);

- claims arising from the recovery of property pursuant to one of the avoiding powers, under §§ 522, 550, or 553, see § 502(h);

- eighth priority tax claims that do not arise until after the commencement of the case, § 502(i); and

- in a converted case, claims that are not entitled to administrative priority that arise after the commencement of the case but before conversion, § 348(d).

The definition of "creditor" also includes an entity that has one of these types of claims. § 101(10)(B).

---

[109] See § 7.5 for a discussion of the rules governing the allowance of contribution and reimbursement claims.

[110] These involuntary gap claims have third priority under § 507(a)(3). See § 7.19.

[111] See § 8.7.

An example will illustrate the operation of one of these relation-back rules. Assume that Debtor owes Creditor $5,000, but then pays Creditor in full 60 days prior to bankruptcy. On the date the petition is filed, Creditor would not have a claim against Debtor. However, if no defenses apply, the $5,000 pre-bankruptcy payment will be avoided as a preference under § 547. Creditor will have to repay the $5,000 to the estate, under § 550. Upon repaying the money, Creditor will be given a prepetition claim for $5,000. See § 502(h). Creditor's claim will be allowed or disallowed as if it arose prior to bankruptcy. If the claim is allowed, Creditor then will share in the bankruptcy distribution (if any). Creditor's claim also will be discharged.

B. PRIORITIES

§ 7.7   Basic Principles

One of the core functions of a bankruptcy case is to distribute the debtor's assets to creditors. This distributional process inevitably entails an ordering function, except in the rare case in which all creditors are paid in full. The first creditors to be paid are those with enforceable claims against estate *property*, such as *secured* creditors[112] or *trust* beneficiaries.[113] Those property claimants are entitled to receive either their property or its value.[114] The remaining assets in the estate then are distributed to all of the general *unsecured* creditors, i.e., to those who do not have any enforceable liens or claims against estate property.[115] For all of the general unsecured creditors, the controlling bankruptcy principle is *equality* of distribution.[116]

The equality principle is only a touchstone, however, rather than a universally applicable rule. The Code's distributional scheme contains many exceptions to the baseline premise of equality. Ten different types of unsecured claims are afforded *priority* over other unsecured claims. § 507(a)(1)–(10). These "priority" claims are entitled to be paid in full before any distribution is made to non-priority unsecured claims. See § 726(a)(1). Furthermore, the priority claims themselves are ranked in § 507(a); higher ranking priorities must be fully paid before payment may be made to lower priorities (subject to an exception discussed below). § 726(a)(1). For example, all second priority claims under § 507(a)(2) must be paid before any distribution is made to third priority claims under § 507(a)(3). Within a priority class, all claims are of equal rank, subject to two exceptions, discussed in the next two paragraphs. Thus, if there are not enough assets in the estate to satisfy a particular priority class in full, all claimants in that class will share on a pro rata basis. § 726(b).

The first exception to the rule that priority claims of the same rank are paid in parity is for the newly reconstituted first priority for domestic support obligations under § 507(a)(1). Within that priority, claims under subsection (A) are paid ahead of claims under subsection (B). The difference is who the claimant is; under (A), the

---

[112] See §§ 7.27–7.34.

[113] See §§ 7.35–7.36.

[114] 11 U.S.C. § 725.

[115] See §§ 7.25–7.26.

[116] See Howard Delivery Service, Inc. v. Zurich American Ins. Co., 547 U.S. 651, 655, 667 (2006); Nathanson v. NLRB, 344 U.S. 25, 29 (1952).

claimant must be a spouse, former spouse, child, or representative of the child; while under (B), the claimant is a governmental unit.

The second exception is where a case is begun under a reorganization chapter (11, 12, or 13) and then converted to a liquidation case under chapter 7. In that event, the administrative expenses incurred in the superseding chapter 7 (colloquially called "burial expenses") are given priority over administrative expenses incurred in the superseded case. § 726(b). The reason is to incentivize people to be willing to participate in the administration of the superseding chapter 7. Otherwise, if administrative claims in the superseded reorganization case exceeded the free assets of the estate, no one would agree to administer the chapter 7 case.

The exception to the rule that priority claims must be paid in the order listed in § 507(a) was grafted onto the Code in 2005, when Congress moved domestic support obligations to first priority.[117] If such claims actually were paid ahead of all administrative expenses, including the cost of paying the bankruptcy trustee, then a scenario could well arise where no one would be willing to serve as the trustee—it is not a job that very many people likely would do for free—which of course would then make it impossible to administer the bankruptcy case at all. Indeed, such is the very reason that until 2005 all administrative expenses had always been paid as the *first* priority. Recognizing this reality, Congress qualified its grant of "first" priority to domestic support obligations by providing that a trustee's expenses, although nominally "second" priority, are in fact to be paid before DSO claims "to the extent that the trustee administers assets that are otherwise available for the payment of" DSO claims. § 507(a)(1)(C). So, for example, if a trustee were to sell unencumbered property of the bankruptcy estate, the trustee would collect his standard fee, as calculated under § 326,[118] out of the proceeds of that sale, before making distribution to any DSO first priority claims. Note that the priority for DSO claims will only be even potentially relevant in cases involving *individual* debtors, since obviously a corporation or a partnership would never owe alimony or support to a spouse, former spouse, or child.

The Code's priority provisions embody a mélange of policy goals. Some of these make sense, such as the need to pay administrative claims first.[119] Otherwise, it would be difficult to induce people to participate in the administration of the bankruptcy case, and the whole system might grind to a halt. Even though administrative expenses are denominated "second" priority, § 507(a)(2), in reality they are almost always paid first: in business cases involving corporate or partnership debtors, by definition there never could be a DSO claim, leaving administrative expenses first; and in cases of individual debtors, the most common administrative expense is that for the trustee, which is paid first.[120] § 507(a)(1)(C).

---

[117] See § 7.9.

[118] See § 7.16.

[119] See § 7.11.

[120] The problem case will be a business case involving an individual debtor who does have DSO claims. In that situation, the administrative expenses incident to running the debtor's business will in fact be paid second, behind DSO claims, since only administrative expenses for the trustee are prioritized over DSO claims in § 507(a)(1)(C). See § 7.9.

Other priority provisions, however, are less easy to justify; some appear to represent blatant congressional favoritism of special interest groups. For example, are the claims of fishermen and grain producers really deserving of priority treatment? See § 507(a)(6).

Courts narrowly construe the priority provisions against the claimant, because such claims mark a departure from the fundamental principle of equality.[121] The putative priority claimant bears the burden of proving its right to the claimed priority.[122] Priorities are strictly statutory, and may only be created by Congress. As the Supreme Court recently explained, a claimant is entitled to receive priority in payment over other unsecured creditors "only when clearly authorized by Congress."[123] In other words, the courts are not free to afford priority status to a claim based upon the court's own ideas of equity[124] in the same way that a court is able to subordinate a claim for equitable reasons.[125] In reorganization cases, some courts have invoked their equity powers to order the priority payment of certain nonpriority unsecured claims, under the controversial "necessity of payment" (or "critical vendor") rule.[126] More recently, courts have tended to limit such "necessity" payments to those business expenses that can be justified directly under § 363(b), eschewing reliance on vague notions of "equity."[127]

The priority rules are found in § 507. That section applies in all chapters except chapters 9 and 15, but the manner of implementation varies depending on whether the case is a liquidation or reorganization. In a chapter 7 liquidation, the assets of the estate are distributed in accordance with § 726(a). Priority claims under § 507(a) are paid first. § 726(a)(1). In reorganization cases under chapters 11, 12, and 13, payments are made according to the terms of the confirmed plan, rather than in a lump sum distribution by the trustee. A reorganization plan may be confirmed by the court only if the plan provides for the full payment of all § 507(a) priority claims. See § 1129(a)(9)

---

[121] See *Howard Delivery*, supra note 116, 547 U.S. at 655, 667.

[122] See Woods v. City Nat'l Bank & Trust Co., 312 U.S. 262, 268 (1941). See also In re Hemingway Transport, Inc., 954 F.2d 1 (1st Cir. 1992).

[123] *Howard Delivery*, supra note 116, 547 U.S. at 655.

[124] This notion was nicely captured by Judge Posner for the Seventh Circuit: "The fact that a proceeding is equitable does not give the judge a free-floating discretion to redistribute rights in accordance with his personal views of justice and fairness, however enlightened those views may be." In re Chicago, Milwaukee, St. Paul & Pacific Railroad Co., 791 F.2d 524, 528 (7th Cir. 1986).

[125] See § 7.23.

[126] See § 11.12. See, e.g., In re Ionosphere Clubs, Inc., 98 B.R. 174 (Bankr. S.D.N.Y. 1989). The legitimacy of this judge-made rule under the Code is open to question. A number of court of appeals decisions have concluded that the courts do not have the power to prefer some claims over others. See, e.g., In re B & W Enterprises, Inc., 713 F.2d 534, 537 (9th Cir. 1983); In re Saybrook Mfg. Co., 963 F.2d 1490, 1495–96 (11th Cir. 1992). The Seventh Circuit decision in *In re Kmart Corp.*, 359 F.3d 866 (7th Cir. 2004), expressly rejected the invocation of "equity" as a basis for affording priority payment to supposedly "critical" vendors. Id. at 871. Instead, that court only allowed payments that could be justified under § 363(b). See infra note 16 and accompanying text. Commentators are divided on the issue. Compare Charles J. Tabb, Emergency Preferential Orders in Bankruptcy Reorganizations, 65 Am. Bankr. L.J. 75 (1991) (arguing against necessity of payment rule) with Russell A. Eisenberg & Frances F. Gecker, The Doctrine of Necessity and Its Parameters, 73 Marq. L. Rev. 1 (1989) (arguing in favor of rule).

[127] The leading case is *Kmart*, supra note 126, 359 F.3d 866. See In re Tropical Sportswear Int'l Corp., 320 B.R. 15 (Bankr. M.D. Fla. 2005).

(chapter 11);[128] § 1222(a)(2) (chapter 12); § 1322(a)(2) (chapter 13). The plan may provide for the full payment of the priority claim over the life of the plan, except that second and third priority claims in chapter 11 must be paid in full in cash on the effective date of the plan. § 1129(a)(9)(A).

Section 507(a) contains ten priorities. These priority categories are ranked ordinally; claims of a higher priority class must be paid in full before claims of a lower priority class are paid. Dollar amounts are effective as of April 1, 2013, and will be indexed every three years thereafter. In order, the priorities are:

First: domestic support obligations (subject to the exception discussed above for trustee expenses), § 507(a)(1); within this priority, claims owed to or recoverable by a spouse, former spouse, or child, or the child's representative, are accorded first rank under subsection (A), followed by like claims that have been assigned to or are owed to or recoverable by a governmental unit, under subsection (B);

Second: administrative expenses, § 503(b),[129] and fees and charges assessed under title 28, chapter 123, including § 1930, see § 507(a)(2);

Third: claims in an involuntary case that arise between the time the petition is filed and bankruptcy relief is ordered, §§ 507(a)(3), 502(f);[130]

Fourth: employee wage claims up to $12,475 each, for the 180 days before the date of tho bankruptcy filing or the date the debtor ceased its business, whichever is earlier, § 507(a)(4);[131]

Fifth: unpaid contributions to employee benefit plans for the 180 days before the earlier of the date of bankruptcy or the closing of the business, up to a dollar cap computed in conjunction with fourth priority claims, § 507(a)(5);

Sixth: grain producer and fishermen claims, up to $6,150 each, § 507(a)(6);

Seventh: consumer "layaway" deposits, up to $2,775 each, § 507(a)(7);

Eighth: prepetition taxes, § 507(a)(8);[132]

Ninth: commitments to maintain the capital of insured depository institutions, § 507(a)(9);

Tenth: claims for death or personal injury resulting from the debtor's operation of a motor vehicle or vessel while unlawfully intoxicated, § 507(a)(10).[133]

---

[128] The chapter 11 confirmation rules are plagued by an inadvertent drafting omission, in that § 1129(a)(9) is entirely silent about the required treatment of ninth and tenth priority claims under § 507(a)(9) and (10). This omission apparently was caused by a failure to amend § 1129(a)(9) to conform to amendments to the numbering of priority claims in § 507(a) in 1994 and 2005, and was not fixed in 2010 (when the same drafting error was fixed in § 726(b)).

[129] See §§ 7.10–7.18.

[130] See § 7.19.

[131] See § 7.20.

[132] See § 7.21.

The priority for claims of the United States under § 3466 of the Revised Statutes, which applies outside of bankruptcy, is not applicable in bankruptcy cases. Thus, for example, a prepetition tax claim of the Internal Revenue Service would be entitled to priority only to the extent provided by § 507(a)(8). This lower priority of federal government claims is sometimes a motive for creditors to supersede a non-bankruptcy collective proceeding (such as an assignment for the benefit of creditors) by filing an involuntary bankruptcy case.

The states are not permitted to establish priorities that will be effective in bankruptcy cases. The federal priority scheme set out in § 507(a) preempts state priorities under the Supremacy Clause of the Constitution. Nor may a state circumvent the ban on creating bankruptcy priorities by designating the priority as a "lien;" under § 545, the bankruptcy trustee is authorized to avoid state statutory liens that operate only in bankruptcy cases.[134]

The Code contains several "super" priorities that trump the priorities specified in § 507(a).[135] Section 507(b) provides a superpriority for the claim of a secured creditor who is given "adequate protection" under §§ 361–364, usually as a form of compensation for using the creditor's collateral, in the event that the protection given later proves to have been *in*adequate. An even higher superpriority can be given to a postpetition lender under § 364(c)(1), as an inducement to loan new money to the bankruptcy estate.[136]

In addition, several Code provisions that are not expressly called "priority" sections have been given a *de facto* priority effect by some courts.[137] This occurs when the court orders payment or performance of specified obligations by the estate prior to the final bankruptcy distribution. The result is that the party who receives payment or performance is effectively paid in full, whether or not they are a priority claimant under § 507(a). For example, the debtor in possession in a chapter 11 case may have to comply with the provisions of a collective bargaining agreement during the pendency of the chapter 11 case, resulting in the payment of wage claims of employees.[138]

§ 7.8 "Super" Priorities and De Facto Priorities

Section 507 of the Code is entitled "Priorities." One logically might conclude that § 507 thus encompasses the full range of the Code's priority rules. Unfortunately, life in the bankruptcy arena is not that simple. Instead, several other sections of the Code directly affect the priority of claims. Some of these sections (§§ 726(b), 364(c)(1), 507(b))

---

[133] This priority, added in 2005, is very similar to the discharge exception for DUI debts. § 523(a)(9). See § 10.24. For some reason, operation of an aircraft while intoxicated is included in the discharge exception, but not in the new priority.

[134] See § 6.50.

[135] See § 7.8.a.

[136] See § 11.10.b.

[137] See § 7.8.b.

[138] 11 U.S.C. § 1113(f). Compare In re Unimet Corp., 842 F.2d 879 (6th Cir. 1988) (employees must be paid notwithstanding § 507) with In re Roth American, Inc., 975 F.2d 949 (3d Cir. 1992) (employees may only be paid in accordance with § 507). For a thoughtful examination of *Unimet* and *Roth* and their progeny, see In re Certified Air Technologies, Inc., 300 B.R. 355 (Bankr. C.D. Cal. 2003).

expressly confer "super" priorities on the claimant. Other sections (§§ 1113(f), 1114(e), 365(d)(3), 365(d)(5), 362(b)(4)) do not appear on their face to establish priorities (or superpriorities) at all, yet have been interpreted to afford *de facto* priority status to certain unpaid claims.

a.   *Superpriorities*

One of the oddities of the Bankruptcy Code is that administrative expense claims are not necessarily first in the bankruptcy distribution line (even apart from DSO claims). An administrative priority can be trumped by even higher priorities, which are known colloquially as "super"[139] priorities. The Code specifically provides for three superpriorities:

1.   When a reorganization case is converted to a liquidation under chapter 7, the administrative expenses in the superseding chapter 7 case (colloquially called "burial" expenses) have priority over the administrative expenses in the superseded chapter 11, 12, or 13 case, § 726(b).

2.   The court may grant a postpetition extender of credit a priority over administrative expenses under § 503(b) and § 507(b) for the postpetition credit extension, § 364(c)(1).[140]

3.   A creditor who was given adequate protection that later proves to have been inadequate is awarded a superpriority over other first priority expenses, 507(b).

"Burial" expenses

The first superpriority arises in the situation where a reorganization case fails and is converted to a liquidation case under chapter 7. In this situation, the normal rule of pro rata treatment between all priority claims of the same class is suspended. Instead, the "burial" administrative expenses incurred in the superseding chapter 7 case are given priority over the administrative expenses incurred in the chapter 11, 12, or 13 case prior to conversion. § 726(b). Without this rule, it would be difficult to induce anyone to participate in the administration of the chapter 7 case following conversion, especially if the administrative expenses already incurred equaled or exceeded the size of the estate. The downside is that affording priority to post-conversion administrative expenses could make it harder to entice people to work for or do business with the estate in a reorganization case.

---

[139]   The ordinal names would not do the job, since "first" is as high as you can go. Golfers might note an analogy to the popular Callaway drivers. The original, called "Big Bertha," was followed by the bigger "Great Big Bertha." Next came "The Biggest Big Bertha" (I am not making this up). Having foolishly painted itself into a superlative corner, Callaway eventually went back to "Big" Bertha, and then added a "Hyper" driver. As of 2013, they appear to have learned their lesson, and now feature two drivers: an "X Hot" and a "RAZR Fit Xtreme."

[140]   See § 11.10.b.

Superpriority credit

A debtor who is operating its business almost always needs to be able to borrow money and otherwise obtain credit and incur debt. Potential lenders and credit extenders are understandably wary, however, about loaning money or extending credit to a bankruptcy debtor. The creditor might perceive a significant risk that the debt will not be repaid. To overcome this natural reluctance and induce the extension of postpetition credit, Congress provided enticements for postpetition lenders and credit extenders in § 364.[141] The basic inducement is the promise that the loan or credit extension will be granted administrative priority status.[142] § 364(a), (b).

The promise of a first priority might not be enough, however, to persuade a reluctant lender or credit extender to make a postpetition loan or to extend credit. There is always the risk of administrative insolvency, i.e., that the estate will not be sufficient to pay all administrative claims in full. And, if the chapter 11 case converts to chapter 7, the post-conversion administrative expenses will be paid first, as discussed above. § 726(b). The Code thus gives the bankruptcy court the power to grant a postpetition lender or credit extender a superpriority under § 364(c)(1). The superpriority debt will be paid in full ahead of all other administrative expenses and the § 507(b) superpriority claims, discussed below. Thus, even if the estate proves to be administratively insolvent, the superpriority creditor might still be repaid in full.

This extraordinary benefit may not be awarded lightly. Granting a superpriority makes it more difficult to induce subsequent parties to deal with the estate on an administrative expense basis, since they will know that the superpriority claim will be paid before them. Notice of the proposed superpriority must be given. The court then may only approve the grant of the superpriority on a showing that the credit is necessary to the estate and, most importantly, that the credit could not be obtained solely on the promise of an administrative priority.

Inadequate protection

The fundamental means by which the Code deals with the rights of secured creditors during the pendency of a bankruptcy case is through "adequate protection."[143] If adequate protection under § 361 is given to the secured creditor, the trustee or debtor in possession can resist relief from the stay under § 362; obtain turnover of the collateral under § 542; use, sell, or lease the collateral under § 363; and even grant a priming lien to a new lender under § 364(d). Adequate protection, though, is based on predictions about the future. What will a replacement lien be worth? How much will collateral depreciate? How much will the collateral appreciate if improvements are made? And so on.

Predictions, though, sometimes do not come true. Bankruptcy judges do not have an infallible crystal ball. What happens if adequate protection is given to a secured creditor under § 361, but subsequent events demonstrate that the protection given was

---

[141] See § 11.10 for a more complete discussion of § 364.

[142] See § 11.10.a.

[143] See §§ 3.18–3.20.

inadequate? For example, assume that the debtor retains collateral valued by the court at $5,000, and the court enters an adequate protection order requiring the debtor to pay the creditor $100 per month for depreciation. Ten months later, the debtor defaults. The collateral is then sold for only $3,500. Thus, the collateral has declined in value by $1,500, but the creditor has been paid only $1,000; the adequate protection fell short by $500.

The intent of Congress in this situation was for § 507(b) to give the disappointed creditor a superpriority over all of the § 507(a) priority claims in the amount of the adequate protection shortfall (in the example, $500).[144] In short, § 507(b) was designed as a "statutory fail-safe system" to back up adequate protection.[145] Adequate protection and § 507(b) thus "enjoy a symbiotic relationship."[146] The § 507(b) claim still would be paid behind a § 364(c)(1) superpriority, however.

Whether the language of § 507(b) always accomplishes the congressional goal is not clear. Perhaps the biggest problem is that the statutory language seems to suggest that the "inadequate protection" claim of the secured creditor must itself qualify for an administrative expense priority. Administrative expense status usually requires proof of an actual, concrete benefit to the estate. The concern is that a court might hold, as the Fourth Circuit did in one case,[147] that retention of collateral by the debtor following a denial of stay relief is not a sufficient benefit to support administrative priority, thus negating the § 507(b) claim entirely. Although perhaps faithful to the literal language of the Code, this result seems unfair to the stayed creditor, and contrary to congressional intent. Other courts have taken a more generous view of § 507(b), applying it to compensate a disappointed secured creditor even absent strict compliance with the terms of the statute.[148]

b. De Facto Priorities

Giving effect to the listed priorities in the Code is challenge enough. Complicating the situation, though, is the fact that courts have interpreted several sections of the Code as having a *de facto* priority or even superpriority status. The fault may not lie with the courts, but with the infelicitous drafting of Congress. This issue has arisen with regard to: interim performance of collective bargaining agreements, see § 1113(f); the payment of retiree benefits, see § 1114(e); performance under unexpired leases, see § 365(d)(3), (5); and the enforcement of the government's police or regulatory powers notwithstanding the stay, see § 362(b)(4).

---

[144] 124 Cong. Rec. H11,095 (daily ed. Sept. 28, 1978) (statement of Rep. Edwards).

[145] In re Marine Optical, Inc., 10 B.R. 893, 894 (B.A.P. 1st Cir. 1981); In re DeSardi, 340 B.R. 790 (Bankr. S.D.Tex. 2006).

[146] In re Callister, 15 B.R. 521, 528 (Bankr. D. Utah 1981), appeal dismissed, 673 F.2d 305 (10th Cir. 1982).

[147] Ford Motor Credit Co. v. Dobbins, 35 F.3d 860 (4th Cir. 1994).

[148] See, e.g., In re Blehm Land & Cattle Co., 859 F.2d 137 (10th Cir. 1988); In re Center Wholesale, Inc., 759 F.2d 1440 (9th Cir. 1985).

Collective bargaining agreements

In 1984, the Supreme Court held in *NLRB v. Bildisco & Bildisco*[149] that a chapter 11 debtor in possession could reject its collective bargaining agreement *and* that the debtor did not commit an unfair labor practice under the National Labor Relations Act by unilaterally modifying the terms of the agreement pending the resolution of the rejection motion. Congress quickly enacted § 1113 in response to the *Bildisco* decision.[150] While Congress largely codified the Court's holding with regard to the issue of the rejection of the collective bargaining agreement, in § 1113(f) Congress clearly overruled the Court's holding with regard to the legality of unilateral interim modifications. Section 1113(f) provides: "No provision of this title shall be construed to permit a trustee to unilaterally terminate or alter any provisions of a collective bargaining agreement prior to compliance with the provisions of this section."

The issue that has arisen concerns the implementation of § 1113(f). The intent of Congress was to strip the debtor of the power to unilaterally effect[151] changes in the labor contract. If the debtor wants changes prior to rejection, court approval must be obtained under § 1113(e). Does that mean, though, that the debtor must continue to perform under the collective bargaining agreement by paying wages and other benefits to union employees, without regard to the priority scheme drafted by Congress? And, if those payments are not made, what is the remedy: does § 1113(f) effectively confer a superpriority on the union employees?

To illustrate, assume that the debtor owed $2,000 to each of 100 union employees for wages earned in the month prior to the bankruptcy filing. Under the labor contract, those wages would come due the week after the bankruptcy filing. The priority section apparently grants the unpaid prepetition wages a fourth priority. § 507(a)(4). Fourth priority claims cannot be paid, obviously, ahead of first, second, and third priority claims. But, if payment must be made on the terms provided in the labor contract, in accordance with § 1113(f), the union employees' wage claims in effect will have jumped ahead of higher priority claims.

The courts are divided on whether § 1113(f) must be read to dictate superpriority treatment of the union claims. Some courts conclude that § 1113(f) must be given its literal effect, and that full compliance with the precise terms of the collective bargaining agreement is mandated.[152] In the above hypothetical, the debtor would have to pay the prepetition wages when due, unless the court authorized an emergency modification of the labor contract under § 1113(e). More courts today, though, refuse to read § 1113(f) as conferring a *de facto* priority on union members, and instead insist that the express priority provisions of the Code must control.[153] Under the latter view,

---

[149] 465 U.S. 513 (1984). See § 8.11.

[150] See § 8.12.

[151] If Congress can split infinitives, see § 1113(f), then so can I.

[152] The leading case is In re Unimet Corp., 842 F.2d 879 (6th Cir. 1988), cert. denied, 488 U.S. 828 (1988).

[153] The leading case is *In re Roth American, Inc.*, 975 F.2d 949 (3d Cir. 1992). In re Certified Air Technologies, Inc., 300 B.R. 355 (Bankr. C.D. Cal. 2003), ably summarizes the debate.

immediate payment of the employee's wages would only be proper if doing so would be consistent with the Code's priority scheme.

Retiree benefits

A similar but not identical problem exists for retiree benefits under § 1114. Congress added § 1114 to the Code in 1988 in response to the attempt of LTV Corporation to escape its obligations to retirees. Subsection (e)(1) of § 1114 provides that a debtor in possession "shall timely pay and shall not modify any retiree benefits," except as therein permitted. Subsection (e)(2) goes on to provide that any required payment of retiree benefits has the status of an administrative expense under § 503.

If a case involves potential administrative insolvency, these two subsections may be at war with each other. Subsection (e)(1) appears to command immediate timely payment of retiree benefits—arguably without regard to whether the estate will have sufficient funds to pay all administrative claims in full. Yet subsection (e)(2) expressly provides that retiree benefits are nothing more than standard administrative expenses—which would mean that they must share pro rata with all other first priority claims. The Code offers no hints at how to solve this conundrum.

Unexpired leases

In 1984 Congress added § 365(d)(3) and (4) to the Code to enhance the protection for nondebtor lessors of nonresidential real property leases.[154] Subsection (d)(4) provides that the lease will be rejected by operation of law if the debtor in possession does not act to assume, reject, or obtain an extension of time within 60 days of the order for relief. Subsection (d)(3) dictates the rights of the nondebtor lessor pending the debtor's decision whether to assume or reject the lease. It provides in part that "the trustee shall timely perform all the obligations of the debtor . . . arising from and after the order for relief . . . until such lease is assumed or rejected, notwithstanding section 503(b)(1)."

This provision changed the old practice, under which a lessor was entitled to an administrative priority only in the amount of a reasonable rental for the premises actually used by the debtor during the bankruptcy case.[155] Now, under § 365(d)(3), the majority view is that the lessor is entitled to full payment at the lease rate for all postpetition obligations, irrespective of whether there is any actual benefit to the estate.[156]

Even under this view, problems arise in determining when an obligation "arises." The difficulty occurs when a bill on the lease comes due postpetition, but covers a period that straddles the petition date. This commonly occurs for rent and tax obligations. Courts differ on whether to use a "proration" or "accrual" theory, only

---

[154] See § 8.26.

[155] See, e.g., In re United Cigar Stores Co., 69 F.2d 513 (2d Cir. 1934), cert. denied, 293 U.S. 566 (1934).

[156] See, e.g., In re Pacific–Atlantic Trading Co., 27 F.3d 401 (9th Cir. 1994). See also In re Burival, 613 F.3d 810 (8th Cir. 2010).

requiring the debtor to pay the portion of the bill attributable to the postpetition period,[157] or a "billing date" theory, requiring the debtor to pay the entire bill if it comes due postpetition.[158] Under the latter approach, the violence to the Code's priority scheme is more dramatic, since part of a lessor's prepetition claim will be paid in full.

If the estate appears to have sufficient assets to pay all administrative claims in full, the courts agree that § 365(d)(3) commands full and immediate payment of lease obligations that come due postpetition and prior to rejection or assumption. What the courts do not agree on is whether the same result is mandated if the estate is administratively insolvent. Some courts take the position that the unqualified directive that the debtor "timely perform" the lease obligations "notwithstanding section 503(b)(1)" plainly does require immediate payment, even in cases of administrative insolvency.[159] Other courts, however, excuse the debtor from the obligation to "timely perform" if the estate will not have enough assets to fully satisfy all first priority claims.[160] The lessor's postpetition lease claims then must share pro rata with all other administrative expenses.

In 1994, Congress extended the principle of § 365(d)(3) to unexpired *personal* property leases. See § 365(d)(5).[161] That subsection requires the trustee to timely perform all the obligations of the debtor arising under an unexpired lease of personal property that arise from and after 60 days after the order for relief until assumption or rejection. Unlike subsection (d)(3), the rule in subsection (d)(5) defers the timely performance obligation for 60 days after the bankruptcy filing. This delay should afford the trustee or debtor in possession an opportunity to reject an unwanted lease before the performance directive takes effect. Furthermore, under subsection (d)(5) the court is given authority to countermand the timely performance rule based on the "equities of the case." Otherwise, though, the issue of de facto priority is the same under (d)(5) as it is under (d)(3).[162]

Police power orders

A de facto superpriority also can result when the trustee or debtor in possession is required to expend estate funds to comply with a governmental order issued pursuant to the government's "police or regulatory powers." In such a case, the automatic stay will not stop the government from enforcing its order. § 362(b)(4). An example would be an order directing the cleanup of environmental pollution.[163] Although the government would still be stayed if it is only enforcing a money judgment, many courts have

---

[157] See, e.g., In re Handy Andy Home Improvement Centers, Inc., 144 F.3d 1125 (7th Cir. 1998).

[158] See, e.g., In re Montgomery Ward Holding Co., 268 F.3d 205 (3d Cir. 2001). See also *Burival*, supra note 156, 613 F.3d 810.

[159] See, e.g., In re C.Q., LLC, 343 B.R. 915 (Bankr. W.D. Wis. 2005); In re Telesphere Commc'ns, Inc., 148 B.R. 525 (Bankr. N.D. Ill. 1992).

[160] See, e.g., In re Joseph C. Spiess Co., 145 B.R. 597 (Bankr. N.D. Ill. 1992).

[161] As enacted, this rule was codified in § 365(d)(10). It was changed to subsection (d)(5) in 2005.

[162] For an application, see In re Midway Airlines Corp., 406 F.3d 229 (4th Cir. 2005).

[163] See, e.g., Penn Terra, Ltd. v. Department of Environmental Resources, 733 F.2d 267 (3d Cir. 1984). See also § 3.11.

narrowly construed the meaning of "money judgment" in this context, and have permitted the government to enforce its order.[164]

§ 7.9 Domestic Support Obligations

Claims for domestic support—obligations such as alimony, maintenance, and child support—are in many circumstances favored under the law. The proverbial "deadbeat dad" can have a much higher percentage of his wages garnished to pay such claims than for any other type of claim. He could be imprisoned for contempt for failure to pay such claims. The list goes on and on, and yet default on such claims remains one of our most pressing and troubling social problems. Bankruptcy law is no exception in providing special benefits to and protections for "domestic support obligations" ("DSO"). DSO claims cannot be discharged, § 523(a)(5);[165] payments on such claims are not avoidable as preferences, § 547(c)(7);[166] DSO claims can be enforced against exempt property, § 522(c)(1);[167] judicial liens securing such debts cannot be avoided even if they impair an exemption, § 522(f)(1)(A);[168] the automatic stay does not prevent the collection of such debts from the debtor, § 362(b)(2)(B);[169] and, as of 1994, such claims were given priority under § 507. As originally enacted, claims for alimony, maintenance, and support were given *seventh* priority.[170]

Not content with the manifold protections already afforded domestic claimants, and never averse to seizing prime opportunities for positive political public relations, in the 2005 amendments Congress enacted a package of amendments that favored DSO claimants.[171] Included in that package was an amendment that elevated the priority for DSO claims from seventh priority to *first* priority, in § 507(a)(1)(A) and (B).[172]

The new first priority actually has two subsidiary priority levels. The key is who the beneficial claimant is. Top billing for the first priority, under subsection (A), is accorded to "[a]llowed unsecured claims for domestic support obligations that, as of the date of the filing of the petition . . . are owed to or recoverable by a spouse, former spouse, or child of the debtor, or such child's parent, legal guardian, or responsible relative." § 507(a)(1)(A). The claim does not necessarily have to actually be filed by that claimant, as long as they are the beneficial party. The second ranking for DSO claims—"subject to claims under subparagraph (A)"—are the same sort of claims as in (A) (*viz.*, allowed unsecured claims for domestic support obligations), but as to which a governmental unit is the beneficial claimant. § 507(a)(1)(B). The governmental unit could enjoy that status either by assignment from the spouse or child (unless done voluntarily for the purpose of collection), or because under non-bankruptcy law that claim is owed to or recoverable by the governmental unit. In such event, the

---

[164] See, e.g., *Penn Terra*, supra note 163, 733 F.2d 267. See also § 3.11.

[165] See § 10.20.

[166] See § 6.23.

[167] See § 9.4.

[168] See § 9.10.

[169] See § 3.14.

[170] Pub. L. No. 103–394, § 304(c), 108 Stat. 4132 (1994).

[171] Pub. L. No. 109–8, Subtit. B, "Priority Child Support," §§ 211–220, 119 Stat. 50–59 (2005).

[172] Id. § 212(9), 119 Stat. 51. See H.R. Rep. No. 109–31 (pt. 1), 109th Cong., 1st Sess. 16, 59–60 (2005).

government's priority is conditioned on making distribution of monies received in accordance with the applicable non-bankruptcy law.

Common to both parts of the first priority is that the claims must be for "domestic support obligations." This is a newly defined term in the 2005 law, codified in § 101(14A). The first part of that definition identifies proper party claimants, § 101(14A)(A), and to that extent is redundant of the priority provision in § 507(a)(1). Importantly, though, note that the inclusion of governmental units as proper beneficial claimants under the new first priority is an extension from prior law, which under the seventh priority was limited to a spouse, former spouse, or child, and did not extend to any other entity.

The next critical definitional limitation of a "domestic support obligation" is that the debt must be *"in the nature of"* alimony, maintenance, or support, § 101(14A)(B). Excluded, then, are debts that are simply a division of assets under a property settlement agreement. There is a huge body of case law under the discharge exception (§ 523(a)(5)) on the issue of whether a debt is in the nature of alimony, maintenance, or support or instead is just a division of property. That case law should be relevant in applying § 507(a)(1) as well. Note that while the definition of "domestic support obligation" can include debts established in a property settlement agreement, § 101(14A)(C)(i), it *also* requires that the debt be "in the nature of" alimony, maintenance, or support. In short, the *nature* of the debt controls, not its source.

The only problem with elevating DSO claims to *first* priority is that it is unworkable to put them ahead of all administrative expenses. Consider an example. Debtor files chapter 7, and has only one unencumbered asset—Thing, with a value of $5,000. Debtor also owes back child support of $8,000 to Child. In the dream world Congress lived in when it was drafting BAPCPA, the hope in moving the child support claim to first priority was that Trustee would sell Thing for $5,000 and turn over all the money to the Child. Oh, but wait—why would Trustee do that, when that means Trustee would not get paid a dime for his troubles? When presented with this practical problem, Congress realized that it had to put in, at the very least, a carveout for trustee expenses ahead of DSO claims, so that in cases like the above hypothetical the Trustee actually would be willing to invest in the time and trouble to sell Thing. Accordingly, under § 507(a)(1)(C), most administrative expenses of a trustee[173] are to be paid ahead of DSO claims under § 507(a)(1)(A) and (B), "to the extent that the trustee administers assets that are otherwise available for the payment of such [i.e., the DSO] claims."[174] So, in the hypothetical, before Child gets paid, the trustee will apply the sale proceeds first to the expenses of the sale, then to payment of his own fee under § 326(a) (which would be up to 25% of the first $5,000 disbursed). Thus, "first" priority DSO claims actually may *not* be first, when it matters. When combined with the reality that about 95% of all consumer chapter 7 cases have no free assets available to pay unsecured creditors (and remember, priority claims are still unsecured), then the much-trumpeted change of moving DSO claims to first priority rings hollow indeed.

---

[173] The administrative expenses covered are those in § 503(b)(1)(A) (actual and necessary costs and expenses of preserving the estate, see § 7.12), § 503(b)(2) (compensation and reimbursement of the fees and expenses of the trustee himself under § 330, see § 7.16), and § 503(b)(6) (fees and mileage).

[174] See H.R. Rep. No. 109–31 (pt. I), 109th Cong., 1st Sess. at 60 (2005).

The one situation where elevating DSO claims to even the qualified "first" priority of § 507(a)(1)(A) and (B) matters, and accordingly is problematic, is in an individual business reorganization case under chapter 11 or 13. As a practical matter, the current expenses of running a business during the pendency of the bankruptcy case must be paid first, in order to induce creditors to do business with the bankruptcy estate. If DSO claims must be paid ahead of such operating business expenses, then creditors may not be willing to deal with the bankruptcy estate. That, in turn, could cause the reorganization to fail, and everyone would be worse off. However, in most business reorganizations, the fact that Congress placed administrative expenses (other than trustee carveout claims) in *second* priority under § 507(a)(2), behind DSO first priority claims, is meaningless. Why? Because by definition the first priority for DSO claims will never exist if the debtor is a *corporation* or a *partnership*. Companies do not have spouses or children, except in a metaphorical sense. Thus, for all business entity debtors, the priority for administrative expenses is in reality still *first*, as it should be.

Having said that, though, a significant problem still remains for business cases involving an *individual* debtor. Individuals of course can have spouses and children, and can owe domestic support obligations. In running their business in chapter 11 or 13, such a debtor will have the same needs as any other business to incur and pay current debt. However, except for the trustee carveout in § 507(a)(1)(C), DSO claims are in fact required to be paid ahead of all administrative expenses. Is there any way out of this foolish box? Perhaps. One possibility is to interpret expansively the trustee carveout as it pertains to "the administrative expenses of the trustee allowed under paragraph[ ] (1)(A)" of § 503(b). Under § 503(b)(1)(A), administrative expenses are allowed for "the actual, necessary costs and expenses of preserving the estate."[175] Courts have construed that section to include the costs of running the debtor's business. In substance, then, it is possible that the reference in § 507(a)(1)(C) could extend to all actual and necessary business expenses. The sticking point, though, is that the carveout in subsection (C) applies only to the administrative expenses "of the trustee" under the referenced sections. Is there any way to read this to allow the trustee to pay *other* current administrative creditors of the bankruptcy estate? While the most natural reading of the language "of the trustee" is that it applies to expenses where the trustee himself is the claimant, it is at least possible to read it as expenses *incurred by* the trustee. If that hurdle is surmounted, there remains the need to show that the payment came from assets that the trustee "administers" to qualify for the carveout. Here the argument would be that the asset "administered" was the debtor's business.

If the tack suggested in the preceding paragraph fails, one other possibility remains for the individual business debtor who needs to obtain current credit for ongoing business expenses in his reorganization case but is hamstrung by first priority DSOs. That debtor might seek to incur credit under § 364(c)(2) or (3).[176] Under those provisions, a trustee (or DIP) can obtain credit or incur debt and grant the credit extender a lien on unencumbered (or under-encumbered) assets of the estate. The showing required is that the trustee is unable to obtain credit as an administrative

---

[175]   See § 7.12.
[176]   See § 11.10.b.

expense under § 503(b)(1). If an individual business debtor is burdened by first priority DSOs, which would come ahead of second priority § 503(b)(1) administrative expenses, then that showing could well be made. By giving the putative administrative creditor a *lien* on estate assets, the trustee effectively would trump the first priority DSOs, since liens are satisfied before priority claims, which are unsecured. Note that the trustee would have to give a lien under subsection (2) or (3) of § 364(c) to effectively elevate the administrative claimant above first priority DSO claims, because the "superpriority" provision in subsection (1) of § 364(c) only trumps "administrative expenses" under § 503(b) or § 507(b), and thus remains subordinate to first priority DSO claims.

§ 7.10   Administrative Expenses: Fundamentals

The second priority is for (1) administrative expenses allowed under § 503(b), and (2) court fees and charges assessed against the estate. § 507(a)(2). An entity claiming an entitlement to an administrative expense must establish its claim under § 503(b). Section 503(b) lists nine different types of expenses that are allowable administrative expenses. § 503(b)(1)–(9). Note that this listing does not signify a priority ranking within the administrative expense class; all administrative expenses are of equal rank. If the estate is not sufficient to pay all administrative expenses in full, i.e., is administratively insolvent, those expenses will share on a pro rata basis. § 726(b). The only exception to this pro rata sharing rule is when a reorganization case is converted to liquidation under chapter 7; in that event, the "burial" expenses in the superseding chapter 7 case are paid before the administrative expenses in the superseded reorganization case.[177]

The list of administrative expenses in § 503(b) is not exclusive, because the statute uses the word "including" as a preface to the list. See § 102(3). Accordingly, in appropriate cases the court has the authority to allow an administrative expense that is not specifically described in § 503(b). This opening has permitted courts to grant first priority to certain claims on "fairness" grounds, even when those claims might not directly benefit the estate.[178] Examples are tort claims[179] and environmental obligations.[180] Having said that, the vast majority of administrative expenses do fall within the described categories in § 503(b).

The courts carefully scrutinize requests for administrative expenses, and strictly construe § 503(b) against the claimant.[181] The reason for this cautious approach is that allowing administrative expenses departs from the normal bankruptcy rule of equality of distribution. A claimant who is awarded an administrative expense will be paid in full before any payment is made to general unsecured non-priority claimants. A strong bankruptcy policy favors maximizing the realizable value of the bankruptcy estate for

---

[177] See § 7.8.a.

[178] See § 7.14.

[179] E.g., Reading Co. v. Brown, 391 U.S. 471 (1968).

[180] E.g., In re Wall Tube & Metal Products Co., 831 F.2d 118 (6th Cir. 1987).

[181] E.g., Trustees of Amalgamated Ins. Fund v. McFarlin's, Inc., 789 F.2d 98 (2d Cir. 1986). See also Sanchez v. Northwest Airlines, Inc., 659 F.3d 671 (8th Cir. 2011); In re Bethlehem Steel Corp., 479 F.3d 167 (2d Cir. 2007).

the benefit of the general unsecured creditors; keeping fees and expenses at a minimum helps preserve as much of the estate as possible for those creditors.[182]

Recognizing the premise for limiting administrative expenses at the same time suggests the principle for allowing those expenses. Administrative expenses should be allowed to the extent that they will benefit the general unsecured creditors and the estate. In short, if it makes sense to have a bankruptcy case, then some types of claims must be afforded priority in order to realize the full benefit of that bankruptcy proceeding. This rationale extends to third parties who will only do business with the estate if promised an administrative priority,[183] and to those persons who will only participate in the administration of the bankruptcy case if compensated on a current basis.[184] The fundamental prerequisites for most administrative expenses therefore are (1) that the claim be incurred postpetition in a transaction with the estate,[185] and (2) that the claim benefit the estate.[186] The principal exception is for "fairness" claims, noted above.

Several types of claims fit this general description. Two generic categories of administrative expenses are (1) actual and necessary operating and preservation expenses of the estate, and (2) compensation and reimbursement of entities that enable the bankruptcy process itself to function. The first category, for "actual, necessary costs and expenses of preserving the estate," § 503(b)(1), encompasses such disparate types of expenses as rent, wages, insurance, utilities, trade credit, contracts, taxes, and so forth.[187] The second category covers items such as the fees and expenses of the bankruptcy trustee,[188] the compensation of attorneys who do work for the estate or for an official committee,[189] and the reimbursement of creditors and committee members who contribute to the administration of the bankruptcy case.[190] §§ 503(b)(2)–(6).

The fact that an expense is awarded an administrative expense priority does not guarantee that it will be paid in full. To begin with, the bankruptcy estate may not be sufficient to pay all administrative priority claims in full. Priority claims are not secured, but must look to payment out of the general unencumbered assets of the estate. In those cases involving individual debtors where domestic support obligations exist, the first priority for the DSOs may drain the estate of funds needed to pay second priority administrative expenses.[191] Furthermore, some types of claims are awarded a "super" priority, such as claims under § 507(b) or § 364(c)(1).[192] Finally, administrative

---

[182] See Otte v. United States, 419 U.S. 43, 53 (1974).

[183] See In re Jartran, Inc., 732 F.2d 584 (7th Cir. 1984). See § 7.11.

[184] See H.R. Rep. No. 95–595, 95th Cong., 1st Sess. 186–87 (1977).

[185] See § 7.11. See also In re Sunarhauserman, Inc., 126 F.3d 811 (6th Cir. 1997).

[186] In re Mammoth Mart, Inc., 536 F.2d 950 (1st Cir. 1976). See § 7.11. See also *Sunarhauserman*, supra note 9, 126 F.3d 811.

[187] See §§ 7.12, 7.15.

[188] See § 7.16.

[189] See § 7.17.

[190] See § 7.18.

[191] See § 7.9.

[192] See § 7.8.a.

expenses incurred in a reorganization case that converts to chapter 7 will be paid after the administrative expenses of the superseding chapter 7 case. § 726(b).

§ 7.11   Administrative Expenses: Postpetition Transaction with Estate

As a general rule, an expense will only be allowed as an administrative expense under § 503(b) if it arises *post*petition during the pendency of the bankruptcy case, in a transaction with the representative of the bankruptcy estate.[193] This limitation furthers the underlying purpose of the first priority, which is to *induce* parties to do business with the estate or to participate in the administration of the case. Applying the rule sometimes creates difficult timing issues. Courts usually focus on when the acts giving rise to the claim were performed. This time may be earlier than when a cause of action would accrue under state law or when the right to payment matures.

A good example of the operation of this principle is the Seventh Circuit's decision in *In re Jartran, Inc.*[194] In *Jartran*, the debtor placed an order for Yellow Pages advertisements *prior* to filing a chapter 11 bankruptcy case. The advertisements were actually published *after* the filing, and thus did provide a benefit to the bankruptcy estate. However, the Seventh Circuit denied priority, reasoning that the creditor had not transacted business with the bankruptcy estate, but with the debtor before bankruptcy.[195] Accordingly, the creditor had not been induced to do business with the estate on the promise of an administrative priority. The basis for the claim was first established prior to bankruptcy, when the debtor placed the irrevocable order for the advertisements.

Another example of the application of this rule involves vacation and severance pay claims of the employees of the debtor. Consider the common situation where the amount of vacation and severance pay is based on the length of employment, but where the employees' entitlement to the pay only vests upon termination of employment or after the expiration of a specified amount of time. What happens when the necessary triggering event for vesting occurs *after* the bankruptcy filing, but some of the labor on which the amount of the claim is computed was performed *prior* to bankruptcy? In this situation most courts have allowed an administrative expense to the employees only to the extent attributable to the postpetition labor performed.[196] The amount attributable to prepetition labor is not awarded administrative priority.

One type of case in which the courts have been more permissive in finding postpetition incurrence sufficient to support administrative priority is in the environmental context. The usual pattern is that the pollution occurs prior to bankruptcy, but the cleanup of the contaminated site has not yet taken place when the bankruptcy case is filed. After bankruptcy, the government either incurs cleanup expenses itself, and seeks reimbursement from the estate as an administrative expense, or orders the representative of the estate to clean up the site. The trustee

---

[193]   See In re Mammoth Mart, Inc., 536 F.2d 950 (1st Cir. 1976).

[194]   732 F.2d 584 (7th Cir. 1984).

[195]   Id. at 587–88.

[196]   See, e.g., In re Mammoth Mart, Inc., 536 F.2d 950 (1st Cir. 1976). See also In re Bethlehem Steel Corp., 479 F.3d 167 (2d Cir. 2007).

could plausibly argue in opposition to this request that the government's claim arose prior to bankruptcy, when the pollution occurred, and thus should not be entitled to priority. However, the courts have almost uniformly awarded administrative priority in this situation.[197] They note that the Supreme Court, in *Midlantic National Bank v. New Jersey Department of Environmental Protection*,[198] limited the ability of the bankruptcy trustee to *abandon* a polluted site. Even though the Supreme Court in *Midlantic* stated that it was not deciding the priority question, courts after *Midlantic* have concluded that an inevitable ramification of that decision is to elevate postpetition cleanup claims to administrative priority status, even if they are traceable to prepetition pollution.

The 2005 amendments introduced two exceptions to the general rule that a claim is entitled to administrative expense priority only to the extent it was incurred in a *post*petition transaction with the bankruptcy estate. First, under new § 503(b)(9), a seller of goods is granted an administrative expense for the value of any goods received by the debtor within 20 days *before* the petition date, as long as the goods were sold to the debtor in the ordinary course of the debtor's business.[199] The seller need take no action (such as sending notice to the debtor) to be entitled to this new administrative expense. Note too that the provision does not require proof either that the debtor received the goods while insolvent, or pursuant to a credit sale. However, it is limited to sellers of *goods*, and thus is of no help to sellers of services or other products besides goods; accordingly, in *Jartran*, the new rule would not have applied to the sale of Yellow Pages advertisements.

The effect of the new rule in § 503(b)(9) will be to relax the "postpetition transaction and benefit" aspect of administrative expense doctrine for sellers of goods for a brief (20 day) period. In essence, the cleavage point for timing the transaction is moved back from the petition date to 20 days prior to bankruptcy. By doing so, Congress has sought to provide further encouragement for sellers of goods to do business with financially distressed debtors, by lessening the worry that an intervening bankruptcy might leave an unpaid seller out of luck.

This new remedy is a cousin of and conceptually derived from the well-known seller's remedy of *reclamation*, where under non-bankruptcy law a seller is given a short window of time to "reclaim" goods sold on credit to an insolvent debtor. U.C.C. § 2–702(2). By reclaiming the goods themselves, rather than being left with an unsecured claim against an insolvent debtor, the seller is afforded full recovery rather than only a few cents on the dollar. The justification for the reclamation remedy is that the debtor essentially has defrauded the seller by accepting goods on credit while insolvent. Receipt of goods on credit is treated as a tacit representation of solvency in commercial law. The fraud-based nature of the non-bankruptcy reclamation remedy is seen further by the fact that, whereas a seller normally must demand reclamation within 10 days after the debtor receives the goods, if the debtor makes a written

---

[197] See, e.g., In re Chateaugay Corp. 944 F.2d 997 (2d Cir. 1991); In re Wall Tube & Metal Products Co., 831 F.2d 118 (6th Cir. 1987).

[198] 474 U.S. 494 (1986). See § 5.15.

[199] Pub. L. No. 109–8, § 1227(b), 119 Stat. 200 (2005).

misrepresentation of solvency within the preceding three months, the 10–day limit does not apply. In effect, U.C.C. § 2–702(2) treats any receipt of goods by the debtor on credit while insolvent as conclusively fraudulent for 10 days, and extends the time if actual fraud, in writing, is shown.

The question arises, though, whether and to what extent a reclamation remedy should be recognized in a *bankruptcy* case. The concern, of course, is that by allowing a seller to reclaim, that seller is paid in full in preference to other unsecured creditors, who are left with recovery of a few cents on the dollar. Is the actual or imputed fraud of the debtor in receiving goods on credit while insolvent enough to justify preferring the defrauded seller over other creditors? The answer in the Bankruptcy Code is found in § 546(c)(1), which enforces a seller's reclamation remedy under certain prescribed conditions.[200] The Code's reclamation provision was substantially amended in 2005 to provide much broader relief for sellers of goods, and was done in tandem with the creation of the new administrative expense allowance provision in § 503(b)(9).[201] In most cases a seller would prefer reclamation over an administrative priority, since in reclamation the seller would obtain the goods themselves, whereas payment of an administrative expense would be dependent on the sufficiency of the funds in the debtor's estate to pay all administrative expenses, which is not a sure thing. The interdependence of the reclamation remedy of § 546(c)(1) and the new administrative priority of § 503(b)(9) is seen by the fact that § 546(c)(2), also added in 2005, expressly provides that if a seller fails to give notice of reclamation as required in § 546(c)(1), "the seller still may assert the rights contained in" § 503(b)(9). Note, though, that the substantive predicates of the two remedies are not identical; reclamation under § 546(c)(1) requires proof that the debtor was insolvent when it received the goods, whereas insolvency is not required under § 503(b)(9).

The second exception to the "postpetition transaction and benefit" rule introduced in 2005 was for back pay awards. Under new § 503(b)(1)(A)(ii), wages and benefits awarded pursuant to a judicial proceeding or by the NLRB as back pay for a violation of state or federal law are allowed as an administrative expense. The back pay award must be attributable to "any period of time occurring after" the bankruptcy case has commenced, but the claimant need not prove either that the debtor's unlawful conduct occurred postpetition or even that any services were actually rendered. Thus neither the "fairness" rationale nor the benefit principle need be satisfied. The court does have discretion to disallow the claimed administrative expense if it finds that allowance would "substantially increase the probability of layoff or termination of current employees." Also, the court may deny the administrative expense allowance if it finds that allowance would increase the risk that a domestic support obligation would not be paid, although how that would occur is puzzling, since DSOs come ahead of administrative expenses in the priority pecking order.

---

[200]   See § 7.37.
[201]   Pub. L. No. 109–8, § 1227(a), 119 Stat. 199–200 (2005).

§ 7.12 Administrative Expenses: Actual and Necessary Expenses of Preserving Estate

A prerequisite to the allowance of many types of administrative expenses under § 503(b) is a showing that the expense was "actual and necessary" to the administration and preservation of the estate. This requirement applies most predominantly with regard to § 503(b)(1)(A), which grants priority to "the actual, necessary costs and expenses of preserving the estate." "Preservation" is interpreted as encompassing both (1) the protection of estate property and (2) the facilitation of the operation of the debtor's business. The focus in construing what is "actual and necessary" is on whether a direct and quantifiable benefit flows to the estate, not on the amount of costs incurred or loss suffered by the claimant.[202] The courts state that the consideration must both be supplied to and be beneficial to the trustee or debtor in possession.[203] The scope of "actual and necessary" expenses is narrowly construed, in keeping with the general policy of keeping administrative expenses to a minimum and preserving the maximum value of the estate for the benefit of general creditors.

A wide variety of expenditures are held to constitute actual and necessary expenses under § 503(b). Most of these arise as an incident to the operation of the debtor's business in a reorganization case under chapter 11. Perhaps the most common such expenses are rent, wages, and taxes attributable to the postpetition period. Other common expenses allowed include trade credit, utilities, insurance, and contracts entered into or assumed by the estate.

Administrative rent historically was allowed to the extent that the bankruptcy estate actually used leased property during the administration of the case.[204] A corollary to this principle was that administrative priority was denied if the trustee or debtor in possession did not use the leased property, because no benefit then accrued to the estate. For example, in one case the debtor had leased 70 rail cars prior to bankruptcy, but never used those cars after the filing, and ultimately returned the cars to the lessor seven months after filing. Administrative priority for the seven months' postpetition rent claim was denied.[205] A minority approach would allow priority to the extent the trustee had the opportunity to use the leased property, even if that opportunity had not been seized.[206] Under the majority view, the amount of the priority allowed was the reasonable value of the leased property to the estate, which is not necessarily identical to the amount of rent specified in the lease.

Today, many of the rent cases are controlled by special pro-lessor rules in § 365(d). In 1984 Congress added § 365(d)(3), which requires the trustee to "timely perform" *all* postpetition obligations arising under a nonresidential real property lease, irrespective of actual use or benefit to the estate, until the lease is rejected. To make plain that

---

[202] E.g., In re Goody's Family Clothing, 610 F.3d 812 (3d Cir. 2010); In re Dant & Russell, Inc., 853 F.2d 700, 706 (9th Cir. 1988).

[203] See In re Bethlehem Steel Corp., 479 F.3d 167, 172 (2d Cir. 2007). See also In re Hemingway Transport, Inc., 954 F.2d 1, 5 (1st Cir. 1992).

[204] The foundational case is *Philadelphia Co. v. Dipple*, 312 U.S. 168 (1941).

[205] In re Mid–Region Petroleum, Inc., 1 F.3d 1130 (10th Cir. 1993).

[206] E.g., In re Fred Sanders Co., 22 B.R. 902 (Bankr. E.D. Mich. 1982).

compliance with the standard rules governing administrative expense allowance is not required in this situation, § 365(d)(3) specifies that the trustee's obligation to "timely perform" all lease obligations applies "notwithstanding section 503(b)(1)." Under § 365(d)(3), the trustee accordingly must pay the full contractual lease rental for the leased premises, even if the property is not used.[207] The only way for the trustee or DIP to stop the running of this obligation is to formally reject the lease.

A similar rule for commercial *personal* property leases was added to the Code in 1994.[208] § 365(d)(5). Thus, today the rail car case mentioned above would require payment of postpetition rent, even though the cars were not used and did not benefit the estate. Unlike the commercial lease rule, however, the personal property lease provision only applies in chapter 11 cases, does not apply to obligations arising during the first 60 days of the bankruptcy case, and may be overridden by court order based on the "equities of the case."

Another major category of actual and necessary administrative expenses is for wages and other forms of compensation owed to employees of the debtor based on postpetition labor. Indeed, the importance of this type of administrative claim is emphasized by the fact that Congress specifically identifies "wages, salaries, and commissions for services rendered after the commencement of the case" as an included form of qualifying actual, necessary costs and expenses in § 503(b)(1)(A)(i). Wages and other benefits based on *pre*petition labor are not entitled to administrative priority, although they may qualify as fourth or fifth priority claims. See § 507(a)(4), (5). The necessity of allowing administrative priority for postpetition wages is apparent; otherwise it would be extremely difficult to persuade the debtor's employees to keep working. Although the priority will be allowed only if the employees' services are necessary and beneficial to the estate, courts routinely grant the priority if the debtor's business is authorized to be operated (as is the norm in chapter 11 cases).

Two significant sets of issues that have arisen in applying the wage priority are (1) identifying what forms of compensation are included, and (2) determining the time that the debt arose. As to the first question, courts now recognize that employees are enticed to work for an employer by the promise of a full range of benefits, and not just wages, and accordingly extend the administrative priority to benefits such as vacation pay, severance pay, and sick leave.

With regard to the second issue, the statute covers wages "for services rendered after the commencement of the case." Thus, priority is to be granted only to the extent that labor has been performed after the filing. To illustrate, assume that employees are paid monthly, and that the employer files bankruptcy in the middle of a month. Only that portion of the employees' wages attributable to the two weeks of *postpetition* work will be afforded administrative priority. This attribution principle has been applied in vacation pay cases as well, presuming that vacation pay accrues on a daily basis.[209] The severance pay cases have presented more difficulty, since by definition the

---

[207] See § 8.26.

[208] See § 8.27.

[209] See, e.g., In re Roth American, Inc., 975 F.2d 949 (3d Cir. 1992).

employee's right to the severance pay does not mature until the employee is terminated. If termination occurs after the bankruptcy filing, during the bankruptcy administration, the employee will argue that the entire severance pay debt arose at that time and should be given first priority.[210] The majority of courts have rejected this argument, however, and have only allowed severance pay claims a first priority in an amount attributable to postpetition service.[211] The Second Circuit has held that the full amount of the severance pay claim is entitled to administrative priority,[212] but in a 2007 decision arguably retreated somewhat from that position, recognizing the possibility of an attribution approach, depending on the terms of the severance pay.[213]

Trade credit is another important type of administrative expense that is commonly allowed in cases where the debtor's business is authorized to be operated postpetition. It would be difficult for any business to function without credit, and yet trade suppliers would be unlikely to extend credit without the guarantee of administrative priority. This guarantee is implemented by § 364(a) and (b), under which credit is afforded an administrative priority.[214] Under § 364(a), credit is entitled to first priority without the necessity for court approval if incurred "in the ordinary course of business." The authorization to carry on the debtor's business is thought to carry with it the implicit authorization to incur credit necessary to that business operation, obviating the need for further court oversight. If, however, extension of the credit would fall outside of the ordinary course of business, then a motion for court approval of the credit must be filed, and other creditors must be notified and given the opportunity to object. § 364(b).

§ 7.13 Administrative Expenses. KERP Limits

One of the most controversial issues that has arisen in large chapter 11 cases concerns the payment of large compensation packages to senior management of the debtor. These "key employee retention plans" ("KERP") offer very enticing incentives to the debtor's top executives to stay with the debtor during the chapter 11 case. In big cases the dollars involved can be quite large; for example, in the WorldCom bankruptcy case the court authorized the debtor to pay up to $25 million in bonuses ranging from $20,000 to $125,000 to 329 designated "key employees" who agreed to stay with the company.[215] Because of their incentive structure, these plans have been called "pay to stay" programs.

In the 2005 Amendments, Congress placed some strict limitations on these KERPs in new § 503(c)(1), which limits the allowability and payment of administrative

---

[210] See, e.g., Matson v. Alarcon, 651 F.3d 404 (4th Cir. 2011).

[211] See, e.g., In re Health Maintenance Foundation, 680 F.2d 619 (9th Cir. 1982).

[212] See Straus–Duparquet, Inc. v. Int'l Bhd. of Elec. Workers, 386 F.2d 649 (2d Cir. 1967), and its progeny.

[213] In re Bethlehem Steel Corp., 479 F.3d 167 (2d Cir. 2007). The court stated: "In determining whether a payment incident to termination is entitled to priority as an administrative expense, the key inquiry is whether it represents a new benefit earned at termination or an acceleration of a benefit the employee earned over the course of his or her employment." Id. at 172. If it is the former, then administrative priority is called for, but if the latter, it is not.

[214] See § 11.10.a.

[215] See David A. Skeel, Jr., Creditors' Ball: The "New" New Corporate Governance in Chapter 11, 152 U. Pa. L. Rev. 917, 927 (2003).

expenses under § 503(b).[216] Congress also placed restrictions on "golden parachute" severance packages to insiders. No severance payments are permitted unless "the payment is part of a program that is generally applicable to all full-time employees" and the "amount of the payment is not greater than 10 times the amount of the mean severance pay given to nonmanagement employees during the calendar year in which the payment is made." § 503(c)(2).

The KERP section has two key parts. The first is the scope provision, which determines when the limiting rule is triggered. It applies to transfers to or obligations incurred (1) for the benefit of an "*insider*" (defined in § 101(31)) and (2) "for the purpose of inducing such person to remain with the debtor's business." For corporate debtors, an "insider" is defined to include a director, officer, or "person in control." § 101(31)(b). Typically, any "pay to stay" plan will be targeted at people who meet the insider definition, so that rarely is in dispute. However, the "purpose" requirement often is vigorously contested, as will be discussed below.

If the limiting rule of § 503(c)(1) is triggered, then no payment whatsoever may be made to the targeted beneficiary, unless two statutory justifications of compelling necessity are proven, § 503(c)(1)(A)–(B), and then, even if so justified, allowance and payment can be made only up to a statutory maximum amount. § 503(c)(1)(C). The required justifications are:

- "the transfer or obligation is essential to retention of the person because the individual has a bona fide job offer from another business at the same or greater rate of compensation," § 503(c)(1)(A); and

- "the services provided by the person are essential to the survival of the business," § 503(c)(1)(B).

The requirement that the targeted beneficiary must actually have a job offer in hand, *and* that the offer be for as much or more compensation as that offered in the debtor's proposed KERP, significantly limits the debtor's ability to implement "pay to stay" plans if the trigger is satisfied—and that is precisely what Congress intended. Certainly WorldCom's 329 "key" employees would not all have gotten offers ranging from $20,000 to $125,000 to move elsewhere. And even if they had, it is hard to imagine that all 329 of them would have been "essential to the survival of the business."

Even if the twin necessity justifications can somehow be established, the debtor is severely limited in what it can pay. Two benchmarks are used. First, no covered transfer may be greater than "10 times the amount of the mean transfer or obligation of a similar kind given to nonmanagement employees for any purpose during the calendar year." § 503(c)(1)(C)(i). If no such transfer was made to non-management employees, then the second and alternative benchmark is that the covered transfer cannot exceed 25 percent of the amount of any similar transfer or obligation made to the insider during the prior calendar year. § 503(c)(1)(C)(ii). In most (all?) pre–2005 cases, the KERP payments would have exceeded these statutory limits. The statute

---

[216] Pub. L. No. 109–8, § 331, 119 Stat. 102–03 (2005).

does not say what happens if no "similar transfers" of the second type were made, leaving no benchmarks at all by which the statutory cap can be computed. The likely result is that no KERP at all could then be paid, as, under benchmark #2, 25% of nothing is nothing.

In short, *if* the KERP limits of § 503(c)(1) are triggered, then almost certainly any plan that the debtor would want would be knocked out. So, the fight is over scope—do the KERP limits in fact apply? The fighting issue is whether the plan had the "purpose of inducing such person to remain with the debtor's business." At some level, this requirement cannot be taken entirely literally, because to some degree *all* forms of compensation induce the beneficiary to stay. Few people would work for free. So, the intent must be that the "purpose" test be closely tied to a specific and direct inducement to stay in a situation where normal compensation schemes would not be enough to retain the targeted person, as contrasted with a more general "if they don't pay me I'll leave" notion.

That said, the difficulties in the litigated cases have been (1) to sort out the classic "form-substance" problem, and (2) to determine the controlling characterization of a "mixed" plan that has elements of both a regulated "retention" plan and an unregulated "incentive" plan.[217] A debtor is free to offer performance incentives to its management, subject only to oversight by the bankruptcy court under the deferential business judgment rule.[218] But if it proposes a retention plan, § 503(c)(1) kicks in. Once Congress enacted § 503(c)(1), no one was ever stupid enough to put forward a plan for approval that actually says "if you will stay, we will pay you a gazillion dollars." Instead, they throw in incentives for performance targets, bonuses, options, retirement benefits, consulting payments, the kitchen sink, smoke, mirrors, and, perhaps, some compensation payments that the beneficiary can collect only if they stick around. So what is a court to do? They must do what courts have always done when smart lawyers and business people try to circumvent regulatory rules: look at all the facts and circumstances and try to determine what the substance of the proffered plan is. The most famous line, by far, in this field is Judge Lifland's quip in the *Dana* case: "If it walks like a duck (KERP) and quacks like a duck (KERP), it's a duck (KERP)."[219] In that case, the judge saw a duck, and held that the proposed plan fell within the proscriptions of § 503(c)(1).[220] Not to worry, though; the parties simply went back to the drawing board, tweaked the original plan ever so slightly to make the "incentive" parts shine a bit brighter and the "retention" parts a bit dimmer, re-presented it to Judge

---

[217] E.g., In re Borders Group, Inc., 453 B.R. 459 (Bankr. S.D.N.Y. 2011).

[218] In the 2005 Amendments, Congress also added § 503(c)(3), which provides that an administrative expense cannot be allowed and paid for "other transfers or obligations that are outside the ordinary course of business and not justified by the facts and circumstances of the case, including transfers made to, or obligations incurred for the benefit of, officers, managers, or consultants hired after the date of the filing of the petition." It is hard to see what this provision adds to the general rules governing transfers outside the ordinary course of business under § 363(b) and the allowance of administrative expenses under § 503(b). If the transfer is "not justified by the facts and circumstances" then presumably it would not have been approved by the court even before 2005. The business judgment rule applies to transfers tested under subsection (c)(3).

[219] In re Dana Corp., 351 B.R. 96, 102 n.3 (Bankr. S.D.N.Y. 2006).

[220] See Jillian K. McClelland, Going "Stealth": Executive Compensation in Ch 11 After *Dana*, Ill. Bus. L.J. (posted Oct. 10, 2006) at http://www.law.illinois.edu/bljournal/post/2006/10/10/Going-Stealth-Executive-Compensation-in-Chapter-11-After-Dana.aspx.

Lifland, and now he saw a duck no more and blessed the plan, free from the inconvenient constraints of § 503(c)(1).[221]

The most prominent decision by far applying the severance pay limitation (§ 503(c)(2)) is *In re AMR Corp.*,[222] arising out of the chapter 11 bankruptcy of American Airlines and AA's merger with U.S. Airways. As part of the merger agreement, the debtor sought the court's permission to pay almost $20 million ($19,875,000, to be exact) in severance pay to AA's CEO, Thomas Horton, who after the merger would become the chairman of the board of the new company ("Newco"). The payment would not be made until after the merger, by Newco, and not out of the funds of the debtor's estate, and thus the debtor argued that § 503(c)(2) should not apply, even though it clearly was a severance payment and Horton was an insider. The bankruptcy court, however, denied approval of the severance payment as violative of § 503(c)(2), noting that the payment was related to Horton's service as CEO of the debtor, not "Newco," and was indeed being made to preserve and realize value *for the debtor*, thus falling squarely within the purpose of the statute; that the fund source argument was a "legal fiction," with 72% of Newco to be comprised of assets of the debtor; and that the statute prohibits not only the payment but also the *allowance* by the court of a severance payment.[223] If Newco wants to pay Horton a big chunk of money after the merger closes, the court acknowledged that it could of course do so without any interference from the bankruptcy court. But the court could not bless the payment in advance.

§ 7.14   Administrative Expenses: Fairness

A claimant seeking to establish an entitlement to administrative expense priority normally must prove that the expense was an actual and necessary cost of preserving the estate.[224] The standard justification for this rule is that the deviation from the fundamental bankruptcy premise of equality of distribution should be allowed only when doing so will redound to the benefit of the general non-priority creditors. This rationale breaks down, however, when the claimed expense does not directly "benefit" the bankruptcy estate, but nevertheless is a cost incurred postpetition by the estate. Examples include tort claims[225] and penalties for violation of environmental and other police power regulations.[226] The question is whether administrative priority should also be extended to these postpetition costs of dubious "benefit."

The classic presentation of this issue came in the Supreme Court case of *Reading Co. v. Brown*.[227] In *Reading*, which arose under the old Act, a receivership under chapter XI (a predecessor to current chapter 11) was initiated. During the pendency of the receivership, a fire caused by the alleged negligence of workmen employed by the

---

[221]   In re Dana Corp., 358 B.R. 567 (Bankr. S.D.N.Y. 2006).

[222]   490 B.R. 158 (Bankr. S.D.N.Y. 2013).

[223]   Id. at *8–9.

[224]   See § 7.12.

[225]   See Reading Co. v. Brown, 391 U.S. 471 (1968).

[226]   See In re N.P. Mining Co., 963 F.2d 1449 (11th Cir. 1992) (punitive civil fine); In re Charlesbank Laundry, Inc., 755 F.2d 200 (1st Cir. 1985) (compensatory civil fine).

[227]   391 U.S. 471 (1968).

receiver caused catastrophic losses, exceeding the value of the entire estate. The issue before the Court was whether the tort claims of the fire victims should be allowed as an administrative expense. Were those tort claims "actual and necessary" costs of operating the debtor's business? The dissenting Justices, taking the narrow view, would have denied priority. They would have limited priority to those expenses that are necessary to the operation of the business or the administration of the estate and which directly benefit the estate.[228]

The majority of the Court held that the tort claims were entitled to administrative priority. Justice Harlan for the Court wrote that another statutory objective must be weighed in the balance: "*fairness* to all persons having claims against an insolvent."[229] According to the Court, the postpetition fire victims "had an insolvent business thrust upon [them] by operation of law."[230] While the award of priority to the tort claimants meant that the general creditors holding prepetition unsecured claims against the debtor would receive nothing, the Court did not believe that such a result was unfair. On the contrary, the receivership, if it had been successful, would have benefited those very prepetition creditors.

In a sense, those prepetition general unsecured creditors could be viewed as the residual "owners" of the insolvent business at the time the bankruptcy was filed. As such, they should have to bear the possible risks as well as the rewards that might materialize during the bankruptcy proceeding. If general creditors do not have to bear *all* of the costs of the business, they might have a skewed incentive to pursue rehabilitation, a result which is both inefficient and unfair. Making this broader point, the *Reading* Court stated in a crucial passage that "'actual and necessary costs' should include costs ordinarily incident to operation of a business, and not be limited to costs without which rehabilitation would be impossible."[231]

An intriguing application of the principles enunciated in *Reading* is found in the Eleventh Circuit case of *In re N.P. Mining Co.*[232] In that case, the debtor carried on strip mining operations in violation of Alabama state law after it had filed chapter 11. Under Alabama law, the violator was liable for substantial noncompensatory civil penalties. The Eleventh Circuit held that the penalties incurred during the postpetition operation of the debtor's business were entitled to administrative priority, even though those penalties did not compensate for actual harm and did not "benefit" the estate. The court concluded that the debtor had a duty to manage its property in compliance with the applicable state law under 28 U.S.C. § 959(b), and should have to bear costs ordinarily incident to that business operation under the rationale of *Reading*.

Not all courts are as receptive to administrative claims under the rationale of *Reading,* however. Instead, these courts (especially the Ninth Circuit) insist more

---

[228] Id. at 491 (Warren, C.J., dissenting).

[229] Id. at 477 (Harlan, J., majority) (emphasis added).

[230] Id. at 478.

[231] Id. at 483.

[232] 963 F.2d 1449 (11th Cir. 1992).

strictly on proof of an actual benefit to the estate,[233] or at the very least the commission of an actionable postpetition tort or a compensable violation of the law,[234] in order to support an award of administrative priority. In short, those courts largely ignore the *Reading* Court's core assertion that "costs ordinarily incident to operation of a business" deserve administrative priority.

A striking example is the Ninth Circuit's decision in the case of *In re Allen Care Centers, Inc.*[235] In that case, the debtor sought to abandon a state-licensed nursing home that was losing money. Under state law, however, the operator of a nursing home cannot just close the doors; in order to protect the patients, at least 60 days' notice must be given. If the operator does not want to run the home for the 60 days before closing, the state will appoint a trustee to oversee the closing process. Not surprisingly, however, the operator then must reimburse the state for the closing costs. The bankruptcy judge allowed abandonment on the express condition that a state-appointed trustee take over. The state did so, and expended $200,000 in closing the home. The state's request for allowance of the $200,000 as an administrative expense was denied, however. According to the Ninth Circuit, the estate had not been benefited by the $200,000 expenditure. *Reading* did not apply, the court suggested, because the debtor had not committed a postpetition tort or violated any state law.

In 2005, Congress added § 503(b)(8) to the list of administrative expenses, allowing the actual, necessary costs of closing a health care business,[236] thus overturning the result on the specific facts in a case such as *Allen Care Centers*. Another 2005 amendment, adding back pay awards to the list of administrative expenses, § 503(b)(1)(A)(ii), overturned the specific result in another dubious Ninth Circuit decision.[237] Unfortunately, Congress's piecemeal approach did not respond to or correct the Ninth Circuit's more fundamental misreading of *Reading*, leaving the door open for further misapplications in cases involving neither health care business closings nor back pay awards.

§ 7.15   Administrative Expenses: Taxes

Taxes are ubiquitous in our society, and bankruptcy is not exempt from the reach of the tax collector. The bankruptcy estate is a separate legal entity, and bears responsibility for its own taxes. Postpetition taxes are a common form of administrative expense. Under § 503(b)(1)(B)(i), "any tax" "incurred by the estate" is entitled to first priority, excepting only taxes that are specifically relegated to eighth priority. This exclusion is intended to limit taxes fairly attributable to the *pre*-bankruptcy period to the eighth priority, even if technically the tax is incurred postpetition by the bankruptcy estate.

The reference to "any tax" is meant to be broadly construed, and courts have done so. For example, a capital gains tax arising from the sale of property by the estate will

---

[233]   See, e.g., In re Dant & Russell, Inc., 853 F.2d 700 (9th Cir. 1988).

[234]   In re Palau Corp., 18 F.3d 746, 751 (9th Cir. 1994).

[235]   96 F.3d 1328 (9th Cir. 1996).

[236]   Pub. L. No. 109–8, § 1103, 119 Stat. 190–91 (2005).

[237]   *Palau*, supra note 234, 18 F.3d 746.

be entitled to administrative priority.[238] In addition, most courts have followed the lead of the pre-Code Supreme Court decision in *Nicholas v. United States*[239] to hold that postpetition interest on administrative priority taxes is also entitled to administrative priority.[240]

An issue that had arisen with considerable frequency in chapter 12 and chapter 13 cases involving individual debtors is how to apply the "incurred by the estate" requirement, given that the bankruptcy estate in those chapters is not treated by the IRS as a separate taxable entity. 26 I.R.C. §§ 1398, 1399. As one court explained the interpretive problem:

> "'Incurred by the estate' could have reference to the time liability for a tax accrues—did the liability arise before or after the creation of the estate under § 541. Or, 'incurred by the estate' could have reference to the entity liable for the tax—is the bankruptcy estate created under § 541 liable for the tax?"[241]

The same court then held, after an exhaustive examination of the legislative history and case precedent, that the "incurred by the estate" language "has reference to the time when tax liability is incurred and not to whether the estate is a separate taxable entity."[242] This reading appears to be consistent with longstanding authority, and is the approach taken in corporate chapter 11 cases.[243] Other courts have insisted that the absence of a separate taxable estate in individual chapter 12 and 13 cases precludes allowance of an administrative tax priority.[244]

The Supreme Court resolved this circuit split in its decision in *Hall v. United States*.[245] In *Hall*, the debtors were farmers who filed bankruptcy under chapter 12, and then sold their farm. They proposed a plan which treated the tax on the capital gains from the sale as an unsecured claim. In affirming the decision of the Ninth Circuit that held for the government and against the farmers, Justice Sotomayor wrote:

> "Chapter 12 estates are not taxable entities. Petitioners, not the estate itself, are required to file the tax return and are liable for the taxes resulting from their postpetition farm sale. The postpetition federal income tax liability is not 'incurred by the estate' and thus is neither collectible nor dischargeable in the Chapter 12 plan."[246]

---

[238] See, e.g., In re Goffena, 175 B.R. 386 (Bankr. D. Mont. 1994).

[239] 384 U.S. 678 (1966).

[240] See, e.g., In re Mark Anthony Constr., Inc., 886 F.2d 1101 (9th Cir. 1989).

[241] In re Dawes, 382 B.R. 509, 515 (Bankr. D. Kan. 2008).

[242] Id. at 517.

[243] E.g., In re L.J. O'Neill Shoe Co., 64 F.3d 1146, 1149 (8th Cir. 1995).

[244] See, e.g., In re Whall, 391 B.R. 1 (Bankr. D. Mass. 2008).

[245] 132 S.Ct. 1882 (2012).

[246] Id. at 1887.

In so holding, the Court plainly was concerned that chapter 12 and chapter 13 cases be treated the same way on this issue,[247] and so *Hall* will control the outcome in chapter 13 cases as well. Note that there was a substantial argument in *Hall* that the two chapters should not be treated alike because of a special statutory provision favoring farm debtors found only in chapter 12 (§ 1222(a)(2)(A)), but the Court found that provision insufficient to trump the "incurred by the estate" predicate in § 503(b).[248]

Often a crucial question relating to the priority status of tax claims concerns *timing*. First priority is limited to taxes "incurred by the estate." The "estate" part was just discussed above; what about the timing implications of that phrase? Clearly, if the tax is incurred prior to bankruptcy, it will not be granted administrative priority, although it might be entitled to an eighth priority. Similarly, if a tax is incurred after the estate is terminated, or the case is closed or dismissed, or the subject property no longer is part of the bankruptcy estate, that tax will not be entitled to priority. A tax incurred after confirmation of a chapter 11 plan will be the responsibility of the reorganized debtor, since confirmation of the plan vests all property of the estate in the debtor.[249] § 1141(b).

The question will be, then, what "incurred" means. When a tax is deemed to be "incurred" will be determined by reference to the tax laws. If a tax is attributable both to the prepetition and postpetition time periods, i.e., the tax "straddles" the bankruptcy petition date, the courts will prorate the priority, limiting administrative priority to that part of the tax attributable to the postpetition period.[250]

In the 2005 amendments, Congress clarified the reach of the "incurred by the estate" administrative tax priority. In amended § 503(b)(1)(B)(i), Congress added that the tax incurred by the estate is entitled to administrative priority "whether secured or unsecured, including property taxes for which liability is in rem, in personam, or both."

Administrative priority is also allowed for an excessive "quickie refund" received by the estate. § 503(b)(1)(B)(ii). In other words, if the IRS allows the estate a tentative carryback adjustment, but then determines upon a full audit that the adjustment was too large, the excess amount is entitled to first priority. This priority applies regardless of the taxable year to which the tax refund relates.

The third type of tax claim to which the Code grants first priority status is for a "fine, penalty, or reduction in credit" relating to a tax that is itself entitled to first priority. § 503(b)(1)(C). Until 1996, a number of circuit courts had evaded the apparent priority mandate of § 503(b)(1)(C) with regard to nonpecuniary loss penalties by equitably subordinating the penalty claim under § 510(c).[251] In *United States v. Noland*,[252] the Supreme Court put a stop to this judicial revision of the legislative priority scheme. According to the Court, "the bankruptcy court may not equitably

---

[247] Id. at 1890–91.

[248] Id. at 1889–90.

[249] See In re Fullmer, 962 F.2d 1463 (10th Cir. 1992).

[250] See In re L.J. O'Neill Shoe Co., 64 F.3d 1146 (8th Cir. 1995).

[251] See, e.g., In re Virtual Network Servs. Corp., 902 F.2d 1246 (7th Cir. 1990).

[252] 517 U.S. 535 (1996).

subordinate claims on a categorical basis in derogation of Congress's scheme of priorities."[253] Rather, subordination may only be premised on case-specific facts that justify departure from the normal rule of priority. For example, a showing that the taxing authority had engaged in some type of misconduct might suffice.

Another 2005 amendment relaxed the procedural burden on taxing authorities seeking administrative priority. The normal procedure for a claimant seeking to have a claim allowed as an administrative priority is to "timely file a request for payment of an administrative expense." § 503(a). The reference to "timely" filing was added in 1994, thus empowering bankruptcy courts to fix enforceable dates for filing administrative expense requests. Under § 503(a), an entity also may "tardily file" its administrative expense request, but only if permitted to do so by the court for "cause." Under the 2005 amendments, taxing authorities are excused from complying with the procedural rules of § 503(a). Now, "a governmental unit shall not be required to file a request for the payment" of an administrative tax claim under § 503(b)(1)(B) or (C) "as a condition of its being an allowed administrative expense." § 503(b)(1)(D). As a practical matter, this means that the bankruptcy trustee or the DIP will need to take the initiative and file requests for allowance of administrative tax claims if the government fails to do so.

§ 7.16   Administrative Expenses: Trustees

Trustees play a central role in administering the bankruptcy system. In order to attract qualified people to serve as trustees, fair compensation must be awarded for services rendered by trustees in performing their duties.[254] Trustees are entitled to administrative priority for the compensation and reimbursement awarded them under § 330(a). § 503(b)(2).

Section 330(a) provides that trustees (and examiners) are entitled to "reasonable compensation for actual, necessary services rendered," § 330(a)(1)(A), as well as "reimbursement for actual, necessary expenses." § 330(a)(1)(B). These awards are to be made only after notice and a hearing, and are expressly made subject to § 326, which specifies limits on the compensation of trustees. In addition, a chapter 7 trustee is to be paid $45 from the filing fee, § 330(b)(1), plus another $15 for cases beginning one year after the enactment of the 1994 Act. § 330(b)(2).

Congress specified a list of factors that courts should consider in determining "reasonable compensation." § 330(a)(3). Before 2005, this list applied to all trustees, but as amended in 2005, only a "trustee under chapter 11" is to have the reasonableness of their compensation assessed under subsection (a)(3). Congress did not explain why it made this change.

Section 326 sets ceilings on trustee compensation. A trustee is not necessarily entitled to receive the full amount specified in § 326, but cannot receive more. The ceilings were raised substantially in 1994, in response to a recommendation made in a

---

[253] Id. at 536.

[254] See Am. Bankr. Inst. Nat'l Report on Prof'l Comp. in Bankr. Cases (G. Ray Warner, Reporter) (1991) ("Warner Report"); H.R. Rep. No. 834, 103d Cong., 2d Sess., at 5 (1994).

report sponsored by the American Bankruptcy Institute.[255] In cases under chapter 7 or chapter 11, a graduated cap is computed, based on the amount of monies disbursed or turned over in the case by the trustee to parties in interest. Monies distributed to the debtor are excluded, but disbursements to secured creditors are included. The trustee may not receive more than: 25% of the first $5,000; 10% of the amounts from $5,000 to $50,000; 5% of amounts from $50,000 to one million dollars; and 3% of amounts in excess of one million dollars. § 326(a).

In chapter 12 or chapter 13 cases, a somewhat different scheme is used. If a standing trustee has not been appointed for the judicial district, and a trustee is appointed for the particular case, the trustee may receive a fee not to exceed 5% of all payments under the plan. § 326(b). A provision added to § 330 in 2005 bears on this situation, stating that "[i]n determining the amount of reasonable compensation to be awarded to a trustee, the court shall treat such compensation as a commission, based on section 326." § 330(a)(7). The probable intent was to treat the stated percentages in § 326(b) as presumptive entitlements.

A different approach is taken if a standing trustee has been appointed for a district for all chapter 12 or chapter 13 cases in that district, pursuant to 28 U.S.C. § 586(b). For standing trustees, compensation will be determined by the Attorney General under 28 U.S.C. § 586(e). The percentage fee specified in subsection (e)(1) is 10% of the payments made under the plan, for debtors who are not family farmers, and, for family farmer debtors, 10% of payments up to $450,000, and 3% of all amounts in excess of $450,000. Subsection (e)(2) provides that the fee shall be collected from payments received by the standing trustee.

Several issues have arisen in interpreting § 586(e). One is whether the trustee's percentage fee applies to payments made "outside" of the plan by the debtor directly to certain creditors. In other words, can the debtor escape payment of part of the trustee's fee by making direct payments to creditors, rather than funneling the monies through the trustee? The courts are divided.[256] Another issue is whether the standing trustee is entitled to collect a fee on all monies received by them, including their own fee, or only on payments that will be distributed to creditors under the plan. Again, the courts have gone both ways.[257]

§ 7.17 Administrative Expenses: Attorneys and Other Professionals

The bankruptcy estate bears the cost of professionals retained to represent the estate or an official committee. Compensation and reimbursement awarded under § 330(a) are allowed as an administrative expense. § 503(b)(2). The trustee has the authority to retain professionals on behalf of the estate, § 327, and official chapter 11 committees are authorized to hire attorneys or accountants. § 1103(a), (b). The

---

[255] See Warner Report, supra note 254.

[256] Compare In re Wagner, 36 F.3d 723 (8th Cir. 1994) (direct payments allowed, and are not subject to trustee's fee) with In re Fulkrod, 973 F.2d 801 (9th Cir. 1992) (direct payments not allowed, because would circumvent trustee's fee). For a helpful review of the case law, see In re Lopez, 372 B.R. 40 (B.A.P. 9th Cir. 2007).

[257] Compare In re BDT Farms, Inc., 21 F.3d 1019 (10th Cir. 1994) (trustee may collect fee on their own fee), with Pelofsky v. Wallace, 102 F.3d 350 (8th Cir. 1996) (trustee may not collect fee on own fee).

retention may be on any reasonable terms and conditions of employment. § 328(a). Permissible terms and conditions include a retainer, an hourly basis, a fixed or percentage fee, or a contingent fee. The employment and its terms are subject to court approval. See Rule 2014. Failure to obtain prior court approval may result in a denial or limitation of fees, although *nunc pro tunc* approval lies within the court's discretion.[258]

"Reasonable compensation" for "actual, necessary services rendered" by a retained professional and "reimbursement for actual, necessary expenses" of the professional may be awarded by the court after notice and a hearing. § 330(a)(1)(A), (B). A detailed application must be filed in support of the requested compensation and reimbursement. Rule 2016(a). Interim compensation may be sought every 120 days by the professional, so that they will not have to wait until the very end of the case for payment. § 331.

The payment of attorneys and other professionals out of the bankruptcy estate is invariably a matter of controversy. Warranted or not, Dickensian images of greedy attorneys bleeding the estate dry while creditors go unpaid persist; Senator Metzenbaum complained in 1994 that "lawyers suck the financial life out of companies by charging exorbitant and often unnecessary fees."[259] But at the same time, attorneys want to get paid, and if fees are lower in bankruptcy than in other fields, there is a concern that the most qualified professionals may flee the bankruptcy arena in search of greener pastures in other areas of the law.[260] The pendulum seems to swing back and forth. Under the prior Bankruptcy Act, the "economy" principle dictated keeping attorneys' fees in bankruptcy at a reduced level.[261] While the Senate preferred to retain the economy principle in the Bankruptcy Code,[262] the contrary House position prevailed in 1978.[263] Under the Code, bankruptcy professionals were to be paid at a market rate, commensurate with what they could earn in other fields.

But in 1994, Congress again tightened up on professional fees in bankruptcy cases. The thrust of the 1994 amendments was not so much to return to the notion of economy as to insist on vigilant monitoring of the reasonableness of fees by the Unites States trustees and the courts. First, § 330(a)(2) was added to make clear that the court, acting *sua sponte* or on motion of any party in interest or the U.S. Trustee, could award compensation in an amount less than requested.

Second, Congress provided specific guidelines for the court to consider in determining the amount of reasonable compensation. Under § 330(a)(3), the court was instructed to "consider the nature, the extent, and the value" of the professional's services, taking into account factors such as: (1) the time spent; (2) the rates charged;

---

[258] See, e.g., In re Aquatic Dev. Grp., Inc., 352 F.3d 671 (2d Cir. 2003). Courts differ on whether the attorney must show "extraordinary circumstances" to justify the failure to get prior approval, see id., or whether simple "excusable neglect" will suffice. See In re Singson, 41 F.3d 316 (7th Cir. 1994).

[259] 140 Cong. Rec. S14,597 (daily ed. Oct. 7, 1994).

[260] H.R. Rep. No. 95–595, 95th Cong., 1st Sess., at 329–30 (1977).

[261] See In re Beverly Crest Convalescent Hosp., Inc., 548 F.2d 817 (9th Cir. 1976).

[262] S. Rep. No. 95–989, 95th Cong., 2d Sess., at 40 (1978).

[263] See 124 Cong. Rec. H11,091–92 (daily ed. Sept. 28, 1978) (statement of Rep. Edwards).

(3) whether the services were necessary or beneficial to the administration or completion of the case; (4) whether the services were performed in a reasonable amount of time, considering the complexity, importance, and nature of the problem; (5) whether the person is board certified or otherwise has demonstrated skill and experience in the bankruptcy field (added in 2005); and (6) whether the compensation was reasonable, based on the customary compensation charged in non-bankruptcy cases by similarly skilled practitioners.

Third, in § 330(a)(4)(A), Congress directed courts not to allow compensation for unnecessary duplication of services or for services that were not reasonably likely to benefit the estate or necessary to the administration of the case.

Fourth, in 28 U.S.C. § 586(a)(3)(A), the United States trustees were instructed to review fee applications in accordance with guidelines adopted by the Executive Office of United States Trustees. Those guidelines were issued on January 30, 1996.

Compensation of professionals under § 330 is subject to § 328. The court is given the discretion to allow compensation different from that originally agreed to if it later appears that the terms of employment were improvident in light of unanticipated developments. § 328(a). Conflicts of interest are dealt with harshly. Subject to listed exceptions, the court may reduce fees or disallow fees entirely if the professional was not a "disinterested person," see § 101(14), or represented or held an interest adverse to the estate with respect to the matter on which the professional was employed.[264] § 328(c).

Special rules govern the fees of an attorney for the debtor. Even if the debtor's attorney is not seeking compensation out of the estate, she must disclose to the bankruptcy court all compensation paid or agreed to be paid for services in connection with the bankruptcy case, after one year before the bankruptcy filing. § 329(a), Rule 2016(b). The court may order the debtor's attorney to disgorge any excessive compensation. § 329(b).

The ability of an attorney for the debtor to be awarded compensation out of the estate under § 330 was inadvertently eliminated by the 1994 amendments, an omission that has been upheld by the Supreme Court.[265] Prior to 1994, "the debtor's attorney" was included in the list of people in § 330(a)(1) who were eligible to be awarded compensation and reimbursement. However, in 1994 this reference was deleted. Taking its place was a specific provision allowing compensation to an attorney for an individual debtor in a chapter 12 or chapter 13 case in § 330(a)(4)(B)—but in doing so Congress apparently forgot to say anything about compensating the debtor's attorney in a chapter 7 or chapter 11 case. Even though the omission of the reference to "the debtor's attorney" was almost certainly a scrivener's error—as evidenced both by the absence of any legislative history whatsoever speaking to a reason for the change, as well as by the fact that after the amendment the statutory text itself grammatically

---

[264] See, e.g., In re Am. Int'l Refinery, Inc., 676 F.3d 455 (5th Cir. 2012); In re Rusty Jones, Inc., 134 B.R. 321 (Bankr. N.D. Ill, 1991).

[265] Lamie v. United States Tr., 540 U.S. 526 (2004).

displayed an obvious drafting mistake[266]—courts split over whether there was any defensible way to read the amended statute so as to escape the force of the fact that debtor's attorneys in chapters 7 and 11 previously had been included on the exclusive list of compensable persons and now no longer were.[267] Any hope that the Congressional mistake could be ignored as just that was dashed in 2004 when the Supreme Court held in *Lamie v. United States Trustee*[268] that the plain language of the 1994 amendments precluded a debtor's attorney in chapter 7 or 11 from being paid out of the estate pursuant to § 330(a). The only real possibility by which the debtor's attorney can then be paid out of the estate is if they are retained as a "professional person" under § 327. That possibility is more realistic in chapter 11, where the debtor also usually will be the debtor in possession, and as such can retain an attorney for the estate under § 327. However, in chapter 7 there usually would be no reason for the trustee to employ the debtor's attorney as a professional person for the estate. Accordingly, in chapter 7, debtor's attorneys must get their fee from the debtor in full before they file the case.

§ 7.18 Administrative Expenses: Compensation of Creditors and Committees

One of the oddities of the bankruptcy system to the uninitiated is that the debtor's assets might be used to pay the fees and expenses of both the debtor *and* those of certain creditors. The norm in the American legal system is for each side to pay its own way; why then is bankruptcy different? The answer lies in an appreciation of the collective nature of the bankruptcy process. Bankruptcy is not inherently adversarial. Upon the filing of a bankruptcy petition, all financially interested parties have an equitable stake in the ultimate bankruptcy distribution. Multiple players may play a positive part in bringing that distribution to pass. If a creditor contributes to the common good, then notions of fairness (viewed *ex post*) and inducement (viewed *ex ante*) dictate permitting that creditor to recoup its costs from the common fund. This recovery comes in the form of an allowance of an administrative expense priority for costs and fees incurred by creditors who make a contribution. See § 503(b)(3), (4).

Specifically, § 503(b)(3) grants administrative priority for the actual, necessary *expenses* incurred by:

- a creditor that files an involuntary petition, § 503(b)(3)(A);

---

[266] Before the amendment, the list of persons in § 330(a)(1) to whom an award could be made out of the estate was "to a trustee, to an examiner, to a professional person employed under section 327 or 1103, *or to the debtor's attorney.*" The 1994 amendment simply dropped the italicized language, leaving the statutory text with a serial listing of eligible persons but with no connecting "or" before what was now the last person on the list. Not only that, but pre-amendment this listing of persons to whom an award could be made was parallel to and consistent with the further listing of persons in subparagraph (A) of § 330(a)(1) who could receive "reasonable compensation," a listing which included "or attorney," but post-amendment the parallelism failed, as "or attorney" remained in subparagraph (A), yet lacked an "attorney" counterpart in the eligibility list.

[267] Compare In re Am. Steel Prod., Inc., 197 F.3d 1354 (11th Cir. 1999) (debtor's attorney may not be paid out of estate), with In re Top Grade Sausage, Inc., 227 F.3d 123 (3d Cir. 2000) (debtor's attorney may be paid out of estate).

[268] 540 U.S. 526 (2004).

- a creditor that, after court approval, recovers for the benefit of the estate property that the debtor had transferred or concealed, § 503(b)(3)(B);

- a creditor in connection with the prosecution of a criminal offense relating to the bankruptcy case or to the debtor's business or property, § 503(b)(3)(C);

- a creditor, indenture trustee, equity security holder, or an unofficial committee that makes a "substantial contribution" in a chapter 9 or 11 case, § 503(b)(3)(D);

- a custodian superseded under § 543, plus compensation for the custodian's services, § 503(b)(3)(E); and

- a member of an official chapter 11 committee, incurred in the performance of committee duties, § 503(b)(3)(F).

Note that the administrative expense allowance is limited to reimbursement of expenses; compensation for services rendered is not authorized. The only exceptions where compensation is allowed are for superseded custodians, § 503(b)(3)(E), and for indenture trustees who make a substantial contribution to a case under chapter 9 or 11. § 503(b)(5).

However, § 503(b)(4) does grant an administrative priority for the professional fees and actual, necessary expenses incurred by an attorney or accountant for an entity whose expenses are allowed under subsection (b)(3), with the exception of a member of an official committee under subsection (b)(3)(F). In other words, even though the creditor cannot receive compensation for services rendered, the creditor's attorney or accountant may be awarded reasonable compensation. Thus, for example, if a creditor makes a "substantial contribution" to a chapter 11 case, or successfully commences an involuntary bankruptcy case, administrative priority is awarded both (1) to the creditor for its expenses and (2) to the professionals who assisted the creditor, for their fees and expenses.

Before 1994, the biggest source of confusion in the application of these provisions concerned whether a member of an official chapter 11 committee could be reimbursed for its expenses as an administrative priority. The Code was silent. Specific provision was made for recovery by a member of an unofficial committee who made a substantial contribution, but nothing was said about official committee members. Some cases seized on this statutory silence and denied reimbursement to official committee members, while a slightly larger number of courts filled in the statutory gap by authorizing reimbursement. In 1994 Congress fixed the problem by adding § 503(b)(3)(F), which specifically provides for administrative priority for the actual, necessary expenses of an official committee member that are incurred in the performance of committee duties. This rule was designed to encourage creditors to participate actively as committee members in a chapter 11 case. Note that when Congress added (F) to the list under subsection (b)(3), it did not correspondingly amend subsection (b)(4), so that it appeared that by inclusion under (b)(3), the attorney for an individual committee member might be able to obtain compensation out of the estate under (b)(4). This loophole was closed in 2005 by limiting (b)(4) to attorneys or accountants for entities listed in subparagraphs (A)–(E) of subsection (b)(3), so now the attorney for an individual committee member cannot get compensated out of the estate.

§ 7.19   Involuntary Gap Claims

An involuntary case is commenced by the filing of an involuntary petition against the debtor by the requisite number of eligible petitioning creditors. § 303(b). Commencement, however, is not the same as the entry of an order for relief in the involuntary setting. A full-fledged bankruptcy case will not be in effect until the entry of an order for relief, either by consent of the debtor or by court order after proof of one of the grounds for bankruptcy relief in § 303(h).

In the "gap" period between the commencement of the involuntary case and the entry of an order for relief, the debtor and its creditors are suspended in a sort of legal limbo.[269] Full freedom of action is not permitted, because of the possibility that bankruptcy relief will be ordered. Thus, a bankruptcy estate is created, § 541(a), and creditors are stayed from taking actions to collect prepetition debts or from pursuing property of the debtor or the estate. § 362(a). Yet, at the same time, some leeway is accorded to the debtor to continue with "business as usual," in order to keep the debtor's business afloat, see § 303(f), because (i) bankruptcy relief might not be ordered, and (ii) even if an order for relief is entered, a reorganization might be attempted.

An integral part of the "business as usual" policy is the need to encourage creditors to keep doing business with the debtor on normal terms.[270] This goal is implemented by affording a *third* priority to the claims of "gap" creditors. §§ 507(a)(3), 502(f). Thus, these gap claims are paid before general claims, but after first priority DSO claims (if any) and second priority administrative expense claims.[271]

Two requirements must be met to qualify for the third priority. First, the claim must be incurred in the gap, i.e., between the time of the commencement of the case (when the petition was filed) and the earlier of the appointment of a trustee or the entry of an order for relief. Second, the claim must be incurred in the "ordinary course" of the debtor's business or financial affairs. The fact that the creditor might know of the bankruptcy case is legally irrelevant to the creditor's entitlement to third priority.

The timing focus is on when the claim is *incurred*. If a claim is incurred prepetition, but paid during the gap period, it will not be entitled to third priority, but will be only a general nonpriority claim. The creditor then will have to disgorge the postpetition payment. § 549(a). If the claim is incurred after the entry of the order for relief, it will be eligible for second priority as an administrative expense, if the requirements of § 503(b) are met.

---

[269] See § 2.10.

[270] H.R. Rep. No. 95–595, 95th Cong., 1st Sess., at 354 (1977).

[271] The ranking of gap claims under the Code actually represents a demotion from their status under the prior Act, where they shared in the first priority.

§ 7.20   Employee Wage and Benefit Claims

Employees of the debtor are a favored class in the bankruptcy priority scheme. They are entitled to a first priority for wages and benefits earned during the pendency of the bankruptcy case. § 503(b)(1)(A). Even for wages and benefits attributable to services rendered *prior* to bankruptcy, employees may be awarded fourth and fifth priority in distribution. § 507(a)(4), (5). The fourth priority is for "wages, salaries, or commissions." This priority includes "vacation, severance, and sick leave pay." The fifth priority is for "contributions to an employee benefit plan."

Several policy reasons support the priority for prepetition claims of the debtor's employees. One rationale is that granting priority to employees' claims will encourage employees not to abandon a financially troubled debtor before bankruptcy occurs, thus enhancing the debtor's chances of recovery.[272] A second justification, offered long ago by the renowned Judge Learned Hand, which is somewhat inconsistent with the first, is that employees "could not be expected to know anything of the credit of their employer, but must accept a job as it comes."[273] Finally, the wage priority reflects a concern for the plight of an employee of a bankrupt business. The Supreme Court observed that the recovery of some back wages will "alleviate in some degree the hardship that unemployment usually brings to workers and their families."[274]

Employees are not entitled to an unlimited priority for prepetition wages and benefits. The fourth and fifth priorities are qualified in the amount, time, and form of employee compensation. The first limitation is that each employee is only entitled to priority for a maximum amount of $12,475. This dollar limit was raised dramatically in the 2005 amendments, from $4,000 to $10,000. It has since been indexed three times: in 2007, 2010, and finally in 2013 to the current $12,475, and will continue to be indexed every three years, in accordance with changes in the Consumer Price Index. § 104(b).

Second, the fourth and fifth priorities only apply for limited periods of time. Both the fourth and fifth priorities are restricted to claims arising from services rendered within the 180 days before the bankruptcy filing or the cessation of the debtor's business, whichever occurs first. Thus, if the debtor ceases to operate its business before the bankruptcy filing, the 180–day wage priority will be counted back from that business closing date, rather than from the petition date. This reach-back period for the fourth priority was expanded from 90 days to 180 days in 2005, and now dovetails with the 180–day reach-back for the fifth priority.

In applying these timing rules, the courts usually look to when the services giving rise to the wage or benefit claim were *performed* by the employee, rather than when the right to payment *vests*. A presumption of daily accrual is utilized. This allows the priority component of an employee's total claim to be attributed proportionately to the 180–day third priority period, irrespective of when vesting occurs. This presumption is

---

[272] H.R. Rep. No. 95–595, 95th Cong., 1st Sess., at 187 (1977).

[273] In re Lawsam Elec. Co., 300 F. 736, 736 (S.D.N.Y. 1924).

[274] United States v. Embassy Rest., Inc., 359 U.S. 29, 32 (1959).

followed for various fringe benefits, such as vacation, severance, or sick leave pay, as well as for wages.[275]

To illustrate, assume that an employee had a vacation pay claim of $2,000, attributable to one year's service, which vested at the beginning of the calendar year. Assume that the debtor-employer filed chapter 11 at the beginning of the fourth quarter (October 1), and that the employee was still working for the debtor when vesting took place on January 1. The employee's $2,000 claim would be divided as follows: (1) the amount attributable to the employee's quarter-year of *postpetition* services ($500) would be entitled to second priority as an administrative expense;[276] (2) the amount attributable to services rendered during the 180–day prepetition period (approximately $1,000) would be entitled to fourth priority; and (3) the balance would be a general nonpriority claim.

Many different forms of compensation are intended to be covered by the fourth priority. Section 507(a)(4)(A) specifies that priority is afforded for "wages, salaries, or commissions, including vacation, severance, and sick leave pay." This broad coverage recognizes the reality that compensation packages must be viewed as a whole. The 1978 Code extended the reach of the fourth priority, which under the prior Act covered only "wages."

Even more problematic under the 1898 Act was that there was no counterpart to the current fifth priority for contributions to an employee benefit plan. The priority for "wages" was all an employee could invoke. In two major decisions, the Supreme Court refused to give the priority for "wages" an encompassing breadth, thereby excluding employee benefit plans. The leading decision was *United States v. Embassy Restaurant, Inc.*,[277] in which the Court held that unpaid contributions to a union welfare plan (which included life insurance, sick benefits, and hospital and surgical benefits) did not qualify for the wage priority. In *Joint Industry Board of the Electrical Industry v. United States*,[278] the Court followed *Embassy Restaurant*, holding that an employer's bargained-for contributions to an employees' annuity plan likewise fell outside of the wage priority.

Responding to those two decisions,[279] Congress added the fifth priority for "contributions to an employee benefit plan" in the 1978 Code. The legislative history emphasized that in labor contract negotiations, fringe benefits may be substituted for wage demands.[280] Congress did not, however, define what qualifies as "employee benefit plans" within the meaning of the fifth priority. Clearly included are all the types of benefits that might be substituted for or supplemental to wages, of the types

---

[275] For an interesting discussion of the difficulties that may occur in identifying when vacation pay is "earned," and a disposition to avoid windfalls to any group, see *In re Northwest Engineering Co.*, 863 F.2d 1313 (7th Cir. 1988).

[276] See § 503(b)(1)(A); see § 7.12.

[277] 359 U.S. 29 (1959).

[278] 391 U.S. 224 (1968).

[279] See Howard Delivery Serv., Inc. v. Zurich Am. Ins. Co., 547 U.S. 651, 658–59 (2006).

[280] S. Rep. No. 95–989, 95th Cong., 2d Sess., at 69 (1978); H.R. Rep. No. 95–595, 95th Cong., 1st Sess., at 357 (1977).

exemplified by *Embassy Restaurant* and *Joint Industry Board*. Accordingly, the fifth priority indisputably includes things such as pension plans, life insurance, annuity plans, disability insurance, and health insurance benefits.[281]

Less clear was whether a debtor's insurer's claim for unpaid premiums for workers' compensation qualified for the fifth priority. In 2006 the Supreme Court resolved the issue, holding in *Howard Delivery Service, Inc. v. Zurich American Insurance Co.*[282] that workers' compensation premiums fell outside of the fifth priority. The Court viewed workers' compensation as different in principle from the sort of classic fringe benefits for which the fifth priority was intended, which are designed purely as a form of compensation for *employees*. By contrast, workers' compensation, while undeniably of some benefit to employees, also significantly benefits the *employer* by removing the threat of tort liability.[283] As such, workers compensation plans are not the type of benefit that is substituted for or supplementary to wages, and thus the Court concluded the reason for the fifth priority was not triggered.

The fourth and fifth priorities are linked at the hip in terms of the manner of computation. The fourth priority, as noted above, is $12,475 per employee (subject to triennial adjustment). The amount of the fifth priority in any given case depends directly on the amount paid under the fourth priority. The *maximum* priority for each employee benefit plan is computed as follows: $12,475 multiplied by the number of employees covered by that plan. § 507(a)(5)(B)(i). As with the fourth priority, the fifth priority ceiling was raised from $4,000 to $10,000 in 2005, and has since been indexed. The actual allowed fifth priority in a particular case, however, may be less; that ceiling amount must be reduced by (1) the aggregate amount actually paid to employees *under the fourth priority* and (2) the aggregate amount paid by the estate on behalf of those employees to any other benefit plan. Looked at another way, the fifth priority is only available to the extent of any unused amounts of the potential maximum of $12,475 for the fourth priority.

One dispute in the case law was resolved by the 1994 Amendments. Before 1994, courts had disagreed over whether the commissions due to an independent contractor qualified for priority. The question was whether the priority should be limited strictly to an individual who could be classified as an employee of the debtor. Section 507(a)(4)(B), added in 1994, compromised by allowing the sales commissions earned by an independent contractor to receive fourth priority, but only if that contractor had earned 75% of its commissions in the prior year from the debtor.

§ 7.21 Prepetition Taxes

General comments

It is scarcely a surprise to note that the government's claim for unpaid prepetition taxes may be afforded priority status in the bankruptcy distribution. Indeed, perhaps the surprise is that the priority for taxes is as low as it is; taxes rank eighth in the

---

[281] *Howard Delivery*, supra note 279, 547 U.S. at 662.

[282] 547 U.S. 651 (2006).

[283] Id. at 662–64.

priority line. § 507(a)(8). Indeed, claims of the United States government rank lower in priority in bankruptcy cases than they would in a non-bankruptcy collective proceeding involving an insolvent debtor, where they must be paid first.[284] Congress made a conscious policy decision to "spread the wealth" to more parties in bankruptcy cases, rather than allowing taxes to consume the entire estate. This policy is further evidenced in chapter 7 cases, where tax liens are partially subordinated to higher ranked priority claims. § 724(b). However, priority tax claims still are paid ahead of general unsecured claims.

Classification of a tax claim as within the coverage of § 507(a)(8) is doubly important to the taxing authority. First, of course, the claim qualifies for priority treatment. Second, that tax debt will not be dischargeable in the case of an individual debtor.[285] § 523(a)(1)(A).

Timing is critical in ascertaining the priority of tax claims. If a tax is incurred *post*-petition, by the estate, it will be allowed as a *second* priority administrative expense.[286] § 503(b)(1)(B). Note, though, that even if a tax is technically incurred postpetition, if it actually relates to the *pre*-petition period, and falls within the coverage of the eighth priority, it will be relegated to the lower *eighth* priority rank. §§ 503(b)(1)(B)(i), 502(i). In determining when a tax is deemed to be incurred for purposes of bankruptcy priority (while ultimately the question is one of federal bankruptcy law), deference usually will be given to the non-bankruptcy tax law.[287]

Timing also is important for priority, looking backward from the date of bankruptcy. Almost all of the eighth priority provisions are limited to taxes that are not too old. In other words, the taxing authority must pursue collection with some diligence, or risk losing priority if the taxpayer files bankruptcy. For example, the general rule for income taxes is that they are only afforded priority for three years. § 507(a)(8)(A)(i). Indeed, the only types of eighth priority tax claims that are not subjected to a time limitation are trust-fund taxes, § 507(a)(8)(C), and compensatory penalties relating to priority taxes. § 507(a)(8)(G). Note, though, that if the government is able to obtain a tax *lien*, then that lien will treated as a secured claim.

---

[284] Act of Sept. 13, 1982, Pub. L. No. 97–258, 96 Stat. 972, codified at 31 U.S.C. § 3713(a)(1), provides:

A claim of the United States Government shall be paid first when—

(A) a person indebted to the Government is insolvent and—

(i) the debtor without enough property to pay all debts makes a voluntary assignment of property;

(ii) property of the debtor, if absent, is attached; or

(iii) an act of bankruptcy is committed; or

(B) the estate of a deceased debtor, in the custody of the executor or administrator, is not enough to pay all debts of the debtor.

The statute specifies that it does not apply to bankruptcy cases under title 11. 31 U.S.C. § 3713(a)(2).

Source, from the Statutes at Large, is R.S. § 3466, Act of Nov. 6. 1978, Pub. L. No. 95–598, § 322(a), 92 Stat. 2678. It is interesting (to me at least) to note that Section 3466 has been in substantially its present form since the Act of March 3, 1797, ch. 20, § 5, 1 Stat. 515.

[285] See § 10.16.

[286] See § 7.15.

[287] See, e.g., In re Lewis, 199 F.3d 249 (5th Cir. 2000); In re King, 961 F.2d 1423 (9th Cir. 1992).

What constitutes a "tax" within the eighth priority is a federal bankruptcy law question. Stated otherwise, the label used in a non-bankruptcy statute is not binding in a bankruptcy case. Even if that other law calls an exaction a "tax," it might not be awarded priority in bankruptcy. The Supreme Court made this point clear in *United States v. Reorganized CF & I Fabricators of Utah, Inc.*[288] In that case, the Court held that the 10% "tax" under 26 U.S.C. § 4971(a) for pension plan funding deficiencies was not an "excise tax" entitled to priority under § 507(a)(8)(E), but a nonpriority "penalty."

The eighth priority is extended to compensatory penalties that relate to priority tax claims. § 507(a)(8)(G). Noncompensatory penalties are not entitled to priority, however, and indeed may even be subordinated in a chapter 7 distribution. § 726(a)(4). In addition, many (but not all) courts have held that *interest* on a prepetition penalty claim is also entitled to an equivalent priority.[289] A claim for an erroneous refund or credit is given the same priority as the tax to which it relates. § 507(c).

Seven types of tax claims are included within the eighth priority. Note that these claims are not ranked *inter se*; all eighth priority claims enjoy the same status. The seven types of eighth priority claims are:

- income and gross receipts taxes, § 507(a)(8)(A);

- property taxes, § 507(a)(8)(B);

- withholding taxes, § 507(a)(8)(C);

- employment taxes, § 507(a)(8)(D);

- excise taxes, § 507(a)(8)(E);

- customs duties, § 507(a)(8)(F); and

- penalties relating to a priority tax claim, § 507(a)(8)(G).

Income taxes

The most important category of eighth priority claims is the first, for income or gross receipts taxes. § 507(a)(8)(A). Income taxes are included in the eighth priority in any of three situations:

1. The tax is for a taxable year for which the return, if required, was *last due* (including extensions) after *three years* before the date of the bankruptcy petition. § 507(a)(8)(A)(i).

2. The tax was *assessed* within *240 days* of the date of the petition. § 507(a)(8)(A)(ii).

---

[288] 518 U.S. 213 (1996).

[289] See, e.g., In re Garcia, 955 F.2d 16 (5th Cir. 1992); In re Crecco, 162 B.R. 382 (Bankr. D.Mass 1993).

3. The tax was not assessed before, but is *assessable after*, the bankruptcy filing. § 507(a)(8)(A)(iii).

The basic priority provision is for income taxes for a taxable year that ended on or before the date of bankruptcy, and for which a required return was last due within three years of the bankruptcy filing. § 507(a)(8)(A)(i). A simple example will illustrate the application of this provision. Assume that Debtor owes income taxes for 2009. If no extensions are granted, the last date for Debtor to file her 2009 income tax return is April 15, 2010. The government's claim for 2009 taxes accordingly will retain priority (and protection from discharge, § 523(a)(1)(A)) for three years after April 15, 2010. In other words, if a bankruptcy case involving Debtor is filed on or before April 15, 2013, the government's claim for 2009 taxes will be an eighth priority claim. In addition, the tax debt will be excepted from discharge. § 523(a)(1)(A). If Debtor obtained an extension to file her 2009 tax return, the three-year period would be correspondingly extended.

Even if the three-year period has expired, if the government has assessed the taxes within 240 days of the bankruptcy filing, priority will be awarded. § 507(a)(8)(A)(ii). This 240–day period does not include any period in which an offer in compromise is pending, plus another 30 days. § 507(a)(8)(A)(ii)(I). What constitutes an "assessment" must be determined by reference to the applicable tax law. Even if the tax has not been assessed, if it remains assessable at the time of bankruptcy, priority still will be granted. § 507(a)(8)(A)(iii). Application of this last provision may depend on the length of the governing statute of limitations.

A question which has arisen with considerable frequency is whether the running of the three-year and the 240–day period is suspended (i.e., tolled) by a prior bankruptcy case involving the debtor. Consider the above hypothetical, involving Debtor's 2009 income tax debt, for which the required return was last due on April 15, 2010. In normal circumstances, the three-year priority period would expire on April 15, 2013. Thus, for example, if Debtor were to file bankruptcy on May 15, 2013, the 2009 taxes would not be entitled to priority (and also would be discharged, see § 523(a)(1)(A)). The filing would come a month too late for the government.

What if, however, the Debtor had filed a previous bankruptcy case on July 1, 2011, which remained open until July 1, 2012? For that year, the government would be stayed from attempting to collect on the prepetition tax claim. § 362(a). By the time of the 2011 bankruptcy filing, the government would have had less than three years in which it could pursue collection of the 2009 taxes. Resolving a circuit split, the Supreme Court held in *Young v. United States*[290] that the three-year period did not run during the time a debtor is the subject of a prior bankruptcy case. The *Young* Court invoked the doctrine of equitable tolling.

In 2005 Congress codified and extended the rule of *Young* in an unnumbered paragraph at the end of § 507(a)(8). Under this new rule, any time period in § 507(a)(8) (not just those for income taxes) is suspended in two situations: first, if the

---

[290] 535 U.S. 43 (2002).

governmental unit is prohibited under applicable non-bankruptcy law from collecting a tax because of the taxpayer's request for a hearing and an appeal of a collection action proposed or taken; and second, if collection was stayed in a prior bankruptcy case, or pursuant to a prior confirmed bankruptcy plan. The tolling of the eighth priority time period is for the period of prior suspension, plus 90 days. Thus, for example, in the hypothetical above, where the government was stayed from collection for exactly one year during the pendency of the Debtor's bankruptcy case (from July 1, 2011 to July 1, 2012), the three-year period would be extended for one year and 90 days. Thus, instead of the three-year period expiring on April 15, 2013, it would run until July 14, 2014 (i.e., one year and 90 days after April 15, 2013).

Other priority taxes

Income taxes are not the only eighth priority tax, of course. Six other types are included in the priority, in addition to penalty claims relating to any other priority tax. Most have time limits for which priority will be allowed.

Property taxes are awarded priority if (1) the tax was incurred[291] prior to bankruptcy and (2) the tax was last payable without penalty within *one year* of bankruptcy. § 507(a)(8)(B). The employer's liability for *employment* taxes relating to the prepetition period is given eighth priority, if the return is last due after *three years* before the bankruptcy filing. § 507(a)(8)(D). *Customs duties* usually retain priority status for *one year* after the subject merchandise enters for consumption or is liquidated, although an exception allows four years if fraud or another justifying excuse is present. § 507(a)(8)(F).

Excise taxes are afforded priority for three years. § 507(a)(8)(E). The excise tax category tends to be the residual "catch-all" tax priority provision—but only if it is a "tax" in the first place. What constitutes an "excise tax" has been the subject of considerable controversy. The Supreme Court gave helpful guidance in *United States v. Reorganized CF & I Fabricators of Utah, Inc.*[292] The Court first determined that deference should not be given to the labels used by the non-bankruptcy tax law. Instead, the court must examine the *attributes* of the exaction. A "tax," the Court stated, "is a pecuniary burden laid upon individuals or property for the purpose of supporting the government."[293] By contrast, a "penalty" (which is not a tax) is "an exaction imposed by statute as punishment for an unlawful act."[294]

The only type of priority tax that is not limited in terms of time is for "a tax required to be collected or withheld and for which the debtor is liable in whatever capacity." § 507(a)(8)(C). These "trust fund" taxes would include, for example, taxes that an employer must withhold from wages. In that situation, a "responsible person" for the employer, such as a high-ranking corporate officer, might be held personally liable for the full amount of the tax. 26 U.S.C. § 6672(a). If the responsible person were

---

[291] In 2005 the trigger was changed from the property tax being "assessed" to it being "incurred."

[292] 518 U.S. 213 (1996).

[293] Id. at 224.

[294] Id.

to file for bankruptcy, their tax liability would be nondischargeable and the tax claim would be afforded priority.

§ 7.22 Other Priorities

The priority statute is a special-interest favorite of Congress. Some of the priorities provided for in § 507(a) might be explained more readily by reference to political pressures or isolated notorious incidents than to wise and coherent bankruptcy policy. Priorities are not costless in bankruptcy cases. They reduce the distribution that may be made to general creditors in chapter 7 cases, and make it more difficult to confirm a chapter 11, 12 or 13 plan.

Grain producers and fishermen

In 1984 Congress added a priority for the claims of (1) grain producers against a debtor who owns or operates a grain storage facility, and (2) United States fishermen against a debtor who operates a fish produce storage or processing facility.[295] After the 2005 amendments, this priority stands sixth. § 507(a)(6). Related provisions were added with regard to reclamation claims made by grain producers and fishermen, § 546(d), and the expedited determination of interests in grain storage assets, § 557 (but not fish).

The sixth priority was enacted in response to an armed rebellion by several hundred farmers in Missouri and Arkansas who did not take kindly to the bankruptcy filing by the operators of thirteen grain storage facilities. Taking the law into their own hands, these farmers ignored the automatic stay and the orders of the bankruptcy court and forcibly recovered "their" grain that they had delivered to the debtors before the bankruptcy filing.[296]

Sixth priority claims are limited to $6,150 per individual. The dollar amount was raised from $2,000 to $4,000 in 1994, and since 1998 has been indexed every three years. § 104(b).

Consumer layaway deposits

The seventh priority affords some protection to consumer creditors who have made a "layaway" deposit or down payment. § 507(a)(7). In the wake of the large retail bankruptcy of W.T. Grant Co. during the 1970s reform effort, Congress recognized that ignorant consumers with little bargaining power who made deposits with retailers or service providers usually were "left holding the bag" in the event of bankruptcy, often without even realizing that they were a creditor.[297] The solution was to provide a $900 priority, which was doubled in 1994 to $1,800 (and since has been indexed every three years; as of 2013, the priority stood at $2,775).

A creditor must prove several elements to establish a seventh priority claim:

---

[295] Pub. L. No. 98–353, tit. III, subtit. B, § 350 (1984).
[296] See In re Cox Cotton Co., 24 B.R. 930 (E.D. Ark. 1982), vacated and remanded in part, 732 F.2d 619 (8th Cir. 1984), cert. denied, 469 U.S. 881 (1984).
[297] H.R. Rep. No. 95–595, 95th Cong., 1st Sess., at 188 (1977).

- the creditor is an individual;

- the claim arose from a prepetition deposit of money;

- the deposit was either in connection with the purchase, lease, or rental of property, or the purchase of services;

- the purchase, lease, or rental was for the personal, family, or household use of such individuals; and

- the property or services were not delivered or provided.

Note that the priority as enacted is not strictly limited to layaway deposits with retail debtors, notwithstanding the origin of the inspiration for the provision. The purchase of service contracts is specifically included, and nothing in the statute limits the type of debtor to which the seventh priority may apply. The only categorical restriction is that the intended use be for consumers, i.e., "for the personal, family, or household use" of the creditor.

Capital maintenance commitments

The ninth priority was enacted in 1990, in response to the savings-and-loan debacles of the 1980s.[298] This priority applies to a claim based upon a commitment by the debtor to a Federal depository institutions regulatory agency to maintain the capital of an insured depository institution. § 507(a)(9). The new priority was part of a package that included two new discharge exceptions,[299] § 523(a)(11), (12), and a provision in the executory contracts statute, § 365(o), that in a chapter 11 case requires the immediate cure of a default in a capital maintenance agreement and deems the agreement to be assumed. These provisions should be read together; unfortunately, the congressional drafting in many particulars leaves much to be desired. One glaring hole left by Congress is in the context of the requirements for confirmation of a chapter 11 plan. Nothing states the manner in which ninth priority claims must be dealt with in the plan. § 1129(a)(9).

DUI claims

In 2005 Congress added a new priority, ranked tenth, for certain DUI claims.[300] This priority is almost (but not completely) identical to the discharge exception for DUI debts in § 523(a)(9), which was first introduced in 1984, and then was amended in 1994.[301] The most obvious (and puzzling) difference between the two is that the discharge exception applies to the debtor's operation while unlawfully intoxicated of a "motor vehicle, vessel, or aircraft," where the tenth priority extends only to the debtor's unlawful operation of a "motor vehicle or vessel," omitting any reference to "aircraft." What is especially curious about the difference is that § 523(a)(9) also was amended in

---

[298]   Pub. L. No. 101–647, § 2522(d), 104 Stat. 4789, 4867 (1990).

[299]   See § 10.26.

[300]   Pub. L. No. 109–8, § 223, 119 Stat. 62 (2005).

[301]   See § 10.24.

2005, with "motor vehicle" replaced by "motor vehicle, vessel, or aircraft,"[302] an amendment made to resolve a split in the case law.

To qualify for the tenth priority, a claimant must show: (1) claim is allowed; (2) claim is for "death or personal injury," thus excluding claims for damage to property; (3) the claim is "resulting from"[303] the operation of (4) a motor vehicle or vessel; and (5) that operation was unlawful because the debtor was intoxicated from using alcohol, a drug, or another substance. § 507(a)(10). Note that the claimant need not prove that the debtor's intoxication itself played a causal role in the injury; rather, all that is required is proof that the death or personal injury resulted from the operation of the motor vehicle or vessel, and that the debtor was unlawfully intoxicated while operating the motor vehicle or vessel.

C. SUBORDINATION

§ 7.23   Equitable Subordination

The bankruptcy court is a court of equity. Perhaps the most striking illustration of the equitable powers of the bankruptcy court is its ability to "subordinate for purposes of distribution all or part of an allowed claim to all or part of another allowed claim or all or part of an allowed interest to all or part of another allowed interest." § 510(c)(1). The statutory distribution scheme thus may be overridden in part by the bankruptcy court to prevent inequitable results. Note, though, that the court's equitable power is limited to *subordination*; it may not disallow a claim or interest entirely.

The doctrine of equitable subordination has been a core part of bankruptcy jurisprudence for a very long time. Inequitable conduct is not a recent innovation. Full recognition of the doctrine came in a series of Supreme Court cases in the 1930s and 1940s. In *Taylor v. Standard Gas & Electric Co.*,[304] the Court announced the "Deep Rock" doctrine, requiring the subordination of the allowed claim of a parent corporation that had grossly mismanaged and undercapitalized the debtor subsidiary. Later that year, the Court applied a similar principle in *Pepper v. Litton*,[305] to subordinate the claim of a dominant and controlling stockholder who had acted inequitably in manipulating the affairs of the now-bankrupt corporation to his own advantage. The Court continued to reaffirm the equitable subordination power in cases such as *Sampsell v. Imperial Paper & Color Corp.*,[306] *Heiser v. Woodruff*,[307] and *Comstock v. Group of Institutional Investors*.[308]

Codification of the doctrine of equitable subordination in § 510(c) of the Code in 1978 was not intended either to alter existing practice or to freeze the doctrine in place.

---

[302] Pub, L. No. 109–8, § 1209(2), 119 Stat. 194 (2005).

[303] The discharge exception requires that the injury be "caused by" the operation, rather than "resulting from." It is not clear whether Congress intended any difference in result.

[304] 306 U.S. 307 (1939).

[305] 308 U.S. 295 (1939).

[306] 313 U.S. 215 (1941).

[307] 327 U.S. 726 (1946).

[308] 335 U.S. 211 (1948).

The statutory delegation of power to the bankruptcy courts refers simply to "principles of equitable subordination." § 510(c)(1). The legislative history emphasizes that the congressional intent in using this term was to "follow existing case law and leave to the courts development of this principle."[309] Thus, while the starting point in identifying the parameters of equitable subordination doctrine is the state of the law as of 1978, Congress also wanted to give the courts some flexibility.[310]

The conditions required to establish equitable subordination were summarized by the Fifth Circuit in the leading case of *In re Mobile Steel Co.*,[311] a 1977 case under the Act, shortly before enactment of the Code:

1.   The claimant must have engaged in some type of inequitable conduct.

2.   The misconduct must have resulted in injury to the creditors of the bankrupt or conferred an unfair advantage on the claimant.

3.   Equitable subordination of the claim must not be inconsistent with the provisions of the Bankruptcy Act.

Although decided under the prior Act, *Mobile Steel* continues to command a devoted following under the Code.[312] Indeed, the Supreme Court in 1996 noted with approval the continuing influence and importance of *Mobile Steel*.[313]

Equitable subordination is not lightly inferred. It is an unusual remedy, and is applied by the courts only in very limited circumstances.[314] The court must make specific findings demonstrating the existence of the conditions supporting subordination.[315]

The courts have identified three general categories of "inequitable conduct" sufficient to satisfy the first prong of the *Mobile Steel* test:

1.   Fraud, illegality or breach of fiduciary duties.

2.   Undercapitalization.

3.   A claimant's use of the debtor as a mere instrumentality or alter ego.[316]

Inequitable conduct sufficient to support a finding of equitable subordination is much easier to establish in the case of a creditor who is an *insider* or an *alter ego* of the

---

[309] 124 Cong. Rec. S17,412 (daily ed. Oct. 6, 1978) (statement of Sen. DeConcini); 124 Cong. Rec. H11,095 (daily ed. Sept. 28, 1978) (statement of Rep. Edwards).

[310] See United States v. Noland, 517 U.S. 535, 540–41 (1996).

[311] 563 F.2d 692, 700 (5th Cir. 1977).

[312] See, e.g., In re Kreisler, 546 F.3d 863, 866 (7th Cir. 2008); In re Merrimac Paper Co., 420 F.3d 53, 59 (1st Cir. 2005).

[313] *Noland*, supra note 310, 517 U.S. at 538–39.

[314] See In re Fabricators, Inc., 926 F.2d 1458 (5th Cir. 1991); In re Bolin & Co., LLC 437 B.R. 731 (Bankr. D. Conn. 2010).

[315] See In re Missionary Baptist Found., Inc., 712 F.2d 206 (5th Cir. 1983).

[316] See, e.g., In re Clark Pipe & Supply Co., 893 F.2d 693, 699 (5th Cir. 1990).

debtor. Most of the foundational Supreme Court cases involved such claimants. The Court repeatedly emphasized the heightened fiduciary duties owed to a corporate debtor by an officer, director, or controlling stockholder. While the fact of a close relationship to the debtor will not by itself require subordination (indeed, Congress declined to adopt such an automatic insider subordination rule in the 1970s), courts will closely and carefully scrutinize the dealings of insiders. If material evidence of unfair conduct by an insider is presented, the burden will shift to the insider to prove the good faith and fairness of its dealings with the debtor.[317]

Conversely, courts are very reluctant to subordinate the claim of a noninsider creditor. Unless it is an insider by status or by reason of an assumption of control over the debtor's affairs, a creditor does not owe a fiduciary duty to the debtor or to other creditors in the collection of its claim.[318] To borrow from an old saying, one might say that "all is fair in love, war, and the collection of claims."

A perfect illustration of the difficulty of subordinating a noninsider's claim is the Fifth Circuit case of *In re Clark Pipe and Supply, Inc.*, in which the court first subordinated the creditor's claim,[319] but then on rehearing changed its mind and held that the creditor's claim should not be subordinated.[320] The creditor in that case steadily reduced its lending to the debtor and pursued a course of conduct that led to the payment of much of its own claim, as the debtor's financial position deteriorated. The Fifth Circuit concluded that the creditor did not exercise such total control over the debtor as to make the debtor its own instrumentality, but instead was merely exercising the rights it possessed under loan agreements that had been executed at arms' length. In so holding the Fifth Circuit followed the lead of the Second Circuit in the case of *In re W.T. Grant Co.*[321] The Seventh Circuit later reached a similar conclusion in *Kham & Nate's Shoes No. 2, Inc. v. First Bank of Whiting.*[322]

The necessity of proving inequitable conduct by the claimant seeking payment in the bankruptcy has been reaffirmed in cases involving *successor* claimants. This situation has arisen where an agency such as the FDIC has taken over a failed savings and loan or thrift. The courts hold that the inequitable conduct of the claimant's predecessor cannot be used to subordinate the successor's claim.[323] In other words, the claimant itself must act inequitably.[324]

Without a doubt inequitable conduct by the claimant normally figures into the equitable subordination calculus, and if combined with injury or unfair advantage will

---

[317] See In re Winstar Commc'ns, 554 F.3d 382, 412 (3d Cir. 2009); In re Lemco Gypsum, Inc., 911 F.2d 1553, 1557 (11th Cir. 1990).

[318] In re W.T. Grant Co., 699 F.2d 599, 609–10 (2d Cir. 1983).

[319] 870 F.2d 1022 (5th Cir. 1989), withdrawn upon reconsideration.

[320] 893 F.2d 693 (5th Cir. 1990).

[321] Id. at 702. See *W.T. Grant,* supra note 318, 699 F.2d at 609–10.

[322] 908 F.2d 1351 (7th Cir. 1990).

[323] See, e.g., In re CTS Truss, Inc., 859 F.2d 357 (5th Cir. 1988), on reconsideration, 868 F.2d 146 (5th Cir. 1989).

[324] Enron Corp. v. Springfield Assocs., LLC (In re Enron Corp.), 379 B.R. 425, 439 (S.D.N.Y. 2007).

be a *sufficient* condition to the imposition of subordination. But is proof of inequitable conduct *always* a *necessary* component of equitable subordination?

A series of cases in the early 1990s held that inequitable conduct was *not* always necessary to equitable subordination. These cases usually involved a nonpecuniary loss tax penalty claim.[325] The courts reasoned that it would be unfair to impose the burden of that penalty on the debtor's creditors, and further noted that the punitive purpose of the penalty would not be served. In deciding that inequitable conduct need not be proven, these courts relied on a passage in the legislative history to the Code in which the sponsors of the bill stated that "a claim is generally subordinated only if [the] holder of such claim is guilty of inequitable conduct, *or the claim itself is of a status susceptible to subordination, such as a penalty. . . .*"[326]

The Supreme Court brought this practice to a screeching halt in 1996 in *United States v. Noland*.[327] In that case the Sixth Circuit had subordinated under § 510(c) the government's postpetition tax penalty claim that otherwise would have been entitled to first priority under § 503(b)(1)(C), without requiring any proof that the government had acted inequitably. Instead, the status of the claim alone was deemed sufficient to support subordination.[328]

The Supreme Court reversed the circuit court's categorical subordination of the tax penalty claim.[329] While the *Noland* Court stopped short of mandating proof of inequitable conduct by the claimant in every case, it did hold that equitable subordination may only be imposed by a court based on the equities of a *particular case*.[330] For a court to subordinate a claim solely based on its status is an impermissible judicial arrogation of the legislative function, here contradicting the congressional judgment to afford priority to tax penalty claims. The Court dismissed the legislative history quoted above as being both an inaccurate statement of the law as of 1978 and incompetent by itself to delegate legislative power to the courts.[331]

§ 7.24   Other Types of Subordination

Equitable subordination is not the only type of subordination authorized by the Bankruptcy Code. Two other types of subordination are provided for in § 510, and other provisions in chapter 7 effectively subordinate certain types of claims. §§ 724(b), 726(a)(3), (4).

Subordination agreements are enforced in bankruptcy cases to the same extent as under non-bankruptcy law. § 510(a). Since subordination agreements are between

---

[325] See, e.g., Burden v. United States, 917 F.2d 115 (3d Cir. 1990); Schultz Broadway Inn v. United States, 912 F.2d 230 (8th Cir. 1990); In re Virtual Network Servs. Corp., 902 F.2d 1246 (7th Cir. 1990).

[326] 124 Cong Rec. H11,095 (daily ed. Sept. 28, 1978) (statement of Rep. Edwards) (emphasis added).

[327] 517 U.S. 535 (1996). The principle of *Noland* was reaffirmed by the Court later in the same term in the case of *United States v. Reorganized CF & I Fabricators of Utah, Inc.*, 518 U.S. 213 (1996).

[328] In re First Truck Lines, Inc., 48 F.3d 210 (6th Cir. 1995), reversed sub. nom. United States v. Noland, 517 U.S. 535 (1996).

[329] *Noland*, supra notes 310 and 327, 517 U.S. at 541–43.

[330] Id. at 540.

[331] Id. at 542.

creditors, respecting the relative priority of their claims, the representative of the bankruptcy estate does not succeed to and cannot enforce on behalf of the estate the subordination rights of creditors.[332] Notwithstanding § 510(a)'s recognition of the enforceability of subordination agreements, the legislative history makes clear that such an agreement can be overridden in a chapter 11 plan by the consent of the beneficiary class.[333]

Securities purchase claims for rescission, damages, or reimbursement or contribution are automatically subordinated under § 510(b) to all claims or interests senior or equal to the claim represented by the security. The situation usually arises where the purchaser of securities was defrauded by the debtor. The subordination rule prevents a purchaser of securities from the debtor from bootstrapping its claim to achieve parity with general creditors. An early Supreme Court case had permitted such a result.[334] In enacting the Bankruptcy Code in 1978, Congress decided that it was more appropriate to allocate the risk of an illegal securities offering to the purchasers than to the general creditors.[335]

Tax liens are subordinated to certain priority claims by § 724(b). This rule is discussed in a later section of this treatise.[336]

In chapter 7 distributions, certain types of claims are subordinated. First, tardily filed claims are subordinated in payment to priority claims and to timely filed claims. § 726(a)(3). The only exception is for tardily filed claims that were filed late through no fault of the creditor, and which are still filed in time to permit payment. § 726(a)(2)(C)

Second, fines, penalties, or forfeitures, or multiple, punitive, or exemplary damages, are subordinated to the extent they are not compensation for actual pecuniary loss. § 726(a)(4). These claims are paid fourth, following priority claims, timely and "excused" tardy claims, and "unexcused" tardy claims. The subordination in subsection (a)(4) applies to secured and unsecured claims. Congress did not want any creditor to recover noncompensatory penalties or multiple damages until all other creditors had been paid in full on their principal claim.

D. PAYMENT OF UNSECURED CLAIMS

§ 7.25   In Chapter 7

In chapter 7 liquidation cases, the holders of allowed unsecured claims are paid strictly in accordance with a statutorily prescribed distribution scheme. § 726. The chapter 7 bankruptcy trustee collects the property of the estate and reduces that property to money, and then distributes the money in the order dictated by § 726(a).

---

[332] In re Kors, Inc., 819 F.2d 19 (2d Cir. 1987).

[333] S. Rep. No. 95–989, 95th Cong., 2d Sess., at 74 (1978); H.R. Rep. No. 95–595, 95th Cong., 1st Sess., at 359 (1977).

[334] Oppenheimer v. Harriman Nat'l Bank & Trust Co., 301 U.S. 206 (1937).

[335] H.R. Rep. No. 95–595, 95th Cong., 1st Sess., at 195 (1977).

[336] See § 7.33.

Not all of the property that initially comes into the estate always ends up being distributed to unsecured creditors pursuant to § 726(a). In fact, studies indicate that well over 90 percent of all chapter 7 cases are "no asset" cases, meaning that "no assets" are available for distribution to general unsecured creditors. How does this happen? To begin with, secured creditors must receive either their collateral or its value, before any distribution is made to unsecured creditors.[337] § 725. While this complete priority treatment of secured creditors over unsecured creditors has at times been somewhat controversial,[338] it remains the law. Other entities with superior claims to specific estate property, such as trust beneficiaries, also will recover their property, either in kind or in equivalent money.[339] In addition, individual debtors may take assets out of the estate by exempting property under § 522. All of these preliminary distributions of estate property reduce the size of the fund potentially distributable under § 726.

Consider a simple example. Assume that Debtor has $20,000 in assets when she files chapter 7. However, those assets are subject to the valid claims of various secured creditors in the amount of $12,000. Satisfaction of those secured claims thus will reduce the available estate to $8,000. Debtor then may claim exemptions in the $8,000 balance under § 522. Assuming that her permissible exemption claims are at least $8,000, no property will be left to distribute to general unsecured creditors.

If, however, estate property remains after all secured claims are satisfied and exempt property is removed from the estate, the trustee will be able to make a distribution to unsecured creditors. The trustee must make the distribution in accordance with § 726(a). The bankruptcy court has no authority to vary the statutory order.[340]

Section 726(a) specifies six levels, or tiers, to which distribution will be made. § 726(a)(1)–(6). All of the claims in each tier must be paid in full before any distribution is made to the next tier. Thus, for example, unless all first-tier priority claims under § 726(a)(1) are paid in their entirety, no distribution may be made to allowed unsecured nonpriority claims in the second tier. If the estate does not have enough assets to satisfy all claims at a particular level in full, then all claims within that level will share pro rata. § 726(b). Assume, for example, that the estate is large enough to pay all first-tier claims in full, leaving $10,000 to distribute to second-tier claims,

---

[337] See §§ 7.27–7.28.

[338] See, e.g., Lucian Arye Bebchuk & Jesse M. Fried, The Uneasy Case for the Priority of Secured Claims in Bankruptcy, 105 Yale L.J. 857 (1996).

[339] See §§ 7.35–7.37.

[340] In one prominent—and controversial—case the First Circuit recognized a narrow exception to this rule. In re SPM Mfg. Corp., 984 F.2d 1305 (1st Cir. 1993). In the *SPM* case, the secured creditor agreed to give up some of its entitlement to nonpriority unsecured creditors, but not to priority creditors. The court held that the sharing agreement was enforceable, even though the nonpriority creditors thereby received a distribution in the chapter 7 case but priority creditors did not, apparently contradicting § 726(a). The court concluded that § 726(a) was not violated, however, because no distribution was made under that section; the secured creditor's share of the estate left nothing to be distributed under § 726(a). The court decided that the secured creditor was free to do what it wished with its own money, even if that decision was to share with nonpriority creditors before priority creditors. Whether *SPM* was correctly decided is open to question; regardless, under the majority view courts have confined it to the chapter 7 context, declining to extend it to chapter 11. See, e.g., In re DBSD N. Am., Inc., 634 F.3d 79, 98 (2d Cir. 2011).

which total $20,000. Each second tier claim will then be paid half of the allowed amount of the claim.

The only exception to the rule of pro rata sharing within a class is for administrative expenses allowed under § 503(b), in the event the case is converted from a reorganization chapter to chapter 7. In that situation, the administrative expenses of the superseding chapter 7 case are paid before the administrative expenses of the superseded reorganization case. § 726(b).

The *first* tier of distribution is for priority claims under § 507. § 726(a)(1). Section 507(a) provides for ten classes of priority claims, which must be paid in descending order.[341]

One problem that arose in applying § 726(a)(1) prior to 1994 involved the scenario in which a priority claim (usually for taxes) was not timely filed. The courts of appeals generally held that the priority creditor was entitled to participate in the first tier of distribution even without a timely claim filing, although they disagreed as to whether the priority creditor had to show that it had missed the filing date due to a lack of notice.[342] The statute at that time did not expressly require timely filing. In the 1994 Amendments, Congress addressed this problem by adding a requirement to § 726(a)(1) that the priority claim must either be timely filed or must be "tardily filed before the date on which the trustee commences distribution."[343] In 2005 Congress added to the tardy filing possibility that the claim must be filed before the earlier of the date that is 10 days after the summary of the trustee's final report is mailed to creditors, § 726(a)(1)(A), or when the trustee commences final distribution, § 726(a)(1)(B).[344]

The *second* level of distribution includes the vast majority of nonpriority unsecured claims. Only in rare cases will any distribution be made beyond the second level. Included in § 726(a)(2) is "any allowed unsecured claim" (other than a priority claim under subsection (a)(1) or a claim subordinated under (a)(3) or (4)), proof of which is timely filed under § 501, or which is tardily filed due to a lack of notice and still in time to permit the payment of the claim. Note that participation in the second tier requires the claim to be "allowed," which is a term of art in the Code.[345] § 502. The exception in § 726(a)(2)(C) for tardily filed claims only applies if both criteria are met,

---

[341] See generally §§ 7.7–7.22.

[342] In *In re Vecchio*, 20 F.3d 555 (2d Cir. 1994), the Second Circuit held that the priority claim had to be paid in the first tier even if the claimant had notice. The Sixth Circuit took the view that the priority claimant was required to demonstrate a lack of notice in order to stay in the first tier. In re Century Boat Co., 986 F.2d 154 (6th Cir. 1993).

[343] Pub. L. No. 103–394, § 213(b), 108 Stat. 4126 (1994). The amendment does not clearly resolve the issue of what happens to a priority claim that is tardily filed after the trustee commences distribution. The statute prohibits paying such a claim in the second tier, because § 726(a)(2) expressly excludes claims "of a kind specified in paragraph (1)." The issue then is whether the claim is to be disallowed entirely, as the 1994 amendment to § 502(b)(9) might suggest, or whether the claim is dropped to the third tier of distribution under § 726(a)(3), which covers most tardily filed claims.

[344] Pub. L. No. 109–8, 119 Stat. 128 (2005).

[345] See §§ 7.1–7.6.

i.e., if the filing occurs before distribution *and* the creditor lacked notice.[346] Otherwise tardily filed claims are relegated to the *third* level under § 726(a)(3).

The *fourth* tier of distribution is for noncompensatory penalty claims. § 726(a)(4). Congress determined that all compensatory claims should be paid before any distribution is made to claims for fines, penalties, or forfeitures. Also, Congress was concerned that penalty claims (especially in tax cases) would swallow up too much of the estate, to the detriment of general claimants, and thus decided to subordinate those penalty claims.

Fifth, if anything is left in the estate after payment of the first four levels, all unsecured creditors will be paid postpetition interest on their allowed claim at the legal rate. § 726(a)(5). Thus, if the debtor is solvent on a liquidation basis, interest is paid on claims. This rule provides a limited exception to the normal rule disallowing claims for postpetition interest. § 502(b)(2). Finally, the *sixth* tier provides for any surplus remaining after full satisfaction of the first five tiers to be returned to the debtor. § 726(a)(6).

Although § 726 only applies directly in chapter 7 liquidation cases, § 103(b), that section nevertheless is important in reorganization cases as well. To be confirmed, a plan under chapters 11, 12, or 13 must provide that all unsecured creditors will receive at least as much under the plan as they would have been paid if the debtor had been liquidated under chapter 7. § 1129(a)(7) (chapter 11); § 1225(a)(4) (chapter 12); § 1325(a)(4) (chapter 13). This is known as the "*best interests*" test. In other words, a plan is only in the "best interests" of creditors if it pays those creditors as much or more than they would have received if the debtor had simply liquidated. In order to apply the best interests test in a reorganization chapter, the court will have to conduct a hypothetical chapter 7 liquidation analysis, using the provisions of § 726.[347] The court will compare the amount that creditors would have received in the hypothetical liquidation with the distributions projected under the reorganization plan.

§ 7.26   In Reorganization Cases

The entire scheme for the payment of unsecured claims is fundamentally different in reorganization cases than in a chapter 7 liquidation. In chapter 7, the trustee distributes the net assets of the estate according to a statutorily-prescribed distribution order.[348] In cases under chapter 11, 12, or 13, by contrast, the norm is for payment to be made to creditors over an extended period of time, out of the debtor's future earnings, in accordance with the terms of the confirmed plan of reorganization. Reorganization cases thus afford much more flexibility in the manner and terms of payment to unsecured creditors than a chapter 7 case. That does not mean that "anything goes" in a reorganization case, however; some basic rules prescribe the permissible parameters for paying unsecured creditors.

---

[346] See, e.g., Fogel v. Zell, 221 F.3d 955, 962 (7th Cir. 2000); In re Coastal Alaska Lines, Inc., 920 F.2d 1428, 1433–34 (9th Cir. 1990).

[347] See § 11.26.

[348] See § 7.25.

Priority claims

The proponent of a plan has the least freedom of action with regard to the treatment of *priority* claims under § 507. Stated otherwise, the holder of a priority unsecured claim has the most protection. The basic protective rule, equally applicable in chapters 11, 12, and 13, is that a plan must provide for *full payment* of all priority claims. The holder of a claim may waive that privilege, however. The means of implementing the full-payment rule vary somewhat as between the different types of priority claims and the different chapters.

The simplest rule is in chapter 13, which in § 1322(a)(2) provides that:

The plan—shall provide for the full payment, in deferred cash payments, of all claims entitled to priority under section 507 of this title, unless the holder of a particular claim agrees to a different treatment of such claim.

Several points may be made about this rule. First, as noted above, full payment of the priority claim is required (subject to one exception, noted below). Second, the payment must be made in *cash*. A distribution of widgets to the priority claimant will not suffice. Third, the payment does *not* have to be paid in a lump sum on the effective date of confirmation, but may be deferred or spread out over the life of the plan. The maximum term of a chapter 13 plan ranges from three to five years, depending on whether the debtor's family income is above or below the state median. § 1322(d). If paid over time, the cash payments will have to be discounted to present value, to reflect the time value of money. In other words, deferral requires the payment of interest at a market rate to the claimant, in addition to full payment of the principal amount of the priority claim. Fourth, an individual holder of a claim may agree to different treatment than that specified by the statute; but, the class of claimants in the same priority have no power to waive the rights of any priority claimant.

The exception to the rule that all priority claims must be paid in full in a chapter 13 plan is for domestic support obligations owed to a governmental unit, which are entitled to priority under § 507(a)(1)(B).[349] For those claims, the plan may provide for less than full payment, but only if the debtor commits all "projected disposable income" to plan payments for five years. § 1322(a)(4). This exception was added in 2005.[350] The same rule applies in chapter 12 as well. § 1222(a)(4).

The chapter 12 rules were identical to chapter 13 until 2005. Two changes were introduced in 2005, one in chapter 13 and one in chapter 12. The chapter 13 amendment moved the standard time period for a plan to five years for debtors with family income at or above the state median, as noted above. In chapter 12, the rule remains the same as before: the standard plan period is three years, unless the court approves a longer period, up to five years, for cause. § 1222(c).

---

[349] See § 7.9.
[350] Pub. L. No. 109–8, § 213(8)(C), 119 Stat. 53 (2005).

The amendment to chapter 12 had to do with the treatment of certain claims owing to the government. Congress introduced a new provision,[351] § 1222(a)(2)(A), which creates an exception to the normal rule that the plan must provide for full payment, in deferred cash payments, of all § 507 priority claims. Under this exception, the normal rule does not apply to "a claim owed to a governmental unit that arises as a result of the sale, transfer, exchange, or other disposition of any farm asset used in the debtor's farming operation." Typically, this would be some sort of tax claim resulting from the sale of farm property (e.g., a capital gains tax). Congress apparently had intended that under the new rule, the tax claim would be "treated as an unsecured claim that is not entitled to priority," but "only if the debtor receives a discharge." Congress made this amendment so that family farmers could make sound business decisions affecting the profitability of their farming operation, such as whether to liquidate unprofitable assets, without having to worry about adverse tax consequences, such as capital gains taxes or depreciation recapture. Unfortunately, in 2012 the Supreme Court held in *Hall v. United States*[352] that as written, this intended "Farm Sale Exception" did not actually accomplish its intended goal, and the individual farmer debtors in that case were not entitled to reclassify the tax as a dischargeable unsecured claim. The problem, the Court held, was that the tax was not a priority claim under § 507 at all, since it was not "incurred by the estate."[353] Note, though, that the exception *would* apply if the chapter 12 debtor were a corporation, instead of an individual.

The rule governing the treatment of priority claimants in chapter 11 is more complex. § 1129(a)(9). Initially, note that any individual holder of a claim may agree to waive the statutory protections and accept different treatment. Absent individual waiver, the statute breaks the priority claimants into three different categories.

The first category is for second or third priority claims (i.e., those specified in § 507(a)(2) and (3)). These claims must be paid (1) in full, (2) in cash, (3) on the effective date of the plan. § 1129(a)(9)(A). There thus is no provision for deferring the payment of these priorities, except as agreed to by individual claimants. These types of priority claims cannot be classified in the plan, § 1123(a)(1), because classification would serve no purpose; there is no provision for class voting to have any effect on individual rights. Since the second priority includes administrative expenses, which can be quite large in some chapter 11 cases, the requirement of immediate payment can be onerous. The "effective date" is not defined in the Code; it usually is specified in the plan to be some point in time shortly after confirmation.

The second category of priority claims in terms of permissible chapter 11 plan treatment covers the first, fourth, fifth, sixth, and seventh priorities (i.e., those

---

[351] Id. § 1003(a), 119 Stat. 186.

[352] 132 S.Ct. 1882 (2012).

[353] In *Hall*, the debtors were farmers who filed bankruptcy under chapter 12, and then sold their farm. They proposed a plan that treated the tax on the capital gains from the sale as an unsecured claim, which they argued was mandated by § 1222(a)(2)(A). In affirming the decision of the 9th Circuit and holding against the debtors, Justice Sotomayor wrote: "Chapter 12 estates are not taxable entities. Petitioners, not the estate itself, are required to file the tax return and are liable for the taxes resulting from their postpetition farm sale. The postpetition federal income tax liability is not 'incurred by the estate' and thus is neither collectible nor dischargeable in the Chapter 12 plan." See also §§ 7.15, 13.15.

specified in § 507(a)(1) and § 507(a)(4) through (7)). These claims may be classified. For these claims, the class may vote under § 1126 to accept *deferred* cash payments. § 1129(a)(9)(B)(i). A dissenting class member will be bound to the class vote. However, if the class does not accept the plan, these claims must be paid in full in cash on the effective date of the plan. § 1129(a)(9)(B)(ii).

The final category of priority claims under a chapter 11 plan is for tax claims entitled to eighth priority under § 507(a)(8). § 1129(a)(9)(C). Like second and third priority claims, these eighth priority claims may not be classified. § 1123(a)(1). However, unlike second and third priority claims, the payment of eighth priority claims may be deferred without the consent of the holder of the claim. The holder of a claim under § 507(a)(8) is entitled to be paid in full in cash in regular installment payments over a period not exceeding *five years* after the date of *the order for relief*. § 1129(a)(9)(C)(i), (ii). The timing rule was amended in 2005; before, the tax claim was to be paid within six years after assessment. Also new in 2005 was a provision that the priority tax claim must be paid "in a manner not less favorable than the most favored nonpriority unsecured claim provided for by the plan." § 1129(a)(9)(C)(iii). If the tax claim is deferred, interest must be paid.

There is a statutory gap regarding the chapter 11 confirmation requirements for two types of priority claims, those under § 507(a)(9) and (10). As the preceding paragraphs indicate, § 1129(a)(9) deals with priority claims under § 507(a) in three different ways. However, that section is silent regarding the required treatment of ninth and tenth priority claims.

Nonpriority claims in chapter 11

The treatment of nonpriority unsecured claims in chapter 11 cases is determined by *class*. The plan must designate classes of claims, specify the treatment of each class, and provide the same treatment for each claim in a particular class (unless a particular claim holder agrees to a less favorable treatment of its claim). § 1123(a)(1)–(4). Only claims that are "substantially similar" may be placed in the same class.[354] § 1122(a). The class then will vote on the plan,[355] § 1126, after receiving a court-approved disclosure statement, § 1125.[356]

If the class votes in favor of the plan, the treatment specified in the plan will govern. A class is permitted to accept almost anything. Flexibility is the watchword. And, if the class votes in favor of the plan, that class waives the protections against unfair discrimination and that the plan be "fair and equitable." § 1129(a)(8), (b). Dissenting members of a class are bound to the class vote.

Even when a class accepts a plan, however, some constraints still apply. The most significant is the "best interests" test.[357] § 1129(a)(7). This rule protects individual class members who vote against the plan. Each holder of a claim in a class is entitled to

---

[354] See § 11.17.
[355] See § 11.21.
[356] See § 11.20.
[357] See § 11.26.

receive or retain "property of a value, as of the effective date of the plan, that is not less than the amount that such holder would so receive or retain if the debtor were liquidated under chapter 7 of this title on such date." § 1129(a)(7)(A)(ii). In other words, the class cannot force an individual claimant to take less under the plan than that claim holder would receive in a chapter 7 liquidation. If, however, the plan distributions are greater than or equal to the liquidation payout, then the plan can be said to be in the "best interests" of the claimant. Of course, a claim holder may agree to receive less than a liquidation payout. § 1129(a)(7)(A)(i).

If the class of unsecured claims does not accept the plan, but instead votes against the plan, a new set of protections are triggered. The plan may only be confirmed over the negative vote of a class if the plan proponent seeks confirmation and satisfies the "cram down" rules of § 1129(b).[358] Under § 1129(b)(1), the plan may only be crammed down "if the plan does not discriminate unfairly, and is fair and equitable" with respect to the dissenting class. What does this mean in practical terms? First, any class that is *senior* to the dissenting class may not be paid more than 100¢ on the dollar. Second, any *equal* class may not be paid more than the dissenting class, absent a fair justification. Finally, and perhaps most significantly, no *junior* class can be paid anything at all unless the dissenting class is paid in full. § 1129(b)(2)(B). This principle is known as the "absolute priority" rule. Note that the payment to the dissenting class does not have to be in cash; for example, the plan may propose to distribute stock in the reorganized debtor to the class.

Nonpriority claims in chapters 12 and 13

The rules for the payment of unsecured nonpriority claims in chapters 12 and 13 are much simpler than in chapter 11. Notably, classes in chapters 12 and 13 do not vote. Thus, the sort of negotiated consensus that is the hallmark of chapter 11 does not exist in chapters 12 and 13. Instead, the debtor will propose a plan, and the court will confirm the plan if the statutory requirements are met. See §§ 1225, 1325. A creditor may object to confirmation. §§ 1224, 1324. Since creditors do not vote, certain protections for creditors are built into the confirmation rules.

For unsecured creditors, several guidelines apply. First, if the debtor classifies claims, the plan must provide the same treatment for each claim in a class. §§ 1222(a)(3), 1322(a)(3). A plan "may not discriminate unfairly" against any class. §§ 1222(b)(1), 1322(b)(1). Taken together, these rules help to ensure that an unsecured creditor will receive roughly the same treatment as similarly situated creditors.

Second, the "best interests" test applies in chapters 12 and 13.[359] §§ 1225(a)(4), 1325(a)(4). As discussed above, under this test a plan may only be confirmed if unsecured creditors will receive at least as much under the plan as they would in a chapter 7 liquidation.

---

[358] See §§ 11.30–11.34.
[359] See § 12.16.

Third and finally, unsecured creditors can insist that the debtor devote all of his "projected disposable income" to payments under the plan for the three to five years.[360] §§ 1225(b), 1325(b). This is sometimes called the "best efforts" test. In chapter 12 the standard payment period is three years but can be extended to up to five years for cause, as noted above, § 1222(c). In chapter 13 cases, the plan period is either three or five years, depending on whether the debtor's income is above the applicable state median income level (determined using the same criteria as § 707(b) means testing).[361] § 1322(d), § 1325(b)(4). Thus, even if a debtor does not have any nonexempt assets, meaning that the best interests test will not require any payments to be made to unsecured creditors, a debtor with excess future income cannot confirm a chapter 12 or 13 plan unless it commits all of that excess income to plan payments.

E. SECURED CLAIMS

§ 7.27 Introduction and Overview

Holders of secured claims are preferred over unsecured creditors in a bankruptcy distribution. Secured creditors are entitled to be paid *in full*, up to the value of the collateral securing their claim, § 506(a), before unsecured claims are paid at all. This bankruptcy priority for secured creditors mirrors the result that would obtain outside of bankruptcy. The legal rule that secured creditors have an enforceable entitlement to designated property of the debtor in preference to unsecured creditors is one of the most basic and important in our entire commercial system. It shapes the behavior of consensual creditors outside of bankruptcy (for better or worse) and establishes the fundamental parameters for the distribution of assets in or out of bankruptcy.

The wisdom of this priority rule has been the subject of extensive academic debate,[362] especially when applied to give secured creditors complete priority over nonconsensual unsecured creditors such as tort victims.[363] However, the reevaluations of the institution of secured credit in the 1990s and 2000s, pursuant to the Article 9 Study Project, the work of the National Bankruptcy Review Commission, and Congressional study leading up to the passage of BAPCPA in 2005, have not led to

---

[360] See § 12.17.

[361] See § 2.15.b.

[362] The debate began in earnest with the publication of an article by Professor Alan Schwartz in 1981 questioning the relevance of secured debt. Alan Schwartz, Security Interests and Bankruptcy Priorities: A Review of Current Theories, 10 J. Legal Stud. 1 (1981). Numerous commentators have attempted to answer Professor Schwartz's challenge to explain and justify secured credit on various grounds. See, e.g., Barry E. Adler, An Equity–Agency Solution to the Bankruptcy–Priority Puzzle, 22 J. Legal Stud. 73 (1993); F.H. Buckley, The Bankruptcy Priority Puzzle, 72 Va. L. Rev. 1393 (1986); Steven L. Harris & Charles W. Mooney, Jr., A Property–Based Theory of Security Interests: Taking Debtors' Choices Seriously, 80 Va. L. Rev. 2021 (1994); Saul Levmore, Monitors and Freeriders in Commercial and Corporate Settings, 92 Yale L.J. 49 (1982); Randal C. Picker, Security Interests, Misbehavior, and Common Pools, 59 U. Chi. L. Rev. 645 (1992); Robert E. Scott, A Relational Theory of Secured Financing, 86 Colum. L. Rev. 901 (1986); Paul M. Shupack, Solving the Puzzle of Secured Transactions, 41 Rutgers L. Rev. 1067 (1989); James J. White, Efficiency Justifications for Personal Property Security, 37 Vand. L. Rev. 473 (1984). Not only does Professor Schwartz remain dubious, see Alan Schwartz, The Continuing Puzzle of Secured Debt, 37 Vand. L. Rev. 1051 (1984); Alan Schwartz, Taking the Analysis of Security Seriously, 80 Va. L. Rev. 2073 (1994); but others have attacked the litany of justifications for secured lending as well. See Lucian Arye Bebchuk & Jesse M. Fried, The Uneasy Case for the Priority of Secured Claims in Bankruptcy, 105 Yale L.J. 857 (1996).

[363] See, e.g., Lynn M. LoPucki, The Unsecured Creditor's Bargain, 80 Va. L. Rev. 1887 (1994).

decisions to alter the fundamental premise of full priority for secured claims.[364] Indeed, in the 2005 law, Congress passed numerous amendments that *strengthened* the position of secured creditors in bankruptcy.[365]

Analyzing the treatment of secured claims in bankruptcy requires answering three questions:

First, does a secured claim *exist* at all, and if so, to what *extent*?

Second, what is the *substantive entitlement* of the secured claim holder?

Third, by what *procedural* means may those substantive rights be *enforced*?

The *first* question, regarding the existence and extent of the secured claim in bankruptcy, may be answered in four steps:

1.   Is the underlying claim "*allowed*"?

2.   Is there a valid *lien* or right of *setoff* under non-bankruptcy law?

3.   Can the trustee in bankruptcy *avoid* that lien?

4.   What is the *value* of the creditor's interest in the collateral?

To participate in the bankruptcy case as an "allowed secured claim," the holder of the secured claim must have its claim "allowed" under § 501 and § 502.[366] A claim normally will only be allowed if a proof of claim is filed under § 501 and if there are no grounds for disallowing the claim under § 502. Note, however, that a secured creditor does *not* necessarily forfeit its rights in the collateral if it chooses to forgo filing a proof of claim, instead opting to stand aloof from the bankruptcy case. Over a century ago, the Supreme Court held in *Long v. Bullard*[367] that a bankruptcy discharge does not destroy the *in rem* rights of a lienholder, which instead pass through bankruptcy unaffected, § 506(d)(2); the discharge only eliminates the debtor's *in personam* liability,

---

[364]   The Report of the Article 9 Study Group, stating "that Article 9 is fundamentally and conceptually sound," did not support devising "radically new priority rules." Permanent Editorial Board Study Group, Uniform Commercial Code Article 9 Report, at 6 (Dec. 1, 1992). Noting the growing academic debate, the Report further observed, "Nor did the Committee's deliberations reflect strong support for making major adjustments in the balance Article 9 now strikes between secured creditors and unsecured creditors." Id. at 9.

[365]   Perhaps no better indicator of Congressional sentiment on the question can be found than in the title to § 306(b), Pub. L. No. 109–8, 119 Stat. 80 (2005): "Restoring the Foundation for Secured Credit." Also revealing is the title to id. § 327, 119 Stat. 99–100: "Fair Valuation of Collateral." In the legislative history the House Report highlighted these and other provisions as needed "Protections for Secured Creditors." H.R. Rep. No. 109–31 (pt. 1), 109th Cong., 1st Sess. 17 (2005).

There are several superb commentaries on the secured creditor provisions of BAPCPA. See, e.g., Jean Braucher, *Rash* and Ride–Through Redux: The Terms for Holding on to Cars, Homes, and Other Collateral Under the 2005 Act, 13 Am. Bankr. Inst. L. Rev. 457 (2005); David Gray Carlson, Cars and Homes in Chapter 13 After the 2005 Amendments to the Bankruptcy Code, 14 Am. Bankr. Inst. L. Rev. 301 (2006); William C. Whitford, A History of the Automobile Lender Provisions of BAPCPA, 2007 U. Ill. L. Rev. 143 (2007).

[366]   See §§ 7.1–7.6 for a discussion of allowance.

[367]   117 U.S. 617 (1886).

§ 524(a). The Supreme Court has continually reaffirmed this general principle that liens survive bankruptcy.[368] Thus, even if a secured creditor does not participate in the bankruptcy case, it will retain its right to be paid the value of its collateral, unless some action is taken in the bankruptcy case to set aside that lien.

Note that the bankruptcy law does not create rights of security; it only enforces rights that arise outside of bankruptcy under applicable non-bankruptcy law. Thus, a claimant asserting in bankruptcy a lien on property of the debtor must be able to prove that it obtained a valid lien outside of bankruptcy. The Bankruptcy Code defines a "lien" as a "charge against or interest in property to secure payment of a debt or performance of an obligation." § 101(37). There are three types of liens: consensual, judicial, and statutory.

A *consensual* lien, referred to generically in the Bankruptcy Code as a *"security interest,"* is a "lien created by an agreement." § 101(51). Consensual liens include security interests in personal property under Article 9 of the Uniform Commercial Code and mortgages or deeds of trust on real estate under applicable state laws. *"Judicial* liens" are "obtained by judgment, levy, sequestration, or other legal or equitable process or proceeding." § 101(36). Examples include execution liens, judgment liens, and garnishment liens.[369] *"Statutory* liens" are liens "arising solely by force of a statute on specified circumstances or conditions." § 101(53). A mechanic's and materialmen's ("M & M") lien or a landlord's lien for distress for rent are common statutory liens.

The Bankruptcy Code also treats a creditor's right of *setoff* as a secured claim. § 506(a)(1). A setoff right exists when two parties owe each other mutual debts.[370] The most common situation in which a right of setoff arises under state law is when a debtor has a checking or savings account at a bank from which the debtor has borrowed money. The bank owes the debtor-depositor a debt for the balance in the account; the debtor owes the bank the amount of the outstanding loan. If the debtor defaults on the loan, the bank may set off the amount due on the loan against the debtor's account, reducing the account balance dollar for dollar. While bankruptcy law does not create a right of setoff, it does preserve a setoff right that arises outside of bankruptcy.[371] § 553.

Once the creditor has established that it has a valid lien or right of setoff under non-bankruptcy law, the question then becomes whether that lien or setoff right can be *avoided*, in whole or in part, in the bankruptcy case. The old adage of *Long v. Bullard* that "liens pass through bankruptcy unaffected"[372] must be qualified by the recognition that the bankruptcy trustee has several statutory "avoiding powers" that may enable the trustee to "avoid," i.e., to set aside, the creditor's lien. Upon avoidance, the creditor is relegated to unsecured status; the collateral that previously secured the creditor's

---

[368]   See *Dewsnup v. Timm*, 502 U.S. 410 (1992).

[369]   See § 1.3.

[370]   See § 6.27.

[371]   See § 6.28.

[372]   See *Dewsnup*, supra note 368, at 417 (stating that the rule originated with *Long v. Bullard*; see supra note 6 and accompanying text).

claim is freed from that creditor's priority entitlement and becomes available for distribution to the general unsecured creditors of the estate. Furthermore, in the reorganization chapters, the confirmed plan may alter the rights of the secured creditor.[373]

Avoiding powers that may be exercised to set aside a lien in bankruptcy include the "strong-arm" clause,[374] § 544(a), and the preference provision.[375] § 547. The strong-arm clause gives the trustee the power to avoid "secret liens," i.e., liens that were not perfected as of the time of the bankruptcy filing. Thus, if a debtor gave a creditor an Article 9 security interest in personal property before the commencement of the debtor's bankruptcy case, but the creditor did not take the steps necessary under Article 9 to perfect that security interest (usually the filing of a financing statement) before the bankruptcy filing, the creditor's security interest could be avoided under § 544(a)(1).[376] Preference law allows the trustee to avoid transfers made shortly before bankruptcy that improve a creditor's position relative to other creditors.

To illustrate, if a debtor initially borrowed money from a creditor on an unsecured basis, but then gave the creditor a security interest to secure that previously unsecured debt within the 90 days before the bankruptcy filing, the transfer of the security interest could be avoided as a preference under § 547. This result would hold even if the creditor perfected its security interest before bankruptcy. A creditor's right of setoff also may be vulnerable to the trustee's avoiding powers under § 553(a) and (b) under limited circumstances.

The scope of a creditor's secured claim must take § 552 into account. Outside of bankruptcy, secured creditors may be able to obtain valid liens against property that the debtor acquires in the future. For example, under Article 9 of the U.C.C., a creditor can obtain a security interest in after-acquired property. U.C.C. § 9–204. Such a security interest is colloquially known as a "floating lien," because the lien "floats" to attach to the after-acquired property. Under § 552(a), the filing of a bankruptcy petition sinks a floating lien. That section provides that property acquired by the estate or the debtor after the commencement of the bankruptcy case is not subject to a lien resulting from a security agreement entered into by the debtor prior to bankruptcy. This rule frees postpetition property from the clutches of prepetition liens.

Even though under § 552(a) a prepetition security interest cannot float to attach to postpetition property, in some circumstances a prepetition secured creditor still may be able to claim a lien against postpetition property. Section 552(b), which is an exception to § 552(a), permits a prepetition security interest to attach to the postpetition proceeds, product, offspring, profits, or rents of prepetition collateral.

If a creditor: (1) has an allowed claim; (2) establishes that it has a valid lien or right of setoff under non-bankruptcy law; and (3) if that lien or setoff right is not

---

[373] See In re Penrod, 50 F.3d 459 (7th Cir. 1995) (confirmation of chapter 11 plan extinguishes lien if lienholder participates in reorganization). See also In re Ahern Enters., Inc., 507 F.3d 817 (5th Cir. 2007).

[374] See §§ 6.3–6.4.

[375] See §§ 6.7–6.26.

[376] The trustee also may avoid unperfected statutory liens under § 545(2).

avoided in bankruptcy, the creditor will be entitled to enforce its "allowed secured claim" in the bankruptcy case. It then becomes necessary to ascertain the *extent* of the creditor's priority entitlement. Section 506(a)(1) provides that the creditor's allowed claim "is a secured claim to the extent of the value of such creditor's interest in the estate's interest in such property, or to the extent of the amount subject to setoff." In plain English, the creditor has a secured claim only to the extent that *value* in the collateral supports the creditor's claim.

Determining that value requires three steps. *First*, the extent of the *bankruptcy estate's interest* in the collateral must be established. If the estate has the full fee simple interest, then obviously the entire value of that property is part of the bankruptcy estate and will be subject to distribution. The estate might, however, have less than a full interest. For example, the debtor may have held property worth $10,000 as a tenant in common with a non-debtor party. When the debtor files, only the debtor's half interest of $5,000 would be part of the estate.

Second, the *secured creditor's interest* in the estate's interest must be ascertained. Assume that the estate has a $10,000 interest in property, subject to two valid liens, securing a first lien debt of $8,000 and a second lien of $3,000. The secured claim of the first lienholder is $8,000, because the collateral has sufficient value to cover that first lien in its entirety. However, the second lien, which is junior to the first lien under non-bankruptcy law, is only a secured claim in bankruptcy to the extent of $2,000 ($10,000 minus $8,000). After satisfaction of the $8,000 first lien, only $2,000 in value remains to secure the second lien. That second lienholder is said to be "*undersecured*."[377]

The *third* and final step in calculating the extent of an allowed secured claim is to *value the collateral* itself. Making this valuation is one of the most pervasive, important, and difficult matters that must be resolved in a bankruptcy case.[378] In the above example we have posited a value of $10,000 for the collateral. But how is that value to be determined? Of particular importance is whether *liquidation* or *going concern* value is to be used. In some contexts the relevant inquiry is described as a choice between selecting *retail* value (also called "*replacement*" value, § 506(a)(2)) or *wholesale* value for collateral.

In 1978 Congress chose to pass the buck entirely to the courts, giving them discretion to allocate the difference between going concern and liquidation value on a case-by-case basis.[379] The last sentence of § 506(a)(1) provides: "Such value shall be determined in light of the purpose of the valuation and of the proposed disposition or use of such property. . . . " In the 2005 amendments, however, Congress took part of the buck back, commanding courts to use the *replacement* value for personal property collateral of individual debtors in chapter 7 and 13 cases.[380] § 506(a)(2).

---

[377] For a discussion of the bankruptcy treatment of undersecured claims, see § 7.32.

[378] See § 7.29.

[379] See H.R. Rep. No. 95–595, 95th Cong., 1st Sess., at 356 (1977).

[380] Pub. L. No. 109–8, § 327(2), 119 Stat. 99–100 (2005). See Braucher, supra note 365, at 463–74; Whitford, supra note 365, at 154–55.

Once the extent of the creditor's "allowed secured claim" is determined, the second major question regarding the bankruptcy treatment of secured claims is to ascertain the *substantive entitlement* of the holder of that allowed secured claim. Outside of bankruptcy, when the debtor defaults, a secured creditor typically has the right to have the collateral seized and sold at foreclosure, and to apply the net proceeds of the foreclosure sale against the outstanding debt. Those specific *procedural* rights may not be preserved in a bankruptcy case.[381] Instead, the secured creditor may be stayed from repossessing the collateral or from foreclosing, and may be compelled to turn collateral over to the trustee (or DIP). The trustee may be permitted to use or even sell the collateral.

So what rights does the secured creditor have? In the legislative history to the 1978 Code, Congress stated that "secured creditors should not be deprived of the benefit of their bargain."[382] Yet, as the preceding paragraph indicates, that statement is not literally true; indeed, the same committee report just quoted goes on to observe that "though the creditor might not receive his bargain *in kind*, . . . the secured creditor [must] receive[ ] *in value* essentially what he bargained for."[383] The focus, then, is on honoring and protecting the *value* of the secured creditor's bargain. Here again, though, neither Congress nor the Supreme Court has required protection of the entire bargain, which would include, for example, the right to foreclose on the collateral immediately upon default.[384] Rather, the emphasis is on protecting *the value of the collateral* securing the claim during the pendency of the bankruptcy case.[385] As Justice Douglas observed in a decision that capped a line of Depression-era cases involving the treatment of secured creditors in bankruptcy: "Safeguards were provided to protect the rights of secured creditors, throughout the proceedings, to the extent of the value of the property. There is no constitutional claim of the creditor to more than that."[386]

To illustrate, assume that a secured creditor has a valid lien on collateral worth $10,000 securing a claim of at least that amount when the debtor files bankruptcy. That creditor has an "allowed secured claim" equal to $10,000 and is entitled to receive a value of $10,000 attributable to that claim, by whatever means. The creditor may not have the right to resort to that specific item of collateral, and the creditor may not have the right to choose how or when it will get paid, but eventually the holder of that secured claim is entitled to receive compensation of $10,000 on behalf of its secured claim.

The final important question with regard to the treatment of secured creditors in bankruptcy cases is, what are the different *procedural* means by which the substantive entitlement of the secured creditor (to receive the value of its collateral) may be

---

[381] See United States v. Whiting Pools, Inc., 462 U.S. 198 (1983).

[382] H.R. Rep. No. 95–595, 95th Cong., 1st Sess., at 339 (1977).

[383] Id. (emphasis added).

[384] See, e.g., United Sav. Ass'n v. Timbers of Inwood Forest Assocs., Ltd., 484 U.S. 365 (1988) (denying undersecured creditor compensation for delay in foreclosure caused by automatic stay). See § 3.19.

[385] See Charles J. Tabb, Credit Bidding, Security, and the Obsolescence of Chapter 11, 2013 U. Ill. L. Rev. 103, 108 (2013); see also S. Rep. No. 95–989, 95th Cong., 2d Sess., at 54 (1978).

[386] Wright v. Union Cent. Life Ins. Co., 311 U.S. 273, 278 (1940) (citations omitted). *Wright* and the other significant Supreme Court cases in that line are discussed in detail in Tabb, supra note 24, at 114–17.

realized? As discussed above, bankruptcy displaces, at least initially, the particular *remedies* of secured creditors, the most important of which is the right to foreclose on the collateral in the event the debtor defaults.[387] The primary mechanism for preserving the secured creditor's claim to value during the pendency of the bankruptcy case is *adequate protection*, which is described (but not defined) in § 361 and which applies in numerous provisions of the Code.[388] See § 362(d)(1) (stay relief), § 363(e) (use, sale, or lease of property), § 364(d) (obtaining credit). In effect, adequate protection replaces the secured creditor's non-bankruptcy remedies, and maintains the value of the secured claim until that claim can ultimately be satisfied. The next section discusses the various means by which a secured claim may be paid.

§ 7.28   The Ways a Secured Claim May Be Satisfied in Bankruptcy

The basic substantive entitlement of the holder of a secured claim is to receive the *value* of its collateral.[389] In a bankruptcy case there are a number of different mechanisms by which this substantive right may be realized. They include:

1. *Relief from the stay* is granted, § 362(d), allowing the secured creditor to foreclose on the collateral.

2. The collateral is *abandoned* to the secured creditor, § 554.

3. The collateral is *sold* by the trustee, § 363, and the net proceeds are distributed to the secured creditor.

4. The collateral is *redeemed* by the debtor, § 722.

5. The secured creditor and the debtor enter into a *reaffirmation* agreement, § 524(c), whereby the debtor waives discharge of the debt and in return is permitted to retain the collateral as long as it makes the required payments to the creditor.

6. The amount of the allowed secured claim is paid in a lump sum or over time pursuant to a confirmed *reorganization plan*.

7. The collateral is *returned* to the secured creditor, §§ 725, 1129(b)(2)(A)(iii), 1225(a)(5)(C), 1325(a)(5)(C).

Before 2005, some courts allowed another, non-statutory, option, wherein a debtor who was not in default would neither redeem nor reaffirm, but simply maintain *regular payments* after bankruptcy, and keep their collateral.[390] This stratagem was referred to as *"ride-through,"* the notion being that the debtor's right to keep the

---

[387] See Tabb, supra note 385, at 109–14.

[388] See §§ 3.18–3.20.

[389] Charles J. Tabb, Credit Bidding, Security, and the Obsolescence of Chapter 11, 2013 U. Ill. L. Rev. 103, 108 (2013).

[390] The pre–2005 court of appeals cases are collected in Jean Braucher, *Rash* and Ride–Through Redux: The Terms for Holding on to Cars, Homes, and Other Collateral Under the 2005 Act, 13 Am. Bankr. Inst. L. Rev. 457, 461 n.17 (2005).

collateral as long as he remained current in payments "rode through" the bankruptcy case. In the 2005 amendments, however, Congress apparently intended to remove that option (at least when the creditor does not acquiesce),[391] §§ 521(a)(2)(B), 521(a)(6), 362(h), although some have argued that the "ride-through" option remains alive and well if the creditor refuses to agree to a reaffirmation.[392]

One of the most prevalent means by which the holder of a secured claim is able to realize on the value of their collateral is by obtaining *relief from the automatic stay* under § 362(d) and then proceeding with its non-bankruptcy remedies, such as foreclosure. Stay relief motions are one of the most common forms of litigation in the bankruptcy courts. The grounds for relief from stay in § 362(d)(1)–(3) attempt to balance the secured creditor's right to adequate protection with the estate's need to use the collateral in the bankruptcy case. The topic of relief from the automatic stay is discussed in detail elsewhere in this treatise.[393]

The bankruptcy trustee as representative of the bankruptcy estate has a fiduciary responsibility to collect and liquidate estate assets and to distribute the proceeds to the holders of allowed claims. § 704(a)(1). A longstanding principle of bankruptcy law is that the trustee will not administer estate property if no useful purpose would be served in doing so. Instead, the trustee will simply *abandon* that property.[394] § 554. Abandonment is authorized if the property is "burdensome to the estate or . . . of inconsequential value and benefit to the estate." § 554(a), (b). In the context of secured claims, abandonment will be appropriate if there is no residual equity in the property for the benefit of unsecured claims after satisfying valid liens of secured creditors and the debtor's exemptions.

For example, assume that a debtor has a car worth $8,000, subject to a valid security interest securing a debt of $6,000. Under the federal exemptions, the debtor would be able to exempt up to $3,675 in value in that car. § 522(d)(2). If the debtor claims that exemption, no value will be left in that car for the general creditors of the estate. The holder of the security interest is entitled to receive the first $6,000 and the debtor will get the remaining $2,000. The trustee will abandon the car.

A note of caution is in order for secured creditors, however. Technically, the automatic stay will remain in effect after abandonment, because § 362(a)(5) stays lien enforcement against property of the debtor with regard to prepetition debts. Upon abandonment, the property will leave the estate and normally will revest in the debtor. Thus, relief from the stay will still be necessary. However, in practice courts often order abandonment directly to the secured creditor, perhaps obviating the need for relief from the stay. The legislative history arguably supports this practice, stating

---

[391] Pub. L. No. 109–8, §§ 304, 305, 119 Stat. 78–80 (2005). See Braucher, supra note 390, at 462; William C. Whitford, A History of the Automobile Lender Provisions of BAPCPA, 2007 U. Ill. L. Rev. 143, 153–54 (2007).

[392] E.g., Braucher, supra note 390, at 477–78.

[393] See §§ 3.17–3.25.

[394] See § 5.14.

that "abandonment may be to any party with a possessory interest in the property abandoned."[395]

A third possibility for satisfying a secured claim is for the trustee or debtor in possession to *sell* the collateral and to distribute the net proceeds to the holder of the secured claim. § 363(b)(1). The Code limits the power of the trustee to sell the property free and clear of liens, but that power does exist in certain instances, such as where the total sale price exceeds the aggregate value of all liens, or where the lienholder consents. § 363(f). A significant right granted the lienholder is the right to "bid in" at the sale, unless the court rules otherwise for cause. § 363(k). "Credit bidding" means that the secured creditor may offset its claim against the purchase price, without having to put up new cash.[396] For example, if a secured creditor has a total claim of $10,000, and it purchases the property for $8,000, it will not actually pay any money to the bankruptcy trustee; instead, its total claim will just be reduced to $2,000. In chapter 11 cases, the right to sell collateral pursuant to a plan exists, but so too does the secured creditor's right to bid in at the sale. § 1129(b)(2)(A)(ii). In 2012, the Supreme Court confirmed in the *RadLAX* case that the secured creditor's right to credit bid under a chapter 11 plan cannot be obviated absent an express bankruptcy court finding of cause under § 363(k).[397] If the lienholder is not the successful bidder in the sale, its lien will attach to the proceeds of the sale. Of course, the costs of the sale must be deducted first.

A fourth means of paying off a secured claim is for the debtor to *redeem* the property pursuant to § 722. Redemption is only available for individual debtors who are seeking to retain tangible personal property intended primarily for personal, family or household purposes. Refrigerator, easy chair, golf clubs, jet ski—things like that. In redemption, the debtor pays the holder of the lien the "amount of the allowed secured claim of such holder that is secured by such lien" and then keeps the property free of the lien. § 722. In the example of the car given above, in which the total debt was $8,000 and the car subject to the lien was worth $6,000, the debtor could redeem by paying the lienholder $6,000 in cash. The debtor does *not* have to pay the entire debt. The $2,000 unsecured balance will be treated as an unsecured claim in the bankruptcy case, and usually will be discharged. The amount that the debtor has to pay to the secured creditor, the value of the collateral, is determined by the bankruptcy judge. In 2005, Congress directed that the standard of valuation required in cases involving individual chapter 7 debtors seeking to retain personal property is replacement value, which for consumer collateral means the retail price for property of like age and condition. § 506(a)(2).

Redemption is not a panacea for debtors, however, although it is a very useful tool when it can be invoked. Perhaps the biggest roadblock is that the debtor somehow must come up with the entire amount of the allowed secured claim in cash. The courts have not permitted debtors to redeem by installment payments.[398] The debtor may not

---

[395] S. Rep. No. 95–989, 95th Cong., 2d Sess., at 92 (1978).

[396] See RadLAX Gateway Hotel, LLC v. Amalgamated Bank, 132 S.Ct. 2065, 2069 (2012).

[397] Id. at 2073. For an in-depth discussion of *RadLAX*, see Tabb, supra note 389, at 136–39.

[398] See In re Bell, 700 F.2d 1053 (6th Cir. 1983) (leading case).

use estate property to redeem, because that estate property no longer belongs to the debtor. The only option in most cases is for the debtor to borrow the redemption money from a new lender (or a family member or really good friend), and doing that of course requires the debtor to persuade the new lender to agree to make the loan.

Furthermore, redemption is only available in somewhat limited circumstances, as noted above. First, only individual debtors may redeem. Second, the collateral being redeemed must be "tangible personal property," must be "intended primarily for personal, family, or household use," and must secure a dischargeable consumer debt. § 722. Thus, redemption cannot be used with regard to real property collateral, or collateral used in a business. Finally, the bankruptcy estate must not have any claim to the property: the property must either have been abandoned by the trustee under § 554 or must have been exempted by the debtor under § 522.

If the debtor cannot redeem the collateral, it might try to retain collateral by entering into a *reaffirmation* agreement with the secured creditor. § 524(c). A debt that is reaffirmed will not be discharged in bankruptcy. Thus, if the debtor defaults in payments to the secured creditor after bankruptcy, the secured creditor may exercise all of its non-bankruptcy remedies with regard to the collateral, including repossession and foreclosure. And, most significantly, the creditor may attempt to collect any deficiency from the debtor, since the debtor will remain personally liable on the underlying debt.

Reaffirmation often is the only feasible means for a chapter 7 debtor to retain possession of desired collateral. Yet, that remedy also has undesirable aspects from the debtor's perspective. To begin with, the creditor is likely to require the debtor to reaffirm the *entire* debt, and not just the amount supported by collateral value. In the example of an $8,000 debt secured by a car worth $6,000, the debtor will have to promise to pay the full $8,000, and often with interest, attorneys' fees, and costs as well. As just noted above, the debtor will be personally liable on this full debt after bankruptcy. To top it all off, the debtor may not even be able to persuade the creditor to agree to the reaffirmation. Reaffirmation cannot be imposed on the creditor, and sometimes creditors prefer simply to cut their losses and terminate a credit relationship with a problematic debtor. Creditors also may be able to condition their agreement on terms unfavorable to the debtor, such as reaffirming other debts that the debtor owes to the creditor.

As mentioned above,[399] prior to 2005 a major debate was carried on in the courts over whether a chapter 7 debtor had yet another option if the debtor was not in default at the time of bankruptcy. The disputed option was for the debtor to retain the collateral and keeping making regular payments, without *either* redeeming or reaffirming. The genesis of this option was in ambiguous language in § 521(2) concerning the obligation of an individual chapter 7 debtor to file a "statement of his intention" with regard to collateral securing consumer debts, and then to perform the stated intention. The only "intentions" listed in the statute were to surrender the collateral, redeem, or reaffirm; "maintaining regular payments" was not one of the

---

[399] See supra notes 390–392 and accompanying text.

choices. However, the statute prior to 2005 did not plainly state that the listed options were exclusive, although perhaps such a restriction was implicit. Also, prior to 2005 the Code did not specify what the remedy would be if the debtor failed to elect one of those options. To further muddy the waters, § 521(2)(C) provided that nothing in that section "shall alter the debtor's or the trustee's rights with regard to such property."

The courts split over the effect of these ambiguous provisions.[400] One view was that § 521(2) essentially accomplished nothing and required nothing, and that no sanction existed for noncompliance. Under this approach (called "ride-through"), a debtor could retain collateral without either redeeming or reaffirming, as long as they were not in default. A cardinal benefit to the debtor was that they achieved the benefits of reaffirmation—collateral retention through installment payments—without incurring the undesirable side effect of ongoing personal liability, which instead was discharged. The competing view interpreted § 521(2) to require the debtor to choose either to redeem, reaffirm, or to relinquish the collateral. Simply keeping the collateral and making payments without redeeming or reaffirming was not an option. This approach forced a debtor who wanted to keep collateral either to pay the full amount of the collateral value up front (redemption), or to assume personal liability if paying over time (reaffirmation). As explained above, in 2005 Congress rejected "ride-through" and adopted the view that the debtor indeed must choose, amending several provisions in the Code (§§ 521(a)(2)(B), 521(a)(6), 362(h))[401] to make clear that if the debtor fails to either redeem or reaffirm within a limited time period, the automatic stay will be lifted and the creditor can proceed to enforce its rights against the collateral.

In the reorganization chapters the debtor may retain collateral if it pays the creditor the amount of the allowed secured claim over time and the creditor keeps its lien on the collateral. § 1129(b)(2)(A)(i) (chapter 11); § 1225(a)(5)(B) (chapter 12); § 12325(a)(5)(B) (chapter 13). This result can be forced on the creditor even without its consent; in the jargon, the plan can be *crammed down* over the secured creditor's objection. The debtor will only have to pay the amount of the "allowed secured claim," which is the value of the collateral, rather than the entire debt. In the car example, the debtor could retain the car by making payments on the $6,000 value of the car, not on the total $8,000 debt. The balance is treated as an unsecured claim. Thus, "*strip down*" of the lien is permitted.[402]

Prior to 2005, the one situation where strip down was *not* permitted in a chapter 11 or chapter 13 reorganization case was for a *home mortgage*. § 1123(b)(5) (chapter 11); § 1322(b)(2) (chapter 13). A debtor could cure a default on a home mortgage and reinstate the original terms of the mortgage, but could not strip down the mortgage, even if the creditor was undersecured.

---

[400] See Braucher, supra note 390, at 461 n. 17 for a collection of circuit court cases.
[401] Pub. L. No. 109–8, §§ 304, 305, 119 Stat. 78–80 (2005).
[402] See § 7.32.

In 2005, this prohibition on strip down was extended to personal property collateral in limited situations in chapter 13 cases, especially for automobiles.[403] Most significantly, strip down was barred for so-called "*910*" claims—purchase money security interests in motor vehicles acquired for the debtor's personal use within 910 days of the bankruptcy petition. See Unnumbered Paragraph following § 1325(a). In other words, if the debtor purchased a car on credit within 910 days of bankruptcy, he could not strip down that car loan. In addition, strip down is not permitted in chapter 13 for *any* type of collateral where the debt was incurred within one year of bankruptcy.

In cramming down a secured claim in a reorganization case, the debtor will have to make payments that have a *present value*, "as of the effective date of the plan," equal to the amount of the allowed secured claim. This means that the debtor will have to pay interest on the principal balance of the allowed secured claim. Otherwise the present value of the stream of payments made over time to the secured creditor would be less than the secured claim. For example, the debtor could not confirm a plan that promised to pay a creditor's $6,000 secured debt in three annual installments of $2,000 each. The future payments of $2,000 are worth less than $2,000 today, because of the time value of money.

One of the most litigated issues under the Code has been over the selection of the appropriate *interest rate* (or discount rate) for plan payments. This issue is discussed in detail in a later section.[404] Before the Supreme Court's 2004 decision in *Till v. SCS Credit Corp.*,[405] a multitude of approaches had been taken. Many courts concluded that the creditor should receive a market rate of interest, similar to that which the creditor would charge for similar loans, on the theory that the plan cram down is analogous to a "*coerced loan*" to the debtor.[406] Other courts, however, believed that such a rate overcompensated the creditor by allowing it to recover some profit. The sounder economic approach, these judges suggested, was to value only the actual deprivation to the creditor resulting from the debtor's retention of the collateral.[407] Those who took this view relegated the creditor to some lower rate of interest designed to capture only the present discounted value of the "claim" itself, and thus looked at the "*cost of funds*" to the creditor itself (on the theory that the creditor could make itself whole even with the forced "loan" to the debtor by borrowing an equivalent sum).[408] A third common view employed the "*contract rate*" of interest in the original agreement between the creditor and debtor as the presumptive rate, subject to rebuttal.[409] Courts in this camp often agreed with the underlying theory of the coerced loan approach, and then identified the parties' own contract rate as the best evidence of the market rate for

---

[403] Pub. L. No. 109–8, § 306(b), 119 Stat. 80 (2005). See David Gray Carlson, Cars and Homes in Chapter 13 After the 2005 Amendments to the Bankruptcy Code, 14 Am. Bankr. Inst. L. Rev. 301, 340–70 (2006); Whitford, supra note 391, at 150–51.

[404] See § 7.30.

[405] 541 U.S. 465 (2004).

[406] See, e.g., Koopmans v. Farm Credit Servs., 102 F.3d 874 (7th Cir. 1996).

[407] In re Till, 301 F.3d 583, 594–95 (7th Cir. 2002) (Rovner, J., dissenting), rev'd, 541 U.S. 465 (2004).

[408] See, e.g., id. The Second Circuit in *In re Valenti*, 105 F.3d 55 (2d Cir. 1997) concluded that the "cost of funds" approach was the most accurate conceptually but rejected it as being too difficult to administer.

[409] See, e.g., GMAC v. Jones, 999 F.3d 63 (3d Cir. 1993).

such "coerced" loans.[410] A slight modification treated the contract rate as a ceiling on the permissible cram down rate.[411] Finally, a fourth common view was what was labeled the *"formula"* method (also called "prime plus"), where the court would begin with a risk-free rate (e.g., United States Treasury rate of interest for the same duration) and then add some premium for risk attributable to the debtor's situation.[412]

In *Till* the Supreme Court "decided" that it could not decide which of the four methods it preferred. Indeed, putting together the various voting alignments, a majority of the Justices rejected every theory. The most votes went for the formula rate, backed by the four Justices in the plurality,[413] and for the presumptive contract rate, advocated by the four dissenting Justices,[414] but a majority of five Justices rejected both theories—the fifth vote in each instance being that of Justice Thomas in concurrence, who advocated instead a purely risk-free rate and thus thought both the formula and contract approaches overcompensate the creditor. However, Justice Thomas voted with the plurality because under his theory the debtors' proposed plan (based on a formula approach) already gave the objecting creditor more than it deserved.[415] Notwithstanding the abject confusion engendered by any effort to make sense of the odd voting cast in *Till,* most post-*Till* courts have concluded that at the very least *Till* binds lower courts to confirm a debtor's proposed plan that uses the formula approach.[416] The voting alignment in *Till* also would dictate that a debtor's proposed plan that uses the presumptive contract rate should be confirmed.

One final option for dealing with a secured claim exists: simply *surrender* the collateral to the creditor. In a chapter 7 case, if the collateral has not been administered during the bankruptcy case, the trustee is directed to "dispose" of the property. § 725. Congress's intention was "to give the court appropriate authority to ensure that collateral or its proceeds is returned to the proper secured creditor."[417] In the reorganization chapters, a plan may be confirmed over the objection of the secured creditor if the collateral is returned to the creditor. In chapter 11 such a return would be considered the "indubitable equivalent" of the secured claim.[418] § 1129(b)(2)(A)(iii). In chapters 12 and 13, the statute plainly states that a plan may be confirmed with regard to a secured creditor if "the debtor surrenders the property securing such claim to such holder." § 1225(a)(5)(C) (chapter 12), § 1325(a)(5)(C) (chapter 13).

---

[410] See *Till,* supra note 407.

[411] See, e.g., United Carolina Bank v. Hall, 993 F.2d 1126 (4th Cir. 1993).

[412] This was the view actually adopted by the Second Circuit in *Valenti,* supra note 21, 105 F.3d at 64.

[413] *Till,* supra note 405, 541 U.S. at 478–79 (Stevens, J., plurality).

[414] Id. at 492 (Scalia, J., dissenting).

[415] Id. at 486–91 (Thomas, J., concurring).

[416] See, e.g., Drive Fin. Servs., L.P. v. Jordan, 521 F.3d 343 (5th Cir. 2008); see also In re Tex. Grand Prairie Hotel Realty, L.L.C., 710 F.3d 324, 337 (5th Cir. 2013) (confirmed plan based on "prime plus" formula, but did acknowledge that "we do not suggest that the prime-plus formula is the only—or even the optimal—method for calculating the Chapter 11 cramdown rate").

[417] H.R. Rep. No. 95–989, 95th Cong. 2d Sess., at 96 (1978).

[418] 124 Cong. Rec. H11,104 (daily ed. Sept. 28, 1978) ("Abandonment of the collateral to the creditor would clearly satisfy indubitable equivalence. . . . ") (statement of Rep. Edwards).

§ 7.29   Valuation of a Secured Claim: *Rash* and Beyond

Given that the primary substantive entitlement of a secured creditor in a bankruptcy case is to receive the *value of its collateral*,[419] and given that several of the means by which the creditor's allowed secured claim may be satisfied depend on a *judicial* valuation of the collateral rather than a market sale, it becomes of the utmost importance to determine how the bankruptcy court should value the secured claim.[420] Until the 2005 amendments, Congress largely left the decision on how to value collateral to the courts,[421] and with virtually no guidance. Furthermore, Congress consciously decided *not* to decide the question of which entity should capture the difference between liquidation value and going concern value, instead calling on the parties themselves and the courts to make the allocation "based on equitable considerations based on the facts of the case."[422]

What is now § 506(a)(1) sets forth the general standards for determining "value" in a multitude of bankruptcy contexts. As explained below, § 506(a)(2) (added in 2005) specifies the required valuation standard (replacement value) for personal property in chapter 7 or chapter 13 cases involving individual debtors.[423]

Many courts have noted that the general valuation provision, § 506(a)(1), may be at war with itself. The first sentence of § 506(a)(1) provides that a claim is a secured claim "to the extent of the *value of such creditor's interest*" in the collateral. (Emphasis added.) The second sentence then states that "[s]uch value shall be determined in light of the *purpose* of the valuation and of the *proposed disposition or use* of such property." (Emphasis added.) This valuation is to be made "in conjunction with any hearing on such disposition or use or on a plan affecting such creditor's interest." § 506(a)(1). A determination of value at one point in the case is not given *res judicata* effect,[424] given the statutory command that the value determination will depend on the purpose of the valuation and the proposed use or disposition of the property. Thus, for example, a valuation at an early stage of the case in connection with a motion to lift the stay or for adequate protection would not be dispositive of a later determination of value in conjunction with the confirmation of the plan of reorganization.

---

[419]   See § 7.27. See Charles J. Tabb, Credit Bidding, Security, and the Obsolescence of Chapter 11, 2013 U. Ill. L. Rev. 103, 108 (2013).

[420]   Several commentators have made valuable contributions in this area. See Lucian Arye Bebchuk & Jesse M. Fried, A New Approach to Valuing Secured Claims in Bankruptcy, 114 Harv. L. Rev. 2386 (2001); Jean Braucher, *Rash* and Ride–Through Redux: The Terms for Holding on to Cars, Homes and Other Collateral Under the 2005 Act, 13 Am. Bankr. Inst. L. Rev. 457 (2005); Jean Braucher, Getting It for You Wholesale: Making Sense of Bankruptcy Valuation of Collateral After *Rash*, 102 Dick. L. Rev. 763 (1997); David Gray Carlson, Secured Creditors and the Eely Character of Bankruptcy Valuations, 41 Am. U. L. Rev. 63 (1991); Chaim J. Fortgang & Thomas Moers Mayer, Valuation in Bankruptcy, 32 UCLA L. Rev. 1061 (1985); Robert M. Lawless & Stephen P. Ferris, Economic and the Rhetoric of Valuation, 5 J. Bankr. L. & Prac. 3 (1995); James F. Queenan, Jr., Standards for Valuation of Security Interests in Chapter 11, 92 Com. L.J. 18 (1987). See also Tabb, supra note 419.

[421]   H.R. Rep. No. 95–595, 95th Cong., 1st Sess., at 356 (1977): "Courts will have to determine value on a case-by-case basis, taking into account the facts of each case and the competing interests in the case."

[422]   Id. at 339.

[423]   Pub. L. No. 109–8, § 327(2), 119 Stat. 99–100 (2005) (codified at 11 U.S.C. § 506(a)(2)). See also H.R. Rep. No. 109–31 (pt. 1), 109th Cong., 1st Sess., at 17, 83 (2005).

[424]   See S. Rep. No. 95–989, 95th Cong., 2d Sess., at 54, 68 (1978).

The proverbial "$64,000 question" under § 506(a)(1) is whether the proper valuation focus is on:

(1)   the rights of the *creditor* in realizing on the collateral through a forced sale (*first* sentence),

or

(2)   the value of the collateral to the *debtor* in its proposed use (*second* sentence)?

In the typical case in which the debtor seeks to *retain collateral* under a reorganization plan, the second alternative would require the debtor to pay "*replacement* value" as the price of keeping the property, an amount that would be higher than the "*foreclosure* value" (or "liquidation" value) produced under the first alternative.

The tension between the two, and the practical difference, is aptly illustrated by the facts in *Associates Commercial Corp. v. Rash*,[425] a 1997 Supreme Court case that directly confronted this central valuation issue. The debtor, Elray Rash, purchased a tractor truck for use in his freight hauling business. When Elray and his wife Jean filed bankruptcy under chapter 13, they owed just over $41,000 on the truck, which they sought to retain under their plan. To do so they had to pay the creditor the full value of the "allowed secured claim,"[426] § 1325(a)(5)(B), which depended on what the truck was worth. The creditor's expert valued the truck at $41,000, applying as the valuation standard what it would cost the Rashes to *replace* the truck with one of like age and condition. The debtors' expert, by contrast, valued the truck at $31,875, applying as the valuation standard what the creditor would be able to realize if it were to sell the truck at *foreclosure*.[427] Thus—assuming the respective experts each were correct, given their assumptions—the truck was worth $41,000 to the debtors but only $31,875 to the secured creditor. When the debtors proposed to "cram down" the creditor's secured claim and keep the truck, whose perspective controlled? In short, did

---

[425]   520 U.S. 953 (1997).

[426]   After 2005, in some situations a chapter 13 debtor would not be able to strip down a secured claim in the way the Rashes attempted. Under the unnumbered "hanging paragraph" following § 1325(a), added in 2005, debtors have to pay the full amount of the claim, not just the secured portion, in order to keep a "motor vehicle" purchased pursuant to a PMSI within 910 days of bankruptcy. See § 7.31.b. While Elray Rash's tractor truck would qualify as a "motor vehicle" under 49 U.S.C. § 30102(a)(6), the Rashes' bankruptcy filing came more than 910 days after Elray had purchased the truck, so the new rule would not have applied to them anyway.

[427]   520 U.S. at 957–58.

Elray and Jean have to pay $31,875 (plus interest) to keep their truck, or $41,000?[428] Or something in between?[429]

Unfortunately for the debtors, the Supreme Court in *Rash* held that when the debtors propose to retain collateral in a chapter 13 plan, "§ 506(a) directs application of the replacement-value standard."[430] According to the Court, the valuation question is governed not by the first sentence of § 506(a), which speaks only to *what* is being valued,[431] but instead by the *second sentence* of § 506(a), which does prescribe *how* to value the collateral. The "how" issue turns on the "*proposed disposition or use*" of the collateral. If the debtors' plan proposes for them to retain and use the collateral, as the Rashes' plan did, then the debtors should have to pay the creditor the *replacement value* of the collateral, the Court decided. When the debtors wish to keep the property, the proper perspective for valuation must be the actual value *to the debtors* (i.e., what they save in not having to go out and buy a replacement in the marketplace), rather than the hypothetical foreclosure value to the creditor. The Court first explained:

"Tying valuation to the actual 'disposition or use' of the property points away from a foreclosure-value standard when a Chapter 13 debtor, invoking cram down power, retains and uses the property. Under that option, foreclosure is averted by the debtor's choice and over the creditor's objection. From the creditor's perspective as well as the debtor's, surrender and retention are not equivalent acts."[432]

The Court then elaborated on the last point in a curious (and troubling) passage:

"If a debtor keeps the property and continues to use it, the creditor obtains at once neither the property nor its value and is exposed to double risks: The debtor may again default and the property may deteriorate from extended use. Adjustments in

---

[428] Note that the secured creditor would still have an unsecured claim for any balance, and that unsecured claim would have to share pro rata with other unsecured claims. Thus, for example, in Rash, if the debtors' valuation of $31,875 controlled, the creditor (Associates) would have an unsecured claim of a little over $9,000 (difference between the $41,171 total claim and the $31,875 secured claim). How much Associates would recover on the unsecured portion of the claim would depend, then, on what percentage dividend the Rashes paid on unsecured claims (none of the opinions say). For the Rashes, though, it would not matter: under § 1325(b), they already would be contributing all of their "projected disposable income" to the plan to pay unsecured creditors, so adding Associates' claim into the unsecured pot would not change the debtors' payment obligations.

[429] The Seventh Circuit split the difference between the two. As discussed in the text below, see infra note 32 and accompanying text, this decision was not arbitrary, but reflected the realities of the respective parties' bargaining positions. In re Hoskins, 102 F.3d 311 (7th Cir. 1996). In *Rash*, however, the Supreme Court declined to adopt the *Hoskins* mid-point presumption as the valuation rule, finding no textual support in the Code for that approach. 520 U.S. at 964–65.

[430] 520 U.S. at 956. Section 506(a) was renumbered as § 506(a)(1) in 2005 when Congress added § 506(a)(2).

[431] "What" is being valued is "the creditor's interest in the estate's interest in such property." 520 U.S. at 960. As the *Rash* Court explained, this language addresses the fact that the creditor's secured claim may be only for "limited or partial interests in collateral." Id. at 961. That is, the estate may not hold the full interest in the property, and the creditor may have a junior lien.

[432] Id. at 962.

the interest rate and secured creditor demands for more 'adequate protection,' 11 U.S.C. § 361, do not fully offset these risks."[433]

Justice Ginsburg's "double risks" statement displays both a shocking misunderstanding of finance theory and a profound distrust of bankruptcy judge's abilities either to value collateral accurately or to select appropriate interest rates. As the next section explores in more detail,[434] under finance theory one of the core components of interest rates is to compensate a creditor for the risk of default. As a leading text explains, *"[a] safe dollar is worth more than a risky one."*[435] Accordingly, the riskier dollar will require a higher interest rate if repayment is deferred. So, too, the central role of an adequate protection determination is to compensate a secured creditor in bankruptcy for the risk of projected collateral depreciation.[436] The Court's statement in *Rash* assumes that both the interest rate and adequate protection determinations will be systematically under-compensatory, and thus appears to intimate that a higher initial collateral valuation is needed to offset that "double risk." If either the interest rate or the amount of adequate protection is fixed appropriately, however, the actual effect of artificially inflating the initial valuation of collateral will be to *over*-compensate the secured creditor, who in effect will have been paid twice for both the default risk and the depreciation risk. As the next section discusses, it appears that at least as regards the interest rate issue, the Supreme Court has chosen (in *Till v. SCS Credit Corp.*)[437] to systematically *under*-compensate secured creditors, apparently thus hoping (at least implicitly) that two wrongs will make a right.

The *Rash* Court continued its justification for choosing replacement value as follows, and perhaps less dubiously than per its "double risko" gaffe:

> Of prime significance, the replacement-value standard accurately gauges the debtor's 'use' of the property. It values 'the creditor's interest' in the collateral in light of the proposed [repayment plan] reality: no foreclosure sale and economic benefit for the debtor derived from the collateral equal to . . . its [replacement] value.' . . . In sum, under § 506(a), the value of property retained because the debtor has exercised the § 1325(a)(5)(B) 'cram down' option is the cost the debtor would incur to obtain a like asset for the same 'proposed . . . use.'[438]

So, the Supreme Court chose "replacement value" as the required valuation standard when the debtors propose to retain collateral in a cram down plan. Ah, but what exactly *is* "replacement value," and how precisely does one calculate that number? Here, as it turns out, the valuation devil really is in the details. To ascribe a value to an asset, one must know exactly which "bundles of sticks" are being included. Importantly, in the cram down context, a debtor who is actually *retaining* property most assuredly is *not* getting exactly the same bundle of value sticks he would be

---

[433] Id. at 962–63.

[434] See § 7.30.

[435] Richard A. Brealey & Stewart C. Myers, Principles of Corporate Finance 18 (6th ed. 2000) (book is now in 10th edition, published in 2011).

[436] See § 3.18.

[437] 541 U.S. 465 (2004).

[438] 541 U.S. 465 (2004).

getting if he were to *purchase* the same item from a retail dealer, or possibly even from a private party.[439] For starters, he would not be getting any warranty, which he might get from a retail dealer, but probably would not get from a private party. Nor would he be getting a reconditioned vehicle, which again, he might get from a dealer. Further, a dealer's retail price includes marketing costs.[440] As such, even using the conceptual premise of *Rash* [that one must use the *debtor's* perspective in valuing the collateral when the debtor proposes to retain the collateral in a cram down plan] does not necessarily dictate adopting a full "retail value."

Importantly, the *Rash* Court recognized the limits of their actually modest holding. In the critical footnote 6, *Rash* substantially took away with one hand that which it seemingly had granted with the other, making clear that "replacement" value does *not* necessarily equal "retail" value:

> Our recognition that the replacement-value standard, not the foreclosure-value standard, governs in cram down cases leaves to bankruptcy courts, as triers of fact, identification of the best way of ascertaining replacement value on the basis of the evidence presented. *Whether replacement value is the equivalent of retail value, wholesale value, or some other value will depend* on the type of debtor and the nature of the property. We note, however, *that replacement value, in this context, should not include certain items.* For example, where the proper measure of the replacement value of a vehicle is its retail value, an adjustment to that value may be necessary: *A creditor should not receive portions of the retail price, if any, that reflect the value of items the debtor does not receive when he retains his vehicle*, items such as warranties, inventory storage, and reconditioning.[441]

Thus, *Rash* left a substantial opening for debtors to propose confirmable chapter 13 plans providing for payment of considerably less than the full "retail" value of collateral. Indeed, the Court specifically directed that the value chosen "should not include" such things as warranties and reconditioning, which, along with marketing

---

[439] See Braucher, supra note 420, 13 Am. Bankr. Inst. L. Rev. at 463–74.

To illustrate the problem, assume a simple hypothetical: applying *Rash*, what is the "value" of a 2005 Honda Accord EX 4–door sedan with 40,000 miles in excellent condition, standardly configured, in Champaign, Illinois? If one were to consult the reputable "Kelley Blue Book" website, one would soon discover that this same car has three different possible "values": (1) a "suggested retail" value of $16,295,[when buying from a dealer; http://www.kbb.com/honda/accord/2005–honda-accord/ex-sedan–4d/?pricetype=retail & vehicleid=859 & intent=buy-used & mileage=40000 & anchor=true] (2) a "private party" value of $14,295 [when selling the car yourself; http://www.kbb.com/honda/accord/2005–honda-accord/ex-sedan–4d/?pricetype=private-party & vehicleid=859 & intent=buy-used & mileage=40000 & anchor=true'true & anchor=true]; and (3) a "trade-in" value of $12,195 [when trading in at a dealership; http://www.kbb.com/honda/accord/2005–honda-accord/ex-sedan–4d/?vehicleid=859 & intent=trade-in-sell & mileage=40000 & anchor=true'true'true]. See http://www.kbb.com (last visited May 13, 2013).

Which of these is the value commanded by *Rash*? As the text explains—it is not clear!

[440] For example, the Kelley Blue Book site explains: "Suggested Retail Value is representative of dealers' asking prices and is the starting point for negotiation between a consumer and a dealer. This value assumes that the vehicle has been fully reconditioned and takes into account the dealers' profit and costs for advertising. The final sale price will likely be less depending on the car's actual condition, popularity, warranty and local market factors." See http://www.kbb.com/honda/accord/2005–honda-accord/ex-sedan–4d/?pricetype=retail & vehicleid=859 & intent=buy-used & mileage=40000 & anchor=true (click the "i" graphic next to the "Suggested Retail" title).

[441] 520 U.S. at 965 n.6 (emphases added).

costs, are the major economic components that differentiate "retail" value from "private party" and "trade-in" values.[442] Post–*Rash* courts have seized on footnote 6; as one commentator noted, "bankruptcy courts have felt free to ignore *Rash* altogether and do whatever they did before."[443] Another observed, "if the Court thought it was giving lower courts streamlined guidance on value, it was mistaken. Currently the practice reflects this difficulty; when pressed, most bankruptcy professionals admit (at least in Chapter 13 cases) to just splitting the difference between wholesale and retail."[444]

Unhappy with this result, secured creditors turned to Congress, and in the 2005 amendments Congress tried to close *Rash*'s footnote 6 loophole, with a new § 506(a)(2).[445] The valuation rule of § 506(a)(2) applies only to: (1) *personal property* collateral securing an allowed claim; (2) of *individual* debtors; and (3) in cases under chapter 7 or chapter 13. Thus, to begin with, § 506(a)(2) has no applicability, and § 506(a)(1)—and thus *Rash*—will continue to control, in any of the following cases: (1) real estate collateral is being valued; (2) the debtor is a business entity (e.g., corporation or partnership); or (3) all collateral in a chapter 11 case. Courts will have to look at the "proposed disposition or use" of the collateral, and make fact-based adjustments as per footnote 6 to arrive at an appropriate value.[446]

For cases covered by § 506(a)(2), that 2005 amendment dictates first that "replacement value" (to be measured as of the petition date) is the appropriate standard of valuation, and then directs that "costs of sale or marketing" are not to be deducted. The prohibition against deducting marketing and sales costs is a direct repudiation of part of footnote 6, because those costs are "items the debtor does not receive when he retains his vehicle."[447] However, note also that by negative implication this provision—which will usually apply only to an individual chapter 13 debtor's personal property collateral used for *business* purposes, as explained below—does *not* overrule the parts of footnote 6 that suggest deducting from retail value all *other* items the debtor does not receive, including warranties and reconditioning. Thus, for an individual debtor's business collateral, full retail price still will not be the standard.

However, the second sentence of § 506(a)(2) provides that for *consumer* collateral—that is, "property acquired for personal, family, or household purposes"— "replacement value shall mean the *price a retail merchant would charge* for property of

---

[442] See notes 21–22 supra. Indeed, looking at the Kelly Blue Book explanations, a good case could be made that "private party" value is the most accurate reflection of what should be included in "replacement value" according to footnote 6 of *Rash*. See http://www.kbb.com/honda/accord/2005–honda-accord/ex-sedan–4d/?pricetype=retail & vehicleid=859 & intent=buy-used & mileage=40000 & anchor=true (click the "i" graphic next to the "Suggested Retail" title).

[443] David Gray Carlson, Cars and Homes in Chapter 13 After the 2005 Amendments to the Bankruptcy Code, 14 Am. Bankr. Inst. L. Rev. 301, 359 (2006).

[444] Lee Dembart & Bruce A. Markell, Alive at 25? A Short Review of the Supreme Court's Bankruptcy Jurisprudence, 1979–2004, 78 Am. Bankr. L.J. 373, 384 (2004).

[445] Pub. L. No. 109–8, § 327(2), 119 Stat. 99–100 (2005) (codified at 11 U.S.C. § 506(a)(2)). For discussion, see Braucher, supra notes 420, 439.

[446] One caveat to the statement in the text: if the case is under chapter 13, and the collateral is either a motor vehicle purchased under a PMSI within 910 days of bankruptcy, or any other collateral purchased in the year before bankruptcy, then the "value" will simply be the full amount of the debt. See Unnumbered paragraph following § 1325(a); see infra note 31 and accompanying text and § 7.31.b.

[447] Assocs. Commercial Corp. v. Rash, 520 U.S. 953, 965 n.6 (1997).

that kind considering the age and condition of the property at the time value is determined." This provision *does* preclude most of the potential downward adjustments from full retail value suggested by *Rash* footnote 6 (with the exception of reconditioning costs, since the statutory language mandates retail price for property of "the age and condition" of the property the debtor proposes to retain[448]). Moreover, because § 506(a)(2) applies in both chapter 7 and chapter 13 cases, it will not only govern cram down valuations under § 1325(a)(5)(B), but will also govern redemption valuations under § 722. As a policy matter, § 506(a)(2)'s consumer collateral valuation rule is very hard to justify, as a consumer debtor who wants to retain such collateral is forced to pay the secured creditor for a value that the creditor could never obtain and which the debtor is not getting. To describe such a "value" as anything other than a windfall to the creditor is disingenuous.

As noted above, the new valuation rules of § 506(a)(2) do not apply to all cases. Excluded are all chapter 11 cases, real property collateral, and cases involving corporate or partnership debtors. Furthermore, the "we really mean full retail value" rule of the second sentence of § 506(a)(2) does not apply to goods acquired for *business* use. Thus, ironically, the second sentence of § 506(a)(2) would not apply on the facts of the *Rash* case itself, where the debtor purchased the collateral at issue for use in his freight-hauling business.

Furthermore, in chapter 13 cases involving motor vehicles purchased under a PMSI within 910 days of bankruptcy, or any other "thing of value" purchased within a year of bankruptcy, another 2005 amendment eliminates the need to make any valuation of the collateral at all.[449] A debtor who wishes to retain such collateral in his chapter 13 plan must pay the creditor the full amount of the debt, irrespective of the value of the collateral.

Another common context in which collateral valuation issues may be quite important is in stay relief litigation. The debtor seeks to use collateral in a reorganization, and the creditor in response moves for relief from the stay or for adequate protection. §§ 362(d), 363(e). These disputes over the debtor's desire to use the property and the creditor's demand for protection again highlight the tension in valuation decisions. A court trying to comply with the *Rash* directive to value the collateral in keeping with the command of § 506(a)(1) to consider the "proposed disposition or use" of the property might succumb to the temptation to use a higher going concern value, reasoning that the proposed "use" is by the debtor in its business. The problem, though, is that § 506(a)(1) *also* requires the valuation to be made "in light of the purpose of the valuation." In this setting, the *purpose* of the valuation is to ascertain whether the creditor is "adequately protected" against the eventuality that the debtor's best laid plans of reorganizing its business may go awry. If the need for the creditor to invoke its adequate protection develops, it will be because the debtor has *not* been able to reorganize successfully, meaning that the creditor's only meaningful protection will be to have recourse to its collateral. In that event, all that the creditor

---

[448] See Braucher, supra note 420, 13 Am. Bankr. Inst. L. Rev. at 466.

[449] Pub. L. No. 109–8, § 306(b), 119 Stat. 80 (2005) (codified in unnumbered paragraph following § 1325(a)). See § 7.31.b.

will receive is the liquidation value of the collateral. Therefore, arguably the better approach in valuing collateral in the adequate protection context—even in keeping with *Rash*—is at the lower foreclosure value.

A parting thought about collateral valuation issues. The preceding discussion has focused on what a debtor can *force* a secured creditor to accept. In practice, though, many cases still will be settled through *negotiations* between the debtor and the secured creditor. In that light, consider—even with the 2005 pro-creditor amendments—the reality of what will happen in negotiations between the debtor and secured creditor concerning collateral valuation (1) in the many chapter 13 cram down cases for which valuation is still relevant or (2) for purposes of a § 722 redemption. The creditor's leverage is to invoke the heightened protections of the 2005 law, and to threaten to object to the debtor's retention of the collateral except upon payment of the higher "replacement" value (whatever that might mean!). But the debtor's negotiating leverage is equally, if not more, powerful—he can threaten just to surrender the collateral to the creditor. In that event, the creditor presumably would not be able to recover more than the lower foreclosure value. Consider again the facts of *Rash*: replacement value of $41,000, and foreclosure value of $31,875. The Court held in favor of replacement value, which we will assume for simplicity's sake (and ignoring footnote 6) to be in fact $41,000. So will this dictate that the creditor will get $41,000 from the debtors as the price of keeping the truck? Probably not—because the debtors can say, "fine, take your truck—and enjoy the $31,875 you'll get at foreclosure." As Judge Posner pointed out in *In re Hoskins*,[450] such a scenario involves a "bilateral monopoly" and (given that neither party really wants to do that which they are threatening) a certain element of the old game of "chicken." The most likely outcome of such bargaining may simply be for the parties to split the difference and agree to a mid-point valuation.

§ 7.30   Cram Down Interest Rate: *Till*

In a reorganization case, a debtor normally is permitted to "cram down" an allowed secured claim by paying the holder of that claim the full value of the secured claim over time. See §§ 1129(b)(2)(A)(i)(II) (chapter 11); 1225(a)(5)(B)(ii) (chapter 12); 1325(a)(5)(B)(ii) (chapter 13). As the *Rash* Court explained, "Under the cram down option, the debtor is permitted to keep the property over the objection of the creditor; the creditor retains the lien securing the claim, see § 1325(a)(5)(B)(i), and the debtor is required to provide the creditor with payments, over the life of the plan, that will total the present value of the allowed secured claim, *i.e.,* the present value of the collateral, see § 1325(a)(5)(B)(ii)."[451]

The preceding section explored how the issue of the *value* of the collateral is to be determined, which tells us the amount of the "*allowed secured claim.*"[452] This section explores the equally difficult and important problem of how to account for the fact that in cram down the debtor is permitted to pay off the secured creditor's allowed secured

---

[450] 102 F.3d 311 (7th Cir. 1996).

[451] 520 U.S. 953, 957 (1997).

[452] See 7.29.

claim *over time.* The "first basic principle of finance" is that "*a dollar today is worth more than a dollar tomorrow.*"[453] Accordingly, it won't do to allow the debtor to pay the secured creditor only the amount of the secured claim over time. A debtor could confirm a cram down plan by paying a secured creditor the entire amount of the allowed secured claim in cash on the effective date of confirmation. When the debtor chooses instead to defer payments to the secured creditor, the present value of those deferred payments should give equivalent value to the secured creditor.

Consider the facts in the 2004 Supreme Court case of *Till v. SCS Credit Corp.*[454] The debtors, Amy and Lee Till, filed chapter 13 and wanted to keep a truck with a stipulated value of $4,000, on which SCS Credit had a security interest. Could the Tills confirm a cram down plan by promising to pay SCS a total of $4,000 over the projected three-year life of the plan? Of course not. Because of the "first basic principle" of finance, the "*present value*" of a stream of payments totaling $4,000, stretched out over three years, plainly would be substantially *less* than $4,000 today. Over that three-year period, the Tills accordingly would have to pay SCS some amount *more* than just $4,000 for the "*present value*" of the payment stream to equal exactly $4,000. The measure of the "more" that the Tills would have to pay is called the *interest rate* or the *discount rate*, depending on whether you look forward or backward in time. "Interest," by definition, is compensation for the use of money over time. It is, in short, the price of money.

The need to utilize a present value analysis—and thus for a debtor to pay interest in cram down—follows not only from principles of finance but from the text of the Bankruptcy Code itself, which requires a debtor to provide the crammed down secured creditor with payments equalling the "value, *as of the effective date of the plan,*" of the creditor's allowed secured claim. § 1129(b)(2)(A)(i)(II) (chapter 11); § 1225(a)(5)(B)(II) (chapter 12); 1325(a)(5)(B)(ii) (chapter 13). Thus, as the Supreme Court observed in another case, "When a claim is paid off pursuant to a stream of future payments, a creditor receives the 'present value' of its claim only if the total amount of the deferred payments includes the amount of the underlying claim plus an appropriate amount of interest to compensate the creditor for the decreased value of the claim caused by the delayed payments."[455]

One of the single most difficult, debated, and litigated questions under the Bankruptcy Code has been how to determine the "appropriate amount of interest" in a cram down plan.[456] Saying that "interest" must be paid to compensate for delay in payment is non-controversial; what *is* controversial is deciding what the interest rate should be.

Consider again the facts in *Till.* When the debtors purchased the truck, they agreed to pay a *contract rate* of interest of 21% (this was a "sub-prime" loan, meaning

---

[453] Richard A. Brealey & Stewart C. Myers, Principles of Corporate Finance 16 (6th ed. 2000) (now in 10th edition, published 2011).

[454] 541 U.S. 465 (2004).

[455] Rake v. Wade, 508 U.S. 464, 472 n.8 (1993).

[456] See David G. Epstein, Don't Go and Do Something *Rash* About Cram Down Interest Rates, 49 Ala. L.Rev. 435, 443–59 (1998).

that Lee and Amy were very bad credit risks). In their chapter 13 plan, they proposed to pay SCS interest of 9.5%. They arrived at this rate using a *"formula"* approach (also called "prime plus"), in which they started with the "prime rate"[457] of 8% and added a 1.5% "risk" factor. SCS objected to the plan, arguing that it was entitled to receive the 21% contract rate, and thus the proposed 9.5% rate was inadequate. Under a present value analysis, if SCS were paid interest of only 9.5%, but the appropriate discount rate was 21%, the value "as of the effective date of the plan" of monthly payments from the Tills over three years would be about $3,400—less than SCS's $4,000 allowed secured claim, and thus the Tills' plan would not be confirmable. The dispositive issue, then, was what the appropriate interest rate should be. What is the best theory for identifying the proper rate? Nothing in the Code itself or in the legislative history speaks to this question.

The many opinions at various levels in the *Till* case serve as a microcosm of the range of approaches that courts had taken over the first quarter century under the Bankruptcy Code in choosing a cram down interest rate. At least four major approaches have been used; each attracted some support at some level in *Till*:

> 1. *"Formula"* (proposed in Tills' plan, approved by bankruptcy court in confirming the plan, approved by four-Justice plurality of Supreme Court[458]).
>
> What is it? Start with the prime rate, then add a *"plus"* premium for the added risk of default for this debtor. Typically courts use a presumptive across-the-board "plus" (e.g., range of 1% to 3%) and then allow the creditor to try to prove more. Given this construct, this method is sometimes called *"prime plus."*
>
> 2. *"Coerced loan"* (district judge adopted in reversing bankruptcy court)
>
> What is it? "[T]he creditor is entitled to the rate of interest it could have obtained had it foreclosed and reinvested the proceeds in loans of equivalent duration and risk."[459] The notion is that this leaves the secured creditor as well off under the cram down plan as if it had been paid in full in cash at confirmation, because it then could have gone out and made a similar market loan with the foreclosure proceeds.
>
> 3. *"Presumptive contract rate"* (majority of Seventh Circuit panel,[460] favored by four-Justice dissent in Supreme Court[461])

---

[457] The plurality in *Till* defined the prime rate as "the financial market's estimate of the amount a commercial bank should charge a creditworthy commercial borrower to compensate for the opportunity costs of the loan, the risk of inflation, and the relatively slight risk of default." 541 U.S. at 479 (Stevens, J., plurality).

[458] Id. at 478–79 (Stevens, J., plurality).

[459] Koopmans v. Farm Credit Servs. of Mid–America, 102 F.3d 874, 875 (7th Cir. 1996). See also *Till*, 541 U.S. at 472 (Stevens, J., plurality).

[460] In re Till, 301 F.3d 583, 592–93 (7th Cir. 2002), rev'd, 541 U.S. 465 (2004).

[461] 541 U.S. at 492 (Scalia, J., dissenting).

What is it? The basic theory is the same as for "coerced loan," with the only difference being that the actual contract rate between the debtor and secured creditor on the loan at issue establishes presumptively the market rate for the "coerced loan." Adjustments up or (more likely) down then can be made upon proof by the creditor or debtor.

4.   *"Cost of funds"* (dissenting judge at Seventh Circuit[462])

What is it? The focus is on what it would cost the creditor to borrow an amount of money equal to the allowed secured claim (i.e., the "cost of funds" to the creditor), the idea being that the creditor in theory could use the borrowed money to make itself whole.

To appreciate the differences in these theories, a brief primer on interest rates would be helpful. Interest rates are the means by which we determine how much more valuable present money is than future money. As noted above, interest is the price of money, and the price of money is determined in the same manner as the price of anything else—by supply and demand in various markets for money. As the price of money, interest reflects the intuitive idea that people generally prefer to receive money sooner rather than later. This preference is not irrational.

Interest rates are comprised of several distinct components. As Justice Stevens explained in his plurality opinion in *Till*:

A debtor's promise of future payments is worth less than an immediate payment of the same total amount because the creditor cannot use the money right away, inflation may cause the value of the dollar to decline before the debtor pays, and there is always some risk of nonpayment.[463]

Of the foregoing, the most fundamental and non-controversial component of interest is the second one stated by Justice Stevens—compensation for *inflation*. In periods of positive inflation, money becomes less valuable over time and, thus, interest compensates those who forego present receipt and enjoyment of money for the devaluation of that money expected to occur over time. For example, ignoring everything else, if inflation is 3% per annum, for the value of $100 one year from now to be equal to $100 today, the future recipient would have to be paid 3% (i.e., $3) in addition to the $100 to be paid in one year. All approaches that courts have used to fix a cram down interest rate include compensation for inflation.

Over and above simple inflation compensation, though, interest rates are a reflection of the basic economic concept of *opportunity cost*. Devoting any resource— including money—to any particular use necessarily means foregoing all other possible uses. A creditor who is denied the immediate use and enjoyment of money through a cram down plan thus must be compensated for that lost opportunity cost. This is the first of the three components identified by Justice Stevens ("the creditor cannot use the

---

[462]   301 F.3d at 595–96 (Rovner, J., dissenting). See also In re Valenti, 105 F.3d 55, 64 (2d Cir. 1997).

[463]   541 U.S. at 474 (Stevens, J., plurality).

money right away"[464]). In terms of measuring the foregone return from other possible uses of money, at a minimum one could always invest money in U.S. Treasury obligations, which are considered "risk free" (or as close to a risk-free investment as there is). The interest rate on U.S. Treasury obligations, therefore, is known as the "*risk-free* rate," which contains compensation for inflation and so-called "pure" interest—compensation for the time value of money and nothing else. Again, all approaches for calculating a cram down interest rate agree that at the very least, the creditor must receive the "risk-free" rate. In the *Till* case, Justice Thomas in concurrence embraced the "risk-free" rate,[465] although none of the other eight Justices believed that rate to be sufficient.

The reason that eight Justices in *Till* rejected the risk-free rate is that it does not fully capture the opportunity cost of most uses of money, as virtually all uses of money of course are *not* risk free. Interest rates above the risk-free rate, thus, contain an additional measure of compensation—a so-called "risk premium"—to account for the risk inherent in the future receipts of money. If the first principle of finance is, as stated above, that "*a dollar today is worth more than a dollar tomorrow*,"[466] then a close second principle is that "*[a] safe dollar is worth more than a risky one*."[467] This is the third component of interest Justice Stevens identified ("there is always some risk of nonpayment"). It is in determining how to calculate the risk premium that the many cram down theories diverge, and the battle is joined.[468]

The theories that have enjoyed the most support in the courts—a support reflected in the Supreme Court in *Till,* where each garnered the support of four Justices—are the "formula" (or "prime plus") approach, on the one hand (favored by the plurality), and some variant of a "coerced loan" (or "contract") theory, on the other (favored by the dissent). As noted above, the latter approach actually has two common alternatives. The only difference between those two alternatives is whether the actual contract rate between the creditor and the debtor is deemed to be presumptively indicative of the appropriate market rate for the "coerced" loan the creditor effectively is being compelled to make to this debtor by forgoing immediate foreclosure and living with a cram down plan. The dissent in *Till* favored the "presumptive contract rate" approach. As will be discussed below, all of these approaches remain viable after *Till.*

A theory that had enjoyed a modicum of support prior to *Till,* but which now appears to be off the table, is the "*cost of funds*" approach. Eight Justices in *Till* (i.e., both the plurality and the dissent) rejected "cost of funds" as a method of fixing a cram down interest rate. The principle driving "cost of funds" was described as follows by Judge Rovner of the Seventh Circuit:

---

[464] Id.

[465] Id. at 487 (Thomas, J., concurring).

[466] See supra note 453 and accompanying text.

[467] Brealey & Myers, supra note 453, at 18.

[468] While Justice Thomas advocated in his concurrence in *Till* that the text of the Bankruptcy Code does not require a creditor to be compensated for risk, none of the other eight Justices agreed, and virtually no lower court has ever adopted a "risk-free" rate for cram down. After *Till,* one of the only things we know for certain is that a risk-free rate will not be enough.

Strictly speaking, the debtor's retention of the collateral does not preclude the creditor from making a new loan, it simply deprives the creditor of an asset that the creditor could convert into money and use to fund the new loan. A straightforward way to account for that deprivation is to ask what it would cost the creditor to obtain the cash equivalent of the collateral from an alternative source.[469]

In other words, the focus is not on the risk of non-payment *by the debtor* but instead on *the creditor's* ability to borrow sufficient money to replace the opportunity cost compelled via cram down. The major problems with cost-of-funds are: (1) it assumes that the crammed down creditor has unlimited borrowing capacity and that forcing a creditor to draw on its supply of credit is costless, both of which are demonstrably false; (2) even if the patent error of ignoring the reality of the creditor's marginal cost of borrowing is put aside for a moment, the practical difficulty for a court to identify the particular creditor's cost of funds is daunting; and (3) it ignores the core reason a cram down interest rate is necessary, which is that there is a positive risk that *this debtor* might default. In other words, as Justice Stevens explained in *Till*, the cost of funds approach "mistakenly focuses on the creditworthiness of the *creditor* rather than the debtor."[470]

Eight Justices of the Supreme Court thus agreed in *Till* that (1) the cram down interest rate must fully compensate the creditor for the risk of default by the debtor and (2) fixing that rate necessitates an inquiry into the market for interest rates in light of the specific risks posed by this debtor. Where they parted ways was over how best to approach the question. The methodological problem is acute because by definition the bankruptcy judge must try to resolve a counterfactual: what is the appropriate interest rate to compensate a secured creditor for the economic risks it suffers because it is not allowed to foreclose on a loan, but instead is forced to wait for full payment? The crammed down secured creditor is not actually making a loan to the debtor via cram down—it is simply not being permitted to collect immediately on a loan it made in the past—but the court must hypothesize as if the creditor were making a loan.

Both *Till* camps used a rule of thumb as a convenient starting point. The plurality favored starting with the prime rate—which is admittedly too low for a bankrupt debtor—and adjusting up, while the dissent preferred starting with the contract rate and possibly adjusting down. In theory the two could come out at the same place—although the reality in debtor-friendly bankruptcy courts is that the contract rate may be substantially higher (recall that in *Till* the contract rate was 21% and the formula method produced a rate of 9.5%).

Indeed, it is worth noting that there is no reason conceptually that the "coerced loan" approach could not be used as well as either the formula or presumptive contract theories, since it drives at exactly the same end result—identifying the proper rate of interest to account for the risk of nonpayment thrust upon this secured creditor by the

---

[469] *Till*, 301 F.3d at 595 (Rovner, C.J., dissenting).
[470] 541 U.S. at 478 (Stevens, J., plurality).

cram down. The only difference is that the coerced loan approach does not use any rules of thumb as a starting point; it simply asks, what is the market rate for a loan of similar duration and risk?

Following on that point, if actual, live lending markets were to develop for financing cram down loans, then there would be no need for judicial intervention at all, because the actual market—rather than the hypothetical market imagined by the judge—could be consulted, as Justice Stevens noted in footnote 14 in *Till*.[471] Drawing on footnote 14 in *Till,* some courts in chapter 11 cases have tried to compute the cram down interest rate by reference to what the actual, live "efficient market" lending rate is for such a chapter 11 debtor.[472] One court explained, "In determining whether there is an efficient market for a cramdown loan, a court must analyze the terms of the restructured debt, the type of collateral, the duration of the loan, and the amount of the loan."[473] If, however, there is no such efficient market, then courts routinely fall back to the formula method.[474]

The plurality opinion in *Till* noted the possible convergence of rates under the different theories, and highlighted the salient differences:

> [I]f all relevant information about the debtor's circumstances, the creditor's circumstances, the nature of the collateral, and the market for comparable loans were equally available to both debtor and creditor, *then in theory the formula and presumptive contract rate approaches would yield the same final interest rate.* Thus, we principally differ with the dissent not over what final rate courts should adopt but over which party (creditor or debtor) should bear the burden of rebutting the presumptive rate (prime or contract, respectively).[475]

Recall that under the formula approach, the beginning rule of thumb is to use the prime rate. Everyone (except Justice Thomas) agrees that number is too low. Only the best credit risks are offered the prime rate, by definition, and a bankrupt debtor is anything but. The risk of nonpayment by the debtor under the cram down plan must then be factored in through the use of the "plus" factor. If the calculation of the "plus" factor were taken seriously by the bankruptcy courts, and they actually tried to compute the likely risk of default for the debtor, then there would be little reason for a secured creditor to complain about the formula method, because the *Till* plurality is surely correct that creditors have access to much of the relevant information. But often the "plus" is not a real adjustment, and therein lies the rub. Because proof is difficult

---

[471] Justice Stevens observed that in chapter 11 there is a live market for DIP financing, which to the extent applicable could be consulted. He noted also that the absence of a similar market metric in chapter 13 compelled judicial estimation of imagined "market" rates. Id. at 476 n.14.

[472] See, e.g., In re Am. HomePatient, Inc., 420 F.3d 559, 568–69 (6th Cir. 2005).

[473] In re SW Boston Hotel Venture, LLC, 460 B.R. 38, 54 (Bankr. D. Mass. 2011) (citing Gen. Elec. Credit Equities, Inc. v. Brice Road Devs., LLC (In re Brice Road Devs., LLC), 392 B.R. 274, 280–81 (B.A.P. 6th Cir. 2008)). This court further observed: "Other courts have looked to tiered financing to determine whether a market interest rate exists. The tiered financing or band of investment approach calls for the court to consider whether the debtor can obtain a loan through a combination of different tranches of financing. The interest rates of these tranches are then blended to determine the appropriate rate." Id.

[474] E.g., *SW Boston Hotel*, supra note 473, at 55 (collecting cases).

[475] 541 U.S. at 484.

and time is short, courts routinely use a presumptive "plus" rate, normally somewhere between 1% and 3%. Justice Scalia saw this; looking at the lack of an evidentiary record supporting the 1.5% "plus" number used in *Till*, he quipped—probably correctly—that "it is impossible to view the 1.5% figure as anything other than a smallish number picked out of a hat."[476]

The Tills are a perfect case in point: in the real world, since they were very bad credit risks, they could only qualify for a subprime rate—21%, in the actual case. Yet they confirmed a "formula" based plan of 9.5%. How? Through the use of two presumptions—8% for the prime rate, and another 1.5% for the "plus"—coupled with a disinclination in the bankruptcy court to adjust any further, despite the obvious evidence that the Tills were far worse credit risks than a 9.5% rate would warrant.

This is the real complaint the *Till* dissent had; Justice Scalia stated, "I believe that, in practice, this approach will systematically undercompensate secured creditors for the true risks of default."[477] When a 21% debtor can get a 9.5% cramdown rate, it is hard to argue against the "undercompensation." point.

The *Till* plurality skirted the question; after noting that the issue of the size of the "plus" was not before the Court (although noting without approbation the routine approval of 1% to 3% "plus" plans in the lower courts), Justice Stevens suggested that the "feasibility" requirement for confirming a plan (e.g., § 1325(a)(6)) somehow mitigated the risk to the creditor.[478] If anything, though, the feasibility argument cuts the other way—a plan that pays too little to a creditor and exposes the creditor to excessive risk is more "feasible" for the debtor to perform. Nothing in the feasibility test speaks to whether *the creditor* is receiving adequate risk compensation; all that test asks is whether the debtor is likely to be able to make the payments called for—a task made easier the smaller those payments are.

Indeed, the real motivation of the plurality, one suspects, is revealed in Justice Stevens' comment that the bankruptcy court should "select a rate high enough to compensate the creditor for its risk *but not so high as to doom the plan*."[479] Interest rates, though, are supposed to compensate the creditor for risk, without taking into account how likely it is that the debtor can bear onerous payments. While the plurality acknowledged that at some level the need to use an "eye-popping" interest rate might simply require the bankruptcy judge to deny confirmation, one senses a judicial thumb

---

[476] Id. at 501 (Scalia, J., dissenting).

[477] Id. at 491–92. After analyzing the factors that appropriately should factor into an appropriate interest rate, Justice Scalia went on to add:

In sum, the 1.5% premium adopted in this case is far below anything approaching fair compensation. That result is not unusual, see, e.g., In re Valenti, 105 F.3d 55, 64 (C.A.2 1997) (recommending a 1%–3% premium over the *treasury* rate—i.e., approximately a 0% premium over prime); it is the entirely predictable consequence of a methodology that tells bankruptcy judges to set interest rates based on highly imponderable factors. Given the inherent uncertainty of the enterprise, what heartless bankruptcy judge can be expected to demand that the unfortunate debtor pay *triple* the prime rate as a condition of keeping his sole means of transportation? It challenges human nature.

Id. at 504 (emphasis in original).

[478] Id. at 480 (Stevens, J., plurality) (emphasis added).

[479] Id.

on the scales favoring plan confirmability, with the risk assessment calculus skewed to cut the debtor a break, rather than to fairly compensate the creditor. It is difficult to believe that the plurality actually thought that 9.5% was fair compensation for the creditor's risk in *Till*. But a 9.5% plan is a lot easier to perform than one paying 21%.

Justice Scalia also wondered about the wisdom and administrability of a system where the "plus" could be such a large potential part of the overall rate—in *Till*, for example, the prime rate was only 8% and the contract rate was 21%, suggesting a possible "plus" range of up to 13%. As he noted, "When the risk premium is the greater part of the overall rate, the formula approach no longer depends on objective and easily ascertainable numbers. The prime rate becomes the objective tail wagging a dog of unknown size."[480]

The approach favored by the *Till* dissent took the parties' *contract rate* (here, 21%) as presumptively indicative of the market rate for a "coerced loan" of "similar" duration and risk, and thus the proper cram down rate. What better objective market criteria could there be than what the parties themselves, operating in the marketplace, had agreed to? If the debtors wanted to argue for a lower rate, on the grounds that the pertinent factors shaping an appropriate market interest rate applicable *now* had changed since the parties first agreed to the contract, they were free to do so. Otherwise, though, "[s]ince that rate is generally a good indicator of actual risk, disputes should be infrequent, and it will provide a quick and reasonably accurate standard."[481]

The only reasons to doubt the accuracy of the contract rate would be: (1) a belief that the market itself is not competitive, and thus the rates charged in contracts are not reflective of actual risk; (2) even if the contract rate was reflective of the market when executed, things have changed to alter the risk assessment; or (3) an assessment that there is something innately different about risks (for better or worse) in a bankruptcy reorganization case. Even if there were some credence in these concerns, it still would be fair to ask why the bankruptcy court could not be trusted to account for the differences and adjust downward, just as the plurality was content to let bankruptcy judges start with a rate they knew to a certainty was too *low*—the prime rate—and adjust up, and whether the risk of *over*-compensation that would result from a "contract minus" adjustment approach would be greater than the risk of *under*-compensation from the "prime plus" system favored by the plurality. When the numbers show a prime rate of 8%, a contract rate of 21%, and an "adjusted" rate of 9.5%, the under-compensation pitch seems to carry more heft.

Much of the difference between the plurality and the dissent in *Till* is likely attributable to their views as to the issues framed in the preceding paragraph, and especially as to whether the subprime market is competitive. Justice Stevens argues that "several considerations suggest that the subprime market is not, in fact, perfectly competitive," and "that unregulated subprime lenders would exploit borrowers'

---

[480] Id. at 499 (Scalia, J., dissenting).
[481] Id. at 492.

ignorance and charge rates above what a competitive market would allow."[482] In contrast, Justice Scalia counters that it is a "reasonable" assumption that

> subprime lending markets are competitive and therefore largely efficient. If so, the high interest rates lenders charge reflect not extortionate profits or excessive costs, but the actual risks of default that subprime borrowers present. Lenders with excessive rates would be undercut by their competitors, and inefficient ones would be priced out of the market.[483]

On this count, the calamitous financial events of 2008 appear to back Justice Scalia's view of the world. If anything, the economic meltdown of 2008 demonstrates that subprime lenders were not charging enough, rather than the other way around. Justice Stevens' suggestion that subprime lenders were able (absent regulation) to charge excessive above-market rates now sounds a sadly quaint, and obviously erroneous, refrain.

The second major point of difference between the plurality and the dissent is over the second and third points above, summed up together in Justice Scalia's "assumption . . . that the expected costs of default in Chapter 13 are normally no less than those at the time of lending."[484] Justice Stevens argues that creditors in cram down bankruptcy plans are better off economically than they are outside of bankruptcy, observing that a true market theory (be it "coerced loan" or "presumptive contract") "overcompensates creditors because the market lending rate must be high enough to cover factors, like lenders' transaction costs and overall profits, that are no longer relevant in the context of court-administered and court-supervised cramdown loans."[485] Apparently for the plurality this "overcompensation" warrants a "haircut" of over half of the contract rate! At the same time, there are many ways in which a debtor that is already in bankruptcy is a *worse* credit risk than outside, a fact demonstrated by the extraordinarily high failure rate of chapter 13 plans. To support a presumptive contract rate, though, one only need agree with the dissent that "it does not strike me as plausible that creditors would *prefer* to lend to individuals already in bankruptcy than to those for whom bankruptcy is merely a possibility—as if Chapter 13 were widely viewed by secured creditors as some sort of godsend. . . . The better assumption is that bankrupt debtors are riskier than other subprime debtors—or, at the very least, not systematically *less* risky."[486]

Looking only at the interest rate issue, the dissent in *Till* appears to have the better of the argument. If you doubt that point, put aside all the economic and legal arguments detailed above, and try to be honest with yourself when you answer the following questions: do you think that interest of 9.5% is fair compensation for a creditor forced to accept payments from a debtor who is already in bankruptcy, on a subprime loan with an original interest rate of 21%? If you were that creditor, would

---

[482] Id. at 481, 482 (Stevens, J., plurality).

[483] Id. at 492 (Scalia, J., dissenting).

[484] Id. at 492–93.

[485] Id. at 477 (Stevens, J., plurality).

[486] Id. at 494 (Scalia, J., dissenting) (emphasis in original).

you be indifferent to being paid cash in full up front or being paid 9.5% over a period of years?

One good thing that can be said about the *Till* plurality's seemingly under-compensatory "formula" approach to setting a cram down interest rate is that it could have the serendipitous effect of two wrongs making a right. Recall that cram down of a creditor's secured claim has *two* components: the amount of the allowed secured claim (which sets the "principal" that must be repaid in cram down), and the rate of interest. In the prior section,[487] this treatise takes the position that the Supreme Court got the wrong answer on the first part in *Associates Commercial Corp. v. Rash*,[488] by requiring a debtor to pay *replacement value* as the creditor's allowed secured claim. Since the creditor could not possibly recover that much if the debtor simply surrendered the collateral to it and the creditor foreclosed, using replacement value arguably *over*-compensates the secured creditor in cram down. So, in cram down the beginning *principal* amount to be paid is too high. *Till*'s plurality decision, though, calls for too little to be paid in *interest*, thus *under*-compensating the secured creditor. Put it all together, and you have too little interest being paid on too much principal—maybe it all comes out right in the end!

So where do we stand after *Till* on cram down interest rates? To recap the bidding, under *Till:*

1. Four Justices (Plurality) approved formula, and rejected cost of funds, risk-free, coerced loan, and presumptive contract.

2. Four Justices (Dissent) approved presumptive contract, and rejected cost of funds, risk-free, and formula; probably amenable to coerced loan.

3. One Justice (Concurrence) approved risk-free, and would uphold, over creditor's objection, anything that paid creditor that much or more.

We thus know that there are eight votes against risk-free and cost of funds, so those go into the legal dustbin. Given the fact that the concurrence (Justice Thomas) will uphold as against the secured creditor's objection any method that proposes to pay the creditor as much or more than risk-free—which of course means every other method still on the table, including formula, presumptive contract, and coerced loan—the odd result is that there would be five votes in the Supreme Court to approve over objection a plan that proposed *any* of the following methods: formula, presumptive contract, and (probably) coerced loan. That oddity means that the plan proponent has enormous power to pick the method that requires them to pay the lowest interest rate.

In chapters 12 and 13, of course, the debtor will always be the plan proponent, and thus can choose which of the three methods carries the lowest interest rate. Note that it is not necessarily the case that "formula" will always be the lowest rate; as interest rates move up and down over time, any of the three possible methods potentially could yield the lowest rate. To give but one example, assume that debtor takes out a car loan

---

[487] See § 7.29.

[488] 520 U.S. 953 (1997).

in the fall of 2012, with a contract rate of 6.6%, and then files bankruptcy under chapter 13 three years later, when market interest rates for loans of similar duration and risk are 9.5%, and when the prime rate is 8%. That debtor should propose a plan using the contract rate of 6.6%, because it would be lower than either the formula or coerced loan methods, both of which likely would require around 9.5%. While the contract rate is only "presumptive," leaving the creditor free to argue for an upward adjustment for risk, good luck persuading a bankruptcy court that a creditor should be able to recover more than their contract rate.

In chapter 11, the plan proponent potentially could be either the debtor *or* another party, if the debtor's exclusive right to file a plan terminates under § 1121(c).[489] The plan proponent could then choose the cram down interest rate that most favored them, and should be able to overcome any objection.

§ 7.31   Postpetition Interest on Secured Claims

The general rule in bankruptcy cases is and long has been that creditors may *not* recover postpetition interest. Section 502(b)(2) disallows a claim for unmatured interest. Prior to 1978, however, case law had recognized an exception to this general rule for consensual oversecured creditors, who were permitted to recover interest, fees, and charges after the bankruptcy filing out of their excess security.[490]The exception was justified on the ground that it protected the reasonable expectations of creditors who had bargained for a security cushion.[491] Nonconsensual liens (typically tax liens), which by definition lacked any such bargained-for expectations, were not awarded postpetition interest or fees under pre-Code law.[492]

This judge-made rule was codified in § 506(b), which provides:

> To the extent that an allowed secured claim is secured by property the value of which, after any recovery under subsection (c) of this section, is greater than the amount of such claim, there shall be allowed to the holder of such claim, interest on such claim, and any reasonable fees, costs, or charges provided for under the agreement or State statute under which such claim arose.

The rule of § 506(b) thus permits an oversecured creditor to recover postpetition interest, to the extent the creditor's claim is oversecured.[493] In addition, a consensual secured creditor may recover out of the excess security reasonable fees, costs, and charges that are provided for in the parties' agreement. Furthermore, after a 2005 amendment added "or State statute" in the final clause,[494] an oversecured creditor may assert a right to fees, costs, or charges that are allowed under a state statute, even

---

[489]   See § 11.15.

[490]   See Vanston Bondholders Protective Comm. v. Green, 329 U.S. 156 (1946); Sexton v. Dreyfus, 219 U.S. 339 (1911).

[491]   See In re Boston & Maine Corp., 719 F.2d 493 (1st Cir. 1983), cert. denied, 466 U.S. 938 (1984).

[492]   See, e.g., United States v. Harrington, 269 F.2d 719 (4th Cir. 1959).

[493]   See David Gray Carlson, Postpetition Interest Under the Bankruptcy Code, 43 U. Miami L. Rev. 577 (1989).

[494]   Pub. L. No. 109–8, § 712(d)(1), 119 Stat. 128 (2005).

without an agreement; Congress apparently was thinking of state tax claims when it passed the amendment.

A simple example will illustrate the application of § 506(b). When Debtor files bankruptcy, it is in default to Creditor on a principal debt of $10,000, with interest of 10% per annum. The agreement entitles Creditor to recover attorneys' fees of five percent if the Debtor is in default. The debt is secured by a lien on collateral worth $15,000. A year into the case, the collateral is sold for a net of $15,000, after deducting the costs of the sale. Creditor is entitled to receive $11,500 of the proceeds: (1) $10,000 for its principal debt; (2) $1,000 for the year of postpetition interest at 10%; and (3) $500 in attorneys' fees.

The biggest dispute under the Code in applying § 506(b) has been over whether the entitlement to interest applies to *nonconsensual* creditors as well as consensual creditors. As noted above, pre-Code law drew a distinction between the two, allowing postpetition interest only to *consensual* lienholders. However, the Supreme Court held in *United States v. Ron Pair Enterprises, Inc.*,[495] that the plain language of § 506(b) indicated a change in the law. According to the *Ron Pair* Court, § 506(b) unambiguously allows nonconsensual lienholders to recover postpetition interest to the extent they are oversecured. The Court placed dispositive significance on the comma between the phrases "interest on such claim" and "and any reasonable fees, costs, or charges provided for under the agreement." The Court concluded that the limitation to what was "provided for under the agreement" did not extend past the comma to qualify "interest on such claim." The four dissenting Justices found it hard to believe that Congress intended to change well-settled pre-Code practice without even a hint in the legislative history through the adroit use of a comma.[496]

Even after *Ron Pair*, an oversecured *nonconsensual* lien will not be entitled to recover any postpetition fees, costs, charges, or penalties,[497] *unless* (after the 2005 amendment) specifically provided for in a state statute. The only other way such charges are allowed is if they are "provided for under the agreement," and of course there is no agreement for nonconsensual liens. Even with regard to interest on nonconsensual liens, some courts have held after *Ron Pair* that in appropriate circumstances, equitable considerations such as estoppel may authorize the bankruptcy court to deny or modify the allowance of postpetition interest.[498]

For consensual liens, fees (such as attorneys' fees), costs and charges may be allowed out of the excess security if provided for in the agreement between the debtor and the creditor. Indeed, most courts have held that the creditor may recover attorneys' fees that were agreed to even if such fees would not be allowed under the

---

[495] 489 U.S. 235 (1989).

[496] Id. at 249–51 (O'Connor, J., dissenting).

[497] See, e.g., In re Brentwood Outpatient, Ltd., 43 F.3d 256 (6th Cir. 1994), cert. denied, 514 U.S. 1096 (1995). See also In re Parr Meadows Racing Ass'n, 880 F.2d 1540 (2d Cir. 1989), cert. denied, 493 U.S. 1058 (1990) (postpetition tax penalties disallowed).

[498] See In re Lapiana, 909 F.2d 221 (7th Cir. 1990).

governing state law.[499] The rationale is that the federal law in § 506(b) preempts inconsistent state law.

Application of the rule of § 506(b) obviously requires a valuation of the creditor's collateral. The entitlement to postpetition interest only applies to the extent that the creditor is oversecured, which can only be determined by comparing the value of the collateral with the amount of the debt. If the creditor is *under*secured, the Supreme Court made clear in the *Timbers* case that postpetition interest is not allowable, even under the guise of "adequate protection."[500] If the collateral is sold in the bankruptcy case, the sales price will dictate the collateral value.[501] Otherwise, the court will have to value the collateral. Valuation will follow either from the standards in § 506(a)(1) and the Supreme Court decision in *Associates Commercial Corp. v. Rash,*[502] or from § 506(a)(2) for personal property collateral for an individual debtor in chapter 7 or 13.[503] That means that if the debtor is retaining the collateral, value will be at "replacement value," which would be retail value in cases governed by subsection (a)(2). If, however, the collateral is being sold in the bankruptcy case, and if subsection (a)(2) is not applicable, then that "proposed disposition" under subsection (a)(1) would dictate a liquidation or foreclosure sale value.

Another important question that arises in applying § 506(b) is identifying the appropriate rate of interest. Most courts have used the contract rate.[504] If the debtor was in default, the issue then will be whether the proper contract rate is the standard rate or the higher default rate. Many courts have allowed use of the default rate, as long as it is not unreasonably high.[505] A few courts reject the contract rate, opting instead for a federal "reasonable" rate of interest, usually at the prevailing market rate.[506]

In 1993 the Supreme Court held in *Rake v. Wade* that an oversecured creditor was entitled to postpetition interest on arrearages under § 506(b) *even if* neither the parties' agreement nor applicable state law provided for interest on arrearages.[507] In 1994, Congress overruled *Rake* in reorganization cases, providing that interest on arrearages will only be allowed to the extent authorized by the agreement of the parties or applicable law. §§ 1123(d), 1222(d), 1322(e). This amendment did not affect the application of *Rake* in chapter 7, however.

---

[499] See, e.g., In re Schrlock Constr., Inc., 104 F.3d 200 (8th Cir. 1997); In re K.H. Stephenson Supply Co., 768 F.2d 580 (4th Cir. 1985).

[500] United Savs. Ass'n of Texas v. Timbers of Inwood Forest Assocs., Ltd., 484 U.S. 365 (1988). See § 3.19.

[501] See Ford Motor Credit Co. v. Dobbins, 35 F.3d 860 (4th Cir. 1994).

[502] 520 U.S. 953 (1997).

[503] See § 7.29.

[504] See, e.g., Gen. Elec. Corp. v. Future Media Prods., Inc. 547 F.3d 956 (9th Cir. 2008); In re Laymon, 958 F.2d 72 (5th Cir.), cert. denied, 506 U.S. 917 (1992).

[505] See, e.g., In re Terry Ltd. P'ship, 27 F.3d 241 (7th Cir. 1994), cert. denied, 513 U.S. 948 (1994).

[506] See, e.g., In re Colegrove, 771 F.2d 119 (6th Cir. 1985).

[507] 508 U.S. 464 (1993).

§ 7.32 Lien Stripping and the Treatment of Undersecured Claims

a. Introduction

A pervasive issue in bankruptcy cases concerns the manner of treating an *undersecured* creditor. A creditor is "undersecured" when the collateral securing the creditor's claim is worth less than the total debt. For example, a debt of $10,000 secured by collateral worth $7,000 is undersecured.

The analysis of undersecured claims must begin with § 506(a)(1) of the Code. That section provides for the *bifurcation* of the undersecured claim into (1) a secured claim up to the value of the collateral[508] and (2) an unsecured claim for the deficiency balance.[509] In the example given above, the creditor would be deemed to hold a secured claim equal to $7,000 (the collateral value) and an unsecured claim equal to $3,000 (the difference between the $10,000 total claim and the $7,000 secured claim).

Note one apparent drafting quirk in the 2005 amendment that added § 506(a)(2), dealing with the valuation of personal property collateral of individual debtors in chapter 7 or 13 cases. That subsection specifies the valuation standard in such cases. It says nothing, however, about *bifurcation* of undersecured claims, and there is no reason to think Congress intended to abolish bifurcation in such cases.[510] Apparently Congress still intended for subsection (a)(2) cases to be governed by the bifurcation principles in subsection (a)(1), notwithstanding the lack of any connecting referents between the two subsections.[511]

As discussed in an earlier section,[512] the basic substantive entitlement of a secured creditor in a bankruptcy case is to receive the value of its collateral.[513] While the secured creditor cannot insist in bankruptcy on exercising the full panoply of procedural rights that it would have outside of bankruptcy (especially repossession on default and foreclosure), the secured creditor does retain the right to be paid in full, ultimately, on the secured portion of its claim. In the above example, the secured creditor has a right to be paid $7,000—the value of its collateral[514]—by some means.[515] As will be discussed in the next subsection of this treatise, there are three exceptions in

---

[508] The relevant part of § 506(a)(1) provides that the claim "is a secured claim to the extent of the value of such creditor's interest in the estate's interest in such property."

[509] Section 506(a)(1) goes on to provide that the creditor's allowed claim "is an unsecured claim to the extent that the value of such creditor's interest . . . is less than the amount of such allowed claim."

[510] Indeed, Congress showed in the 2005 amendments that it did know how to abolish bifurcation, because it did precisely that for cases covered by the "hanging paragraph" following § 1325(a).

[511] Textual support for this conclusion lies in the use of the words "such value" in subsection (a)(2), which can only refer to subsection (a)(1), there being no antecedent reference to "value" in subsection (a)(2) itself for the "such" to modify.

[512] See § 7.27.

[513] The Supreme Court held in *Wright v. Union Cent. Life Ins. Co.*, 311 U.S. 273, 278 (1940) that secured creditors are entitled to be protected "to the extent of the value of the property. There is no constitutional claim of the creditor to more than that." See Charles J. Tabb, Credit Bidding, Security, and the Obsolescence of Chapter 11, 2013 U. Ill. L. Rev. 103, 108, 115–17 (2013).

[514] The problems involved in valuing collateral are discussed in § 7.29.

[515] The different ways that a secured claim may be satisfied in bankruptcy are discussed in § 7.28.

reorganization cases where an undersecured creditor is supposed to be paid the full amount of the debt, rather than the just the value of the collateral.

b. *Reorganization Cases*

In reorganization cases, the norm is for the debtor to retain the collateral and to pay the secured creditor the value of the allowed secured claim over time.[516] The payments made under the plan on the secured claim must be discounted to insure that the present value of those payments is at least as much as the collateral value. In practice, this means that interest must be paid on the secured claim under the plan. This reorganization treatment of secured claims is referred to colloquially as "cram down," the idea being that the plan is "crammed down" the secured creditor's throat, whether they like it or not. Two issues predominate in cram down: what is the value of the collateral,[517] and what is the proper interest rate?[518] The Supreme Court in *Rash* summarized the reorganization cram down rules as follows: "Under the cram down option, the debtor is permitted to keep the property over the objection of the creditor; the creditor retains the lien securing the claim, and the debtor is required to provide the creditor with payments, over the life of the plan, that will total the present value of the allowed secured claim, *i.e.,* the present value of the collateral."[519]

In the example in the preceding subsection (assuming none of the exceptions apply), the creditor in a chapter 11, 12, or 13 case would be entitled to retain its lien on the collateral and to receive payments on a principal secured debt of $7,000 (the value of the collateral) plus an appropriate interest rate. Alternatively, the debtor could simply return the collateral to the secured creditor. § 1129(b)(2)(A)(iii) (chapter 11) (surrender = "indubitable equivalent"); § 1225(a)(5)(C) (chapter 12); § 1325(a)(5)(C) (chapter 13). Finally, of course, it is always possible for the secured creditor to agree to different treatment. § 1129(a)(8), (b)(1) (chapter 11); § 1225(a)(5)(A) (chapter 12); § 1325(a)(5)(A) (chapter 13)

A crucial feature of this approach to undersecured claims in the reorganization chapters is that it permits the debtor to *"strip down"* the secured claim to the judicially appraised value of the collateral, even if the total allowed claim is greater. In the example, a debtor who is able to confirm a reorganization plan no longer is required to pay the creditor based on a $10,000 claim; instead, the *principal* balance of the claim has been stripped down to the $7,000 collateral value. The claim for the unsecured balance of $3,000 will be treated separately, in accordance with the rules applicable to the payment of unsecured claims.[520]

Some special rules in the reorganization chapters limit the ability of the debtor to effectuate a strip down in limited circumstances. There are three exceptions to the

---

[516] See § 11.32 (discussing cram down of secured claims in chapter 11 cases pursuant to § 1129(b)(2)(A) and related provisions); § 12.18 (same for chapter 13 cases, pursuant to § 1325(a)(5)). The rights of secured creditors in chapter 12 are much the same as in chapter 13, subject to some exceptions in chapter 13 that do not apply in chapter 12. See § 1225(a)(5).

[517] See § 7.29.

[518] See § 7.30.

[519] 520 U.S. 953, 957 (1997).

[520] See § 7.26.

standard cram down rules explained above. One is in chapter 11 only; one is for home mortgages, in chapter 11 or 13; and one is in chapter 13 only.

The first is if a secured creditor in chapter 11 makes the "§ 1111(b) election." In chapter 11, an undersecured class is entitled to elect to have their entire claim treated as secured and to waive the unsecured portion of their claim.[521] § 1111(b)(2). However, an undersecured class that makes the § 1111(b)(1) election is only entitled to receive payments with a *present value*, as of the effective date of the plan, equal to the value of the collateral. § 1129(a)(7)(B). In our example, an electing class would be entitled to payments under the plan totaling $10,000 (the total allowed claim) but which are worth only $7,000 (the collateral value) when discounted to present value. The benefit of electing under § 1111(b) is that the creditor avoids strip down and obtains thereby the benefit of any post-confirmation appreciation in (or correction for judicial under-valuation of) the value of the collateral if the debtor defaults. In our example, assume that the debtor defaults on payments under the plan, at a time when the collateral securing the claim has increased to $9,000 in value. Without the election, the creditor would be entitled to assert a secured claim against only $7,000 of that collateral value, since the plan would have previously stripped the allowed secured claim down to $7,000. With the election, however, the creditor's "allowed secured claim" is still $10,000, and the entire $9,000 value of the collateral will be subject to that claim. The *quid pro quo* for making the election is that the undersecured creditor must waive its entire unsecured claim.

The second exception to strip down, applicable in both chapters 11 and 13, is for *home mortgages*.[522] As a general rule, a plan may modify the rights of holders of secured claims, as long as the underlying value of the secured claim is eventually paid. Strip down of an undersecured lien is a common type of modification. Strip down is prohibited, however, with regard to "a claim secured only by a security interest in real property that is the debtor's principal residence." § 1123(b)(5) (chapter 11); § 1322(b)(2) (chapter 13). In other words, the rights of the holder of a home mortgage may not be modified in chapter 13 or chapter 11. This special rule was adopted for chapter 13 cases in the Code in 1978 in order to protect the flow of capital into the home lending market. The rule was extended to chapter 11 cases in 1994.

The 111th Congress seriously considered several bills that would for the first time allow a debtor to modify her home mortgage—including strip down—in chapter 13 (but not in chapter 11). President Obama campaigned for such a change in the bankruptcy law in the 2008 election, in order to afford distressed homeowners an opportunity to save their homes. His campaigning on these issues was unsuccessful, however, and strip down is still not allowed in chapter 11 or 13.

Prior to 1993, the case law was divided over whether § 1322(b)(2) did in fact operate to prevent strip down in chapter 13 cases. Most circuit courts had held that the

---

[521] This election is discussed in Tabb, supra note 513, at 121–23.

[522] Political junkies may recall that the home mortgage anti-strip-down rule was raised in the 2008 presidential campaign, in the wake of the economic collapse of 2008. Then—Senator Obama advocated repealing this rule, so that homeowners would be able to modify their mortgages in bankruptcy. See http://www.ontheissues.org/senate/barack_obama.htm.

anti-modification rule of § 1322(b)(2) for home mortgages only applied to the *secured* portion of the claim.[523] On this view, strip down would be permissible. The reasoning of those courts was that (1) § 506(a)(1) automatically bifurcates an undersecured claim into a "secured claim" up to the value of the collateral and an "unsecured claim" for the balance, and (2) the anti-modification provision in § 1322(b)(2) refers only to "secured claims," as defined in § 506(a)(1).

In 1993, the Supreme Court held in *Nobelman v. American Savings Bank*[524] that § 1322(b)(2) does prevent the modification of an undersecured home mortgage. The Nobelmans owed the bank a total debt of over $71,335 on a Dallas condominium worth only $23,500. The debtors proposed a plan that would pay the mortgagee a total present value of $23,500, the amount of the "allowed secured claim." The Supreme Court concluded that the prohibition on modification referred to the *rights* of the holder of the secured claim, rather than just the secured claim itself.[525] Those rights included, among other things, the right to be paid the full principal balance of the debt (i.e., the $71,335), with interest over the agreed term. The Court did not see how the debtor could at the same time strip down the principal balance of the secured claim to $23,500 and yet not "modify" any of the rights of the mortgagee. Something—the term of the payments, the amount of the monthly payment, or the interest rate—would have to be changed, and that would constitute an impermissible modification.[526] Therefore, the Nobelmans could confirm their chapter 13 plan only if they paid the bank the full $71,335 under the plan, on the original terms of the note. The only relief allowed to debtors regarding a home mortgage is to cure a default and, if the creditor had accelerated the balance due, to reinstate the original maturity. § 1124(2) (chapter 11); § 1322(b)(3), (5), (c)(1) (chapter 13). Strip down, however, is prohibited.

In a curious aftermath to *Nobelman*, Congress apparently partially overruled that decision in the 1994 amendments to the Code.[527] In the 1994 legislation, Congress added § 1322(c)(2), which applies to short-term home mortgages, i.e., ones that mature before the final payment is due under the chapter 13 plan. For example, if a home mortgage loan has four years left to run, and the debtor proposes a five-year plan, § 1322(c)(2) would apply. Significantly, (c)(2) applies "notwithstanding subsection (b)(2)"—which is the anti-modification provision that was given effect in *Nobelman*. Since (c)(2) has primacy over (b)(2), the anti-modification rule enforced by *Nobelman* will not apply to cases within the ambit of (c)(2)'s coverage. When applicable, § 1322(c)(2) allows the debtor's plan to "provide for the payment of the claim as modified pursuant to section 1325(a)(5)"—the cram down provision. Modification of the creditor's "claim" under § 1325(a)(5) would permit strip down of an undersecured home mortgage.

---

[523] See, e.g., In re Bellamy, 962 F.2d 176 (2d Cir. 1992); In re Hart, 923 F.2d 1410 (10th Cir. 1991); Wilson v. Commonwealth Mortg. Corp., 895 F.2d 123 (3d Cir. 1990); In re Hougland, 886 F.2d 1182 (9th Cir. 1989).

[524] 508 U.S. 324 (1993).

[525] Id. at 328–29.

[526] Id. at 331–32.

[527] Pub. L. No. 103–393, § 301, 108 Stat. 4106, (1994).

The "plain meaning" of § 1322(c)(2) thus appears to allow the strip down of an undersecured home mortgage that will mature (under the original payment schedule) before the end of the plan. Most courts have given the statute this literal effect and allow strip down of short-term undersecured home mortgages in chapter 13 where the original maturity is before the last payment due under the plan.[528] A few courts have not, and have read the statutory text more narrowly, so that the "as modified" language modifies only "payment," rather than the immediate antecedent, "claim."[529] Under this minority view, the debtor may cure defaults on short-term mortgages and modify the payment schedule so that payments may be made over the life of the plan, but may not strip down an undersecured home mortgage.

Whatever the impact of § 1322(c)(2), there is no doubt that *Nobelman* still controls and that § 1322(b)(2) prevents the strip down of an undersecured home mortgage for home mortgages that mature *after* the last payment is due under the plan. For such mortgages, § 1322(c)(2) does not apply. As a practical matter, this general rule still should apply in most cases, for the simple reason that a mortgage with less than five years left to run is not likely to be undersecured, unless it calls for a large final balloon payment.

An ongoing issue in the courts is whether the *Nobelman* anti-strip-down rule for home mortgages applies when the creditor's "allowed secured claim" is completely worthless. This could happen to a *second mortgage* where the collateral value is less than the amount of the first mortgage. Assume, for example, a second mortgage that secures a $25,000 claim, which is junior to a first mortgage that secures a $200,000 claim. When the debtor files bankruptcy, the home is worth only $195,000. Under § 506(a)(1), the "allowed secured claim" of the second mortgagee is $0, because the first mortgage consumes the entire collateral value. In this scenario, a substantial majority of courts, including all circuit courts to decide the question, have held that strip down (which in this situation they refer to as "strip *off*") is permitted and that *Nobelman* does not apply.[530] For those courts, the second mortgagee cannot fairly be considered a "holder of [a] secured claim" within the meaning of § 1322(b)(2), because by reference to § 506(a)(1) the second mortgagee does not have a "secured" claim at all. Courts embracing the minority view,[531] that strip down is prohibited even for valueless home mortgages, emphasize that the *Nobelman* Court focused on the reference in § 1322(b)(2) to the "rights" of the holder of a secured claim, rather than on the value (if any!) of the secured claim itself. Those minority courts conclude that the second

---

[528] E.g., In re Paschen, 296 F.3d 1203 (11th Cir. 2002); In re Eubanks, 219 B.R. 468 (B.A.P. 6th Cir. 1998); In re Young, 199 B.R. 643 (Bankr. E.D. Tenn. 1996).

[529] E.g., In re Witt, 113 F.3d 508 (4th Cir. 1997). These courts rely heavily on the legislative history, which gives no indication that Congress thought it was altering the *Nobelman* result, even in part. To the contrary, in another part of the 1994 bill, Congress extended the chapter 13 anti-modification rule for home mortgages to chapter 11. See § 1123(b)(5). The stated purpose of § 1322(c)(2) was to overrule a Third Circuit decision that had nothing to do with the *Nobelman* problem. H.R. Rep. No. 103–835, 103rd Cong., 2d Sess. at 52 (1994).

[530] See In re Zimmer, 313 F.3d 1220 (9th Cir. 2002); In re Lane, 280 F.3d 663 (6th Cir. 2002); In re Pond, 252 F.3d 122 (2d Cir. 2001); In re Tanner, 217 F.3d 1357 (11th Cir. 2000); In re Bartee, 212 F.3d 277 (5th Cir. 2000); In re McDonald, 205 F.3d 606 (3d Cir.), cert. denied, 531 U.S. 822 (2000). A subsequent Eleventh Circuit panel said that it would have decided the other way, but was constrained by circuit precedent (*Tanner*). See In re Dickerson, 222 F.3d 924 (11th Cir. 2000).

[531] See, e.g., In re Barnes, 207 B.R. 588 (Bankr. N.D. Ill. 1997).

mortgagee in our example plainly has "rights" in the collateral, even if those rights might prove valueless at the present. Under the majority view, note that valuation could play a momentous role. In our example, if the court valued the home at $200,001, rather than at $195,000, then the second mortgagee *would* be the "holder of a secured claim" (in the amount of $1!) and then indisputably under *Nobelman* would have to be paid in full.

The third and final exception to the general strip down rule, applicable only in chapter 13, was added in 2005 as an unnumbered paragraph (now commonly known as the "hanging paragraph") following § 1325(a).[532] The primary probable intent of the "hanging paragraph" was to limit strip down for car loans,[533] although respected commentators debate whether Congress successfully accomplished that goal.[534] The provision is sufficiently confusing to merit inclusion here in full:

> For purposes of paragraph (5), section 506 shall not apply to a claim described in that paragraph if the creditor has a purchase money security interest securing the debt that is the subject of the claim, the debt was incurred within the 910–day period preceding the date of the filing of the petition, and the collateral for that debt consists of a motor vehicle (as defined in section 30102 of title 49) acquired for the personal use of the debtor, or if collateral for that debt consists of any other thing of value, if the debt was incurred during the 1–year period preceding that filing.

The hanging paragraph's scope is limited. It applies in two alternative scenarios: (1) where the creditor has a "purchase money security interest"; the debt was incurred within 910 days of bankruptcy (about 2½ years); the collateral is a "motor vehicle"; and the collateral was purchased for the "personal use" of the debtor; or (2) for any collateral that is a "thing of value" (what would *not* qualify?), and the debt was incurred within one year of bankruptcy. The predominant congressional focus was on the first type, which was to protect relatively new car purchase loans, now called "910" claims in recognition of the look-back period.

The probable intended operation of the hanging paragraph, to be effected through its provision that "section 506 shall not apply" for purposes of § 1325(a)(5), is to preclude the bifurcation of undersecured claims that fall within the scope of the hanging paragraph, and accordingly to stop the strip down of undersecured claims (especially "910" car PMSI loans) under § 1325(a)(5)(B). Bifurcation normally occurs

---

[532] Pub. L. No. 109–8, § 306(b), 119 Stat. 80 (2005).

[533] See William C. Whitford, A History of the Automobile Lender Provisions of BAPCPA, 2007 U. Ill. L. Rev. 143, 150–51 (2007). See also David Gray Carlson, Cars and Homes in Chapter 13 After the 2005 Amendments to the Bankruptcy Code, 14 Am. Bankr. Inst. L. Rev. 301, 340–41 (2006). Professor Whitford exhaustively examines the history of BAPCPA, and explains that the "hanging paragraph" was first introduced early in the reform process by Senator Abraham of the state of Michigan, acting at the behest of the automobile finance industry. 2007 U. Ill. L. Rev. at 177–78. It is virtually certain that the intent was to block strip down of car loans covered by the amendment.

Furthermore, the title of the amendment in BAPCPA is "Restoring the Foundation for Secured Credit," which suggests rather strongly a pro-creditor intention. See note 25.

[534] See Jean Braucher, *Rash* and Ride–Through Redux: The Terms for Holding on to Cars, Homes, and Other Collateral Under the 2005 Act, 13 Am. Bankr. Inst. L. Rev. 457, 469–74 (2005).

because of the language in § 506(a)(1) that a claim "is a secured claim to the extent of the value of such creditor's interest in the estate's interest in such property . . . and is an unsecured claim to the extent that the value of such creditor's interest . . . is less than the amount of such allowed claim." The thinking of the auto industry in pushing for this amendment likely was that by providing that "section 506 shall not apply" under § 1325(a)(5), bifurcation would not be possible, and the entire allowed claim would then be secured. A debtor who wanted to cram down an auto lender under § 1325(a)(5)(B) and retain the collateral then would have to pay the creditor the full amount of the debt (plus interest), rather than just the stripped-down collateral value. Certainly many courts have so interpreted this provision.[535]

One could debate whether simply providing that "section 506 shall not apply" was sufficient to get the intended job done.[536] First, observe that § 1325(a)(5) *does* still apply. Second, cram down of an "allowed secured claim" is still permitted, and the present value of the amount to be paid in cram down is "not less than the allowed amount of *such* claim." § 1325(a)(5)(B)(ii). Grammatically, "such" can only refer to the prior reference to "allowed secured claim." Thus, *even after* the enactment of the hanging paragraph, a chapter 13 debtor may cram down a "910" car lender under § 1325(a)(5)(B) by paying the creditor the present value amount of the "allowed secured claim." Note that this certainly means that the debtor does not necessarily have to pay contract interest; instead, a cram down interest rate using a lower "formula" method (as in *Till*[537]) would be permissible.[538] Third, the only thing that the hanging paragraph actually does is prevent a bankruptcy court from looking at § 506(a) to determine the amount of the "allowed secured claim." But Congress put nothing in the place of § 506(a); all that remains is a statutory gap. Nature and the law both abhor a vacuum. Is saying that a court cannot look at § 506(a) to determine the amount of the allowed secured claim necessarily the same thing as saying that "the allowed secured claim is equal to the allowed claim"? Admittedly, the vast majority of courts have held that the effect of the hanging paragraph in collateral retention cases is to deem the collateral to be worth the amount of the debt. But the statutory language does not compel that result. A court arguably could look elsewhere, such as general equitable principles, to fix the amount of the allowed secured claim. That inquiry might lead a court to decide that the allowed secured claim was indeed less than the allowed claim, in which case the 2005 amendment would not have accomplished its intended aim.

Indeed, it could be even worse than that for the auto lender—with chapter 13 cram down divorced entirely from § 506, auto lenders would not be able to invoke the beneficial valuation rules of § 506(a)(2) and of the *Rash* case,[539] as well as the entitlement to postpetition interest under § 506(b) if oversecured.[540] Indeed, a court could say that, with § 506 out of the picture, the auto lender does not have an "allowed secured claim" and thus would not be entitled to recover any interest, even over the life

---

[535] See, e.g., In re Johnson, 337 B.R. 269 (Bankr. M.D.N.C. 2006).

[536] See Braucher, supra note 534.

[537] 541 U.S. 465 (2004).

[538] In re Trejos, 352 B.R. 249 (Bankr. D. Nev. 2006).

[539] 520 U.S. 953 (1997). See § 7.29.

[540] See Carlson, supra note 533, at 348. See § 7.31.

of the plan; while it might recover as principal the total amount of its claim, no "present value" protection would remain.[541] Or possibly worst of all, if a court were to read the elimination of § 506 from the calculus as precluding *any* assertion of an "allowed secured claim," reasoning that such is determined solely by reason of § 506(a), then the auto lender would be relegated entirely to *unsecured* status. Countering that position is the view that the lender's security rights under state law still remain, even in bankruptcy.[542] At the end of the day, the reality is that Congress indisputably sought to benefit auto lenders with the hanging paragraph, and most (but not all) courts are likely to try to effectuate that intent, even though it was very, very badly executed.

The discussion of the hanging paragraph so far has assumed (as Congress almost certainly did) that cram down under § 1325(a)(5)(B) is the desired end. But what happens to a "910" claim covered by the hanging paragraph when, instead of *retaining* the car, the debtor chooses instead to *surrender* the collateral to the auto lender under § 1325(a)(5)(C)? The question is whether the debtor's surrender of the collateral fully satisfies the creditor's entire claim, including any *unsecured* deficiency if the creditor was undersecured. When the debtor surrender's the car, the debtor does not then need to provide for the creditor's unsecured claim in the chapter 13 plan, because the creditor would not have an unsecured claim after the full-satisfaction surrender. It appears that Congress was careless in drafting the hanging paragraph and did not think of the surrender possibility.

The argument for the debtor is simple: if the effect of the hanging paragraph, by barring reference to § 506, is to preclude bifurcation of an undersecured "910" claim and deem that the allowed secured claim is equal to the allowed claim—as most courts have held when considering cram down under § 1325(a)(5)(B)—that then necessarily dictates that the same result must occur upon surrender under § 1325(a)(5)(C).[543] Indeed, the confirmation requirements for a secured claim under subsection (5) of § 1325(a) are presented as equivalent alternatives. If "910" collateral is conclusively presumed to equal the amount of the debt, no unsecured claim remains after surrender. Nothing in the hanging paragraph differentiates between different subsections of § 1325(a)(5)—it simply says that "section 506 shall not apply." The

---

[541] See Carlson, supra note 533, at 344–45. Similarly, a court might treat a claim covered by the hanging paragraph in similar fashion as pertains under the § 1111(b) election, and, while requiring that the total of plan payments equal the allowed claim, permit the present value of those payments to equal the collateral value—thus effectively accomplishing strip down. See id. at 343–44.

[542] See, e.g., *Trejos*, supra note 538. See Carlson, supra note 533, at 347.

[543] The leading case for this view is *In re Pinti*, 363 B.R. 369 (Bankr. S.D.N.Y. 2007). Even after the run of court of appeals decisions going the other way, see infra note 545, Judge Morris reaffirmed her decision in *Pinti* in *In re Tompkins*, 391 B.R. 560 (Bankr. S.D.N.Y. 2008).

One court explained this result as follows:

> The effect of the hanging paragraph is that a debtor no longer has this bifurcation tool at his or her disposal. If a creditor files a secured claim relating to 910 property and that claim is allowed under § 502, the debtor must treat the claim as fully secured. In a sense, a fiction arises that the 910 collateral is worth the exact amount of the proof of claim. So when a debtor proposes to retain the collateral, the debtor must propose to pay the entire claim as filed. Likewise, where the debtor proposes to surrender the collateral, the fiction created by the hanging paragraph serves to render the secured claim completely satisfied.

In re Durham, 361 B.R. 206, 209 (Bankr. D. Utah 2006).

secured creditor gets the same bankruptcy deal in retention or surrender cases, namely, the collateral is treated as equal in value to the amount of the debt. The necessary corollary to that result is that the creditor does *not* have an unsecured claim, and that corollary holds for surrender cases just as it does for retention cases. Accordingly, "[t]he majority of bankruptcy courts have concluded that, by eliminating the application of § 506(a) to 910 claims, the hanging paragraph ensures that such creditors are without a remedy to bifurcate their loans into secured and unsecured portions, therefore rendering their loans non-recourse regardless of what the parties' contract allows."[544]

The courts of appeals, however, universally have rejected what had been the majority view in the bankruptcy courts, and instead have held "that, after a debtor satisfies the requirements for plan confirmation under § 1325(a)(5)(C) by surrendering his 910 vehicle, the parties are left to their contractual rights and obligations, and the creditor may pursue an unsecured deficiency claim under state law."[545] The leading case espousing this view—a "retention I win, surrender you lose" approach—is the Seventh Circuit's decision in *In re Wright*.[546] The heart of the *Wright* court's reasoning, adopted by all subsequent circuit courts (but one[547]) is as follows:

> [B]y knocking out § 506, the hanging paragraph leaves the parties to their contractual entitlements. True enough, § 506(a) divides claims into secured and unsecured components. . . . Yet it is a mistake to assume, as the majority of bankruptcy courts have done, that § 506 is the *only* source of authority for a deficiency judgment when the collateral is insufficient. The Supreme Court held in *Butner v. United States* . . . that state law determines rights and obligations when the Code does not supply a federal rule. . . . Creditors don't need § 506 to create, allow, or recognize security interests, which rest on contracts (and the UCC) rather than federal law.[548]

The *Wright* court bolstered its holding by looking at legislative history, drawing the conclusion that in adding the hanging paragraph Congress sought to benefit secured creditors, and thus the amendment should be interpreted in that light.[549]

Wright is wrong. Congress may have intended that result, but that is not the statute they passed. The problem in surrender cases governed by the hanging paragraph is finding a basis for recognizing an allowed unsecured claim that is

---

[544] Tidewater Fin. Co. v. Kenney, 531 F.3d 312, 317–18 (4th Cir. 2008).

[545] Id. at 318. See also AmeriCredit Fin. Servs., Inc. v. Tompkins, 604 F.3d 753 (2d Cir. 2010); In re Barrett, 543 F.3d 1239 (11th Cir. 2008); In re Ballard, 526 F.3d 634 (10th Cir. 2008); In re Long, 519 F.3d 288 (6th Cir. 2008); Capital One Auto Fin. v. Osborn, 515 F.3d 817 (8th Cir. 2008); In re Wright, 492 F.3d 829 (7th Cir. 2007).

[546] 492 F.3d 829 (7th Cir. 2007).

[547] The Sixth Circuit in *Long*, supra note 545, 519 F.3d at 291 took a different tack, recognizing the insurmountable textual problems with the *Wright* reasoning. That court, which just could not believe that Congress could have intended for a secured creditor to get stuck with the car and nothing else, decided that the best approach was to create a uniform *federal* rule recognizing a deficiency claim, relying heavily on the legislative history.

[548] *Wright*, supra note 545, 492 F.3d at 832–33.

[549] Id. at 832.

enforceable in the federal bankruptcy case. The central fallacy of *Wright* is to say that under *Butner* the creditor can invoke state law to create an unsecured claim that is "allowed" in bankruptcy, even with § 506(a) off the table. Not so. *Butner* does speak to the question of whether the creditor has a claim at all. It does *not* speak to the question of whether that claim is "allowed" in a bankruptcy case and, more significantly, how that claim is allocated in bankruptcy as between secured and unsecured portions.[550] On those questions, there *is* governing federal law—§ 506(a) and the hanging paragraph of § 1325(a). Bankruptcy bifurcation depends on § 506(a). Otherwise, § 506(a) would be superfluous. When § 506(a) does not apply because of the mandate of the hanging paragraph, no basis exists in a bankruptcy case for dividing a claim into secured and unsecured portions. In such a situation, even the *Butner* Court would concede (as it must under the Supremacy Clause) that state law must yield.[551] Looking to state law is a red herring.

This is not a case where there is a vacuum of federal law that leaves the field open to state law. Congress did not say "nothing" here; quite to the contrary, Congress made it clear in the hanging paragraph that § 506 bifurcations were off-limits in § 1325(a)(5) cases. That is, the import of the hanging paragraph is not to say "no federal law applies here"; instead, the import is, "no bifurcation of undersecured claims is allowed here." We believe that Congress really meant it in cases involving retention under § 1325(a)(5)(B), so why not also in § 1325(a)(5)(C)? As noted above, there is absolutely no statutory basis for making a distinction between cases under subsections (B) and (C) in terms of the effect of the hanging paragraph. The result of *Wright* is to create just such a distinction. Under the Seventh Circuit view, the "910" lender in a retention case under § 1325(a)(5)(B) is permitted to insist on a fiction that the collateral is worth the full amount of the debt, even though it plainly is not; whereas in a surrender case under § 1325(a)(5)(C) the debtor is not entitled to invoke the same fiction.

Is it likely that Congress meant to deprive undersecured creditors of a deficiency claim in surrender cases? No. But it did. If it wants a different result, it can amend the Code. Courts do not enjoy the same privilege.

c. *Chapter 7: Redemption, Reaffirmation, Ride–Through, and Dewsnup*

The situation with regard to undersecured claims is much different in a chapter 7 liquidation case than it is in the reorganization chapters. The major problem for the debtor is that chapter 7 does not provide any mechanism analogous to the cram down rules found in the reorganization chapters by which the debtor may retain the property and pay the creditor over time, without the creditor's consent. The debtor must either redeem the property in a lump sum cash payment, § 722, or persuade the creditor to enter into a reaffirmation agreement. § 524(c). Importantly, the debtor cannot

---

[550] See Keith M. Lundin, Chapter 13 Bankruptcy, 451.5–12, 13 (3d ed. 2000 & Supp.2007–1).

[551] In announcing its rule of deference to state law, the *Butner* Court included an oft-forgotten but critical qualifier—"*Unless some federal interest requires a different result.*" 440 U.S. 48, 55 (1979). Congress's detailed treatment of undersecured claims in § 506(a)(1), and its prohibition against looking to that section in cases governed by the hanging paragraph, codifies such a "federal interest."

otherwise strip down the creditor's lien to the amount of the secured claim, pursuant to the Supreme Court's 1992 decision in *Dewsnup v. Timm*.[552]

Reaffirmation of the debt will enable the debtor to keep the collateral, but will not permit the debtor to strip down an undersecured claim to the value of the collateral. The reason is simple: the creditor probably will not agree to a reaffirmation unless the debtor agrees to pay the *entire* debt. For example, if a debt of $10,000 is secured by collateral worth $7,000, the creditor would insist that the debtor promise in the reaffirmation agreement to repay the total $10,000 debt, not just the $7,000 secured portion.

The only strip down provision available to a debtor in chapter 7, then, is redemption under § 722. A debtor may redeem collateral by paying the creditor "the amount of the allowed secured claim." Under § 506(a), the allowed secured claim is the value of the collateral. In our example, that would be $7,000. However, redemption is a limited tool. It is only available: (1) to individual debtors; (2) with regard to "tangible *personal* property"; (3) that is "intended primarily for personal, family, or household use," i.e., is a consumer item; (4) that secures a dischargeable consumer debt; and (5) if the property is either abandoned by the trustee under § 554 or exempted under § 522. Thus, redemption under § 722 is never available with regard to undersecured *real* property. Furthermore, the courts have concluded that redemption must be done in a single lump sum cash payment, i.e., installment redemption is not allowed.[553] As a practical matter the debtor may have difficulty finding enough money to pay off the secured creditor.

The limits on redemption and the undesirability of reaffirmation led debtors to search for another way to strip down undersecured claims to the value of the collateral in chapter 7 cases. Until *Dewsnup*, debtors thought they had found the answer in § 506(d), which provides in relevant part:

> To the extent that a lien secures a claim against the debtor that is not an allowed secured claim, such lien is void. . . .

Debtors urged that the plain meaning of this provision, in conjunction with § 506(a), mandated strip down. "Allowed secured claim" is a term of art in § 506(a), meaning that portion of the total claim supported by collateral value. The unsecured balance of the claim, by necessity, is "not an allowed secured claim." Thus, a plain reading of § 506(d) arguably suggests that an undersecured creditor's lien is "void" "to the extent" it is unsecured. In the example we have been using, where the creditor's total claim of $10,000 is secured by collateral worth only $7,000, the interaction of § 506(a) and (d) would result in the voiding of the creditor's lien for any amount in excess of the $7,000 "allowed secured claim," effectively stripping the lien down to the $7,000 value. Many courts gave effect to this plain reading of the statute and authorized strip down.[554]

---

[552] 502 U.S. 410 (1992).

[553] The leading case is *In re Bell*, 700 F.2d 1053 (6th Cir. 1983).

[554] The leading case was *Gaglia v. First Fed. Sav. & Loan Assoc.*, 889 F.2d 1304 (3d Cir. 1989). Some commentators argued that strip down was the proper result, see Margaret Howard, Stripping Down Liens:

Other courts, however, recoiled from this result, and found ways to sidestep strip down. The case of *Dewsnup v. Timm* settled the dispute. In that case the debtor, Aletha Dewsnup, owned two parcels of farmland worth only $39,000 when she filed bankruptcy, but the total debt secured by that land was $120,000. Under § 506(a), the creditor had a secured claim equal to $39,000 and an unsecured claim for the $81,000 balance. The debtor sought to strip down the creditor's lien to $39,000 by voiding the lien under § 506(d) to the extent it exceeded $39,000. She then would be able to satisfy that lien by paying the creditor $39,000.

The Tenth Circuit rejected strip down, however, reasoning that once the collateral was abandoned by the bankruptcy trustee, it ceased to be "property of the estate," and § 506(a) and (d) therefore were no longer applicable.[555] The court further supported its decision by asserting that strip down (1) would give debtors in chapter 7 a better result than they could achieve in the reorganization chapters, contrary to congressional intent to promote the use of those chapters, and (2) would render redemption under § 722 largely superfluous.

In a landmark decision, the Supreme Court affirmed the Tenth Circuit. The Court in *Dewsnup* held that § 506(d) does not allow a chapter 7 debtor to "'strip down' a creditor's lien on real property to the value of the collateral, as judicially determined, when that value is less than the amount of the claim secured by the lien."[556] The Court's reasoning differed sharply from that of the court of appeals, however. Instead of adopting the abandonment theory, the Court embraced a strained reading of the statutory text, justifying its tortured construction by resort to history and policy. Finding the statute to be ambiguous, the *Dewsnup* Court interpreted § 506(d) to provide that a lien is voided only if the underlying claim has been disallowed. In other words, if a claim has been "allowed" and if that claim is "secured" at all, it is an "allowed secured claim" for purposes of § 506(d) and may not be voided.[557] Since Louis Timm's claim (1) was allowed and (2) was secured (for $39,000), under the Court's syllogism it could not be voided even to the extent undersecured.

In so holding, the Court consciously chose not to give "allowed secured claim" the same meaning in § 506(d) that the term indisputably has in § 506(a).[558] The Court did so because it was "not convinced that Congress intended to depart from the pre-Code rule that liens pass through bankruptcy unaffected."[559] Prior to the enactment of the current Bankruptcy Code in 1978, strip down of liens could not be effected except in the reorganization chapters. It is not plausible that Congress would have made such a

---

Section 506(d) and the Theory of Bankruptcy, 65 Am. Bankr. L.J. 373 (1991), while others disagreed. See Joann Henderson, The *Gaglia–Lowry* Brief: A Quantum Leap From Strip Down to Chapter 7 Cram Down, 8 Bankr. Dev. J. 131 (1991).

[555]   908 F.2d 588 (10th Cir. 1990), affirmed on other grounds, 502 U.S. 410 (1992).

[556]   502 U.S. 410, 412, 417 (1992).

[557]   Id. at 417.

[558]   The dissenting Justices were particularly appalled at what they derided as the Court's "one-subsection-at-a-time approach to statutory exegesis," id. at 423 (Scalia, J., dissenting), instead of following the normal presumption that identical terms used in the same act of Congress have the same meaning.

[559]   Id. at 417 (Blackmun, J., majority). The origin of this rule is said to be the case of *Long v. Bullard*, 117 U.S. 617 (1886), which held that a bankruptcy discharge does not affect in rem obligations such as liens, but only eliminates the debtor's in personam liability.

radical change in bankruptcy law, the Court explained, without a clear statement in the Code or in the legislative history.

Furthermore, the *Dewsnup* Court asserted that "basic bankruptcy principles" dictated rejecting the idea of a chapter 7 lien strip down. The Court surmised that the better policy was that any appreciation in the value of the collateral until the time of foreclosure should redound to the benefit of the secured creditor, not to the debtor. Strip down, conversely, would give any such increase in value to the debtor. Venturing onto dangerous ice, the Court stated that "the creditor's lien stays with the real property until the foreclosure."[560] Without strip down, Timm would be able to assert his *in rem* lien on the farmland after bankruptcy up to the full amount of the debt. If that land magically increased in value (to $60,000, for example) before Timm foreclosed, he could capture that entire increase.

Commentators after *Dewsnup* have expressed considerable consternation about the holding of that case, but even more so about the Court's rationale.[561] The Court's suggestion that the creditor's lien stays with the property until foreclosure, if taken seriously, would wreak havoc on numerous provisions of the Bankruptcy Code. To give one example, lien stripping in the reorganization chapters would seem to be in doubt under the Court's theory, even though the statutory provisions in those chapters plainly seem to authorize strip down. Fortunately, most lower courts after *Dewsnup* have chosen to ignore the Court's premise and have confined the case to its factual home in chapter 7. Strip down thus remains alive and well in reorganization cases,[562] although the risk remains that courts will extend the Supreme Court's lien "pass-through" notion and prohibit lien stripping even in the reorganization context.[563]

§ 7.33   Tax Liens

Tax liens deserve special consideration. They are probably the most important and certainly the most ubiquitous type of statutory lien, and pose unique policy issues. On the one hand, the government's interest in protecting the public fisc through the collection of taxes merits protection. Yet, the countervailing concern is that tax liens could consume a disproportionate share of the bankruptcy estate, thereby impeding reorganization efforts and harming other creditors in a liquidation.

The Code partially addresses these problems in several provisions. The trustee may avoid a tax lien to the extent a bona fide purchaser would take free of the lien.[564] § 545(2). In chapter 7, tax liens are subordinated to higher priority claims.[565] § 724(b).

---

[560]   502 U.S. at 417.

[561]   The leading critic has been Professor Howard. See Margaret Howard, Secured Claims in Bankruptcy: An Essay on Missing the Point, 23 Capital U. L. Rev. 313 (1994); Margaret Howard, Dewsnupping the Bankruptcy Code, 1 J. Bankr. L. & Prac. 513 (1992).

[562]   See, e.g., In re Heritage Highgate, Inc., 679 F.3d 132 (3d Cir. 2012); In re Dever, 164 B.R. 132 (Bankr. C.D. Cal. 1994).

[563]   In the case of *In re Taffi*, the district court did extend *Dewsnup* to chapter 11, 1993 WL 558844 (C.D. Cal. Oct. 7, 1993), but the Ninth Circuit reversed on other grounds. 68 F.3d 306 (9th Cir. 1995), vacated, reinstated, 96 F.3d 1190 (9th Cir. 1996) (en banc).

[564]   See § 6.52.

[565]   See § 7.24.

In 2005, an exception to the § 724(b) subordination rule was created with regard to perfected, unavoidable tax liens arising in connection with an ad valorem tax.[566]

In a chapter 11 reorganization case, the Supreme Court held that § 542(a) requires the government to turn over to the debtor in possession property seized by the government prior to bankruptcy in attempting to enforce its tax lien.[567] In return, the debtor must provide adequate protection to the government.

The federal tax lien statute gives the United States a lien in the amount of the tax on all of the debtor-taxpayer's property if the debtor neglects or refuses to pay the tax after demand. 26 U.S.C. § 6321. The lien arises when the assessment is made. 26 U.S.C. § 6322. Until notice of the lien is filed in the proper place, the lien is not valid against any purchaser or judgment lien creditor. 26 U.S.C. § 6323(a). As a result, the trustee will be able to avoid an unfiled federal tax lien under § 545(2) or § 544(a). However, tax liens are not vulnerable as preferences. A special exception excludes the fixing of a statutory lien from preference liability.[568] § 547(c)(6).

Even if a tax lien is not avoided, it may be partially subordinated in a chapter 7 case under § 724(b). That section provides that property subject to a tax lien first must be distributed to claims with a higher priority than the tax claim secured by the lien. § 724(b)(2). Many prepetition taxes are accorded eighth priority in § 507(a)(8).[569] The effect of § 724(b) is that claims in the first seven priority classes will be paid first out of the property subject to the tax lien, but only up to the amount of the tax claim, and subject to one exception added in 2005. After that amount is paid to the higher priority claims, any residue will be paid to the tax claim. This subordination provision does not benefit the holders of general unsecured non-priority claims, though, since the subordination is only to claims with a priority higher than that of the tax claim. The 2005 exception provides that the subordination of the tax lien to administrative expense claims[570] is limited to chapter 7 expenses and to expenses for wages, salaries, and commissions in chapter 7.[571]

Furthermore, another 2005 amendment[572] requires the trustee, before subordinating a tax lien, to exhaust the unencumbered assets of the estate, § 724(e)(1), and to recover from the collateral the reasonable, necessary costs and expenses of preserving or disposing of such property. § 724(e)(2). In addition, fourth and fifth priority claims may be paid from property securing a tax lien, notwithstanding the ad valorem tax lien exception. § 724(f).

---

[566] Pub. L. No. 109–8, § 701(a)(1), 119 Stat. 124 (2005).

[567] United States v. Whiting Pools, Inc., 462 U.S. 198 (1983). See § 5.14.

[568] See § 6.22.

[569] See § 7.21.

[570] There used to be a drafting error in 724(b); the amendment carves out a set of expenses from § 507(a)(1)(C) or 507(a)(2), but it used to read only "§ 507(a)(1)." By the expenses listed it is obvious that Congress meant to reference § 507(a)(2), forgetting here to correct for the fact that elsewhere in the 2005 Act a new first priority was introduced, bumping what had been § 507(a)(1) to second priority. This was fixed in 2010. Pub. L. No. 111–327, § 2(a)(27), 124 Stat. 3560 (2010).

[571] Pub. L. No. 109–8, § 701(a)(2), 119 Stat. 124 (2005).

[572] Id. § 701(a)(3).

As discussed in an earlier section, the holder of a tax lien may be entitled to postpetition interest to the extent the debt is oversecured.[573] § 506(b). In *United States v. Ron Pair Enterprises, Inc.*,[574] the Supreme Court held that the Code changed the law on this point. However, prior to 2005 the taxing authority still was not entitled to recover postpetition penalties.[575] A 2005 amendment added the possibility of recovery under § 506(b) for "any reasonable fees, costs, or charges" provided for in a "State statute."[576]

In limited respects the government is exempted from the automatic stay to pursue the collection of tax claims and the creation of a tax lien. Under § 362(a)(9), the government may conduct an audit to determine tax liability, issue the debtor a notice of tax deficiency, make a demand for tax returns, and make an assessment for any tax and issue a notice and demand for payment of that assessment. However, a tax lien only attaches to property by reason of such an assessment if the tax is a debt of the debtor that will not be discharged (see § 523(a)(1)), and the property or its proceeds are transferred out of the estate to or otherwise revested in the debtor.

§ 7.34 Surcharging Secured Creditors

Secured creditors may not always recover the full value of their collateral. Under § 506(c), they may be charged with expenses necessary to preserve or dispose of the collateral.[577] Section 506(c) provides:

> The trustee may recover from property securing an allowed secured claim the reasonable, necessary costs and expenses of preserving, or disposing of, such property to the extent of any benefit to the holder of such claim.

For such a short statute, § 506(c) has given rise to a surprisingly large number of issues. The reason is simple: claimants are always trying to find a way to get paid. When the estate does not have sufficient unencumbered funds to pay all administrative expenses in full, the collateral of a secured creditor presents a very tempting target.

The first disputed issue under § 506(c) concerns *standing*. The statute says that "the trustee" may recover from collateral; that language suggests rather strongly that "the trustee" is the proper (and *only*) party with standing to assert a § 506(c) surcharge. In a chapter 11 case, the debtor in possession performs the functions of a trustee, and thus would have § 506(c) standing. § 1107(a). But must the statute inevitably be given its literal reading, if the trustee (or debtor in possession) does not act, and an administrative expense claimant attempts to invoke § 506(c) so that they may be paid? The issue invariably is presented when a particular administrative expense claimant files a motion to surcharge collateral to pay its administrative expenses. The argument in favor of expanding standing is that the particular claimant

---

[573] See § 7.29.

[574] 489 U.S. 235 (1989).

[575] See In re Parr Meadows Racing Ass'n, 880 F.2d 1540 (2d Cir. 1989).

[576] Pub. L. No. 109-8, § 712(d)(1), 119 Stat. 128 (2005).

[577] See David Gray Carlson, Secured Creditors and Expenses of Bankruptcy Administration, 70 N.C. L. Rev. 417 (1992).

may be the only party with a financial incentive to request a § 506(c) surcharge, and that denying them standing would allow the secured creditor a windfall.

The Supreme Court settled this question in *Hartford Underwriters Insurance Co. v. Union Planters Bank, N.A.*, holding that the plain language of § 506(c) limits standing to a trustee, excluding thereby an administrative expense claimant.[578] Note, though, that the Court did not decide whether a frustrated claimant who had asked the trustee to seek a surcharge under § 506(c), but to no avail, could petition the court for permission to act *derivatively* in the trustee's stead, as representative of the estate.[579] By leaving that possibility open, the Court minimized the risk that a secured creditor could enjoy a windfall at the expense of a deserving administrative claimant. Every Court of Appeals to consider the issue after *Hartford* has concluded that because of footnote 5, the Court did not foreclose derivative standing in bankruptcy, and then has held that derivative standing is available on a proper showing.[580]

An important subsidiary issue was not decided by the Supreme Court in *Hartford*: "who ultimately receives the recovery obtained by a trustee under § 506(c)"?[581] Does it go directly to the administrative claimant, or does it go into the estate, with the claimant relegated to seeking recovery for its priority expense out of the general assets of the estate? The answer would matter if the estate were administratively insolvent. The right answer should be that the recovery goes into the estate, and not directly to the claimant; otherwise, the claimant would enjoy a *de facto* superpriority under § 506(c).

Once the standing threshold is crossed, the substantive issue still remains: in what circumstances is it appropriate to surcharge the secured creditor's collateral to pay the expenses of other parties? The basic policy behind § 506(c) is the equitable notion that the secured creditor should not enjoy a windfall at someone else's expense.[582] Thus, a § 506(c) surcharge against collateral will be allowed in one of two situations: first, if the secured creditor is *benefited* by the claimed expenditure; or second, if the secured creditor *consents* to the expenditure. In the event of either benefit or consent, it would be inequitable not to surcharge the creditor's collateral. The statute itself mandates that the expenses must be "reasonable" and "necessary," and the surcharge is authorized only "to the extent of any benefit to the holder" of the secured claim.

While the general policy may be readily apparent, the difficulty lies in the application to specific circumstances. What sort of "benefit" will suffice? What constitutes "consent"? Some cases (too few) are easy. These usually involve a direct, obvious, and quantifiable benefit to the secured party, or express consent by the secured creditor. For example, if the creditor's collateral is being sold, costs directly related to the sale may be paid out of the sale proceeds under § 506(c). These are costs

---

[578] 530 U.S. 1, 6, 13 (2000).

[579] Id. at 13 n.5.

[580] See In re Trailer Source, Inc., 555 F.3d 231, 239–43 (6th Cir. 2009) (collecting cases).

[581] Id. at 11 n.4.

[582] See Internal Revenue Serv. v. Boatmen's First Nat'l Bank, 5 F.3d 1157, 1159 (8th Cir. 1993); In re Felt Mfg. Co., 402 B.R. 502 (Bankr. D.N.H. 2009).

that necessarily must be incurred to effect the sale. Even if the creditor were to make the sale, rather than the trustee, the creditor would have to incur the same types of expenses. Examples might include appraisal fees, auctioneer fees, advertising and marketing costs, storage expenses, and the like.

The fights occur when an attempt is made to surcharge the secured creditor's collateral with some of the more generalized costs of the bankruptcy or reorganization proceeding. The "benefit" in such cases is less direct, and more remote. Yet the argument is put forth that the benefit to the secured creditor is just as surely present. For instance, the plea often is made that the expense incurred helped the debtor to reorganize, and that keeping the debtor afloat as a going concern enhanced the value of the secured creditor's collateral. In a liquidation, the creditor's collateral might have brought much less. The claim then is made that the expenses that allowed the secured creditor to capture that going concern premium in fairness should be charged against that extra value. The principle urged is that the secured creditor should not be allowed to enjoy the benefits of the reorganization without bearing any of the costs.

Much the same argument may be cast in terms of "implied consent." Here, the assertion is that the secured creditor, by participating in the reorganization and cooperating with the debtor, thereby impliedly consented to help pay the freight for the expenses incurred in the course of that reorganization effort. The lienholder should not be allowed to enjoy the benefits of a reorganization without shouldering any of the costs. If the secured party is aware all along that the estate may not have enough general funds to pay administrative expenses, the § 506(c) demand starts to take on the flavor of estoppel.

Creative as these "indirect benefit" and "implied consent" arguments are, most circuit courts have found them insufficient to support a surcharge under § 506(c).[583] The general rule is that the administrative costs and expenses of a bankruptcy or reorganization case are payable only out of the unencumbered assets of the estate, not out of collateral.[584] If collateral can be charged for anything more than directly beneficial expenses, or when express consent is given, administrative creditors effectively will have priority over secured creditors.[585] Therefore, the prevailing view limits § 506(c) recoveries to cases involving direct and immediate benefits to the creditor's collateral.[586] Furthermore, "consent" will not be lightly inferred; cooperation in the reorganization effort will not suffice.[587] Having said that, some thoughtful lower

---

[583] See, e.g., In re Visual Indus., Inc., 57 F.3d 321, 325–26 (3d Cir. 1995) (benefit which trade creditor provided to debtor's primary secured creditor, in supplying debtor with raw materials that it needed to continue its operations and to generate income to pay down its debt to secured creditor, was not the kind of "direct benefit" required for surcharging of secured creditor's collateral.); In re Flagstaff Foodservice Corp., 762 F.2d 10, 12 (2d Cir. 1985).

[584] See, e.g. In re Flagstaff Foodservice Corp., 739 F.2d 73, 76 (2d Cir. 1984).

[585] See *Visual Industries*, supra note 583, 57 F.3d at 327.

[586] See, e.g., In re C.S. Assocs., 29 F.3d 903 (3d Cir. 1994); In re Glasply Marine Indus., Inc., 971 F.2d 391 (9th Cir. 1992). See also In re K & L Lakeland, Inc., 128 F.3d 203 (4th Cir. 1997).

[587] See, e.g., In re Ferncrest Court Partners, Ltd., 66 F.3d 778 (6th Cir. 1995); *Flagstaff Foodservice*, supra note 583, 762 F.2d at 12.

court opinions have expressed greater sympathy for imposing general administrative costs on a secured creditor under § 506(c).[588]

F. TRUSTS AND OTHER PROPERTY CLAIMS

§ 7.35   Express Trusts and Statutory Trusts

It is hardly a remarkable proposition to state that creditors of a debtor are entitled to be paid only out of the debtor's property. When the debtor files bankruptcy, all of the debtor's property becomes property of the bankruptcy estate.[589] § 541(a). In a liquidation bankruptcy, property of the estate is distributed to creditors in the order of priority of their allowed claims. In reorganization cases, while creditors are paid under a plan out of the debtor's future income, the baseline entitlement of creditors is determined by reference to the amount of property in the estate. In effecting a bankruptcy distribution, then, it becomes critical to identify what constitutes the property of the estate.

A corollary principle to the foregoing is that property that is *not* in the bankruptcy estate cannot be distributed to creditors of the debtor. Instead, that property should be returned to its rightful owner. In a sense, this return of property is a form of "payment" to that property claimant. A claimant with a superior interest in property who obtains the turnover of their property from the bankruptcy estate effectively realizes a complete "priority" in payment with regard to that returned property.

In the simplest cases (which never happen) this "return of property" principle is self-evident and noncontroversial. For example, assume that a debtor borrows a friend's golf clubs. After playing a round, the debtor stops by the federal courthouse and files bankruptcy. Although the debtor still has a possessory interest in the clubs, the friend has a superior claim to the clubs. The clubs of course should be returned to the friend; it would be absurd to sell the clubs, distribute the proceeds to the debtor's creditors, and leave the unlucky friend with only an unsecured claim.

The cases that arise in the real world are not so easy. Usually the debtor (and thus the estate upon filing) also has some form of entitlement to the subject property; the difficulty then is sorting out and balancing the respective rights of the debtor and the other party. There are four primary categories of cases in which claimants assert a form of "property" claim against property held by the bankruptcy estate.

The first, and most important, involves *secured* claims. A lien is a form of property. The many special issues confronting secured claims in bankruptcy have been discussed in other sections of this book.[590]

---

[588] See, e.g., In re AFCO Enters., 35 B.R. 512 (Bankr. D. Utah 1983).

[589] See chapter 5 for a discussion of property of the estate.

[590] See §§ 7.27–7.34. See also the treatment of issues regarding relief from the automatic stay in §§ 3.17–3.25.

Second, *joint* property claimants may assert rights against property in which the estate shares an interest. Examples include community property, joint tenancies, tenancies by the entirety, and so forth.

The third category of property cases involve *trusts*—express trusts and statutory trusts, discussed in this section, and (possibly) constructive trusts, discussed in the following section. In trust cases the property claimant is asserting either legal title or, more often, equitable title to the property. The Code expressly excludes from the reach of property of the estate any non-debtor equitable interests in property, limiting the estate to the debtor's legal title.[591] § 541(d).

Finally, sellers who seek to *reclaim* property they sold to the debtor are making a form of property claim.[592]

Express trusts

If the debtor is the trustee of an express trust, the non-debtor beneficiary's equitable interest in the trust res will not become property of the estate. § 541(d). Instead, the beneficiary's equitable interest will be turned over to them. However, if the relationship between the debtor and the claimant is not trustee-beneficiary, but debtor-creditor, then (1) the property will come into the bankruptcy estate and (2) the claimant will share pro rata with all other creditors.

The difficult question in many cases is determining whether the legal relationship between the debtor and the claimant is that of a trust or a debt. If the debtor expressly executes a trust instrument as settlor of the trust, identifies and segregates a trust res, and designates a beneficiary, then the relationship obviously is a trust. However, if all of the traditional elements of an express or implied trust are not plainly satisfied, the outcome is more doubtful. Courts usually look to the governing non-bankruptcy law to determine whether the property claimant has carried its burden of proving that a trust exists. Even if the claimant proves the existence of a trust, they still must identify and trace the trust funds.

Consider a scenario that has arisen with some frequency in department store bankruptcy cases. A specialized vendor (e.g., a seller of furs, or tires, or glasses) leases space in the store from the debtor department store. The usual terms of the lease agreement are that the vendor will turn over all sale proceeds to the debtor, who deducts a rental or royalty fee and then remits the net proceeds back to the vendor on a periodic basis. The agreement may or may not be denominated a "trust," and may or may not require the debtor to retain the proceeds in a segregated account. The dispute arises when the debtor files bankruptcy in the middle of a period, after collecting proceeds from the vendor but before remitting the net proceeds back to the vendor. The vendor, of course, wants to recover the proceeds. The legal issue is whether the vendor is a beneficiary of a trust with regard to those proceeds or a creditor; i.e., is the legal relationship between the parties that of a trust or just a debt? The cases have gone

---

[591] See § 5.8.
[592] See § 7.37.

both ways, although most courts have been very reluctant to find a trust in this situation.[593]

Statutory trust

Perhaps even more common is the situation in which a claimant asserts that they are the beneficiary of a *statutory* trust and thus entitled to the turnover of trust funds. The scenario in which this arises most often is with regard to state or federal tax claims. The tax laws often provide that monies that a debtor is supposed to collect or withhold, such as for employees' wages[594] or sales taxes,[595] are held "in trust" for the government. See, e.g., 26 U.S.C. § 7501.

Another common statutory trust situation involves the bankruptcy of general contractors. State law may provide that the property owner is entitled to retain funds until the general contractor pays the subcontractors.[596] Also, state law may create a "trust" in favor of subcontractors for monies paid over to the general contractor by the property owner.

In both the tax and the contractor cases, the standard approach of the courts is to look first to the governing non-bankruptcy law to determine whether a "trust" has in fact been created. If it has, the second step is to identify the trust funds. Only if a trust exists and the trust res is identified may the claimant recover or retain the alleged trust funds.

The leading statutory trust case is the Supreme Court's decision in *Begier v. United States*.[597] In *Begier*, the trust issue arose in the context of the bankruptcy trustee's attempt to recover payments made to the IRS by the debtor during the preference period. The government's defense was that the money paid was not property of the debtor, but was held in a statutory trust for the United States. The statute in question was 26 U.S.C. § 7501, which provides that "the amount of tax [required to be] collected or withheld shall be held to be a special fund in trust for the United States."

The Supreme Court held for the government. First, the Court found that § 7501, the governing non-bankruptcy law, created a trust. That finding alone did not conclude the question, however, because the government still had to prove that the specific dollars paid were the funds held in trust; in other words, the alleged trust beneficiary had to trace the trust res.[598] Some nexus between the collected or withheld taxes and the alleged trust funds must be established. Common law tracing rules would not help, since they require identification of a specific corpus. The *Begier* Court held that a special federal tracing rule could be invoked by the United States; the debtor's act of

---

[593] Compare In re Sakowitz, Inc., 949 F.2d 178 (5th Cir. 1991) (not a trust), with In re Goldblatt Bros., Inc., 33 B.R. 1011 (N.D. Ill. 1983), app. dismissed, 758 F.2d 1248 (7th Cir. 1985) (implied trust found).

[594] See, e.g., City of Farrell v. Sharon Steel Corp., 41 F.3d 92 (3d Cir. 1994).

[595] See, e.g., In re Al Copeland Enters., Inc., 991 F.2d 233 (5th Cir. 1993).

[596] See, e.g., In re Modular Structures, Inc., 27 F.3d 72 (3d Cir. 1994); In Re Caribbean Resort Constr. & Maint., Inc., 318 B.R. 241 (Bankr. D.P.R. 2003).

[597] 496 U.S. 53 (1990). See discussion also in § 6.11.

[598] 496 U.S. at 62.

making the payments to the government constituted the debtor's identification of the trust property.[599] This conclusion suggests, though, that if no payment is made, tracing still might pose a problem for the government in asserting a right to "trust" property held by the debtor.

§ 7.36   Constructive Trusts

Claimants may seek to bypass the Code's priority scheme by asserting a property interest in estate property pursuant to a *constructive trust*. A constructive trust is an equitable remedy imposed under state law to give effect to the equitably superior property claim of the non-debtor party. In the bankruptcy context the constructive trust question often arises when the claimant alleges that the debtor defrauded it out of property, and requests that the subject property be transferred to it pursuant to a constructive trust. Claimants seeking relief via a constructive trust invariably point to § 541(d) of the Code, which provides that property of the estate does not include property in which the debtor holds only legal title.[600]

A major battle that has been fought in many cases concerns the interaction between the claimant's assertion of an equitable property right under a constructive trust, supposedly enforceable against the estate under § 541(d), and the trustee's invocation of the strong-arm power as a hypothetical bona fide purchaser under § 544(a)(3).[601] The claimant argues that the property subject to the constructive trust in its favor should be excluded from the estate under § 541(d) and turned over to it. The trustee counters that the claimant's unrecorded equitable interest should be avoided under § 544(a)(3), freeing the property from the equitable interest and leaving the claimant with only an unsecured claim.

Some courts have taken the position that the claimant's superior equities should prevail and that § 541(d) should "control" § 544(a)(3).[602] These courts reason that it would be an unmerited windfall to the debtor's other creditors to permit them to profit from the debtor's fraud. The prevailing view today, however, is that the constructive trust claimant will lose in this situation. For example, in *Belisle v. Plunkett*,[603] the debtor defrauded several real estate limited partnership investors by taking their money and purchasing and recording property in his own name, rather than in the name of the partnership. When the debtor filed bankruptcy, the bankruptcy trustee successfully invoked § 544(a)(3) to avoid the investors' equitable interests. Under applicable law, a bona fide purchaser would take free of the investors' equitable claims, and thus the bankruptcy trustee could set aside those interests under the strong-arm clause. The investors were left with an unsecured claim in the debtor's bankruptcy.

---

[599]   Id. at 66–67.

[600]   For discussions of constructive trusts in bankruptcy, see Emily L. Sherwin, Constructive Trusts in Bankruptcy, 1989 U. Ill. L. Rev. 297 (1989). See also Carlos J. Cuevas, Bankruptcy Code Section 544(a) and Constructive Trusts: The Trustee's Strong Arm Powers Should Prevail, 21 Seton Hall L. Rev. 678 (1991); Jeffrey Davis, Equitable Liens and Constructive Trusts in Bankruptcy: Judicial Values and the Limits of Bankruptcy Distribution Policy, 41 Fla. L. Rev. 1 (1989).

[601]   See §§ 5.8, 6.4.

[602]   See, e.g., In re Quality Holstein Leasing, 752 F.2d 1009 (5th Cir. 1985).

[603]   877 F.2d 512 (7th Cir.), cert. denied, 493 U.S. 893 (1989).

The supposed "conflict" between § 541(d) and § 544(a)(3) only comes into play if the non-debtor claimant has a cognizable equitable property interest in the first place. In an important decision, the Sixth Circuit in *In re Omegas Group, Inc.*[604] called into question the underlying assumption that a defrauded claimant has an equitable property right. In *Omegas Group*, the debtor allegedly defrauded the claimant by pocketing over a million dollars that was supposed to be used to purchase computers for the claimant. The unhappy claimant asked the bankruptcy court to impose a constructive trust, and to turn over the money to the trust.

The Sixth Circuit said no. Even if state law would recognize a constructive trust in this situation, the circuit court explained that the state law was preempted by the supreme federal bankruptcy law's policy favoring equality of distribution between claimants. The court observed, "To permit a creditor, no matter how badly he was 'had' by the debtor, to lop off a piece of the estate under a constructive trust theory is to permit that creditor to circumvent completely the Code's equitable system of distribution."[605] Unless a constructive trust or equitable lien had already been imposed by a court prior to bankruptcy, or a trust had been created by statute,[606] according to *Omegas Group* the claimant has no property right *at all*. The prospective *remedy* of a constructive trust did not constitute "property." The claimant was just an unsecured creditor, and had to share with everyone else.

The *Omegas Group* decision did leave an opening for the recognition of constructive trusts in bankruptcy if a court had already imposed the trust or equitable interest prior to bankruptcy. In that situation, the claimant would have an enforceable property right under state law at the time of bankruptcy. The vitality of this small loophole in *Omegas Group* was demonstrated by the case of *In re McCafferty*,[607] in which the same Sixth Circuit did enforce a constructive trust. The debtor's ex-wife asserted a property right in the debtor's pension benefits pursuant to a prepetition state court divorce decree that created the constructive trust. Under state law her interest was superior to that of her ex-husband's creditors. The ex-wife prevailed in the bankruptcy case, and was able to obtain the turnover of the subject property.

The Sixth Circuit's hostile view towards constructive trusts in bankruptcy is controversial, and has been criticized.[608] Numerous courts in other circuits have applied constructive trusts in bankruptcy,[609] and in many ways have limited and qualified the reach of *Omegas Group*. The criticisms are apt. As Professor Kull cogently explains, the fundamental error of *Omegas Group* is its failure to recognize that in appropriate circumstances the law of restitution recognizes and enforces the claimant's underlying rights *in property,* which are superior under non-bankruptcy law to the claims not only of the debtor but of the debtor's creditors as well. The equities of

---

[604] 16 F.3d 1443 (6th Cir. 1994).

[605] Id. at 1453.

[606] See § 7.35.

[607] 96 F.3d 192 (6th Cir. 1996).

[608] See Andrew Kull, Restitution in Bankruptcy: Reclamation and Constructive Trust, 72 Am. Bankr. L.J. 265 (1998).

[609] See, e.g., In re Leitner, 236 B.R. 420, 423–24 (Bankr. D. Kan. 1999) (disagreeing with *Omegas* and recognizing constructive trust on home debtor purchased with embezzled funds).

restitution are perfectly congruent with the equities of bankruptcy.[610] Claimants who do have a valid non-bankruptcy restitutionary claim are *not* similarly situated to the debtor's general creditors. A "constructive trust" often is simply a means to give effect to the claimant's superior right *in property*. And when a restitutionary claim cannot be established vis-à-vis the debtor's creditors *outside* of bankruptcy—as, for example, when the claimant cannot trace his property—then likewise a constructive trust claim *in* bankruptcy would and should fail.

To see these points, assume that the debtor stole Ralph's wallet (stuffed with cash) on the way to the courthouse to file bankruptcy. Surely even the Sixth Circuit would give Ralph back his wallet;[611] it is, after all, *his* wallet; Ralph isn't a "creditor" of the debtor, on a par with the credit card company, the chiropractor, and the cleaners. Should the result change if debtor took the cash out of Ralph's wallet and bought a trombone before filing bankruptcy?[612] Again, it is hard to fathom why that should be the case. Now the bankruptcy trustee can't give Ralph his cash back, because the debtor already spent it, but the equities clearly demand that a "constructive trust" be imposed in Ralph's favor on the traceable fruits of the stolen money, the trombone. To do otherwise would unfairly give a windfall to the debtor's creditors at Ralph's expense. If, however, the debtor used the cash to buy (and eat) a lot of hot dogs, and threw the wallet in the river, then poor Ralph is just out of luck in terms of obtaining restitutionary relief, because there is no property on which the restitutionary claim can be fastened. Ralph is left with a "claim" simply because we have nothing else to give him.

And yet, the danger exists that courts blindly following the Sixth Circuit's blanket dismissal of constructive trusts in bankruptcy might get it terribly wrong. Kull gives the following appalling example:

> The best illustration so far of the practical harm done by *Omegas Group* is a 1996 decision in the *Dow Corning* case. Because of simple clerical errors, a buyer of goods from Dow Corning was invoiced twice for an order worth $300,000; both invoices were paid shortly before Dow Corning's bankruptcy. The buyer sought to recover the second $300,000 as money paid by mistake. The bankruptcy court denied the claim on the authority of *Omegas Group*. Because the remedy of constructive trust had been declared "anathema to the equities of bankruptcy," the other creditors of Dow Corning were allowed to divide up an extra $300,000 which, by common sense and at common law, was merely the misplaced property of the claimant.

> Such an outcome is impossible to square with our basic notions of property. Because ownership is not ordinarily destroyed when property is transferred by mistake, the result in *Dow Corning* makes bankruptcy an instrument of confiscation. No accepted principle of bankruptcy mandates such indifference to underlying questions of ownership. On the contrary, the usual precept is that

---

[610] Kull, supra note 608, at 276–77.

[611] Id. at 279.

[612] In essence, this is like the *Leitner* case, supra note 609, where the debtor embezzled money from the claimant and then used the embezzled money to buy a home.

bankruptcy respects state-law property rights except where they have been specifically reallocated.[613]

To that one can only say, "amen." Bankruptcy should not be "an instrument of confiscation." What courts must do is carefully apply long-established principles of the law of restitution, and when that non-bankruptcy law dictates returning a claimant's property to him—*even when a debtor is insolvent and has competing creditors*—then that is the proper result, whether the "property" returned be the very thing itself that was misappropriated, or instead just the traceable fruits of that thing via a "constructive trust."

§ 7.37   Reclamation by Sellers

A particular type of implied fraud by the debtor may permit a trade creditor to *reclaim* goods in kind from the bankruptcy estate. The situation in which reclamation may be permitted is where the creditor-seller ships goods to the debtor-buyer on credit, not realizing that the debtor was *insolvent* at the time it received the goods. By definition, then, the debtor was unable to pay for the goods when it took delivery of them. Under commercial practice, receipt of goods on credit amounts to a tacit business representation of solvency, and thus the debtor's credit receipt while insolvent is deemed fraudulent against the seller.[614] If the creditor makes a prompt demand for the return of the goods, both the Uniform Commercial Code and the Bankruptcy Code permit reclamation (or an equivalent substitute).

A seller's reclamation right is recognized by § 2–702(2) of the Uniform Commercial Code and antecedent common law. Under § 2–702(2), reclamation will lie if: (1) the seller discovers (2) that the buyer received goods on credit while insolvent, and (3) the seller makes demand for reclamation within 10 days of the buyer's receipt. The U.C.C. excuses compliance with the 10–day rule if the buyer made a written misrepresentation of solvency within the three months before delivery of the goods.

Prior to enactment of the Bankruptcy Code in 1978, the cases were in hopeless disarray over the extent to which a seller's U.C.C. reclamation right could be enforced in a federal bankruptcy case. Congress sought to clarify this problem by enacting § 546(c), which as originally enacted provided that the trustee's avoiding powers (except those to set aside fraudulent transfers) were "subject to any statutory or common law right" of the seller to reclaim goods, with some additional bankruptcy requirements included. Courts generally agreed that § 546(c) itself did not create a federal right of reclamation, but simply incorporated non-bankruptcy reclamation entitlements as limitations on the bankruptcy trustee's avoiding powers. Courts debated, however, whether under this original formulation § 546(c) was the *exclusive* basis for a seller to reclaim goods from the bankruptcy estate, or merely provided a complying seller with a safe harbor from the trustee's avoiding powers, leaving the possibility that a seller who did not comply with § 546(c) still might escape avoidance.

---

[613] Kull, supra note 608, at 275–76 (citing In re Dow Corning Corp., 192 B.R. 428 (Bankr. E.D. Mich. 1996)).

[614] U.C.C. § 2–702, Official Comment 2.

Even before the 2005 amendments, the courts generally read § 546(c) as *exclusive*,[615] and compliance with that section's terms as mandatory to establish an enforceable bankruptcy reclamation right.

In 2005, Congress amended § 546(c)(1) by deleting the reference to the "statutory or common law" right of reclamation.[616] At a minimum, this amendment should make clear that reclamation in bankruptcy may occur only if the seller complies with all the requirements of § 546(c)(1). As will be seen, § 546(c)(1) varies in several important particulars from § 2–702(2) of the U.C.C. Less obvious, though, is whether this 2005 deletion changes the landscape and renders non-bankruptcy reclamation rights—and restrictions—completely irrelevant, and creates instead only an independent federal right of reclamation. Most courts have held that amended § 546(c)(1) does not establish an independent federal reclamation right, and that non-bankruptcy reclamation rules and limitations remain viable.[617] The issue is particularly critical in determining, for example, whether the seller's reclamation right in bankruptcy is subject to the rights of a buyer in the ordinary course of business or other good faith purchaser, as it is under the U.C.C., but which is not referenced in § 546(c)(1).[618] Even if so, courts may disagree as to the *application* of those limitations; for example, does a DIP lender in bankruptcy qualify as a good faith purchaser, so that if the goods subject to reclamation are also subject to the DIP lien, and are sold, with the proceeds distributed to the DIP lender, is the reclamation claim rendered valueless?[619]

Perhaps it is possible that § 2–702(2) of the U.C.C. and the attendant judicial gloss thereon still complement § 546(c)(1) to the extent there is no conflict. However, to the extent § 546(c)(1) and § 2–702(2) conflict, then the federal provision of course controls. For example, the fact that a seller demands reclamation within 45 days after the debtor's receipt of the goods, as permitted by the federal law, but not within 10 days after receipt, as required by the U.C.C., plainly would not be a basis for denying reclamation under § 546(c)(1).

To establish a right of reclamation under § 546(c)(1), a seller must carry the burden of proving the following statutory elements:

1. The seller sold the goods to the debtor in the *ordinary course* of the seller's business.

2. The debtor was *insolvent* (as defined in § 101(32)) at the time it received the goods.

3. The debtor received the goods *within 45 days* before the filing of the bankruptcy petition.

---

[615] See In re Julien Co., 44 F.3d 426, 432 (6th Cir. 1995).

[616] Pub. L. No. 109–8, § 1227(a), 119 Stat. 199–200 (2005).

[617] See In re Dana Corp., 367 B.R. 409, 416 (Bankr. S.D.N.Y. 2007).

[618] Id. at 417–18.

[619] Compare Phar–Mor, Inc. v. McKesson Corp.,534 F.3d 502, 507–08 (6th Cir. 2008) (reclamation claim still valid, and may be compensated with administrative expense priority), with In re Dairy Mart Convenience Stores, Inc., 302 B.R. 128, 136 (Bankr. S.D.N.Y. 2003) (reclamation claim valueless).

4. The seller made a *written demand* for return of the goods.

5. The demand was made not later than 45 days after the debtor received the goods, § 546(c)(1)(A), or, if the 45–day period expired after the commencement of the bankruptcy case, the demand was made not later than 20 days after the bankruptcy case was commenced, § 546(c)(1)(B).

Furthermore, implicit in the remedy of reclaiming "such goods" are the requirements that:

1. The goods are identifiable as those sold to the debtor.

2. The goods are still in the possession or control of the trustee or debtor in possession at the time of the demand.

Complementing the seller's reclamation right under § 546(c)(1) is an administrative expense priority under § 503(b)(9), added in 2005.[620] If the seller fails to provide the notice required by § 546(c)(1), it still may assert the rights to an administrative priority in § 503(b)(9). § 546(c)(2). Under § 503(b)(9), administrative priority is awarded for the *value* of goods received by the debtor within *20 days* before bankruptcy (rather than the 45–day period allowed in § 546(c)(1)) if the goods were sold to the debtor in the *ordinary course* of the debtor's business. Indeed, assuming that the bankruptcy estate is administratively solvent, a prospective reclamation seller may simply choose to file a request for administrative priority for goods that the debtor received within the 20 days before bankruptcy, rather than bother with reclamation under § 546(c)(1). Interestingly, there is no statutory requirement in § 503(b)(9) that the seller claiming an administrative expense priority prove that the debtor received the goods while insolvent, as there is in § 546(c)(1).

Furthermore, even if reclamation of the goods themselves is impossible under § 546(c)(1) because, for example, the goods cannot be identified (because commingled) or are no longer in the debtor or trustee's possession (because sold), the ordinary course seller would be able to fall back on an administrative priority claim under § 503(b)(9).[621] As noted, the look-back period for the priority is only for goods received by the debtor within 20 days of bankruptcy, whereas reclamation is permitted for goods received within 45 days before bankruptcy.

If the seller's right to reclamation under § 546(c)(1) is established, the seller is entitled to reclaim the goods in kind. In a chapter 7 case, this means that the trustee will surrender the goods themselves to the seller. See § 725. In a chapter 11 case, if the debtor is still operating its business as a debtor in possession, the debtor may wish to retain the goods. In order to do so, the debtor essentially will have to again "purchase" the goods from the seller. This postpetition purchase of the reclaimed goods presumably will be an ordinary course transaction requiring no prior court approval for the debtor's payment of the purchase price. See § 363(c)(1).

---

[620] Pub. L. No. 109–8, § 1227(b), 119 Stat. 200 (2005).

[621] See, e.g., *Phar–Mor*, supra note 619.

Section 546(c)(1), as amended in 2005, now expressly provides that a seller's reclamation right is "subject to the prior rights of a holder of a security interest in such goods or the proceeds thereof." This amendment codified, in part, prevailing case law under pre–2005 law. The legislative history to the 1978 Code emphasized that nothing in the Bankruptcy Code's recognition of a seller's reclamation right was intended to change the relative non-bankruptcy priorities of creditors to the debtor's goods, and thus the bankruptcy "right is subject to any superior rights of other creditors."[622] A creditor with a perfected security interest in the debtor's inventory, for example, thus would defeat a seller's reclamation right under § 546(c)(1) if non-bankruptcy law would accord priority to the secured creditor. Resolving a fight between a reclamation seller and an inventory lender thus will require resort to applicable non-bankruptcy law.

A curious, and perhaps unintended, consequence of the addition in 2005 of the specific reference to the prior rights of a secured creditor is to raise doubts as to whether *other* "superior rights of other creditors" under non-bankruptcy law no longer trump the seller's bankruptcy reclamation right, as they surely did prior to 2005. One plausibly could make an *expressio unius est exclusio alterius* ("expression of one thing is the exclusion of another") statutory construction argument, to the effect that by specifically referencing the prior right of a secured creditor in § 546(c)(1), but not mentioning any other superior rights, the latter were no longer viable. Otherwise, why bother taking the trouble to mention the prior rights of a secured creditor (especially since such a creditor would have prevailed over a reclamation claimant under pre–2005 law anyway)? This matters especially vis-à-vis buyers in the ordinary course of business ("BOCB"), who do defeat reclamation claimants outside of bankruptcy under the U.C.C. While certainly open to question, it is most probable that the intent of Congress in 2005 was not to take away any non-bankruptcy "superior rights" of other parties (such as a BOCB) but simply to remove any doubt about the priority accorded to secured creditors. Indeed, if a BOCB from the debtor were vulnerable to a reclamation seller if the debtor filed bankruptcy, the dislocation on the world of commerce would be extreme. Nor is there any bankruptcy-specific reason to alter the non-bankruptcy pecking order between those competing claimants. Finally, nothing in the history of the 2005 law suggested that Congress believed it was effecting such a sea change in the relative rights of competing claimants.

As mentioned above, the seller's right of reclamation as enforced under Bankruptcy Code § 546(c)(1) differs in several significant ways from § 2–702(2) of the Uniform Commercial Code. First, the definition of "insolvency" is different in the two codes. In particular, under the U.C.C., a person may be "insolvent" in the "equity" sense either if he has "generally ceased to pay debts in the ordinary course of business," U.C.C. § 1–201(23)(A), or is "unable to pay debts as they become due." U.C.C. § 1–201(23)(B). In bankruptcy, equity insolvency does not apply in the reclamation context; instead, only a "balance sheet" insolvency test is used, so that a seller must prove that the buyer's debts exceeded its assets. § 101(32). The U.C.C. now also includes a balance sheet test of insolvency in addition to the "equity insolvency" tests of subsection (A) and (B) of 1–201(23), noted above, by reference to the

---

[622] H.R. Rep. No. 95-595, 95th Cong., 1st Sess. 372 (1977). See also S. Rep. No. 95–989, 95th Cong., 2d Sess., at 86 (1978) ("[R]ight is subject to any superior rights of *secured* creditors.") (emphasis added).

bankruptcy definition: the definition of "insolvent" includes "being insolvent within the meaning of federal bankruptcy law." U.C.C.§ 1–201(23)(C). A second significant difference between Bankruptcy Code § 546(c)(1) and § 2–702(2) of the Uniform Commercial Code is that § 546(c)(1) requires a *written* demand for reclamation, while § 2–702(2) would also permit an oral demand to suffice. In bankruptcy, an oral demand will not be enough.[623] Third, the Bankruptcy Code, unlike the U.C.C., does not excuse the seller from compliance with the time limits for making the reclamation demand if the buyer made a written misrepresentation of solvency within three months.[624] Fourth, under § 546(c)(1), the sale must have been made in the ordinary course of the seller's business, while no such constraint applies under § 2–702(2).

A final difference is the time periods within which the demand must be made. Under § 2–702(2), the seller must make the demand within 10 days of the debtor's receipt of the goods (subject to the misrepresentation excuse, noted above). Originally the Bankruptcy Code also required demand within 10 days. In 1994, though, Congress amended the statute to allow the seller to make demand *either* within 10 days, *or* within 20 days, if the 10–day period expired after the commencement of the bankruptcy case. The change was made in response to the complaints of trade creditors who said they did not have sufficient notice to exercise their reclamation rights when the debtor took delivery of the goods just before bankruptcy was filed.[625] In 2005, Congress again changed the time periods within which demand had to be made, considerably liberalizing those requirements to the benefit of sellers, who now have *45 days* to demand reclamation, or, if bankruptcy intervenes within the 45–day demand period, 20 days after the bankruptcy filing to make their demand.

Even if the seller otherwise jumps through all of the hoops presented by § 2–702(2) and § 546(c), it still might not recover the goods. The debtor may have already transferred the goods to a third party. If the debtor no longer has the goods, the seller will be denied reclamation, and, prior to 2005, under the majority view could not obtain a compensating administrative expense claim or replacement lien to make up for the loss.[626] An exception was allowed if the debtor still had the goods when the demand was made, but ignored the demand and sold the goods to a third party.[627] The addition of the new administrative expense priority in 2005 in § 503(b)(9) enables the seller to recover a priority for the "value" of goods received within 20 days of bankruptcy, even if reclamation in kind is not possible.

Prior to 2005, even if the reclaiming seller fully complied with § 546(c) and U.C.C. § 2–702(2), and the debtor still had the goods, and no other creditors had rights superior to the reclaiming seller, the Bankruptcy Code *still* gave the bankruptcy court the power to deny reclamation in kind under an earlier version of § 546(c)(2). For example, the court might do so if the debtor needed the goods to reorganize.[628] If the

---

[623] See *Julien*, supra note 615, 44 F.3d 426.

[624] See In re Marin Motor Oil, Inc., 740 F.2d 220 (3d Cir. 1984).

[625] See H.R. Rep. No. 103–834, 103d Cong., 2d Sess., at 23 (1994).

[626] See Collingwood Grain, Inc. v. Coast Trading Co., 744 F.2d 686 (9th Cir. 1984).

[627] See In re Griffin Retreading Co., 795 F.2d 676 (8th Cir. 1986).

[628] See Eagle Indus. Truck Mfg., Inc. v. Cont'l Airlines, 125 B.R. 415 (Bankr. D. Del. 1991).

court denied reclamation, it then had to give the seller either an administrative expense priority under § 503(b) or secure the seller's claim with a lien. In 2005, Congress repealed the provision that gave the bankruptcy court the power to deny a valid reclamation claim.

The Code contains two other return-of-goods provisions. As part of the 1984 amendments that gave grain producers and fishermen a priority in payment, Congress also added § 546(d), which spells out a reclamation right for grain producers and fishermen. In 1994, Congress added § 546(h), which permits the debtor to return goods to a creditor and allows the creditor to offset the purchase price of the goods against its prepetition claim. This action must be approved by the court, after notice and a hearing, must be taken within 120 days of the commencement of the case, and the creditor must consent.

Chapter 8

EXECUTORY CONTRACTS AND
UNEXPIRED LEASES

A. OVERVIEW

§ 8.1   Summary of § 365

One of the most confused, difficult, and misunderstood areas in bankruptcy law is that of "executory contracts." Executory contracts are a special type of property that bankruptcy debtors bring to their bankruptcy estates.[1] What makes the treatment of contracts in bankruptcy difficult is that the *property* right in the contract is tied to an attendant *liability*; that is, the bankruptcy estate cannot obtain the right to the asset without incurring the contractual obligation. So it does not suffice simply to say that the contract passes into the estate via § 541 as property of the estate, because the rub is whether the asset is worth the concomitant liability. So what happens in bankruptcy to the debtor's contracts? The answers are found not in § 541, but instead in § 365, the Code section governing executory contracts and unexpired leases (which are just a subset of executory contracts).

Section 365 has mutated into an almost impenetrable legal thicket. Part of the problem is that § 365 has been a lightning rod for congressional tinkering and special interest legislation. After the dust had settled from the 1994 and 2005 Amendments, § 365 comprised sixteen subsections, many of considerable detail. It is difficult to quibble with the conclusions of the National Bankruptcy Conference's Code Review Project that "more reworking is required here than in other places in the Code,"[2] or of a leading article that "[t]he law of executory contracts is in need of a thorough rethinking."[3] Unfortunately, no such reworking or rethinking has occurred. More colorful, as well as more apt in capturing the nature of executory contract law, is the assessment of it as the most "psychedelic" part of a bankruptcy law "that might have been written by Lewis Carroll"[4] (author of "Alice in Wonderland").

---

[1]   Some of the best scholarship in the bankruptcy area has been written regarding executory contracts. The foundational work, written with respect to the law under the prior Bankruptcy Act but still relevant, was the monumental two-part article by Professor Vern Countryman, Executory Contracts in Bankruptcy (pt. I), 57 Minn. L. Rev. 439 (1973); id. (pt. II), 58 Minn. L. Rev. 479 (1974). Then in the late 1980s a trio of excellent works were published: Michael T. Andrew, Executory Contracts in Bankruptcy: Understanding "Rejection," 59 U. Colo. L. Rev. 845 (1988); Thomas H. Jackson, chapter 5, "Executory Contracts in Bankruptcy: The Combination of Assets and Liabilities," in The Logic and Limits of Bankruptcy Law, at 105–121 (Harvard 1986); Jay Lawrence Westbrook, A Functional Analysis of Executory Contracts, 74 Minn. L. Rev. 227 (1989).

[2]   National Bankruptcy Conference, Reforming the Bankruptcy Code 191 (1994).

[3]   Andrew, supra note 1, at 849. Another scholar described the situation with regard to executory contracts as "one approaching legal chaos." Morris G. Shanker, Bankruptcy Asset Theory and its Application to Executory Contracts, 1992 Ann. Surv. Bankr. L. 97, 97.

[4]   Westbrook, supra note 1, at 228.

Before delving into some of the unpleasant nuances of executory contract law, it might be helpful to have some sense of the overall outline and composition of § 365. As a threshold matter, the special rules of § 365 only apply to an executory contract or an unexpired lease. Yet, the Code nowhere defines "executory contract." Courts have had to fill in the gap and ascertain what constitutes an executory contract within the meaning of § 365.[5]

Executory contract law can be analyzed in light of:

1. The *options* the trustee has with regard to an executory contract;

2. The *limits* that constrain the trustee's choice; and

3. The legal *effects* of electing any particular option.

Much of § 365 goes to answering those questions. Section 365 also describes in some detail the procedures governing the trustee's exercise of the relevant options.[6] As discussed below,[7] the trustee has four basic choices with regard to an executory contract:

1. Reject the contract;[8]

2. Assume the contract;[9]

3. Assign the contract, after first assuming it;[10] or

4. Do nothing.[11]

The basic choice of the trustee[12] to *assume or reject* the contract, subject to court approval, is spelled out in § 365(a). The further option of assuming and then *assigning* the contract is dealt with by § 365(f).

The limits on the trustee's powers to assume an executory contract are addressed by subsections (b) and (c). A crucial *non*-limitation is stated by § 365(e), which invalidates "ipso facto" clauses. Ipso facto clauses would terminate or modify the contract automatically upon the filing of bankruptcy or the occurrence of insolvency, or give the non-debtor party the option to terminate or modify.[13] The restrictions on assignment are embodied in § 365(f). Because a contract must first be assumed in order

---

[5]   See § 8.2.

[6]   See §§ 8.4–8.5.

[7]   See § 8.3.

[8]   See §§ 8.6–8.13.

[9]   See §§ 8.14–8.20.

[10]   See §§ 8.21–8.24.

[11]   See §§ 8.25–8.27.

[12]   Note that references to the "trustee" include the "debtor in possession" in a chapter 11 case. § 1107(a).

[13]   See § 8.17.

to be assigned, § 365(f)(2)(A), all of the conditions to assumption apply with equal force to assignments.

As originally enacted, § 365(d) dealt primarily with some of the procedural rules governing the trustee's election, the most important of which were the time limits within which the trustee must act.[14] Since 1978 this subsection has been a particular favorite of Congress in wielding its special interest legislative pen. The amendments to subsection (d) have generally conferred extraordinary benefits on favored classes (lessors of commercial real estate, airports (repealed in 2005), equipment lessors, and so forth). Many of those benefits apply during the gap period after the filing of the petition but prior to the trustee's decision to assume or reject the contract.

Considerable attention is given in § 365 to the legal effects of a decision to reject the contract.[15] Some persuasive scholarship has suggested that much of this focus on the legal effects of rejection is "profoundly confused."[16] Be that as it may, the section as it currently reads does address the effects of rejection in depth; subsections (g), (h), (i), (j), (n) and (p) all cover that subject. In addition, two sections applicable only in chapter 11 cases deal with the rejection of special types of contracts: § 1113 governs the rejection of collective bargaining agreements,[17] and § 1114 covers retiree benefits.[18]

Much less is said in § 365 about the legal effect of assumption[19] or assignment.[20] While parts of subsections (b) and (g) do bear on assumption, much of the operative law has been developed by the courts. The ramifications of assignment are specified in § 365(k) and (l).

§ 8.2 Definition of an Executory Contract

Given the existence of the many special rules governing executory contracts in § 365, it becomes a matter of considerable importance to define an "executory contract." Many courts have grappled with the question of whether a contract is "executory" and thus within the purview of § 365 and its many rules—the most important of which is that the contract, if "executory," can be assumed or rejected by the trustee. Some courts attempt to bypass the threshold requirement of "executoriness," and instead focus directly on the results of allowing assumption or rejection of the contract. If determining executoriness under the traditional tests (explained below) would lead to an undesirable result, courts have utilized alternative analyses. Particularly troubling

---

[14] See § 8.4.

[15] See §§ 8.7–8.10.

[16] Andrew, supra note 1, at 848. Another influential article on this topic is Westbrook, supra note 1, 74 Minn. L. Rev. 227. Andrew responded to the Westbrook article in Michael T. Andrew, Executory Contracts Revisited: A Reply to Professor Westbrook, 62 U. Colo. L. Rev. 1 (1991). Professor Shanker also has made significant contributions. See Shanker, supra note 3; Morris G. Shanker, A Proposed New Executory Contract Statute, 1993 Ann. Surv. Bankr. L. 129. For a thoughtful earlier article, see Raymond T. Nimmer, Executory Contracts in Bankruptcy: Protecting the Fundamental Terms of the Bargain, 54 U. Colo. L. Rev. 507 (1983).

[17] See §§ 8.11–8.12.

[18] See § 8.13.

[19] See § 8.14.

[20] See § 8.21.

are cases where the debtor's contract rights and obligations are left in limbo: because the contract is held to be non-executory it can neither be assumed or rejected within the formal confines of § 365, and the results that follow from this "non" status are quite unpredictable.[21] For now, though, most courts approach issues regarding the treatment of the debtor's contracts in bankruptcy on the assumption that § 365 applies if and only if those contracts can be classified as "executory" within the meaning of that section.

Congress, however, has not defined "executory contract" in the Code. The legislative history suggests somewhat vaguely that "[t]hough there is no precise definition of what contracts are executory, it generally includes contracts on which performance remains due to some extent on both sides."[22] For bankruptcy law purposes, this description in the legislative history is of little greater interpretive assistance than Professor Williston's observation that "[a]ll contracts to a greater or lesser extent are executory. When they cease to be so, they cease to be contracts."[23]

This definitional void was filled by Professor Vern Countryman in a widely cited law review article, *Executory Contracts in Bankruptcy*.[24] Defining "executory contract" in light of the *purposes* to be served by the bankruptcy trustee's assumption or rejection of the contract, Professor Countryman excluded contracts that have been substantially performed by either the debtor or the non-debtor party to the contract. This is known as the "*material breach*" test. The "Countryman" definition of an "executory contract" is:

> a contract under which the obligation of both the bankrupt and the other party to the contract are so far unperformed that the failure of either to complete performance would constitute a material breach excusing the performance of the other.[25]

The rationale of this definition can be gleaned from a simple example. Assume that Debtor and Other Party enter into a contract prior to bankruptcy, pursuant to which Debtor agrees to buy and Other Party to sell 1,000 hats at a price of $5 each, with delivery to be made in 30 days. This contract, before either party has performed, can be viewed as an "asset coupled with a liability." For either side to obtain the promised benefit—the asset—that party must itself perform, which is the liability. Indeed, such is the essence of the whole concept of a contract.

In our hypothetical, consider first the case in which Other Party has already performed by the time Debtor files bankruptcy. In the hypothetical, this would mean that Other Party has delivered the hats to Debtor prior to the bankruptcy filing. The contract between Debtor and Other Party is no longer "executory" for bankruptcy

---

[21]   See Jay Lawrence Westbrook, A Functional Analysis of Executory Contracts, 74 Minn. L. Rev. 227, 239 (1989).

[22]   H.R. Rep. No. 95–595, 95th Cong., 1st Sess., at 347 (1977).

[23]   1 Samuel Williston, Contracts § 14 (3d ed. 1957) (quoted in Vern Countryman, Executory Contracts in Bankruptcy (pt. I), 57 Minn. L. Rev. 439, 450 (1973)).

[24]   The article was published in two parts: 57 Minn. L. Rev. 439 (1973) (pt. I), and 58 Minn. L. Rev. 479 (1974) (pt. II).

[25]   57 Minn. L. Rev. 439, 460 (1973).

purposes, because no function would be served by classifying it as such. Assumption of the contract is not necessary for the bankruptcy estate to obtain the benefit of the contract, since the estate already has that benefit (the hats). Nor would rejection do anything, since Other Party already has a claim for the unpaid purchase price. In short, the contract now is only a liability of the estate (and a "claim" for Other Party).

Now assume that Debtor has performed but that Other Party has not performed by the time the Debtor files bankruptcy. In the hypothetical, Debtor therefore has prepaid the purchase price but Other Party has not delivered the hats. Again, the contract would not be considered executory within the meaning of § 365, because again no purpose would be served by dealing with the contract under § 365. Assumption would not give the estate any greater rights than it already has under § 541; the Debtor having paid for the hats, the estate succeeds to Debtor's right either to delivery of the hats or to a remedy for breach against Other Party if Other Party fails to deliver. Rejection, which is treated as a deemed breach by Debtor, § 365(g), would be particularly nonsensical, for the simple reason that Debtor did not breach, but fully performed. It would be absurd to give Other Party a claim against the estate. In this situation, the contract is only an asset of the estate, without an accompanying liability.

Finally, consider the case in which neither party has performed its material obligations under the contract: Debtor has not paid, and Other Party has not delivered. This contract is "executory" for bankruptcy purposes. Treating it as such has bankruptcy consequences. Assumption of the contract by the trustee on behalf of the estate is necessary for the estate to capture the benefit of that contract, namely, delivery of the hats. In return, the estate becomes obligated to pay the purchase price as an expense of administration. If the contract is not beneficial, however, the trustee will not assume the contract, but instead will reject it. The estate will not enjoy the benefit of the contract, but neither will the estate be liable for the purchase price as a priority claim. Other Party will be left with only a general unsecured damages claim for breach. § 365(g)(1). This example demonstrates that a contract is dealt with as "executory" in bankruptcy only if at the time of the bankruptcy filing, that contract from the estate's perspective is an *asset coupled with a liability*.

The Countryman definition has been widely adopted in the courts, although not universally.[26] Obviously, many contracts are significantly more complex than the simple contract for sale described above, and perhaps no single definition can capture perfectly the exact universe of contracts with which bankruptcy must deal in a special way. Many of the decisions in which the courts have declined to use the Countryman test have been ones in which the court did not like the result that would follow under § 365 if the contract were treated as executory. Often the problem lies in the effect of

---

[26]   Currently, the Countryman test has been explicitly adopted in the Third, Fourth, Fifth, Seventh, Eighth, Ninth, and Tenth circuits, respectively. See, e.g., In re Baird, 567 F.3d 1207 (10th Cir. 2009); In re Liljeberg Enters., Inc., 304 F.3d 410 (5th Cir. 2002); In re Columbia Gas Sys., 50 F.3d 233 (3d Cir. 1995); In re Streets and Beard Farm P'ship, 882 F.2d 233 (7th Cir. 1989); Lubrizol Enters., Inc. v. Richmond Metal Finishers, Inc., 756 F.2d 1043 (4th Cir. 1986); In re Select–A–Seat Corp., 625 F.2d 20 (9th Cir. 1980); In re Knutson, 563 F.2d 916 (8th Cir. 1977). The remaining circuits have not explicitly adopted an approach; courts in those circuits may use the Countryman definition, but may utilize alternative analyses as well. For an example from the Second Circuit, see *In re Bradlees Stores, Inc.*, 2001 WL 1112308, at *6–7 (S.D.N.Y. Sept. 20, 2001).

rejection of that contract, which if done under § 365 seems blatantly unfair to the non-debtor party. The opposite problem also rears its head; in a number of scenarios (an option contract, for example), a finding of non-executoriness could prevent the estate from realizing the benefits of a valuable contract. Courts that have eschewed the Countryman test typically desire to reach a result that they deem preferable to that which § 365 would dictate.[27]

In light of the manifest confusion and uncertainty, some commentators and law reformers have urged a fundamental rethinking of the whole issue of "executoriness." Michael Andrew concluded that executoriness was meaningful only as applied to assumption, not rejection.[28] He suggested defining an executory contract as

> a contract under which (a) debtor and non-debtor each have unperformed obligations, and (b) the debtor, if it ceased further performance, would have no right to the other party's continued performance.[29]

Andrew's test is generally referred to as the "exclusionary" approach (because of his view that executory contracts do not automatically pass into the estate). His main goal was to prevent the erroneous use of "rejection" as a means of unfairly harming the non-debtor party. Some courts have used Andrew's approach.[30]

Professor Westbrook took Andrew's idea and went one step further: he proposed *eliminating the threshold requirement of "executoriness" altogether*, as what he called a "rule without a reason."[31] Westbrook explained that the bankruptcy trustee should be able to act as needed with respect to the respective rights and obligations that comprise the debtor's contracts that pass to the estate without having to pass a preliminary executoriness test:

> The trustee must abandon or realize upon each contract right in the estate and must perform or breach each contract obligation. When contract law makes certain rights and obligations interdependent, the trustee's right to realize upon the rights

---

[27]   For example, a widely cited decision under the former Bankruptcy Act that declined to follow the Countryman test is *In re Jolly*, 574 F.2d 349 (6th Cir.), cert. denied, 439 U.S. 929 (1978). In *Jolly*, a chapter XIII debtor wished to reject a contract to purchase burial plots as to which he was in default, and thereby avoid the cemetery's claim. The Sixth Circuit refused to allow rejection, and observed that "the key . . . is to work backward, proceeding from an examination of the purposes rejection is expected to accomplish. If those objectives have already been accomplished, or if they can't be accomplished through rejection, then the contract is not executory." Id. at 351.

An even more blatant result-oriented approach was taken in *In re Booth*, 19 B.R. 53 (Bankr. D. Utah 1982). Judge Ralph Mabey in that case recharacterized a contract for deed as a secured transaction in order to prevent the rejection of the contract and the forfeiture that would ensue. In doing so, Judge Mabey observed that "executory contracts are measured not by a mutuality of commitments but by the nature of the parties and the goals of reorganization. . . . Thus, it is the consequences of applying § 365 to a party . . . which controls." Id. at 57.

[28]   Michael T. Andrew, Executory Contracts in Bankruptcy: Understanding "Rejection," 59 U. Colo. L. Rev. 845, 889–894 (1988).

[29]   Id. at 893.

[30]   See, e.g., In re Family Snacks, Inc., 257 B.R. 884, 905 (B.A.P. 8th Cir. 2001).

[31]   Westbrook, supra note 21, at 282–85.

will be dependent upon performance of the obligations, as for any other contract party.[32]

The 1997 National Bankruptcy Review Commission agreed with Westbrook, and recommended to Congress that "Title 11 should be amended to delete all references to "executory" in section 365 and related provisions, and "executoriness" should be eliminated as a prerequisite to the trustee's election to assume or breach a contract."[33] Alas, with Congress making extensive revisions to the Bankruptcy Code in 2005 and with no change in the basic conceptions underlying § 365, including the need to pass through the "executory" door to play the § 365 game, it appears unlikely that any change is forthcoming. Courts thus will have to persist in their struggles to divine the meaning of an "executory contract." In doing so, they should try to keep their eyes on the ball, namely, to ask, what is the *function* that is to be served by the decision in a particular case, and does it make sense for the bankruptcy trustee to be able to deal with the rights or obligations of a contract that has passed into the estate?

The Countryman definition has proven difficult to apply especially in the context of certain kinds of agreements where a material breach analysis does not appropriately define the true nature of the contract. The concern is that application of the Countryman definition to such agreements creates a larger hurdle to assumption or rejection by the trustee than Congress intended, and may without any evident justification either harm the estate or give it a windfall, with a correspondingly unwarranted windfall or harm to the non-debtor.

This issue is especially apparent in the treatment of option contracts. Using the Countryman definition, an option contract simply cannot be executory. Because there is no affirmative duty on the part of the optionee to exercise the option, the optionee is technically incapable of causing a material breach. Some courts have relied on alternative tests to get around the harsh result caused by the application of the Countryman definition.[34] Other courts have drawn a bright-line rule based on timing. Under this second approach, an option contract may be executory only where the optionee has elected to exercise the option, but performance is still due on both sides.[35] Although this approach has the benefit of consistency, one criticism is that it makes an

---

[32] Id. at 281. The National Bankruptcy Conference also has recommended discarding the terms "rejection" and "executory contract" altogether. National Bankruptcy Conference, Reforming the Bankruptcy Code 203–07 (1994).

Professor Shanker likewise has argued that "focusing on whether a contract is or is not executory is the wrong approach." Morris G. Shanker, Bankruptcy Asset Theory and its Application to Executory Contracts, 1992 Ann. Surv. Bankr. L. 97, 101. Instead, the focus should be on whether the *debtor* has future contractual obligations, which the trustee then must decide whether to perform or not. Whether the Other Party has future obligations is irrelevant, Shanker asserts. Id. at 101–02.

[33] National Bankruptcy Review Commission, Final Report: Bankruptcy: The Next Twenty Years, Recommendation 2.4.4 at 21 (1997).

[34] See, e.g., In re Waldron, 36 B.R. 633 (Bankr. S.D. Fla. 1984) (finding that an option contract could be executory under the "some performance due" language contained in the legislative history). In this case, the court assumed the optionee would elect the option. The "performance due" for the optionor referred to both the obligation to keep the option open, and then to ultimately perform once the option was exercised.

[35] See, e.g., In re Robert L. Helms Constr. & Dev. Co., Inc., 139 F.3d 702 (9th Cir. 1998).

arbitrary distinction, with harsh results; an option elected the day before filing may be assumed or rejected, whereas an option elected the day after may not.[36]

The other concern is that strict adherence to the Countryman definition is open to manipulation and can lead to uncertainty in application. This can be seen in the context of licensing agreements. The issue arises where the main obligation of the license agreement, usually the payment of money, has been performed, but each side has some remaining obligations under the agreement. The query then becomes whether these remaining obligations are significant enough to give rise to a material breach under the Countryman definition. Riding on the outcome of the "executoriness" decision is whether the estate then can "assume" (and thus capture the value of a beneficial contract) or "reject" (and thus escape a disadvantageous contract).

Two recent cases, decided by two courts of appeals in 2012 on very similar facts— but reaching opposing results—illustrate the issue. In *In re Exide Technologies*,[37] the court held that a licensing agreement was *not* an executory contract where the licensee had already substantially performed by paying the purchase price. The court found that the licensee's remaining obligations under the license, such as quality control and trademark use restrictions, were not substantial enough to cause a material breach. Because the agreement was not "executory," rejection was not permitted.[38]

By contrast, the court in *In re Interstate Bakeries*,[39] dealt with a similar licensing agreement but reached a very different result. There, the licensee also had already substantially performed by paying the purchase price, but was still subject to a quality control provision. The court distinguished this case from *Exide*, however, mainly because the contract itself provided that the quality control provision was in fact material. Thus, because the licensee had at least one remaining obligation that could give rise to a material breach, the license was held to be executory and thus subject to assumption or rejection under § 365.

Taken together, these cases illustrate some of the key problems in applying the Countryman definition to licensing agreements—and indeed, highlight the basic foolishness of imposing a threshold test of "executoriness" in the first place. First, the outcome may be unpredictable; although both courts were dealing with interpreting the materiality of a quality control provision, they came to opposite results. Second, the standard may allow for manipulation by the parties. Simply by specifying in the contract that a provision is material, the parties in *In re Interstate Bakeries* were able to render the agreement executory. And at the end of the day, the most basic question remains: what is the point of going through this threshold game of "pin the executory tail on the bankruptcy donkey" at all? It has taken on a meaningless yet critically important life of its own.

The executoriness issue also has proven difficult in the context of negative covenants, such as non-compete clauses. Courts have grappled with whether an

---

[36]   See, e.g., In re Bergt, 241 B.R. 17, 21 (D. Alaska 1999).

[37]   607 F.3d 957 (3d Cir. 2012).

[38]   Id. at 964.

[39]   690 F.3d 1069 (8th Cir. 2012).

obligation *not* to do something can rise to the level of materiality required by the Countryman definition.[40] It may be that a negative covenant can be executory even under a strict Countryman standard where it is central to the bargained-for agreement.[41] However the courts decide the question, though, it is hard to justify why the question is worth asking in the first place. The better approach is simply to consider the state law dealing with the impact of negative covenants, when performed or not, and then ask directly whether a federal bankruptcy policy requires reaching a different result than would obtain under the non-bankruptcy law. Hiding such an inquiry behind the smokescreen of "executoriness" is at best confusing and unhelpful, and can be pernicious if valuable contracts are lost or burdensome ones linger.

§ 8.3   The Trustee's Options

Assuming that a contract is "executory,"[42] the critical question facing the bankruptcy trustee (or debtor in possession)[43] is what choice to make with regard to that contract.[44] Even if the contract is viewed as a special form of property of the estate,[45] the obligations under that contract do not automatically bind the estate. This basic concept has been a cornerstone of executory contract law since the 1818 English case of *Copeland v. Stephens*.[46] The options the trustee has are to:

1.   *Assume* the contract;

2.   *Reject* the contract;

3.   *Assign* the contract after first assuming it; or

4.   *Do nothing.*

Section 365(a) sets forth the basic choice, providing that "the trustee, subject to the court's approval, may assume or reject any executory contract or unexpired lease of the debtor." *"Assumption"* means that the estate itself becomes obligated on the

---

[40]   See, In re Spectrum Information Techs., Inc., 190 B.R. 741, 748 (Bankr. E.D.N.Y. 1996) ("remaining obligations of confidentiality and non-interference are vestiges of that agreement that do not rise to a level of material future performance"); But see In re Rovine Corp., 5 B.R. 402, 404 (Bankr. W.D. Tenn. 1980) ("an obligation not to do a particular thing . . . falls squarely in the definition of executory contracts. . . . ").

[41]   E.g., In re WorldCom, Inc., 343 B.R. 486 (Bankr. S.D.N.Y. 2006).

[42]   See § 8.2.

[43]   In a chapter 11 case, the debtor in possession is the representative of the estate vested with the power to decide what to do about executory contracts. § 1107(a).

[44]   See Jesse M. Fried, Executory Contracts and Performance Decisions, 46 Duke L.J. 517 (1996).

[45]   There is some debate as to whether an executory contract passes into the estate under § 541. Michael Andrew asserts that contracts do not automatically become part of the estate; this is known as the "exclusionary" approach. See Michael T. Andrew, Executory Contracts in Bankruptcy: Understanding "Rejection," 59 U. Colo. L. Rev. 845, 856–66 (1988); Michael T. Andrew, Executory Contracts Revisited: A Reply to Professor Westbrook, 62 U. Colo. L. Rev. 1, 4–5, 19–23 (1991). Professors Westbrook and Shanker argue that contracts do become property of the estate. Jay L. Westbrook, A Functional Analysis of Executory Contracts, 74 Minn. L. Rev. 227, 248–49, 323–32 (1989); Morris G. Shanker, Bankruptcy Asset Theory and its Application to Executory Contracts, 1992 Ann. Surv. Bankr. L. 97, 104–08. All agree, though, that the contract only binds the estate if the trustee acts to "assume" that contract.

[46]   106 Eng. Rep. 218 (K.B. 1818).

contract.[47] It is a decision of the estate representative to perform the contract. By doing so the estate will become entitled to obtain the benefit of the contract; in return, the claim of the non-debtor party will be elevated to priority status as an administrative expense of the estate.

"Rejection" is best understood as a decision by the trustee not to assume the contract.[48] By rejecting the contract the trustee has chosen not to obligate the estate on the contract. Rejection is treated as a prepetition breach of the contract, thus leaving the non-debtor party with only a general unsecured claim for damages. § 365(g)(1). Of course, if the trustee rejects the contract, the estate will not receive the benefit of that contract.

A third option, essentially a corollary to assumption but not mentioned in § 365(a), is for the trustee to assume and then *assign* the contract to a third party.[49] § 365(f). Assignment allows the estate to capture the value of a profitable contract by selling the contract. Upon assignment the estate will be relieved of any further liability on the contract. § 365(k).

A final option, which is only implicitly recognized in the statute, is for the trustee to *do nothing.* In other words, the trustee might not take any action to assume, assign, or reject. Often the trustee has a strong incentive to delay making an election as long as possible, thereby preserving the possibility of reaping the benefit of the contract through assumption or assignment if it ultimately appears that doing so will be in the best interest of the estate, but also preserving the option of rejection as well. During this limbo period in which no decision has been made, the trustee can compel the other party to continue performing, even though the trustee is not strictly bound to the contract unless the contract is ultimately assumed.[50] Colloquially put, during this limbo period the trustee on behalf of the bankruptcy estate is free to drive down a one-way street of enforceability. In chapter 7 cases or cases involving leases of nonresidential real property, if the trustee fails to act within specified time periods, the contract will be deemed rejected.[51] § 365(d)(1), (4). In these instances, if the trustee does not act, the law makes the choice for the estate. In a chapter 11 case, any contract other than a nonresidential real property lease will not be deemed rejected if the trustee fails to act; the Code gives the trustee until the time of confirmation of the plan to assume or reject. § 365(d)(2). If the trustee does not do so, the contract will "ride through" the reorganization and be binding on the debtor after confirmation.[52]

---

[47] See § 8.14. See Daniel J. Bussel & Edward A. Friedler, The Limits on Assuming and Assigning Executory Contracts, 74 Am. Bankr. L.J. 321 (2000).

[48] See § 8.7.

[49] See § 8.21. See Bussel & Friedler, supra note 47.

[50] See Douglas W. Bordewieck, The Postpetition, Pre–Rejection, Pre–Assumption Status of an Executory Contract, 59 Am. Bankr. L.J. 197 (1985).

[51] See § 8.4.

[52] Although the Code itself is silent as to the treatment of a contract that has been neither assumed nor rejected by the debtor, courts have applied a judicially created "ride through" or "pass through" doctrine. This doctrine provides that if a contract is neither assumed nor rejected it will pass through the bankruptcy unaffected. See, e.g., In re National Gypsum Co., 208 F.3d 498 (5th Cir. 2000) (citing Federal's, Inc. v. Edmonton Inv. Co., 555 F.2d 577, 579 (6th Cir.1977) (decided under prior Bankruptcy Act)).

Which choice should the trustee make? The ultimate question is whether the contract will be beneficial to the estate.[53] Many factors may affect the answer to that question. The hypothetical discussed in the preceding section will serve to illustrate the trustee's exercise of her discretion in a fairly simple setting. In that contract Debtor agreed to buy and Other Party to sell 1,000 hats at $5 each, with delivery in 30 days. If the Debtor files bankruptcy while the contract is still "executory," i.e., before either party has substantially performed, the contract will pass to the bankruptcy estate.

In our hypothetical the trustee's choice will depend primarily on the current market price of hats. If the price has declined, to $4 for example, the trustee will not want to assume the contract, but will reject the contract. Even if the estate needs hats, it can go out and purchase them in the market for less than the contract price. The Other Party will have an unsecured claim for its damages, but that claim will only be paid in "bankruptcy dollars" out of the bankruptcy distribution. For example, if general creditors are paid 30¢ on the dollar in the bankruptcy case, the Other Party's claim of $1,000 (contract price minus market price) will only result in a $300 payment in bankruptcy.

If, however, the market price of hats has risen, for example to $6, the trustee will want to assume the contract. The $5 contract price is very favorable compared to the market price. If the estate actually wants the hats, it is obviously better off paying $5 each for them instead of $6. Even if the estate does not need hats, the trustee probably could assume and then assign the contract to a third party at the higher market price. The premium of one dollar per hat over contract price will be captured by the estate.

B. PROCEDURES

§ 8.4   Timing

The bankruptcy trustee's decision whether to assume, assign, or reject an executory contract often is of considerable importance, both to the estate and to the non-debtor party to that contract. Given the importance of the trustee's decision, the question of *when* the trustee must decide becomes critical. The interests of the trustee and the non-debtor party often diverge sharply with regard to the timing issue.

The non-debtor party usually prefers a rapid decision. If the trustee's election is to assume, the non-debtor party will enjoy several benefits, notably the curing of any existing defaults, § 365(b), and the ability to enforce the obligations due under the contract against the estate as an expense of administration. § 365(g)(2). Furthermore, the non-debtor party can rely on the continued existence of the contract in making future business plans. Even if the trustee's decision is to reject, the non-debtor party may prefer to learn of that choice sooner rather than later. Knowing that the estate will not assume the contract enables the non-debtor party to make alternative business arrangements. The only benefit of a delayed rejection for the non-debtor party would be if the estate were paying currently for benefits received under the contract, pending the trustee's decision, and the non-debtor could not readily replace that source of income.

---

[53]   See Fried, supra note 44.

By contrast, the trustee almost invariably will prefer delay. Delay gives the trustee greater flexibility. The trustee may not know early in the case which contracts will be beneficial to the estate. Circumstances may change, and it may take time to gather complete information. Making a final decision to reject or assume commits the trustee. If the choice is to reject, the trustee cannot change her mind later. The potential benefit of that contract will be lost to the estate. Conversely, if the trustee assumes the contract, the estate will become obligated on the contract. If the assumption later appears to have been unwise, the estate either will have to perform on an unprofitable contract or pay damages as an administrative priority for breach.[54]

A detailed series of rules in § 365(d) attempt to balance the competing interests of the estate and the non-debtor party with regard to the time within which the trustee's decision to assume or reject must be made. In almost every instance, the bankruptcy court retains the power to extend or shorten the time; the difference in the various statutory provisions is in the default rule. In some situations the trustee must persuade the court to grant an extension based on a showing of "cause," see § 365(d)(1), (4)(B), whereas in other cases the non-debtor party must convince the court to compel the trustee to make an earlier decision. § 365(d)(2).

When the court is deciding whether to extend or to shorten the time for the trustee to decide, it will balance the competing interests of the parties. Some of the potentially pertinent factors were mentioned above. The party asking the court to override the default rule will bear the burden of persuasion. In reality, it usually is much easier for the trustee or debtor in possession to persuade the court to grant it an extension of time than it is for the non-debtor party to obtain an order shortening the time. The trustee is acting on behalf of the estate, and therefore represents the interests of many creditors and other affected parties, whereas the non-debtor party stands alone. Cognizant of this fact, and of the irreversible consequences of the assumption or rejection choice, courts are hesitant to force the trustee to move too quickly. A non-debtor party asking for a reduction in time will need to show particularized and substantial harm to it resulting from delay, along with a minimum of prejudice to the estate. If the non-debtor party is being paid on a current basis postpetition while the trustee is pondering her decision, it becomes even more difficult for the non-debtor party to prevent delay of the trustee's final decision. In short, courts tend to favor the estate's interest over that of the non-debtor party.

Which default rule applies depends on the application of several factors, including the applicable chapter and the nature of the contract. In a chapter 7 case, the trustee has *60 days* to act. § 365(d)(1). Within that 60–day period, the trustee must either assume or reject, or must obtain an extension of time from the court. If the trustee fails to act by the 60–day deadline, the contract is deemed rejected as a matter of law. This presumptive 60–day rule applies to all types of executory contracts and unexpired leases in chapter 7 cases (except for nonresidential real property leases, which have their own rule, § 365(d)(4)).

---

[54]   In re Klein Sleep Prods., Inc., 78 F.3d 18 (2d Cir. 1996). In a 2005 amendment, Congress limited the amount of the administrative priority in this situation to two years' rent. § 503(b)(7).

In any type of reorganization proceeding, whether under chapter 9, 11, 12, or 13, the trustee is not constrained by an initial 60–day period. Instead, the statute gives the trustee until *confirmation of the plan* to decide. § 365(d)(2). The trustee (or debtor in possession) may not know which contracts it will want to retain until the plan has been finally formulated. The courts have long recognized that a trustee in a reorganization case should have a reasonable time to weigh the relative burdens and benefits of an executory contract.[55] As the Supreme Court noted in *NLRB v. Bildisco & Bildisco*, "this difference between the two types of proceedings reflects the considered judgment of Congress that a debtor-in-possession seeking to reorganize should be granted more latitude in deciding whether to reject than should a trustee in liquidation."[56] Thus the burden is on the non-debtor party to seek an order to compel the trustee or debtor in possession to make a final decision at some time prior to confirmation of the plan.

One type of contract was excepted from these general rules, however, as part of the 1984 Amendments, and as further modified in the 2005 Amendments.[57] Responding to a determined lobbying effort by commercial lessors, Congress added § 365(d)(3) and (4) to govern nonresidential leases of real property, i.e., commercial real estate leases. Subsection (d)(3) deals with the interim treatment of such leases pending the trustee's decision, and is discussed in more detail in a subsequent section.[58] Subsection (d)(4), as amended in 2005, addresses the time constraints applicable to the trustee's decision to assume or reject such nonresidential real estate property leases, and the special timing rule in § 365(d)(4) applies in any case under any chapter. That rule provides that (unless plan confirmation in a chapter 9, 11, 12, or 13 cases occurs earlier, in which case the trustee or debtor in possession must act to assume or reject the lease by the date of plan confirmation) the trustee must act within *120 days* after the date of the order for relief.

One issue that has come up is the applicability of this special protective timing rule where the nonresidential real property lease is indivisibly integrated with other agreements, so that the trustee must assume or reject the combined agreement as a single whole. Is the entire "mixed" agreement imbued with the special protective quality of the nonresidential real property lease, or does the tainting of that special lease with unprotected elements destroy the protection for the whole? For example, in the context of franchising, the nonresidential real property lease may be integrated with the overall franchise agreement if it is found to be part of the same underlying transaction. The issue then is whether the trustee should be forced to comply with the

---

[55]   Note that some courts have even allowed the trustee to assume or reject *after* confirmation of the plan under certain circumstances. For example, in one decision the Seventh Circuit allowed the debtor to reject executory agreements after confirmation of the plan where the debtor's plan explicitly included a reserved right to reject executory contracts up to 15 days after plan confirmation. In re UAL Corp., 635 F.3d 312 (7th Cir. 2011).

[56]   465 U.S. 513, 529 (1984).

[57]   Also, prior to the 2005 Amendments, another series of detailed provisions in § 365(d)(5) through (9) governed procedures with regard to airport gate leases. These rules applied only to cases involving an "affected air carrier" pending between September 1992 and 1993. Rail Safety Enforcement and Revenue Act, Pub. L. No. 102–365, § 19, 106 Stat. 982 (1992). These rules were enacted to address concerns that Senator Danforth had in the TWA bankruptcy regarding the detrimental effect of delay on the St. Louis airport. However, the 2005 Amendments eliminated these provisions from the Code.

[58]   See § 8.26.

strict 120–day requirement of subsection (d)(4) for the entire agreement, including both the nonresidential real property lease *and* those parts of the agreement that by themselves would not enjoy special rights. One court determined that where a nonresidential real property lease is integrated with a franchise agreement, the trustee should be afforded the "more generous" deadline under subsection (d)(2).[59] In short, that court opted for the "tainting" view. To keep the protective coating of § 365(d)(4), the nonresidential real estate lease must stand alone. The court drew upon the purposes of the Code, to give the debtor the opportunity to effectively reorganize. The court further reasoned that to apply the more stringent requirement of (d)(4) would give the creditor undue leverage to pressure the debtor to make a quick decision as to the entire franchise agreement, merely by incorporation of the lease.

Even more significantly, extension of this 120–day period is severely limited. Congress changed the rule in 2005 so that only one 90–day extension, for cause shown, is permitted without the lessor's consent. Any additional extensions may be granted "only upon prior written consent of the lessor in each instance." § 365(d)(4)(B)(ii). Failure to act within the specified time frame results in deemed rejection of the lease. The practical ramification of this limitation on the extension of commercial real estate leases in a chapter 11 case (where it will matter the most) is to force the debtor in possession to make a hard choice, often before the debtor in possession has enough information to do so prudently: procure the lessor's consent, which likely will cost money; go ahead and assume the lease, which would make the future rent payments an administrative priority; or reject a lease that might later prove to be valuable. The risk of the assumption choice was somewhat softened by another 2005 amendment, which capped the amount of the administrative priority for a rent claim on an assumed lease that is later rejected, limiting that priority to two years' rent, rather than the total remaining rent due. § 503(b)(7).

One interesting problem has arisen in applying § 365(d)(4)(A), typified by the Ninth Circuit case of *In re Southwest Aircraft Services, Inc.*[60] The debtor in possession in that case filed a motion for an extension of time prior to the expiration of the initial period (at that time, 60 days), but the court did not act on the motion within the 60–day time period. The question was whether the lease was deemed rejected as a matter of law under subsection (d)(4) when day 60 passed without the entry of a court order extending the time. Relying on its view of the better policy and ignoring the plain language of the statute (over a vigorous dissent), the Ninth Circuit held that the filing of the motion within the 60 days was sufficient to prevent automatic rejection.[61] Presumably the same result would obtain in a chapter 7 case under subsection (d)(1). A

---

[59]   In re FPSDA I, LLC, 450 B.R. 392 (Bankr. E.D.N.Y. 2011).

[60]   831 F.2d 848 (9th Cir. 1987), cert. denied, 487 U.S. 1206 (1988). Accord, In re Beautyco, Inc., 307 B.R. 225 (Bankr. N.D. Okla. 2004).

[61]   See also In re Treasure Isles HC, Inc., 462 B.R. 645 (B.A.P. 6th Cir. 2011). There, the debtor initially filed a motion for an extension within the 120–day period, and then filed a second motion for another extension during the additional 90–day period. When the lessor of the property objected to the second extension, the debtor moved to assume the lease 3 days before the 90–day extension expired. Although the hearing on the motion to assume the lease occurred seventeen days after the expiration of the 90–day period, the bankruptcy court determined, and the Bankruptcy Appellate Panel affirmed, that the filing of the motion to assume within the 90–day period was sufficient to allow assumption of the lease after the 90–day period expired.

few courts have held, however, that under the plain language of the statute, the court actually must grant the extension within the 60–day period.[62]

A similar question of application is whether the court under subsection (d)(1) may grant a *second* extension of time, after the expiration of the initial 60–day period, but within the initially extended period. For example, assume that on day 60 the court extends the time for the trustee to decide for another 120 days (i.e., to day 180 of the case). Does the court have the power to enter a second extension after day 60 but prior to the expiration of day 180? The plain language of subsection (d)(1) again suggests that the court would not have that power, indicating that the court may grant extensions only within the first 60 days. However, the reasoning of *Southwest Aircraft Services* would support a finding that the court has the power to grant subsequent extensions, and most courts have so held.[63] The 2005 Amendments codified the ability of the court to grant a subsequent extension of time for nonresidential real property under subsection (d)(4)(B)(ii), but *only* if the lessor gives prior written consent to the extension. Before the 2005 amendment, subsection (d)(4) presented the same issue as subsection (d)(1) with regard to multiple extensions. The propensity of courts to grant numerous extensions under (d)(4) is what motivated Congress to impose an absolute limitation of one extension without the lessor's consent.

§ 8.5   Court Approval

The trustee is not given unfettered discretion to decide whether to assume or reject an executory contract. Section 365(a) states that "the trustee, *subject to the court's approval*, may assume or reject an executory contract." Thus, the Code expressly contemplates that the bankruptcy court must approve the trustee's decision to assume or reject. In addition, a decision to assign the contract must be approved by the court, since a prerequisite of assignment is assumption. § 365(f)(2)(A). Furthermore, the court will only approve an assignment if it finds that the assignee has provided adequate assurance of future performance. § 365(f)(2)(B).

As discussed in the preceding section, this apparently absolute requirement of court approval does not in fact always apply. If the case is one under chapter 7, § 365(d)(1), or if the contract in question is a nonresidential real property lease, § 365(d)(4), then the trustee's failure to act by the statutorily prescribed deadline will result in the contract being rejected automatically, by operation of law. Thus, in these situations a trustee who wants to reject effectively could circumvent court supervision by doing nothing and letting the statutory deadline pass. In cases outside of chapter 7, all executory contracts other than nonresidential real property leases will still be subject to the requirement of court approval.

The inclusion of the express provision for court approval in § 365(a) overrules a line of decisions under the prior Bankruptcy Act which authorized *implied* assumption.[64] The factual scenario in which the non-debtor party would argue that the

---

[62]   DeBartolo Prop. Mgmt., Inc. v. Devan, 194 B.R. 46 (D. Md. 1996). Accord, In re DCT, Inc., 283 B.R. 442 (Bankr. E.D. Mich. 2002).

[63]   See, e.g., In re Channel Home Ctrs., Inc., 989 F.2d 682 (3d Cir.), cert. denied, 510 U.S. 865 (1993).

[64]   See, e.g., In re Italian Cook Oil Corp., 190 F.2d 994 (3d Cir. 1951).

trustee had impliedly assumed the contract was when the trustee knowingly had performed and accepted benefits under the contract during the pendency of the bankruptcy case. The non-debtor would assert that the trustee thus should be equitably estopped from later rejecting the same contract and depriving the non-debtor of a priority claim under the contract. In effect, the argument was that actions speak louder than words, and that the trustee should be compelled to adhere to the de facto decision to assume. Even under the Act, the implied assumption theory was denounced by many courts.[65] The debate was settled by § 365(a). Now the non-debtor's argument that the trustee's acceptance of benefits mandates assumption and precludes rejection is plainly out of court.[66]

The Code does not provide any guidance with regard to the standards that the court should apply in deciding whether to approve the trustee's decision to assume or reject. As will be discussed in the next section, the courts have adopted a "business judgment" test for deciding whether to approve the trustee's decision to reject an executory contract.[67] By inference, a similar deference is given to the trustee's decision to assume, since rejection is nothing more than a choice not to assume.

C. REJECTION

§ 8.6   Standards for Rejection

The bankruptcy trustee has the power, subject to the court's approval, to assume or reject any executory contract of the debtor. § 365(a). However, with only one exception, nothing in the Code states what *standard* governs the trustee's choice, and the court's review of that choice. The exception is for collective bargaining agreements; § 1113(c)(3) specifies that the balancing of the equities must clearly favor rejection.[68] Given the statutory silence, the courts have had to develop a standard.

The trustee's power to reject an executory contract follows from the fact that a debtor's performance obligations under an executory contract do not automatically become obligations of the estate. A choice must be made by the trustee, and that choice may be not to assume, i.e., to "reject." If the contract is rejected, the estate will not succeed to either the asset or the liability represented by that contract. By declining to accept the property interest embodied in the contract, the trustee is in effect "abandoning" that property. Since the late nineteenth century, the courts have understood the trustee's power of rejection as analogous to the trustee's power to abandon burdensome property.[69] Consequently, a trustee clearly may reject a contract that is *burdensome*.

---

[65]   See, e.g., Texas Importing Co. v. Banco Popular de Puerto Rico, 360 F.2d 582 (5th Cir. 1966).

[66]   See, e.g., In re Whitcomb & Keller Mortg. Co., 715 F.2d 375 (7th Cir. 1983).

[67]   See In re Minges, 602 F.2d 38, 43 (2d Cir. 1979).

[68]   See § 8.12 for further discussion of the special case of collective bargaining agreements under § 1113.

[69]   *American File Co. v. Garrett*, 110 U.S. 288 (1884) is a foundational case. Recent commentators have suggested that the power of rejection actually is not derived from the power of abandonment, but instead predates abandonment and flows from the earlier notion that the bankruptcy trustee must act affirmatively to adopt (or "assume") on behalf of the estate the liabilities under a contract of the debtor. See Michael T.

Viewing the rejection decision as hinging upon proof of *burden* to the estate is likely to lead one astray, however. Although courts sometimes speak in terms of burden, the meaning they give to "burden" belies the common understanding of that term. It is more accurate to say that a trustee will only assume a contract that will provide a net *benefit* to the estate, and thus will reject a contract that will not affirmatively benefit the estate. Thus, "burden" is equated with "not beneficial," rather than with "net loss."

The significance of this point may be demonstrated by considering the case of a contract that is profitable, i.e., is not a losing contract, but with respect to which the estate could make an even larger profit by rejecting the contract and taking other actions. The fact that damages for rejecting the original contract will be paid only in "cents on the dollar" (depending on the degree of the debtor's insolvency) makes this option a realistic possibility. Non-debtor parties to such contracts have argued that rejection should not be allowed, given that the estate cannot prove a net loss from assumption. A large majority of courts have concluded that rejection *should* be approved in this situation, since the rejection will benefit the estate, and thus the entire body of creditors. The Supreme Court made this point clear in a railroad reorganization case in 1943,[70] and a leading Second Circuit decision in 1979 clarified that the same principle applied to all types of reorganization cases.[71]

A small minority of courts do require proof that a contract actually will be burdensome to the estate, in the sense that its performance will result in a net loss to the estate.[72] Also, some courts have intimated that the interests of the non-debtor party to the contract should be considered. Under this approach, the benefits to the estate of rejection must be balanced against the harm to the non-debtor party, and if the harm greatly outweighs the benefit, rejection will be denied.[73] Most courts, however, look only at the impact *on the estate* of the rejection decision.

The vast majority of courts take a very deferential approach to the trustee's decision whether to assume or reject. Except for union contracts, the trustee's choice will be gauged by the *"business judgment"* standard.[74] Thus, the court will approve the decision of the trustee unless it appears that the trustee acted in bad faith or grossly abused her discretion.[75]

Judged by this standard, in most cases the only reason that the trustee's decision to reject would not be approved is if the trustee misapprehended the legal effects of rejection. In other words, the trustee may believe erroneously that rejection would

---

Andrew, Executory Contracts in Bankruptcy: Understanding "Rejection," 59 U. Colo. L. Rev. 845, 856–66 (1988). However, the distinction does not make a difference in the legal standard the courts will apply in deciding whether to approve the trustee's rejection decision.

[70] Grp. of Inst. Inv. v. Chicago, M., St. P. & P. R.R., 318 U.S. 523, 549–50 (1943).

[71] In re Minges, 602 F.2d 38, 43 (2d Cir. 1979)

[72] See, e.g., In re Stable Mews Assocs., Inc., 41 B.R. 594 (Bankr. S.D.N.Y. 1984)

[73] See, e.g., In re Huang, 23 B.R. 798 (B.A.P. 9th Cir. 1982).

[74] *Minges*, supra note 71, 602 F.2d at 43.

[75] Lubrizol Enters., Inc. v. Richmond Metal Finishers, Inc., 756 F.2d 1043 (4th Cir. 1985), cert. denied, 475 U.S. 1057 (1986).

bring certain benefits to the estate; if that is not true, however, then the reason for rejection disappears. In the notorious case of *Lubrizol Enterprises, Inc. v. Richmond Metal Finishers, Inc.*,[76] for example, whether rejection would be beneficial and thus approved by the court depended on whether rejection would deprive the non-debtor party of the right to use licensed technology.[77] In other cases the dispute has been whether rejection would free the debtor from the constraints of a covenant not to compete.[78] In short, then, the battle usually will not be over the proper legal *standard*, but over the *effects* of rejection. If rejection will benefit the estate, the court will allow it.

As mentioned above, union contracts are treated differently than other types of executory contracts. In all other types of contracts little solicitude is shown for the possible harm to the non-debtor party that might result from rejection, as noted. For collective bargaining agreements, however, the interests of the union employees and the goals of the labor laws are given independent weight. A showing that the trustee exercised business judgment will not suffice. Section 1113 requires proof that the balancing of the equities clearly favors rejection.[79] his statutory standard codifies part of the result in *NLRB v. Bildisco & Bildisco*,[80] in which the Supreme Court held that the trustee must show that the labor contract is burdensome and that the balancing of the equities favors rejection.[81]

In some narrow circumstances, the court may apply a higher standard where rejection implicates public policy. For example, in *In re Mirant Corp.*,[82] Mirant, a large public utility company going through reorganization, sought to reject a contract to purchase electricity. The court concluded that "use of the business judgment standard would be inappropriate . . . because it would not account for the public interest inherent in the transmission and sale of electricity."[83] The court drew upon the Supreme Court's ruling in *Bildisco* to conclude that a higher standard is warranted based on the "special nature" of the agreements.[84] However, the contours of this exception are difficult to define and rarely applied. The higher standard is not utilized in every situation where a public policy is implicated, and it is unclear exactly when a public policy exception is warranted.[85]

A standard higher than business judgment might also be required in circumstances in which the directors or managers of the debtor are not disinterested.

---

[76]   Id.

[77]   For a fuller discussion of this case, see § 8.8.

[78]   Compare In re Carrere, 64 B.R. 156 (Bankr. C.D. Cal. 1986) (not allow rejection because would not relieve debtor of possible negative injunction to enforce covenant not to compete against her), with In re Taylor, 913 F.2d. 102 (3d Cir. 1990) (allow rejection of personal services contract).

[79]   See § 8.12.

[80]   465 U.S. 513 (1984).

[81]   The *Bildisco* case is discussed more fully in § 8.11.

[82]   378 F.3d 511 (5th Cir. 2004).

[83]   Id. at 524.

[84]   Id. The court did not require that the lower court use the *Bildisco* standard on remand, but suggested that it might.

[85]   See, e.g., In re Pilgrim's Pride Corp., 403 B.R. 413, 425 (N.D. Tex. 2009) (declining to invoke the public policy exception where "health and safety of the public are not threatened by rejection.").

In these cases, the "entire fairness" standard may be applied.[86] Under this standard, proof of fair dealing, price, and terms must be provided. For example, in *In re Los Angeles Dodgers, LLC*, the debtor in possession sought postpetition financing, with the debtor's sole shareholder to pay a lender's fee of $5.25 million if the financing was not approved. However, the court found that the potential personal liability of the debtor and sole shareholder compromised the debtor's judgment.[87] This was based on the debtor's refusal to negotiate with Major League Baseball, which was willing to extend an unsecured debtor-in-possession loan on better terms than debtor's proposed financing with another lender, because of the shareholder's poor relationship with the baseball Commissioner. Relying on the "entire fairness" standard, the court denied the debtor's motion for the proposed financing.[88] While the *Dodgers* case did not involve rejection of an executory contract, the motion sought similarly involved presumptive application of a business judgment standard, and, more importantly, the reasons that the court used the stricter "entire fairness" test should apply with equal force in the rejection context. The bottom line is that in some situations, the debtor management's business judgment is not fully trusted.

§ 8.7   Effects of Rejection: General Principles

Perhaps the most troublesome aspect of executory contract doctrine has concerned the effects of rejection. If any area of the law of executory contracts is to be reformed in the coming years, the law on the consequences of rejection has to be a leading candidate.[89] The problem stems from a fundamental misapprehension by many courts of the nature of rejection.

Perhaps paradoxically, rejection can best be understood by viewing it negatively: it is *not assumption*. The importance of this basic point derives from the fact that the bankruptcy estate does not automatically become a party to a pre-bankruptcy contract of the debtor. This principle has been recognized since the foundational 1818 English case of *Copeland v. Stephens*.[90] The estate only becomes liable for the obligations and entitled to the benefits under a contract of the debtor if the trustee or debtor in possession chooses to assume the contract. Rejection is nothing more or less than a decision by the trustee *not to assume* (and, thus, not become a party to) the contract. It is not some special power to terminate, cancel, or rescind a contract, or to avoid certain liabilities under the contract;[91] it is just a choice not to assume. Stripped to its essence, rejection becomes more easily understood—and much less important than many courts

---

[86]   In re L.A. Dodgers, L.L.C., 457 B.R. 308, 313 (Bankr. D. Del. 2011).

[87]   Id.

[88]   Id. at 314.

[89]   Some useful critiques and suggestions are made in National Bankruptcy Review Commission, Final Report: Bankruptcy: The Next Twenty Years, at 459–463 and Recommendation 2.4.1 (1997); Michael T. Andrew, Executory Contracts in Bankruptcy: Understanding "Rejection," 59 U. Colo. L. Rev. 845 (1988); Morris G. Shanker, Bankruptcy Asset Theory and its Application to Executory Contracts, 1992 Ann. Surv. Bankr. L. 97 (hereinafter "Asset Theory"); Jay L. Westbrook, A Functional Analysis of Executory Contracts, 74 Minn. L. Rev. 227 (1989); National Bankruptcy Conference, Reforming the Bankruptcy Code 191–220 (1994).

[90]   106 Eng. Rep. 218 (K.B. 1818).

[91]   See, e.g., Thompkins v. Lil' Joe Records, Inc., 476 F.3d 1294 (11th Cir.), cert. denied, 128 S. Ct. 613 (2007); In re Lavigne, 114 F.3d 379 (2d Cir. 1997); In re Austin Dev. Co., 19 F.3d 1077 (5th Cir.), cert. denied, 513 U.S. 874 (1994).

have made it. Indeed, some leading experts have advocated eliminating the term "rejection" entirely, because it is not that important and spawns more confusion than it is worth.[92]

Since rejection is "not assumption," the first important legal effect of rejection is that the bankruptcy estate will not become liable to perform under the contract. The estate will not be required to perform (or pay as an administrative expense) the future obligations of the debtor under the contract. Consider the hypothetical used in earlier sections,[93] where Debtor prior to bankruptcy entered into a contract to buy 1,000 hats from Other Party for $5 each, with delivery in 30 days. If Debtor files bankruptcy and the trustee rejects that contract, the estate will not have to pay the $5,000 price for the hats. Nor will Other Party be able to claim its damages for nonperformance as an administrative expense priority. Such a claim would occur only if the trustee assumed the contract.[94] § 365(g)(2). This result means that the non-debtor party to the contract will not be treated as a favored creditor and elevated over all other creditors in the distribution of the property of the estate.

The second legal consequence of rejection, which is a corollary to the first, is that the estate will not be entitled to receive the benefits of that contract. In the hypothetical, upon rejection of the contract, the estate forfeits the right to demand delivery of the hats from Other Party. The Other Party is excused from rendering performance to the estate.

These first two effects of rejection follow from the first principle of rejection law, namely, that rejection is "not assumption." That principle alone, however, does not fully resolve the rights of all affected parties, although it largely takes care of the interests of the estate. Still to be determined are the rights of the debtor and the non-debtor party after rejection. The crucial remaining question is whether the non-debtor party will have a claim cognizable in bankruptcy.

The Supreme Court settled this issue in the leading 1916 case of *Central Trust Co. v. Chicago Auditorium Association*.[95] In *Chicago Auditorium*, the Court laid the second cornerstone of rejection doctrine, holding that rejection constituted a *breach* of the contract that gave rise to a bankruptcy claim. To enhance clarity, and minimize the risk of misguided judicial interpretations, the 1997 Commission Report actually recommended that the term "rejection" be replaced with "election to breach."[96] While Congress did not adopt that suggestion, the principle remains valid. This principle of rejection-as-breach is codified today in § 365(g), which provides that "rejection of an executory contract or unexpired lease of the debtor constitutes a breach of such contract or lease . . . (1) immediately before the date of the filing of the petition." This rule applies *even if* the contract is not in default at the time of the bankruptcy filing. In

---

[92]   Commission Report, supra note 89, at 459–63; National Bankruptcy Conference, supra note 89, at 203–07; Morris G. Shanker, A Proposed New Executory Contract Statute, 1993 Ann. Surv. Bankr. L. 129, 130.

[93]   See §§ 8.2, 8.3.

[94]   See § 8.14.

[95]   240 U.S. 581 (1916).

[96]   Commission Report, supra note 89, Recommendation 2.4.1., at 20, 459.

effect, rejection of the contract in bankruptcy is treated as an anticipatory repudiation of the contract.[97] The "rejection as breach" rule leads directly to the third and fourth consequences of rejection.

The third effect of rejection is that the non-debtor party is deemed to have a *general unsecured prepetition claim* in the bankruptcy case. Section 365(g)(1), just quoted, specifies that rejection constitutes a *prepetition* breach. The non-debtor party's claim from rejection is allowed as if it arose prior to bankruptcy. § 502(g). Thus, while the non-debtor party is not treated *better* than any of the debtor's other general creditors (because it does not have a priority claim), neither is it treated *worse* as a consequence of rejection; it is deemed to have a claim just like all other general creditors. In the hypothetical, Other Party's claim for breach of the sales contract for hats should be treated as if Debtor anticipatorily repudiated the contract before filing bankruptcy. Without the rejection-as-breach rule, it might be possible to conclude that the non-debtor party did not have a claim in bankruptcy, and thus would not be able to share in the bankruptcy distribution at all. It bears noting that some of the claim disallowance provisions do place limits on the amount of the contract rejection claim that may be allowed, but for various policy reasons that have nothing to do with basic rejection doctrine.[98] See § 502(b)(6), (7).

Recognizing that rejection gives rise to a prepetition claim leads to the fourth consequence of rejection, which is that the debtor will be able to *discharge* that claim. Only "debts" are discharged in bankruptcy, and "debt" is defined as "liability on a claim." § 101(12). To the extent that a breach of the contract gives rise to a "right to payment," and thus is a "claim," § 101(5), that claim will be discharged. This rule provides an important benefit to the debtor, because without discharge, the non-debtor party could attempt to obtain satisfaction of its claim against the debtor personally after bankruptcy. Thus, in our hypothetical, Other Party's claim for breach would be paid pro rata as a general claim in Debtor's bankruptcy, and then would be discharged.

As explained above, it is settled law that rejection of an executory contract gives the non-debtor party a general unsecured claim in the bankruptcy case. By a legal fiction, even though the rejection actually occurs after the bankruptcy filing, the rejection (and thus "breach") is deemed to have occurred immediately prior to the bankruptcy filing. But how far does that legal fiction extend? Does it mean that the *calculation* of the non-debtor's rejection claim should be based on economic conditions existing immediately prior to bankruptcy, rather than at the actual time of rejection? If market prices move dramatically in the interim between the time of the bankruptcy filing and the time of rejection, which time period is used to calculate the non-debtor's claim could make an enormous difference. For example, in a case in the Enron bankruptcy arising out of the rejection of a contract for the sale of electricity, the non-debtor buyer would have had a claim for well over $6 million if the actual time of rejection was used, but no claim at all if the bankruptcy petition date was used to compute its claim.[99] This result is explained by the simple fact that the market shifted:

---

[97]　See Shanker, Asset Theory, supra note 89, at 110–12.

[98]　See § 7.4.

[99]　In re Enron Corp., 330 B.R. 387 (Bankr. S.D.N.Y. 2005), aff'd, 354 B.R. 652 (S.D.N.Y. 2006).

at the time of bankruptcy, the contract price was above market price, but by the time of rejection—over a year after the bankruptcy filing—market price exceeded the contract price.

Under the prior Bankruptcy Act, courts understood that the proper date to use to calculate the non-debtor's rejection claim was the *actual date of rejection*.[100] The only function of the relation back fiction was to give the non-debtor a claim that could participate in the bankruptcy case; it was never intended to alter or affect the *amount* of such claim. Instead, non-bankruptcy law (typically state law) governs the computation of the amount of claims against the estate. Bankruptcy, recall from *Butner*,[101] takes property interests of and claims against the debtor as it finds them, as determined by non-bankruptcy law, absent a bankruptcy-specific reason to change the result. There is no special bankruptcy reason to change the amount of rejection claims against the estate. Where Congress perceived the need for special bankruptcy limitations on claims, it so provided in the claims allowance provision (§ 502(b)).[102]

Unfortunately, some recent courts have taken a wrong turn, and have read language in § 502(g)(1),[103] which is the provision that gives the non-debtor party to a rejected contract a bankruptcy claim, as changing the prior law and commanding that rejection claims be calculated as of the day immediately preceding the bankruptcy filing, rather than at the time of rejection.[104] In *Enron*, that meant that the non-debtor had a claim of *zero*, even though its *actual* damages from the rejection indisputably were $6.6 million. This approach is manifestly unfair to non-debtor parties to executory contracts: it effectively gives the bankruptcy estate a free option to speculate at the expense of the non-debtor party. Assume a case like *Enron*, where the debtor was the buyer, and the contract price was at or above the market price at the time of bankruptcy. If the market price goes up from the contract price while the debtor is in bankruptcy, the estate will assume the contract. Fair enough; the non-debtor cannot complain about the performance of a contract it made; such is the inherent risk of any contract to be performed over time. But if the market price goes down, the estate will reject the contract, and buy at the lower market price—and yet the non-debtor party will have no claim at all for damages from that rejection, since its damages would be computed at the fictional date pre-bankruptcy when there were no damages!

---

[100] See, e.g., In re Good Hope Chem. Corp., 747 F.2d 806 (1st Cir. 1984), cert. denied, 471 U.S. 1102 (1985).

[101] 440 U.S. 48 (1979).

[102] Indeed, two disallowance provisions deal specifically with rejection claims. § 502(b)(6), (7).

[103] The language is:

A claim arising from the rejection, under section 365 of this title or under a plan under chapter 9, 11, 12, or 13 of this title, of an executory contract or unexpired lease of the debtor that has not been assumed shall be determined, and shall be allowed under subsection (a), (b), or (c) of this section or disallowed under subsection (d) or (e) of this section, the same as if such claim had arisen before the date of the filing of the petition.

The courts have seized on the word "determined" as effecting this momentous change in the law. That reading, however, is very dubious.

[104] See In re Am. HomePatient, Inc., 414 F.3d 614 (6th Cir.2005), cert. denied, 547 U.S. 1019 (2006); *Enron*, supra note 99.

For certain types of financial contracts, a 2005 amendment changes the foregoing result and requires that damages be calculated at the date of the actual rejection or, if earlier, the date the contract was terminated, liquidated, or accelerated. § 562(a). This special rule applies to a swap agreement, securities contract, forward contract, commodity contract, repurchase agreement, or master netting agreement. For these contracts, the calculation of rejection damages therefore cannot be made as of the filing date, as in *Enron*.[105]

§ 8.8　　Effects of Rejection: More than Breach?

If the courts would consistently apply the two cornerstone principles of rejection identified in the preceding section—and no more—executory contract law would be much fairer, less controversial, and far less important. To review, the first principle is that *"rejection is 'not assumption,'"* and the second is that *"rejection is breach."* Unfortunately, courts have muddied the waters by ascribing greater effect to the rejection of an executory contract than the foregoing principles would dictate. In response, Congress has enacted a series of special rules to counter a few misguided court decisions.[106] However, in doing so, Congress has further complicated the law, and, perhaps even worse, has created a possible negative inference that all cases not covered by a special rule are subject to the erroneous rationales of the misguided decisions.[107]

The fundamental error that some courts have committed is to view rejection as *more than breach*.[108] Courts have interpreted rejection as tantamount to a termination, cancellation, or rescission of the contract, and indeed even as a quasi-avoiding power capable of recapturing property for the benefit of the estate. The impact of these decisions is that bankruptcy suddenly becomes an attractive option for some debtors solely because of the extraordinary "rejection powers" supposedly available. With the consequences of rejection looming like the Damoclean sword, the importance of whether a contract can be classified as executory and whether rejection should be authorized is greatly magnified; indeed, the rejection decision can be the pivotal event in the entire bankruptcy case.

The king of all bad executory contract cases is *Lubrizol Enterprises, Inc. v. Richmond Metal Finishers, Inc.*,[109] which was decided by the Fourth Circuit in 1985. The specific result of *Lubrizol* was overruled by Congress in 1988 with the addition of

---

[105]　Indeed, cases such as *Enron* use the fact of the 2005 enactment of § 562 as evidence that the rule under § 502(g) was, and is, different than that announced in § 562—otherwise, why bother with the amendment? See 354 B.R. at 657–59. The obvious, and surely correct, answer is: to clarify the law for certain types of contracts whose participants successfully lobbied Congress for that certainty. Furthermore, § 562(a) is not superfluous even under the "why bother" approach, because it specifies the *alternative* date for computing damages as the date of termination, liquidation, or acceleration, § 562(a)(2), in contrast to the standard date of rejection, § 562(a)(1).

[106]　See § 8.10.

[107]　Indeed, the very real danger of courts making such an inference is demonstrated in the preceding section in the *Enron* case, as discussed in note 105 of § 8.7.

[108]　The seminal article that exposed the fallacies of numerous court decisions in the rejection area is Michael T. Andrew, Executory Contracts in Bankruptcy: Understanding "Rejection," 59 U. Colo. L. Rev. 845 (1988).

[109]　756 F.2d 1043 (4th Cir. 1985), cert. denied, 475 U.S. 1057 (1986).

§ 365(n),[110] but the fallacious reasoning of that decision can still be applied in other contexts. In *Lubrizol*, the debtor, Richmond Metal Finishers (RMF), had granted Lubrizol a nonexclusive license to use a metal coating process technology owned by RMF. This technology was RMF's principal asset, and the sale or licensing of that technology was the primary source of revenue for RMF. The license with Lubrizol contained a "most favored licensee" clause, which meant that its royalty payments had to be reduced to match any lower royalty rate agreement that RMF reached with another licensee.

RMF filed chapter 11 and sought to reject the license with Lubrizol. The reason RMF wanted to reject was that it believed that it would be better able to sell or license the technology to others if it could strip Lubrizol of the right to keep using the technology. The bankruptcy court approved the rejection, but the district court declined to do so, concluding that rejection would not have the effect desired by RMF. The district court properly determined that rejection would not deprive Lubrizol of the right to use the technology.

The Fourth Circuit reversed, and held that RMF could reject the license.[111] As a threshold matter, the court had to find that the license was an "executory contract" and therefore was subject to rejection. On this issue, the court groped to identify sufficient remaining unperformed obligations on both sides so that it could label the license as "executory." Unbelievably, the court concluded that Lubrizol's duties to deliver quarterly sales reports and to keep books of account rendered the license executory as to Lubrizol and thus subject to rejection. Apparently, if Lubrizol had not had these minimal duties, it would not have lost the right to use the technology!

Having surmounted this preliminary hurdle, the Fourth Circuit then had to decide the crucial issue: would rejection take away from Lubrizol the right to use the technology? The standard for rejection, the business judgment rule,[112] would plainly be satisfied if rejection would have this extraordinary effect, for the debtor had presented uncontroverted evidence that its business prospects would be enhanced by stripping the right to use the technology from Lubrizol.

However, if rejection were viewed simply as the equivalent of a breach of contract, Lubrizol would be able to keep using the technology. Outside of bankruptcy, RMF by anticipatorily repudiating the license agreement would not be able to take the technology away from Lubrizol. Lubrizol would have a claim for any damages it suffered from RMF's breach, but also would be entitled to retain the technology even after RMF's breach. That technology had in effect been conveyed to Lubrizol in the license agreement. As discussed in the preceding section, § 365(g) codifies earlier case law and treats rejection as breach, which enables a non-debtor party to claim damages in the bankruptcy case. That section does not, however, support an inference that the

---

[110] An Act to keep secure the rights of intellectual property licensors and licensees which come under the protection of title 11 of the United States Code, the Bankruptcy Code, Pub. L. No. 100–506, 102 Stat. 2538 (1988).

[111] *Lubrizol*, supra note 109, 756 F.2d at 1047–48.

[112] See § 8.6.

damages claim is the *exclusive* right given to the non-debtor party. Thus, the Fourth Circuit should have held for Lubrizol.

Instead, the *Lubrizol* court turned § 365(g) on its head and misread the legislative history, and concluded that, upon rejection, Lubrizol *only* had a claim for damages. The court recognized the unfairness of this result to Lubrizol, but inferred from the absence of a special protective rule in § 365 for technology licensees that Congress did not intend to afford them such a privilege. In the court's view, Lubrizol lost the right to keep using the technology when RMF rejected the license agreement. By rejecting the license, RMF had effectively recovered the technology property for the benefit of the estate. Rejection thus was treated as the equivalent of an avoiding power.

The special rules that the court had in mind cover cases where the debtor is the lessor of real property, § 365(h), or the vendor of real property, § 365(i). In those cases the Code affords special rights to the non-debtor lessee or vendee who is in possession of the property.[113] These rules were added to the Code in 1978 partially in response to a pre-Code decision, *In re New York Investors Mutual Group, Inc.*[114] In *New York Investors*, the debtor was the vendor under a contract for the sale of real estate. The non-debtor vendee had equitable title, and outside of bankruptcy could have enforced the contract by specific performance. The district court held that rejection defeated the vendee's rights and left it only with a claim for damages. The court justified this result by noting the overriding policy of equitable distribution among creditors, apparently forgetting that bankruptcy law also differentiates among creditors based upon their different property rights.

Both *Lubrizol* and *New York Investors* go off the track by allowing rejection to be used as a means of recovering for the benefit of the estate property that has been conveyed by the debtor to another party prior to bankruptcy. While the special rules of § 365 mitigate the harshness of this view in the specific situations covered therein, the problems raised by this fundamental misconception of the nature of rejection continue in other contexts. For example, assume that the debtor is the lessor of a true lease of *personal* property, and that the non-debtor lessee is in possession of the property at the time the debtor files bankruptcy. If the debtor rejects the lease, will the lessee have to return the property to the estate? For *real property* leases, § 365(h) would allow the lessee to retain possession, but that section does not apply to a personal property lease. Under the "rejection-as-avoiding-power" view espoused by courts such as *Lubrizol* and *New York Investors*, the lessee would only have a claim for damages and would have to return the property to the debtor. Yet, if rejection is treated only as a breach, recovery of the property would not be warranted; under non-bankruptcy law, a lessor cannot terminate a lease and recover the leased property by unilaterally repudiating the lease.

Rejection also poses a possible threat in cases where a third party holds an interest in the property that is the subject of the contract or lease at issue. For example, the third party may hold a security interest or mortgage in the debtor's interest in a leasehold. If rejection is viewed as rescission or termination, then

---

[113]   See § 8.10.
[114]   143 F. Supp. 51 (S.D.N.Y. 1956).

arguably the security interest would be extinguished. Fortunately, however, some courts are starting to recognize that rejection does not terminate or rescind the underlying lease, and thus that the security interest or mortgage is not destroyed.[115]

Another situation not covered expressly by § 365 is a franchise agreement, which also includes trademarks. Consider the case where the debtor is the franchisor, files bankruptcy, and then rejects the franchise agreement. For example, assume that the debtor franchises "Big Burger" restaurants. Does rejection mean that the non-debtor franchisee will be prohibited from continuing to operate and hold itself out as a Big Burger restaurant? Under the erroneous "rejection-as-rescission" view, the franchisee would lose all rights under the agreement, except for a damages claim. The result instead should turn on whether, under applicable non-bankruptcy contract law, the franchisee normally could continue operations as a Big Burger restaurant after repudiation by the franchisor.

Numerous courts have grappled with this issue. One view (which, let me be clear, is *wrong*!) is that because § 365(n) does not address trademarks specifically, the section does not apply to them, and by negative inference, the protections of that section cannot be extended to contracts not specifically listed therein.[116] Such reasoning is exactly the worry I voiced above. Under this view, since the section does not apply, a licensor can unilaterally terminate a trademark license, depriving the licensee of all of his rights under the agreement, and leaving him with nothing but a damages claim.[117] This is the result under the dubious "rejection-as-rescission" theory. Of course, saying that § 365(n) does not apply should not then countenance allowing rejection to be used to recover property already conveyed! Implicitly, courts who take this errant view assume that the fundamental reasoning of *Lubrizol* was correct, with only the specific outcome changed by statute. As explained above, though, *Lubrizol* was not correct, but was totally misguided. What a terrible irony to see the very congressional action taken to reverse that dreadful outcome being used to validate the underlying defective reasoning!

Thankfully, however, several courts have disagreed with this approach. In *In re Exide Technologies*, the Third Circuit held that a license agreement was not an "executory" contract at all and thus could not be rejected, and of course that meant the court did not have to decide the effects of rejection.[118] In a thoughtful concurrence, though, Judge Thomas Ambro expressed the view that the courts' equitable power should be used to allow a trademark licensee to retain its rights even when a franchisor rejects the license agreement. Thus, even if rejection had been allowed, he argued, it would not have availed the debtor, who could not achieve its goal of denying the licensee the use of the trademark. Significantly, Judge Ambro declined to fall for

---

[115] See, e.g., Leasing Serv. Corp. v. First Tenn. Bank Nat'l Ass'n, 826 F.2d 434 (6th Cir. 1987); see also In re Austin Dev. Co., 19 F.3d 1077 (5th Cir. 1994).

[116] See, e.g., In re Deel, L.L.C., 2011 WL 9012049, at *7 (Bankr. D. Del. Feb. 8, 2011) (finding that § 365(n) was inapplicable to the trademark in the franchise agreement and that the franchisee's only remedy was a claim for breach of contract); In re Old Carco, L.L.C., 406 B.R. 180, 211 (Bankr. S.D.N.Y. 2009) (finding that § 365(n) does not protect trademarks because they are not a specifically protected form of intellectual property under the Code).

[117] See *Deel*, supra note 116, at *7; In re HQ Global Holdings, 290 B.R. 507, 513 (Bankr. D. Del. 2003).

[118] In re Exide Techs., 607 F.3d 957, 964 (3d Cir. 2010).

the negative inference argument noted above.[119] His following cogent observation is worth repeating:

> Courts may use § 365 to free a bankrupt trademark licensor from burdensome duties that hinder its reorganization. They should not—as occurred in this case— use it to let a licensor take back trademark rights it bargained away. This makes bankruptcy more a sword than a shield, putting debtor-licensors in a catbird seat they often do not deserve.[120]

Most recently, the Seventh Circuit agreed with Judge Ambro's position in *Sunbeam Products, Inc. v. Chicago American Manufacturing, LLC*.[121] There, the court rejected the *Lubrizol* analysis and held that the rejection of the underlying contract did not abrogate the licensee's right to sell fans it manufactured with the debtor's trademark on them.[122] The court based its reasoning on an examination of § 365(g), which classifies rejection of an executory contract as a breach, thereby "establish[ing] that in bankruptcy, as outside of it, the other party's rights remain in place."[123] And, because outside of bankruptcy, a licensor's breach of a contract does not terminate the licensee's right to use the intellectual property at stake, the result is the same in bankruptcy.[124]

Another major area of controversy regarding the consequences of rejection is the extent to which the non-debtor party to the contract will be able to enforce *equitable* remedies after the rejection. This issue can arise in various contexts. One common situation is where the debtor is subject to a covenant not to compete. Such a covenant may be included in an employment contract, where the debtor is the employee,[125] or in a franchise agreement, where the debtor is the franchisee.[126] In these cases, even after the debtor rejects the agreement that contains the non-compete clause, the non-debtor party wants to obtain or enforce a negative injunction to enforce the covenant against the debtor. Another case is where the non-debtor party would have a right of specific performance of the contract outside of bankruptcy, and wants to obtain specific performance in bankruptcy as well.

The disposition of these equitable remedy cases is easy (but wrongheaded) in jurisdictions that follow the *Lubrizol* theory that rejection leaves the non-debtor *only* with a damages claim. Under this view, the non-debtor would not be able to enforce equitable remedies after rejection.

---

[119] Id. at 965–68 (Ambro, J., concurring).

[120] Id. at 967–68.

[121] Sunbeam Prods., Inc. v. Chicago Am. Mfg., LLC, 686 F.3d 372 (7th Cir. 2012), cert. denied, 133 S. Ct. 790 (U.S. 2012).

[122] Id. at 375.

[123] Id. at 377.

[124] Id. at 376–77.

[125] See, e.g., In re Udell, 18 F.3d 403 (7th Cir. 1994); In re Ortiz, 400 B.R. 755 (C.D. Cal. 2009). See also Kennedy v. Medicap Pharmacies, Inc., 267 F.3d 493, 497 (6th Cir. 2001).

[126] See, e.g., In re Register, 95 B.R. 73 (Bankr. M.D. Tenn.), aff'd, 100 B.R. 360 (M.D. Tenn. 1989); In re Rovine Corp., 6 B.R. 661 (Bankr. W.D. Tenn. 1980).

The proper approach to the equitable remedy cases is much more complex.[127] To begin with, and most importantly, the ultimate resolution does *not* lie in executory contract law under § 365. All that § 365 establishes in these circumstances is that "rejection is breach." That merely gets the analysis started, rather than concluding it, as some courts wrongly have done. Properly understood, once the rejection-as-breach point is acknowledged, the next, and critically important, question that must be answered is this: outside of bankruptcy (likely under state law), upon breach, could the non-debtor party obtain a negative injunction to enforce the covenant not to compete? Or could the non-debtor get an order of specific performance in appropriate cases (to purchase a Van Gogh painting, for example). State law may say "no" to the injunction or to specific performance, and then rejection only gives the non-debtor party a claim. The reason, though, is because the non-debtor party has no injunctive right under the governing non-bankruptcy law in the first place—*not* because § 365(g) and § 502(g) say "rejection = breach = only a claim." For example, in one case a well-known rapper, Ricardo Brown Jr. (much better known as "Kurupt" and a member of the rap group The Dogg Pound) had signed a contract with Death Row Records that contained a covenant not to compete. He was able to reject the contract and discharge Death Row's claim, free from injunctive constraint, because he had not been a celebrity when he signed the contract, and under California law the Death Row Records of the world can only get an injunction when the other party had celebrity status at the time the contract was signed.[128]

Then, if and only if the non-bankruptcy law would give the non-debtor party an equitable remedy in the event of the debtor's breach, bankruptcy policy must be considered to determine the ultimate effect of rejection. That is, even if the non-debtor would enjoy an equitable remedy outside of bankruptcy they ultimately might not prevail in bankruptcy, because there may be *other* bankruptcy policies that supersede the non-debtor's equitable remedies.

One such bankruptcy policy is the fresh start, and another is equality of treatment of creditors. For an individual debtor, the fresh start policy embodied in the discharge may trump a covenant not to compete. This result could be reached by classifying the equitable remedy of a negative injunction as a "claim" under § 101(5)(B), estimating that claim under § 502(c), and then discharging that claim.[129] Again, though, saying that "rejection = breach" has nothing to do with this analysis. The question is whether under federal bankruptcy law, that equitable remedy should be classified as a dischargeable claim.

The availability of specific performance should depend on whether the non-debtor party could enforce that right not only against the debtor, but against all of the debtor's creditors as well. This focus is appropriate, because if specific performance is granted, that creditor will be preferred over the other creditors, who have only a pro rata claim against the debtor's assets. If the specific performance right can be converted into a claim under § 101(5)(B), it is fairer to all creditors and more faithful to the equality

---

[127] An excellent analysis can be found in *Ortiz*, supra note 125, 400 B.R. 755.

[128] In re Brown, 1997 WL 786994 at *5–6 (E.D. Pa. Nov. 26, 1997).

[129] National Bankruptcy Conference, Reforming the Bankruptcy Code 202 (1994).

principle to deny specific performance and allow that creditor only a pro rata share as well. If, however, the creditor has an unavoidable interest in property represented by the specific performance right, then that property interest should be respected in bankruptcy. Thus, the test should be whether the non-debtor's entitlement to specific performance could be avoided by the trustee under the avoiding powers, especially § 544(a).[130] Nothing about "rejection," though, should be relevant to the analysis.

§ 8.9   Effects of Rejection: Individual Debtors

Another area in which the effects of rejection are uncertain is with regard to the contracts and leases of an *individual debtor*, especially in chapter 7. For example, what happens to the apartment lease for an individual debtor when he files chapter 7? As regards the position of the bankruptcy *estate*, the debtor's residential real property lease is subject to the assume-reject-assign decision of Code § 365, but absent unusual circumstances, the trustee is unlikely to assume the debtor's lease. If not, then the lease will be deemed rejected under § 365(d)(1) when the trustee fails to act within 60 days of the filing. The estate then will neither be obligated to pay rent nor entitled to possession. The lessor will have a claim for damages for the deemed breach under § 365(g)(1) and § 502(g)(1). But what happens to the debtor? Does he now have to move out? Can he stay as long as he pays rent? Will his obligation to pay rent be discharged? Can the lessor recover possession?

Note that these issues will not arise, or at least are readily answered, in the case of a *corporate* debtor. Once a corporate debtor files bankruptcy, the bankruptcy estate succeeds to all of the corporate debtor's assets as property of the bankruptcy estate, and the corporate debtor ceases to exist and function as an entity separate and distinct from the debtor's bankruptcy estate. Assume, for example, that a corporate debtor files chapter 7 bankruptcy, goes out of business, and the trustee rejects a real estate lease. The leased premises will revert to the lessor—there being no one else with any possible claim to the premises. The lessor also will be left with a claim in the bankruptcy case. By contrast, an individual debtor *does* continue to exist notwithstanding the intervention of bankruptcy. After rejection of the lease by the estate, the leased premises in theory could be deemed to be abandoned by the trustee either to the lessor or to the debtor. That is, with a live debtor continuing to exist post-rejection, there is a competing residual claimant who has a possible interest in the leasehold.

Executory contracts and leases pose a particular conceptual difficulty for cases involving individuals because of the unique character of those contracts and leases as a form of property that is tied to an accompanying liability. For most types of "property," the bankruptcy analysis is straightforward, even for individual debtors. All of the debtor's property initially passes into the estate under § 541. The trustee then decides what to do with that property: some of it may be returned to the debtor if properly claimed as exempt under § 522; some may be abandoned if it has no net value for the estate under § 554, such as collateral for an undersecured claim; and the rest will be

---

[130] See §§ 6.3, 6.4. For further discussion, see National Bankruptcy Conference, supra note 24, at 199–202; Michael T. Andrew, Executory Contracts Revisited: A Reply to Professor Westbrook, 62 U. Colo. L. Rev. 1, 26–28 (1991); Jay Lawrence Westbrook, A Functional Analysis of Executory Contracts, 74 Minn. L. Rev. 227, 255–57 (1989).

sold under § 363, with the net proceeds used to pay allowed claims. But for contracts and leases, enjoyment of the right to the asset is conditioned on ongoing performance of the attendant obligations. The trustee may not want to perform, and thus may prefer simply to reject the contract or lease, taking the estate out of the equation. But the contract or lease remains, just with the estate out of the picture.

In sorting out the ramifications of a rejection in cases involving individual debtors, the first step is to recognize that the rejection is deemed to be a *breach* and accordingly gives the non-debtor party (the lessor in our apartment example) a prepetition claim.[131] § 365(g)(1), 502(g)(1). As such, the lessor's "claim" is subject to *discharge* under § 727(b). If nothing else happens, the debtor no longer will be personally liable on the rent obligation. The lessor would be able to share in any bankruptcy distribution.

Who gets possession of the leased premises? This question is much more difficult, and the Code does not provide a clear answer. The starting point is to recognize that "breach" is *not* synonymous with "termination."[132] If it were, then of course the lessor would be entitled to recover possession. But since "breach" does not automatically terminate the lease, to determine the parties' rights after breach "we must turn to state law."[133]

Differentiating "breach" from "termination" is particularly important in the case of an individual debtor's unexpired real property lease, because landlord-tenant law is governed largely by *property* law principles, not by contract law. The common law rule is that "the parties to a lease have . . . no general power to terminate for the other party's breach of a lease covenant."[134] Because of this, most courts have concluded that a chapter 7 trustee's "rejection breach" of an individual debtor's lease does *not* automatically terminate the debtor's leasehold interest and give the lessor the right to possession.

Instead, the lessor would have to resort to whatever state law termination remedies are available, which in turn depends upon the nature of the debtor's breach. Every state by statute permits a lessor to evict a tenant for failure to pay rent. Except for the § 362 automatic stay, nothing about a bankruptcy case should stand in the way of the lessor's eviction action. With the estate out of the picture, there is no reason why the bankruptcy court should not grant the lessor relief from the stay under § 362(d)(1) to pursue eviction against a non-paying tenant; also, some stay exceptions under § 362(b) may apply. The discharge of the debtor's obligation to pay rent under the lease only bars actions by the lessor "to collect, recover or offset any such debt as a *personal liability* of the debtor." § 524(a)(2). In short, "[d]espite the discharge, a landlord can still avail itself of its statutory remedy to recover possession of premises for nonpayment of rent."[135]

---

[131] See § 8.7.

[132] In re Austin Dev. Co., 19 F.3d 1077, 1083 (5th Cir.), cert. denied, 513 U.S. 874 (1994).

[133] In re Lavigne, 114 F.3d 379, 387 (2d Cir. 1997).

[134] William B. Stoebuck & Dale A. Whitman, The Law of Property § 6.10, at 253 & § 6.78, at 392 (3d ed. 2000).

[135] In re Hepburn, 27 B.R. 135, 136 (Bankr. E.D.N.Y. 1983).

Thus, if the lease is not only rejected, but after rejection the debtor fails to pay rent, the lessor should be entitled to recover the leased premises and evict the debtor. But what if the debtor is *current* on his rent, and has expressed his intent to retain possession and keep paying rent? In such a situation, eviction for nonpayment of rent would be unavailable to the lessor. The only "breach" of the lease in such a case is the "technical breach arising from the failure [of the trustee] to assume" the lease.[136] For lease breaches *other* than a failure to pay rent, the lessor's ability to terminate the lease depends upon the existence of a termination clause in the lease agreement itself. Outside of bankruptcy, such clauses are generally given effect. However, in bankruptcy such a termination clause is rendered unenforceable by the Code's ban on *ipso facto* clauses.[137] § 365(e)(1). The lessor now may be out of luck—no statutory right to evict for nonpayment of rent (because rent *is* being paid), and no contractual right to terminate (because of the anti-*ipso facto* rule). The debtor thus may be able to preserve its rights under the lease by continuing to perform according to its terms. If so, the lessor's non-bankruptcy "deal" has been dramatically altered: permitting the debtor to retain possession of the leased premises, at the same time that his personal liability for future rent obligations is discharged, effects a transformation of the lease from a recourse to a *nonrecourse* lease!

In some states, the lessor may have a better chance of avoiding this result, because of a difference in the underlying state law. The important difference in those states is that they have abandoned the traditional property law approach and have adopted instead the rule of the Restatement (Second) of Property that makes lease termination rights analogous to the "material breach" principles of contract law.[138] Under the Restatement, even without a termination clause in the lease, a tenant's breach gives the lessor the power to terminate the lease if "the landlord is deprived of a significant inducement to the making of the lease."[139] Some courts have suggested that a "rejection breach," standing alone, might satisfy this termination standard, because of the fact that the debtor is no longer personally liable:

> "Of course, it could be argued that the failure affirmatively to assume the lease *has* materially affected the landlord's rights, since the debtors' contractual obligation to pay rent has been discharged. Thus, the tenants are no longer on the hook to the landlord until the expiration of the lease term but are free to stop paying rent and to turn the keys back to the landlord at any time."[140]

If the landlord is permitted to terminate the lease on this basis, the debtor could remain in possession of the leased premises only by negotiating a new lease or reaffirming their continuing personal liability on the old lease under § 524(c).

Although the most common context in which it is necessary to determine an individual debtor's lease rights upon rejection of the lease by the debtor's chapter 7 trustee is in the case of *residential* real property leases, some individual debtors also

---

[136] See In re Park, 275 B.R. 253, 256 (Bankr. E.D. Va. 2002).

[137] See § 8.17.

[138] See Stoebuck & Whitman, supra note 134, § 6.10, at 254 & n.4.

[139] See Restatement (Second) of Property § 13.1(1).

[140] *Park*, supra note 6, 275 B.R. at 257.

have commercial real estate leases. For those leases, § 365(d)(4) complicates things even more, providing that, upon deemed rejection for the trustee's failure to act within the requisite time period, *"the trustee shall immediately surrender that nonresidential real property to the lessor."* Despite the courts' general agreement that a trustee's rejection of a residential real property lease does not automatically terminate the debtor's leasehold estate, the "shall immediately surrender" language in § 365(d)(4) has led a majority of courts to conclude that rejection of a *commercial* real estate lease *does* effect a termination of the debtor's leasehold estate.[141]

Other courts, however, have rejected this interpretation of § 365(d)(4).[142] These courts reason that § 365(d)(4) does not use the term "termination," a telling omission given that other provisions of § 365 *do* provide that rejection in certain situations allows the non-debtor party to "terminate" the contract or lease. See Bankruptcy Code § 365(h)(1)(A)(i), (h)(2)(A)(i), (i)(1) & (n)(1)(A). Moreover, "while § 365(d)(4) . . . expressly requires the *trustee* to surrender the property to the landlord, it is silent as to an individual debtor who is not a debtor in possession."[143] In other words, § 365(d)(4) only purports to govern the rights of the bankruptcy *estate* vis-à-vis the non-debtor party and does not speak directly to the rights of an individual debtor. These courts therefore hold that an individual chapter 7 debtor's rights under a rejected lease are essentially the same with respect to both residential and commercial real property leases.

Such was the state of the law before the 2005 amendments, which enacted § 365(p) to address expressly this issue of the individual debtor's continuing rights under a rejected lease. The first thing to note about § 365(p) is that by its terms it applies only to *personal property* leases.[144] Whether it will have an indirect effect on the treatment of real property leases—and if so whether the effect would be to presume the same rule as subsection (p) or, by negative inference, the *opposite* rule—is an open question.

When it does apply, the first effect of § 365(p), in subsection (1), is to provide for automatic termination of the stay. Note that this rule applies in all cases, not just those involving individual debtors. However, § 365(p)(1) does not have anything to say about what happens to the rights of the *debtor* after the stay is lifted if the debtor is current on rent.[145] Thus it is consistent with any of the pre–2005 lines of case authority discussed above.

Subsection (p)(2) applies to cases involving individual debtors under chapter 7. It *probably* also applies only to personal property leases, although that subsection lacks a specific cross-reference to subsection (p)(1), which does reference personal property

---

[141] See, e.g., Sea Harvest Corp. v. Riviera Land Co., 868 F.2d 1077, 1080–81 (9th Cir. 1989).

[142] See *Austin Development*, supra note 132, 19 F.3d 1077; *Park*, supra note 6.

[143] *Park*, supra note 136, 275 B.R. at 258.

[144] See discussion in note 146 infra and accompanying text for the possible application of § 365(p)(2) to real estate leases for individual chapter 7 cases.

[145] See In re Mortensen, 444 B.R. 225 (Bankr. E.D.N.Y. 2011) (allowing a debtor who had remained current on her motor vehicle lease payments throughout bankruptcy to reopen her case to file a lease assumption agreement where she had notified the lessor of her intent to assume the lease and make payments according to its terms).

leases.[146] Under § 365(p)(2), an individual chapter 7 debtor can notify the lessor that he wants to "assume" the lease. The lessor then has the option to agree—or not[147]—to the debtor's proposed assumption, and may condition that assumption on the cure of any defaults. § 365(p)(2)(A). On an agreed assumption by the debtor, obviously the debtor would be entitled to retain possession of the leased property. The *quid pro quo*, though, is that the debtor would have to take on personal liability for all lease obligations.

In interpreting this new section, courts have noted that assumption is consensual between the lessor and the debtor.[148] The point is to allow the debtor and lessor to agree to terms that allow the debtor to remain in possession of the property.[149] The process is intended to take place outside of court, and does not require court approval or the filing of an assumption agreement.[150] During this time, the lessor is provided with a safe harbor so that it may contact the debtor regarding its acceptance or rejection of the debtor's proposed assumption of the lease and to negotiate terms of a cure without violating the automatic stay under § 362 or the discharge injunction under § 524(a)(2).[151]

However, a dispute exists between courts as to whether more than a mere agreement between the lessor and debtor is required so that the debtor is liable for the lease obligations, and so that those obligations are not subject to discharge. That is, must the parties execute and process through the court a formal reaffirmation agreement that satisfies § 524(c)? Some courts take the position that § 365(p) binds the debtor to the lease terms and that the discharge does not affect the assumed obligation.[152] Conversely, other courts have held that when there is assumption without a reaffirmation agreement, the debtor's assumed obligation under § 365(p) is dischargeable.[153]

---

[146] Subsection (p)(2)(A) refers to "the" lease, without any preceding "lease" to which the "the" might be referring, suggesting the possibility that the reference is back to subsection (1), which speaks of "personal property" leases. Note, though, that subsection (p)(3), which deals with individual debtors in chapters 11 and 13, does include a specific reference to "personal" property, raising at least a possible argument that Congress knew how to limit application to personal property leases when it wanted to.

Under subsection (p)(3), if a personal property lease is not assumed in the debtor's plan, it is deemed rejected and the stay is terminated.

[147] In re Ebbrect, 451 B.R. 241, 245 (Bankr. E.D.N.Y. 2011) (providing that under § 365(p) a lessor is not obliged to accept the debtor's offer).

[148] See, e.g., In re Farley, 451 B.R. 235, 238 (Bankr. E.D.N.Y. 2011).

[149] Thompson v. Credit Union Fin. Group, 453 B.R. 823, 827 (W.D. Mich. 2011).

[150] See *Mortensen*, supra note 145, 444 B.R. at 230; In re Robinson, Case No. 07–54058, 2007 Bankr. LEXIS 3020 at *3 (Bankr. S.D. Ohio Aug. 13, 2007).

[151] See *Ebbrect*, supra note 147, 451 B.R. 241 at 245; *Farley*, supra note 148, 451 B.R. at 239.

[152] See, e.g., *Mortensen*, supra note 145, 444 B.R. 225 at 230; see also *Ebbrecht*, supra note 147, 451 B.R. at 247 (reasoning that assumption under § 365(p) and affirmation under § 524 are different procedures and that § 365(p) creates a binding obligation on the debtor that is not subject to discharge, and therefore need not be reaffirmed).

[153] See, e.g., *Thompson*, supra note 149, 453 B.R. at 827; see also In re Eader, 426 B.R. 164, 167 (Bankr. D. Md. 2010) (finding that "the personal obligation of the debtor under the assumed agreement is subject to the discharge provided by Section 524(a) unless the debtor reaffirms the indebtedness under the lease in compliance with Section 524(c) *et. seq.*"); In re Crawford, Case No. 10–80397, 2010 Bankr. LEXIS 1746 at *4 (Bankr. M.D.N.C. May 19, 2010) ("Absent a reaffirmation agreement, the personal obligation of a debtor under a lease which has been assumed pursuant to § 365(p) is subject to discharge."); In re Walker, Case No. 06–11514C–7G, 2007 Bankr. LEXIS 1547, at *2 (Bankr. M.D.N.C. April 27, 2007) (finding that

Interestingly, though, the statute does not say what happens if the debtor does not propose assumption or if the debtor proposes it but the lessor refuses. The implication that lessors would urge is that absent such an agreed assumption, the debtor cannot retain possession. But debtors would argue that all that would happen is that the stay would terminate, leaving the lessor to its state law rights, and if under *state* law a lessor could not terminate, as discussed above, then nothing in § 365(p)(2) dictates otherwise. Perhaps the debtor can simply continue making regular lease payments and retain possession of the leased property thereby, while at the same time being discharged from any personal liability to make all lease payments.

§ 8.10   Effects of Rejection: Special Cases

The failure of some courts to ascribe the appropriate limited effect to rejection[154] has forced Congress to enact some special rules in § 365 to protect the legitimate interests of non-debtor parties to contracts or leases in the event of rejection. See § 365(h), (i), (j), (n). The basic problem is that some decisions have treated rejection as equivalent to the rescission or termination of the contract or lease, leaving the non-debtor party with nothing more than a claim for damages, *and* have required the non-debtor party to return to the estate any property conveyed to it under that contract or lease.

If all courts properly understood rejection, the special rules of § 365 discussed in this section would not be necessary. An unfortunate side effect of these special statutory provisions is that in omitted cases not specifically covered by a protective rule, courts might draw an inference that similar protections for the non-debtor party may not be inferred. Indeed, the Fourth Circuit made that precise argument in *Lubrizol*, bolstering its decision against the non-debtor licensee in that case by noting that "no comparable special treatment is provided for technology licensees such as Lubrizol."[155]

Three types of cases are dealt with by the special rules of § 365:

- the debtor is lessor and the non-debtor is lessee under a real estate lease, § 365(h);

- the debtor is vendor and the non-debtor is a vendee in possession under a contract for the sale of real estate, § 365(i), (j); and

- the debtor is licensor and the non-debtor is a licensee of a right to intellectual property (i.e., the *Lubrizol* situation), § 365(n).

The operative premise of the Code in each of these three situations is the same: even if the trustee rejects the lease or contract, the non-debtor has the option to retain its property interest. In short, unless the non-debtor consents, rejection cannot be used

---

assumption under § 365(p) does not necessarily lead to waiver of discharge); In re Creighton, 427 B.R. 24, 27 (Bankr. D. Mass. 2007) (holding that an assumption agreement under § 365(p) is a "species of reaffirmation agreement" under § 524(c), and that if not complied with, is dischargeable).

[154]   See § 8.8.

[155]   756 F.2d 1043, 1048 (4th Cir. 1985), cert. denied, 475 U.S. 1057 (1986).

to strip property from the non-debtor. Of course, as noted earlier, this should be the outcome even without any special rules; but, given cases like *Lubrizol* and *In re New York Investors Mutual Group, Inc.*,[156] congressional action was needed.

Section 365(h) applies when the debtor is the lessor and the non-debtor is the lessee under a lease of real estate.[157] For example, assume that the debtor leases office space on the tenth floor in Tall Towers to a lessee, and that the lease has not expired when the debtor files bankruptcy. If the trustee rejects the unexpired lease, and if rejection amounts to a breach that would entitle the lessee to treat the lease as terminated, the lessee is given a choice by § 365(h). The first option for the lessee is to treat the lease as terminated. § 365(h)(1)(A)(i). If the lessee makes that choice, the lessee must relinquish possession of the premises; but the lessee also will have a claim in the bankruptcy case for all of its damages arising from the rejection. §§ 365(g)(1), 502(g)(1).

The other option for the non-debtor lessee is to retain its rights under the lease. § 365(h)(1)(A)(ii). Thus, for example, the lessee may choose to remain in possession of the premises, notwithstanding the rejection. The lessee is privileged to retain these rights for the balance of the lease term, as well as for any enforceable renewal or extension periods. If this option is selected, the lessee must keep paying rent and otherwise must perform its obligations under the lease. However, the lessee may offset against the rent any damages caused by the lessor's nonperformance. § 365(h)(1)(B). Note that neither the debtor nor the trustee will be obligated to perform under the lease. Thus, in the Tall Towers hypothetical, the debtor will not have to provide elevator service, heat, electricity, or water, or maintain common areas, and so forth. Other than the right of offset against rent for such damages, a lessee who elects to retain its rights waives all other claims against the debtor and the estate. A non-debtor lessee in a shopping center who retains its rights also will still be subject to any restrictions pertaining to tenant mix, use, radius, and so forth. § 365(h)(1)(C).

The 1994 Amendments clarified the scope of § 365(h). Prior to the amendments, § 365(h) applied to a lessee who was "in possession of the leasehold," which raised some doubts as to whether the retention option existed when the lessee had sublet the premises or assigned its rights.[158] The amendment to subsection (h) made clear what Congress had intended all along, namely that the lessee was entitled to retain all rights in or appurtenant to the real property, even if it sublet or assigned its rights.[159]

The second set of special rules in § 365 applies to real estate (or timeshare) sale contracts, in which the debtor is the vendor and the non-debtor is the vendee, and the vendee is already in possession. Section 365(i) is modeled after § 365(h), and gives the

---

[156] 143 F. Supp. 51 (S.D.N.Y. 1956). See § 8.8 for further discussion.

[157] Actually, § 365(h)(1) applies to the case of a real property lease, and § 365(h)(2) applies to a timeshare interest under which the debtor is the seller. The operative rules are essentially the same, however, and for simplicity the discussion in the text focuses on the lease case.

[158] See In re Carlton Rest., Inc., 151 B.R. 353 (Bankr. E.D. Pa. 1993) (tenant may not assign lease); In re Harborview Dev. 1986 Ltd. Partnership, 152 B.R. 897 (D.S.C. 1993) (actual physical possession by tenant required). But see In re Lee Road Partners, Ltd., 169 B.R. 507 (E.D.N.Y. 1994) (section applies even if property sublet).

[159] See H.R. Rep. No. 103–834, 103d Cong., 2d Sess., at 21–22 (1994).

non-debtor vendee similar protection to that embodied in (h).[160] If the real estate sale contract remains executory at the time the debtor files bankruptcy, and the trustee rejects the contract, the purchaser is given a choice: it may treat the contract as terminated, or it may remain in possession. § 365(i)(1).

Again, then, the non-debtor party cannot be involuntarily dispossessed of the property and deprived of its interest. If the purchaser chooses to treat the contract as terminated, it will have a claim for its damages arising from the rejection. §§ 365(g)(1), 502(g)(1). To the extent the purchaser has already paid part of the purchase price, it also automatically is granted a lien on the debtor's interest in the real property to secure the recovery of the price paid. § 365(j). If the purchaser elects to remain in possession, it will have to continue to make all payments due under the contract. The purchaser is entitled to offset against such payments any post-rejection damages caused by the debtor's nonperformance, but it waives all other claims. § 365(i)(2)(A). The debtor and the trustee have no obligations under the contract, except that the trustee must deliver title to the purchaser in accordance with the terms of the contract.

If the purchaser is not in possession when the debtor files bankruptcy, it does not have the choice given by § 365(i). In the event of rejection by the trustee, such a disappointed purchaser is given a lien to secure any payments it has already made on the price, § 365(j), and also may assert a claim for its damages for breach.

The final protective rule in § 365 for non-debtor parties to rejected contracts is § 365(n). This subsection was added to the Code in 1988[161] to overrule the Fourth Circuit's infamous decision in the *Lubrizol* case.[162] Recall that in *Lubrizol*, the court held that rejection of the license agreement had the effect of depriving the non-debtor licensee of the right to continue using the technology, leaving the licensee only with a claim for damages. Under § 365(n), a licensee of intellectual property is given a choice upon rejection of the license by the trustee. The licensee may opt to treat the license as terminated and simply claim its damages. § 365(n)(1)(A). Alternatively, the licensee may elect to retain its rights to the intellectual property for the duration of the license term and any extension periods. § 365(n)(1)(B). This second option is the one that the *Lubrizol* court concluded the licensee did not have.

If the licensee chooses to retain its rights to the intellectual property, it must act to do so within a reasonable amount of time following rejection or within a court-imposed deadline, or it risks waiver of its rights.[163] In addition, it must continue to

---

[160] H.R. Rep. No. 95–595, 95th Cong., 1st Sess., at 349 (1977).

[161] An Act to keep secure the rights of intellectual property licensors and licensees which come under the protection of title 11 of the United States Code, the Bankruptcy Code, Pub. L. No. 100–506, 102 Stat. 2538 (1988).

[162] Lubrizol Enters., Inc. v. Richmond Metal Finishers, Inc., 756 F.2d 1043 (4th Cir. 1985), cert. denied, 475 U.S. 1057 (1986). See § 8.8 for further discussion; see also In re Exide Techs., 607 F.3d 957, 965 (3d Cir. 2010) (Ambro, J., concurring) (stating that 365(n) was enacted to address the unfavorable precedent set in *Lubrizol*, which would allow an intellectual property licensor to unilaterally terminate a licensee's ability to use its intellectual property).

[163] Hitachi Global Storage Techs. Neth., B.V. v. Read–Rite Corp. (In re Read–Rite Corp.), 393 Fed. Appx. 535, (9th Cir. 2010) (stating in dicta that even if there had been a valid contract between the debtor and transferee in the first place, the transferee relinquished its rights under § 365(n) when it waited more than a year after the court-imposed deadline to assert its rights).

make all royalty payments[164] due under the contract. § 365(n)(2)(B). The licensee also waives any right of setoff it may have under the contract and any claim for administrative expenses. § 365(n)(2)(C). The trustee must allow the licensee to exercise its rights, § 365(n)(2)(A), and also must supply any intellectual property covered by the license to the licensee and not interfere with the licensee's rights. § 365(n)(3).

Note that a licensee has the option to retain its rights even after it has ceased to do business with the debtor.[165] Such was the case in *Apple, Inc. v. Spansion, Inc.,* where the debtor rejected a prepetition patent license it had granted to Apple, and Apple moved to retain its rights under § 365(n).[166] The bankruptcy court denied Apple's motion.[167] On appeal, the District Court for the District of Delaware reversed the denial of Apple's motion to retain its rights, finding that although the two companies had ceased to do business with one another, the purpose behind the license continued to exist.[168]

In one high profile case, *In re Qimonda AG Bankruptcy Litigation,* the courts have examined the applicability of § 365(n) to a foreign main proceeding. There, a foreign debtor in a chapter 15 proceeding sought to reject patent licenses under the authority of German insolvency law, and deprive the licensee of the right to use the licensed technology[169]—in short, what happened in *Lubrizol*. The licensee objected, arguing that § 365(n) applied and thus precluded depriving it of the use of the licensed technology.[170] The district court determined that § 365(n) does not automatically apply in chapter 15 proceedings, but does so only in the discretion of the bankruptcy court.[171] The district court then remanded the case to determine whether the application of German insolvency law in this situation would violate United States public policy, and thus should not be allowed pursuant to 11 U.S.C. § 1506.[172] The bankruptcy court on remand held that rejection and termination of the licensee's rights would contravene the public policy exception of 1506, and denied the motion.[173] As this book went to press, the case had been certified for direct appeal to the Fourth Circuit to determine whether German insolvency law or § 365(n) should apply in a chapter 15 case involving a foreign main proceeding.[174]

---

[164] The Ninth Circuit held that the label the parties use is not dispositive of what constitutes a "royalty payment," and concluded that "license fees" must be treated as royalty payments under the statute. In re Prize Frize, 32 F.3d 426 (9th Cir. 1994).

[165] Apple, Inc. v. Spansion, Inc. (In re Spansion Inc.), 09–1069 KJC, 2011 WL 3268084 (D. Del. July 28, 2011).

[166] Id. at *2.

[167] Id. at *3.

[168] Id. at *9.

[169] In re Qimonda AG Bankruptcy Litigation, 433 B.R. 547, 553 (E.D. Va. 2010).

[170] Id.

[171] Id. at 561.

[172] Id. at 570–71.

[173] In re Qimonda AG, 462 B.R. 165 (Bankr. E.D. Va. 2011).

[174] In re Qimonda AG, 470 B.R. 374 (E.D. Va. 2012).

§ 8.11   Collective Bargaining Agreements: *Bildisco*

Perhaps the most controversial case decided by the Supreme Court under the Bankruptcy Reform Act of 1978 has been the Court's 1984 ruling in *NLRB v. Bildisco & Bildisco*.[175] In *Bildisco*, the Court decided two separate questions. First, the Court unanimously held that a chapter 11 debtor in possession could reject its collective bargaining agreement.[176] Second, the Court decided by a narrow five-to-four margin that the debtor had not committed an unfair labor practice by unilaterally modifying its labor contract pending the bankruptcy court's decision on the rejection motion.[177] Congress reacted quickly to the *Bildisco* decision, enacting § 1113 as part of the 1984 Amendments just a few months later.[178] In § 1113, Congress largely codified the *Bildisco* holding on the rejection issue, § 1113(b), (c), but overturned the Court's holding on the unilateral modification question, § 1113(e), (f).

Bildisco & Bildisco was a partnership in the business of distributing building supplies. Prior to filing chapter 11, Bildisco had entered into a collective bargaining agreement with a union. The debtor defaulted on many of its obligations under that labor contract, both before and after it filed for relief under chapter 11. After filing chapter 11, the debtor unilaterally modified the terms of the agreement, and requested and was granted permission to reject the contract. The union appealed that authorization. The union also complained to the National Labor Relations Board that the debtor's unilateral modification of the agreement was unlawful. The Board agreed, finding that the debtor had committed an unfair labor practice, and petitioned the Third Circuit for enforcement of its order. The Third Circuit upheld the rejection of the contract and refused to enforce the Board's order. The Supreme Court granted certiorari and then affirmed.

The issue of a chapter 11 debtor's ability to reject a collective bargaining agreement had been a hot issue in the courts for about a decade prior to the Supreme Court's *Bildisco* decision. The first prominent decision was that of the Second Circuit in 1975 in *Shopmen's Local Union No. 455 v. Kevin Steel Products, Inc.,*[179] in which the court held that a labor contract under the National Labor Relations Act could be rejected pursuant to a balancing of the equities standard. The very same year, the Second Circuit also addressed a similar question under the Railway Labor Act in *Brotherhood of Railway, Airline & Steamship Clerks v. REA Express, Inc.,*[180] and announced a stricter standard for rejection. In *REA Express*, the court required proof

---

[175]   465 U.S. 513 (1984). An avalanche of law review articles discussed the *Bildisco* decision. For a sampling, see, e.g., Vern Countryman, Is the National Labor Policy Headed for Bankruptcy?, 1984 Ann. Surv. Bankr. L. 159; Glenn George, Collective Bargaining in Chapter 11 and Beyond, 95 Yale L.J. 300 (1985); David L. Gregory, Labor Contract Rejection in Bankruptcy: The Supreme Court's Attack on Labor in *NLRB v. Bildisco*, 25 B.C. L. Rev. 539 (1984).

[176]   *Bildisco*, 465 U.S. at 516, 521–27 (Rehnquist, J., majority); id. at 535 (Brennan, J., concurring in part and dissenting in part). Joining Justice Rehnquist in the majority were Chief Justice Burger and Justices Powell, Stevens, and O'Connor. Joining Justice Brennan concurring in part and dissenting in part were Justices White, Marshall, and Blackmun.

[177]   Id. at 516–17, 527–34 (Rehnquist, J., majority); id. at 535–54 (Brennan, J. concurring in part and dissenting in part).

[178]   See § 8.12 for a discussion of § 1113.

[179]   519 F.2d 698 (2d Cir. 1975).

[180]   523 F.2d 164 (2d Cir.), cert. denied, 423 U.S. 1017 (1975).

that rejection was necessary to save the debtor's business from failing. Subsequent decisions, including that of the Third Circuit in *Bildisco*[181] and the Eleventh Circuit,[182] favored the *Kevin Steel* "balancing of the equities" standard over the *REA Express* "business failure" standard.

The Supreme Court in *Bildisco* held unanimously that the labor contract could be rejected. The Court first established that the bankruptcy court had the power to approve the rejection of the labor contract, pursuant to the general rejection power in § 365.[183] Next, and most centrally, the Court held that the appropriate standard for rejection was a showing that the contract was burdensome and that the balancing of the equities favored rejection.[184] The stricter "business failure" test of *REA Express*, the Court felt, was "fundamentally at odds with the policies of flexibility and equity" embodied in chapter 11.[185]

The Court gave some guidance as to the factors that courts should consider in balancing the equities. Bearing in mind always the goal of promoting the debtor's chances for a successful reorganization, a court considering a rejection motion should weigh the qualitative differences in the hardships faced by the debtor, creditors, and employees under the alternative choices of rejection or assumption.[186] The Court emphasized, however, that "the Bankruptcy Code does not authorize freewheeling consideration of every conceivable equity, but rather only how the equities relate to the success of the reorganization."[187] Since Congress adopted the "balancing of the equities" standard in § 1113(c)(3), the Court's discussion of this point remains relevant to the consideration of rejection motions today.

The Supreme Court went on to discuss when a rejection motion would be ripe for determination by the bankruptcy court. Foreshadowing the detailed procedural mechanisms later built into § 1113, the Court suggested that the court should only get involved late in the day, if negotiations had been tried and had failed to result in a voluntary settlement.[188]

The second major issue in *Bildisco* was whether the debtor had committed an unfair labor practice by unilaterally modifying the terms of the collective bargaining agreement prior to the bankruptcy court's ruling on the rejection motion. As noted above, the Court split five-to-four on this question, with the majority holding in the debtor's favor.[189] The position urged in Justice Brennan's dissent ultimately prevailed, however: in the 1984 Amendments, Congress prohibited unilateral interim modifications by the trustee or debtor in possession in § 1113(f). Now an interim

---

[181]   682 F.2d 72 (3d Cir. 1982), aff'd, 465 U.S. 513 (1984).

[182]   In re Brada Miller Freight Sys., 702 F.2d 890 (11th Cir. 1983).

[183]   *Bildisco*, supra note 175, 465 U.S. at 521–23. Now § 1113 governs the rejection of collective bargaining agreements. See § 8.12.

[184]   *Bildisco*, 465 U.S. at 523–27; Id. at 535 (Brennan, J., concurring in part and dissenting in part).

[185]   Id. at 525 (Rehnquist, J., majority).

[186]   Id. at 527.

[187]   Id.

[188]   Id. at 526–27.

[189]   Id. at 527–34.

change must be approved by the bankruptcy court, and then only on proof that the modification is "essential to the continuation of the debtor's business, or in order to avoid irreparable damage to the estate."[190] § 1113(e).

The *Bildisco* majority concluded that the debtor had not violated the labor laws by unilaterally altering the terms of the agreement. The problem facing the debtor was that outside of bankruptcy, the federal labor laws prohibit an employer from implementing unilateral changes while a collective bargaining agreement is in effect.[191] According to the majority, bankruptcy changes that result. The Court's basic premise was that the debtor must have the right to modify in order to preserve the potential benefit of rejection.[192]

The Court circumvented the labor law proscription against unilateral changes by concluding that the collective bargaining agreement is "not an enforceable contract" after a bankruptcy petition is filed, unless and until the trustee or debtor in possession formally assumes that agreement.[193] In other words, the specific terms of the contract cannot be enforced against the estate before assumption. This part of the *Bildisco* opinion, discussing the nature of an executory contract pending the trustee's decision, remains important today for all types of executory contracts. The Court stressed the importance to the reorganization of giving the debtor in possession time to decide whether to assume or reject contracts, and perceived that enforcing the terms of the labor contract prior to that decision might force the debtor's hand. The majority gave primacy to the policy favoring bankruptcy reorganization over labor law policies.

The dissent looked at the issue from the opposite perspective.[194] Justice Brennan began with the premise that the labor laws should be enforced as written, and then looked at whether anything in the bankruptcy law required a different result. Not surprisingly, the dissent found no such mandate in the Bankruptcy Code. The majority's "no enforceable contract" theory was rejected by the dissent, which instead concluded that the labor contract continued "in effect" after the bankruptcy filing, and therefore remained subject to the labor laws until formal rejection.

§ 8.12　Collective Bargaining Agreements: After *Bildisco*

Congress responded to the Supreme Court's decision in *Bildisco* by enacting § 1113 in July, 1984.[195] That section now governs the rejection or modification of collective bargaining agreements in bankruptcy cases.[196] § 1113(a). Note that § 1113 only applies in a chapter 11 case. § 103(g).

---

[190]　See § 8.12.

[191]　29 U.S.C. § 158(a)(5), (d).

[192]　*Bildisco*, supra note 175, 465 U.S. at 529.

[193]　Id. at 532. The Court did not, however, agree with the view of the Third Circuit that the debtor in possession was a "new entity". Id. at 528.

[194]　Id. at 535–54 (Brennan, J., concurring in part and dissenting in part).

[195]　Pub. L. No. 98–353, § 541(a), 98 Stat. 390 (1984).

[196]　Many commentators have analyzed the provisions of § 1113. Some of these include Daniel L. Keating, The Continuing Puzzle of Collective Bargaining Agreements in Bankruptcy, 35 Wm. & Mary L. Rev.

Recall from the previous section that the Court decided two primary issues in *Bildisco*: first, that the debtor in possession could reject the collective bargaining agreement upon proof that the contract was burdensome and that the balancing of the equities favored rejection; and second, that the debtor did not commit an unfair labor practice by unilaterally modifying the collective bargaining agreement pending the bankruptcy court's decision on the rejection motion. In § 1113, Congress clearly overturned the Court's holding on the unilateral modification question, § 1113(e), (f), but (according to the prevailing view) largely codified *Bildisco* on the rejection issue. § 1113(b), (c).

The issue that divided the *Bildisco* Court was whether a debtor in possession had the power unilaterally to modify a labor contract without following the governing provisions in the National Labor Relations Act. The majority concluded that the debtor did have that power, as a necessary incident to the rejection power, while the dissent reached the opposite conclusion, finding the labor laws controlling.

Consider a simple example. Assume that Debtor and Union entered into a collective bargaining agreement prior to bankruptcy, in which the Union employees are to be paid $15 per hour and are granted generous vacation, medical and other benefits. After the agreement is signed, the Debtor's industry is deregulated, and the Debtor no longer can compete effectively on those terms. Market wages drop to $10 an hour, and fringe benefits become much more modest. Debtor files chapter 11. May Debtor start paying the employees $10 an hour and slash benefits?

Under *Bildisco*, the answer was yes. Under § 1113, the answer is no. Subsection (f) states: "No provision of this title shall be construed to permit a trustee to unilaterally terminate or alter any provisions of a collective bargaining agreement prior to compliance with the provisions of this section." "Compliance with the provisions of this section" means going to the bankruptcy court and asking for permission to cut wages and benefits.

The bankruptcy court is authorized to approve an interim modification. § 1113(e). The standard for approving the requested changes is more demanding than that for ultimate rejection, however. Under § 1113(e), the strict "business failure" test from *REA Express* is resurrected: interim modifications may only be authorized "if essential to the continuation of the debtor's business, or in order to avoid irreparable damage to the estate." Furthermore, the court may act only "after notice and a hearing," although to accommodate the possibility of true emergencies, "any hearing under this section shall be scheduled in accordance with the needs of the trustee."

Even if the court approves the requested changes, the debtor is not home free. The rejection motion is not mooted by the modification, and thus rejection could be denied. The debtor still has the duty to bargain with the union in good faith under the terms of the labor laws. And the union retains the right to strike, a right that the bankruptcy court cannot interfere with.

---

503 (1994); S. Elizabeth Gibson, The New Law on Rejection of Collective Bargaining Agreements in Chapter 11: An Analysis of 11 U.S.C. § 1113, 58 Am. Bankr. L.J. 325 (1984).

Some unanswered questions persist with regard to interim changes. One is whether a rejection motion must already be pending when the request for modifications under § 1113(e) is made. Some courts have required a pending rejection motion, except in extreme emergencies,[197] while other courts conclude that changes may be sought prior to asking for rejection.[198] Another issue is whether union employees have a claim for wages lost due to interim changes. Courts also struggle with whether § 1113 gives the court authority to modify a collective bargaining agreement that has expired by its own terms. Some courts have held that § 1113 is not applicable in such a scenario because the *Bildisco* decision explicitly applies to *unexpired* collective bargaining agreements.[199] Other courts have held that § 1113 is applicable to expired collective bargaining agreements, drawing on the intended purpose of the section.[200] Because *Bildisco* was intended to allow a debtor to modify or reject a collective bargaining agreement, "it would be an odd result to find that § 1113, enacted specifically to codify and modify *Bildisco,* did not allow a debtor to modify its residual obligations if it followed § 1113's procedures."[201]

Even more crucial is whether § 1113(f) institutes a *de facto* superpriority for prepetition claims of the union members under the collective bargaining agreement. For example, assume that the debtor has not paid the employees' wages for the two weeks prior to filing for chapter 11. Those prepetition wages would be entitled to a fourth priority. § 507(a)(4). The union will argue, however, that § 1113(f) requires the employer to pay currently all wages covered by the labor contract, including the unpaid prepetition wages. Failure to do so, the union asserts, would be a prohibited unilateral alteration of the contract. A minority of courts have agreed, and have held that covered prepetition claims are entitled to superpriority status under § 1113(f).[202] The clear majority position, though, is that § 1113(f) does not give rise to a priority claim independent of that conferred by § 507(a).[203] Note, though, that the question of priority only arises if the employer does not abide by § 1113(f) and actually *pay* the prepetition wages in accordance with the terms of the collective bargaining agreement; if payment is made, the priority question is mooted.

The heart of § 1113 is the treatment of the employer's motion to reject the collective bargaining agreement. The public outcry following *Bildisco* focused on the Court's holding that an employer could reject a labor contract in bankruptcy, and triggered congressional action. Ironically, in view of its impetus, § 1113 does not substantially change the debtor employer's ability to reject a collective bargaining agreement. The rules of the game are spelled out in considerable detail, but the range of possible outcomes is hardly affected. Those rules may be grouped into three major

---

[197] See In re Ionosphere Clubs, Inc., 139 B.R. 772 (S.D.N.Y. 1992).

[198] See Beckley Coal Mining Co. v. United Mine Workers of Am., 98 B.R. 690 (D. Del. 1988).

[199] See, e.g., In re Sullivan Motor Delivery, Inc., 56 B.R. 28 (Bankr. E.D. Wis. 1985).

[200] See, e.g., In re Karykeion, Inc., 435 B.R. 663 (Bankr. C.D. Cal. 2010).

[201] Id. at 675.

[202] See In re Unimet Corp., 842 F.2d 879 (6th Cir.), cert. denied, 488 U.S. 828 (1988).

[203] See In re Roth Am., Inc., 975 F.2d 949 (3d Cir. 1992). Accord, Peters v. Pikes Peak Musicians Ass'n, 462 F.3d 1265 (10th Cir. 2006); Adventure Res., Inc. v. Holland, 137 F.3d 786 (4th Cir.), cert, denied, 525 U.S. 962 (1998); In re Ionosphere Clubs, Inc., 22 F.3d 403 (2d Cir. 1994).

categories: (1) the pre-rejection negotiation procedures, § 1113(b), (c)(1), (c)(2); (2) the standard for rejection, § 1113(c)(3); and (3) the hearing timetable, § 1113(d).

Some courts have compiled the statutory negotiation procedures and the rejection standard into a nine-part test by which to judge a rejection motion.[204] This test is nothing more than a restatement of the statutory requirements spelled out in § 1113(b) and (c). The nine requirements are:

1. The debtor in possession must "make a proposal" to the union to modify the collective bargaining agreement, § 1113(b)(1)(A);

2. The proposal must be "based on the most complete and reliable information available at the time" of the proposal, § 1113(b)(1)(A);

3. The proposal must provide "for those necessary modifications" that are "necessary to permit the reorganization of the debtor," § 1113(b)(1)(A);

4. Those proposed modifications also must assure "that all creditors, the debtor and all of the affected parties are treated fairly and equitably," § 1113(b)(1)(A);

5. The debtor must provide the union "such relevant information as is necessary to evaluate the proposal," § 1113(b)(1)(B), subject to the court's power to enter a protective order with regard to confidential information, § 1113(d)(3);

6. Between the time of making the proposal and the hearing on the rejection motion, the debtor must meet with the union at reasonable times, § 1113(b)(2);

7. At those meetings, the debtor must "confer in good faith in attempting to reach mutually satisfactory modifications," § 1113(b)(2);

8. The union must refuse to accept the proposal "without good cause," § 1113(c)(2); and

9. The "balance of the equities clearly favors rejection" of the collective bargaining agreement, § 1113(c)(3).

The detailed provisions commanding pre-rejection negotiations reflect the spirit of the *Bildisco* admonition that a voluntary settlement is greatly to be preferred over an adversarial resolution in court. This approach draws heavily on the labor law policies of avoiding labor strife and encouraging collective bargaining, and imports those ideas into the specialized arena of bankruptcy.

Of these statutory requirements, the most controversial and important has been the third, that the proposal must provide only for those "necessary" modifications that are "necessary" to permit the reorganization. § 1113(b)(1)(A). The obvious question is:

---

[204] The first court to spell out this nine-part test was *In re American Provision Co.*, 44 B.R. 907 (Bankr. D. Minn. 1984).

what does "necessary" mean? In particular, the courts have disagreed on the issues of (1) necessary *to what end*, and on (2) *how* necessary the modifications must be to that end. The Third Circuit has interpreted the "necessary" provisions as requiring proof that the modifications proposed are the bare minimum needed to stave off immediate liquidation of the debtor.[205] In essence, this view asserts that § 1113(b) resurrects the strict "business failure" test from *REA Express*. The opposing view, adhered to by a majority of courts, is that "necessary" is not so narrow a concept. Instead, as the Second Circuit has held, the debtor may propose modifications that go beyond the absolute minimum that is required to avoid immediate liquidation, and may urge changes to the labor contract that will help to ensure the long-term viability of the debtor's business.[206] This view was taken by the Southern District of New York in the American Airlines bankruptcy. Embracing the majority test for "necessity," the court granted American Airlines' motion to reject its labor contract with its pilots.[207] It did so based on a finding that the labor contract was burdensome and that American's proposed modifications were necessary to permit reorganization.[208] Obviously, the majority view is much more generous to the debtor employer.

Another important component of the debtor's proposal is that it must assure fair and equitable treatment to all directly affected parties—union employees, nonunion employees, creditors, the debtor, and management. § 1113(b)(1)(A). The point of this requirement is that the union employees cannot be forced to bear the brunt of all of the "belt tightening" needed to see the debtor through its financial straits. To some extent all impacted parties must "share the pain," although courts do allow some variance in the exact degree of sacrifice imposed on each group. Thus, if the debtor proposes to cut union employees' wages by 20 percent, the proposal would not necessarily have to involve a 20 percent cut in management and nonunion salaries as well—but a court would surely look askance at a proposal that left management salaries untouched. Furthermore, courts will take into account any concessions made by an affected group prior to bankruptcy.

The statute also requires meetings to be held between management and labor interests after the proposal has been made to the union. § 1113(b)(2). These meetings must occur at reasonable times, and good faith is required. These terms leave much to the discretion of the courts. Congress did not intend to require proof that the parties have "bargained to impasse," within the meaning of the labor laws, but simply wanted to give the parties a viable chance to reach a voluntary accord.

The union then must reject the debtor's proposal "without good cause." § 1113(c)(2). It is difficult to fathom what this requirement adds to the other provisions. If the debtor (1) has made a proposal that satisfies the requirements of § 1113(b)(1), i.e., is fair and equitable to all parties and proposes only necessary modifications, and is based on complete information that is provided to the union, and

---

[205] Wheeling–Pittsburgh Steel Corp. v. United Steelworkers, 791 F.2d 1074 (3d Cir. 1986).

[206] See Truck Drivers Local 807 v. Carey Transp., Inc., 816 F.2d 82 (2d Cir. 1987).

[207] In re AMR Corp., 478 B.R. 599 (Bankr. S.D.N.Y. 2012).

[208] Id.

(2) has met with the union as required by § 1113(b)(2), then what "good cause" could the union have to reject the proposal?

Only if all of the foregoing hoops are jumped through will the court be required to render a decision on the rejection motion. Codifying the *Bildisco* standard (and rejecting the "business failure" test), Congress in § 1113(c)(3) authorizes rejection if the "balance of the equities clearly favors rejection." It is thus not enough for the debtor to demonstrate that rejection will be beneficial, as is the case for other types of executory contracts. An explicit balancing of interests is commanded. Courts applying the "balancing of the equities" test must bear in mind the Supreme Court's caution in *Bildisco* that the Code "does not authorize freewheeling consideration of every conceivable equity, but rather only how the equities relate to the success of the reorganization."[209] The bankruptcy court's inquiry thus is limited to weighing the impact of rejection of the labor contract on those parties that would be directly affected, in light of how rejection will bear on the probable success of the debtor's reorganization. Rejection is most likely to be approved if the high cost of the labor contract places the debtor at a severe competitive disadvantage. The hypothetical used earlier, where the debtor's labor costs under the collective bargaining agreement are 50 percent over current market wages due to deregulation, might be such a case.

The fact that the bankruptcy court authorizes the rejection of a union contract does not end the labor chess game for the debtor. The national labor laws still remain very much in effect. Thus, the debtor still has a duty to bargain collectively with the union. The union retains the right to strike. Indeed, the prospect of a strike may be considered by the bankruptcy court when pondering whether or not to approve the rejection.

Another important aspect of § 1113 is the detailed timetable for considering a rejection motion. § 1113(d). If the debtor insists on strict compliance with the statutory rules and does not agree to any extensions, the whole matter should be concluded within no more than 51 days. A hearing must be scheduled within 14 days after the filing of the rejection motion, on at least ten days' notice to all interested parties. § 1113(d)(1). The court has the power to extend the time for commencement of the hearing for seven days, but no more. Then, the court must rule on the rejection application within 30 days after the commencement of the hearing. § 1113(d)(2). If the court fails to rule within that time, the debtor in possession is empowered to implement changes in "any provisions" of the collective bargaining agreement pending the court's ruling. § 1113(d)(2).

Recently, the applicability of § 1113 to a chapter 9 municipality bankruptcy came into play. While going through a chapter 9 case, the city of Vallejo, California sought to reject four collective bargaining agreements, with police officers, fire fighters, electrical workers, and other administrative employees.[210] The unions argued that § 1113 and *Bildisco* were inapplicable because of heightened protection for union employees available under California labor laws. The court rejected this contention, and held that

---

[209]   NLRB v. Bildisco & Bildisco, 465 U.S. 513, 527 (1984).
[210]   In re City of Vallejo, 432 B.R. 262 (E.D. Cal. 2010).

the city could reject the contracts simply by meeting the requirements of *Bildisco* and the Bankruptcy Code.[211]

§ 8.13   Retiree Benefits

In 1988 Congress enacted § 1114 and § 1129(a)(13) to protect the insurance benefits of retired employees.[212] The 1988 law was prompted by the LTV bankruptcy case, in which LTV sought to cut off medical benefits for retirees. Actually, the 1988 legislation made permanent the stop-gap measures promulgated by Congress in response to the LTV case.[213] The 2005 Amendments added a provision extending the protection for retirees into the pre-bankruptcy time period.[214] § 1114(l). Section 1114 is a complex provision, although it is modeled closely after § 1113. Many commentators have questioned how effectively that section accomplishes the congressional aims that motivated its passage.[215]

The primary thrust of § 1114 is to prevent a chapter 11 debtor in possession (or trustee) from unilaterally terminating or modifying insurance benefits for retired employees (as LTV attempted to do). Thus, the heart of the section is subsection (e), which provides that the debtor in possession "shall timely pay and shall not modify any retiree benefits." § 1114(e)(1). Furthermore, the liability for those payments is expressly accorded status as an administrative expense priority, thereby avoiding the ambiguity on that issue that plagues § 1113. § 1114(e)(2). Section 1129(a)(13) complements § 1114(e) by requiring a confirmed plan to provide for the continued payment of retiree benefits.

A permanent modification in retiree benefits may only be obtained if the bankruptcy court so orders, § 1114(e)(1)(A), (g), or if the authorized representative of the retirees agrees to the changes. § 1114(e)(1)(B). Congress established procedures and standards for permanent modification that mirror those contained in § 1113. Thus, the debtor in possession must first make a qualifying proposal to the authorized representative for the retirees, and negotiations must be held. § 1114(f). Only if negotiations fail to produce a voluntary accord will the court get involved. If the debtor in possession makes a qualifying proposal and the retirees' representative rejects the proposal without good cause, the court may order modification if necessary to permit the debtor's reorganization, the modification treats all affected parties fairly and equitably, and the balancing of the equities clearly favors the modification. § 1114(g). All of these standards are borrowed from § 1113.

---

[211]   Id. at 272.

[212]   Retiree Benefits Bankruptcy Protection Act, Pub. L. No. 100–334, 102 Stat. 610 (1988).

[213]   See Pub. L. No. 99–591, § 608, 100 Stat. 3341–74 (1986); Pub. L. No. 100–99, 101 Stat. 716 (1987); Pub. L. No. 100–41, 101 Stat. 309 (1987).

[214]   Pub, L. No. 109–8, § 1403, 119 Stat. 215 (2005).

[215]   Professor Daniel L. Keating has been the most notable critic. See Daniel Keating, Bankruptcy Code § 1114: Congress' Empty Response to the Retiree Plight, 67 Am. Bankr. L.J. 17 (1993); Daniel Keating, Good Intentions, Bad Economics: Retiree Insurance Benefits in Bankruptcy, 43 Vand. L. Rev. 161 (1990). For similar criticisms, see Leslie T. Gladstone, Retiree Benefit Bankruptcy Protection Act of 1988: Welfare Benefits in Need of Reform, 65 Am. Bankr. L.J. 427 (1991).

However, the legislative history to § 1114 indicates that Congress favored a pro-retiree interpretation of the standards for modification that is reflected by the minority view of § 1113.[216] Specifically, a sponsor of § 1114 stated that Congress intended to adopt the view espoused by the Third Circuit that "necessary to permit reorganization" implemented a "business failure" test,[217] rather than the position of the Second Circuit that the debtor could make changes that went beyond the bare minimum required for survival.[218]

As is also the case with collective bargaining agreements under § 1113, temporary changes in retiree benefits may be ordered by the court under § 1114 pending resolution of the request for permanent modification. Just as in § 1113, interim modifications will only be authorized if the continuation of the debtor's business demands such action, or if irreparable damage to the estate will otherwise result. § 1114(h)(1).

The protection regarding interim modifications was extended in 2005 to go back 180 days before bankruptcy. Under that provision, if the debtor during the 180 days before bankruptcy (1) modified retiree benefits and (2) was insolvent when it did so, on motion of a party in interest the court shall reinstate the benefits as of the date of the modification, "unless the court finds that the balance of the equities clearly favors such modification." § 1114(l).

Section 1114 is not by its terms limited to union employees. Instead, the benefits of that section extend to "retired employees and their spouses and dependents" who have an entitlement to the types of retiree benefits covered by § 1114. § 1114(a). Retirees with annual income of $250,000 or more for the year prior to the bankruptcy are normally excluded, however. § 1114(m). "Retiree benefits" are defined as "medical, surgical, or hospital care benefits, or benefits in the event of sickness, accident, disability, or death under any plan, fund, or program . . . maintained or established . . . by the debtor." § 1114(a).

The protections of § 1114 and § 1129(a)(13) are in some ways ephemeral. Several cases have pointed out that the rights of the retirees under those sections are no greater than the underlying rights granted by the plan that provides the benefits in the first place. Thus, if the debtor employer reserves in the plan itself the right to terminate the plan by giving notice or to modify the terms of the plan, nothing in § 1114 or § 1129(a)(13) limits the debtor's power to exercise its contractual rights.[219] Furthermore, the major problem, which is the lack of mandatory prefunding of such plans, is not addressed by the Bankruptcy Code.[220] Finally, the payments required by § 1114(e) can only be made from available cash that is not subject to a valid lien.[221] As

---

[216] See 134 Cong. Rec. S6825 (daily ed. May 26, 1988) (statement of Sen. Metzenbaum).

[217] In re Wheeling–Pittsburgh Steel Corp., 791 F.2d 1074 (3d Cir. 1986).

[218] Truck Drivers Local 807 v. Carey Transp., Inc., 816 F.2d 82 (2d Cir. 1987).

[219] See, e.g., LTV Steel Co. v. United Mine Workers (In re Chateaugay Corp.), 945 F.2d 1205 (2d Cir. 1991), cert. denied, 502 U.S. 1093 (1992); In re Doskocil Cos., 130 B.R. 870 (Bankr. D. Kan. 1991); In re Federated Dep't Stores, Inc., 132 B.R. 572 (Bankr. S.D. Ohio 1991). But see In re Visteon Corp., 612 F.3d 210 (3d Cir. 2010) (statute followed despite contract language).

[220] See Keating, supra note 215, 67 Am. Bankr. L.J. at 18.

[221] E.g., In re Jones & Lamson Mach. Co., 102 B.R. 12 (Bankr. D. Conn. 1989).

one observer noted, "the fundamental flaw with § 1114 is that it attempts to create new wealth where none exists."[222]

D. ASSUMPTION

§ 8.14   Effects of Assumption

The debtor's bankruptcy estate does not automatically become a party to an executory contract of the debtor. In effect, the status of the contract vis-à-vis the estate is in limbo until the representative of the bankruptcy estate makes a decision whether to assume or reject that contract. The effects of rejection were discussed in previous sections.[223] This section explains the effects of *assumption*.

The primary effect of assumption is that the bankruptcy estate becomes a party to the executory contract. In essence, the estate is substituted for and takes the debtor's place under that contract. Two primary consequences follow. First, the estate after assumption is entitled to obtain the benefit of the other party's performance to the contract. Second, and concomitant to the first, the estate promises to perform in full all of the debtor's obligations under the contract.

The promise to perform first requires the estate to *cure* almost all existing defaults under the contract, or to provide adequate assurance of prompt cure.[224] § 365(b)(1)(A). For example, if the debtor had fallen behind in payments due under the contract prior to bankruptcy, the trustee will have to cure (or assure the prompt cure of) those defaults as a condition of assumption. Note that this cure will have the effect of preferring the non-debtor party's unpaid prepetition claim over other unsecured creditors. If the contract is not assumed, the non-debtor party will be left with a general unsecured claim against the estate for the amounts in default, to be paid pro rata in the bankruptcy distribution. In addition to curing defaults, the trustee must compensate (or provide assurance of compensation to) the non-debtor party for any damages for actual pecuniary loss resulting from the default. § 365(b)(1)(B).

The non-debtor party also is entitled to future performance by the estate after assumption. Upon assumption, the non-debtor party has an administrative priority claim against the estate on the assumed contract.[225] The situation is treated as if the estate entered into a *new contract* with the non-debtor party during the bankruptcy administration. Thus, if the estate breaches or later rejects the contract, the other party's damages will be an administrative priority claim. § 365(g)(2). Furthermore, because that claim would be an administrative expense allowed under § 503 rather than § 501, the limits on allowance of claims in § 502(b) do not govern.[226] The only limitation on the amount of the administrative priority claim if an assumed contract is

---

[222] Keating, supra note 215, 67 Am. Bankr. L.J. at 47.

[223] See §§ 8.7–8.10.

[224] See § 8.16. The 2005 Amendments supplemented § 365(b)(1)(A) by providing that a trustee does not have to cure a default arising from any failure to perform a nonmonetary obligation under an unexpired lease of real property, if it is impossible to do so. Pub. L. No. 109–8, § 328(a)(1)(A), 119 Stat. 100 (2005). See H.R. Rep. No. 109–31 (pt. 1), 109th Cong., 1st Sess. 87 (2005). See § 8.16.

[225] See In re Klein Sleep Prods., Inc., 78 F.3d 18 (2d Cir. 1996).

[226] Id.

later rejected is for commercial real estate leases; in 2005 Congress added a rule capping such a claim at two years' rent.[227] § 503(b)(7). If the contract to be assumed was in default prior to assumption, the estate must provide adequate assurance of future performance. § 365(b)(1)(C). Note, though, that adequate assurance need not be provided (as, for instance, under U.C.C. § 2–609) absent an existing default.

A logical corollary to the cure right and the entitlement to administrative priority is that assumption insulates the non-debtor party from any possible liability for prepetition payments received under the contract. For example, the debtor may have made otherwise preferential payments to the non-debtor party shortly before filing bankruptcy. Since assumption entitles the non-debtor to full performance on the contract, both retroactively and prospectively, preference liability under § 547 is precluded.[228]

In short, assumption places the non-debtor party on a fundamentally different footing than other general estate creditors. The non-debtor party is entitled to keep otherwise preferential payments, to have defaults cured, and to obtain administrative priority for future obligations. These striking effects are thought to be only fair as the *quid pro quo* to the non-debtor for compelling that party to render future performance under the contract to the bankruptcy estate. However, the practical result is that the trustee or debtor in possession will seek to postpone assumption as long as possible, especially if the court will force the non-debtor party to continue performing during the limbo period prior to assumption or rejection.[229] Indeed, the Second Circuit has concluded that bankruptcy courts in chapter 11 cases should routinely refuse to approve assumptions until the last possible moment, precisely because of the momentous effects of assumption.[230]

Another legal effect of assumption should be noted. Assumption must be "*cum onere*," i.e., with all the burdens. In other words, the trustee or debtor in possession must assume the *entire* contract, including provisions that are less favorable to the estate. The trustee may not selectively choose only those contractual provisions that would benefit the estate. This all-or-nothing approach seeks to protect the legitimate interests of the non-debtor party. The only exception to this principle is that "*ipso facto*" clauses, which would permit the non-debtor to terminate the contract solely because of the debtor's bankruptcy filing or financial status, are not enforced in bankruptcy.[231] § 365(b)(2), (e)(1).

Assumption is also important because it is a precondition to assignment.[232] § 365(f)(2)(A). Assignment may allow the estate to capture the premium value of a profitable contract, without obligating the estate itself to perform that contract.[233] Realization of this benefit is only possible, though, if the trustee assumes the contract.

---

[227] Pub. L. No. 109–8, § 445(3), 119 Stat. 117–18 (2005).

[228] See In re Superior Toy & Mfg. Co., 78 F.3d 1169 (7th Cir. 1996).

[229] See §§ 8.25–8.27.

[230] *Klein Sleep*, supra note 225, 78 F.3d at 29.

[231] See § 8.17.

[232] See § 8.22.

[233] See § 8.21.

One important ramification is that existing defaults (including those that arose prior to bankruptcy) either must be cured or adequate assurance of prompt cure must be given. Also, contracts that cannot be assumed for various reasons, see § 365(c), likewise cannot be assigned.

§ 8.15   Limits on Assumption: Contract in Existence

A basic limitation on the bankruptcy trustee's power to assume an executory contract is that the contract still must be *in existence* when the bankruptcy case is filed by the debtor. The trustee cannot assume what does not exist. This rule is a logical application of the concepts that contracts are a form of estate property, and that property of the estate is limited to property interests that the debtor had at the time of filing.[234] § 541(a)(1). Thus, if the debtor's interest in a contract or lease was finally terminated under governing non-bankruptcy law prior to bankruptcy, assumption by the bankruptcy trustee is not an available option.[235] A specific statute codifies this rule for nonresidential real property leases, § 365(c)(3), but the same principle holds for all other types of contracts and leases, even though not expressly codified.

Default is not equivalent to termination, however. The rule prohibiting assumption only applies if the contract was completely terminated prior to bankruptcy. For example, under the contract the debtor's default might give the non-debtor party the right to terminate the contract only if it gives the debtor ten days' notice and opportunity to cure. Termination will not be effective until the notice is given and the ten days has run without the debtor curing the default. If the debtor files bankruptcy any time before the expiration of the ten days, the contract is still alive and subject to assumption by the trustee. If state law provides a redemption period or anti-forfeiture period within which the debtor may cure the default and thereby revive the contract, that period must have expired before the bankruptcy filing.

In order to prevent forfeitures and to preserve potentially valuable contracts for the estate, courts will construe non-bankruptcy termination provisions or anti-forfeiture provisions strictly against the non-debtor party and in favor of the estate.[236] Yet, a clearly drafted termination clause will be given effect. The only exception is for "*ipso facto*" clauses, which are not enforced in bankruptcy.[237] Thus, the current rules reward a non-debtor party for drafting draconian termination clauses and for acting promptly to effect a termination.

If bankruptcy ensues before the contract terminates, the trustee will be afforded time to cure the default. There is some question as to how much time the trustee then will have to act. For example, assume that the non-debtor mailed a ten-day termination notice, and the debtor filed bankruptcy on day nine. Must the trustee cure by the next day? Under the Bankruptcy Act, the answer may have been yes: cases held that the trustee was limited to the debtor's rights, and thus had only the contractual

---

[234]   See § 5.2.

[235]   A well-known early Code case reaching this conclusion is *In re Mimi's of Atlanta, Inc.*, 5 B.R. 623 (Bankr. N.D. Ga. 1980), aff'd, 11 B.R. 710 (N.D. Ga. 1981).

[236]   E.g., In re Waterkist Corp., 775 F.2d 1089 (9th Cir. 1985).

[237]   See § 8.17.

period to act.[238] Under the Code, however, the trustee's options are not so limited. At a minimum, the trustee would be entitled to the time provided by § 108(b), namely, the later of the time provided for cure in the contract or applicable law, or 60 days after the bankruptcy filing. The better view, though, is that even § 108(b) does not restrict the trustee's time to cure defaults. Instead, the trustee is constrained only by the timing provisions of § 365 itself, which specifically governs assumption and cure.[239] Especially in a chapter 11 case, the trustee may have until the time of confirmation of the plan to act. § 365(d)(2).

A related question is whether the contract can terminate or be terminated *post-petition* so as to prevent assumption by the estate. The court should not be able to prevent the contract from expiring of its own force after the filing of the petition.[240] To illustrate, if the debtor entered into a one-year supply contract for gizmos with the non-debtor party prior to bankruptcy, and that one year period will expire a week after the bankruptcy filing, the bankruptcy court will be powerless to extend the contractual period.

However, after bankruptcy is filed, the non-debtor party may be barred from taking affirmative steps to terminate the contract based on the failure of the debtor in possession to comply with the terms of the contract, even if the contract gives the non-debtor a termination right.[241] The Code, however, is not explicit on this issue. According to the Supreme Court, after bankruptcy is filed, an executory contract is not "enforceable" against the trustee or debtor in possession until assumption.[242] Allowing the non-debtor to terminate based on the DIP's action or inaction arguably would be tantamount to a *de facto* enforcement of the contract against the DIP, and would undermine the DIP's right to a reasonable time to decide whether to assume or reject the contract.

An intriguing question is whether the non-debtor party may terminate a contract postpetition by exercising a contractual termination right that is independent of any action or inaction of the DIP. For example, an insurance company may have the contractual right to cancel an insurance policy by giving 30 days' notice. If the insured files bankruptcy, may the insurer still cancel by giving notice? Even if the contract were to be assumed, the trustee or DIP would not obtain any greater rights than the debtor had under the contract, suggesting that the insurance company's privilege of cancellation would persist. Yet, most courts have interpreted such a termination as an

---

[238] See, e.g., Schokbeton Indus., Inc. v. Schokbeton Prods. Corp., 466 F.2d 171 (5th Cir. 1972).

[239] E.g., Moody v. Amoco Oil Co., 734 F.2d 1200 (7th Cir.), cert. denied, 469 U.S. 982 (1984). See § 8.4 for a discussion of the time limits for assumption.

[240] See Gloria Mfg. Corp. v. Int'l Ladies' Garment Workers' Union, 734 F.2d 1020 (4th Cir. 1984).

[241] For a good discussion of this question, see Douglas W. Bordewieck, The Postpetition, Pre–Rejection, Pre–Assumption Status of an Executory Contract, 59 Am. Bankr. L.J. 197, 203–13 (1985). See also Daniel J. Bussel & Edward A. Friedler, The Limits on Assuming and Assigning Executory Contracts, 74 Am. Bankr. L.J. 321 (2000).

[242] See NLRB v. Bildisco & Bildisco, 465 U.S. 513, 532 (1984).

act to obtain property from the estate or to exercise control over property of the estate, and thus as prohibited by the automatic stay of § 362(a).[243]

Earlier it was noted that the prohibition against assuming expired contracts is analogous to the presumptive rule defining the scope of property of the estate under § 541(a) as of the time of commencement of the bankruptcy case. Yet, as discussed in Chapter 6, several avoiding powers enable the trustee to augment the estate by recapturing property transferred prior to the bankruptcy case. Can a similar recapture be effected for valuable contracts terminated shortly before bankruptcy (and thus analogous to a preference) or without fair compensation when the debtor was insolvent (and thus analogous to a fraudulent conveyance)? Conceptually, the argument for recapture would appear to be plausible, if the trustee can surmount the hurdle of characterizing the termination as a "transfer of property." Yet, courts have been reluctant to extend the avoiding powers to reach contractual terminations.[244]

§ 8.16   Limits on Assumption: Defaults

The trustee's power to assume an executory contract is qualified on compliance with certain statutory conditions if the debtor is in *default*. § 365(b). Specifically, before the trustee may assume a defaulted contract, the trustee must:

- *cure* the default, or provide adequate assurance of prompt cure, § 365(b)(1)(A);

- *compensate* the non-debtor party to the contract for any actual pecuniary loss resulting from the default, or provide adequate assurance of prompt compensation, § 365(b)(1)(B); and

- provide *adequate assurance* of future performance under the contract, § 365(b)(1)(C).

The provisions in § 365(b)(1) reflect Congress' concern with protecting the legitimate interests of the non-debtor party to an executory contract or lease. When that contract or lease is in default, the non-debtor's position becomes more tenuous, and special protections are needed to assure that the non-debtor will receive full performance of its contractual expectations.

The rules of § 365(b)(1) do not, however, apply to *every* type of default under a contract. In some circumstances Congress deemed the need to enable the trustee to assume a beneficial contract to be more important than enforcing the entire bargain. In a major change from prior law,[245] Congress made *"ipso facto"* or "bankruptcy" clauses unenforceable in bankruptcy.[246] § 365(b)(2)(A)–(C), (e)(1). Such clauses declare the filing of bankruptcy, or some similar financial condition (such as the onset of

---

[243] E.g., In re Amber Lingerie, Inc., 30 B.R. 736 (Bankr. S.D.N.Y. 1983); see also Eric Lam, Cancellation of Insurance: Bankruptcy Automatic Stay Implications, 59 Am. Bankr. L.J. 267 (1985). See generally § 3.6.

[244] See, e.g., In re Metro Water & Coffee Servs., Inc., 157 B.R. 742 (Bankr. W.D.N.Y. 1993) (refusing to apply fraudulent conveyance law).

[245] H.R. Rep. No. 95–595, 95th Cong.,1st Sess., at 347 (1977).

[246] See § 8.17.

insolvency), to be an event of default under the contract, which then would terminate the contract or allow the non-debtor party to terminate or take other action under the contract. The trustee will not have to cure a default under an ipso facto clause as a condition of assuming the contract.

In 1994, Congress further qualified the trustee's absolute duty to cure under the contract. If the default arose from the debtor's failure to perform nonmonetary obligations, the trustee will not have to satisfy "penalty" rates or penalty provisions in order to assume. § 365(b)(2)(D). In other words, the trustee can assume the contract by simply remedying the defective performance itself (cure) and compensating the non-debtor party for actual pecuniary loss caused by the default, without payment of contractual default penalties (that are *not* compensation for actual pecuniary loss). Cure is permitted at the nondefault rate in such a situation.[247]

In 2005, Congress again further qualified the trustee's absolute duty to cure defaults as a prerequisite to assumption, with amendments to § 365(b)(1)(A) addressing *nonmonetary defaults*.[248] Cure of such a default is not required if the default is impossible to cure. Furthermore, § 365(b)(1)(A) now provides that a default provision prohibiting "a failure to operate in accordance with non-residential real property lease," a so-called "going dark" default, is considered cured by resuming operations as required in the lease upon assumption. Moreover, the 2005 Amendments make clear that excusing the cure of incurable non-monetary defaults does not excuse compliance with the § 365(b)(1)(B) requirement of compensating the non-debtor party for any actual pecuniary loss caused by the default, and excusing the cure of the incurable nonmonetary default also does not affect the § 365(b)(1)(C) requirement of providing adequate assurance of future performance according to the terms of the contract or lease.

Nor does the trustee's power to cure depend on the existence of a contractual provision conferring such a right. Even if the contract itself is silent about cure, the trustee is granted that privilege by the express terms of the Bankruptcy Code.[249]

The statutory rule conferring the right to cure on the trustee leaves a number of questions open. When must the trustee cure? On what terms? And what if the default is incurable? Except for the last, the Code is silent on all of these issues.

The issue of the *time* within which the trustee must cure is critical. Note initially that the statute does not require immediate cure: it provides that the trustee either must cure *or* provide adequate assurance that the trustee will "promptly" cure. § 365(b)(1)(A). Courts have noted the significant potential for slippage in a term such as "promptly," and in some cases cure has been allowed over a year after assumption.[250]

---

[247] 140 Cong. Rec. H10,768 (daily ed. Oct. 4, 1994).

[248] Pub. L. No. 109–8, § 328(a)(1)(A), 119 Stat. 100 (2005).

[249] See, e.g., In re Sigel & Co., 923 F.2d 142 (9th Cir. 1991).

[250] See, e.g., In re Valley View Shopping Ctr., 206 B.R. 10 (D. Kansas 2001) (finding that two years constituted a prompt cure in light of the circumstances).

Another timing question concerns when cure must be effected if either the contract itself or applicable non-bankruptcy law provides a period for cure. Must the trustee comply with that time period? For example, consider the example given in the preceding section of this book, where the contract allows the non-debtor party to terminate the contract if it gives the debtor ten days' notice and opportunity to cure, the notice is given, and the debtor files bankruptcy on day nine. How long does the trustee have to cure?[251] Under the prior Act, some cases had held that the trustee had to act within the original time period[252]—here by day ten. As mentioned in the preceding section, though, the Code expands the trustee's rights. At the very least, the trustee would be entitled to cure within the longer of 60 days after the filing of bankruptcy or the contractual time period. § 108(b). The Code may give the trustee even more time than suggested by § 108(b). To the extent that the time for assumption under § 365(d) extends beyond the § 108(b) time period,[253] the time for the trustee to exercise her cure right likewise may be extended along with the time for assumption.[254] Otherwise the trustee's assumption right would be implicitly curtailed.

The Code is also silent on the *terms* of the cure that the trustee must effect. Here the courts must be sensitive to balance the need to protect the expectations of the non-debtor party against the importance of allowing the trustee to assume beneficial contracts on reasonable terms. Most courts have permitted the trustee to go beyond the terms provided by the contract itself, and to cure in a manner that protects the essential rights of the non-debtor. Otherwise non-debtor parties could, by careful drafting, make the cure right an illusory privilege.

Other than the provision added in 2005 regarding nonmonetary defaults on real estate leases, nothing in the Code answers the Delphic inquiry of whether a trustee is required to cure even an incurable default before assuming. If so, that contract would be unassumable, because the trustee would be unable to comply with all of the predicates to assumption. For example, the debtor may have failed to take an action under the contract by a required time. Even bankruptcy courts cannot roll back the calendar. Thus, a strict reading of § 365(b)(1)(A) would suggest that the contract could not be assumed, unless it fell within the specific exception added by the 2005 Amendments.

Having said that, the reality is that courts typically hold that only material and economically substantial nonmonetary defaults must be cured.[255] The test to determine whether a term is material or economically substantial depends on "whether the term is integral to the bargain struck between the parties (its materiality) and whether

---

[251] For a good discussion of this and related problems, see Douglas W. Bordewieck, The Postpetition, Pre–Rejection, Pre–Assumption Status of an Executory Contract, 59 Am. Bankr. L.J. 197 (1985). See also Daniel J. Bussel & Edward A. Friedler, The Limits on Assuming and Assigning Executory Contracts, 74 Am. Bankr. L.J. 321 (2000).

[252] E.g., Schokbeton Indus., Inc. v. Schokbeton Prods. Corp., 466 F.2d 171 (5th Cir. 1972).

[253] See § 8.4.

[254] E.g., Moody v. Amoco Oil Co., 734 F.2d 1200 (7th Cir.), cert. denied, 469 U.S. 982 (1984). This is the position espoused by Bordewieck, supra note 7.

[255] See, e.g., In re New Breed Realty Enters., Inc., 278 B.R. 314, 321 (Bankr. E.D.N.Y. 2002) ("Where the default is non-monetary and is not curable, the debtor is precluded from assuming an executory contract only if the default was material or if the default caused 'substantial economic detriment.'").

performance of that term gives a party the full benefit of his bargain (its economic significance)."[256] Accordingly, in order to preserve a valuable contract for the estate, courts tend to read the "cure" requirement as applying only to the realm of the possible, unless doing otherwise plainly undermines the essence of the non-debtor party's bargain. Under this view, a court would allow assumption if the trustee could compensate the non-debtor party for its damages suffered because of the default, and could give adequate assurance of future performance.

The requirement of adequate assurance of future performance is borrowed from the Uniform Commercial Code, which allows a party to a sales contract to demand such assurances if it has reasonable grounds for insecurity. U.C.C. § 2–609. Note, though, that in bankruptcy the non-debtor is entitled to assurances *only* if the debtor is in default on the contract. While the non-debtor might argue that § 2–609 still would apply, and that the fact of the debtor's bankruptcy constitutes reasonable grounds for insecurity, that view would render as surplusage the supreme federal command that only if the debtor is in default must adequate assurance of future performance be given. The content of the assurances would depend on the nature of the default, and must be construed in light of the congressional purpose to give the non-debtor party the essential benefit of their bargain. In most cases, some type of concrete and substantial financial evidence that the estate will be able to perform the contract in the future probably will be required. Note that assurances must always be given when the trustee is assigning the contract under § 365(f).[257]

A special set of rules governs the issue of adequate assurance of future performance when the contract to be assumed is a shopping center lease.[258] § 365(b)(3). The need to safeguard the interests of the other tenants in the shopping center dictates giving less deference to the special concerns of the bankruptcy estate in assuming a shopping center lease. Thus, the estate will have little leeway to escape the rigors of compliance with the terms of the master contract.

In some types of contracts the concern with protecting the expectations of the non-debtor party are paramount. Examples include personal service contracts and contracts to make a loan. Congress has chosen to address this problem by prohibiting the assumption of such contracts entirely,[259] § 365(c), rather than by trying to condition assumption on the provision of assurances.

§ 8.17   Limits on Assumption: Ipso Facto Clauses

At bottom, contract law is about protecting the legitimate expectations of the parties to that contract. To some extent, Congress has crafted § 365 in a way that will protect the expectancy interests of the non-debtor party to a contract. That protection, though, is not complete; the goals of contract law in some instances give way to the policies of the bankruptcy laws. Whether accurate or not, many commercial entities probably perceive a greater insecurity and risk of default pursuant to an executory

---

[256] In re Fleming Cos., 499 F.3d 300, 305–306 (3d Cir. 2007).

[257] See § 8.24.

[258] See § 8.18.

[259] See §§ 8.19–8.20.

contract with a debtor that is in bankruptcy—even under the scheme detailed in § 365. Given their choice, many non-debtor parties probably would prefer not to have to go forward with a contract with a bankrupt entity. At a minimum, they would like to have the choice whether to proceed or not, and on what terms.

Prior to the enactment of the Bankruptcy Code in 1978, an escape route was available. The non-debtor party could draft the default provisions of the contract so that the filing of bankruptcy itself, "*ipso facto*," was an event of default, terminating or authorizing termination of the contract. With the contract terminated, nothing was left for the bankruptcy trustee to assume. Because many of the same concerns about doing business with a financially troubled debtor might exist even if the debtor had not yet filed bankruptcy, additional "ipso facto" clauses were created. These clauses deemed defaults to occur on the onset of insolvency, or if a custodian or trustee was appointed for the debtor's assets, or if certain of the debtor's financial ratios fell below a prescribed level. Taken together, these ipso facto clauses offered non-debtor parties a convenient way to avoid entanglement with a financially distressed debtor. For the most part, the courts enforced these clauses, although on rare occasions a court exercised its equitable powers to refuse enforcement.[260]

One of the most significant changes Congress made in the 1978 Code was to bar the enforcement of ipso facto clauses in bankruptcy cases.[261] § 365(b)(2), (e)(1). Extensive testimony made plain that the prior practice of enforcing these clauses had deprived bankruptcy estates of valuable contracts that could have facilitated reorganization or increased the value of the estate for all creditors. Congress decided that the parochial interests of the non-debtor party could not justify such a result. At the same time, Congress recognized that "the unenforceability of ipso facto or bankruptcy clauses . . . will require the courts to be sensitive to the rights of the nondebtor party."[262]

Thus, the Code now provides that (1) a contract may not be terminated or modified solely because of the operation of the described types of ipso facto clauses,[263] § 365(e)(1), and (2) the special default rules of subsection (b) need not be complied with solely because of a default under one of those clauses, § 365(b)(2). The clauses included within the Code prohibition are those conditioned on:

- the insolvency or financial condition of the debtor at any time before the case is closed, § 365(b)(2)(A), (e)(1)(A);

- the commencement of a case under the Code, § 365(b)(2)(B), (e)(2)(B); and

- the appointment of or taking possession by a bankruptcy trustee or a custodian prior to bankruptcy, § 365(b)(2)(C), (e)(2)(C).

---

[260] E.g., Queens Boulevard Wine and Liquor Co. v. Blum, 503 F.2d 202 (2d Cir. 1974).

[261] H.R. Rep. No. 95–595, 95th Cong. 1st Sess., at 347–48 (1977).

[262] Id. at 348.

[263] See, e.g., In re Lehman Bros. Holdings, 422 B.R. 407, 419–20 (Bankr. S.D.N.Y. 2010).

§ 8.18   Limits on Assumption: Shopping Center Leases

As discussed in the preceding sections, Congress has balanced the interests of the estate and of the non-debtor party with respect to executory contracts and leases, and generally has come down in favor of the estate, subject only to a baseline assurance of protection for the non-debtor. The power to make the balancing judgment is vested in the bankruptcy court; the non-debtor cannot escape the clutches of bankruptcy by careful drafting. For leases in *shopping centers*, though, Congress has decreed a diametrically opposite rule. For such leases, ultimate power generally is ceded to the non-debtor lessor; *strict enforcement* of lease terms is the norm. § 365(b)(3). The reason for this dramatically different approach is that the other side of the balancing scales in a shopping center situation is weighted down with the cumulative interests of not only the non-debtor lessor, but of all of the other tenants in the shopping center as well. Congress concluded that only rigorous enforcement of all of the terms of a shopping center lease and master lease agreement could adequately safeguard the rights of all tenants. [264]

The statutory vehicle by which the special shopping center rules are implemented is through the definition of "*adequate assurance of future performance.*" § 365(b)(3). The need for a trustee (or debtor in possession) to demonstrate such assurances is triggered either when the trustee seeks to assume a lease that is in default, § 365(b)(1)(C), or to assign a lease. § 365(f)(2)(B). For shopping center leases, adequate assurance of future performance "includes"[265] adequate assurance:

- of the source of rent, § 365(b)(3)(A);

- in an assignment, that the financial condition and operating performance of the assignee and its guarantors is similar to that of the debtor and its guarantors, as of the time the debtor first became lessee, § 365(b)(3)(A);

- that any percentage rent will not decline "substantially," § 365(b)(3)(B);

- that assumption or assignment will be subject to *all* the provisions of the lease, including provisions such as radius, location, use, and exclusivity, *and* will not breach any such provision in any *other* lease, financing agreement, or master agreement relating to that shopping center, § 365(b)(3)(C); and

- that assumption or assignment will not disrupt *any* tenant mix or balance in the shopping center, § 365(b)(3)(D).

As originally enacted in 1978, this set of rules contained considerably more leeway for the trustee seeking to assume or assign a shopping center lease. With regard to provisions such as radius, location, use, exclusivity, and tenant mix, § 365(b)(3)(C), (D), all that was required was that the assumption or assignment not *substantially* breach or disrupt those provisions. Experience proved, however, that the congressional goal of

---

[264]   S. Rep. No. 65, 98th Cong., 1st Sess., at 68 (1983).

[265]   "Includes" is a Code term of art that signifies that it is "not limiting." § 102(3).

assuring "a landlord of his bargained for exchange"[266] was not being realized; the opening created by the "substantiality" requirement proved too wide, allowing trustees effectively to ignore important provisions of the lease, to the detriment of other tenants.[267]

In response, Congress in 1984 deleted the qualifier "substantially" in both subsections (C) and (D) of § 365(b)(3). Now exact compliance with all terms of the lease is demanded. In addition, the 1984 Amendments added the provision in subsection (A) that the assignee's financial condition and operating performance must be similar to that of the debtor at the time the debtor became lessee. The overall effect has been to make it much more difficult for a trustee to assume or assign a shopping center lease. The balance of power has been shifted radically in favor of non-debtor lessors, in a manner akin to that which prevailed when ipso facto clauses were enforced under the old Act.[268] As the Fourth Circuit observed in one case, in blocking an attempted assignment to an assignee who would not have complied with a use restriction requiring that the space be sued for an auto parts store, "Section 365(b)(3)(C) simply does not allow the bankruptcy court or us to modify West Town's *original* bargain with the debtor.'"[269] The court so held even though no auto parts supplier bid on the lease, the proposed assignee (an apparel merchandiser) had offered $80,000 to buy out the lease, and the bankruptcy court found that the tenant mix would not be significantly disrupted.[270]

Given the fundamental difference in the applicable rules and range of possible outcomes depending on whether a lease is subject to the special shopping center rules, determining whether those rules apply is of tremendous importance. Congress has not, however, defined what constitutes a *"shopping center."* In the legislative history to the 1978 Code, Congress did give some general guidance, noting that "a shopping center is often a carefully planned enterprise, and though it consists of numerous individual tenants, the center is planned as a single unit, often subject to a master lease or financing agreement."[271] The report went on to emphasize the importance of tenant mix, the nature of the business, projected levels of gross sales, and location.[272]

Some cases are easy, of course; no one would doubt that a large shopping mall, with all stores under one roof, common parking, and with all leases subject to a master agreement with one landlord, would qualify. But what about a downtown streetfront block of stores, not subject to a master lease, lacking common areas and joint advertising, but with a single landlord?

---

[266] H.R. Rep. No. 95–595, 95th Cong., 1st Sess., at 348 (1977).

[267] S. Rep. No. 65, 98th Cong., 1st Sess., at 67–68 (1983).

[268] See Leslie Cohen, Shopping Center Leases in Bankruptcy and the Impact of BAPCPA, 30 Cal. Bankr. J. 31 (2009).

[269] In re Trak Auto Corp., 367 F.3d 237, 244 (4th Cir. 2004) (quoting S.Rep. No. 98–65, at 67–68 (1983) (emphasis in original)).

[270] Id. at 240.

[271] H.R. Rep. No. 95–595, 95th Cong., 1st Sess., at 348 (1977).

[272] Id. at 348–49.

In such borderline cases, much will depend on the court's attitude about how broadly or narrowly to apply the shopping center rules. The Seventh Circuit took a narrow view, finding that the absence of a master lease, fixed hours, common areas, joint advertising, and a developed plot plan dictated a holding that the stores were not part of a shopping center.[273] The Third Circuit, however, in perhaps the best known shopping center case, evinced much greater willingness to find the existence of a shopping center in a doubtful case.[274] The court in *Joshua Slocum* resolved the doubt in favor of the landlord and non-debtor tenants, finding a strong congressional purpose in the 1984 Amendments to protect those non-debtor interests. In that case, the court held the lease in question was part of a shopping center, even though there was no master lease, no joint advertising, no right for tenants to terminate if the anchor tenant did so, and a physical configuration at odds with the normal understanding of a shopping center. The Third Circuit did find, however, that most of the other common indicia of a shopping center were present.[275] At bottom, the key was the practical interdependence of the various tenants on each other. Having found that the shopping center rules applied, the court then held that the trustee could not assign the lease without complying with an average sales clause, meaning that in reality the lease was not assignable. The net result was that the value of a profitable lease could not be captured by the bankruptcy estate.

§ 8.19   Limits on Assumption: Nondelegable Contracts

Contract law generally permits the assignment of contractual rights and the delegation of contractual duties. Assignment and delegation may be limited, however. First, the contracting parties might expressly prohibit assignment and delegation in the contract itself; outside of bankruptcy such clauses typically are enforced. Second, even if the contract itself contains no such express prohibitions, some contractual duties may not be delegable, either (1) because the other party has a substantial interest in performance by the original obligor rather than a delegate, or (2) because of limiting legislation.

Consider three examples. Example One is a contract for Debtor to supply bricks for a private construction project. Example Two is a government contract for Debtor Contractor to supply bricks to the United States Government. Example Three is a

---

[273] In re Goldblatt Bros., Inc., 766 F.2d 1136 (7th Cir.1985).

[274] In re Joshua Slocum, Ltd., 922 F.2d 1081 (3d Cir. 1990).

[275] The Third Circuit identified no fewer than fourteen criteria that were relevant to determining the existence of a shopping center, although none of the criteria were found to be dispositive:

A combination of leases; (2) all leases held by one landlord; (3) all tenants are commercial retailers; (4) common parking; (5) development as a shopping center; (6) master lease; (7) fixed hours; (8) joint advertising; (9) contractual interdependence of tenants, evidenced by restrictive use provisions; (10) percentage rent clauses; (11) right of tenants to terminate if anchor tenant terminates; (12) joint participation in maintenance; (13) tenant mix; and (14) physical contiguity of stores.

Id. at 1087–88. The most important characteristic, the court found, was "a combination of leases held by a single landlord, leased to commercial retail distributors of goods, with the presence of a common parking area." Id. at 1088 (quoting Collier on Bankruptcy ¶ 365.04[3]).

contract for Picasso Jr.[276] to paint bricks for a wealthy private patron. In each instance the obligor wishes to delegate its duties to a third person. May it do so?

The Debtor's duties in Example One would be delegable. Bricks are bricks, and presumably performance by a delegate would not vary materially from that of the original obligor. If the other party really does want bricks supplied only by Debtor, it would have to prohibit delegation of the brick-supplying duty expressly in the contract. Such a contractual prohibition would be enforced.

In Example Two, the Debtor's duties would *not* be delegable, even though bricks are still just bricks. Here, though, a specific statute in the United States Code prohibits a party to a government contract from transferring such a contract without the government's consent. 41 U.S.C. § 6305. The statutory prohibition applies irrespective of whether the contract itself bars delegation.[277]

Finally, in Example Three, Picasso could not delegate his duty to paint bricks to a third party. Undoubtedly, the brick art patron contracted for Picasso's personal skill and expertise, and has a substantial interest in performance by Picasso. As with the government contract, the patron would not have to include an anti-delegation clause in the contract; such a bar is read into the contract, based on the nature of the duties involved.

The pertinent question for bankruptcy cases is the extent to which these non-bankruptcy anti-delegation rules are given effect in bankruptcy, when the *obligor* files bankruptcy. The question is an important one, because the answer may dictate whether the estate will obtain the benefit of a valuable contract. The issue comes up in four distinct settings: (1) assignment to a third person;[278] (2) assumption by the trustee; (3) assumption by a debtor in possession; and (4) an attempt by a non-debtor party to enforce an ipso facto clause. Unfortunately, the relevant Code rules do not provide entirely clear and satisfactory answers.[279]

The Code sections that bear on the problem are: § 365(c)(1) (regarding assumption); § 365(f)(1) (regarding assignment); and § 365(e)(2)(A) (regarding enforcement of ipso facto clauses). Subsection (c)(1)(A) provides in part that "the trustee may not assume or assign any executory contract . . . if applicable law excuses a party, other than the debtor, . . . from accepting performance from or rendering performance to an entity other than the debtor or the debtor in possession," and twice emphasizes that the excuse must apply independent of any contractual anti-

---

[276] This is an example of "professorial license:" while there may not be a "Picasso Jr.," the hypothetical had to address the fact that "the" Picasso died in 1973, and yet still use the name of a famous artist to make the point.

[277] 41 U.S.C. § 6305 (2011) (Pub.L. 111–350, § 3, Jan. 4, 2011, 124 Stat. 3804) (formerly codified at 41 U.S.C. § 15) states in pertinent part: "The party to whom the Federal Government gives a contract or order may not transfer the contract or order, or any interest in the contract or order. A purported transfer in violation of this subsection annuls the contract or order so far as the Federal Government is concerned, except that all rights of action for breach are reserved to the Federal Government."

[278] See § 8.23.

[279] For helpful analyses, see Daniel J. Bussel & Edward A. Friedler, The Limits on Assuming and Assigning Executory Contracts, 74 Am. Bankr. L.J. 321 (2000); Brett W. King, Assuming and Assigning Executory Contracts: A History of Indeterminate "Applicable Law," 70 Am. Bankr. L.J. 95 (1996).

assignment clauses. Subsection (f)(1), which is expressly made subject to subsection (c), allows assignment of a contract "notwithstanding a provision in an executory contract or unexpired lease of the debtor, *or in applicable law*," that prohibits or conditions assignment. Subsection (e)(2)(A) provides an exception to the general rule of § 365(e)(1) that prohibits enforcement of ipso facto clauses. It permits enforcement of such a clause in language that tracks § 365(c)(1) except that the applicable law must excuse the non-debtor party from accepting performance from or rendering performance to "the trustee or to an assignee" of such contract or lease, rather than to "a party other than the debtor or the debtor in possession," as provided in subsection (c)(1). Until the 1984 Amendments, subsection (c)(1) and (e)(2)(A) were identical; in 1984, (c)(1) was changed to read as it is now.

Some cases are readily resolved by application of these statutory rules. If the *only* bar to assignment or delegation is a *contractual* anti-assignment clause, both assumption and assignment are allowed in bankruptcy notwithstanding that clause. Accordingly, in Example One, the private brick supply contract could be assumed by the trustee or the debtor in possession, and also could be assigned, even if the contract itself prohibited assignment. The contractual anti-assignment clause would not be honored under § 365(c)(1), (f)(1) or (e)(2)(A), since the debtor's duties under the contract are neither inherently nondelegable nor is their assignment prohibited by statute.

Examples Two and Three, where the bar to delegation is not dependent on a contractual clause, but arises in one case from limiting legislation and in the other from the personal nature of the obligations, can be more difficult to resolve. The debtor's duties under these contracts could not be delegated under non-bankruptcy law without the consent of the other party to the contract, irrespective of whether the contracts prohibit delegation. This fact seems to bring the contracts squarely within the prohibition of § 365(c)(1)(A) and the exclusion of § 365(e)(2)(A). Thus, on the face of the statutes, Picasso's trustee could neither assume the painting contract on behalf of the estate, nor assign that contract to a third party. To do so would deprive the non-debtor party to the contract of their right to have Picasso himself paint the bricks. Similarly, the government contract could not be assumed by the trustee or assigned to another contractor; otherwise the government's right under 41 U.S.C. § 6305 to insist on performance by the debtor would be eviscerated.

Two problems remain. The first is a possible dissonance between subsections (c) and (f) in assignment cases; the second deals with assumption by a debtor in possession. The first problem is addressed in a later section.[280] For now, just note that the reference to "applicable law" in (f) is hard to square with the similar reference in (c). Some courts have resolved the problem in favor of prohibiting assignment in bankruptcy if assignment is prohibited outside of bankruptcy by statutory or common law, but not if the only bar to assignment is in the contract. Under that approach, the contracts in Examples Two and Three would not be assignable in bankruptcy.

It makes sense to conclude that Picasso's trustee could not assign Picasso's painting contract to a third person, and that the United States could block the

---

[280] See § 8.23.

assignment of a government contract to a different entity. But what if Picasso *himself* files chapter 11, and continues as debtor in possession? Or if the debtor government contractor does likewise? May Picasso or the contractor acting as debtor in possession *assume* the contract, even though they could not assign it? Common sense says yes. The reason for the non-bankruptcy prohibition on delegation of duties would not apply in either case, since the original obligor was going to perform. The brick art patron would be getting bricks painted personally by Picasso; the United States would be receiving bricks from the original contractor.

There is a hitch, however. Common sense may say "yes," but the statute may say "no." Congress may have made a drafting error (and have failed twice to correct it!). The problem is that § 365(c)(1) states that the trustee (or, by application of § 1107(a), the debtor in possession) may not *assume* a contract "*if*" applicable non-bankruptcy law would excuse the other party from accepting performance from a third party (someone "other than the debtor or the debtor in possession"). In other words, the statute appears to enact a "*hypothetical*" test: a contract cannot be assumed if it cannot be assigned. Applying this hypothetical test would mean that neither Picasso nor the contractor could assume their contract, because they could not assign that contract to a third party. A number of courts have so held, finding no ready escape from the apparent "plain language" of the statute.[281]

Other courts have rejected the hypothetical test, and have concluded that § 365(c)(1) should be interpreted as providing an "*actual*" test: is the entity seeking to assume the contract *actually* someone "other than the debtor or debtor in possession"?[282] If so, assumption should be barred. If, however, the entity seeking to assume is actually the original obligor (e.g., Picasso, or the brick contractor), assumption should be permitted. The non-bankruptcy rights of the other party (e.g., brick art patron, or the U.S. government) would be respected, and a potentially valuable contract could be captured for the bankruptcy estate. The same interpretive problem inheres in the ipso facto exclusion of § 365(e)(2)(A).[283]

Bankruptcy courts in the Southern District of New York have in some instances taken a different approach to the issue. The so-called *Footstar* analysis seeks to effectuate the purposes of § 365(c)(1), in a manner consistent with the "actual test,"

---

[281] The first major circuit decision was *In re West Elecs., Inc.*, 852 F.2d 79 (3d Cir. 1988). The leading case for the hypothetical test is *In re Catapult Entertainment, Inc.*, 165 F.3d 747 (9th Cir.), cert. denied, 528 U.S. 924 (1999). See also In re Sunterra Corp., 361 F.3d 257 (4th Cir. 2004). For an interesting application, see *In re EBC I, Inc.*, 382 Fed.Appx. 135, 137 (3d Cir. 2010) (debtor's pre-paid purchase of advertising services was not assumable or assignable under the hypothetical test, and thus debtor "did not receive less than 'reasonably equivalent' value when those rights reverted to the [ISP] upon termination of the contract").

[282] See Institut Pasteur v. Cambridge Biotech Corp., 104 F.3d 489 (1st Cir.), cert. denied, 521 U.S. 1120 (1997), abrogated on other grounds by Hardemon v. City of Boston, 144 F.3d 24 (1st Cir.1998); Summit Inv. & Dev. Corp. v. Leroux, 69 F.3d 608 (1st Cir. 1995). A thoughtful propounding of the actual test is found in *In re Hartec Enter., Inc.*, 117 B.R. 865 (Bankr. W.D. Tex. 1990). Judge Clark points out in *Hartec* that the hypothetical test renders the phrase "or debtor in possession" in § 365(c)(1)(A) as surplusage, and ignores congressional amendments in 1984 and 1986 that sought to remedy the problem.

[283] See *Summit*, supra note 282. But see In re Mirant Corp., 440 F.3d 238 (5th Cir. 2006) (holding that subsection (e) calls for an actual test whereas subsection (c) uses a hypothetical test).

while avoiding the statutory criticisms associated with that test.[284] How does it manage this clever trick? Through a "plain meaning" gambit of its own. The *Footstar* analysis emphasizes that the statute explicitly prohibits assumption only by *the trustee*, not the "debtor" or "debtor in possession".[285] Thus under this interpretation, where the debtor itself is the debtor in possession and has not been replaced by a trustee, *assumption* is permitted even where *assignment* is not.[286] Of course, the statutory criticism that could be leveled against this test is that it may run afoul of § 1107(a), which gives the debtor in possession virtually all powers and rights of a trustee.

The consequences of this division in the case law is illustrated in the context of intellectual property licenses, such as patent, trademark, and copyright licenses. Often such a license might be the most important asset a debtor has. However, well-established federal law severely limits a licensee's ability to assign its interest in an intellectual property license.[287] Thus, in courts that utilize the "hypothetical test," where the rule is "no right to assign means you also cannot assume," a debtor licensee may also be prevented from *assuming* valuable intellectual property rights, which can prove disastrous to a reorganization.[288] This unfortunate and unsupportable result has caused some commentators to suggest that § 365 should be revised to contain an explicit carve-out for intellectual property licenses, by prohibiting assignment but not assumption of such licenses.[289]

Of course, the even better result is for Congress to fix the statute so it plainly provides for an actual test, no matter what sort of contract is under consideration. There is no policy justification whatsoever for the hypothetical test.

Even if the assumption hurdle can be surmounted, one final problem with assumption bears noting in the case of nondelegable contracts involving *individual* debtors. As mentioned above, such a contract could not be assumed by the *trustee*, because of § 365(c)(1). Perhaps, though, the individual acting as *debtor in possession* could assume the contract, as just discussed. But will such assumption do any good? Until 2005, § 541(a)(6) excluded *post*-petition earnings attributable to the services of an individual debtor from the bankruptcy estate, except in chapter 13.[290] Now the exclusion only applies in chapter 7 (or 12), and not in chapter 11 or 13. When applicable, this principle helps to implement the individual debtor's fresh start. Because of this exclusionary rule, some courts have concluded that personal service contracts of individual debtors cannot be dealt with at all in § 365.[291] Other courts,

---

[284] In re Footstar, Inc., 323 B.R. 566 (Bankr. S.D.N.Y. 2005) ("Footstar I"), as reiterated in In re Footstar, Inc., 337 B.R. 785, 788 (Bankr.S.D.N.Y.2005) ("Footstar II").

[285] 323 B.R. at 570–74.

[286] The "*Footstar*" analysis was adopted by Judge Gerber in In re Adelphia Communications Corp., 359 B.R. 65 (S.D.N.Y. 2007).

[287] See, e.g., Gardner v. Nike, Inc., 279 F.3d 774 (9th Cir. 2002) (discussing federal law limiting assignability of a copyright license).

[288] See, e.g., *Catapult Entertainment*, supra note 281.

[289] For an example of this proposition, see Warren E. Agin, Assuming Intellectual Property Licenses, 31 Am. Bankr. Inst. J. 46 (2012).

[290] See § 5.9.

[291] E.g., In re Carrere, 64 B.R. 156 (Bankr. C.D. Cal. 1986).

however, have declined to categorically exclude all such contracts from § 365.[292] Under the pre–2005 law, even if the debtor as chapter 11 debtor in possession were to assume and then perform under the contract, his creditors would have no claim to the postpetition earnings the debtor received. However, in the 2005 Amendments Congress enacted § 1115(a)(2), which brings an individual debtor's post-petition earnings into the bankruptcy estate in a chapter 11 case. Now assumption would be meaningful for a chapter 11 individual debtor, and it becomes necessary to resolve the issue of whether § 365(c)(1) calls for an actual or a hypothetical test.

§ 8.20 Limits on Assumption: Contracts to Make a Loan

Congress singled out one class of contracts as being ineligible in all circumstances to be assumed or assigned by the trustee in a bankruptcy case: contracts to make a loan, or to extend other debt financing or financial accommodations. § 365(c)(2). Consequently, ipso facto clauses are enforceable with regard to such contracts. § 365(e)(2)(B). In short, a lender cannot be compelled to make a loan to a bankrupt, even if the lender committed to make that loan prior to bankruptcy. In this situation, the need to protect the legitimate interests of the non-debtor party conclusively outweigh the estate's interest in obtaining the loan.

Furthermore, a new extension of credit, with administrative priority for the lender, implicates the interests of the entire body of unsecured creditors. The new loan must be paid in full before general claims are paid. Thus, a loan contract is not assumable even if the lender consents.[293] Instead, a loan or extension of credit in bankruptcy can be authorized only under § 364.[294] That section contains detailed rules for notice to creditors, court approval, and the standards governing that approval. Another possible way for a bankruptcy estate to obtain working capital is to use "cash collateral" pursuant to § 363(c)(2).[295] Assuming or assigning loan contracts, though, is not an option.

The issue sometimes arises as to whether a contract falls within the prohibited class of contracts. The Code does not define "loan," "debt financing," or "financial accommodation." In the legislative history, Congress indicated that the exclusion was to be construed narrowly:

> Characterization of contracts to make a loan, or extend other debt financing or financial accommodations, is limited to the extension of cash or a line of credit and is not intended to embrace ordinary leases or contracts to provide goods or services with payments to be made over time.[296]

The courts have had some difficulty determining the scope of the statute, and in framing an acceptable test. In a sense almost all executory contracts involve at least an incidental extension of credit; indeed, the essence of a contract is mutual promises to

---

[292] E.g., In re Taylor, 913 F.2d 102 (3d Cir. 1990).

[293] In re Sun Runner Marine, Inc., 945 F.2d 1089 (9th Cir. 1991).

[294] See § 11.10.

[295] See § 5.18.

[296] 124 Cong. Rec. H11,093 (daily ed. Sept. 28, 1978) (statement of Rep. Edwards).

perform in the future. The legislative history just quoted indicates, though, that Congress intended for § 365(c)(2) to have a much narrower reach. On one extreme, a loan commitment, such as for a construction loan, obviously would be nonassumable. On the other extreme, an ordinary contract to deliver goods or to lease property in exchange for regular monthly payments would be assumable; such contracts are the standard fare of § 365. But what about cases that fall in the middle? Generalizations are difficult; the prevailing view appears to be that if the financing is only an incidental part of the contract, assumption will be permitted; however, if the credit extension is a central and significant aspect of the contract, assumption will be denied. The cases consider the extent and nature of the risk that assumption would impose on the non-debtor party.

For example, the Ninth Circuit held in *In re Easebe Enterprises, Inc.*,[297] that an option to purchase was nonassumable. The terms were that the debtor could purchase the property for $800,000, with $75,000 down and the balance financed by the seller over five years. The court concluded that a contract that required money or other property to be delivered in exchange for a promise to pay was nonassumable.

In another case, the Eleventh Circuit read § 365(c)(2) more favorably to the estate. In *In re Thomas B. Hamilton Co.*,[298] the court held that a credit card merchant agreement with a chapter 11 retail debtor was not a financial accommodations contract and therefore could be assumed. This agreement did involve some financing, in that the debtor had an obligation to repay the merchant bank for monies previously advanced on credits that later were validly charged back. However, the court of appeals concluded that such financing was incidental, and using a "primary purpose" test, found that § 365(c)(2) was not implicated. Under that test, the question is whether the "primary purpose" of the contract is the extension of credit, or instead whether the credit extension is merely incidental to the transaction.

E. ASSIGNMENT

§ 8.21   Effects of Assignment

One of the options a bankruptcy trustee has with regard to an executory contract or unexpired lease is to assume and then *assign* that contract or lease to a third party. For example, assume that the debtor was the lessee under a long-term real property lease, and files bankruptcy with several years left to run on the lease, at a time when market rents for similar property have risen. The trustee will assign the lease and capture the increase in the market rents for the benefit of the bankruptcy estate.

What is the legal effect of the assignment? Outside of bankruptcy, the debtor would remain liable on the lease, unless released by the lessor. Thus, if the assignee were to breach the lease, the lessor could look to the debtor for payment. It is a

---

[297] 900 F.2d 1417 (9th Cir. 1990). On the issue of whether an option contract is an "executory" contract under § 365, this case was overruled by *In re Robert L. Helms Constr. & Dev. Co.*, 139 F.3d 702 (9th Cir. 1998), but remains good law on the nonassignability issue. See In re Whiteprize, LLC, 275 B.R. 868, 873 (Bankr. D. Ariz. 2002).

[298] 969 F.2d 1013 (11th Cir. 1992).

fundamental principle of contract law that an assignor cannot relieve itself of liability for contractual duties by delegating those duties to another.

In bankruptcy, however, this basic rule changes: § 365(k) provides that assignment "relieves the trustee and the estate from any liability for any breach of such contract or lease occurring after such assignment." The debtor's liability also will be discharged. Thus, if the assignee were to default on the lease after a bankruptcy assignment, the lessor would *not* be able to collect from *either* the debtor or the estate. Nor can the non-debtor escape this rule by prohibiting assignment in the contract; such anti-assignment clauses are invalid in bankruptcy.[299] § 365(f)(1).

Instead, the *only* party responsible for future obligations under a contract or lease after assignment will be the *assignee*. Actually, § 365 does not expressly impose such liability on the assignee, but that liability is implicit in the section and is consistent with contract law. Because only the assignee will be liable after a bankruptcy assignment, the essential protection for the non-debtor party is the requirement in § 365(f)(2)(B) that the assignee provide "*adequate assurance of future performance*" as a condition to the assignment.[300] Such assurances must be provided even if the contract is *not in default*. The non-debtor's bargain has been altered without its consent by the substitution of a new obligor; the *quid pro quo* is assurance of performance by that obligor.

Note that an "assignment" is different from a "sublease." The special rules of § 365(f) and (k) apply only to assignments, not subleases.[301] Thus, a trustee could assume a lease and then sublease to a third party and thereby realize any appreciation in the value of the lease. In subleasing the property, the sublessee would *not* be required to provide adequate assurances of future performance under subsection (f)(2)(B); by contrast, an assignee would have to provide assurances. Even in a sublease case, assurances would be required from the trustee in order to assume the lease, but only if the lease were in default. § 365(b)(1)(C). One downside of a sublease is that the estate will remain liable on the lease, because § 365(k) only relieves the estate of liability after an assignment. Also, the anti-assignment rule of § 365(f)(1) would not prohibit anti-subletting clauses in the lease.

§ 8.22   Limits on Assignment: Assumption

Assignment is a significant power for a bankruptcy trustee. By an assignment the trustee can cash in the profit of a favorable contract, and yet simultaneously escape further liability on that contract. Exercising this privilege requires compliance with two conditions. First, the trustee must *assume* the contract. § 365(f)(2)(A). Second, the assignee must provide adequate assurance of future performance.[302] § 365(f)(2)(B).

---

[299] See § 8.23.

[300] See § 8.24.

[301] E.g., In re Lafayette Radio Elec., 8 B.R. 528 (Bankr. E.D.N.Y. 1981).

[302] See § 8.24.

The prerequisite of assumption means that an assignment is subject to all of the limitations on assumption, discussed in earlier sections.[303] For example, defaults on the contract generally must be cured, or assurance of prompt cure must be given. § 365(b)(1)(A). Also, the non-debtor must be compensated for any damages resulting from that default. § 365(b)(1)(B). The cure and compensation rules insure that the non-debtor party will at least be brought current on the contract at the time of the assignment. Thereafter, the non-debtor must look to the assignee for performance. The assignee also will take the contract subject to all of its terms and conditions, since assumption must be *"cum onere."*

Some contracts may not be assignable because they are not assumable. Nondelegable contracts fall into this category,[304] § 365(c)(1), as do contracts to make a loan or to provide financial accommodations.[305] § 365(c)(2). The next section discusses the enforceability of non-bankruptcy restrictions on assignment.

§ 8.23   Limits on Assignment: Non–Bankruptcy Restrictions

Outside of bankruptcy, the parties to a contract or lease generally are free to prohibit or condition assignment of the contract. By the use of such anti-assignment clauses, contracting parties retain control over the parties with whom they will do business. Furthermore, anti-assignment provisions may prevent the other party to the contract from capturing the increased value of a beneficial contract via assignment, meaning that the enhanced value of the contract or lease defaults to the party in whose favor the bar on assignment operates.

In bankruptcy, however, restrictions on assignment are viewed with suspicion. If enforced, anti-assignment rules might prevent the bankruptcy estate as successor to the debtor from realizing the premium on a profitable contract. Consider a simple example. Debtor leases space in a commercial building for a period of three years, at a rental of $10,000 per year, and operates a hardware store on the premises. After two years, Debtor files bankruptcy. When the Debtor files, the market rental for similar space has increased to $14,000 per year. The trustee for Debtor in theory could assign the lease for $4,000 ($14,000 minus $10,000, for the remaining year). However, if the Debtor's lease prohibits Debtor from assigning its interest without the lessor's consent, and if such a clause were enforced in bankruptcy, the trustee could not assign the lease and make the $4,000 profit. The lessor instead would be able to relet the premises at the higher market rate.

The Bankruptcy Code does not enforce such contractual anti-assignment clauses, however. Section 365(f)(1) states that the trustee may assign a contract or lease "notwithstanding a provision in an executory contract or lease of the debtor, or in applicable law, that prohibits, restricts, or conditions the assignment of such contract or lease." In our example, then, Debtor's trustee could assign the lease and make $4,000 for the estate.

---

[303] See §§ 8.15–8.20.

[304] See § 8.19.

[305] See § 8.20.

Unhappy with this outcome, non-debtor lessors and other contracting parties have tried to devise ways to draft limitations on assignment that will not run afoul of § 365(f)(1) but that will still allow them to keep the appreciation in the value of a contract or lease. Consider, for example, the case of *In re Standor Jewelers West, Inc.*,[306] in which the lease required the lessee to pay 75 percent of the appreciation of the lease to the lessor as a condition of assignment. Applied to our hypothetical, the lessor would be entitled to receive $3,000 of the $4,000 increase. Not surprisingly, the court invalidated the 75% provision as a violation of § 365(f)(1), and permitted the estate to keep the entire profit from the assignment.

Another means of circumventing the "no-anti-assignment" rule of § 365(f)(1) is through the utilization of very specific and detailed "use" clauses. In our hypothetical, assume that the lease required the premises to be used only for a hardware store of a type that described the debtor's business exactly. If the trustee seeks to assign the lease to an assignee who would not comply precisely with the terms of the use clause, the lessor will protest, arguing that the terms of the lease are being violated. Assignment in bankruptcy requires assumption, § 365(f)(2)(A),[307] and assumption normally must be "*cum onere*," i.e., with all the terms of the contract. Furthermore, an assignee must demonstrate adequate assurance of future performance,[308] § 365(f)(2)(B), which it cannot do if it would be in breach of a valid use clause. The only types of contractual provisions that the Code allows the trustee to ignore are ipso facto clauses,[309] § 365(b)(2), (e)(1), and anti-assignment clauses. § 365(f)(1). The use clause, the lessor would argue, is neither, and thus must be honored. Yet, if the lessor's argument is accepted, the debtor's valuable lease would be essentially non-assignable, and the bankruptcy estate thus would not be able to capture the profit on that lease.

Courts have not always permitted non-debtor lessors to escape by the clever employment of use clauses. One approach is to require the lessor to demonstrate the "*actual and substantial detriment*" that it would suffer if the court approved an assignment that deviated from strict compliance with the use clause.[310] For example, if the trustee wanted to assign the lease to a sporting goods store, what harm would the lessor suffer? Yet, courts must be careful not to go too far in ignoring bona fide use restrictions. The lessor may have valid business reasons to restrict the use of the premises to a hardware store. Congress did indicate that the non-debtor party should receive "the full benefit of his bargain."[311] The challenge for courts is to prevent deft evasion of the Code's prohibition of anti-assignment clauses without depriving the non-debtor party of its legitimate interests. Recall, by the way, that in a shopping center, the trustee must strictly comply with the terms of a use clause,[312] § 365(b)(3)(C), and thus assignment in our hypothetical to anything other than a hardware store would not be possible.

---

[306] 129 B.R. 200 (B.A.P. 9th Cir. 1991).

[307] See § 8.22.

[308] See § 8.24.

[309] See § 8.17.

[310] E.g., In re U.L. Radio Corp., 19 B.R. 537 (Bankr. S.D.N.Y. 1982).

[311] H.R. Rep. No. 95–595, 95th Cong., 1st Sess., at 348 (1977).

[312] See § 8.18.

An earlier section noted an apparent conflict between subsections (c) and (f) in assignment cases, where the non-bankruptcy prohibition on assignment is found somewhere other than in the contract itself. A common example is 41 U.S.C. § 6305, which prohibits the assignment of any contract with the United States government without the government's consent. Many state statutes similarly limit or condition assignment of special classes of contracts. As just discussed, § 365(f)(1) overrides anti-assignment provisions in a contract or lease "*or in applicable law.*" No one doubts that purely contractual anti-assignment provisions are invalid in bankruptcy and cannot block the estate's assignment of a valuable contract. The puzzling question, though, is what the reference to "applicable law" in subsection (f)(1) means.[313]

Looking just at subsection (f), one would assume that the reference to "applicable law" would extend to any sort of "applicable" anti-assignment law other than ones found just in the contract itself. Thus, for example, one might think that subsection (f) would negate all statutory and common law anti-assignment laws, and permit assignment in bankruptcy notwithstanding such laws. But that cannot be right. Subsection (f) applies "*except* as provided in subsection . . . (c)." And subsection (c)(1)(A) provides that a contract cannot be assumed—which, recall, is a prerequisite to assignment—if an "applicable law" (other than an anti-assignment clause in the contract itself) *excuses* the non-debtor party from accepting performance from or rendering performance to someone other than the debtor or debtor in possession, *unless* the non-debtor party *consents* to the assignment, under subsection (c)(1)(B). In short, under subsection (c), which trumps subsection (f), "applicable" anti-assignment laws that do not depend on contract clauses, which would seem to include prohibitions in statutes (such as for government contracts) and in common law (such as for unique personal services) are *enforced* so as to preclude assumption.[314] That being the case, what sorts of "applicable law" anti-assignment rules could subsection (f) possibly be referring to? What is left? Unless Congress simply made a gross drafting error, and the "applicable law" anti-assignment rule of § 365(f)(1) is meaningless, the scope of "applicable law" in subsection (c)(1)(A) must be more circumscribed than in subsection (f)(1). But in what way? Despite the linguistic gyrations indulged in by some courts, the plain fact is that the statutory language itself offers few helpful clues to resolving the puzzle.[315]

---

[313] See Daniel J. Bussel & Edward A. Friedler, The Limits on Assuming and Assigning Executory Contracts, 74 Am. Bankr. L.J. 321 (2000); Brett W. King, Assuming and Assigning Executory Contracts: A History of Indeterminate "Applicable Law," 70 Am. Bankr. L.J. 95 (1996); Morris W. Macey & James R. Sacca, Reconciling Sections 365(1)(1) and (f)(1) of the Bankruptcy Code: Should Anti–Assignment Laws Prohibit Assumption of Contracts by a Debtor in Possession, 100 Com. L.J. 117 (1995).

[314] See § 8.19.

[315] In a pleasing, albeit surprising display of honesty, one court confessed:

"I cannot say with any sense of intellectual honesty that I believe that traditional approaches to legal analysis will lead to a principled conclusion. In my view the reality is that in attempting to accommodate competing policy interests, all of which are of substantial weight, Congress has enacted statutes which impose conflicting mandates and has created a statutory scheme leaving interstices which the courts necessarily must fill on a case by case basis. Under these circumstances I will not ornament my holding with a facade of precedent or references to what I deem to be inconclusive statutory language."

In re Antonelli, 148 B.R. 443, 447 (D. Md. 1992), aff'd, 4 F.3d 984 (4th Cir. 1993).

At a minimum, courts agree that if the nature of the debtor's contractual obligations is such that the non-debtor party, unless it consents, would inherently be excused from accepting performance from anyone other than the debtor, whether or not the contract blocks assignment, and no matter who the assignee is, then bankruptcy assignment is prohibited.[316] Here, subsection (c)(1) indisputably applies and controls the outcome. The references to "excuse" in subsection (c)(1)(A) and to "consent" in (c)(1)(B) are telling. As a matter of contract law, the question is whether the *delectus personae* (the choice of the person) is material; that is, does the non-debtor party have a "substantial interest" in having the original obligor perform, and no one else?[317] Thus contracts that are uniquely *personal* in nature would not be assignable in bankruptcy without the consent of the non-debtor party. If Debtor is engaged to be married, and then files bankruptcy, his trustee cannot assign the contract to be married, even if the assignee might be a "better catch" than the Debtor himself. If I were to file bankruptcy, my trustee could not assign my job as a law professor; amazing as it may seem, my employer bargained for me, and no one else, to teach my classes and write books such as this.

Beyond the obviously nondelegable "personal" contracts just discussed, the courts have struggled mightily to reconcile the apparent conflict between subsections (c) and (f), with little success. One approach has been to enforce those anti-assignment rules that would be effective *independent* of contractual anti-assignment clauses, but to deny enforcement if the "applicable law" simply validates contractual prohibitions on assignment. The leading case espousing this view is *In re Pioneer Ford Sales, Inc.*,[318] a First Circuit decision authored by Justice Breyer during his tenure on the Court of Appeals. *Pioneer Ford* involved a Rhode Island statute that prohibited the assignment of a car dealership without the manufacturer's consent, as long as that consent was not unreasonably withheld. The First Circuit concluded that the state statute must be given effect in bankruptcy, and assignment was prohibited (the court finding that the manufacturer's consent was not unreasonably withheld, as required by the state statute). According to *Pioneer Ford*, the two subsections do not conflict; the key, the court said, is that § 365(c)(1) "refers to state laws that prohibit assignment 'whether or not' the contract is silent, while (f)(1) contains no such limitation."[319] Thus, "[a]pparently (f)(1) includes state laws that prohibit assignment only when the contract is not silent; that is to say, state laws that enforce contract provisions prohibiting assignment."[320] Courts and commentators alike have criticized this facile reconciliation as reading a limitation into subsection (f) that it does not contain.[321]

In *Magness* the Sixth Circuit tried another tack.[322] At issue in that case was whether a golfing membership in a country club could be assigned, even though the

---

[316] See, e.g., In re Magness, 972 F.2d 689, 699–700 (6th Cir. 1992) (Guy, J., concurring);

[317] See E. Allan Farnsworth, Contracts § 11.10 at 719–20 (4th ed. 2004). See Restatement (2nd) of Contracts § 318(2).

[318] 729 F.2d 27 (1st Cir. 1984).

[319] Id. at 29.

[320] Id.

[321] See, e.g., *Magness*, supra note 316, 972 F.2d at 695 (Joiner, J. majority opinion); Bussel & Friedler, supra note 313, at 328–29; King, supra note 313, at 107–08.

[322] 972 F.2d 689 (6th Cir. 1992).

club's rules prohibited assignment, a prohibition enforced under Ohio law. The Sixth Circuit attempted to reconcile subsections (f) and (c) as follows:

"At first, it might seem that they are not consistent, but a careful parsing of the provisions suggests that § 365(f) contains the broad rule and § 365(c) contains a carefully crafted exception . . .

Subsection (f) states that although the contract or applicable law prohibits assignment, these provisions do not diminish the broad power to assume and assign executory contracts. . . . In other words, a general prohibition against the assignment of executory contracts, i.e., by contract or "applicable law," is ineffective against the trustee. . . . However, subsection (f), by specific reference to subsection (c), allows one specific circumstance in which the power of the trustee may be diminished. Subsection (c) states that if the attempted assignment by the trustee will impact upon the rights of a non-debtor third party, then any applicable law protecting the right of such party to refuse to accept from or render performance to an assignee will prohibit assignment by the trustee. While subsections (f) and (c) appear contradictory by referring to "applicable law" and commanding opposite results, a careful reading reveals that each subsection recognizes an "applicable law" of markedly different scope.

. . . As required in § 365(c), the applicable law of controlling significance to the solution of this problem addresses the interests of the non-debtor third parties, rather than law relating to general prohibitions or restrictions on assignment of executory contracts covered by § 365(f)."[323]

The solution, in short, depends on whether the applicable non-bankruptcy law upholds the right of the non-debtor party to refuse performance from anyone other than the debtor.[324] Under Ohio law, the Sixth Circuit in *Magness* found that the country club membership was the sort of "personal" contract that could not be assigned without the club's consent. If you know the movie *Caddyshack*, think of the Rodney Daingerfield character and you might be able to imagine why club members should not have Rodney foisted on them without their consent. If, however, the prohibition on assignment would be enforceable outside of bankruptcy only if contained in the club's rules, then bankruptcy assignment would be allowed.

Under this view, the emphasis, then, is on whether the non-debtor party has an absolute right to block assignment, no matter what. Stated otherwise, is the situation one where the *only* way that the contract can be assigned is if the other party consents? Only in that circumstance will subsection (c)(1)'s prohibition be triggered and bankruptcy assignment be precluded. As Bussel and Friedler point out,[325] there are very few situations in the law where the other party to a contract actually enjoys such an absolute right to block assignment. Unique personal service contracts, federal

---

[323] Id. at 695–96.

[324] For a similar policy analysis in the context of sales of property under § 363, see *In re Dewey Ranch Hockey, LLC*, 414 B.R. 577 (Bankr. D. Ariz. 2009) (holding that the National Hockey League had the right to admit only members that met its "good character" and other written requirements).

[325] Bussel & Friedler, supra note 313, at 334–36, 335 n.61.

government contracts, and patent and copyright licenses are the most common examples. By comparison, a statute such as that involved in *Pioneer Ford Sales* would not qualify under this approach, because the non-debtor party does *not* enjoy an absolute privilege to withhold consent and bar assignment; instead, they may not unreasonably withhold consent.

§ 8.24   Limits on Assignment: Adequate Assurance of Future Performance

The signal effect of a bankruptcy assignment is that the estate is relieved of liability for future performance under the contract.[326] § 365(k). Only the assignee is liable after assignment. Nor can the non-debtor avoid this outcome by including an ipso facto clause,[327] § 365(b)(2), (e)(1), or an anti-assignment clause,[328] § 365(f)(1), in the contract. Thus, the critical protection for a non-debtor party to a contract that the trustee wants to assign is this: the assignee must provide *adequate assurance of future performance*.[329] § 365(f)(2)(B).

A similar assurance requirement applies to assumption, but only if the contract is in default.[330] § 365(b)(1)(C). For assignments, however, the assurance requirement applies in *all* cases, even if the contract is not in default.[331] The universal applicability of the assurance requirement in the assignment context is mandated by the fact that the non-debtor is being compelled to deal exclusively with a stranger to the original contract. The congressional concern that the non-debtor receive "the full benefit of his bargain"[332] is strained to the limit in assignments. Indeed, that directive cannot literally be fulfilled, since part of the non-debtor's "bargain" was to choose the party with whom to contract.

The phrase "adequate assurance of future performance" was new to the bankruptcy law in 1978. Congress lifted the term from Article 2 of the Uniform Commercial Code, governing Sales. Under U.C.C. § 2–609, a party to a sales contract is entitled to "adequate assurance of 'due' performance" if "reasonable grounds for insecurity arise" with respect to the other party's performance. In essence, the Bankruptcy Code conclusively deems the assignment of contractual obligations to a new party, without recourse against the original contracting party, to constitute reasonable grounds for insecurity.

The Code does not define "adequate assurance," and the legislative history gives no guidance. Comments 3 and 4 to § 2–609 of the U.C.C. discuss the meaning and give examples of adequate assurance in the sales context, and by analogy should provide

---

[326] See § 8.21.

[327] See § 8.17.

[328] See § 8.23.

[329] For a discussion, see David B. Simpson, Leases and the Bankruptcy Code: The Protean Concept of Adequate Assurance of Future Performance, 56 Am. Bankr. L.J. 233 (1982).

[330] See § 8.16.

[331] See, e.g., In re Res. Tech. Corp., 624 F.3d 376 (7th Cir. 2010) (denying the proposed assumption and assignment of energy conversion contracts where the assignee was unable to provide adequate assurance of its ability to finance the obligations assigned to it under the contract).

[332] H.R. Rep. No. 95–595, 95th Cong., 1st Sess., at 348 (1977).

some assistance to bankruptcy courts applying § 365(f)(2)(B).[333] Those Comments emphasize the fact-specific nature of the inquiry, and the examples demonstrate that the gravamen of the matter is evidence of the financial ability of the obligor to meet future obligations.

The cases under the Bankruptcy Code adopt a pragmatic approach to the adequate assurance question, and generally are sensitive to the legitimate concerns of the non-debtor party. The nature of the contract and the risks facing the non-debtor are pertinent. Courts demand concrete proof that the assignee has the financial wherewithal to perform. Evidence that would be relevant to such a showing includes financial statements, demonstrated access to sufficient working capital, cash reserves, contingency plans, personal guarantees, reasonable projections, financial history, market studies, and so forth. Since the non-debtor is not given the choice whether to do business with this assignee, the court, acting on behalf of the non-debtor, must not subject that party to greater risks than the non-debtor undertook in the original bargain. At the same time, the court must not give the non-debtor more than it bargained for, and must recognize the potential benefit to the estate and all creditors resulting from assignment.

In some cases Congress has spoken with more specificity with regard to what constitutes adequate assurance. For leases, a non-debtor lessor is authorized to require a deposit or other security substantially the same as the lessor would demand if it leased voluntarily to a similar tenant. § 365(l). For leases in shopping centers, the whole panoply of special rules in § 365(b)(3) apply.[334] Recall that the trustee has little flexibility in shopping center cases. The non-debtor is able to demand strict compliance with provisions regarding tenant mix, use, radius, location, exclusivity, and the like, and substantial assurance that percentage rents will not be adversely affected and that the source of rent will be secure.

In cases not involving shopping centers, courts may have more leeway to permit assignments that deviate in some degree from the precise terms of the original contract or lease. The question often arises in connection with use clauses. If strictly enforced, a narrowly drafted use clause might effectively block any assignment; yet, in some instances, the lessor has a legitimate interest in enforcing the use clause. Courts have tried to accommodate these conflicting concerns. One approach has been to allow deviation from a use clause, unless the non-debtor can demonstrate "actual and substantial detriment" from the proposed nonconforming use.[335] Another approach has been to allow deviation from the contract only where the term is not "material and economically significant," which focuses on the importance of the term in the context of the overall agreement.[336] Given the presumptive norm in bankruptcy of *cum onere* compliance with all contractual terms, other than those expressly invalidated in the

---

[333] See *Resource Technology*, supra note 331, 624 F.3d at 383.

[334] See § 8.18.

[335] E.g., In re U.L. Radio Corp., 19 B.R. 537 (Bankr. S.D.N.Y. 1982). See also In re Martin Paint Stores, 199 B.R. 258 (Bankr. S.D.N.Y. 1996).

[336] In re Fleming Companies, Inc., 499 F.3d 300 (3d Cir. 2007).

Code (such as ipso facto and anti-assignment clauses), courts perhaps should place the burden on the trustee to justify the deviation, rather than the other way around.

F. THE "LIMBO" PERIOD PRIOR TO ASSUMPTION OR REJECTION

§ 8.25 The Generally Applicable Rules

The Code in § 365 addresses in excruciating detail three options a trustee has with regard to an executory contract or unexpired lease: assume, assume and then assign, or reject. The trustee has one final option, however, about which the Code is virtually silent, but which is of enormous practical importance: *do nothing*. What are the rights of the bankruptcy estate and the parties with regard to an executory contract or unexpired lease during the "limbo" period after the filing of the bankruptcy petition, but before the trustee takes formal action to assume, assign, or reject?[337] Congress has enacted a few special rules to govern the treatment during this gap period of nonresidential real property leases,[338] § 365(d)(3)–(4), and commercial personal property leases,[339] § 365(d)(5), but has not addressed the basic issue more broadly. Thus, the generally applicable rules in this area, apart from the special cases just noted, are the product of judicial development.

That judicial development has proven to be markedly pro-debtor, and remarkably unsympathetic to the concerns of the non-debtor party to the contract. Indeed, this pronounced pro-debtor orientation of the courts fueled the special interest legislation in favor of non-debtor lessors of real property leases in 1984 and 2005 and of commercial personal property leases in 1994. In those instances, Congress was persuaded that the default rules created by the courts were too unfair to the non-debtor parties. However, in all other cases, though, the pro-debtor judicial rules remain in effect.

The first principle governing the status of limbo contracts is that "the filing of the petition in bankruptcy means that the [contract] is no longer immediately enforceable, and may never be enforceable again. . . . We conclude that from the filing of a petition in bankruptcy until formal acceptance, the [contract] is not an enforceable contract."[340] This statement in the Supreme Court's 1984 decision in *NLRB v. Bildisco & Bildisco*, although directed specifically at collective bargaining agreements, is not limited in conception or application to labor contracts, but is a proposition about the general nature of limbo period contracts in bankruptcy. Point one, then, is that an executory contract is *not enforceable* against the estate prior to formal assumption.

In other words, the particular terms of the contract, including default clauses, timing deadlines, and so forth, cannot be enforced against the estate, even indirectly.

---

[337] An excellent article on this issue is by Douglas W. Bordewieck, The Postpetition, Pre–Rejection, Pre–Assumption Status of an Executory Contract, 59 Am. Bankr. L.J. 197 (1985). Another useful article is Howard Buschman, Benefits and Burdens: Postpetition Performance of Unassumed Executory Contracts, 5 Bankr. Dev. J. 341 (1988).

[338] See § 8.26.

[339] See § 8.27.

[340] NLRB v. Bildisco & Bildisco, 465 U.S. 513, 532 (1984).

The courts have concluded that the trustee or debtor in possession must have a reasonable time to decide whether to assume or reject the contract, and that this right to make a carefully considered decision is paramount to the non-debtor party's right to enforce the precise contractual terms. The non-debtor party cannot eliminate or impair the trustee's right to decide by terminating the contract or disposing of the subject matter of the contract during the gap period.

At the same time, the executory contract continues in existence, and may be enforced *against* the *non-debtor* party during the gap period. That is, the non-debtor may be compelled to continue performing prior to assumption of the contract.[341] Nor does this compelled performance result in the *de facto* assumption of the contract by the estate; assumption requires formal court approval.[342] In short, the power to enforce an unassumed executory contract is a one-way street: the estate can force the non-debtor to perform, but the non-debtor cannot compel the estate to perform.

What rights, then, does the non-debtor party have during the limbo period? Most significantly, to the extent the estate elects to enforce the contract, the non-debtor is entitled to compensation as an *administrative expense* priority for the reasonable value of all benefits actually provided to the estate during bankruptcy.[343] This reasonable value may be measured by what is specified in the contract, but need not necessarily be computed according to the contract terms; payment is only for the *benefit* received by the estate—which may not be the full contractual amount—rather than for the loss suffered by the non-debtor party. Furthermore, under the majority view, potential but unrealized benefits under the contract are not compensable absent formal assumption.[344] A minority approach would allow priority even for potential benefits.[345]

The administrative expense compensation rule may be illustrated by the following hypothetical. Assume that prior to bankruptcy the debtor leased 30 cars for use in its business. After filing for chapter 11, the debtor, as debtor in possession, uses only ten of those cars; the other 20 are left idle in the company parking garage. Under the majority view, the non-debtor lessor would be entitled to an administrative priority for the reasonable rental value of only the ten cars used, for the period of use.[346] No "benefit" was realized by the estate for the 20 cars that the debtor in possession chose not to use. The minority approach requires administrative priority for all 30 cars, by defining the estate's benefit as the opportunity to use the cars, rather than actual use. All courts agree, though, that the non-debtor has no priority claim for future rents due under an unassumed lease after the trustee or debtor in possession rejects the lease.

---

[341] E.g., In re Whitcomb & Keller Mortgage Co., 715 F.2d 375 (7th Cir. 1983).

[342] Id. See § 365(a). See § 8.5.

[343] See NLRB v. Bildisco & Bildisco, 465 U.S. 513, 531 (1984) (citing *Philadelphia Co. v. Dipple*, 312 U.S. 168 (1941); *In re Public Ledger*, 161 F.2d 762 (3d Cir. 1947)).

[344] E.g., In re Mid–Region Petroleum, 1 F.3d 1130 (10th Cir. 1993).

[345] E.g., In re Fred Sanders Co., 22 B.R. 902 (Bankr. E.D. Mich. 1982).

[346] Ignore the impact of § 365(d)(5) for now. As discussed below, that section alters the general rule in a chapter 11 case and requires full performance of a commercial personal property lease, beginning 60 days after the order for relief. See § 8.27.

The other basic right that the non-debtor party has during the limbo period is to file a motion requesting the bankruptcy court to compel the trustee or debtor in possession to decide whether to assume or reject. In a chapter 11 case, the trustee or debtor in possession otherwise would have until the time of confirmation of the plan to make that decision.[347] § 365(d)(2). The only exception is for nonresidential real property leases, which will be deemed rejected if the trustee fails to act within 120 days, unless the court extends the time by no more than 90 days, for cause, or the lessor agrees to an extension § 365(d)(4).

In deciding how long to give the trustee to decide, the court must balance the competing interests of the non-debtor and the estate.[348] The non-debtor is often prejudiced by being left in limbo. It might not be compensated currently for all opportunity costs (e.g., the 20 unused cars in the hypothetical); it cannot make substitute arrangements with another party, because the trustee might later assume the contract; and yet the non-debtor cannot make reliable future business plans, because the trustee also might reject the contract. While the non-debtor will prefer an earlier decision, the trustee usually will want to delay the decision as long as possible. Assumption will require the estate to cure any defaults, compensate the non-debtor for damages resulting from the defaults, and provide adequate assurance of future performance.[349] § 365(b)(1). Furthermore, assumption will convert future contractual obligations into an administrative priority claim.[350] Rejection, conversely, will deprive the estate forever of the potential value of the contract.

The operation of the foregoing rules is illustrated by the case of *In re Whitcomb & Keller Mortgage Co.*[351] In that case the debtor, a mortgage banker, had an executory contract with Data–Link Systems, Inc., pursuant to which Data–Link was to provide computer services to the debtor, for a fee. At the time of the debtor's chapter 11 filing, the debtor was about $13,000 in arrears. During the chapter 11 case, Data–Link ceased providing services. The bankruptcy court ordered Data–Link to resume providing services, in exchange for payment for current services by the estate, but without ordering the estate to cure the prepetition arrearage. Later, the debtor in possession rejected the contract. The Seventh Circuit held that the bankruptcy court acted properly in ordering Data–Link to provide postpetition services prior to assumption, and that Data–Link was entitled to priority only for actual postpetition services provided. Neither the prepetition amount in default nor future post-rejection damages were entitled to administrative status; the order to perform did not constitute an order to assume the contract.

§ 8.26   Special Rules: Nonresidential Real Property Leases

In the 1984 Amendments, Congress enacted some special rules to afford greater protection to a non-debtor lessor of nonresidential real property (i.e., commercial real

---

[347] See § 8.4.

[348] This problem is discussed in detail in § 8.4.

[349] See § 8.16.

[350] E.g., In re Klein Sleep Prods., Inc., 78 F.3d 18 (2d Cir. 1996).

[351] 715 F.2d 375 (7th Cir. 1983).

estate) during the limbo period prior to assumption or rejection.[352] § 365(d)(3), (4). The first rule, in (d)(3), entitles the lessor to full performance of all obligations of the debtor lessee during the gap; the second, in (d)(4), which was amended in 2005, places the burden on the trustee or debtor in possession to act within 120 days or to obtain an extension. This latter timing rule is discussed in an earlier section in this Chapter.[353]

The heart of the 1984 nonresidential real property changes is § 365(d)(3), which states in part that "the trustee shall timely perform all the obligations of the debtor" that arise after the order for relief, until the lease is assumed or rejected. The court may extend the time for the trustee's performance up to 60 days after the order for relief, but not beyond. The only obligations that need not be performed by the trustee are those arising under ipso facto clauses described in § 365(b)(2).

The statute further provides that the trustee's obligation to perform exists "notwithstanding section 503(b)(1)." Most courts have read this language to excuse the lessor from showing actual use and benefit to the estate, as required by § 503(b)(1).[354] A small number of courts still require proof of compliance with § 503, however.[355]

An example will demonstrate the impact of § 365(d)(3). Assume that prior to bankruptcy, a debtor leased three floors of office space from a lessor at a rental of $10,000 per floor per month. After filing for relief under chapter 11,[356] the debtor as debtor in possession continued to occupy two of the three floors. Under the general rule in effect prior to the adoption of § 365(d)(3), the bankruptcy estate would only be liable for rent for the two floors used, and only at a reasonable rate.[357] Thus, administrative rent would be $20,000 per month (or perhaps even less, if market rents were lower than the lease rental). Under § 365(d)(3), however, the debtor in possession would have to pay the lessor the full lease rental of $30,000 per month for the postpetition period, until assumption or rejection. In addition to rent, the debtor in possession would have to perform all other lease obligations arising postpetition, such as the payment of taxes and the maintenance of insurance. With court approval, the trustee or debtor in possession can delay postpetition performance, but only up to 60 days after the order for relief.

Section 365(d)(3) does not require the trustee to cure any prepetition defaults, however; that obligation only arises upon formal assumption of the lease. § 365(b)(1)(A). Section 365(d)(3) only mandates performance of *post*-petition obligations. An obligation may come due postpetition, but relate to both the prepetition and postpetition worlds. For example, if the debtor in the above hypothetical filed bankruptcy exactly in the middle of the month, half of the monthly rent would be

---

[352] In construing these amendments, many courts have given weight to remarks made in the legislative history by Senator Hatch. See 130 Cong. Rec. S8895 (daily ed. June 29, 1984) (statement of Sen. Hatch).

[353] See § 8.4.

[354] See In re Pacific–Atlantic Trading Co., 27 F.3d 401 (9th Cir. 1994).

[355] E.g., In re Palace Quality Servs. Indus., Inc., 283 B.R. 868 (Bankr. E.D. Mich. 2002); In re Mr. Gatti's, Inc., 164 B.R. 929 (Bankr. W.D. Tex. 1994).

[356] Note that § 365(d)(3), unlike § 365(d)(5) (discussed in § 8.27), does not apply only in chapter 11 cases. Instead, (d)(3) applies in cases under all chapters.

[357] Philadelphia Co. v. Dipple, 312 U.S. 168 (1941).

attributable to the prepetition period and half to the postpetition time. A similar problem often arises with tax bills. The courts are divided on whether to prorate the (d)(3) obligation in such cases. Those that do not prorate, but require full payment, adopt a "billing date" approach, and reason that the entire obligation arises (and thus must be "timely performed" in full under (d)(3)) when it comes due under the lease.[358] Consider, for example, the case of *In re Burival*.[359] In that case, the debtors (foolishly) declared bankruptcy just two days before their second bi-annual payment of $91,000 on leased farmland was due.[360] The court adopted the billing date approach and thus held that the non-debtor landlord was entitled to payment of the entire $91,000 as an administrative expense, even though much of the time frame to which the payment applied fell during the pre-bankruptcy period.[361] Other courts do prorate, and embrace instead an "accrual" theory.[362] Under that approach, only the ratable post-petition portion of the time period to which the payment applies is required to be performed under (d)(3). So, for example, in *Burival*, the bankruptcy court had adopted the accrual method, and would have only allowed the landlord about $50,000 on its rent claim, instead of the full $91,000 due under the lease.

What if, however, the timing falls the *other* way, that is, the due date for the bill is *prior* to the filing of bankruptcy, but a portion of the time period to which that bill applies comes after the bankruptcy filing? This is the well-known and oft-litigated "stub rent" problem. The facts in the Third Circuit case of *In re Goody's Family Clothing, Inc.*[363] are typical. Rent was due up front, on the first of every month, for the following month. Debtor filed on June 9. On July 1, debtor paid the July rent in accordance with § 365(d)(3). But what about the rent attributable to the "stub" period of June 9–June 30? Under the lease, that bill had fallen due on June 1—prior to bankruptcy, and thus, under the billing date approach, not within the protective coverage of § 365(d)(3). Of course, under an accrual approach, this would not be a problem; whatever portion of the rent accrued postpetition would be entitled to payment under (d)(3). But not so under the billing date method. Did that mandate, then, that the entire rent for the month of June—including the postpetition period from June 9 to June 30—was just a general non-priority claim? The Third Circuit held "no." Even though § 365(d)(3) did not apply by its terms to mandate payment of the June rent, the court concluded that the non-debtor lessors still could look to the general protection of § 503(b)(1) and recover a portion of the June rent as an administrative expense for any actual benefits provided to the estate.[364] Of course, the lessors then must prove actual benefit to the estate, rather than having an automatic entitlement as provided for in § 365(d)(3).

Section 365(d)(3) has a number of other gaps. The most telling of these is the absence of any provision in (d)(3) for a *remedy* in the event the trustee does not "timely

---

[358] See, e.g., In re Montgomery Ward Holding Corp., 268 F.3d 205 (3d Cir. 2001).

[359] Burival v. Creditor Comm. (In re Burival), 406 B.R. 548 (B.A.P. 8th Cir. 2009), aff'd, 613 F.3d 810 (8th Cir. 2010).

[360] Id. at 551.

[361] Id. at 553.

[362] See, e.g., In re Handy Andy Home Improv. Centers, Inc., 144 F.3d 1125 (7th Cir. 1998).

[363] 610 F.3d 812 (3d Cir. 2010).

[364] Id. at 818–19.

perform" all the debtor's obligations.[365] For example, in the hypothetical given at the beginning of this section, what happens if day 61 arrives and the debtor in possession has *not* paid the lessor any postpetition rent? The *Burival* case raised the remedy problem as well; whatever the landlord's entitlement, the fact was that the debtors had paid nothing for the post-petition period. What then? Section 365(d)(3) does not clearly answer the question, so the courts have had to fill in the statutory void. A common solution has been for the court to order the trustee to make the accrued postpetition payment to the lessor.[366] In the hypothetical, the court might order the debtor in possession to pay $60,000 (the two months postpetition rent). Failing payment, the court might order the debtor in possession to vacate and surrender the premises to the lessor,[367] or the court might lift the stay to permit the lessor to pursue its remedies in state court.[368] The trustee's failure to comply with § 365(d)(3) should *not* be deemed to terminate or reject the lease automatically, however, or to give the lessor the power to terminate.

A serious problem has arisen when it appears that the estate might not have enough assets to pay all administrative expense claims in full, and the trustee has not performed under § 365(d)(3). Facing the prospect of administrative insolvency, should the court nevertheless order the trustee to make immediate payment under (d)(3)? If the court so orders, the practical effect would be to confer a *de facto* superpriority over other administrative claimants on the non-debtor lessor. In this situation, most courts have concluded that payment should not be ordered, reasoning that the trustee's obligation to perform under § 365(d)(3) is just a special form of administrative priority, and should be ranked on a par with all other administrative expenses.[369] A minority of courts have ordered immediate payment irrespective of administrative solvency, however, concluding that § 365(d)(3) does indeed effectively grant a superpriority to the lessor.[370]

A closely related issue concerns the status of the non-debtor lessor's unpaid post-petition rent claim. Is that rent claim automatically entitled to status as an administrative expense priority? Or is the claim simply one for which payment is mandated by the statute, but which is not necessarily entitled to any sort of priority status if payment is not forthcoming? The confusion follows from the qualifying clause in the first sentence of § 365(d)(3), "notwithstanding section 503(b)(1) of this title." As many courts have noted, linguistically that clause could have a number of different, and indeed opposing, meanings.[371] The overwhelming majority view is that an unpaid rent claim under § 365(d)(3) is given administrative expense status.[372] Under the

---

[365] See In re Midway Airlines Corp., 406 F.3d 229 (4th Cir. 2005).

[366] E.g., In re Buyer's Club Mkts., Inc., 115 B.R. 700 (Bankr. D. Colo. 1990).

[367] E.g., In re Orvco, Inc., 95 B.R. 724 (B.A.P. 9th Cir. 1989).

[368] E.g., In re Granada, Inc., 88 B.R. 369 (Bankr. D. Utah 1988).

[369] E.g., In re Wingspread Corp., 116 B.R. 915 (Bankr. S.D.N.Y. 1990), aff'd, 145 B.R. 784 (S.D.N.Y. 1992), aff'd without op., 992 F.2d 319 (2d Cir. 1993). See *Midway Airlines*, supra note 365.

[370] E.g., In re Telesphere Commc'ns, Inc., 148 B.R. 525 (Bankr. N.D. Ill. 1992).

[371] The majority and dissenting opinions in the BAP decision in *Burival*, supra note 359, ably explain the different possible interpretations.

[372] See, e.g., id., 406 B.R. at 554–55, and cases cited therein, e.g., In re Cukierman, 265 F.3d 846, 850 (9th Cir.2001); In re Furr's Supermarkets, Inc., 283 B.R. 60, 69 (B.A.P. 10th Cir. 2002).

minority view, (d)(3) has nothing at all to do with administrative expense status; all that the quoted clause means is that "timely *payment*" must be made of the postpetition rent claim under (d)(3) even though that claim does *not* otherwise enjoy administrative expense status. Under this view, if the disappointed lessor who is not timely paid under (d)(3) needs and wants to establish administrative expense status, it must do so under § 503(b) by showing an actual benefit conferred on the estate.[373]

Another difficulty in applying § 365(d)(3) is to determine *when* the special priority period stops running. The statute says that the trustee shall timely perform all obligations of the debtor "until such lease is assumed or rejected." When is the lease "rejected"? In our hypothetical, assume that the debtor in possession files a motion to reject the lease the very same day that the debtor files bankruptcy, but that the court does not formally approve the rejection until a month later. Is the rejection effective to stop the clock under (d)(3) when the DIP files the motion to reject, or only when the court approves the rejection? The answer dictates whether the non-debtor lessor will receive full payment for the period between the filing of the motion and court approval; in the hypothetical, the difference would be $30,000 in rent. Most courts, relying on the provision in § 365(a) that rejection is "subject to the court's approval," and on the congressional purpose to favor lessors in § 365(d)(3), have held that rejection occurs when the court approves the motion to reject.[374] Under this view, the lessor in the example would be entitled to $30,000 in postpetition rent, even though the estate never occupied the premises postpetition and the debtor in possession filed an immediate motion for rejection. Some courts have taken the view that, while rejection does not occur until court approval, nevertheless the bankruptcy court has the equitable power to give that rejection *retroactive effect*, and thus to defeat the non-debtor lessor's claim for postpetition, pre-rejection rent under § 365(d)(2).[375]

§ 8.27   Special Rules: Commercial Personal Property Leases

In the 1994 Amendments, Congress again acted to provide additional protection for the non-debtor lessor on certain types of unexpired leases during the gap period prior to assumption or rejection.[376] The special rules of § 365(d)(5) to "an unexpired lease of *personal* property (other than personal property leased to an individual primarily for personal, family, or household purposes)," i.e., to commercial personal property leases. Most of these are equipment leases; consumer leases are excluded. The section only applies in chapter 11 cases. Section 365(d)(5) borrows in part from § 365(d)(3),[377] but does not exactly mirror that section.

The primary protection afforded by § 365(d)(5) is that the "trustee shall timely perform all of the obligations of the debtor . . . first arising from or after 60 days after

---

[373] See *Burival,* supra note 359, 406 B.R. at 556–57 (Kressel, J., dissenting).

[374] See In re Thinking Machines Corp., 67 F.3d 1021 (1st Cir. 1995). The *Thinking Machines* court further suggested in dicta, though, that the bankruptcy court had the equitable power to give rejection retroactive effect. The best-known cases embracing the minority view, that rejection is effective for purposes of § 365(d)(3) on the filing of the motion, is In re Joseph C. Spiess Co., 145 B.R. 597 (Bankr. N.D. Ill. 1992).

[375] See In re At Home Corp., 392 F.3d 1064 (9th Cir. 2004). The *Thinking Machines* court first suggested this possibility. See supra note 374.

[376] Bankruptcy Reform Act, Pub. L. No. 103–394, § 219(b), 108 Stat. 4128 (1994).

[377] See § 8.26.

the order for relief, . . . until such lease is assumed or rejected." However, the court may override this rule, with respect either to the debtor's obligations or the time for performance, "based on the equities of the case." No guidance is given, in the Code or the legislative history, as to what the "equities of the case" might include.

The most obvious effect of § 365(d)(5) is that the trustee or debtor in possession will have to pay the non-debtor lessor the full lease rental for all property leased, whether or not that property is actually used by the estate. To revisit a hypothetical used in an earlier section,[378] assume that the debtor prior to bankruptcy entered into a lease for 30 cars to be used in its business. After filing chapter 11, the debtor uses ten of the cars and leaves 20 cars idle. Under the general rule followed by a majority of courts prior to the enactment of § 365(d)(5), the lessor would only be entitled to administrative rent for the ten cars actually used by the debtor in possession. Furthermore, the rental would be at a reasonable rate, and not necessarily the lease rate. Section 365(d)(5) mandates that the DIP pay the full lease rent for all 30 cars. In addition, the DIP will have to perform any other obligations of the debtor on the lease, such as the maintenance of insurance on the leased property.

Unlike the special rule for nonresidential real property leases in § 365(d)(3), the full performance obligation of the trustee for personal property leases does not begin immediately upon the bankruptcy filing. Instead, that obligation only starts to run 60 days after filing. In theory, this gives the trustee or debtor in possession some time to evaluate the lease and to reject it without incurring any administrative obligation, thereby avoiding in part a problem that has plagued § 365(d)(3).

Given that § 365(d)(5) is derived in concept from § 365(d)(3), it is not surprising that some of the issues arising under subsection (d)(3) also exist under subsection (d)(5). Cases interpreting the former section should be persuasive authority on the latter.[379] One such issue is whether the non-debtor lessor can obtain administrative priority even without complying with § 503(b)(1). The majority approach under § 365(d)(3) is that compliance with § 503(b)(1) is *not* required.[380] Thus, actual use and benefit by the estate need not be shown.

A second issue common to (d)(3) and (d)(5) is how long the special priority period continues. The answer turns on when "rejection" occurs, which is either at the time the trustee files the motion to reject, or when the court actually approves the rejection. Under § 365(d)(3), most courts have concluded that rejection does not occur until the court acts.[381] Under (d)(5), this second issue may be somewhat less critical, since the trustee has an initial 60–day grace period to act. In addition, under (d)(5) the court can invoke the "equities of the case" to deny payment to the lessor, an escape route not available under (d)(3).

---

[378] See § 8.25.

[379] See, e.g., In re Midway Airlines Corp., 406 F.3d 229 (4th Cir. 2005) (case under (d)(5) drew extensively on (d)(3) case law).

[380] E.g., In re Pacific–Atlantic Trading Co., 27 F.3d 401 (9th Cir. 1994). Contra In re Orvco, Inc., 95 B.R. 724 (B.A.P. 9th Cir. 1989) (overruled by subsequent Ninth Circuit decision in *PATCO*).

[381] E.g., In re Thinking Machines Corp., 67 F.3d 1021 (1st Cir. 1995).

A third common issue is what the remedy is for noncompliance. The court can order the trustee to make payments (if the estate is administratively solvent) or return the leased property. If the trustee does not comply, the court will face the question of whether (d)(5) creates a *de facto* superpriority for rental obligations covered by the section. A majority of courts under (d)(3) have held that the lessor's claim for unpaid rent is entitled to priority, but not to superpriority;[382] a minority, though, have concluded that (d)(3) commands superpriority.[383] The result should be the same under both subsections, because (1) each contains identical language that the "trustee shall timely perform all [of] the obligations of the debtor," and (2) each was motivated by a similar desire to accord special protection to non-debtor lessors.

---

[382] E.g., In re Wingspread Corp., 116 B.R. 915 (Bankr. S.D.N.Y. 1990), aff'd, 145 B.R. 784 (S.D.N.Y. 1992), aff'd without op., 992 F.2d 319 (2d Cir. 1993). See *Midway Airlines*, supra note 355.

[383] E.g., In re Telesphere Commc'ns, Inc., 148 B.R. 525 (Bankr. N.D. Ill. 1992).

Chapter 9

EXEMPTIONS

A. EXEMPTION LAW AND PRACTICE

§ 9.1 Function and Purpose of Exemption Laws

Exemption laws are one of the most important protections for individual debtors, in or out of bankruptcy. Exemption laws give an individual debtor the privilege of keeping certain property from his creditors *even if* those creditors are not paid. That property thus is said to be "exempt" from the claims of the debtor's creditors. In other words, most creditors have a right to collect their debts only out of the *non*-exempt property of the debtor. In a bankruptcy case, exempt property is removed from the bankruptcy estate and returned to the debtor, and thus is not available for distribution to general creditors.

Every state affords individual debtors the right to retain some property as exempt by statute. Many states even grant exemption rights in the state constitution.[1] The extent of the generosity to the debtor of a state exemption law varies greatly from state to state.[2] A few states have a set of general exemptions available to all residents, and a separate set of exemptions available only to debtors in bankruptcy.[3] Also, some federal laws that create property rights simultaneously create exemption privileges in that property.[4] The Bankruptcy Code contains its own scheme of exemptions,[5] § 522(d), but almost always permits debtors to elect the exemptions available under state law instead.[6] § 522(b)(1), (3).

Why do we have exemption laws?[7] Permitting an individual debtor to retain enough property to carry on his or her daily life is in the best interests of the debtor

---

[1] To give one example, Florida provides several exemptions in their state constitution for homestead and personal property. Fla. Const. art. 10, § 4.

[2] For instance, Florida, Iowa, Kansas and Texas only limit their homestead exemption by the size of land, rather than dollar amount. Fla. Const. art. 10, § 4; Iowa Code Ann. § 561.2; Kan. Stat. An. § 60–2301; Tex. Prop. Code Ann. § 41.002. Conversely, most other states limit the homestead exemption by dollar amount. See, e.g., 27 V.S.A. § 101 (Vermont, $125,000). Notably, Illinois only provides for a $15,000 homestead exemption per individual, up to $30,000 for two or more individuals. 735 ILCS 5/12–901.

[3] See Mich. Comp. Laws § 600.6023 (general exemptions); Mich. Comp. Laws § 600.5451 (debtor exemptions). The Sixth Circuit held that Michigan did not violate the supremacy clause with its bankruptcy-specific exemptions, nor did it fail to meet the uniformity requirement of the Bankruptcy Clause in the Constitution. In re Shafer, 689 F.3d 601 (6th Cir. 2012). See also In re Westby, 473 B.R. 392 (Bankr. D. Kan. 2012); § 9.15.

[4] For example, an individual's interest in the civil service retirement fund is automatically exempted through the federal statute, which creates the civil service retirement fund. 5 U.S.C. § 8346(a).

[5] See § 9.3.

[6] See § 9.2.

[7] See Alan N. Resnick, Prudent Planning or Fraudulent Transfer? The Use of Nonexempt Assets to Purchase or Improve Exempt Property on the Eve of Bankruptcy, 31 Rutgers L. Rev. 615, 621 (1978):

"Current state and federal exemption laws promote five distinct social policies. Each specific exemption should further one or more of the following policies:

and the debtor's dependents, as well as society as a whole. Public policy would not be served by rendering a debtor and the debtor's family completely destitute. Not only would such a result be inhumane, it would be unwise. If creditors could strip every item of property from a debtor, the debtor would become either a ward of the state or the object of private charity. Do we really want creditors to be able to literally take the clothes off a debtor's back, and throw the debtor in the street? Even when English law allowed fraudulent bankrupts to be put to death, the bankruptcy law also allowed the debtor to keep necessary wearing apparel, tools of the trade, and necessary household goods and furniture.[8] People do not forfeit their right to retain at least a modicum of human dignity by going into debt. One of my students captured the spirit of this principle by quoting a classic passage from the television series "Seinfeld," where Jerry admonishes his friend George, telling him, "George, we're trying to have a civilization here."[9]

Furthermore, the exemption laws are an integral part of the *"fresh start"* policy.[10] In bankruptcy cases the exemption and discharge laws work hand-in-glove to promote the debtor's financial fresh start: the discharge frees the product of the debtor's future labors from the claims of past creditors,[11] and exempt property retained provides the debtor with the minimum "grubstake" that will enable the debtor to work most effectively. A debtor who is permitted to keep some property may be better able to resume his or her place as a productive member of society. For example, exemption laws usually allow a debtor to keep "professional books" or the "tools of the trade," as noted above. § 522(d)(6). The fable of the golden goose might be invoked as a useful analogy; the debtor's exempt property might be the equivalent of the debtor's golden-egg laying goose. This very book might be exempt property for a bankruptcy attorney! If a single creditor could seize the debtor's income-producing property, that creditor might harmfully impose a negative externality on all of the debtor's other creditors.

The foregoing policies generally are thought to outweigh the parochial interests of the debtor's creditors. In some situations, however, protecting the interests of a particular creditor may be more important than promoting the general exemption policy. For example, a minor child's claim for support and an ex-spouse's claim for alimony are enforceable against exempt property in many states[12] (and under the Bankruptcy Code, § 522(c)(1)). However, courts are split on whether the section in the Bankruptcy Code that renders a debtor's exempt property liable to certain tax debts

---

(1) To provide the debtor with property necessary for his physical survival;

(2) To protect the dignity and the cultural and religious identity of the debtor;

(3) To enable the debtor to rehabilitate himself financially and earn income in the future;

(4) To protect the debtor's family from the adverse consequences of impoverishment;

(5) To shift the burden of providing the debtor and his family with minimal financial support from the society to the debtor's creditors."

[8]   5 Geo. 2, ch. 30, § 1 (1732).

[9]   See http://www.seinology.com/scripts/script–160.shtml (episode 160, "The Blood," season 9, episode 4, broadcast date Oct. 16, 1997). Kudos to Jacob Jost, J.D. 2013, for the perfect reference.

[10]   But see § 2.15.c.3 for a discussion on a possible emerging view from the Supreme Court restricting the "fresh start" policy.

[11]   See § 10.3.

[12]   See, e.g., Alaska Stat. § 09.38.065(1)(A); N.C. Gen. Stat. § 1C–1601(e)(1)(9); R.I. Gen. Laws § 9–26–4.1(a)(4).

and domestic support obligations trumps state law that otherwise shields such exempted property from those claims.[13]

Outside of bankruptcy under state collection law, exemption laws operate by blocking creditor collection efforts against exempt property. For example, a creditor would not have the right to have the sheriff seize exempt property pursuant to a writ of execution. If the exempt property were seized, the debtor would have a valid action for conversion. Judicial liens in favor of the creditor, such as execution liens or judgment liens, will not attach to exempt property. Note, though, that a *consensual* lien on exempt property (for example, a home mortgage), typically *is* enforceable against that property.[14]

In a bankruptcy case, "an exemption is an interest withdrawn from the estate (and hence from the creditors) for the benefit of the debtor."[15] Property that might be exempt is initially included in the bankruptcy estate under § 541(a), representing a change in approach from the practice under the prior Bankruptcy Act, which excluded property needed for the debtor's fresh start from the estate at the outset of the case.[16] Under the Bankruptcy Code, the debtor (or a dependent of the debtor), must file a list of exempt property.[17] § 522(l); Rule 4003(a). Property that is not claimed as exempt remains in the estate.[18] If exemptions are claimed and are either not contested or withstand a contest, the exempted property then is taken out of the bankruptcy estate and returned to the debtor. Once withdrawn from the estate, the exempt property will not be distributed to creditors in a chapter 7 case. § 726(a).

Even in rehabilitation cases, such as chapter 13, in which estate property is not distributed to creditors, exemptions play an important role. To explain, unsecured creditors in a chapter 13 case have a baseline entitlement to be paid at least the amount they would receive in a liquidation, which is computed by reference to the amount of nonexempt assets in the estate.[19] Accordingly, in order to confirm a plan under chapter 13, the court must first determine that the debtor's plan satisfies this requirement. § 1325(a)(4). This is the same for chapter 11 cases involving individual debtors too, under § 1129(a)(7)(A)(ii). This liquidation analysis is known as the "best interest of the creditors" test.

Nor may most creditors of a bankruptcy debtor enforce their claims against exempt property in the debtor's hands after the bankruptcy case is over.[20] § 522(c).

---

[13]　Compare In re Quezada, 368 B.R. 44 (Bankr. S.D. Fla. 2007) (holding that§ 522(c)(1) preempts state law that protects exempted property from DSO and tax debts), with In re McCombs, 659 F.3d 503 (5th Cir. 2011) (citing Art. 16, §§ 50–51 of the Texas Constitution to deny executing DSO claims against exempted homestead property, noting that § 522(c)(1) does not preempt state law).

[14]　See, e.g., Cal. Code Civ. Proc. § 688.030; Mich. Comp. Laws Ann. § 600.6023.

[15]　Owen v. Owen, 500 U.S. 305, 308 (1991).

[16]　See Lockwood v. Exchange Bank, 190 U.S. 294 (1903). The legislative history shows that Congress intended to overrule *Lockwood* in the Code. S. Rep. No. 95–989, 95th Cong., 2d Sess., at 82 (1978); H.R. Rep. No. 95–595, 95th Cong., 1st Sess., at 368 (1977).

[17]　See § 9.6.

[18]　See Taylor v. Freeland & Kronz, 503 U.S. 638 (1992).

[19]　See § 12.16.

[20]　See § 9.4.

This prohibition applies even against debts that are not discharged in the bankruptcy case. The only exceptions are claims for nondischargeable taxes, domestic support obligations, and certain debts relating to insured depository institutions. § 522(c)(1), (3). However, unavoided liens may be enforced against exempt property. § 522(c)(2). Exempt property generally is not liable for the administrative expenses of the bankruptcy case. § 522(k).

Exemptions are a personal privilege of the debtor, and as such generally may be waived. Outside of bankruptcy, this may be done either directly, by waiving the right to assert exemptions against a creditor, or indirectly, by granting the creditor a consensual lien on the exempt property, as noted above. The creditor then will be entitled to foreclose that lien to collect its debt, without being constrained by the exemption laws. Probably the most common example is that a mortgagee may foreclose a defaulted mortgage against a debtor's home, notwithstanding the homestead exemption.

In bankruptcy, however, the debtor's freedom to waive the privilege of exemptions is much more circumscribed. This protective approach is justified on the grounds (1) that debtors need paternalistic protection against coercive creditor tactics, and (2) a debtor's waiver of exemptions might create negative externalities. An outright waiver of exemptions is not enforceable in a bankruptcy case.[21] § 522(e). A debtor still can effectively waive exemptions simply by not claiming property as exempt—but even then a dependent of the debtor may claim the exemptions on the debtor's behalf. § 522(l).

As noted above, a creditor can enforce an unavoided lien against property that was exempted in bankruptcy. § 522(c)(2). However, the Bankruptcy Code gives the debtor or the trustee significant powers to avoid the fixing of liens that impair exemptions to which the debtor would be entitled, § 522(f). Additionally, § 522(g)–(j) empower the debtor to claim exemptions in property recovered post-petition, and also allow the debtor to act on avoidable transferred exempt property if the trustee fails to do so.[22]

The extent of an individual debtor's exempt assets will be an important factor for the debtor to consider in deciding which chapter of the Bankruptcy Code to file for relief under. For example, if a debtor has substantial nonexempt assets, the debtor may prefer to retain his or her property and make payments to creditors in a repayment plan under chapter 13. Conversely, if a debtor does not have any nonexempt assets, the debtor may prefer instead to file for immediate liquidation under chapter 7, if eligible. In such a "no-asset" case the debtor will not have to relinquish any property to the trustee for distribution to creditors, but still remains eligible to receive a discharge of his or her debts.

§ 9.2   Exemption Laws Available to Bankruptcy Debtors

One of the most important exemption law issues in bankruptcy cases is identifying the exemption law or laws available to the debtor when some of the debtor's property

---

[21]   See § 9.12.

[22]   See §§ 9.7–9.11.

may be exempt under one body of law but not another. Exemption laws remain far from uniform—even in federal bankruptcy cases. To illustrate, a debtor in Illinois may exempt only a $15,000 homestead, while a Massachusetts debtor may exempt $500,000, and debtors in Florida and Texas are not subject to *any* dollar limit on their homestead exemption.[23] The applicable law issue implicates important and difficult problems of federalism, uniformity, and fairness. The basic questions are (1) whether the governing exemption law will be state or federal law, and (2) whether all bankruptcy debtors will be entitled to retain at least a minimum amount of property as exempt.

These issues are more difficult than they need to be, because of two factors: (1) a last-minute compromise in connection with the passage of the Bankruptcy Code in 1978, and then (2) the convoluted 2005 amendments.[24] Some historical background might be helpful.[25] The United States bankruptcy laws enacted prior to 1978 vacillated over whether to incorporate the exemption laws of the states, create a separate federal exemption law in bankruptcy cases, or do both. The 1800 and 1841 bankruptcy laws utilized federal exemptions,[26] while the 1867 bankruptcy law allowed debtors for the first time to claim those exemptions made available under the law of the state in which the debtor resided, *in addition to* the federal exemptions.[27] In the 1898 Act, which remained in force for 80 years until the current Bankruptcy Code was enacted, the law came full circle: *only* state exemptions could be used.[28] The Supreme Court upheld the constitutionality of the 1898 Act against a challenge that it rendered the bankruptcy law nonuniform.[29]

In the reform effort of the 1970s, the House and Senate took different positions with respect to the applicable law issue. The Senate was content to continue the practice followed under the 1898 Act, in which the debtor could claim only the exemptions offered by the state of his or her domicile (in addition to exemptions in non-bankruptcy federal laws, such as for Social Security benefits).[30] The House, however, took the position that *all* debtors should be entitled to claim *either* the state and "other federal" exemptions *or*, in the alternative, a minimum level of exemptions provided in the federal bankruptcy law itself.[31] The House position was driven by concern over the

---

[23] See 735 I.L.C.S. 5, § 12–901 (Illinois); Mass. Gen. Laws Ann. ch. 188, § 1 (Massachusetts); Fla. Const. art. 10, § 4(a)(1) (Florida); Tex. Const. art. 16 § 51 (Texas). To give but one example of the possibilities for debtors who plan carefully, former baseball commissioner Bowie Kuhn established residence in Florida before filing bankruptcy, and claimed a very large homestead exemption. Charles Jordan Tabb, The Death of Consumer Bankruptcy in the United States?, 18 Bankr. Dev. J. 1, 43 (2001). Some of these possibilities were foreclosed by the 2005 amendments discussed below.

[24] For an excellent analysis of the 2005 amendments relating to exemptions, see Margaret Howard, Exemptions Under the 2005 Bankruptcy Amendments: A Tale of Opportunity Lost, 79 Am. Bankr. L.J. 397 (2005).

[25] See generally Charles Jordan Tabb, The Historical Evolution of the Bankruptcy Discharge, 65 Am. Bankr. L.J. 325 (1991).

[26] Bankruptcy Act of 1800, ch. 19, §§ 5, 18, 2 Stat. 23, 27 (1800) (repealed 1803); Bankruptcy Act of 1841, ch. 9, § 3, 5 Stat. 442–43 (1841) (repealed 1843).

[27] Bankruptcy Act of 1867, ch. 176, § 14, 14 Stat. 523 (1867) (repealed 1878).

[28] Bankruptcy Act of 1898, § 6, 30 Stat. 548 (1898) (repealed 1978).

[29] Hanover Nat'l Bank v. Moyses, 186 U.S. 181 (1902). See also § 9.15.

[30] S. Rep. No. 95–989, 95th Cong., 2d Sess., at 75 (1978).

[31] H.R. Rep. No. 95–595, 95th Cong., 1st Sess., at 360 (1977).

seemingly inadequate exemptions offered to debtors in some states. Pennsylvania, for example, does not offer a separate homestead exemption at all, but allows a debtor to exempt just $300 in any property.[32] The federal bankruptcy provision, by comparison, offers a $22,975 homestead exemption. § 522(d)(1).

The House and Senate reached a compromise: (1) to allow a debtor to elect either the state and other federal exemptions *or* the federal bankruptcy exemptions in § 522(d) (the House position), *unless* (2) the state in which the debtor resides passes a law specifically prohibiting its debtors from using the § 522(d) bankruptcy exemptions, thus (3) leaving available to those debtors only the state and non-bankruptcy federal exemptions (thereby giving effect to the Senate position). § 522(b)(2). In other words, a state may "*opt out*" of the federal exemptions of § 522(d), and limit resident debtors to the exemptions available under state law and other federal law, making the § 522(d) exemptions inapplicable to them. The problem is that, as of 2013, 34 states had opted out of the federal scheme, rendering § 522(d) a dead letter in much of the nation.[33] It is important to note, though, that a state's power to opt out is limited to § 522(d), and does not extend to the rest of § 522, the provisions of which therefore remain applicable even in opt-out states.[34]

Accordingly, under current law, the first question to ask is whether the state in which the debtor resides[35] has opted out of the federal bankruptcy exemptions. If the state *has* opted out, the debtor is limited to (1) state exemptions; (2) non-bankruptcy federal exemptions; (3) exemptions applicable to property held as tenants by the entirety or joint tenants; and (4) certain tax-exempt retirement funds. § 522(b)(3). The non-bankruptcy federal exemptions, which are not listed in the Bankruptcy Code, cover a wide range of property, ranging from special pensions for Medal of Honor winners,[36] to wage garnishments,[37] to the assignment of Social Security benefits,[38] to benefits for survivors of Lighthouse Service providers.[39]

If the state has *not* opted out of the federal exemptions, then the debtor may choose either the federal exemptions in § 522(d), or the state and non-bankruptcy federal exemptions.[40] If the debtor selects the federal bankruptcy exemptions, the debtor cannot also claim the exemptions available under other federal laws.[41]

---

[32]   See 42 Pa. Cons. Stat. Ann. § 8123.

[33]   The states that have chosen to opt out, as of 2013, are Alabama, Arizona, California, Colorado, Delaware, Florida, Georgia, Idaho, Illinois, Indiana, Iowa, Kansas, Kentucky, Louisiana, Maine, Maryland, Mississippi, Missouri, Montana, Nebraska, Nevada, New York, North Carolina, North Dakota, Ohio, Oklahoma, Oregon, South Carolina, South Dakota, Tennessee, Utah, Virginia, West Virginia, and Wyoming.

[34]   See § 9.16.

[35]   It actually is more complicated than this. See infra notes 45–61 and accompanying text, § 522(b)(2), (3)(A). In most cases, though, the applicable state is the one in which the debtor lives when he files bankruptcy.

[36]   38 U.S.C. § 1562(c).

[37]   15 U.S.C. § 1673.

[38]   42 U.S.C. § 407.

[39]   33 U.S.C. § 775.

[40]   See §§ 522(b)(2), (3).

[41]   See In re Kochell, 732 F.2d 564 (7th Cir. 1984).

In a joint case involving an individual debtor and the debtor's spouse, both spouses must choose the same exemption scheme. In other words, one debtor may not choose the federal exemptions and the other the state exemptions. § 522(b)(1). This forbidden practice is referred to as "stacking" exemptions. Other than the prohibition against stacking, the exemption law applies separately with respect to each spouse. § 522(m). This means that the dollar limits in § 522(d) would be doubled in a joint case. If the spouses cannot agree whether to select the state or federal exemption scheme, then they are deemed to have selected the federal exemptions. § 522(b)(1). Of course, if the debtors' state has opted out of the federal exemptions, this selection problem will not arise.

The exemptions available to a debtor are determined as of the date of the filing of the bankruptcy petition.[42] Thus, for example, a debtor cannot take advantage of exemptions that come into effect after the bankruptcy filing, nor may a debtor exempt the postpetition appreciation of his homestead. Further, where a debtor converts from one chapter to another, most courts have held that the debtor's exemptions are limited to those available on the date of the original bankruptcy filing, rather than on the date of conversion,[43] although some early Bankruptcy Code authority went the other way.[44]

The discussion above has couched the debtor's exemption choice as federal (if no opt out) or state. But *which* state? One might think that the applicable state exemption law would be that of the state where the debtor resided or was domiciled at the time he filed bankruptcy. But in fact the law is not, and indeed has never been, quite that simple, in the case where the debtor *moved* to another state within a limited time period before filing bankruptcy. Even before the 2005 amendments, to be discussed below, the operative state for a debtor's bankruptcy exemption choice was the place in which the debtor's domicile had been located for 180 days before the bankruptcy filing, *or*, if the debtor had moved in that 180–day period, the place where the debtor had been domiciled for the "longer portion" of the 180 days. Thus, to be assured of being able to claim the state exemptions of the state to which he was moving, the pre–2005 debtor had to spend 91 days in the new state before filing.[45] Otherwise, the exemption laws of the old state (where the debtor had been domiciled for the longer portion of the 180–day period) would still apply, even though the debtor no longer lived there.

The fact that the debtor might be forced to claim state law exemptions for a state in which the debtor no longer was domiciled, and in which the debtor might own no property, has raised the puzzling question of whether the exemption laws of the *old* state can be applied extraterritorially to property of the debtor located in the *new* state. The issue is particularly sticky for *real property*, given the general principle that state

---

[42] See, e.g., Owen v. Owen, 500 U.S. 305, 314 n.6 (1991); In re Alsberg, 68 F.3d 312 (9th Cir. 1995), cert. denied, 517 U.S. 1168 (1996); In re Petersen, 897 F.2d 935 (8th Cir. 1990); In re Hutton, 893 F.2d 1010 (8th Cir. 1990); In re Armenakis, 406 B.R. 589 (Bankr. S.D.N.Y. 2009); In re Gillenwater, 479 B.R. 711 (Bankr. W.D. Va. 2012). This timing rule does not apply to involuntary cases, where the operative date is when the court enters an order for relief. See, e.g., In re Hodes, 402 F.3d 1005 (10th Cir. 2005).

[43] See, e.g., In re Sandoval, 103 F.3d 20 (5th Cir. 1997); In re Marcus, 1 F.3d 1050 (10th Cir. 1993).

[44] See In re Lindberg, 735 F.2d 1087 (8th Cir. 1984), cert. denied, 469 U.S. 1073 (1984).

[45] See, e.g., In re Tanzi, 287 B.R. 557 (Bankr. W.D. Wash. 2002), aff'd, 297 B.R. 607 (B.A.P. 9th Cir. 2003) (debtors could not claim $985,000 Florida homestead as exempt when they had lived in Florida for less than 90 days).

real property laws do not have extraterritorial effect. For example, to take the facts of one well-known case, assume that the debtors moved from Minnesota to Arizona less than 90 days before they filed bankruptcy (in Minnesota, because of the venue statute, 28 U.S.C. § 1408(1)), and then sought to claim their *Arizona* homestead of $181,000 as fully exempt under the *Minnesota* exemption law (which allowed up to $200,000 in a homestead).[46] Can they do that? Maybe so. Given that the Minnesota homestead statute was silent about extraterritorial effect, the Eighth Circuit applied it liberally so as to extend to the debtors' Arizona homestead.[47] Ultimately, though, the issue is one of interpretation of the applicable state exemption law; if that law is limited either by its terms or by judicial construction to homesteads located within that state, then extraterritorial application is precluded in bankruptcy.[48] If so, then the debtor's claimed state law exemption fails entirely. Prior to 2005, if the state also had opted out of the federal exemptions under § 522(d), the debtor would have no exemption law available to claim a homestead.

The pre–2005 limitation on the ability of a debtor to take advantage of more favorable exemption laws elsewhere was important, but also modest—as long as a debtor waited just 91 days to file bankruptcy in the new state, he was able to claim the state law exemptions of the new state. Florida and Texas, with their unlimited homestead exemptions, were particularly popular destinations for debtors with substantial assets that they hoped to shield from their creditors.[49] O.J. Simpson (although he has not filed bankruptcy) undoubtedly has been the most famous debtor to seek asylum in the welcoming arms of the unlimited Florida homestead exemption.[50]

Seeking to curb this "exemption-planning-by-moving" strategy, in 2005 Congress added an important limitation on a debtor's ability to select *state* exemptions.[51] A debtor now must move and establish a new domicile *two years* (730 days) before bankruptcy in order to claim the exemptions of the state to which he has moved. § 522(b)(3)(A). If the debtor was not domiciled in that state for the *entire* 2–year period preceding the bankruptcy filing—not just the "longer portion"—then the applicable state exemption law for bankruptcy purposes is the state in which the debtor was

---

[46]   In re Drenttel, 403 F.3d 611 (8th Cir. 2005).

[47]   Id. at 614–15. Accord, In re Arrol, 170 F.3d 934 (9th Cir. 1999) (California exemption law applied to Michigan property).

[48]   For example, Texas exemption law is limited by its terms to in-state homesteads. See In re Peters, 91 B.R. 401 (Bankr. W.D. Tex. 1988). Kansas law, while silent about extraterritorial application, has been limited by Kansas courts to in-state property. See In re Ginther, 282 B.R. 16 (Bankr. D. Kan. 2002). Both types of limitations have been applied in bankruptcy. Iowa's unlimited homestead exemption, on the other hand, is not limited to in-state property, and has been applied to exempt property in California. In re Roberts, 450 B.R. 159 (N.D. Iowa 2011).

[49]   See Tabb, supra note 23, at 42–43. Iowa and Kansas also have unlimited homestead exemptions, but for some reason have not been as popular a destination for debtors as Florida and Texas. For a classic example of the sort of behavior Congress sought to curtail, see *Havoco of Am., Ltd. v. Hill*, 197 F.3d 1135 (11th Cir. 1999), on certification, 790 So. 2d 1018 (Fla.), aff'd, 255 F.3d 1321 (11th Cir. 2001). The debtor, a resident of Tennessee, paid cash for a $650,000 fully exempt homestead in Florida, just 3 days before a $15 million judgment against him became enforceable. The Florida Supreme Court and the Eleventh Circuit upheld the debtor's homestead claim, even assuming that his purchase was made with the specific intent to defraud his creditors.

[50]   After his 2008 criminal conviction, Simpson now has taken up residence in a less desirable "home" in Nevada state prison.

[51]   Pub. L. No. 109–8, § 307(1), 119 Stat. 81 (2005). See also Howard, supra note 24, at 411–12.

domiciled during the 180–day period *before* the 2–year prepetition period (*i.e.*, the period between 2½ and 2 years before the petition date). If the debtor was domiciled in more than one state during this earlier 6–month period, then the applicable state is that in which the debtor was domiciled for a greater portion of the 6–month period than in any other state. Note that there is no *intent* requirement in this new rule; even if a debtor moved for the most benign of motives (or even disadvantageously!), the debtor is precluded from claiming exemptions in the new state.

Many, many baffling issues arise out of this complicated scheme, especially when overlaid on the possibility of some (but not all) states "opting out" of the federal bankruptcy exemptions. For example, the dueling state exemption issue arises when a debtor relocates from an "opt-out" state (e.g., one that does not permit debtors to select the federal bankruptcy exemptions) to a state that has not opted out less than 730 days before filing bankruptcy. Here, the question is whether the debtor, bound by their previous state's exemptions, must use them because the state has not opted out. For example, if Debtor moves from Arizona, an opt-out state, to Massachusetts, a state that has not opted out, and files for bankruptcy in Arizona (due to venue constraints in 28 U.S.C. § 1408(1)), may the Debtor elect the federal exemptions? Or is he bound by the Arizona exemptions, as Arizona has opted out of the federal exemptions, even though he is no longer an Arizona resident? The Bankruptcy Court for the District of Arizona held that the debtor was free to elect the federal exemptions because the Arizona statute only applied to its own residents.[52] The Fifth Circuit has also adopted this position.[53]

Or consider a Kansas case, in which the debtor moved from Nebraska (an opt-out state) to Kansas (also opt-out), and filed for bankruptcy in Kansas before living there at least 730 days (but long enough to file there under the venue statute).[54] Thus, the debtor was in a position where she could not elect *either* Kansas' exemptions (because of the 730–day residency rule) *or* Nebraska's exemptions (because the statute only applied to residents of Nebraska), *and* both states had tried to block debtors from electing the federal bankruptcy exemptions! Is such a debtor rendered "exemption-less"? No. A savings clause following § 522(b)(3) provides that such a debtor can then elect the federal exemptions of § 522(d).

Note, though, that notwithstanding the cases just discussed, courts are split on whether a debtor who moves to a new state and files within 730 days may still use his old state's exemption laws, even when that state's exemption laws are, like the two cases above, limited to residents. Some courts do not give effect to the state's limitation to residents, but instead hold that § 522(b) preempts state exemption statues that attempt to impose such a residency restriction. Under this view, those states' exemption laws—including any opt-out provisions—still determine debtors' available exemptions, regardless of whether debtors meet the statute's territorial requirements.[55] For example, when a debtor moved from Illinois (an opt-out state) to

[52]   In re Rody, 468 B.R. 384 (Bankr. D. Ariz. 2012).
[53]   In re Camp, 631 F.3d 757 (5th Cir. 2011).
[54]   In re Long, 470 B.R. 186 (Bankr. D. Kan. 2012).
[55]   See, e.g., In re Garrett, 435 B.R. 434 (Bankr. S.D. Tex. 2010).

Indiana, and filed for bankruptcy within 730 days, the Bankruptcy Court for the Northern District of Indiana required the debtor to abide by Illinois' exemption statute, which forbade residents from electing federal exemptions.[56] Even though the debtor was not a resident of Illinois when she filed, the court still bound her to Illinois' exemption law, and did not permit her to elect the federal exemption laws.

Another 2005 amendment also curbed the exemption-by-moving strategy as it pertains to state homestead exemption claims.[57] Under new § 522(p)(1), a cap of $125,000 was imposed on the homestead to the extent that the interest claimed as exempt was acquired within the 1215–day period (i.e., about three years and four months) prior to bankruptcy. The amount of that cap since has been indexed upward to $155,675, as of 2013. While there is an exception for amounts rolled over from a prior residence, that exception is limited to in-state rollovers. § 522(p)(2)(B). Thus, if the debtor moves to a new state within 1215 days of bankruptcy, and then purchases a home there and attempts to claim that homestead as exempt under the new state law, the debtor's exemption will be limited to $155,675.

By extending the domiciliary requirement from (effectively) 91 days to 730 days (or, in some circumstances, 1215 days!) in 2005, Congress has greatly increased the importance of the issue of whether the debtor can claim state law exemptions from a past domiciliary state (*viz.,* the state in which the debtor resided for the longer portion of the 180 days before the 730 days before bankruptcy, i.e., from days 731–910, counting backward from filing). As before,[58] whether the old state's law will apply to property in the new state will depend on whether the old state's courts have interpreted the law to have extraterritorial effect. Now, though, as noted above, there is at least a savings clause, so that debtors will not be rendered exemption-less in opt out states. Under the "postamble" to § 522(b)(3), if the effect of the new domiciliary test "is to render the debtor ineligible for any exemption," then the debtor is permitted to claim the federal bankruptcy exemptions under § 522(d), *even if* the debtor is located in a state that has otherwise opted out of the federal exemptions. This has been called a "stealth override" of state opt out.[59] Note an ambiguity lurking in the savings clause, though: it provides that the debtor must be rendered ineligible for "any" exemption. What, then, if the state law would disallow extraterritorial application of its homestead exemption, but *would* permit exemption claims on personal property? Does the savings clause apply? It is not entirely clear.[60] In at least one case where a debtor moved from one state to another, and was required to use his old state's exemptions limiting the homestead exemption to in-state property, the court allowed the debtor to use the bankruptcy homestead exemption in addition to the personal property exemptions under state law.[61]

---

[56]   In re Shell, 478 B.R. 889 (Bankr. N.D. Ind. 2012).

[57]   Pub. L. No. 109–8, § 322(a), 119 Stat. 96–97 (2005).

[58]   See supra notes 23–28 and accompanying text.

[59]   See Howard, supra note 24, at 412.

[60]   See id.

[61]   In re Kelsey, 477 B.R. 870 (Bankr. M.D. Fla. 2012).

One final exemption eligibility question: what if the debtor has not been domiciled in *any* state during the 730–day pre-bankruptcy period? In other words, what if the debtor either was a resident alien without an established U.S. domicile, or was a U.S. citizen who had been living abroad? In that situation, the debtor would be able to claim the federal exemptions. Section 522(b)(2) provides that the debtor may claim the federal exemptions under § 522(d) "unless the State law that is applicable to the debtor under paragraph (3)(A) specifically does not so authorize." If the debtor has *no* state law domicile under the rules of (3)(A) discussed above, then by definition there is no state that can preclude the debtor from claiming the federal exemptions.

§ 9.3   The Bankruptcy Exemption Law and Issues of Application

In or out of bankruptcy, one of the most commonly litigated issues involving individual debtors concerns the *application* of exemption laws. The answer determines who gets the property at issue—the debtor or his creditors. Can the debtor *really* keep the Porsche for himself without paying his creditors?[62] Exemption laws are purely creatures of statute (or, in some states, the state constitution). Those laws usually exempt some or all of the following types of property, although variations between states are considerable (especially in exemptible dollar amounts): homestead; motor vehicle; wearing apparel; household goods and furnishings; jewelry; health aids; professional books and "tools of the trade"; life insurance; pension benefits; and other social insurance benefits. In addition, many states have a general "catch-all" allowance, or "wildcard" exemption, for any personal property up to a certain dollar amount. The debtor who seeks to claim property as exempt must show, if challenged, that the claimed property falls within one of the statutory (or, if applicable, constitutional) exemption categories. Courts generally give exemption laws a liberal construction, in favor of debtors, the protected class.[63]

An individual debtor in bankruptcy *always* may choose the governing *state* exemption law.[64] In addition, the Bankruptcy Code in § 522(d) provides a schedule of exemptions that individual debtors may select as an *alternative* to state exemptions. As discussed in the preceding section, states may "opt out" of the federal exemptions and limit resident debtors to the state and non-bankruptcy federal exemptions. § 522(b)(2). As of 2013, 34 states had opted out,[65] leaving § 522(d) in effect in only 16 states and the District of Columbia.[66]

---

[62] This was an actual case I litigated (on behalf of a creditor) when I was in practice. Happily I can report that the answer was "no."

[63] See, e.g., In re Johnson, 480 B.R. 305, 311 (Bankr. N.D. Ill. 2012) (holding that exemption laws should be construed in the way most favorable to debtors, as the statutes' purpose was to provide debtors with assistance during tough economic times) (citing *In re Barker*, 768 F.2d 191, 195–96 (7th Cir. 1985)); In re McMillin, 414 B.R. 348 (Bankr. D. Ore. 2010).

[64] There are limited exceptions. One is for the rare debtor who has no state of domicile, as discussed in the last paragraph of § 9.2; another is for debtors who file bankruptcy in a new state before living there for two years, and their previous state limits its exemptions to "residents only." For the latter group of debtors, remember that courts are split on whether to apply debtors' previous resident state's exemption laws despite the fact they are no longer residents there.

[65] Alabama, Arizona, California, Colorado, Delaware, Florida, Georgia, Idaho, Illinois, Indiana, Iowa, Kansas, Kentucky, Louisiana, Maine, Maryland, Mississippi, Missouri, Montana, Nebraska, Nevada, New

Notwithstanding the limited availability of § 522(d), the exemptions provided in that section are worthy of study for several reasons. First, they represent a thoughtful model exemption law; Congress derived § 522(d) from the 1976 Uniform Exemptions Act.[67] Many of the issues that arise when applying and interpreting any state or federal exemption law are illustrated by the provisions of § 522(d). Second, the movement to make a uniform set of exemptions available to all bankruptcy debtors remains strong,[68] and may well bear fruit someday.

In summary, the twelve categories of exemptions in § 522(d) are, in order:

1.   Homestead.

2.   Motor vehicle.

3.   Household furnishings and goods, wearing apparel, etc.

4.   Jewelry.

5.   "Wild card" dollar exemption.

6.   Professional books and tools of the trade.

7.   Life insurance contract.

8.   Rights under life insurance contract.

9.   Health aids.

10. Right to receive various benefits, such as social security.

11. Right to receive certain payments, such as for wrongful death, personal injury, or life insurance.

12. Tax-exempt retirement funds, under certain described Internal Revenue Code sections.

Both state law exemptions and the exemptions provided in subsections (1) through (12) of § 522(d) are limited in the following four different possible ways:

•   limitation by *amount*;

•   limitation by the *type* of property;

York, North Carolina, North Dakota, Ohio, Oklahoma, Oregon, South Carolina, South Dakota, Tennessee, Utah, Virginia, West Virginia, and Wyoming.

[66]   Alaska, Arkansas, Connecticut, District of Columbia, Hawaii, Massachusetts, Michigan, Minnesota, New Hampshire, New Jersey, New Mexico, Pennsylvania, Rhode Island, Texas, Vermont, Washington, Wisconsin.

[67]   See H.R. Rep. No. 95–595, 95th Cong., 1st Sess., at 361 (1977).

[68]   For further discussion, see Daniel A. Austin, Bankruptcy and the Myth of "Uniform Laws", 42 Seton Hall L. Rev. 1081 (2012); Victor D. Lopez, State Homestead Exemptions and Bankruptcy Law: Is it Time for Congress to Close the Loophole?, 7 Rutgers Bus. L.J. 143 (2010).

- limitation by the *use* of property; and

- limitation by the debtor's *need* for the property.

More than one limitation may apply to the same exemption. For example, the federal exemption for household furnishings and goods (§ 522(d)(3)) is limited in amount ($575 for one item, and $12,250 for all in the category), by type of property ("household furnishings," "household goods," and several more types), and by use ("personal, family, or household use").

Dollar limits

Many of the exemptions in § 522(d) are limited to stated dollar maximums. § 522(d)(1)–(6), (8), (11)(D). The listed dollar amounts all were doubled in the 1994 amendments. These amounts now are indexed to changes in the Consumer Price Index, and are adjusted every three years, § 104(b); as of this writing, the last adjustment was April 1, 2013. For example, the homestead exemption was raised from $7,500 to $15,000 in 1994, and as of 2013 was indexed up to $22,975.

In applying the exemptions with dollar limits, several points must be borne in mind. First, the court may have to value the claimed property. Second, the value is computed as of the date of the filing of the bankruptcy petition, not the date a party objects to the exemption. Note a possible risk a debtor may bear if the property appreciates post-bankruptcy, discussed below. As will be seen, the estate, not the debtor, may enjoy the fruits of that appreciation in value. Third, the dollar amount of these exemptions is keyed to the *debtor's interest*. The "debtor's interest" is the *net* equity amount remaining *after* accounting for valid liens and other interests in the property. This means that exemptions are available only to the extent that the debtor possesses equity in the property. Fourth, if the debtor and the debtor's spouse file a joint case, each may separately claim the exemptions. § 522(m). That means that the dollar amounts will be doubled. Fifth, if a wild card exemption applies (such as § 522(d)(5)), that may be added to the exemptible dollar total. Finally, when taking all competing interests into account, the property may be only *partially* exempt, with both the debtor *and* competing claimants entitled to some piece of the property pie.

In *Schwab v. Reilly*,[69] the Supreme Court emphasized the limited nature of what the debtor exempts under such dollar-limited exemptions. Importantly, the debtor does *not* get an exemption in the *thing itself*, but *only* is entitled to dollars; as the Court stated, these exemptions "define the 'property' a debtor may 'clai[m] as exempt' as the debtor's 'interest'—up to a specified dollar amount—in the assets described in the category, *not* as the assets themselves."[70] Why this might matter is illustrated by the Ninth Circuit's decision in the *Gebhart* case.[71] The debtors in that case had equity of $89,703 in their home, which they claimed as fully exempt under Arizona's $100,000 homestead exemption, and the trustee did not object. The debtors continued living in the home and even refinanced their mortgage. *Three years later*, the home having

---

[69]   130 S.Ct. 2652 (2010).

[70]   Id. at 2661–62 (emphasis in original).

[71]   621 F.3d 1206 (9th Cir. 2010).

appreciated substantially in value, so that the debtors had equity in excess of the exempt amount, the bankruptcy trustee sought to sell the Gebhart's home and capture that excess value for the estate. Amazingly, the trustee won. The Ninth Circuit relied on *Schwab* for the proposition that *the home itself* was at all times property of the bankruptcy estate (until either the case was closed or the home abandoned); all that the debtors exempted, in effect, was a charge against that home for a stack of cash equal to $89,703.[72]

If the value of the "debtor's interest" in the item *exceeds* the exempt amount, what happens? (i.e., think about my Porsche case mentioned above!). This was the situation in *Schwab*. The debtor has some choices, but keeping all of the property as exempt is not one of them. The choices are: (1) the trustee will sell the property and remit the exempt amount to the debtor; (2) the debtor will use the "wild card" exemption in § 522(d)(5) to make up the nonexempt amount; or (3) the court may permit the debtor to pay the nonexempt amount to the trustee and retain the item.

If the value of the debtor's interest in the property is *less* than the exemption, then you have the *Gebhart* scenario. The debtor can claim the entire value in the property as of the date of bankruptcy as exempt, and accordingly file a motion to compel the trustee to *abandon* the property to the debtor under § 554. The debtor would argue that there is no reason for the trustee to administer the property, because by definition there is no net value remaining for the estate after taking into account the debtor's exemption and any valid liens on the property. The trustee's counter, of course, as illustrated by *Gebhart*, is that even if there is no value for the estate *now*, perhaps the property will subsequently appreciate in value, and the estate is entitled to enjoy that appreciation. Courts will have to determine whether to countenance such a "wait and see" gambit that seriously burdens the debtor's fresh start. Of course, even if the debtor persuades the court to compel abandonment, if a valid lien remains on the item, the debtor still will have to deal with the secured creditor even after abandonment. Unavoided liens are enforceable against exempt property. § 522(c)(2). If the property is of a type subject to redemption under § 722, the debtor can pay off the secured creditor. Otherwise, the debtor will have to work out an agreement with the lienholder.

The foregoing rules may be illustrated by a simple example involving an automobile. Debtor is entitled to exempt up to $3,675 in value in one motor vehicle. § 522(d)(2). Assume that Debtor claims a Chevy Blazer as totally exempt. The first step will be to value the vehicle; for the purpose of the hypothetical, assume that the court finds that the Blazer is worth $15,000. The second step is to deduct the amount of all valid liens on the vehicle; assume that Bank has a security interest securing an $11,000 debt. That reduces the "Debtor's interest" to $4,000, of which $3,675 is exempt. In sum, then, the $15,000 value of the Blazer is divided as follows: (1) $11,000 to Bank for the secured claim; (2) $3,675 for Debtor as an exemption; and (3) $325 to the bankruptcy estate. The trustee would not abandon the Blazer to Debtor, because net value remains for the benefit of the estate. Debtor might be able to exempt the $325 balance by using part of the "wild card" exemption in subsection (d)(5). Otherwise, the trustee would sell the vehicle and remit $3,675 to the Debtor for Debtor's exempt

---

[72]   Id. at 1210–11.

share. Debtor could try to pay $325 to the estate and keep the vehicle itself, although after *Schwab*, as discussed above, the trustee might not have to accept that deal, if the trustee preferred to wait and see if the property appreciates in value. Regardless, Debtor then would have to deal with Bank and do something about the lien and the debt owed to Bank.

If Debtor and Debtor's spouse own the vehicle jointly, and if they file a joint bankruptcy case, both can claim an exemption, meaning that together they would be entitled to a $7,350 motor vehicle exemption (2 times $3,675). Then together their interest (of $4,000) would be totally exempt under § 522(d)(2), and it is likely that the trustee would abandon the vehicle. Of course, Debtor and Debtor's spouse still would have to do something with Bank's lien, but that is not a concern of the trustee.

Wild card exemption

One of the dollar exemptions alluded to above deserves special comment. The "wild card" exemption in § 522(d)(5) permits the debtor to apply the amount specified therein to exempt *any* property. Many state exemption statutes have similar provisions. Often the debtor will apply the wild card in part to make up for shortfalls in specific exemption allowances, such as in the Chevy Blazer example above. The debtor in that hypothetical had a $4,000 interest in a motor vehicle, but the motor vehicle exempt amount was only $3,675. The debtor might be able to use $325 from the wild card and exempt the vehicle in full.

The amount of the wild card under the federal scheme depends on the amount of the homestead exemption the debtor actually uses under subsection (d)(1). The wild card amount is computed as follows (as indexed to 2013): (1) $1,225 + (2) up to $11,500 of the *unused* amount of the homestead exemption. § 522(d)(5). The homestead exemption is $22,975. To illustrate, assume that a debtor claims a $12,000 homestead under § 522(d)(1). That leaves $10,975 unused, which, when added to the base $1,225 amount, entitles the debtor to a $12,200 wild card exemption. The debtor can apply that $12,200 to exempt any property, or a part thereof. Now assume instead that the debtor claims only $8,000 on the homestead, leaving $14,975 unused under subsection (d)(1). The debtor in this second example can use only $11,500 of that unused amount, which, when added to the $1,225 base, gives the maximum wild card of $12,725. Congress allowed debtors to use part of their unused homestead exemption "in order not to discriminate against the non-homeowner."[73]

Property type limits

Except for the wild card exemption just discussed, all of the exemptions in § 522(d) apply to described *types* of property. Thus, issues may arise in *classifying* the property. This is a common type of exemption litigation. Are cows and bulls "tools of the trade" under subsection (d)(6)?[74] Can a houseboat be a "residence"?[75] What about a truck

---

[73]   H.R. Rep. No. 95–595, 95th Cong., 1st Sess., at 361 (1977).

[74]   Compare In re Parrotte, 22 F.3d 472 (2d Cir. 1994) (yes), with In re Patterson, 825 F.2d 1140 (7th Cir. 1987) (no).

[75]   In re Norris, 499 F.3d 443 (5th Cir. 2007) (no).

driver's cab?[76] Is a pistol a "household good"?[77] In attempting to answer these imponderables, courts focus both on the language of the statute and the perceived reason for the exemption. In addition, these classification issues often are interwoven with *use* issues, discussed next. For example, whether the truck driver's cab is his "residence" under subsection (d)(1) may depend on how the driver uses the cab. The many gun cases look closely at the way the debtor uses the gun.[78]

What happens if property classified as exempt is combined inextricably with nonexempt property? One interesting case decided by the Eighth Circuit presented the problem of a debtor selling his homestead and claiming the proceeds as exempt when the sale of the homestead was bundled with nonexempt property. In *In re Danduran*,[79] the debtor sold his real estate (exempt property) along with some nonexempt personal property (pool table, hot tub, washer/dryer, BBQ grill, area rugs, mirrors, a wreath, etc.). The debtor claimed the total sale price of his home as exempt, including the nonexempt personal property items. Not surprisingly, the trustee objected, asserting that a "significant portion" of the proceeds from the sale were from nonexempt personal property. The Eighth Circuit held that nonexempt proceeds from personal property sold with a homestead were converted to exempt proceeds of the homestead.

Property use limits

A few of the exemptions in § 522(d) apply only if a particular *use* is made of the claimed item. See § 522(d)(1), (3), (4), (6). The same exact item of property may or may not be exempt, depending on how the debtor uses that item. For example, the homestead exemption only extends to real or personal property that the debtor or a dependent of the debtor "*uses as a residence.*" § 522(d)(1). A houseboat could be exempt if the debtor lives in it,[80] but not if the debtor uses it only on vacations.

Two of the exemptions are limited to consumer usages, i.e., "the personal, family, or household use" of the debtor or a dependent. Section 522(d)(3) applies to "household furnishings, household goods, wearing apparel, appliances, books, animals, crops, or musical instruments" held primarily for "personal, family, or household use." Section 522(d)(4) covers "jewelry" held primarily for personal, family, or household use. Both of these provisions also are subject to a dollar limit: $575 per item and $12,250 overall for (d)(3), and $1,550 in the aggregate under (d)(4).

---

[76] See In re Laube, 152 B.R. 260 (Bankr. W.D. Wis. 1993) (yes).

[77] Compare In re Raines, 161 B.R. 548 (Bankr. N.D. Ga. 1993) (yes) with In re Barrick, 95 B.R. 310 (Bankr. M.D. Pa. 1989) (no).

[78] See In re McGreevy, 955 F.2d 957 (4th Cir. 1992) (holding that guns were not "household goods" when the debtor lived in a townhouse and firearms were usually used away from home for hunting or target practice); In re Heath, 318 B.R. 115 (Bankr. W.D. Ky. 2004) (allowing debtor to exempt one of five guns under "household good" exemption when debtor's son used gun to hunt and supply meat for the family); In re Karaus, 276 B.R. 227 (Bankr. D. Neb. 2002) (allowing debtor to exempt a shotgun and pistol to protect his home, but not allowing exemptions for guns part of the debtor's "gun collection").

[79] In re Danduran, 657 F.3d 749 (8th Cir. 2011).

[80] Movie aficionados will recall that Tom Hanks lived in a houseboat with his son in "Sleepless in Seattle." I confess that it is one of my favorite movies. But then, so too is "Die Hard." I have eclectic tastes.

The final use category is for "implements, professional books, or tools" of the debtor's "trade." § 522(d)(6). An aggregate dollar limit of $2,300 applies. This category has been the focus of endless litigation. What is a "trade"? What constitutes a "tool" of that trade? Can a debtor have more than one trade? What happens if the debtor temporarily ceases working in that trade, but intends to return? A commonly litigated question is whether a debtor's car can be a tool of the debtor's trade. Some courts take the position that the existence of the specific exemption category for motor vehicles (in subsection (d)(2)) implicitly negates allowing motor vehicles to be exempted under another provision.[81] Many courts, though, do allow the debtor to exempt a motor vehicle as a tool of the trade if it is necessary for and used in connection with the debtor's trade.[82] A traveling salesperson probably could exempt his car as a tool of the trade, while a debtor who simply used her car to commute to work could not.[83]

Necessity limits

The final type of limitation on exemption categories is for *necessity*. See § 522(d)(10)(D), (10)(E), (11)(B), (11)(C), (11)(E). Each of these exemptions applies to the debtor's "right to receive" certain payments, but *only* "to the extent reasonably necessary for the support of the debtor and any dependent of the debtor." The types of payments to which the necessity limitation applies include: alimony, support, or maintenance; pensions; wrongful death awards; life insurance benefits; and compensation for loss of future earnings. In making the very fact-specific determination of what constitutes "reasonable need," courts weigh a long list of factors, such as the debtor's other anticipated income, the debtor's projected expenses, the debtor's age and health, and so on.[84] Courts focus on the basic needs and responsibilities of the debtor and the debtor's dependents, and do not attempt to maintain the debtor in the lifestyle to which he was accustomed.

§ 9.4   Limitations on the Protective Reach of Exemptions

What good does it do a debtor to be able to claim property as "exempt"? First, exempt property will not be distributed to creditors in a chapter 7 bankruptcy distribution, since by definition the act of exemption removes the property from the bankruptcy estate. In reorganization cases, where estate property is not distributed to creditors, the debtor still benefits from exemptions. The minimum amount the debtor must pay to unsecured creditors under the plan is determined by reference to the amount of the hypothetical chapter 7 liquidation distribution, see §§ 1129(a)(7), 1225(a)(4), 1325(a)(4), which would be net of exemptions.

Second, exempt property generally is not liable for the payment of any administrative expenses in the bankruptcy case. § 522(k). The only exceptions are that the debtor's exempt property is liable for the aliquot share of the costs of avoiding a

---

[81]   See, e.g., In re Van Pelt, 83 B.R. 617 (Bankr. S.D. Iowa 1987).

[82]   See, e.g., In re Cleaver, 407 B.R. 854 (B.A.P. 8th Cir. 2009); In re Taylor, 861 F.2d 550 (9th Cir. 1988); In re Gaydos, 441 B.R. 102 (Bankr. N.D. Ohio 2010).

[83]   See, e.g., In re King, 451 B.R. 884 (Bankr. N.D. Iowa 2011) (disallowing exemption of a car as a "tool of the trade" when it was only used to commute to job).

[84]   See In re Flygstad, 56 B.R. 884 (Bankr. N.D. Iowa 1986).

transfer of property that the debtor then exempts, or the unpaid costs of avoiding a lien or transfer under § 522 itself, or of recovering property under that section. § 522(k)(1), (2).

Third, exempt property is forever immunized from collection with respect to most pre-bankruptcy debts, aside from four types enumerated in § 522(c). Notably, this protection applies even to most types of nondischargeable debts. For example, if a debtor defrauded a creditor, and the creditor's debt was held nondischargeable under § 523(a)(2), even after the bankruptcy case was over the creditor could not enforce its fraud debt against the debtor's exempt property.

The general rule of immunity for exempt property from prepetition debts is subject to a few exceptions. First, if the bankruptcy case is *dismissed*, the protective rule of § 522(c) evaporates.

Second, four types of debts may be enforced against exempt property:

- nondischargeable taxes, see §§ 522(c)(1), 523(a)(1);

- nondischargeable domestic support obligations, §§ 522(c)(1), 523(a)(5);

- unavoided liens against the exempt property, § 522(c)(2)(A), and tax liens against the property, if notice is properly filed, § 522(c)(2)(B); and

- nondischargeable debts relating to insured depository institutions, owed to a federal regulatory agency, § 522(c)(3).

The first exception, for taxes that are nondischargeable under § 523(a)(1), is narrower than under prior law, which allowed even dischargeable taxes to be enforced against exempt property. While the Senate preferred to continue the old rule,[85] Congress instead opted for the House position in enacting the Bankruptcy Code, which was limited to nondischargeable taxes.[86]

The provision allowing unavoided liens and tax liens to be enforced against exempt property, § 522(c)(2), follows the venerable 1886 precedent of *Long v. Bullard*.[87] The general principle that unavoided liens may be enforced against exempt property opens debtors up to the possible loss of their exemptions to the extent that creditors are able to obtain liens against that property. To protect debtor's exemption rights against this eventuality, Congress also provided in § 522 for limited avoidance of certain types of liens that would impair the debtor's exemptions. Once a lien is avoided, the underlying debt no longer will be enforceable against exempt property. Exemption lien avoidance is discussed below.[88]

---

[85]   S. Rep. No. 95–989, 95th Cong., 2d Sess., at 76 (1978).

[86]   124 Cong. Rec. H11,095 (daily ed. Sept. 28, 1978) (statement of Rep. Edwards). See also H.R. Rep. No. 95–595, 95th Cong., 1st Sess., at 361 (1977).

[87]   117 U.S. 617 (1886). See S. Rep. No. 95–989, 95th Cong., 2d Sess., at 76 (1978); H.R. Rep. No. 95–595, 95th Cong., 1st Sess., at 361 (1977).

[88]   See §§ 9.7–9.11.

The protective rule of § 522(c) and the exceptions thereto are matters of *federal* law, preempting inconsistent state laws, as demonstrated by the Fifth Circuit's series of decision in *Davis v. Davis* and Congress's reaction to those decisions. The bankruptcy and district courts in *Davis* held that, notwithstanding § 522(c)(1), an ex-spouse could not enforce her claim for alimony, maintenance, and support against the debtor's exempt homestead, since Texas law did not allow the ex to enforce such a claim against the homestead.[89] The Fifth Circuit panel reversed, concluding that the preemptive federal policy expressed in § 522(c)(1) permitted the ex-spouse to enforce the claim for alimony, maintenance, or support against the homestead, even though the underlying state law was to the contrary.[90] That decision, though, was vacated,[91] and on rehearing en banc, the Fifth Circuit reinstated the bankruptcy and district court decisions giving effect to Texas law over § 522(c).[92] In the 2005 amendments, however, Congress added a clarification to § 522(c)(1) embracing the approach taken by the Fifth Circuit panel and rejecting the approach of the en banc court, thereby giving primacy to the federal exemption law.[93] A state through "opt-out" may define which property may be exempted, the *Davis* panel had explained, but the state cannot dictate how exemptions in bankruptcy are *enforced*. Under this view, a debtor who files bankruptcy may be *worse* off than a debtor who does not file.

The rule for debts relating to insured depository institutions was added as part of a package of amendments in 1990 that responded to the savings and loan debacle of the 1980s. The policy behind § 522(c)(3) was expressed by then-Senator Biden, who explained that the new rule "specifically preempts State homestead laws, which would otherwise allow S & L crooks to retain lavish homes through the excessive protections in some State bankruptcy laws."[94]

Finally, some courts have authorized surcharging exempt property to remedy a debtor's misconduct in concealing non-exempt property that is now unavailable for distribution to creditors. Retired Supreme Court Justice Souter, sitting by designation on a panel of the First Circuit, allowed such a surcharge in the 2012 case of *Malley v. Agin*.[95] Malley, the debtor, willfully concealed $25,000 from the trustee in his chapter 7 case. Once the trustee discovered this concealment, Malley subsequently failed to comply with the bankruptcy court's order to turn over the funds, claiming he had already spent the money. Meanwhile, Malley had validly claimed the entire value of a $9,000 truck as exempt under various provisions with no objections, and the trustee sought to "surcharge" this exempt property to cover the missing $25,000 and the accompanying administrative costs associated with uncovering Malley's concealment. The First Circuit in *Malley* authorized the surcharge under the provisions of § 105(a),

---

[89]   170 B.R. 892 (Bankr. N.D. Tex. 1994), aff'd, 188 B.R. 544 (N.D. Tex. 1995).

[90]   105 F.3d 1017 (5th Cir. 1997).

[91]   131 F.3d 1120 (5th Cir. 1997).

[92]   170 F.3d 475 (5th Cir. 1999), cert. denied, 528 U.S. 822 (1999).

[93]   The operative statutory language in § 522(c)(1) is "(in which case, notwithstanding any provision of applicable nonbankruptcy law to the contrary, such property shall be liable for a debt of a kind specified in such paragraph)."

[94]   136 Cong. Rec. S17,602 (Oct. 27, 1990).

[95]   Malley v. Agin, 693 F.3d 28 (1st Cir. 2012).

but courts are far from agreement on the subject.[96] Furthermore, despite its appeal on an equitable level, allowing a surcharge remedy seems inconsistent with the Court's holding in *Taylor v. Freeland & Kronz*, discussed in § 9.6 below.

§ 9.5   Limitations on Exemptions: Pre–Bankruptcy Planning and Homesteads

a. *Fraud*

One of the most intractable problems involving exemptions arises when a debtor converts nonexempt property to exempt property shortly before filing bankruptcy. The effect of this action is to allow the debtor to keep for himself property that otherwise would have been distributed to the debtor's creditors. Can a debtor do that? If not, what is the sanction?[97]

For example, assume that the day before filing bankruptcy, Debtor transfers $50,000 from his nonexempt money market account to Bank to pay off the mortgage on his homestead, Homeacre. State law (a major culprit in this whole controversy) permits debtors to exempt an unlimited homestead amount.[98] The payment to Bank is not recoverable as a preference, because the payment of a secured claim does not have a preferential effect.[99] See § 547(b)(5). If Debtor is allowed to retain the full $50,000 enhancement of his exempt homestead interest in Homeacre, his bankruptcy creditors correspondingly are out the same $50,000. Alternatively, a debtor may simply purchase a larger amount of exempt property shortly before filing bankruptcy. A variation on this exemption planning strategy is for a debtor to *move* to a state with more generous exemptions, and then purchase exempt property there.[100]

Such eve-of-bankruptcy conversions of nonexempt to exempt property raise two issues. First, is the debtor entitled to keep the exemption in the converted property?[101] Second, will the debtor's discharge be denied under § 727(a)(2) on the ground that the debtor made a "fraudulent transfer"?[102]

---

[96]   For the opposite view, see the Tenth Circuit's decision in *In re Scrivner*, 535 F.3d 1258 (10th Cir. 2008). See also In re Mazon 395 B.R. 742 (M.D. Fla. 2008); In re Campbell, 475 B.R. 622 (Bankr. N.D. Ill. 2012).

[97]   The issues raised by eve-of-bankruptcy conversions have spawned some excellent academic commentary. See, e.g., Thomas H. Jackson, The Logic and Limits of Bankruptcy Law 275–78 (1986); Theodore Eisenberg, Bankruptcy Law in Perspective, 28 U.C.L.A. L. Rev. 953, 992–96 (1981); Steven L. Harris, A Reply to Theodore Eisenberg's "Bankruptcy Law in Perspective," 30 U.C.L.A. L. Rev. 327, 339–45 (1982); Alan N. Resnick, Prudent Planning or Fraudulent Transfer? The Use of Nonexempt Assets to Purchase or Improve Exempt Property on the Eve of Bankruptcy, 31 Rutgers L. Rev. 615 (1978); Lawrence Ponoroff & F. Stephen Knippenberg, Debtors Who Convert Their Assets on the Eve of Bankruptcy: Villains or Victims of the Fresh Start?, 70 N.Y.U. L. Rev. 235 (1995).

[98]   Such a law is not a figment of a professor's imagination, but is the constitutional policy of some Southern states, notably Texas and Florida. See discussion in § 9.2.

[99]   See § 6.16.

[100]   Some of the limitations on the "exemption-planning-by-moving" strategy were discussed in § 9.2.

[101]   E.g., Hanson v. First Nat'l Bank, 848 F.2d 866 (8th Cir. 1988).

[102]   E.g., Norwest Bank Nebraska, N.A. v. Tveten, 848 F.2d 871 (8th Cir. 1988).

In cases where the exemption claimed is provided by state law, the court will first look to *state* law to determine the first issue, whether to allow the exemption;[103] but the second issue, whether to deny the debtor's discharge, is always a question of *federal* law.[104] Back to the first issue, the 2005 amendments imposed some federal limitations, discussed below,[105] on the extent to which a homestead exemption can be claimed in bankruptcy, even under state law. Even apart from those provisions, it is worth noting that resolution of the state law exemption question is not dispositive of the federal discharge issue, and vice versa. In other words, even if the state law would allow the debtor to keep the exemption, it is still possible for the debtor to lose his discharge in the federal bankruptcy case.[106] Conversely, it would be possible for the bankruptcy court to grant the debtor a discharge, and yet still find that under state law the exemption should be disallowed.[107] Having said that, it is jarring for inconsistent results to be reached, especially in the case where the state law permits the exemption.[108] The standard for proving fraud by the debtor is the same under state and federal law,[109] as discussed below, and the propriety of imposing the draconian sanction of loss of discharge on a debtor who acts entirely in accordance with applicable non-bankruptcy law is open to question.

Congress addressed the exemption conversion issue in the legislative history to the 1978 Bankruptcy Code, apparently endorsing the legitimacy of the practice:

> As under current law, the debtor will be permitted to convert nonexempt property into exempt property before filing a bankruptcy petition. The practice is not fraudulent as to creditors, and permits the debtor to make full use of the exemptions to which he is entitled under the law.[110]

The seeming congressional ratification of conversion is not as unqualified as might appear at first blush. The introductory statement, "as under current law," incorporates the existing practice under the 1898 Act. Case law under the Act recognized (1) that "mere" conversion of nonexempt to exempt property, by itself, was not fraudulent, and would neither defeat the debtor's exemption nor trigger a loss of discharge, but also (2)

---

[103] A good example of this point is *Havoco of America, Ltd. v. Hill*, 197 F.3d 1135 (11th Cir. 1999), on certification, 790 So. 2d 1018 (Fla.), aff'd, 255 F.3d 1321 (11th Cir. 2001). In that case, the debtor, a resident of Tennessee, paid cash for a $650,000 fully exempt homestead in Florida, just 3 days before a $15 million judgment against him became enforceable, and then filed bankruptcy. The Eleventh Circuit certified to the Florida Supreme Court the question of whether the debtor's homestead claim would be valid *under Florida law*, even assuming that his purchase was made with the specific intent to defraud his creditors. The Florida court answered that it would still be exempt even if fraudulent.

[104] See In re Laughlin, 602 F.3d 417 (5th Cir. 2010) (citing *In re Reed*, 700 F.2d 986, 990–91 (5th Cir. 1983)).

[105] See § 9.5.b.

[106] See id.

[107] See Jackson, supra note 97, at 277.

[108] See id.

[109] See *Tveten*, supra note 102, 848 F.2d at 874. Accord, In re Addison, 540 F.3d 805, 816 n.14 (8th Cir. 2008).

[110] S. Rep. No. 95–989, 95th Cong., 2d Sess., at 76 (1978); H.R. Rep. No. 95–595, 95th Cong., 1st Sess., at 361 (1977).

that proof of *extrinsic fraud* by the debtor beyond the simple act of conversion would suffice to deny the exemption and perhaps the discharge as well.[111]

The cases under the Bankruptcy Code continue to recite with the pride of schoolchildren these black-letter platitudes—but the results in the cases belie the very maxims the courts seemingly hold dear. "Black-letter" principle number one is this:

"Mere conversion of property from nonexempt to exempt on the eve of bankruptcy—even though the purpose is to shield the asset from creditors—is not enough to show fraud."[112]

The first principle, however, must always be considered in conjunction with its qualifier, "black-letter" principle number two:

"This blanket approval of conversion is qualified, however, . . . if there was extrinsic evidence of the debtor's intent to defraud creditors."[113]

And, in applying principle number two, jurists caution that "extrinsic" evidence means evidence *other than* the act of converting the assets into exempt form, while insolvent, for the purpose of putting the property beyond the reach of creditors.[114]

So what type of "extrinsic" evidence will suffice to establish that the debtor acted with actual fraudulent intent? Some courts use statutory guidance and look to listed indicia of fraud under state law.[115] The easiest cases are those in which the debtor affirmatively misled or even lied to his creditors.[116] In our original hypothetical, in which the debtor transferred $50,000 out of his money market account to pay off the mortgage on his homestead, that fact alone would not establish fraud under principle number one. But assume in addition that a judgment creditor, taking the debtor's deposition, had asked the debtor if he had any money in money market accounts, and the debtor lied and said no—and then immediately went out and transferred the money. Such deceit would be extrinsic evidence of fraud sufficient to satisfy principle number two.

A good example of extrinsic fraud is the Fifth Circuit case of *In re Reed*.[117] The debtor in that case operated a men's clothing store, which became insolvent. The debtor

---

[111] See, e.g., Crawford v. Sternberg, 220 F. 73 (8th Cir. 1915) (holding that transferring money for exemption purposes the day before adjudication was not fraudulent); Kangas v. Robie, 264 F. 92 (8th Cir. 1920) (holding that *Crawford*'s exemption rule does not apply if fraud is shown); Wudrick v. Clements, 451 F.2d 988 (9th Cir. 1971) ("[P]urposeful conversion of nonexempt assets to exempt assets on the eve of bankruptcy is not fraudulent per se.").

[112] Ford v. Poston, 773 F.2d 52, 54 (4th Cir. 1985). Accord, *Tveten*, supra note 102, 848 F.2d at 874; *Reed*, supra note 104, 700 F.2d at 990–91.

[113] *Tveten*, supra note 102, 848 F.2d at 874. Accord, *Reed*, supra note 104, 700 F.2d at 990–91; In re Thomas, 477 B.R. 778, 782 (Bankr. D. Idaho 2012) (citing *Wudrick*, supra note 111).

[114] See *Hanson*, supra note 101, 848 F.2d at 870 (Arnold, J., concurring); see also Smiley v. First Nat'l Bank, 864 F.2d 562, 567 (7th Cir. 1989).

[115] In re Cipolla, 476 Fed.Appx. 301 (5th Cir. 2012) (looking to the Texas Uniform Fraudulent Transfer Act to determine whether a debtor intended to defraud his creditors when he transferred value of nonexempt asset to an exempt asset).

[116] E.g., McCormick v. Sec. State Bank, 822 F.2d 806, 807–08 (8th Cir. 1987).

[117] 700 F.2d 986 (5th Cir. 1983).

entered into an agreement with his creditors, inducing them to postpone collection efforts for one year in exchange for his promise to turn over management of the business to a consulting firm. Having lulled his creditors into inaction, the debtor then embarked on a rapid, comprehensive, and secretive scheme to divert monies from his business to a secret account, purchase and then liquidate antiques and valuable coins (some perhaps for less than full value), and use the cash proceeds to pay down two mortgages on his exempt homestead.[118] Even though Texas state law apparently permitted the debtor to retain the full amount of the homestead exemption, notwithstanding his deceit,[119] the Fifth Circuit held that the debtor's bankruptcy discharge should be denied on the ground of actual fraud.[120]

Lying, misleading, concealing—these all are satisfactory extrinsic evidence of fraud. But what about just being very, very greedy? In colloquial terms, the issue is whether in exemption conversion cases there is a corollary "principle of too much," i.e., is it true that "when a pig becomes a hog it is slaughtered"?[121] Does the debtor-hog get slaughtered if he converts too much nonexempt property to exempt property in contemplation of bankruptcy?

The classic case presenting this question is the Eighth Circuit decision in *Norwest Bank Nebraska, N.A. v. Tveten*.[122] Reduced to basics, the operative facts were that Omar Tveten, a physician who owed almost $19 million in the wake of failed real estate deals, consulted a bankruptcy attorney and then, shortly before filing bankruptcy, proceeded to liquidate virtually all of his nonexempt property and purchase $700,000 of life insurance and annuity contracts with the Lutheran Brotherhood, which he thought was entirely exempt under state law.[123] Even though there was no evidence of any extrinsic fraud other than greed, Tveten lost his discharge. According to the Eighth Circuit, he was a hog who deserved to get slaughtered; taking advantage of an unlimited exemption law in contemplation of bankruptcy fulfilled the "potential for unlimited abuse," going "well beyond the purpose for which exemptions are permitted."[124] The *Tveten* premise, properly rejected by some courts,[125] is that a debtor should only be permitted to convert into exempt assets an amount deemed by the court after the fact to have been "reasonable" in light of the purposes of the exemption laws.

The result in *Tveten* can be, and always is, compared to a decision handed down by the very same panel of three judges on the exact same day, *Hanson v. First National Bank*.[126] The debtors in *Hanson*, like Omar Tveten, also consulted a bankruptcy

---

[118] Id. at 988–89.

[119] Id. at 990 & n.2.

[120] Id. at 991–92.

[121] This catchy phrase has been recycled through many judicial opinions on the subject, including by Judge Arnold in his dissent in *Tveten*, supra note 102, 848 F.2d at 879, discussed in the text.

[122] 848 F.2d 871 (8th Cir. 1988).

[123] Actually, poor Omar also lost his exemption, because the state supreme court held in his case that the unlimited exemption law violated the state constitution. In re Tveten, 402 N.W.2d 551 (Minn. 1987) (discussed in *Tveten*, 848 F.2d at 879 n.3 (Arnold, J., dissenting)).

[124] *Tveten,* supra note 102, 848 F.2d at 876.

[125] See Smiley v. First Nat'l Bank, 864 F.2d 562, 567 (7th Cir. 1989).

[126] 848 F.2d 866 (8th Cir. 1988).

attorney, liquidated nonexempt assets (selling them *to their son* for the appraised value), and purchased exempt property with the proceeds on the eve of bankruptcy. But the same Eighth Circuit panel held that the Hansons had done nothing fraudulent, and were entitled to their exemptions.[127] How can these two cases be distinguished? As explained by Judge Arnold, who concurred in *Hanson* and dissented in *Tveten*, the only apparent differences were (1) the Hansons were farmers and Tveten was a physician; (2) the Hansons converted $31,000 of nonexempt property into exempt property, while Tveten converted $700,000; and (3) the state exemption laws used by the Hansons were limited in amount, but the state law invoked by Tveten was unlimited.[128] The legal relevance of any of these facts as evidence of the debtor's actual fraudulent intent is hard to grasp.[129]

The Eighth Circuit to this day remains committed to a "not too much" premise for determining fraudulent conversion into exempt assets—*even though* the debtor is only taking advantage of exemptions made available by the state legislature. In a 2008 case, the Eighth Circuit revisited *Tveten* and distinguished it from the case before the court on the following basis:

> *Tveten* differs markedly from the present case. Unlike *Tveten*, Addison did not attempt to convert "almost his entire net worth" into exempt assets prior to bankruptcy. Rather, Addison left substantial nonexempt assets for his creditors to recover. In fact, the Trustee-initiated auction of some of Addison's nonexempt assets brought in proceeds in excess of $10,000. Moreover, the total amount of converted assets at issue in this case is less than $20,000, only a fraction of the amount present in *Tveten*.[130]

The "slaughtered hog" problem highlighted by *Tveten* only arises because of the arguably excessive exemptions allowed by some states. If bankruptcy debtors were limited to a more modest uniform set of exemptions, debtors would not be able to progress past the "pig" stage. The National Bankruptcy Review Commission in 1997 recommended limiting debtors to a uniform set of federal exemptions,[131] which would eliminate the conversion problem except in the case of real fraud of the sort present in *Reed*. But Congress has made the policy choice to continue to allow bankruptcy debtors to take advantage of state exemption laws. §§ 522(b)(1), (3)(A). Judges who second-guess the appropriateness of the quantum of state exemptions allowed in a bankruptcy case, and disallow exemptions or deny discharge in exemption conversion cases on that basis alone, are improperly usurping the legislative function. Knowledgeable debtors who do nothing more than take advantage of what the law allows may be punished, while ignorant debtors, by contrast, may escape unscathed. In the meantime, if

---

[127] Id. at 869. The issue of discharge was not presented in *Hanson*, as it was in *Tveten*, although it seems clear from the court's reasoning in *Hanson* that the court would have granted the debtors a discharge as well.

[128] See id. at 870 (Arnold, J., concurring).

[129] For further discussion on these two cases, see Juliet M. Moringiello, Distinguishing Hogs from Pigs: A Proposal for a Preference Approach to Pre–Bankruptcy Planning, 6 Am. Bankr. Inst. L. Rev. 103, 109–20 (1998).

[130] *Addison*, supra note 109, 540 F.3d at 817.

[131] National Bankruptcy Review Commission Final Report, Bankruptcy: The Next Twenty Years, Recommendations 1.2.1–1.2.6, at 117–44 (1997).

conscious pre-bankruptcy exemption planning can lead to a loss of discharge, if some judge later thinks the debtor took "too much," any semblance of certainty, consistency and reliability in the law is lost. It is fair to tell debtors contemplating bankruptcy not to lie, but it is not fair to make them guess how much an unknown judge thinks is too much.

The "conversion" issue can arise also in the situation where the debtor *moves* from one state to another, and then seeks to takes advantage of more generous exemptions in the new domiciliary state.[132] Note that in this scenario, in order to take advantage of the new state's exemptions, the debtor might be purchasing new property that falls within an exemption category in that state, but also might not be purchasing anything new. It would be possible for the debtor to try to claim as exempt under the new state's laws property that he already owned, and which now would be potentially exempt for the first time.

Consider two possibilities for a hypothetical Debtor who decamps from Illinois (which has both a very cold climate and a miserly $15,000 homestead exemption) to Florida (which has both warm weather and an unlimited homestead exemption). Hypothetical One is that Debtor sells his $500,000 Illinois home (of which $485,000 is not exempt under Illinois law), and uses all of that money to buy a homestead in Florida after moving there. Hypothetical Two is that Debtor lived in an apartment in Illinois and already owned a $500,000 second home in Florida while he was domiciled in Illinois, and upon moving permanently to Florida established as his domicile what had been his vacation home, and declared the Florida home as his homestead and claimed it as exempt. In terms of the economic impact on Debtor and his creditors, these two situations are remarkably similar. But would these situations be treated alike in bankruptcy?

As discussed in a previous section,[133] one significant limitation in these sorts of cases on the debtor's ability to claim the exemptions of the state to which he moves is the 730–day domiciliary rule of § 522(b)(3)(A). That provision, amended in 2005 (effectively increasing the required in-state pre-bankruptcy domiciliary time period from 91 days to 730 days), precludes the debtor from selecting the exemptions of the new state unless he has been domiciled there for the entire 730–day period prior to bankruptcy. Thus, in the hypotheticals in the preceding paragraph, if Debtor changed his domicile from Illinois to Florida within 730 days of filing bankruptcy, he would not be able to claim the Florida homestead as exempt in bankruptcy under either scenario presented. The reason for Debtor's move is irrelevant; there is no requirement that Debtor have changed his domicile with any sort of bad intent. The fact of changing domicile within 730 days, standing alone, is sufficient to defeat the exemption claim in the new state.

If, however, Debtor moved to Florida *more* than 730 days before bankruptcy, the limiting domiciliary rule of § 522(b)(3)(A) would not apply. What then? First, with

---

[132] In re Primack, 89 B.R. 954 (Bankr. S.D. Fla. 1988) (rejecting the trustee's argument that there was "conceivable fraud" in connection with the debtors' move to Florida and homestead purchase).

[133] See § 9.2.

regard to *homestead* exemption claims (such as in the hypothetical), several new limiting rules were enacted in 2005. See § 522(o), (p), (q). The impact and application of those provisions is discussed in the following subsection of this treatise. To sum them up quickly here, the upshot is that in the sell-and-buy scenario (Hypothetical One), Debtor would be limited to a $155,675 homestead if he acquired the Florida homestead within 1215 days of bankruptcy (§ 522(p)), or he might be deprived of $485,000 of that homestead exemption if the court found that his conversion from nonexempt to exempt assets was done with actual fraudulent intent, in which case the prohibitory period reaches back ten years before bankruptcy, § 522(o). Under Hypothetical Two, where he already owned the Florida property, neither of those limitations would apply, depending on when he purchased that property.

If the debtor's "exemption-planning-by-moving" strategy involves property *other than* a homestead, none of the new 2005 rules in § 522(o)–(q) would apply. The 730–day domiciliary requirement of § 522(b)(3)(A) would still apply, of course, and, quite frankly, would eliminate most of the perceived cases of abuse, where intimations of *fraud* might lurk as a result of the debtor's propitious move to a state with considerably more generous exemptions than he had previously enjoyed. Indeed, as an anti-abuse measure, § 522(b)(3)(A) is wildly over-inclusive, since it applies irrespective of the debtor's intent, and indeed is not even subject to rebuttal. Even if a debtor is transferred against his will by his employer "kicking and screaming" to the new state, and the facts show that the debtor much would have preferred to remain in the first state, the 730–day rule will still apply.

If the debtor's move occurred more than 730 days before bankruptcy, then supposedly it would be open to the courts to review the move on the grounds of fraud, and disallow exemptions claimed in pursuit of that fraudulent scheme. In such a situation, the court would look at all the facts and circumstances, including the debtor's financial situation at the time of the move, what actions the debtor took to claim the new exemptions, the amount of nonexempt property converted to exempt property, and so forth. Having said that, the reality is that in most cases it is a bit far-fetched to say that a debtor acted with an actual fraudulent intent to hinder, delay, or defraud creditors by taking advantage of more generous exemptions available in the new state, when the debtor changed domicile more than 730 days before bankruptcy. Two years is a really long time for a financially troubled debtor to stay out of bankruptcy.

Another issue arises when a debtor transfers nonexempt property to a third party to keep it out of creditors' reach. However, such a situation is dealt with in § 548, which allows the trustee to avoid the transfer, if fraudulent, and then recover the property or its value for the benefit of the estate using § 550.[134] Note, though, that even if the trustee recovers the property under § 550, the debtor may still exempt the property if he did not voluntarily transfer the property and also did not conceal it, § 522(g) (though it is hard to think of a situation where a transfer was found to be fraudulent under § 548, and yet the debtor still meets the requirements of subsection (g)).

---

[134] See §§ 548, 550.

By the same token, if a debtor acquires exempt property by a method tainted with fraud, courts will not allow the debtor to exercise exemption rights with regards to such property. The principle in play here is that "a homestead cannot be a haven for wrongfully obtained money or properties because such property does not belong to the wrongdoer."[135] Indeed, it is well settled that exemption laws were never intended to be a shelter for wrongfully obtained money or property.[136]

b. *Homestead Limitations*

The 2005 amendments added several provisions designed to close the much-maligned "800–pound gorilla of loopholes"[137]—the "mansion loophole." These provisions in various ways limit a debtor's ability to claim extremely large state law homestead exemptions in a bankruptcy case[138]—particularly in one of the five states that do not place a cap on a homestead exemption, sarcastically referred to by Congress as "debtors' paradises."[139] As one bankruptcy judge in Miami stated, "you could shelter the Taj Mahal in this state and no one could do anything about it."[140] At the outset, it is worth noting what Congress did *not* do, even though it had been recommended by the National Bankruptcy Review Commission: adopt a *uniform ceiling* on the homestead exemption, at a fair dollar amount, applicable in all cases.[141] In fact, Congress rejected a proposal to place an absolute cap on homestead exemptions, even at $1,000,000.[142] If the amount of the homestead exemption allowable in a bankruptcy case can be no more than an amount that is fair and reasonable for a debtor's housing needs, then virtually all of the concerns and issues about fraudulent conversion, or exemption planning, and so forth, fall away. By whatever means the debtors arrive at their homestead exemption, be it moving, cashing out a money market account, paying down a mortgage—absent gross fraud of the sort in *Reed*—it does not matter, because as a matter of policy we actually *want* debtors to be able to live in adequate housing. The cap would keep debtors from insulating an unfair amount from their creditors. Sadly, though, Congress did not take this tack, despite the House Report advocating its implementation.[143] It bowed instead to the states' rights pressures of several powerful

---

[135] See In re Gamble–Ledbetter (E.D. Tex. 2009) (citing *Maryland Casualty Co. v. Schroeder*, 446 S.W.2d 117, 121 (Tex.Civ.App. 1969)). See also In re Huie, 2007 WL 2317152 (Bankr. E.D. Tex. 2007) (disallowing the debtor's use of § 522(f) to avoid a lien on his homestead purchased with fraudulently obtained funds because of the requirement that "the lien must impair an exemption to which the debtor would have been entitled").

[136] See Baucum v. Texam Oil Corp., 423 S.W.2d 434, 441–42 (Tex.Civ.App. 1967).

[137] Charles Jordan Tabb, The Death of Consumer Bankruptcy in the United States?, 18 Bankr. Dev. J. 1, 42 (2001).

[138] See Margaret Howard, Exemptions Under the 2005 Bankruptcy Amendments: A Tale of Opportunity Lost, 79 Am. Bankr. L.J. 397, 398–408. (2005).

[139] H.R. Rep. No. 109–31,109th Cong., 1st Sess., at 593 (2005).

[140] Larry Rohter, Rich Debtors Finding Shelter Under a Populist Florida Law, The New York Times, July 25, 1993, accessible at http://www.nytimes.com/1993/07/25/us/rich-debtors-finding-shelter-under-a-populist-florida-law.html?pagewanted=all & src=pm (quoting Judge A. Jay Cristol).

[141] See Commission Report, supra note 131, Recommendation 1.2.2, at 125–33. The Commission suggested a ceiling of $100,000, but the exact dollar amount is less important than the fact of setting *some* reasonable limit, which applies in *all* cases.

[142] H.R. Rep. No. 109–31,109th Cong., 1st Sess., at 591 (2005).

[143] Id. at 596 ("If Congress is serious about curbing abuse, a national, absolute dollar amount cap, without any loopholes, is the only way to do it.").

states—especially Texas and Florida—with extraordinarily large homestead exemptions, who wanted to keep their status as a potential exemption haven for the rich and famous alive and well.[144]

Instead of a straightforward, simple, across-the-board homestead cap, in 2005 Congress gave us a potpourri of confusing, awkward amendments, which address the mansion loophole in various and incomplete ways. Some of these 2005 changes—in particular the 730–day domiciliary requirement in § 522(b)(3)(A)—have already been discussed.[145] The legislative history proudly summarizes these provisions:

> The bill also restricts the so-called "mansion loophole." Under current bankruptcy law, debtors living in certain states can shield from their creditors virtually all of the equity in their homes. In light of this, some debtors actually relocate to these states just to take advantage of their "mansion loophole" laws. S. 256 closes this loophole for abuse by requiring a debtor to be a domiciliary in the state for at least two years before he or she can claim that state's homestead exemption; the current requirement can be as little as 91 days. The bill further reduces the opportunity for abuse by requiring a debtor to own the homestead for at least 40 months before he or she can use state exemption law; current law imposes no such requirement. S. 256 prevents securities law violators and others who have engaged in criminal conduct from shielding their homestead assets from those whom they have defrauded or injured. If a debtor was convicted of a felony, violated a securities law, or committed a criminal act, intentional tort, or engaged in reckless misconduct that caused serious physical injury or death, the bill overrides state homestead exemption law and caps the debtor's homestead exemption at $125,000. To the extent a debtor's homestead exemption was obtained through the fraudulent conversion of nonexempt assets (e.g., cash) during the ten-year period preceding the filing of the bankruptcy case, S. 256 requires such exemption to be reduced by the amount attributable to the debtor's fraud.[146]

Thus, the four limitations added in 2005 that restrict the debtor's ability to claim a large state law homestead exemption are:

1. The *730–day domiciliary requirement* in § 522(b)(3)(A).[147] Recall from earlier discussions that a debtor who changes domicile within 730 days of filing bankruptcy is precluded from using the state law exemptions of the state to which he moved. No fraudulent intent need be shown.

2. A *$155,675 cap* on a state law homestead exemption if the debtor acquired the property in which he is claiming the homestead exemption within *1215 days*

---

[144] Those who thought that then-President George W. Bush, a native Texan, would ever sign a bankruptcy bill that imposed a uniform federal ceiling on homestead exemptions, thus negating the unlimited Texas homestead exemption in bankruptcy cases, were, to put it kindly, extreme optimists. Another key advocate for retaining the option of large state homestead exemptions was Senator Grassley of Iowa, which also has an unlimited homestead exemption.

[145] See §§ 9.2, 9.5.a.

[146] H.R. Rep. No. 109–31, 109th Cong., 1st Sess., at 15–16 (2005).

[147] Pub. L. No. 109–8, § 307(1), 119 Stat. 81 (2005).

before bankruptcy.[148] § 522(p)(1). While an exception applies if the debtor within the 1215–day period simply rolled over the proceeds from the sale of a prior residence that he had acquired prior to the 1215–day period, that exception only applies if the former and current residences are in the *same state.* § 522(p)(2). Thus, if the debtor used proceeds from the sale of a residence in one state to acquire a homestead in another state (the classic "move to Florida" gambit) within the 1215–day period, the $155,675 cap applies.

3. A *$155,675 cap* on a state law homestead exemption if the debtor did something bad—either was convicted of a felony that demonstrates that the bankruptcy filing was an abuse, § 522(q)(1)(A), or owes a debt arising from the violation of a securities law, for fiduciary or securities fraud, for a civil remedy under RICO,[149] or for a criminal act, intentional tort, or willful or reckless behavior that caused physical injury or death in the past five years, § 522(q)(1)(B).[150] This is the so-called "Enron" provision, as it was inspired by political pressure to stop Enron executives from claiming large homesteads if they filed bankruptcy.

4. A *10–year disallowance* for exemptions that were obtained by the *fraudulent conversion* of nonexempt to exempt assets, § 522(o).[151]

i. *Section 522(p)*

Other than the 730–day domiciliary rule, the 2005 "mansion loophole" antidote that has been invoked most often and that has received the most judicial attention is the 1215–day homestead acquisition rule of § 522(p). The obvious intent of Congress was as stated in the House Report, quoted above—to let the debtor only take advantage of a state homestead exemption larger than $125,000 if the debtor has owned the property for more than forty months (1215 days) before bankruptcy.[152] The dollar amount was indexed to 155,675 in 2013, and will continue to be indexed every three years. Subsection (m) directs that subsection (p) should apply separately to joint debtors. Some courts see this as a green light to double the dollar amount in the case of joint debtors.[153]

Note initially that this is a very incomplete "closing" of the so-called "mansion loophole." It only stops a debtor who buys the homestead within forty months of bankruptcy. That means, of course, that it does *not* apply to a debtor who bought the homestead *more* than forty months before bankruptcy. If a wealthy debtor *already*

---

[148] Id., § 322(a), 119 Stat. 96–97.

[149] 18 U.S.C. §§ 1961–1968.

[150] 119 Stat. 97.

[151] Id. § 308(2); 119 Stat. 81.

[152] Note that § 522 does not contain any "primary residence" requirement for the homestead exemption, so a debtor owning two homes at the time of filing may select either for exemption. See In re Demeter, 478 B.R. 281 (Bankr. E.D. Mich. 2012).

[153] In re Gentile, 483 B.R. 50 (Bankr. D. Mass. 2012); In re Rasmussen, 349 B.R. 747 (Bankr. M.D. Fla. 2006).

lived in Texas or Florida and owned an expensive home, nothing about § 522(p) would keep him from claiming his entire homestead as exempt in bankruptcy; the $155,675 cap would not apply. As Senator Kohl of Wisconsin pointed out to his fellow Senators, in urging them to adopt an across-the-board homestead cap rather than the more limited restrictions they did pass, "Ken Lay [chairman and CEO of Enron before its demise], for example . . . intends to retain his $7.1 million, 13,000–square–foot condominium in the finest apartment building in Houston."[154] Furthermore, a debtor who already resides in one of the big-exemption states is free to roll over his home equity into a new homestead in the same state within the 40–month period. § 522(p)(2)(B). Thus, under subsection (p)(2)(B), Lay could have sold his $7.1 million condo and purchased another fully exempt homestead in Texas with the sale proceeds. The only prohibition is on acquiring a new homestead in *another* state.

The limitation in subsection (p) also apparently would not apply to Hypothetical Two in the preceding subsection where Debtor *already* owned a $500,000 vacation home in Florida at the 40–month mark, even though Debtor then was domiciled in Illinois. Debtor's establishment of domicile in Florida within the 40–month mark and claim of the $500,000 home there as exempt would not be covered by subsection (p), because that subsection only bars the debtor's exemption of an amount beyond the cap in "any . . . interest that was acquired by the debtor during the 1215–day period." The reference is to when the debtor *acquired* the interest, not to when that interest took on an exempt character.[155]

In a similar vein, courts and commentators have pondered whether subsection (p) applies to an increase in the debtor's effective homestead exemption within the 1215–day period due to (1) the debtor making regularly scheduled mortgage payments or (2) an appreciation in the value of the debtor's homestead. Considering both the statutory text ("interest that was acquired") and the history of the section, it is hard to imagine that Congress intended subsection (p) to apply in either of these situations. The focus of subsection (p) is not on whether the debtor's exemption interest increases, but on whether the debtor actually acquires property within the 1215–day period that the debtor then seeks to exempt. Even in the mortgage payment situation, it is a stretch of the statutory language and purpose to say that the debtor has "acquired" an "interest;"[156] the debtor already owned the "interest," namely, the property, and is simply paying a debt owed on that property. Nonetheless, at least one court entertained the idea (in dicta) that subsection (p) applies not only when the debtor actually acquires legal title to the property within the 1,215–day period, but also when the debtor increases his equity by making mortgage payments, or even making improvements to the property.[157]

---

[154] Lay was the CEO of Enron. Letter from Sen. Herb Kohl to U.S. Senators (April 9, 2002), at http://www.abiworld.org/AM/Template.cfm?Section=Home&TEMPLATE=/CM/ContentDisplay.cfm&CONTENTID=52814.

[155] See In re Rogers, 513 F.3d 212 (5th Cir. 2008). Contra, In re Greene, 346 B.R. 835 (Bankr. D. Nev. 2006).

[156] See In re Burns, 395 B.R. 756 (Bankr. M.D. Fla. 2008).

[157] In re Nestlen, 441 B.R. 135 (B.A.P. 10th Cir. 2010).

Subsection (p) is subject to two exceptions. As discussed above, one is for amounts rolled over from an interest in the debtor's principal residence, as long as the prior residence (1) is in the same state and (2) was acquired before the 1215–day period. § 522(p)(2)(B). The other exception is for "family farmers"—there is no cap for a principal residence of a family farmer. § 522(p)(2)(A).

In addition, the introductory clause to subsection (p) states that it applies, "except as provided in sections 544 and 548," which are the two sections that give the trustee the power to avoid fraudulent transfers. It is utterly unclear what the exception for these avoiding powers means, or why it is in the statute.[158] Indeed, § 522(o), also added in 2005, already provides that a debtor will lose his homestead exemption to the extent attributable to a fraudulent conversion of nonexempt to exempt assets within ten years before bankruptcy, which is a much longer period than either § 544(b) or § 548 would encompass. Perhaps Congress simply wanted to make it abundantly clear that nothing in subsection (p) was to be interpreted as a positive grant of an entitlement to a homestead exemption that would trump even a fraud challenge.

One of the most intriguing and puzzling issues in the courts over the application of § 522(p) has been figuring out when that section actually *applies*. The culprit is in the trigger language, which provides that "*as a result of electing* under subsection (b)(3)(A) to exempt property under state or local law," the amount a debtor can claim under the state homestead exemption might be limited. In a state that has opted out of the federal exemptions, a debtor technically does not "elect" to exempt property under state law; instead, that is the only option available. However, only a handful of states that have not opted out have homestead exemptions over $155,675,[159] so, if the statute means what it might be read to say, § 522(p) would apply only in those few states. Some hyper-technical courts have held that this "plain meaning" of § 522(p) must control, and thus there is no cap at all in an "opt out" state.[160] If so, the provision would not apply in Florida, which was the state most often mentioned by legislators as the primary "mansion loophole" destination that needed to be closed. As Judge Markell observed, after looking closely at the historical development of the section, "it is inconceivable that Congress intended such a limited result, and it is demonstrably not what members of Congress thought they were implementing when they voted for the bill."[161] He thus held that the statute as written constituted a "scrivener's error" and should be interpreted as Congress "undeniably intended," namely that § 522(p) would apply to impose a $125,000 cap (now $155,675) in every state, whenever a debtor sought to claim a state homestead exemption for property acquired within 1215 days of bankruptcy.[162] Other courts have reached the same result, although some have found the statute ambiguous and have resorted to legislative history to resolve the ambiguity,[163] while others have read the "as a result of electing" language to refer to

---

[158] See Howard, supra note 138, at 405–06.

[159] According to *In re Kane*, 336 B.R. 477, 484 & n. 13 (Bankr. D. Nev. 2006), as of the date of that opinion (and when the dollar amount was lower, at $125,000) those states were Texas, Massachusetts, Minnesota, and Rhode Island, as well as the District of Columbia.

[160] The best-known case advocating this position is *In re McNabb*, 326 B.R. 785 (Bankr. D. Ariz. 2005).

[161] *Kane,* supra note 159, 336 B.R. at 484.

[162] Id. at 485–89.

[163] See, e.g., In re Kaplan, 331 B.R. 483 (Bankr. S.D. Fla. 2005).

the debtor's act of actually claiming the state law homestead exemption.[164] I think this last reading is in fact what Congress *thought* it was doing. However a court gets there, though, the right answer should be that the $155,675 cap applies in all jurisdictions whenever the debtor elects the state homestead exemption.

ii.   Section 522(q)

This is the so-called "Enron" provision. It acquired that name because it supposedly captures some of the types of wrongdoings various Enron executives were accused of, and would prevent those "bad guys" from claiming a huge homestead exemption. Under this section, a debtor who trips any of the listed triggers in the statute is limited to a homestead exemption of $155,675 (as of 2013) under state law. § 522(q)(1). This amount is indexed every three years.

There is no timing limitation in subsection (q) of the sort in § 522(p) or § 522(b)(3)(A). If the section applies, the debtor's state homestead exemption is capped no matter how long the debtor has been domiciled in the state or has owned the subject property and claimed it as a homestead.

Preliminarily, note that the same "as a result of electing" scope problem, just discussed in conjunction with subsection (p), afflicts subsection (q) as well. The better view, again, is that notwithstanding the inartful verbiage used, the section should apply to a debtor who attempts to claim a state homestead exemption in any state in excess of $155,675.

Notably, one exception may apply to the homestead cap found in § 522(q). The court has the discretion to override the statutory cap to the extent it believes that a larger homestead exemption is "reasonably necessary for the support" of the debtor or the debtor's dependents. § 522(q)(2). It is curious that Congress would allow a necessity override when the cap is based on the debtor's bad acts (subsection (q)), but not when all the debtor did wrong was buy the homestead within forty months of bankruptcy (subsection (p)).

If § 522(q) applies, it may have negative consequences for the debtor beyond an exemption restriction. The debtor's *discharge* may be impacted as well. All chapters provide for delay of a debtor's discharge if there is reasonable cause to believe two things: (1) that § 522(q)(1) "may be applicable to the debtor" and (2) a proceeding is pending in which the debtor may be found guilty of a felony of the type described in (q)(1)(A) or liable for a debt of the kind described in (q)(1)(B). See § 727(a)(12) (chapter 7); § 1141(d)(5)(C) (chapter 11); § 1228(f) (chapter 12); § 1328(h) (chapter 13). While the wording of these discharge sections is confusing, the probable intent is to delay entry of the debtor's discharge until the issue of the debtor's exemption under § 522(q) is resolved. This is the view taken by the revised Bankruptcy Rules, which provide that upon expiration of the time limit for objecting to discharge, the court shall enter the discharge order "unless a motion *to delay or postpone* discharge under § 727(a)(12) is pending." Rule 4004(c)(1)(I).

---

[164]   See, e.g., In re Virissimo, 332 B.R. 201 (Bankr. D. Nev. 2005).

The principal interpretive issues in applying § 522(q) are figuring out exactly what the triggers mean. There are two alternative triggers. The first, in subsection (q)(1)(A), applies if the court determines "that the debtor has been convicted of a felony (as defined in section 3156 of title 18) which under the circumstances, demonstrates that the filing of the case was an abuse of the provisions of this title." The one thing we know for sure from subsection (q)(1)(A) is that the debtor must be convicted of a "felony," which by the reference to 18 U.S.C. § 3156 means "an offense punishable by a maximum term of imprisonment of more than one year." What is not clear is the further requirement that the fact of the debtor's felony conviction "demonstrates that the filing of the case was an abuse." What sort of nexus between the felony conviction and the bankruptcy case did Congress have in mind here? The legislative history is unhelpful and to date no reported cases have elucidated the point. The fact of a felony conviction alone is not enough to trigger the cap; in some way that conviction must be related to a finding that the bankruptcy filing was an abuse. One example of a possible linkage is if the convicted felon debtor sought to discharge in the bankruptcy case civil liabilities to the victims of his crime.

The more commonly invoked trigger under subsection (q) is the second one, that the debtor owes a certain type of debt attributable to a listed bad act. Note first that a final judgment adjudicating the debtor's liability for the debt is not necessary; the statute simply requires that the debtor "owes a debt." Indeed, the references in the discharge statutes to § 522(q)(1)(B) speak of a "pending" proceeding in which the debtor could be found liable for one the listed types of debts, demonstrating that Congress contemplated the possibility that the debtor's liability for the debt could be fixed after the bankruptcy case commenced.

Four categories of debts are listed in § 522(q)(1)(B), namely, those arising from any of the following:

1. Violation of federal or state securities laws, § 522(q)(1)(B)(i). This provision in particular was inspired by the Enron case.

2. "[F]raud, deceit, or manipulation in a fiduciary capacity or in connection with the purchase or sale" of any registered security, § 522(q)(1)(B)(ii).

3. Any civil remedy under RICO (18 U.S.C. § 1964), § 522(q)(1)(B)(iii).

4. "[A]ny criminal act, intentional tort, or willful or reckless misconduct that caused serious physical injury or death" to another individual in the past five years, § 522(q)(1)(B)(iv).

To date relatively few cases have interpreted these provisions. In one circuit court case, a debtor who pled guilty to negligent vehicular homicide had her homestead exemption capped under the "criminal act" provision, the court rejecting the debtor's argument that a heightened *mens rea* limitation qualified the "criminal act" trigger.[165] A number

---

[165] In re Larson, 513 F.3d 325 (1st Cir. 2008).

of courts have had to construe the meaning of "reckless" misconduct that led to physical injury, and generally look to state law torts principles.[166]

iii. *522(o)*

The final homestead limitation added in 2005 is for cases where the debtor fraudulently converted nonexempt property into exempt homestead property within ten years of bankruptcy. § 522(o). The exemption disallowance is imposed to the extent of the fraudulent conversion. The elements to establishing a limitation under § 522(o) are:

> (1) the debtor disposed of property within the 10 years preceding the bankruptcy filing; (2) the property that the debtor disposed of was nonexempt; (3) some of the proceeds from the sale of the nonexempt property were used to buy a new homestead, improve an existing homestead, or reduce the debt associated with an existing homestead; and (4) the debtor disposed of the nonexempt property with the intent to hinder, delay or defraud a creditor.[167]

In the homestead context, § 522(o) gives statutory recognition to the longstanding judicial practice of limiting exemptions based on the debtor's fraudulent conversion of nonexempt property into exempt property, discussed in the preceding subsection of the treatise.[168] As such, the same principles should apply in determining what is and what is not fraud,[169] namely, that (1) "mere" conversion of nonexempt to exempt property will not suffice but (2) "extrinsic evidence" of fraud will suffice.[170] Having said that, "pig-becomes-a-hog" courts (such as the Eighth Circuit) may be inclined to find "fraud" based on what they see as the debtor's greed in taking too much exempt property. So, Iowa debtors (where there is both an unlimited homestead and a lot of hogs and pigs), beware!

One of the most notable aspects of § 522(o) is that it allows a 10–year look-back in assessing whether the debtor's exemption conversion was fraudulent. That is a very long time indeed, and makes it unlikely that a debtor could plan far enough ahead for the fraudulent conversion to work. Compare the much more limited one-year look-back period for denying a debtor a discharge under § 727(a)(2) based on the same fraudulent conversion.

An intriguing question under § 522(o) is what effect it will have in those states, such as Florida,[171] where the state exemption law has been construed to mean that the debtor is entitled to claim the full homestead exemption *even if* the debtor obtained the homestead through actual fraud. A powerful argument can be made that § 522(o)

---

[166] See, e.g., *Burns*, supra note 156, 395 B.R. at 765–66.

[167] In re Corbett, 478 B.R. 62 (Bankr. D. Mass. 2012) (citing *In re Presto*, 376 B.R. 554, 568 (Bankr. S.D. Tex. 2007)).

[168] See § 9.5.a.

[169] See *Addison,* supra note 109, 540 F.3d at 811–12.

[170] See, e.g., In re Cook, 460 B.R. 911 (Bankr. N.D. Fla. 2011) (holding that mere conversion of nonexempt assets to exempt, without evidence of intrinsic fraud, is not enough to trigger § 522(o)).

[171] See Havoco of Am., Ltd. V. Hill, 197 F.3d 1135 (11th Cir. 1999), on certification, 790 So. 2d 1018 (Fla.), aff'd, 255 F.3d 1321 (11th Cir. 2001). See supra note 7 and accompanying text.

changes the law in those states in bankruptcy cases, as § 522(o) imposes an independent *federal* limitation on the amount of the allowable exemption. In other words, the better interpretation would seem to be that while the debtor initially might have a claim to an unlimited homestead exemption under state law, notwithstanding the fraud, the independent federal cap of § 522(o) nevertheless would then be levied, and of course would control under the Supremacy Clause. So far, bankruptcy courts in each district in Florida have taken this approach, and have held that § 522(o) trumps Florida's otherwise generous homestead exemption.[172]

§ 9.6   Exemption Procedures

The process for determining which property the debtor may retain as exempt is fairly straightforward. Congress implemented a new procedure in the 1978 Bankruptcy Code. Under the prior Bankruptcy Act, exempt property never came into the estate.[173] The bankruptcy trustee would file a report of exempt property that did not come into the estate, and the debtor had the burden of objecting to the trustee's report.

The Bankruptcy Code reversed this basic approach, and mandates that all property initially comes into the estate under § 541(a). The debtor then has to claim property as exempt and thereby take that property out of the estate.[174] § 522(l). The trustee will have the burden of objecting to the debtor's claimed exemptions.

Step one in the exemption process under the Bankruptcy Code, then, is that the potentially exempt property comes into the bankruptcy estate under § 541(a). Step two is the claim of exemptions by or on behalf of the debtor. § 522(l); Rule 4003(a). The debtor must file a list of property claimed as exempt in the initial bankruptcy schedule of assets. That schedule must be filed within fourteen days of the filing of the petition. Rules 1007(b), (c), 4003(a). If the debtor does not file a claim of exemptions within that time, a dependent of the debtor may file on behalf of the debtor within the next thirty days. § 522(l); Rule 4003(a).

Standing to claim exemptions is limited to the debtor or a dependent of the debtor. The right to exemptions is a personal privilege of the debtor. Sometimes creditors seek to assert exemptions on behalf of the debtor. For example, in a Ninth Circuit case, the debtor paid the creditor during the preference period with property that the debtor would have been entitled to claim as exempt.[175] The creditor defended the preference on the ground that the property would have been exempt. The court held against the creditor, ruling that the creditor did not have standing to assert the debtor's right to claim exemptions, and that the debtor was free to waive exemptions prior to bankruptcy, as it did in that case.

---

[172] In re Osejo, 447 B.R. 352 (Bankr. S.D. Fla. 2011); In re Cook, 460 B.R. 911 (Bankr. N.D. Fla. 2011) ("Section 522(o) was enacted to preclude Florida's "virtually limitless" homestead exemption in instances of fraud."); In re Booth, 417 B.R. 820 (Bankr. M.D. Fla. 2009).

[173] Lockwood v. Exch. Bank, 190 U.S. 294 (1903). See also S. Rep. No. 95–989, 95th Cong., 2d Sess., at 82 (1978); H.R. Rep. No. 95–595, 95th Cong., 1st Sess., at 368 (1977).

[174] S. Rep. No. 95–989, 95th Cong., 2d Sess., 75–76 (1978); H.R. Rep. No. 95–595, 95th Cong., 1st Sess., at 360 (1977).

[175] In re Noblit, 72 F.3d 757 (9th Cir. 1995).

Once the debtor (or a dependent) has filed the list of exempt property, step three is for the trustee or any creditor to object to any claimed exemptions that might be unwarranted. Rule 4003(b). The objection must be filed within thirty days of the conclusion of the statutory meeting of creditors under § 341(a), unless the court extends the time to object. The trustee has the duty to examine the debtor's exemption claims and object to any exemptions the trustee believes are improper.

What happens in step four depends on whether an objection is filed. If no objections are filed, the property passes out of the estate and goes to the debtor. "Unless a party in interest objects, the property claimed as exempt on such list is exempt." § 522(l). The legislative history reiterates that Congress meant what it said, *viz*, that absent a timely objection, the listed property is exempted.[176] This result holds even if the exemption claimed may not have been proper. If there was any doubt about the absolute necessity to file a timely objection in order to prevent the debtor from obtaining the claimed property as exempt, the Supreme Court initially removed that doubt in *Taylor v. Freeland & Kronz* in 1992.[177] However, the Supreme Court also recognized a loophole in this otherwise strict objection deadline in its 2010 decision in *Schwab v. Reilly*, discussed below.[178]

If a timely objection is filed to the debtor's listed exemptions, a hearing on notice will be held by the court to determine the debtor's entitlement to the contested exemptions. The objecting party (usually the trustee) has the burden of proof. Rule 4003(c). In effect, the debtor establishes a prima facie case by filing a list of exempt property, which the trustee must rebut. If the trustee carries this burden, then the disputed property remains in the bankruptcy estate; if not, the debtor takes the property.

Prior to 1992, the courts were divided over how to deal with the problem of "exemption by declaration." The question was how to deal with the case where the debtor claimed an exemption to which she was not entitled, but for some reason no one filed a timely objection. In *Taylor v. Freeland & Kronz*,[179] the debtor claimed as entirely exempt the proceeds from a pending employment discrimination action. Importantly, she had no statutory basis for that exemption. At the creditors' meeting, the trustee was informed that the action might be worth as much as $90,000. Nevertheless, the trustee did not object to the exemption claim or obtain an extension of time in which to object, probably assuming that the action was worthless. As it turned out, the trustee was wrong, and $110,000 was paid to settle the claim (of which $71,000 was paid to the debtor's attorneys). The trustee then sued the attorneys to recover the $71,000 on behalf of the estate. The attorneys defended by arguing that the property had been exempted by the debtor, and thus was no longer property of the estate.

Prior to *Taylor*, the courts had taken three different approaches in these types of cases. The first was to follow the literal meaning of the statute and hold that the listed

---

[176] S. Rep. No. 95–989, 95th Cong., 2d Sess., at 71 (1978); H.R. Rep. No. 95–595, 95th Cong., 1st Sess., at 363 (1977).

[177] 503 U.S. 638 (1992).

[178] 130 S. Ct. 2652 (2010).

[179] 503 U.S. 638 (1992).

property was exempt, irrespective of the merits of the underlying exemption claim. The second approach, diametrically opposed to the first, only allowed meritorious exemptions to stand, even if the objection to the exemption was filed late. The third, and majority line of cases, took the middle ground and allowed the debtor to keep the property as exempt if the claim had been made in good faith, but denying the exemption if the debtor did not have a colorable basis for making the claim.

The debtor's asserted exemption in *Taylor* probably would have failed to pass muster under either the second or third approaches. The Supreme Court, however, opted for the first view, resting on the plain meaning of the Bankruptcy Code and Bankruptcy Rules. The statute says that the property listed as exempt "is exempt" unless an objection is filed, § 522(l), and Rule 4003(b) specifies when the objection must be made. Accordingly, the Court decided that if a timely objection is not filed, the debtor is absolutely entitled to the exemption.[180] The Court rejected the prevailing compromise position on the ground that the courts "have no authority to limit the application of § 522(l) to exemptions claimed in good faith."[181] Furthermore, the Court found that the plain meaning of the statute was not absurd, but was supported by the policies of expedition and finality that are so important to bankruptcy proceedings.[182] The Court did leave open the possibility that a bankruptcy court could invoke its equitable powers under § 105(a) to disallow exemptions claimed fraudulently or in bad faith.[183]

Taylor should not be read as an invitation to debtors to act with impunity in trying to exempt property without a colorable statutory basis. As the Court noted, such an attempt might meet with a request for sanctions under Rule 9011, could lead to a denial of discharge, and even could trigger criminal prosecution for perjury or under 18 U.S.C. § 152.[184] Indeed, as the Court later illustrated in *Schwab*, there are still limits to what property a debtor may exempt even absent any objections. Furthermore, the exemption claim itself might be disallowed under the court's equitable powers, a question left open in *Taylor*, as noted above. Nor is it likely that a brazen "exemption by declaration" scheme would work. Prompted by the Court's demand for vigilance in *Taylor*, trustees should be more careful either to file a timely objection or to request an extension of time.

The statutory language at issue in *Taylor* may not be as "plain" as the Court suggested. As Justice Stevens pointed out in his dissent,[185] § 522(l) is triggered only if the debtor claims property as exempt "under subsection (b)" (which in turn refers either to the federal exemptions in subsection (d) or state exemptions). If the debtor has no colorable basis for the claimed exemption, she might fail to pass the threshold test of claiming an exemption "under" a statute. Indeed, the Court's reasoning in *Schwab* arguably supports this view, even though the Court there protested that it was

---

[180] Id. at 643–44.
[181] Id. at 645.
[182] Id. at 644.
[183] Id. at 645–46.
[184] Id. at 644.
[185] Id. at 651 (Stevens, J., dissenting).

not overruling *Taylor*.[186] For example, assume that a debtor claims her interest in a "boat" as exempt under an exemption statute that on its face applies only to "farm animals." One could conclude that the purported exemption claim was a legal nullity, accomplishing nothing. Nothing in *Taylor* prevents a court from determining whether the property in dispute is the property described as exempt. Calling a "boat" a "farm animal" does not make it so. In a case decided after *Taylor,* the First Circuit reached this conclusion when the debtor claimed a $50,000 personal injury settlement as totally exempt, without any statutory basis for claiming more than $7,500.[187] The debtor crafted his schedules in such a way to "disguise" this total amount, and list the settlement in several different areas as an allowable expense, so as to not "raise any red flags." The court disallowed the $42,500 balance, despite the trustee's failure to object, finding no reason to require the trustee to object in such a situation. As a subsequent First Circuit court observed, "*Taylor* does not tell us *what* has been claimed as exempt—only that *whatever* has been claimed as exempt is beyond the estate's grasp once the deadline has elapsed. In this case the focus is on the 'threshold question . . . whether the property in dispute is *in fact* the property of the estate listed as exempt.'"[188]

In 2010 the Supreme Court visited a similar scenario in *Schwab v. Reilly*.[189] The debtor in *Schwab* was entitled to a "wildcard" exemption of $10,225, as well as an exemption for tools of the trade up to $1,850, for a total of $12,075. On her Schedule B form, the debtor included a list of "business equipment" with a total estimated market value of $10,718. On her Schedule C form, she claimed that same list of business equipment as exempt with $1,850 exempt under the wildcard provision (§ 522(d)(5)) and $8,868 exempt under the tools of the trade provision (§ 522(d)(6)). The debtor again listed the current market value of the business equipment as $10,718. Thus, the debtor's evident intent as reflected on the face of her schedules was to claim the *entire* value in the business equipment as exempt, and thus to remove *the business equipment itself* from the estate and keep all of it for her own use in her one-woman catering business.[190]

Despite an appraisal revealing the equipment to be worth as much as $17,200, the trustee did not object to the exemptions within the 30–day window, though he advised the debtor of his intent to sell the equipment. However, since no formal objection to debtor Nadejda Reilly's exemption claim was filed, under *Taylor* it would seem that whatever the debtor had claimed as exempt now was indeed irrefutably exempt. But, and here is the rub that ultimately sank Reilly's claim—*what was it that she had claimed as exempt?*

After the objection period had ended, the trustee moved the bankruptcy court for permission to auction off the restaurant equipment so that he could distribute to

---

[186]   130 S.Ct. at 2665–67.

[187]   See Mercer v. Monzack, 53 F.3d 1 (1st Cir. 1995), cert. denied, 517 U.S. 1103 (1996).

[188]   In re Barroso–Herrans, 524 F.3d 341, 344 (1st Cir. 2008) (quoting *Mercer*, supra note 187).

[189]   Schwab v. Reilly, 130 S.Ct. 2652 (2010). For a superb discussion of the case and its implications, see David Gray Carlson, The Role of Valuation in Federal Bankruptcy Exemption Process: The Supreme Court Reads Schedule C, 18 Am. Bankr. Inst. L. Rev. 461 (2010).

[190]   130 S.Ct. at 2671–72 (Ginsburg, J., dissenting).

creditors the value of the equipment in excess of the $10,718 claimed by the debtor. Nice try, the debtor countered, but under *Taylor*, too late. She asserted, and all the lower courts agreed,[191] that *Taylor* mandated that her exemption claim of all the business equipment had become final, because the trustee had been on notice that she intended to exempt the equipment's *full value* by equating the "Value of Claimed Exemption" and "Current Market Value of Property" columns on the Schedule C form. Thus, she argued, under *Taylor* the trustee had forfeited any claim to the value in excess by not objecting within the required time period.

The debtor lost. The Supreme Court held that because the debtor listed the value of her exemptions within the dollar amount range allowed by the Bankruptcy Code, the trustee was not required to object to the exemptions in order to preserve the estate's right to retain any value in the equipment beyond the value of the exempt interest.[192] Thus, unlike in *Taylor*, the claimed exemption was not plainly invalid on its face.[193] Quite the contrary, the Court explained: the exemption she claimed was valid; there was nothing for the trustee to object to. That conclusion depends, though, on identifying exactly *what* it was that Nadejda Reilly had exempted, and that is the central importance of the Court's opinion. The Court emphasized that the exemptions under § 522(d)(5) and (6) allow a debtor to exempt only an *interest* in the claimed property up to the statutorily allowed amount. Subsequent to the trustee's failure to object, then, the "property claimed as exempt" under § 522(l) that became exempt under the *Taylor* rationale was only the dollar value of the property up to $10,718. Most significantly, the *actual property itself*, and any value of that property above $10,718, was not rendered exempt by the trustee's failure to object.

Schwab thus clarifies that a trustee must object to a debtor's claimed exemption only if the debtor's listed exemption value exceeds the statutorily allowed amount, or is otherwise facially invalid. Nor can the debtor use a dollar-limited exemption to exempt the entire property in kind, even if the valuations listed on the schedules indicate that the debtor is trying to claim the entire value as exempt. Stated otherwise, the trustee's obligation to object to the debtor's exemption claims does not extend to issues of valuation.

The Court suggested in dicta that the solution for debtors who do wish to retain specific property in kind is to state the property's "current market value" on Schedule C as something along the lines of "full fair market value," or "100% of FMV." Only such an obvious and unambiguous claim of the entire value, the Court indicated, would trigger the trustee's obligation to object within 30 days.[194] Of course, this "trick" is far from intuitive, nor, more importantly, is it ever likely to work. All that the trustee need do is to object to this form of exemption—which is completely unauthorized statutorily—and force the debtor to list an actual value, whereupon the debtor's exemption right again will be only for the dollar value claimed. Innumerable lower court decisions post-*Schwab* have shown the futility of the Court's suggested

---

[191] 403 B.R. 336 (Bankr. M.D. Pa.2006), aff'd, 534 F.3d 173 (3d Cir. 2008), rev'd, 130 S.Ct. 2652 (2010).

[192] 130 S.Ct. at 2661–62.

[193] Id. at 2665–67.

[194] Id. at 2668.

circumventions; indeed, most courts conclude that a "full FMV" or "100% of FMV" type of exemption claim is facially invalid and uphold the trustee's objection without even requiring a hearing.[195]

As the debtor in the Third Circuit post-*Schwab* case *In re Orton* found out, even listing the *actual* fair market value of the asset you wish to exempt may not be good enough.[196] In *Orton*, the debtor claimed wild-card exemptions for the fair market value of his interests in two assets—an underlying interest in vacant land and an accompanying interest in the oil and gas lease to which the land was subject. The value of both interests was well within the wild-card exemption limit under § 522(d)(5).[197] The trustee did not object to these claimed exemptions within the 30–day period. Nonetheless, the trustee eventually moved to close the chapter 7 case *but* to retain the debtor's interest in the lease so that any future royalties would benefit the estate. The debtor, of course, argued that because no party had objected to his exemptions those assets were no longer part of the estate and were free from creditors' claims. Drawing on the Court's reasoning in *Schwab*, the Third Circuit disagreed with this assessment. Despite successfully exempting a dollar amount equal to the full fair market value of the assets he wished to retain, the Court determined that the debtor in this case had not in fact exempted the *assets* themselves, but only his interest in them. Like the Court in *Schwab*, the Third Circuit came to this conclusion from the language of § 522(d)(5).[198] Accordingly, although the debtor "retains an interest in his lease; the lease itself is property of the Estate."

The court in *Orton* also noted that even if the debtor had used the phrase "full fair market value" or "100% of FMV" instead of listing the assets' actual fair market value (as suggested by the Court in *Schwab!*), the debtor *still* probably would not be able to exempt the actual assets *in kind*.[199] Essentially, then, debtors who wish to exempt an actual asset itself may need to resort to requesting or filing a motion to compel the trustee to abandon the asset. For exemptions allowing debtors only their "interest" in the listed property, abandonment is the only remaining road to finality.

B. PRESERVING THE DEBTOR'S EXEMPTIONS

§ 9.7   Avoiding Powers of the Debtor and the Trustee

Exempt property is protected from the collection efforts of most unsecured creditors. § 522(c). Indeed, even creditors with nondischargeable debts are barred from proceeding against exempt property. Only nondischargeable tax, family support, and

---

[195]   See, e.g., In re Massey, 465 B.R. 720, 728–30 (B.A.P. 1st Cir. 2012) (collecting cases).

[196]   In re Orton, 687 F.3d 612 (3d Cir. 2012).

[197]   Note that as no well had been drilled on the property, the current fair market value for these assets was fairly low—only $1 for the debtor's interest in the oil and gas lease—but with the potential to increase exponentially if a well were ever drilled successfully in the future.

[198]   As discussed above, § 522(d)(5) allows debtors to exempt their "aggregate interest in any property" up to the statutory amount. Compare this with § 522(d)(9) which allows debtors to exempt "[p]rofessionally prescribed health aids." Courts have reasoned that the health aids themselves can be removed from the estate by exemption, whereas only the *debtor's interest* in wild-card property is exemptible.

[199]   Id. at 628 n.1.

financial institution claims are excepted.[200] § 522(c)(1), (3). However, this comprehensive prophylactic rule is subject to one glaring weak spot: it does not apply at all to the holders of *secured* claims. A creditor with a lien on exempt property is allowed to enforce that lien against the debtor's exempt property. § 522(c)(2).

The apparent impotence of the exemption-protection rule against liens, without more, could undermine the policy favoring exemptions. Liens could be the Trojan horse that slides through the exemption wall. A general creditor with leverage against the debtor could compel the debtor to grant the creditor a global security interest in all of the debtor's assets, including exempt property. The debtor may not even be aware of the legal significance of the form he signs. Or the creditor might obtain a judicial lien against the debtor's exempt property. If the debtor failed to pay the creditor, and filed bankruptcy, the creditor still would be able to enforce its lien against the debtor's exempt property after bankruptcy. The benefit of the exemption law to the debtor would be chimerical. In reality, what would be likely to happen is that the creditor could coerce the debtor into signing a reaffirmation agreement, with the debtor waiving the discharge of that debt.[201]

To prevent the evisceration of the exemption policy through the use of liens, Congress gave the debtor the power to *avoid* certain types of liens that impair the debtor's exemptions. § 522(f). Once the lien is avoided, the creditor no longer will be able to enforce that lien against the exempt property. However, in giving debtors a lien-avoidance power to protect exemptions, Congress had to be careful not to go too far. Some types of liens *should* be enforceable against exempt property. It often is in the *debtor's* interest to be able to grant to a creditor a valid and enforceable lien on exempt property. If all liens that impaired exemptions could be set aside in bankruptcy, creditors soon would either cease extending credit on the strength of such liens altogether, or would increase the cost of that credit substantially because of the bankruptcy-avoidance risk. The cure could be worse than the disease. For example, debtors would find it very hard to obtain home mortgage loans if the mortgage on the homestead could be avoided in bankruptcy. The challenge for Congress in crafting the lien avoidance provisions in § 522 was to empower debtors to avoid liens that impaired exemptions without destroying the ability of debtors to obtain meaningful secured credit.

The lien-avoidance balancing act that Congress adopted permits debtors to avoid two types of liens. First, *judicial* liens on any type of otherwise exempt property may be avoided.[202] § 522(f)(1)(A). Second, liens that (i) are nonpossessory and nonpurchase-money, and (ii) are on certain types of personal collateral, such as household goods or tools of the trade, that are thought to be valuable primarily for the leverage they give the creditor, are avoidable.[203] § 522(f)(1)(B).

---

[200] See § 9.4.

[201] The threat posed by liens to the debtor's full enjoyment of available exemptions is discussed in H.R. Rep. No. 95–595, 95th Cong., 1st Sess., at 126–27 (1977).

[202] See § 9.10.

[203] See § 9.11.

In addition, debtors are given the power to *redeem* otherwise unavoidable liens on exempted tangible personal property that secures consumer debts.[204] § 722. To guard against a related abusive practice, outright *waivers* of exemptions are made unenforceable in bankruptcy.[205] § 522(e).

In the 1994 Amendments, two modifications were made to the § 522(f) avoidance rules. Congress carved out from the types of judicial liens that could be avoided those liens that secure a family support debt of the kind specified in § 523(a)(5). § 522(f)(1)(A). Congress amended this rule slightly in 2005. The second modification made in 1994 was to prevent the avoidance of liens on tools of the trade and related types of collateral to the extent the value of the collateral was more than $5,000 (since indexed to $6,225). § 522(f)(3). In 2005, Congress added a detailed definition of "household goods" for purposes of avoidance under subsection (f)(1)(B). § 522(f)(4).

Two significant qualifications affect the operation of the lien avoidance rules of § 522(f)(1). First, the debtor can only "avoid the *fixing* of a lien on an interest of the debtor in property."[206] According to the Supreme Court in *Farrey v. Sanderfoot*,[207] the fixing requirement permits the debtor to avoid a lien only if the debtor had an interest in the property *before* the lien was affixed to the property. The second critical characteristic of avoidance under § 522(f)(1) is that the debtor may only avoid the lien to the extent that lien impairs an exemption to which the debtor otherwise would have been entitled.[208] The import of the "would have been entitled" formulation as it pertains to the effect of a state's choice to "opt out" of the federal exemptions was explained by the Supreme Court in 1991 in *Owen v. Owen*.[209] In the 1994 Amendments, Congress clarified some uncertainties in the computation of the extent of impairment of the lien. § 522(f)(2).

Subsection (f) is not the only avoidance provision in § 522, although it is by far the most important. Under subsection (h), a debtor is permitted to step into the shoes of the trustee and bring actions to avoid transfers or recover a setoff that the trustee chooses not to pursue. The debtor's substituted avoiding power under § 522(h) is limited to the extent that the debtor can exempt the property avoided or recovered. The avoidance rule of § 522(h) is necessary to give full effect to the debtor's exemption rights, because the trustee will not have much incentive as the representative of the estate to avoid a transfer and recover property if the debtor then will exempt the recovered property.

Other provisions in § 522 give the debtor supplementary rights to claim exemptions in property that has been recovered after avoidance by the debtor under subsections (f) or (h), or by the trustee under any of the trustee's avoiding powers. Under subsection (g), the debtor may exempt property that is recovered by the trustee, but only if the transfer that the trustee avoided was involuntary as to the debtor (such

---

[204] See § 9.13.

[205] See § 9.12.

[206] Scc § 9.8.

[207] 500 U.S. 291 (1991).

[208] See § 9.9.

[209] 500 U.S. 305 (1991).

as by the fixing of a judicial lien), and the debtor did not conceal the property. Subsection (i) gives the debtor the powers (1) to recover property after avoidance by the debtor, and (2) to claim exemptions in the recovered property. These supplementary exemption rules in § 522(g) and (i) must be applied in conjunction with the general grant of exemptions in § 522(b). § 522(j). In other words, additional exemptions will only be permitted under subsections (g) and (i) to the extent the debtor has not claimed the full amount of exemptions available under subsection (b).

§ 9.8   "Fixing" of Liens and *Farrey*

The power given to the debtor to avoid liens in § 522(f) is subject to two general restrictions:

- the debtor may avoid the "*fixing* of a lien on an interest of the debtor in property," and

- the lien may be avoided only "to the extent that such lien impairs an exemption to which the debtor would have been entitled."

This section discusses the "fixing" requirement, and the next section analyzes impairment. The Supreme Court has given interpretive assistance with regard to both questions, in two decisions handed down on exactly the same day in 1991.[210] In *Farrey v. Sanderfoot*,[211] the Court held that the "fixing" provision requires the debtor to have had an interest in the subject property *before* the lien attached. In *Owen v. Owen*,[212] the Court held that the "would have been entitled" language refers to the hypothetical state of affairs that would exist if there were no lien. That ruling effectively prevents states from defining away the lien avoidance rules in § 522(f) by how they characterize the exemption entitlement in the context of a lien.

The *Farrey* case involved a debtor's attempt to avoid a lien that had been granted to his ex-wife in a state court divorce decree. This situation had arisen with some frequency prior to *Farrey*, with the courts reaching inconsistent results. In the division of the marital property, the Wisconsin divorce court awarded the husband, Gerald Sanderfoot, most of the couple's marital assets, including their home. In return, he was ordered to pay half the value of the property (about $29,000) to the wife, Jeanne Farrey. To secure his obligation to his ex-wife, the court ordered that a lien be placed on the marital residence for the amount of the debt.

Sanderfoot never paid Farrey a penny. Instead, he sought to use bankruptcy as a convenient tool to escape his obligations. He filed chapter 7, claimed the homestead as exempt under Wisconsin law to the extent of $40,000, and sought to avoid Farrey's lien

---

[210] For an interesting article discussing these cases, see C. Robert Morris, Bankrupt Fantasy: The Site of Missing Words and the Order of Illusory Events, 45 Ark. L. Rev. 265 (1992). The two cases also are discussed in Charles Jordan Tabb & Robert M. Lawless, Of Commas, Gerunds, and Conjunctions: The Bankruptcy Jurisprudence of the Rehnquist Court, 42 Syracuse L. Rev. 823, 866–73 (1991).

[211] 500 U.S. 291 (1991).

[212] 500 U.S. 305 (1991).

under § 522(f)(1).[213] He argued that her lien was a "judicial lien" which impaired his homestead exemption, and thus under the plain language of the statute was avoidable. The Seventh Circuit agreed with Sanderfoot,[214] although Judge Posner dissented, lamenting that the result contravened "layman's justice."[215]

Other courts had reached a different result than the Seventh Circuit, denying avoidance. One view was that the lien did not attach to an interest of the debtor in property, but rather was a means of protecting the non-debtor spouse's own preexisting interest in the marital property.[216] In other words, the lien was in the nature of an equitable charge, attributable to and in compensation for the non-debtor's own interest. In essence, the divorce decree simply partitioned the property of the divorcing spouses.[217]

Another rationale for denying avoidance was to reject the threshold assertion that the marital lien was a "judicial" lien at all.[218] Although technically imposed pursuant to a court order, in substance the lien in favor of the non-debtor spouse was more like a *consensual* lien. Consensual liens cannot be avoided under § 522(f)(1)(A). Gerald Sanderfoot essentially purchased Jeanne Farrey's half interest in the marital home, and gave her a mortgage to secure the debt, albeit at the court's instigation. If, instead of imposing the lien directly pursuant to the divorce decree, the court had ordered Sanderfoot to execute a mortgage, the inappropriateness of attempting lien avoidance would have been more evident, although the substance of the arrangement would not have been any different.

The Supreme Court reversed the Seventh Circuit, and held that the lien in Farrey's favor could *not be avoided* under § 522(f)(1).[219] The ex-wife did not contest the conclusion that the lien was properly classified as a "judicial" lien, and thus the Court did not address that question.[220] As an alternative basis for its holding, the Court adopted the view that Farrey's lien fastened only to what had been her preexisting interest.[221]

The heart of the Court's reasoning, however, focused on the statutory grammar and issues of timing. The exact language of the statute is that "the debtor may avoid the fixing of a lien on an interest of the debtor in property." Justice White explained what the Court thought this language meant:

---

[213] Note that the section allowing the avoidance of judicial liens that impair exemptions has been renumbered from § 522(f)(1) to § 522(f)(1)(A).

[214] 899 F.2d 598 (7th Cir., 1990), rev'd, 500 U.S. 291 (1991).

[215] Id. at 607 (Posner, J., dissenting).

[216] See, e.g., Boyd v. Robinson, 741 F.2d 1112 (8th Cir. 1984); see also Parker v. Donahue, 862 F.2d 259 (10th Cir. 1989). This was the approach taken by the Bankruptcy Court in *Farrey*. 83 B.R. 564 (Bankr. E.D. Wis. 1988).

[217] See Morris, supra note 210, at 284–85.

[218] See, e.g., In re McCormmach, 111 B.R. 330 (Bankr. D. Ore. 1990).

[219] *Farrey*, supra note 211, 500 U.S. at 292.

[220] Id. at 295.

[221] Id. at 300. Justice Scalia did not join in that conclusion. Id. at 300 n.4.

[T]he statute expressly states that the debtor may avoid "the fixing" of a lien on the debtor's interest in property. The gerund "fixing" refers to a temporal event. That event—the fastening of a liability—presupposes an object onto which the liability can fasten. The statute defines this pre-existing object as "an interest of the debtor in property." Therefore, unless the debtor had the property interest to which the lien attached at some point before the lien attached to that interest, he or she cannot avoid the fixing of the lien under the terms of § 522(f)(1).[222]

Relying on misguided legislative history regarding the purpose of the judicial lien avoiding power,[223] the Court stated that its interpretation of the statute was consistent with the policy of countering the effects of a race to the courthouse, since no such race had taken place here.[224]

Having concluded that the debtor may only avoid a lien under § 522(f) if the debtor had an interest in the property *before* the lien attached, the Court then applied its newly-announced legal rule. Did the debtor have an interest in the property now subject to the ex-wife's lien before that lien attached? The Court held that he did not.[225] Looking at applicable state law and the terms of the divorce decree, the Court concluded that the decree extinguished the preexisting interests of both parties in the home, and replaced them with new interests: fee simple ownership for the debtor, and a secured claim for the non-debtor. Since these interests were created simultaneously, the debtor did not have the preexisting interest required for avoidance under § 522(f)(1).[226]

The Court's reasoning is most unfortunate. Justice White makes an unexplained and unsupported logical leap from the unremarkable proposition that the statute "presupposes an object onto which the liability can fasten" to the radical conclusion that this object must be *preexisting*. In doing so, the Court ignored the nature of lien attachment and unnecessarily limited the reach of the exemption lien-avoiding power in the context of after-acquired liens. Preliminarily (and irrelevantly), the Court was correct in observing that a lien may not be avoided under § 522(f) when that lien attached to the property *before* the debtor acquired an interest in the property.[227]

But the Court failed to explain why a lien cannot "fix" on the debtor's interest in property when the lien and the debtor's interest arise *at the same time*. As one court of appeals judge explained prior to *Farrey*, in a simultaneous creation situation the lien must have fixed on the debtor's interest; indeed, no one else has an interest in the property.[228] In cases ranging from tax liens, to judgment liens, to after-acquired property clauses in personal property security interests, it is commonplace for a creditor's lien to "fix" on a debtor's interest in property at the very instant the debtor

---

[222] Id. at 296.

[223] See § 9.10 for a discussion of the purposes of the judicial lien avoiding power, and an explanation of why the accompanying legislative history makes no sense.

[224] *Farrey*, 500 U.S. at 300–01.

[225] Id. at 299–301.

[226] Id. at 299–300.

[227] See id. at 298–99.

[228] See *Boyd*, supra note 7, 741 F.2d at 1115 (Ross, J., dissenting).

acquires the interest. Under the Court's reasoning in *Farrey*, however, in all of these types of cases a debtor will not be able to avoid the simultaneous lien, because the debtor did not have a *prior* interest.[229] The Court did not in any way limit its logic to the unique case of liens in divorce decrees. This substantial gap in the lien avoidance power will weaken the exemption rights of debtors.

Ironically, however, the Court's approach failed to afford complete protection to non-debtor spouses even in the special case of divorce decrees.[230] Jeanne Farrey prevailed only because of the Court's conclusion that the divorce decree extinguished Gerald Sanderfoot's prior interest and created a new interest in its place. However, the Court could have interpreted the divorce decree in the following way: as (1) allowing Sanderfoot to retain his existing half interest in the home; (2) conveying Farrey's half interest to him; and (3) giving Farrey a lien on the entire property. Under this reading, the Court's own approach would allow the debtor to avoid the half of Farrey's lien that "fixed" on his preexisting interest.

In 1994 Congress attempted a partial cure for the special problem of judicial liens in divorce decrees. In § 522(f)(1)(A), Congress carved out from the category of voidable judicial liens those liens that secure a nondischargeable debt to a spouse, former spouse or child for alimony, maintenance, or support. In 2005 this exclusion was amended to encompass judicial liens that secure any debt of the kind specified in § 523(a)(5), thereby removing the requirement that the debt be payable *to* the spouse, former spouse, or child to qualify for the exclusion, and further bringing assigned debts of the requisite "kind" within the exclusion. The 1994 and 2005 amendments were part of packages of provisions intended to strengthen the protection of these types of family support debts. However, neither the 1994 nor the 2005 amendment contradicts the basic reasoning of *Farrey*. The *Farrey* requirement for avoidance that the debtor have an interest in property before the challenged lien affixes to the property remains unaffected. Thus, all types of after-acquired liens in which creation of the lien is simultaneous with the debtor's acquisition of the property remain unavoidable under § 522(f)(1).

§ 9.9   Impairment of Exemptions

The debtor's power to avoid liens of the types described in § 522(f)(1) is not unlimited. Since the purpose of the avoiding power is to preserve the debtor's entitlement to his or her exemptions, avoidance is permitted only to the extent that the challenged lien "impairs an exemption to which the debtor would have been entitled." This statutory language has generated two sets of related issues: (1) how to calculate the extent of impairment, and (2) the significance of the "would have been entitled" clause.

---

[229] See Morris, supra note 210, at 289–92.

[230] The concurring Justices recognized this problem. *Farrey*, supra note 211, 500 U.S. at 302–04 (Kennedy, J., concurring).

a.   *The Extent of Impairment*

Calculating the extent that a lien impairs an exemption is not as simple as might appear at first blush. To make the impairment computation, the court must know whether to give effect to the *actual* state of affairs with all the liens in place, or the *hypothetical* state of affairs that would exist without the challenged lien. This issue implicates the meaning of the "would have been entitled" language, discussed below.

Prior to 1994, the courts reached conflicting results in a variety of situations. Looking at the actual state of affairs, a minority of courts denied or limited avoidance on the ground that the debtor's exemption rights were not impaired by the lien or were only partially impaired.[231] Fortunately, in the 1994 Amendments Congress cleared up much of the confusion by enacting § 522(f)(2), which provides the formula to determine the extent to which a lien may be avoided. The legislative history to subsection (f)(2) is quite helpful.[232] The 1994 Amendment adopted a hypothetical test, explained below.

Section 522(f)(2) utilizes an arithmetic test to calculate the extent of impairment. Under this test,

A lien impairs an exemption to the extent that:

> A.   *The sum of:*
>
> > *(i) the challenged lien +*
> >
> > *(ii) all other liens on the property +*
> >
> > *(iii) the amount of the exemption the debtor could claim if there were no liens*
>
> *exceeds*
>
> B.   *The value that the debtor's interest in the property would have in the absence of any liens.*

Consider some examples. In each, assume that Debtor's homestead, Homeacre, has a value of $80,000 in the absence of any liens. The applicable homestead exemption is provided by § 522(d)(1), which (as of 2013) allows an individual debtor to exempt $22,975. The challenged judicial lien secures a debt of $30,000. There also is an unavoidable mortgage on Homeacre, which is senior to all other liens. The amount of the debt secured by this first mortgage varies in the following examples, to illustrate the different applications of § 522(f)(2).

---

[231] See, e.g., In re Simonson, 758 F.2d 103 (3d Cir. 1985). See also In re Chabot, 992 F.2d 891 (9th Cir. 1992).

[232] See Bankruptcy Reform Act of 1994, Section-by-Section Description, § 303, 140 Cong. Rec. H10,769–70 (Oct. 4, 1994). The amendment adopted a simple arithmetic test in a decision, In re Brantz, 106 B.R. 62 (Bankr. E.D. Pa. 1989), that was cited favorably by the Supreme Court in Owen v. Owen, 500 U.S. 305, 313 n.5 (1991).

Example One

The senior mortgage secures a debt of $80,000. In other words, Debtor has no equity in Homeacre over and above the unavoidable first mortgage, and as of the time of the bankruptcy case the judicial lien is valueless. Prior to 1994, some courts had held that, since the Debtor had no equity, Debtor in actuality had no exemptible homestead interest, and thus the judicial lien did not impair an exemption to which the Debtor would have been entitled. The problem, though, is that this outcome left the judicial lien in place on Homeacre, and any equity the Debtor subsequently acquired in Homeacre after bankruptcy (either by appreciation in the realty or by making payments on the senior mortgage debt) would be captured by the still-intact judicial lien. In effect, the judicial lien impairs the debtor's homestead exemption *prospectively*. After the 1994 clarification, there is no question that under § 522(f)(2), the judicial lien can be avoided in its entirety.

Application of the formula in § 522(f)(2) to Example One is as follows:

[Sum of (i) challenged lien ($30,000) + (ii) all other liens ($80,000) + (iii) exemption ($22,975)] = $132,975

exceeds

[value of debtor's interest absent any liens] = $80,000

*Impairment = **$52,975*** ($132,975 minus $80,000).

Since the judicial lien impairs the exemption by an amount in excess of the amount of the lien, the entire judicial lien can be avoided. Now, if the debtor in the future acquires equity in Homeacre, as, for example, by making mortgage payments, that equity interest will be free of the now-avoided judicial lien.

Example Two

The senior mortgage secures a debt of $57,025. In this example, the Debtor has equity, and the judicial lien is partially secured. In a case like this, some courts prior to 1994 held that the Debtor could only avoid $22,975 of the judicial lien (i.e., the extent the exemption actually is impaired).[233] However, this left the judicial lien partially intact, and exposed the Debtor's post-bankruptcy equity to the judicial lien.

Under § 522(f)(2), added in 1994, the judicial lien again can be totally avoided, as follows:

[Sum of (i) challenged lien ($30,000) + (ii) all other liens ($57,025) + (iii) exemption ($22,975)] = $110,000

exceeds

[value of debtor's interest absent any liens] = $80,000

---

[233] See, e.g., *Chabot*, supra note 231, 992 F.2d 891.

Impairment = $30,000 ($110,000 minus $80,000).

Since the extent of impairment is equal to the amount of the judicial lien, that judicial lien can be avoided in full.

Example Three

The senior mortgage secures a debt of $40,000. In this example, the Debtor has equity and, but for the exemption, the judicial lien would be fully secured. In this situation only part of the judicial lien will be avoidable, as follows:

[Sum of (i) challenged lien ($30,000) + (ii) all other liens ($40,000) + (iii) exemption ($22,975)] = $92,975

exceeds

[value of debtor's interest absent any liens] = $80,000

Impairment = $12,975 ($92,975 minus $80,000).

In this third example, only $12,975 of the judicial lien can be avoided (thus leaving $17,025 intact). The intuitive correctness of this result can be seen by examining what would happen without avoidance. The $80,000 property would be subject to liens of $40,000 (first mortgage) and $30,000 (judicial lien), for a total of $70,000, leaving $10,000 for the debtor to claim as exempt. This $10,000 exemption is $12,975 less than the maximum homestead exemption of $22,975.

Example Four

The senior mortgage secures a debt of $50,000, and is followed in priority by the $30,000 judicial lien *and* an unavoidable second mortgage securing a debt of $30,000. In this situation, then, the Debtor would not have any equity in the property even if the judicial lien were avoided, because of the presence of the unavoidable second mortgage. Again, some courts prior to 1994 looked only at the actual state of affairs, and, finding no impairment, did not avoid the judicial lien.[234] This result too was changed by § 522(f)(2), as follows:

[Sum of (i) challenged lien ($30,000) + (ii) all other liens ($80,000, i.e., $50,000 first mortgage + $30,000 second mortgage) + (iii) exemption ($22,975)] = $132,975

exceeds

[value of debtor's interest absent any liens] = $80,000

Impairment = $52,975 ($132,975 minus $80,000).

Since the extent of impairment exceeds the amount of the judicial lien, the entire judicial lien is avoided. What will happen is that the amount of the avoided judicial

---

[234] See *Simonson*, supra note 231, 758 F.2d 103.

lien will be *preserved* for the benefit of the Debtor, § 522(i)(2), allowing the Debtor to claim the full $22,975 homestead exemption, § 522(i)(1). After this sequence of events, the $80,000 value in Homeacre will be allocated as follows: (1) the first $50,000 to the unavoidable first mortgage; (2) the next $22,975 to the Debtor as exempt property; and (3) the $7,025 balance to the unavoidable second mortgage. In effect the Debtor steps into the shoes of the avoided judicial lien and claims an exemption out of that amount.

Example Five

Debtor claims the homestead as exempt under *state* exemption law, which allows an *unlimited* homestead exemption. Under state law, a judicial lien that arises after the homestead is established attaches to the property but is simply *unenforceable* against the property while it maintains its homestead character. Does the existence of an unenforceable judicial lien "impair" the Debtor's exemption?

The courts took different positions prior to 1994. One view was that the judicial lien did not deprive the Debtor of any rights under state law, could not be enforced while the property remained a homestead, and thus did not impair any exemption.[235] The competing view held that the debtor's exemption was impaired, because of the cloud on title attributable to the judicial lien.[236] Under the arithmetic test of § 522(f)(2), the latter view will control. The judicial lien is counted in the computation of impairment without regard to its present enforceability.

b. *"Would Have Been Entitled"*

The preceding discussion demonstrates that the meaning of "impairment" must be considered in the context of the exemptions "to which the debtor would have been entitled." That statutory language naturally leads to the question, "would have been entitled *but for what?*"[237] An important interpretive dispute under § 522(f) was whether the "would have been entitled" test is to be applied in the context of the *actual* situation or some *hypothetical* state of affairs. If the actual situation governs, in a variety of scenarios the debtor will not be able to avoid a lien, because the debtor will not have an exemption.

One such case is where the dollar amounts of all of the liens on the property, if unavoided, would leave the debtor without an exemptible interest. As discussed above, the addition of § 522(f)(2) in 1994 resolved this problem in the debtor's favor, mandating the use of a hypothetical test.

The second common situation in which the "would have been entitled" language has proven important is where the state has "opted out" of the federal exemptions (thereby limiting resident debtors to available state exemptions), and also has *defined* the available state exemptions so that the extent of the debtor's exemption rights is limited by the liens. The creditor then will argue that the question of impairment should be judged in light of the debtor's actual exemptions, as limited by the liens,

---

[235] See, e.g., In re Sanders, 39 F.3d 258 (10th Cir. 1994).

[236] See In re Henderson, 18 F.3d 1305 (5th Cir. 1994).

[237] See *Owen*, supra note 232, 500 U.S. at 311.

which invariably would dictate that avoidance should be denied. In other words, the creditor would assert that the *actual* impact of the liens on the subject property should be given full effect *before* considering the impairment issue.

For example, many states define a debtor's exemptions in terms of the value of the debtor's net interest in property. The value of the debtor's interest, in turn, is defined as the *equity* the debtor has in the property *after* taking valid liens into account. For example, assume that the state exemption law allows a debtor to exempt "$5,000 in 'value' in any personal property," and further provides that "*value* is the fair market value of the debtor's interest in the property, less the amount of any valid liens on that property." Assume also that the state has opted out of the federal exemptions.

Assume further that (1) Debtor has personal property valued at $5,000, without taking liens into account, and (2) Creditor has a nonpossessory, nonpurchase-money security interest in that property, of the type listed in § 522(f)(1)(B), to secure a debt of $7,000. Creditor would argue (1) that the "value" of the property under the state exemption law is *zero* (since the secured debt exceeds the fair market value of the property); (2) that the amount of Debtor's available exemption under state law therefore also is zero; (3) Debtor thus has no exemption at all which is being "impaired" by the security interest; and (4) avoidance therefore cannot be ordered under § 522(f)(1). Prior to 1991, some courts agreed with this line of reasoning,[238] although others did not.[239]

A second line of cases held for the creditor in these situations, based on a probable misreading of the meaning of the state's exemption law. In these cases, the courts interpreted the state law to provide that property that is subject to a lien is not exempt *at all*.[240] While in theory a state could so provide in its exemption law, the more likely meaning of the state law is that the property is exempt, but the particular lienholder may enforce its lien against the otherwise exempt property.

The dispositive question in all of these state exemption cases is whether the impairment issue should be considered in light of the *actual* or *hypothetical* state of affairs. If actual, the lien will first be given effect, and then the debtor will not have an exemption, and impairment will not be found. If, however, the court considers the hypothetical situation that would exist if there were no liens on the property in determining if the debtor has an exemption, impairment will be found. In the above example, without the $7,000 security interest, the Debtor would have been able to claim a $5,000 personal property exemption under state law. Under a hypothetical test, then, the Creditor's security interest could be avoided under § 522(f)(1)(B).

The Supreme Court settled the debate in 1991 in *Owen v. Owen*[241] in favor of the debtor, finding that impairment must be determined under a *hypothetical* test. The "would have been entitled *but for what*" question was answered by the Court to mean

---

[238] See, e.g., In re Pine, 717 F.2d 281 (6th Cir. 1983).
[239] See In re Leonard, 866 F.2d 335 (10th Cir. 1989).
[240] See, e.g., In re McManus, 681 F.2d 353 (5th Cir. 1982).
[241] 500 U.S. 305 (1991).

"would have been entitled *but for the lien at issue.*"[242] Even if state exemption law defines away a debtor's exemption rights in the context of a lien, the federal avoidance rule in § 522(f)(1) controls. The irony, though, is that *Owen* was the wrong case, on the facts, to decide this issue. The real problem in *Owen* was one of timing, not whether a state that has opted out may define the nature of the exemption in a way that defeats lien avoidance. And, to add to the irony, the timing problem in *Owen* apparently was controlled by the Court's decision in *Farrey v. Sanderfoot*,[243] handed down the very same day.

Owen, like *Farrey,* involved a deadbeat husband's attempt to avoid a judicial lien in favor of his ex-wife. Helen Owen obtained a judgment for $160,000 against Dwight Owen, her former husband, and recorded the judgment in Sarasota County, Florida. At the time of recordation, the debtor did not own any real property in that county. Eight years later, he purchased a condominium in the county. Because of the after-acquired nature of judgment liens,[244] Helen's judgment lien attached to Dwight's interest in the condominium at the exact instant that he acquired the property. At that time, the Florida exemption law did not allow a debtor to claim a condominium as an exempt homestead. Later, Florida amended its homestead exemption law to include condominiums within its coverage. Florida law also provided, however, that a homestead exemption could not displace a preexisting lien on property that attached before the property acquired homestead status. Thus, under Florida law, (1) the debtor would be able to claim the condominium as an exempt homestead, (2) but the ex-wife's judgment lien could still be enforced against the property, notwithstanding the exemption.

The debtor then filed bankruptcy and sought to avoid his ex-wife's lien under what is now § 522(f)(1)(A). Helen argued that her lien did not impair an exemption to which the debtor "would have been entitled," on the ground that the debtor was not entitled under the applicable state exemption law to enforce the exemption as against her preexisting lien. Since Florida had opted out of the federal exemptions, only Florida exemption law was available to the debtor. The Eleventh Circuit agreed with Helen.[245]

The Supreme Court reversed and remanded.[246] Justice Scalia for the Court concluded that the "would have been entitled" language in § 522(f)(1) requires consideration of what exemptions the debtor would have been entitled to "but for the lien at issue."[247] Since the debtor would have been entitled to claim a homestead exemption in the condominium but for his ex-wife's judgment lien, the ex-wife could not rely on the state's exclusion of her lien from the force of his homestead as a basis for escaping avoidance under § 522(f)(1).[248] Once a state creates a homestead exemption, the state cannot then limit the scope of lien avoidance under § 522(f)(1) by further providing that the exemption is not valid as against liens that otherwise could

---

[242] Id. at 311–12.

[243] 500 U.S. 291 (1991). See § 9.8.

[244] See § 1.3.c.

[245] 877 F.2d 44 (11th Cir. 1989), rev'd, 500 U.S. 305 (1991).

[246] 500 U.S. 305 (1991).

[247] Id. at 311.

[248] Id. at 313–14.

be avoided (here, preexisting liens). In short, a state under the guise of opt-out cannot define away § 522(f) lien avoidance.

This holding settled the hypothetical-versus-actual debate in interpreting when a lien impairs an exemption to which the debtor would have been entitled. A hypothetical analysis is to be used. However, in *Owen* the majority of the Court failed to discern that the real issue in that case was whether avoidance should be allowed when the creditor's lien attaches to the property *before* the property was exempt.[249] This was not a case where the state tried to define away an existing exemption right. As Justice Stevens explained in dissent, the proper approach would have been to use a hypothetical test, but to apply that test at the time the lien attached to the property.[250] As it stands, though, for purposes of the "would have been entitled" test, the hypothetical analysis will be applied at the time of the bankruptcy filing, irrespective of the order in which the lien and the exemption arose.

Timing, though, still matters in some situations. Indeed, the ultimate outcome in *Owen* was controlled by the Court's reasoning in *Farrey v. Sanderfoot*.[251] *Farrey* held that a lien may only be avoided under § 522(f)(1) if it fixed on the debtor's interest in property, meaning that the debtor must have an interest in the property *before* the lien attaches. The *Owen* Court remanded for a consideration of the fixing question.[252] Here, however, since the judgment lien and the debtor's interest arose at the same instant, the lower court on remand held that the debtor did not have a prior interest, the "fixing" requirement of *Farrey* was not satisfied, and Helen's lien was not avoidable.[253]

The reasoning of *Owen* can, however, lead to avoidance of a lien under § 522(f)(1) in some cases where the exemption postdates the lien. For example, assume that (1) the debtor in *Owen* had owned the condominium *before* his ex-wife's judicial lien attached; (2) when that lien attached the property was not exempt; (3) the state then changed the law to permit the exemption of the property; and (4) the debtor then filed bankruptcy and sought to avoid the lien. Since the debtor had an interest in the property prior to the attachment of the lien, *Farrey's* "fixing" requirement would be satisfied. Under *Owen*, application of the hypothetical "would have been entitled" test as of the time of bankruptcy leads to the conclusion that the debtor would have been entitled to claim a homestead exemption but for the judicial lien. Thus, the judicial lien may be avoided. No bankruptcy policy, though, supports avoidance in this situation, where the creditor obtained a lien on the property before the property was exempt.

§ 9.10   Judicial Liens

To assist debtors in realizing the full benefit of their exemption rights, Congress in § 522(f) gave debtors the power to avoid certain types of liens that impair

---

[249] Only Justice Stevens in dissent noted the importance of the distinction between antecedent and subsequent liens. Id. at 314–15.

[250] Id. at 321.

[251] 500 U.S. 291 (1991). See also § 9.8.

[252] 500 U.S. 305, 314 (1991).

[253] See In re Owen, 961 F.2d 170 (11th Cir. 1992).

exemptions.[254] The preceding two sections discussed two aspects of this lien avoidance power: first, that a debtor may only avoid the "fixing of a lien on an interest of the debtor in property;"[255] and second, that avoidance is permitted only to the extent that the lien impairs an exemption to which the debtor would have been entitled.[256] Subject to these rules, two types of liens may be avoided under § 522(f)(1): (1) judicial liens, other than liens securing domestic support obligations (discussed in this section), § 522(f)(1)(A); and (2) nonpossessory, nonpurchase-money security interests in described types of personal collateral (discussed in the next section), § 522(f)(1)(B).[257]

A "judicial lien" is defined as a "lien obtained by judgment, levy, sequestration, or other legal or equitable proceeding."[258] § 101(36). For example, an execution lien or a judgment lien obtained by a judgment creditor against property of the judgment debtor would be classified as a judicial lien.

The reason for the lien avoidance power with regard to judicial liens is somewhat difficult to fathom. The legislative history explanation is:

> The debtor may void any judicial lien on exempt property . . . The first right allows the debtor to undo the actions of creditors that bring legal action against the debtor shortly before bankruptcy. Bankruptcy exists to provide relief for an overburdened debtor. If a creditor beats the debtor into court, the debtor is nevertheless entitled to his exemptions.[259]

This explanation makes no sense. The trustee's power to avoid preferences (which the debtor can invoke if the trustee does not, § 522(h)) already remedies the problem of the "rush to the courthouse."[260] § 547. If the creditor obtains a judicial lien against the debtor's exempt property within 90 days of the bankruptcy filing, that lien can be avoided under § 547. Even though involuntary, the fixing of the judicial lien is still considered a "transfer" under the Bankruptcy Code.[261] § 101(54). While one might question as a normative matter whether a transfer of *exempt* property is the sort of property transfer that should be implicated by the preference laws, which are concerned primarily with the relative distributional rights between creditors, the courts nevertheless have held that transfers of exempt property are subject to avoidance under § 547.[262]

If the power to avoid judicial liens that impair exemptions is not predicated on a need to reverse the outcome of a pre-bankruptcy race of diligence, then what purpose does § 522(f)(1)(A) serve? The puzzle deepens when one considers that in most states a judicial lien will not even attach to exempt property in the first place. For example, to

---

[254] See § 9.7.

[255] See § 9.8.

[256] See § 9.9.

[257] See § 9.11.

[258] See § 1.3.

[259] II.R. Rep. No. 95–595, 95th Cong., 1st Sess., at 126–27 (1977).

[260] See § 6.7.

[261] See § 6.10.

[262] See § 6.11.

the extent a debtor has established a homestead exemption, a judgment lien will not attach to the homestead. The immunity from judicial liens is one of the defining attributes of what it means for property to be exempt. Thus, the problem supposedly remedied by § 522(f)(1)(A) will not even occur in the normal course of events.

One possible key to the puzzle of the role of judicial lien avoidance is the non-uniformity of the nature of state exemption laws. While judicial liens do not attach to exempt property at all in many states, they do attach to exempt property in some jurisdictions. In those states, the lien attaches, but simply is not enforceable by foreclosure as long as the property retains its exempt character. In those states, then, there would be a judicial lien on exempt property that could be avoided under § 522(f)(1)(A).

Avoidance in bankruptcy could be an important protection for the debtor in this situation if the state law provides that the exemption insulates a debtor's equity in the property only in the event of a *forced* execution sale and *not* in the event of a *voluntary* sale. Some state exemption laws treat a voluntary sale of exempt property as equivalent to an abandonment of the exemption. If so, the creditor's judicial lien will attach to the debtor's property *and* will follow the property into the hands of a purchaser, unless satisfied from proceeds of the sale. Absent avoidance of the lien, the debtor could not sell the exempt property after bankruptcy unless he paid "the lienholder out of equity that should have been protected as exempt property."[263] By permitting a bankruptcy debtor to avoid such an exemption-impairing judicial lien, § 522(f)(1)(A) preserves the full amount of the debtor's state exemption from *any* subsequent sale of the homestead property, whether involuntary *or* voluntary.

Another situation in which a judicial lien could encumber otherwise exempt property relates to the temporal ordering of (1) the attachment of the lien and (2) the exempting of the debtor's property. The chronology contemplated by the legislative history is for the debtor to have the property first, unencumbered by the judicial lien, with the judicial lien attaching later. As explained above, in most states the judicial lien will not even attach to previously exempt property. The judicial lien could attach to the property, however, if the lien came *first*, i.e., if the lien attached, and then the property acquired exempt status. This could occur either (1) if property already encumbered by a judicial lien was conveyed to the debtor, who sought to claim the property as exempt, or (2) if the debtor owned nonexempt property and a judicial lien attached to the property while it was nonexempt, but later the property became eligible for exemption due to an amendment in the governing exemption law. The latter situation is what occurred in *Owen v. Owen*.[264] In the former event, the Supreme Court's decision in *Farrey v. Sanderfoot*,[265] which interpreted § 522(f) to require the debtor to have an interest in the property *before* the lien "fixed," would eliminate the possibility of avoidance.

---

[263] 140 Cong. Rec. H10752–01 (1994) (statement of Rep. Jack Brooks, Chairman of the Judiciary Committee).

[264] 500 U.S. 305 (1991). Florida amended its homestead laws after the debtor had acquired the property and the judicial lien had attached, to provide for the first time that a condominium could be exempted as a homestead. See § 9.9.

[265] 500 U.S. 291 (1991). See § 9.8.

The final situation in which § 522(f)(1)(A) could have an effect, and the one that perhaps best explains why Congress included the judicial lien avoidance provision in § 522(f), is where the bankruptcy debtor elects the *federal* exemptions under § 522(b)(2) and (d). Of course, the debtor can only make that election if the state has not opted out of the federal scheme, § 522(b)(2), and 34 states had opted out as of 2013. The debtor would want to make that election if the federal exemptions were more favorable than the state exemptions. Indeed, Congress included the federal scheme of exemptions (at the behest of the House) because of a concern about the inadequacy of state exemption laws.[266]

The federal bankruptcy exemptions of course are not operative *prior* to the initiation of a bankruptcy case. To the extent that the state exemption law that was in effect prior to bankruptcy did not protect property of the debtor that would be exempt under § 522(d), a judicial lien could attach to the property before bankruptcy. For example, if the debtor resided in a state that does not provide a homestead exemption, a judicial lien could attach to the debtor's home prior to bankruptcy. In bankruptcy, though, the debtor would want to exempt up to $22,975 in the homestead under § 522(d)(1). Avoidance of the judicial lien that had previously attached to the homestead under state law then would be necessary to give full effect to the federal exemptions provided in § 522(d).

§ 9.11 Nonpossessory, Nonpurchase–Money Security Interests in "Leverage" Collateral

In the 1978 Bankruptcy Code Congress gave debtors the power to avoid two types of liens that impair exemptions. § 522(f)(1). As discussed in the preceding section, the reason for authorizing the avoidance of judicial liens in § 522(f)(1)(A) is not entirely clear, and the explanation given in the legislative history does not make sense.[267] The same cannot be said for the second lien avoidance provision. The purpose behind § 522(f)(1)(B), which allows the avoidance of nonpossessory, nonpurchase-money security interests in various types of personal collateral, is quite clear and does make sense. Congress wanted to stop an abusive creditor practice that was depriving debtors of the full benefit of their exemptions. The problem is that the statutory language adopted implements the stated purpose only imperfectly.

Liens may be enforced against exempt property, unless avoided.[268] § 522(c)(2). Under pre-Code law, creditors often took advantage of superior bargaining power or debtor ignorance to obtain comprehensive security interests on virtually everything the debtor owned. In short, these "consensual" liens bordered on being contracts of adhesion. Indeed, the Federal Trade Commission decided that it was an unfair trade practice for a creditor to take nonpossessory, nonpurchase-money security interests in household goods and similar items. These global security interests covered household goods and furnishings, wearing apparel, appliances, and other personal consumer items.

---

[266] See H.R. Rep. No. 95–595, 95th Cong., 1st Sess., at 126 (1977).

[267] See § 9.10.

[268] See § 9.4.

The primary value of the security interest in such personal goods to the creditor was not the monetary value that the collateral might bring upon foreclosure, but the *leverage* that the *threat* of repossession and sale gave the creditor.[269] While the creditor might not get much money from selling all of the debtor's clothes and pots and pans, the debtor certainly would not want to have their home and closets cleaned out. The prospective cost and inconvenience to the debtor to replace everything put enormous pressure on the debtor to reaffirm its debt to the creditor. Congress sought to stamp out this abusive tactic by authorizing the debtor in § 522(f)(1)(B)[270] to avoid these security interests to the extent they impair the debtor's exemptions.

To avoid a security interest under § 522(f)(1)(B), the debtor must show:

1. The security interest was fixed on an interest of the debtor in property (the temporal requirement);[271]

2. The security interest impairs an exemption to which the debtor would have been entitled;[272]

3. The security interest is not possessory;

4. The security interest is not "purchase-money"; and

5. The collateral is one of the following types of exempt property:

    A. "Household furnishings, household goods, wearing apparel, appliances, books, animals, crops, musical instruments, or jewelry held primarily for the personal, family, or household use of the debtor" or a dependent.[273] § 522(f)(1)(B)(i).

    B. "Implements, professional books, or tools, of the trade of the debtor or the trade of a dependent."[274] § 522(f)(1)(B)(ii).

    C. "Professionally prescribed health aids for the debtor or a dependent."[275] § 522(f)(1)(B)(iii).

The first two elements of avoidance, fixing and impairment, are discussed in previous sections. The provision that only *nonpossessory* security interests may be avoided refers to *possession by the secured party*. In other words, if the debtor has possession of the collateral, as is almost invariably the case, this element is satisfied.

---

[269] H.R. Rep. No. 95–595, 95th Cong., 1st Sess., at 126–28 (1977). See also United States v. Sec. Indus. Bank, 459 U.S. 70, 84 (1982) (Blackmun, J., concurring).

[270] As originally enacted, this avoiding power was codified in § 522(f)(2). In 1994, the section was renumbered, and this provision was moved to § 522(f)(1)(B).

[271] See § 9.8.

[272] See § 9.9.

[273] This category covers the exemptions provided for in §§ 522(d)(3) and (4).

[274] This category covers the exemptions provided for in § 522(d)(6).

[275] This category covers the exemptions provided for in § 522(d)(9).

The requirement that the security interest be *nonpurchase-money* causes more problems. A purchase-money security interest is one in which the creditor either takes a security interest in the very item sold by the creditor to the debtor, or loans the debtor the money to enable the debtor to buy the collateral. U.C.C. § 9–103. A nonpurchase-money security interest, as the name suggests, is one that is not purchase-money. Purchase-money security interests do not implicate the same concern about creditor abuse as do nonpurchase-money security interests. If the creditor extended the credit to enable the debtor to buy the very item at issue, it is not unfair to permit the creditor to retake that property upon the debtor's default. The creditor is out real money up front in exchange for the collateral, and the extent of the creditor's purchase-money security interest is linked directly to and limited by the amount of the property sold. These same built-in protections do not exist for nonpurchase-money security interests. A creditor could take a nonpurchase-money security interest in all of a debtor's belongings.

In many instances the purchase-money character of the security interest is evident and avoidance is unavailable. Debtor buys a piano for his home from The Piano Shop on credit, and grants The Piano Shop a security interest to secure the debt for the piano. That is a purchase-money obligation and security interest, and lien avoidance under § 522(f)(1)(B) is not possible, nor should it be.

In one situation, however, a purchase-money secured creditor who tries to work with a financially troubled debtor inadvertently may end up being exposed to lien avoidance under § 522(f)(1)(B). The trap arises if the debtor seeks to *refinance* what was originally a purchase-money obligation. If the form of the refinancing is that the original obligation is paid off and a new debt substituted in its place, most courts have held that the purchase-money character of the security interest is lost.[276] The new money advanced does not enable the debtor to "purchase" the collateral, which the debtor already owned at the time of the refinancing. The only way for the secured creditor to preserve the purchase-money character of the security interest is to keep the *original obligation* alive, rather than replacing it with a new debt.

Avoidance under § 522(f)(1)(B) is available only with regard to certain types of collateral. These collateral types are those specified in the federal exemption categories in § 522(d)(3), (4), (6), and (9). In 2005, Congress added an extremely detailed definition of what does and what does not qualify as "household goods" for purposes of avoidance under subsection (f)(1)(b). § 522(f)(4). So, for example, we now know that jewelry worth more than $650 in aggregate does not qualify, except for wedding rings. § 522(f)(4)(A)(xiv), (B)(iv). A debtor can avoid liens on one television, one radio, and one VCR,[277] but otherwise electronic equipment is capped at $650, and so forth. § 522(f)(4)(A)(iv), (v), (vi), (B)(ii).

---

[276] See, e.g., In re Matthews, 724 F.2d 798 (9th Cir. 1984).

[277] The specific reference to a "VCR" is an example of the perils of obsessively detailed drafting. Almost before the ink was dry on the 2005 legislation, VCRs were becoming obsolete, and have largely been replaced by DVD players and DVRs. Would a debtor now be able to avoid a lien to the extent that it impairs an exemption on a DVD player? One court held that a DVD player was a "household good," although the BAPCPA amendments only refer to a VCR, because "technology had changed since BAPCPA was drafted,

Even though the types of collateral for which avoidance is possible are those listed in several subsections of the federal exemptions in § 522(d), note that avoidance also is possible with regard to exemptions claimed under *state* law, as long as the property is one of the *types* described. The theory supposedly underlying avoidance of security interests in these types of collateral, as discussed above, is that the only real value to the creditor is the leverage it gives the creditor to coerce a reaffirmation, rather than any significant monetary foreclosure value of the collateral.[278] For some of the described items, such as household goods and wearing apparel, this is probably true.

The problem, though, is that the categories included in subsections (i) through (iii) of § 522(f)(1)(B) are extremely overbroad in effectuating the stated congressional purpose. Literal application of these provisions may enable a debtor to avoid extremely valuable security interests, taken by a secured creditor for their actual economic value, rather than just for the leverage they would give the creditor. This threat is especially pronounced when the debtor is invoking *state* exemptions, which may allow much more generous exemptions in the described types of collateral than do the federal exemptions in § 522(d). Indeed, some state exemptions in these types of property have no dollar limit.

A good illustration of the risk to lenders and the overbreadth of § 522(f)(1)(B) is the Tenth Circuit case of *In re Liming*.[279] In *Liming*, the debtor was able to avoid a security interest in a $30,000 tractor. The tractor was a tool of the debtor's trade (farming), and the applicable state exemptions allowed an unlimited dollar exemption in such items. Even though the purpose of the avoidance provision was not implicated at all (indeed, the abusive party in the case was the *debtor*, who had defrauded the creditor), the court felt bound by the plain language of the statute.

Congress added § 522(f)(3) to the Bankruptcy Code in 1994 in an effort to deal with this problem.[280] The thrust of the amendment is to limit avoidance in cases such as *Liming* to $5,000, a cap that was increased by indexing to $6,225 in 2013. Any excess value of the lien over $6,225 cannot be avoided. Subsection (f)(3) only applies if the debtor voluntarily uses the *state* exemptions rather than the federal exemptions or is forced to use the state exemptions because the state has opted out of the federal exemptions. § 522(f)(3)(A). Furthermore, the $6,225 avoidance cap only applies if state law allows an unlimited exemption, or prohibits the avoidance of consensual liens on otherwise exempt property. § 522(f)(3)(B). In addition, this limiting rule does not extend to all of the types of collateral potentially avoidable under § 522(f)(1)(B). Instead, it only applies to (1) implements, professional books, or tools of the trade, or (2) farm animals or crops.

Another major interpretive problem that plagued the avoiding power for nonpossessory, nonpurchase-money security interests in the early years of the

---

and the reference to a VCR could reasonably be interpreted to include a DVD player." In re Zieg, 409 B.R. 917, 920 (Bankr. W.D. Mo. 2009).

[278] See H.R. Rep. No. 95–595, 95th Cong., 1st Sess., at 126–28 (1977).

[279] 797 F.2d 895 (10th Cir. 1986).

[280] See H.R. Rep. No. 103–834, 103d Cong., 2d Sess., at 42 (1994).

Bankruptcy Code concerned the effect and extent of opt-out.[281] The issue that arose was whether the security interest "impaired" an exemption to which the debtor would have been entitled. Some state statutes either defined the exemption in terms of the "debtor's interest," net of consensual liens, or were interpreted as providing that property subject to a security interest was not exempt at all. In either situation, some courts held that the debtor did not have an exemption in the property that was being impaired, and thus avoidance was not possible.[282]

However, the Supreme Court effectively settled this debate in favor of the debtor and against the creditor (albeit on completely different facts) in *Owen v. Owen* in 1991.[283] Under *Owen*, whether a debtor's exemption is "impaired" is to be judged against the hypothetical state of affairs that would exist absent the lien. Under these state statutes, the debtor would have an exemption if the security interest did not exist. After *Owen*, then, states cannot opt out and define away a debtor's lien avoidance rights with regard to nonpossessory, nonpurchase-money security interests.

§ 9.12 Waiver Restrictions

The debtor's right to retain some property as exempt in a bankruptcy case is considered a fundamental part of the debtor's financial fresh start in life.[284] Nor are the benefits of the exemption law limited to the debtor personally. The dependents of the debtor share the debtor's need for minimal asset protection. Furthermore, society as a whole has an interest in assisting the debtor in making a fresh start.[285]

Under pre-Code law, however, debtors generally were free to waive the benefits of the exemption law in favor of their creditors. Creditors with significant bargaining power were able to take advantage of this loophole and exact exemption waivers from consumer debtors. These routine waivers favored creditors at the expense of debtors, dependents of the debtor, and the public interest.

In 1978, Congress decided to remedy this problem and strengthen the exemption policy. Accordingly, Congress changed the law in the Bankruptcy Code by making agreements by the debtor to waive exemptions in favor of creditors unenforceable in bankruptcy. § 522(e). In addition, an agreement by the debtor to waive the power to avoid liens or recover avoided property under § 522 was rendered unenforceable by § 522(e). Blanket exemption waiver clauses in adhesion contracts now have no legal force and effect in bankruptcy cases.

The banning of exemption waiver agreements does not mean, however, that the debtor always will obtain the full benefit of all possible exemptions in a bankruptcy case. First, the debtor still can effectively waive an exemption by granting a creditor a

---

[281] See § 9.16.

[282] See, e.g., In re Pine, 717 F.2d 281 (6th Cir. 1983); In re McManus, 681 F.2d 353 (5th Cir. 1982).

[283] 500 U.S. 305 (1991). See § 9.9.

[284] See § 9.1.

[285] See, e.g., In re N. Shore Nat'l. Bank of Chicago, 17 B.R. 867, 869 (Bankr. N.D. Ill. 1982) ("The fresh start concept of the Code ultimately benefits society because the debtor has an opportunity to be a self-sufficient entity rather than a continuing burden on society.").

valid lien on exempt property. Unless the lien is avoided on some basis (which might be possible for certain types of liens that impair exemptions),[286] the lienholder will be entitled to enforce the lien against the exempt property.[287] § 522(c)(2). The anti-waiver rule in § 522(e) is carefully limited to waivers executed in favor of *unsecured* creditors.

Second, a debtor can forfeit his exemptions by the simple expedient of not claiming those exemptions in the first place. Under the Bankruptcy Code, the burden is on the debtor to claim property as exempt.[288] § 522(l), Rule 4003(a). Otherwise, the property remains in the estate. As a partial remedy to this informal "do nothing" form of waiver, Congress authorized a dependent of the debtor to claim exemptions if the debtor fails to do so. § 522(l).

Third, a debtor can give up his right to exemptions by transferring exempt property to creditors shortly before bankruptcy. Although the bankruptcy trustee may be able to avoid the transfer and recover the property for the estate, the debtor will not then be able to claim an exemption in the recovered property. Although the debtor may claim an exemption in recovered property in some circumstances, that privilege only applies when the original transfer was involuntary as to the debtor. § 522(g)(1)(A).

§ 9.13   Redemption under § 722

The congressional policy to enable a debtor to enjoy the full range of available exemptions is further buttressed by the provision allowing an individual debtor to *redeem* tangible personal property intended for consumer use from a lien securing a dischargeable consumer debt, if the property has been exempted or abandoned. § 722. In redemption, the debtor satisfies the secured claim in full by paying the lienholder the amount of the allowed secured claim. If the debt is undersecured, the lienholder has an allowed unsecured claim to the extent of the deficiency.

For example, assume that Debtor purchases a refrigerator from Creditor for $800, and grants Creditor a purchase-money security interest in the refrigerator as security. When Debtor files chapter 7, the refrigerator is worth $400,[289] but the total debt is $600. Debtor claims the refrigerator as exempt under § 522(d)(3). However, Debtor cannot avoid Creditor's security interest under § 522(f)(1)(B), because it is a purchase-money security interest. Since Debtor needs the refrigerator and wants to keep it, and would prefer not to incur the transaction and purchase costs associated with replacing the item, Creditor would have substantial leverage to persuade Debtor to enter into a reaffirmation agreement under § 524(c). To reaffirm, Debtor undoubtedly would have to agree to pay the full $600 debt to Creditor, even though the refrigerator is only worth $400.

Redemption steps in to save the day for Debtor. Under § 722, Debtor can discharge Creditor's security interest by paying Creditor $400—the value of the collateral. All of

---

[286] See § 522(f). See §§ 9.7–9.11.

[287] See § 9.4.

[288] See § 9.6.

[289] Note that valuation of the collateral for purposes of redemption will require application of § 506(a)(2), which dictates that "replacement value" must be used. See § 7.29.

the requirements for redemption are met: (1) Debtor is an individual; (2) the property is tangible personal property; (3) the property is "intended primarily for personal, family, or household use"; (4) the property secures a dischargeable consumer debt; and (5) the property has been exempted. Debtor will have to make the payment in cash, in a lump sum; installment redemption is not allowed.[290] But still Debtor is better off; instead of paying $600 to keep the exempt refrigerator, Debtor only has to pay $400. Creditor will be left with a $200 unsecured claim. Debtor can redeem without Creditor's consent. Creditor's leverage to coerce a reaffirmation is eliminated.[291]

Redemption thus complements the lien avoidance rule of § 522(f)(1)(B), which only allows avoidance of nonpossessory, nonpurchase-money security interests. Under § 722, the debtor can retain exempt property for its current value. The purchase-money creditor is better off than in the case of outright avoidance; the creditor does at least get paid the value of the collateral. But the creditor cannot obtain an unfair reaffirmation agreement.

C.   CONSTITUTIONAL ISSUES

§ 9.14   Retroactivity: *Security Industrial Bank*

Whether a statute applies prospectively or retroactively depends on the intent of Congress. A familiar canon of statutory construction provides that statutes normally only operate prospectively. Bankruptcy laws, however, test this canon, because by their very nature such laws usually affect the *preexisting* rights of creditors, in order to provide relief to troubled debtors with respect to preexisting obligations. Indeed, most bankruptcy laws in United States history have been passed in direct response to a major financial crisis.

The Supreme Court has held that Congress has the power pursuant to the Bankruptcy Clause to impair retrospectively *contractual* obligations.[292] With respect to the impairment of *property* rights, however, the Court has held that the Fifth Amendment prohibitions against uncompensated takings and against deprivation of property without due process of law limit the congressional exercise of the Bankruptcy Clause.[293]

The issues of (1) prospective versus retrospective operation of a statute and (2) the constitutionality of retroactively impairing liens under the Bankruptcy Clause were brought together by the enactment of the lien avoiding powers of § 522(f) in the 1978 Bankruptcy Code. Prior law did not contain any similar avoiding power for security

---

[290] See In re Bell, 700 F.2d 1053 (6th Cir. 1983). In 2005 Congress codified this view that the entire redemption payment had to be made up front, adding the language "in full at the time of redemption."

[291] The policy behind redemption and its interaction with the exemption section is discussed in H.R. Rep. No. 95–595, 95th Cong., 1st Sess., at 127–28 (1977).

[292] Hanover Nat'l Bank v. Moyses, 186 U.S. 181 (1902).

[293] Louisville Joint Stock Land Bank v. Radford, 295 U.S. 555 (1935). Some have questioned whether the Fifth Amendment property protections should be construed to limit the operation of the Bankruptcy Clause. See James S. Rogers, The Impairment of Secured Creditors' Rights in Reorganization: A Study of the Relationship Between the Fifth Amendment and the Bankruptcy Clause, 96 Harv. L. Rev. 973 (1983). However, as will be discussed in the text, the Supreme Court reaffirmed the continuing vitality of *Radford* in *United States v. Sec. Indus. Bank*, 459 U.S. 70, 76–78 (1982).

interests;[294] thus, under pre-Code law, liens of the type described in § 522(f) were valid and could be enforced against exempt property of the debtor. Indeed, it was precisely because of congressional concern about abusive creditor practices with regard to these types of liens, and the negative impact of those practices on a debtor's exemption rights, that Congress enacted § 522(f) in 1978.[295]

Application of the § 522(f) avoiding power posed no problems of retroactive application or constitutional concern with regard to liens that were created *after* the *effective date* of the new Bankruptcy Code, October 1, 1979. Such liens obviously were subject to the new law, and creditors taking liens of the types made vulnerable by § 522(f) were on notice of the potential for avoidance. Even for liens that were created after the *enactment date* of the Code (November 6, 1978), a strong argument could be made that application of the new avoiding power would withstand constitutional scrutiny, again because of the advance notice to creditors that such liens would be vulnerable under the already-enacted legislation.[296]

Liens that were created *before* the enactment of the Bankruptcy Code were another matter entirely. At the time those liens arose, they were valid and enforceable even in a bankruptcy case. Inevitably, after the Code became effective, individual debtors filed bankruptcy and sought to avoid pre-enactment liens under § 522(f). The challenged liens typically were nonpossessory, nonpurchase-money security interests in household furnishings and appliances, which under the Code are voidable to the extent they impair the debtor's exemptions under § 522(f)(1)(B).[297]

Two issues had to be decided. First, did Congress *intend* for § 522(f) to be applied retroactively to permit debtors to avoid pre-enactment liens? Second, if Congress did intend retroactive application, was that *constitutional* under the Fifth Amendment's Due Process and Takings Clauses? The Supreme Court addressed these questions in the 1982 case of *United States v. Security Industrial Bank.*[298]

Prior to the Court's decision in *Security Industrial Bank*, all circuit courts that considered the question had concluded that Congress did intend for § 522(f) to apply retrospectively.[299] The circuit courts had not agreed, however, on whether retroactive application violated the Fifth Amendment. With regard to the Due Process clause, courts had little trouble finding that § 522(f) was valid as a rational exercise of

---

[294] Judicial liens, the target of avoidance under § 522(f)(1)(A), were avoidable under the old Bankruptcy Act in certain circumstances. See 1898 Bankruptcy Act § 67(a).

[295] See H.R. Rep. No. 95–595, 95th Cong., 1st Sess., at 126–28 (1977).

[296] See In re Webber, 674 F.2d 796 (9th Cir.), cert. denied, 459 U.S. 1086 (1982).

[297] Until 1994, this avoiding power was numbered § 522(f)(2). See Bankruptcy Reform Act of 1994, Pub. L. No. 103–394, 108 Stat. 4132 (1994).

[298] 459 U.S. 70 (1982). For a discussion of this decision, see Charles Jordan Tabb, The Bankruptcy Reform Act in the Supreme Court, 49 U. Pitt. L. Rev. 477, 497–507 (1988). See also Rogers, supra note 293.

[299] See In re Gifford, 688 F.2d 447, 449–51 (7th Cir. 1982); In re Webber, 674 F.2d 796, 801–02 (9th Cir.), cert. denied, 459 U.S. 1086 (1982); In re Ashe, 669 F.2d 105 (3d Cir.), vacated, 459 U.S. 1082 (1982); Rodrock v. Sec. Indus. Bank, 642 F.2d 1193, 1196–97 (10th Cir. 1981), aff'd on other grounds sub. nom. United States v. Sec. Indus. Bank, 459 U.S. 70 (1982). Judge Pell dissented from the Seventh Circuit's decision in *Gifford,* presaging the Supreme Court's decision in *Security Industrial Bank* by arguing that prospective application should be presumed given the doubtful constitutionality of applying the statute retroactively.

legislative power.[300] The Takings Clause presented a harder case, since the destruction of the creditor's security interest was total. The circuit courts had divided over the constitutionality of retroactive application.[301]

The Supreme Court in *Security Industrial Bank* affirmed the decision of the Tenth Circuit that the creditor's pre-enactment security interests could not be avoided under § 522(f), but on different grounds.[302] The Tenth Circuit had held that Congress intended to apply § 522(f) retroactively, but that doing so violated the Takings Clause.[303] The Supreme Court held that Congress did *not intend* to apply § 522(f) retroactively, given the substantial constitutional doubt of the validity of retroactive application.[304] Three Justices concurred on the ground that prospective application was dictated by early Supreme Court precedent interpreting prior bankruptcy laws.[305] The concurring Justices noted, though, that if they were "writing on a clean slate," they would hold that Congress intended § 522(f) to operate retroactively, and that such application was constitutional.[306]

Perhaps the most important part of the Court's opinion in *Security Industrial Bank* is the dictum on the construction of the Fifth Amendment Takings Clause in the context of liens in bankruptcy cases.[307] Significantly, the Supreme Court reaffirmed the validity of a 1935 takings decision,[308] stating that "[t]he bankruptcy power is subject to the Fifth Amendment's prohibition against taking private property without compensation."[309] The Court agreed with the lower courts that § 522(f) was a rational exercise of Congress's power under the Bankruptcy Clause,[310] but that conclusion did not resolve the distinct takings problem.

In discussing the takings problem, the Court in dictum rejected each of the arguments that lower courts had relied on in finding that retroactive application of § 522(f) was constitutional. As noted, the concurring Justices would have upheld the constitutionality of the retroactive operation of § 522(f).[311] The first issue was whether the creditor's nonpossessory, nonpurchase-money security interest in household furnishings and appliances was a valuable property interest entitled to protection under the Takings Clause. The argument that it was not was based on the assertion that this type of collateral had little monetary worth, but was valuable to the creditor primarily for the leverage it gave the creditor in coercing the debtor to reaffirm

---

[300] See, e.g., *Gifford*, supra note 299, 688 F.2d at 453–55; *Ashe*, supra note 299, 669 F.2d at 110–11.

[301] Compare *Gifford*, 688 F.2d at 453–60 (constitutional) and *Ashe*, 669 F.2d at 110–11 (same) with *Rodrock*, supra note 8, 642 F.2d at 1197–98 (unconstitutional).

[302] 459 U.S. 70 (1982).

[303] 642 F.2d at 1196–98.

[304] 459 U.S. at 82.

[305] Id. at 84–85 (Blackmun, J., concurring). The concurring Justices relied on *Holt v. Henley*, 232 U.S. 637 (1914), and also on *Auffm'ordt v. Rasin*, 102 U.S. 620 (1881).

[306] 459 U.S. at 83–84 (Blackmun, J., concurring).

[307] Id. at 75–78 (Rehnquist, J., majority).

[308] Louisville Joint Stock Land Bank v. Radford, 295 U.S. 555 (1935).

[309] United States v. Sec. Indus. Bank, 459 U.S. 70, 75 (1982).

[310] Id. at 74.

[311] Id. at 84 (Blackmun, J., concurring).

debts.[312] The majority in *Security Industrial Bank* nevertheless indicated that these security interests were "property" entitled to Fifth Amendment protection, relying on the characterization of these security interests as property under state law.[313]

The second takings issue focused on the economic impact of avoidance on the property interest involved. Those favoring constitutionality asserted that § 522(f) was a permissible economic regulation that had an insignificant impact on the creditor's legitimate expectations. The Court in *Security Industrial Bank* again disagreed, noting that § 522(f) completely destroyed the creditor's property right.[314] Finally, the Court rejected the argument that the Takings Clause applied only to takings for a public use, and did not apply when a property right was transferred from one private party (the creditor) to another (the debtor).[315]

Having gone to the brink of finding that retroactive application of § 522(f) would violate the Takings Clause of the Fifth Amendment, the Court then backed off from rendering that holding. Instead, the Court invoked the "cardinal principle that this Court will first ascertain whether a construction of the statute is fairly possible by which the constitutional question may be avoided."[316] The Court made that possibility a reality by holding that Congress had not intended for § 522(f) to have retrospective effect.[317] The Court reached this conclusion by invoking the general presumption that statutes operate only *prospectively*, and refusing to infer, absent a clear congressional directive, that Congress intended to depart from the presumptive norm when doing so might be unconstitutional.[318] The Court also relied on old Supreme Court precedent applying a bankruptcy statute prospectively.[319]

As noted above, all circuit courts to consider the issue, including the Tenth Circuit in *Security Industrial Bank,* had held that Congress had intended for § 522(f) of the Code to apply retroactively. If the Code did not apply to pre-enactment liens, these courts believed that there would be a statutory gap, because the old Bankruptcy Act had been repealed. The Supreme Court finessed this gap argument, concluding that the remainder of the new Code still could be applied to pre-enactment liens, even though § 522(f) could not.[320] One might protest that it is improbable in the extreme that Congress intended for part but not all of the new Code to apply to pre-enactment liens, but by relying on this obvious fiction the Court was able to avoid a transitional constitutional problem.

---

[312] See H.R. Rep. No. 95–595, 95th Cong., 1st Sess., at 126–27, discussed in § 9.11.

[313] 459 U.S. at 76–78.

[314] Id. at 75–76.

[315] Id. at 78.

[316] Id. (quoting Lorillard v. Pons, 434 U.S. 575 (1978), quoting *Crowell v. Benson*, 285 U.S. 22 (1932)).

[317] Id. at 82.

[318] Id. at 78–80. The Court also noted that an earlier version of the 1978 statute did have a clear retroactivity provision, which was deleted after a witness raised constitutional concerns about retroactive destruction of liens. Id. at 81.

[319] Id. at 81. The concurring Justices would have based the decision on precedent alone. Id. at 84–85 (Blackmun, J., concurring).

[320] Id. at 78–79 (Rehnquist, J., majority).

The problem that so troubled the Court in *Security Industrial Bank* has been held not to exist with regard to *judicial* liens. In a Third Circuit case decided the year after *Security Industrial Bank*, the court held that § 522(f) could constitutionally be applied retroactively to avoid judicial liens.[321] One important difference between judicial liens (avoidable under § 522(f)(1)(A))[322] and security interests (avoidable under § 522(f)(1)(B))[323] is that the pre-Code Bankruptcy Act *had* provided for the avoidance of judicial liens in some circumstances. See 1898 Act § 67(a). The pre-enactment judicial lien creditor thus could not have the same sort of vested expectations as would the holder of a pre-enactment security interest.

A second difference between judicial liens and security interests is that judicial liens are in the nature of a general remedial charge on the debtor's property for the purpose of satisfying the judgment, rather than a specific and tangible property interest. The essentially remedial nature of judicial liens has led some courts to conclude that the lienholder does not have vested rights deserving of constitutional protection while the lien remains unexercised. For example, a court found no constitutional infirmity when a state amended its exemption laws after a creditor obtained a judicial lien, effectively enabling the debtor to avoid a larger portion of the lien under § 522(f)(1)(A).[324]

§ 9.15 Uniformity

The Bankruptcy Clause of the Constitution (Article I, § 8, clause 4) gives Congress the power "To establish uniform Laws on the subject of Bankruptcies throughout the United States." What does it mean for a federal bankruptcy law to be "*uniform*"? A plausible interpretation of the constitutional grant of power would be that the same laws must apply to every bankruptcy debtor in the United States. Such an approach might be called "true" uniformity, or "personal" (i.e., to each debtor) uniformity.

The uniformity issue is particularly significant in the context of exemptions.[325] Under the current Bankruptcy Code, debtors are permitted to claim *state* exemptions, as an alternative to the federal exemptions offered in § 522(d). § 522(b)(1), (3). In addition, states may "opt out" of the federal exemptions, and limit resident debtors to the state exemptions.[326] § 522(b)(2). The Code's utilization of state exemptions poses a serious threat to uniformity, because exemption laws vary tremendously from state to state. For example, a debtor who resides in Florida or Texas may claim a homestead exemption of unlimited value,[327] while a Pennsylvania debtor is offered no homestead exemption at all. If these nonuniform state exemption laws are used in federal bankruptcy cases, does that violate the constitutional command of uniformity? If the

---

[321] In re Ashe, 712 F.2d 864 (3d Cir. 1983).

[322] See § 9.10.

[323] See § 9.11.

[324] See Bartlett v. Giguere, 168 B.R. 488 (Bankr. D.N.H. 1994).

[325] For an excellent discussion of this issue, see Judith S. Koffler, The Bankruptcy Clause and Exemption Laws: A Reexamination of the Doctrine of Geographic Uniformity, 58 N.Y.U. L. Rev. 22 (1983). See also § 1.10.c.

[326] See §§ 9.2, 9.16.

[327] See Fla. Const. art. 10, § 4(a)(1); Tex. Const. art. 16, § 51.

constitutional grant is construed to require "true" or "personal" uniformity, then obviously the answer would be yes.

The answer, however, is no. In 1902, the Supreme Court held in *Hanover National Bank v. Moyses*[328] that for the purposes of the Bankruptcy Clause, all that the Constitution requires is "that uniformity is geographical and not personal."[329] The *Moyses* Court upheld the incorporation of state exemption laws in the Bankruptcy Act of 1898, holding that

> [T]he system is, in the constitutional sense, uniform throughout the United States, when the trustee takes in each State whatever would have been available to the creditors if the bankrupt law had not been passed. The general operation of the law is uniform although it may result in certain particulars differently in different States.[330]

Although *Moyses* has been criticized on the ground that it was incorrectly decided,[331] the Supreme Court has never retreated in bankruptcy cases from the rule announced in *Moyses*. In its most recent bankruptcy uniformity decision (which did not deal with exemption laws), the Court in dictum restated with apparent approval the rule of *Moyses* "that Congress can give effect to the allowance of exemptions prescribed by state law without violating the uniformity requirement."[332] The Court in that case further observed that "a bankruptcy law may be uniform and yet 'may recognize the laws of the State in certain particulars, although such recognition may lead to different results in different States.'"[333]

Courts have relied on *Moyses* and its progeny to hold that the exemption provisions in § 522(b) of the Bankruptcy Code do not violate the constitutional requirement of uniformity.[334] This result is not incontrovertible, however, *even if* one concedes that the Court would still follow *Moyses* today.[335] The approach to exemptions in § 522(b) might be described as "*Moyses redux* and redoubled." Unlike the 1898 Act, which only allowed debtors to use state exemptions, the 1978 Code does offer debtors a choice between state and federal exemptions—*but also* allows the states to *opt out* of the federal exemptions. The Bankruptcy Code, in short, not only permits the states to fix exemption levels for its debtors, but also gives states the power to decide whether

---

[328]   186 U.S. 181 (1902).

[329]   Id. at 188.

[330]   Id. at 190.

[331]   For a persuasive attack on the decision in *Moyses*, see Koffler, supra note 325. In particular, the Court in *Moyses* relied on two lower court decisions that had upheld the exemption provisions of the 1867 Bankruptcy Act against a uniformity challenge. The *Moyses* Court failed to note, however, a crucial distinction between the 1867 and 1898 laws: the 1867 Act also allowed debtors to select a uniform set of federal exemptions, while the 1898 Act did not, but allowed debtors to claim *only* state exemption laws. In addition, the Court's approach in *Moyses* in the bankruptcy context is inconsistent with the Court's approach to uniformity in the taxation and naturalization cases.

[332]   Ry. Labor Execs. Ass'n v. Gibbons, 455 U.S. 457, 469 (1982).

[333]   Id. (quoting *Stellwagen v. Clum*, 245 U.S. 605, 613 (1918) (upholding the use of state fraudulent conveyance laws in bankruptcy cases)).

[334]   The leading case is *In re Sullivan*, 680 F.2d 1131 (7th Cir.), cert. denied, 459 U.S. 992 (1982).

[335]   See especially the criticisms in Koffler, supra note 325, at 87–101. See also Frank R. Kennedy, Bankruptcy and the Constitution, U. Mich. L. Quad. 40, 44 (1989).

the federal exemptions of § 522(d) can be used by resident debtors. Thus, a debtor who files for bankruptcy in one state may be allowed to claim the federal exemptions, but a debtor who resides in another state may be deprived of that privilege. Even under the exceedingly liberal standard of uniformity embraced by the *Moyses* Court, opt-out would seem to render the bankruptcy law nonuniform. Considering the precise tests used by *Moyses*, under the opt-out scheme the "general operation of the law" *does* differ from state to state, and the trustee does *not* necessarily take "in each State whatever would have been available to the creditors if the bankrupt law had not been passed."[336]

The nonuniformity constitutional attack on § 522(b) could be cast instead as a challenge that § 522(b) is an impermissible *delegation* of congressional power to the states. The Bankruptcy Clause grants *Congress* the power to establish uniform bankruptcy laws—not the states. The essence of opt-out, however, is that the *states* are given the power to choose what bankruptcy exemption law may be used by resident debtors. No standards whatsoever govern the states' exercise of this delegated opt-out power.

Notwithstanding the plausible delegation concern, most courts to consider the issue have rejected the delegation attack, again following *Moyses*[337] and finding no distinction between the exemption provisions of the 1898 Bankruptcy Act and the 1978 Bankruptcy Code.[338] These courts sidestep the delegation problem, reasoning that since the states themselves have the residual power to enact bankruptcy laws that do not conflict with the federal legislation,[339] § 522(b)(2) does not affect an unconstitutional delegation of congressional power.[340] That theory, however, fails to grapple with the problem that Congress has in fact delegated to the states the power to decide as a threshold matter whether part of the federal bankruptcy law will apply at all.

Furthermore, several states have one set of general exemptions available to all residents, and a separate set of exemptions available only to debtors in bankruptcy.[341] Although there would seem to be particularly compelling arguments for unconstitutionality in these circumstances, courts facing this issue have disagreed, and uphold the constitutionality of separate bankruptcy-only exemptions. Recently the Sixth Circuit joined the Fourth Circuit,[342] Tenth Circuit,[343] and the B.A.P. for the Ninth Circuit[344] in finding no constitutional problems, holding that Michigan's bankruptcy-specific exemptions do not violate the Supremacy Clause and do not fail to meet the Bankruptcy Clause's uniformity requirement.[345] The Sixth Circuit reasoned

---

[336] *Moyses*, supra note 328, 186 U.S. at 190.

[337] See id.

[338] See, e.g., *Sullivan*, supra note 334, 680 F.2d at 1136–37.

[339] See Sturges v. Crowninshield, 17 U.S. (4 Wheat.) 122, 195–96 (1819).

[340] *Sullivan*, supra note 334, 680 F.2d at 1136.

[341] See, e.g., Mich. Comp. Laws § 600.6023 (general exemptions); Mich. Comp. Laws § 600.5451 (debtor exemptions). California, Colorado, Georgia, Indiana, Montana, New York, Ohio, and West Virginia also have exemptions applicable only to debtors in bankruptcy.

[342] Sheehan v. Peveich, 574 F.3d 248 (4th Cir. 2009).

[343] In re Kulp, 949 F.2d 1106 (10th Cir. 1991).

[344] In re Applebaum, 422 B.R. 684 (B.A.P. 9th Cir. 2009).

[345] In re Shafer, 689 F.3d 601 (6th Cir. 2012), cert. denied, 133 S.Ct. 1244 (2013). See also In re Westby, 473 B.R. 392 (Bankr. D. Kan. 2012).

that the state opt-out provision in § 522(b)(2) gives states the ultimate authority to enact laws relating to exemptions, unrestricted by any requirement that state exemptions apply equally to both bankruptcy and non-bankruptcy cases.

In summary, the prevailing view is that the use of different state exemptions laws in bankruptcy cases (even bankruptcy-specific state laws), and the possibility of opt-out, do not render the bankruptcy exemption law in § 522(b) unconstitutional as nonuniform or as an impermissible delegation of congressional power. Having said that, strong arguments can be made that the result should be otherwise.

§ 9.16   Limits of Opt-Out

In § 522(b)(1), Congress gave bankruptcy debtors the power to choose between state exemptions and the federal exemptions provided in § 522(d). What Congress gave with one hand, however, it took away with the other, further providing that a state may "opt out" of the federal exemptions and limit debtors domiciled in the state to the exemptions provided by state law. § 522(b)(2). The opt-out provision was added to the 1978 Bankruptcy Code at the last minute as a compromise to resolve differences between the House, which wanted debtors to be able to choose between state and federal exemptions, and the Senate, which wanted debtors to be restricted to state exemptions.[346] As of 2013, 34 states had opted out.

The opt-out provision has been tested at many levels. Most fundamentally, it has been challenged on constitutional grounds. Debtors limited to state exemptions less generous than those provided in the § 522(d) federal scheme have argued that opt-out is invalid on enough grounds to fill an entire course in constitutional law, claiming that: (1) opt-out renders the bankruptcy law *nonuniform*; (2) it is an impermissible *delegation* of congressional power to the states; (3) it violates the *Supremacy* Clause; (4) opt-out deprives debtors of *due process* of law; (5) debtors are deprived of *equal protection* of the laws; and (6) allowing states to opt out violates the *Privileges and Immunities* Clause. Although an occasional lower court has accepted one or more of these arguments, at the circuit level the constitutionality of opt-out has been consistently upheld.[347]

The preceding section discussed the uniformity and delegation issues.[348] A 1902 Supreme Court decision is still held to be controlling on those questions.[349] The due process and equal protection arguments are doomed by the fact that bankruptcy laws, as an economic regulation rather than a fundamental right, are judged according to a rational basis test.[350] Courts have little trouble in finding that Congress acted

---

[346] Compare H.R. Rep. No. 95–595, 95th Cong., 1st Sess., at 126, 360 (1977) (choice between state and federal exemptions), with S. Rep. No. 95–989, 95th Cong., 2d Sess., at 75 (1978) (state exemptions only). The compromise is noted in 124 Cong. Rec. H11,095 (daily ed. Sept. 28, 1978) (statement of Rep. Edwards).

[347] See, e.g., Storer v. French (In re Storer), 58 F.3d 1125 (6th Cir.), cert. denied, 516 U.S. 990 (1995) (rejecting challenges based on (1) privileges and immunities; (2) supremacy; (3) delegation; (4) due process; and (5) equal protection); In re Sullivan, 680 F.2d 1131 (7th Cir.), cert. denied, 459 U.S. 992 (1982) (rejecting challenges based on (1) uniformity; (2) supremacy; and (3) delegation).

[348] See § 9.15.

[349] See Hanover Nat'l Bank v. Moyses, 186 U.S. 181 (1902).

[350] See United States v. Kras, 409 U.S. 434, 446 (1973).

rationally in permitting states to decide that debtors domiciled within the state's borders should have the same exemptions available to them in or out of bankruptcy.[351]

Finally, the supremacy and the privileges and immunities arguments fall apart in light of the explicit congressional delegation of the opt-out power to the states in § 522(b)(2).[352] The gravamen of these challenges is that opt-out permits a state to contradict the congressional decision to provide a minimum floor of exemptions.[353] The fatal weakness in that argument, though, noted by many courts,[354] is that such an intention can be attributed only to the House. The Senate did not acquiesce in the House view, and the opt-out compromise negates an inference that the House policy prevailed. Indeed, as the Supreme Court noted in *Owen*, "Nothing in subsection (b) (or elsewhere in the Code) limits a State's power to restrict the scope of its exemptions; indeed, it could theoretically accord no exemptions at all."[355]

If opt-out is constitutional, as the prevailing view holds it is, does that then mean that opt-out is absolute? In other words, may a state through opt-out craft its exemption laws in such a way so as to effectively undermine other parts of § 522? The answer is no. All that opt-out sanctions is for a state to prevent a domiciliary debtor from using the federal exemptions in § 522(d). All of the other provisions of § 522 remain fully operative, even in a state that has opted out. The Supreme Court made this point clear in *Owen*, stating "We have no basis for pronouncing the opt-out policy absolute, but must apply it along with whatever other competing or limiting policies the statute contains."[356]

In *Owen*, the Court held that a state cannot define away the lien avoidance provisions of § 522(f).[357] Prior to *Owen*, a few circuit courts had held that a state that had opted out could prevent lien avoidance by defining the debtor's exemption rights in a way that preserved the creditor's lien or security interest.[358] The Supreme Court in *Owen* concluded that opt-out did not have such an all-encompassing reach. The "would have been entitled" language in § 522(f), the lien-avoiding provision, required consideration of the debtor's available exemptions in the absence of any liens. A state by opting out under subsection (b)(1) of § 522 could not affect the operation of this separate rule in subsection (f).

In a similar vein, it has been held that a state that has opted out cannot thereby preclude the application of subsection (c)'s rules on the enforcement of debts against exempt property.[359] In a Fifth Circuit case, the court was confronted with Texas state law that did not allow an ex-spouse to enforce a claim in the nature of alimony,

---

[351] See *Storer*, supra note 347, 58 F.3d at 1129–30.

[352] See id. at 1127–29. See also *Sullivan*, supra note 347, 680 F.2d at 1135–36.

[353] See Rhodes v. Stewart (In re Rhodes), 14 B.R. 629, 634 (M.D. Tenn. 1981), rev'd, 705 F.2d 159 (6th Cir.), cert. denied, 464 U.S. 983 (1983).

[354] See, e.g., *Sullivan*, supra note 347, 680 F.2d at 1135.

[355] 500 U.S. 305, 308 (1991).

[356] Id. at 313.

[357] See § 9.9.

[358] See, e.g., In re Pine, 717 F.2d 281 (6th Cir. 1983); In re McManus, 681 F.2d 353 (5th Cir. 1982).

[359] See In re Davis, 105 F.3d 1017 (5th Cir. 1997), vacated, 131 F.3d 1120 (5th Cir. 1997).

maintenance, or support against a debtor's exempt homestead. The federal rule, however, that provides that property exempted in a bankruptcy case generally is not liable for prepetition debts, carves out an exception and does permit the enforcement of alimony, maintenance, and support debts against exempt property.[360] § 522(c)(1). In short, the bankruptcy rule and the Texas rule are diametrically opposed. The Fifth Circuit first held that the federal enforcement rule preempted the state law, opt-out notwithstanding.[361] The enforcement issue, the court determined, was solely a matter of federal law. However, that panel decision was vacated, and on rehearing en banc, the Fifth Circuit changed course, and upheld the Texas state law, finding no implied preemption of the Texas law.[362] Congress, however, preferred the view of the Fifth Circuit panel, and in 2005 amended the statute at issue (§ 522(c)(1)) to make clear that the *federal* rule allowing enforcement by a DSO against the homestead applies, irrespective of any state law rules to the contrary.

In one area, courts have reached conflicting decisions on the impact of opt-out on other subsections of § 522. Subsection (m) provides that "this section shall apply separately with respect to each debtor in a joint case." For example, if joint debtors elected the federal exemptions (assuming the state had not opted out, of course), each debtor could claim a $22,975 homestead exemption under § 522(d)(1), meaning that the total homestead exemption available to the joint debtors would be $45,950.

The problem arises when a state that has opted out of the federal exemptions defines a *joint* exemption in a way that precludes doubling the exemption available to a *single* debtor. For example, in the Ninth Circuit case of *In re Granger*,[363] the Oregon state exemption law permitted *one* debtor to claim a $15,000 homestead as exempt, but only allowed *joint* debtors who were members of the same household to exempt $20,000 in a homestead. In a Fourth Circuit case, *In re Cheeseman*,[364] Virginia law allowed a "householder or head of a family" to exempt $5,000 in a homestead, and arguably under state law it would be impossible for *both* spouses to be the qualifying "householder or head." In the face of these limited state joint exemptions, does § 522(m) require doubling the exemption available to a single debtor? If so, the *Granger* debtors could exempt $30,000 in a homestead, even though the state law maximum would be $20,000, and the *Cheeseman* debtors could exempt $10,000, not the $5,000 available under state law.

The two circuit courts reached opposite conclusions. The Ninth Circuit held that the debtors were limited to the state-provided joint exemption of $20,000.[365] The Fourth Circuit, however, interpreted § 522(m) as allowing the joint debtors to exempt twice the permissible state law amount.[366] In light of the Supreme Court's determination in *Owen v. Owen* that opt-out is not absolute, and that a state cannot circumvent the application of the other provisions of § 522, the Fourth Circuit's

---

[360] See § 9.4.

[361] *Davis*, supra note 359, 105 F.3d at 1022–23.

[362] 170 F.3d 475 (5th Cir. 1999), cert. denied, 120 S.Ct. 67 (1999).

[363] Granger v. Watson (In re Granger), 754 F.2d 1490 (9th Cir. 1985).

[364] Cheeseman v. Nachman (In re Cheeseman), 656 F.2d 60 (4th Cir. 1981).

[365] *Granger*, supra note 363, 754 F.2d at 1491–92.

[366] *Cheeseman*, supra note 364, 656 F.2d at 63–64.

approach is probably correct. If so, even in a state that has opted out of the federal exemptions, debtors in a joint case may be permitted to claim more property as exempt than they could under state law.

Chapter 10

THE DISCHARGE

A. INTRODUCTION

§ 10.1   Overview of Discharge

Most individual debtors file bankruptcy to take advantage of the bankruptcy discharge. The debtor does not have to pay discharged debts, and creditors may not try to collect debts that are discharged. Any property that the debtor earns or acquires after bankruptcy is free from discharged debts. The debtor thus is said to have a *"fresh start"* in life, in an economic sense. Several sections of the Code implement this fundamental policy. In a chapter 7 liquidation case, § 727(b) provides that a discharge under § 727(a) "discharges the debtor from all debts that arose before the date of the order for relief."[1] That date usually is the date the debtor files the bankruptcy case. A creditor need not share in the bankruptcy distribution to have its claim discharged; under § 727(b) the discharge operates even if the creditor does not file a proof of claim and even if a filed claim is not allowed.

The discharge is enforced automatically by § 524(a).[2] The debtor does not have to do anything to take advantage of the discharge. First, a discharge voids any judgment that determines the debtor's personal liability for a discharged debt. § 524(a)(1). Second, creditors are enjoined by the Code from attempting to collect discharged debts as a personal liability of the debtor. § 524(a)(2). Third, § 525 complements § 524 by protecting the debtor from discriminatory treatment inflicted solely because the debtor filed bankruptcy.[3] For example, an employer could not fire an employee for filing bankruptcy. Section 525 thus attempts to limit indirect pressures that might chill the debtor's willingness to resort to bankruptcy and obtain a fresh start.

That is the good news for debtors, but it is not the whole story. The Bankruptcy Code, while favorable to debtors, is not completely one-sided. The right to a discharge and the scope of the discharge are far from absolute. The first limitation is that the discharge only applies to *pre-bankruptcy debts*.[4] § 727(b). Creditors are entitled to collect any debts incurred after bankruptcy. It is sometimes said that the debtor is entitled to a "fresh start," but not a "head start." Furthermore, a debtor can only receive a bankruptcy discharge every *eight years*.[5] § 727(a)(8), (9). Thus, post-bankruptcy creditors have ample opportunity to collect their debts before a debtor can find sanctuary in bankruptcy court again.

---

[1]   This coverage extends to those debts, which actually arise after the petition is filed but which are deemed by § 502 to arise prior to the filing of the petition.

[2]   See § 10.31.

[3]   See § 10.32.

[4]   See § 10.2.

[5]   See § 10.11.

Second, not all debtors receive a discharge. Section 727(a) lists twelve exclusive grounds for *denial* of a discharge.[6] If any one of the § 727(a) grounds is found, none of the debtor's debts are discharged. Yet, the debtor still must turn over all of his nonexempt property for distribution to creditors. Denial of discharge thus is a draconian "lose-lose" situation for debtors. The premise behind most of the discharge denial provisions is that only a financially honest debtor deserves a fresh start in life. Section 727(a) attempts to make the bankruptcy process a meaningful collection system for creditors, by requiring debtors to cooperate in the bankruptcy proceeding in order to receive a discharge. Thus, for example, a debtor who has hidden assets from his creditors will not be discharged.

A third limitation is that even a debtor who does receive a general discharge under § 727(b) may have some of her specific debts *excepted* from the operation of that discharge. Section 523(a) enumerates twenty-one different categories of debts that are not discharged.[7] Those discharge exceptions represent a hodge-podge of policy decisions by Congress either to punish the debtor for assorted bad acts (most intentional torts, for example) or to reward certain "worthy" creditors (such as taxing authorities and alimony and child support claimants). A creditor whose debt is excepted from discharge under § 523(a) may attempt to collect that debt from the debtor after the debtor's bankruptcy case is over. That creditor also shares in the bankruptcy distribution. The debtor is protected from all other creditors, however, whose claims are still discharged. From the debtor's viewpoint, the sanction of excluding a single debt from discharge under § 523(a) is less severe than a denial of discharge of all debts under § 727(a).

An implicit fourth limitation on the availability of a chapter 7 discharge is the "*abuse*" test in § 707(b), which directs the bankruptcy court to dismiss a chapter 7 case if it finds that granting relief would be an abuse of the provisions of that chapter. As amended in 2005, the "abuse" test employs a detailed "means test" to determine whether the debtor has the capacity to repay a certain amount of his debts out of future income in a chapter 13 plan.[8] If so, the debtor's chapter 7 case will be dismissed, leaving the debtor with the choice whether to forego bankruptcy relief altogether or to proceed under a chapter 13 payment plan. In chapter 13, the debtor would have to commit all of his "projected disposable income" for three to five years to the payment of creditor claims. § 1325(b). Thus, a debtor with few current assets and large debts, but with the prospect of substantial future earnings, may not be allowed to discharge those debts at little price in chapter 7 and then keep for himself the full fruits of his future labors. Creditors get to share some of that future income.

Fifth, the debtor may choose to "*reaffirm*" debts that otherwise would be discharged.[9] § 524(c), (d). A valid reaffirmation agreement makes the debtor personally

---

[6]   See §§ 10.4–10.14.

[7]   See §§ 10.15–10.27. In addition to the discharge exclusions in § 523(a), Congress has sprinkled some nondischargeability rules through other parts of the United States Code. Examples include certain student loans, 42 U.S.C. § 292f(g) (Health Education Assistance Loan); 42 U.S.C. § 254o(d)(93) (National Health Service Corps loans); 37 U.S.C. § 301d(c)(3) (Armed Forces medical officers); bonus pay for an Armed Forces physician reservist, 37 U.S.C. § 302g(d), (e); and fines owed to the United States, 18 U.S.C. § 3613(e).

[8]   See § 2.15.

[9]   See §§ 10.34–10.36.

liable for the reaffirmed debt, notwithstanding the general discharge. The creditor is allowed to pursue collection if the debtor later defaults on the reaffirmed debt. While at first blush it seems absurd for a debtor to reaffirm, there are plausible reasons why debtors reaffirm. Most often the debtor wants to keep property subject to a valid lien, such as a car. A debtor also may choose voluntarily to repay a discharged debt, even without reaffirming the debt. § 524(f).

A final limitation is that valid *liens* and encumbrances on the debtor's property are not discharged, but continue to be enforceable against that property. The Supreme Court established this principle over a century ago in *Long v. Bullard*.[10] The § 524(a) discharge injunction only halts the collection of debts that represent a personal liability of the debtor. *In rem* liability remains. Thus, if specific property is subject to the debt, the secured creditor may enforce its lien. However, the secured creditor is limited to its collateral; recourse against the debtor personally for any deficiency claim is barred by the discharge.

The discharge rules change a bit when the debtor proceeds under one of the reorganization or debt adjustment chapters.[11] In chapter 11, the critical discharge event is the *confirmation* of the plan of reorganization (except in cases where the chapter 11 debtor is an individual). Section 1141(d)(1) provides that confirmation discharges the debtor from all debts that arose prior to the date of confirmation. Note that this is a later cutoff point than in chapter 7, which draws the discharge line at the time of the initial order for bankruptcy relief. Except in cases involving individual debtors, performance under the confirmed chapter 11 plan is not a prerequisite to discharge; confirmation of the plan is all that is required. For cases where the debtor is an individual, the chapter 11 discharge rules were amended in 2005 to conform more closely to chapter 13. For individuals, discharge normally occurs not at plan confirmation, but instead only after completion of all payments required by the plan, although the court has the power to order otherwise in certain circumstances. § 1141(d)(5). For individual debtors, the exceptions to discharge in § 523(a) apply in chapter 11 just as in chapter 7. § 1141(d)(2). However, the chapter 7 grounds for denial of discharge in § 727(a) only apply in a chapter 11 case in the event that the debtor is liquidating rather than reorganizing. § 1141(d)(3).

Chapter 13 is different still. Confirming a plan is much simpler than in chapter 11. However, discharge is not granted on confirmation, as it is in chapter 11 (except for individuals). Instead, a chapter 13 debtor receives a discharge under § 1328(a) only when she completes all payments under the confirmed plan. The only exception is that the court has the discretion to grant a "hardship" discharge under § 1328(b) to a debtor who fails to complete performance under the plan.

Until 2005, a full-compliance discharge under § 1328(a) was considerably broader than a chapter 7 discharge; many types of debts that are excluded from a chapter 7 discharge under § 523(a) (such as for fraud or taxes) were discharged under § 1328(a). For this reason the chapter 13 discharge was referred to as a "super" discharge.

---

[10]   117 U.S. 617 (1886).

[11]   See §§ 10.37–10.39.

However, in 2005, Congress amended the full-compliance chapter 13 discharge by taking away most of the "super" provisions; now, almost all of the important § 523(a) exceptions are excluded from discharge in chapter 13 as well. A § 1328(b) hardship discharge is and always has been subject to all of the § 523(a) exceptions. § 1328(c)(2). Long-term debts, i.e., those that extend beyond the life of the chapter 13 plan, are not discharged by the completion of plan payments under either type of chapter 13 discharge. § 1328(a)(1), (c)(1).

Until 2005, none of the chapter 7 grounds for discharge denial in § 727(a) applied in a chapter 13 case. In 2005, Congress added three grounds for denying (or delaying) a chapter 13 discharge that mirror similar rules in chapter 7. First, a restriction on discharges in successive cases was introduced for the first time. Now, a chapter 13 discharge is barred if the debtor received a discharge in a previous case under chapter 7, 11, or 12 that was filed during the previous four years, § 1328(f)(1), or in a prior chapter 13 case filed in the past two years, § 1328(f)(2). These time periods are shorter than those in chapter 7. § 727(a)(8), (9) (eight and six years). Second, the debtor must complete a course in personal financial management, unless excused. § 1328(g); compare § 727(a)(11). Finally, the debtor's discharge may be delayed if there is reason to believe that § 522(q) might be applicable to the debtor. §§ 1328(h), 727(a)(12).

Chapter 12, which provides for the adjustment of debts of family farmers, closely tracked chapter 13's discharge provisions until 2005. § 1228. One difference from the chapter 13 discharge is that in chapter 12, all of the § 523(a) discharge exceptions have always applied with full force. With the substantial changes to the chapter 13 discharge in 2005, there now are several more differences in the discharge provisions of the two chapters. There is no limitation in chapter 12 on receiving discharges in successive cases, as there now is in chapter 13. Nor is there a requirement in chapter 12 that the debtor complete a course in personal financial management, as in chapter 13. However, chapter 12 does also now require the court to delay the discharge if there is a possible pending action under § 522(q). § 1228(f).

A discharge may not necessarily be permanent. For a limited time (180 days in chapter 11, one year in all the other chapters), the court has the power to revoke the discharge. This drastic action, which is rarely invoked, usually is based on the debtor's fraud in procuring the discharge. §§ 727(d), (e), 1144, 1228(d), 1328(e).

Most discharge litigation takes place in the bankruptcy court.[12] This makes sense, given that discharge is entirely a federal bankruptcy policy. The bankruptcy court is the exclusive forum for resolution of all issues relating to the denial of a chapter 7 discharge under § 727(a).[13] Rule 4004(a). Likewise, complaints asserting that a debt is excepted from discharge under § 523(a)(2), (4), or (6) may be brought only in the bankruptcy court.[14] § 523(c)(1); Rule 4007(c). However, collateral estoppel may

---

[12] Under 28 U.S.C. § 157(b)(2)(I)–(J), objections to discharge under § 727(a) and dischargeability determinations under § 523(a) are core proceedings, which the bankruptcy court may "hear and determine" by entering a final order, reviewable only on appeal. See also Stern v. Marshall, 131 S.Ct. 2594 (2011). If the district court withdraws the reference of a case to the bankruptcy court under 28 U.S.C. § 157(d), it then serves as the trial court for core proceedings.

[13] See § 10.28.

[14] See § 10.29.

effectively foreclose litigation of discharge issues in the bankruptcy court when the debtor and creditor had previously litigated those issues in a non-bankruptcy forum.[15] Non-bankruptcy courts have concurrent jurisdiction with bankruptcy courts to hear issues under the remaining subsections of § 523(a).[16] However, discharge revocation issues must be tried solely in the bankruptcy court.

§ 10.2 The Scope of the Discharge

The discharge has a broad but not unlimited scope. In a chapter 7 liquidation case, § 727(b) governs the scope of the discharge. In the reorganization chapters, the discharge may have an even greater reach. Section 727(b) contains four basic premises:

1. Those debts listed in § 523(a) are excepted from the general discharge;

2. All other "debts" are discharged, provided that:

3. The debt arose or is deemed to arise prior to bankruptcy, and

4. Creditors do not have to share in the bankruptcy distribution for their debt to be discharged.

The exclusions from the discharge in § 523(a) are discussed at length later in this chapter.[17] In a chapter 7 case or a chapter 12 case, § 523(a) applies in its entirety. § 727(b) (chapter 7), § 1228(a)(2) (chapter 12). In chapter 11, § 523(a) applies to individual debtors only, thereby excluding corporate and partnership debtors from its coverage (except for a few types of tax debts, § 1141(d)(6)). § 1141(d)(2). Finally, until 2005, in chapter 13 many of the § 523(a) debts were discharged if the debtor completed performance under the plan. However, in 2005, Congress substantially amended the chapter 13 discharge provisions. Now, most important § 523(a) debts are excluded from discharge in chapter 13 as well, even if the debtor receives a "full compliance" discharge under § 1328(a).[18] § 1328(a)(2)–(4). A chapter 13 debtor who does not complete plan payments but receives a hardship discharge is subject to all of the § 523(a) exceptions. § 1328(c)(2). A chapter 13 discharge does not apply to long-term debts paid beyond the life of the plan. § 1328(a)(1), (c)(1).

The second limitation on the reach of the discharge is that only "*debts*" are discharged. This restriction applies in all chapters. "Debt" is a term of art in bankruptcy. Section 101(12) defines "debt" as "liability on a claim"; "claim," in turn, is defined in § 101(5). The operative principle of the § 101(5) definition is that any "right to payment" existing at the time of bankruptcy constitutes a claim cognizable in bankruptcy, and thus is potentially dischargeable.[19] A right to payment is still a claim even if it is unliquidated, contingent, unmatured, or disputed. § 101(5). Even rights to equitable remedies may be discharged if an alternative right to payment exists.[20]

---

[15] See § 10.30.

[16] 28 U.S.C. § 1334(b).

[17] See §§ 10.15–10.27.

[18] See § 10.38.

[19] See §§ 7.1–7.2.

[20] See § 7.3.

§ 101(5)(B). The amount of any of these types of uncertain claims may have to be fixed or estimated during the bankruptcy case, § 502(c), but that does not defeat their status as a claim. The Bankruptcy Code significantly expands the concept of claims from that which prevailed under prior law. The legislative history to the Code expresses the congressional intent "that all legal obligations of the debtor, no matter how remote or contingent, will be able to be dealt with in the bankruptcy case."[21]

The Supreme Court has implemented this legislative directive by giving "debt" and "claim" the broadest possible construction. In *Ohio v. Kovacs*, the Court held that a debtor's environmental cleanup obligation constituted a dischargeable debt, noting that the only performance sought by the state was the payment of money by the debtor.[22] In 1990 the Court held in *Pennsylvania Department of Public Welfare v. Davenport* that a criminal restitution obligation was a debt dischargeable in a chapter 13 case.[23] A year later in *Johnson v. Home State Bank* the Court concluded that a mortgage constituted a claim in chapter 13 even though the debtor's personal liability had previously been discharged in a chapter 7 case, reasoning that the mortgagee still had a right to payment through foreclosure of the mortgaged property.[24]

Not every conceivable legal obligation is a debt, however. A right to *payment* must exist as part of that obligation. This limitation has been most important in excluding certain types of equitable remedies from the debt definition, and thus from the discharge, when under applicable law a right to payment may not be substituted for the equitable relief. For example, an order commanding the debtor to clean up polluted property has been held not to be a debt if the environmental agency does not have the option of accepting a monetary payment in lieu of the cleanup.[25] Similarly, an employer's right to an injunction to enforce a covenant not to compete has been held not to be a claim dischargeable in bankruptcy if under state law money damages cannot be substituted for injunctive relief.[26]

The third limitation on the scope of the discharge relates to the timing of when the debt arose. Generally, the bankruptcy filing operates as the point of cleavage: pre-bankruptcy debts are discharged, while those arising after bankruptcy are not. In chapter 7 the discharge applies to "debts that arose before the date of the order for relief under this chapter." § 727(b). In the typical voluntary case filed by the debtor, the order for relief is the date the original bankruptcy petition is filed. § 301. Note that some types of claims that actually arise postpetition are deemed for bankruptcy purposes to arise prepetition, and accordingly are also covered by the discharge.

---

[21]   H.R. Rep. No. 95–595, 95th Cong., 1st Sess., at 309 (1977); S. Rep. No. 95–989, 95th Cong., 2d Sess., at 22 (1978).

[22]   469 U.S. 274, 285 (1985). The debtor had been dispossessed prior to bankruptcy by a receiver, and thus could not personally effect the cleanup of the polluted property.

[23]   495 U.S. 552, 564 (1990).

[24]   501 U.S. 78 (1991). The Court's decision thus opened up the possibility of a "chapter 20" case (i.e., chapter 7 + chapter 13), in which a debtor first files chapter 7 to discharge personal liability, and then files chapter 13 to restructure the secured claim.

[25]   See, e.g., United States v. Apex Oil Co., Inc., 579 F.3d 734 (7th Cir. 2009); In re Torwico Elecs., Inc., 8 F.3d 146 (3d Cir. 1993); In re Chateaugay Corp., 944 F.2d 997 (2d Cir. 1991). See also § 7.3.b.

[26]   See, e.g., In re Udell, 18 F.3d 403 (7th Cir. 1994). See also Kennedy v. Medicap Pharms., Inc., 267 F.3d 493 (6th Cir. 2001). See also § 7.3.c.

§ 502(f)–(i). For example, the trustee may reject an executory contract during the bankruptcy case, giving rise to a breach of contract claim by the other party to the contract. §§ 365(g)(1), 502(g). That claim is treated as a prepetition claim in the bankruptcy case.

The order for relief comes at a later date in an involuntary case or in a case converted to chapter 7 from another chapter, and thus some debts that arise after the initial bankruptcy filing may be discharged. In an involuntary case, the bankruptcy filing by the petitioning creditors does not constitute an order for relief. Instead, the order for relief is entered later by the court if it finds that grounds exist for the bankruptcy case to go forward. § 303(h). The result is that debts that arise after the filing of the bankruptcy petition but before the order for relief in an involuntary case are discharged. For converted cases, the conversion order constitutes the chapter 7 order for relief. § 348(a), (b). Thus, all pre-conversion debts are discharged.

A later discharge cutoff date governs in chapter 11 reorganization cases. All debts that arise before the date the plan of reorganization is confirmed are discharged. § 1141(d)(1)(A). In other words, all debts that arise during the pendency of the chapter 11 case are subject to discharge. Chapters 12 and 13 do not have a similar blanket discharge of pre-confirmation claims. In those chapters, discharge applies to all debts "provided for by the plan." §§ 1228(a), 1328(a). Typically only pre-bankruptcy debts will be provided for by the plan, thus effectively limiting the discharge to such debts. In chapter 13, however, certain types of postpetition claims may be allowed and dealt with in the plan, and thus discharged. § 1305.

Sometimes it is quite difficult to determine when a debt "arose." A difficult timing issue is created when the underlying acts that lead to the creation of the claim all occur prior to the bankruptcy case, but nevertheless under state law a cause of action is not cognizable until after the bankruptcy is filed. This scenario often arises for tort claims. The asbestos cases present a good example. The claimants were exposed to asbestos long before the filing of the bankruptcy case, but often did not manifest injury until many decades later, after bankruptcy. On a simpler level, a dentist may commit negligent malpractice prior to filing for bankruptcy, but the patient may not discover the injuries until after the dentist has filed.[27] The states vary on when the tort cause of action accrues in this type of situation, and may postpone accrual until manifestation of an injury.

Several approaches have been taken to deal with these timing problems.[28] Under the "conduct" test, a claim is deemed to arise for bankruptcy purposes if the conduct of the debtor that gives rise to the claim occurs prior to bankruptcy.[29] This approach moves the claim determination up to the earliest possible point in time. A discredited

---

[27] See In re Edge, 60 B.R. 690 (Bankr. M.D. Tenn. 1986).

[28] See § 7.2.

[29] See, e.g., Grady v. A.H. Robins Co., 839 F.2d 198 (4th Cir. 1988), cert. denied, 487 U.S. 1260 (1988). Prior to the bankruptcy filing of A.H. Robins Co., a Dalkon Shield IUD manufactured by Robins was inserted into Rebecca Grady; however, she did not manifest symptoms until after the filing. The court held that she had a claim, which was barred by the automatic stay. Note, though, that Grady *also* had been exposed to the defective product prior to bankruptcy, so she would have had a claim under the now-prevailing "prepetition relationship" test as well. See also Wright v. Corning, 679 F.3d 101 (3d Cir. 2012).

minority view, the "accrued state law theory," defers to the states by linking the concept of a bankruptcy claim to the accrual of a state law cause of action.[30] In contrast to the conduct test, the accrued state law theory postpones recognition of a claim. In between these two polar positions is the now dominant "prepetition relationship" test, which recognizes a claim if the claimant had a sufficient relationship with the debtor at the time of filing.[31] Conduct alone by the debtor would not be enough, but conduct coupled with exposure to a defective product might be, even if injuries are not manifested until after bankruptcy. Due process also may preclude the recognition of a claim and its discharge before the creditor even becomes aware that she has a claim.[32]

Environmental claims present a similar timing problem. The debtor may pollute prior to bankruptcy, but will not have cleaned up the property in accordance with the state or federal environmental law when the bankruptcy petition is filed. Thus, at the time of filing, cleanup obligations remain. The prospective environmental liability may still be undiscovered at the time bankruptcy is filed. Adding to the confusion is the fact that pollution is not a static act, but may instead present an ongoing threat. Once pollutants have been discharged, they may continue to be released, leaking into surrounding lands or water. The courts have had trouble in determining when a claim arises in these situations.[33] A common approach is to find a claim only if the environmental agency had "fair contemplation" of the environmental threat at the time of filing.[34]

A final important principle is that the discharge of debts is not dependent on the distribution of a dividend to the creditor. The discharge is effective against a debt even if no proof of claim is filed or if a claim is filed but not allowed. This rule applies in cases under all the chapters. § 727(b) (chapter 7); § 1141(d)(1)(A) (chapter 11); § 1228(a), (c) (chapter 12); § 1328(a), (c) (chapter 13). The creditor therefore does not have the ability to opt out of the bankruptcy discharge by forgoing a dividend in bankruptcy.

---

[30] In re M. Frenville Co., 744 F.2d 332 (3d Cir. 1984), cert. denied, 469 U.S. 1160 (1985). In *Frenville,* a claim for contribution was brought against a debtor after bankruptcy. The contribution claim did not accrue under state law until the party seeking contribution had itself been sued, which took place after the bankruptcy filing. However, all of the debtor's acts which gave rise to the contribution claim were performed prior to bankruptcy. The Third Circuit held there was no claim. The Third Circuit now has abandoned *Frenville.* See In re Grossman's Inc., 607 F.3d 114, 121, 125 (3d Cir. 2010):

Courts have declined to follow *Frenville* because of its apparent conflict with the Bankruptcy Code's expansive treatment of the term 'claim'. . . .

Irrespective of the title used, there seems to be something approaching a consensus among the courts that a prerequisite for recognizing a "claim" is that the claimant's exposure to a product giving rise to the "claim" occurred pre-petition, even though the injury manifested after the reorganization. We agree and hold that a "claim" arises when an individual is exposed pre-petition to a product or other conduct giving rise to an injury, which underlies a "right to payment" under the Bankruptcy Code.

[31] Epstein v. Official Comm. of Unsecured Creditors of Piper Aircraft Corp., 58 F.3d 1573 (11th Cir. 1995).

[32] See, e.g., Wright v. Corning, 679 F.3d 101 (3d Cir. 2012); Lemelle v. Universal Mfg. Corp., 18 F.3d 1268 (5th Cir. 1994).

[33] See Kathryn R. Heidt, Environmental Obligations in Bankruptcy: A Fundamental Framework, 44 Fla. L. Rev. 153 (1992).

[34] See, e.g., ZiLOG, Inc. v. Corning, 450 F.3d 996 (9th Cir. 2006) (adopting a "fair contemplation" test, which is similar to the pre-petition relationship test); In re Jensen, 995 F.2d 925, 930 (9th Cir. 1993).

§ 10.3   The Policy Behind the Discharge

A discharge of debts is not a necessary or inevitable part of a bankruptcy law. The essence of a bankruptcy proceeding, as with any other collective collection mechanism, is only that the nonexempt assets of the debtor be collected, liquidated, and distributed in a fair manner to the debtor's creditors. This task can be accomplished without a discharge.

Bankruptcy history illustrates that a freely available discharge is not required.[35] The first bankruptcy law in Anglo–American jurisprudence was passed in England in 1543,[36] but no discharge was offered until 1706.[37] Even then the debtor could not file a voluntary bankruptcy case to avail himself of the discharge; only creditors could commence a bankruptcy case. Debtors could not file a voluntary bankruptcy case in order to receive a discharge until the 1841 United States law[38]—almost 300 years after the passage of the first bankruptcy law. Even today, most other "civilized" countries do not offer the debtor as liberal a discharge from his debts as does the United States.

No single explanation can be offered for the current United States discharge policy. In fact, the policy justifications for the discharge and for exceptions to that discharge often are self-contradictory.[39] The most fundamental policy statement is that of the United States Supreme Court in the famous *Local Loan* case: that the bankruptcy discharge is designed to give "the honest but unfortunate debtor . . . a new opportunity in life and a clear field for future effort, unhampered by the pressure and discouragement of preexisting debt."[40] One may ask why a debtor needs or deserves such a fresh start.

Two primary justifications usually are given. First, it is considered humane not to require the debtor to spend the rest of his life buried under the weight of hopeless insolvency. Second, being humane to the debtor by discharging his debts actually indirectly benefits the rest of society. This social utility occurs because the debtor who has been freed from his debts has an incentive to work more and be a productive member of society, because he may keep from his creditors the product of his labors. As Justice Sutherland explained in *Local Loan,* where the Court held that William Hunt was freed from his pre-bankruptcy assignment of wages by his bankruptcy discharge:

---

[35]   See Charles J. Tabb, The Historical Evolution of the Bankruptcy Discharge, 65 Am. Bankr. L.J. 325 (1991).

[36]   34 & 35 Hen. 8, c. 4 (1542).

[37]   4 Anne, c. 17 (1705). See John C. McCoid, II, Discharge: The Most Important Development in Bankruptcy History, 70 Am. Bankr. L.J. 163 (1996).

[38]   Bankruptcy Act of 1841, ch. 9, §§ 1, 4, 5 Stat. 441, 443–44 (repealed 1843). See John C. McCoid, II, The Origins of Voluntary Bankruptcy, 5 Bankr. Dev. J. 361 (1988).

[39]   The justifications for discharge are explored in more detail in Charles J. Tabb, The Scope of the Fresh Start in Bankruptcy: Collateral Conversions and the Dischargeability Debate, 59 Geo. Wash. L. Rev. 56, 89–103 (1990). See also Margaret Howard, A Theory of Discharge in Consumer Bankruptcy, 48 Ohio St. L.J. 1047 (1987). For further discussions, see Barry Adler, Ben Polak, & Alan Schwartz, Regulating Consumer Bankruptcy: A Theoretical Inquiry, 29 J. Legal Stud. 585 (2000); Richard M. Hynes, Why (Consumer) Bankruptcy?, 56 Alal. L. Rev. 121 (2004).

[40]   Local Loan Co. v. Hunt, 292 U.S. 234, 244 (1934).

When a person assigns future wages, he, in effect, pledges his future earning power. The power of the individual to earn a living for himself and those dependent upon him is in the nature of a personal liberty quite as much if not more than it is a property right. To preserve its free exercise is of the utmost importance, not only because it is a fundamental private necessity, but because it is a matter of great public concern. From the viewpoint of the wage-earner there is little difference between not earning at all and earning wholly for a creditor. Pauperism may be the necessary result of either. . . . The new opportunity in life and the clear field for future effort, which it is the purpose of the Bankruptcy Act to afford the emancipated debtor, would be of little value to the wage-earner if he were obliged to face the necessity of devoting the whole or a considerable portion of his earnings for an indefinite time in the future to the payment of indebtedness incurred prior to his bankruptcy.[41]

The generous discharge right that the *Local Loan* Court was construing had been passed by Congress in 1898,[42] directly in response to the devastating Panic of 1893.[43] In an 1897 Report, the House of Representatives explained the justifications for this discharge provision in very human terms:

This vast number constitutes an army of men crippled financially—most of them active, aggressive, honest men who have met with misfortune in the struggle of life, and who, if relieved from the burden of debt, would reenter the struggle with fresh hope and vigor and become active and useful members of society. . . .

[T]he passage of a bankrupt law . . . will lift these terrible and hopeless burdens, and restore to the business and commercial circles of the country the active and aggressive elements that have met with misfortune and are now practically disabled for the battle of life. . . .

[W]hen an honest man is hopelessly down financially, nothing is gained for the public by keeping him down, but, on the contrary, the public good will be promoted by having his assets distributed ratably as far as they will go among his creditors and letting him start anew.[44]

The statements in *Local Loan* and the House Report also point out the basic restriction of the fresh start policy: that it is only available to "honest but unfortunate" debtors. Bankruptcy is not intended to be a haven for crooks and other bad actors.

---

[41] Id.

[42] Bankruptcy Act of 1898, ch. 541, 30 Stat. 550, §§ 14, 17 (1898) (repealed 1978).

[43] See Tabb, supra note 35, at 362–63.

[44] Id. at 365 n.21, (quoting H.R. Rep. No. 65, 55th Cong., 2d Sess., at 30–32 (1897) (incorporating H.R. Rep. No. 1228, 54th Cong., 1st Sess. (1896)).

Tabb further notes:

In a similar vein, Representative Henderson of Iowa, the House manager of the bill, argued, "Is it not better for the creditors to divide among them fairly what these poor fellows have and let them once more hold up their heads among their fellow-men and join their energies to those of the rest of the community for the common welfare?" Speech of Hon. David B. Henderson, in the House of Representatives, Feb. 16, 1898, in A National Bankruptcy Law, at 16.

Id.

Some of the grounds for denial of discharge in § 727(a) and most of the exceptions to discharge in § 523(a) are intended to withhold the benefits of the discharge from debtors who are not honest and just unfortunate, in order to deter the debtor's bad behavior. However, it appears somewhat inconsistent with the humanity and social utility rationales to keep even dishonest debtors bound eternally to their debts.

Another justification for our discharge policy may be labeled the "debtor cooperation" theory. The discharge is seen as a carrot offered to the debtor to entice him to cooperate in the bankruptcy case, so that more assets may be recovered for distribution to creditors. Those creditors basically are willing to forego the possibility of post-bankruptcy recovery later in the hope of a larger bankruptcy dividend now. Most of the discharge denial provisions in § 727(a) are directly related to the debtor's lack of cooperation in the bankruptcy case itself. The discharge originally came into English and American law to serve this induced compliance function. The debtor compliance rationale does not, however, mesh well with discharge exceptions, which undermine the debtor's incentive to cooperate.

These are not the only rationales for the discharge offered by scholars and courts. It has been suggested that the discharge is necessary to correct systematic overborrowing by debtors who are unable to control their impulses to take on too much credit and who are unable to project in advance their inability to repay their debts.[45] These phenomena may explain why the discharge is made nonwaivable in advance. § 727(a)(10). Others have posited that the bankruptcy discharge may operate as a form of limited liability for individuals. This argument leads to the question of whether the discharge is economically efficient, the answer to which depends largely on whether one believes the creditor or the debtor to be the superior risk-bearer.[46]

Unfortunately, Congress and the courts have not always clearly elucidated the policies supporting the discharge. Until recently, most courts had viewed the discharge as a fundamental debtor benefit, and accordingly had construed statutory limitations on the free grant of the discharge narrowly. This traditional pro-debtor orientation was redirected somewhat by the Supreme Court's 1991 decision in *Grogan v. Garner*, which, in holding that a preponderance of the evidence standard was proper under § 523(a), emphasized that the restriction to "honest but unfortunate" debtors was in fact intended to be a meaningful limitation on the fresh start policy.[47] The decline of the fresh start policy became more evident with the passage of BAPCPA in 2005, with its numerous provisions designed specifically to curtail the debtor's fresh start, substituting instead a policy "intended to ensure that debtors repay creditors the maximum they can afford."[48] In some cases, it appears that the Supreme Court has

---

[45] Thomas Jackson first expressed this view in Thomas H. Jackson, The Fresh–Start Policy in Bankruptcy Law, 98 Harv. L. Rev. 1393 (1985), and repeated it in Thomas H. Jackson, The Logic and Limits of Bankruptcy Law 232–48 (1986).

[46] Compare Theodore Eisenberg, Bankruptcy Law in Perspective, 28 UCLA L. Rev. 953 (1981) (arguing that the debtor is best able to assess the risk of default, and thus should not be offered a freely available discharge), with Margaret Howard, supra note 5, and Steven L. Harris, A Reply to Theodore Eisenberg's Bankruptcy Law in Perspective, 30 UCLA L. Rev. 327 (1982) (asserting that the creditor may be a better risk monitor and that discharge should be broadly available).

[47] 498 U.S. 279, 286–87 (1991).

[48] H.R. Rep. No. 109–31, 109th Cong., 1st Sess., at 2 (2005).

taken Congress at its word, interpreting the Bankruptcy Code in a way that in cases of doubt does not further the fresh start policy as much as the "make the debtor pay" policy.[49] As the Sixth Circuit has concluded, "[w]e believe it is now clear that . . . we must, as the Supreme Court did, . . . apply the interpretation that has the best chance of fulfilling [the] . . . purpose of maximizing creditor recoveries."[50] And yet, in a 2013 case, *Bullock v. BankChampaign, N.A.*,[51] the Supreme Court reaffirmed its longstanding policy of narrowly construing exceptions to discharge, so as to promote the fresh start, denying it usually only in instances of knowing and clear debtor fault.

B. GROUNDS FOR DENIAL OF A CHAPTER 7 DISCHARGE: § 727

§ 10.4 Individual Debtors Only

The first limitation on the grant of the discharge is that only an individual debtor is eligible. § 727(a)(1). A corporation or a partnership may file a chapter 7 case, but will not receive a discharge. Since the business entity is being liquidated, and will not continue to exist after bankruptcy, a discharge is unnecessary. Only people need a "fresh start" in life; they do continue to exist after a bankruptcy liquidation. An individual who is a partner in a partnership thus needs to file personal bankruptcy to discharge his personal responsibility for partnership debts. Causing the partnership alone to go through chapter 7 will not relieve the individual partner of liability for partnership debts. This first limitation on the discharge right, unlike most in § 727(a), is self-executing; Rule 4004(c)(1) requires the court to refuse the discharge if the debtor is not an individual, even if no complaint objecting to discharge is filed.

§ 10.5 Actual Fraudulent Transfers

The current Bankruptcy Code follows centuries of precedent in demanding that a debtor who seeks the privilege of a discharge in bankruptcy must not intentionally attempt to frustrate the collection efforts of creditors prior to and in that bankruptcy case. Section 727(a)(2) bars the discharge of a debtor who has made actual fraudulent transfers within a year of the bankruptcy or in the case itself. Several elements must be proven by a party objecting to the debtor's discharge under that section.

First, the requisite "intent to hinder, delay, or defraud" of the debtor must be established. This evil intent must be directed at either a creditor, typically one seeking to collect a debt prior to bankruptcy, or an officer in the bankruptcy case charged with custody of estate property, typically the bankruptcy trustee. Actual fraudulent intent must be proven; constructive fraud is not enough.[52] Evidence of surrounding circumstances—"badges of fraud"—may be considered to help prove actual fraudulent intent. Common indicia of fraud include transfers for no consideration or for nominal

---

[49]   See, e.g., Ransom v. FIA Card Servs., N.A., 131 S.Ct. 716 (2011). See also § 2.15.c.

[50]   Baud v. Carroll, 634 F.3d 327, 356 (6th Cir. 2011).

[51]   133 S.Ct. 1754 (2013). The issue before the Court was the scope of the term "defalcation" in § 523(a)(4). See § 10.19.

[52]   See, e.g., In re Miller, 39 F.3d 301 (11th Cir. 1994). See also In re Herman, 396 Fed. Appx. 108, 110 (5th Cir. 2010) ("A plaintiff must prove actual fraud—not constructive fraud. . . . ").

consideration; transfers to relatives, friends, or business associates; transfers made at suspicious times, such as shortly before filing bankruptcy or after a creditor files a lawsuit; the debtor's continued possession and use of the supposedly transferred property; secrecy in the transaction; and so forth. While circumstantial evidence is helpful, fraudulent intent nevertheless is not lightly found.

A common defense debtors raise when challenged under § 727(a)(2) is that they did not have the requisite fraudulent intent because they were relying on someone else's advice—their attorney, or their accountant, or their spouse.[53] Courts have been surprisingly receptive to such self-serving claims of innocence in many cases, at least if the alleged reliance is even remotely reasonable. An unsophisticated debtor is most likely to be granted lenity in these cases.

The second element of a § 727(a)(2) case is that the property must be "transferred, removed, destroyed, mutilated, or concealed." The statutory list is designed to be broad, in order to encompass a variety of acts that potentially could frustrate collection efforts. It is the possibility of harm to the creditor that is relevant, not the benefit to the debtor. For example, if something is done to the property with the requisite intent so as to make it unavailable to both the creditor and the debtor, the statute is satisfied. The last category, concealment, is of particular relevance in the bankruptcy case itself. The debtor must be totally forthcoming in his bankruptcy schedules and at the meeting of creditors regarding the description and location of his assets.

While in most cases the actor effectuating the transfer, destruction, or the like will be the debtor himself, such is not an absolute requirement. The statute is met if the debtor "permitted" any such activity. In other words, the debtor cannot hide behind the facade of an agent or intermediary, but is held fully responsible for the authorized acts of that agent.

Third, the property affected must be property which either before or in the bankruptcy case would have been available for distribution to creditors but for the fraudulent activity. Otherwise no harm to creditors (even theoretically) could occur, and no reason exists to deprive the debtor of his discharge. The property must be that of the debtor with regard to pre-bankruptcy activities, or property of the bankruptcy estate for activities occurring after the bankruptcy is filed.

An intriguing question that has arisen is whether a debtor can effectively "undo" a fraudulent transfer before bankruptcy and thereby avoid denial of discharge under § 727(a)(2). This might occur if the debtor initially has gotten extremely bad advice—to make a fraudulent transfer (e.g., quitclaim Blackacre to your spouse)—from an attorney, and then learns the truth from another attorney before filing, and thus reverses the deed. The argument that the debtor should still receive a discharge is that this will encourage debtors to "come clean" and restore property for the benefit of their creditors before bankruptcy.[54] The more literal reading of the Code language, however,

---

[53]   See, e.g., Gregory E. Maggs, Consumer Bankruptcy Fraud and the "Reliance on Advice of Counsel" Argument, 69 Am. Bankr. L.J. 1 (1995).

[54]   See, e.g., In re Retz, 606 F.3d 1189 (9th Cir. 2010); In re Adeeb, 787 F.2d 1339 (9th Cir. 1986).

points the other way; if the debtor makes a fraudulent transfer, the discharge right is lost, no matter what happens thereafter.[55]

Finally, § 727(a)(2) only has a limited reach-back in time. The fraudulent act must have occurred within *one year* of the bankruptcy petition to bar the debtor's discharge. A two-year limitation exists for the avoidance of fraudulent transfers by the bankruptcy trustee under § 548, and a trustee also may be able to avoid transfers more than two years old by resort to state fraudulent transfer law under § 544(b). Under § 727(a)(2), however, the one-year limit is set in stone, and cannot be circumvented by resort to longer state law periods. Having said that, in some situations the one-year period in § 727(a)(2) may as a practical matter be stretched a bit. For example, if the debtor delayed recording or perfecting the fraudulent transfer (e.g., the proverbial quitclaim deed of Blackacre to the debtor's spouse), the time of the transfer may be deemed to occur at the time of recordation or perfection, see § 548(d), not when the transfer actually occurred. A second illustration is that a fraudulent transfer that was originally made more than a year prior to bankruptcy may be brought within the one-year period if the debtor actively concealed the transfer in that year. On the other end of the time spectrum, the debtor has a continuing responsibility during the bankruptcy case not to deal fraudulently with estate property. However, the debtor's postpetition actions with regard to his own property cannot serve as a basis for discharge denial. This is because a debtor's postpetition property, which does not go into the estate, is not distributed to the bankruptcy creditors anyway.

A debtor who makes a preferential transfer to a creditor generally is not brought within the scope of § 727(a)(2). A preference, while perhaps avoidable in its own right under § 547, is not fraud that will deprive a debtor of his discharge. In contrast, a debtor who makes a preferential transfer to an "insider" may face some risk of classification of the transfer as a fraudulent conveyance[56] and thus within § 727(a)(2). Most likely, however, such a transfer would constitute only constructive and not actual fraud, and would thus be outside the ambit of § 727(a)(2).

An area of controversy under § 727(a)(2) concerns a debtor who converts nonexempt property to exempt property shortly before bankruptcy. The legislative history suggests that such a practice is not necessarily fraudulent:

> As under current law, the debtor will be permitted to convert non-exempt property into exempt property before filing a bankruptcy petition. The practice is not fraudulent as to creditors, and permits the debtor to make full use of the exemptions to which he is entitled under the law.[57]

Courts differ on whether such activity is simply prudent planning by the debtor or fraud within the meaning of § 727(a)(2). While courts agree that "mere" conversion of nonexempt to exempt property is not enough to prove fraud, they differ on how much

---

[55]   See, e.g., In re Davis, 911 F.2d 560 (11th Cir. 1990). See also San Jose v. McWilliams, 284 F.3d 785 (7th Cir. 2002).

[56]   See Unif. Fraudulent Conveyance Act § 5(b).

[57]   H.R. Rep. No. 95–595, 95th Cong., 1st Sess., at 361 (1977); S. Rep. No. 95–989, 95th Cong. 2d Sess., at 76 (1978).

more must be shown. Perhaps the clearest illustration of the hopelessly confused state of the law is found in two decisions handed down by the Eighth Circuit on the very same day that reached opposite results. The only apparent differences were that in one case the debtor was a doctor who converted over $700,000 into exempt assets and sought to discharge $19 million,[58] whereas in the other the debtor was a farmer who converted only a few thousand dollars and had much smaller total debts.[59] The disparate results are best summed up in the homespun expression that "when a pig becomes a hog it is slaughtered."[60] If the debtor has actively misled creditors in connection with the exemption conversion scheme, however, courts have no trouble in finding fraud and denying the discharge.[61] In short, exemption planning poses a risk to the debtor's discharge.[62]

§ 10.6 Unjustified Failure to Keep Proper Books and Records

A debtor may be denied a discharge if she has unjustifiably failed to keep books and records that are adequate to permit creditors and the bankruptcy trustee to ascertain the true status of the debtor's financial condition and her past business transactions. § 727(a)(3). Complete disclosure is thus a condition of the discharge. Interested parties must be able to figure out, at least roughly, what when wrong. They do not, however, have to be happy with what they discover.

Section 727(a)(3) may be triggered either by an act or omission of the debtor. The objecting party must prove either an act—that the debtor "has concealed, destroyed, mutilated, [or] falsified" financial records—or an omission—that the debtor has "failed to keep or preserve" such records. Thus, a debtor has both an affirmative duty to keep proper records in the first place and to refrain from using the paper shredder. Unlike § 727(a)(2), the objecting party does *not* have to prove any culpable mental state of the debtor in connection with the requisite act or omission. Also unlike § 727(a)(2), the "bad books" exception does not on its face extend to the acts (or omissions) of an authorized agent of the debtor, although courts have held the debtor responsible for an agent's acts or omissions under § 727(a)(3) as well.[63]

The section is noticeably and perhaps intentionally vague about exactly what kind of financial records the debtor must have. "[A]ny recorded information, including books, documents, records, and papers," may qualify, depending on whether they would have served the function of assisting in ascertaining "the debtor's financial condition or business transactions." Note that non-business consumer debtors are covered by the reference to "financial condition." Courts have fleshed out the section by requiring records of a type typical for someone in the debtor's circumstances—in effect a

---

[58] In re Tveten, 848 F.2d 871 (8th Cir. 1988).
[59] Hanson v. First Nat'l Bank, 848 F.2d 866 (8th Cir. 1988).
[60] In re Swift, 3 F.3d 929 (5th Cir. 1993).
[61] See, e.g., In re Reed, 700 F.2d 986 (5th Cir. 1983).
[62] See § 9.5.
[63] See, e.g., In re Sherod, Bankr. No. 89–2007–C H, 1990 WL 10593998 (S.D. Iowa Nov. 2, 1990).

"reasonable financial record-keeper" standard.[64] Application of this standard will vary depending on the debtor's line of work, education, business sophistication, and the like. For those to whom much is given, much is expected.[65]

Even if the court finds that the objecting party has established that the debtor's records were inadequate, the final clause of § 727(a)(3) offers the debtor an escape hatch. The debtor still may receive a discharge if the court finds the debtor's failure was *justified* in light of the surrounding circumstances of the case. For example, an "innocent" spouse may be able to establish justification by showing they relied on the other spouse to keep the records,[66] or one partner may show that he justifiably relied on another partner to maintain partnership records.[67]

Courts have differed over whether the debtor has the burden of proving justification once the creditor or trustee has proven inadequate records, or whether the objecting party still has to prove the absence of justification. The two-step burden-shifting approach now appears to be the prevailing view.[68] In any event, justification can be difficult to establish. The debtor must come forward with a convincing explanation as to why she should not be held accountable for a very real failure that indisputably has interfered with the efficacious administration of the bankruptcy case.

§ 10.7 Bankruptcy Crimes

The fourth ground for denial of discharge is the commission by the debtor of a bankruptcy crime "in or in connection with the case." Section 727(a)(4) specifies four different acts that, when done "knowingly and fraudulently," will bar discharge. If the United States Attorney chooses to pursue the matter (and the bankruptcy court has a duty to inform the United States Attorney when it believes a bankruptcy crime has been committed), the debtor may face an even more unpleasant prospect than loss of discharge: conviction of a federal felony under 18 U.S.C. § 152. Such a conviction carries a possible penalty of a fine or five years in prison, or both. Of course, not every debtor whose discharge is denied under § 727(a)(4) will end up serving time. The United States Attorney may choose not to prosecute, and the standard of proof is higher in the criminal proceeding (beyond a reasonable doubt) than in the bankruptcy discharge trial (preponderance). A criminal conviction would be conclusive in a subsequent bankruptcy discharge proceeding through application of collateral estoppel.[69]

The acts contained in the statutory list of § 727(a)(4)(A)–(D) all pertain in some way to the fair and effective operation of the bankruptcy process. They give content to

---

[64] See, e.g., In re Banks, 420 B.R. 579 (Bankr. M.D. Fla. 2009) (excusing folk artist-debtor's failure to keep adequate records); In re Sigust, 255 B.R. 822 (Bankr. W.D. La. 2000) (requiring debtor with MBA do more than retain tax returns).

[65] See, e.g., Meridian Bank v. Alten, 958 F.2d 1226 (3d Cir. 1992). See also In re Womble, 108 Fed. Appx. 993 (5th Cir. 2004).

[66] E.g., In re Cox, 41 F.3d 1294 (9th Cir. 1994).

[67] E.g., In re Cacioli, 463 F.3d 229 (2d Cir. 2006).

[68] See id.

[69] E.g., In re Raiford, 695 F.2d 521 (11th Cir. 1983). See also In re Jasper, 312 F.App'x. 97 (10th Cir. 2008).

the requirement in early bankruptcy laws that the debtor must "conform" to the bankruptcy law in order to receive his discharge. A party objecting to discharge under § 727(a)(4) need only prove one of the four specified grounds to prevail.

The first act is probably of the greatest practical importance: making a false oath or account in the bankruptcy case. The debtor has a duty to prepare and file detailed schedules and statements of affairs. The trustee and the creditors then can pore over those schedules, which are a matter of public record, and question the debtor at the meeting of creditors about his financial affairs. Any misstatement or omission by the debtor exposes him to possible loss of discharge under § 727(a)(4), subject to proof of the requisite *mens rea*. Courts also have required the mistake to be material.[70] For example, a common scenario involves the debtor's failure to list a valuable asset on his schedules.[71] Harm to creditors need not be proven, however.[72]

The other acts under § 727(a)(4) occur—or at least are litigated—much less frequently than subsection (A). Subsection (B) proscribes presenting or using a false claim in the case. The third subsection, (C), prohibits a discharge in the event of the debtor's extortion, bribery, or attempts at the same. The final subsection, (D), bars the discharge for withholding books and records relating to the debtor's property and financial affairs from an officer of the estate. The close relationship between this ground and § 727(a)(3) is apparent.

The hard proof for a party objecting to discharge under § 727(a)(4) is proof of the requisite mental state of the debtor. The specified act must be committed "*knowingly and fraudulently*" by the debtor. An honest or even a negligent mistake will not deprive the debtor of the benefits of a discharge. A debtor may argue that the mistake was not his but that of his attorney or accountant. Courts try to determine whether the mistake should have been evident to the debtor, who is ultimately responsible for his schedules. There is a limit to the "see no evil, hear no evil" attitude behind which courts will permit debtors to hide. At some point, an extreme reckless disregard for the truth will suffice to block the discharge.

§ 10.8   Failure to Explain Loss of Assets

Debtors who end up in bankruptcy court usually have lost a considerable portion of their property, and no longer have sufficient assets to meet their liabilities. The fifth ground for denial of discharge requires the debtor to "explain satisfactorily" how this financial situation came to pass. § 727(a)(5). This explanation requirement is presented in the statements of affairs that the debtor has to file, and in the official meeting of creditors.

---

[70] See In re Tripp, 224 B.R. 95 (Bankr. N.D. Iowa 1998). In *Tripp*, the debtors failed to list illegal marijuana on their property schedules. The court rejected the debtors' argument that this omission was not material since no value could be realized for the estate by the sale of the illegal drug. The court explained that the debtor's obligation is to disclose all of their property.

[71] See, e.g., Stamat v. Neary, 635 F.4d 974 (7th Cir. 2011); In re Calder, 907 F.2d 953 (10th Cir. 1990).

[72] E.g., In re Bressler, 387 B.R. 446 (Bankr. S.D.N.Y 2008) ("Omitted or incorrect information may be 'material' for purposes of section 727(a)(4)(A) even if the failure to disclose was not prejudicial to creditors."); *Tripp*, supra note 70, 224 B.R. 95.

The critical question under § 727(a)(5) is what constitutes a "satisfactory" explanation. The Code itself is silent on the issue; much is left to the discretion of the court in the particular case.[73] The objecting party usually establishes a prima facie case by showing a significant loss of assets or general insolvency. The debtor then has the burden of going forward with a satisfactory explanation of what happened. To be "satisfactory" the debtor's explanation does not have to convince the court that the loss was not the debtor's fault, or that the debtor acted properly in the past in incurring the to-be-explained loss. All that § 727(a)(5) asks of the debtor is that he shed sufficient light on what transpired in the past that the trustee and the creditors know what happened, even though they may not be too happy with what they have learned. For example, a debtor who testifies credibly that he bet all of his savings on "Lucky Star" to win in the seventh race at Louisiana Downs should be granted a discharge. Courts most often find explanations to be unsatisfactory when they are very general or vague ("spent everything on drugs"), or of suspect credibility ("the dog ate my bearer bonds").[74] The lack of documentation or other independent corroboration also may be quite important. The debtor who bet on Lucky Star will fare better in court if he still has the losing race ticket.

In some ways § 727(a)(5) has a broader scope than some of the other grounds in § 727(a). Noticeable by its absence is any requirement of a particular intent or mental state on the part of the debtor. Even if the court believes the debtor is doing the very best job he can to reconstruct the details of his financial downfall, if the debtor fails in that task his discharge will be denied. The section also does not contain any limitation on how far back in time the loss that is to be explained can have occurred, although a few courts have read in a two-year limit, perhaps as a sort of "penumbra" from other parts of § 727(a).[75] The farther back in time the debtor has to go to explain losses, the more difficult his job becomes.

§ 10.9 Refusal to Testify or Obey Lawful Court Order

The debtor's duty to cooperate in the bankruptcy case is reinforced by § 727(a)(6), which bars the discharge if the debtor refuses to testify in the bankruptcy case or to obey lawful court orders. The debtor will be required to testify at the § 341 meeting of creditors, and may have to testify thereafter at a variety of court proceedings or depositions. The court also may order the debtor to take certain actions in the case, such as to turn over property, amend schedules, produce documents, appear in court or at a deposition, and so on. If the order is lawful,[76] the debtor must comply or lose his discharge under subsection (A). The debtor might try to squirm off the hook by arguing that his failure to comply was not a "refusal," but rather only an oversight, or was

---

[73] See, e.g., In re Martin, 698 F.2d 883, 886 (7th Cir. 1983) ("Section 727(a)(5) is broadly drawn and clearly gives a court broad power to decline to grant a discharge in bankruptcy where the debtor does not adequately explain a shortage, loss, or disappearance of assets.").

[74] See, e.g., In re D'Agnese, 86 F.3d 732 (7th Cir. 1996). In *D'Agnese*, the debtor was unable to remember what had happened to over $300,000 in assets, which included various pieces of jewelry, Waterford crystal decanters, and sterling silver serving pieces.

[75] See, e.g., In re Lindemann, 375 B.R. 450, 472 (Bankr. N.D. Ill. 2007) (noting that a focus on the two years prior to the bankruptcy filing is common).

[76] An order would usually be unlawful only in the rare event that the bankruptcy court exceeded its jurisdiction.

subject to forces beyond his control, thereby reading an element of willful disobedience into the statute. Some courts have accepted this interpretation of the statute.[77]

A major change was made by Congress in the 1978 Bankruptcy Reform Act with regard to the debtor's refusal to testify. Under prior law, the debtor had to choose between invoking his Fifth Amendment privilege against self-incrimination, in which case he lost his discharge, or testifying in order to receive a discharge. Under the current Bankruptcy Code the debtor no longer faces this dilemma. He may invoke his constitutional privilege against self-incrimination and still receive a discharge. § 727(a)(6)(B). If, however, the debtor is granted immunity, he then must testify or lose his discharge. The immunity given is use immunity, not transactional immunity.[78]

The statute does not permit any basis for refusal to answer other than invocation of the Fifth Amendment privilege. It has been held, contrary to the apparent facial meaning of § 727(a)(6)(C), that a debtor may invoke any privilege contained in Rule 501 of the Federal Rules of Evidence without losing his discharge. If a debtor does refuse to answer a question, the other party must then go to the bankruptcy court and get the question approved as material, at which point the debtor is again given the opportunity to answer and preserve his discharge. A final line of defense for the debtor will be that he has not "refused" to answer, if he has given equivocal and evasive answers. When "I can't remember" becomes the equivalent of "I refuse to answer" is a matter for the court's sound discretion.

§ 10.10 Commission of Prohibited Acts in Bankruptcy of an Insider

The seventh ground for denial of discharge goes beyond prior law, making a debtor responsible for the consequences of his actions not just in his own bankruptcy case, but also in the bankruptcy case of an "insider." § 727(a)(7). An individual debtor is denied discharge in his own case if he committed any of the acts specified in subsections (2), (3), (4), (5), or (6) of § 727(a) in an insider's bankruptcy case. One court noted that the section "strengthens the court's ability to prevent abuse to the system as a whole and provides additional means to defeat a discharge of those who may damage the integrity of the bankruptcy system through impropriety in a prior case."[79]

Section 727(a)(7) applies to acts committed up to one year prior to the debtor's own case, and continues to apply throughout the debtor's case. Section 101(31)(A) defines who is an "insider" to an individual debtor. Included are close personal or business associates: the debtor's relatives, relatives of a general partner of the debtor, a partnership of which the debtor is the general partner, a general partner of the debtor, or a corporation of which the debtor is an officer, director, or control person. Thus, even if the debtor in his own individual case acts in a totally exemplary manner, he still will be denied a discharge in his personal case if he commits a proscribed act in the

---

[77] See, e.g., Standiferd v. U.S. Trustee, 641 F.3d 1209, 1212 (10th Cir. 2011) ("Ultimately, the court may not deny discharge under § 727(a)(6)(A) unless it finds that the debtor's non-compliance was willful."); In re Jordan, 521 F.3d 430, 433 (4th Cir. 2008) (noting that a majority of courts have found that the word "refused" requires the showing of a willful or intentional act).

[78] See generally Kastigar v. United States, 406 U.S. 441 (1972) (discussing the difference between use immunity and transactional immunity).

[79] Am. Savs. & Loan Ass'n v. Weber (In re Weber), 99 B.R. 1001, 1015 (Bankr. D. Utah 1989).

bankruptcy case involving his business.[80] Note, however, that a debtor cannot be an "insider" of himself (this is bankruptcy, not psychiatry), so that if a debtor commits a prohibited act in his own case, which is then dismissed, that earlier malfeasance will not bar his discharge in a subsequent case.

§ 10.11 Time Bar on Successive Discharges

One of the principal restrictions on the availability of the discharge is that a debtor may only avail himself of the discharge privilege every *six* or *eight* years (depending on which bankruptcy chapter he received a discharge under in the prior case). Prior to the 2005 amendments, the time bar was six years in all instances. The time bar is intended to prevent abuse of the bankruptcy system, and to avoid having a habitual debtor class. Early bankruptcy laws approached the problem of successive bankruptcies by conditioning the discharge in the second case on the payment of a significant minimum dividend to creditors in the first case.[81] Current law does not prevent the filing and processing of a second bankruptcy case within six or eight years of a prior case; it simply does not permit a discharge in that second case.

The six or eight-year time bar applies only when the *second case* is a *chapter 7*. The debtor can cut the time limit by filing a chapter 13 case the second time around, instead of a chapter 7. Section 727(a) does not apply in chapter 13. A chapter 13 debtor will be denied discharge if the debtor received a discharge in a case filed under Chapter 7, 11, or 12 in the *four years* preceding the second filing, § 1328(f)(1), or in a chapter 13 case in the past two years, § 1328(f)(2). The 2005 amendments imposed a time bar in chapter 13 for the first time.[82] A debtor may avoid the time bar entirely by reorganizing under chapter 11 in the second case. However, if the debtor liquidates in chapter 11, § 1141(d)(3) reimposes the time limitation.

There are two possible time bars (six years or eight years) when the second case is a chapter 7, depending on what chapter the debtor received a discharge under in the first case. Subsection (8) of § 727(a) addresses the situation where the *first* case was under *chapter 7* or *chapter 11*. If the debtor received a discharge in the first case, he is absolutely precluded from receiving a discharge in a second case under chapter 7 commenced within *eight years*. § 727(a)(8). This time period was extended from six to eight years in 2005.[83] Rule 4004(c) apparently requires an objection to be filed alleging a violation of the eight-year bar, even though the times of the respective filings would seem to be a fact of which a court could take judicial notice.

The eight-year period is computed from the date of the *commencement* of case 1 to the commencement of case 2, *not* from discharge to discharge. Thus, if the second case is *filed* more than eight years after the first case was filed, § 727(a)(8) will not bar discharge, irrespective of whether the discharges were granted within eight years of

---

[80] E.g., In re Krehl, 86 F.3d 737, 743 (7th Cir. 1996); In re Adams, 31 F.3d 389 (6th Cir. 1994), cert. denied, 513 U.S. 1111 (1995).

[81] See Charles J. Tabb, The Historical Evolution of the Bankruptcy Discharge, 65 Am. Bankr. L.J. 325 (1991).

[82] Pub. L. No. 109–8, § 312(2), 119 Stat. 87 (2005).

[83] Id. § 312(1), 119 Stat. 86–87.

each other. Even if the debtor did not receive a discharge in the first case (thereby rendering § 727(a)(8) inapplicable), § 523(a)(10) will prevent him from discharging in the second case the debts not discharged in the first case.

Section 727(a)(9) provides a slightly different rule for the situation where the first case was a debt adjustment case under *chapter 13* or *chapter 12*. Assuming again that the debtor did receive a discharge in the first case (even a hardship discharge, i.e., one in which plan payments were not completed), whether the discharge in the subsequent chapter 7 case is barred under § 727(a)(9) depends on what happened in the first case. Unlike subsection (8), subsection (9) does not impose an absolute bar, and the time limit is *six years*, not eight. Like subsection (8), the six-year time between cases is computed between filing dates, not discharge dates.

The debtor may receive his discharge in a chapter 7 case following a chapter 13 or chapter 12 case in one of two circumstances. First, if unsecured creditors were paid 100% on their claims in the original debt adjustment case, § 727(a)(9)(A) permits discharge in the ensuing liquidation case. The full payout case cannot be considered an abuse of the bankruptcy system, and the creditors were not harmed in that first case. Even if the debtor did not pay 100% on unsecured claims in the first chapter 13 or 12 case, he still may receive a discharge if 70% was paid on unsecured claims in the first case *and* that 70% plan was proposed in good faith by the debtor and represented the debtor's best efforts. § 727(a)(9)(B). The confirmation of the chapter 13 plan in the first case must contain a finding of good faith, § 1325(a)(3), and the legislative history suggests that debtors likewise should be able to obtain a "best efforts" finding in the confirmation order.[84] Those findings in the first case should clear the way for a discharge in a subsequent chapter 7.

§ 10.12 Waiver of Discharge

The bankruptcy discharge privilege is offered to most individual debtors for most debts, but not all eligible debtors choose to accept the discharge offer. Instead, for a variety of reasons, a few debtors elect to waive the discharge. This waiver is valid and enforceable against the debtor, pursuant to § 727(a)(10), subject to a few important restrictions.

By far the most important and meaningful restriction is that the discharge is not waivable *in advance*. Waiver is only valid when executed *after* the bankruptcy case is commenced. This prevents creditors from obtaining blanket discharge waivers as a matter of course at the time credit is extended. The nonwaivability of the discharge is one of the cornerstones of the United States consumer bankruptcy system.

Section 727(a)(10) also requires the waiver to be in *writing*, thus obviating any argument either of "implied waiver" from the debtor's actions or of an oral waiver. Finally, the court is required to approve the waiver, which is a change from prior law. It should be noted that the statute does not elucidate any standard pursuant to which the court may choose not to approve the executed waiver, and Rule 4004(c) likewise

---

[84]   124 Cong. Rec. H11,098 (daily ed. Sept. 28, 1978) (statement of Rep. Edwards); 124 Cong. Rec. S17,415 (daily ed. Oct. 6, 1978) (statement of Sen. DeConcini).

does not suggest any basis for the court to exercise its discretion to decline to approve a waiver. This is to be contrasted with the substantive requirements for court approval of agreements to reaffirm particular debts in certain circumstances under § 524(c). The approval limitation thus may only demand that the court ascertain that the waiver in fact was knowingly and voluntarily made, although some courts will undertake a more substantive paternalistic review of the wisdom of the debtor's choice.

§ 10.13 Failure to Complete Personal Financial Management Course

The 2005 amendments added a series of provisions to the Code imposing requirements of "credit counseling" for individual debtors.[85] The new provisions require an individual debtor to get counseling *twice*: first, *before* filing bankruptcy, as a condition of eligibility to file bankruptcy at all, under any chapter,[86] § 109(h), and then again *after* filing, during the case, as a condition of receiving a discharge in a case under chapter 7 (§ 727(a)(11)) or chapter 13 (§ 1328(g)). These debtor education requirements were proudly hailed as significant *"Consumer Debtor Bankruptcy Protections."*[87] Given that the only consequence of non-compliance in both cases is to harm the debtor—first, by barring the debtor from filing bankruptcy, and second, by denying the debtor a discharge—debtors might prefer a little less "protection." Perhaps Congress also contemplated some "protection" for *creditors*, who would be exposed to fewer credit risks if dealing with a more financially savvy debtor class.

The purported idea behind the new discharge rule was stated in the House Report: "The bill also requires debtors, after they file for bankruptcy relief, to receive financial management training that will provide them with guidance about how to manage their finances, so that they can avoid future financial difficulties."[88] Congress must have been inspired by the old Confucian proverb, "give a man a fish, you feed him for a day; teach a man to fish, you feed him for a lifetime" (and, perhaps, given the function of § 727(a)(11)—"if he won't learn how to fish, you throw him overboard"!).

To avoid the discharge bar of § 727(a)(11) (in chapter 7) or § 1328(g) (in chapter 13), the debtor must complete an approved "instructional course concerning personal financial management." The debtor then must file a certificate of completion (following Official Form 23) with the court, within 60 days of the first date set for the § 341 meeting of creditors. Rule 1007(b)(7), (c). Note that the course *must* be completed *after* the bankruptcy filing, and, in order to receive the discharge, before the discharge hearing. Most courts have allowed a debtor who failed to complete the course to reopen their case, take the course, and then receive a discharge.[89] The statute does not appear to allow a debtor who took an approved course *prior* to filing to count that course for purposes of avoiding the discharge bar.

A new § 111 provides detailed requirements regulating approved credit counseling agencies and the financial management instructional services to be offered. The United

---

[85]   Pub. L. No. 109–8, 119 Stat. 37–42 (2005).

[86]   See § 2.3.b.

[87]   H.R. Rep. No. 109–31 (pt. 1), 109th Cong., 1st Sess., at 17–18 (2005).

[88]   Id. at 18.

[89]   See, e.g., In re Meaney, 397 B.R. 390 (Bankr. N.D. Ill. 2008).

States trustee supervises the approval of counseling agencies and instructional courses. The only statutory standard regarding the content of the required courses is that they must assist debtors in "understanding personal financial management." While the agencies may charge a reasonable fee, counseling services must be provided "without regard to [the debtor's] ability to pay the fee." § 111(c)(2)(B). Counseling may be done over the telephone or Internet. No guidance is given as to how long or how detailed the course must be.

The discharge denial rule is subject to limited, and exclusive, exceptions: (1) for debtors described in § 109(h)(4), e.g., debtors who are "incapacitated" (which is defined to mean a mental disability); "disabled" (defined to mean physical inability to take advantage of counseling services); or on active military duty in a military combat zone; or (2) if the United States trustee determines that adequate approved instructional courses are not available in the district in which the debtor resides. As to the latter exception, since telephonic or Internet-based instruction is allowed, one wonders how this could ever come to pass in any district.

§ 10.14 Delay of Discharge Due to Possible Proceeding under § 522(q)

In 2005, Congress added a provision, which delays entry of the discharge order if the court finds that there is reasonable cause to believe that the debtor is subject to a pending proceeding that might give rise to a limitation of the homestead exception under § 522(q).[90] § 727(a)(12). The same rule applies in all chapters: chapter 7 (§ 727(a)(12)); chapter 11 (§ 1141(d)(5)(c)); chapter 12 (§ 1228(f)); and chapter 13 (§ 1328(h)). Under § 522(q), a debtor who elects a state law homestead exception in bankruptcy is limited to a homestead exemption of $155,675 (as indexed to 2013) if either (1) the debtor has been convicted of a felony which demonstrates that the filing of the bankruptcy case was an abuse, or (2) the debtor owes a debt arising from a securities law violation, racketeering, fiduciary fraud, or a criminal act or intentional tort that caused death or personal injury in the past 5 years.[91] Although, as one court observed, "It would strain the faculties of the layperson and the lawyer alike to try to understand why Congress linked these statutes together in the manner provided by § 727(a)(12),"[92] the bankruptcy courts must try to give effect to the new rule.

The effect of the new discharge rule apparently is to *postpone* the debtor's discharge until the proceeding that could impact § 522(q) is completed and the exemption issue resolved, although the statute does not clearly say that in so many words. It does not appear that the rule effects a *permanent* denial of discharge. The Bankruptcy Rules, as revised in December 2008, take this view, providing that the court is to enter a discharge upon expiration of the time for objecting "unless a motion *to delay or postpone* discharge under § 727(a)(12) is pending." Rule 4004(c)(1)(I). Once the § 522(q) matter is settled, then the debtor's exemption is capped (or not), and the court can then go ahead and enter the debtor's discharge. So, for example, if the debtor

---

[90] Pub. L. No. 109–8, § 330(a)(3), 119 Stat. 101 (2005).

[91] See § 9.5.b.

[92] In re Jacobs, 342 B.R. 114, 115 (Bankr. D.D.C. 2006).

is the defendant in a pending action alleging that the debtor is liable for securities fraud, and has claimed a homestead exemption under state law in excess of $155,675, and the date set for entry of the discharge is approaching, the court (within ten days before the entry of the discharge order[93]) must not enter the discharge order. Instead, the court should wait until the securities fraud action is concluded (which may require the court to lift the automatic stay), allowing the bankruptcy court to make a determination under § 522(q) whether to cap the exemption claim. Having done that, the court then is free to enter the discharge; § 727(a)(12) will no longer bar the discharge, because no § 522(q)-related proceeding will be "pending."

Note that the § 727(a)(12) rule (and the similar rules in the other chapters) can only apply if (1) the debtor has elected a homestead exemption under *state* law, and (2) that exemption claim exceeds $155,675. If either of those conditions is not satisfied, then there is no possible application of § 522(q), which is a prerequisite to the invocation of § 727(a)(12).[94]

Furthermore, the statute specifically requires that the proceeding that might affect § 522(q) must already be *pending*. § 727(a)(12)(B). If literally applied, this limitation seems to say that the court cannot delay entry of the discharge order in a situation where the debtor is *alleged* to have committed a felony within the meaning of § 522(q)(1)(A) or to be liable for a debt of the type described in § 522(q)(1)(B), but no proceeding to prosecute the debtor for the felony or to hold the debtor liable for the debt has yet been filed. That is, can the debtor preclude a § 727(a)(12) problem by winning a race to the courthouse? Probably not, notwithstanding the apparent possibility if the statutory language were to be rigidly construed. Under the revised Bankruptcy Rules, the court "shall forthwith grant the discharge" upon expiration of the time for filing objections to discharge or to dismiss the case, "unless . . . a motion to delay or postpone discharge under § 727(a)(12) *is pending*." Rule 4004(c)(1)(I). The time period by which the proceeding must be "pending" is just 60 days after the first date set for the meeting of creditors, unless extended within that time. Rule 4004(a). Note also that except for criminal proceedings, no action to hold the debtor liable for a debt may be filed once a bankruptcy case is commenced, because of the automatic stay. Yet, one suspects that if faced with this situation, a court would exercise its equitable powers to defer entry of the discharge (to the extent possible under the strict language of Rule 4004), and then either grant relief from the stay to permit the proceeding against the debtor to be filed, so it then would be "pending," or would simply deem the claim filed against the debtor to be the "pending" proceeding.

---

[93] Note the "Alice in Wonderland" impossibility of complying literally with the statute on this procedural point. How can a court enter an order within ten days *before* the *entry* of an order it will not be able to enter once it has entered the first order? It is likely that Congress *meant* to fix the referent date as the date *scheduled* for the bankruptcy court to enter the discharge order under Rule 4004, but for the interposition of the § 522(q) pending proceeding problem that triggers § 727(a)(12).

[94] See, e.g., *Jacobs*, supra note 92, at 114–15.

C. EXCEPTIONS TO DISCHARGE UNDER § 523: NONDISCHARGEABLE DEBTS

§ 10.15 Overview

A debtor who receives a general discharge from his debts under § 727 still may not exit bankruptcy with a full financial fresh start in life. Specific debts may be excepted from the operation of the general discharge pursuant to § 523, leaving those creditors free to pursue collection from the debtor after bankruptcy. All other creditors will still be bound by the discharge, however. The debts excepted under § 523 are similar to those enumerated in § 17 of the 1898 Act. Section 523(a) contains the complete and exclusive list of excepted debts in the Code;[95] a bankruptcy court has no power to exercise its equitable discretion to create new discharge exceptions.

Section 523(a) applies only to the debts of *individual* debtors. This restriction is congruent with the limitations of chapter 7, in which only individual debtors may receive a discharge at all, § 727(a)(1), and chapter 13, in which only individuals may be debtors in the first place. § 109(e). Corporate and partnership debtors may receive a discharge, however, in chapter 11 and in chapter 12. Section 1141(d)(2) coordinates the chapter 11 discharge with § 523(a) by specifying that an individual debtor is not discharged from a § 523(a) debt. By negative inference, corporate and partnership debtors thus will be discharged in chapter 11 even from debts under § 523(a). One exception to this general rule was added in 2005, whereby corporate debtors are not discharged in chapter 11 from fraud debts or from tax debts as to which the debtor either filed a fraudulent return or willfully attempted to evade or defeat the tax. § 1141(d)(6).

The marriage between § 523 and chapter 12 for corporate and partnership debtors is less tidy. Section 1228, which governs the discharge in chapter 12, provides that no chapter 12 debtor is discharged from a § 523(a) debt. § 1228(a)(2), (c)(2). This would extend the scope of § 523(a) to corporate and partnership debtors, who are eligible for chapter 12 relief. § 109(f), § 101(18)(B). As just mentioned above, however, § 523 by its terms is limited to individual debtors. What Congress intended to do in chapter 12 cases is not clear.[96]

Section 523 applies in all types of cases. Subject to the limitation to individual debtors just discussed, the section operates with full force not only in a chapter 7 case, but also in chapter 11 and in chapter 12.

In chapter 13, however, all of the § 523(a) exceptions apply only in the event a *"hardship"* discharge is granted. § 1328(b), (c)(2). Before 2005, in the event the debtor was granted a full-compliance discharge under § 1328(a), the only § 523(a) debts *not* discharged were for family support debts, educational loans, DWI liabilities, and criminal fines and restitution obligations. § 1328(a)(2), (3). Congress has made steady inroads into this so-called Chapter 13 "super" discharge, however, suggesting a move in

---

[95]   Some discharge exceptions are located in other titles of the United States Code.

[96]   Courts have held that corporate debtors in chapter 12 are precluded from obtaining a discharge of debts excepted under § 523(a). E.g., In re JRB Consol., Inc. 188 B.R. 373 (Bankr. W.D. Tex. 1995).

Congressional policy towards conforming chapter 13 to the other chapters and applying all § 523(a) exceptions uniformly. In 2005, Congress added to the list of nondischargeable debts even in a chapter 13 full-compliance discharge the following: (1) some types of debts for taxes (§ 523(a)(1)(B) & (C), § 507(a)(8)(C), § 1328(a)(2)); (2) fraud debts (§ 523(a)(2), § 1328(a)(2)); (3) unscheduled debts (§ 523(a)(3), § 1328(a)(2)); (4) debts for fiduciary fraud or defalcation, larceny, or embezzlement (§ 523(a)(4), § 1328(a)(2)); and (5) debts for restitution or damages awarded in a civil action where the debtor was found to have acted willfully or maliciously and caused death or personal injury (§ 1328(a)(4), see also § 523(a)(6)).

The only significant debts that still remain as part of the chapter 13 "super" discharge are: (1) income taxes due more than three years before bankruptcy, if the debtor filed a timely and non-fraudulent return, and if the debtor did not try to evade the tax (§ 523(a)(1)(A));[97] (2) debts for willful and malicious injury to property (§ 523(a)(6)); and (3) debts arising from property settlements in divorce or separation proceedings. (§ 523(a)(15)). All of the discharge exceptions in § 523(a)(10)–(19) are still covered by the current version of the "super" discharge of § 1328(a).

§ 10.16 Taxes

The policy of giving an honest debtor a fresh start in life is subordinated to the goal of protecting the public fisc through a discharge exception for certain taxes by § 523(a)(1). In addition, § 523(a)(7) makes some tax penalties nondischargeable.[98] These exceptions are automatic, requiring no action to be taken by the taxing authority in the bankruptcy case to preserve its rights. Some diligence may be required of the government, however, in attempting to collect its taxes in order to bring the debt within the scope of § 523(a)(1).

The first of the three categories of nondischargeable tax debts in subsection (1) is for those tax debts which are entitled to either third or eighth priority under § 507(a)(3) or § 507(a)(8). § 523(a)(1)(A). Since priority claims by definition are paid prior to general unsecured claims, the amount of the tax for which the debtor ultimately will be responsible after bankruptcy because of the discharge exception is reduced by the priority treatment given the same claim in the bankruptcy. Third priority taxes are those taxes incurred in the ordinary course of the debtor's business or financial affairs in an involuntary case during the gap period between the commencement of the case and the entry of the order for bankruptcy relief or the appointment of a trustee. §§ 507(a)(3), 502(f).

Eighth priority taxes are much more comprehensive in their reach and much more important in the normal case.[99] Included are income or gross receipts taxes, property taxes, withholding taxes, employment taxes, excise taxes, and customs duties. Many of these taxes enjoy priority only if not stale; others have no time limitation. An example

---

[97] The tax exception does not help the debtor, though, because tax debts under § 523(a)(1)(A) are those which are entitled to priority under § 507(a)(3) or (8), and to confirm a chapter 13 plan the debtor must provide for full payment of all priority debts. § 1322(a)(2).

[98] See § 10.22.

[99] See § 7.21.

of the latter type is a "trust fund" withholding tax, which enjoys priority and nondischargeability no matter how long before bankruptcy it was incurred. § 507(a)(8)(D).

The most common example of the time-sensitive taxes is income taxes. The income tax priority generally includes only those taxes for which a required return was last due within *three years* of the bankruptcy case. § 507(a)(8)(A)(i). Alternatively, a tax that is assessed within 240 days of bankruptcy will be granted priority and excepted from discharge, § 507(a)(8)(A)(ii), as will a tax that remains assessable at the time of bankruptcy. § 507(a)(8)(A)(iii).

A tax debt that is older than the statutorily-prescribed period is denied priority and is therefore dischargeable. Congress intended to place some duty of diligence on the government in collecting taxes. For example, income taxes for the 2010 tax year normally would be due on April 15 of the following year (2011). If the taxpayer-debtor filed bankruptcy anytime on or before April 15, 2014, the debt for the 2010 income taxes would be entitled to priority and would therefore not be dischargeable under § 523(a)(1)(A). If the debtor filed after April 15, 2014, however, the 2010 tax debt would be discharged and not entitled to priority.

An issue that has arisen with considerable frequency is whether the pendency of a prior bankruptcy case suspends the running of the three-year period. For example, in the above hypothetical, assume that the debtor filed bankruptcy on April 20, 2014—more than four years after the due date for filing the 2010 tax return. Without more, the 2010 tax debt would be discharged. However, what if the debtor had been in bankruptcy previously, from May 2011 until May 2013? The taxing authority would have been prevented by the automatic stay from attempting to collect the tax during the prior bankruptcy case, and thus would not have enjoyed three "stay-free" years to try to collect. Until 2002, in the face of statutory silence on the tolling question, the courts were split over whether a prior bankruptcy case tolled the three-year period.[100]

The Supreme Court settled the issue in 2002 in the case of *Young v. United States*, holding that the running of the three-year period is equitably tolled during the pendency of a bankruptcy case.[101] In 2005, Congress codified a tolling rule with regard to the 240–day assessment priority provision, suspending that time period for any time that the government was prohibited from collecting under non-bankruptcy law or pursuant to a bankruptcy case, plus an additional 90 days. § 507(a)(8)(A)(ii)(II). There is no reason to believe that by codifying tolling for the 240–day assessment priority but not doing so for the general three-year priority, Congress intended to overturn the *Young* holding.

The second category of nondischargeable tax claims is those for which a required return (or equivalent report or notice) either was not filed at all prior to bankruptcy or was filed late and within two years of bankruptcy or thereafter. § 523(a)(1)(B). The tax year to which the return applies is irrelevant. This subsection thus balances the

---

[100] CompareIn re Taylor, 81 F.3d 20 (3d Cir. 1996) (toll), with In re Quenzer, 19 F.3d 163 (5th Cir. 1993) (not toll).

[101] 535 U.S. 43 (2002).

dilatoriness of the taxpayer-debtor in filing the return (or not) against that of the taxing authority in pursuing the taxpayer. The government is never time-barred in the case of the non-filing debtor, but once a late return is filed, the government has only two years to take action, such as obtaining a tax lien.

The final category of nondischargeable tax claims covers those claims as to which the debtor either (1) filed a fraudulent return or (2) in any way willfully attempted to evade or defeat the tax. § 523(a)(1)(C). No time bar exists for these claims. Most of the litigation has concerned the second prong, that of willful evasion. Courts note that "[t]he willful attempt to evade prong of 523(a)(1)(C) includes 'both a conduct requirement (that the debtor sought 'in any manner to evade or defeat' his tax liability) and a mental state requirement (that the debtor did so 'willfully')."[102] One of the issues courts have struggled with is where the debtor's "conduct" is simply choosing to pay other debts before he pays his back taxes; is that enough of an "evasion"? If the *only* "conduct" of the debtor is not paying the tax, that should not be enough to constitute evasion;[103] otherwise almost every tax debt would, by definition, be nondischargeable. However, if nonpayment is coupled with even the slenderest of reeds of affirmative dubious conduct, courts will find the tax debt nondischargeable,[104] assuming the requisite mental state can be established. A debtor who can do so but who intentionally fails to file a return and pay a tax may be considered a tax evader within the meaning of the exception.[105] As to the mental state requirement, "the proper test is whether, in the case of a debtor who is financially able to pay his taxes but chooses not to do so, (1) the debtor had a duty under the law, (2) the debtor knew he had that duty, and (3) the debtor voluntarily and intentionally violated that duty."[106] Under that test, debtors have almost no chance of prevailing.

An important practical question is whether *interest* continues to accrue on an unpaid tax liability even after the filing of a bankruptcy petition. As against the bankruptcy estate itself, a claim for postpetition interest is only paid in the rare case in which the estate is solvent.[107] §§ 726(a)(5), 502(b)(2). However, if the underlying tax debt is nondischargeable as to the debtor, then the debtor himself remains personally liable for postpetition interest, under the rule laid down by the Supreme Court in *Bruning v. United States*.[108]

---

[102] In re Griffith, 206 F.3d 1389, 1396 (11th Cir. 2000) (en banc) (quoting *In re Birkenstock*, 87 F.3d 947, 951 (7th Cir. 1996)).

[103] In re Haas, 48 F.3d 1153 (11th Cir. 1995), abrogated on other grounds by *Griffith*, supra note 102. The Eleventh Circuit sitting en banc in *Griffith*, while abrogating the conclusion of the *Haas* court that evading *payment* of the tax could never be nondischargeable, still reaffirmed *Haas* on the point that nonpayment by itself was not enough to constitute evasion. 206 F.3d at 1395.

[104] See, e.g., *Griffith*, supra note 102, 206 F.3d at 1396; In re Bruner, 55 F.3d 195, 200 (5th Cir. 1995). See also United States v. Coney, 689 F.3d 365, 375 (5th Cir. 2012) (holding that the debtor's attempts to "structure cash transactions to avoid federal reporting requirements" and "obstruct the Government's investigation of his activities" satisfied the conduct requirement of § 523(a)(1)(C)).

[105] In re Toti, 24 F.3d 806 (6th Cir. 1994). See also In re Fretz, 244 F.3d 1323, 1329–30 (11th Cir. 2001).

[106] *Bruner*, supra note 104, 55 F.3d at 197. See also *Coney*, supra note 104, 689 F.3d at 374.

[107] New York v. Saper, 336 U.S. 328 (1949) (disallowing postpetition interest on tax claim against bankruptcy trustee).

[108] 376 U.S. 358, 360 (1964). See, e.g., In re Hanna, 872 F.2d 829, 830–31 (8th Cir.1989).

A new dischargeability exception relating to tax debts was added to the Code in 1994. Under § 523(a)(14), a debt that is incurred to pay a tax to the United States that itself would be nondischargeable under § 523(a)(1) is likewise deemed nondischargeable. In 2005, a similar provision was added for debts incurred to pay nondischargeable taxes to a governmental unit other than the United States, i.e., state and local taxes. § 523(a)(14A). These rules prevent debtors from converting a nondischargeable debt into a dischargeable debt by using their credit cards shortly before filing bankruptcy to pay a tax debt that would be excepted from discharge and then filing bankruptcy and discharging the credit card debt. The new rule should facilitate the ability of debtors to use their credit cards to pay tax debts.[109]

§ 10.17 Fraud

By far the most important and most litigated discharge exception is § 523(a)(2), for debts based on fraud. The purposes of the fraud exception are "to punish egregious debtor misconduct and to protect the interests of innocent parties victimized by fraud."[110] Section 523(a)(2) is set up in a somewhat awkward fashion. Subsection (A) applies to all types of nondischargeable fraud debts *except* those based on false financial statements, which are covered by subsection (B). Subsections (A) and (B) therefore are mutually exclusive. However, most (but not all) of the elements necessary to establish the exception are the same under either (A) or (B). As will be explained below, the primary difference is whether the creditor must prove reasonable reliance or justifiable reliance. Finally, subsection (C) establishes a rebuttable presumption of fraud under subsection (A) in the specific context of eve-of-bankruptcy "load-ups" by consumers.

Some other provisions of § 523 are designed to alleviate possible creditor abuse of the fraud exception. Section 523(c)(1) requires the creditor to file the fraud complaint in the bankruptcy court. Bankruptcy Rule 4007(c) puts the creditor on a short time leash to file—within 60 days of the first meeting of creditors. Section 523(d) exposes a creditor who loses a § 523(a)(2) action to possible liability to a consumer debtor for costs and attorneys' fees incurred in that action, if the creditor's position "was not substantially justified," unless the court finds that "special circumstances would make the award unjust." The current version of § 523(d) has been watered down significantly from the original version contained in the 1978 Bankruptcy Reform Act, which provided for judgment to be granted against the losing creditor in every § 523(a)(2) case, "unless such granting of judgment would be clearly inequitable."[111]

The statute spells out in detail the elements of a cause of action under § 523(a)(2)(B). As the Supreme Court explained in *Field v. Mans*,[112] this specificity in subsection (B) is necessary because the false financial statement provision is entirely a

---

[109] Section-by-Section Analysis, commentary on § 221 of Bankruptcy Reform Act of 1994, 140 Cong. Rec. H10,769 (daily ed. Oct. 4, 1994).

[110] Luther Zeigler, The Fraud Exception to Discharge in Bankruptcy: A Reappraisal, 38 Stanford L. Rev. 891, 899 (1986).

[111] Bankruptcy Reform Act of 1978, Pub. L. No. 95–598, § 523(d), 92 Stat. 2592.

[112] 516 U.S. 59, 68–69 (1995).

product of congressional creation, without an obvious analogue in the common law of torts. The elements under (B) are that the debt must be obtained by:

> use of statement in writing—(i) that is materially false; (ii) respecting the debtor's or an insider's financial condition; (iii) on which the creditor to whom the debtor is liable . . . reasonably relied; and (iv) that the debtor caused to be made or published with intent to deceive.

In contrast to subsection (B), § 523(a)(2)(A) does not delineate the elements that the creditor must prove. The Supreme Court in *Mans* explained that such statutory specificity is unnecessary in subsection (A), because Congress intended to incorporate by reference the elements of common law fraud as generally understood when the Bankruptcy Code was enacted in 1978.[113]

A creditor seeking to establish a nondischargeable fraud debt must prove that the debtor by their fraud obtained "money, property, services, or an extension, renewal, or refinancing of credit" from the creditor. § 523(a)(2). This statutory definition of what may be obtained is quite broad; broader in fact than under prior law, especially due to the specific inclusion of "services."[114] At the same time, Congress, by using the phrase "to the extent obtained by," intended that only what was so obtained should escape discharge. The language "to the extent" limits the exception to that portion of the debt directly traceable to the fraud. This problem often arises in the case of a refinancing.

The word "obtained" is construed strictly to mean that some form of pecuniary benefit must be procured directly by reason of the fraud. It does not extend to consequential losses caused by the debtor's misrepresentations. In the *Mans* case, Justice Ginsburg in her concurrence raised a question as to whether the debt in question was "obtained by" the claimed fraud.[115] In that case, the debtor fraudulently omitted to disclose to the creditors that he had already sold property and thereby triggered a due-on-sale clause. The debt had been created previously, without any taint of fraud. The only effect of the debtor's fraud was to lull the creditors into not pursuing collection of the accelerated debt. Such inaction might not be enough to satisfy the "obtained by" requirement. A related question, on which the courts have split, is whether the debtor personally must receive the obtained benefit, or whether the exception applies even if a third person receives the benefit, as long as the debtor was the fraudulent actor.[116]

One context in which the "obtained by" limitation has proven quite important is where the original debt arguably was obtained by fraud, but the parties then enter into a settlement agreement and release that says nothing about fraud, and that itself was not the product of fraud. The classic fact scenario is outlined by the Supreme Court in

---

[113]　Id.

[114]　The Code thus overrules *Gleason v. Thaw*, 236 U.S. 558 (1915).

[115]　516 U.S. 59, at 78–79 (Ginsburg, J., concurring).

[116]　Compare In re Sabban, 600 F.3d 1219 (9th Cir. 2010) (noting there is no requirement that the debtor receive a benefit from his or her fraudulent activity to violate § 523(a)(2)(A)), with In re Rountree, 478 F.3d 215 (4th Cir. 2007) (holding that a debtor must obtain something through fraud for the § 523(a)(2)(A) exception to apply).

Archer v. Warner:[117] "(1) *A* sues *B* seeking money that (*A* says) *B* obtained through fraud; (2) the parties settle the lawsuit and release related claims; (3) the settlement agreement does not resolve the issue of fraud, but provides that *B* will pay *A* a fixed sum; (4) *B* does not pay the fixed sum; (5) *B* enters bankruptcy; and (6) *A* claims that *B*'s obligation to pay the fixed settlement sum is nondischargeable because, like the original debt, it is for 'money . . . obtained by . . . fraud.'" The Court held that, for purposes of the fraud exception to discharge, the original character of the debt as fraudulent survived the execution of a settlement agreement and release.[118] The *Archer* Court found that the case was controlled by its earlier decision in *Brown v. Felsen*,[119] in which the Supreme Court rejected a *res judicata* argument and allowed a creditor to try to prove fraud even though the original, allegedly fraudulent debt had been reduced prior to bankruptcy to a state court consent judgment that was silent as to fraud.

The requirement that something of value be obtained from the creditor is really secondary to the essential focus of the exception, however. The vast majority of claims by definition involve the procurement of some form of property or credit from the creditor by the debtor, and most of those claims nevertheless are discharged. What makes claims under § 523(a)(2) nondischargeable is the debtor's fraudulent activity in obtaining that property or credit. Such fraud, with resulting nondischargeability, is not lightly found, but only applies "to actual or positive fraud rather than fraud implied in law."[120]

Under subsection (A), unlike subsection (B), the representation does not have to be in writing, but may be oral. Silence as to or concealment of a material fact is held to be sufficient by the overwhelming majority of courts, although a small minority insist on an actual overt false representation. In *Mans* the Court implicitly approved the majority view, as the Court addressed the reliance issue on the merits without expressing any concern over the fact that the representation was not overt but was by omission.[121] The misrepresented fact cannot be as to the financial condition of the debtor or an insider, however, which is covered exclusively by subsection (B). Since § 523(a)(2)(B) also requires a writing, this means that an oral misrepresentation as to financial condition is dischargeable.

A common problem is whether a debtor's statement is one of fact, and thus potentially within the discharge exception, or just the expression of an opinion—mere "puffery"—in which case the exception fails. This problem often arises when the debtor makes a statement as to the value of property to the creditor in connection with the obtaining of property or credit, which later proves to be wildly inaccurate.

---

[117] 538 U.S. 314, 316 (2003).

[118] Id. at 323.

[119] 442 U.S. 127 (1979).

[120] 124 Cong. Rec. H11,096 (daily ed. Sept. 28, 1978) (statement of Rep. Edwards); 124 Cong. Rec. S17,412 (daily ed. Oct. 6, 1978) (statement of Sen. DeConcini). These excerpts from the legislative history show the intent of Congress to codify thereby the holding of *Neal v. Clark*, 95 U.S. 704 (1877), that actual fraud is required.

[121] 516 U.S. 59 (1995)

The scienter requirement has been construed with some sympathy toward the creditor's inherent difficulty in proving a case predicated on the other party's actual state of mind. Circumstantial evidence of the debtor's intent to deceive is permissible. Furthermore, most courts allow recklessness as to the truth of a statement to satisfy the intent element.

The courts have had substantial difficulty in resolving the case in which the debtor issues a check for goods or services and the check is then dishonored. Some courts have held that the issuance of a check constitutes an implied representation that there are sufficient funds in the account to cover the check, and that fraud is thus established upon further proof that the debtor knew at the time the check was issued that sufficient funds in fact were lacking. Other courts, however, have held that the mere issuance of a bad check is not in and of itself a fraudulent misrepresentation sufficient to establish a cause of action under § 523(a)(2). These cases rely on the non-bankruptcy Supreme Court case of *Williams v. United States*.[122] The Court in *Williams* stated that, "a check is not a factual assertion at all, and therefore cannot be characterized as 'true' or 'false.'"[123] Those courts that rely on *Williams* require something more to trigger § 523(a)(2), such as an additional oral representation that the check will be honored or the intentional issuance of the bad check to forestall imminent collection efforts.

Perhaps the most common, difficult and contentious question courts have faced under the fraud exception is the situation where the debtor runs up a *credit card* debt and then shortly thereafter files bankruptcy. While at first blush such a debtor's behavior seems obviously fraudulent, on closer examination the nature of a credit card case makes for an awkward fit for fraud. Given the way credit cards are used and approved, it often is problematic to find several of the elements of fraud, including (1) a *representation* of fact by the debtor to the credit card issuer as to either the debtor's ability to pay or intent to pay; (2) the debtor's *intent* to deceive the creditor; and (3) actual and justifiable *reliance* by the creditor.[124]

As to the representation issue, the credit card case is difficult to distinguish from the bad check case, and thus arguably should be controlled by *Williams*. As one prominent bankruptcy judge observed in concluding that "[t]he use of a credit card to incur debt in a typical credit card transaction involves no representation, express or implied," the force of *Williams* is inescapable:

> The similarities between the issuance of a check and the use of a credit card are sufficient to make it illogical to conclude that the use of a credit card in an ordinary credit transaction necessarily invokes a representation, when the issuance of a bad check does not, per se, involve a representation. Just as the

---

[122]   458 U.S. 279 (1982).

[123]   Id. at 284–85.

[124]   *In re Stearns*, 241 B.R. 611 (Bankr. D. Minn. 1999), thoughtfully examines the difficulties in proving fraud from the mere use of a credit card. See also In re Mercer, 246 F.3d 391 (5th Cir. 2001); In re Anastas, 94 F.3d 1280 (9th Cir. 1996).

Supreme Court has held a check is not capable of being true or false, using a credit card to incur debt in of itself is not capable of being true or false.[125]

Nevertheless, the vast majority of courts have held that the debtor, by using the credit card, *is* making an *implied* representation that he at least has the *intent* to repay the debt.[126] Thus, to give an extreme example to illustrate the point, a debtor who stops on the way to the federal courthouse to file bankruptcy and charges $5,000 on his credit card obviously never intended to repay that credit card debt, and most courts are going to exclude that debt from discharge under § 523(a)(2)(A). A debtor who wantonly "runs up" a substantial credit card debt in the days and weeks before filing bankruptcy is a prime candidate to be caught under the fraud exception. But the debtor who simply gets in over her head, and keeps getting in deeper and deeper, all the while hoping against hope that she can "turn it around" and pay off her debts, might escape.[127] Such debtor may be a fool, but she is not a crook.

Some courts have even concluded that the debtor's use of a credit card is an implied representation that the debtor has the *ability* to repay the debt, but that view should be plainly foreclosed under the Code's scheme. The representation of "ability" to pay is a representation as to *financial condition* and thus can be dealt with only under subsection (B) of § 523(a)(2), which requires a written—not an implied—representation by the debtor.[128]

Assuming that a court is willing, as a matter of law, to follow the implied misrepresentation of intent to repay approach, the challenging task remains of determining whether such an intent can be shown on the facts. The creditor must prove that at the time the card was used the debtor did not have a present intent to repay; the fact that the charges ultimately were not paid is not sufficient proof by itself. Section 523(a)(2)(C), discussed below, now may ease the creditor's proof problems in the case of pre-bankruptcy spending sprees.

Most courts have resorted to examination of a variety of objective surrounding circumstantial factors to determine the subjective *intent* of the debtor, both in determining the intent to repay and the intent to deceive. In other words, these courts assess the "totality of the circumstances,"[129] weighing various factors in an effort to divine whether the debtor has been engaged in an overall pattern of deceptive conduct.[130] In effect, courts employ "badges of fraud" tailored to the specific

---

[125] In re Alvi, 191 B.R. 724, 732 (Bankr. N.D. Ill. 1996).

[126] See, e.g., cases cited supra note 124.

[127] See, e.g., *Stearns,* supra note 124, at 624.

[128] See In re Ortiz, 441 B.R. 73, 83 (Bankr. W.D. Tex. 2010).

[129] See, e.g., In re Morrison, 555 F.3d 473, 482 (5th Cir. 2009); In re White, 128 Fed. Appx. 994, 999 (4th Cir. 2005); In re Massa, 187 F.3d 292, 297 (2d Cir. 1999); In re Rembert, 141 F.3d 277, 282 (6th Cir. 1998); Palmacci v. Umpierrez, 121 F.3d 781, 789 (1st Cir. 1997); In re Eashai, 87 F.3d 1082, 1087 (9th Cir. 1996).

[130] See *Eashai,* supra note 129, 87 F.3d at 1087–88 (citing *In re Dougherty,* 84 B.R. 653 (B.A.P. 9th Cir. 1988)) (incorporating the twelve *Dougherty* factors, used to establish the element of intent to deceive, into an approach which also considers all of the elements of common law fraud). The twelve factors from *Dougherty* are:

    1. The length of time between the charges made and the filing of bankruptcy;

circumstances of credit card use. At some point the objective unlikelihood of repayment casts enough doubt on the credibility of the debtor's protestations of subjective innocence that the creditor will prevail. But the possibility of an "empty head, pure heart" defense remains.

A competing minority approach is the "assumption of risk" test. Under this view, the credit card issuer is assigned more responsibility to monitor the activities of the debtor. Discharge of the debt will be denied only if the charges were made after the card was revoked, or if a known credit limit was exceeded.[131] Otherwise, the creditor is said to assume the risk that the debtor will incur charges that it cannot repay.

Assuming that the creditor can surmount the misrepresentation and intent hurdles, it still must prove that it actually and justifiably *relied* on the debtor's implied representation of intent to repay.[132] Here again, given the reality of how credit card transactions are approved and processed, finding specific reliance by the credit card issuer in any particular transaction is essentially fictional. In effect, courts must imply a reliance on an implied representation—a house of legal cards that is hard to square with the notion that actual fraud must be established. As one court noted, "In a dischargeability proceeding based on a depersonalized and open-ended credit relationship like that on today's charge card accounts, identifying just how a creditor 'relies' should be done only in focus, after a finding of active wrongdoing on the part of the account holder."[133] What many courts do is infer reliance unless the creditor has reason to know otherwise: "the credit card issuer justifiably relies on a representation of intent to repay as long as the account is not in default and any initial investigations into a credit report do not raise red flags that would make reliance unjustifiable."[134]

The litigated cases often turn on the nature and degree of the creditor's reliance on the fraudulent statement. In cases involving a false financial statement under subsection (B), the Code expressly requires the creditor to prove *reasonable* reliance. Under this objective test, the courts often will only deny discharge of the debt if the creditor made reasonable efforts to investigate the truth of the debtor's statements.

---

2. Whether or not an attorney has been consulted concerning the filing of bankruptcy before the charges were made;
3. The number of charges made;
4. The amount of the charges;
5. The financial condition of the debtor at the time the charges are made;
6. Whether the charges were above the credit limit of the account;
7. Whether the debtor made multiple charges on the same day;
8. Whether or not the debtor was employed;
9. The debtor's prospects for employment;
10. Financial sophistication of the debtor;
11. Whether there was a sudden change in the debtor's buying habits; and
12. Whether the purchases were made for luxuries or necessities.

[131] First Nat'l Bank v. Roddenberry, 701 F.2d 927 (11th Cir. 1983). See also AT & T Universal Card Servs. Corp. v. Pakdaman, 210 B.R. 886, 888 (D. Mass. 1997).

[132] See *Mercer*, supra note 124, 246 F.3d at 403.

[133] *Stearns*, supra note 124, 241 B.R. at 627.

[134] *Anastas*, supra note 124, 94 F.3d at 1286 (citing *Eashai*, supra note 129, at 1091).

Subsection (A) is silent on the reliance issue, however. Until the Supreme Court settled the issue in 1995 in *Field v. Mans*,[135] this silence in (A), contrasted with the express requirement of reasonable reliance in (B), gave rise to considerable disagreement as to whether reasonableness was also required under (A). Prior to *Mans,* the majority of courts did demand proof that the creditor's reliance was reasonable in (A) as well as in (B).[136] A few courts held that only actual reliance need be proved under (A).[137] An intermediate view was that the creditor's reliance must be "justifiable," which is a subjective test that takes account of the particular facts and circumstances applicable to this creditor's case.[138] While the creditor under this intermediate test did not have to live up to the standard of diligence and inquiry demanded of an objectively reasonable person, that creditor could not go out of its way to avoid discovering the truth.[139]

In *Field v. Mans* the Supreme Court adopted the *justifiable* reliance standard for fraud cases under § 523(a)(2)(A).[140] The Court reasoned that Congress, by using a well-understood term of art in (A), had intended to incorporate the common law meaning of fraud. The prevailing common law view in fraud cases in 1978 (when the Code was enacted) was to require proof only of subjectively justifiable reliance, rather than objectively reasonable reliance. As the Court observed, though, reasonableness is not entirely irrelevant, because extremely unreasonable behavior by the creditor raises serious doubts as to the existence of actual reliance in fact. The Court's holding in *Mans* creates the anomaly (which the Court frankly admitted)[141] that the creditor has a more demanding proof burden when the debtor's fraud is incorporated in a written financial statement. The Court explained this oddity by showing that in the legislative history to the Code Congress expressed concern about creditor abuses with regard to false financial statements.[142]

The creditor trying to prove reliance must establish a proper temporal relation between the false statement and the credit decision. If the statement was made after the credit decision, then reliance obviously is negated; at the same time, it has been held that a creditor cannot reasonably or justifiably rely upon an extremely old and outdated statement.[143] Furthermore, if the creditor knows that the information is false, or should see "red flags" raised by the statement, then reliance on the truthfulness of the statement is unjustified. Many courts assessing reasonableness look to objective factors such as the creditor's normal business practices, the standards and customs of the industry, past relationships between the parties, the amount of the loan, and the sophistication of the lender, all viewed in light of the circumstances surrounding the specific transaction.

---

[135]   516 U.S. 59 (1995).

[136]   E.g., In re Mullet, 817 F.2d 677 (10th Cir. 1987) (abrogated by *Field v. Mans*, 516 U.S. 59 (1995)).

[137]   E.g., In re Mayer, 51 F.3d 670 (7th Cir. 1995); In re Ophaug, 827 F.2d 340 (8th Cir. 1987).

[138]   In re Kirsh, 973 F.2d 1454, 1460 (9th Cir. 1992)

[139]   Id. at 1461.

[140]   516 U.S. at 74–75.

[141]   Id. at 76–77.

[142]   Id. at 447 & n.13 (quoting H.R. Rep. No. 95–595, 95th Cong., 1st Sess., at 130–31 (1977)).

[143]   See, e.g., In re Baratta, 272 B.R. 501, 506 (Bankr. M.D. Fla. 2001).

One set of issues unique to § 523(a)(2)(B) addresses what constitutes a writing "respecting the debtor's . . . financial condition." Although the normal § 523(a)(2)(B) case involves the familiar formal financial statement, such is not absolutely required by Congress. Any writing that concerns the debtor's financial condition will be enough.

The test of the materiality of the falsehood usually is stated as a "but-for" issue, i.e., whether the creditor would have made the loan even if the truth about the debtor's financial condition had been known. The willingness of courts to allow creditors to prevail on the lesser showing that the false statement was only one contributing factor to the decision to lend is more problematic. Whatever test is used, bankruptcy courts are skeptical of self-serving statements by credit officials regarding the supposedly great import of picayune misstatements or omissions by the debtor.

Section 523(a)(2)(C), added by the 1984 amendments and amended in 1994 and 2005, improves the creditor's ability to win one particular type of dischargeability case: eve-of-bankruptcy consumer spending sprees. That subsection applies by its terms to subsection (A) cases only, and not to subsection (B) cases. The important litigation benefit to the complaining creditor is that in the described situation a *presumption* of nondischargeability is raised, which the debtor then may try to rebut. The presumption applies to two types of "load-ups" by consumers: (1) debts for luxury goods and services totaling more than $650 incurred in the 90 days preceding bankruptcy, and (2) cash advances under an open end credit plan totaling more than $925 in the 70 days preceding bankruptcy. Much of the litigation under subsection (C) concerns what is and what is not a "luxury" item. The statute itself states that a luxury item does "not include goods or services reasonably necessary for the support or maintenance of the debtor or a dependent of the debtor." § 523(a)(2)(C)(ii)(II).

§ 10.18 Unscheduled Debts

The debtor is responsible for scheduling creditors so that they may be notified of the deadlines for filing claims and § 523(c)(1) lawsuits. § 521(1); Rule 1007. A creditor's claim usually will not be allowed if a proof of claim is not filed by the set bar date; and if the claim is not allowed it will not be paid in the ultimate distribution. §§ 501, 502, 726(a). Yet, the discharge under § 727(b) operates as to all prepetition claims, whether or not a proof of claim was filed or the claim was allowed. It would be most unfair to exclude a creditor from the bankruptcy distribution (or prevent the creditor from contesting dischargeability) because the debtor failed to list the creditor properly in the schedules, but nevertheless to discharge that creditor's claim. There are three possible solutions: pay the creditor anyway; not discharge the debt; or both.

Attempting to pay a creditor who has not timely filed a claim usually will not be a viable response to the unscheduled creditor problem. Finding such a creditor may be difficult in the first place. Furthermore, waiting to discover the unknown creditor undermines the goal of distributing the bankruptcy estate to known creditors as promptly as possible. The court may not retroactively extend the time for filing claims to include the omitted creditor.[144] Even though the innocent unscheduled creditor thus

---

[144] In re Smith, 21 F.3d 660 (5th Cir. 1994).

may be deprived of the benefit side of a liquidation bankruptcy, the discharge (the detriment side) can easily be avoided as to such a creditor by the simple expedient of excepting the unscheduled debt from discharge. This is the solution the Code adopts in § 523(a)(3).

Section 523(a)(3) operates in a straightforward way. The debt is not discharged if it was not listed in the debtor's schedules in time to permit the creditor to file a proof of claim or a complaint alleging nondischargeability under § 523(a)(2), (4), or (6). The proper listing of the creditor in the schedules must include the correct name and address of the creditor, if known or discoverable by debtor through the exercise of reasonable diligence. §§ 523(a)(3), 521(1); Rule 1007(a), (b). If the debtor accurately lists the creditor, but the creditor is not notified due to the failure of the clerk's office or the mails, the discharge will be effective.

A major exception to the operation of § 523(a)(3)'s nondischargeability rule is when the creditor "had notice or actual knowledge" of the bankruptcy case in time to file the proof of claim or dischargeability complaint. The knowledge referred to is of the bankruptcy case generally, and not of the specific bar dates. The debt of such a creditor is discharged in all events, scheduled or not. The rationale is that a creditor with actual knowledge of the bankruptcy case possesses the ability to inquire further and preserve her rights. The usual question that arises is what constitutes "notice or actual knowledge." Creditors are not required to follow up on unsubstantiated rumors. However, notice to an agent or attorney of the creditor typically will be imputed to the creditor. Although a plausible argument can be made that § 523(a)(3) is unconstitutional under the due process clause, based on the Supreme Court's 1953 decision in *City of New York v. New York, New Haven & Hartford Railroad Co.*,[145] the courts under the Code have upheld the constitutionality of that section.[146]

Another question concerns how § 523(a)(3) applies in a no-asset case.[147] In such a case, which occurs with great frequency, creditors are usually notified that it is unnecessary to file a proof of claim. Rule 2002(e). Many courts have permitted the debtor to amend his schedules or reopen a case to include an omitted creditor, as long as the original omission was not fraudulent or intentional, and thereby discharge the creditor's claim.[148] Those courts reason that the creditor was not harmed by the omission, since no dividend was payable anyway, and further state that § 523(a)(3) is not triggered by its terms, since "timely filing" of a proof of claim is inapposite in a no-asset case in which creditors have been instructed not to file claims. The rationale of these cases, where the only "right" lost by not being scheduled was the meaningless filing of a proof of claim, would not seem to apply equally to cases where the lost right is the timely filing of a dischargeability complaint as required by § 523(c)(1) and Rule 4007(c). Other courts reject the "no harm" theory, reasoning that the purpose of the

---

[145] 344 U.S. 293, 297 (1953).

[146] See In re Medaglia, 52 F.3d 451 (2d Cir. 1995); Yukon Self Storage Fund v. Green (In re Green), 876 F.2d 854, 856–57 (10th Cir. 1989).

[147] See Lauren A. Helbling & Christopher M. Klein, The Emerging Harmless Innocent Omission Defense to Nondischargeability Under Bankruptcy Code § 523(a)(3)(A): Making Sense of the Confusion Over Reopening Cases and Amending Schedules to Add Omitted Debts, 69 Am. Bankr. L.J. 33, 42–43 (1995).

[148] E.g., In re Stone, 10 F.3d 285 (5th Cir. 1994).

notice to creditors is not just to allow them to file a proof of claim, but also to participate fully in the bankruptcy case, such as by attending the § 341 creditors' meeting and questioning the debtor, voting for the trustee, and the like. The latter view is more prevalent in chapter 11 cases, where creditor participation may actually be meaningful.

§ 10.19 Fiduciary Fraud or Defalcation, Embezzlement, Larceny

Section 523(a)(4) excepts from discharge debts "for fraud or defalcation while acting in a fiduciary capacity, embezzlement, or larceny." The requirement that the debtor be acting in a fiduciary capacity applies only to the acts of fraud or defalcation; any debtor, fiduciary or not, found to have incurred a debt by embezzlement or larceny will not have that debt discharged. Complaints asserting nondischargeability under § 523(a)(4) must be brought within 60 days of the first meeting of creditors and only in the bankruptcy court. § 523(c)(1); Rule 4007(c).

Relatively fewer cases involve allegations of embezzlement or larceny than fiduciary misconduct. Both embezzlement and larceny involve the fraudulent appropriation of the money or property of another by the debtor with the intent to convert that property to the debtor's own use. The difference is that in larceny the initial taking itself must have been wrongful, whereas in embezzlement the debtor's original possession is lawful, with the misappropriation occurring subsequent thereto. Regardless, both constitute crimes, and a prior criminal conviction will be given collateral estoppel effect on the dischargeability issue.

Many more cases address the fiduciary wrongdoings, although courts narrowly construe both the requirements of (1) a fiduciary relationship and (2) fraud or defalcation. The necessary fiduciary relationship, determined as a matter of federal law, must arise out of a technical or express trust, and must exist independently of the alleged wrongdoing.[149] Implied or constructive trusts are not enough. Usually a contract or statute (state or federal) creating the fiduciary relationship is required. Misfeasance in the context of ordinary commercial relationships normally will not suffice.

Common types of litigated cases involve the conversion of a secured party's collateral by a debtor; the misapplication of funds collected by an insurance agent; the diversion of payments by a building contractor; or a failure to make required contributions to an ERISA plan. In the collateral conversion case, courts almost never except the debt under § 523(a)(4),[150] although § 523(a)(6) remains a possibility.[151] In the insurance cases the creditor stands a better chance, depending on the terms of the contract and on the existence of a state statute.[152] The builder cases often turn on the specific terms of the governing state statute,[153] but often the contractor is found to be a

---

[149] Davis v. Aetna Acceptance Co., 293 U.S. 328 (1934).

[150] Id.

[151] See, e.g., In re Tinkler, 311 B.R. 869 (Bankr. D. Colo. 2004).

[152] E.g., In re Coley, 354 B.R. 813 (Bankr. N.D. Tex. 2006).

[153] E.g., In re Johnson, 691 F.2d 249 (6th Cir. 1982).

fiduciary.[154] In some situations courts will ignore a state statute that purports to make the debtor a fiduciary to the state itself, reasoning that the statute is nothing more than the state's attempt to make its own claim nondischargeable in bankruptcy.[155] Creditors rarely prevail in the ERISA cases, either because the unpaid contributions are not considered plan assets, or because the debtor who is the plan administrator is not deemed a sufficient fiduciary for purposes of § 523(a)(4).[156]

Even if a fiduciary relationship is found, the creditor must also prove that the debtor committed "fraud" or "defalcation" while acting in that capacity. An early Supreme Court case, *Neal v. Clark*, which arose under the Bankruptcy Act of 1867, concluded that "fraud" had the same meaning in the fourth exception as under the second exception, namely that it "means positive fraud, or fraud in fact, involving moral turpitude or intentional wrong, . . . and not implied fraud, or fraud in law, which may exist without the imputation of bad faith or immorality."[157] Justice Harlan for the Court came to this conclusion in part because of the grouping of "fraud" with "embezzlement," which does require intentional wrongdoing, and in part to further "the object and intention of Congress in enacting a general law by which the honest citizen may be relieved from the burden of hopeless insolvency."[158]

The meaning of "defalcation," by contrast, was the subject of widespread disagreement for well over a century. Courts differed sharply over what mental state had to be proven. The leading historical exposition of the development and meaning of the "defalcation" rule was by Judge Learned Hand in a 1937 case, *Central Hanover Bank & Trust Co. v. Herbst*.[159] While far from crystalline, that opinion at the very least appeared to stand for the proposition that "defalcation" required *less* of a culpable mental state than its statutory companions in the fourth exception (fraud, misappropriation, and embezzlement under the Bankruptcy Act then in effect).[160] As to how much less, though, Hand equivocated; he observed both that "'defalcation' may demand some portion of misconduct" and yet also acknowledged the possibility that a prior version of the statute "may have included innocent defaults."[161]

Hand's equivocation was repeated endlessly in hopelessly conflicting circuit court decisions for the next three-quarters of a century, both under the Bankruptcy Act and the 1978 Bankruptcy Code now in effect, until finally settled by the Supreme Court in 2013. The Courts of Appeals embraced at least three different standards. The least demanding was that even an innocent mistake, or at the most negligence, would

---

[154] See, e.g., In re Patel, 565 F.3d 963 (6th Cir. 2009).

[155] See, e.g., In re Marchiando, 13 F.3d 1111 (7th Cir.), cert. denied, 512 U.S. 1205 (1994) (lottery agent who failed to remit proceeds of lottery sales discharged).

[156] See, e.g., In re Halpin, 566 F.3d 286 (2d Cir. 2009); In re Bucci, 493 F.3d 635 (6th Cir. 2007), cert. denied, 553 U.S. 1093 (2008); In re Luna, 406 F.3d 1192 (10th Cir. 2005). But see In re Hemmeter, 242 F.3d 1186 (9th Cir. 2001).

[157] 95 U.S. 704, 709 (1878).

[158] Id.

[159] 93 F.2d 510 (2d Cir. 1937).

[160] Id. at 512.

[161] Id. at 511–12.

suffice.[162] The middle view, which commanded the largest following, required proof that the debtor acted recklessly, judged objectively.[163] The most demanding standard was extreme recklessness.[164]

In 2003 the Supreme Court opted for the most demanding standard of culpability in *Bullock v. BankChampaign, N.A.*[165] As it had in *Neal v. Clark*, the *Bullock* Court presumed that the various terms in the fourth exception—*including* "defalcation"—carried similar culpability requirements, all necessitating proof of scienter.[166] The Court in *Bullock* accordingly held that "the term 'defalcation' . . . includes a culpable state of mind requirement akin to that which accompanies application of the other terms in the same statutory phrase. We describe that state of mind as one involving knowledge of, or gross recklessness in respect to, the improper nature of the relevant fiduciary behavior."[167] The Court pointed out that this heightened standard requiring scienter would be especially beneficial to "*nonprofessional* trustees, perhaps administering small family trusts potentially immersed in intrafamily arguments that are difficult to evaluate in terms of comparative fault."[168] Furthermore, again as it had in *Neal* 135 years earlier, the Court gave the exclusion from discharge the most narrow possible reading, so as to preserve and promote the "fresh start" policy for the debtor's benefit, excepting only cases involving clear wrongdoing and fault.[169]

Randy Bullock was almost the perfect candidate for the Court to construe § 523(a)(4) in the most favorable way for debtors. He was a nonprofessional trustee of a small family trust (indeed, until the settlor asked him to take out a loan from the trust, he was not even aware that he was the trustee!), his only wrongdoing was technical self-dealing (borrowing from the trust in excess of the authorization specifically granted—and as noted, one of the loans was taken at the instance of the settlor, his father, and another was on behalf of his mother), and he repaid all monies borrowed, with interest! But in the finest Dickensian fashion, his greedy brothers had sued him successfully in Illinois state court for a breach of fiduciary duty under state law, and,

---

[162] See, e.g., In re Strack, 524 F.3d 493 (4th Cir. 2008); In re Banks, 263 F.3d 862 (9th Cir. 2001); In re Cochrane, 124 F.3d 978, 984 (8th Cir. 1997).

[163] See, e.g., Bullock v. BankChampaign, N.A. (In re Bullock), 670 F.3d 1160, 1166 (11th Cir. 2012), vacated and remanded, 133 S.Ct. 1754 (2013); In re Harwood, 637 F.3d 615, 624 (5th Cir. 2011); In re Berman, 629 F.3d 761, 765 n.3 (7th Cir. 2011); In re Patel, 565 F.3d 963, 970 (6th Cir. 2009). See also Meyer v. Rigdon, 36 F.3d 1375, 1385 (7th Cir. 1994).

[164] See, e.g., In re Hyman, 502 F.3d 61 (2d Cir. 2007); In re Baylis, 313 F.3d 9 (1st Cir. 2002).

[165] 133 S.Ct. 1754 (2013).

[166] Id. at 1759–60. This canon parades under the very fancy name of "*noscitur a sociis*," which is Latin meaning "known by its associates"; the point is that the meaning of a word in a statutory text can be gleaned by comparison to other words in the same statutory context.

[167] Id. at 1755. The Court elaborated:

> Thus, where the conduct at issue does not involve bad faith, moral turpitude, or other immoral conduct, the term requires an intentional wrong. We include as intentional not only conduct that the fiduciary knows is improper but also reckless conduct of the kind that the criminal law often treats as the equivalent. Thus, we include reckless conduct of the kind set forth in the Model Penal Code. Where actual knowledge of wrongdoing is lacking, we consider conduct as equivalent if the fiduciary "consciously disregards" (or is willfully blind to) "a substantial and unjustifiable risk" that his conduct will turn out to violate a fiduciary duty.

> Id. at 1759. This meaning is similar to what the Court has required in the securities fraud area.

[168] Id. at 1761 (emphasis in original).

[169] Id. at 1760–61.

even though that court acknowledged that Randy did not have a malicious motive, the brothers got a judgment imposing a constructive trust on the benefits the debtor obtained from the loans, over and above the principal and interest that he had fully repaid. When he could not pay off the judgment debt (in part because the Bank, the successor trustee, blocked him from selling one of the properties he had purchased with one of the loans), he filed bankruptcy and sought to discharge the Illinois judgment debt. The lower courts had all held that the debt was not dischargeable under the middle standard (objective recklessness), since Bullock "should have known that he was engaging in self-dealing."[170] Under the Supreme Court's heightened standard, though, it is highly likely that Randy Bullock will be able to discharge the debt. So too will many other debtors who find themselves technically cast in a fiduciary role (such as, for example, a building contractor) and who make some mistakes in exercising their duties, nevertheless still be able to obtain a discharge unless they knowingly breached those duties in a manner that substantiates a finding of clear fault.

It is worth noting that the Court's approach in *Bullock* is quite favorable to debtors, and strongly furthers the fresh start policy. Looking beyond the specific context of the decision, *Bullock* should be powerful authority for an expansive interpretation of the reach of the fresh start policy and for a very narrow scope for exclusions therefrom. *Bullock*'s limitation of the discharge exception to cases involving knowing debtor fault mirrors its approach taken to other exceptions, such as, for example, its decision in *Kawaauhau v. Geiger*[171] requiring proof of a subjective intent to injure to constitute willful and malicious injury under § 523(a)(6). In other areas (e.g., the means test of chapter 7 and the best efforts test of chapter 13), the Court seems unsympathetic to the light of individual debtors. But *Bullock* suggests that the fresh start policy perhaps is not dead quite yet.

§ 10.20 Domestic Support Obligations

Bankruptcy is not a haven for debtors hoping to discharge obligations to support their family. Even before a specific exception to discharge embodied this principle, the Supreme Court refused to permit the discharge of such obligations.[172] Sections 523(a)(5) and 523(a)(15) subordinate the fresh start goal for the individual debtor to the policy that family support debts must be paid. Debts covered by § 523(a)(5) are even excepted from a chapter 13 full-compliance discharge, § 1328(a)(2), and may be enforced against the debtor's exempt property. § 522(c)(1).

In a new § 101(14A), the 2005 amendments introduced the new term "domestic support obligation," which is used throughout the Code, including in § 523(a)(5). Domestic support obligations are defined broadly to include almost all types of debts in the nature of alimony, maintenance, or support owed to the debtor's spouse or former spouse, child, parent or guardian of the debtor's child, or a governmental unit. However, unless voluntarily assigned by the debtor for the purpose of collection, a debt assigned to a non-governmental entity is not a domestic support obligation.

---

[170] 670 F.3d at 1166.

[171] 523 U.S. 57 (1998). See also § 10.21.

[172] Wetmore v. Markoe, 196 U.S. 68 (1904).

§ 101(14A)(D). Domestic support obligations can be established pursuant to a separation agreement, property settlement, divorce decree, or court order, and include debts accruing at any point before, on or after the order for relief, including all accrued interest. § 101(14A).

Before 1994 the most important scope limitation of the fifth exception was that the debt had to be "actually in the nature of alimony, maintenance, or support."[173] A property division or property settlement obligation is not excluded from discharge under § 523(a)(5), and until 1994 was always dischargeable. Also dischargeable before 1994 were "hold harmless" debts, in which the debtor spouse agreed to pay certain marital debts and hold the non-debtor spouse harmless from such debts. In the 1994 amendments Congress added § 523(a)(15), which makes property settlement debts and hold harmless agreements nondischargeable as well. Thus, the issue of whether a domestic debt is actually in the nature of alimony, maintenance, or support (and thus potentially within the fifth exception) now is less critical, given the possible fall-back of the fifteenth exception. In 2005, BAPCPA amended 523(a)(15) to remove the affirmative defenses previously included, making all property settlements arising from divorce or separation nondischargeable. Note, though, that fifth exception debts are not discharged in chapter 13[174] and are enforceable against exempt property, but fifteenth exception debts enjoy neither benefit. The distinction between a marital debt that is covered by § 523(a)(5) and one that is only covered by § 523(a)(15) thus remains important, although considerably less so than before 1994.

Drawing the line between debts that are and those that are not actually in the nature of alimony, maintenance or support has proven difficult for courts. Most have resorted to consideration of a long laundry list of factors. It is important to determine that the obligation be based on an enforceable duty of support.[175] The intent of the parties at the time of the decree is important.[176] However, the label placed on the debt by the parties themselves or by the state court is not controlling. The bankruptcy court must determine the nature of the debt as a matter of *federal* law.[177] Of course, bankruptcy courts undoubtedly will borrow heavily from state domestic relations law in making this determination. Until 2005, the applicability of the fifteenth exception had to be litigated exclusively in the bankruptcy court, but that restriction was dropped in BAPCPA. Now, state courts have concurrent jurisdiction to decide whether either § 523(a)(5) or § 523(a)(15) applies. Thus, a creditor can wait to litigate the applicability of a marital debt until after bankruptcy, and proceed in state court.

One question is whether the bankruptcy court's inquiry extends to a consideration of changed circumstances. While the vast majority of courts look only at the nature of the debt at the time of the original decree, and thus refuse to take changed

---

[173] Bankruptcy Reform Act of 1978, Pub. L. No. 95–598, § 523(a)(5)(B), 92 Stat. 2549 (amended 1994).

[174] 11 U.S.C. § 1328(a)(2).

[175] See Audubon v. Shufeldt, 181 U.S. 575 (1901).

[176] See, e.g., In re Zamos, 300 Fed. Appx. 451, 452 (9th Cir. 2008); In re Evert, 342 F.3d 358, 368 (5th Cir. 2003); In re Brody, 3 F.3d 35 (2d Cir. 1993); In re Sampson, 997 F.2d 717 (10th Cir. 1993).

[177] See In re Brody, 3 F.3d 35, 39 (2d Cir. 1993); H.R. Rep. No. 95–595, 95th Cong., 1st Sess., at 364 (1977), reprinted in 1978 U.S.C.C.A.N. 5963, 6320; S. Rep. No.989, 95th Cong., 2d Sess., at 79 (1978), reprinted in 1978 U.S.C.C.A.N. 5787, 5865.

circumstances into account,[178] the Sixth Circuit in *In re Calhoun* held that the court should consider how the financial circumstances of the respective parties may have changed in the interim since that original decree.[179] Doing so would create a heavy burden for the bankruptcy courts, and likely would cause more debts to be discharged.

The final limitation of § 523(a)(5) (through § 101(14A)(C)) is that the debt must be based on a separation or property settlement agreement, a divorce decree, other court order, or a determination made by a governmental unit under applicable non-bankruptcy law. This makes dischargeable common law support obligations which are not embodied in one of the cited vehicles, as well as other contractual debts for necessaries and the like not part of an actual separation or property settlement agreement.

§ 10.21 Willful and Malicious Injury

Ever since the passage of the Bankruptcy Act of 1898, Congress has excepted from discharge debts stemming from "willful and malicious" injuries by the debtor.[180] The current exception is § 523(a)(6). The bankruptcy court has exclusive jurisdiction (under § 523(c)(1)) to determine dischargeability issues under § 523(a)(6), although this exception (along with fraud) is a prime candidate for application of collateral estoppel. The section prevents the discharge of debts based on intentional torts ("willful") that contain some aggravating features ("malicious"). Exactly how aggravating has proven to be difficult to pin down. Punitive damages, which are often awarded on proof of malice, may be excepted from discharge under this section.[181]

Two elements must be proved to establish the § 523(a)(6) exception. First, the debtor's actions must have been *willful*," which, as the legislative history emphasizes, means "deliberate or intentional."[182] Cases allowing a "reckless disregard" standard to suffice were intended to be overruled by the 1978 Code. Behavior that is merely negligent (or even reckless) would not give rise to a nondischargeable debt under the sixth exception. For the most part, this part of the statutory formulation has caused relatively little trouble for the courts. Perhaps the most difficulty has come in the drunk driving cases. In 1984, however, Congress added a separate discharge exception for DUI debts for death or personal injury, § 523(a)(9), which does not require proof of intent.[183] In DUI property damage cases, however, to which (9) does not apply, subsection (6) remains important.

---

[178] E.g., Forsdick v. Turgeon, 812 F.2d 801, 803 (2d Cir. 1987); In re Harrell, 754 F.2d 902, 906–07 (11th Cir. 1985).

[179] 715 F.2d 1103, 1109–10 (6th Cir. 1983). The Sixth Circuit itself has expressed regret that *Calhoun* has been read more broadly than intended, and relief that other jurisdictions have not taken that course. See In re Fitzgerald, 9 F.3d 517, 520 (6th Cir. 1993).

[180] See Charles Jordan Tabb, The Scope of the Fresh Start in Bankruptcy: Collateral Conversions and the Dischargeability Debate, 59 Geo. Wash. L. Rev. 56 (1990).

[181] See, e.g., In re Scarborough, 171 F.3d 638 (8th Cir. 1999); In re McNallen, 62 F.3d 619 (4th Cir. 1995).

[182] H.R. Rep. No. 95–595, 95th Cong., 1st Sess., at 365 (1977), reprinted in 1978 U.S.C.C.A.N. 5963, 6320; S. Rep. No. 95–989, 95th Cong., 2d Sess., at 79 (1978), reprinted in 1978 U.S.C.C.A.N. 5787, 5865.

[183] See § 10.24.

Most of the interpretive difficulty has come from the second element of § 523(a)(6), that the debtor's actions must have been "*malicious*." Until 1998, courts differed widely on the proper meaning of malice. The issue has arisen most often in three types of cases: (1) the debtor converts the secured creditor's collateral for the debtor's own benefit and then dissipates the collateral proceeds; (2) the debtor inflicts an injury driving a vehicle while intoxicated; and (3) a physician commits particularly egregious malpractice.

The question is whether the section requires proof of "*special* malice"—i.e., that the debtor *intended to injure* the creditor—or whether it is sufficient to prove "*implied* malice"—i.e., that the debtor intentionally committed an act knowing that the act was wrongful and was likely to harm the creditor, without just cause or excuse. The Supreme Court misleadingly framed the question in the leading 1998 case of *Kawaauhau v. Geiger* (one of the "bad doctor" cases) as follows: "We confront this pivotal question concerning the scope of the "willful and malicious injury" exception: Does § 523(a)(6)'s compass cover acts, done intentionally, that cause injury (as the [debtors] urge), or only acts done with the actual intent to cause injury?"[184] The Court opted for the latter reading. In so holding, the Court (if taken at its word) could have caused harm to intentional tort victims who will stand helpless as their debts are discharged, because they will be unable to prove that the debtor acted with the actual subjective intent to injure them, even though the debtor may have acted intentionally, knowing that what he did was wrong and was substantially certain to injure the creditor, but nevertheless was not motivated by any personal animus to the creditor.

The *Geiger* Court omitted a third plausible, and indeed preferable, interpretation (and one that had prevailed for almost a century): that the debtor intentionally committed an act that caused injury, knowing that the act was wrongful and substantially certain to cause injury, without justification or excuse. The important additions of this preferred interpretation to the Court's "straw man" first alternative (that the debtor intentionally committed an act that caused injury) are that the debtor (1) knew the act it committed was wrongful, (2) knew the act was substantially certain to cause injury, and (3) in so acting, had no justification or excuse. As will be discussed below, post-*Geiger*, many lower courts have "read" *Geiger* as allowing exception to discharge on proof of the elements of this third formulation.

In deciding *Geiger,* the Court was not writing on a clean slate. The original interpretation, in the 1904 Supreme Court case of *Tinker v. Colwell*, required only *implied* malice.[185] Thus, Charles Tinker was unable to discharge a $50,000 judgment

---

[184]   523 U.S. 57, 61 (1998).

[185]   193 U.S. 473 (1904). The Court explained:

> There may be cases where the act has been performed without any particular malice towards the husband, but we are of opinion that, within the meaning of the exception, it is not necessary that there should be this particular, and, so to speak, personal malevolence toward the husband, but that the act itself necessarily implies that degree of malice which is sufficient to bring the case within the exception stated in the statute. The act is wilful, of course, in the sense that it is intentional and voluntary, and we think that it is also malicious within the meaning of the statute.

based on "criminal conversation" (adultery) with Frederick Colwell's wife, irrespective of whether Tinker was driven by malevolence toward Frederick or just passion for Frederick's wife. Instead, according to the *Tinker* Court, "[m]alice, in common acceptation, means ill will against a person; but in its legal sense it means a wrongful act, done intentionally, without just cause or excuse."[186] Thus, the Court in *Tinker* concluded that a "wilful disregard of what one knows to be his duty, an act which is against good morals, and wrongful in and of itself, and which necessarily causes injury and is done intentionally, may be said to be done wilfully and maliciously, so as to come within the exception."[187]

While *Tinker* established that special malice need not be shown, the 1934 Supreme Court case of *Davis v. Aetna Acceptance Co.*[188] illustrated that not every intentional tort falls within the exception. The creditor objected to discharge of a debt following the debtor's conversion of the creditor's collateral. Even though the lower courts had found that the debtor's act did constitute a legal conversion, which indisputably is an intentional tort, the Court concluded that not every conversion was excluded from discharge, but that aggravating features were required.[189] In that case, the debtor mistakenly but innocently believed that he had authority to sell the collateral and use the proceeds. Such a technical conversion, while done intentionally, is not "malicious," the Court held, and the resulting debt was held to be dischargeable.[190]

In *Geiger*, the Supreme Court confronted a case in which the debtor, Dr. Paul Geiger, had committed particularly egregious malpractice by knowingly and admittedly prescribing a course of antibiotic treatment for an infection that he knew to be less effective than a viable alternative, and then cavalierly canceling that treatment altogether, causing Margaret Kawaauhau to have her leg amputated. Margaret argued that Geiger's knowing malpractice met the *Tinker* standard of "willful disregard of what one knows to be his duty, an act which is against good morals, and wrongful in and of itself, and which necessarily causes injury and is done intentionally."

The *Geiger* Court disagreed. Having framed the question of the section's scope as a false choice between the alternatives of encompassing every act done intentionally by a debtor that causes injury or only acts done with the intent to cause injury, the Court chose the latter. It held that "nondischargeability takes a deliberate or intentional *injury,* not merely a deliberate or intentional *act* that leads to injury."[191] The Court relied heavily on the statutory text, observing that "[t]he word 'willful' in (a)(6)

> In order to come within that meaning as a judgment for a wilful and malicious injury to person or property, it is not necessary that the cause of action be based upon special malice, so that without it the action could not be maintained.
>
> Id. at 485.

[186] Id. at 485–86.

[187] Id. at 487.

[188] 293 U.S. 328 (1934).

[189] Id. at 333.

[190] Id.

[191] Kawaauhau v. Geiger, 523 U.S. 57, 61 (1998).

modifies the word 'injury.'"[192] Thus, the Court held "that debts arising from recklessly or negligently inflicted injuries do not fall within the compass of § 523(a)(6)."[193] This last holding, standing alone, might not work mischief, but the earlier statement, that a "deliberate or intentional injury" is required, could.

The *Geiger* Court sought to limit subsection (6) to *intentional torts*,[194] which is a defensible interpretation of the section, but the way they did so—by also requiring an *intent to injure*—went too far, and much farther than needed to decide the case. By doing so they created the potential for unfair results in certain recurring cases (especially the collateral conversion cases), as explained below. The Supreme Court could have decided against Margaret Kawaauhau simply by saying that the debtor, Dr. Paul Geiger, did not commit a "willful" (or "intentional") tort, but at most acted with gross negligence (or even a "reckless disregard"). The 1978 legislative history, reacting to a spate of drunk driving cases that had gone against the debtor, makes clear that Congress thought that the section required an intentional tort.[195] Indeed, even in *Tinker* the Court had taken pains to note that a debtor who merely acts negligently, and not intentionally, would not come within the exception.[196] The way the Court in *Geiger* read subsection (6), though, not only requires an intentional tort, but an intentional tort in which the debtor also intends to injure the victim. Taking the Court at its word, this further and entirely unnecessary elaboration effectively overturns the *implied malice* standard of *Tinker*, and puts a *special malice* standard in its place. The essence of "special" malice is a subjective intent to cause injury.

The Court in *Geiger* distinguished *Tinker* on the ground that *Tinker* involved an intentional tort.[197] Fair enough. But in finding that Dr. Geiger had not committed an intentional tort, the Supreme Court did not also need to throw out *Tinker's* implied malice standard and require proof of intent to injure. Indeed, under the new *Geiger* standard, Tinker's chances of receiving a discharge for his debt to the cuckolded husband would be much greater, since Colwell would have to show that Tinker *intended to injure* him by having an affair with his wife. That Tinker knew that what he was doing was wrong, knew that by doing so he was substantially certain to cause injury to Colwell, and knew that he had no justification for doing so, would not seem to suffice under *Geiger*.

The *Geiger* opinion seems to conflate the separate elements of willfulness and malice into a single unitary test of "intent to injure." Indeed, under the Court's formulation, it is entirely unclear what the word "malicious" adds. It is exceedingly difficult to think of many (any?) cases in which a debtor who inflicted a "willful . . . injury" (meaning, as the *Geiger* Court asserts, an "actual intent to cause injury") would not *also* have acted with malice.

---

[192] Id.

[193] Id. at 64.

[194] Id. at 61.

[195] See supra note 182 and accompanying text.

[196] 193 U.S. 473, 489 (1904).

[197] Geiger, 523 U.S. at 63.

After *Geiger*, we at least do know how to resolve two of the three types of common cases. Debts arising in the "bad doctor" cases involving horrific medical malpractice will be *discharged*, unless the victim can prove both that the doctor's malpractice rose to the level of an intentional tort (battery, perhaps?) *and* that the physician acted with an intent to injure the victim (or, as explained below, knew that his actions were substantially certain to cause injury). Debts arising from drunk driving will also fall outside the scope of the § 523(a)(6) exception (but § 523(a)(9) remains possibly available).

That leaves collateral conversion cases. Literally thousands of § 523(a)(6) cases involve the conversion by the debtor of a secured party's collateral.[198] There also have been a considerable number of cases involving misappropriation of trade secrets, which are similar to the conversion cases in that they also involve the taking of another's property. It is in these sorts of situations that *Geiger's* "intent-to-injure" formulation could work the most harm. The Supreme Court established early on that conversion cases could come within the exception,[199] although the Court also made clear, as noted above, that innocent conversions were not covered.[200] Prior to *Geiger,* a majority of courts applied the implied malice standard, and concluded that the conversion debt should not be discharged if the debtor acted with knowledge that the conversion was impermissible and had no justification or excuse,[201] as contrasted with an innocent conversion, such as in *Davis v. Aetna Acceptance.*[202] So, for example, an ignorant consumer who sells his used refrigerator and keeps the proceeds, not realizing that doing so violates the security interest of the store that sold him the refrigerator on credit, is not acting with "implied malice" because he does not realize that his sale is unauthorized. His debt will be discharged.

After *Geiger,* the result in the innocent conversion cases will not change—those have always been dischargeable, even under an implied malice test—but the outcome in the *knowing* conversion cases might. What if, for example, a sophisticated business debtor takes the money from a secured creditor's collateral account and, instead of using that money to pay the secured creditor (as he knows he is supposed to under the terms of the security agreement) he wrongfully pays off other business debts with that money, but does so not with a malevolent desire to injure the secured creditor, but inspired by wishful thinking that he might thereby be able to save his business? Under an implied malice test, the debtor should not be able to discharge the debt to the secured creditor, because he knew that what he was doing was illegal and was substantially certain to harm the secured creditor, even though he was not driven by ill motives toward the secured creditor—just as Charles Tinker knew it was wrong to sleep with Frederick Colwell's wife, and was likely to harm Colwell, and accordingly was denied discharge of the resulting debt.[203] But under the *Geiger* approach, if the secured creditor must prove that the business debtor converted the collateral "with the

---

[198] See Tabb, supra note 180.

[199] McIntyre v. Kavanaugh, 242 U.S. 138, 141 (1916).

[200] See Davis v. Aetna Acceptance Co., 293 U.S. 328 (1934), supra note 188.

[201] The leading case was *United Bank of Southgate v. Nelson*, 35 B.R. 766 (N.D. Ill. 1983).

[202] 293 U.S. 328 (1934). See supra notes 188 and 198 and accompanying text.

[203] Tinker v. Colwell, 193 U.S. 473 (1904).

actual intent to cause injury,"[204] the creditor could well lose—assuming that lower courts give effect only to what the Court actually said in *Geiger* and require proof of "actual intent to cause injury."

As it turns out, that assumption might be unwarranted. In *Geiger*, the Court relied on the definition of "intent" in § 8A of the Restatement of Torts, that the actor must "intend the consequences of an act."[205] However, the Court omitted the alternative meaning, also in § 8A: "*or that he believes that the consequences are substantially certain to result from it.*"[206] Post–*Geiger*, many lower courts have adopted this alternative meaning of "intent" and have read *Geiger* as allowing an exception to discharge if the creditor can prove that the debtor acted knowing that his actions entailed an "objective substantial certainty of harm,"[207] even if the creditor could not prove that the debtor acted with a *subjective* motive to cause harm. Under this alternative formulation, a creditor can prevail *either* by showing that the debtor "will[ed] or desire[d] harm" *or* "believe[d] injury is substantially certain to occur as a result of his behavior."[208] This alternative reading gives the creditor whose collateral has been knowingly (rather than innocently) converted much more hope of blocking the discharge of the resulting debt. The key issues will be whether the debtor knew that the conversion was unauthorized and whether the debtor believed that his conversion was substantially certain to cause harm to the secured creditor. A showing of subjective personal malevolence toward the secured creditor would not be required. Even Charles Tinker would be likely to lose under the alternative reading, since he would have known that his affair with Frederick Colwell's wife was wrong and was substantially certain to harm Colwell. So, perhaps we have simply come full circle.

§ 10.22 Governmental Fines and Penalties, Criminal Restitution

Section 523(a)(7) excepts from discharge a debt that is (1) "for a fine, penalty, or forfeiture"; (2) is "payable to and for the benefit of a governmental unit"; and (3) "is not compensation for actual pecuniary loss." Although the section was drafted principally, although not entirely, to cover the dischargeability of tax penalties, the most interesting litigation has been with regard to criminal restitution obligations. The exception from discharge under § 523(a)(7) occurs automatically, without the need for the creditor to litigate the dischargeability issue in the bankruptcy court.

The dischargeability of a tax penalty is linked directly to the dischargeability of the underlying tax. § 523(a)(7)(A). Thus, if the underlying tax is discharged, then so too is the penalty. If the tax is not discharged under § 523(a)(1), then the penalty likewise is excepted from discharge. § 523(a)(7)(A). However, this discharge exception is subject to the further limitation that the penalty must relate to a transaction or event that

---

[204] Geiger, 523 U.S. at 61.

[205] Id. at 61–62.

[206] Restatement (Second) of Torts § 8A (1965).

[207] See, e.g., In re Shcolnik, 670 F.3d 624, 629 (5th Cir. 2012); In re Williams, 337 F.3d 504, 508–09 (5th Cir. 2003); In re Miller, 156 F.3d 598, 606 (5th Cir. 1998), cert. denied, 526 U.S. 1016 (1999). But see In re Su, 290 F.3d 1140 (9th Cir. 2002) (holding that the willful injury requirement of § 523(a)(6) is governed by a subjective standard).

[208] In re Markowitz, 190 F.3d 455, 465 n.10 (6th Cir. 1999).

occurred within three years of the bankruptcy filing.[209] The legislative history also makes clear that tax "penalties" that in reality are merely pecuniary loss penalties designed to collect the underlying tax are "compensation for actual pecuniary loss" and thus dischargeable.[210] Postpetition interest on a nondischargeable tax debt is excluded from the discharge.[211]

The unexpected problem that developed under the Code was whether *criminal restitution* obligations were nondischargeable under § 523(a)(7). At least two aspects of those obligations made application of § 523(a)(7) uncertain. First, the requirement that the penalty not be *compensation* for actual pecuniary loss was troublesome, especially in states where the restitution obligation was measured directly by the amount of loss the victim had suffered. Second, the limitation that the *government* be the payee and beneficiary of the penalty seemed to be a barrier, particularly under state statutes directing payment directly to the victim and giving the victim the right to enforce the restitution obligation in the civil courts.

Despite these problems, however, in 1986 the Supreme Court in *Kelly v. Robinson*[212] held that criminal restitution obligations are excepted from discharge under § 523(a)(7). The Court avoided a literalistic reading of the statute, and focused instead on the historical exclusion of such debts from the discharge, and on the state's overriding interest in implementing its criminal justice system unfettered by the constraints of bankruptcy. The semantic difficulties in applying § 523(a)(7) were answered by finding that the essential purpose of the state's restitution scheme was to further the state's "interests in rehabilitation and punishment," for the benefit of "society as a whole."[213]

Kelly v. Robinson did not completely end the problem, however. By declining to hold that the restitution obligation was not a debt, the Court left open the possibility that such an obligation could be discharged in a chapter 13 case, where (at that time) § 523(a)(7) did not apply if the debtor completed performance under the plan and received a discharge under § 1328(a). Exactly that scenario came before the Supreme Court in *Pennsylvania Department of Public Welfare v. Davenport*[214] in 1990, and the Court held that the restitution obligation was a debt and could be discharged in the chapter 13 case. Congress then moved immediately to reverse the result in *Davenport*, excepting criminal restitution obligations from a full-compliance chapter 13 discharge. § 1328(a)(3). Now a criminal debtor has no way to discharge such a restitution debt in bankruptcy.

Some courts have held, however, that restitution that is designed *solely* to compensate the victim does not come within the § 523(a)(7) exception, notwithstanding *Kelly*. In cases involving federal crimes some courts pointed out that the federalism rationale of *Kelly* does not apply, although most courts nevertheless refused to

---

[209] 11 U.S.C. § 523(a)(7)(B). See, e.g., In re Roberts, 906 F.2d 1440 (10th Cir. 1990).

[210] S. Rep. No. 95–989, 95th Cong., 2d Sess., at 73 (1978), reprinted in 1978 U.S.C.C.A.N. 5787, 5859.

[211] See In re Burns, 887 F.2d 1541 (11th Cir. 1989).

[212] 479 U.S. 36 (1986).

[213] Id. at 52–53.

[214] 495 U.S. 552, 564 (1990).

discharge federal restitution obligations. In 1994, Congress responded to these decisions by adding § 523(a)(13) to the list of discharge exceptions. The new exception covers a debt "for any payment of an order of restitution" issued under the federal Criminal Code, title 18. Thus, the new rule unequivocally makes all restitution obligations for federal crimes nondischargeable.

Not content with previous efforts to shore up the bankruptcy-immune status of fines and penalties, Congress acted again in 1996, adding a bankruptcy discharge exception to the federal Criminal Code as part of, intriguingly, the "Antiterrorism and Effective Death Penalty Act of 1996."[215] Under amended 18 U.S.C. § 3613(e), the bankruptcy discharge does not discharge "liability to pay a fine" owed to the United States. In addition, a lien filed with regard to such a fine cannot be avoided in bankruptcy.

§ 10.23 Educational Loans

Student loans are excepted from discharge, unless the debtor can demonstrate "undue hardship." § 523(a)(8). In addition, a number of other federal laws outside of the Bankruptcy Code make specific types of student loans under federal grant programs nondischargeable in bankruptcy, often under an even more demanding standard for the debtor.[216] The policy behind the eighth exception (and its counterparts outside title 11) is to prevent abuse of the educational loan system.[217]

To explain this "abuse," the legislative history behind § 523(a)(8) illustrates Congress's concern about debtors with large amounts of educational loans, few other debts, and well-paying jobs, who then file for bankruptcy to discharge their educational loans shortly after school and before any loans become due.[218] The House Report further describes this concern, noting that because "more and more students are turning to the bankruptcy courts as a relatively easy way to solve their debt problems," then "[i]t is possible that if educational debts are the main reason for filing, and if this practice is allowed under the law, then it might create a disincentive for other student borrowers to repay their loans."[219]

Congress has been zealous in implementing this policy, continually amending § 523(a)(8) to make discharge of student loans more difficult. Among other changes, § 523(a)(8) now applies to except educational loans from discharge in chapter 13. § 1328(a)(2). Furthermore, as originally enacted, student loans were only nondischargeable for five years, but that time period was extended from five years to

---

[215] Pub. L. No. 104–132, 110 Stat. 1214 (1996).

[216] See 42 U.S.C. § 292f(g) (Health Education Assistance Loan); 42 U.S.C. § 254o(d)(3) (National Health Service Corps loans); 37 U.S.C. § 301d(c)(3) (Armed Forces medical officers). To discharge a loan under HEAL or NHSC, a debtor must show that not discharging the debt would be "unconscionable," an even higher standard than "undue hardship" under § 523(a)(8). See also Mathews v. Pineo, 19 F.3d 121 (3d Cir. 1994).

[217] H.R. Rep. No. 95–595, 95th Cong., 1st Sess., at 131–34 (1977).

[218] Id. at 133 ("A few serious abuses of the bankruptcy laws by debtors with large amounts of educational loans, few other debts, and well-paying jobs, who have filed bankruptcy shortly after leaving school and before any loans became due, have generated the movement for an exception to discharge.").

[219] Id. at 136.

seven years, and then repealed altogether in 1998. Even for loans taken out prior to 1998, courts usually apply the current, less debtor-friendly statute to bankruptcy cases filed after the amendment to § 523(a)(8).[220] Finally, in 2005, Congress amended § 523(a)(8) to make student loans nondischargeable regardless of the type of lender if the loan debt is tax-deductible, meaning that most loans from non-governmental and profit-making organizations are nondischargeable.[221]

A student loan may be characterized in theory as an enabling loan to the debtor, helping her to make productive the human capital that the discharge permits the debtor to keep free from pre-bankruptcy creditors.[222] This enabling loan in fairness then should be repaid before permitting the debtor to enjoy the fruits of that enhanced human capital. To illustrate, a newly certified eye surgeon, who currently has no tangible assets but shortly will earn a six-figure income, should not be able to discharge the student loan that put her through medical school.

Section 523(a)(8) has two basic parts, an inclusive portion (in subsections (A) and (B)) and an exception for "undue hardship." Unless the debt falls within the inclusive provision, there is no need to consider the undue hardship question. If, however, the debt is one of the types covered in subsection (A) or (B), the question of undue hardship then would be ripe.

The inclusive provision, which defines which educational loans are nondischargeable, is quite broad, and now covers most educational loans. First, an "educational loan" or an "educational benefit overpayment" is nondischargeable if made directly by or if insured or guaranteed by any governmental unit. § 523(a)(8)(A)(i). The definition of "governmental unit" includes state and local governments as well as the federal government. § 101(27). Second, dischargeability is denied for any loan made under a "program" funded at all by a governmental unit *or* by a nonprofit institution. § 523(a)(8)(A)(i). Additionally, a debtor may not discharge "an obligation to repay funds received as an educational benefit, scholarship, or stipend." § 523(a)(8)(A)(ii). Finally, 523(a)(8)(B) (which was added in 2005) provides that "any other educational loan that is a qualified educational loan" is nondischargeable if incurred by an individual debtor. A "qualified educational loan" means a loan debt that is tax-deductible under § 221 of the Internal Revenue Code.[223]

---

[220] See, e.g., In re Lewis, 506 F.3d 927 (9th Cir. 2007) (rejecting the debtor's argument that they had a right to rely on the statute in effect when they took out loans, and holding that application of the current, harsher version of § 523(a)(8) applies).

[221] Bankruptcy Abuse Prevention and Consumer Protection Act of 2005, Pub. L. No. 109–8, 119 Stat. 23 § 220.

[222] Indeed, the legislative history in 1977 described student loans as "a mortgage on the debtor's future." See H.R. Rep. No. 95–595, 95th Cong., 1st Sess., at 133 (1977).

[223] This statute defines a "qualified education loan" as any debt incurred solely to pay qualified higher education expenses: 1) incurred on behalf of the taxpayer, taxpayer's spouse, or any dependent of the taxpayer; 2) paid or incurred within a reasonable period of time before or after the debt is incurred; and 3) attributable to education received during a time when the recipient was an eligible student. Exceptions to qualified student loans include any debt owed to a person related to the debtor, or any loan under a qualified employer plan. 26 U.S.C. § 221(d)(1).

Note that the IRC definition requires the loan be incurred on behalf of a taxpayer, or someone related to a taxpayer. This requirement lead the court in *In re LeBlanc* to conclude that a nonresident alien debtor

Some dispute has arisen over what constitutes a "governmental unit." For example, many courts have debated whether a credit union qualifies. The First Circuit held that a federal credit union is a governmental unit and thus protected from the discharge of student loans under the eighth exception, even though the credit union is not a nonprofit institution.[224]

Most courts have held that § 523(a)(8) applies to *debts,* and not to specific debtors.[225] In other words, the bankruptcy debtor to whom the section applies need not be the primary obligor on the educational loan (i.e., the student), or even receive the educational benefit of the student loan; discharge of a secondary liability on the loan is prevented as well. This issue comes up typically in the case of a parent who co-signs the loan and then files bankruptcy.[226] A minority of courts have disagreed, reasoning that the "enabling loan" policy does not apply to a debtor other than the student themself.

The most interesting and difficult issues under § 523(a)(8) are raised by the provision that an otherwise nondischargeable educational loan nevertheless may be discharged if not discharging that debt "would impose an undue hardship on the debtor and the debtor's dependents." The student loan exception thus specifies a standard of nondischargeability, rather than a rule. Curiously, Congress left the term "undue hardship" undefined, exposing the term to much debate in student loan cases. However, that statute's use of "undue" suggests that Congress viewed garden-variety hardships an insufficient excuse to discharge student loans.[227] Thus, the exception gives considerable discretion to the bankruptcy judge to tailor the fresh start policy of the Code to the vagaries of specific fact situations, and to find in effect that in the totality of the circumstances there was no abuse of the system. For example, the premise of abuse hardly would be sustained if the hypothetical eye surgeon referred to above suffered a career-ending illness or injury and then filed bankruptcy.

Courts are not, however, lenient to debtors in finding "undue hardship," to put it mildly. The debtor bears the burden of proof.[228] The leading test of "undue hardship" is the three-part test announced by the Second Circuit in *Brunner*:

1. That the debtor cannot maintain, based on current income and expenses, a "minimal" standard of living for herself and her dependents if forced to repay the loans;

---

from Canada was not a "taxpayer" as defined by the IRC because the debtor did not file a United States income tax return during the pertinent timeframe, and therefore the loans she received were not "qualified education loans" as defined by the IRC and thus not subject to the Code's student loan discharge exception. 404 B.R. 793 (Bankr. M.D. Pa. 2009).

[224] TI Fed. Credit Union v. DelBonis, 72 F.3d 921 (1st Cir. 1995).

[225] In re Pelkowski, 990 F.2d 737 (3d Cir. 1993).

[226] See, e.g., Cockels v. Mae, 414 B.R. 149 (E.D. Mich. 2009) (holding student loan exception applies to parent co-signer).

[227] See Educ. Credit Mgmt. Corp v. Frushour (In re Frushour), 433 F.3d 393, 399 (4th Cir. 2005); Rifino v. United States (In re Rifino), 245 F.3d 1083, 1087 (9th Cir. 2001); Brunner v. N.Y. State Higher Educ. Servs. Corp (In re Brunner), 46 B.R. 752, 753 (S.D.N.Y. 1985).

[228] See, e.g., In re Hixson, 450 B.R. 9, 19 (Bankr. S.D.N.Y. 2011); In re Wells, 360 B.R. 652, 658 (Bankr. N.D.N.Y. 2007).

2. That additional circumstances exist indicating that this state of affairs is likely to persist for a significant portion of the repayment period of the student loans; and

3. That the debtor has made good faith efforts to repay the loans.[229]

The Eighth and First Circuits are the only two circuits not to adopt the *Brunner* test. The Eighth Circuit has embraced instead a "totality of the circumstances" approach,[230] which it believes to be less restrictive than the *Brunner* test, and to give bankruptcy judges more discretion. The court made clear in *In re Nash*, the only First Circuit case citing *Brunner*, that it did not endorse a preferred method of identifying a case of "undue hardship."[231] Additionally, although the Tenth Circuit ultimately adopts the *Brunner* test over the totality of the circumstances approach, one court in the circuit noted that as applied, the *Brunner* test does not always further the "fresh start" policy for debtors, as courts apply it with undue restriction.[232] However, the same court also acknowledged that the totality of the circumstances approach may not fare better for debtors. In adopting the *Brunner* test, the court stated that, "[w]e do not read *Brunner* to rule out consideration of all the facts and circumstances,"[233] thus adopting a sort of hybrid of the two approaches.

The critical difference between the *Brunner* test and the "totality of the circumstances" approach to interpreting and applying the undue hardship standard in § 523(a)(8), is that for courts applying the *Brunner* test, the debtor must meet *all three* factors or the court will not find undue hardship and discharge the debtor's student loans. Conversely, in courts adopting the totality of the circumstances approach, no single factor is determinative, making the approach more flexible to allow or deny a student loan discharge in light of the facts. Regardless of the test or approach used in determining whether repayment of student loans would constitute undue hardship, at a minimum courts focus on two issues: (1) the economic prospects of the debtor, and (2)

---

[229] Brunner v. New York State Higher Educ. Servs. Corp., 831 F.2d 395, 396 (2d Cir. 1987). Accord, In re Mosko, 515 F.3d 319 (4th Cir. 2008); Educ. Credit Mgmt. Corp. v. Polleys, 356 F.3d 1302 (10th Cir. 2004); In re Gerhardt, 348 F.3d 89 (5th Cir. 2003); In re Cox, 338 F.3d 1238 (11th Cir. 2003), cert. denied, 541 U.S. 991 (2004); In re Pena, 155 F.3d 1108 (9th Cir.1998); In re Faish, 72 F.3d 298 (3d Cir. 1995), cert. denied, 518 U.S. 1009 (1996); In re Cheesman, 25 F.3d 356 (6th Cir.1994), cert. denied, 513 U.S. 1081 (1995); In re Roberson, 999 F.2d 1132 (7th Cir. 1993).

[230] In re Andrews, 661 F.2d 702 (8th Cir.1981). Even after virtually all other circuits had adopted *Brunner*, the Eighth Circuit has continued to reaffirm its totality test. See In re Reynolds, 425 F.3d 526 (8th Cir. 2005), cert. denied, 549 U.S. 811 (2006); In re Long, 322 F.3d 549 (8th Cir. 2003). The Eighth Circuit's "totality" test is as follows:

"In evaluating the totality-of-the-circumstances, our bankruptcy reviewing courts should consider: (1) the debtor's past, present, and reasonably reliable future financial resources; (2) a calculation of the debtor's and her dependent's reasonable necessary living expenses; and (3) any other relevant facts and circumstances surrounding each particular bankruptcy case. Simply put, if the debtor's reasonable future financial resources will sufficiently cover payment of the student loan debt—while still allowing for a minimal standard of living—then the debt should not be discharged. Certainly, this determination will require a special consideration of the debtor's present employment and financial situation—including assets, expenses, and earnings—along with the prospect of future changes—positive or adverse—in the debtor's financial position."

Id. at 554–55.

[231] In re Nash, 446 F.3d 188, 190–91 (1st Cir. 2006).

[232] Educ. Credit. Mgmt. Corp. v. Polleys, 356 F. 3d 1302 (10th Cir. 2004).

[233] Id. at 1308.

whether the conduct of the debtor disqualifies the debtor from taking advantage of the exception.[234]

An intriguing use of the court's equitable powers has come in cases in which the court has Solomonically "split the baby" by discharging part of the student loan under the undue hardship provision, concluding that an all-or-nothing approach is too restrictive. Smacking even more of unbridled judicial activism is the decision of the Sixth Circuit to *defer* the final dischargeability decision for 18 months, thus introducing the concept of a *suspended* discharge.[235] A related issue concerns the *res judicata* effect of a determination of no undue hardship. Should a debtor be permitted to reopen her case and relitigate the issue of undue hardship based on an allegation of changed circumstances since the first determination?

§ 10.24 DUI Debts for Death or Personal Injury

The national tragedy of drunk driving has spilled over into the bankruptcy courts. Drivers who cause injury or death while driving under the influence of alcohol or drugs have attempted to discharge the resulting liabilities in bankruptcy. Prior to 1984, drunk driving victims had to bring their nondischargeability complaint under § 523(a)(6), where they encountered considerable difficulty in proving that the debtor's actions had been both "willful" and "malicious."[236] The Supreme Court's 1998 decision in *Kawaauhau v. Geiger*,[237] which requires proof under (a)(6) that the debtor intended to injure the victim, now makes it extremely difficult for a creditor to prevail under that subsection in a drunk driving case.

To make it easier for drunk driving victims to avoid discharge, Congress in 1984 added § 523(a)(9) to the list of excepted debts. That section specifically precludes the discharge of DUI debts for death or personal injury without the necessity of proving either willfulness or malice; only unlawful intoxication must be established. Further amendments in 1990 rendered chapter 13 unavailable as a means to discharge these debts. § 1328(a)(2).

The 1990 amendments also cleared up the principal interpretive difficulty of the section as originally enacted in 1984, which was that debts could be excepted only if arising from "a judgment or consent decree entered in a court of record." This language apparently made a pre-bankruptcy judgment a condition of nondischargeability, which if given effect would enable a debtor to avoid the operation of the exception by the simple expedient of filing bankruptcy before final entry of such a judgment. Most courts simply ignored the plain language of the section and denied dischargeability even if no judgment had yet been entered, reasoning that Congress could not have

---

[234] In re Weir, 269 B.R. 710, 716 (Bankr. E.D. Va. 2002) (citations omitted).

[235] *Cheesman*, supra note 229, 25 F.3d 356.

[236] Compare In re Adams, 761 F.2d 1422 (9th Cir. 1985) (intentional act of driving while intoxicated both willful and malicious under § 523(a)(6)), with In re Compos, 768 F.2d 1155 (10th Cir. 1985) (intentional act of driving while intoxicated shows only reckless disregard for others, and thus is not within § 523(a)(6)).

[237] 523 U.S. 57 (1998). See also § 10.21.

meant what it said.[238] In 1990 Congress conformed the statute to the prevailing judicial interpretation by dropping the judgment or consent decree limitation.

To establish nondischargeability under § 523(a)(9), then, all that the creditor must prove is that (1) death or personal injury (2) was caused by the debtor's operation of a motor vehicle, vessel, or aircraft (3) while unlawfully intoxicated from alcohol, drugs, or another substance. "Unlawful" intoxication is to be determined by reference to the applicable state law. Note that the creditor does not have to prove that the debtor's intoxication actually caused the injury, only that the injury was caused by the debtor's operation of a motor vehicle while intoxicated. A debtor's proof that he can "hold his liquor" would thus be irrelevant if his blood alcohol level exceeded legal limits.

Before the 2005 amendments, some courts questioned what qualified as a "motor vehicle." In other words, if a debtor gets drunk and drives a motorboat, snowmobile, or airplane, and kills someone, would § 523(a)(9) apply? In 2005, Congress settled this question by adding the words "vessel or aircraft" to § 523(a)(9) to indicate that the exception should apply broadly to all debts arising from "drunk driving," not just those debts related to the driving of automobiles.

In another important respect the ninth exception is limited. The 1990 amendments clarified that only debts for "death or personal injury" are excepted from discharge. This amendment excluded claims for damage to "property" alone, as well as debts for related items such as insurance surcharges and replacement rentals. For property damage claims the creditor is relegated to the willful and malicious injury exception under § 523(a)(6) which, as noted above, will be very hard to establish under the stringent requirements of the *Geiger* case. The ninth exception still should cover both compensatory and punitive damages if the injury suffered is death or personal injury.

Debts covered by this exception, like those for most nondischargeable taxes and for federal depository claims, also are given a statutory priority in distribution of the debtor's bankruptcy estate. § 507(a)(10). The tenth priority was added in 2005. Curiously (and inexplicably), the tenth priority does not include debts arising from the operation of an aircraft while unlawfully intoxicated, while the discharge exception in § 523(a)(9) does, as noted above.

§ 10.25   Debts From Prior Bankruptcy Case in Which Discharge Was Waived or Denied

A debtor only gets one bite at the discharge apple. If a debtor files a liquidation bankruptcy case and either waives his discharge or is denied a discharge (for any reason other than the time bar on successive discharges), then the debtor may not discharge in a subsequent bankruptcy case the debts that were not discharged in the first case. § 523(a)(10). In effect, the tenth exception imposes a statutory *res judicata* rule for discharge.

---

[238]   E.g., In re Hudson, 859 F.2d 1418 (9th Cir. 1988).

The operation of § 523(a)(10) is not all-encompassing. It does not apply when the second case is a chapter 13, although the court may consider the debtor's attempt to discharge previously undischarged debts as a factor in assessing the good faith of the debtor's chapter 13 plan under § 1325(a)(3). Nor will § 523(a)(10) operate to prevent the discharge of a specific debt that was reaffirmed in the first case. Furthermore, § 523(a)(10) does not apply to prevent the discharge in a second case of debts that were only *excepted* from discharge in a prior case. In most cases, however, that limitation is irrelevant; the other § 523(a) exceptions are still available, and collateral estoppel principles should prevent the discharge in the second case of most types of previously excepted debts.

Only in limited instances may a debt be discharged in a second case despite a prior determination of nondischargeability under § 523(a). Under § 523(b), the court may revisit in the second case dischargeability determinations under § 523(a)(1), (3), or (8). What explains these provisions? They cover situations where the exception in the first case depended on a time limit (e.g., taxes) which has expired by the time the second case is filed;[239] where the original discharge exception was for failure to schedule debts, a failing that is curable in a subsequent case; or where the discharge determination depends upon the court's assessment of the debtor's current circumstances (educational loans).

§ 10.26 Relating to Federal Depository Institutions

The 1980s crisis in the banking and savings and loan industries spawned legislation in 1990 seeking to shore up the position of the FDIC and other federal agencies in bankruptcy cases.[240] In the dischargeability context, two new exceptions to discharge were created, subsections 523(a)(11) and (12), along with a host of explanatory definitions.

Section 523(a)(11) excepts from discharge debts arising from fiduciary fraud or defalcation in connection with an insured depository institution (defined in § 101(35)) or an insured credit union (defined in § 101(34)). Not all such debts are excepted, however, but only those provided for in a final judgment, unreviewable order, or consent decree of a court, or issued by a federal depository institutions regulatory agency (defined in § 101(21B)), or in a settlement agreement entered into by the debtor. This limitation creates the same interpretive problems raised by § 523(a)(9) before the 1990 amendments eliminated the "court order" restriction in that section. Courts are likely to respond in the same fashion, that is, by ignoring the statute.

---

[239] Section 523(b) continues to reference § 523(a)(8), an inclusion originally attributable to the fact that subsection (8) also contained a time limit on the exception to discharge. Thus, that time limit might have expired by the time a second bankruptcy case was filed, even if it had not when the first case was filed, and if so, then the educational loan debt would be discharged in the second case. Now, however, subsection (8) does not contain a time limit, so that justification for including the reference to subsection (a)(8) in § 523(b) no longer holds. However, there still may be reason to revisit the (a)(8) issue in the second case, in that the undue hardship assessment could be different in the second case than it was in the first.

[240] See Crime Control Act of 1990, Pub. L. No. 101–647, § 2522, 104 Stat. 4789, 4865–68 (1990). These amendments became effective on November 29, 1990.

The necessity of § 523(a)(11) is unclear. Section 523(a)(4) already excepted all debts for fiduciary fraud or defalcation, and would seem to cover all cases now covered by section (11). Nor does it appear that Congress intended to preclude the FDIC and others from asserting subsection (4), since specific reference to that subsection as it applies to federal depository institutions is made in § 523(c)(2) and § 523(e). The probable reason for the enactment of the 1990 law is to overrule those cases that narrowly construed the "fiduciary" element in § 523(a)(4) as applied to depository institutions, and thereby discharged the obligation. However, Congress achieved this result via § 523(e).

Procedurally, the federal agency is relieved in certain circumstances from the strict time limits and operation of § 523(a)(3)(B) and Rule 4007(c) regarding the filing of dischargeability complaints under subsections (2), (4), and (6). Section 523(c)(2) excuses compliance with those provisions if the federal agency did not have time reasonably to comply with the deadlines.

Debtors also are precluded from discharging certain debts arising from their failure to fulfill capital maintenance commitments made to a federal depository institutions regulatory agency with respect to an insured depository institution. § 523(a)(12). This failure must be "malicious or reckless" to fall within the section. An exception is made if the capital maintenance commitment would otherwise be terminated due to the act of the federal agency. This twelfth exception, unlike its companion eleventh exception, goes beyond any of the previously existing exceptions. Proof of fraud is not required (as it would be under subsection (2)), and merely reckless behavior will suffice (but would not under subsection (6)). The exception in § 523(a)(12) is self-executing, since it is not included in § 523(c) with those exceptions that must be litigated exclusively in the bankruptcy court. Debts covered by this exception, like those for most nondischargeable taxes and for DUI claims that result in death or personal injury, also are given a statutory priority in distribution of the debtor's bankruptcy estate. § 507(a)(9).

§ 10.27 Other Exceptions

Congress cannot seem to resist the temptation to keep adding exceptions to the discharge. The subjects covered range widely across the imaginable spectrum. As of 2013, the official count in § 523(a) was twenty-one exceptions, and several other exclusions are scattered throughout the United States Code. One of the amendments, for fines owing to the United States, under 18 U.S.C. § 3613(e), is mentioned in the section on fines and penalties.[241] Yet another 1996 entry in the nondischargeable category is for the obligation to repay a "special pay" bonus received by a health care professional in the Selected Reserves, if the recipient does not serve the full time commitment promised in exchange for the bonus.[242]

In BAPCPA in 2005, Congress continued this trend, adding additional exceptions from discharge. The new exceptions are listed in § 523(a)(14A), which excepts from

---

[241] See § 10.22.

[242] National Defense Authorization Act, Pub. L. No. 104–106, 110 Stat. 186 (1996), codified at 37 U.S.C. § 302g(d), (e).

discharge obligations incurred to pay a nondischargeable tax to a governmental entity other than the United States, and § 523(a)(14B), which excepts fines or penalties incurred under Federal election law (but not under state law). The previous § 523(a)(18), which dealt with family support obligations, was also deleted and replaced with an unrelated exception. The new § 523(a)(18) provides that debts owed to retirement plans and employee benefit funds for permitted loans are not dischargeable.

Congress also tightened the screws on prisoners, as part of the Prison Litigation Reform Act of 1995.[243] That Act was intended to limit the perceived abuse of frequent (endless) federal court filings by prisoners. One way courts can attempt to cut down on such filings is to impose court costs and fees on prisoners, and to prohibit further filings until outstanding costs are paid; in short, only allow access to the court system for prisoners who "pay their own way." The concern that was addressed by § 523(a)(17) was that prisoners would simply file bankruptcy and discharge the debt to pay those court costs and fees. Section 523(a)(17) precludes the discharge of a debt "for a fee imposed by a court for the filing of a case, motion, complaint, or appeal, or for other costs and expenses assessed with respect to such filing," and then makes clear that the exclusion applies "regardless of an assertion of poverty . . . or the debtor's status as a prisoner." In 2005, Congress added language to clarify that this exception is limited to prisoner cases, and does not apply to all debts for court costs, fees and expenses.

Congress added another discharge exception to the Code in 1994, for condominium or cooperative fees and assessments that come due after the filing of the bankruptcy petition and that relate to the postpetition period. § 523(a)(16). According to the legislative history, this amendment was necessary to prevent the discharge of those obligations, which would be unfair to other owners of the association.[244] Congress acted in response to a Seventh Circuit decision that had held that such postpetition fees and assessments constituted dischargeable prepetition claims, on the theory that they arose from the debtor's prepetition contract with the condominium association.[245]

Congress may have acted prematurely, however. In 1994 a competing line of case authority emerged that held that such postpetition assessments did not constitute dischargeable prepetition claims.[246] These cases reasoned that the claim did not arise prepetition, when the debtor signed the condominium contract, but only arose when assessed after the bankruptcy filing. As a postpetition claim, the obligation would not be dischargeable. These courts reached this result by treating the claim for fees and assessments as one rooted in the property itself, i.e., as an obligation that "runs with the land," rather than one based in contract.

The hasty action of Congress may not be harmless, either. Section 523(a)(16) is limited in its scope. Before BAPCPA, the discharge exception only applied if the debtor had received some tangible benefit from their ownership of the unit in the postpetition

---

[243] Pub. L. No. 104–140 (renumbered from 104–134), 110 Stat. 1327 (1996), codified at 11 U.S.C. § 523(a)(17).

[244] Section-by-Section Analysis, commentary on § 309 of the Bankruptcy Reform Act of 1994, 140 Cong. Rec. H10,770 (daily ed. Oct. 4, 1994).

[245] In re Rosteck, 899 F.2d 694 (7th Cir. 1990).

[246] E.g., In re Rosenfeld, 23 F.3d 833 (4th Cir. 1994).

period, either by physically occupying the unit or by receiving rental payments. BAPCPA expanded this exemption somewhat, to include fees or assessments "for as long as the debtor or the trustee has a legal, equitable, or possessory ownership interest in such unit, such corporation, or such lot. . . . " § 523(a)(16). If no such interest exists, then the debt would still be dischargeable under the approach taken by the Seventh Circuit, which treats the postpetition assessment as a prepetition claim. Nothing in the 1994 amendment alters the time when the claim is deemed to arise. Of course, those jurisdictions that follow the competing view and deem the claim as arising postpetition still will not discharge the debt. However, because Congress in the 1994 legislative history also suggested that the Seventh Circuit view was correct,[247] other jurisdictions now may be hesitant to embrace the contrary line of cases.

D. PROCEDURES

§ 10.28 Procedures for Denial of Discharge in Chapter 7

An individual chapter 7 debtor does not have to take any affirmative steps to obtain his discharge. In olden times a debtor had to apply for his discharge, but today the onus is on others to object. Subject to some exceptions detailed in the Bankruptcy Rules, the bankruptcy court will automatically grant an individual debtor a discharge "forthwith" upon expiration of the time for filing objections to discharge or to move to dismiss the case. Rule 4004(c)(1).

There are several exceptions to the automatic discharge entry rule in Rule 4004(c)(1). The court may take judicial notice of the fact that the debtor is not an individual, and thus not eligible for discharge, § 727(a)(1), and should not enter the discharge order. Rule 4004(c)(1)(A). If the debtor has waived the discharge in a manner allowed under § 727(a)(10), no discharge order will be entered. Rule 4004(c)(1)(C). Nor should a discharge order be entered if there is a pending motion objecting to discharge, seeking to dismiss the case, or asking to extend the time to make either motion. Rule 4004(c)(1)(B), (D)–(F). The debtor also must have paid all required fees before he can receive his discharge. Rule 4004(c)(1)(G). The Rules, as revised through December 2011, also implement several aspects of the 2005 legislation as they relate to the debtor's right to a discharge. The court should not enter the discharge order if the debtor has not filed a statement that he has completed the course in personal financial management, as required under § 727(a)(11). Rule 4004(c)(1)(H). In accordance with § 727(a)(12), the bankruptcy court may delay the entry of a discharge order if it appears that a § 522(q) homestead exemption limitation proceeding is pending. Rule 4004(c)(1)(I). The court also should delay entry of the discharge order if a presumption has arisen that a reaffirmation agreement is an undue hardship under § 524(m), Rule 4004(c)(1)(J), or if the debtor has not yet filed all tax documents required under § 521(f). Rule 4004(c)(1)(K).

Standing to contest the discharge is limited to the trustee, creditors, and the United States trustee. § 727(c)(1). The court itself may not act *sua sponte* to deny the discharge, although if requested to do so it may order the trustee to investigate the

---

[247] "Except to the extent that the debt is nondischargeable under this section, obligations to pay such fees would be dischargeable." Section-by-Section Analysis, supra note 244.

merits of a discharge objection. § 727(c)(2). The trustee has a statutory duty to object to discharge if advisable. § 704(a)(6).

Most objections to discharge must be litigated in an adversary proceeding in the bankruptcy court. Rules 4004(d), 7001(4). The applicable rules are those in Part VII of the Federal Rules of Bankruptcy Procedure, which largely track the Federal Rules of Civil Procedure. The only exceptions are for objections under §§ 727(a)(8), 727(a)(9), and 1328(f), which are handled as contested matters under Part IX and commenced by motion. Rule 4004(d). The complaint or motion must be filed in the court where the bankruptcy case is pending. Rule 5005(a).

Parties considering objecting to discharge have a very limited time to file their complaint: *60 days* after the first date set for the § 341 meeting of creditors. Rule 4004(a). The rule is strictly construed—the clock starts running from the first date *set* for the creditors' meeting, even if it is not then held, and the complaint actually must be *received* by the bankruptcy clerk by the deadline. The trustee and creditors will receive at least 28 days notice of this bar date in the initial notice of the bankruptcy. Rules 4004(a), 2002(f)(4). The Rules were amended in 2011 to allow a party to move to extend the time to object to discharge even after the time for objection has expired, and before the discharge is granted, in very limited circumstances: the objection is based on facts that would support revocation of discharge under § 727(d), and the movant did not know of those facts in time to object. Rule 4004(b)(2).

Although the discharge objection deadline of Rule 4004(a) is stated in absolute terms, the Supreme Court held in *Kontrick v. Ryan*[248] that the deadline is not jurisdictional. In that case, the Court allowed the bankruptcy court to decide an untimely discharge objection when the debtor failed to object in his responsive pleading to the tardy filing.

Prior to the promulgation of Rule 4004(b)(2) in 2011, some courts had invoked their equitable powers to allow an objection to be filed after the deadline despite the language of the Rules upon proof of equitable defenses, such as (1) that the debtor fraudulently concealed the grounds for objection, or (2) that the clerk's office mailed an incorrect bar date notice.[249] Other courts, however, concluded that they possessed no discretion to permit a late filing.[250] It is unclear how the 2011 amendment to the Rules, adding a specific narrow exception allowing out-of-time motions under Rule 4004(b)(2), will impact this split in the case law. On one side, the argument will be that the enactment of a specific exception in the Rules now precludes the exercise of judicial discretion recognizing additional exceptions not embodied in the Rules, under an *expression unius* theory. The counter-argument would be that judicial discretion is not constrained as to cases not covered by the new rule; instead, the Rules Committee

---

[248] 540 U.S. 443 (2004), limited by Kay v. Sec'y of Health and Human Servs., 80 Fed. Cl. 601, 605 (2008) (noting that to the extent *Kontrick* and similar cases "indicate that the issue of timeliness is not properly a question of the court's jurisdiction in an action brought pursuant to a waiver of sovereign immunity, they unquestionably have been overruled by the Supreme Court's holding in *John R. Sand & Gravel*").

[249] See, e.g., In re Themy, 6 F.3d 688 (10th Cir. 1993) (incorrect notice). See also Farouki v. Emirates Bank Intern., Ltd., 14 F.3d 244 (4th Cir. 1994) (fraudulent concealment).

[250] See In re Chalasani, 92 F.3d 1300 (2d Cir. 1996).

simply wanted to make certain that cases that do fall within the exception are protected. In *Kontrick*, the Court made clear that it was *not* deciding whether an untimely discharge objection could be entertained based on equitable grounds;[251] it held only that the debtor waived his objection to untimeliness by failing to raise the defense in his responsive pleadings.

If a party needs more time to decide whether to file a discharge objection, it must apply for an extension of time within the original 60–day period, and the court then in its discretion may extend the time for filing the complaint. Rules 4004(b), 9006(b)(3). Merely filing the motion for the extension does not toll the bar date. Except as provided in the exception under Rule 4004(b)(2), discussed above, a party who files late may not receive an out-of-time extension to file, even upon proof of excusable neglect (although, as noted above, the possibility of equitable defenses remains an open question). Even if a complaint alleging some grounds for denial of discharge is timely filed, the 60–day bar still applies to any additional grounds for objection, which may not be added later by amendment.

If no complaints have been filed by the expiration of the 60–day period or any timely extensions thereof, the bankruptcy court "shall forthwith" grant the debtor a discharge, unless the debtor is not an individual or filed a waiver, or one of the new 2005 exceptions discussed above applies. Rule 4004(c)(1). However, the debtor may ask the court to defer granting the discharge for 30 days. Rule 4004(c)(2). A debtor might do this if he is negotiating a reaffirmation agreement, because a reaffirmation must be agreed to prior to the granting of the discharge. § 524(c)(1).

If an objection to discharge is timely filed, then the adversary proceeding is tried (or, for motions under §§ 727(a)(8), 727(a)(9), and 1328(f), a contested matter is heard). The Federal Rules of Evidence will apply at trial, Rule 9017, and the ultimate burden of proof at trial is on the plaintiff who is objecting to the debtor's discharge. Rule 4005. The issue of which party has the burden of going forward is left to case development. The burden of going forward might be placed on the debtor under § 727(a)(3), where the debtor may have to justify his otherwise inadequate books, and § 727(a)(5), where the debtor may have to explain losses.

Rule 4005 also says nothing about the *standard* of proof. The lower courts have divided over whether the appropriate standard is preponderance of the evidence or clear and convincing. The Supreme Court's 1991 decision in *Grogan v. Garner*, holding that *preponderance* is the proper standard in a § 523(a)(2) discharge exception case, has influenced many courts to adopt a preponderance standard in § 727 cases as well.[252] The court in *Grogan* stated in dictum that the proper standard under § 727(a)(4) was preponderance, relying on a statement in the legislative history.[253] On the other hand, courts may take the position that total denial of discharge under § 727

---

[251] 540 U.S. at 457–58.

[252] See, e.g., In re Scott, 172 F.3d 959, 966–67 (7th Cir. 1999). See also In re Harwood, 637 F.3d 615, 619 (5th Cir. 2011); In re Pisculli, 408 F.App'x. 477, 479 (2d Cir. 2011); In re Adams, 31 F.3d 389 (6th Cir. 1994), cert. denied, 513 U.S. 1111 (1995).

[253] 498 U.S. 279, 289 (1991) (citing H.R. Rep. No. 95–595, 95th Cong., 1st Sess., at 384 (1977), and S. Rep. No. 95–989, 95th Cong., 2d Sess., at 98 (1978)).

is a much more drastic penalty than exception of a single debt under § 523, thus rendering *Grogan* inapposite.

Once action has been taken either to grant or deny the discharge, creditors again are notified. A copy of the order of discharge is mailed to creditors. Rule 4004(g). This puts creditors on notice of the § 524(a) discharge injunction. The debtor may enforce the discharge nationwide, both by using nationwide service of process, Rule 7004, and by registering the discharge order in any federal district. Rule 4004(f). On the other hand, if the discharge is denied, the clerk must mail creditors a notice of no discharge. Rule 4006. This notice enables creditors to pursue collection of nondischarged debts in a timely manner. Statutes of limitations that had been tolled by the bankruptcy begin running again 30 days after the discharge is denied. §§ 108(c)(1), 362(c)(2).

§ 10.29 Procedures for Discharge Exceptions

The procedure governing the adjudication of a discharge exception depends initially on the subsection of § 523(a) within which the affected debt falls. Two basic categories exist: those that have to be litigated exclusively in the bankruptcy court, and those that do not. Section 523(c)(1) requires discharge exception actions under § 523(a)(2) (fraud), § 523(a)(4) (fiduciary fraud or defalcation, embezzlement, larceny), and § 523(a)(6) (willful and malicious injury), to be brought in the bankruptcy court in a limited time period or be discharged. Until the 2005 amendments, property settlement debts under § 523(a)(15) also had to be litigated in bankruptcy court, but BAPCPA dropped that restriction. All of the § 523(a) exceptions other than (2), (4), and (6) need not be litigated in the bankruptcy court. In effect they are self-executing, although litigation in a bankruptcy or a non-bankruptcy forum (most likely state court) ultimately may be required to settle a controversy.

Many of the procedures regarding the § 523(c)(1) discharge exceptions track the procedures for discharge objections. A complaint to determine dischargeability under § 523(a)(2), (4), or (6) must be filed in the bankruptcy court within 60 days of the first date set for the § 341 meeting of creditors, unless the court grants an extension pursuant to a motion filed within the 60–day period. Rule 4007(c). It has been held that the trustee has standing to obtain an extension under Rule 4007(c) for the benefit of all creditors.[254] The court lacks the authority to grant an out-of-time extension, even for excusable neglect. Rule 9006(b)(3). However, the reasoning of the *Kontrick v. Ryan* Court, in holding that the Rule 4004 deadline for filing an objection to discharge can be waived if the debtor does not move to dismiss the complaint in a timely fashion, would seem to apply as well to the deadline for filing a dischargeability complaint under § 523(c)(1) and Rule 4007(c).[255]

Creditors must be given 30 days notice of the bar date. Rules 4007(c), 2002(f)(5). As with discharge exceptions, the clock begins to run from the first date set for the creditors' meeting, and the complaint must be filed with the bankruptcy clerk by the bar date.

---

[254] In re Brady, 101 F.3d 1165 (6th Cir. 1996).

[255] 540 U.S. 443 (2004).

A debt will not be discharged if the debtor failed to list the creditor on the schedules, and the creditor did not receive notice of the bankruptcy case and lacked actual knowledge of the case in time to file a discharge exception complaint within the 60 day filing deadline. § 523(a)(3)(B). A creditor seeking to invoke § 523(a)(3)(B) also may have to show that it had a meritorious dischargeability objection that it would have alleged if given the chance.

The 60 day limit of Rule 4007(c) applies in all cases under all chapters, but is modified slightly under chapter 13. The differential treatment in chapter 13 cases is necessary because some debts under § 523(a)(6) are discharged if the chapter 13 debtor completes performance under her plan.[256] § 1328(a). In that context, then, the idea of an "exception" to discharge is meaningless. However, if a chapter 13 debtor cannot complete performance under the plan, and seeks a hardship discharge, all discharge exceptions do apply. § 1328(b) and (c). In that situation, the court must fix a time for filing dischargeability complaints under § 523(a)(6) and § 523(c)(1), and give 30 days notice of that judicially fixed bar date. Rule 4007(c) and (d). Until the 2005 amendments, this exception in chapter 13 extended to debts under § 523(a)(2) and (4) as well, since those also must be litigated in the bankruptcy court under § 523(c)(1) and were discharged in chapter 13 if the debtor received a full-compliance discharge under § 1328(a), but not if the debtor sought a hardship discharge under § 1328(b). However, in 2005 the exceptions in § 523(a)(2) and (4) were made nondischargeable even in a full-compliance discharge under § 1328(a).

Once a complaint under Rule 4007 is filed, an adversary proceeding is commenced. Rule 7001(6). Only the affected creditor and the debtor have standing to file the complaint; the trustee does not. Rule 4007(a). The bankruptcy court may defer action on the discharge exception lawsuit until the discharge itself has either been granted or denied under Rule 4004 and § 727, because a complete denial of discharge would moot any necessity to rule on the dischargeability of particular claims.

The creditor has the burden of proof. The Supreme Court in *Grogan v. Garner* held that the proper standard of proof is *preponderance* of the evidence,[257] thereby rejecting the widespread view in the lower courts that a "clear and convincing" standard was appropriate. While *Grogan* only involved a complaint under § 523(a)(2), the Court made clear that the same standard of proof applied to all § 523(a) exceptions, apparently even those that might be litigated in a forum other than the bankruptcy court.[258]

A completely different scenario exists for § 523(a) discharge exceptions other than (2), (4), or (6). These do not have to be litigated in the bankruptcy court, although they

---

[256] Some debts that might fall within § 523(a)(6) are excluded from the chapter 13 full-compliance discharge under § 1328(a)(4), but there is no explicit reference to § 523(a)(6), and the match between the two provisions is incomplete. The exclusion in § 1328(a)(4) covers debts for restitution or damages awarded in a civil action against the debtor as a result of a willful or malicious injury by the debtor that caused personal injury or death. This provision is narrower than § 523(a)(6), since it requires an award in a civil action, and is limited to personal injury and death claims. There also is a disconnect in that § 1328(a)(4) covers debts from a willful "or" malicious injury, whereas § 523(a)(6) requires a willful "and" malicious injury.

[257] 498 U.S. 279, 291 (1991).

[258] Id. at 287–88.

may be. If not, a creditor may wait until the termination of the § 362 automatic stay and then sue the debtor in state court on the debt. The permanent injunction of § 524(a) against debt collection should not apply to debts excepted automatically from the discharge under § 523(a), although the creditor in suing on the debt is taking the chance that it is right on the § 523(a) issue. If it is wrong it may be liable for damages for violating the § 524(a) injunction. The debtor in the state court action might raise the bankruptcy discharge as a defense, and the creditor would respond by asserting a § 523(a) discharge exception. The state court then would try the § 523(a) issue. Presumably the same burden and standard of proof would apply to the § 523(a) issue as when trial is in the bankruptcy court. For debts not covered by § 523(c)(1) but possibly within another § 523(a) exception, the debtor may prefer to file a complaint to determine dischargeability in the bankruptcy court instead of waiting for later resolution in a non-bankruptcy forum, relying on the possibly greater pro-debtor sympathies of the bankruptcy judge.

§ 10.30 Collateral Estoppel and Res Judicata

Dischargeability litigation under § 523 may be affected by a pre-bankruptcy suit between the creditor and debtor in a non-bankruptcy forum, through application of the doctrines of collateral estoppel or res judicata.[259] The Supreme Court has held in the creditor's favor as to each doctrine. In *Brown v. Felsen* the Court held that *res judicata* does not apply,[260] whereas in *Grogan v. Garner* the Court held that collateral estoppel does apply.[261]

The *res judicata* issue typically arises in the following way. The creditor first obtains a judgment against the debtor in a pre-bankruptcy lawsuit, but in that suit does not seek or obtain a finding of fraud, malice, or the like, even where such was potentially available to the creditor. Then, after the debtor files bankruptcy, the creditor files a dischargeability complaint, and the debtor raises the defense of *res judicata*. After a final judgment on the merits, *res judicata* usually bars a party from litigating grounds for or defenses to a cause of action that were previously available to that party, even if not asserted or determined in the first suit.

The Supreme Court in 1979 in *Brown v. Felsen*, however, expressly rejected the *res judicata* argument of the debtor on these basic facts.[262] The bankruptcy court in the later § 523(a) action thus is not limited to a consideration of the record in the prior case, and the creditor is free to litigate the fraud or malice issue for the first time in bankruptcy. The Court in *Brown* opined that the creditor in the pre-bankruptcy lawsuit may lack an incentive to litigate fraud, since its primary interest is simply to collect the debt, and a judgment for the debt can be obtained even without asserting fraud. To force the creditor to litigate fraud on the chance that the debtor later might file bankruptcy and thereby interpose a new barrier to collection would be wasteful. Furthermore, forcing the creditor to litigate all possible future dischargeability issues

---

[259] See Jeffrey Thomas Ferriell, The Preclusive Effect of State Court Decisions in Bankruptcy, 58 Am. Bankr. L.J. 349 (1984) (pt. 1), 59 Am. Bankr. L.J. 55 (1985) (pt. 2).

[260] 442 U.S. 127, 138–39 (1979).

[261] 498 U.S. 279, 284 & n.11, 290 (1991).

[262] *Brown*, supra note 260, 442 U.S. at 138–39.

in state court would undermine the congressional determination that some dischargeability issues should be tried exclusively in the bankruptcy court. Thus, after *Brown*, a creditor is free to choose not to press issues of fraud, malice, or the like in a pre-bankruptcy suit on the debt, and by doing so does not in any way damage its chances to have that debt excepted from discharge in a subsequent bankruptcy case.

What if the creditor chooses, on the contrary, to go ahead and litigate the fraud or malice issue in the initial state court lawsuit? The creditor might want to do this to obtain a punitive damages award. It also might want to procure a finding of fraud or malice in state court in advance of a possible bankruptcy filing by the debtor in order to insure via collateral estoppel that the judgment debt will be excepted from any future discharge.

Until 1991, the creditor's ability to invoke collateral estoppel in this situation was uncertain. The Supreme Court in *Brown* had expressly left open the question of the applicability of collateral estoppel.[263] Bankruptcy scholars had expressed the concern, noted by the *Brown* court in dictum, that giving collateral estoppel effect to a prior state court determination undermined the 1970 congressional decision to remit certain dischargeability issues exclusively to the bankruptcy court. Another hurdle to the application of collateral estoppel was that most bankruptcy courts required the creditor to prove the elements of a § 523(a) action by clear and convincing evidence. This prevented the use of collateral estoppel unless the prior state court judgment also was predicated on the clear and convincing standard.

The creditor prevailed in *Grogan v. Garner*[264] on the collateral estoppel issue. The Supreme Court determined that the proper standard of proof in all discharge exception actions was *preponderance* of the evidence, rejecting the majority view requiring clear and convincing proof. This holding opened the door to application of collateral estoppel:

> If the preponderance standard also governs the question of nondischargeability, a bankruptcy court could properly give collateral estoppel effect to those elements of the claim that are identical to the elements required for discharge and which were actually litigated and determined in the prior action.[265]

After noting the prior uncertainty, the Court concluded that "[w]e now clarify that collateral estoppel principles do indeed apply in discharge exception proceedings pursuant to § 523(a)."[266] Surprisingly, the Court did not even discuss the argument that application of collateral estoppel would undermine the reservation of some dischargeability issues exclusively to the bankruptcy court.

One limit on *Grogan's* reach, suggested by the Court itself in dictum, is that the prior judgment must actually determine all issues necessary to the § 523(a) action. In a fraud case under § 523(a)(2), this would include a finding that the money, property or services were actually obtained by the fraud; proof of damages caused by the fraud is

---

[263] Id. at 139 n.10.
[264] 498 U.S. 279 (1991).
[265] Id. at 284.
[266] Id. at 284 n.11.

not enough.[267] Of course, if the creditor also obtained a finding of malice in the first lawsuit, collateral estoppel could be applied to except the debt under § 523(a)(6).

Brown and *Grogan* together tell the creditor that it will not be prevented from asserting fraud in a later bankruptcy case if it chooses not to raise it in the pre-bankruptcy action, but that if it does successfully assert fraud in that first suit, that finding will be given preclusive effect in bankruptcy. The only possible scenario, then, in which all the cards might not be in the creditor's hand would seem to be where the creditor does litigate fraud in the first action, but loses. For example, assume that the creditor proves breach of contract, and is awarded judgment for actual damages, but the state court finds against the creditor on the fraud issue, which was asserted in an attempt to obtain punitive damages. Here the Court's reasoning in *Grogan* seemingly could be turned against the creditor, so that collateral estoppel would block the creditor's assertion of fraud as an exception to discharge in the bankruptcy case. This assumes, of course, that the standard of proof in the state court suit was preponderance. If a clear and convincing test was applied in state court, as is in fact the case in many states with regard to fraud, then a finding against the creditor under that higher standard would not preclude the creditor from trying to prove fraud in the bankruptcy case by the lower preponderance standard approved by the Court in *Grogan*.

E. ENFORCING THE DISCHARGE

§ 10.31 The Discharge Injunction

As with any legal privilege, the practical utility of the discharge to the debtor depends on how that privilege can be enforced. History has shown creditors to be adept at circumventing the effect of the discharge, through post-discharge collection efforts or coercive reaffirmations. Discharged debtors also have suffered various forms of discrimination, which chills their desire to obtain a discharge. In the Code Congress has attempted to address these problems and make the debtor's "fresh start" more effective.

The discharge first became a part of Anglo–American bankruptcy jurisprudence in 1706.[268] However, until 1970 the debtor had the burden of raising the discharge as an affirmative defense in a post-bankruptcy suit by the creditor in state court to collect the discharged debt. Empirical studies confirmed that many debtors suffered enforceable default judgments on discharged debts, because of ignorance, lack of money for legal fees, questionable service of process, and other reasons. Congress drastically changed this practice in 1970 by eliminating the *"affirmative defense"* theory of discharge enforcement and replacing it in § 14f of the Bankruptcy Act with provisions that *automatically* (1) voided any judgment obtained at any time on a discharged debt, and (2) enjoined creditors from taking any formal action to collect discharged debts as

---

[267] Id. at 282 n.2.

[268] 4 Anne, c. 17 (1705). See also Charles Jordan Tabb, The Historical Evolution of the Bankruptcy Discharge, 65 Am. Bankr. L.J. 325 (1991).

personal liabilities of the debtor.[269] This amendment permitted debtors to ignore post-discharge collection efforts. In § 524(a) of the Code, Congress has continued the policy of former § 14f, and even expanded to some extent the debtor's protection.

Thus, *the debtor does not have to do anything to enforce the discharge*. In summary, upon entry of the discharge order:

- the discharge *voids any judgment* to the extent it determines the debtor's personal liability for a discharged debt, and

- the creditor is *automatically enjoined* from taking any formal or informal action to collect a discharged debt as a personal liability of the debtor.

To elaborate, § 524(a)(1) provides that the discharge "voids any judgment at any time obtained" as to discharged debts, to the extent that the judgment determines the debtor's personal liability. This is true even if the debtor purports to "waive" discharge of the particular debt. Only a waiver of discharge entirely in compliance with § 727(a)(10), or a binding reaffirmation agreement as to the particular debt under § 524(c), may be enforced by the creditor against the debtor.

Section 524(a)(2) contains the statutory injunction against creditor efforts to collect discharged debts. Creditors are given mail notice of the § 524(a)(2) injunction. Rule 4004(g). A creditor who *knowingly* violates the injunction may be punished for civil *contempt* by an award of damages to the debtor, including costs, attorneys' fees, and even punitive damages. As under the 1970 law, the creditor is enjoined from taking any formal collection action. If a creditor violates this injunction and sues to recover a discharged debt, any judgment the creditor might obtain would be *void*. The debtor need not lift a finger. This is true even if the creditor made an honest mistake.

In addition, Congress in § 524(a)(2) has gone a step beyond the 1970 law by enjoining *any* "act" to collect the debt, intending to prohibit dunning calls and letters as well as any and all indirect collection activities with regard to the discharged debt. In short, "the injunction is to give complete effect to the discharge and to eliminate any doubt concerning the effect of the discharge as a total prohibition on debt collection efforts."[270] Courts have taken Congress at its word, and have given the § 524(a)(2) injunction against informal collection actions a broad scope. For example, a creditor's failure to update the information provided to credit reporting agencies to show that a debt has been discharged and is no longer due and owing may violate the discharge injunction.[271]

Although extremely broad, § 524(a)(1) and (2) do not have an unlimited reach. First, those sections only prohibit collection efforts to the extent those efforts are directed at the *debtor's personal liability*. The discharge "does not affect the liability of

---

[269] Pub. L. No. 91–467, § 3, 84 Stat. 991 (1970). See Vern Countryman, The New Dischargeability Law, 45 Am. Bankr. L.J. 1 (1971).

[270] H.R. Rep. No. 95–595, 95th Cong., 1st Sess., at 365 (1977), reprinted in U.S.C.C.A.N. 5963, 6322; S. Rep. No. 95–989, 95th Cong., 2d Sess., at 80 (1978), reprinted in U.S.C.C.A.N. 5787, 5865.

[271] See, e.g., In re Torres, 367 B.R. 478 (Bankr. S.D.N.Y. 2007).

any other entity on, or the property of any other entity for, such debt." § 524(e). Thus, for example, a co-debtor, guarantor, surety, or insurer would remain liable on the debt. The debtor may even be joined in a post-discharge action against a third party on a discharged debt if he is a necessary party to that suit, although the debtor would not be personally liable for the debt.

Second, valid and unavoided *liens* against property are not discharged. They are said to "ride through" the discharge. This is a continuation of the nineteenth century rule of *Long v. Bullard*.[272] The lienholder thus may foreclose on the lien after discharge of the underlying debt, but may not recover any deficiency from the debtor. Discharge, then, operates to relieve the debtor's *in personam* liability, but does not expunge *in rem* liability.

Third, the debtor may *voluntarily repay* the discharged debt. § 524(f). The underlying premise is that the debt remains a moral obligation of the debtor. Absent a binding reaffirmation agreement under § 524(c), a creditor may not enforce a promise by the debtor to repay a discharged debt, and under § 524(a)(2) the creditor is prohibited from even requesting the debtor to pay. If, however, the debtor does in fact pay a discharged debt, the creditor is legally entitled to keep that payment, and could successfully resist a subsequent action by the debtor seeking restitution of the payment.

One judicial exception to § 524(a)(2) is when the debtor is required by a *criminal* court to make *restitution* of a discharged debt as a condition of parole. The debtor then must choose between paying the discharged debt or going to prison. Despite the obvious infringement of the fresh start policy, the federal courts have taken the view that the government's interest in the unfettered operation of the criminal justice system is paramount to the debtor's interest in a fresh start in bankruptcy, and generally have refused to interfere with the criminal proceeding.[273] When the criminal action is in the state courts, this reluctance to intervene is heightened by federalism concerns, as emphasized by the Supreme Court in *Younger v. Harris*.[274] Debtors nevertheless sometimes ask the bankruptcy court to enjoin a state court criminal action if the "principal motivation" of the criminal proceeding is nothing more than a disguised attempt to collect a discharged debt, and occasionally have succeeded.[275] Today, though, almost all federal bankruptcy courts refuse to enjoin state criminal proceedings, even if "principally motivated" by a desire to collect a discharged debt, unless the facts support invocation of the extremely stringent "bad faith" exception to *Younger*.[276] However, if the bankruptcy case is filed *before* the state criminal action has

---

[272] 117 U.S. 617 (1886).

[273] One of the strongest recent pronouncements on this point is the Ninth Circuit's decision in the related context of the § 362 automatic stay. In re Gruntz, 202 F.3d 1074 (9th Cir. 2000). See also United States v. Colasuonno, 697 F.3d 164 (2d Cir. 2012).

[274] 401 U.S. 37 (1971).

[275] See In re Brown, 39 B.R. 820, 827 n.12, 830 (Bankr. M.D. Tenn. 1984); In re Wise, 25 B.R. 440, 442 (Bankr. E.D. Va. 1982).

[276] See, e.g., In re Jones, 277 B.R. 816 (Bankr. M.D. Ga. 2001); cf. In re Batel, 404 B.R. 584, 590 (B.A.P. 1st Cir. 2009) (no bad faith exception to § 362(b)(1)).

been commenced, the bankruptcy court could enjoin *the creditor* from asking the state prosecutor to bring the criminal proceeding.[277]

Special enforcement problems are raised in community property states when only one spouse goes through bankruptcy and receives a discharge. The hard issue is whether community creditors of the non-debtor spouse will be precluded from collecting from after-acquired community property. In § 524(a)(3) and § 524(b) Congress compromised, and gave such creditors the ability to reach that community property, but only when the non-debtor spouse individually would not have been able to discharge his debts. In such a case the non-debtor as a practical matter is attempting to obtain a discharge they otherwise could not have had by hiding behind the discharge of the honest spouse. The result is that the honest spouse loses some of the benefit of their own discharge.

The 2005 amendments added two provisions to § 524. The first new rule, § 524(i), strengthens the discharge injunction in reorganization cases. That section provides that the willful failure of a creditor to credit payments received under a confirmed plan violates the discharge injunction if the act of the creditor to collect and failure to credit payments caused "material injury" to the debtor. This rule does not apply if the confirmation order is revoked; the plan is in default; or the creditor has not received required payments.

The second new section, § 524(j), provides that the discharge injunction does not apply to a creditor who holds a home mortgage if the creditor communicates with the debtor in the ordinary course of business, and the communication is limited to seeking or obtaining periodic payments associated with that home mortgage, in lieu of seeking *in rem* relief to enforce the lien.

§ 10.32   The Prohibition Against Discrimination

The full enjoyment of a discharge in bankruptcy can be undermined by more than just post-discharge collection activities by disappointed creditors, which are prohibited by § 524. A debtor who will be fired from his job if he discharges his debts in bankruptcy, or who will lose his driver's license if he does not pay a discharged debt, may be hesitant to avail himself of the discharge privilege, and even if he does go through bankruptcy will not exit the bankruptcy process with a full financial fresh start. Section 525 prohibits some forms of discrimination against debtors based on their bankruptcy filing, thereby facilitating the fresh start policy.[278]

The genesis of § 525 is the 1971 Supreme Court case of *Perez v. Campbell*.[279] The Court in *Perez* struck down an Arizona statute that would have required the debtors to pay a tort judgment that had been discharged in bankruptcy as a condition of keeping their driver's licenses. The state statute was held to violate the Supremacy Clause by undermining the federal fresh start policy expressed in the bankruptcy discharge.

---

[277] See In re Byrd, 256 B.R. 246 (Bankr. E.D.N.C. 2000).

[278] See Douglass G. Boshkoff, Bankruptcy–Based Discrimination, 66 Am. Bankr. L.J. 387 (1992).

[279] 402 U.S. 637 (1971).

Section 525 codifies and extends the rationale of *Perez*. The section is comprised of three subsections, each of which prohibits different forms of discrimination by different entities. Courts have found § 525 difficult to apply. Three concerns tend to recur: scope, causation, and justification.

The first major question is determining the *scope* of the anti-discrimination ban. That is, is the form of discrimination alleged prohibited under § 525, either expressly or by judicial extension? The section specifically proscribes certain forms of discrimination by certain entities, as discussed below. However, Congress did not intend the statutory listing to be exclusive. The committee reports accompanying the 1978 Code state that "the section is not exhaustive. The enumeration of various forms of discrimination against former bankrupts is not intended to permit other forms of discrimination."[280] However, Congress at the same time chose not to take the path of prohibiting by statute all discrimination, thereby suggesting that some discrimination might be allowed. The task of developing "the contours of the anti-discrimination provision" was left instead to the courts. Notwithstanding the invitation in the legislative history to expand the reach of the anti-discrimination rule beyond that spelled out in the text of § 525, courts for the most part have been reluctant to venture beyond the express statutory prohibitions. Indeed, even with respect to interpretation of the specified prohibitions, courts often have construed the statute narrowly.

The first subsection, which originally comprised the entire section, bars a *governmental unit* from engaging in two types of discrimination. First, codifying *Perez,* a governmental unit may not discriminate in any manner with respect to "a license, permit, charter, franchise, or other similar grant," solely because of the debtor's bankruptcy. § 525(a). So, for example, an attorney could not be denied or stripped of a law license solely because she had filed bankruptcy. However, most courts have interpreted this language as strictly limited to the described items or others of a similar nature. The Sixth Circuit in one well-known case held that a home improvement loan by a state agency was not an "other similar grant" and thus the state's policy to refuse to even consider an applicant for a loan for three years after the receipt of a bankruptcy discharge was not prohibited.[281] That court viewed the enumerated items as "benefits conferred by government that are unrelated to the extension of credit."[282]

Secondly, a governmental unit may not discriminate in *employment* solely because of the debtor's bankruptcy. This prohibition extends to discrimination in (1) hiring, (2) firing, and (3) with respect to the terms of employment.

The second subsection, added in 1984, provides that *private employers* may not fire an employee or discriminate in employment solely because of a debtor's bankruptcy. § 525(b). Note, though, that unlike the government employment anti-discrimination rule in subsection (a), private employers are not specifically barred by the statute from

---

[280]   H.R. Rep. No. 95–595, 95th Cong., 1st Sess., at 367 (1977), reprinted in U.S.C.C.A.N. 5963, 6323; S. Rep. No. 95–989, 95th Cong., 2d Sess., at 81 (1978), reprinted in U.S.C.C.A.N. 5787, 5867.

[281]   Toth v. Mich. State Hous. Dev. Auth., 136 F.3d 477 (6th Cir. 1998), cert. denied, 524 U.S. 954 (1998).

[282]   Id. at 480.

discriminating in *hiring* because of bankruptcy. Given that the statutory prohibitions are not an exhaustive list, courts could accept the congressional invitation in the legislative history to extend the prohibited forms of discrimination to cover discrimination in hiring, but have declined to do so.[283] Indeed, the Ninth Circuit narrowly construed even the explicit statutory ban on discrimination in firing, finding no violation when an employer fired an employee just *before* that employee filed bankruptcy, even though the debtor was fired because he told his employer that he was planning to file bankruptcy.[284] The court did not even consider the possibility of judicially extending the reach of § 525, as contemplated in the legislative history.

Finally, in 1994 subsection (c) was added, to prohibit discrimination with regard to *student loans,* by a governmental unit or by a person engaged in the student loan business, because of a bankruptcy filing or failure to pay a dischargeable debt. The stated purpose of § 525(c) was to overrule a Second Circuit case that had upheld the state's refusal to guarantee a student loan to a debtor because the debtor had not repaid a prior loan, even though the earlier loan debt had been discharged in bankruptcy.[285]

Another problem in applying § 525, apart from the scope issues just discussed, is determining whether the governmental unit or private employer has impermissibly discriminated. The difficulty lies in ascertaining both (1) *causation* and (2) *justification.* That is, even if the discrimination alleged falls within the scope of acts prohibited, the debtor still must prove that the discrimination occurred "*solely because*" of the debtor's bankruptcy. Furthermore, the discrimination may be justified in some instances because the non-debtor entity is permitted to take certain factors into account, especially evidence of the debtor's future financial responsibility.

Thus, in application, § 525 may not be nearly as favorable to debtors as might be expected. Three possible "bad" reasons for discriminating are specified in the statute: that the debtor was a bankruptcy debtor; that the debtor was insolvent prior to or during the bankruptcy case, up to the time of the discharge determination; or that the debtor has not paid a dischargeable debt. However, subsections (a) and (b) require a debtor asserting a violation of § 525 to show that he suffered a prohibited form of discrimination "*solely* because" of one of the forbidden reasons. Subsection (c) omits the reference to "solely," and thus apparently adopts a slightly easier causation test for student loan discrimination. In any event, the statute clearly is designed to provide that if *other* factors besides consideration of the debtor's bankruptcy also played a part in the discrimination, the statute is not violated.

A special issue of justification and causation comes up under subsection (a) with respect to the governmental grant anti-discrimination provision. The question is the extent to which the bankruptcy filing or failure to pay a discharged debt can be considered as evidence of the debtor's future financial responsibility in situations

---

[283] See, e.g., Myers v. TooJay's Mgmt. Corp., 640 F.3d 1278 (11th Cir. 2011); Rea v. Federaed Investors, 627 F.3d 937 (3d Cir. 2010); Fiorani v. CACI, 192 B.R. 401 (E.D. Va. 1996).

[284] In re Majewski, 310 F.3d 653 (9th Cir. 2002).

[285] In re Goldrich, 771 F.2d 28 (2d Cir. 1985). See also Section-by-Section Analysis, commentary to § 313, Bankruptcy Reform Act of 1994, 140 Cong. Rec. H10,771 (daily ed. Oct. 4, 1994).

where financial responsibility might be material to the decision whether to grant the debtor the benefit sought. The legislative history states that "future financial responsibility or ability" may be considered.[286] As the Sixth Circuit observed in the case discussed above, in upholding the denial of a home improvement loan to a debtor, "[a] reckoning of an applicant's financial responsibility is an essential part of any lender's evaluation of a post-discharge application for a loan or extension of credit."[287] Courts have encountered difficulty, though, in determining when various forms of "financial responsibility" laws, such as to obtain or keep a driver's license,[288] or to receive a government loan,[289] permissibly deny those privileges as a consideration of "future financial responsibility." Courts have tended to uphold laws that operate in a neutral and nondiscriminatory manner against all affected parties, irrespective of whether they have gone through bankruptcy or not.[290] However, at a minimum the congressional policy would seem to prohibit a law that conclusively deems a former bankruptcy debtor to be, *for that reason alone*, financially irresponsible in the future.

In applying subsection (c), which specifically prohibits discrimination with respect to student loans because of a debtor's bankruptcy filing or failure to pay a discharged debt, courts will have little latitude to permit consideration of the bankruptcy filing or failure to pay a discharged debt as evidence of the debtor's *prospective* financial responsibility; the loan decision is inextricably bound up in the question of prospective financial capacity, and yet Congress expressly prohibited discrimination with regard to student loans. Certainly a blanket discriminatory policy, such as one denying all future student loans if any prior loan remains unpaid—even if previously discharged in bankruptcy—would be violative of subsection (c). Indeed, it could be argued that the addition of subsection (c) undermines the prevalent tendency in the courts to give considerable weight to a debtor's bankruptcy as evidence of projected financial responsibility with regard to loan programs *other than* student loans, which are not specifically covered in § 525(c). The courts, though, even after the 1994 addition of subsection (c), have continued to uphold denial of loans other than student loans to formerly bankrupt debtors.[291] Such loans remain outside the ambit of § 525 both because of the scope issue discussed above, as not an "other similar grant" under subsection (a), and because of the causation and justification reasons speaking to future financial responsibility.

Exemplifying the problems in applying § 525 is the Supreme Court case of *Federal Communications Commission v. NextWave Personal Communications, Inc.*[292] That case involved a governmental license that was also intertwined with a governmental loan or extension of credit. The debtor in *NextWave* was a successful bidder at an FCC auction of PCS licenses. Pursuant to FCC regulations, the debtor paid 10% of its auction bid in cash, and executed a promissory note to the FCC for the balance, secured by a

---

[286] H.R. Rep. No. 95–595, 95th Cong., 1st Sess., at 367 (1977), reprinted in U.S.C.C.A.N. 5963, 6323; S.Rep. No. 989, 95th Cong., 2d Sess., at 81 (1978), reprinted in U.S.C.C.A.N. 5787, 5867.

[287] *Toth*, supra note 281, 136 F.3d at 480.

[288] E.g., Duffey v. Dollison, 734 F.2d 265 (6th Cir. 1984).

[289] E.g., *Goldrich*, supra note 285, 771 F.2d 28.

[290] E.g., *Duffey*, supra note 288, 734 F.2d 265.

[291] See, e.g., *Toth*, supra note 281, 136 F.3d 477.

[292] 537 U.S. 293 (2003).

perfected security interest in the licenses themselves. The terms of the licenses provided that the licenses would be cancelled if the debtor defaulted in any of its payment obligations to the FCC. Thereafter, the debtor experienced financial difficulties and, *before* defaulting on its payment obligations to the FCC, filed a chapter 11 petition in an attempt to restructure its payment obligations to the FCC under a plan of reorganization. *After* the debtor's bankruptcy filing, though, the FCC contended that the debtor's PCS licenses were automatically cancelled according to their terms by the debtor's post-bankruptcy default in payment. The debtor challenged this action as violating § 525(a), and won.

The FCC contended that its cancellation of the debtor's PCS licenses was not "solely because" of the debtor's failure to pay its debt to the FCC; rather, the cancellation was at least in part, if not primarily, to further the FCC's valid regulatory objectives in licensing the spectrum. The Supreme Court, however, rejected this argument:

> In our view, that factor is irrelevant. When the statute refers to failure to pay a debt as the sole cause of cancellation ('solely because'), it cannot reasonably be understood to include, among the other causes whose presence can preclude application of the prohibition, the governmental unit's *motive* in effecting the cancellation. Such a reading would deprive § 525 of all force. It is hard to imagine a situation in which a governmental unit would not have some further motive behind the cancellation—assuring the financial solvency of the licensed entity, *e.g., Perez v. Campbell*, 402 U.S. 637 (1971) . . . or punishing lawlessness, . . . or even (quite simply) making itself financially whole. Section 525 means nothing more or less than that the failure to pay a dischargeable debt must alone be the proximate cause of the cancellation—the act or event that triggers the agency's decision to cancel, whatever the agency's ultimate motive in pulling the trigger may be.[293]

The FCC also argued that conditions necessary to maintenance of the debtor's PCS licenses are not "a debt that is dischargeable" in bankruptcy, within the meaning of § 525(a). Again, the Supreme Court disagreed:

> This is nothing more than a retooling of [the FCC's] recurrent theme that 'regulatory conditions' should be exempt from § 525. No matter how the Commission casts it, the argument loses. Under the Bankruptcy Code, 'debt' means 'liability on a claim,' 11 U.S.C. § 101(12), and 'claim,' in turn, includes any 'right to payment,' § 101(5)(A). We . . . have held that the 'plain meaning of a "right to payment" is nothing more nor less than an enforceable obligation, regardless of the objectives the State seeks to serve in imposing the obligation,' *Pennsylvania Dept. of Public Welfare v. Davenport*, 495 U.S. 552, 559 (1990). See also *Ohio v. Kovacs*, 469 U.S. 274 (1985). In short, a debt is a debt, even when the obligation to pay it is also a regulatory condition.[294]

---

[293] Id. at 301–02.

[294] Id. at 302–03.

Thus, the debtor succeeded in invoking § 525(a) to prevent the government from revoking its PCS licenses for non-payment.

§ 10.33 Revocation of the Chapter 7 Discharge

A debtor who is granted a discharge is not necessarily out of the financial woods for at least a year, because of the possibility that the discharge will be revoked. § 727(d), (e). A complaint to revoke the debtor's discharge must be filed either by the trustee, the United States trustee, or a creditor. Although a debtor conceivably might want to revoke a discharge in order to reaffirm a particular debt or to file a new case so as to discharge new debts, the debtor lacks standing to apply for revocation. Nor may the court act *sua sponte* to revoke a discharge.

The grounds for revoking a discharge under § 727(d) are not surprising. The first ground is that the "discharge was obtained through the fraud of the debtor." § 727(d)(1). Actual or positive fraud is required. Often the fraud involves omission of property from the debtor's schedules and an ongoing concealment by the debtor. A plaintiff invoking the first ground must show that it did not learn of the debtor's fraud until after the discharge had been granted. Otherwise, an objection to discharge should have been filed. A complaint asserting revocation under § 727(d)(1) must be filed within one year of the entry of the discharge order. § 727(e)(1). This is an absolute time limit; the bankruptcy court has no power to entertain a complaint to revoke filed after the one year period. Rules 9006(b)(2), 9024. Some courts, however, have been receptive to pleas to invoke their equity powers to toll the running of the one-year period because of the debtor's fraudulent activities.[295]

The second ground for revocation is that the debtor acquired or became entitled to acquire property of the estate, but knowingly and fraudulently failed to report such property and to turn it over to the trustee. § 727(d)(2). This provision is a necessary supplement to § 727(a)(2), because under § 541(a) certain forms of property that the debtor may acquire after the commencement of the bankruptcy case, and perhaps even after the initial granting of the discharge, become property of the estate. The debtor has a duty to file a supplementary schedule as to such property. Rule 1007(h).

The third ground for revoking a discharge incorporates § 727(a)(6). § 727(d)(3). That provision bars a debtor's discharge because of a refusal to obey a court order or a refusal to testify for any reason other than invocation of the self-incrimination privilege. This ground must be carried over into the revocation provisions because of the procedural fact that the discharge is entered early in the case. Without § 727(d)(3), an already discharged debtor might have considerably less incentive to cooperate during the remainder of the bankruptcy case.

Although the statute does not expressly bar a plaintiff with pre-discharge knowledge of the debtor's misdeeds from raising § 727(d)(2) or (3), as it does under subsection (d)(1), courts nonetheless have read such a requirement into those

---

[295] See, e.g., In re Stedham, 327 B.R. 889, 900–03 (Bankr. W.D. Tenn. 2005).

subsections as well.[296] The time limit for bringing a complaint under (d)(2) or (d)(3) is longer than under (d)(1): one year from the later of the granting of the discharge or the closing of the case. § 727(e)(2). This longer time period is used because a discharge is entered before the case is closed, and the subsection (d)(2) and (d)(3) grounds concern possible post-discharge actions of the debtor.

The final ground for revocation relates to a debtor's failure to cooperate in an audit, either by making a material misstatement or by failing to provide requested records, if the debtor is randomly selected for an audit by a bankruptcy administrator or United States auditor pursuant to 28 U.S.C. § 586(f). § 727(d)(4). The audit referred to is authorized by a different provision added by Congress in 2005 that requires the United States Trustee to conduct random audits in not less than 1 out of every 250 cases in each Federal judicial district. 28 U.S.C. § 603(a)(2).

F. REAFFIRMATION

§ 10.34 Effects of Reaffirmation

A bankruptcy debtor may voluntarily choose to forego a discharge of all of his debts by filing a written waiver of the discharge with the court after the bankruptcy case has commenced. § 727(a)(10). Much more common than total waiver is a partial negation of the discharge privilege, through an agreement to *reaffirm* a particular debt. A reaffirmation agreement is a contract between the debtor and a creditor pursuant to which the debtor promises to pay the debt notwithstanding the discharge. Under contract law the debtor's promise is supported by valid consideration. Restatement (2d) of Contracts § 83 (1979). In return the creditor may promise to permit the debtor to retain collateral as long as the debtor remains current in his payments, or may agree to settle a dischargeability complaint. If the contract complies with the statutory restrictions on enforceability (specified in detail § 524(c), (d), (k)–(m)), then the discharge enforcement provisions of § 524(a)(1) and (2) do not apply to the reaffirmed debt. That debt is reinstated in full (often with postpetition interest and attorney's fees), and the creditor is entitled to invoke the full panoply of collection remedies under state law to enforce payment of that debt thereafter.

§ 10.35 Reasons Why Debtors Reaffirm

Why would a debtor ever do such a crazy thing? Empirical studies have shown that a surprisingly high percentage of individual consumer debtors reaffirm otherwise dischargeable debts. A study under the prior Bankruptcy Act found that over one-third of the interviewed debtors reaffirmed some debts,[297] and more recent studies under the Bankruptcy Code showed reaffirmation rates ranging from 19% to as high as 52% of all consumer cases.[298] With over a million consumer filings every year, that is a lot of reaffirmed debts. This high rate of reaffirmation raises serious questions about the

---

[296] E.g., In re Lyons, 23 B.R. 123, 125–26 (Bankr. E.D. Va. 1982). See, e.g., In re Dietz, 914 F.2d 161, 163 (9th Cir. 1990).

[297] David T. Stanley & Marjorie Girth, Bankruptcy: Problem, Process, Reform 60 (1971).

[298] National Bankruptcy Review Commission Final Report, Bankruptcy: The Next Twenty Years 152 & nn. 319–20 (1997).

efficacy of the fresh start. The evidence shows that the major repeat consumer creditors (VISA, Sears, etc.) routinely request reaffirmation agreements. The issue for Congress is how to protect ignorant consumer debtors from agreeing to foolish reaffirmations without depriving those debtors of the freedom to enter into advantageous agreements.

By far the most common reason that debtors reaffirm is to *keep encumbered property*, especially the family car or large household appliances. Since unavoided liens ride through bankruptcy and may be enforced after bankruptcy, a debtor who wants to prevent the seizure and sale of his car, refrigerator, or other secured item must find some way to pay the secured creditor. Reaffirmation is one possibility. Other means may exist, however. One option is to *redeem* the item under § 722, but substantive restrictions on redemption, especially the requirement that a single lump-sum cash payment for the entire value of the item must be made to the secured creditor,[299] limit the practical availability of redemption for many debtors. Before BAPCPA, in some jurisdictions the debtor was able to retain encumbered property without reaffirming or redeeming, simply by remaining current on payments on the secured debt. The 2005 amendments, however, took away that option.[300]

A second reason for reaffirming a debt is the debtor's desire to *preserve a relationship* with a particular creditor. This may be done so that the creditor will extend credit in the future to the debtor, or just out of personal or moral motives. The debtor may feel the creditor has been fair, lenient, or the like, and deserves to be paid.

Third, a reaffirmation agreement may be entered into in *settlement of dischargeability litigation*. The debtor may see the handwriting on the wall, and, since the debtor believes the debt ultimately will not be discharged anyway, may at least want to avoid incurring additional attorney's fees in the dischargeability action. The provision granting costs and attorney's fees to a debtor who prevails in a § 523(a)(2) fraud case in certain circumstances was intended to lessen the creditor's leverage to obtain reaffirmations by contesting dischargeability. § 523(d). The 1984 amendments, however, took much of the teeth out of § 523(d). The 1978 Code also required the court to pass on the good faith of a reaffirmation agreement entered as a settlement of dischargeability litigation, but that provision was repealed in 1984.

A final common reason for reaffirming a debt is to *protect a co-debtor* from having to pay the debt. A debtor whose aged grandmother co-signed the debtor's note may feel a moral compulsion to keep the finance company off of grandma's back. The 1978 reform effort attempted to reduce the motivation to reaffirm for this reason by offering debtors who proceed under chapter 13 a stay against co-debtors. § 1301. A similar co-debtor stay was included in chapter 12. § 1201.

---

[299] See In re Bell, 700 F.2d 1053 (6th Cir. 1983). See also In re Price, 370 F.3d 362, 367 (3d Cir. 2004).
[300] See § 7.32.c.

§ 10.36 Restrictions on Enforceability of Reaffirmations

One of the biggest debates in the entire field of consumer bankruptcy centers on the extent to which enforceable reaffirmations should be allowed.[301] Contract law does not bar the enforcement of an agreement to repay a debt discharged in bankruptcy; the moral obligation to pay is good consideration for that agreement.[302] Bankruptcy law prior to the 1978 reform freely allowed and enforced reaffirmations. Because of the large number of reaffirmations and the concomitant erosion of the federal fresh start policy, the House originally wanted to eliminate enforceable reaffirmations altogether, limiting creditors to voluntary repayments by debtors.[303] The Code as enacted in 1978 did allow for reaffirmation agreements, but imposed a number of restrictions on enforceability that limited the usefulness of this technique for creditors seeking to avoid the effects of discharge. These restrictions were cut back in 1984, opening up the availability of reaffirmations a bit more. Creditors have seized the opportunity, and today reaffirmations again are widely used.

The substantive restrictions on enforceable reaffirmation agreements are set forth in § 524(c) and (k)–(m), and the applicable procedure in § 524(d) and Rule 4008. Concerned that creditors were still abusing reaffirmations, in 2005 Congress added significant new regulations on reaffirmation agreements, in a provision entitled "Discouraging Abuse of Reaffirmation Agreement Practices."[304] The new regulations are located in § 524(k), (l), and (m), and, among other things, specify the form that an enforceable reaffirmation agreement must take. The mandated form includes very clear warnings and disclosures. Furthermore, even if the required form is used, a presumption of "undue hardship" is raised if the debtor's financial statements show that the reaffirmed debt exceeds the debtor's disposable income, and unless the presumption is rebutted, the bankruptcy court will not approve the agreement. § 524(m)(1). The restrictions and the implementing procedure all are paternalistically designed to protect debtors from improvident reaffirmations. Before the 2005 amendments, it was not clear that the congressional goal was being achieved. The jury is still out on whether the 2005 amendments will make a significant difference.

An agreement that does not comply with all of the substantive regulations of § 524 and which does not follow the proper procedures for approval is entirely *void* and unenforceable. If the creditor *does* attempt to enforce a void agreement, that creditor is in violation of the § 524(a) discharge injunction and will be subject to sanctions for contempt.[305]

Initially it should be noted that an *agreement* is necessary, which means that both the debtor and the creditor must be willing parties. A creditor may be unwilling to reaffirm when the debt is secured by collateral and the creditor would prefer to proceed with foreclosure of the collateral immediately, before its value depreciates. The creditor

---

[301] The topic is thoroughly discussed in the 1997 Commission Report. See National Bankruptcy Review Commission Final Report, Bankruptcy: The Next Twenty Years 145–65 (1997).

[302] Restatement (Second) of Contracts § 83 (1979).

[303] H.R. Rep. No. 95–595, 95th Cong., 1st Sess., at 164 (1977), reprinted in U.S.C.C.A.N. 5963, 6125.

[304] Pub. L. No. 109–8, § 203, 119 Stat. 43–49 (2005).

[305] See, e.g., In re Latanowich, 207 B.R. 326 (Bankr. D. Mass. 1997).

also may be able to exact the debtor's agreement to reaffirm multiple debts as a condition of the creditor consenting to the reaffirmation of the debt the debtor actually wants to reaffirm.

The Code's restrictions on enforcing reaffirmations include *all* of the following:

1. *Timing*

There are two significant timing restrictions on when an enforceable reaffirmation agreement can be made. First, the agreement must be entered into *after* the bankruptcy filing. An agreement is enforceable only if the debtor receives all required disclosures under subsection (k) of § 524 before signing. Thus, a pre-bankruptcy agreement to reaffirm is not enforceable, which means that a creditor cannot slip an enforceable promise to reaffirm in the event of a future bankruptcy filing into the boilerplate terms of the initial credit agreement. Second, the agreement must be made *before* the discharge is granted.[306] § 524(c)(1). A creditor who asks a debtor to reaffirm a discharged debt after bankruptcy therefore violates the discharge injunction, and might be sanctioned.

2. *Filing*

The agreement must be filed with the bankruptcy court. § 524(c)(3). This requirement enables the court to determine whether the reaffirmation regulations are being followed and to conduct an independent review of the reaffirmation when the debtor does not have an attorney. The policy of Sears not to file reaffirmation agreements with the bankruptcy courts was part of their nationwide scheme to circumvent the reaffirmation rules, and led to a fine of over $400 million.[307]

3. *Warnings and disclosures*

The heart of the 2005 amendments regarding reaffirmations was to expand significantly the disclosures a creditor must give a debtor, in new subsection (k) of § 524. The required disclosures and warnings, which must be clear and conspicuous, are spelled out in considerable detail in § 524(k)(1)–(3), with § 524(k)(3) providing the exact form and language that must be used. Some of the most important warnings and disclosures are: that the debtor is not required to reaffirm; that the debtor has a right to rescind; and what the legal effect is if the debtor reaffirms, and the consequences of default. § 524(k)(3)(J)(i). If the debtor has an attorney, then that attorney also must inform the debtor of the legal ramifications of the reaffirmation agreement. § 524(c)(3)(C). If the debtor is not represented by an attorney, the debtor must go to court and hear it from the judge at the discharge hearing. § 524(d)(1).

---

[306] This requirement motivates the rule that a debtor may request a delay in the entry of a discharge, in case a reaffirmation is still being negotiated. See Rule 4004(c).

[307] See *Latanowich*, supra note 305.

4.　*Debtor affirmations*

The debtor must follow very specific guidelines to affirm the agreement, the required form of which is given in § 524(k)(4). To affirm the agreement the debtor must (1) sign the agreement after receiving all required disclosures from the creditor; (2) state the amount of her monthly take home pay and other income, her current monthly expenses, and the amount available to make payments on the debt being reaffirmed; and (3) affirm that entering into the agreement will not impose an undue hardship, and if a presumption of undue hardship arises, state how the debtor will make payments. § 524(k)(6).

5.　*Rescission*

The debtor can rescind the agreement by notifying the creditor, at any time *prior to discharge*, or within *60 days* after the reaffirmation agreement is filed with the court, whichever is later. § 524(c)(4). Thus, note that a debtor could still rescind the reaffirmation after the discharge is entered, if the agreement was filed with the court within 60 days of the discharge hearing. The debtor's rescission right is reinforced by the requirement that the reaffirmation agreement itself must contain a clear and conspicuous *disclosure* to the debtor of the fact that the debtor may rescind. § 524(k)(2), (3)(J)(i).

6.　*Independent review*

An independent third party must pass on the agreement on the debtor's behalf. Exactly who and how are matters that Congress has waffled over, however. Originally, the 1978 Code placed the onus on the bankruptcy judge, demanding that the court find (1) that the agreement was in the debtor's *best interests* and (2) that it did not impose an *undue hardship* on the debtor. From the creditor's perspective, this requirement blocked too many reaffirmations, because courts were not very willing to make the required findings. In 1984, the "guardian" function was shifted in most cases from the court to the *debtor's attorney*. That attorney now must file an affidavit stating (1) that the debtor's agreement is fully informed and voluntary, (2) does not impose an undue hardship on the debtor or the debtor's dependents, and (3) that the attorney has advised the debtor of the legal ramifications of the reaffirmation agreement. § 524(c)(3). Section 524(k)(5)(A) now provides the exact form an attorney's certification in § 524(c)(3) must take.[308] Furthermore, if a presumption of undue hardship arises under subsection (m) (discussed below), the attorney must further certify that in the attorney's opinion the debtor will be able to make the required payments. § 524(k)(5)(B). The attorney does not have to certify that he believes that the reaffirmation is in the debtor's "best interests." If an attorney did not represent the debtor in negotiating the reaffirmation agreement, and the debt is not a consumer debt secured by real property, the court then must make the findings of no undue hardship and best interests. § 524(c)(6), (d)(2). The 1994 amendments clarified that the debtor only must go to court if not represented by an attorney.

---

[308] Courts have struggled to interpret the 2005 regulations when the exact forms are either not followed, or are filled out incorrectly or incompletely. For a useful discussion, see *In re Mendoza*, 347 B.R. 34 (Bankr. W.D. Tex. 2006).

7. *Presumption of undue hardship*

Another important protection added in 2005 is a presumption of undue hardship. For the 60 days after the agreement is filed, a reaffirmation agreement is presumed to create an undue hardship on the debtor if the debtor's financial schedules show that the net of the debtor's current monthly income minus expenses (i.e., the debtor's disposable income) is *less* than the scheduled payments under the reaffirmation agreement. § 524(m)(1). In such a case, the debtor may rebut the presumption by identifying additional sources of funds. The court may disapprove the reaffirmation agreement if the presumption of undue hardship is not rebutted to its satisfaction.[309] Section 524(m)(2) exempts from this provision reaffirmation agreements where the creditor is a credit union.

One practical issue was clarified in 2005. New § 524(l)(1) makes clear that the creditor may accept payments from the debtor both before and after the filing of a reaffirmation agreement. § 524(l)(1). However, the creditor's privilege of accepting payments from the debtor is qualified by the further requirement that the creditor believes in "good faith" that the reaffirmation agreement is effective. § 524(l)(2).

Somewhat confusingly, § 524(l)(3) provides that "the requirements of subsections (c)(2) and (k) shall be satisfied if disclosures required under those subsections are given in good faith." This section could be read in two opposite ways—one providing the creditor with a safe harbor, and the other (more likely) imposing an additional requirement on the creditor. The statutory language could be interpreted to mean that the formal requirements of subsections (c)(2) and (k) "shall be satisfied"—even if as a formal matter they are *not* satisfied—as long as the disclosure was given in "good faith." However, such a reading would undermine the protective purpose of the disclosure requirements. More probably, the intent of Congress was to mandate that the disclosure requirements would be satisfied *only if* the disclosures were made in "good faith," *in addition* to meeting all the formal requirements of subsections (c)(2) and (k). Under this view, a creditor who gave disclosures in bad faith would not satisfy the requirements of (c)(2) and (k) even if the formal requirements were met.

G. THE DISCHARGE IN THE REORGANIZATION AND DEBT ADJUSTMENT CHAPTERS

§ 10.37 The Discharge in Chapter 11

A debtor may be granted a discharge in chapter 11. Fewer restrictions inhibit the chapter 11 discharge than in chapter 7. The obligations assumed under the chapter 11 plan are substituted for the debtor's prior debts. In a sense, confirmation of the plan serves as a novation of the previously existing obligations.

The first difference from chapter 7 is that the chapter 11 discharge is not limited to individual debtors. Corporations and partnerships also may be discharged, assuming

---

[309] See, e.g., In re Laynas, 345 B.R. 505 (Bankr. E.D. Pa. 2006).

that the corporation or partnership is reorganizing in chapter 11 and not liquidating.[310] Since the debtor's business entity will exist after the completion of a bankruptcy reorganization, the discharge of prior claims is of paramount importance to the feasibility of that reorganization. The breadth of the chapter 11 discharge for business debtors is underscored by the fact that virtually all debts are discharged for corporate and partnership debtors, even debts that fall within the § 523(a) exceptions to discharge. Indeed, until the 2005 amendments, no § 523(a) debts were excluded from a chapter 11 discharge for a corporation or partnership, and that rule still holds for partnerships. For corporate debtors, Congress added an exclusion to the chapter 11 discharge in 2005 for (1) fraud debts owed to a governmental unit and for (2) tax or customs debts as to which the debtor either made a fraudulent return or willfully attempted to evade or defeat the tax. § 1141(d)(6).

An *individual* debtor will not be able to escape liability for § 523(a) debts by proceeding under chapter 11, however. § 1141(d)(2). A creditor asserting a § 523(c)(1) ground against an individual debtor in chapter 11 must file the complaint within 60 days of the § 341 meeting of creditors, just as in chapter 7. Rule 4007(c). The individual debtor who reorganizes and does not liquidate in chapter 11 will not, however, be subject to the § 727(a) discharge denial grounds. § 1141(d)(3). This exemption does not give the debtor free rein to be uncooperative in the bankruptcy case, though, because to confirm the plan of reorganization the debtor must comply with the provisions of the bankruptcy law and must propose the plan in good faith. § 1129(a)(2), (3).

The time bar on successive discharges does not apply when the second case is a reorganizing chapter 11, but a chapter 11 discharge will count towards the eight-year bar in a later chapter 7. If the debtor is liquidating in chapter 11, thereby bringing the § 727(a) grounds back into play, § 1141(d)(3), a complaint objecting to discharge must be filed by the first date set for the confirmation hearing. Rule 4004(a). The creditors would be aware by that time that a liquidating plan was being proposed. Section 1141(d)(4) copies § 727(a)(10) by permitting a debtor to waive the discharge in writing after the case is filed.

For corporations and partnerships, the discharge in chapter 11 is an incident of and effective upon the *confirmation* of the reorganization plan. Before 2005, discharge occurred immediately upon confirmation in all chapter 11 cases, unlike in chapters 12 and 13, where discharge is deferred pending the debtor's performance under the plan. BAPCPA, however, changed the rule for individual chapter 11 debtors, postponing the discharge until the completion of all payments under the confirmed plan. § 1141(d)(5)(A). A court may grant an individual debtor a "hardship" discharge even if performance under the plan is not completed, if creditors have been paid at least as much as they would have in a chapter 7 and if modification of the plan is not practical. § 1141(d)(5)(B). As under all other chapters, an individual debtor may have his chapter 11 discharge delayed if a § 522(q) exemption proceeding is pending. § 1141(d)(5)(C).

---

[310] Section 1141(d)(1)(A) discharges "the debtor," which in a chapter 11 can include corporations and partnerships, see § 109(d) ("person" eligible), and § 101(41) ("person" includes corporation and partnership). Under § 1141(d)(3), the § 727(a)(1) restriction of discharge to individual debtors is applied in a liquidating chapter 11.

The chapter 11 discharge operates against all debts that arise up to the date of *confirmation*, § 1141(d)(1)(A), whereas in chapter 7 only debts that arise before the initial filing of the case are discharged. As in chapter 7, however, creditor participation is not required for discharge, as the discharge operates against all debts, even if no proof of claim is filed, a filed claim is not allowed, or the creditor votes against the plan. § 1141(d)(1)(A)(i)–(iii). Although § 1141(d)(1) suggests that the discharge is absolute, numerous courts have held that as a matter of due process creditors who do not receive notice of the case are not affected thereby.[311]

Finally, a chapter 11 discharge may be revoked, but only if the order confirming the plan was procured by fraud. § 1144. This provision is not limited to fraud by the debtor. Non-performance under the plan is not a basis for revoking confirmation. Revocation may be sought by a "party in interest," which under § 1109(b) includes a broader class of parties than those who have standing to seek revocation in chapter 7. The time limit to seek revocation in chapter 11 is shorter than in chapter 7, being only 180 days from the confirmation order. Also, a clever party may not attempt to circumscribe the 180–day limit by moving under Federal Rule of Civil Procedure 60, made applicable by Bankruptcy Rule 9024, as the latter specifically carves out an applicability exception for § 1144. Courts have also limited revocation to cases where the movant did not learn of the fraud until after the plan was confirmed, and courts generally adopt an "all or nothing approach," and refuse to cherry pick components of a plan confirmation order to revoke.[312]

§ 10.38 The Discharge in Chapter 13

Historically, the chapter 13 discharge must be considered in light of the congressional policy in the 1978 Code to encourage individual consumer debtors to proceed under that chapter instead of under chapter 7, so that unsecured creditors would get paid more. One of the major incentives designed to persuade debtors to file voluntarily under chapter 13 was the broader discharge available in chapter 13, colloquially known as the "super-discharge." The 2005 amendments dramatically altered this approach, however, by (1) mandating that debtors with sufficient repayment capacity be excluded from chapter 7 under the § 707(b) "abuse" rule, thereby leaving only chapter 13 as a viable bankruptcy choice, and concomitantly (2) largely eliminating the "super" discharge. Of course, relief under chapter 13 ultimately remains voluntary with the debtor.

There are still several important differences between the discharge under chapter 7 and under chapter 13. To begin with, § 727(a) is inapplicable in chapter 13. Indeed, creditors are not even permitted to object to the debtor's discharge in chapter 13. However, creditors may object to confirmation of the debtor's plan, and one requirement for confirmation is the good faith of the debtor. § 1325(a)(3).

Perhaps the most important difference is that discharge in chapter 13 normally is granted only when the debtor *completes his payments* under a confirmed plan.

---

[311] This view stems from *City of New York v. New York, New Haven, & Hartford R.R. Co.*, 344 U.S. 293 (1953). See, e.g., Reliable Elec. Co. v. Olson Constr. Co., 726 F.2d 620 (10th Cir. 1984).

[312] See, e.g., In re Motors Liquidation Co., 462 B.R. 494 (Bankr. S.D.N.Y. 2012).

§ 1328(a). Confirmation alone does not trigger the discharge, as it did in chapter 11 for individuals prior to 2005. The chapter 13 plan period will be from three to five years. § 1322(d). If a debtor encounters difficulty in meeting his obligations under the plan, he may seek modification of the plan, § 1329, and will receive a "full-compliance" discharge under § 1328(a) upon completion of the modified plan.

If modification of the plan is not practicable, the debtor still may be able to receive a chapter 13 discharge. A "hardship" discharge may be granted by the court if it finds that modification is not practicable, that creditors actually received as much under the plan as they would have if the debtor had liquidated under chapter 7, and that the debtor's failure to make all the scheduled payments under the plan "is due to circumstances for which the debtor should not justly be held accountable." § 1328(b). Section 727(a) still does not apply even if a hardship discharge is granted.

Discharge in chapter 13 is operative against debts that are provided for by the chapter 13 plan, or that are not provided for but are disallowed under § 502. One exception made necessary by the relatively short lifespan of a chapter 13 plan is for debts for which the last payment is due after the termination of the plan period. §§ 1328(a)(1), 1322(b)(5).

Until 1990, almost all of the § 523(a) debts were discharged by a chapter 13 full-performance discharge under § 1328(a), excepting only family support obligations under § 523(a)(5). This was the so-called "super" discharge referred to above, intended to entice debtors to choose to file under chapter 13 instead of chapter 7. The breadth of the full-performance discharge was confirmed by the Supreme Court in *Pennsylvania Department of Public Welfare v. Davenport*,[313] when it held that a criminal restitution obligation was dischargeable in chapter 13. However, some courts circumvented the congressional scheme by holding that a debtor who proceeds under chapter 13 in order to discharge § 523(a) debts lacks "good faith" and thus should not be able to confirm a plan under § 1325(a)(3).[314]

The breadth of the full-performance discharge has been almost unceasingly controversial, and *Davenport* provided the occasion for Congress to begin retrenching on the scope of § 1328(a), a retrenchment that now, after the sea change effected by the 2005 amendments, is almost complete. Today, many of the most important types of debts excepted from the discharge under § 523(a) are also excluded even under a chapter 13 full-performance discharge under § 1328(a). In 1990 Congress added educational loans under § 523(a)(8), DUI injuries under § 523(a)(9), and criminal restitution obligations to the list of debts excepted from the § 1328(a) discharge.[315] In 2005, in § 1328(a)(2) and (4) Congress added several more exceptions to this list,[316] including debts for: fraud (§ 523(a)(2)); unscheduled claims (§ 523(a)(3)); fiduciary fraud or defalcation, embezzlement, or larceny (§ 523(a)(4)); withholding taxes (§ 507(a)(8)(C)); taxes as to which the debtor did not file a return, filed late, filed a

---

[313]   495 U.S. 552 (1990).

[314]   E.g., In re LeMaire, 898 F.2d 1346 (8th Cir. 1990).

[315]   See Criminal Victims Protection Act of 1990, Pub. L. No. 101–647, §§ 3101–04, 104 Stat. 4916 (1990) (codified at § 1328(a)(2)–(3)).

[316]   Pub. L. No. 109–8, § 314(b), 119 Stat. 88 (2005).

fraudulent return, or willfully attempted to evade or defeat (§ 523(a)(1)(B), (C)); and for restitution or damages awarded in a civil action for willful or malicious injury that caused personal injury or death (this partially tracks § 523(a)(6)).

One common type of debt covered by the discharge exceptions that *is* still discharged by a full-performance discharge under § 1328(a) are tax debts under § 523(a)(1)(A). These are debts for taxes that enjoy priority under § 507(a)(3) or (8), and which are excepted from discharge for that reason. Since they are priority debts, the debtor must provide for full payment of these debts in the chapter 13 plan, § 1322(a)(2), and thus the fact of "discharge" is meaningless.

That leaves only two common types of § 523(a) debts as still subject to the full-performance discharge under § 1328(a): property settlement debts, under § 523(a)(15), and debts for "willful and malicious injury" to property, under § 523(a)(6). Willful or malicious injury debts that result in personal injury (or death) are excluded from the chapter 13 discharge by § 1328(a)(4), also added in 2005. A curiosity of the 2005 amendments is that § 1328(a)(4) only imperfectly tracks the exception in § 523(a)(6).[317] First, it covers debts for "willful *or* malicious injury," rather than "willful *and* malicious injury," as under § 523(a)(6). No explanation for the difference was given by Congress, nor is any evident. Also odd is the fact that § 1328(a)(4) only applies to debts as to which restitution or damages have been "awarded in a civil action against the debtor," which appears to mandate that a judgment already have been entered.[318] If applied as written, this provision could lead to a "race to the courthouse," as debtors rush to file bankruptcy before a judgment can be entered in a civil action. There is no apparent reason to limit the reach of § 1328(a)(4) in this way, but the language seems clear (although at least two courts disagree[319]). This is the same flaw that originally afflicted the DUI exception (§ 523(a)(9)), until Congress wised up there and eliminated the requirement of a prior judgment. Apparently such wisdom is fleeting.

Hardship discharges, where the debtor does not complete performance under the plan but successfully petitions the court to enter a discharge anyway, have always been subject to all of the § 523(a) exceptions. § 1328(c)(2). If a debtor files an application for a hardship discharge, then Rule 4007(d) requires the court to give creditors 30 days notice of the time fixed for filing complaints under § 523(c)(1).

Most debts "provided for by the plan" and thus dischargeable are prepetition debts. § 1328(a). However, under § 1305(a) claims for postpetition taxes and necessary consumer debts may be filed and then dealt with in the plan. Postpetition consumer debts are only discharged if prior approval to incur the debt was obtained from the chapter 13 trustee. § 1328(d).

A chapter 13 discharge is not as restrictive as a chapter 7 discharge with regard to limiting relief in successive bankruptcy cases. Until 2005, there was no such bar when the *second* case was under chapter 13. In 2005, Congress amended § 1328 to include a

---

[317] See § 10.21.

[318] See In re Byrd, 388 B.R. 875 (Bankr. C.D. Ill. 2007).

[319] In re Taylor, 388 B.R. 115 (Bankr. M.D. Pa. 2008). See also In re Wang, 418 B.R. 373 (B.A.P. 9th Cir. 2009).

new subsection (f), which provides that a chapter 13 debtor will be denied discharge if the debtor received a discharge under chapter 7, 11, or 12 in the *four years* prior to the chapter 13 filing. § 1328(f)(1). This four-year bar is measured from the date the previous case was filed, not the date when a discharge was granted. If the first case was under chapter 13, a *two-year* discharge bar is in effect. § 1328(f)(2). The wisdom of these successive filing restrictions is dubious at best when the second case is under chapter 13. To receive a discharge under chapter 13, the debtor must pay all of his priority debts in full and must pay all of his disposable income to creditors for several years.

A chapter 13 discharge in the first case does trigger the six-year bar in a later chapter 7 case, although not if the chapter 13 plan either paid 100 percent on unsecured claims, or 70 percent in a good faith, best efforts plan. § 727(a)(9). The debtor also could preserve the ability to obtain a subsequent discharge by waiving discharge in the chapter 13 case. The discharge in chapter 13 does not preclude a discharge in a subsequent chapter 11 case, unless it is a liquidating chapter 11 filed within six years.

The 2005 amendments added provisions that qualify the chapter 13 discharge that are identical to changes made in the other chapters. Thus, a debtor must complete a course in personal financial management after the filing of the bankruptcy case in order to receive his chapter 13 discharge. § 1328(g). Also, if a § 522(q) exemption limitation proceeding is pending, the chapter 13 discharge must be deferred until the exemption matter is resolved. § 1328(h).

As with discharges under chapters 7 and 11, a chapter 13 discharge may be revoked. Revocation is possible within one year after the discharge is granted. § 1328(e). A party in interest must prove that the discharge was obtained by the debtor's fraud and that the requesting party did not have pre-discharge knowledge of the fraud.

§ 10.39 The Discharge in Chapter 12

Most of what has been said with regard to the chapter 13 discharge applies with equal force to the discharge in chapter 12, which makes sense given that chapter 12 is modeled on chapter 13. The chapter 12 discharge section, § 1228, closely mirrors the chapter 13 discharge provision, § 1328. Examples of discharge rules in chapter 12 that follow chapter 13 principles include: discharge follows completion of payments under a three-to-five year plan, § 1228(a), § 1222(c); plan modification is possible, § 1229; domestic support obligations must be paid, § 1228(a); a hardship discharge may be available, § 1228(b); § 727(a) does not apply, § 103(b); written waiver of discharge is allowed, § 1228(a); debts provided for by the plan and disallowed debts are discharged, id.; long-term debts exceeding the life of the plan are not discharged, § 1228(a)(1); the time bar in a subsequent chapter 7 depends on the performance in the prior chapter 12, § 727(a)(9); the discharge may be delayed in a § 522(q) exemption limitation proceeding is pending, § 1228(f); and revocation is authorized for fraud, § 1230(a).

A few differences in the discharge between chapters 12 and 13 should be noted, however. Until 2005, the most significant was that all of the § 523(a) exceptions apply in chapter 12, even for a full-performance discharge. § 1228(a)(2), (c)(2). Congress is not trying to induce family farmers to go under chapter 12, as it is trying to steer individual consumers into chapter 13. Rather, chapter 12 was enacted as a temporary haven for farmers who had difficulty proceeding under chapter 11. The need for a broader discharge in chapter 12 thus does not exist. With the substantial amendment of the reach of the chapter 13 discharge in 2005, however, which made many of the § 523(a) exceptions nondischargeable even in a full-performance chapter 13 discharge, this difference has been largely eliminated.

Second, chapter 12 is not limited to individuals. A "family farmer" is an eligible debtor under § 109(f), and "family farmer" is defined in § 101(18)(B) to include a corporation or partnership. One statutory incongruity is that § 523(a) on its face is limited to individual debtors, but chapter 12 purports to apply § 523(a) fully, even though chapter 12 relief is available to corporations and partnerships as well as individuals. The resolution of this inconsistency is unclear.[320]

Another difference is that chapter 12 does not provide for the treatment of postpetition tax and necessary consumer claims, as does chapter 13. Administrative expenses and other § 507 priority claims are to be paid in full under the plan, § 1222(a)(2), and will be discharged.

Finally, the chapter 12 discharge is not conditioned on the debtor's completion of a course in personal financial management, as it is in chapter 13.

---

[320] Courts have held that corporate debtors in chapter 12 are precluded from obtaining a discharge of debts excepted under § 523(a). E.g., In re JRB Consol., Inc. 188 B.R. 373 (Bankr. W.D. Tex. 1995). See also In re Breezy Ridge Farms, Inc., 2009 WL 1514671 (Bankr. M.D. Ga. May 29, 2009).

Chapter 11

REORGANIZATION UNDER CHAPTER 11

A. INTRODUCTION

§ 11.1 Theory and Purposes of Reorganization

In both its original conception and in common parlance, "bankruptcy" connotes the idea of *liquidation* of the bankrupt debtor's present assets, and distribution of those assets to creditors on an equitable basis. Chapter 7 of the Code provides a statutory scheme for such a bankruptcy liquidation. However, while chapter 7 may be a fair and efficient means of liquidating and distributing the debtor's current assets, a bankruptcy liquidation may not always be the best approach to dealing with a debtor's financial distress. In some circumstances, a *reorganization* may be the better approach.

Chapter 11 is the general business reorganization chapter of the Code. The premise underlying chapter 11 is that everyone—creditors, the debtor, stockholders, employees, suppliers, the community—can benefit if a debtor's financial affairs are restructured at an acceptable cost. As the legislative history to the Code explained:

> The purpose of a business reorganization case, unlike a liquidation case, is to restructure a business's finances so that it may continue to operate, provide its employees with jobs, pay its creditors, and provide a return for its stockholders. The premise of a business reorganization is that assets that are used for production in the industry for which they were designed are more valuable than those same assets sold for scrap.[1]

In essence, chapter 11 is based on the idea "that a business is worth more alive than dead—i.e., it is worth more as a going concern than in a forced sale liquidation."[2] Liquidation has solely a present "balance sheet" focus—debts and assets. But the financial value and worth of a debtor should not always be judged by the balance sheet alone; a debtor's projected income statement should be considered as well.

If the debtor's projected earnings exceed expenses, it might not make sense to liquidate that debtor's assets. As long as the debtor can utilize its assets profitably, to produce positive net income, economically it could be more efficient for the debtor to *reorganize* its business, i.e., to retain its property and produce profits through continued business operation. The focus is on *current* income and expenses; if *past* debts are taken into account, the debtor still may have negative net earnings. But what is past is past; in deciding how to deploy the debtor's assets most efficiently, only future profitability should matter. If the debtor can utilize those assets to produce

---

[1]   H.R. Rep. No. 95–595, 95th Cong., 1st Sess., at 220 (1977).

[2]   See Charles J. Tabb, The Future of Chapter 11, 44 S.C. L. Rev. 791, 804 (1993); see also Lynn M. LoPucki & William C. Whitford, Corporate Governance in the Bankruptcy Reorganization of Large, Publicly Held Companies, 141 U. Pa. L. Rev. 669, 758 (1993).

positive earnings, creditors holding past debts can be paid out of those future earnings. Those creditors will benefit from a future payment plan if the present value of those payments equals or exceeds the amount that creditors would have received in an immediate liquidation. Of course, if the debtor is operating inefficiently, liquidation will be the most prudent course.

Reorganization, then, might offer an opportunity for a viable business to realize a "going concern" premium over liquidation value. Indeed, it is a condition of confirmation of a chapter 11 plan that unsecured creditors be paid at least as much as they would receive in a liquidation.[3] § 1129(a)(7)(A)(ii). Much of the negotiations that occur in chapter 11 are over how to *allocate* this premium between various stakeholders.

Opting for reorganization instead of liquidation may be a better solution for the debtor as well as for creditors. The debtor will be able to keep its property and its business, and this approach may preserve value for the residual owners. Individual debtors also are eligible for chapter 11 relief, and may benefit from it.[4] An individual debtor may opt for chapter 11 in order to keep more of her property, and also to maintain a better credit rating. However, with the increased debt ceilings for chapter 13 since 1994, and with chapter 13 generally more favorable to debtors than chapter 11, relatively few individual debtors are likely to file under chapter 11.[5] For example, in the 12–month period ending March 31, 2012, 396,175 cases were filed under chapter 13, while a mere 1,723 individual chapter 11 cases were filed.[6]

As mentioned, reorganization, rather than liquidation, also may benefit other constituencies beyond the debtor and the creditors. For example, employees of a business obviously have a strong interest in keeping their jobs, while suppliers want to keep a customer; the failure of a business inevitably has a negative ripple effect on those entities that did business with that debtor. More indirectly, the community in which the debtor operates may have an interest in keeping the business operating.[7]

In some cases it might be possible to obtain the benefits of a reorganization in a liquidation. As noted above, the basic premise underlying a reorganization is that the *going concern* value of the business exceeds the *liquidation* value, and reorganizing allows financially interested parties to capture that going concern premium. In theory,

---

[3]   See § 11.26.

[4]   Toibb v. Radloff, 501 U.S. 157 (1991).

[5]   Before 1994, a debtor was eligible to file for relief under chapter 13 only if she owed unsecured debts of no more than $100,000 and secured debts of no more than $350,000. Beginning in 1994, and as most recently indexed in 2013, those limits have been raised to $383,175 in unsecured debts and $1,149,525 in secured debts. § 109(e).

The 2005 amendments, which imported many of the negative (for individual debtors) aspects of chapter 13 into chapter 11, such as deferring the discharge and including postpetition property in the estate, make chapter 11 an even less appealing choice than before for individuals.

[6]   United States Courts Statistics, U.S. Bankruptcy Courts—Business and Nonbusiness Cases Commences, by Chapter of the Bankruptcy Code, During the 12–Month Period Ending March 31, 2012, http://www.uscourts.gov/uscourts/Statistics/BankruptcyStatistics/BankruptcyFilings/2012/0312_f2.pdf (last visited Jan. 14, 2013).

[7]   See Karen Gross, The Need to Take Community Interests Into Account in Bankruptcy: An Essay, 72 Wash. U. L. Rev. 1031 (1994).

however, the debtor's assets possibly could be *sold* intact to a third party purchaser for a price that reflects the going concern value of the asset package.

Chapter 11 does authorize the debtor's assets to be sold, in part or in their entirety. In other words, partial or total liquidations are permitted in chapter 11. § 1123(b)(4). Some commentators have even argued for a *mandatory* auction system in this context.[8] These reformers are concerned about the inefficiencies of chapter 11, and have greater faith in the markets. However, it is not obvious that markets would work more efficiently than chapter 11 in allowing the realization of the going concern surplus.

Critics (especially those associated with the "law and economics" camp) attacked chapter 11 in the 1980s and 1990s, suggesting that chapter 11 might do more harm than good, and proposed various solutions, ranging from reform to repeal.[9] Despite the

---

[8]   See Douglas G. Baird, Revisiting Auctions in Chapter 11, 36 J. L. & Econ. 633, 634 (1993) ("[W]hen large, publicly traded firms enter Chapter 11, they should be put on the auction block and sold to the highest bidder. A speedy sale separates the question of how to use the assets from the question of how rights to them will be allocated among creditors, shareholders, and others."); Douglas G. Baird, The Uneasy Case for Corporate Reorganizations, 15 J. Legal Stud. 127, 139–45 (1986) (discussing the sale of assets under chapter 11); Thomas H. Jackson, The Logic and Limits of Bankruptcy Law 218–24 (1986).

[9]   The halcyon era of the "whither reorganization?" debate was from 1986 (begun with Jackson's and Baird's 1986 works, see supra note 8) through 1993, with the "end game" of that round of commentary being the 1992 article by Michael Bradley & Michael Rosenzweig, The Untenable Case for Chapter 11, 101 Yale L.J. 1043 (1992), and the ensuing replies (see infra note 10).

A second round of debate, focused on the notion of "contract bankruptcy," was triggered in 1992 by the publication of Robert K. Rasmussen, Debtor's Choice: A Menu Approach to Corporate Bankruptcy, 71 Tex. L. Rev. 51 (1992), and ran through 1999, largely ending with a series of articles, replies, and surreplies in the Yale Law Journal by Alan Schwarz and Lynn LoPucki, cited below, and infra note 10.

Then, in 2003, Baird and Rasmussen questioned whether chapter 11 was even relevant anymore as a vehicle for effecting large corporate reorganizations. Douglas G. Baird & Robert K. Rasmussen, The End of Bankruptcy, 55 Stan. L. Rev. 751 (2002). LoPucki again responded. Lynn M. LoPucki, The Nature of the Bankrupt Firm: A Response to Baird and Rasmussen's *The End of Bankruptcy*, 56 Stan. L. Rev. 645 (2003).

In addition to the foregoing, notable critics, some of whom suggest drastic reforms or alternatives to chapter 11, include: Barry E. Adler, A Theory of Corporate Insolvency, 72 N.Y.U. L. Rev. 343 (1997); Barry E. Adler, A World Without Debt, 72 Wash. U. L. Q. 811 (1994); Barry E. Adler, Finance's Theoretical Divide and the Proper Role of Insolvency Rules, 68 S. Cal. L. Rev. 401 (1994); Barry E. Adler, Financial and Political Theories of American Corporate Bankruptcy, 45 Stan. L. Rev. 311 (1993); Barry E. Adler, Bankruptcy and Risk Allocation, 77 Cornell L. Rev. 439 (1992); Philippe Aghion et. al., The Economics of Bankruptcy Reform, J.L. Econ. & Org. 523 (1992); Baird, supra note 8, *Revisiting Auctions*; Baird, supra note 8, *Uneasy Case*; Lucian Arye Bebchuk, A New Approach to Corporate Reorganizations, 101 Harv. L. Rev. 775 (1988); James W. Bowers, Rehabilitation, Redistribution, or Dissipation: The Evidence for Choosing Among Bankruptcy Hypotheses, 72 Wash. U. L. Q. 955 (1994); James W. Bowers, The Fantastic Wisconsylvania Zero–Bureaucratic Cost School of Bankruptcy Theory: A Comment, 91 Mich. L. Rev. 1773 (1993); James W. Bowers, Groping and Coping in the Shadow of Murphy's Law: Bankruptcy Theory and the Elementary Economics of Failure, 88 Mich. L. Rev. 2097 (1990); Jackson, supra note 8, at 209–24; Thomas H. Jackson, Bankruptcy, Nonbankruptcy Entitlements and the Creditors' Bargain, 91 Yale L.J. 857 (1982); Robert K. Rasmussen & David A. Skeel, Jr., The Economic Analysis of Corporate Bankruptcy Law, 3 Am. Bankr. Inst. L. Rev. 85 (1995); Robert K. Rasmussen, The Ex Ante Effects of Bankruptcy Reform on Investment Incentives, 72 Wash. U. L. Q. 1159 (1994); Robert K. Rasmussen, The Efficiency of Chapter 11, 8 Bankr. Dev. J. 319 (1991); Mark J. Roe, Bankruptcy and Debt: A New Model for Corporate Reorganizations, 83 Colum. L. Rev. 527 (1983); Alan Schwartz, A Contract Theory Approach to Business Bankruptcy, 107 Yale L.J. 1807 (1998); Alan Schwartz, Contracting About Bankruptcy, 13 J. L. Econ. & Org. 127 (1997); Alan Schwartz, Bankruptcy Workouts and Debt Contracts, 36 J.L. & Econ. 595 (1993); Michelle J. White, Does Chapter 11 Save Economically Inefficient Firms? 72 Wash. U. L. Q. 1319 (1994).

critics, chapter 11 has had just as many devout defenders.[10] The academic furor now has largely subsided. While in some shape the debate probably will continue,[11] it is worth noting that, as of 2013, neither Congress nor the Supreme Court had ever endorsed any radical revisions to the basic shape of chapter 11 relief. Indeed, in recent years the most dramatic change in the reorganization landscape, especially evident in the aftermath of the 2008 economic debacle, has been the trend of large companies directly seeking bailouts from the federal government, in lieu of (or in addition to) seeking relief in the federal bankruptcy court.[12] Note that the American Bankruptcy Institute, through its Chapter 11 Commission, is studying and will propose potential reforms for chapter 11.[13] The Commission held five public meeting in 2012 to collect input from interested parties, in order to create a final report on the matter, with expected completion by April 2014.[14]

One of the main criticisms of chapter 11 is that it failed to achieve its stated goals at an acceptable cost,[15] although more recent empirical scholarship has questioned that assertion.[16] Another critique, noted above, is that the going concern premium could be reaped in a market sale, obviating the need to resort to the inefficient processes of a court-supervised reorganization.[17] Yet another criticism is that chapter 11 creates

---

[10]   See John D. Ayer, Through Chapter 11 With Gun or Camera, But Probably Not Both: A Field Guide, 72 Wash. U. L. Q. 883 (1994); John D. Ayer, Bankruptcy as an Essentially Contested Concept: The Case of the One–Asset Case, 44 S.C. L. Rev. 863 (1993); Jean Braucher, Bankruptcy Reorganization and Economic Development, 23 Cap. U. L. Rev. 499 (1994); David Gray Carlson, Bankruptcy Theory and the Creditors' Bargain, 61 U. Cin. L. Rev. 453 (1992); Hon. Frank H. Easterbrook, Is Corporate Bankruptcy Efficient?, 27 J. Fin. Econ. 411 (1990); Christopher W. Frost, Bankruptcy Redistributive Policies and the Limits of the Judicial Process, 74 N.C. L. Rev. 75 (1995); Donald R. Korobkin, The Unwarranted Case Against Corporate Reorganization: A Reply to Bradley and Rosenzweig, 78 Iowa L. Rev. 669 (1993); Donald R. Korobkin, Contractarianism and the Normative Foundations of Bankruptcy Law, 71 Tex. L. Rev. 541 (1993); Donald R. Korobkin, Rehabilitating Values: A Jurisprudence of Bankruptcy, 91 Colum. L. Rev. 717 (1991); Lynn M. LoPucki, Contract Bankruptcy: A Reply to Alan Schwartz, 109 Yale L.J. 317 (1999); Lynn LoPucki, Strange Visions in a Strange World: A Reply to Professors Bradley and Rosenzweig, 91 Mich. L. Rev. 79 (1992); Lawrence Ponoroff, Enlarging the Bargaining Table: Some Implications of the Corporate Stakeholder Model for Federal Bankruptcy Proceedings, 23 Cap. U. L. Rev. 441 (1994); Tabb, supra note 2; Elizabeth Warren & Jay Lawrence Westbrook, Contracting Out of Bankruptcy: An Empirical Intervention, 118 Harv. L. Rev. 1197 (2005); Elizabeth Warren, Bankruptcy Policymaking in an Imperfect World, 92 Mich. L. Rev. 336 (1993); Elizabeth Warren, The Untenable Case for the Repeal of Chapter 11, 102 Yale L.J. 437 (1992); Elizabeth Warren, Bankruptcy Policy, 54 U. Chi. L. Rev. 775 (1987); William C. Whitford, What's Right About Chapter 11, 72 Wash. U. L. Q. 1379 (1994).

[11]   A useful review of the debate and a critique of the earlier reform proposals is found in David A. Skeel, Jr., Markets, Courts, and the Brave New World of Bankruptcy Theory, 1993 Wis. L. Rev. 465. The "contract bankruptcy" debate is assessed in Steven L. Schwarcz, Rethinking Freedom of Contract: A Bankruptcy Paradigm, 77 Tex. L. Rev. 515 (1999). See also Susan Block–Lieb, The Logic and Limits of Contract Bankruptcy, 2001 U. Ill. L. Rev. 503.

[12]   For example, Chrysler, American Express, General Motors, Freddie Mac, Fannie Mae, are all among large companies that received a "bail-out" from the federal government. See Matthew Ericson, Elaine He & Amy Schoenfeld, Tracking the $700 Billion Bailout, N.Y. Times, http://www.nytimes.com/packages/html/national/200904_CREDITCRISIS/recipients.html (last visited June 2, 2013).

[13]   ABI Commission to Study the Reform of Chapter 11, http://commission.abi.org (last visited Jan. 14, 2013). See also Kenneth N. Klee & Richard Levin, Rethinking Chapter 11, 21 J. Bankr. L. & Prac. 5 Art. 1 (2012).

[14]   See Ch. 11 Commission Field Hearing at NCBJ, 31–JAN Am. Bankr. Inst. J. 10 (2013).

[15]   See Lawrence A. Weiss, Bankruptcy Resolution: Direct Costs and Violation of Priority of Claims, 27 J. Fin. Econ. 285 (1990).

[16]   See Stephen P. Ferris & Robert M. Lawless, The Expenses of Financial Distress: The Direct Costs of Chapter 11, 61 U. Pitt. L. Rev. 629 (2000).

[17]   See supra note 8 and accompanying text.

perverse incentives and encourages strategic risk-taking.[18] The redistributional tendencies of chapter 11 have been questioned.[19] Furthermore, some critics assert that "extraneous" interests (such as preserving jobs, aiding suppliers, and assisting communities) should not be taken into account, but that the only appropriate determinants of bankruptcy policy are value maximization and optimal asset deployment.[20] Finally, chapter 11 has been assailed as a weak "second-best" political compromise that should be replaced with a free market contract-based structure.[21]

Whatever the theoretical niceties, in the real world many financially troubled debtors try to restructure their debts, instead of just liquidating. Often this restructuring is accomplished outside of the bankruptcy court, in a workout agreement.[22] Perhaps the relevant question to ask is why a reorganization ever needs to take place under the protection of a court.[23]

However, consensual out-of-court workouts do not always work. One reason is that dissenting creditors cannot be bound to the restructuring agreement. A dissenter is free to invoke its state law collection remedies against the debtor, such as levying against the debtor's assets. These actions might make it difficult for the debtor to continue in business. A "holdout problem" then arises: even if a workout would be better for the creditors as a group, the holdout dissenting creditor can "extort" more than its fair share from the debtor by threatening to undermine the whole reorganization.

Chapter 11 solves the holdout problem. The first necessary component of the solution is to enjoin dissenting creditors from exercising their state law collection remedies against the debtor. The second element is to bind the dissenters to the terms of the restructuring agreement. Some type of court process is needed to implement these two remedies. The original mechanism used was the equity receivership.[24] Today, chapter 11 does the job. A reorganization under chapter 11 enjoys the benefits of both a stay provision, § 362, and a rule binding dissenters to the terms of the plan agreed to by the necessary majority of creditors. § 1141(a).

§ 11.2 Historical Antecedents

Chapter 11 has three parents: chapter X, chapter XI, and chapter XII. These three chapters, offering different forms of reorganization relief, were enacted as part of the

---

[18] See John D. Ayer, Goodbye to Chapter 11: The End of Business Bankruptcy as We Know It, 5 Norton Bankr. L. Adviser 2 (2001).

[19] See Bruce A. Markell, Clueless on Classification: Toward Removing Artifical Limits on Chapter 11 Claim Classification, 11 Bankr. Dev. J. 1 (1995).

[20] For a discussion on these competing views, see Christopher W. Frost, The Theory, Reality and Pragmatism of Corporate Governance in Bankruptcy Reorganizations, 72 Am. Bankr. L.J. 103 (1998).

[21] See generally Robert J Keach & Albert Togut, Commission to Explore Overhauling Chapter 11, 30–JUN Am. Bankr. Inst. J. 36 (2011).

[22] See § 1.4; Stuart C. Gilson et al., Troubled Debt Restructurings: An Empirical Study of Private Reorganization of Firms in Default, 27 J. Fin. Econ. 315 (1990).

[23] For a fuller discussion, see Tabb, supra note 2, at 804–07.

[24] See David A. Skeel, Jr., Debt's Dominion: A History of Bankruptcy Law in America 56–60 (2001); see also Garrard Glenn, The Basis of the Federal Receivership, 25 Colum. L. Rev. 434 (1925); Oliver H. Bassuener, Bankruptcy—Reorganizations—Equity Receiverships, 20 Marq. L. Rev. 156 (1936).

Chandler Act of 1938.[25] One of the most significant decisions Congress made in 1978 was to merge the three business reorganization chapters into a single chapter, chapter 11.[26]

Chapter X was intended to provide for the reorganization of large public companies. Enacted against a backdrop of perceived abuse of public creditors and investors under then-current reorganization laws, chapter X's overriding theme and purpose was paternalistic protection. The net result was an extremely cumbersome and expensive procedure. Some of the most salient features of chapter X were:

- The judge had to approve the petition, if satisfied that it complied with the chapter's requirements and was filed in good faith. Bankruptcy Act § 141.

- An independent trustee was appointed in every case, and management of the debtor was ousted. The only exception was if debts were less than $250,000. Bankruptcy Act § 156.

- Any party in interest could file a plan. Bankruptcy Act § 169.

- The court had to approve the plan after a formal hearing, *before* the plan could be submitted to creditors and stockholders for a vote. Bankruptcy Act §§ 169, 174.

- After the approval hearing, and before the court approved the plan, the Securities and Exchange Commission prepared and filed an "advisory" report on the plan. Bankruptcy Act § 172.

- The plan could only be confirmed if it was "fair and equitable." Bankruptcy Act § 221(2). The "fair and equitable" test was a term of art meaning that the plan satisfied the "absolute priority" rule. The absolute priority rule required full payment (but no more than full payment) of senior creditors before anything could be paid to junior creditors, and full payment (but no more) to junior creditors before anything could go to equity. In practice, to determine if the plan complied with the "fair and equitable" test, the court had to value the reorganized business.[27]

Chapter XI offered none of the laborious protections of chapter X, but at the same time did not offer as much relief.[28] Titled "Arrangements," the supposed purpose of chapter XI was to permit a smaller business to compose its *unsecured* trade debts. The definition of an "arrangement" spoke in terms of a "plan of a debtor for the settlement, satisfaction, or extension of the time of payment of his unsecured debts." Bankruptcy Act § 306(1). The definitions of "creditors" and of "debts" referred only to unsecured debts. Bankruptcy Act § 307(1), (2). The plan under chapter XI could not affect secured

---

25   Ch. 575, 52 Stat. 840 (1938).

26   H.R. Rep. No. 95–595, 95th Cong., 1st Sess., at 223 (1977).

27   See § 11.31.

28   See H.R. Rep. No. 95–595, 95th Cong., 1st Sess., at 225–26 (citing to relevant sections of the Bankruptcy Act, stating chapter XI plans were restricted in relief and did not permit adjustment of secured debt or of equity).

debts or equity; the arrangement could only modify or alter the rights of unsecured creditors. Bankruptcy Act § 356.

So why did over 90% of all business debtors choose to proceed under chapter XI instead of chapter X?[29] In contrast to the unfavorable provisions of chapter X, chapter XI provided that:

- The debtor presumptively was continued as debtor in possession, Bankruptcy Act § 342, Rule 11–18(b); a receiver or trustee was only appointed if the need for one was established.

- The debtor had the exclusive right to file a plan as long as its chapter XI case was pending. Bankruptcy Act § 323, Rule 11–36.

- The plan of arrangement did *not* have to comply with the absolute priority rule; instead, it only had to be in the "best interests of creditors," Bankruptcy Act § 366(2), meaning that unsecured creditors would receive liquidation value under the plan. This meant that the debtor could retain the entire going concern surplus over liquidation value for itself.

In a nutshell, then, under chapter XI the debtor could (i) retain control of the business and the plan, (ii) capture the going concern surplus to the exclusion of creditors, and (iii) do it all much more quickly and inexpensively. They just could not modify secured claims and equity. In addition to these features, there was a growing appreciation by professionals that in chapter XI cases, bankruptcy courts might "liberally construe the bankruptcy law beyond its original intent," in the debtor's favor.[30] Little wonder, then, that even large public companies such as W.T. Grant sought relief under chapter XI instead of chapter X. Conversion from XI to X could be ordered, but even public corporations were not excluded automatically from chapter XI. According to the Supreme Court, the test for which chapter should be used turned on a nebulous "needs to be served" standard.[31]

Chapter XII, titled "Real Property Arrangements by Persons other than Corporations," was a peculiar vehicle designed for individuals or other noncorporate entities to deal with encumbered real estate. In form it was modeled after chapter XI, but the primary purpose of the plan was to alter or modify "debts secured by real property." Bankruptcy Act § 406(1). Chapter XII was enacted initially to accommodate a unique method of real estate financing in Chicago, Illinois.[32]

---

[29] H.R. Rep. No. 95–595, 95th Cong., 1st Sess., at 222 (1977).

[30] Harvey R. Miller, Bankruptcy and Reorganization Through the Looking Glass of 50 Years (1960–2010), 19 J. Bankr. L. & Prac. 3 Art. 1 (2010) (listing the perceived advantages as bankruptcy courts construing the law to "(a) enjoin secured creditors from exercising remedial rights for extended periods of time; (b) enjoin all unsecured creditors and others from taking any actions against the debtor and its property [ ]; (c) construe rejection and assumption of executory contracts, including collective bargaining agreements and unexpired leases to favor debtors in possession or trustees, and (d) allow dilution of equity interests").

[31] Gen. Stores Corp. v. Shlensky, 350 U.S. 462, 466 (1956) ("The essential difference is not between the small company and the large company but between the needs to be served.").

[32] H.R. Rep. No. 95–595, 95th Cong., 1st Sess. 223–24 (1977).

In the 1978 Bankruptcy Code, Congress decided to merge the three chapters, concluding that any justification for separate chapters had disappeared.[33] The goal in crafting the single reorganization chapter was to "adopt[ ] much of the flexibility of chapter XI of current law, and incorporate[ ] the essence of the public protection features of current chapter X."[34] As things stood when the current Bankruptcy Code was enacted, Congress observed that "chapter X has become an unworkable procedure, and chapter XI is inadequate to fill the void."[35] As will be discussed in subsequent sections, the single chapter 11 sought to take the middle ground between chapters X and XI, although favoring the flexibility of chapter XI, by including provisions such as:

- The debtor is presumptively continued as debtor in possession, §§ 1101(1), 1107(a), but may be replaced by a trustee for cause. § 1104(a).[36]

- The debtor is given the exclusive right to file the plan for an initial period of time, but not forever. § 1121.[37]

- The court does not have to preapprove the plan, and the role of the SEC is greatly reduced.[38]

- The best interests liquidation test of chapter XI must always be satisfied, § 1129(a)(7),[39] but the absolute priority rule of chapter X is triggered only if a class votes against the plan, § 1129(b).[40] This compromise permits creditors and equity holders to bargain over the allocation of reorganization value.

- The interests of creditors and equity security holders are protected by (i) committee representation, §§ 1102, 1103;[41] (ii) the right to vote, § 1126;[42] (iii) limits on classification, § 1122, 1123(a);[43] and (iv) the right to receive an approved disclosure statement before voting. § 1125.[44]

Chapters X, XI, and XII were not the first reorganization provisions of the bankruptcy law. Composition agreements were introduced as early as 1874.[45] The 1874 law permitted the debtor to retain his property and to propose a plan that would pay creditors a stated percentage of the debts over time. If accepted by a majority in number and three-fourths in value of the creditors, the plan could be confirmed and would bind all creditors, even those who voted against the plan. This composition law died with the rest of the Bankruptcy Act when it was repealed in 1878.

---

[33] Id. at 223.

[34] Id. at 224.

[35] Id. at 223.

[36] See §§ 11.4, 11.6.

[37] See § 11.15.

[38] See § 11.9.

[39] See § 11.26.

[40] See §§ 11.30–11.34.

[41] See § 11.8.

[42] See § 11.21.

[43] See § 11.17.

[44] See § 11.20.

[45] Ch. 390, § 17, 18 Stat. 182–84 (1874).

A similar composition provision was included in § 12 of the Bankruptcy Act of 1898, which required a majority of creditors in number and value to accept the plan, and that the plan was in the best interests of creditors (the liquidation test), before a court could confirm it.[46] Confirmation of a composition agreement discharged a debtor from his debts, other than those debts a debtor failed to pay pursuant to the composition agreement. Bankruptcy Act § 14c.

During the Great Depression of the 1930s, several reorganization provisions were enacted by Congress before the adoption of chapters X, XI, and XII in 1938.[47] First, in 1933 Congress made compositions more widely available in § 74.[48] The same law authorized agricultural compositions[49] and railroad reorganizations.[50] The very next year, corporate reorganizations were authorized in § 77B.[51] A municipal reorganization law also was passed in 1934.[52] While the Supreme Court overturned this first municipal reorganization law,[53] a second such law, passed in 1937,[54] was upheld by the Court.[55] Congress sought to help farmers keep their farms in the Frazier–Lemke Act of 1934,[56] but the Supreme Court held that act unconstitutional in 1935.[57] A revised version was enacted in just a few weeks,[58] which the Court then upheld.[59] Both the railroad reorganization provision, § 77, and the corporate reorganization section, § 77B, were amended in the same long summer of 1935.[60] The Supreme Court upheld the constitutionality of the railroad reorganization law in a critical decision.[61] In the Chandler Act of 1938, Congress split the corporate reorganization law into the tripartite scheme of chapters X, XI, and XII, a schism that was to be healed 40 years later.

A review of the historical treatment of the reorganization laws, and an appreciation of the roots of some modern provisions of chapter 11, also must take into account the heritage of the federal equity receiverships of the late nineteenth and early twentieth centuries.[62] Equity receiverships were used as a means of keeping the

---

[46] Ch. 541, § 12, 30 Stat. 544, 549 (1898).

[47] For discussion, see Charles Jordan Tabb, The History of the Bankruptcy Laws in the United States, 3 Am. Bankr. Inst. L. Rev. 5, 28 (1995). See also David A. Skeel, Jr., Debt's Dominion: A History of Bankruptcy Law in America, pt. 2, "The Great Depression and New Deal," 73–127 (2001).

[48] Act of March 3, 1933, ch. 204, 47 Stat. 1467.

[49] Id., 47 Stat. at 1470–74 (§ 75).

[50] Id., 47 Stat. at 1474–82 (§ 77).

[51] Act of June 7, 1934, ch. 424, 48 Stat. 911.

[52] Act of May 24, 1934, ch. 345, 48 Stat. 798 (chapter IX).

[53] Ashton v. Cameron Cnty. Water Improvement Dist. No. 1, 298 U.S. 513 (1936).

[54] Act of Aug. 16, 1937, ch. 657, 50 Stat. 653.

[55] United States v. Bekins, 304 U.S. 27 (1938).

[56] Ch. 869, 48 Stat. 1289 (1934) (amending § 75).

[57] Louisville Joint Stock Land Bank v. Radford, 295 U.S. 555 (1935).

[58] Act of Aug. 28, 1935, ch. 792, 49 Stat. 942.

[59] Wright v. Vinton Branch, 300 U.S. 440 (1937).

[60] Act of Aug. 27, 1935, ch. 774, 49 Stat. 911 (amending § 77); Act of Aug. 19, 1935, ch. 809, 49 Stat. 965 (amending § 77B).

[61] Cont'l Illinois Nat'l Bank & Trust Co. v. Chicago, Rock I. & P. Ry., 294 U.S. 648 (1935).

[62] For discussion, see Tabb, supra note 47, at 21–23; see also Skeel, supra note 47, ch. 2, "Railroad Receivership and the Elite Reorganization Bar," 48–70.

railroads running, and were extended to provide for corporate reorganization prior to the enactment of § 77B in 1934.[63]

A receivership normally was commenced by a creditor's petition to the federal court to exercise its equity jurisdiction and appoint a receiver to assume control of the debtor corporation's assets. The receiver would take title to the assets, halting creditor collection efforts. Furthermore, the receiver had the power to continue operating the debtor's business while searching for a buyer of the assets, thus preserving the ability to obtain going concern value for the assets. Creditors were paid out of the proceeds of the receiver's foreclosure sale of the assets.

Eventually insiders came to dominate receiverships, and abuses became pervasive.[64] Exorbitant fees were paid to professionals, many of whom were cronies of the debtor's managers. Old management would effectively retain control of the debtor by purchasing the debtor's assets through the guise of a "protective committee" which the insiders dominated. Several judicial doctrines were developed to limit such abuses. The most important for modern purposes was the "absolute priority" rule, which precluded old shareholders from retaining any interest in the debtor unless all creditors were paid in full.[65] This requirement that the transaction be "fair and equitable" was carried over in chapter X in 1938, and is incorporated in current chapter 11 if a class of unsecured creditors or equity holders does not accept the plan.[66] § 1129(b).

§ 11.3 Planning: Weighing the Chapter 11 Alternative

Filing for relief under chapter 11 has become a business-planning tool of choice for many business debtors. But why? What are the merits and demerits of filing under chapter 11? To answer that question, one must compare chapter 11 with the alternatives a financially troubled debtor faces. Those alternatives include: (1) do nothing formal; (2) attempt an out-of-court workout; (3) liquidate; or (4) file for relief under another chapter of the Bankruptcy Code.

Chapter 11 versus "doing nothing"

Sometimes the best step to take is none at all. While chapter 11 can provide meaningful relief to many debtors, it poses risks and costs as well. A debtor might be able to avoid filing by persuading its most persistent creditors to hold off in collection efforts while the debtor restructures its business outside of court, sells off unprofitable divisions, refocuses marketing efforts, or the like. If enough creditors can be convinced to stay their hand, if the debtor's business problems are fixable, and if major debt restructuring is not required, doing nothing formal might work.

---

[63] See Garrard Glenn, The Basis of the Federal Receivership, 25 Colum. L. Rev. 434 (1925).

[64] See Jacob Trieber, The Abuses of Receiverships, 19 Yale L.J. 275 (1910).

[65] See N. Pacific Ry. Co. v. Boyd, 228 U.S. 482 (1913).

[66] See §§ 11.30–11.34.

Chapter 11 versus an out-of-court workout

By the time a debtor gets to the threshold of actively considering chapter 11, the "do nothing" option usually will have been thoroughly exhausted. More drastic measures probably are necessary. Assuming that the debtor wants to continue business operations rather than liquidate, but needs to restructure its debts in order to survive both in the short term and the long term, the debtor has two primary choices: reorganize under the supervision of a court in chapter 11, or attempt an out-of-court workout. Studies have shown that about half of the major business debt reorganizations are accomplished out of court, and about half in court. What are the pros and cons of each?

The primary benefits of chapter 11 over an out-of-court workout are:

- Automatic stay of all creditor collection efforts is in place while a debtor is reorganizing, and until the debtor emerges from bankruptcy. § 362. This prevents creditors from upsetting the applecart by levying on the debtor's assets during the restructuring.

- Dissenting creditors are bound to the terms of a confirmed plan.[67] § 1141(a). This rule overcomes the "holdout" problem that plagues out-of-court workouts.

- Plan may be confirmed over objection of an entire class. § 1129(b). This power is known as "cram down."[68]

- Payment of current interest is suspended during case. § 502(b)(2). Not having to pay interest during the pendency of the case gives the chapter 11 debtor a significant competitive advantage.[69]

- Unwanted contracts can be rejected or assigned. § 365(a).[70] The debtor's rejection power even extends to collective bargaining agreements.[71] § 1113.

- Financing can be obtained on favorable terms, and prior liens can be subordinated.[72] § 364.

- Avoiding powers of the trustee[73] can be exercised by the debtor acting as debtor in possession. § 1107(a). For example, a debtor in possession may set aside unperfected liens, § 544(a), and also avoid and recover preferential transfers. §§ 547, 550.

---

[67] See § 11.35.

[68] See §§ 11.30–11.34.

[69] See Charles J. Tabb, The Future of Chapter 11, 44 S.C. L. Rev. 791, 837–38 (1993).

[70] One study sampling large, public company filings between 1991 and 2004 showed that firms with relatively high levels of leased assets were more likely to file for chapter 11 than restructure out of court, suggesting the ability to reject leases incentivized decisions to file. Yung–Yu Ma & Elizabeth Tashijan, Executory Contracts and Chapter 11 Restructuring Incentives (Working Paper, Nov. 1, 2012), available at http://ssrn.com/abstract=2170132.

[71] See §§ 8.11–8.12.

[72] See § 11.10.

[73] See § 6.2.

- Debtor's management retains control (at least initially).[74] The debtor will be continued as debtor in possession,[75] §§ 1101(1), 1107(a), and will be permitted to use, sell, or lease property of the estate in the ordinary course of business without court oversight.[76] § 363(c)(1). However, transactions out of the ordinary course require bankruptcy court approval, whereas such a limitation would not constrain a workout (although creditors may ask for similar oversight privileges). § 363(b). The bankruptcy court will give substantial deference to the business judgment of the debtor's management.[77]

- Property may be sold free and clear of liens and interests, either outside of the plan or pursuant to the plan.[78] §§ 363(f), 1123(a)(5)(D).

- An acceleration can be reversed, defaults cured, and the original terms of an obligation reinstated.[79] § 1124(2).

- Debtor retains the exclusive right to propose a plan for a limited period of time.[80] § 1121.

- Dramatic restructuring may be effected through the plan. The scope of relief possible in a plan is extremely broad, including sales of assets, corporate mergers, the issuance of stock, modification of claims or curing of defaults, and so forth.[81] § 1123(a)(5).

- Confirmation of plan discharges pre-bankruptcy obligations (except for individual debtors). § 1141(d).

- Centralized venue and supervision by an experienced bankruptcy judge who is likely to have marked "pro-debtor" tendencies.

---

[74]   See, e.g., In re Bayou Grp., L.L.C., 363 B.R. 674, 686 (S.D.N.Y. 2007), aff'd, 564 F.3d 541 (2d Cir. 2009) ("The management of a bankrupt entity that filed in Chapter 11 is automatically authorized to act as the debtor-in-possession, since under the Bankruptcy Code, the term "debtor-in-possession" quite simply "means debtor." (citing 11 U.S.C. § 1101(1))).

[75]   See § 11.4.

[76]   See §§ 5.16–5.18, 11.13.

[77]   See, e.g., In re Spansion, Inc., 426 B.R. 114, 141 (Bankr. D. Del. 2010) ("Absent some demonstrable impropriety in the confirmation process, it is not for the Court to supplant the Debtor's business judgment with its own."); In re Taub, 427 B.R. 208, 225 (Bankr. E.D.N.Y. 2010) ("A debtor-in-possession should be permitted to operate within the broad parameters of sound business judgment, and the debtor-in-possession's performance should not be assessed solely with the benefit of hindsight.").

[78]   In certain circumstances, a § 363 sale may also shield an asset-buyer from any successor liability that might otherwise arise. See, e.g., In re Grumman Olson Indus., Inc., 467 B.R. 694, 703 (S.D.N.Y. 2012) ("Section 363(f) can be used to sell property free and clear of claims that could otherwise be assertable against the buyer of the assets under the common law doctrine of successor liability.").

[79]   See § 11.18.

[80]   See § 11.15.

[81]   See § 11.16.

- The foregoing benefits might be realized expeditiously through a "prepackaged" plan, in which acceptances of the plan are solicited prior to bankruptcy, and then used to confirm a chapter 11 plan.[82] § 1126(b).

With so many factors pointing to the benefits of chapter 11, one can readily see why so many debtors have taken that route. Before jumping in with both feet, however, debtors should weigh the potential downsides of filing chapter 11, and the relative benefits of attempting an out-of-court workout:

- Workout is likely to cost less. In chapter 11, a plan must provide full payment for administrative expenses. §§ 1129(a)(9), 507(a)(2), 503(b). These include professional fees for the debtor *and* all official committees. §§ 327, 330, 1103. The United States trustee's fee also must be paid. 28 U.S.C. § 1930(a)(6). In large cases, administrative expenses may run into the millions of dollars. By engaging in a workout rather than filing chapter 11, professional fees will be reduced due to avoided reporting requirements and extraneous litigation that otherwise accompanies a chapter 11.

- Workout is likely to take less time. Even though chapter 11 is more streamlined than old chapter X,[83] it still can be a relatively cumbersome procedure compared to an out-of-court workout.[84]

- The "hassle" factor is much higher in chapter 11. A chapter 11 debtor must: file voluminous schedules and statements of financial affairs at the outset of the case; be subjected to an examination at an initial meeting of creditors, § 341, and potentially at examinations under Rule 2004; file numerous reports with the United States trustee's office every month; and obtain court approval for many types of business transactions, § 363(b), as well as for most forms of legal relief sought.

- Filing chapter 11 may trigger hostile reactions from trade creditors, banks, labor unions, or other interested parties. A bankruptcy filing, and the negative publicity and fear that follow, could hurt the debtor's business prospects and scare away customers.

- The court must approve the plan as "feasible," even if all classes of creditors and equity holders approve the plan.[85] § 1129(a)(11). Thus, a workout may offer parties more freedom to negotiate.

- The debtor's management risks losing control in chapter 11. Against the debtor's wishes, any of the following scenarios are possible, although none are mandatory: (1) case might be converted to chapter 7, § 1112(b); (2) trustee could

---

[82] See § 11.23.

[83] See § 11.2.

[84] For example, an out-of-court workout avoids the need to obtain court approval for various conduct, as required in chapter 11. See 11 U.S.C. §§ 363, 364, 1125(b), 1129; Fed. R. Bankr. P. 2002, 3017, 3018.

[85] See § 11.28.

be appointed and debtor's management ousted, § 1104(a);[86] (3) hostile plan could be filed, § 1121(c), and confirmed; (4) takeover could be effected through purchase of claims; or (5) equity interests could be forfeited through application of absolute priority rule in cram down, § 1129(b).

Chapter 11 versus liquidation

Preliminarily, a common misconception needs to be put to rest: a debtor is *not* required to reorganize in chapter 11. Liquidation *is* permitted in chapter 11. § 1123(a)(5)(D). A debtor might choose to liquidate in chapter 11 in order to retain control over the liquidation process. For example, Lehman Brothers, the largest bankruptcy case ever filed (in 2008), filed chapter 11 with the purpose of liquidation, not reorganization. Assuming, though, that the choice is reorganization versus liquidation, what factors should influence a debtor's selection?

If the debtor is solvent, even on a liquidation valuation, so that the residual ownership interests of equity retain some value, but the debtor's business prospects are not favorable, the debtor might consider cashing out up front so that it can realize that value. Otherwise, a prolonged and unsuccessful attempt at reorganization under chapter 11 could dissipate the residual value of the company. For example, the Eastern Airlines debacle, in which hundreds of millions of dollars in value were frittered away in chapter 11, is a leading case in point, demonstrating that even chapter 11 cannot salvage a business that is not operationally viable.

Chapter 11 versus chapter 12 or chapter 13

Some debtors will be eligible for relief under both chapter 11 and chapter 12, or both chapter 11 and chapter 13. For debtors of substantial size, the debt limits in chapter 13[87] and chapter 12[88] will preclude relief under those chapters. However, assuming the debtor is eligible, and wants to reorganize, it then must decide which chapter to use. In the vast majority of cases, debtors will prefer either chapter 12 or 13 to chapter 11.[89] Those chapters are much more streamlined and impose fewer burdens on the debtor, allow only the debtor to file a plan, do not allow creditors to vote, and do not have the absolute priority rule. Chapter 13 also offers debtors a broader discharge. § 1328(a).

Chapter 11 may be preferable in some situations, although for individual debtors many of these advantages were taken away in 2005. First, consider the advantages prior to 2005. Unlike chapters 12 and 13, the discharge in chapter 11 was not deferred until the completion of the plan, but was entered upon confirmation of the plan. § 1141(d)(1). Furthermore, chapter 11 did not require debtors to commit all projected disposable income to the plan for three to five years, as do chapters 12 (§ 1225(b)) and 13 (§ 1325(b)). Although the debtor retains his property, a trustee is appointed and

---

[86]   See § 11.6.

[87]   A debtor is only eligible for chapter 13 relief if she has noncontingent, liquidated unsecured debts of no more than $383,175 and secured debts of no more than $1,149,525. § 109(e).

[88]   The debt limit in chapter 12 is $4,031,575 in the aggregate. § 101(18).

[89]   See § 12.3 (chapter 13 compared to chapter 11), § 13.2 (chapter 12 compared to chapter 11).

oversees the debtor in every case under chapter 12 or chapter 13. §§ 1202(a), 1302(a). Conversely, in chapter 11, a trustee is appointed only in rare situations. § 1104(a). The debtor must move much more rapidly to file and obtain confirmation of her plan in chapter 12 or 13, and in chapter 13 must even start paying on the plan prior to confirmation. § 1326(a)(1). Modification of the plan after confirmation may be ordered by the court on the request of a party other than the debtor in chapters 12 or 13, §§ 1229(a), 1329(a), but not in chapter 11. § 1127. Finally, chapter 11 enables a debtor to effect a much more comprehensive restructuring than in chapter 12 or 13. § 1123(a)(5).

In 2005, Congress changed several of the foregoing rules for *individual debtors* to bring chapter 11 more into line with chapter 13, thus reducing the chapter 11 advantage. However, the benefits of chapter 11 versus chapter 12, as discussed above, still apply for corporate or partnership debtors.

The first 2005 change that was prejudicial to individual debtors in chapter 11 concerned postpetition property. Prior to 2005, an individual debtor in chapter 11 could retain for himself property acquired postpetition, including all earnings arising from postpetition services, whereas in chapter 13 such property would come into the estate. § 1306(a). In 2005, however, Congress added § 1115, which essentially copies the chapter 13 rule, bringing all postpetition property into the estate in an individual chapter 11, including earnings from services performed by the individual debtor. § 1115(a).

A second 2005 change that eliminated a chapter 11 advantage over chapter 13 for individuals concerns the discharge rule. Prior to 2005, all chapter 11 debtors received a discharge upon confirmation of the plan, whereas in chapter 13, discharge is deferred until the debtor completed performance under the plan. § 1328(a). In 2005, the rule was amended for individual chapter 11 debtors, who now receive a discharge only upon completion of plan performance, just as in chapter 13, rather than upon confirmation. § 1141(d)(5).

A third change regards the "projected disposable income" test for confirmation. Until 2005, as noted, a chapter 13 debtor had to commit all of his projected disposable income to plan payments in certain circumstances, § 1325(b), whereas an individual debtor in chapter 11 faced no such requirement for confirmation. The 2005 amendments also took away this chapter 11 advantage, adding a projected disposable income test to chapter 11 for individual debtors. § 1129(a)(15). Under this test, if the holder of an allowed unsecured claim objects to confirmation, either: (1) the plan must provide for their payment in full, i.e., the value of the claim as of the effective date of the plan of property to be distributed on account of the claim cannot be less than the amount of such claim; or (2) the value of property to be distributed under the plan is not less than the projected "disposable income" of the debtor (defined in § 1325(b)(2)) to be received during the five-year period beginning the date the first payment is made, or during the period provided by the plan, whichever is longer.

Fourth, the 2005 amendments also altered the plan modification rules for individual debtors, to bring those rules more in line with chapter 13 practice. Now, an individual debtor's plan may be modified at the request of any party in interest, at any time after confirmation, whether or not the plan has been substantially consummated, as long as all payments have not been completed. § 1127(e). The plan may be modified to increase or reduce the amount of payments, extend or reduce the time period for payments, or alter the amount of distribution to a creditor. § 1127(e).

B. CONTROL AND MANAGEMENT OF THE REORGANIZATION CASE

§ 11.4 Two Hats: Debtor and Debtor in Possession

The leading character in the chapter 11 drama is the *"debtor in possession."* The debtor in possession, commonly known as the DIP, is a hybrid creature. The debtor in possession is defined as "debtor except when a person that has qualified under section 322 of this title is serving as trustee in the case." § 1101(1). In plain English, that means that the DIP *is* the chapter 11 debtor (and *vice versa*), but *also* must perform the duties of the bankruptcy trustee. Upon the filing of a chapter 11 case, the debtor schizophrenically assumes two roles. The first is as debtor-*qua*-debtor; the second is as debtor-*qua*-trustee.[90] The debtor is itself, obviously, and is also the fiduciary representative of the bankruptcy estate.[91] All duties, rights and powers of the trustee (except investigating the debtor!) are to be exercised by the debtor as the DIP.[92] § 1107(a). The debtor ceases to be DIP only in the relatively rare event that an independent trustee is appointed under § 1104(a).[93] One of the critical policy decisions that Congress made in the 1978 Code was to leave the debtor in possession as the norm.[94] In doing so, Congress adopted the approach of old chapter XI and rejected the requirement of an independent trustee imposed by old chapter X.[95]

In its dual status as debtor and DIP, the debtor must carry out at least three distinct functions: (1) operate the business; (2) administer the estate; and (3) seek to confirm a plan.

First, the debtor will continue to run the business. A central premise of chapter 11 is to permit financially interested parties to capture the going concern value of the debtor's business; therefore, that value must be preserved before it can be parceled out to creditors and equity holders. In chapter 11, continued operation of the debtor's business is the norm. § 1108.[96] No court order is needed to authorize business operation; if a party in interest wants to curtail the debtor's power to continue the business, that party bears the burden of going into court and requesting the court to

---

[90]   The ramifications of the debtor's dual role are explored in Daniel B. Bogart, Liability of Directors of Chapter 11 Debtors in Possession: "Don't Look Back–Something May be Gaining on You," 68 Am. Bankr. L.J. 155 (1994).

[91]   See, e.g., In re Reliant Energy Channnelview LP, 594 F.3d 200, 210 (3d Cir. 2010) ("[D]ebtors-in-possession have a fiduciary duty to maximize the value of the estate. . . . "); In re Grasso, 490 B.R. 500 (Bankr. E.D. Pa. 2013) (discussing the debtor's violation of his fiduciary obligations as a DIP).

[92]   See S. Rep. No. 95–989, 95th Cong., 2d Sess., at 116 (1978); H.R. Rep. No. 95–595, 95th Cong., 1st Sess., at 404 (1977).

[93]   See § 11.6.

[94]   H.R. Rep. No. 95–595, 95th Cong., 1st Sess., at 232–34 (1977).

[95]   See § 11.2.

[96]   Note that § 1108 permits DIPs to continue operations, and also allows them to modify or cease operations if appropriate under the circumstances. See, e.g., In re Saint Vincents Catholic Med. Ctrs. of New York, 429 B.R. 139, 151 (Bankr. S.D.N.Y. 2010).

impose limits. § 1108. Nor will the debtor in its capacity as business operator need court authority to engage in transactions in the ordinary course of business. § 363(c)(1). Again, a party in interest must obtain a court order to restrain the debtor from entering into ordinary course business transactions. And obtaining such an order will not be easy; the court will give substantial deference to the debtor's business judgment.[97] Only if the complainant can show clear mismanagement, a significant risk of injury to creditors, or abuse of discretion will the court enter a limiting order. Thus, the debtor will be able to continue flying planes, or selling violas, or servicing computers—whatever its business entails.

The debtor also may enter into transactions out of the ordinary course, but only after notice and a hearing. § 363(b). This does not necessarily mean that an actual hearing will be held, but only that notice of the proposed action will be sent to interested parties, who then will have an opportunity to object. If no objection is timely filed, the court may go ahead and approve the requested action without holding a formal evidentiary hearing. § 102(1). The power to make non-ordinary business decisions can be crucial to the debtor's reorganization attempt. Not only may the debtor need to modify its legal obligations through the chapter 11 plan, but the debtor may need to restructure its business operations as well. All of the debt revision in the world will not save the debtor if the underlying business is not made healthy. Perhaps an unprofitable division needs to be sold, or a product line refocused, or a labor agreement renegotiated, or layoffs made. Whatever needs to be done to the business can be done while under court supervision in chapter 11.

As the DIP, the debtor carries out the functions of a trustee. § 1107(a). The trustee is the fiduciary officer of the estate who is charged with primary responsibility for performing the *administrative* tasks relating to the case. § 1106(a). Thus, the DIP must keep accounts of all property, file reports, examine proofs of claims and object to ones it believes are improper, file tax returns, and respond to requests for information. §§ 704, 1106(a), 1107(a). The DIP is the representative of the estate, with the power to sue and be sued. § 323. Furthermore, the DIP as the "trustee" has primary standing to bring avoidance actions, such as contest preferential transfers (§ 547), set aside unperfected liens (§ 544(a)), and challenge fraudulent transfers (§§ 544(b), 548). In carrying out its administrative responsibilities, which is the *second* major role of the DIP, the debtor should be able to count on the local office of the United States trustee for assistance and guidance. 28 U.S.C. § 586(a)(3).

The restructuring of the debtor's business and the administration of the estate are only part of the challenge facing the debtor, however. Presumably (or hopefully) business revision efforts are already underway, or at least in contemplation, by the time the debtor arrives at the chapter 11 door. By that time, though, the debtor needs a more radical form of surgery than mere business revision can accomplish. The debtor needs to reorganize not only its business, but also its legal obligations. The plan of reorganization is the means by which the debtor's debts and equity interests are reordered. Confirmation of a plan replaces the old obligations with the new. § 1141.

---

[97]   See, e.g., In re Dilley, 378 B.R. 1, 6 (Bankr. D. Maine 2007) ("A court will not entertain objections to a trustee's conduct of the estate where that conduct involves a business judgment made in good faith, upon a reasonable basis, and within the scope of his authority under the Code.").

The *third* principal task facing the debtor as DIP, then, is to restructure debt and equity. To do this the debtor must file a plan, §§ 1106(a)(5), 1107(a), 1121, and get the plan confirmed. § 1129. Pragmatically, the ultimate goal of chapter 11 is to confirm a plan. The debtor as DIP has the duty to try to bring that goal to fruition.

In seeking to confirm a plan, the debtor will not have unfettered authority. Most significantly, the debtor must *negotiate* the terms of the plan with the official committee of unsecured creditors, and any other official committees that are appointed, §§ 1102(a), 1103(c)(3), and with the major secured creditors. Although a "cram down" plan is possible, at bottom, chapter 11 is based on the ideal of *consensus*. If the debtor's exclusive period to file a plan under § 1121 expires, other parties in interest may file a hostile plan. § 1121(c). Furthermore, the debtor's management has to be aware that in chapter 11, perhaps more than anywhere else, "uneasy lies the head that wears a crown."[98] The managers could be fired by the board of directors. Studies have shown a very high rate of turnover for the managers of a chapter 11 debtor.[99] Alternatively, the shareholders could replace the board itself[100]—and the new board then could fire the managers. Finally, the court might decide to oust the debtor as DIP and appoint an independent trustee.[101] § 1104(a).

The debtor in its fiduciary capacity as DIP is subject to several duties.[102] First, the DIP is bound by a duty of *care* owed to its creditors, to exercise the care, diligence and skill of a reasonably prudent person acting under similar circumstances. Second, the debtor has a duty of *loyalty*.[103] Thus, the debtor as DIP must avoid conflicts of interest, refrain from self-dealing, treat all parties fairly, and attempt to maximize the value of the estate. Some courts have held, however, that the duty of loyalty is measured by the "corporate fiduciary" standard, rather than the more stringent "common law trustee" standard.[104] Thus, a circuit court held that a DIP did not violate his fiduciary duties to creditors when he sold property to his parents for the appraised price of $7,000 pursuant to § 363(b), without first disclosing that he had received a higher offer that had then been withdrawn (for $45,000) from a third party prior to bankruptcy.[105]

§ 11.5   Corporate Governance and the Role of Shareholders

Chapter 11 is based in part on the premise that the reorganization of a viable business under court protection might preserve a going concern premium over and

---

[98]   William Shakespeare, Henry IV, part 2, Act III, scene 1, line 30.

[99]   See Stuart C. Gilson, Bankruptcy, Boards, Banks, and Blockholders, 27 J. Fin. Econ. 355 (1990); Stuart C. Gilson, Management Turnover and Financial Distress, 25 J. Fin. Econ. 241 (1989); Lynn M. LoPucki & William C. Whitford, Corporate Governance in the Bankruptcy Reorganization of Large, Publicly Held Companies, 141 U. Pa. L. Rev. 669 (1993).

[100]   See § 11.5.

[101]   See § 11.6.

[102]   See, e.g., In re McConville, 110 F.3d 47, 50 (9th Cir. 1997) (stating that DIPs are "fiduciaries of their own estate owing a duty of care and loyalty to the estate's creditors,"), cert. denied, 522 U.S. 966 (1997).

[103]   Wolf v. Weinstein, 372 U.S. 633 (1963).

[104]   See, e.g., In re Schipper, 933 F.2d 513 (7th Cir. 1991). See also In re Engman, 395 B.R. 610, 626 (Bankr. W.D. Mich. 2008) ("[C]ourts implicitly, if not explicitly, pass upon the trustee's separate fiduciary duty of loyalty whenever a trustee affirmatively represents, as he must, that he has no personal interest. . . . ").

[105]   *Schipper*, 933 F.2d 513.

above liquidation value.[106] The game then is to allocate that premium in the plan of reorganization between the various financially interested parties—different classes of creditors and equity holders. Since the "debtor" is presumptively left in control as "debtor in possession,"[107] §§ 1101(1), 1104(a), 1107(a), and as such is given wide discretion to make business decisions, as well as the power to negotiate with creditors and the initial exclusive right to propose the plan,[108] § 1121, the debtor's management plays a crucial role in shaping the distribution of reorganization value. Who has the power to select those managers thus assumes considerable importance.

Outside of bankruptcy, shareholders have ultimate control of a corporation. They elect the board of directors, which in turn selects the managers of the corporation. But outside of bankruptcy, a corporate debtor normally is beholden only to itself, and for the most part is free to promote its own selfish interests as it sees fit. In bankruptcy, as discussed in the previous section, the debtor has a dual role as both debtor and debtor in possession, and in the latter role is a fiduciary for the body of creditors. Does this dual role negate or minimize the presumptive control of corporate shareholders? Stated otherwise, to what extent does the filing of chapter 11 interfere with the normal processes of corporate governance?[109]

The general rule is that the non-bankruptcy state law rules regarding matters of corporate governance continue to apply in a chapter 11 reorganization.[110] Included is the right of shareholders to hold an annual meeting of shareholders, or to call special meetings, and elect a new board of directors. Presumptively, then, a chapter 11 debtor's shareholders would have the right to call a meeting and elect a new board that the shareholders believe would better serve their interests.

As with all general rules, however, exceptions exist. In chapter 11, the bankruptcy court has the power to enjoin a shareholders meeting if it finds that holding the meeting would be a "clear abuse" and is likely to cause "irreparable injury."[111] The question then, of course, is what constitutes "clear abuse" and "irreparable injury."

---

[106] See § 11.1.

[107] See § 11.4.

[108] See § 11.15.

[109] Many excellent articles have been written on this topic. See Edward S. Adams, Governance in Chapter 11 Reorganizations: Reducing Costs, Improving Results, 73 Boston U.L. Rev. 581 (1993); Daniel B. Bogart, Liability of Directors of Chapter 11 Debtors in Possession: "Don't Look Back–Something May be Gaining on You," 68 Am. Bankr. L.J. 155 (1994); Mark E. Budnitz, Chapter 11 Business Reorganizations and Shareholder Meetings: Will the Meeting Please Come to Order, or Should the Meeting be Canceled Altogether?, 58 Geo. Wash. L. Rev. 1214 (1990); Anna Y. Chou, Corporate Governance in Chapter 11: Electing a New Board, 65 Am. Bankr. L.J. 559 (1991); Christopher W. Frost, Running the Asylum: Governance Problems in Bankruptcy Reorganizations, 34 Ariz. L. Rev. 89 (1992); Lynn M. LoPucki & William C. Whitford, Corporate Governance in the Bankruptcy Reorganization of Large, Publicly Held Companies, 141 U. Pa. L. Rev. 5669 (1993); Thomas G. Kelch, Shareholder Control Rights in Bankruptcy and the Withering Mirage of Corporate Democracy, 52 Md. L. Rev. 264 (1993).

[110] See Manville Corp. v. Equity Sec. Holders Comm. (In re Johns–Manville Corp.), 801 F.2d 60, 64 (2d Cir. 1986); In re J.P. Linahan, Inc., 111 F.2d 590 (2d Cir. 1940); In re Bush Terminal Co., 78 F.2d 662 (2d Cir. 1935); In re Saxon Indus., Inc., 39 B.R. 49 (Bankr. S.D.N.Y. 1984); In re Lionel Corp. 30 B.R. 327 (Bankr. S.D.N.Y. 1983); Saxon Indus., Inc. v. NKFW Partners, 488 A.2d 1298 (Del. 1985).

[111] See *Manville*, supra note 110, 801 F.2d at 64, 68; *Linahan*, supra note 110, 111 F.2d 50.

Note, though, that whatever board is serving, be it the "old" board or a newly elected board, it is subject to the fiduciary duties of care and loyalty. While shareholders thus might be able to elect a new board during a chapter 11 case, they do *not* have the right to put a board in place that can shed its DIP hat, along with the fiduciary duties towards creditors, and act solely to promote the parochial interests of the shareholders.

The leading case addressing these issues is the Second Circuit's opinion in *Manville Corp. v. Equity Security Holders Committee (In re Johns–Manville Corp.).*[112] The *Manville* case involved an attempt to deal with billions of dollars in liability for asbestos-related injuries. It was one of the most complex chapter 11 cases in history. More than three years into the case, after endless negotiations, a "fragile consensus" was reached and the debtor filed a plan. The debtor's exclusive right to file a plan had been kept in place. The debtor's shareholders, however, did not like the plan. They wanted to call a meeting of shareholders and elect a new board that would file a plan that the shareholders believed would be more favorable to them. Under state corporate law the shareholders had a right to call the meeting. The management of the debtor sought to enjoin the meeting. The bankruptcy court granted the injunction and the district court affirmed. These courts concluded that the Equity Committee, representing the debtor's shareholders, was willing to threaten to "torpedo" the reorganization in order to advance their own selfish desire to grab a larger share of the pot.

The Second Circuit reversed the summary judgment granting the injunction and remanded for further findings. In its opinion, the Second Circuit emphasized that the bankruptcy court should be very reluctant to enjoin a shareholders' meeting.[113] The Equity Committee's desire to obtain more bargaining power in the formulation of the plan, standing alone, was not sufficient to show "clear abuse," as to authorize a bankruptcy court to enjoin a shareholder meeting.[114] This held true even if the shareholders wanted to force the reorganization to "take an entirely different turn." Nor was the three-year delay in requesting a meeting plainly abusive, although delay could be a factor in proving abuse.[115] In short, the *Manville* court made very clear that a debtor's shareholders have a strong presumptive right to elect a board of directors that continues in reorganization, even if their motivation is selfish and could result in delaying the reorganization process.[116]

So what *would* constitute a clear abuse (and, at the same time, indicate the likelihood of irreparable injury)? The focus, the *Manville* court said, should be on the seriousness of the threat to the viability of the reorganization itself, rather than simply whether the reorganization would be delayed. If the reorganization was "seriously threatened," or put in "real jeopardy," an injunction against the shareholders meeting

---

[112]   801 F.2d 60 (2d Cir. 1986).

[113]   Id. at 64.

[114]   Id. at 64–65. The court cited with approval the earlier Second Circuit decision in *In re Bush Terminal Co.*, 78 F.2d 662 (2d Cir. 1935).

[115]   801 F.2d at 66 & n.7.

[116]   Indeed, the court even stated that, "the shareholders' natural wish to participate in this matter of corporate governance be respected." Id. at 64.

would be warranted.[117] The same circuit in 1979 had approved an injunction of a shareholders meeting in a case where the showing was that holding the meeting could sound the "death knell" for rehabilitation.[118] Delay is permissible, apparently, but death is not.

On remand, the bankruptcy judge in *Manville* entered the injunction.[119] He found that holding the shareholders meeting would in fact seriously jeopardize the reorganization. Years had been devoted to achieving a delicate and fragile consensus on a plan in a case involving billions of dollars and people's health at stake. Thus, the shareholders' desire to enforce their state law rights and attempt to get a bigger slice of the pie had to yield to the reorganization imperative at this late date.

An intriguing question was broached but not decided by the Second Circuit in the *Manville* case: what happens to the shareholders' right to call a meeting and elect a board if the debtor is *insolvent*? In such a situation, the stock would be worthless. Does it then make any sense for the primary agents of the reorganization (the management of the DIP) to be selected by a group that has little if any financial interest in the outcome? A group that comes in last in the distribution line, and whose shares are usually cancelled in the reorganization plan? In dictum, the Second Circuit suggested not; if the debtor were insolvent, the court opined that denying the right to call a meeting would be proper, because the shareholders would not then be "real parties in interest."[120]

But is that assertion correct? It might be *if* the "absolute priority" rule were always enforced in a reorganization case. But it is not.[121] Creditors who receive less than 100% of their claims can waive the absolute priority rule, and approve a reorganization plan that gives something to equity holders. Only if a class of creditors votes against the plan is the absolute priority rule triggered. § 1129(b). Even for a debtor that is obviously insolvent, then, equity holders have the right to negotiate with creditors to seek a waiver of the absolute priority rule. And that assumes that the debtor's insolvency could easily be ascertained. If an "insolvency exception" exists to the shareholder's presumptive right to call a meeting under state corporate law, the bankruptcy court would be forced to value the company to determine whether the debtor is solvent. That, however, flies directly in the face of the congressional decision to eliminate the need for a valuation of the debtor in reorganization unless a class votes against the plan. Other courts have disagreed with the rationale underlying the *Manville* dictum, and have stated that the debtor's insolvency does not automatically negate the shareholder's right to call a meeting.[122]

---

[117] Id. at 66, 67, 69.

[118] In re Potter Instrument Co., 593 F.2d 470 (2d Cir. 1979).

[119] 66 B.R. 517 (Bankr. S.D.N.Y. 1986).

[120] 801 F.2d at 65 n.6. The rationale supporting this dicta also applies to cases like *In re Williams Communications Group, Inc.*, 281 B.R. 216 (Bankr. S.D.N.Y. 2002), which hold that "hopelessly insolvent" debtors' shareholders' are not entitled to having an equity committee appointed.

[121] See Lynn M. LoPucki, The Myth of the Residual Owner: An Empirical Study, 82 Wash. U. L. Rev. 1341 (2004).

[122] See, e.g., Saxon Indus., Inc. v. NKFW Partners, 488 A.2d 1298 (Del. 1985). See also In re Saxon Indus., 39 B.R. 49 (Bankr. S.D.N.Y. 1984) ("However, the issue of whether the insolvency of Saxon and the

§ 11.6   Appointment and Role of a Trustee

One of the most fundamental decisions Congress made in the 1978 Bankruptcy Code was *not* to require an independent trustee in every case. Instead, the norm is for the debtor to continue in possession, and to fulfill the fiduciary role of the trustee.[123] § 1107(a). A trustee will only be appointed if the requisite need is shown. § 1104(a).

Under the prior Act, a trustee was required in chapter X, in cases where the debts exceeded $250,000. Bankruptcy Act § 156. In chapter XI, however, the debtor was continued as debtor in possession. Protection of the public interest and the interests of creditors was the watchword in chapter X, while chapter XI promoted flexibility for the benefit of creditors and debtors.[124] In merging the two chapters into the single chapter 11, Congress had to decide which it deemed more important. Flexibility won. The need to protect public creditors from insider abuses or debtor mismanagement was not perceived to be pervasive enough to warrant requiring a trustee in every case, as the "serious abuses of the 1930's" had largely been cured by the adoption and enforcement of other laws.[125] Instead, problem cases could be dealt with individually, Congress thought, by having the court appoint a trustee only when needed.[126] The Senate had wanted to require a trustee for all public companies,[127] but the House position providing for the purely discretionary appointment of a trustee ultimately prevailed.

One uninitiated in reorganization practice might assume that routinely appointing a trustee to take the place of the existing management of the debtor would be a wise idea. After all, current management led the debtor into bankruptcy in the first place, whether by incompetence, fraud, or neglect. Is it really a sound idea to retain the very managers who were responsible for the debtor's descent into bankruptcy, and give them the leading role in reorganizing the debtor? Furthermore, if managers know that they will not lose their jobs or control of the company if they drive the debtor into bankruptcy, might they not be encouraged *ex ante* to take excessive business risks, knowing that if things do not work out a soft landing waits in bankruptcy court? Proponents of this line of reasoning assert that the factors that drive a company into bankruptcy court might be more likely to be attributable to endogenous decisions than to exogenous forces if management survival is the norm.

---

proximity to confirmation should preclude the holding of shareholders' meeting is not before the court at this time. This court will not preclude the equity committee from resorting to all available legal remedies. . . . ").

[123] See § 11.4. See also H.R. Rep. No. 95–595, 95th Cong., 1st Sess., at 234 (1977) ("[T]he Bill adopts the flexible approach of leaving the debtor in possession of the business unless a request is made for the appointment of a trustee.").

[124] See § 11.2. See also H.R. Rep. No. 95–595, 95th Cong., 1st Sess., at 232 (1977) ("The twin goals of the standard for the appointment of a trustee should be protection of the public interest and the interests of creditors, as contemplated in current chapter X, and facilitation of a reorganization that will benefit both the creditors and the debtors, as contemplated in current chapter XI.").

[125] H.R. Rep. No. 95–595, 95th Cong., 1st Sess., at 233 (1977) ("The serious abuses of the 1930s have largely been cured by the adoption of the securities laws, and their vigorous enforcement by the Securities and Exchange Commission. Most often today, the need for reorganization results from business cycles or honest mismanagement of the company.").

[126] Id. at 232–34.

[127] S. Rep. No. 95–989, 95th Cong., 2d Sess., at 115 (1978).

Congress, however, concluded after careful deliberation that the costs of a mandatory trustee system outweighed the benefits. First, Congress discounted the degree of management fault, observing that "simple business reverses" often caused the debtor's need for reorganization, rather than "fraud, dishonesty, or gross mismanagement."[128] Chapter X had been enacted in 1938, in a climate where reorganization abuses were viewed as widespread. In 1978, Congress perceived that the landscape had fundamentally changed, and abuses no longer were commonplace. Furthermore, even where the debtor's management was to blame, the "bad guys" often had *already* been replaced by new managers *before* the bankruptcy filing, and it made no sense to throw out the replacement team. In short, the *benefits* of a mandatory trustee appointment could fairly be questioned.

Second, the *costs* of a mandatory trustee regime would be substantial.[129] The direct costs would be significant; the trustee and the trustee's professionals all have to be paid. In addition, the indirect costs of a trustee must be taken into account. An independent trustee would take time to learn the debtor's business. While the new trustee is working her way through the learning curve, the debtor's already troubled business might die on the vine. Existing debtor management, while perhaps not candidates for the business "hall of fame," at least would already know the nuances of the business, and would not miss a beat while the reorganization was progressing. For these reasons, Congress stated that, "very often, the creditors will be benefited by continuation of the debtor in possession."[130] And, if existing management were in fact stupid or dishonest, they could be replaced for cause.

A further indirect cost of a mandatory trustee system would be that debtors would be *deterred* from filing for chapter 11 relief in the first place.[131] No one likes to put themselves out of a job. Congress noted that debtors flocked in droves to chapter XI, where the management retained possession, in preference to chapter X, where they would be replaced. In short, if the debtor's management had some assurance that they would be able to keep their jobs, they might be willing to file for chapter 11 relief while the debtor's business was still salvageable.

The end result in the 1978 Code was a congressional decision that a court should only appoint a trustee and oust the debtor from possession on a case-by-case basis, "if the protection afforded by a trustee is needed and the costs and expenses of a trustee would not be disproportionately higher than the value of the protection afforded."[132] Under § 1104(a), as amended in 2005, one of three showings must be made to support the appointment of a trustee:[133]

1. *"Cause"* exists, "including *fraud, dishonesty, incompetence,* or *gross mismanagement* of the affairs of the debtor by current management, either before or after the commencement of the case, or similar cause." § 1104(a)(1) (emphasis

---

[128] H.R. Rep. No. 95–595, 95th Cong., 1st Sess., at 233 (1977).
[129] Id.
[130] Id.
[131] Id. at 233–34.
[132] Id. at 234.
[133] See Barry L. Zaretsky, Trustees and Examiners in Chapter 11, 44 S.C. L. Rev. 907 (1993).

added). Note that the statute goes on to expressly negate as "cause" any bright-line test based on the number of securities holders of the debtor or the amount of the debtor's assets or liabilities.

2.   Appointment would be "in the *interests*" of creditors, equity security holders, or other interests. § 1104(a)(2).

3.   When "grounds exist to convert or dismiss the case" under § 1112, but the court determines instead that the appointment of a trustee or an examiner is in the "best interests of creditors and the estate." § 1104(a)(3) (this final ground was added in 2005).

If the expressed desire for a trustee is based on the perception that the debtor's financial affairs need to be investigated, the preferred course is not to appoint a trustee, but to appoint an examiner instead under § 1104(c).[134] The examiner will not displace the debtor, but can perform the more limited investigatory role.[135] § 1106(b). "The standards for determining whether to order the appointment of an examiner are the same as those for appointment of a trustee: the protection must be needed and the cost not disproportionately high."[136]

The congressional intention to provide for the discretionary appointment of a trustee in chapter 11 cases where needed has been perverted by the courts. In practice, it is extremely difficult to succeed in having a trustee appointed. Courts announce and apply a very strong presumption against appointing a trustee, proclaim that naming a trustee is an "extraordinary" remedy, and insist that "clear and convincing" evidence must be presented.[137] Some degree of incompetence or mismanagement is magnanimously forgiven by the courts.[138] But it is not clear that Congress intended for the bar to be set so high in trying to get a trustee appointed; in 1978 Congress simply decided that a system of *mandatory* trustees would be unwise. If the creditors and equity holders would be better off with a trustee than with current management, a trustee arguably should be appointed. The debtor's management has no vested right to maintain control.

In some egregious cases a trustee might be appointed under § 1104(a). For example, if the evidence showed outright fraud by the debtor's managers, a trustee would be warranted.[139] In the Eastern Airlines case, a trustee eventually was appointed (albeit too late).[140] The debtor's management in that case had underestimated ongoing losses by hundreds of millions of dollars, and completely lost

---

[134] H.R. Rep. No. 95–595, 95th Cong., 1st Sess., at 234 (1977).

[135] See § 11.7.

[136] H.R. Rep. No. 95–595, 95th Cong., 1st Sess., at 234 (1977).

[137] See, e.g., In re Bayou Grp., LLC, 564 F.3d 541 (2d Cir. 2009). But see In re Veblen W. Dairy LLP, 434 B.R. 550, 555–56 (Bankr. D.S.D. 2010) ("[A] party seeking the appointment of a chapter 11 trustee bears the burden of persuasion by the preponderance of the evidence, not by clear and convincing evidence."); In re Keely & Grabanski Land P'ship, 455 B.R. 153 (B.A.P. 8th Cir. 2011) (same).

[138] Indeed, § 1104(a)(1) only requires appointment of a trustee for "gross mismanagement," rather than mere mismanagement.

[139] See, e.g., In re Bibo, Inc., 76 F.3d 256 (9th Cir.), cert. denied, 519 U.S. 817 (1996).

[140] In re Ionosphere Clubs, Inc., 113 B.R. 164 (Bankr. S.D.N.Y. 1990).

the confidence of the creditors. Note too that the list of possible factors in § 1104(a)(1) is not exclusive; other reasons, such as an irremediable conflict of interest, or a failure to keep proper books and records, might support the appointment of a trustee.

In 2005 Congress added a new rule, providing that the United States trustee is *required* to move for the appointment of a trustee if there are "reasonable grounds to suspect" that current members of management "participated in actual fraud, dishonesty, or criminal conduct" in managing the debtor or the debtor's public financial reporting. § 1104(e). This was passed in response to the uproar caused by notorious scandals such as Enron and WorldCom. Even before Congress added subsection (e), if a court found the facts of a case to support the appointment of a trustee, the court was without discretion, and must appoint a trustee.[141]

Although there has been considerable debate on the question, the better view is that the court may act *sua sponte* to order the appointment of a trustee.[142] The bankruptcy judge will not actually make the appointment; that task is left to the United States trustee, subject to the court's approval. § 1104(d). In 1994, Congress amended the Code to allow for the *election* of a trustee by creditors in lieu of appointment by the United States trustee. § 1104(b). The election would only occur, though, if the court first ordered the appointment of a trustee under § 1104(a).[143]

The trustee's appointment is not necessarily permanent. The court has the authority to order the debtor to be restored to possession and management of property of the estate and of the operation of the business. § 1105. This would typically only be done based on a showing of a significant change in circumstances since the trustee appointment was initially ordered, or if new evidence becomes available that shows the decision to appoint a trustee was improvidently made.[144]

If a chapter 11 trustee is appointed or elected, the trustee takes over for the debtor in possession. As such the trustee has two overriding responsibilities. The first is to operate the debtor's business during the pendency of the case. § 1108. Second, the trustee has the duty to file a plan of reorganization "as soon as practicable," or explain why he is not filing a plan. § 1106(a)(5). In putting together a plan, the trustee should consult with creditors and other interested parties, in the hope of forging a consensual plan.[145] In order to perform these duties, the trustee may investigate the debtor's business and financial affairs, and is to file a report of his findings. § 1106(a)(3), (4). The trustee also must perform the administrative tasks incident to the processing of the bankruptcy case, such as filing reports and tax returns, examining claims, and the like. § 1106(a)(1), (2), (6)–(8). As representative of the estate, the trustee has the power to sue and be sued, § 323, and to bring avoidance actions on behalf of the estate.

---

[141] 11 U.S.C. § 1104(a) ("[T]he court *shall* order the appointment of a trustee . . . " (emphasis added)).

[142] See, e.g., In re Basil St. Partners, LLC, 477 B.R. 856 (Bankr. M.D. Fla. 2012); Allen v. King, 461 B.R. 709 (D. Mass. 2011); In re U.S. Mineral Prods. Co., 105 Fed.Appx. 428 (3d Cir. 2004); *Bibo*, supra note 17, 76 F.3d 256.

[143] H.R. Rep. No. 95–595, 95th Cong., 1st Sess., at 234 (1977) ("If the court determines that a trustee is to be appointed in the case, the bill separates the court from the appointment process.").

[144] See id. at 403 ("This section would permit the court to reverse its decision to order the appointment of a trustee in light of new evidence."); In re Taub, 441 B.R. 211, 215–16 (Bankr. E.D.N.Y. 2010).

[145] H.R. Rep. No. 95–595, 95th Cong., 1st Sess., at 404 (1977).

Section 1116 was added in 2005, applying exclusively to small businesses. A debtor in possession or trustee must, in addition to the other duties required by chapter 11, append all recent financial statements, attend all bankruptcy proceedings scheduled by the court (unless otherwise excused), file all postpetition financial and other reports, timely file all tax returns and other government filings and allow the United States trustee to inspect its business including the premises and records.[146] §§ 1116, 308(b). A "small business case" is one involving a "small business debtor," § 101(51C), and a "small business debtor" is one with less than $2,490,925 in noncontingent liquidated secured and unsecured debt. § 101(51D)(A).

§ 11.7   Appointment and Role of an Examiner

In chapter 11 an examiner may be appointed instead of a trustee.[147] § 1104(c). The examiner's fees and expenses will be paid out of the estate as an expense of administration. §§ 330(a), 503(b)(2). The examiner's duty usually is to perform an investigation of the debtor as directed by the court. § 1106(b). For example, in the 1980s and 1990s, examiners were appointed in some of the large leveraged buyout cases to investigate the possible existence of fraudulent conveyance actions that could be brought on behalf of the estate.

In carrying out this investigative role, an examiner may obviate the need for a trustee. Congress concluded in the 1978 reforms that where the primary need was to *investigate* the debtor, the preferred course would be to forego appointing a trustee at the outset, and to appoint an examiner instead for the limited purpose of carrying out the investigation.[148] The costs and dislocation attendant to the appointment of a trustee thus could be avoided, yet pre-bankruptcy misdeeds would not escape undetected.

If the examiner does uncover evidence of "fraud, dishonesty, incompetence, misconduct, mismanagement, or irregularity in the management of the affairs of the debtor," § 1104(c), the court might then choose to appoint a trustee under § 1104(a). Otherwise, the debtor would be left in possession. The examiner herself is barred from serving as trustee in the case, however, § 321(b), nor may the examiner be employed by the trustee. § 327(f). Congress wanted to ensure the absolute impartiality of the examiner, by eliminating any temptation for the examiner to suggest that a trustee was needed so that she could obtain lucrative employment for herself.

The Code specifies two grounds for the appointment of an examiner. One is discretionary and general, the other mandatory and specific. The discretionary ground is that an examiner may be appointed if "such appointment is in the interests of creditors, any equity security holders, and other interests of the estate." § 1104(c)(1). This broad standard obviously gives the court considerable discretion. The legislative history explained that the court should make the appointment if "the protection [is]

---

[146] Note that in 2013 as this book went to press, a bill was pending in the Senate, which if passed, would, *inter alia*, relax these reporting requirements in small business cases. Small Business Reorganization Efficiency and Clarity Act, S. 2370, 112th Cong. (2012).

[147] See Barry L. Zaretsky, Trustees and Examiners in Chapter 11, 44 S.C.L. Rev. 907 (1993).

[148] H.R. Rep. No. 95–595, 95th Cong., 1st Sess., at 402–03 (1977).

needed, and the costs and expenses [would] not be disproportionately high."[149] While the cost-benefit balancing task is the same in principle as that for the appointment of a trustee, the application will be different for an examiner, because the examiner normally would have a more limited role than a trustee.

The second ground for the appointment of an examiner is that the court "shall order" the appointment if "the debtor's fixed, liquidated, unsecured debts, other than debts for goods, services, or taxes, or owing to an insider, exceed $5,000,000." § 1104(c)(2). This apparently mandatory directive to appoint an examiner in large cases is part of the 1978 compromise in which Congress decided not to require the appointment of a trustee in every such case, which had been the practice under chapter X and which the Senate wanted to continue. The deal that was struck was that an examiner initially would be appointed in large cases (as defined by the amount of debt), and that a trustee would be appointed only if the examiner's report showed a need for a trustee in the case.

Notwithstanding the expressed intention of Congress that an examiner always be appointed if the unsecured debt threshold is crossed, many courts have refused to enforce the command of § 1104(c)(2). Hoping to avoid the costs or delay of an examiner in cases where the judge sees no need for one, courts grasp onto the straw of other parts of § 1104(c) to read "*shall* order" as "*may* order."[150] These courts point out that the appointment is only to be made on the request of a party in interest, after notice and a hearing, and that the examiner is only to make such investigation "as is appropriate." What purpose is to be served by the hearing, the courts ask, if appointment of an examiner is required? And what if the "appropriate" degree of investigation, considering the costs and benefits, is *no* investigation? Did Congress really want to force courts to appoint an examiner, and then direct the examiner not to do anything at all?

The foregoing arguments can be answered in two ways. First, the statute is constructed so that the qualifying and explanatory language about the examiner appointment process and the scope of the investigation modifies *both* the discretionary *and* the mandatory appointment grounds. All of that language is directly relevant and important to the implementation of the discretionary ground, and thus is neither superfluous nor absurd. Furthermore, the statutory reference to the need for a party in interest to request the appointment of an examiner does *not* preclude the court from making the appointment on its own motion.[151] § 105(a).

Second, the language of the Code is plain, and the Supreme Court repeatedly has instructed that courts are not free to rewrite what they perceive to be unwise statutes; § 1104(c)(2) clearly states without qualification that "the court shall order the appointment of an examiner . . . [if the] fixed, liquidated, unsecured debts . . . exceed $5,000,000." The legislative history reinforces that Congress really meant what it said

---

[149] Id. at 403.

[150] See, e.g., In re Dewey & LeBoeuf LLP, 478 B.R. 627 (Bankr. S.D.N.Y. 2012); In re Residential Capital, LLC, 474 B.R. 112 (Bankr. S.D.N.Y. 2012); In re Spansion, Inc., 426 B.R. 114 (Bankr. D. Del. 2010).

[151] See, e.g., In re Michigan BioDiesel, LLC, 466 B.R. 413 (Bankr. W.D. Mich. 2011); In re Pub. Serv. Co., 99 B.R. 177 (Bankr. D.N.H. 1989); In re UNR Indus., 72 B.R. 789 (Bankr. N.D. Ill. 1987).

in the statutory language, emphasizing that "an examiner is required to be appointed" in cases exceeding the debt limits.[152] Some courts have recoiled against the revisionist trend and have held that the plain language of § 1104(c)(2) must be enforced as written.[153] That an examiner must be appointed, however, does not dictate the *scope* of the examiner's investigation; the bankruptcy court still retains "the authority to limit examiner investigations to 'appropriate' subjects, methods, and duration."[154]

As noted, the normal role for an examiner is to conduct an "appropriate" investigation of the debtor and to report her findings. § 1106(b), (a)(3), (4). What is "appropriate" is determined by the bankruptcy court. The examiner does not usually operate the debtor's business, negotiate or file a plan, or otherwise carry out any of the duties of the debtor in possession. Unlike the appointment of a trustee, the appointment of an examiner does not divest the debtor from its status as debtor in possession.

The Code also gives the court considerable flexibility to expand and tailor the examiner's duties to fit the needs of the particular case. To explain, the examiner may perform "any other duties of the trustee that the court orders the debtor in possession not to perform." § 1106(b). Furthermore, the investigation may inquire into "any other matter relevant to the case or to the formulation of a plan." § 1106(a)(3). Thus, in some large cases, courts have appointed an examiner to facilitate and mediate the formulation of a reorganization plan.[155] Examiners have been authorized to bring suits on behalf of the estate, including the power to seek the recovery of preferences and fraudulent conveyances.[156]

§ 11.8 Creditors' Committees and Equity Committees

The norm in chapter 11 cases is to leave the debtor in control as debtor in possession, or DIP.[157] §§ 1101(1), 1107(a). Appointment of an independent trustee is the exception, not the rule.[158] § 1104(a). Nor is an examiner appointed in every case.[159] § 1104(c). Does this scheme mean that the debtor as DIP is left free to act alone as an unchecked benevolent chapter 11 dictator? No. Congress is not that foolish. A counterweight to the DIP is needed for the chapter 11 system to function fairly and for the interests of creditors and other interested parties to be properly represented in the formulation of the plan and other matters.

---

[152] 124 Cong. Rec. S17,417 (daily ed. Oct. 6, 1978) (remarks of Sen. DeConcini); 124 Cong. Rec. H11,100 (daily ed. Sept. 28, 1978) (remarks of Rep. Edwards).

[153] See, e.g., In re Revco D.S., Inc., 898 F.2d 498 (6th Cir. 1990); Walton v. Cornerstone Ministries Invs., Inc., 398 B.R. 77 (N.D. Ga. 2008); In re UAL Corp., 307 B.R. 80 (Bankr. N.D. Ill. 2004).

[154] *UAL*, supra note 153, 307 B.R. at 86.

[155] See, e.g., In re A.H. Robins Co., 828 F.2d 1023 (4th Cir. 1987), cert. denied, 485 U.S. 969 (1988); In re Pub. Serv. Co., 99 B.R. 177 (Bankr. D.N.H. 1989).

[156] See Williamson v. Roppollo, 114 B.R. 127 (W.D. La. 1990). See also In re Carnegie Int'l Corp., 51 B.R. 252 (Bankr. S.D. Ind. 1984).

[157] See § 11.4.

[158] See § 11.6.

[159] See § 11.7.

That role is filled by the official committee of unsecured creditors.[160] Other than the DIP, the unsecured creditors' committee often is the most important player in the chapter 11 game. The creditors' committee negotiates with the debtor over the plan and generally monitors the progress of the case. § 1103(c). The members of the creditors' committee are fiduciaries to the constituents they represent.[161] As a designated participant in the chapter 11 scheme, the committee is paid for out of the estate. §§ 330(a), 503(b)(2).

The Code mandates the appointment of an unsecured creditors' committee in all chapter 11 cases. § 1102(a)(1). The only exception is for "small business"[162] cases, in which the court is given the discretion to dispense with the creditors' committee for "cause."[163] § 1102(a)(3). In small cases, having a committee might be an unwarranted expense for the estate.

Additional committees of creditors or equity security holders may be appointed as well. The United States trustee has broad discretion to appoint such additional committees as he "deems appropriate." § 1102(a)(1). The court may order the appointment of additional committees "if necessary to assure adequate representation of creditors or of equity security holders." § 1102(a)(2). In all events, the actual members on all officially sanctioned committees, mandatory and optional, are appointed by the United States trustee, not the court.

In 2005 Congress amended the Code to make clear that the court not only has the power to order the appointment of additional committees, but also has the power to order the United States trustee to *change the membership* of an existing committee if necessary to ensure adequate representation of creditors or equity security holders. § 1102(a)(4). Factors a court considers when deciding whether to change membership of an existing committee include: (1) the ability of the committee to function; (2) the nature of the case; (3) standing and desires of the various constituencies; (4) ability for creditors to participate in the case without the official committee; (5) possibility that classes would be treated differently under plan and require representation; (6) motivations of movant; and (7) whether the committee members have any conflicts of interest.[164]

The court may also order the United States trustee to increase the number of members on a committee to include a creditor that is a small business concern. § 1102(a)(4). These 2005 amendments closed a serious and confounding statutory gap

---

[160] See Kenneth N. Klee & K. John Shaffer, Creditors' Committees Under Chapter 11 of the Bankruptcy Code, 44 S.C.L. Rev. 995 (1993). See also Daniel J. Bussel, Coalition–Building Through Bankruptcy Creditors' Committees, 43 UCLA L. Rev. 1547 (1996).

[161] See In re SPM Mfg. Corp., 984 F.2d 1305 (1st Cir. 1993); In re Commercial Mortg. & Fin., Co., 414 B.R. 389 (Bankr. N.D. Ill. 2009).

[162] A "small business" is defined as one with less than $2,490,925 in noncontingent, liquidated debts. § 101(51D). Businesses whose primary activity is owning or operating real property are excluded from the definition, even if they satisfy the debt ceiling.

[163] See In re Haskell–Dawes, Inc., 188 B.R. 515 (Bankr. E.D. Pa. 1995), for a discussion of what constitutes cause to do away with the creditors' committee.

[164] E.g., In re ShoreBank Corp., 467 B.R. 156, 160–61 (Bankr. N.D. Ill. 2012).

that the repeal of a prior authorizing provision in 1986 created.[165] Still left open after 2005 is the question whether the court also has the power to *abolish* an existing discretionary committee that it previously had ordered to be created.[166] Regardless, the court would not have the power to dispense with the mandatory official unsecured creditors' committee. With regard to additional committees, the better view is that the court does enjoy the power of abolition, as a logical and necessary corollary to the court's power to order the creation of new committees in order to ensure adequate representation.

Whether additional committees should be appointed usually comes down to a comparison of costs and benefits.[167] The costs are clear: all official committees are paid for out of the estate. A committee is allowed to hire counsel and other professionals, and those professional fees are allowable administrative expenses. §§ 1103(a), 330(a), 503(b)(2). The expenses of the committee members are also accorded administrative expense status. § 503(b)(3)(F). In addition, creating another official committee can delay the plan negotiation process. The reason for appointing the committee in the first place is to give a voice to a group that previously had not been adequately represented, so that new committee will have to be given a seat at the bargaining table, and is likely to make new demands on behalf of their constituency.

The countervailing benefit that would justify appointing a committee in the face of these costs will be that a separate committee is needed to assure the *"adequate representation"* of a particular group.[168] In the case of unsecured creditors, the question

---

[165] Until 1986, the court's power to abolish or reconstitute an existing committee was plainly conferred by § 1102(c). However, in 1986 § 1102(c) was repealed as part of the expansion of the United States trustee system, in which administrative matters (such as the appointment of committees) were vested exclusively in the United States trustee's office. Prior to 2005, the courts took three divergent views on the issue of the court's residual power to revise or abolish appointed committees. One view was that the repeal of § 1102(c) left the court powerless to interfere with the composition of committees, save only the remaining statutory authority in § 1102(a)(2) to order the appointment of additional committees. See, e.g., In re New Life Fellowship, Inc., 202 B.R. 994 (Bankr. W.D. Okla. 1996). At the opposite extreme was the view that the court inherently retained plenary authority to review the decisions of the United States trustee, and to alter or eliminate committees. See, e.g., In re Pub. Serv. Co., 89 B.R. 1014 (Bankr. D.N.H. 1988). The third approach, as one might suspect, took the middle ground—the court had authority, but only to correct actions by the United States trustee that were "arbitrary and capricious," and represented an "abuse of discretion." See, e.g., In re Barney's, Inc., 197 B.R. 431 (Bankr. S.D.N.Y. 1996); In re Columbia Gas Sys., Inc., 133 B.R. 174 (Bankr. D. Del. 1991). For example, this high standard might be met if the United States trustee's actions were based on a clear legal error (such as appointing a non-creditor to the committee), had no evidentiary support in the record, or were "patently unreasonable, arbitrary, or fanciful." See, e.g., *Barney's*, 133 B.R. at 439.

[166] By restoring the court's power to reconstitute a committee and to increase the number of members of the committee in 2005, but by saying nothing about the power of abolition, which had been present in pre–1984 § 1102(c), Congress left open the possibility that courts will find that courts still lack the abolition power. As stated in the text, though, the better view is that the power to abolish committees is tied up in the creation power.

See also In re Dewey & Leboeuf LLP, 2012 WL 5985325, at *5 (Bankr. S.D.N.Y. Nov. 29, 2012) ("[T]he Court need not reach the issue whether section 1102 implicitly confers on the Court the authority to order an official committee appointed by the UST to be disbanded based on subsequent changed circumstances, or whether sections 105 and 1102 when applied together provide such authority. . . . ").

[167] See, e.g., In re Eastman Kodak Co., 2012 WL 2501071 (Bankr. S.D.N.Y. June 28, 2012); In re Spansion, Inc., 421 B.R. 151 (Bankr. D. Del. 2009); In re Pilgrim's Pride Corp., 407 B.R. 211 (Bankr. N.D. Tex. 2009); In re Wang Labs., Inc., 149 B.R. 1 (Bankr. D. Mass. 1992); In re Orfa Corp., 121 B.R. 294 (Bankr. E.D. Pa. 1990).

[168] See In re SPM Mfg. Corp., 984 F.2d 1305 (1st Cir. 1993).

is whether the subject group is not being adequately served by the official unsecured creditors' committee, and whether the need for a voice could be satisfied by the appointment of a member to that committee, instead of appointing an entirely new committee. Conflicts in reorganization goals between different groups do not necessarily dictate creating a separate committee for each group; some tension on the official committee is expected and acceptable.

Despite the Code's grant of discretion to appoint additional official committees, courts are hesitant to grant creditors such relief. Thus, the burden imposed on parties moving for an additional committee has been described as a "high standard," even requiring moving parties to show that an additional committee is "absolutely required," "essential," or "indispensable."[169]

For equity security holders, the unsecured creditors' committee obviously will not represent their interests. The management of the debtor might, however—and it is possible for shareholders to oust the board and replace it with a group that will be more responsive to shareholder needs.[170] The debtor, though, as DIP must act as a fiduciary for all creditors, and thus is not free entirely to represent only the selfish desires of equity. With creditors permitted to waive the absolute priority rule in favor of equity holders, an equity committee could play an important role in negotiating a share of reorganization value for equity interests.[171] But equity committees usually are only appointed in large and complex cases with numerous shareholders, or in the event of a debtors' possible solvency.[172]

Given the importance of the official unsecured creditors' committee and other committees in the chapter 11 process, parties who are interested in influencing the outcome of the reorganization may have a strong desire to serve on an official committee—or to have other entities removed. The United States trustee plays the primary role in determining committee composition, although under § 1102(a)(4) the bankruptcy court can order a change a membership. As noted above, the United States trustee actually appoints the members of all committees. § 1102(a)(1), (2). The members of the unsecured creditors' "ordinarily" will consist of the seven unsecured creditors holding the largest claims who are willing to serve. § 1102(b)(1). The rationale for this presumption is that the largest creditors (i) will be the most interested in the case because of their financial stake and (ii) will need to be on board for a plan to be confirmed. To identify these creditors, the United States trustee will look at the list of the 20 largest unsecured creditors that the debtor must file. Rule 1007(d). A *prepetition* committee may be continued as the official bankruptcy committee if that committee was "fairly chosen" and is "representative." Appointing such a committee, which

---

[169] See, e.g., In re Residential Capital, LLC, 480 B.R. 550, 558 (Bankr. S.D.N.Y. 2012); In re Eastman Kodak, 2012 WL 2501071, at *2 (Bankr. S.D.N.Y. June 28, 2012); In re ShoreBank Corp., 467 B.R. 156, 164–65 (Bankr. N.D. Ill. 2012); In re Oneida Ltd., 351 B.R. 79, 83 (Bankr. S.D.N.Y. 2006).

[170] See § 11.5.

[171] See Lynn M. LoPucki & William C. Whitford, Bargaining Over Equity's Share in the Bankruptcy Reorganization of Large, Publicly Held Companies, 139 U. Pa. L. Rev. 125 (1990).

[172] See In re Pilgrim's Pride Corp., 407 B.R. 211, 216 (Bankr. N.D. Tex. 2009) (applying the following factors to determine whether to appoint an equity committee: "(1) whether Debtors are likely to prove solvent; (ii) whether equity is adequately represented by stakeholders already at the table; (iii) the complexity of the Debtors' cases; and (iv) the likely cost to Debtors' estates of an equity committee").

already has been negotiating with the debtor over the terms of a workout, may be efficient. For equity committees, the United States trustee will examine the list of equity security holders, Rule 1007(a)(3), and will "ordinarily" appoint the seven largest holders who are willing to serve.

The statute appears to require that only "creditors" may serve on the unsecured creditors' committee. A creditor is an entity that has a "claim" against the debtor, § 101(10), and a "claim" is a "right to payment." § 101(5). This means that agents of a creditor, such as an attorney, might be able to serve on a committee in their representative capacity, but should not be permitted to serve themselves as committee members.[173] In one prominent case, the Third Circuit held that a labor union as the collective bargaining representative had a "right to payment" and thus could serve on a committee.[174] Notwithstanding the clear statutory limitation to creditors, some courts have allowed agents to serve as committee members. Note, though, a "claim" may be a "contingent" right to payment, and that the holder of such a contingent claim should be eligible for committee membership.[175]

Since committee members are fiduciaries to their constituents, an entity who labors under a serious conflict of interest should not be appointed to (or if appointed, should be removed from) a committee. Having said that, courts do not mandate that every member of a committee speak with a single voice; discordant and dissenting views are permitted and even encouraged. Indeed, the fact that a committee member might urge the liquidation of the debtor is not disqualifying; that might even be the best course. But if liquidation is urged because that would enhance the competitive position of the entity, a conflict arises.

Committees serve their constituents in a representative role. As such, they should take whatever steps are appropriate in the circumstances to keep their constituents apprised of developments and obtain the input of class members. These duties were codified in 2005 in § 1102(b)(3), which requires that a committee both provide access to information to and solicit and receive comments from class members who are not on the committee. Also, of course, the committee must comply with any court order that compels any additional reports or disclosures to be made to class members.

The duties of an official chapter 11 committee are broad. § 1103(c). The trustee (or DIP) is required by statute to meet with the committee as soon as practicable after the committee is appointed "to transact such business as may be necessary and proper." § 1103(d). The most important role for the committee is to "participate in the formulation of the plan, advise those represented by such committee of such committee's determination as to any plan formulated, and collect and file with the court acceptances or rejections of a plan." § 1103(c)(3). In most chapter 11 cases in which a plan is confirmed, the debtor and the official committees reach a consensus on the terms of the plan, and the committees then send out the plan and ballot to the body of creditors or interest holders with a recommendation to vote in favor of the plan. If

---

[173] See In re Dow Corning Corp., 194 B.R. 121 (Bankr. E.D. Mich. 1996), rev'd on other grounds, 194 B.R. 121 (E.D. Mich. 1997); In re Charter Co., 42 B.R. 251, 253 (Bankr. M.D. Fla. 1984).

[174] In re Altair Airlines, Inc., 727 F.2d 88 (3d Cir. 1984).

[175] See In re Barney's, Inc., 197 B.R. 431 (Bankr. S.D.N.Y. 1996).

the unsecured creditors' committee does not agree with the debtor's plan, cram down under § 1129(b) is the only realistic possibility to confirm that plan.

The duties of committees are not limited to the plan negotiation and confirmation process. They also may consult with the DIP or trustee, § 1103(c)(1), and have standing to appear and be heard on any issue in the case. § 1109(b). The bankruptcy judge normally gives considerable weight to the position of official committees. A committee is entitled to obtain information from the DIP, especially with regard to proposed non-ordinary transactions.[176]

Committees may investigate the debtor's business and financial affairs. § 1103(c)(2). The possibility of a preliminary committee investigation may persuade the court to refrain from appointing an examiner up front, waiting instead for the results of the committee's inquiry. Based upon that investigation, the committee may seek the appointment of a trustee or examiner, §§ 1103(c)(4), 1104, move that the case be dismissed or converted to chapter 7, § 1112(b), seek permission to file their own plan, § 1121(c), (d), or take other action.

Committees are vested with a catch-all authority to "perform such other services as are in the interest of those represented." § 1103(c)(5). The fact that the estate foots the bill for committee work dictates, however, that the "other services" be limited to activities directly related to the bankruptcy case itself. For example, in the *Dow Corning* breast implant case, the court declined to permit the tort claimants' committee to lobby for changes in the law to benefit the tort victims.[177]

An issue that sometimes arises is whether a committee has standing to bring an action, such as an avoidance action, on behalf of the estate. Direct standing appears to be foreclosed by the language of the Code, which only authorizes the "'trustee" (which would include the DIP, § 1107(a)) to bring actions on behalf of the estate. That the statute means what it says here is supported by the Supreme Court's decision in another context in *Hartford Underwriters Insurance Co. v. Union Planters Bank, N.A.*, that the plain language of § 506(c) does indeed limit standing to a "trustee."[178]

But what if the estate appears to have a meritorious action, and the trustee or DIP refuses to sue? Committees have been granted *derivative standing* to sue on behalf of the estate in one of two ways—without the consent of the trustee or DIP, or with it. Nothing in *Hartford* should preclude allowing derivative standing; indeed, the Supreme Court made clear that it was not deciding that question.[179] To obtain derivative standing against the DIP's or trustee's wishes, the committee must show: (1) that the estate has a colorable claim; (2) demand to sue was made on the DIP or trustee; (3) the DIP or trustee unjustifiably refused to bring the action; and (4) the court granted leave to the committee to bring the action.[180] But if the committee brings

---

[176] See, e.g., In re Structurlite Plastics Corp., 91 B.R. 813 (Bankr. S.D. Ohio 1988).

[177] See In re Dow Corning Corp., 199 B.R. 896 (Bankr. E.D. Mich. 1996).

[178] 530 U.S. 1, 6, 13 (2000).

[179] Id. at 13 n.5.

[180] See, e.g., In re First Capital Holding Corp., 146 B.R. 7 (Bankr. C.D. Cal. 1992). Accord Fogel v. Zell, 221 F.3d 955, 965 (7th Cir. 2000); In re Gibson Group, Inc., 66 F.3d 1436, 1438 (6th Cir. 1995).

an action without obtaining leave of court, the members of the committee might be sanctioned.[181] Additionally, consensual derivative standing requires proof that: "(1) the committee has the consent of the debtor in possession or trustee, and (2) the court finds that suit by the committee is (a) in the best interest of the bankruptcy estate, and (b) is 'necessary and beneficial' to the fair and efficient resolution of the bankruptcy proceedings."[182]

Much of the committee's work is conducted through professionals retained by the committee, particularly through the committee's counsel. § 1103(a). The professionals retained by the committee are paid out of the bankruptcy estate on an administrative priority basis. §§ 503(b)(2), 330(a). An attorney or accountant employed by the committee is prohibited from representing another entity with an "adverse interest" in connection with the bankruptcy case. § 1103(b). However, the mere fact that the attorney or accountant represents one or more individual creditors in the represented class does not as a *per se* matter constitute a disqualifying adverse interest.[183]

The members of a committee have qualified immunity with regard to actions taken within the scope of their authority. However, the immunity does not extend to protect committee members in the case of "willful misconduct," or with regard to *ultra vires* actions.[184]

§ 11.9   Securities and Exchange Commission

Under chapter X of the prior Bankruptcy Act, the Securities and Exchange Commission played a very important role. Before the court would approve a plan of reorganization, the SEC would file an advisory report on the merits of the plan. Bankruptcy Act § 172. The SEC's primary concern was to protect the interests of public creditors and public investors. If the SEC had any problems with the plan, revisions probably would have to be made before the court would approve the plan. The plan would not even be sent out for a vote until the laborious approval process, including the preparation of and reaction to the SEC's report, was concluded. This process was very cumbersome, slow, and costly.

In the 1978 Code, Congress decided to jettison in large part the chapter X approach. Replacing the chapter X paradigm of paternalistic protection (by the trustee, court and SEC) was the concept of "informed suffrage." The SEC no longer files an advisory report, the court does not preapprove the plan, and an independent trustee is not always appointed. Instead, the heart of the protective process under the current law is that a court-approved disclosure statement is sent to creditors and equity

---

[181]   See In re Gen. Homes Corp., 181 B.R. 870 (Bankr. S.D. Tex. 1995).

[182]   In re Commodore Int'l, Ltd., 262 F.3d 96, 100 (2d Cir. 2001). See also Plan Comm. v. PricewaterhouseCoopers, LLP, 335 B.R. 234 (D.C. 2005).

[183]   See, e.g., In re Enron Corp., 2002 WL 32034346, at *6 (Bankr. S.D.N.Y. May 23, 2002) ("Section 1103(b) is the only statutory provision that concerns the committee's right to select counsel. . . . This section does not require an attorney to cease representing creditors in matters that (i) are unrelated to the bankruptcy case, (ii) are not adverse to the committee's interests in the bankruptcy case, or (iii) per-date the professional's employment by the committee").

[184]   See Luedke v. Delta Air Lines, Inc., 159 B.R. 385 (S.D.N.Y. 1993); In re Walnut Equip. Leasing Co., Inc., 2000 WL 1456951 (Bankr. E.D. Pa. Sept. 22, 2000).

holders before they vote. That disclosure statement must contain "adequate information."[185] § 1125. As the legislative history explained:

> The premise underlying the consolidated chapter 11 of this bill is the same as the premise of the securities law. If adequate disclosure is provided to all creditors and stockholders whose rights are to be affected, then they should be able to make an informed judgment on their own, rather than having the court or the Securities and Exchange Commission inform them in advance of whether the proposed plan is a good plan.[186]

What role is left for the SEC today in reorganization cases? The SEC is given the power to raise any issue and appear and be heard on any issue in a chapter 11 case, but does not have standing to appeal. § 1109(a). Nor is the SEC a "party in interest," meaning, for example, that it has no right to file a plan. § 1121(c). Notices that are required to be sent to creditors must be sent to the SEC if the Commission has filed a notice of appearance in the case or a written request to receive notices. Rule 2002(j)(1). The proposed plan and disclosure statement must be mailed to the SEC before the disclosure statement approval hearing. Rule 3017(a). In practice, in cases involving public debt or equity, the SEC may scrutinize the plan and disclosure statement and make any objections it deems proper at the disclosure statement hearing. The court typically will give substantial weight to the Commission's comments, and often will send the disclosure statement back to the proponent with instructions to respond to the SEC's concerns.

The Commission has determined as a matter of policy, however, not to get involved in the chapter 11 process in particular cases as a matter of course. Instead, it has decided to leave to committees and the United States trustee the responsibility to represent the interests of diverse public creditors and investors in most cases, and to ensure the fair operation of the disclosure and solicitation process. Only if the committee structure leaves a protective gap in a case, or if broader legal or policy issues are at stake, will the Commission get deeply involved.

C.   OPERATING THE BUSINESS IN CHAPTER 11

§ 11.10   Obtaining Financing and Credit: § 364

The trustee (or DIP, § 1107(a)) is authorized to obtain credit and to incur debt, i.e., to borrow money, or accept goods on credit, on behalf of the estate. § 364. It is difficult to operate any business without working capital, and chapter 11 debtors are no exception. Indeed, the very financial problems that drove the debtor to chapter 11 may make the chapter 11 debtor's need especially acute. Obtaining financing normally is one of the first matters a DIP must attend to after filing for reorganization. "DIP financing" has become one of the most important practical tools in large chapter 11

---

[185]   See § 11.20.

[186]   H.R. Rep. No. 95–595, 95th Cong., 1st Sess., at 226 (1977).

reorganizations.[187] Section 364 of the Code "governs all obtaining of credit and incurring of debt by the estate."[188]

Prepetition loan agreements cannot be assumed by the DIP.[189] § 365(c)(2). A creditor must voluntarily agree to extend new credit to a chapter 11 debtor, and is not bound by any pre-bankruptcy promises. The debtor can, however, obtain authorization from the court to use "cash collateral" as a form of working capital without the creditor's consent, § 363(c)(2), but then must provide the creditor with "adequate protection" of its lien interest.[190] Trade creditors perhaps can be ordered to continue shipping goods to the debtor, but only on a C.O.D. (cash (or collect) on delivery) basis.[191]

In many cases, then, the debtor must persuade lenders and creditors to make new loans and extend new credit to the debtor operating as DIP in chapter 11. At first blush, one might wonder why any creditor would take the seemingly foolish step of loaning new money to a debtor who is already in bankruptcy court. Three general concerns arise from a lender's standpoint regarding postpetition financing: (1) if also a prepetition lender, protection of the prepetition security interest and adequate protection; (2) financing terms on the postpetition loan, including an agreement on exit financing, or full payment upon confirmation; and (3) what the postpetition lender's rights and remedies upon default will be.

Not surprisingly, Congress designed § 364 to overcome any initial reluctance of creditors to extend credit to a chapter 11 debtor, by offering a progressive hierarchy of inducements, and at the same time to protect existing creditors from the debtor improvidently incurring excessive new debt. The latter objective is addressed by requiring all borrowing or obtaining of credit out of the ordinary course of business to be approved by the court, after notice to creditors and the opportunity for a hearing. § 364(b)–(d). Ordinary course transactions do not require separate court approval; the authorization to operate the business carries with it the implied authority to engage in ordinary course transactions. § 364(a).

Section 364 offers significant incentives to entice lenders to loan money, or otherwise extend credit to a DIP operating its business in chapter 11. The most basic carrot held out to a prospective creditor or lender is an administrative priority, on a par with other second priority claims.[192] § 364(a), (b). If the offer of an administrative priority is not a big enough carrot, the new lender may be granted a "superpriority,"

---

[187] See David A. Skeel, Jr., The Past, Present, and Future of Debtor-in-Possession Financing, 25 Cardozo L. Rev. 1905 (2004); David A, Skeel, Jr., Creditors' Ball: The "New" New Corporate Governance in Chapter 11, 152 U. Penn. L. Rev. 917 (2003). For an excellent analysis of DIP financing, see George G. Triantis, A Theory of the Regulation of Debtor-in-Possession Financing, 46 Vand. L. Rev. 901 (1993).

[188] S. Rep. No. 95–989, 95th Cong., 2d Sess., at 57 (1978); H.R. Rep. No. 95–595, 95th Cong., 1st Sess., at 346 (1977).

[189] See § 8.20. See also In re Sun Runner Marine, Inc., 945 F.2d 1089 (9th Cir. 1991).

[190] See § 5.18.

[191] See, e.g., In re Docktor Pet Ctr., Inc., 144 B.R. 14 (Bankr. D. Mass. 1992) (finding adequate protection in § 365(b)(1)(C) met when debtor assumed and assigned contract, and the trade creditor dealt with the debtor's assignee on collect on delivery terms).

[192] See § 11.10.a.

i.e., a priority even over all other administrative claims.[193] § 364(c)(1). Furthermore, liens may be granted on unencumbered property or equity in property of the estate to secure chapter 11 loans.[194] § 364(c)(2), (3). If even a superpriority and liens on available property are not enough to prompt a necessary postpetition loan, the new chapter 11 lender may be given a "priming" lien on estate property, i.e., a first lien that subordinates prior lienholders.[195] § 364(d). Some form of "adequate protection" must then be given to the displaced lienholder. § 364(d)(1)(B). All of these incentives are buttressed by the provision for statutory "mootness": an appellate reversal of the grant of a priority or lien under § 364 will not affect the validity of the debt incurred or the priority or lien awarded if the lender acted in good faith, assuming that the financing order was not stayed pending appeal.[196] § 364(e).

In some cases prospective chapter 11 lenders have sought benefits not expressly authorized by the terms of § 364. An example of a controversial practice is "cross-collateralization."[197] Cross-collateralization gives the chapter 11 lender a lien on property of the *post*-petition estate to secure not only the postpetition loan, but also the lender's unsecured *pre*-petition claim. The legality of cross-collateralization is uncertain.[198]

a. *Administrative Priority*

The first inducement that may be offered to postpetition credit extenders is an administrative priority. § 364(a), (b). This grant of second priority may be authorized in two ways, one implicit and one explicit. First, if the DIP is authorized to operate its business, which is the presumptive norm in chapter 11, § 1108, the DIP may obtain unsecured credit or incur unsecured debt in the *ordinary course* of business. § 364(a). Second, if general business operation is not authorized, or if the credit extension or loan is not in the ordinary course of business, the court may approve the transaction after notice and a hearing. § 364(b).

---

[193] See § 11.10.b.

[194] See id.

[195] See § 11.10.c.

[196] See § 11.10.d.

[197] See § 11.11.

[198] The only court of appeals decision squarely on point held that cross-collateralization is illegal. In re Saybrook Mfg. Co., 963 F.2d 1490 (11th Cir. 1992). Other circuit courts have implicitly found that cross-collateralization is not illegal per se, in holding that the appeal of a cross-collateralization order was moot under § 364(e), as the lenders and debtor acted in good faith regarding the postpetition lending transaction. See In re Ellingsen MacLean Oil Co., 834 F.2d 599 (6th Cir. 1987), cert. denied, 488 U.S. 817 (1988); In re Adams Apple, Inc., 829 F.2d 1484 (9th Cir. 1987). See also In re Texlon Corp., 596 F.2d 1092, 1098 (2d Cir. 1979) ("In order to decide this case we are not obliged, however, to say that under no conceivable circumstances could 'cross-collateralization' be authorized."); In re Revco D.S., Inc., 901 F.2d 1359 (6th Cir. 1990) (regarding the adequate protection requirement when the DIP lenders receive a superpriority lien, subordinating prepetition liens from them and another creditor, and the DIP financing agreement provides for the DIP lender to receive prepetition interest).

The position adopted by the Eleventh Circuit in *Saybrook* was advocated by the author of this book in a series of articles, including Charles J. Tabb, Lender Preference Clauses and the Destruction of Appealability and Finality: Resolving a Chapter 11 Dilemma, 50 Ohio St. L.J. 109 (1989) (hereafter "Lender Preference Clauses"); Charles J. Tabb, A Critical Reappraisal of Cross–Collateralization in Bankruptcy, 60 S. Cal. L. Rev. 109 (1986).

The implied authorization for a DIP to obtain credit or incur debt in the ordinary course of business inheres in the general grant of authority to operate the business. In effect it is a "lesser included" power. The efficiency of allowing the debtor to enter into ordinary course transactions without express court approval was recognized in equity receiverships and in reorganizations under the prior Act.[199] The important question under § 364(a) will be whether a loan or credit extension was in the ordinary course of business.

Since the "ordinariness" of the transaction in subsection (a) substitutes for notice to creditors and court approval in subsection (b), the test for whether a transaction qualifies as ordinary should turn on whether notice to creditors and court oversight of this particular transaction would serve a useful purpose. If approval would be virtually automatic, there is no point in incurring the time and expense of sending out notices. If the only objections creditors might interpose speak to the threshold question of the wisdom of continued business operations, their concerns should be aired in a general motion to restrict operations, not in objections to transactions ordinarily incident to the running of the business.

Courts have used a two-prong test to ascertain whether a transaction is in the ordinary course of business.[200] There is some dispute whether *both* prongs must be satisfied, or whether either will suffice; the prevailing view appears to require that both be met.[201] The first prong is the *"vertical dimension"* test, which focuses on the reasonable expectations of a hypothetical creditor: is this type of transaction one that such a creditor would expect a debtor in this business to enter into, or would that transaction expose such a creditor to economic risks of a different nature than generally accepted? For example, a major loan might not be ordinary, but routine credit extensions from a longtime trade supplier would be. The second prong of the test looks at the *"horizontal dimension"* of the transaction in the context of the industry, by comparing the debtor's business to other businesses in the same industry: is this type of loan or credit normal for similarly situated businesses? If so, that supports a finding of ordinariness.

Some courts reject the two-prong test, and instead adopt the *"reasonable expectations"* test,[202] which closely resembles the *"vertical dimension"* test from the

---

[199] See Chicago Deposit Vault Co. v. McNulta, 153 U.S. 554 (1894); In re Avorn Dress Co., 78 F.2d 681, modified, 79 F.2d 337 (2d Cir. 1935).

[200] See, e.g., Braunstein v. McCabe, 571 F.3d 108 (1st Cir. 2009); In re Straightline Inv., Inc., 525 F.3d 879 (9th Cir. 2008).

[201] Compare In re Enron Corp., 2003 WL 1562202, at *16 (Bankr. S.D.N.Y. 2003) ("[B]oth elements of this inquiry must be satisfied in order for a transaction to be within the ordinary course of business." (citing *In re Crystal Apparel, Inc.*, 220 B.R. 816, 831 (Bankr. S.D.N.Y. 1998))), with In re Husting Land & Dev., Inc., 255 B.R. 772, 780 (Bankr. D. Utah 2000) (rejecting the horizontal test, and only requiring a party to meet the vertical dimension test).

[202] These courts reject the two-prong test, specifically the "horizontal dimension" test, as a matter of statutory construction when comparing § 364(a) with § 547(c)(2). In short, § 547c(2), prior to 2005, required a creditor to prove that three elements fell within the ordinary course of business: (1) the underlying debt; (2) the debtor's payment, subjectively, between the parties; and (3) the debtor's payment, objectively, as compared to industry standards. By contrast, § 364(b) only requires proof of one of those elements—that the underlying debt was incurred in the ordinary course of business. See, e.g., In re 211 Waukegan, LLC, 479 B.R. 771 (Bankr. N.D. Ill. 2012); In re Ockerlund Const. Co., 308 B.R. 325, 329 n.1 (Bankr. N.D. Ill. 2004); In re Garofalo's Finer Foods, Inc., 186 B.R. 414, 429 (N.D. Ill. 1995).

two-prong test. Under this test, courts contemplate the reasonable expectations of a creditor who deals with the debtor as to the types and terms of transactions into which the debtor might enter.[203] To make this determination, the court's primary focus is the debtor's prepetition conduct, as a means to inform and develop expectations of its postpetition conduct.[204]

If the transaction falls outside of the ordinary course of business, court approval must be obtained, after notice and a hearing.[205] § 364(b). Rule 4001(c) governs motions to obtain credit. The hearing cannot be held on less than 14 days' notice, except to deal with an emergency. If no objections to the proposed loan or credit are filed, court approval is typically routine.

If the transaction is not in the ordinary course of business, but prior approval is not obtained, the creditor may request *nunc pro tunc* approval of the transaction. The standard for obtaining such approval is quite stringent,[206] and usually such relief is denied, leaving the lender with a general nonpriority claim. Courts consider four factors when determining whether to exercise its equitable discretion to grant *nunc pro tunc* approval of postpetition financing: (1) whether the financing transaction benefits the bankruptcy estate; (2) whether the creditor has adequately explained its failure to seek prior authorization, or proves it otherwise acted in good faith; (3) whether there is full compliance with the requirements of § 364; and (4) whether the circumstances of the case present a rare situation in which retroactive authorization is appropriate.[207]

Since § 364(a) and (b) specifically authorize the granting of an administrative priority under § 503(b)(1), as a threshold matter, the credit or debt must meet the requirements of § 503(b)(1). That means that the credit be extended, or the debt incurred, for the actual and necessary costs and expenses of "preserving the estate," which has been construed to include operation of the debtor's business. Benefit to the estate and a transaction with the DIP must be shown.

b.   *Superpriority and Non–Priming Liens*

The promise of an administrative priority may not be enough to induce a creditor or lender to extend credit or make a loan to a chapter 11 debtor.[208] The prospective credit extender may consider the possibility of administrative insolvency to be too great a risk. If so, and if the financing is necessary to the debtor's business, the court after notice and a hearing may approve even greater protection for the credit extender. § 364(c). The court may approve: (1) a "superpriority" for the debt or credit, with

---

[203]   See *211 Waukegan*, supra note 202, 479 B.R. at 779.

[204]   *Garofalo's Finer Foods*, supra note 202, 186 B.R. at 425.

[205]   In re Azevedo, 485 B.R. 596, 601 n.6 (Bankr. D. Idaho 2013) (describing the § 364(b) option as the "fail-safe" approach for a creditor to protect its rights).

[206]   See In re Am. Cooler Co., 125 F.2d 496 (2d Cir. 1942); In re Living Hope Sw. Med. SVCS, LLC, 450 B.R. 139 (Bankr. W.D. Ark. 2011).

[207]   E.g., In re Harbin, 486 F.3d 510, 523 (9th Cir. 2007).

[208]   See, e.g., In re Mayco Plastics, Inc., 379 B.R. 698 (Bankr. E.D. Mich. 2008) ("However, in many instances, the benefits afforded by the Bankruptcy Code to the holder of an allowed administrative expense claim under § 503(b)(1) are not sufficiently attractive to induce a party to make a loan or extend credit to a Chapter 11 debtor.").

priority over all administrative expenses under § 503(b) and § 507(b); (2) a lien on unencumbered estate property; or (3) a lien on the equity in property of the estate that is already subject to a lien.

Before approving a superpriority or liens, the court must be convinced that the necessary loan or credit cannot be obtained simply on the promise of an administrative expense.[209] Furthermore, the debtor must show why the funds are needed, and for what purpose. At bottom, the debtor must establish that the proposed financing is in the best interests of creditors. This general showing can be made by proof that the debtor has reasonable prospects for reorganization with the financing, and that the requested credit or debt is the most prudent way to preserve that possibility. Courts examine whether the relief requested in § 364(c) is an appropriate exercise of the debtor's business judgment.[210]

The provision for a superpriority in § 364(c)(1) adopts the practice that developed under chapter XI of the Act.[211] The new lender is entitled to be repaid out of the unencumbered assets of the estate before all other administrative expenses, including the superpriority under § 507(b) for "inadequate" adequate protection.

Note, though, that even a superpriority does not guarantee repayment. The estate still must have sufficient free assets to repay the debt. If all estate property is subject to liens, the superpriority debt will not be paid.[212] Furthermore, if the case is converted to chapter 7, most courts have held that under § 726(b) the administrative expenses incurred in the superseding chapter 7 case have priority over the pre-conversion expenses, even those under § 364(c)(1).[213] Another risk a postpetition creditor takes is that the court will allow interim payment of professional fees under § 331, leaving nothing for the superpriority creditor.[214] Other courts have held, however, that interim fees cannot trump a § 364(c)(1) superpriority claim.[215]

Courts are especially reluctant to approve superpriority loans, and unsecured creditors may oppose such a grant. The problem is that once a superpriority is granted, it may be difficult for the estate to persuade later creditors to do business with the estate on a simple administrative expense basis, because the superpriority debt must be repaid first. That creates a risk that the debtor's reorganization will fail. Thus, approval might be granted only if failure *without* the superpriority loan would be

---

[209] See, e.g., In re Los Angeles Dodgers LLC, 457 B.R. 308 (Bankr. D. Del. 2011) ("The Court may not approve any credit transaction under [§ 364(c)] unless the debtor demonstrates that it has attempted, but failed, to obtain unsecured credit under § 364(a) or (b).").

[210] See In re AMR Corp., 485 B.R. 279, 287 (Bankr. S.D.N.Y. 2013).

[211] See White Chem. Co. v. Moradian, 417 F.2d 1015 (9th Cir. 1969).

[212] See In re Mayco Plastics, Inc., 379 B.R. 691, 701 (Bankr. E.D. Mich. 2008) ("[T]here is nothing in § 364(c)(1) that states that such debt is secured by an interst in property of the estate, in stark contrast to debt authorized to be secured under §§ 364(c)(2) or (3) or § 364(d).").

[213] See, e.g., In re Visionaire Corp., 290 B.R. 348 (Bankr. E.D. Mo. 2003). On appeal the Eighth Circuit Bankruptcy Appellate Panel affirmed the part of the order that gave priority to § 726(b) over § 364(c)(1), but reversed in part on other grounds. 299 B.R. 530 (B.A.P. 8th Cir. 2003). See also In re Summit Ventures, Inc., 135 B.R. 478 (Bankr. D. Vt. 1991).

[214] See In re Callister, 15 B.R. 521 (Bankr. D. Utah 1981), appeal dismissed, 673 F.2d 305 (10th Cir. 1982), aff'd, 1984 WL 249787, 13 B.C.D. 21 (10th Cir. 1984).

[215] See In re Flagstaff Foodservice Corp., 739 F.2d 73 (2d Cir. 1984).

likely. Some courts have insisted that the superpriority lender agree to a "carve-out" from its superpriority for the fees and expenses of professionals, because otherwise the administration of the estate might grind to a halt.[216] It is not clear, however, that a carve-out in favor of a selected group of administrative claimants to the exclusion of others in the same priority class is permissible.

In addition to or in lieu of granting a superpriority, § 364(c)(1), the court may approve the granting of a senior lien on unencumbered property of the estate or a junior lien on encumbered property. § 364(c)(2), (3). These liens "do not interfere with existing property rights."[217] Liens give an added measure of protection to the lender. If the chapter 11 case succeeds, the priority will suffice, because all second priority claims must be paid in full on the effective date of the plan. § 1129(a)(9)(A). However, if the chapter 11 case fails, the lender's lien will survive dismissal or conversion of the case. Furthermore, the lender whose claim is secured will be entitled to adequate protection of that secured claim throughout the bankruptcy case. The downside for unsecured creditors is that previously unencumbered property is removed from the estate. The question is whether the upside, the influx of new money to the estate to assist the debtor in operating the business, is worth the price.

c. *Priming Liens*

Even a superpriority or liens on equity or on unencumbered property under § 364(c) may not be sufficient to entice a lender to make a loan to a chapter 11 DIP or trustee. For example, if most of the assets of the estate are already subject to valid liens, the new loan would be subordinate to the prior liens, and would not be assured of repayment. In such cases, where the DIP needs to borrow money, but the inducements of § 364(c) are not enough to enable the DIP to obtain credit, the final possibility is to grant the new lender a "priming" lien. Under § 364(d), the court, after notice and a hearing, may authorize the DIP to obtain credit or incur debt "secured by a senior or equal lien on property of the estate that is subject to a lien."

In other words, the bankruptcy court has the power to subordinate a preexisting, prepetition senior lien in favor of the postpetition lender, granting the postpetition lender the senior, or first lien. The new senior lien is said to "prime" the prior first lien, which now is relegated to junior lien status. For example, assume that when Debtor files chapter 11, First Bank has a perfected first lien on all of Debtor's property, including Blackacre. Second Bank agrees to make a postpetition loan to Debtor, but only if it is granted a first lien on Blackacre. Notwithstanding the minor inconvenience that First Bank *already* has a first lien on Blackacre, § 364(d) permits the court to grant Second Bank the first lien on Blackacre as security for the postpetition loan, and to demote First Bank's lien to junior status below Second Bank's lien.

What showing must be made to support such a dramatic intrusion on the legal rights of the subordinated lienholder? Pre–Code law also permitted the practice of granting priming liens, although courts differed markedly over the strength of the

---

[216]   See In re Ames Dep't Stores, Inc., 115 B.R. 34 (Bankr. S.D.N.Y. 1990).

[217]   S. Rep. No. 95–989, 95th Cong., 2d Sess., at 58 (1978); H.R. Rep. No. 95–595, 95th Cong., 1st Sess., at 347 (1977).

proof needed to support the grant.[218] Under § 364(d), a priming lien may be awarded: (1) only with court approval, after notice and a hearing; (2) if the DIP is unable to obtain credit under § 364(c); and (3) if the subordinated lienholder's interest is "adequately protected." Courts will only grant postpetition financing on a priming basis as a last resort.[219]

The "inability" requirement usually is established by introducing evidence that the debtor made unsuccessful efforts to obtain a necessary postpetition loan under § 364(c), i.e., solely on the promise of a superpriority, liens on unencumbered property, or junior liens on encumbered property. Only reasonable good faith efforts to obtain such financing need be established. The debtor does not have to contact every conceivable lender, especially if time is of the essence.[220] Given that most lenders insist on a first lien position, if the debtor's assets are heavily encumbered, proof of inability often will not be difficult.

The real crux of the § 364(d) dispute will be on the issue of *adequate protection* of the primed lender's interest. In the above hypothetical, the Debtor would have to show that First Bank's interest is adequately protected, even though its lien on Blackacre is demoted from first to second position, behind the Second Bank lien. The DIP has the burden of proof on the adequate protection issue. § 364(d)(2). How can this be done? In practice, priming liens are granted most often in two types of cases: first, where the debtor has a sizable equity cushion, sufficient to cover both the priming lien and the primed lien;[221] and second, where the debtor persuades the court that the new money will enable the debtor to enhance the value of the collateral, so that both liens will be fully secured.[222]

To illustrate the first situation, assume that First Bank's claim is $75,000, and that Second Bank will loan the DIP $50,000. If the Debtor can show that the collateral, Blackacre, has a value of substantially more than $125,000, adequate protection may be established. The trick, of course, is fixing the value of Blackacre, which requires the court both to weigh the credibility of competing expert appraisals, and to decide whether to value the property at a higher going concern value or a lower liquidation value. The court also must decide how much cushion to give First Bank.

---

[218] See In re Chicago, R.I. & P. R.R. Co., 545 F.2d 1087 (7th Cir. 1976); Melniker v. Lehman (In re Third Ave. Transit Corp.), 198 F.2d 703 (2d Cir. 1952); In re Prima Co., 88 F.2d 785 (7th Cir. 1937).

[219] In re YL W. 87th Holdings I LLC, 423 B.R. 421, 441 (Bankr. S.D.N.Y. 2010).

[220] See, e.g., In re Snowshoe Co., 789 F.2d 1085 (4th Cir. 1986); Suntrust Bank v. Den–Mark Const., Inc., 406 B.R. 683 (E.D.N.C. 2009).

[221] See, e.g., In re Dunes Casino Hotel, Inc., 69 B.R. 784 (Bankr. D.N.J. 1986); In re Strug–Division LLC, 380 B.R. 505, 513 (Bankr. N.D. Ill. 2008) ("An 'equity cushion' seems to be the preferred test of adequate protection required to prime a first mortgage under 11 U.S.C. § 364(d)(1)."). Note, though, the mere presence of an equity cushion alone will not be determinative of whether there is adequate protection. See, e.g., In re Olde Prairie Block Owner, LLC, 448 B.R. 482 (Bankr. N.D. Il. 2011); In re Stoney Creek Techs., LLC, 364 B.R. 882 (Bankr. E.D. Pa. 2007).

[222] See, e.g., In re Fontainebleau Law Vegas Holdings, LLC, 434 B.R. 716, 753–54 (S.D. Fla. 2010) (noting that there is adequate protection if a priming lien would enhance the value of assets in a greater amount than the decrease in value of a creditor's interest in the property caused by the priming lien); In re 495 Cent. Park Ave. Corp., 136 B.R. 626 (Bankr. S.D.N.Y. 1992).

To demonstrate the second common scenario in which adequate protection is found under § 364(d), assume the same debts ($75,000 for First Bank, and $50,000 for Second Bank), but that the collateral, Blackacre, is worth only $100,000 at the time of the new loan. At that value, First Bank's lien would not be adequately protected if subordinated. However, the Debtor may offer proof that it will use the $50,000 to be borrowed from Second Bank to make improvements on Blackacre, which it asserts will increase the value of Blackacre by more than enough to cover First Bank's subordinated lien in full.

Courts grant relief sparingly under § 364(d), because of the obvious risk to and interference with the property rights of the primed lienholder. But even with such judicial caution taken as a given, one can argue that § 364(d) logically makes no sense, but is internally inconsistent. Substantively, two critical proofs must be made: that no one will make the loan voluntarily without being granted a first lien, and that the lienholder who is relegated to second lien status is adequately protected. Consider those two points. Taken together, they reveal that the primed lienholder is being made to accept as "adequate" protection that which no voluntary lender would accept. The only other possibility is that other lenders would have been willing to accept a subordinated position—but then the "inability" test would fail. In our example, if the lending market believed that the equity cushion in Blackacre that presently existed or that would be generated was ample to cover both the $75,000 debt of First Bank and the $50,000 new loan, a voluntary loan should have been obtainable under § 364(c)(3).

d. Mootness

Lenders who are considering making a loan to a chapter 11 DIP obviously care about the priority and security for the repayment of the debt. But granting the lien or priority in the financing order is not enough. If the lender is at risk of losing its priority or lien if an appellate court reverses the financing authorization, no rational lender would be willing to advance funds until all appeals had been exhausted. Otherwise the lender could be out the money, but with no priority or security for the debt. As the Seventh Circuit observed, "[i]f creditors fear that the rug will be pulled out from under them, they will hesitate to lend."[223] In the meantime, the desperate debtor might die for lack of necessary funds. The problem, then, is how to protect the rights of other creditors and financially interested parties to challenge a financing order that they believe was entered in error, and yet not kill any hopes that the debtor might have for reorganizing.

The resolution of this dilemma is found in § 364(e).[224] Under that section, the reversal or modification on appeal of a financing order does not affect the validity of the debt incurred, or the validity of any priority or lien granted, if the lender acted in good faith, *unless* the financing order was *stayed* pending appeal. In other words, a creditor who wishes to challenge a financing order has the burden of obtaining a stay of the order while the appeal is pending. If the financing order is stayed, the lender will not advance funds, and thus incurs no risk. If no stay is obtained, and the lender advances

---

[223] Kham & Nate's Shoes No. 2, Inc. v. First Bank of Whiting, 908 F.2d 1351, 1355 (7th Cir. 1990).

[224] See Tabb, Lender Preference Clauses, 50 Ohio St. L.J. 109, supra note 198.

funds, the appeal will effectively be mooted, and the lender will be protected. The statutory mootness rule of § 364(e) is a powerful weapon in the debtor's arsenal, because in practice it is extremely difficult to persuade a court that has just granted the debtor's motion to obtain necessary financing to turn around and stay that order.

The safe harbor of § 364(e) is not inviolable, however. First, it offers no protection for a lender who has acted in bad faith. An explicit finding of good faith is required.[225] In a leading case, the Seventh Circuit held that a lender who *knew* that the loan and priority were illegal, but proceeded anyway in the hope that the transaction would slide through, failed the good faith test, and thus lost the protection of § 364(e).[226] Second, § 364(e) might not apply to protect the lender with regard to illegal "extra-statutory" provisions, such as cross-collateralization. The courts of appeals have gone both ways on this question of whether subsection (e) may protect transactions not otherwise authorized by § 364.[227] Finally, an appellate court may review a financing order and fashion partial relief that does not interfere with the lender's priority or lien for funds advanced.[228]

§ 11.11 Obtaining Financing: Cross-Collateralization

Obtaining financing and credit is a critical need for a reorganizing debtor. Section 364 responds to this need by enabling the debtor in possession to obtain credit or to incur debt.[229] Under § 364, prospective postpetition lenders or creditors can be offered a wide range of enticements to extend credit or make a loan to the DIP, progressing from an administrative priority,[230] § 364(a), (b); to a superpriority or a lien on unencumbered property or on equity in property already subject to a lien,[231] § 364(c); and finally to the granting of a "priming" lien ahead of an existing lien.[232] § 364(d). Postpetition creditors are given additional comfort by the statutory mootness rule that the grant of a priority or lien under § 364 to a good faith lender cannot be disturbed unless the financing order is stayed. § 364(e).[233]

But what if the prospective lender demands more? What if the debtor desperately needs money to stay afloat, and the only lender who will deal with the debtor refuses to make the postpetition loan unless the debtor not only secures and grants priority for

---

[225] See, e.g., In re Cooper Commons, LLC, 430 F.3d 1215 (9th Cir. 2005); In re Swedeland Dev. Group, Inc., 16 F.3d 552 (3d Cir. 1994); In re Revco D.S., Inc., 901 F.2d 1359 (6th Cir. 1990).

[226] In re EDC Holding Co., 676 F.2d 945 (7th Cir. 1982).

[227] Compare In re Saybrook Mfg. Co., 963 F.2d 1490 (11th Cir. 1992) (section 364(e) does not protect illegal extra-statutory provisions), with In re Ellingsen MacLean Oil Co., 834 F.2d 599 (6th Cir. 1987), cert. denied, 488 U.S. 817 (1988), and In re Adams Apple, Inc., 829 F.2d 1484 (9th Cir. 1987) (section 364(e) applies to all parts of financing order, even those provisions not authorized by § 364). The Ninth Circuit has reaffirmed its position in *Adams Apple*, and rejected the contrary view of *Saybrook*. In re Cooper Commons, LLC., 430 F.3d 1215 (9th Cir. 2005). For discussion, see Tabb, Lender Preference Clauses, 50 Ohio St. L.J. 109 (1989), supra note 198 (arguing for the "no mootness" position later adopted in *Saybrook*).

[228] See In re Swedeland Dev. Group, Inc., 16 F.3d 552 (3d Cir. 1994). See also In re Fountainebleau Las Vegas Holdings, LLC, 434 B.R. 716 (S.D. Fla. 2010).

[229] See § 11.10.

[230] See § 11.10.a.

[231] See § 11.10.b.

[232] See § 11.10.c.

[233] See § 11.10.d.

the *post*-petition loan, but also secures and grants priority for the lender's unsecured *pre*-petition claim as well? May the court approve a grant of collateral or priority out of the estate for an unsecured prepetition claim, in exchange for a postpetition loan? The practice of granting a lien on collateral out of the postpetition bankruptcy estate to secure a lender's prepetition unsecured claim is referred to as "*cross-collateralization.*"[234] Debtors agree to such clauses because they have no choice; if they want the money, cross-collateralization is the cost.

Cross-collateralization has been extremely controversial under the Code; the legality of the practice is in doubt.[235] Some local bankruptcy rules specifically state that absent compelling circumstances, courts will deny provisions granting cross-collateralization.[236] At a minimum, many local rules require debtors to locate, highlight, and justify provisions that grant cross-collateralization.[237]

Two examples, taken from leading circuit court cases, will illustrate the operation of cross-collateralization. In each, the essence is that postpetition assets secure a prepetition unsecured claim. The first case is the 1979 Second Circuit case, *Otte v. Manufacturers Hanover Commercial Corp. (In re Texlon Corp.).*[238] In *Texlon*, decided under the prior Bankruptcy Act, a cross-collateralization order in favor of the prepetition lender was entered *ex parte* on the day the debtor filed for relief under chapter XI. The lender was granted a security interest in the inventory, equipment, and accounts of the debtor's bankruptcy estate to secure the postpetition advances *and* the lender's unsecured prepetition claim. During the ten weeks that the debtor remained in chapter XI before converting to a liquidation case under chapter VII, the lender advanced $667,000 to the debtor. In that short time, enough assets were generated to repay the $667,000 in full, with another $267,000 left over. The effect of the cross-collateralization clause would have been to give this entire $267,000 to the lender for its prepetition claim, in preference to all other unsecured creditors. Absent the cross-collateralization provision, all prepetition unsecured claims would have shared the $267,000 on a pro rata basis.

The second example is the 1992 Eleventh Circuit case of *Shapiro v. Saybrook Manufacturing Co. (In re Saybrook Manufacturing Co.).*[239] In *Saybrook*, the debtor's

---

[234] Sometimes this practice is specifically referred to as "forward cross-collateralization," distinguishable from mere cross-collateralization, which might just be securing post-petition debts with pre-petition assets. However, unless otherwise noted, the term cross-collateralization generally refers to the practice of securing a pre-petition debt on post-petition assets.

[235] For an in-depth discussion and criticism of cross-collateralization, see Charles J. Tabb, A Critical Reappraisal of Cross–Collateralization in Bankruptcy, 60 S. Cal. L. Rev. 109 (1986) (hereafter "Critical Reappraisal"); Charles J. Tabb, Lender Preference Clauses and the Destruction of Appealability and Finality: Resolving a Chapter 11 Dilemma, 50 Ohio St. L.J. 109 (1989) (hereafter "Lender Preference Clauses"); Charles J. Tabb, Emergency Preferential Orders in Bankruptcy Reorganizations, 65 Am. Bankr. L.J. 75 (1991) (hereafter "Emergency Preferential Orders"); Charles J. Tabb, Requiem for Cross–Collateralization, 2 J. Bankr. L. & Prac. 109 (1993) (hereafter "Requiem"). See also Karen M. Gebbia & Lawrence E. Oscar, *Saybrook Manufacturing*: Is Cross–Collateralization Moot in Chapter 11 Cases?, 2 J. Bankr. L. & Prac. 163 (1993).

[236] See, e.g., M.D. Fla. Bankr. L. R. 2081–1(e)(1)(ii)(1).

[237] See, e.g., Del. Bankr. L. R. 4001–2(1)(i)(A) (2011).

[238] 596 F.2d 1092 (2d Cir. 1979).

[239] 963 F.2d 1490 (11th Cir. 1992).

prepetition lender had a total claim of $34 million, of which only $10 million was secured, leaving an unsecured prepetition claim of $24 million. The lender agreed to advance $3 million to the debtor in the chapter 11 case, and in return was granted a security interest in all of the debtor's assets to secure both the postpetition loan *and* the prepetition debt. At the time the financing order was entered, the debtor's estate had $2 million in unencumbered inventory, which by virtue of the cross-collateralization clause became collateral for the lender's prepetition and postpetition claims. The immediate effect of the cross-collateralization order thus was to decrease the lender's prepetition unsecured claim by $2 million, from $24 million to $22 million, and to increase the secured claim from $10 million to $12 million.

Both courts of appeals struck down the cross-collateralization provision, but on somewhat different grounds. The historical progress between the two cases is intriguing. In *Texlon*, the Second Circuit, after condemning cross-collateralization on the merits in dictum as "a post-adjudication preference,"[240] rested its holding on procedural grounds, concluding that "a financing scheme so contrary to the spirit of the Bankruptcy Act should not have been granted by an *ex parte* order."[241] Amazingly, post-*Texlon* cases read that decision as implicitly *authorizing* cross-collateralization, as long as the procedural requisites of notice and a hearing were satisfied.[242] The leading case then announced a four-part test for approving cross-collateralization:[243]

1. The debtor's business would fail without the proposed financing;

2. The debtor cannot obtain alternative financing on acceptable terms;

3. The lender will not accede to less preferential terms; and

4. The financing is in the best interests of all creditors.

With this four-part test in place to guide bankruptcy judges weighing the merits of cross-collateralization orders, the action on cross-collateralization then shifted to the procedural issue of the mootness of an appeal of a financing order containing a cross-collateralization provision. Two circuit courts, the Sixth[244] and the Ninth,[245] held that § 364(e)[246] mooted the appeal of an unstayed cross-collateralization financing order.[247] Since bankruptcy judges invariably would refuse an appellant's request to stay a cross-collateralization order, which by definition would only be entered if the debtor's need

---

[240]   596 F.2d at 1097.

[241]   Id. at 1098.

[242]   This development is discussed in Tabb, Critical Reappraisal, supra note 235, at 116–19. See also In re Monach Circuit Indus., Inc., 41 B.R. 859, 861–62 (Bankr. E.D. Pa. 1984) (noting that "[s]everal bankruptcy courts have construed [*Texlon*] as providing that 'cross-collateralization provisions may not be approved *ex parte*, but only after notice and a hearing'" (collecting cases)).

[243]   In re Vanguard Diversified, Inc., 31 B.R. 364, 366 (Bankr. E.D.N.Y. 1983).

[244]   Unsecured Creditors' Comm. v. First Nat'l Bank & Trust Co. (In re Ellingsen MacLean Oil Co.), 834 F.2d 599 (6th Cir. 1987), cert. denied, 488 U.S. 817 (1988).

[245]   Burchinal v. Cent. Washington Bank (In re Adams Apple, Inc.), 829 F.2d 1484 (9th Cir. 1987).

[246]   See § 11.10.d.

[247]   These decisions were criticized in Tabb, Lender Preference Clauses, supra note 235, at 116–35.

for immediate financing was compelling, this mootness view effectively made cross-collateralization orders unreviewable.

The entire legal scene regarding cross-collateralization orders shifted dramatically in 1992 with the Eleventh Circuit's decision in *Saybrook*.[248] The court first held that the appeal was *not* moot under § 364(e).[249] As the *Saybrook* court explained, § 364(e) by its terms only applies to protect liens and priorities that are "authorized under this section," i.e., authorized under § 364. The decisive question, then, is whether cross-collateralization is "authorized under § 364." To conclude as the Sixth and Ninth Circuits did that the appeal is moot with regard to *all* provisions in a financing order, whether or not those provisions are authorized, would "put the cart before the horse," according to the Eleventh Circuit.[250]

That does not mean, however, that the entire financing order is open to appellate revision. Only those portions that are not authorized under § 364 would be vulnerable. Significantly, that limitation protects a lender's *post*-petition advances in full, because § 364 does expressly authorize granting liens and priorities to assure the repayment of postpetition advances.

The *Saybrook* court then turned to the merits of cross-collateralization clauses, and held that cross-collateralization was *per se* illegal.[251] According to the Eleventh Circuit:

"We conclude that cross-collateralization is inconsistent with bankruptcy law for two reasons. First, cross-collateralization is not authorized as a method of post-petition financing under section 364. Second, cross-collateralization is beyond the scope of the bankruptcy court's inherent equitable power because it is directly contrary to the fundamental priority scheme of the Bankruptcy Code."[252]

Saybrook thus unequivocally rejected the arguments that had been made to support cross-collateralization. The primary supporting arguments were that (1) the court has the inherent equitable power under § 105(a) to approve cross-collateralization, because doing so might enhance the chances of a successful reorganization; (2) cross-collateralization might benefit all creditors, even those not preferred, by facilitating a reorganization; and (3) a cross-collateralization provision is just part of the price of the postpetition financing.

As the critical quoted passage above from *Saybrook* reveals, the Eleventh Circuit concluded that the court lacks the *power* to enter a cross-collateralization order. The equitable powers of the bankruptcy court cannot contradict the Code itself, and the direct effect of a cross-collateralization order is to alter the Code's priority scheme, by elevating the lender's prepetition unsecured claim ahead of all other unsecured

---

[248] 963 F.2d 1490 (11th Cir. 1992). For a detailed discussion of this case, see Tabb, Requiem, supra note 235, and Gebbia & Oscar, supra note 235.

[249] 963 F.2d at 1492–93.

[250] Id. at 1493.

[251] Id. at 1494–96. In so holding, the court relied on Tabb, Critical Reappraisal, supra note 235.

[252] 963 F.2d at 1494–95.

claims.[253] Although the *Saybrook* court agreed that "rehabilitation is the primary purpose of chapter 11," it went on to emphasize that "this end, however, does not justify the use of any means."[254] Thus, if a postpetition lender wishes to extract a high price in exchange for its postpetition loan, it must do so directly, through permissible means, not by rearranging the Code's priorities.

The rationale of the *Saybrook* decision could draw into question the legality of the whole gamut of "emergency preferential orders."[255] Cross-prioritization clauses, in which a lender is granted *priority* for a prepetition claim in exchange for postpetition financing, rather than collateral, would clearly be proscribed under the *Saybrook* doctrine. So too does the decision cast doubt on the legitimacy of the practice of paying the prepetition claims of employees and trade creditors at the outset of a reorganization case under the supposed authority of the "necessity of payment" rule, a practice that today parades under the name of "critical vendor" orders.[256]

§ 11.12 The Necessity of Payment Rule and Critical Vendor Orders

Congress prescribed a very specific scheme of priority for the payment of claims in bankruptcy cases.[257] Secured claims are paid the value of their collateral.[258] Unsecured claims are paid out of the residue of the estate, after secured claims are satisfied. The universe of unsecured claims is divided into *priority* and *nonpriority* claims. The complete and exclusive listing of priority claims is contained in § 507.[259] In a chapter 7 case, priority claims must be paid in full before nonpriority claims are paid. § 726(a)(1). Nonpriority unsecured claims then share equally on a pro rata basis out of any remaining estate funds.[260] § 726(a)(2), (b).

In a chapter 11 case, § 1129(a)(9) requires that plans provide for the full payment of all priority claims under § 507 before being confirmed, but the Code contains no such mandate for nonpriority unsecured claims. For nonpriority unsecured claims, in order to be confirmed, a plan must only provide for payment equal to what they would receive in a liquidation.[261] § 1129(a)(7). While a plan may classify unsecured claims separately, and treat those classes differently if all affected classes consent, if a class votes against the plan, confirmation is possible only if the plan "does not discriminate unfairly, and is fair and equitable."[262] § 1129(b).

Most significantly, the Code contains *no express authority* for a bankruptcy court to create new priorities or otherwise alter the priority scheme, apart from the power to

---

[253] Id. at 1496.

[254] Id. See also In re Kaib, 448 B.R. 373, 376 n.2 (Bankr. W.D. Pa. 2011) ("Cross collateralizing is generally disallowed in a bankruptcy context" (citing *Saybrook*)).

[255] For a detailed discussion of these orders, see Tabb, Emergency Preferential Orders, supra note 235.

[256] See § 11.12.

[257] See Chapter 7 of this treatise for a detailed discussion of the payment of claims.

[258] See § 7.27.

[259] See § 7.7.

[260] See § 7.25

[261] See §§ 7.26, 11.26, 11.29.

[262] See §§ 11.17, 11.33.

equitably *subordinate* claims in § 510(c).[263] Nor does any provision in the Code authorize the court to order the early payment of some unsecured claims in preference to other claims of the same class.

Notwithstanding the absence of any statutory authority in the Code to rearrange the priority scheme or to pay some unsecured claims in preference to others, many bankruptcy courts have invoked their residual "equitable" powers under § 105(a) to order the payment of certain unsecured claims in the early days of a chapter 11 reorganization.[264] Often included as part of a package of "first day orders," these orders typically direct the payment of the prepetition claims of employees of the debtor and key trade creditors. The rationale behind the payments is that these crucial claims need to be paid in order to preserve the debtor's chances of reorganizing, and that the paramount end of reorganization justifies any means. If employees and critical suppliers are not paid for their pre-bankruptcy claims, the reasoning goes, they might cease working for or doing business with the debtor, crippling the debtor's chances for business survival. This is true, supposedly, *even if* such creditors are paid in full for current services rendered or goods sold during the reorganization case. In short, these claimants are perceived to have leverage over the debtor that enables them to "extort" (a strong word, but it seems to describe the phenomenon) payment of their pre-bankruptcy claims in preference to other creditors and in contravention of the Code's priority scheme. The practice of paying these sorts of "necessary" claims has been called the "*necessity of payment rule*" or the "doctrine of necessity,"[265] and today is often discussed under the rubric of "*critical vendor orders.*" As Judge Easterbook explained when writing for the majority in the Seventh Circuit's decision in *In re Kmart Corporation*, the "'doctrine of necessity' is just a fancy name for a power to depart from the Code."[266]

The necessity of payment rule originated in federal equity receiverships for railroad reorganizations in the late nineteenth century.[267] These decisions relied heavily on the *public interest* in keeping the railroads running to justify the inequality in treatment of creditors.[268] The Necessity of Payment Rule was not a rule of priority, but a rule of payment, in which the equity courts bowed to the necessity of paying creditors who were able to apply economic sanctions to coerce payment.[269] By contrast,

---

[263] See § 7.23. In railroad reorganizations only, priority rules recognized in equity receiverships are incorporated into the Code. See § 1171(b).

[264] See, e.g., In re Berry Good, LLC, 400 B.R. 741, 746 (Bankr. D. Ariz. 2008); In re Just for Feet, Inc., 242 B.R. 821 (D. Del. 1999); In re Chateaugay Corp., 80 B.R. 279 (S.D.N.Y. 1987); In re Ionosphere Clubs, Inc., 98 B.R. 174 (Bankr. S.D.N.Y. 1989). See also In re CoServ, LLC, 273 B.R. 487 (Bankr. N.D. Tex. 2002) (holding that payment of prepetition debts "other than pursuant to a plan" might be allowed, but only under "extraordinary circumstances").

[265] See *Ionosphere Clubs*, supra note 264, 98 B.R. at 176. For an article explaining and justifying the doctrine, see Russell A. Eisenberg & Frances F. Gecker, The Doctrine of Necessity and Its Parameters, 73 Marguette L. Rev. 1 (1989). For criticism of the doctrine, see Charles J. Tabb, Emergency Preferential Orders in Bankruptcy Reorganizations, 65 Am. Bankr. L.J. 75 (1991).

[266] 359 F.3d 866, 871 (7th Cir. 2004).

[267] See Miltenberger v. Logansport, C. & S.W. Ry. Co., 106 U.S. (16 Otto) 286 (1882).

[268] See id. at 312. See also Thomas Finletter, The Law of Bankruptcy Reorganization 379 (1939).

[269] See In re B & W Enters., Inc., 713 F.2d 534, 537 (9th Cir. 1983).

the "Six Months Rule" was a rule of priority that also developed in railroad cases.[270] The Six Months Rule permits the payment of necessary current operating expenses incurred in the ordinary course of business in the six months before the filing of the petition. That rule is based on principles of equitable restitution, on the theory that the current assets of the debtor are attributable in part to the credit extended in the six months preceding the filing. The Six Months Rule is incorporated into the Code in railroad reorganization cases only. § 1171(b). Nothing in the Code, however, incorporates the Necessity of Payment Rule. Until the 2004 *Kmart* decision,[271] discussed below, it was universally assumed that the only possible source of authority for ordering "necessary" payments was the court's general equitable powers under § 105(a).

As noted above, a number of bankruptcy courts have determined that they do possess such a general power under § 105(a), in order to foster the debtor's chances of reorganizing.[272] Until the Seventh Circuit's decision in *Kmart*, every court of appeals to consider the issue had held that the courts have *no power* to interfere with the Code's priority scheme by ordering the early payment of selected prepetition unsecured claims.[273] These courts followed the Supreme Court's reasoning that whatever equitable powers the bankruptcy courts possess may only be exercised in a manner consistent with the express provisions of the Code.[274] Importantly, determining the relative payment rights of creditors in bankruptcy is a core *legislative* function, not amenable to equitable redetermination by the courts, other than "under principles of equitable subordination," pursuant to § 510(c). The Supreme Court has emphasized that "[d]ecisions about the treatment . . . of claims in bankruptcy proceedings . . . are not dictated or illuminated by principles of equity,"[275] and that "reordering of priorities . . . takes place at the legislative level of consideration [and] is beyond the scope of judicial authority."[276] Thus, given the Code's comprehensive priority provisions, the

---

[270] See Fosdick v. Schall, 99 U.S. (9 Otto) 235 (1879). For more recent applications, see In re Boston & Maine Corp., 634 F.2d 1359 (1st Cir. 1980), cert. denied, 450 U.S. 982 (1981); In re Penn Cent. Transp. Co., 458 F. Supp. 1234, 1319 (E.D. Pa. 1978), aff'd in part & remanded, 596 F.2d 1102 (3d Cir. 1979), supp. op., 596 F.2d 1127 (3d Cir. 1979), cert. denied, 444 U.S. 834 (1979); In re New York, New Haven & Hartford R.R. Co., 278 F. Supp. 592 (D. Conn. 1967), aff'd, 405 F.2d 50 (2d Cir. 1968), cert. denied, 394 U.S. 999 (1969).

[271] 359 F.3d 866 (7th Cir. 2004).

[272] See cases in supra note 264.

[273] The decision most squarely on point is *B & W Enterprises, Inc. v. Goodman Oil Co. (In re B & W Enterprises, Inc.)*, 713 F.2d 534 (9th Cir. 1983), in which the Ninth Circuit flatly rejected the argument that postpetition payments to suppliers could be justified by the Necessity of Payment Rule, concluding that the "Rule" did not apply outside of railroad cases (if even there) and that the bankruptcy court had no power to approve such a payment.

For other decisions in which a court of appeals held or observed that bankruptcy courts have no power to order payments to some prepetition creditors, see In re Oxford Mgmt., Inc., 4 F.3d 1329 (5th Cir. 1993); Official Comm. of Equity Sec. Holders v. Mabey, 832 F.2d 299 (4th Cir. 1987), cert. denied, 485 U.S. 962 (1988); Southern Ry. v. Johnson Bronze Co. (In re Johnson Bronze Co.), 758 F.2d 137 (3d Cir. 1985); In re Crowe & Assocs., Inc., 713 F.2d 211 (6th Cir. 1983). In addition, the Eleventh Circuit's rationale for rejecting cross-collateralization in *In re Saybrook Manufacturing. Co.*, 963 F.2d 1490 (11th Cir. 1992), that the bankruptcy court does not have the equitable power to alter the Code's priority scheme, would apply with equal force to the Necessity of Payment Rule. See § 11.11.

[274] Norwest Bank Worthington v. Ahlers, 485 U.S. 197, 206 (1988).

[275] United States v. Noland, 517 U.S. 535, 541 (1996) (quoting *Burden v. United States*, 917 F. 2d 115, 122 (3d Cir. 1990)).

[276] United States v. Reorganized CF & I Fabricators of Utah, Inc., 518 U.S. 213, 229 (1996).

payment of some nonpriority unsecured claims in preference to other claims transgresses the fundamental limitations on the scope of the court's equitable powers. Under this view, the Necessity of Payment Rule (or the "Doctrine of Necessity") is an illegal expansion of the bankruptcy court's powers, with no justifiable place in reorganization practice today. In short, critical vendor orders simply lie outside the scope of the bankruptcy court's powers.

The Seventh Circuit in *Kmart* agreed that the bankruptcy court could not invoke its general equitable powers under § 105(a) to rewrite the statutory priority scheme.[277] However, it then went on to speculate in dicta that possible authority for "critical vendor orders" might lie in § 363(b)(1),[278] which authorizes the trustee to use, sell, or lease property of the estate other than in the ordinary course of business. The *Kmart* court held, however, that even if in principle it was conceivable that § 363(b)(1) might support critical vendor orders, on the record before the court, insufficient proof had been made: "We need not decide whether § 363(b)(1) could support payment of some pre-petition debts, because *this* order was unsound no matter how one reads § 363(b)(1)."[279] Nevertheless, the court's further musings on what *might* constitute sufficient proof under § 363 has set the agenda by which bankruptcy courts—anxious to find any hook on which to hang their hat in order to enter orders they believe in their infinite wisdom to be necessary and prudent—will assess whether to approve critical vendor orders. That the Seventh Circuit expressly stated that it was *not* deciding whether § 363 did or did not authorize critical vendor orders has been conveniently ignored.

The facts in *Kmart* are typical of what has become the practice in large reorganization cases, and demonstrate the stark disconnect between what the law *says* and what courts actually *do*. Here, the bankruptcy judge entered an extremely open-ended "critical vendor order" on the first day of the case, without notifying any disfavored creditors, without taking any pertinent evidence, and without making any findings as to the impact on the disfavored creditors. The order gave the debtor the unilateral discretion to pay in full the pre-bankruptcy claims of *any* of its suppliers that it deemed "critical," in exchange for an agreement to ship on "customary trade terms" for the next two years. Kmart exercised this remarkable power to pay a total of $300 million in satisfaction of the *pre-petition debts* of 2,330 suppliers (that is a *lot* of "critical" vendors!). Another 2,000 suppliers, however, did not get designated as "critical," a tough break indeed, since along with 43,000 other unsecured creditors, they eventually received only a dime on the dollar for their pre-bankruptcy claims.[280] One of the disfavored creditors appealed, wondering how it could be that some (thousands of) similarly situated creditors could get paid in full while it got paid a measly 10%, even though the Code's priority scheme appears to require equal payment, unless the unequal treatment is approved in a confirmed reorganization plan either by consent of all classes, or through the exercise of the rigorous "cram down" rules, none of which happened.

---

[277] 359 F.3d at 871.

[278] Id. at 872.

[279] Id. (emphasis in original).

[280] Id. at 869–70.

The district court reversed and held that the critical vendor order was illegal, following the unbroken line of circuit court authority[281] that has found no statutory or equitable power to order the payment of "critical" vendors, stating "we cannot ignore the Bankruptcy Code's statutory scheme of priority in favor of 'equity'. . . . [T]hese payments . . . simply are not authorized by the Bankruptcy Code. Congress has not elected to codify the doctrine of necessity or otherwise permit pre-plan payment of prepetition unsecured claims."[282] The Seventh Circuit then affirmed, but created much mischief with its unwarranted and unprecedented speculations that § 363(b)(1) may provide authority for critical vendor orders "if the record shows the prospect of benefit to the other creditors."[283]

Before turning to § 363, Judge Easterbrook for the Seventh Circuit quickly concluded that § 105(a) provides no authority for critical vendor orders, stating that "[a] 'doctrine of necessity' is just a fancy name for a power to depart from the Code," and that the court's equitable power under § 105(a) "is one to implement rather than override."[284] In order to override the Code's clear priority scheme, then, the Seventh Circuit insisted that some specific statutory authority be invoked. After rejecting suggestions that § 364 or § 503 might do the job, the *Kmart* court turned to § 363(b), and found it "more promising," reasoning that "satisfaction of a pre-petition debt in order to keep 'critical' supplies flowing is a use of property other than in the ordinary course of administering an estate in bankruptcy."[285]

This suggestion is grievously wrong. Section 363(b) has *nothing* to do with the priority of distributions. Yet the *Kmart* court's suggestion that it does turns § 363(b) into the debtor's ultimate priority trump card. Any court-approved "use" of property to pay pre-bankruptcy claims is *ipso facto* valid, even if doing so completely contradicts the express, specific statutory priority scheme spelled out in the Code. Normal statutory interpretation principles would dictate that the more specific provisions must control.[286] Under Judge Easterbrook's theory, however, a bankruptcy court has total authority and discretion to rewrite the Code's carefully conceived priority ordering as it sees fit, happily relying on the simple all-powerful justification that doing so is nothing more than a "use" of property under § 363. Even more mischievous is the fact that invoking a specific statutory provision as the basis for this supposed über-authority to rewrite priorities lends a false impression of legitimacy to the decision. At least when courts invoked § 105(a) they (and everyone else) knew that was a "Code" signal for the fact that they were skating on thin ice and basically making stuff up, but it was really important so everyone complicitly agreed to look the other way. It is deeply ironic that the *Kmart* court purported to denigrate the legitimacy of invoking a court's equitable powers to reorder the statutory priority scheme, but then turned around and did far worse by misreading § 363. Courts should not follow the *Kmart* lead; section 363(b) is

---

[281]   See cases cited supra note 273.

[282]   Capital Factors, Inc. v. Kmart Corp., 291 B.R. 818, 823 (N.D. Ill. 2003).

[283]   359 F.3d at 874.

[284]   Id. at 871.

[285]   Id. at 872.

[286]   E.g., RadLAX Gateway Hotel, LLC v. Amalgamated Bank, 132 S.Ct. 2065 (2012); Morales v. Trans World Airlines, Inc., 504 U.S. 374 (1992).

not a legitimate source of authority to enter critical vendor orders. But they will follow it, because it gives them what they want.[287]

Having opened Pandora's box, the Seventh Circuit then at least partially closed the lid, stating that "it is prudent to read, and use, § 363(b)(1) to do the least damage possible to priorities established by contract and by other parts of the Bankruptcy Code."[288] The court then effected this damage control by imposing several minimum evidentiary requirements that must be *proven* (and not just alleged) before a critical vendor order can be approved, even under the dubious authority of § 363(b):

1. "the disfavored creditors were at least as well off as they would have been had the critical-vendors order not been entered;"[289]

2. "the supposedly critical vendors would have ceased deliveries if old debts were left unpaid;"[290] and

3. "discrimination among unsecured creditors was the only way to facilitate a reorganization."[291]

The overarching requirement that the court cited in summation is that "preferential payments to a class of creditors are proper only if the record shows the prospect of benefit to the other creditors."[292]

The *Kmart* court's list of proofs required to approve a critical vendor order bears a very close resemblance to the judicial test that came to be used to approve cross-collateralization orders: (1) that the debtor's business would fail without the financing (thus mirroring the third *Kmart* element); (2) the debtor cannot get alternative financing on acceptable terms (implicit in the second and third *Kmart* elements); (3) the lender will not agree to less preferential terms (thus mirroring the second *Kmart* element); and (4) the financing is in the best interests of all creditors (thus mirroring the first *Kmart* element).[293]

Just as with the cross-collateralization test, the *Kmart* tests collapse upon closer examination.[294] Judge Easterbrook himself noted some of the flaws. For one, he observed that to say that suppliers would not be willing to furnish *new* goods and

---

[287] See, e.g., In re News Publ'g Co., 488 B.R. 241 (Bankr. N.D. Ga. 2013); In re Orion Ref. Corp., 372 B.R. 688 (Bankr. D. Del. 2007); In re Tropical Sportswear Int'l Corp., 320 B.R. 15 (Bankr. M.D. Fla. 2005).

[288] *Kmart*, 359 F.3d at 872.

[289] Id. at 874. The court earlier described this element in a slightly different fashion, "the disfavored creditors *will* be as well off with reorganization as with liquidation." Id. at 873 (emphasis in original). The difference in the two formulations is that the one in the footnote implicitly assumes that failure to enter the critical vendor order will lead to liquidation, whereas the one in the text does not.

[290] Id. at 873.

[291] Id. at 874.

[292] Id.

[293] See In re Vanguard Diversified, Inc., 31 B.R. 364 (Bankr. E.D.N.Y. 1983). See also § 11.11.

[294] See Charles J. Tabb, A Critical Reappraisal of Cross–Collateralization in Bankruptcy, 60 S. Cal. L. Rev. 109 (1986); Charles J. Tabb, Lender Preference Clauses and the Destruction of Appealability and Finality: Resolving a Chapter 11 Dilemma, 50 Ohio St. L.J. 109 (1989); Charles J. Tabb, Emergency Preferential Orders in Bankruptcy Reorganizations, 65 Am. Bankr. L.J. 75. (1991).

services—which is the only thing that could possibly be relevant to the debtor's prospects for reorganization—*even if guaranteed payment for the new deliveries*, unless paid for *old* deliveries, would be economically irrational.[295] Yes it would—but not if the court is willing to cave in to the extortionate demands of the critical supplier that old debts be paid as well as being guaranteed payment for the new deliveries. By opening up even the prospect of approving a critical vendor order, the critical vendor's economic decision to insist on payment of both new *and* old debts is quite rational. Importantly, it is virtually impossible to test the credibility of a vendor's assertion that element #2 is satisfied, *viz.*, that it will not ship—even for cash!—unless old debts are paid. Since it is in the vendor's obvious economic interest to say that, how can a court tell who is bluffing? And, if the vendor truly is "critical" to the debtor's survival, then neither the debtor nor the bankruptcy court will be willing to call that bluff. In short, it will be an extremely difficult task as a practical matter for the courts to figure out when payment really is "necessary."

Furthermore, overlooked in this analysis is the fact that a pre-petition creditor's threat to cut off deliveries unless paid in full for its pre-bankruptcy claims appears to be a blatant violation of the automatic stay's proscription against "any act to collect, assess, or recover a claim against the debtor that arose before the commencement of the case." § 362(a)(6).

Nor will it be an easy matter to determine which vendors are "critical." The truncated process by which the issue is resolved gives great power to the debtor to make the call, and makes it difficult for the court to second-guess the debtor's determination.[296] Relevant issues include how easily the debtor can acquire alternative products or services elsewhere, how essential this particular vendor's products or services are to the debtor's operations, and the extent to which the debtor can resist the vendor's demand for payment of its prepetition claims. The most extreme case would be one where the "critical" vendor is the only source for a good or service without which the debtor's business cannot operate. For example, if unpaid, the vendors would refuse to deal with the debtor, and as a result, the debtor would be unable to continue in

---

[295] *Kmart*, 359 F.3d at 873.

[296] One court, in considering the impact of Kmart, developed a three-prong test to determine critical vendor status: (1) the vendor must be necessary for the successful reorganization of the debtor; (2) the transaction must be in the "sound business judgment" of the debtor; and (3) the favorable treatment of the critical vendor must not prejudice other unsecured creditors. In re United Am., Inc., 327 B.R. 776, 782 (Bankr. E.D. Va. 2005). Note that the third prong of this test conflicts with *Kmart's* third, minimum evidentiary requirement that: "discrimination among unsecured creditors was the only way to facilitate a reorganization." *Kmart*, 359 F.3d at 874. Thus, this might signal that in the wake of *Kmart*, courts continue to perform damage control by means of narrowing the circumstances of when critical vendor orders will be approved, while still acknowledging there might exist a time and place when appropriate. Indeed, *United American*, immediately prior to announcing the three-prong test, stated: "The Doctrine of Necessity can be easily abused. *Kmart Corp.* reflects the extent to which a narrowly constructed remedy became over time a routine appeasement of creditors. If there is to be a Doctrine of Necessity, it must be narrowly construed and sparingly applied." 327 B.R. at 782.

See also In re Corner Home Care, Inc., 438 B.R. 122 (Bankr. W.D. Ky. 2010) (applying *United's* test); In re Ionosphere Clubs, Inc., 98 B.R. 174, 175–77 (Bankr. S.D.N.Y. 1989) (articulating the same factors, pre-*Kmart*, when discussing the doctrine of necessity).

business.[297] Likely, then, very few vendors would ever be considered "critical" to such a degree—certainly not 2,330 of them! Nor is it likely that other unsecured creditors would object to the payment of such a vendor. Indeed, one could fairly wonder why the debtor had not *already* paid a vendor who was that essential to survival.

Thus, the strong likelihood is that most supposedly "critical" vendors whom the debtor seeks to pay may be *important* to the debtor's business, but in fact would not satisfy a "reorganization failure" test. If a court were to take the third *Kmart* test seriously, few would pass muster. It is among this overwhelmingly preponderant intermediate mass of the debtors' vendors that the relative leniency or stringency of the "necessity" standard will determine how many vendors are considered "critical." How effective the demands of these "sort-of-critical" vendors for payment will be depends in large part on how much resistance they can expect from the debtor—which in turn depends on the legal permissibility of paying prepetition claims. The easier it is to obtain authorization to pay prepetition claims pursuant to a critical vendor order, the more leverage more vendors will have to demand and receive such payment. Thus, an inherent problem for courts assessing critical vendor order requests is that their assessment is in substantial part circular and self-determining.

The first element of the *Kmart* test is problematic as well. To say that the disfavored creditors are as well off with the order as not paternalistically substitutes the *court's* determination of what is good for the disfavored creditors for the decision of those creditors themselves. Obviously those creditors who objected did not think that the order was in their interest. Why does the court know better? The *Kmart* court stated that "If paying the critical vendors would enable a successful reorganization and make even the disfavored creditors better off, then all creditors favor payment whether or not they are designated as 'critical.'"[298] The problem with that statement is that it is demonstrably false—all creditors do *not* favor payment.

Nor is this a determination that can be made pursuant to a defensible *process*. One of the most disturbing aspects of critical vendor orders is that they are entered on the first day of the case, with virtually no notice to adversely affected parties, little or no chance to object, no meaningful opportunity to be heard, and certainly no opportunity to vote. The court decides for them, and does so very much "under the gun" of urgency. It is significant that the Code's scheme *does* allow for differential treatment between unsecured creditors in a chapter 11 plan—*if* all of the confirmation safeguards are met, including both procedural and substantive protections. Creditors get a disclosure statement and they get to vote on a plan, and if a class votes against a plan, then confirmation is possible only if the rigorous cram down rules are satisfied. But *none* of those protections exists in the context of entry of a first-day critical vendor order.

Thus, Judge Easterbrook goes astray when he opines that a critical vendor order might be allowed pursuant to "a use of § 363(b)(1) similar to the theory underlying a

---

[297] See, e.g., In re News Publ'g Co., 488 B.R. 241, 244 (Bankr. N.D. Ga. 2013) ("The foundation of a critical vendors order is that unpaid vendors will refuse to deal with the debtor, and as a result, the debtor will not be able to continue in business.").

[298] *Kmart*, 359 F.3d at 872.

plan crammed down the throats of an impaired class of creditors: if the impaired class does at least as well as it would have under a Chapter 7 liquidation, then it has no legitimate objection and cannot block the reorganization."[299] First, as just explained, *none* of the critical *procedural* protections built into the chapter 11 plan confirmation (and cram down) process are preserved. This fact alone casts grievous doubts on the legitimacy of critical vendor orders, and undermines Easterbrook's cram down analogy.

Second, the *Kmart* court gets the substantive cram down test wrong. What Judge Easterbrook cites as the cram down test—that the impaired class does as well as it would in a liquidation—is in fact the *best interests* test of § 1129(a)(7), and is a right that is enjoyed by and can be asserted by an *individual* unsecured creditor, even if that creditor's class votes in favor of the plan.[300] It is not a "class" protection at all, but a protection for minority class members, and must be satisfied in *all* cases (unless waived by every single creditor), not just in cram down cases. Cram down, by contrast, occurs when an entire class votes against a plan, and necessitates showings both that the plan (1) does not "discriminate unfairly" and (2) is "fair and equitable"—meaning that the absolute priority rule must be satisfied.[301] In the context of critical vendor orders, it is quite doubtful whether either the "no unfair discrimination" test or the absolute priority rule would be satisfied.

An intriguing postscript to *Kmart* concerns the impact of the 2005 Amendments. While nothing in those amendments directly deals with critical vendor orders or the Necessity of Payment Rule, two important amendments do address the underlying problem that partially motivated the impetus for critical vendor orders, by enhancing the likelihood that prepetition vendors will get paid for their pre-bankruptcy claims. First, the *reclamation* rights of a supplier of goods under § 546(c) were greatly expanded.[302] Second, the *administrative expense* priority entitlement for such suppliers was enhanced under § 503(b)(9).[303]

Under amended § 546(c), assuming that the debtor was insolvent at the time of delivery, an unpaid seller may be able to "reclaim" the actual goods delivered to the debtor in the ordinary course of business for 45 days prior to bankruptcy—and thus receive in effect full "payment" on its claim. A debtor who wished to keep the goods would be forced to pay off the creditor's reclamation claim in full, essentially mirroring the "critical vendor" payment. Note, though, that § 546(c) law imposes no "criticality" test; rather, *all* unpaid suppliers are entitled to reclamation if they meet the tests of ordinary course, delivery while insolvent, and timing.[304]

---

[299] Id. at 872–73.

[300] See § 11.26.

[301] See § 11.33.

[302] See § 7.37.

[303] See id.

[304] Though note, if the debtor enters into a DIP financing order proposing to use goods subject to the reclamation right at collateral for the postpetition financing, if the party with such reclamation right fails to object, its interest may be distinguished. See In re Circuit City Stores, Inc., 441 B.R. 496 (Bankr. E.D. Va. 2010).

The second powerful new payment right given to trade suppliers in 2005 was an enhanced administrative expense priority for *all* unpaid sellers of goods for the value of goods (1) sold to the debtor in the ordinary course of business and (2) received by the debtor within 20 days of bankruptcy. § 503(b)(9). This administrative priority does not even require proof that the debtor received the goods while insolvent, and, like the reclamation provision, does not require proof that the vendor was "critical." Also, a creditor who meets the requirements for reclamation but who failed to give the required notice still is entitled to the administrative priority. § 546(c)(2). Now, a debtor can effectively pay vendors who qualify for the priority early in the reorganization case, without running afoul of the equality principle, since Congress has afforded statutory priority to such creditors. Courts routinely allow early payment of administrative claims during the pendency of a reorganization case, differing only on what to do if the estate later proves administratively insolvent.

The interesting question in the wake of the 2005 Amendments is whether these new statutory rules designed to protect unpaid vendors should be interpreted as *replacing* critical vendor orders entered under the dubious authority of § 363(b). The argument can be made that Congress now has directly addressed the core "unpaid vendor" problem, and that it would be even more indefensible than it currently is to give § 363(b) an expansive interpretation to go beyond what Congress has expressly permitted. The only factual situations in which critical vendor orders now might operate that are not already covered by the 2005 rules would be if one of the requirements for reclamation or the administrative priority was not met. These scenarios would include cases where the goods were delivered to the debtor (1) out of the ordinary course of business; (2) more than 45 days before bankruptcy; or (3) or more than 20 days before bankruptcy, while the debtor was solvent. One could fairly wonder whether a supposedly "critical vendor" payment *should* be ordered in such cases; doing so would substantially minimize the importance and relevance of those specific limitations that Congress enacted in 2005.

As a final note, another "extraordinary" chapter 11 practice, that of offering substantial retention packages to designated "key employees," was curtailed sharply in the 2005 Amendments.[305] Under new § 503(c), strict regulations now govern such "KERP" agreements with insiders. For retention agreements, the court must find (1) that the transfer or obligation is essential to retention because the person has a bona fide job offer from another business at the same pay or more; (2) the services provided are essential to the business's survival; and (3) the pay cannot exceed specified caps on amount. Severance payments are not permitted unless part of a general program for all employees and the amount is capped at ten times the mean severance pay to non-management employees. Indisputably, after 2005 a bankruptcy court would not have the authority to approve a key employee retention plan that did not comply with § 503(c) under either its equitable powers, § 105(a), or under § 363(b).

---

[305] See § 7.13.

§ 11.13 Use, Sale or Lease of Property of the Estate

In chapter 11, continued operation of the debtor's business is the norm. § 1108. In fact, a party seeking to restrict business operations has the burden of obtaining a limiting order from the bankruptcy court. The debtor normally continues as debtor in possession (DIP), § 1101(1), and as DIP, retains control and management of its business and possession of property of the estate. The DIP is vested with the rights, powers, and duties of a trustee.[306] § 1107(a). For cause, a trustee may replace the debtor as DIP,[307] § 1104(a), who then will take possession of estate property and assume responsibility for operating the debtor's business. During the reorganization process, the estate representative (either trustee or DIP) not only will operate the business, but also might restructure that business. Both in operating and in restructuring the debtor's business, the estate representative of necessity will have to be able to deal with estate property. Section 363 governs the use, sale, or lease of property of the estate by the DIP or trustee.[308]

The statutory authorization for the debtor to use, sell, or lease estate property is found in subsections (b) and (c) of § 363. The principal difference in these subsections is whether the debtor must obtain court approval of the proposed use, sale, or lease of property, after notice and a hearing. The answer turns on whether the proposed transaction is in the *ordinary course of business*. If it is not in the ordinary course, then the debtor must obtain court approval. § 363(b)(1). The debtor does not need to send notice or obtain court approval of ordinary course transactions, however. § 363(c)(1). The general authorization in § 1108 for the debtor to operate the debtor's business necessarily carries with it the authorization to engage in all transactions and activities necessary and essential to that business operation, including the use, sale, or lease of property of the estate. The only exception is for "cash collateral," which the DIP or trustee may use only if the lienholder consents, or after court approval. § 363(c)(2)–(4).[309]

Whether a particular transaction is in the ordinary course of the debtor's business depends on whether the transaction is one as to which creditors presumably would want prior notice and the opportunity to be heard. Courts have framed two tests for judging the ordinary course inquiry: first, whether the transaction is ordinary as compared to the debtor's own prepetition operations (the "vertical dimension" test); and second, whether that transaction is ordinary compared to other businesses in the industry (the "horizontal dimension" test).[310] Each test focuses in a different way on the reasonable expectations of the debtor's creditors. If a DIP or trustee makes a transfer outside of the ordinary course of business, then a party may challenge the transaction as an unauthorized postpetition transfer. § 549. Additionally, if a court finds that a

---

[306] See § 11.4.

[307] See § 11.6.

[308] See §§ 5.16–5.18.

[309] See § 5.18.

[310] See, e.g., Braunstein v. McCabe, 571 F.3d 108, 124–26 (1st Cir. 2009); In re Lavigne, 114 F.3d 379 (2d Cir. 1997); In re Roth Am., Inc., 975 F.2d 949 (3d Cir. 1992); In re Straightline Invs., Inc., 525 F.3d 870 (9th Cir. 2008).

DIP made an unauthorized transfer under § 549, then an order replacing said DIP may not be too far behind.[311] § 1104.

Even for transactions that are not in the ordinary course, an actual court hearing will not always be required. The phrase "after notice and a hearing" means "such notice as is appropriate in the particular circumstances and such opportunity for a hearing as is appropriate in the particular circumstances," § 102(1)(A), and recognizes that an act may be taken without a hearing if notice is given, and either no party in interest timely requests a hearing or an emergency dictates dispensing with a prior hearing. § 102(1)(B). The Bankruptcy Rules implement this "negative notice" approach, dispensing with the hearing if no objection to a proposed use, sale, or lease is filed and served after notice is given. Rule 6004.

The most basic constraint on the debtor's authority to use, sell, or lease estate property is found in § 363(e), which provides that an entity with an interest in property that the debtor proposes to use, sell, or lease is entitled to *adequate protection* of its interest. The court will prohibit or condition the use, sale, or lease of estate property as is necessary to provide adequate protection. What constitutes adequate protection is dealt with by § 361.[312] The adequate protection issue usually arises with respect to secured parties, who are entitled to maintain and preserve the value of their collateral during the bankruptcy case. The debtor has the burden of proving adequate protection. § 363(p)(1).

The debtor may want to sell some (or all) property of the estate. Many sales are in the ordinary course of business, and will not need court approval. § 363(c)(1). For example, a retail debtor obviously may continue to sell its inventory. The debtor also may want to sell property out of the ordinary course of business.[313] For example, the debtor's business restructuring plan might call for selling some unprofitable stores. Court approval is needed for such sales. Under the conditions specified in § 363(f), property may be sold free and clear of the interests of others. Sales of property also may be effected through the plan itself. § 1123(a)(5)(D), (b)(4).

As mentioned above, the Code's general rules in § 363 allowing a debtor to use, sell, or lease estate property are subject to special limitations for "cash collateral." § 363(c)(2)–(4). For cash collateral, the interest of the non-debtor party in the property is given significant protection because of the risk that the cash collateral will be dissipated by the debtor. The debtor must segregate and account for any cash collateral in its possession, custody, or control. § 363(c)(4). Furthermore, the debtor is barred from using, selling, or leasing the cash collateral unless *prior permission* is obtained from either the secured creditor or the court. § 363(c)(2). The dispositive issue at a cash collateral hearing before the court usually is whether the secured creditor's interest in the cash collateral is being adequately protected. See §§ 363(e), 361.

In many chapter 11 cases, the debtor's need for cash collateral at the outset of the case is compelling. Section 363(c)(3) provides a specialized hearing procedure that

---

[311] See § 11.6.

[312] See §§ 3.18–3.20 for a discussion of adequate protection.

[313] See § 5.17.

enables the debtor to obtain emergency relief, and yet also safeguards the critical interests of the secured creditor. A cash collateral hearing often is the first significant contested matter in a chapter 11 case.

A question that has arisen is the extent to which § 363 can be used to sell *all or substantially all* of the property of the estate, instead of selling the property pursuant to a confirmed plan. This question was discussed in great detail in an earlier chapter, and I will not repeat that extended discussion here, but it is of course relevant.[314] The reality is that "the new 'chapter 3' reorganization"[315] is here to stay, although commentators differ as to whether we should applaud or decry that development.[316] The most notorious (in all senses of the word) § 363 sale cases have been the sale/reorganizations of General Motors[317] and Chrysler[318] in 2009.[319] In addition to the two auto cases, the largest § 363 sale in history occurred in the fall of 2008, when less than a week after filing chapter 11, Lehman Brothers sold its investment banking and trading businesses to Barclays for over a billion dollars.

Two related concerns arise when a debtor sells all or substantially all of its assets through a § 363 sale, one procedural and one substantive. The procedural concern is that the debtor is attempting to dispose of its assets and fix the payment to creditors without a formal disclosure statement, plan, ballot, or meaningful opportunity for creditors to participate in the bankruptcy process, other than by appearing at a court hearing and complaining. In short, debtors might use a § 363 sale to circumvent the more stringent and time-consuming procedural requirements of the chapter 11 plan confirmation process. On the substantive side, the worries are first, that this may not be the best deployment of the debtor's assets, and second, that the "sale" will subvert distributional entitlements. The first concern (deployment) is less problematic than the second (distribution), and might well be manageable in a sale setting. However, even if a prompt sale is the most efficient and value-enhancing way of deploying the debtor's assets, and even if the judge can make that determination wisely at a sale hearing,

---

[314] See id.

[315] Charles J. Tabb & Ralph Brubaker, Bankruptcy Law: Principles, Policies, and Practice 719 (3d ed. 2010).

[316] See, e.g., Ralph Brubaker & Charles Jordan Tabb, Bankruptcy Reorganization and the Troubling Legacy of *Chrysler* and *GM*, 2010 U. Ill. L. Rev., 1375 (2010). See also Barry E. Adler, A Reassessment of Bankruptcy Reorganization After *Chrysler* and *General Motors*, 18 Am. Bankr. Inst. L. Rev. 305 (2010); Douglas G. Baird & Robert K. Rasmussen, The End of Bankruptcy, 55 Stan. L. Rev. 751 (2002); Todd L. Friedman, The Unjustified Business Justification Rule: A Reexamination of the *Lionel* Canon in Light of the Bankruptcies of *Lehman*, *Chrysler*, and *General Motors*, 11 U.C. Davis Bus. L.J. 181 (2010); Melissa B. Jacoby & Edward J. Janger, Ice Cube Bonds and the Price of Process in Chapter 11 Bankruptcy, ___ Yale L.J. ___ (forthcoming 2014); Stephen J. Lubben, No Big Deal: The *GM* and *Chrysler* Cases in Context, 83 Am. Bankr. L.J. 531 (2009); Stephen J. Lubben, The "New and Improved" Chapter 11, 93 Ky. L.J. 839 (2005); Mark J. Roe & David Skeel, Assessing the *Chrysler* Bankruptcy, 108 Mich. L. Rev. 727 (2010); David A. Skeel, Jr., Creditors' Ball: The "New" New Corporate Governance in Chapter 11, 152 U. Pa. L. Rev. 927 (2003).

[317] In re Gen. Motors Corp. 407 B.R. 463 (Bankr. S.D.N.Y. 2009).

[318] In re Chrysler LLC, 405 B.R. 84, 111 (Bankr. S.D.N.Y. 2009), aff'd, 576 F.3d 108, 123–26 (2d Cir. 2009), vacated as moot sub. nom. Ind. State Police Pension Trust v. Chrysler LLC, 130 S.Ct. 1015 (2009).

[319] For discussion of these cases, see Brubaker & Tabb, supra note 316; see also Adler, supra note 316; Douglas G. Baird, Lessons from the Automobile Reorganizations, 4 J. Leg. Analysis 271 (2012); Lubben, *No Big Deal*, supra note 316, Roe & Skeel, supra note 316; A. Joseph Warburton, Understanding the Bankruptcies of Chrysler and General Motors: A Primer, 60 Syracuse L. Rev. 531 (2010).

that deployment choice should not be allowed to bleed over into the "who gets what" question—but it often does. How to make the pie the biggest and who gets how big a slice are critically different questions. Regardless of how a company disposes of its property—whether by plan or sale—courts should keep their primary focus on the need to preserve distributional norms and the entitlements of stakeholders.[320] It bears noting, of course, that the procedural and substantive concerns are linked: if the more protective plan confirmation procedures are not followed, but instead the § 363 path is taken, it may be more difficult for the bankruptcy court to make a wise decision on the deployment and distributional questions.

Courts agree that a preplan sale of all estate assets is permitted under some circumstances, but disagree on what those circumstances are. Under the largely abandoned restrictive view, a § 363 sale of all assets is allowed only if there is an emergency that would prevent the debtor from complying with the time-consuming chapter 11 confirmation procedures.[321] The much more permissive and now overwhelming majority approach rejects the "emergency only" view, and permits a proposed preplan sale of all or substantially all of the estate assets if the sale proponent offers a "*good business reason*" for the sale.[322] While courts talk in such flowery and catchy terms as "melting ice cubes," in truth the bar is not terribly high. Perhaps "stale bread" or "lukewarm coffee" would be more apt. A "good business reason" is a modest hurdle indeed.

The two gigantic auto cases have resolved this dispute (to the extent there even still was one) in favor of allowing free and clear sales of substantially all the debtor's property, pursuant to the generous "good business reason" test,[323] as long as the supposed sale is not really a "*sub rosa*" plan.[324] It is difficult indeed formally to distinguish between reorganization by plan and reorganization by sale—any reorganization lawyer worth her salt can make a plan look like a sale, and vice versa[325]—which means that seeking to ferret out and condemn "*sub rosa*" sale-plans, as courts are wont to do, is both a fools' errand and a red herring. The real threat is to distributional entitlements. As the discussion in chapter 5 explains, what is the most troubling about *Chrysler* and *GM* is that they conflate the deployment and distributional questions—and in *GM*, distributional entitlements were undermined.[326] Union workers got a much bigger share than did other unsecured creditors, which *could* be allowed in a plan cram down if sufficient justification for the discrimination in treatment were shown, but because the court believed the canard that "the allocation of ownership interests in the new enterprise is irrelevant to the estates' economic

---

[320] Brubaker & Tabb, supra note 316, at 1379.

[321] See, e.g., In re White Motor Credit Corp., 14 B.R. 584 (Bankr. N.D. Ohio 1981).

[322] See In re Lionel Corp., 722 F.2d 1063 (2d Cir. 1983). The *Lionel* test was reaffirmed in the auto cases.

[323] In re Chrysler LLC, 405 B.R. 84, 111 (Bankr. S.D.N.Y. 2009), aff'd, 576 F.3d 108, 123–26 (2d Cir. 2009), vacated as moot sub. nom. Ind. State Police Pension Trust v. Chrysler LLC, 130 S.Ct. 1015 (2009); In re Gen. Motors Corp. 407 B.R. 463 (Bankr. S.D.N.Y. 2009).

[324] In re Braniff Airways, Inc., 700 F.2d 935 (5th Cir. 1983).

[325] See Brubaker & Tabb, supra note 316, at 1379.

[326] See id. at 1406–07.

interests,"[327] the justification question was never even asked.[328] Yet, a bedrock principle of reorganization law, dating back to the origins of the "fair and equitable" test and the absolute priority rule, in venerable foundational cases such as *Northern Pacific Railway Co. v. Boyd,*[329] is that the value doled out in the reorganized new enterprise must respect the distributional entitlements to the debtor's estate; the two are obviously and necessarily equivalent.[330]

D. THE PLAN

§ 11.14 What a Plan Is and Why Confirmation Matters

The ultimate goal of a chapter 11 case is to confirm a plan of reorganization. While the debtor's business normally will operate in the interim while the terms of plan are worked out, § 1108, Congress did not intend for the debtor to remain in chapter 11 in perpetuity.[331] At some point either a plan must be confirmed, with the debtor or a successor then emerging from chapter 11, or the case should be dismissed or converted to a liquidation under chapter 7. If a plan is confirmed, the terms of the plan will serve as the blueprint for the debtor's financial obligations from that point forward. Upon confirmation, all prior claims and interests against the debtor are replaced by the provisions of the plan.[332] § 1141.

A plan of reorganization is a combination of (1) a *contract* between the debtor, creditors, and equity, and (2) an *investment* in the reorganized debtor by creditors and equity holders. It is a contract in the sense that a plan normally is assented to by all classes of creditors and interest holders, who agree to relinquish their prior claims or interests in exchange for the treatment offered by the plan and the like agreement of other classes. A plan is an investment in the sense that those creditors and interest holders decide to "invest" in the reorganized debtor or its successor by trading their pre-bankruptcy claims or interests for the claims or interests offered by the plan, after receiving adequate disclosure about the plan.[333]

Chapter 11 is premised on the ideal of capturing the premium of going concern value over liquidation value.[334] Congress decided to let the financially interested parties bargain over how to allocate that premium:

---

[327] In re Gen. Motors Corp. 407 B.R. 463, 497 (Bankr. S.D.N.Y. 2009) (quoting In re Chrysler LLC, 405 B.R. 84, 99 (Bankr. S.D.N.Y. 2009)). See Brubaker & Tabb, supra note 11, at 1402–03.

[328] See Brubaker & Tabb, supra note 316, at 1403–04.

[329] 228 U.S. 482 (1913). See § 11.33.

[330] See Brubaker & Tabb, supra note 316, at 1402–03.

[331] Ideally, a chapter 11 reorganization proceeding will not be pending for seven years. See Grp. of Inst. Investors v. Chicago, M., St. P. & P.R. Co., 318 U.S. 523 (1943).

[332] See § 11.35.

[333] Whether a proponent of a plan provides adequate disclosure to creditors and parties in interest depends on whether the plan's disclosure statement would provide a hypothetical reasonable investor with information that would enable them to evaluate what impact the plan would have on their claims and the outcome of the case, so as to decide what course of action to take. See, e.g., In re Ferguson, 474 B.R. 466, 470–71 (Bankr. D.S.C. 2012) (citations omitted).

[334] See § 11.1.

The parties are left to their own to negotiate a fair settlement. The question of whether creditors are entitled to the going-concern or liquidation value of the business is impossible to answer. . . . Instead, negotiation among the parties after full disclosure will govern how the value of the reorganizing company will be distributed among creditors and stockholders. The bill only sets the outer limits on the outcome: it must be somewhere between the going-concern value and the liquidation value.[335]

A reorganization plan is not a pure contract in the classic sense, however. One difference from a normal contract is that non-assenting parties are bound to the plan's terms. § 1141(a), (d)(1). However, those dissenting parties are protected from the tyranny of the majority by the rule that they are entitled to receive at least the liquidation value of their claim or interest.[336] § 1129(a)(7). Also, the parties are not entirely autonomous; the court will only confirm a plan if a number of statutory requirements in addition to party assent are satisfied. For example, the court must find that the plan is feasible, even if all classes accept the plan.[337] § 1129(a)(11).

Notwithstanding these important differences, a plan still is largely contractual in nature. It is a product of consensus. The terms of a plan almost always are arrived at through negotiations with the various classes of creditors and equity security holders. The dynamics of plan negotiation can be complicated, especially in larger cases. In those cases, multiple committees may be appointed,[338] and all will assert a voice in the bargaining process. The primary negotiating body for unsecured creditors is the official creditors' committee.[339] § 1103(c)(3). If the unsecured creditors' committee agrees to the plan, a positive vote by the entire body of unsecured creditors is almost a certainty. However, if the creditors' committee opposes the plan, the unsecured creditors are likely to reject the plan.

Creditors and interest holders are dealt with in a plan by classes.[340] The plan must classify claims, § 1123(a)(1), and only similar claims may be classified together.[341] § 1122(a). All claims in the same class must receive the same treatment. § 1123(a)(4). All impaired classes will vote on whether to accept the plan,[342] § 1126, after receiving a court-approved disclosure statement.[343] § 1125. Classes that are not impaired,[344] § 1124, are deemed to accept the plan. § 1126(f). If all classes either are not impaired or vote in favor of the plan, § 1129(a)(8), and the court finds that the other confirmation standards are met, the plan will be confirmed. At least one impaired class must accept

---

[335] H.R. Rep. No. 95–595, 95th Cong., 1st Sess., at 224 (1977).

[336] See § 11.26.

[337] See § 11.28.

[338] 11 U.S.C. § 1102(a)(2). For a case analyzing the process of appointing an additional creditors' committee, see In re Residential Capital, LLC, 480 B.R 550 (Bankr. S.D.N.Y. 2012).

[339] See § 11.8.

[340] See § 11.17.

[341] When creditors are placed in separate classes with different distribution percentages, the plan proponent must justify this difference in treatment. See, e.g., In re UAL Corp., 468 F.3d 456, 461 (7th Cir. 2006).

[342] See § 11.21.

[343] See § 11.20.

[344] See § 11.18.

the plan, unless all classes are unimpaired.[345] § 1129(a)(10). If an impaired class votes against the plan, the plan may only be confirmed under the "cram down" rules of § 1129(b).[346] To be crammed down, a plan must "not discriminate unfairly," and must be "fair and equitable."[347] § 1129(b).

In addition to the bargaining component inherent in the formulation of reorganization plans, Congress emphasized the investment character of a plan. The legislative history explicitly states that "the premise underlying the consolidated chapter 11 of this bill is the same as the premise of the securities law,"[348] namely, allowing affected parties to make informed decisions after receiving adequate information about their options. The decision is made by a creditor or interest holder when it votes on the plan, and the adequate information is contained in the court-approved disclosure statement.

§ 11.15 Exclusivity

One of the most critical aspects of the balance of power in a chapter 11 reorganization concerns who has the right to file a plan of reorganization. Will the debtor have the exclusive right to file a plan, or will other interested parties, such as creditors, have the right to file rival plans? Confirmation of a plan is the ultimate goal of a chapter 11 case. A confirmed plan is the formal document that defines the legal rights of all stakeholders in the reorganization.[349] Only those entities with the right to propose a plan and seek confirmation of that plan possess the specific power to shape the ultimate outcome of the case in a positive way. Parties who do not have the right to file a plan may be able to exert a negative influence, by threatening to veto any plan proposed, and may comment on and bargain over the plans proposed by others, but cannot directly achieve the ends they desire. Thus, defining who may file a plan impacts strongly on the tenor of plan bargaining dynamics.

The exclusivity issue was another point of contention that was implicated in the merger of chapters X, XI, and XII into a single reorganization chapter in 1978. Under chapter X, any party in interest could file a plan. Bankruptcy Act § 169. This rule logically followed from the requirement that an independent trustee be appointed in every case; it would not make much sense to appoint a trustee but not allow the trustee to propose a plan. In chapter XI, by contrast, where the debtor remained in possession, the debtor concomitantly retained the exclusive right to file a plan; creditors were permanently excluded. Bankruptcy Act § 323.

In choosing the best rule on who should have the right to file a plan when it merged the reorganization chapters in 1978, Congress had to weigh competing concerns. If the debtor is given the perpetual exclusive right to propose a plan, as in old chapter XI, the debtor will have significant leverage to coerce creditors into accepting

---

[345] See § 11.27.

[346] See §§ 11.30–11.34.

[347] See § 11.18.

[348] H.R. Rep. No. 95–595, 95th Cong., 1st Sess., at 226 (1977). It is for this reason that courts require plans to contain a disclosure statement with adequate information.

[349] See § 11.14.

its terms on a "take-it-or-leave-it" basis.[350] Since creditors are not paid interest on their claims during the pendency of the case, § 502(b)(2), the debtor can "wait out" the creditors, who effectively lose money each day the case drags on. All that creditors can do to counter the debtor's delaying tactic is to move for the appointment of a trustee, § 1104(a); seek to convert the case to chapter 7 or to dismiss the case, § 1112(b); or vote against any plan the debtor proposes. §§ 1126, 1129(a)(8).

Allowing the debtor to have permanent exclusivity thus could cause serious problems. However, Congress was concerned that the opposite rule, in which the debtor is given no exclusive right to file a plan, also would create significant difficulties.[351] In short, a "free for all" in filing plans would not be the palliative for all evils. One concern is that debtors would be reluctant to file chapter 11 in the first place if they knew that creditors could file hostile plans, and thus might forego an opportunity to reorganize and save the business until it was too late. Furthermore, even if the debtor did overcome that initial reluctance and file chapter 11, the absence of exclusivity might contribute to a breakdown of negotiations. Instead of sitting down at the bargaining table and trying to work things out, different groups might simply go off and file their own plan. Consensus might never be realized.

Congress compromised, and sought to capture the best of both worlds. The solution was to give the debtor *limited* exclusivity. The balance struck in § 1121 is to give the debtor an *initial* exclusive period of 120 days to file a plan (and 180 days to obtain acceptances of that plan, § 1121(c)(3)), but thereafter to permit any party in interest to file a plan. § 1121(b), (c)(2). In the interests of flexibility, the court is given the power, on a showing of cause, to extend (or contract) the debtor's exclusivity. § 1121(d)(1). Under this compromise, which gives the debtor the first chance to put an acceptable plan together, the debtor hopefully will not be deterred from filing for needed chapter 11 relief, and at the outset all parties will be forced to sit down together at the bargaining table. However, the debtor is not given the power to stall creditors into submission. In the rare case in which a trustee is appointed, the exclusive period will be terminated, § 1121(c)(1), which is logical because one of the primary duties of a trustee is to formulate a plan. § 1106(a)(5).

The congressional compromise has been honored in the breach. Courts routinely grant debtors multiple extensions of the exclusive period.[352] Thus, in many cases a practice of *de facto* permanent debtor exclusivity has developed. This is not what Congress intended.[353] The legislative history explains that "[i]n most cases, 120 days will give the debtor adequate time to negotiate a settlement, without unduly delaying creditors," and that extensions normally would be needed only "if an unusually large company were to seek reorganization."[354] Many commentators have pointed out that

---

[350] H.R. Rep. No. 95–595, 95th Cong., 1st Sess., at 231 (1977).

[351] Id. at 231–32.

[352] See, e.g., In re AMR Corp., 477 B.R. 384, 414 (Bankr. S.D.N.Y. 2012) ("American [the debtor] sought, and received, its second extension of its exclusive filing period. . . . "). But see In re Borders Grp., Inc., 460 B.R. 818, 821 (Bankr. S.D.N.Y. 2011) ("A court's decision to extend a debtor's exclusive periods is a serious matter; extensions are not granted routinely or cavalierly." (citations omitted)).

[353] See Charles J. Tabb, The Future of Chapter 11, 44 S.C. L. Rev. 791, 825 (1993).

[354] H.R. Rep. No. 95–595, 95th Cong., 1st Sess., at 232 (1977).

indefinite exclusivity has been one of the biggest problems in chapter 11 practice under the Code, causing delay, driving up costs, and pressuring creditors into capitulating to unfavorable plans.[355] When coupled with the debtor's right to propose a "new value" cram down plan,[356] exclusivity arguably has tilted the balance of power too heavily in the debtor's favor. Suggestions were made to impose an absolute limit on the debtor's exclusivity, or at least to raise the standard required to obtain an extension.

This problem was partially addressed with respect to small business cases in the 1994 reforms, but was not dealt with in large cases—where it has been a bigger problem—until 2005. Now, the 120–day period to file may not be extended beyond a date that is *18 months* after the date of the order for relief. § 1121(d)(2)(A). The 180–day period to obtain acceptances may not be extended beyond 20 months of the date of the order of relief. § 1121(d)(2)(B). These appear to be absolute deadlines, with the bankruptcy court enjoying no discretion to extend them.[357] It is a sad commentary that Congress believed that the courts so abused the discretion given them that it felt the need to impose an absolute deadline on the debtor's exclusivity.

In a small business case, the debtor has a longer initial exclusive period: 180 days to file a plan. § 1121(e)(1). No matter who files, the plan and disclosure statement (if any) may not be filed later than 300 days after the date of order for relief. § 1121(e)(2). These time periods may be extended on a proper showing. § 1121(e)(3). The absolute caps of 18 months and 20 months in subsection (d) do not appear to apply to small business cases. These small business rules mark a change from the direction taken for small businesses in 1994, pursuant to which such debtors were given a shorter 100–day exclusive period, all plans had to be filed within 160 days, and extensions were granted only if the debtor could show the need to do so was caused by "circumstances for which the debtor should not be held accountable."

Whether the case is a small business case governed by the special rules of § 1121(e), or a normal case governed by the remaining rules of § 1121, the crucial question in practice typically is what sort of showing the debtor must make to keep the exclusive period in effect. The legislative history suggests that cause for an extension "might include an unusually large case, ... or recalcitrance among creditors."[358] The rarer instance of cause for a reduction might be "an unusually small case, [or] delay by the debtor."[359] In moving for an extension, the debtor will have the burden of establishing cause.[360] Courts typically demand a particularized demonstration of cause. Factors that will support a debtor's extension request include: the case is large and

---

[355] See Edward I. Altman, Evaluating the Chapter 11 Bankruptcy–Reorganization Process, 1993 Colum. Bus. L. Rev. 1, 4; Lynn M. LoPucki, The Trouble With Chapter 11, 1993 Wis. L. Rev. 729, 753; Marvin J. Whitman et. al., A Rejoinder to "The Untenable Case for Chapter 11," 2 J. Bankr. L. & Prac. 839, 860 (1993).

[356] See § 11.34.

[357] See In re Randi's, Inc., 747 B.R. 783, 787 (Bankr. S.D. Ga. 2012) (holding that a court may not invoke § 105 to extend the deadlines in § 1121).

[358] H.R. Rep. No. 95–595, 95th Cong., 1st Sess., at 406 (1977).

[359] Id.

[360] See In re Borders Grp., Inc., 460 B.R. 818, 821 (Bankr. S.D.N.Y. 2011) ("The burden of proving cause to reduce or increase exclusivity is on the moving party...." (citing In re R.G. Pharmacy, Inc., 374 B.R. 484, 487 (Bankr. D. Conn. 2007))).

complex; plan negotiations are active and ongoing, and offer a reasonable probability of success; and the debtor is negotiating in good faith, and has not been stalling.[361] In short, courts are willing to give the debtor the benefit of the doubt, and will grant an extension in large cases, and if progress is being made. But if the parties are at an impasse, or the debtor is not negotiating in good faith, the court may refuse to extend exclusivity. The standard for extension in small business cases is clearly set forth. After giving notice to parties in interest, the debtor must demonstrate "by a preponderance of the evidence that it is more likely than not that the court will confirm a plan within a reasonable period of time." § 1121(e)(3)(A).

§ 11.16 The Contents of a Plan: Mandatory and Permissive Provisions

The watchword in chapter 11 is flexibility. Nowhere is that more true than with regard to the contents of a plan. Congress intended for the parties to have considerable freedom to negotiate whatever plan best serves their interests. Few restrictions are placed on what a plan may provide. At the same time, parties are given substantial power in a chapter 11 plan to effect a comprehensive and radical restructuring of the debtor's financial affairs. In short, the powers of old chapter X are combined with the flexibility of old chapter XI. The result is an impressive legal weapon for change.

The parameters of the contents of a plan are spelled out in § 1123.[362] The *mandatory* provisions of a plan are listed in subsection (a). Subsection (b) describes the *permissive* terms of a plan.

Mandatory provisions

The Code lists eight provisions that a plan "shall" contain, "[n]otwithstanding any otherwise applicable nonbankruptcy law."[363] § 1123(a)(1)–(8). The first four of these highlight the chapter's emphasis on *class* treatment of claims and interests.[364] First, the plan is required to designate classes of claims and interests. § 1123(a)(1). This classification must comply with § 1122, which only permits "substantially similar" claims to be classified together. Classification is not required for second, third or eighth priority claims, however, which instead must be dealt with individually in the plan. § 1129(a)(9)(A), (C).

The next two requirements for classes are that the plan must specify which classes are not impaired,[365] § 1123(a)(2), and the treatment of any class that is impaired. § 1123(a)(3). A class that is not impaired will not vote on the plan, but instead will be deemed to accept the plan. § 1126(f). The heart of the plan usually is the specification of the treatment of impaired classes. The possibilities are almost endless: the holders of

---

[361] See, e.g., In re Adelphia Commc'ns Corp., 352 B.R. 578, 586–87 (Bankr. S.D.N.Y. 2006).

[362] See S. Rep. No. 95–989, 95th Cong., 2d Sess., at 118–20 (1978); H.R. Rep. No. 95–595, 95th Cong., 1st Sess., at 406–07 (1977).

[363] See In re Federal–Mogul Global Inc., 684 F.3d 355 (3d Cir. 2012) (expressly holding that the "notwithstanding applicable nonbankruptcy law" language preempts state law, and allowed a plan to provide for the assignment of insurance policy rights despite an anti-assignment clause).

[364] See § 11.17.

[365] See § 11.18. Impairment is dealt with in 11 U.S.C. § 1124.

claims or interests in a class may be paid in full, in part, or not at all; in cash, property, or stock; over time or in a lump sum, and so forth.

Finally, the plan must provide the same treatment for each claim or interest in a given class, unless a particular holder agrees to less favorable treatment. § 1123(a)(4). In other words, nonconsensual discrimination within a class is prohibited. Note, though, that discrimination *between* classes may be permitted, subject to the limits on classification, § 1122; voting, § 1126; and the cram down prohibition against unfair discrimination. § 1129(b).

A plan is supposed to work. Thus, the fifth requirement is that the plan "provide adequate means for the plan's implementation." § 1123(a)(5). The extraordinary breadth of powers conferred on the parties and the extent of restructuring possible in a chapter 11 plan are strikingly demonstrated by the illustrative list of possible implementing means. § 1123(a)(5)(A)–(J). While no particular one of these illustrations is required to be in every plan, by inclusion in § 1123(a)(5) the listed means are authorized as permissible provisions of a plan. Among other things, a plan may provide for: the debtor to retain or transfer property; the merger or consolidation of the debtor with one or more entities; the sale of estate property, subject to or free of any lien; satisfaction or modification of liens; curing or waiving of any defaults; extension of maturity dates or change of interest rates; amendment of the debtor's charter; or the issuance of securities. Note that a complete liquidation of the debtor is possible. § 1123(a)(5)(d), (b)(4).

The Supreme Court has held that a debtor may designate that plan payments must first be applied to "trust fund" tax liabilities on which the debtor's principals would be personally liable, notwithstanding a contrary policy of the Internal Revenue Service, if necessary to the plan's success.[366] In the case of liquidating plans, however, the courts have taken different views on whether such a designation is permissible.[367] Absent a designation in the plan, the taxing authority's rule that plan payments are "involuntary" and therefore must be applied as directed by the IRS will continue in effect.[368]

The power to cure defaults was limited by a 1994 amendment that added § 1123(d). In *Rake v. Wade*,[369] the Supreme Court had held that interest had to be paid in order to cure mortgage arrearages *even if* neither state law nor the parties' original agreement required such payments. Under § 1123(d), the amount required to cure a default is to be determined in accordance with the parties' agreement and the applicable non-bankruptcy law.

A plan involving a reorganized corporate debtor must provide for the inclusion in the corporate charter of a provision prohibiting the issuance of nonvoting securities.

---

[366] United States v. Energy Res., Inc., 495 U.S. 545 (1990).

[367] Compare In re Kare Kemical, Inc., 935 F.2d 243 (11th Cir. 1991) (not permissible), with In re Deer Park, Inc., 10 F.3d 1478 (9th Cir. 1993) (permissible).

[368] See In re Fullmer, 962 F.2d 1463 (10th Cir. 1992), abrogated on other grounds by Raleigh v. Ill. Dep't of Rev., 530 U.S. 15 (2000).

[369] 508 U.S. 464 (1993).

Furthermore, voting power must be distributed "appropriately" between the various classes. § 1123(a)(6).

The plan must include only provisions that are consistent with the interests of creditors and equity security holders and with public policy with respect to the selection of officers, directors, and trustees under the plan, and their successors. § 1123(a)(7).

Finally, in the case of individual debtors, the 2005 amendments added a requirement that the plan must provide for payment to creditors of all or part of the debtor's earnings from personal services performed after commencement of the case or other future income as necessary to execute the plan. § 1123(a)(8).[370] This change brings individual chapter 11 requirements more in line with chapter 13.

Permissive provisions

The terms that are permitted, but not required, to be in a plan are listed in § 1123(b). Obviously, these provisions cannot contradict the mandatory terms of subsection (a). The powers made available to the parties in a plan in subsection (b) are very broad.

First, the plan may impair or leave unimpaired any class of claims or interests. § 1123(b)(1). Significantly, this power of impairment extends to secured claims, addressing one of the perceived shortcomings of old chapter XI. In addition, under § 1123(b)(5), the plan may provide for the modification of the rights of holders of secured claims. However, in 1994 the modification power was eliminated with regard to mortgages on a debtor's primary residence, as Congress decided to extend the chapter 13 anti-modification rule (§ 1322(b)(2)) to chapter 11. An issue that then arises is whether that anti-modification provision applies to property that the debtor also uses for his business, or what date (loan or petition) is used to determine whether the mortgage is on a primary residence.[371] Congress has considered changing this rule to permit home mortgage modification in chapter 13; however such bills have not been successful in the past, and the pending bills would not change the chapter 11 rule, leaving intact the anti-modification rule in that chapter.

Executory contracts or leases may be assumed, rejected, or assigned in the plan, if that contract or lease has not already been rejected during the case. § 1123(b)(2). This provision may even permit a creditor to require a debtor to assume an executory contract through a proposed plan.[372] A prior assumption is not final however; that contract or lease could still be rejected in the plan, although the other party to the contract or lease would then have an administrative expense claim for all damages (except as limited under § 503(b)(7) for commercial real estate leases). Note that the

---

[370] See also 11 U.S.C. § 1115(a)(2).

[371] See In re Wages, 479 B.R. 575 (Bankr. D. Idaho 2012) (holding that anti-modification provision applies to debtor's principal place of residence, even if they operated a business on it, and that courts should use the petition date to determine a particular land's use).

[372] See In re Nickels Midway Pier, LLC, 452 B.R. 156 (D.N.J. 2011) (holding that plan proposed by lessee could require debtor to assume an executory contract).

terms of § 365, which is the specific section governing the treatment of executory contracts and unexpired leases, will still apply at confirmation. Plans commonly contain a provision that all contracts or leases not expressly assumed in the plan are rejected. If this is not done, a contract or lease that is not mentioned in the plan may "ride through" confirmation and be binding on the reorganized debtor.

The plan may provide for the settlement of any claim belonging to the debtor or the estate. § 1123(b)(3)(A). Alternatively, such a claim may be retained, with post-confirmation enforcement rights vested in the debtor, trustee, or a designated representative. § 1123(b)(3)(B). For example, the plan might transfer the responsibility for litigating all preference actions on behalf of the estate to a liquidating trustee. However, the power to bring post-confirmation actions (1) must be expressly provided for in the plan,[373] and (2) is only available if potential recoveries would benefit the estate.[374]

As mentioned above, Congress expressly authorized liquidating plans. Under § 1123(b)(4), the plan may provide for the sale of all or substantially all of the property of the estate. Liquidation might be pursued in chapter 11 rather than in chapter 7 so that the debtor's management can supervise an orderly sale of property, perhaps in a more efficient and less expensive way than would be possible with an independent trustee.

Finally, a catch-all section authorizes the plan to "include any other appropriate provision not inconsistent with the applicable provisions of this title."[375] § 1123(b)(6). For example, several courts have concluded that plans creating trusts and channeling injunctions may be authorized under this provision and § 105(a) to address a debtor's mass tort liabilities.[376]

§ 11.17 Classification

Classification of claims and interests is central to the chapter 11 plan confirmation process.[377] Indeed, it is difficult to overstate the importance of classification in chapter

---

[373] See, e.g., In re SI Restructuring Inc., 714 F.3d 860, (5th Cir. 2013) ("For a reservation to be effective, it 'must be specific and unequivocal'—blanket reservations of 'any and all claims' are insufficient." (citation omitted)); Harstad v. First Am. Bank, 39 F.3d 898, 902 (8th Cir. 1994); In re Mako, Inc., 985 F.2d 1052, 1055 (10th Cir. 1993).

[374] See, e.g., In re Paige, 685 F.3d 1160, 1191–92 (10th Cir. 2012); In re Texas Gen. Petroleum Corp., 52 F.3d 1330, 1335–36 (5th Cir. 1995).

[375] See In re Lehman Bros. Holdings Inc., 487 B.R. 181, 190 (Bankr. S.D.N.Y. 2013) ("Section 1123(b)(6) is a broadly-worded, open-ended invitation to the creativity of those who are engaged in drafting plan language. . . . This amounts to a green light for those engaged in plan negotiations. Just about anything can be included, provided that the terms of the plan do not run afoul of applicable bankruptcy law.").

[376] See, e.g., In re Global Indus. Techs., Inc., 645 F.3d 201 (3d Cir. 2011); In re Dow Corning Corp., 280 F.3d 648 (6th Cir. 2002); In re Drexel Burnham Lambert Grp., Inc., 960 F.2d 285 (2d Cir. 1992); In re A.H. Robins Co., 880 F.2d 694 (4th Cir. 1989).

[377] For helpful discussions of classification in chapter 11, see John C. Anderson, Classification of Claims and Interests in Reorganization Cases Under the New Bankruptcy Code, 58 Am. Bankr. L.J. 99 (1984); William Blair, Classification of Unsecured Claims in Chapter 11 Reorganizations, 58 Am. Bankr. L.J. 197 (1984); David Gray Carlson, The Classification Veto in Single–Asset Cases under Bankruptcy Code Section 1129(a)(10), 44 S.C.L. Rev. 565 (1993); Bruce A. Markell, Clueless on Classification: Toward Removing Artificial Limits on Chapter 11 Claim Classification, 11 Bankr. Dev. J. 1 (1995); Peter E. Meltzer, Disenfranchising the Dissenting Creditor Through Artificial Classification or Artificial Impairment, 66 Am.

11. Claims and interests are dealt with by classes.[378] The main purpose of classifying claims is to recognize a difference in the repayment rights of creditors, which accordingly warrant a difference in treatment.[379] The proponent of a plan is required to designate classes, § 1123(a)(1); specify any class that is not impaired, § 1123(a)(2); specify the treatment of impaired classes, § 1123(a)(3); and provide the same treatment for all claims or interests in a class, unless a particular holder agrees to less favorable treatment. § 1123(a)(4). Classes vote on the proposed plan,[380] § 1126; classes may be impaired,[381] § 1124; and for a plan to be confirmed, all classes must either vote in favor of the plan, be unimpaired, or be crammed down.[382] § 1129(a)(8), (b). The dissenting members of a class are bound by the vote of the required majority. § 1126(c), (d). If all classes are either unimpaired or accept the plan, the plan will not have to comply with the "absolute priority" rule, § 1129(a)(8), (b), which means that a costly valuation of the debtor will be avoided. In any event, at least one impaired class must accept the plan, if any class is impaired.[383] § 1129(a)(10). Aside from the voting aspect of classifying claims, improper classification of claims results in the court denying confirmation of the plan.[384] In short, who is placed in which class is a matter of tremendous significance in a chapter 11 case.

So what are the rules that govern the classification of claims and interests? Analysis of this issue may be divided into two distinct components: first, which claims *may* be placed in the same class, and second which claims *must* be placed in the same class? The Code speaks directly to the first issue, § 1122, but is largely silent as to the second.

The primary limitation on permissible classification is that only *"substantially similar"* claims or interests may be placed in the same class. § 1122(a). Stated in the negative, § 1122(a) prohibits dissimilar claims or interests from being placed in the same class.[385] Similarity is determined by reference to the nature of the claims or interests being classified.[386] In other words, what matters is the legal character and effect of the claim or interest against the debtor. The nature and identity of the holder

---

Bankr. L.J. 281 (1992); Scott F. Norberg, Classification of Claims Under Chapter 11 of the Bankruptcy Code: The Fallacy of Interest Based Classification, 69 Am. Bankr. L.J. (1995); Linda J. Rusch, Single Asset Cases and Chapter 11: The Classification Quandary, 1 Am. Bankr. Inst. L. Rev. 43 (1993); Linda J. Rusch, Gerrymandering the Classification Issue in Chapter Eleven Reorganization, 63 U. Colo. L. Rev. 163 (1992).

[378] The only exception is for priority claims under § 507(a)(2), (3), and (8), which are not required to be classified. § 1123(a)(1). Each holder of one of these types of priority claims is entitled to be paid in full under the plan. § 1129(a)(9)(A), (C).

[379] See, e.g., SPCP Grp., LLC v. Biggins, 465 B.R. 316, 323 (M.D. Fla. 2011).

[380] See § 11.21.

[381] See § 11.18.

[382] See §§ 11.25, 11.30–11.34.

[383] See § 11.27.

[384] See In re Multiut Corp., 449 B.R. 323, 333 (Bankr. N.D. Ill. 2011) ("The improper classification of claims results in denial of confirmation under § 1129(a)(1).").

[385] See In re Zante, Inc., 467 B.R. 216, 219 (D. Nev. 2012) ("Section 1122(a) permits substantially similar claims to be classed differently, so long as claims that are not substantially similar are not classed together." (citations omitted)). Note that while § 1122(a) does not prohibit classifying similar claims in different classes, § 1122(b) requires a rational reason for doing so.

[386] S. Rep. No. 95–989, 95th Cong., 2d Sess., at 118 (1978); H.R. Rep. No. 95–595, 95th Cong., 1st Sess., at 406 (1977). See also In re Johnston, 21 F.3d 323, 327 (9th Cir. 1994).

is irrelevant. Indeed, the same entity might hold claims or interests in more than one class. Additionally, claims are not required to be classified based on their value alone.[387] Similarity in legal entitlements is critical, since a class votes together (with dissenters bound by the class vote) and the same treatment must be afforded to each member of a class. It would be illogical and unfair to lump dissimilar claims or interests together and permit a binding unitary vote by a nonunitary class. A helpful rule of thumb to use in judging similarity is to ask whether it would be fair for all members of the class to be bound by the class vote.

The similarity requirement is gauged primarily by the *relative priority in payment* against the debtor's assets enjoyed by the holder of the claim or interest.[388] Thus, secured claims and unsecured claims are legally dissimilar, because a secured claim has a right to payment out of specific collateral, while unsecured claims have only a general right to payment out of the residual assets of the estate. Unsecured claims against the debtor, in turn, are not similar to equity interests in the debtor, such as stock or partnership interests. Claims are entitled to be paid in full before equity interests receive anything.

Within the universe of secured claims, claims are dissimilar if they (1) are secured by different collateral, or (2) have a different rank against the same collateral.[389] A claim secured by Blackacre is not similar to a claim secured by inventory. Nor is the first lien on Blackacre similar to the second lien on Blackacre.

Within the ranks of unsecured claims, several tiers of classification may exist. Some unsecured claims will be entitled to priority under the Code, § 507, and accordingly cannot be classified with non-priority claims. And each level of priority is distinct from the others; for instance, a fourth priority claim under § 507(a)(4) could not be grouped with a seventh priority claim under § 507(a)(7).[390] For non-priority unsecured claims, some claims may be senior debt, while others may be subordinated. Those different types of claims will fall into different classes. For example, subordination agreements are enforceable under the Code, § 510(a), which dictates the need for separate classification of the subordinated claims.

Generally, though, the vast majority of non-priority unsecured claims will be "substantially similar," and thus *may* be placed in the same class. This is true whether the claim is for trade debt, or the undersecured portion of a secured claim, or arose because of the recovery of preference, or from the rejection of an executory contract. However, this does not necessarily mean that all unsecured claims *must* be placed in the same class; that critical issue is discussed below.

---

[387] See, e.g., In re Multiut Corp., 449 B.R. 323, 334–35 (Bankr. N.D. Ill. 2011) (citation omitted).

[388] See, e.g., In re Save Our Springs (S.O.S.) Alliance, Inc., 632 F.3d 168, 174 (5th Cir. 2011); In re W.R. Grace & Co., 475 B.R. 34, 109–10 (D. Del. 2012); In re Frascella Enters., Inc., 360 B.R. 435, 442 (Bankr. E.D. Pa. 2007) ("The similarity of claims is not judged by comparing creditor claims *inter se*. Rather, the question is whether the claims in a class have the same or similar legal status in relation to the assets of the debtor." (citations omitted)).

[389] See, e.g., In re A.O.V. Indus. Inc., 792 F.2d 1140 (D.C. Cir. 1986); In re Commercial W. Fin. Corp., 761 F.2d 1329 (9th Cir. 1985).

[390] As noted above, priority claims under § 507(a)(2), (3), and (8) are not classified.

The same priority separation holds true for equity interests. For example, the holders of preferred stock would have to be placed in a different class from the holders of common stock.

Substantial similarity of claims or interests is an important limitation on classification. It governs which claims or interests may be classified together. However, by far the more commonly litigated issue is which claims *must* be classified together. In other words, to what extent is the proponent of a plan free to place claims or interests that *are* substantially similar into *different* classes? The question almost always arises with regard to unsecured claims.

One might wonder what difference it makes. Why would a plan proponent ever want to put unsecured creditors in different classes? One reason is administrative convenience. For creditors with very small claims, it is hardly worth the time and expense to send them the plan and a ballot and solicit their votes. If those small claims can be paid in full, such costs might be avoided, on the theory that the fully paid claimants are deemed to accept the plan, and thus do not have to vote.

However, after the 1994 Amendments, this result may no longer be possible. In 1994, Congress repealed § 1124(3), which had provided that a claim was not "impaired" if it was paid in full in cash. A claim that is not impaired is conclusively deemed to accept the plan. § 1126(f). With the repeal of § 1124(3), however, a claim still should be considered "impaired" even if cashed out in full, and as such would be entitled to vote.[391]

Congress expressly authorized the separate classification of small administrative convenience classes. § 1122(b). Beyond that, however, the Code says nothing about placing similar claims in separate classes. Separate classification is neither expressly prohibited nor permitted. The only pertinent statutory restrictions speak to the *treatment* afforded classes, specifically, that (1) the members of the same class are entitled to receive the same treatment, § 1123(a)(4), and (2) if a class votes no, the plan may "not discriminate unfairly" against that class, and must be "fair and equitable." § 1129(b). Accordingly, courts generally agree that it is at least *possible* for similar claims to be placed in different classes.[392] What they disagree on is what showing is required to make that possibility a reality.

Aside from the administrative convenience situation, the most likely reason why a plan proponent might seek to separately classify similar claims is to try to satisfy § 1129(a)(10), which requires one impaired class to vote in favor of the plan. The proponent of the plan might want to put a large dissenting creditor in a separate class from other unsecured creditors, increasing the chances that the remaining members of the unsecured class will vote in favor of the plan, with the dissenter's class then to be dealt with via cram down.

To illustrate, assume that Debtor has unsecured trade debt of $500,000, dispersed among 20 creditors. Bank Five has a total claim of $3 million against Debtor, which is

---

[391] See §§ 11.18, 11.21.

[392] See, e.g., In re Jersey City Med. Ctr., 817 F.2d 1055 (3d Cir. 1987).

secured by collateral worth $2.4 million. Under § 506(a)(1), Bank Five is deemed to hold two claims against Debtor: a secured claim for the value of the collateral ($2.4 million), and an unsecured claim for the balance ($600,000). Bank Five's secured and unsecured claims must be separately classified. If Bank Five's unsecured claim cannot be classified separately from the unsecured trade debt, Bank Five effectively will be able to block confirmation.

Why? Because Bank Five holds a controlling voice over the unsecured class, and if the single unsecured class votes no, the requirement of § 1129(a)(10) that at least one impaired class vote in favor of the plan is not likely to be met. Under § 1126(c), an affirmative vote of a class of claims requires the assent of two-thirds in amount of the class. In the example, Bank Five, with over half of the total unsecured debt, controls more than enough to prevent an affirmative class vote. If, however, Bank Five is placed in its on class, the class with $500,000 in trade debt might vote in favor of the plan, satisfying § 1129(a)(10). Even though Bank Five could still vote its separate unsecured class against the plan, the proponent could attempt to cram down the plan under § 1129(b).

Whether such "gerrymandering" of classes to obtain a positive class vote is permissible has been one of the most hotly debated issues under the Code. The problem often arises in single asset real estate cases, where the major lender is undersecured, and thus would control the unsecured class, as in the example. A significant number of courts of appeals have *not* allowed separate classification for the sole purpose of creating an impaired class that will vote in favor of the plan.[393] As the Fifth Circuit stated in the leading case of *In re Greystone III Joint Venture*, the "one clear rule" is that "thou shalt not classify similar claims differently in order to gerrymander an affirmative vote on a reorganization plan."[394] To justify separate classification, some other more legitimate reasons must be advanced.[395] Other courts, however, have criticized the "one clear rule" reading of § 1122(a), and instead have given that section a more expansive and permissive interpretation.[396] As a practical matter, the issue became less important after the Supreme Court in 1999 limited the ability of a single asset debtor to confirm a "new value" cram down plan in *Bank of America National Trust and Savings Association v. 203 North LaSalle Street Partnership*,[397] because even if separate classification of the objecting undersecured creditor's unsecured claim is permitted, the plan still can be confirmed only via cram down.

---

[393] See, e.g., In re Barakat, 99 F.3d 1520 (9th Cir. 1996), cert. denied, 520 U.S. 1143 (1997); In re Boston Post Road Ltd. P'ship, 21 F.3d 477 (2d Cir. 1994), cert. denied, 513 U.S. 1109 (1995); John Hancock Mut. Life Ins. Co. v. Route 37 Bus. Park Assocs., 987 F.2d 154 (3d Cir. 1993); In re Lumber Exch. Bldg. Ltd. P'ship, 968 F.2d 647 (8th Cir. 1992); In re Bryson Props., XVIII, 961 F.2d 496 (4th Cir.), cert. denied, 506 U.S. 866 (1992); In re Pac. Lumber Co., 584 F.3d 229, (5th Cir. 2009); In re Greystone III Joint Venture, 948 F.2d 134, corrected and reinstated, 995 F.2d 1274 (5th Cir.), cert. denied 506 U.S. 821 (1992). See also In re Heritage Org., L.L.C., 375 B.R. 230, 298 (Bankr. N.D. Tex. 2007) ("A Debtor's motives must be scrutinized to prevent the possibility of vote manipulation." (citations omitted)).

[394] 995 F.2d at 1279.

[395] See In re W.R. Grace & Co., 475 B.R. 34, 110 (D. Del. 2012) ("[S]ubstantially similar claims may not be classified separately when it is done for an illegitimate reason." (citation omitted)).

[396] See, e.g., In re Dow Corning Corp., 244 B.R. 634 (Bankr. E.D. Mich. 1999); In re Crosscreek Apts., Ltd., 213 B.R. 521 (Bankr. E.D. Tenn. 1997).

[397] 526 U.S. 434 (1999). See § 11.34. The classification issue was not presented to the Supreme Court, which made clear that it was not deciding the permissibility of separate classification. 526 U.S. at 439 n.7.

The decisions in which separate classification has been allowed usually find either that the separation is based on "good business reasons" (stated otherwise, a "legitimate business or economic justification") or that the claimant who is separated has distinct, non-creditor interests that provide it with different motivations than other unsecured creditors.[398] For example, courts have held that the interests of a utility, a municipality, and a labor union are sufficiently distinct to warrant being placed in their own class.[399]

The right of a nonrecourse creditor in § 1111(b)(1)(A) to have its claim treated as recourse has caused some dissension in the courts as to the propriety of separate classification. A "nonrecourse" claim is one in which the creditor cannot sue the debtor personally for a debt, but is limited to recovery against the collateral. Nonrecourse financing is common in single asset real estate financing. Under § 1111(b)(1)(A), the nonrecourse creditor is given recourse unless it elects to have its entire claim treated as secured. The reason is to limit the ability of debtors to cram down single asset lenders in a depressed real estate market. The effect of giving the lender recourse is that the lender will have an unsecured claim for the deficiency in the value of the collateral as compared to the total debt. The question is whether this "artificial" unsecured claim that is purely a creature of statute may (or must!) be classified separately from traditional unsecured claims. Most courts have held that the fact that a claim is created by § 1111(b)(1)(A) is *not* a sufficient justification for separate classification.[400] In the context of chapter 11, that statutory unsecured claim has the same right to payment as does an unsecured claim that arises under non-bankruptcy law. However, a small minority of courts have held that the legal rights of a creditor holding an unsecured claim solely by virtue of § 1111(b)(1)(A) are so different from the rights of general unsecured claims that separate classification is not only permitted, but may actually be mandated by the "substantial similarity" rule of § 1122(a).[401]

Yet another reason why a plan proponent may attempt separate classification of similar claims is that the proponent may not want to provide the same treatment for all unsecured claims, but runs into the roadblock that § 1123(a)(4) entitles all members of a class to the same treatment. For example, the proponent might want to pay one group of unsecured creditors a larger dividend than another group, or pay one group in cash and another in stock. The only way around the restriction of § 1123(a)(4)—other than obtaining a waiver from every single class member that receives less favorable treatment—is to create separate classes.

---

[398] See In re Red Mountain Mach. Co., 448 B.R. 1 (Bankr. D. Ariz. 2011); In re Trenton Ridge Invs., LLC, 461 B.R. 440 (Bankr. S.D. Ohio 2011).

[399] See In re Wabash Valley Power Ass'n, 72 F.3d 1305 (7th Cir. 1995), cert. denied, 519 U.S. 965 (1996); In re Briscoe Enters., Ltd. II, 994 F.2d 1160 (5th Cir.), cert. denied, 510 U.S. 992 (1993); In re U.S. Truck Co., 800 F.2d 581 (6th Cir. 1986).

[400] See, e.g., *Barakat*, supra note 393, 99 F.3d 1520; *Boston Post Road*, supra note 393, 21 F.3d 477; *Greystone III Joint Venture*, supra note 393, 995 F.2d 1274, In re RYYZ, LLC, 490 B.R. 29 (Bankr. E.D.N.Y. 2013).

[401] See, e.g., In re Woodbrook Assocs., 19 F.3d 312 (7th Cir. 1994); In re Greenwood Point, LP, 445 B.R. 885 (Bankr. S.D. Ind. 2011); In re SM Ltd., 160 B.R. 202 (Bankr. S.D. Fla. 1993). The Supreme Court in *203 North LaSalle Street* did not decide this issue. 526 U.S. at 439 n.7.

This motivation for creating separate classes might pass muster, if a good business or economic reason supported the distinction.[402] For example, some institutional creditors may have restrictions on how much stock they are permitted to hold in other companies, and thus will not want to receive stock under the plan. The bigger problem for the proponent, if a sound reason supports separation, might be the difference in treatment. If the disfavored class votes against the plan, confirmation is possible only if the difference in treatment is not found to be an "unfair" discrimination, and if the plan is "fair and equitable." § 1129(b).

§ 11.18 Impairment

Chapter 11 plans are structured primarily around *classes* of claims and interests.[403] A central concept governing the treatment of classes in a chapter 11 plan is *"impairment."* Impairment is dealt with in § 1124. A class must either be impaired or unimpaired. The proponent of the plan is required to specify which classes are not impaired. § 1123(a)(2). For the plan to be confirmed without going to cram down, every class must either (1) be unimpaired, or (2) accept the plan. § 1129(a)(8). If a class is impaired and does not accept the plan, confirmation is only available if the cram down standards are met with regard to that class. § 1129(b).

A primary effect of finding that a class is not impaired, then, is that the necessary confirmation protection for that class is satisfied. § 1129(a)(8)(B). Furthermore, that standard is met without the plan proponent having to solicit the votes of the members of the unimpaired class. A class that is not impaired is *conclusively* deemed to accept the plan. § 1126(f). This saves the plan proponent the time and expense of soliciting those votes, and avoids the risk of a negative class vote.

The members of an unimpaired class have no right to vote—even if they can prove that they would have voted against the plan. This rule is not a matter of academic curiosity, but is an important benefit to debtors, and was not clarified until the 1984 Amendments. When would it matter whether an unimpaired class may vote? Usually, it matters if the debtor renders a secured creditor unimpaired under § 1124(2), as discussed below, by curing a default and reinstating a below-market interest rate. In such a situation, the creditor would prefer immediate foreclosure to confirmation, because the creditor then could lend the money currently tied up in the debtor at the higher market rates.

Another potentially significant effect of the impairment concept on confirmation concerns the effect of § 1129(a)(10), which requires at least one impaired class to accept the plan, but only if any class is impaired.[404] Thus, if *all* classes are unimpaired, § 1129(a)(10) will not stand in the way of confirmation of the plan. If, however, any

---

[402] See, e.g., In re Draiman, 450 B.R. 777, 790 (Bankr. N.D. Ill. 2011) ("Claims may also be separately classified if there are good business reasons to do so or if the claimants have sufficiently different interests in the plan." (quoting *In re Wabash Valley Power Ass'n, Inc.*, 72 F.3d 1305, 1321 (7th Cir. 1995))). See also In re Unbreakable Nation Co., 437 B.R. 189 (Bankr. E.D. Pa. 2010) ("Classification of claims by the debtor must be reasonable." (citations omitted)).

[403] See § 11.17.

[404] See § 11.27.

classes are impaired, the plan proponent will have to comply with § 1129(a)(10), and obtain the affirmative vote of an impaired class.

Impairment is primarily important as a means of dealing with classes of claims or interests, but it also has significance for the individual holders of claims or interests in a class. The principal protection at confirmation for the individual class members is the "best interests" test, which provides that each holder of a claim or interest either must accept the plan or must receive at least as much under the plan as they would have received in a hypothetical liquidation under chapter 7.[405] § 1129(a)(7)(A). However, the best interests test does *not apply* to the members of classes that are not impaired, but rather applies only to impaired classes. Because of this, a member of an unimpaired class will lose the benefit of special chapter 7 rules that might be more favorable to them than the chapter 11 rules.

For example, chapter 7 contains a "solvency exception" to the general rule that postpetition interest is not paid on claims. § 726(a)(5). Under that exception, if the estate is solvent after paying all claims in full, postpetition interest will be paid on claims before a distribution is made to the debtor. However, until the 1994 Amendments, a solvent debtor could avoid paying postpetition interest in chapter 11 by proposing in the plan to pay all claims in full.[406] Under old § 1124(3), classes that were paid in full were not impaired, and the best interests test of § 1129(a)(7) therefore did not apply. The best interests reference to chapter 7 is the only vehicle for invoking a solvency exception in chapter 11, which does not contain any such exception. Those unimpaired classes could not vote against the plan, because of the conclusive presumption of acceptance. § 1126(f). Thus, the fully paid "unimpaired" classes got less than they would have received in chapter 7. Congress responded to this particular problem by repealing § 1124(3) in 1994, so that even fully paid classes are impaired.[407] Still, though, other rules that are unique to chapter 7 (such as the partnership rules, § 723, or the subordination of tax liens, § 724(b)) will continue to be unavailable to members of classes that are unimpaired under § 1124.

The effects of a class being impaired are, of course, the opposite of the effects of a class being unimpaired. First, the members of an impaired class will be entitled to vote on the plan. § 1126. If the requisite majority of the impaired class does not accept the plan, confirmation will only be possible under the cram down rules. Second, if any class is impaired, at least one of the impaired classes must vote in favor of the plan. § 1129(a)(10). Finally, the individual members of an impaired class are entitled to invoke the protections of the best interests test of § 1129(a)(7)(A).

It is thus extremely important to know whether a class is impaired or not. Section 1124 contains the exclusive list of means by which a class may be unimpaired under a

---

[405] See § 11.26.

[406] See, e.g., In re New Valley Corp., 168 B.R. 73 (Bankr. D.N.J. 1994).

[407] H.R. Rep. No. 103–835, 103d Cong. 47–48 (1994) ("In a recent Bankruptcy Court decision (*New Valley*), unsecured creditors were denied the right to receive post petition interest. . . . In order to preclude this unfair result in the future, the Committee finds it appropriate to delete section 1124(3) from the Bankruptcy Code. As a result of this change, if a plan proposed to pay a class of claims in cash in the full allowed amount of the claims, the class would be impaired, entitling creditors to vote for or against the plan of reorganization.").

plan. Two options are stated. The plan must comply with only one of the two to render the class unimpaired, i.e., the two choices are stated in the disjunctive. The two options are: (1) leave all rights unaltered, or (2) cure and compensate for defaults and reinstate an accelerated obligation. § 1124(1), (2).

The first way that a class may be deemed unimpaired is if the plan "leaves unaltered the legal, equitable, and contractual rights" of the holder of the claim or interest. § 1124(1). Congress meant what it said in § 1124(1)—the plan must not alter the rights of the class holders at all. *Any* alteration will be an impairment, even if the court believes that the class would be better off under the plan than before.[408] That decision is for the class to make in voting on the plan. If the class votes against the plan, the proponent could then invoke the cram down rules of § 1129(b). But impairment is not a substitute for cram down. Congress in § 1124(1) thus departed significantly from prior law, under which a class was impaired only if "materially and adversely affected."[409] A situation in which § 1124(1) might be satisfied is where the debtor is not in default on a secured debt, has continued regular payments during the case, and proposes in the plan simply to keep paying on the original terms.[410]

But what if the debtor *is* in default on a secured obligation, and the creditor has exercised its right to accelerate the debt, but the debtor would like to keep the benefit of the original terms? For example, the debtor may have a below-market interest rate. The answer for such a debtor in default is § 1124(2), which permits the debtor to "deaccelerate" the obligation. Under that provision, a class will not be impaired even if the debtor is in default and the creditor has accelerated if the plan proposes to do the following:

- cure the default (other than those specified in § 365(b)(2));

- reinstate the maturity as it existed before the default;

- compensate the creditor for damages suffered because of reasonable reliance on the acceleration provision;

- if the claim or interest arises from any failure to perform a nonmonetary obligation, other than a default arising from a failure to operate a commercial real estate lease subject to § 365(b)(1)(A),[411] compensates the creditor for actual pecuniary loss incurred as a result; and

- otherwise leave the creditor's rights unaltered.

---

[408] See, e.g., In re Vill. at Camp Bowie I, L.P., 710 F.3d 239 (5th Cir. 2013); In re L & J Anaheim Assocs., 995 F.2d 940 (9th Cir. 1993).

[409] Bankruptcy Act § 107 ("Creditors or stockholders or any class thereof shall be deemed to be 'affected' by a plan only if their or its interest shall be materially and adversely affected thereby. . . . ").

[410] See In re Tex. Rangers Baseball Partners, 434 B.R. 393, 406–07 (Bankr. N.D. Tex. 2010) ("[I]f a creditor receives under the plan everything to which the creditor would be entitled in a judgment entered immediately following the plan's effective date, the creditor is receiving treatment that, as required by section 1124(1), honors all the creditor's 'legal, equitable, and contractual rights.'").

[411] This is the provision added in 2005 that excuses the cure of defaults in commercial real estate leases that are incurable, and that allows the cure of a so-called "going dark" default by resuming operation in accordance with the lease terms. See § 8.16.

The power to deaccelerate under § 1124(2) is a powerful weapon for debtors. It minimizes the incentive for creditors to try to move quickly and accelerate before the debtor can file for relief under chapter 11, because the debtor can reverse that acceleration in chapter 11. Indeed, a creditor might unwittingly force a debtor to file chapter 11 by hastily accelerating.

The right to cure under § 1124(2) persists even if the creditor has obtained a foreclosure judgment.[412] Only when the collateral is sold at foreclosure sale does it become too late for the debtor to "put Humpty Dumpty back together again." To cure, though, the debtor must pay full compensation for the default on the effective date of the plan. Furthermore, both prepetition and postpetition defaults must be cured. The debtor will not have to cure defaults under "ipso facto" clauses, though, which are predicated on the debtor's bankruptcy filing or financial condition.[413] Nor will the debtor have to cure incurable nonmonetary defaults on commercial real estate leases.

Other than curing the defaults and reinstating the original maturity, a debtor cannot otherwise modify or alter the obligation under § 1124(2). If the debtor wants to extend the time for payment, strip down an undersecured debt, or otherwise modify the rights of the class, it might be able to do so, but the class will have a right to vote, and if it votes no, the plan will have to satisfy the cram down rules. Again, impairment is not a substitute for cram down.

As mentioned above, before 1994 there were three options under § 1124. The third, in old § 1124(3), provided that a class was not impaired if the members of the class were paid the full amount of their allowed claim in cash on the effective date of the plan. That subsection was repealed in 1994, however. The intended effect of the repeal of § 1124(3) was to make available to fully paid classes the protections of both the best interest test of § 1129(a)(7)(A) and the absolute priority rule of § 1129(b).

However, one unintended effect of the repeal was to make it easier for a debtor to satisfy § 1129(a)(10). Now a class that is paid in full still will be deemed impaired, will accordingly be permitted to vote on the plan, and if it votes in favor of the plan will satisfy the requirement in (a)(10) that one impaired class accept the plan.[414] Because of this, plan proponents will not have to resort to such tricks as "artificial impairment," where they would impair the rights of a fully paid class in a trivial way (such as by delaying payment for a few days, or paying 99% on claims) and thereby hope to qualify that "impaired" class as the accepting class under (a)(10).[415] Congress has done the work for the plan proponents, who may pay a class in full and yet still use that class for (a)(10).

---

[412] See, e.g., In re Madison Hotel Assocs., 749 F.2d 410 (7th Cir. 1984).

[413] See, e.g., Gen. Elec. Capital Corp. v. Future Media Prods., Inc., 547 F.3d 956, 960 (9th Cir. 2008) ("[T]he provision allowing 'cures' under § 1124(2)(A) 'authorizes a plan to *nullify all* consequences of default, including avoidance of default penalties such as higher interest.'" (citation omitted, emphasis in original)).

[414] See In re Atlanta–Stewart Partners, 193 B.R. 79 (Bankr. N.D. Ga. 1996).

[415] See, e.g., In re Combustion Eng'g, Inc., 391 F.3d 190 (3rd Cir. 2004) (remanding case to determing whether use of "stub claims" of asbestos claimants who participated in prepetition settlement constituted an artificial impairment); In re Windsor on the River Assocs., Ltd., 7 F.3d 127 (8th Cir. 1993) (holding that a class "artificially impaired" by a short delay in payment could not be used to satisfy § 1129(a)(10)).

At the same time, though, the fact that a fully paid class will be considered impaired means that the class will have the right to vote, which will necessitate the expense of sending the disclosure statement, plan, and ballot to those class members, and create the risk of a negative vote. Apparently even the votes of an administrative convenience class created under § 1122(b) will have to be solicited, since the class will be impaired.

§ 11.19 Modification

The proponent of a plan may want to modify that plan after the plan has been filed. The rules governing the modification of a plan depend entirely on *when* in the chapter 11 process the modification is sought. Confirmation of the plan is the principal dividing line; *pre*-confirmation modifications are much easier to effect than *post*-confirmation modifications. § 1127(a), (b). And for modifications prior to confirmation, it makes a difference whether votes have been solicited yet or not.

Prior to confirmation, modifications are commonplace. The negotiation of the terms of a plan is an ongoing process, and as the consensus changes, the filing of a modified plan will become necessary. Until a disclosure statement is approved and votes on a plan are solicited, the proponent is free to file a modified plan. The modified plan then becomes "the plan." § 1127(a). The proponent then will pursue confirmation of the plan as modified. The disclosure statement will be based on the modified plan, and votes will be solicited with regard to the modified plan. Of course, the modified plan must meet the requirements of §§ 1122 and 1123, § 1127(a), and will have to comply with the disclosure requirements of § 1125. § 1127(c), (f)(2). The 2005 Amendments made clear that all of the requirements of §§ 1121 through 1129 apply to pre-confirmation modifications. § 1127(f)(1).

If the proponent has already solicited votes on a plan, but has not yet confirmed the plan, the situation becomes trickier if the proponent then wants to modify the plan. The obvious problem is that creditors and interest holders voted on a plan that is not the same as the modified plan. Perhaps they would not vote the same way on the plan as modified. The challenge is to protect the legitimate interests of those voting on the plan without incurring unnecessary expense and delay. Several provisions in the Code and Rules attempt to strike this balance.

First, the holder of a claim or interest is entitled to change its vote on the modified plan. § 1127(d). If it does not affirmatively change its vote within the time fixed by the court, though, it will be deemed to have kept its vote the same on the modified plan. Twenty-one days' notice of the time fixed to accept or reject a proposed modification must be sent to all creditors, Rule 2002(a)(5), and such notice as the court may direct must be sent to equity security holders. Rule 2002(d)(7).

However, Rule 3019 may contradict § 1127(d). Under Rule 3019(a), if the court finds that a proposed modification does not "adversely change" the treatment of the claim or interest of a holder who has not accepted the modification in writing, the modified plan shall be deemed accepted by all creditors and equity security holders who have already accepted the plan. The intention of Rule 3019(a) is to permit the proponent of a plan to make minor modifications without having to go through the whole notification process. Since the Rules cannot change the Code, however, Rule

3019(a) should not be able to preclude a claim or interest holder from changing their vote, as § 1127(d) entitles them to do, even if the modification does not adversely change the treatment of any claim or interest who has not yet accepted the plan.

The second major provision affecting a pre-confirmation modification is that the proponent of the modification is required to comply with § 1125, "with respect to the plan as modified." § 1127(c). Section 1125 deals with disclosure and solicitation.[416] At a minimum, § 1127(c) means that a disclosure statement on the modified plan must be sent to holders of claims and interests that have not yet voted on the plan. The legislative history does not clarify whether § 1127(c) requires a new disclosure statement to be sent to prior voters, but rather the House Report on § 1127(c) states that if the plan modifications are minor, "the court might determine that additional disclosure was not required under the circumstances."[417] It is possible that prior voters still need "adequate information" so they can decide whether to change their vote, as permitted by § 1127(d).[418] Probably, though, they are not entitled to a new disclosure statement, because the proponent of the plan is not soliciting their vote under § 1125(b).[419] They have already voted, and under § 1127(d) that vote will stand unless the holder changes their vote. The 2005 Amendments clarify that there must be such disclosure under § 1125 "as the court may direct," § 1127(f)(2), which gives the court the express power to tailor the necessary disclosure in such instances, which then would be binding.

Post-confirmation modifications stand on a completely different footing than pre-confirmation modifications. The power to modify a confirmed plan is very limited. § 1127(b). First, modification is only possible before "*substantial consummation*" of the plan. Substantial consummation occurs quite early in the plan implementation process. Under § 1101(2), "substantial consummation" is defined to mean:

- the transfer of all or substantially all of the property proposed by the plan to be transferred;

- assumption by the debtor or the debtor's successor of the business or the management of the property dealt with by the plan; and

- commencement of distribution under the plan.

Thus, once the reorganized debtor or its successor is in place, property has been transferred, and distributions have begun, modification is no longer possible. Note that the completion of distributions is not required—only that such distributions have commenced.

---

[416] See § 11.20.

[417] H.R. Rep. No. 95–595, 95th Cong., 1st Sess. 411 (1977).

[418] See, e.g., In re GAC Storage El Monte, LLC, 489 B.R. 747 (Bankr. N.D. Ill. 2013); In re Young Broad., Inc., 430 B.R. 99, 120 (Bankr. S.D.N.Y. 2010).

[419] See, e.g., In re Boylan Int'l, Ltd., 452 B.R. 43 (Bankr. S.D.N.Y. 2011) (holding that proposed modification of plan did not require additional disclosure and re-solicitation of votes).

Even if substantial consumation has not yet occurred, modification of a confirmed plan is not a matter of right. Only the proponent of the plan or the reorganized debtor may seek a post-confirmation modification. The court then must find that circumstances warrant the modification, and after notice and a hearing must reconfirm the plan, as modified, under § 1129. § 1127(b). Prior votes will stand, however, unless the holder of the claim or interest changes their vote within the time fixed by the court. § 1127(d).

The 2005 Amendments altered the modification rules for individual debtors. As with most of the 2005 changes affecting individual debtors in chapter 11, the amendments brought the chapter 11 practice for individuals more into line with that in chapter 13. Prior to 2005, it was not possible for anyone other than the chapter 11 plan proponent or the reorganized debtor to propose a modification to the plan. In contrast, in chapter 13 the trustee or an unsecured creditor also could propose a modification. § 1329(a). The 2005 Amendments made it possible for a chapter 11 plan modification to be proposed by the trustee, the United States trustee, or the holder of an allowed unsecured claim, in addition to the debtor. § 1127(e). Also, the modification may be proposed at any time after confirmation as long as it is before all payments have been completed, whether or not the plan has been substantially consummated.

§ 11.20 Obtaining Acceptances: Disclosure and Solicitation

After a plan is filed, the proponent of the plan will solicit votes on the plan. Within modest limits, chapter 11 is based on a model of flexibility, open bargaining, and freedom of contract.[420] The basic premise is that the stakeholders in the reorganization are free to carve up reorganization value in whatever manner they see fit—as long as they do so advisedly. This approach marks a sea change from old chapter X, which was predicated on a model of paternalistic oversight by various benevolent watchdogs, such as the court, the independent trustee, and the Securities and Exchange Commission.[421]

In keeping with the new paradigm, one of the core principles of chapter 11 is *informed suffrage*.[422] Before they cast their ballots, those creditors and equity security holders who are entitled to vote on the plan must be given enough information to enable them to make a considered choice. In fact, the Code generally prohibits solicitation of votes from claim holders prior to the transmission of adequate information, as described by § 1125(a)(1).[423] The vehicle by which this goal is achieved is to require the plan proponent to send a court-approved *disclosure statement* to creditors and equity security holders when soliciting votes. § 1125(b), Rule 3017. Voters then will be able to use the information in the disclosure statement to assist them in making an intelligent decision whether to accept or reject the plan.

The first step in the process is to obtain court approval of the disclosure statement. The proponent of a plan will file a disclosure statement with the plan or within a time fixed by the court. Rule 3016(b). The court then will hold a hearing to

---

[420] See §§ 11.1, 11.14.

[421] See § 11.2.

[422] See H.R. Rep. No. 95–595, 95th Cong., 1st Sess., at 226 (1977).

[423] See, e.g., In re Autobacs Strauss, Inc., 473 B.R. 525, 584 (Bankr. D. Del. 2012).

approve the disclosure statement, on at least 28 days' notice to the debtor, creditors, equity security holders, committees, the SEC, the IRS, the United States trustee, and other parties in interest. Rules 3017(a), 2002(b)(1), (i), (j), (k). The plan and the disclosure statement will not automatically be mailed with the notice to all creditors and equity security holders, but only to those who request them; however, the plan and disclosure statement will be mailed to the debtor, any trustee, committees, the SEC, and the United States trustee. The notice of the disclosure statement hearing will inform parties of the date fixed for filing objections to the disclosure statement. Rule 3017(a).

At the hearing, the court will consider the objections to the disclosure statement, and will decide whether the statement should be approved as containing "adequate information." § 1125(a), (b); Rule 3017(b). The court may conditionally approve the disclosure statement, subject to the proponent amending the disclosure statement as directed by the court before mailing out the disclosure statement with the ballots. On or before the approval of the disclosure statement, the court will fix two more dates. The Rules require courts to fix a date for holders of claims or interests to accept or reject the plan, and permit courts to fix a date for the confirmation hearing. Rule 3017(c).

Once the court has approved the disclosure statement, all holders of claims and interests entitled to vote will be sent a package of materials that will include: the approved disclosure statement; a copy of the court opinion approving the disclosure statement (or a summary of the opinion); a ballot for voting; the plan or a court-approved summary of the plan; notice of the time to file ballots; notice of the time fixed for filing objections to confirmation of the plan; and notice of the time fixed for the confirmation hearing. § 1125(b); Rule 3017(d).

The court may order that the plan and disclosure statement not be sent to the members of any unimpaired class, Rule 3017(d), because such a class will not vote, since it is conclusively deemed to accept the plan. § 1126(f). However, the members of an unimpaired class must be informed that their class has been designated as unimpaired, and given an opportunity to procure a copy of the plan and disclosure statement. Rule 3017(d).

It is common for official committees to assume the responsibility for mailing the package of materials to their constituents, along with the committee's recommendation on whether to vote for or against the plan. The committee also may collect the ballots from their constituents. § 1103(c)(3).

The procedure for approving the disclosure statement, soliciting votes, and confirming a plan can be much more streamlined in a case in which the debtor is a "small business," as defined by § 101(51C). § 1125(f), Rule 3017.1. The option to place a small business case on a "fast track" was added to the Code in 1994, and further amended in 2005. The most significant feature of the fast track rules of § 1125(f) is that the court may combine the hearing on the disclosure statement with the confirmation hearing, § 1125(f)(3)(C), thereby saving time and money. Under the fast track rules, there are three ways a court may deal with the disclosure statement. The court may even determine that a separate disclosure statement is not necessary at all, if the plan itself provides adequate information. § 1125(f)(1). The court also may approve a disclosure statement submitted on a standard form either approved by the court or adopted as an official form under 28 U.S.C. § 2075. § 1125(f)(2). Finally, the court may conditionally approve the disclosure statement as containing adequate information before votes are solicited, and the conditionally approved statement must be mailed not later than 25 days before the confirmation hearing. § 1125(f)(3)(A), (B).

The procedures specified for soliciting votes are not optional. Because of the centrality of the disclosure process to the chapter 11 regime, Congress took special care to put strong enforcement teeth into the disclosure and solicitation rules. First, any votes that are solicited or procured without complying with the foregoing rules may be "*designated*," meaning those votes will not be counted. § 1126(e). Second, the plan may not be confirmed. Under § 1129(a)(2), the proponent must comply with the applicable provisions of the Code in order to confirm the plan, and thus a failure to comply with the disclosure and solicitation rules of § 1125 could be fatal. Third, a person who solicits votes on a plan without following the prescribed rules forfeits the protection of the safe harbor in § 1125(e) from liability for securities fraud.[424]

The 2005 Amendments added an important qualification to the general rule that votes may not be solicited before the disclosure statement is sent out. Under the new rule, an acceptance or rejection of a plan can be solicited if it complies with applicable non-bankruptcy law and is solicited *before* the commencement of the bankruptcy case. § 1125(g). This exception was intended to facilitate "pre-arranged" plans involving "lock-up" agreements with creditors who before bankruptcy agree to vote in favor of a plan that will be filed post-petition. These are in contrast to "pre-packaged" bankruptcies, in which the plan is approved entirely by pre-bankruptcy solicitation and voting.[425]

It is important to note that the foregoing rules apply with equal force to solicitations of acceptances *or rejections* of the plan. § 1125(b). Thus, an opponent of the plan must be careful not to lobby against the plan in a way that would be considered the "solicitation" of a rejection of the plan until the court-approved disclosure statement is sent to voters. If rejections are solicited before a disclosure statement is sent, any dissenting votes that are procured will not be counted.[426] § 1126(e). However, in a very important decision, the Third Circuit held in *Century Glove, Inc. v. First American Bank*[427] that a party who solicits rejections does *not* have to obtain court approval of all information it sends to those solicited, as long as the voters have already received a court-approved disclosure statement. In *Century Glove*, a creditor who opposed the debtor's plan sent several large creditors a copy of its own "draft" plan after the debtor's plan and the approved disclosure statement had been sent to the creditors. The court refused to designate the negative votes of those creditors. It concluded that the operative Code policy is to assure that creditors receive at least a

---

[424] H.R. Rep. No. 95–595, 95th Cong., 1st Sess., at 410 (1977) ("The subsection protects only persons that solicit in good faith and in compliance with the applicable provisions of the reorganization chapter."). For one example of an application of this rule, see *In re Tucker Freight Lines, Inc.*, 62 B.R. 213 (Bankr. W.D. Mich. 1986).

[425] See § 11.23.

[426] See, e.g., In re California Fidelity, Inc., 198 B.R. 567 (B.A.P. 9th Cir. 1996).

[427] 860 F.2d 94 (3d Cir. 1988).

sufficient minimum amount of information before voting—not that all information be blessed as accurate by the Court.

The crucial question with regard to the sufficiency of a disclosure statement is whether it contains "*adequate information.*" § 1125(b). "Adequate information" is a defined term of art in the Code, meaning:

> [I]nformation of a kind, and in sufficient detail, as far as is reasonably practicable in light of the nature and history of the debtor and the condition of the debtor's books and records, including a discussion of the potential material Federal tax consequences of the plan to the debtor, any successor to the debtor, and a hypothetical investor typical of the holders of the claims or interests in the case, that would enable such a hypothetical investor of the relevant class to make an informed judgment about the plan, but adequate information need not include such information about any other possible or proposed plan and in determining whether a disclosure statement provides adequate information, the court shall consider the complexity of the case, the benefit of additional information to creditors and other parties in interest, and the cost of providing additional information.

§ 1125(a)(1). Several important points may be gleaned from this statutory definition. The balance sought is to give voters enough information to vote, but within realistic bounds, considering that the debtor is in bankruptcy

First, the focus is functional—will voters have enough information to be able to make an informed judgment about how to vote in the plan? That is the ultimate role of the disclosure statement.

Second, the targeted "consumer" of the information is carefully limited to a "hypothetical investor typical of holders" in the particular class.[428] That typical investor is further defined as someone who is in the class, has the relationship with the debtor that holders in the class "generally" have, and also has the ability to obtain "other" information that class members generally have. § 1125(a)(2). Thus, the disclosure is not intended for the public at large, but only members of the class, and even then does not have to be pitched to the most ignorant class member (or the most informed), but only to a "typical" member. Furthermore, disclosure can differ between classes; the same disclosure statement does not have to be sent to all classes. § 1125(c). Nor does the disclosure statement itself have to be a sufficient stand-alone document that contains all relevant information. Available extraneous sources of information may be relied upon to supplement the disclosure statement.

Third, the fact that the debtor is in bankruptcy may be taken into account. The Code expressly provides that the adequacy of disclosure is a *bankruptcy* question, and is not to be governed by non-bankruptcy disclosure rules, such as the securities laws. § 1125(d). A full-blown securities prospectus is not required. Creating such a document might be virtually impossible, and even if not might not be worth the expenditure of time and money given the exigencies of time and the debtor's limited resources. The

---

[428] See, e.g., In re Ferguson, 474 B.R. 466, 470–71 (Bankr. D.S.C. 2012).

SEC and similar agencies do have a right to be heard on the adequacy of disclosure, but may not appeal from an order approving a disclosure statement. § 1125(d).

The preeminence of *bankruptcy* law with regard to the disclosure rules in chapter 11 cases is underscored by the safe harbor rule of § 1125(e). This protective rule is a logical corollary of the provision in § 1125(d) that securities laws do not govern the adequacy of disclosure. Under § 1125(e), a person that solicits votes on a plan or participates in the offer or issuance of securities under the plan, in good faith and in compliance with the rules prescribed in § 1125, is protected from liability under the securities laws. This safe harbor rule permits parties involved in the plan approval process to rely on the bankruptcy court's order approving the disclosure statement. The safe harbor of § 1125(e) is tied to the exemption in § 1145 from registration under the securities laws of securities issued under a plan.

In considering what is "reasonably practicable" to be disclosed in the case of a bankruptcy debtor, the court is given considerable flexibility and discretion to consider such matters as the "nature and history of the debtor" and the "condition of the debtor's books and records." § 1125(a)(1). In 2005 Congress further elucidated the pragmatic nature of the "adequate information" test, providing that "the court shall consider the complexity of the case, the benefit of additional information to creditors and other parties in interest, and the cost of providing additional information." § 1125(a)(1). If the impossible were required, the reorganization might be doomed to failure. Discussion of the potential material federal tax consequences is required, though. § 1125(a)(1). The adequate information standard is substantive, not procedural, and will be highly fact-specific in any given case.

Congress emphasized that "[c]ourts will take a practical approach as to what is necessary under the circumstances of each case, such as the cost of preparation of the statements, the need for relative speed in solicitation and confirmation, and, of course, the need for investor protection."[429] The standard for determining whether the plan proponent has provided adequate information under § 1125 as whether "hypothetical reasonable investors receive such information as will enable them to evaluate for themselves what impact the information might have on their claims and the outcome of the case, and to decide for themselves what course of action to take."[430] Additionally, some courts use the factors laid out in *In re Metrocraft Pub Services, Inc.*,[431] to evaluate the adequacy of a disclosure statement:

(1)   the events leading up to the petition date;

(2)   a description of the available assets and their value;

---

[429] H.R. Rep. No. 95–595, 95th Cong., 1st Sess., at 408–09 (1977).

[430] See, e.g., H.R. Rep. No. 95–595, 95th Cong., 1st Sess., at 409 (1977) ("In other words, the adequacy of disclosure is measured against the typical investor, not an extraordinary one."); In re Ferguson, 474 B.R. 466, 470–71 (Bankr. D.S.C. 2012) (citations omitted).

[431] 39 B.R. 567 (Bankr. N.D. Ga. 1984). For courts applying the *Metrocraft* factors, see, e.g., In re Cypresswood Land Partners, I, 409 B.R. 396, 424 (Bankr. S.D. Tex. 2009); In re Phoenix Petroleum Co., 278 B.R. 385, 393 (Bankr. E.D. Pa. 2001); In re U.S. Brass Corp., 194 B.R. 420, 424–25 (Bankr. E.D. Tex. 1996); In re Ferretti, 128 B.R. 16, 18–19 (Bankr. D.N.H. 1991); In re Cardinal Congregate I, 121 B.R. 760, 765 (Bankr. S.D. Ohio 1990).

(3)   the anticipated future of the company;

(4)   the source of information stated in the disclosure statement;

(5)   a disclaimer;

(6)   the present condition of the debtor;

(7)   the scheduled claims;

(8)   the estimated return to creditors under a chapter 7 liquidation;

(9)   the accounting method utilized to produce financial information and the name of the accountants responsible for such information;

(10) the future management of the debtor;

(11) the chapter 11 plan or a summary thereof;

(12) the estimated administrative expenses, including attorneys' and accountants' fees;

(13) the collectability of accounts receivable;

(14) financial information, data, valuations, or projections relevant to a creditor's decision to accept or reject the plan;

(15) information relevant to the risks posed to creditors under the plan;

(16) the actual or projected realizable value from recover of avoidable transfers;

(17) litigation likely to arise in a nonbankruptcy context;

(18) tax attributes of the debtor; and

(19) the relationship of the debtor with affiliates.[432]

Recognizing that courts have considerable flexibility to prescribe what information is "adequate" in any given case, certain types of information tend to be included in most disclosure statements as a matter of practice. Initially there usually is a brief statement describing what a disclosure statement is and how it fits into the chapter 11 confirmation process. A disclaimer reminds readers that the accuracy of projections and estimates cannot be guaranteed. The disclosure statement will give some background about the nature and business of the debtor, why it ended up in chapter 11, and the history of the case. Then the disclosure statement will provide a summary of the operative provisions of the plan and how classes will be treated under the plan.

---

[432] *Metrocraft*, supra note 431, 39 B.R. at 568 (collecting factors from various cases, and adding its own).

With the plan on the table, the disclosure statement then usually will devote considerable discussion to the debtor's financial situation and its projected ability to perform under the plan. This analysis often takes a "before and after" form, with confirmation the point of demarcation. What are the assets and liabilities of the debtor now, and what will they look like after confirmation? How is the capital structure arranged now, and how will that change under the plan? What are the current income and expenses of the debtor, and what are they projected to be after confirmation? Who will be the debtor's post-confirmation management, and what is their projected compensation? What are the most important risk factors? The bottom line is this: what will different classes be paid, and how likely is it that the plan will work?

Most disclosure statements also contain a description of the primary alternatives available to creditors and equity security holders if this plan were not to be confirmed. A liquidation analysis, describing the projected distribution to various classes in chapter 7, invariably will be included. However, the Code expressly provides that the disclosure statement does not have to provide information about any other possible or proposed plan. § 1125(a)(1). Nor is a full going-concern valuation of the debtor or an appraisal of the debtor's assets required. § 1125(b).

A disclosure statement is a legal document, prepared in the context of a judicial proceeding. It is not formally binding, though, in the same way that a confirmed plan is binding.[433] Having said that, the doctrine of judicial estoppel may preclude the proponent of the plan from taking a position later that contradicts the disclosure statement. For example, the failure to disclose a known cause of action may bar the reorganized debtor from pursuing that cause of action after confirmation.[434]

§ 11.21 Obtaining Acceptances: Voting

Voting by creditors and equity security holders plays an important but not dispositive role in the confirmation of a plan. Since chapter 11 is premised largely on consensus, and a plan in many respects is contractual in nature, the need to permit affected parties to vote whether to accept or reject the plan is apparent. Voting is done by classes. § 1126(c), (d). Claims and interests are separated into "classes," with only "substantially similar" claims or interests in the same class.[435] §§ 1122(a), 1123(a)(1). One of the requirements for a non-cram-down confirmation of a plan is that every class either (1) affirmatively vote in favor of the plan, or (2) be unimpaired under § 1124,[436]

---

[433] See In re Bridgepoint Nurseries, Inc., 190 B.R. 215 (Bankr. D.N.J. 1996).

[434] See Payless Wholesale Distribs., Inc. v. Alberto Culver, Inc., 989 F.2d 570 (1st Cir.), cert. denied, 510 U.S. 931 (1993); In re Goodman Bros. Steel Drum Co., Inc., 247 B.R. 604 (Bankr. E.D.N.Y. 2000).

Courts are split on whether a general claim reservation in a disclosure statement provides adequate disclosure as to preserve claims, or whether specific claims or potential defendants must be included. Compare Westland Oil Dev. Corp. v. MCorp Mgmt. Solutions, Inc. v. FDIC, 157 B.R. 100, 103–04 (S.D. Tex. 1993) (holding confirmation of debtor's chapter 11 plan barred debtor from subsequently asserting breach of contract and fraud claims against a creditor because, in part, the general retention clauses in the disclosure statement failed to adequately disclose the present action), with In re Ampace Corp., 279 B.R. 145, 157–58 (Bankr. D. Del. 2002) (holding that avoidance action was not barred, even though disclosure statement only contained a general reservation for avoidance actions, because creditor knew or should have known that it received payment from the debtor within the preference period).

[435] See § 11.17.

[436] See § 11.18.

in which case the class is deemed to accept the plan under § 1126(f). § 1129(a)(8). Furthermore, if any class is impaired under the plan, at least one impaired class must vote in favor of the plan.[437] § 1129(a)(10).

However, perhaps surprisingly, an affirmative or deemed acceptance of the plan by every class is *neither* a necessary nor a sufficient condition for confirmation. Even if every class votes or is deemed to vote in favor of the plan, the plan still will only be confirmed if all of the remaining confirmation requirements in § 1129(a) are satisfied. And even if a class is impaired and does not accept the plan, the plan still can be confirmed under the cram down provisions of § 1129(b). Indeed, the *only* confirmation requirement in § 1129(a) that does *not* have to be met is § 1129(a)(8), regarding acceptance or deemed acceptance by a class.

Only the members of classes that are partially impaired may vote on a plan. If a class is not impaired under § 1124, the class (and each holder in the class) is *conclusively* presumed to have accepted the plan, and will not vote. § 1126(f). In 1984 Congress clarified that the presumption of acceptance by an unimpaired class is conclusive. An unimpaired class actually might prefer to reject the plan, as, for example, if the debtor were curing a default and reinstating an obligation with a below-market interest rate. Such an unwilling but unimpaired class does not have the privilege of rejection.

Nor will a class be permitted to vote on the plan if it is totally impaired. § 1126(g). Instead, if the plan provides that the members of a class will not receive or retain any property under the plan on account of their claims or interests, that class is deemed to reject the plan. For example, if a plan cancels a class of stock, the Code assumes this class rejected the plan. In this situation, since § 1129(a)(8) cannot be satisfied as to such a totally impaired class, the plan can only be confirmed if the cram down standards of § 1129(b) are met as to that class.

Thus, only the members of partially impaired classes vote. Within such classes, eligible voters are those who are (1) the holder of a claim or interest (2) that is allowed under § 502. § 1126(a). A "claim" is defined as a "right to payment."[438] § 101(5). Issues that might arise with regard to the existence of a claim include identifying the time when a claim arises[439]—future tort claims would be an example—or determining whether an equitable remedy constitutes a claim.[440] While "interest" is not defined directly in the Code, by indirection one can ascertain that it is a share in a corporation, a limited partnership interest, or a warrant or right regarding those two forms of "equity security."[441] § 101(16). A special rule is included for claims or interests of the United States; the Secretary of the Treasury is empowered to vote on behalf of the government. § 1126(a).

---

[437] See § 11.27.

[438] See § 7.1.

[439] See § 7.2.

[440] See § 7.3.

[441] Under § 501(a), an "equity security holder" is authorized to file a proof of "interest." Under § 101(17), "equity security holder" is defined as the holder of an equity security of the debtor. "Equity security," in turn, is defined as noted in the text. § 101(16).

Not all claims or interests may vote on a plan, however. The claim or interest also must be "allowed" under § 502.[442] To be allowed, a proof of claim or interest must be filed or be deemed filed, §§ 501, 1111(a); Rules 3002(a), 3003–3005, and must survive any timely objections. § 502(a); Rule 3007. In chapter 11 cases, claims and interests that are scheduled and are not listed as disputed, contingent, or unliquidated are deemed filed without the holder actually having to file a proof of claim or interest. § 1111(a). If an objection to a claim or interest is filed, the court generally must resolve the dispute, and may disallow the claim. § 502(b). However, when an objection is filed, the court has the power to temporarily allow the claim or interest in an amount the court deems proper for the purpose of voting on the plan, Rule 3018(a), while reserving the final decision on allowance for later. In the case of contingent or unliquidated claims, the court also has the power to estimate the amount of the claim for the purpose of allowance, § 502(c), and the holder then would be entitled to vote the claim in the estimated amount.

In confirming a plan it is critical to ascertain when a class votes in favor of the plan. If all classes accept the plan, cram down will be avoided. Dissenting individual members in a class will be bound to the terms of a confirmed plan. § 1141(a). The required vote for acceptance by classes of claims is spelled out in § 1126(b), and the required vote for classes of interests is identified in § 1126(c).

For *claims*, an affirmative class vote requires acceptance of the plan by creditors that hold:

- a majority in number, and

- two-thirds in amount,

of the allowed claims in the class that actually voted on the plan. § 1126(c). The votes of creditors who are "designated" under § 1126(e) are excluded entirely from the calculation.

For *interests*, an affirmative class vote requires acceptance of the plan by the holders of interests that hold:

- two-thirds in amount

of the allowed interests that actually voted on the plan, again excluding those holders who are designated under § 1126(e). § 1126(d). Note that the Code does not contain a numerosity requirement for interests, unlike claims.

Several points about the manner of counting a class vote bear emphasis. First, the calculation is based only on creditors or interest holders who *actually vote* on the plan. This is a major change from the prior Act, which counted all claims or interests, whether they voted or not. Under that system, voter apathy (which was prevalent) worked against confirmation. Second, only *allowed* claims or interests are counted.

---

[442] See §§ 7.4, 7.5.

Finally, votes that are *designated* under § 1126(e) are excluded, both from the numerator (the acceptances) and the denominator (the total votes cast).

An example will demonstrate the importance of the shift in the Code to count only those ballots actually cast. Assume that a class is comprised of 100 claims, which total $100,000. Only 60 holders vote, holding $70,000 in claims, but of those 60 voting holders, 45 vote in favor of the plan, holding $56,000 in claims. If the percentage vote were computed by reference to all claims, the class would not accept the plan: only 45 out of 100 holders accepted, holding only $56,000 out of $100,000 in claims. However, under the Code, the class does accept the plan: more than one-half in number of those voting (45 out of 60), and at least two-thirds in amount ($56,000 out of $70,000—or 80%) accepted the plan.

Much of the litigation with regard to plan voting concerns whether to "designate" votes under § 1126(e). Since designated votes are excluded from the calculation, the designation of accepting votes might change a class acceptance to a rejection, and the designation of rejecting votes might have the opposite effect. The court is empowered to designate any entity whose acceptance or rejection (1) was "not in good faith," or (2) was not solicited or procured in good faith or in accordance with the provisions of the Code. Congress explained this subsection as permitting a court to designate any vote that, with respect to its class, suffers from "a conflict of interest that is of such nature as would justify exclusion of that person's claim or interest from the amounts and number" requirements for confirmation.[443] As discussed in the preceding section,[444] § 1126(e) puts teeth into the disclosure and solicitation rules of § 1125 by permitting the designation of votes that were improperly solicited.

A difficult question courts face is determining when an entity voted in bad faith or was solicited in bad faith. Obviously, what constitutes bad faith cannot be readily distilled or easily identified. The court's task is especially challenging because by definition an inquiry must be made into the voter's motives. Either a positive or a negative vote will be allowed to stand if cast for the right reasons, but will be designated if cast for the wrong reasons. But what motivations are improper?

Obviously, a creditor or equity security holder that simply does not like the terms of the plan is free to vote against the plan. There is general agreement that voters are allowed to indulge their own selfish motivations. Indeed, creditors and equity holders are expected to try to get all that they can under the plan, and may vote against a plan that does not give them as large a slice of the reorganization pie as they want. The fundamental nature of plan negotiations is that different groups of claimants and equity holders will threaten to vote against a plan unless their share is sweetened, and making such threats is not bad faith.[445]

While voters thus need not be saints, they cannot be sinners either. The assumption implicit in the whole scheme of classifying "substantially similar" claim

---

[443] H.R. Rep. No. 95–595, 95th Cong., 1st Sess., at 411 (1977) (further stating that an example of such a conflict would be where a person holds a claim or interest in more than one class).

[444] See § 11.20.

[445] See, e.g., In re Adelphia Commc'ns Corp., 359 B.R. 54 (Bankr. S.D.N.Y. 2006).

together, § 1122(a), and then voting by classes, is that the members of a class will make voting decisions on plans principally on the merits of the plan *as it relates to their class*. If that assumption is belied, bad faith might be found. Otherwise it would be unfair to bind the other members of the class to the class vote that is tainted by a voter with mixed motives or a conflict of interest. For example, a creditor who holds claims in more than one class might labor under an irremediable conflict of interest in voting one of the claims, and its vote on that claim could be designated.[446] To illustrate, the plan might propose to pay class 3 more, at the expense of class 4; Creditor X, holding claims in both classes, could vote the class 3 claim, but perhaps not the class 4 claim.

Voters are not permitted to abuse the bankruptcy system. Thus, a creditor who votes against a plan solely to try to drive the debtor as a competitor out of business, or acts out of pure malice, or resorts to blackmail, or attempts to obtain an ulterior advantage, would not be acting in good faith.[447] A creditor is allowed to cast its vote, but not to sell it or use it as a club.

A situation in which bad faith may be raised is when a creditor purchases a large block of claims, and then attempts to vote those claims.[448] Such a claims purchaser is sometimes referred to as a "vulture" investor. The issue of whether such a claims purchaser has acted in bad faith is particularly likely to arise if the purchaser acquires a large enough block of claims to control the vote of an important class, and thus obtains the power to dictate the terms of the reorganization. The courts have divided over whether it is bad faith to acquire a controlling share of a class for the express purpose of influencing the shape of the plan.[449]

Sometimes a debtor will put together a workout agreement and obtain acceptances for that plan prior to bankruptcy, and then seek to confirm that plan in a "prepackaged" chapter 11.[450] The debtor in a prepackaged plan wants to be able to use the prepetition acceptances in the chapter 11 case, without having to resolicit the votes. This tactic is permitted by § 1126(b), but only if the prepetition disclosure either complied with applicable non-bankruptcy disclosure laws, such as the securities laws, or, if no such law applied, the disclosure contained "adequate information" within the meaning of § 1125.

---

[446] H.R. Rep. No. 95–595, 95th Cong., 1st Sess., at 411 (1977). Note that this option could remedy the problem discussed in § 11.17 regarding separate classification of similar claims.

[447] See Young v. Higbee Co., 324 U.S. 204 (1945) (interpreting a similar rule under the Bankruptcy Act); In re DBSD N. Am., Inc., 634 F.3d 79 (2d Cir. 2011); In re Fed. Support Co., 859 F.2d 17 (4th Cir. 1988); In re Landing Assocs., Ltd., 157 B.R. 791 (Bankr. W.D. Tex. 1993).

[448] See § 11.22.

[449] Compare In re Allegheny Int'l Inc., 118 B.R. 282 (Bankr. W.D. Pa. 1990) (holding bad faith); In re Mangia Pizza Invs., LP, 480 B.R. 669 (Bankr. W.D. Tex. 2012) (same), with In re 255 Park Plaza Assocs. Ltd. P'ship, 100 F.3d 1214 (6th Cir. 1996) (holding not bad faith); In re Marin Town Ctr., 142 B.R. 374 (N.D. Cal. 1992) (same); In re Pleasant Hill Partners, 163 B.R. 388 (Bankr. N.D. Ga. 1994) (same).

[450] See § 11.23.

§ 11.22   Obtaining Acceptances: Trading in Claims

There is a market, it seems, for everything—even claims against a bankruptcy debtor. The practice of purchasing bankruptcy claims is known as "trading in claims."[451] A more colorful name for this practice is "vulture investing," supposedly because the purchaser is like a vulture, picking over the carcass of the chapter 11 debtor (who is not yet entirely dead, however!).

Why would anyone voluntarily buy a claim against a debtor that is already in bankruptcy? Vulture investors normally purchase claims at a substantial discount to their face amount. Creditors often are happy to sell, in order to avoid the risk and delay in collecting on their claims. The purchaser then may vote the purchased claims on the plan, § 1126(a), and will receive any distributions made under the plan to the members of the class. If the purchaser acquires enough claims, it may be able to control the class vote, and thus the terms of the reorganization, and possibly reap huge profits.[452] In essence, a vulture investor could effectuate a hostile takeover of the debtor through the purchase of chapter 11 claims.

Even apart from the "control profit" available by purchasing claims, a vulture purchaser with more information about the value of a claim than the creditor-seller might be able to pay less than fair value for the claim and reap an immediate windfall. For example, a claim may have a value of 50 cents on the dollar, but a claim holder without reliable information about the debtor's finances might be willing to sell that claim for 25 cents on the dollar. The potential to capture such profits sparked the creation of numerous "vulture funds" in the 1980s and 1990s.

Vulture investing is not without risk, however. The biggest threat is that the court will deny the purchaser the right to vote the acquired claims under § 1126(e). That section gives the court the power to "designate" (i.e., to disallow) any vote that was not made in good faith.[453] The pivotal issue in the courts has been whether the avowed purchase of a "blocking" position (i.e., a block of votes large enough to control the vote of a class under § 1126(b) or (c)) is bad faith. The leading case holding that purchasing a blocking position *is* bad faith and that the vote of the claims acquired therefore should not be counted is *In re Allegheny International, Inc.*[454] In that case, the purchaser bought the claims after the debtor had proposed its plan, and then circulated

---

[451] See, e.g., Scott K. Charles, Trading Claims in Chapter 11 Cases: Legal Issues Confronting the Postpetition Investor, 1991 Ann. Surv. Am. L. 261; Joy F. Conti et. al., Claims Trafficking in Chapter 11–Has the Pendulum Swung Too Far?, 9 Bankr. Dev. J. 300 (1992); Chaim J. Fortgang & Thomas M. Mayer, Trading Claims and Taking Control of Corporations in Chapter 11, 12 Cardozo L. Rev. 1 (1990); Christopher W. Frost, Chapter 11 Acquisition Strategies: Good Faith, Bad Faith, and the Motivations of Claim Buyers, 31 No. 5 Bankr. L. Letter 1 (2011); Adam J. Levitin, Bankruptcy Markets: Making Sense of Claims Trading, 4 Brook. J. Corp. Fin. & Comm. L. 67 (2009); Richard Lieb, Vultures Beware: Risks of Purchasing Claims Against a Chapter 11 Debtor, 48 Bus. Law. 915 (1993); Herbert P. Minkel, Jr. & Cynthia A. Baker, Claims and Control in Chapter 11 Cases: A Call for Neutrality, 13 Cardozo L. Rev. 35 (1991).

[452] As one commentator explained, "Vulture investors may control the terms for the reorganization of a debtor in chapter 11 by means of the purchase at bargain prices of a blocking vote position in a significant debt class. This could enable a vulture investor to dictate the terms of the reorganization, which could result in very large rewards for the investor." Lieb, supra note 451, at 917.

[453] See § 11.21.

[454] 118 B.R. 282 (Bankr. W.D. Pa. 1990).

a competing plan that would give the purchaser a much larger interest. Another case, however, held that purchasing a blocking share was not bad faith, and that the purchaser was entitled to vote the claims.[455] Although the court in the second case purported to distinguish *Allegheny* on the factual grounds that the purchase was made before the debtor proposed a plan, and the purchaser was not proposing a competing plan, the tenor of the opinion indicates a more permissive attitude about the propriety of claims trading.

Another possible risk is that the court will either subordinate the purchased claim or limit the amount of the allowed claim to the purchase price paid. These sanctions might be imposed if the purchaser was an insider who violated a fiduciary duty. In one case, an insider paid $10 million for $60 million in claims. After a complicated procedural case history, the Third Circuit subordinated these claims for inequitable conduct relating to a breach of fiduciary duty.[456]

The Code and Rules do not contain any provisions that directly address the merits of claims trading. As a procedural matter, Rule 3001(e) requires evidence of the transfer to be filed by the transferee. If the transferor has already filed a proof of claim, notice of the filed evidence of transfer will be sent to the transferor, who then has 21 days to object to the alleged transfer. The rule was amended in 1991, though to make clear that it is neutral on the substantive legitimacy of trading in claims. If the transferor has already voted on the plan, the transferee will only be able to change the vote if it can establish cause. Rule 3018(a). The mere fact that the identity of the holder has changed will not suffice as cause.

§ 11.23 Obtaining Acceptances: Prepackaged Plans

A chapter 11 plan is in many cases nothing more than a consensual workout agreement that is blessed by the federal bankruptcy court. Many financially distressed debtors, perhaps as many as half, restructure their debts outside of bankruptcy. Out-of-court workouts often avoid much of the cost and delay that tends to plague many chapter 11 cases. But out-of-court agreements do not always work, in large part because creditors who do not assent to the agreement cannot be bound to its terms. The best of both worlds, it seems, would be to enjoy the speed and efficiency of an out-of-court restructuring, and yet still bind dissenting creditors. Such a magical device exists—the "*prepackaged*" plan, also known as a "prepack."[457]

In a prepackaged plan, the terms of the plan are agreed to, and acceptances of the plan are solicited and obtained, *before* the debtor files chapter 11. The chapter 11 case is filed in order to confirm the previously agreed-to plan, and thereby bind the dissenting creditors to the plan's terms under § 1141. In the confirmation process, the debtor uses the acceptances that were obtained prior to bankruptcy. A variation is the "*pre-arranged*" plan, in which votes are solicited and obtained under a "lock-up" agreement before the bankruptcy filing, but the plan itself is not filed until after

---

[455] In re Marin Town Ctr., 142 B.R. 374 (N.D. Cal. 1992).

[456] Citicorp Venture Capital, Ltd. v. Comm. of Creditors Holding Unsecured Claims., 160 F.3d 982 (3d Cir. 1998).

[457] See Charles J. Tabb, The Future of Chapter 11, 44 S.C.L. Rev. 791, 848–50 (1993).

bankruptcy is commenced. A 2005 amendment allows such votes to be counted if they were solicited in accordance with applicable non-bankruptcy law. § 1125(g).[458]

The problem with a "prepack" is the risk that the disclosure and solicitation protections in § 1125 of the Code might be circumvented.[459] Debtors should not be able to realize the substantial benefits of chapter 11 without affording affected creditors and equity security holders the safeguards that lie at the heart of the Code's chapter 11 regime. At the same time, a too-rigid insistence on adherence to every technical Code requirement might cause the loss of opportunities to save substantial amounts of time and money with little offsetting gain.

The Code's Solomonic resolution of this delicate balancing act is found in § 1126(b). Under that section, prepetition acceptances may be used for the purpose of voting on and confirming a chapter 11 plan *if* the prepetition disclosure and solicitation of those acceptances was adequate. The prepetition disclosure and solicitation will pass muster if (1) the solicitation complied with any applicable non-bankruptcy disclosure laws (such as the securities laws), or (2) if no such laws apply, the solicitation came after the disclosure of "adequate information" within the meaning of § 1125(a). Furthermore, the Rules require the plan to have been transmitted to substantially all creditors or equity security holders of the same class, and bar the use of prepetition acceptances if an "unreasonably short time" was prescribed for voting. Rule 3018(b).

In attempting a prepack, a debtor encounters several points of uncertainty.[460] First, the debtor cannot know for sure in advance whether "adequate information" was disseminated to those creditors and equity security holders from whom votes were solicited. If the court later finds that adequate information was not given, the prepetition votes cannot be used, and the debtor will have to go back through the entire disclosure and solicitation process in chapter 11. In a chapter 11 case, by contrast, the court approves the disclosure statement as containing adequate information before the proponent of the plan solicits votes. § 1125(b). Second, a court considering a prepack might conclude that an "unreasonably short time" was given for creditors or equity security holders to vote, and if so, the prepetition votes again will not be counted.

A third problem with prepacks is that the debtor must comply with applicable non-bankruptcy disclosure laws, such as the securities laws, if such laws apply. This requirement is more rigorous than in chapter 11 itself. The Code makes clear that a disclosure statement in the bankruptcy case does *not* have to comply with non-bankruptcy disclosure laws. § 1125(d). Thus, the disclosure required to confirm a prepackaged plan might be much more onerous than that required otherwise in chapter 11. Also, an entity that solicits acceptances prior to bankruptcy will not have the safe harbor from securities liability offered to a good faith solicitor under § 1125(e).

As a practical matter, prepackaged plans are the most useful in cases where the debtor does not need to revise its business, but simply needs to overhaul its capital

---

[458] See also 11 U.S.C. § 1126(b).

[459] See § 11.20.

[460] These uncertainties reared their ugly head in the case of *In re Southland Corp.*, 124 B.R. 211 (Bankr. N.D. Tex. 1991), in which the court refused to approve a prepackaged plan.

structure. For example, if the debtor has a sound business, but is laboring under a crushing debt load as a result of the issuance of junk bonds pursuant to a leveraged buyout, the debtor would be a prime candidate for a prepack. In such a case, an exchange offer would be made prior to the chapter 11 filing to the junk bond holders; if the needed percentage accepts the offer, the debtor will file chapter 11 and attempt to confirm the prepackaged plan. However, a debtor who needs to rework its business to survive, by rejecting contracts, selling off major assets, and the like, will not be suitable for a prepack. That debtor will need to avail itself of the full panoply of the Code's remedial opportunities.

§ 11.24 Confirmation Requirements: Overview

The ultimate goal of a chapter 11 case is the confirmation of a plan under § 1129. Confirmation follows approval of the disclosure statement and the solicitation and collection of votes.[461] The only exception is in a "small business" case, in which the hearing to approve the disclosure statement and the confirmation hearing may be combined. § 1125(f)(3).

The bankruptcy court must hold a confirmation hearing. § 1128(a). Any party in interest may object to confirmation. § 1128(b). The right to object applies even if a party is not entitled to vote. The court is required to hold a confirmation hearing even if no objection is filed. However, absent timely objection, the court may determine that the plan was proposed in good faith and not by any means forbidden by law without taking evidence on those issues. Rule 3020(b)(2).

At least 28 days' notice of the time fixed for filing objections to confirmation and the time set for the hearing on confirmation must be sent to the debtor, the trustee, all creditors and indenture trustees, and notice of those times also must be sent to all equity security holders, committees, the SEC, the District Director for the IRS, and the United States trustee. Rule 2002(b), (d)(7), (i), (j), (k). Objections must be filed and served on the debtor, the trustee, the proponent of the plan, any committee, the United States trustee, and any other entity the court designates. Rule 3020(b)(1).

Sixteen statutory requirements must be satisfied before a consensual plan may be confirmed. § 1129(a)(1)–(16). If all sixteen requirements are met, the court "shall" confirm the plan, § 1129(a); confirmation is not discretionary. However, the court may only confirm one plan (in the rare event where there are competing plans and more than one plan meets all the requirements). § 1129(c). It is not enough for a plan to be accepted or deemed accepted by all classes.[462] In fact, the only requirement in § 1129(a) that is not mandatory for confirmation is class acceptance, under § 1129(a)(8). If the

---

[461] See §§ 11.20, 11.21.

[462] See, e.g., In re Multiut Corp., 449 B.R. 323, 332–33 (Bankr. N.D. Ill. 2011) ("Even absent the filing of an objection to a plan, the proponent must affirmatively demonstrate that the plan is confirmable. Additionally, regardless of whether an objection to confirmation has been raised, the court must determine whether the requirements of § 1129(a), and if applicable § 1129(b), have been met." (internal citations omitted)).

rest of § 1129(a) is satisfied, the plan proponent still would have the option to seek to confirm the plan under the cram down rules.[463] § 1129(a)(8), (b).

The plan confirmation requirements weave together many policy threads. As is true throughout chapter 11, in the confirmation rules Congress sought to retain maximum flexibility while still providing a minimum level of protection for classes and for individual class members, and protecting the court's jurisdiction and the integrity of the process. Since a confirmed chapter 11 plan carries the imprimatur of the federal courts, and is imbued with the public interest, a variety of public policy goals are implicated.

The statutory requirements for confirmation are:

1.   The plan complies with the applicable provisions of the Code. § 1129(a)(1).

2.   The plan proponent complies with the applicable provisions of the Code. § 1129(a)(2).

3.   The plan has been proposed in good faith, and not by any means forbidden by law. § 1129(a)(3).

4.   Any payments for services in connection with the case by the debtor, plan proponent, or person issuing securities or acquiring property, are approved by the court as reasonable. § 1129(a)(4).

5.   The identity of post-confirmation management is disclosed and is consistent with the interests of creditors and equity security holders and with public policy, and the identity of and compensation to be paid to any insider who will be employed by the reorganized debtor are disclosed. § 1129(a)(5).

6.   Governmental regulatory rate approvals are or will be obtained. § 1129(a)(6).

7.   Each holder of a claim or interest of an impaired class either accepts the plan or will receive the liquidation value of their claim or interest. § 1129(a)(7). This is known as the "best interests" test.[464]

8.   Each class either accepts the plan or is not impaired.[465] § 1129(a)(8).

9.   Priority claims will be paid in full under the plan. § 1129(a)(9). Whether payment must be on the effective date of the plan or may be deferred depends on the priority class.

10.   If a class of claims is impaired, at least one impaired class has accepted the plan, not counting insider acceptances.[466] § 1129(a)(10).

---

[463] See §§ 11.30–11.34.
[464] See § 11.26.
[465] See § 11.25.
[466] See § 11.27.

11. Confirmation is not likely to be followed by liquidation or further reorganization, unless it is a liquidating plan. § 1129(a)(11). This is known as the "feasibility" test.[467]

12. Fees payable to the United States trustee under 28 U.S.C. § 1930 are paid or will be paid on the plan's effective date. § 1129(a)(12).

13. Retiree benefits under § 1114 will continue to be paid for the obligated period.[468] § 1129(a)(13).

14. Postpetition domestic obligations must be paid. § 1129(a)(14).

15. At the insistence of any unsecured creditor, an individual debtor must pay to creditors under the plan all of his "disposable income" for a period of not less than five years. § 1129(a)(15).

16. Transfers of property must comply with applicable provisions of non-bankruptcy law that govern the transfer of property by a corporation or trust that is not a moneyed, business, or commercial corporation or trust. § 1129(a)(16).

§ 11.25 Confirmation Requirements: Class Protection

Chapter 11 plans are structured around *classes* of creditors and equity security holders. The operative paradigm in chapter 11 is to permit the various classes of claims and interests to bargain over the allocation of reorganization value, given full and adequate disclosure.[469] The differing classes are not required to adhere slavishly to their non-bankruptcy entitlements, as would be dictated by an unwaivable application of the absolute priority rule, but may relinquish value to other classes.

Thus, the requisite statutory protection of a class of claims or interests will be satisfied if the class votes to accept the plan. § 1129(a)(8)(A). The freedom of a class to consent to the terms of a plan rests on several cornerstones. The classification rules limit class membership to claims or interests that are "substantially similar," § 1122(a), and all members of a class must receive the same treatment, unless they agree to less favorable treatment.[470] § 1123(a)(4). Before the class votes, the members of the class must receive a court-approved disclosure statement.[471] § 1125(b). The vote of any class member that is cast in bad faith or whose vote is solicited in bad faith or by impermissible means will not be counted. § 1126(e). These restrictions help assure the fairness of the class vote. Subject to these protections, all class members, even those individual members who reject the plan, are bound by the affirmative vote of the necessary supermajority of voting class members.[472] § 1126(c), (d).

---

[467] See § 11.28.

[468] See § 8.13.

[469] H.R. Rep. No. 95–595, 95th Cong., 1st Sess., at 224 (1977).

[470] See § 11.17.

[471] See § 11.20.

[472] See § 11.21.

A class is not always entitled to vote, however. The proponent of a plan has the power to prevent a class vote if the class is not impaired under § 1124.[473] A class that is not impaired is conclusively presumed to accept the plan. § 1126(f). If a class is not impaired, the statutory requirement for class protection is satisfied. § 1129(a)(8)(B). Under § 1124, a class may be unimpaired in one of two alternative ways. The first is if the plan leaves unaltered the legal, equitable, and contractual rights of the class holders. § 1124(1). The second is if the plan cures defaults, compensates the creditor for damages suffered, reinstates the original maturity of the obligation, and otherwise leaves the creditor's rights unaltered. § 1124(2).

In the event that § 1129(a)(8) is satisfied, either by an affirmative class vote or because the class is not impaired, the class is not entitled to invoke the privileges of the cram down rules of § 1129(b). This means that the class that is taken care of under § 1129(a)(8) cannot be heard to complain about the relative allocation of reorganization value to other classes.

However, the cram down rules are extremely important in determining the rights of a class. Unless a class is not impaired, that class will be negotiating with other classes over the terms of the plan with an understanding of the rights that the class could insist on by voting against the plan. In short, the bargaining dynamics are directly affected by the ultimate entitlements of each class in cram down. The fact that a class is free to waive those rights does not minimize the significance of those rights in the negotiation process.

Reserving for later a more detailed discussion of the cram down rules,[474] a brief overview here will highlight the critical protections for each class. The general cram down standard is that the plan "does not discriminate unfairly, and is fair and equitable" with respect to each impaired dissenting class. § 1129(b)(1). The prohibition against unfair discrimination will protect a class against the proponent creating other classes of the same legal rank and then providing more favorable treatment in the plan to those other classes. A plan that created two classes of unsecured claims, and proposed to pay one such class 10 cents on the dollar and pay the other in full, would run into serious problems with the unfair discrimination restriction, absent a very impressive justification for the differential treatment.

The "fair and equitable" test imports the "absolute priority rule" into the Code with respect to a dissenting class. In essence, the absolute priority rule simply dictates that the non-bankruptcy priority ordering of various classes against the debtor and the debtor's property be preserved under the plan. For secured classes, the fair and equitable test generally requires the class to receive the value of their collateral under the plan.[475] § 1129(b)(2)(A).

For unsecured claims and for equity security holders, the absolute priority rule boils down to two critical factors.[476] § 1129(b)(2)(B), (C). Unless the dissenting class is

---

[473] See § 11.18.

[474] See §§ 11.30–11.34.

[475] See § 11.32.

[476] See § 11.33.

paid in full, no class *junior* to the dissenting class is entitled to receive or retain anything under the plan. For example, if unsecured creditors are not paid in full, equity security holders, who are behind unsecured creditors in priority, must take nothing. The second component of the fair and equitable rule for unsecured and equity classes is that no class *senior* to the dissenting class may be paid more than in full. An exception exists for individual debtors who are allowed to retain property of the estate included in § 1115. § 1129(b)(2)(B)(ii).

In summary, then, a class is entitled to threaten to invoke the absolute priority rule and the prohibition against unfair discrimination when negotiating the terms of a plan. That strategy may be preempted, however, if the class is not impaired under the plan.

§ 11.26   Confirmation Requirements: Best Interests Test

Chapter 11 is designed to maximize the value of a debtor's assets for the benefit of all interested constituencies.[477] However, a cardinal principle of chapter 11 is that this primary goal may not be achieved at the expense of any entity with a direct financial interest in the debtor without their consent. Promoting the "greater good" of the group as a whole does not justify treating any stakeholder worse than they would be treated in a liquidation. Thus, if any holder of a claim or interest would receive more on its claim or interest in a chapter 7 liquidation than under the proposed chapter 11 plan, and does not vote in favor the plan, that plan cannot be confirmed. § 1129(a)(7). All creditors and interest holders thus possess a limited veto power over the terms of a chapter 11 plan. This baseline rule of protection for every financially interested party is known as the "*best interests*" test. The best interests financial standard is derived from chapter XI of the prior Act. Bankruptcy Act § 336(2). The plan is said to be in the "best interests" of all creditors and interest holders in the sense that they will receive at least as much under the plan as they would have received if the debtor had liquidated under chapter 7.

The best interests test of § 1129(a)(7) is intended to provide a floor of protection for dissenting members of a class.[478] Chapter 11 plans are principally structured around the treatment of creditors and interest holders as members of *classes*.[479] The plan will place creditors and interest holders in various classes,[480] propose treatment of the claims and interests as a class, and voting will be done on a class-wide basis.[481] If a class accepts or is deemed to accept a plan, the absolute priority rule will not be invoked as to that class. § 1129(a)(8), (b). Dissenting creditors generally are bound by the decision of the class, and likewise will be bound by the terms of the plan if confirmed. § 1141(a). Even if the class votes in favor of a plan, however, *every single*

---

[477]   See § 11.1.

[478]   See 124 Cong. Rec. H11,103 (daily ed. Sept. 28, 1978); 124 Cong. Rec. S17,420 (daily ed. Oct. 6, 1978).

[479]   See § 11.25.

[480]   See § 11.17.

[481]   See § 11.21.

member of the class is entitled to insist on compliance with the best interests test.[482] Thus, this is an individual creditor right, rather than a creditor class right.

An individual claim holder or interest holder may waive the best interest test. § 1129(a)(7)(A)(i). In a class of any size, however, it would be unusual to obtain a 100 percent acceptance rate. The waiver provision thus typically only applies in the real world to a class comprised of a single secured creditor.

Notably, the best interests test also will not apply if the class is *unimpaired*.[483] "Impairment" is a term of art in the Code.[484] § 1124. In general, a class is unimpaired if the plan does not alter the legal or equitable rights of that class, or if defaults are cured and the original contract terms are reinstated. One major change was made to § 1124 in the 1994 Amendments, to address a problem that arose in applying the impairment rules in the best interests context. One court had held that a solvent debtor did not have to pay postpetition interest in order to confirm a chapter 11 plan, even though in chapter 7 interest would have had to be paid since the estate was solvent.[485] § 726(a)(5). Prior to the 1994 Amendments, a class was not considered impaired if it was cashed out in full under the plan. The 1994 change deleted that provision (former § 1124(3)), meaning that the plan proponent no longer can avoid the best interests test by proposing to cash out the principal amount of the claims of a class.[486]

Application of the best interests test requires the court to engage in a *hypothetical chapter 7 liquidation analysis*, and to compare the distribution that would be made to each class of claims and interests in that liquidation with the payout proposed under the terms of the chapter 11 plan.[487] If the hypothetical chapter 7 distribution would exceed the proposed payout in chapter 11 for a given class, the best interests test is not satisfied and confirmation must be denied (unless every single member of that class accepts the plan).

In making the liquidation analysis, the court must apply the Code provisions relevant to a chapter 7 distribution.[488] Thus, the primary chapter 7 distributional rule must be consulted,[489] § 726, as well as applicable subordination provisions.[490] §§ 510, 724(b), 726(a)(3), (4). The plan proponent must introduce concrete evidence of the likely estate assets that would be available for distribution in chapter 7 and their value, as

---

[482]   See, e.g., Bank of Am. Nat'l Trust & Savs. Assoc. v. 203 N. LaSalle St. P'ship, 526 U.S. 434, 442 n.13 (1999).

[483]   The Code states that this rule applies "[w]ith respect to each impaired class of claims or interests." 11 U.S.C. § 1129(a)(7).

[484]   See § 11.18.

[485]   In re New Valley Corp., 168 B.R. 73 (Bankr. D.N.J. 1994).

[486]   H.R. Rep. No. 103–835, 103rd Cong., at 47–48 (1994) (expressly overruling *New Valley*, so that "if a plan proposed to pay a class of claims in cash in the full allowed amount of the claims, the class would be impaired, entitling creditors to vote for or against the plan of reorganization").

[487]   See, e.g., In re W.R. Grace & Co., 475 B.R. 34, (D. Del. 2012) ("The bankruptcy courts determine this liquidation value by conjuring up a hypothetical Chapter 7 liquidation that would be conducted on the effective date of the plan." (internal quotations and citation omitted)).

[488]   H.R. Rep. No. 95–595, 95th Cong., 1st Sess., at 412 (1977).

[489]   See § 7.25.

[490]   See §§ 7.23, 7.24.

well as a comprehensive assessment of the estimated claims in each class. In many cases a fairly detailed financial analysis will be necessary,[491] although the courts recognize that constructing the hypothetical liquidation is not an exact science and must in part be based on reasonable assumptions and best guesses.[492]

Both the asset and debt sides of the ledger may be different in the hypothetical chapter 7 liquidation than they actually are in the chapter 11 case. Courts recognize that some assets may bring less if sold at foreclosure in a liquidation under chapter 7.[493] Thus, the total "pie" available for distribution might be smaller in the hypothetical liquidation. At the same time, the debts may be greater. For example, in a chapter 7 liquidation, the debtor might reject executory contracts and leases that it would assume if it were continuing its business in chapter 11, and the rejection of those contracts and leases would give rise to damage claims. The liquidation analysis also would have to factor in projected administrative expenses that would arise in the chapter 7 case.

In determining what the creditors and interest holders would receive in a chapter 7 liquidation, the courts generally limit their inquiry to what those parties would receive *in* the bankruptcy case itself. In other words, a court does not ask whether the creditor or interest holder would be better off overall if the debtor were to liquidate, but only compares the *bankruptcy distributions* in chapter 7 versus chapter 11. For example, a creditor that has made a long-term loan at what are now below-market interest rates would be financially better off if it could get its money out of the loan immediately, in a chapter 7 liquidation, and then lend that money out at the higher market rates. That economic truth does not mean, however, that the best interests test of § 1129(a)(7) is violated, as long as the chapter 11 distribution to the creditor is as much as the chapter 7 distribution would have been.

The distributional comparison between the actual chapter 11 and the hypothetical chapter 7 must be made as of the same point in time to be valid. The Code identifies that date as the "effective date of the plan." § 1129(a)(7)(A)(ii). The Code does not define what the "effective date" is; usually the plan and the order confirming the plan will identify the effective date. For the purposes of computing the amount of the distribution under the proposed chapter 11 plan, the requirement that the value be fixed "as of the effective date of the plan" means that plan payments must be discounted to present value. Plan payments that will be received in the future are worth less than payments received in the present; a dollar today is worth more than a dollar received a year from now. The measure of this difference is the discount rate, or, viewed from the other perspective, the interest rate. To illustrate, if a claim would be paid $5,000 in chapter 7, and the chapter 11 plan proposes to make a series of five annual principal payments of $1,000 each, the plan will only be confirmable if it also provides for the payment of interest during that five year payout period. Picking the appropriate interest rate has proven to be a matter of considerable debate and

---

[491] See, e.g, In re Multiut Corp., 449 B.R. 323 (Bankr. N.D. Ill. 2011); In re Hockenberry, 457 B.R. 646 (Bankr. S.D. Ohio 2011). See also In re Adelphia Commc'ns Corp., 361 B.R. 337 (S.D.N.Y. 2007).

[492] See In re Chicago Invs., LLC, 470 B.R. 32 (Bankr. D. Mass. 2012); In re Crowthers McCall Pattern, Inc., 120 B.R. 279 (Bankr. S.D.N.Y. 1990).

[493] See, e.g., In re Landing Assocs., Ltd., 157 B.R. 791 (Bankr. W.D. Tex. 1993).

difference of opinion; courts have used measures such as the formula rate (prime rate plus a risk premium), contract rate, the market rate for similar loans, the legal rate of interest, and others.

One exception to the best interests test is for undersecured creditors who make an election under § 1111(b)(2). § 1129(a)(7)(B). The § 1111(b)(2) election permits a class of undersecured creditors to choose to have the total amount of their claim treated as a secured claim in the chapter 11 case. For example, if a total claim of $10,000 is secured by collateral worth $8,000, if the § 1111(b)(2) election is made, the claim will be treated as a $10,000 secured claim. In making the election, however, that class waives the unsecured portion of their claim ($2,000 in the example), and accordingly will not receive any distribution on that unsecured claim. The unsecured claim thus receives less in the chapter 11 case than it would have in the hypothetical chapter 7 case, if any dividend at all would have been paid in a liquidation to unsecured claims. The electing class must choose, however, between making the § 1111(b) election and invoking the benefit of the best interests test. If the choice is to elect under § 1111(b), then the best interests test only requires that the plan provide for payments with a present value equal to the value of the collateral. In the example, the discounted value of the payments to be made to the electing creditor under the plan would have to be at least $8,000.

§ 11.27 Confirmation Requirements: One Consenting Impaired Class

If any class of claims is impaired under the plan, at least one impaired class must accept the plan.[494] § 1129(a)(10). The acceptance of that impaired class must be calculated without including the acceptance of any insider. The (a)(10) requirement cannot be overridden by a cram down under § 1129(b), but is an independent limit on confirmation that must be satisfied in every case. The only way to escape the mandate of § 1129(a)(10) is to leave *all* classes unimpaired under the plan. The essence of § 1129(a)(10) is that the debtor cannot have a total cram down plan. Some expression of affirmative approval of the plan by impaired non-insiders must be garnered.

The exclusion of insider votes means that the class vote must be retabulated using only non-insider votes. Who is an "insider" is determined by reference to § 101(31). Interestingly, though, insiders are not automatically excluded from the class vote for purposes of satisfying § 1129(a)(8), although it is possible that an insider's vote could be "designated" under § 1126(e) because of a conflict of interest. Nevertheless, it is possible to have the anomalous situation in which a class accepts the plan for purposes of (a)(8) but not for (a)(10). That class thus could not be used to satisfy (a)(10), but would not have to be crammed down under § 1129(b) if another impaired class accepted the plan and thereby eliminated the (a)(10) problem.

---

[494] See Ralph Brubaker, Artificial Impairment and the Single–Asset Real Estate Debtor, 33 No. 4 Bankr. L. Letter 1 (2013); David Gray Carlson, The Classification Veto in Single–Asset Cases under Bankruptcy Code Section 1129(a)(10), 44 S.C.L. Rev. 565 (1993); Bruce A. Markell, Clueless on Classification: Toward Removing Artificial Limits on Chapter 11 Claim Classification, 11 Bankr. Dev. J. 1 (1995); Linda J. Rusch, Single Asset Cases and Chapter 11: The Classification Quandary, 1 Am. Bankr. Inst. L. Rev. 43 (1993); Linda J. Rusch, Gerrymandering the Classification Issue in Chapter Eleven Reorganization, 63 U. Colo. L. Rev. 163 (1992).

The confirmation commandment of § 1129(a)(10) has been particularly significant in blocking the confirmation of "single asset" real estate cases. In those cases, the operative facts often are that the secured lender holds the great majority of the debt, and, as an undersecured creditor, is able to control the votes of both the secured class *and* the unsecured class. For example, assume that Debtor has $100,000 in trade debt, and owes $4 million to Bank, secured by real estate valued at $3 million. Even if the original obligation to Bank was nonrecourse, § 1111(b)(1)(A) converts the unsecured portion of the debt into an allowable unsecured claim in the chapter 11 case. Bank thus has a $3 million secured claim and a $1 million unsecured claim. If Bank votes both its secured and unsecured claims against the plan, and its unsecured claim is classified with the general unsecured trade debt, confirmation will not be possible, because Bank controls the class vote in both classes. The Debtor could not confirm the plan under the § 1129(b) cram down rules, because cram down is available only if all requirements in § 1129(a) other than (a)(8) are satisfied; in other words, § 1129(a)(10) *must* be complied with. On these facts, classes are impaired, and no impaired class has voted in favor of the plan.

Debtors have tried different strategies to get around this result. The most common is to classify the Bank's unsecured claim separately from the trade debt. Then, the separate trade debt class can be impaired and vote in favor of the plan. Most circuit courts, though, have not permitted such "gerrymandering" of classes in order to escape the dictates of (a)(10).[495] Unless some good business reason for the separate classification can be given, most courts require all unsecured debt to be classified together in this type of case. A minority view would permit separate classification, on the theory that the Bank's unsecured claim that is purely a creature of statute and exists only in a chapter 11 case is not "substantially similar" (see § 1122(a)) to the trade debt.[496]

The proponent of a plan cannot use the *deemed* acceptance of the plan under § 1126(f) by an *unimpaired* class to satisfy § 1129(a)(10). Prior to the 1984 Amendments, there was a split in the case law on whether a deemed acceptance would suffice. In 1984 Congress clarified that the qualifying acceptance for purposes of (a)(10) must be by "a class of claims that is impaired under the plan." Thus, the impairment rules of § 1124 assume importance under (a)(10) for two reasons. The first is that the plan proponent will not have to comply with (a)(10) if *all* classes are unimpaired. The second is that if any class is impaired, one of the impaired classes must affirmatively accept the plan.

Prior to 1994, plan proponents often were tempted to "artificially" impair a class in order to qualify that class for purposes of § 1129(a)(10). For example, the plan might

---

[495] The leading case is *Phoenix Mut. Life Ins. Co. v. Greystone III Joint Venture (In re Greystone III Joint Venture)*, 948 F.2d 134, corrected and reinstated, 995 F.2d 1274 (5th Cir.), cert. denied, 506 U.S. 821 (1992). For other cases taking this restrictive classification view, see, e.g., In re Barakat, 99 F.3d 1520 (9th Cir. 1996), cert. denied, 520 U.S. 1143 (1997); Boston Post Rd. Ltd. P'ship v. FDIC, 21 F.3d 477 (2d Cir. 1994), cert. denied, 513 U.S. 1109 (1995); John Hancock Mut. Life Ins. Co. v. Route 37 Bus. Park Assocs., 987 F.2d 154 (3d Cir. 1993); In re Lumber Exch. Bldg. Ltd. P'ship, 968 F.2d 647 (8th Cir. 1992); In re Bryson Props., XVIII, 961 F.2d 496 (4th Cir. 1992). See also § 11.17.

[496] See, e.g., In re Woodbrook Assocs., 19 F.3d 312 (7th Cir. 1994); In re SM Ltd., 160 B.R. 202 (Bankr. S.D. Fla. 1993).

promise to pay the members of a class 99% on their claims, or might delay payment for a few days after the effective date of the plan. In either case, the class technically would be "impaired." Courts did not respond favorably to such artificial impairment schemes, however, recognizing the blatant attempt to circumvent the strictures of § 1129(a)(10).[497]

Now, however, such sleight-of-hand is not necessary. In 1994 Congress repealed § 1124(3), which had provided that a class was not impaired if it was paid in full in cash on the effective date of the plan. With § 1124(3) gone, though, a class that is to be paid in full in cash on the effective date will be impaired, will get to vote, and should be counted for purposes of complying with (a)(10). One suspects that the chance of an affirmative vote by a class that is fully cashed out up front is quite high.

Indeed, the repeal of § 1124(3) may even give single asset real estate debtors a way to escape the classification hurdle that has so often been held to bar passage through (a)(10), as described in the hypothetical in the text above.[498] Under § 1122(b), a plan is expressly authorized to designate a separate class of small unsecured claims for administrative convenience purposes. The rationale is to permit those small claims to be cashed out, so their votes will not have to be solicited. Now, however, since a class that is cashed out is still impaired, the administrative convenience class apparently would be impaired, would get to vote, and their affirmative vote should satisfy § 1129(a)(10).

§ 11.28 Confirmation Requirements: Feasibility

The bankruptcy court has an independent veto power over a chapter 11 plan. Even if all other requirements for confirmation in § 1129(a) are met—including the affirmative vote of all impaired classes—the plan will not be confirmed unless the court finds that the plan is *feasible*. Under § 1129(a)(11), the court must find that confirmation of the plan "is not likely to be followed by the liquidation, or the need for further financial reorganization" of the debtor or the debtor's successor. The only exception is if the plan itself actually proposes liquidation or further reorganization. The feasibility test of § 1129(a)(11) is derived from the reorganization chapters under the Act, which simply required the court to find that the plan was "feasible."[499]

The requirement in (a)(11) that the court find that the plan is feasible is one of the primary remaining vestiges under the Code of the old view of the bankruptcy court's role in reorganization cases as an independent watchdog. The feasibility requirement at confirmation complements the court's power to dismiss or convert a chapter 11 case for "cause" under § 1112(b); such "cause" might include the lack of reasonable prospects for rehabilitation. In a sense, § 1129(a)(11) is conceptually at odds with the controlling chapter 11 paradigm of freedom of contract, adding a paternalistic overlay to that

---

[497] See, e.g., In re Windsor on the River Assocs., Ltd., 7 F.3d 127 (8th Cir. 1993) (holding that class that was impaired only because of a short delay in payment could not be used to satisfy § 1129(a)(10)). But see In re L & J Anaheim Assocs., 995 F.2d 940 (9th Cir. 1993) (recognizing impairment, whether discretionary or economically driven).

[498] See, e.g., In re Vill. at Camp Bowie I, L.P., 710 F.3d 239 (5th Cir. 2013).

[499] See Bankruptcy Act § 221(2) (chapter X); § 366(2) (chapter XI); § 472(2) (chapter XII).

consent-based model. Even if every class accepts the plan after adequate disclosure, or is unimpaired, the court still can—indeed, must—block confirmation if it concludes that the plan is not feasible.

Why? Does it make sense to give a disinterested judicial officer the power and mandate to second-guess the financial stakeholders themselves, whose money is actually on the line? Congress did not attempt to explain or rationalize the feasibility test in the legislative history to the 1978 Code. The test was carried forward without question from prior law. Under the Act, courts took the view that the feasibility requirement could be justified on the premise that a federal court "is not bound to clog its docket with visionary or impracticable schemes for resuscitation."[500] Under the Code, courts continue to parrot the mantra of the policy against allowing "visionary schemes" to proceed.[501]

Such a policy certainly makes sense prior to confirmation. At that point in time, the court's docket is being "clogged" with the case. More importantly, though, creditors and equity security holders stand to lose money in a failed attempt at reorganization. Horror stories such as the Eastern Air Lines case are graphic demonstrations. It is telling that a ground for a court to dismiss or convert a chapter 11 case (under § 1112(b)(4)(A)) is the "absence of a reasonable likelihood of rehabilitation" (i.e., the feasibility issue), *but only* if coupled with proof of "substantial or continuing loss to or diminution of the estate." The real concern, then, is less with "clogging" and more with the protection of creditors and equity security holders. In the early stages of a chapter 11 case, those parties are *not* entitled to *vote* on whether the case should proceed; the court of necessity must step in and play the role of protector.

At the point of confirmation, though, the need for a court protector is less obvious, precisely because creditors and equity security holders do have the power to vote, and are entitled to receive a court-approved disclosure statement that contains "adequate information" before they cast their ballots. It is generally agreed that part of the "adequate information" that a disclosure statement must contain is a discussion of the risks of plan failure.[502] In short, when creditors and equity security holders vote, in theory at least they are doing so with a fair appreciation of the relevant risks. If the classes vote in favor of the plan, but the court concludes that the plan is not feasible, in effect the court is substituting its own judgment for that of the financial stakeholders.

It is possible, though, that the confirmation feasibility requirement plays a defensible role in protecting the rights of *dissenting individual class members*. Those dissenters are protected, of course, by the right to receive at least the liquidation value of their claim or interest under the plan.[503] § 1129(a)(7)(A). However, the requirement that the plan *propose* to pay creditors or equity security holders liquidation value does

---

[500] Tennessee Pub. Co. v. Am. Nat'l Bank, 299 U.S. 18, 22 (1936) (explaining feasibility requirement in § 77B corporate reorganizations).

[501] See, e.g., In re Danny Thomas Props. II Ltd. P'ship, 241 F.3d 959, 963 (8th Cir. 2001); In re Pikes Peak Water Co., 779 F.2d 1456, 1460 (10th Cir. 1985); In re Pizza of Hawaii, Inc., 761 F.2d 1374, 1382 (9th Cir. 1985).

[502] See § 11.20.

[503] See § 11.26.

not guarantee that they actually will *receive* that value. If the plan fails, they may not receive the liquidation value of their claim or interest. The harm suffered by the affected creditor or interest holder then could be quite high, since their rights will have been permanently altered by confirmation of the plan. In all chapter 11 cases other than those involving individual debtors, confirmation effects an immediate novation of all claims or interests, § 1141, whether or not the plan is consummated. Perhaps the court should be able to provide a countermajoritarian protection against such a risk for minority class members, by passing independently on the feasibility of the plan.

This explanation is not completely satisfactory, however, because the feasibility requirement cannot be waived, even by a unanimous vote of creditors and equity security holders. Thus, at some level, the requirement of court approval of a plan can only be explained by a policy of protecting the jurisdiction and integrity of the federal courts.

In its application, the feasibility requirement is not very rigorous. The threshold of proof is said to be "relatively low." The plan proponent only must demonstrate a "reasonable assurance" or "reasonable prospect" of success; "[s]uccess need not be guaranteed."[504] The mere potential that the plan will fail is not enough to defeat confirmation.[505] In short, success only need be shown to be "more probable than not" to establish feasibility.

Having said that, the court's finding of feasibility cannot be based on pure speculation. In making a feasibility determination, a court may examine: (1) adequacy of capital structure; (2) earning power of debtor's business; (3) economic conditions; (4) ability of management; (5) probability of continuation of same management; and (6) any other matter that may affect the debtor's ability to perform the plan.[506] At the very least, some evidence of the future viability of the reorganized debtor (or its successor) must be introduced.[507]

The crucial question will be whether the reorganized debtor is likely to be able to pay its obligations under the plan while funding ongoing operations. Expert testimony is usually introduced, complete with fancy financial projections about expected cash flow and profits. Projected earnings, economic conditions, the identity of management, and the debtor's capital structure all may bear on the court's decision.[508] If an asset

---

[504] See, e.g., Kane v. Johns–Manville Corp., 843 F.2d 636, 649 (2d Cir. 1988). See also In re Acequia, Inc., 787 F.2d 1352, 1364 (9th Cir. 1986) (finding the feasibility requirement satisfied when the debtor presented evidence to demonstrate the plan's "reasonable probability of success"); In re Briscoe Enters., Ltd., II, 994 F.2d 1160, 1166 (5th Cir.), cert. denied, 510 U.S. 992 (1993) (upholding confirmation when bankruptcy court found only a "marginal prospect of success"); In re Pikes Peak Water Co., 779 F.2d 1456, 1460 (10th Cir. 1985).

[505] See, e.g., In re Drexel Burnham Lambert Grp., Inc., 138 B.R. 723 (Bankr. S.D.N.Y. 1992); In re Mayslake Vill.–Plainfield Campus, Inc., 441 B.R. 309 (Bankr. N.D. Ill. 2010); In re Tribune Co., 464 B.R. 126 (Bankr. D. Del. 2011).

[506] In re GAC Storage Lansing, LLC, 485 B.R. 174, 182 (Bankr. N.D. Ill. 2013) (citing *In re U.S. Truck Co., Inc.*, 800 F.2d 581, 589 (6th Cir. 1986)); In re Trans Max Techs., Inc., 349 B.R. 80, 92 (Bankr. D. Nev. 2006).

[507] See, e.g., In re Walker, 165 B.R. 994 (E.D. Va. 1994).

[508] See, e.g., In re Am. Consol. Transp. Cos., Inc., 470 B.R. 478, 489 (Bankr. N.D. Ill. 2012) (explaining that determining whether a proposed plan meets the feasibility requirement necessitates a complex

sale is an important component of the plan, the projected value of the property to be sold obviously is critical. The longer the payout term is under the plan, the more difficult the feasibility showing becomes, because of the uncertainty and speculation inherent into making projections many years down the road.[509]

Risk factors must be taken into account. For example, the failure to provide for the realistic possibility that a large judgment might be entered against the reorganized debtor defeated feasibility in one well-known case.[510] However, if adequate contingency plans are included to address the possible occurrence of known risks, the feasibility test might be met. The need to accommodate future risks has posed a major problem in the mass tort cases, especially those with substantial "future" claims.

As long as there is some evidence supporting feasibility, the ultimate decision will rest almost entirely with the bankruptcy judge. Feasibility is a fact-intensive inquiry, and appellate reversal would be possible only on proof of clear error.[511]

§ 11.29 Confirmation Requirements: Other Requirements

The confirmation rules governing classes,[512] § 1129(a)(8), individual class members,[513] § 1129(a)(7), acceptance by an impaired class,[514] § 1129(a)(10), and feasibility,[515] § 1129(a)(11), while of great importance, comprise only four of the sixteen requirements in § 1129(a). A plan must meet all of the other statutory tests in § 1129(a) (except, perhaps, subsection (a)(8), under a cram down plan) before a court will confirm it.

Plan complies with applicable provisions of Code

The first requirement is that the *plan* complies with the applicable provisions of the Code. § 1129(a)(1). This provision is the means by which the rules on classification,[516] § 1122, and on the mandatory and permissible contents of the plan,[517] § 1123, are made applicable to the confirmation of the plan.[518] This rule also might preclude the confirmation of a plan that attempts to include provisions that are not authorized by the Code, such as an injunction in favor of non-debtor third parties.[519]

---

evaluation of available data concerning the past, present, and proposed future operations of the debtor (citation omitted)).

[509] See, e.g., In re White, 36 B.R. 199 (Bankr. D. Kan. 1983).

[510] *Pizza of Hawaii*, supra note 501, 761 F.2d 1374.

[511] See, e.g., In re DBSD N. Am., Inc., 634 F.3d 79, 106 (2d Cir. 2011); In re Harbin, 486 F.3d 510, 517 (9th Cir. 2007); In re Save Our Springs (S.O.S.) Alliance, Inc., 632 F.3d 168, 172 (5th Cir. 2011).

[512] See § 11.25.

[513] See § 11.26.

[514] See § 11.27.

[515] See § 11.28

[516] See § 11.17.

[517] See § 11.16.

[518] See H.R. Rep. No. 95–595, 95th Cong., 1st Sess., at 412 (1977).

[519] See In re Riverbend Leasing LLC, 458 B.R. 520 (Bankr. S.D. Iowa 2011) (denying plan confirmation for failure to comply with § 1129(a)(1) when plan provided for release of claims against insider

Proponent complies with applicable provisions of Code

The *proponent* of the plan also is required to comply with the Code's applicable provisions. § 1129(a)(2). This second requirement helps to enforce the disclosure, solicitation, and voting rules of § 1125[520] and § 1126,[521] by making it impossible for a plan proponent to bypass those rules and confirm a plan.[522]

Good faith

The third confirmation requirement is that the plan is proposed "in good faith," and "not by any means forbidden by law." § 1129(a)(3). This requirement has a long history tracing back to the reorganization chapters under prior bankruptcy laws, and much of the "received wisdom" from prior law should help inform the meaning of the current provision.[523] Obviously, "good faith" is a broad and open-ended standard, incapable of precise definition; but such flexibility and generality is necessary, because of the myriad circumstances in which the bona fides of a plan legitimately may be drawn into question.

At bottom, the good faith confirmation requirement is a means to assure that chapter 11 plans further the underlying purposes of the chapter. In other words, the plan must seek to achieve a result that is consistent with the objectives and policies behind chapter 11.[524] Chapter 11 is intended to be a mechanism to facilitate the reorganization (or liquidation, if appropriate) of a financially distressed debtor, and to enable that debtor to deal with its creditors and equity security holders in a fundamentally fair way. If the plan is not being proposed to serve these underlying goals, confirmation should be denied, as such a plan is an abuse of the legal process,[525] and should not be countenanced. If, however, the proponent has a legitimate and honest purpose to reorganize, and a reasonable hope of success, good faith should be found.[526]

---

guarantees). For an thorough discussion on the interplay between § 1129(a)(1) and § 524(e), see In re Linda Vista Cinemas, L.L.C., 442 B.R. 724 (Bankr. D. Ariz. 2010).

[520] See § 11.20.

[521] See § 11.21.

[522] See H.R. Rep. No. 95–595, 95th Cong., 1st Sess. 412 (1977).

[523] See In re Buttonwood Partners, Ltd., 111 B.R. 57, 59 (Bankr. S.D.N.Y. 1990) ("Section 1129(a)(3) is derived from § 221(3) of the Bankruptcy Act which stated that the court could confirm a plan if it satisfied that 'the proposal of the plan and its acceptance are in good faith and have not been made or procured by means or promises forbidden by this Act.' Consequently, given the relationship between § 221(3) of the Act and § 1129(a)(3), it must be construed that the term 'means forbidden by law' subsumes some conduct in connection with obtaining confirmation of such proposal.").

[524] See, e.g., In re South Beach Sec., Inc., 606 F.3d 366 (7th Cir. 2010); In re Sylmar Plaza, L.P., 314 F.3d 1070 (9th Cir. 2002); In re PWS Holding Corp., 228 F.3d 224 (3d Cir. 2000); In re Madison Hotel Assocs., 749 F.2d 410 (7th Cir. 1984).

[525] See, e.g., In re Plant Insulation Co., 485 B.R. 203 (N.D. Cal. 2012) ("A proposed plan does not meet the good faith standard, however, if it is intended 'to obtain tactical litigation advantages' that are 'not within the legitimate scope of the bankruptcy laws.'" (quoting In re SGL Carbon Corp., 200 F.3d 154, 165 (3d Cir. 1999))).

[526] See In re Vill. at Camp Bowie I, L.P., 710 F.3d 239 (5th Cir. 2013); In re Bd. of Dirs. of Telecom Argentina, S.A., 528 F.3d 162 (2d Cir. 2008); Kane v. Johns–Manville Corp., 843 F.2d 636 (2d Cir. 1988).

Stating such broad platitudes is relatively easy, of course, but applying them can be much more difficult. Equally unhelpfully, but understandably, courts emphasize that the "totality of the circumstances" must be weighed in judging good faith.[527] This inquiry is largely fact-intensive, and thus the bankruptcy court's determination will be reversed only if clearly erroneous.[528]

A hostile liquidation plan filed by a competitor for the purpose of driving the debtor out of business might be bad faith.[529] However, a creditor's liquidating plan might pass muster if it was proposed in an honest belief that liquidation was the best course to take.[530] Much depends on the motivations of the plan proponent.

It has been held that the alleged "bad faith" of the proponent must affect the bankruptcy administration in some way. For example, in one case the Eleventh Circuit held that it was not bad faith that the plan proponent had invoked his Fifth Amendment privilege against self-incrimination in a related adversary proceeding, when he had filed all schedules and complied diligently with all aspects of the plan confirmation process.[531]

However, if the plan is being interposed merely to delay creditors from enforcing their rights, bad faith may be found.[532] So, too, if the debtor does not have a real business to reorganize, or any significant debt, or has incorporated a new business for the purpose of cleansing its financial obligations without exposing its assets, a finding of bad faith may be warranted. Proof that the plan is intended primarily as a tax avoidance scheme should preclude a holding of good faith.[533] However, the Ninth Circuit held that a plan proposed by solvent debtors, solely for the purpose of reducing their obligation to a creditor by roughly $1 million, is not per se "lacking in good faith."[534]

Good faith has been raised as an issue in many of the single asset real estate cases, on the premise that the dispute is primarily between only two parties—the debtor and the secured lender. Chapter 11, the argument goes, was not intended to be a federal mortgage foreclosure law. The absence of a so-called "common pool" problem involving multiple creditors, the filing of the case to delay foreclosure, the fact that the debtor may have few employees, and other factors are cited to support bad faith. Courts have come down all over the board in resolving this debate. It seems, however, that the intent of Congress, for better or worse, plainly was to allow single asset real

---

[527] See, e.g., In re PPI Enters. (U.S.), Inc., 324 F.3d 197 (3d Cir. 2003); In re T–H New Orleans Ltd. P'ship, 116 F.3d 790 (5th Cir. 1997); In re McCormick, 49 F.3d 1524 (11th Cir. 1995); In re Sun Country Dev., Inc., 764 F.2d 406 (5th Cir. 1985).

[528] See, e.g., In re Combustion Eng'g, Inc., 391 F.3d 190 (3d Cir. 2004); In re Cajun Elec. Power Co-op., Inc., 150 F.3d 503 (5th Cir. 1998).

[529] See In re Unichem Corp., 72 B.R. 95 (Bankr. N.D. Ill. 1987), aff'd, 80 B.R. 448 (N.D. Ill. 1987).

[530] See Hanson v. First Bank of S. Dakota, N.A., 828 F.2d 1310 (8th Cir. 1987).

[531] See In re McCormick, 49 F.3d 1524 (11th Cir. 1995).

[532] See, e.g., In re Am. Capital Equip., LLC, 688 F.3d 145 (3d Cir. 2012); In re Pikes Peak Water Co., 779 F.2d 1456 (10th Cir. 1985).

[533] See, e.g., In re S. Beach Sec., Inc., 421 B.R 456 (N.D. Ill. 2009); In re Maxim Indus., Inc., 22 B.R. 611 (Bankr. D. Mass. 1982).

[534] In re Sylmar Plaza, L.P., 314 F.3d 1070 (9th Cir. 2002).

estate debtors to use chapter 11, and therefore seeking to confirm a plan in such a case usually should not be found to be bad faith. Some of the provisions in chapter 11 are drafted primarily with real estate cases in mind (§ 1111(b), for example), and chapter 11's lineage goes back to old chapter XII, which was designed entirely to deal with real estate cases.

Most of the foregoing concerns might be raised early in the case, prior to confirmation, in a motion under § 1112(b) to dismiss the chapter 11 case or convert it to chapter 7 for cause.[535] However, the court may be more willing in the incipient stages of a case to give the debtor a chance to show why an opportunity to obtain chapter 11 relief is merited. Many courts will give the debtor the opportunity to "get religion" and "cure" an initial bad faith filing with the subsequent filing of a good faith plan, although other courts hold that an initial bad faith taint cannot be removed. Confirmation, though, is the final act in the case, and the effects of confirmation are momentous.[536] The court thus must be diligent in not permitting a suspect plan to be confirmed.

Courts also must be cautious not to conflate the good faith and feasibility tests. Under prior law, many courts in weighing the good faith of a *petition* under chapter X considered whether the debtor had reasonable reorganization prospects as a component of "good faith." Under chapter 11, good faith is not an express requirement of filing, and concerns over feasibility may be addressed either by converting or dismissing the case for "cause" under § 1112(b) or denying confirmation under § 1129(a)(11).[537]

Payments for services reasonable

The fourth requirement polices the fees charged for services rendered in connection with the case. This rule continues the longstanding policy guarding against abuses by professionals in "milking" the estate for excessive fees. All payments already made or to be made after confirmation for such fees for services rendered or for costs and expenses must be disclosed, and then approved by the bankruptcy court as "reasonable." § 1129(a)(4). Implicit in this provision is the power of the court to disallow fees that are unreasonable. No guidelines are suggested in either the Code or legislative history with regard to how reasonableness is to be determined. The payments covered are those that are made by the debtor, the plan proponent (if other than the debtor), any person issuing securities under the plan, and any person acquiring property under the plan. The services, costs, or expenses to which the rule applies are those in connection with the case or with the plan. In many instances, such as for professional fees charged against the estate, the court may already have approved the fees under § 330. Whatever "reasonable" may or may not mean in this

---

[535] See § 2.17.

[536] See § 11.35.

[537] See, e.g., In re Vill. at Camp Bowie I, L.P., 710 F.3d 239 (5th Cir. 2013) ("Here, the bankruptcy court determined that the [debtor] had not run afoul of § 1129(a)(3), as it had proposed a feasible cramdown plan for the legitimate purposes of reorganizing its debts. . . . ").

context, reasonable fees do not include fee premiums or enhancements for advancing one's own interests at the expense of other creditors.[538]

Disclosure and approval of management and insiders

The post-confirmation management of the reorganized debtor or its successor must be disclosed, along with the "affiliations" of those individuals. § 1129(a)(5)(A)(i). In addition, the court must approve the disclosed slate of officers and directors as being consistent (1) with the interests of creditors and equity security holders and (2) with public policy. § 1129(a)(5)(A)(ii). These requirements will permit both plan voters and the court to protect against the post-confirmation employment of incompetent, biased, or dishonest management. Even if interested parties cannot easily replace undesirable management with a trustee during the case, § 1104(a), they can effectively vote them out of office on confirmation. This rule supplements the § 1129(a)(11) feasibility determination; knowing the identity of post-confirmation officers and directors will assist the court in determining whether a plan meets the feasibility requirement.

The plan proponent also must disclose the identity of any insider that will be employed or retained by the reorganized debtor after confirmation, as well as the compensation to be paid to that insider. § 1129(a)(5)(B). This disclosure rule minimizes the possibility of insider abuses. Note, though, that court approval of the proposed compensation is not required.

Regulatory approvals

The sixth requirement applies only in cases in which the debtor must obtain the approval of a government regulatory agency of rate changes. Utilities are an obvious example. Under § 1129(a)(6), the primary jurisdiction of the regulatory agency over rate changes is preserved. The plan must provide for the approval of any proposed rate changes by that agency.

Priority claims

Priority claims are dealt with by § 1129(a)(9). Subject to the possible waiver of rights by any individual priority claimant, the ninth confirmation requirement provides for the *full payment in cash* of all priority claims. However, this full payment rule is implemented in three different ways, depending on the priority category. There is a gap in the Code, however—§ 1129(a)(9) does not indicate which of the three approaches applies to ninth or tenth priority claims under § 507(a)(9) and (10).

The first type of treatment is for second and third priority claims, i.e., those that arise after the filing of the petition. These claims are not classified, § 1123(a)(1), and must be paid in full in cash on the effective date of the plan. § 1129(a)(9)(A).

Prepetition priority tax claims (i.e., those dealt with in § 507(a)(8)) also are not classified, § 1123(a)(1), but are not entitled to be cashed out up front. Instead, the plan may pay those eighth priority claims in regular cash installments over a period of not

---

[538]   See, e.g., In re Adelphia Commc'ns Corp., 441 B.R. 6 (Bankr. S.D.N.Y. 2010).

later than 5 years after the date of the order for relief. § 1129(a)(9)(C). Those payments may not be in a manner less favorable than the most favored non-priority unsecured claim provided for by the plan. § 1129(a)(9)(C)(iii). Interest must be paid on the deferred claims, so that the present value of all the payments equals the allowed amount of the claim. The 2005 amendments added § 1129(a)(9)(D), which provides that secured claims that would qualify as eighth priority tax claims, but for the fact that they are secured, are entitled to be cashed out in the same manner as those priority tax claims in accordance with § 1129(a)(9)(C).

The other type of priority claim treatment is for claims in the first priority and fourth through seventh priority categories. § 1129(a)(9)(B). These priorities are classified. Each priority level will constitute a separate class. If the class accepts the plan, payments may be deferred, with interest. If the class rejects the plan, however, deferral is not permitted, and the full claim must be cashed out on the plan's effective date.

United States trustee fees paid

The twelfth requirement, § 1129(a)(12), is a nagging reminder of either (1) the difficulty of drafting a comprehensive Code without making mistakes or (2) the incompetence of Congress. This section is totally unnecessary. Under subsection (a)(12), the plan must provide that all fees payable under 28 U.S.C. § 1930 have been or will be paid. The most significant of the fees in 28 U.S.C. § 1930 are the quarterly fees that are payable to the United States trustee, as calculated according to a sliding scale that is tied to the level of disbursements. 28 U.S.C. § 1930(a)(6). These same fees, however, are accorded second priority under § 507(a)(2), and thus are already dealt with by § 1129(a)(9)(A), discussed above, which requires full cash payment of those priority fees.

Retiree benefits

Section 1129(a)(13) was added in 1988 as part of a package of provisions that sought to improve the lot of retirees.[539] Under this section, the plan must provide for the continuation of retiree benefits for the duration of the period for which the debtor has obligated itself to provide benefits. The level of benefits that must be supplied is established by reference to § 1114, which prescribes detailed rules governing any desired modifications.

Domestic support obligations

In 2005, the Code was amended to require that the debtor "has paid" all *post*-petition domestic support obligations that are payable under a judicial or administrative order or a statute. § 1129(a)(14). Pre-petition DSOs would qualify as first priority expenses under § 507(a)(1) and thus would be dealt with under § 1129(a)(9)(B). The statutory wording in (a)(14) suggests that a proposal to pay the

---

[539] See Bankruptcy Retiree Benefits Act of 1988, Pub. L. No. 100–334, 102 Stat. 610 (1988). The primary other addition to the Code was § 1114, which requires the treatment of retiree benefits in a manner similar to that for collective bargaining agreements in § 1113. See § 8.13.

post-petition DSOs in the plan itself would not suffice, since the plan proponent must show that the debtor "has paid" such obligations.

BAPCPA added additional language to § 1129(b)(2)(B)(ii), referencing § 1129(a)(14). Known as the "absolute priority rule," § 1129(b)(2)(B)(ii) allows a creditor to object to a plan if another creditor holding a claim junior to theirs receives any distribution under the plan, while the objecting creditor does not receive 100% of their claim.[540] The absolute priority rule makes an exception, however, for individual debtors, allowing them to retain property included into the estate under § 1115, "subject to the requirements of subsection (a)(14)." However, some courts and commentators hold that this reference to subsection (a)(14) was a drafting error, and really Congress meant to reference (a)(15).

Projected disposable income test for individual debtors

Applicable only to individual debtors, Congress in 2005 added a "projected disposable income test" confirmation requirement. § 1129(a)(15). This change is part of a whole package of 2005 amendments that sought to make chapter 11 for individual debtors more like chapter 13.[541] Prior to 2005, chapter 13 had a projected disposable income test while chapter 11 did not, making chapter 11 potentially more attractive to individual debtors. § 1325(b). No more. Under the new chapter 11 plan requirements, if the holder of an allowed unsecured claim objects to confirmation, either (1) they have to be paid in full, i.e., the value of the claim as of the effective date of the plan of property to be distributed on account of the claim cannot be less than the amount of such claim, or (2) the value of property to be distributed under the plan is not less than the *"projected disposable income"* of the debtor (defined in § 1325(b)(2)) to be received during the 5–year period beginning when payments are made, or during the period for payments provided by the plan, whichever is longer. This requirement might require a court to investigate the credibility of a debtor's financial information, before declaring a plan meets § 1129(a)(15).[542]

Transfers of property

The final confirmation requirement provides that all transfers of property must be made in accordance with applicable non-bankruptcy law that governs transfers of property by corporations or trusts that is not a moneyed, business, or commercial corporation or trust. § 1129(a)(16). Note that subsection (a)(16) only applies to

---

[540] See 11.33.

[541] See, e.g., In re Friedman, 466 B.R. 471, 484 (B.A.P. 9th Cir. 2012) ("[C]learly, the drafters of § 1129(a)(15) tried to create symmetry between chapters 11 and 13 for individual debtors."); In re Shat, 424 B.R. 854, 862 (Bankr. D. Nev. 2010) ("[I]t appears that Congress inserted the individual chapter 11 provisions to ensure no easy escape from means testing. The template for this effort was to adopt and adapt as much of chapter 13 as possible with respect to individual debtors.").

[542] See In re Gbadebo, 431 B.R. 222, 226–27 (Bankr. N.D. Cal. 2010) (holding that debtor failed to meet the § 1129(a)(15) requirement, although his statement of income and expenses showed a negative number, because he treated his company as his personal "piggy bank").

nonprofit entities.[543] Additionally, at least one court has held that equity is not the type of "asset" affected by this section.[544]

§ 11.30 Cram Down: Overview

If a plan satisfies all of the confirmation requirements in § 1129(a) *except* § 1129(a)(8), which requires each class either to be unimpaired or to accept the plan,[545] the proponent of the plan still might be able to confirm the plan. § 1129(b)(1). The proponent may (but is not required to) request that the plan be confirmed under § 1129(b), notwithstanding the dissenting vote of an impaired class. Confirmation of a plan over a class dissent is known as *cram down* of the plan,[546] because the plan is "crammed down" the throat of the dissenting class.

The cram down rules of § 1129(b) represent a central part of the compromise by which chapters X and XI were merged into a single reorganization chapter in 1978. Under chapter X, the financial standard was the "*absolute priority*" rule, which required the plan to adhere strictly to the non-bankruptcy priority entitlements of the different classes of creditors and equity security holders. Bankruptcy Act § 221(2). Senior classes had to be paid in full before any distribution could be made to lower priority classes. Application of the absolute priority rule required a costly valuation of the debtor in every case. Chapter XI (and XII), by comparison, did not require compliance with the absolute priority rule, but only required the plan to satisfy the "*best interests*" test. Bankruptcy Act § 366(2) (chapter XI), § 472(2) (chapter XII). These rules meant that in chapter X the full going concern reorganization value was allocated to creditors in the order of their priorities, whereas in chapter XI creditors were entitled only to liquidation value.[547]

In the 1978 Code, Congress decided to let the different classes of creditors and equity security holders bargain over how to distribute the difference between liquidation and going concern value.[548] As long as all classes agree, or are not impaired, the absolute priority rule will not apply. § 1129(a)(8), (b)(1). The need to value the debtor would be obviated.

However, if an impaired class does vote against the plan, it triggers the absolute priority rule, assuming that the plan proponent wishes to proceed to cram down. § 1129(b)(1). Cram down is not automatic, but must be requested by the proponent. Also, the court may not rewrite the plan so that it will meet the statutory

---

[543] See, e.g., In re Rubicon U.S. REIT, Inc., 434 B.R. 168, 179 (Bankr. D. Del. 2010); In re Cypresswood Land Partners, I, 409 B.R. 396, 433 (Bankr. S.D. Tex. 2009); In re Hawaiian Telcom Commc'ns, Inc., 430 B.R. 564, 598–99 (Bankr. D. Haw. 2009).

[544] In re Seasons Partners, LLC, 439 B.R. 505, 516 (Bankr. D. Ariz. 2010).

[545] See § 11.25.

[546] For excellent discussions of cram down, see Richard L. Broude, Cramdown and Chapter 11 of the Bankruptcy Code: The Settlement Imperative, 39 Bus. Law. 441 (1984); Kenneth N. Klee, All You Ever Wanted to Know About Cram Down Under the New Bankruptcy Code, 53 Am. Bankr. L.J. 133 (1979); Kenneth N. Klee, Cram Down II, 64 Am. Bankr. L.J. 229 (1990).

[547] See § 11.31.

[548] H.R. Rep. No. 95–595, 95th Cong., 1st Sess., at 224 (1977).

requirements, but must simply decide whether the statute is satisfied.[549] The absolute priority rule only applies, though, *from the dissenting class down*. This is a major change from practice under chapter X of the Act, in which the rule was applied to all classes.[550] Under the Code, classes senior to the dissenting class will not be subject to the rule. In short, "senior accepting classes are permitted to give up value to junior classes as long as no dissenting intervening class receives less than the amount of its claims in full."[551]

The basic statement of the absolute priority rule is found in § 1129(b)(1). Continuing the language of retired chapter X (Bankruptcy Act § 221(2)), which in turn was drawn from older statutes and precedents, the Code provides that a plan may be confirmed over the opposition of an impaired class only if the plan "*does not discriminate unfairly, and is fair and equitable.*" § 1129(b)(1). This requirement arises only with respect to each class of claims or interests that is impaired and has not accepted the plan.

The Code elaborates on the meaning of the "fair and equitable" test. § 1129(b)(2). Section 1129(b)(2)(A) describes the "fair and equitable" test in detail with regards to secured creditors, while § 1129(b)(2)(B) provides the test for unsecured creditors. Note, though, that the statutory exposition in (b)(2) of the meaning of "fair and equitable" is neither exclusive nor comprehensive, but is intended to be illustrative only. The rich body of case law precedent interpreting the "fair and equitable" standard over the decades will continue to apply in cases under the Code, even if not expressly incorporated in the statute. For example, the rule that a class senior to the dissenting class may not be paid more than 100% on its claims is not included in the Code, but the legislative history makes clear that this longstanding rule will apply with full force in chapter 11.[552] A similar rule fashioned by courts and confirmed by the legislative history is that where an estate is solvent, all creditors must be paid in full, including postpetition interest, before equity holders may participate in any recovery.[553]

The meaning of the fair and equitable test is first described for secured claims.[554] § 1129(b)(2)(A). In a nutshell, the secured class must retain their liens and receive the present value of their collateral in one manner or another. For dissenting classes of unsecured claims, § 1129(b)(2)(B) elucidates the fair and equitable standard.[555] Unless the unsecured class is paid in full, no junior class may receive or retain any property under the plan on account of their claim or interest. The same absolute priority rule— full payment or the exclusion of junior classes—applies to classes of interest holders.[556] § 1129(b)(2)(C). An exception to the absolute priority rule exists for *individual debtors,*

---

[549]   Id. at 414.

[550]   See N. Pac. Ry. Co. v. Boyd, 228 U.S. 482, 508 (1913) ("[T]he creditors were entitled to be paid before the stockholders could retain [the property] for any purpose whatever.").

[551]   124 Cong. Rec. S17,420 (daily ed. Oct. 6. 1978) (remarks of Sen. DeConcini); 124 Cong. Rec. H11,104 (daily ed. Sept. 28, 1978) (remarks of Rep. Edwards).

[552]   See id.

[553]   See H.R. Rep. No. 103–835, 103d Cong., at 47 (1994).

[554]   See § 11.32.

[555]   See § 11.33.

[556]   See id.

who are allowed to retain property included in the estate under § 1115, which brings postpetition property and earnings into the estate.[557] § 1129(b)(2)(B)(ii).

A major controversy that has arisen under the Code is whether a junior class of equity can escape the dictates of the absolute priority rule and retain their interest in the reorganized debtor by invoking the "new value" doctrine.[558] Under that supposed "exception" to the absolute priority rule, the equity class makes a contribution of new value to the reorganized debtor, and receives an interest in the debtor in exchange for that new contribution—not on account of the old interest. Whether this strategy is permissible under the Code remains open to debate, as the Supreme Court twice (in 1988 and 1999) has held that proposed "new value" plans did not pass muster on the facts presented, but expressly declined both times to decide the threshold issue of whether a new value exception exists at all.[559]

§ 11.31 Cram Down: History

Cram down has a long if not storied history. In 1978 Congress adopted some aspects of prior law, while also making important changes. An appreciation of pre-Code law informs an understanding of the application of the current cram down rules in § 1129(b).[560]

Reorganizations of incorporated entities began in earnest soon after the Civil War, with attempts being made to restructure the debts of railroads. At that time no statutory authority existed to permit corporate reorganizations. Resort was had to the federal courts, however, which exercised their equitable powers to appoint receivers for the corporate debtors. The receiver would take title to the debtor's assets and sell that property at foreclosure. Often these sales were made in pursuance of a prearranged contractual agreement between stockholders and senior debt to distribute value to each, as specified in the contract. Priority issues inevitably arose—particularly when raised by nonassenting creditors who were squeezed out of the "deal" cut between senior debt and equity.[561]

As early as 1869, the Supreme Court held in *Railroad Co. v. Howard*[562] that a contract which attempted to give stockholders a share of the sale proceeds without full

---

[557] See id.

[558] See § 11.34.

[559] Bank of Am. Nat'l Trust & Sav. Ass'n v. 203 North LaSalle St. P'ship, 526 U.S. 434, 443 (1999) ("We do not decide whether the statute includes a new value corollary or exception, but hold that on any reading respondent's proposed plan fails to satisfy the statute"); Norwest Bank Worthington v. Ahlers, 485 U.S. 197, 203 n.3 (1988) ("We need not reach this question to resolve the instant dispute. . . . [W]e think it clear that even if the *Los Angeles Lumber* exception to the absolute priority rule has survived enactment of the Bankruptcy Code, this exception does not encompass respondents' promise to contribute their 'labor, experience, and expertise' to the reorganized enterprise.").

[560] For useful discussions of cram down and absolute priority under pre-Code law, see Walter J. Blum & Stanley A. Kaplan, The Absolute Priority Doctrine in Corporate Reorganizations, 41 U. Chi. L. Rev. 651 (1974); Walter J. Blum, The Law and Language of Corporate Reorganization, 17 U. Chi. L. Rev. 565 (1950). See also John D. Ayer, Rethinking Absolute Priority After Ahlers, 87 Mich. L. Rev. 963 (1989).

[561] For a brief overview of the history of equity receiverships, and how the absolute priority rule developed, see Ralph Brubaker & Charles Jordan Tabb, Bankruptcy Reorganizations and the Troubling Legacy of *Chrysler* and *GM*, 2010 U. Ill. L. Rev.1375, 1400–03 (2010).

[562] 74 U.S. 392 (1869).

payment to nonassenting unsecured creditors was ineffective against those creditors. The unpaid creditors were entitled in equity to charge the fund received by the stockholders, which was held in trust for the benefit of creditors. Thirty years later, the Court held in *Louisville Trust Co. v. Louisville, New Albany & Chicago Railway Co.*[563] that an order decreeing a foreclosure sale had to be set aside to determine whether that sale was made in pursuance of an illegal contract between bondholders and stockholders to preserve the rights of both and destroy the rights of unsecured creditors. While recognizing the practical reality that inquiry could be made beyond the "technical rights" of the parties, the Court nevertheless reaffirmed that foreclosure proceedings could not "be rightfully carried to consummation which recognize and preserve any interest in the stockholders without also recognizing and preserving the interests, not merely of the mortgagee, but of every creditor of the corporation."[564] Any sale, which attempts to preserve the interests of the stockholders, "must necessarily secure and preserve the prior rights of general creditors," because of "the familiar rule that the stockholder's interest in the property is subordinate to the rights of creditors."[565] An agreement between senior debt and stockholders to preserve each of their rights and yet exclude unsecured creditors would be a "travesty" that comes "within judicial denunciation" and could not "be tolerated."[566]

But what if it is alleged that the property of the debtor is fully encumbered and is worth less than the senior secured debt, so that the claims of the excluded unsecured creditors apparently are *valueless*? In that event, may the senior creditors relinquish value to stockholders to persuade them to consent to the sale, and leave unsecured creditors out? In the landmark equity receivership case of *Northern Pacific Railway Co. v. Boyd*,[567] the lower court in charge of the foreclosure sale made such a finding of insolvency prior to the sale; after the sale, stock in the new company was issued to the stockholders of the old debtor. Proponents of this arrangement sought to distinguish the *Louisville Trust* case by urging that Boyd, though a nonassenting unsecured creditor, "cannot complain if worthless stock in the new company was given for worthless stock in the old."[568]

In a momentous decision, the Supreme Court in a narrow 5–4 vote rejected this justification and held in favor of Boyd. The Court announced that the distribution of value in a corporate reorganization had to be done "according to a fixed principle."[569] That "fixed principle" mandated the payment of unsecured creditors before any property could be received or retained by stockholders—in short, the "absolute priority" rule. In perhaps the most famous (and important) passage in the history of corporate reorganization law, the *Boyd* Court observed:

"If the value of the road justified the issuance of stock in exchange for old shares, the creditors were entitled to the benefit of that value, whether it was present or

---

[563] 174 U.S. 674 (1899).

[564] Id. at 683.

[565] Id. at 684.

[566] Id.

[567] 228 U.S. 482 (1913). See Brubaker & Tabb, supra note 561, 2010 U. Ill. L. Rev. at 1402–03.

[568] 228 U.S. at 507.

[569] Id.

prospective, for dividends or only for purposes of control. In either event it was a right of property out of which the creditors were entitled to be paid before the stockholders could retain it for any purpose whatever."[570]

The Court in *Boyd* did note that the "fixed principle" did not "require the impossible," *viz.*, the payment of unsecured creditors in cash as a condition of the stockholders retaining an interest; instead, creditors could be paid in bonds or in preferred stock.[571] In a later equity decision, the Court elaborated in *Kansas City Terminal Railway Co. v. Central Union Trust Co.*[572] on the practical necessity of "cooperation between bondholders and stockholders" in securing a purchaser of the assets of a large corporation, and confirmed that a "fair and open arrangement" could be made to achieve that result.[573] In dictum, the *Kansas City Terminal* Court recognized that "other arrangements" might be authorized by a court of equity when necessary to preserve the prior rights of unsecured creditors, even if a "reasonable adjustment" of rights occurred.[574] In particular, the Court noted the possibility that stockholders might be permitted to contribute additional funds to the enterprise and retain a valuable interest in exchange.[575] This suggestion planted the seeds of the "new value" exception to the absolute priority rule.[576]

Corporate reorganizations were first authorized by *statute* in § 77B of the Bankruptcy Act, enacted in 1934. Under § 77B(f)(1), the judge was authorized to confirm a plan if "it is fair and equitable and does not discriminate unfairly in favor of any class of creditors or stockholders." In 1939, the Supreme Court confirmed in *Case v. Los Angeles Lumber Products Co.*[577] that the "fixed principle" of absolute priority announced in *Boyd* and other cases was imported into § 77B by the use of the "fair and equitable" language, which had become a term of art.[578] In *Case*, the Court likewise reaffirmed the continued vitality of the "new value" doctrine, observing that where necessary to the success of the reorganization, if "stockholders make a fresh contribution and receive in return a participation reasonably equivalent to their contribution, no objection can be made."[579] The Court held, though, that the stockholders' pledge of such intangibles as "continuity of management" and "financial standing and influence in the community" did not constitute an adequate "contribution in money or money's worth."[580]

When the Chandler Act was enacted in 1938, reorganizations were split into three chapters: chapter X for corporate reorganizations, chapter XI for "arrangements," and chapter XII for real property arrangements. Only chapter X carried forward the

---

[570] Id. at 508.

[571] Id.

[572] 271 U.S. 445 (1926).

[573] Id. at 453–54.

[574] Id. at 455.

[575] Id. at 454–55.

[576] See § 11.34.

[577] 308 U.S. 106 (1939).

[578] Id. at 118–19.

[579] Id. at 121.

[580] Id. at 122–23.

absolute priority rule requiring a plan to be *"fair and equitable."* Bankruptcy Act § 221(2). The confirmation standard in chapters XI and XII required only that the plan be in the *"best interests"* of the creditors, Bankruptcy Act §§ 366(2), 472(2), meaning that creditors were entitled to be paid only the *liquidation* value of their claims. Under that more permissive standard, no objection could be raised to stockholders retaining an interest in the reorganized debtor based on the premium of going concern over liquidation value; as long as creditors were paid liquidation value, the plan could be confirmed.

Over time, dissatisfaction with the absolute priority scheme of chapter X grew. Debtors voted with their feet, flocking to chapter XI in droves in preference to chapter X. The perceived need to use the absolute priority rule to protect public investors from the machinations of corporate insiders dwindled as investment patterns shifted; whereas in 1938, when chapter X was enacted, public securities were usually senior bonds, which were preferred under the absolute priority rule, by 1978 public investors more often purchased subordinated debentures and stock, which fell at the bottom of the priority ladder.[581]

But the criticisms of the absolute priority rule were even more basic. *Applying* the rule was a nightmare. In order to implement the absolute priority rule, the going concern *"reorganization value"* of the debtor's property and business first had to be determined.[582] The classes of claimants then had to be arranged in order of priority, so that participation rights in the reorganized debtor could be distributed in descending order. All claimants who fell below the judicially determined level of "reorganization value" then had to be excluded entirely from participation.

The required judicial proceeding to establish the debtor's reorganization value was time-consuming and expensive. Delay could be fatal for a troubled enterprise. Even worse, the necessary underlying "premise of a valid and reliable valuation is specious or inflexible or illusory."[583] In an oft-quoted phrase, the valuation was *"a guess compounded by an estimate."*[584] The basis for the criticism is this. Valuation of the enterprise often was done on a "capitalized earnings" basis. Two variables had to be established to capitalize earnings: (1) the projected future earnings of the reorganized debtor, and (2) the capitalization rate. The earnings (E) would be multiplied by the capitalization rate (R) to determine reorganization value (V): $E \times R = V$.

---

[581]   H.R. Rep. No. 95–595, 95th Cong., 1st Sess., at 222 (1977).

[582]   See id.; Blum & Kaplan, supra note 560, at 655.

[583]   Blum & Kaplan, supra note 560, at 655.

[584]   Peter Coogan wrote that catchy language, which is quoted in H.R. Rep. No. 95–595, 95th Cong., 1st Sess., at 222 (1977).

In a famous passage from an unreported opinion in the *King Resources* bankruptcy, where the company's value depended on the value of 600 drilling permits in the Canadian Arctic, the district judge sarcastically stated:

"My final conclusion . . . is that it is worth somewhere between $90 million and $100 million as a going concern, and to satisfy the people who want precision on the value, I fix the exact value of the company at the average of those, $96,856,850, which of course is a total absurdity that anybody could fix a value with that degree of precision, but for the lawyers who want me to make that fool estimate, I have just made it."

Chaim J. Fortgang & Thomas Moers Mayer, Valuation in Bankruptcy, 32 U.C.L.A. L. Rev. 1061, 1132 (1985) (quoting Citibank v. Baer, 651 F.2d 1341, 1347 (10th Cir. 1980) (quoting district court opinion)).

The capitalization rate established the relationship of the debtor's annual earnings to the total value of the enterprise. For example, if annual earnings were 20% of the company's value, capitalization would be at 20%, or a rate of 5 times earnings.[585] Neither variable could be computed with any certainty, however; each was predicated on a host of assumptions, predictions, and surmises. A slight modification of either the projected earnings (E) or the capitalization rate multiplier (R) would necessarily change the product, the value (V) of the enterprise. The right to participate in the reorganization under the absolute priority rule hinged entirely on a comparison of "V" to the amount of debts or interests in each class in the priority ladder.

For example, assume a simple case, in which a debtor had secured debts of $5 million and unsecured debts of $3 million, for a total of $8 million. For stockholders of the debtor to be allowed to retain an interest in the reorganized enterprise under the absolute priority rule, the debtor would have to be valued at more than $8 million. Assume that the valuation hearing projected the reorganized debtor's annual earnings (E) to be $1.3 million, and determined that the proper multiplier (R) for this debtor was 6; the value (V) of the debtor would be $7.8 million ($1.3 million x 6). Stockholders would have to be excluded under the absolute priority rule. However, if future annual earnings were projected to be $1.35 million, the stockholders could retain an interest in the reorganized debtor; the value would be greater than the $8 million in debts: V = $1.35 million × 6 = $8.1 million. Or, if a multiplier of 6.2 were used, instead of 6, stockholders again would not have to be excluded: V = $1.3 million × 6.2 = $8.06 million.

Critics charged that the valuation process in practice proceeded backwards: the trustee and the court first decided which classes should be allowed to share in the reorganization, and then selected an earnings figure and a capitalization rate that would achieve the predetermined result.[586] In a number of notorious cases, stockholders were excluded, and yet soon after confirmation the stock of the reorganized debtor traded for much more than had been projected.

In the end, Congress in 1978 asked the basic question of whether the game of inexorably applying the absolute priority rule in corporate reorganization cases was worth the candle. The answer: only if the classes of creditors and equity security holders *could not agree* on how to divide up reorganization value. Thus, under the Code the absolute priority rule will be invoked *only* if a class is (1) impaired and (2) votes against the plan, and (3) the plan proponent still requests confirmation. § 1129(b)(1). And even then, the absolute priority rule will be applied only *from the dissenting class down*, permitting senior classes to give up value to each other. If all classes either are unimpaired or accept the plan, § 1129(a)(8), the absolute priority rule will not be applied. As the legislative history explained:

> The bill does not impose a rigid financial rule for the plan. The parties are left to their own to negotiate a fair settlement. . . . [N]egotiation among the parties after full disclosure will govern how the value of the reorganizing company will be

---

[585] See Blum & Kaplan, supra note 560, at 656.

[586] See id. at 657.

distributed among creditors and stockholders. The bill only sets the outer limits on the outcome: it must be somewhere between the going-concern value and the liquidation value.

> Only when the parties are unable to agree on a proper distribution of the value of the company does the bill establish a financial standard. . . . Simply put, the bill requires that the plan pay any dissenting class in full before any class junior to the dissenter may be paid at all. The rule is a partial application of the absolute priority rule.[587]

Under the Code, then, the venerable history of the absolute priority rule may still be carried forward in any given case—but only if a consensus cannot be reached and the plan proponent is game for attempting cram down.

§ 11.32 Cram Down: Dissenting Secured Classes

Chapter 11 presents an ongoing tension between the need of the reorganizing debtor to retain and use collateral and the desire of lienholders to keep their rights against the collateral and ultimately to be paid. During the pendency of the case, this tension is played out in the arena of motions for turnover,[588] § 542(a), relief from the automatic stay,[589] § 362(d), and adequate protection.[590] §§ 362(d)(1), 363(e), 361. The operative principle during the case is that the value of the lienholder's secured claim must be maintained. The creditor's lien must be kept intact and the collateral value preserved; but the secured creditor has no right to any more than that. Most significantly, the lienholder is not entitled to be compensated for the costs of delay caused by the continuation of the case, except to the extent the creditor bargained for extra security.[591]

The *interim* suspension and preservation of the lienholder's rights while the reorganization case is pending stands on an entirely different footing from the situation attending the *final* fixing of rights pursuant to the confirmed chapter 11 plan. "The reorganized debtor," the Supreme Court has counseled, "is supposed to stand on his own two feet."[592] The protection afforded the lienholder at the conclusion of the case thus must be "completely compensatory,"[593] as measured by the creditor's collateral. If such "complete compensation" can be provided to the secured creditor, the reorganized debtor may retain the collateral after confirmation, even if the secured creditor does not consent to the plan.

A plan may be confirmed with respect to a class of secured claims in one of three ways: (1) the secured class *accepts* the plan, §§ 1129(a)(8)(A), 1126(c); (2) the class is

---

[587] H.R. Rep. No. 95–595, 95th Cong., 1st Sess., at 224 (1977).

[588] See § 5.12.

[589] See §§ 3.21–3.25.

[590] See §§ 3.18–3.20.

[591] United Savs. Ass'n v. Timbers of Inwood Forest Assocs., Ltd., 484 U.S. 365 (1988). See § 3.19.

[592] *Timbers*, 484 U.S. at 378.

[593] See In re Arnold & Baker Farms, 85 F.3d 1415, 1422 (9th Cir. 1996), cert. denied, 519 U.S. 1054 (1997); In re Murel Holding Corp., 75 F.2d 941, 942 (2d Cir. 1935).

not impaired, §§ 1129(a)(8)(B), 1124; or (3) the *cram down* standards of § 1129(b)(2)(A) are satisfied. Acceptance by the class is self-explanatory. Even if the class does not favor the plan, the plan still may be confirmed if the class is unimpaired or crammed down.[594]

A class of secured claims may be unimpaired in one of two ways.[595] The first is to leave unaltered all legal, equitable, and contractual rights of the creditor class. § 1124(1). This alternative might be used if the debtor is not in default on the secured debt and simply proposes to leave the secured debt unaffected by the reorganization plan. Second, even if the debt is in default and has been accelerated, the plan may propose to cure the default, reverse the acceleration, and reinstate the original maturity of the obligation, but otherwise leave the creditor's rights intact.[596] § 1124(2). This second option is particularly beneficial to debtors who want to keep an attractive interest rate on the debt. In either event, the secured class is getting essentially what it originally bargained for, and thus will not be heard to complain.

A third means by which a class could be unimpaired was repealed in 1994. Under § 1124(3), a class was not impaired if it was paid the full amount of its allowed claim in cash on the effective date of the plan. For a secured class, the application of this third alternative required the cash payment of the value of the collateral, *unless* the class elected the application of § 1111(b). Under § 1111(b), an undersecured class could elect to have its total claim treated as an allowed secured claim, but in doing so forfeited its unsecured deficiency claim. However, making this election prevented the debtor from cashing out the secured creditor under § 1124(3) for just the value of the collateral; instead, the debtor had to pay the full amount of the debt. With the repeal of § 1124(3) in 1994, debtors no longer have the option to render a secured class unimpaired by cashing out the allowed secured claim; a cash-out plan that is not accepted by the secured class must be confirmed under the cram down rules.

If a secured class is impaired and does not accept the plan, confirmation of the plan is only possible if the secured class is crammed down under § 1129(b)(2)(A). The essence of the cram down standard for a secured class is that the class must (1) retain its liens and (2) be paid the full value of its "allowed secured claim," calculated as of the plan's effective date. If these guidelines are satisfied, the treatment of the secured class will be "completely compensatory." The Code describes three alternative ways in which this complete compensation may be achieved under a plan:

1.   The lienholder (A) will retain its liens, to the extent of its allowed secured claim, and (B) will be paid deferred cash payments that (1) total the allowed secured claim, and (2) have a present value equal to the value of the collateral. § 1129(b)(2)(A)(i).

2.   The collateral will be sold free and clear, but (A) the creditor's lien will attach to the sales proceeds, and (B) the secured creditor has a right to bid in at the sale. § 1129(b)(2)(A)(ii).

---

[594]   H.R. Rep. No. 95–595, 95th Cong., 1st Sess., at 413 (1977).
[595]   See § 11.18.
[596]   See, e.g., In re Madison Hotel Assocs., 749 F.2d 410 (7th Cir. 1984).

3.   The lienholders will realize the "indubitable equivalent" of their secured claims. § 1129(b)(2)(A)(iii).[597]

The first cram down option is probably the most commonly invoked: the debtor may retain the collateral if it pays the creditor the amount of the allowed secured claim over time and the creditor keeps its lien on the collateral to secure its allowed secured claim. § 1129(b)(2)(A)(i). Application of this deceptively simple rule requires some careful parsing of the statute.

First, the creditor must retain its lien "to the extent of the allowed amount" of its secured claim. § 1129(b)(2)(B)(i)(I). After confirmation, the creditor's lien will secure a debt that will not necessarily be measured by the total debt, as before, but only by the "allowed secured claim," which could be less if the debt was greater than the value of the collateral. § 506(a).

Second, the amount to be paid over time to the creditor, in deferred cash payments, must satisfy two separate tests: the "*principal amount*" test and the "*present value*" test. § 1129(b)(2)(B)(i)(II). Under the "principal amount" test, the *total* amount of the payments proposed to be made to the secured creditor under the plan must equal the "allowed amount of such claim," meaning the allowed secured claim. Under the "present value" test, the stream of payments when discounted to present value as of the effective date of the plan must equal the value of the collateral. These two tests are required because of the possibility that the "allowed secured claim" will be greater than the value of the collateral, if an undersecured creditor elects the application of § 1111(b)(2), as explained below.

An example might help. Assume that Creditor has a total claim of $100,000, which is secured by collateral that the bankruptcy court has valued at $70,000. Under § 506(a)(1), the creditor would have a secured claim equal to the value of the collateral ($70,000), and an unsecured claim for the deficiency ($30,000). However, a special rule, applicable only in chapter 11, comes into play. Under § 1111(b)(2), an undersecured creditor may elect to have its *entire* claim treated as an allowed secured claim. In the example, that would give Creditor an allowed secured claim of $100,000. The *quid pro quo* for making the election is that the undersecured creditor must give up its unsecured claim.

Assume first that Creditor does *not* make the § 1111(b)(2) election. Its allowed secured claim thus will be $70,000, which is the value of the collateral. Creditor's $30,000 unsecured claim will be classified separately from the secured claim, and dealt with under the confirmation rules governing unsecured claims. Significantly (especially in single asset real estate cases), an undersecured creditor is given an unsecured claim for any deficiency by § 1111(b)(1) even if the original claim was "non-recourse." A claim is non-recourse when the debtor is not personally liable for the debt, and the creditor's only rights are against the collateral. The effect of § 1111(b)(1) is to convert a non-recourse claim into a recourse claim.

---

[597] For a discussion of these three alternatives, and how they work together, see Charles J. Tabb, Credit Bidding, Security, and the Obsolescence of Chapter 11, 2013 U. Ill. L. Rev. 103 (2013).

With regard to Creditor's $70,000 allowed secured claim, the plan must allow Creditor to retain its liens on collateral to secure a debt of $70,000. The total of payments to be made to Creditor over the life of the plan must be at least $70,000 (the principal amount test), and those payments when discounted to present value must equal at least the $70,000 value of the collateral (the present value test).

Now assume that Creditor does elect the application of § 1111(b)(2). Creditor will have an allowed secured claim of $100,000, and no unsecured claim. The plan must provide for Creditor to retain liens to secure a debt equal to its allowed secured claim of $100,000 (not just $70,000). The payments to Creditor under the plan must total $100,000 (the principal amount test), but still only need to have a discounted present value equal to the collateral value of $70,000.

What factors will a creditor weigh in deciding whether to make the election under § 1111(b)(2)? It would be a mistake to assume that an undersecured creditor should always make the election, just because its allowed secured claim then would equal the total debt, rather than just the lower value of the collateral. Remember that the price of making the election is forfeiture of the creditor's unsecured claim. If the plan proposes to pay a dividend to unsecured classes, an electing creditor would be giving up the value of that dividend. For example, if the plan proposed a 40% dividend to unsecured claims, the Creditor in our hypothetical would be relinquishing $12,000 (40% × $30,000). And, *if* the debtor completes the payments proposed by the plan on the secured claim, the present value of the payments received by Creditor will be the same—$70,000—whether it makes the § 1111(b)(2) election or not.

So perhaps the question should be why a creditor ever *would* elect under § 1111(b)(2). The reason is this: by making the election, a creditor preserves the possibility of recovering after confirmation more than the judicially determined value of the collateral, up to the total amount of its claim. How could that happen, if the bankruptcy court concluded that the collateral was worth less than the total debt? There are two main possibilities. One is that the valuation by the bankruptcy court was too low. The other is that the property appreciates in value after confirmation. In either event, a creditor who makes the election under § 1111(b)(2) retains the possibility of an upside recovery, but a creditor who does not elect is frozen at the judicially determined amount. The difference will be important if the debtor defaults, attempts to refinance the collateral, or sells the collateral before completing payments under the plan.

In our example, assume that a year after confirmation, Debtor gets an offer to sell the collateral securing Creditor's claim for $85,000. If Creditor did not elect under § 1111(b)(2), its secured claim would only be $70,000, meaning that the Debtor could accept the $85,000 offer, pay off Creditor for $70,000, and pocket the $15,000 surplus. However, if Creditor did make the election, its secured claim would be $100,000, and the entire $85,000 in sales proceeds would have to be paid to Creditor. The real importance of the § 1111(b)(2) election is to protect a secured creditor against the risk that a debtor will file chapter 11 and cram down the secured claim at a low value determined by the bankruptcy court, at a time when the market is temporarily depressed.[598]

The cram down of a secured class under the first option of § 1129(b)(2)(A) requires the court to ascertain both (1) the value of the collateral, and (2) what discount rate should be used in the present value analysis. In the above example, it was simply assumed that the collateral was worth $70,000. In real cases, of course, the collateral valuation is not presented on a silver platter. One of the most hotly contested issues in cram down, indeed, will be valuing the collateral.

The secured creditor wants to establish a high value (and the debtor, of course, wants a low value), because that value sets the floor of payments, which the creditor is entitled to receive, and the amount of the secured claim. In our example, if the court had valued the collateral at $85,000 instead of $70,000, Creditor would have had an $85,000 secured claim even without making the election under § 1111(b)(2), and the present value of payments to Creditor under the plan would have had to equal $85,000, not $70,000. The Code eschews any hard-and-fast rules with regard to valuation, giving the bankruptcy court the discretion to determine value on a case-by-case basis, considering "the purpose of the valuation" and "the proposed disposition or use of such property." § 506(a)(1). If the debtor is proposing to retain the collateral in its business, the quoted language would suggest that the court probably should favor valuing the creditor's collateral more in line with going-concern value, rather than at a lower liquidation value.

Even if the collateral value can be determined, the court will still have to conduct a present value analysis. The debtor is permitted to make deferred cash payments to the secured creditor. § 1129(b)(2)(A)(i)(II). However, under the "present value" test, those deferred payments must have a value as of the effective date of the plan that is at least equal to the value of the creditor's collateral. Because of the time value of money, a payment to be made in the future is worth less than the same amount paid today. Interest is the measure of the difference.[599] Thus, to satisfy the present value test, the debtor will have to pay an adequate rate of interest on the principal balance of the debt. Otherwise, the present value of the deferred payments to the secured creditor will be less than the value of the collateral, and the plan could not be crammed down over the secured creditor's dissent.

In our example, the present value of payments to Creditor must equal at least $70,000. Thus, the debtor could not confirm a plan that promised to pay Creditor $10,000 on the effective date of the plan, $30,000 in a year, and the remaining $30,000 in two years. The present value of the two future payments would be less than $30,000 each, because of time value. To compensate, interest would have to be paid.

---

[598] One of the most notorious Bankruptcy Act cases, *In re Pine Gate Assocs., Ltd.*, 10 C.B.C. 581 (Bankr. N.D. Ga. 1976), involved such a cram down at the judicially appraised collateral value in a chapter XII case. Section 1111(b) and the accompanying special cram down rules were enacted in reaction to the *Pine Gate* result. See Tabb, supra note 597, at 117–22, for discussion of *Pine Gate* and how the Code was drafted in light of that decision.

[599] See *Murel Holding*, supra note 593, 75 F.2d at 942.

One of the most litigated issues under the Code has been over the appropriate method for fixing the rate of interest for deferred plan payments in a cram down. Ascertaining this "cram down rate" has caused headaches and confusion.[600] The leading case, although decided in the context of a chapter 13 cram down, is the Supreme Court's 2004 decision in *Till v. SCS Credit Corp.*[601] Unfortunately, the Court in *Till* did not garner a majority for any approach, meaning that at least three commonly used methods are potentially still on the table. In theory, all of these methods attempt by different means to determine an appropriate *market* rate of interest. Indeed, the Supreme Court in *Till* explained that if a competitive market exists for bankruptcy financing, then recourse to that market is the fairest and most accurate method to use to determine the interest rate, and accordingly might warrant a different result in chapter 11 cases (where there is a more active DIP financing market) than in chapter 13, where there is no such market: "Thus, when picking a cramdown rate in a Chapter 11 case, it might make sense to ask what rate an efficient market would produce."[602]

In *Till,* the four-Justice plurality approved the "formula" (or "prime plus") approach,[603] under which the court starts with the "prime rate" of interest[604] and then adjusts upward by adding in a risk premium. However, the concurring Justice (Thomas) did not believe that *any* compensation for risk was required, but concurred with the plurality because the debtor had proposed a formula-based cram down interest rate, which Justice Thomas believed overcompensated the secured creditor.[605] The four-Justice dissent in *Till* preferred the "presumptive contract rate" approach,[606] which uses the actual contract interest rate between the debtor and secured creditor as the starting point, and then allows either party to argue for adjustments up or down in that rate to reflect the actual risk involved in the debtor's cram down. Since this method also incorporates a risk compensation component, Justice Thomas would have concurred if the debtor had proposed a plan using the presumptive contract method, so this approach likewise remains viable after *Till*. The final possible method that is still possible after *Till* is the "coerced loan" method, which is really just a variant of the presumptive contract rate approach. Under the coerced loan approach, "the creditor is entitled to the rate of interest it could have obtained had it foreclosed and reinvested the proceeds in loans of equivalent duration and risk."[607] The notion is that this leaves the secured creditor as well off under the cram down plan as if it had been paid in full in cash at confirmation, because it then could have gone out and made a similar market loan with the foreclosure proceeds.

---

[600] See, e.g., In re Texas Grand Prairie Hotel Realty, L.L.C., 710 F.3d 324 (5th Cir. 2013); In re Am. HomePatient, Inc., 420 F.3d 559 (6th Cir. 2005).

[601] 541 U.S. 465 (2004). See § 7.30 for a detailed discussion of cram down interest rates and of *Till.*

[602] 541 U.S. at 476 & n.14.

[603] Id. at at 478–79 (Stevens, J., plurality).

[604] The plurality in *Till* defined the prime rate as "the financial market's estimate of the amount a commercial bank should charge a creditworthy commercial borrower to compensate for the opportunity costs of the loan, the risk of inflation, and the relatively slight risk of default." Id. at 479.

[605] Id. at 487 (Thomas, J., concurring).

[606] Id. at 492 (Scalia, J., dissenting).

[607] Koopmans v. Farm Credit Servs. of Mid–Am., 102 F.3d 874, 874–75 (7th Cir. 1996). See also *Till,* supra note 14, 541 U.S. at 472 (Stevens, J., plurality).

An intriguing issue that has arisen with regard to the cram down of a secured class under the first option is whether the plan may provide for the *negative amortization* of the secured debt. In negative amortization, interest is deferred initially and added to the principal balance, meaning that in the early part of the repayment period the principal debt actually increases. In the early years of the Code, some courts took the view that as a *per se* matter a negative amortization plan could not be crammed down over the objection of a secured class.[608] The prevailing current view, however, is to allow negative amortization cram down in limited circumstances, weighing numerous factors that bear on the extent of risk to the secured creditor.[609]

The second cram down option addresses the situation where a debtor wants to *sell* the collateral securing a creditor's claim. § 1129(b)(2)(A)(ii). The secured creditor is protected in two different ways in such a case. First, even though the sale of the collateral will be "free and clear" of the creditor's lien, meaning that the purchaser will take the asset free from the lien, the creditor's lien will be transferred to the *proceeds* of the sale. Then, the lien on the proceeds will be dealt with either under the deferred cash payment or indubitable equivalent cram down options. Second, any concern that the lienholder might have that the sale might not bring a fair price for the collateral is assuaged by the privilege of the lienholder to bid at the sale itself, and to offset its claim against the purchase price. §§ 363(k), 1129(b)(2)(A)(ii). The right to credit bid at a sale is the essential protection for secured creditors against being cashed out at too low a valuation,[610] thus serving the same function in sale cases as the § 1111(b) election serves in collateral retention cases.[611] In *RadLAX Gateway Hotel, LLC v. Amalgamated Bank*,[612] discussed below, the Supreme Court upheld the presumptive right of secured creditors to credit bid when their collateral is being sold, absent an express finding of cause.

In the third and final option, the plan proponent is given the catch-all authorization to cram down a dissenting secured class by providing the class with the "indubitable equivalent" of their secured claims. § 1129(b)(2)(A)(iii). This somewhat stilted and inscrutable phrase is taken from Judge Learned Hand's opinion in the *Murel Holding* case, in which he opined that a senior lienholder could not be forced in a plan to accept a substitute of anything but "the most indubitable equivalence."[613] For example, the legislative history to the Code explains that abandonment of the collateral to the creditor would satisfy the indubitable equivalent standard.[614] So too would a replacement lien on similar collateral be enough.[615] However, a present cash

---

[608] See In re McCombs Props. VIII, Ltd., 91 B.R. 907 (Bankr. C.D. Cal. 1988).

[609] See Great W. Bank v. Sierra Woods Group, 953 F.2d 1174 (9th Cir. 1992).

[610] In *RadLAX Gateway Hotel, LLC v. Amalgamated Bank*, 132 S.Ct. 2065, 2070 n.2 (2012), the Supreme Court observed that "[t]he ability to credit-bid helps to protect a creditor against the risk that its collateral will be sold at a depressed price."

[611] See Tabb, supra note 597, at 122–24.

[612] 132 S. Ct. 2065 (2012).

[613] 75 F.2d 941, 942 (2d Cir. 1935).

[614] 124 Cong. Rec. S17,421 (daily ed. Oct. 6, 1978) (remarks of Sen. DeConcini); 124 Cong. Rec. H11,104 (daily ed. Sept. 28, 1978) (remarks of Rep. Edwards).

[615] H.R. Rep. No. 95–595, 95th Cong. 6475 (1977).

payment of less than the secured claim would not suffice, nor would the issuance of unsecured notes or equity securities in exchange for the secured claim.[616]

Until the credit bidding furor erupted (see below), the indubitable equivalent issue probably arose most often in the situation in which the debtor proposed to relinquish collateral to the secured creditor—sometimes called "dirt for debt" plans. If *all* of the creditor's collateral is abandoned to it, then the indubitable equivalence test is plainly met. The Supreme Court in *RadLAX* confirmed that collateral surrender cases were the standard scenario in which the indubitable equivalent option would be applicable.[617] Also, if part of the collateral is abandoned, and the creditor retains its lien on the remaining collateral, cram down is possible. However, courts do not permit the debtor to cram down a secured creditor by turning over *part* of the creditor's collateral in *full* satisfaction of the debt, with no other liens to be retained by the creditor.[618]

What if the debtor wishes to sell property encumbered by a creditor's lien free and clear? The second option for cramming down a plan, found in § 1129(b)(2)(A)(ii), clearly contemplates this situation. But may the debtor alternatively sell the collateral without allowing the secured creditor to credit bid, by using the third option, § 1129(b)(2)(A)(iii), arguing that cram down is allowed if the secured creditor realizes the "indubitable equivalent" of its claim—notwithstanding denial of the credit bid right? In 2012, the Supreme Court decisively said "no" in *RadLAX Gateway Hotel, LLC v. Amalgamated Bank*.[619]

In *RadLax*, the debtors sought to cram down a plan that provided for the sale of assets securing the bank's claim free and clear of all liens, and moved for approval of bid procedures that would not allow the bank to credit bid the amount of its claim. Recall that § 1129(b)(2)(A)(ii), addressing the free and clear sale of property encumbered by a lien, permits the lienholder to bid at the auction, absent a finding of cause. The debtors in *RadLAX*, however, relied on two recent appellate court cases, from the Third and Fifth Circuits, which had concluded that a secured creditor did not have a right to credit bid in an asset sale, as long as it received "the indubitable equivalent" of its claim.[620] In other words, the Third and Fifth Circuits held that a debtor could cram down a plan providing for the free and clear sale of property under § 1129(b)(2)(A)(iii)—which does not necessarily include a credit bid right—rather than § 1129(b)(2)(A)(ii), which does. Noting that the three subsections in § 1129(b)(2)(A) are joined by the disjunctive "or," those courts read the three cram down options as

---

[616] Id.

[617] 132 S.Ct. at 2072.

[618] See In re Arnold & Baker Farms, 85 F.3d 1415 (9th Cir. 1996), cert. denied, 519 U.S. 1054 (1997).

[619] 132 S. Ct. 2065 (2012). For an in depth analysis of this issue, see Tabb, supra note 597, 2013 U. Ill. L. Rev. 103; see also Ralph Brubaker, Cramdown of an Undersecured Creditor Through Sale of the Creditor's Collateral: Herein of Indubitable Equivalence, the § 1111(b)(2) Election, Sub Rosa Sales, Credit Bidding, and Disposition of Sale Proceeds, 29 No. 12 Bankr. L. Letter 1 (2009).

[620] In re Philadelphia Newspapers, LLC, 599 F.3d 298 (3d Cir. 2010); In re Pac. Lumber Co., 584 F.3d 229 (5th Cir. 2009). In *Philadelphia Newspapers*, Judge Ambro issued a lengthy, thoughtful dissent, relying heavily on Professor Brubaker's article, cited supra note 32. 599 F.3d at 319 (Ambro, J., dissenting).

alternatives. If the sale procedures and the auction price fairly valued the creditor's collateral, that would suffice as the "indubitable equivalent," they concluded.[621]

In *RadLAX*, the bankruptcy court[622] and then the Seventh Circuit below rejected the approach adopted by the Third and Fifth Circuits, and held that a court could not replace a secured creditor's right to credit bid with a judicial estimation of indubitable equivalence.[623] The Seventh Circuit reasoned that denying secured creditors the right to credit bid removes a "crucial check against undervaluation," and increases the risk that the lender would not receive the current market value of the encumbered assets.[624] Thus, the circuit court noted (without deciding the issue) that *even if* it were possible to try to cram down a free and clear sale under the indubitable equivalent third option, a non-credit-bid sale very possibly might not provide the lender with the "indubitable equivalent" of their claim, and thus could not be confirmed under subsection (iii) regardless. However, the Seventh Circuit then held that free and clear sales could *only* be crammed down under subsection (ii), because of the statutory construction canon that the specific controls the general, and because otherwise subsection (ii) as a practical matter would be superfluous.[625]

The Supreme Court granted certiorari to resolve the split between the Third, Fifth and Seventh Circuits, to determine "[w]ether a debtor may pursue a chapter 11 plan that proposes to sell assets free of liens without allowing the secured creditor to credit bid, but instead providing it with the indubitable equivalent of its claim under Section 1129(b)(2)(A)(iii) of the Bankruptcy Code."[626] In a short and (way too) simple opinion, the Court affirmed the Seventh Circuit and held that "debtors may not sell their property free of liens under § 1129(b)(2)(A) without allowing lienholders to credit-bid, as required by clause (ii)."[627] Thus, the Court determined that "the RadLAX debtors may not obtain confirmation of a Chapter 11 cramdown plan that provides for the sale of collateral free and clear of the Bank's lien, but does not permit the Bank to credit-bid at the sale."[628]

Finding no textual ambiguity,[629] the Court declined to consider history, policy, or the purposes of the Code, but instead relied almost entirely on the canon of

---

[621] Scholarly commentary following the Fifth and Third Circuit opinions was extensive and almost uniformly harshly critical of those decisions. See, e.g., Brubaker, supra note 32. See also Jason S. Bookner, *Pacific Lumber* and *Philadelphia Newspapers*: The Eradication of a Carefully Constructed Statutory Regime Through Misinterpretation of Section 1129(b)(2)(A) of the Bankruptcy Code, 85 Am. Bankr. L.J. 127 (2011); Alan N. Resnick, Denying Secured Creditors the Right to Credit Bid in Chapter 11 Cases and the Risk of Undervaluation, 63 Hastings L.J. 323, 354 (2012).

[622] In re River Rd. Hotel Partners, LLC, 2010 WL 6634603 (Bankr. N.D. Ill. 2010), aff'd, 651 F.3d 642 (7th Cir. 2011), aff'd, 132 S. Ct. 845 (2011).

[623] In re River Rd. Hotel Partners, LLC, 651 F.3d 642 (7th Cir. 2011), aff'd, 132 S. Ct. 845 (2011).

[624] Id. at 651.

[625] Id. at 652–53.

[626] Petition for Writ of Certiorari, RadLAX Gateway Hotel, 132 S. Ct. 2065 (No. 11–166), cert. granted, 132 S. Ct. 845 (2011).

[627] *RadLAX*, 132 S. Ct. at 2072.

[628] Id. at 2073.

[629] Indeed, the Fifth and Third Circuits had held that the plain meaning dictated exactly the opposite result, and the Seventh Circuit found the text of the statute ambiguous.

construction "that the specific governs the general."[630] In this situation, "[t]he general/specific canon explains that the 'general language' of clause (iii), 'although broad enough to include it, will not be held to apply to a matter specifically dealt with' in clause (ii)."[631] Justice Scalia, writing for the majority, explained that reading the statute in this way was necessary to avoid superfluity. Otherwise, if a debtor could effectuate a free and clear cram down sale using subsection (iii)'s indubitable equivalence test, sans credit bidding, it would eliminate any realistic role for subsection (ii), which only allows a free and clear sale with credit bidding.[632] The court interpreted the cram down section for secured claims (§ 1129(b)(2)(A)) as providing three different rules, with the relevant rule dependent on the proposed treatment of the collateral, so "that (i) is the rule for plans under which the creditor's lien remains on the property, (ii) is the rule for plans under which the property is sold free and clear of the creditor's lien, and (iii) is a residual provision covering dispositions under all other plan."[633]

The Court did not consider whether "cause" existed under subsection (ii) (and thus by reference § 363(k)) to deny credit bidding, as the debtors had lost that issue in the bankruptcy court and had not appealed that question to the Supreme Court. After *RadLAX,* the only way a free and clear collateral sale can be made without allowing credit bidding is if the bankruptcy court finds "cause" under § 363(k) to deny that right.[634] Very little case law exists on this question. If the secured creditor acted unfairly in its dealings with the debtor prior to bankruptcy, or if the legitimacy of their secured claim is in doubt, some courts have suggested that cause might be found. Debtors have argued (as did the debtor in *RadLAX*) that the prospect of credit bidding "chills" other prospective bidders from participating in the auction, and that should be sufficient cause. It is unlikely that future debtors will have much more luck with the chilling argument than did the *RadLAX* debtor.

§ 11.33 Cram Down: Dissenting Unsecured and Equity Classes

If a class of unsecured creditors or equity holders votes against the plan, and the proponent of the plan seeks to confirm the plan under § 1129(b) over the objection of the dissenting class, the plan will only be confirmed if the plan complies with the *"absolute priority"* rule.[635] "In very general terms, this means that a junior interest may

---

[630] Id. at 2071.

[631] Id. at 2071–72 (quoting *D. Ginsberg & Sons, Inc. v. Popkin*, 985 U.D. 204, 208 (1932)).

[632] Id. at 2071.

[633] Id. at 2072.

[634] See Tabb, supra note 597, at 138–39.

[635] See John D. Ayer, Rethinking Absolute Priority After *Ahlers*, 87 Mich. L. Rev. 963 (1989); Douglas G. Baird & Thomas H. Jackson, Bargaining After the Fall and the Contours of the Absolute Priority Rule, 55 U. Chi. L. Rev. 738 (1988); Douglas G. Baird and Robert K. Rasmussen, *Boyd's* Legacy and Blackstone's Ghost, 1999 Sup. Ct. Rev. 393; David Gray Carlson & Jack F. Williams, The Truth About the New Value Exception to Bankruptcy's Absolute Priority Rule, 21 Cardozo L. Rev. 1303 (2000); Allen C. Eberhart et al., Security Pricing and Deviations from the Absolute Priority Rule in Bankruptcy Proceedings, 45 J. Fin. 1457 (1990); Lynn M. LoPucki & William C. Whitford, Bargaining Over Equity's Share in the Bankruptcy Reorganization of Large, Publicly Held Companies, 139 U. Pa. L. Rev. 125 (1990); Bruce A. Markell, Owners, Auctions, and Absolute Priority in Bankruptcy Reorganization, 44 Stan. L. Rev. 69 (1991); Raymond T. Nimmer, Negotiated Bankruptcy Reorganization Plans: Absolute Priority and New Value Contributions, 36 Emory L.J. 1009 (1987); David A. Skeel, Jr., The Uncertain State of an Unstated Rule: Bankruptcy

not be retained unless claims of senior interests are fully satisfied."[636] The confirmation cram down standard is spelled out in § 1129(b)(1): from the perspective of the dissenting class, the plan may be confirmed if it "*does not discriminate unfairly, and is fair and equitable.*"

For unsecured classes, the requirement that the plan be "fair and equitable" is explicated in part in § 1129(b)(2)(B). Under that provision, the plan will be fair and equitable with respect to a dissenting class of unsecured claims only in one of two alternative scenarios:

- the dissenting class is paid in full, § 1129(b)(2)(B)(i); or

- no class junior to the dissenting class gets anything under the plan on account of its claim or interest, § 1129(b)(2)(B)(ii).

For classes of interests, the fair and equitable rule has the same functional meaning. Under § 1129(b)(2)(C), a plan is fair and equitable only if:

- the dissenting class is paid the greater of its full value, or the amount of a fixed liquidation preference or fixed redemption price, § 1129(b)(2)(C)(i); or

- no class junior to the dissenting class gets anything under the plan on account of its claim or interest, § 1129(b)(2)(C)(ii).

The effect of § 1129(b)(2)(B) and (C) is to require the plan to adhere to the order of priority entitlements against the debtor's assets between classes of unsecured claims and equity interests under applicable non-bankruptcy law. This should be a familiar concept. Indeed, the essential meaning of "priority" is the right to be paid in full before a class of lower rank is paid anything. Most basically, the *creditors* of a firm are entitled to be paid in full before the equity *owners* of a firm take anything. Filing bankruptcy does not alter that basic relationship. The Supreme Court's recognition and enforcement of this fundamental allocation of rights between creditors and stockholders formed the basis of the first pronouncements of the "absolute priority" rule in equity receiverships in the nineteenth century.[637] Today the crucial premise that creditors must be paid before owners remains unchanged, in or out of bankruptcy.[638] The only difference in a bankruptcy reorganization is that creditors are *permitted*, but not *required*, to waive their priority rights.

To apply the absolute priority rule with respect to the dissenting class, the essential first step is to identify the entire class priority ladder from the perspective of that class. The priority rankings are determined by reference to non-bankruptcy law,

---

Contribution Rule After Ahlers, 63 Am. Bankr. L.J. 221 (1989); Elizabeth Warren, A Theory of Absolute Priority, 1991 Ann. Surv. Am. L. 9 (1991).

[636] H.R. Rep. No. 95–595, 95th Cong. 251 (1977).

[637] See Louisville Trust Co. v. Louisville, N.A. & C. Ry., 174 U.S. 674, 683–84 (1899). See § 11.31 for a detailed discussion of the historical development of the absolute priority rule.

[638] See, e.g., Commodity Futures Trading Comm'n v. Lake Shore Asset Mgmt. Ltd., 646 F.3d 401, 407 (7th Cir. 2011) ("[C]reditors are usually paid ahead of shareholders in insolvency proceedings, whether the proceedings take the form of bankruptcy, or of receivership.").

with respect to the relative order and source of payment if the debtor's assets were to be liquidated. The requirement in chapter 11 that only claims and interests that are "substantially similar" may be classified together,[639] § 1122(a), recognizes and implements these non-bankruptcy priority rights. The "similarity" referred to in the Code is a similarity in liquidation payment entitlements.

The categories of "creditors" and "equity" sometimes are subdivided into multiple priority rankings. Within the unsecured creditor ranks, in addition to general unsecured trade debt, there may be senior debt and subordinated debt. Subordination agreements are enforced in bankruptcy, § 510(a), and principles of equitable subordination also may be enforced. § 510(c). Within the equity universe, several layers of stock may be issued, with different liquidation preferences. For example, preferred stock must be paid before common stock.

It is important to emphasize that under the Code the absolute priority rule is enforced and applied from the perspective of the dissenting class. It is for this reason that the Code's approach is sometimes referred to as a "modified" or "relative" absolute priority rule. Assume, for example, that there are three classes of unsecured claims: trade debt, senior debt, and subordinated debt. The senior debt is senior only to the subordinated debt, pursuant to a subordination agreement; both senior and subordinated debt are on a par with the trade debt. Application of the absolute priority rule would depend on which class voted against the plan. For instance, if the trade debt class votes against the plan, that class would not be entitled to be paid in full before anything was paid to subordinated debt, because the subordinated debt is not junior to the trade debt. However, if the senior debt class dissented from the plan, the subordinated debt class would have to be cut out of the plan unless senior debt was paid in full, because the subordinated class is junior to the senior debt. In cases such as this, the additional cram down prohibition against "unfair discrimination" (discussed below) will have significance.

The significance of the relative application of the absolute priority rule is underscored by the fact that the rule is only applied from the dissenting class down. Senior classes are free to waive the absolute priority rule and give up value to each other, even if a junior class dissents. However, a senior class would not be permitted to give value to a class junior to the dissenting class; that, indeed, is the heart of the absolute priority rule. Assume, for example, that there are four classes, ranked by priority from 1 (highest) to 4 (lowest). If class 3 votes against the plan, class 1 would still be allowed to relinquish value to class 2, but class 4 must be excluded from participation unless class 3 is paid in full.

In short, a senior class cannot give up property to a junior class and skip over a dissenting intervening class, unless the dissenting class is paid in full. Indeed, absolute priority would be violated even if there were two classes of *equal* priority and one of the two equal classes proposed to give up property to a junior class.[640]

---

[639] See § 11.17.

[640] See In re Armstrong World Indus., Inc., 432 F.3d 507 (3d Cir. 2005). For further discussion, see Ralph Brubaker, Taking Chapter 11's Distribution Rules Seriously: "Inter–Class Gifting Is Dead! Long Live

If the "give up" is from a senior class of *secured* creditors to a class junior to the dissenting unsecured class, however, the issue of whether absolute priority is violated has been more hotly debated, and some authority upholding such give-ups developed. The conceptual genesis of this give-up doctrine, also called "inter-class gifting," is, curiously enough, a chapter 7 case. In *In re SPM Manufacturing Corp.*, the First Circuit allowed a senior secured class to "gift" part of its chapter 7 distribution to general unsecured creditors, bypassing priority tax claims.[641] The theory, basically, was that the tax claims were out of the money anyway and that the senior class could do whatever it wished with its bankruptcy distribution. After *SPM*, the always creative chapter 11 bar extended the *SPM* theory to chapter 11 plans and sought to cram down plans under which a secured creditor gave up some of its entitlement to equity, bypassing a dissenting unsecured class.

However, in 2011, the Second Circuit rejected the gifting doctrine in *In re DBSD North America, Inc.*,[642] even though the gift was being made by a secured class, and even though that secured creditor supposedly was entitled to the full residual value of the debtor. The Second Circuit looked at the text of the Code, and found no basis for escaping the conclusion that the absolute priority rule was violated under the proposed plan: the dissenting unsecured class had not accepted the plan, was not being paid in full, and the old equity holders were receiving property on account of their stock.[643] Furthermore, the *DBSD* court looked at history, and found considerable comfort in the Supreme Court's absolute priority jurisprudence, both in its foundational cases involving railroad receiverships and in its post–1978 Code cases.[644] Indeed, the critical facts in the Court's early cases were strikingly similar to those in *DBSD* (secured creditor holds lien for debt in excess of value of debtor, and that secured creditor proposes to give up value to shareholders, skipping over unsecured creditors), and yet the Supreme Court repeatedly held that such a plan violated absolute priority.[645] As the DBSD court observed, the "fixed principle" of absolute priority the Supreme Court announced in that long series of cases had "the aim of stopping the very sort of transaction that the appellees propose here."[646] In the final analysis, the Second Circuit concluded that "although Congress did soften the absolute priority rule in some ways, it did not create any exception for 'gifts' like the one at issue here."[647]

This, I submit, is the best result. As one commentator, Amy Timm, noted, "it is clear from the text of § 1129(b)(2)(B)(ii), the historical line of case law preceding the 1978 Code, and relevant legislative history that Congress did not intend to allow for a

---

Inter–Class Gifting!," 31 No. 4 Bankr. L. Letter 1 (April 2011); Amy S. Timm, The Gift that Gives Too Much: Invalidating a Gifting Exception to the Absolute Priority Rule, 2013 U. Ill. L. Rev. 1649 (2013).

[641]   984 F.2d 1305 (1st Cir. 1993).

[642]   634 F.3d 79 (2d Cir. 2011). See the excellent analyses in Brubaker, supra note 6; Timm, supra note 6.

[643]   634 F.3d at 95–97.

[644]   Id. at 94, 97–99.

[645]   See, e.g., R.R. Co. v. Howard, 74 U.S. 392 (1868); Louisville Trust Co. v. Louisville, N.A. & C. Ry. Co., 174 U.S. 674 (1899); N. Pac. R. Co. v. Boyd, 228 U.S. 482 (1913).

[646]   634 F.3d at 99.

[647]   Id. at 100.

gifting exception to the rule within the plan context."[648] Furthermore, Timm went on to say, "Any such exception, no matter how conducive to a more efficient reorganization, would necessarily lead to either arbitrary, court-made limits or to an exception so large that the rule is meaningless."[649]

Nor can one ignore the problems inherent in valuing the debtor; the linchpin proposition underlying a gifting exception, that "it's all the secured creditor's property anyway," depends on making an accurate judicial valuation of an often uncertain enterprise. As Professor Brubaker pointed out, "As the *Boyd* Court indicated, the virtue in the absolute priority rule (without any 'gifting' exception) is that it obviates any judicial assessment of the value of the reorganized enterprise for purposes of resolving the unsecured creditors' contention that enterprise value is being improperly funneled to old equity holders. As with so many aspects of the absolute priority rule, then, rejection of a 'gifting' exception provides an important procedural check on the vagaries of judicial valuations."[650]

Brubaker also noted the knotty problem of distinguishing legitimate "bargaining" from insider holdups: "It is virtually impossible to penetrate the real reasons for the 'gift' to old equity: Is it really because they will provide substantial value to the reorganized entity, or is it simply because they have substantial control over the reorganization process, and a 'gift' to them is necessary to grease the reorganization skids?"[651]

Returning to the operation of the absolute priority rule, it is important to note that identifying the various priority categories is only the first step in applying the absolute priority rule to unsecured or equity classes. The crucial next step is to ascertain who is being paid what under the plan. This analysis is necessary for three reasons. First, a dissenting class may be crammed down if the plan provides for each holder of a claim or interest in that class to receive or retain property equal to the allowed amount of the claim or interest. § 1129(b)(2)(B)(i), (C)(i). In other words, if a class is paid in full, the absolute priority rule is satisfied as to that class, irrespective of what the plan provides for other classes. Second, if a dissenting class is not being paid in full, the "who gets what" issue is relevant to determine if any class *junior* to the dissenting class is receiving or retaining under the plan anything on account of their claims or interests, which would violate the absolute priority rule. § 1129(b)(2)(B)(ii), (C)(ii). Third, if a dissenting class is not being paid in full, the absolute priority rule demands that no class *senior* to the dissenting class is paid *more* than in full. Although this aspect of the "fair and equitable" standard was not expressly mentioned in the Code, the legislative history makes clear that Congress nevertheless intended for the longstanding prohibition against paying a senior class more than its full value to continue to be enforced with full vigor under the Code.[652]

---

[648] Timm, supra note 640, at 1678.

[649] Id.

[650] Brubaker, supra note 640.

[651] Id.

[652] H.R. Rep. No. 95–595, 95th Cong., 414 (1977) ("One requirement applies generally to all classes before the court may confirm under this subsection. No class may be paid more than in full."); 124 Cong. Rec.

The bad news is that application of these principles usually will require a full valuation of the reorganized debtor.[653] A valuation is necessary to determine which classes are entitled to share in the distribution of reorganization value. To give a simple example, if the total secured and unsecured debt is $8 million, and the reorganized debtor is found to be worth $9 million, then the debtor's equity interests could not be cancelled; of necessity, the plan must be proposing to pay some senior class more than in full.

The need for a valuation of the debtor is thought to be "bad news" for at least two reasons. One is that the valuation process is time-consuming and expensive. A full-blown judicial hearing is required, and the interested parties will have to pay attorneys, accountants, and other experts. Indeed, one of the main reasons the drafters of the Code permitted classes to waive application of the absolute priority rule was to permit them to avoid the costly valuation hearing. This possibility has led to the common practice, particularly in larger cases, of giving equity at least a small share, in order to avoid cram down.[654] If a class of equity is cancelled, it is considered totally impaired, and as such is conclusively deemed to reject the plan, § 1126(g), requiring the application of the absolute priority rule of the proponent wishes to confirm the plan.

The second big problem with a valuation of the debtor is that it is incredibly speculative and imprecise.[655] In many cases, a debtor's business will be valued by capitalizing earnings. Making this computation requires the court to ascertain two highly uncertain variables: the debtor's projected earnings, and the appropriate capitalization rate. Slight alterations in either variable can change the outcome of whether a class is included or excluded under the absolute priority rule. If the debtor's assets were being sold and converted into a pot of cash, which then could be handed out to claimants in order of their priority, there would not be a problem. That, of course, is not happening in a reorganization; in most cases the debtor plans to continue operating its business after confirmation of the plan. To further complicate matters, the plan may propose to pay some classes with stock in the reorganized debtor. As explained in the section discussing the historical evolution of the absolute priority rule,[656] the imprecision of the valuation of a reorganizing debtor was one of the main factors that led Congress in 1978 to authorize classes to waive the application of the absolute priority rule.

In the application of the exclusionary aspect of the absolute priority rule, that no class junior to the dissenting class may receive or retain anything under the plan on account of their claims or interests, a raging debate has been carried on with regard to

---

S17,420 (daily ed. Oct. 6, 1978) (remarks of Sen. DeConcini); 124 Cong. Rec. H11,104 (daily ed. Sept. 28, 1978) (remarks of Rep. Edwards).

[653] H.R. Rep. No. 95–595, 95th Cong., 1st Sess., at 414 (1977) ("While section 1129(a) does not contemplate valuation of the debtor's business, such a valuation will almost always be required under section 1129(b) in order to determine the value of the consideration to be distributed under the plan.").

[654] See LoPucki & Whitford, *supra* note 635.

[655] H.R. Rep. No. 95–595, 95th Cong., 1st Sess., at 222 (1977).

[656] See § 11.31.

whether a "new value" exception exists.[657] Under that supposed exception, a class junior to the dissenting class would be permitted to take an interest in the reorganized debtor if they were doing so on account of a contribution of "new value" to the reorganized debtor, rather than on account of their old equity interest. The new value doctrine will be explored in more detail in the next section.

In some cases, a junior class seeks to avoid the proscription of the requirement that classes junior to the dissenting class not receive or retain any "property" on account of their claims or interests by arguing that the interest they have retained in the reorganized debtor is valueless and thus is not "property." Some courts have even chased and swallowed that red herring.[658] The Supreme Court finally put the "no value" argument to rest, however, in *Norwest Bank Worthington v. Ahlers*.[659] Even if the equity interest a junior class seeks to retain does not have a positive current market value, the power to control the reorganized debtor and the right to share in potential future profits both indicate that the interest is "property." In so holding, the Court reaffirmed the position it had taken long ago in *Northern Pacific Railway Co. v. Boyd*.[660] Indeed, the *Ahlers* Court acknowledged that common sense suggested that the interest proposed to be retained must have value if the parties are fighting over it.[661]

In some cases the proponent of the plan will seek to avoid the application of the absolute priority rule by paying a dissenting class in full. If a class is paid the full value of its claims or interests, there is no bar to permitting classes of lower rank to take an interest in the reorganized debtor. Several aspects of the full payment rule should be noted. First, the payment may be *deferred* over the life of the plan. With deferral, however, interest must be paid. The Code requires calculation of the value of the payments to the dissenting class "as of the effective date of the plan," which means that payments to be made in the future must be discounted to present value. Identifying the rate that should be used to discount future payments has been extremely controversial; perhaps the prevailing view today is that the class should be paid a market rate of interest, as determined by reference to loans of similar length and risk.[662]

A second significant point regarding the full payment option is that the payment can be made in any form of *property*—in short, the Code does *not* require the payment of *cash* to cram down a class. The permissibility of paying a dissenting class in property other than cash has been recognized ever since the landmark 1913 Supreme Court decision in *Northern Pacific Railway Co. v. Boyd*.[663] In that equity receivership case, the Court noted that the absolute priority rule did not "require the impossible," i.e., the payment of creditors in cash, but allowed payment to be made in bonds or in stock of the reorganized debtor.[664] If securities are used to pay a class in full, the court of course

---

[657] See § 11.34.

[658] See In re Star City Rebuilding, Inc., 62 B.R. 983 (W.D. Va. 1986).

[659] 485 U.S. 197, 207–09 (1988).

[660] 228 U.S. 482, 508 (1913).

[661] 485 U.S. at 209.

[662] See, e.g., Fed. Nat'l Mortg. Ass'n v. Vill. Green I, GP, 483 B.R. 807 (W.D. Tenn. 2012).

[663] 228 U.S. 482 (1913).

[664] Id. at 508.

will have to value those securities. In making that often difficult valuation, the court only has to find that there is a "reasonable likelihood" that the value will be enough to effect full payment.[665]

For unsecured classes, the amount that must be paid is the "allowed amount" of the unsecured claims. Reference must be paid to § 502 to determine allowance. For classes of interests, the amount to be paid is somewhat more complex. One possibility is that the plan will pay the interest "the value of such interest." § 1129(b)(2)(C)(i). If the debtor is insolvent, then by definition the value of the equity interest would be zero. If the class of interests is entitled to be paid a fixed liquidation preference or a fixed redemption price, then that fixed amount must be paid in order to cram down that class under the "paid-in-full" option, even if the interest is valueless.

The cram down requirement that a plan be "fair and equitable" addresses the rights of a dissenting class vis-à-vis other classes that are junior or senior to that dissenting class. However, the rights of a dissenting class with respect to classes of the *same* rank are dealt with by the cram down prohibition against unfair discrimination.[666] § 1129(b)(1). For example, if a plan divides unsecured claims into more than one class,[667] and does not provide the same treatment for the different classes of the same rank, the unfair discrimination rule will be at issue.

It is critical to emphasize that the statute does not prohibit any form of discrimination between similarly situated classes. All that is banned is *unfair* discrimination. By inference, discrimination between equal classes will be permitted if it is "fair."[668] The task then, of course, is to figure out what sorts of discrimination are fair and which are not.

Many courts have adopted a four-part test for measuring the fairness of discrimination: (1) whether the discrimination is supported by a reasonable basis; (2) whether the debtor can confirm and consummate a plan without the discrimination; (3) whether the discrimination is proposed in good faith; and (4) the treatment of the classes that are being discriminated against.[669] This four-part test has been criticized, however. Other courts have stated the governing test more succinctly, as requiring

---

[665] 124 Cong. Rec. S17,421 (daily ed. Oct. 6, 1978) (remarks of Sen. DeConcini); 124 Cong. Rec. H11,104–05 (daily ed. Sept. 28, 1978) (remarks of Rep. Edwards).

[666] See H.R. Rep. No. 95–595, 95th Cong.,1st Sess., at 417 (1977) ("The criterion of unfair discrimination is not derived from the fair and equitable rule or from the best interests of creditors test. Rather it preserves just treatment of a dissenting class from the class's own perspective.").

[667] Whether that separate classification will be permitted is a difficult and controversial issue. While § 1122(a) provides that only "substantially similar" claims or interests may be placed in the same class, it does not expressly require all substantially similar claims to be placed in the same class. Courts have permitted some separate classification of same rank claims or interests, but usually require proof of a good reason for the classification. See § 11.17.

[668] See, e.g., In re Armstrong World Indus., Inc., 348 B.R. 111, 121 (D. Del. 2006) ("The pertinent inquiry is not whether the plan discriminates, but whether the proposed discrimination is 'unfair.'" (citing *In re Jim Beck, Inc.*, 214 B.R. 305, 307 (W.D. Va. 1997))).

[669] This test was formulated in a chapter 13 case, *In re Aztec Co.*, 107 B.R. 585 (Bankr. M.D. Tenn. 1989), and has been cited favorably in many chapter 11 cases. See, e.g., In re Bryson Props. XVIII, 961 F.2d 496 (4th Cir), cert. denied, 506 U.S. 866 (1992).

proof that the proposed discrimination has a reasonable and legally supportable basis, and that the discrimination is necessary for the reorganization.[670]

The difference in treatment between the classes may be with regard to the terms of payment, or the amount of payment, or the status of the claims, or identity of the claimholders. If the only difference is in the terms of the payment, such as (i) when the claims will be paid or (ii) what form of property will be distributed, the courts are more likely to uphold the discrimination, assuming that a good reason is given for the different treatment. If a different amount is proposed to be paid to classes of similar rank, the need for the discrimination becomes more difficult to justify. However, even then confirmation is possible. For example, the debtor might show that the cooperation of a certain group of creditors (such as necessary suppliers or union workers) was extremely important to the viability of the reorganization, thus meriting paying those creditors more. Another example would be where the court confirms a plan providing for different amounts of payments to similar classes when the difference is minor or immaterial.[671]

Cases involving subordinated debt cause particular problems in applying the unfair discrimination test.[672] The tricky part is that often the subordinated debt will not be subordinated to all unsecured claims, but only to a specific group of claims, which then in comparison to the subordinated debt will be senior debt. Both the senior and subordinated debt will be on the same rank, though, as general trade debt. Thus, the trade debt is equal to senior and subordinated debt, but the subordinated debt is junior to the senior debt. The unfair discrimination calculation must be made by comparing the ratio of the trade debt to the overall unsecured debt, and determining whether that ratio is preserved in the proposed plan distribution.

The Curious Case of Individual Debtors and Absolute Priority After BAPCPA

An area of controversy with regards to the absolute priority rule involves the exception for *individual debtors,* who are allowed to retain property included in the estate under § 1115, which brings postpetition property and earnings into the estate.[673] § 1129(b)(2)(B)(ii). That is, in § 1129(b)(2)(B)(ii), which is the subsection providing that, unless a dissenting class is paid in full, cram down requires that "the holder of any claim or interest that is junior to the claims of such class will not receive or retain under the plan on account of such junior claim or interest any property," the 2005 amendments then carved out an exception for individual debtors, "except that in a case

---

[670] See In re 203 N. LaSalle St. Ltd. P'ship, 190 B.R. 567 (Bankr. N.D. Ill. 1995), aff'd, 195 B.R. 692 (N.D. Ill. 1996), overruled on other grounds, 526 U.S. 434 (1999).

[671] See, e.g., In re Tribune Co., 472 B.R. 223 (Bankr. D. Del. 2012); In re Unbreakable Nation Co., 437 B.R. 189 (Bankr. E.D. Pa. 2010); In re Greate Bay Hotel & Casino, Inc., 251 B.R. 213 (Bankr. D.N.J. 2000).

[672] For a detailed discussion of the application of the unfair discrimination rule in the context of subordinated debt, see H.R. Rep. No. 95–595, 95th Cong., 1st Sess., at 416–17 (1977); Christopher W. Frost, Subordination of Securities Claims in Bankruptcy: What is the Scope of Section 510(b)?, 27 No. 2 Bankr. L. Letter 1 (2007).

[673] For a thorough discussion, see Ralph Brubaker, The Absolute Priority Rule for Individual Chapter 11 Debtors: To Be or Not to Be?, 32 No. 10 Bankr. L. Letter 1 (2012); Ralph Brubaker, Individual Chapter 11 Debtors, BAPCPA, and the Absolute Priority Rule, 30 Bankr. L. Letter No. 4, 1 (Apr. 2010); Bruce A. Markell, The Sub Rosa Subchapter: Individual Debtors in Chapter 11 After BAPCPA, 2007 U. Ill. L. Rev. 67, 88–90 (2007).

in which the debtor is an individual, the debtor may retain property included in the estate under section 1115, subject to the requirements of subsection (a)(14) of this section." So, the question, of course, is what is the "property included in the estate under § 1115"?

The 2005 amendment has courts questioning: "has the absolute priority rule been abrogated with regards to individual debtors?" The answer to this question depends on what property § 1115 includes. The courts are hopelessly divided. Section 1115, added by the 2005 amendments, states in pertinent part:

> (a) In a case in which the debtor is an individual, property of the estate *includes, in addition to the property specified in section 541*—

> (1) all property of the kind specified in section 541 that the debtor acquires after the commencement of the case . . . and

> (2) earnings from services performed by the debtor after the commencement of the case.[674]

The word in contention, and causing the split of authority, is "includes." What exactly does "includes" include? Clearly it includes *postpetition* property, and thus under the absolute priority rule exception in § 1129(b)(2)(B)(ii), individual debtors need not comply with the absolute priority rule as regards that postpetition property. But that is nothing new. Of course, for that postpetition property, the debtor must comply with the "projected disposable income" test (also known as the "best efforts" test) of § 1129(a)(15), and commit all of her disposable postpetition income to pay creditors. Note that the "subject to" reference in the absolute priority rule exception is a drafting error; instead of "subsection (a)(14)," the reference is supposed to be to "subsection (a)(15)." So, for postpetition property, the rule thus is: no absolute priority rule (and thus debtor can retain property without paying dissenting creditor class in full), but must comply with the projected disposable income test. That treatment of postpetition property is precisely what is done in chapter 13, which the 2005 amendments sought to mirror in chapter 11 for individual debtors.

The difficult issue is what to do about *prepetition* property, which but for § 1115 would be (and always was) included in the estate under § 541. Is that prepetition property "include[d]" under § 1115 for purposes of the exception in § 1129(b)(2)(B)(ii) (and thus freed from the absolute priority rule), or is it "included" under § 541, and only noted by reference under § 1115 (and thus still subject to the absolute priority rule)? To be frank, the statute admits of either reading, although on a purely grammatical basis, the better reading is that § 1115 itself "includes" prepetition property under § 541, since it says "includes" "*in addition to*" the § 541 property, which necessarily infers that the § 541 property itself is "include[d]" in § 1115.

With this ambiguity, two approaches have emerged: the "*narrow*" interpretation (under which courts find that the absolute priority rule still applies to individual

---

[674] 11 U.S.C. § 1115(a) (emphasis added).

debtors with regard to prepetition property), and the "*broad*" interpretation (which holds that the absolute priority rule has been abrogated as to individual debtors).

Courts subscribing to the narrow interpretation hold that the absolute priority rule remains unchanged as applied to individual debtors, and still applies in full force to prepetition property brought into the estate by § 541.[675] These courts reason that the bankruptcy estate already included property added by § 541, and thus § 1115 can only *include* property to the estate that which was not *already* included. Notably, the only circuit courts to address this issue favored the narrow interpretation.[676]

Conversely, courts subscribing to the broad interpretation hold that the absolute priority rule no longer applies to individual debtors.[677] These courts adhere to a straightforward reading of the Code, to reason that § 1115 expressly includes, by its terms, all § 541 property in the estate, and thus the absolute priority rule no longer restricts an individual debtor from retaining *any* property of the estate. Furthermore, the 2005 amendments sought to bring chapter 11 more in line with chapter 13 for individual debtors, and no absolute priority rule exists in chapter 13.[678] Indeed, if the narrow interpretation were to prevail, an individual chapter 11 debtor would get the worst of all possible deals: absolute priority rule applies, preventing her from retaining any prepetition property at all unless dissenting unsecured creditor class is paid in full, *and* a projected disposable income test requires the debtor to pay every last cent of her disposable postpetition earnings to creditors. Under chapter 13, only the second constraint applies, and for all corporate and partnership chapter 11 debtors, only the first is applicable. There is no evident reason why Congress would have wanted to stick it to an individual chapter 11 debtor quite that severely.

§ 11.34 Cram Down: New Value Exception

The mandate of the absolute priority rule, that no junior class may receive or retain anything under the plan on account of their pre-bankruptcy claims or interests unless a dissenting senior class is paid in full,[679] is subject to an important qualification. Note that the statutory language carefully limits the prohibition to what the class may receive or retain under the plan "*on account of*" their claim or interest. § 1129(b)(2)(B)(ii), (C)(ii). One of the most hotly debated issues under the Code has been whether this formulation of the rule leaves an opening for a junior class to take something under the plan "on account of" a contribution of *new value* to the reorganized debtor, rather than "on account of" their pre-bankruptcy claim or

---

[675] See, e.g., In re Stephens, 704 F.3d 1279 (10th Cir. 2013); In re Maharaj, 681 F.3d 558 (4th Cir. 2012); In re Arnold, 471 B.R. 578 (Bankr. C.D. Cal. 2012); In re Draiman, 450 B.R. 777 (Bankr. N.D. Ill. 2011); In re Lee Min Ho Chen, 482 B.R. 473 (Bankr. D.P.R. 2012).

[676] In re Stephens, 704 F.3d 1279 (10th Cir. 2013); In re Maharaj, 681 F.3d 558 (4th Cir. 2012).

[677] See, e.g., In re Friedman, 466 B.R. 471 (B.A.P. 9th Cir. 2012); In re Tucker, 479 B.R. 873 (Bankr. D. Ore. 2012); SPCP Grp., LLC v. Biggins, 465 B.R. 316 (M.D. Fla. 2011); In re Shat, 424 B.R. 854 (Bankr. D. Nev. 2010).

[678] See, e.g., In re Roedemeier, 374 B.R. 264, 275 (Bankr. D. Kan. 2007); *Shat*, supra note 43, 424 B.R. at 862.

[679] See § 11.33.

interest.[680] While the Code does not expressly authorize such a new value participation, neither does it plainly prohibit a junior class from sharing based on a new contribution. This statutory silence, in conjunction with important changes from prior law in the structure of the reorganization chapter, has made the debate intractable. Is there a "new value" exception to the absolute priority rule under the Code? The Supreme Court (twice) has raised but then declined to answer that question, but in each instance has found that the proposed plan was not confirmable even if there were such an exception.[681]

A brief history review is necessary to appreciate the debate. The Supreme Court first established the contours of the absolute priority rule in equity receivership cases in the late nineteenth and early twentieth centuries.[682] The leading pronouncement of the rule came in 1913 in *Northern Pacific Railway Co. v. Boyd*.[683] Just thirteen years later, while reaffirming the "fixed principle" of absolute priority in *Boyd*, the Court in *Kansas City Terminal Railway Co. v. Central Union Trust Co.*[684] laid the cornerstone of the "new value" exception to the absolute priority rule. The Court, recognizing the practical difficulties that often plagued attempts to reorganize, made the following observation in dictum:

> "Generally, additional funds will be essential to the success of the undertaking, and it may be impossible to obtain them unless stockholders are permitted to contribute and retain an interest sufficiently valuable to move them. In such or similar cases the chancellor may exercise an informed discretion concerning the practical adjustment of the several rights."[685]

After another thirteen years passed, the Court revisited the absolute priority rule and the new value exception, this time in a case construing the confirmation requirements of § 77B of the Bankruptcy Act, which had been enacted in 1934. The 1934 law imported the principles of absolute priority that had been developed in the equity cases, under the "fair and equitable" standard. Justice Douglas' 1939 opinion for the Court in *Case v. Los Angeles Lumber Products Co.*[686] remains relevant today in debates over the existence and application of the new value doctrine. In *Case*, even though the debtor was insolvent, and though all bondholders did not consent to the

---

[680] See John D. Ayer, Rethinking Absolute Priority After Ahlers, 87 Mich. L. Rev. 963 (1989); Douglas G. Baird & Thomas H. Jackson, Bargaining After the Fall and the Contours of the Absolute Priority Rule, 55 U. Chi. L. Rev. 738 (1988); Douglas G. Baird and Robert K. Rasmussen, *Boyd's* Legacy and Blackstone's Ghost, 199 Sup. Ct. Rev. 393; David Gray Carlson & Jack F. Williams, The Truth About the New Value Exception to Bankruptcy's Absolute Priority Rule, 21 Cardozo L. Rev. 1303 (2000); Bruce A. Markell, Owners, Auctions, and Absolute Priority in Bankruptcy Reorganization, 44 Stan. L. Rev. 69 (1991); Raymond T. Nimmer, Negotiated Bankruptcy Reorganization Plans: Absolute Priority and New Value Contributions, 36 Emory L.J. 1009 (1987); David A. Skeel, Jr., The Uncertain State of an Unstated Rule: Bankruptcy Contribution Rule After Ahlers, 63 Am. Bankr. L.J. 221 (1989); Elizabeth Warren, A Theory of Absolute Priority, 1991 Ann. Surv. Am. L. 9 (1991).

[681] Norwest Bank Worthington v. Ahlers, 485 U.S. 197 (1988). Bank of Am. Nat'l Trust & Savs. Ass'n v. 203 N.LaSalle St. P'ship, 526 U.S. 434 (1999).

[682] See § 11.31.

[683] 228 U.S. 482 (1913).

[684] 271 U.S. 445 (1926).

[685] Id. at 455.

[686] 308 U.S. 106 (1939).

plan and were not paid in full, the plan nevertheless gave 23% of the assets and voting power in the reorganized debtor to old stockholders. The old stockholders did not make any "fresh contribution" to the reorganized debtor in exchange for this interest. Instead, the district court confirmed the plan because it found that it would be an asset of value to the reorganized debtor to retain the old stockholders, who would be able to provide "continuity of management" as well as their "financial standing and influence in the community."[687]

The Court rejected the proposed plan. Three aspects of the Court's opinion in *Case* are significant for present purposes. First, Justice Douglas in dictum reaffirmed the existence of a "new value" exception to the absolute priority rule. Second, the Court described the parameters of the new value rule. Finally, the Court found that the proposed contribution did not suffice to satisfy that exception. As to the first two points, the *Case* opinion stated:

> "It is, of course, clear that there are circumstances under which stockholders may participate in a plan of reorganization of an insolvent debtor. . . . Especially in the [*Kansas City Terminal*] case did this Court stress the necessity, at times, of seeking new money "essential to the success of the undertaking" from the old stockholders. Where that necessity exists and the old stockholders make a fresh contribution and receive in return a participation reasonably equivalent to their contribution, no objection may be made. . . . In view of these considerations we believe that to accord "the creditor his full priority against the corporate assets" where the debtor is insolvent, the stockholder's participation must be based on a contribution in money or money's worth, reasonably equivalent in view of all the circumstances to the participation of the stockholder."[688]

Thus, according to *Case*, (1) a new value rule exists, but (2) for that rule to be satisfied, the proponents of the plan must prove the following:

- the necessity of the contribution;

- a fresh contribution;

- made in money or money's worth; and

- the extent of the participation in the reorganized entity is reasonably equivalent to the value of the contribution.[689]

Applying these criteria, the Court in *Case* held that the old stockholders' intangible promises of "continuity of management," "financial standing and influence," and the like did not rise to the level of a "money's worth" contribution that could justify a 23% equity participation in the new entity. Justice Douglas observed that these promises "have no place in the asset column of the balance sheet of the new company.

---

[687] Id. at 112–13. See also In re Los Angeles Lumber Prods. Co., 24 F.Supp. 501, 513–16 (S.D. Cal. 1938).

[688] 308 U.S. at 121–22.

[689] Id.

They reflect merely vague hopes or possibilities. As such, they cannot be the basis for issuance of stock to otherwise valueless interests."[690]

Although chapter X replaced § 77B, the identical "fair and equitable" language was carried forward. At the time the Code was enacted in 1978, it was a generally accepted tenet of the reorganization gospel that *Case* was still good law, in all respects—as to its statement of the absolute priority rule, its recognition of the new value exception, its delineation of the contours of that exception, and its application of the relevant criteria. For better or worse, Congress said nothing about the new value doctrine when it adopted the Code. It considered but did not adopt a proposal to make the new value rule explicit in the Code. The congressional silence has been interpreted in two diametrically opposed ways: as an affirmation of the continued vitality of the new value rule, or as a repudiation of that doctrine. The latter argument is weak, since in 1978 Congress made it quite clear that it was not codifying all aspects of the fair and equitable standard, but nevertheless intended for the many judicially developed contours of that rule to continue to apply.

In numerous cases, the Supreme Court has announced and applied a principle of statutory construction to the effect that well-settled pre-Code bankruptcy law doctrines are presumed to continue in effect under the Code, unless Congress clearly manifested a contrary intention.[691] If that canon of interpretation were to be applied in this context, one might conclude that the new value rule would still exist. Indeed, it has been tellingly argued that the so-called new value "exception" is in truth not an exception at all, but just a logical corollary and application of the general principle of absolute priority.[692]

However, when the Supreme Court confronted the "history" argument in 1999 in *Bank of America National Trust and Savings Association v. 203 North LaSalle Street Partnership*,[693] the majority found that history to be equivocal and ultimately of little interpretive assistance. Why? First, the Court emphasized that the old law on "new value" was not very well-settled.[694] To begin with, Justice Douglas' famous statement of the new value exception in *Case* was pure dictum. Compounding the weakness of the *Case* dictum was the fact that no court had ever confirmed a new value plan in a reported case prior to the enactment of the Code. Second, the Court found the drafting history of the absolute priority rule in the Code to be unhelpful.[695] That Congress had considered but did not enact an expansion of the new value rule said nothing one way or the other about the continued validity of a new value rule. Furthermore, Justice Souter for the majority pointed out that "the Code does not codify any authoritative pre-Code version of the absolute priority rule."[696] Indeed, the Code for the first time

---

[690] Id. at 122–23.

[691] E.g., Dewsnup v. Timm, 502 U.S. 410, 419 (1992); United Sav. Ass'n of Texas v. Timbers of Inwood Forest Assocs., Ltd., 482 U.S. 365, 366 (1988); Midlantic Nat'l Bank v. New Jersey Dep't of Envtl. Prot., 474 U.S. 494, 501 (1986).

[692] See Markell, supra note 680.

[693] 526 U.S. 434 (1999).

[694] Id. at 445–46. See Ayer, supra note 680, at 1016; Markell, supra note 680, at 92.

[695] 526 U.S. at 446–49.

[696] Id. at 448.

fleshed out the particulars of the absolute priority rule. Since the Code's absolute priority rule thus may differ from prior law in at least some respects, but says nothing specifically regarding the new value principle, it is impossible to say whether a new value rule is or is not supported by history. Justice Souter noted "that this history does nothing to disparage the possibility apparent in the statutory text, that the absolute priority rule . . . may carry a new value corollary."[697] At the same time, though, the Court also did not find that history made a compelling case in favor of the new value rule.

The *203 North LaSalle* Court could have further discounted any relevance of history to the new value issue by pointing out the substantial differences in the confirmation rules under old law and current law. One could argue that the Code's reorganization scheme is so radically different from the Act that meaningful comparisons between the two cannot be made. In the confirmation context as it relates to a possible new value plan, two major changes were made in the Code. First, cramdown is only required and the absolute priority rule triggered when a *class* of creditors rejects the plan, whereas under prior law a single dissenting creditor could trigger application of the absolute priority rule. Second, under the Code the debtor normally remains in possession and retains an exclusive right to file a reorganization plan, whereas under the old law an independent trustee was appointed and there was no exclusivity. As will be explained below, the Supreme Court in *203 North LaSalle* found the linkage of new value with exclusivity to be fatal to the debtor's effort to confirm a new value plan, unless some sort of external market test otherwise validates the debtor's proffered "new" contribution.

Even if the new value doctrine exists, it is still not easy to satisfy. Taking their cue from the delineation of the doctrine in *Case*, courts recognizing the new value exception require proof that:

- new value (a "fresh contribution") is being given;

- the new value is in "money or money's worth;"

- the new value is "substantial;"

- the new value is being given "up front;"

- the contribution is necessary for a successful reorganization; and

- the value given is reasonably equivalent to the value of the interest received or retained.[698]

In addition, after the Supreme Court's 1999 decision in *203 North LaSalle*, to be discussed in depth below, some sort of a market test of the new value contribution

---

[697] Id. at 449.

[698] See, e.g., In re Ambanc La Mesa Ltd. P'ship, 115 F.3d 650 (9th Cir. 1997); In re RYYZ, LLC, 2013 WL 1338178 (Bankr. E.D.N.Y. April 4, 2013). But see In re Coltex Loop Cent. Three Partners, L.P., 138 F.3d 39, 43 (2d Cir. 1998) (holding that the *Case* framework for evaluating new value is not applicable under the Code).

must be made. That is, the debtor cannot confirm a new value plan if it retains the exclusive right to make the new value contribution, unless the interest that the old debtor is purchasing in the reorganized debtor's property is opened up in some fashion to competitive market bidding. Also, in the case of individual debtors, *if* there even is an absolute priority rule, courts disagree whether the new value must come from a source other than the debtor, though the predominant view is that it must.[699]

It is clear that promises of future services or other intangible, non-capital contributions will not suffice. The leading case is *Norwest Bank Worthington v. Ahlers*, decided by the Supreme Court in 1988.[700] The Court in *Ahlers* did not decide whether a new value exception existed under the Code, although it pointedly raised the question;[701] instead, the Court held that even if such a doctrine persisted under the Code, it was not satisfied in that case. In *Ahlers*, a farmer promised future contributions of "labor, experience, and expertise" in exchange for keeping his farm. As had the Court half a century before in *Case*, the Supreme Court in *Ahlers* rejected the plea that such promises were "money or money's worth." According to Justice White, the debtor's "promise of future services is intangible, inalienable, and, in all likelihood, unenforceable," "has no place in the asset column of the balance sheet," and "cannot be exchanged in any market for something of value to the creditors *today*."[702] The promise of "sweat equity" could not support an exception to the operation of the absolute priority rule.[703]

Even if something more tangible than future services is offered, courts carefully police the equivalency and substantiality of the value promised. For example, a guarantee of a future loan is not adequate,[704] and neither is a promise to obtain a release of a lien.[705] Even if hard cash is offered, the court will insist that a sufficient amount be given to justify the debtor's retention of an equity interest.[706] Many courts are quite demanding in gauging substantiality and equivalency.

The "last word" on the new value exception today remains the Supreme Court's 1999 decision in *Bank of America National Trust and Savings Association v. 203 North LaSalle Street Partnership*.[707] The issue, according to Justice Souter, writing for a six-Justice majority, was:

---

[699] See In re Lee Min Ho Chen, 482 B.R. 473 (Bankr. D.P.R. 2012); In re Draiman, 450 B.R. 777 (Bankr. N.D. Ill. 2011). But see In re Arnold, 471 B.R. 578 (Bankr. C.D. Cal. 2012); In re Lively, 467 B.R. 884 (Bankr. S.D. Tex. 2012).

[700] 485 U.S. 197 (1988).

[701] Id. at 203–04 n.3 (1988).

[702] Id. at 204 (emphasis in original).

[703] Id. at 206.

[704] See Kham & Nate's Shoes No. 2. Inc. v. First Bank of Whiting, 908 F.2d 1351, 1360–62 (7th Cir. 1990).

[705] See In re Snyder, 967 F.2d 1126, 1130–31 (7th Cir. 1992).

[706] See, e.g., In re Woodbrook Assocs., 19 F.3d 312 (7th Cir. 1994).

[707] 526 U.S. 434 (1999). Much of the ensuing textual discussion of the *203 North LaSalle* case comes from Charles Jordan Tabb, Creditor Wins New Value Case, 19 Bankr. L. Letter 1 (June 1999). I have not attempted herein to cite all references from that article.

"[W]hether a debtor's prebankruptcy equity holders may, over the objection of a senior class of impaired creditors, contribute new capital and receive ownership interests in the reorganized entity, when that opportunity is given exclusively to the old equity holders under a plan adopted without consideration of alternatives."[708]

And the Supreme Court held:

"[O]ld equity holders are disqualified from participating in such a 'new value' transaction by the terms of 11 U.S.C. § 1129(b)(2)(B)(ii), which in such circumstances bars a junior interest holder's receipt of any property on account of his prior interest."[709]

The debtor, 203 North LaSalle Street Partnership, an Illinois real estate limited partnership, owned one primary asset: 15 floors of a Chicago office building. The debtor's principal creditor was its lender, Bank of America National Trust and Savings Association (Bank). Bank loaned debtor $93 million, secured by a nonrecourse first mortgage on the debtor's real estate. Debtor defaulted, Bank started foreclosure proceedings, and debtor filed chapter 11 to trigger the automatic stay. In short, *203 North LaSalle* was a typical single asset real estate case, with bankruptcy filed to stop foreclosure. The limited partners of the debtor had an acute desire to retain their ownership and to avoid foreclosure: if the Bank foreclosed, the limited partners would suffer $20 million in tax liabilities.

So the debtor proposed a plan that would allow its partners to retain ownership, cramming the plan down over the Bank's objection. The plan initially was filed while the debtor retained the exclusive right under § 1121(b) to file a plan; later, the bankruptcy judge extended the debtor's exclusive right. The bankruptcy judge denied the Bank's motion to terminate exclusivity so that the Bank could file its own competing liquidating plan. The bankruptcy judge valued the property at $54.5 million. Since a nonrecourse claim is afforded recourse under chapter 11, the Bank elected under § 1111(b) to retain its statutory unsecured claim and thus bifurcate its total $93 million claim into a secured claim equal to the value of the property ($54.5 million), and an unsecured claim for the balance ($38.5 million). The Bank opposed the plan. The salient aspects of the debtor's plan were:

• Bank's $54.5 million secured claim was to be paid in full 7–10 years after the original 1995 due date.

• Bank's $38.5 million unsecured claim was placed in its own class, and was to be paid approximately 16% (a little over $6 million) on a present value basis. This figure was calculated by taking the expected proceeds of $19 million on a projected sale or refinancing in 10 years and discounting that figure to present value.

---

[708] 526 U.S. at 437.

[709] Id.

• All other unsecured claims (mostly trade debt), totaling about $90,000, were placed in a separate class, and were to be paid in full, without interest, on the effective date of the plan.

• The limited partners of the Old Debtor were given the *exclusive* opportunity to purchase the entire ownership interest in the Reorganized Debtor for new capital contributions totaling $6.125 million over 5 years, which was worth about $4.1 million on a present value basis.

The trade debt accepted the plan, satisfying § 1129(a)(10), and the bankruptcy judge found that all of the other requirements for plan confirmation under § 1129(a) were met as well—except, of course, § 1129(a)(8), because the Bank voted against the plan. To confirm the plan the debtor thus had to resort to "cramdown" under § 1129(b). That meant that the plan had to be "fair and equitable" with respect to the dissenting impaired class (the Bank), § 1129(b)(1), and with respect to a dissenting unsecured class (such as the Bank), the fair and equitable test requires either that the dissenting class must be paid in full (§ 1129(b)(2)(B)(i)), or that junior classes (i.e., the limited partners here) must not get anything under the plan on account of their junior interest (§ 1129(b)(2)(B)(ii)).

Since the plan proposed to pay the Bank only about 16% on its unsecured claim, the first option for satisfying the absolute priority rule (full payment) obviously was not met. The only chance left was the second option—that old equity (the limited partners) be cut out of the plan. But they are not, the Bank objected, pointing to the inescapable fact that the plan provided for the debtor's limited partners to obtain the ownership of the Reorganized Debtor. Perhaps so, the bankruptcy judge answered, rejecting the Bank's plea, but the plan nevertheless does not run afoul of the absolute priority rule. Why not? Because the equity interest in the Reorganized Debtor that the Old Debtor's limited partners were purchasing under the plan was being obtained in exchange for the *new value* they were contributing, and not because of their status as pre-bankruptcy owners. The Bank appealed. It lost in the district court[710] and then in the Seventh Circuit.[711]

The Supreme Court then granted the Bank's petition for certiorari. The circuits were split on the question, and the lower courts had gone in every direction in scores and scores of decisions. Most single asset real estate cases depend on a new value rule for the debtor's plan to be confirmed over the lender's objection. In finding that a new value exception does exist and that an exclusive right to contribute does not violate the absolute priority rule, the Seventh Circuit agreed with the Ninth Circuit[712] and parted company with the Second Circuit[713] and Fourth Circuit,[714] each of which had held that an exclusive privilege to contribute new capital constituted "property" and thus contravened the absolute priority rule.

---

[710] 195 B.R. 692 (N.D. Ill. 1996).

[711] 206 F.3d 955 (7th Cir. 1997).

[712] In re Bonner Mall P'ship, 2 F.3d 899 (9th Cir. 1993), cert. granted sub nom., 510 U.S. 1039, motion to vacate denied and appeal dismissed as moot, 513 U.S. 18 (1994).

[713] In re Coltex Loop Cent.Three Partners, LLP, 138 F.3d 39 (2d Cir. 1998).

[714] In re Bryson Props. XVIII, 961 F.2d 496 (4th Cir. 1992), cert. denied, 506 U.S. 866 (1992).

So what *exactly* does the statute say? In cramdown, § 1129(b)(1) states the general rule that "the court . . . shall confirm the plan . . . if the plan does not discriminate unfairly, and is fair and equitable, with respect to each class of claims that is impaired under, and has not accepted, the plan." Fleshing out this general rule, § 1129(b)(2) then provides that:

> "[T]he condition that a plan be fair and equitable with respect to a class includes the following requirements . . . (B) With respect to a class of unsecured claims—(i) the plan provides that each holder of a claim of such class receive or retain on account of such claim property of a value, as of the effective date of the plan, equal to the allowed amount of such claim, or (ii) *the holder of any claim or interest that is junior to the claims of such class will not receive or retain under the plan on account of such junior claim or interest any property.*"[715]

The precise issue in *203 North LaSalle* was what the italicized language means in the context of an exclusive new value plan. When the debtor's limited partners have an exclusive right to purchase the ownership in the reorganized debtor, but must commit new money in order to make that purchase, in an amount adjudged to represent the value of the purchased interest, is the statutory absolute priority rule violated? The Seventh Circuit had said "no." The Supreme Court said "yes."

The Court held that the debtor's plan ran afoul of § 1129(b)(2)(B)(ii),[716] and thus the Bank won. Significantly, though, the Court took pains to emphasize that it did "not decide whether the statute includes a new value corollary or exception."[717] It held only that *this* plan was "doomed . . . by its provision for vesting equity in the reorganized business in the debtor's partners without extending an opportunity to anyone else either to compete for that equity or to propose a competing reorganization plan."[718] In short, it was the *exclusive* character of the *opportunity* to make the new value contribution that the Court found objectionable, rather than the actual fact of the new value purchase of ownership itself. A market test of some sort (although the Court declined to decide just what sort of market test) was necessary. The Court ultimately decided that the exclusive chance to purchase, in and of itself, constituted "property" that could not be given to old equity in the fact of the absolute priority rule.

The outcome of the case turned on the interpretation of three seemingly benign little words in § 1129(b)(2)(B)(ii): "*on account of.*" The clear mandate of the statute prohibits junior interest holders from receiving or retaining any "property" under the plan, not absolutely, but only "on account of" their junior interest. "On account of" suggests some sort of causal link, but what?

The debtor proposed that "on account of" should be read to mean "in exchange for." According to the debtor, since the "property" in question was the ownership interest in the Reorganized Debtor, and since the limited partners got that interest "in exchange

---

[715] 11 U.S.C. § 1129(b)(2) (emphasis added).

[716] 526 U.S. at 437.

[717] Id. at 443.

[718] Id. at 454.

for" their contribution of new money, and not in exchange for their old equity interest, the absolute priority rule of subsection (b)(2)(B)(ii) was not violated.

The Court rejected the debtor's proposed interpretation. The Court's first concern was textual. The statutory prohibition extends to the interest holders "retain[ing]" property on account of their prior interest; the Court thought it an "exceedingly odd" construction to speak of someone "retaining" property "in exchange for" something.[719] The unlikelihood of such a reading was reinforced by the fact that elsewhere in the chapter 11 confirmation rules (§ 1123(a)(5)(J)) the Code explicitly uses the phrase "in exchange for." So one would think that if Congress had meant "in exchange for" in § 1129(b)(2)(B)(ii), it would have used the same phrase.

Second, the Court found a practical difficulty with a rule that would depend on how substantial the partners' new value contribution was. Under the debtor's proposed reading, if the receipt of equity in the Reorganized Debtor was predicated on a substantial contribution, the absolute priority rule would not be broken, but if the same equity interest was based on an insubstantial contribution, the rule would be violated. The Court found it hard to justify an "absolute" priority rule that was so "variable" that it had to be "measure[d] by the Lord Chancellor's foot."[720]

So the debtor's argument that "on account of" meant "in exchange for" was rejected by the Court. Instead, the Court took the view that the more likely meaning of "on account of" was "because of."[721] This was the obvious meaning of that phrase in other parts of the Code, and in interpreting statutes the presumption is that identical phrases carry the same meaning throughout. In sum, the Court determined "that a causal relationship between holding the prior claim or interest and receiving or retaining property is what activates the absolute priority rule."[722] For all practical purposes, that determination was the end of the game as far as this plan was concerned. However, the Court still had to consider what *degree* of causation between the prior interest and the new interest would upset the absolute priority apple cart.

Two main possibilities had been suggested. As the Court explained, this plan actually failed under either alternative. However, which of those readings the Court favored would be important for future cases in ascertaining the extent of the anti-new value ban. The most extreme view is that *any* degree of causation would suffice. In other words, if old equity *ever* ended up with property in the reorganized debtor, then, "*res ipsa loquitur*," there had to be some causation, which would violate the absolute priority rule.[723] On this view, any form of new value plan, even one that did not afford old equity an exclusive right, would be *verboten*.

The Court thought this was a bit much, and instead did leave the door open for some types of new value plans. As a textual mater, the Court objected that the extremist reading would render the "on account of" language superfluous (which is a

---

[719] Id. at 450.

[720] Id.

[721] Id.

[722] Id. at 451.

[723] Id.

bad thing in statutory construction). As a practical matter, the majority wondered what policy reason would inspire Congress to exclude *only* old equity from the class of prospective purchasers, when old equity might be the very ones most willing and inclined to give a go at reorganization.[724]

That left "a less absolute statutory prohibition,"[725] in which the requisite causation to trigger the absolute priority rule would depend on the *price* paid by old equity for the new property. A "truly full value transaction" would be permissible, the Court opined.[726] Such a reading would "reconcile the two recognized policies underlying Chapter 11, of preserving going concerns and maximizing property available to satisfy creditors."[727] A rule of thumb the Court suggested for measuring the sufficiency of the price paid is that it would "always" be too low if the price was less than would have been paid by a third party. In dictum, the Court intimated, without deciding, that the price *still* might be too low, unless old equity paid *more* than anyone else would have paid—otherwise old equity's contribution would not be necessary.[728]

In the case before it, though, the Court concluded that the plan failed even on the "less absolute" reading, because of the fact that old equity had the *exclusive* right to purchase the new equity.[729] Exclusivity was the fatal flaw. While the Court conceded that the debtor's statutory exclusive right to propose a plan under § 1121(b) is not itself a form of "property" within the prohibition of § 1129(b)(2)(B)(ii), what seemed to trouble the Court was that the debtor "took advantage" of that statutory right to propose a plan that gave the debtor's partners the exclusive right to purchase the new equity. It was that exclusive privilege in the plan, which was the forbidden "property" fruit. The concurrence agreed. The Court thus cast its lot with the views of the Fourth and the Second Circuits, which in *Bryson Properties* and *Coltex Loop* also had held that an exclusive opportunity to purchase new equity is a form of property that cannot be given to old equity over a dissenting unsecured class's objection. The Court likened this exclusive right to purchase to an exclusive purchase option or to a right of first refusal, both of which are generally considered to be property.[730]

Having decided that the exclusive option was "property," the Court found it inescapable that this property right was given to old equity "on account of" their prior interest, and thus violated the absolute priority rule. Justice Souter pointed out a logical bind. If old equity truly was putting more money up to buy the new equity than anyone else would have, then the protection of exclusivity would be unnecessary. But if not, then "there is no apparent reason for giving old equity a bargain," unless of course that *is* precisely the purpose—to give old equity a bargain—which would contravene

---

[724] Id. at 452–53.

[725] Id. at 453.

[726] Id. at 453–54.

[727] Id. at 453.

[728] Id. at 453 n.26.

[729] Id. at 454.

[730] Id. at 454–55.

the very purpose of the absolute priority rule of preventing distributions of value to junior interests "on account of" their status as old equity holders.[731]

The key, the Court explained, was that a "competitive choice"—a "market test"[732]—had to be offered. Even if the bankruptcy judge in this case did a very fine job in valuing the property, still a market valuation is preferable; apparently, so preferable as to be mandated by the Code's "on account of" language. The current Court's exaltation of the market and distrust of judicial valuations thus continued. The Court did not decide exactly what sort of market test would suffice, but suggested either (1) allowing competing plans to be filed (i.e., terminating exclusivity) or (2) auctioning off the new equity.[733] In summation, the majority left the matter thusly:

> "It is enough to say, assuming a new value corollary, that plans providing junior interest holders with exclusive opportunities free from competition and without benefit of market valuation fall within the prohibition of § 1129(b)(2)(B)(ii)."[734]

The Court's reasoning responded to the reality of what often had upset creditors about a new value plan, namely, the fact that they had no say in the matter, and no chance to offer a competing plan, or to bid. Instead, they were entirely at the mercy of the court's assessment of the equivalency of the contribution made by the debtor to the value of the interest retained.

The obvious question after *203 North LaSalle* is what it means for the future of the new value exception, especially in the single asset real estate context. We know from the Court's opinion that a "new value" cramdown plan in which old equity has the *exclusive* opportunity to bid and where no "market test" occurs is off the table. But at the same time, the Court did not impose a *per se* ban on old equity participating in the reorganization based on a contribution of new money. It just cannot be an exclusive option to buy. The most plausible reading of the Court's opinion is that a *non*-exclusive new value cramdown plan would be acceptable to the Court, assuming that the contribution of old equity was for a fair and adequate price and was in "money or money's worth." The Court's real concern was that the price be subjected to competitive forces.

Applying the dictates of *203 North LaSalle,* the Seventh Circuit held in *In re Castleton Plaza, LP*,[735] that this requirement of competition applies even when the proposed "new value" plan is in favor of an insider (the debtor's wife) rather than the debtor himself. At bottom, "[c]ompetition is essential whenever a plan of reorganization leaves an objecting creditor unpaid yet distributes an equity interest to an insider."[736] Responding to the argument that the value proposed was fair, the court responded in the same way Justice Souter had: if such were the case, then surely the insider bidder would win the open auction that the court was now requiring.

---

[731] Id. at 456.

[732] Id. at 458.

[733] Id.

[734] Id.

[735] 707 F.3d 821, 821–24 (7th Cir. 2013).

[736] Id. at 821–22.

Assuming that old equity might be permitted to bid on new equity, as long as that right is not exclusive, additional issues present themselves. First, what types of competition will suffice to assuage the Court's market-test sensibilities? The Court itself expressly declined to state anything definitive on that score. But, as noted above, the Court did give very strong hints that either of the following would suffice: (1) terminate exclusivity and allow competing plans to be filed, or (2) hold an open auction for the equity interest in the reorganized debtor. Indeed, subsequent cases have so held.[737] The evidence from the surprisingly scarce case law in the years since *203 North LaSalle* was decided initially showed little appetite or inclination to hold auctions; the more common tactic was to terminate exclusivity and allow competing plans to be filed. Yet, decisions such as the Seventh Circuit's 2013 ruling in *Castleton Plaza* may indicate a preference for competitive open auctions, rather than merely allowing competing plans to be considered. The dissenting secured lender in that case had put its own plan on the table, but the bankruptcy judge confirmed the debtor's insider new value plan instead. The Seventh Circuit required an auction, explaining that "competition helps prevent the funneling of value from lenders to insiders, no matter who proposes the plan or when. An impaired lender who objects to *any* plan that leaves insiders holding equity is entitled to the benefit of competition."[738]

With regard to the competing plan scenario, one issue is whether the debtor's plan may then reserve the right to purchase new equity exclusively to old equity, *if* the judge has terminated exclusivity and allowed other plans to be filed that provide otherwise. The debtor could argue that the Supreme Court's "competitive" concern would be squarely satisfied. Yet, the reality is that the bankruptcy judge (1) can only confirm one plan, and (2) is vested with discretion to decide which plan to confirm. Assume that exclusivity is terminated and the bank files a liquidating plan (as the Bank wished to do in *203 North LaSalle*). But then assume that the bankruptcy judge chooses to confirm the debtor's cramdown new value plan that only allows old equity to purchase, and further the *amount* of the debtor's contribution is set by the judge's valuation. Is the Bank any better off than before? (Probably not—and that practical reality drove the Seventh Circuit's decision in *Castleton Plaza*, noted above). Do we care? Lenders certainly do.

And if competing plans are allowed, but exclusive new value plans are also countenanced, what will happen to the judicial requirements for confirming the new value plan? Must the bankruptcy judge still conclude that the new value contribution is "necessary"? "Substantial"? Or does the fact that the bankruptcy judge could have confirmed a competing plan—but did not—excuse compliance with such requirements, whose real function was only to serve as surrogates for an absent market? Here the

---

[737] See, e.g., In re Ralph Roberts Realty, LLC, 487 B.R. 480 (Bankr. E.D. Mich. 2012); In re Cypresswood Land Partners, I, 409 B.R. 396 (Bankr. S.D. Tex. 2009); In re Global Ocean Carriers, Ltd., 251 B.R. 31 (Bankr. D. Del. 2000).

[738] 707 F.3d at 824.

evidence suggests that courts still tend to hew to the old "necessity" and "substantiality" tests.[739]

If one worries that such lingering doubts will lead courts to move in the direction of *always* requiring an auction (a worry that has proven unfounded so far), problems exist under that scenario as well. An initial query is whether old equity must *beat* any other bidder. The Court hinted in a footnote at such a requirement. If that is the case, then in a situation such as that presented in *203 North LaSalle*, where the old partners have very compelling tax worries driving them to try to win the bid, the bank could effectively put the screws on old equity and keep forcing them up. All the bank would have to do is keep matching old equity's bid.

And what about the terms of the bidding? For example, will the bank be allowed to "credit bid" its claim in vying for the new equity?[740] Even if not, in a case in which the bank holds almost all of the debt, it effectively would be bidding with "play money" anyway, just moving dollars from one pocket to another. That would mean that it would be very hard for old equity to outbid the bank.

The real impact of *203 North LaSalle* likely is hidden to some degree, and hard to quantify, because the Court's clear rejection of a common strategy in single asset real estate cases—cram down an exclusive new value plan—is simply off the table. It is an unknowable counterfactual how many single asset debtors there are who would have crammed down a new value plan but for *203 North LaSalle* but instead did not even try because they knew it would be futile even to try. One judge observed that the Supreme Court "hog-tied" the new value doctrine in *203 North LaSalle*,[741] which is probably an apt characterization. We do know that few single asset cram down cases have appeared in the published reports since the Supreme Court's decision. Perhaps we should at the very least be thankful for that gift.

E. POST-CONFIRMATION ISSUES

§ 11.35 The Effects of Confirmation

Confirmation of a chapter 11 plan has a profound legal effect.[742] The confirmed plan is the operative legal document that dictates the financial structure and obligations of the reorganized debtor, replacing the pre-confirmation regime. The

---

[739] See, e.g., In re Hoffinger Indus., Inc., 321 B.R. 498, 511 (Bankr. E.D. Ark. 2005) (noting that although a competing plan had been filed, the "appropriateness and sufficiency of the new value tendered has been raised and subjected to Court scrutiny").

[740] The court in *Beal Bank, S.S.B. v. Water's Edge Ltd. P'ship*, 248 B.R. 668 (Bankr. D. Mass. 2000) did not permit a credit bid. However, the Supreme Court's decision in *RadLAX Gateway Hotel, LLC v. Amalgamated Bank*, 132 S.Ct. 2065 (2012), requiring that a secured creditor be offered the chance to credit bid when being crammed down via a free and clear auction sale, might support a determination that credit bidding should be allowed when the plan provides for the debtor to be "sold" for new value. Perhaps, though, if it is structured as an inside private sale to old equity rather than a public sale at auction, the court might find "cause" to deny the credit bid right under § 363(k).

[741] Wilkow v. Forbes, Inc., 241 F.3d 552, 554 (7th Cir. 2001).

[742] See Frank R. Kennedy & Gerald K. Smith, Postconfirmation Issues: The Effects of Confirmation and Postconfirmation Proceedings, 44 S.C. L. Rev. 621 (1993). This article is an encyclopedic review of most significant post-confirmation issues.

operative effects of confirmation are governed by § 1141. Under that provision, confirmation has four primary legal effects:

1. The terms of the plan are *binding* on the debtor, all creditors, equity holders, or general partners of the debtor, as well as on any entity issuing securities or acquiring property under the plan. This binding effect applies whether or not the affected party is impaired under the plan or voted in favor of the plan. § 1141(a).

2. All property of the estate is *vested* in the debtor, except as otherwise provided in the plan or confirmation order. § 1141(b).

3. Property dealt with by the plan is *free and clear* of all claims and interests, except as provided in the discharge rules and except as provided in the plan or confirmation order. § 1141(c).

4. The debtor is *discharged* from any pre-confirmation debt, and all rights and interests of equity security holders or general partners provided for by the plan are terminated. The discharge is effective whether or not the creditor filed a proof of claim, had its claim allowed, or voted in favor of the plan. § 1141(d)(1). This discharge rule does not apply to individual debtors, who are not released until all payments under the plan have been made. § 1141(d)(5)(A). Other exceptions to this broad discharge are provided for (i) nondischargeable § 523 debts for an individual debtor, § 1141(d)(2); (ii) corporate debts owing to a domestic governmental unit under sections 523(a)(2)(A) or (B), to persons as a result of an action filed under subchapter III of chapter 37 or any similar State statute, or for a tax or customs duty for which the debtor made a fraudulent return or attempted to evade tax or customs, § 1141(d)(6); (iii) the case of a liquidating plan, if the debtor would not have received a discharge under § 727(a), § 1141(d)(3); and (iv) a written waiver of discharge executed by the debtor after the entry of the order for relief in the bankruptcy case, § 1141(d)(4).

Binding effect

The rule that the provisions of a confirmed plan are binding on all affected parties is essential to the operation of the chapter 11 system. § 1141(a). The order confirming the plan must be accorded finality, and that finality effect must be globally applied and enforced. A confirmed plan binds all parties to the reorganization proceeding, whether or not their claims or interests are impaired, and whether or not they accepted the plan. It is this unique feature of a chapter 11 plan that distinguishes it from out-of-court workouts, which cannot bind dissenting creditors or equity security holders. A confirmation order, as a final order of a federal court, is given res judicata effect, and cannot be collaterally attacked.[743]

---

[743] Stoll v. Gottlieb, 305 U.S. 165, 170–71 (1938). See § 11.38.

Vesting of property

Upon the filing of a bankruptcy petition, all property of the debtor becomes property of the estate. § 541(a). This property of the bankruptcy estate is under the exclusive jurisdiction of the bankruptcy court, 28 U.S.C. § 1334(e), and is protected by the § 362(a) automatic stay from the collection efforts of creditors and any extrinsic efforts to control that property. These protective measures are only intended to be temporary, however, to assist the debtor in pursuing without interference or hindrance its reorganization efforts during the pendency of the bankruptcy case. When a plan is confirmed, the debtor in common parlance is said to "emerge" from chapter 11, and the Supreme Court has noted that a reorganized debtor must "stand on his own two feet."[744] Part of this two-footed "emergence" is effected by § 1141(b), which vests all property of the estate in the debtor, unless the plan or confirmation order provide otherwise. Thus, upon confirmation, property of the estate is magically transformed back into the debtor's property, and in doing so loses the benefits of the stay and the exclusive jurisdiction of the bankruptcy court. The vesting of property in the debtor is generally beneficial to the reorganized debtor, however. To engage in business, obtain credit, and the like, the debtor needs to be able to deal with its property as its own, without the cocoon of court protection. As noted above, though, the rule vesting estate property in the debtor is just a default rule, and can be overridden by a contrary provision in the plan or confirmation order. For example, the plan may provide for the transfer of estate property to a third party.

Free and clear

If property is dealt with by the plan, upon confirmation that property is "free and clear" of all claims and interests. § 1141(c). Those pre-confirmation claims and interests only retain those rights against property that are expressly reserved to them under the terms of the plan. This free and clear rule applies whether the plan transfers the property to a third party or provides for its retention by the debtor. As with the vesting rule, the rule freeing property dealt with by the plan from all claims and interests is only a default rule, and can be overridden by a contrary provision in the plan or confirmation order. Also, debts that are excluded from the chapter 11 discharge under § 1141(d)(2)–(6) are of necessity excepted from the operation of the free and clear rule.

In two situations the rule of § 1141(c) has caused some controversy. The first is the extinguishing of liens, and the second is successor liability. With regard to liens, an ancient principle of bankruptcy law, dating to the 1886 decision of the Supreme Court in *Long v. Bullard*,[745] is that liens "ride through" a bankruptcy case unaffected. To a limited extent this remains true under chapter 11: if the lienholder declines to file a claim, and remains aloof from the bankruptcy case, its *in rem* lien claim should not be affected, even by confirmation.[746] This remains true for situations where a debtor

---

[744] United Savs. Ass'n v. Timbers of Inwood Forest Assocs., Ltd., 484 U.S. 365, 378 (1988).

[745] 117 U.S. 617 (1886).

[746] See In re Greater Am. Land Res., Inc., 452 B.R. 532, 544 (Bankr. D.N.J. 2011) ("Because this court has determined that [the creditor] did not 'participate' in the Debtor's bankruptcy sufficiently to allow its lien . . . to be extinguished . . . [the creditor's] lien survives *in rem* pursuant to § 506(d).").

improperly denies the creditor's claim, or treats it incorrectly, as an unsecured claim.[747] However, if a lienholder participates in the chapter 11 case, and is dealt with under the plan, the only rights the lienholder will have after confirmation are those accorded to it in the plan.[748] In the case where a secured creditor receives sufficient notice of the bankruptcy proceeding to file a claim and "participate," but declines in favor of having its lien ride through and avoid dealing with the bankruptcy case, a debtor may file a proof of claim on behalf of the secured creditor.[749]

If the plan deals with the secured creditor, but does *not* provide for the creditor to retain its lien, the plain language of § 1141(c) dictates that the creditor's pre-confirmation liens will be extinguished.[750] In other words, four requirements must be met in order for a lien to be extinguished through the plan confirmation process: (1) the plan must be confirmed; (2) the plan must deal with property encumbered by the lien; (3) the lienholder must participate in the reorganization; and (4) the plan must not preserve the lien.[751] Debtors must be careful with the second requirement that their plan *deals* with the encumbered property. What exactly does "deals with" mean in this context? Courts require that the plan itself give some indication that it either compensates the creditor for extinguishing its lien, or otherwise affects the creditor's interest through Code-provided powers (e.g., exchange, extinguish, impair, modify, etc.).[752] A diligent secured creditor should be able to protect its rights, however. If a proposed plan deals with the creditor but fails to provide for the creditor to retain its lien, the creditor would have a valid objection to confirmation of the plan, because the secured creditor is entitled to retain its lien, either through the impairment or the cram down rules. §§ 1124, 1129(b)(2)(A).

The successor liability issue arises when the debtor's assets are transferred in the plan to another entity, and the conditions for the imposition of successor liability under nonbankruptcy law otherwise are met (such as continuation of an ongoing enterprise under the same name). The question is whether the post-confirmation successor to the debtor is freed from liability for claims and interests against the debtor by § 1141(c).[753] The literal terms of subsection (c) suggest that successor liability will not survive a chapter 11 confirmation. The better view, embraced by most courts, is that the Code

---

[747] See In re Be–Mac Transp. Co., Inc., 83 F.3d 1020 (8th Cir. 1996).

[748] See In re WorldCom, Inc., 382 B.R. 610, 621 (Bankr. S.D.N.Y. 2008) ("The 'default rule' is that section 1141(c) extinguishes liens, since they are 'interests,' unless the bankruptcy plan otherwise preserves them."), aff'd, 2011 WL 1496378 (S.D.N.Y. 2011), aff'd, 466 Fed. Appx. 28 (2d Cir. 2012).

[749] See In re S. White Transp., Inc., 473 B.R. 695, 703 (S.D. Miss. 2012); 11 U.S.C. § 501(c).

[750] See In re Penrod, 50 F.3d 459 (7th Cir. 1995). Accord In re Ahern Enter., Inc., 507 F.3d 817 (5th Cir. 2007); In re Reg'l Bldg. Sys, Inc., 254 F.3d 528 (4th Cir. 2001).

[751] See, e.g., In re S. White Transp., Inc., 473 B.R. 695, 700 (S.D. Miss. 2012) (quoting In re Ahern Enters., Inc., 507 F.3d 817, 822 (5th Cir. 2007)).

[752] See, e.g., In re Airadigm Commc'ns, Inc., 519 F.3d 640, 649 (7th Cir. 2008). In *Airadigm*, the creditor held a lien on the debtor's licenses. All parties involved, even the bankruptcy court, erroneously assumed that the licenses had been validly cancelled, and thus the plan only addressed payment to the creditor where the licenses were reinstated. However, the Code does not allow a licensor to cancel its license just because the licensee entered bankruptcy, § 525. Thus, the Seventh Circuit held that the plan did not "deal" with the encumbered property, and thus the creditor's lien was never extinguished.

[753] For a superb discussion, see David Gray Carlson, Successor Liability in Bankruptcy: Some Unifying Themes of Intertemporal Creditor Priorities Creating by Running Covenants, Products Liability, and Toxic–Waste Cleanup, 50 Law & Contemp. Probs. 119 (Spring 1987).

indeed preempts state successor liability rules.[754] However, in products liability cases, in which the tort victim either does not know of the bankruptcy case before confirmation or does not suffer injury until after confirmation, a few courts have imposed successor liability, notwithstanding § 1141(c).[755]

While this judicial sympathy for innocent tort victims is laudable, such a result can only be squared with the Code if the victim is a future claimant and thus not a "creditor" within the meaning of the Code. § 101(10). Tort claimants that are "creditors" would seem to be barred by § 1141(c). Indeed, even if a party might be found only to have an "interest in property," the clear trend is to find that successor liability is eliminated; this issue has arisen primarily in the context of all-asset sales under § 363(f).[756] Of course, if a claimant lacked notice of the bankruptcy case, the constitutional requirement of due process might override § 1141(c) and preserve the claimant's successor liability claim.

Discharge

In chapter 11, the critical discharge event (except for individual debtors) is the *confirmation of the plan* of reorganization. § 1141(d)(1). Confirmation *immediately* discharges corporate and partnership debtors from all debts that arose prior to the date of confirmation, and replaces those debts with the obligations assumed in the plan. Note that debts that arise postpetition but prior to confirmation are also discharged in chapter 11, as contrasted to chapter 7, where only prepetition debts are discharged. § 727(b). For individual debtors, the discharge rule was changed in 2005 to mirror that of chapter 13; now, discharge for individuals occurs upon completion of performance under the plan, rather than confirmation. § 1141(d)(5).

Unlike chapters 12 and 13, §§ 1228(a), 1328(a), performance under a confirmed chapter 11 plan is not a prerequisite to discharge for corporate and partnership debtors; confirmation of the plan is all that is required. Even if the debtor defaults under the plan, creditors are left with only their reduced rights under the confirmed plan. Only in the rare case in which the discharge is revoked for fraud under § 1144 will creditors be able to resurrect their pre-confirmation claims.[757] As noted above, though, in 2005 individual debtors in chapter 11 were relegated to the deferred discharge scheme of chapters 12 and 13.

Creditors do not have to participate in or assent to the chapter 11 plan for their claims to be discharged. Indeed, the power to bind and discharge nonassenting creditors is one of the critical functions served by chapter 11. In one notable case, however, the Ninth Circuit held that a creditor's pre-confirmation setoff right under

---

[754] See, e.g., In re White Motor Credit Corp., 75 B.R. 944 (Bankr. N.D. Ohio 1987); In re PBBPC, Inc., 484 B.R. 860 (B.A.P. 1st Cir. 2013); MPI Acquisition, LLC v. Northcutt, 14 So.3d 126 (Ala. 2009). But see Chicago Truck Drivers, Helpers & Warehouse Workers Union (Indep.) Pension Fund v. Tasemkin, Inc., 59 F.3d 48 (7th Cir. 1995).

[755] See, e.g., In re Savage Indus., Inc., 43 F.3d 714 (1st Cir. 1994); Lemelle v. Universal Mfg. Corp., 18 F.3d 1268 (5th Cir. 1994); In re Grumman Olson Indus., Inc., 467 B.R. 694 (S.D.N.Y. 2012).

[756] See, e.g., In re Trans World Airlines, Inc., 322 F.3d 283 (3d Cir. 2003).

[757] See § 11.36.

§ 553, which was not provided for in the plan, survived the confirmation discharge.[758] That decision arguably ignored the strong policy of finality that underlies § 1141.[759]

Corporate and partnership debtors are able to receive a discharge in chapter 11, unless the plan provides for the liquidation of all or substantially all of the estate property.[760] § 1141(d)(3)(A). Indeed, the discharge for corporations and partnerships is not even subject to the § 523 exceptions, although those exceptions will apply to an individual debtor. § 1141(d)(2). Notwithstanding these provisions, a corporate debtor will not receive a discharge upon confirmation from any debt of a kind specified in section 523(a)(2)(A) or (B) "that is owed to a domestic governmental unit, or owed to a person as the result of an action filed under subchapter III of chapter 37 of title 31 or any similar State statute." § 1141(d)(6)(A). Corporate debtors also are not discharged upon confirmation from a tax or customs duty in which the debtor made a fraudulent return or attempted to evade or defeat that tax or customs duty. § 1141(d)(6)(B). The legislative history makes clear that the omission of corporate and partnership debtors from (d)(2) was intentional, stating that "[i]t is necessary for a corporation or partnership undergoing reorganization to be able to present its creditors with a fixed list of liabilities upon which the creditors or third parties can make intelligent decisions."[761] The courts have upheld this distinction in treatment between individual and corporate debtors in § 1141(d)(2) against constitutional challenges, reasoning that the congressional choice had a rational basis.

For all chapter 11 debtors, including individuals, the chapter 7 grounds for denial of discharge in § 727(a) do not usually apply. The only exception is in the rare event that the debtor is liquidating in chapter 11, § 1123(b)(4), rather than reorganizing. § 1141(d)(3). The eight-year bar on successive bankruptcy discharges thus does not apply when the second case is a reorganizing chapter 11. A chapter 11 discharge will trigger the eight-year bar in a later chapter 7 case, however. § 727(a)(8). Section 1141(d)(4) copies § 727(a)(10) by permitting a debtor to waive the discharge in writing after the case is filed.

The seemingly absolute discharge language of the Code in some cases will have to bow to the constitutional dictates of due process. Creditors who do not receive any notice of the bankruptcy case cannot constitutionally be discharged.[762] However, cases that have held that due process requires giving actual notice to known creditors, even

---

[758] Carolco Television Inc. v. Nat'l Broad. Co. (In re De Laurentiis Entm't Group, Inc.), 963 F.2d 1269 (9th Cir. 1992), cert. denied, 506 U.S. 918 (1992). See also United States v. Munson, 248 B.R. 343, 346–47 (C.D. Ill. 2000) (same, in the context of chapter 13).

[759] See In re Lykes Bros. S.S. Co., Inc., 217 B.R. 304, 310 (Bankr. M.D. Fla. 1997) ("[T]his Court concludes that facilitating the reorganization process is the overriding policy in this case and that, therefore, the provisions of Section 1141 take precedence over Section 553.").

[760] See e.g., In re SunCruz Casinos LLC, 342 B.R. 370, 380 (Bankr. S.D. Fla. 2006) ("The net effect of the provisions of § 1141(d)(3) is that a corporate debtor which is liquidated under chapter 11 and does not continue in business after its chapter 11 plan goes into effect does not receive a bankruptcy discharge.").

[761] 124 Cong. Rec. S17,422 (daily ed. Oct. 6, 1978) (remarks of Sen. DeConcini); 124 Cong. Rec. H11,105 (daily ed. Sept. 28, 1978) (remarks of Rep Edwards).

[762] This view stems from *City of New York v. New York, N.H., & H. R.R. Co.*, 344 U.S. 293 (1953). See also In re Grossman's Inc., 607 F.3d 114 (3d Cir. 2010); Reliable Elec. Co. v. Olson Constr. Co., 726 F.2d 620 (10th Cir. 1984); In re Chance Indus., Inc., 367 B.R. 689 (Bankr. D. Kan. 2006); DPWN Holdings (USA), Inc. v. United Air Lines, Inc., 871 F.Supp.2d 143 (E.D.N.Y. 2012).

if those creditors have actual knowledge of the pendency of the bankruptcy case,[763] have been criticized on a variety of grounds.[764] The constitutional due process limitation poses particular problems in cases involving attempts to discharge unmanifested future tort claims. The constitutional mandate might be satisfied, however, by a combination of publication notice and the appointment of a representative for the class.[765]

§ 11.36 Attacking Confirmation: Revocation

Once confirmed, a chapter 11 plan is difficult to attack. Even if the confirmation order is appealed, the appeal may become moot if the debtor makes substantial distributions under the plan, because the appellate court would not be able to grant effective relief.[766] Collateral attack on a confirmed plan is extremely difficult.[767] The doctrine of res judicata has been applied with particular rigor in this area.[768] The concern here regards protecting innocent third parties who relied on the confirmation order.[769]

A confirmed plan may be set aside, however, if the court *revokes* the order of confirmation on the ground that the order was procured by fraud. § 1144. Notably, a bankruptcy court only has the power to fully revoke a confirmed plan, and may not partially revoke it.[770] Fraud is the exclusive basis on which a court may revoke a confirmation order, and courts have construed the statute to require proof of actual, rather than constructive, fraud.[771] The fact that the debtor failed to perform under the terms of the plan would not be a basis for revoking confirmation; the alleged fraud must be on the court.[772] The statute does not limit revocation to cases where the debtor or plan proponent perpetrated the fraud, as long as it can be shown that confirmation

---

[763] See, e.g., *Reliable Electric*, supra note 762, 726 F.2d 620.

[764] See Kennedy & Smith, supra note 742, at 659–664; Kenneth N. Klee & Frank A. Merola, Ignoring Congressional Intent: Eight Years of Judicial Legislation, 62 Am. Bankr. L.J. 1 (1988). See also Laura B. Bartell, Due Process for the Unknown Future Claim in Bankruptcy—Is This Notice Really Necessary?, 78 Am. Bankr.L.J. 339 (2004).

[765] See In re Mansaray–Ruffin, 530 F.3d 230, 239 n.7 (3d Cir. 2008) ("[I]t is well established that notice of bankruptcy proceedings by publication is generally sufficient to protect the procedural due process rights of unknown creditors, but not those of known creditors." (citations omitted)). See also Bartell, supra note 23; Ralph R. Mabey & Jamie Andra Gavrin, Constitutional Limitations on the Discharge of Future Claims in Bankruptcy, 44 S.C. L. Rev. 745 (1993).

[766] See § 11.37.

[767] See § 11.38.

[768] See Stoll v. Gottlieb, 305 U.S. 165 (1938).

[769] See In re Genesis Health Ventures, Inc., 355 B.R. 438 (Bankr. D. Del. 2006); In re Trico Marine Servs., 337 B.R. 811 (Bankr. S.D.N.Y. 2006).

[770] In re Motors Liquidation Co., 462 B.R. 494 (Bankr. S.D.N.Y. 2012). But see In re Northfield Labs. Inc., 467 B.R. 582, 588 (Bankr. D. Del. 2010) ("The plain language of section 1144, however, only provides for revocation of an entire confirmation order. It is unclear whether partial revocation is permissible pursuant to section 1144 and Plaintiffs have cited no case law in this regard.").

[771] See, e.g., In re Tenn–Fla Partners, 226 F.3d 746 (6th Cir. 2000) (agreeing with the bankruptcy court's analysis, which concluded that "fraud" in § 1144 means actual, as opposed to constructive fraud); In re Level Propane Gases, Inc., 438 B.R. 354 (B.A.P. 6th Cir. 2010).

[772] E.g., *Motors Liquidation*, supra note 746, 462 B.R. 494.

was procured by fraud.[773] For example, it would suffice to show that the debtor's attorney carried out the fraud.[774]

Fraud in procuring confirmation might be established by showing that the debtor failed to disclose the existence of valuable assets in the disclosure statement,[775] or misrepresented the value of assets.[776] Concealing the existence of potential purchasers of the debtor's assets could constitute fraud.[777] Presenting false financial information at confirmation might be sufficient fraud. However, not every nondisclosure or inaccuracy in the disclosure statement or in the testimony at the confirmation hearing will result in setting aside the confirmation order.[778] Not only must the representation or concealment be false, and with regard to a material fact, but must be made (or withheld) with scienter.[779]

Revocation of confirmation must be sought by a party in interest within 180 days after the entry of the confirmation order. The 180–day time limit is absolute and may not be extended. Rule 9024. This is true even if the fraud was not discovered until after the 180–day period expired. In fact, one court stated that 180 days is the outside window, while for "cases with more complicated plans of reorganization that impact greater numbers of interested parties, the time frame within which a request for revocation should be made necessarily shortens because the level of difficulty required to comply with the statute and protect innocent third parties in a revocation order increases exponentially."[780] This policy favoring the finality of confirmation orders, protecting innocent third parties, is very strong. The statute does not, however, require the party requesting revocation to prove that they did not know or have reason to know of the fraud until after confirmation of the plan.

A moving party who misses the 180–day deadline might try to circumvent this requirement by using Federal Rule of Civil Procedure 60(b), which contains a more lenient timing requirement of one year. However, Rule 9024, which makes Federal Rule of Civil Procedure 60(b) applicable to bankruptcy proceedings, contains an express limitation for § 1144 complaints to revoke confirmation orders. Rule 9024 squashes any hope a debtor may have of gaming the system, and requires § 1144 complaints to be filed within the time prescribed by the statute—180 days. Rule 9024.

Even though a motion to revoke confirmation must be brought within a relatively short time period after confirmation, it is still very possible that implementation of the plan may have begun before revocation. In the implementation process, third parties may have acquired rights in good faith, relying on the confirmation order. For example,

---

[773] See In re Northfield Labs. Inc., 467 B.R. 582 (Bankr. D. Del. 2010).

[774] See In re Baron's Stores, Inc., 390 B.R. 734 (Bankr. S.D. Fla. 2008).

[775] See, e.g., In re Giguere, 165 B.R. 531 (Bankr. D.R.I. 1994).

[776] See, e.g., In re Kostoglou, 73 B.R. 596 (Bankr. N.D. Ohio 1987).

[777] See, e.g., In re Tenn–Fla Partners, 170 B.R. 946 (Bankr. W.D. Tenn. 1994), aff'd in part, rev'd in part, 229 B.R. 720 (W.D. Tenn. 1999), aff'd, 226 F.3d 746 (6th Cir. 2000).

[778] See In re Longardner & Assocs., Inc., 855 F.2d 455 (7th Cir. 1988), cert. denied, 489 U.S. 1015 (1989); *Genesis Health*, supra note 745, 355 B.R. 438.

[779] See *Motors Liquidation*, supra note 746, 462 B.R. at 506.

[780] In re Delta Air Lines, Inc., 386 B.R. 518, 533 (Bankr. S.D.N.Y. 2008).

property may have been transferred to a good faith purchaser for value. In conjunction with the revocation order, the bankruptcy court is required to issue whatever orders are necessary to protect such good faith reliance parties.[781] § 1144(1). Indeed, if it is sufficiently difficult to "put Humpty Dumpty back together again" and unwind the actions taken under a confirmed plan, a court may exercise its discretion to refuse to revoke confirmation, even if fraud is proven. Indeed, some courts construe the word "*shall*" before § 1144(1) to mean that if a court cannot fashion a revocation order that protects innocent parties, then the court is barred from revoking the confirmation order, even if the order was procured by fraud.[782] The statute says that the court "may" revoke for fraud, thus indicating that whether to revoke or not falls within the court's discretion; revocation is not mandatory upon proof of fraud.[783] If the court cannot revoke the plan confirmation order, either because of third party protection issues or 180 days has passed, the court may still accord other relief to parties injured by the fraud, such as damages.[784]

The court also is required to revoke the debtor's discharge when it revokes an order of confirmation. § 1144(2). Recall that in chapter 11, unlike chapters 12 and 13, the debtor's discharge is entered upon confirmation of the plan, not at the completion of performance under the plan, unless the debtor is an individual. § 1141(d). Revocation of the debtor's discharge will serve to reinstate the claims of creditors to their pre-confirmation amounts.

What happens after a confirmation order is revoked? One possibility is for a party in interest to request the court to dismiss the case. Revocation of confirmation constitutes cause for dismissal. § 1112(b)(4)(L). An alternative to dismissal would be for the court to convert the case to chapter 7. Neither remedy is required, however; the court is vested with discretion to choose the course of action that is in the best interests of creditors and the estate. The court could retain the case in chapter 11 and appoint a trustee under § 1104(a). The plan could be modified and an attempt made to reconfirm the plan (hopefully without fraud this time), but only if the plan had not yet been substantially consummated, and only if the plan proponent or the debtor requested the modification.[785] § 1127(b).

§ 11.37 Attacking Confirmation: Appeal and Mootness

An order confirming a chapter 11 plan is a final order. The proper means by which a party in interest should challenge a confirmation order is to appeal the order. Unless the confirmation order is reversed or modified on a direct appeal, that order will be accorded *res judicata* effect, and may not later be collaterally attacked.[786] A notice of appeal must be filed within fourteen days after entry of the confirmation order. Rule 8002(a).

---

[781] See *Trico Marine*, supra note 745, 343 B.R. 68.

[782] *Delta Air Lines*, supra note 756, 386 B.R. at 532 ("[T]he statute bars revocations of the confirmation order in this case because an order satisfying the mandatory statutory predicate cannot be drafted.").

[783] See id.

[784] See Savoy Senior Hous. Corp. v. TRBC Ministries, LLC, 401 B.R. 589, 597–98 (S.D.N.Y. 2009).

[785] See § 11.19.

[786] See § 11.38.

The right to appeal a confirmation order may be more ephemeral than real, however. If the appellant does not obtain a stay of the confirmation order, there is a significant risk that the plan will be consummated, at least in part, and the appeal will become moot. An unstayed confirmation order is final, and parties are entitled to act pursuant to such a plan, even if an appeal is pending. Indeed, it is common for the plan proponent to move swiftly to commence implementing a plan after entry of the confirmation order, in order to enhance the likelihood of mooting any appeal.

An appellant has a right to request a stay of a confirmation order pending the disposition of the appeal. Rule 8005. If a stay is granted, the plan may not be implemented, and the appeal will not become moot. However, two factors make the right to seek a stay almost meaningless in many cases. First, the bankruptcy court is not required to grant a stay. Often the court will conclude that the potential harm from staying implementation of the plan outweighs the risk of mootness. Even though an appellant then has a right to seek a stay from the appellate court, the same hesitancy to derail the reorganization train will afflict that court. A second problem, related to the first, is that the court to whom a stay request is presented may require the appellant to post a supersedeas bond as a condition of the stay. The cost of such a bond could be astronomical in large corporate reorganizations, where millions or even billions of dollars are at stake. As a practical matter, then, obtaining a stay may be impossible. The fact that an appellant requests but is denied a stay of the confirmation order is not an excuse precluding application of the mootness doctrine.[787]

The term "mootness" is actually used in two different senses in the context of the appeal of a chapter 11 plan confirmation order. An appeal will be "moot" under Article III of the Constitution if it is impossible for the appellate court to grant meaningful or effective relief on appeal. In such a situation, there is no longer a live "case or controversy" before the federal courts.[788] However, an appeal is not moot in this constitutional sense merely because the appellate court cannot fully restore the parties to the *status quo ante*. If the court can fashion some form of meaningful relief, even if it only partially redresses the grievances of the prevailing party, the appeal is not constitutionally moot.[789]

However, even if an appeal is not constitutionally moot, because some form of relief can be given, the appellate court nevertheless may dismiss the appeal on "equitable" or "prudential" grounds. As the Second Circuit explained, "[e]quitable mootness is a doctrine distinct from constitutional mootness, though they have been discussed in the same breath. Equitable mootness is a prudential doctrine that is invoked to avoid disturbing a reorganization plan once implemented."[790] Courts also use "mootness" to describe this phenomenon, although in this context that term is

---

[787] E.g., In re Charter Commc'ns, Inc., 691 F.3d 476 (2d Cir. 2012); In re UNR Indus., 20 F.3d 766 (7th Cir.), cert. denied, 513 U.S. 999 (1994).

[788] See Church of Scientology v. United States, 506 U.S. 9, 12 (1992). The seminal case is *Mills v. Green*, 159 U.S. 651, 653 (1895).

[789] See, e.g., In re Thorpe Insulation Co., 677 F.3d 869 (9th Cir. 2012); In re Pac. Lumber Co., 584 F.3d 229 (5th Cir. 2009); In re Chateaugay Corp., 10 F.3d 944 (2d Cir. 1993). See generally In re Cont'l Airlines, 91 F.3d 553, 558 (1996) (en banc), cert. denied, 519 U.S 1057 (1997).

[790] In re Metromedia Fiber Network, Inc., 416 F.3d 136 (2d Cir. 2005).

misleading. As Judge Easterbrook observed in *In re UNR Industries*, "[t]here is a big difference between *inability* to alter the outcome (real mootness) and *unwillingness* to alter the outcome ('equitable mootness'). Using one word for two different concepts breeds confusion."[791]

What factors will an appellate court consider in determining whether to dismiss an appeal on equitable grounds? Those most commonly invoked include:[792]

- whether the reorganization plan has been substantially consummated;

- whether a stay has been obtained;

- whether the relief requested would affect the rights of parties not before the court;

- whether the relief requested would affect the success of the plan; and

- the public policy of affording finality to bankruptcy judgments.

Of these five factors, the most important consideration is whether the reorganization plan has been substantially consummated.[793] In fact, the Second Circuit presumes an appeal is equitably moot where the plan has been substantially consummated.[794] "Substantial consummation" does not mean that substantially *all* plan distributions have been made; it only requires the *commencement* of distribution under the plan, the transfer of property, and the assumption of control by the reorganized debtor or its successor. § 1101(2). These steps could take place within days after the entry of the confirmation order.[795] The emphasis on finding an appeal to be moot on equitable grounds is especially compelling in cases where the reorganization plan is complex and involves numerous intricate transactions, or where third parties have taken actions in reliance on the confirmation of the plan, such as by purchasing or selling assets, issuing or acquiring securities, entering into contracts or leases, and so forth.[796] Indeed, as mentioned earlier, one court stated that for "cases with more complicated plans of reorganization that impact greater numbers of interested parties, the time frame within which a request for revocation should be made necessarily

---

[791] 20 F.3d at 769 (emphasis in original).

[792] *Continental Airlines*, supra note 789, 91 F.3d at 560. See also In re Am. HomePatient, Inc., 420 F.3d 559 (6th Cir. 2005); In re Idearc, Inc., 662 F.3d 315 (5th Cir. 2011).

[793] See *Pacific Lumber*, supra note 789, 584 F.3d at 242 ("[P]lan consummation may often be dispositive of the question of equitable mootness."); *UNR Industries*, supra note 787, 20 F.3d 766.

[794] See *Charter Communications*, supra note 787, 691 F.3d at 482. Note that this presumption can be overcome if five factors are met: (1) the court can still order some effective relief; (2) such relief will not affect the re-emergence of the debtor as a revitalized corporate entity; (3) such relief will not unravel intricate transactions as to knock the props out from under the authorization for every transaction that has taken place and create an unmanageable, uncontrollable situation for the court; (4) the parties who would be adversely affected by the modification have notice of the appeal and an opportunity to participate; and (5) the appellant pursued all available remedies to obtain a stay of execution of the objectionable order if the failure to do so creates a situation rendering it inequitable to reverse the orders appealed from. Id.

[795] As they did in *Pacific Lumber*, supra note 789, 584 F.3d at 242.

[796] *Continental Airlines*, supra note 789, 91 F.3d at 560.

shortens because the level of difficulty required to comply with the statute and protect innocent third parties in a revocation order increases exponentially."[797]

Since both the complexity and third party reliance factors are common in large cases, as a practical matter it may be almost impossible for an appellant to avoid dismissal of the appeal on equitable mootness grounds. This is especially true if the challenge to the plan is global. An appellant has the best chance of avoiding mootness if their attack on the plan is narrow. An appellate court that would not be willing to upset the entire reorganization apple cart might be willing to take one or two apples out of that cart.

§ 11.38 Attacking Confirmation: Collateral Attack and Res Judicata

The provisions of a confirmed chapter 11 plan bind the debtor and any creditor, equity security holder, or general partner of the debtor, and any party issuing securities or acquiring property under the plan.[798] § 1141(a). The order confirming the plan is a final order. A party who wants to challenge a confirmation order and avoid the binding effect of confirmation should do so by appealing the order. Because of the considerable difficulty of obtaining a stay pending appeal, however, and the concomitant risk of mootness (whether "true" mootness or "equitable" mootness), a direct appellate challenge to the merits of a confirmation order may be unavailing.[799] May a disgruntled party, convinced that the confirmation order was entered in error, and perhaps even beyond the court's jurisdiction, collaterally attack the merits of the order confirming the plan?

The answer is no. Courts usually do not permit collateral attack of a final order of confirmation. Instead, a confirmation order will be given *res judicata* effect. The doctrine of res judicata bars parties who were before the court that entered the contested order from raising issues that were actually decided or that could have been decided by that court.[800] Res judicata is based on the need for finality in judicial proceedings.[801] In bankruptcy court, just as in any other court, parties are not entitled to a second bite at the judicial apple.[802]

The elements of res judicata, as described in a case that barred a collateral attack on a confirmed bankruptcy plan, are as follows: "[T]he parties must be identical in both

---

[797] In re Delta Air Lines, Inc., 386 B.R. 518, 533 (Bankr. S.D.N.Y. 2008).

[798] See § 11.35.

[799] See § 11.37.

[800] See In re Szostek, 886 F.2d 1405, 1408 (3d Cir. 1989).

[801] See Stoll v. Gottlieb, 305 U.S. 165, 172 (1938) ("It is just as important that there should be a place to end as that there should be a place to begin litigation. After a party has his day in court, with opportunity to present his evidence and his view of the law, a collateral attack upon the decision as to jurisdiction there rendered merely retries the issue previously determined.").

[802] As the Supreme Court observed in *Celotex Corp. v. Edwards*, 514 U.S. 300, 313 (1995):

"We have made clear that it is for the court of first instance to determine the question of the validity of the law, and until its decision is reversed for error by orderly review, either by itself or by a higher court, its orders based on its decision are to be respected. . . . If dissatisfied with the Bankruptcy Court's ultimate decision, respondents can appeal. . . . Respondents chose not to pursue this course of action, but instead to collaterally attack the Bankruptcy Court's [order]. This they cannot be permitted to do without seriously undercutting the orderly process of the law."

suits, the prior judgment must have been rendered by a court of competent jurisdiction, there must have been a final judgment on the merits, and the same cause of action must be involved in both cases."[803]

The foregoing recitation of the elements of res judicata suggests one situation in which the doctrine will not apply—when the complaining party was *not* before the court, and could not have raised the issue presented, because the claim later raised was based on acts that occurred *after* the confirmation of the plan. In short, actions that arise post-confirmation are not subject to the res judicata bar.[804]

The requirement that the order for which res judicata effect is being sought "must have been rendered by a court of competent jurisdiction" might be thought to indicate that a collateral attack on a final order would succeed if it could be shown that the order entered was beyond the subject matter jurisdiction of the bankruptcy court. This avenue seems especially attractive in those cases where the challenge is to a provision in a confirmed plan that purports to discharge and release *non-debtors*. So, for example, some courts have held that granting such non-debtor releases is beyond the powers of the bankruptcy court, and therefore orders purporting to do so should not be given binding effect.[805] While the majority view upholds non-debtor releases on the merits,[806] the important question here is whether a non-debtor release order should be protected from collateral attack *even if* the bankruptcy court order was erroneous on the merits. The answer should be yes.

Those decisions that hold otherwise misperceive the nature and operation of the res judicata inquiry, and ignore two prominent Supreme Court opinions, *Stoll v. Gottlieb*[807] and *Chicot County Drainage District v. Baxter State Bank*.[808] *Stoll* is of particular relevance, because the plan challenged in that case purported to release claims against a non-debtor guarantor. While the Court in *Stoll* recognized that "a court does not have the power, by judicial fiat, to extend its jurisdiction over matters beyond the scope of the authority granted to it by its creators,"[809] it went on to hold that "after a Federal court has decided the question of the jurisdiction over the parties as a contested issue, the court in which the plea of res judicata is made has not the power to inquire again into that jurisdictional fact."[810] The Court thus rebuffed the creditor's attempt to collaterally attack the release by suing the guarantor in state court. In *Stoll*, the parties had actually litigated the jurisdictional issue. *Chicot County* goes one step further, and makes clear that the bar of res judicata cannot be avoided by declining to challenge the court's jurisdiction at the time of confirmation.[811] Thus, if a

---

[803] Republic Supply Co. v. Shoaf, 815 F.2d 1046, 1051 (5th Cir. 1987).

[804] See, e.g., Donaldson v. Bernstein, 104 F.3d 547 (3d Cir. 1997); In re Pavlovich, 952 F.2d 114 (5th Cir. 1992).

[805] See, e.g., Underhill v. Royal, 769 F.2d 1426 (9th Cir. 1985); Union Carbide Corp. v. Newboles, 686 F.2d 593 (7th Cir. 1982).

[806] E.g., In re Metromedia Fiber Network, Inc., 416 F.3d 136 (2d Cir. 2005); In re Dow Corning Corp., 280 F.3d 648 (6th Cir.), cert. denied, 537 U.S. 816 (2002).

[807] 305 U.S. 165 (1938).

[808] 308 U.S. 371 (1940).

[809] 305 U.S. at 171.

[810] Id. at 172.

[811] 308 U.S. at 375. The Court in *Chicot County* further elaborated:

party believes that the bankruptcy court is acting beyond the scope of its jurisdictional authority in approving a particular term of the plan, under *Stoll* and *Chicot County* that party is required to raise the issue before the bankruptcy court, and appeal an adverse decision.

The bar of res judicata also has been applied after confirmation of a chapter 11 bankruptcy plan to preclude the debtor or its successor from suing parties after confirmation on causes of action that arose before confirmation, but which were not disclosed prior to the entry of the confirmation order.[812] These rulings prevent a debtor from unfairly surprising a party who might have consented to the chapter 11 plan without knowing of the debtor's intention later to bring suit against them.

§ 11.39 Implementation of a Plan and Distribution

Confirmation of a plan, while certainly the goal of a chapter 11 case, is not the end of the case. A bankruptcy case remains open until the court formally closes the case under § 350(a). Rule 3022 provides that the court shall enter a final decree closing the chapter 11 case only "[a]fter an estate is fully administered." In the chapter 11 context, closing may not occur for some years after confirmation, as full administration of a chapter 11 case could take a long time. The reorganized debtor or its successor must perform under the terms of the plan.

Some statutory assistance and encouragement regarding this task is provided by § 1142, concerning the implementation of the plan. Under § 1142(a), the debtor and any entity organized or to be organized to carry out the plan are given two directives: first, they "shall carry out the plan"; and second, they "shall comply with any orders of the court." Non-bankruptcy laws relating to financial condition are expressly preempted by § 1142(a). Under Rule 3021, after a plan is confirmed, "distribution shall be made" to creditors and indenture trustees with allowed claims, and to those security holders of record at the time distribution commences whose claims or interests have not been disallowed.

The court is given the discretionary power to facilitate implementation of the plan in § 1142(b), by directing the debtor and any other necessary party (1) to execute and deliver any instrument required to transfer property under the plan, and (2) to perform any other act necessary for consummation of the plan, such as the satisfaction of a lien. The bankruptcy court's general equitable powers under § 105(a) also support the entry

---

"The lower federal courts are all courts of limited jurisdiction, that is, with only the jurisdiction which Congress has prescribed. But none the less they are courts with authority, when parties are brought before them in accordance with the requirements of due process, to determine whether or not they have jurisdiction to entertain the cause and for this purpose to construe and apply the statute under which they are asked to act. Their determinations of such questions, while open to direct review, may not be assailed collaterally. . . . The court has the authority to pass upon its own jurisdiction and its decree sustaining jurisdiction against attack, while open to direct review, is res judicata in a collateral action. Whatever the contention as to jurisdiction may be, whether it is that the boundaries of a valid statute have been transgressed, or that the statute itself is invalid, the question of jurisdiction is still one for judicial determination."

Id. at 376–77.

[812] See, e.g., Eubanks v. FDIC, 977 F.2d 166 (5th Cir. 1992); Sure–Snap Corp. v. State St. Bank & Trust Co., 948 F.2d 869 (2d Cir. 1991).

of orders by the court after confirmation to help effectuate the plan. Furthermore, Rule 3020(d) provides that "[n]otwithstanding the entry of the order of confirmation, the court may issue any other order necessary to administer the estate."

Section 1143 prescribes a time limit on the acts that must be taken by a party to participate in a plan distribution. If the plan requires presentment or surrender of a security, or the performance of any other act as a condition of participation, that act must be taken within five years after the confirmation order is entered. If the party does not act within five years, it forfeits its right to participate in the distribution.

A question that has led to a difference of opinion in the courts concerns the extent of the bankruptcy court's subject matter jurisdiction after confirmation. The fundamental point of disagreement is whether the plan must specifically provide for the retention of jurisdiction (as was the practice under old chapter XI), or whether full jurisdiction continues even without specification in the plan (as was the practice under old chapter X). Stated otherwise, is the bankruptcy court's post-confirmation jurisdiction inherently more circumscribed than its pre-confirmation jurisdiction? Many disputes, issues, and problems may arise in the months or years after confirmation that may be required to make distributions, transfer property, recover assets, prosecute actions, and complete performance under the plan. While retention-of-jurisdiction provisions in plans are commonplace, are they a necessity?

A minority line of authority has taken the mistaken view that post-confirmation jurisdiction is narrower than pre-confirmation jurisdiction, and that generally the bankruptcy court only has the jurisdiction after confirmation to implement the specific terms of the plan, except to the extent the plan expressly reserves a broader jurisdiction.[813] This perception of a constriction of the bankruptcy court's subject matter jurisdiction at the instant of confirmation is a mirage, and contradicts the plain meaning of the relevant jurisdictional statutes.[814] Under 28 U.S.C. § 1334(b), the district court is given jurisdiction "of all civil proceedings arising under title 11, or arising in or related to cases under title 11." Under 28 U.S.C. § 157, the bankruptcy court is given the power to exercise the jurisdiction conferred on the district court. Nothing in § 1334(b) suggests a difference in the scope of the subject matter jurisdiction in bankruptcy before and after confirmation. The only relevant question should be whether the action "arises under" title 11, "arises in" title 11, or is "related to" a title 11 case. While it may be that some post-confirmation actions involving the reorganized debtor would not have an effect on the bankruptcy case, and do not arise under or in a title 11 case, and thus would not be within the jurisdiction conferred by § 1334(b), the absence of jurisdiction is predicated on the failure to meet the statutory requirements of arising under, arising in, or related to—not on some judicial gloss regarding a narrowed jurisdiction. By the same token, then, an action that clearly does

---

[813] See, e.g., Alderwoods Grp., Inc. v. Garcia, 682 F.3d 958 (11th Cir. 2012); In re DPH Holdings Corp., 448 Fed.Appx 134 (2d Cir. 2011); In re Craig's Stores of Texas, Inc., 266 F.3d 388 (5th Cir. 2001); In re Johns–Manville Corp., 7 F.3d 32, 34 (2d Cir. 1993); Goodman v. Phillip R. Curtis Enters., Inc., 809 F.2d 228 (4th Cir. 1987).

[814] See In re In re Gainey Corp., 447 B.R. 807 (Bankr. W.D. Mich. 2011); Thickstun Bros. Equip. Co., Inc., 344 B.R. 515 (B.A.P. 6th Cir. 2006); Harstad v. First Am. Bank, 155 B.R. 500 (Bankr. D. Minn. 1993), aff'd, 39 F.3d 898 (8th Cir. 1994). See also Frank R. Kennedy & Gerald K. Smith, Postconfirmation Issues: The Effects of Confirmation and Postconfirmation Proceedings, 44 S.C. L. Rev. 621, 630–44 (1993).

arises under title 11, such as an action to recover a preference under § 547, would fall within the subject matter jurisdiction of the bankruptcy court, whether brought before or after confirmation, irrespective of whether jurisdiction was retained in the plan.[815]

That the court might have jurisdiction does not necessarily mean that the post-confirmation lawsuit will be allowed to proceed, however. On three different grounds, prosecution of the action may be barred. The first is *res judicata*.[816] If the action existed before confirmation, but was not mentioned in the plan, res judicata may preclude the debtor from asserting the existence of the cause of action after confirmation.[817] A second and related ground for dismissal is judicial estoppel. The putative defendant may have been misled by the plan's silence regarding the action.[818] Finally, the reorganized debtor may not have standing to prosecute the action, if the plan did not specifically provide for the retention of the cause of action, as permitted by § 1123(b)(3).[819]

§ 11.40   Serial Cases: "Chapter 22"

Before a chapter 11 plan can be confirmed, the bankruptcy court must find that "confirmation of the plan is not likely to be followed by the liquidation, or the need for further financial reorganization, of the debtor or any successor to the debtor under the plan." § 1129(a)(11). In short, the court must find that the plan is "feasible."[820] A finding of feasibility, of course, is not a guarantee of success—as the statistics starkly reveal. A fairly high percentage of confirmed plans fail; studies have found post-confirmation failure rates ranging from 25% to 40% of all confirmed cases.[821] If the reorganized debtor defaults under a confirmed plan, what happens next?

One possibility is for the debtor or plan proponent to attempt to modify the plan under § 1127(b), to make it easier for the reorganized debtor to comply with the plan obligations.[822] In most cases, however, post-confirmation modification will not be an available remedy, because (except for individual debtors) the modification must be effected before "substantial consummation" of the plan, which occurs quite soon after confirmation of the plan and the commencement of distribution. Another option would be for the court to dismiss the chapter 11 case or to convert the case to chapter 7, whichever is in the best interests of creditors and the estate. Material default under the plan would constitute "cause" for dismissal or conversion. § 1112(b)(4)(N). A third

---

[815]   See generally In re Diabetes Am., Inc., 485 B.R. 340 (Bankr. S.D. Tex. 2012).

[816]   See § 11.38.

[817]   See Eubanks v. FDIC, 977 F.2d 166 (5th Cir. 1992).

[818]   See Payless Wholesale Distribs., Inc. v. Alberto Culver, Inc., 989 F.2d 570 (1st Cir.), cert. denied, 510 U.S. 931 (1993).

[819]   *Harstad*, supra note 814, 39 F.3d 898.

[820]   See § 11.28.

[821]   See, e.g., Elizabeth Warren & Jay Lawrence Westbrook, The Success of Chapter 11: A Challenge to the Critics, 107 Mich. L. Rev. 603, 610 (2009); Edith S. Hotchkiss, Post–Bankruptcy Performance and Management Turnover, 50 J. Fin. 3 (1995); Susan Jensen–Conklin, Do Confirmed Chapter 11 Plans Consummate? The Results of a Study and Analysis of the Law, 97 Com. L.J. 297 (1992); Lynn M. LoPucki & William C. Whitford, Patterns in the Bankruptcy Reorganization of Large, Publicly Held Companies, 78 Cornell L. Rev. 597 (1993).

[822]   See § 11.19.

possibility would be to appoint a trustee to replace the debtor. § 1104(a). Unless the order confirming the plan was procured by fraud, however, the court would not have the power to revoke the confirmation order.[823] § 1144.

A significant number[824] of defaulting chapter 11 debtors have taken yet another course: file a *second* chapter 11 petition, while still attempting to carry out the terms of the plan confirmed in the *first* case. This tactic is known as a "chapter 22" filing (derived, of course, by adding the second chapter "11" case to the first and still open chapter "11" case). May a debtor make such a "serial" "chapter 22" bankruptcy filing? There is no express Code prohibition against this sort of repeat filing. The only repetitive filing bar is § 109(g), which precludes a debtor from refiling within 180 days after taking a voluntary dismissal in a previous bankruptcy case under certain circumstances. That ban obviously does not apply to a second chapter 11 filing.

In the early years of the Code, a few bankruptcy courts announced what amounted to a *per se* rule against successive chapter 11 filings.[825] These courts were concerned about the potential for abuse by debtors and by the possible evasion of the limits on post-confirmation modification in § 1127(b). In 1989, however, the Seventh Circuit upheld a serial chapter 11 filing in *In re Jartran, Inc.,*[826] rejecting the *per se* ban and finding that the bankruptcy court had not abused its discretion in finding that the debtor had filed the second chapter 11 case in "good faith." In *Jartran,* the second case proposed a liquidating plan, and the court found that this was a new and permissible purpose that had not been pursued in the first case. The court emphasized that the debtor was not trying to restructure its plan obligations. Furthermore, the Seventh Circuit relied on the absence of a statutory ban on refiling akin to that in § 109(g).

A similar line of reasoning was adopted by the Supreme Court in 1991 in a related context in *Johnson v. Home State Bank,*[827] in holding that a "chapter 20" filing (chapter 7 followed by chapter 13) was not *per se* invalid, but had to be tested in the crucible of good faith. The Fifth Circuit agreed in *In re Elmwood Development Co.*[828] that serial "chapter 22" filings were not absolutely banned, but should be policed via a good faith scrutiny. In *Elmwood,* however, the court held that the debtor had acted in bad faith in filing the second case. In that case, the debtor filed the second chapter 11 just before a "drop dead" date in the confirmed plan would have permitted the major creditor to foreclose.

If a debtor can show an "unanticipated change of circumstances" after the plan in the first case was confirmed, the court might be more willing to find that the second

---

[823] See § 11.36.

[824] There were 197 chapter 22 cases filed between 1984 and 2008, though there were nineteen repeat filers in 2008 (more than any prior year), suggesting this may be an upward trend. Edward I. Altman et al., Post–Chapter 11 Bankruptcy Performance: Avoiding Chapter 22, 21 J. Applied Corp. Fin. 53 (2009).

[825] See In re AT of Maine, Inc., 56 B.R. 55 (Bankr. D. Me. 1985); In re Northampton Corp., 37 B.R. 110 (Bankr. E.D. Pa. 1984).

[826] 886 F.2d 859 (7th Cir. 1989).

[827] 501 U.S. 78, 87 (1991).

[828] 964 F.2d 508 (5th Cir. 1992).

filing was made in good faith.[829] In that event, the second filing would be consistent with the purposes and policies of chapter 11. If the alleged "changes" were readily foreseeable at the time the first plan was confirmed, though, the court will cast a skeptical eye on the debtor's protestations of good faith. More than a mere shift in market conditions must be shown. For example, one court held that the recent decline in the economy was not an unforeseeable and changed circumstance substantially impairing the debtor's ability to perform under the first confirmed case, as to justify a second chapter 11 filing.[830] As evidenced by *Jartran*, courts also may be more receptive to a second filing that proposes only to liquidate the debtor.

If the second case is upheld, the obligations that will be dealt with must be judged by reference to the second filing. Thus, in *Jartran* the administrative claim of a claimant in the first case was not accorded priority status in case number two, as the previous administrative expense claim arose prior to the second filing, and did not benefit the estate in the second one.[831]

---

[829]   See, e.g., In re 1633 Broadway Mars Rest. Corp., 388 B.R. 490 (Bankr. S.D.N.Y. 2008); In re Motel Props., Inc., 314 B.R. 889 (Bankr. S.D. Ga. 2004); In re Casa Loma Assocs., 122 B.R. 814 (Bankr. N.D. Ga. 1991); In re Garsal Realty, Inc., 98 B.R. 140 (Bankr. N.D.N.Y. 1989).

[830]   In re Caviata Attached Homes, LLC, 481 B.R. 34 (B.A.P. 9th Cir. 2012).

[831]   886 F.2d at 870–71.

Chapter 12

INDIVIDUAL DEBT ADJUSTMENTS
UNDER CHAPTER 13

A. INTRODUCTION

§ 12.1   Theory and Purposes of Chapter 13

Congress intended for chapter 13 to function as the primary rehabilitation chapter for individual consumer debtors.[1] For individuals needing bankruptcy relief, the choice usually is between liquidating under chapter 7 and reorganizing under chapter 13, rather than whether to reorganize under chapter 11 or 13.[2] Chapter 13 permits a debtor to retain her property and repay her creditors pursuant to a court-approved plan over three to five years.

Congress has expressed the belief that chapter 13 could benefit both the debtor and her creditors.[3] For creditors, the obvious attraction of chapter 13 is the prospect of getting paid more on their claims. To be confirmed, a chapter 13 plan must provide that unsecured creditors will be paid at least as much as they would receive in a chapter 7 liquidation,[4] § 1325(a)(4), and secured creditors must be paid the value of their collateral (and in some cases the full amount of the debt).[5] § 1325(a)(5). Chapter 13 supposedly offers several benefits to the debtor. First, the debtor may keep her non-exempt property; in chapter 7, that property either would be turned over to the trustee for distribution to creditors, or would be subject to foreclosure by secured creditors. Chapter 13 gives a debtor a chance to retain her house, car, and other property, even if the debtor currently is in default and facing foreclosure. Second, a debtor who pays more on her debts in chapter 13 may emerge from bankruptcy with a better credit rating.[6] Finally, Congress thought that debtors might prefer to avoid the stigma of straight bankruptcy.

Congress may have indulged in some wishful thinking. Most debtors would prefer to liquidate immediately under chapter 7, receive a discharge, and move on.[7] The "opportunity" to pay creditors more money for several years under chapter 13 is one that many consumer debtors happily ignore. The chapter 13 option is particularly unappealing to a debtor who has few if any nonexempt assets (and thus little to lose in chapter 7), but substantial future earning capacity (and thus much to lose in chapter

---

[1]   H.R. Rep. No. 95–595, 95th Cong., 1st Sess., at 118 (1977).

[2]   Section 12.3 discusses the merits of chapter 13 versus chapters 7 or 11.

[3]   H.R. Rep. No. 95–595, 95th Cong., 1st Sess., at 118 (1977).

[4]   See § 12.16.

[5]   See § 12.18.

[6]   See H.R. Rep. No. 95–959, 95th Cong., 1st Sess., at 118 (1977) ("Chapter 13 also protects a debtor's credit standing far better than a straight bankruptcy, because he is viewed by the credit industry as a better risk.").

[7]   See § 12.3.

13). If allowed to do so, such a debtor could gain the unfettered enjoyment of her future earnings through a chapter 7 discharge, in exchange for relinquishing only her few nonexempt assets. Even if the debtor wanted to retain secured property, the debtor could seek just to reaffirm that one secured debt,[8] or to redeem the collateral if possible.[9] Chapter 13 is needed only if the creditor will not agree to reaffirm, the debtor cannot redeem, or the debtor needs to cure a default or reverse an acceleration. One could make a defensible argument that chapter 13 so rarely benefits a consumer debtor, and so often is chosen to the debtor's disadvantage due to misinformation, that from the perspective of debtors, chapter 13 should be repealed.[10] Nor does chapter 13 even work very often. Empirical studies show a relatively low rate of chapter 13 completion, with an accordingly low percentage of debtors actually receiving a discharge.[11]

Furthermore, unlike the "old days," credit often is readily available even for recent bankrupts. Indeed, the time bar on successive discharges[12] may make a recent bankrupt a safer credit risk than a debtor who is free to file bankruptcy and receive a discharge at any time. Finally, only the naive or quaintly moralistic would consider the so-called "stigma"[13] of bankruptcy a legitimate policy determinant in an era in which over one million Americans file for bankruptcy relief every year.[14]

In light of the reality that debtors exercising their unrestrained self-interest would choose chapter 7 over chapter 13 much more often than Congress would like, the question for legislators is how to respond. One possibility is to concede defeat, and gripe about the moral bankruptcy of fiscal bankrupts. Congress has not opted for that course—nor would the consumer credit industry let it do so.

A second possibility is to make debtors proceed under chapter 13, whether they like it or not. In short, Congress could permit creditors to file involuntary chapter 13 cases, or move to convert chapter 7 cases to chapter 13. Congress has not opted for the compulsion approach either, although it came much closer in 2005. Even in the post-BAPCPA world, though, an involuntary chapter 13 case cannot be commenced, § 303(a), and a case cannot be converted from another chapter to chapter 13, except on the debtor's request. §§ 706(c), 707(b)(1), 1112(d). This prohibition holds even if a debtor's chapter 7 case is subject to dismissal for "abuse" under § 707(b)(1); it still

---

[8] See §§ 10.34–10.35.

[9] See §§ 7.32.c., 9.13.

[10] See, e.g., Jean Braucher, Lawyers and Consumer Bankruptcy: One Code, Many Cultures, 67 Am. Bankr. L.J. 501, 506 n.19 (1993); William C. Whitford, Has the Time Come to Repeal Chapter 13?, 65 Ind. L.J. 85 (1989).

[11] Jean Braucher, An Empirical Study of Debtor Education in Bankruptcy: Impact on Chapter 13 Completion Not Shown, 9 Am. Bankr. L. Rev. 557, 571–74 (2001).

[12] See § 10.11. See also 11 U.S.C. § 727(a)(8), (9).

[13] See H.R. Rep. No. 95–595, 95th Cong., 1st Sess., at 118 (1977) ("In addition, it satisfied many debtors' desire to avoid the stigma attached to straight bankruptcy and to retain the pride attendant on being able to meet one's obligations.").

[14] For example, in 2012, there were 1,219,132 nonbusiness bankruptcy petitions filed. United States Courts, Bankruptcy Cases Filed, Terminated, and Pending, Fiscal Years 2008–2012, Table 6 (2013), available at http://www.uscourts.gov/Statistics/JudicialBusiness/2012/us-bankruptcy-courts.aspx.

Compare this number with the 34,873 petitions (including business) filed in 1952. See Charles Elihu Nadler, The Problem of the Insolvent Wage Earner, 16 Bus. Law. 390, 390 (1961).

remains the debtor's choice whether to consent to a conversion to chapter 13, or to just let the court go ahead and dismiss. The "voluntariness" of chapter 13 is further reinforced in that the debtor is even free to change her mind after filing chapter 13, and move either to dismiss the case or convert it to chapter 7.[15] § 1307(a), (b).

In rejecting the use of a mandated chapter 13 procedure in 1978, Congress determined that involuntary repayment plans (1) raise constitutional issues regarding involuntary servitude, and (2) are unlikely to be successful anyway if the debtor does not want to perform.[16] Having said that, the amendments in 2005 that do allow involuntary *chapter 11* cases to be filed against individual debtors, § 303(a), and which otherwise conform chapter 11 to chapter 13 in most important respects for individual debtors,[17] undercut the force of that earlier congressional policy determination.[18] In short, if Congress can do what it did to chapter 11 for individuals, there is little reason not to also allow involuntary chapter 13 cases as well.

Instead, however, Congress has adopted a "carrot and stick" approach to try to influence debtors to "choose" chapter 13. Originally, one important "carrot" was the debtor's ability to modify and write down secured claims, §§ 1322(b)(2), 1325(a)(5), and retain collateral in chapter 13. § 1306(b). Another big carrot was the chapter 13 "superdischarge." § 1328(a). As enacted in 1978, the Code allowed a debtor who completed performance under the chapter 13 plan to discharge many types of debts that would not be dischargeable in chapter 7, even including debts based on fraud or on a willful and malicious injury.[19] However, Congress has steadily nibbled away at the most important chapter 13 carrots ever since enacting the Code in 1978, until now there is hardly more than the stem of a carrot left. With regard to secured claims, a debtor now cannot strip down an undersecured claim either on her home, § 1322(b)(2), or on many car loans, § 1325(a)(5), which are of course by far the most important forms of collateral to debtors. Similarly, Congress has created more and more exceptions to

---

[15]   See § 2.16. However, note that after the Supreme Court's decision in *Marrama v. Citizen's Bank*, 549 U.S. 365 (2007), the courts divide over the question of whether this right to convert or dismiss from chapter 13 is absolute, or is qualified by the authority of a bankruptcy court to deny a debtor's request on grounds of bad-faith conduct. Compare In re Procel, 467 B.R. 297 (S.D.N.Y. 2012) (holding that the right is absolute, pursuant to a pre-*Marrama* case, *In re Barbieri*, 199 F.3d 616 (2d Cir. 1999)), with In re Jacobsen, 609 F.3d 647 (5th Cir. 2010) (holding that the right is not absolute); In re Rosson, 545 F.3d 764 (9th Cir. 2008) (same).

[16]   H.R. Rep. No. 95–595, 95th Cong., 1st Sess., at 120–21 (1977).

[17]   For example, § 1115 brings post-petition property into the estate just like § 1306(a), § 1129(a)(15) operates the same as § 1325(b)(1)(B) by permitting a debtor to overcome objections to their plan by pledging all projected disposable income, and like § 1322(a)(1), § 1123(a)(8) requires a debtor's plan to provide creditors with payment from their post-petition earnings.

[18]   See Margaret Howard, Bankruptcy Bondage, 2009 U. Ill. L. Rev. 191, 234–35 (2009).

[19]   See § 12.23.

the superdischarge.[20] Furthermore, debtors now must commit all of their "projected disposable income" to plan payments.[21] § 1325(b)(1)(B).

The biggest "stick" is the "abuse" test of § 707(b),[22] which bars access to chapter 7 for many consumer debtors with a modest ability to repay debts. As modified in 2005 and indexed through 2013, this test creates a presumption of abuse in cases where a debtor with income above the state median has sufficient excess income to repay her unsecured creditors at least $124.59 to $207.92 a month (depending on the amount of debt). If an abuse is found the chapter 7 case must be dismissed, unless the debtor "consents" instead to a conversion to chapter 13. § 707(b)(1).

Curiously, Congress also professes to persist in the belief that many more debtors would choose chapter 13 if they just had all of the facts.[23] One example of this view is § 341(d)(2), which requires the trustee to tell the debtor at the chapter 7 meeting that the debtor could file under another chapter. The (probably vain) hope is that the debtor will "see the light" and convert to chapter 13. In 2005 Congress added two provisions that seek to educate individual consumer debtors about the possible benefits of chapter 13 even before they file bankruptcy. The bankruptcy clerk must give the debtor a notice describing the various chapters and the benefits of each. § 342(b)(1)(A).

§ 12.2   Historical Antecedents and Areas of Reform

The forerunner of chapter 13 was chapter XIII of the prior Bankruptcy Act.[24] Congress enacted chapter XIII in the Chandler Act of 1938,[25] providing "Wage Earners' Plans," which allowed individual wage earners to retain their property and compose their debts through a plan that was accepted by creditors. Practice under chapter XIII varied widely throughout the country. In some regions, it was used extensively, while in others it was virtually a dead letter.[26]

In the bankruptcy reforms of the 1970s, Congress determined that chapter XIII was not working well. As the House Report explained, "an overly stringent and formalized chapter XIII (wage earner plans) has discouraged overextended debtors

---

[20]   Debts which were added to the exclusions from the superdischarge from 1978 to 2005 were for: educational loans, §§ 523(a)(8), 1328(a)(2); drunk driving, §§ 523(a)(9), 1328(a)(2); and restitution or criminal fines, § 1328(a)(3). In 2005, BAPCA added exclusions for debts for: certain taxes, § 523(a)(1)(B) & (C), § 507(a)(8)(C), § 1328(a)(2); fraud, § 523(a)(2), § 1328(a)(2); unscheduled debts, § 523(a)(3), § 1328(a)(2); fiduciary fraud or defalcation, larceny or embezzlement, § 523(a)(4), § 1328(a)(2); and willful or malicious injury, § 1328(a)(4). See also § 12.23.

[21]   See § 12.17.

[22]   See § 2.15.

[23]   Also, Congress added a requirement that before individual consumer debtors can be eligible to file bankruptcy at all, they must obtain financial counseling. § 109(h). Part of the thinking was that upon being counseled, many debtors would select chapter 13 instead of chapter 7. Interestingly, the "Bankruptcy Basics" materials available on the United States Courts website contains a separate section for "Advantages of Chapter 13" under chapter 13 materials, while the chapter 7 section contains an "Alternatives to Chapter 7" section instead, further highlighting advantages of chapter 13. United States Courts, Bankruptcy Basics, http://www.uscourts.gov/FederalCourts/Bankruptcy/BankruptcyBasics.aspx (last visited June 2, 2013).

[24]   Bankruptcy Act §§ 601–686, codified at 11 U.S.C. §§ 1001–1086 (repealed 1979).

[25]   Ch. 575, 52 Stat. 840 (1938).

[26]   Charles Elihu Nadler, The Problem of the Insolvent Wage Earner, 16 Bus. Law. 390, 398 (1961).

from attempting to arrange a repayment plan."[27] The Senate Report lamented that chapter XIII "has been one of the least understood and most erratically applied of all federal statutes dealing with bankruptcy or social welfare."[28] In particular, Congress identified six major problems with chapter XIII, and came up with the accompanying solutions (some of which have been modified substantially since 1978):[29]

1.   Eligibility for relief was too narrow. Only a "wage earner," defined as "an individual whose principal income is derived from wages, salary, or commissions," Act § 606(8), was eligible. Excluded were small business owners, self-employed individuals, or social welfare recipients. Congress pointed out that "the distinction between a barber, grocer, or worm-digger who is self-employed from one who is an employee is slight."[30]

The solution in the 1978 Code? Expand eligibility to include *any* "individual with regular income," from whatever source, with debts below a stated amount. § 109(e).

2.   A "hardship" discharge could only be granted after three years had elapsed. Act § 661. In addition, all of the exceptions to discharge applied with full force in chapter XIII, even if the debtor received a full-compliance discharge. Act § 660.

Solution: Permit the court to grant a hardship discharge "at any time" after confirmation of the plan,[31] § 1328(b), and exclude many of the discharge exceptions from the full-compliance discharge.[32] § 1328(a). Since 1978, Congress has retreated substantially from the latter policy.

3.   "Secured creditors [were] dealt with erratically, tediously, and uncertainly."[33]

Solution: Clarify the treatment of secured creditors, and permit modification, cure, and cram down.[34] §§ 1325(a)(5), 1322(b)(2), (3), (5).

4.   Creditors were able to exert leverage against the debtor and obtain favorable treatment by pressuring accommodation codebtors for payment.

Solution: Provide for a stay of actions against individual codebtors on consumer debts.[35] § 1301.

5.   Creditors were entitled to vote on plans, with a plan being confirmable only if a majority of unsecured creditors and all secured creditors accepted the plan. Act § 652.

---

[27]   H.R. Rep. No. 95–595, 95th Cong., 1st Sess., at 117 (1977).

[28]   S. Rep. No. 95–989, 95th Cong., 2d Sess., at 12 (1978).

[29]   Id. at 13; H.R. Rep. No. 95–595, 95th Cong., 1st Sess., at 116–25 (1977). For a discussion of the differences in the new and old chapters, see Hon. Joe Lee, Chapter 13 nee Chapter XIII, 53 Am. Bankr. L.J. 303 (1979).

[30]   H.R. Rep. No. 95–595, 95th Cong., 1st Sess., at 119 (1977).

[31]   See § 12.24.

[32]   See § 12.23.

[33]   S. Rep. No. 95–989, 95th Cong., 2d Sess., at 13 (1978).

[34]   See §§ 12.12, 12.18.

[35]   See § 12.8.

This resulted in the rejection of feasible plans by creditors, the filing of unrealistic plans or a premature resort to liquidation by debtors, and the imposition of substantial costs on the process with little benefit.

Solution: Eliminate creditor voting, substituting the best interests and projected disposable income tests for unsecured creditors,[36] §§ 1325(a)(4), 1325(b)(b)(1), and modification and cram down for secured creditors.[37] §§ 1322(b)(2), 1325(a)(5).

6.　　There was no time limit on the length of plans, with some plans going for as long as ten years. This undermined the debtor's fresh start, as well as creating serious feasibility problems.

Solution: Limit plans to three years in length, unless the court for cause extends the plan period, with an absolute maximum of five years. § 1322(d). In 2005, Congress changed the presumptive plan length to five years for debtors with incomes above the state median.[38]

Congress retained some features of chapter XIII practice. The basic structure of the chapter, as a repayment plan carried out by an individual debtor, who retained possession of her property subject to court protection, and whose discharge was entered after the completion of payments, was kept. Additionally, Congress continued the rules that relief under chapter 13 is purely voluntary with the debtor, § 303(a),[39] and that only the debtor may propose a plan. § 1321.[40]

§ 12.3　　Planning: Weighing the Chapter 13 Alternative

Congress intended for chapter 13 to be the chapter of choice for individual consumer debtors.[41] Not only might chapter 13 be beneficial to some debtors, creditors also normally will get paid more under a repayment plan than in a straight liquidation. For most consumer debtors, the alternative to filing for relief under chapter 13 would be to liquidate under chapter 7. Whether to proceed under chapter 13 is purely voluntary with the debtor. § 303(a). Below, the pros and cons of chapter 13 versus chapter 7 for the debtor are highlighted.

In 1984, Congress sought to influence the debtor's "choice" between chapter 13 and chapter 7 by empowering the court to dismiss a chapter 7 case on the ground of "substantial abuse." In 2005, in BAPCPA Congress replaced this old substantial abuse test with a more detailed, more draconian, and less discretionary "abuse" test,[42] § 707(b)(1), with presumptive abuse being established pursuant to a "means" test. § 707(b)(2). This means test seeks to bar supposed "can pay" debtors from chapter 7, and to ensure that debtors repay creditors the maximum they can afford.[43] If abuse is

---

[36]　See § 12.16.

[37]　See §§ 12.12, 12.18.

[38]　See § 12.14.

[39]　See H.R. Rcp. No. 95–595, 95th Cong., 1st Sess., at 120–21 (1977).

[40]　Id. at 123.

[41]　H.R. Rep. No. 95–595, 95th Cong., 1st Sess., at 118 (1977).

[42]　See § 2.15.

[43]　See H.R. Rep. No. 109–31(I), 109th Cong., 1st Sess., at 89 (2005).

found, the debtor must choose between letting the court dismiss the chapter 7 case or "consent" to conversion to chapter 13.

For some debtors engaged in business, or debtors who are ineligible for chapter 13 because of excessive debt[44] but want to retain their property and reorganize, chapter 11 may be an alternative to chapter 13. As will be discussed, most debtors would select chapter 13 over chapter 11. The few advantages chapter 11 enjoyed over chapter 13 for individual consumer debtors were largely eliminated in 2005. A family farmer debtor who meets the eligibility requirements for both chapters may choose between seeking relief under chapter 13 or chapter 12. In most cases, however, chapter 12 will be the preferred choice for a family farmer.[45]

Chapter 13 versus chapter 7: Benefits of chapter 13

As noted above, Congress hoped and intended that most consumer debtors would choose chapter 13 over chapter 7.[46] Selecting chapter 13 relief is voluntary with the debtor, however. Assuming that a debtor actually has a choice (which she may not because of the chapter 7 abuse test), what factors should a debtor weigh in deciding whether to file under chapter 7 or chapter 13? Chapter 13 has many benefits over chapter 7. These include:

- Debtor will retain her nonexempt property in chapter 13, § 1306(b), but in chapter 7 must turn over nonexempt property to trustee for liquidation and distribution to creditors.[47] § 704(a)(1).

- Chapter 13 debtor can retain some types of collateral by paying the secured creditor only the value of the collateral, even if less than the debt owed, in installments.[48] § 1325(a)(5). In chapter 7, however, the debtor can only retain collateral by reaffirming, § 524(c), which usually requires payment of the total debt, or by redeeming, § 722, which cannot be done in installments. As of 2005, though, this advantage had been substantially curtailed, as the "strip down" of an undersecured claim is allowed neither with respect to home mortgages nor to many security interests in automobiles—in short, the most important collateral to debtors.

- Debtor's ability to retain collateral in chapter 13 is further aided by the power to cure defaults, § 1322(b)(3), reverse an acceleration, § 1322(b)(5), and modify secured claims, § 1322(b)(2).[49] Conversely, in chapter 7, none of these remedies are available. The only exceptions in chapter 13 to these beneficial rules are

---

[44] To be eligible for chapter 13 a debtor may not have more than $383,175 in noncontingent, liquidated unsecured debts and $1,149,525 in noncontingent, liquidated secured debts. § 109(e). These debt limits were raised dramatically in 1994 (and again in 2005) and have been indexed triannually, most recently in April 2013. Prior to 1994, a debtor was ineligible for chapter 13 if she had more than $100,000 in unsecured or $350,000 in secured debts.

[45] See § 13.2.

[46] § 12.1.

[47] H.R. Rep. No. 95–595, 95th Cong., 1st Sess., at 118 (1977).

[48] See § 12.18.

[49] See § 12.12.

for, first, a home mortgage loan, which can be cured and deaccelerated, but which cannot be modified, § 1322(b)(2), and second, for certain security interests in cars and other personal property, as to which the full debt must be repaid, even if greater than the collateral value. § 1325(a)(5).

- Debtor can cure defaults and modify unsecured claims in chapter 13. § 1322(b)(2), (3), (5).

- A chapter 13 debtor who completes performance under the plan will receive a "superdischarge," § 1328(a), which discharges some types of debts under § 523(a) that are excluded from a chapter 7 discharge.[50] However, BAPCPA eliminated some of the most important debts that were previously included in the "superdischarge," although chapter 13 debtors can still receive a discharge of certain debts that are not dischargeable under chapter 7. Prior to 2005, some courts limited the debtor's power to take advantage of this privilege by holding that a debtor who seeks to use chapter 13 to discharge otherwise nondischargeable debts has acted in bad faith.[51] § 1325(a)(3). After BAPCPA, the need for such judicial policing has been greatly reduced.

- Debtor will be allowed (indeed, required, § 1322(a)(2)) to pay nondischargeable domestic support obligations in full over the life of the chapter 13 plan, in preference to other unsecured claims.

- If court allows separate classification and treatment,[52] a debtor in chapter 13 may be able to pay other debts that are nondischargeable in chapter 13 (such as student loans) in full under the plan, in preference to other unsecured claims.

- Discharge in chapter 13 will be denied only for nonperformance or failure to complete the required debtor education under § 1328(g), unlike chapter 7, which provides numerous grounds for denying discharge. § 727(a).

- Debtor who pays 100% of unsecured claims in chapter 13, or 70% in good faith and as the debtor's best effort, will not be subject to six-year bar to discharge in a subsequent chapter 7 case. § 727(a)(9).

- If debtor pays unsecured debts in full in chapter 13, she will emerge from bankruptcy with a better credit rating than if she liquidates and creditors are not paid in full.[53]

- A debtor may reject or assign unfavorable or unnecessary contracts in chapter 13. § 1322(b)(7).

---

[50] See § 12.23.

[51] See § 12.15.

[52] See § 12.11.

[53] H.R. Rep. No. 95–595, 95th Cong., 1st Sess., at 118 (1977) ("Chapter 13 also protects a debtor's credit standing far better than a straight bankruptcy, because he is viewed by the credit industry as a better risk.").

- By proceeding under chapter 13, debtor may obtain the benefit of a stay of collection actions against individual codebtors.[54] § 1301.

- Chapter 13 as a consolidation loan, under which the debtor makes plan payments to the trustee who then makes distributions to creditors; debtors may avoid all direct contact with creditors while under chapter 13 protection.

- Finally, to the extent such a thing exists any more, a debtor can avoid the "stigma" of bankruptcy by filing under chapter 13 and repaying creditors.[55]

Chapter 13 versus chapter 7: Benefits of chapter 7

The foregoing list suggests that debtors sometimes might want to select chapter 13 instead of liquidating under chapter 7. Yet, many debtors do not choose chapter 13, but opt for chapter 7; indeed, this preference for chapter 7 motivated the enactment of the chapter 7 "substantial abuse" provision in 1984, and then the revised "abuse" test in 2005 (§ 707(b)(1)). Why might debtors prefer chapter 7 relief?

The most basic reason a debtor would opt for chapter 7 over chapter 13 inheres in the essential nature of relief under the two chapters. In chapter 13, the debtor must pay creditors all of her projected disposable income for three to five years, § 1325(b), and will not receive a discharge until she does so, § 1328(a). In chapter 7, by contrast, a debtor can receive an *immediate discharge* without paying creditors any of her future income. Thus, if the debtor (1) does not have significant nonexempt assets that she must turn over to the trustee, (2) can work out her problems, if any, with secured creditors, and (3) does not need the superdischarge, chapter 7 looks a lot more attractive than chapter 13. This simple calculus dictates that the vast majority of rational consumer debtors would choose chapter 7 over chapter 13.

Chapter 13 versus chapter 11: Benefits of chapter 13

Some debtors may want to reorganize and retain their property rather than liquidate, but may either be ineligible for chapter 13 or unable to obtain the full relief they need in chapter 13. For such debtors, chapter 11 may provide an option. Usually, though, eligible debtors will prefer chapter 13 over chapter 11, for the following reasons:

- Creditors do not get to vote on the plan in chapter 13, but do have that right in chapter 11. § 1126.[56]

- Because there is no right to vote in chapter 13, there also is no disclosure statement, as there is in chapter 11. § 1125.[57]

---

[54] See § 12.8.

[55] H.R. Rep. No. 95–595, 95th Cong., 1st Sess., at 118 (1977) ("In addition, it satisfies many debtors' desire to avoid the stigma attached to straight bankruptcy and to retain the pride attendant on being able to meet one's obligations.").

[56] H.R. Rep. No. 95–595, 95th Cong., 1st Sess., at 123–24 (1977). See also § 11.21.

[57] See § 11.20.

- There are no committees of creditors in chapter 13, unlike chapter 11. §§ 1102, 1103.[58] For small business debtors, however, it is possible to dispense with committees in chapter 11 as well. § 1102(a)(3).

- The debtor may retain her business and her property without paying unsecured creditors in full in chapter 13, but in chapter 11 is subject to the "absolute priority rule," § 1129(b)(2)(B)(ii), which does not allow the owner of the business to retain control of property over the objection of a dissenting unsecured class that is not paid in full.[59]

- In chapter 13 a debtor has the exclusive right to file a plan forever, § 1321, but in chapter 11 the debtor's exclusivity is limited. § 1121.[60]

- A debtor can strip down a secured claim (other than a home mortgage or certain car loans) to the value of the collateral in chapter 13, § 1325(a)(5),[61] but in chapter 11 the secured creditor may elect to have the entire debt treated as secured. § 1111(b).

- In chapter 13 a debtor may obtain a "superdischarge,"[62] § 1328(a), but in chapter 11 the debtor is subject to all § 523(a) exceptions. § 1141(d)(2).

- Priority claims may be paid in full in chapter 13 over time without interest, § 1322(a)(2), but in chapter 11 priority claims either must be paid in full in cash on the effective date of the plan, or interest must be paid if installment payments are used. § 1129(a)(9).

- A chapter 13 debtor has the benefit of a codebtor stay,[63] § 1301, but a chapter 11 debtor does not.

Chapter 13 versus chapter 11: Benefits of chapter 11

What benefits does chapter 11 offer that chapter 13 does not? The first is eligibility. A debtor who has unsecured debts exceeding $383,175, and secured debts exceeding $1,149,525, exceeds the debt ceiling in § 109(e) and cannot file under chapter 13, but may file under chapter 11, which does not contain debt prohibitions.

Even if a debtor is eligible under both chapters, there are (even after 2005) some benefits to chapter 11 over chapter 13:

---

[58] See § 11.8.

[59] See §§ 11.33–11.34. Though note, some courts have held that the absolute priority rule does not apply to cases filed by individual chapter 11 debtors. E.g., In re Tucker, 479 B.R. 873 (Bankr. D. Ore. 2012). However, that the absolute priority rule continues to apply in individual chapter 11 cases remains the majority view. E.g., In re Lively, 717 F.3d 406 (5th Cir. 2013); In re Maharaj, 681 F.3d 558 (4th Cir. 2012); In re Stephens, 704 F.3d 1279 (10th Cir. 2013).

[60] See § 11.15.

[61] See § 12.18.

[62] See § 12.23.

[63] See § 12.8.

- A debtor in chapter 13 cannot delay, but must file a plan with the petition or within 14 days thereafter, Rule 3015(b), and then begin making payments within 30 days after filing the plan or commencing the case. § 1326(a)(1). In chapter 11, a debtor may not have to file a plan or make any payments for many months.

- A trustee will not be appointed in every chapter 11 case,[64] § 1104, but a trustee will serve in every chapter 13 case.[65] § 1302(a). Even though a chapter 13 trustee does not normally take possession of the debtor's property, §§ 1303, 1304(b), 1306(b), the trustee will investigate the debtor, monitor the debtor's performance, advise the debtor, and appear at hearings. § 1302(b).

Congress eliminated one advantage of chapter 11 versus chapter 13 in 1994. Before the enactment of § 1123(b)(5), a chapter 11 debtor could modify a home mortgage, which is not allowed in chapter 13. § 1322(b)(2). In 1994, however, Congress extended chapter 13's anti-modification rule to chapter 11.

In 2005, Congress eliminated most of the most important benefits of chapter 11 over chapter 13. In BAPCPA, Congress enacted a whole series of chapter 11 amendments designed to mirror the chapter 13 scheme for individual debtors. In particular:

- In chapter 11, the discharge was entered immediately on confirmation of the plan, § 1141(d), while the chapter 13 discharge has always been delayed until plan payments have either been made or attempted.[66] § 1328(a), (b). Now, discharge in chapter 11 is likewise deferred for individual debtors. § 1141(d)(5).

- A debtor in chapter 13 has always had to devote all projected disposable income to plan payments for three to five years,[67] § 1325(b), whereas Chapter 11 did not contain such a requirement prior to 2005. Now it does. § 1129(a)(15)(B).

- A chapter 13 plan may be modified after confirmation at the request of the trustee or an unsecured creditor,[68] § 1329, but prior to 2005 those parties did not have standing to request modification of a chapter 11 plan. Again, that rule has been changed to follow the chapter 13 practice. § 1127(d). The 2005 change also permits modification of chapter 11 plans even if the plan has been substantially consummated.

- Prior to 2005, an individual chapter 11 debtor kept for herself virtually all of her postpetition property and earnings, whereas such property and earnings have always been included in the chapter 13 estate. § 1306(a). In 2005, the chapter 11 rule was amended to conform to chapter 13, making the individual

---

[64] See § 11.6.

[65] See § 12.5.

[66] See §§ 12.23, 12.24.

[67] See § 12.17.

[68] See § 12.21.

debtor's earnings and property acquired postpetition during the pendency of the case part of the chapter 11 estate. § 1115(a).

Chapter 13 versus chapter 12

Chapter 12 was enacted in 1986 for the benefit of family farmers. Chapter 12 was modeled closely after chapter 13. When chapter 12 was enacted, chapter 13 eligibility was limited to debtors with unsecured debts of $100,000 or less and secured debts of $350,000 or less. The chapter 12 debt ceiling of $1.5 million, amended and indexed (as of 2013) to the current amount of $4,031,575 under § 101(18), thus opened up relief to many farm debtors. With the enlargement of the chapter 13 debt limits (as of 2013) to $383,175 in unsecured debt and $1,149,525 in secured debt, § 109(e), the imperative for chapter 12 has been reduced in many cases.

Even aside from the differences in the debt ceiling, however, in many respects chapter 12 is preferable to chapter 13.[69] For example, the debtor is subject to less oversight by the trustee in chapter 12, as the chapter 12 debtor may extend the payment of secured claims beyond the plan period, § 1222(b)(9); a home mortgage can be modified in chapter 12, § 1222(b)(2); property may be sold free and clear of interests more readily in chapter 12, § 1206; the debtor has at least 90 days from the order of relief to file a plan in chapter 12, § 1221, while a chapter 13 debtor has 14 days, Rule 3015(b); and the debtor does not have to make plan payments prior to confirmation in chapter 12. Perhaps the main benefit of chapter 13 over chapter 12 prior to 2005 was the "superdischarge." In chapter 12, a debtor who completes performance under the plan is still subject to all of the § 523(a) discharge exceptions, but a chapter 13 debtor is not. §§ 1228(a), 1328(a). However, in 2005 this advantage was greatly lessened, as many of the most important discharge exceptions (especially those for fraud and for willful "or" malicious injury), were made applicable to the chapter 13 full-compliance discharge as well.

B. DISTINCTIVE ASPECTS OF CHAPTER 13

§ 12.4   Role of Debtor

A chapter 13 debtor is a hybrid creature—part debtor, part trustee. This dual nature inheres in the form and function of a chapter 13 case. The core of chapter 13 is that the debtor may keep her property and pay her creditors over time, pursuant to a court-approved plan.[70] The debtor in chapter 13 is not usually liquidating her property, and thus is more than just a "debtor." At the same time, however, chapter 13 lacks some of the important creditor protection provisions of chapter 11, and the debtor therefore is not given full and unfettered fiduciary responsibility for the administration of the case, but is placed under the general supervision of the chapter 13 trustee.[71]

One of the prime attractions of chapter 13 for debtors is that they may retain possession of their property. Although the filing of the bankruptcy petition transforms

---

[69]   See § 13.2.

[70]   See § 12.1.

[71]   See § 12.5 for a discussion of the role of a chapter 13 trustee.

the debtor's property into property of the estate, § 541(a), in chapter 13 the debtor remains in possession of property of the estate. § 1306(b). Then, upon confirmation of the chapter 13 plan, all estate property vests in the debtor, unless otherwise provided in the plan or the confirmation order.[72] § 1327(b).

The chapter 13 debtor also is given all of the critical corollary powers to deal with estate property. § 1303. The debtor has these powers exclusive of the chapter 13 trustee. Thus, the debtor alone has the powers to use, sell, or lease property of the estate out of the ordinary course of business under § 363(b), or to sell property free and clear under § 363(f), and is given these rights without the hindrance of ipso facto clauses under § 363(l). In exercising these rights with regard to estate property, the debtor is made subject to the countervailing protections for creditors, such as the provision of adequate protection under §§ 363(e) and 361, and the granting of relief from the stay under §§ 363(d) and 362(d).

If the debtor is engaged in business, additional powers are conferred on the debtor. § 1304. These powers are triggered if the debtor is self-employed and incurs trade credit in the production of income from that employment. § 1304(a). The debtor is empowered to operate the business; to use, sell, or lease property of the estate in the ordinary course of that business under § 363(c); and to obtain credit or incur debt under § 364. § 1304(b). As the operator of the business, the debtor must file all required business summaries and reports as provided in § 704(8). § 1304(c).

The debtor has the exclusive right, forever, to file a chapter 13 plan.[73] § 1321. Unlike chapter 11,[74] there is no provision for creditors or other interested parties to file a chapter 13 plan. The only way a chapter 13 debtor could have an involuntary plan forced upon her would be if the case first were converted to chapter 11. If a conversion motion were made, the debtor could forestall conversion by exercising her absolute right to dismiss the chapter 13 case. § 1307(b). The debtor must act expeditiously in filing the chapter 13 plan, however; the Bankruptcy Rules require the debtor to file the plan with the petition or within 14 days thereafter, unless an extension is granted for cause. Rule 3015(b). Failure to file a plan on time would be cause for dismissal or conversion of the case. § 1307(c)(3). A debtor also retains the right to modify her plan at any time before the plan is confirmed. § 1323(a).

The debtor has other obligations as well. Chapter 13 relief is not costless for the debtor. Most importantly, of course, the debtor must make payments under a chapter 13 plan. The debtor's obligation to begin making payments commences within 30 days after the plan is filed or the order for relief, whichever comes first, § 1326(a)(1), even if the plan is not yet confirmed. The trustee will retain the payments and make the plan distributions if the plan is confirmed. § 1326(a)(2). Again, the debtor's failure to begin making timely payments would be cause for dismissal or conversion. § 1307(c)(4).

The debtor's fresh start is delayed in chapter 13 because the debtor's postpetition earnings become property of the estate. § 1306(a)(2). Meanwhile, the debtor's discharge

---

[72]   See § 12.20.

[73]   See S. Rep. No. 95–989, 95th Cong., 2d Sess., at 141 (1978).

[74]   See § 11.15.

is not granted until the debtor either completes performance under the plan, § 1328(a), or is awarded a hardship discharge, § 1328(b). However, a chapter 13 debtor may claim exemptions, § 522(b), and may avoid liens that impair her exemptions, § 522(h).[75]

The chapter 13 debtor has many of the initial responsibilities placed upon chapter 7 debtors. For example, the debtor in chapter 13 must file a list of creditors and all required schedules. § 521(a)(1), Rule 1007(b). The debtor also must appear at the initial meeting of creditors and be examined under oath. § 343. At all times the debtor must cooperate with the trustee. § 521(a)(3).

While a chapter 13 trustee definitely has standing,[76] there has been substantial controversy over whether the chapter 13 debtor has standing concurrent with the trustee to bring avoidance actions on behalf of the estate. The statutory language arguably suggests not, but courts nevertheless divide on whether the debtor may act in the capacity of the trustee and bring avoidance actions.[77] Except for the power to avoid liens that impair exemptions, see § 522(h), the avoiding powers all provide that "the trustee" may bring the avoiding action. Simply put, the "debtor" is not a "trustee"; the only "trustee" in a chapter 13 case is the chapter 13 trustee. Furthermore, while §§ 1303 and 1304 do give the chapter 13 debtor some of the rights and powers of a trustee, as discussed above, those sections do *not* empower the debtor to exercise the trustee's avoiding powers, giving rise to a possible negative inference that the debtor does not have standing to bring avoidance actions. Indeed, §§ 1303 and 1304 are conspicuously different in structure from § 1107(a), which confers all rights, powers, and duties of a trustee on a chapter 11 debtor in possession, except for those specifically excluded.

However, another plausible negative inference to draw from §§ 1303 and 1304 is that all of the powers of a trustee which are not given exclusively to the chapter 13 debtor in those sections also may be exercised by the trustee. That does not necessarily mean, though, that the debtor cannot *share* with the trustee the nonexclusive power to exercise other trustee powers. In other words, the real importance of §§ 1303 and 1304 may be in giving some rights *exclusively* to the debtor, rather than in limiting which trustee powers the debtor may utilize. The legislative history supports this interpretation, stating that the enumeration of the debtor's exclusive rights and powers "does not imply that the debtor does not also possess other powers concurrently with the trustee."[78] Many courts have given weight to this legislative history and have weighed the practicalities of the situation, and, reasoning that the chapter 13 debtor is the party with the most incentive to bring avoidance actions on behalf of the estate, have allowed the debtor to act.[79] Moreover, even if a court holds that a chapter 13

---

[75]   See §§ 9.1, 9.7.

[76]   See, e.g., In re Cecil, 488 B.R. 200 (Bankr. M.D. Fla. 2013).

[77]   The majority of cases do not permit chapter 13 debtors to prosecute avoidance actions. See, e.g., In re Binghi, 299 B.R. 300 (Bankr. S.D.N.Y. 2003); In re Lee, 432 B.R. 212 (D.S.C. 2010); In re Mouton, 479 B.R. 55 (Bankr. E.D. Ark. 2012); In re Richardson, 311 B.R. 302 (Bankr. S.D. Fla. 2004); In re Ryker, 315 B.R. 664 (Bankr. D.N.J. 2004); In re Smith, 459 B.R. 571 (Bankr. M.D. Pa. 2011); In re Turner, 490 B.R. 1 (Bankr. D.C. 2013).

[78]   124 Cong. Rec. S17,423 (daily ed. Oct. 6, 1978) (remarks of Sen. DeConcini); 124 Cong. Rec. H11,106 (daily ed. Sept. 28, 1978) (remarks of Rep. Edwards).

[79]   See, e.g., In re Hamilton, 125 F.3d 292 (5th Cir. 1997).

debtor may not bring avoidance actions, a court may nonetheless find standing for debtors to prosecute avoidance actions if a confirmed plan grants such avoidance powers to a debtor.[80]

§ 12.5   Role of Chapter 13 Trustee

A trustee serves in every chapter 13 case. § 1302(a). However, the chapter 13 trustee is a much different animal than the traditional chapter 7 trustee. Most significantly, since a chapter 13 case contemplates a payment plan rather than a liquidation, the chapter 13 trustee does not take possession of and liquidate the debtor's nonexempt property.[81] The chapter 13 trustee is the "principal administrator" of the chapter 13 case.[82] The primary but not exclusive role of the chapter 13 trustee is to serve as the *disbursing agent* for monies paid by the debtor under the plan. What normally happens is that the debtor makes her monthly plan payment to the trustee, who then makes the distributions to each individual creditor provided for by the plan. § 1326(a)(2), (c). The trustee also is charged with various duties related to the debtor's performance under the plan, such as ensuring that the debtor begins making timely plan payments, § 1302(b)(5), advising the debtor on financial matters, and assisting and supervising the debtor's performance under the plan. § 1302(b)(4).

In the interest of efficiency, one individual is usually appointed by the United States trustee to serve as the "standing trustee" for *all* of the chapter 13 cases in a district or region. § 1302(a); 28 U.S.C. § 586(b). That individual then is able to process funds received from debtors and issue checks to creditors on a centralized basis. Consolidating administration of all chapter 13 cases in a district or region under a single individual also permits the adoption of uniform guidelines relating to chapter 13 plans and procedures in a given locality. The standing trustee must qualify as a trustee under § 322. The standing trustee is supervised by the United States trustee, who in turn functions under the general supervision of the Attorney General. 28 U.S.C. § 586(b), (c).

A trustee under chapter 13 has some additional duties beyond serving as disbursing agent and overseeing the plan process. § 1302. Many of the duties of a chapter 7 trustee are also imposed on a chapter 13 trustee. § 1302(b)(1). These include the duties to examine and object to claims, to investigate the debtor's financial affairs, and to object when advisable to the debtor's discharge. The trustee also has standing to appear and be heard at hearings concerning the value of property subject to a lien, the confirmation of the plan, or the modification of a confirmed plan. § 1302(b)(2). Additionally, in any case in which there is a claim for a domestic support obligation, the trustee must provide to both the claimant and to the applicable state child support enforcement agency statutory notices designed to assist and facilitate ongoing

---

[80]   See In re Hearn, 337 B.R. 603 (Bankr. E.D. Mich. 2006).

[81]   This conclusion is deduced from the absence of a statutory directive to the chapter 13 trustee to superintend a liquidation. In particular, § 1302(b)(1) specifies those duties that a chapter 13 trustee shares with a chapter 7 trustee, and conspicuously omits a reference to § 704(a)(1), which is the provision that gives the chapter 7 trustee the duty to liquidate the debtor's property.

[82]   S. Rep. No. 95–989, 95th Cong., 2d Sess. 139 (1978).

collection of domestic support obligations from the debtor and the debtor's estate. § 1302(b)(6), (d).

The chapter 13 trustee does not, however, take possession of the debtor's property; run the debtor's business; use, sell, or lease property; obtain credit or incur debt; or propose a plan. In short, many of the most important duties of a chapter 11 trustee are not imposed on a chapter 13 trustee. Nor does the chapter 13 trustee file business operating reports. All of these rights and duties are reserved exclusively to the debtor.[83] §§ 1303, 1304. If the debtor is not performing satisfactorily, the trustee may move to dismiss or convert the case, § 1307(c), (d), or to modify the plan. § 1329(a).

In one area the courts have had some difficulty in determining whether the debtor or the chapter 13 trustee is the appropriate actor. The uncertainty concerns who has standing to bring avoidance actions, such as actions to set aside and recover preferences or fraudulent conveyances. The statutory scheme apparently confers *exclusive* standing on the chapter 13 trustee, and a number of courts have held that this plain meaning must be given effect.[84] At a minimum it is agreed that the chapter 13 trustee does have standing, even if that standing is not exclusive of the debtor.[85] As discussed in the previous section, many courts have chosen to ignore the statutory language and have permitted the chapter 13 debtor to bring avoidance actions on behalf of the estate.[86]

The compensation of a chapter 13 trustee depends initially on whether a standing trustee has been appointed.[87] If not, then the trustee appointed for the single case may receive a fee not to exceed 5% of all payments under the plan. § 326(b). In the more common situation where a standing trustee is serving, the trustee's compensation is governed by 28 U.S.C. § 586(e). That section allows the Attorney General to fix the trustee's maximum annual compensation, which is based on a reference to level V of the Executive Schedule *and* a percentage fee of plan payments. In chapter 13, the standard percentage is 10%, 28 U.S.C. § 586(e)(1)(B)(i), which is to be collected from payments made under the plans.

§ 12.6   Postpetition Property

In a chapter 7 liquidation bankruptcy case, the presumptive rule is that the bankruptcy estate is fixed at the time of the filing of the case.[88] § 541(a)(1). In other words, as a general rule, the estate does *not* include property acquired or earned by the debtor *after* the commencement of the case. Instead, subject only to a handful of

---

[83]   See § 12.4.

[84]   See, e.g., In re Binghi, 299 B.R. 300 (Bankr. S.D.N.Y. 2003); In re Lee, 432 B.R. 212 (D.S.C. 2010); In re Mouton, 479 B.R. 55 (Bankr. E.D. Ark. 2012); In re Richardson, 311 B.R. 302 (Bankr. S.D. Fla. 2004); In re Ryker, 315 B.R. 664 (Bankr. D.N.J. 2004); In re Smith, 459 B.R. 571 (Bankr. M.D. Pa. 2011); In re Turner, 490 B.R. 1 (Bankr. D.C. 2013).

[85]   See, e.g., In re Cecil, 488 B.R. 200 (Bankr. M.D. Fla. 2013).

[86]   In re Barbee, 461 B.R. 711 (B.A.P. 6th Cir. 2011); United States v. Dewes, 315 B.R. 834 (N.D. Ind. 2004).

[87]   See § 7.16 for a discussion of the compensation of trustees.

[88]   See § 5.2.

statutory exceptions,[89] property that the debtor obtains postpetition belongs to the debtor, free from the debtor's creditors. For individual debtors, the right to retain property acquired after bankruptcy is a critical component of the debtor's fresh start, operating hand-in-glove with the discharge. This policy is especially strong with regard to the debtor's *postpetition earnings*.[90] § 541(a)(6).

The general presumption against a "perpetual" bankruptcy estate does not apply in a chapter 13 case. The rule in chapter 12 is the same,[91] and, as of 2005, in individual chapter 11 cases as well. § 1115(a). In chapter 13, the governing rule is that all postpetition property acquired during the pendency of the case, whether by the debtor or by the estate, becomes property of the estate. § 1306(a). Significantly, this inclusive rule extends even to postpetition *earnings* of the debtor. § 1306(a)(2). Specifically, the expanded chapter 13 estate includes:

- all property of the kind specified in § 541 that the debtor acquires *after* the commencement of the case and *before* the case is closed, dismissed, or converted, § 1306(a)(1); and

- all earnings from postpetition services performed by the debtor after the commencement of the case and before the case is closed, dismissed, or converted, § 1306(a)(2).

A *quid pro quo* for obtaining the benefits of chapter 13 thus is that the debtor must defer her fresh start until the conclusion of the bankruptcy case. This policy of delaying the debtor's enjoyment of the fresh start is also manifested in the postponement of the chapter 13 discharge until the debtor has completed performance under the plan, or been excused by the court for failing to do so. § 1328.

At the same time, keeping the estate open during the pendency of a chapter 13 case is not always as onerous to the debtor as might first appear. The debtor remains in possession of estate property in chapter 13, § 1306(b), unlike chapter 7, where the debtor must turn over nonexempt property to the trustee for liquidation and distribution to creditors. § 521(a)(4). In chapter 13, by contrast, if all goes well the debtor's property will never be liquidated.

Indeed, the inclusion in the estate of property acquired postpetition can even be beneficial to a chapter 13 debtor. With the property included in the estate, creditors are *stayed* under § 362(a) from seeking to collect their claims out of that property. For example, creditors would not be entitled to garnish the debtor's wages during the pendency of a chapter 13 case. This stay applies even to the enforcement of *postpetition* claims against estate property. § 362(a)(3). Application of the stay thus may help the debtor carry out the terms of the plan.

However, the stay of actions against postpetition property can be a two-edged sword. To explain, because of the stay, the debtor may find it difficult to obtain

---

[89]   See § 5.3.

[90]   See § 5.9.

[91]   See § 13.4.

postpetition credit. Softening the blow is the provision in § 1327(b) that confirmation of the debtor's plan vests all property of the estate in the debtor, unless the plan provides otherwise.[92] Since confirmation occurs very early in a chapter 13 case, a literal reading of § 1327(b) suggests that the stay will not bar the collection of postpetition claims after confirmation,[93] although the cases are divided. A debtor could elect to keep the stay in effect by providing in the plan that estate property will not vest in the debtor upon confirmation.

Given the relatively high failure rate of chapter 13 cases,[94] perhaps a greater concern to the debtor is the effects of the expanded chapter 13 estate in the event of a *conversion* of the chapter 13 case to another chapter.[95] The debtor's potential problem is that property acquired during the pendency of the chapter 13 case becomes property of the estate only because of the special rule in § 1306(a), and yet may be included in the estate *after* conversion. If so, the debtor could end up worse off than if she had never attempted to pay creditors under a chapter 13 plan, because the postpetition property would not have come into the estate if the debtor had originally filed under chapter 7.

The 1994 Amendments addressed this problem in chapter 13. As will be discussed in the next chapter, however, the 1994 Amendments did not address the identical problem in the chapter 12 setting.[96] When the case is originally filed under chapter 13, and then converts, property of the estate *after* conversion will consist *only* of property of the estate as of the date of the filing of the petition—excluding therefore property acquired postpetition and pre-conversion—and which remains in the possession and under the control of the debtor on the date of conversion. § 348(f)(1)(A). If, however, the debtor converts in *bad faith*, the property of the estate in the converted case will consist of the property of the estate as of the date of conversion, rather than the date of filing. § 348(f)(2).

§ 12.7   Postpetition Claims

The general rule is that both the allowable claims of creditors and the extent of property of the estate are determined as of the commencement of the case. Just as chapter 13 contains a special rule that provides for postpetition property to be brought into the estate,[97] § 1306, so too does chapter 13 permit the allowance and payment of certain types of postpetition claims in the chapter 13 case. § 1305. Unlike the property inclusion rule, the postpetition claims rule is not global in operation, but is limited in scope to two types of claims: tax claims, § 1305(a)(1), and necessary consumer debts, § 1305(a)(2). In addition, domestic support obligations that first become payable after the date of the bankruptcy filing must be paid in full by the debtor as a condition of

---

[92]   See § 12.20.

[93]   The collection of prepetition claims will still be stayed. §§ 362(a)(1), (2), (6), 524(a)(1), (2). Such claims may not be collected even against property of the debtor.

[94]   Statistically, only one-third of chapter 13 cases succeed. See Katherine Porter, The Pretend Solution: An Empirical Study of Bankruptcy Outcomes, 90 Tex. L. Rev. 103, 107–08 (2011).

[95]   For a more detailed discussion of the effects of conversion, see § 2.22.

[96]   See § 13.4.

[97]   See § 12.6.

confirming a chapter 13 plan. § 1325(a)(8). All other creditors with claims that arise postpetition normally are not dealt with at all in the bankruptcy case; they do not receive distributions in the bankruptcy case, but neither are their claims discharged. Postpetition creditors usually look solely to the assets of the postpetition debtor for payment.

The special rule of § 1305 intentionally blurs the line between prepetition and postpetition claims in order to benefit the two types of postpetition claim holders covered by § 1305(a). Holders of claims for postpetition taxes or for postpetition necessary consumer debts are given a choice. They are permitted (but not required) to file their claim in the chapter 13 bankruptcy case, § 1305(a), have their claim allowed, § 1305(b), and participate in the distribution. Alternatively, the postpetition claimant may elect to wait and seek to collect from the debtor after the conclusion of the chapter 13 case (or after estate property vests in the debtor, § 1327(b)), and forego participation in the bankruptcy case. If the postpetition claimant does not choose to file a claim, no one else has the right to file a claim on behalf of that creditor.[98]

What choice should the postpetition claimant make? For the tax claimant, § 1305(a)(1), there is little reason not to file its claim in the chapter 13 case and participate in the chapter 13 plan payout if possible. As a priority claim, the tax claim must be paid in full under the chapter 13 plan. § 1322(a)(2). If the chapter 13 case does not succeed, and the tax claim is not paid in full, that claim will not be discharged. §§ 523(a)(1), 1328(c)(2). The taxing authority may still proceed against the debtor.

The second type of debt covered by § 1305 is a necessary postpetition consumer debt, under § 1305(a)(2). This category applies to debts for property or services "necessary for the debtor's performance under the plan." Examples given in the legislative history are "auto repairs in order that the debtor will be able to get to work, or medical bills."[99] In order to protect the debtor (and other creditors) from the debtor's own improvidence, the claim of such a postpetition creditor will be disallowed in the chapter 13 case if the claimant knew or should have known that prior approval by the trustee of the debtor incurring the debt was practicable and was not obtained. § 1305(c). In addition, the claim will not be discharged. § 1328(d). For example, before the debtor gets auto repairs done, the chapter 13 trustee should be contacted for preapproval. However, the provision of emergency medical services to the debtor may be required before the trustee's approval can be obtained.

Whether to file a claim in the chapter 13 bankruptcy case or not is a harder call for the holder of a claim for necessary consumer property or services than for a tax claimant. The benefit of filing the claim is that if the claim is allowed, §§ 1305(b), 502, the claimant may participate in the payout under the chapter 13 plan. Since the chapter 13 plan could be in effect for up to five years,[100] § 1322(d), and since the postpetition claimant might not easily be able to collect from the debtor until the plan period is finished, the claimant may want to get some money sooner rather than later.

---

[98] The provisions in § 501 that permit another entity or the debtor to file a claim on behalf of the claimant do not apply to postpetition claims, because the postpetition claimant is not a "creditor."

[99] H.R. Rep. No. 95–595, 95th Cong., 1st Sess. 427–28 (1977).

[100] See § 12.14.

That being said, why would the holder of a claim covered by § 1305(a)(2) ever *not* want to file a claim? The risk is that the debt will be *discharged* even if it is not paid in full. If the creditor files a claim as authorized by § 1305(a)(2), and the claim is allowed under § 1305(b) and § 502, the debtor is permitted to provide for that postpetition claim in her plan. § 1322(b)(6). Under § 1328(a) and (c), the chapter 13 discharge applies to all "debts provided for by the plan." The debtor thus could receive a discharge of the postpetition debt without paying that debt in full.

If, however, the postpetition claimant chooses not to file a claim, the debt cannot be discharged. The unfiled claim would not be allowed, could not be provided for by the debtor in her plan, and therefore could not be discharged. In short, the postpetition claimant would retain the right to pursue the debtor for the full amount of the claim after bankruptcy.

§ 12.8   Codebtor Stay

As in any other type of bankruptcy case, creditors in chapter 13 are stayed from attempting to collect their debts from the debtor, the debtor's property, or property of the estate during the case. § 362(a). The § 362(a) stay, however, only applies to protect the debtor. A person who is liable with the bankruptcy debtor, i.e., a *codebtor*, does not have the benefit of the § 362(a) stay, unless that person also is the subject of a bankruptcy case. In cases under chapters 7 or 11, creditors are free to pursue codebtors while the debtor's case is pending. Indeed, the risk of bankruptcy is one of the reasons that creditors demand guarantors and sureties in the first place.

The rule in chapter 13 is radically different. The reformers of the 1970s found that creditors used the threat of collection against codebtors as a means of leverage to coerce bankruptcy debtors into either paying or reaffirming the debt.[101] These codebtors often were friends or family members, who may not have fully understood the consequences of cosigning or guaranteeing the debtor's obligation. When the debtor would default and file bankruptcy, the creditor in effect would say, "pay or reaffirm the debt to me, or Grandma pays." Faced with that moral pressure, the debtor would give that creditor preferential treatment, undermining the debtor's fresh start and giving that creditor an advantage over other creditors.[102]

To prevent such tactics in chapter 13 cases, Congress enacted the "codebtor stay" in § 1301. The codebtor stay prevents creditors from attempting to collect a consumer debt from an individual who is a codebtor with the bankruptcy debtor during the pendency of the bankruptcy case. § 1301(a). Relieved of the indirect threat of collection from the codebtor, the bankruptcy debtor can deal with that creditor on the same basis as other creditors, obtaining a more complete fresh start. The codebtor obviously benefits from the § 1301 stay, but this protection is an incidental byproduct of the congressional attempt to provide full protection for the bankruptcy debtor.

The codebtor stay is not absolute. Congress carefully attempted to limit its scope to the abusive cases described above. Thus, the codebtor stay only protects (1) an

---

[101]   H.R. Rep. No. 95–595, 95th Cong., 1st Sess. 122 (1977).

[102]   Id. at 121–22.

individual codebtor; (2) who is liable with the debtor on a *consumer* debt, § 1301(a); (3) during the pendency of the chapter 13 case. § 1301(a)(2). Consumer debts are defined as debts incurred by an individual for personal, family, or household purposes. § 101(8). For example, it has been held that a loan taken out for a business opportunity[103] and a tax debt[104] are not a consumer debt to which the codebtor stay applies. Most other debts incurred by individual debtors who are not operating a business would qualify as consumer debts, however.

Furthermore, the codebtor stay does not apply if the individual codebtor became liable on the debt in the ordinary course of the individual's business. § 1301(a)(1). In other words, the codebtor stay would not extend to commercial guarantors and sureties.[105] A creditor also is permitted to present a negotiable instrument and give notice of dishonor. § 1301(b).

The creditor also may request relief from the codebtor stay. An expedited procedure for resolving some of those requests is provided. § 1301(d). The codebtor stay is automatically terminated 20 days after a request for relief is filed under subsection (c)(2), unless the debtor or any individual that is liable on the debt with the debtor files a written objection. § 1301(d).

Three grounds are provided for granting relief from the codebtor stay. § 1301(c). The first is if the "codebtor" actually received the consideration for the debt, i.e., the bankruptcy debtor is really the codebtor, rather than the other way around. § 1301(c)(1).

The creditor also can obtain relief from the codebtor stay during the pendency of the bankruptcy case to the extent the bankruptcy debtor does not propose to pay the creditor in full. § 1301(c)(2). The legislative history gives the example of a $100 debt, of which the debtor proposes to pay $70 under the plan.[106] The creditor would be able to obtain relief to proceed against the codebtor for the remaining $30.[107] The codebtor stay is not intended to preclude the creditor from obtaining full satisfaction, but only to keep it from getting an unfair advantage in the bankruptcy case itself. Indeed, the creditor may collect not only the principal amount of the debt, but also all interest, fees, charges, and penalties to which it is entitled.

The final situation in which the creditor may obtain stay relief to proceed against the codebtor is if the creditor's interest would be "irreparably harmed" by continuation of the stay. § 1301(c)(3). This ground for relief also reflects the policy that the creditor's legitimate interests be protected. Thus, if the codebtor's own financial situation is deteriorating, or if the codebtor is about to leave the jurisdiction, the creditor should be able to get relief.[108]

---

[103] In re Chrisman, 27 B.R. 648 (Bankr. S.D. Ohio 1982).

[104] E.g., In re Pressimone, 39 B.R. 240 (N.D.N.Y. 1984).

[105] H.R. Rep. No. 95–595, 95th Cong., 1st Sess. 122 (1977).

[106] Id.

[107] Id.

[108] Id.

C. THE CHAPTER 13 PLAN

§ 12.9   Plan Process

One of the major attractions of chapter 13 for debtors is the speed and simplicity of the process. Unlike chapter 11, chapter 13 is not predicated on the concept of a consensual plan. Instead, in chapter 13 the debtor proposes the terms of the plan, which the court judges against prescribed statutory standards. If those statutory tests are met, the court will confirm the plan, whether the creditors like it or not. In chapter 13, creditors do not vote on the plan, like they do in chapter 11.[109] The only direct input that creditors have in the chapter 13 plan confirmation process is (1) they may object to confirmation, § 1324, Rule 3015(f), and (2) a secured creditor may (but need not) accept the plan, § 1325(a)(5)(A).[110] The lack of creditor voting eliminates the need for a disclosure statement and the solicitation of votes, both of which are required in chapter 11,[111] and therefore largely obviates the need for the debtor to negotiate with creditors over the terms of the plan.

The chapter 13 process unfolds rapidly in a series of well-defined steps:

Step 1: Debtor files voluntary petition for relief under chapter 13, or voluntarily converts from another chapter to chapter 13.

Step 2: Debtor files plan. In chapter 13 only the debtor is permitted to file a plan. § 1321. The debtor may, and often does, file the plan at the outset of the case, with the petition. The debtor must file the plan within 14 days after the filing of the petition, or obtain an extension for cause. Rule 3015(b).

Step 3: Notice and plan sent to creditors and trustee. After the plan is filed, 28 days' notice of the confirmation hearing and the time fixed for filing objections to confirmation is sent to the trustee and all creditors. Rule 2002(b). The plan or a summary of the plan must be included. Rule 3015(d). The plan or a summary also must be sent to the local United States trustee. Rule 3015(e).

Step 4: Debtor commences making payments. After filing the plan, the debtor is required to start making the payments proposed by the plan and payments to lessor and secured creditors not later than 30 days after the date of filing of the plan or the order for relief, whichever is earlier (in short, 30 days after the order for relief). § 1326(a)(1). The debtor sends the payments called for by the plan to the chapter 13 trustee, § 1326(a)(1)(A), who holds the money until confirmation. If the plan is confirmed, the trustee will then distribute the monies in accordance with the terms of the plan. If not, the trustee will return the money to the debtor. § 1326(a)(2). In addition, the 2005 amendments require the debtor to commence making payments directly to personal property lessors, § 1326(a)(1)(B), and adequate protection payments to creditors secured by personal property collateral, § 1326(a)(1)(C), both for amounts due postpetition. Any payments made directly to lessors and to secured

---

[109] See § 11.21.

[110] See § 12.18.

[111] See § 11.20.

creditors are to be deducted from the amount paid to the trustee. The court has the power to alter the amount of pre-confirmation payments. § 1326(a)(3).

The debtor also is obligated to provide proof of insurance to lessors and secured creditors not later than 60 days after filing. § 1326(a)(4).

Step 5. Filing of prepetition tax returns. Not later than one day before the meeting of creditors, debtor must file with the appropriate authorities all tax returns for all taxable periods ending during the 4–year period prior to the date the petition was filed. § 1308(a). Failure to do so requires the court to either dismiss the case or convert the case to chapter 7. § 1307(e).

Step 6: Meeting of creditors held. § 341(a). The meeting must be scheduled not earlier than 21 days and not later than 50 days after the order for relief. Rule 2003(a).

Step 7: Objections to confirmation filed. After receiving a copy of the plan and notice of the confirmation hearing, a party in interest may file an objection to confirmation. § 1324(a), Rule 3015(f). The grounds for objecting are that one or more of the requirements of § 1325 are not met. As noted above, the opportunity to object is the only say that creditors have in the process; they do not get to vote. The only exception is for secured creditors, who are permitted to accept a plan. § 1325(a)(5)(A).

Step 8: Confirmation hearing. At the scheduled time, the court must hold a hearing on confirmation. § 1324(a). The confirmation hearing may be held no earlier than 20 days, nor later than 45 days, after the meeting of creditors, except that the court may approve an earlier hearing if it is in the best interest of the creditors and the estate. § 1324(b). A hearing is mandated even if no one objects to confirmation. However, absent an objection, the court may determine that the plan was proposed in good faith and not by any means forbidden by law, without taking evidence on those matters.

Optional Step [before 9]: Pre-confirmation modification of plan by debtor. The debtor is freely permitted to modify the plan at any time before confirmation. § 1323(a). The modified plan becomes the operative plan. § 1323(b). The debtor does not have to obtain a new acceptance of the plan from a secured creditor who has already accepted the plan, unless the modification changes the secured claim holder's rights under the plan. § 1323(c).

Step 9: Court confirms plan. If the plan complies with all of the requirements of § 1325, the court is required to confirm the plan. The court does have some discretion, however, in that it must determine that the plan is feasible.[112] § 1325(a)(6).

Optional Steps [after 9]:

A.   Court revokes confirmation. If confirmation was obtained by fraud, the court has the power to revoke the confirmation order.[113] § 1330(a). A party in interest must request revocation within 180 days after the entry of the confirmation order.

---

[112] See § 12.19.

B. Plan modified post-confirmation. The plan may be modified after confirmation.[114] § 1329. Unlike pre-confirmation modification, a post-confirmation request for modification may be made by the trustee or an unsecured creditor, as well as the debtor. § 1329(a). A modification may be proposed because of changed circumstances (for better or worse).

C. Case converted or dismissed. The debtor has an absolute right to convert the case to chapter 7 or to dismiss the case at any time.[115] § 1307(a), (b). A party in interest also may request conversion or dismissal, on a showing of cause. § 1307(c), (d).

Step 10: Trustee makes payments under plan. After the plan is confirmed, the trustee begins making the distributions to creditors under the plan. § 1326(c). The plan may provide for the debtor to make some payments directly to creditors, outside of the plan process, rather than funneling the payments through the trustee. The 2005 amendments contemplate that this will be done for payments to personal property lessors and secured creditors. The trustee also must pay administrative priority expenses and the percentage fee of the standing trustee, as well as any allowable compensation to a chapter 7 trustee due to the conversion or dismissal of a prior chapter 7 case. § 1326(b)(3), (d).

Step 11: Performance completed (or not), discharge granted. The final step is the completion of performance under the plan by the debtor. Under Chapter 13, the debtor's discharge is not entered at the time the plan is confirmed, but is deferred to see if the debtor can perform under the plan. If the debtor does successfully carry out the terms of the plan (even as modified under § 1329), the debtor then will receive a "superdischarge." § 1328(a). This full-compliance discharge is effective even with regard to some debts that would be excluded from discharge in chapter 7.[116] If the debtor cannot complete performance under the plan, the debtor may ask the court to grant a "hardship discharge" anyway. § 1328(b). A hardship discharge, which is not a matter of right, is subject to all of the discharge exceptions in § 523(a).[117] § 1328(c).

§ 12.10 Mandatory and Prohibited Provisions

The Code specifies in considerable detail: (1) what provisions are *required* to be in the plan, § 1322(a); (2) what provisions are *permitted* to be in the plan,[118] § 1322(b); (3) what plan provisions are *prohibited*; and (4) what statutory requirements must be satisfied for the plan to be confirmed.[119] § 1325. Since creditors do not vote on the plan,

---

[113] See § 12.22.

[114] See § 12.21.

[115] See § 2.16. However, as mentioned in a previous section, note that after the Supreme Court's decision in *Marrama*, the courts divide over the question of whether this right to convert or dismiss from chapter 13 is absolute, or is qualified by the authority of a bankruptcy court to deny a debtor's request on grounds of bad-faith conduct. Compare In re Procel, 467 B.R. 297 (S.D.N.Y. 2012) (holding that the right is absolute, pursuant to a pre-*Marrama* case, *In re Barbieri*, 199 F.3d 616 (2d Cir. 1999)), with In re Jacobsen, 609 F.3d 647 (5th Cir. 2010) (holding that the right is not absolute); In re Rosson, 545 F.3d 764 (9th Cir. 2008) (same).

[116] See § 12.23.

[117] See § 12.24.

[118] See §§ 12.11–12.13.

[119] See §§ 12.15–12.19.

this statutory scheme plays a critical role in both protecting the rights and interests of creditors and yet still offering necessary relief to the debtor.

Mandatory provisions

Only three *mandatory* plan requirements are imposed. § 1322(a). First, the plan must provide for the submission of sufficient future income or earnings to the trustee to enable the plan to be carried out. § 1322(a)(1). This rule works in conjunction with the feasibility test. The Code separately requires the court to find that the debtor in fact will be able to make the payments called for by the plan, i.e., that the plan is feasible,[120] § 1325(a)(6); the mandatory rule of § 1322(a)(1) dictates that on paper the plan payments will be adequately funded. Note that the requirement that the debtor provide for adequate funding of the plan does not prohibit the debtor from making some payments directly to creditors outside of the plan.[121] Furthermore, all submissions do not have to come directly from the debtor; it is commonplace for the plan to provide for payments by third parties (such as an employer) directly to the trustee. Indeed, after confirmation the court may order any entity from whom the debtor receives income to pay any part of that income to the trustee. § 1325(c).

The second mandatory provision of a chapter 13 plan is that the plan must provide for the full payment of all priority claims under § 507. § 1322(a)(2). Payment must be in cash, but may be deferred over the life of the plan. Although all priority claims must be paid in full over the life of the plan, there is no additional requirement that those claims be paid temporally in the order of their priority. For example, the debtor could provide that all eighth priority tax claims be paid first. Furthermore, if payments are to be made over time, the plan does *not* have to provide for the payment of interest. The statute does not specify that the full cash payment must be "as of the effective date of the plan." The holder of a given priority claim may waive the protections of § 1322(a)(2) and agree to different treatment of their claim.

The only exception to the foregoing is that the plan may provide for less than full payment of priority domestic support obligations under § 507(a)(1)(B). Those are DSOs payable to someone other than the spouse or child (e.g., to a governmental unit). However, if it does so, the plan must provide that debtor will devote all of his projected disposable income to plan payments for a period of five years, beginning on the date the first payment is due under the plan. § 1322(a)(4).

The final mandatory provision is that the plan must provide the same treatment for each claim within a particular class. § 1322(a)(3). Classification of claims is not mandatory, but permissive,[122] § 1322(b)(1), but if the debtor does elect to classify claims, then claims in the same class must receive the same treatment. If the debtor wants to provide different treatment for similar claims, it therefore must place those claims in separate classes. The test then will be whether the differential treatment unfairly discriminates against any class. § 1322(b)(1).

---

[120] See § 12.19.

[121] See, e.g., In re Aberegg, 961 F.2d 1307 (7th Cir. 1992); In re Mendoza, 111 F.3d 1264 (5th Cir. 1997).

[122] See § 12.11.

Prohibited provisions

The Code gives the debtor considerable flexibility in crafting the terms of a plan, subject to certain fundamental guidelines.[123] A few provisions are prohibited, however. One sort of prohibition is simply the reverse of a required provision. In other words, if the Code says that a plan must do "X," then the debtor's plan could not provide for "not X." For example, the plan must propose that unsecured creditors will receive at least as much as they would in a chapter 7 liquidation.[124] § 1325(a)(4). The plan accordingly could not provide for unsecured creditors to receive less than they would in a liquidation.

The other type of prohibition is of the more direct "thou shalt not" variety. There are four such proscribed provisions. First, the plan may not discriminate unfairly against any class that the debtor chooses to designate.[125] § 1322(b)(1).

Second, the plan may not modify a home mortgage.[126] § 1322(b)(2).

Third, a plan may not "materially alter" the terms of a loan described in § 362(b)(19). § 1322(f). The referenced loans are retirement fund loans. This provision was added in 2005. The new rule further provides that amounts required to repay such loans do not count as "disposable income" under § 1325.

The final prohibition concerns the *length* of a chapter 13 plan. In a significant departure from pre-Code law, designed to protect debtors from the burden of having to perform under a plan for an excessively long time, the Code imposes a maximum plan period. As amended in 2005, the maximum plan period is either three years or five years.[127] Which cap applies depends on whether the current monthly income of the debtor and the debtor's spouse is greater than or less than the median family income of the debtor's state for the same family size; if their income is above median, then the maximum plan period is five years, § 1322(d)(1), but if not, then the maximum plan period is three years (although the court may approve a five year period for cause). § 1322(d)(2).

§ 12.11 Permissive Provisions: Classification of Unsecured Claims

Congress extended the range of permissible plan provisions in 1978 when it authorized debtors to designate classes of unsecured claims. § 1322(b)(1). Classification was not permitted under old chapter XIII. Granting debtors the power to classify claims is part of the general move in the Code to afford debtors greater flexibility in crafting their plans.

Classification is a limited right, however. First, classification is permitted "as provided in § 1122." § 1322(b)(1). Under § 1122,[128] only claims that are "substantially

---

[123] H.R. Rep. No. 95–595, 95th Cong., 1st Sess., at 123 (1977).

[124] See § 12.16.

[125] See § 12.11.

[126] See §§ 12.12, 12.18.

[127] See § 12.14.

[128] See § 11.17.

similar" may be classified together, § 1122(a), except that small claims may be grouped together and paid in full for administrative convenience, § 1122(b). Note that the statute does *not* require *all* substantially similar claims to be placed in the same class, but only mandates that claims within a particular class must be substantially similar. In practical effect, this means that separate classes of unsecured claims are possible. A debtor could not, however, place a secured creditor in the same class as unsecured creditors.

The Code does expressly permit one type of separate classification. Resolving a split in the case law, § 1322(b)(1) specifies that consumer debts on which the debtor is liable with a codebtor may be treated differently than other unsecured claims. The generous classification rule for cosigned consumer debts further implements the policy underlying the codebtor stay of § 1301,[129] believing a debtor from indirect leverage that could be asserted by the creditor by pressuring the codebtor.

A second limitation on classification is that each claim within a particular class must be given the same treatment. § 1322(a)(3). Although classification is permissive, if the debtor chooses to classify claims, the Code requires the same treatment for class members.

Third, the utility to a debtor of separate classification is restricted by the rule that the plan may not "discriminate unfairly" against any class of unsecured claims. Since a chapter 13 debtor does not need to obtain favorable class votes, as is the case in chapter 11, usually the only reason a debtor would be interested in separately classifying unsecured claims is precisely because the debtor wants to discriminate against one or more classes in the plan. For example, the debtor might want to pay 100 cents on the dollar on a nondischargeable student loan debt, but pay other unsecured claims only 20 cents each. Is this permitted? *Some* discrimination must be allowed, since the statute prohibits only *"unfair"* discrimination. The crux of chapter 13 classification fights, then, is over what constitutes an "unfair" discrimination.

Hundreds of cases have litigated the meaning of the unfair discrimination restriction. A four-part test for judging the fairness of the proposed discrimination has found favor with many courts:[130]

(1)   Does the discrimination have a reasonable basis?

(2)   Could the debtor carry out the plan without the discrimination?

(3)   Is the discrimination proposed in good faith?

(4)   Is the degree of discrimination directly related to the basis for the discrimination?

---

[129]   See § 12.8.

[130]   See, e.g., In re Leser, 939 F.2d 669, 672 (8th Cir. 1991) (citing *In re Wolff*, 22 B.R. 510, 512 (B.A.P. 9th Cir. 1982)).

As some courts have noted, the foregoing four-part test, while facially appealing, arguably begs the crucial questions.[131] In particular, the requirements that the discrimination have a reasonable basis, and that the debtor propose the discrimination in good faith, presuppose a stable referent of what goals are legitimate. Take, for instance, the student loan example given above. The debtor wants to classify the nondischargeable student loan separately and pay that debt in full, while paying only a small percentage to all other unsecured creditors. Does such a discrimination have a reasonable basis, and is it proposed in good faith; in short, is it "fair"?

The answer depends on what values are deemed most important. If we value (1) giving a chapter 13 debtor a more complete "fresh start" after bankruptcy (by paying off nondischargeable debts), and (2) protecting the financial integrity of the student loan system (by paying loan debts in full), then the discrimination in favor of student loans would be reasonable, in good faith, and fair. Some courts have so held.[132] Those courts further explain that the creditors who are being discriminated against still have the baseline protections of the best interests and disposable income tests.[133]

However, if we value equality between creditors, and look at the discrimination issue from the perspective of creditors as a group rather than the debtor, the discrimination in favor the student loan creditor is anything but fair and reasonable. Because the disposable income test requires the debtor to devote all excess income to plan payments, the total pot of money available for all creditors under the plan is a fixed amount. That being true, the allocation of monies as between creditors is a "zero-sum" game; every nickel used to pay the favored student loan creditor is a nickel taken out of the pockets of the other creditors. And even without the plan discrimination, that student loan creditor would be better off than other creditors, since it would be free to pursue the debtor after bankruptcy on the nondischargeable debt. A substantial majority of courts accordingly have concluded that the debtor's desire to pay off a nondischargeable debt pursuant to the chapter 13 plan is not a legitimate basis for discriminating in favor of the creditor holding the nondischargeable debt.[134]

Prior to 1994, alimony and child support cases proved especially contentious. Because of the strong public policy favoring the payment of those needy and deserving creditors, courts were inclined to allow separate classification and more favorable treatment of alimony and support claims.[135] This precise issue went away in 1994, though, when alimony and support claims were accorded priority status under § 507(a)(7); in 2005, that priority standing was elevated to first under § 507(a)(1). A chapter 13 plan is required to provide for the full payment of all priority claims,

---

[131] See In re Crawford, 324 F.3d 539, 542 (7th Cir. 2003) ("With respect, this test is empty. . . . ").

[132] See, e.g., In re Boscaccy, 442 B.R. 501 (Bankr. N.D. Miss. 2010); In re Johnson, 446 B.R. 921 (Bankr. E.D. Wis. 2011); In re Kalfayan, 415 B.R. 907 (Bankr. S.D. Fla. 2009); In re King, 460 B.R. 708 (Bankr. N.D. Tex. 2011); In re Pracht, 464 B.R. 486 (Bankr. M.D. Ga. 2012); In re Sharp, 415 B.R. 803 (Bankr. D. Colo. 2009).

[133] See, e.g., In re Abaunza, 452 B.R. 866 (Bankr. S.D. Fla. 2011); In re Orawsky, 387 B.R. 128 (Bankr. E.D. Pa. 2008); In re Stull, 489 B.R. 217 (Bankr. D. Kan. 2013).

[134] See, e.g., Crawford, supra note 131, 324 F.3d 539; In re Groves, 39 F.3d 212 (8th Cir. 1994); In re Belda, 315 B.R. 477 (N.D. Ill. 2004); In re Colley, 260 B.R. 532 (Bankr. M.D. 2000); In re Edmonds, 444 B.R. 898 (Bankr. E.D. Wis. 2010).

[135] See, e.g., In re Leser, 939 F.2d 669 (8th Cir. 1991).

§ 1322(a)(2), although a domestic support obligation that has been assigned and thus is payable to someone other than the spouse or child may be paid less than in full if all disposable income is devoted to plan payments for five years, § 1322(a)(4).[136]

Courts might be more willing to approve separate classification and more favorable treatment for one class of unsecured creditors if it appeared that doing so could benefit the creditors as a group, rather than just the debtor and the favored creditor. Such a situation might arise if separate classification made it easier for the debtor to perform under the plan, by obtaining necessary business credit from a critical supplier, or required medical treatment from the only readily available doctor.[137] However, if the creditor was requiring the debtor to repay a prepetition debt in full as a condition of providing future services, that creditor arguably would be violating the automatic stay, and could be held in contempt, and perhaps ordered to provide necessary services in exchange for current payment.

§ 12.12 Permissive Provisions: Modification, Cure, and Deacceleration

The debtor's need for bankruptcy relief often may arise because the debtor is unable to make full and timely payments on all of her current obligations. Although the debtor may have regular income, her disposable income may not be sufficient to pay everyone in full. Or, the debtor may have defaulted in payments on a major loan, such as for her home or car, and may not have enough cash on hand to cure the default immediately, opening the door to a possible foreclosure of a valuable asset.

Yet, if the debtor could stay creditors while she made payments over time, and scale back or extend some obligations, she might be able to retain her property and make meaningful payments to her creditors. Such, indeed, is the essence of chapter 13. Some of the most important tools necessary to enable the debtor to effect such a restructuring and repayment plan are the provisions permitting the debtor to modify claims, § 1322(b)(2), cure or waive defaults, § 1322(b)(3), and cure defaults and maintain payments on a long-term debt, § 1322(b)(5).

In fact, even a "chapter 20 debtor" (one that receives a discharge of her personal liability in an initial chapter 7 case, then files a second case under chapter 13 to deal with secured debts) may utilize these provisions, even if she is ineligible for a discharge in the 13 because she filed too soon after the chapter 7 case.[138] Note, though, that even if a court permits a chapter 20 debtor to modify her lien, the result may be ephemeral, as the lien may be reinstated if the second chapter 13 case is dismissed.[139]

---

[136] Note now the issue has become how far courts are willing to go to find a DSO obligation. For example, in one case, a court rejected a chapter 13 plan that did not provide for full payment of the debtor's obligation to hire his ex-wife as a consultant at an annual salary of $33,800. In re Ashby, 485 B.R. 567 (Bankr. W.D. Ky. 2013). The court held that the nature of this obligation was a DSO claim, recognizing that the provision in the marital settlement agreement laying out the obligation did not designate it as maintenance purely for tax reasons.

[137] See, e.g., In re Sutherland, 3 B.R. 420 (Bankr. W.D. Ark. 1980); see also In re Terry, 78 B.R. 171 (Bankr. E.D. Tenn. 1987).

[138] See In re Casey, 428 B.R. 519 (Bankr. S.D. Cal. 2010).

[139] See In re Victorio, 454 B.R. 759 (Bankr. S.D. Cal. 2011).

The most basic power the debtor needs is to be able to cure defaults. For example, assume that Debtor owns her home, subject to a mortgage in favor of Creditor to secure a $80,000 debt. Monthly payments are $800. Prior to filing for relief under chapter 13, Debtor misses two payments, and thus is $1600 in arrears. Creditor notifies Debtor that if she does not cure the default within 10 days, it will accelerate the note and foreclose on the mortgage. Debtor does not have $1600 available to pay Creditor. If Debtor files chapter 13, she may propose a plan that will cure the $1600 default to Creditor over the life of the plan. In a three-year plan, Debtor would have to pay only $44.44 a month plus interest to cure the default, in addition to maintaining the regular payments. Creditor's consent to this arrangement is not required.

One question that has arisen with regard to the cure provisions of § 1322(b)(3) and (5) is whether the debtor must pay *interest* on the arrearages being cured. Prior to 1993, most courts of appeals had held that interest did not have to be paid.[140] In 1993, however, the Supreme Court held in *Rake v. Wade*[141] that an oversecured creditor was entitled to postpetition interest on arrearages both before and after confirmation, even though neither the mortgage documents nor state law entitled the mortgagee to such interest. Congress overturned the holding in *Rake* in 1994 in § 1322(e), which provides that the amount necessary to cure a default is to be determined in accordance with the underlying agreement and applicable nonbankruptcy law. After *Rake* and the enactment of § 1322(e), then, the debtor will have to pay postpetition interest to cure a default if either the loan documents or state law so provides, but not otherwise.

In our hypothetical, assume that Creditor did accelerate the balance due on the note before Debtor filed chapter 13. Does that mean that cure is no longer possible? The answer is no. The cure provisions of § 1322(b) also permit the debtor to reverse an acceleration, i.e., to "deaccelerate," and to reinstate the original payment schedule.[142] After deaccelerating, Debtor will be able to cure just the amount in default over the life of the plan. The debtor's power to deaccelerate is very significant in influencing the behavior of parties when the debtor is in default. The creditor knows (1) that it cannot terminate the debtor's cure rights by rushing to accelerate before the debtor can file chapter 13, and (2) that if it does accelerate, it is likely to push the debtor into chapter 13.

At some point, though, the debtor's right to "cure" a default must end. The courts agree that a debtor no longer can cure once the debt has been accelerated, a foreclosure judgment has been entered, and the collateral has been sold at a foreclosure sale that has become final. Prior to 1994, most circuit courts had held that the debtor's cure right did extend beyond the entry of a foreclosure judgment, being terminated only when the property actually was sold at foreclosure.[143] The Third Circuit, however, disagreed, and took the view that entry of the foreclosure judgment extinguished the

---

[140] See, e.g., Landmark Fin. Servs. v. Hall, 918 F.2d 1150 (4th Cir. 1990).

[141] 508 U.S. 464 (1993).

[142] See, e.g., In re Taddeo, 685 F.2d 24 (2d Cir. 1982); Grubbs v. Houston First Am. Savs. Ass'n, 730 F.2d 236 (5th Cir. 1984); In re Clark, 738 F.2d 869 (7th Cir. 1984); In re Litton, 330 F.3d 636 (4th Cir. 2003); In re Metz, 820 F.2d 1495 (9th Cir. 1987).

[143] See, e.g., In re Glenn, 760 F.2d 1428 (6th Cir. 1985), cert. denied, 474 U.S. 849 (1985).

debtor's right to cure.[144] Congress rejected the Third Circuit's holding in 1994, enacting § 1322(c)(1), which provides that for home mortgages, cure may be effected until the time of the foreclosure sale. The legislative history further explained that if state law allows the debtor more extensive cure rights, such as through a later redemption period, that more beneficial state law may be invoked by the debtor.[145]

The debtor's rights to cure defaults and reverse an acceleration permit the debtor to reinstate and maintain the original payment terms, and forestall an immediate foreclosure. To fully resolve her financial difficulties, however, the debtor may need more drastic relief. In our hypothetical, the Debtor's problem may not just be curing the $1600 default, but making the $800 monthly payments in the first place. In short, the Debtor may need to *modify* the original terms of the obligation, and either extend the time for payments, reduce the amount of the payments, or both. Section 1322(b)(2) permits the debtor to do just that; under that section, the debtor's plan may modify the rights of the holder of a secured claim or an unsecured claim, with one very important exception. That exception is for home mortgages, which may not be modified. § 1322(b)(2).

Assume first that the collateral securing Debtor's obligation is *not* her home. The Debtor then would be free to modify the terms of the obligation, subject only to the limitations of § 1325(a)(5) for the secured portion of the claim[146] and § 1325(a)(4)[147] and (b)[148] for the unsecured portion. For example, if the property were worth only $60,000, the $80,000 debt would be bifurcated under § 506(a)(1) into a secured claim for $60,000 and an unsecured claim for $20,000. Debtor could strip down the secured claim to the $60,000 value, and then cram down that $60,000 claim under § 1325(a)(5). Debtor also could change the term of the repayments required and modify the interest rate. Debtor's required monthly payments obviously would drop substantially.

A 2005 amendment took away some of the debtor's power to write down certain types of undersecured claims, as described in the preceding paragraph. The "hanging paragraph" following § 1325(a) provides that "section 506 shall not apply" to (1) purchase money security interests where the debt was incurred in the 910 days before bankruptcy if the collateral is a motor vehicle purchased for the debtor's personal use,[149] or to (2) collateral "of any other thing of value"[150] for debts incurred in the year before bankruptcy. Since § 506 is the section that provides for the bifurcation of undersecured claims into secured and unsecured portions, the apparent intent of this amendment was to preclude the debtor from stripping down an undersecured claim in the described categories and providing for payment of only the lower value of the

---

[144] See In re Roach, 824 F.2d 1370 (3d Cir. 1987).

[145] 140 Cong. Rec. H10,769 (Oct. 4, 1994).

[146] See § 12.18.

[147] See § 12.16.

[148] See § 12.17.

[149] Courts generally determine whether a debtor acquired a vehicle for personal use by looking at his actual use of the motor vehicle shortly after purchase. E.g., In re Maushart, 483 B.R. 627 (Bankr. M.D. Pa. 2012).

[150] For example, courts hold that vehicles purchased for non-personal use (for example, a semi-truck tractor) within the past one-year period fall within this catchall provision. See In re Tanguay, 427 B.R. 663 (Bankr. E.D. Tenn. 2010).

collateral in satisfaction of the *secured* claim under § 1325(a)(5). Instead, the debtor would be forced to pay the full amount of the debt under that section.[151] So, for example, assume that the debtor purchased a new car on credit two years before bankruptcy, and when she filed chapter 13, the car was worth $10,000 but the debt was $12,000. To comply with § 1325(a)(5) and the hanging paragraph, the debtor would have to promise the secured creditor payments with a present value of $12,000, rather than $10,000, as before. Note, though, that the anti-modification rule of § 1322(b)(2) poses no bar to the debtor either extending the term of the payment schedule or modifying the interest rate, or to curing defaults; the debtor simply cannot change the principal amount due.

One issue that comes up is whether a creditor, otherwise protected under the hanging paragraph, has a purchase money security interest in "negative equity" of a trade-in vehicle. To illustrate, suppose Debtor wants to trade in his old Volkswagen, worth $7,000, for a new Mercedes, worth $50,000. However, Debtor still owes $15,000 on the Volkswagen. Thus, there is $8,000 "negative equity" on the Volkswagen. So, Lender applies a $7,000 credit for the trade-in, but pays down the $15,000 still owed by Debtor, and adds it to the balance, bringing the total bill for the Mercedes to $58,000. Does Lender have a purchase money security interest in the $8,000 negative equity, as to allow him to demand that portion over the course of a chapter 13 plan? The Ninth Circuit says no; noting that the Code does not define "purchase money security interest," the court looked to state law, and found that under California Law, the PMSI did not encompass negative equity.[152] However, most circuit courts have taken the other view, including the Second, Fifth, Sixth, Seventh, Eighth and Tenth Circuits, and hold that a creditor does in fact have a PMSI in any negative equity.[153]

If the collateral securing the debt is Debtor's *home*, the rules change. Modification is out. A special rule protects mortgagees whose claim is secured only by a security interest in the debtor's principal residence. § 1322(b)(2). The rights of those creditors may not be stripped down and modified, although defaults may be cured.[154]

Prior to 1993, the courts disagreed as to whether § 1322(b)(2) did in fact prevent strip down in chapter 13 cases. Several courts of appeals held that the anti-modification rule of § 1322(b)(2) for home mortgages only applied to the *secured* portion of the claim,[155] and that strip down thus was permissible. Those courts explained that

---

[151] Thus, if a debtor surrenders the vehicle and the proceeds from the sale still do not bring in the full value of the claim, a lender would be able to maintain an unsecured claim for the deficiency. E.g., AmeriCredit Fin. Servs., Inc. v. Tompkins, 604 F.3d 753 (2d Cir. 2010).

[152] In re Penrod, 611 F.3d 1158 (9th Cir. 2010). See also In re Hayes, 376 B.R. 655 (Bankr. M.D. Tenn. 2007) (holding that a lender's security interest in payments forwarded to debtor to cover negative equity and insurance payments on new vehicle did not constitute PMSIs); In re White, 417 B.R. 102 (Bankr. S.D. Ind. 2009).

[153] See, e.g., In re Dale, 582 F.3d 568 (5th Cir. 2009); In re Ford, 574 F.3d 1279 (10th Cir. 2009); In re Howard, 597 F.3d 852 (7th Cir. 2010); In re Mierkowski, 580 F.3d 740 (8th Cir. 2009); In re Peaslee, 585 F.3d 53 (2d Cir. 2009); In re Westfall, 599 F.3d 498 (6th Cir. 2010); In re Morey, 414 B.R. 473 (Bankr. E.D. Wis. 2009); In re Padgett, 408 B.R. 374 (B.A.P. 10th Cir. 2009).

[154] One court permitted modification when the creditor's lien was on a parcel of land, and the debtor's residence straddled such land with an adjacent lot. In re LaFata, 483 F.3d 13 (1st Cir. 2007).

[155] See, e.g., In re Bellamy, 962 F.2d 176 (2d Cir. 1992); In re Hougland, 886 F.2d 1182 (9th Cir. 1989).

§ 506(a) automatically bifurcates an undersecured claim into a "secured claim" up to the value of the collateral and an "unsecured claim" for the balance, and that the anti-modification provision in § 1322(b)(2) refers only to "secured claims," as defined in § 506(a).

In 1993, however, the Supreme Court held in *Nobelman v. American Savings Bank*[156] that § 1322(b)(2) does prevent the modification of an undersecured home mortgage. The Nobelmans owed the mortgagee a total debt of over $71,000 on property worth only $23,500. The Court decided that the prohibition on modification referred to the *rights* of the holder of the secured claim, rather than just the secured claim itself.[157] Those rights included the right to be paid the full principal balance of the debt (i.e., the $71,000), with interest over the agreed term. The Court pointed out that it was impossible for the debtor to strip down the principal balance of the secured claim to $23,500 and yet not "modify" any of the rights of the mortgagee. Something would have to be altered—the term of the payments, the amount of the monthly payment, or the interest rate—and that would constitute an impermissible modification.[158] Therefore, the debtors could only confirm their chapter 13 plan if they paid the mortgagee the full $71,000 under the plan.

One limitation on this special protective rule is that it applies only where the creditor's claim is secured *only* by a security interest in the debtor's principal residence. In other words, if the creditor has additional security (such as in personal property), it forfeits the protection of the special rule.[159] Creditors who include boiler-plate dragnet security provisions in their home mortgage documents thus through their greed may forfeit the protections of § 1322(b)(2). However, creditors who have a security interest on rents derived from a debtor's residence are not excluded thereby from the anti-modification provision.[160]

A related issue that the courts have had to resolve is whether the home mortgage anti-modification rule applies to a *multi-unit* property, where some but not all of the units are the debtor's principal residence. For example, assume that the collateral in question is a duplex, and the debtor lives in one unit and rents out the other. Courts have held that the debtor may modify such a claim in a chapter 13 plan, notwithstanding the anti-modification rule, because the creditor's claim is not secured "only" by a security interest in the debtor's principal residence, but by the rental unit as well.[161]

In *Nobelman*, the mortgagee had $23,500 in value on the $71,000 debt, and the Court thus had no trouble concluding that the mortgagee was still "the holder of a

---

[156]   508 U.S. 324 (1993).

[157]   Id. at 328–29.

[158]   Id. at 331–32.

[159]   See Hammond v. Commonwealth Mortg. Corp. of Am. (In re Hammond), 27 F.3d 52 (3d Cir. 1994).

[160]   See, e.g., In re Ferandos, 402 F.3d 147 (3d Cir. 2005); In re Rolle, 218 B.R. 636 (Bankr. S.D. Fla. 1998). But see In re Thomas, 344 B.R. 386 (Bankr. W.D. Pa. 2006) (allowing debtor to modify mortgage when creditor took security interest in the property's escrow fund).

[161]   See In re Scarborough, 461 F.3d 406 (3d Cir. 2006); Lomas Mortg., Inc. v. Louis, 82 F.3d 1 (1st Cir. 1996).

secured claim" and its rights thus immune from modification under § 1322(b)(2).[162] But what if the mortgagee's claim were totally valueless? For example, assume that Debtor had granted a first mortgage to Bank One to secure a debt of $80,000, and a second mortgage to Bank Two to secure a debt of $30,000, at a time when the home was worth $130,000. Subsequently, though, housing prices collapse, and when Debtor files chapter 13, the home is alleged to be worth only $75,000. If that valuation is accurate, then Bank Two's $30,000 claim is totally unsecured, since the collateral value is insufficient to pay off the first mortgage of $80,000. The question is whether Bank Two's valueless mortgage can be modified notwithstanding § 1322(b)(2). This practice is called "strip off," as contrasted with "strip down." A clear majority of courts, and all but one of the circuit courts to consider the issue,[163] hold that the valueless home mortgage can be modified; that is, they conclude that the anti-modification rule of § 1322(b)(2) does not apply. Their reasoning is that the underwater mortgagee is not a "holder of [a] secured claim" at all under § 506(a), and thus does not fall within the scope of § 1322(b)(2) as a threshold matter. Note, though, that if the court concluded that there were even *a penny* of value securing the mortgage, then the *entire* mortgage would be protected from modification by § 1322(b)(2), because then the mortgagee would be the "holder of a secured claim" (albeit for one cent!), and thus its *rights* could not be modified under the *Nobelman* Court's interpretation of the anti-modification rule. So, in the example given, if the bankruptcy court disagreed with Debtor's proposed valuation of $75,000, and found instead a value of $80,000.01, then Debtor could not modify Bank Two's mortgage at all.

Another limitation on the anti-modification rule of § 1322(b)(2) is that after 1994, it apparently does not apply to short-term home mortgage loans. In the 1994 legislation, Congress enacted § 1322(c)(2), which on its face applies to home mortgages that mature before the final payment is due under the chapter 13 plan. For example, if a home mortgage loan has four years left to run, and the debtor proposes a five-year plan, § 1322(c)(2) would apply. This would arise most often when the debtor took out a short-term loan with a balloon payment at the end. Significantly, (c)(2) applies "notwithstanding subsection (b)(2)"—which is the anti-modification provision that was given effect in *Nobelman*. Since (c)(2) controls (b)(2), the anti-modification rule does not apply to cases covered by subsection (c)(2). The new subsection permits the debtor to provide in the plan for the payment of a covered home mortgage claim "as modified" under the cram down provision (§ 1325(a)(5)). Modification under § 1325(a)(5) would permit strip down of an undersecured home mortgage.

The "plain meaning" of § 1322(c)(2) thus appears to allow the strip down and modification of an undersecured home mortgage that will mature before the end of the

---

[162] 508 U.S. at 329.

[163] In re Zimmer, 313 F.3d (9th Cir. 2002); In re Lane, 280 F.3d 663 (6th Cir. 2002); In re Pond, 252 F.3d 122 (2d Cir. 2001); In re Tanner, 217 F.3d 1357 (11th Cir. 2000); In re Bartee, 212 F.3d 277 (5th Cir. 2000); In re McDonald, 205 F.3d 606 (3d Cir.), cert. denied, 531 U.S. 822 (2000). But see In re Woolsey, 969 F.3d 1266 (10th Cir. 2012) (applying *Nobelman*'s rationale to preclude stripping down a wholly unsecured junior mortgage). See also TD Bank, N.A. v. Landry, 479 B.R. 1 (D. Mass. 2012) (holding that proper time for valuing residential property to decide whether junior mortgagee is undersecured or holds a claim wholly unsecured, for purposes of determining application of the anti-modification provision, is the petition date).

A subsequent Eleventh Circuit panel said that it would have decided the other way, but was constrained by circuit precedent (*Tanner*). See In re Dickerson, 222 F.3d 924 (11th Cir. 2000).

plan. Courts, always looking for ways to get around the home mortgage anti-modification rule, have given the statute its literal effect and allow modification.[164] The oddity, though, is that there is no evidence in the legislative history to the 1994 amendments that Congress was even aware that it was altering the outcome in *Nobelman,* which had been decided just the year before. Indeed, in another section of the 1994 bill, Congress extended the chapter 13 anti-modification rule for home mortgages to chapter 11. See § 1123(b)(5). The stated purpose of § 1322(c)(2) was to overrule a Third Circuit decision that had nothing to do with the *Nobelman* problem.[165]

§ 12.13 Permissive Provisions: Other Provisions

The statutory authorization for a debtor in a chapter 13 plan to classify claims,[166] § 1322(b)(1), and to modify claims and cure defaults,[167] § 1322(b)(2), (3), (5), are of great importance in enabling debtors to obtain necessary relief in chapter 13. Those are not the only permissive provisions that a plan may include, however. Section 1322(b) is designed to afford the debtor considerable flexibility in framing the terms of a plan, so that each debtor can tailor her plan to deal with her own individual circumstances.[168]

First, the debtor is given flexibility in providing for the *order* in which claims may be paid under the plan. Under prior law, there was a view that secured claims had to be paid before unsecured claims. That premise is negated by § 1322(b)(4), which specifies that payments may be made on any unsecured claim concurrently with payments on any secured claim or other unsecured claims. The only explicit temporal limitation on when claims must be paid is § 1326(b), which mandates that "before or at the time of" "each payment" to creditors under the plan, second priority claims, the standing chapter 13 trustee's percentage fee, and any compensation owed to a chapter 7 trustee under a converted or dismissed case, shall be paid.

A debtor is permitted to provide for the payment of postpetition claims allowed under § 1305. § 1322(b)(6). The two types of claims that may be allowed under § 1305 are tax debts and necessary consumer debts.[169] By providing for the payment of these claims in the plan, the debtor may be able to discharge those claims in the chapter 13 case. § 1328(a), (c). If the holder of the claim chooses not to file a proof of claim, however, the claim will not be "allowed," § 1305(b), and the debtor will not be able to provide for the claim in the plan, since the statutory authorization in § 1322(b)(6) only extends to allowed claims.

The debtor is given a final opportunity to deal with executory contracts and unexpired leases in the plan, by assuming, assigning, or rejecting the contract or lease. § 1322(b)(7). Under § 365, action also may be taken with regard to the contract or lease

---

[164] E.g., In re Paschen, 296 F.3d 1203 (11th Cir. 2002). But see In re Witt, 113 F.3d 508 (4th Cir. 1997) (denying bifurcation of an undersecured mortgage that becomes due prior to the final payment under the plan).

[165] See 140 Cong. Rec. H10,769 (Oct. 4, 1994) (referring to *First Nat'l Fidelity Corp. v. Perry,* 945 F.2d 61 (3d Cir. 1991)).

[166] See § 12.11.

[167] See § 12.12.

[168] H.R. Rep. No. 95–595, 95th Cong., 1st Sess., at 123 (1977).

[169] See § 12.7.

outside of the plan. An amendment to the Code in 1984 clarified that actions regarding contracts or leases in a chapter 13 plan are still subject to the many special rules and limitations of § 365. For example, a lease of nonresidential real property is governed by special rules as to interim performance and timing. § 365(d)(3), (4). Note, though, that the special protections for commercial personal property leases in § 365(d)(5) do not apply in chapter 13, but only in chapter 11.

Another provision affording the debtor flexibility in drafting a plan is § 1322(b)(8), which allows the debtor to provide for the payment of a claim from property of the estate or from property of the debtor. Furthermore, § 1322(b)(9) permits the debtor to control the vesting of property of the estate. In § 1327(b), the default rule is that confirmation of the plan vests all property of the estate in the debtor.[170] For various reasons, however, the debtor may want to override that rule. For example, the debtor may want to defer the vesting of certain property of the estate, in order to maintain the automatic stay in effect as to that property. The debtor then could provide that the described property would not vest in the debtor until the completion of payments under the plan, or on a debt secured by the property. Additionally, BAPCPA added a provision that allows the debtor to pay postpetition interest accruing on nondischargeable unsecured claims, but only if the debtor still has disposable income available after paying all allowed claims in full. § 1322(b)(10).

Finally, a catch-all provision empowers the debtor to include in the plan "any other appropriate provision[171] not inconsistent with this title." § 1322(b)(11). While Congress in the specific grants of permissive authority in § 1322(b) tried to cover the most common situations that individual debtors might encounter in trying to repay their debts, it is impracticable in a Code to cover every imaginable scenario. The grant of residual authority in § 1322(b)(11) is an important cog in the confirmation scheme, because under § 1325(a)(1), the plan may only be confirmed if it complies with the provisions of the Code. The congressional intent in subsection (b)(11) plainly was to give debtors considerable latitude in creating their plans. At the same time, the "not inconsistent" limitation will require courts to be sensitive to the rights of creditors and other parties in interest, and to be alert to implicit and indirect conflicts with specific statutory sections. Provisions approved by bankruptcy courts under § 1322(b)(1) include: including enhanced reporting requirements,[172] authorizing the debtor to exercise a trustee's avoiding powers,[173] establishing reserve funds to pay utilities in event of default,[174] and paying taxes in a particular order.[175]

---

[170] See § 12.20.

[171] One court read "appropriate provision" as a limitation to deny confirmation of a plan that included provisions "serving no useful purpose," but merely "cluttered" the plan. In re Madera, 445 B.R. 509 (Bankr. D.S.C. 2011).

[172] See In Re Monroy, 650 F.3d 1300 (9th Cir. 2010).

[173] See In re Hearn, 337 B.R. 603 (Bankr. E.D. Mich. 2006).

[174] See In re Epling, 255 B.R. 549 (Bankr. S.D. Ohio 2000).

[175] See In re Klaska, 152 B.R. 248 (Bankr. C.D. Ill. 1993).

§ 12.14 Length of Chapter 13 Plans

Under the prior Act, local practice varied greatly in the administration of chapter XIII wage earner plans. One of the areas in which national uniformity was most notably absent was with regard to the *length* of chapter XIII plans.[176] In some regions, plans might extend as long seven to ten years, making them "a way of life for certain debtors," as well as "the closest thing there is to indentured servitude."[177] This situation, Congress decided in 1978, was unacceptable. Not only was practice not uniform, lengthy repayment plans often were not feasible, they were too harsh on debtors, and they discouraged debtors from choosing to proceed under a debt repayment plan in the first place. In short, creditors and debtors alike suffered from the use of extremely long plan periods.

Congress remedied these problems in the 1978 Code by imposing a time limit on the length of chapter 13 plans. Under § 1322(d) as originally enacted, the plan could not provide for payments over a period that is longer than *three years*, unless the court approved a longer period, not to exceed five years, based on a showing of "cause." In 2005, this rule was changed for debtors with a family income at or above the state median income. Today, the maximum length of the plan is either three or five years, depending on the debtor's income level. If the current monthly income of the debtor and the debtor's spouse, when multiplied by twelve, is not less than the median annual income for a similar family size in the debtor's state, then the maximum plan term is *five years*. § 1322(d)(1). If, however, that annualized income is *less* than the state median, the old rule applies (three year limit, subject to extension to five years for cause). § 1322(d)(2). A plan that provides for payments over a longer period than allowed by § 1322(d) cannot be confirmed.

Nor may the plan time limits of § 1322(d) be circumvented by a post-confirmation modification. A modification cannot provide for payments for a period that expires after the "applicable commitment period" under § 1325(b)(1)(B) (which period will be either three years or five years, depending again on whether the debtor's family income is above or below the state median) after the first payment was due under the plan as originally confirmed. Again, the court for cause may approve a longer period (although never longer than five years). § 1329(c).

There is no *minimum* plan period directly required by the Code. However, the projected disposable income test indirectly comes into play. Under § 1325(b)(1)(B), the debtor must apply all disposable income to plan payments for the applicable commitment period (three to five years, depending on debtor's income) after the first payment under the plan is due. In combination, § 1322(d) and § 1325(b)(1)(B) thus tend to establish either three years or five years (depending again on whether debtor's family income is above or below the state median) as the presumptive norm for a chapter 13 plan period, unless the debtor can repay all unsecured claims in full in a shorter time period.

---

[176] S. Rep. No. 95–989, 95th Cong., 2d Sess., at 13 (1978).

[177] H.R. Rep. No. 95–595, 95th Cong., 1st Sess., at 117 (1977).

The Code is not clear on when the clock starts running on the permissible plan period. Both the modification rule (§ 1329(c)) and the disposable income test (§ 1325(b)(1)(B)) refer to when the first payment under the plan was due as the starting point in the calculation, but § 1322(d) is silent on the issue. One possibility, of course, is to count from when the first plan payment is due after confirmation, but this is not certain, given that the debtor must commence making payments prior to confirmation. § 1326(a)(1). If the first post-confirmation payment due date were used, the debtor thus would effectively have to make payments for more than three years.

A fighting issue under § 1322(d) is what constitutes "cause" to support an extension beyond the three-year period. This issue does not arise with presumptive five-year periods for above-median debtors, because that period cannot be extended; it is only if the debtor is below the median that the three-year period is used (and thus subject to possible extension). Most fundamentally, it should not qualify as "cause" that the debtor would be able to pay more to creditors over a longer period,[178] though some courts disagree and take the broader view.[179] That will always be true, and if the courts permitted a "greater payment" justification, the five-year exception would swallow up the three-year rule; five-year plans would become the norm, even for below-median debtors. The case against finding "cause" for a longer plan period based on a debtor's projected payment ability became even more compelling in 2005, when Congress amended the law to provide that above median debtors could be subject to five-year plans without a showing of cause.

Instead of focusing the cause inquiry on benefit to creditors, the proper focus should be on whether the *debtor* would benefit from an extension beyond three years. At first blush one might wonder why it would ever be in the debtor's interests to pay creditors more money. In fact, though, a benefit might accrue to the debtor from an extended repayment period in several situations.

First, allowing the debtor to make payments for more than three years might enable the debtor to confirm a plan. For example, the debtor might not be able to pay priority claims or allowed secured claims in full over three years, which would preclude confirmation. See §§ 1322(a)(2), 1325(a)(5)(B). That same debtor might have enough disposable income to pay those priority and secured claims in full over five years, though, and thereby confirm the plan. Allowing the extension beyond three years thus would help the debtor.

Second, even if a debtor could confirm a plan, it might not be able to obtain complete relief in a three-year plan. For example, the debtor might only be able to cure a default under § 1322(b)(3) or (5) if she could make payments against the arrearages for more than three years. Permitting the extended cure period might enable the debtor to retain valuable property.

Finally, some courts have authorized a debtor to make payments for more than three years if the debtor is thereby able to pay unsecured claims in full, or at least 70%

---

[178] See, e.g., In re Greer, 60 B.R. 547 (Bankr. C.D. Cal. 1986)

[179] See, e.g., In re Pierce, 82 B.R. 874 (Bankr. S.D. Ohio. 1987); In re Ward, 456 B.R. 766 (Bankr. E.D. Mich. 2010).

on those claims. Achieving those repayment amounts can be important for the debtor, because it frees the debtor from the constraint of the six-year bar on a subsequent bankruptcy discharge. § 727(a)(9). For example, a debtor who paid 65% on her unsecured debts could not receive a chapter 7 discharge in a case filed within six years, but that debtor would be eligible for a discharge in less than six years if she paid unsecured claims 70% in a good faith, best efforts plan.

D. CONFIRMATION REQUIREMENTS

§ 12.15 Good Faith

Chapter 13, like the rest of the Bankruptcy Code, is intended for the relief of honest debtors and the equitable treatment of creditors, not as a haven for dishonest debtors. As originally enacted in 1978, the liberal discharge provisions in chapter 13, along with the lack of any rigorous payment tests for unsecured claims other than the "best interests" test of § 1325(a)(4), created potential for debtor abuse, and generated a need for careful policing. To a considerable extent this policing need now has been addressed by the subsequent enactment of specific laws targeted at those specific problems, especially the virtual evisceration of the "superdischarge" in § 1328(a) and the requirement in § 1325(b) that debtors commit all projected disposable income to pay off their unsecured creditors. Apart from those specific policing rules, though, the broader vehicle by which the court is empowered to screen out bad faith debtors is § 1325(a)(3), which requires as a condition of confirmation that the court find that "the plan has been proposed in good faith and not by any means forbidden by law." In addition, in 2005 Congress added a further good faith requirement (already embraced judicially by the courts in considering dismissal for cause under § 1307(c)),[180] that the debtor's action in *filing* the case itself had to be in good faith. § 1325(a)(7).

The debtor has the burden of showing that it proposed the plan in good faith.[181] If a creditor objects to confirmation on the ground that the debtor has acted in bad faith, an evidentiary hearing may be required,[182] although some courts permit the bankruptcy court to dispense with a hearing in limited circumstances.[183] In any event, if good faith is challenged, the court must make specific findings of fact on the good faith issue in confirming a plan.[184]

The dispositive question in every contested case is, of course, what constitutes "good faith"? Just as obviously, it is impossible to capture the full meaning of a concept as broad and as vague as "good faith" in a tidy phrase or test. Most courts have recognized the hopelessness of such a task, and have fallen back on the essentially useless general admonition that the "totality of the circumstances" must be

---

[180] See, e.g., In re Alt, 305 F.3d 413 (6th Cir. 2002); In re Smith, 286 F.3d 461 (7th Cir. 2002); In re Young, 237 F.3d 1168 (10th Cir. 2001).

[181] See, e.g., In re Stanley, 224 Fed.Appx. 343 (5th Cir. 2007); In re Welsh, 711 F.3d 1120, 1124 (9th Cir. 2013).

[182] See, e.g., In re Schaitz, 913 F.2d 452 (7th Cir. 1990).

[183] See, e.g., Noreen v. Slattengren, 974 F.2d 75 (8th Cir. 1992).

[184] See, e.g., In re Robinson, 987 F.2d 665 (10th Cir. 1993); In re Tucker, 989 F.2d 328 (9th Cir. 1993).

considered.[185] At a minimum, courts demand that the debtor have "honest intentions,"[186] assuming that the debtor's intentions somehow can be divined. One lodestar many courts hew to is that the debtor must act with "fundamental fairness."[187] Having said that, it is hard to see how using such a catchphrase has moved the ball any closer to the goal line of clarity.

To assuage the feeling of being adrift in an uncharted sea, courts have gravitated to the comfortable tendency to develop lengthy laundry lists of factors to be weighed in the good faith calculus. For example, one such list suggests consideration of no fewer than a dozen criteria:[188]

(1)   the amount of the proposed payments and the amount of the debtor's surplus;

(2)   the debtor's employment history, ability to earn and likelihood of future increase in income;

(3)   the probable or expected duration of the plan;

(4)   the accuracy of the plan's statements of the debts, expenses and percentage repayment of unsecured debt and whether any inaccuracies are an attempt to mislead the court;

(5)   the extent of preferential treatment between classes of creditors;

(6)   the extent to which secured claims are modified;

(7)   the type of debt sought to be discharged and whether any such debt is nondischargeable in chapter 7;

(8)   the existence of special circumstances such as inordinate medical expenses;

(9)   the frequency with which the debtor has sought relief under the Bankruptcy Reform Act;

(10) the motivation and sincerity of the debtor in seeking chapter 13 relief;

(11) the burden which the plan's administration would place upon the trustee; and,

(12) whether the debtor is attempting to abuse the spirit of the Code.

---

[185]   See, e.g., In re Cranmer, 697 F.3d 1314 (10th Cir. 2012); In re Flores, 692 F.3d 1021 (9th Cir. 2012); In re Smith, 286 F.3d 461 (7th Cir. 2002).

[186]   See, e.g., Barnes v. Whelan, 689 F.2d 193 (D.C. Cir. 1982); In re Smith, 848 F.2d 813 (7th Cir. 1988).

[187]   See, e.g., In re Rimgale, 669 F.2d 426, 432–33 (7th Cir. 1982) (citing In re Beaver, 2 B.R. 337, 340 (Bankr. S.D. Cal. 1980)).

[188]   In re Caldwell, 895 F.2d 1123, 1126–27 (6th Cir. 1990). The Seventh Circuit, by contrast, has proffered but five factors (although explaining that these five are but illustrative, not exclusive):

Another formulation of the factors relevant to the "totality of the circumstances" inquiry was expressed in a 1995 Fourth Circuit case, which identified the following:

"The percentage of proposed repayment to creditors, the debtor's financial situation, the period of time over which creditors will be paid, the debtor's employment history and prospects, the nature and amount of unsecured claims, the debtor's past bankruptcy filings, the debtor's honesty in representing the facts of the case, the nature of the debtor's pre-petition conduct that gave rise to the debts, whether the debts would be dischargeable in a Chapter 7 proceeding, and any other unusual or exceptional problems the debtor faces."[189]

Courts recognize that such lists are neither self-executing nor, despite their impressive length, all-encompassing. Good faith still must be evaluated on a case-by-case basis in light of the general purposes of Chapter 13, imposing a significant responsibility on and vesting wide discretion in the bankruptcy court.[190] Because of the inherently fact-intensive nature of the good faith inquiry, the bankruptcy court's determination usually will only be reversed if clearly erroneous.

Notwithstanding the long lists of factors, and the concomitant exhortation to weigh the totality of the circumstances based on the facts of the individual case, certain fact patterns and decisional models emerge. Two types of behavior by debtors have been especially likely to trigger protestations of bad faith by creditors: first, using chapter 13 in an attempt to discharge debts of a type listed in § 523(a) that would not be dischargeable in chapter 7; and second, proposing to pay unsecured creditors nothing at all in the chapter 13 plan, or only a very minimal dividend. In combination, these two facts may provoke a firestorm of complaints.

A third situation in which good faith is likely to be questioned, but which arises less frequently than the other two, is when the debtor has filed multiple bankruptcy cases, with the current chapter 13 proceeding but the latest in the series. Here courts tend to hold that the fact of serial filings does not constitute bad faith on a *per se* basis, but is a factor that can be considered.[191] In dictum the Supreme Court approved this view, noting in *Johnson v. Home State Bank*[192] that a serial filing *could* run afoul of the good faith requirement, but was not *automatically* impermissible. Courts should tread lightly, though, in inferring bad faith from multiple filings, given that Congress has put a specific remedy in the Code to deal with repetitive filings. § 109(g).[193]

In the early years of the Code, one of the most litigated issues was whether a zero-payment or minimal-payment plan violated the good faith requirement. Some courts held flatly that a zero-payment plan could not be confirmed under any circumstances.[194] If the plan proposed to pay only a nominal percentage to unsecured creditors, some courts again refused to confirm the plan, or at the least took the paltry

---

[189] In re Solomon, 67 F.3d 1128, 1134 (4th Cir. 1995).

[190] See, e.g., In re Puffer, 674 F.3d 78 (1st Cir. 2012).

[191] See, e.g., In re Bateman, 515 F.3d 272 (4th Cir. 2008); In re Johnson, 708 F.2d 865 (2d Cir. 1983).

[192] 501 U.S. 78, 87 (1991).

[193] § 2.3.

[194] See, e.g., In re Terry, 630 F.2d 634 (8th Cir. 1980).

percentage being repaid into account as a factor to be weighed in assessing good faith.[195] Other courts, however, recoiled at imposing a payment requirement where Congress had not, and rejected the premise that the amount paid under the plan could be considered in the good faith equation.[196]

The use of § 1325(a)(3)'s good faith test as a vehicle for monitoring the quantum of payments to unsecured creditors, questionable from the outset, clearly became untenable with the enactment of the projected disposable income test (also known as the "best efforts" test) of § 1325(b) in 1984. To confirm a plan, a debtor not only must show that the unsecured creditors will be paid at least as much as they would have received in a liquidation (the so-called "best interests" test),[197] § 1325(a)(4), but also must commit all of her projected disposable income for the applicable commitment period of three to five years to plan payments.[198] § 1325(b)(1)(B). Congress added the projected disposable income test for the specific purpose of preventing debtors with substantial excess income but few distributable assets from proposing minimal repayment plans. Now, if a debtor is applying *all* of her projected disposable income for the entire life of the plan to payments under the plan, it is difficult in most cases to see how the fact that unsecured creditors still might not be receiving a substantial dividend can be counted as "bad faith." Indeed, by definition the debtor would not be able to pay a penny more. Thus, future payment ability almost always should be dealt with solely under the projected disposable income test, not under a general "good faith" assessment.[199] The only circumstance in which a debtor's putative payment ability still even conceivably might be relevant under "good faith" and not under "best efforts" is where the debtor in bad faith has chosen *not* to maximize her income, eschewing taking a readily available higher-paying job, and yet can count only her actual lower-paying job's wages towards the best efforts test.

The use of chapter 13 to escape nondischargeable debts remains controversial, although the occasion for the debate has been reduced dramatically with the 2005 evisceration of the "superdischarge." The problem is as follows. If a debtor completes payments under the plan, she will be discharged from all debts provided for by the plan, *including* some types of debts under § 523(a) that would be excepted from a chapter 7 discharge.[200] § 1328(a). Before 2005, the full-compliance chapter 13 discharge even applied to debts for *fraud* and for *willful and malicious injury*. Congress created this "superdischarge" on purpose, intending it to be an incentive for debtors to opt for voluntary relief under chapter 13 instead of liquidating under chapter 7.

So, assume that prior to 2005 a debtor who faced a substantial debt that was indisputably based on fraud decided to proceed under chapter 13 instead of chapter 7, specifically because the debtor wanted to be able to discharge that fraud debt. Is that "bad faith"? Notwithstanding the avowed congressional policy to permit debtors to

---

[195] See, e.g., *Rimgale*, supra note 187, 669 F.2d 426.

[196] See, e.g., In re Puffer, 674 F.3d 78 (1st Cir. 2012).

[197] See § 12.16.

[198] See § 12.17.

[199] See, e.g., In re Cranmer, 967 F.3d 1314 (10th Cir. 2012); In re Ragos, 700 F.3d 220 (5th Cir. 2012); In re Mancl, 381 B.R. 537 (W.D. Wis. 2008).

[200] See § 12.23.

discharge otherwise nondischargeable debts in chapter 13, creditors and courts have bristled at the wisdom of the statutory scheme. Many courts have sought to ameliorate the problem by holding that a debtor who invokes chapter 13 for the express purpose of escaping from a nondischargeable debt has acted in bad faith, and cannot confirm a chapter 13 plan. The debtor then must turn to either chapter 7 or chapter 11 for relief, if at all, and under those chapters will not be able to discharge the objectionable debt.

The best-known example of this judicial activism is the Eighth Circuit's decision in *Handeen v. LeMaire (In re LeMaire).*[201] The debtor in that case had tried to *murder* Handeen with a rifle. Handeen obtained a civil judgment against LeMaire, which LeMaire, after being released from prison, sought to discharge in chapter 13. The debt to Handeen, although obviously for willful and malicious injury within the meaning of § 523(a)(6), and thus not dischargeable in a chapter 7 case, would have been dischargeable (at that time) in chapter 13 if LeMaire made all payments under the plan. The Eighth Circuit held that LeMaire had acted in bad faith, and chapter 13 relief should be denied. The dissent complained that it cannot be bad faith to use the statute exactly as it is written, and indeed for the very reason it was written that way, and explained that the majority's holding effectively eviscerated the superdischarge.

The dissent, it would seem, plainly has the better of the argument. If Congress wants debtors to be able to discharge debts for willful and malicious injury, or for fraud, in chapter 13, with the statutory *quid pro quo* being that the debtor must make payments to creditors for a period of three to five years, and indeed must commit every dime of his projected disposable income over and above necessary living expenses to repay creditors for that multi-year period, then the judiciary should respect that legislative decision as a matter of separation of powers. Nor is it a fair "interpretation" of the statute to invoke a general test such as "good faith" to effectively trump a more specific statutory provision that defines the scope of the discharge.

After the 2005 amendments, this issue has become considerably less important, since many more of the § 523(a) debts now are excluded from discharge in chapter 13 even if the debtor completes performance under the plan. For example, fraud debts now cannot be discharged, § 1328(a)(2), and neither can debts for "willful or malicious injury" that caused personal injury or death, if a civil judgment has been entered.[202] § 1328(a)(4). Today, then, LeMaire would be out of luck in chapter 13 as well—but that suggests even more strongly that it was inappropriate for the Eighth Circuit to use the "good faith" test to second-guess Congress's decision at the time to allow a chapter 13 debtor to discharge such debts, since Congress has shown that if its legislative choice was foolish, it can fix its mistakes. Post–2005, with Congress having revisited the issue of the superdischarge in BAPCPA, and having made substantial changes in its scope, it

---

[201] 898 F.2d 1346 (8th Cir. 1990) (en banc).

[202] Curiously, Congress did not simply incorporate § 523(a)(6), but instead opted for the exclusion described in the text. Query, then, what if a debtor had committed an act that likely was a "willful or malicious injury" (such as attempted murder!) but the victim had not yet gotten a civil judgment for restitution or damages, as § 1328(a)(4) requires, before the debtor filed chapter 13. Would a court be warranted in ruling that the debtor acted in "bad faith"? Here, when Congress has revisited the statute and drafted with extreme specificity, and has distinguished between cases where the victim has and has not gotten a judgment, it would be especially troubling for a court to undermine that legislative choice by invoking a general good faith rubric.

now would be an even more egregious arrogation of power for a court to hold that a debtor who uses chapter 13 to take advantage of the miserly not-so-"super"-discharge still left has acted in bad faith.

§ 12.16 Best Interests Test

Unsecured creditors in chapter 13 cases lack many of the protections that they have in chapter 11 cases. Notably, they do not have the right to *vote* on the debtor's proposed plan. A chapter 13 plan is not a product of negotiation, as is often the case in chapter 11, but rather is dictated entirely by the debtor, subject only to the specific constraints of the Code. Unsecured creditors are not represented by an official committee in chapter 13, as they are in chapter 11, and indeed there would be little for a chapter 13 committee to do. Finally, classes of unsecured creditors in chapter 13 cannot invoke the absolute priority rule, meaning that the debtor is free to retain her property and any equity interests therein.

The absence of many of the important chapter 11 safeguards in chapter 13 heightens the importance of the statutory protections that unsecured creditors do have in chapter 13. The two most important statutory rights of unsecured creditors are that the plan be in their "best interests," § 1325(a)(4), considered in this section, and that the debtor devote all of his or her "projected disposable income" to payments under the plan (also known as the "best efforts" test), § 1325(b), discussed in the next section.[203] The "best interests" test means that the unsecured creditors must receive at least much in payments under the plan as they would if the debtor were to liquidate under chapter 7. The best interests test is also a requirement for confirmation of a plan under chapter 11,[204] § 1129(a)(7), and chapter 12. § 1225(a)(4). The statutory tests are very similar under the different reorganization chapters.

The chapter 13 best interests test varies in some particulars from the test as framed in chapter 11. Importantly, the application of the test cannot be waived by individual creditors in chapter 13 as it can in chapter 11. This distinction is not surprising, since creditors do not vote on chapter 13 plans. Thus, in every chapter 13 case the debtor is required to carry the burden of proving that the best interests test is satisfied as to all unsecured creditors.

Another difference between the chapter 13 and chapter 11 tests is that in chapter 13 there is no exception for "unimpaired" classes of creditors, as there is in chapter 11. Impairment is solely a chapter 11 concept, and does not apply in the chapter 13 context, where creditors do not vote. In addition, the chapter 11 exception to the best interests test for undersecured creditors who make an election to be treated as fully secured, see § 1111(b)(2), has no counterpart in chapter 13.

The application of the best interests test in chapter 13 requires the court to compare (1) the distribution that unsecured creditors would receive in a hypothetical chapter 7 liquidation with (2) the payments that those creditors will receive pursuant to the terms of the debtor's proposed chapter 13 plan. The manner of making that

---

[203] See § 12.17.

[204] See § 11.26.

calculation will generally be the same in chapter 13 as in chapter 11. The first value to be computed is the amount that unsecured creditors would be paid in the hypothetical chapter 7. This computation requires the debtor to introduce evidence demonstrating what the value of the distributable non-exempt estate assets would have been in chapter 7 and what the amount of debts would have been.[205] Then the chapter 7 rules of distribution must be applied to determine the order in which the allowed claims would have been paid. See § 726. Subordination principles must be consulted in this exercise as well. See §§ 510, 726(a)(3), (4).

The asset side of the equation in the hypothesized chapter 7 might not be the same as it actually is in the chapter 13 case. To begin with, the liquidation value of the property may be less than its going concern value in the hands of the chapter 13 debtor. Furthermore, the special chapter 13 rule that includes the debtor's postpetition earnings as property of the estate,[206] § 1306(a), does not apply in chapter 7. The chapter 7 estate only includes that property described in § 541. A crucial component of the hypothetical calculation is the deduction of the debtor's claimed exemptions from property of the estate, because in a chapter 7 case exempt property is not distributed to creditors. Indeed, in a very large percentage of cases, where the debtor does not have any nonexempt property, the application of the debtor's exemptions ends the best interests inquiry. These cases are known as "no asset" cases. The test in no asset cases is easily satisfied: in chapter 7, unsecured creditors would get nothing; and you cannot get less than nothing in chapter 13. The courts generally have concluded, appropriately, that even a zero payment chapter 13 plan can satisfy the best interests test of § 1325(a)(4) (although the debtor may run into other obstacles to plan confirmation).[207]

One question that the courts have had some trouble resolving is in fixing the date as of which the hypothetical chapter 7 asset valuation should be made. The statute refers only to the "effective date" of the plan for making the comparison. Many courts recognize, however, that the property of the estate that would be available for distribution to creditors in a chapter 7 case is only that included under § 541, which for the most part only includes property that the debtor had at the time the bankruptcy petition was filed. This principle suggests that the petition date should be used, at least for defining *which property* is in the hypothetical chapter 7 estate. In other words, property that actually comes into the chapter 13 estate during the case, pursuant to § 1306(a), should not be counted. That conclusion does not necessarily mean, however, that the *value* of the property included under § 541 also should be limited to the value as of the petition date. For example, what if the property appreciates in value between the time of the bankruptcy filing and the date of the confirmation hearing? Should the property's value be fixed at the time of filing, with postpetition appreciation going to the debtor, without factoring into the best interests test, or vice versa? The courts have

---

[205] See, e.g. Baud v. Carroll, 634 F.3d 327, 352 n.19 (6th Cir. 2011).

[206] See § 12.6.

[207] For example, a plan that proposes to pay nothing to creditors would likely fail the requirement that a plan be proposed in good faith. See In re Terry, 630 F.2d 634 (8th Cir. 1980). One court permitted a below-median-income debtor, with no disposable income, to extend her plan beyond the 36–month applicable commitment period, as needed, as to satisfy the best interests of creditors test. In re Boyd, 487 B.R. 669 (Bankr. E.D.N.C. 2013).

gone both ways, although the preferred view adopts the petition date as the operative valuation date.[208]

On the expense side of the equation in computing the hypothetical chapter 7 liquidation amount, the court must count those expenses that would have arisen in a liquidation even if those expenses are not actually incurred in chapter 13. Administrative expenses, such as the trustee's fee, are an example. One interesting illustration of this point is in cases where the debtor would realize a capital gain if property were liquidated, and would be liable for a capital gains tax. In that situation the courts have decided that the amount of the estimated capital gains tax that would have been incurred in a liquidation has to be deducted as an expense of the chapter 7 liquidation.[209]

The amount of the distribution that would be made in the hypothetical chapter 7 case then must be compared to the amount that the chapter 13 plan proposes to make to the various classes of unsecured creditors. As noted above, this second half of the inquiry will not be necessary if no distribution would be made to unsecured creditors in chapter 7. If, however, some payout would be made in chapter 7 to unsecured creditors, the chapter 13 computation must be made.

As is true in chapter 11, the stream of payments proposed to be made to unsecured creditors in the chapter 13 plan must be reduced to present value, as of the effective date of the plan. A dollar paid a year after confirmation is worth less than a dollar paid immediately. The requirement that plan payments be reduced to present value requires the court to apply a discount rate to future payments. Looked at the other way, the debtor's plan must pay postpetition interest on the principal amount of the claims that would be paid in chapter 7. To illustrate, assume that a creditor would be paid $900 in a hypothetical chapter 7 distribution. If the debtor's plan proposes three annual payments of $300 each to that creditor, the plan also must pay provide for the payment of interest on the claim. If no interest is provided for, the plan will not be confirmed.[210] The courts are in disagreement as to what the appropriate rate of interest should be; measures that have been selected include the market rate for similar debts, the contract rate, and the legal rate.

The chapter 13 "superdischarge," § 1328(a), has raised a recurring question in connection with the best interests test: is the test satisfied with regard to a creditor who holds a claim that would *not* be dischargeable in chapter 7, but which *is* dischargeable in chapter 13? The question arises because some of the discharge exceptions in § 523(a) do not apply in chapter 13. The creditor holding the claim that would not be discharged in chapter 7 but which would be discharged in chapter 13, will argue that the best interests test is not satisfied, because the creditor would be better off in chapter 7, where it could pursue collection of the debt from the debtor *after* the

---

[208] The courts using the petition date as the operative date then discount the net present value of the hypothetical liquidation to the effective date of the plan. See, e.g., In re Hardy, 755 F.2d 75 (6th Cir. 1985) (using plan date to value property, requiring present value analysis); In re Hockenberry, 457 B.R. 646 (Bankr. S.D. Ohio 2011).

[209] E.g., In re Card, 114 B.R. 226 (Bankr. N.D. Cal. 1990).

[210] See In re Hardy, 755 F.2d 75 (6th Cir. 1985).

conclusion of the bankruptcy case. Notwithstanding the common sense appeal of this argument, the courts have uniformly rejected it in favor of confirming the debtor's chapter 13 plan, by focusing closely on what the statutory language of § 1325(a)(4) actually says. The statutory test requires the court to compare only the distributions that the creditor would receive *in* the bankruptcy case itself. Thus, if the payments to be made in chapter 13 are at least equal to the distribution that the creditor would receive from the bankruptcy estate in the hypothetical chapter 7 case, then the best interests test is met, without regard to whether the creditor might be able to collect additional amounts from the debtor outside of bankruptcy.[211]

§ 12.17 Projected Disposable Income Test

In the Code as originally enacted in 1978, the primary protection for unsecured creditors in chapter 13 was the "best interests" test, which required a plan to propose to pay unsecured creditors at least as much as they would receive in a chapter 7 liquidation.[212] § 1325(a)(4). The best interests test offered meaningful succor to unsecured creditors *if* the debtor had significant nonexempt assets that would have been distributed to creditors in chapter 7. For example, if the chapter 7 dividend would have been 40%, then under § 1325(a)(4) the present value of plan payments also would have to equal at least 40%.

However, § 1325(a)(4) did not aid unsecured creditors in the fairly common situation in which the debtor had few, if any, unencumbered, nonexempt assets. If all of the debtor's assets were either exempt or fully encumbered, unsecured creditors would receive nothing in a chapter 7 distribution, and the chapter 13 best interests test therefore would be satisfied even if the plan offered to pay little or nothing to unsecured creditors. The use of minimal-payment or even zero-payment chapter 13 plans was particularly galling to unsecured creditors if the debtor (1) was discharging debts in chapter 13 that would not have been dischargeable in chapter 7, or (2) the debtor had significant income in excess of expenses, and thus *could* have made substantial payments to unsecured creditors in chapter 13. Some courts attempted to police these alleged "abuses" under the "good faith" requirement of § 1325(a)(3),[213] but such efforts were uneven, controversial, and labor-intensive.

Congress moved to remedy the foregoing problem by adding the "projected disposable income" (also called "ability to pay" or "best efforts") test to the Code in 1984. § 1325(b). The premise of this test is that the debtor must pay every free penny over and above necessary living expenses to unsecured creditors over the life of the plan. Thus, creditors get the best of both worlds: the best interests test assures them that they are paid the full value of the debtor's current nonexempt assets at the time of filing, and then the disposable income test captures the debtor's future income during the plan period. Short of keeping the debtor in perpetual debt bondage, you cannot really ask any more of the debtor than that. They can only pay what they have or what they earn. In the 2005 act, Congress made some important changes in how the

---

[211] See, e.g., In re Rimgale, 669 F.2d 426 (7th Cir. 1982).

[212] See § 12.16.

[213] See § 12.15.

projected disposable income test is calculated, as well as the time period for which it applies (the "applicable commitment period"), in conjunction with and as a complement to the significant amendments made to the § 707(b) "abuse" test in chapter 7.

Under the projected disposable income test, if the trustee or the holder of an allowed unsecured claim objects to confirmation, then the debtor must show either: (1) that the plan proposes to pay the objecting unsecured claim in full, § 1325(b)(1)(A), or (2) that *all* of the debtor's *"projected disposable income"* which is *"to be received"* will be applied to payments under the plan for the "applicable commitment period." § 1325(b)(1)(B). This requirement must be met even if the best interests test is also satisfied.

The "applicable commitment period" will be either three years or five years, depending on whether the debtor's family income is, respectively, below or above the state median for a family of the same size. § 1325(b)(4)(A). This comparison to state median income, and the expectation that above-median debtors should be compelled to devote their extra income to payments to creditors for five years (rather than just three), was added in 2005 and mirrors similar concepts found in the § 707(b) abuse test. Prior to 2005, the required payment period was only three years. Now only below-median debtors can get by with paying all disposable income for just three years. The only statutory exception whereby a commitment period shorter than three or five years is allowed is if the debtor's plan provides for *full payment* of all allowed unsecured claims during the shorter period. § 1325(b)(4)(B).

Some courts have also interpreted the statute to mean that there is *no* commitment period if the debtor has no disposable income.[214] A majority, though, conclude that the language of § 1325(b)(1)(B) and (b)(4) unconditionally imposes a temporal requirement of either a three-year or five-year plan (depending on whether the debtor's income is above or below median), subject only to the single statutory exception for full payment just noted, *even if the debtor has no projected disposable income!*[215]

If one believes the consumer credit industry's protestations of debtor abuse, the projected disposable income (or "best efforts") test makes some sense as a matter of bankruptcy policy. It does seem unsavory to allow a debtor who has sizable debts and no current nonexempt assets that could be distributed to creditors, but who has just been hired as a physician at $200,000 a year, to discharge her debts without paying anything to creditors out of her future income. The philosophy may be sound (although one wonders how many actual debtors fit the profile just described), but the mechanics of implementation are more problematic.

As noted above, the best efforts test complements the best interests test. A debtor with significant unencumbered, nonexempt assets will have to make substantial

---

[214] See, e.g., In re Kagenveama, 541 F.3d 868 (9th Cir. 2008); In re Davis, 392 B.R. 132 (Bankr. E.D. Pa. 2008). See also In re Flores, 692 F.3d 1021 (9th Cir. 2012) (permitting above-median income debtor with no disposable income to decrease applicable plan period from five to three years).

[215] See, e.g., Baud v. Carroll, 634 F.3d 327 (6th Cir. 2011); In re Frederickson, 545 F.3d 652 (8th Cir. 2008); In re Tennyson, 611 F.3d 873 (11th Cir. 2010).

payments to unsecured creditors because of § 1325(a)(4). A debtor who does not have much in the way of distributable current assets, but who does have a significant positive future earning capacity, will have to make meaningful payments to unsecured creditors because of § 1325(b). It is worth emphasizing that the introduction of the projected disposable income test in § 1325(b) in 1984 made it even more obviously inappropriate for a court to consider the debtors' ability to pay debts as a factor in applying the general "good faith" test in § 1325(a)(3).

The projected disposable income requirement effectively sets both a floor and a ceiling on the debtor's plan payments. The floor is that all projected disposable income must be devoted to plan payments for the applicable commitment period. At the same time, given the definition of disposable income, and the fact that the test requires devotion of *all* of that disposable income to plan payments, that also is the maximum that the debtor could pay. The reason is that if the debtor proposes to pay *more* than her disposable income under the plan, the plan would not be *feasible*, and thus could not be confirmed because of noncompliance with § 1325(a)(6).

The key question in applying the best efforts test is, as one might expect, how to calculate the debtor's "projected disposable income." The "disposable" part is easy enough to understand—how much does "income" exceed "expenses"? That excess is, in concept, "disposable," and the command of § 1325(b)(1)(B) is that the debtor must deliver that excess to creditors for the required period. Computing "income" and "expenses" (and especially the latter) has been more difficult and controversial. It was here (as well as in imposing a five-year term) that BAPCPA made significant changes. Again, the tenor of those amendments mirrors what was done in the chapter 7 "abuse" test in 2005, namely, prescribing with considerably more specificity what counts as income and what living expenses can be allowed to the debtor, intending thereby to restrict the discretion formerly exercised by bankruptcy judges. As will be seen below, though, a 2010 Supreme Court decision effectively revived, à la Lazarus, the need for the judge to exercise considerable discretion on a regular basis.

The starting point in looking for "disposable income" is the debtor's schedules and forms. One of the debtor's initial obligations is to file schedules of current income and current expenditures. § 521(a)(1)(B)(ii); Rule 1007(b)(1)(B); Official Form 6, Schedules I and J. Under BAPCPA, a debtor also must file a schedule of current monthly income and calculation of commitment period. Rule 1007(b)(6); Official Form B22C. These documents help the chapter 13 trustee and creditors to ascertain whether the debtor, by her own admission, has income in excess of expenses, i.e., "disposable income."[216] Whether what the debtor claims as income and as expenses will be allowed is, of course, ultimately up to the bankruptcy judge.

---

[216] Many cases have grappled with the problem that the calculation of disposable income under Form B22C may differ, often dramatically, from that produced by a comparison of Schedules I and J. Without question the starting point for the disposable income calculation under the Code is Form B22C, since "disposable income" is defined in § 1325(b)(2) by reference to "current monthly income" as well as (for above-median debtors) to the means test expense allowances of § 707(b)(2). The problem arises when the B22C calculation of disposable income varies markedly from what a comparison of Schedules I and J shows. This difficulty is played out in deciding what the "applicable commitment period" is and also in ascertaining what "projected" disposable income is in such cases. See, e.g., *Kagenveama*, supra note 214, 541 F.3d 868.

Prior to 2005, under the test as originally enacted in 1984, the bankruptcy courts were in the business of being both a financial prognosticator and a board of budget review. To apply § 1325(b), the court had to be able to project the debtor's income and expenses for the next three years, and further had to decide which of those projected expenses were "reasonably necessary" for the maintenance and support of the debtor and the debtor's dependents. Especially troublesome was the expense side of the equation. Even for categories of expenses that all would concede are "necessary" (such as food, clothing shelter, utilities, transportation, etc.), this statutory assignment required the court to exercise very specific financial oversight of the amount of the debtor's projected expenses on a case-by-case basis. How much does a family of four need to spend on groceries each month? How much on clothing? How much for rent or the mortgage? The list could go on and on. With the large number of bankruptcy filings, making the bankruptcy judges engage in this sort of extremely fact-intensive inquiry was a questionable use of judicial resources.

An even more fundamental objection to this whole enterprise was that adjudicating which expenses were reasonably necessary inevitably placed the court in the position of having to make sensitive value-laden judgments about the appropriate lifestyle of the debtor. Inevitably, too, the outcome was that like debtors were not treated alike. The Code itself gave no guidance on the standards the court should apply in making those subjective assessments. There was general judicial agreement that debtors should neither be permitted to live like a prince nor be condemned to live like a pauper; but between the two is a wide chasm in which the court had much discretion in drawing the lines. Should debtors be required to sell their cars and take the bus to work? Or can a family have one car? Or two, if both spouses work? How fancy a car can it be? How new? Can the debtor's family ever eat dinner out? How often? Where? Can they ever go to a movie? Matinee or full price? Are magazine subscriptions out? Does it depend on which magazine? May the debtors send their children to private school? May the debtors pledge money to their church? To United Way? What about going to a Cubs game? Smart phone? Cheap phone?

The 2005 amendments effected a sea change in the law, and (especially for debtors above the state median income for their family size) purported to remove much of the discretion judges formerly had to exercise. Consistent with (and indeed incorporating by reference) the approach taken in chapter 7 for calculating the presumption of abuse under the "means test" in § 707(b)(2), Congress carefully defined "projected disposable income." § 1325(b)(2). The "income" side of the equation is defined as "*current monthly income*" which is "received by the debtor," minus a few exclusions (child support, foster care, or disability for a dependent child). Significantly (and, as will be explained, problematically), "current monthly income" is a defined term.[217] § 101(10A).

That income definition has two components: the *types* or *sources* of income that will be counted, and a *temporal* element. The included sources of income are broad indeed: first, "the income from all sources that the debtor receives (or in a joint case the debtor and the debtor's spouse receive) without regard to whether such income is taxable," § 101(10A)(A); and second, "any amount paid by any entity other than the

---

[217] See § 2.15.c.(2).

debtor . . . on a regular basis for the household expenses of the debtor or the debtor's dependents." § 101(10A)(B). The *only* exclusions from the "current monthly income" definition are for Social Security benefits or (less commonly) payments to victims of war crimes or terrorism. Note that even tax-exempt income is included. So too is income that would be exempt from the claims of creditors, such as workers compensation benefits.[218] The debtor even has to count monies they regularly receive from someone else to help defray household expenses, so if Grandma has been giving you $50 a month to help you pay your bills, that counts. The temporal element is that income from the six full months *before* bankruptcy is counted. I say more below on the difficulty raised by incorporating a backward-looking timing perspective into a forward-looking payment system. Aside from that glitch, though, the 2005 amendments on the "income" side did not change much, other than to give some added clarity, and to bring in amounts regularly contributed by a third party. Courts already were counting just about everything as income.

Also, as before, income counts only if it is "to be received" by the debtor during the commitment period. In an intriguing pre-BAPCPA case, the Fourth Circuit had to decide whether to count as income those distributions from an IRA that the debtor was eligible to receive without penalty but which the debtor had not yet elected to, and could not yet be compelled to, start receiving.[219] The debtor's obvious intention was to delay taking the IRA distributions until after the completion of the plan. The court held that the unreceived IRA distributions could not be counted as projected disposable income. However, such a plan could still be challenged under the good faith requirement of § 1325(a)(3).

On the expense side of the ledger, the basic test is that the debtor can deduct "amounts reasonably necessary to be expended—(A)(i) for the maintenance or support of the debtor or a dependent of the debtor." § 1325(b)(2)(A). In addition, the debtor can deduct: domestic support obligations that arise postpetition, § 1325(b)(2)(A)(i); charitable contributions to a qualified religious or charitable entity, up to 15% of the debtor's gross income, § 1325(b)(2)(A)(ii): and, if the debtor is engaged in business, expenses necessary for the "continuation, preservation, and operation" of the business. § 1325(b)(2)(B).

In determining the basic expense deduction, for "amounts reasonably necessary to be expended for the maintenance or support of the debtor or a dependent," the guidelines that govern the judge's task depend initially—again—on the debtor's family income. If the debtor's family income is *below* the state median for a family of that size, then the game is the same as it was before 2005, namely, the judge exercises her discretion. If, however, the debtor's income is *greater* than the state median income for that family size, then the expense allowances are governed by the "means test" rules in subparagraphs (A) and (B) of § 707(b)(2).[220] This cross-reference makes sense, because the whole premise of the means test in chapter 7 as applied to above-median debtors is that if the debtor has sufficient repayment capacity, that debtor is only allowed to

---

[218] See, e.g., In re Koch, 109 F.3d 1285 (8th Cir. 1997).

[219] In re Solomon, 67 F.3d 1128 (4th Cir. 1996).

[220] See § 2.15.c.(3).

proceed under chapter 13; therefore, the chapter 13 calculations must be consistent. The incorporation of the means test rules means that the debtor will be limited to (but also entitled to) IRS living expenses, along with the other allowances permitted in § 707(b)(2). Note that *Ransom v. FIA Card Services,*[221] the leading Supreme Court case interpreting the expense allowances under the means test rules of § 707(b)(2), arose in the chapter 13 context.

Assuming that the court is able to ascertain income and expenses and therefore arrive at the debtor's "disposable" income, the next big problem in applying § 1325(b)(1)(B) is to *project* that disposable income over the plan period. Prior to the 2005 amendments, courts normally handled the projection task by extrapolating the debtor's *current* income over the next 36 months, and then assessing how much of that income was "disposable."[222] However, this simple multiplication act was not inexorable; courts noted that "consideration of future events is at times appropriate in evaluating projected future income."[223] Courts tried to make their best guess as to what the debtor's financial future held. If things nevertheless changed after confirmation, then those changes could readily be accommodated through a motion to *modify* the terms of the plan under § 1329.[224]

The projection task got greatly confused with the passage of BAPCPA in 2005. Indeed, how projection works under § 1325(b)(1)(B) has proven to be one of the most controversial and debated issues under the new law. For better or worse, the Supreme Court has resolved the projection question, adopting in *Hamilton v. Lanning*[225] the "forward-looking" approach, under which the bankruptcy court must take into account expected post-confirmation "changes in the debtor's income or expenses that are *known or virtually certain* at the time of confirmation."[226] In so deciding, the Court rejected the "mechanical" test, under which the bankruptcy court would simply multiply the income/expense differential by the number of months in the applicable commitment period. While the Court's holding was a sensible and pragmatic interpretation, the statutory basis for the Court's decision was more tenuous than the Court admitted.

The problem is that the statutory provisions do not mesh in a coherent way, and read strictly appear to be at war with each other. Recall first that the core requirement is that the debtor must commit all of her "*projected* disposable income" which is "*to be received*" during the applicable commitment period to plan payments. § 1325(b)(1)(B). That language—in relevant part carried forward without change from pre-BAPCPA law—seems to require a *forward*-looking assessment. As noted above, prior to BAPCPA, that was indeed how courts interpreted the text. So too does that

---

[221]   131 S.Ct. 716 (2012).

[222]   See, e.g., In re Anderson, 21 F.3d 355 (9th Cir. 1994); In re Killough, 900 F.2d 61 (5th Cir. 1990).

[223]   Spalding v. Truman, 2008 WL 4566459 (N.D. Tex. Oct. 14, 2008) (discussing *Killough,* supra note 222, in which the Fifth Circuit considered whether to require the debtor to commit projected future overtime pay to plan payments; although the *Killough* court ultimately did not make the debtors count overtime, they did so after a fact-specific assessment, and made it plain that requiring such an inclusion was at least possible).

[224]   See § 2.21.

[225]   130 S.Ct. 2464 (2010).

[226]   Id. at 2478 (emphasis added).

interpretation make sense as a functional matter, because under a chapter 13 plan the debtor must make payments in the future, out of the net disposable income the debtor actually will have available. As noted, in *Lanning* the Supreme Court adopted post-BAPCPA the forward-looking approach yet again.

However, the fly in the ointment is this: the term "disposable income" itself is defined by reference to "current monthly income," § 1325(b)(2), which in turn calculates a debtor's income by looking *backward* in time at the six full months prior to bankruptcy. § 101(10A)(A). Further complicating the matter is that for above-median debtors, expense allowances are computed by reference to the allowances in the means test of § 707(b)(2), which in many respects may diverge from a debtor's actual expenses. With income calculated solely by reference to the past, and with expense allowances not necessarily tied to actual expenses, the upshot is that a debtor's calculation of "disposable income" on Form B22C may depart dramatically from what the debtor's actual projected disposable income to be received appears to be, as reflected on Schedules I and J. The departure could run either way.[227] In one direction, literally applying the statutory calculation in § 1325(b)(2) would suggest that a debtor has much more disposable income than she really does, and if so applied would require the impossible, rendering the plan unconfirmable because it would not be feasible.[228] Conversely, the debtor's Form B22C might show little or no apparent "disposable income," whereas the reality is that the debtor has ample future repayment capacity; here, the debtor would not have to pay anything to her creditors, even though she obviously could.[229] While the temptation in such cases is simply to resort to Schedules I and J, which more closely project the expected future reality, that approach seemingly renders superfluous the 2005 congressional enactment of the "disposable income" definition in § 1325(b)(2).

As noted above, in 2010 the Supreme Court clarified how to interpret the "projected disposable income" test in *Hamilton v. Lanning*,[230] adopting the "forward-looking" test. In effect, the Court said to use Form B22C's formula most of the time, unless it doesn't work, in which case the bankruptcy court should just use Schedules I and J (or something like them), just like in the good old days. That makes practical sense, but hash of the statute—as Justice Scalia pointed out in dissent.[231] As he noted,

---

[227] For discussions of this problem pre- and post-*Lanning,* see Christopher Frost, Nagging Problems under BAPCPA post *Lanning* and *Ransom,* 32 No. 11 Bankr. L. Letter 1 (2012) (post-*Lanning*); Christopher Frost, Inching Toward Workability: The Supreme Court Adds to Its BAPCPA Jurisprudence, 31 No. 3 Bankr. L. Letter 1 (2011) (post-*Lanning*); Christopher Frost, Plain Meaning and Unintended Results Under BAPCPA: *In re Kagenveama,* 28 No. 8 Bankr. L. Letter 1 (2008).

[228] Thus, in *In re Lanning,* 545 F.3d 1269 (10th Cir. 2008), aff'd, 130 S.Ct. 2464 (2010), the debtor's Form B22C showed a disposable income of $1,114 a month, whereas her real disposable income, as revealed by Schedules I and J, was only $149 a month. The difference arose because the debtor had received a large one-time buyout during the pre-bankruptcy six-month period in which "current monthly income" was computed. Obviously the debtor could not pay $1,114 a month in her chapter 13 plan, because she was not going to have that much money available.

[229] Thus, in *Kagenveama,* supra note 214, 541 F.3d 868, the debtor's Form B22C showed "disposable income" as a negative $4.04, meaning (if the statute were applied literally) that she would not be required to pay anything to her creditors under § 1325(b)(1)(B), even though her Schedules I and J showed actual disposable income of $1,523 per month, which would mean that she actually could pay over $90,000 to her creditors over the 60–month commitment period.

[230] 130 S.Ct. 2464 (2010).

[231] Id. at 2479 (Scalia, J., dissenting).

"That interpretation runs aground because it either renders superfluous text Congress included or requires adding text Congress did not."[232] He concludes that "[t]he Court, in short, can arrive at its compromise construction only by rewriting the statute."[233] In fairness, though, neither does Scalia's proffered interpretation work under the statute either, because how, pray tell, can a debtor apply her projected disposable income "to be received in the applicable commitment period" during the life of the plan, as § 1325(b)(1)(B) commands, when she is not going to receive that income!

The difficulty in *Lanning* was how to apply § 1325(b) when the debtor's actual situation during the projected chapter 13 plan period demonstrably was going to differ substantially from the formulaic projection suggested by a mechanical application of the "current monthly income" definition. Because of a large one-time buyout the debtor received prior to bankruptcy, the mechanical test showed that she had almost a thousand dollars more a month available to pay her debts than she really did. Obviously, then, if the mechanical test were applied, it would have been impossible for her to confirm a chapter 13 plan, because the required plan would of course not be feasible (as the debtor might find it difficult to make payments out of money no longer coming in!).[234] The Court found it hard to believe that Congress could have intended such a "senseless result[ ],"[235] and thus added the interpretive gloss that "the court may account for changes in the debtor's income or expenses that are known or virtually certain at the time of confirmation."[236]

Thus, the Court made it possible for the Lannings of the world (whose actual payment ability is less than the formula suggests) to confirm and carry out a chapter 13 plan. But the shoe often (more often, perhaps?) will be on the other foot. The Court's embrace of the forward-looking *also* forces a debtor whose actual payment ability is *greater* than the formula suggests (such as in *Kagenveama*) to pay creditors the larger amount. The *Lanning* Court *also* thought it would be a "senseless result" that Congress surely did not intend if "[i]n cases in which the debtor's disposable income is higher during the plan period, the mechanical approach would deny creditors payments that the debtor could easily make."[237] The Court thought it much more likely that Congress intended such a can-pay debtor to pay up. If the statute has to be rewritten a little to get there, so be it.

After *Lanning*, the game has focused on the application of this "known or virtually certain" test in case after case. As Justice Scalia perceived,[238] if courts are allowed to

---

[232] Id.

[233] Id.

[234] Indeed, the debtor might not have even been able to have eschewed chapter 13 and filed under chapter 7, because she might have flunked the chapter 7 means test, due to this one-time buyout (subject to rebuttal of course for special circumstances).

[235] Id. at 2476–77 (Alito, J., majority opinion).

[236] Id. at 2478.

[237] Id. at 2476

[238] Id. at 2479 (Scalia, J., dissenting): "If the statute authorizes estimations, it authorizes them in *every* case, not just those where changes to the debtor's income are both 'significant' and either 'known or virtually certain. *Ibid.* If the evidence indicates it is merely more likely than not that the debtor's income will increase by some minimal amount, there is no reading of the word 'projected' that permits (or requires) a court to ignore that change."

ignore the mechanical CMI formula in some cases because the statutory modifier "projected" authorizes a sneak peek at reality, there is really no reason to limit that peek, assuming the court has sufficient confidence in the projections as to the post-confirmation facts. The extensive post-*Lanning* case law indicates that courts are indeed willing to tweak the disposable income projection (on either the income or expense side) on a regular basis, and even when the changes from the mechanical formula are much more modest than Stephanie Lanning's thousand dollar a month shortfall. A common scenario has been where a debtor has secured debt payments that will cease at some point during the plan period, either because the debtor will complete payments or because the debtor intends to surrender the collateral. Courts now routinely invoke *Lanning* to require the debtor's plan to "step up" payments to unsecured creditors once the secured debt payments will end.[239] Many, many other examples could be given; for instance, some courts have forced debtors to count projected tax refunds[240] or likely bonuses[241] as income under *Lanning*'s forward projection.

While if one is intellectually honest there is no way to make sense of the warring statutes, the most sensible result, I believe, is what the Court came up with in *Lanning*, and to look, ultimately, at projections of future reality. That approach best effectuates Congressional intent and as a practical matter is the most workable solution. As a practical matter, we have almost come back full circle to where we were prior to BAPCPA, *viz.*, the bankruptcy courts look at what exactly the debtor realistically can pay on a case-by-case basis. So what if that is not exactly what the statute says; deal with it. Sometimes even Congress needs a bit of an assist from the Court.

§ 12.18 Treatment of Secured Claims

Secured creditors are different from unsecured creditors for one very fundamental reason: secured claims, by definition, are supported by collateral. The required treatment of allowed secured claims in chapter 13 plans reflects that critical fact. Under § 1325(a)(5), one of three alternatives must be satisfied for each allowed secured claim:

- the holder of the secured claim has *accepted* the plan, § 1325(a)(5)(A);

- the plan provides that (i) the holder of the secured claim retains its lien until the debt is paid or discharged, (ii) the value of property distributed under the plan is not less than the allowed amount of such claim, and (iii) if property is distributed in the form of periodic payments, they shall be equal monthly payments, and if the claim is secured by personal property, the amount of the monthly payments shall be sufficient to provide the claimholder adequate protection for the duration of the plan, § 1325(a)(5)(B); or

---

[239] See, e.g., In re Quigley, 673 F.3d 269 (4th Cir. 2012) (surrender);

[240] See, e.g., In re Grier, 464 B.R. 839 (Bankr. N.D. Iowa 2011); In re Skougard, 438 B.R. 738 (Bankr. D. Utah 2010); In re Barbutes, 436 B.R. 518 (Bankr. M.D. Tenn. 2010).

[241] In re O'Neill Miranda, 449 B.R. 182 (Bankr. D. P.R. 2011).

- the debtor will *surrender* the collateral to the secured creditor, § 1325(a)(5)(C).

In effect, the basic premise of § 1325(a)(5) is that the plan must propose to give the holder of the secured claim the full value of its secured claim, which usually is just the value of the collateral, unless the secured creditor agrees to different treatment. Significantly, if this collateral value is provided by the plan to the secured creditor, the *consent* of the secured creditor is *not* necessary, although it is sufficient. In the jargon, the plan can be "*crammed down*" over the secured creditor's objection. Subsection (B) is the "cram down" option. Collateral value can be provided in one of two ways: the debtor can either (1) surrender the collateral to the secured creditor (subsection (C)), or (2) retain the collateral and distribute to the creditor property during the plan period that has a present value equal to the collateral value (subsection (B)).[242]

In most cases, of course, the debtor will want to retain the collateral. Indeed, one of the most common reasons for a debtor to choose to proceed under chapter 13 is so that the debtor can keep encumbered property. Few legal issues arise under either of the other two options under § 1325(a)(5); the secured creditor can hardly complain if it accepts the plan, or if the debtor surrenders the collateral to the secured creditor. The main issue that has arisen under the "surrender" option concerns the impact on 910–day car loans of the 2005 amendment which added the "hanging paragraph" following § 1325(a); more on that below. One question under the "acceptance" option has been whether the secured creditor's failure to object constitutes acceptance; many courts have held that it does.[243] Most of the critical issues have arisen in applying § 1325(a)(5)(B), the "cram down" option.

Consider an example. Prior to bankruptcy, Debtor purchased a car from Creditor for $20,000, and gave Creditor a security interest to secure the unpaid purchase price. Debtor signed a note promising to pay the balance over five years, with interest at 12% per annum. When the Debtor filed for relief under chapter 13, there were two years remaining on the note, and the total debt to Creditor was $10,000. The car, however, was worth less; how much less depends on the valuation standard chosen. Under the higher retail value, the car was worth $7,500, while the lower wholesale value was $6,000. Also, assume that market interest rates for similar car loans had dropped to 8% by the time of the bankruptcy filing.

If the Debtor wanted to keep the car in a chapter 7 case, she would have two primary options.[244] One would be to *redeem* the car under § 722 by paying the Creditor the actual current value of the car ($6,000 wholesale, or $7,500 retail) in a lump sum cash payment. The main problem for the Debtor would be coming up with that much

---

[242] For excellent discussions of the treatment of secured claims in chapter 13 after the 2005 amendments see Jean Braucher, *Rash* and Ride–Through Redux: The Terms for Holding on to Cars, Homes, and Other Collateral Under the 2005 Act, 13 Am. Bankr. Inst. L. Rev. 457 (2005); David Gray Carlson, Cars and Homes in Chapter 13 After the 2005 Amendments to the Bankruptcy Code, 14 Am. Bankr. Inst. L. Rev. 301 (2006); William C. Whitford, A History of the Automobile Lender Provisions of BAPCPA, 2007 U. Ill. L. Rev. 143 (2007).

[243] See, e.g., In re Jones, 530 F.3d 1284 (10th Cir. 2008); In re Szolek, 886 F.2d 1405 (3d Cir. 1989). But see In re Bateman, 331 F.3d 821 (11th Cir. 2003) (not requiring creditor to object to confirmation when filed proof of claim differed from the amount indicated in the plan).

[244] See § 7.32.c.

money; installment redemption is not permitted. The other option for Debtor would be to *reaffirm* the car debt under § 524(c), and keep the car with Creditor's agreement. The problem with reaffirmation, apart from obtaining Creditor's agreement, is that the price of Creditor's consent may well be that Debtor must promise to pay the entire $10,000 debt, even though the car is worth considerably less.

Chapter 13 "cram down" under § 1325(a)(5)(B) gives the Debtor the best of both worlds. Without having to obtain Creditor's consent, the Debtor may retain the car and (i) pay Creditor only the actual value of the car, rather than the total debt, and (ii) make the payments in installments over the life of the chapter 13 plan, which can be as long as five years. Furthermore, the Debtor does not necessarily have to pay interest at the contract rate, but might be able to invoke the lower market rate, or some other measure. The Debtor is permitted to modify the Creditor's rights in the plan. § 1322(b)(2).

The net results of the many benefits offered by chapter 13 cram down are that the Debtor can (i) write down the secured debt to the value of the collateral, and (ii) drastically reduce the monthly payments. In the example, at the time of filing, the Debtor owed $10,000, payable in two years, at 12% interest. Under a chapter 13 plan, § 1325(a)(5)(B) arguably permits the Debtor to pay $7,500,[245] over up to five years, at 8% interest. It does not take a mathematical genius to deduce that the Debtor's payments will be much lower under the chapter 13 plan (on the facts presented, the monthly payments would drop from almost $500 to about $150). That drastic reduction in payments could well be the difference between the debtor being able to make the payments and keep the car or have to admit defeat and give up the car.

The unsecured portion of the creditor's claim will be treated as a separate unsecured claim under § 506(a)(1). In the example above, if the $7,500 collateral value is used as the basis for the allowed secured claim (as § 506(a)(2) likely requires), the Creditor holding a total claim of $10,000 would have a $2,500 unsecured claim. That claim then would be entitled to the protections for unsecured claims, namely, the best interests test of § 1325(a)(4)[246] and the projected disposable income test of § 1325(b).[247]

In cramming down a secured claim under § 1325(a)(5)(B), in addition to providing for the secured creditor to *retain its lien* for the secured claim, § 1325(a)(5)(B)(i), the debtor will have to distribute property to the creditor that have a present value, as of the effective date of the plan, equal to the amount of the allowed secured claim. § 1325(a)(5)(B)(ii). Note that the debtor does not necessarily have to pay cash to the creditor, although that is the norm, but is permitted to distribute any "property" of sufficient value. This statutory formula has two crucial components: (1) the interest rate required to provide present value; and (2) the amount of the allowed secured claim, which is in effect the new principal amount of the secured debt. Each has been the subject of great controversy.

---

[245] This figure is used, rather than the lower $6,000 wholesale value, on the assumption that § 506(a)(2), added in 2005, would require use of the retail price on these facts.

[246] See § 12.16.

[247] See § 12.17.

First, the statutory requirement in § 1325(a)(5)(B)(ii) that the value paid to the secured creditor must be computed "as of the effective date of the plan" requires the plan payments to be discounted to present value as of that date. Courts usually determine present value as of the date of confirmation of the plan.[248] Discounting to present value means that the debtor will have to pay *interest* on the principal balance of the allowed secured claim. Otherwise, the present value of the stream of payments made over time to the secured creditor would be less than the secured claim. In the car example, the debtor could not confirm a plan that promised to pay the creditor's $7,500 secured debt in three annual installments of $2,500 each. The future payments of $2,500 are worth less than $2,500 today, because of the time value of money.

One of the most litigated issues under the Code has been identifying the appropriate rate of interest, i.e., the discount rate, for plan payments. The identical issue arises in cram downs under the other reorganization chapters, see § 1129(b)(2)(A)(i)(II) (chapter 11), § 1225(a)(5)(B)(ii) (chapter 12). Before the Supreme Court's 2004 decision in *Till v. SCS Credit Corp.*,[249] many approaches were taken. A popular view was that the creditor should receive a *market* rate of interest, similar to what the creditor would charge for similar loans. The theory supporting this view was that the plan cram down is in effect a "coerced loan" to the debtor, and in fairness to the creditor should be measured by the rate for such loans.[250] A related view used the contract rate as presumptively establishing the market rate, although subject to rebuttal.[251] Other courts, however, believed that either the market rate or contract rate overcompensated the creditor, and looked instead to a below-market rate of interest, calculated, for example, by reference to the debtor's cost of borrowing the money[252] or the cost of funds to the creditor.[253] The final commonly utilized approach was the "*formula*" method (also called "prime plus"), where the court would begin with a risk-free rate (e.g., the United States Treasury rate of interest for same duration) and then add some premium for risk attributable to the debtor's situation.[254]

In *Till* (which is discussed in detail in chapter 7 on claims),[255] the Supreme Court squarely confronted this issue. Unfortunately, none of the various approaches were able to command a majority of the Court. Indeed, putting together the various voting alignments, a majority of the Justices rejected every theory! Two theories commanded four votes each: the formula rate, backed by the four Justices in the plurality,[256] and the presumptive contract rate, advocated by the four dissenting Justices.[257] Oddly,

---

[248] See, e.g., In re Marsh, 475 B.R. 892 (N.D. Ill. 2012).

[249] 541 U.S. 465 (2004). See § 7.30.

[250] See, e.g., Koopmans v. Farm Credit Servs., 102 F.3d 874 (7th Cir. 1996).

[251] See, e.g., GMAC v. Jones, 999 F.2d 63 (3d Cir. 1993).

[252] See, e.g., In re Fowler, 903 F.2d 694 (9th Cir. 1990).

[253] See, e.g., In re Jordan, 130 B.R. 185 (Bankr.D.N.J. 1991). See also In re Till, 301 F.3d 583, 594–95 (7th Cir. 2002) (Rovner, J., dissenting), rev'd, 541 U.S. 465 (2004). The Second Circuit in *In re Valenti*, 105 F.3d 55 (2d Cir. 1997) concluded that the "cost of funds" approach was the most accurate conceptually but rejected it as being too difficult to administer.

[254] This was the view actually adopted by the Second Circuit in *Valenti*, supra note 253, 105 F.3d at 64.

[255] See § 7.30.

[256] *Till*, supra note 249, 541 U.S. at 478–79 (Stevens, J., plurality).

[257] Id. at 492 (Scalia, J., dissenting).

though, a majority of five Justices rejected both theories—the fifth vote in each instance being that of Justice Thomas in concurrence, who advocated instead a purely risk-free rate, and thus concluded that both the formula and contract approaches overcompensate the creditor. However, Justice Thomas voted to concur with the plurality because under his theory the debtors' proposed plan (which used the formula approach) gave the objecting creditor more than it deserved, so the creditor's objection was ill-founded.[258] Notwithstanding the difficulty of making sense of the odd voting cast in *Till,* post-*Till* courts have concluded that at the very least, *Till* binds lower courts to confirm a debtor's proposed plan that uses the formula approach.[259] The voting alignment in *Till* also would dictate that if the debtor proposes a plan that uses the presumptive contract rate, that plan also should be confirmed. The reason is that a majority of the Court would hold that the creditor could not complain about the debtor's proposed use of the presumptive contract rate—the four dissenting Justices (who think the presumptive contract rate is appropriate) and the concurring Justice (Thomas) who would hold that the contract rate overcompensates the complaining creditor, whose objection therefore should be rejected.

The second critical issue in cram down is determining the *amount* of the allowed secured claim. In most cases, the amount of the "allowed secured claim" is the *value of the collateral*. In Code parlance, the collateral value normally is "the value of such creditor's interest in the estate's interest in such property."[260] § 506(a)(1). The point of debate has been what *standard* should be used to value the collateral when the debtor proposes to retain the collateral in the chapter 13 case.[261] Section 506(a) controls the valuation issue. Putting aside for a moment the special rule of § 506(a)(2), added in 2005, let us consider the general valuation rules of § 506(a)(1). The first sentence of that subsection, just quoted, identifies the allowed secured claim by reference to the "creditor's interest" in the estate's interest in the collateral. The second sentence of § 506(a)(1) specifies that value is to be "determined in light of the purpose of the valuation and of the proposed disposition or use of such property."

In the car example above, the retail value (what it would cost the debtor to replace the collateral) is $7,500, while the wholesale value (what the creditor could get at foreclosure) is $6,000. Prior to the Supreme Court's 1997 decision in *Associates Commercial Corp. v. Rash*,[262] the courts of appeals took three, and perhaps four, different views. One view was that the debtor must pay the higher replacement cost if she proposes to retain the collateral, emphasizing the second sentence of § 506(a).[263] At the opposite end of the spectrum, focusing on the first sentence of § 506(a), which refers to the "creditor's interest," was the position that the debtor only needed pay the lower

---

[258] Id. at 486–91 (Thomas, J., concurring).

[259] See, e.g., Drive Fin. Servs., L.P. v. Jordan, 521 F.3d 343 (5th Cir. 2008).

[260] The more complicated statutory language is used because: (1) the debtor may not have an undivided and unencumbered interest in the entire property, or (2) the creditor may not have the only lien on the property.

[261] See § 7.29.

[262] 520 U.S. 953 (1997).

[263] See In re Taffi, 96 F.3d 1190 (9th Cir. 1996) (en banc); In re Winthrop Old Farm Nurseries, Inc., 50 F.3d 72 (1st Cir. 1995).

wholesale cost, because that is all that the creditor could realize on foreclosure.[264] Still other courts proposed simply to split the difference between the two, and take the midpoint.[265] Finally, one court suggested that there was no standard at all, and that bankruptcy courts thus were free to fix any value that they believed appropriate in a given case.[266]

The Supreme Court attempted to settle the debate in *Associates Commercial Corp. v. Rash*.[267] In *Rash*, the Court held that the debtor must pay the higher *replacement* cost when the debtor proposes to *retain* the property in the plan. The dispositive statutory provision, the Court concluded, is the second sentence of § 506(a), which requires the courts to value collateral in light of the "proposed disposition or use of such property." Where the "use" proposed is retention by the debtor, the debtor must pay what it would cost the debtor to obtain that item. The *Rash* court defined replacement value as "the price a willing buyer in the debtor's trade, business, or situation would pay to obtain like property from a willing seller."[268] Thus, under *Rash*, the creditor's "allowed secured claim" presumptively would be the higher $7,500 retail value, rather than the lower $6,000 wholesale value. Having said that, and as discussed in detail in the chapter dealing with claims,[269] the Supreme Court recognized in a crucial footnote 6 that a debtor who is retaining collateral is not actually getting everything that a retail buyer gets: "For example, where the proper measure of the replacement value of a vehicle is its retail value, an adjustment to that value may be necessary: *A creditor should not receive portions of the retail price, if any, that reflect the value of items the debtor does not receive when he retains his vehicle*, items such as warranties, inventory storage, and reconditioning."[270]

Thus, *Rash* left an opening for a debtor to propose a confirmable chapter 13 plan providing for payment of considerably less than the full "retail" value of collateral, even when the debtor plans to retain the collateral. As just quoted above, the Court specifically directed that the value chosen should not include such things as warranties and reconditioning, which, along with marketing costs, are the major economic components that differentiate "retail" value from lower values that more nearly approximate wholesale value, such as "private party" and "trade-in" values. After *Rash,* courts have taken full advantage of the loophole left by footnote 6 and have confirmed cram down plans using considerably less than retail price to fix collateral value. One commentator noted, "bankruptcy courts have felt free to ignore *Rash* altogether and do whatever they did before."[271]

---

[264] See In re Rash, 90 F.3d 1036 (5th Cir. 1996) (en banc), rev'd, 520 U.S. 953 (1997); In re Mitchell, 954 F.2d 557 (9th Cir. 1992).

[265] In re Hoskins, 102 F.3d 311 (7th Cir. 1996).

[266] *Valenti*, supra note 253, 105 F.3d 55.

[267] 520 U.S. 953 (1997).

[268] Id. at 960.

[269] See § 7.29.

[270] 520 U.S. at 965 n.6 (emphases added).

[271] Carlson, supra note 242, at 359.

In the 2005 amendments, Congress tried to close *Rash*'s footnote 6 loophole, with a new § 506(a)(2).[272] The valuation rule of § 506(a)(2) applies only to: (1) personal property collateral securing an allowed claim; (2) of individual debtors; and (3) in cases under chapter 7 or—significant for the purposes of the present chapter—chapter 13. Accordingly, for present purposes, even in chapter 13, the new rule of § 506(a)(2) will not apply if the collateral is real estate. In that event, § 506(a)(1)—and thus *Rash*—will continue to control.

For cases covered by § 506(a)(2), which in chapter 13 would be all cram down cases involving *personal property collateral* (except for those cases covered by the so-called "hanging paragraph," as discussed below), the 2005 amendment dictates first that "*replacement value*" (to be measured as of the petition date) is the appropriate standard of valuation. Next, the statute directs that "costs of sale or marketing" are not to be deducted from that value, a proviso that directly repudiates part of *Rash's* footnote 6. Note, though, the negative inference is that the remainder of footnote 6 is not repudiated, thus arguably validating the exclusion from retail value of all *other* items the debtor does not receive, including warranties and reconditioning.

Importantly, though, the second sentence of § 506(a)(2) provides that for *consumer* collateral—that is, "property acquired for personal, family, or household purposes"— "replacement value shall mean the *price a retail merchant would charge* for property of that kind considering the age and condition of the property at the time value is determined." This provision *does* preclude most of the potential downward adjustments from full retail value suggested by footnote 6. Note that the valuation rule of the second sentence will not govern where the collateral is acquired for *business* use. Thus, for an individual debtor's business collateral, full retail price still will not be the standard.

The debtor's powers to modify the rights of the holder of a secured claim and cram down that secured claim are subject to two important exceptions. First, the debtor may not modify the rights of the holder of "a claim secured only by a security interest in real property that is the debtor's principal residence." § 1322(b)(2). In other words, the debtor may not modify and cram down a home mortgage.

To illustrate the operation of the home mortgage rules, assume that Debtor owes Creditor $80,000 on Debtor's home, secured by a mortgage on the home. At the time of bankruptcy, the home is worth only $60,000. The question is whether Debtor may strip down the secured claim to the $60,000 value of the collateral, and pay the Creditor under § 1325(a)(5)(B) based on the $60,000 secured debt, or whether Debtor must continue to pay Creditor based on the full $80,000 debt. The Supreme Court held in *Nobelman v. American Savings Bank*[273] that § 1322(b)(2)'s anti-modification clause prevents strip down under § 1325(a)(5)(B), and requires the debtor to pay the mortgagee the full amount of the debt, even if it is undersecured.

---

[272] Pub. L. No. 109–8, § 327(2), 119 Stat. 99–100 (2005) (codified at 11 U.S.C. § 506(a)(2)). For discussion, see Braucher, supra note 242.

[273] 508 U.S. 324 (1993). See §§ 7.32.b., 12.12.

If the creditor's claim is totally underwater, though, post-*Nobelman* courts have held that the anti-modification rule does not apply, reasoning that in such a situation the creditor does not hold a "secured claim" at all.[274] In our hypothetical, this would be the case for a *second* mortgage on the home: the first mortgage secures a debt of $80,000, yet the home is worth only $60,000, and thus the second mortgage is completely valueless.

The anti-modification rule of § 1322(b)(2) also applies only if the creditor's claim is secured "only" by the home mortgage. Thus, if the creditor has additional security, such as personal property, or other housing units that the debtor does not himself use as a residence (e.g., the debtor finances a duplex and lives in only one of the units), modification and cram down are permissible.[275] Some courts might ignore "boiler-plate" clauses claiming a security interest in rents and fixtures, however.[276]

In 1994, Congress enacted § 1322(c)(2), which apparently overrules *Nobelman* in a narrow class of cases. Under that section, if the last payment on the original payment schedule on a home mortgage loan is due before the date of the last plan payment—i.e., during the life of the chapter 13 case—the plan may provide for the payment of the secured claim "as modified" pursuant to § 1325(a)(5). This scenario could arise if the debtor financed a home under a short-term note with a final balloon payment. As discussed above,[277] it is possible (indeed, likely) that § 1322(c)(2) was a congressional mistake, since the legislative history made no reference at all to *Nobelman*, which had been decided just the year before. Nevertheless, the courts have given effect to the plain meaning of the statutory text.[278]

The second major exception to the standard cram down rules is found in the so-called "hanging paragraph" that was added by the 2005 amendments.[279] The new rule, tacked on to the end of § 1325(a) (and thus the moniker "hanging paragraph"), applies in two situations: first, a purchase money security interest in a motor vehicle acquired for the debtor's personal use within 910 days before bankruptcy (often called "910 claims"); or second, where the collateral is "any other thing of value," securing a debt incurred within one year before bankruptcy. Virtually all of the decided cases (of which

---

[274] See, e.g., In re Zimmer, 313 F.3d 1220 (9th Cir. 2002); In re Lane, 280 F.3d 663 (6th Cir. 2002); In re Pond, 252 F.3d 122 (2d Cir. 2001); In re Tanner, 217 F.3d 1357 (11th Cir. 2000); In re Bartee, 212 F.3d 277 (5th Cir. 2000); In re McDonald, 205 F.3d 606 (3d Cir.), cert. denied, 531 U.S. 822 (2000). But see In re Woolsey, 969 F.3d 1266 (10th Cir. 2012) (applying *Nobelman*'s rationale to preclude stripping down a wholly unsecured junior mortgage). See also TD Bank, N.A. v. Landry, 479 B.R. 1 (D. Mass. 2012) (holding that proper time for valuing residential property to decide whether junior mortgagee is undersecured or holds a claim wholly unsecured, for purposes of determining application of the anti-modification provision, is the petition date).

[275] See, e.g., In re Hammond, 27 F.3d 52 (3d Cir. 1994).

[276] See, e.g., In re Ferandos, 402 F.3d 147 (3d Cir. 2005); In re Davis, 989 F.2d 208 (6th Cir. 1993); In re Rolle, 218 B.R. 636 (Bankr. S.D. Fla. 1998). But see In re Thomas, 344 B.R. 386 (Bankr. W.D. Pa. 2006) (allowing debtor to modify mortgage when creditor took security interest in the property's escrow fund).

[277] See § 12.12.

[278] E.g., In re Paschen, 296 F.3d 1203 (11th Cir. 2002).

[279] Pub. L. No. 109–8, § 306(b), 119 Stat. 80 (2005).

there have been many) have dealt with the car loan situation; the legislative history demonstrates that such was plainly the preoccupation of Congress.[280]

The substance of the new rule is short and simple (although in some situations the application is anything but): for the covered types of secured claims, the hanging paragraph says that "For purposes of paragraph (5), section 506 shall not apply to a claim described in that paragraph." Since § 506(a)(1) is the provision that divides undersecured claims into secured and unsecured portions, the obvious intent of Congress was to preclude bifurcation of an undersecured claim for purposes of § 1325(a)(5), and thereby prevent the "strip down" of that undersecured claim under the cram down provision of § 1325(a)(5)(B). Instead, Congress expected that the amendment would force the debtor to provide for payment of the total amount of the debt due the creditor under the cram down provision, rather than just the value of the collateral. Thus, for example, if the debt was $10,000, and the collateral value only $7,500, then Congress intended for the debtor to have to propose payments to the creditor with a present value of $10,000. Before the amendment, in such a situation the debtor could cram down the creditor by proposing payments with a present value of only $7,500, since that was the amount of the "allowed secured claim" after the bifurcation effected by § 506(a)(1). In the subsection (B) cram down situation, for claims covered by the hanging paragraph (most importantly 910–day car claims), most courts have given effect to this apparent intent of Congress.[281] It should be noted, though, as discussed in detail in the chapter dealing with secured claims,[282] that a plausible reading of the statutory text itself does not necessarily command the "no strip down" result that Congress almost certainly intended.[283]

---

[280] See Whitford, supra note 242, for an in-depth discussion. He points out that the impetus for the provision came from Michigan legislators, seeking to protect the home-state industry. 2007 U. Ill. L. Rev. at 177–78. See also Braucher, supra note 242, at 469–74; Carlson, supra note 242, at 340–41.

[281] See, e.g., In re Johnson, 337 B.R. 269 (Bankr. M.D.N.C. 2006).

[282] This new rule is discussed extensively in § 7.32.b.

[283] See Braucher, supra note 242, at 469–74. The argument basically is as follows. First, § 1325(a)(5) still applies. Second, cram down of an "allowed secured claim" is still permitted, and the present value of the amount to be paid in cram down is "not less than the allowed amount of such claim." § 1325(a)(5)(B)(ii). Grammatically, "such" can only refer to the prior reference to "allowed secured claim." Thus, a chapter 13 debtor still may cram down a "910" car lender under § 1325(a)(5)(B) by paying the creditor the present value amount of the "allowed secured claim." Third, the only thing that the hanging paragraph actually does is prevent a bankruptcy court from looking at § 506(a) to determine the amount of the "allowed secured claim." But Congress put nothing in the place of § 506(a). A statutory gap thus remains. It is possible that a court could look elsewhere—such as state law, perhaps, or principles of equity—to ascertain the amount of the secured claim—and then conclude that the amount of the secured claim is less than the total debt.

Indeed, as explained in chapter 7 of this treatise, it could be even worse than that for the auto lender. With chapter 13 cram down divorced entirely from § 506, auto lenders would not be able to invoke the beneficial valuation rules of § 506(a)(2) and the *Rash* case, or the entitlement to postpetition interest under § 506(b) if oversecured. A court could even say that, with § 506 out of the picture, the auto lender does not have an "allowed secured claim" and thus would not be entitled to recover any interest, even over the life of the plan; while it might recover as principal the total amount of its claim, no "present value" protection would obtain. See, e.g., In re Taranto, 344 B.R. 857 (Bankr. N.D. Ohio 2006); Carlson, supra note 242, at 344–45. Even worse, if a court were to read the elimination of § 506 as precluding any assertion of an "allowed secured claim," reasoning that such is determined solely by reason of § 506(a), then the auto lender would be relegated entirely to unsecured status. Countering that position is the view that the lender's security rights under state law still obtain, even in bankruptcy. See In re Trejos, 352 B.R. 249 (Bankr. D. Nev. 2006); Carlson, supra note 242, at 347.

A significant controversy has arisen over what surely is an unintended possible effect of the hanging paragraph, namely, what happens when the debtor proposes to *surrender* the collateral to the secured creditor in accordance with subsection (C) of § 1325(a)(5), and the value of the collateral is less than the amount of the creditor's total claim? The issue is whether the debtor's surrender of the collateral fully satisfies the creditor's entire claim, eliminating thereby any *unsecured* deficiency claim. If so, then the debtor of course would not need to provide for the creditor's unsecured claim in the chapter 13 plan at all, for the excellent reason that the creditor would not *have* any unsecured bankruptcy claim remaining after the debtor returned the collateral to the creditor. In sum, it is possible that the hanging paragraph converted claims covered thereunder from recourse to non-recourse claims.

The debtor's argument focuses on the fact that the hanging paragraph precludes any application of § 506 to § 1325(a)(5). Since § 506(a)(1) is the bankruptcy provision that bifurcates an undersecured claim into secured and unsecured portions, with § 506 out of the picture for "910" claims, there is no apparent statutory basis for the undersecured creditor to assert an unsecured deficiency claim in conjunction with the chapter 13 plan confirmation process. In the context of cram down under subsection (B) of § 1325(a)(5), Congress undeniably intended that the import of the § 506 exclusion be to deem the "allowed secured claim" to be equal to the total allowed claim, even if the creditor actually was undersecured, and as just discussed most courts have so held when considering cram down under § 1325(a)(5)(B). However, nothing in the hanging paragraph differentiates between different subsections of § 1325(a)(5)—it simply says that "section 506 shall not apply." Arguably, then, the same result must obtain upon surrender of the collateral under § 1325(a)(5)(C)—namely, the collateral is conclusively deemed to be worth the amount of the debt.[284] Structurally this makes sense as well, because the confirmation requirements for a secured claim under § 1325(a)(5) are presented as equivalent alternatives. The secured creditor gets the same chapter 13 deal in retention or surrender cases: the collateral is treated as equal in value to the amount of the debt. That then means, of course, that the creditor does *not* have an unsecured claim, a proposition that holds for surrender cases and cram down cases alike. Accordingly, as one appellate court observed, "[t]he majority of bankruptcy courts have concluded that, by eliminating the application of § 506(a) to 910 claims, the hanging paragraph ensures that such creditors are without a remedy to bifurcate their loans into secured and unsecured portions, therefore rendering their loans non-recourse regardless of what the parties' contract allows."[285]

The courts of appeals, however, have gone the other way and have held for the secured creditor, concluding "that, after a debtor satisfies the requirements for plan confirmation under § 1325(a)(5)(C) by surrendering his 910 vehicle, the parties are left to their contractual rights and obligations, and the creditor may pursue an unsecured deficiency claim under state law."[286] The leading case espousing this view is the

---

[284] The leading case espousing this view is *In re Pinti*, 363 B.R. 369 (Bankr. S.D.N.Y. 2007). See also In re Tompkins, 391 B.R. 560 (Bankr. S.D.N.Y. 2008); In re Durham, 361 B.R. 206, 209 (Bankr. D. Utah 2006).

[285] Tidewater Fin. Co. v. Kenney, 531 F.3d 312, 317–18 (4th Cir. 2008).

[286] Id. at 318. See also In re Barrett, 543 F.3d 1239 (11th Cir. 2008); DaimlerChrysler Fin. Servs. Ams. LLC v. Ballard, 526 F.3d 634 (10th Cir. 2008); In re Long, 519 F.3d 288 (6th Cir. 2008); Capital One Auto

Seventh Circuit's decision in *In re Wright*.[287] The *Wright* court's reasoning, adopted by several courts of appeals, asserts that "it is a mistake to assume . . . that § 506 is the *only* source of authority for a deficiency judgment when the collateral is insufficient."[288] Instead, the court asserted that when, as here, the Code does not provide a federal rule, *state law* should control.[289] The state law governing contracts and security interests provides that the debtor is responsible for any deficiency that results after the sale of the collateral, and that state law therefore provides the basis for finding that the undersecured creditor retains an unsecured claim following surrender of the collateral under § 1325(a)(5)(C), notwithstanding the hanging paragraph. The *Wright* court relied further on legislative history, which indicated that in adding the hanging paragraph Congress sought to benefit secured creditors.[290]

As discussed in detail in chapter 7, this reasoning of the *Wright* court is flawed. The deference to state law is appropriate only when no federal bankruptcy interest provides otherwise. Here, though, Congress has legislated specifically—it provided that § 506, which is the bankruptcy provision dealing specifically with the bifurcation of undersecured claims, "shall not apply." In so doing, Congress intended to preclude such bifurcation, at least in cram down cases under § 1325(a)(5)(B). Furthermore, there is no statutory basis for distinguishing between cases under subsections (B) and (C) with regard to the hanging paragraph's anti-bifurcation effect. The result of *Wright* and its progeny is to create just such a distinction. Under this view, the "910" lender in a retention case under § 1325(a)(5)(B) is permitted to benefit from a fiction that the collateral is worth the full amount of the debt, even though in reality it is not, because of the hanging paragraph; whereas in a surrender case under § 1325(a)(5)(C) the debtor is not entitled to the benefit of the same fiction.

The Sixth Circuit in *In re Long*[291] agreed with the ultimate holding of *Wright* and the other circuits courts, but its reasoning was markedly different. The *Long* court recognized the insurmountable textual problems with the *Wright* reasoning, and rejected the idea that Congress intended for state law to apply in the absence of § 506. However, the Sixth Circuit looked at the pro-creditor legislative history and found it unlikely that Congress could have intended for the secured creditor to lose its deficiency claim in surrender cases under § 1325(a)(5)(C). All that Congress meant to do with the hanging paragraph was prevent strip down in cram down cases, but in trying to do so Congress made a drafting mistake. Accordingly, the *Long* court decided that the best approach was to ignore the drafting error, and recognize a uniform *federal* rule recognizing a deficiency claim in surrender cases.

Fin. v. Osborn, 515 F.3d 817 (8th Cir. 2008); In re Wright, 492 F.3d 829 (7th Cir. 2007). See also In re Smith, 465 B.R. 350 (Bankr. D. Mass. 2012).

[287] 492 F.3d 829 (7th Cir. 2007).
[288] Id. at 832.
[289] Id. at 832–33.
[290] Id. at 832.
[291] 519 F.3d 288 (6th Cir. 2008).

§ 12.19 Feasibility and Other Requirements

The bankruptcy court should not confirm a chapter 13 plan that is destined to fail. Accordingly, to confirm the plan the court is required to find that "the debtor will be able to make all payments under the plan and to comply with the plan." § 1325(a)(6). Similar requirements are found in chapter 11[292] (§ 1129(a)(11)) and chapter 12 (§ 1225(a)(6)).

In chapter 13 (as in chapter 12), this safeguard is especially important for creditors, who are not entitled to vote on the plan. The feasibility test for confirmation is logically linked with the threshold eligibility requirement that a debtor have "regular income," § 109(e), which is defined as "income [that] is sufficiently stable and regular to enable such individual to make payments under a plan." § 101(30).

In making the feasibility determination, the court will rely heavily on the advice of the chapter 13 trustee. The trustee has the duty to investigate the financial circumstances of the debtor, §§ 704(4), 1302(b)(1); to advise and assist the debtor with regard to the plan, § 1302(b)(4); and to appear and be heard at the confirmation hearing, § 1302(b)(2)(B). The schedules of current expenses and current income that the debtor must file at the outset of the case, Official Form B22C, and the statement of financial affairs, § 521(a)(1), together with testimony gathered at the § 341 meeting of creditors, will assist the trustee in this financial investigation.

What happens if the court determines at confirmation that the debtor's plan is not feasible? One possibility would be to dismiss the case or convert it to chapter 7. § 1307(c). Such radical measures rarely would be warranted, however. The better practice in the vast majority of cases would be for the debtor to *modify* her plan as permitted by § 1323 to respond to the court's specific concerns, and then to seek confirmation of the modified plan. Note that since this modification would take place prior to the entry of a confirmation order, § 1323 governs, not § 1329, meaning that the debtor may modify as a matter of right, and that no one else may propose a modification.

On the merits, how should the court resolve feasibility issues that may arise? To begin with, the court probably will be somewhat lenient to the debtor, and give the debtor the benefit of the doubt. This reality probably helps to explain the high failure rate of confirmed chapter 13 cases. Assuming that the debtor is willing, there is not a major downside to attempting performance under an ambitious plan. Confirmation in chapter 13 does not result in an immediate discharge. The permanent composition of creditor's claims is conditioned on the debtor's performance under the plan. If the debtor ends up having difficulty making plan payments, modification of the plan under § 1329 is readily available.[293] Accordingly, courts may indulge the debtor's reasonable optimistic forecasts about the course of future events. For example, in one case the

---

[292] See § 11.28.

[293] See § 12.21.

court confirmed a plan that was predicated on the assumption that the debtor would find permanent employment before unemployment benefits ended.[294]

That being said, the court must carry out its statutory duty, and should not confirm a plan where it is more probable than not that the debtor will not be able to make payments. Courts look for certain "red flags" to signal feasibility problems. One, obviously, is if the debtor's budget on its face reveals insufficient disposable income to make the plan payments.[295] Note that for debtors with family incomes above the state median income for the same family size, the 2005 amendments dramatically reduced the flexibility afforded debtors in framing their budget, incorporating the expense allowances of the chapter 7 means test. § 1325(b)(3). Even if the budget is facially sufficient, courts look to certain factors to determine if that budget is patently unrealistic. For example, many courts will not confirm a plan that does not provide a reserve fund for unexpected contingencies.[296] A third question courts will ask is whether the debtor will be able to take care of his primary obligations to his dependents. The legislative history made clear that such a finding is incumbent on the courts.[297] Fourth, if performance of the debtor's plan is dependent on outside sources of income, even the debtor's spouse, the court will take a close look at feasibility.[298] Finally, courts are wary of "balloon" payment plans, especially if the source of the balloon payment is unknown.[299] Many of these cases are predicated on a proposed future sale of property, such as the debtor's home. In assessing feasibility in such cases, the court will look at how soon the debtor plans to sell the property, what market contingencies could adversely affect value in the interim, and how much equity the debtor now has and how much the debtor will need to fund the plan.[300]

A peculiar feasibility problem was created by the 2005 amendments to the projected disposable income test of § 1325(b). As discussed in detail above,[301] that test incorporates the definition of "current monthly income," which looks retrospectively at the debtor's historical income. Prior to the Supreme Court's decision in *Lanning*, courts debated whether that historical income should be used to project forward into the future for the purpose of applying the disposable income test, or whether the court should make adjustments for expected future reality. Jurisdictions that do embrace the use of historical income as conclusive, such as the Ninth Circuit,[302] create the

---

[294] In re Compton, 88 B.R. 166 (Bankr. S.D. Ohio 1988). And in another case, the court predicated confirmation on amending the plan to include wage attachment to ensure that available funds would be used not only for the plan itself, but for marketing for the sale of the debtor's boat. In re Capodanno, 94 B.R. 62 (Bankr. E.D. Pa. 1988). However, another court did not permit confirmation of a plan in which the success hinged upon the debtor's successful appeal of a judgment, and successful prosecution of a pending malpractice action. In re Shelly, 458 B.R. 740 (Bankr. N.D. Ohio 2011).

[295] See, e.g., In re Wilson, 117 B.R. 714 (Bankr. M.D. Fla. 1990).

[296] See, e.g., In re Greer, 60 B.R. 547 (Bankr. C.D. Cal. 1986).

[297] H.R. Rep. No. 95–595, 95th Cong., 1st Sess. 124 (1977).

[298] See, e.g., In re Olp, 29 B.R. 932 (Bankr. E.D. Wis. 1983).

[299] See, e.g., In re Brunson, 87 B.R. 304 (Bankr. D.N.J. 1988). However, for cases where the court confirmed a plan as feasible under the circumstances where the debtor proposed a balloon payment, see *In re Wagner*, 259 B.R. 694 (B.A.P. 8th Cir. 2001) , and *In re Groff*, 131 B.R. 703 (Bankr. E.D. Wis. 1991).

[300] Compare In re Hogue, 78 B.R. 867 (Bankr. S.D. Ohio 1987) (sale plan not feasible), with In re Gregory, 143 B.R. 424 (Bankr. E.D. Tex. 1992) (sale plan feasible).

[301] See § 12.17.

[302] In re Kagenveama, 541 F.3d 868 (9th Cir. 2008).

possibility of a "Catch–22" whereby a debtor apparently could not satisfy both the projected disposable income test and the feasibility test. This could occur in situations where the debtor's actual projected disposable income (as shown on Schedules I and J) is less than the historical income, as computed under Form B22C. For example, in *Lanning*,[303] the debtor's Form B22C showed a disposable income of $1,114 a month, whereas her real disposable income, as revealed by Schedules I and J, was only $149 a month. The difference arose because the debtor had received a large one-time buyout during the pre-bankruptcy six-month period in which "current monthly income" was computed. Obviously the debtor could not pay $1,114 a month in her chapter 13 plan, because she was not going to have that much money available. Faced with this practical problem, the Supreme Court did not demand rigid adherence to Form B22C, but if it had, it is hard to see how the debtor could have proposed a feasible plan.

Section 1325(a) has a few additional confirmation requirements that have not been discussed so far in this treatise. Under § 1325(a)(1), the plan must comply with the provisions of chapter 13 and with the other applicable provisions of title 11. That rule puts teeth in the provisions of § 1322 that dictate the mandatory and permissive provisions of the plan. Next, § 1325(a)(2) requires that "any fee, charge, or amount required under chapter 123 of title 28, or by the plan, to be paid before confirmation, has been paid." The 2005 amendments added three confirmation requirements. First, the debtor's action in filing the petition must be in good faith. § 1325(a)(7). This good faith requirement complements the additional requirement that the plan be proposed in good faith.[304] Second, the debtor must have paid in full by the time of confirmation all domestic support obligations that arise postpetition, if the debtor is required to pay that DSO by a judicial or administrative order or by statute. § 1325(a)(8). Note that prepetition DSOs are first priority claims and thus the plan must provide for full payment of those claims under § 1322(a)(2). Finally, the debtor must have filed all tax returns as required by § 1308. § 1325(a)(9).

E. CONFIRMATION AND BEYOND

§ 12.20 Effects of Confirmation

Confirmation of the debtor's plan occurs very early in the chapter 13 process.[305] Confirmation is not the final step, but more of an important way station along the road to the completion of payments to creditors. Nevertheless, confirmation is a significant step. Indeed, if the plan is not confirmed, and the debtor does not file another plan or modify the plan, the court may convert the case to chapter 7 or dismiss the case. § 1307(c). If the plan is confirmed, the debtor will attempt to perform under the plan's terms, and upon completing performance will receive a discharge. § 1328(a).

The entry of a confirmation order has several immediate and important legal ramifications. § 1327. First, the terms of a confirmed plan *bind* the debtor and all creditors. § 1327(a). The plan is binding on each creditor even if the creditor's claim was not provided for by the plan, and irrespective of whether the creditor objected to,

---

[303] 130 S.Ct. 2464 (2010).

[304] See § 12.15.

[305] See § 12.9.

accepted, or rejected the plan. The confirmed plan is given *res judicata* effect, and cannot be collaterally attacked.[306]

The debtor cannot use § 1327(a) as a way to bypass the other provisions in the Code, however, and adversely affect creditor's claims. For example, if a creditor has properly filed a secured proof of claim, many courts conclude that the debtor cannot seek to void that claim or reduce the amount of the claim in the plan if the debtor did not object to the filed claim as required by § 502(a) prior to confirmation of the plan.[307] Other courts do, however, permit post-confirmation claim objections.[308]

It is important to emphasize that, notwithstanding the binding effect of the plan, the composition of creditors' claims effected by the plan is not permanent at the time of confirmation. If the debtor fails to perform under the plan, does not receive a discharge, and the case is converted or dismissed, the claims of creditors will be restored to their original amount (less any payments actually made on those claims under the chapter 13 plan, of course).

Second, confirmation *vests* all property of the estate in the debtor. § 1327(b). This result is only a default rule, and can be overridden in the plan or in the confirmation order. A debtor is permitted in the plan to provide for vesting of estate property in the debtor or another entity at the time of confirmation or at a later date. § 1322(b)(9). A debtor might want to defer the vesting of estate property to retain the protection of the § 362(a) automatic stay, even against postpetition claims. However, if the debtor does provide that estate property will not vest upon confirmation, it may be more difficult for the debtor to obtain postpetition credit, since potential creditors would be aware that their collection efforts would be stayed until the completion of the chapter 13 case.

Section 1327(b) must be read in conjunction with § 1306(a), which provides that property acquired by the debtor during the pendency of the chapter 13 case, until the case is closed, dismissed, or converted, becomes estate property.[309] Courts have struggled to reconcile these two sections, noting that the cutoff date for § 1306(a)—the date the case is closed, dismissed, or converted—typically will come *after* confirmation. Three views have developed.[310] One is that § 1327(b) means what it says, and that all property of the estate vests in the debtor at confirmation, unless the plan or confirmation order provides otherwise.[311] The second view uses the time of confirmation as a dividing line, holding that all property or earnings acquired *after* confirmation remain property of the estate (thus effectuating § 1306(a), in part), whereas the property that existed at the time of confirmation does vest in the debtor (thus partly upholding § 1327(b)).[312] This is probably the majority view. The third

---

[306] See, e.g., In re Evon, 489 B.R. 88 (Bankr. N.D. Ill. 2013); In re McLemore, 426 B.R. 728 (Bankr. S.D. Ohio 2010).

[307] See In re Bateman, 331 F.3d 821 (11th Cir. 2003); In re Simmons, 765 F.2d 547 (5th Cir. 1985).

[308] See, e.g., In re Morton, 298 B.R. 301 (B.A.P. 6th Cir. 2003); In re Shank, 315 B.R. 799 (Bankr. N.D. Ga. 2004).

[309] See § 12.6.

[310] See United States v. Harchar, 371 B.R. 254 (N.D. Ohio 2007).

[311] See, e.g., In re Toth, 193 B.R. 992 (Bankr. N.D. Ga. 1996); In re Petrucelli, 113 B.R. 5 (Bankr. S.D. Cal. 1990).

[312] See In re Waldron, 536 F.3d 1239 (11th Cir. 2008); Barbosa v. Soloman, 235 F.3d 31 (1st Cir. 2000).

approach Solomonically "splits the baby" and holds (albeit without any apparent textual support) that only the post-confirmation property that the debtor needs to fund the plan remains property of the estate.[313]

The third and final legal effect of confirmation of a chapter 13 plan is that the property that vests in the debtor under subsection (b) is *free and clear* of any claim or interest of any creditor provided for by the plan. § 1327(c). This rule, like the vesting rule of (b), is presumptive only, and can be changed by a contrary provision in the plan or confirmation order.

A controversy that has arisen under subsection (c) is whether the plan can void the lien of a creditor if the plan provides for the creditor's claim but eliminates the creditor's lien in the plan. As a threshold matter, under the literal language of § 1327(c), the plan must "provide for" the creditor's claim in order to vest the collateral in the debtor free and clear of the encumbrance; otherwise, the lien rides through confirmation.[314] In the chapter 11 setting, the Seventh Circuit has held that confirmation can void liens, and a number of circuits have followed suit.[315] In a chapter 13 case, the Fourth Circuit took a different view, and held that a creditor's lien could not be extinguished by fiat in a chapter 13 plan, unless the plan made express provision for the payment of the secured amount.[316] The court explained that a lien normally may only be avoided in an adversary proceeding, under Rule 7001. Other courts, though, disagree with the Fourth Circuit, and follow the view that by providing for a secured creditor's claim in the plan but not also preserving the creditor's lien thereunder, confirmation voids that lien.[317]

§ 12.21 Performance under the Plan and Modification

After the debtor's chapter 13 plan is confirmed under § 1325, the next step in the process is for the debtor to *perform* under the terms of the plan. The debtor actually must begin making payments proposed by a plan to the trustee *prior* to confirmation, not later than 30 days after the plan is filed or the order for relief, whichever is earlier. § 1326(a)(1). The trustee holds those funds, and if the plan is confirmed, distributes the payments to creditors. § 1326(a)(2). After confirmation, the debtor continues to make payments to the trustee, who in turn makes the distributions to creditors under the plan. § 1326(c). The debtor alternatively may provide in the plan or the confirmation order to make payments directly to creditors, rather than through the trustee. At the time of each payment to creditors under the plan, there must be paid any priority claim under § 507(a)(2) and the standing trustee's percentage fee. § 1326(b)(1)–(2). Additionally, if there is compensation due a chapter 7 trustee from a converted or dismissed case, that compensation must be paid at the time of payment to creditors. § 1326(b)(3).

---

[313] See In re Price, 130 B.R. 259 (N.D. Ill. 1991).

[314] See In re Thomas, 883 F.2d 991 (11th Cir. 1989), cert. denied, 497 U.S. 1007 (1990).

[315] In re Penrod, 50 F.3d 459 (7th Cir. 1995). See also In re Ahern Enters., Inc., 507 F.3d 817 (5th Cir. 2007).

[316] Cen–Pen Corp. v. Hanson, 58 F.3d 89 (4th Cir. 1995).

[317] See, e.g., In re Harnish, 224 B.R. 91 (Bankr. N.D. Iowa 1998).

Performance under the terms of the plan is critical for the debtor as well as for creditors. The debtor in chapter 13 does not receive a discharge at the time of confirmation.[318] The chapter 13 discharge is not granted until "completion by the debtor of all payments under the plan."[319] § 1328(a). If the debtor cannot complete performance under the plan, and cannot modify the plan under § 1329 or obtain a hardship discharge under § 1328(b),[320] the court may dismiss the chapter 13 case or convert the case to chapter 7. § 1307(c). Creditors' claims will be reinstated to their original amounts, less any payments made during the chapter 13 case.

If the debtor does complete performance under the plan, and certifies that all required domestic support obligations have been paid, the discharge will be entered as soon as practicable. § 1328(a). But what happens if, as so often occurs, the debtor encounters difficulty in making payments under the terms of a confirmed chapter 13 plan? Studies have shown a significant failure rate for chapter 13 cases, ranging from one-third to one-half of all cases. The debtor has several options when problems arise in making payments under the plan.

First, the debtor can simply give up, and exercise her absolute right to either convert the case to chapter 7, § 1307(a), or dismiss the case. § 1307(b). Other interested parties may file a motion requesting the court to dismiss the case or convert it to chapter 7, § 1307(c), although the granting of such relief is discretionary with the court. After confirmation, conversion to either chapter 11 or chapter 12 is not permitted. § 1307(d).

A second and perhaps more palatable option for the debtor is to attempt to *modify* the plan under § 1329. If the debtor is able to complete all payments under the plan as modified, which now is "the plan," § 1329(b)(2), the debtor will receive a full-compliance discharge under § 1328(a). If the debtor instead wants to seek a "hardship" discharge under § 1328(b) without first attempting to modify the original plan under § 1329, the debtor will have to show that modification was not practicable. § 1328(b)(3).

Post-confirmation modification is different from pre-confirmation modification under § 1323 in several important respects. Prior to confirmation, the debtor alone has the right to propose modifications, § 1323(a), and court approval of the modification is not required; the plan as modified simply becomes the plan, § 1323(b), but of course still must be confirmed under § 1325.

After confirmation, and before the completion of payments under the plan, some of the rules governing modification change. First, the debtor no longer has the exclusive right to propose modifications; in addition to the debtor, the chapter 13 trustee or the holder of an allowed unsecured claim also may request modifications. § 1329(a). The debtor usually would want to modify the plan to make it easier to perform, such as by reducing plan payments. The trustee or unsecured creditors, by contrast, normally

---

[318] See § 12.20.

[319] See § 12.23.

[320] See § 12.24.

would request a modification if the debtor's situation had improved, and they might seek to increase plan payments.[321]

A second difference is that a post-confirmation modification is subject to court oversight. At least 21 days' notice of the proposed modification and the time fixed for filing objections to the modification must be sent to the debtor, the trustee, and all creditors. Rule 3015(g). If an objection is filed, the court will have to resolve the dispute. If the court disapproves the modification, it is ineffective. § 1329(b)(2). If, however, no objections to the modification are filed, or if the court approves the modification over filed objections, the plan as modified becomes "the plan." Id.

Under § 1329(a), a plan may be modified after confirmation to: (1) increase or reduce plan payments; (2) extend or reduce the time for making plan payments; (3) alter the distribution to a creditor whose claim is provided for by the plan to take account of payments on that claim other than under the plan; or (4) reduce the amount paid under the plan to allow the debtor to purchase health insurance for himself and any dependents. § 1329(a)(1)–(4). There has been some dispute in the courts as to whether the debtor may reduce the total amount to be paid to creditors, or whether the debtor may just reduce the amount of each payment, with the total amount to be paid remaining the same. The sounder view permits the debtor to reduce the total amount to be paid.[322]

The modified plan also must comply with the statutory provisions governing plans, such as § 1322 and 1325. § 1329(b)(1). For example, the Eleventh Circuit held that a debtor could modify a plan after confirmation to cure post-confirmation defaults, as permitted by § 1322(b)(5).[323] Note that the "best interests" test of § 1325(a)(4)[324] will have to be recalculated as of the date of the proposed modification.[325]

The modification may not provide for payments for more than the applicable commitment period under § 1325(b)(1)(B) after the first payment was due under the original confirmed plan, unless the court approves a longer period. § 1329(c). This restriction prevents parties from using modifications to circumvent the time limits on the length of chapter 13 plans in § 1322(d).

Courts have disagreed over the showing necessary to support a post-confirmation modification. The statute does not require proof of "cause" or any other predicate. This statutory omission has been construed by many courts to permit the *debtor* to modify freely after confirmation without showing cause, subject of course to the need to comply with all of the statutory rules in § 1322 and § 1325. Usually, though, the debtor only modifies for a good reason; for example, the debtor might show that his family had incurred unexpected medical expenses, or that he had lost his job. However, one court did not allow a debtor to modify his confirmed plan based on the debtor showing his

---

[321] See, e.g., In re Witkowski, 16 F.3d 739 (7th Cir. 1994).

[322] See In re Frost, 123 B.R. 254 (S.D. Ohio 1990).

[323] In re Hoggle, 12 F.3d 1008 (11th Cir. 1994).

[324] See § 12.16.

[325] H.R. Rep. No. 95–595, 95th Cong., 1st Sess., at 431 (1977).

motor vehicle did not pass inspection, and thus would require costly repairs and could not be driven on the road.[326]

For modifications proposed by someone *other* than the debtor, i.e., by the trustee or an unsecured creditor, the rule may be different. In such cases, the traditional understanding has been that, because of the binding *res judicata* nature of the entry of a confirmation order,[327] § 1327(a), the proponent of a modification must prove *changed circumstances* since confirmation.[328] For example, the trustee or an unsecured creditor might show that the debtor had gotten a new job entailing a large raise, or that projected medical expenses were no longer required, or that the debtor received a substantial tax refund. Some courts require not only that there be a change in the debtor's financial condition, but further that the change be both (1) substantial and (2) unanticipated.[329] For example, one court held that a trustee's post-confirmation discovery of debtor's surrender of residence warranted an amendment to the plan.[330] An emerging competing view, however, disagrees with the traditional view that the proponent of a modification must show that circumstances have changed.[331] According to these courts, the statute expressly permits post-confirmation modifications in § 1329 without requiring any such proof, negating the *res judicata* argument. However, this view may read too much into statutory silence and give insufficient weight to the binding nature of a confirmation order on other parties.

§ 12.22 Revocation of Confirmation

Entry of an order confirming the debtor's chapter 13 plan has several important consequences, as discussed in a previous section.[332] § 1327. A confirmation order may be *revoked*, however, upon proof that the debtor procured confirmation by *fraud*. § 1330(a). The other reorganization chapters contain similar provisions. § 1144 (chapter 11);[333] § 1230 (chapter 12).[334] The chapter 12 rule is identical to the chapter 13 provision.

Proof of actual fraud is required to revoke the confirmation order. Note that the statute does not necessarily limit revocation to cases in which the *debtor* carried out the fraud, although that would be the most typical scenario. Examples of fraud that might warrant revoking confirmation include the debtor misrepresenting his eligibility for chapter 13 relief, misstating the debts owing, or falsely identifying or hiding sources of income. One court held that the debtor's failure to disclose a pending

---

[326] In re Palmer, 419 B.R. 162 (Bankr. N.D.N.Y. 2009).

[327] See § 12.20.

[328] See, e.g., In re Arnold, 869 F.2d 240 (4th Cir. 1989).

[329] See, e.g., In re Murphy, 474 F.3d 143 (4th Cir. 2007); In re Eckert, 485 B.R. 77 (Bankr. M.D. Pa. 2013).

[330] In re Justice, 418 B.R. 342 (Bankr. W.D. Miss. 2009).

[331] See, e.g., In re Meza, 467 F.3d 874 (5th Cir. 2006); Barbosa v. Soloman, 235 F.3d 31 (1st Cir.2000); In re Witkowski, 16 F.3d 739 (7th Cir. 1994).

[332] See § 12.20.

[333] See § 11.36.

[334] See § 13.11.

criminal proceeding against him was not fraud that warranted revocation of the confirmation order.[335]

A party in interest must request revocation of the confirmation order. § 1330(a). This request must be brought within 180 days after the entry of the confirmation order. Since confirmation in chapter 13 normally occurs very early in the case, creditors must be vigilant in pursuing revocation of confirmation. Note, though, that the time to seek revocation of *discharge* extends much later, since that is tied to the time the discharge is granted, which does not occur until the end of the chapter 13 case.[336] § 1328(e). A request to revoke confirmation must be brought as an adversary proceeding. Rule 7001(5).

Unlike the rule for revoking a discharge under § 1328(e),[337] the statutory rule for revoking confirmation does not expressly require a party requesting revocation to prove that they did not know of the fraud prior to entry of the court's order. The statutory omission would not prevent a court from invoking equitable principles such as estoppel, however.

What are the effects of revocation of a confirmation order? To begin with, the effects of confirmation in § 1327 will be reversed. Importantly, the claims of creditors which were modified by the now-revoked chapter 13 plan are reinstated in full. For example, if the debtor's plan proposed to pay unsecured creditors 10% on their claims, a creditor with a $500 claim would after revocation still have a $500 claim, rather than just a $50 claim.

A decision then will have to be made about the future of the case. One option is for the court to fix a time for the debtor to *modify* the plan under § 1329,[338] and then, if the debtor does so, to confirm the modified plan if it meets the statutory requisites. § 1330(b). At first blush it might seem to be a toothless sanction to revoke confirmation but then permit the debtor to modify the plan, and ultimately perhaps receive a discharge. The reason for the modification option, though, is that *creditors* may fare best (i.e., get more money) if the debtor stays in chapter 13 and performs under a modified plan. The nature of the necessary modification will depend on the fraud committed. For example, if the debtor's fraud consisted of failing to disclose a significant source of income, the modified plan probably will require larger payments by the debtor to creditors. § 1329(a)(1).

If the plan is not modified and confirmed as modified after revocation of confirmation, the court is required to proceed under § 1307. § 1330(b). Under § 1307(c)(7), revocation of confirmation constitutes "cause" for the court either to *dismiss* the case or *convert* the case to chapter 7. Whether to dismiss or convert depends on which is in the "best interests" of the creditors and the estate. Note that the court does not have the option to convert to chapter 11.

---

[335] In re Leverett, 486 B.R. 391 (Bankr. W.D. Tex. 2013).

[336] See § 12.25.

[337] See id.

[338] See § 12.21.

§ 12.23　Full-Compliance Discharge

In chapter 13, confirmation of the debtor's plan is one of the *first* steps in the process, rather than the culmination of the case. Unlike chapter 11 cases involving corporate and partnership debtors, § 1141(d)(1)(A), in chapter 13 the debtor's discharge is not granted on confirmation. Instead, a chapter 13 debtor receives a discharge under § 1328(a) at the *end* of the case, when she *completes* all payments under the confirmed plan. The only exception is that the court may grant a "hardship" discharge under § 1328(b) to a debtor who fails to complete performance under the plan, but can justify that failure.[339] A debtor who modifies the confirmed plan,[340] § 1329, and then successfully completes payments under the plan as modified, will receive a full discharge under § 1328(a).

As originally enacted, the full-compliance discharge under § 1328(a) was one of the primary incentives Congress created to entice debtors to opt for chapter 13 instead of liquidating under chapter 7. Even now, a full discharge in chapter 13 is somewhat broader in scope than a chapter 7 discharge. A few types of debts that are excluded from a chapter 7 discharge under § 523(a) are discharged under § 1328(a). Originally, though, *most* types of § 523(a) debts were dischargeable in chapter 13, including even debts for fraud and for willful and malicious injury. For this reason, the chapter 13 discharge was sometimes referred to as a "*superdischarge.*" However, if the debtor is unable to complete performance under the plan, and settles for a hardship discharge under § 1328(b), all of the exceptions to discharge in § 523(a) will apply. § 1328(c)(2).

Congress has been chipping away at the scope of the superdischarge, and after 2005 there is little of it left. Until 1990, the *only* types of debts that were excluded from a chapter 13 full-compliance discharge were:

- Long-term debts on which the last payment is due after the end of the plan period, §§ 1328(a)(1), 1322(b)(5); and

- debts for domestic support obligations under § 523(a)(5), § 1328(a)(2).

The breadth of the superdischarge was confirmed by the Supreme Court in *Pennsylvania Department of Public Welfare v. Davenport*,[341] when it held that a criminal restitution obligation was a "debt" and as such was dischargeable in chapter 13. *Davenport*, it seems, woke Congress up to the potential for abuse inherent in the incredibly broad chapter 13 discharge, and the legislature immediately began cutting back on the scope of the superdischarge. In 1990, Congress added educational loans under § 523(a)(8), drunk driving debts under § 523(a)(9), and criminal restitution obligations and criminal fines to the list of debts excepted from the § 1328(a) discharge.[342]

---

[339] See § 12.24.

[340] See § 12.21.

[341] 495 U.S. 552 (1990).

[342] See Criminal Victims Protection Act of 1990, Pub. L. No. 101–647, §§ 3101–04, 104 Stat. 4916 (1990) (codified at § 1328(a)(2)–(3)).

In 2005, BAPCPA added the following to the list of excluded debts:

- certain types of tax debts under § 523(a)(1)(B) and (C) and § 507(a)(8)(C), § 1328(a)(2);

- fraud debts under § 523(a)(2), § 1328(a)(2);

- unscheduled debts under § 523(a)(3), § 1328(a)(2);

- debts for fiduciary fraud or defalcation, larceny, or embezzlement under § 523(a)(4), § 1328(a)(2); and

- debts for restitution or damages awarded in a civil action against the debtor as a result of willful or malicious injury by the debtor that caused death or personal injury, § 1328(a)(4).

After BAPCPA, then, the only relatively common types of debts that are still left as part of the so-called "super" discharge are for (1) income taxes due more than three years before bankruptcy, for which the debtor actually filed a timely return that was not fraudulent, and which tax the debtor did not attempt to evade or defeat (§ 523(a)(1)(A)); (2) debts arising from property settlements in divorce or separation proceedings (§ 523(a)(15)); and (3) non-criminal fines and penalties (§ 523(a)(7)).

The chapter 13 superdischarge has been controversial from the day it was enacted. When it was still actually "super," some courts circumvented the congressional scheme by holding that a debtor who proceeded under chapter 13 in order to discharge § 523(a) debts lacked "good faith" and thus should not be able to confirm a plan under § 1325(a)(3). Perhaps the most famous example was the Eighth Circuit's decision in *Handeen v. Lemaire (In re LeMaire).*[343] The debtor in that case had attempted to murder Handeen by shooting him at point-blank range with a bolt-action rifle, hitting him five times and seriously wounding him. After the debtor emerged from the penitentiary, Handeen obtained a civil judgment against him for over $50,000. The debt, obviously based on a "willful and malicious injury," would have been excluded from a chapter 7 discharge by § 523(a)(6). The debtor, however, filed for relief under chapter 13, hoping to take advantage of the § 1328(a) superdischarge, which would discharge willful and malicious injury debts covered by § 523(a)(6). Looking at the totality of the circumstances and public policy considerations, the Eighth Circuit held that LeMaire's chapter 13 filing was in bad faith and his plan could not be confirmed.

The *LeMaire* court's discomfort with the notion that a person who tried to murder someone could discharge a civil judgment arising out of that murderous attempt certainly is understandable. But one might ask whether it was an appropriate exercise of *judicial* power to deny that criminal/debtor relief under chapter 13, given the clear *legislative* directive that debtors in chapter 13 were permitted to discharge debts based on a willful and malicious injury? To invoke the general "good faith" talisman of § 1325(a)(3) to prevent a debtor from discharging debts in chapter 13 which would be nondischargeable in chapter 7, based on that fact alone, undermines the specific

---

[343]   898 F.2d 1346 (8th Cir. 1990) (en banc).

congressional determination that a debtor may do just that and ignores the fundamental principle of separation of powers. Can it be "bad faith" for a debtor to do exactly what the law expressly authorizes him to do, without more? Nor was this aspect of chapter 13 the product of an inadvertent drafting error by Congress; to the contrary, it was one of the cornerstones of their initial construct of the chapter 13 model.

The argument that courts should not use "good faith" to subvert a debtor's attempted use of the superdischarge, absent proof of other facts suggesting bad faith, became even more powerful after the 2005 amendments. Congress revisited the superdischarge and made a host of changes, ultimately leaving far fewer debts still eligible for the superdischarge. For example, after 2005 the murderous debtor in *LeMaire* would not even be eligible for the superdischarge, his debt being based on a willful or malicious injury that caused personal injury or death, for restitution or damages awarded in a civil action. § 1328(a)(4). That congressional action underscores the need for courts to respect the legislative decisions made with respect to those debts that *are* still eligible for the superdischarge. Congress has demonstrated that it can fix problematic statutes; the courts should not sit as a board of legislative review. After 2005, what if a debtor tried to kill someone with a rifle, but filed chapter 13 before the victim was able to obtain a judgment in a civil action? In that event, the debt would not be excluded from the superdischarge under § 1328(a)(4), which requires an award in a civil action. Or what if, when the debtor tried to murder the intended victim with a high-powered rifle, he missed the target, but hit the target's Mercedes, causing $20,000 in property damage? In § 1328(a)(4), the discharge exclusion applies only to a willful or malicious injury that causes personal injury or death—and thus not if the only debt caused is for property damage. For a court to decide that the debtor was acting in bad faith and thus should not be able to confirm a chapter 13 plan would render meaningless the statutory distinctions that Congress itself made in 2005.

The chapter 13 full-compliance discharge is effective against all debts that are "provided for by the plan," or that are disallowed. § 1328(a). Some question has arisen as to whether a debt is "provided for" if it is referred to in a plan that proposes to pay nothing on the debt, or whether some payment must be made. In *Rake v. Wade*,[344] the Supreme Court explained that a plan "provides for" a debt by "making a provision" for, "dealing with," or "referring to" the debt, even if no payment is proposed, assuming that affected claimants have notice of the plan and an opportunity to object.

Most debts "provided for by the plan" and thus dischargeable are prepetition debts. However, under § 1305(a), claims for postpetition taxes and necessary consumer debts may be filed and then dealt with in the plan.[345] § 1322(b)(6). Postpetition consumer debts are only allowed, § 1305(c), and then discharged if prior approval to incur the debt was practicable and was obtained from the chapter 13 trustee. § 1328(d).

The grounds for objecting to a chapter 7 discharge under § 727(a) do not apply at all in chapter 13. § 103(b). Thus, for example, a chapter 13 discharge is not barred even

---

[344]   508 U.S. 464 (1993).
[345]   See § 12.7.

if the debtor made a fraudulent transfer shortly before bankruptcy. The debtor may *waive* the chapter 13 discharge, though, by executing a written waiver of discharge after the commencement of the bankruptcy case. § 1328(a).

The 2005 amendments for the first time provided for denial of discharge in chapter 13—even if the debtor completes payments under the plan and receives a full-compliance discharge—if the debtor obtained a discharge in a prior bankruptcy case. § 1328(f). Previously, there was no limitation on receiving a discharge in successive bankruptcy cases when the second case was under chapter 13, except that the court might take the fact of the prior bankruptcy case into account in assessing good faith under § 1325(a)(3). However, under BAPCPA, discharge in a chapter 13 case is denied if the debtor received a discharge (1) in a prior chapter 7, 11, or 12 case filed within *four years* before the filing of the current chapter 13 case, or (2) in a prior chapter 13 case filed within *two years* before the filing of the current chapter 13. Note that the latter prohibition apparently applies even if all creditors were paid in full in the first chapter 13 case! The justification for such a harsh policy is hard to fathom.

If the chapter 13 case is filed first, then there is a conditional six-year bar on receiving a discharge in a subsequent chapter 7 case. The condition is that the debtor may receive a discharge in the chapter 7 case in less than six years only if the payout on unsecured claims in the original chapter 13 case was either (1) 100%, or (2) at least 70%, the plain was proposed in good faith, and was the debtor's best effort. § 727(a)(9).

BAPCPA also added a provision denying discharge to a debtor who fails to complete an instructional course concerning personal financial management after filing the petition. § 1328(g)(1). A similar rule was added to chapter 7 in 2005. This post-filing debtor education rule is in addition to the debtor eligibility rule of § 109(h), which requires a debtor to receive credit counseling within 180 days prior to filing a petition in order to be eligible for bankruptcy relief. Exceptions to the chapter 13 educational requirement for various hardship cases are provided on the same basis as for the prepetition counseling requirement, see § 109(h)(4), or if the United States trustee determines that adequate instructional services are not available in the judicial district. § 1328(g)(2).

Finally, BAPCPA now limits the homestead exemption to $155,675 if the debtor is convicted of a felony which demonstrates that the filing of the bankruptcy case was an abuse, or the debtor owes a debt arising from a securities law violation, racketeering, fiduciary fraud, or crimes or intentional or reckless torts that caused death or personal injury in the past five years. § 522(q). If there is reasonable cause to believe that § 522(q) might apply to the debtor, or if there is a pending proceeding against the debtor for such a felony or debt, then under § 1328(h) the court must delay entry of the discharge until the § 522(q) matter is resolved.

§ 12.24 Hardship Discharge

The overriding goal of a debtor who files for relief under chapter 13 usually is to obtain a discharge. If the debtor completes all payments under the plan, and completes the personal financial management instruction, the court then will grant the debtor a full discharge under § 1328(a). This full-compliance discharge is sometimes called the "superdischarge" because it is effective even against some debts listed in § 523(a) that would be excluded from discharge under chapter 7, 11, or 12.[346] A debtor who has difficulty making payments under the plan as originally confirmed may attempt to modify the plan under § 1329 and complete performance under the plan as modified, and upon doing so will receive a full-compliance discharge.[347]

If modification of the plan is not practicable, however, the debtor still may be able to receive a chapter 13 discharge, even if the debtor has not completed the payments under the plan. § 1328(b). The only other options available to a defaulting debtor would be to dismiss the case or convert to chapter 7. § 1307(a), (b). A "hardship" discharge may be granted by the court under § 1328(b) only if the court finds that:

1) The debtor's failure to complete plan payments is "due to circumstances for which the debtor should not justly be held accountable," § 1328(b)(1);

2) The amount *actually paid* on unsecured claims under the chapter 13 plan is not less than the amount that those claims *would have been paid* if the debtor's estate had been liquidated under chapter 7 on the effective date of the plan, i.e., the "best interests" test of § 1325(a)(4) is carried out, § 1328(b)(2); *and*

3) Modification of the plan under § 1329 is not practicable, § 1328(b)(3).

If the debtor is able to meet all three of those statutory criteria, she may receive a discharge. It is worth noting, though, that the debtor may have difficulty showing *both* that the failure to meet plan payments is due to circumstances for which the debtor should not be held accountable *and* that the modification of the plan is impracticable. Recall that a modification can call for a reduction in plan payments. § 1329(a)(1). The debtor must show why reducing plan payments will not be workable. One reason that courts have accepted is that the debtor has died.[348] At less of an extreme, if the debtor's reasonably necessary current expenses exceed the debtor's income, leaving the debtor with no disposable income, the debtor would not be able to make any plan payments, and modification would be impossible. For example, the legislative history suggests that modification might be impracticable if "the problems, such as a natural disaster, a long-term layoff, or family illness or accidents with attendant medical bills, are severe enough."[349]

The hardship discharge will cover all unsecured debts that are provided for by the plan, or that are disallowed under § 502. It does not apply to secured debts. However, the debtor will lose the prospective benefit of the § 1328(a) "superdischarge." A "hardship" discharge under § 1328(b) is subject to all of the § 523(a) discharge exceptions. § 1328(c)(2). Thus, a debtor who has debts that would be discharged under a full-compliance discharge, but not under a hardship discharge, has a strong incentive to try to modify the plan under § 1329 and complete performance under the modified plan. Of course, since the 2005 amendments largely gutted the superdischarge, there

---

[346] See § 12.23.

[347] See § 12.21.

[348] See, e.g., In re Graham, 63 B.R. 95 (Bankr. E.D. Pa. 1986).

[349] H.R. Rep. No. 95–595, 95th Cong., 1st Sess., at 125 (1977).

will be fewer cases where the difference in discharge exceptions will be relevant to the debtor.

A hardship discharge also does not apply with regard to long-term debts on which payments will be made after the end of the plan period, as authorized by § 1322(b)(5). § 1328(c)(1). This exclusion from discharge for long-term debts applies even if the debtor receives a full-compliance discharge. § 1328(a)(1).

The Code permits a debtor to file an application for a hardship discharge at any time after confirmation of the plan. This represents a change from prior law, which forced the debtor to try to perform under the plan for three years before becoming eligible for a hardship discharge.[350] If a debtor files an application for a hardship discharge, then Rule 4007(d) requires the court to give creditors 30 days' notice of the time fixed for filing complaints objecting to the dischargeability of a debt under § 523(c)(1).

§ 12.25 Revocation of Discharge

The individual debtor's ultimate goal in chapter 13 is to obtain a discharge. As discussed in the preceding sections, the court will grant the debtor a discharge (1) if the debtor completes all payments under the plan,[351] § 1328(a), or (2) even if the debtor does not complete performance under the plan, if the court finds that entry of a "hardship" discharge is warranted.[352] § 1328(b). Having reached the promised land of discharge, the debtor is not always entitled to remain; an order granting a chapter 13 debtor a discharge is not necessarily final.

As with discharges under chapter 7[353] (§ 727(d)), chapter 11[354] (§ 1144), and chapter 12 (§ 1228(d)), a chapter 13 discharge may be revoked. § 1328(e). The chapter 12 revocation provision is a verbatim copy of the chapter 13 rule. The showing required to revoke the discharge is the same in all chapters,[355] including chapter 13: the debtor obtained the discharge through *fraud*. § 1328(e)(1). Proof of *actual* fraud is required. For example, one court granted a revocation request based upon fraud when the debtor failed to disclose a nearly $100,000 inheritance.[356]

In addition, the party requesting revocation must prove that they did not know of the debtor's fraud until after the discharge was granted. § 1328(e)(2). Again, the rule is the same in all the other chapters. In effect, prior knowledge of the fraud estops a party from seeking revocation. However, the fact that some parties were aware of the debtor's fraud and did not act in a timely manner does not necessarily mean that the

---

[350] Id.; S. Rep. No. 95–989, 95th Cong., 2d Sess., at 13 (1978).

[351] See § 12.23.

[352] See § 12.24.

[353] See § 10.33.

[354] See § 11.36.

[355] Technically, in chapter 11 the required showing is that the debtor procured the confirmation order by fraud. Upon revocation of confirmation, the debtor's chapter 11 discharge is revoked. § 1144.

[356] In re Knupp, 461 B.R. 351 (Bankr. W.D. Va. 2011).

debtor will escape the consequences of his fraudulent behavior. Any party in interest who did not know of the fraud may request revocation.

Revocation must be requested no later than *one year* after the discharge is granted. § 1328(e). Again, this follows the practice in the other chapters. An action to revoke the debtor's discharge commences an adversary proceeding. Rule 7001(4). In chapter 11, however, a request to revoke confirmation must be brought within 180 days. § 1144. In applying the one-year time limitation in chapter 13, it is important to remember that the discharge is *not* entered at the time the plan is confirmed, but is deferred until the debtor has completed performance under the plan, or made an appropriate showing as to why nonperformance should be excused. § 1328(a), (b). In chapter 11, by contrast, the discharge is entered upon confirmation, except for individual debtors.[357] § 1141(d). Thus, revocation of a debtor's discharge in chapter 13 might occur several years after entry of the order of confirmation. Revocation of *confirmation* is a separate issue in a chapter 13 case.[358] § 1330.

---

[357] See § 11.35.
[358] See § 12.22.

Chapter 13

FAMILY FARMER DEBT ADJUSTMENTS UNDER CHAPTER 12

A. INTRODUCTION

§ 13.1   Rationale for Chapter 12

Congress added Chapter 12 to the Bankruptcy Code in 1986 as a temporary emergency chapter to provide relief to family farmers.[1] The paramount purpose was "to give family farmers facing bankruptcy a fighting chance to reorganize their debts and keep their land."[2] One senator explained, "We must stop the bleeding on the farm."[3] As an emergency measure, Chapter 12 originally was scheduled to expire in 1993, but the "sunset" period later was extended to October 1998. Chapter 12 became a permanent part of the Bankruptcy Code effective July 1, 2005, as part of the Bankruptcy Abuse Prevention and Consumer Protection Act of 2005 (BAPCPA).[4] Additionally, BAPCPA expanded chapter 12 to include family fishermen.[5]

Chapter 12 basically is a chapter 13 clone tailored to fit the needs of family farmers and fishermen.[6] Family farmers are permitted to keep their land and fishermen are permitted to keep the property used in their fishing operation if they make payments under a three-to-five year plan. By enacting chapter 12, Congress continued its long history of special bankruptcy treatment for farmers. The most prominent previous examples of farm-bankruptcy legislation were the Frazier–Lemke Acts of the Great Depression.[7]

A family farmer is not necessarily limited to chapter 12. In theory a farm debtor could use either chapter 13 or chapter 11 to restructure his obligations. However,

---

[1]   Bankruptcy Judges, United States Trustees, and Family Farmer Bankruptcy Act of 1986, Pub. L. No. 99–554, 100 Stat. 3088 (1986).

[2]   Joint Explanatory Statement of the Committee of the Conference, 132 Cong. Rec. H8999 (daily ed. Oct. 2, 1986).

[3]   132 Cong. Rec. S15,076 (daily ed. Oct. 3, 1986) (remarks of Sen. Grassley).

[4]   Pub. L. No. 109–8, § 1001, 119 Stat. 185–86 (2005).

[5]   Id. § 1007, 119 Stat. 187–88. See Katherine M. Porter, Phantom Farmers: Chapter 12 of the Bankruptcy Code, 79 Am. Bankr. L.J. 729, 735–37 (2005).

[6]   Joint Explanatory Statement of the Committee of the Conference, 132 Cong. Rec. H8999 (daily ed. Oct. 2, 1986).

[7]   For a discussion, see John C. Anderson, An Analysis of Pending Bills to Provide Family Farm Debtor Relief Under the Bankruptcy Code, reprinted in 132 Cong. Rec. S15,076–91 (daily ed. Oct. 3, 1986); see also Porter, supra note 5, at 730–33. Congress enacted the first Frazier–Lemke Act in 1934. Ch. 869, 48 Stat. 1289 (1934). The Supreme Court struck down that law as a violation of the Fifth Amendment rights of mortgagees in *Louisville Joint Stock Land Bank v. Radford*, 295 U.S. 555 (1935). Congress responded by enacting the second Frazier–Lemke Act. Ch. 792, 49 Stat. 942 (1935). The Supreme Court upheld the constitutionality of the second act. Wright v. Vinton Branch, 300 U.S. 440 (1937); Wright v. Union Cent. Life Ins. Co., 311 U.S. 273 (1940). For a discussion of these cases, see Charles J. Tabb, Credit Bidding, Security, and the Obsolescence of Chapter 11, 2013 U. Ill. L. Rev. 103, 114–17 (2013).

Congress enacted chapter 12 because it believed that, for different reasons, chapters 11 and 13 did not adequately address the needs of family farmers.[8] Chapter 13 would be fine, for the most part, *if* the debtor were eligible. The problem, though, is with the debt limit on chapter 13 eligibility. Prior to 1994, to be eligible for chapter 13 a debtor had to be under the debt limit of $100,000 in unsecured and $350,000 in secured debt. Accordingly, few farmers could qualify. Today, even though the chapter 13 ceilings have been raised substantially, chapter 12 still has much higher debt limits than chapter 13. As of 2013, the debt ceilings are $4,031,575 for chapter 12 (one combined figure for both secured and unsecured debt) and $383,175 in unsecured and $1,149,525 in secured debts for chapter 13.

The problems with chapter 11 for farmers were not so much with eligibility as with the legal hurdles in chapter 11 itself that made it difficult for farmers to retain their farms. Congress eliminated several of these obstacles in chapter 12. For example, a farm debtor can write down the secured debt on the farmland in chapter 12 and cash out the mortgagee, and can do so beyond the life of the plan. §§ 1222(b)(2), 1222(b)(9), 1225(a)(5). In chapter 11, however, the secured creditor can elect under § 1111(b) to have its entire claim treated as secured, effectively precluding cash out. Chapter 11 also poses procedural problems for farmers, with the burdens of disclosure and voting, and the possibility of creditor plans. None of these exist in chapter 12. Nor is a chapter 12 debtor who seeks to retain his farm forced to comply with the absolute priority rule, as he would in chapter 11 if a class of unsecured creditors dissented from the plan.[9] A chapter 12 farm debtor also is given greater rights than in chapter 11 to sell farmland, farm equipment, or commercial fishing property (including fishing vessels) free and clear of liens.[10] § 1206.

It is important to remember that bankruptcy is a purely voluntary remedy for farmers. § 303(a). Creditors are barred not only from filing an involuntary case against a family farmer under chapter 12, but also from filing involuntary bankruptcy against a farmer or family farmer under *any* chapter. The unique concern that farmers should not be forced into bankruptcy against their wishes dates from the nineteenth century. Creditors also cannot place a family farmer in chapter 12 by seeking to convert to that chapter a case voluntarily filed by the farmer under chapter 7, 11, or 13, unless the farmer consents to the conversion to chapter 12. §§ 706(c), 1112(d), 1307(e). Furthermore, a family farmer who voluntarily files under chapter 12 has an absolute right to convert to chapter 7 or to dismiss the case entirely.[11] § 1208(a), (b). The prohibitions against filing an involuntary chapter 12, converting involuntarily to chapter 12, and permitting voluntary dismissal or conversion also apply with regards

---

[8]   The Joint Explanatory Statement of the Committee of the Conference elaborated:

Most family farmers have too much debt to qualify as debtors under Chapter 13 and are thus limited to relief under Chapter 11. Unfortunately, family farmers have found Chapter 11 needlessly complicated, unduly time-consuming, inordinately expensive and, in too many cases, unworkable.

132 Cong. Rec. H8998 (daily ed. Oct. 2, 1986).

[9]   See §§ 11.30–11.34.

[10]   See § 13.14.

[11]   The courts are divided, however, on the issue of whether the debtor's absolute right to dismiss under § 1208(b) must give way to a creditor's motion to convert a chapter 12 case to chapter 7 under § 1208(d) based on the alleged fraud of the debtor.

to a family fisherman. However, a family fisherman does not enjoy protection from an involuntary chapter 7 or 11 case.

§ 13.2   Planning: Weighing the Chapter 12 Alternative

Congress enacted chapter 12 in 1986 as an emergency measure to help family farmers. Although farmers were (and still are) entitled to seek relief under chapter 11, that chapter is not well-suited to the special circumstances facing small farm debtors. Chapter 12, which in many respects is a virtual chapter 13 clone, differs from chapter 11 in a number of ways that greatly benefit the farmer debtor. Chapter 12 is not an unalloyed boon to farmers, however; in exchange for the special benefits of chapter 12, farmers have to give up certain features of chapter 11 that are more desirable. A comparison of the critical differences between the two chapters follows.

Chapter 12 versus chapter 11: Benefits of chapter 12

Most of the rules in chapter 11 that made it difficult for family farm debtors to succeed in chapter 11 are changed in chapter 12. Yet, the chapter 12 debtor retains the basic and crucial privileges of retaining possession of his farm, § 1207(b), and continuing to manage and operate the farm as debtor in possession. § 1203. Chapter 12 is more favorable than chapter 11 to debtors for many reasons:

- The debtor has the exclusive right to file a plan in chapter 12. § 1221. In chapter 11, by comparison, the debtor can lose exclusivity in various ways.[12] § 1121.

- Creditors do not get to vote on a chapter 12 plan, like they do in chapter 11.[13] § 1126.

- Because creditors do not vote in chapter 12, the debtor does not have to prepare a disclosure statement, or solicit acceptances, both of which are required in chapter 11.[14] § 1125.

- There are no committees of creditors or interest holders in chapter 12, as there are in chapter 11.[15] §§ 1102, 1103.

- The "absolute priority" rule in chapter 11, which prohibits the debtor from retaining any property (e.g., the farm) over the objection of a class of unsecured creditors unless that class is paid in full,[16] § 1129(b)(2)(B), is not included in chapter 12. As long as unsecured creditors are paid liquidation value, § 1225(a)(4), and the debtor commits all projected disposable income to plan payments, § 1225(b), the chapter 12 debtor can retain his farm without paying unsecured creditors 100 cents on the dollar. The difficulties the chapter 11

---

[12] See § 11.15.

[13] See § 11.21.

[14] See § 11.20.

[15] See § 11.8.

[16] See §§ 11.33, 11.34.

absolute priority rule poses for a farmer debtor were demonstrated in a Supreme Court case that held that the farmer's promise to contribute future labor to the farming operation did not justify a departure from the absolute priority rule that would allow the farmer to keep his farm.[17]

- The debtor has much more flexibility in dealing with secured claims in chapter 12 than in chapter 11:

    1. The debtor may restructure the secured debt over a period longer than the life of the plan. § 1222(b)(9).

    2. A chapter 12 debtor may modify all secured claims, *including* the mortgage on the debtor's home. § 1222(b)(2). In chapter 11, modification of a home mortgage is prohibited. § 1123(b)(5).

    3. The secured creditor cannot elect to have its entire claim treated as secured in chapter 12, as it can in chapter 11. § 1111(b). This election in chapter 11 is especially troublesome for a farmer if the farmer plans to sell or refinance the farm shortly after confirmation.[18] In chapter 12, the debtor can strip down the secured claim to the value of the collateral. § 1225(a)(5)(B).

- In chapter 12 a debtor has broad power to sell farmland, farm equipment, and commercial fishing property free and clear of liens and interests.[19] § 1206. In chapter 11, a debtor must comply with § 363(f) to sell property free and clear.

- Priority claims may be paid in installments without interest in chapter 12. § 1222(a)(2). In chapter 11, by comparison, priority claims either must be cashed out up front, or interest must be paid. § 1129(a)(9).

- In chapter 12, postpetition tax claims arising from the debtor's sale of farm assets used in a farming operation are not entitled to priority treatment, but may instead be treated as nonpriority unsecured claims. § 1222(a)(2)(A). Chapter 11 contains no equivalent rule. Note, though, that the Supreme Court's 2012 decision in *Hall v. United States,*[20] discussed below,[21] limits the scope and utility of this special rule.

- A chapter 12 debtor is given the benefit of a codebtor stay, § 1201, which is not available in chapter 11.

---

[17]   Norwest Bank Worthington v. Ahlers, 485 U.S. 197 (1988). Even though the case was decided after chapter 12 became part of the Code, the case had originally been filed under chapter 11, prior to the enactment of chapter 12.

[18]   See 132 Cong. Rec. S15,081 (daily ed. Oct. 3, 1986).

[19]   See § 13.14. The legislative history emphasized the importance of this power. Joint Explanatory Statement of the Committee of the Conference, 132 Cong. Rec. H8999 (daily ed. oct. 2, 1986).

[20]   132 S.Ct. 1882 (2012).

[21]   See §§ 13.7, 13.15.

- After confirmation it is much easier for the debtor to modify the plan in chapter 12, § 1229, than it is in chapter 11.[22] § 1127. At the same time, the debtor has substantial protection against prejudicial *ex post* modifications sought by other parties, particularly after the 2005 amendments. [23] § 1229(d).

One of the supposed benefits of chapter 12 at the time it was enacted was that a special adequate protection rule was made available to family farm debtors.[24] § 1205. The congressional aim was to free debtors from having to pay time value compensation to undersecured creditors.[25] As it happened, the Supreme Court fixed the problem, holding in a landmark 1988 case that time value compensation did not have to be paid as part of adequate protection.[26]

Chapter 12 versus chapter 11: Benefits of chapter 11

Chapter 11 still has some features that may be preferable for debtors. However, for individual debtors in chapter 11, many of the advantages were taken away in the 2005 amendments. The possible chapter 11 advantages are:

- Discharge is granted immediately on confirmation in chapter 11, for corporate and partnership debtors, § 1141(d)(1), but is deferred in chapter 12 until performance under the plan has been completed or excused.[27] § 1228(a), (b). For individual chapter 11 debtors, the discharge rule was changed in 2005 to mirror the chapter 12 rule. § 1141(d)(5).

- The exceptions to discharge in § 523(a) *might* be applicable to corporate and partnership debtors in chapter 12, § 1228(a)(2), (c)(2), but only apply to individual debtors in chapter 11.[28] § 1141(d)(2).

- The debtor must commit all projected disposable income to plan payments for three years in chapter 12, and perhaps longer if the court finds cause, § 1225(b)(1)(B), while chapter 11 does not contain a projected disposable income requirement for corporate and partnership debtors. Here again, the rule for individual debtors in chapter 11 was amended in 2005 to require the commitment of projected disposable income, as in chapter 12. § 1129(a)(15)(B).

- Unsecured creditors and the trustee may request post-confirmation modification of a plan in chapter 12,[29] § 1229(a), but do not have that right in chapter 11, except with regard to individual chapter 11 debtors. § 1127.

---

[22] See §§ 13.9, 11.39.

[23] Pub. L. No. 109–8, § 1003, 119 Stat. 186 (2005).

[24] See § 13.13.

[25] Joint Explanatory Statement of the Committee of the Conference, 132 Cong. Rec. H8999 (daily ed. Oct. 2, 1986).

[26] United Savs. Ass'n v. Timbers of Inwood Forest Assocs., Ltd., 484 U.S. 365 (1988). See § 3.19.

[27] See § 13.10.

[28] The Code is ambiguous on this point in chapter 12. The section governing discharge exceptions, § 523(a), states expressly that it applies to individual debtors only. However, chapter 12 is open to corporate and partnership debtors, yet § 1228(a)(2) and (c)(2) purport to exclude from discharge for all chapter 12 debtors those debts of the types listed in § 523(a). See § 13.10 for more discussion.

- A debtor must proceed more rapidly in chapter 12 than in chapter 11. In chapter 12, the debtor must file his plan within 90 days, unless a good excuse is given for an extension, § 1221, and the hearing on confirmation must be concluded within 45 days after the plan is filed, unless cause is shown. § 1224. In chapter 11, extensions of the debtor's exclusive period to file a plan beyond the initial 120–day period are common.[30] § 1121(d).

- A trustee serves in every chapter 12 case,[31] § 1202(a), but is only appointed in chapter 11 if cause is shown.[32] § 1104(a).

- In unusual farm cases, the debtor may need to take advantage of the special chapter 11 rules granting an exemption from the securities laws, § 1145, or permitting the debtor to reject a collective bargaining agreement. § 1113. Chapter 12 offers neither.

Chapter 12 versus chapter 13

Chapter 12 was largely copied from chapter 13. Thus, it is not surprising that the two chapters are almost identical in many areas. There are a few notable differences though.

First, the debt limit in chapter 12 is considerably higher ($4,031,575 aggregate, § 101(18), versus $383,175 in unsecured and $1,149,525 in secured debts, § 109(e)). Thus, some farmers will be eligible only under chapter 12. Note, though, that it is possible for a farmer to be eligible only under chapter 13, if he has substantial contingent or unliquidated debts, because those debts do count against the chapter 12 debt ceiling, but do not count in chapter 13.

The chapter 12 rules that are more beneficial to the debtor than chapter 13 are:

- The trustee has fewer duties in chapter 12 than in chapter 13; notably, the trustee in chapter 12 is not required to investigate the debtor in every case.[33] §§ 1202, 1302.

- The chapter 12 debtor may pay secured claims for a period longer than the life of the plan, § 1222(b)(9), but does not have a similar privilege in chapter 13.

- A home mortgage may be modified in chapter 12, § 1222(b)(2), but not in chapter 13. § 1322(b)(2).

- The debtor has greater power to sell farmland, farm equipment, and commercial fishing property free and clear of interests and liens in chapter 12,[34] § 1206, than in chapter 13, which is subject to § 363(f).

---

[29]   See § 13.9.
[30]   See § 11.15.
[31]   See § 13.3.
[32]   See § 11.6.
[33]   See §§ 12.5, 13.3.

- In chapter 12 the debtor does not have to make payments prior to confirmation, as is required in chapter 13. § 1326(a)(1).

- The debtor is given more time to file a plan in chapter 12 than in chapter 13 (90 days, § 1221, versus 14 days, Rule 3015(b)).

- As of 2005, the chapter 12 disposable income test cannot be modified after the fact to require the debtor to commit a higher *actual* disposable income to plan payments than provided for as *projected* up front in the plan.[35] § 1225(b)(1)(C). Chapter 13's statutory provisions on this point are more ambiguous and the courts often have interpreted them to require the payment of actual disposable income.

Chapter 13 is preferable to chapter 12 in the following ways, although in both instances Congress made important changes to chapter 13 in 2005 that made the chapter 13 "advantage" much less important:

- The discharge in chapter 12 is subject to all discharge exceptions, even if the debtor completes performance under the plan, § 1228(a)(2), but a chapter 13 full-compliance discharge is not subject to some § 523(a) debts.[36] § 1328(a). Prior to 2005, the chapter 13 full-compliance discharge was much broader, but in that year Congress added numerous exceptions. Now there are few significant § 523(a) debts that would be discharged in chapter 13 but not in chapter 12. Probably the most important is for stale income taxes under § 523(a)(1)(A).

- In chapter 12 the court has the power to order the debtor to devote all projected disposable income to the plan for more than three years, up to a maximum of five years, § 1225(b)(1)(B), but in chapter 13 three years is the limit for debtors whose family income is below the state median income for the same family size.[37] § 1325(b)(1)(B). Here again, Congress made chapter 13 less advantageous in 2005, by exposing above-median debtors to a presumptive commitment period of five years for the best efforts test.

B.   COMPARISON TO CHAPTER 13

§ 13.3   Roles of Debtor and Trustee

The chapter 12 debtor possesses attributes of both a chapter 13 debtor [38] and a chapter 11 debtor in possession. [39] Even though chapter 12 was patterned after chapter 13, in many ways the chapter 12 debtor bears a closer resemblance to the chapter 11 DIP. Upon filing the petition, the debtor in chapter 12 acquires the status of debtor in

---

[34]   See § 13.14.

[35]   Pub. L. No. 109–8, § 1006, 119 Stat. 187 (2005). See also Katherine M. Porter, Phantom Farmers: Chapter 12 of the Bankruptcy Code, 79 Am. Bankr. L.J. 729 738–39 (2005).

[36]   See §§ 12.23, 13.10.

[37]   See § 12.17.

[38]   See § 12.4.

[39]   See § 11.4.

possession. As such, the chapter 12 debtor-as-DIP is given all of the rights, powers, functions, and duties of a trustee serving in a chapter 11 case. § 1203. The only exceptions are the duty to investigate the debtor, of course, and the right to compensation under § 330. This blanket conferral of all of the trustee's powers on the chapter 12 DIP is taken directly from the chapter 11 provision, § 1107(a), as compared to the more limited chapter 13 grant in §§ 1303 and 1304.

In one respect chapter 12 is ambiguous regarding the allocation of power between the debtor in possession and the trustee. The explicit wording of § 1203 only confers on the chapter 12 debtor in possession the rights of a trustee serving in a case *under chapter 11*. While this grant is sufficient to cover most matters, it does not dispose of those powers of a trustee that are *specific to chapter 12*. For example, the adequate protection rule [40] (§ 1205) and the authorization to sell free of interests [41] (§ 1206) refer to "the trustee," and arguably these powers are not given to the chapter 12 debtor in possession by § 1203. Having said that, it is hard to understand why Congress would not want the debtor in possession to exercise those powers.

As debtor in possession, the chapter 12 debtor presumptively retains possession of his property, § 1207(b), and is entitled to continue operating his farm or commercial fishing operation. § 1203. The debtor will have the powers to use, sell, or lease property in or out of the ordinary course of business, § 363; obtain credit and incur debt, § 364; make decisions regarding executory contracts and leases, § 365; bring avoidance actions; and so forth. At the same time, the debtor will be subject to competing concerns, such as providing creditors with adequate protection under § 1205.[42] Unless provided otherwise in the plan or confirmation order, confirmation of a chapter 12 plan vests all property of the estate in the debtor. § 1227(b).

The chapter 12 debtor in possession may be dispossessed for cause, such as fraud, dishonesty, incompetence, or gross mismanagement. § 1204(a). If the debtor is removed, the chapter 12 trustee will step into the debtor's shoes, take possession of estate property, and assume responsibility for operating the farm and all related matters. §§ 1202(b)(5), 1207(b). The court has the power to reinstate a dispossessed debtor as debtor in possession. § 1204(b). In these ways the chapter 12 scheme is like that in chapter 11.[43]

Unlike a chapter 11 trustee, however, §§ 1106(a)(5), 1121(c)(1), the trustee in chapter 12 does not have the right to file a plan, even if the debtor is dispossessed. [44] Only the debtor has the right to file a chapter 12 plan. § 1221. This permanent right of debtor exclusivity is an important component of the purely voluntary nature of chapter 12, and is drawn from the identical rule in chapter 13. See § 1321. Congress did not want family farmers to be subjected to involuntary payment plans. If a party in

---

[40]   See § 13.13.

[41]   See § 13.14.

[42]   See § 13.13. Note that § 361 does not apply in chapter 12 cases, § 1205(a), but is replaced by the special adequate protection rules in § 1205(b).

[43]   See Joint Explanatory Statement of the Committee of the Conference, 132 Cong. Rec. H8999 (daily ed. Oct. 2, 1986).

[44]   See id.

interest moves to convert a chapter 12 case to chapter 11, the debtor may dismiss the case, § 1208(b), thereby avoiding the possibility of confirmation of an involuntary payment plan under that chapter. The debtor also has the right to modify the plan at any time before confirmation of the plan. § 1223(a).

Because of the potentially more complex financial nature of chapter 12 cases, the debtor in chapter 12 is given substantially more time to file a plan than is his chapter 13 counterpart. In chapter 12 a debtor has 90 days to file a plan, § 1221, as compared to the 14–day requirement in chapter 13. See Rule 3015(b). In either chapter, the debtor may file a plan with the petition. Rule 3015(a), (b). The chapter 12 debtor may obtain an extension of time in which to file a plan, but only if the court finds that "the need for an extension is attributable to circumstances for which the debtor should not justly be held accountable." § 1221.

Like chapter 13, § 1302(a), and unlike chapter 11, § 1104(a), a trustee serves in every chapter 12 case. § 1202(a). In most districts or regions the United States trustee appoints a single individual to serve as the "standing trustee" for all chapter 12 cases in that district or region. See § 1202(a); 28 U.S.C. § 586(b). Standing trustees are governed by most of the same rules in chapter 12 as they are in chapter 13. [45] One exception is the compensation scheme, which only allows standing trustees in chapter 12 to collect a fee of 10% on plan payments up to $450,000, with a three percent fee for payments in excess of $450,000. 28 U.S.C. § 586(e)(1)(B)(ii).

As noted above, the chapter 12 trustee only takes possession of the debtor's property and operates the debtor's farm in the unusual case where the debtor is dispossessed for cause under § 1204(a). § 1202(b)(5). In the normal case, the chapter 12 trustee's functions are similar to the trustee in chapter 13. The trustee serves primarily as a disbursing agent for plan payments. § 1226(c). In addition, the trustee is charged with ensuring that the debtor begins making timely payments required by a confirmed plan. § 1202(b)(4). Note, though, that in chapter 12 the debtor does not have to make payments prior to confirmation, as does a chapter 13 debtor. See § 1326(a)(1). The chapter 12 trustee also does not advise and assist the debtor with regard to the plan, as the chapter 13 trustee is required to do. See § 1302(a)(4).

Trustees in chapters 12 and 13 alike are charged with the duty to appear and be heard at any hearing on the valuation of collateral, confirmation of the plan, or modification of the plan. §§ 1202(b)(3), 1302(b)(2). In addition, the chapter 12 trustee must appear and be heard at hearings on the sale of property of the estate. § 1202(b)(3)(D). This role is necessitated by the more generous provisions in chapter 12 for sales free of interests, see § 1206, than in other types of cases. [46]

The trustee in chapter 12 is not required to investigate the debtor's business and financial affairs in every case, as is the chapter 13 trustee, see § 1302(b)(1), (c). Instead, an investigation of the debtor is required in chapter 12 only if the court so orders, for cause shown. § 1202(b)(2). Other than the investigatory function, though,

---

[45] See § 12.5.

[46] See § 13.14.

the chapter 12 trustee has the same types of general trustee duties as the chapter 13 trustee, such as examining proofs of claims, objecting to the discharge if advisable, accounting for property, and filing a final report. §§ 1202(b)(1), 1302(b)(1). Additionally, both the chapter 12 and the chapter 13 trustee must provide the applicable notices required for any claim for domestic support. §§ 1202(b)(6), 1302(b)(6).

§ 13.4   Postpetition Property

Chapter 12 mirrors chapter 13[47] (§ 1306(a)) by providing for the inclusion in the bankruptcy estate of property acquired by the debtor and the debtor's earnings from services during the pendency of the chapter 12 case. § 1207(a). The case law construing § 1306(a) should be persuasive for interpretation of § 1207(a) as well. Chapters 12 and 13 (and 11 for individual debtors) thus depart from the general rule of § 541(a) that the bankruptcy estate does not include postpetition property.[48] In chapters 12 and 13, and chapter 11 for individual debtors, the debtor's "fresh start" is deferred during the pendency of the case, with the discharge delayed until completion of the case, §§ 1228, 1328, and with postpetition property and earnings included in the estate.

However, the debtor normally remains in possession of this property, § 1207(b), and estate property will not be liquidated and distributed to creditors in chapter 12. Postpetition property and earnings that are brought into the estate by § 1207(a) are protected from the reach of creditors by the automatic stay of § 362(a). This protection applies even against claims that arose after the commencement of the case. The debtor thus may be better able to perform under the terms of the plan. Upon confirmation, though, the general rule is that estate property vests in the debtor.[49] § 1227(b). If given its literal effect, this provision would terminate the application of the stay with regard to postpetition claims. The debtor may override the vesting rule of § 1227(b) by a provision in the plan, and thereby keep the stay in effect. Doing so might make it harder for the debtor to obtain postpetition credit, though.

The chapter 12 rules with regard to the expanded estate differ from chapter 13 in a few ways. First, in chapter 12 the debtor may be divested of possession of estate property. §§ 1207(b), 1204. If the chapter 12 debtor is dispossessed, the chapter 12 trustee will take possession of estate property and assume operation of the debtor's farm. § 1202(b)(5). In that respect, a chapter 12 debtor faces more risk from the inclusion of postpetition property in the estate than does a chapter 13 debtor.

The chapter 12 debtor's risks from the expanded estate are heightened by the prospect that postpetition property will be included in the estate if the chapter 12 case is converted to chapter 7. § 1207(a). That postpetition property then would be liquidated and distributed to creditors in the converted chapter 7 case. Ironically, if the debtor had not attempted to reorganize under chapter 12 first, the property acquired postpetition probably would not have been included in the estate, rendering the debtor worse off for trying to pay creditors more. While § 348(f) deals with the conversion

---

[47]   See § 12.6.
[48]   See §§ 5.3, 5.4.
[49]   See § 13.8.

problem in a chapter 13 case by excluding property acquired postpetition from the estate in the converted case unless the debtor acted in bad faith, there is no similar protective rule applicable to chapter 12 cases.

Perhaps the difference in rules can be attributed in part to the fact that a chapter 12 case can be converted only at the request of the *debtor*, unless the debtor committed fraud. § 1208(a), (d). A chapter 13 case, by comparison, may be converted to chapter 7 on the request of a party in interest or the United States trustee. § 1307(c). Furthermore, a chapter 12 debtor has an absolute right to *dismiss* the chapter 12 case at any time, § 1208(b), meaning that the debtor probably could prevent a chapter 7 liquidation of postpetition property. However, some courts have held that a debtor's apparently absolute dismissal right under § 1208(b) might not be available if a creditor has moved for conversion to chapter 7 under § 1208(d) on the ground that the debtor has committed fraud.[50] The Supreme Court's 2007 decision in *Marrama v. Citizens Bank*,[51] limiting a debtor's apparently absolute right to convert in another context due to bad faith, supports an analogous limitation in the chapter 12 setting. Under that view, the debtor does bear some risk of involuntary liquidation of postpetition property.

In some respects, the rule in chapter 12 including postpetition property and earnings in the estate may be less important than in chapter 13. In chapter 13, the individual debtor's postpetition earnings often are the primary source of plan payments. In chapter 12, by comparison, the plan may be funded by profits from the operation of the farm, rather than from the debtor's earnings. Furthermore, if the chapter 12 debtor is not an individual, then § 541(a)(6) already may bring into the estate some postpetition earnings, to the extent they represent the proceeds or product of estate property.

§ 13.5   Codebtor Stay

Chapter 12 tracks chapter 13 in providing for a codebtor stay. § 1201. A creditor may not attempt to collect a consumer debt from an individual that is liable with the debtor on the debt during the pendency of the chapter 12 case, § 1201(a), unless the creditor can establish one of the three grounds for relief from the stay in § 1201(c). Since § 1201 is almost a verbatim copy of the chapter 13 provision, § 1301, case authority under chapter 13 should be relevant to the interpretation of the codebtor stay in chapter 12.[52]

The rationale for the enactment of the codebtor stay in chapter 13 in the 1978 Code was to prevent creditors from bringing indirect pressure on an individual bankruptcy debtor to pay or reaffirm a consumer debt by threatening to collect from an individual (often a friend or relative of the debtor) who was liable with the debtor on the debt.[53] Presumably, the same justification supports the imposition of the codebtor stay in chapter 12.

---

[50]   The leading case is *In re Graven*, 936 F.2d 378 (8th Cir. 1991).

[51]   549 U.S. 365 (2007).

[52]   See § 12.8 for a discussion of the codebtor stay in chapter 13.

[53]   H.R. Rep. No. 95–595, 95th Cong., 1st Sess., at 121–22 (1977).

In practice, however, the codebtor stay probably is much less important in chapter 12 than it is in chapter 13. To begin with, the codebtor stay will not apply at all in chapter 12 if the family farmer bankruptcy debtor is a corporation or a partnership, rather than an individual. The codebtor stay only applies to consumer debts, and by definition, a "consumer debt" can only be incurred by an individual debtor. § 101(8). Furthermore, the stay will not apply if the codebtor is not an individual. § 1201(a). Thus, if a family farm corporation or partnership is the codebtor, the § 1201 stay will not apply, even if the bankruptcy debtor is an individual.

The "consumer debt" definition highlights another significant limitation on the availability of the codebtor stay in chapter 12 cases. Under that definition, a consumer debt is one that is incurred for "personal, family, or household" purposes. § 101(8). A key question in determining the applicability of § 1201 in family farm bankruptcy cases is whether debts relating to the debtor's *farming operation* qualify as consumer debts. Those farm-related debts obviously are the most significant ones facing a chapter 12 debtor in the bulk of the cases. Virtually all courts to consider the issue have agreed that farming debts are *not* "consumer" debts, and thus the codebtor stay does not apply. [54] Courts do not buy the creative argument that a debt relating to the "family" farm necessarily must be for "family" purposes, and thus be deemed a "consumer" debt. These courts' conclusion surely is correct. The codebtor stay never has been intended to interfere with the collection of debts relating to the debtor's *business* operations, and the chapter 12 debtor's farm operation *is* their business.

The three grounds for stay relief in § 1201(c) are identical to the chapter 13 provision. They are: (1) the codebtor actually received the consideration, not the bankruptcy debtor, §§ 1201(c)(1), 1301(c)(1); (2) the plan filed by the debtor does not propose to pay the creditor's claim in full, §§ 1201(c)(2), 1301(c)(2); and (3) keeping the stay in effect would irreparably harm the creditor's interest, §§ 1201(c)(3), 1301(c)(3). If the creditor requests relief under the second ground, the stay will terminate automatically after 20 days unless the debtor or an individual that is liable with the debtor on the debt files a written objection. §§ 1201(d), 1301(d).

§ 13.6   Plan: Process

The chapter 12 process is modeled closely after the simplified and expeditious chapter 13 scheme[55] rather than the cumbersome chapter 11 rules. Indeed, the legislative history explains that one of the primary reasons for enacting chapter 12 in the first place was that for family farmers chapter 11 was "needlessly complicated, unduly time-consuming, inordinately expensive, and in too many cases, unworkable." [56] Thus, like chapter 13 but unlike chapter 11, the chapter 12 confirmation process is not inherently consensual. The chapter 12 plan is not negotiated, but presented by the debtor; if the plan meets the statutory requirements it will be confirmed. In chapter 12, creditors do not receive a disclosure statement, and are not entitled to vote on the plan; committees of creditors are abolished; and creditors may not file rival plans.

---

[54]   See, e.g., In re Smith, 189 B.R. 11 (Bankr. C.D. Ill. 1995).

[55]   See § 12.9.

[56]   Joint Explanatory Statement of the Committee of the Conference, 132 Cong. Rec. H8998 (daily ed. Oct. 2, 1986).

Although very similar in basic design to the chapter 13 process, the chapter 12 plan process is not identical in all respects to chapter 13. Significant differences are:

- The debtor has more time to file a plan–90 days after the petition in chapter 12, § 1221, versus 14 days in chapter 13, Rule 3015(b). The time to file a plan in chapter 12 thus is much closer to the exclusivity period in chapter 11[57] (120 days, or 180 for small business debtors, § 1121) than the chapter 13 period.

- The standard to obtain an extension of time to file a plan is stricter in chapter 12 than in chapter 13. In chapter 12, the debtor must show that the need for an extension is "attributable to circumstances for which the debtor should not justly be held accountable," § 1221, while a chapter 13 debtor only needs to show "cause," Rule 3015(b).

- In chapter 12 the debtor is permitted to but is not required to begin making plan payments prior to confirmation, as is required in chapter 13, §§ 1226(a), 1326(a)(1).

- "Expedited" notice must be sent in chapter 12. § 1224. The Rules have implemented this statutory command by requiring only 21 days' notice to creditors and the trustee in chapter 12 of the confirmation hearing and the time fixed for filing objections, Rule 2002(a)(8), compared to 28 days in chapter 13, Rule 2002(b)(2).

- The chapter 12 confirmation hearing must be concluded not later than 45 days after the filing of the plan, unless the court extends the time for cause. § 1224. Prior to 2005, chapter 13 did not impose any such requirement. In 2005, Congress added § 1324(b), which requires the chapter 13 confirmation hearing to be "held" (but perhaps not then necessarily "concluded," as in chapter 12?) not earlier than 20 days or later than 45 days after the first meeting of creditors.

- Even if the debtor completes performance under the chapter 12 plan, the debtor will not receive a "superdischarge," as in chapter 13, § 1328(a), but remains subject to all discharge exceptions in § 523(a). [58] § 1228(a)(2).

Notwithstanding those differences between the chapter 12 and chapter 13 processes, the basic structure in the two chapters is the same. To summarize, the chapter 12 process, from start to finish, is:

Step 1: Debtor files plan, with petition or within 90 days, unless the court extends the time. § 1221, Rule 3015(a).

Step 2: Twenty-one days' notice is sent to creditors and the trustee of the time fixed for filing objections and the confirmation hearing. Rule 2002(a)(9).

---

[57] See § 11.15.

[58] See § 13.10.

Step 3: Objections to confirmation may be filed by a party in interest, the trustee, or the United States trustee. § 1224, Rule 3015(f).

Step 4: Confirmation hearing is held. The hearing must be concluded not later than 45 days after the plan is filed, unless the time is extended for cause. § 1224.

Optional Step [before 5]: Debtor modifies plan before confirmation. § 1223.

Step 5: Court confirms plan. § 1225.

Optional Steps [after 5]:

A.   Court revokes confirmation for fraud, on motion filed within 180 days.[59] § 1230.

B.   Plan is modified post-confirmation, on request of debtor, trustee, or unsecured creditor.[60] § 1229.

C.   Case is converted to another chapter or dismissed, on motion of debtor or party in interest. § 1208.

Step 6: Trustee makes payments to creditors under plan, unless debtor provides in plan to make direct payments to creditors. § 1226(c). Trustee also must pay administrative priority claims and the standing trustee's percentage fee. § 1226(b).

Step 7: Performance under plan is completed (or not), and debtor receives discharge (or not). § 1228.

§ 13.7   Plan: Confirmation

The statutory provisions on what provisions are required to be in the plan, § 1222(a), what terms are permitted to be in the plan, § 1222(b), limits on the length of a plan, § 1222(c), and what requirements must be satisfied for the plan to be confirmed, § 1225, are very similar to, but are not completely identical with, the chapter 13 rules.

The chapter 12 rules that are essentially the same as the chapter 13 provisions are:

Mandatory plan provisions:[61]

- The plan shall provide for submission of sufficient future earnings or income of debtor to trustee to permit execution of plan, § 1222(a)(1);

- The same treatment must be provided for all claims and interests in the same class, § 1222(a)(3); and

---

[59]   See § 13.11.

[60]   See § 13.9.

[61]   See § 12.10 for chapter 13 rules.

- The plan must provide for full payment, in deferred cash payments, of § 507 priority claims, § 1222(a)(2), unless the claim holder agrees to different treatment, except for assigned domestic support obligations under § 507(a)(1)(B), which need not be paid in full if the debtor commits all disposable income to plan payments for five years, § 1222(a)(4).

However, an important 2005 amendment added an exception to the priority claims full payment requirement in chapter 12, if the claim is owed to a governmental unit resulting from the "sale, transfer, exchange, or other disposition" of farm assets.[62] § 1222(a)(2)(A). Such a claim may be treated as a nonpriority unsecured claim. Chapter 13 does not contain an equivalent rule. However, in *Hall v. United States*,[63] decided in 2012, the Supreme Court largely undermined the intent of the 2005 amendment by holding that that the individual farmer debtors in that case were not entitled to reclassify the tax as a dischargeable unsecured claim. The problem was that the tax was not a priority claim under § 507 at all, since it was not "incurred by the estate."

Permissive plan provisions:

- classification is allowed, subject to prohibition against unfair discrimination, § 1222(b)(1). Just as in chapter 13, these classifications are permitted "as provided in section 1122."[64]

- modification of rights of holders of claims is permitted, § 1222(b)(2);[65]

- any default may be cured or waived, § 1222(b)(3);[66]

- unsecured claims may be paid concurrently with secured claims, § 1222(b)(4);

- cure defaults and maintain payments on long-term debt on which last payment is due after date of final plan payment, § 1222(b)(5);[67]

- assume, reject, or assign executory contracts and unexpired leases, § 1222(b)(6);

- pay claims from property of estate or property of debtor, § 1222(b)(7);

- provide for vesting of property of estate on confirmation or later, in debtor or any other entity, § 1222(b)(10);

- provide for payment of post-petition interest accrued on non-dischargeable, unsecured claims, § 1222(b)(11);[68] and

---

[62] Pub. L. No. 109–8, § 1003, 119 Stat. 186 (2005). See § 13.15.

[63] 132 S.Ct. 1882 (2012).

[64] See § 12.11.

[65] See § 12.12.

[66] See id.

[67] See id.

[68] See § 12.13

- include any other appropriate provision not inconsistent with Code, § 1222(b)(12).

Length of plan period:

- maximum of three-year plan period, unless court approves longer period for cause, with absolute maximum of five years, § 1222(c).[69] After 2005, the same rule pertains in chapter 13 *only* for debtors with a family income below the state median income for the same family size. For above-median debtors in chapter 13, five years is the presumptive commitment period. § 1322(d).

Plan confirmation requirements:

- plan complies with provisions of chapter 12 and other applicable provisions of title 11, § 1225(a)(1);

- fees and charges required under chapter 123 of title 28 must be paid before confirmation, § 1225(a)(2);

- plan proposed in good faith, and not by any means forbidden by law, § 1225(a)(3);[70]

- unsecured claims paid at least as much as in liquidation, i.e., the "best interests" test is met, § 1225(a)(4);[71]

- secured claims are crammed down by retention of lien and payment of allowed secured claim, or collateral is surrendered, or secured creditor accepts plan, § 1225(a)(5).[72] Note, though, that in 2005 Congress added some requirements to the chapter 13 cram down rule that are not contained in the chapter 12 rule.

- plan is feasible, § 1225(a)(6);[73] and

- all projected disposable income applied to plan, if objection is filed, § 1225(b).[74]

As is evident, chapters 12 and 13 are near-clones in many respects. There are, however, some very critical differences between the confirmation rules in the two chapters. The crucial distinctions are:

- chapter 12 does *not* prohibit the modification of home mortgages in § 1222(b)(2), as chapter 13 does. Additionally, while chapter 13 prohibits strip down of certain purchase money security interests,[75] § 1325(a), chapter 12

---

[69] See § 12.14.

[70] See § 12.15.

[71] See § 12.16.

[72] See § 12.18; See In re Heath, 483 B.R. 708, 711 (Bankr. E.D. Ark. 2012) (also extending the lien retention requirement to include cross-collateralized property).

[73] See § 12.19; In re Ellis, 478 B.R. 132 (Bankr. N.D.N.Y. 2012).

[74] See § 12.17.

[75] See § 12.18.

contains no such provision. This means that a chapter 12 debtor is free to "strip down" an undersecured lien for any type of debt to the value of the collateral;[76]

- there are no provisions in chapter 12 for dealing with postpetition claims under the plan, as is true in chapter 13 for taxes and necessary consumer debts, in §§ 1305, 1322(b)(6);

- the sale of all or any part of the property of the estate is permitted in chapter 12, § 1222(b)(8);

- in chapter 12 the debtor not only may cram down and strip down secured claims, but may pay the modified secured claims for a period extending beyond the life of the plan, § 1222(b)(9); and

- the court in chapter 12 has the power to compel the debtor to devote projected disposable income to plan payments for more than three years, up to a maximum of five years, § 1225(b)(1)(B). In chapter 13, the projected disposable income test only runs for three years for a debtor whose family income is below the state median; a five-year commitment period is required only for above-median debtors.

§ 13.8 Plan: Effects of Confirmation

Confirmation of a chapter 12 plan has almost exactly the same legal effects as the confirmation of a chapter 13 plan,[77] § 1327. There are also many similarities to the effects of confirmation of a plan in chapter 11, § 1141, but there is one significant difference.[78] In chapter 12, confirmation has three primary consequences:

- the provisions of the plan are *binding* on the debtor and all creditors, § 1227(a);

- property of the estate *vests* in the debtor, unless the plan or confirmation order provides otherwise, § 1227(b); and

- property vests in the debtor *free and clear* of any claim or interest of a creditor provided for by the plan, again unless the plan or confirmation order provides to the contrary, § 1227(c).

Significantly, confirmation of a chapter 12 plan does *not* result in the immediate *discharge* of debts, as is true in chapter 11 for corporate and partnership debtors, § 1141(d)(1). Chapter 13 provides for a similar delay in discharge,[79] § 1328(a), (b), as does chapter 11 as applied to individual debtors, § 1141(d)(5). A chapter 12 discharge is only entered when the debtor *completes* payments under the plan, § 1228(a), unless the court grants the debtor a hardship discharge under § 1228(b).[80] The practical

---

[76] See, e.g., Harmon v. United States, 101 F.3d 574 (8th Cir. 1996); In re Hand, 2010 WL 745624, at *1 (Bankr. M.D. Fla. Feb. 4, 2010).

[77] See § 12.20.

[78] See § 11.35.

[79] See §§ 12.23, 12.24.

[80] See § 13.10.

importance of this deferral of discharge is that the restructuring of creditors' claims proposed by the chapter 12 plan is not given permanent effect at the time of confirmation, as is the case in chapter 11 (for corporate and partnership debtors). If the debtor fails to complete plan performance in chapter 12, and is not awarded a hardship discharge, the creditors' claims will "spring back" to their original amount (less any payments already made during the chapter 12 case).[81]

Other than the conditional effect of the composition of creditors' claims, though, the provisions of a confirmed plan are given *res judicata* effect, and may not be collaterally attacked.[82] § 1227(a). A similar rule applies in both chapter 11, § 1141(a), and chapter 13, § 1327(a). If the debtor is a corporation or a partnership, the *res judicata* effect of confirmation applies to the debtor, each creditor, and each equity security holder or general partner, as the case may be.

Confirmation of a chapter 12 plan vests all property of the estate in the debtor. § 1227(b). Again, the same rule applies in chapters 11 (§ 1141(b)) and 13 (§ 1327(b)). The vesting rule is not inexorable, however; the debtor can provide for delayed vesting in the plan or confirmation order. § 1222(b)(10). The legislative history shows that Congress was concerned that family farmer debtors be able to obtain credit while they were operating in chapter 12 under court protection. Congress believed that the vesting rule in § 1227(b) would help farmers obtain such credit by using re-vested property as security for postpetition loans. [83] If vesting is deferred, the property will remain subject to the automatic stay of § 362(a).

The final effect of confirmation of a chapter 12 plan is that property vests in the debtor free and clear of any claim or interest of a creditor provided for by the plan. § 1227(c). As with the vesting rule, the debtor can provide otherwise in the plan or confirmation order. Furthermore, as reflected by the reference to § 1228(a), the debtor takes the property subject to claims that are not discharged. A similar rule is in effect in chapter 11 (§ 1141(c)) and chapter 13 (§ 1327(c)). The free-and-clear provision is triggered only with regard to creditors whose claims are provided for by the plan.

§ 13.9   Plan: Performance and Modification

After a family farm debtor's chapter 12 plan is confirmed, the debtor must attempt to perform under the terms of the plan. Unlike chapter 11's rule for corporate and partnership debtors, § 1141(d)(1), the discharge is not entered in chapter 12 at the time of confirmation. Instead, discharge is deferred until the debtor completes performance under the plan.[84] § 1228(a). In performing under the plan, the debtor either makes payments to the trustee, who then makes the distributions to creditors, or the debtor pays creditors directly, outside of the plan. § 1226(c).

---

[81]   See, e.g., In re Hoffman Farms, 195 B.R. 80 (D.S.D. 1996).

[82]   See, e.g., In re Watkins, 240 B.R. 735, 738 (Bankr. C.D. Ill. 1999).

[83]   Joint Explanatory Statement of the Committee of the Conference, 132 Cong. Rec. H8999 (daily ed. Oct. 2, 1986).

[84]   See § 13.10.

If the debtor is not able to complete performance under the plan as originally confirmed, the debtor faces several options:

- modify the plan under § 1229, and perform under the plan as modified, upon the completion of which a discharge will be entered under § 1228(a);

- seek a hardship discharge under § 1228(b), but which is only permitted if modification is impracticable, § 1228(b)(3); or

- exercise the debtor's absolute right to convert the case to chapter 7, § 1208(a), or to dismiss the case, § 1208(b).

Modification of a plan in chapter 12 is allowed after confirmation of the plan. § 1229. The provision governing post-confirmation modification in chapter 12 is similar to the chapter 13 provision, § 1329.[85] Case authority under chapter 13 should be helpful in construing the chapter 12 modification rule. The ability to modify a chapter 11 plan after confirmation is more limited. § 1127.

Post-confirmation modification in chapter 12 under § 1229 differs from pre-confirmation modification under § 1223 in three important respects. First, only the debtor may modify prior to confirmation, § 1223(a), but after confirmation, modification may be sought by the debtor *or* the trustee or any unsecured creditor. § 1229(a). Second, the court may have to approve a post-confirmation modification, but is not involved at all in a pre-confirmation modification. Notice of the proposed post-confirmation modification and the time fixed for filing objections must be sent to the debtor, the trustee, and all creditors. Rule 3015(g). If an objection is filed, the court will have to rule on whether the modification should be allowed. The modified plan becomes "the plan" unless the court disapproves the modification. § 1229(b)(2). Third, the types of modifications permitted are spelled out for post-confirmation modifications, § 1229(a)(1)–(3), and post-confirmation modifications are prohibited under certain circumstances, § 1229(d)(1)–(3). However, no such limits are imposed on pre-confirmation modifications.

For both pre-confirmation and post-confirmation modifications, the plan as modified must comply with all of the statutory requirements governing plans. §§ 1223(a), 1229(b)(1). The time limits on chapter 12 plans imposed by § 1222(c) must be strictly observed, even if the plan is modified. § 1229(c).

Modifications after confirmation may be more commonplace in chapter 12 than in chapter 13 because of the greater difficulty of projecting with complete accuracy the net profits from the debtor's farming operations over the next three to five years. If the farm proves more profitable than expected, the trustee or an unsecured creditor could request a modification to provide for greater payments to creditors, albeit subject to the new limiting rule of § 1229(d) enacted in 2005. On the other hand, if the debtor's profits are lower than projected, the debtor may request a modification to reduce payments. Even though the statute does not specify that "cause" must be shown to support a

---

[85] See § 12.21.

modification, courts generally require some showing of a change in circumstances.[86] Otherwise parties could effectively circumvent the binding effect of the confirmation order, § 1227(a), by requesting modification.

In 2005 Congress amended the chapter 12 rules to prohibit the retroactive assessment of disposable income.[87] Under new § 1229(d), together with § 1225(b)(1)(C), three protections for debtors were implemented. First, the plan may not be modified to increase the amount of any payment due before the modified plan becomes the effective plan. § 1229(d)(1). Second, only the *debtor* is permitted to increase the amount of payments to unsecured creditors in a given month, based on an increase in the debtor's disposable income, if doing so would result in total payments for that month exceeding the debtor's disposable income. § 1229(d)(2). Finally, in the last year of the plan, only the debtor is allowed to modify the plan in such a way that would leave the debtor with insufficient funds to carry on the farming operations *after* the completion of the plan.

§ 13.10 Discharge

The discharge rules applicable in chapter 12 under § 1228 are in many respects similar to the rules in chapter 13.[88] However, chapter 12 differs fundamentally from the chapter 11 discharge scheme, which (for corporate and partnership debtors) provides for the entry of the discharge on confirmation of the plan, § 1141(d)(1). In chapter 12, the discharge is not entered at the time of plan confirmation, but only when the debtor either completes performance under the plan or receives a hardship discharge. § 1228(a), (b).

Chapter 12 mirrors chapter 13 in the following discharge rules:

- discharge is not granted on confirmation, but after completion of performance under the plan, § 1228(a);

- a debtor may modify the plan and receive a discharge after completing payments under the modified plan, § 1229;

- a debtor who does not complete payments under the plan, either as originally confirmed or as modified, still can receive a "hardship" discharge if modification was impracticable, the debtor should not justly be held accountable for the failure to complete payments, and unsecured creditors were paid at least liquidation value on their claims, § 1228(b);

- the grounds for objecting to a discharge in § 727(a) do not apply in chapter 12, § 103(b);

- the discharge extends to debts "provided for by the plan" or disallowed under § 502, § 1228(a), (c);

---

[86] In re Mattson, 456 B.R. 75 (Bankr. W.D. Wash. 2011) (discussing the required showing for modification in a chapter 13).

[87] Pub. L. No. 109–8, § 1006, 119 Stat. 187 (2005). See also Katherine M. Porter, Phantom Farmers: Chapter 12 of the Bankruptcy Code, 79 Am. Bankr. L.J. 729, 738–39 (2005).

[88] See §§ 12.23–12.25 for a discussion of the chapter 13 discharge rules.

- long-term debts on which the last payment is due after the end of the plan period are excluded from the discharge, §§ 1228(a)(1), (c)(1), 1222(b)(5), (b)(9);

- the debtor may waive the discharge in a writing executed after the order for relief, § 1228(a);

- a chapter 12 discharge will not bar a discharge in a subsequent chapter 7 case if the debtor paid unsecured claims 100% in the chapter 12 case, or 70% in good faith, if that represented the debtor's best efforts, § 727(a)(9);

- the discharge may be revoked for fraud within one year, § 1228(d); and

- discharge may also be deferred if there is reasonable cause to believe that the homestead exemption limitation rule of § 522(q)(1) may be applicable to the debtor or if there is a pending proceeding in which the debtor may be found guilty of a felony or liable for a debt described in § 522(q)(1). § 1228(f).

The discharge provisions are not identical in chapters 12 and 13, however. The most significant difference is that *all* of the § 523(a) discharge exceptions apply in chapter 12, even for a full-compliance discharge. § 1228(a)(2), (c)(2). In other words, chapter 12 does not offer debtors the lure of a "superdischarge." All debts that would be nondischargeable in chapter 7 are similarly nondischargeable in chapter 12. § 1228(a)(2), (c)(2). The difference in treatment between chapter 12 and 13 probably is due to a difference in statutory purpose. Congress originally intended for the superdischarge to be a carrot to entice consumer debtors to opt for a repayment plan under chapter 13, thus benefiting creditors, in lieu of liquidating under chapter 7. Chapter 12, however, was created for the benefit of family farm debtors, as an alternative to chapter 11.

This rule highlights a possible advantage of chapter 11 over chapter 12 for corporate or partnership debtors, because the § 523(a) exceptions only apply to *individual* debtors in chapter 11. § 1141(d)(2). In chapter 12, however, the statute applies the discharge exceptions in § 523(a) to all debtors. § 1228(a)(2), (c)(2). Since corporate and partnership debtors may qualify as a "family farmer" eligible for chapter 12 relief, §§ 109(f), 101(18)(B), the statute appears to extend § 523(a) to corporate and partnership debtors.

This may be a congressional mistake, however. Section 523(a) by its terms only applies to "individual" debtors. The unqualified incorporation of § 523(a) in chapter 12, which as just stated is open to corporate and partnership debtors as well as individuals, thus makes no sense. Congress gave no hint how to resolve this statutory ambiguity.

Another difference between chapter 12 and chapter 13 is that chapter 12 does not provide for the treatment of postpetition tax and necessary consumer claims, as does chapter 13. §§ 1305, 1322(b)(6), 1328(d).

Finally, a chapter 12 full-compliance discharge expressly covers administrative expenses allowed under § 503. § 1228(a). A hardship discharge does not apply to § 503 expenses. Chapter 13 contains no reference to the discharge of expenses allowed under § 503. In chapter 12, the plan must provide for the full payment of priority claims,

§ 1222(a)(2), and payments must be made on first priority claims before or at the time of each payment to creditors under the plan. § 1226(b)(1). Thus, if plan performance is completed, the § 503 expenses should be fully paid, and the discharge provided by § 1228(a) will be unobjectionable.

§ 13.11 Revocation of Confirmation and Discharge

Chapter 12 tracks chapter 13 in permitting (i) revocation of the order of confirmation, § 1230, and (ii) revocation of the debtor's discharge. § 1228(d). Both chapter 12 sections copy the corollary chapter 13 rule word-for-word, and thus interpretations of the chapter 13 provisions should inform construction of the chapter 12 clone rules.[89]

The chapter 12 order of confirmation may be revoked on request of a party in interest within 180 days of the entry of the confirmation order. § 1230(a). Note that in chapter 12, confirmation may occur somewhat later than in chapter 13, since the debtor is given more time to file a chapter 12 plan. See § 1221. Nevertheless, confirmation still occurs fairly early in a chapter 12 case, and precedes entry of discharge. Confirmation will only be revoked upon proof that the confirmation order was procured by *fraud*. § 1230(a).

Upon revocation of confirmation, the effects of the confirmation order (§ 1227) will be undone. This means that creditors' claims that were modified or compromised by the plan will be reinstated in full. After confirmation, a choice must be made whether to (i) confirm a modified plan under § 1229, or (ii) proceed under § 1208.[90] § 1230(b). The option chosen will turn on what is best for creditors. Under § 1208, the court either may (i) dismiss the case, § 1208(c)(7), or (ii) convert the case to chapter 7, if the debtor committed fraud. § 1208(d). Although conversion to chapter 7 is not normally permitted in chapter 12, § 1208(c), the instance of debtor fraud is the single exception.

Revocation of the debtor's discharge in chapter 12 will occur much later in the case than revocation of confirmation. Recall that in chapter 12 (as in chapter 13), discharge is not entered on confirmation of the plan, but is deferred until the debtor either completes performance under the plan or is granted a hardship discharge.[91] § 1228(a), (b). In chapter 11, by comparison, entry of the confirmation order does result in the immediate entry of discharge for corporate and partnership debtors, without waiting to see if the debtor performs under the plan.[92] § 1141(d)(1). A party in interest must request revocation of the chapter 12 discharge within *one year* after entry of the discharge order. § 1228(d).

To revoke the discharge in chapter 12, the party requesting revocation must prove that the debtor obtained the discharge by *fraud*. § 1228(d)(1). Furthermore, that party

---

[89] For a discussion of the chapter 13 rules, see § 12.22 (revocation of confirmation) and § 12.25 (revocation of discharge).

[90] The Code actually refers to § 1207, not § 1208, but this reference is a typographical error.

[91] See § 13.10.

[92] See § 11.35.

must show that they were not aware of the debtor's fraud at the time the discharge was granted. § 1228(d)(2).

C. SPECIAL RULES AND ISSUES

§ 13.12 Definitional Problems and Eligibility for Relief

Chapter 12 is extremely favorable to debtors as compared to chapter 11.[93] Accordingly, Congress strictly defined the eligibility requirements for chapter 12 relief in order to limit relief to those relatively small family farmers whose need prompted the emergency enactment in the first place, and small fishermen who were added in 2005. Only a "family farmer or family fisherman with regular annual income" may obtain relief under chapter 12. § 109(f). This eligibility rule has two principal components, each of which is separately defined in the Code: first, that the debtor be a "family farmer," § 101(18), or "family fisherman," § 101(19A); and second, that the debtor have "regular annual income," §§ 101(19), (19B). When chapter 12 was made a permanent part of the Code in 2005, Congress opened up the eligibility rules, making chapter 12 accessible to many more farm debtors, and providing eligibility to family fishermen for the first time.[94]

The "regular annual income" part of the eligibility criteria is borrowed directly from chapter 13, except that in chapter 12 the reference is to regular "annual" income, to take account of the seasonal nature of the farming business. As in chapter 13, regular income is defined functionally; the test is whether the farmer's or fisherman's "income is sufficiently stable and regular" to enable the debtor to make payments under the chapter 12 plan. §§ 101(19), (19B). Given the periodic nature of farm income, and the evident congressional purpose to provide relief to small farmers, courts give farm debtors considerable latitude in applying the regular income test.

The more critical limitation on chapter 12 eligibility is that the debtor must be a "family farmer" or "family fisherman" as defined in considerable detail in § 101(18) and § 101(19A). The primary elements of the "family farmer" definition are:

- total debts cannot exceed $4,031,575 (as indexed to 2013), § 101(18)(A), (B)(ii);

- the "family" component—the debtor must either be:

- an individual or an individual and spouse, § 101(18)(A), or

- a corporation or partnership that is: majority-owned by one family and the family relatives, § 101(18)(B); not publicly traded, § 101(18)(B)(iii); the farming operation is conducted by that family, § 101(18)(B); and more than 80% of the value of the assets relate to the farming operation, § 101(18)(B)(i);

---

[93]   See § 13.2.

[94]   See Katherine M. Porter, Phantom Farmers: Chapter 12 of the Bankruptcy Code, 79 Am. Bankr. L.J. 729, 733–37 (2005).

- 50% of the debts (excluding the debt on the debtor's residence) must be attributable to "farming operations,"[95] § 101(18)(A), (B)(ii); and

- at least half of the debtor's gross income must come from the farming operation, § 101(18)(A), (B).

The primary elements of the "family fisherman" definition are essentially the same as those for the family farmer, with just two differences. § 101(19A). Those differences are:

- Total debts cannot exceed $1,868,200 (as indexed to 2013), § 101(19A)(A)(i), (B)(ii)(II); and

- 80% of debts (excluding the debt on the debtor's residence) must be attributable to commercial fishing operations, § 101(19A)(A)(i), (B)(ii)(II).

The debt ceiling of $1.5 million imposed when chapter 12 was first enacted greatly exceeded the chapter 13 limits prior to the 1994 amendments, and thus opened up relief to many farm debtors whose debts were too large for them to qualify for chapter 13.[96] Before 1994, chapter 13 eligibility was restricted to debtors with no more than $100,000 in unsecured and $350,000 in secured debts, so the chapter 12 limit of $1.5 million more than tripled the overall ceiling. This differential was greatly reduced by the 1994 amendment that increased the chapter 13 ceiling to $250,000 in unsecured and $750,000 in secured debts. Since then, the debt ceilings have increased again, with the chapter 12 ceiling now (as of 2013) substantially higher than the chapter 13 limit, to $4,031,575 for chapter 12 and $383,175 in unsecured and $1,149,525 in secured debts for chapter 13.

At the same time, Congress did not want a substantial "agribusiness" to be eligible for the streamlined chapter 12 procedures. In those larger cases, with debts exceeding $4,031,575, Congress believed that fairness to creditors dictated forcing a debtor to reorganize under chapter 11.

The debt ceiling in chapter 12 is not separated into unsecured and secured components, but a single aggregate number is used. Furthermore, unlike the chapter 13 debt ceiling, § 109(e), the chapter 12 calculation is not limited to noncontingent and liquidated debts; in other words, contingent, unliquidated, and disputed debts would have to be counted in determining eligibility. The $4,031,575 ceiling amount includes the debt for the debtor's principal residence, even though that home debt is excluded from the "50% farm debts" limitation.[97] Note also that spouses cannot double the debt limit by filing separately.[98]

---

[95] The 50% figure was adopted in 2005, Pub. L. No. 109–8, § 1004, 119 Stat. 186 (2005), reflecting a major change from prior law, which imposed a much more stringent 80% requirement. See Porter, supra note 2, at 734.

[96] See Joint Explanatory Statement of the Committee of the Conference, 132 Cong. Rec. H8998 (daily ed. Oct. 2, 1986).

[97] See In re Reiners, 846 F.2d 1012 (5th Cir. 1988).

[98] See In re Johnson, 73 B.R. 107 (Bankr. S.D. Ohio 1987).

Several of the definitional elements are linked to the "farming operation" or "commercial fishing operation." "Farming operation" is defined broadly in § 101(21), as including[99] "farming, tillage of the soil, dairy farming, ranching, production or raising of crops, poultry, or livestock, and production of poultry or livestock products in an unmanufactured state." The term "commercial fishing operation" is likewise broadly defined as "the catching and harvesting of fish, shrimp, lobsters, urchins, seaweed, shellfish, or other aquatic species or products of such species." § 101(7A)(A). Also included in this definition are "aquaculture activities consisting of raising" any of these species. § 101(7A)(B).

Courts have differed over whether a debtor who as a lessor rents out farmland to others is thereby engaged in a "farming operation." In all events, the debtor must be engaged in the farming operation at the time of the bankruptcy filing, although the courts may give the debtor some leeway if it appears that the debtor has only temporarily ceased farming, and will soon resume farming operations.

The requirement that 50% of the debtor's gross income must be attributable to the farming or fishing operation is governed by the tax year preceding the taxable year in which the filing took place, §§ 101(18)(A)(i), 101(19A)(A)(ii), *or*, as provided in a notable 2005 amendment applicable only to farmers and not to fishermen, in the second and third taxable years preceding the filing, § 101(18)(A)(ii).[100] "Gross income" is given the same meaning as under the tax law.[101] Most courts simply use the debtor's tax return to determine if the 50% requirement is satisfied. In determining whether the requisite percentage of the debts were attributable to farming or fishing operations, courts look both at the purpose for which the debts were incurred and the uses actually made of the funds obtained.

§ 13.13　Adequate Protection

Chapter 12 contains its own rule for adequate protection. § 1205. Section 361, the adequate protection provision that applies to the rest of the Code, is not applicable in a chapter 12 case. § 1205(a). Today, § 1205 is an historical anomaly. Congress crafted a special adequate protection rule in 1986 to free family farmers from the force of circuit court decisions that were overruled by the Supreme Court two years later, in 1988. Years later, though, § 1205 steadfastly remains on the books.

When chapter 12 was enacted, some circuit courts had held that adequate protection under § 361 required a debtor to compensate an undersecured creditor for the "lost opportunity cost" resulting from the automatic stay of foreclosure.[102] The amount required to be paid was the interest the creditor could have earned on the realized value of the collateral after foreclosure. Congress concluded that many farm

---

[99]　The use of the word "includes" signifies that the statutory list of activities that qualify as farming operations is not exclusive. § 102(3).

[100]　Pub. L. No. 109–8, § 1005, 119 Stat. 186–87 (2005). See Porter, supra note 2, at 734–35.

[101]　See In re Fonke, 310 B.R. 809 (Bankr. S.D. Tex 2004) (chapter 13 case involving farmer; interpretation equally applicable to chapter 12); In re Wagner, 808 F.2d 542 (7th Cir. 1986); See also In re DeGour 478 B.R. 1, 4–5 (Bankr. C.D. Ca. 2012).

[102]　See, e.g., In re Am. Mariner Indus., Inc., 734 F.2d 426 (9th Cir. 1984).

debtors could not afford to pay lost opportunity costs, making effective chapter 11 relief unattainable.[103]

To remedy the problem, and assist family farm debtors in their reorganization efforts, Congress enacted § 1205, which (i) made § 361 inapplicable in chapter 12, § 1205(a); (ii) eliminated the references to the creditor's "interest" in property and "indubitable equivalent" that circuit courts had relied on to compel the payment of lost opportunity costs;[104] and (iii) provided debtors with a new option for adequate protection, the payment of reasonable market rent.[105] § 1205(b)(3). These helpful legislative efforts proved unnecessary when the Supreme Court in 1988 held in *United Savings Association v. Timbers of Inwood Forest Associates, Ltd.*[106] that adequate protection under § 361 did *not* require the payment of lost opportunity costs to an undersecured creditor.[107]

Section 1205(b) provides four alternative methods of adequate protection. Two are taken directly from § 361: the making of cash payments, § 1205(b)(1), and the granting of additional or replacement liens, § 1205(b)(2). The only difference is that what is being protected against in § 1205 is a decrease in the value of "such property" (i.e., the collateral), rather than in the value of the creditor's "interest" in the property. After *Timbers*, though, there is no legal difference between the two formulations.

The third and final alternative in § 361, the provision of an "indubitable equivalent," § 361(3), is jettisoned from § 1205 in favor of a slightly different catch-all rule that permits granting "such other relief . . . as will adequately protect" the value of the collateral. § 1205(b)(4). Again, after *Timbers* there should be no legal difference between § 361(3) and § 1205(b)(4). As is true with § 361, Congress made clear in § 1205(b)(4) that the granting of an administrative expense priority under § 503(b) is *not* sufficient to qualify as adequate protection.

The only real difference between adequate protection under § 361 and under § 1205, then, is that § 1205(b)(3) permits adequate protection to be provided by paying the creditor a "reasonable rent" for the use of farmland. Note, though, that the payment of rent is not mandatory, but is just one of the options for providing adequate protection. Thus, if another of the adequate protection methods suffices, the debtor will not have to pay rent. An example would be if the farmland was not depreciating in value.[108] If rent had to be paid whenever the debtor used farmland, even if the land was not depreciating, the congressional purpose to assist farm debtors would be undermined.

---

[103] Joint Explanatory Statement of the Committee of the Conference, 132 Cong. Rec. H8999 (daily ed. Oct. 2, 1986).

[104] The statutory language in § 1205(b) now refers to protecting the creditor from a "decrease in the value of property" securing its claim.

[105] Joint Explanatory Statement of the Committee of the Conference, 132 Cong. Rec. H8999 (daily ed. Oct. 2, 1986).

[106] 484 U.S. 365 (1988).

[107] See § 3.19.

[108] See, e.g., In re Anderson, 88 B.R. 877 (Bankr. N.D. Ind. 1988).

If the rental option is used, the rent is to be calculated based on what is "customary in the community where the property is located, based upon the rental value, net income, and earning capacity of the property." § 1205(b)(3). The statute does not specify when rent is to be paid; the courts have permitted debtors to pay in advance, in installments, or at the end of the season.[109]

If rent is paid under § 1205(b)(3), an issue that has arisen is whether the creditor must then apply that rent to the total debt. If it does not have to do so, the debtor will be *worse* off than it would be in chapter 11, where, after *Timbers*, time-value costs do not have to be paid. If the creditor in chapter 12 may keep the rent without applying that rent to the principal debt, the creditor effectively is getting a form of lost opportunity cost compensation that it would not be entitled to in chapter 11. Because of this, many courts have held that the creditor must apply the rent to the debt.[110]

In general, adequate protection is a less significant issue in chapter 12 cases than in chapter 11. The reason is that a chapter 12 plan normally is confirmed much earlier in the case than a chapter 11 plan. Upon confirmation, the secured creditor's rights are fixed by the plan itself, and adequate protection no longer comes into play.

§ 13.14 Sales Free of Interests

One provision that is unique to chapter 12 is the power to sell "farmland, farm equipment, or property used to carry out a commercial fishing operation" free and clear of another entity's interest without having to comply with the restrictive rules of § 363(f). § 1206. Under § 363(f), a free-and-clear sale is authorized only if one of five tests is met.[111] Significantly, § 363(f) normally precludes a sale free and clear if the lienholder does not consent to the sale, § 363(f)(2), assuming there is no equity in the property. § 363(f)(3).

In enacting chapter 12, Congress determined that the restrictive sale rule in § 363(f) hampered the ability of a family farmer to reorganize. For a family farm reorganization to be successful, Congress thought it was critical that the debtor be able to scale down the size of the farming operation by selling unnecessary farm property, without having to comply with § 363(f).[112] In other words, Congress wanted family farm debtors to be able to sell (figuratively) underwater farm property without the consent of the secured creditor. This special privilege does not extend to all property of the estate, but is limited to farmland, farm equipment, and commercial fishing property.

The special rule in § 1206 permitting free-and-clear sales without the lienholder's consent does not mean that Congress was insensitive to the rights of the lienholder. The last clause of § 1206 makes clear that the lien will attach to the *proceeds* of the

---

[109] See, e.g., In re Kocher, 78 B.R. 844 (Bankr. N.D. Ind. 1987).

[110] See, e.g., In re Rennich, 70 B.R. 69 (Bankr. D.S.D. 1987).

[111] The alternative tests are: (1) applicable nonbankruptcy law permits a free and clear sale; (2) the holder of the interest or lien consents to the sale: (3) the sale price exceeds the value of all liens on the property; (4) the interest is the subject of a bona fide dispute; or (5) the entity asserting the interest could be compelled in a legal or equitable proceeding to accept money satisfaction of the claim.

[112] Joint Explanatory Statement of the Committee of the Conference, 132 Cong. Rec. H8999 (daily ed. Oct. 2, 1986).

sale. Furthermore, the legislative history emphasizes that the lienholder still has the right to bid in at the sale, in accordance with § 363(k), and offset its claim against the purchase price.[113]

A sale under § 1206 may be effected during the case or pursuant to the plan. A chapter 12 plan permits the debtor to sell all or part of its property. § 1222(b)(8). Thus, unlike chapter 13, but like chapter 11, total or partial liquidations are authorized in chapter 12. A sale under § 1206 outside of the plan must be on notice to interested parties, with court approval required. Rules 6004, 2002(a)(2), (c)(1).

A point of confusion in applying § 1206 concerns which party has standing to request the sale. The logical party to seek a sale is the family farmer debtor, who presumptively is continued as debtor in possession, §§ 1203, 1207(b), and as such continues to operate the farm. The legislative history, which speaks of allowing "family farmers to sell assets" under this new rule,[114] apparently contemplates a sale by the debtor. The problem, though, is that the Code specifies that "the trustee" may sell property under § 1206. While references to "the trustee" usually will be deemed to apply to the chapter 12 debtor in possession because of the conferral of the trustee's powers on the DIP in § 1203,[115] the § 1203 grant may be defective with regard to trustee powers that are specific to chapter 12. The reference in § 1203 is only to the powers of a trustee serving in a case "under chapter 11," which would not pick up trustee powers that do not apply in chapter 11—such as the sale of interests in § 1206. Notwithstanding the strict reading of the statutory language, most courts have held that the chapter 12 debtor in possession may exercise the power in § 1206 to sell property free and clear of interests.[116]

§ 13.15 Tax Provisions

Chapter 12 contains two special tax provisions in § 1231. These rules are quite similar to chapter 11's tax provisions in § 1146. First, an exemption from stamp taxes or similar taxes is included in § 1231(a) for the issuance, transfer, or exchange of a security, or the making or delivery of an instrument of transfer, if done under a confirmed chapter 12 plan. Second, the court may authorize the chapter 12 debtor to obtain a determination of the tax consequences of the plan from any government authority with income tax responsibility. § 1231(b). In 2005 Congress repealed two other tax rules. The first had provided that the taxable period of an individual debtor terminated on the date the case was filed, for state and local income tax purposes only. The other special rule applicable to state and local income taxes required the trustee to make a return for an individual debtor for each taxable period after the order for relief, while the case was pending.

---

[113] Id.

[114] Id.

[115] See § 13.3.

[116] See, e.g., In re Brileya, 108 B.R. 444 (Bankr. D. Vt. 1989); In re Pew, LLC., 391 B.R. 25, 45 (B.A.P. 9th. Cir. 2008) (stating in dicta that a trustee or DIP may sell property free and clear of an interest so long as that interest attaches to the proceeds).

In 2005 a significant amendment was made to the treatment of tax claims arising from the sale of a farm asset used in the debtor's farming operation. Prior to 2005, tax claims arising from the debtor's postpetition disposition of farm property (typically capital gains taxes) had to be paid in full for the plan to be confirmed.[117] This rule proved to be a major roadblock for farm debtors who hoped to raise needed working capital by selling some farm assets. In 2005, an exception was added to the general rule of § 1222(a)(2) that priority claims must be paid in full in order for the plan to be confirmed. Under the exception, a claim owed to a governmental unit that arises from the sale or other disposition of a farm asset used in the debtor's farming operation may be treated as a non-priority unsecured claim, subject only to the condition that the debtor receives a discharge.[118] § 1222(a)(2)(A). Typically, this would be some sort of tax claim resulting from the sale of farm property (e.g., a capital gains tax). Congress made this amendment so that family farmers could make sound business decisions affecting the profitability of their farming operation, such as whether to liquidate unprofitable assets, without having to worry about adverse tax consequences, such as capital gains taxes or depreciation recapture.

Unfortunately, in 2012 the Supreme Court held in *Hall v. United States*[119] that as written, this intended "Farm Sale Exception" did not actually accomplish its intended goal, and the individual farmer debtors in that case were not entitled to reclassify the tax as a dischargeable unsecured claim. The problem, the Court held, was that the tax was not a priority claim under § 507 at all, since it was not "incurred by the estate."[120] Note, though, that the exception *would* apply if the chapter 12 debtor were a corporation, instead of an individual.

---

[117] See Katherine M. Porter, Phantom Farmers: Chapter 12 of the Bankruptcy Code, 79 Am. Bankr. L.J. 729, 737–38 (2005).

[118] Pub. L. No. 109–8, § 1003(a), 119 Stat. 186 (2005).

[119] 132 S.Ct. 1882 (2012).

[120] In *Hall*, the debtors were farmers who filed bankruptcy under chapter 12, and then sold their farm. They proposed a plan that treated the tax on the capital gains from the sale as an unsecured claim, which they argued was mandated by § 1222(a)(2)(A). In affirming the decision of the Ninth Circuit and holding against the debtors, Justice Sotomayor wrote: "Chapter 12 estates are not taxable entities. Petitioners, not the estate itself, are required to file the tax return and are liable for the taxes resulting from their postpetition farm sale. The postpetition federal income tax liability is not 'incurred by the estate' and thus is neither collectible nor dischargeable in the Chapter 12 plan." See also §§ 7.15, 13.15.

Table of Cases

Table of Bankruptcy Code Sections

Table of Bankruptcy Rules

Table of Other Statutes

Index

References are to Pages

CHAPTER 12 CASES

CHAPTER 15 CASES

CHAPTER 20 CASES

CHAPTER 22 CASES

CHARITABLE CONTRIBUTIONS

CHECK PAYMENTS, PREFERENCES

CONSUMER BANKRUPTCIES

CONTEMPT POWERS

CONTESTED MATTERS

CONTINGENT CLAIMS

CONTRACT LAW

CONVERSIONS

CONVEYANCES

DEEDS OF TRUST

See also Mortgages, this index
Definition, 12

DEFAULTS

Workouts, 32

DEFINITIONS

A/B/C, 33
Abuse test, 9
Accord and satisfaction, 33
Act of bankruptcy, 157
Adequate protection, 289, 293
After notice and a hearing, 441
Alias writ, 15
Allowance, 638
Allowed claim, 75
Assurance of payment, 139
Automatic stay, 6
Avoidance, 463
BAFJA, 47
Bankrupt, 1
BAP, 380
Baseline dividend, 391
BFP, 474
BOCB, 779
Bona fide dispute, 155
Cash collateral property, 458
Choate liens, 16
Classes of claims, 97
Clearing bank, 107
Collateral, 12
Composition, 31
Consensual lien, 12
Contested matter, 76
Conveyance, 574
Core bankruptcy issue, 319
Core proceeding, 84
Corporation, 81, 122
Cram down, 729, 754
Crammed down plan, 92
Creditor, 81
Custodian, 431
Debt relief agency, 206
Debtor, 1, 80
Debtor in possession, 81
Deed of trust, 12
Derivative title principle, 464
DIP, 81
Discharge of debts, 3
Dormant judgment, 15
Dormant lien, 18
DSO, 673
Earmarked, 497
Emergence from chapter 11, 1178
Equity cushion, 303
Equity insolvency test, 159
Execution, 13
Execution lien, 15
Executory contract, 785
Extension, 31
Face sheet petition, 283
Family farmer, 10
Family fishermen, 10

Financing statement, 20
Floating lien, 543
Floor plan financing, 543
Foreign proceeding, 125
Future creditor, 622
Garnishor and garnishee, 24
General lien, 22
Grab law, 4
Grab rule, 113
Hanging paragraph, 102
In custodia legis property, 17
Inchoate lien, 16
Individual, 122
Insolvency, 509, 591
Ipso facto clause, 409
Judgment lien, 20
Judicial lien, 11, 918
KERP, 683
Levy, 16
Levy of writ, 14
Lien, 11
Lien stripping, 753
Limbo period, 856
Liquidation bankruptcy, 1, 2
Lis pendens, 28
Means test, 9
Mortgage, 12
Municipality, 81
Negative notice, 441
910 claims, 102
No-asset cases, 89
Novations, 33
Offset, 563
Ordinary course transactions in estate property, 439
Perfection, 20
Perpetual estate, 397
Person, 80, 122
Pluries writ, 15
PMSI, 255
Preference, 482
Present creditor, 622
Procedural consolidation, 231
Property claim, 771
Property of the estate, 78
Recovery, 463
Regular annual income, 1299
Rejection, 792
Rooted payment, 398, 421
Sale free and clear, 444
SARE, 314
Security interest, 12
Setoff, 563, 564
Small business case, 286
Statutory lien, 11, 627
Straight bankruptcy, 2
Strip down, 729
Stripping down, 102
Subrogation, 25
Substantial abuse test, 9
Substantive consolidation, 231
Transfer, 573
Unexpired lease, 783
Unimpaired classes of claims, 97
Upset price, 18
Voluntary bankruptcy, 87

DISCRIMINATION

DISMISSAL

EXAMINERS

EXECUTION SALES

EXECUTORY CONTRACTS

EXEMPTION LAWS

FINANCING STATEMENTS

FINES AND PENALTIES

FIRST IN TIME PRINCIPLE

FLOOR PLAN FINANCING

FORECLOSURE

FORMS

FRACTIONAL INTEREST TRANSFERS

FRAUD

FRAUDULENT TRANSFERS

FREEZES

FRESH START PRINCIPLE

FUTURE EARNINGS

GAP PERIODS

GARNISHMENT

GOOD FAITH

GRAB LAW

GUARANTORS

HANGING PARAGRAPH

HARDSHIP

HEALTH INSURANCE BENEFITS

HEARINGS

HOMESTEADS

INDIVIDUAL

INDIVIDUAL DEBT ADJUSTMENT

INHERITANCES

INJUNCTIONS

INSIDERS

PLANS, REORGANIZATION

POLICE POWER ORDERS

POLLUTED PROPERTY

PONZI SCHEMES

POST–BANKRUPTCY CLAIMS

POSTPETITION ASSETS

PREJUDGMENT REMEDIES

PRE–PACKAGED BANKRUPTCIES

PRIOR BANKRUPTCIES

PRIORITIES

PRISON LITIGATION REFORM ACT

PRIVATE BANKRUPTCY LAWS

PROCEDURE

PROFESSIONAL FEES

PROJECTED DISPOSABLE INCOME TEST

PROPERTY LAW

See State Law, this index

PURCHASE MONEY SECURITY INTERESTS (PMSI)

RAILROAD REORGANIZATIONS

REPLEVIN

RES JUDICATA

RESIDENTIAL MORTGAGEES

RESTITUTION OBLIGATIONS

RETIREMENT FUNDS

REVOCATION

RIDE–THROUGH DEBTORS

SALES

STATUTE OF ANNE

STATUTES OF LIMITATIONS

STATUTORY LIENS

STAYS

STIGMA OF BANKRUPTCY

STOCKBROKER LIQUIDATIONS